SOCIAL SECURITY LEGISLATION 2021/2022

VOLUME V:
INCOME SUPPORT AND THE LEGACY BENEFITS

SOCIAL SECURITY LEGISLATION 2021/2022

General Editor
Nick Wikeley, M.A. (Cantab)

VOLUME V:
INCOME SUPPORT AND THE
LEGACY BENEFITS

Commentary By

**John Mesher, B.A., B.C.L.
(Oxon), LL.M. (Yale)**
Retired Judge of the Upper Tribunal

Richard Poynter, B.C.L., M.A. (Oxon)
Judge of the Upper Tribunal

Nick Wikeley, M.A. (Cantab)
Judge of the Upper Tribunal
Emeritus Professor of Law, University of Southampton

Consultant Editor
Child Poverty Action Group

SWEET & MAXWELL THOMSON REUTERS

Published in 2021 by
Thomson Reuters trading as Sweet & Maxwell
Registered in England & Wales, Company No 1679046.
Registered Office and address for service:
5 Canada Square, Canary Wharf,
London E14 5AQ

Typeset by Servis Filmsetting Ltd, Stockport, Cheshire
Printed and bound by CPI Group (UK) Ltd,
Croydon, CR0 4YY

No natural forests were destroyed to make this product.
Only farmed timber was used and re-planted.

For further information on our products and services,
visit www.sweetandmaxwell.co.uk

No natural forests were destroyed to make this product.
Only farmed timber was used and re-planted.

A CIP catalogue record for this book is
available from the British Library

ISBN (print): 978-0-414-09132-0
ISBN (e-book): 978-0-414-09134-4
ISBN (print and e-book): 978-0-414-09133-7

CHILD POVERTY ACTION GROUP

The Child Poverty Action Group (CPAG) is a charity, founded in 1965, which campaigns for the relief of poverty in the United Kingdom. It has a particular reputation in the field of welfare benefits law derived from its legal work, publications, training and parliamentary and policy work, and is widely recognised as the leading organisation for taking test cases on social security law.

CPAG is therefore ideally placed to act as Consultant Editor to this 5-volume work—Social Security Legislation 2021/2022. CPAG is not responsible for the detail of what is contained in each volume, and the authors' views are not necessarily those of CPAG. The Consultant Editor's role is to act in an advisory capacity on the overall structure, focus and direction of the work.

For more information about CPAG, its rights and policy publications or training courses, its address is 30 Micawber Street, London, N1 7TB (telephone: 020 7837 7979—website: *http://www.cpag.org.uk*).

FOREWORD

I thoroughly commend these latest volumes of the Social Security Legislation. With the accompanying commentaries, they remain an essential source of information and guidance to those who are involved in First-tier Tribunal proceedings in this most complex area of legislation and continually developing jurisprudence. We remain indebted to the publishers and to all those who contribute their knowledge and expertise to these volumes and, in so doing, assist us in delivering justice.

Judge Kate Markus QC
Chamber President of the First-tier Tribunal,
Social Entitlement Chamber

PREFACE

Income Support and the Legacy Benefits is Volume V of the series *Social Security Legislation 2021/22*. The companion volumes are Hooker, Mesher, Mitchell, Ward and Wikeley, Volume I: *Non-Means Tested Benefits*; Mesher, Poynter and Wikeley, Volume II: *Universal Credit, State Pension Credit and the Social Fund*; Rowland and Ward, Volume III: *Administration, Adjudication and the European Dimension*; and Wikeley, Mitchell, Hooker and Rowland, Volume IV: *HMRC-administered Social Security Benefits and Scotland*. The "year" in the title refers to the tax/contribution year and indicates the period the books, including the subsequent Supplement, are designed to cover.

Each of the volumes in the series provides a legislative text, clearly showing the form and date of amendments, up to date to April 12, 2021, with explanatory commentary. The commentary sometimes includes references to later case law as well as to later administrative guidance and to expected legislative changes, particularly in relation to the coronavirus provisions.

This year's Volume V is very different from last year's Volume V. This is because of the substantial restructuring of the series that has been undertaken this year. The position has now been reached where for virtually all practical purposes it is impossible to make a new claim for any of the so-called "legacy" means-tested benefits replaced by universal credit: income support, income-based jobseeker's allowance, income-related employment and support allowance, housing benefit for those under pension age, child tax credit and working tax credit. Someone whose other income is insufficient now has only universal credit as a choice for a means-tested benefit to claim. Accordingly, we draw the attention of readers to the separate Note on Restructuring the *Social Security Legislation* series that follows this Preface. We urge all readers, and especially seasoned readers of these Volumes (who may now not find material where they expected it to be), to read that Note. It explains in more detail how we have this year begun the process of restructuring the series to reflect the fact that universal credit has now become the default means-tested benefit for new claims in the social security system.

This restructuring has resulted in some re-ordering of material across the volumes to provide readers with a clear and coherent explanation (at least so far as we can) of the various social security benefits. The substantive legislation and associated commentary on universal credit has been moved to the new Volume II (which also covers state pension credit and the social fund, as before). This new Volume V is devoted to the legacy benefits replaced by universal credit. Thus, Part I covers the primary legislation governing the legacy benefits while Parts II, III and IV deal with income support, old-style income-based JSA and old-style income-related ESA respectively. Part V includes the Commencement Orders for the Welfare Reform At 2012, which introduced universal credit but now have a limited shelf-life, while Part VI encompasses minor savings provisions related to the introduction of universal credit. Part VII is devoted to immigration status as relevant to legacy benefits and the right to reside rules. Tax credits are still the province of Volume IV. The other main legacy benefit, housing benefit, as administered by local authorities, is not covered by this series: see *CPAG's Housing Benefit and Council Benefit Legislation*. Although a final decision has yet to be taken, we anticipate that this Volume V will be a 'one off' publication this year, although it will continue to be updated.

This year, revising and updating the legislative text and commentary while starting the restructuring process has required even more than the customary flexibility on the part of the publisher and a great deal of help from a number of sources, including CPAG as advisory editor to the series. We remain grateful for this assistance in our task of providing an authoritative reflection on the current state of the law. Users of the series, and its predecessor works, have over the years contributed to their effectiveness by providing valuable comments on our commentary, as well as pointing out where the text of some provision has been omitted in error, or become garbled, or not been brought fully up to date. In providing such feedback, users of the work have helped to shape the content and ensure the accuracy of our material, and for that we continue to be grateful. That is all the more important given the major restructuring that has taken place. We therefore hope that users of the work will continue to provide such helpful input and feedback. Please write to the General Editor of the series, Professor Nick Wikeley, c/o School of Law, University of Southampton, Highfield, Southampton SO17 1BJ, email: njw@soton.ac.uk, and he will pass on any comments received to the appropriate commentator.

Our gratitude also goes to the President of the Social Entitlement Chamber of the First-tier Tribunal and her colleagues there for continuing the now long tradition of help and encouragement in our endeavours.

Finally, this year's books are unfortunately the last with which our colleague Richard Poynter will be involved. He has been contributing to the series for more than 20 years, in which time he has not only provided pithy commentary on the legislation, often illuminating and elucidating particularly difficult and technical areas, but has also been instrumental in keeping the editors in general in touch with needs of, and problems faced by, users within all parts of the tribunal system. His expertise and insight will be greatly missed by the remaining editors.

August 28, 2021

John Mesher
Nick Wikeley

NOTE ON RESTRUCTURING THE *SOCIAL SECURITY LEGISLATION* SERIES

The advent of Universal Credit (UC) has changed the landscape of the modern social security system and especially the role of the previous 'legacy' means tested benefits. The phased introduction of UC has presented a major challenge to commentators such as ourselves. To start with, our response was simply to prepare a stand-alone separate Volume in the series, namely (in previous years) *Volume V: Universal Credit*. However, the existing mapping of social security benefits across the five volumes has become increasingly difficult to sustain as UC has become the default means-tested benefit across the country rather than in selected postcode areas. Indeed, we did not anticipate that a five Volume series would continue indefinitely, but our plans for restructuring the whole series have been repeatedly delayed over recent years in keeping with the protracted roll out of UC itself. This year, however, we have begun the process of restructuring the series to reflect the 'new normal' in social security provision. In doing so we have sought to combine both intellectual coherence and practical utility in our treatment of the various aspects of the benefits system.

The principal change in the series for this year (and going forward) is that the arrangement of material as between Volumes II and V has been fundamentally re-organised to reflect the default position for today's means-tested benefits, namely that new claimants applying for a means tested benefit claim UC and not one of the legacy benefits. Accordingly, the main change in the series is that most of the UC material has been moved from Volume V to Volume II. The legislative material and commentary on Income Support and income-based Jobseeker's Allowance (or old-style JSA) has made the reverse journey from Volume II to Volume V. At the same time, and as part of this rationalisation, the income-related Employment and Support Allowance (or old style ESA) material has been transferred from Volume I over to Volume V so that it sits alongside the other legacy benefits. Our present thinking is that this new Volume V featuring the legacy benefits is a 'one off' publication for this year only, but with some form of updating supplement in future years.

As a result, Volume II has been renamed *Universal Credit, State Pension Credit and the Social Fund* while Volume V has been retitled *Income Support and the Legacy Benefits*. Thus, Volume II deals with UC and the other current means tested benefits for new claimants (pension credit and the social fund), while Volume V covers Income Support, old-style ESA and JSA, the UC Commencement Orders and other legacy issues (including immigration status and right to reside). The restructuring has therefore principally affected Volumes II and V in the series. There have, however, been knock on consequences for the other three Volumes.

So far as Volume I is concerned, and as already noted, old-style ESA material has been moved from Volume I to Volume V so that it sits with the other legacy benefits. However, as part of the process of ensuring all non means tested benefits are grouped together in Volume I, the material covering the new-style JSA (a contributory benefit) has been transferred to Volume I from Volume II, so joining new-style ESA in Volume I. For the convenience of readers, Volume I also includes a new Part covering limited capability for work and limited capability for work-related activity for old-style ESA cases.

So far as Volume III is concerned, the contents have been re-organised and re-ordered to reflect the post-Brexit realities, and so are arranged thus: Part I: Social Security Statutes, Part II: Social Security Regulations, Part III: Tribunals, Part IV: Human Rights and Part V: The European Dimension.

So far as Volume IV is concerned, Parts I to XII are essentially as before, covering tax credits and HMRC-administered social security benefits, with the addition of a new Part XI dealing with the Tax-Free Childcare Regulations. However, new Parts XIII and XIV bring together in one place the existing material relating exclusively to the Scottish social security system and previously found in Volumes II and III. In recognition of this reorganisation, and putting to one side theological arguments about whether tax credits are social security benefits, the Volume has been retitled as *Volume IV: HMRC-administered Social Security Benefits and Scotland*. In due course, the replacement of tax credits by universal credit will result in further changes to this Volume.

CONTENTS

PART I
SOCIAL SECURITY STATUTES

PART II
INCOME SUPPORT REGULATIONS

PART III
OLD STYLE JOBSEEKER'S ALLOWANCE REGULATIONS

Contents

PART IV
OLD STYLE EMPLOYMENT AND SUPPORT ALLOWANCE REGULATIONS

PART V
UNIVERSAL CREDIT COMMENCEMENT ORDERS

Contents

Contents

Contents

PART VI
TRANSITIONAL, SAVINGS AND MODIFICATIONS PROVISIONS

Contents

Contents

PART VII
IMMIGRATION STATUS AND THE RIGHT TO RESIDE

USING THIS BOOK: AN INTRODUCTION TO LEGISLATION AND CASE LAW

Introduction

This book is not a general introduction to, or general textbook on, the law relating to social security but it is nonetheless concerned with both of the principal sources of social security law—*legislation* (both primary and secondary) and *case law*. It sets out the text of the most important legislation, as currently in force, and then there is added commentary that refers to the relevant case law. Lawyers will be familiar with this style of publication, which inevitably follows the structure of the legislation.

This note is designed primarily to assist readers who are not lawyers to find their way around the legislation and to understand the references to case law, but information it contains about how to find social security case law is intended to be of assistance to lawyers too.

Primary legislation

Primary legislation of the United Kingdom Parliament consists of *Acts of Parliament* (also known as *Statutes*). They will have been introduced to Parliament as *Bills*. There are opportunities for Members of Parliament and peers to debate individual clauses and to vote on amendments before a Bill is passed and becomes an Act (at which point the clauses become sections). No tribunal or court has the power to disapply, or hold to be invalid, an Act of Parliament, although, until December 31, 2020, that could be done if it was inconsistent with European Union law.

An Act is known by its "short title", which incorporates the year in which it was passed (e.g. the Social Security Contributions and Benefits Act 1992), and is given a chapter number (abbreviated as, for instance, "c.4" indicating that the Act was the fourth passed in that year). It is seldom necessary to refer to the chapter number but it appears in the running headers in this book.

Each *section* (abbreviated as "s." or, in the plural, "ss.") of an Act is numbered and may be divided into *subsections* (abbreviated as "subs." and represented by a number in brackets), which in turn may be divided into *paragraphs* (abbreviated as "para." and represented by a lower case letter in brackets) and *subparagraphs* (abbreviated as "subpara." and represented by a small roman numeral in brackets). Subparagraph (ii) of para.(a) of subs. (1) of s.72 will usually be referred to simply as "s.72(1)(a)(ii)". Upper case letters may be used where additional sections or subsections are inserted by amendment and additional lower case letters may be used where new paragraphs and subparagraphs are inserted. This accounts for the rather ungainly s.109B(2A)(aa) of the Social Security Administration Act 1992.

Sections of a large Act may be grouped into a numbered *Part*, which may even be divided into *Chapters*. It is not usual to refer to a Part or a Chapter unless referring to the whole Part or Chapter.

Where a section would otherwise become unwieldy because it is necessary to include a list or complicated technical provisions, the section may simply refer to a *Schedule* at the end of the Act. A Schedule (abbreviated as "Sch.") may be divided into paragraphs and subparagraphs and further divided into heads and subheads. Again, it is usual to refer simply to, say, "para.23(3)(b) (ii) of Sch.3". Whereas it is conventional to speak of a section *of* an Act, it is usual to speak of a Schedule *to* an Act.

Secondary legislation

Secondary legislation (also known as *subordinate legislation* or *delegated legislation*) is made by *statutory instrument* in the form of a set of *Regulations* or a set of *Rules* or an *Order*. The power to make such legislation is conferred on ministers and other persons or bodies by Acts of Parliament. To the extent that a statutory instrument is made beyond the powers (in Latin, *ultra vires*) conferred by primary legislation, it may be held by a tribunal or court to be invalid and ineffective. Secondary legislation must be laid before Parliament. However, most secondary legislation is not debated in Parliament and, even when it is, it cannot be amended although an entire statutory instrument may be rejected.

A set of Regulations or Rules or an Order has a name indicating its scope and the year it was made and also a number, as in the Social Security (Disability Living Allowance) Regulations 1991 (SI 1991/2890) (the 2890th statutory instrument issued in 1991). Because there are over a thousand statutory instruments each year, the number of a particular statutory instrument is important as a means of identification and it should usually be cited the first time reference is made to that statutory instrument.

Sets of Regulations or Rules are made up of individual *regulations* (abbreviated as "reg.") or *rules* (abbreviated as "r." or, in the plural, "rr."). An Order is made up of *articles* (abbreviated as "art."). Regulations, rules and articles may be divided into paragraphs, subparagraphs and heads. As in Acts, a set of Regulations or Rules or an Order may have one or more Schedules attached to it. The style of numbering used in statutory instruments is the same as in sections of, and Schedules to, Acts of Parliament. As in Acts, a large statutory instrument may have regulations or rules grouped into Parts and, occasionally, Chapters. Statutory instruments may be amended in the same sort of way as Acts.

Scottish legislation

Most of the social security legislation passed by the United Kingdom Parliament applies throughout Great Britain, i.e. in England, Wales and Scotland, but a separate Scottish social security system is gradually being developed and relevant legislation is included in Volume IV in this series. Acts of the Scottish Parliament are similar to Acts of the United Kingdom Parliament and Scottish Statutory Instruments are also similar to their United Kingdom counterparts. One minor difference is that "schedule" usually has a lower case "s" and references are to a schedule *of* an Act, rather than *to* an Act.

Northern Ireland legislation

Most of the legislation set out in this series applies only in Great Britain, social security not generally being an excepted or reserved matter in relation to Northern Ireland. However, Northern Irish legislation—both primary legislation, most relevantly in the form of *Orders in Council* (which, although statutory instruments, had the effect of primary legislation in Northern Ireland while there was direct rule from Westminster and still do when made under the Northern Ireland (Welfare Reform) Act 2015) and *Acts of the Northern Ireland Assembly*, and subordinate legislation, in the form of *statutory rules*—largely replicates legislation in Great Britain so that much of the commentary in this book will be applicable to equivalent provisions in Northern Ireland legislation. Although there has latterly been a greater reluctance in Northern Ireland to maintain parity with Great Britain, one example of which led to some delay in enacting legislation equivalent to the Welfare Reform Act 2012, this is usually resolved politically by, for instance, the allocation of funds to allow the effects of some of the changes to be mitigated in Northern Ireland while the broad legislative structure remains similar.

European Union legislation

European Union primary legislation is in the form of the *Treaties* agreed by the Member States. Relevant subordinate legislation is in the form of *Regulations*, adopted to give effect to the provisions of the Treaties, and *Directives*, addressed to Member States and requiring them to incorporate certain provisions into their domestic laws. Directives are relevant because, where a person brings proceedings against an organ of the State, as is invariably the case where social security is concerned, that person may rely on the Directive as having direct effect if the Member State has failed to comply with it. Treaties, Regulations and Directives are divided into *Articles* (abbreviated as "Art.").

While the United Kingdom was a Member State of the European Union, United Kingdom legislation that was inconsistent with European Union legislation had to be disapplied. The United Kingdom ceased to be a Member State on January 31, 2020, but the effect of the European Union (Withdrawal Act) 2018, as amended in 2020, is that, with very limited exceptions, European Union law continued to apply in the United Kingdom during the implementation period ending on December 31, 2020. After that date, European Union law remains relevant only to the extent that United Kingdom legislation so provides. For instance, the 2018 Act, as amended, provides for the enforcement of the Withdrawal Agreement, under which rights acquired by individuals before the end of the implementation period may be retained.

Finding legislation in this book

If you know the name of the piece of legislation for which you are looking, use the list of contents at the beginning of each volume of this series which lists the pieces of legislation contained in the volume. That will give you the paragraph reference to enable you to find the beginning of the piece of legislation. Then, it is easy to find the relevant section, regulation, rule, article or Schedule by using the running headers on the right hand pages. If you do not know the name of the piece of legislation, you will probably need to use the index at the end of the volume in order to find the relevant paragraph number but will then be taken straight to a particular provision.

The legislation is set out as amended, the amendments being indicated by numbered sets of square brackets. The numbers refer to the numbered entries under the heading "AMENDMENTS" at the end of the relevant section, regulation, rule, article or Schedule, which identify the amending statute or statutory instrument. Where an Act has been consolidated, there is a list of "DERIVATIONS" identifying the provisions of earlier legislation from which the section or Schedule has been derived.

As regards the European Union, United Kingdom legislation concerned with the consequences of the United Kingdom's withdrawal is set out in Part V of Volume III in this series, together with relevant extracts from the Withdrawal Agreement and the Social Security Protocol to the Trade and Cooperation Agreement. Following the extracts from the Withdrawal Agreement is up-dating commentary on the European Union legislation that is set out in Part III of the 2020-21 edition of Volume III. Readers are encouraged to retain that volume so as to be able to find the main text of relevant European Union legislation there.

Finding other legislation

United Kingdom legislation and legislation made by the legislatures in Scotland, Wales and Northern Ireland may now be found on *http://www. legislation.gov.uk* in both its original form and (usually) its amended form. Northern Ireland social security legislation may also be found at *https:// www.communities-ni.gov.uk/services/law-relating-social-security-northern-ire-land-blue-volumes*. European Union legislation may be found at *https:// eur-lex.europa.eu/homepage.html*.

Interpreting legislation

Legislation is written in English (or, at least, there is an official English version) and generally means what it says. However, languages being complicated, more than one interpretation is often possible. Most legislation itself contains definitions. Sometimes these are in the particular provision in which a word occurs but, where a word is used in more than one place, any definition will appear with others. In an Act, an interpretation section is usually to be found towards the end of the Act or of the relevant Part of the Act. In a statutory instrument, an interpretation provision usually appears near the beginning of the statutory instrument or the relevant Part of it. In the more important pieces of legislation in this series, there is included after every section, regulation, rule, article or Schedule a list of "DEFINITIONS", showing where definitions of words used in the provision are to be found.

However, not all words are statutorily defined and there is in any event more to interpreting legislation than merely defining its terms (see the note to s.3(1) of the Tribunals, Courts and Enforcement Act 2007 in Part III of Volume III of this series). Decision-makers and tribunals need to know how to apply the law in different types of situations. That is where case law comes in.

Case law and the commentary in this book

In deciding individual cases, courts and tribunals interpret the relevant law and incidentally establish legal principles. Decisions on questions of legal principle of the superior courts and appellate tribunals are said to be binding on decision-makers and the First-tier Tribunal, which means that decision-makers and the First-tier Tribunal must apply those principles. Thus the judicial decisions of the superior courts and appellate tribunals form part of the law. The commentary to the legislation in this series, under the heading "GENERAL NOTE" after a section, regulation, rule, article or Schedule, refers to this *case law*.

Most case law regarding social security benefits is in the form of decisions of the Upper Tribunal (Administrative Appeals Chamber), to which the functions of the former Social Security Commissioners and Child Support Commissioners in Great Britain were transferred on November 3, 2008. However, decisions of those Commissioners remain relevant, as are decisions of the Commissioners who still sit in Northern Ireland.

The commentary in this series is not itself binding on any decision-maker or tribunal because it is merely the opinion of the author. It is what is actually said in the legislation or in the judicial decision that is important. The legislation is set out in this series, but it will generally be necessary to look elsewhere for the precise words used in judicial decisions. The way that decisions are cited in the commentary enables that to be done.

The reporting of decisions of the Upper Tribunal and Commissioners

A few of the most important decisions of the Administrative Appeals Chamber of the Upper Tribunal are selected to be "reported" each year in the Administrative Appeals Chamber Reports (AACR), using the same criteria as were formerly used for reporting Commissioners' decisions in Great Britain. The selection is made by an editorial board of judges and decisions are selected for reporting only if they are of general importance and command the assent of at least a majority of the relevant judges. The term "reported" simply means that they are published in printed form as well as on the Internet (see *Finding case law*, below) with headnotes (i.e. summaries) and indexes, but reported decisions also have a greater precedential status than ordinary decisions (see *Judicial precedent* below).

A handful of Northern Ireland Commissioners' decisions are also selected for reporting in the Administrative Appeals Chamber Reports each year, the selection being made by the Chief Social Security Commissioner in Northern Ireland.

Citing case law

As has been mentioned, much social security case law is still to be found in decisions of Social Security Commissioners and Child Support Commissioners, even though the Commissioners have now effectively been abolished in Great Britain.

Reported decisions of Commissioners were known merely by a number or, more accurately, a series of letters and numbers beginning with an "R". The type of benefit in issue was indicated by letters in brackets (e.g. "IS" was income support, "P" was retirement pension, and so on) and the year in which the decision was selected for reporting or, from 2000, the year in which it was published as a reported decision, was indicated by the last two digits, as in *R(IS) 2/08*. In Northern Ireland there was a similar system until 2009, save that the type of benefit was identified by letters in brackets after the number, as in *R 1/07 (DLA)*.

Unreported decisions of the Commissioners in Great Britain were known simply by their file numbers, which began with a "C", as in *CIS/2287/2008*. The letters following the "C" indicated the type of benefit in issue in the case. Scottish and, at one time, Welsh cases were indicated by a "S" or "W" immediately after the "C", as in *CSIS/467/2007*. The last four digits indicated the calendar year in which the case was registered, rather than the year it was decided. A similar system operated in Northern Ireland until 2009, save that the letters indicating the type of benefit appeared in brackets after the numbers and, from April 1999, the financial year rather than the calendar year was identified, as in *C 10/06-07 (IS)*.

Decisions of the Upper Tribunal, of courts and, since 2010, of the Northern Ireland Commissioners are generally known by the names of the parties (or just two of them in multi-party cases). In social security and some other types of cases, individuals are anonymised through the use of initials in the names of decisions of the Upper Tribunal and the Northern Ireland Commissioners. Anonymity is much rarer in the names of decisions of courts. In this series, the names of official bodies are also abbreviated in the names of decisions of the Upper Tribunal and the Northern Ireland Commissioners (e.g. "SSWP" for the Secretary of State for Work and Pensions, "HMRC" for Her Majesty's Revenue and Customs, "CMEC" for the Child Maintenance and Enforcement Commission, "DSD" for the Department for Social Development in Northern Ireland and "DC" for the Department for Communities in Northern Ireland). Since 2010, such decisions have also been given a "flag" in brackets to indicate the subject matter of the decision, which in social security cases indicates the principal benefit in issue in the case. Thus, the name of one universal credit case is *SSWP v AJ (UC)*.

Any decision of the Upper Tribunal, of a court since 2001 or of a Northern Ireland Commissioner since 2010 that has been intended for publication has also given a neutral citation number which enables the decision to be more precisely identified. This indicates, in square brackets, the year the decision was made (although in relation to decisions of the courts it sometimes merely indicates the year the number was issued) and also indicates the court or tribunal that made the decision (e.g. "UKUT" for the Upper Tribunal, "NICom" for a Northern Ireland Commissioner, "EWCA Civ" for the Civil Division of the Court of Appeal in England and Wales, "NICA" for the Court of Appeal in Northern Ireland, "CSIH" for the Inner House of the Court of Session (in Scotland), "UKSC" for the Supreme Court and so on). A number is added so that the reference is unique and finally, in the case of the Upper Tribunal or the High Court in England and Wales, the relevant chamber of the Upper Tribunal or the relevant division or other part of the High Court is identified (e.g. "(AAC)" for the Administrative Appeals Chamber, "(Admin)" for the Administrative Court and so on). Examples of decisions of the Upper Tribunal and a Northern Ireland Commissioner with their neutral citation numbers are *SSWP v AJ (UC)* [2020] UKUT 48 (AAC) and *AR v DSD (IB)* [2010] NICom 6.

If the case is reported in the Administrative Appeals Chamber Reports or another series of law reports, a reference to the report usually follows the neutral citation number. Conventionally, this includes either the year the case was decided (in round brackets) or the year in which it was reported (in square brackets), followed by the volume number (if any), the name of the series of reports (in abbreviated form, so see the Table of Abbreviations at the beginning of each volume of this series) and either the page number or the case number. However, before 2010, cases reported in the Administrative Appeals Chamber Reports or with Commissioners' decisions were numbered in the same way as reported Commissioners' decisions. *Abdirahman v Secretary of State for Work and Pensions* [2007] EWCA Civ 657; [2008] 1 W.L.R. 254 (also reported as *R(IS) 8/07*) is a Court of Appeal decision, decided in 2007 but reported in 2008 in volume 1 of the Weekly Law Reports at page 254 and also in the 2007 volume of reported Commissioners' decisions. *NT v SSWP* [2009] UKUT 37 (AAC); *R(DLA) 1/09* is an Upper Tribunal case decided in 2009 and reported in the Administrative Appeals Chamber Reports in the same year. *Martin v Secretary of State for Work and Pensions* [2009] EWCA Civ 1289; [2010] AACR 9 is a decision of the Court of Appeal that was decided in 2009 and was the ninth decision reported in the Administrative Appeals Chamber Reports in 2010.

It is usually necessary to include the neutral citation number or a reference to a series of reports only the first time a decision is cited in any document. After that, the name of the case is usually sufficient.

All decisions of the Upper Tribunal that are on their website have neutral citation numbers. If you wish to refer a tribunal or decision-maker to a decision of the Upper Tribunal that does not have a neutral citation number, contact the office of the Administrative Appeals Chamber (*adminappeals@ justice.gov.uk*) who will provide a number and add the decision to the website.

Decision-makers and claimants are entitled to assume that judges of both the First-tier Tribunal and the Upper Tribunal have immediate access to reported decisions of Commissioners or the Upper Tribunal and they need not provide copies, although it may sometimes be helpful to do so. However, where either a decision-maker or a claimant intends to rely on an unreported decision, it will be necessary to provide a copy of the decision to the judge and other members of the tribunal. A copy of the decision should also be provided to the other party before the hearing because otherwise it may be necessary for there to be an adjournment to enable that party to take advice on the significance of the decision.

Finding case law

The extensive references described above are used so as to enable people easily to find the full text of a decision. Most decisions of any significance since the late 1990s can be found on the Internet.

Decisions of the Upper Tribunal may be found at *https://www.gov.uk/ administrative-appeals-tribunal-decisions*. The link from that page to "decisions made in 2015 or earlier" leads also to decisions of the Commissioners in Great Britain. This includes reported decisions since 1991 and other decisions considered likely to be of interest to tribunals and tribunal users since about 2000, together with a few older decisions. Decisions of Commissioners in Northern Ireland may be found on *https://iaccess.communities-ni.gov.uk/NIDOC*.

The Administrative Appeals Chamber Reports are also published by the Stationery Office in bound volumes which follow on from the bound volumes of Commissioners' decisions published from 1948.

Copies of decisions of the Administrative Appeals Chamber of the Upper Tribunal or of Commissioners that are otherwise unavailable may be obtained from the offices of the Upper Tribunal (Administrative Appeals Chamber) or, in Northern Ireland, from the Office of the Social Security and Child Support Commissioners.

Decisions of a wide variety of courts and tribunals in the United Kingdom may be found on the free website of the British and Irish Legal Information Institute, *http://www.bailii.org*. It includes all decisions of the Supreme Court and provides fairly comprehensive coverage of decisions given since about 1996 by the House of Lords and Privy Council and most of the higher courts in England and Wales, decisions given since 1998 by the Court of Session and decisions given since 2000 by the Court of Appeal and High Court in Northern Ireland. Some earlier decisions have been included, so it is always worth looking and, indeed, those decisions dating from 1873 or earlier and reported in the English Reports may be found through a link to *http://www.commonlii.org/uk/cases/EngR/*.

Decisions of the Court of Justice of the European Union are all to be found at *https://curia.europa.eu*.

Decisions of the European Court of Human Rights are available at *https://www.echr.coe.int*.

Most decisions of the courts in social security cases, including decisions of the Court of Justice of the European Union on cases referred by United Kingdom courts and tribunals, are reported in the Administrative Appeals Chamber Reports or with the reported decisions of Commissioners and may therefore be found on the same websites and in the same printed series of reported decisions. So, for example, *R(I)1/00* contains Commissioner's decision *CSI/12/1998*, the decision of the Court of Session upholding the Commissioner's decision and the decision of the House of Lords in *Chief Adjudication Officer v Faulds*, reversing the decision of the Court of Session. The most important decisions of the courts can also be found in the various series of law reports familiar to lawyers (in particular, in the *Law Reports*, the *Weekly Law Reports*, the *All England Law Reports*, the *Public and Third Sector Law Reports*, the *Industrial Cases Reports* and the *Family Law Reports*) but these are not widely available outside academic or other law libraries, or subscription-based websites. See the Table of Cases at the beginning of each volume of this series for all the places where a decision mentioned in that volume is reported.

If you know the name or number of a decision and wish to know where in a volume of this series there is a reference to it, use the Table of Cases or the Table of Commissioners' Decisions 1948–2009 in the relevant volume to find the paragraph(s) where the decision is mentioned.

Judicial precedent

As already mentioned, decisions of the Upper Tribunal, the Commissioners and the higher courts in Great Britain become case law because they set binding precedents which must be followed by decision-makers and the First-tier Tribunal in Great Britain. This means that, where the Upper Tribunal, Commissioner or court has decided a point of legal principle, decision-makers and appeal tribunals must make their decisions in conformity with the decision of the Upper Tribunal, Commissioner or court, applying the same principle and accepting the interpretation of the law contained in the decision. So a decision of the Upper Tribunal, a Commissioner or a superior court explaining what a term in a particular regulation means, lays down the definition of that term in much the same way as if the term had been defined in the regulations themselves. The decision may also help in deciding what the same term means when it is used in a different set of regulations, provided that the term appears to have been used in a similar context.

Only decisions on points of law set precedents that are binding and, strictly speaking, only decisions on points of law that were necessary to the overall conclusion reached by the Upper Tribunal, Commissioner or court are binding. Other parts of a decision (which used to be known as obiter dicta) may be regarded as helpful guidance but need not be followed if a decision-maker or the First-tier Tribunal is persuaded that there is a better approach. It is particularly important to bear this in mind in relation to older decisions of Social Security Commissioners because, until 1987, most rights of appeal to a Commissioner were not confined to points of law.

Where there is a conflict between precedents, a decision-maker or the First-tier Tribunal is generally free to choose between decisions of equal status. For these purposes, most decisions of the Upper Tribunal and decisions of Commissioners are of equal status. However, a decision-maker or First-tier Tribunal should generally prefer a reported decision to an unreported one unless the unreported decision was the later decision and the Commissioner or Upper Tribunal expressly decided not to follow the earlier reported decision. This is simply because the fact that a decision has been reported shows that at least half of the relevant judges of the Upper Tribunal or the Commissioners agreed with it at the time. A decision of a Tribunal of Commissioners (i.e. three Commissioners sitting together) or a decision of a three-judge panel of the Upper Tribunal must be preferred to a decision of a single Commissioner or a single judge of the Upper Tribunal.

A single judge of the Upper Tribunal will normally follow a decision of a single Commissioner or another judge of the Upper Tribunal, but is not bound to do so. A three-judge panel of the Upper Tribunal will generally follow a decision of another such panel or of a Tribunal of Commissioners, but similarly is not bound to do so, whereas a single judge of the Upper Tribunal will always follow such a decision.

Strictly speaking, the Northern Ireland Commissioners do not set binding precedent that must be followed in Great Britain but their decisions are relevant, due to the similarity of the legislation in Northern Ireland, and are usually regarded as highly persuasive with the result that, in practice, they are generally given as much weight as decisions of the Great Britain Commissioners. The same approach is taken in Northern Ireland to decisions of the Upper Tribunal on social security matters and to decisions of the Great Britain Commissioners.

Decisions of the superior courts in Great Britain and Northern Ireland on questions of legal principle are almost invariably followed by decision-makers, tribunals and the Upper Tribunal, even when they are not strictly binding because the relevant court was in a different part of the United Kingdom or exercised a parallel – but not superior – jurisdiction.

Decisions of the Court of Justice of the European Union come in two parts: the Opinion of the Advocate General and the decision of the Court. It is the decision of the Court which is binding. The Court is assisted by hearing the Opinion of the Advocate General before itself coming to a conclusion on the issue before it. The Court does not always follow its Advocate General. Where it does, the Opinion of the Advocate General often elaborates the arguments in greater detail than the single collegiate judgment of the Court. Within the European Union, courts and tribunals must apply decisions of the Court of Justice of the European Union, where relevant to cases before them, in preference to other authorities binding on them. This is no longer so in the United Kingdom, but it will still be necessary for courts and tribunals in the United Kingdom to take account of such decisions when issues of European Union law are relevant, and they are arguably bound by a decision of the Court of Justice on the interpretation of the Citizens' Rights provisions of the Withdrawal Agreement.

The European Court of Human Rights in Strasbourg is quite separate from the Court of Justice of the European Union in Luxembourg and serves a different purpose: interpreting and applying the European Convention on Human Rights, which is incorporated into United Kingdom law by the Human Rights Act 1998. Since October 2, 2000, public authorities in the United Kingdom, including courts, Commissioners, tribunals and decision-makers have been required to act in accordance with the incorporated provisions of the Convention, unless statute prevents this. They must take into account the Strasbourg case law and are required to interpret domestic legislation, so far as it is possible to do so, to give effect to the incorporated Convention rights. Any court or tribunal may declare secondary legislation incompatible with those rights and, in certain circumstances, invalidate it. Only the higher courts can declare a provision of primary legislation to be incompatible with those rights, but no court, tribunal or Upper Tribunal can invalidate primary legislation. The work of the Strasbourg Court and the impact of the Human Rights Act 1998 on social security are discussed in the commentary in Part IV of Volume III of this series.

See the note to s.3(2) of the Tribunals, Courts and Enforcement Act 2007 in Part III of Volume III of this series for a more detailed and technical consideration of the rules of precedent.

Other sources of information and commentary on social security law

For a comprehensive overview of the social security system in Great Britain, CPAG's *Welfare Benefits and Tax Credits Handbook*, published annually each spring, is unrivalled as a practical introduction from the claimant's viewpoint.

From a different perspective, the Department for Work and Pensions publishes the 14-volume *Decision Makers' Guide* and the newer *Advice for Decision Making*, which covers personal independence payment, universal credit and the "new" versions of Jobseeker's Allowance and Employment and Support Allowance (search for the relevant guide by name at *https://www.gov.uk* under the topic "Welfare"). Similarly, Her Majesty's Revenue and Customs publish manuals relating to tax credits, child benefit and guardian's allowance, which they administer, see *https://www.gov.uk/government/collections/hmrc-manuals*. (Note that the *Child Benefit Technical Manual* also covers guardian's allowance.) These guides and manuals are extremely useful but their interpretation of the law is not binding on tribunals and the courts, being merely internal guidance for the use of decision-makers.

There are a number of other sources of valuable information or commentary on social security case law: see in particular publications such as the *Journal of Social Security Law*, CPAG's *Welfare Rights Bulletin*, *Legal Action* and the *Adviser*. As far as online resources go there is little to beat *Rightsnet* (*https://www.rightsnet.org.uk*). This site contains a wealth of resources for people working in the welfare benefits field but of special relevance in this context are Commissioners'/Upper Tribunal Decisions section of the "Toolkit" area and also the "Briefcase" area which contains summaries of the decisions (with links to the full decisions). Sweet and Maxwell's online subscription service *Westlaw* is another valuable source (*https://legalsolutions. thomsonreuters.co.uk/en/products-services/westlaw-uk.html*), as is LexisNexis Lexis (*https://www.lexisnexis.co.uk*).

Conclusion

The internet provides a vast resource but a search needs to be focused. Social security schemes are essentially statutory and so in Great Britain the legislation which is set out in this series forms the basic structure of social security law. However, the case law shows how the legislation should be interpreted and applied. The commentary in this series should point the way to the case law relevant to each provision and the Internet can then be used to find it where that is necessary.

EFFECTIVE DATES OF CHANGES TO UNIVERSAL CREDIT LEGISLATION

Once universal credit has been awarded, the general rule is that a superseding decision based on a change of circumstances, takes effect from the first day of the assessment period in which that change occurred or is expected to occur (see the Decisions and Appeals Regulations 2013 reg.35 and Sch.1, Pt.III). This follows the rule for the "legacy" benefits (IS, HB, JSA(IB), and ESA(IR)) in which changes took effect from the first day of the benefit week in which they occurred or were expected to occur (see, e.g., the Social Security and Child Support (Decisions and Appeals) Regulations 1999 Schs 3A and 3C).

The administrative advantages of having a bright line rule about the effective dates for changes in circumstances are obvious: it avoids having to carry out more than one benefit calculation for each period by reference to which entitlement is administered.

However, the "legacy" benefits were paid on a weekly basis, so claimants could neither gain nor lose more than a week's benefit if a change in circumstances was taken into account early. By contrast, universal credit is administered by reference to monthly assessment periods. Having an adverse change that occurs towards the end of an assessment period taken into account up to a month early can have serious consequences for claimants (e.g., where a claimant ceases to be liable to pay rent and therefore to be eligible for the housing costs element).

It is therefore important to note that where the change in circumstances is a change in *legislation* the opposite rule often applies. In such cases, the amending Regulations may contain a provision in the following (or similar terms):

> "(2) Where the amendments made by these Regulations apply in respect of an existing award of universal credit, they have effect for the purposes of that award—
>
> (a) on [date] if there is an assessment period for that award that begins on that day; or
>
> (b) if sub-paragraph (a) does not apply, on the first day of the next assessment period for the award beginning after that day.
>
> (3) For the purposes of this regulation, "existing award of universal credit" means an award of universal credit that exists on [date]."

The effect is that the amended law apples to new claims for universal credit from the outset. However, where there is an existing award of universal credit, the amendment takes effect from the first day of the following assessment period.

In such cases, the Amendment sections of the commentary in this volume refer to "Assessment periods beginning on or after" the date on which the amending regulation comes into force (or similar), rather than just stating that date.

TABLE OF CASES

TABLE OF COMMISSIONERS' DECISIONS

TABLE OF ABBREVIATIONS USED IN THIS SERIES

1975 Act	Social Security Act 1975
1977 Act	Marriage (Scotland) Act 1977
1979 Act	Pneumoconiosis (Workers' Compensation) Act 1979
1986 Act	Social Security Act 1986
1996 Act	Employment Rights Act 1996
1998 Act	Social Security Act 1998
2002 Act	Tax Credits Act 2002
2004 Act	Gender Recognition Act 2004
2006 Act	Armed Forces Act 2006
2008 Act	Child Maintenance and Other Payments Act 2008
2013 Act	Marriage (Same Sex Couples) Act 2013
2014 Act	Marriage and Civil Partnership (Scotland) Act 2014
A1P1	Art.1 of Protocol 1 to the European Convention on Human Rights
A2 Regulations	Accession (Immigration and Worker Authorisation) Regulations 2006
A8 Regulations	Accession (Immigration and Worker Registration) Regulations 2004
AA	Attendance Allowance
AA 1992	Attendance Allowance Act 1992
AAC	Administrative Appeals Chamber
AACR	Administrative Appeals Chamber Reports
A.C.	Law Reports, Appeal Cases
A.C.D.	Administrative Court Digest
Admin	Administrative Court
Admin L.R.	Administrative Law Reports
Administration Act	Social Security Administration Act 1992
Administration Regulations	Statutory Paternity Pay and Statutory Adoption Pay (Administration) Regulations 2002
AIP	assessed income period
All E.R.	All England Reports
All E.R. (E.C.)	All England Reports (European Cases)
AMA	Adjudicating Medical Authorities
AO	Adjudication Officer
AOG	*Adjudication Officers Guide*
art.	article

Art.	Article
ASD	Autistic Spectrum Disorder
ASPP	Additional Statutory Paternity Pay
A.T.C.	Annotated Tax Cases
Attendance Allowance Regulations	Social Security (Attendance Allowance) Regulations 1991
AWT	All Work Test
BA	Benefits Agency
Benefits Act	Social Security Contributions and Benefits Act 1992
B.H.R.C.	Butterworths Human Rights Cases
B.L.G.R.	Butterworths Local Government Reports
Blue Books	*The Law Relating to Social Security*, Vols 1–11
B.P.I.R.	Bankruptcy and Personal Insolvency Reports
B.T.C.	British Tax Cases
BTEC	Business and Technology Education Council
B.V.C.	British Value Added Tax Reporter
B.W.C.C.	Butterworths Workmen's Compensation Cases
c.	chapter
C	Commissioner's decision
C&BA 1992	Social Security Contributions and Benefits Act 1992
CA (Civ Div)	Court of Appeal (Civil Division)
CAA 2001	Capital Allowances Act 2001
CAB	Citizens Advice Bureau
CAO	Chief Adjudication Officer
CB	Child Benefit
CBA 1975	Child Benefit Act 1975
CBJSA	Contribution-Based Jobseeker's Allowance
C.C.L. Rep.	Community Care Law Reports
CCM	HMRC *New Tax Credits Claimant Compliance Manual*
C.E.C.	European Community Cases
CERA	cortical evoked response audiogram
CESA	Contribution-based Employment and Support Allowance
CFF payment	Children's Funeral Fund payment
CFS	chronic fatigue syndrome
Ch.	Chancery Division Law Reports; Chapter
Citizenship Directive	Directive 2004/38/EC of the European Parliament and of the Council of April 29, 2004
CJEC	Court of Justice of the European Communities
CJEU	Court of Justice of the European Union
CJRS	Coronavirus Job Retention Scheme
Claims and Payments Regulations	Social Security (Claims and Payments) Regulations 1987

Claims and Payments Regulations 1979	Social Security (Claims and Payments) Regulations 1979
Claims and Payments Regulations 2013	Universal Credit, Personal Independence Payment, Jobseeker's Allowance and Employment and Support Allowance (Claims and Payments) Regulations 2013
CM	Case Manager
CMA	Chief Medical Adviser
CMEC	Child Maintenance and Enforcement Commission
C.M.L.R.	Common Market Law Reports
C.O.D.	Crown Office Digest
COLL	*Collective Investment Schemes Sourcebook*
Community, The	European Community
Computation of Earnings Regulations	Social Security Benefit (Computation of Earnings) Regulations 1978
Computation of Earnings Regulations 1996	Social Security Benefit (Computation of Earnings) Regulations 1996
Consequential Provisions Act	Social Security (Consequential Provisions) Act 1992
Contributions and Benefits Act	Social Security Contributions and Benefits Act 1992
Contributions Regulations	Social Security (Contributions) Regulations 2001
COPD	chronic obstructive pulmonary disease
Coronavirus SEISS	Coronavirus Self-Employed Income Support Scheme
CP	Carer Premium; Chamber President
CPAG	Child Poverty Action Group
CPR	Civil Procedure Rules
Cr. App. R.	Criminal Appeal Reports
CRCA 2005	Commissioners for Revenue and Customs Act 2005
Credits Regulations 1974	Social Security (Credits) Regulations 1974
Credits Regulations 1975	Social Security (Credits) Regulations 1975
Crim. L.R.	Criminal Law Review
CRU	Compensation Recovery Unit
CSA 1995	Children (Scotland) Act 1995
CSIH	Inner House of the Court of Session (Scotland)
CSM	Child Support Maintenance
CS(NI)O 1995	Child Support (Northern Ireland) Order 1995
CSOH	Outer House of the Court of Session (Scotland)
CSPSSA 2000	Child Support, Pensions and Social Security Act 2000
CTA	Common Travel Area
CTA 2009	Corporation Tax Act 2009
CTA 2010	Corporation Tax Act 2010
CTB	Council Tax Benefit

CTC	Child Tax Credit
CTC Regulations	Child Tax Credit Regulations 2002
CTF	child trust fund
CTS	Carpal Tunnel Syndrome
DAC	Directive 2011/16/ EU (Directive on administrative co-operation in the field of taxation)
DAT	Disability Appeal Tribunal
dB	decibels
DCA	Department for Constitutional Affairs
DCP	Disabled Child Premium
Decisions and Appeals Regulations 1999	Social Security Contributions (Decisions and Appeals) Regulations 1999
Dependency Regulations	Social Security Benefit (Dependency) Regulations 1977
DfEE	Department for Education and Employment
DHSS	Department of Health and Social Security
Disability Living Allowance Regulations	Social Security (Disability Living Allowance) Regulations
DIY	do it yourself
DLA	Disability Living Allowance
DLA Regs 1991	Social Security (Disability Living Allowance) Regulations 1991
DLAAB	Disability Living Allowance Advisory Board
DLADWAA 1991	Disability Living Allowance and Disability Working Allowance Act 1991
DM	Decision Maker
DMA	Decision-making and Appeals
DMG	*Decision Makers' Guide*
DMP	Delegated Medical Practitioner
DP	Disability Premium
DPT	diffuse pleural thickening
DPTC	Disabled Person's Tax Credit
DRO	Debt Relief Order
DSD	Department for Social Development (Northern Ireland)
DSM IV; DSM-5	Diagnostic and Statistical Manual of Mental Disorders of the American Psychiatric Association
DSS	Department of Social Security
DTI	Department of Trade and Industry
DWA	Disability Working Allowance
DWP	Department for Work and Pensions
DWPMS	Department for Work and Pensions Medical Service
EAA	Extrinsic Allergic Alveolitis
EAT	Employment Appeal Tribunal

EC	European Community
ECHR	European Convention on Human Rights
ECJ	European Court of Justice
E.C.R.	European Court Reports
ECSC	European Coal and Steel Community
ECSMA	European Convention on Social and Medical Assistance
EEA	European Economic Area
EEC	European Economic Community
EESSI	Electronic Exchange of Social Security Information
E.G.	Estates Gazette
E.G.L.R.	Estates Gazette Law Reports
EHC plan	education, health and care plan
EHIC	European Health Insurance Card
EHRC	European Human Rights Commission
E.H.R.R.	European Human Rights Reports
EL	employers' liability
E.L.R	Education Law Reports
EMA	Education Maintenance Allowance
EMP	Examining Medical Practitioner
Employment and Support Allowance Regulations	Employment and Support Allowance Regulations 2008
EPS	extended period of sickness
Eq. L.R.	Equality Law Reports
ERA	evoked response audiometry
ERA scheme	Employment, Retention and Advancement scheme
ES	Employment Service
ESA	Employment and Support Allowance
ESA Regs 2008	Employment and Support Allowance Regulations 2008
ESA Regs 2013	Employment and Support Allowance Regulations 2013
ESA Regulations	Employment and Support Allowance Regulations 2008
ESA WCAt	Employment and Support Allowance Work Capability Assessment
ESA(IR)	income-related employment and support allowance
ESC	employer supported childcare
ESE Scheme	Employment, Skills and Enterprise Scheme
ESE Regulations	Jobseeker's Allowance (Employment, Skills and Enterprise Scheme) Regulations 2011
ESES Regulations	Jobseeker's Allowance (Employment, Skills and Enterprise Scheme) Regulations 2011
ETA 1973	Employment and Training Act 1973

ETA(NI) 1950	Employment and Training Act (Northern Ireland) 1950
ETS	European Treaty Series
EU	European Union
Eu.L.R.	European Law Reports
EWCA Civ	Civil Division of the Court of Appeal (England and Wales)
EWHC Admin	Administrative Court, part of the High Court (England and Wales)
FA 1993	Finance Act 1993
FA 1996	Finance Act 1996
FA 2004	Finance Act 2004
Fam. Law	Family Law
FAS	Financial Assistance Scheme
F.C.R.	Family Court Reporter
FEV	forced expiratory volume
FIS	Family Income Supplement
FISMA 2000	Financial Services and Markets Act 2000
F.L.R.	Family Law Reports
FME	further medical evidence
F(No.2)A 2005	Finance (No.2) Act 2005
FOTRA	Free of Tax to Residents Abroad
FRAA	flat rate accrual amount
FRS Act 2004	Fire and Rescue Services Act 2004
FSCS	Financial Services Compensation Scheme
FTT	First-tier Tribunal
General Benefit Regulations 1982	Social Security (General Benefit) Regulations 1982
General Regulations	Statutory Shared Parental Pay (General) Regulations 2014
GMCA	Greater Manchester Combined Authority
GMFRA	Greater Manchester Fire and Rescue Authority
GMP	Guaranteed Minimum Pension
GMWDA	Greater Manchester Waste Disposal Authority
GNVQ	General National Vocational Qualification
GP	General Practitioner
GRA	Gender Recognition Act 2004
GRB	Graduated Retirement Benefit
GRP	Graduated Retirement Pension
HB	Housing Benefit
HB (WSP) R (NI) 2017	Housing Benefit (Welfare Social Payment) Regulations (Northern Ireland) 2017
HBRB	Housing Benefit Review Board
HCA	Homes and Communities Agency
HCD	House of Commons Debates
HCP	healthcare professional

HCV	Hepatitis C virus
Health Service Act	National Health Service Act 2006
Health Service (Wales) Act	National Health Service (Wales) Act 2006
HIV	Human Immunodeficiency Virus
HL	House of Lords
H.L.R.	Housing Law Reports
HMIT	Her Majesty's Inspector of Taxes
HMRC	Her Majesty's Revenue and Customs
HMSO	Her Majesty's Stationery Office
HO	Home Office
Hospital In-Patients Regulations 1975	Social Security (Hospital In-Patients) Regulations 1975
HP	Health Professional
HPP	Higher Pensioner Premium
HRA 1998	Human Rights Act 1998
H.R.L.R.	Human Rights Law Reports
HRP	Home Responsibilities Protection
HSE	Health and Safety Executive
IAC	Immigration and Asylum Chamber
IAP	Intensive Activity Period
IB	Incapacity Benefit
IB PCA	Incapacity Benefit Personal Capability Assessment
IB Regs	Social Security (Incapacity Benefit) Regulations 1994
IB Regulations	Social Security (Incapacity Benefit) Regulations 1994
IB/IS/SDA	Incapacity Benefits Regime
IBJSA	Income-Based Jobseeker's Allowance
IBS	Irritable Bowel Syndrome
ICA	Invalid Care Allowance
I.C.R.	Industrial Cases Reports
ICTA 1988	Income and Corporation Taxes Act 1988
IFW Regulations	Incapacity for Work (General) Regulations 1995
IH	Inner House of the Court of Session
I.I.	Industrial Injuries
IIAC	Industrial Injuries Advisory Council
IIDB	Industrial Injuries Disablement Benefit
ILO	International Labour Organization
ILR	indefinite leave to remain
Imm. A.R.	Immigration Appeal Reports
Incapacity for Work Regulations	Social Security (Incapacity for Work) (General) Regulations 1995
Income Support Regulations	Income Support (General) Regulations 1987
Income Support General Regulations	Income Support (General) Regulations 1987

IND	Immigration and Nationality Directorate of the Home Office
I.N.L.R.	Immigration and Nationality Law Reports
I.O.	Insurance Officer
IPPR	Institute of Public Policy Research
IRESA	Income-Related Employment and Support Allowance
I.R.L.R.	Industrial Relations Law Reports
IS	Income Support
IS Regs	Income Support Regulations
IS Regulations	Income Support (General) Regulations 1987
ISA	Individual Savings Account
ISBN	International Standard Book Number
ITA 2007	Income Tax Act 2007
ITEPA 2003	Income Tax, Earnings and Pensions Act 2003
I.T.L. Rep.	International Tax Law Reports
I.T.R.	Industrial Tribunals Reports
ITS	Independent Tribunal Service
ITTOIA 2005	Income Tax (Trading and Other Income) Act 2005
IVB	Invalidity Benefit
IW (General) Regs	Social Security (Incapacity for Work) (General) Regulations 1995
IW (Transitional) Regs	Incapacity for Work (Transitional) Regulations
Jobseeker's Allowance Regulations	Jobseeker's Allowance Regulations 1996
Jobseeker's Regulations 1996	Jobseeker's Allowance Regulations 1996
JSA	Jobseeker's Allowance
JSA 1995	Jobseekers Act 1995
JSA (NI) Regulations	Jobseeker's Allowance (Northern Ireland) Regulations 1996
JSA (Transitional) Regulations	Jobseeker's Allowance (Transitional) Regulations 1996
JSA Regs 1996	Jobseeker's Allowance Regulations 1996
JSA Regs 2013	Jobseeker's Allowance Regulations 2013
JSA(IB)	income-based jobseeker's allowance
JS(NI)O 1995	Jobseekers (Northern Ireland) Order 1995
J.S.S.L.	Journal of Social Security Law
J.S.W.L.	Journal of Social Welfare Law
K.B.	Law Reports, King's Bench
L.& T.R.	Landlord and Tenant Reports
LCW	limited capability for work
LCWA	Limited Capability for Work Assessment
LCWRA	limited capability for work-related activity
LDEDC Act 2009	Local Democracy, Economic Development and Construction Act 2009
LEA	local education authority

LEL	Lower Earnings Limit
LET	low earnings threshold
L.G. Rev.	Local Government Review
L.G.L.R.	Local Government Reports
L.J.R.	Law Journal Reports
LRP	liable relative payment
L.S.G.	Law Society Gazette
Luxembourg Court	Court of Justice of the European Union (also referred to as CJEC and ECJ)
MA	Maternity Allowance
MAF	Medical Assessment Framework
MAN	Mandatory Activity Notification
Maternity Allowance Regulations	Social Security (Maternity Allowance) Regulations 1987
MDC	Mayoral development corporation
ME	myalgic encephalomyelitis
Medical Evidence Regulations	Social Security (Medical Evidence) Regulations 1976
MEN	Mandatory Employment Notification
Mesher and Wood	*Income Support, the Social Fund and Family Credit: the Legislation* (1996)
M.H.L.R.	Mental Health Law Reports
MHP	mental health problems
MIF	minimum income floor
MIG	minimum income guarantee
Migration Regulations	Employment and Support Allowance (Transitional Provisions, Housing Benefit and Council Tax Benefit (Existing Awards) (No.2) Regulations 2010
MP	Member of Parliament
MRSA	methicillin-resistant Staphylococcus aureus
MS	Medical Services
MWA Regulations	Jobseeker's Allowance (Mandatory Work Activity Scheme) Regulations 2011
MWAS Regulations	Jobseeker's Allowance (Mandatory Work Activity Scheme) Regulations 2011
NCB	National Coal Board
NDPD	Notes on the Diagnosis of Prescribed Diseases
NHS	National Health Service
NI	National Insurance
N.I..	Northern Ireland Law Reports
NICA	Northern Ireland Court of Appeal
NICom	Northern Ireland Commissioner
NICs	National Insurance Contributions
NINO	National Insurance Number
NIRS 2	National Insurance Recording System
N.L.J.	New Law Journal

NMC	Nursing and Midwifery Council
Northern Ireland Contributions and Benefits Act	Social Security Contributions and Benefits (Northern Ireland) Act 1992
N.P.C.	New Property Cases
NRCGT	non-resident capital gains tax
NTC Manual	Clerical procedures manual on tax credits
NUM	National Union of Mineworkers
NUS	National Union of Students
OCD	obsessive compulsive disorder
Ogus, Barendt and Wikeley	A. Ogus, E. Barendt and N. Wikeley, *The Law of Social Security* (1995)
Old Cases Act	Industrial Injuries and Diseases (Old Cases) Act 1975
OPB	One Parent Benefit
O.P.L.R.	Occupational Pensions Law Reports
OPSSAT	Office of the President of Social Security Appeal Tribunals
Overlapping Benefits Regulations	Social Security (Overlapping Benefits) Regulations 1975
P	retirement pension case
P. & C.R.	Property and Compensation Reports
para.	paragraph
Pay Regulations	Statutory Paternity Pay and Statutory Adoption Pay (General) Regulations 2002; Statutory Shared Parental Pay (General) Regulations 2014
PAYE	Pay As You Earn
PC	Privy Council
PCA	Personal Capability Assessment
PCC	Police and Crime Commissioner
PD	Practice Direction; prescribed disease
PENP	post-employment notice pay
Pens. L.R.	Pensions Law Reports
Pensions Act	Pension Schemes Act 1993
PEP	Personal Equity Plan
Persons Abroad Regulations	Social Security Benefit (Persons Abroad) Regulations 1975
Persons Residing Together Regulations	Social Security Benefit (Persons Residing Together) Regulations 1977
PIE	Period of Interruption of Employment
PILON	pay in lieu of notice
Pilot Scheme Regulations	Universal Credit (Work-Related Requirements) In Work Pilot Scheme and Amendment Regulations 2015
PIP	Personal Independence Payment
P.I.Q.R.	Personal Injuries and Quantum Reports
Polygamous Marriages Regulations	Social Security and Family Allowances

	(Polygamous Marriages) Regulations 1975
PPF	Pension Protection Fund
Prescribed Diseases Regulations	Social Security (Industrial Injuries) (Prescribed Diseases) Regulations 1985
PSCS	Pension Service Computer System
PSED	Public Sector Equality Duty
Pt	Part
PTA	pure tone audiometry
P.T.S.R.	Public and Third Sector Law Reports
PTWR 2000	Part-time Workers (Prevention of Less Favourable Treatment) Regulations 2000
PVS	private and voluntary sectors
Q.B.	Queen's Bench Law Reports
QBD	Queen's Bench Division
QCS Board	Quality Contract Scheme Board
QEF	qualifying earnings factor
QYP	qualifying young person
r.	rule
R	Reported Decision
R.C.	Rules of the Court of Session
REA	Reduced Earnings Allowance
reg.	regulation
RIPA	Regulation of Investigatory Powers Act 2000
RMO	Responsible Medical Officer
rr.	rules
RR	reference rate
RSI	repetitive strain injury
RTI	Real Time Information
R.V.R.	Rating & Valuation Reporter
s.	section
S	Scottish Decision
SAP	Statutory Adoption Pay
SAPOE Regulations	Jobseeker's Allowance (Schemes for Assisting Persons to Obtain Employment) Regulations 2013
SAWS	Seasonal Agricultural Work Scheme
SAYE	Save As You Earn
SB	Supplementary Benefit
SBAT	Supplementary Benefit Appeal Tribunal
SBC	Supplementary Benefits Commission
S.C.	Session Cases
S.C. (H.L.)	Session Cases (House of Lords)
S.C. (P.C.)	Session Cases (Privy Council)
S.C.C.R.	Scottish Criminal Case Reports
S.C.L.R.	Scottish Civil Law Reports

Sch.	Schedule
SDA	Severe Disablement Allowance
SDP	Severe Disability Premium
SEC	Social Entitlement Chamber
SEISS	Self-Employed Income Support Scheme
SEN	special educational needs
SERPS	State Earnings Related Pension Scheme
ShPP	statutory shared parental pay
ShPP Regulations	Statutory Shared Parental Pay (General) Regulations 2014
SI	Statutory Instrument
SIP	Share Incentive Plan
S.J.	Solicitors Journal
S.J.L.B.	Solicitors Journal Law Brief
SLAN	statement like an award notice
S.L.T.	Scots Law Times
SMP	Statutory Maternity Pay
SMP (General) Regulations 1986	Statutory Maternity Pay (General) Regulations 1986
SPC	State Pension Credit
SPC Regulations	State Pension Credit Regulations 2002
SPCA 2002	State Pension Credit Act 2002
SPL Regulations	Shared Parental Leave Regulations 2014
SPP	Statutory Paternity Pay
ss.	sections
SS (No.2) A 1980	Social Security (No.2) Act 1980
SSA 1975	Social Security Act 1975
SSA 1977	Social Security Act 1977
SSA 1978	Social Security Act 1978
SSA 1979	Social Security Act 1979
SSA 1981	Social Security Act 1981
SSA 1986	Social Security Act 1986
SSA 1988	Social Security Act 1988
SSA 1989	Social Security Act 1989
SSA 1990	Social Security Act 1990
SSA 1998	Social Security Act 1998
SSAA 1992	Social Security Administration Act 1992
SSAC	Social Security Advisory Committee
SSAT	Social Security Appeal Tribunal
SSCBA 1992	Social Security Contributions and Benefits Act 1992
SSCB(NI)A 1992	Social Security Contributions and Benefits (Northern Ireland) Act 1992
SSCPA 1992	Social Security (Consequential Provisions) Act 1992

SSD	Secretary of State for Defence
SSHBA 1982	Social Security and Housing Benefits Act 1982
SSHD	Secretary of State for the Home Department
SSI	Scottish Statutory Instrument
SS(MP)A 1977	Social Security (Miscellaneous Provisions) Act 1977
SSP	Statutory Sick Pay
SSP (General) Regulations	Statutory Sick Pay (General) Regulations 1982
SSPA 1975	Social Security Pensions Act 1975
SSPP	statutory shared parental pay
SSWP	Secretary of State for Work and Pensions
State Pension Credit Regulations	State Pension Credit Regulations 2002
S.T.C.	Simon's Tax Cases
S.T.C. (S.C.D.)	Simon's Tax Cases: Special Commissioners' Decisions
S.T.I.	Simon's Tax Intelligence
STIB	Short-Term Incapacity Benefit
subpara.	subparagraph
subs.	subsection
T	Tribunal of Commissioners' Decision
T.C.	Tax Cases
TCA 1999	Tax Credits Act 1999
TCA 2002	Tax Credits Act 2002
TCC	Technology and Construction Court
TCEA 2007	Tribunals, Courts and Enforcement Act 2007
TCGA 1992	Taxation of Chargeable Gains Act 2002
TCTM	*Tax Credits Technical Manual*
TEC	Treaty Establishing the European Community
TENS	transcutaneous electrical nerve stimulation
TEU	Treaty on European Union
TFC	tax-free childcare
TFEU	Treaty on the Functioning of the European Union
TIOPA 2010	Taxation (International and Other Provisions) Act 2010
TMA 1970	Taxes Management Act 1970
T.R.	Taxation Reports
Transfer of Functions Act	Social Security Contributions (Transfer of Functions etc.) Act 1999
Tribunal Procedure Rules	Tribunal Procedure (First-tier Tribunal)(Social Entitlement Chamber) Rules 2008
UB	Unemployment Benefit
UC	Universal Credit
UC Regs 2013	Universal Credit Regulations 2013
UCITS	Undertakings for Collective Investments in Transferable Securities

UKAIT	UK Asylum and Immigration Tribunal
UKBA	UK Border Agency of the Home Office
UKCC	United Kingdom Central Council for Nursing, Midwifery and Health Visiting
UKFTT	United Kingdom First-tier Tribunal Tax Chamber
UKHL	United Kingdom House of Lords
U.K.H.R.R.	United Kingdom Human Rights Reports
UKSC	United Kingdom Supreme Court
UKUT	United Kingdom Upper Tribunal
UN	United Nations
Universal Credit Regulations	Universal Credit Regulations 2013
URL	uniform resource locator
USI Regs	Social Security (Unemployment, Sickness and Invalidity Benefit) Regulations 1983
USI Regulations	Social Security (Unemployment, Sickness and Invalidity Benefit) Regulations 1983
UT	Upper Tribunal
VAT	Value Added Tax
VCM	vinyl chloride monomer
Vol.	Volume
VWF	Vibration White Finger
W	Welsh Decision
WCA	Work Capability Assessment
WCAt	limited capability for work assessment
WFHRAt	Work-Focused Health-Related Assessment
WFI	work-focused interview
WFTC	Working Families Tax Credit
Wikeley, Annotations	N. Wikeley, "Annotations to Jobseekers Act 1995 (c.18)" in *Current Law Statutes Annotated* (1995)
Wikeley, Ogus and Barendt	Wikeley, Ogus and Barendt, *The Law of Social Security* (2002)
Withdrawal Act	European Union (Withdrawal) Act 2018
Withdrawal Agreement Act	European Union (Withdrawal Agreement) Act 2020
W.L.R.	Weekly Law Reports
WLUK	Westlaw UK
Workmen's Compensation Acts	Workmen's Compensation Acts 1925 to 1945
WP	Widow's Pension
WPS	War Pensions Scheme
WRA 2007	Welfare Reform Act 2007
WRA 2009	Welfare Reform Act 2009
WRA 2012	Welfare Reform Act 2012
W-RA Regulations	Employment and Support Allowance (Work-Related Activity) Regulations 2011
WRAAt	Work-Related Activity Assessment

PART I

SOCIAL SECURITY STATUTES

Child Support Act 1991

(1991 c.48)

SECTION REPRODUCED

43.   Recovery of child support maintenance by deduction from benefit.   1.1

SCHEDULE REPRODUCED

Sch.1, paras 4 and 8

GENERAL NOTE

This book does not deal directly with the system of child support maintenance.   1.2
For a full treatment, see E. Jacobs, *Child Support: the Legislation.*

From its inception the child support legislation provided for certain income-related benefits to be reduced where a parent on benefit failed to cooperate in the process of assessing maintenance from an absent parent (now referred to as a non-resident parent) (see ss.6 and 46 of the Child Support Act 1991). However, s.6 and s.46 were both repealed with effect from July 14, 2008 (see Child Maintenance and Other Payments Act 2008 (c.6) s.15(a) and (b) and s.58 and Sch.8 so far as it relates to the repeal of ss.6 and 46, and the Child Maintenance and Other Payments Act 2008 (Commencement) Order 2008 (SI 2008/1476) (c.67) arts 2(2)(a) and (c) and 2(3) (a) and (c)). Article 2(4) of the Commencement Order provided that the repeal of s.6 did not apply in relation to "existing cases" (i.e. those where immediately before July 14, 2008 a maintenance calculation was in force or an effective date had been set (art.2(5)). Thus those claimants were still subject to the s.6 compulsion but as s.46 had been repealed they could not be penalised for failing to apply for child support. However, with effect from October 27, 2008 art.3(a) of the Child Maintenance and Other Payments Act 2008 (Commencement No.3 and Transitional and Savings Provisions) Order 2008 (SI 2008/2548) (c.110) brought s.15(a) fully into force and art.4 of that Order provides that "existing cases" are to be treated as if the parent with care had made an application under s.4 of the Child Support Act 1991. The consequence of the repeal of s.46 is that all reduced benefit decisions ceased to have effect on July 14, 2008.

In addition, the original child support scheme ("the 1993 scheme") provided that where an absent parent was on income support or income-based JSA, a deduction could be made from his income support or income-based JSA as a contribution towards child support maintenance. This deduction still applies in cases which have not yet been "converted" to the "new" child support scheme ("the 2003 scheme") introduced by the Child Support, Pensions and Social Security Act 2000 (see below) and since October 6, 2003 and October 27, 2008 has also applied to state pension credit and income-related ESA respectively. (This deduction can also be made from an absent parent's contribution-based JSA/contributory ESA if he would be entitled to income-based JSA/income-related ESA at the same rate but for the fact that he is getting contribution-based JSA/contributory ESA; in addition, deductions for arrears of child support maintenance can be made from contribution-based JSA/contributory ESA in certain circumstances (see further the note to s.43).) There is also provision for the deduction to be made from universal credit (see para.10 of Sch.6 to the Universal Credit, Personal Independence Payment, Jobseeker's Allowance and Employment and Support Allowance (Claims and Payments) Regulations 2013 (SI 2013/380) in Vol.III in this series).

1.3   However, for those cases to which the 2003 scheme applies, a deduction of £5 in respect of the flat rate of child support maintenance can be made from a greatly expanded list of benefits (see further the note to s.43). In relation to the third child support scheme ("the 2012 scheme") (see below) the deduction is £7.

Those parts of the child support legislation relevant to the deduction are included in this book. Readers are referred to the 2002 edition of this volume for the provisions relating to deductions as a contribution towards child maintenance under the 1993 scheme.

On March 3, 2003 the long-delayed changes to the child support scheme introduced by the Child Support, Pensions and Social Security Act 2000 finally came into force (see the Child Support, Pensions and Social Security Act 2000 (Commencement No.12) Order 2003 (SI 2003/192), as amended by the Child Support, Pensions and Social Security Act 2000 (Commencement No.13) Order 2003 (SI 2003/346)). The "new" rules only applied to all new (and non-linking) child support applications (a new application was one with an effective date on or after March 3, 2003); most existing cases were to be "converted" at a future date, although some may transfer earlier. Thus, for example, if after March 3, 2003, a person with a existing child support assessment made a new application for a different child with a different non-resident parent the "new" scheme applied to both applications. For full details of the 2003 scheme and when it applies, see E. Jacobs, *Child Support: the Legislation*.

Further substantial reform to the child support system has been made by the Child Maintenance and Other Payments Act 2008. For the details of this see E. Jacobs, *Child Support: the Legislation*. This third child support scheme ("the 2012 scheme") applied to certain new applications made on or after December 10, 2012 and certain cases linked to those applications. It was extended to certain other new cases on July 29, 2013. It commenced for all other new cases on November 25, 2013 but only started to apply to existing cases in 2014.

[¹ Applications by those claiming or receiving benefit

1.4   **6.**—[² . . .]]

AMENDMENTS

1. Child Support, Pensions and Social Security Act 2000 s.3 (March 3, 2003).
2. Child Maintenance and Other Payments Act 2008 (c.6) s.15(a), s.58 and Sch.8 (July 14, 2008 and October 27, 2008).

Special cases

[¹ Recovery of child support maintenance by deduction from benefit

1.5   **43.**—[² (1) The power of the Secretary of State to make regulations under section 5 of the Social Security Administration Act 1992 by virtue of subsection (1)(p) of that section may be exercised with a view to securing the making of payments in respect of child support maintenance by a non-resident parent.

(2) The reference in subsection (1) to the making of payments in respect of child support maintenance includes the recovery of—

(a) arrears of child support maintenance, and

(b) fees payable under section 6 of the Child Maintenance and Other Payments Act 2008.]

(3) For the purposes of this section, the benefits to which section 5 of the 1992 Act applies are to be taken as including war disablement pensions

and war widows' pensions (within the meaning of section 150 of the Social Security Contributions and Benefits Act 1992 (interpretation)).]

AMENDMENTS

1. Child Support, Pensions and Social Security Act 2000 s.21 (March 3, 2003).
2. Welfare Reform Act 2012 s.139 (February 4, 2014).

DEFINITIONS

"child support maintenance"—see Child Support Act 1991 s.54.
"non-resident parent"—*ibid.*

GENERAL NOTE

The long-delayed changes to the child support scheme introduced by the Child   1.6
Support, Pensions and Social Security Act 2000 finally came into force on March 3, 2003. The changes were implemented in stages depending on the type of case (see the note at the beginning of the Child Support Act 1991 above). They included the substitution of this section and of Pt I of Sch.1 to the 1991 Act. The new form contained some significant differences from the previous provisions.

This form of s.43 and para.4 of Pt I of Sch.1 to the 1991 Act apply in those cases to which the "new" child support scheme applies ("the 2003 scheme") (see art.3 of and the Schedule to the Child Support, Pensions and Social Security Act 2000 (Commencement No.12) Order 2003 (SI 2003/192)—broadly these are applications for child support maintenance with an effective date on or after March 3, 2003 and certain cases where there is an existing assessment).

Note that there is now a third child support scheme ("the 2012 scheme"). See the note at the beginning of the Child Support Act 1991 above for when this applies and see further below.

Note also that s.43 was further amended on February 4, 2014. The main effect of   1.7
the amendments is to also allow for the recovery by deduction from benefit of fees payable under s.6 of the Child Maintenance and Other Payments Act 2008 by the non-resident parent (subs.(2)(b)).

Under the 2003 scheme, unless the nil rate is applicable, a £5 flat rate of child support maintenance applies for non-resident parents in receipt of certain prescribed benefits (although a different amount may apply under the transitional arrangements when a case converts to the new system). (For when the nil rate is applicable see para.5 of Sch.1 to the 1991 Act and reg.5 of the Child Support (Maintenance Calculations and Special Cases) Regulations 2000 (SI 2001/155) in E. Jacobs, *Child Support: the Legislation.*)

This section, Sch.1 paras 4 and 8 and reg.4 of the Child Support (Maintenance Calculations and Special Cases) Regulations 2000, together with Sch.9B to the Claims and Payments Regulations 1987 (see Vol.III of this series), provide for the deduction of the £5 flat rate from the non-resident parent's benefit and its payment to the parent with care. The deduction will be made if either the non-resident parent or his partner is getting income support, income-based JSA, income-related ESA, state pension credit or universal credit. It is halved if the non-resident parent's partner is also a non-resident parent with a child support maintenance calculation in force. The flat-rate deduction will also be made if the non-resident parent is in receipt of any of the following: contribution-based JSA, contributory ESA, incapacity benefit, severe disablement allowance, retirement pension, carer's allowance, maternity allowance, industrial injuries benefit, bereavement allowance, widowed mother's allowance, widowed parent's allowance, widow's pension, war disablement pension, war widow's or widower's pension, an Armed Forces Compensation Payment, a social security benefit paid by a country other than the UK, or a training allowance (other than work-based learning for young people or, in Scotland, Skillseekers training). In addition, except where income support, income-based JSA, income-related ESA or state pension credit is payable to the non-resident parent or his partner, a deduction of £1 for arrears of child support maintenance can be made from any of those benefits or allowances. A deduction can only be made from one benefit in any one week (para.2(2) of Sch.9B to the Claims and Payment Regulations). No deduction will be made if this would result in less than 10p of the benefit remaining payable (para.2(3) of Sch.9B). Note also that if the non-resident parent is regarded as having "shared care" (i.e. for at least 52 nights in a year), the amount of child support maintenance payable will be nil and no deduction will be made (see para.8(2) of Sch.1 to the 1991 Act). For a discussion of the priority to be given to the flat-rate deduction in relation to other deductions, see the note to reg.35 of the Claims and Payments Regulations in Vol.III of this series.

1.8   Under the 2012 scheme (the third child support scheme—see the note at the beginning of the Child Support Act 1991 as to when this applies), the rules for deductions from benefit were originally the same as under the 2003 scheme (in relation to the 2012 scheme see reg.44 of the Child Support Maintenance Calculations Regulations 2012 (SI 2012/2677) rather than reg.4 of the Child Support (Maintenance Calculations and Special Cases) Regulations 2000). However, from November 25, 2013, the deduction from benefit where maintenance liability has been assessed under the 2012 scheme was increased from £5 to £7. This increased rate does not apply to cases assessed under the 2003 scheme.

There is a right of appeal to a tribunal against a decision to make deductions from benefit in respect of child support maintenance, although there may be little scope for argument if the legislation has been correctly applied.

For the previous form of s.43, Sch.1 para.5(4) and regs 13 and 28 and Schs 4 and 5 of the Child Support (Maintenance Assessments and Special Cases) Regulations 1992, under which (together with para.7A of Sch.9 to the Claims and Payments Regulations 1987 (see Vol.III of this series)) a deduction of £7.40 can be made from the income support, income-based JSA, income-related ESA, or state pension credit of an absent parent (or contribution-based JSA/contributory ESA if the absent parent would be entitled to income-based JSA/income-related ESA at the same rate but for the fact that he is getting contribution-based JSA/contributory ESA, or if the absent parent is getting both contribution-based and income-based JSA/contributory ESA and income-related ESA and his income-based JSA/income-related ESA is insufficient for the deduction to be made: see para.1(1), definition of "specified benefit", and para.1(2) and (3) of Sch.9 to the Claims and Payments Regulations 1987 in Vol.III of this series) as a contribution towards the maintenance of his children, see the 2002 edition of this volume. These provisions still apply for existing cases that have not been converted to the "new" child support scheme (see the note at the beginning of the Child Support Act 1991, above). Note also that in existing cases deductions for arrears of child support maintenance can be made from contribution-based JSA/contributory ESA (even where there would be no entitlement to income-based JSA/income-related ESA) in certain circumstances (see para.7B of Sch.9 to the Claims and Payments Regulations). If the full £7.40 cannot be deducted because other deductions are being made which have a higher priority, £3.70 can be deducted (see paras 7A(4), 8(1) and 9 of Sch.9 to the Claims and Payments Regulations). Contributions towards child maintenance are seventh in priority (out of 10) of the deductions covered by Sch.9.

1.9   In *CCS/16904/1996* the Commissioner conducted a detailed analysis of the legislation on deductions in place of child support maintenance. He referred to the fact that s.43(2) allowed regulations to be made for deducting payments in place of child support maintenance from various benefits and reg.28(2) of the Child Support (Maintenance Assessments and Special Cases) Regulations 1992 (SI 1992/1815) (see the 2002 edition of this volume for this regulation) defined the amount of the payments (now see para.4 of Sch.1, together with reg.4(3) of the Child Support (Maintenance Calculations and Special Cases) Regulations) but there was nothing that in so many words imposed an obligation on an absent parent to make such payments. He concluded that the legal basis for liability to make payments in place of child support maintenance was provided by the general duty to maintain a child under s.1 of the 1991 Act. This required the payment of such "maintenance" (not just child support maintenance) as determined in accordance with the provisions of the Act. Thus if it was decided that s.43 applied, this gave rise to a liability on the absent parent to make payment and a corresponding entitlement of the parent with care to receive the amounts deducted by the Secretary of State. The decision was appealed to the Court of Appeal under the name of *Dollar v Child Support Officer*, reported as *R(CS) 7/99*, but there was no specific challenge to the Commissioner's conclusion on this issue. The Court of Appeal proceeded on the basis that there was a liability to make the payments identified in s.43(2). The Commissioner states in *R(CS) 5/05* that he therefore sees no reason to depart from what he said in *CCS/16904/1996*.

Note also *R. (Plumb) v Secretary of State for Work and Pensions* [2002] EWHC 1125 (Admin), March 22, 2002, unreported (Admin. Ct). The claimant contended that the £5.10 deduction (as it then was) from his JSA made as a contribution towards the maintenance of his child affected the quality and extent of his contact with his daughter and thus was in breach of art.8 of the European Convention on Human Rights (right to family life). The Court accepted that such a deduction was capable of amounting to an interference with an art.8 right but on the facts of this case this was far from being established. Furthermore, any interference with the claimant's right under art.8(1) was justified under art.8(2).

[¹ Reduced benefit decisions

46.—[² . . .]]   1.10

AMENDMENTS

1. Child Support, Pensions and Social Security Act 2000 s.19 (March 3, 2003).
2. Child Maintenance and Other Payments Act 2008 (c.6) s.15(b) s.58 and Sch.8 (July 14, 2008).

SCHEDULE 1   **Section 11**

MAINTENANCE CALCULATIONS

[¹ PART I

CALCULATION OF WEEKLY AMOUNT OF CHILD SUPPORT MAINTENANCE

Flat rate

4.—(1) Except in a case falling within sub-paragraph (2), a flat rate of [³£7] is payable if the   1.11
nil rate does not apply and—
    (a) the non-resident parent's [² gross] weekly income is £100 or less; or
    (b) he receives any benefit, pension or allowance prescribed for the purposes of this paragraph of this sub-paragraph; or
    (c) he or his partner (if any) receives any benefit prescribed for the purposes of this paragraph of this sub-paragraph.
  (2) A flat rate of a prescribed amount is payable if the nil rate does not apply and—
    (a) the non-resident parent has a partner who is also a non-resident parent;
    (b) the partner is a person with respect to whom a maintenance calculation is in force; and
    (c) the non-resident parent or his partner receives any benefit prescribed under sub-paragraph (1)(c).
  (3) The benefits, pensions and allowances which may be prescribed for the purposes of sub-paragraph (1)(b) include ones paid to the non-resident parent under the law of a place outside the United Kingdom.

[Paras 5 to 7 not reproduced.]

Shared care—flat rate

8.—(1) This paragraph applies only if—   1.12

(a) the rate of child support maintenance payable is a flat rate; and

(b) that rate applies because the non-resident parent falls within paragraph 4(1)(b) or (c) or 4(2).

(2) [⁴ If the care of a qualifying child is, or is to be, shared] as mentioned in paragraph 7(2) for at least 52 nights during a prescribed 12-month period, the amount of child support maintenance payable by the non-resident parent to the person with care of that child is nil.]

[The rest of the Schedule has not been reproduced.]

AMENDMENTS

1. Child Support, Pensions and Social Security Act 2000 s.1(3) and Sch.1 (March 3, 2003).

2. Child Maintenance and Other Payments Act 2008 Sch.4 para.2 (October 8, 2012 for the purpose of making regulations and other dates).

3. Child Maintenance and Other Payments Act 2008 Sch.4 para.4(b) (November 25, 2013 subject to savings specified in SI 2013/2947 art.3).

4. Child Maintenance and Other Payments Act 2008 Sch.4 para.7 (October 8, 2012 for the purpose of making regulations and other dates).

Social Security Contributions and Benefits Act 1992

(1992 c.4)

SECTIONS REPRODUCED

PART VII

INCOME-RELATED BENEFITS

General

1.13   123.   Income-related benefits.

Income support

124.   Income support.
125.   *Repealed.*
126.   Trade disputes.
127.   Effect of return to work.

Family credit

128.   *Repealed.*

Disability working allowance

129.   *Repealed.*

8

General

PART VIII

THE SOCIAL FUND

PART XIII

GENERAL

Interpretation

Subordinate legislation

Short title, commencement and extent

PART VII

INCOME-RELATED BENEFITS

General

Income-related benefits

123.—(1) Prescribed schemes shall provide for the following benefits (in   **1.14**
this Act referred to as "income-related benefits")—
    (a) income support;

   (b) [⁴. . .];
   (c) [⁴. . .];
   (d) housing benefit; and
[¹(e) council tax benefit.]
   (2) The Secretary of State shall make copies of schemes prescribed under subsection (1)(a), (b) or (c) above available for public inspection at local offices of [³ the Department of Work and Pensions] at all reasonable hours without payment.

[Subss. (3)–(4) omitted as applying only to housing benefit and council tax benefit.]

AMENDMENTS

   1. Local Government Finance Act 1992 Sch.9 para.1(1) (April 1, 1993).
   2. Tax Credits Act 1999 Sch.1 paras 1 and 2(f) (October 5, 1999).
   3. Secretaries of State for Education and Skills and for Work and Pensions Order 2002 (SI 2002/1397) art.12 and Sch. para.9 (June 27, 2002).
   4. Tax Credits Act 2002 s.60 and Sch.6 (April 8, 2003).

Income support

Income support

1.15   **124.**—(1) A person in Great Britain is entitled to income support if—
   [¹(a) he is of or over the age of 16;]
[⁴(aa) he has not attained the qualifying age for state pension credit;]
   (b) he has no income or his income does not exceed the applicable amount;
   (c) he is not engaged in remunerative work and, if he is a member of a [⁶ couple], the other member is not so engaged; [¹. . .]
   [¹(d) except in such circumstances as may be prescribed, he is not receiving relevant education;
   (e) he falls within a prescribed category of person; [⁵ . . .]
   (f) he is not entitled to a jobseeker's allowance and, if he is a member of a [⁶ couple], the other member of the couple is not [³, and the couple are not,] entitled to an income-based jobseeker's allowance.] [⁴ [⁹. . .]
   (g) if he is a member of a [⁶ couple], the other member of the couple is not entitled to state pension credit.] [⁸ ; and
   (h) he is not entitled to an employment and support allowance and, if he is a member of a couple, the other member of the couple is not entitled to an income-related employment and support allowance.]
   [¹⁰(1A) Regulations under paragraph (e) of subsection (1) must secure that a person who-
   (a) is not a member of a couple, and
   (b) is responsible for, and a member of the same household as, a child under the age of 5,
falls within a category of person prescribed under that paragraph.]
   (2) [². . .].
   (3) [². . .].
   (4) Subject to subsection (5) below, where a person is entitled to income support, then—

(a) if he has no income, the amount shall be the applicable amount; and

(b) if he has income, the amount shall be the difference between his income and the applicable amount.

(5) Where a person is entitled to income support for a period to which this subsection applies, the amount payable for that period shall be calculated in such manner as may be prescribed.

(6) Subsection (5) above applies—

(a) to a period of less than a week which is the whole period for which income support is payable; and

(b) to any other period of less than a week for which it is payable.

[[8] (7) In this section, "income-related employment and support allowance" means an income-related allowance under Part 1 of the Welfare Reform Act 2007 (employment and support allowance).]

AMENDMENTS

1. Jobseekers Act 1995 Sch.2 para.30 (October 7, 1996).
2. Jobseekers Act 1995 Sch.3 (October 7, 1996).
3. Welfare Reform and Pensions Act 1999 Sch.8 para.28 (March 19, 2001).
4. State Pension Credit Act 2002 s.14 and Sch.2 paras 1 and 2 (October 6, 2003).
5. State Pension Credit Act 2002 s.21 and Sch.3 (October 6, 2003).
6. Civil Partnership Act 2004 s.254(1) Sch.24 para.42 (December 5, 2005).
7. Welfare Reform Act 2007 s.28 and Sch.3 para.9 (October 27, 2008).
8. Welfare Reform Act 2007 s.28 and Sch.3 para.10 (October 27, 2008).
9. Welfare Reform Act 2007 s.67 and Sch.8 (October 27, 2008).
10. Welfare Reform Act 2009 s.3(1) (May 21, 2012). (Note that s.3(1) had been amended before it came into force. Section 58(1) and (2) of the Welfare Reform Act 2012, brought into force on March 20, 2012 by art.2(1)(c) of the Welfare Reform Act 2012 (Commencement No. 1) Order 2012 (SI 2012/863) replaced "7" with "5" in the new subs.(1A)(b)).

DEFINITIONS

"Great Britain"—see s.172(a).
"income-based jobseeker's allowance"—see s.137(1) and Jobseekers Act s.35(1).
"couple"—see s.137(1).
"prescribed"—*ibid.*
"qualifying age for state pension credit"—*ibid.*

GENERAL NOTE

Subsection (1)

Here the general conditions of entitlement to income support are set out. Note the amendments made on October 7, 1996, on October 6, 2003, and on October 27, 2009 as a consequence of the introduction of, respectively, jobseeker's allowance ("JSA"), state pension credit ("SPC") and employment and support allowance ("ESA") (see below). All of the conditions must be satisfied for there to be entitlement to income support (*CIS 166/1994*). There is also a capital test under s.134(1). 1.16

If there is entitlement under this subsection, the amount of income support is laid down in subss.(4)–(6).

There is no contributions test or requirement of citizenship (but see s.115 of the Immigration and Asylum Act 1999 on "persons subject to immigration control"). However, although a person qualifies if he is in Great Britain, an habitual residence condition was introduced on August 1, 1994 and a right to reside condition on May

1, 2004. See the definition of "person from abroad" in reg.21AA of the Income Support (General) Regulations and the notes to that definition. Regulation 4 of the Income Support Regulations allows an award to continue for a short period of temporary absence from Great Britain, but otherwise income support cannot be paid to a person outside Great Britain. See *R(IS) 4/99* and *R(IS) 9/98*, which hold that income support is not a social security benefit within art.4(1) of EC reg.1408/71. Although income support has been listed by the UK Government as included in the new category of "special non-contributory benefits" to which reg.1408/71 applies from June 1, 1992 (see art.4(2a) and Annex IIa), such benefits cannot be "exported" (i.e. paid where the claimant is in another Member State) (art.10a). Article 10a provides for the granting of such benefits "exclusively in the territory of the Member State in which [the person] reside[s], in accordance with the legislation of that State". ("Resides" means "habitually resides": art.1(h).) It was argued in *Perry v Chief Adjudication Officer, The Times*, October 20, 1998, also reported as part of *R(IS) 4/99*, that art.10a conferred a positive right to income support on the claimant because of his habitual residence in the UK, and that he remained entitled to income support by virtue of that right, even during periods of temporary absence. However, the Court of Appeal rejected this argument. The language of art.10a made it clear that special non-contributory benefits were to be granted in accordance with the domestic law of the Member State. Presence in Great Britain was a requirement of the UK's legislation (subject to the exceptions in reg.4 of the Income Support Regulations) and this was not incompatible with art.10a. The Court of Appeal also agreed with the Commissioner that the claimant could not rely on art.2(4) of EC Regulation 1247/92 (the Regulation which introduced the June 1992 amendment) to export an entitlement to income support in respect of periods before June 1, 1992.

Paragraph (a)

1.17   From October 7, 1996 the minimum age for income support is again 16 (as it was until September 1988 before most 16- and 17-year-olds were excluded). But to be entitled a person must fall within a prescribed category (para.(e)). See reg.4ZA of and Sch.1B to the Income Support Regulations for these categories. Note that a person aged 16 to 18 in relevant education is still only entitled to income support in certain circumstances (para.(d) and reg.13 of the Income Support Regulations).

The reduction in the lower age limit is a consequence of the replacement from October 7, 1996 of income support by income-based JSA for people who are required to be available for work as a condition of receiving benefit. To be entitled to income-based JSA a person must in general be at least 18 (Jobseekers Act s.3(1)(f)(i)), although there are exceptions, which are similar, but not identical, to those that used to operate for income support (see the 1996 edition of J. Mesher and P. Wood, *Income Support, the Social Fund and Family Credit: the Legislation* for reg.13A of and Sch.1A to the Income Support Regulations and the further escape under s.25; these provisions were revoked on October 7, 1996). Entitlement to JSA, SPC or ESA excludes entitlement to income support (paras (f)–(h)).

Paragraph (aa)

1.18   State Pension Credit was introduced on October 6, 2003. Paragraph (aa) rules out any possibility that a claimant could be entitled to both state pension credit and income support by providing that no person who has reached "the qualifying age for state pension credit" can be entitled to income support. "The qualifying age for state pension credit" is defined by s.137(1) below. The effect of that definition is that the qualifying age was 60 for both men and women until April 2010 and will now increase by stages to 65 in line with the increase in pensionable age for a woman. It remains possible for the partner of a person over 60 to claim income support in some circumstances—see para.(g) below.

Paragraph (b)

1.19   The person's income (which includes the income of the claimant's family) must be less than the applicable amount (effectively the figure set for the family's requirements under s.135). However, note that as a consequence of the removal of amounts for children from income support (with effect from April 6, 2004, except in "transitional cases"—see the note to reg.17 of the Income Support Regulations), only a partner's income will count as that of the claimant and the applicable amount will no longer include any personal allowances for children, the family premium, the disabled child premium or an enhanced disability premium for a child.

CIS 166/1994 confirms that the conditions in subs.(1) are cumulative. The fact that the claimant was not working in his business and so para.(c) did not apply, did not mean that income from that business could not potentially disentitle him under para.(b). See the notes to reg.30 of the Income Support Regulations.

Paragraph (c)

The introduction of the condition in para.(c) marked an important change from the supplementary benefit rules. If either the claimant or his partner is in remunerative work (defined in regs 5 and 6 of the Income Support Regulations) there is no entitlement to income support. For supplementary benefit, this condition was only applied to the claimant. The transitional protection announced on April 28, 1988 (see p.198 of the 1998 edition of *Mesher and Wood*) has remained on an extra-statutory basis.

Note that from October 7, 1996 the limit for remunerative work in the case of a partner is 24 hours or more a week (Income Support Regulations reg.5(1A)). It remains 16 or more for the claimant.

1.20

Paragraph (d)

See regs 12 and 13 of the Income Support Regulations.

1.21

Paragraph (e)

From October 7, 1996 only certain categories of people are entitled to income support. See reg.4ZA of and Sch.1B to the Income Support Regulations for these categories. They are similar to those groups who formerly were exempt from the requirement to be available for work for the purposes of income support (see Sch.1 to the Income Support Regulations which was revoked on October 7, 1996), but there are some differences.

1.22

Paragraph (f)

Entitlement to JSA excludes entitlement to income support (any "top-up" to a person's contribution-based JSA will be by way of income-based JSA, not income support); if the claimant is a member of a couple, he will also not qualify for income support if his partner is entitled to income-based JSA or if he and his partner are entitled together to "joint-claim" JSA. But although entitlement to income support and JSA is mutually exclusive, some people may be eligible for either, i.e. those who fall into a prescribed category for income support but who also satisfy the labour market conditions for JSA. See the notes to reg.4ZA of the Income Support Regulations for discussion of the position of such claimants and of the fact that the raising of the limit for remunerative work for partners to 24 hours a week from October 7, 1996 may create a "better-off" problem for some claimants.

1.23

Paragraph (g)

By virtue of para.(aa) above, a claimant who has reached the qualifying age for state pension credit cannot be entitled to income support. Claimants who have not themselves reached the qualifying age for state pension credit, but who have partners above that age, may claim income support as long as their partners are not actually entitled to state pension credit. Since, under s.1 SSAA 1992, there can be no entitlement to state pension credit without making a claim, the effect is that couples with one member who has reached the qualifying age for state pension credit and one member who has not (and who are not already in receipt of state pension credit) can choose to claim either income support, JSA, or ESA (according to the circumstances of the member who has not reached pensionable

1.24

age), or state pension credit. It will normally be advantageous to claim state pension credit.

Paragraph (h)

1.25   Entitlement to ESA excludes entitlement to IS (as does a partner's entitlement to income-related (but not contribution-related) ESA). See the note on the Introduction of ESA in the commentary to para.7 of Sch.1B (below).

Subsection (1A)

1.26   See para.1 of Sch.IB to the Income Support Regulations and the notes to that paragraph.

Subsection (4)

1.27   This provision sets out the basic means test calculation for income support. Providing that the conditions of entitlement imposed by subs.(1) and the capital test under s.134(1) are satisfied, the claimant's income is set against his applicable amount, calculated according to regs 17–22 of the Income Support (General) Regulations. The difference is the amount of benefit. The claimant's income includes that of the other members of his family, except in prescribed cases (s.136(1)). Note that as a consequence of the removal of amounts for children from income support (with effect from April 6, 2004, except in "transitional cases"—see further the note to reg.17 of the Income Support Regulations), only a partner's income will count as that of the claimant.

Subsections (5) and (6)

1.28   These provisions allow regulations to deal with entitlement for part-weeks. See regs 73–77 of the Income Support (General) Regulations.

Severe hardship cases

1.29   **125.**—[¹. . .]

AMENDMENT

1. Jobseekers Act 1995 Sch.3 (October 7, 1996).

Trade disputes

1.30   **126.**—(1) This section applies to a person, other than a child or a person of a prescribed description—
(a) who [² is prevented from being entitled to a jobseeker's allowance by section 14 of the Jobseekers Act 1995 (trade disputes)]; or
(b) who would be so [² prevented] if otherwise entitled to that benefit, except during any period shown by the person to be a period of incapacity for work [¹ . . .] or to be within the maternity period.
(2) In subsection (1) above "the maternity period" means the period commencing at the beginning of the 6th week before the expected week of confinement and ending at the end of the 7th week after the week in which confinement takes place.
(3) For the purposes of calculating income support—
(a) so long as this section applies to a person who is not a member of a family, the applicable amount shall be disregarded;
(b) so long as it applies to a person who is a member of a family but is not a member of a [⁴ couple], the portion of the applicable amount which is included in respect of him shall be disregarded;
(c) so long as it applies to one of the members of a [⁴ couple]—

      (i) if the applicable amount consists only of an amount in respect of them, it shall be reduced to one half; and

      (ii) if it includes other amounts, the portion of it which is included in respect of them shall be reduced to one-half and any further portion of it which is included in respect of the member of the couple to whom this section applies shall be disregarded;

(d) so long as it applies to both members of a [⁴ couple]—

      (i) if neither of them is responsible for a child or person of a pre-scribed description who is a member of the same household, the applicable amount shall be disregarded; and

      (ii) in any other case, the portion of the applicable amount which is included in respect of them and any further portion of it which is included in respect of either of them shall be disre-garded.

(4) Where a reduction under subsection (3)(c) above would not produce a sum which is a multiple of 5p, the reduction shall be to the nearest lower sum which is such a multiple.

(5) Where this section applies to a person for any period, then, except so far as regulations provide otherwise—

(a) in calculating the entitlement to income support of that person or a member of his family the following shall be treated as his income and shall not be disregarded—

      (i) any payment which he or a member of his family receives or is entitled to obtain by reason of the person to whom this section applies being without employment for that period; and

      (ii) without prejudice to the generality of sub-paragraph (i) above, any amount which becomes or would on an application duly made, become available to him in that period by way of repay-ment of income tax deducted from his [³ taxable earnings (as defined by section 10 of the Income Tax (Earnings and Pensions) Act 2003 under PAYE regulations]; and

(b) any payment by way of income support for that period or any part of it which apart from this paragraph would be made to him, or to a person whose applicable amount is aggregated with his—

      (i) shall not be made if the weekly rate of payment is equal to or less than the relevant sum; or

      (ii) if it is more than the relevant sum, shall be at a weekly rate equal to the difference.

(6) In respect of any period less than a week, subsection (5) above shall have effect subject to such modifications as may be prescribed.

(7) Subject to subsection (8) below, the "relevant sum" for the purposes of subsection (5) above shall be [⁵£41.00].

(8) If an order under section 150 of the Administration Act (annual up-rating) has the effect of increasing payments of income support, from the time when the order comes into force there shall be substituted, in subsection (5)(b) above, for the references to the sum for the time being mentioned in it references to a sum arrived at by—

(a) increasing that sum by the percentage by which the personal allow-ance under paragraph 1(1) of Part I of Schedule 2 to the Income Support (General) Regulations 1987 for a single person aged not less than 25 has been increased by the order; and

(b) if the sum so increased is not a multiple of 50p, disregarding the remainder if it is 25p and, if it is not, rounding it up or down to the nearest 50p,

and the order shall state the substituted sum.

AMENDMENTS

1. Social Security (Incapacity for Work) Act 1994 Sch.1 para.31 (April 13, 1995).
2. Jobseekers Act 1995 Sch.2 para.31 (October 7, 1996).
3. Income Tax (Earnings and Pensions) Act 2003 Sch.6 Pt 2 para.179 (April 6, 2003).
4. Civil Partnership Act 2004 s.254 and Sch.24 para.43 (December 5, 2005).
5. Social Security Benefits Up-rating Order 2020 (SI 2020/234) art.23 (April 6, 2020).

DERIVATION

Social Security Act 1986 s.23.

DEFINITIONS

"child"—see s.137(1).
"couple"—*ibid.*
"family"—*ibid.*
"prescribed"—*ibid.*
"the Administration Act"—see s.174.

GENERAL NOTE

1.31   The trade dispute rule, long an important part of the supplementary benefit scheme, was considerably simplified in the income support rules, although most of the stringency remains.

Subsection (1)

1.32   The rule applies to anyone other than a child or qualifying young person (Income Support Regulations reg.14) who is disentitled to old style JSA, or would be disentitled, under s.14 of the old style Jobseekers Act 1995. Thus the income support rule depends directly on the JSA rule. Note that if the decision-maker considers that there is not enough information to decide this question, it will be assumed that the person is involved in the trade dispute (Decisions and Appeals Regulations 1999 reg.13(2)).

The rule does not apply when the person involved is incapable of work. The rule also does not apply in the maternity period, defined in subs.(2).

If the rule applies there are consequences for the way in which applicable amounts are calculated. This is dealt with in subs.(3). There are also consequences for the way in which income is calculated. This is dealt with in subs.(5) and in a number of regulations. The most immediate effect is that the person is treated as in remunerative work for the seven days following the first day of the stoppage of work or the day on which the claimant withdrew their labour (Income Support Regulations reg.5(4)). The result is that neither the person nor their partner can be entitled to income support at all for those days (s.124(1)(c)).

Subsection (3)

1.33   This provision sets out the effect on the applicable amount if the claimant is not excluded by the conditions of entitlement.

(a) A single claimant with no child or qualifying young person in the household is to have no applicable amount, and so cannot be entitled to any benefit.

16

(b) For a single claimant with a child or qualifying young person in the house-hold, the "portion of the applicable amount included in respect of" the claimant is disregarded. It is clear that the personal allowance for the claimant is taken out, and so is any premium payable on account of the claimant's disability or age or because of being a carer. For the small number of claimants who could still qualify for the family premium on a transitional basis following its abolition in April 2004 (see the notes to reg.17 of the Income Support Regulations and reg.83 of the JSA Regulations 1996) that premium is not regarded as being "in respect of" the claimant.

(c) For a couple where the trade dispute rule applies to only one of them, if they have no premiums on top of their personal allowance, that allowance is reduced by a half. This is a different rule from supplementary benefit, which would have left the other partner with the appropriate personal allowance for a single claimant. If there are any premiums, then the rule in para.(b) applies. Thus any premium payable solely for the person involved in the dispute (e.g. a carer premium) is taken out, but according to para.32642 of the *Decision Makers Guide* such a premium will be included in full if it is for the person not involved in the dispute. Any premium paid for the couple (e.g. a pensioner premium) is reduced by half. For the small number of claimants who could still qualify for the family premium on a transitional basis following its abolition in April 2004 (see the notes to reg.17 of the Income Support Regulations and reg.83 of the JSA Regulations 1996) that premium is not regarded as being "in respect of" the claimant.

(d) For a couple where the trade dispute rule applies to both of them, the applicable amount is nil if there is no child or qualifying young person in the house-hold. If there is a child or qualifying young person, then any family premium and any premium paid for that person's disability is allowed on top of the personal allowance for that person.

Note that housing costs are payable, provided that at least one member of the family (e.g. a child or qualifying young person) is not involved in the dispute. The housing costs are treated as the responsibility of the member or members not involved in the dispute (Income Support Regulations Sch.3 para.2(2)).

Subsection (5)

If the trade dispute rule applies, the normal rules about income are modified. Under para.(a) any payment that a member of the family receives, or is entitled to obtain by reason of the person involved in the trade dispute being without employment, must be taken into account. In *R(SB) 29/85* a loan from a local authority Social Work Department (the Scottish equivalent of a Social Services Department) to meet arrears of hire purchase repayments was held to be capable of being such a payment. The claimant had not been in arrears before the dispute and the loan was to be repaid on his return to work. However, on the facts it was a payment of capital, not income. Regulation 41(3) of the Income Support Regulations (now only still in force in "transitional cases"—see further the note to reg.41(3)) secures that, in trade dispute cases, payments under ss.17, 23B, 23C or 24A of the Children Act 1989 or s.12 of the Social Work (Scotland) Act 1968 or s.29 or s.30 of the Children (Scotland) Act 1995 (payments to families to prevent children being taken into care, etc.) are to be treated as income, not capital. Nor does the disregard of such income in para.28 of Sch.9 to the Income Support Regulations apply in trade dispute cases. Other categories of income normally disregarded but counted here are income in kind (para.21) and charitable, voluntary or personal injury payments (para.15). Holiday pay paid more than four weeks after the termination of employment (normally capital) is earnings (reg.35(1)(d)).

The other main category under para.(a) is income tax refunds paid or due. The effect of reg.48(2) is that in trade dispute cases refunds do not count as capital. The

1.34

assumption is then that they count as income, but this does not seem to be provided for expressly.

Under para.(b) there is the final automatic deduction of the "relevant sum." This is the sum specified in subs.(6), as increased in future years under subs. (7). The sum was increased in April 2020 to £41.00, from £40.50, where it had stood since April 2015. The relevant sum is often called "assumed strike pay," but is deducted regardless of whether the person involved is entitled to strike pay, a member of a union, or even on strike.

The "compensation" for this rule is that any payment from a trade union up to the amount of £41.00 is disregarded (Income Support Regulations Sch.9 para.34).

The cumulative result of these income rules, plus the reductions in applicable amounts, is that even married strikers will often receive very little benefit indeed (if any).

Effect of return to work

1.35   **127.**—If a person returns to work with the same employer after a period during which section 126 above applies to him, and whether or not his return is before the end of any stoppage of work in relation to which he is or would be [¹ prevented from being entitled to a jobseeker's allowance]—

(a) that section shall cease to apply to him at the commencement of the day on which he returns to work; and

(b) until the end of the period of 15 days beginning with that day section 124(1) above shall have effect in relation to him as if the following paragraph were substituted for paragraph (c)—"(c) in the case of a member of a [² couple], the other member is not engaged in remunerative work; and"; and

(c) any sum paid by way of income support for that period of 15 days to him or, where he is a member of a [² couple], to the other member of that couple, shall be recoverable in the prescribed manner from the person to whom it was paid or from any prescribed person or, where the person to whom it was paid is a member of a [² couple], from the other member of the couple.

AMENDMENTS

1. Jobseekers Act 1995 Sch.2 para.32 (October 7, 1996).
2. Civil Partnership Act 2004 s.254 and Sch.24 para.44 (December 5, 2005).

DERIVATION

Social Security Act 1986 s.23A.

DEFINITIONS

"couple"—see s.137(1).
"prescribed"—*ibid.*

GENERAL NOTE

1.36   This section allows income support to be paid for the first 15 days following a return to work from a trade dispute. Normally the work would exclude entitlement to benefit under s.124(1)(c) regardless of whether any wages were payable or not. The rules about the relevant sum and income tax refunds under s.126 do not apply, but the other adjustments to the income rules do apply. Applicable amounts are calculated in the ordinary way. Note that any advance of earnings or loan made by the employer counts as earnings (Income Support Regulations, reg.48(5) and (6)). In addition, any payment of benefit under this section is recoverable under subs.(c) and Pt VIII of the Payments Regulations.

Family credit

Family credit

128.—[¹ . . .]   1.37

AMENDMENT

1. Tax Credits Act 2002 s.60 and Sch.6 (April 8, 2003).

Disability working allowance

Disability working allowance

129.—[¹ . . .]   1.38

AMENDMENT

1. Tax Credits Act 2002 s.60 and Sch.6 (April 8, 2003).

General

Exclusions from benefit

134.—(1) No person shall be entitled to an income-related benefit if his   1.39
capital or a prescribed part of it exceeds the prescribed amount.

(2) Except in prescribed circumstances the entitlement of one member of a family to any one income-related benefit excludes entitlement to that benefit for any other member for the same period.

(3) [¹ . . .]

(4) Where the amount of any income-related benefit would be less than a prescribed amount, it shall not be payable except in prescribed circumstances.

AMENDMENT

1. Local Government Finance Act 1992 Sch.9 para.7 (April 1, 1993).

DERIVATION

Subs.(1): Social Security Act 1986 s.22(6).
Subs.(2): 1986 Act s.20(9).
Subs.(4): 1986 Act s.21(7).

DEFINITIONS

"family"—see s.137(1).
"prescribed"—*ibid.*

GENERAL NOTE

Subsection (1)

The capital limit for income support was raised to £16,000 for all claimants on   1.40
April 10, 2006 (Income Support Regulations reg.45). See the 2005 edition of what

was then Vol.II of this series for the different capital limits that applied for most claimants before that date. That brought the capital limit for income support (and income-based JSA, which was increased to £16,000 from April 10, 2006—see reg.107 of the JSA Regulations 1996) into line with that which applies for housing benefit and until the abolition of council tax benefit on April 1, 2013 applied for that benefit. The same capital limit applies for income-related ESA (see reg.110 of the ESA Regulations 2008) and for universal credit (see reg.18 of the Universal Credit Regulations in Vol.II of this series). There is no capital limit for working tax credit and child tax credit, nor for state pension credit (although there capital over £10,000 generates notional income).

Since the capital rule operates as an exclusion to benefit it is arguable that the burden of proof that a claimant's capital exceeds the limit is on the Secretary of State. The Tribunal of Commissioners in *CIS 417/1992*, reported as part of *R(IS) 26/95*, treat satisfaction of the capital rule as part of what the claimant has to prove in showing entitlement to income support on a claim. However, the contrary argument was not put to the Tribunal. But once it has been shown that the claimant possesses an item of capital, it is for them to prove that one of the disregards in Sch.10 applies (*CIS 240/1992*). Similarly, it has long been established that if the claimant is the legal owner of a property, the burden is on them to show that the beneficial ownership does not follow the legal ownership (see *VMcC v SSWP (IS)* [2018] UKUT 63 (AAC)). And once it is established that the claimant possesses some capital asset(s) the burden shifts to them to show that they no longer possess it or them (*R(SB) 38/85*).

These decisions, however, need to be read in the light of the House of Lords' judgment in *Kerr v Department of Social Development for Northern Ireland* [2004] UKHL 23; [2004] 1 W.L.R. 1372, also reported as *R 1/04 (SF)*, in which Baroness Hale emphasised that the process of adjudication for social security benefits is a co-operative one in which both the Department and the claimant should play their part and that normally it ought not to be necessary to resort to more formal concepts such as the burden of proof.

In *MB v Royal Borough of Kensington & Chelsea (HB)* [2011] UKUT 321 (AAC) the claimant relied on *Chichester DC v B and SSWP* [2009] UKUT 34 (AAC) in which it was stated that it was for the Council to show that the claimant had a beneficial interest in the capital at issue (see para.28). Judge Wikeley, however, considered that the answer to this lay in the point made by Baroness Hale in *Kerr* that it was for each party (claimant or Department) to provide such information as they reasonably can. The claimant in *MB* was the one who had exclusive knowledge about the purchase of the property in issue and the mortgage payments and thus it was her responsibility to marshal what evidence she could to show that, although she was the legal owner, she was not the sole beneficial owner of the property. The same can be said about most, if not all, items of capital.

Subsection (4)

1.41   See reg.26(4) of the Claims and Payments Regulations in Vol.III of this series.

The applicable amount

1.42   **135.**—(1) The applicable amount, in relation to any income-related benefit, shall be such amount or the aggregate of such amounts as may be prescribed in relation to that benefit.

(2) The power to prescribe applicable amounts conferred by subsection (1) above includes power to prescribe nil as an applicable amount.

(3) [¹[³ . . .

(4) . . .]

(5) [⁴ . . .] The applicable amount for a severely disabled person shall include an amount in respect of his being a severely disabled person.

(6) Regulations may specify circumstances in which persons are to be treated as being or as not being severely disabled.

AMENDMENTS

1. To be omitted until s.9 of the Social Security Act 1990 is brought into force: Social Security (Consequential Provisions) Act 1992 s.6 and Sch.4 Pt I.
2. Local Government Finance Act 1992 Sch.9 para.8 (April 1, 1993).
3. Health and Social Care Act 2001 s.67(2) and Sch.6 Pt 3 (April 15, 2002).
4. Tax Credits Act 2002 s.60 and Sch.6 (April 8, 2003).

DERIVATION

Social Security Act 1986 s.22(1)–(4).

DEFINITION

"prescribed"—see s.137(1).

GENERAL NOTE

Subsection (1)

See regs 17–22A of, and Sch.2 and Sch.7 to, the Income Support (General) Regulations.

CIS 683/1993 confirms that a claimant's applicable amount can only consist of elements specified in the relevant regulations. It cannot be increased by the amount of maintenance (or insurance premiums) the claimant is required to pay.

1.43

Subsection (2)

See reg.21 of and Sch.7 to the Income Support Regulations.

1.44

Subsections (5) and (6)

See para.13 of Sch.2 to the Income Support (General) Regulations. A provision requiring the payment of a community care addition to income support to very severely disabled people was put into the 1986 Act when it was going through the House of Lords. Although the Government did not wish to have this requirement in the legislation it did not seek to remove its spirit when the Bill returned to the House of Commons. However, it put in its own amendments, which have now become subss.(5) and (6).

In *R(IS) 22/93* the Commissioner held that s.22(4) of the 1986 Act (the predecessor of subs.(6)) did not authorise the making of regulations prescribing conditions to be satisfied before a person counts as severely disabled other than conditions relating to the extent of that person's disablement. Otherwise, the mandatory provision of s.22(3) (the predecessor of subs.(5)) would be undermined. He therefore went on to hold that heads (ii) and (iii) of para.13(2)(a) of Sch.2, on the severe disability premium, were not validly part of the General Regulations. This was because they referred to the presence of a non-dependant in the claimant's household and to the receipt of invalid care allowance by another person, and not to the claimant's disability.

On appeal, the majority of the Court of Appeal took the opposite view, that s.22(4) gave the Secretary of State power to specify financial and domestic conditions as part of the circumstances in which a person was or was not to be treated as severely disabled (*Chief Adjudication Officer v Foster* [1992] Q.B. 31; [1991] 3 All E.R. 846). Therefore the provisions were valid. Lord Donaldson MR dissented trenchantly, saying that if s.22(4) allowed regulations to specify conditions not relating to the severity of disability this would "emasculate the imperative contained in subs.(3) and indeed . . . render it otiose."

1.45

The House of Lords ([1993] A.C. 754; [1993] 1 All E.R. 705) also held the provisions to be valid. Lord Bridge agreed that subs.(3) (now subs.(5)) required the applicable amount for a severely disabled person to include some amount in respect of being such a person. But subs.(4) (now subs.(6)) was a deeming provision that allowed the Secretary of State to define who was to be treated as severely

1.46

disabled. He could do this by reference to circumstances that either related to the degree of disability or affected the extent of need for income support arising from the disability. If the only power intended to be given by subs.(4) was a power to define the degree of disability that qualified as severe, the language used was totally inappropriate for that purpose (especially compared with the precise code for determining the degree of disability which qualified someone for severe disablement allowance).

Lord Bridge would have reached this conclusion without looking at the Parliamentary history of the subsections in Hansard, but following *Pepper v Hart* [1993] A.C. 593; [1992] 3 W.L.R. 1032 this could be consulted. The statements of Ministers in both Houses of Parliament on the government amendments made clear that it was intended to use the regulation-making power to prescribe that the severe disability premium should only be applicable where the person was receiving the higher rate of attendance allowance, was living in a household with no other adult able to care for him and had no-one eligible for invalid care allowance in respect of him. Therefore, the ambiguity in the regulation-making power was to be resolved so as to authorise that use of the power.

The House of Lords' decision settled the scope of subss.(5) and (6). See the notes to para.13 of Sch.2 to the Income Support (General) Regulations for the conditions for the severe disability premium. On the powers of the Social Security Commissioners, tribunals and decision-makers to determine the validity or otherwise of regulations, see Vol.III of this series.

Income and capital

1.47   **136.**—(1) Where a person claiming an income-related benefit is a member of a family, the income and capital of any member of that family shall, except in prescribed circumstances, be treated as the income and capital of that person.

(2) Regulations may provide that capital not exceeding the amount prescribed under section 134(1) above but exceeding a prescribed lower amount shall be treated, to a prescribed extent, as if it were income of a prescribed amount.

(3) Income and capital shall be calculated or estimated in such manner as may be prescribed.

(4) A person's income in respect of a week shall be calculated in accordance with prescribed rules; and the rules may provide for the calculation to be made by reference to an average over a period (which need not include the week concerned).

(5) Circumstances may be prescribed in which—
   (a) a person is treated as possessing capital or income which he does not possess;
   (b) capital or income which a person does possess is to be disregarded;
   (c) income is to be treated as capital;
   (d) capital is to be treated as income.

DEFINITIONS

   "family"—see s.137(1).
   "prescribed"—*ibid.*

GENERAL NOTE

Subsection (1)

1.48   This provides that the general rule for income support is that all of the family's (as defined in s.137(1)) income and capital should be aggregated together and treated as the claimant's. The modifications to this rule for children and young persons were in regs 44 and 47 of the Income Support Regulations (see the 2003 edition of what was then Vol.II of this series for those regulations and the notes to those regulations). However, as a consequence of the removal of amounts for children and young persons from income support (with effect from April 6, 2004, except in "transitional cases"— see the note to reg.17 of the Income Support Regulations), a child's income and capital will be totally ignored and only a partner's income and capital will count as that of the claimant (see the amended form of reg.23(1) of the Income Support Regulations).

Subsection (2)

See reg.53 of the Income Support Regulations. From April 10, 2006 this pro-   **1.49**
vides for an income to be assumed to be produced from capital between £6,000 and £16,000 (see the 2005 edition of what was then Vol.II of this series for the different lower and upper capital limits that applied for most claimants before that date). However, for claimants who live permanently in a care home, Abbeyfield Home, Polish Resettlement home or independent hospital (for the definitions of these terms see reg.2(1) of the Income Support Regulations) the tariff income rule only applies to capital over £10,000 (see reg.53(1A)).

Subsections (3)–(5)

Large parts of the regulations deal with the matters covered by these subsections.   **1.50**

Interpretation of Part VII and supplementary provisions

137.—(1) In this Part of this Act, unless the context otherwise requires —   **1.51**
[¹"billing authority" has the same meaning as in Part I of the Local Government Finance Act 1992;]
"child" means a person under the age of 16;
[¹. . .]
[⁴ [⁷ ⁸ "couple" means—
  (a) two people who are married to, or civil partners of, each other and are members of the same household; or
  (b) two people who are not married to, or civil partners of, each other but are living together [⁹ as if they were a married couple or civil partners] otherwise than in prescribed circumstances;]]
"dwelling" means any residential accommodation, whether or not consisting of the whole or part of a building and whether or not comprising separate and self-contained premises;
"family" means—
  (a) a [⁴ couple];
  (b) a [⁴ couple] and a member of the same household for whom one of them is or both are responsible and who is a child or a person of a prescribed description;
  (c) except in prescribed circumstances, a person who is not a member of a [⁴ couple] and a member of the same household for whom that person is responsible and who is a child or a person of a prescribed description;
[²"income-based jobseeker's allowance" has the same meaning as in the Jobseekers Act 1995;]
"industrial injuries scheme" means a scheme made under Schedule 8 to this Act or section 159 of the 1975 Act or under the Old Cases Act;
[¹ ⁵ . . .]
[⁶ "local authority" in relation to Scotland means a council constituted under section 2 of the Local Government etc. (Scotland) Act 1994;]

[⁴ . . .]

[³"pensionable age" has the meaning given by the rules in paragraph 1 of Schedule 4 to the Pensions Act 1995 (c.26);]

"prescribed" means specified in or determined in accordance with regulations;

[³"state pension credit" means state pension credit under the State Pension Credit Act 2002;

[⁴ . . .]

"the qualifying age for state pension credit" is (in accordance with section 1(2)(b) and (6) of the State Pension Credit Act 2002)—

(a) in the case of a woman, pensionable age; or

(b) in the case of a man, the age which is pensionable age in the case of a woman born on the same day as the man;]

[⁴ . . .]

"war pension scheme" means a scheme under which war pensions (as defined in section 25 of the Social Security Act 1989) are provided;

"week", in relation to [¹council tax benefit], means a period of seven days beginning with a Monday.

[⁴ (1A) [⁷ . . .]]

(2) Regulations may make provision for the purposes of this Part of this Act—

(a) as to circumstances in which a person is to be treated as being or not being in Great Britain;

(b) continuing a person's entitlement to benefit during periods of temporary absence from Great Britain;

(c) as to what is or is not to be treated as remunerative work or as employment;

[²(d) as to circumstances in which a person is or is not to be treated as engaged or normally engaged in remunerative work;]

(e) as to what is or is not to be treated as relevant education;

(f) as to circumstances in which a person is or is not to be treated as receiving relevant education;

(g) specifying the descriptions of pension increases under war pension schemes or industrial injuries schemes that are analogous to the benefits mentioned in section 129(2)(b)(i) to (iii) above;

(h) as to circumstances in which a person is or is not to be treated as occupying a dwelling as his home;

(i) for treating any person who is liable to make payments in respect of a dwelling as if he were not so liable;

(j) for treating any person who is not liable to make payments in respect of a dwelling as if he were so liable;

(k) for treating as included in a dwelling any land used for the purposes of the dwelling;

(l) as to circumstances in which persons are to be treated as being or not being members of the same household;

(m) as to circumstances in which one person is to be treated as responsible or not responsible for another.

AMENDMENTS

1. Local Government Finance Act 1992 Sch.9 para.9 (April 1, 1993).
2. Jobseekers Act 1995 Sch.2 para.35 (October 7, 1996).

3. State Pension Credit Act 2002 s.14 and Sch.2 paras 1 and 4 (October 6, 2003).

4. Civil Partnership Act 2004 s.254(1) and Sch.24 para.46 (December 5, 2005).

5. Local Government etc. (Scotland) Act 1994 s.180 and Sch.13 para.174(5) and Sch.14 (April 1, 1996).

6. Welfare Reform Act 2007 Sch.5 para.1(4) (July 3, 2007).

7. Marriage (Same Sex Couples) Act 2013 (Consequential and Contrary Provisions and Scotland) Order 2014 (SI 560/2014) art.2 and Sch.1 para.22(8) (March 13, 2014).The amendment extends to England and Wales only (see SI 2014/107 art.1(4)).

8. Marriage and Civil Partnership (Scotland) Act 2014 and Civil Partnership Act 2004 (Consequential Provisions and Modifications) Order 2014 (SI 2014/3229) art.5(3) and Sch.4 para.2(13) (December 16, 2014). The amendment relates only to Scotland (see (SI 2014/3229) art.3(4)) but is in the same terms as the amendment made in relation to England and Wales by SI 2014/107 (see point 7 above).

9. Civil Partnership (Opposite-sex Couples) Regulations 2019 (SI 2019/1458) reg.41 and Sch.3 Pt.1 para.14 (December 2, 2019).

DEFINITIONS

"the 1975 Act"—see s.174.
"the Old Cases Act"—*ibid.*

GENERAL NOTE

Subsection (1)

These definitions are important throughout the income support scheme: 1.52

"*Child*". Note the restricted definition that gives rise to the need to define "young persons" in regulations, to describe those aged 16 and over.

"*Couple*". See the notes to the definition in reg.2(1) of the Income Support Regulations.

"*Dwelling*". See the notes to the definition of "dwelling occupied as the home" in reg.2(1) of the Income Support Regulations.

"*Family*". The definition effectively covers couples with or without children and single claimants with children. It may be that some contexts in the regulations require that single claimants without children are also included where a "family" is referred to.

Paragraph (b) covers couples and any child or young person (see reg.14 of the Income Support Regulations) in the household for whom one of the couple is responsible. On the general test of membership of the household and children, see *England v Secretary of State for Social Services* [1982] 3 F.L.R. 222; *R(FIS) 4/83* and *R(SB) 14/87*. There are deeming rules in reg.16 of the Income Support Regulations.

Paragraph (c) covers a single claimant who is responsible for a child in the same household.

"*Income-based jobseeker's allowance*". See ss.35(1) and 1(4) of the Jobseekers Act.

"*The qualifying age for state pension credit*". See note to s.124(1)(aa) above.

PART VIII

THE SOCIAL FUND

Payments out of the social fund

[¹ **138.**—(1) There may be made out of the social fund, in accordance 1.53
with this Part of this Act—

(a) Payments of prescribed amounts, whether in respect of prescribed items or otherwise, to meet, in prescribed circumstances, maternity expenses and funeral expenses; and

(b) . . . *[Omitted as relating solely to the discretionary social fund.]*]

(2) Payments may also be made out of that fund, in accordance with this Part of this Act, of a prescribed amount or a number of prescribed amounts to prescribed descriptions of persons, in prescribed circumstances, to meet expenses for heating, which appear to the Secretary of State to have been or to be likely to be incurred in cold weather.

(3) . . . *[Omitted as relating solely to the discretionary social fund.]*

(4) In this section "prescribed" means specified in or determined in accordance with regulations.

[² (4A) This section has effect in or as regards Scotland as if—

(a) references in subsections (1)(a) and (2) to the making of payments out of the social fund were to the making of payments by the Scottish Ministers,

(b) the reference in subsection (2) to the Secretary of State were to the Scottish Ministers, and

(c) the reference in subsection (4) to regulations were to regulations made by the Scottish Ministers.

(4B) Where regulations are made by the Scottish Ministers under this section—

(a) sections 175(2) and (7) and 176 do not apply, and

(b) the regulations are subject to the negative procedure (see section 28 of the Interpretation and Legislative Reform (Scotland) Act 2010).

(4C) The power to make an Order in Council under section 30(3) of the Scotland Act 1998 is exercisable for the purposes of this section as it is exercisable for the purposes of that Act.]

(5) . . . *[Omitted as relating solely to the discretionary social fund.]*

AMENDMENT

1. Social Security Act 1998 s.70 (April 5, 1999).

2. Scotland Act 2016 s.23(5) (May 17, 2017 for the purpose of making regulations: see SI 2017/405 reg.2(b)(iii). The amendment will not come into force for other purposes until April 1, 2022: see SI 2017/405 reg.3 as substituted by SI 2019/1438 reg.2).

GENERAL NOTE

Subsection (1)(a)

1.54   Subsection (1)(a) is re-enacted by s.70(1)(a) of the 1998 Act with effect from April 5, 1999. This part of the social fund scheme was originally brought into operation in April 1987 to enable payments to be made for maternity and funeral expenses. These are made under the ordinary system of adjudication and under regulations required to be made by subs.(1)(a). They are not subject to any budget. See the Social Fund Maternity and Funeral Expenses (General) Regulations 2005. The death grant and the maternity grant, formerly payable under the Social Security Act 1975, were abolished (1986 Act ss.38 and 41) and the provisions for maternity and funeral expenses under the supplementary benefit regulations were removed in April 1987 (General Regulations regs 13–15).

Subsection (1)(a) does little more than provide the framework for the detailed entitlement set out in the General Regulations. See s.78(4) of the Administration Act on the recovery of funeral payments from the estate of the deceased.

New restrictions on payments for funeral expenses were introduced on June 5,

1995 and there was further clarification and tightening-up of the rules on April 7, 1997 (see regs 7 and 7A of the General Regulations and the notes to those regulations). Note also the changes introduced on November 17, 1997.

The argument that maternity (or funeral) expenses that do not qualify under subs. (1)(a) can be met from the discretionary social fund under subs.(1)(b) was rejected in *R. v Social Fund Inspector, Ex p. Harper*, High Court, February 7, 1997. Harrison J held that subss.(1)(a) and (b) provided mutually exclusive methods of meeting particular needs and that maternity and funeral expenses were only intended to be met to the extent laid down in the General Regulations.

Subsection (2)

Although the predecessor of this subsection was in force from April 1988, the regulations it required were not in place until November 7, 1988 (Social Fund Cold Weather Payments (General) Regulations 1988). The form of the scheme, as embodied in the 1988 Regulations, has been amended several times. The current form does not require a separate claim to be made for a severe weather payment. As for maternity and funeral expenses, the decisions are made by decision-makers, with appeals to a tribunal, and are not subject to any budget.

See also the notes to the Social Fund Winter Fuel Payment Regulations 2000.

1.55

Subsections (4A)-(4C)

These subsections make provision for the operation of the social fund in Scotland.

1.56

PART XIII

GENERAL

Interpretation

Application of Act in relation to territorial waters

172.—In this Act—

(a) any reference to Great Britain includes a reference to the territorial waters of the United Kingdom adjacent to Great Britain;

(b) any reference to the United Kingdom includes a reference to the territorial waters of the United Kingdom.

1.57

Age

173.—For the purposes of this Act a person—

(a) is over or under a particular age if he has or, as the case may be, has not attained that age; and

(b) is between two particular ages if he has attained the first but not the second;

and in Scotland (as in England and Wales) the time at which a person attains a particular age expressed in years is the commencement of the relevant anniversary of the date of his birth.

1.58

References to Acts

174.—In this Act—

"the 1975 Act" means the Social Security Act 1975;

"the 1986 Act" means the Social Security Act 1986;

"the Administration Act" means the Social Security Administration Act 1992;

1.59

"the Consequential Provisions Act" means the Social Security (Consequential Provisions) Act 1992;

"the Northern Ireland Contributions and Benefits Act" means the Social Security Contributions and Benefits (Northern Ireland) Act 1992;

"the Old Cases Act" means the Industrial Injuries and Diseases (Old Cases) Act 1975; and

"the Pensions Act" means the [¹ Pension Schemes Act 1993].

AMENDMENT

1. Pension Schemes Act 1993 s.190 Sch.8 para.41.

Subordinate legislation

Regulations, orders and schemes

1.60   **175.**—(1) Subject to [²subsection (1A) below], regulations and orders under this Act shall be made by the Secretary of State.

[²(1A) Subsection (1) above has effect subject to—

(a) any provision [³ . . .] providing for regulations or an order to be made by the Treasury or by the Commissioners of Inland Revenue, [³ . . .]

[³ . . .]

(2) Powers under this Act to make regulations, orders or schemes shall be exercisable by statutory instrument.

(3) Except in the case of an order under section 145(3) above and in so far as this Act otherwise provides, any power under this Act to make regulations or an order may be exercised—

(a) either in relation to all cases to which the power extends, or in relation to those cases subject to specified exceptions, or in relation to any specified cases or classes of case;

(b) so as to make, as respects the cases in relation to which it is exercised—

(i) the full provision to which the power extends or any less provision (whether by way of exception or otherwise),

(ii) the same provision for all cases in relation to which the power is exercised, or different provision for different cases or different classes of case or different provision as respects the same case or class of case for different purposes of this Act;

(iii) any such provision either unconditionally or subject to any specified condition;

and where such a power is expressed to be exercisable for alternative purposes it may be exercised in relation to the same case for any or all of those purposes; and powers to make regulations or an order for the purposes of any one provision of this Act are without prejudice to powers to make regulations or an order for the purposes of any other provision.

(4) Without prejudice to any specific provision in this Act, any power conferred by this Act to make regulations or an order (other than the power conferred in section 145(3) above) includes power to make thereby such incidental, supplementary, consequential or transitional provision as appears to the [² person making the regulations or order] to be expedient for the purposes of the regulations or order.

(5) Without prejudice to any specific provisions in this Act, a power conferred by any provision of this Act except—

(a) sections 30, 47(6), [¹25B(2)(a)] and 145(3) above and paragraph 3(9) of Schedule 7 to this Act;

(b) section 122(1) above in relation to the definition of "payments by way of occupational or personal pension"; and

(c) Part XI,

to make regulations or an order includes power to provide for a person to exercise a discretion in dealing with any matter.

(6) *[Omitted as relating only to housing benefit and community charge benefit.]*

(7) Any power of the Secretary of State under any provision of this Act, except the provisions mentioned in subsection (5)(a) and (b) above and Part IX, to make any regulations or order, where the power is not expressed to be exercisable with the consent of the Treasury, shall if the Treasury so direct be exercisable only in conjunction with them.

(8) and (9) *[Omitted as relating only to ss.116 to 120.]*

(10) Any reference in this section or section 176 below to an order or regulations under this Act includes a reference to an order or regulations made under any provision of an enactment passed after this Act and directed to be construed as one with this Act; but this subsection applies only so far as a contrary intention is not expressed in the enactment so passed, and without prejudice to the generality of any such direction.

AMENDMENTS

1. Social Security (Incapacity for Work) Act 1994 Sch.1 para.36 (April 13, 1995).

2. Social Security Contributions (Transfer of Functions, etc.) Act 1999 s.2 and Sch.3 para.29 (April 1, 1999).

3. Tax Credits Act 2002 s.60 Sch.6 (April 1, 2003).

DERIVATION

Social Security Act 1986 ss.83(1) and 84(1).

Parliamentary control

176.—(1)–(2c) *[Omitted as not applying to income-related benefits.]*   **1.61**

(3) A statutory instrument—

(a) which contains (whether alone or with other provisions) any order, regulations or scheme made under this Act by the Secretary of State, [¹the Treasury or the Commissioners of Inland Revenue,] other than an order under section 145(3) above; and

(b) which is not subject to any requirement that a draft of the instrument shall be laid before and approved by a resolution of each House of Parliament,

[² (bb) regulations prescribing a percentage rate for the purposes of—

(i) paragraph 3B(3) or 7B(3) of Schedule 5, or

(ii) paragraph 5(3) of Schedule 5A;]

shall be subject to annulment in pursuance of a resolution of either House of Parliament.

AMENDMENTS

1. Social Security Contributions (Transfer of Functions, etc.) Act 1999 s.2 and Sch.3 para.30 (April, 1999).

2. Pensions Act 2004 ss.297(4) and 322(3) and Sch.3 para.11 (April 6, 2005).

DERIVATION

Social Security Act 1986 s.83(4).

[Short title, commencement and extent]

Short title, commencement and extent

1.62   **177.**—(1) This Act may be cited as the as the Social Security Contributions and Benefits Act 1992.

(2) This Act is to be read, where appropriate, with the Administration Act and the Consequential Provisions Act.

(3) The enactments consolidated by this Act are repealed, in consequence of the consolidation, by the Consequential Provisions Act.

(4) Except as provided in Schedule 4 to the Consequential Provisions Act, this Act shall come into force on 1st July 1992.

(5) The following provisions extend to Northern Ireland—

section 16 and Schedule 2;

section 116(2); and

this section.

(6) Except as provided by this section, this Act does not extend to Northern Ireland.

DEFINITIONS

"the Administration Act"—see s.174.
"the Consequential Provisions Act"—*ibid.*

Jobseekers Act 1995

(1995 C.18)

SECTIONS REPRODUCED

PART I

THE JOBSEEKER'S ALLOWANCE

Entitlement

PART II

BACK TO WORK SCHEMES

PART III

MISCELLANEOUS AND SUPPLEMENTAL

SCHEDULES

An Act to provide for a jobseeker's allowance and to make other provision to promote the employment of the unemployed and the assistance of persons without a settled way of life. [June 28, 1995]

GENERAL NOTE

1.64   Readers who wish to consult a brief overview of the introduction in 1996 of jobseeker's allowance (JSA) as a single benefit taking two forms – contribution-based JSA (CBJSA) and income-based JSA (IBJSA) – followed by the tacking on in 2001 of the joint-claim couple provisions (as a form of IBJSA) should consult the notes to the old style Jobseekers Act 1995 in the 2020/21 edition of what was then Vol. II of this series: *Income Support, Jobseeker's Allowance, State Pension Credit and the Social Fund.*
    What is now set out here is the form of the Jobseekers Act 1995 unamended by the Welfare Reform Act 2012 (WRA 2012), but omitting the provisions that apply only to CBJSA. That form of the Act is called the old style Jobseekers Act 1995. The same has been done for the Jobseeker's Allowance Regulations 1996 (JSA Regulations 1996). The WRA 2012 amendments create a different form of JSA based on contributions that is called new style JSA. The amended form of the Act is called the new style Jobseekers Act 1995 and is set out in Vol.I of this series: *Non-Means Tested Benefits*, with its associated regulations, the Jobseeker's Allowance Regulations 2013 (the JSA Regulations 2013).
    The position has now been reached where for all intents and purposes any new claim for JSA can only be for new style JSA under the 1995 Act as amended by the WRA 2012. The circumstance that brings about the abolition of IBJSA for new claims under s.33(1)(a) of the WRA 2012 and the coming into force of the amendments to the 1995 Act under various later provisions is the making of a new claim for JSA (or for other benefits including universal credit and ESA) in an area where "full service" universal credit has been rolled out and where the particular claimant is legally able to make a claim for universal credit (see arts 4(1) and (2) of the Welfare Reform Act 2012 (Commencement No.9 and Transitional and Transitory Provisions and Commencement No.8 and Savings and Transitional

Provisions (Amendment)) Order 2013 (SI 2013/983) as further applied in later Commencement Orders). The Orders are now set out so far as still relevant later in this Volume. The position was reached in December 2018 where the universal credit rollout had extended to the whole of Great Britain. Some prohibitions on claiming universal credit remained, in particular the so-called SDP gateway, where a claimant who was entitled to an income-related benefit including the severe disability premium was prohibited from claiming universal credit (reg.4A of the Universal Credit (Transitional Provisions) Regulations 2014 (SI 2014/1230)). That prohibition was removed by the revocation of reg.4A with effect from January 27, 2021. The only prohibitions that remain as at April 2021 are under reg.4 of the Transitional Provisions Regulations 2014, where the Secretary of State determines (to safeguard efficient administration or to ensure efficient testing of systems of administration) that no claims for universal credit are to be accepted in an area or category of case, and under art.4(11) of the Welfare Reform Act 2012 (Commencement No.32 and Savings and Transitional Provisions) Order 2019 (SI 2019/167) where the claimant is a "frontier worker" (i.e. a person who is "in Great Britain" for the purposes of s.4(1)(c) of the WRA 2012 but does not reside in Great Britain or Northern Ireland. The emergency discretion to stop accepting claims and the frontier worker rule have such a limited practical effect that to all intents and purposes the situation has now been reached when any new claim for JSA can only be for new style JSA.

Entitlement to old style JSA can only now exist as part of a continuing award made earlier. Since entitlement to old style CBJSA was limited to 182 days in any jobseeking period (s.5 of the old style Jobseekers Act 1995), no award made at a time when a new claim for old style JSA was still generally possible could survive long after April 2021. In practice, continuing awards will overwhelmingly be awards of IBJSA. Accordingly, while the provisions of the old style Jobseekers Act 1995 that are not relevant to IBJSA have not been repealed, they have been omitted from this book as irrelevant to new claims. In so far as those provisions might possibly be relevant to a continuing award of old style CBJSA, previous editions of what was then Vol.II of this series can be consulted.

Some of the more historical discussion in previous editions, for instance about the transition from unemployment benefit to JSA in 1996, has also been omitted, but much long-standing discussion of general principles and issues has been retained.

PART I

THE JOBSEEKER'S ALLOWANCE

Entitlement

The jobseeker's allowance

1.—(1) An allowance, to be known as a jobseeker's allowance, shall be payable in accordance with the provisions of this Act.   **1.65**

(2) Subject to the provisions of this Act, a claimant is entitled to a jobseeker's allowance if he—

(a) is available for employment;
(b) has entered into a jobseeker's agreement, which remains in force;
(c) is actively seeking employment;
[¹(d) satisfies the conditions set out in section 2;]
(e) is not engaged in remunerative work;
[⁴(f) does not have limited capability for work;]
(g) is not receiving relevant education;

(h) is under pensionable age; and

(i) is in Great Britain.

[¹(2A) Subject to the provisions of this Act, a claimant who is not a member of a joint-claim couple is entitled to a jobseeker's allowance if he satisfies—

(a) the conditions set out in paragraphs (a) to (c) and (e) to (i) of subsection (2); and

(b) the conditions set out in section 3.

(2B) Subject to the provisions of this Act, a joint-claim couple are entitled to a jobseeker's allowance if—

(a) a claim for the allowance is made jointly by the couple;

(b) each member of the couple satisfies the conditions set out in paragraphs (a) to (c) and (e) to (i) of subsection (2); and

(c) the conditions set out in section 3A are satisfied in relation to the couple.

(2C) Regulations may prescribe circumstances in which subsection (2A) is to apply to a claimant who is a member of a joint-claim couple.

(2D) Regulations may, in respect of cases where a person would (but for the regulations) be a member of two or more joint-claim couples, make provision for only one of those couples to be a joint-claim couple; and the provision which may be so made includes provision for the couple which is to be the joint-claim couple to be nominated—

(a) by the persons who are the members of the couples, or

(b) in default of one of the couples being so nominated, by the Secretary of State.]

(3) A jobseeker's allowance is payable in respect of a week.

(4) In this Act—

"a contribution-based jobseeker's allowance" means a jobseeker's allowance entitlement to which is based on the claimant's satisfying conditions, which include those set out in section 2; [². . .]

"an income-based jobseeker's allowance" means a jobseeker's allowance entitlement to which is based on the claimant's satisfying conditions, which include those set out in section 3 [¹ or a joint-claim jobseeker's allowance;

"a joint-claim couple" means a [³ couple] who—

(a) are not members of any family whose members include a person in respect of whom a member of the couple is entitled to child benefit, and

(b) are of a prescribed description;

"a joint-claim jobseeker's allowance" means a jobseeker's allowance entitlement to which arises by virtue of subsection (2B).]

AMENDMENTS

1. Welfare Reform and Pensions Act 1999 Sch.7 para.2 (March 19, 2001).
2. Welfare Reform and Pensions Act 1999 Sch.13 Pt V (April 2, 2000).
3. Civil Partnership Act 2004 s.254 and Sch.24 Pt 7 para.118 (December 5, 2005).
4. Welfare Reform Act 2007 Sch.3 para.12 (October, 27, 2008).

DEFINITIONS

"actively seeking employment"—see s.7(1).
"available for employment"—see s.6(1).
"claimant"—see s.35(1).
"couple"—see s.35(1).
"employment"—see s.35(1) and JSA Regulations 1996 reg.3.

"employment" (in section 7)—see s.7(8).
"entitled"—see s.35(1) and SSAA 1992 ss.1 and 68.
"Great Britain"—see s.35(1).
"jobseeker's agreement"—see ss.9(1) and 35(1).
"limited capability for work"—see s.35(2) and Sch.1 para.2 and SSCBA 1992 Pt XIIA.
"pensionable age"—see s.35(1) and JSA Regulations 1996 reg.3 and SSCBA 1992 s.122(1).
"relevant education"—see s.35(2) and Sch.1 para.14 and JSA Regulations 1996 reg.54.
"remunerative work"—see s.35(2) and Sch.1 para.1 and JSA Regulations 1996 reg.51.
"week"—see s.35(1).
"work"—*ibid.*

GENERAL NOTE

This section provides the legislative basis for the payment of old style JSA, a weekly **1.66** benefit (subs.(3)) and a single benefit taking two forms. Subsection (2) sets out the conditions of entitlement to contribution-based JSA (CBJSA) and subss. (2A) (standard claimants) and (2B) (joint-claim couples) set out the conditions of entitlement to income-based JSA (IBJSA). Although provisions no longer relevant to IBJSA have been omitted, all of the conditions in subs.(2), except for the condition of satisfying the contribution conditions in s.2, are incorporated into the conditions for IBJSA, so need consideration. The additional condition for IBJSA in subss. (2A) and (2B) is to satisfy the income-based conditions in s.3.

Subsection (2)
Temporary Coronavirus Provisions

Regulation 7 of the Social Security (Coronavirus) (Further Measures) Regulations **1.67** 2020 (SI 2020/371) (see Pt III of this volume) provided that for the three months beginning with March 30, 2020 anyone with an award of old style JSA was to be treated as available for employment (see subs.(2)(a)) and as actively seeking employment (see subs.(2)(c)). It is arguable that, by virtue of reg.15(5) of the JSA Regulations 1996, the deeming of non-availability in reg.15 trumps the effect of reg.7 except where modified by reg.4 of the Social Security (Coronavirus) (Prisoners) Regulations 2020 (SI 2020/409) (temporary release of English and Welsh prisoners: see the notes to reg.15). The power to extend the three-month period was not exercised before it expired. The overall effect of reg.7 expired at the end of November 12, 2021 (reg.10(2)).

For the period initially running to November 12, 2020, later extended to May 12, and again to August 31, 2021 (reg.10(2B) of the Further Measures Regulations), reg.8 of the Further Measures Regulations provides that anyone who has an award of old style JSA and satisfies all the conditions of entitlement in s.1(2) apart from para.(f) (does not have limited capability for work) is to be treated as capable of work or as not having limited capability for work, but only in three specified circumstances. Those are that the person is: (a) infected or contaminated with coronavirus disease (defined in reg.1(2) of the Further Measures Regulations to mean COVID-19); (b) in isolation (defined there to mean the separation of the person from any other person in such a manner as to prevent infection or contamination with coronavirus disease); or (c) caring for a child or qualifying young person who is a member of their household and falls within (a) or (b). Isolation is presumably intended only to cover to those who are not leaving the place where they are living at all ("self-isolating"), not those who are leaving that place but maintaining social distancing from others while out (that is the view in para.16 of Memo ADM 04/20). But there must be doubt because the crucial word in the definition is "separation", whose ordinary meaning is a good deal wider than "isolation", and it must cover separations for precautionary purposes between persons who are not definitely known to be infected or contaminated with COVID-19, but may be. Paragraph 16 of that Memo stresses that a person may be in isolation although other people live in the same household.

It is not clear whether the restriction of the effect of regs 7 and 8 to those who have an award of old style JSA means that on a new claim (insofar as a claim for old style JSA, as opposed to new style JSA and universal credit, is still possible) the availability and actively seeking employment and not having limited capability for work conditions are to be applied in determining initial entitlement. It appears that in practice little if any attention was given to "conditionality" during the period affected. Although there was no legislative change to the condition in s.1(2)(b) of having entered into a jobseeker's agreement (see below), until the reintroduction of the requirement for new claimants and reviews for existing claimants from July 1, 2020 (Parliamentary answer of July 1, 2020 (WQ 62431) by the Under-Secretary of State, Mims Davies) the condition was probably treated as satisfied under reg.34 of the JSA Regulations 1996 (see the notes to s.9 below).

1.68   *Subsection (2)* sets out the basic conditions of entitlement to old style JSA, in either of its forms, either directly or by reference. It is merely a "framework", amplified by other sections of and Schedules to the Act (this begins, "Subject to the provisions of this Act") and in the detail of the JSA Regulations 1996. In relation to IBJSA, only the conditions in paras (a)-(c) and (e)-(i) are relevant, with the additional condition of satisfying the relevant income-based condition in s.3 ("standard" claimants) or s.3A (joint-claim couples) (subss. (2A) and (2B)). For joint-claim couples both members must satisfy all the conditions (subs.(2B)(b)). Only the IBJSA conditions are set out below. They are very much a framework, with detailed content provided in the rest of the Act and the JSA Regulations 1996.

All of the conditions must be satisfied for there to be entitlement, but para.8 of Sch.1 allows regulations to be made prescribing when claimants can be entitled to regular IBJSA without being available for work, having entered into a jobseeker's agreement or actively seeking employment. Paragraph 8A allows regulations to be made prescribing circumstances in which a joint-claim couple can be entitled without satisfying any of the subs.(2) conditions. Other sections of the Act authorise regulations to prescribe circumstances in which those "labour market" conditions are to be treated as satisfied or not satisfied.

(1) "*Is available for employment*" (para.(a)): see further s.6 and the JSA Regulations 1996 Pt II, Chs I and II (regs 4–17). This "labour market" condition is one aspect of the central underlying principle, common to regimes of benefit for unemployed people, that the claimant's unemployment must be involuntary.

1.69   (2) "*Has entered into a jobseeker's agreement which remains in force*" (para.(b)): see further ss.9–10 and the JSA Regulations 1996 (regs 31–40). Note, in particular, that a claimant is to be treated as having satisfied this condition in any of the circumstances set out in JSA Regulations 1996 reg.34 (a provision probably used during the 2020 coronavirus outbreak: see the notes to s.9). This is a further aspect of the underlying principle, common in regimes of benefit for the unemployed, that the claimant's unemployment must be involuntary: being a jobseeker, looking to return to work, and agreeing a programme of activity, the better to enable doing so. The jobseeker's agreement is an integral part of identifying what steps back to work are appropriate for claimants and to enable regular and effective monitoring of their activities to that end, reviewing and altering the terms of the agreement as necessary over a period. Note, in particular, that "employment officers" (usually Jobcentre Plus personnel: see the notes to the s.35(1) definition and s.9(13)) cannot enter into an agreement the terms of which are such that the claimant acting in accordance with them would fail to satisfy either of the key requirements to be available for and actively seeking work, thus placing such officers at the heart of policing these central requirements of the system (s.9(5)). See the notes to s.9 below for when an agreement has validly been entered into and the notes to s.10 for when it remains in force.

(3) "*Is actively seeking employment*" (para.(b)): see further s.7 and the JSA Regulations 1996 regs 18–22. This second "labour market" condition is a further aspect of the

central underlying principle, common to regimes of benefit for unemployed people, that the claimant's unemployment must be involuntary. In any week a person is actively seeking employment if during that week they take such steps as they can reasonably be expected to take in order to have *the best prospects of securing employment*, thereby stressing the requirements of taking positive action to secure work.

(4) *"Is not engaged in remunerative work"*, (para.(e)): see further s.21 and Sch.1 para.1, which together enabled the making of the amplificatory regulations, the JSA Regulations 1996 regs 51–53. It may seem obvious that those who have a job cannot be said to be unemployed. But previous regimes had always catered for partial unemployment, and it is inevitably a matter of controversy at what point a line is to be drawn saying claimants are working to such an extent that they cannot properly be said to be unemployed and need state support. The remunerative work rules draw that line; once the threshold is reached the old style JSA system will no longer regard a working claimant as "unemployed". The remunerative work rules as applicable to IBJSA set the threshold for the claimant at 16 hours per week: "remunerative work" means in the case of the claimant, work in which they are engaged or, where hours of work fluctuate, are engaged on average, for not less than 16 hours per week; and work here means work for which payment is made or which is done in expectation of payment (JSA Regulations 1996 reg.51(1)(a)). Provision is made in JSA Regulations 1996 reg.51(2) and (3) for determining the number of hours for which a person is engaged in work, essentially along the same line as provisions applicable to the issue in income support prior to its replacement as a benefit for unemployed people (Income Support (General) Regulations 1987 reg.5).

Regulation 52 of the JSA Regulations 1996 prescribes categories who are to be treated as engaged in remunerative work, regardless of whether they are actually undertaking any activities, in particular those absent from what would be remunerative work on holiday or without good reason (excluding absence on maternity etc leave or through illness). Regulation 53 protects a variety of claimants by treating them as not engaged in remunerative work when they might actually be, in particular people carrying out many worthy or voluntary activities, some caring responsibilities and on various official work-related schemes. **1.70**

A claimant who is a member of a couple (but not within the meaning of joint-claim couple) will be excluded from IBJSA, despite not being engaged (or treated as engaged) in remunerative work, if the partner is so engaged (or treated as so engaged), but the hours' threshold in respect of the partner is 24 rather than 16 (s.3(1)(e) and JSA Regulations 1996 reg.51(1)(b)). As regards a joint-claim couple, both must satisfy the remunerative work condition. Failure of one to do so would, in principle, be expected to result in disentitlement of both. But see JSA Regulations 1996 reg.3E, enabling the other member of a joint-claim couple to claim as a "standard" ss.1(2A) and 3 claimant in certain circumstances where the other member fails to meet one or more of the conditions of entitlement in s.1(2)(a)–(c) and (e)–(i). One such circumstance is where the "failing" member is engaged, or has agreed to be engaged, in remunerative work for more than 16 but less than 24 hours per week (JSA Regulations 1996 reg.3E(2)(g)).

(5) *"Does not have limited capability for work"* (para.(f)): this represents, as in the past, a demarcation line between benefits for those able to work but unable to find employment and benefits for those incapable of work (incapacity benefit and ESA). However, complications inevitably did occur when claimants had to transfer from one type of benefit to the other, particularly in respect of periods of short-term incapacity. Hence the demarcation is no longer as strict as in the past; s.21 and Sch.1 para.2 enabled the making of JSA Regulations 1996 reg.55, which allows someone to remain in receipt of old style JSA whilst incapable of work for up to two weeks. No more than two such periods are permitted in any jobseeking period of less than 12 months. Where a jobseeking period lasts longer than 12 months, in effect one is entitled to no more than two such "short-term incapacity periods" in any 12 months. Regulation 55A now allows receipt to continue for a more extended period of up to 13 weeks in total, but only once in any 12 months. **1.71**

1.72   (6) *"Is not receiving relevant education"* (para.(g)): see further s.21 and Sch.1 para.14 and the regulation they enabled, JSA Regulations 1996 reg.54, which defines it to cover only full-time education, not being a course of advanced education, which is undertaken by a child or young person. Someone treated as a child for child benefit purposes or who is receiving full-time education as far as the child benefit system is concerned (see SSCBA 1992 s.142) is treated as receiving full-time education for the purposes of jobseeker's allowance (JSA Regulations 1996 reg.54(2)). As this exclusion covers persons under 19, the effect of the contribution conditions (the claimant's insurance record) is to make this in practice a hurdle much more relevant to income-based than contribution-based JSA. Those on a full-time course of advanced education, it should be noted, will be excluded from old style JSA because they are treated as not available for employment (see s.6 and JSA Regulations 1996 regs 1(3) and 15(a)).

    (7) *"Is under pensionable age"* (para.(h)): "pensionable age" is defined as in the SSCBA 1992 s.122(1) (see s.35(1) and JSA Regulations 1996 reg.3).

    (8) *"Is in Great Britain"* (para.(i)): see further s.21 and Sch.1 para.11, which enabled JSA Regulations 1996 reg.50 to treat temporary absence for certain specified purposes (e.g. to attend an employment interview) as presence in Great Britain and the amendment effected by JSA Regulations 1996 reg.165 to reg.11 of the Persons Abroad Regulations 1975 to enable entitlement notwithstanding absence in the circumstances covered by reg.11.

1.73   See reg.85A of and para.14 of Sch.5 to the JSA Regulations 1996 for the rule making the IBJSA applicable amount nil for a "person from abroad", i.e. a person who is not habitually resident in the common travel area (UK, Channel Islands, Isle of Man and Republic of Ireland) under the special rules in reg.85A, that in general require that the person has a right to reside in one of those places. In addition, s.115(1) of the Immigration and Asylum Act 1999 prevents "a person subject to immigration control", as defined in s.115(9), from being entitled to IBJSA, along with many other benefits, unless within limited exceptions. See the notes to regs.85 and 85A of the JSA Regulations 1996 and, in particular, to regs. 21 and 21AA of the Income Support Regulations.

Subsection (2A)

1.74   This deals with what is termed in this commentary the "standard" claimant for IBJSA: that is, the claimant who is not a member of a joint-claim couple (on "joint-claim couple" see notes to subs.(4), below). In other words, broadly speaking, being a single person or a member of a couple with children (now that any childless couple where one partner is aged at least 18 now counts as a joint-claim couple). This claimant must meet the common conditions of entitlement in s.1(2)(a)–(c) and (e)–(i), plus the income-based conditions in s.3.

Subsection (2B)

1.75   This deals with the entitlement of a joint-claim couple (see notes to subs.(4)) to IBJSA. The couple must make a claim for the allowance jointly. Each member of the couple must meet the common conditions of entitlement in s.1(2)(a)–(c) and (e)–(i), plus the income-based conditions in s.3A. An allowance, entitlement to which is obtained pursuant to this subsection, is called a "joint-claim jobseeker's allowance" (subs.(4)).

Subsection (2C)

1.76   This rule-making power enables regulations to stipulate circumstances in which a member of a joint-claim couple (see further notes to subs.(4)) is instead to be treated as a "standard" claimant under subs.(2A). JSA Regulations 1996 reg.3E is the product of the exercise of this power. It enables one member of a joint-claim couple to claim as a "standard" ss.1(2A) and 3 claimant in certain circumstances where the other member (described here as the "failing" member) does not satisfy one or more of the conditions of entitlement in s.1(2)(a)–(c) and (e)–(i). One such circumstance is where the "failing" member is engaged, or has agreed to be engaged, in remunerative work for more than 16 but less than 24 hours per week (JSA Regulations 1996 reg.3E(2)(g)). Others include where the "failing" member is pregnant and claiming maternity allowance or statutory maternity pay (reg.3E(2) (h)); or in receipt of statutory sick pay (reg.3E(2)(k)); or who is over pensionable age (reg.3E(2)(f)). See further the notes to that regulation.

Subsection (2D)

This power enables regulations to be made where someone would otherwise be   **1.77**
a member of two joint-claim couples. JSA Regulations 1996 reg.3(2) is the product of the exercise of this power. Where someone would otherwise be a member of more than one joint-claim couple, he will be regarded as a member of the couple he nominates or (in default) that the Secretary of State nominates. That nominated couple operates to the exclusion of any other couple of which he may be a member.

Subsection (3)

This stipulates that old style JSA is paid in respect of a week, whereas UB was,   **1.78**
of course, a daily benefit. Note, however, that s.21 and Sch.1 para.5 enable the making of regulations to permit payment of JSA for a period of less than a week. The circumstances in which this may be done are contained in JSA Regulations 1996 regs 150–155.

Subsection (4)

This specifies that there are two types of jobseeker's allowance: (1) a   **1.79**
"contribution-based jobseeker's allowance", entitlement to which depends on fulfilling the common conditions in subs.(2) plus the specific ones in s.2; and (2) an "income-based jobseeker's allowance", entitlement to which is dependent on meeting the particular conditions set out in s.3 (standard claimant) or s.3A (joint-claim couple) as well as the common conditions in subs.(2). It is not now necessary to examine the complicated provisions on the amount of benefit when a claimant was entitled to both CBJSA and IBJSA.

The subsection also defines "joint-claim couple" as a couple, *of a prescribed description*, who are not members of any family that includes someone for whom one of the members of the couple is entitled to child benefit. JSA Regulations 1996 reg.3A, as amended from February 25, 2008, gives the prescribed description: where one of the members of the couple was born after October 28, 1947, but being 18 or over. Thus any couple where the members are over 18 and below pensionable age is now covered. Such a couple, however, will not be of a prescribed description if:

(a) under JSA Regulations 1996 reg.77(3), one of its members is treated as responsible for a child or young person (where no one is as yet entitled to child benefit, for example, because a claim has only just been made);

(b) the couple has care of a child or young person in one or more of the circumstances mentioned in JSA Regulations 1996 reg.78(4) (where they are fosterers or the child has been placed with them for adoption); and

(c) a child or young person is living with the couple in the circumstances mentioned in JSA Regulations 1996 reg.78(8) (a child living with the couple when he is away from home while at school).

"Joint-claim jobseeker's allowance" is also defined in this subsection. It means an   **1.80**
allowance entitlement to which arises through subs.(2B), above. It then falls within the definition of IBJSA.

The contribution-based conditions

1.81   **2.**— [*Omitted as not applying to income-based JSA*]

The income-based conditions

1.82   **3.**—(1) The conditions referred to in [¹ section 1(2A)(b)] are that the claimant—

(a) has an income which does not exceed the applicable amount (determined in accordance with regulations under section 4) or has no income;

(b) is not entitled to income support [²[⁴, state pension credit or an income-related employment and support allowance]];

(c) is not a member of a family one of whose members is entitled to income support;

(d) is not a member of a family one of whose members is entitled to an income-based jobseeker's allowance;

[² (dd) is not a member of a [³ couple] the other member of which is entitled to state pension credit;]

[⁴ (de) is not a member of a couple the other member of which is entitled to an income-related employment and support allowance;]

(e) is not a member of a [³ couple] the other member of which is engaged in remunerative work; and

(f) is a person—

(i) who has reached the age of 18; or

(ii) in respect of whom a direction under section 16 is in force; or

(iii) who has, in prescribed circumstances to be taken into account for a prescribed period, reached the age of 16 but not the age of 18.

(2) Regulations may provide for one or both of the following conditions to be included in the income-based conditions, in the case of a person to whom subsection (1)(f)(ii) or (iii) applies—

(a) a condition that the claimant must register for employment;

(b) a condition that the claimant must register for training.

(3) In subsection (1)(f)(iii) "period" includes—

(a) a period of a determinate length;

(b) a period defined by reference to the happening of a future event; and

(c) a period of a determinate length but subject to earlier determination upon the happening of a future event.

(4) Regulations under subsection (2) may, in particular, make provision by reference to persons designated by the Secretary of State for the purpose of the regulations.

AMENDMENTS

1. Welfare Reform and Pensions Act 1999 s.59 and Sch.7 para.4(1) (March 19, 2001).

2. State Pension Credit Act 2002 s.14 and Sch.2 para.37 (October 6, 2003).

3. Civil Partnership Act 2004 s.254 and Sch.24 para.119 (December 5, 2005).

4. Welfare Reform Act 2007 s.28(1) and Sch.3 para.12(3) (October 27, 2008).

DEFINITIONS

"claimant"—see s.35(1).
"couple"—*ibid.*
"employment"—*ibid.* and JSA Regulations 1996 reg.4.

"family"— see s.35(1).
"income-based conditions"—*ibid.*
"income-based jobseeker's allowance"—see s.1(4).
"prescribed"—see s.35(1).
"training"—*ibid.*

GENERAL NOTE

Subsection (1)

This contains the further conditions for entitlement to income-based JSA for a   1.83
claimant who is not a member of a "joint-claim couple" in addition to those in s.1
and the capital rule under s.13(1). See s.3A for the further conditions of entitlement
for a joint-claim couple. For who constitutes a "joint-claim couple", see s.1(4) and
reg.3A(1) of the JSA Regulations 1996.

Under para.(a), the person's income (which includes the income of any partner:
s.13(2) and reg.88(1) of the JSA Regulations 1996) must be less than the applicable
amount (effectively the figure set for the family's requirements under s.4(5)). Note that
as a consequence of the removal of amounts for children from income-based JSA (with
effect from April 6, 2004, except in "transitional cases"—see the note to reg.17 of the
Income Support Regulations and the note to reg.83 of the JSA Regulations 1996), only
a partner's income will count as that of the claimant and the applicable amount will no
longer include any personal allowances for children, the family premium, the disabled
child premium or the enhanced disability premium for a child.

The person must in general be at least 18 (para.(f)(i)), unless within certain categories (para.(f)(iii)), or the Secretary of State has directed that he will otherwise suffer
severe hardship (para.(f)(ii) and s.16). (See regs 57–68 of the JSA Regulations 1996 for
those 16- and 17-year-olds who are entitled to income-based JSA and the conditions of
their eligibility.) If the person is a member of a couple, the partner must not be engaged
in remunerative work (in the case of a partner remunerative work is work of 24 hours or
more a week: reg.51(1)(b) of the JSA Regulations 1996) (para.(e)). Paragraphs (b) and
(c) confirm that income-based JSA is not payable if the claimant, or any member of the
family, is entitled to income support. See the corresponding amendment to s.124(1)
of the SSCBA 1992 as regards the conditions of entitlement to income support. In
addition, para.(d) excludes entitlement if another member of the family is entitled to
income-based JSA. Following the introduction of state pension credit on October 6,
2003, entitlement to income-based JSA is also excluded if the claimant is entitled to
state pension credit (para.(b)) or is a member of a couple and his partner is entitled to
state pension credit (para.(dd)). Similarly, from October 27, 2008, as a consequence
of the start of the ESA scheme, entitlement is excluded if the claimant is entitled to
income-related ESA (para.(b)) or if he is a member of a couple and his partner is entitled to income-related ESA (para.(de)).

Subsection (2)

See reg.62 of the JSA Regulations 1996.   1.84

[¹ The conditions for claims by joint-claim couples

3A.—(1) The conditions referred to in section 1(2B)(c) are—   1.85
(a) that the income of the joint-claim couple does not exceed the applicable amount (determined in accordance with regulations under
section 4) or the couple have no income;
(b) that no member of a family of which the couple are members is entitled to income support;
(c) that no member of any such family (other than the couple) is entitled
to an income-based jobseeker's allowance;
[² (cc) that neither member of the couple is entitled to state pension credit;]

[³ (cd) that neither member of the couple is entitled to an income-related employment and support allowance;]

     (d) that at least one member of the couple has reached the age of 18; and

     (e) that if only one member of the couple has reached the age of 18, the other member of the couple is a person—

          (i) in respect of whom a direction under section 16 is in force; or

          (ii) who has, in prescribed circumstances to be taken into account for a prescribed period, reached the age of 16.

     (2) Subsections (2) and (4) of section 3 shall apply in relation to a member of the couple to whom subsection (1)(e)(i) or (ii) above applies as they apply in relation to a claimant to whom subsection (1)(f)(ii) or (iii) of that section applies.

     (3) In subsection (1)(e)(ii) above "period" shall be construed in accordance with section 3(3).]

AMENDMENTS

     1. Welfare Reform and Pensions Act 1999 s.59 and Sch.7 para.4(2) (March 19, 2001).

     2. State Pension Credit Act 2002 s.14 and Sch.2 para.38 (October 6, 2003).

     3. Welfare Reform Act 2007 s.28(1) and Sch.3 para.12(4) (October 27, 2008).

DEFINITIONS

     "claimant"—see s.35(1).
     "family"—*ibid.*
     "income-based jobseeker's allowance"—see s.1(4).
     "joint-claim couple"—*ibid.*
     "prescribed"—see s.35(1).

GENERAL NOTE

Subsection (1)

1.86   In addition to the requirements in s.1 and the capital rule under s.13(1), this sets out the further conditions for entitlement to income-based JSA in the case of a joint-claim couple (defined in s.1(4) and see reg.3A(1) of the JSA Regulations 1996). For a claimant for income-based JSA who is not a member of a joint-claim couple, see. s.3.

     The conditions in subs.(1) more or less mirror those in s.3(1), with the necessary adjustments in the wording due to the fact that this section is only concerned with claims by a couple who both have to meet the conditions (except in certain circumstances—see reg.3E of the JSA Regulations 1996). The amendment made on October 6, 2003 as a consequence of the introduction of state pension credit excludes entitlement to income-based JSA in the case of a joint-claim couple if either member of the couple is entitled to state pension credit (para.(cc)). A similar amendment was made on October 27, 2008 following the start of the ESA scheme excluding entitlement if either member of the couple is entitled to income-related ESA (para.(cd)).

[¹ Joint-claim couples: the nominated member

1.87   **3B.**—(1) Where a joint-claim couple make a claim for a joint-claim jobseeker's allowance, they may nominate one of them as the member of the couple to whom the allowance is to be payable.

     (2) In default of one of them being so nominated, the allowance shall be payable to whichever of them is nominated by the Secretary of State.

     (3) Subsections (1) and (2) have effect subject to section 4A(4) and (7).

     (4) In this Act references to the nominated member of a joint-claim couple are, except where section 20A(7) applies, to the member of the couple nomi-

nated under subsection (1) or (2) above; and where section 20A(7) applies, references to the nominated member of such a couple are to the member of the couple to whom section 20A(7) provides for the allowance to be payable.

(5) Nothing in this section or section 20A(7) affects the operation of any statutory provision by virtue of which any amount of the allowance is required or authorised to be paid to someone other than the nominated member of the couple.]

AMENDMENT

1. Welfare Reform and Pensions Act 1999 s.59 and Sch.7 para.4(2) (March 19, 2001).

DEFINITIONS

"joint-claim couple"—see s.1(4).
"joint-claim jobseeker's allowance"—*ibid.*

Amount payable by way of jobseeker's allowance

4.— (1) – (2) [*Omitted as not applying to income-based JSA*]   1.88
(3) In the case of an income-based jobseeker's allowance[¹ (other than a joint-claim jobseeker's allowance)], the amount payable shall be—
  (a) if a claimant has no income, the applicable amount;
  (b) if a claimant has an income, the amount by which the applicable amount exceeds his income.
[¹(3A) In the case of a joint-claim jobseeker's allowance, the amount payable in respect of a joint-claim couple shall be—
  (a) if the couple have no income, the applicable amount;
  (b) if the couple have an income, the amount by which the applicable amount exceeds the couple's income.]
(4) Except in prescribed circumstances, a jobseeker's allowance shall not be payable where the amount otherwise payable would be less than a prescribed minimum.
(5) The applicable amount shall be such amount or the aggregate of such amounts as may be determined in accordance with regulations.
(6) – (11A) [*Omitted as not applying to income-based JSA*]
(12) Regulations under subsection (5) may provide that, in prescribed cases, an applicable amount is to be nil.

AMENDMENT

1. Welfare Reform and Pensions Act 1999 Sch.7 para.5 (March 19, 2001).

DEFINITIONS

"claimant"—see s.35(1).
"income-based jobseeker's allowance"—see s.1(4).
"joint-claim couple"—*ibid.*
"prescribed"—see s.35(1).

GENERAL NOTE

Subsection (3)
This provision sets out the basic means test calculation for income-based JSA   1.89
(other than a joint-claim jobseeker's allowance). Provided that the conditions of entitlement imposed by ss.1 and 3 and the capital test under s.13(1) are satisfied,

the claimant's income is set against his applicable amount, calculated according to regs 82–87 of the JSA Regulations 1996. The difference is the amount of benefit. Claimants' income includes that of the other members of their family (s.13(2)). However, as a consequence of the removal of amounts for children and young persons from income-based JSA (with effect from April 6, 2004, except in "transitional cases"—see further the note to reg.17 of the Income Support Regulations and the note to reg.83 of the JSA Regulations 1996), a child's income and capital will be totally ignored and only a partner's income and capital will count as that of the claimant (see the amended form of reg.88(1) of the JSA Regulations 1996).

Subsection (3A)

1.90   This sets out the basic means test calculation for a joint-claim jobseeker's allowance. Provided that the conditions of entitlement imposed by ss.1 and 3A–B and the capital test under s.13(1) are satisfied, the joint-claim couple's income is set against its applicable amount, calculated according to regs 86A–C of the JSA Regulations 1996. The difference is the amount of benefit, so that, if the couple has no income the amount payable is its applicable amount.

Subsection (4)

1.91   See reg.87A of the JSA Regulations 1996.

Subsection (5)

1.92   See regs 82 to 87 of, and Schs 1, 2, 5 and 5A to, the JSA Regulations 1996. These adopt the income support model, although there are some changes to the premiums to reflect the fact that people over pensionable age have never been entitled to JSA.

Subsection (12)

1.93   See regs 85 and 85A of, and Schs 5 and 5A to, the JSA Regulations 1996.

Amount payable in respect of joint-claim couple

1.94   **4A.** [*Omitted as not applying to income-based JSA*]

Duration of a contribution-based jobseeker's allowance

1.95   **5.** [*Omitted as not applying to income-based JSA*]

Jobseeking

Availability for employment

1.96   **6.**—(1) For the purposes of this Act, a person is available for employment if he is willing and able to take up immediately any employed earner's employment.

(2) Subsection (1) is subject to such provisions as may be made by regulations; and those regulations may, in particular, provide that a person—

(a) may restrict his availability for employment in any week in such ways as may be prescribed; or

(b) may restrict his availability for employment in any week in such circumstances as may be prescribed (for example, on grounds of conscience, religious conviction or physical or mental condition or because he is caring for another person) and in such ways as may be prescribed.

(3) The following are examples of restrictions for which provision may be made by the regulations—

(a) restrictions on the nature of the employment for which a person is available;

(b) restrictions on the periods for which he is available;

(c) restrictions on the terms or conditions of employment for which he is available;

(d) restrictions on the locality or localities within which he is available.

(4) Regulations may prescribe circumstances in which, for the purposes of this Act, a person is or is not to be treated as available for employment.

(5) Regulations under subsection (4) may, in particular, provide for a person who is available for employment—

(a) only in his usual occupation,

(b) only at a level of remuneration not lower than that which he is accustomed to receive, or

(c) only in his usual occupation and at a level of remuneration not lower than that which he is accustomed to receive,

to be treated, for a permitted period, as available for employment.

(6) Where it has been determined [¹ . . .] that a person is to be treated, for the purposes of this Act, as available for employment in any week, the question whether he is available for employment in that week may be subsequently determined [¹under section 9 or 10 of the Social Security Act 1998].

(7) In this section "permitted period", in relation to any person, means such period as may be determined in accordance with the regulations made under subsection (4).

(8) Regulations under subsection (4) may prescribe, in relation to permitted periods—

(a) the day on which any such period is to be regarded as having begun in any case;

(b) the shortest and longest periods which may be determined in any case;

(c) factors which [²the Secretary of State] may take into account in determining the period in any case.

(9) For the purposes of this section "employed earner's employment" has the same meaning as in the Benefits Act.

AMENDMENTS

1. Social Security Act 1998 Sch.7 para.134(1) (October 18, 1999).
2. Social Security Act 1998 Sch.7 para.134(2) (October 18, 1999).

DEFINITIONS

"the Benefits Act"—see s.35(1).
"claimant"—*ibid.*
"employed earner's employment"—see subs.(9) and SSCBA 1992 s.2(1)(a).
"employment"—see s.35(1) and JSA Regulations 1996 reg.4.
"prescribed"—see s.35(1).
"regulations"—*ibid.*
"week"—*ibid.*

GENERAL NOTE

This section and ss.7-10 expand on the "labour market conditions" for entitlement to old style JSA in s.1(2)(a)–(c). However, much of the key detail remains in the

1.97

45

regulations made under these sections (see Pt II of the JSA Regulations 1996). Note that regulations made under ss.6 and 7 are subject to the affirmative procedure (s.37(1)(c)). See also s.19B for the possibility of a reduction in benefit on a new claim after the termination of entitlement because of ceasing to be available for employment.

Note that there can be no entitlement to regular IBJSA at the beginning of a claim until the decision-maker is satisfied that the claimant meets the availability condition in s.1(2)(a). However, there may be eligibility for payments under the hardship provisions in regs 140–146H of the JSA Regulations 1996. In addition, if the issue is ultimately resolved in favour of the claimant, full benefit is to be paid from the date of claim.

The interaction of the hardship provisions and the rules on suspension of payment of benefit is complex. There appear to be two stages at the beginning of a claim. First, the decision-maker may defer the making of any decision until satisfied that there is sufficient evidence to do so, within the limits of reasonableness under s.8(1) of the SSA 1998 (see the annotation in Vol.I). In those circumstances, if the sole reason for the delay is that an issue arises as to satisfaction of one of the "labour market" conditions in s.1(2)(a)–(c) (reg.141(2) of the JSA Regulations 1996 and the equivalent provision for joint-claim couples in regs 146A–146H, not separately noted below) and the claimant falls into one of the vulnerable groups specified in reg.140(1), the claimant is to be treated as entitled to IBJSA at the hardship rate after the expiry of the seven waiting days. A person outside the vulnerable groups, if in hardship (reg.140(2)), can be so treated from the 15th day after the claim (reg.142). However, there seems a limited need for any delay in making a decision in such circumstances because reg.141(4), made under para.8 of Sch.1 to the old style Jobseekers Act 1995, allows a person within a s.140(1) vulnerable group, except where there is deemed non-availability under reg.15 of the JSA Regs 1996, to be entitled to IBJSA at the hardship rate without satisfying the conditions in s.1(2)(a)–(c), provided that the other conditions in s.1(2) are satisfied. There is no similar provision in reg.142. If a decision on entitlement can then be made under reg.141(4), the second stage comes into play. On the face of it, reg.16(2) of the Decisions and Appeals Regulations 1999 requires the Secretary of State to suspend payment of any benefit whenever an issue arises as to whether a JSA claimant is or was available for employment or is or was actively seeking employment. However, reg.141(5) specifically excludes the effect of that provision in the circumstances where reg.141(4) applies. These second-stage rules also apply where an issue as to availability arises during the course of an award of JSA.

1.98   The benefits regimes for unemployed people have always embodied an underlying principle that the unemployment must be involuntary, one aspect of which is that a claimant without work must want to and seek to return to the world of employment. One element giving effect to that principle has been the requirement that the claimant, as a condition of receiving benefit, must be "available for employment" (examined here). The other is that the claimant must actively be seeking employment (examined in the annotations to s.7).

This section, amplifying the basic statement of availability as a condition of entitlement to IBJSA set out in s.1(2)(a), gives a basic definition of the "available for employment" requirement (subss.(1) and (9)). But that relatively straightforward approach, encapsulating the essence of previous case law, is itself made "subject to such provisions as may be made by regulations" made under the other provisions of this section, which consist of rule-making powers (subss.(2)–(5)), definitions (subss.(7) and (9)), and one dealing with the scope of revision or supersession of a decision that a person is to be treated as available (subs.(6)). The regulations made under this section are the JSA Regulations 1996 regs 4 and 5–17, which are detailed and rendered complex by "legislation by reference" and the manner in which they often qualify each other.

Temporary Coronavirus Provisions

Regulation 7 of the Social Security (Coronavirus) (Further Measures) Regulations 2020 (SI 2020/371) (see Pt III of this volume) provided that for the three months beginning with March 30, 2020 anyone with an award of old style JSA was to be treated as available for employment. It is arguable that, by virtue of reg.15(5) of the JSA Regulations 1996, the deeming of non-availability in reg.15 trumps the effect of reg.7 except where modified by reg.4 of the Social Security (Coronavirus) (Prisoners) Regulations 2020 (SI 2020/409) (temporary release of English and Welsh prisoners: see the notes to reg.15). The effect of reg.7 of the Further Measures Regulations expired at the end of November 12, 2020 (reg.10(2)). The power to extend the three-month period was not exercised before it expired.

1.99

It is not clear whether the restriction of the effect of reg.7 to those who had an award of old style JSA meant that on a new claim (insofar as a claim for old style JSA, as opposed to new style JSA and universal credit, is still possible) the availability condition was to be applied in determining initial entitlement. The mechanism suggested for new style JSA in the notes to s.6E of the new style Jobseekers Act 1995 (Vol.I of this series) cannot work for old style JSA because the availability and actively seeking work conditions are imposed directly by the legislation as conditions of entitlement. It appears that in practice little if any attention was given to "conditionality" during the period affected.

Subsection (1)

This sets out what might be called the general principle of availability; in effect a statutory endorsement of the basic case law propositions that to be available a claimant must be prepared to accept at once any offer of suitable employment brought to his notice (*R(U) 1/53*) and must be able to accept such an offer (*Shaukat Ali v CAO*, appendix to *R(U) 1/85*). The general principle stated in the subsection requires a claimant:

1.100

(i)   to be *willing* to take up *any employed earner's employment*;

(ii) to be *able* to take it up; and

(iii) to be willing and able to do so *immediately*.

Each of these elements requires some further comment, undertaken below. It must be recalled, however, that this general statement, important as it is in emphasising requirements to be flexible to meet the needs of the labour market, is qualified by regulations. The essence of those qualifications is set out in the annotation to this section, with the detail being reserved for the annotations to the particular regulations.

Now that s.7 imposes the discrete condition of entitlement of actively seeking employment there can be no room for the application to s.6 of the proposition in para.14 of *R(U) 5/80* that being available means being available in an active, positive sense and that "availability implies some active step by the person concerned to draw attention to his availability" (*RL v SSWP (JSA)* [2018] UKUT 177 (AAC) paras.22-25). However, as Judge Lane suggests there, many non-entitlement decisions may still be being based wrongly on failure to fulfil the availability condition when the proper ground would be failure to meet the actively seeking work condition.

Non-availability precludes entitlement to old style JSA (see s.1(2)(a)). It was not entirely clear at the outset whether the legislation required the matter to be looked at on a weekly basis or, like unemployment benefit, a daily basis, although it was always the Department's view that the provision in s.1(3) that old style JSA is payable in respect of a week means that to be entitled a claimant has to be available on all the days of the week. The subsequent case law puts the matter beyond doubt. In *Secretary of State for Social Security v David*, reported as part of *R(JSA) 3/01* (see the more detailed discussion in the notes to regs 7(3) and 13(3) of the JSA Regulations 1996), the claimant had been held in police custody for two days

1.101

out of a benefit week and been found not available for employment for the whole of the benefit week. Commissioner Levenson had accepted that a claimant was either available for employment throughout a particular week or was not, but concluded that Mr David was available for the two days in police custody because of the rule allowing a restriction of availability as reasonable in the light of a claimant's physical or mental condition. On appeal, the Court of Appeal rejected that way out and said nothing to indicate any disagreement with Commissioner Levenson's adoption of the weekly basis. Indeed, the concern expressed by Simon Brown LJ in para.27 of his judgment about the unfairness of a claimant (presumed innocent) losing a whole week's benefit through two days' detention (which eventually led to the introduction of reg.14(1)(s) of the JSA Regulations 1996) was predicated on that basis. Further, that basis was implicitly adopted by Judge Rowland in *AT v SSWP (JSA)* [2013] UKUT 73 (AAC) (see para.1.106 below), in his acceptance that the claimant there would have failed to meet the condition of availability for the whole of a benefit week by reason of going away on holiday in the evening of the last day if it had not been for the making of a retrospective variation of his jobseeker's agreement. That approach is consistent with the decision in *R(JSA) 2/07*, which on its facts dealt with a more long-standing expressed unwillingness to work on a day on which the jobseeker's agreement currently in force required him to be available. Such an unwillingness can be regarded as existing throughout the week and is far less problematic than a suddenly intervening event or change of mind.

1.102   *"Any employed earner's employment"*: As was the case with the previous regime of benefits for unemployed people *(R(U)14/51)*, availability for self-employment does not suffice; the section requires availability for employed earner's employment, on the definition of which see subs.(9) and SSCBA 1992 ss.2(1)(a) and 122(1). Note in contrast that in some circumstances claimants can confine their jobsearch to self-employment and still be actively seeking employment under s.7 and JSA Regulations 1996 reg.20. But the claimant must always still be available for *employment* as opposed to *self-employment*.

The rubric refers to *"any"* employed earner's employment. The apparent width of this indicates graphically the need for claimants to be flexible in a changing labour market. Yet, subs.(2) and resultant regulations enable the imposition of a range of restrictions on availability, for the generality of claimants throughout their claim (JSA Regulations 1996 regs 7 and 8), for the generality of claimants during a "permitted period" of up to 13 weeks (JSA Regulations 1996 reg.16), for those laid off or kept on short-time (JSA Regulations 1996 reg.17) and for particular groups of claimants (JSA Regulations 1996 regs 13 and 13A), examined in more depth in the annotations to the particular regulations themselves.

1.103   The reasoning in *GP v SSWP (JSA)* [2015] UKUT 476 (AAC), reported as [2016] AACR 14, discussed in the notes to s.7(1) below, would indicate that only availability for employed earner's employment in Great Britain can be required.

Under the previous regime of benefits for the unemployed, being available for part-time work only did not of itself necessarily preclude availability *(CU109/48(KL); CU22/91,* paras 9 and 10). That is *not* the position under old style JSA. Subject to regulations enabling restriction of hours to less, in order to be regarded as available for employment, a person must be willing and able (see below) to take up employment for a minimum of 40 hours per week (JSA Regulations 1996 reg.6(1)) but also be willing and able to take up employment of less than 40 hours per week (JSA Regulations 1996 reg.6(2)). In other words, being available merely for part-time employment (less than 40 hours per week) does not suffice, but to be available one must not only be available for full-time employment (40 hours or more per week) but also be willing and able to accept part-time employment (less than 40 hours per week), if offered. Generally, no claimant is able to restrict availability to less than the 40 hours minimum (JSA Regulations 1996 reg.7(1)), although there are exceptions for those with caring responsibilities (reg.13(4) and (5)), for certain lone parents (reg.13A), for those on short-time (reg.17(2)) and for anyone whose physical or mental condition makes such a restriction reasonable (reg.13(3)). Furthermore, JSA Regulations 1996 reg.7 allows a claimant to agree a pattern of availability ("the times at which he is available to take up employment") for 40 hours or more across a week, even though this may effect some reduction in his prospects of securing employment, provided that the pattern of availability is such as to afford him reasonable prospects of securing employment and that those prospects are not reduced considerably by the restriction embodied in the pattern of availability.

A claimant who is in part-time employment, not excluded from entitlement under s.1(2)(e) by being engaged in "remunerative work", i.e. for more than 16 hours a week, is nonetheless required to be available for employment for at least 40 hours a week (or any lesser number as allowed under the rules just discussed). But the person need only be willing to accept such employment after expiry of any statutory period of notice needed to terminate the part-time contract (JSA Regulations 1996 reg.5(3) and see under *Immediately* below).

"Willing . . . to take up": What claimants are willing and not willing to do can, of **1.104** course, most obviously be judged from their professions of willingness on claim forms, in interviews with Jobcentre Plus, and in their jobseeker's agreement. But it can also be inferred from conduct (see *R(U)4/53*). There the claimant had shown by his long practice of not taking up the option of working voluntary shifts on Saturdays that he was not available for work on Saturdays. Reference is sometimes made to the statement in para.14 of *R(U) 5/80* that availability implies some active step by the claimant to draw attention to their availability. However, as pointed out by Judge Lane in para.24 of *RL v SSWP (JSA)* [2018] UKUT 177 (AAC), that statement was made at a time when the legislation did not contain a separate condition of entitlement of actively seeking work or employment. Thus, a failure to take reasonable steps to seek employment or to agree a jobseeker's agreement committing to such steps would in general be better dealt with by reference to that condition rather than availability.

"Able to take up": Problem areas under previous regimes of benefits for unemployed **1.105** people afford likely instances where this requirement will prove problematic. Because of the different wording of the primary legislation, and the detail of new specific regulations, however, it cannot readily be assumed that the case law solutions propounded under the old UB regime will necessarily carry over into the new. But, bearing that very much in mind, obvious instances of inability to take up employment are where immigration law precludes the claimant working (*Shaukat Ali v CAO*, Appendix to *R(U)1/85*), or where the claimant is about to go abroad (*R(U)2/90(T)*—dealing with the position of wives of servicemen about to join their husbands for a posting abroad), or is contractually bound to another employer (*R(U)11/51*), for example, to be on call each working day. As regards this last category, note, however, the specific rules treating "a person who is laid-off " and "a person who is kept on short time" (both terms specifically defined in JSA Regulations 1996 reg.4) as available in certain circumstances (reg.17). Thus, it is arguable that a person subject to a zero hours contract who is given no hours of work could be available for employment but probably not if the contract contained an exclusivity clause (not made ineffective until the coming into force of s.153 of the Small Business, Enterprise and Employment Act 2015 on May 26, 2015). By the same token, it is arguable that a person "furloughed" under the Coronavirus Job Retention Scheme, which by its initial terms only prohibits employment by the furloughing employer, is available for alternative employment unless the contract of employment prohibits that. Such a person might also be able to take advantage of reg.17 on workers who are laid off, if the circumstances amount to "temporary adverse industrial conditions".

Another instance of possible inability would be going away on holiday. The position as respects UB, of course, was that claimants could still be regarded as available if, having made prior arrangements with the Employment Service, they could be readily contacted, would be willing and able to cut short the holiday to accept employment and could show that there was nothing to prevent them accepting such suitable employment as might be notified *(R(U)1/55)*. But there is now in the legislation itself an explicit statutory requirement of being able to take up *immediately* any employment, with only a few exceptions enshrined in legislation (JSA Regulations 1996 regs 5, 11 and 12). So it would appear that a harsher approach may have to be taken than under the UB regime (see *CJSA/1279/1998*). However, the existence of other provisions deeming claimants to be available for employment and to be actively seeking employment in certain circumstances may also be relevant to potential entitlement (regs 14 and 19).

On the general approach, there is helpful guidance on the relationship between the condition of availability and the contents of the jobseeker's agreement in *R(JSA) 2/07* and *AT v SSWP (JSA)* [2013] UKUT 73 (AAC). The critical provisions are regs 5(4) and 7(2) of the JSA Regulations 1996. Regulation 5(4) provides that claimants who in accordance with reg.7 or some other provisions are only available for employment at certain times are not required to be able to take up employment at a time at which they are not available, provided that they are willing and able to take up employment immediately they are available. Regulation 7(2) allows claimants to restrict the number of hours per week for which they are available, subject to a minimum of 40 hours except where use can be made of the exceptions in reg.7(1), if that pattern of availability leaves reasonable prospects of securing employment and (sub-para.(b)) the pattern of availability is recorded in the jobseeker's agreement, as originally signed or as varied. The great majority of claimants will have imposed such a restriction, by stating that they are not available every day of the week or for some hours out of the 24 or for some maximum weekly hours no less than 40. It was decided in *R(JSA) 2/07* that, for reg.7(2)(b) to have any practical application, it has to entail that a claimant whose actual pattern of availability is more restricted than recorded in the jobseeker's agreement (e.g. by going away on holiday and becoming unable to take up employment immediately) ceases to satisfy the conditions of entitlement in s.1(2)(a). And ceasing to satisfy that condition on one day in the benefit week eliminates entitlement for the whole week.

1.106   The application of those principles is well illustrated in *AT*, along with a very limited way out through the possibility of a retrospective amendment of the jobseeker's agreement. The Secretary of State decided that the claimant there had not been available for employment and therefore not entitled to JSA for the two benefit weeks ending on December 31, 2009 and January 7, 2010. After the Jobcentre had closed on December 31, 2009, the claimant decided to go away to Yorkshire, intending to return on January 3, 2010. Bad weather stopped him returning until January 8, 2010, so that he missed signing on on January 7, although he had informed the Jobcentre of the position on January 5. Judge Rowland agreed that the claimant had not been available for employment in the benefit week ending on January 7, 2010, but accepted the Secretary of State's submission that, since the claimant had been available for all of the week ending December 31, 2009 until the evening of that day, his travelling to Yorkshire did not significantly reduce his prospects of securing employment, so that there should be a retrospective variation of his jobseeker's agreement (which had originally contained no restriction on days or times of availability, only a maximum of 40 hours per week) to accord with the actual pattern of availability in that week. The claimant had also no doubt done enough in the week ending December 31, 2009 to satisfy the condition of actively seeking employment.

The circumstances of *AT* were unusual so that, while the decision shows a way out in a limited number of hard cases, it does not provide any great inroad into the basic holiday rule. It is possible that some exceptions and deemings might assist a wider range of claimants, in which case reg.7(2) of the JSA Regulations 1996 will not be a problem. Under reg.5(1), a person who has caring responsibilities for anyone needing care who is in the same household or a close relative need only be willing and able to take up employment on being given one week's notice and to attend an interview on 48 hours' notice. Under reg.5(1A), where the caring responsibilities are for a child and they would make it unreasonable for the claimant to keep to the para.(1) limits, the notice periods are extended to 28 and 7 days respectively. The definition of "caring responsibilities" in reg.4 does not require a person to have sole or main or even any particular degree of responsibility for caring for the child or other person. So could a claimant with a child or a relative etc who needs care, even if they have a partner, argue that while away on holiday they are to be regarded as available for employment if they can be called back for an interview or employment within the relevant limits? In addition, reg.14(1)(t) deems claimants to be available for employment while looking after a child for whom they have caring responsibilities during a school holiday or similar vacation period, if it is unreasonable to make other arrangements for care. Claimants who can take the benefit of any of those provisions might still have a problem with the condition of actively seeking employment, but reg.19(1)(p) deems claimants to be actively seeking employment in any week in respect of which they have given notice to an employment officer that they do not intend to be actively seeking employment and intend to be residing away from home (subject to a limit of two weeks in any 12 months in an ordinary holiday case). Regulation 19(1)(p) appears to require advance notice, as would obviously be sensible for anyone who wanted to take advantage of any of the provisions on availability.

"Immediately": The old style JSA statutory formulation of availability generally requires willingness and ability to take up *immediately* any employed earner's employment. A person is able to take up employment immediately even if they first have to obtain clearance in respect of any job, where that clearance is more or less a formality and normally a telephone call would suffice (*CSU 182/1997*, which concerned a former Inland Revenue employee who had taken early retirement and so was subject to the "Rules on the acceptance of outside appointments by Crown Servants"). See the helpful remarks of Simon Brown LJ in *Secretary of State for Social Security v David*, reported in *R(JSA) 3/01*, and discussed in the notes to reg.7(3) of the JSA Regulations 1996:

1.107

> "No doubt the requirement for immediate availability allows the claimant time to wash, dress and have his breakfast, but strictly it would seem to be inconsistent with, say, a claimant's overnight stay with a friend or relative, or attendance at a weekend cricket match, or even an evening at the cinema (unless perhaps he had left a contact number and had not travelled far)".

Those latter examples could of course only bite if they occurred during hours in which the claimant had undertaken to be available, as explained below.

However, exceptions are provided in JSA Regulations 1996 reg.5, made under the width of the enabling power in subs.(2), below. The exceptions give claimants varying periods of grace within which they must be willing and able to take up employment, for a range of groups: (a) for persons with caring responsibilities; (b) for those engaged in voluntary work; (c) for others providing a service with or without remuneration; and (d) for certain persons employed for less than 16 hours per week and under a specific statutory obligation to provide notice. It also prevents the "immediately" requirement being used to negate the protective effect of regs 7, 13 or 17, allowing certain claimants periods of non-availability (in effect agreeing a "pattern of availability") by providing that the "immediately" condition cannot be used to require a claimant to be available at a time of permitted non-availability pursuant to his pattern of availability, so long as he is willing and able to take up employment immediately that permitted spell ends. See further the annotations to JSA Regulations 1996 reg.5.

Subsections (2) and (3)

Subsection (2) enables the basic availability rule in subs.(1) to be modified by regulations, particularly (but not exclusively) by enabling claimants to restrict their availability in prescribed ways and by enabling them to restrict their availability both in prescribed circumstances (e.g. on grounds of their physical or mental

1.108

condition) and in prescribed ways. Subsection (3) sets out examples of restrictions which can be provided for in regulations: on the nature of employment; on periods of availability; on terms and conditions of employment; and on the locality or localities of availability. But clearly neither subsection so limits the modifications that can be made in regulations.

Leaving aside the "deemed available" and "deemed not available" regulations examined under subs.(4), the regulations made: (a) provide for exceptions to the "immediately" available requirements (JSA Regulations 1996 reg.5), and (b) set out permitted restrictions (JSA Regulations 1996 regs 6–13A and 17). The former have been noted in the annotation to subs.(1). The latter set a standard minimum hours (40) per week requirement and enable a claimant to place a range of restrictions on availability in a week without endangering entitlement through failure to surmount the availability hurdle (see in particular regs 7, 8, 13, 13A and 17). Some groups of claimants are allowed more restrictions than others. See further the annotations to the specific regulations, but note here a central requirement (not applicable to those who impose only restrictions reasonable in light of physical or mental condition and in some other circumstances) that the claimant establish that they have reasonable prospects of securing employment despite (generally all) the restrictions he has imposed.

Subsections (4), (5), (7) and (8)

1.109   Subsection (4) enables the making of regulations treating someone either as available or, as the case may be, not available for old style JSA purposes, whatever might be the result of applying the standard test of actual availability. See further JSA Regulations 1996 regs 14 and 14A (treated as available) and 15 (treated as not available, i.e. excluded from JSA), as temporarily modified during the 2020 coronavirus outbreak (see the notes to reg.15). See also reg.7 of the Social Security (Coronavirus) (Further Measures) Regulations 2020 (SI 2020/371) (Pt III of this volume) providing that for the three months beginning with March 30, 2020, anyone with an award of old style JSA was to be treated as available for and actively seeking employment (see the notes to s.1(2)). The effect of reg.7 expired at the end of November 12, 2020 (reg.10(2)). The power to extend the three-month period was not exercised before it expired.

Subsection (5) provides that regulations under subs.(4) can in particular enable claimants to restrict their availability to their usual occupation for a "permitted period", defined in subs.(7) as "in relation to any person, such period as may be determined in accordance with regulations", which regulations, pursuant to subs. (8), can prescribe the day on which the period begins, its minimum and maximum lengths and the factors that a decision-maker may take into account in determining the period in any particular case. JSA Regulations 1996 reg.16 is the product. There is a specific "deeming" regulation dealing with those laid-off or kept on short time (reg.17). Other "deeming" regulations deal with full-time students following a "qualifying course" (an employment related course of further or higher education, or a standard above that, lasting no more than 12 months) (reg.17A) and lone parents with care of children aged 5 (reg.17B).

Subsection (6)

1.110   This provides that where it had been decided that a person is to be treated as available for employment in any benefit week, a subsequent revision or supersession of that decision can embrace also the question whether, in that week, the person was actually available for employment.

Subsection (9)

1.111   This stipulates that "employed earner's employment" has the same meaning for purposes of this section as it does in SSCBA 1992, s.2.

See *GP v SSWP (JSA)* [2015] UKUT 476 (AAC), reported as [2016] AACR 14, discussed in para.1.103 above and in detail in the notes to s.7(1) below.

Actively seeking employment

7.—(1) For the purposes of this Act, a person is actively seeking employ- 1.112
ment in any week if he takes in that week such steps as he can reasonably
be expected to have to take in order to have the best prospects of securing
employment.

(2) Regulations may make provision—

(a) with respect to steps which it is reasonable, for the purposes of subsection (1), for a person to be expected to have to take in any week;

(b) as to circumstances (for example, his skills, qualifications, abilities and
physical or mental limitations) which, in particular, are to be taken
into account in determining whether, in relation to any steps taken by
a person, the requirements of subsection (1) are satisfied in any week.

(3) Regulations may make provision for acts of a person which would
otherwise be relevant for purposes of this section to be disregarded in such
circumstances (including circumstances constituted by, or connected with,
his behaviour or appearance) as may be prescribed.

(4) Regulations may prescribe circumstances in which, for the purposes
of this Act, a person is to be treated as actively seeking employment.

(5) Regulations under subsection (4) may, in particular, provide for a
person who is actively seeking employment—

(a) only in his usual occupation,

(b) only at a level of remuneration not lower than that which he is accustomed to receive, or

(c) only in his usual occupation and at a level of remuneration not lower
than that which he is accustomed to receive,

to be treated, for the permitted period determined in his case for the purposes of section 6(5), as actively seeking employment during that period.

(6) Regulations may provide for this section, and any regulations made
under it, to have effect in relation to a person who has reached the age of 16
but not the age of 18 as if "employment" included "training".

(7) Where it has been determined [¹. . .] that a person is to be treated, for the
purposes of this Act, as actively seeking employment in any week, the question
whether he is actively seeking employment in that week may subsequently be
determined [¹under section 9 or 10 of the Social Security Act 1998].

(8) For the purposes of this section—

"employment" means employed earner's employment or, in prescribed
circumstances—

(a) self-employed earner's employment; or

(b) employed earner's employment and self-employed earner's employment;

and "employed earners employment" and "self-employed earner's employment" have the same meaning as in the Benefits Act.

AMENDMENT

1. Social Security Act 1998 Sch.7 para.135 (October 18, 1999).

DEFINITIONS

"the Benefits Act"—see s.35(1).
"employed earner's employment"—see subs.(8) and SSCBA 1992 ss.2(1)(a) and
122(1).
"prescribed"—see s.35(1).

"regulations"—*ibid.*
"self-employed earner's employment"—see subs.(8) and SSCBA 1992 ss.2(1)(b) and 122(1).
"training"—see s.35(1); JSA Regulations 1996 reg.65(6).
"week"—see s.35(1); JSA Regulations 1996 reg.4.

General Note

1.113   The actively seeking employment test as a "labour market" condition of entitlement to old style JSA (s.1(2)(c)), like availability for employment (the other "labour market" condition) set out in s.6, is a concrete manifestation of the underlying principle governing benefit regimes for unemployed people that the unemployment must be involuntary. Dropped from the regime in the 1930s, it was reintroduced amidst considerable controversy in 1989. Contrary to expectations, it did not generate a flood of appeals to tribunals. Note the possibility under s.19B of a reduction in benefit on a new claim after the termination of entitlement because of ceasing to be actively seeking employment.

Note that there can be no entitlement to regular IBJSA at the beginning of a claim until the decision-maker is satisfied that the claimant meets the condition in s.1(2)(c). However, there may be eligibility for payments under the hardship provisions in regs 140–146H of the JSA Regulations 1996. In addition, if the issue is ultimately resolved in favour of the claimant, full benefit is to be paid from the date of claim.

The interaction of the hardship provisions and the rules on suspension of payment of benefit is complex. There appear to be two stages at the beginning of a claim. First, the decision-maker may defer the making of any decision until satisfied that there is sufficient evidence to do so, within the limits of reasonableness under s.8(1) of the SSA 1998 (see the annotation in Vol. III). In those circumstances, if the sole reason for the delay is that an issue arises as to satisfaction of one of the "labour market" conditions in s.1(2)(a)–(c) (reg.141(2) of the JSA Regulations 1996 and the equivalent provision for joint claim couples in regs 146A–146H, not separately noted below) and the claimant falls into one of the vulnerable groups specified in reg.140(1), the claimant is to be treated as entitled to IBJSA at the hardship rate after the expiry of the seven waiting days. A person outside the vulnerable groups, if in hardship (reg.140(2)), can be so treated from the 15th day after the claim (reg.142). However, there seems a limited need for any delay in making a decision in such circumstances because reg.141(4), made under para.8 of Sch.1 to the old style Jobseekers Act 1995, allows a person within s.140(1), except where there is deemed non-availability under reg.15 of the JSA Regulations 1996, to be entitled to IBJSA at the hardship rate without satisfying the conditions in s.1(2)(a)–(c), provided that the other conditions in s.1(2) are satisfied. There is no similar provision in reg.142. If a decision on entitlement can then be made under reg.141(4), the second stage comes into play. On the face of it, reg.16(2) of the Decisions and Appeals Regulations 1999 requires the Secretary of State to suspend payment of any benefit whenever an issue arises as to whether a JSA claimant is or was available for employment or is or was actively seeking employment. However, reg.141(5) specifically excludes the effect of that provision in the circumstances where reg.141(4) applies. These second stage rules also apply where an issue as to actively seeking employment arises during the course of an award of JSA.

Note that regs 19–21B of the JSA Regulations 1996, made under subs.(4), prescribe circumstances in which a claimant is deemed to satisfy the actively seeking employment test and that reg.18, made under subs.(2), amplifies the test in subs.(1).

Temporary Coronavirus Provisions

1.114   Regulation 7 of the Social Security (Coronavirus) (Further Measures) Regulations 2020 (SI 2020/371) (see Pt III of this volume) provided that for the three months beginning with March 30, 2020 anyone with an award of old style JSA was to be treated as actively seeking employment (see the notes to s.1(2)), as well as available for employment. The effect of reg.7 expired at the end of November 12, 2020 (reg.10(2)). The power to extend the three-month period was not exercised before it expired.

It is not clear whether the restriction of the effect of reg.7 to those who had an award of old style JSA meant that on a new claim (insofar as a claim for old style JSA, as opposed to new style JSA and universal credit, was still possible) the actively seeking employment condition was to be applied in determining initial entitlement. The mechanism suggested for new style JSA in the notes to s.6D of the new style Jobseekers Act 1995 in Vol.I of this series cannot work for old style JSA because the availability and actively seeking work conditions are imposed directly by the legislation as conditions of entitlement. It appears that in practice little if any attention was given to "conditionality" during the period affected.

Subsection (1)

The UB test for actively seeking work was contained in subordinate legislation: to be actively seeking work in any week, persons had to take such steps, reasonable in their case, as to offer them *the best prospects of receiving offers of employment*. For old style JSA, this subsection contains a similarly formulated test: in any week persons are actively seeking employment if during that week they take such steps as they can reasonably be expected to take in order to have *the best prospects of securing employment*, perhaps thereby stressing more strongly the requirement of taking positive action to secure work.

1.115

Note that here "employment" is not confined to "employed earner's employment" but can in some circumstances embrace self-employment (subs.(8)): see further JSA Regulations 1996 regs 18(3)(i), 19(1)(r) and 20(2) and (3)). However, it is significant that the definition of "employed earner's employment" in s.2(1)(a) of the SSCBA 1992, specifically imported into s.7 (and therefore the regulations made under it) by subs.(8) as part of the definition of "employment", is restricted to such employment in Great Britain. In *GP v SSWP (JSA)* [2015] UKUT 476 (AAC), reported as [2016] AACR 14, Judge Gray held that that means that steps directed to securing employment that is not in Great Britain cannot count for the purpose of satisfying the test in s.7(1). In the particular case, the claimant was a highly qualified research scientist who, having been unsuccessful in seeking work in the UK in her field or in more menial jobs, was looking only for jobs in China and had in the period in question arranged two interviews there. The judge decided that the claimant's entitlement to JSA was rightly terminated. She mentioned the oddity that the s.2(1) definition is restricted to Great Britain, rather than the UK. That would on its face exclude from entitlement claimants taking steps only to secure employment in Northern Ireland. If that conclusion cannot be right, could it be argued that, despite the specific terms of s.7(8), the restriction to employment in Great Britain should be ignored? There is the further oddity that under reg.19(1)(m) of the JSA Regulations 1996 a person who is temporarily absent from Great Britain for at least three days in any week to attend an interview for employment, having notified an employment officer in writing, is deemed to be actively seeking employment for that week (and see regs 14(1)(a) and 50(6)). In that context, "employment" cannot sensibly be restricted to employment in Great Britain. It would be ludicrous if reg.19(1)(m) were restricted to interviews abroad for jobs in Great Britain. Is this a case where the context requires a different meaning from that specified in s.7(8) or does it indicate that that definition properly extends to something that would be employed earner's employment if carried on in Great Britain? There is no similar restriction in relation to the work search requirement in new style JSA.

It is for claimants to establish that they are actively seeking employment. As Northern Ireland Commissioner Brown stated in *C1/00–01 (JSA)* and *C2/00–01 (JSA)*, "it is . . . in the claimant's interest to keep a record and to have as far as possible further corroborative proof of the steps he has taken to seek employment" (see para.29). Note, however, that claimants' oral or written statements that they did this or that constitutes "evidence", so that in that case the tribunal erred insofar as it appeared to have rejected the claimant's statement merely because it was uncorroborated: "a claimant does not have to produce corroborative evidence though obviously his case will be strengthened if he can do so" (see para.30). These principles were followed and applied in *PC v SSWP (JSA)* [2016] UKUT 277 (AAC) and *RL v SSWP (JSA)* [2017] UKUT 282 (AAC), where it was suggested that the approach should now be based on *Kerr v Department for Social Development* [2004] UKHL 23, [2004] 1 W.L.R. 1372, *R 1/04 (SF)*. Commissioner Brown continued:

> "the tribunal was of course entitled to reject any evidence if it did not find it reliable. What it was not entitled to do however was to conclude that the claimant's evidence was not evidence. The claimant's evidence could have been accepted by the Tribunal and could, at its height, have, if accepted, established that he was actively seeking work. Instead, however, the Tribunal appeared to ignore this evidence and appeared to have the view that corroborative evidence must always be produced" (see para.34).

1.116   As Commissioner Williams rightly points out in *CJSA/1814/2007* (at paras 9–15), this subsection requires the application of a positive rather than a negative test. It asks what the claimant did in the week in question, rather than what they did not do. It is not a matter of whether each of the steps in the claimant's jobseeker's agreement was taken, but rather whether the tests in s.7(1) and JSA Regulations 1996 reg.18(1) were met by what the claimant actually did in the week at issue. The questions to be answered were thus:

> "(a) Should the claimant be expected to take at least three jobsearch steps that week, or is it reasonable that only one or two be taken?
> (b) What steps were taken?
> (c) In the light of that reasonable expectation and those findings, were the steps taken by the claimant "such steps as he can reasonably be expected to have to take in order to have the best prospects of securing employment" (s.7(1))?
> If the steps by the claimant taken [sic] meet that test, it is irrelevant that the claimant did not also take some other step, whether or not it is in the jobseeker's agreement". (at para.15)

That approach and the terms of reg.18 in general indicate that the stress should be more on reasonableness than on a view that there will always be something more that could be done to have the best prospects of securing employment. *CJSA/1814/2007* was followed and applied in *CJSA/3146/2009* in finding that a tribunal had gone wrong in law in focusing on whether the claimant had met the requirements of his jobseeker's agreement rather than on whether the steps that he had taken were such as he could reasonably have been expected to take to have the best prospects of securing employment. By the same token, although it was suggested in *PG v SSWP (JSA)* [2017] UKUT 388 (AAC) that it might take very cogent reasoning to justify a person having to take very well in excess of the three steps a week that is the starting point under reg.18(1) (the tribunal had said that there was no objection in principle to requiring a claimant to engage in actively searching for work as a full-time task), that would seem to underplay the effect of the fundamental test in s.7(1).

1.117   Despite the general obligation on the claimant to show the positive steps taken in a week, if the Secretary of State asserts to a tribunal that the claimant has failed to take particular steps that were open, supporting evidence may be necessary, particularly where the relevant information is within the DWP's control. So, where it was asserted that there were suitable roles on the Universal Jobmatch website that the claimant could have applied for, but did not, the Secretary of State needed to produce evidence of such availability to validate that assertion (para.11 of *RD v SSWP (JSA)* [2015] UKUT 702 (AAC)).

In Commissioner's decision *CJSA/2162/2001* (see the notes to s.9 below), it was suggested that there might be circumstances in which the application of the s.7(1) test would result in a conclusion that there were no steps that it was reasonable for the claimant to take in a particular week, so that the test could be satisfied by taking no steps. It is now submitted that the endorsement of that view in past editions was wrong. Despite the view expressed there by Commissioner Williams that reg.18 read as a whole did not preclude such a conclusion, it is hard to read reg.18(1) as requiring anything less than an absolute minimum of one step in any week to satisfy s.7(1). See further the notes to reg.18 and note the deeming in reg.19.

Subsection (2)

This enabling power authorises regulations to be made with respect to the steps it is reasonable for someone to be expected to have to take in order to be regarded as actively seeking employment and as to the circumstances that in particular are to be taken into account in determining whether the steps actually taken by a person are such as to satisfy the actively seeking employment test.   **1.118**

See the detailed provision in reg.18 and the notes to that provision. The non-exhaustive list in reg.18(2) of things that might count as reasonable steps is probably less significant than the non-exhaustive list in reg.18(3) of circumstances of the particular case to which regard is to be had in deciding whether the claimant has taken all reasonable steps in a week. As well as the claimant's skills, qualifications and abilities and physical or mental limitations, as specifically mentioned in subs. (2), account must be taken of the claimant's past work experience and the lapse of time since last working, steps taken in previous weeks and their effectiveness, the availability and location of employment vacancies and the special circumstances of homeless claimants. Taking part in various worthy activities and being deemed available for employment under reg.14 are relevant. More generally, time engaged in voluntary work (see reg.4) and the extent to which it may have improved prospects of employment is to be taken into account (reg.18(3)(g)).

Subsection (3)

This remarkable and controversial provision had no direct parallel in the predecessor provisions on actively seeking work that governed UB and income support for unemployed people. It enables regulations to be made prescribing circumstances in which acts of a person that would otherwise be relevant in applying the actively seeking employment test are to be disregarded. Those circumstances include ones constituted by, or connected with, the person's behaviour or appearance, but the range of circumstances is not restricted to those categories. The aim was to "enable a person's jobseeking activity to be disregarded if he behaves or presents himself in such a way as deliberately to reduce or extinguish his chance of receiving offers of employment" (DSS, *Notes on Clauses* [with respect to the Jobseekers Bill]). JSA Regulations 1996 reg.18(4) is the material provision. It provides that an otherwise relevant act of a person is to be disregarded unless the circumstances were due to reasons beyond his control: (i) where in taking the act he acted in a violent or abusive manner; (ii) where the act comprised the completion of an application for employment and he spoiled the application; and (iii) where, by his behaviour or appearance he otherwise undermined his prospects of securing the employment in question.   **1.119**

The regulation, particularly in head (iii), thus involves a more explicit "policing" of behaviour, appearance and, possibly, form-filling competence by Jobcentre Plus personnel, decision-makers and tribunals. The concept of "spoiled the application" in head (ii) is by no means crystal clear. The saving for reasons beyond one's control will presumably protect the dyslexic and the illiterate, but what about the semi-literate? Electoral law, of course, has the concept of the "spoilt ballot paper", which covers the situation in which the voter has inadvertently dealt with his ballot paper in such a manner that it cannot conveniently be used as a ballot paper, but whether that in any way provides a valid analogy for "spoiled" in this regulation remains to be seen. See also the decisions in *CJSA/4665/2001* and in *CJSA/2082/2002* and *CJSA/5415/2002*, discussed in the notes to s.19(2)(c) below. Given the aim of the provision, it might have been better to have worded it "deliberately spoiled". A further sanction for some such behaviour lies in the preclusion of payment of benefit under s.19(2)(d) in respect of the person having, without a good reason, neglected to avail themself of a reasonable opportunity of employment; the equivalent provision in the UB regime enabled disqualification of a claimant who had attended an interview for a job as a parcel porter in a "dirty and unshaven state" (*R(U)28/55*). Care will have to be taken to avoid applying the provision in a manner discriminatory on grounds of sex or race (e.g. to penalise men with long hair or Rastafarians with dreadlocks). Many other difficult cases can be envisaged, like those of claimants with visible tattoos or who wish to wear overt symbols of religious faith or political affiliation.

Arguably, the power in subs.(3) is unnecessary, because in any circumstances that it covers the claimant will not have taken such steps as they could reasonably have been expected to take to have the best prospects of securing employment.

Subsections (4) and (5)

1.120   Subsection (4) enables the making of regulations treating a person as actively seeking employment. Subsection (5) amplifies this by providing that such regulations can, for the "permitted period" for availability purposes (see s.6(5) and JSA Regulations 1996 reg.16), enable persons to be treated as actively seeking employment where they are actually doing so only in their usual occupation, or only at a level of remuneration not lower than that which they are accustomed to receive, or only in that occupation and at such a level of remuneration. See JSA Regulations 1996 regs 19–21B. See now reg.7 of the Social Security (Coronavirus) (Further Measures) Regulations 2020 (SI 2020/371) (above, under *Temporary Coronavirus Provisions*).

There is a wide range of cases of deemed actively seeking employment specified in reg.19(1) (possibly subject to conditions in reg.19(2) or (2A)), which need to be looked at carefully. Some mirror cases of deemed availability for employment under regs 14 or 14A. Of particular interest is reg.19(1)(p), covering any week in respect of which the claimant has given (advance) notice to an employment officer of not intending to be actively seeking employment and intending to reside away from home (subject to varying limits within any 12 months: reg.19(2)).

Subsection (6)

1.121   This enables regulations to be made so that in respect of payment of IBJSA to 16 and 17-year-olds "employment" for actively seeking work purposes extends to training. See further JSA Regulations 1996 reg.65.

Subsection (7)

1.122   This deals with the situation where in accordance with the Act it has been decided that a person is to be treated as actively seeking employment in any week. It enables a subsequent revision or supersession of that decision to embrace also the question whether in that week the person was actually actively seeking employment.

Subsection (8)

1.123   This makes clear that employment, for actively seeking work purposes, covers both employed earner's and self-employed earner's employment. For definitions of these terms, see SSCBA 1992 ss.2(1) and 122(1).

See the discussion of *GP v SSWP (JSA)* [2015] UKUT 476 (AAC), reported as [2016] AACR 14, in the notes to s.7(1) above, in relation to employment outside Great Britain.

See the somewhat unconvincing decision of the Court of Appeal in *Hakki v Secretary of State for Work and Pensions and Blair* [2014] EWCA Civ 530 on the application of the SSCBA 1992 definition of self-employed earner's employment in the child support context. The Court accepted the agreement on behalf of the mother with the Secretary of State's view that, despite the terms of s.2(1) of the SSCBA 1992 and the approach of the Upper Tribunal in *HH v CMEC (CSM)* [2011] UKUT 60 (AAC), the definition for child support and social security purposes should be the same as for income tax purposes, meaning that a person had to be engaged in a trade, profession, employment or vocation. In the case of a "professional" poker player it held, on the particular facts found by the First-tier Tribunal, that he did not have a sufficient degree of organisation in relation to his poker playing to constitute a trade. However, it was accepted that it was possible to conceive of cases in which there was sufficient organisation for a gambler's winnings to be taxable and for the person therefore to be a self-employed earner. The reasoning has been somewhat uncritically endorsed in the further child support case of *French v SSWP and another* [2018] EWCA Civ 470; [2018] AACR 25.

Attendance, information and evidence

8.—(1) Regulations may make provision for requiring a claimant [²(other than a joint-claim couple claiming a joint-claim jobseeker's allowance)]—   1.124

   (a) to [⁴participate in an interview in such manner, time and place] as [¹an employment officer] may specify; and

   (b) to provide information and such evidence as may be prescribed as to his circumstances, his availability for employment and the extent to which he is actively seeking employment.

[²(1A) Regulations may make provision—

   (a) for requiring each member of a joint-claim couple claiming a joint-claim jobseeker's allowance to attend at such place and such time as [⁵an employment officer] may specify;

   (b) for requiring a member of such a couple to provide information and such evidence as may be prescribed as to his circumstances, his availability for employment and the extent to which he is actively seeking employment;

   (c) for requiring such a couple to jointly provide information and such evidence as may be prescribed as to the circumstances of each or either member of the couple, the availability for employment of each or either member of the couple and the extent to which each or either member of the couple is actively seeking employment;

   (d) where any requirement to provide information or evidence is imposed on such a couple by virtue of paragraph (c), for the joint obligation of the couple to be capable of being discharged by the provision of the information or evidence by one member of the couple.]

(2) Regulations under subsection (1) or [²(1A)] may, in particular, [⁵provide for entitlement to a jobseeker's allowance to cease at such time as may be determined in accordance with any such regulations if, when a person fails to comply with such regulations, that person (or, if that person is a member of a joint-claim couple, either member of the couple) does not make prescribed contact with an employment officer within a prescribed period of the failure]

   [³(ca)] [⁶ . . .]

   [³(d)] [⁶ . . .]

   [³(2A)] [⁶ . . .]

   [¹(3)] [⁶ . . .]

AMENDMENTS

1. Welfare Reform and Pensions Act 1999 s.70 and Sch.8 para.29 (November 11, 1999).

2. Welfare Reform and Pensions Act 1999 Sch.7 para.7 (March 19, 2001).

3. Welfare Reform Act 2009 s.33 (February 10, 2010).

4. Welfare Reform Act 2012 s.45 (October 8, 2012).

5. Welfare Reform Act 2012 s.48 and Sch.7 para.2 (October 22, 2012), replacing paras (a)–(c) of subs.(2).

6. Welfare Reform Act 2012 s.147 and Sch.14 Pt 3 (October 22, 2012).

"a joint-claim couple"—see s.1(4).
"a joint-claim jobseeker's allowance"—see s.1(4).
"claimant"—see s.35(1).
"employment"—see s.35(1) and JSA Regulations 1996 reg.4.
"employment officer"—see s.35(1).
"prescribed"—*ibid*
"regulations"—*ibid*.

GENERAL NOTE

1.125   This section provides a range of rule-making powers with respect to requiring claimants (and each member of a joint-claim couple) to participate in an interview in such manner, time and place as an employment officer may specify and to provide information and evidence on their circumstances, availability for employment and the extent to which they are actively seeking employment (subs.(1)). In short, to provide through participation, etc. the wherewithal whereby the claim can continue to be monitored and assessed. The change from "attend" to "participate in", effected from October 8, 2012, as well as reflecting enhanced conditionality, also enables interviews to be conducted remotely.

The provision made under subs.(1)(a) is reg.23 of the JSA Regulations 1996 (subs.(1A)(a) and reg.23A for joint-claim couples). The provision made under subss.(1)(b) and (1A)(b)–(d) is reg.24, augmented by regs 24A and 24B. The immediate consequences of failing to comply with a requirement under s.8 are set out in regs 25–27. Subject to conditions, failures to participate in a properly notified interview or to provide a signed declaration under reg.24(6) and (10) (but not failures to comply with any other part of reg.24) lead to the ceasing of entitlement to old style JSA. A failure without a good reason to comply with regulations made under s.8(1) or (1A) is also a sanctionable failure under s.19A(2)(a), potentially leading to reduction of benefit for fixed periods under reg.69A of the JSA Regulations 1996. However, reg.70A(2) prevents there being a reduction in benefit for any failure to comply with any part of reg.24 and for many failures to comply with reg.23 or 23A. See the notes to regs 25 and 70A for the interaction between the sanction and the ceasing of entitlement under regs 25–27.

In *CS v SSWP (JSA)* [2015] UKUT 61 (AAC) Judge Wikeley drew an analogy in cases under regs 25–27 with the sanctions regime, so that the same principle as he had suggested in *DL v SSWP (JSA)* [2013] UKUT 295 (AAC) should apply, that the legislation should be construed strictly, giving the claimant the benefit of any doubt that might reasonably apply before imposing a penalty.

The jobseeker's agreement

1.126   **9.**—(1) An agreement which is entered into by a claimant and an employment officer and which complies with the prescribed requirements in force at the time when the agreement is made is referred to in this Act as "a jobseeker's agreement".

(2) A jobseeker's agreement shall have effect only for the purposes of section 1.

(3) A jobseeker's agreement shall be in writing and be signed by both parties.

[³(3A) The agreement may be in electronic form and signed by means of an electronic signature (within the meaning given in section 7(2) of the Electronic Communications Act 2000).]

(4) A copy of the agreement shall be given to the claimant.

(5) An employment officer shall not enter into a jobseeker's agreement with a claimant unless, in the officer's opinion, the conditions mentioned in section

1(2)(a) and (c) would be satisfied with respect to the claimant if he were to comply with, or be treated as complying with, the proposed agreement.

(6) The employment officer may, and if asked to do so by the claimant shall forthwith, refer a proposed jobseeker's agreement to [¹the Secretary of State] for him to determine—

(a) whether, if the claimant concerned were to comply with the proposed agreement, he would satisfy—
   (i) the condition mentioned in section 1(2)(a); or
   (ii) the condition mentioned in section 1(2)(c); and
(b) whether it is reasonable to expect the claimant to have to comply with the proposed agreement.

(7) [¹On a reference under subsection (6) the Secretary of State]—

(a) shall, so far as practicable, dispose of it in accordance with this section before the end of the period of 14 days from the date of the reference;
(b) may give such directions, with respect to the terms on which the employment officer is to enter into a jobseeker's agreement with the claimant, as [¹the Secretary of State] considers appropriate;
(c) may direct that, if conditions as he considers appropriate are satisfied, the proposed jobseeker's agreement is to be treated (if entered into) as having effect on such date, before it would otherwise have effect, as may be specified in the direction.

(8) Regulations may provide—

(a) for such matters as may be prescribed to be taken into account by [¹the Secretary of State] in giving a direction under subsection (7)(c); and
(b) for such persons as may be prescribed to be notified of—
   (i) any determination of [¹ the Secretary of State] under this section;
   (ii) any direction given by [¹ the Secretary of State] under this section.

(9) [¹ . . .].

(10) Regulations may provide that, in prescribed circumstances, a claimant is to be treated as having satisfied the condition mentioned in section 1(2)(b).

(11) Regulations may provide that, in prescribed circumstances, a jobseeker's agreement is to be treated as having effect on a date, to be determined in accordance with the regulations, before it would otherwise have effect.

(12) Except in such circumstances as may be prescribed, a jobseeker's agreement entered into by a claimant shall cease to have effect on the coming to an end of an award of a jobseeker's allowance made to him [²or to a joint-claim couple of which he is a member.].

(13) In this section and section 10 "employment officer" means an officer of the Secretary of State or such other person as may be designated for the purposes of this section by an order made by the Secretary of State.

AMENDMENTS

1. Social Security Act 1998 Sch.7 para.136 (October 18, 1999).
2. Welfare Reform and Pensions Act 1999 Sch.7 para.8 (March 19, 2001).
3. Social Security (Electronic Communications) Order 2011 (SI 2011/1498) art.2(2) (February 1, 2012).

DEFINITIONS

"a joint-claim couple"—see s.1(4).
"a joint-claim jobseeker's allowance"—see s.1(4).

"claimant"—see s.35(1).
"employment officer"—*ibid.*
"prescribed"—*ibid.*
"regulations"—*ibid.*

GENERAL NOTE

1.127   This section, containing and enabling the making of further important provisions on the jobseeker's agreement, needs to be read in the light of the amplification and clarification provided by JSA Regulations 1996 regs 31–36, made under it; and of s.10 supplemented by regs 37–40, which provide for the variation of a jobseeker's agreement. This note attempts to blend the provisions of this section and the JSA Regulations 1996 with statements in the 1994 White Paper (*Jobseeker's Allowance*, Cmnd. 2687) and/or in Parliament on the administrative process, to give a coherent account of how the arrangements with respect to jobseeker's agreements operate. On some points of finer detail, however, readers will have to scrutinise closely the exact terms of the regulations referred to. It is important to keep in mind that, although a "claimant commitment" approach has been imported into old style JSA (see para.1.131 below), the legislation has not been amended and there remain important differences between the nature and effect of a claimant commitment in new style JSA and universal credit and that of a jobseeker's agreement in old style JSA.

Perhaps the most obvious and striking difference between UB and old style JSA is the central requirement that, in order to be entitled to JSA, the claimant must have entered into a jobseeker's agreement that remains in force (s.1(2)(b)). Note, however, that a person may be treated as having done so in any of the circumstances set out in JSA Regulations 1996 reg.34. This provision covers various cases in which the claimant has not yet had an interview with an employment officer, for instance at the beginning of a claim that was allowed to be made without attending a Jobcentre Plus office (reg.34(a)), as well as some cases in which the claimant is deemed to be available for employment (reg.34(c) and (g)). Could an example of the application of reg.34(d) (normal operation of provisions or practice as to claiming impracticable or unduly difficult because of circumstances not peculiar to the claimant) be circumstances where the office is overwhelmed by claims on the closure of a town's major employer? Another example might be given by the circumstances during the 2020 coronavirus outbreak and the closure of jobcentres. For new claimants, reg.34(a) would probably also have applied.

If reg.34 applies, s.1(2)(b) is satisfied and the actual absence of a signed agreement is not an obstacle to an award of old style JSA. If reg.34 does not apply, there cannot be any award of regular benefit until a jobseeker's agreement is signed (although, as seen below, the agreement may then operate from the date of claim and benefit will be payable after the waiting days if the other conditions of entitlement are satisfied). However, there may be eligibility for payments under the hardship provisions in regs 140–146H of the JSA Regulations 1996.

1.128   The interaction of the hardship provisions and the rules on suspension of payment of benefit is complex. There appear to be two stages at the beginning of a claim. First, the decision-maker may defer the making of any decision until satisfied that there is sufficient evidence to do so, within the limits of reasonableness under s.8(1) of the SSA 1998 (see the annotation in Vol. III). In those circumstances, if the sole reason for the delay is that an issue arises as to satisfaction of one of the "labour market" conditions in s.1(2)(a)–(c) (reg.141(2) of the JSA Regulations 1996 and the equivalent provision for joint claim couples in regs 146A–146H, not separately noted below) and the claimant falls into one of the vulnerable groups specified in reg.140(1), the claimant is to be treated as entitled to IBJSA at the hardship rate after the expiry of the seven waiting days. A person outside the vulnerable groups, if in hardship (reg.140(2)), can be so treated from the 15th day after the claim (reg.142). However, there seems a limited need for any delay in making a decision in such circumstances because reg.141(4), made under para.8 of Sch.1 to the old style

Jobseekers Act 1995, allows a person within s.140(1), except where there is deemed non-availability under reg.15 of the JSA Regulations 1996, to be entitled to IBJSA at the hardship rate without satisfying the conditions in s.1(2)(a)–(c), provided that the other conditions in s.1(2) are satisfied. There is no similar provision in reg.142. If a decision on entitlement can then be made under reg.141(4), the second stage of possible suspension of payment could come into play. However, it appears that reg.16(1) and (3) of the Decisions and Appeals Regulations 1999 allowing the Secretary of State to suspend payment of any benefit whenever an issue arises as to whether a condition of entitlement is satisfied cannot bite in these circumstances. Unless and until a jobseeker's agreement is signed, there is no doubt that the condition of entitlement in s.1(2)(b) is not met, so that no "issue" arises. Thus the specific effect of reg.141(5) of the JSA Regulations 1996 in excluding the operation of reg.16 where reg.141(4) applies appears not to be necessary in the present context.

A jobseeker's agreement has effect only for the purposes of entitlement to JSA ("the purposes of section 1") (subs.(2)) and hence does not give rise to any contractual or other private law obligations or relationship. Now see *RL v SSWP (JSA)* [2017] UKUT 282 (AAC), *RL v SSWP (JSA)* [2018] UKUT 177 (AAC) and *CH v SSWP (JSA) (No.2)* [2018] UKUT 320 (AAC). Claimants continue (understandably) not to grasp that a jobseeker's agreement is not an agreement.

Nor does a restriction in the jobseeker's agreement of availability to employment paying at least the national minimum wage prevent the application of s.17A and relevant regulations to require a claimant to participate in a Mandatory Work Activity scheme (*AW v SSWP (JSA)* [2016] UKUT 387 (AAC)). Note that there is no direct sanction for a claimant's failure to comply with the commitments recorded in the jobseeker's agreement. The condition of entitlement in s.1(2)(b) is met by the mere existence of the agreement and there is nothing in ss.19–19B that specifically refers to the jobseeker's agreement. There is a link to the condition of entitlement in s.1(2)(a) (availability) through the requirement in reg.7(2)(b) of the JSA Regulations 1996 that the claimant at least keeps to the pattern of availability recorded in the agreement, discussed in para.1.131 below. There is also a link to the condition of entitlement in s.1(2)(c) (actively seeking employment) in that a failure to carry out the work-search steps recorded in the agreement *might* lead to a conclusion that that condition is not satisfied, but the test is that set out in s.7(1) above and reg.18 of the JSA Regulations 1996 (basically whether the claimant has taken such steps as can reasonably be expected to have the best prospects of employment), not merely falling below the level specified in the agreement (see the notes to s.7(1)).

Subsection (1) defines "a jobseeker's agreement" as one entered into by a claimant and an "employment officer", complying with the "prescribed requirements" as in force at the time it is made. "Employment officer" is defined in subs.(13) in the same terms as in s.35(1) (see the notes on the definition there). The jobseeker's agreement must be in writing and signed by both parties to it (the claimant and the employment officer) (subs.(3)) or in electronic form with electronic signatures (subs.(3A)). Claimants sign a declaration that they understand and agree to the conditions set out in the agreement (White Paper para.4.19), but the declaration is not specified in regulations as one of the "prescribed requirements".

1.129

The "prescribed requirements" are listed in JSA Regulations 1996 reg.31. The agreement must contain: (i) the claimant's name; (ii) unless the claimant is available for any hours at any times, the total number of hours for which he is available for employment and any pattern of availability ("the times at which he is available to take up employment": see reg.7); (iii) any restrictions on availability as permitted by the scheme; (iv) a description of the type of employment being sought; (v) the action the claimant will take to seek employment and to improve the prospects of finding employment; (vi) the start and finish of the "permitted period" in which he is allowed to restrict his availability and jobsearch to his usual occupation and/or his usual rate of remuneration; (vii) a statement of his rights to have a proposed agreement referred to the Secretary State (decision-maker), to have a decision-maker's decision and/or directions reviewed by another decision-maker, and of his right of appeal to a tribunal in respect of the decision and/or direction given on that review; and (viii) the date of the agreement. A copy of the agreement must be given to the claimant (subs.(4)). The requirements are thus a mixture of the formal, of statements by the claimant as to availability and steps proposed for actively seeking employment and elements that depend on an acceptance by the employment officer that if the claimant acts in accordance with them the conditions of entitlement to old style JSA will be met (e.g. restrictions on availability and length of permitted period).

It must be the case that, if an agreement that has been entered into by a claimant does not contain one or more of the prescribed requirements, the claimant does not necessarily fail to satisfy the condition of entitlement in s.1(2)(b). Whether that outcome follows would depend on the nature of the requirement concerned and on the circumstances. In the case of most of the prescribed requirements, no doubt in practice the employment officer would decline to enter into the agreement if the claimant had not co-operated so as to allow the necessary matters to be recorded. But if, say, the jobseeker's agreement failed properly to inform the claimant about the rights to have the proposed agreement referred to the Secretary of State, etc. that could not possibly on its own lead to the conclusion that the claimant did not satisfy s.1(2)(b) (see *CH v SSWP (JSA)* [2015] UKUT 373 (AAC), reported as [2016] AACR 28, where Judge Ward found the form of agreement (ES3JP 05/11) in use from 2012 to 2014 in breach of reg.31(g)). The decision in an appeal to the Upper Tribunal (*CJSA/1116/2015* and *1118/2015*) that was thought to raise the issue of whether the form of "claimant commitment" (i.e. in law a jobseeker's agreement) in use from 2014 onwards is affected by the same defect as identified in *CH* in relation to the earlier form did not in the event decide that issue.

1.130   However, it is not clear how far a jobseeker's agreement as such may contain other matters than those prescribed in reg.31. No doubt the document can contain additional useful material. The White Paper (para.4.17) mentioned information on the facilities offered by Jobcentre Plus and the standards of service claimants are entitled to receive. It could also helpfully show what information or changes of circumstances a claimant is required to notify and how. Since the definition in s.9(1) and reg.31 only sets out what the agreement is required to contain in a non-exhaustive way, there is nothing to prevent the document containing such information.

But it is more difficult to say whether further requirements can be imposed on a claimant in a jobseeker's agreement. The decision in *PT v SSWP (JSA)* [2015] UKUT 703 (AAC), not in itself of citable authority because it was given by consent of both parties, records the following interesting proposition put forward by the Secretary of State. He accepted that the proper purpose of a jobseeker's agreement is to set out the details of the claimant's jobseeking, not to include "sanctionable activities". Thus, it was said that a requirement to attend a "skills conditionality for [Universal Jobmatch]/CV workshop" should not have been proposed to become part of a varied agreement: any condition of opening a Universal Jobmatch account should be imposed through a jobseeker's direction under s.19A(2)(c) below and any requirement to attend a skills conditionality scheme should be imposed through reg.3(7) of the Jobseekers Allowance (SAPOE) Regulations 2013 (Pt III below). It might be queried whether such conditions could not be notified to a claimant in a jobseeker's agreement. However, if so, their force and the consequences in terms of sanctions for non-compliance, would stem, not from their inclusion in the jobseeker's agreement (which has the limited consequences discussed above), but from the particular provisions enabling their imposition. For instance, if an employment officer insisted on a jobseeker's agreement including a statement that the claimant would open a Universal Jobmatch account, which could be said to fall within reg.31(e) (action the claimant will take to seek employment and improve the prospects of finding employment), failure to open the account would carry no consequences in respect of being a breach of the terms of the agreement and would only lead to non-entitlement under ss.1(2)(c) and 7 if the other steps taken in any week fell short of what the claimant could reasonably have been expected to do. For the sanction under s.19A(2)(c) to be available, the employment officer would have to have given a direction as defined in s.19A(11). That can be in such manner as the employment officer thinks fit, so could in terms of the legislation be done in the jobseeker's agreement. Bearing in mind the difference in the consequences of a failure to comply and the formality of the process required to vary a jobseeker's agreement, it would appear at least sensible to keep such specific and perhaps short-term requirements separate from a jobseeker's agreement as such. The position is rather different in new style JSA, where all of a claimant's responsibilities are to be recorded in a claimant commitment.

The jobseeker's agreement is an integral part of identifying what steps back to work are appropriate for claimants and to enable regular and effective monitoring of their activities to that end, reviewing and altering the terms of the agreement as necessary over a period (see White Paper para.4.16, and ss.10 and 11). Note, in particular, that "employment officers" cannot enter into an agreement the terms of which are such that the claimant acting in accordance with them would fail to satisfy either of the key requirements to be available for and actively seeking employment, thus placing such officers at the heart of policing these central requirements of the system (subs.(5)).

According to para.5 of Ch.1 of the *Government's response to the Independent review of the operation of Jobseeker's Allowance sanctions validated by the Jobseekers Act 2013* (Cmnd. 8904, July 2014), the "claimant commitment approach" has been rolled out to JSA from October 2013, with the rollout completed in April 2014. It is not clear what this means in relation to old style JSA when there has been no change in the legislation. There is reference in that document to improved claimant understanding of the requirements placed on them and to a new personalised approach to job search, centring on active discussion between advisers and claimants leading to detailed plans of actions, tailored to and owned by individual claimants. **1.131**

The jobseeker's agreement is supposed not to be a standard pro forma document but one which aims to reflect the particular claimant's circumstances on availability. JSA Regulations 1996 reg.7(2)(b) requires that to be available the claimant must adhere in practice to the pattern of availability (either strictly or by following an even less restrictive pattern) embodied in the jobseeker's agreement unless and until that agreement is varied pursuant to s.10 (*R(JSA)2/07*, para.14). So, in *R(JSA)2/07*, the claimant who had agreed to Saturday working in his jobseeker's agreement, but followed an actual pattern which excluded Saturday, was not protected by reg.7(2) and so was not available. If claimants are unhappy about the pattern proposed for the agreement, they have a number of choices. First, they can refuse to sign and request that the proposed agreement be referred to the Secretary of State, hoping that the Secretary of State will agree with them about its terms and will backdate the agreement so that the claimant, without benefit until the matter is decided, will not have lost but merely postponed benefit. Alternatively, they can sign under protest and immediately seek a variation of the agreement. But if they do so, they must, if they are to retain benefit pending the variation, adhere to the "agreed" pattern set out in the agreement.

The basic rule on when the agreement comes into effect would appear to be that it does so on the day it is signed, but that is a deduction from the effect of other rules rather than finding expression in a particular provision. In some cases, no doubt, the claimant and the employment officer will reach ready agreement on the terms of the jobseeker's agreement, which will be signed on the day of claim, and take effect then. Where it is not signed until a date later than the day of claim, JSA Regulations 1996 reg.35, made pursuant to subs.(11), provides that the agreement is to be automatically backdated to the day of claim, unless the agreement (in reality a proposed agreement) is referred to the Secretary of State (decision-maker) in accordance with subs.(6). Note, though, the possible effect of reg.34 in treating an agreement as having been made, especially in certain circumstances at the beginning of a claim.

The most common situation in which a proposed jobseeker's agreement will be referred to a decision-maker is likely to be where there is a dispute between the parties over the availability and/or actively seeking work aspects of it or over whether it is reasonable to expect the claimant to have to comply with it. In such a situation, the employment officer *must* refer the proposed agreement to a decision-maker if the claim- **1.132** ant asks them to do so (subs.(6)). In addition, the employment officer always has power to refer such matters to the decision-maker (subs.(6)), and doubtless will do so particularly where they are unsure about the availability and/or actively seeking work aspects.

If a proposed agreement is referred to a decision-maker, the reference must, so far as is practicable, be disposed of (determined) within 14 days (subs.(7)(a)). The determination must deal with the questions set out in subs.(6), in particular whether it is reasonable to expect the claimant to have to comply with the proposed agreement and may include directions about the terms on which the employment officer is to enter into an agreement with the claimant and about the date on which the agreement, if entered into, takes effect (subs.(7)(b) and (c)), which allows backdating. The automatic backdating of the effect of an agreement to the date of claim under reg.35 of the JSA Regulations 1996 does not apply where there has been a reference under s.9(6). *CH v SSWP (JSA)* [2015] UKUT 373 (AAC), reported as [2016] AACR 28, discusses the nature of the proper procedure under s.9(6) and (7) when a claimant is not prepared to accept an initial jobseeker's agreement in the terms proposed by the employment officer. It also criticises some of the administrative guidance in operation at the dates in question there. If there is a reference to the Secretary of State, either at the claimant's request or under the employment officer's discretion, the decision on the reference cannot go beyond determining the questions under s.9(6) and giving directions under s.9(7). In *CH*, it appeared that the decision given by the Secretary of State did not deal with those questions, but went straight to a decision that the claimant was not entitled to JSA because he had not entered into a jobseeker's agreement. That decision had to be set aside for the reference procedure to be followed. There can only be a decision on entitlement once the claimant has had notice of the outcome of the reference and has had the opportunity to consider a proposed agreement prepared in accordance with the determination and any directions. Judge Ward noted in para.39 that the Secretary of State accepted that any physical or mental limitations on a claimant's jobseeking ability should be considered under s.9(6).

CH is a confirmation of Commissioner Williams' early identification in *CJSA/2162/2001* that:

> "a valid jobseeker's agreement continues in force until it is varied or brought to an end in accordance with the 1995 Act and the Jobseeker's Allowance Regulations. It cannot unilaterally be ignored by the Secretary of State."

1.133   On the question of whether it is reasonable to expect the claimant to comply with the terms of a proposed agreement, see *CH v SSWP (JSA) (No.2)* [2018] UKUT 320 (AAC), which concerned the appeal from the decision of the Secretary of State on the reference of the questions in s.9(6) directed to be referred by Judge Ward in *CH* (above). There were a number of modifications in the revised initial agreement proposed by the employment officer, as compared with the proposed agreement that had been before Judge Ward. Although the types of job to be looked for were the same, the requirement to access the jobseekers.direct.gov.uk site was reduced from three times to twice a week and the requirement to access the internet daily was reduced to weekly, such access being for periods acceptable to the claimant in view of his problems with spending too long in front of a screen. A right of review by a disability employment adviser at the request of either party was also written in. The First-tier Tribunal had erred in law by failing to explain why it considered that it was reasonable to expect the claimant to comply with the proposed agreement. In substituting his own decision that the claimant was not entitled to old style JSA for the weeks in question (by reason of not having entered into a jobseeker's agreement) Judge Wikeley first concluded that compliance would mean that the claimant satisfied the conditions of entitlement of availability for and actively seeking employment. The jobs listed were appropriate and realistic in the light of the claimant's experience and the proposed hours and travelling time were not onerous. The job search activities were suitably calibrated to the claimant's circumstances. By contrast, the qualifications and restrictions suggested by the claimant would not have allowed him to satisfy those conditions. As to reasonableness, the proposed agreement was not unduly onerous or insufficiently focused on the claimant's individual suitability for types of work and did not rely on standard-form job search requirements. It was a reasonably bespoke agreement for the claimant's own circumstances. The claimant had failed to explain how it would be unreasonable to expect him to comply with it.

See also *PG v SSWP (JSA)* [2017] UKUT 388 (AAC). That case stemmed from an employment officer's proposal to vary a jobseeker's agreement to include the provision "Search Universal Jobmatch via Gov.UK to identify and apply for jobs you can do – 5 times per week minimum" (see the notes to s.10 for the variation process), but the principles are equally applicable to s.9. It was apparently accepted on behalf of the Secretary of State that the claimant's objection to applying for jobs through Universal Jobmatch, on the basis that that would require registration on a site that he believed was not secure and was open to fraud, would have made it unreasonable to require him to comply with an agreement including such a requirement (see ss.9(6)(b) and 10(5)(b)). But it was argued that the requirement was only to search for jobs on the site, to which the claimant had no objection, and did not necessarily involve applying for them through that method, so that compliance was reasonable. Judge Wright remitted the issue of whether some jobs listed on Universal Jobmatch could only be applied for through the site to a new tribunal for determination as a matter of fact, although he suspected that by inference the proposed provision did require registration. He also suggested (paras 15 and 23) that it might be unreasonable to require a claimant to comply with an agreement whose terms were too uncertain, without indicating how that test might apply to the circumstances of *PG*. Last, in response to the First-tier Tribunal's statement that there was no objection in principle to requiring a claimant to engage in actively seeking work as a full-time task, the judge stated that it might take very cogent reasoning to justify a person having to take very well in excess of the three steps per week that are the starting point under reg.18(1) of the JSA Regulations 1996 on actively seeking employment. However, the fundamental test in s.7(1) of the old style Jobseekers Act 1995 is in terms of the steps that the claimant can reasonably be expected to have to take to secure the best prospects of securing employment, with reg.18(1) merely fixing a minimum of three steps per week (or one or two if reasonable), so such cogent reasoning may not be too difficult to find. That would especially be the case if, as seems to be correct, taking the same step five days a week (e.g. checking a website) counts as five steps.

From May 14, 2018 Universal Jobmatch has been replaced by the Find a job service, run by Adzuna.

In considering whether back-dating is appropriate, JSA Regulations 1996 reg.32   **1.134** (made under subs.(8)(a)) stipulates that the decision-maker must take into account all relevant matters, including those specifically listed in the regulation (i.e. that list is not exhaustive). The matters so listed are: (i) whether the claimant was reasonable in refusing to accept the proposed agreement; (ii) whether the terms of the agreement which the claimant has indicated, to the decision-maker or the employment officer, that he is prepared to accept, are reasonable; (iii) the fact that the claimant has signified to the decision-maker or the employment officer that he is prepared to accept the proposed agreement; (iv) the date on which, taking account of all the circumstances, the decision-maker considers the claimant was prepared to enter into an agreement the decision-maker considers reasonable; and (v) the fact that the date on which the claimant first had an opportunity to sign a jobseeker's agreement was later than the date of claim. Notification of the decision-maker's determination and any directions given by him will doubtless be given to the employment officer as a matter of the arrangements within the old style JSA administrative structure, and must be given to the claimant under JSA Regulations 1996 reg.33. Any determination of the Secretary of State (decision-maker) under this section is binding (subs.(9)) but not final, because of the possibility of revision and appeal under the DMA arrangements. The right of appeal is created by para.8 of Sch.3 to the Social Security Act 1998.

Generally, a jobseeker's agreement ceases to have effect when the claimant's award of JSA comes to an end (subs.(12)). JSA Regulations 1996 reg.36 prescribes the circumstances in which a jobseeker's agreement shall not so cease to have effect (for example, where a further claim for JSA is made within 14 days of the previous award coming to an end: see reg.36(a)). Note in particular that a mere failure by a claimant to sign a varied jobseeker's agreement directed by the Secretary of State under s.10(6)(b) does not allow the immediate termination of the existing agreement and the consequent ending of entitlement until the claimant has had the 21 days specified under s.10(6)(c) to sign the varied agreement. See the notes to s.10 for further details.]

Variation of jobseeker's agreement

1.134.1

10.—(1) A jobseeker's agreement may be varied, in the prescribed manner, by agreement between the claimant and any employment officer.

(2) Any agreement to vary a jobseeker's agreement shall be in writing and be signed by both parties.

[²(2A) Any agreement to vary a jobseeker's agreement may be in electronic form and signed by means of an electronic signature (within the meaning given in section 7(2) of the Electronic Communications Act 2000).]

(3) A copy of the agreement, as varied, shall be given to the claimant.

(4) An employment officer shall not agree to a variation of a jobseeker's agreement, unless, in the officer's opinion, the conditions mentioned in section 1(2)(a) and (c) would continue to be satisfied with respect to the claimant if he were to comply with, or be treated as complying with, the agreement as proposed to be varied.

(5) The employment officer may, and if asked to do so by the claimant shall forthwith, refer a proposed variation of a jobseeker's agreement to [¹the Secretary of State] for him to determine—

(a) whether, if the claimant concerned were to comply with the agreement as proposed to be varied, he would satisfy—
   (i) the condition mentioned in section 1(2)(a), or
   (ii) the condition mentioned in section 1(2)(c); and
(b) whether it is reasonable to expect the claimant to have to comply with the agreement as proposed to be varied.

(6) [¹On a reference under subsection (5) the Secretary of State]—

(a) shall, so far as practicable, dispose of it in accordance with this section before the end of the period of 14 days from the date of the reference;
(b) shall give such directions as he considers appropriate as to—
   (i) whether the jobseeker's agreement should be varied, and
   (ii) if so, the terms on which the claimant and the employment officer are to enter into an agreement to vary it;
(c) may bring the jobseeker's agreement to an end where the claimant fails, within a prescribed period, to comply with a direction given under paragraph (b)(ii);
(d) may direct that, if—
   (i) the jobseeker's agreement is varied, and
   (ii) such conditions as he considers appropriate are satisfied,
   the agreement as varied is to be treated as having effect on such date, before it would otherwise have effect, as may be specified in the direction.

(7) Regulations may provide—

(a) for such matters as may be prescribed to be taken into account by [¹the Secretary of State] in giving a direction under section (6)(b) or (d); and

(b) for such persons as may be prescribed to be notified of—
  (i) any determination of [¹the Secretary of State] under this section;
  (ii) any direction given by [¹the Secretary of State] under this section.
(8) [¹ . . .].

AMENDMENTS

1. Social Security Act 1998 Sch.7 para.137 (October 18, 1999).
2. Social Security (Electronic Communications) Order 2011 (SI 2011/1498) art.2(3) (February 1, 2012).

DEFINITIONS

"claimant"—see s.35(1).
"employment officer"—see s.9(13).
"jobseeker's agreement"—see ss.35(1) and 9(1).
"prescribed"—see s.35(1).
"regulations"—*ibid.*

GENERAL NOTE

This section enables a jobseeker's agreement to be varied, with the aim of ensur- **1.135** ing that it reflects the claimant's changing circumstances and the labour market. The section also provides for the mode and manner of decision-making and is amplified by JSA Regulations 1996 regs 37–40.

A jobseeker's agreement can, on the proposal of either the employment officer or the claimant, be varied with the consent of both parties (subs.(1); JSA Regulations 1996 reg.37). An agreement to vary must, like the varied agreement itself, be in writing and signed by both parties (subs.(2); JSA Regulations 1996 reg.37) or in electronic form with electronic signatures (subs.(2A)). The claimant must get a copy of the varied agreement (subs.(3)). An employment officer cannot agree a variation unless satisfied that under its terms the claimant would continue to be available for and actively seeking employment (subs.(4)), once more emphasising the central role for Jobcentre Plus personnel in monitoring those crucial "labour market" conditions of entitlement.

Section 10 appears to envisage both a written agreement to vary that must be signed and a written copy of the jobseeker's agreement as varied (that presumably must also be signed under the general requirement in s.9(3)). Presumably those could be incorporated into one document.

Some cases will be the subject of decisions and directions of decision-makers. **1.136** The most common situation in which a proposed variation of a jobseeker's agreement will be referred to a decision-maker is likely to be where there is a dispute between the parties over the availability and/or the actively seeking work aspects of it, or over whether it is reasonable to expect the claimant to have to comply with it. In such a situation, the employment officer *must* refer the proposed variation of the agreement to a decision-maker if the claimant asks him to do so (subs.(5)). In addition, employment officers always have power to refer such matters to the decision-maker (subs.(5), and doubtless will do so particularly where they are unsure about the availability and/or the actively seeking work aspects.

Decision-makers are, so far as is practicable, to determine the reference within 14 days. They must give such directions as they consider appropriate as to whether the agreement should be varied and if so the terms on which the parties are to agree a varied agreement. Should the claimant fail to do so within 21 days of the direction, the decision-maker can bring the existing jobseeker's agreement to an end, thus disentitling the claimant to old style JSA since s.1(2)(b) requires a jobseeker's agreement to be in force (subs.(6)(a)–(c)). The decision-maker can also backdate the varied agreement (subs.(6)(d)). In giving directions under subs.(6)(b) or (d) the decision-maker must take into account the preference of the claimant if he considers that both the claimant's proposals and those of the employment officer meet the requirements of subs.(5) (the "labour market" conditions and the "reasonableness" requirement) (JSA Regulations 1996 reg.38).

In *HS v SSWP (JSA)* [2015] UKUT 701 (AAC), the claimant refused to sign a new jobseeker's agreement (under the title of a claimant commitment), not being satisfied with its terms (on the basis accepted by Judge Turnbull). The employment officer referred the matter to the Secretary of State, who gave a decision that the claimant was not entitled to old style JSA because he had not entered into a job-seeker's agreement. As agreed by the Secretary of State before the Upper Tribunal, the claimant's refusal to sign the new agreement did not entitle the making of a decision to terminate entitlement. Under s.10(5) and (6)(b) the Secretary of State could only decide on the reference whether the proposed agreement was compatible with the requirements of availability for employment and actively seeking employment and whether it was reasonable to expect the claimant to comply with the proposed terms and give directions about whether the agreement should be varied and the terms on which it was to be entered into. The existing jobseeker's agreement could not be brought to an end under s.10(6)(c) (so ending satisfaction of the condition of entitlement in s.1(2)(b)) until the expiry of the period of 21 days specified under s.10(6)(c) for the claimant to sign the varied agreement.

1.137   See *PG v SSWP (JSA)* [2017] UKUT 388 (AAC), discussed in the notes to s.9, for some general, although inconclusive, opinions on the general approach to when it is reasonable to expect the claimant to comply with the agreement as proposed to be varied and for the specific case of a claimant who objected to having to register for a Universal Jobmatch account on the basis that he considered the site insecure and open to fraud. The Secretary of State apparently accepted that it would have been unreasonable to require the claimant to register for an account, but a dispute whether the terms of the proposed agreement ("Search Universal Jobmatch via Gov.UK to identify and apply for jobs you can do") necessarily entailed registration in order to apply for jobs was sent to a new tribunal for determination. The claimant had not objected to searching on Universal Jobmatch, which did not require registering for an account. From May 14, 2018 Universal Jobmatch has been replaced by the Find a job service, run by Adzuna.

Commissioner Mesher considered the matter of directions in *R(JSA)2/07*. In the absence of a statutory provision specifying when a varied agreement should be treated as having effect, he thought that in most, if not all, cases a direction needed to be given. As to when the agreement should start, that could be the date of signature or the date the proposal to vary the agreement was made. He thought that where the proposal to vary came from the claimant, then, given the difficult choices faced by a claimant unhappy with the agreement (see commentary to s.9 and JSA Regulations 1996 reg.7(2)), that indicated that the date of the proposal was the more appropriate (see para.30).

Retrospective variation is permissible *(R(JSA)2/07; AT v SSWP (JSA)* [2013] UKUT 73 (AAC), see para.10).

1.138   Notification of the decision-maker's determination and any directions given by them will doubtless be given to the employment officer as a matter of the arrangements within the JSA administrative structure, and must be given to the claimant under JSA Regulations 1996 reg.40, made pursuant to subs.(7)(b). A right of appeal against the determination is created by para.8 of Sch.3 to the Social Security Act 1998.

A decision-maker can bring a jobseeker's agreement to an end (thus denying benefit) where, within 21 days, a claimant has not agreed the terms of a varied agreement as indicated by the decision-maker. In *CJSA/4435/1998*, Commissioner Levenson was of the view that an appeal against the decision-maker's direction on the terms of the agreement necessarily involved also an appeal against his decision to terminate the agreement (see para.8). In the particular case, dealing only with the type of work for which the claimant should be available, he noted that the relevant standard was that of "reasonable prospects of employment", notwithstanding imposed restrictions, pursuant to JSA Regulations 1996 regs 8 and 10. The tribunal applied a different test of "good prospects" when rejecting his appeal, and so erred in law in imposing on the claimant a higher degree of proof than that stipulated in the regulations.

Jobseeker's agreement: reviews and appeals

11.—[¹ . . .].   1.139

1. Social Security Act 1998 Sch.7 para.138 (October 18, 1999).

Income and capital

Income and capital: general

12.—(1) In relation to a claim for a jobseeker's allowance, the income   1.140
and capital of a person shall be calculated or estimated in such manner as
may be prescribed.

(2) A person's income in respect of a week shall be calculated in accordance with prescribed rules.

(3) The rules may provide for the calculation to be made by reference
to an average over a period (which need not include the week concerned).

(4) Circumstances may be prescribed in which—

(a) a person is treated as possessing capital or income which he does not
    possess;

(b) capital or income which a person does possess is to be disregarded;

(c) income is to be treated as capital;

(d) capital is to be treated as income.

DEFINITIONS

"prescribed"—see s.35(1).
"week"—*ibid.*

GENERAL NOTE

This section is very similar to subss.(3)–(5) of s.136 of the SSCBA 1992 and   1.140.1
contains extensive powers to prescribe how a claimant's capital and income is to be
calculated for the purposes of old style JSA. See Pt VIII of, and Schs 6, 6A, 7 and 8
to, the JSA Regulations 1996.

See also s.13.

Income and capital: income-based jobseeker's allowance

13.—(1) No person shall be entitled to an income-based jobseeker's allow-   1.141
ance if his capital, or a prescribed part of it, exceeds the prescribed amount.

(2) Where a person claiming an income-based jobseeker's allowance is a
member of a family, the income and capital of any member of that family
shall, except in prescribed circumstances, be treated as the income and
capital of the claimant.

[¹(2A) Subsections (1) and (2) do not apply as regards a joint-claim jobseeker's allowance; but a joint-claim couple shall not be entitled to a joint-
claim jobseeker's allowance if the couple's capital, or a prescribed part of it,
exceeds the prescribed amount.

(2B)Where a joint-claim couple claim a joint-claim jobseeker's allowance—

(a) the couple's income and capital includes the separate income and capital of each of them; and

(b) the income and capital of any other person who is a member of any family of which the couple are members shall, except in prescribed circumstances, be treated as income and capital of the couple.]

(3) Regulations may provide that capital not exceeding the amount prescribed under subsection (1) [¹or (2A)], but exceeding a prescribed lower amount, shall be treated, to a prescribed extent, as if it were income of a prescribed amount.

AMENDMENT

1. Welfare Reform and Pensions Act 1999 s.59 and Sch.7 para.9 (March 19, 2001).

DEFINITIONS

"claimant"—see s.35(1).
"family"—*ibid.*
"income-based jobseeker's allowance"—see s.1(4).
"joint-claim couple"—*ibid.*
"joint-claim jobseeker's allowance"—*ibid.*
"prescribed"—see s.35(1).
"regulations"—*ibid.*

GENERAL NOTE

1.142   The provisions in this section are similar to those in ss.134(1) and 136(1) and (2) of the SSCBA 1992. Note the amendments made on March 19, 2001 relating to the introduction of joint claims for old style JSA for certain childless couples (see the notes at the beginning of this Act and to s.1(4)). Since February 25, 2008, all childless couples (unless they are exempt) have been required to make a joint claim (see reg.3A of the JSA Regulations 1996).

Subsection (1)
1.143   The capital limit for income-based JSA was raised to £16,000 for all claimants on April 10, 2006 (JSA Regulations 1996, reg.107). See the 2005 edition of this volume for the different capital limits that applied for most claimants before that date and see the note to s.134(1) of the SSCBA 1992.

Subsection (2)
1.144   This provides that the general rule for income-based JSA (as for income support) is that all of the family's (as defined in s.35(1)) income and capital is aggregated together and treated as the claimant's. The modifications to this rule for children and young persons were in regs 106 and 109 of the JSA Regulations 1996. However, as a consequence of the removal of amounts for children and young persons from income-based JSA (with effect from April 6, 2004, except in "transitional cases"— see the note to reg.17 of the Income Support Regulations and the note to reg.83 of the JSA Regulations 1996), a child's income and capital will be totally ignored and only a partner's income and capital will count as that of the claimant (see the amended form of reg.88(1) of the JSA Regulations 1996).

Subsections (2A) and (2B)
1.145   Subsections (1) and (2) do not apply to joint-claim JSA but the effects of subss. (2A) and (2B) is to apply similar rules to those in subss.(1) and (2) to joint-claim JSA. On subs.(2B), see reg.88ZA of the JSA Regulations 1996.

Subsection (3)

This enables a similar "tariff income" rule to the one that operates for income support to be applied to income-based (including joint-claim) JSA. Regulation 116 of the JSA Regulations 1996 provides for an income to be assumed to be produced from capital between £6,000 and £16,000 (£10,000 and £16,000 in the case of claimants living permanently in a care home, Abbeyfield Home, Polish Resettlement home or independent hospital).

Trade disputes

Trade disputes

14.—(1) Where—
  (a) there is a stoppage of work which causes a person not to be employed on any day, and
  (b) the stoppage is due to a trade dispute at his place of work,
that person is not entitled to a jobseeker's allowance for the week which includes that day unless he proves that he is not directly interested in the dispute.

(2) A person who withdraws his labour on any day in furtherance of a trade dispute, but to whom subsection (1) does not apply, is not entitled to a jobseeker's allowance for the week which includes that day.

(3) If a person who is prevented by subsection (1) from being entitled to a jobseeker's allowance proves that during the stoppage—
  (a) he became bona fide employed elsewhere;
  (b) his employment was terminated by reason of redundancy within the meaning of [¹section 139 of the Employment Rights Act 1996,] or
  (c) he bona fide resumed employment with his employer but subsequently left for a reason other than the trade dispute,
subsection (1) shall be taken to have ceased to apply to him on the occurrence of the event referred to in paragraph (a) or (b) or (as the case may be) the first event referred to in paragraph (c).

(4) In this section "place of work", in relation to any person, means the premises or place at which he was employed.

(5) Where separate branches of work which are commonly carried on as separate businesses in separate premises or at separate places are in any case carried on in separate departments on the same premises or at the same place, each of those departments shall, for the purposes of subsection (4), be deemed to be separate premises or (as the case may be) a separate place.

AMENDMENT

1. Employment Rights Act 1996 Sch.1 para.67(2)(a) (August 22, 1996).

DEFINITIONS

"employment"—see s.35(1) and JSA Regulations 1996 reg.4.
"entitled"—see s.35(1).
"trade dispute"—*ibid.*
"week"—*ibid.*

GENERAL NOTE

This section denies entitlement to old style JSA to certain persons affected by or involved in trade disputes in two situations. First, where a stoppage of work due to a trade dispute at the claimant's place of work causes them not to be employed on any day, they will not be entitled to JSA for the week which includes that day, unless either they can establish that they are not directly interested in the dispute or they can invoke one of the escape routes provided by subs.(3) (subs.(1)). The second situation where entitlement is denied throughout a week is where in furtherance of a trade dispute the claimant withdraws their labour on any day in that week, but not in such a way as to be caught by subs.(1) (the first situation of denial of entitlement) (subs.(2)).

In many respects the section replicates the trade dispute disqualification from UB in SSCBA 1992 s.27 and, as noted below, case law interpreting that and its precursor provisions will still be relevant in interpreting this old style JSA provision. There has been some change of terminology without apparent change of meaning (e.g. "place of work" rather than "place of employment"). That one day affected bars title for the whole week rather than just for the day, as would have been the case with UB, is unsurprising; it reflects the change from a daily benefit (UB) to a weekly benefit (JSA). Like the trade dispute disqualification from UB, this provision denies entitlement. Hence weeks ruled out do not form part of a jobseeking period (JSA Regulations 1996 reg.48(3)(e)), but nor did they erode the 182-day maximum period of entitlement to CBJSA founded on a contribution record in a single set of two tax/contribution years. This is in marked contrast to the double penalty suffered by the person who, for example, loses their job through misconduct, precluded from payment of JSA by s.19, who not only is denied payment but has the 182-day period eroded by the period of preclusion imposed under that section. This differential can to some degree be rationalised on the basis that the role of ss.19–19B is to preclude payment to those who are in some way responsible for their own unemployment, whereas, as shown below, the trade dispute preclusion can catch the innocent, and in part the trade dispute preclusion in denying benefit to those affected is said to manifest state neutrality in the dispute, the merits of which should not concern the benefit system.

Subsection (1)

1.149   To bring the trade dispute preclusion in subs.(1) into operation, subject to the escape routes discussed at the end of this note, the Secretary of State (decision-maker) must prove on the balance of probabilities that:

(1) there was a *trade dispute*;

(2) at the claimant's *place of work*;

(3) which resulted in a *stoppage of work*; and

(4) that stoppage caused the claimant not to be employed on a day.

This adapts for this section the approach to the unemployment benefit trade dispute disqualification set out in *R(U)17/52(T)*.

Each of these conditions contains terms (highlighted above) whose interpretation is vital to the correct application of the section's denial of entitlement to JSA.

Trade dispute

1.150   Determining the existence of a trade dispute seems logically the first task of the adjudicating authorities, because in the absence of a trade dispute the other conditions cannot apply. The basic definition, which is very broad, is now to be found in s.35(1), rather than in the section itself, as was the case in UB, but the definitions are identical. The definition clearly includes strikes, whether official or unofficial (*R(U)5/59*), lockouts (*R(U)17/52*) and demarcation disputes (*R(U)14/64*). There is no requirement that the claimant be a party to the trade dispute: *R(U)3/69* and see below. It has been held that there can be a trade dispute between an employer and employees of another employer who picket the employer's premises and persuade its employees to strike: *R(U)1/74*. There is a requirement in the definition of trade dispute in s.35(1) that the dispute concern employment or non-employment of persons or conditions or terms of employment. Disputes outside these parameters are not trade disputes for the purpose of this section. It is now clearly established that a dispute about safety procedures is within the definition: *R(U)3/71, R(U)5/77* and *R. v National Insurance Commissioner, Ex p. Thompson* (1977), reported as an Appendix to *R(U)5/77*. In *R(U)5/87* Commissioner Rice held that the words "any dispute . . . which is connected with the employment . . . of any person" are wide enough to include any dispute connected with the manner in which the employment is carried out, and in that case covered the dispute over the employees' "go slow". In most cases establishing the existence of a trade dispute is unlikely to be problematic. But note that in *R(U)21/59*, para.6, the Commissioner indicated that a dispute between an employer and an employee must have reached "a certain stage of contention before it may properly be termed a [trade] dispute". The Commissioner was clearly satisfied that evidence that the workforce had met to consider their response to their employer's rejection of their claims concerning their terms of employment amounted to a trade dispute and suggested that one may well have existed some time before the meeting took place.

It should be noted that in determining the existence of a trade dispute it is no part of the adjudicating authorities' task to make any assessment of the merits of the dispute: *Ex p. Thompson* (cited above) and *R(SSP)1/86*. It may be necessary to make findings of fact about when the trade dispute started and ended, but it should be remembered that the more important dates relate to when the stoppage of work started and ended. This is discussed below. There is a clear distinction to be drawn between a trade dispute and a stoppage of work under the section.

Place of work

The trade dispute must be at the claimant's place of work as defined in subs.(4).   1.151
Read with subs.(5) this allows some separation of departments within a range of employment operated by a single employer. It will usually be a straightforward task to identify the premises or place at which the claimant is employed. Obviously each case must be determined on its own facts. How broadly or narrowly the place will be defined will vary according to the circumstances of each case. In *R(U)4/58* the place of employment of an employee loading ships was held to be the whole of the docks.

Where the decision-maker shows on the balance of probabilities a place of work, it will be for the claimant to prove on the balance of probabilities that there are separate branches of work and that the trade dispute is not at his place of work so construed: *R(U)1/70*, at para.14. The escape route in accord with the terms of subss.(4) and (5) is complex because the claimant, who may not be best placed to do so, must adduce evidence to show that:

(a) there are separate branches of work; a claimant is unlikely to succeed unless he can show that the branch is engaged in work that is not part of an integrated process of production: *R(U)4/62*, para.7;

(b) the separate branches of work are commonly carried on as separate businesses in separate premises or at separate places; this necessarily involves adducing evidence as to patterns in other similar businesses: *R(U)4/62* and *R(U)1/70*, para.17; and

(c) at his place of employment the branches of work are in fact carried out in separate departments at the same premises or place.

In cases involving such arguments, clear findings of fact are obviously vital. *CU/66/1986(T)* affords an illustration. There the claimant successfully appealed her trade dispute disqualification to a Tribunal of Commissioners. She was a colliery canteen worker at Frickley Colliery, laid off during the miner's strike in 1984–1985. The Commissioners held that there was carried on in the canteen a separate branch of work, and one which is commonly carried on as a separate business in separate premises or at a separate place. But was the canteen a separate department? The evidence of the NUM Branch Secretary at the colliery was that the canteen was inside the colliery gates and had been attached to or added to the pit-head baths that had been built in

1937. It was managed by the manageress who was appointed by and answerable to the NCB Catering Manager at Doncaster. While applications for jobs at the canteen would be made to the colliery's personnel manager, the area canteen manager would be responsible for making the appointment. As regards disciplinary matters with respect to canteen workers, again, the area manager would be involved but the colliery manager would also have to be informed. Profits and losses in the canteen did not appear to feature in figures about the profitability of the colliery. The Commissioners, in the light of this evidence, decided that the work carried on in the canteen was a separate branch of work carried on in a separate department on the same premises or at the same place as the colliery. Accordingly, since the trade dispute that caused the stoppage of work was not at the claimant's place of employment she would not be disqualified from benefit. The Commissioners also referred to an Umpire's decision (Case 2185/29, *Umpires Decisions*, Vol.VIII, p.88) under the equivalent provision in s.8(1) of the Unemployment Insurance Act 1920. There, a blacksmith employed in the blacksmiths' department at a colliery, which department did both wagon repairing and general colliery work, was able to rely on the escape route, notwithstanding that only some work in that department was carried on as a separate department from coal-mining.

Stoppage of work

1.152   Generally defining a stoppage of work is relatively easy. But defining when it begins may be more problematic and a useful approach may be to adopt the reverse of the principles laid down in the decisions on the ending of stoppages of work discussed below. The starting point will always be to consider the definition given by the Tribunal of Commissioners in *R(U)17/52(T)*:

"A stoppage of work must be in the nature of a strike or lockout, that is to say it must be a move in a contest between an employer and his employees, the object of which is that employment shall be resumed on certain conditions."

In *R(U)7/58* it was held that a stoppage of work occurred when 38 production workers out of a total of 90 withdrew their labour. In *R(U)1/87* Commissioner Skinner said that "stoppage of work" means "a situation in which operations are being stopped or hindered otherwise than to a negligible extent" (para.7). There the closure of the furriers' fleshing shop on May 2, 1984, causing a 60 per cent loss of production, resulted in a stoppage from that date. In *R(U)1/65*, following a long line of Commissioners' decisions, it was held that where there was a trade dispute and subsequently the employer indicates that he will never re-employ the strikers, the stoppage of work continues to be due to the trade dispute despite the high improbability that the strikers will be re-employed and despite their acceptance of that position. In effect the disqualification can only end when they become bona fide employed elsewhere or when the stoppage ends. In *R(U)25/57*, the Commissioner adopted the approach taken by the Umpire in 1926 as establishing the principles to be applied in determining when the end of a stoppage of work occurred:

"A stoppage of work may come to an end without any settlement of the dispute, by the workers returning to work in a body, or by driblets, or by their places being taken by other men. In such cases the stoppage of work comes to an end when the employers have got all the workers they require, that is, when work is no longer being stopped or hindered by the refusal of workers to work on the employer's terms or the refusal of employers to employ the workers on the workers' terms . . . When work is again proceeding normally and is not being held up, either by the men holding back or by circumstances directly resulting from the stoppage of work, the stoppage of work is at an end." (para.6)

This approach was cited with approval in *R(U)1/65*. It is consistent with this approach that, where a dispute had ended but work was needed to industrial plant to carry out repairs necessitated by the stoppage, a lay-off while those repairs were carried out was a part of the stoppage due to the trade dispute: *R. v National Insurance Commissioner Ex p. Dawber* (published as an Appendix to *R(U)9/80*).

The stoppage causes the claimant not to be employed on a day

If the stoppage causes the claimant not to be employed on any day, entitlement to   1.153
old style JSA is lost for the week including that day (unless one of the escape routes
can be invoked), a change reflecting the weekly character of JSA as opposed to the
daily benefit structure of UB.

It has already been noted that the claimant need not be a party to the trade dispute
to be caught by the disqualification. Claimants are caught if the stoppage is the effective cause of their not working. So, if enough people stay away from work for a stoppage to occur, all those losing days of employment, whether by their own choice or
by force of circumstances, such as picketing or being laid off by the employer, are to
be regarded as having lost their employment by reason of the stoppage.

Escape routes

There are four escape routes for avoiding the preclusive effect of subs.(1): the   1.154
proviso in the subsection itself and the three exceptions set out in subs.(3).

(1) The proviso: Claimants can avoid the disqualification by proving that they have no   1.155
direct interest in the trade dispute. In determining what constitutes a direct interest
in the trade dispute, it is necessary to look no further than the decision of the House
of Lords in *Presho v Insurance Officer* [1984] 1 All E.R. 97 (published as Appendix
2 to *R(U)1/84*), followed by the Court of Appeal in *Cartlidge v Chief Adjudication
Officer* [1986] 2 All E.R. 1, appendix to *R(U)5/86*. In *Presho* Lord Brandon said that
the words should be given their natural and ordinary meaning, and continued:

> "Where different groups of workers, belonging to different unions, are employed
> by the same employers at the same place of work and there is a trade dispute
> between the common employers and one of the unions to which one of the groups
> of workers belong, those in the other groups of workers belonging to other unions
> are directly, and not merely indirectly, interested in that trade dispute provided
> that two conditions are fulfilled. The first condition is that, whatever may be the
> outcome of the trade dispute, it will be applied by the common employers not only
> to the group of workers belonging to the one union participating in the dispute,
> but also to the other groups of workers belonging to the other unions concerned.
> The second condition is that the application of the outcome of the dispute 'across
> the board' . . . should come about automatically as a result of one or other of
> three things: first, a collective agreement which is legally binding; or, second, a
> collective agreement which is not legally binding; or, third, established industrial
> custom and practice at the place of work concerned. [These issues involve] a
> question of fact of a kind which insurance officers, local tribunals and the commis-
> sioner, are by reason of their wide knowledge and experience of matters pertaining
> to industrial relations, exceptionally well qualified to answer." (At 101–102.)

In *Cartlidge,* the Commissioners had found that the miners' dispute concerned both
pay and pit closures, and so Mr Cartlidge, the amount of whose redundancy payment
on his impending leaving could thereby be affected, was directly interested in the
trade dispute. It follows that it will be extremely difficult for claimants to take advantage of this escape route. However, the fact that the claimant was at one time directly
interested in the trade dispute (and thus then unable to invoke the proviso) does not
preclude him from successfully invoking it later during the stoppage should he cease
to have a direct interest. The proviso is not invocable once and once only during a
stoppage *(R(U)1/87,* para.9, relying on *R(U)5/86(T),* paras 15–28 where a Tribunal
of Commissioners disapproved statements to the contrary in *R(U)4/79(T)* because a
line of Commissioners' authority running contrary to that relied on in *R(U)4/79(T)*
had not been cited or considered). A claimant initially directly interested in the trade
dispute (and therefore rightly denied benefit) can cease to be so interested and thus

claim the benefit of the proviso to conclude the period of denial, where his dismissal by his employer genuinely indicates the employer's intention to sever all relations with him and is not just a tactical manoeuvre in the dispute. In *R(U)1/87* the hindsight available to the Commissioner showed that the claimant's dismissal on the first day of the stoppage was part of plans to trim the size of the workforce and thus a genuine severance of all relations with the claimant rather than a tactical move in the dispute. Accordingly, the claimant was not subject to disqualification after that first day. Of course, were that case being decided now, with respect to old style JSA, the whole week in which that day occurred would be ruled out by subs.(1).

1.156 *(2) Bona fide employment elsewhere (subs.(3)(a)):* If someone caught by the subs. (1) preclusion proves that during the stoppage he became bona fide employed elsewhere, subs.(1) is to be taken to cease to apply to him from the point at which he became so employed elsewhere.

The burden of proof is on the claimant to establish the bona fide nature of the employment. Bona fide means that the employment must not merely be a device to avoid the disqualification; both the employment and the reason for taking it must be genuine *(R(U) 6/74)*. There is no objection to the taking of temporary employment so long as it is genuine. It will usually be necessary to show that the relationship with the former employer with whom there was a trade dispute has been permanently severed. So a former boiler-maker who obtained intermittent work in his usual occupation in a different port, but returned to his former employer on the ending of the dispute was held not to have established that he was bona fide employed elsewhere *(R(U)39/56)*.

1.157 *(3) Employment terminated by reason of redundancy (subs.(3)(b)):* If someone caught by the subs.(1) preclusion proves that during the stoppage his employment was terminated by reason of redundancy within the meaning of s.139(1) of the Employment Rights Act 1996, subs.(1) is to be taken to have ceased to apply to him from the point of such termination. As to "by reason of redundancy within the meaning of section 139(1)", termination will be by reason of redundancy if it is attributable wholly or mainly to: (a) the fact that the employer has ceased, or intends to cease, to carry on that business in the place where the employee [the JSA claimant] was employed, or (b) the fact that the requirements of that business for employees to carry out work of a particular kind, or for employees to carry out work of a particular kind in the place where [the claimant] was employed, have ceased or diminished or are expected to cease or diminish.

The precursor of this provision was inserted into the UB trade dispute disqualification scheme, to remove the injustice perceived to exist in the *Cartlidge* case. Mr Cartlidge had volunteered for redundancy prior to the start of the miners' dispute in 1984. Between receiving his notice of redundancy and its taking effect, a stoppage due to a trade dispute at his place of work caused him to not to be employed on some days. He had tried to work and had done so for much of the period but had lost some days' work because of the picketing of his pit. The Court of Appeal reluctantly held that the trade dispute disqualification extended beyond the termination of his employment because the stoppage of work was still continuing (the relevant provision then disqualified "for any day during the stoppage"). The effect of this provision is that subs.(1) can have no preclusive effect beyond the point of termination of employment by reason of redundancy.

1.158 *(4) Bona fide resumption of employment and subsequent leaving for another reason (subs.(3)(c)):* If someone caught by the subs.(1) preclusion proves that during the stoppage they bona fide resumed employment with their employer, subs.(1) is to be taken to have ceased to apply to them from the point at which they bona fide resumed their employment.

This is an escape route for claimants who have withdrawn their labour, subsequently returned to work, but then left it for a reason unconnected with the trade dispute. The reason will usually be something other than leaving their job to take another: subs.(3)(a) would there afford an easier escape route. Bona fide is to be interpreted as in subs.(3)(a). But otherwise it is not easy to see how this provision will work in practice. Does resumption mean that the employment was terminated and re-employment offered, or merely that the claimant returned to work during the trade dispute, or both? There appears to be no case law on the precursor of this provision, so many points await interpretation.

Subsection (2)

This subsection makes it clear that anyone not falling within subs.(1) who withdraws their labour on any day in furtherance of a trade dispute is not entitled to old style JSA for the week which includes that day. It fills a gap in the test in subs.(1)(a) because it does not require any stoppage of work to have occurred; nor does it require the trade dispute to be at the claimant's place of employment. As long as the withdrawal of labour is in furtherance of a trade dispute, the preclusion operates. It could require the authorities to draw a distinction between a "withdrawal of labour" and a "lock-out" (*Ogus, Barendt and Wikeley, The Law of Social Security*, p.141), risking an opinion on the merits of the dispute.

    1.159

The rule can only be applied to claimants who have withdrawn their labour. That would cover straightforward strikes or refusals to carry out some significant part of contractual duties, even if the latter led to the employer sending the employees home completely. On the other hand, refusals to work voluntary overtime or works-to-rule would not be covered. And if an employer has initiated a lock-out before the occurrence of anything that would otherwise count as a withdrawal of labour it would seem that the employees could not be regarded as a having withdrawn their labour. A withdrawal must involve a voluntary choice not to work. Much more troublesome would be cases where employees decline to cross picket lines. Being physically prevented from entering work premises or being subjected to threats of violence against self or others would no doubt negate the necessary element of voluntary choice. At the other end of the spectrum, agreeing to polite and reasoned requests not to cross a picket line would also no doubt be regarded as a withdrawal of labour. But there will be many circumstances in the middle where the question will be very difficult to answer. If there are many pickets, with shouted insults and imprecations or more, when do spirited attempts at persuasion turn into intimidation?

    1.160

The rule also requires that the individual's withdrawal of labour is in furtherance of a trade dispute, as defined in s.35(1). There is no requirement that the dispute has led to any stoppage of work or similar, nor that the claimant potentially caught by subs.(2) has any material interest in the outcome of the dispute. Presumably a trade dispute has to be in existence before a withdrawal of labour can be in furtherance of it. In para.6 of *R(U) 21/59* the Commissioner indicated that a dispute between an employer and an employee must have reached "a certain stage of contention before it may properly be termed a [trade] dispute". He was clearly satisfied that evidence that the workforce had met to consider their response to their employer's rejection of their claims concerning their terms of employment amounted to a trade dispute and suggested that one may well have existed some time before the meeting took place. However, in the UB and JSA context such problems have tended to be short-circuited by the question of whether there had been a stoppage of work as a result of any trade dispute at the claimant's place of work.

"Furtherance" presumably points towards whatever subjective intention behind the withdrawal of labour can properly be attributed to the claimant, rather than whether the withdrawal is likely to have any practical influence on the outcome of the trade dispute. That would be consistent with the inherent principle that a solo withdrawal of labour can trigger the application of subs.(2). It is not necessary for the claimant to have acted in concert with others, provided that the withdrawal of labour was in furtherance of a trade dispute.

It is not clear whether the rule must continue to apply to weeks after the claimant's contract of employment has been terminated. If it is the employer who dismisses the clamant it must be arguable that the claimant is no longer withdrawing their labour. There is nothing to withdraw from.

Effect on other claimants

1.161   **15.**—(1) Except in prescribed circumstances, subsection (2) applies in relation to a claimant for an income-based jobseeker's allowance where a member of his family ("A") is, or would be, prevented by section 14 from being entitled to a jobseeker's allowance.

(2) For the purposes of calculating the claimant's entitlement to an income based jobseeker's allowance—

(a) any portion of the applicable amount which is included in respect of A shall be disregarded for the period for which this subsection applies to the claimant;

(b) where the claimant and A are a [² couple], any portion of the applicable amount which is included in respect of them shall be reduced to one half for the period for which this subsection applies to the claimant;

(c) except so far as regulations provide otherwise, there shall be treated as the claimant's income—

(i) any amount which becomes, or would on an application duly made become, available to A in relation to that period by way of repayment of income tax deducted from A's [¹ taxable earnings (as defined by section 10 of the Income Tax (Earnings and Pensions) Act 2003 under PAYE regulations]; and

(ii) any other payment which the claimant or any member of his family receives or is entitled to obtain because A is without employment for that period; and

(d) any payment by way of a jobseeker's allowance for that period or any part of it which apart from this paragraph would be made to the claimant—

(i) shall not be made, if the weekly rate of payment ("the rate") would be equal to or less than the prescribed sum; and

(ii) shall be at a weekly rate equal to the difference between the rate and the prescribed sum, if the rate would be more than the prescribed sum.

(3) Where a reduction under subsection (2)(b) would not produce a sum which is a multiple of 5p, the reduction shall be to the nearest lower sum which is such a multiple.

(4) Where A returns to work with the same employer after a period during which subsection (2) applied to the claimant (whether or not his return is before the end of any stoppage of work in relation to which he is, or would be, prevented from being entitled to a jobseeker's allowance), subsection (2) shall cease to apply to the claimant at the commencement of the day on which A returns to work.

(5) In relation to any period of less than a week, subsection (2) shall have effect subject to such modifications as may be prescribed.

(6) Subsections (7) to (9) apply where an order made under section 150 of the Administration Act (annual up-rating of benefits) has the effect of increasing the sum prescribed in regulations made under section 4(5) as the personal allowance for a single person aged not less than 25 ("the personal allowance").

(7) For the sum prescribed in regulations made under subsection (2)(d) there shall be substituted, from the time when the order comes into force, a sum arrived at by increasing the prescribed sum by the percentage by which the personal allowance has been increased by the order.

(8) If the sum arrived at under subsection (7), is not a multiple of 50p—

(a) any remainder of 25p or less shall be disregarded;

(b) any remainder of more than 25p shall be rounded up to the nearest 50p.

(9) The order shall state the sum substituted for the sum prescribed in regulations made under subsection (2)(d).

(10) Nothing in subsection (7) prevents the making of further regulations under subsection (2)(d) varying the prescribed sum.

AMENDMENTS

1. Income Tax (Earnings and Pensions) Act 2003 Sch.6 Pt 2 para.229 (April 6, 2003).

2. Civil Partnership Act 2004 s.254 and Sch.24 para.120 (December 5, 2005).

MODIFICATIONS

Section 15(2)(d) is modified by reg.155(1), in relation to an income-based allowance, and reg.155(2), in relation to a joint-claim allowance, of the JSA Regulations 1996 (SI 1996/207) for the purpose of adapting its provisions to entitlement for part-weeks. See the text of reg.155 in Pt III for the details of the modifications.

DEFINITIONS

"applicable amount"—see s.35(1).
"the Administration Act"—*ibid.*
"claimant"—*ibid.*
"couple"—*ibid.*
"employment"—*ibid.* and JSA Regulations 1996 regs 3 and 4.
"family"—see s.35(1).
"income-based jobseeker's allowance"—*ibid.*, and s.1(4).
"prescribed"—see s.35(1).

GENERAL NOTE

Subsection (1)

This provision applies where the partner of an income-based JSA claimant is involved in a trade dispute. Although subs.(1) refers to a member of the claimant's family, the effect of reg.171(b)(i) of the JSA Regulations 1996 is that subs. (2) can only apply to the claimant's partner. Note that benefit will not be affected if the claimant's partner is incapable of work or within the "maternity period" (six weeks before and seven weeks after confinement) (reg.171(b)(ii)), or has limited capability for work (reg.171(b)(iii)). If the *claimant* is involved in a trade dispute see s.14.

Note also reg.52(2) of the JSA Regulations 1996, which treats a partner as in remunerative work for seven days beginning on the first day of the stoppage of work or the first day on which the partner withdrew his labour if the claimant was not entitled to income-based JSA when the partner became involved in the dispute. The result is to disentitle the claimant for those days (s.3(1)(e)). The partner is not treated as in remunerative work outside this period (reg.53(g)).

1.162

Subsection (2)

This follows the rules for income support in s.126(3)(c) and (5) of the SSCBA 1992. See the notes to s.126. The basic principle is that where the claimant's partner is involved in a trade dispute, no benefit is payable in respect of him (paras (a) and (b)). The "prescribed sum" for the purposes of para.(d) is £41.00 from April 6, 2020 (reg.172 of the JSA Regulations 1996). This sum had not previously been up-rated since April 2015.

1.163

Subsection (4)

1.164   Subsection (2) ceases to apply from the day the claimant's partner returns to work.

[¹Trade disputes: joint-claim couples

1.165   **15A.**—(1) Sections 14 and 15 shall, in relation to a joint-claim couple claiming a joint-claim jobseeker's allowance, apply in accordance with this section.

(2) Where each member of the couple is prevented by section 14 from being entitled to a jobseeker's allowance, the couple are not entitled to a joint-claim jobseeker's allowance.

(3) But where only one member of the couple is prevented by that section from being entitled to a jobseeker's allowance, the couple are not for that reason alone prevented from being entitled to a joint-claim jobseeker's allowance.

(4) Section 15(1) does not have effect in relation to the couple but, except in prescribed circumstances, section 15(2) applies for the purposes of calculating the couple's entitlement to a joint-claim jobseeker's allowance where—

(a) a member of the couple, [³ . . .]

(b) [³ . . .]

is, or would be, prevented by section 14 from being entitled to a jobseeker's allowance.

(5) Where section 15(2) applies in relation to the couple by virtue of subsection (4) above, that provision and section 15(4) apply with the following modifications—

(a) references to the claimant are to be taken as references to the couple;

(b) references to "A" are to the person mentioned in subsection (4)(a) or (b) above;

(c) [³ . . .] and

(d) section 15(2)(c)(ii) has effect as if for "of his family" there were substituted "of any family of which the couple are members".]

AMENDMENTS

1. Welfare Reform and Pensions Act 1999 s.59 and Sch.7 para.10 (March 19, 2001).

2. Civil Partnership Act 2004 s.254 and Sch.24 para.121 (December 5, 2005).

3. Welfare Reform Act 2012 s.147 and Sch.14 Pt 2 (May 8, 2012).

DEFINITIONS

"claimant"—see s.35(1).
"couple"—*ibid.*
"family"—*ibid.*
"joint-claim couple"—see s.1(4).
"joint-claim jobseeker's allowance"—*ibid.*

GENERAL NOTE

1.166   This applies the rules in ss.14 and 15 (subject to minor modifications, see subss. (4) and (5)) to joint-claim couples (i.e. since February 25, 2008, all childless couples (unless they are exempt), see reg.3A of the JSA Regulations 1996).

Persons under 18

Severe hardship

16.—(1) If it appears to the Secretary of State—   1.167
  (a) that a person—
      (i) has reached the age of 16 but not the age of 18;
      (ii) is not entitled to a jobseeker's allowance or to income support; and
      (iii) is registered for training but is not being provided with any training; and
  (b) that severe hardship will result to him unless a jobseeker's allowance is paid to him,
the Secretary of State may direct that this section is to apply to him.
  (2) A direction may be given so as to have effect for a specified period.
  (3) The Secretary of State may revoke a direction if—
  (a) it appears to him that there has been a change of circumstances as a result of which failure to receive a jobseeker's allowance need no longer result in severe hardship to the person concerned;
  [¹(b) it appears to him that the person concerned has, without [² a good reason]—
      (i) neglected to avail himself of a reasonable opportunity of a place on a training scheme; or
      (ii) after a place on such a scheme has been notified to him by an employment officer as vacant or about to become vacant, refused or failed to apply for it or to accept it when offered to him; or]
  (c) he is satisfied that it was given in ignorance of some material fact or was based on a mistake as to some material fact and considers that, but for that ignorance or mistake, he would not have given the direction.
  [¹(4) In this section—
"employment officer" means an officer of the Secretary of State or such other person as may be designated for the purposes of this section by an order made by the Secretary of State;
"period" includes—
  (a) a period of a determinate length;
  (b) a period defined by reference to the happening of a future event; and
  (c) a period of a determinate length but subject to earlier determination upon the happening of a future event;
"training scheme" has such meaning as may be prescribed.]

AMENDMENTS

  1. Social Security Act 1998 s.86(1) and Sch.7 para.139 (October 18, 1999).
  2. Welfare Reform Act 2012 s.48 and Sch.7 para.3 (October 22, 2012).

DEFINITION

  "training"—see s.35(1) and JSA Regulation 1996 reg.57(1).

GENERAL NOTE

Subsections (1) and (2)

1.168   This provision is similar to the former s.125 of the Contributions and Benefits Act (revoked on October 7, 1996), which dealt with income support severe hardship directions.

Subsection (1) requires that the person under 18 is not entitled to income support or JSA, so the person must fall outside the categories covered in regs 59–61 of the JSA Regulations and not be eligible for income support under reg.4ZA of and Sch.1B to the Income Support Regulations. (He must also not be entitled to contribution-based JSA, but this is very unlikely in the case of a person under 18.) The other main conditions are that the person is registered for, but not receiving, training and that severe hardship will (not may) result if JSA is not paid. The question of whether these conditions are satisfied is for the Secretary of State, and even if they are, there is a discretion whether or not to allow benefit. There is no right of appeal to an appeal tribunal from the Secretary of State's decision.

To claim JSA on the grounds of severe hardship, the person should first register for work and training with the Careers Service where he will be given an ES9 referral form to take to the JobCentre (but see reg.62 of the JSA Regulations for the exceptions to this rule). Staff are instructed that all 16- and 17-year-old claimants should be allowed to make an application for JSA and should not be turned away by the JobCentre. An initial check will be made to see if the young person is eligible for JSA as of right (see regs 59–61 of the JSA Regulations). If not, and the application on the grounds of severe hardship fails at this stage, it will automatically be referred to the Severe Hardship Claims Unit for consideration. The Employment Service has produced detailed guidance on JSA for 16- and 17-year-olds (*Employment Service Guidance, JSA for 16 and 17 year olds*). Chapter 7, which deals with the severe hardship interview, states that the young person should be informed of the need to contact parents, whether or not the young person is living with them, or a third party, in order to verify the information he or she has given. The young person's consent to do this is required, but refusal of permission without good reason may mean that there will not be enough evidence on which to make a direction (although all such potential "nil" decisions still have to go to the Severe Hardship Claims Unit). At the same time no "undue pressure" is to be placed on the young person to give permission. This could be difficult to implement in practice. However, the guidance also states (more flexibly) that evidence from a responsible third party (e.g. a relative, social worker or voluntary worker), either in person, by telephone or in writing, may mean that contact with the young person's parents is not necessary.

A direction may be made for a definite period (subs.(2)) (usually eight weeks, but this can be varied according to the circumstances). It can be renewed and it may be revoked if any of the conditions in subs.(3) apply. If a direction is made the decision-maker must consider all the other conditions of entitlement.

Note that the three-day waiting period for JSA does not apply if a s.16 direction has been made (reg.46(1) of the JSA Regulations).

Subsection (3)

1.169   Once a direction is made under this section the claimant satisfies s.3(1)(f) (iii). If the claimant ceases to satisfy the other conditions of entitlement, entitlement will cease. The Secretary of State has a general discretion to revoke a direction whenever there is a change of circumstances, which means that severe hardship no longer need follow from non-payment of JSA (para.(a)). This emphasises the strictness of the test under subs.(1). If severe hardship will not definitely follow from the non-payment of JSA subs.(1) cannot operate. It appears that the revocation of the direction may be retrospective from the date of the change of circumstances, and, if there was a failure to disclose facts constituting the change, the overpayment is recoverable under s.71A of the Administration Act. A direction may also be revoked if it was originally given in ignorance of or under a mistake as to a material fact that would have altered the decision on the inevitability of severe hardship (para.(c)). If there was misrepresentation of or failure to disclose that material fact, recovery under s.71A may arise.

In addition, para.(b) allows for revocation of a direction where the person has failed to pursue or refused a training opportunity without good cause ("good cause" for these purposes is not defined, so the existing case law on its meaning will be relevant).

Note that in such a case the sanctions provided for in s.19(5) do not apply (s.20(2)). The young person's "offence" will be dealt with by revocation of the direction, if this is considered appropriate, or by reduction of his JSA under reg.63(1)(b), if this applies. If a direction is revoked the young person can apply for another severe hardship direction to be made but it seems that it will be subject to a 40 per cent reduction (20 per cent if the young person is pregnant or seriously ill) of the appropriate personal allowance under para.1 of Sch.1 to the JSA Regulations for the first two weeks (s.17(3)(a) and reg.63(1)(a)). See the notes to s.17 and reg.63. **1.170**

Note that the sanctions in s.19(5) also do not apply if a young person who is the subject of a severe hardship direction commits the lesser "misdemeanour" of failing to complete a training course without good cause (s.20(2)). Instead his JSA will be reduced in accordance with s.17 and reg.63 of the JSA Regulations, if applicable. But note that the sanctions in s.19(6) do apply.

Reduced payments

17.—(1) Regulations may provide for the amount of an income-based jobseeker's allowance [³ payable in respect of] any young person to whom this section applies to be reduced— **1.171**

   (a) in such circumstances;

   (b) by such a percentage; and

   (c) for such a period.

as may be prescribed.

[²(1A) Regulations may provide for the amount of a joint-claim job-seeker's allowance payable in respect of any joint-claim couple where a member of the couple is a young person to whom this section applies to be reduced—

   (a) in such circumstances;

   (b) by such a percentage; and

   (c) for such a period,

as may be prescribed.]

  (2) This section applies to any young person in respect of whom—

   (a) a direction is in force under section 16; and

   (b) [¹ any] of the conditions mentioned in subsection (3) is satisfied.

  (3) The conditions are that—

   (a) the young person was previously entitled to an income-based job-seeker's allowance and that entitlement ceased by virtue of the revocation of a direction under section 16;

[¹(b) he has given up a place on a training scheme, or failed to attend such a scheme on which he has been given a place, and no certificate has been issued to him under subsection (4);

   (c) he has lost his place on such a scheme through misconduct.

  (4) Where a young person who has given up a place on a training scheme, or failed to attend such a scheme on which he has been given a place—

   (a) claims that there was [⁴ a good reason] for his doing so; and

   (b) applies to the Secretary of State for a certificate under this subsection, the Secretary of State shall, if he is satisfied that there was good cause, issue a certificate to that effect and give a copy of it to the young person.

(5) In this section—

"training scheme" has such meaning as may be prescribed;

"young person" means a person who has reached the age of 16 but not the age of 18.]

AMENDMENTS

1. Social Security Act 1998 s.86(1) and Sch.7 para.140 (October 18, 1999).
2. Welfare Reform and Pensions Act 1999 s.70 and Sch.8 para.29 (November 11, 1999).
3. Welfare Reform and Pensions Act 1999 Sch.7 para.11 (March 19, 2001).
4. Welfare Reform Act 2012 s.48 and Sch.7 para.3 (October 22, 2012).

GENERAL NOTE

1.172   Under this section regulations can provide for JSA that is being paid because a severe hardship direction is in force to be paid at a reduced rate. See reg.63 of the JSA Regulations that has been made under this section. Note that although subs.(3)(a) refers to revocation of a s.16 direction generally, it is only where a direction has been revoked under s.16(3)(b) that a reduction will be applied under reg.63 (see reg.63(1)(a)).

    Note the escape-route in para.(4) whereby the Secretary of State can decide that the young person had a good reason for failing to complete the training and issue a certificate to that effect. A decision as to whether or not to issue such a certificate is one against which there is no right of appeal (para.1(b) of Sch.2 to the Social Security Act 1998). See reg.7(24) of the Decisions and Appeals Regulations in relation to supersessions where a sanction has been imposed under reg.63 of the JSA Regulations but the Secretary of State then issues a certificate under s.17(4).

1.173   Note also that if a young person who is the subject of a severe hardship direction fails to pursue or refuses a training opportunity without a good reason (so that the direction is liable to be revoked under s.16(3)(b)), or fails to complete a training course without a good reason, or loses his place through misconduct, the sanctions provided for in s.19(5) do not apply (s.20(2)). The young person's "offence" will be dealt with under s.16, or this section and reg.63 of the JSA Regulations, as appropriate. See the notes to reg.63.

[¹ "Work for your benefit" schemes etc.

Schemes for assisting persons to obtain employment: "work for your benefit" schemes etc.

1.174   **17A.**—(1) Regulations may make provision for or in connection with imposing on claimants in prescribed circumstances a requirement to participate in schemes of any prescribed description that are designed to assist them to obtain employment.

(2) Regulations under this section may, in particular, require participants to undertake work, or work-related activity, during any prescribed period with a view to improving their prospects of obtaining employment.

(3) In subsection (2) "work-related activity", in relation to any person, means activity which makes it more likely that the person will obtain or remain in work or be able to do so.

(4) Regulations under this section may not require a person to participate in a scheme unless the person would (apart from the regulations) be
required to meet the jobseeking conditions.

(5) Regulations under this section may, in particular, make provision—

(a) for notifying participants of the requirement to participate in a
scheme within subsection (1);

(b) for securing that participants are not required to meet the jobseeking
conditions or are not required to meet such of those conditions as are
specified in the regulations;

(c) for suspending any jobseeker's agreement to which a person is a
party for any period during which the person is a participant;

(d) [² . . .]

(e) [² . . .]

(f) [² . . .]

(6) [² . . .]

(7) [² . . .]

(8) [² . . .]

(9) [² . . .]

(10) In this section—

"claimant", in relation to a joint- claim couple claiming a joint- claim jobseeker's allowance, means either or both of the members of the couple;

"the jobseeking conditions" means the conditions set out in section 1(2)
(a) to (c);

"participant", in relation to any time, means any person who is required
at that time to participate in a scheme within subsection (1).]

AMENDMENTS

1. Welfare Reform Act 2009 s.1 (November 12, 2009).
2. Welfare Reform Act 2012 s.147 Sch.14 Pt 3 (October 22, 2012).

GENERAL NOTE

This provision enables the Secretary of State to make regulations requiring   1.175
claimants to participate in schemes that are designed to assist them to obtain
employment, including requiring them to undertake work or work-related activity (activity which would make it more likely that the participant will obtain or
remain in work or be able to do so) as part of a "work for your benefit" scheme.
Section 20E(3)(a) and (4) allows regulations to provide for any functions of the
Secretary of State under regulations under s.17A to be contracted out to any
person.

Under the penalty provisions originally in s.17A, benefit was not payable for a
period of between one and 26 weeks where a claimant failed without good cause to
comply with regulations. Those were replaced with effect from October 22, 2012
by the possibility of a sanction under s.19 or 19A. A failure without a good reason
to participate in a scheme under s.17A(1) can attract a higher-level sanction under
s.19(2)(e) but only if the scheme is prescribed for the purposes of s.19. The only
scheme so prescribed (in reg.70B of the JSA Regulations 1996) is Mandatory Work
Activity (see the MWAS Regulations, below), although the scheme has ceased to
operate after April 2016. The relevant potential sanction for other schemes is therefore that under s.19A(2)(b) for failing without a good reason to comply with regulations under s.17A, which requires sanctions of fixed periods of four and 13 weeks for
first and second "offences" within a year (see reg.69A of the JSA Regulations 1996).

Section 20E(3)(a) allows the Secretary of State to contract out certain functions under regulations under s.17A to such persons (thus including companies or local authorities) and their employees as are authorised for the purpose. In practice the Secretary of State has contracted out the giving of notices of the requirement to participate in schemes under s.17A or the ceasing of that requirement to the scheme providers and their employees (see reg.17 of the SAPOE Regulations and regs.20 and 18 respectively of the now redundant MWAS Regulations and ESES Regulations). See the notes to s.19A(2)(b) for discussion of what evidence of authorisation and of the giving of notices needs to be provided by the Secretary of State in any sanction appeal.

1.176 Section 17A schemes were piloted in limited geographical areas from 2010, to assess their effectiveness (Jobseeker's Allowance (Work for Your Benefit Pilot Scheme) Regulations 2010 (SI 2010/1222), originally operative for three years from November 22, 2010 but revoked on March 1, 2012).

The other regulations, mainly without geographical limit, made under s.17A are:

- the Jobseeker's Allowance (Mandatory Work Activity Scheme) Regulations 2011 (SI 2011/688) ("the MWAS Regulations") (the scheme has not operated since April 2016);

- the Jobseeker's Allowance (Employment, Skills and Enterprise Scheme) Regulations 2011 (SI 2011/917) ("the ESES Regulations");

- the Jobseeker's Allowance (Schemes for Assisting Persons to Obtain Employment) Regulations 2013 (SI 2013/276) ("the SAPOE Regulations");

- the Jobseeker's Allowance (Supervised Jobsearch Pilot Scheme) Regulations 2014 (SI 2014/1913) (which expired after April 29, 2015 and are not included in Part III below, only in the Supplement to the 2014/15 edition); and

- the Jobseeker's Allowance (18–21 Work Skills Pilot Scheme) Regulations 2014 (SI 2014/3117) (not included in Part III as only operating in limited areas but set out in the Supplement to the 2014/15 edition).

The Jobseekers (Back to Work Schemes) Act 2013 validated retrospectively the ESES Regulations that had been declared ultra vires by the Court of Appeal in *R (Reilly and Wilson) v Secretary of State for Work and Pensions* [2013] EWCA Civ 66; [2013] 1 W.L.R. 2239 on the ground that the regulations failed to describe, rather than merely name, the schemes they purported to bring within s.17A. The Act was passed on the day on which the Secretary of State sought permission to appeal to the Supreme Court. On the day of the Court of Appeal's judgment (February 12, 2013) the ESES Regulations were replaced by the SAPOE Regulations, which set out the details of the schemes that had been named in the ESES Regulations. See the notes to the 2013 Act for discussion of the effect of the decisions of the Supreme Court in *Reilly and Wilson*, the three-judge panel of the Upper Tribunal in *SSWP v TJ (JSA)* [2015] UKUT 56 (AAC) and the Court of Appeal in *SSWP v Reilly and Hewstone and SSWP v Jeffrey and Bevan* [2016] EWCA Civ 413; [2017] Q.B. 657; [2017] AACR 14.

1.177 The 2013 Act also provided that notices given for the purposes of the ESES Regulations were to be treated as having complied with regs 4(2)(c) and (e) (details of requirements to participate and information about consequences of failure to participate) if fairly minimal conditions were satisfied. But see para.21 of *SSWP v CN (JSA)* [2020] UKUT 26 (AAC) where it was said to be arguable that the appointment letter in that particular case did not satisfy the condition in reg.4(2)(c) of the ESES Regulations on the details of what the claimant had to do even when read with the "sanitising" effect of s.1(4)(a) of the 2013 Act.

In *R (Reilly No 2 and Hewstone) v Secretary of State for Work and Pensions* [2014] EWHC 2182 (Admin) Lang J granted a declaration that the 2013 Act was incompatible with art.6 of the ECHR in that its retrospective effect meant that it interfered with the claimants' right to a fair trial. That decision was confirmed by the Court of Appeal in *SSWP v Reilly and Hewstone* and *SSWP v Jeffrey and Bevan*. See the introductory notes to the 2013 Act for a full discussion, including its amendment from October 2020 by a Remedial Order.

The 2013 Act also sought to protect the operation of the MWAS Regulations from challenge on the basis that notices given to claimants under reg.4 were invalid in the same way as notices under reg.4 of the ESES Regulations in *Reilly and Wilson*, on which now see the decision of the Supreme Court ([2013] UKSC 68; [2013] 1 A.C. 453). However, the 2013 Act gave no protection to the MWAS Regulations against a vires challenge on the same grounds as in *Reilly and Wilson*. Such a challenge was rejected by Hickinbottom J in *R (Smith) v Secretary of State for Work and Pensions* [2014] EWHC 843 (Admin). He held that there was sufficient description of the scheme to meet the standard required by the Supreme Court. The reasons included that the prescription of the period of the scheme was relevant to its description under s.17A(1) and was not relevant only to subs.(2). That conclusion and reasoning was in essence endorsed by the Court of Appeal on the claimant's appeal ([2015] EWCA Civ 229).

Section 17A: supplemental

17B.—(1) For the purposes of, or in connection with, any scheme within section 17A(1) the Secretary of State may—   1.178

    (a) make arrangements (whether or not with other persons) for the provision of facilities;

    (b) provide support (by whatever means) for arrangements made by other persons for the provision of facilities;

    (c) make payments (by way of fees, grants, loans or otherwise) to persons undertaking the provision of facilities under arrangements within paragraph (a) or (b);

    (d) make payments (by way of grants, loans or otherwise) to persons participating in the scheme;

    (e) make payments in respect of incidental expenses.

(2) For the purposes of, or in connection with, any scheme within section 17A(1)—

    (a) the Scottish Ministers, and

    (b) the Welsh Ministers,

may make payments (by way of fees, grants, loans or otherwise) to persons (including the Secretary of State) undertaking the provision of facilities under arrangements within subsection (1)(a) or (b) if the following condition is met.

(3) The condition is that the Scottish Ministers or the Welsh Ministers consider that the facilities are capable of supporting the training in Scotland or Wales of persons for employment.

(4) Unless the Scottish Ministers or Welsh Ministers otherwise specify, the payments may be used by the person to whom they are made for the provision of any of the facilities provided under the arrangements.

(5) In subsections (1) to (4) "facilities" includes services, and any reference to the provision of facilities includes the making of payments to persons participating in the scheme.

(6) The power of the Secretary of State to make an order under section 26 of the Employment Act 1988 (status of trainees etc) includes power to make, in relation to—

    (a) persons participating in any scheme within section 17A(1), and

    (b) payments received by them by virtue of subsection (1) above,

provision corresponding to any provision which (by virtue of section 26(1) or

(2) of that Act) may be made in relation to persons using such facilities, and to such payments received by them, as are mentioned in section 26(1) of that Act.

AMENDMENT

1. Welfare Reform Act 2009 s.1 (November 12, 2009).

DEFINITION

"person"—see Interpretation Act 1978 Sch.1.

GENERAL NOTE

1.179   This contains provisions supplemental to s.17A that relate to the practical operation of the "work for your benefit" schemes prescribed under that section. It provides support for any contractual arrangements the Secretary of State may make regarding the delivery of such schemes (e.g. with non-governmental organisations, including private-sector companies, or for paying transport costs for participants).

Persons dependent on drugs etc.

Persons dependent on drugs etc.

1.180   **17C.**—[¹ . . .]

AMENDMENT

1. Welfare Reform Act 2012 s.60(1) (May 8, 2012).

Recovery of overpayments

1.181   **18.**—*[Omitted. See s.71A of the Social Security Administration Act 1992 in Vol. III.]*

Denial of jobseeker's allowance

[¹**Higher-level sanctions**

1.182   **19.**— (1) The amount of an award of a jobseeker's allowance is to be reduced in accordance with this section in the event of a failure by the claimant which is sanctionable under this section.

(2) It is a failure sanctionable under this section if a claimant—

(a) through misconduct loses employment as an employed earner;

(b) without a good reason voluntarily leaves such employment;

(c) without a good reason refuses or fails to apply for, or accept if offered, a situation in any employment which an employment officer has informed him is vacant or about to become vacant;

(d) without a good reason neglects to avail himself of a reasonable opportunity of employment;

(e) without a good reason fails to participate in any scheme within section 17A(1) which is prescribed for the purposes of this section.

(3) For the purposes of subsection (2)(b), in such circumstances as may be prescribed, including in particular where a person has been dismissed by his employer by reason of redundancy within the meaning of

section 139(1) of the Employment Rights Act 1996 after volunteering or agreeing to be so dismissed, a person who might otherwise be treated as having left his employment voluntarily is to be treated as not having left voluntarily.

(4) Regulations are to provide for—

(a) the amount of a reduction under this section;

(b) the period for which such a reduction has effect, not exceeding three years in relation to any failure sanctionable under this section.

(5) Regulations under subsection (4)(b) may in particular provide for the period of a reduction to depend on either or both of the following—

(a) the number of failures by the claimant sanctionable under this section;

(b) the period between such failures.

(6) Regulations may provide—

(a) for cases in which no reduction is to be made under this section;

(b) for a reduction under this section made in relation to an award that is terminated to be applied to any new award made within a prescribed period of the termination.

(7) During any period for which the amount of a joint-claim jobseeker's allowance is reduced under this section by virtue of a failure by one of the claimants which is sanctionable under this section, the allowance is payable to the other member of the couple.

AMENDMENT

1. Welfare Reform Act 2012 s. 46(1) (October 22, 2012).

DEFINITIONS

"a joint-claim jobseeker's allowance"—see s.1(4).
"claimant"—see s.35(1).
"employed earner"—see s.35(1); JSA Regulations 1996 reg.75(4); SSCBA 1992 s.2(1)(a) and 122(1).
"employment"—see s.35(1); JSA Regulations 1996 reg.75(4).
"employment officer"—see s.35(1).
"prescribed"—*ibid.*
"regulations"—*ibid.*

GENERAL NOTE

Subsection (1)

Since 1911, state benefits for unemployment have contained sanctions in respect **1.183** of voluntary unemployment whether in terms of conduct bringing about a loss of employment or conducing to the continuance of a claimant's unemployment. In the unemployment benefit regime, the sanction of disqualification from benefit for a period was most recently found in SSCBA 1992. Until the October 2012 changes, the previous version of s.19 afforded sanctions by precluding, for varying periods, payment of JSA to which the claimant was otherwise entitled where the claimant fell within the circumstances covered in either subs.(5) or (6) of that section.

Subsection (5) provided grounds for precluding payment which were concerned with the claimant's failure to comply with a jobseeker's direction issued by an employment officer or with avoidable loss or refusal of a training scheme or employment programme opportunity. The successor to those grounds is not the new s.19, but the new s.19A, dealing with "other sanctions", examined below.

Subsection (6) of the previous version of s.19, essentially echoing the "heads" of disqualification from UB in SSCBA 1992 s.28(1)(a)–(c), provided grounds for precluding payment of JSA which were concerned with the avoidable loss or refusal of employment (e.g. loss of a job through misconduct; voluntarily leaving a job without just cause, etc.). That was the ancestor of this "new" s.19 which deals with the imposition of "higher-level sanctions" (drastic reduction of old style JSA for much longer periods than before) in respect of—with one addition— essentially the same conduct bringing about unemployment or conducing to its continuance, now referred to as "a failure by the claimant sanctionable under this section". What constitutes such a failure is set out in subs.(2).

1.184   It cannot be stressed enough that "higher-level sanctions" represented a very much more stringent sanctions regime than those previously applicable. The old UB and early JSA disqualification regime was sometimes justified on the basis of the "causal theory", that the basic purpose was "to provide against the misfortune of unemployment happening against a person's will" (*R(U) 20/64*). So claimants should not be compensated for unemployment caused by their own unreasonable conduct. That was said to be supported by the then maximum length of disqualification of six weeks, said to represent the length of unemployment that could fairly be attributed to the claimant's conduct, rather than the state of the labour market. Although the grounds for sanction under s.19 are much the same, the greatly increased periods of denial of benefit under the 2012 form of reg.69 of the JSA Regulations 1996 mean that the causal theory can no longer hold water. Sanctions cannot be regarded as anything other than a penalty, even though they are designed to encourage responsible behaviour. As such, it was suggested by Judge Wikeley in *DL v SSWP (JSA)* [2013] UKUT 295 that the legislation on sanctions should be construed strictly and that claimants should be given the benefit of any doubt that might reasonably arise.

On May 9, 2019, the Secretary of State (Amber Rudd) made a written statement to Parliament (HCWS1545) that she had decided to remove three-year sanctions for third or subsequent failures and reduce the maximum sanction length to six months by the end of the year. That commitment was carried out by the amendment of reg.69 of the JSA Regulations 1996 with effect from November 27, 2019 (reg.2 of the Jobseeker's Allowance and Universal Credit (Higher-Level Sanctions) (Amendment) Regulations 2019 (SI 2019/1357)), making the length of the sanction 26 weeks in cases that had previously attracted 156 weeks. See the notes to reg.69 for the detailed effect. It is submitted that nonetheless old style JSA sanctions must still be seen as penalties.

Subsection (2)

1.185   This sets out the conduct by the claimant ranking as a failure sanctionable under this section (subs.(1)).

Paragraph (a): "through misconduct loses employment as an employed earner"

1.186   "Loses employment": this concept is not confined to dismissal, but can also embrace persons claiming benefit while suspended from work for misconduct (*R(U)10/71*) and the person who accepts the chance to resign rather than be dismissed as a result of his misconduct (*R(U)2/76*, where the claimant used a company car without permission to give driving lessons and was found at home in the bath when he should have been out selling). In *CU/056/1989*, Commissioner Heggs, dealing with a situation in which the claimant had been allowed to resign rather than be dismissed, noted in para.7:

"In Decision *R(U)17/64* it was held that 'loss of employment' is a more comprehensive phrase than 'leaving voluntarily' because loss of employment may result either from voluntarily leaving or from dismissal. In considering whether employment has been lost through misconduct, therefore, it is not always necessary to determine categorically whether the claimant left voluntarily or was dismissed. In the present case the tribunal, in my view, correctly concluded that the claimant lost his employment through misconduct"

The claimant had been allowed to resign rather than be dismissed after he had been caught eating company products (pies) at his workplace in violation of a general prohibition on eating company products in the production area. He had previously violated this rule and been warned about his conduct. He had also received a final written warning that future misconduct would result in his summary dismissal. Unfortunately, the SSAT decision was erroneous in law because it contained no explanation of why the claimant's admitted conduct constituted misconduct.

"As an employed earner": see s.35(1); JSA Regulations 1996 reg.3; SSCBA 1992 s.2(1)(a). The disqualification does not cover misconduct in self-employment. Nor, if the reasoning in *GP v SSWP (JSA)* [2015] UKUT 476 (AAC), reported as [2016] AACR 14, discussed in the notes to s.7(1) above, is correct, does it cover misconduct in employment outside Great Britain, which would include employment in Northern Ireland.

According to the then Minister of State Esther McVey (House of Commons written answers April 2, 2014), guidance to Jobcentre Plus staff is that if a JSA claimant leaves a zero hours contract there should be no sanction for misconduct or voluntarily ceasing work. However, it is hard to see the legal basis for such guidance. If a claimant was employed (even if under a zero hours contract) and committed an act of misconduct that led to its loss, that would appear to be a sanctionable failure requiring a reduction of benefit in the absence of any legislative exemption. **1.187**

"Through misconduct": the loss of employment must be brought about because of the claimant's misconduct. The change from "his misconduct" in SSCBA 1992 s.28(1)(a) to merely "misconduct" in para.(a), as in its immediate predecessor (the "old" s.19(6)(a)), cannot, it is submitted, be read so as to justify penalising claimants who lost their job through someone else's misconduct. Any such reading would be absurd and unjust and contrary to the aim of penalising "voluntary unemployment".

Authorities directly in point because they deal with the situation where there were several reasons for the loss of employment state that misconduct need not be the sole cause of the loss of employment so long as it is a contributory cause, a necessary element in bringing about the loss (*R(U)1/57; R(U)14/57; CU/34/92*). Suggestions that it must be the main cause in order to ground disqualification read too much into *R(U)20/59*, where the Commissioner's statement that misconduct (trouble with the police) was there the main cause seems to be no more than a finding of fact in that particular case in which the multiple cause point was not really an issue. A Northern Ireland authority (*R8/60(UB)*) requiring that misconduct be the decisive cause cannot stand against British authorities directly in point, being of persuasive authority only.

The meaning and scope of misconduct. "Misconduct" is not statutorily defined. Case law offers such definition as there is. The term has to be interpreted in a common-sense manner and applied with due regard to the circumstances of each case (*R(U)24/56; R(U)8/57*, para.6). It is narrower than unsatisfactory conduct (*R124/51 (UB)*). Misconduct is "conduct which is causally but not necessarily directly connected with the employment, and having regard to the relationship of employer and employee and the rights and duties of both, can fairly be described as blameworthy, reprehensible and wrong" (*R(U)2/77*, para.15). The Commissioner in *R(U)2/77*, para.6, saw nothing wrong with a tribunal's description of it as an indictment of the claimant's character as an employee. A useful test, particularly where the conduct in question occurred away from work, would be: was the claimant's blameworthy, reprehensible and wrong conduct such as would cause a reasonable employer to dispense with their services on the ground that, having regard to this conduct they were not a fit person to hold that appointment (*R(U)7/57*, para.6). **1.188**

The act or omission alleged to constitute misconduct need not have been deliberate or intentional, although such might often be the case. Misconduct can consist in carelessness or negligence, but there it is necessary to discriminate between that type and degree of carelessness which may have to be put up with in human affairs, and the more deliberate or serious type of carelessness which justifies withholding benefit because the claimant has lost their employment through their own avoidable fault. In *R(U)8/57* the claimant, a manager of a branch pharmacy, was dismissed for "negligence in the discharge of responsible duties" when a number of cash shortages were discovered over a period of weeks. Serious carelessness could legitimately be inferred and his disqualification was upheld, notwithstanding his acquittal on a charge of embezzlement arising out of the same situation. A claimant who acts on a genuine misunderstanding cannot properly be said to be guilty of misconduct; the behaviour cannot there be described as "blameworthy, reprehensible and wrong" (*CU/122/92*, para.6, citing *R(U)14/56*).

Where the conduct grounding the loss of employment might be regarded as whistleblowing (public interest disclosure) the public interest disclosure provisions in the Employment Rights Act 1996 (ss.43A–43L, 47B and 103) should be considered since the question of whether the disclosure was a protected one is relevant to the question of whether the conduct was blameworthy, reprehensible and wrong. Judge Mesher so held in *AA v SSWP (JSA)* [2012] UKUT 100 (AAC), reported as [2012] AACR 42 (see especially paras 10–15). There it had been appropriate for the claimant School Manager to refer concerns about the head teacher's expenses claim to the appropriate LEA officer and probably to the school governors. However, the misconduct found by the disciplinary panel and grounding the dismissal (the "loss of employment") was his disclosure to several other employees to whom, under the legislation, it was not reasonable to disclose the matter. So that, while the tribunal had erred in law by not considering the public interest disclosure provisions, that error was not material. Note that with effect from June 25, 2013 s.43B(1) of the Employment Rights Act has been amended to add the specific condition that the disclosure is made in the public interest (see *Chesterton Global Ltd v Nurmohamed* [2017] EWCA Civ 979; [2018] I.C.R. 731). In *Kilraine v London Borough of Wandsworth* [2018] EWCA Civ 1436, [2018] I.C.R. 1850 it is clarified that, to qualify, a disclosure must in its context have sufficient factual content to count as a disclosure of "information".

1.189
Misconduct which occurred before the claimant took up the employment, the loss of which is under consideration but which caused its loss, cannot disqualify them: see *R(U)26/56*, where an accountant was dismissed when his employers learned of a conviction for fraud which occurred before he commenced employment with them. In *R(U)26/56*, *both* the conduct and its consequences (the criminal conviction) occurred before the employment was taken up. *R(U)1/58*, however, also applies the non-preclusion principle where the conduct occurred before the taking-up of the employment, but the consequences came after its commencement. There a civil engineer and buyer was awaiting trial for certain acts committed before he entered the employment. By agreement with his employer he ceased work pending the result of the trial. On conviction he simply did not return to the employment. Nor, however, was he pressed to do so. The Commissioner held that "acts or omissions occurring before the commencement of the employment do not constitute 'misconduct'" (at para.4), citing *R(U)26/56*, so the only matter remaining was the issue of voluntary leaving without just cause. The leaving was not voluntary: "he merely anticipated a decision by his employers to dispense with his services; he was not altogether a free agent when deciding or agreeing not to attend further at his place of business" (at paras 5 and 6). So, to refer to a case of interest notified to the authors, an SSAT was correct at the time in holding that a van driver, dismissed after conviction of a drink-driving offence and disqualification from driving, could not be disqualified from benefit because the conduct constituting the offence had taken place before he took up the employment in question, even though the conviction came after he had done so.

It may perhaps be arguable that the authority discussed in the previous paragraph depended to an extent on an adoption (whether explicit or implicit) of the "causal theory" of UB disqualifications, that the primary object was not to penalise the claimant, but more to discourage avoidable claims against the fund from which benefit was paid. As it was put in *R(U) 20/64*, the "basic purpose of unemployment benefit is to provide against the misfortune of unemployment happening against a person's will." Thus there was a responsibility on a claimant to do what was reasonable to avoid becoming a burden on the fund that could only arise once the claimant became employed. The causal theory was in the past bolstered by the limitation of the period of disqualification to a maximum of six weeks, after which time it was said that the primary cause of continued unemployment was the state of the labour market, rather than the claimant's act of misconduct or leaving employment voluntarily or whatever. Now that the sanctions regime gives every appearance of imposing penalties, with more extensive periods of exclusion from benefit possible, it might be argued that it is irrelevant to whether such penalties are deserved or not that the misconduct occurred before the claimant started the employment that was later lost. However, it is submitted that to constitute misconduct an act still has to be "blameworthy" in the context of the employment relationship and that there cannot be blameworthiness in that sense if the person has not yet taken up the employment in question.

Subject to that, the causal connection with the employment need not be direct (*R(U) 2/77*, para.15). The conduct need not have taken place at work, though cases where it did will be common.

In *R(U) 1/71* the Chief Commissioner upheld the disqualification of a local authority parks' gardener dismissed for an act of gross indecency with another man, away from work and out of working hours (although apparently not in private within the meaning of s.1 of the Sexual Offences Act 1967), but reduced the period of disqualification to one week (an option not available under the current legislation). The Commissioner said in para.10:

1.190

> "If a person loses his employment by reason of misconduct which has a sufficient connection with the employment it may not matter that it was committed outside the employment. Common examples are those of the man employed as a motor vehicle driver who loses his licence as a result of his driving outside his employment and is disqualified from driving: there is an obvious link between the misconduct and the work. [See, e.g. *R(U) 7/57* and *R(U) 24/64*.] Similarly a person who commits offences of dishonesty outside his work may be disqualified [. . .], since most employers regard a thief as unsuitable to have about their premises. [See, e.g. *R(U) 10/53*.]" (Case references added by annotator.)

Sexual offences outside the employment were said by the Commissioner in para.11 to present considerable difficulty but could rank as misconduct in special circumstances where they could be said to have something to do with the employment:

> "The commercial traveller's case [*CU/381/51*] is a good instance. The employers may well have thought that there was a real danger that when visiting houses trying to sell ribbons, probably to women who might often be alone in the house, the claimant might attempt some sort of liberties. Further, there are some employments where the employer has a legitimate interest in the conduct of employees even outside the employment. One example may be that of a person who holds a special position, e.g. a school teacher. Another may be that of an employee of a government department or a local authority, who rightly feel that their employees should maintain a high standard of conduct at all times."

In *R(U) 1/71* itself, even though the claimant did not work in public parks, the Commissioner, in a case he thought close to the line, was not prepared to overturn the tribunal's view that the claimant had lost his employment through misconduct, though substantially reducing the period of disqualification. Modern sensibilities might make the assessment of such circumstances more complex. On the one hand there is a widespread feeling that no opprobrium should attach to the acts involved in the offence concerned. On the other, there is perhaps a more widespread feeling than in the past that actions and opinions outside employment are relevant to whether that employment should continue.

1.191   *Examples of misconduct.* Apart from those already noted, instances have been: persistent absenteeism without permission (*R(U)22/52, R(U)8/61*); unauthorised absence through ill health and/or domestic circumstances when coupled with failure to notify the employer (*R(U)23/58; R(U)11/59*); repeated unauthorised absence to seek work more suited to the claimant's state of health in circumstances in which the claimant gave the employer no reasons for his absences and he had received previous warning about his conduct (*R(U)8/61*); overstaying a holiday without permission (*R(U)2/74; R(U)11/59*). Theft from fellow workers at a works' social function has been held to be misconduct (*R(U)10/53*). So has offensive behaviour to fellow employees, consisting of obscene language and an element of what would now be termed sexual harassment (suggestive remarks to and, in their presence, about female colleagues) (*R(U)12/56*). By analogy, one would today expect racial abuse and discrimination to be capable of constituting misconduct. Recklessly or knowingly making false allegations about superiors or colleagues can be misconduct, and where a false criminal charge is so laid it would plainly be misconduct (*R(U)24/55*, para.13), but it was not enough to prove misconduct to show that the employee's charge of assault by his supervisor had been dismissed in the magistrates' court (*ibid.*). Refusal to obey a reasonable instruction *in line with the claimant's contract of employment* (e.g. a refusal to work overtime) has been held to be misconduct (*R(U)38/58*), even where obeying the instruction would conflict with trade union policies (*R(U)41/53*). However, disobedience of such an order due to a genuine misunderstanding has been held not to constitute misconduct (*R(U)14/56*), and not every breach of every trivial rule would suffice (*R(U)24/56*). And, of course, the claimant can legitimately refuse to obey instructions not contractually stipulated for without its constituting misconduct (*R(U)9/59; R9/60(UB)*). Where an employee was dismissed for refusing to join a trade union as part of a closed-shop arrangement negotiated after his employment commenced, he did not lose his job through misconduct (*R(U)2/77*).

1.192   *Establishing misconduct, matters of proof and the duties of the statutory authorities; decision-makers, First-tier Tribunals and the Upper Tribunal.* The Secretary of State (decision-maker) bears the onus of proof of establishing misconduct, and it must be clearly proved by the best available evidence. As a general rule, of course, hearsay evidence can be accepted by the statutory authorities, but particularly where a claimant is charged with misconduct and he disputes the facts which are alleged to constitute it, "it is desirable that the most direct evidence of those facts should be adduced, so that the allegations may be properly tested" (*R(U)2/60*, para.7).

Officers of the Secretary of State now have extensive powers to require employers to provide information (see e.g. ss.109A and 109B of the SSAA 1992) and First-tier Tribunals have power to summons witnesses and/or require them to produce documents and answer questions (reg.16 of the Tribunal Procedure (First-tier Tribunal) (Social Entitlement Chamber) Rules 2008, Vol.III of this series). Nevertheless, the use of such powers is often considered out of proportion if, say, an employer is reluctant to supply much detail on request and it may be difficult to get to the truth of the matter. In some cases the statutory authorities may be able to have regard to what has happened in other legal or disciplinary proceedings arising out of the same situation now said to show misconduct. Where such proceedings are pending one option in difficult cases where the available evidence about the relevant conduct conflicts would be to postpone a decision on the "sanctionable failure" issue until the outcome of such proceedings as are pending is known. There is no obligation to await their outcome (*R(U)10/54* and see *AA v SSWP (JSA)* [2012] UKUT 100

(AAC), reported as [2012] AACR 42, above at para.1.188), and one must always keep in view the relationship between those proceedings and the tasks of the tribunals dealing with old style JSA issues.

Another option would be to try to resolve the matter by weighing and comparing the evidence available (e.g. does the tribunal believe the direct evidence given by the claimant it has seen and questioned and how does that compare with the indirect and/or hearsay evidence in any written material from the employer or others which is relied on by the decision-maker) and ultimately, where doubts persist, allow the matter to be settled by application of the rules on onus of proof. It would presumably be open to the decision-maker to revise or supersede the tribunal's decision if new material facts came to light in the course of those other proceedings. The other legal proceedings could be criminal proceedings, court proceedings for breach of contract, or complaints of unfair dismissal heard in employment tribunals. Disciplinary proceedings may take place before a much wider variety of bodies. An important issue is what is the relationship to the decision-making task of the JSA decision-makers and tribunals, of decisions given by these other bodies on a matter relevant to the claimant's case?

While in varying degrees decisions given by such bodies certainly can constitute relevant evidence for the statutory authorities, they are not, legally speaking, conclusive of the outcome before the JSA authorities, who are duty bound to make up their own minds as to what constitutes misconduct grounding reduction of benefit, irrespective of the conclusions reached by employers, the courts or other tribunals or disciplinary bodies (*R(U)10/54*, para.6; *R(U)2/74*, para.15). The other proceedings do not deal with the exact issue dealt with by the JSA decision-makers and tribunals. For example, a motoring conviction as a private motorist which did not attract a ban from driving would not necessarily constitute misconduct warranting the disqualification of a lorry-driver who had been sacked by his employer as a result. It would depend on the nature of the conduct constituting the offence: the claimant might be able to show that notwithstanding the conviction his conduct was not "blameworthy" (*R(U)22/64*, para.6). It must be remembered too that the standard of proof of guilt in criminal cases is proof beyond reasonable doubt, a higher standard than that applicable here—proof on the balance of probabilities. So an acquittal on a criminal charge arising out of the conduct now said to constitute misconduct does not necessarily preclude a finding of misconduct. Thus in *R(U)8/57*, where the manager of the branch pharmacy was acquitted of embezzlement in relation to the cash shortages, he nonetheless lost his employment through misconduct since his inadequate supervision of staff amounted to serious carelessness. Similarly, there are important differences between proceedings before First-tier Tribunals on the one hand, and unfair dismissal proceedings in the employment tribunal on the other. In unfair dismissal, while the employee's conduct is relevant, the main issue before the employment tribunal concerns the employer's behaviour in consequence. Before the tribunals dealing with JSA, in contrast, the emphasis is more on the employee's conduct, although that of the employer is also relevant. The issue of loss of employment through misconduct raises issues of what is fair between claimant and the other contributors to the insurance fund and not what is fair as between employer and employee. Commissioners stressed that social security tribunals when dealing with misconduct cases should not express their decisions in such terms as fair or unfair dismissal or proper or improper dismissal. The onus of proof in employment tribunal proceedings may not be the same on issues relevant to the JSA tribunals' task as they are in proceedings before those JSA tribunals. Equally, while the issue before the JSA tribunals is one of substance, the employment tribunal can find a dismissal unfair on procedural grounds. Hence, while the decision of the employment tribunal is conclusive of the matters it had to decide, it does not conclude anything in proceedings before the JSA decision-makers and tribunals authorities, and its findings of fact are not binding on them, even where some of the facts before the employment tribunals are identical with facts relevant to the JSA proceedings:

1.193

"There will, therefore, be cases where a claimant succeeds before an [employment] tribunal on the unfair dismissal question, but the relevant adjudicating authority has decided that disqualification [from benefit] must be imposed by reason of misconduct, and *vice versa*" (per Commissioner Rice in *CU/90/1988*, para.4).

The findings of fact in the employment tribunal are, however, cogent evidence on which JSA decision-makers and tribunals can act (*CU/17/1993*), since it may well be that with both employer and employee present and examined the employment tribunal, a judicial authority presided over by a lawyer, reaching its deliberate findings of fact after due inquiry, is better placed than the JSA decision-makers and tribunals to fully investigate the facts of the matter. But the JSA decision-makers and tribunals are not bound to decide the facts in the same way as the employment tribunal (*R(U)2/74*, paras 14 and 15 and see generally on the relationship between the two sets of proceedings: *R(U)4/78* and *R(U)3/79*).

For similar reasons of ability to obtain and to probe evidence, decisions of the criminal courts on matters relevant to the case before the JSA decision-makers and tribunals are entitled to great respect. Thus where it is clear that a criminal court has decided the identical issue which the claimant needs to reopen before the judicial authorities (First-tier or Upper Tribunal) in order to succeed in his appeal, the decision of that court is likely *in practice* to be dispositive of the issue before those authorities. This is almost certainly so if one follows the view of the Commissioner in *R(U)24/55* that in such a situation, save in exceptional cases, the statutory authorities must treat a conviction by a criminal court as conclusive proof that the act or omission which constitutes the offence was done or made. It is also likely to be so if one prefers to *R(U)24/55* the later view of a Commissioner in a sickness benefit case dealing with a similar issue (*R(S)2/80*). Now see the helpful discussion, not necessary to the decision, in *KL v SSWP (DLA)* [2015] UKUT 222 (AAC), an overpayment recoverability case, of the case law on when it would be found to be an abuse of process for a claimant to seek to argue before a tribunal a point decided against him in the criminal proceedings. It has always been for the person relying on it to prove the fact of a conviction, and it is preferably done through official certification (*R(U)24/64*). In *R(S)2/80* it was said that the initial onus was on the adjudication officer [now Secretary of State/decision-maker] to show that the conviction directly related to points at issue in the appeal, and if that were done the onus passed to the claimant to show on the balance of probabilities that he was nevertheless entitled to the benefit; that is, by analogy in this context, that he did not lose his job through misconduct (e.g. by showing that the true facts were not as found by the court or, if they were, that they do not constitute misconduct).

1.194   Where the decisions of disciplinary bodies (which may well examine a wide range of witnesses) are concerned, it appears that although never binding on the JSA decision-makers and tribunals, they are entitled to an increasing degree of respect the more their proceedings approximate to proceedings in a court of law. Thus a finding by a chief constable after police disciplinary proceedings was cogent evidence that the claimant had committed particular acts (*R(U)10/63*), but a decision by a hospital management committee, the precise reasons for which were not disclosed to the Commissioner, was not so regarded (*R(U)7/61*).

Whether one is concerned with decisions of the courts, of employment tribunals or disciplinary proceedings it is submitted that crucial questions for the JSA decision-makers and tribunals will be: what was the decision; by what sort of body, how, by what process, and on what sort(s) of evidence was the decision made; and how closely does the matter involved in that decision relate to that before the JSA decision-makers and tribunals? See also the discussion in the notes to s.3 of the Tribunals, Courts and Enforcement Act 2007 under the heading *Relying on decisions of other bodies* in Vol.III of this series.

1.195   *Paragraph (b): "without a good reason voluntarily leaves such employment"*
Note at the outset that s.20(3) and JSA Regulations 1996 reg.74 made under it protect from sanction under this head or under that in subs.(2)(d) certain persons

who leave employed earner's employment voluntarily and without good reason at any time within the "trial period" (that is, between the beginning of the fifth week and the end of the twelfth week of the employment in question, with some provision to ignore certain weeks). The approach to such cases must be first to consider, in the light of the case law principles elaborated below, whether the claimant voluntarily left without a good reason and, if he did so, then to consider whether s.20(3) and JSA Regulations 1996 reg.74 protect him from preclusion of payment of JSA.

In *CJSA/3304/1999*, Commissioner Levenson considered the case of someone who had left employment A for unspecified reasons, then found employment with employer B, from which he was dismissed, and only then claimed JSA. The tribunal allowed the claimant's appeal against preclusion of payment founded on his having voluntarily left employment A without just cause. Commissioner Levenson upheld the tribunal. A preclusion of payment can only be made where a claim for benefit has been made and only "in respect of the employment immediately preceding the claim" (at para.16). Insofar as *R(U)13/64* might be thought to say otherwise, Commissioner Levenson, drawing support from Commissioner Goodman in para.9 of *CU/64/1994*, declined to follow it.

"*Such employment*". The restriction ("such" referring back to para.(a)) to   **1.196** employed earners' employment means that leaving self-employment cannot ground disqualification under this head. Nor, if the reasoning in *GP v SSWP (JSA)* [2015] UKUT 476 (AAC), reported as [2016] AACR 14, discussed in the notes to s.7(1) above, is correct, can it be grounded by leaving employment outside Great Britain, thus including employment in Northern Ireland.

According to the then Minister of State Esther McVey (House of Commons written answers April 2, 2014), guidance to Jobcentre Plus staff is that if a JSA claimant leaves a zero hours contract there should be no sanction for misconduct or voluntarily ceasing work. However, it is hard to see the legal basis for such guidance. Ceasing such employment would appear to bring the legislation into play, although the terms of the contract might contribute to a good reason for ceasing the employment.

Onus of proof. Those who assert that the claimant left employment voluntarily must   **1.197** prove it. Once done the onus passes to the claimant to prove that they had "a good reason" for so leaving. In both cases the onus is discharged on the balance of probabilities (*R(U)20/64(T)*). See further, below.

"*Voluntarily leaves*": The commonest case of voluntarily leaving will be when the   **1.198** claimant of their own accord handed in their notice or otherwise terminated their contract of employment. Indeed, in many cases there will be no dispute about this aspect of the case; the real issue will be that of 'good reason'. But voluntarily leaving also embraces other means by which employment was lost. So the actors who threatened to leave unless certain demands were met and were then treated by their employers as having given notice left voluntarily (*R(U)33/51*). It is still voluntarily leaving where the employment ends because the employer refuses to accept the claimant's withdrawal of notice (*R(U)27/59*). It can also embrace in limited instances cases where the loss of employment took the form of a dismissal brought about by conduct of the claimant which would inevitably lead to termination of the employment (*R(U)16/52; R(U)2/54, R(U)9/59, R(U)7/74*), but such situations must be looked at with caution and restraint (*R(U)2/77*). Thus, in *R(U)16/52* the claimant's appointment was conditional on her completing a satisfactory medical. She refused to undergo X-ray examination and was given notice. The Commissioner stated as a general rule of unemployment insurance law that if a person deliberately and knowingly acts in a way that makes it necessary for his employer to dismiss him, he may be regarded as having left his employment voluntarily. But another Commissioner later made clear in *R(U)7/74* that "this would normally require a finding that the employee had acted, or was threatening to act, in a manner involving a deliberate repudiation of his contract of employment". So in that case an employee whose written terms of employment made no reference to a requirement to work overtime, did not leave voluntarily when he was dismissed for refusing to work overtime (cf. *R(U)9/59*). Similarly, dismissal of an existing employee for refusal to join a trade union when a closed shop agreement was negotiated was not voluntary leaving (*R(U)2/77*). Nor was dismissal for refusing for good reason to pay a trade union subscription (*R(U)4/51*). Leaving was not voluntary where the claimant who departed had no effective choice but to quit, e.g. because dismissal appeared inevitable (*R(U)1/58:* cf. *R(U)2/76*). In *R(U)1/96*, Commissioner Goodman considered the case of a female nursery assistant who gave her employer four weeks' notice, was prepared to work out those weeks, but whose employer, after an unsuccessful attempt to persuade her to stay on, told her to leave after two days. The Commissioner considered and applied *CU/155/50* and *R(U)2/54* so as to reject the argument that the claimant had not left voluntarily but had been dismissed (and could therefore only be disqualified if misconduct could be proved). He regarded *British Midland Airways v Lewis* [1978] I.C.R. 782 (a decision of the Employment Appeal Tribunal in the context of dismissal under labour legislation) as not laying down "any categorical proposition of law" but as merely being a decision on the facts of that case, and continued:

> "In my view the ruling in *CU/155/50* and *R(U)2/54* that there is a voluntary leaving applies equally, whether it is a case of an employer not allowing an employee to work out his or her notice or whether it is a case of actual notice to leave given first by the employee, followed by a notice of termination given during the currency of the employee's notice by the employer. In the latter case, once the employee has given in his notice to leave it is a unilateral termination of the employment contract and cannot be withdrawn without the consent of the employer (*Riordan v War Office* [1959] 1 W.L.R. 1046). It follows that in the present case, when the claimant gave her four weeks notice in on Wednesday December 9, 1992 she had herself terminated the employment and thereby left it voluntarily. Even if what the employer did on Friday December 11, 1992 can be construed as giving in a counter-notice requiring her to leave on that day and not to work out her four weeks notice, that does not, in my view, alter the fact that the effective termination of the employment was a voluntary leaving by the claimant." (At para.12.)

1.199   *Taking early retirement* can constitute voluntarily leaving (*R(U)26/51, R(U)20/64, R(U)4/70, R(U)1/81*). Even where a schoolteacher retired three years early in response to the generalised encouragement to take early retirement offered to teachers in his position by his local education authority, which further certified that his retirement was in the interests of the efficient discharge of the education authority's functions, it was still voluntarily leaving (*Crewe v Social Security Commissioner* [1982] 2 All E.R. 745 CA, published as an Appendix to *R(U)3/81*). However, in *R(U)1/83* the Commissioner distinguished *Crewe* and held that a civil servant who acceded to his employer's specific request that *he* retire early should not be regarded as having left his employment voluntarily. Since these cases were decided, subs.(3) (s.19(7) in previous JSA legislation) has been added to the section, enabling regulations to be made treating someone who might otherwise be regarded as having left his employment voluntarily as not having left voluntarily. Whether this in effect exempts from preclusion under this head a claimant on the *Crewe* side of the line depends on whether in the circumstances of his particular case, including the nature and terms of his early retirement scheme, he can bring himself within the terms of the protection for voluntary redundancy set out in JSA Regulations 1996 reg.71, a matter explored below in the annotations to reg.71. For early retirement cases not saved by that regulation and subsection, the fine distinction between the *Crewe* type of case and those of the type considered in *R(U)1/83* may still be important. In *CSU/22/94*, Commissioner Mitchell applied *R(U)1/83* in favour of a claimant (a principal teacher) who had been pressured by his employers to accept an early retirement package, in a context in which his only alternative was to accept a lower status position (albeit one without loss of income) (being placed on a long-term supply teacher basis). That alternative was one which "a teacher of the claimant's experience and standing could not reasonably be expected to accept" (at para.5). The decision thus stresses the need for tribunals carefully to consider whether the claimant can be said to have left voluntarily before moving on to the "without a good reason" aspect.

In *CU/70/94*, Commissioner Rice made it clear that one cannot base a finding of voluntary leaving without a good reason on the notion that the claimant who left, not considering herself up to the job for medical reasons, ought to have found out more about, or to have known more about, the demands of the job before she accepted it.

"Without a good reason". There is no definition of "good reason" in the Act, just as   1.200
there was none of "just cause" in previous legislation dealing with disqualification from benefit or preclusion of payment of JSA. Nor do any of the JSA Regulations 1996 clarify its meaning with respect to this para. (contrast reg.72 with respect to paras (c) and (d), below). Like "just cause" or "good cause" in the previous scheme of sanctions, "good reason" affords claimants a chance to explain and justify their conduct, whether that be an act or omission. The *Explanatory Memorandum* accompanying the amending regulations stated that "good reason" would be applied in the same way as the predecessor terms, but noted that "in the revised regime regulations will not set out particular circumstances or situations for the Decision Maker leaving him to take into account all reasons considered relevant when determining good reason" (para.7.18). See further *http://www.legislation.gov.uk/uksi/2012/2568/pdfs/uksiem_20122568_en.pdf* [Accessed June 17, 2013]. The House of Commons Work and Pensions Committee (report of November 6, 2018 on *Benefit Sanctions* (HC 995 2017–19), para.111) recommended that regulations be introduced containing a non-exhaustive list of circumstances that could constitute good reason. The DWP (House of Commons Work and Pensions Committee, *Benefit Sanctions: Government Response* (HC 1949 2017–19, February 11, 2019), paras 66–9) rejected that recommendation as undermining flexibility, while noting that a list of good reasons is available in the *DMG* and on GOV.uk (the link provided in the response is to chapter K2 of the *ADM* for universal credit).

On that basis, the approach in this annotation (subject to the doubt expressed at the end of the next paragraph) is that court, Commissioners' and Upper Tribunal decisions on "just cause" and "good cause" in UB and previous JSA sanctions regimes are relevant authorities with respect to the interpretation of "good reason". Those decisions avoided laying down hard and fast rules for all circumstances, something fully harmonising with the policy intention expressed in the *Explanatory Memorandum*.

"Just cause" was regarded as requiring a balancing of the interests of the claimant with those of the community of fellow contributors to the National Insurance Fund. It was not a matter simply of what is in the best interests of the claimant, or of what is just as between employee and employer, or of what is in the public interest generally. To establish that they did not leave without just cause (that phraseology giving the proper emphasis) claimants had to show that in leaving they acted reasonably in circumstances that made it just that the burden of their unemployment should be cast on the National Insurance Fund (*Crewe v Social Security Commissioner* [1982] 2 All E.R. 745, per Slade LJ, at 752; per Donaldson LJ, at 750–751, explaining *R(U)20/64(T)*, para.8; per Lord Denning MR, at 749). Was what the claimant did right and reasonable in the context of the risk of unemployment? Was the voluntary leaving such as to create an unreasonable risk of unemployment, bearing in mind that there may be circumstances that leave a person no reasonable alternative but to leave employment (per Donaldson LJ, at 750)? Establishing just cause may well be a heavier burden than showing "good cause" (per Slade LJ, at 751). In *R(U)4/87*, Commissioner Monroe stated that "the analogy with insurance seems now the paramount criterion of just cause" (para.8). His examination of decisions on the matter led him "to think that in general it is only where circumstances are such that a person has virtually no alternative to leaving voluntarily that he will be found to have had just cause for doing so, rather as a person who throws his baggage overboard to make room in the lifeboat can claim on his baggage insurance" (para.9). There is therefore a faint suggestion in the earlier authority that there may be some difference in the ordinary use of language between "good cause" and "just cause". It may also be arguable that the formula "without a good reason" shifts the focus away from the notion of a balance between the interests of the claimant and those of the community of contributors to the fund from which benefit is paid towards more emphasis on the interests of the claimant. That would make it easier for a claimant to avoid the imposition of a sanction. In *SA v SSWP (JSA)* [2015] UKUT 454 (AAC), a decision on s.19A(2) (c) and failing to carry out a jobseeker's direction, Judge Knowles accepted the Secretary of State's submission that in determining whether a good reason had been shown for the failure all the circumstances should be considered and that the question was whether those circumstances would have caused a reasonable person (with the characteristics of the claimant in question) to act as the claimant did. Expressing the approach in such terms tends to point away from the notion of a balance.

1.201   *S v SSWP (UC)* [2017] UKUT 477 (AAC) actually decides only a relatively short point about the meaning of "for no good reason" in ss.26 and 27 of the WRA 2012 on universal credit (see Vol.II of this series) The First-tier Tribunal had said that the claimant's professed ignorance of the effect of work (including part-time work) on his universal credit entitlement could not amount to a good reason for failing to undertake all reasonable work search action because ignorance of the law was no defence. On the claimant's appeal to the Upper Tribunal the Secretary of State accepted that, by analogy with the well-established case law on good cause for a delay in claiming, ignorance of the law was capable of constituting a good reason. Judge Mitchell agreed that the tribunal had erred in law, but concluded that the error was not material because the only proper conclusion on the evidence was that the claimant could reasonably have been expected to raise with his work coach or other DWP official any concerns or confusions over the financial implications on his universal credit award of taking any of the sorts of work he had agreed to search for. Thus, even on the correct approach the claimant did not have a good reason for what the tribunal had concluded was a failure under s.27(2)(a).

It may be that the analogy with good cause in *S* and in *SA* (indeed in para.57 of *S* the judge said that "good reason" expressed the same concept as "good cause" but in more modern language) is misleading or at least incomplete. That is because when considering good cause for a delay in claiming there is no difficulty in adopting the general meaning approved in *R(SB) 6/83* of some fact that, having regard to all the circumstances (including a claimant's state of health and the information that he had or might have obtained), would probably have caused a reasonable person of the same age and experience to act or fail to act as the claimant had done. It was in that context that the principle that a reasonable ignorance or mistaken belief as to rights could constitute good cause was established. But the question there is what a reasonable person could be expected to do to secure an advantage to them in the form of the benefit claimed late. In the context of universal credit and JSA sanctions, the notion of reasonableness carries a distinctly different force. So when considering what circumstances could justify a voluntary leaving, the notion of a good reason must be based on whether it is reasonable to place the burden of the claimant's unemployment on the community that funds old style JSA. Although many personal circumstances are relevant to s.19(2)(b), the notion of a balance between those circumstances and the claimant's proper responsibilities is not captured by the traditional concept of "good cause" in the context of delay in claiming. The better analogy would seem to be with "just cause" as used in unemployment benefit and in old style JSA before the 2012 amendments (or with "good cause" as used in some of those provisions). The adoption of the "good cause" approach in relation to claimed ignorance of rights in *S* cannot be taken as excluding such an approach to s.19(2) (b). The full meaning of "without a good reason" remains to be worked out.

Whether the claimant succeeds in discharging the burden of showing a good reason depends essentially on all the circumstances of the case, including the reasons for leaving and such matters as whether they had another job to go to, whether before they left they had made reasonable inquiries about other work or its prospects, or whether there were in their case good prospects of finding other work. Such elements should not be considered in water-tight compartments *(R(U)20/64(T))*, para.9). The previous claims record is not directly relevant *(R(U)20/64(T))* para.18). In *R(U) 4/87* Commissioner Monroe, following para.10 of *R(U)3/81* (approved in *Crewe*), ruled as remote from and irrelevant to the just cause issue long-term considerations prayed in aid by the claimant who had "urged that his leaving had in the long run actually benefited the national insurance fund, in that he had made available a vacancy for someone who would otherwise have continued unemployed, and that he was now earning more so that he was paying higher contributions" (at para.10).

Such factors had nothing to do with the issue of being forced to leave *(ibid.)*. In *CU/048/90*, Commissioner Sanders considered the appeal of a claimant who had, as a result of his employer's attitude, become dissatisfied with his employment and had sought alternative employment by circulating his curriculum vitae to 30 companies. During interviews with Barclays Bank he was given the impression that his application for a particular post would be successful, and he resigned from his employment. In the event he was not offered the other post. Commissioner Sanders considered the correct approach to "just cause" to be that set out in *R(U)4/87* (para.9). He thought that the "circumstances have to be very demanding before a claimant can establish just cause for leaving" (para.3). It seemed to the Commissioner "that in the circumstances of the case the claimant had reason to leave because he thought he was not progressing in his career" but took the view "that the circumstances were not so pressing as to justify his leaving, from an unemployment benefit point of view, before he had secured the job with Barclays Bank even though he had been led to believe that his application for that job would be successful" *(ibid.)*. He agreed with the SSAT that the claimant did not have just cause for leaving voluntarily and had to be disqualified.

In some cases, probably rare in practice, an actual promise of immediate suitable new employment (which then falls through after the employment was left or the start of which is delayed) may afford a good reason in the absence of other justificatory circumstances *(R(U)20/64(T)*, para.17; *Crewe*, per Donaldson LJ, para.750). However, there was no rule of law saying that just cause cannot be established where the claimant leaves without another job to go to. Indeed, in *R(U)20/64(T)* a Tribunal of Commissioners suggested that there could be circumstances in the claimant's personal or domestic life which become so pressing that they justify leaving employment "without regard to the question of other employment" (para.12) and they cited as illustrations *R(U)14/52*, *R(U)19/52* and *R(U)31/59*, all noted below. Equally, it was clearly established that some feature of the claimant's existing employment may justify leaving it immediately without any regard to the question of other employment (para.11) and here the Commissioners quoted as instances *CU248/49*, *R(U)15/53*, *R(U)38/53* and *R(U)18/57*, considered below. But there must be some urgency in the matter and, as regards the latter class of case, the circumstances must be so pressing that it cannot be reasonable to expect the claimant to take such steps as are open to him to resolve before leaving the grievance connected with work through the proper channels of existing grievance procedures. *CU106/1987* makes it clear that a tribunal cannot merely rely on the Secretary of State's (decision-maker's) suggestion that there would be such a grievance procedure in the circumstances of the claimant's employment. It was wrong in law to take account of a suggested grievance procedure to reject the claimant's appeal without having proper findings of fact as to its existence. One would equally have thought that a tribunal should also consider whether any procedure found to exist could cover the claimant's complaint and whether it was reasonable in the circumstances to expect the claimant to have resort to it.

A simple desire to change jobs is not usually enough to warrant putting the burden of one's unemployment on the Fund. Nor does moving house without more constitute just cause; it depends on the reasons for the move *(R(U)20/64(T)*, para.15).

1.202

Rather than approaching the just cause issue from the angle of considering it necessary for the claimant to be assured of suitable alternative employment, unless there were circumstances justifying him in leaving without it (the approach in *R(U)14/52*), the Commissioners in *R(U)20/64(T)* preferred a different perspective. They preferred to look: (1) at whether the reasons for leaving themselves amounted to just cause (i.e. leaving aside the matter of alternative employment or its prospects); and (2) where the reasons did not of themselves establish just cause to then consider whether the "promises or prospects of other employment may be effective as an *additional* factor which may help the claimant establish just cause. For example, where a man *almost* establishes just cause [in relation to, e.g. pressing personal or domestic circumstances] the fact that he has a promise or prospects of other employment may serve to tip the scale in his favour . . . In considering these matters of course the strength of his chances of employment and the gap, if any, likely to occur between the two employments must be taken into account" (para.17).

1.203 The Commissioners stated:

> "that it is impossible to lay down any period of time representing a gap between employments, or any degree of probability of fresh employment which will give an automatic answer to the question whether the claimant has shown just cause for leaving."

They drew:

> "a distinction between on the one hand, having suitable employment to go to, as where there is an actual promise of employment, and having only prospects of employment on the other. It may be reasonable to expect a claimant who has only prospects to take some steps before leaving, such as communicating with the employment exchange to see whether his prospects cannot be made more certain."

It is probably true to say that the claimant's chances of establishing a good reason under the current provisions are stronger where there are promises or good prospects of employment, or where the reasons for leaving are in themselves quite strong and he can show efforts made to ascertain job prospects before leaving the old employment.

A number of cases concerning, on the one hand, grievances about existing employment and, on the other, personal or domestic circumstances, can usefully be quoted as *instances* in which just cause was established, and it may be useful to note in contrast a number of examples in each category where it was not. But the importance of looking to the precise circumstances of each and every case cannot be too strongly stressed. Note that whether a given set of facts constitutes a good reason for leaving is a question of mixed fact and law, making it one that the Upper Tribunal can deal with under their jurisdiction to correct errors of law by tribunals (*CU/53/1991*), depending on the nature of the error invoked.

1.204 *(i) Grievances about work*. In *R(U)/15/53* a piece-worker who lost his job when he refused to accept a substantial reduction in earnings thrust on him by his employer had just cause for leaving. In *R(U)38/53* the claimant left after subjection to pressure to join a trade union and was able to establish just cause; it would have been intolerable if he had to remain. In *R(U)18/57* an apprentice ordered to do work clearly outside the scope of his apprenticeship had only the options of doing as he was told or leaving immediately. In choosing the latter he had just cause. It may be now that working under a zero hours contract, especially if it had an enforceable exclusivity clause, could contribute towards a good reason for ceasing the employment (and see the guidance mentioned above under "such employment"). But mere failure to get on with colleagues (*R(U)17/54*) or strained relations with one's employer (*R(U)8/74*) has been held not enough. Not feeling oneself capable of the work, where one's employer was satisfied, is unlikely to be enough without clear medical evidence of that fact (*R(U)13/52*), but leaving employment during a probationary period because the claimant considered himself unsuited to the work and that it was unfair to his employer to continue training him was more generously treated in *R(U)3/73*.

Indeed, in *CU/43/1987* Commissioner Davenport said that "a person who is experimenting in trying a new line of work should not lightly be penalised if that experiment fails". Persons should be encouraged to try new types of employment where work in their usual field is not available:

> "It must be recognised that in such circumstances a person may find that he cannot stay in his employment and it may be that he is reasonable in leaving that employment, whereas a person who had more experience in the field in question would not be held to have acted reasonably if he gave up the employment. Not everyone finds that new and unfamiliar employment is such that she or he can reasonably stay in it". (At para.7.)

CU/90/91 further illustrates that persons who leave employment as unsuitable after a trial period can have just cause for doing so and be protected from preclusion of payment without having to rely on the time-limited "trial period" concept found in s.20(3) and JSA Regulations 1996 reg.74. Commissioner Hallett stated:

> "It is clear from the evidence, which I accept, that the claimant took the job with Fords (which would have been permanent) on trial, conditionally on his being able to obtain accommodation in the area. It is well-settled in social security unemployment law that claimants should be encouraged to take jobs on trial and that if, after trial, the job proves unsuitable, they do have just cause for leaving. It is in the interests of the national insurance fund, and of public policy, to encourage persons to obtain employment and not penalise them if, after fair trial, the job proves unsuitable". (At para.10.)

The claimant had just cause for leaving.

There is no such well-settled principle applying to leaving a job taken, not on trial, but as a "stop-gap" pending something better turning up (*R(U) 40/53*; *CJSA/63/2007*, para.15).

(ii) Personal or domestic circumstances. In *R(U)14/52* the claimant had just cause for leaving his job in order to be with his elderly and sick wife who lived alone. It was not possible for her to move to live with him so as to be near enough to his work. He also thought his chances of employment would be good in his wife's area, but there was little evidence in the case of searching inquiries about those prospects. In *R(U)19/52* the claimant who left her job to move with her service-man husband to a new posting, likely to be more than short-term, had just cause. Had the posting been short-term, however, she would have had to make inquiries about job prospects in the new area before leaving. See further *R(U)4/87* and *CU110/1987*. In *CU110/1987* the claimant's service-man husband received telephone notice of posting to Germany on February 14, 1986. He went there on March 1, 1986. On February 14, 1986, the claimant gave the one week's notice required under her contract of employment and ceased work on February 21, claiming benefit the next day. She had to be available to vacate the married quarters in Aldershot from March 1. However, she did not join her husband in Germany until March 25, since repairs were needed to the married quarters there. Commissioner Monroe held that in these circumstances she had just cause for leaving when she did [February 21] rather than later. That, rather than whether she should have left at all, was the real issue in the case, since in the Commissioner's view it could hardly be said that she did not have just cause to leave (whenever she could) to join her husband in Germany. She was not to be disqualified from benefit. Actual entitlement to benefit, however, would turn on the unresolved matter of her availability for work. On this issue of

1.205

availability in that context, see *R(U)2/90(T)*. In *R(U)31/59* the reason for leaving was the move to a new home, too far from the job, because the existing home (two small attic rooms) was wholly unsuitable for the claimant's family. By contrast, in *R(U)6/53* the 21-year-old girl who left her job to move with her rather strict parents to a new area did not have just cause; it was reasonable to expect her to live alone, at least until she could find work in the new area. In *CJSA/2507/2005*, Commissioner Williams applied Commissioner Monroe's statement at para.9 of *R(U)4/87*, quoted in 1.219 above, to dismiss the 28-year-old claimant's appeal against a tribunal-imposed three week disqualification for voluntary leaving (the decision-maker had imposed eight weeks). He had left to join his fiancée and get married, but had no job to go to. The three-week disqualification represented the period up to the marriage. The Commissioner also noted the need to treat with some caution decisions on this area which are 50 years' old, reflecting a very different job market and attitudes to married women, and given when appeal to the Commissioners covered fact and law.

Leaving for a financial advantage (e.g. to draw a marriage gratuity only payable on resignation (*R(U)14/55*), or to take early retirement, even where this was encouraged by the employer and might be said to be in the public interest in terms of opening the way for younger teachers and promoting the efficiency of the education service, has been held not to rank as just cause (*Crewe v Social Security Commissioner* [1982] 2 All E.R. 745; *R(U)26/51*; *R(U)23/59*; *R(U)20/64(T)*; *R(U)4/70*; *R(U)1/81*). However, if "good reason" has different nuances of meaning from "just cause", as discussed above, that might justify more emphasis on what was reasonable in the claimant's own interests. Further, it may be that a different approach is justified where a claimant leaves a job to avoid hardship rather than to pursue extra money (as suggested in *CJSA/1737/2014*, where one of the claimant's arguments was that the cost of travel to and from work was prohibitive).

Subsection (3) and JSA Regulations 1996 reg.71, below, may provide significant assistance for some such claimants by treating them as not having left voluntarily thus obviating the good reason issue.

Paragraph (c)

1.206   *"Without a good reason refuses or fails to apply … is vacant or about to become vacant"*: This head of preclusion covers the claimant who has been informed by an "employment officer" that a situation in any employment is vacant or about to become so. The penalty applies where, without a good reason, (i) the claimant has refused to apply for that situation, (ii) has failed to apply for it, or (iii) has refused to accept it when offered.

Since para.(c) refers to "any employment", not to "any such employment" (compare para.(b)), it appears that the term covers self-employment as well as employment as an employed earner (the definition of employment in reg.75(4) of the JSA Regulations 1996 applying, since the reg.4 definition does not apply to s.19). However, there must be something that amounts to a "situation", which points towards forms of self-employment that are analogous to employed earner's employment. In *MT v SSWP (JSA)* [2016] UKUT 72 (AAC) doubts were expressed whether registration with an employment agency could fall within para.(c), at least without evidence of some specific vacancy. If the reasoning in *GP v SSWP (JSA)* [2015] UKUT 476 (AAC), reported as [2016] AACR 14, discussed in the notes to s.7(1) above, is correct, only employment in Great Britain can be in issue. If para.(c) is not applicable because there is no situation vacant or about to become vacant, para.(d) should be considered separately (*CJSA/4179/1997* and *MT*), but if that possibility is raised for the first time before a First-tier Tribunal the claimant must be given a fair opportunity to deal with the altered case.

The claimant must have been "informed" of the situation that is vacant or about to become vacant by an employment officer. The previous form of this provision used the term "notified", as had been the case since the 1930s. If there is any difference in meaning it can only be slight, as it had long been accepted that in the nature of things the official doing the notification/informing may have limited information to pass on and that provided that the broad nature of the situation had been made clear there was notification for these purposes *(R(U) 32/52)*. In *MT* (above) the Secretary of State referred to "exact details" of a vacancy not having been given, but since in fact no details of anything that could be regarded as a vacancy had been given that phrase cannot be taken as laying down any test. It is then up to claimants to ascertain such further particulars as they require. The informing can be done orally *(CU/40/1987)*, although good practice and the potential need for acceptable proof of the information given to the claimant in the light of the principle that the claimant should in sanctions cases be given the benefit of any doubt that might reasonably arise *(DL v SSWP (JSA)* [2013] UKUT 295 (AAC)), must surely point to the need for written or computer records to be kept and to be available to the claimant for reference. In practice something called a Mandatory Employment Notification ("MEN") is used.

See the notes to the definition of "employment officer" in s.35(1) for the extension beyond Jobcentre Plus employees for the purpose of subs.(2)(c) to employees of "prime contractors" engaged by the Secretary of State to provide services or facilities in relation to the schemes concerned and employees of "approved subcontractors". The DMG Memos relevant to the Orders mentioned there that remain in force (now incorporated into the internet version of the DMG) say that an employment officer, including such employees, can inform claimants of reasonable vacancies or employment opportunities, gather evidence to send to decision-makers and make higher-level sanction referrals to a decision-maker if a claimant refuses or fails to comply. They also say that they can "mandate a claimant to attend a job interview". It is not clear what is intended here. For the purposes of subs.(2)(c) it must be implied that a vacancy actually exists or is shortly to exist, but employment officers within the extended meaning given by the Orders in question have no power to give jobseeker's directions under s.19A(2)(a) and (11)(a). So the mandation can only be in the form of a threat of referral for a sanction if the claimant refuses or fails to attend the interview. Such action can properly be regarded as a refusal or failure to apply for the situation that is vacant.

According to the then Minister of State Esther McVey (House of Commons written answers April 2, 2014 and September 1, 2014), guidance to Jobcentre Plus staff is that JSA claimants (in contrast to universal credit claimants) are not to be mandated to apply for vacancies for zero hours contracts, apparently whether there is an enforceable exclusivity clause or not. Thus no sanction under s.19(2)(c) should arise from a failure to apply for such a vacancy. If one did, then it would be arguable that the terms of the contract constituted a good reason for failing to apply. See also the prohibition in s.20(1) below of any reduction in benefit for refusing to seek employment in a situation vacant because of a stoppage of work due to a trade dispute.

"Refusal" clearly covers outright rejection of an offer or of the opportunity to apply for the post. Accepting an offer but then telling lies which caused the employer to withdraw it was treated as refusal in a Northern Ireland decision *(R6/50(UB))*. On the meaning of "accept a situation in any employment", see *CSU 7/1995*. The claimant accepted the offer of a job of a lampshade maker at a wage of £79 per week, having been informed of the vacancy by the Employment Service. But she changed her mind and did not start the job because the wage was too low to meet her commitments. The tribunal decided that since she did accept the offer of employment, s.28(1)(b) of SSCBA 1992 (whose terms were substantially similar to subs.(2)(c)) did not operate to disqualify her from receiving UB. However, the Commissioner held that although, normally, acceptance of an offer of a situation would be tantamount to accepting the situation it could not have been intended that it would be possible to defeat the operation of s.28(1)(b) by an acceptance in theory but a repudiation in practice. The claimant had not "accepted the situation" within the meaning of s.28(1)(b).

See also *CJSA 4179/1997* in which the claimant was offered a "trial" as a part-time car washer. The tribunal dealt with the case under the equivalent of subs.(2)(c) but the Commissioner expressed doubt as to whether the "trial" was an offer of a "situation in any employment". The tribunal should have investigated what the trial involved.

1.207

1.208

If that provision did not apply, the equivalent of subs.(2)(d) should then have been considered.

A failure properly to complete an application form can amount to a failure to apply (*CJSA 2692/1999* and see *R(U)32/52*). However, where the applicant disputed the necessity of including a photograph on the employer's application form, contending that it would be accepted without one, the employment officer, without clear information to the contrary from the employer, should have tested the matter by forwarding the form without photograph to see if that indeed was the case. The officer had not done so and, in *CJSA/2082/2002* and *CJSA/5415/2002*, Commissioner Rowland allowed the appeal against the sanction imposed.

In *CJSA/4665/2001*, Commissioner Howell held that the "failed to apply" head could not catch someone who had filled in application forms which the Employment Service then refused to pass on because of criticisms of the Employment Service and government training initiatives, on the faith of which he had left his last job and felt badly let down. Since the forms were otherwise properly completed, and there was no evidence of any intention to spoil his chances or that any employers had been or would be put off by the comments from considering him for employment, it had not been shown that he had "failed to apply" for the posts in question. The Commissioner noted that the claimant might be wise to take the advice of the Employment Service and remove the comments so as to maximise his chances of employment. He noted also that there will be other cases:

"where the way a claimant completes or spoils a job application will be unsatisfactory and unfit to be put in front of any employer so as to prevent it counting as a genuine application at all, so that he or she will have 'failed to apply': it is all a question of fact." (para.5.)

1.209   In *CJSA/2931/2003*, Commissioner Howell upheld a tribunal decision disqualifying the claimant for 18 weeks as fully justified on the facts. It had doubted the claimant's credibility in claiming that he had telephoned and been told that the vacancy was filled whereas in fact it had remained open. The sanction imposed was well within the bounds of reasonableness in a case where a long-term claimant was found to have made no real effort to follow up a vacancy notified to him.

There is now no requirement that the employment be "suitable", but there is, across all the sub-heads of the paragraph, a saving for "good reason". On "good reason" see the annotation to para.(b), above. Note, however, that JSA Regulations 1996 reg.72, below, stipulates that "good reason" in respect of para.(c) cannot be founded on travel time to and from work of less than an hour and a half each way "unless in view of the health of the person, or any caring responsibilities of his, that time was or is unreasonable".

In the past, however, questions of the suitability of the employment and of "good cause" (now replaced by good reason but intended to operate in the same way) for the refusal or failure to apply, or refusal or failure to accept, tended to intertwine. The case authorities tended not to distinguish between them (see, e.g. *R(U)26/52*) to the extent that it almost appeared that the sole basis for "good cause", at least as reflected in reported decisions, was the non-suitability of the employment in the claimant's circumstances.

1.210   A general merging of the suitability and good cause heads was evident in the case authorities. The heads focused on such matters as the location of the employment (*R(U)41/51*, *R(U)34/58*), the claimant's personal and family circumstances (*R(U)13/52*, *R(U)20/60*, *R(U)2/77*, *R2/63(UB)*) and on the terms of the employment. That intertwining of the issues may mean that some issues sometimes characterised as "suitability" issues in the past may still be raised, despite the deletion of "suitable" from the statutory text, as "good reason" issues, save where regulations dictate otherwise.

In *PL v DSD (JSA)* [2015] NI Com 72 (followed and applied in *PO'R v DFC (JSA)* [2018] NI Com 1), the Chief Commissioner for Northern Ireland has approved and applied the obiter suggestion of Judge Ward in *PL v SSWP (JSA)* [2013] UKUT 227 (AAC) (on the pre-October 2012 form of the Great Britain legislation) that, in deciding whether a claimant had good cause for failing to avail himself of a reasonable opportunity of a place on a training scheme or employment programme, a tribunal erred in law, where the circumstances raised the issue, in failing to consider the appropriateness of the particular scheme or programme to the claimant in the light of his skills and experience and previous attendance on any placements. Judge Ward's suggestion had been that the test was whether the claimant had reasonably considered that what was provided would not help him. It seems likely that a similar general approach will be taken to the issue of "good reason" under s.19(2)(c) and the appropriateness of the situation in question, as also suggested in *MT* (above). It may though still need to be sorted out how far the issue turns on the claimant's subjective view, within the bounds of reasonableness, in the light of the information provided at the time, as against a tribunal's view of the appropriateness of the situation in employment. The Chief Commissioner made no comment in *PL* on the treatment of the claimant's refusal to complete and sign forms with information about criminal convictions and health, that the First-tier Tribunal had found were reasonably required by the training provider as part of its application process for the scheme, as a failure by the claimant to avail himself of a reasonable opportunity of a place on the training scheme.

See as an example of a potential good reason on its own facts (and no more than that), *GR v SSWP (JSA)* [2013] UKUT 645 (AAC), where it was held that a claimant with a genuinely held fear that prevented him going to the town where a course was to take place had good cause (under reg.7 of the Jobseeker's Allowance (Employment, Skills and Enterprise Scheme) Regulations 2011) for failing to participate in the scheme in question. A further example might be that the vacancy was for employment under a zero hours contract (see above).

Paragraph (d)

"*Without a good reason neglects to avail himself of a reasonable opportunity of employ-* 1.211
ment": Note at the outset that s.20(3) and JSA Regulations 1996 reg.74 made under it protect from sanction under this head or under that in subs.(2)(b) certain persons who leave employed earner's employment voluntarily and without a good reason at any time within the "trial period" (that is, between the beginning of the fifth week and the end of the twelfth week of the employment in question, with some provision to ignore certain weeks). In short, in cases covered by s.20(3) and reg.74, characterising (as one could) the voluntary leaving as a "neglect to avail" will be pointless; those provisions will prevent preclusion.

Since para.(d) refers to "any employment", not to "any such employment" (compare para.(b)), it appears that the term covers self-employment as well as employment as an employed earner (the definition of employment in reg.75(4) of the JSA Regulations 1996 applying, since the reg.4 definition does not apply to s.19). However, there is considerable doubt what might amount to a "reasonable opportunity" outside the familiar context of job as an employee. In that context the judge in *MT v SSWP (JSA)* [2016] UKUT 72 (AAC) cited the DMG guidance (para.34757) that "reasonable" should have its ordinary meaning of sensible or likely, although the examples given of unreasonableness are nowhere near the dividing line. If the reasoning in *GP v SSWP (JSA)* [2015] UKUT 476 (AAC), reported as [2016] AACR 14, discussed in the notes to s.7(1) above, is correct, only employment in Great Britain can be in issue. See also the prohibition in s.20(1) below of any reduction in benefit for refusing to seek employment in a situation vacant because of a stoppage of work due to a trade dispute, which must be taken to apply to this paragraph as much as to para.(c).

This head of sanction overlaps somewhat with para.(c). Preclusion is to be 1.212
imposed where claimants have neglected to avail themselves of a reasonable opportunity of employment. There is now a saving for "good reason", on which see also the notes to paras (b) and (c), above, and JSA Regulations 1996 reg.72 (noted more

fully, and covering this head in the same way as in para.(c)). The submission made in the note to para(c) on the relevance of suitability/good cause case law also applies here, so that decisions like *R(U)2/77* which protected the person, who could have had his old job back if he would, contrary to his convictions, join a trade union, would still be relevant. In *R(U)5/71* an excusing factor was a conscientious objection to a job, connected with religion or morals.

This head of sanction seems designed to cater in part for the person who literally complies with subs.(2)(c) in that they apply for the post, and do not explicitly refuse it, but who behave in such a way that they would never get it, for example, by turning up at an interview in a dirty or unkempt condition, unwashed and unshaved (*R(U)28/55*). See also s.7(3) and JSA Regulations 1996 reg.18(4) on deeming acts not to count for the purposes of actively seeking employment. Neglect to avail will also cover an explicit refusal to take a job or to fulfill a key condition for getting it (e.g. the requirement in Scotland that teachers be registered: *R(U)5/71*).

If para.(c) is not applicable because there is no situation vacant or about to become vacant, para.(d) should be considered separately (*CJSA/4179/1997* and *MT*), but if that possibility is raised for the first time before a First-tier Tribunal, a cautious approach should be taken in the light of the principle in *DL* (see notes to subs.(1)) and the claimant must be given a fair opportunity to deal with the altered case (*MT*).

See the notes to para.(c) above for "good reason" and the relevance of the suitability of the opportunity in question for the particular claimant.

Paragraph (e)

1.213

"*Without a good reason fails to participate in any scheme within section 17A(1) which is prescribed for the purposes of this section*": This is a new head of sanction. On "good reason", including the relevance of the appropriateness of the scheme for the claimant, see the annotation to para.(b), above. Note that JSA Regulations 1996 reg.72 has no application to this head of sanction. On schemes "within s. 17A(1) . . . prescribed for the purposes of this section", see the annotations to s.17A and JSA Regulations 1996 reg.70B. Mandatory Work Activitiy is the only scheme to have been prescribed. The scheme ceased to operate after April 2016.

AW v SSWP (JSA) [2016] UKUT 387 (AAC) confirms that a requirement to participate in a Mandatory Work Activity scheme was not invalidated by the fact that the claimant's jobseeker's agreement restricted his availability for employment to work that paid at least the national minimum wage. Participation in the scheme was not employment and satisfaction of the conditions of entitlement in paras (a) to (g) of s.1(2) of the old style Jobseekers Act 1995 did not prevent the imposition of requirements under s.17A, as s.1(2) is subject to the provisions of the Act as a whole. Note that the decision quotes an out-of-date version of s.19(2)(e) referring to good cause instead of a good reason.

SN v SSWP (JSA) [2018] UKUT 279 (AAC) discusses, from para.42 onwards, what can amount to a failure to participate in a scheme (at a time when the consequent sanction was under reg.8 of the Jobseeker's Allowance (Mandatory Work Activity Scheme) Regulations 2011, rather than s.19(2)(e)). It confirms that conduct of the claimant related to the ordinary requirements of the work activity in question leading to the termination of their placement can amount to a failure to participate. In particular, it is held in paras 59–62 that actions before the start of the scheme can be relevant. In *SN* the claimant was required to work for four weeks as a retail assistant in a charity shop. As found by Judge Wright in substituting a decision on the appeal, the claimant visited the shop about a week before the placement was due to start, to find out what would be entailed. During the visit he used offensive language to one member of staff and about the nature of the work involved, that was unreasonable in any work setting. He attended at the shop at the specified time for the start of the placement, but, as the representative of the programme provider was not to arrive for about 20 minutes, retired to a changing cubicle to sit down, took off his shoes and appeared to go to sleep. When the representative arrived, the deputy manager of the shop told him that the claimant would not be allowed to work there in view of his earlier offensive conduct. The judge concludes that the combination of the claimant's behaviour on the earlier visit and his attitude of antagonism and lack of interest on the first day of the placement meant that he had failed to meet the notified requirements for participation in the scheme. There was no good cause for the failure.

CS v SSWP (JSA) [2019] UKUT 218 (AAC) directly concerned s.19A(2)(b)   **1.214** rather than s.19(2)(e), but the principle would be equally applicable here. Judge Hemingway accepted that it was legitimate for a scheme provider to require an attender to verify their identity before starting the scheme, so that a refusal to do so would usually amount to a failure to participate in the scheme. However, in this particular case the claimant had declined to verify various items of information about him appearing on a computer screen, largely because of misguided views about the effect of the Data Protection Act 1998, but also because of concerns about the security of social security information held by scheme providers. The judge held that the tribunal had erred in law by failing to make findings of fact about whether the claimant had been offered the opportunity to verify his identity by other means, e.g. by producing a passport or driving licence or other document in addition to the appointment letter that he had already produced. In the absence of such findings, the tribunal had not been entitled to conclude that the claimant had refused to confirm his identity rather than merely having refused to confirm it by the method initially put forward by the scheme provider. It might in other cases be relevant to enquire what the appointment letter or other documents say or do not say about confirming identity.

See the note to the Jobseekers (Back to Work Schemes) Act 2013 for full discussion of the "prior information duty", as elucidated by the Court of Appeal in *SSWP v Reilly and Hewstone and SSWP v Jeffrey and Bevan* [2016] EWCA Civ 413; [2017] Q.B. 657; [2017] AACR 14. *NM v SSWP (JSA)* [2016] UKUT 351 (AAC) shows that the duty may be relevant both to whether a claimant has validly been referred to a scheme and to whether there was a good reason for not complying with a requirement to participate in it.

In *DH v SSWP (JSA)* [2016] UKUT 355 (AAC), a case about the SAPOE Regulations, it was held that the First-tier Tribunal erred in law in apparently dismissing the claimant's objections to attending a Work Programme run by a particular provider (on the grounds that staff of the company concerned had lied in a police statement and in court about whether travel expenses had been refunded to him and had bullied him) as, even if true, irrelevant to whether he had a good reason for failing to comply with requirements to attend. The tribunal had said that the claimant's remedies were to contact the police and to use appropriate complaints procedures, not to refuse to attend interviews or courses. The judge asked the rhetorical question in para.20 what could amount to good reason if such matters did not. The circumstances are to be distinguished from those in *R(JSA) 7/03*, not mentioned in *DH*, where the claimant's objection was a generalised one to the involvement of private companies in the provision of such schemes.

A further example of a potential good reason on its own facts (and no more   **1.215** than that), *GR v SSWP (JSA)* [2013] UKUT 645 (AAC), where it was held that a claimant with a genuinely held fear that prevented him going to the town where a course was to take place had good cause (under reg.7 of the Jobseeker's Allowance (Employment, Skills and Enterprise Scheme) Regulations 2011) for failing to participate in the scheme in question.

See also *SA v SSWP (JSA)* [2015] UKUT 454 (AAC), discussed in the notes to s.19A(2)(c) below, on when turning up late (or some similarly minor infraction of the scheme's requirements) might not amount to a failure to participate in the scheme, regardless of issues of good reason. Some doubt about the result in *SA* was expressed in para.45 of *SN* (above).

Subsection (3)

1.216   This enables regulations to provide that certain situations that would otherwise be treated as "voluntarily leaving without a good reason" are not to be so treated. Specifically mentioned is voluntarily agreeing to be dismissed by reason of redundancy. See JSA Regulations 1996 reg. 71.

Subsections (4)–(7)

1.217   The sanction for a sanctionable failure comes in the form of a reduction of a JSA award (on which see JSA Regulations 1996, new reg.70 (subs.(1)). Basically, this means a reduction of 100 per cent for a single claimant and where each member of a joint-claim couple commits a sanctionable failure, with a lesser reduction where the sanctionable failure is only by one member of such a couple. The greater stringency from October 2012 came in the increased length of the period for which a sanction can be imposed, in which there is no discretion as to the length: broadly speaking, 13 weeks for a first offence; 26 weeks for a second within a year; and 156 weeks (three years) for a third to within a year (see JSA Regulations 1996 new reg.69). That final period was reduced to 26 weeks with effect from November 27, 2019, in fulfilment of an undertaking given by the then Secretary of State, Amber Rudd, in May 2019 (see the notes to reg.69). The principles previously applying to the fixing of the length of a period of disqualificaton for UB and JSA are thus not applicable to the new regime. Reg.69(6) stipulates when the period of reduction begins.

    Subsection (6) enables regulations to provide for cases in which no reduction is to be made under s.19. See JSA Regulations 1996 new reg.70A(1). It also enables regulations to provide for a sanction applied to an old style JSA award which has terminated to then be applied to a new JSA award. See JSA Regulations 1996 new reg.70C.

    Note in addition that, as before, under s.20 as amended, nothing in s.19 or regulations made under it can authorise reduction merely because the claimant "refuses to seek or accept employment in a situation vacant because of a stoppage of work due to a trade dispute".

[¹Other sanctions

1.218   **19A.**— (1) The amount of an award of a jobseeker's allowance is to be reduced in accordance with this section in the event of a failure by the claimant which is sanctionable under this section.

    (2) It is a failure sanctionable under this section if a claimant—

    (a) without a good reason fails to comply with regulations under section 8(1) or (1A);

    (b) without a good reason fails to comply with regulations under section 17A;

    (c) without a good reason refuses or fails to carry out a jobseeker's direction which was reasonable having regard to his circumstances;

    (d) without a good reason neglects to avail himself of a reasonable opportunity of a place on a training scheme or employment programme;

    (e) without a good reason refuses or fails to apply for, or accept if offered, a place on such a scheme or programme which an employment officer has informed him is vacant or about to become vacant;

    (f) without a good reason gives up a place on such a scheme or programme or fails to attend such a scheme or programme having been given a place on it;

    (g) through misconduct loses a place on such a scheme or programme.

    (3) But a failure is not sanctionable under this section if it is also sanctionable under section 19.

    (4) Regulations are to provide for—

(a) the amount of a reduction under this section;

(b) the period for which such a reduction has effect.

(5) Regulations under subsection (4)(b) may provide that a reduction under this section in relation to any failure is to have effect for—

(a) a period continuing until the claimant meets a compliance condition specified by the Secretary of State,

(b) a fixed period not exceeding 26 weeks which is—

(i) specified in the regulations, or

(ii) determined in any case by the Secretary of State, or

(c) a combination of both.

(6) In subsection (5)(a) "compliance condition" means—

(a) a condition that the failure ceases, or

(b) a condition relating to—

(i) future compliance with a jobseeker's direction or any requirement imposed under section 8(1) or (1A) or 17A of this Act, or

(ii) future avoidance of the failures referred to in subsection (2)(d) to (g).

(7) A compliance condition specified under subsection (5)(a) may be—

(a) revoked or varied by the Secretary of State;

(b) notified to the claimant in such manner as the Secretary of State may determine.

(8) The period fixed under subsection (5)(b) may in particular depend on either or both of the following—

(a) the number of failures by the claimant sanctionable under this section;

(b) the period between such failures.

(9) Regulations may provide—

(a) for cases in which no reduction is to be made under this section;

(b) for a reduction under this section made in relation to an award that is terminated to be applied to any new award made within a prescribed period of the termination.

(10) During any period for which the amount of a joint-claim jobseeker's allowance is reduced under this section by virtue of a failure by one of the claimants which is sanctionable under this section, the allowance is payable to the other member of the couple.

(11) In this section—

(a) "jobseeker's direction" means a direction given by an employment officer (in such manner as he thinks fit) with a view to achieving one or both of the following—

(i) assisting the claimant to find employment;

(ii) improving the claimant's prospects of being employed;

(b) "training scheme" and "employment programme" have such meaning as may be prescribed.]

AMENDMENT

1. Welfare Reform Act 2012 s.46(1) (October 22, 2012).

DEFINITIONS

"claimant"—see s.35(1).

"employment officer"—*ibid.*

"employment programme"—see JSA Regulations 1996 reg.75(1)(a).

"regulations"—see s.35(1).
"training scheme"—see subs.(11)(b) and JSA Regulations 1996 reg.75(1)(b).
"week"—see JSA Regulations 1996 reg.75(3).

GENERAL NOTE

Subsection (1)

1.219   This covers a different set of grounds, set out in subs.(2), from those in the new form of s.19 in respect of which failure is sanctionable by a reduction of an old style JSA award. The reductions under s.19A are for considerably shorter periods than those for higher-level sanctions under s.19 (see the notes to subss.(4) – (9)).

Subsection (2)

1.220   The grounds set out in paras (c)–(g) correspond with those set out in the previous s.19(5) but also encompass two new grounds in subs.(2)(a) and (b).

    Notions of "without good cause" no longer apply, being replaced by "without a good reason" in paras (a)–(f), on which see the annotation to the new s.19(2)(b), above. JSA Regulations 1996 reg.72 applies only in respect of para.(c). Otherwise what ranks as "good reason" depends on all the circumstances of the case.

1.221   *Paragraph (a): "without a good reason fails to comply with regulations under section 8(1) or (1A)*: Subsections (1) and (1A) of s.8, dealing respectively with single claimants and joint claim couples, require participation in interviews and the provision of information and evidence on availability for and actively seeking employment. See JSA Regulations 1996 regs 23–27. Non-compliance with these provisions is in some circumstances a failure sanctionable under s.19A, but see the complicated relationship with the result of cessation of entitlement discussed in the notes to reg.25.

1.222   *Paragraph (b): "without a good reason fails to comply with regulations under section 17A"*: Section 17A enables regulations to provide for or in connection with the imposition on claimants of a requirement to participate in schemes designed to assist them to obtain employment. See the Jobseeker's Allowance (Mandatory Work Activity Scheme) Regulations 2011 (SI 2011/688), the Jobseeker's Allowance (Employment, Skills and Enterprise Scheme) Regulations 2011 (SI 2011/917), the Jobseeker's Allowance (Schemes for Assisting Person to Obtain Employment) Regulations 2013 (SI 2013/276) and the annotations to s.17A. Non-compliance with these provisions without a good reason is a failure sanctionable under s.19A, except in relation to the Mandatory Work Activity Scheme, failure without good reason to participate in which fell within s.19(2)(e) (higher-level sanctions) while the scheme was running.

    SSWP v DC (JSA) [2017] UKUT 464 (AAC); [2018] AACR 16 concerned two sanctions imposed in August 2013 for failures, without good cause, to participate in a Scheme as required under reg.4 of the ESES Regulations in June and August 2012. By August 2013 the Regulations had been revoked, but continued to apply in relation to failures to participate that occurred while they were in force. For the same reason, the sanctions provisions in reg.8 (revoked with effect from October 22, 2012) applied in *DC*, rather than s.19A of the old style Jobseekers Act 1995. The principles will be applicable to the other regulations made under s.17A.

    The first appeal (in relation to August 2012) raised the issue of the effect of the Secretary of State being unable to provide to the First-tier Tribunal, as directed, a copy of the appointment letter known as a Mandatory Activity Notification (MAN) sent or handed to the claimant in respect of the appointment that he failed to attend. The tribunal had allowed the claimant's appeal on the basis that the Secretary of State had failed to show that the claimant had been properly notified in accordance with the conditions in reg.4(2). In concluding that there was no error of law in that, Judge Rowland held that this was not a matter of the drawing of adverse inferences, but of the Secretary of State simply having failed to come forward with evidence on a matter on which the burden of proof was on him. Although there was evidence before the tribunal that the claimant had been given an appointment letter, that evidence did not go beyond showing the date and time of the appointment. It did not show where the claimant was to attend or what other information was provided and how it was expressed. The judge rejected the Secretary of State's submission relying on the presumption of regularity and the "inherent probabilities". Although the tribunal could, using its specialist experience, properly have concluded that the letter had contained enough information to make it effective, it was not bound to do so, given that it is not unknown for documents to be issued in an unapproved form or to use language that is not intelligible to an uninitiated recipient. The judge agreed with the tribunal that a copy of the appointment letter should have been in the tribunal bundle: a decision-maker might be able to rely on the presumption of regularity, but on an appeal (where it is not known what issues may eventually emerge) a copy of the letter should be provided. Much the same approach was taken by the Chief Commissioner in Northern Ireland in *PO'R v DFC (JSA)* [2018] NI Com 1, where it was said that the tribunal there should not have decided against the claimant without having adjourned to obtain a copy of the appointment letter.

If a copy of the appointment letter was not in the bundle, then Judge Rowland's view was that a tribunal could, using its inquisitorial jurisdiction in an area where unrepresented claimants in particular could not be expected to identify such technical points, properly exercise its discretion under s.12(8)(a) of the SSA 1998 to direct that a copy be provided. It would not be fair to decide the case against the Secretary of State without giving that opportunity to provide the evidence. But where, as in *DC*, the evidence directed was not provided, the tribunal could properly conclude that the Secretary of State had failed to come forward with evidence on a matter on which the burden of proof was on him. There is therefore no formal incompatibility with the decision of Judge Wright in *SSWP v CN (JSA)* [2020] UKUT 26 (AAC), discussed in the introductory note to the Jobseekers (Back to Work Schemes) Act 2013, although there was less emphasis there on the inquisitorial role of the tribunal.

1.223

Judge Rowland accepted that the tribunal in *DC* had erred in law in deciding against the Secretary of State on the authorisation point (discussed below) without giving him an opportunity to provide relevant evidence, but that error was not material as, even if there was evidence that the provider was authorised to issue reg.4 notices, the tribunal would have been entitled to allow the claimant's appeal on the basis of the lack of necessary evidence that an effective notice had been given.

The second appeal (in relation to June 2012) raised the issue of whether the tribunal had been entitled to conclude that the Secretary of State had not shown that the Scheme provider in question had been authorised under reg.18 of the ESES Regulations to give reg.4 notices when he was unable to produce a copy of a letter of authorisation. Judge Rowland held that the tribunal had gone wrong in law. Regulation 18 did not specify the form in which authorisation had to be given, so that it was a matter of fact and degree. So authority could be found to exist in evidence as to the conduct of those concerned, including what they have said and written over a period. The tribunal did not consider that possibility, raised by the provider acting as though authorised and the Secretary of State asserting that authority had been given. The judge went on to re-make the decision on the appeal. It had emerged that, by an administrative mistake, no formal letter of authority had ever been issued, but the existence of a contract between the Secretary of State and the main contractor for the sub-contractor to act in the area in question and a draft authorisation letter was sufficient to satisfy reg.18. He found that the claimant had been properly notified and had not shown good cause for his failure to participate, so that a sanction was to be imposed. On close analysis of reg.8 the sanction was to be for four weeks, rather than the 26 that had originally been imposed.

In *CS v SSWP (JSA)* [2019] UKUT 218 (AAC) Judge Hemingway accepted that it was legitimate for a scheme provider to require a person attending to verify their identity before starting the scheme, so that a refusal to do so would usually amount to a failure to participate in the scheme (and so, it would seem, to a failure to comply with regulations made under s.17A within this paragraph). However, in the particular case the claimant had declined to verify various items of information about him appearing on a computer screen, largely because of misguided views about the effect of the Data Protection Act 1998, but also because of concerns about the security of social security information held by scheme providers. The judge held that the tribunal had erred in law by failing to make findings of fact about whether the claimant had been offered the opportunity to verify his identity by other means, e.g. by producing a passport or driving licence or other document in addition to the appointment letter that he had already produced. In the absence of such findings, the tribunal had not been entitled to conclude that the claimant had refused to confirm his identity rather than merely having refused to confirm it by the method initially put forward by the scheme provider. It might in other cases be relevant to enquire what the appointment letter or other documents say or do not say about confirming identity.

See the note to the Jobseekers (Back to Work Schemes) Act 2013 for full discussion of the "prior information duty", as elucidated by the Court of Appeal in *SSWP v Reilly and Hewstone and SSWP v Jeffrey and Bevan* [2016] EWCA Civ 413; [2017] Q.B. 657; [2017] AACR 14. *NM v SSWP (JSA)* [2016] UKUT 351 (AAC) shows that that duty may be relevant both to whether a claimant has validly been referred to a scheme and to whether there was a good reason for not complying with a requirement to participate in it.

1.224   *Paragraph (c): "without a good reason refuses or fails to carry out a jobseeker's direction which was reasonable having regard to his circumstances"*: This provision constitutes the only statutory authority for the giving of a jobseeker's direction, by making it a sanctionable failure to refuse or fail to carry one out. "Jobseeker's direction" is defined in subs.(11)(a) in fairly wide but not open-ended terms. It must be given by an "employment officer" (defined in s.35(1): see the notes to that definition for discussion, which shows that the extension beyond Jobcentre Plus employees does not apply for the purposes of s.19A(2)(c)). It can be given in whatever manner the employment officer thinks fit. Thus, there is no requirement that the direction be given in writing or in any other permanent form. However, good practice, plus the potential need for acceptable proof of the existence and terms of the direction in the light of the principle that the claimant should in sanctions cases be given the benefit of any doubt that might reasonably arise (*DL v SSWP (JSA)* [2013] UKUT 295 (AAC)), must surely point to the need for written or computer records to be kept and to be available to the claimant for reference. See the notes to s.9 around *PT v SSWP (JSA)* [2015] UKUT 703 (AAC) for the reasons why it is at the least good practice not to give a direction as part of a jobseeker's agreement. The control comes in the provision that the direction be made with a view to assisting the claimant to find employment or to improving the claimant's prospects of being employed or both. That formulation must require that the direction can objectively be found to have such a purpose, not merely that the particular employment officer subjectively believes that it has. Within that constraint any kind of personal behaviour or activity involving any kind of third party could potentially come within the definition in subs.(11). However, in practice the requirement in subs.(2)(c) that the direction be reasonable before a sanction can be imposed provides a further limit. Claimants faced with directions that they think are unreasonable are nonetheless put in the dilemma that refusing to comply will probably lead to an immediate loss of benefit for at least four weeks (unless they can persuade the employment officer or the Secretary of State on mandatory reconsideration of the unreasonableness), which a successful appeal will not reinstate for many months.

See the note to the Jobseekers (Back to Work Schemes) Act 2013 for full discussion of the "prior information duty", as elucidated by the Court of Appeal in *SSWP v Reilly and Hewstone and SSWP v Jeffrey and Bevan* [2016] EWCA Civ 413; [2017] Q.B. 657; [2017] AACR 14. *NM v SSWP (JSA)* [2016] UKUT 351 (AAC) shows that that duty may be relevant both to whether a claimant has validly been referred to a scheme and to whether there was a good reason for not complying with a requirement to participate in it. The requirements of fairness at the base of the Court of Appeal's decision would equally require that claimants should have sufficient information to enable them to make meaningful representations about whether a direction should be given and, if so, its terms.

The references to "the claimant" and to having regard to the claimant's circumstances require that the purpose prescribed in subs.(11) must be linked to the particular claimant's employment prospects. In *DM v SSWP (JSA)* [2015] UKUT 67 (AAC), Judge Rowley cited some relevant parts of the DMG as follows:

> "7. Under paragraph 34904 of the [DMG] it is provided that a Jobseeker's Direction should be (amongst other things):
> (1) linked to action to improve the claimant's chances of finding work;
> (2) personalised and appropriate to that individual claimant;
> (3) related to labour market activities.
> 8. It is further provided (under paragraph 34905) that the issue of a Jobseeker's Direction must be tailored to each individual claimant's requirements.
> 9. The [DMG] also provides guidance on certain sessions which are known as Group Information Sessions. Under paragraph 34911 it is said that 'generally a claimant cannot be mandated to attend a Group Information Session. There needs to be a clearly identified and tangible benefit to the individual claimant in terms of improving their employment prospects by attending the session'."

In *DM*, the claimant, who had been registered unemployed for nearly four years, **1.225** was issued with a document describing itself as a jobseeker's direction directing him to attend and participate fully in a Group Information Session ["General" at para.10 may be a typo] at a specified date, time and place. The reason for the direction was said to be to attend the work programme returnees' information session to improve his chances of employment. It was stated that he would receive additional information to help him look for work, to ensure that he had the correct job goals and improve his CV, although Judge Rowley apparently accepted the claimant's contention that the session was in fact about the sanctions regime. The claimant attended at the right time but was asked to leave the session shortly before the end because he was said to be disrupting it by asking questions and heckling. It was then decided that he was in breach of the direction by failing to participate fully in the session, that the direction was reasonable and that he had not had good reason for failing to comply with the direction, so that he was made subject to a sanction for four weeks. On appeal, the First-tier Tribunal concluded that the jobseeker's direction was reasonable having regard to the claimant's circumstances and confirmed the sanction decision. Judge Rowley held that the tribunal had gone wrong in law by reaching that decision in the absence of any evidence to show why the Group Information Session would have assisted the particular claimant to find employment or to improve his prospects of being employed. Nor was there any evidence to suggest that the conditions in para.34904 were met. She substituted her own decision that the sanction should not have been imposed.

There will inevitably be some overlap between the requirement that the direction be "reasonable, having regard to the claimant's circumstances" and the "good reason" exemption, so that "excusing" factors might be argued as constituting "good reason" for the refusal/failure or as rendering the direction "unreasonable". However, as the circumstances of *DM* (above) show, there may be a discrepancy between what is set out in a direction and what is actually provided to the claimant. The direction itself may be quite reasonable. But what are claimants to do who, having, say, been directed to "participate fully" in a particular course or session, find that it is not in fact directed to their own circumstances or to improving prospects of employment? Can that in itself amount to a good reason for not completing the course or session or should the claimant, having started the course or session, complete it even if under protest or challenge? The approach adopted in *PL v DSD (JSA)* [2015] NI Com 72 by the Chief Commissioner for Northern Ireland, approving and applying the obiter suggestion of Judge Ward in *PL v SSWP (JSA)* [2013] UKUT 227 (AAC) (see notes to para.(d) below) would suggest that the appropriateness of whatever was directed would be relevant.

In *SA v SSWP (JSA)* [2015] UKUT 454 (AAC) the claimant, who had hearing difficulties and wore a hearing aid in one ear, was directed by an employment officer to attend and complete a CV writing course with Learn Direct two days later from 11.15 a.m. to 12.15 p.m. He was given a letter to confirm the time and date. The claimant arrived at 11.25 a.m. and was told that he was too late and so had been deemed to have missed his appointment. He immediately went to the Jobcentre Plus office to rebook an appointment for the course and explained that he had misheard the time for the appointment as 11.50 a.m., the time that he normally signed on. A fixed four-week sanction for failing, without a good reason, to carry out a reasonable job-seeker's direction was imposed. On appeal the claimant said that at the meeting with the employment officer he had not been wearing his hearing aid and that he had not thought to check the time of the appointment on the letter as he genuinely thought that it was the same as his two previous appointments. The First-tier Tribunal regarded it as clear that the direction had been reasonable and that the claimant had failed to comply with it, so that the sole question was whether he had had a good reason for the failure. On that question, the tribunal concluded that, although the error was genuine, that did not in itself give him a good reason and that he had failed to take reasonable steps to confirm the time of the appointment and dismissed his appeal. In setting aside the tribunal's decision and substituting her own decision reversing the imposition of the sanction (as had been suggested by the Secretary of State), Judge Knowles held that the tribunal had erred in law by failing to consider the question of whether the claimant had failed to comply with the direction. In the substituted decision, she concluded that, the claimant not having refused to carry out the direction and taking into account that his error was genuine and that he took immediate steps to rebook, it was disproportionate to treat his late arrival in isolation as amounting to a failure to comply with the direction. That can only be regarded as a determination on the particular facts that does not constitute any sort of precedent to be applied as a matter of law in other cases. The outcome may have reflected an understandable desire in a deserving case to get around the absence of any scope for varying the fixed period of four weeks for a s.19A sanction for a "first offence". However, there could have been nothing unreasonable about a conclusion that arriving 10 minutes after the beginning of a course that only lasted for an hour amounted to a failure to comply with a direction to attend and complete the course, no matter how genuine the error that led to the late arrival. Some doubt about the result in *SA* was expressed in para.45 of *SN v SSWP (JSA)* [2018] UKUT 387 (AAC) (see para.1.213 for the facts of the case).

1.226   In discussing whether the tribunal had also approached the question of good reason properly, Judge Knowles accepted the Secretary of State's submission that all the circumstances should be considered and that the question was whether those circumstances would have caused a reasonable person to act as the claimant did, provided that the reasonable person was given the characteristics of the claimant in question. See the notes to s.19(2)(b) above for further discussion of good reason.

Note that JSA Regulations 1996 reg.72 stipulates with respect to this head of sanction that "good reason" cannot be founded on travel time to and from work of less than an hour and a half each way "unless in view of the health of the person, or any caring responsibilities of his, that time was or is unreasonable".

1.227   *Paragraph (d): "without a good reason neglects to avail himself of a reasonable opportunity of a place on a training scheme or employment programme"*: Note that in *CSJSA/495/2007* and *CSJSA/505/2007*, Commissioner May rejected as unarguable the claimant's arguments that the application to him of sanctions for failing to take up a place on an intensive activity period employment programme infringed art.4 ECHR (freedom from slavery or forced labour). Nor was there an arguable case of discrimination. A similar argument for the application of art.4 was comprehensively rejected by the Supreme Court in *R (Reilly and Wilson) v Secretary of State for Work and Pensions* [2013] UKSC 68; [2014] 1 A.C. 453. There is a saving for "good reason".

In *PL v DSD (JSA)* [2015] NI Com 72 (followed and applied in *PO'R v DFC (JSA)* [2018] NI Com 1), the Chief Commissioner for Northern Ireland has approved and applied the obiter suggestion of Judge Ward in *PL v SSWP (JSA)* [2013] UKUT 227 (AAC) (on the pre-October 2012 form of the Great Britain legislation) that in deciding whether a claimant had good cause for failing to avail himself of a reasonable opportunity of a place on a training scheme or employment programme a tribunal erred in law, where the circumstances raised the issue, in failing to consider the appropriateness of the particular scheme or programme to the claimant in the light of his skills and experience and previous attendance on any placements. Judge Ward's suggestion had been that the test was whether the claimant had reasonably considered that what was provided would not help him. It seems likely that a similar general approach will be taken to issues of "good reason" under s.19A(2)(d)–(f). It may though still need to be sorted out how far the issue turns on the claimant's subjective view, within the bounds of reasonableness, in the light of the information provided at the time, as against a tribunal's view of the appropriateness of what was to be provided. The Chief Commissioner made no comment on the treatment of the claimant's refusal to complete and sign forms with information about criminal convictions and health, that the First-tier Tribunal had found were reasonably required by the training provider as part of its application process for the scheme, as a failure by the claimant to avail himself of a reasonable opportunity of a place on the training scheme.

Paragraph (e): "without a good reason refuses or fails to apply for, or accept if offered, a place on such a scheme or programme which an employment officer has informed him is vacant or about to become vacant": This covers the situation, after an employment officer has informed a claimant of a vacant place on such a scheme or programme, of refusal or failure to apply for such a place or to accept it when offered. There is a saving for "good reason". The extended meaning of "employment officer" mentioned in the notes to para.(c) above does not apply for the purposes of para.(e).   1.228

Paragraph (f): "without a good reason gives up a place on such a scheme or programme or fails to attend such a scheme or programme having been given a place on it" *R(JSA)* 2/06 held that turning up late could rank as "failure to attend", but see *SA v SSWP (JSA)* [2015] UKUT 454 (AAC), discussed in the notes to para.(c) above. There is a saving for "good reason".   1.229

Paragraph (g): "through misconduct loses a place on such a scheme or programme" On the meaning and scope of "misconduct", see the annotation to s.19(2)(a), above. There is no saving for "good reason".   1.230

Subsection (3)

A failure under s.19A is not sanctionable under this section if it also sanctionable under the higher level sanctions regime in the "new" s.19.   1.231

Subsections (4)–(9)

The period for which a sanction can apply is set by regulations made under subs. (4)(b) read with subss.(5)–(8). See JSA Regulations 1996 new reg.69A. Section 19A allows: a fixed period of not more than 26 weeks as set by regulations or determined in a particular case by the Secretary of State; a period (in principle able to be longer that than the 26-week maximum) lasting until the claimant complies with a compliance condition set by the Secretary of State (that failure ceases and/or future failures are avoided); or a combination of both (see subs.(5)). However, reg.69A used only a small part of that power. The sanction is of fixed periods of 4 weeks for a first offence and 13 weeks for a second within a year. The power in subs.(5)(a) to make the period continue to run until a compliance condition has been met has not been exercised. Regulation 69A(3) stipulates when the period of reduction begins.   1.232

The amount of the reduction is set, pursuant to subs.(4)(a), by the JSA Regulations 1996 new reg.70 and parallels that with respect to higher-level sanctions. Basically, this means a reduction of 100 per cent for a single claimant and where each member of a joint-claim couple commits a sanctionable failure, with a lesser reduction where the sanctionable failure is only by one member of such a couple.

JSA Regulations 1996 reg.70A(2)–(5) set out circumstances in which no reduction is to be made under s.19A, although those do not remove the status of sanctionable failure (but note reg.69(2)(a) and reg.69A(2)(a)).

Subsection (10)

1.233   As regards joint-claim couples where only one of the claimants is subject to a sanction, JSA continues to be paid to the compliant member.

[¹Claimants ceasing to be available for employment etc

1.234   **19B.**— (1) Regulations may make provision for reduction of the amount of an award of a jobseeker's allowance other than a joint-claim jobseeker's allowance if the claimant—

    (a) was previously entitled to such an allowance or was a member of a couple entitled to a joint-claim jobseeker's allowance, and

    (b) ceased to be so entitled by failing to comply with the condition in section 1(2)(a) or (c) (availability for employment and actively seeking employment).

(2) Regulations may make provision for reduction of the amount of a joint-claim jobseeker's allowance if one of the claimants—

    (a) was previously entitled to a jobseeker's allowance other than a joint-claim jobseeker's allowance, and

    (b) ceased to be so entitled by failing to comply with the condition in section 1(2)(a) or (c).

(3) Regulations may make provision for reduction of the amount of an award of joint-claim jobseeker's allowance if—

    (a) the couple were previously entitled to a joint-claim jobseeker's allowance but ceased to be so entitled by either or both of them failing to comply with the condition in section 1(2)(a) or (c), or

    (b) either member of the couple was a member of another couple previously entitled to such an allowance and that couple ceased to be so entitled by that person failing to comply with the condition in section 1(2)(a) or (c).

(4) Regulations are to provide for—

    (a) the amount of a reduction under this section;

    (b) the period for which such a reduction has effect.

(5) The period referred to in subsection (4)(b) must not include any period after the end of the period of 13 weeks beginning with the day on which the claimant's previous entitlement ceased.

(6) Regulations under subsection (4)(b) may in particular provide for the period of a reduction to depend on either or both of the following—

    (a) the number of occasions on which a claimant's entitlement has ceased as specified in subsection (1), (2) or (3);

    (b) the period between such occasions.

(7) Regulations may provide for a reduction under this section made in relation to an award that is terminated to be applied to any new award made within a prescribed period of the termination.

(8) During any period for which the amount of a joint-claim jobseeker's allowance is reduced under this section by virtue of a failure by one of the claimants to comply with the condition in section 1(2)(a) or (c), the allowance is payable to the other member of the couple.

AMENDMENT

1. Welfare Reform Act 2012 s.46(1) (October 22, 2012).

DEFINITIONS

"a joint-claim jobseeker's allowance"—see s.1(4).
"claimant"— see s.35(1).

GENERAL NOTE

This section enables regulations to provide for an award of old style JSA to be   1.235
reduced in respect of a claim for a period not exceeding 13 weeks where a previous
JSA entitlement had ended because of failing to be available for or actively seeking
employment. Section 19B does not apply when the reason for the termination of the
previous award was that there ceased to be a jobseeker's agreement in effect. When
a reduction is to apply is set out in JSA Regulations 1996 new reg.69B(1)–(5). The
period of reduction is set by paras (6) and (7) of that provision (broadly speaking,
four weeks for a first offence and 13 weeks for a second within a year) and its commencement stipulated as the date of claim (reg.69(8)). The amount of reduction
is set by JSA Regulations 1996 new reg.70 and parallels that with respect to higher
level sanctions. Basically, this means a reduction of 100 per cent for a single claimant and where each member of a joint-claim couple commits a sanctionable failure,
with a lesser reduction where the sanctionable failure is only by one member of such
a couple.

[¹Hardship payments

19C.— (1) Regulations may make provision for the making of payments   1.236
("hardship payments") by way of a jobseeker's allowance to a claimant
where—
   (a) the amount of the claimant's award is reduced under sections 19 to
      19B, and
   (b) the claimant is or will be in hardship.
   (2) Regulations under this section may in particular make provision as
to—
   (a) circumstances in which a claimant is to be treated as being or not
      being in hardship;
   (b) matters to be taken into account in determining whether a claimant
      is or will be in hardship;
   (c) requirements or conditions to be met by a claimant in order to
      receive hardship payments;
   (d) the amount or rate of hardship payments;
   (e) the period for which hardship payments may be made;
   (f) whether hardship payments are recoverable.]

AMENDMENT

1. Welfare Reform Act 2012 s.46(1) (June 19, 2017).

GENERAL NOTE

It would appear on close examination that this section was not brought into   1.237
force on October 22, 2012. Although s.46 of the WRA 2012 (inserting ss.19–
19C) was originally brought into force by art.2(6) of the Welfare Reform Act 2012
(Commencement No.2) Order (SI 2012/1246) as from October 14, 2012, art.2(6)

was revoked by art.2(7) of the Welfare Reform Act 2012 (Commencement No.4) Order 2012 (SI 2012/2530). Although art.2(2)(a) of the No.4 Order indeed brought s.46(1) of the WRA 2012 into force on October 22, 2012, its commencement was limited to the "purposes of the substitution of sections 19 to 19B of the Jobseekers Act 1995", thus, on a strict reading, suggesting that s.19C was not included. The text of the "Blue Volumes", however, incorporated s.19C as in force, as did Westlaw, and the Explanatory Notes to the Welfare Reform Bill which became the 2012 Act clearly envisaged that ss.19–19C would be in force until transfer to universal credit was completely rolled out. Since s.19C only confers rule–making powers (on which see regs 140–146H of the JSA Regulations 1996) enabling the making of hardship payments, no-one is likely to complain about the possible invalidity of those regulations, especially since there appear to be alternative powers to make the regulations in s.20(4) and (6). In view of the dubious situation, the text of s.19C was originally included in this volume, but in italics. Now art.15 of the Welfare Reform Act 2012 (Commencement No.29 and Commencement No.17, 19, 22, 23 and 24 and Transitional and Transitory Provisions (Modification)) Order 2017 (SI 2017/664) has appointed June 19, 2017 as the day for the coming into force of s.46(1) in relation to s.19C.

Exemptions from section 19 [³ and 19A]

1.238   **20.**—(1) Nothing in section 19, or in regulations under that section, shall be taken to [³authorise reduction] of a jobseeker's allowance merely because the claimant refuses to seek or accept employment in a situation which is vacant in consequence of a stoppage of work due to a trade dispute.

(2) Section [³19A] does not apply, in the circumstances mentioned in subsection [³(2)(c) to (g)] of that section, if—

(a) a direction is in force under section 16 with respect to the claimant; and

(b) he has acted in such a way as to risk—

(i) having that direction revoked under subsection (3)(b) of section 16; or

(ii) having the amount of his jobseeker's allowance reduced by virtue of section 17, because [¹the condition mentioned in section 17(3)(b) or (c) is satisfied].

(3) Regulations shall make provisions for the purpose of enabling any person of a prescribed description to accept any employed earner's employment without falling within section [³19(2)(b) or (d)] should he leave that employment voluntarily and without [³ good reason] at any time during a trial period.

(4) In such circumstances as may be prescribed, an income-based jobseeker's allowance shall be [²payable in respect of] a claimant even though section 19 prevents payment of a jobseeker's allowance to him.

(5) A jobseeker's allowance shall be payable by virtue of subsection (4) only if the claimant has complied with such requirements as to the provision of information as may be prescribed for the purposes of this subsection.

(6) Regulations under subsection (4) may, in particular, provide for a jobseeker's allowance payable by virtue of that subsection to be—

(a) payable at a prescribed rate;

(b) payable for a prescribed period (which may differ from the period fixed under section 19(2) or (3)).

(7) In subsection (3), "trial period" has such meaning as may be prescribed.

(8) Regulations may make provision for determining, for the purposes of

this section, the day on which a person's employment is to be regarded as commencing.

AMENDMENTS

1. Social Security Act 1998, Sch.7 para.142 (October 18, 1999).
2. Welfare Reform and Pensions Act 1999 s.70 and Sch.8 para.29 (November 11, 1999).
3. Welfare Reform Act 2012 Sch.7 para.5 (October 22, 2012).

DEFINITIONS

"claimant"—see s.35(1).
"employment"—see s.35(1) and JSA Regulations 1996 reg.4.
"income-based jobseeker's allowance"—see ss.1(4) and 35(1).
"jobseeker's agreement"—see ss.9(1) and 35(1).
"regulations"—see s.35(1).
"trade dispute"—*ibid.*
"trial period"—see JSA Regulations 1996 reg.74(4).

GENERAL NOTE

This section affords a number of exemptions from the preclusive effect of ss.19 and 19A and enables the making of regulations providing for hardship payments of a reduced rate of IBJSA for those precluded from full old style JSA by ss.19 or 19A. See further JSA Regulations 1996 regs 140–146D.　　　　1.239

Subsection (1)
This provides that nothing in s.19 or regulations made under it can prevent payment of old style JSA merely because the claimant refuses to seek or accept employment vacant in consequence of a stoppage of work due to a trade dispute. On the definition of "trade dispute", see s.35(1) and the notes to s.14(1). On "stoppage of work", see the notes to s.14(1).　　　　1.240

This maintains the traditional "neutral" approach to trade disputes taken in social security law. A claimant is not required to be a strike-breaker and so will not be sanctioned for refusing work that is vacant because of a trade dispute.

Subsection (2)
If a young person who is the subject of a severe hardship direction fails to pursue or refuses a training opportunity without a good reason or fails to complete a training course without a good reason, or loses his place through misconduct, s.19A(2) (c)–(g) does not apply. The young person's "offence" will be dealt with by revocation of the direction under s.16(3) or reduction in his old style JSA under s.17 as appropriate. See reg.63 of the JSA Regulations 1996.　　　　1.241

Subsections (3), (7) and (8)
This provision and JSA Regulations 1996 reg.74 made under it protect certain persons who leave employment voluntarily without good reason at any time during a trial period from preclusion from old style JSA under the voluntarily leaving employment without a good reason head of s.19(2)(b) or under s.19(2)(d) (neglect to avail oneself of a reasonable opportunity of employment). Regulation 74(4) defines "trial period". See further the annotations to s.19(2)(b) and (d).　　　　1.242

Subsections (4), (5) and (6)
In the past a claimant suspended or disqualified from UB under s.28(1) of the SSCBA 1992, or who would have been so disqualified if otherwise entitled, could (if eligible) receive reduced payments of income support. Now there is no automatic entitlement to reduced income-based JSA where a sanction is imposed under　　　　1.243

s.19. Benefit will only be paid if hardship can be shown. There can be no hardship payment if the claimant is sanctioned under ss.19A or 19B.

See regs 140–146H of the JSA Regulations 1996 for the rules governing hardship payments and the notes to those regulations.

[¹ **Denial or reduction of joint-claim jobseeker's allowance**

1.244   **20A.**—[² . . .]

AMENDMENTS

1. Welfare Reform and Pensions Act 1999 s.59 and Sch.7 para.13 (March 19, 2001).
2. Welfare Reform Act 2012 s.147 and Sch.14 Pt 3 (October 22, 2012).

GENERAL NOTE

1.245   This section, together with s.20B below, made provision corresponding to that made by the former ss.19 and 20 in relation to a joint-claim jobseeker's allowance. For further details see pp.122–123 of Vol.II of the 2012/13 edition. Both sections have now been repealed because the rules for imposing sanctions on joint-claim couples are included in the new ss.19–20.

1.246   [¹**20B.**— [² . . .]

AMENDMENTS

1. Welfare Reform and Pensions Act 1999 s.59 and Sch.7 para.13 (March 19, 2001).
2. Welfare Reform Act 2012 s.147 and Sch.14 Pt 3 (October 22, 2012).

GENERAL NOTE

See p.124 of Vol.II of the 2012/2013 edition.

Miscellaneous

[¹**Contracting out**

1.247   **20E.**—(1) *[Not yet in force]*
        (2)   *[Not yet in force]*
        (3)   Regulations may provide for any of the following functions of the Secretary of State to be exercisable by, or by employees of, such person (if any) as the Secretary of State may authorise for the purpose—
        (a) any function under regulations under section 8, [² . . .] 17A [² . . .] [³ . . .], except the making of an excluded decision (see subsection (4));
        (b) *[Not yet in force]*
        (c) *[Not yet in force]*
        (d) *[Not yet in force]*.
        (4)   Each of the following is an "excluded decision" for the purposes of subsection (3)—
        (a) a decision about whether a person has failed to comply with a requirement imposed by regulations under section 8, [² . . .], [⁴ . . .] [³ . . .];
        (b) a decision about whether a person had good cause for failure to comply with such a requirement;

(c) a decision about not paying or reducing a jobseeker's allowance in consequence of a failure to comply with such a requirement.

(5) Regulations under subsection (3) may provide that a function to which that subsection applies may be exercised—

(a) either wholly or to such extent as the regulations may provide,

(b) either generally or in such cases as the regulations may provide, and

(c) either unconditionally or subject to the fulfilment of such conditions as the regulations may provide.

(6) An authorisation given by virtue of any provision made by or under this section may authorise the exercise of the function concerned—

(a) either wholly or to such extent as may be specified in the authorisation,

(b) either generally or in such cases as may be so specified, and

(c) either unconditionally or subject to the fulfilment of such conditions as may be so specified;

but, in the case of an authorisation given by virtue of regulations under subsection (3), this subsection is subject to the regulations.

(7) An authorisation given by virtue of any provision made by or under this section—

(a) may specify its duration,

(b) may be revoked at any time by the Secretary of State, and

(c) does not prevent the Secretary of State or any other person from exercising the function to which the authorisation relates.

(8) Anything done or omitted to be done by or in relation to an authorised person (or an employee of that person) in, or in connection with, the exercise or purported exercise of the function concerned is to be treated for all purposes as done or omitted to be done by or in relation to the Secretary of State or (as the case may be) an officer of the Secretary of State.

(9) But subsection (8) does not apply—

(a) for the purposes of so much of any contract made between the authorised person and the Secretary of State as relates to the exercise of the function, or

(b) for the purposes of any criminal proceedings brought in respect of anything done by the authorised person (or an employee of that person).

(10) Any decision which an authorised person makes in exercise of a function of the Secretary of State has effect as a decision of the Secretary of State under section 8 of the 1998 Act.

(11) Where—

(a) the authorisation of an authorised person is revoked at any time, and

(b) at the time of the revocation so much of any contract made between the authorised person and the Secretary of State as relates to the exercise of the function is subsisting,

the authorised person is entitled to treat the contract as repudiated by the Secretary of State (and not as frustrated by reason of the revocation).

(12) In this section—

(a) "the 1998 Act" means the Social Security Act 1998;

(b) "authorised person" means a person authorised to exercise any function by virtue of any provision made by or under this section;

(c) references to functions of the Secretary of State under any enactment (including one comprised in regulations) include functions which the Secretary of State has by virtue of the application of section 8(1) (c) of the 1998 Act in relation to the enactment.]

AMENDMENTS

1. Welfare Reform Act 2009 s.32(1) and (2) (March 9, 2011) but only for the purposes of enabling under subss.(3)(a) and (4)–(12) of s.20E the ability to contract out within limits certain of the Secretary of State's functions in regulations made under s.17A. See further the commentary to s.17A.

2. Welfare Reform Act 2012 s.147 and Sch.14 Pt 2 (amending Welfare Reform Act 2009 s.32(2) inserting s.20E) (May 8, 2012).

3. Welfare Reform Act 2012 s.147 and Sch.14 Pt 6 (amending Welfare Reform Act 2009 s.32(2) inserting s.20E) (May 8, 2012).

4. Welfare Reform Act 2012 s.48 and Sch.7 para.16(1) and (2)(c) (amending Welfare Reform Act 2009 s.32(2) inserting s.20E) (October 22, 2012).

Supplementary provisions

1.248   **21.**—Further provisions in relation to a jobseeker's allowance are set out in Schedule 1.

Members of the forces

1.249   **22.**—(1) Regulations may modify any provision of this Act, in such manner as Secretary of State thinks proper, in its application to persons who are or have been members of Her Majesty's forces.

(2) The regulations may, in particular, provide for [¹ section 19(2)(b)] not to apply in relation to a person who is discharged from Her Majesty's forces at his own request.

(3) For the purposes of this section, Her Majesty's forces shall be taken to consist of such establishments and organisations in which persons serve under the control of the Defence Council as may be prescribed.

AMENDMENT

1. Welfare Reform Act 2012 s.48 and Sch.7 para.7 (October 22, 2012).

Recovery of sums in respect of maintenance

1.250   **23.**—(1) Regulations may make provision for the court to have power to make a recovery order against any person where an award of income-based jobseeker's allowance has been made to that person's spouse [¹ or civil partner].

(2) In this section "recovery order" means an order requiring the person against whom it is made to make payments to the Secretary of State or to such other person or persons as the court may determine.

(3) Regulations under this section may make provision for the transfer by the Secretary of State of the right to receive payments under, and to exercise rights in relation to, a recovery order.

(4) Regulations made under this section may, in particular, include provision—

(a) as to the matters to which the court is, or is not, to have regard in determining any application under the regulations; and

(b) as to the enforcement of recovery orders.

(5) In this section, "the court" means—

(a) in relation to England and Wales, [² the family court]; and

(b) in relation to Scotland, the sheriff.

AMENDMENTS

1. Civil Partnership Act 2004 s.254 and Sch.24 para.122 (December 5, 2005).
2. Crime and Courts Act 2013 (Family Court: Consequential Provision) Order 2014 (SI 2014/605) art.21(1) (April 22, 2014).

DEFINITIONS

"income-based jobseeker's allowance"—see s.1(4).
"regulations"—see s.35(1).

GENERAL NOTE

This section is concerned with the enforcement of a person's liability to maintain his spouse or civil partner where an award of JSA has been made to that spouse or civil partner (compare s.106 of the Administration Act in relation to income support). It is not known how often these powers to recover such maintenance are in fact used since the child support maintenance system first introduced by the Child Support Act 1991 has been in operation.   1.251

PART II

BACK TO WORK SCHEMES

The back to work bonus

26.—*[Omitted].*   1.252

GENERAL NOTE

Section 26 remains in force but has been omitted from this work because it has not been possible to make a claim under the back to work bonus scheme that was made under the section since January 29, 2005. See pp.138–140 of Vol.II of the 2019/20 edn for further details.   1.253

Pilot schemes

29.—(1) Any regulations to which this subsection applies may be made so as to have effect for a specified period not exceeding [³ 36 months].   1.254

(2) Any regulations which, by virtue of subsection (1), are to have effect for a limited period are referred to in this section as "a pilot scheme".

(3) A pilot scheme may provide that its provisions are to apply only in relation to—

(a) one or more specified areas or localities;

(b) one or more specified classes of person;

(c) persons selected—

(i) by reference to prescribed criteria; or

(ii) on a sampling basis.

(4) A pilot scheme may make consequential or transitional provision with respect to the cessation of the scheme on the expiry of the specified period.

(5) A pilot scheme ("the previous scheme") may be replaced by a further pilot scheme making the same, or similar, provision (apart from the specified period) to that made by the previous scheme.

(6) Subject to subsection (8), subsection (1) applies to—

    (a) regulations made under this Act, other than—
        (i) regulations made under section 4(2) or (5) which have the effect of reducing any age-related amount or applicable amount; or
        (ii) regulations made under section 27;
    (b) regulations made under the Administration Act, so far as they relate to a jobseeker's allowance;
    (c) regulations made under Part VII of the Benefits Act (income-related benefits), other than any mentioned in subsection (7); and
    (d) regulations made under the Administration Act, so far as they relate to income-related benefits payable under Part VII of the Benefits Act.

(7) The regulations referred to in subsection (6)(c) are—
    (a) [² . . .]
    (b) [² . . .]
    (c) regulations under section 130(4) of that Act which have the effect of reducing the appropriate maximum housing benefit;
    (d) regulations under section 131(10)(a) of that Act which have the effect of reducing the appropriate maximum council tax benefit; and
    (e) regulations reducing any of the sums prescribed under section 135(1) of that Act.

(8) Subsection (1) applies only if the regulations are made with a view to ascertaining whether their provisions will, or will be likely to, encourage persons to obtain or remain in work or will, or will be likely to, [³ make it more likely that persons will obtain or remain in work or be able to do so].

AMENDMENTS

    1. Tax Credits Act 1999 Sch.1 paras 1 and 6(h) (October 5, 1999).
    2. Tax Credits Act 2002 s.60 and Sch.6 (April 8, 2003).
    3. Welfare Reform Act 2009 s.28(1) (November 12, 2009).

DEFINITIONS

    "the Administration Act"—see s.35(1).
    "the Benefits Act"—*ibid.*
    "regulations"—*ibid.*

GENERAL NOTE

1.255   This important provision contains the power to "pilot" changes in regulations across particular geographical areas and/or specified categories of claimants for a period of up to (from November 12, 2009) three years (this period can be extended: see subs.(5)). The power can only be exercised in relation to the types of regulations listed in subs.(6) and with a view to assessing whether the proposed changes are likely to encourage people to find or remain in work or make it more likely that they will do so, or be able to do so (subs.(8)). Regulations made under this section are subject to the affirmative resolution procedure (s.37(1)(c)). See the use of this power, as well as that in s.17A(1), in the making of the Jobseeker's Allowance (Supervised Jobsearch Pilot Scheme) Regulations 2014 (SI 2014/1913), set out only in the Supplement to the 2014/15 edition because they ceased to have effect on April 30, 2015, and of the Jobseeker's Allowance (18–21 Work Skills Pilot Scheme) Regulations 2014 (SI 2014/3117), also set out only in that Supplement because they only apply to claimants in limited areas of the country and ceased to have effect on November 25, 2016.

PART III

MISCELLANEOUS AND SUPPLEMENTAL

Termination of awards

31.—(1) Regulations may make provision allowing, in prescribed cir- cumstances, an award of income support to be brought to an end by [¹ the Secretary of State] where the person to whom it was made, or where he is a member of a [³ couple] his partner [² or the couple], will be entitled to a jobseeker's allowance if the award is brought to an end.

(2) Regulations may make provision allowing, in prescribed circum- stances, an award of a jobseeker's allowance to be brought to an end by[¹ the Secretary of State] where the person to whom it was made, or where he is a member of a [³ couple] his partner, [² or where the award was made to a couple a member of the couple,] will be entitled to income support if the award is brought to an end.

(3) In this section "partner" means the other member of the couple con- cerned.

AMENDMENTS

1. Social Security Act 1998 s.86(1) and Sch.7 para.143 (October 18, 1999).
2. Welfare Reform and Pensions Act 1999 s.59 and Sch.7 para.14 (March 19, 2001).
3. Civil Partnership Act 2004 s.254 and Sch.24 para.123 (December 5, 2005).

DEFINITION

"couple"—see s.35(1).

Interpretation

35.—(1) In this Act—
[² . . .]
"the Administration Act" means the Social Security Administration Act 1992;
"applicable amount" means the applicable amount determined in accord- ance with regulations under section 4;
"benefit year" has the meaning given by section 2(4);
"the Benefits Act" means the Social Security Contributions and Benefits Act 1992;
"child" means a person under the age 16;
"claimant" means a person who claims a jobseeker's allowance; [³except that in relation to a joint-claim couple claiming a joint-claim jobseek- er's allowance it means the couple, or each member of the couple, as the context requires;]
"continental shelf operations" has the same meaning as in section 120 of the Benefits Act;
"contribution-based conditions" means the conditions set out in section 2;
"contribution-based jobseeker's allowance" has the meaning given in section 1(4);
[⁴ [¹³ ¹⁴ "couple" means—

1.256

1.257

129

(a) two people who are married to, or civil partners of, each other and are members of the same household; or

(b) two people who are not married to, or civil partners of, each other but are living together [¹⁵ as if they were a married couple or civil partners] otherwise than in prescribed circumstances;]]

"employed earner" has the meaning prescribed for the purposes of this Act;

"employment", except in section 7, has the meaning prescribed for the purposes of this Act;

[¹¹ "employment officer", for any purpose of this Act, means an officer of the Secretary of State or such other person as may be designated for that purpose by an order made by the Secretary of State;]

"entitled", in relation to a jobseeker's allowance, is to be construed in accordance with—

(a) the provisions of this Act relating to entitlement; and

(b) [²section 1 of the Administration Act and section 27 of the Social Security Act 1998]

"family" means—

(a) a [⁵ couple];

(b) a [⁵ couple] and a member of the same household for whom one of them is, or both are, responsible and who is a child or a person of a prescribed description;

(c) except in prescribed circumstances, a person who is not a member of a [⁵ couple] and a member of the same household for whom that person is responsible and who is a child or a person of a prescribed description;

[⁸ "FAS payments" means payments made under the Financial Assistance Scheme Regulations 2005;]

"Great Britain" includes the territorial waters of the United Kingdom adjacent to Great Britain;

"income-based conditions" means the conditions set out in section 3;

"income-based jobseeker's allowance" has the meaning given in section 1(4);

[¹⁰ "income-related employment and support allowance" means an income-related allowance under Part 1 of the Welfare Reform Act 2007 (employment and support allowance);]

"jobseeker's agreement" has the meaning given by section 9(1);

[¹² "jobseeker's direction" has the meaning given by section 19A;]

"jobseeking period" has the meaning prescribed for the purposes of this Act;

[³"joint-claim couple" and "joint-claim jobseeker's allowance" have the meanings given by section 1(4);]

[⁶ . . .];

[³ "the nominated member", in relation to a joint-claim couple, shall be construed in accordance with section 3B(4);]

"occupational pension scheme" has the same meaning as it has in the Pension Schemes Act 1993 by virtue of section 1 of that Act;

"pensionable age" has the meaning prescribed for the purposes of this Act;

"pension payments" means—

(a) periodical payments made in relation to a person, under a personal pension scheme or, in connection with the coming to an end of an employment of his, under an occupational pension scheme or a public service pension scheme; and

(b) such other payments as may be prescribed;

"personal pension scheme" means—

(a) a personal pension scheme as defined by section 1 of the Pension Schemes Act 1993;

[⁹ (b) an annuity contract or trust scheme approved under section 620 or 621 of the Income and Corporation Taxes Act 1988 or a substituted contract within the meaning of section 622(3) of that Act which is treated as having become a registered pension scheme by virtue of paragraph 1(1)(f) of Schedule 36 to the Finance Act 2004; and

(c) a personal pension scheme approved under Chapter 4 of Part 14 of the Income and Corporation Taxes Act 1988 which is treated as having become a registered pension scheme by virtue of paragraph 1(1)(g) of Schedule 36 to the Finance Act 2004;]

[⁸ "PPF payments" means any payments made in relation to a person—

(a) payable under the pension compensation provisions as specified in section 162(2) of the Pensions Act 2004 or Article 146(2) of the Pensions (Northern Ireland) Order 2005 (the pension compensation provisions); or

(b) payable under section 166 of the Pensions Act 2004 or Article 150 of the Pensions (Northern Ireland) Order 2005 (duty to pay scheme benefits unpaid at assessment date etc.);]

"prescribed" [¹, except in section 27 (and in section 36 so far as relating to regulations under section 27),] means specified in or determined in accordance with regulations;

"public service pension scheme" has the same meaning as it has in the Pension Schemes Act 1993 by virtue of section 1 of that Act;

"regulations" [¹, except in section 27 (and in section 36 so far as relating to regulations under section 27),] means regulations made by the Secretary of State;

"tax year" means the 12 months beginning with 6th April in any year;

"trade dispute" means any dispute between employers and employees, or between employees and employees, which is connected with the employment or non-employment or the terms of employment or the conditions of employment of any persons, whether employees in the employment of the employer with whom the dispute arises, or not;

"training" has the meaning prescribed for the purposes of this Act and, in relation to prescribed provisions of this Act, if regulations so provide, includes assistance to find training or employment, or to improve a person's prospects of being employed, of such a kind as may be prescribed;

[⁶...];

"week" means a period of 7 days beginning with a Sunday or such other period of 7 days as may be prescribed;

"work" has the meaning prescribed for the purposes of this Act;

"year", except in the expression "benefit year", means a tax year.

[⁷ (1A) [¹³ ¹⁴...]]

(2) The expressions [¹⁰ "limited capability for work"], "linked period", "relevant education" and "remunerative work" are to be read with paragraphs 2, 3, 14 and 1 of Schedule 1.

(3) Subject to any regulations made for the purposes of this subsection, "earnings" is to be construed for the purposes of this Act in accordance with section 3 of the Benefits Act and paragraph 6 of Schedule 1 to this Act.

AMENDMENTS

1. Social Security Contributions (Transfer of Functions, etc.) Act 1999 s.2 and Sch.3 para.62 (April 1, 1999).

2. Social Security Act 1998 Sch.7 para.144 (October 18, 1999).

3. Welfare Reform and Pensions Act 1999 s.59 and Sch.7 para.15 (March 19, 2001).

4. Civil Partnership Act 2004 s.254 and Sch.24 para.124(2) (December 5, 2005).

5. Civil Partnership Act 2004 s.254 and Sch.24 para.124(3) (December 5, 2005).

6. Civil Partnership Act 2004 s.254 and Sch.24 para.124(4) (December 5, 2005).

7. Civil Partnership Act 2004 s.254 and Sch.24 para.124(5) (December 5, 2005).

8. Pensions Act 2004 (PPF Payments and FAS Payments) (Consequential Provisions) Order 2006 (SI 2006/343) art.2 and Sch. Pt 2 para.2(2) (February 14, 2006).

9. Taxation of Pension Schemes (Consequential Amendments) Order 2006 (SI 2006/745) art.12 (April 6, 2006).

10. Welfare Reform Act 2007 s.28(1) and Sch.3 para.12(5) (October 27, 2008).

11. Welfare Reform Act 2012 s.44(5) (June 10, 2012).

12. Welfare Reform Act 2012 s.48 and Sch.7 para.8 (October 22, 2012).

13. Marriage (Same Sex Couples) Act 2013 (Consequential and Contrary Provisions and Scotland) Order 2014 (SI 560/2014) art.2 and Sch.1 para.26 (March 13, 2014).The amendments extend to England and Wales only (see SI 2014/107 art.1(4)).

14. Marriage and Civil Partnership (Scotland) Act 2014 and Civil Partnership Act 2004 (Consequential Provisions and Modifications) Order 2014 (SI 2014/3229) art.29 and Sch.5 para.12 (December 16, 2014). The amendments relate only to Scotland (see SI 2014/3229 art.3(4)) but are in the same terms as the amendments made in relation to England and Wales by SI 2014/107 (see point 13 above).

15. Civil Partnership (Opposite-sex Couples) Regulations 2019 (SI 2019/1458) reg.41 and Sch.3 Pt.1 para.14 (December 2, 2019).

GENERAL NOTE

1.258 This section defines certain terms used in the legislation, but leaves some to be construed in accordance with specified paragraphs of Sch.1 and others to be defined through regulations, some of which definitions relate to the whole of the JSA Regulations (see regs 1(3) and 3) and some of which only apply to specified Parts.

"*Child*". The restriction to a person under 16 gives rise to the need to define "young person" in the JSA Regulations to cater for the over-15s (see JSA Regulations 1996 regs 57(1) and 76(1)).

"*Couple*". See the notes to the definition in reg.2(1) of the Income Support Regulations.

"*Employed earner*". See reg.3 of the JSA Regulations.

"*Employment*". This is defined for purposes of "actively seeking employment" in s.7(8) to cover both employed and self-employed earner's employment as those terms are used in SSCBA 1992, but otherwise "employment" has the meaning prescribed in regulations: see JSA Regulations 1996 regs 3, 4 and 75(4).

"*Employment officer*". This is an important definition for many purposes within the old style JSA scheme but in particular for the sanction under s.19A(2) (c) for refusing or failing, without a good reason, to carry out a reasonable jobseeker's direction. Section 19A(11) defines a jobseeker's direction as a direction given by an employment officer with a view to assisting the claimant to find employment, to improving the claimant's prospects of being employed or both. See the notes to s.19A(2)(c) for discussion of those conditions. Other important functions of employment officers include entering into and varying jobseeker's agreements (for which the same definition is provided by s.9(13)) and specifying the time, place and manner of interviews under regs 23 and 23A of the JSA Regulations 1996 and s.8(1). In many places, action by an employment officer forms part of the background (e.g. informing a claimant of a vacancy, failure to apply for which or accept if offered can attract a sanction under s.19(2)(c)). Sometimes action must be approved by an employment officer (e.g. reg.14(1)(a)). Occasionally a determination of an issue of entitlement is to be made by an employment officer, rather than the Secretary of State. Examples are reg.13(6) of the JSA Regulations 1996 (whether a person with caring responsibilities for a child does not have reasonable prospects of securing employment if restricting availability to hours left after fulfilling the caring responsibilities, so as to be exempted from the reasonable prospects test) and reg.17A(3) (whether a claimant may undertake a qualifying course and therefore still be treated as available for employment).

The definition appears to cover any officer of the Secretary of State. Apparently, all Jobcentre Plus employees are regarded as employment officers. It is trickier to pin down just how far the Secretary of State's power to extend the meaning to other persons has in fact been exercised.

The designation of other persons (which can, by virtue of Sch.1 to the Interpretation Act 1978, include corporate and unincorporated associations, such as companies, as well as natural persons) must be made by an order and must be for a purpose of the old style Jobseekers Act 1995. An order under s.9(13) (meaning of employment officer for purposes of jobseeker's agreement) or s.16(4) (meaning for the purposes of hardship payments) falls outside the requirement in s.36(1) for any power under the Act to make orders to be exercisable by statutory instrument. The other provisions mentioned in s.36(1) as exempted no longer exist. However, at the time of writing no orders under ss.9(13) or 16(4) have been identified. Section 36(1A) exempts any order relating to employment officers under s.35(1) from the s.36(1) requirement.

Four Orders have been made in recent years but only for the purposes of s.19(2)(c) (see above). They are the Jobseeker's Allowance (Supervised Jobsearch Pilot Scheme) (Employment Officers) Designation Order 2014 (in force from October 2, 2014 to April 30, 2015), the Jobseeker's Allowance (Community Work Placements) (Employment Officers) Designation Order 2014 (in force from October 27, 2014), the Jobseeker's Allowance (Work Programme) (Employment Officers) Designation Order 2014 (also in force from October 27, 2014) and the Jobseeker's Allowance (Work and Health Programme) (Employment Officers) Designation Order 2018 (in force from April 1, 2018).

The Community Work Placements Order relates to the scheme described in reg.3(8A) of the Jobseeker's Allowance (Schemes for Assisting Persons to Obtain Employment) Regulations 2013. Regulation 3(8A) has been revoked with effect from November 20, 2017. The Work Programme Order relates to the scheme described in reg.3(8). The Work and Health Programme Order relates to the scheme described in reg.3(8C). See the notes to reg.3 of the SAPOE Regulations. The Orders are deposited in the House of Commons Library and can be accessed on the Parliament website. Their effect is now dealt with in the internet version of the DMG, having previously been the subject of Memos. Each Order designates employees of "prime contractors" and "approved sub-contractors" as employment officers. Prime contractors are organisations specified in a schedule to the Order in question which have been appointed by the Secretary of State to provide services or facilities for the scheme in question. Approved sub-contractors are organisations engaged by a prime contractor to perform its obligations under a relevant contract and which are approved by the Secretary of State.

"Family". The definition is the same as in s.137(1) of the Contributions and Benefits Act 1992. See the notes to that definition. For "person of a prescribed description" see reg.76(1) of the JSA Regulations.

"FAS payments". "PPF payments" (see below) are not available in respect of pension schemes that wound up before April 6, 2005. Payments under the Financial Assistance Regulations are intended to cover defined benefits

occupational pension schemes that wound up between January 1997 and April 2005 because of employer insolvency.

"*Occupational pension scheme*". Section 1(1) of the Pension Schemes Act 1993 (as amended by s.239 of the Pensions Act 2004 with effect from September 22, 2005 in the case of an occupational pension scheme that has its main administration in the UK and with effect from April 6, 2006 in all other cases (see art.2(7) of the Pensions Act 2004 (Commencement No.6, Transitional Provisions and Savings) Order 2005 (SI 2005/1720), and as further amended with effect from November 26, 2007 by reg.2(b) of the Occupational Pension Schemes (EEA States) Regulations 2007 (SI 2007/3014)) defines an "occupational pension scheme" as:

"a pension scheme—
(a) that—
(i) for the purpose of providing benefits to, or in respect of, people with service in employments of a description, or
(ii) for that purpose and also for the purpose of providing benefits to, or in respect of, other people,
is established by, or by persons who include, a person to whom subsection (2) applies when the scheme is established or (as the case may be) to whom that subsection would have applied when the scheme was established had that subsection then been in force, and
(b) that has its main administration in the United Kingdom or outside the EEA states,
or a pension scheme that is prescribed or is of a prescribed description".

Section 1(2)–(5) provides:

1.259   "(2) This subsection applies—
(a) where people in employments of the description concerned are employed by someone, to a person who employs such people,
(b) to a person in an employment of that description, and
(c) to a person representing interests of a description framed so as to include—
(i) interests of persons who employ people in employments of the description mentioned in paragraph (a), or
(ii) interests of people in employments of that description.

(3) For the purposes of subsection (2), if a person is in an employment of the description concerned by reason of holding an office (including an elective office) and is entitled to remuneration for holding it, the person responsible for paying the remuneration shall be taken to employ the office-holder.

(4) In the definition in subsection (1) of "occupational pension scheme", the reference to a description includes a description framed by reference to an employment being of any of two or more kinds.

(5) In subsection (1) "pension scheme" (except in the phrases "occupational pension scheme", "personal pension scheme" and "public service pension scheme") means a scheme or other arrangements, comprised in one or more instruments or agreements, having or capable of having effect so as to provide benefits to or in respect of people—
(a) on retirement,
(b) on having reached a particular age, or
(c) on termination of service in an employment."

"*Pensionable age*". See reg.3 of the JSA Regulations.

"*Personal pension scheme*". The meaning in s.1(1) of the Pension Schemes Act 1993 (as amended by s.239 of the Pensions Act 2004 with effect from April 6, 2006 (see art.2(7) of the Pensions Act 2004 (Commencement No.6,

Transitional Provisions and Savings) Order 2005 (SI 2005/1720), and as further amended with effect from April 6, 2007 by the Finance Act 2007 Sch.27 Pt 3(2) para.1) is

"a pension scheme that—
(a) is not an occupational pension scheme, and
(b) is established by a person within section 154(1) of the Finance Act 2004".

Section 1(5) further provides that "pension scheme" in s.1(1) means "a scheme or other arrangements, comprised in one or more instruments or agreements, having or capable of having effect so as to provide benefits to or in respect of people—
(a) on retirement,
(b) on having reached a particular age, or
(c) on termination of service in an employment."

"PPF payments". The Pension Protection Fund ("PPF") was set up under the Pensions Act 2004 in order to provide protection for members of defined benefits (i.e. normally final salary) occupational pension schemes and in relation to the defined elements of hybrid pension schemes in the event of the employer's insolvency. For the complex provisions see Pt 2 of the Pensions Act 2004.
"Public service pension scheme". A "public service pension scheme" is:

"an occupational pension scheme [as defined above] established by or under an enactment or the Royal prerogative or a Royal charter, being a scheme (a) all the particulars of which are set out in, or in a legislative instrument made under, an enactment, Royal warrant or charter, or (b) which cannot come into force, or be amended, without the scheme or amendment being approved by a Minister of the Crown or government department or by the Scottish Ministers".

The term includes:

"any occupational pension scheme established, with the concurrence of the Treasury, by or with the approval of any Minister of the Crown or established by or with the approval of the Scottish Ministers and any occupational pension scheme prescribed by regulations made by the Secretary of State and the Treasury jointly as being a scheme which ought in their opinion to be treated as a public service pension scheme for the purposes of this Act". (Pension Schemes Act 1993 s.1)

"Training". See reg.57(1) of the JSA Regulations.

Regulations and orders.

36.—(1) Any power under this Act to make regulations or orders, other than an order under [² section [³ 8(3),] 9(13), 16(4) or 19(10)(a)] shall be exercisable by statutory instrument.   1.260

[⁷ (1A) Subsection (1) does not apply to an order under section 35(1) in relation to employment officers.]

(2) Any such power may be exercised—
(a) either in relation to all cases to which it extends, or in relation to those cases subject to specified exceptions, or in relation to any specified cases or classes of case;
(b) so as to make, as respects the cases in relation to which it is exercised—
   (i) the full provision to which the power extends or any less provision (whether by way of exception or otherwise),
   (ii) the same provision for all cases in relation to which it is exercised, or different provision for different cases or different

classes of case or different provision as respects the same case or class of case for different purposes of this Act,

(iii) any such provision either unconditionally or subject to any specified condition.

(3) Where any such power is expressed to be exercisable for alternative purposes it may be exercised in relation to the same case for any or all of those purposes.

(4) Any such power includes power—

(a) to make such incidental, supplemental, consequential or transitional provision as appears to the Secretary of State [¹ , or (in the case of regulations made by the Treasury) to the Treasury,] to be expedient; and

(b) to provide for a person to exercise a discretion in dealing with any matter.

[⁴ (4A) Without prejudice to the generality of the provisions of this section—

(a) regulations under section 17A [⁵ ⁶ . . .] may make different provision for different areas;

(b) regulations under section 17A [⁵ ⁶ . . .] may make provision which applies only in relation to an area or areas specified in the regulations.]

(5) Any power to make regulations or an order for the purposes of any provision of this Act is without prejudice to any power to make regulations or an order for the purposes of any other provision.

AMENDMENTS

1. Social Security Contributions (Transfer of Functions, etc.) Act 1999 s.2 and Sch.3 para.63 (April 1, 1999).

2. Social Security Act 1998 s.86(1) and Sch.7 para.145 (October 18, 1999 for purposes specified in SI 1999/2860 art.2 and Sch.1).

3. Welfare Reform and Pensions Act 1999 s.70 and Sch.8 para.29(6) (November 11, 1999).

4. Welfare Reform Act 2009 s.1(3) (November 12, 2009).

5. Welfare Reform Act 2009 s.11 and Sch.3 paras 3(1) and (2) (November 12, 2009).

6. Welfare Reform Act 2012 s.147 and Sch.14 Pt. 6 (May 8, 2012).

7. Welfare Reform Act 2012 s.48 and Sch.7 para.9 (October 22, 2012 note that art.2(6) of SI 2012/1246, which originally provided for Sch.7 para.9 to come into force on October 1, 2012 was revoked by SI 2012/2530 art.2(7)).

DEFINITION

"regulations"—see s.35(1).

GENERAL NOTE

1.261   See s.37 for the regulations which require approval by affirmative resolution.

Parliamentary control

1.262   **37.**—(1) Subsection (2) applies in relation to the following regulations (whether made alone or with other regulations)—

(a) regulations made under, or by virtue of, any provision of this Act other than—

(i) section 6, 7, 26, 29 or 40,

(ii) paragraph (b) of the definition of "pension payments" in section 35(1), or

(iii) paragraph 17 of Schedule 1,

before the date on which jobseeker's allowances first become payable;

[⁶ (aa) the first regulations to be made under section 6J or 6K;]

[⁵ (ab) the first regulations to be made under sections 19 to 19C;]

   (b) the first regulations to be made under section 26;

   (c) regulations made under section [³ . . .] 29, paragraph (b) of the definition of "pension payments" in section 35(1) [¹ [⁴ . . .]] or paragraph [²8B or] 17 of Schedule 1.

(2) No regulations to which this subsection applies shall be made unless a draft of the statutory instrument containing the regulations has been laid before Parliament and approved by a resolution of each House.

(3) Any other statutory instrument made under this Act, other than one made under section 41(2), shall be subject to annulment in pursuance of a resolution of either House of Parliament.

AMENDMENTS

1. Welfare Reform Act 2009 s.11 and Sch.3 paras 3(1) and (3) (November 12, 2009).

2. Welfare Reform Act 2009 s.29(2) (January 19, 2012 as SI 2012/68).

3. Welfare Reform Act 2012 s.47 (March 20, 2012).

4. Welfare Reform Act 2012 s.147 and Sch.14 Pt. 6 (May 8, 2012).

5. Welfare Reform Act 2012 s.46(2) (June 10, 2012).

6. Welfare Reform Act 2012 s.49(6) (February 25, 2013).

DEFINITIONS

"pension payments"—see s.35(1).
"regulations"—*ibid.*

GENERAL NOTE

Note in particular that regulations governing availability for, and actively seeking, employment, pilot schemes and requirements for people who are dependent on drugs have to be approved by affirmative resolution (subs.(1)(c)).   1.263

General financial arrangements

38.—*[Omitted as not relevant.]*   1.264

Provision for Northern Ireland

39.—*[Omitted as not relevant.]*   1.265

Transitional provisions

40.—(1) The Secretary of State may by regulations make such transitional   1.266 provision, consequential provision or savings as he considers necessary or expedient for the purposes of or in connection with—

   (a) the coming into force of any provision of this Act; or

   (b) the operation of any enactment repealed or amended by any such provision during any period when the repeal or amendment is not wholly in force;

(2) Regulations under this section may in particular make provision—

   (a) for the termination or cancellation of awards of unemployment benefit or income support;

(b) for a person whose award of unemployment benefit or income support has been terminated or cancelled under regulations made by virtue of paragraph (a) to be treated as having been awarded a jobseeker's allowance (a "transitional allowance")—

    (i) of such a kind,

    (ii) for such period,

    (iii) of such an amount, and

    (iv) subject to such conditions,

as may be determined in accordance with the regulations;

(c) for a person's continuing entitlement to a transitional allowance to be determined by reference to such provision as may be made by the regulations;

(d) for the termination of an award of a transitional allowance;

(e) for the review of an award of a transitional allowance;

(f) for a contribution-based jobseeker's allowance not to be payable for a prescribed period where a person is disqualified for receiving unemployment benefit;

(g) that days which were days of unemployment for the purposes of entitlement to unemployment benefit, and such other days as may be prescribed, are to be treated as having been days during which a person was, or would have been, entitled to a jobseeker's allowance;

(h) that days which were days of entitlement to unemployment benefit, and such other days as may be prescribed, are to be treated as having been days of entitlement to a contribution-based job-seeker's allowance;

(i) that the rate of a contribution-based transitional allowance is to be calculated by reference to the rate of unemployment benefit paid or payable.

DEFINITIONS

"contribution-based jobseeker's allowance"—see s.1(4).
"prescribed"—see s.35(1).
"regulations"—*ibid.*

GENERAL NOTE

1.267   See the Jobseeker's Allowance (Transitional Provisions) Regulations 1996 (SI 1996/2657) which are consolidating regulations that replaced the Jobseeker's Allowance (Transitional Provisions) Regulations 1995 (SI 1995/3276), as amended, from November 4, 1996. The text and commentary can be found in the 2000 edition of this volume.

Short title, commencement, extent etc.

1.268   **41.**—(1) This Act may be cited as the Jobseekers Act 1995.

(2) Section 39 and this section (apart from subsections (4) and (5)) come into force on the passing of this Act, but otherwise the provisions of this Act come into force on such day as the Secretary of State may by order appoint.

(3) Different days may be appointed for different purposes.

(4) Schedule 2 makes consequential amendments.

(5) The repeals set out in Schedule 3 shall have effect.

(6) Apart from this section, section 39 and paragraphs 11 to 16, 28, 67 and 68 of Schedule 2, this Act does not extend to Northern Ireland.

GENERAL NOTE

Subsections (4) and (5)

The amendments and repeals effected by, respectively, Schs 2 and 3 have been taken into account in the appropriate places in this book.   1.269

SCHEDULE A1

[Repealed by the Welfare Reform Act 2012 s.60(1) with effect from May 8, 2012]

SCHEDULE 1

SUPPLEMENTARY PROVISIONS

Remunerative work

1.—(1) For the purposes of this Act, "remunerative work" has such meaning as may be prescribed.   1.270

(2) Regulations may prescribe circumstances in which, for the purposes of this Act—
  (a) a person who is not engaged in remunerative work is to be treated as engaged in remunerative work; or
  (b) a person who is engaged in remunerative work is to be treated as not engaged in remunerative work.

[⁶ Limited capability for work

2.—(1) The question whether a person has, or does not have, limited capability for work shall be determined, for the purposes of this Act, in accordance with the provisions of Part 1 of the Welfare Reform Act 2007 (employment and support allowance) [¹² or Part 1 of the Welfare Reform Act 2012 (universal credit) as the Secretary of State considers appropriate in the person's case].   1.271

(2) References in Part 1 of the Welfare Reform Act 2007 to the purposes of that Part shall be construed, where the provisions of that Part have effect for the purposes of this Act, as references to the purposes of this Act.]

[¹² (3) References in Part 1 of the Welfare Reform Act 2012 to the purposes of that Part are to be construed, where the provisions of that Part have effect for the purposes of this Act, as references to the purposes of this Act.]

Linking periods

3.—Regulations may provide—   1.272
  (a) for jobseeking periods which are separated by not more than a prescribed number of weeks to be treated, for purposes of this Act, as one jobseeking period;
  (b) for prescribed periods ("linked periods") to be linked, for purposes of this Act, to any jobseeking period.

Waiting days

4.—Except in prescribed circumstances, a person is not entitled to a jobseeker's allowance in respect of a prescribed number of days at the beginning of a jobseeking period.   1.273

5.—Regulations may make provision in relation to—
  (a) entitlement to a jobseeker's allowance, or
  (b) the amount payable by way of such an allowance, in respect of any period of less than a week.

Employment protection sums

6.—(1) In relation to any contribution-based jobseeker's allowance, regulations may make provision—   1.274
  (a) for any employment protection sum to be treated as earnings payable by such person, to such person and for such period as may be determined in accordance with the regulations; and
  (b) for any such period, so far as it is not a period of employment, to be treated as a period of employment.

(2) In this paragraph "employment protection sum" means—

(a) any sum, or a prescribed part of any sum—
    (i) payable, in respect of arrears of pay, under an order for reinstatement or re-engagement made under[¹the Employment Rights Act 1996];
    (ii) payable, by way of pay, under an order made under that Act for the continuation of a contract of employment;
    (iii) payable, by way of remuneration, under a protective award made under section 189 of the Trade Union and Labour Relations (Consolidation) Act 1992; and
(b) any prescribed sum which the regulations provide is to be treated as related to any sum within paragraph (a).

Pension payments

1.275   **7.**—Regulations may make provision, for the purposes of any provision of, or made under, this Act—
(a) for such sums by way of pension payments to be disregarded for prescribed purposes;
(b) as to the week in which any pension payments are to be treated as having begun;
(c) for treating, in a case where—
    (i) a lump sum is paid to a person in connection with a former employment of his or arrangements are made for a lump sum to be so paid; or
    (ii) benefits of any description are made available to a person in connection with a former employment of his or arrangements are made for them to be made so available; or
    (iii) pension payments to a person are assigned, reduced or postponed or are made otherwise than weekly,
such payments as being made to that person by way of weekly pension payments as are specified in or determined under the regulations;
(d) for the method of determining whether pension payments are made to a person for any week and their amount.

Exemptions

1.276   **8.**—Regulations may prescribe circumstances in which a person may be entitled to an income-based jobseeker's allowance without—
(a) being available for employment;
(b) having entered into a jobseeker's agreement; or
(c) actively seeking employment.

[⁴ **8A.**—(1) Regulations may prescribe circumstances in which a joint-claim couple may be entitled to a joint-claim jobseeker's allowance without each member of the couple satisfying all the conditions referred to in section 1(2B)(b).

(2) Regulations may prescribe circumstances in which, and a period for which, a transitional case couple may be entitled to a joint-claim jobseeker's allowance without having jointly made a claim for it.

(3) In sub-paragraph (2)—
(a) "a transitional case couple" means a joint-claim couple a member of which is entitled to an income-based jobseeker's allowance on the coming into force of Schedule 7 to the Welfare Reform and Pensions Act 1999; and
(b) "period" shall be construed in accordance with section 3(3).]

[⁸ **8B.** —(1) This paragraph applies if domestic violence has been inflicted on or threatened against a person ("V") in prescribed circumstances.

(2) The Secretary of State must exercise the powers to make regulations under sections 6(4) and 7(4) so as to secure that, for an exempt period, V is treated as—
(a) being available for employment; and
(b) actively seeking employment.

(3) If V has not entered into a jobseeker's agreement before the exempt period begins, the Secretary of State must also exercise the power to make regulations under section 9(10) so as to secure that V is treated as having entered into a jobseeker's agreement which is in force for the exempt period.

(4) In this paragraph—
    "domestic violence" has such meaning as may be prescribed;
    "exempt period" means a period of 13 weeks beginning no later than a prescribed period after the date (or last date) on which the domestic violence was inflicted or threatened.

(5) Regulations may make provision for the purposes of this paragraph prescribing circumstances in which domestic violence is, or is not, to be regarded as being inflicted on or threatened against a person.]

9.—Regulations may provide—
- (a) for an income-based jobseeker's allowance to which a person is entitled by virtue of regulations under paragraph 8 [4 or 8A] to be payable at a prescribed rate;
- (b) for it to be payable for a prescribed period.

[4 Continuity of claims and awards: persons ceasing to be a joint-claim couple

9A.—(1) Regulations may make provision about the entitlement to a jobseeker's allowance of persons ("ex-members") who cease to be members of a joint-claim couple.   **1.277**
(2) Regulations under this paragraph may, in particular, provide—
- (a) for treating each or either of the ex-members as having made any claim made by the couple or, alternatively, for any such claim to lapse;
- (b) for any award made in respect of the couple to be replaced by an award (a "replacement award") in respect of each or either of the ex-members of the couple or, alternatively, for any such award to lapse.

Continuity of claims and awards: persons again becoming a joint-claim couple

9B.—(1) Regulations may make provision about the entitlement to a jobseeker's allowance of persons ("ex-members") who, having ceased to be members of a joint-claim couple, again become the members of a joint-claim couple.   **1.278**
(2) Regulations under this paragraph may, in particular, provide—
- (a) for any claim made by the ex-members when they were previously a joint-claim couple to be revived or otherwise given effect as a claim made by the couple;
- (b) for any award made in respect of the ex-members when they were previously a joint-claim couple to be restored;
- (c) for any such award, or any replacement award (within the meaning of paragraph 9A) made in respect of either of them, to be replaced by an award (a "new award") in respect of the couple.

Continuity of claims and awards: couple becoming a joint-claim couple

9C.—(1) Regulations may make provision about the entitlement to a jobseeker's allowance of persons who become members of a joint-claim couple as a result of the [5 couple] of which they are members becoming a joint-claim couple.   **1.279**
(2) Regulations under this paragraph may, in particular, provide—
- (a) for any claim made by either member of the couple before the couple became a joint-claim couple to be given effect as a claim made by the couple;
- (b) for any award, or any replacement award (within the meaning of paragraph 9A), made in respect of either member of the couple before the couple became a joint-claim couple to be replaced by an award (a "new award") in respect of the couple.

Paragraphs 9A to 9C: supplementary

9D.—(1) Regulations may provide, in relation to any replacement award (within the meaning of paragraph 9A) or new award (within the meaning of paragraph 9B or 9C)—   **1.280**
- (a) for the award to be of an amount determined in a prescribed manner;
- (b) for entitlement to the award to be subject to compliance with prescribed requirements as to the provision of information and evidence.
(2) In paragraphs 9A to 9C and this paragraph—
"award" means an award of a jobseeker's allowance;
"claim" means a claim for a jobseeker's allowance.]

Claims yet to be determined and suspended payments

[4 **10.**—(1) In such circumstances as may be prescribed—   **1.281**
- (a) a claimant for a jobseeker's allowance other than a joint-claim jobseeker's allowance;
- (b) a joint-claim couple claiming a joint-claim jobseeker's allowance; or
- (c) a member of such a couple,

may be treated as being entitled to an income-based jobseeker's allowance before his or (as the case may be) the couple's claim for the allowance has been determined.]

(2) In such circumstances as may be prescribed, an income-based jobseeker's allowance shall be [³ payable in respect of]

[⁴ (a) a claimant for a jobseeker's allowance other than a joint-claim jobseeker's allowance;
(b) a joint-claim couple claiming a joint-claim jobseeker's allowance; or
(c) a member of such a couple,

even though payment to him or (as the case may be) the couple] of a jobseeker's allowance has been suspended by virtue of regulations under [² section 21(2) of the Social Security Act 1998].

(3) A jobseeker's allowance shall be payable by virtue of sub-paragraph (1) or (2) only if the claimant [⁴ or (as the case may be) the couple or the member of the couple] has complied with such requirements as to the provision of information as may be prescribed for the purposes of this paragraph.

(4) Regulations may make provision for a jobseeker's allowance payable by virtue of sub-paragraph (1) or (2) to be—

(a) payable at a prescribed rate;
(b) payable for a prescribed period;
(c) treated as being a contribution-based jobseeker's allowance for the purposes of section 5 of this Act.

(5) Regulations may make provision—

(a) for the recovery, by prescribed means and in prescribed circumstances, of the whole or part of any amount paid by virtue of sub-paragraph (1) or (2);
(b) for the whole or part of any amount paid by virtue of sub-paragraph (1) to be treated, if an award is made on the claim referred to there, as having been paid on account of the jobseeker's allowance awarded;
(c) for the whole or part of any amount paid by virtue of sub-paragraph (2) to be treated, if the suspension referred to there is lifted, as having been paid on account of the suspended allowance.

[⁹(6) References in sub-paragraphs (1) and (2) to an income-based jobseeker's allowance include a payment by way of such an allowance under section 19C.]

Presence in and absence from Great Britain

1.282   **11.**—(1) Regulations may provide that in prescribed circumstances a claimant who is not in Great Britain may nevertheless be entitled to a contribution-based jobseeker's allowance.

(2) Regulations may make provision for the purposes of this Act as to the circumstances in which a person is to be treated as being or not being in Great Britain.

Households

1.283   **12.**—Regulations may make provision for the purposes of this Act as to the circumstances in which persons are to be treated as being or not being members of the same household.

Responsibility for another person

1.284   **13.**—Regulations may make provision for the purposes of this Act as to the circumstances in which one person is to be treated as responsible or not responsible for another.

Relevant education

1.285   **14.**—Regulations may make provision for the purposes of this Act—

(a) as to what is or is not to be treated as relevant education; and
(b) as to the circumstances in which a person is or is not to be treated as receiving relevant education.

[¹⁰**14AA.**—For any purpose of this Act regulations may provide for—

(a) circumstances in which a person is to be treated as having or not having a good reason for an act or omission;
(b) matters which are or are not to be taken into account in determining whether a person has a good reason for an act or omission.]

Calculation of periods

1.286   **15.**—Regulations may make provision for calculating periods for any purpose of this Act.

Employment on ships etc.

16.—(1) Regulations may modify any provision of this Act in its application to any person   **1.287**
who is, has been, or is to be—
    (a) employed on board any ship, vessel, hovercraft or aircraft,
    (b) outside Great Britain at any prescribed time or in any prescribed circumstances, or
    (c) in prescribed employment in connection with continental shelf operations,
so far as that provision relates to a contribution-based jobseeker's allowance.
    (2) The regulations may in particular provide—
    (a) for any such provision to apply even though it would not otherwise apply;
    (b) for any such provision not to apply even though it would otherwise apply;
    (c) for the taking of evidence, in a country or territory outside Great Britain, by a British
        consular official or other prescribed person;
    (d) for enabling payment of the whole, or any part of a contribution-based jobseeker's
        allowance to be paid to such of the claimant's dependants as may be prescribed.

Additional conditions

17.—Regulations may require additional conditions to be satisfied with respect to the   **1.288**
payment of a jobseeker's allowance to any person who is, has been, or is to be, in employment
which falls within a prescribed description.

Benefits Act purposes

18.—Regulations may provide for—   **1.289**
    (a) a jobseeker's allowance;
    (b) a contribution-based jobseeker's allowance; or
    (c) an income-based jobseeker's allowance,
to be treated, for prescribed purposes of the Benefits Act, as a benefit, or a benefit of a prescribed description.

[[7] Treatment of information supplied as information relating to social security

19.—Information supplied in pursuance of any provision made by or under this Act [[11] . . .]   **1.290**
shall be taken for all purposes to be information relating to social security.]

AMENDMENTS

    1. Employment Rights Act 1996 Sch.1 para.67(3) (August 22, 1996).
    2. Social Security Act 1998 Sch.7 para.146 (October 18, 1999).
    3. Welfare Reform and Pensions Act 1999 Sch.8 para.29(7) (October 18, 1999).
    4. Welfare Reform and Pensions Act 1999 Sch.7 para.16 (March 19, 2001).
    5. Civil Partnership Act 2004 s.254 and Sch.24 Pt 7 para.125 (December 5, 2005).
    6. Welfare Reform Act 2007 s.28(1) and Sch.3 para.12(6) (October 27, 2008).
    7. Welfare Reform Act 2009 s.34(3) and Sch.3 Pt 1 para.3(4) (January 12, 2010).
    8. Welfare Reform Act 2009 s.29(1) (January 19, 2012).
    9. Welfare Reform Act 2012 Sch.7 para.10(1), (3) (October 22, 2012).
    10. Welfare Reform Act 2012 s.46(3)(b) (June 10, 2012).
    11. Welfare Reform Act 2012 s.147 and Sch.14 Pt 6 (May 8, 2012).
    12. Universal Credit (Consequential, Supplementary, Incidental and Miscellaneous
Provisions) Regulations 2013 (SI 2013/630) reg.10 (April 29, 2013).

DEFINITIONS

    "a joint-claim couple"—see s.1(4).
    "a joint-claim jobseeker's allowance"—*ibid.*
    "a transitional case couple"—see para.8A(3).
    "the Benefits Act"—see s.35(1).
    "contribution-based jobseeker's allowance"—see ss.35(1) and 1(4).
    "couple"—see s.35(1).
    "employment"—*ibid.*
    "employment protection sum"—see para.6(2).
    "ex-members"—see paras 9A(1) and 9B(1).

"Great Britain"—see s.35(1).
"income-based jobseeker's allowance"—see ss.35(1) and 1(4).
"jobseeker's agreement"—see ss.35(1) and 9(1).
"jobseeking period"—see s.35(1) and JSA Regulations 1996 reg.47.
"pension payments"—see s.35(1).
"PPF payment"—*ibid.*
"prescribed"—*ibid.*
"regulations"—*ibid.*
"week"—*ibid.*

GENERAL NOTE

Paragraph 1

1.291   Where a claimant is engaged in remunerative work, there can be no entitlement to old style JSA (s.1(2)(e)). If only a partner is so engaged, the claimant cannot be entitled to IBJSA (s.3(1)(c) and see ss.1(2)(e) and (2B)(b) for a joint-claim couple). This provision enables regulations to define "remunerative work" (in fact setting a threshold of 16 hours for the claimant and 24 hours for a partner). Those regulations can also define situations in which, despite not being so engaged, a person is to be treated as if engaged in remunerative work and, conversely, to prescribe situations in which someone who would on the usual rules be regarded as being in remunerative work is to be treated as if he were not. See further JSA Regulations 1996 regs 51–53.

Paragraph 2

1.292   To be entitled to old style JSA, a claimant must not have limited capability for work (s.1(2)(f)). This provision ensures that the assessment of capacity for work is to be determined in accordance with the rules for ESA or universal credit.

Paragraph 3

1.293   This makes provision that benefits those whose unemployment is intermittent, interspersed with, say, periods of employment, of incapacity for work, of training for work or periods when pregnant, by providing, somewhat after the fashion of UB and its notion of "period of interruption of employment" ("PIE"), for the concepts of "linking" and "linked periods" whereby apparently separate jobseeking periods are fused into one and certain periods ("linked periods") do not "break" a jobseeking period.

"Linking", and through it the creation of a single jobseeking period, is important for the purposes of IBJSA only because the "waiting days" (see para.4 below) only have to be served once in any jobseeking period. The concept also had importance for the purposes of CBJSA in determining the relevant benefit year when identifying the last two complete contribution years in which the contribution conditions had to be satisfied. Those conditions no longer need to be explored here, but "linking" still needs some unpacking.

A "jobseeking period" is basically any period throughout which the claimant satisfies (or is treated as satisfying) the conditions of entitlement to old style JSA set out in s.1(2)(a)–(c) and (e)–(i): available for employment; a current jobseeker's agreement; actively seeking employment; not in remunerative work; not receiving relevant education; under pensionable age; and in Great Britain (s.35(1); JSA Regulations 1996 reg.47(1)). Where a hardship payment under Pt IX of those Regulations is paid to a claimant who does not satisfy a labour market condition (any of the conditions in s.1(2)(a)–(c): availability; actively seeking; jobseeker's agreement), he is to be treated as satisfying them for purposes of applying the above definition of jobseeking period (JSA Regulations 1996 reg.47(2)). He was also treated as satisfying the conditions in s.1(2)(a)–(c) and (e)–(i) when entitled to JSA under reg.13(3) of the JSA (Transitional) Regulations (JSA Regulations 1996 reg.47(2A)). Certain periods cannot constitute, or be part of, a jobseeking period: (i) any period in which no claim for JSA has been made or treated as made; (ii) any period before the day on which a claim is made or before the earliest date in which good cause for a late claim is shown; (iii) a period caught by the 12-month limit on backdating entitlement under s.1(2) of the SSAA 1992; (iv) a period of disentitlement under JSA Regulations 1996 regs 25 and 26; and (v) any week of disentitlement because the claimant is caught by the trade dispute rule in s.14 (JSA Regulations 1996 reg.47(3)). Note also JSA Regulations 1996 reg.47A on periods of interruption of employment prior to October 7, 1996.

"Linked periods" comprise: (i) any period throughout which the claimant is, or is treated as, incapable of work under Pt XIIA of the SSCBA 1992; (ii) any period of limited capability for work for the purposes of employment and support allowance; (iii) any period throughout which she was entitled to a maternity allowance under s.35 of that Act; (iv) any period throughout which the claimant was engaged in training for which a training allowance is payable; (v) (but only for contributions conditions purposes) any period throughout which the claimant was entitled to a carer's allowance under s.70 of the SSCBA 1992; (vi) a period of attending court in response to a jury summons, which period includes October 6, 1996 and was immediately preceded by a period of entitlement to unemployment benefit; (vii) certain periods of participation in the Self-employed Employment Option, the Voluntary Sector Option or the Environment Task Force Option of the New Deal and various Intensive Activity Period Programmes; and (viii) certain periods of participation in an employment zone programme (JSA Regulations 1996 reg.48(2), (3)).

Two or more jobseeking periods "link" and are treated as one jobseeking period where they are separated by a period comprising only: (i) one of 12 weeks; (ii) a linked period; (iii) a period of not more than 12 weeks falling between any two linked periods or between a jobseeking period and a linked period; and (iv) any period in respect of which the claimant is summoned for jury service and is required to attend court (JSA Regulations 1996 reg.48(1)).

Paragraph 4

UB was a daily benefit payable in respect of a six-day week. Old style JSA is a weekly benefit. Nonetheless, through this provision, as amplified by JSA Regulations 1996 reg.46(2), it deploys the concept of "waiting days", familiar from UB but never part of income support, whereby, despite meeting the other conditions of entitlement to JSA, there is no entitlement to it for a number of days (initially three but extended to seven from October 27, 2014) at the start of a jobseeking period. On "jobseeking period" and the effect of "linking", see notes to para.3, above. Note further that the "waiting days" rule does not apply where the claimant's entitlement to JSA begins within 12 weeks of the ending of an entitlement to income support, incapacity benefit, employment and support allowance or carer's allowance, nor where the claim for IBJSA has to be determined by reference to s.3(1)(f)(ii), (i.e. the person is 16 or 17, registered for training but is not being provided with any, severe hardship will result to him if JSA is not paid, and the Secretary of State directs that s.16 is to apply to him) (JSA Regulations 1996 reg.46(1)).

Paragraph 5

Although old style JSA is a weekly rather than a daily benefit, provision is made through regulations made under this paragraph for entitlement to JSA and the amount payable in respect of a period less than a week. See JSA Regulations 1996 regs 150–155 on IBJSA.

Paragraph 6

This paragraph is not relevant to IBJSA.

1.294

1.295

1.296

1.297

Paragraph 7

1.298   This enables regulations to deal with the listed aspects of taking into account pension payments.

Paragraphs 8, 8A, and 9

1.299   These enable regulations to allow access to reduced rates of income-based JSA for "persons in hardship", both in respect of standard cases and those of joint-claim couples, without having to meet the "labour market" conditions (availability; actively seeking; jobseeker's agreement). See further, JSA Regulations 1996 regs 140–146 (standard cases) and regs 146A–146H (joint-claim couples). In addition, para.8A enables the making of regulations for a "transitional case couple" to be entitled to a joint-claim jobseeker's allowance for a period without having made a claim for it. A "transitional case couple" is a "joint-claim couple" where one member was entitled to income-based JSA when the joint claim changes came into effect (March 19, 2001). JSA Regulations 1996 reg.3F was the product of the exercise of this rule-making power.

Paragraph 8B

1.300   This requires the Secretary of State to make regulations under ss.6(4), 7(4) and 9(10) of the Act providing for victims of domestic violence who are claiming a jobseeker's allowance to be treated as available for and actively seeking work for a set 13-week period, and if the claimant has not completed a jobseeker's agreement before the 13-week period begins, to be treated as having entered into a jobseeker's agreement which is in force for the 13-week period. Paragraph 8B enables the regulations to specify the circumstances in which domestic violence must have been inflicted or threatened in order for the exemption to apply, to prescribe the circumstances in which domestic violence is, or is not, to be regarded as having been inflicted or threatened and to define "domestic violence". See reg.14A of the JSA Regulations 1996 inserted with effect from April 23, 2012 and amended, with a new definition of "domestic violence", from October 29, 2013.

Paragraphs 9A–9D

1.301   These rule-making powers deal with matters of continuity where a couple cease to be a joint-claim couple (e.g. because of the birth of a child) (a "replacement award") (para.9A), where a couple again become a joint-claim couple (e.g. because of the death of a child) (para.9B) and where two people newly become one (e.g. because a child has become 16 and left education) (para.9C) (in both cases a "new award"). See further JSA Regulations 1996 regs 3B (ceasing to be a joint-claim couple), 3C (a couple again or newly becoming a joint-claim couple).

Paragraph 10

1.302   This enables regulations to allow access to reduced rate payments of IBJSA for a "person in hardship" before the claim or the joint-claim for JSA has been determined and where payment of JSA has been suspended by virtue of regulations under s.5(1)(n) or (nn) of the SSAA 1992. See further JSA Regulations 1996 regs 140–146 (standard cases) and 146A–146H (joint-claim couples).

Paragraph 11

1.303   Generally, to be entitled to old style JSA, a claimant must be in Great Britain (s.1(2) (i)). Sub-paragraph (1) enables regulations to be made prescribing circumstances in which someone not in Great Britain can nevertheless be entitled to CBJSA. See JSA Regulations 1996 regs 165 and 166. The former effected amendments to reg.11 of the Persons Abroad Regulations (see below). The latter amended the Social Security (Mariners' Benefits) Regulations 1975, which are not reproduced in this book.

Sub-paragraph (2) enables the making of regulations treating a person as being, or as not being, in Great Britain. See JSA Regulations 1996 reg.50, which in the circumstances there set out treats someone temporarily absent from Great Britain as if they were present in Great Britain, thus enabling them to remain eligible for old style JSA while temporarily absent.

Paragraph 12

This enables the making of regulations to set out when persons are or are not to be regarded for JSA purposes as members of the same household. See reg.78 of the JSA Regulations 1996.

1.304

Paragraph 13

This enables the making of regulations setting out when someone is to be treated as responsible for a child or young person. See reg.77 of the JSA Regulations 1996.

1.305

Paragraph 14

A person cannot be entitled to old style JSA if receiving relevant education (s.1(2) (g)). This paragraph enables regulations to provide for what does and does not constitute relevant education and for when someone is, or is not, to be treated as receiving it. See further JSA Regulations 1996 reg.54, which defines it to cover only full-time education, not being a course of advanced education, which is undertaken by a child or young person. Someone treated as a child for child benefit purposes or who is receiving full-time education as far as the child benefit system is concerned (see SSCBA 1992 s.142), is treated as receiving full-time education for purposes of jobseeker's allowance (JSA Regulations 1996 reg.54(2)). As this exclusion covers persons under 19, the effect of the contribution conditions (the claimant's insurance record) is to make this in practice a hurdle much more relevant to IBJSA than to CBJSA. Those on a full-time course of advanced education, it should be noted, will be excluded from JSA because treated as not available for employment (see s.6 and JSA Regulations 1996 regs 1(3) and 15(a)).

1.306

Paragraph 14AA

In many areas of old style JSA involving sanctions "good cause" or "just cause" has been replaced by "good reason". This paragraph enables the making of regulations setting out, for any purposes of the Jobseekers Act 1995, circumstances in which someone is or is not to be treated as having a "good reason" for any act or omission. It also enables regulations to stipulate matters which are or are not to be taken into account in determining whether someone has a "good reason" for an act or omission. See reg.72 of the JSA Regulations 1996, in relation only to ss.19(2)(c) and (d) and 19A(2)(c).

1.307

Paragraph 16

This paragraph is not relevant to IBJSA.

1.308

Paragraph 17

This enables regulations to require additional conditions to be satisfied with respect to payment of old style JSA to those in, or who have been in, or who are to be in, employment of a prescribed description. See further JSA Regulations 1996 Pt XII (not reproduced in this work), dealing with share fishermen and persons outside Great Britain, including mariners.

1.309

Children (Leaving Care) Act 2000

(2000 c.35)

SECTIONS REPRODUCED

GENERAL NOTE

1.311   The Children (Leaving Care) Act 2000, which came into effect on October 1, 2001, placed new duties on local authorities in connection with the provision of support and assistance to those who are leaving local authority care (i.e. whom the local authority is ceasing to "look after"). The Act replaced the arrangements previously contained in s.24 of the Children Act 1989. Its provisions were amplified in the Children (Leaving Care) (England) Regulations 2001 (SI 2001/2874) and the Children (Leaving Care) (Wales) Regulations 2001 (SI 2001/2189), both of which also came into force on October 1, 2001.

However, the Children (Leaving Care) (England) Regulations were revoked and partly replaced with effect from April 1, 2011 by the Care Leavers (England) Regulations 2010 (SI 2010/2571). These regulations replace the provisions in the 2001 Regulations relating to relevant children (see below). Provisions relating to eligible children (see below) are now in the Care Planning, Placement and Case Review (England) Regulations 2010 (SI 2010/959) which also came into force on April 1, 2011. See pp.760–762 for the relevant provisions of both these sets of Regulations.

In addition, the Children (Leaving Care) (Wales) Regulations 2001 (SI 2001/2189) were revoked and partly replaced with effect from April 6, 2016 by the Care Leavers (Wales) Regulations 2015 (SI 2015/1820). These Regulations replace the provisions in the 2001 Regulations relating to relevant children who are now referred to as "category 2 young persons". Provisions relating to "category 1 young persons" (previously referred to as eligible children) are now in the Care, Planning, Placement and Case Review (Wales) Regulations 2015 (SI 2015/1818) which also came into force on April 6, 2016. See pp.762–764 for the relevant provisions of both these sets of Regulations.

1.312   The Act does not apply to Scotland, with the exception of s.6. It was originally intended that equivalent legislation would be introduced in Scotland in 2002. However, a decision was taken to delay the implementation of the changes in Scotland and the relevant provisions (see the Support and Assistance of Young People Leaving Care (Scotland) Regulations 2003 (SSI 2003/608)) only came into force on April 1, 2004.

The effect of s.6 of the Act is to exclude an "eligible child" (defined in para.19B of Sch.2 to the Children Act 1989, inserted by s.1) or a "relevant child" (defined in s.23A of the 1989 Act, inserted by s.2) from entitlement to income-based JSA, income support and housing benefit. From April 6, 2016, this exclusion also applies to a "category 1 young person" within the meaning of s.104(2) of the Social Services and Well-being (Wales) Act 2014 or a "category 2 young person" within the meaning of s.104(2). Section 6(3) allows regulations to provide for exceptions to this rule: see the Children (Leaving Care) Social Security Benefits Regulations 2001 (SI 2001/3074) (p.764). In addition regulations under s.6(4) can extend the exclusion from these benefits to children who have been looked after by a local authority in Scotland. Such regulations have been made and came into force on April 1, 2004 (see the Children (Leaving Care) Social Security Benefits (Scotland) Regulations 2004 (SI 2004/747)) (p.768).

Note that s.6(1) has not been amended following the introduction of ESA on October 27, 2008 so as to exclude entitlement to income-related ESA. This would appear to be an oversight as a purported amendment to reg.2(1) of the Children (Leaving Care) Social Security Benefits Regulations 2001 has been made to include a reference to income-related ESA. However, in view of the fact that s.6 has not been amended to exclude an "eligible child" or a "relevant child" from entitlement to ESA, such an amendment to the 2001 Regulations is not necessary (and is ultra vires).

For a discussion of s.6 and of the relevant definitions, see the note to reg.2 of the Children (Leaving Care) Social Security Benefits Regulations 2001 (p.765). See also the note to reg.2 of the Children (Leaving Care) Social Security Benefits (Scotland) Regulations 2004 (p.770).

Further duties of local authorities towards children whom they are looking after

1.—In Part II of Schedule 2 to the Children Act 1989 ("the 1989 Act"), which contains provision as to children being looked after by local authorities, after paragraph 19 insert—   1.313

"*Preparation for ceasing to be looked after*
19A.—*[Omitted.]*
19B.—(1) A local authority shall have the following additional functions in relation to an eligible child whom they are looking after.
(2) In sub-paragraph (1) "eligible child" means, subject to subparagraph (3), a child, who—

(a) is aged sixteen or seventeen; and
(b) has been looked after by a local authority [² or by a local authority in Wales] for a prescribed period, or periods amounting in all to a prescribed period, which began after he reached a prescribed age and ended after he reached the age of sixteen.

(3) The [¹ [² Secretary of State]] may prescribe—

(a) additional categories of eligible children; and
(b) categories of children who are not to be eligible children despite falling within sub-paragraph (2).

(4)–(8) *[Omitted.]*
19C.—*[Omitted.]*."

AMENDMENTS

1. Children and Young Persons Act 2008 Sch.3 para.27(3) (November 13, 2008).
2. Social Services and Well-being (Wales) Act 2014 (Consequential Amendments) Regulations 2016 (SI 2016/413) reg.115 (April 6, 2016).

Additional functions of local authorities in respect of certain children

2.—(1) The 1989 Act is amended as follows.   1.314
(2) *[Omitted.]*
(3) In the heading before section 24, at the end insert "and young persons".
(4) After that heading insert the following new sections—

"The responsible authority and relevant children.

1.315 **23A.**—(1) The responsible local authority shall have the functions set out in section 23B in respect of a relevant child.

(2) In subsection (1) 'relevant child' means (subject to subsection (3)) a child who—

(a) is not being looked after [² by any local authority in England or by any local authority in Wales];

(b) was, before last ceasing to be looked after, an eligible child for the purposes of paragraph 19B of Schedule 2; and

(c) is aged sixteen or seventeen.

(3) The [¹ [² Secretary of State]] may prescribe—

(a) additional categories of relevant children; and

(b) categories of children who are not to be relevant children despite falling within subsection (2).

(4)–(5) *[Omitted.]*
23B.—*[Omitted.]*
23C.—*[Omitted.]*"

AMENDMENTS

1. Children and Young Persons Act 2008 Sch.3 para.8(2) (November 13, 2008).
2. Social Services and Well-being (Wales) Act 2014 (Consequential Amendments) Regulations 2016 (SI 2016/413) reg.74 (April 6, 2016).

Exclusion from benefits

1.316 **6.**—(1) No person is entitled to income-based jobseeker's allowance under the Jobseekers Act 1995, or to income support or housing benefit under the Social Security Contributions and Benefits Act 1992, while he is a person to whom this section applies.

(2) Subject to subsection (3), this section applies to—

(a) an eligible child for the purposes of paragraph 19B of Schedule 2 to the Children Act 1989;

(b) a relevant child for the purposes of section 23A of that Act; and

[¹ (ba) a category 1 young person within the meaning of section 104 of the Social Services and Well-being (Wales) Act 2014;

(bb) a category 2 young person within the meaning of section 104 of the Social Services and Well-being (Wales) Act 2014;]

(c) any person of a description prescribed in regulations under subsection (4).

(3) The Secretary of State may by regulations provide that this section does not apply to a person who falls within subsection (2)(a) or (b) but who also falls within such category or description, or satisfies such conditions, as may be prescribed in the regulations.

(4) The Secretary of State may make regulations prescribing descriptions of persons who do not fall within subsection (2)(a) or (b) but who—

(a) have been looked after by a local authority in Scotland (within the meaning of section 17(6) of the Children (Scotland) Act 1995); and

(b) otherwise correspond (whether or not exactly) to eligible or relevant children.

(5) The Secretary of State may in regulations make such transitional, consequential and saving provision as he considers necessary or expedient in connection with the coming into force of this section.

(6) Section 175(3) to (5) of the Social Security Contributions and Benefits Act 1992 (supplemental power in relation to regulations) applies to regulations made under this section as it applies to regulations made under that Act.

(7) Powers to make regulations under this section include power to make different provision for different areas.

(8) Powers to make regulations under this section are exercisable by statutory instrument.

(9) No statutory instrument containing regulations under subsection (4) is to be made unless a draft of the instrument has been laid before Parliament and approved by a resolution of each House of Parliament.

(10) A statutory instrument containing regulations under subsection (3) or (5) shall be subject to annulment in pursuance of a resolution of either House of Parliament.

AMENDMENT

1. Social Services and Well-being (Wales) Act 2014 (Consequential Amendments) Regulations 2016 (SI 2016/413) reg.178 (April 6, 2016).

GENERAL NOTE

Section 104(2) of the Social Services and Well-being (Wales) Act 2014 provides that a category 1 young person is a child who (a) is aged 16 or 17; (b) is being looked after by a local authority; and (c) has been looked after by a local authority or a local authority in England for a specified period, or periods amounting in all to a specified period, which began after the child reached a specified age and ended after the child reached the age of 16. This definition replicates the definition of an "eligible child" in para.19B(2) of Sch.2 to the Children Act 1989). A category 2 young person is a child who (a) is aged 16 or 17; (b) is not being looked after by a local authority or a local authority in England; and (c) immediately before ceasing to be looked after was a category 1 young person. This definition replicates the definition of a "relevant child" in s.23A(2) of the 1989 Act.

1.317

Welfare Reform Act 2007

(2007 C.5)

ARRANGEMENT OF SECTIONS

PART 1

EMPLOYMENT AND SUPPORT ALLOWANCE

Entitlement

1.318

SCHEDULES

An Act to make provision about social security; to amend the Vaccine Damage Payments Act 1979; and for connected purposes.

[3rd May 2007]

PART 1

EMPLOYMENT AND SUPPORT ALLOWANCE

Entitlement

Employment and support allowance

1.—(1) An allowance, to be known as an employment and support allowance, shall be payable in accordance with the provisions of this Part.   1.319

(2) Subject to the provisions of this Part, a claimant is entitled to an employment and support allowance if he satisfies the basic conditions and either—

    (a) the first and the second conditions set out in Part 1 of Schedule 1 (conditions relating to national insurance) or the third condition set out in that Part of that Schedule (condition relating to youth), or

    (b) the conditions set out in Part 2 of that Schedule (conditions relating to financial position).

(3) The basic conditions are that the claimant—

    (a) has limited capability for work,

[⁴ (aa) has accepted a claimant commitment]

    (b) is at least 16 years old,

    (c) has not reached pensionable age,

    (d) is in Great Britain,

    (e) is not entitled to income support, and

    (f) is not entitled to a jobseeker's allowance (and is not a member of a couple who are entitled to a joint-claim jobseeker's allowance).

[¹(3A) After the coming into force of this subsection no claim may be made for an employment and support allowance by virtue of the third condition set out in Part 1 of Schedule 1 (youth).]

(4) For the purposes of this Part, a person has limited capability for work if—

153

(a) his capability for work is limited by his physical or mental condition, and

(b) the limitation is such that it is not reasonable to require him to work.

(5) An employment and support allowance is payable in respect of a week.

(6) In subsection (3)—

"joint-claim jobseeker's allowance" means a jobseeker's allowance entitlement to which arises by virtue of section 1(2B) of the Jobseekers Act 1995 (c. 18);

"pensionable age" has the meaning given by the rules in paragraph 1 of Schedule 4 to the Pensions Act 1995 (c. 26).

[³(6A) In subsection (3)(f), in relation to a contributory allowance, the reference to a couple entitled to a joint-claim jobseeker's allowance does not include a couple so entitled by virtue of regulations under paragraph 8A of Schedule 1 to the Jobseekers Act 1995.]

(7) In this Part—

"contributory allowance" means an employment and support allowance entitlement to which is based on subsection (2)(a) [² (and see section 1B(2))];

"income-related allowance" means an employment and support allowance entitlement to which is based on subsection (2)(b).]

AMENDMENTS

1. Welfare Reform Act 2012 s.53 (May 1, 2012).
2. Welfare Reform Act 2012 s.52(2) (May 1, 2012).
3. Welfare Reform Act 2012 s.50(1) (May 8, 2012).
4. Welfare Reform Act 2012 s.54(2) (April 29, 2013 and various dates).

MODIFICATIONS

Section 1(2) is modified by Sch.1 para.2 of the Employment and Support Allowance (Transitional Provisions, Housing Benefit and Council Tax Benefit) (Existing Awards) (No.2) Regulations 2010 (SI 2010/1907) (as amended) for the purposes specified in reg.6(1).

Section 1(2) is modified by Sch.2 para.2(a) of the Employment and Support Allowance (Transitional Provisions, Housing Benefit and Council Tax Benefit) (Existing Awards) (No. 2) Regulations 2010 (SI 2010/1907) (as amended) for the purposes specified in reg.16(1).

Section 1(7) is modified by Sch.2 para.2(b) of the Employment and Support Allowance (Transitional Provisions, Housing Benefit and Council Tax Benefit) (Existing Awards) (No.2) Regulations 2010 (SI 2010/1907) (as amended) for the purposes specified in reg.16(1).

For details of the modifications, see the text of those Regulations, below.

DEFINITIONS

"contributory allowance"—see subs.(7).
"income-related allowance"—see subs.(7).
"joint-claim jobseeker's allowance"—see subs.(6).
"pensionable age"—see subs.(6).

GENERAL NOTE

Subsection (1)

1.320 This establishes Employment and Support Allowance (ESA), which is payable in accordance with the terms set out in the remainder of Part I of the Act, a framework clothed with the detail afforded by several sets of regulations:

154

- *Employment and Support Allowance Regulations 2008 (SI 2008/794) (ESA Regulations) (as amended)*
  Like the JSA and IS Regs which in many respects they emulate, these set out the key detailed rules on ESA.

- *Employment and Support Allowance (Transitional Provisions) Regulations 2008 (SI 2008/795) (as amended)*
  These deal with the transition to ESA (key rules for "existing customers" of the IB/IS/SDA incapacity benefits' regime).

- *Employment and Support Allowance (Consequential Provisions) Regulations 2008 (SI 2008/1082)*
  These effect amendments to Housing and Council Tax benefits and are not reproduced.

- *Employment and Support Allowance (Consequential Provisions) (No. 2) Regulations 2008 (SI 2008/1554)*
  These effect a variety of changes to legislation covered in *Social Security Legislation*.

- *Employment and Support Allowance (Consequential Provisions) (No. 3) Regulations 2008 (SI 2008/1879)*
  These effect a variety of changes to tax credits and child benefit.

A brief overview of ESA and its purpose may be useful to place the detailed rules and commentary in context.

State support towards the income replacement needs of those incapable of work has been the province of incapacity benefit (IB), income support (IS), or a mixture of both, since the non-contributory incapacity benefit, Severe Disablement Allowance (SDA), was closed to new claimants from April 6, 2001. From October 27, 2008 (the "appointed day", "commencement") both were closed to new claimants who claimed benefit on the basis of a health condition or disability which so affects their ability to work that it is not reasonable to expect them to do so. From then, any such claim was treated as one for Employment and Support Allowance (ESA), claimed to be less complex and easier to claim. "Existing customers" (those already in receipt of those benefits, or whose claim for a new spell of incapacity links back to a period of incapacity for work prior to commencement) were able to retain entitlement to them after the appointed day, but lost it once the relevant period of incapacity for work came to an end without linking to another which started prior to commencement. All new claimants (and those "existing customers" unable to link in that way) had to look for income replacement to the new ESA. Thus yet another client group has been removed from IS, leaving it very much as a residual benefit, ultimately to be abolished and replaced by universal credit. Indeed, now that universal credit has been rolled out nationwide, in most cases it is no longer possible to get income-related ESA on a new claim.

Like old style JSA, old style ESA is a single benefit with two forms: contributory ESA (CESA) and income-related ESA (IRESA). A claimant may be entitled to one or the other or, in some cases, both. See further *LH v SSWP (ESA)* [2014] UKUT 480 (AAC); [2015] AACR 14, where Judge Rowland confirmed that employment and support allowance is a single benefit with two routes to qualification and that it is not necessary to make separate claims for each of the contributory allowance and the income-related allowance (para. 12); see also *DS v SSWP* [2018] UKUT 270 (AAC). On the standard claim form a claimant has the opportunity to indicate which of the types s/he seeks (both types or one or the other), something which has advantages both for the claimant (no need to disclose details of financial position if seeking only CESA) and for the Secretary of State (no need to check contribution records where someone seeks only IRESA). However, as Judge Rowland stated

> "despite the language usually used, an indication that one or other of the allowances is not "claimed" amounts to a waiver of the need for the Secretary of State

1.320.1

to consider entitlement to that element of employment and support allowance, rather than amounting to a true failure to claim it. The legislation does not actually contemplate there being a claim for only one element of the allowance" (para.13).

Where someone has initially sought only one form and later wishes to seek the other form as well, the matter should be raised not through a new claim but through an application for supersession under SSA 1998 s.10 or through revision under SSA 1998 s.9 or a subsequent appeal under SSA 1998 s.12 (para.15).

ESA, payable in respect of a week, is a benefit to provide support to those clearly unable to work, through a "support component" paid in addition to their basic allowance, and to require those capable of work-related activity to engage in it in return (at least for claims made before April 3, 2017) for a "work-related activity component" on top of their basic allowance, the hope being that they will eventually return to the labour force. ESA is a benefit with similarities to JSA, but initially had no time limit on either its contributory or income related forms, save that entitlement ceased on reaching pensionable age (s.1(3)(c)).

1.321   The conditions of entitlement common to the basic allowance aspect of both forms of ESA are that the claimant is at least 16; has not reached pensionable age; is in Great Britain; is not entitled to IS; is not entitled to JSA in his own right or as part of a joint-claim couple; and has limited capability for work (see subs.(3)). The matter of capacity is either assessed by a work-related capability assessment (a functional test similar to the IB personal capability assessment or all work test), involving a medical examination, or, is deemed to exist for a much reduced set of "exempt" groups. Generally, three "waiting days" of non-entitlement have to be served (s.22, Sch.2 para.4; ESA Regs reg.144). During the (generally 13-week) assessment period, only basic allowance ESA is payable. Additional components (support or work-related activity) depend on the claimant being assessed or treated as having limited capability for work/work-related activity respectively (albeit not for (broadly speaking) new claims made on or after April 3, 2017). The personal allowance aspect of ESA basic allowance (a lower rate for those under 25) is based on the personal allowances in JSA (single person, lone parent or couple), but those able to qualify for IRESA can also access applicable premiums. After the assessment period ends (when the claimant has been assessed or treated as having limited capacity for work), claimants become eligible for one (but not both) of two additional components: the *support* component; or the *work-related activity* component. However, the work-related activity component is not payable on (broadly speaking) new claims made on or after April 3, 2017. To be eligible for the *support* component, claimants must have limited capability for work-related activity (capacity for that must be limited by their physical or mental condition to such an extent that it is not reasonable to require them to undertake such activity). If they do not have limited capacity for work-related activity (i.e. capability for work-related activity is not limited by physical or mental condition or, if it is, the limitations are not such as to render it unreasonable to undertake such activity), they will be eligible for the work-related activity component on top of the basic allowance (at least for claims made before April 3, 2017), provided they meet prescribed conditions on work-related activity. Should they not do so, they can be sanctioned by progressive reduction (ultimately removal) of the amount of that component to which they would otherwise be entitled.

As with IB/IS, claimants entitled to ESA can be disqualified from it where their conduct conduces to their incapacity (e.g. because of misconduct in bringing it about or in refusing treatment which would alleviate it) or their failure to adhere to prescribed rules of behaviour (s.18; ESA Regs regs 157, 159). "Persons in hardship" cannot be disqualified but receive a reduced rate of personal allowance (ESA Regs reg.158, Sch.5, para.14). Absences from Great Britain (other than certain temporary absences) preclude entitlement to ESA (s.18(4), Sch.2 paras 5, 6, 8; ESA Regs regs 151–155).

ESA is part of a broader governmental strategy to assist people with a health condition or disability. Government is convinced that benefit dependency, particularly strong in respect of benefits for incapacity, is a major element in hardship and deprivation, and that work is the route out of poverty. The measures set out in its 2006 Green Paper (Cm 6730) were intended to increase the numbers who are able to remain in work when they fall sick or become disabled; to raise the numbers moving from benefits into employment; and better to meet the needs of those requiring extra help and support because of a health condition. Unlike IB (rather caricatured by a Government determined like its predecessors to reduce the cost to the public purse of supporting the once favourably-treated group—those incapable of work), ESA does not automatically assume incapacity for work merely because someone has a significant health condition or disability. It was built on experience with the pilots of the Pathways to Work project which was rolled out nationally in April 2008. It was claimed that this initiative had significantly increased the IB claimants being helped into work, and that "these pilots have demonstrated that, with the right help and support, many people on incapacity benefits can move back into work, reinforcing the view that labelling people on incapacity benefits as 'incapable of work' is wrong and damaging". Government considered that no lesser approach than ESA would provide the necessary cultural shift, from a benefits package based on "incapacity for work" to one founded firmly on what a person can do.

Government expected that ESA would have a significant and wide-ranging positive impact on disabled people and people with health conditions who were out of work. ESA was a benefit designed to help these people overcome barriers, and where appropriate move into work and improve their lives. The Work Capability Assessment (WCA) sought to relate more accurately to modern context than the 12-year-old IB/IS system, and to focus more on what people can do, rather on what they are unable to do. The conditionality regime for those with limited capability for work sought to engage customers placed in the work-related activity group. It afforded them access to employment and condition management programmes. But ESA recognises the needs of those in the Support Group; their entitlement to the support component is not conditional on work-related activity but they can engage, if they wish, with those programmes. ESA seeks better to reflect the aspirations of disabled people, and improve the "customer experience" of individuals on the benefit.

1.322

ESA in outline was broadly welcomed as to its purpose of, and potential for, helping disabled people fulfil their aspiration to work, by spokespersons across all parties, and as a potential route out of poverty by groups representing the disabled. But concerns (becoming stronger as more detail emerged) were nonetheless expressed about a range of aspects: conditionality (sanctions welcomed and seen as vital by some to "persuade" the reluctant to engage with help and knowledge, seen as problematic or unnecessary by others); the impact on persons with a variety of conditions (mental health problems, cancer sufferers, Asperger's syndrome), particularly fluctuating ones, and on the terminally ill; which groups would be exempt from the WCA; what would be the categories of permitted work so vital to building confidence that someone could return to work; the nature of the law-making process leaving too much to secondary legislation or ministerial fiat; adding to the complexity of the benefits system with a supposed single benefit involving six rates; the nature and interrelationship of two capability assessments with different criteria; and, crucially, the other side of the coin—the provisions deal with the attitude of the disabled to work but leave untouched the attitude of employers to the disabled would-be worker.

Note that for the purpose of making "conversion decisions" under the "Migration Regulations" from November 1, 2010, subs.(2) is to be read as if there were substituted the text set out in Sch.1 para.2 of those Regulations: see the Employment and Support Allowance (Transitional Provisions, Housing Benefit and Council Tax Benefit) (Existing Awards) (No. 2) Regulations 2010 (SI 2010/1907). After a conversion decision has been made, subs.(2) is to be read as modified by reg.16(1) and Sch.2 para.(2)(a) to those Regulations.

From October 1, 2010, after a conversion decision has been made under the

"Migration Regulations", subs.(7) is to read as if there were substituted the text contained in Sch.2 para.(2)(b) to those Regulations.

Since ESA was introduced in October 2008, there have been a series of amendments to the secondary legislation governing the descriptors that apply for the purposes of the WCA. These changes are discussed below in the commentary to Sch.2 and Sch.3 to the Employment and Support Allowance Regulations 2008 (SI 2008/794). There have also been two major changes since the 2007 Act to the framework in the primary legislation. The first has been the gradual introduction of universal credit under the Welfare Reform Act 2012, which increasingly is replacing income-related ESA in affected areas. The second has been the abolition of the work-related activity component in ESA for (broadly speaking) claims made on or after April 3, 2017.

The National Audit Office report *Investigation into errors in Employment and Support Allowance* (March 2018) examined DWP errors in converting people's existing IB claims into ESA awards where claimants were only awarded contribution-based ESA despite being entitled to income-related ESA. It is estimated some 70,000 people had not been paid the full amount of ESA that they were entitled to (on average underpayments were £5,000). The Public Accounts Committee is holding an inquiry into the DWP's handling of these errors.

Subsections (2), (3A), (7)

1.323   As with JSA, read together these envisage two ways of gaining title to ESA: the "contributory route" to the "contributory allowance" (CESA); and the "income-related" route to "income-related allowance" (IRESA). They provide that entitlement to CESA is grounded on satisfaction of the "basic conditions" in subs.(3) plus *either* (a) satisfaction of the national insurance contribution conditions (Sch.1 Pt 1) *or* (b) that the claimant is someone incapacitated in youth (Sch.1 Pt 1). But no new claims for CESA on the grounds of youth (see subs.(2)(a) and Pt 1 of Sch.1) may be made on or after May 1, 2012 (subs.(3A). Those claimants who would have been entitled on those grounds will instead have to meet the usual National Insurance contribution conditions for a claim for CESA. Entitlement to IRESA is grounded on satisfaction of the basic conditions in subs.(3) plus those relating to financial position (Sch.1 Pt 2).

Subsection (3)

1.324   This stipulates the "basic conditions" which must be satisfied where the claimant claimed old style ESA. The claimant must:

- *be at least 16*

    this is the current school-leaving age and so this lower limit is apt for a benefit that is an earnings replacement one;

- *be under pensionable age*

    "pensionable age" is here defined according to the rules in Pensions Act 2004, Sch.4, para.1 (see subs.(6)). It thus links to the sliding scale of pensionable ages found there as the pensions system moves steadily towards equal pension ages for men and women;

- *be in Great Britain*

    absences from Great Britain (other than certain temporary absences) preclude entitlement to ESA. See further s.18(4), Sch.2 paras 5, 6, 8; ESA Regs 2012 regs 88–92. Essentially this is a presence rather than a residence test;

- *not be entitled to IS (under SSCBA 1992, s.124)*

    this establishes the mutual exclusivity of old style ESA and IS;

- *not be entitled to JSA (under JSA 1995)*

    this establishes the mutual exclusivity of old style ESA and JSA;

- *have limited capability for work*

the basic test for this is set out in subs.(4): claimants will have limited capa-   1.325
bility for work where their capability for work is limited by their physical
or mental condition and that limitation is such that it is not reasonable to
require them to work. ESA Regs 2013 reg.15(1) elaborates that this is to be
determined on the basis of a limited capability for work assessment. This is:

> "an assessment of the extent to which a claimant who has some specific
> disease or bodily or mental disablement is capable of performing the activi-
> ties prescribed in Schedule 2 [to the ESA Regs] or is incapable by reason
> of such disease or bodily or mental disablement of performing those activi-
> ties" (ESA Regs reg.15(2)).

The claimant is to be matched, in the light of all the evidence, by the decision-maker or tribunal against a range of activities and descriptors, and an
appropriate "score" awarded. The threshold "score" for entitlement is 15
points, but as regards its computation see further the commentary to s.8 and
to ESA Regs 2013 Pt 4 (regs 15–29) and Sch.2.

- *have accepted a claimant commitment*

This condition, inserted by s.54(2) of the WRA 2012, initially applied only to
new style ESA in universal credit areas. It was then implemented more widely
as from the summer of 2017. It replaces the conditionality requirement in the
original version of the WRA 2007.

Subsection (4)

This sets out the basic definition of "limited capability for work". See commen-   1.326
tary to subs.(3), s.8 and to ESA Regs Pt 5 (regs 19–33) and Sch.2.

Subsection (5)

Emulating JSA, ESA is a weekly benefit, one paid in respect of a week. For cases   1.327
of part-week entitlement see s.22, Sch.2 para.3 and ESA Regs Pt 14 (regs 165–169).

Subsection (6)

This defines, by reference to other legislation, "joint-claim jobseeker's allowance"   1.328
and "pensionable age".

Subsection (7)

Another definition provision. See commentary to subss.(2), (7), above.   1.329

[¹ Duration of contributory allowance

1A. [*Omitted as not applying to income-related ESA*]

General Note

As noted in the annotation to WRA 2007 s.1, this has the effect that for *those not in*   1.330
the support group CESA—whether obtained by the contributory route (subs.(2)) or as
a person incapacitated in youth (subs.(4))—is from May 1, 2012 time-limited to 365
days (counting days of entitlement before, on and after that date), even if the period
of limited capability for work exceeds this period. Termination on this ground is
appealable, and in any such appeal termination can be contested on the basis that the
claimant at the point of termination, although not regarded by the Secretary of State
as being in the support group, ought to have been because the claimant at that point

in fact had limited capability for work-related activity (or was to be treated as such) (*MC and JH v SSWP (ESA)* [2014] UKUT 125 (AAC)). Note that the Secretary of State can by order increase the time-limit (subss.(2)(b) and (4)(b)). To requalify for a further period of entitlement to CESA the conditions in subs.(3) must be met with the second contribution condition being met in at least one tax year later than the second of the two tax years by reference to which (under the second contribution condition) his previous period of entitlement to CESA had been based.

Since someone may move from the support group to the work-related activity group and back again, calculating when the maximum period of entitlement to CESA is reached can be more complicated than simply counting 365 days of entitlement. Hence, the days stipulated in subs.(5) do not count in calculating the maximum period of entitlement.

[¹ Further entitlement after time-limiting

1.331   **1B.** [*Omitted as not applying to income-related ESA*]

GENERAL NOTE

1.332   This has the effect that where a person's contributory ESA ceased under s.1A as a result of time limiting, but their health condition has deteriorated so that they are later placed in the support group, they will be able to re-qualify for an award of CESA (see subs.(2) which ranks it as such) if the three conditions in subs.(1) are satisfied:

- the person has not ceased to have (or be treated as having) limited capability for work;
- the person satisfies the basic conditions (see WRA 2007 s.1(3)); and
- the person has (or is treated as having) limited capability for work-related activity.

Entitlement to the award only subsists for as long as the person has (or is treated as having) limited capability for work-related activity (and so falls into the support group). If a subsequent work capability assessment places the recipient in the work related activity group, then entitlement to an award arising by virtue of this section ceases.

Amount of contributory allowance

1.333   **2.** [*Omitted as not applying to income-related ESA*]

Deductions from contributory allowance: supplementary

1.334   **3.**— [*Omitted as not applying to income-related ESA*]

Amount of income-related allowance

1.335   **4.**—(1) In the case of an income-related allowance, the amount payable in respect of a claimant shall be—

(a) if he has no income, the applicable amount;
(b) if he has an income, the amount by which the applicable amount exceeds his income.

(2) Subject to subsection (3), the applicable amount for the purposes of subsection (1) shall be calculated by—

(a) taking such amount, or the aggregate of such amounts, as may be prescribed, and

(b) if in the claimant's case the conditions of entitlement to the support component [¹ . . .] are satisfied, adding the amount of that component.

(3) Regulations may provide that, in prescribed cases, the applicable amount for the purposes of subsection (1) shall be nil.

(4) The conditions of entitlement to the support component are—

(a) that the assessment phase has ended,

(b) that the claimant has limited capability for work-related activity, and

(c) that such other conditions as may be prescribed are satisfied.

(5) [¹ . . .]

(6) Regulations may—

(a) prescribe circumstances in which paragraph (a) of subsection (4) [¹ . . .] is not to apply;

(b) prescribe circumstances in which entitlement under subsection (4) [¹ . . .] is to be backdated;

(c) make provision about the amount of the component under subsection (4) [¹ . . .].

AMENDMENT

1. Welfare Reform and Work Act 2016 s.15(3) (April 3, 2017).

MODIFICATION

Section 4 is modified by Sch.1, para.4 of the Employment and Support Allowance (Transitional Provisions, Housing Benefit and Council Tax Benefit) (Existing Awards) (No. 2) Regulations 2010 (SI 2010/1907) (as amended) for the purposes specified in reg.6(1) and by Sch.2 para.4 of those Regulations for the purposes specified in reg.16(1). For details of the modification, see the text of those Regulations below.

DEFINITIONS

"assessment phase"—s.24(2)
"income-related allowance"—ss.24(1) and 1(7).
"limited capability for work-related activity"—ss.24(1) and 2(5).
"prescribed"—s.24(1).
"regulations"—*ibid*.

GENERAL NOTE

This section is similar in effect to ss.124(4) and 135(1)–(2) of the Contributions and Benefits Act and ss.3(1)(a) and (4) of the Jobseekers Act. Applicable amounts (including the work-related activity component and the support component) are prescribed by regs 67–70 of, and Schs 4 and 5 to, the ESA Regulations. Income (including tariff income from capital) is governed by s.17 and Pt 10 of, and Schs 7, 8 and 9 to, the ESA Regs.　**1.336**

Subsections (4) and (5)

On the repeal of subs. (5) with effect from April 3, 2017, see the annotation to the former s.2(3) above (see further s.15(3) of the Welfare Reform and Work Act 2016 and reg.3(a) of the Pensions Act 2014 (Commencement No. 9) and the　**1.337**

Welfare Reform and Work Act 2016 (Commencement No. 4) Regulations 2017 (SI 2017/111)).

The requirement that the claimant should have (or should not have) limited capability for work-related activity in s.4(4)(b) (and, before it was repealed, s.4(5)(b)) was considered by the Upper Tribunal in *SSWP v PT (ESA)* [2011] UKUT 317 (AAC); [2012] AACR 17. In that case, the claimant had been entitled to ESA with the work-related activity component but his entitlement ended when he resumed full-time work. However, his job ended after nine days. He reclaimed ESA and was awarded benefit at the basic rate (i.e. *without* the work-related activity component). The Secretary of State submitted that the component could not be paid until there had been a fresh work capability assessment because, although s.4(5)(a) was disapplied by ESA Regs, reg.7(1)(b) (made under the powers conferred by s.4(6)(a)), the claimant did not satisfy s.4(5)(b): the condition of not having limited capability for work-related activity could only be satisfied after the question of whether or not the claimant had such limited capability had been freshly determined in an assessment for that purpose. Rejecting that submission, Upper Tribunal Judge Mesher stated (at para.15):

> "15. I do not accept the submissions for the Secretary of State. I go back to the plain words of section 4(4)(b) and (5)(b) of the 2007 Act. Looked at in isolation the natural and obvious meaning is that together the two provisions exhaust all possibilities in relation to limited capability for work-related activity. Providing that paragraph (a) on the ending of the assessment phase is satisfied or does not apply, either a claimant is so limited, in which case section 4(4)(b) applies, or is not, in which case section 4(5)(b) applies. ... If someone in the circumstances of the claimant here cannot be said to have limited capability for work-related activity because there has not yet been an assessment, so as not to fall within section 4(4)(b), then the person falls within section 4(5)(b). The person does not have limited capability for work-related activity because it has not yet been determined that the person does have such limited capability."

Advance award of income-related allowance

1.338   **5.**—(1) This section applies to claims for an employment and support allowance by a person who—

    (a) would be entitled to an income-related allowance, but for the fact that he does not satisfy the condition in paragraph 6(1)(a) of Schedule 1,

    (b) would satisfy that condition if he were entitled to the component mentioned in section 4(4) or (5), and

    (c) is not entitled to a contributory allowance.

(2) In relation to claims to which this section applies, section 5(1) of the Administration Act (regulations about claims for benefit) shall have effect as if—

    (a) in paragraph (d) (power to permit an award on a claim for benefit for a future period to be made subject to the condition that the claimant satisfies the requirements for entitlement when the benefit becomes payable under the award), there were inserted at the end "and to such other conditions as may be prescribed", and

    (b) in paragraph (e) (power to provide for such an award to be revised or superseded under the Social Security Act 1998 (c. 14) if any of those requirements are found not to have been satisfied), for "any of those requirements" there were substituted "any of the conditions to which the award is made subject".

(3) Regulations may, in relation to claims to which this section applies,

make provision enabling an award to be made on terms such that the time at which benefit becomes payable under the award is later than the start of the period for which the award is made.

MODIFICATION

Section 5 is modified by Sch.1 para.5 of the Employment and Support Allowance (Transitional Provisions, Housing Benefit and Council Tax Benefit) (Existing Awards) (No.2) Regulations 2010 (SI 2010/1907) (as amended) for the purposes specified in reg.6(1). For details of the modification, see the text of those Regulations below.

DEFINITIONS

"Administration Act"—s.65.
"contributory allowance"—ss.24(1) and 1(7).
"income-related allowance"—*ibid.*

GENERAL NOTE

The support component and, at least for claims predating April 3, 2017, work-related activity component (see s.4(4) and (5) above) are only paid after the end of the assessment phase. During that phase, there will be some claimants who are not entitled to income-related ESA because their income exceeds their applicable amount, who would be so entitled if their applicable amount included the support component or work-related activity component. This section allows an advance award to be made in such a case. See also reg.146 of the ESA Regulations.

Amount payable where claimant entitled to both forms of allowance

6.—(1) This section applies where a claimant is entitled to both a contributory allowance and an income-related allowance.

(2) If the claimant has no income, the amount payable by way of an employment and support allowance shall be the greater of—

(a) his personal rate, and

(b) the applicable amount.

(3) If the claimant has an income, the amount payable by way of an employment and support allowance shall be the greater of—

(a) his personal rate, and

(b) the amount by which the applicable amount exceeds his income.

(4) Where the amount payable to the claimant by way of an employment and support allowance does not exceed his personal rate, the allowance shall be treated as attributable to the claimant's entitlement to a contributory allowance.

(5) Where the amount payable to the claimant by way of an employment and support allowance exceeds his personal rate, the allowance shall be taken to consist of two elements, namely—

(a) an amount equal to his personal rate, and

(b) an amount equal to the excess.

(6) The element mentioned in subsection (5)(a) shall be treated as attributable to the claimant's entitlement to a contributory allowance.

(7) The element mentioned in subsection (5)(b) shall be treated as attributable to the claimant's entitlement to an income-related allowance.

(8) In this section—

1.339

1.340

"applicable amount" means the amount which, in the claimant's case, is the applicable amount for the purposes of section 4(1);

"personal rate" means the amount calculated in accordance with section 2(1).

DEFINITIONS

"applicable amount"—see subs.(8), s.4(1).
"claimant"—see s.24(1).
"contributory allowance"—see s.1(7).
"income-related allowance"—see s.1(7).
"personal rate"—see subs.(8), s.2(1).

GENERAL NOTE

1.341   This is similar to Jobseekers Act 1995 s.4(6)–(12), where, as with ESA, JSA has both a contributory element and an income related element. Like those provisions, this section deals with situations where a claimant is entitled to both a contributory allowance (CESA) and an income-related allowance (IRESA). Here, the amount calculated under s.2(1) (amount of CESA) is referred to as the "personal rate". The applicable amount for IRESA is made up of an amount in respect of the claimant and any partner, plus applicable premiums plus eligible housing costs (see s.4(1); ESA Regs reg.67(1)). If the claimant has no income and the personal rate is higher than the applicable amount (the amount for the purposes of IRESA), the claimant receives the personal rate (the CESA amount). If the claimant has no income and the applicable amount exceeds the personal rate, he will receive the personal rate, topped up with an additional amount of IRESA equal to the excess. If the person has an income, the amount payable will be the greater of the personal allowance and the amount by which his applicable amount exceeds his income.

Exclusion of payments below prescribed minimum

1.342   7.—Except in such circumstances as regulations may provide, an employment and support allowance shall not be payable where the amount otherwise payable would be less than a prescribed minimum.

DEFINITIONS

"prescribed"—see s.24(1).
"regulations"—see s.24(1).

GENERAL NOTE

1.343   ESA is not payable where it falls below the minimum amount prescribed in regulations. This amount is set at 10p in the Claims and Payments Regs 1987 reg.26C(6), inserted with effect from October 27, 2008 by reg.21 of the ESA (Consequential Provisions) (No.2) Regs 2008 (SI 2008/1554). Compare JSA Regs reg.87A.

Assessments relating to entitlement

Limited capability for work

1.344   8.—(1) For the purposes of this Part, whether a person's capability for work is limited by his physical or mental condition and, if it is, whether the limitation is such that it is not reasonable to require him to work shall be determined in accordance with regulations.

(2) Regulations under subsection (1) shall—

(a) provide for determination on the basis of an assessment of the person concerned;

(b) define the assessment by reference to the extent to which a person who has some specific disease or bodily or mental disablement is capable or incapable of performing such activities as may be prescribed;

(c) make provision as to the manner of carrying out the assessment.

(3) Regulations under subsection (1) may, in particular, make provision—

(a) as to the information or evidence required for the purpose of determining the matters mentioned in that subsection;

(b) as to the manner in which that information or evidence is to be provided;

(c) for a person in relation to whom it falls to be determined whether he has limited capability for work to be called to attend for such medical examination as the regulations may require.

(4) Regulations under subsection (1) may include provision—

(a) for a person to be treated as not having limited capability for work if he fails without good cause—

(i) to provide information or evidence which he is required under such regulations to provide,

(ii) to provide information or evidence in the manner in which he is required under such regulations to provide it, or

(iii) to attend for, or submit himself to, a medical examination for which he is called under such regulations to attend;

(b) as to matters which are, or are not, to be taken into account in determining for the purposes of any provision made by virtue of paragraph (a) whether a person has good cause for any act or omission;

(c) as to circumstances in which a person is, or is not, to be regarded for the purposes of any such provision as having good cause for any act or omission.

(5) Regulations may provide that, in prescribed circumstances, a person in relation to whom it falls to be determined whether he has limited capability for work, shall, if prescribed conditions are met, be treated as having limited capability for work until such time as—

(a) it has been determined whether he has limited capability for work, or

(b) he falls in accordance with regulations under this section to be treated as not having limited capability for work.

(6) The prescribed conditions referred to in subsection (5) may include the condition that it has not previously been determined, within such period as may be prescribed, that the person in question does not have, or is to be treated as not having, limited capability for work.

DEFINITIONS

"limited capability for work"—see s.1(4).
"medical examination"—
"prescribed"—see s.24(1).
"regulations"—see s.24(1).

GENERAL NOTE

Subsections (1), (2)

1.345　　A key condition of entitlement to ESA is that the claimant has limited capability for work, namely that his capability for work is limited by his physical or mental condition such that it is not reasonable to require him to work (s.1(3)(a), (4)). This section provides that whether this is so is to be determined in accordance with regulations made under subss.(2)–(6) of this section. The regulations are Pt 5 of the ESA Regs, regs 19–33. These embody the first element in the Work Capability Assessment, governing entitlement to ESA, an analogue of the Personal Capability Assessment (PCA) in the previous incapacity benefits' regime (Incapacity Benefit/Income Support/Severe Disablement Allowance). But while there are many similarities with the PCA there are some significant differences as regards activities/descriptors, those exempt from the test and the system of scoring. The approach taken here, however, is that where terminology and basic issues are the same as with the PCA, the extensive case law interpreting and applying the PCA will carry over into the interpretation and application of comparable provisions and the resolution of comparable issues with this first element of the WCA. The second element, which differs from the PCA, is the work-related activity assessment, designed to assess whether a claimant has limited capability for work-related activity. Claimants who have limited capability for work are placed in the work-related activity group while those with limited capability for work-related activity are placed in the support group.

　　Note that payment of the separate work-related activity component has not been available for new claims to ESA since April 3, 2017 (subject to transitional provisions): see the annotation to the former s.2(3) above (and see further section 15(2) and (3) of the Welfare Reform and Work Act 2016 and regulation 3(a) of the Pensions Act 2014 (Commencement No. 9) and the Welfare Reform and Work Act 2016 (Commencement No. 4) Regulations 2017 (SI 2017/111)).

Subsections (3), (4)

1.346　　Note that whether the claimant has good cause for failure to comply with the information-gathering and examination aspects of that assessment is to some extent structured by regulations in that ESA Regs, reg.24 provides an non-exhaustive list of matters to be taken into account in determining that good cause issue. No regulations have yet been made under para.(4)(c) to determine what does, or does not, rank as good cause.

Limited capability for work-related activity

1.347　　**9.**—(1) For the purposes of this Part, whether a person's capability for work-related activity is limited by his physical or mental condition and, if it is, whether the limitation is such that it is not reasonable to require him to undertake such activity shall be determined in accordance with regulations.

　　(2) Regulations under subsection (1) shall—

　　(a) provide for determination on the basis of an assessment of the person concerned;

　　(b) define the assessment by reference to such matters as the regulations may provide;

　　(c) make provision as to the manner of carrying out the assessment.

　　(3) Regulations under subsection (1) may, in particular, make provision—

　　(a) as to the information or evidence required for the purpose of determining the matters mentioned in that subsection;

　　(b) as to the manner in which that information or evidence is to be provided;

　　(c) for a person in relation to whom it falls to be determined whether he has limited capability for work-related activity to be called to attend for such medical examination as the regulations may require.

(4) Regulations under subsection (1) may include provision—

(a) for a person to be treated as not having limited capability for work-related activity if he fails without good cause—

    (i) to provide information or evidence which he is required under such regulations to provide,

    (ii) to provide information or evidence in the manner in which he is required under such regulations to provide it, or

    (iii) to attend for, or submit himself to, a medical examination for which he is called under such regulations to attend;

(b) as to matters which are, or are not, to be taken into account in determining for the purposes of any provision made by virtue of paragraph (a) whether a person has good cause for any act or omission;

(c) as to circumstances in which a person is, or is not, to be regarded for the purposes of any such provision as having good cause for any act or omission.

Definitions

"regulations"—see s.24(1).
"work-related activity"—see ss.24(1), 13(7).

General Note

Subsections (1), (2)

Whether an ESA claimant is entitled to the more generous support component or, at least for claims predating April 3, 2017, the less generous work-related activity component in addition to his basic allowance turns on whether he does (support component) or does not (work-related activity component) have limited capability for work-related activity (s.2(2), (3)). He has "limited capability for work-related activity" where his capability for such activity is limited by his physical or mental condition such that it is not reasonable to require him to undertake it (s.2(5)). "Work-related activity" is activity which makes it more likely that he will obtain or remain in work or be able to do so (ss.24(1), 13(7)). This section provides that whether or not he has such limited capability is to be determined in accordance with regulations under subss.(2), (4) of this section. The regulations in question are ESA Regs, Pt 6, regs 34–39. These flesh out the second element in the new three element Work Capability Assessment: the work related activity assessment (WRAAt).   1.348

Subsections (3), (4)

Note that whether the claimant has good cause for failure to comply with the information-gathering and examination aspects of that assessment is to some extent structured by regulations in that ESA Regs, reg.39 provides an non-exhaustive list of matters to be taken into account in determining that good cause issue. No regulations have yet been made under para.(4)(c) to determine what does, or does not, rank as good cause.   1.349

Report

10.—The Secretary of State shall lay before Parliament an independent report on the operation of the assessments under sections 8 and 9 annually for the first five years after those sections come into force.   1.350

1.351   The new capability assessments in respect of work and work related activity were controversial. So this section provides—but only for the first five years after commencement—for independent annual review of their operation, a report on which must be laid before Parliament by the Secretary of State.

Conditionality

Work-focused health-related assessments

1.352   [*omitted*]

GENERAL NOTE

1.353   This section has been omitted because work-focused health related assessments were suspended for a period of two years from July 19, 2010 pending reconsideration of its purpose and delivery. Following that review and from June 1, 2011 the ESA Regs governing it (regs 47–49, 51–53) were revoked (see Employment and Support Allowance (Work-Related Activity) Regulations 2011 (SI 2011/1349), reg.11).

Work-focused interviews

1.354   **12.**—(1) Regulations may make provision for or in connection with imposing on a person who is—

    (a) entitled to an employment and support allowance, and

    (b) not a member of the support group [¹or a lone parent of a child under the age of one],

a requirement to take part in one or more work-focused interviews as a condition of continuing to be entitled to the full amount payable to him in respect of the allowance apart from the regulations.

(2) Regulations under this section may, in particular, make provision—

    (a) prescribing circumstances in which such a person is subject to a requirement to take part in one or more work-focused interviews;

    (b) for notifying such a person of any such requirement;

    (c) prescribing the work-focused interviews in which a person who is subject to such a requirement is required to take part;

    (d) for determining, in relation to work-focused interviews under the regulations, when and how the interview is to be conducted and, if it is to be conducted face to face, where it is to take place;

    (e) for notifying persons who are required under the regulations to take part in a work-focused interview of what is determined in respect of the matters mentioned in paragraph (d);

    (f) prescribing circumstances in which a person who is a party to a work-focused interview under the regulations is to be regarded as having, or not having, taken part in it;

    (g) for securing that the appropriate consequence follows if a person who is required under the regulations to take part in a work-focused interview—

        (i) fails to take part in the interview, and

        (ii) does not, within a prescribed period, show that he had good cause for that failure;

    (h) prescribing matters which are, or are not, to be taken into account in determining whether a person had good cause for any failure to comply with the regulations;

  (i) prescribing circumstances in which a person is, or is not, to be regarded as having good cause for any such failure.

(3) For the purposes of subsection (2)(g), the appropriate consequence of a failure falling within that provision is that the amount payable to the person in question in respect of an employment and support allowance is reduced in accordance with regulations.

(4) Regulations under subsection (3) may, in particular, make provision for determining—

  (a) the amount by which an allowance is to be reduced,

  (b) when the reduction is to start, and

  (c) how long it is to continue,

and may include provision prescribing circumstances in which the amount of the reduction is to be nil.

(5) Regulations under this section shall include provision for a requirement to take part in one or more work-focused interviews to cease to have effect if the person subject to the requirement becomes a member of the support group.

(6) Regulations under this section may include provision—

  (a) that in such circumstances as the regulations may prescribe a requirement to take part in a work-focused interview that would otherwise apply to a person by virtue of such regulations is not to apply, or is to be treated as not having applied;

  (b) that in such circumstances as the regulations may prescribe such a requirement is not to apply until a prescribed time;

  (c) that in such circumstances as the regulations may prescribe matters mentioned in subsection (2)(d) may be redetermined.

(7) In this section, "work-focused interview" means an interview by the Secretary of State conducted for such purposes connected with getting the person interviewed into work, or keeping him in work, as may be prescribed.

AMENDMENT

1. Welfare Reform Act 2009 s.3(3) (October 31, 2011).

DEFINITIONS

"appropriate consequence"—see subs.(3).
"entitled"—see s.24(1).
"prescribed"—see s.24(1).
"regulations"—see s.24(1).
"support group"—see s.24(4).
"work-focused interview"—see subs.(7).

GENERAL NOTE

This section covers those claimants, entitled to ESA, who do not have limited capability for work-related activity and who are thus entitled not to the support component (they are not part of the "support group" (see s.24(4)). Those only with limited capability for work but not limited capability for work-related activity must comply with certain conditions—the regime is one of "conditionality" (stipulating required behaviour and using sanctions to regulate and change behaviour). One of these conditions is participation in one or more work-focused interviews conducted either by Jobcentre Plus or (as envisaged by s.16) one of the contractors in the private or voluntary sectors (PVS).

1.355

A "work-focused interview" is one conducted for such purposes connected with keeping the interviewee in work or getting him into work, as may be set out in regulations (subs.(7)).

This section enables the making of regulations to impose the requirement of participation in such an interview and to exempt persons from it, whether totally or delaying its application for a particular period (subss.(1), (5), (6)); to deal with the process of carrying out such an interview, and with the consequences of not participating in one without good cause (subs.(2)). Subsection (3) stipulates that a reduction in the amount of ESA otherwise payable is the appropriate consequence, and that subsection and subs.(4) enable the making of regulations determining the amount and period of the reduction and the circumstances in which the reduction is to be nil. Subsection (5) enables regulations to provide that the requirement shall cease to have effect if the person becomes a member of the support group, that is, if it is determined that he has, or is to be treated as having, limited capability for work-related activity.

The relevant regulations are the ESA Regs, Pt 8 (Conditionality) Ch.2 (work-focused interviews), regs 54–62. Despite the width of the rule-making power (which would appear to authorise reduction in the amount of ESA payable) the sanction originally (at least until December 2012) operated only by reduction of the work-related activity component of ESA, rather than on the whole allowance. It would appear that this has always been the policy intention, but, if so, it would have been better in terms of compliance with Convention Rights so to confine the rule-making power (see JHRC, *Second Report of Session 2006–07*, HL 34/HC 263 (2006–07), para.3.18). That recommendation has been given added force by subsequent developments. In December 2012 the sanctions regime was amended so the reduction in benefit applied to the whole of the basic amount or personal allowance for a single claimant (but did not operate on the work-related activity component). However, the abolition of the work-related activity component for (broadly speaking) new claims since April 3, 2017 means that if a new claimant in the work-related activity group is sanctioned they would lose the entirety of their standard ESA benefit.

Note that whether the claimant has good cause for failure to participate in a work-focused health-related interview is to some extent structured by regulations in that ESA Regs, reg.61(3) provides a non-exhaustive list of matters which may be taken into account by decision-maker or appeal tribunal in determining that good cause issue. No regulations have yet been made under para.(2)(i) to determine what does, or does not, rank as good cause.

Work-related activity

1.356
13.—(1) Regulations may make provision for or in connection with imposing on a person who is subject to a requirement imposed under section 12(1) a requirement to undertake work-related activity in accordance with regulations as a condition of continuing to be entitled to the full amount payable to him in respect of an employment and support allowance apart from the regulations.

(2) Regulations under this section may, in particular, make provision—

(a) prescribing circumstances in which such a person is subject to a requirement to undertake work-related activity in accordance with regulations;

(b) for notifying such a person of any such requirement;

(c) prescribing the time or times at which a person who is subject to such a requirement is required to undertake work-related activity and the amount of work-related activity he is required at any time to undertake;

(d) prescribing circumstances in which a person who is subject to such a requirement is, or is not, to be regarded as undertaking work-related activity;

(e) for securing that the appropriate consequence follows if a person who is subject to such a requirement—

    (i) fails to comply with the regulations, and

    (ii) does not, within a prescribed period, show that he had good cause for that failure;

(f) prescribing the evidence which a person who is subject to such a requirement needs to provide in order to show that he has complied with the regulations;

(g) prescribing matters which are, or are not, to be taken into account in determining whether a person has complied with the regulations;

(h) prescribing matters which are, or are not, to be taken into account in determining whether a person had good cause for any failure to comply with the regulations;

(i) prescribing circumstances in which a person is, or is not, to be regarded as having good cause for any such failure.

(3) For the purposes of subsection (2)(e), the appropriate consequence of a failure falling within that provision is that the amount payable to the person in question in respect of an employment and support allowance is to be reduced in accordance with regulations.

(4) Regulations under subsection (3) may, in particular, make provision for determining—

(a) the amount by which an allowance is to be reduced,

(b) when the reduction is to start, and

(c) how long it is to continue,

and may include provision prescribing circumstances in which the amount of the reduction is to be nil.

(5) Regulations under this section shall include provision for a requirement to undertake work-related activity in accordance with regulations to cease to have effect if the person subject to the requirement becomes a member of the support group.

(6) Regulations under this section may include provision that in such circumstances as the regulations may provide a person's obligation under the regulations to undertake work-related activity at a particular time is not to apply, or is to be treated as not having applied.

(7) In this Part, "work-related activity", in relation to a person, means activity which makes it more likely that the person will obtain or remain in work or be able to do so.

[[1](8) The reference to activity in subsection (7) includes work experience or a work placement.]

AMENDMENT

1. Welfare Reform Act 2012 s.55 (December 3, 2012).

DEFINITIONS

    "appropriate consequence"—see subs.(3).

    "regulations"—see s.24(1).

    "support group"—see s.24(4).

    "work-related activity"—see subss.(7), (8).

1.357   This section applies only to those subject to a requirement to participate in a work-focused interview ("a requirement imposed under s.12(1)"). It thus covers those claimants, entitled to ESA, who do not have limited capability for work-related activity and who are thus entitled not to the support component (they are not part of the "support group" (see s.24(4)), who have not been exempted from the requirement or had it delayed. Those only with limited capability for work but not limited capability for work-related activity must comply with certain conditions in order to retain entitlement—the regime is one of "conditionality" (stipulating required behaviour and using sanctions to regulate and change behaviour). The first envisaged condition was participation in a work-focused health related assessment", but that was suspended from July 19, 2010 and the ESA Regs dealing with it revoked from June 1, 2011 (s.11). The second is participation in a work-focused interview (s.12). This section enables the imposition on those subject to the second of a third condition: a requirement to undertake work-related activity. That is to undertake activity which makes it more likely that the person to be subjected to the condition will obtain or remain in work or be able to do so (ss.24(1), 13(7), (8)).

This section enables the making of regulations to impose the requirement to undertake such activity and to exempt persons from it, whether totally or delaying its application for a particular period (subss.(1), (5), (6)); to deal with the process of imposition of the requirement, and with the consequences of not undertaking it without good cause (subs.(2)). Subsection (3) stipulates that a reduction in the amount of ESA otherwise payable is the appropriate consequence, and that subsection and subs.(4) enable the making of regulations determining the amount and period of the reduction and the circumstances in which the reduction is to be nil. Subsection (5) enables regulations to provide that the requirement shall cease to have effect if the person becomes a member of the support group, that is, if it is determined that he has, or is to be treated as having, limited capability for work-related activity.

No such regulations have ever been made, but regulations laid in May 2011 and operative from June 1, 2011 enable the Secretary of State to require ESA claimants in the work-related activity group to undertake work-related activity. They do not apply to lone parents with a child under five or to ESA claimants also receiving carer's allowance or carer's premium. See the Employment and Support Allowance (Work-Related Activity) Regulations 2011 (SI 2011/1349). Activities envisaged are work tasters; programmes to manage health in work; job search assistance; and programmes to assist in stabilising the individual's life (*Explanatory Notes to the Welfare Reform Act 2007*, paras 86–91). Information presented to the Commons by the DWP when the Welfare Reform Bill was being considered there indicated that claimants would be asked to participate in a minimum amount of work-related activity (e.g. one activity) in a given time period (e.g. four weeks), and in between each period they would in their work-focused interview review what they had done and discuss what they would like to do in the next period (DWP, *Welfare Reform Bill: Draft Regulations and Supporting Material*, January 2007). That same material stressed that no-one would be forced to undertake a particular activity; the requirement is to participate in some work-related activity. Perhaps an appropriate analogy may be with the proper approach to the question in JSA of whether a claimant is actively seeking work (see commentary to Jobseekers Act 1995 ss.7, 9; and to JSA Regs regs 18. Note also the power to direct that specific activity will not count a work-related activity for a particular person (s.15).

Despite the width of the rule-making power (which would appear to authorise reduction in the amount of ESA payable) it was originally envisaged that, as with that applicable to the other elements in respect of work-related activity "conditionality' (see ss.11, 12, above), the sanction would operate only by reduction of the work-related activity component of ESA, rather than on the whole allowance. It would appear that this has always been the policy intention, but, if so, it would have been better so to confine the rule-making power (see JHRC, *Second Report of Session 2006–07*, HL 34/HC 263 (2006–07), para.3.18). That recommendation has been given added force by subsequent developments. In December 2012 the sanctions regime was amended so the reduction in benefit applied to the whole of the basic amount or personal allowance for a single claimant (but did not operate on the work-related activity component). However, the abolition of the work-related activity component for (broadly speaking) new claims since April 3, 2017 means that if a new claimant in the work-related activity group is sanctioned they would lose the entirety of their standard ESA benefit.

Action plans in connection with work-focused interviews

14.—(1) The Secretary of State shall in prescribed circumstances provide a person subject to a requirement imposed under section 12(1) with a document prepared for such purposes as may be prescribed (in this section referred to as an action plan).

1.358

(2) Regulations may make provision about—
(a) the form of action plans;
(b) the content of action plans;
(c) the review and updating of action plans.

(3) Regulations under this section may, in particular, make provision for action plans which are provided to a person who is subject under section 13 to a requirement to undertake work-related activity to contain particulars of activity which, if undertaken, would enable the requirement to be met.

(4) Regulations may make provision for reconsideration of an action plan at the request of the person to whom the plan is provided and may, in particular, make provision about—
(a) the circumstances in which reconsideration may be requested;
(b) the period within which any reconsideration must take place;
(c) the matters to which regard must be had when deciding on reconsideration whether the plan should be changed;
(d) notification of the decision on reconsideration;
(e) the giving of directions for the purpose of giving effect to the decision on reconsideration.

DEFINITIONS

"action plan"—see subs.(1).
"prescribed"—see s.24(1).
"regulations"—see s.24(1).
"work-related activity"—see ss.24(1), 13(7).

GENERAL NOTE

Note that the relevant regulation (ESA Regs, reg.58) has now been repealed.

1.359

Directions about work-related activity

15.—[1(1) In prescribed circumstances, the Secretary of State may by direction given to a person subject to a requirement imposed under section 13(1) provide that the activity specified in the direction is—

1.360

   (a) to be the only activity which, in the person's case, is to be regarded as being work-related activity; or

   (b) to be regarded, in the person's case, as not being work-related activity.

(1A) But a direction under subsection (1) may not specify medical or surgical treatment as the only activity which, in any person's case, is to be regarded as being work-related activity.

(2) A direction under subsection (1) given to any person—

   (a) must be reasonable, having regard to the person's circumstances;

   (b) must be given to the person by being included in an action plan provided to the person under section 14; and

   (c) may be varied or revoked by a subsequent direction under subsection (1).]

(3) Where a direction under subsection (1) varies or revokes a previous direction, it may provide for the variation or revocation to have effect from a time before the giving of the direction.

AMENDMENT

1. Welfare Reform Act 2009 s.10 (February 10, 2010).

DEFINITIONS

"prescribed"—see s.24(1).
"work-related activity"—see ss.24(1), 13(7).

GENERAL NOTE

1.361   For ESA claims made before April 3, 2017, engagement in work-related activity is a condition of entitlement to work-related activity component for most of the claimants who are not in the support group. Failure to engage in such activity can be sanctioned by reduction or removal of work-related activity component, leaving such a claimant reliant solely on basic allowance ESA. This section enables a written direction to be given to a claimant with the effect that the activity specified in the direction will in his case be treated as not being work-related activity. The DWP envisages that this power will only be used in limited circumstances "where a given activity was wholly inappropriate for the claimant" (DWP, *Welfare Reform Bill: Draft Regulations and Supporting Material*, January 2007). Since engagement in work-related activity will not be an operative part of "conditionality" until resources permit (probably not before 2011 (see commentary to s.13), the regulations envisaged by subs.(1), setting out the circumstances, in which a direction can be given, have not yet been made

[¹ Persons dependent on drugs etc.

Persons dependent on drugs etc.

1.362   **15A.** [² *Repealed.*]]

AMENDMENT

1. Welfare Reform Act 2009 s.11 and, Sch.3 para.6 (November 12, 2009).
2. Welfare Reform Act 2012 ss.60(2), 150(2)(b) (May 8, 2012).

Contracting out

16.—(1) The following functions of the Secretary of State may be exercised by, or by employees of, such person (if any) as the Secretary of State may authorise for the purpose, namely—
  (a) conducting interviews under section 12;
  (b) providing documents under section 14;
  (c) giving, varying or revoking directions under section 15;
  [¹ (d) . . .]
  [¹ (e) . . .]
  [¹ (f) . . .]
(2) Regulations may provide for any of the following functions of the Secretary of State to be exercisable by, or by employees of, such person (if any) as the Secretary of State may authorise for the purpose—
  (a) any function under regulations under any of sections 11 to 15 [¹ . . .], except the making of a decision to which subsection (3) applies (an "excluded decision");
  (b) the function under section 9(1) of the Social Security Act 1998 (c. 14) (revision of decisions), so far as relating to decisions, except excluded decisions, that relate to any matter arising under such regulations;
  (c) the function under section 10(1) of that Act (superseding of decisions), so far as relating to decisions, except excluded decisions, of the Secretary of State that relate to any matter arising under such regulations;
  (d) any function under Chapter 2 of **Part 1** of that Act (social security decisions), except section 25(2) and (3) (decisions involving issues that arise on appeal in other cases), which relates to the exercise of any of the functions falling within paragraphs (a) to (c).
(3) This subsection applies to the following decisions—
  (a) a decision about whether a person has failed to comply with a requirement imposed by regulations under section 11, 12 or 13 [¹ . . .];
  (b) a decision about whether a person had good cause for failure to comply with such a requirement;
  (c) a decision about reduction of an employment and support allowance in consequence of failure to comply with such a requirement.
(4) Regulations under subsection (2) may provide that a function to which that subsection applies may be exercised—
  (a) either wholly or to such extent as the regulations may provide,
  (b) either generally or in such cases or areas as the regulations may provide, and
  (c) either unconditionally or subject to the fulfilment of such conditions as the regulations may provide.
(5) An authorisation given by virtue of subsection (1), or by virtue of regulations under subsection (2), may authorise the exercise of the function concerned—
  (a) either wholly or to such extent as may be specified in the authorisation,
  (b) either generally or in such cases or areas as may be so specified, and
  (c) either unconditionally or subject to the fulfilment of such conditions as may be so specified.
(6) In the case of an authorisation given by virtue of regulations under subsection (2), subsection (5) is subject to the provisions of the regulations.

1.363

(7) An authorisation given by virtue of subsection (1), or by virtue of regulations under subsection (2)—

(a) may specify its duration,

(b) may be revoked at any time by the Secretary of State, and

(c) shall not prevent the Secretary of State or any other person from exercising the function to which the authorisation relates.

(8) Where a person is authorised to exercise any function by virtue of subsection (1), or by virtue of regulations under subsection (2), anything done or omitted to be done by or in relation to him (or an employee of his) in, or in connection with, the exercise or purported exercise of the function shall be treated for all purposes as done or omitted to be done by or in relation to the Secretary of State.

(9) Subsection (8) shall not apply—

(a) for the purposes of so much of any contract made between the authorised person and the Secretary of State as relates to the exercise of the function, or

(b) for the purposes of any criminal proceedings brought in respect of anything done or omitted to be done by the authorised person (or an employee of his).

(10) Any decision which a person authorised to exercise any function by virtue of subsection (1), or by virtue of regulations under subsection (2), makes in exercise of the function shall have effect as a decision of the Secretary of State under section 8 of the Social Security Act 1998.

(11) Where—

(a) a person is authorised to exercise any function by virtue of subsection (1), or by virtue of regulations under subsection (2), and

(b) the authorisation is revoked at a time when a relevant contract is subsisting,

the authorised person shall be entitled to treat the relevant contract as repudiated by the Secretary of State (and not as frustrated by reason of the revocation).

(12) In subsection (11), the reference to a relevant contract is to so much of any contract made between the authorised person and the Secretary of State as relates to the exercise of the function.

(13) In this section, references to functions of the Secretary of State under—

(a) an enactment contained in, or in regulations under, this Part, or

(b) an enactment contained in Chapter 2 of Part 1 of the Social Security Act 1998,

include a reference to any function which the Secretary of State has by virtue of the application in relation to that enactment of section 8(1)(c) of that Act (decisions under certain enactments to be made by the Secretary of State).

AMENDMENT

1. Welfare Reform Act 2012 ss.147, 150(2)(b), Sch.14 Pt 6 (May 8, 2012).

DEFINITIONS

"regulations"—see s.24(1).

GENERAL NOTE

This section authorises, to such a degree as is specified in regulations and/or an 1.364
authorisation (subss.(5), (6)), the contracting out of certain functions vested in the
Secretary of State (DWP/JobCentre Plus decision-makers and Personal Advisers)
in respect of the conditionality aspect of membership to the work-related activity
group, and of a wide (but not unlimited) range of decisions related to the exercise
of those functions.

Those functions are conducting work-focused interviews under s.12; providing
documents under s.14 (action plans in connection with work-focused interviews);
and giving, varying or revoking directions under s.15 (subs.(1)). The functions can
be exercised by the contractor ("such person as the Secretary of State may authorise
for the purpose") or by employees of the contractor (subs.(1)). Anything done (or
omitted to be done) by them must be treated as if done (or omitted to be done) by
the Secretary of State (subss.(8), (9)). Their decisions in respect of the authorised
functions are to be given effect as ones of the Secretary of State under s.8 SSA 1998
(subs.(10). Revocation of the authorisation may be treated as a repudiation of the
contract by the Secretary of State and not as a matter of frustration of the contract
(subss.(11, (12)).

In addition, subs.(2) enables the making of regulations authorising a number of
other functions to be so exercisable by the contractor or the contractor's employees.
The regulations can authorise the exercise of any functions under ss.11–15, above
(subs.(2)(a)), other than "excluded decisions" which are enumerated in subs.(3).
Put shortly, this prevents authorising contractors or their employees to make decisions in respect of the sanctioning aspect of "conditionality" as regards entitlement
to the work-related activity component, although information and material from
them will perforce feed into and inform decisions on these matters made by DWP/
JobCentre Plus decision-makers. Thus subs.(3) provides that regulations cannot
enable the making by contractors or their employees of decisions on whether
the claimant has failed to comply with requirements, set out in regulations, on
work-focused health-related assessments (s.11), work-focused interviews (s.12) or
work-related activity (s.13) (para.(a)). Regulations cannot authorise them to make
decisions on whether the claimant had good cause for any failure to comply with
such a requirement (para.(b)), or on whether failure to comply must be sanctioned
by reduction or removal of the amount of work-related activity component to which
the claimant would otherwise be entitled (para.(c)). But, save so far as they relate
to excluded decisions, regulations can authorise contractors or their employees to
exercise powers of revision and supersession under ss.9 and 10, respectively, of the
Social Security Act 1998, in respect of any functions under ss.11–15 (subs.(2)(b),
(c)). Subsection (2)(d) enables regulations to authorise them also to exercise, in
respect of those functions, any function under Ch.2 of Pt I of that 1998 Act, other
than ones under ss.25(2) and (3) of it (decisions involving issues that arise on appeal
in other cases).

The ESA regime envisages that helping claimants return to work or to the
labour market need not solely be the task of the DWP or Jobcentre Plus,
important as their role is. Contractors in the private and voluntary sector (PVS)
have specialist knowledge and innovative approaches which, properly harnessed
and deployed, may well ensure the best possible support for claimants in the
work-related activity group. As with the Provider Led Pathways aspect of the
Pathways to Work project on which the ESA approach was built, JobCentre Plus
will conduct the first work-focused interview. It will be recalled that a "work-
focused interview" is one conducted for such purposes connected with keeping
the interviewee in work or getting him into work, as may be set out in regulations (s.12(7)). A secondary purpose will be to provide information on benefit
and service entitlement. This renders it appropriate that it be done by JobCentre
Plus. But a principal reason for its staff doing so is that at that stage, very early
in a claim, eligibility for ESA will not have been determined by the medical test.

Although interviews after the claimant's first work-focused interview may well be carried out by PVS providers, JobCentre Plus will during the lifetime of the claim exercise functions relating to entitlement to benefit, sanctioning decisions and processing of benefit payments.

[¹ Hardship payments

1.365   **16A.**—(1) Regulations may make provision for the making of payments ("hardship payments") by way of an employment and support allowance to a person where—

(a) the amount otherwise payable to the person in respect of an employment and support allowance is reduced by virtue of regulations under section 11(3), 12(3) or 13(3), and

(b) the person is or will be in hardship.

(2)   Regulations under this section may in particular make provision as to—

(a) circumstances in which a person is to be treated as being or not being in hardship;

(b) matters to be taken into account in determining whether a person is or will be in hardship;

(c) requirements or conditions to be met by a person in order to receive hardship payments;

(d) the amount or rate of hardship payments;

(e) the period for which hardship payments may be made.]

AMENDMENT

1. Welfare Reform Act 2012 s.56 (November 26, 2012).

GENERAL NOTE

Regulations 64A–64D of the ESA Regulations (see below) were made under the powers conferred by this section.

Miscellaneous

Income and capital: general

1.366   **17.**—(1) In relation to a claim for an employment and support allowance, the income and capital of a person shall be calculated or estimated in such manner as may be prescribed.

(2) A person's income in respect of a week shall be calculated in accordance with prescribed rules, which may provide for the calculation to be made by reference to an average over a period (which need not include the week concerned).

(3) Circumstances may be prescribed in which—

(a) a person is to be treated as possessing capital or income which he does not possess;

(b) capital or income which a person does possess is to be disregarded;

(c) income is to be treated as capital;

(d) capital is to be treated as income.

(4) Regulations may provide that a person's capital shall be deemed for the purposes of this Part to yield him an income at a prescribed rate.

DEFINITIONS

"prescribed"—see s.24(1).
"regulations"—*ibid.*
"week"—*ibid.*

GENERAL NOTE

This section is very similar to s.136(3)–(5) of the Contributions and Benefits Act   1.367
and s.12 of the old style Jobseekers Act 1995.

It enables the Secretary of State to introduce detailed regulations governing the
treatment of income and capital for the purposes of old style ESA. See Pt 10 of and
Schs 7, 8 and 9 to the ESA Regulations 2008.

See also para.6(2) of Sch.1 which contains the "aggregation rule" for the purposes of income-related ESA, i.e., that where the claimant is a member of a couple,
the partner's income and capital counts as that of the claimant (except in prescribed
circumstances).

Disqualification

18.—(1) Regulations may provide for a person to be disqualified for   1.368
receiving an employment and support allowance, or treated for such purposes as the regulations may provide as not having limited capability for
work, if—

  (a) he has become someone who has limited capability for work through
      his own misconduct,
  (b) he remains someone who has limited capability for work through his
      failure without good cause to follow medical advice, or
  (c) he fails without good cause to observe any prescribed rules of behav-
      iour.

(2) Regulations under subsection (1) shall provide for any such disqualification, or treatment, to be for such period not exceeding 6 weeks as may
be determined in accordance with Chapter 2 of Part 1 of the Social Security
Act 1998 (c. 14).

(3) Regulations may prescribe for the purposes of subsection (1)—

  (a) matters which are, or are not, to be taken into account in determin-
      ing whether a person has good cause for any act or omission;
  (b) circumstances in which a person is, or is not, to be regarded as
      having good cause for any act or omission.

(4) Except where regulations otherwise provide, a person shall be disqualified for receiving a contributory allowance for any period during which he is—

  (a) absent from Great Britain, or
  (b) undergoing imprisonment or detention in legal custody.

DEFINITIONS

"contributory allowance"—see s.1(7).
"limited capability for work"—see s.1(4).
"prescribed"—see s.24(1).
"regulations"—see s.24(1).
"week"—see s.24(1).

GENERAL NOTE

Subsections (1)–(3)

Like previous incapacity benefits' regimes (compare SSCBA 1992 s.171E and   1.369
IW (General) Regs reg.18), ESA embodies disqualification from benefit, or treat-

ing someone as not having limited capability for work, for a period not exceeding six weeks as sanctions in respect of conduct which conduces to a person's limited capability for work either by bringing it about through misconduct (subs.(1)(a)) or by remaining someone with limited capacity by failing without good cause to follow medical advice (subs.(1)(b)) or by failing without good cause to adhere to prescribed rules of behaviour (subs.(1)(c)). These subsections provide rule-making power for the regime of disqualification. The relevant regulations are the ESA Regs regs 157–158. Note the protection from disqualification for a "person in hardship" (regs 157(3)(a), 158) and someone disqualified from receiving ESA because of regulations made pursuant to s.7 of the Social Security Fraud Act 2001 (reg.157(3) (b); for that section and the consequent Social Security (Loss of Benefit) Regs 2001, see Vol.III).

Although subs.(3) enables regs to be made dealing with aspects of the "good cause" issue (matters to take into or leave out of account; things which do or do not rank as "good cause"), no such regs have yet been made. "Good cause" thus remains a matter for the decision-maker or tribunal, circumscribed by case law on analogous provisions.

Subsection (4)

1.370   This mandates for the ESA regime disqualification from CESA in respect of periods of absence from GB or of imprisonment or detention in legal custody. Exceptions from disqualification can be afforded by regs : see ESA Regs regs 151–155 (temporary absence from GB), 160, 161 (imprisonment or detention in legal custody). Compare, with respect to incapacity benefit, SSCBA 1992 s.113.

Pilot schemes

1.371   **19.**—(1) Any regulations to which this subsection applies may be made so as to have effect for a specified period not exceeding [¹36 months].

(2) Subject to subsection (3), subsection (1) applies to—

(a) regulations which are made under any provision of this Part, other than sections 3, 8 and 9;

(b) regulations which are made under the Administration Act, so far as they relate to an employment and support allowance.

(3) Subsection (1) only applies to regulations if they are made with a view to ascertaining whether their provisions will or will be likely to—

(a) encourage persons to obtain or remain in work, or

(b) make it more likely that persons will obtain or remain in work or be able to do so.

(4) Regulations which, by virtue of subsection (1), are to have effect for a limited period are referred to in this section as a "pilot scheme".

(5) A pilot scheme may provide that its provisions are to apply only in relation to—

(a) one or more specified areas;

(b) one or more specified classes of person;

(c) persons selected—

(i) by reference to prescribed criteria, or

(ii) on a sampling basis.

(6) A pilot scheme may make consequential or transitional provision with respect to the cessation of the scheme on the expiry of the specified period.

(7) A pilot scheme may be replaced by a further pilot scheme making the same or similar provision.

AMENDMENT

1. Welfare Reform Act 2009 s.28(2) (November 12, 2009).

DEFINITIONS

"Administration Act"—see. s.65.
"prescribed"—see. s.24(1).
"regulations"—*ibid.*

GENERAL NOTE

This is similar to s.29 of the old style Jobseekers Act 1995. From November 12, 2009 the initial period for which a pilot scheme can run has been extended to three years; in addition such a scheme can be repeated (see subs.(7)). Any regulations under Pt 1 of the Act or associated rules under the SSAA 1992 may be piloted, other than regulations concerning deductions from contributory ESA (s.3), limited capability for work (s.8) and limited capability for work-related activity (s.9). Regulations made under this section are subject to the affirmative resolution procedure (s.26(1)(c)).
1.372

The power under s.29 of the old style Jobseekers Act 1995 has been used on a fairly regular basis to test in particular changes to "conditionality" and it seems likely that this will also be the case for ESA.

Relationship with statutory payments

20.—(1) A person is not entitled to an employment and support allowance in respect of a day if, for the purposes of statutory sick pay, that day—
1.373
(a) is a day of incapacity for work in relation to a contract of service, and
(b) falls within a period of entitlement (whether or not it is a qualifying day).

(2) Except as regulations may provide, a woman who is entitled to statutory maternity pay is not entitled to a contributory allowance in respect of a day that falls within the maternity pay period.

(3) Regulations may provide that—
(a) an amount equal to a woman's statutory maternity pay for a period shall be deducted from a contributory allowance in respect of the same period,
(b) a woman shall only be entitled to a contributory allowance if there is a balance after the deduction, and
(c) if there is such a balance, a woman shall be entitled to a contributory allowance at a weekly rate equal to it.

(4) Except as regulations may provide, a person who is entitled to statutory adoption pay is not entitled to a contributory allowance in respect of a day that falls within the adoption pay period.

(5) Regulations may provide that—
(a) an amount equal to a person's statutory adoption pay for a period shall be deducted from a contributory allowance in respect of the same period,
(b) a person shall only be entitled to a contributory allowance if there is a balance after the deduction, and
(c) if there is such a balance, a person shall be entitled to a contributory allowance at a weekly rate equal to it.

(6) Except as regulations may provide, a person who is entitled to addi-

tional statutory paternity pay is not entitled to a contributory allowance in respect of a day that falls within the additional paternity pay period.

(7) Regulations may provide that—

(a) an amount equal to a person's additional statutory paternity pay for a period shall be deducted from a contributory allowance in respect of the same period,

(b) a person shall only be entitled to a contributory allowance if there is a balance after the deduction, and

(c) if there is such a balance, a person shall be entitled to a contributory allowance at a weekly rate equal to it.

(8) In this section—

"the additional paternity pay period" has the meaning given in section 171ZEE(2) of the Contributions and Benefits Act;

"the adoption pay period" has the meaning given in section 171ZN(2) of that Act;

"the maternity pay period" has the meaning given in section 165(1) of that Act.

DEFINITIONS

"the additional paternity pay period"—see subs.(8).
"the adoption pay period"—see subs.(8).
"Contributions and Benefits Act"—see s.65.
"contributory allowance"—see s.1(7).
"entitled"—see s.24(1).
"the maternity pay period"—see subs.(8).

GENERAL NOTE

1.374   This deals with the relationship between ESA and certain other "employer paid" statutory payments, the overall responsibility for them lying with HMRC. The payments covered by this section are statutory sick pay (SSP), statutory maternity pay (SMP), statutory adoption pay (SAP) and additional statutory paternity pay (ASPP). They are dealt with in *Vol.IV: Tax Credits and HMRC-administered Social Security Benefits*. The relationships are not all of a piece. ESA cannot be paid in respect of days for which there is SSP entitlement (subs.(1)). As regards SMP, SAP and ASPP, the interrelationship only concerns CESA. The general rule is that CESA cannot be payable at the same time as any of these other payments, but exceptions can be made by regulations (subss.(2)–(7)). The relevant regs are the ESA Regs, regs 80 (SMP), 81 (SAP) and 82 (ASPP). Where they operate to enable ESA to be paid, however, the amount of CESA payable is reduced by the amount of the relevant statutory payment, and only any balance of CESA remaining is payable.

Deemed entitlement for other purposes

1.375   **21.**—Regulations may provide for a person who would be entitled to an employment and support allowance but for the operation of any provision of, or made under, this Part, the Administration Act or Chapter 2 of Part 1 of the Social Security Act 1998 (c. 14) (social security decisions and appeals) to be treated as if entitled to the allowance for the purposes of any rights or obligations (whether his own or another's) which depend on his entitlement, other than the right to payment of it.

DEFINITIONS

"Administration Act"—see s.65.
"regulations"—see s.24(1).

GENERAL NOTE

This section is identical to SSCBA 1992 s.113(3). It enables regs to be made   1.376
enabling someone to be treated as still entitled to ESA, though not to payment of
it, even though provisions of or made under this Part of the WRA, the AA 1992 or
SSA 1998, Pt I Ch.2 operate to disentitle him. The person will only be treated as
entitled in this way to enable him or someone else to retain rights and obligations
under social security law more generally.

Supplementary provisions

22.—Schedule 2 (which contains further provisions in relation to an   1.377
employment and support allowance) has effect.

GENERAL NOTE

This provides the basis for giving effect to the detailed provisions on ESA set out   1.378
in Sch.2. These concern rule making in respect of: treating someone as having or
not having limited capability for work/work-related activity (as the case may be),
waiting days, linking periods, payments of benefit for less than a week, presence in
GB, entitlement to CESA by persons not in GB, retained entitlement to IRESA
after someone has left GB, modifying entitlement to CESA in respect of employment on ships, vessels, aircraft or hovercraft, the effect of work, treating ESA as
"benefit", attribution of reductions where someone is entitled both to CESA and
IRESA, ESA information to be treated as social security information, the making of
advance claims, and modifying provisions in respect of ESA as regards Members of
Her majesty's forces.

Recovery of sums in respect of maintenance

23.—(1) Regulations may make provision for the court to have power to   1.379
make a recovery order against any person where an award of income-related
allowance has been made to that person's spouse or civil partner.
   (2) The reference in subsection (1) to a recovery order is to an order requiring the person against whom it is made to make payments to the Secretary of
State or to such other person or persons as the court may determine.
   (3) Regulations under subsection (1) may include—
   (a) provision as to the matters to which the court is, or is not, to have
       regard in determining any application under the regulations;
   (b) provision as to the enforcement of orders under the regulations;
   (c) provision for the transfer by the Secretary of State of the right to
       receive payments under, and to exercise rights in relation to, orders
       under the regulations.
   (4) In this section, "the court" means—
   (a) in relation to England and Wales, a magistrates' court;
   (b) in relation to Scotland, the sheriff.

DEFINITIONS

"income-related allowance"— see s.1(7).
"regulations"— see s.24(1).

GENERAL NOTE

1.380   This is similar to the powers in relation to income-based JSA in s.23 of the Jobseekers Act. For the powers in relation to income support and universal credit, see s.106 of the Administration Act (to be found in Vol.III in this series).

General

Interpretation of Part 1

1.381   **24.**—(1) In this Part—

"claimant" means a person who has claimed an employment and support allowance;

"contributory allowance" has the meaning given by section 1(7);

"employment" and "employed" have the meanings prescribed for the purposes of this Part;

"entitled", in relation to an employment and support allowance, is to be construed in accordance with—

(a) the provisions of this Act,

(b) section 1 of the Administration Act (entitlement dependent on making of claim), and

(c) section 27 of the Social Security Act 1998 (c. 14) (restrictions on entitlement in certain cases of error);

"income-related allowance" has the meaning given by section 1(7);

"income support" means income support under section 124 of the Contributions and Benefits Act;

"limited capability for work" shall be construed in accordance with section 1(4);

"limited capability for work-related activity" shall be construed in accordance with section 2(5);

"period of limited capability for work" has the meaning prescribed for the purposes of this Part;

"prescribed" means specified in, or determined in accordance with, regulations;

"regulations" means regulations made by the Secretary of State;

"week" means a period of 7 days beginning with a Sunday or such other period of 7 days as may be prescribed;

"work-related activity" has the meaning given by section 13(7).

(2) For the purposes of this Part, the assessment phase, in relation to a claimant, is the period—

(a) beginning, subject to subsection (3), with the first day of the period for which he is entitled to an employment and support allowance, and

(b) ending with such day as may be prescribed.

(3) Regulations may prescribe circumstances in which the assessment phase is to begin with such day as may be prescribed.

[¹(3A) For the purposes of this Part, a person is a lone parent if the person—

(a) is not a member of a couple (within the meaning given by section 137(1) of the Contributions and Benefits Act), and

(b) is responsible for, and a member of the same household as, a person under the age of 16.

(3B) For the purposes of subsection (3A)(b) regulations may make provision—

(a) as to circumstances in which one person is to be treated as responsible or not responsible for another;

(b) as to circumstances in which persons are to be treated as being or not being members of the same household.]

(4) For the purposes of this Part, a person is a member of the support group if he is a person in respect of whom it is determined that he has, or is to be treated as having, limited capability for work-related activity.

AMENDMENT

1. Welfare Reform Act 2009 s.3(5) (October 6, 2011 (regulation-making purposes) and October 31, 2011 (all other purposes)).

DEFINITIONS

"Administration Act"—see s.65.
"Contributions and Benefits Act"—see s.65.

GENERAL NOTE

This defines, sometimes by referring the reader to other provisions or leaving   1.382
the meaning to be set out in regulations, a number of key terms in respect of
ESA. Note in particular that the "assessment phase", during which there can
generally only be entitlement to basic allowance ESA, is generally to begin on the
first such day of entitlement and to end in accordance with regulations (subss.(2),
(3)). See on this ESA Regs regs (4)–(7). Note also that membership of the support
group, and thus eligibility for the more generous "support component" in addition
to basic allowance ESA, is dependent on a determination that the person has, or
is to be treated as having, limited capability for work-related activity (subs.(4)).

General

Regulations [² and orders]

25.—(1) Any power under this Part to make regulations [² or an order]   1.383
shall be exercisable by statutory instrument.

(2) Any such power may be exercised—

(a) in relation to all cases to which it extends,

(b) in relation to those cases subject to specified exceptions, or

(c) in relation to any specified cases or classes of case.

(3) Any such power may be exercised so as to make, as respects the cases in relation to which it is exercised—

(a) the full provision to which the power extends or any less provision (whether by way of exception or otherwise);

(b) the same provision for all cases in relation to which it is exercised, or different provision for different cases or different classes of case or different provision as respects the same case or class of case for different purposes of this Part;

(c) any such provision either unconditionally or subject to any specified condition.

(4) Where any such power is expressed to be exercisable for alternative purposes, it may be exercised in relation to the same case for all or any of those purposes.

(5) Any such power includes power—

(a) to make such incidental, supplementary, consequential or transitional provision or savings as appear to the Secretary of State to be expedient;

(b) to provide for a person to exercise a discretion in dealing with any matter.

(6) Without prejudice to the generality of the provisions of this section, regulations under any of sections 11 to 15 [¹ ³ . . .] may make provision which applies only in relation to an area or areas specified in the regulations.

(7) The fact that a power to make regulations is conferred by this Part is not to be taken to prejudice the extent of any other power to make regulations so conferred.

AMENDMENT

1. Welfare Reform Act 2009 s.11 and Sch.3 para.8(3) (November 12, 2009).

2. Welfare Reform Act 2012 s.51(2) (March 20, 2012 (regulation-making purposes); May 1, 2012 (all other purposes)).

3. Welfare Reform Act 2012 s.147 and Sch.14 Pt 6 para.1 (May 8, 2012).

GENERAL NOTE

1.384   This section is similar to s.175 of the Contributions and Benefits Act and s.36 of the Jobseekers Act.

Parliamentary control

1.385   **26.**—(1) None of the following regulations shall be made unless a draft of the statutory instrument containing them has been laid before, and approved by a resolution of, each House of Parliament—

(a) regulations under section 2(2)(c) or (3)(c) or 4(4)(c) or (5)(c);

[⁴ (aa) the first regulations under section 11D(2)(d) or 11J;]

(b) the first regulations under section 13;

(c) regulations which by virtue of section 19(1) are to have effect for a limited period.

[¹ ³ . . .]

(2) A statutory instrument that—

(a) contains regulations made under this Part, and

(b) is not subject to a requirement that a draft of the instrument be laid before, and approved by a resolution of, each House of Parliament,

shall be subject to annulment in pursuance of a resolution of either House of Parliament.

[² (3) A statutory instrument containing an order under section 1A shall be subject to annulment in pursuance of a resolution of either House of Parliament.]

AMENDMENT

1. Welfare Reform Act 2009 s.11 and Sch.3 para.8(4) (November 12, 2009).
2. Welfare Reform Act 2012 s.51(3) (March 20, 2012 (regulation-making purposes); May 1, 2012 (all other purposes)).
3. Welfare Reform Act 2012 s.147 and Sch.14 Pt 6 para.1 (May 8, 2012).
4. Welfare Reform Act 2012 s.57(6) (February 25, 2013).

GENERAL NOTE

This section is similar to s.176 of the Contributions and Benefits Act and s.37 of the Jobseekers Act.   **1.386**

Financial provisions relating to Part 1

27.—(1) There shall be paid out of the National Insurance Fund so   **1.387**
much of any sums payable by way of employment and support allowance as
is attributable to entitlement to a contributory allowance.
(2) There shall be paid out of money provided by Parliament—
(a) so much of any sums payable by way of employment and support allowance as is attributable to entitlement to an income-related allowance, and
(b) any administrative expenses of the Secretary of State or the Commissioners for Her Majesty's Revenue and Customs in carrying this Part into effect.
(3) The Secretary of State shall pay into the National Insurance Fund sums estimated by him to be equivalent in amount to sums recovered by him in connection with payments of contributory allowance.
(4) The Secretary of State shall pay into the Consolidated Fund sums estimated by him to be equivalent in amount to sums recovered by him in connection with payments made by way of income-related allowance.

DEFINITIONS

"contributory allowance"—ss.24(1) and 1(7).
"income-related allowance"—*ibid*.

GENERAL NOTE

This section is similar to s.163 of the Administration Act, s.38 of the Jobseekers   **1.388**
Act and s.20 of the State Pension Credit Act.

Consequential amendments relating to Part 1

28.—(1) Schedule 3 (which makes amendments consequential on this   **1.389**
Part) has effect.
(2) Regulations may make provision consequential on this Part amending, repealing or revoking any provision of—
(a) an Act passed on or before the last day of the Session in which this Act is passed, or
(b) an instrument made under an Act before the passing of this Act.
(3) In subsection (2), "Act" includes an Act of the Scottish Parliament.

DEFINITIONS

"Act"—see subs.(3).
"regulations"—see s.24(1).

Subsection (1)

1.390   This gives effect to a range of consequential amendments of other Acts of Parliament set out in Sch.3 incorporated elsewhere in this book.

Subsection (2)

1.391   This enables the making of consequential regulations amending Acts (including ones of the Scottish Parliament) passed on or before the last day of the 2006–07 Westminster parliamentary session (the one in which the WRA 2007 was passed) (para.(a), subs.(3)). It also enables consequential regulations to amend subordinate legislation, already made before the passing of the WRA 2007, under Acts (including those of the Scottish Parliament) (para.(b), subs.(3)).

Transition relating to Part 1

1.392   **29.**—Schedule 4 (which makes provision with respect to transition in relation to this Part) has effect.

GENERAL NOTE

1.393   This gives effect to Sch.4, reproduced in full with provisions not yet in force set out in italics. That Schedule embodies rule-making powers for pre- and post-commencement claims, awarding ESA in respect of a pre-commencement period, converting existing awards of IB/IS/SDA to ESA, the post-commencement up-rating of IB/SDA, and a general power to provide for transitional matters with respect to ESA. The regulations so made are the Employment and Support Allowance (Transitional Provisions) Regulations 2008 (SI 2008/795) and the Employment and Support Allowance (Transitional Provisions, Housing Benefit and Council Tax Benefit) (Existing Awards) (No.2) Regulations 2010 (SI 2010/1907).

Sections 30–63 Omitted

PART 5

GENERAL

Northern Ireland

1.394   **64.**—(1) This section applies to an Order in Council under paragraph 1(1) of the Schedule to the Northern Ireland Act 2000 (c. 1) (legislation for Northern Ireland during suspension of devolved government) which contains a statement that it is made only for purposes corresponding to those of this Act.

(2) Such an Order—

(a) is not subject to paragraph 2 of that Schedule (affirmative resolution of both Houses of Parliament), but

(b) is subject to annulment in pursuance of a resolution of either House of Parliament.

GENERAL NOTE

1.395   Part I of the WRA 2007 dealing with ESA applies only to Great Britain (England, Wales and Scotland). This is true of the social security system generally. But comparable provision in respect of social security for Northern Ireland is always made by Order in Council under its devolution Act. This section deals with parliamentary scrutiny and control over such an Order. It provides that any such Order, stated to be made only for purposes corresponding to those of the WRA 2007, is to be subject to annulment by either House of Parliament rather than to the affirmative resolution procedure that would otherwise be applicable.

General interpretation

65.—In this Act— 1.396
"Administration Act" means the Social Security Administration Act 1992 (c. 5);
"Contributions and Benefits Act" means the Social Security Contributions and Benefits Act 1992 (c. 4).

Financial provisions: general

66.—(1) There shall be paid out of money provided by Parliament— 1.397
(a) any expenditure incurred by the Secretary of State in consequence of Parts 2 to 4 of this Act, and
(b) any increase attributable to this Act in the sums payable out of money so provided under any other enactment.
(2) There shall be paid into the Consolidated Fund any increase attributable to this Act in the sums payable into that Fund under any other enactment.

Repeals

67.—The enactments specified in Schedule 8 are hereby repealed to the 1.398
extent specified.

Section 68 omitted

Extent

69.—(1) Subject to the following provisions, this Act extends to England 1.399
and Wales and Scotland only.
(2) The following provisions extend to England and Wales only—
(a) sections 42(1) to (10) and 43, and
(b) paragraphs 6, 11(2) and 16 of Schedule 3.
(3) Paragraphs 1, 2, 4, 11(3), 14 and 22 of Schedule 3 extend to Scotland only.
(4) The following provisions also extend to Northern Ireland—
(a) sections 33(7), 49, 56, 57, 61, 64, 65, 68, this section and sections 70 and 71,
(b) paragraph 15 of Schedule 2, and sections 22 and 24 to 26 so far as relating thereto,
(c) paragraphs 5, 10(1) and (28), 17(1) and (2), 19, 23(1) to (3) and (6) to (8) and 24 of Schedule 3, and section 28 so far as relating thereto,
(d) paragraph 1 of Schedule 7, and section 63 so far as relating thereto, and
(e) Schedule 8, so far as relating to the Vaccine Damage Payments Act 1979 (c. 17), the Income and Corporation Taxes Act 1988 (c. 1), the Disability (Grants) Act 1993 (c. 14), section 2 of the Social Security

Act 1998 (c. 14) and the Income Tax (Earnings and Pensions) Act 2003 (c. 1), and section 67 so far as relating thereto.

(5) The following provisions extend to Northern Ireland only—

(a) section 45, and

(b) Schedule 8, so far as relating to the Social Security Administration (Northern Ireland) Act 1992 (c. 8), and section 67 so far as relating thereto.

(6) The following provisions also extend to the Isle of Man—

(a) sections 56 and 57, section 68, this section and sections 70 and 71,

(b) paragraph 1 of Schedule 7, and section 63 so far as relating thereto, and

(c) Schedule 8, so far as relating to the Vaccine Damage Payments Act 1979, and section 67 so far as relating thereto.

GENERAL NOTE

1.400 Only subs.(1) concerns ESA. It means that the ESA scheme under Pt I of the Act applies only to England, Wales and Scotland. Comparable provision can be made for Northern Ireland through Order in Council under the devolution legislation (s.64). The devolution arrangements and the complicated political background in Northern Ireland may, however, mean that relevant legislation may have to be enacted by the Northern Ireland Assembly.

Commencement

1.401 **70.**—(1) The following provisions shall come into force at the end of the period of 2 months beginning with the day on which this Act is passed—

(a) sections 41(2) and (3), 44, 45, 54, 55, 59, 61(1)(b) and (2) to (6) and 62,

(b) paragraphs 1 to 4, 10, 11 and 14 of Schedule 5, and section 40 so far as relating thereto,

(c) paragraphs 2(1) and (3), 3 and 4 of Schedule 7, and section 63 so far as relating thereto, and

(d) Schedule 8, so far as relating to—

(i) section 3(5) of the Pneumoconiosis etc. (Workers' Compensation) Act 1979 (c. 41),

(ii) section 140(1A) of the Contributions and Benefits Act,

(iii) sections 71(5), 71ZA(2), 134(8)(a) and 168(3)(d) of the Administration Act,

(iv) section 69(5) of the Social Security Administration (Northern Ireland) Act 1992,

(v) Schedule 13 to the Local Government etc. (Scotland) Act 1994 (c. 39), (vi) section 38(7)(a) of, and paragraph 81(2) of Schedule 7 to, the Social Security Act 1998 (c. 14), and

(vii) paragraph 65 of Schedule 24 to the Civil Partnership Act 2004 (c. 33), and section 67 so far as relating thereto.

(2) The remaining provisions of this Act, except—

(a) this section,

(b) sections 64, 65, 66, 68, 69 and 71, and

(c) paragraph 8 of Schedule 5, and section 40 so far as relating thereto, shall come into force on such day as the Secretary of State may by order made by statutory instrument appoint, and different days may be so appointed for different purposes.

GENERAL NOTE

The key operative date for the ESA regime is October 27, 2008.

1.402

Short title

71.—This Act may be cited as the Welfare Reform Act 2007.

1.403

SCHEDULES

SCHEDULE 1   **Section 1**

EMPLOYMENT AND SUPPORT ALLOWANCE: ADDITIONAL CONDITIONS

PART 1

CONTRIBUTORY ALLOWANCE

Conditions relating to national insurance

1.— [*Omitted as not applying to income-related ESA*]

1.404

PART 2

INCOME RELATED ALLOWANCE

6.—(1) The conditions are that the claimant–

1.405

(a) has an income which does not exceed the applicable amount or has no income;
(b) does not have capital which, or a prescribed part of which, exceeds the prescribed amount;
(c) is not entitled to state pension credit;
(d) is not a member of a couple the other member of which is entitled to an income-related allowance, state pension credit, income support or an income-based job-seeker's allowance;
(e) is not engaged in remunerative work;
(f) is not a member of a couple the other member of which is engaged in remunerative work;
(g) is not receiving education.

(2) Where the claimant is a member of a couple, the income and capital of the other member of the couple shall, except in prescribed circumstances, be treated for the purpose of this paragraph as income and capital of the claimant.

(3) Regulations may prescribe circumstances in which, for the purposes of sub-paragraph (1)(e) and (f)—

(a) a person who is not engaged in remunerative work is to be treated as engaged in remunerative work; or
(b) a person who is engaged in remunerative work is to be treated as not engaged in remunerative work

(4) Regulations may—

(a) make provision about when, for the purposes of sub-paragraph (1)(g), a person is, or is not, to be treated as receiving education;
(b) prescribe circumstances in which sub-paragraph (1)(g) does not apply.

(5) In this paragraph—

"applicable amount" means the amount which, in the claimant's case, is the applicable amount for the purposes of section 4(1);

[² [¹ "couple" means-

(a) two people who are married to, or civil partners of, each other and are members of the same household; or

(b) two people who are not married to, or civil partners of, each other but are living together [³ as if they were a married couple or civil partners] otherwise than in pre-scribed circumstances;]]

"education" has such meaning as may be prescribed;

"income-based jobseeker's allowance" has the same meaning as in the Jobseekers Act 1995(c.18);

"remunerative work" has such meaning as may be prescribed.

(6) [² [¹ . . .]]

(7) Regulations may make provision for the preceding provisions of this paragraph to have effect with prescribed modifications in a case where—

(a) the claimant is a husband or wife by virtue of a marriage entered into under a law which permits polygamy,

(b) either party to the marriage has for the time being any spouse additional to the other party, and

(c) the claimant, the other party to the marriage and the additional spouse are members of the same household.

(8) Regulations may make provision for the purposes of this paragraph as to circumstances in which people are to be treated as being or not being members of the same household.

AMENDMENTS

1. Marriage (Same Sex Couples) Act 2013 (Consequential and Contrary Provisions and Scotland) Order 2014 (SI 2014/560) art.2 and Sch.1, para.32 (March 13, 2014). The amendment extends to England and Wales only (see SI 2014/560 art.6(1)).

2. Marriage and Civil Partnership (Scotland) Act 2014 and Civil Partnership Act 2004 (Consequential Provisions and Modifications) Order 2014 (SI 2014/3229) art.29 and Sch.5, para. 17 (December 16, 2014). The amendment only relates to Scotland (see SI 2014/3229 art.3(4)) but is in the same terms as the amendment made in relation to England and Wales by SI 2014/560 (see above).

3. Civil Partnership (Opposite-sex Couples) Regulations 2019 (SI 2019/1458) reg.41(a) and Sch.3, para.30 (December 2, 2019).

MODIFICATIONS

Paragraph 6 is modified by Sch.1, para.6(b) of the Employment and Support Allowance (Transitional Provisions, Housing Benefit and Council Tax Benefit) (Existing Awards) (No. 2) Regulations 2010 (SI 2010/1907) (as amended) for the purposes specified in reg.6(1) of the 2010 Regulations and by Sch.2, para.4A for the purposes specified in reg.16(1) of those Regulations. For details of the modi-fications, see the text of those Regulations in Pt IX. The modifications are further modified in those cases in relation to which universal credit has come into force— see the General Note to the 2010 Regulations.

DEFINITIONS

"civil partner"—see Interpretation Act 1978 Sch.1
"education"—see ESA Regulations 2008 reg.14.
"prescribed"—see s.24(1).
"regulations"—*ibid.*
"remunerative work"—see ESA Regulations 2008 regs 2(1), 41 and 42.

GENERAL NOTE

Sub-paragraph (1)

1.406   This sets out the extra conditions for entitlement to income-related ESA that are additional to the basic conditions of entitlement for ESA in s.1(3). All of the conditions in sub-para.(1) must be satisfied for there to be entitlement to income-related ESA.

Under head (a) the claimant's income (which includes the income of any partner (sub-para.(2)) must not exceed the applicable amount (effectively the figure set for the claimant's, or the claimant's and any partner's, requirements under s.4).

Head (b) contains the capital test. The capital limit for income-related ESA is the same as for income support and income-based JSA, i.e., £16,000 (see reg.110 of the ESA Regulations 2008). See further the note to s.134(1) of the SSCBA 1992. For capital that is disregarded for the purposes of income-related ESA see Sch.9 to the ESA Regulations 2008.

Entitlement to state pension credit excludes entitlement to income-related ESA (head (c)). If a claimant has reached the qualifying age for state pension credit (between April 2010 and November 2018 this will increase by stages to 65 in line with the increase in pensionable age for a woman from April 2010) but has not reached pensionable age (currently 65 for a man and from April 2010 increasing by stages from 60 to 65 in November 2018 for a woman), it will normally be advantageous to claim state pension credit rather than income-related ESA. Note that the equalisation of the state pension age for men and women was previously to have been completed by April 5, 2020 but the timetable for this in the Pensions Act 1995 is being accelerated with effect from April 2016 so that the women's state pension age will now be 65 by November 2018; in addition, the increase in state pension age to 66 for both men and women has been brought forward—it will start to rise from 65 in December 2018 to reach 66 by October 2020 (see s.1 of the Pensions Act 2011). Between 2026 and 2028 it will rise to 67 (see s.26 of the Pensions Act 2014).

A claimant who is a member of a couple (defined in sub-para.(5)) will also not qualify for income-related ESA if the partner is entitled to state pension credit, income support, income-based JSA or income-related ESA (head (d)). The definition of "couple" in sub-para.(5) was amended (and sub-para.(6) was omitted) with effect from March 13, 2014 in England and Wales, and from December 16, 2014 in Scotland, as a consequence of the Marriage (Same Sex Couples) Act 2013 and the Marriage and Civil Partnership (Scotland) Act 2014 respectively. The further amendment with effect from December 2, 2019 was to take account of the amendment of the definition of "civil partner" in the Civil Partnerships Act 2004, to include partners of the opposite sex. The latter amendment accordingly altered the definition in Sch.1 to the Interpretation Act 1978.

Under heads (e) and (f) if either the claimant or any partner is in remunerative work there is no entitlement to income-related ESA. However note that the meaning of "remunerative work" is not the same for the claimant as it is for the partner. Regulation 41 of the ESA Regulations 2008 sets out the test for the claimant; the test for the partner is in reg.42 of those Regulations. See the notes to regs 41 and 42, and note also regs 40 and 43–45.

In addition claimants are excluded from entitlement to income-related ESA if they are receiving education (head (g)). See further regs 14–18 of the ESA Regulations 2008 (made under sub-para.(4)) and the notes to those regulations. See in particular reg.18 which provides that head (g) does not apply if the claimant is entitled to disability living allowance ("DLA"), personal independence payment ("PIP") or armed forces independence payment (see reg.2(1) for the definition of "armed forces independence payment").

Note that head (g) does not apply in the case of claimants who had an existing award of income support by virtue of reg.13(2)(b) or (bb) (persons in relevant education who are ill or disabled) of, or paras 10 or 12 (disabled or deaf students) of Sch.1B to, the Income Support Regulations (see the 2015/16 edition of what was then Vol.II in this series for these provisions) and who have been transferred to ESA as a result of a conversion decision under the Employment and Support Allowance (Transitional Provisions, Housing Benefit and Council Tax Benefit) (Existing Awards) (No. 2) Regulations 2010 (SI 2010/1907) (as amended) (see Pt IX for these Regulations). The modifications to s.1(2) of the Act made by Sch.1, para.2 and Sch.2, para.2 of the 2010 Regulations mean that such claimants will be able to get ESA while in education even if they do not get DLA, PIP or armed forces independence payment.

Sub-paragraph (2)

1.407 This provides that the general rule for income-related ESA is that where the claimant is a member of a couple (defined in sub-para.(5)) both the claimant's and any partner's income and capital are aggregated together and treated as the claimant's.

[¹ SCHEDULE 1A   **Section 15A**

Persons dependent on drugs etc.

1.408 [² *Repealed.*]]

AMENDMENTS

1. Welfare Reform Act 2009 s.11 and Sch.3 para.7 (November 12, 2009).
2. Welfare Reform Act 2012 ss.60(2), 150(2)(b) (May 8, 2012).

SCHEDULE 2

Employment and Support Allowance: Supplementary Provisions

Limited capability for work

1.409 **1.**—Regulations may make provision—
   (a) for a person to be treated in prescribed circumstances as having, or as not having, limited capability for work;
   (b) for the question of whether a person has limited capability for work to be determined notwithstanding that he is for the time being treated by virtue of regulations under sub-paragraph (a) as having limited capability for work;
   (c) for the question of whether a person has limited capability for work to be determined afresh in prescribed circumstances.

Waiting days

1.410 **2.**—Except in prescribed circumstances, a person is not entitled to an employment and support allowance in respect of a prescribed number of days at the beginning of a period of limited capability for work.

Periods of less than a week

1.411 **3.**—Regulations may make provision in relation to—
   (a) entitlement to an employment and support allowance, or
   (b) the amount payable by way of such an allowance,
in respect of any period of less than a week.

Linking periods

1.412 **4.**—(1) Regulations may provide for circumstances in which a period of limited capability for work which is separated from another period of limited capability for work by not more than a prescribed length of time is to be treated for the purposes of this Part as a continuation of the earlier period.

(2) Regulations may provide, in relation to periods which are linked by virtue of regulations under sub-paragraph (1), that a condition which was satisfied in relation to the earlier period is to be treated for the purposes of this Part as satisfied in relation to the later period.

[² 4A Regulations may prescribe circumstances in which a person may be entitled to employment and support allowance without having accepted a claimant commitment.]

Presence in Great Britain

5.—Regulations may make provision for the purposes of this Part as to the circumstances in which a person is to be treated as being, or not being, in Great Britain.

1.413

Contributory allowance: entitlement in case of absence from Great Britain

6.—Regulations may provide that in prescribed circumstances a claimant who is not in Great Britain may nevertheless be entitled to a contributory allowance.

1.414

Contributory allowance: modification in relation to employment on ships etc.

7.—(1) Regulations may modify any provision of this Part, so far as relating to a contributory allowance, in its application to any person who is, has been, or is to be—
    (a) employed on board any ship, vessel, hovercraft or aircraft,
    (b) outside Great Britain at any prescribed time or in any prescribed circumstances, or
    (c) in prescribed employment in connection with continental shelf operations.
(2) Regulations under this paragraph may, in particular, provide—
    (a) for any provision of this Part to apply even though it would not otherwise apply;
    (b) for any such provision not to apply even though it would otherwise apply;
    (c) for the taking of evidence, in a country or territory outside Great Britain, by a consular official or other prescribed person;
    (d) for enabling the whole, or any part, of a contributory allowance to be paid to such of the claimant's dependants as may be prescribed.
(3) In this paragraph, "continental shelf operations" has the same meaning as in section 120 of the Contributions and Benefits Act.

1.415

Income-related allowance: entitlement in case of absence from Great Britain

8.—(1) Regulations may provide that in prescribed circumstances a claimant who is entitled to an income-related allowance immediately before ceasing to be in Great Britain continues to be entitled to such an allowance after ceasing to be in Great Britain.
(2) Regulations may modify any provision of this Part, so far as relating to an income-related allowance, in its application to a person who is entitled to such an allowance by virtue of regulations under sub-paragraph (1).
(3) Regulations under sub-paragraph (2) may, in particular, provide—
    (a) for any provision of this Part to apply even though it would not otherwise apply;
    (b) for any such provision not to apply even though it would otherwise apply.

1.416

Limited capability for work-related activity

9.—Regulations may make provision—
    (a) for a person to be treated in prescribed circumstances as having, or as not having, limited capability for work-related activity;
    (b) for the question of whether a person has limited capability for work-related activity to be determined notwithstanding that he is for the time being treated by virtue of regulations under sub-paragraph (a) as having limited capability for work-related activity;
    (c) for the question of whether a person has limited capability for work-related activity to be determined afresh in prescribed circumstances.

1.417

Effect of work

10.—Regulations may prescribe circumstances in which a person is to be treated as not entitled to an employment and support allowance because of his doing work.

1.418

Treatment of allowance as "benefit"

11.—Regulations may provide for—
    (a) an employment and support allowance,
    (b) a contributory allowance, or
    (c) an income-related allowance,
to be treated, for prescribed purposes of the Contributions and Benefits Act, as a benefit, or a benefit of a prescribed description.

1.419

Attribution of reductions in cases where allowance taken to consist of two elements

1.420   12.—Where an employment and support allowance is taken by virtue of section 6(5) to consist of two elements, any reduction in the amount payable in respect of the allowance which falls to be made by virtue of—

    (a) section 11,

    (b) section 12,

    (c) section 13,

  [[1](ca) Schedule 1A,]

    (d) section 2AA of the Administration Act (full entitlement to certain benefits conditional on work-focused interview for partner),

shall be treated as reducing such of those elements by such amount as may be prescribed.

Treatment of information supplied as information relating to social security

1.421   13.—Information supplied in pursuance of regulations under any of sections 8, 9 and 11 to 13 [[1](, or under any paragraph of Schedule 1A other than paragraph 8,] shall be taken for all purposes to be information relating to social security.

Advance claims

1.422   14.—This Part shall have effect with prescribed modifications in relation to cases where a claim to an employment and support allowance is by virtue of regulations under section 5(1) (c) of the Administration Act (advance claims) made, or treated as if made, for a period wholly or partly after the date on which it is made.

Members of the forces

1.423   15.—(1) Regulations may modify—

    (a) any provision of this Part, or

    (b) any corresponding provision made for Northern Ireland,

in its application to persons who are or have been members of Her Majesty's forces.

(2) For the purposes of this paragraph, Her Majesty's forces shall be taken to consist of prescribed establishments and organisations in which persons serve under the control of the Defence Council.

AMENDMENTS

1. Welfare Reform Act 2009 s.11 and Sch.3 para.8(5) (November 12, 2009).
2. Welfare Reform Act 2012 s.54(1) and (6) (February 25, 2013).

DEFINITIONS

    "Administration Act"—see s.65.

    "continental shelf operations"—see para.7(3).

    "Contributions and Benefits Act"—see s.65.

    "contributory allowance"—see s.1(7).

    "employed"—see s.24(1).

    "employment"—see s.24(1).

    "entitled"—see s.24(1).

    "Her Majesty's forces"—see para.15(2).

    "income-related allowance"—see s.1(7).

    "limited capability for work-related activity"—see s.2(5).

    "period of limited capability for work"—see s.24(1).

    "prescribed"—see s.24(1).

    "regulations"—see s.24(1).

    "week"—see s.24(1).

    "work-related activity"—see ss.24(1), 13(7).

GENERAL NOTE

Paragraph 2 (waiting days)

1.424   See ESA Regs reg.144. The general rule, as with previous contributory incapacity benefit regimes, is that there is no entitlement to ESA in respect of a number of "waiting days" at the beginning of a period of limited capability for work. The general rule has a number of exceptions set out in reg.144(2). In addition, the general rule is, of course, affected by the "linking rules" (on which see reg.145) in a case of intermittent incapacity where those rules fuse into one ostensibly separate spells of limited capability for work: the "waiting days" only have to be served once in a period of limited capability for work. Regulation 144 originally set the number of these days of non-entitlement ("waiting days") at three. From October 27, 2014 that was increased to seven with respect to a new claim in respect of a waiting period starting on or after that date.

Paragraph 3 (periods of less than a week)

Like JSA, ESA is a weekly benefit, paid in respect of a week of limited capability   **1.425** for work. It is paid fortnightly in arrears, and the day of the week on which payment is to be made is determined by reference to the last two digits of the claimant's national insurance number (Claims and Payments Regs, reg.26C (see updating material with respect to Vol.III). This para of Sch.2 enables regs to make provision for payment in respect of periods of less than a week: see ESA Regs, regs 165–169.

Paragraph 4 (linking periods)

See ESA Regs, reg.145. The linking rules are crucial for those suffering from   **1.426** intermittent incapacity. They impact, to the claimant's benefit, as regards "waiting days"; those days of non-entitlement (see para.(2) and ESA Regs reg.144) only have to be served once in any period of limited capability for work. They are also relevant to determining the relevant benefit year and hence the appropriate tax years to which to have regard with respect to the application of the national insurance contribution conditions (see further the commentary to Sch.1 Pt 1 paras 1–3).

The linking rule works on the basis that two ostensibly separate spells of limited capability for work will be fused into one where the separation period between the spells is not more than 12 weeks. This fusing does not, however, mean that days in the separation period thereby become ones of limited capability for work (*Chief Adjudication Officer v Astle* (Court of Appeal, judgment of March 17, 1999, available on LEXIS and noted in [1999] 6 J.S.S.L. 203). See further for more detail the commentary to SSCBA 1992, s.30C(1)(c) (the "linking" rule)). A period of limited capability for work can only be formed of days of actual limited capability for work and/or ones which the legislative scheme treats as ones of limited capability for work.

Note that the Employment and Support Allowance (Amendment of Linking Rules) Regulations 2012 (SI 2012/919) regs 5 and 6 heavily amended the linking rules and a variety of other rules in the ESA Regs and the Migration Regs with effect from May 1, 2012.

Paragraph 5 (presence in Great Britain)

Entitlement to ESA generally requires presence in Great Britain (s.1(3)(d)). This   **1.427** paragraph enables regulations to treat someone, whatever the actual reality in terms of presence or absence, as being or not being in Great Britain. See ESA Regs reg.11 (condition relating to youth—residence or presence).

Paragraph 6 (entitlement to CESA when absent from Great Britain)

Entitlement to CESA generally requires presence in Great Britain (s.1(3)(d)).   **1.428** This para. enables regulations to give entitlement where the claimant is not in Great Britain. See ESA Regs regs 151–155, dealing with periods of temporary absence. Note also that CESA is an exportable benefit for purposes of EC law.

Paragraph 7 (Modification of CESA for those employed on ships etc)

This enables regulations to modify the rules on entitlement to CESA as regards   **1.429** those who are, have been or are to be, employed on any ship, vessel, hovercraft or aircraft; outside Great Britain; or in prescribed employment in connection with continental shelf operations. See the various amendments made with effect from

October 27, 2008 by the Employment and Support Allowance (Consequential Provisions) (No.2) Regulations 2008 (SI 2008/1554), regs 65 and 67, respectively to the Social Security (Airmen's Benefits) Regulations 1975 (SI 1975/494), Social Security (Mariners' Benefits) Regulations 1975 (SI 1975/529).

Paragraph (8) (retaining entitlement to IRESA when absent from Great Britain)

1.430   See ESA Regs regs 151–155.

Paragraph 10 (effect of work)

1.431   Unsurprisingly, in a benefits regime founded on limited capability for work, the general rule in respect of ESA is that the doing of any work negatives limited capability: see ESA Regs, reg.40, precluding entitlement to ESA in any week in which a claimant does work. But like the previous incapacity benefit regime, the general preclusive rule is modified to permit engagement in a range of work without loss of benefit. This recognizes that work can assist recovery or help the claimant into thinking about work and a possibility to return to work, or merely not wanting to exclude the sick and disabled from participation in civic office or a range of voluntary or charitable work. Under ESA, unlike its predecessor regime, the rules more fully protect through more generous earnings disregards those only in receipt of the income related form of the benefit as well as those receiving its contributory form. See ESA Regs regs 41–46.

Paragraph 12 (attribution of deductions from ESA)

1.432   A claimant may be entitled to CESA to IRESA or to both. Where someone is entitled to both IRESA and CESA, this para enables the making of regulations to provide for which component or components is or are to be reduced because of provisions enabling reduction set out in the specified provisions dealing with ESA conditionality (ss.11–13) or where, under SSAA 1992 s.2AA, entitlement depends on the claimant's partner complying with conditions in respect of work-focused interviews. See ESA Regs reg.63. See also, in Vol.III, with respect to SSAA 1992 s.2AA, the Social Security (Jobcentre Plus Interviews for Partners) Regs 2003 (SI 2003/1886), reg.11, as amended with effect from October 27, 2008, by reg.71 of the Employment and Support Allowance (Consequential Provisions) (No.2) Regs 2008 (SI 2008/1554).

Paragraph 14 (Advance claims)

1.433   See ESA Regs reg.66.

Paragraph 15 (members of Her Majesty's forces)

1.434   This enables regulations to modify the rules on entitlement to ESA in respect of persons who are or have been members of those forces. See ESA Regs regs 155 and Sch.1. See also the Social Security (Benefit) (Members of the Forces) Regs 1975 (SI 1975/493) as amended with effect from October 27, 2008 by reg.66 of the Employment and Support Allowance (Consequential Provisions) (No.2) Regs 2008 (SI 2008/1554).

SCHEDULE 3   **Section 28**

CONSEQUENTIAL AMENDMENTS RELATING TO PART 1

1.435   Insofar as the provisions in this Schedule amend legislation contained in the main volumes, these amendments have been taken into account in preparing the legislative text.

SCHEDULE 4   **Section 29**

TRANSITION RELATING TO PART 1

General power to provide for transition relating to Part 1

1.—(1) Regulations may make such provision as the Secretary of State considers necessary   **1.436**
or expedient—
  (a) in connection with the coming into force of any provision of, or repeal relating to, this
      Part, or
  (b) otherwise for the purposes of, or in connection with, the transition to employment and
      support allowance.
(2) The following provisions of this Schedule are not to be taken as prejudicing the generality of sub-paragraph (1).

Pre-commencement claims

2.—Regulations may—   **1.437**
  (a) make provision for a claim for incapacity benefit, income support or severe disable-
      ment allowance which is made before the appointed day to be treated wholly or partly
      as a claim for an employment and support allowance;
  (b) make provision for the purpose of enabling claims for an employment and support
      allowance to be made before the appointed day for a period beginning on or after that
      day.

Post-commencement claims

3.—Regulations may—   **1.438**
  *(a) make provision excluding the making of a claim for incapacity benefit or severe disablement
       allowance on or after the appointed day;*
  (b) make provision for a claim for incapacity benefit, income support or severe
      disablement allowance which is made on or after the appointed day to be treated in
      prescribed circumstances as a claim for an employment and support allowance;
  (c) make provision for a claim for an employment and support allowance to be treated
      wholly or partly as a claim for incapacity benefit, income support or severe disable-
      ment allowance;
  (d) make provision excluding the making of a claim for an employment and support
      allowance by a person who is entitled to an existing award.

Award of employment and support allowance for pre-commencement period

4.—*Regulations may*—   **1.439**
  *(a) make provision for an employment and support allowance of such a kind as the regulations
       may provide to be awarded in prescribed circumstances for a period before the appointed day;*
  *(b) make provision with respect to conditions of entitlement in relation to an award under sub-
       paragraph (a) and the amount payable by way of an allowance under such an award.*

Matching of awards of employment and support allowance

5.—*(1) For the purposes of this paragraph, an award of an employment and support allowance is   **1.440**
one that falls to be made on matching terms if—*
  *(a) it is made in pursuance of a claim by a person who was previously entitled to an existing
       award, and*
  *(b) had it continued to be possible to make an award of incapacity benefit, income support on
       grounds of incapacity for work, or severe disablement allowance, the award which would
       have been made to him ("the hypothetical award") would have been made on the basis of
       the linking of periods of incapacity for work.*
(2) Regulations may—
  *(a) make provision for the purpose of securing that an award of an employment and support
       allowance that falls to be made on matching terms is made on terms which match in whole or
       part the hypothetical award;*
  (b) make provision for the modification of matched awards for the purpose of securing that the

person with the award is put in the position he would have been had he been made the hypothetical award which was then the subject of conversion under paragraph 7.

*(3) In sub-paragraph (2)(b), the reference to matched awards is to awards of an employment
and support allowance that have been the subject of matching in pursuance of regulations under sub-
paragraph (2)(a).*

6.—*(1) For the purposes of this paragraph an award of an employment and support allowance is
one which falls to be made on matching terms if—*

> *(a) it is made in pursuance of a claim by a person who was previously entitled to an existing award,*
> *(b) had he continued to be entitled to that award, it would have been the subject of conversion
> under paragraph 7 before the date of his claim for an employment and support allowance, and*
> *(c) had it continued to be possible to make an award of incapacity benefit, income support on grounds
> of incapacity for work, or severe disablement allowance, the award which would have been made
> to him would have been made on the basis of the linking of periods of incapacity for work.*

*(2) Regulations may make provision for the purpose of securing that an award of an employment
and support allowance that falls to be made on matching terms is made on terms which match in whole
or part the award that would have resulted from conversion under paragraph 7 had entitlement to the
existing award continued.*

Treatment of existing awards

1.441 **7.**—(1) Regulations may—

> (a) make provision for converting existing awards into awards of an employment and
> support allowance, and with respect to the terms of conversion;
> (b) make provision for the termination of existing awards in prescribed circumstances.

(2) Regulations under sub-paragraph (1)(a) may, in particular—

> (a) make provision for conversion of an existing award—
>> (i) on application, in accordance with the regulations, by the person entitled to the
>> award, or
>> (ii) without application;
> (b) make provision about the conditions to be satisfied in relation to an application for
> conversion;
> (c) make provision about the timing of conversion;
> (d) provide for an existing award to have effect after conversion as an award of an employ-
> ment and support allowance—
>> (i) of such a kind,
>> (ii) for such period,
>> (iii) of such an amount, and
>> (iv) subject to such conditions,
>> as the regulations may provide;
> (e) make provision for determining in connection with conversion of an existing award
> whether a person has limited capability for work-related activity.
> [¹(f) make provision modifying the application of section 1A in relation to awards of an
> employment and support allowance to persons previously entitled to existing awards.]

(3) Regulations under sub-paragraph (1)(a) may, in relation to existing awards which have
been the subject of conversion under this paragraph, include provision about revision under
section 9 of the Social Security Act 1998 (c. 14), or supersession under section 10 of that Act
in respect of the period before conversion.

Transitional allowances

1.442 **8.**—(1) Regulations may—

> (a) make provision for a person's continuing entitlement to an employment and support
> allowance awarded by virtue of regulations under paragraph 7 (a "transitional allowance")
> to be determined by reference to such provision as may be made by the regulations;
> (b) make provision for the review of an award of a transitional allowance;
> (c) make provision for the termination of an award of a transitional allowance;
> (d) make provision for this Part, or any other enactment relating to social security, to have
> effect with prescribed modifications in relation to a person with a transitional allowance;
> (e) make provision for the purpose of enabling a transitional allowance to be revised under
> section 9 of the Social Security Act 1998 (c. 14) or superseded under section 10 of that
> Act.

(2) In this paragraph "enactment" includes an enactment contained in subordinate legislation (within the meaning of the Interpretation Act 1978 (c. 30)).

9.—*(1) Regulations may prescribe circumstances in which a person who is entitled to a transitional allowance immediately before reaching pensionable age is to be treated as having satisfied the condition in paragraph 5(2) of Schedule 3 to the Contributions and Benefits Act (first contribution condition for entitlement to state pension).*

(2) In this paragraph, "pensionable age" has the meaning given by the rules in paragraph 1 of Schedule 4 to the Pensions Act 1995 (c. 26).

1.443

Post-commencement up-rating of incapacity benefit and severe disablement allowance

10.—Regulations may provide for section 150 of the Administration Act (annual up-rating of benefits), so far as relating to—
  (a) incapacity benefit under section 30A of the Contributions and Benefits Act, or
  (b) severe disablement allowance,
    to have effect with prescribed modifications in relation to tax years beginning on or after the appointed day.

1.444

Interpretation

11.—In this Schedule—
"appointed day" means the day appointed for the coming into force of section 1;
"existing award" means—
  (a) an award of incapacity benefit,
  (b) an award of severe disablement allowance, and
  (c) an award of income support made to a person to whom regulation 6(4)(a) or 13(2)(b) or (bb) of, or paragraph 7(a) or (b), 10, 12 or 13 of Schedule 1B to, the Income Support (General) Regulations 1987 (S.I. 1987/1967) (persons incapable of work or disabled) applies;
"incapacity benefit" (except in paragraph 10(a)) means—
  (a) incapacity benefit under section 30A, 40 or 41 of the Contributions and Benefits Act,
  (b) long-term incapacity benefit under regulation 11(4) of the Social Security (Incapacity Benefit) (Transitional) Regulations 1995 (S.I. 1995/310) (former sickness benefit), and
  (c) invalidity benefit which has effect by virtue of regulation 17(1) of those regulations as if it were long-term incapacity benefit;
"severe disablement allowance" means severe disablement allowance under section 68 of that Act (as it has effect by virtue of article 4 of the Welfare Reform and Pensions Act 1999 (Commencement No. 9, and Transitional and Savings Provisions) Order 2000 (S.I. 2000/2958) (C. 89));
"transitional allowance" has the meaning given by paragraph 8(1)(a).

1.445

AMENDMENT

1. Welfare Reform Act 2012 s.51(4) (March 20, 2012).

DEFINITIONS

"Administration Act"—see s.65.
"appointed day"—see para.11.
"Contributions and Benefits Act"—see s.65.
"enactment"—see para.8(2).
"existing award"—see para.11.
"the hypothetical award"—see para.5(1)(b).
"incapacity benefit" (except in paragraph 10(a))—see para.11.
"income support"—see s.24(1).
"limited capability for work-related activity"—see s.2(5).
"pensionable age"—see para.9(2).
"prescribed"—see s.24(1).
"regulations"—see s.24(1).
"severe disablement allowance"—see para.11.
"transitional allowance"—see paras 11, 8(1)(a).
"work-related activity"—see ss.24(1), 13(7).

GENERAL NOTE

Provisions in italics were not yet in force as at April 8, 2019.

1.446

Paragraphs 1–3

1.447   See further the Employment and Support Allowance (Transitional Provisions) Regs 2008, regs 1–4 of which entered into force on July 27, 2008.

Paragraphs 7–8

1.448   See the Employment and Support Allowance (Transitional Provisions, Housing Benefit and Council Tax Benefit) (Existing Awards) (No. 2) Regulations 2010 (SI 2010/1907), the key provisions of which came into force on October 1, 2010. Put shortly, these Regulations provide for the migration to ESA of most of those people with current awards of benefit on incapacity grounds (IB, SDA and IS on the grounds of incapacity). The Regulations make appropriate transitional provision, where appropriate, for those whose awards qualify for conversion. The Explanatory Note for the No. 2 Regulations (SI 2010/1907) identifies the policy intent, timetable for and effects of, the migration process:

> "The policy intent is, with few exceptions, for existing incapacity benefits customers to go through the migration process between October 2010 and the end of March 2014. This will determine if they qualify for Employment and Support Allowance and will eventually enable the other incapacity benefit schemes to be wholly wound down.
>
> Migration to the Employment and Support Allowance regime, (to which the Government committed in the December 2008 White Paper), will align and simplify the benefit system, by ensuring that, over time, all customers with a health condition or disability in similar circumstances will be treated equally, receiving support to get into to work and the same level of financial help.
>
> Some current incapacity benefits customers will be found fit for work and disallowed benefit on grounds of incapacity. They may claim Jobseeker's Allowance or remain on Income Support if they qualify on grounds other than incapacity" (paras 7.2–7.4 (footnotes omitted)).

The exceptions mentioned include those who reach state pension age during migration and those over pension age in receipt of SDA. The migration of existing "national insurance credits only" claimants will take place when the main migration has been completed.

ESA rates are different from those of the benefits it replaced. The governmental commitment was that transferees would not suffer a cash reduction at the point of change. The Regulations envisage the following situations:

- Where someone receives more from their existing benefit than the amount they would otherwise receive by way of ESA, this level will be frozen on a mark-time basis; and they will receive a 'transitional addition' that will make their ESA up to the level of their old benefit entitlement until the earlier of either the ESA rate catching up or April 5, 2020.

- Where someone's existing award is the same amount as the amount of ESA receivable, the transferee will get ESA at the same rate from the effective date of migration.

- Where someone receives less on their existing benefit than the amount they would receive by way of ESA, they will receive the appropriate ESA rate on migration.

(2013 c.17)

Jobseekers (Back to Work Schemes) Act 2013

(2013 C.17)

An Act to make provision about the effect of certain provisions relating to participation in a scheme designed to assist persons to obtain employment and about notices relating to participation in such a scheme.[26th March 2013]

GENERAL NOTE

In *R (Reilly and Wilson) v Secretary of State for Work and Pensions* [2013] EWCA   **1.450**
Civ 66; [2013] 1 W.L.R. 2239, the Court of Appeal quashed as unlawful the Jobseeker's Allowance (Employment, Skills and Enterprise Scheme) Regulations 2011 (SI 2011/917) ("the ESES Regulations") under which some of the "Back to Work" schemes operated, because the Secretary of State acted ultra vires in failing to provide sufficient decription of the various schemes in the Regulations to satisfy s.17A(1) of the Jobseekers Act 1995. The Court also held that notices sent to claimants advising them that they were required to take part in a programme within the ESES Scheme did not comply with the requirements of reg.4 of the ESES Regulations. The effect of the decision was that the DWP had no right to impose a sanction on claimants who had failed to meet their requirements. The Court, however, upheld the general policy principle of the employment programmes comprised in the ESES Regulations and also ruled that they did not breach art.4(2) of the ECHR (prohibiting forced or compulsory labour). The Court of Appeal's reasoning was subsequently upheld in substance by the Supreme Court in *R (Reilly and Wilson) v Secretary of State for Work and Pensions* [2013] UKSC 68; [2014] 1 A.C. 453, but because of the retrospective validation of the ESES Regulations by this Act, it was indicated that that would have to be reflected in the order made. It emerges from the judgment of Lang J in *R (Reilly No 2 and Hewstone) v Secretary of State for Work and Pensions* [2014] EWHC 2182 (Admin) that the order was to allow the Secretary of State's appeal on the *ultra vires* point on the basis that the 2013 Act had come into force. The order apparently also allowed the appeal on the point about breach of the notification requirements, which was accepted on behalf of the Secretary of State in *Reilly (No 2)* to have been wrong, so that the declaration in Miss Reilly's favour remained in force.

The DWP on the day of the Court of Appeal's judgment issued the Jobseeker's Allowance (Schemes for Assisting Persons to Obtain Employment) Regulations 2013 (SI 2013/276) ("the SAPOE Regulations"), which came into effect at 18.45 on February 12, 2013 so that sanctions could be applied from the date those new Regulations came into force.

This Act came into force on March 26, 2013, the day on which the Secretary of State sought permission to appeal against the decision of the Court of Appeal in *Reilly and Wilson*, the Bill having been fast-tracked through Parliament. Section 1(14) provides that the ESES Regulations are to be treated as having been revoked by the SAPOE Regulations on the coming into force of the latter.

1.451   This Act is designed retrospectively to validate the impugned ESES Regulations making actions which related to participation in these employment programmes effective, and providing that notices served under those Regulations informing claimants of requirements as to participation, and about consequences of failing to meet requirements, were effective. The provisions affect claimants where sanctions have been applied for failures to comply with the ESES Regulations and cases where the claimant has failed to comply with a requirement of the ESES Regulations but a decision to impose a sanction has not yet been taken. It aims to ensure that any such decisions cannot be challenged on the grounds that the ESES Regulations were invalid or the notices inadequate, notwithstanding the Court of Appeal's judgment, so that benefit sanctions already imposed or to be imposed stand, saving the public purse some £130 million which would otherwise have to be paid to claimants who had been, if the Court of Appeal decision had stood, treated unlawfully. The Act also aims to protect from challenge on the basis of the reasoning in *Reilly and Wilson* about the validity of notices under the Jobseeker's Allowance (Mandatory Work Activity Scheme) Regulations 2011 (SI 2011/688).

The compatibility of the 2013 Act with the ECHR was challenged in *Reilly (No 2)* (above), on the basis that the purported retrospective validation of the ESES Regulations breached the claimants' right to a fair trial under art.6 in relation to the proceedings in existence as at March 26, 2013 (the challenges to Ms Reilly's favourable judgment in the Court of Appeal and to Mr Hewstone's favourable decisions from a First-tier Tribunal against which the Secretary of State had appealed to the Upper Tribunal). Mr Hewstone also had one decision pending and "stockpiled" before the Secretary of State). The only remedy sought by the claimants was a declaration of incompatibility under s.4 of the Human Rights Act 1998, which cannot affect the validity or continuing operation of the provision declared incompatible. At one time, when the staying of other cases to await the outcome of *Reilly (No 2)* was put into operation, it was thought that there was to be a challenge on the basis of European Union law, which could in principle, if successful, have led to a conclusion that the 2013 Act or parts of it had to be disapplied. However, no such challenge was maintained before Lang J.

Lang J granted the declaration of incompatibility with art.6 of the ECHR, having concluded that art.1 of Protocol 1 was not engaged (so that Mr Hewstone could not rely on the ECHR in relation to his stockpiled claim). She had no doubt that the Act had a preclusive retrospective effect on the claimants' pending proceedings. Indeed, she went so far as to say that the Upper Tribunal would be bound in Mr Hewstone's case to allow the Secretary of State's appeal because the only tenable defect in the application of the ESES Regulations in his case had been retrospectively validated. The Judge's view was that there were not the required "compelling grounds of public interest" in order to justify the retrospective interference with the claimants' rights. She rejected the Secretary of State's argument that giving the decision in *Reilly* what was in practice a prospective effect in other cases, through the impact of the 2013 Act, was merely giving effect to the general principle contained in s.27 of the SSA 1998 in relation to decisions of the Upper Tribunal on appeal or of higher courts on further appeal, starkly exposing the misunderstanding of the effect of s.27 involved. If *Reilly and Wilson* is regarded as the test case, s.27 did not prevent its application to the claimant who brought the test case (Ms Reilly), to claimants whose appeals to the First-tier Tribunal or cases before the Upper Tribunal or higher were pending at the date of the test case decision (e.g. Mr Hewstone) or to claimants for whom decisions had been stockpiled under s.25 of the SSA 1998 pending the decision in the test case. Nor could it be accepted that the flaws identified in *Reilly and Wilson* were mere technicalities, that the 2013 Act was restoring the original intentions of Parliament or that the effect was to prevent claimants enjoying an undeserved windfall.

1.452   The Secretary of State's appeal against Lang J's decision was heard by the Court of Appeal at the end of November 2015 and judgment was given on April 28, 2016, there having been some post-hearing submissions (*SSWP v Reilly and Hewstone* and

SSWP v Jeffrey and Bevan [2016] EWCA Civ 413; [2017] Q.B. 657; [2017] AACR 14). That appeal was heard at the same time as that of the Secretary of State against the decision of the three-judge panel in February 2015 in *SSWP v TJ (JSA)* [2015] UKUT 56 (AAC), where the cases of three claimants had been selected to attempt to resolve issues left outstanding by *Reilly and Wilson* and *Reilly (No.2)*. There was a detailed description and discussion of the decision in *TJ* in the 2015/16 edition of this volume, which need not now all be repeated here in the light of the Court of Appeal's decision.

The three cases before the Upper Tribunal all stemmed from decisions of the Secretary of State, made before the amendment of the ESES Regulations by the Jobseeker's Allowance (Sanctions) (Amendment) Regulations 2012, to impose a sanction of non-payment of JSA on the claimants under reg.8 for having failed without good cause to participate in a scheme under the ESES Regulations (in two cases the Work Programme and in one the Community Action Programme). Regulation 8 as in existence at the time is set out at p.1257 of Vol.II (2012/13 edition). Two tribunals allowed the claimants' appeals on the ground that, following the High Court decision in *Reilly and Wilson*, the notifications requiring participation did not meet the requirements of reg.4. The Secretary of State was given permission to appeal to the Upper Tribunal. The other tribunal disallowed the claimant's appeal without reference to *Reilly and Wilson*.

The central element of the decision of the majority of the Upper Tribunal (Judges Rowland and Wright; Charles J dissenting on this element) was that the 2013 Act, despite the provision in s.1(1) that the ESES Regulations are to be treated "for all purposes" as made under s.17A of the old style Jobseekers Act 1995, was to be construed either under ordinary canons of statutory construction or as "read down" under s.3 of the Human Rights Act 1998 so as to be compatible with art.6 of the ECHR, as not applying retrospectively to claimants who had already brought appeals to the First-tier Tribunal prior to March 26, 2013. That conclusion was fairly shortly rejected by the Court of Appeal in *Jeffrey and Bevan*. The Court of Appeal took the view that the phrase "for all purposes" was in essence the beginning and end of the analysis (para.131 of the judgment of the court). It agreed with Charles J in that respect and also in the view that s.27 of the SSA 1998 (the "anti-test-case" rule) played no part in informing the intention underlying the 2013 Act. The Court of Appeal further rejected the argument made for the claimants that s.12(8)(b) of the SSA 1998 (tribunals not to take into account any circumstances not obtaining at the time when the decision appealed against was made) would prevent any First-tier Tribunal that was considering any appeal pending as at March 26, 2013 from giving effect to the 2013 Act because its enactment would, notwithstanding its retrospective effect, constitute a circumstance not obtaining at the date of the sanction decision. The Upper Tribunal had treated this as a separate issue, but counsel for Ms Jeffrey said that the argument was intended to support the construction point. The Court of Appeal held (para.137) that the effect of s.12(8)(b) could not be to nullify subsequent explicitly retrospective legislation that would otherwise govern the tribunal's decision and that the decision in *CAO v McKiernon*, reported as *R(I) 2/94* (extensively discussed by the majority in the Upper Tribunal) was not authority to the contrary, having been concerned with a wholly different question. The Court of Appeal agreed with the conclusion and reasoning in para.175 of the Upper Tribunal's decision to the effect that it would be improper to use the discretion in s.12(2)(a) of the Tribunal, Courts and Enforcement Act 2007 not to set aside a decision of a First-tier Tribunal found to have involved an error of law to avoid a result incompatible with art.6 of the ECHR. To do so would be to ignore the binding effect of the 2013 Act and the fact that even a declaration of incompatibility under s.4 of the Human Rights Act 1998 does not affect the validity or continuing operation of primary legislation.

Since the Court of Appeal took that view of the main parts of the Upper Tribunal decision, the central issue (although it appears in the judgment first) became whether Lang J was right or wrong about incompatibility with art.6 of the

1.453

ECHR. Following an exhaustive review of the Strasbourg and other authorities it concluded that she had been right. The retrospective provision was, in relation to claimants who had commenced proceedings (appeal or judicial review) prior to March 26, 2013, incompatible with art.6 as designed to influence the judicial determination of those disputes contrary to the *Zielinski* principle (*Zielinski v France* (2001) 31 EHRR 19) as properly understood. There were not the compelling grounds of the general interest to constitute justification for that interference with the right to a fair trial. The Court comprehensively rejected the six grounds, some fairly desperate, to the contrary put forward by the Secretary of State. Very much in brief, it was held that:

(1) it was not necessary that there be an intention to target any particular claimant, but that there is a breach of the *Zielinski* principle if part of the intention is to interfere with the outcome of a class of claims generally, as was plainly the case for the 2013 Act;

(2) although there was no substantive interference with Ms Reilly's access to the court, as she had not been sanctioned, there was in Mr Hewstone's case and it did not matter that he had not in his appeals expressly raised the ground of challenge to notices that eventually succeeded in the Supreme Court or had other arguable grounds (e.g. good cause) on which he could rely;

(3) and (4) the failures in the ESES Regulations that the 2013 Act was designed to correct retrospectively were not merely technical drafting loopholes; even if the fact that claimants with good cause for failing to participate in a scheme could escape sanction meant that protection from the retrospective effect would go to the undeserving, that did not outweigh the value of protecting the integrity of the judicial process; the financial impact, as only claimants who had commenced proceeding were to be protected, would be limited to about £1.3 million; it did not matter that those in a similar position who had not commenced proceedings would not be protected; and the existence of s.27 of the SSA 1998 assisted the claimants rather than the Secretary of State;

(5) under the heading of justification, the effect of the 2013 Act on existing appeals was not "only incidental"; and

(6) although in places Lang J might have transgressed the principle in art.9 of the Bill of Rights that proceedings in Parliament ought not to be impeached or questioned in any court, there was no such transgression in the Court of Appeal's reasoning.

1.454   A remedial Order, the Jobseekers (Back to Work Schemes Act 2013) (Remedial) Order 2020 (SI 2020/1085), was eventually approved by Parliament, after many convolutions described in the notes to the 2020/21 edition of what was then Vol.II of this series, to come into effect on October 3, 2020. The Order inserts new ss.1A and 1B into the 2013 Act. The new s.1A is designed to resolve the limited incompatibility with art.6 of the ECHR of the effect of s.1 in relation to the ESES Regulations, as held by the Court of Appeal, in appeals against Secretary of State decisions lodged before March 26, 2013 and still pending. The new s.1B does the same for certain appeals lodged before March 26, 2013 against MWAS Regulations penalties (attention having been drawn to this issue in *SSWP v DM (rule 17) (JSA)* [2018] UKUT 424 (AAC)). That covers cases where the deeming of the validity of notices by s.1(7) would have applied. In the cases covered, the Secretary of State, if revising their own decision, is required to disregard the specified parts of s.1. If the appeal has been determined by a tribunal, the Secretary of State is required to supersede the tribunal decision and to disregard the specified provisions. Any tribunal or court dealing with either an original appeal or an appeal following a revision or supersession must also disregard the specified provisions. Memo DMG 23/20 gives helpful guidance on the carrying out of the required revisions and supersessions.

MB v SSWP (JSA) [2021] UKUT 69 contains discussion of the background to and operation of the Remedial Order and confirms that, even if a claimant had an appeal to the Upper Tribunal pending, the Secretary of State is obliged to supersede the First-tier Tribunal decision. That led to the dismissal of the claimant's appeal in *MB*.

The Court of Appeal rejected the argument on behalf of Mr Hewstone that   **1.455**
claimants who had been sanctioned under reg.8 of the ESES Regulations before
March 26, 2013 but who had not by that date appealed or started other legal
proceedings had been deprived of a "possession" under art.1 of Protocol 1 of the
ECHR. It appears that that argument was put in two ways: that in any period for
which such a claimant satisfied the conditions of entitlement in s.1(2) of the old style
Jobseekers Act 1995 the right to receive JSA was a possession and, alternatively, that
after the decisions of Foskett J and the Court of Appeal in *Reilly and Wilson*, they
had a legitimate expectation of receiving a "repayment" of the JSA withheld during
the sanction period which constituted a possession. The Court agreed with Lang J
that the first alternative did not work because each sanction decision had the effect
that benefit was not payable for a period in the future, so that no possession was ever
acquired that was then removed. It may be arguable that that reasoning overlooks
the fact that claimants continue to be entitled to old style JSA through a period of
a sanction, so that they are deprived of the normal consequence of entitlement,
which is that benefit is payable. The Court held that the second alternative did not
work under the Strasbourg authority because the claim to "repayment" was not sufficiently supported by settled national case-law as at March 26, 2013 to constitute
an asset or possession.

The final issue dealt with in relation to the Upper Tribunal's decision in Mr Bevan's
case was its guidance on the so-called prior information requirement (see para.74 of
the judgment of the Supreme Court in *Reilly and Wilson*), a failure to comply with
which might vitiate the requirement to participate in a scheme. The Upper Tribunal
had concluded, in the terms of its own summary in para.13(vi), that in the case of
schemes which were mandatory both at the stages of referral onto them and once
on them, no basis could be identified on which *meaningful* representations could be
made prior to the decision to refer, in the sense of those representations being able
to affect the decision to refer. In the 2015/16 edition of this volume there was some
criticism of the Upper Tribunal's use of the word "mandatory" in this context.

The Court of Appeal first held that the Upper Tribunal had been right on the particular facts of Mr Bevan's case (where his complaint was that he could not afford
the bus fare to attend the appointment given, so needed payment in advance rather
than a refund) to find that it would have made no difference to what he would have
said to the provider about the fares if he had known about what *The Work Programme
Provider Guidance* issued by the DWP said about ability to use transportation.

So far as the Upper Tribunal's general guidance is concerned, the Court said this
in para.172 about the submission that the Upper Tribunal had erred in saying that
there was no scope for making representations in connection with a decision to refer
a claimant to the Work Programme since referral was mandatory:

> "We do not believe that that is a fair reading of what the Tribunal said; and if it is
> properly understood there does not seem to be any dispute of principle between
> the parties. The Tribunal was not laying down any absolute rule. The Secretary of
> State's policy, embodied in the guidance, is that referral to the Programme should
> be automatic (ignoring the specified exceptions) if the criteria are met. All that the
> Tribunal was doing was to point out that, that being so, any representations would
> have to address the question why he should depart from the policy; and that it was
> not easy to see what such representations might be. That seems to us an obvious
> common sense observation, particularly since referral to the Work Programme
> does not as such involve any specific obligation: see para.151 above. But it does
> not mean that there could never be such cases, and indeed para.224 is expressly
> addressed to that possibility. The Tribunal did not depart from anything that the
> Supreme Court said in [*Reilly and Wilson*]. It was simply considering its applica-
> tion in the particular circumstances of referral to the Work Programme."

The Court considered that in the real world application of the prior informa-   **1.456**
tion duty was unlikely to be important at the point of initial referral to the Work

Programme, as claimants were unlikely to object at that stage, before any specific requirements were imposed. Problems were likely to emerge when particular requirements were imposed on claimants that they considered unreasonable or inappropriate. The Upper Tribunal had appeared to say in para.249 of its decision that there was little or no scope for the operation of the duty at that stage. The Court of Appeal says this in paras 177 and 178:

> "177. Mr de la Mare [counsel for Mr Bevan] submitted that that is wrong. If it is indeed what the Tribunal meant, we agree. So also does Ms Leventhal [counsel for the Secretary of State], who explicitly accepted in her written submissions that 'the requirements of fairness continue to apply after referral'. In principle, JSA claimants who are required, or who it is proposed should be required, under the Work Programme to participate in a particular activity should have suffi- cient information to enable them to make meaningful representations about the requirement – for example, that the activity in question is unsuitable for them or that there are practical obstacles to their participation. The fact that participation is mandatory if the requirement is made is beside the point: the whole purpose of the representations, and thus of the claimant having the relevant information to be able to make them, is so that the provider may be persuaded that the require- ment should <u>not</u> be made, or should be withdrawn or modified.
> 178. However we should emphasise that the foregoing is concerned with the position in principle. It is quite another matter whether the Work Programme as operated in fact fails to give claimants such information. The Secretary of State's evidence before the Tribunal was that the relevant guidance in fact provides for them to be very fully informed. We have already referred to the Tribunal's findings about the information given at the referral interview. But it was also the evidence that at the initial interview with the provider post-referral, which is designed to find out how the claimant can be best supported, and in the subse- quent inter-actions between claimant and provider claimants are supposed to be given both information and the opportunity to make representations. Whether in any particular case there has nevertheless been a failure to give information nec- essary to enable the claimant to make meaningful representations will have to be judged on the facts of the particular case. Tribunals will no doubt bear in mind the point made in [*Reilly and Wilson*] that it is important not to be prescriptive about how any necessary information is provided: see para.74 of the judgment of Lord Neuberger and Lord Toulson."

It is understood that Mr Bevan, who had been represented by CPAG, abandoned the possibility of applying for permission to appeal to the Supreme Court against the Court of Appeal's decision, having been unable to obtain legal aid. The Supreme Court refused Mr Hewstone's application for permission to appeal on the ground that it did not raise a point of law that deserved consideration at that point, as the outcome would not have affected the position of the parties to the case. That was because the claimants had succeeded on the point on art.6 of the ECHR and had only been seeking a declaration of incompatibility with the ECHR. The judges did indicate, though, that the issue whether the 2013 Act breached art.1 of Protocol 1 of the ECHR might deserve consideration in another case in which its resolution could affect the outcome.

The prior information duty was applied in *NM v SSWP (JSA)* [2016] UKUT 351 (AAC). Judge Wright held, as eventually conceded by the Secretary of State, that the inability to show that relevant DWP guidance had been considered before the claimant was given notice to participate in a Mandatory Work Activity scheme meant either that the claimant should not have been referred to the scheme (because the officer either would have followed the guidance or could have been persuaded to do so on representations from the claimant) or that he had good reason for not participating in the scheme. The appeal related to a sanction for failing to participate, through behaviour on the scheme. The guidance, in something called *Mandatory Work Activity Guidance* or *Operational Instructions – Procedural Guidance – Mandatory Work Activity – January 2012*, was relevant because at the time it instructed that claimants should not be considered for referral to Mandatory Work Activity if, among other circumstances, they were currently working (paid or voluntary). The claimant had been volunteering in a Sue Ryder shop, which activity he had to give up to attend the required scheme as a volunteer in a Salvation Army shop. The Secretary of State submitted that the guidance had since been changed to introduce an element of discretion about referral of claimants doing voluntary work. Judge Wright held that this would not excuse a failure by an officer of the Secretary of State to consider his own guidance or, on any appeal, a failure to provide the guidance to a First-tier Tribunal in accordance with the principles of natural justice.

Judge Wright has since emphasised some important elements of the applica-   **1.457**
tion of the prior information duty, that should serve to rein in an over-enthusiastic use of the principle in some First-tier Tribunals, but only when properly placed in context. In *SSWP v SD (JSA)* [2020] UKUT 39 (AAC) he stressed, by reference both to the Supreme Court in *Reilly and Wilson* and the Court of Appeal in *Reilly and Hewstone* and *Jeffrey and Bevan*, that even if there has been a breach of the duty at the stage of initial referral to the Work Programme the notice of referral would only be invalidated if the breach was material. In this particular case, the claimant had never objected to his referral, and his appeal against a sanction for failing to participate by non-attendance at a notified appointment was solely based on the ground that he had previously been told not to attend by his work coach. The tribunal, which had raised and sought evidence on the prior information point on its own initiative, failed to explain why it considered any breach of the duty material. In substituting a decision, the judge rejected any unfairness in the referral to the Work Programme and rejected on the evidence the claimant's contention about the appointment.

In *SSWP v CN (JSA)* [2020] UKUT 26 (AAC), a case to which the 2013 Act applied, the claimant's sole ground of appeal against a sanction for failing to participate in the Work Programme by not attending an appointment was that she had never failed to keep an appointment (i.e. implicitly that she could not have received the notice of the appointment and/or had good cause under the ESES Regulations). The tribunal allowed her appeal on the ground that the bundle did not contain a copy of the notice referring her to the Work Programme (i.e. the WP05) so that it was not satisfied that she had properly been notified of the requirement to participate. The tribunal appeared to think that that issue was one "raised by the appeal" within s.12(8)(a) of the SSA 1998, which it manifestly was not as the Secretary of State's submission in the bundle was that there was no dispute that the claimant was referred to the Work Programme. Nor did it give any explanation, if it had exercised its discretion under s.12(8)(a) to consider the issue, as to why it did so and how it was clearly apparent from the evidence so as to be capable of being dealt with under that discretion. Even if those hurdles had been overcome, the Secretary of State had not been given a fair opportunity to deal with the point. It is not necessary for the Secretary of State in all sanctions cases to provide evidence in the appeal bundle that all preconditions for the imposition of the sanction are satisfied. It depends what issues have been put in dispute in the appeal. Having therefore set the tribunal's decision aside, the judge substituted a decision finding on the evidence that the claimant had received the letter notifying her of the appointment in question. Unfortunately, in doing so the judge did not explain how that conclusion was compatible with what he stated at para.21 was arguable, that the appointment letter did not satisfy the condition in reg.4(2)(c) of the ESES Regulations on details of what the claimant had to do even when read with the "sanitising" effect of s.1(4)(a) of the 2013 Act.

The judge's statement that the Secretary of State need not in all sanctions cases provide evidence in the appeal bundle to support the satisfaction of all the preconditions to imposing a sanction, must be read in the light of the approach in *SSWP v DC (JSA)* [2017] UKUT 464 (AAC), reported as [2018] AACR 16, and *PO'R v DFC (JSA)* [2018] NI Com 1 (see the notes to s.19A of the old style Jobseekers Act

1995). There it was said that the Secretary of State should in all cases involving a failure to participate in some scheme or interview where notice of certain details of the scheme, etc. was required to be given, as well as notice of date, time and place, include in the appeal bundle a copy of the appointment letter, whether the claimant had raised any issue as to the terms of the letter or not. That was on the basis that unrepresented claimants could not be expected to identify technical issues about the validity of notices, and it could not be predicted what particular issues might arise in the course of an appeal. If the letter was not included in the initial bundle, the decisions approved the action of tribunals in directing its production as a proper exercise of their inquisitorial jurisdiction. That exercise must rest on a use of the discretion in s.12(8)(a) to consider issues not raised by the appeal. The resolution of the approaches is no doubt that whenever a tribunal exercises that discretion, it must do so consciously and explain why it has done so in any statement of reasons. It may be that an adequate explanation is to be found more readily when it is a notice of a specific appointment in issue rather than an initial reference to a scheme.

1.458   There was no challenge in the Court of Appeal to the Upper Tribunal's conclusion that, under reg.7 of the ESES Regulations, to avoid a sanction for failure to participate in a scheme good cause had to be shown within five working days of the claimant's being notified of the failure. Nor was there any challenge to its conclusion that a requirement to give notice under reg.4(2) of the ESES Regulations was met by the provision of a WP05 ("start notification") letter from the Secretary of State, but might be constituted by more than one document (such as, in addition or alternatively, an "opportunity letter" or an "appointment letter" from the scheme provider). In *SN v SSWP (JSA)* [2018] UKUT 279 (AAC), para.91, it was confirmed that, despite the failure to issue the claimant with a MWA05 letter, he had been sufficiently notified of the requirement to participate in a mandatory work activity scheme within reg.4 of the Jobseeker's Allowance (Mandatory Work Activity Scheme) Regulations 2011 by a combination of information given in an interview with an adviser and a letter from the programme provider about the specific placement as a retail assistant in a charity shop.

The report required by s.2 was produced by Matthew Oakley in July 2014 "(Independent review of the operation of Jobseeker's Allowance sanctions validated by the Jobseekers Act 2013)" and the government's response was published as Cmnd.8904. An update on improvements to communications was published by the DWP on December 18, 2014. There have been several further official reports on sanctions policy (extending beyond those under s.17A of the old style Jobseekers Act 1995), in particular the House of Commons Work and Pensions Committee, "Benefits Sanctions policy beyond the Oakley Review", HC 814 2014–15 (March 24, 2015), "Benefit Sanctions: Beyond the Oakley Review: Government Response to the Committee's Fifth Report of Session 2014–15", HC 557 2015–16 (October 22, 2015) and subsequent letters between the Secretary of State and the chairman of the Committee. There is an excellent summary of this and other literature from many sources as at November 30, 2015 in a House of Commons Debate Pack on Benefit Sanctions produced by the House of Commons Library (CDP-0113). The Scottish Government has also issued a number of updates on benefit sanctions in Scotland.

On November 30, 2016 the National Audit Office published a report on *Benefit sanctions* (HC 628 2016-17) concluding that the system could not be said to provide value for money while the Department did not understand the reasons for the inconsistency in the application of sanctions. Those points were taken up by the House of Commons Public Accounts Committee in its report of February, 21 2017 on *Benefit sanctions* (HC 775 2016-17), which recommended that the Department should review its use of sanctions, which had increased in severity over recent years.

1.459   In its October 2017 response to the Public Accounts Committee's report (Treasury Minutes, Cm 9505) the government accepted the recommendations on better monitoring and gathering of statistics, undertaking to report progress by January 2018, and said that it would undertake a feasibility study into a trial of a pre-sanction 14-day warning system (the so-called "yellow card" proposal). However, it warned that legislative amendments would be necessary before a trial could be implemented. The absence of space for such amendments was the justification in the January 2018 Progress Report (Treasury Minutes, Cm 9566) for not currently proceeding with the feasibility study. But the "spirit" of the proposal would be kept in mind. In April 2018 the House of Commons Work and Pensions Committee launched an enquiry into sanctions, including the non-implementation of the yellow card feasibility study and whether the recommendations of the Oakley Review had improved the sanctions regime. A May 2018 report on a trial of an early warning system in 2016 concluded that it made little difference to the outcomes (JSA sanctions early warning trial evaluation—final report (DWP ad hoc research report no. 63)). The feasibility of a trial that could be introduced without the need for legislation was apparently still being explored in the context of a first sanctionable failure to participate in a work-search review.

There is much valuable further information, as well as a distinctly critical evaluation, in the House of Commons Work and Pensions Committee's report of November 6, 2018 on "Benefit Sanctions" (HC 995 2017–19). Although the scope of the committee's enquiry went widely into the principle of conditionality across the benefit system, particularly focusing on universal credit and what could be done to protect potentially vulnerable groups subject to conditionality there, much is relevant to old style and new style JSA. In particular, the committee recommended: more rigorous evaluation of the effectiveness of the conditionality and sanctions regime and its effect on claimants' well-being; the reduction of the length of higher level sanctions to two, four and six months; further detailed exploration of allowing a warning for any first sanctionable failure, coupled with any sanction decision first being made provisionally to give the claimant the opportunity to respond.

The government's initial response (House of Commons Work and Pensions Committee, "Benefit Sanctions: Government Response" (HC 1949 2017–19, February 11, 2019), while in general acknowledging the validity of the issues raised, gave little in the way of specific concessions. The recommendation to evaluate the effectiveness of sanctions was accepted, but to be focused on whether the universal credit sanctions regime is effective in supporting claimants to search for work. The recommendation to reduce the length of sanctions was rejected, though subject to reconsideration if the evidence base about the effectiveness of longer sanctions in moving people into work developed further (and now see the next paragraph). The recommendation on a warning system was partially accepted. A "proof of concept" trial, to lead to further testing, was to begin in Spring 2019, but with no commitment to legislation before May 2019. The recommendation on provisional decisions was rejected. The 2016 test of the early warning system showed that only 13 per cent of affected claimants took advantage of the chance to produce more evidence of good reason.

On May 9, 2019, the Secretary of State (Amber Rudd) made a written statement to Parliament (HCWS1545) including the following:

> "I have reviewed my Department's internal data, which shows that a six-month sanction already provides a significant incentive for claimants to engage with the labour market regime. I agree with the Work and Pensions Select Committee that a three-year sanction is unnecessarily long and I feel that the additional incentive provided by a three-year sanction can be outweighed by the unintended impacts to the claimant due to the additional duration. For these reasons, I have now decided to remove three year sanctions and reduce the maximum sanction length to six months by the end of the year."

The necessary amendment to reg.69 of the JSA Regulations 1996 took effect on November 27, 2019, applying to sanctions in operation at that date as well as to future impositions. For old style JSA the result is that a person can never have a sanction of longer than 26 weeks outstanding at any time (see the notes to reg.69). That is not so for new style JSA and universal credit.

Regulations and notices requiring participation in a scheme

1.460   **1.**—(1) The 2011 Regulations are to be treated for all purposes as regulations that were made under section 17A of the Jobseekers Act 1995 and other provisions specified in the preamble to the 2011 Regulations and that came into force on the day specified in the 2011 Regulations.

(2) The Employment, Skills and Enterprise Scheme mentioned in the 2011 Regulations is to be treated as having been, until the coming into force of the 2013 Regulations, a scheme within section 17A(1) of the Jobseekers Act 1995.

(3) The following are to be treated as having been, until the coming into force of the 2013 Regulations, programmes of activities that are part of the Employment, Skills and Enterprise Scheme—

(a) the programmes described in regulation 3(2) to (8) of the 2013 Regulations, and

(b) the programme known as the Community Action Programme,

and references to the scheme are to be read accordingly.

(4) A notice given for the purposes of regulation 4(1) of the 2011 Regulations (requirement to participate and notification) is to be treated as a notice that complied with regulation 4(2)(c) (details of what a person is required to do by way of participation in scheme) if it referred to—

(a) the Employment, Skills and Enterprise Scheme, or

(b) a programme of activities treated under subsection (3) as part of the scheme.

(5) A notice given for the purposes of regulation 4(1) of the 2011 Regulations is to be treated as a notice that complied with regulation 4(2)(e) (information about the consequences of failing to participate) if it described an effect on payments of jobseeker's allowance as a consequence or possible consequence of not participating in the scheme or a programme of activities.

(6) Regulation 4(3) of the 2011 Regulations (notice of changes in what a person is required to do by way of participation in scheme) is to be treated as if at all times—

(a) it required the person in question to be notified only if the changes in the requirements mentioned in regulation 4(2)(c) were such that the details relating to those requirements specified in—

(i) a notice given to the person under regulation 4(1), or

(ii) a notice given to the person under regulation 4(3) on an earlier occasion, were no longer accurate, and

(b) it required the person to be notified only of such changes as made the details inaccurate.

(7) A notice given for the purposes of regulation 4(1) of the Mandatory Work Activity Scheme Regulations is to be treated as a notice that complied with regulation 4(2)(d) (details of what a person is required to do by way of participation in scheme) if it referred to—

(a) the Mandatory Work Activity Scheme, or

(b) a placement described as Mandatory Work Activity.

(8) A notice given for the purposes of regulation 4(1) of the Mandatory Work Activity Scheme Regulations is to be treated as a notice that complied with regulation 4(2)(f) (information about the consequences of failing to participate) if it described an effect on payments of jobseeker's allowance as a consequence or possible consequence of not participating in the scheme or placement.

(9) Regulation 4(3) of the Mandatory Work Activity Scheme Regulations is to be treated as if at all times—

(a) it required the person in question to be notified only if the changes in the requirements mentioned in regulation 4(2)(d) were such that the details relating to those requirements specified in—

(i) a notice given to the person under regulation 4(1), or

(ii) a notice given to the person under regulation 4(3) on an earlier occasion, were no longer accurate, and

(b) it required the person to be notified only of such changes as made the details inaccurate.

(10) The penalty provisions are to be treated (notwithstanding the amendments made by the 2012 Regulations) as having effect after the relevant time as they did before the relevant time, in relation to a failure to comply with the 2011 Regulations or, as the case may be, the Mandatory Work Activity Scheme Regulations that occurred or began to occur before the relevant time

(11) In subsection (10) and this subsection—
"the penalty provisions" means—

(a) in the case of a failure to comply with the 2011 Regulations, the provisions relating to the imposition of a penalty for such a failure that had effect before the relevant time;

(b) in the case of a failure to comply with the Mandatory Work Activity Scheme Regulations, the provisions relating to the imposition of a penalty for such a failure that had effect before the relevant time;

"the relevant time" means the time at which the 2012 Regulations came into force.

(12) A penalty imposed on a person before or after the coming into force of this Act for—

(a) failing to participate in a scheme within section 17A(1) of the Jobseekers Act 1995, or

(b) failing to comply with regulations under section 17A of that Act,
is to be treated as lawfully imposed if the only ground or grounds for treating it as unlawfully imposed is or are removed by subsections (1) to (10).

(13) Subsection (12) does not affect a person's ability to apply for a revision or supersession of, or to appeal against, a decision to impose a penalty by reference to other grounds.

(14) Subject to subsection (10), the 2011 Regulations are to be treated as having been revoked by the 2013 Regulations on the coming into force of the 2013 Regulations.

(15) In this section—
"the 2011 Regulations" means the provisions known as the Jobseeker's Allowance (Employment, Skills and Enterprise Scheme) Regulations 2011 (SI 2011/917);

"the 2012 Regulations" means the Jobseeker's Allowance (Sanctions) (Amendment) Regulations 2012 (S.I. 2012/2568);

"the 2013 Regulations" means the Jobseeker's Allowance (Schemes for Assisting Persons to Obtain Employment) Regulations 2013 (SI 2013/276);

"the Mandatory Work Activity Scheme Regulations" means the Jobseeker's Allowance (Mandatory Work Activity Scheme) Regulations 2011 (SI 2011/688).

[¹1A Certain appeals against penalties under the 2011 Regulations

1.461

(1) This section applies where—

(a) the Secretary of State has made a decision imposing on a claimant for jobseeker's allowance a penalty for failing to comply with the 2011 Regulations ("the penalty decision"), and

(b) the claimant lodged an appeal against the penalty decision before 26 March 2013, and the appeal had not been finally determined, abandoned or withdrawn before 26 March 2013.

(2) If the Secretary of State revises the penalty decision under section 9 of the Social Security Act 1998, in making the revised decision, the Secretary of State must disregard subsections (1) to (6) of section 1 of this Act and subsection (12) of section 1 so far as it relates to those subsections.

(3) Subsection (4) applies where a tribunal has decided the appeal before this section comes into force.

(4) In a case where the tribunal decided to uphold the penalty decision (in whole or in part), the Secretary of State must make a decision superseding the tribunal's decision.

(5) In making a superseding decision under subsection (4), the Secretary of State must disregard subsections (1) to (6) of section 1 and subsection (12) of section 1 so far as it relates to those subsections.

(6) Section 10(1)(b) of the Social Security Act 1998 (power of the Secretary of State to supersede a tribunal decision) does not apply in a case where subsection (4) applies.

(7) A superseding decision made under subsection (4) is to be treated for all purposes as if it were a superseding decision made under section 10 of the Social Security Act 1998.

(8) Subsection (9) applies where, after this section has come into force, a court or tribunal is considering—

(a) the appeal mentioned in subsection (1)(b),

(b) an appeal against a revised decision made under section 9 of the Social Security Act 1998 by virtue of subsection (2), or

(c) an appeal against a superseding decision made under subsection (4).

(9) In considering the appeal, the court or tribunal must disregard subsections (1) to (6) of section 1 and subsection (12) of section 1 so far as it relates to those subsections.

(10) A revised decision made by virtue of subsection (2) and a superseding decision made under subsection (4) are to be treated as having effect from the date on which the penalty decision had effect (other than for the purposes of any rule as to the time allowed for bringing an appeal).

(11) In this section—

"the 2011 Regulations" has the same meaning as in section 1;

"court" means the Court of Appeal, the Court of Session or the Supreme Court;

"tribunal" means the First-tier Tribunal or the Upper Tribunal.]

AMENDMENT

1. Jobseekers (Back to Work Schemes Act 2013) (Remedial) Order 2020 (SI 2020/1085) art.2 (October 3, 2020).

GENERAL NOTE

See *MB v SSWP (JSA)* [2021] UKUT 69, which contains discussion of the back-   **1.462**
ground to and operation of the Remedial Order. It confirms, as eventually agreed
on behalf of the Secretary of State, that, even if a claimant had an appeal to the
Upper Tribunal pending, the Secretary of State is obliged by s.1A(4) to supersede
the First-tier Tribunal decision. That led to the dismissal of the claimant's appeal
in *MB*.

[¹1B Certain appeals against penalties under the Mandatory Work Activity Scheme Regulations

(1) This section applies where—   **1.463**
   (a) the Secretary of State has made a decision imposing on a claimant
       for jobseeker's allowance a penalty for failing to comply with the
       Mandatory Work Activity Scheme Regulations ("the penalty deci-
       sion"), and
   (b) the claimant lodged an appeal against the penalty decision before 26
       March 2013, and the appeal had not been finally determined, aban-
       doned or withdrawn before 26 March 2013.

(2) If the Secretary of State revises the penalty decision under section 9 of
the Social Security Act 1998, in making the revised decision, the Secretary
of State must disregard subsections (7) to (9) of section 1 of this Act and
subsection (12) of section 1 so far as it relates to those subsections.

(3) Subsection (4) applies where a tribunal has decided the appeal before
this section comes into force.

(4) In a case where—
   (a) the tribunal decided to uphold the penalty decision (in whole or in
       part), and
   (b) the Secretary of State decides that subsection (7), (8) or (9) of
       section 1 or subsection (12) of section 1 so far as it relates to those
       subsections may be relevant to the tribunal's decision,
the Secretary of State must make a decision superseding the tribunal's
decision.

(5) In making a superseding decision under subsection (4), the Secretary
of State must disregard subsections (7) to (9) of section 1 and subsection
(12) of section 1 so far as it relates to those subsections.

(6) Section 10(1)(b) of the Social Security Act 1998 (power of the
Secretary of State to supersede a tribunal decision) does not apply in a case
where subsection (4) applies.

(7) A superseding decision made under subsection (4) is to be treated for
all purposes as if it were a superseding decision made under section 10 of
the Social Security Act 1998.

(8) Subsection (9) applies where, after this section has come into force, a
court or tribunal is considering—
   (a) the appeal mentioned in subsection (1)(b),
   (b) an appeal against a revised decision made under section 9 of the
       Social Security Act 1998 by virtue of subsection (2), or

(c) an appeal against a superseding decision made under subsection (4).

(9) In considering the appeal, the court or tribunal must disregard subsections (7) to (9) of section 1 and subsection (12) of section 1 so far as it relates to those subsections.

(10) A revised decision made by virtue of subsection (2) and a superseding decision made under subsection (4) are to be treated as having effect from the date on which the penalty decision had effect (other than for the purposes of any rule as to the time allowed for bringing an appeal).

(11) In this section—

"the Mandatory Work Activity Scheme Regulations" has the same meaning as in section 1;

"court" has the same meaning as in section 1A; and

"tribunal" has the same meaning as in section 1A]

AMENDMENT

1. Jobseekers (Back to Work Schemes Act 2013) (Remedial) Order 2020 (SI 2020/1085) art.2 (October 3, 2020).

Report

1.464   **2.**—(1) The Secretary of State must appoint an independent person to prepare a report on the operation of the provisions relating to the imposition of a penalty during the period of a year beginning with the day on which this Act comes into force, so far as that operation relates to relevant penalties.

(2) The person must complete the preparation of the report and send it to the Secretary of State as soon as reasonably practicable after the end of the period mentioned in subsection (1).

(3) On receiving the report, the Secretary of State must lay a copy of it before Parliament.

(4) In this section—

"penalty" means a penalty that may be imposed for—

   (a) failing to participate in a scheme within section 17A(1) of the Jobseekers Act 1995, or

   (b) failing to comply with regulations under section 17A of that Act;

"relevant penalty" means a penalty that, but for section 1 of this Act, would not be or would not have been lawfully imposed on a person.

Extent, commencement and short title

1.465   **3.**—(1) This Act extends to England and Wales and Scotland.

(2) This Act comes into force on the day on which it is passed.

(3) This Act may be cited as the Jobseekers (Back to Work Schemes) Act 2013.

European Union (Withdrawal Agreement) Act 2020

2020 c.1

PART 3

CITIZENS' RIGHTS

RIGHTS IN RELATION TO ENTRY AND RESIDENCE

Rights related to residence: application deadline and temporary protection

7.—(1) A Minister of the Crown may by regulations make such provision   1.466
as the Minister considers appropriate for any of the following purposes—
  (a) specifying the deadline that applies for the purposes of—
     (i) the first sub-paragraph of Article 18(1)(b) of the withdrawal
          agreement (deadline for the submission of applications for the
          new residence status described in Article 18(1));
     (ii) the first sub-paragraph of Article 17(1)(b) of the EEA EFTA
          separation agreement (deadline for the submission of applica-
          tions for the new residence status described in Article 17(1));
     (iii) the first sentence of Article 16(1)(b) of the Swiss citizens' rights
          agreement (deadline for the submission of applications for the
          new residence status described in Article 16(1));
  (b) implementing Article 18(2) of the withdrawal agreement (protec-
       tion for Union citizens etc. in the period prior to the deadline for the
       submission of applications for the new residence status described in
       Article 18(1));
  (c) implementing Article 17(2) of the EEA EFTA separation agreement
       (protection for EEA EFTA nationals etc. in the period prior to the
       deadline for the submission of applications for the new residence
       status described in Article 17(1));
  (d) implementing Article 16(2) of the Swiss citizens' rights agreement
       (protection for Swiss nationals etc. in the period prior to the dead-
       line for the submission of applications for the new residence status
       described in Article 16(1));
  (e) implementing Article 18(3) of the withdrawal agreement (protection
       for Union citizens etc. pending a final decision on an application for
       the new residence status described in Article 18(1));
  (f) implementing Article 17(3) of the EEA EFTA separation agreement
       (protection for EEA EFTA nationals etc. pending a final decision
       on an application for the new residence status described in Article
       17(1));
  (g) implementing Article 16(3) of the Swiss citizens' rights agreement
       (protection for Swiss nationals etc. pending a final decision on an
       application for the new residence status described in Article 16(1)).
  (2) If the Minister considers it appropriate, regulations under subsection
(1) relating to the implementation of a provision mentioned in subsection
(1)(b), (c) or (d) may be made so as to apply both to—
  (a) persons to whom the provision in question applies, and
  (b) persons to whom that provision does not apply but who may be

granted leave to enter or remain in the United Kingdom by virtue of residence scheme immigration rules (see section 17) and who do not have such leave.

(3) If the Minister considers it appropriate, regulations under subsection (1) relating to the implementation of a provision mentioned in subsection (1)(e), (f) or (g) may be made so as to apply both to—

   (a) persons to whom the provision in question applies, and

   (b) persons to whom that provision does not apply but who make an application for leave to enter or remain in the United Kingdom by virtue of residence scheme immigration rules.

(4) The power to make regulations under subsection (1) may (among other things) be exercised by modifying any provision made by or under an enactment.

Frontier workers

1.467   **8.**—(1) A Minister of the Crown may by regulations make such provision as the Minister considers appropriate for the purpose of implementing any of the following—

   (a) Articles 24(3) and 25(3) of the withdrawal agreement (rights of employed and self-employed frontier workers) other than as regards rights enjoyed as workers (see section 14(1));

   (b) Articles 23(3) and 24(3) of the EEA EFTA separation agreement (rights of employed and self-employed frontier workers) other than as regards rights enjoyed as workers (see section 14(2));

   (c) Article 20(2) of the Swiss citizens' rights agreement (rights of frontier workers to enter and exit).

(2) A Minister of the Crown may by regulations make such provision as the Minister considers appropriate for the purpose of implementing any of the following—

   (a) Article 26 of the withdrawal agreement (issue of documents);

   (b) Article 25 of the EEA EFTA separation agreement (issue of documents);

   (c) Article 21(1)(a) and (2) of the Swiss citizens' rights agreement (issue of documents).

(3) The power to make regulations under subsection (1) or (2) may (among other things) be exercised by modifying any provision made by or under the Immigration Acts.

Restrictions of rights of entry and residence

1.468   **9.**—(1) A Minister of the Crown may by regulations make such provision as the Minister considers appropriate for the purpose of implementing any of the following—

   (a) Article 20(1), (3) and (4) of the withdrawal agreement (restrictions of the rights of entry and residence);

   (b) Article 19(1), (3) and (4) of the EEA EFTA separation agreement (restrictions of the rights of entry and residence);

   (c) Articles 17(1) and (3) and 20(3) of the Swiss citizens' rights agreement (restrictions of the rights of entry and residence).

(2) If the Minister considers it appropriate, regulations under subsection (1) relating to the implementation of a provision mentioned in subsection (1)(a), (b) or (c) may be made so as to apply both to—

(2020 c.1 reg.9)

(a) persons to whom the provision in question applies, and

(b) persons to whom that provision does not apply but who—

  (i) have entry clearance granted by virtue of relevant entry clearance immigration rules (see section 17),

  (ii) have leave to enter or remain in the United Kingdom granted by virtue of residence scheme immigration rules (see section 17), or

  (iii) otherwise have leave to enter granted after arriving with entry clearance granted by virtue of relevant entry clearance immigration rules.

(3) In subsection (2)(b), references to a person who has entry clearance or leave to enter or remain include references to a person who would have had entry clearance or leave to enter or remain but for—

(a) the making of a deportation order under section 5(1) of the Immigration Act 1971, or

(b) the making of any other decision made in connection with restricting the right of the person to enter the United Kingdom.

(4) The power to make regulations under subsection (1) may (among other things) be exercised by modifying any provision made—

(a) by or under the Immigration Acts, or

(b) under other primary legislation.

Co-ordination of social security systems

13. [*See Vol.III*]   1.469

Non-discrimination, equal treatment and rights of workers etc.

14. [*See Vol.III*]   1.470

Independent Monitoring Authority for the Citizens' Rights Agreements

15. [*See Vol.III*]   1.471

Regulations: supplementary

16. (1) In sections 7, 8, 9 and 14—

(a) a power to make provision for the purpose of implementing a provision of the withdrawal agreement includes power to make provision to supplement the effect of section 7A of the European Union (Withdrawal) Act 2018 in relation to that provision of the agreement,

(b) a power to make provision for the purpose of implementing a provision of the EEA EFTA separation agreement includes power to make provision to supplement the effect of section 7B of that Act in relation to that provision of the agreement, and

(c) a power to make provision for the purpose of implementing a provision of the Swiss citizens' rights agreement includes power to make provision to supplement the effect of section 7B of that Act in relation to that provision of the agreement.

(2) The conferral of a power on a Minister of the Crown under section 7, 8, 9 or 11 does not affect the extent of any power of a devolved authority under section 12, 13 or 14 which overlaps with a power under section 7, 8, 9 or 11 by virtue of section 17(4).

219

(3) Regulations under this Part may not provide for the conferral of functions (including the conferral of a discretion) on, or the delegation of functions to, a person who is not a public authority (but may so provide if the person is a public authority).

(4) In subsection (3), 'public authority' means a person who exercises functions of a public nature.

Interpretation: Part 3

1.472 17. (1) In this Part, 'residence scheme immigration rules' means—

(a) Appendix EU to the immigration rules except those rules, or changes to that Appendix, which are identified in the immigration rules as not having effect in connection with the residence scheme that operates in connection with the withdrawal of the United Kingdom from the EU, and

(b) any other immigration rules which are identified in the immigration rules as having effect in connection with the withdrawal of the United Kingdom from the EU.

(2) In this Part, 'relevant entry clearance immigration rules' means any immigration rules which are identified in the immigration rules as having effect in connection with the granting of entry clearance for the purposes of acquiring leave to enter or remain in the United Kingdom by virtue of residence scheme immigration rules.

(3) In this Part, references to having leave to enter or remain in the United Kingdom granted by virtue of residence scheme immigration rules include references to having such leave granted by virtue of those rules before this section comes into force.

(4) In this Part, a reference to a Chapter, Title, Part or other provision of the withdrawal agreement, EEA EFTA separation agreement or Swiss citizens' rights agreement includes a reference to—

(a) any other provision of the agreement in question so far as relating to that Chapter, Title, Part or other provision, and

(b) any provision of EU law which is applied by, or referred to in, that Chapter, Title, Part or other provision (to the extent of the application or reference).

(5) In this Part—

'entry clearance' has the meaning given by section 33(1) of the Immigration Act 1971 (interpretation);

'immigration rules' has the same meaning as in the Immigration Act 1971.

PART II

INCOME SUPPORT

The Income Support (General) Regulations 1987

(SI 1987/1967) (AS AMENDED)

Made by the Secretary of State under ss.20(1), (3)(d), (4), (9), (11) and (12), 22(1), (2), (4) and (5) to (9), 23(1), (3) and (5), 51(1)(n) and 84(1) of the Social Security Act 1986 and ss.114, 166(1) to (3A) of the Social Security Act 1975

ARRANGEMENT OF REGULATIONS

PART I

GENERAL

2.1

PART II

CONDITIONS OF ENTITLEMENT

PART III

MEMBERSHIP OF A FAMILY

223

Part VI

Applicable Amounts and Assessment of Income and Capital in Urgent Cases

Part VII

Calculation of Income Support for Part-Weeks

Schedules

Part I

General

Citation and commencement

1. These Regulations may be cited as the Income Support (General) Regulations 1987 and shall come into force on 11th April 1988.   2.2

Interpretation

2.3   **2.**—(1) In these Regulations, unless the context otherwise requires

[⁸⁸ "the 2012 Act" means the Welfare Reform Act 2012;]

[⁵⁹ "Abbeyfield Home" means an establishment run by the Abbeyfield Society including all bodies corporate or incorporate which are affiliated to that Society;]

"the Act" means the Social Security Act 1986;

[⁴⁸ "adoption leave" means a period of absence from work on ordinary or additional adoption leave by virtue of section 75A or 75B of the Employment Rights Act 1996;]

[¹⁰⁶ "approved blood scheme" means a scheme established or approved by the Secretary of State, or trust established with funds provided by the Secretary of State, for the purpose of providing compensation in respect of a person having been infected from contaminated blood products;]

[⁵⁷ "the Armed Forces and Reserve Forces Compensation Scheme" means the scheme established under section 1(2) of the Armed Forces (Pensions and Compensation) Act 2004;]

[⁸⁹ "armed forces independence payment" means armed forces independence payment under the Armed Forces and Reserve Forces (Compensation Scheme) Order 2011;]

"attendance allowance" means:—

(a) an attendance allowance under section 35 of the Social Security Act [SSCBA, s.64];

(b) an increase of disablement pension under section 61 or 63 of that Act [SSCBA, s.104 or 105];

(c) a payment under regulations made in exercise of the power conferred by section 159(3)(b) of that Act;

(d) an increase of an allowance which is payable in respect of constant attendance under section 5 of the Industrial Injuries and Diseases (Old Cases) Act 1975;

(e) a payment by virtue of articles 14, 15, 16, 43 or 44 of the Personal Injuries (Civilians) Scheme 1983 or any analogous payment; or

(f) any payment based on need for attendance which is paid as part of a war disablement pension;

[⁷² "basic rate", where it relates to the rate of tax, has the same meaning as in the Income Tax Act 2007 (see section 989 of that Act)]

[²⁶"the benefit Acts" means the Contributions and Benefits Act [⁶⁹, the Jobseekers Act 1995 [⁸⁸ , Part 1 of the Welfare Reform Act [¹⁰⁰, Part 4 of the 2012 Act and Part 1 of the Pensions Act 2014]]];]

"benefit week" has the meaning prescribed in paragraph 4 of Schedule 7 to the Social Security (Claims and Payments) Regulations 1987 [⁴and for the purposes of calculating any payment of income and of regulation 74(2)(a) "benefit week" shall also mean the period of 7 days ending on the day before the first day of the first benefit week following the date of claim or the last day on which income support is paid if it is in payment for less than a week;]

[⁶"board and lodging accommodation" means—

(a) accommodation provided to a person or, if he is a member of a family, to him or any other member of his family, for a charge which is inclusive of the provision of that accommodation and at least some cooked or prepared meals which both are cooked or prepared (by a person other than the person to whom the accommodation is provided or a member of his family) and are consumed in that accommodation or associated premises; or

(b) accommodation provided to a person in a hotel, guest house, lodging house or some similar establishment,

except accommodation provided by a close relative of his or of any other member of his family, or other than on a commercial basis;]

[59"care home" in England [107 ...] has the meaning assigned to it by section 3 of the Care Standards Act 2000, [107 in Wales means a care home service within the meaning of Part 1 of the Regulation and Inspection of Social Care (Wales) Act 2016 which is provided wholly or mainly to persons aged 18 or over] and in Scotland means a care home service within the meaning assigned to it by [81 paragraph 2 of schedule 12 to the Public Services Reform (Scotland) Act 2010];]

[49"child tax credit" means a child tax credit under section 8 of the Tax Credits Act 2002;]

[31"the Children Order" means the Children (Northern Ireland) Order 1995;]

"claimant" means a person claiming income support;

"close relative" means a parent, parent-in-law, son, son-in-law, daughter, daughter-in-law, step-parent, step-son, step-daughter, brother, sister, [60 or, if any of the preceding persons is one member of a couple, the other member of that couple]

[19 70 ...]

"concessionary payment" means a payment made under arrangements made by the Secretary of State with the consent of the Treasury which is charged either to the National Insurance Fund or to a Departmental Expenditure Vote to which payments of benefit [71 or tax credits under the benefit Acts or the Tax Credits Act 2002] are charged;

[19the "Contributions and Benefits Act" means the Social Security Contributions and Benefits Act 1992;]

[90 "contribution-based jobseeker's allowance" means an allowance under the Jobseekers Act 1995 as amended by the provisions of Part 1 of Schedule 14 to the 2012 Act that remove references to an income-based allowance, and a contribution-based allowance under the Jobseekers Act 1995 as that Act has effect apart from those provisions;]

[84 "the Contributions Regulations" means the Social Security (Contributions) Regulations 2001;]

[69 [90 "contributory employment and support allowance" means an allowance under Part 1 of the Welfare Reform Act as amended by the provisions of Schedule 3, and Part 1 of Schedule 14, to the 2012 Act that remove references to an income-related allowance, and a contributory allowance under Part 1 of the Welfare Reform Act as that Part has effect apart from those provisions;]]

"co-ownership scheme" means a scheme under which a dwelling is let by a housing association and the tenant, or his personal representative, will, under the terms of the tenancy agreement or of the agreement under which he became a member of the association, be entitled, on his ceasing to be a member and subject to any condition stated in either agreement, to a sum calculated by reference directly or indirectly to the value of the dwelling;

[60 [92 94 "couple" means—

(a) two people who are married to, or civil partners of, each other and are members of the same household; or

(b) two people who are not married to, or civil partners of, each other but are living together [¹⁰⁸ as if they were a married couple or civil partners];]]

[³⁸"course of study" means any course of study, whether or not it is a sandwich course (within the meaning prescribed in regulation 61(1)) and whether or not a grant is made for attending or undertaking it;]

"Crown tenant" means a person who occupies a dwelling under a tenancy or licence where the interest of the landlord belongs to Her Majesty in right of the Crown or to a government department or is held in trust for Her Majesty for the purposes of a government department, except (in the case of an interest belonging to Her Majesty in right of the Crown) where the interest is under the management of the Crown Estate Commissioners [¹⁰⁴ or a relevant person];

[²²"date of claim" means the date on which the claimant makes, or is treated as making, a claim for income support for the purposes of regulation 6 of the Social Security (Claims and Payments) Regulations 1987;]

[¹⁵"disability living allowance" means a disability living allowance under section 37ZA of the Social Security Act [SSCBA, s.71];

[⁴⁹ . . .]

"dwelling occupied as the home" means the dwelling together with any garage, garden and outbuildings, normally occupied by the claimant as his home including any premises not so occupied which it is impracticable or unreasonable to sell separately, in particular, in Scotland, any croft land on which the dwelling is situated;

"earnings" has the meaning prescribed in regulation 35 or, as the case may be, 37;

[²⁸ [⁵⁸. . .]]

[²⁸ [⁵⁸. . .]]

"employed earner" shall be construed in accordance with section 2(1)(a) of the Social Security Act [SSCBA, s.2(1)*a*];

[⁴"employment" except for the purposes of section 20(3)(d) of the Act [SSCBA, s.124(1)(d)], includes any trade, business, profession, office or vocation;]

[⁶⁹ "the Employment and Support Allowance Regulations" means the Employment and Support Allowance Regulations 2008;]

[⁷⁹ ⁸⁵ . . .]

[³⁷"employment zone" means an area within Great Britain designated for the purposes of section 60 of the Welfare Reform and Pensions Act 1999 and an "employment zone programme" means a programme established for such an area or areas designed to assist claimants for a jobseeker's allowance to obtain sustainable employment;

"employment zone contractor" means a person who is undertaking the provision of facilities in respect of an employment zone programme on behalf of the Secretary of State for Education and Employment;]

[⁷⁴ "enactment" includes an enactment comprised in, or in an instrument made under, an Act of the Scottish Parliament [⁹¹ or the National Assembly for Wales];]

[⁵²[⁵⁴ . . .]]

[⁹⁸ "first year of training" means a period of time beginning with a person's first day of training.]

[³⁹"full-time student" has the meaning prescribed in regulation 61(1);]

[¹¹⁰ "Grenfell Tower payment" means a payment made to a person because that person was affected by the fire on 14th June 2017 at Grenfell Tower, or a payment to the personal representative of such a person—

(a) from the £5 million fund announced on 16th June 2017 for the benefit of certain persons affected by the fire on 14th June 2017 at Grenfell Tower and known as the Grenfell Tower Residents' Discretionary Fund;

(b) by the Royal Borough of Kensington and Chelsea; or

(c) by a registered charity;]

[⁵⁷ "a guaranteed income payment" means a payment made under article 14(1)(b) or article 21(1)(a) of the Armed Forces and Reserve Forces (Compensation Scheme) Order 2005;]

[⁷⁰ "Health Service Act" means the National Health Service Act 2006; "Health Service (Wales) Act" means the National Health Service (Wales) Act 2006;]

"housing association" has the meaning assigned to it by section 1(1) of the Housing Associations Act 1985;

[³⁰"housing benefit expenditure" means expenditure in respect of which housing benefit is payable as specified in [⁶² regulation 12(1) of the Housing Benefit Regulations 2006] but does not include any such expenditure in respect of which an amount is applicable under regulation 17(1)(e) or 18(1)(f) (housing costs);]

[³⁵"Immigration and Asylum Act" means the Immigration and Asylum Act 1999;]

[³⁵ . . .]

[⁶⁹ "income-related employment and support allowance" means an income-related allowance under Part 1 of the Welfare Reform Act (employment and support allowance);]

[⁵⁹ [⁷⁸ "independent hospital"—

(a) in England, means a hospital as defined by section 275 of the National Health Service Act 2006 that is not a health service hospital as defined by that section;

(b) in Wales, has the meaning assigned to it by section 2 of the Care Standards Act 2000; and

(c) in Scotland, means an independent healthcare service as defined in [⁸¹ section 10F(1)(a) and (b) of the National Health Service (Scotland) Act 1978];]]

[⁴³ ⁶⁸ . . .]

"invalid carriage or other vehicle" means a vehicle propelled by petrol engine or by electric power supplied for use on the road and to be controlled by the occupant;

[³⁸"last day of the course" has the meaning prescribed in regulation 61(1);]

"liable relative" has the meaning prescribed in regulation 54;

[⁸⁷ "local welfare provision" means occasional financial or other assistance given by a local authority, the Scottish Ministers or the Welsh Ministers, or a person authorised to exercise any function of, or provide a service to, them, to or in respect of individuals for the purpose of—

(a) meeting, or helping to meet, an immediate short term need—

(i) arising out of an exceptional event, or exceptional circumstances; and

    (ii) that requires to be met in order to avoid a risk to the well-being of an individual; or
- (b) enabling individuals to establish or maintain a settled home, where those individuals have been or, without the assistance, might otherwise be—
    (i) in prison, hospital, a residential care establishment or other institution; or
    (ii) homeless or otherwise living an unsettled way of life;]

[⁶¹ "the London Bombings Relief Charitable Fund" means the company limited by guarantee (number 5505072) and registered charity of that name established on 11th July 2005 for the purpose of (amongst other things) relieving sickness, disability or financial need of victims (including families or dependants of victims) of the terrorist attacks carried out in London on 7th July 2005;]

[¹⁰⁵ "the London Emergencies Trust" means the company of that name (number 09928465) incorporated on 23rd December 2015 and the registered charity of that name (number 1172307) established on 28th March 2017;]

"lone parent" means a person who has no partner and who is responsible for, and a member of the same household as, a child or young person;

"long tenancy" means a tenancy granted for a term of years certain exceeding twenty one years, whether or not the tenancy is, or may become, terminable before the end of that term by notice given by or to the tenant or by re-entry, forfeiture (or, in Scotland, irritancy) or otherwise and includes a lease for a term fixed by law under a grant with a covenant or obligation for perpetual renewal unless it is a lease by sub-demise from one which is not a long tenancy;

[⁶³ "long-term patient" means a person who—
(a) is a patient within the meaning of regulation 21(3); and
(b) has been such a patient for a continuous period of more than 52 weeks;]

[⁶ ⁶⁷ . . .]

[⁷⁹ "the Mandatory Work Activity Scheme" means a scheme within section 17A of the Jobseekers Act 1995, known by that name and provided pursuant to arrangements made by the Secretary of State that is designed to provide work or work-related activity for up to 30 hours per week over a period of four consecutive weeks with a view to assisting claimants to improve their prospects of obtaining employment;]

[²²"maternity leave" means a period during which a woman is absent from work because she is pregnant or has given birth to a child, and at the end of which she has a right to return to work either under the terms of her contract of employment or under [⁶⁶ Part VIII of the Employment Rights Act 1996];]

[¹⁰² "member of the support group" means a claimant who has or is treated as having limited capability for work-related activity under either—
(a) Part 6 of the Employment and Support Allowance Regulations 2008; or
(b) Part 5 of the Employment and Support Allowance Regulations 2013;]

[¹⁰² "member of the work-related activity group" means a claimant who has or is treated as having limited capability for work under either—

(a) Part 5 of the Employment and Support Allowance Regulations 2008 other than by virtue of regulation 30 of those Regulations; or

(b) Part 4 of the Employment and Support Allowance Regulations 2013 other than by virtue of regulation 26 of those Regulations;]

[⁷⁵ "MFET Limited" means the company limited by guarantee (number 7121661) of that name, established for the purpose in particular of making payments in accordance with arrangements made with the Secretary of State to persons who have acquired HIV as a result of treatment by the NHS with blood or blood products;]

[⁷¹ . . .]

"mobility supplement" means any supplement under [⁷¹ article 20 of the Naval, Military and Air Forces Etc. (Disablement and Death) Service Pensions Order 2006] including such a supplement by virtue of any other scheme or order or under Article 25A of the Personal Injuries (Civilians) Scheme 1983;

[¹¹⁰ "the National Emergencies Trust" means the registered charity of that name (number 1182809) established on 28th March 2019;]

"net earnings" means such earnings as are calculated in accordance with regulation 36

"net profit" means such profit as is calculated in accordance with regulation 38;

[⁴¹"the New Deal options" means the employment programmes specified in regulation 75(1)(a)(ii) of the Jobseeker's Allowance Regulations 1996 and the training scheme specified in regulation 75(1)(b)(ii) of those Regulations;]

"non-dependant" has the meaning prescribed in regulation 3;

"non-dependant deduction" means a deduction that is to be made under regulation 17(*e*) and paragraph [⁷⁰ 18] of Schedule 3;

[⁵⁹ . . .]

"occupational pension" means any pension or other periodical payment under an occupational pension scheme but does not include any discretionary payment out of a fund established for relieving hardship in particular cases;

[¹⁰⁹ "parental bereavement leave" means leave under section 80EA of the Employment Rights Act 1996;]

"partner" means where a claimant—

(a) is a member of [⁶⁰a couple], the other member of that couple;

(b) is married polygamously to two or more members of his household, any such member;

[^{48 82} "paternity leave" means a period of absence from work on [⁹⁶ . . .] paternity leave by virtue of section 80A or 80B of the Employment Rights Act 1996 [⁹⁶ . . .]]

"payment" includes a part of a payment;

[²³"pay period" means the period in respect of which a claimant is, or expects to be, normally paid by his employer, being a week, a fortnight, four weeks, a month or other shorter or longer period as the case may be;]

[²⁵"pension fund holder" means with respect to a personal pension scheme or [⁶⁴ an occupational pensions scheme], the trustees, managers or scheme administrators, as the case may be, of the scheme [⁶⁴ . . .] concerned;]

[³⁸ "period of study" means the period beginning with the date on which a person starts attending or undertaking a course of study and ending with the last day of the course or such earlier date (if any) such as he finally abandons it or is dismissed from it;]

[⁸⁸ "personal independence payment" means personal independence payment under Part 4 of the 2012 Act;]

[²² ⁶⁴ "personal pension scheme" means—

(a) a personal pension scheme as defined by section 1 of the Pension Schemes Act 1993;

(b) an annuity contract or trust scheme approved under section 620 or 621 of the Income and Corporation Taxes Act 1988 or a substituted contract within the meaning of section 622(3) of that Act which is treated as having become a registered pension scheme by virtue of paragraph 1(1)(f) of Schedule 36 to the Finance Act 2004;

(c) a personal pension scheme approved under Chapter 4 of Part 14 of the Income and Corporation Taxes Act 1988 which is treated as having become a registered pension scheme by virtue of paragraph 1(1)(g) of Schedule 36 to the Finance Act 2004;]

"policy of life insurance" means any instrument by which the payment of money is assured on death (except death by accident only) or the happening of any contingency dependent on human life, or any instrument evidencing a contract which is subject to payment of premiums for a term dependent on human life;

[⁵"polygamous marriage" means any marriage during the subsistence of which a party to it is married to more than one person and the ceremony of marriage took place under the law of a country which permits polygamy;]

[⁴⁴. . .]

[⁷⁴ "public authority" includes any person certain of whose functions are functions of a public nature;]

¹⁶"qualifying person" means a person in respect of whom [¹¹⁰ a Grenfell Tower payment has been made or] payment has been made from the Fund [²¹[⁵⁶ the Eileen Trust [⁷⁵ , MFET Limited] [⁶¹, the Skipton Fund [⁸⁰ , the Caxton Foundation] [¹⁰³, the Scottish Infected Blood Support Scheme] [¹⁰⁶, an approved blood scheme] [¹⁰⁵, the London Emergencies Trust, the We Love Manchester Emergency Fund] [¹¹⁰, the National Emergencies Trust] or the London Bombings Relief Charitable Fund]]]

[²⁶. . .]

"relative" means close relative, grand-parent, grand-child, uncle, aunt, nephew or niece;

"relevant enactment" has the meaning prescribed in regulation 16(8)(a);

[¹⁰⁴ "relevant person", in relation to any property, rights or interests to which section 90B(5) of the Scotland Act 1998 applies, means the person who manages that property or those rights or interests;]

"remunerative work" has the meaning prescribed in regulation 5;

[⁵⁹ . . .]

[¹⁸[⁵⁰ . . .]]

[⁵⁹ . . .]

[²⁵ [⁶⁴ . . .]]

[¹⁰¹ "Scottish basic rate" means the rate of income tax of that name calculated in accordance with section 6A of the Income Tax Act 2007;

[103 "Scottish Infected Blood Support Scheme" means the scheme of that name administered by the Common Services Agency (constituted by section 10 of the National Health Service (Scotland) Act 1978);]

"Scottish taxpayer" has the same meaning as in Chapter 2 of Part 4A of the Scotland Act 1998;]

"self-employed earner" shall be construed in accordance with section 2(1)(b) of the Social Security Act [SSCBA, s.2(1)(b)];

[40 55 "self employment route" means assistance in pursuing self-employed earner's employment whilst participating in—

(a) an employment zone programme; or

(b) a programme provided or other arrangements made pursuant to section 2 of the Employment and Training Act 1973 (functions of the Secretary of State) or section 2 of the Enterprise and New Towns (Scotland) Act 1990 (functions in relation to training for employment etc.)]

[74 [93 . . .]]

[95 "shared parental leave" means leave under section 75E or 75G of the Employment Rights Act 1996;]

"single claimant" means a claimant who neither has a partner nor is a lone parent;

"Social Security Act" means the Social Security Act 1975;

[34"sports award" means an award made by one of the Sports Councils named in section 23(2) of the National Lottery etc. Act 1993 out of sums allocated to it for distribution under that section;]

[66 72 . . .]

[38 . . .]

[37"subsistence allowance" means an allowance which an employment zone contractor has agreed to pay to a person who is participating in an employment zone programme;]

"supplementary benefit" means a supplementary pension or allowance under section 1 or 4 of the Supplementary Benefits Act 1976;

"terminal date" in respect of a claimant means the terminal date in his case for the purpose of regulation 7 of the Child Benefit (General) Regulations 1976;

[80 "the Caxton Foundation" means the charitable trust of that name established on 28th March 2011 out of funds provided by the Secretary of State for the benefit of certain persons suffering from hepatitis C and other persons eligible for payment in accordance with its provisions;]

[21"the Eileen Trust" means the charitable trust of that name established on 29th March 1993 out of funds provided by the Secretary of State for the benefit of persons eligible for payment in accordance with its provisions;]

[16"the Fund" means moneys made available from time to time by the Secretary of State for the benefit of persons eligible for payment in accordance with the provisions of a scheme established by him on 24th April 1992 or, in Scotland, on 10th April 1992;]

[20 70]

[2 70]

[20 70]

[^{65} "the Independent Living Fund (2006)" means the Trust of that name established by a deed dated 10th April 2006 and made between the Secretary of State for Work and Pensions of the one part and Margaret Rosemary Cooper, Michael Beresford Boyall and Marie Theresa Martin of the other part;]

[$^{20\,70}$]

[^{9}"the Macfarlane (Special Payments) Trust" means the trust of that name, established on 29th January 1990 partly out of funds provided by the Secretary of State, for the benefit of certain persons suffering from haemophilia;]

[^{13}"the Macfarlane (Special Payments) (No.2) Trust" means the trust of that name, established on 3rd May 1991 partly out of funds provided by the Secretary of State, for the benefit of certain persons suffering from haemophilia and other beneficiaries;]

[^{1}"the Macfarlane Trust" means the charitable trust, established partly out of funds provided by the Secretary of State to the Haemophilia Society, for the relief of poverty or distress among those suffering from haemophilia;]

[^{56}"the Skipton Fund" means the ex-gratia payment scheme administered by the Skipton Fund Limited, incorporated on 25th March 2004, for the benefit of certain persons suffering from hepatitis C and other persons eligible for payment in accordance with the scheme's provisions;]

"training allowance" means an allowance (whether by way of periodical grants or otherwise) payable—

(a) out of public funds by a Government department or by or on behalf of the [^{12} Secretary of State [^{99} ...] [^{11}, [^{73} Skills Development Scotland,] Scottish Enterprise or Highlands and Islands Enterprise] [^{42}, [^{83} ... [^{77} ...] [^{99} ...] or the [^{71} Welsh Ministers]];

(b) to a person for his maintenance or in respect of a member of his family; and

(c) for the period, or part of the period, during which he is following a course of training or instruction provided by, or in pursuance of arrangements made with, that department or approved by that department in relation to him or so provided or approved by or on behalf of [^{12}the Secretary of State [^{99} ...] [^{11}, [^{73} Skills Development Scotland,] Scottish Enterprise or Highlands and Islands Enterprise], [^{42} or the [^{71} Welsh Ministers]]

but it does not include an allowance paid by any Government department to or in respect of a person by reason of the fact that he is following a course of full-time education [^{7}, other than under arrangements made under section 2 of the Employment and Training Act 1973,] or is training as a teacher;

[^{90} "universal credit" means universal credit under Part 1 of the 2012 Act;]

[^{24}"voluntary organisation" means a body, other than a public or local authority, the activities of which are carried on otherwise than for profit;]

[$^{45\,71}$ ...]

[^{71} "war disablement pension" means any retired pay or pension or allowance payable in respect of disablement under an instrument specified in section 639(2) of the Income Tax (Earnings and Pensions) Act 2003(14);

"war pension" means a war disablement pension, a war widow's pension or a war widower's pension;

"war widow's pension" means any pension or allowance payable to a woman as a widow under an instrument specified in section 639(2) of the Income Tax (Earnings and Pensions) Act 2003 in respect of the death or disablement of any person;

"war widower's pension" means any pension or allowance payable to a man as a widower or to a surviving civil partner under an instrument specified in section 639(2) of the Income Tax (Earnings and Pensions) Act 2003 in respect of the death or disablement of any person;]

[[19]"water charges" means—

(a) as respects England and Wales, any water and sewerage charges under Chapter 1 of Part V of the Water Act 1991;

(b) as respects Scotland, any water and sewerage charges under Schedule 11 to the Local Government Finance Act 1992;

in so far as such charges are in respect of the dwelling which a person occupies as his home.]

[[105] "the We Love Manchester Emergency Fund" means the registered charity of that name (number 1173260) established on 30th May 2017;]

[[69] "the Welfare Reform Act" means the Welfare Reform Act 2007;]

[[32]"welfare to work beneficiary" means a person—

(a) to whom regulation 13A(1) of the Social Security (Incapacity for Work) (General) Regulations 1995 applies; and

(b) who again becomes incapable of work for the purposes of Part XIIA of the Contributions and Benefits Act 1992;]

[[49]"working tax credit" means a working tax credit under section 10 of the Tax Credits Act 2002;]

[[49] . . .]

[[23]"year of assessment" has the meaning prescribed in section 832(1) of the Income and Corporation Taxes Act 1988;]

"young person" has the meaning prescribed in regulation 14,

[[3] "[70] . . . [[12] . . . youth training]" means—

(a) arrangements made under section 2 of the Employment and Training Act 1973 (functions of the Secretary of State); or

(b) arrangements made by the Secretary of State for persons enlisted in Her Majesty's forces for any special term of service specified in regulations made under section 2 of the Armed Forces Act 1966 (power of Defence Council to make regulations as to engagement of persons in regular forces),

for purposes which include the training of persons who, at the beginning of their training, are under the age of 18.]

[[44] (1A) For the purposes of these Regulations, where a person's principal place of residence is a [[59] care home, an Abbeyfield Home or an independent hospital and he is temporarily absent from that home or hospital, he shall be regarded as continuing to reside in that home or hospital]—

(a) where he is absent because he is a patient, for the first [[51] 52] weeks of any such period of absence and for this purpose—

(i) "patient" has the meaning it has in Schedule 7 by virtue of regulation 21(3); and

(ii) periods of absence separated by not more than 28 days shall be treated as a single period of absence equal in duration to all those periods; and

(b) for the first three weeks of any other period of absence.]

[93 (1B) References in these Regulations to a claimant participating as a service user are to—

(a) a person who is being consulted by or on behalf of—

    (i) a body which has a statutory duty to provide services in the field of health, social care or social housing; or

    (ii) a body which conducts research or undertakes monitoring for the purpose of planning or improving such services,

in their capacity as a user, potential user, carer of a user or person otherwise affected by the provision of those services;

[97 (ab) a person who is being consulted by or on behalf of—

    (i) the Secretary of State in relation to any of the Secretary of State's functions in the field of social security or child support or under section 2 of the Employment and Training Act 1973; or

    (ii) a body which conducts research or undertakes monitoring for the purpose of planning or improving such functions,

in their capacity as a person affected or potentially affected by the exercise of those functions or the carer of such a person;] or

(b) the carer of a person consulted under [97 sub-paragraphs (a) or (ab)].]

(2) In these Regulations, unless the context otherwise requires, a reference—

(a) to a numbered Part is to the Part of these Regulations bearing that number;

(b) to a numbered regulation or Schedule is to the regulation in or Schedule to these Regulations bearing that number;

(c) in a regulation or Schedule to a numbered paragraph is to the paragraph in that regulation or Schedule bearing that number;

(d) in a paragraph to a lettered or numbered sub-paragraph is to the sub-paragraph in that paragraph bearing that letter or number.

(3) Unless the context requires otherwise, any reference to the claimant's family or, as the case may be, to being a member of his family, shall be construed for the purposes of these Regulations as if it included in relation to a polygamous marriage a reference to any partner and any child or young person who is treated as the responsibility of the claimant or his partner, where that child or young person is a member of the claimant's household.

[29(4) [58 . . .]]

AMENDMENTS

1. Income Support (General) Amendment Regulations 1988 (SI 1988/663) reg.2 (April 11, 1988).

2. Family Credit and Income Support (General) Amendment Regulations 1988 (SI 1988/999) reg.4 (June 9, 1988).

3. Income Support (General) Amendment No.3 Regulations 1988 (SI 1988/1228) reg.2 (August 29, 1988).

4. Income Support (General) Amendment No.4 Regulations 1988 (SI 1988/1445) reg.2 (September 12, 1988).

5. Income Support (General) Amendment No.5 Regulations 1988 (SI 1988/2022) reg.2(*b*) (December 12, 1988).

6. Income Support (General) Amendment No.5 Regulations 1988 (SI 1988/2022) reg.2(*a*) (April 10, 1989).

7. Income Support (General) Amendment No.2 Regulations 1989 (SI 1989/1323) reg.2 (August 21, 1989).

8. Income Support (General) Amendment Regulations 1989 (SI 1989/534) Sch.I para.1 (October 9, 1989).

9. Income-related Benefits Schemes Amendment Regulations 1990 (SI 1990/127) reg.3 (January 31, 1990).

11. Enterprise (Scotland) Consequential Amendments Order 1991 (SI 1991/387) art.9 (April 1, 1991).

12. Income Support (General) Amendment Regulations 1991 (SI 1991/236) reg.2 (April 8, 1991).

13. Income-related Benefits Schemes and Social Security (Recoupment) Amendment Regulations 1991 (SI 1991/1175) reg.5 (May 11, 1991).

15. Disability Living Allowance and Disability Working Allowance (Consequential Provisions) Regulations 1991 (SI 1991/2742) reg.11(2) (April 6, 1992).

16. Income-related Benefits Schemes and Social Security (Recoupment) Amendment Regulations 1992 (SI 1992/1101) reg.6(2) (May 7, 1992).

17. Income-related Benefits Schemes (Miscellaneous Amendments) (No.3) Regulations 1992 (SI 1992/2155) reg.12 (October 5, 1992).

19. Income-related Benefits Schemes (Miscellaneous Amendments) Regulations 1993 (SI 1993/315) reg.3 (April 12, 1993).

20. Social Security Benefits (Miscellaneous Amendments) (No.2) Regulations 1993 (SI 1993/963) reg.2 (April 22, 1993).

21. Income-related Benefits Schemes and Social Security (Recoupment) Amendment Regulations 1993 (SI 1993/1249) reg.4 (May 14, 1993).

22. Income-related Benefits Schemes (Miscellaneous Amendments) (No.4) Regulations 1993 (SI 1993/2119) reg.2 (October 4, 1993).

23. Income-related Benefits Schemes (Miscellaneous Amendments) (No.5) Regulations 1994 (SI 1994/2139) reg.22 (October 3, 1994).

24. Income-related Benefits Schemes (Miscellaneous Amendments) Regulations 1995 (SI 1995/516) reg.17 (April 10, 1995).

25. Income-related Benefits Schemes and Social Security (Claims and Payments) (Miscellaneous Amendments) Regulations 1995 (SI 1995/2303) reg.6(2) (October 2, 1995).

26. Income Support (General) (Jobseeker's Allowance Consequential Amendments) Regulations 1996 (SI 1996/206) reg.2 (October 7, 1996).

28. Income-related Benefits Schemes and Social Fund (Miscellaneous Amendments) Regulations 1996 (SI 1996/1944) reg.13 and Sch. para.1 (October 7, 1996).

29. Income-related Benefits Schemes and Social Fund (Miscellaneous Amendments) Regulations 1996 (SI 1996/1944) reg.13 and Sch. para.2 (October 7, 1996).

30. Income-related Benefits and Jobseeker's Allowance (Miscellaneous Amendments) Regulations 1997 (SI 1997/65) reg.4(1) (April 7, 1997).

31. Social Security (Miscellaneous Amendments) Regulations 1998 (SI 1998/563) reg.5(1) and (2)(e) (April 6, 1998).

32. Social Security (Welfare to Work) Regulations 1998 (SI 1998/2231) reg.13(2) (October 5, 1998).

33. Social Security and Child Support (Tax Credits) Consequential Amendments Regulations 1999 (SI 1999/2566) reg.2(3) and Sch.2 Part III (October 5, 1999).

34. Social Security Amendment (Sports Awards) Regulations 1999 (SI 1999/2165) reg.2(1) and 2(e) (August 23, 1999).

35. Social Security (Immigration and Asylum) Consequential Amendments Regulations 2000 (SI 2000/636) reg.3(2) (April 3, 2000).

37. Social Security Amendment (Employment Zones) Regulations 2000 (SI 2000/724) reg.2 (April 3, 2000).

38. Social Security Amendment (Students) Regulations 2000 (SI 2000/1981) reg.5(1) and (2) (July 31, 2000).

39. Social Security Amendment (Students) Regulations 2000 (SI 2000/1981) reg.5(1) and (2)(b) (July 31, 2000). The new definition was moved to its present—and alphabetically correct—place in the regulation by the Social Security (Students

and Income-related Benefits) (No.2) Regulations 2000 (SI 2000/ 2422) reg.4 (October 9, 2000).

40. Social Security Amendment (Employment Zones) (No.2) Regulations 2000 (SI 2000/2910) reg.2(1) and (2) (November 27, 2000).

41. Social Security (Miscellaneous Amendments) Regulations 2001 (SI 2001/ 488) reg.2 (April 9, 2001).

42. Social Security (Miscellaneous Amendments) (No.2) Regulations 2001 (SI 2001/652) reg.2 (March 26, 2001).

43. Social Security Amendment (New Deal) Regulations 2001 (SI 2001/ 1029) reg.15(2) and (3)(c) (April 9, 2001).

44. Social Security Amendment (Residential Care and Nursing Homes) Regulations 2001 (SI 2001/3767) reg.2 and Sch. Pt I para.1 (April 8, 2002).

45. Social Security (Miscellaneous Amendments) Regulations 2002 (SI 2002/ 841) reg.2 (April 8, 2002).

46. Income Support (General) and Jobseeker's Allowance Amendment Regulations 2002 (SI 2002/1411) reg.2 (June 17, 2002).

47. Social Security Amendment (Employment Programme) Regulations 2002 (SI 2002/2314) reg.3(2) (October 14, 2002).

48. Social Security (Paternity and Adoption) Amendment Regulations 2002 (SI 2002/2689) reg.2 (December 8, 2002).

49. Income-related Benefits and Jobseeker's Allowance (Working Tax Credit and Child Tax Credit) (Amendment) Regulations 2002 (SI 2002/2402) reg.2 and Sch.1 para.1 (April 6, 2003).

50. Social Security (Removal of Residential Allowance and Miscellaneous Amendments) Regulations 2003 (SI 2003/1121) reg.2 and Sch.1 (October 6, 2003).

51. Social Security (Hospital In-Patients and Miscellaneous Amendments) Regulations 2003 (SI 2003/1195) reg.3(2) (May 21, 2003).

52. Social Security (Miscellaneous Amendments) (No.2) Regulations 2003 (SI 2003/2279) reg.2(2) (October 1, 2003).

53. Social Security (Miscellaneous Amendments) Regulations 2004) (SI 2004/565) reg.2(2) (April 1, 2004).

54. Social Security (Miscellaneous Amendments) Regulations 2004 (SI 2004/565) reg.2(2) (April 1, 2004).

55. Social Security (Income-Related Benefits Self-Employment Route Amendment) Regulations 2004 (SI 2004/963) reg.2 (May 4, 2004).

56. Social Security (Miscellaneous Amendments) (No.2) Regulations 2004 (SI 2004/1141) reg.2 (May 12, 2004).

57. Social Security (Miscellaneous Amendments) Regulations 2005 (SI 2005/574) reg.2 (April 4, 2005).

58. Social Security (Miscellaneous Amendments) Regulations 2005 (SI 2005/574) reg.3 (April 4, 2005).

59. Social Security (Care Homes and Independent Hospitals) Regulations 2005 (SI 2005/2687) reg.2 and Sch.1 para.1 (October 24, 2005).

60. Civil Partnership (Pensions, Social Security and Child Support) (Consequential, etc. Provisions) Order 2005 (SI 2005/2877) art.2(3) and Sch.3 para.13(2) (December 5, 2005).

61. Income-related Benefits (Amendment) (No.2) Regulations 2005 (SI 2005/3391) reg.2 (December 12, 2005).

62. Housing Benefit and Council Tax Benefit (Consequential Provisions) Regulations 2006 (SI 2006/217) reg.5 and Sch.3 para.1 (March 6, 2006).

63. Social Security (Miscellaneous Amendments) Regulations 2007 (SI 2007/719) reg.2(2) (April 9, 2007).

64. Social Security (Miscellaneous Amendments) (No.3) Regulations 2007 (SI 2007/1749) reg.2(2) (July 17, 2007).

65. Independent Living Fund (2006) Order 2007 (SI 2007/2538) reg.2(2) (October 1, 2007).

66. Social Security (Miscellaneous Amendments) (No.5) Regulations 2007 (SI 2007/2618) reg.5(2) (October 1, 2007).

67. Social Security (Miscellaneous Amendments) (No.5) Regulations 2007 (SI 2007/2618) reg.2 and Sch. (October 1, 2007).

68. Social Security (Miscellaneous Amendments) Regulations 2008 (SI 2008/698) reg.2(2) (April 14, 2008).

69. Employment and Support Allowance (Consequential Provisions) (No.2) Regulations 2008 (SI 2008/1554) reg.2(1) and (2) (October 27, 2008).

70. Social Security (Miscellaneous Amendments) (No.6) Regulations 2008 (SI 2008/2767) reg.2(1) and (2) (November 17, 2008).

71. Social Security (Miscellaneous Amendments) (No.7) Regulations 2008 (SI 2008/3157) reg.2(1) and (2) (January 5, 2009).

72. Social Security (Miscellaneous Amendments) Regulations 2009 (SI 2009/583) reg.2(1) and (2) (April 6, 2009).

73. Social Security (Miscellaneous Amendments) Regulations 2009 (SI 2009/583) reg.2(1) and (3) (April 6, 2009).

74. Social Security (Miscellaneous Amendments) (No.4) Regulations 2009 (SI 2009/2655) reg.2(1) and (2) (October 26, 2009).

75. Social Security (Miscellaneous Amendments) (No.2) Regulations 2010 (SI 2010/641) reg.2 (April 6, 2010).

76. Housing and Regeneration Act 2008 (Consequential Provisions) (No.2) Order 2010 art.4 and Sch.1 para.9 (April 1, 2010).

77. Apprenticeships, Skills, Children and Learning Act 2009 (Consequential Amendments to Subordinate Legislation) (England) Order 2010 (SI 2010/1941) reg.3(1) and (2) (September 1, 2010).

78. Health and Social Care Act 2008 (Miscellaneous Consequential Amendments) Order 2010 (SI 2010/1881) regs 2 and 5 (October 1, 2010).

79. Social Security (Miscellaneous Amendments) (No.2) Regulations 2011 (SI 2011/1707) reg.4(2)(a) and (3) (August 5, 2011).

80. Social Security (Miscellaneous Amendments) (No.3) Regulations 2011 (SI 2011/2425) reg.7(1) and (2) (October 31, 2011).

81. Public Services Reform (Scotland) Act 2010 (Consequential Modifications of Enactments) Order 2011 (SI 2011/2581) art.2 and Sch.2 para.14 (October 28, 2011).

82. Social Security (Miscellaneous Amendments) Regulations 2012 (SI 2012/757) reg.3(1) and (2) (April 1, 2012).

83. Young People's Learning Agency Abolition (Consequential Amendments to Subordinate Legislation) (England) Order 2012 (SI 2012/956) reg.3(2) (May 1, 2012).

84. Social Security (Miscellaneous Amendments) (No. 2) Regulations 2012 (SI 2012/2575) reg.2(2) (November 5, 2012).

85. Jobseeker's Allowance (Schemes for Assisting Persons to Obtain Employment) Regulations 2013 (SI 2013/276) reg.13(a) (February 12, 2013).

86. National Treatment Agency (Abolition) and the Health and Social Care Act 2012 (Consequential, Transitional and Saving Provisions) Order 2013 (SI 2013/235) art.9 and Sch.1 para.10(1) and (2) (April 1, 2013).

87. Social Security (Miscellaneous Amendments) Regulations 2013 (SI 2013/443) reg.2(1) and (2) (April 2, 2013).

88. Personal Independence Payment (Supplementary Provisions and Consequential Amendments) Regulations 2013 (SI 2013/388) reg.8 and Sch. para.11(1) and (2) (April 8, 2013).

89. Armed Forces and Reserve Forces Compensation Scheme (Consequential Provisions: Subordinate Legislation) Order 2013 (SI 2013/591) art.7 and Sch. para.4(1) and (2) (April 8, 2013).

90. Universal Credit (Consequential, Supplementary, Incidental and Miscellaneous Provisions) Regulations 2013 (SI 2013/630) reg.28(1) and (2) (April 29, 2013).

91. Social Security (Miscellaneous Amendments) (No.3) Regulations 2013 (SI 2013/2536) reg.4(1) and (2) (October 29,2013).

92. Marriage (Same Sex Couples) Act 2013 (Consequential Provisions) Order 2014 (SI 2014/107) reg.2 and Sch.1 para.9 (March 13, 2014). The amendment extends to England and Wales only (see SI 2014/107 art.1(4)).
93. Social Security (Miscellaneous Amendments) Regulations 2014, (SI 2014/591) reg.2(1) and (2) (April 28, 2014).
94. Marriage and Civil Partnership (Scotland) Act 2014 and Civil Partnership Act 2004 (Consequential Provisions and Modifications) Order 2014 (SI 2014/3229) art.29 and Sch.6 para.5 (December 16, 2014). The amendment relates only to Scotland (see SI 2014/3229 art.3(4)) but is in the same terms as the amendment made in relation to England and Wales by SI 2014/107 (see point 92 above).
95. Shared Parental Leave and Statutory Shared Parental Pay (Consequential Amendments to Subordinate Legislation) Order 2014 (SI 2014/3255) art.5(1) and (2)(b) (December 31, 2014).
96. Shared Parental Leave and Statutory Shared Parental Pay (Consequential Amendments to Subordinate Legislation) Order 2014 (SI 2014/3255) art.5(1) and (2)(a) (April 5, 2015). The amendment is subject to the transitional provision in art.35 of SI 2014/3255, which is reproduced below.
97. Social Security (Miscellaneous Amendments) Regulations 2015 (SI 2015/67) reg.2(1)(a) and (2) (February 23, 2015).
98. Social Security (Members of the Reserve Forces) (Amendment) Regulations 2015 (SI 2015/389) reg.2(1) and (2) (April 6, 2015).
99. Deregulation Act 2015 (Consequential Amendments) Order 2015 (SI 2015/971) art.2 and Sch.3 para.2(1) and (2) (May 26, 2015).
100. Pensions Act 2014 (Consequential, Supplementary and Incidental Amendments) Order 2015 (SI 2015/1985) art.8(1) and (2) (April 6, 2016).
101. Social Security (Scottish Rate of Income Tax etc.) (Amendment) Regulations 2016 (SI 2016/233) reg.2(1) and (2) (April 6, 2016).
102. Employment and Support Allowance and Universal Credit (Miscellaneous Amendments and Transitional and Savings Provisions) Regulations 2017 (SI 2017/204) reg.7(1) and Sch.1, Pt.1, para.1(1) and (2) (April 3, 2017).
103. Social Security (Scottish Infected Blood Support Scheme) Regulations 2017 (SI 2017/329) reg.3(1) and (2) (April 3, 2017).
104. Crown Estate Transfer Scheme 2017 (SI 2017/524) para.8 and Sch.5, Pt.3, para.67 (April 1, 2017).
105. Social Security (Emergency Funds) (Amendment) Regulations 2017 (SI 2017/689) reg.2(1) and (2) (June 19, 2017).
106. Social Security (Infected Blood and Thalidomide) Regulations 2017 (SI 2017/870) reg.2(1) and (2) (October 23, 2017).
107. Social Security and Child Support (Regulation and Inspection of Social Care (Wales) Act 2016) (Consequential Provision) Regulations 2018 (SI 2018/228) reg.2 (April 2, 2018).
108. Civil Partnership (Opposite-sex Couples) Regulations 2019 (SI 2019/1458) reg.41 and Sch.3 Pt.2 para.40 (December 2, 2019).
109. Parental Bereavement Leave and Pay (Consequential Amendments to Subordinate Legislation) Regulations 2020 (SI 2020/354) reg.5(1) and (2) (April 6, 2020).
110. Social Security (Income and Capital) (Miscellaneous Amendments) Regulations 2020 (SI 2020/618) reg.2(1) and (2) (July 15, 2020).

DEFINITIONS

"dwelling"—see SSCBA s.137(1).
"family"—*ibid.*
"occupational pension scheme"—see PSA s.1.

GENERAL NOTE

2.4   The significance of most of these definitions is mentioned in the notes to the regulations in which they occur. A few points are noted here.

"Armed Forces and Reserve Forces Compensation Scheme": This scheme replaced the   2.5
War Pensions Scheme ("WPS") for those who suffer injuries, ill health or death
due to service in the Armed Forces on or after April 6, 2005. However, the WPS
continues to operate for existing beneficiaries and for claims where the cause of the
injury, illness or death is due to service before April 6, 2005. Originally the new
scheme, as set out in the Armed Forces and Reserve Forces (Compensation Scheme)
Order 2005 (SI 2005/439), made three types of payment: tariff based lump sums,
regular "guaranteed income payments" and bereavement grants. See the definition
of "guaranteed income payment" below which covers payments made to the injured
person under art.14(1)(b) of the Armed Forces and Reserve Forces (Compensation
Scheme) Order 2005 and payments to "a surviving spouse, civil partner or his
surviving adult dependant" under art.21(1)(a) of the Order. A "surviving adult
dependant" means someone with whom the deceased was "cohabiting as partners
in a substantial and exclusive relationship" (see art.22 of and Sch.1 to the Order).

However, the 2005 Order was revoked and replaced, with modifications, by
the Armed Forces and Reserve Forces (Compensation Scheme) Order 2011 (SI
2011/517) with effect from May 9, 2011. The amended scheme provides for
additional payments, including a supplementary award, a fast payment and a
payment for medical expenses. "Guaranteed income payments" are now made
under art.15(1)(c) of the 2011 Order or art.29(1)(a) in the case of payments to "a
surviving spouse, civil partner or his surviving adult dependant" (s.17(2)(a) and
s.23(2) of the Interpretation Act 1978 will apply) . "Surviving adult dependant" is
defined in art.30 of, and Sch.1 to, the 2011 Order and is broadly the same definition
as in the 2005 Order.

The £10 disregard that applies to war disablement, war widows and war widowers' pensions paid under the WPS scheme also applies to guarantee income payments (see para.16(cc) of Sch.9). No special provision is made in respect of the
lump sum payments but since they are made in respect of personal injury presumably they will be treated in the same way as other personal injury payments (see the
disregards in para.15 of Sch.9 and paras 12 and 12A of Sch.10).

The 2011 Order scheme was further amended by the Armed Forces and Reserve   2.6
Forces (Compensation Scheme) (Amendment) Order 2013 (SI 2013/436) with
effect from April 8, 2013. This provides for a new benefit, "armed forces independence payment", which is payable to a person who is entitled to a guaranteed income
payment at the rate of at least 50 per cent. An award of armed forces independence
payment precludes entitlement to disability living allowance, attendance allowance
and personal independence payment. Armed forces independence payment is fully
disregarded (see para.76A of Sch.9).

The Armed Forces and Reserved Forces (Compensation Scheme) (Amendment)
Order 2014 (SI 2014/412) made further amendments to the 2011 Order on April 7,
2014, as did the Armed Forces and Reserve Forces (Compensation Scheme) (Amendment) Order 2015 (SI 2015/413) on April 6, 2015. These amendments included
the uprating of the amount of the armed forces independence payment (not uprated
in April 2016).

"Armed forces independence payment": see under *"Armed Forces and Reserve Forces*   2.7
Compensation Scheme".

"Board and lodging accommodation": Since April 1989 there are no special calcula-   2.8
tions of benefit for claimants in board and lodging accommodation and therefore the
definition is of less significance than in the past. Either the accommodation must be
in some establishment like a hotel or lodging house or the charge must include the
provision of some cooked or prepared meals in the accommodation or associated
premises. The requirement in para.(a) that a charge is made for the accommodation
has logically to be considered before the exclusion of non-commercial arrangements.
In *CSB 1163/1988* the claimant moved with her two children into a house owned
by the Jesus Fellowship Church (Baptist), where 17 other people also lived. Meals
were provided. The terms of her occupation were that she should put all her income

into a "common purse." A basic charge to cover food, accommodation and running costs was set, but any excess of the claimant's income was regarded as a donation to the Church. The Commissioner holds that the claimant was not a boarder because she did not pay a "charge." She was one of a joint community of persons, all sharing their income and outgoings. See also *R. v Sheffield Housing Benefits Review Board, Ex p. Smith, Rugby BC Housing, Benefits Review Board, Ex p. Harrison and Daventry DC Housing Benefits Review Board, Ex p. Bodden*, below. Some family arrangements may be of this kind. Similarly, if a person makes a contribution of whatever he can afford week by week to the household expenses, this is probably not a charge. On the other hand, a fixed, but low, amount may require the non-commercial basis exception to be examined. Cases on the meaning of "board" in the Rent Acts (e.g. *Otter v Norman* [1988] 2 All E.R. 897 HL) indicate that merely providing the ingredients will not amount to preparing a meal. This was specifically decided in the supplementary benefit context in *CSB 950/1987*. The argument that getting a packet of cornflakes out of a cupboard constituted preparation was rejected.

If this primary definition is met there is an exclusion either if the accommodation is provided by a close relative (see definition below) of the claimant or any member of his family (see s.137(1)) or if it is provided on other than a commercial basis. Provision by a limited company, of which a close relative of the resident is a director or a shareholder, is not provision by a close relative (*R(SB) 9/89*). In this case the company was formed well before the resident went into the home. It might be different if the company was a mere facade or had been formed for a fraudulent or improper purpose. In *R(IS) 2/91* the claimant became a resident in a nursing home of which his daughter was the sole proprietor. He was actually cared for by the staff employed by his daughter. Nonetheless, his accommodation and meals were "provided" by his daughter. "Provided" means "made available".

What is a commercial basis is unclear, although the *Decision Makers Guide* suggests that the phrase should be interpreted broadly, not simply that a profit has to be made (Ch.24, App.5, paras 49–50). If the charge and the arrangements are as one would expect in a commercial relationship it can clearly be argued that the basis is commercial. The *DMG* considers that if the intention is to cover the cost of food plus a reasonable amount for accommodation, the arrangement should also be regarded as commercial. This approach is confirmed by *CSB 1163/1988* (above), where the tribunal had decided that "commercial basis" contained an element of profit. The Commissioner holds that this was an error of law and that the phrase means a basis that is intended to be more or less self-financing and not provided as part of a quasi "family" setting. On the facts, the lack of the intention to make a profit by the Church did not prevent the basis being commercial, but the "community" nature of the arrangement did. It was probable that if the claimant paid no income in for at least a short time, she would not have been asked to leave. In *R. v Sheffield Housing Benefits Review Board, Ex p. Smith, Rugby BC Housing Benefits Review Board, Ex p. Harrison and Daventry DC Housing Benefits Review Board, Ex p. Bodden* (1996) 28 H.L.R. 36 (housing benefit cases which also concerned the Jesus Fellowship Church) Blackburne J reaches a similar conclusion. In deciding whether an arrangement was on a commercial basis, it was necessary to look at the arrangement as a whole. It was not correct only to consider the amount payable for the accommodation and to ignore the other terms of the agreement. See also *Campbell v (1) South Northamptonshire DC (2) SSWP* [2004] EWCA Civ 409, reported as *R(H) 8/04* (the appeal from *CH/5125, CH/5126, CH/5129* and *CH/5130/02*) which again concerned the Jesus Fellowship.

2.9   As far as family arrangements are concerned, all the circumstances must be considered. If money has been spent adapting accommodation to a disabled person's needs, this may be relevant. It is not the case, as is often argued by decision-makers, that if a person enters into an arrangement with a friend or a non-close relative it is automatically non-commercial. In *CIS 1951/1991* (confirmed in *R(IS) 17/94* and in *R(IS) 11/98*) whether a family arrangement was on a commercial basis is held to be entirely a question of fact for the tribunal, which has to consider whether it is similar to that which might have been arranged with a paying lodger (see the notes to reg.3).

See further the notes to reg.9(1)(a) of the Housing Benefit Regulations 2006 in CPAG's *Housing Benefit and Council Tax Benefit Legislation* for the extensive case law on the meaning of "on a commercial basis" in the housing benefit context.

"Care home". The definition in s.3 of the Care Standards Act 2000 reads as follows: 2.10

"3 Care homes
(1) For the purposes of this Act, an establishment is a care home if it provides accommodation, together with nursing or personal care, for any of the following persons.
(2) They are—
(a) persons who are or have been ill;
(b) persons who have or have had a mental disorder;
(c) persons who are disabled or infirm;
(d) persons who are or have been dependent on alcohol or drugs.
(3) But an establishment is not a care home if it is—
(a) a hospital;
(b) an independent clinic; or
(c) a children's home,
or if it is of a description excepted by regulations."

In Scotland s.2(3) of the Registration of Care (Scotland) Act 2001 defines a "care home service" as:

"a service which provides accommodation, together with nursing, personal care or personal support, for persons by reason of their vulnerability or need; but the expression does not include—
(a) a hospital;
(b) a public, independent or grant-aided school;
(c) an independent health care service; or
(d) a service excepted from this definition by regulations."

SA v SSWP (IS) [2010] UKUT 345 (AAC) confirms that if an establishment satisfies the conditions in the definition of "care home" then it falls to be treated as a care home even if it is also an educational establishment. Those terms are not mutually exclusive and a care home does not cease to be a care home merely by virtue of fulfilling some other function.

"Close relative": The words "brother" and "sister" include half-brothers and half- 2.11
sisters (*R(SB) 22/87*). The same decision confirms that if a child is adopted it becomes the child of its adoptive parents and ceases to have any legal relationship with its natural parents or brothers or sisters. It is legal relationships which are referred to in the definition of "close relative." In *Bristol City Council v JKT (HB)* [2016] UKUT 517 (AAC), a case on the equivalent housing benefit definition, Judge Ward points out that what was said in *R(SB) 22/87* about "brother" and "sister" including half-brothers and sisters was obiter but then goes on to reach the same conclusion that half-siblings fall within the definition of "close relative".
From December 5, 2005, references to "step" relationships and "in laws" are to be read as including relationships arising through civil partnership in any provision to which s.246 of the Civil Partnership Act 2004 applies. Section 246 is applied to the definition of "close relative" in reg.2(1) by art.3 of and para.21 of the Schedule to the Civil Partnership Act 2004 (Relationships Arising Through Civil Partnership) Order 2005 (SI 2005/3137).

"Couple": Whether or not two people are to be treated as a couple for the purposes 2.12
of IS (and IBJSA) has a number of important consequences. First, if two people are a couple then neither can be a "lone parent", which may mean that neither falls

within the "prescribed categories" in Sch.1B. Secondly, the applicable amount for a couple is less than that for two single claimants. Thirdly, a claimant is excluded from entitlement to income support if her partner (i.e. the other member of the couple) is in remunerative work (see the notes to reg.5) and, fourth, a couple's income and capital are aggregated for the purposes of the means test (see reg.23). Note, however, that a finding that two people are a couple does not, by itself, affect either's right to benefit and it cannot simply be assumed that non-entitlement to benefit will be the automatic consequence of such a finding. In other words, such a determination is merely one step in a chain of reasoning that may eventually lead to the "outcome decision" that the claimant is or is not entitled to benefit but is not itself an outcome decision and therefore cannot be appealed until the outcome decision is taken—see *CIS/1720/2004* and *CPC/3891/2004*.

A new definition of "couple" was introduced on December 2, 2019, the day on which the Civil Partnership (Opposite-sex Couples) Regulations (SI 2019/1458) came into force. Two people are now treated as a couple if:

- they are married to, or civil partners of, each other and are members of the same household; or if

- they are neither married to, nor civil partners of, each other but are living together as if they are a married couple or civil partners.

Spouses and civil partners

2.13   If two people are legally married, or have formally registered a civil partnership, whether or not they are a couple depends upon whether they are "members of the same household". In *Santos v Santos* [1972] 2 All E.R. 246 at 255, it was said that "household" refers to "people held together by a particular kind of tie". According to *R(SB) 4/83*, the concept of a household is a matter of commonsense and common experience.

If, in practice, two people each have exclusive occupation of separate accommodation, then they do not live in the same household. But the reverse does not necessarily apply: a single house can contain a number of households. In *CSB/463/1986*, for example, two claimants physically shared one room in a house as well as other facilities, but otherwise lived separately. They were in separate households. Thus a husband and wife can maintain separate households under the same roof. If the couple have decided to live apart in the same house, there can be separate households even if the husband is still maintaining the wife (*CIS/72/1994*). In *CIS/671/1992* the claimant and his wife shared a room for the mentally ill. Both suffered from senile dementia and they did not understand that they were husband and wife. It is held that there must be some communality, something that can be identified as a domestic establishment. Mere presence in the same room did not turn them into a household. It is a question of fact in each case. In *CIS/81/1993* the same Commissioner similarly concludes that a husband and wife (who were not mentally incapacitated) were not members of the same household where they lived in separate rooms in a nursing home, were billed separately and had only limited contact with each other. In *CIS/671/1992* the Commissioner also considers whether the claimant and his wife could be said to be members of some other household (the home as a whole). He refers to the decision of the House of Lords in *Simmons v Pizzey* [1979] A.C. 37 (occupants of a woman's refuge not a single household), and concludes that all the residents of the home were not one household. These decisions are followed in *R(IS) 1/99*, which also concerned a married couple who shared a double room in a residential home (for which they were billed separately). The room was furnished with their own furniture and they had a kettle and a toaster to make breakfast, although they ate their main meals in the communal dining room. They spent much of their time together and were able to wash and dress themselves, apart from needing assistance to get out of the bath. They had entered the home because it was becoming difficult to cope on their own and so they needed someone else to undertake the organisation of their domestic and personal activities. The Commissioner agrees with *CIS/671/1992* that for there to be a "household" there had to be a domestic establishment. This meant two or more people living together as a unit and enjoying a reasonable level of independence and self-sufficiency. If the degree of independence and self-sufficiency fell below a certain level, there was no longer a domestic establishment and therefore no longer a household. The point at which this occurred was a matter for the common sense of the tribunal. The tribunal had correctly concluded in this case that the claimants were not members of the same household.

A person under 16 cannot be a member of a couple (*CFC/7/1992*).

If a person maintains, and from time to time lives in the same house as, his or her lawful spouse there is an initial presumption that they form a couple.   **2.14**

Difficult issues can arise where one (or both) of the parties might be said to live in more than one place. In *R(SB) 30/83*, the Commissioner holds that the issue is not decided on a week-by-week basis. So where the woman was absent during University terms living in a rented bed-sit, the couple were living together throughout. This principle was implicitly applied in *R(SB) 8/85*. The claimant lived with a Mr G, whose employment brought him to the area and was said to go back to his wife at weekends. The Commissioner holds that a person can only be a member of one couple, and so of one household, at a time. This appears to leave open, to be determined according to the circumstances, whether Mr G was living with the claimant for five days a week and with his wife for two days, or with only one of them. *CIS/11304/1995* explicitly states that there can be two households in these circumstances. Mr K lived with his wife in Zimbabwe for six months of the year and with the claimant in England for the other half of the year. Although Mr K could not simultaneously have two households, he could spend six months of the year in one household and six in another.

Once two people have become a couple (which requires a common household to have been established), reg.16 of the Income Support Regulations (reg.78 of the Jobseeker's Allowance Regulations) treats them as continuing to be members of that household during some periods of temporary absence.

Unmarried partners

Under what used to be known as the "cohabitation rule", two people who are not married to each other, or civil partners of each other, are treated as a couple for benefit purposes if they are "living together as if they were a married couple or civil partners", which is the test that has now replaced the long-standing "living together as husband and wife" test. The application of the latter test to individual cases was among the most contentious issues in the whole of social security law. The new test does not reflect any change of social security policy but only the facts that, (1) since the introduction of same sex marriages, it has been possible for two people to be a "married couple" without also being "husband and wife", and (2) that civil partners can be either the same sex or opposite sexes. The case law about the former test will therefore be highly persuasive authority on the interpretation of the current one.   **2.15**

The first point to note is that the income support scheme recognises other ways of living together and has specific rules for determining the entitlement of claimants who live in someone else's household or have someone else living in their household. As Webster J stated in *Robson v Secretary of State for Social Services* [1982] 3 F.L.R. 232 at 236:

> "the legislation provides for three different situations: two persons who are living together being husband and wife is the first; two persons living together as husband and wife is the second; and two persons living together not as husband and wife is the third. It seems to me that where the facts show that there are two persons living together not being husband and wife, then both the second and third situations must be considered."

Thus to show that a couple are living together is only the first step, not the final one, as so often happens in practice (see also, e.g. *Crake v SBC, Butterworth v SBC* [1982] 1 All E.R. 498 at 502, SB 38).

There have been a number of Commissioner's decisions on a similar rule in widow's benefit (the test is held to be the same in *R(SB) 17/81* and *R(G) 3/81* and the same principles will apply for the income-related benefits), but the position reached is fairly vague. Early attempts to obtain a judicial definition of "cohabitation" were unsuccessful ("for my part it is so well-known that nothing I could say about it could possibly assist in its interpretation hereafter", Lord Widgery CJ in *R. v S.W. London A.T., Ex p. Barnett*, SB 4). The examination of three main matters is required in deciding if two people are cohabiting: "(1) their relationship in relation to sex: (2) their relationship in relation to money: (3) their general relationship. Although all three are as a rule relevant, no single one of them is necessarily conclusive" *(R(G) 3/71)*. In *CIS/87/1993*, however, the Commissioner expresses the view that it is the parties' general relationship that is most important (see below).

2.16   In response to criticisms about the operation of the cohabitation rule the Supplementary Benefits Commission produced published guidelines. The last formulation in summary form was in the 1984 edition of the Supplementary Benefits Handbook. A previous form of these guidelines had been approved as "an admirable signpost; the approach cannot be faulted" (Woolf J in *Crake v SBC, Butterworth v SBC*, above) and were found to correspond to the *R(G) 3/71* test in *R(SB) 17/81*. The Handbook said (para.2.13) that the main criteria are:

"*1. Members of the same household*
The couple must be living in the same household and neither partner will usually have any other home where they normally live. This implies that the couple live together, apart from absences necessary for employment, visits to relatives, etc.

2. Stability
Living together as husband and wife clearly implies more than an occasional or very brief association. When a couple first live together, it may be clear from the start that the relationship is similar to that of husband and wife (for example, if the woman has taken the man's name and borne his child), but in cases where at the outset the nature of the relationship is less clear it may be right not to regard the couple as living together as husband and wife until it is apparent that a stable relationship has been formed.

3. Financial support
In most husband and wife relationships one would expect to find financial support of one party by the other, or sharing of household expenses, but the absence of any such arrangement does not of itself prove that a couple are not living together.

4. Sexual relationship
Similarly, a sexual relationship is a normal part of a marriage and therefore of living together as husband and wife. But its absence at any particular time does not necessarily prove that a couple are not living as husband and wife.

5. Children
When a couple are caring for a child of their union, there is a strong presumption that they are living together as husband and wife.

6. Public acknowledgment
Whether the couple have represented themselves to other people as husband and wife is relevant. However, many couples living together do not wish to pretend that they are actually married. The fact that they retain their identity publicly as unmarried people does not mean that they cannot be regarded as living together as husband and wife."

The Handbook was wrong to claim that these guidelines had been approved by courts and a Commissioner, for there had been changes in form. The most important, in the paragraph on "sexual relationship", are devastatingly set out by the Commissioner in *R(SB) 35/85*. It was the 1979 version that was approved in *Crake* and *Butterworth* and in *R(SB) 17/81* and that referred to a sexual relationship as an important as well as a normal part of marriage and also noted that the presence of a sexual relationship did not necessarily prove that a couple were living as husband and wife. The 1982 edition added a new sentence: "However, if a couple have never had such a relationship it is most unlikely that they should be regarded as living together as husband and wife." The 1983 edition "watered down" that sentence to suggesting that "it may be wrong" to regard the couple as living together as husband and wife in such circumstances. In the 1984 edition this final sentence disappeared altogether, along with the suggestion that the presence of a sexual relationship does not necessarily prove that a couple are living as husband and wife. In the meantime, the law has remained exactly the same.

However, it is correct to stress that there is no single way by which the issue can be decided in every case. For the signposts tend not to help in making the basic distinction between couples living together as husband and wife and those living together in other ways. As *CIS/87/1993* and *CIS/4156/2006* emphasise, it is important to consider *why* the couple are living together. The issues are now dealt with in Ch.11 of the DMG, where the issues are discussed quite fully and with reference to a range of decisions. It is notable that in para.11108 a sexual relationship is now described as an important part of marriage, and the presence of a sexual relationship is said not to be conclusive in itself of living together as husband and wife.

For a helpful discussion of the practical difficulties of following the "admirable signposts" in individual cases, an account of the developments in the case law in the higher courts since *Crake* and *Butterworth*, and guidance on the importance of also identifying "any relevant features of the emotional relationship between the parties" in order to reduce the extent that the result given by the signposts is equivocal, see the decisions of the Upper Tribunal in *PP v Basildon DC (HB)* [2013] UKUT 505 (AAC) and *KJ v SSWP (IS)* [2019] UKUT 312 (AAC); and the decision of the Inner House of the Court of Session in *DK v SSWP* (2016) CSIH 84.

Household

See the notes under the heading Spouses and Civil Partners, above.   2.17

Stability

Stability of a relationship is only of great weight if the relationship is one like   2.18
husband and wife. There is no reason why a stable landlady-lodger relationship or flat-sharing relationship should not last for many years (see, for example, *CP/8001/1995*). However, it is sometimes suggested that an element of permanency in a relationship may differentiate it from, say, an employer-housekeeper relationship (e.g. *Campbell v Secretary of State for Social Services* [1983] 4 F.L.R. 138, where the "housekeeper" had sold her furniture and intended to apply for a joint local authority tenancy with the man). This forward-looking approach does make sense. But, as *CP/8001/1995* points out, even if an arrangement has become an established and settled one after some years, it does not follow that it has been on the same footing since the couple first started living together.

Financial support

The approach to financial support seems to make almost any arrangement point   2.19
the same way, except a very clearly fixed commercial payment. If one member of the alleged couple pays a lot, s/he is supporting the other. If s/he pays very little, this shows that the relationship is more than a commercial one. This makes it very difficult for parties who are friends, or where the man pays what he can afford, where the proper conclusion may merely be that the two people share a household.

Sexual relationship

2.20   There has been an attempt to decrease reliance on the existence of a sexual relationship, partly in response to criticism of "sex snoopers" and methods of investigation. Officers are now instructed not to initiate questions about sexual relationships and not to seek to inspect sleeping arrangements, but to note statements and evidence presented by the claimant. However, if a rule is to distinguish people living together as husband and wife from people living together in some other way it seems impossible not to give great significance to the nature of the sexual relationship. By playing down its importance, either as being present or absent, the Handbook inevitably shifted the test closer to one which simply tested whether the couple were living together in one household. The Commissioner in *CIS/87/1993* considers that where there has never been a sexual relationship, strong alternative grounds are needed to reach the conclusion that the relationship is akin to that of husband and wife. In his view, the instruction to DSS officers not to ask about the physical aspects of the relationship is inappropriate in an inquisitorial system, and if the information is not volunteered, such questions may have to be asked. But care will need to be taken to prevent any such investigation becoming over-intrusive. In *CSB/150/1985* the Commissioner held that an unmarried couple who refrained on principle from any sexual relationship could not be described as living together as husband and wife. The claimant and his fiancée lived in the same house, but were Mormons. That religion forbids sexual relationships before marriage.

In *CIS/4156/2006*, the Deputy Commissioner considered a situation where the alleged partners had previously cohabited at a different address but had separated because of the man's violent behaviour and had subsequently lived apart for nearly 15 years. He approved as helpful the guidance in Vol.I of the 2006 edition that in such circumstances "it may be proper to test the re-created relationship as if they had not formerly been married (e.g. in relation to the sexual relationship)". The Deputy Commissioner also expressed the view that the expression "living together as husband and wife" did not extend to include a relationship "akin to . . . a so-called open marriage" in which at least one party was free to conduct sexual liaisons with others.

Children and public acknowledgment

2.21   The shared care of children, especially children of the couple, and public acknowledgment are obviously important factors. In *R(G) 1/79*, the adoption of the same name on the electoral register was decisive. Other elements might be whether the couple visit relatives or friends, or go on holiday, together. What these points come to is that the so-called "objective facts" of a relationship may be capable of being interpreted either way. This, then, leaves the authorities in a difficulty, although it is clear that the burden of proof (where relevant: see *CIS/317/1994* below) is on the Secretary of State, at least when the rule operates as a disqualification.

In two decisions the Divisional Court has stressed the importance of looking at the intention of the parties in explaining the "objective facts". In *Butterworth v SBC*, above, the claimant was disabled following a serious accident, and invited the man, whom she had known for five years, to move into her house, since she was then on her own. The man had his own bedroom, with a lock on the door. He did the cooking and household tasks, and they lived as one household. Woolf J says:

> "If the only reason that [the man] went to that house temporarily was to look after Mrs. Butterworth in her state of illness and, albeit, while doing so, acted in the same way as an attentive husband would behave towards his wife who suffered an illness, this does not amount to living together as husband and wife because it was not the intention of the parties that there should be such a relationship. Looked at without knowing the reason for the man going to live there, it would appear that they were living together as husband and wife, but when the reason was known that would explain those circumstances."

In *Robson's* case (above), the parties were both seriously disabled, needing wheel-chairs and invalid cars. They had been friends for a long time before they were widowed. They moved together into a two-bedroom maisonette at their social worker's suggestion. They lived as one household. As so often the SBAT assumed that this was conclusive, and this was an error of law. In order to provide guidance to tribunals, Webster J says that often it is only possible to decide into which cat-egory a relationship falls by considering the objective facts,

> "because usually the intention of the parties is either unascertainable, or, if ascer-tainable, is not to be regarded as reliable. But if it is established to the satisfaction of the tribunal that the two persons concerned did not intend to live together as husband and wife and still do not intend to do so, in my judgment it would be a very strong case indeed sufficient to justify a decision that they are, or ought to be treated as if they are, husband and wife."

Although subsequent Divisional Court decisions (e.g. *Kaur v Secretary of State for Social Services* [1982] 3 F.L.R. 237) have not referred to intention as a factor, it has not been rejected either. However, in *R(SB) 17/81* the Commissioner says that Webster J's words are of no real assistance to tribunals. For, he says, it is "the conduct of the person concerned to which regard has to be paid", i.e. "what he or she does or says at the relevant time." If *R(SB) 17/81* is taken as deciding that only the "objective facts" as identified by the Handbook criteria are relevant, and that the intention of the parties is not relevant, it need not be followed as being inconsist-ent with persuasive decisions of the Divisional Court. If *R(SB) 17/81* is taken as a reminder of the difficulties of establishing intention it is in line with those decisions, although evidence of intention should not be as limited as suggested. On the facts of *R(SB) 17/81* the couple shared a sexual relationship and one household, but said that there was nothing permanent about the relationship. The Commissioner points out that the fact that they did not intend to marry did not mean that they did not intend to live together as though they were married. It is the second view of *R(SB) 17/81* that seems to have been applied in recent Commissioners' deci-sions, although decision-makers commonly rely on the first view in submissions to tribunals. *CSSB/145/1983* is a decision on facts reminiscent of *Robson's* case. Two disabled people living in a sheltered housing scheme moved into one flat to share living expenses and provide mutual support. At the beginning the housing association running the flats did not have the funds to divide the one bedroom. There was no sexual relationship. The SSAT had decided that the situation was no different from that of a married couple where one partner had a serious disability. The Commissioner holds this to be a wrong approach. A sharing of expenses and mutual support can arise between people of the same sex, or between brother and sister, and does not in itself amount to living together as husband and wife. In *R(SB) 35/85* the claimant was a widow in her seventies. She had taken over the tenancy of her bungalow in 1976, on the death of her brother, with whom she had lived for some years. In 1974, Mr W, who needed care and help, had moved into the household. By August 1984, he was a widower. The claimant did the cooking and there was a sharing of household expenses. The Commissioner holds that the SSAT, in finding the claimant and Mr W to be living together as husband and wife, had failed to see that the existence of a common household was only one ingre-dient in the decision. He adopts as helpful guidance the approach of Woolf J in *Butterworth* that it is impossible to categorise all the kinds of explanation of why two people were sharing a household, which would mean that the two were not living together as husband and wife. In *CIS/87/1993* the claimant maintained that the only relationship between him and Mrs B, with whom he was living, was that of patient and carer. The Commissioner decides that the SSAT had failed to consider their general relationship and why they were living together. He expresses reservations about the "criteria" relied upon by AOs in cohabitation cases. He points out that Woolf J in *Crake* and *Butterworth* considered it wrong to refer to them as "criteria"

2.22

and preferred the description "admirable signposts". There was nothing in *R(SB) 17/81* to suggest that only these admirable signposts had to be considered. In the Commissioner's view, the admirable signposts failed to emphasise the significance of the parties' "general relationship". It was arguable that it was the parties' general relationship that was of paramount importance and that their sexual and their financial relationship were only relevant for the light they threw upon the general relationship. The importance of looking at the totality of the parties' relationship and of not simply using the criteria as items on a checklist to be ticked off one by one is emphasised in *CP/8001/1995*. The claimant was a widow who had taken in a lodger. He paid her rent and a contribution towards expenses, but they did not pool resources, even though she had a right to draw cheques on his bank account. As time passed, they became friends, watched TV and ate together and went on holiday together with a group of friends. There was no sexual relationship, but on occasion they went halves on a twin-bedded room when staying in a hotel. The Commissioner decides that even though there were elements in the arrangement that matched those found in a normal marriage, it was equally akin to that of a brother and sister living in the same household, and that the totality of the evidence did not add up to a husband and wife relationship.

Burden of proof

2.23   In *CIS/317/1994* the Commissioner decides that the question of onus of proof did not arise where the question of whether the claimant was living together as husband and wife with her alleged partner fell to be determined on an initial claim for income support. What had to be considered was all the relevant facts. He pointed to the duty on the claimant to provide such information as may be required to decide the claim (see reg.7(1) of the Claims and Payments Regulations). The Commissioner also considered that although living together as husband and wife operated as a disqualification for widow's benefit it did not do so for income support. But, with respect, this distinction seems more apparent than real. Even though cohabitation is not an automatic bar in all cases, if the claimant's alleged partner is in remunerative work, or has income or capital that disentitles them to income support, or has himself already claimed income support, the effect of a living together decision will be to disqualify the claimant from income support. Thus it is suggested that the burden of proof (on the decision-maker) may come into play in marginal cases (if the claimant otherwise satisfies the conditions of entitlement to income support), even on initial claims. If benefit is stopped on a revision or supersession on the grounds of alleged cohabitation, the burden of proof will be on the DM. However, as pointed out above, it is often not so much the facts that may be at issue as the interpretation of those facts. Here the intention of the parties and the reason why they are living together may be the deciding factors (and see *CIS/87/1993* above).

2.24   *"Date of claim"*: See the notes to reg.6 of the Social Security (Claims and Payments) Regulations in Vol.III of this series.

2.25   *"Dwelling occupied as the home"*: "Home" is no longer defined, but the present definition contains many similarities to that of "home" in the old Supplementary Benefit (Requirements) Regulations and (Resources) Regulations. Instead of referring to accommodation, it refers to a dwelling, but since the definition of "dwelling" in s.137(1) of the Contributions and Benefits Act refers to residential accommodation, there is probably not much difference. The s.137(1) definition does specify that a dwelling can be the whole or part of a building and need not comprise separate and self-contained premises. The dwelling must be normally occupied as the home by the claimant. There is no reference here to the claimant's family, but presumably if the claimant has a family within s.137(1) of the Contributions and Benefits Act, the family's home will normally be his home, although see *CIS 81/1991* below.

In *OR v SSWP & Isle of Angelsey CC* [2013] UKUT 65 (AAC) the claimant was not occupying a night shelter as his home, given the very transient nature of his stays there, the fact that he was not allowed to remain there or leave any personal possessions there during the day, and the fact that he had no right to stay there on the following or any given night (if the shelter was full when he arrived he would be turned away). However, as the Upper Tribunal Judge emphasised, this case turned on its own particular facts and did not mean that other users of night shelters (or similar accommodation) are not entitled to housing benefit.

The question whether the reference to "the dwelling" means that only one dwelling at a time can meet the definition or whether in certain circumstances two physically separate buildings may constitute one dwelling has been the subject of several decisions. *R(SB) 30/83* decided that two completely separate units could not constitute one home. However, *R(SB) 10/89* held that two units about 600 yards apart, neither of which on their own could accommodate the assessment unit were one home. The Commissioner relied on some Rent Act cases on when something is let as a separate dwelling (in particular, *Langford Property Co Ltd v Goldrich* [1949] 1 K.B. 511). She took account of the fact that the mode of life of the assessment unit was such that one house was an "extension" or "annexe" of the other, that the two houses were within walking distance of each other, and that neither had been purchased as an investment. In *CIS 299/1992* it was held that a bungalow and an adjoining caravan constituted one dwelling. But in *CIS 81/1991*, where the claimant lived in one house and members of his family slept in another, the second house did not come within the definition in reg.2(1). This was because it was not occupied by the *claimant* as his home. The Commissioner distinguished *R(SB) 10/89* on the grounds that it was decided in relation to what in his view was the significantly different definition of "home" in the Supplementary Benefit Regulations, which referred to ". . . the accommodation . . . normally occupied by the *assessment unit* (emphasis added). . .". On the wording of the definition in reg.2(1), this decision is probably correct where only members of the claimant's family live in the other property. However, where the claimant personally occupies two physically separate properties, there seemed to be no reason why both should not constitute the dwelling normally occupied as his home.

This has now been confirmed by the Court of Appeal in *Secretary of State for Work and Pensions v Miah* [2003] EWCA Civ 1111; [2003] 4 All E.R. 702, also reported as *R(JSA) 9/03*. The Commissioner in that case had disagreed with *CIS 81/1991* and concluded that a "dwelling occupied as the home" could comprise more than one building. He had directed the new tribunal to have particular regard to para.13 of *R(SB) 10/89* and to consider whether the situation was in effect that of a single home on a split site. Occasional use of the second house by the claimant would not suffice, since the second house also had to be "normally" occupied by the claimant as his home. The Court of Appeal upheld the Commissioner's approach. It took the view that the use of the phrase "dwelling occupied as the home" indicated that the focus should be the functions served by the concept of a dwelling rather than its constituent elements and that function was a place serving as a home for the claimant. Common sense, justice and fairness also supported this approach. If the claimant had been living in one property which was large enough to accommodate him and his family then it would have been disregarded. It could not be fair that he should suffer when the purpose of having two properties was exactly the same. The Court also pointed to the difficulties, if the disregard only applied to one property, of determining which of the properties was to be disregarded in a case where the claimant was occupying both as his home (which, as the Court pointed out, was not the situation in *CIS 81/1991*).

2.26

See also *London Borough of Hackney v GA* [2008] UKUT 26 (AAC), reported as *R(H) 5/09*, in which two flats owned by different landlords constituted one dwelling and *Birmingham CC v IB* [2009] UKUT 116 (AAC), in which the additional room rented by a disabled student at university for his carer was held to be part of the dwelling occupied by him.

In *MM v SSWP (IS)* [2012] UKUT 358 (AAC) the claimant was the joint-owner of No.65 with his wife. However, for a number of years the claimant and his wife had stayed at No.16 (his father's house) in order to provide care for his father. The claimant's evidence was that (a) he returned to No.65 every day; (b) he had carried out repairs on No.65; (c) he paid gas and electricity bills in respect of No.65; (d) he kept food at No.65 and occasionally ate snacks there; (e) he kept clothes at both addresses; (f) his bank and insurance statements went to No.65 but other mail was delivered to No.16; and (g) he had not let No.65, in part because he wanted to use the house every day.

2.27   Judge Wikeley concluded that the tribunal had not made sufficient findings of fact and had not applied the correct legal test, i.e. whether the claimant normally occupied No.65 as his home, and in particular had not considered the "two proper-ties/one home issue" (see *Miah* and *R(SB) 10/89*). This issue was not confined to the situation where one property alone was not large enough to accommodate the family unit as a whole. The test under the legislation, as interpreted by the case law, was whether or not the claimant himself in effect used No.65 as an annex to No.16 and so had "a single home on a split site".

The issue in *CH/1786/2005*, a case on the meaning of "dwelling normally occupied as his home" in reg.5(1) of the Housing Benefit Regulations 1987, was whether the claimant, who after his father died stayed with his sister for much of the time, had ceased to occupy his flat as his home. Upholding the tribunal's decision that the claimant's flat remained the dwelling normally occupied as his home, the Commissioner concludes that it is a mistake to try and chop up what is essentially a single factual question into a series of individual tests for particular factors. In his view, identifying a person's "centre of interests" was not a separate test to be applied in determining where a person was truly making his normal home but really an expression of the overall conclusion after looking at all the facts.

In *PJ v SSWP (SPC)* [2014] UKUT 152 (AAC) the claimant was not normally occupying his home when he had gone to live in his daughter's home in order to avoid liability for council tax (and had remained there for three years). His other daughter remained in the family home because she was a student and so was exempt from council tax. The claimant visited at weekends and also stayed there at night for 50 per cent. of the time during a three month period in order to care for his daughter who was ill at that time but this did not mean that he was normally occupying the family home as his home.

2.28   Paragraph 3(6) of Sch.3 allows payments to be made for two homes in limited circumstances.

It also appears that accommodation cannot be normally occupied until some person has actually moved in (*R(SB) 27/84, R(SB) 7/86*), given the special rule created in para.3(7) for periods before anyone moves in. But this raises the ques-tion as to what is meant by "moved in" (and see *R(H) 9/05* below). In an uns-tarred decision, *CIS 4/1990*, the Commissioner doubts the existence of a rule that occupation requires residence. The same point was made in the supplementary benefit context in *CSB 524/1985* (not quoted by the Commissioner) and *CSSB 34/1987*. While it is right that the word used in the legislation is "occupy" and not "reside," it must also be noted that the definition requires not simply occupation, but occupation as the home. This point was the basis of *R(SB) 7/86* also not men-tioned in *CIS 4/1990*. However, it is suggested that the issue of what is sufficient to amount to occupation will be one of fact depending on the particular circumstances of the case. Thus, for example in *CH 2521/2002*, a case on the meaning of "dwell-ing normally occupied as his home" in reg.5(1) of the Housing Benefit Regulations 1987, the Commissioner decided that the claimant did not so occupy a flat when he only slept there a few nights a week while he was decorating it and had not moved in any clothing or possessions (other than a cooker which he did not use and a camp bed).

However, in *R(H) 9/05*, the Deputy Commissioner reached a different con-clusion on the facts. The claimant, who was elderly and disabled, entered into a tenancy agreement of a flat near her relatives on February 12, 2004, intending to move in on March 15, 2004 after the flat had been adapted to meet her needs. The work was carried out and her furniture was moved in on March 15, 2004. The claimant gave up her previous accommodation but did not physically go to the flat herself on March 15 because she had been admitted to hospital. Following a rehabilitation period the claimant went to live in the flat on August 9, 2004. The Deputy Commissioner holds that the claimant was normally occupying the flat as her home from March 15, 2004. She was not occupying any other home from that date and the flat had become her new permanent address. The local authority had contended that normal occupation involved physical presence in a property but since the claimant had a physical presence in the shape of her furniture it was difficult to see how she could be said not to have occupied it. As a matter of general law occupation did not require the personal presence of the tenant if the property was under her control and being used by her to store her goods and for no other purpose. The Deputy Commissioner therefore rejected the local authority's submission that it was necessary (but sufficient) for the claimant to spend one night at the property in order to normally occupy it as her home. In his view, if "normally" was intended to refer to some degree of regularity of occupation, far more than one night would be needed. But he did not consider that the word "normally" was directed to any question of length of occupation but was being used to deal with the case where there might be more than one dwelling that was the claimant's home. The local authority had also relied on various references in other parts of reg.5 of the Housing Benefit Regulations 1987 (which contained similar, although not identical, provisions to para.3 of Sch.3) to the claimant moving into the property as inferring that occupation meant physically moving in. But "moving in" was not part of the definition in reg.5(1) (the equivalent of para.3(1)). The subsequent paragraphs modified the general rule in reg.5(1) by spelling out certain circumstances in which a claimant could be treated as occupying a dwelling as her home for housing benefit purposes before she had moved in. But this did not answer the question as to what a claimant had to do in order to "move into" a property. In the Deputy Commissioner's view the claimant in this case had moved into the flat on the date that she removed her furniture from her previous home and moved it into her new flat. A more significant argument in his view was the fact that for the claimant to take advantage of the temporary absence provisions in reg.5(8B) and (8C) (the equivalent of para.3(11) and (12)) she had to be said to intend to *return* to occupy the flat as her home after her stay in hospital. However, the Deputy Commissioner concludes that because she had occupied the flat through the acts of her agents moving her furniture in she could be said to be returning there when she left hospital. Although this strained the use of the word "return", the alternative construction would be to draw an artificial distinction between a person who spent 10 minutes at the property before becoming unwell and a person who became unwell before arriving in person at the property.

The definition extends to any garden or outbuildings which are occupied as   2.29
part of the home (like the toilet and coalstore in outbuildings in *R(SB) 13/84* or the "development land" in *R(SB) 27/84* which might have been part of the garden). *CIS 427/1991* holds that the line between a garden and other land occupied with a dwelling is to be drawn according to the view of the ordinary man in the street.

If a building or a garden is occupied as part of the home it does not matter that they could be sold separately. This only comes into play when some buildings or land are not so occupied. Then those premises still count as part of the home if it is impracticable or unreasonable to sell them separately. (Note *C3/99-00(FC) (T)* which draws attention to the different definition in the Northern Ireland legislation.) A potential limit to this extension is exposed by *CSB 965/1986*, where the claimant was a tenant of a council house and owned a half-share in a smallholding two fields away. The small-holding was clearly not occupied as part of the home. The Commissioner holds that the extension could not apply since the home could not be sold and therefore the question of separate sale could not arise. This decision seems dubious, especially since the definition refers by way of example to croft land in Scotland, where the crofter is often only a tenant. Perhaps *CSB 965/1986* can be supported on the basis that if the small-holding was the only premises actually owned by the claimant it could not be unreasonable or impracticable to sell it separately. In *CIS 427/1991* the Commissioner holds that *R(SB) 13/84* was wrong in suggesting that property outside Scotland which is comparable to croft land is to be treated on the same principles. In considering reasonableness and practicability all the circumstances must be considered, including the use to which the premises are put, any profit made from them, etc. (*R(SB) 13/84* and *R(SB) 27/84*). In *CIS 427/1991* the state of health of the claimant's wife was a factor of which account could be taken in assessing whether it was unreasonable to sell land held with the home but not occupied as the home (she was a manic depressive who needed the adjoining fields for therapeutic walking). Medical evidence as to the therapeutic benefit would obviously be highly desirable in these circumstances.

CIS 616/1992 holds that the common parts of a block of flats (e.g. the entrance hall or staircases) do not come within the definition. It is not impracticable or unreasonable to sell such areas separately but quite simply impossible to do so.

2.30   *"Employed earner"*: The meaning in s.2(1)(a) of the Contributions and Benefits Act 1992, as amended by the Income Tax (Earnings and Pensions) Act 2003 Sch.6 Pt 2 para.171 with effect from April 6, 2003, and the National Insurance Contributions Act 2014 s.15(1) with effect from May 13, 2014, is "a person who is gainfully employed in Great Britain either under a contract of service, or in an office (including elective office) with earnings."

On the tests for deciding whether a person is an employed earner or in self-employment, see *CJSA 4721/2001*.

2.31   *"A guarantee income payment"*: See the note to *"the Armed Forces and Reserve Forces Compensation Scheme"* above.

2.32   *"Independent hospital"*: s.2 of the Care Standards Act 2000 defines an "independent hospital" as a "hospital which is not a health service hospital". In Scotland, an independent healthcare service is defined by s.2(5) of the Regulation of Care (Scotland) Act 2001 as an independent hospital, a private psychiatric hospital, an independent clinic and an independent medical agency (unless it is excepted from that definition by regulations).

2.33   *"Nursing home"*: The definition of "nursing home" was revoked on October 24, 2005. For the text of, and a note to, the former definition see pp.209 and 221 of Vol.II of the 2005 edition. For the period from October 5, 2005 until its revocation, the definition was modified (in relation to Scotland) by art.2 of, and para.3(1) of the Schedule to, the Mental Health (Care and Treatment) (Scotland) Act 2003 (Modification of Subordinate Legislation) Order 2005 (SSI 2005/445) and, in relation to England and Wales, by art.15 of, and para.3(2) of Sch.2 to, the Mental Health (Care and Treatment) (Scotland) Act 2003 (Consequential Provisions) Order 2005 (SI 2005/2078). The modification consisted of the substitution of the words "an independent health care service within the meaning of section 2(5) of the Regulation of Care (Scotland) Act 2001" for the words "a private hospital within the meaning of section 12 of the Mental Health (Scotland) Act 1984 (private hospitals)".

2.34   *"Occupational pension"*: Section 1(1) of the Pension Schemes Act 1993 (as amended by s.239 of the Pensions Act 2004 with effect from September 22, 2005 in the case of an occupational pension scheme that has its main administration in the UK and with effect from April 6, 2006 in all other cases (see art.2(7) of the Pensions Act 2004 (Commencement No.6, Transitional Provisions and Savings) Order 2005

(SI 2005/1720), and as further amended with effect from November 26, 2007 by reg.2(b) of the Occupational Pension Schemes (EEA States) Regulations 2007 (SI 2007/3014)) defines an "occupational pension scheme" as

"a pension scheme—

(a) that—

(i) for the purpose of providing benefits to, or in respect of, people with service in employments of a description, or

(ii) for that purpose and also for the purpose of providing benefits to, or in respect of, other people,

is established by, or by persons who include, a person to whom subsection (2) applies when the scheme is established or (as the case may be) to whom that subsection would have applied when the scheme was established had that subsection then been in force, and

(b) that has its main administration in the United Kingdom or outside the EEA states,

or a pension scheme that is prescribed or is of a prescribed description".

Section 1(2)–(5) provides:

"(2) This subsection applies—

(a) where people in employments of the description concerned are employed by someone, to a person who employs such people,

(b) to a person in an employment of that description, and

(c) to a person representing interests of a description framed so as to include—

(i) interests of persons who employ people in employments of the description mentioned in paragraph (a), or

(ii) interests of people in employments of that description.

(3) For the purposes of subsection (2), if a person is in an employment of the description concerned by reason of holding an office (including an elective office) and is entitled to remuneration for holding it, the person responsible for paying the remuneration shall be taken to employ the office-holder.

(4) In the definition in subsection (1) of "occupational pension scheme", the reference to a description includes a description framed by reference to an employment being of any of two or more kinds.

(5) In subsection (1) "pension scheme" (except in the phrases "occupational pension scheme", "personal pension scheme" and "public service pension scheme") means a scheme or other arrangements, comprised in one or more instruments or agreements, having or capable of having effect so as to provide benefits to or in respect of people—

(a) on retirement,

(b) on having reached a particular age, or

(c) on termination of service in an employment."

"Personal pension scheme": The meaning in s.1(1) of the Pension Schemes Act 1993 (as amended by s.239 of the Pensions Act 2004 with effect from April 6, 2006 (see art.2(7) of the Pensions Act 2004 (Commencement No.6, Transitional Provisions and Savings) Order 2005 (SI 2005/1720), and as further amended with effect from April 6, 2007 by the Finance Act 2007 Sch.27 Pt 3(2) para.1) is   2.35

"a pension scheme that—

(a) is not an occupational pension scheme, and

(b) is established by a person within section 154(1) of the Finance Act 2004".

Section 1(5) further provides that "pension scheme" in s.1(1) means "a scheme or other arrangements, comprised in one or more instruments or agreements, having or capable of having effect so as to provide benefits to or in respect of people—

    (a) on retirement,

    (b) on having reached a particular age, or

    (c) on termination of service in an employment."

2.36   *"Self-employed earner"*: The meaning in s.2(1)(b) of the Contributions and Benefits Act 1992 is "a person who is gainfully employed in Great Britain otherwise than in employed earner's employment (whether or not he is also employed in such employment)."

    On the tests for deciding whether a person is an employee or self-employed see *CJSA 4721/2001*.

2.37   *"Self-employment route"*: The new form of the definition of *"self-employment route"* is intended to encompass assistance in pursuing self-employed earner's employment while participating in *any* programme provided or other arrangement made under s.2 of the Employment and Training Act 1973 or s.2 of the Enterprise and New Towns (Scotland) Act 1990 (it has been introduced so as to avoid the need to amend the definition each time a new scheme is created). It also covers such assistance while taking part in an employment zone programme (such programmes, which no longer operate, did not come under those provisions but s.60 of the Welfare Reform and Pensions Act 1999). A person who is receiving assistance under the self-employment route is not regarded as being in remunerative work (this was previously achieved by Orders made by the Secretary of State under s.26 of the Employment Act 1988 in relation to individual schemes under s.2 of the 1973 Act but now see the new sub-para.(dd) of reg.6(1) and the amended form of reg.53(bb) of the JSA Regulations 1996).

    The other main consequence of participating in programmes under the self-employment route is that the normal rules for the treatment of income do not apply to receipts from trading (see reg.23A); such receipts are only to be taken into account as income in accordance with regs 39A–39D. Note the disregards in para.64 of Sch.9 and para.6(3) and (4) and para.52 of Sch.10 and of discretionary payments for those who were participating in an employment zone programme in para.72 of Sch.9 and para.58 of Sch.10.

    See also para.13 of Sch.9 which from April 1, 2004 has provided for a single disregard of the various allowances, grants and other payments made under s.2 of the Employment and Training Act 1973 or s.2 of the Enterprise and New Towns (Scotland) Act 1990 to people participating in New Deals and other training and welfare to work schemes. For the capital disregard see para.30 of Sch.10. These disregards have replaced, among other provisions, para.62 of Sch.9 and para.50 of Sch.10 which had previously contained a disregard of top-up grants for people participating in the self-employment route; such grants will now be ignored under the blanket provisions in para.13 of Sch.9 and para.30 of Sch.10.

2.38   *"The Skipton Fund"*: This is government-funded and has been set up to make lump sum ex-gratia payments to people (or their dependants if the person died after August 29, 2003) who have contracted hepatitis C from NHS blood, blood products or tissue. Such payments are fully disregarded (see para.39 of Sch.9 for the income disregard and para.22 of Sch.10 for the capital disregard).

2.39   *"The Caxton Foundation"*: this charitable trust is also government-funded. It was established on March 28, 2011 to provide additional discretionary financial support to people who have been infected with hepatitis C as a result of National Health Service treatment. Payments from the Caxton Foundation are fully disregarded (see para.39 of Sch.9 for the income disregard and para.22 of Sch.10 for the capital disregard).

"Training allowance": *R(IS) 10/98* holds that payments from the European   2.40
Social Fund can fall within this definition. As part of his part-time course the
claimant went on a two-week placement in Brussels and Strasbourg, for which
funds were provided by the European Social Fund. The Commissioner decided
that this meant that he was in receipt of a training allowance and so could
continue to be paid income support during his absence abroad (under reg.4(2)(c)
(i) and para.11 of Sch.1 in force at that time; see the 1996 edition of J. Mesher
and P. Wood, *Income-Related Benefits: The Legislation*). The payment from the
European Social Fund was out of "public funds" administered in the UK by the
Department of Employment and so could be said to be made "by or on behalf of
the Secretary of State for Employment"; the Secretary of State would also have
to have been satisfied that the course, or at least the placement, came within the
ambit of the European Social Fund and so could be said to have "approved" the
course.

In *R(TC) 1/03* the "training allowance" paid to the claimant was funded from
the local authority's budget, not by external funding. It therefore did not fall within
the definition in reg.2(1) of the Family Credit Regulations (which paralleled this
definition) (see Vol.II of the 2002 edition for the Family Credit Regulations which
were revoked in April 2003).

"Welfare to work beneficiary": See the notes to this definition, which was relevant to   2.41
incapacity for work, in Vol.II of the 2015/16 edition. The ESA equivalent is a "work
or training beneficiary", see para.1(3A)–(3C) and para.15(15) of Sch.6 to the ESA
Regulations 2008 below.

Paragraph (1B)
Until April 28, 2014 reg.2(1) included a definition of "service user group."   2.42
However, that definition has been omitted and replaced by para.(1B). The main
effect of the change is to clarify that carers who are paid expenses because the person
for whom they care participates as a service user are covered by this provision.
Paragraph (1B) was further amended on February 23, 2015 to include claimants
who are participating in research conducted by or on behalf of (i) the DWP in connection with its social security, child support or labour market functions, or (ii) a
body who undertakes research or monitoring in relation to such functions, as well
as those who are research participants in the areas of health, social care and social
housing.

Payment of expenses that result from a "claimant participating as a service user"
are disregarded (see para.2A of Sch.9 and the note to that paragraph); reg.35(2)(f)
ensures that they do not count as earnings.

Paragraph (3)
Note that special provision is only made for polygamous marriages. The defini-   2.43
tion of "family" in s.137(1) of the Contributions and Benefits Act will apply in
other situations, e.g. civil partnerships or living together as husband/wife or civil
partners.

[¹Disapplication of section 1(1A) of the Administration Act

2A.—Section 1(1A) of the Administration Act (requirement to state   2.44
national insurance number) shall not apply—

    (a) [³ . . .]

    (b) to a partner in respect of whom a claim for income support is made
        or treated as made before [² 5th October 1998].]

[⁴ (c) to a person who—
        (i) is a person in respect of whom a claim for income support is
            made;

(ii) is subject to immigration control within the meaning of section 115(9)(a) of the Immigration and Asylum Act;

(iii) is not entitled to any income support for the purposes of section 124 of the Contributions and Benefits Act; and

(iv) has not previously been allocated a national insurance number.]

AMENDMENTS

1. Social Security (National Insurance Number Information: Exemption) Regulations 1997 (SI 1997/2676) reg.10 (December 1, 1997).

2. Social Security (National Insurance Number Information: Exemption) (No.2) Regulations 1997 (SI 1997/2814) reg.2 (December 1, 1997).

3. Social Security (Working Tax Credit and Child Tax Credit) (Consequential Amendments) Regulations 2003 (SI 2003 No.455) reg.2 and Sch.1 para.1 (April 6, 2004, except in "transitional cases" and see further the note to reg.17 of the Income Support Regulations).

4. Social Security (National Insurance Number Information: Exemption) Regulations 2009 (SI 2009/471) reg.5 (April 6, 2009).

DEFINITION

"partner"—see reg.2(1).

GENERAL NOTE

2.45   Subsection (1A), together with subss.(1B) and (1C), was inserted into s.1 of the Administration Act by s.19 of the Social Security Administration (Fraud) Act 1997 and came into force on December 1, 1997. The effect of these provisions is that where s.1(1)(a) of the Administration Act (no entitlement to benefit unless a claim for it is made) applies, i.e. generally, there will also be no entitlement to benefit unless the claimant provides a national insurance (NI) number, together with information or evidence to show that it is his, *or* provides evidence or information to enable his NI number to be traced, *or* applies for a NI number and provides sufficient information or evidence for one to be allocated to him. This is known colloquially as the "NINO requirement". A P45 or P60 form will be evidence of a person's NI number but these may not always be available; other evidence which shows the person's number should also be sufficient. The NINO requirement applies to both the claimant and any person for whom he is claiming, except in prescribed circumstances (subss.(1A) and (1C)). The effect of reg.2A is that where a claim for income support was made, or treated as made, before October 5, 1998 (but not on or after that date) the national insurance number requirement did not apply to any partner of the claimant. Between December 1, 1997 and April 5, 2004 any child or young person included in the claim was also exempt from the requirement under para.(a). That exemption became unnecessary—and para.(a) was therefore repealed—on April 6, 2004 when support for children and young persons was removed from income support and transferred to child tax credit. See the note to reg.17 for the circumstances in which para.(a) remains in force on a transitional basis.

Note *CIS 345/2003* which confirms that a decision refusing to allocate an NI number (or alternatively if such a refusal is a determination, not a decision, a decision denying income support on the basis of such a determination) is appealable (*CIS 3692/2001* which decided that a tribunal only had a restricted jurisdiction as regards such a decision not followed). The Commissioner considered that the new tribunal would find the following observations from an officer on behalf of the Secretary of State helpful:

"It is to be hoped that the Secretary of State's representatives in the claimant's local social security office will in the meantime reconsider its refusal to provide to the tribunal the evidence on which its refusal of the claimant's claim under section 1(1B) of the Social Security [Administration Act 1992 was based]. If not, the new tribunal will, in my submission, be at liberty firstly to direct the Secretary of State to produce the evidence in question and secondly, in the event of a refusal to comply with that direction, to consider whether the Secretary of State is thereby seeking to shelter from scrutiny an indefensible decision."

The addition of para.(c) reverses the actual decision of the Court of Appeal in *SSWP v Wilson* [2006] EWCA Civ 882; R(H) 7/06 (see p.226 of Vol.II of the 2008 edition). It applies where:

- the claimant is the partner of a person subject to immigration control (see s.115 Immigration and Asylum Act 1999 and reg.21(3)) and is therefore a special case and entitled to IS at the single person rate only under para.16A(a) of Sch.7, or

- the claimant is a member of a polygamous marriage which includes one or more members who is a person subject to immigration control and is therefore entitled to IS only for him/herself and those members of the marriage who are not subject to immigration control under para.16A(b) of Sch.7.

The effect is that, from April 6, 2009, it is not necessary for the person subject to immigration control to satisfy the NINO requirement unless that person has previously been allocated a national insurance number. Note, however, that the amendment does not affect the reasoning of the Court that "[a]s a matter of ordinary language, benefit is claimed 'in respect of' a person if the benefit claimed is in some way referable to that person, as where the benefit or some component of it is defined or quantified by reference to that person".

Definition of non-dependant

3.—(1) In these Regulations, "non-dependant" means any person, except someone [³ to whom paragraph (2), (2A) or (2B) applies], who normally resides with a claimant [⁴or with whom a claimant normally resides.]   2.46

[³(2) This paragraph applies to—

(a) any member of the claimant's family;

(b) a child or young person who is living with the claimant but who is not a member of his household by virtue of regulation 16 (circumstances in which a person is to be treated as being or not being a member of the household);

(c) a person who lives with the claimant in order to care for him or for the claimant's partner and who is engaged for that purpose by a charitable or [⁵voluntary organisation] which makes a charge to the claimant or the claimant's partner for the care provided by that person;

(d) the partner of a person to whom sub-paragraph (c) applies.

(2A) This paragraph applies to a person, other than a close relative of the claimant or the claimant's partner,—

(a) who is liable to make payments on a commercial basis to the claimant or the claimant's partner in respect of his occupation of the claimant's dwelling;

(b) to whom the claimant or the claimant's partner is liable to make payments on a commercial basis in respect of his occupation of that person's dwelling;

(c) who is a member of the household of a person to whom sub-paragraph (a) or (b) applies.

(2B) Subject to paragraph (2C), this paragraph applies to—

(a) a person who jointly occupies the claimant's dwelling and who is either—

   (i) a co-owner of that dwelling with the claimant or the claimant's partner (whether or not there are other co-owners); or

   (ii) jointly liable with the claimant or the claimant's partner to make payments to a landlord in respect of his occupation of that dwelling,

(b) a partner of a person whom sub-paragraph (a) applies.

(2C) Where a person is a close relative of the claimant or the claimant's partner, paragraph (2B) shall apply to him only if the claimant's, or the claimant's partner's, co-ownership, or joint liability to make payments to a landlord in respect of his occupation, of the dwelling arose either before 11th April 1988, or, if later, on or before the date upon which the claimant or the claimant's partner first occupied the dwelling in question.]

(3) [² . . .].

(4) For the purposes of this regulation a person resides with another only if they share any accommodation except a bathroom, a lavatory or a communal area [¹ but not if each person is separately liable to make payments in respect of his occupation of the dwelling to the landlord].

(5) In this regulation "communal area" means any area (other than rooms) of common access (including halls and passageways) and rooms of common use in sheltered accommodation.

AMENDMENTS

1. Income Support (General) Amendment Regulations 1989 (SI 1989/534) reg.2 (April 10, 1989).

2. Income Support (General) Amendment Regulations 1989 (SI 1989/534) Sch.1 para.2 (October 9, 1989).

3. Income Support (General) Amendment No.6 Regulations 1991 (SI 1991/2334) reg.2 (November 11, 1991).

4. Income-related Benefits Schemes (Miscellaneous Amendments) (No.6) Regulations 1994 (SI 1994/3061) reg.2(2) (December 2, 1994).

5. Income-related Benefits Schemes (Miscellaneous Amendments) Regulations 1995 (SI 1995/516) reg.18 (April 10, 1995).

DEFINITIONS

"child"—see SSCBA s.137(1).
"claimant"—see reg.2(1).
"dwelling"—see SSCBA s.137(1).
"family"—*ibid.*
"partner"—see reg.2(1).
"voluntary organisation"—*ibid.*
"young person"—*ibid.*, and reg.14.

GENERAL NOTE

Paragraph (1)

2.47   The definition of "non-dependant" is important for a number of purposes, particularly deductions from housing costs and qualification for the severe disability premium. Its use for different purposes causes difficulties. What might be a sensible test for determining when a contribution towards accommodation costs ought to be assumed from an independent person who shares the claimant's accommodation might be less sensible in determining a severely disabled person's financial needs.

A person who normally resides with the claimant, or with whom the claimant normally resides, (*Chief Adjudication Officer v Bate* [1996] 2 All E.R. 790 HL also reported as *R(IS) 12/96*), unless within the important exceptions in paras (2)–(2C), is a non-dependant.

The December 1994 amendment to para.(1) was the government's immediate (within 48 hours) response to the Court of Appeal's decision in *Bate v Chief Adjudication Officer and Secretary of State for Social Security* on November 30, 1994 (*The Times*, December 12, 1994). Ms Bate was a severely disabled person who lived in her parents' home. The Court of Appeal decided that because her parents were the "householders", in the sense that it was they who jointly occupied the home as tenants, they did not normally reside with *her*, but she normally resided with *them*. Thus they did not come within the definition of non-dependant at all. The Court recognised that this construction did not fit easily with the amendment to reg.3(2)(d) on April 10, 1989 (now recast in para.(2A)), but did not consider that the meaning of the initial regulation could be determined by later amendments. The April 1989 amendment simply showed that the draftsman had assumed that "residing with the claimant" had the meaning which the Court had rejected. However, the House of Lords disagreed, holding that "resides with" meant no more than that the claimant and the other person lived in the same dwelling. It was not limited to the situation where it was the *claimant's* household or dwelling.

The December 2, 1994 regulations (SI 1994/3061) were introduced without first being referred to the Social Security Advisory Committee. Section 173(1)(a) of the Administration Act permits this if the Secretary of State considers it inexpedient to refer proposed regulations by reason of urgency. The failure to refer these proposed regulations was challenged by Ms Bate (see Welfare Rights Bulletin 125). It was argued that the Court of Appeal had decided that it was Parliament's intention that people in Ms Bate's position should be entitled to a severe disability premium (and therefore it intended that financial provision should be made for this) and so the Secretary of State could not say that it was urgent that payment of the premium should stop. In addition, the Secretary of State should not be allowed to sidestep the consultation procedure, which Parliament clearly considered important, in this way. (See the comment of Hobhouse LJ in *Chief Adjudication Officer v Palfrey* (reported as part of *R(IS) 26/95*) that one reason at least for the consultation procedure is the "remarkable latitude" given to the maker of regulations in the Social Security Acts.) But leave to bring judicial review was refused both by the High Court and the Court of Appeal.

Paragraphs (4) and (5) provide a partial definition of "resides with." In its original form, para.(4) put forward only one necessary, but not on its own sufficient, condition about sharing accommodation. But the general test of para.(1) still had to be satisfied. On "sharing of accommodation" see *CSIS 185/1995* in the note to para. (4). The post-April 1989 form of para.(4) specifically excludes from the definition a situation where co-residents are separately liable to make payments to a landlord. Such a person is already paying for accommodation costs. "Landlord" does not require there to be a tenancy; licensees can come within the exclusion (*CSIS 43/1992*).

Outside this exclusion the arrangement must still come within the general meaning of "residing with" and be the normal situation to come within the definition in para. (1). In *CSIS 100/1993* the claimant's daughter sometimes stayed in her mother's home and used that address for official correspondence. The Commissioner says that where correspondence is sent is a possible indicator that the daughter normally resided with the claimant, but equally, having regard to the other places the daugh-

2.48

ter stayed, it could be that she had no "fixed abode" (and thus did not normally reside with the claimant). This is further expanded on in *CIS 14850/1996* where the Commissioner states that for a person to be "normally resident" it was necessary for him to have lived in the house concerned, if not permanently, for a sufficient length of time for it to be regarded as his usual abode. The question of normal residence was a practical one to be determined in the light of common sense (see *CSIS 76/1991*). It would be relevant to consider why the residence started, its duration, the relationship, if any, between the people concerned, including its history; the reason why the residence had been taken up and whether it had lasted longer than its original purpose; and whether there was any alternative residence the person could take up. In that case a woman who was previously unknown to the claimant but who may have been his daughter came to live with him on the breakdown of her marriage. The matrimonial proceedings were protracted and she was also waiting for a council house. When the claimant applied for his income support to be reviewed to include a severe disability premium she had been living in his house for nine months. The Commissioner considered that since they had not previously known each other normal residence might take longer to establish and even longer if they were not in fact close relatives. If "the daughter" was waiting for alternative accommodation her residence could be quite lengthy without necessarily becoming normal. Questions such as what steps she had taken to find other accommodation, or with regard to her former matrimonial home, would also need to be investigated. In *CH/4004/2004* a destitute cousin staying temporarily with the claimant was not "normally" residing with her. See also *AM v SSWP* [2011] UKUT 387 (AAC).

Paragraphs (2)–(2C)

2.49   These provisions except those who would otherwise count as non-dependants from coming within that category. The exceptions have been through a convoluted series of forms, whose meaning has been a matter of great controversy. The convolutions are traced in previous editions of J. Mesher and P. Wood, *Income-related Benefits: the Legislation*, and great care must be taken in identifying what form of the regulation is in effect at particular dates which may be relevant to outstanding claims and appeals. See *CIS 20034/1997* for a useful summary of the position in relation to each of the periods from October 9, 1989 for a severely disabled claimant living with his family. The House of Lords in *Foster v Chief Adjudication Officer* [1993] A.C. 754; [1993] 1 All E.R. 705 holds that the amendment made on October 9, 1989 (to add the conditions now substantially contained in para.(2B)(a) (i) and (ii)) was not ultra vires on the ground of irrationality.

Note that regs 4–6 of the Income Support (General) Amendment No.6 Regulations 1991 provide transitional protection for claimants who were entitled to the severe disability premium before October 21, 1991, by virtue of the pre-November 1991 form of reg.3 (see p.1752).

In *R(IS) 17/94* a Tribunal of Commissioners states that tribunals, when considering, for example, a claimant's right to a severe disability premium, should deal with the position from the date of claim down to the date when the issues are finally decided (preferring the approach of *R(IS) 26/95* to that of *CIS 649/1992*, where the Commissioner held that an adjudicating authority should only consider the position as at the date from which benefit is sought). *CIS 649/1992* is also inconsistent with, for example, *R(IS) 13/93* (see the notes to reg.23(2) of the Adjudication Regulations). But in relation to appeals lodged on or after May 21, 1998, note the effect of s.22(8) of the Administration Act inserted by para.3 of Sch.6 to the Social Security Act 1998 where there is a change of circumstances after the date of the decision under appeal, and now see s.12(8)(b) of the 1998 Act. In addition, *R(IS) 17/94* dealt with an argument that once a claimant had acquired a right to a severe disability premium, its removal by subsequent amendment of reg.3(2) was prevented by s.16(1)(c) of the Interpretation Act (protection of acquired rights). Section 16 applies unless the contrary intention appears. The Commissioners hold that the words "shall come into force in relation to a particular claimant" in reg.1(1) of SI 1989/534 (the regulations at issue) indicated that the regulations were intended to apply to existing claimants. A claim made after the regulations came into force would be subject to them without the need for these words. Thus they were clearly intended to provide for existing claimants.

Paragraph (2)

These four categories excluded from the definition of non-dependant have been in the regulation since 1988 and are relatively straightforward. They cover those who are not sufficiently independent of the claimant to be a non-dependant.   2.50

(a) A member of the family. This, by reference to s.137(1) of the Contributions and Benefits Act, covers children and 16–18-year-olds treated as in full time secondary level education as well as partners, but only if members of the same household.

(b) Children who are not members of the family under the operation of the special rules in reg.16.

(c) Certain carers provided at a charge by charities or voluntary bodies, plus the carer's partner.

Paragraph (2A)

This is a recasting in November 1991 of the previous para.(2)(d)–(db). The difference is that a close relative (defined in reg.2(1)) of the claimant or his partner does not come within para.(2A). Thus, for instance, the parents of a severely disabled person may no longer come within para.(2A). If they are not to be non-dependants from November 1991, they must come within paras (2B) and (2C). Outside the close relative exception, the effect of para.(2A) now is that where the relationship between the claimant (or the claimant's partner) and the other person (or a member of that person's household) is a commercial one, that person is not a non-dependant. No further contribution to accommodation costs is therefore appropriate.   2.51

There must be a legal liability (as distinct from a moral or ethical obligation *(CIS 754/1991)*) to make payments for accommodation, i.e. rent or a board and lodging charge, on a commercial basis. The first question is whether there is a liability to pay. It has been held on the pre-November 1991 version of para.(2A) that a severely disabled claimant living with, for example, his parents can be their licensee and therefore liable to pay for his accommodation in the sense that if no payment is made the licence could terminate *(CIS 195/1991, CIS 754/1991)*. In deciding whether such a liability exists there would need to be findings as to the terms on which a claimant lives in his parents' home, the amount and regularity of the payments and the use made of the claimant's contributions. If the payments go towards rent or a mortgage that would be a stronger case than if they are used for the claimant's own personal needs *(CIS 754/1991)*, however, they need not be applied directly to accommodation costs. If the claimant's contributions go into a general fund used for household costs (including accommodation) that will suffice *(R(IS)17/94)*. It will then be necessary to conclude on the basis of the relevant findings whether there was an intention to create legal relations. Such an intention can be inferred from a course of conduct (see Scarman LJ in *Horrocks v Forray* [1976] 1 W.L.R. 230 at 239). *CIS 754/1991* holds that this might not be too difficult to infer where an adult member of the family is making regular payments in respect of his occupation. It may be easier to infer where the parents depend on the claimant's contributions because of their own financial circumstances. In his directions to the new SSAT in *CIS 754/1991* the Commissioner concludes:

"In essence there should be what I might call a broad approach to satisfaction of the condition keeping in mind that the AO has throughout accepted that in

[*CIS 195/1991*] it was right to conclude that the claimant [had a liability to make payments in respect of his occupation]. I should have thought that the facts in many of the cases are likely to be essentially indistinguishable from those in [*CIS/195/1991*]."

The facts in *CIS/195/1991* were that the claimant's parents took £20 per week from his benefit. The rest of the money was used for his own needs. The SSAT found that the claimant lived in his parents' house as a licensee and paid them £20 in respect of his occupation of it.

But what of the situation where there can be no contractual liability because one of the parties lacks the capacity to make a contract? In *CIS 195/1991* the claimant was held to be capable of incurring a liability to make payment, despite his mental disability. Under English law the contract was voidable because of his mental disability, not void. However, in Scottish law an "incapax" is not capable of making any personal contract. *R(IS) 17/94* holds that in Scottish cases ATs must first consider whether a claimant is so mentally incapacitated as to be incapax. Although, if this is the case, the doctrine of recompense may well apply to establish a liability on the incapax, so that the result is similar in practical terms to that in *CIS 195/1991* (see 1993 Supplement for fuller discussion of *R(IS) 17/94*, the reported version of *CSIS 28/1992* and *CSIS 40/1992*). The doctrine of recompense is also considered in *CSIS 641/1995*, although on the particular facts of that case (see the summary in the 1998 Supplement to J. Mesher and P. Wood, *Income-related Benefits: the Legislation*) it did not apply. In *CIS 754/1991* the Commissioner expresses the *obiter* view that where a person has no contractual capacity at all, the doctrine of restitution does not seem available to assist claimants in England in the way that recompense can in Scotland. Thus in English cases for mentally disabled claimants it will generally be necessary for there to be a finding of sufficient contractual capacity. On the facts of both *CIS 195/1991* and *CIS 754/1991* the capacity required does not seem to be of a very high order. The claimant in *CIS 754/1991* was found to have sufficient contractual capacity despite having Downs syndrome and needing an appointee to act for her in social security matters.

2.52 Since October 1, 1990, the liability to pay has had to be on a commercial basis. The words "commercial basis" govern the nature of the liability, not just the quality of the payments made (*R(IS) 17/94*). For a discussion of "commercial basis" see *CSB 1163/1988* and the notes to the definition of "board and lodging accommodation" in reg.2(1). In *CIS 195/1991* (approved in *R(IS) 17/94*) the Commissioner held that the question of whether an arrangement is on a commercial basis was entirely one of fact for the SSAT. What has to be considered is whether the arrangement is the sort that might have been entered into if the parents had taken in a lodger, instead of, in *CIS 195/1991*, their physically and mentally handicapped son. This approach was also expressly approved by another Tribunal of Commissioners in *R(IS) 11/98*. The claimant, who was severely disabled, lived with her parents and paid them £25 per week. The Commissioners emphasise that *CIS 195/1991* had only considered that a commercial arrangement in a family situation was unlikely, not that it was impossible or even improbable. They also confirm that a profit element is not necessary, nor was it relevant whether the family depended financially on the payments or whether they would take any action if the claimant did not pay (although these last two factors were relevant to the question of whether there was a liability to make payments, see *CIS 754/1991*). The Commissioners rejected the AO's contention that in considering the adequacy of the claimant's payments a deduction should be made for the value of the care provided by the parents, pointing out that reg.3 referred to payments in respect of the *occupation* of the dwelling.

Although there might still be some scope for structuring an informal relationship to get within para.(2A), the requirement of a commercial basis (since October 1, 1990) and the exclusion of close relatives (from November 11, 1991) provide quite a stringent control. Note the transitional protection in regs 4–6 of the Income

Support (General) Amendment No.6 Regulations 1991 (see p.1752) for claimants entitled to the severe disability premium before October 21, 1991.

Tribunals faced with sorting out severe disability premium entitlement, in particular for the periods October 9, 1989 to September 30, 1990 and October 1, 1990 to November 10, 1991, will need to pay particular regard to the Commissioners' decisions discussed above. There is a useful summary of the position in relation to each of the periods from October 9, 1989 in *CIS 20034/1997*.

Paragraphs (2B)–(2C)

These provisions replace the previous para.(2)(c) on joint occupiers, and impose a considerably stricter test. The biggest change in November 1991 was to exclude joint occupiers who are close relatives (see reg.2(1)) from the operation of para. (2B) except in restricted circumstances. This is done by para.(2C). If the close relative met the conditions of para.(2B) either before April 11, 1988, or as soon as the claimant or partner moved to the current home, then advantage can be taken of para.(2B). The aim is to exclude arrangements made within a family (in the non-income support sense) designed to take advantage of the definition of a non-dependant. The thinking is that if the arrangement was the basis on which the occupation of the home by the claimant started it is likely to be a genuine one. Existing claimants excluded by this rule may particularly benefit from the transitional protection mentioned above. *CIS 80/1994* rejects the argument that para.(2C) is invalid on the ground that it operates retrospectively. The Commissioner states that para.(2C) imposes a new condition of future eligibility (though with reference to past events). Thus it does not take away any vested right or create any new obligation in regard to events that have already passed.

In *CIS 650/1993* the claimant had been a joint tenant of her home with her husband. When he died in 1990 she became the sole tenant. Later her sister came to live with her and they became joint tenants. The Commissioner rejects the claimant's contention that the previous joint liability of the claimant and her husband meant that para.(2C) was satisfied. In the context of reg.3, para.(2C) only referred to the joint liability of the claimant and the person currently residing with her and not to any other joint liability.

In *CIS 216/1997* the claimant who was in receipt of the severe disability premium gave up the tenancy of her local authority home (with effect from January 22, 1995) and went to live with her daughter and her family. She moved to her daughter's home on January 16, 1995 and became a joint tenant with her of that home on January 23, 1995. During the week from January 16–22, the claimant was moving her belongings from her old home to her new, although she slept at her daughter's home from January 16. The Commissioner decides that the claimant was to be regarded as having "first occupied" her new home when she first normally resided there. It was clear from the evidence that arrangements for the joint tenancy had been made with the local authority before the claimant moved in with her daughter. The move and the creation of the joint tenancy were inextricably linked. In his view the claimant did not finally become an occupier of her new home until January 23, 1995 and so para.(2C) applied.

The rest of para.(2B) is based on the provisions in force from October 1989. First, there must be joint occupation of the claimant's home. In *CIS 180/1989* the claimant was a single woman in receipt of attendance allowance, severe disablement allowance and income support. She lived with her parents, who owned the house. The Commissioner held that "jointly occupies" is not to be given a technical meaning, but its ordinary meaning. The phrase applies where "persons who normally reside together jointly occupy the premises in the sense of equality of access and use as distinct from a situation where restrictions are imposed in relation to those matters." It did not matter, under the legislation in force at the relevant time, that the claimant did not have any proprietary interest in the house. *CIS 180/1989* (approved by the Tribunal of Commissioners in *R(IS)17/94*) has governed the position, particularly in severe disability premium cases, for the period before

2.53

2.54

October 9, 1989, when amendments to impose the extra conditions now substantially contained in para.(2B)(a)(i) and (ii) were made. Indeed, it has been usual for AOs to concede that for the period before October 9, 1989, parents or other family members are not non-dependants.

It might be objected that the approach of *CIS 180/1989* expanded the exception on joint occupation so far that it excluded everyone who would be caught by the primary definition of a non-dependant. This is not so. People can reside together, but without the equality of access and use stressed by the Commissioner. The House of Lords in the *Foster* case, where it was conceded that the claimant's parents were joint occupiers up to October 9, 1989, expressed similar doubts that the exception, if widely construed, might eat up the rule, but did not reach any authoritative conclusion. In a decision on the equivalent housing benefit provision (*Fullwood v Chesterfield BC, The Times*, June 15, 1993) the Court of Appeal specifically rejected the basis of *CIS 180/1989*, holding that "jointly occupies" is a technical legal phrase, meaning "occupies by right jointly with one or more persons". Thus, joint occupation entails either a joint tenancy or joint liability to make payments under an agreement for occupation. This decision strictly only related to housing benefit, but both the Court of Appeal and the House of Lords in *Bate* (see above) accepted that the phrase should be given the same meaning for the purposes of income support. It connoted a legal relationship and not merely factual co-residence.

From October 9, 1989, it has been specifically provided that one of two extra conditions must be satisfied. One is that the claimant (or partner) is a "co-owner" of the home with the other person (or partner), a concept that can include at least some beneficial owners who are not also legal owners: see *SSWP v HB (SPC)* [2015] UKUT 389 (AAC). This is unchanged since October 9, 1989. The other condition is that there is joint liability to make payments in respect of the occupation of the home to a landlord. This was changed in November 1991 from the October 9, 1989 form to specify that the payments must be to a landlord. The result is broadly to confirm the outcome of *CIS 299/1990* (discussed in the 1991 edition of J. Mesher and P. Wood, *Income-related Benefits: the Legislation*) and to remove the problem of interpretation addressed in that decision. These conditions narrowed the scope of para.(2B) considerably. Where there is separate, rather than joint, liability a person is deemed not to be residing with the claimant (para.(4)).

Paragraph (3)

2.55   The revocation removes the special rule for boarders and hostel-dwellers.

Paragraph (4)

2.56   The original form of para.(4) merely meant that if accommodation other than bathroom, lavatory or a communal area was not shared, one person was not "residing with" another. It did not mean that the person was "residing with" the other just because such accommodation was shared. The general test of para.(1) still has to be satisfied. See *R(IS) 12/06*, *CSIS/100/1993*, *CIS/14850/1996*, and also *Kadhim v London Borough of Brent Housing Benefit Review Board* (CA, unreported, December 20, 2000) which reaches the same view on the similar provision in reg.3(4) of the Housing Benefit Regulations. Paragraph 4 now also excludes from the definition of non-dependant a person who is separately liable to make payments to the landlord. See *CSIS 43/1992* above. Joint tenants and co-owners (other than close relatives of the claimant or partner) are excluded by para.(2B)(a).

CSIS 185/1995 holds that a person does not share a kitchen with another if it is not used physically by him but only by a third party to prepare food on his behalf. The Commissioner also points out that the issue is whether there is a "sharing of *accommodation*". So deciding whether the claimant shared a room simply because some of her clothes were stored there, would depend on what use, if any, the claimant made of the room, by considering what was stored there, in what, and to what extent, if any, the claimant herself went in and out of the room to deal with her property.

[¹Permitted period

3A.—(1) For the purposes of regulation 17(6), [². . .], paragraph 7(6)   2.57
of Schedule 3A, paragraph 6(3) of Schedule 3B and paragraphs 4 and 6
of Schedule 8 (applicable amounts, mortgage interest, protected sums and
earnings to be disregarded), where a claimant has ceased to be entitled to
income support—

  (a) because he or his partner becomes engaged in remunerative work the
       permitted period, [³. . .] shall be 12 weeks; or
  (b) for any other reason, the permitted period shall be eight weeks.

  (2) [³. . .].
  (3) [³. . .].

AMENDMENTS

1. Income Support (General) Amendment No.3 Regulations 1989 (SI 1989/
1678) reg.2 (October 9, 1989).
2. Social Security (Income Support, Claims and Payments and Adjudication)
Amendment Regulations 1995 (SI 1995/2927) reg.4 (December 12, 1995).
3. Income Support (General) (Jobseeker's Allowance Consequential Amendments) Regulations 1996 (SI 1996/206) reg.3 (October 7, 1996).

GENERAL NOTE

Regulation 3A provides a definition of the maximum permitted period of break in   2.58
entitlement for the application of the various provisions set out in para.(1).

The omission of paras (2) and (3) is a consequence of the introduction of jobseeker's allowance on October 7, 1996.

Schedules 3A and 3B were revoked by SI 2006/588 with effect from April 3,
2006. However, para.(1) has not been amended to reflect that change.

PART II

CONDITIONS OF ENTITLEMENT

[¹Prescribed categories of person

4ZA.—(1) Subject to the following provisions of this regulation, a person   2.59
to whom any paragraph of Schedule 1B applies falls within a prescribed category of person for the purposes of section 124(1)(e) of the Contributions
and Benefits Act (entitlement to income support).

  (2) Paragraph (1) does not apply to a [⁴ full-time student] during the
period of study.

  (3) A[⁴ full-time student] during the period of study falls within a prescribed category of person for the purposes of section 124(1)(e) of the
Contributions and Benefits Act only if—

  (a) [¹¹ . . .]
  (b) paragraph 1, 2, [¹⁰ . . .] 11, [¹⁰ . . .] [⁸ 15A,] or 18 of Schedule 1B
       applies to him; or
  [⁷ (c) any other paragraph of Schedule 1B applies to him and—
          (i) in the case of a person with a partner, the partner is also a full-
              time student and either he or his partner is treated as responsi-
              ble for a child or young person, or

(ii) in any other case, he is treated as responsible for a child or young person,

but this provision applies only for the period of the summer vacation appropriate to his course; [⁹ . . .]

[⁶ (d) [⁹ . . .]]

[⁵(3A) Paragraph (1) does not apply to a person to whom section 6 of the Children (Leaving Care) Act 2000 (exclusion from benefits) applies.]

[²(4) A person who falls within a prescribed category in Schedule 1B for the purposes of this regulation for any day in a benefit week, shall fall within that category for the whole of that week.]

AMENDMENTS

1. Income Support (General) (Jobseeker's Allowance Consequential Amendments) Regulations 1996 (SI 1996/206) reg.4 (October 7, 1996).

2. Income-related Benefits and Jobseeker's Allowance (Amendment) (No.2) Regulations 1997 (SI 1997/2197) reg.5(2) (October 6, 1997).

3. Social Security (Immigration and Asylum) Consequential Amendments Regulations 2000 (SI 2000/636) reg.3(3) (April 3, 2000).

4. Social Security Amendment (Students) Regulations 2000 (SI 2000/1981) reg.5(5) and Sch. (July 31, 2000).

5. Children (Leaving Care) Act 2000 (Commencement No.2 and Consequential Provisions) Order 2001 (SI 2001/3070) art.3(2) and Sch.1 para.(a) (October 1, 2001).

6. Social Security (Adult Learning Option) Amendment Regulations 2006 (SI 2006/2144) reg.2 (September 1, 2006).

7. Social Security (Students Responsible for Children or Young Persons) Amendment Regulations 2008 (SI 2008/1826) reg.2 (July 9, 2008).

8. Social Security (Miscellaneous Amendments) Regulations 2009 (SI 2009/583) reg.2(4) (April 6, 2009).

9. Social Security (Miscellaneous Amendments) (No.4) Regulations 2009 (SI 2009/2655) reg.2(3) (October 26, 2009).

10. Income Support (Prescribed Categories of Person) Regulations 2009 (SI 2009/3152) reg.3(2)(a) and 3(7) (December, 30, 2009). Regulation 3(2)(a) omitted "10," and "12," in reg.4ZA(3)(b) with effect from December 30, 2009 but reg.3(7) provided that this did not apply in the case of a person who was subject to the saving provisions in reg.2(2) of those Regulations. See the 2015/16 edition of this volume for these Regulations and the notes to them.

11. Social Security (Miscellaneous Amendments) (No.3) Regulations 2013 (SI 2013/2536) reg.4(3) (October 29, 2013).

DEFINITIONS

"child"—see SSCBA s.137(1).
"benefit week"—see reg.2(1).
"full-time student"—see reg.61(1).
"partner"—see reg.2(1).
"period of study"—*ibid.*
"young person"—see reg.14.

GENERAL NOTE

Paragraph (1)

2.60 As a consequence of the introduction of JSA on October 7, 1996, the income support scheme had to undergo a fundamental restructuring. Income support was no longer available to people who are claiming benefit because they are unemployed.

People who have to be available for, and actively seeking, work as a condition of receiving benefit have to claim JSA. Since October 7, 1996, in order to qualify for income support a person has to fall within a "prescribed category" (see SSCBA s.124(1)(e)). These categories are set out in Sch.1B. When Sch.1B was first introduced the categories broadly resembled most of those in the former Sch.1 (people not required to be available for employment) which was revoked on October 7, 1996, but there were some differences. See the notes to Sch.1B. For the position of full-time students, see paras (2) and (3). Note also para.(3A) (see below).

Schedule 1B provides an exhaustive list of the circumstances in which a person will be entitled to income support. There is no category of analogous circumstances or provision for a reduced rate of benefit on the ground of hardship for people who do not come within these categories (compare the former reg.8(3), see the 1996 edition of J. Mesher and P. Wood, *Income-related Benefits: the Legislation*). Moreover, the provision for hardship payments under JSA is considerably restricted (see regs 140–146 of the JSA Regulations 1996 and the notes to those regulations (regs 146A–146H in the case of joint-claim couples)). Pt VI of the Income Support Regulations, which formerly contained some very limited provision for urgent cases outside the normal scope of the income support rules, was revoked (subject to three savings: see the note to Pt VI) with effect from January 25, 2010.

Note that entitlement to income support and JSA is mutually exclusive, although some people may be eligible for either. Section 124(1)(f) of the Contributions and Benefits Act provides that entitlement to JSA excludes entitlement to income support (any "top-up" to a person's contribution-based JSA will be by way of income-based JSA). Similarly, a person will not be entitled to JSA (contribution- or income-based) if he is entitled to income support (ss.2(1)(d) and 3(1)(b) of the Jobseekers Act). However, there is nothing to prevent a person who qualifies for income support claiming JSA if he also fulfils the conditions of entitlement for JSA. But in most circumstances it will be better for him to claim income support so as to avoid the risk of being "sanctioned" for not complying with the labour market conditions. If the claimant is a member of a couple he will not be entitled to income support if his partner is claiming *income-based* JSA (SSCBA s.124(1)(f)). If his partner is claiming *contribution-based* JSA he will be able to claim income support if he is eligible for this, or his partner (or, from March 19, 2001, he and his partner in the case of most (since February 25, 2008, all, unless exempt) childless couples) can claim income-based JSA. Before October 27, 2008, if the claimant was incapable of work it was better for him to claim income support in order to qualify for the disability premium under para.12(1)(b) of Sch.2 after serving the appropriate waiting period. This was because if the only basis for qualifying for the premium was incapacity for work for 364 days (or 196 days if he was terminally ill), his partner would not be able to get a JSA disability premium for him (see para.14 of Sch.1 to the JSA Regulations 1996). However, following the introduction of ESA on October 27, 2008 *new* claims for income support on the ground of incapacity for work were no longer possible (see further the note to para.7 of Sch.1B in the 2015/16 edition of this volume). Finally, note the "better-off" problem for some claimants as a result of the limit for remunerative work for partners being 24 hours a week from October 7, 1996 (see reg.5(1A) and reg.51(1)(b) JSA Regulations 1996). The consequence of this is that if the claimant's partner is working between 16 and 24 hours a week the couple will have to consider whether they will gain more by claiming working tax credit; see further Vol.IV of this series.

A further substantial contraction in the number of people covered by income support occurred on October 6, 2003 when the state pension credit scheme commenced. Claimants who have reached "the qualifying age for state pension credit" are not entitled to income support (see s.124(1)(aa) of the Contributions and Benefits Act 1992) and have to claim state pension credit. "The qualifying age for state pension credit" is defined in s.137(1) of the Contributions and Benefits Act 1992—the effect of that definition is that the qualifying age was 60 but from April 2010 it will gradually rise in line with the staged increase in pensionable age for women until it reaches 65 in November 2018 (this equalisation of the state pension age for men and women was

2.61

previously to have been completed by April 5, 2020 but the timetable for this in the Pensions Act 1995 has been accelerated with effect from April 2016 so that women's state pension age will now be 65 by November 2018; in addition, the increase in state pension age to 66 for both men and women has been brought forward—it will start to rise from 65 in December 2018 to reach 66 by October 2020 (see s.1 of the Pensions Act 2011) and between 2026 and 2028 it will rise to 67 (see s.26 of the Pensions Act 2014)). A claimant whose partner is entitled to (i.e. who has claimed and been awarded) state pension credit is also ineligible (s.124(1)(g) of the 1992 Act). Thus a couple with one member over the qualifying age for state pension credit and the other under that age (who are not already in receipt of state pension credit) can chose to claim either income support (or JSA, or from October 27, 2008, ESA, if eligible) or state pension credit. It will normally be advantageous to claim state pension credit. For an overview of the state pension credit scheme see the Introduction and General Note at the beginning of the State Pension Credit Act 2002.

Note also that with effect from April 6, 2004 when the process of transferring all financial support for children and young persons from income support to child tax credit began, income support has in effect become an "adults only benefit" for many claimants. The transfer of "the child elements" to child tax credit for existing claimants was intended to start in October 2004 but has been repeatedly delayed and it now seems that the transfer process will not take place at all and the situation will be resolved by the abolition of income support and child tax credit and their replacement by universal credit. See further the note to reg.17.

Most recently, the year 2008 saw two substantial changes to the categories of people who can claim income support that will limit eligibility for this benefit still further. The first was the commencement on October 27, 2008 of the ESA scheme, which replaced incapacity benefit, severe disablement allowance and income support on the grounds of incapacity or disability for most (but not all) new claimants. Existing claimants who were receiving income support on the grounds of incapacity or disability continued to be entitled to this, although the process of "migrating" these claimants (and incapacity benefit and severe disablement claimants) to ESA began on a national basis (there had been a pilot in Aberdeen and Burnley from October 2010) on February 28, 2011. See the Employment and Support Allowance (Transitional Provisions, Housing Benefit and Council Tax Benefit) (Existing Awards) (No.2) Regulations 2010 (SI 2010/1907) (as amended) ("the Migration Regulations") in Vol.I of this series, which establish the framework within which most "existing awards" will either be converted to awards of ESA or terminated, and the notes to those Regulations. "Existing award" is defined in para.11 of Sch.4 to the Welfare Reform Act 2007 and covers awards of incapacity benefit, severe disablement allowance and income support under regs 6(4)(a) or 13(2) (b) or (bb), or paras 7(a) or (b), 10, 12 or 13 of Sch.1B. Note that reg.6(4)(a) (disabled workers) was revoked on January 25, 2010 (although there is some transitional protection: see the note to reg.6(4)(a)). In addition, reg.6(4)(a) was not included in the definition of "income support on the grounds of disability" in reg.1(4) of the Employment and Support Allowance (Transitional Provisions) Regulations 2008 (SI 2008/795) (as amended) (see Vol.I of this series for these Regulations). The result is that *claims* (see the notes to the Income Support (Prescribed Categories of Person) Regulations 2009 (SI 2009/3152) in the 2015/16 edition of this volume) under reg.6(4)(a) made in respect of a period on or after October 27, 2008 did not fall within the linking provisions in reg.2(2) of the Transitional Provisions Regulations because they were not claims for income support "on the grounds of disability" and so were treated as claims for ESA. However, a claimant who still has a transitionally protected award of income support under reg.6(4)(a) will be subject to the conversion process. For further details of claimants who (until converted) are still eligible for income support under reg.13(2)(b) or (bb), or paras 7(a) or (b), 10, 12 or 13 of Sch.1B, see the note to the respective provision in the 2015/16 edition of this volume.

2.62   It was intended that the conversion process to ESA would be completed by the end of March 2014 but it is not clear whether this was achieved.

The second significant development was that with effect from November 24,

2008 lone parents with an only or youngest child aged 12 or over were no longer entitled to income support solely on the grounds of being a lone parent (this change was introduced in stages for existing claimants). This was extended to exclude lone parents whose only or youngest child was aged 10 or over from October 26, 2009 and those whose only or youngest child was aged seven or over from October 25, 2010. From May 21, 2012 entitlement to income support solely on the grounds of being a lone parent has been limited to those lone parents whose sole or youngest child is aged under five (although note that since that date any lone parent who is under 18 will be eligible for income support (regardless of the age of her child)). See further the note to para.1 of Sch.1B.

In view of the sustained and continuing reduction in the coverage of the income support scheme, s.9 of the Welfare Reform Act 2009, which made provision for the abolition of income support when "the Secretary of State considers that it is no longer appropriate" for there to be any prescribed categories of people who qualify for income support, came as no great surprise. Section 9 has not been brought into force and has been overtaken by the provisions in the Welfare Reform Act 2012 to introduce a new benefit for working-age claimants—universal credit—which will replace income support, income-based JSA, income-related ESA, housing benefit, working tax credit and child tax credit. It was originally intended that this would be introduced on a national basis from October 2013. However, in the event it was not until April 2016 that new claims were extended to the whole of the country and then only for a restricted category of claimant. See further the note to reg.1 of the JSA Regulations 2013 in Pt VI of this book.

Paragraphs (2) and (3)

The effect of paras (2) and (3) is to exclude most full-time students (defined in reg.61(1)) from entitlement to income support from the beginning of their course to the end (see the definition of period of study in reg.2(1)).

A full-time student will only be entitled during his/her period of study if s/he is a lone parent whose youngest child is under five, or if s/he is under 18 (regardless of the age of her/his child), a single foster parent, a person who is in non-advanced education and entitled under para.15A of Sch.1B, or a refugee learning English (para.(3)(b); note that para.11 of Sch.1B, also listed in para.(3)(b), is no longer relevant as it applied to disabled full-time students who did not fall under para.7 of the former Sch.1 following its amendment on September 1, 1990).

Until December 30, 2009 para.(3)(b) also included students to whom paras 10 or 12 of Sch.1B applied, although as a consequence of the introduction of ESA, *new* claims for income support on these grounds were no longer possible from October 27, 2008, except in certain circumstances. Paragraph 10 covered students who qualified for the disability or severe disability premium, or had been incapable of work, or treated as incapable of work, or treated as capable of work by virtue of reg.18 of the Incapacity for Work Regulations (disqualification for misconduct, etc.), or entitled to statutory sick pay, for at least 28 weeks (two or more periods separated by not more than eight weeks counted as continuous). Paragraph 12 covered students who were receiving a disabled student's allowance on the grounds of deafness. Both paragraphs were revoked on December 30, 2009, subject to a saving provision. See pp.256–257 of the 2015/16 edition of this volume under "Consequences of the introduction of ESA", "Revocation of paragraphs 10 and 12 on December 30, 2009" and "Migration to ESA" for further details.

Under the new form of para.(3)(c) (introduced on July 9, 2008 as a consequence of the decision in *CJSA/2663/2006* (see the note to reg.15 of the JSA Regulations 1996) in order to remove the discrimination previously contained in para.(3)(c)), a student who is a single person with responsibility for a child or young person is eligible for income support during the summer vacation on the same basis as a student couple with responsibility for a child or young person. The student (or the claimant for the student couple) must come within one of the categories of people who can claim income support. Similar amendments have been made to reg.15 of the JSA Regulations 1996.

2.63

2.64

Sub-paragraph (d), which provided for a further category of exempt student to cover a person who was taking part in the "Adult Learning Option" scheme (part of the "New Deal for Skills"), was revoked on October 26, 2009 because that scheme ceased in 2008.

Similarly, sub-para.(a), which covered a full-time student who had limited leave to enter or remain in the UK without recourse to public funds but who was temporarily without funds because remittances from abroad had been interrupted, was revoked on October 29, 2013. This is because entitlement to income support in those circumstances (under reg.2(1) of and para.1 of Pt I of the Schedule to the Social Security (Immigration and Asylum) Consequentional Amendments Regulations 2000 (SI 2000/636)) was abolished with effect from October 29, 2013.

Paragraph (3A)

2.65   Section 6 of the Children (Leaving Care) Act 2000 (p.150) excludes certain 16- and 17-year-olds who have been looked after by a local authority in England or Wales on or after October 1, 2001, or by a local authority in Scotland on or after April 1, 2004, from entitlement to income support, income-based JSA and housing benefit. Regulation 2 of the Children (Leaving Care) Social Security Benefits Regulations 2001 (SI 2001/3074) and reg.2 of the Children (Leaving Care) Social Security Benefits (Scotland) Regulations 2004 (SI 2004/747) provide for exceptions to the exclusion from income support and income-based JSA (but not housing benefit). For a discussion of s.6, the relevant definitions and the exceptions, see the notes to reg.2 of the Children (Leaving Care) Social Security Benefits Regulations 2001 (p.956) and to reg.2 of the Children (Leaving Care) Social Security Benefits (Scotland) Regulations 2004 (p.770).

Note that s.6(1) of the 2000 Act has not been amended following the introduction of ESA on October 27, 2008 as to exclude entitlement to income-related ESA. This would appear to be an oversight as a purported amendment to reg.2(1) of the Children (Leaving Care) Social Security Benefits Regulations 2001 (SI 2001/3074) has been made to include a reference to income-related ESA. However, in view of the fact that s.6 has not been amended to exclude entitlement to ESA, such an amendment to the 2001 Regulations is not necessary (and is ultra vires).

Note also that reg.2 of the 2001 Regulations has not been amended to take account of the changes in Wales to s.6 made by the Social Services and Well-being (Wales) Act 2014. Thus, as things stand at the moment, the exceptions to the s.6 exclusion do not apply in Wales with effect from April 6, 2014.

Paragraph (4)

2.66   This confirms that if a person satisfies any of the paragraphs in Sch.1B on any day in a benefit week, he is treated as doing so for the whole of that week.

Temporary absence from Great Britain

2.67   **4.**—(1) Where a claimant is entitled to income support for a period immediately preceding a period of temporary absence from Great Britain, his entitlement to income support [² shall continue only—

    (a) in the circumstances specified in paragraph (2), during the first 4 weeks of that period of temporary absence; and

    (b) in the circumstances specified in paragraph (3), during the first 8 weeks of that period.]

(2) The circumstances in which a claimant's entitlement to income support is to continue during the first four weeks of a temporary absence from Great Britain are that—

    (a) the period of absence is unlikely to exceed 52 weeks; and

    (b) while absent from Great Britain, the claimant continues to satisfy the other conditions of entitlement to income support; and

(c) any one of the following conditions apply—
   (i) the claimant falls within one or more of the prescribed categories of person listed in Schedule 1B other than paragraphs 7, 15, 20, 21, 24, 25, 26 or 27 of that Schedule; or
   (ii) the claimant falls within paragraph 7 of Schedule 1B (persons incapable of work) and his absence from Great Britain is for the sole purpose of receiving treatment from an appropriately qualified person for the incapacity by reason of which he satisfies the conditions of that paragraph; or]
   (iii) he is in Northern Ireland; or
   (iv) he is a member of a couple and he and his partner are both absent from Great Britain, and a premium referred to in paragraphs 9, [⁵9A,] 10, 11 or 13 of Schedule 2 (applicable amounts) is applicable in respect of his partner; [¹ or
   [³(v) on the day on which the absence began he had satisfied the provisions of [⁴paragraph 7 of Schedule 1B] (persons incapable of work) for a continuous period of not less than—
      (aa) 196 days in the case of a claimant who is terminally ill within the meaning of section 30B(4) of the Contributions and Benefits Act, or who is entitled to the highest rate of the care component of disability living allowance[⁹ , armed forces independence payment] [⁸ or the enhanced rate of the daily living component of personal independence payment]; or
      (bb) 364 days in any other case,
and for this purpose any two or more separate periods separated by a break of not more than 56 days shall be treated as one continuous period.]]
[²(3) The circumstances in which a claimant's entitlement to income support is to continue during the first 8 weeks of a temporary absence from Great Britain are that—
   (a) the period of absence is unlikely to exceed 52 weeks; and
   (b) the claimant continues to satisfy the other conditions of entitlement to income support; and
   (c) the claimant is, or the claimant and any other member of his family are, accompanying a member of the claimant's family who is a child or young person solely in connection with arrangements made for the treatment of that child or young person for a disease or bodily or mental disablement; and
   (d) those arrangements relate to treatment—
      (i) outside Great Britain;
      (ii) during the period whilst the claimant is, or the claimant and any member of his family are, temporarily absent from Great Britain; and
      (iii) by, or under the supervision of, a person appropriately qualified to carry out that treatment.
[⁶(3A) A claimant's entitlement to income support shall continue during a period of temporary absence from Great Britain if—
   (a) he satisfied the conditions of entitlement to income support immediately before the beginning of that period of temporary absence; and
   [⁷(b) that period of temporary absence is for the purpose of the claimant receiving treatment at a hospital or other institution outside Great Britain where the treatment is being provided—

(i) under section 6(2) of the Health Service Act (performance of functions outside England) or section 6(2) of the Health Service (Wales) Act (performance of functions outside Wales);

(ii) pursuant to arrangements made under section 12(1) of the Health Service Act (Secretary of State's arrangements with other bodies), section 10(1) of the Health Service (Wales) Act (Welsh Minister's arrangements with other bodies), paragraph 18 of Schedule 4 to the Health Service Act (joint exercise of functions) or paragraph 18 of Schedule 3 to the Health Service (Wales) Act (joint exercise of functions); or

(iii) under any equivalent provision in Scotland or pursuant to arrangements made under such provision.]]

(4) In paragraphs (2) and (3) "appropriately qualified" means qualified to provide medical treatment, physiotherapy or a form of treatment which is similar to, or related to, either of those forms of treatment.]

AMENDMENTS

1. Income Support (General) Amendment Regulations 1988 (SI 1988/663) reg.3 (April 11, 1988).

2. Income Support (General) Amendment Regulations 1990 (SI 1990/547) reg.3 (April 9, 1990).

3. Disability Working Allowance and Income Support (General) Amendment Regulations 1995 (SI 1995/482) reg.5 (April 13, 1995).

4. Income Support (General) (Jobseeker's Allowance Consequential Amendments) Regulations 1996 (SI 1996/206) reg.5 (October 7, 1996).

5. Income-related Benefits Schemes and Social Fund (Miscellaneous Amendments) Regulations 1996 (SI 1996/1944) reg.6(3) (October 7, 1996).

6. Social Security (Income Support and Jobseeker's Allowance) Amendment Regulations 2004 (SI 2004/1869) reg.2 (October 4, 2004).

7. Social Security (Miscellaneous Amendments) (No.6) Regulations 2008 (SI 2008/2767) reg.2(1) and (3) (November 17, 2008).

8. Personal Independence Payment (Supplementary Provisions and Consequential Amendments) Regulations 2013 (SI 2013/388) reg.8 and Sch. para.11(1) and (3) (April 8, 2013).

9. Armed Forces and Reserve Forces Compensation Scheme (Consequential Provisions: Subordinate Legislation) Order 2013 (SI 2013/591) art.7 and Sch. para.4(1) and (3) (April 8, 2013).

DEFINITIONS

"claimant"—see reg.2(1).
"couple"—*ibid.*
"disability living allowance"—*ibid.*
"partner"—*ibid.*

GENERAL NOTE

2.68   This provision takes over from reg.3 of the old Conditions of Entitlement Regulations a limited right to benefit during the claimant's absence from Great Britain (normally excluded by s.124(1) of the Contributions and Benefits Act; 1986 Act, s.20(3)); see *Perry v Chief Adjudication Officer, The Times*, October 20, 1998, also reported as *R(IS) 4/99*, in the note to s.124(1)). Great Britain means England, Scotland and Wales. If it is the claimant's partner who is temporarily absent, see Sch.7 para.11.

Paragraph (1)

The absence must be temporary, on the meaning of which see *Chief Adjudication Officer v Ahmed, The Times*, April 6, 1994 (Court of Appeal). In *R. v Social Security Commissioner Ex p. Akbar, The Times*, November 6, 1991, Hodgson J had decided that temporary meant "not permanent". The Court of Appeal in *Ahmed* says that this is wrong, although the decision in *Akbar* itself was correct. However, the Court does agree with Hodgson J that an absence can be temporary, even though the intended date for return remains uncertain. Thus *R(S) 1/85* should not be followed on this point. The Court of Appeal holds that the decision as to whether a person is temporarily absent is one of fact for the adjudicating authority concerned. Relevant factors include the claimant's intention (although this is not decisive) and the length of the absence. If a person initially has the intention of not returning or an intention to stay for some fixed period which goes beyond the temporary (e.g. a matter of years), the absence is not temporary from the outset. In practice, the 52-week period referred to in paras (2)(a) and (3)(a) is likely to be the most important test.

The claimant must have been entitled to income support immediately before the temporary absence. Since the reference is to entitlement, it does not seem that income support must actually have been received. But a claim must have been made for that period before entitlement can arise (Administration Act s.1).

If the conditions set out in para.(2) are met, entitlement at the rate which would have been payable if the claimant had remained in Great Britain, can continue for the first four weeks of the temporary absence. If the conditions of para.(3) are met, entitlement can continue for the first eight weeks of absence. When calculating periods of absence from Great Britain the day of leaving and the day of return are both days on which the person is in Great Britain (see para.070642 of the *Decision Makers Guide* and *R(S) 1/66*).

If the claimant does not satisfy the conditions for continuing entitlement or the four or eight weeks are exhausted, any partner remaining in Great Britain may claim. If the absence is temporary, the couple ought on principle to remain members of the same household (although the effect of reg.16(3)(d) is obscure).

2.69

Paragraph (2)

Sub-paragraphs (a) and (b) are self-explanatory. It is important that all the other conditions of entitlement must continue to be satisfied. The five conditions in sub-para.(c) are alternatives.

Head (i) covers claimants eligible for income support, apart from by reason of incapacity for work (but see (ii) and (v)), secondary education, trade disputes or being a person from abroad.

Some of the conditions which lead to eligibility for income support will obviously continue during absence abroad (e.g. pregnancy) but others may not (e.g. temporarily looking after children, if the children are left behind). Since the October 1993 change in the test of responsibility for a child, a lone parent who goes abroad temporarily without her children should continue to be eligible for income support under para.1 of Sch.1B. This is because reg.15(1) now makes receipt of child benefit the primary test of responsibility. Child benefit can continue to be paid while a claimant is temporarily absent from Great Britain for up to eight weeks. Only if no claim for child benefit has been made is the person with whom the child usually lives treated as responsible under reg.15(2)(a). The matter has to be tested week by week (*CIS 49/1991*). See the 1993 edition of J. Mesher and P. Wood, *Income-related Benefits: the Legislation* for the potential problems for lone parents absent abroad prior to October 4, 1993.

Head (ii) covers incapacity for work, but only subject to these conditions (as applied to incapacity benefit by reg.2(1) of the Social Security (Persons Abroad) Regulations 1975). See *R(S) 2/86* and *R(S) 1/90* for the conditions and head (v). Paragraph (4) defines when the person providing treatment is appropriately qualified.

2.70

2.71

Head (iii) is self explanatory.

Head (iv) refers to the pensioner and disability premiums, but only applies to couples who are both abroad. It requires the premium to be "applicable". It is clearly arguable that "applicable" means "ought to be applied", so that entitlement to the premium, even if it is not actually in payment, will do.

Head (v) allows those incapable of work for at least 52 weeks, or 28 weeks if they are terminally ill (i.e. expected to die from a progressive disease within six months) or entitled to the highest rate care component of disability living allowance, the enhanced rate of the daily living component of personal independence payment, or armed forces independence payment, to use the regulation free of the conditions of head (ii). Two or more periods of incapacity count as one continuous period unless there is a break of more than eight weeks. Before April 13, 1995 the minimum period was 28 weeks for all claimants, but it has been increased for most claimants in line with the changes following the introduction of incapacity benefit. For the details of incapacity benefit see Vol.I of this series. Note reg.8(1) of the Income-related Benefits Schemes and Social Security (Claims and Payments) (Miscellaneous Amendments) Regulations 1995 (p.1758), which provides that in deciding whether a claimant can satisfy head (v) on or after October 2, 1995, a period of incapacity immediately before April 13, 1995 can count towards the 52 (or 28) weeks, provided it is linked to, or part of, the current period. See also the transitional provision in reg.27(2) of the Income Support (General) (Jobseeker's Allowance Consequential Amendments) Regulations 1996 (p.1759) in relation to the October 1996 changes to income support that are a consequence of the introduction of JSA.

Paragraph (3)

2.72   The conditions in heads (a) and (b) are the same as in para.(2)(a) and (b). Then the effect of heads (c) and (d) is that where the claimant is accompanying a child or young person in their family abroad for that child or young person to receive treatment, entitlement can continue for eight weeks. The claimant's absence must be solely for that purpose. The treatment must be for a medical condition and be carried out by an appropriately qualified person within the meaning of para.(4). There seems to be no reason why a claimant accompanying a child should be more deserving than a claimant going abroad for treatment for himself.

Paragraph (3A)

2.73   From October 4, 2004 claimants who are temporarily absent from Great Britain in order to receive NHS treatment at a hospital (or similar institution) in another country, and who were entitled to IS immediately before their departure, continue to be so entitled during their absence.

Persons treated as engaged in remunerative work

2.74   **5.**—(1) Subject to the following provisions of this regulation, for the purposes of section 20(3)(c) of the Act [SSCBA, s.124(1)(*c*)] (conditions of entitlement to income support), remunerative work is work in which a person is engaged, or, where his hours of work fluctuate, he is engaged on average, for [⁶not less than 16 hours] a week being work for which payment is made or which is done in expectation of payment.

[⁹(1A) In the case of any partner of the claimant paragraph (1) shall have effect as though for the words "16 hours" there were substituted the words "24 hours".]

(2) [⁸Subject to paragraph (3B),] the number of hours for which a person is engaged in work shall be determined—

   (a) where no recognisable cycle has been established in respect of a person's work, by reference to the number of hours or, where those hours are likely to fluctuate, the average of the hours, which he is expected to work in a week;

(b) where the number of hours for which he is engaged fluctuate, by reference to the average of hours worked over—
  (i) if there is a recognisable cycle of work, the period of one complete cycle (including, where the cycle involves periods in which the person does no work, those periods but disregarding any other absences);
  (ii) in any other case, the period of five weeks immediately before the date of claim or the date [[11] on which a superseding decision is made under section 10 (decisions superseding earlier decisions) of the Social Security Act 1998] or such other length of time as may, in the particular case, enable the person's average hours of work to be determined more accurately.

(3) A person shall be treated as engaged in remunerative work during any period for which he is absent from work referred to in paragraph (1) if the absence is either without good cause or by reason of a recognised, customary or other holiday.

[[7](3A) A person shall not be treated as engaged in remunerative work on any day on which the person is on maternity leave [[14], paternity leave [[17], adoption leave [[18], shared parental leave or parental bereavement leave]]] or is absent from work because he is ill.]

[[8](3B) Where for the purpose of paragraph (2)(b)(i), a person's recognisable cycle of work at a school, other educational establishment or other place of employment is one year and includes periods of school holidays or similar vacations during which he does not work, those periods and any other periods not forming part of such holidays or vacations during which he is not required to work shall be disregarded in establishing the average hours for which he is engaged in work.]

(4) A person who makes a claim and to whom or whose partner section 23 of the Act [SSCBA, s.126] (trade disputes) applies [[1]or applied] shall, for the period of seven days following the date on which the stoppage of work due to a trade dispute at his or his partner's place of work commenced or, if there is no stoppage, the date on which he or his partner first withdrew his labour in furtherance of a trade dispute, be treated as engaged in remunerative work.

(5) [[15] Subject to paragraph (5A), a person], who was or was treated as being, engaged in remunerative work and in respect of that work earnings to which [[4] regulation [[16] 35(1)(b) and (d)]] (earnings of employed earners) applies are [[3]paid] shall be treated as engaged in remunerative work for the period for which those earnings are taken into account in accordance with Part V.

[[15] (5A) Paragraph (5) shall not apply to earnings disregarded under paragraph 1 of Schedule 8 to these regulations.]

[[2](6) For the purposes of this regulation, in determining the number of hours in which a person is engaged or treated as engaged in remunerative work, no account shall be taken of any hours in which the person is engaged in an employment or a scheme to which [[12]. . . regulation 6(1)] (persons not treated as engaged in remunerative work) applies.]

[[5](7) For the purposes of paragraphs (1) and (2), in determining the number of hours for which a person is engaged in work, that number shall include any time allowed to that person by his employer for a meal or for refreshment, but only where that person is, or expects to be, paid earnings in respect of that time.]

[[13](8)–(10) . . .]

AMENDMENTS

1. Income Support (General) Amendment Regulations 1988 (SI 1988/663) reg.4 (April 11, 1988).
2. Income Support (General) Amendment No.4 Regulations 1988 (SI 1988/1445) reg.3 (September 9, 1988).
3. Income Support (General) Amendment No.5 Regulations 1988 (SI 1988/2022) reg.3 (December 12, 1988).
4. Income Support (General) Amendment No.2 Regulations 1989 (SI 1989/1323) reg.3 (October 9, 1989).
5. Income Support (General) Amendment Regulations 1990 (SI 1990/547) reg.4 (April 9, 1990).
6. Income Support (General) Amendment No.4 Regulations 1991 (SI 1991/1559) reg.3 (April 7, 1992).
7. Income-related Benefits Schemes (Miscellaneous Amendments) (No.4) Regulations 1993 (SI 1993/2119) reg.3 (October 4, 1993).
8. Income-related Benefits Schemes (Miscellaneous Amendments) Regulations 1995 (SI 1995/516) reg.19 (April 10, 1995).
9. Income-related Benefits Schemes and Social Fund (Miscellaneous Amendments) Regulations 1996 (SI 1996/1944) reg.6(4) (October 7, 1996).
10. Social Security (Miscellaneous Amendments) (No.2) Regulations 1999 (SI 1999/2556) reg.2(2) (October 4, 1999).
11. Social Security Act 1998 (Commencement No.12, and Consequential and Transitional Provisions) Order 1999 (SI 1999/3178) art.3(5) and Sch.5 para.1 (November 29, 1999)
12. Social Security (Miscellaneous Amendments) Regulations 2000 (SI 2000/681) reg.2(a) (April 3, 2000).
13. Social Security (Miscellaneous Amendments) Regulations 2001 (SI 2001/488) reg.3 (April 9, 2001).
14. Social Security (Paternity and Adoption) Amendment Regulations 2002 (SI 2002/2689) reg.2 (December 8, 2002).
15. Social Security (Miscellaneous Amendments) (No. 5) Regulations 2007 (SI 2007/2618) reg.5(5) (October 1, 2007).
16. Social Security (Miscellaneous Amendments) Regulations 2008 (SI 2008/698) reg.2(3) (April 14, 2008).
17. Shared Parental Leave and Statutory Shared Parental Pay (Consequential Amendments to Subordinate Legislation) Order 2014 (SI 2014/3255) art.5(1) and (3) (December 31, 2014).
18. Parental Bereavement Leave and Pay (Consequential Amendments to Subordinate Legislation) Regulations 2020 (SI 2020/354) reg.5(1) and (3) (April 6, 2020).

DEFINITIONS

"the Act"—see reg.2(1).
"adoption leave"—*ibid.*
"date of claim"—*ibid.*
"maternity leave"—*ibid.*
"partner"—*ibid.*
"paternity leave"—*ibid.*

GENERAL NOTE

2.75   Under s.124(1)(c) of the SSCBA 1992, and ss.1(2)(e) and 3(1)(e) of the Jobseekers Act 1995, it is a condition of entitlement to income support and income-based JSA that neither the claimant nor her/his partner is in remunerative work. It is also a condition of entitlement to contribution-based JSA that the claimant should not be in remunerative work. Remunerative work is also relevant to the amount of any non-dependant deduction from the claimant's housing costs (see para.18 of Sch.3) and (in transitional cases, see the note to reg.17) to whether the earnings of certain children and young persons are disregarded under para.15 of Sch.8.

The rules governing remunerative work are set out, for income support purposes, in this regulation and reg.6, and, for income-based JSA purposes, in regs 51–53 of the JSA Regulations, which are in similar—though not identical—terms. Since the introduction of JSA on October 7, 1996, the principal rule has been that a claimant (and, where relevant, a non-dependant or a child or young person) is in remunerative work if s/he works for not less than 16 hours a week and the claimant's partner is in remunerative work if s/he works for not less than 24 hours a week (except in those cases where the couple is obliged to make a joint claim for JSA, in which case the 16-hour rule applies to both members because both are claimants). Where the hours of work fluctuate, an average is taken using the rules in para.(2).

In cases (other than joint-claim JSA cases) where the claimant's partner is working between 16 and 24 hours a week, it may be possible for the couple to claim both working tax credit (see Vol.IV) and income support or income-based JSA. In such cases, there is an automatic entitlement to maximum WTC but the claimant's IS or income-based JSA will be reduced pound for pound by the WTC that is paid.

Because income support is normally paid in arrears, the disentitlement applies immediately a person starts remunerative work, regardless of whether wages have been paid or when they will be paid. This situation is specifically mentioned in the Social Fund Guide as one in which a crisis loan might be payable if no other resources are available. The details of the test are therefore important. Note the exceptions in reg.6, brought in by para.(6).

Paragraph (1)

First note that the test is in terms of work, not employment. Therefore, the   2.76
precise categorisation of the activities carried out may not be crucial. This is illustrated in two family credit decisions (remunerative work was a qualification for family credit). In *CFC 7/1989* the claimant's husband was working in connection with Moral Re-Armament, a Christian charity, for about 38 hours a week. He received payment by persuading individuals to covenant income to him. He was not employed by Moral Re-Armament or the covenantors, nor did he contract with them on a self-employed basis. But this did not matter, because what he did was undoubtedly work and he was paid for it. In *R(FC) 2/90* both the claimant and her husband were officers of the Salvation Army. It was accepted, following the decision of the Court of Appeal in *Rogers v Booth* [1937] 2 All E.R. 751, that the relationship of officers to the Salvation Army is spiritual, not contractual. Nevertheless, the onerous duties of officers were "work."

Remunerative

Work is remunerative if payment is made for it, or it is done in the expectation of   2.77
payment. There is a significant difference from the common law test (on which see *R(FIS) 1/83*), because the mere hope of or desire for payment is not the same as expectation (although note that in *R(IS) 13/99* the Commissioner comments that he did not see any fundamental distinction between "hope of" and "expectation of" payment). Thus in *CFC 3/1989*, the claimant's husband, who regarded himself as a self-employed writer, but who had not sold any manuscripts and did not anticipate any sales in the next six months, was not in remunerative work. The Commissioner puts forward a rule of thumb, not a binding principle, that for work to be done in the expectation of payment some payment must be expected within 26 weeks of the relevant date. This was based partly on the length of a family credit award, but there clearly should be one dividing line between the income support and family credit systems. In *R(IS) 1/93* the Commissioner holds that the guiding principle on when there is an expectation of payment should be common sense and an appreciation of the realities of the situation. The claimant, another writer, had sent several works to publishers, but had had negligible success in selling anything. She was working

"on spec", with only the hope of payment, not an expectation. In *Kevin Smith v Chief Adjudication Officer (R(IS) 21/95)* the claimant's partner, who was in receipt of an enterprise allowance, wished to establish herself as an agent for pop groups and spent a lot of time building up contacts in the pop music world. The Court of Appeal, having said that the question is really one of fact, distinguishes between work done to set up a business, which is not done in expectation of payment, and work carried out once the business is established, which it would be reasonable to infer was done in expectation of payment. On the facts of that case the claimant's partner was not engaged in remunerative work. On the other side of the line, see *CIS 434/1994* in which a person who had started an estate agent's business and was working without pay until the business became profitable was held to be in remunerative work. In *CIS 929/1995* the two or three hours a freelance musician spent practising each day did not count as hours of work for the purposes of reg.5(1).

In *R(IS) 22/95* the claimant's wife worked in a general shop owned by the two of them. For several months she had worked without pay and had no expectation of receiving any in the future because the business was making a loss. The Commissioner holds that the SSAT had been correct in concluding that on the facts she was not in remunerative work. This decision was upheld by the Court of Appeal in *Chief Adjudication Officer v Ellis* (reported as part of *R(IS) 22/95*). In *Ellis* the Court gives some general guidance on the questions to be considered when deciding whether a person is in remunerative work. In particular, the Court draws a distinction between a person providing a service (such as the claimant carrying on a translation agency in *Perrot v SBC* [1980] 3 All E.R. 110 where the unprofitability of her business was irrelevant) and the position of a retail shop. The Court points out that the price paid for goods sold in a shop is not payment for the work of the salesman, but the price of the goods sold. Thus simply carrying on a retail business did not necessarily mean that a person was in remunerative work (so *CSIS 39/1994* should not be followed on this point). But if the person was not expecting to make any money the question had to be asked why the shop was being kept open. In this case the answer was clear. The claimant's wife was carrying on the business in the hope of disposing of the goodwill. She was not in remunerative work.

In *R(IS) 5/95* the claimant who was both a director and an employee of a small limited company had also worked for some months without pay, due to financial difficulties. The Commissioner states that it was necessary to consider in relation to each week whether he was working in his capacity as an employee or a director (although the functions of a director of a small private company were quite slight (*R(U) 1/93*, para.5)). If this work had been done as an employee it was only remunerative if any payment expected was in that capacity (although reg.42(6) (notional earnings) would also need to be considered). Moreover expectation of payment meant payment for current work. It may be that this is not the case for the self-employed, although the Court of Appeal in *Ellis* states that the question of whether work is done in expectation of payment is to be decided at the time the work is done, not at the end of the year or other accounting period.

2.78 If a claimant deliberately arranges to work for no remuneration (and therefore has no expectation of payment) then, unsurprisingly, that work does not qualify as remunerative work. In *CTC 626/2001* a husband went into partnership with his wife. He worked 30 hours a week in the partnership business and she worked six. However, in order to save income tax the partners agreed that 100 per cent of the profits was allocated to the wife leaving the husband with no income from the business. The Commissioner upheld the decision of the tribunal that there was no entitlement to WFTC: the wife was in remunerative work but for less than 16 hours a week and the husband, though he worked far more than 16 hours a week, was not in remunerative work at all. As *CTC 626/2001* related to a tax credit the conclusion that the husband was not in remunerative work was to his disadvantage. However, one logical consequence of the decision is the possibility that a similar arrangement could be used by a self-employed claimant who was in fact working for more than 16 hours a week to retain entitlement to IS or income-based JSA. It is suggested that such an arrangement would not in fact be effective because, following the remarks of Millet LJ in *Ellis*, it would be appropriate in such circumstances "to treat the partnership as a single economic unit just as if it were carried on by a sole trader".

The payment must be in return for the work (*R(FIS) 1/86*), but need not derive from an employer. Thus the payments by covenantors in *CFC 7/1989* (see above) counted. So too did the payments from the Salvation Army in *R(FC) 2/90*, although they were not paid under contract and were aimed at providing for the officers' actual needs. There was a distinction from the maintenance grant paid to a student. Provision for actual needs went beyond mere maintenance. A grant is not in return for work (*R(FIS) 1/86*), so that students and trainees (*R(FIS) 1/83*) will still not be said to be in remunerative work. The argument that enterprise allowance is paid in return for work was rejected by the Court of Appeal in *Kevin Smith v Chief Adjudication Officer* (above). The Court holds that it is a payment to enable people to establish themselves in business, not for work. This conclusion was indicated both by the terms of the enterprise allowance scheme and reg.37(1). If receipt of enterprise allowance by itself meant that a person had to be treated as engaged in remunerative work, the inclusion in reg.37(1) of enterprise allowance as earnings was unnecessary since the calculation stage envisaged by reg.37 would never be reached.

A payment in kind will count in the same way as a payment in cash. In *CFC 33/1993* the provision of rent-free accommodation and the payment of gas and electricity bills meant that the claimant's work was done for payment.

Engaged in work

It is hours during which the person is engaged in work and is paid (or at least expects payment) which are crucial. The calculation is usually relatively easy for employees. Thus in *CIS 3/1989* the claimant's paid one hour lunch break did not count towards the limit. He was not "engaged in" work for that hour. The precise result is reversed from April 1990, by para.(7), but the principle might apply in other situations. *R(FC) 1/92* suggests that where the nature of the job requires a person to work beyond the contractually specified hours, the longer hours count. However, it is not clear just how this translates from the old family credit provision to income support. For the self-employed the test is not of hours costed and charged to a client, but of hours of activities which are essential to the undertaking (*R(FIS) 6/85*). Thus time spent in preparation, research, doing estimates and accounts, travel for the purposes of the undertaking, keeping a shop open, etc. must all count. But activities carried on merely in the hope, rather than expectation, of payment are not remunerative. The actual hours of work must be considered. In *R(IS) 22/95*, although the shop in which the claimant's wife worked was open from 08:30–18:30 Monday to Friday, she only spent three hours a day in it. The rest of the time she was in her home (which was in the same premises), ready to go into the shop if the shop bell rang. The Commissioner expresses the view (without finally deciding the point) that on the particular facts of that case (a small shop with little stock and fewer customers) the hours "on call" may not be hours of work. The decision in *R(IS) 22/95* was upheld by the Court of Appeal in *Chief Adjudication Officer v Ellis* (see above), but the Court of Appeal does not deal with this particular point. But in *R(IS) 13/99* the same Commissioner decides that the time spent by a self-employed minicab driver waiting at the cab office for potential customers (which he was not obliged to do) was work done in expectation of payment. This seems somewhat dubious, in that it was not essential to his work for him to spend that time there. However, the decision was upheld by the Court of Appeal (*Kazantzis v Chief Adjudication Officer*, reported as part of *R(IS) 13/99*). In *R(IS) 12/95* all the hours that a share fisherman was at sea (including those that he was not on watch or was sleeping) counted. The Commissioner referred to *Suffolk CC v Secretary of State for the Environment* [1984] I.C.R. 882 in which the House of Lords had distinguished between a regular fireman required to remain in the station while on duty and a retained fireman free to do as he pleases until called upon. The claimant could not do as he pleased during his rest period. He had to stay on the trawler

2.79

and could be summoned to assist if, for example, there was a storm. In the *Suffolk* case the House of Lords held that a retained fireman's waiting time could not be taken into account in calculating his contractual hours of employment. The claimant in *R(IS) 13/99* had attempted to rely on this decision but the Commissioner points out that the circumstances were not analogous. The issue under para.(1) was not whether the claimant was employed during his waiting time but whether he was "at work" during that time.

CIS 514/1990 holds that although recipients of enterprise allowance must undertake to work for at least 36 hours a week in their business, that does not mean that they must automatically be treated as doing so for benefit purposes (see *Kevin Smith v Chief Adjudication Officer (R(IS) 21/95)*) above on whether enterprise allowance is paid in return for work).

Paragraphs (2)–(3A)

2.80   Where a person works a fixed number of hours, week in, week out, there is no difficulty in applying the weekly limits in para.(1) to his or her claim. Although, what if a person does not work the same hours each week? What, indeed, if there are some weeks in which s/he does no work at all? This is the problem addressed by paras (2)–(3A) and also, for those who work in schools or other places of education and who wish to claim income support (but not JSA) during school holidays, by para. (3B) (see the note on "Term-time only workers" below).

Although these provisions (and those that preceded them) have been the subject of a considerable number of Commissioners' decisions, consideration of paras (2) to (3A) must now begin with the decision of the Tribunal of Commissioners in *R(JSA) 5/03*, dealing with the equivalent provisions of regs 51 and 52 of the JSA Regulations. The appeals before the Tribunal of Commissioners concerned people who were employees and the principles laid down in its decision must be seen in that context. Other considerations may be relevant in cases where the claimant is "self-employed" (see below).

The Tribunal's starting point was that:

"11. Defining 'remunerative work' as being work in which someone is engaged for not less than 16 hours a week (24 hours in the case of a claimant's partner) is simple enough. But how do you arrive at the appropriate number of hours when the working hours fluctuate? And how do you deal with those periods during most people's working year, when for some reason or other they are absent from work (and, therefore, not engaged in work at all)?

12. The first step in any analysis is to recognise that periods when a person does no work fall into various categories. Consideration of regulations 51(2) and 52(1) suggests that the relevant categories are:

 (a) periods during which someone is without work because he or she is between jobs,
 (b) periods of no work (other than holidays) during which someone is without work because work is not provided by his or her employer,
 (c) periods during which someone can properly be regarded as being on holiday,
 (d) periods of absence due to sickness and maternity leave.
 (e) periods of unauthorised absence 'without good cause'.

In these appeals, we are not concerned with periods of absence due to sickness or maternity leave, but it is apparent from the terms of regulation 52(1) that a person who is otherwise in remunerative work ceases temporarily to be so engaged during such absences. We are also not concerned with periods of absence without good cause, but it is equally apparent that such absences are to be treated in the same way as holidays."

2.81   The Tribunal's approach to those issues was to look first at whether the person's employment had ended. In doing so, "regard should be had to reality" (at para.25) and not just to the formal legal position:

"22. In our view, the approach taken by decision-makers should be as follows. Where a contract of employment comes to an end at the beginning of what would be a period of absence from work even if the contract continued, the person should be taken still to be in employment if is expected that he or she will resume employment after that period, either because there is some express arrangement, though not necessarily an enforceable contract, or because it is reasonable to assume that a long standing practice of re-employment will continue."

If it is determined that the person is no longer in employment then no question of remunerative work arises. If, on the other hand, the employment relationship is—as a matter of reality—still subsisting, it becomes necessary to decide whether the person is absent from work due to a holiday or for some other reason. This issue is to be decided on the basis that a person is on holiday during those periods of absence for which they are entitled to be paid—either by contract or, from October 1, 1998, under the Working Time Regulations 1998.

The Tribunal continues:

"28. Applying regulation 51(2) [i.e. of the JSA Regulations—equivalent to reg.5(2) of the IS Regulations] is relatively straightforward once it has been established that a person is still engaged in employment and his or her entitlement to holidays has been ascertained. If he works the same number of hours each week when not on holiday, that is the number of hours to be taken into account for the purpose of regulation 51(1). If the number of hours fluctuates, an average is taken. How the average is calculated when there is no cycle of work is determined under regulation 51(2)(b)(ii) [or reg.5(2)(b)(ii)] which allows some discretion as to the period over which the average is to be calculated. Regulation 51(2)(b)(i) [or reg.5(2)(b)(i)] makes more specific provision in a case where there is a recognisable cycle of work."

Specifically, when there is a recognisable cycle of work of one year the requirement in reg.51(2)(b)(i) [or 5(2)(b)(i)] to calculate the average taking into account "periods in which the person does no work . . . but disregarding other absences" means: 2.82

"dividing the total number of hours worked . . . by 52 less the number of weeks of holiday to which the particular claimant is entitled. The result determines whether the person concerned is in remunerative work or not for the whole period of the cycle (*R(IS) 8/95*) so that it is not necessary where there is a cycle to attribute the holiday entitlement to any particular weeks."

The same approach should presumably be adopted to established cycles of work of less than 52 weeks but which include periods in which the person does no work.

On that basis, unpaid "holidays" are "periods in which the person does no work" for the purposes of reg.51(2)(b)(i) [reg.5(2)(b)(i)] and paid holidays and periods of absence through sickness, etc. are "other absences". In cases which pre-date the Working Time Regulations 1998—or to which those Regulations do not apply, see for example *CJSA/4764/2002*—in which the employee has no holiday entitlement, neither the fact that payment of their salary may be spread over the year in equal monthly instalments nor the fact that the rate at which they are paid has been enhanced to reflect the absence of any formal holiday entitlement alters the position that there is no holiday entitlement (although the latter circumstance is relevant to the issue of the claimant's earnings (see para.42)).

In consequence, the Tribunal of Commissioners held that the reasoning in (though not the result of) *R(IS) 15/94* was incorrect and that *R(IS) 7/96* which had followed that reasoning was wrongly decided and should no longer be followed.   2.83

For an instructive example of the workings of a complex remunerative work calculation, see *NS v SSWP (IS)* [2015] UKUT 423 (AAC).

Seasonal workers (other than term-time only workers)

2.84   The position of seasonal workers (other than term-time only workers claiming income support—see below) was considered by the Commissioner in *R(JSA) 1/07* and in *CJSA/3832/2006*.

In the former case, the claimants had, for several years, been able to obtain casual work during the summer season in holiday resorts on the Lincolnshire coast but had been unable to find work during the winter months. The Secretary of State refused their claims for JSA on the basis that they had to be treated as having a cycle of work extending over the whole calendar year. The tribunal rejected that argument and found that they were not in a cycle of work at all during periods when they were not in employment. Confirming that decision, the Commissioner held that whether there was an "expectation" that the claimant would resume his or her employment (i.e. under the test in *R(JSA) 5/03*—see above) was a matter of fact for the tribunal and that "there would need to be some element of mutuality in the arrangement or understanding between employer and employee" before such an "expectation" could be found to exist. The Secretary of State's construction was

> "an attempt to start with the calculation provisions by assuming that the whole year is to be included, and then work backwards to distort the meaning of regulation 51(1) [i.e. of the JSA Regulations and, by implication, also of reg.5(1)] as if it contained a deeming provision making people count as in work when in fact they are not".

2.85   The recurrence of an inability to get work at all during the winter months did not turn the whole calendar year into one continuous period of the claimant being "engaged in work" for the purposes of reg.51 so as to be able to call the whole year a recognisable cycle of work. Regulation 51(2) was concerned with the calculation of a numerical average of hours *at* work over a period while a person continues to be *in* work.

In *CJSA/3832/2006*, the claimant worked as a cleaner during university terms only. At the end of each term his contract of employment was terminated and he and his colleagues were told that if they were interested in re-employment from the beginning of the following term they should contact the facilities manager during the preceding week. The Commissioner stated:

> "As was recently stressed in *CJSA/1390/2006* [now *R(JSA) 1/07*], the real question is whether the person claiming benefit can properly be regarded as being 'in' work at the material time. There must be some sort of continuing relationship between the employer and employee, even if it is not technically a subsisting employment relationship. Unless the circumstances show some commitment to a resumption of the employment relationship by a former worker upon which an employer might reasonably place some reliance, it is difficult to see how a person can be regarded as being in employment between periods of work when his contract of employment has expressly been terminated. It seems to me that there needs to be a 'tacit understanding' or a mutual expectation such as was found in *R(U) 1/66* and *R(U) 8/68*, discussed in *R(JSA) 5/03*. In my judgment, the tribunal erred in apparently not distinguishing between a cycle involving periods of employment and periods of unemployment and a cycle of employment involving periods of work and periods of no work."

As there was no evidence of any expectation by the employer that the claimant would resume employment, and as it would not be difficult to find other cleaners if he did not apply in the week before the next term, the claimant was not in remunerative work during the vacation.

In the light of the requirement in *R(JSA) 1/07* for the "expectation" to be mutual to both employer and employee, it is suggested that the result should have been the same if the evidence had shown that the claimant did not have an expectation of being re-employed if he were to apply.

Term-time only workers—para. (3B)

For JSA the position of those who only work during term-time is governed by reg.51(2)(a) and (b) of the JSA Regulations as interpreted by the decision of the Tribunal of Commissioners in *R(JSA) 5/03*. This is because, in *R(JSA) 4/03*, reg.51(2)(c) of the JSA Regulations was held by the same Tribunal to be of no legal effect because it discriminated indirectly against women and could not be objectively justified by reference to factors other than sex. It was therefore inconsistent with EC Directive 79/7 (see Vol.III). However, unlike JSA, income support is not within the material scope of that Directive because it provides protection against poverty rather than against any of the risks listed in art.3 of the Directive—see *Jackson and Cresswell v Chief Adjudication Officer* (C-63/91 and C-64/91) [1992] E.C.R. I-4737 (also reported as an appendix to *R(IS) 10/91*). Therefore reg.5(3B) of the Income Support Regulations (equivalent to reg.52(2)(c)) is unaffected by the decision in *R(JSA) 4/03* and needs to be applied.

2.86

In the past the application of reg.5 to term-time-only workers has been a matter of acute controversy and readers are referred to the more detailed historical note at pp.213-219 of Vol.II of the 2000 edition. The law as it relates to income support has, however, now been settled by the decision of the House of Lords in *Chief Adjudication Officer v Stafford and Banks* [2001] UKHL 33 HL, June 28, 2001 (also reported as *R(IS) 15/01*).

The issue in *Stafford and Banks* may conveniently be illustrated using the facts of Mr Banks' appeal. He was employed as an assistant for children with special needs at a junior school. During the 38 weeks of term time each year, he worked a regular 20- hour week but during the 14 weeks of the school holidays he did not work at all and was not paid. He had a continuing contract of employment with the same employer and all parties approached the case on the basis that he had a recognisable cycle of work of one year including both term-time and school holidays. It was common ground that in these circumstances, the combined effect of para.(2)(b)(i) and (3B) (which had been introduced to reverse the effect of the decision in *R(IS) 15/94*) was to average Mr Banks' working hours across the cycle but that school holidays had to be disregarded when calculating that average. The effect was that Mr Banks' hours were averaged over term-time only and were accordingly 20 hours a week (20 3 38 4 38) rather than 14.6 hours per week (20 3 38 ÷ 52) which would have been the case if they had been averaged over the whole year including school holidays.

Up to this point, there was no dispute. What divided the parties and the House of Lords was whether or not—in addition to this averaging process—*the two paragraphs also had the effect of treating Mr Banks as being engaged in remunerative work during the 14 weeks of school holiday when he was not actually working*. In other words, was it possible for Mr Banks to say that he was not engaged in remunerative work at all during those weeks in the cycle which had not been included in the calculation of his average hours?

2.87

The majority of the House of Lords (Lord Slynn, Hope and Millet) held that it was not. The disregard in para.(3B) only applied to the calculation of the average number of hours and did not alter the length of the cycle of work. The decision as to whether or not the claimant was engaged in remunerative work was to be applied to the full period of the cycle. The decision is, perhaps, best summarised in the judgment of Lord Millet (at paras 63 and 65):

". . . To my mind the critical point is that paras (2)(b)(i) is not replaced by paragraph (3B) but merely made subject to it. Paragraph 2(b) remains in full force save only to the extent to which it is modified by paragraph (3B). The two paragraphs must be read together. They are both concerned with persons who have a regular cycle of work. Neither of them is concerned with the question when a person is to be treated as being engaged in work, but only with the determination of the average number of hours for which he is engaged in work for the purpose of determining whether the work (in which ex hypothesi he must be treated as being engaged) is remunerative work. Paragraph 2(b)(i) directs that the average number of hours is to be determined by reference to a complete cycle including periods during which he does no work, and there is nothing in paragraph (3B) which modifies this. It does not affect the duration of the cycle or exclude periods during which he does no work. In the case of the present claimant, therefore, the cycle of work remains the complete year . . . and the claimant continues to be treated (by paragraph (2)(b)(i)) as engaged in work throughout the cycle including periods when he does no work. Paragraph (3B) directs that the school holidays are to be disregarded, not for the purpose of determining when a person is to be treated as engaged in work, but merely for the purpose of establishing the average number of hours worked during the cycle."

In the circumstances, the decision of the Commissioner in *CSJSA/395/1998* must be followed in preference to the decisions in *CIS/1118/1997, CIS/3216/1997* and *CJSA/3218/1997* which had held (with Lord Cooke who dissented in *Stafford and Banks*) that para.(3B) restricted the weeks during which a claimant is treated as engaged in remunerative work to those which were included in the averaging calculation. Similarly, the persuasive dissent of Lord Scott (who would have held that neither para.(2) nor para.(3B) had the effect of treating a claimant as being engaged in remunerative work when he was not actually working) cannot be taken as representing the law.

2.88   The decision of the majority in *Stafford and Banks* considerably narrows the scope for further dispute about the benefit entitlements of term-time only workers. However, it should be noted that para.(3B) (and hence the *Stafford and Banks* ruling) only applies if it is first established that there is a "recognisable cycle of work". In three appeals decided since the decision of the House of Lords in *Stafford and Banks (R(JSA) 8/03, CIS/914/1997* and *CJSA/2759/1998)*, Commissioner Rowland held that such a cycle had not been established. The Commissioner pointed out that where a person is employed on a casual or relief basis "it may be clear that [he or she] will not work during school holidays *but it may not be clear that he or she will work during the whole of the terms* and for that reason a cycle may not be established" (emphasis added). There may come a time when a pattern of regular employment in practice will establish an annual cycle but in *CIS/914/1997* the Commissioner refused to accept that this had occurred when the claimant had only worked for part of a year before claiming benefit and in *CJSA/2759/1998* he expressed the view that establishing a cycle in practice "is likely to require the completion of two cycles".

It should also be noted that in *Stafford and Banks*, the House of Lords was dealing with a case in which it was not disputed that the employment relationship between the claimant and his employer continued to exist over the holiday period. This issue must now be approached in accordance with *R(JSA) 5/03* (above), i.e. by having regard to the reality of the position rather than a strict analysis of the status of the contract of employment. Even so, there may be cases in which it will not be reasonable to expect that the person will resume employment. In such cases, any recognisable cycle of work that may have been established will be broken with the effect that *Stafford and Banks* no longer applies.

Self-employment

2.89   In the case of a self-employed worker who has periods of work interspersed with periods of no work the position is less clear. Paragraph (1) does not state what is the appropriate period to look at when determining whether a person is engaged in remunerative work. Each case will therefore depend to some extent on its own facts. If, for example, a person carries on a business for six months of the year and does no work in connection with that business for the rest of the year, it must be arguable that the period to be looked at is the six months when his business is dormant and that during that time he is not engaged in work. This was the approach originally taken in the *Decision Makers Guide* (but now see para.20340). However, this is not the conclusion reached by the Commissioner in *CIS 493/1993*.

The claimant ran a guest house with a six-month season and did a minimal amount of work during the closed season. The claimant had argued that there were two cycles, or periods, one in which he worked more than 16 hours every week and the second during which he was not engaged in work at all. The Commissioner states that the first question was whether there was a recognisable cycle, and the second was whether the claimant's hours fluctuated within that cycle. The basis of this approach seems to have been that para.(2) is to be used to determine the number of hours for which a person is engaged in work. But para.(2) does not provide a rule for deciding the number of hours worked per week in all cases. It applies in the circumstances described in the opening words of sub-paras (a) and (b) (*R(IS) 8/95*). It is suggested that the first question is what is the appropriate period for deciding whether a claimant is engaged in remunerative work, which will depend on the facts of each case, before going on to consider whether the particular circumstances referred to in para.(2) apply. Note that para.(3B) would not seem to apply to the self-employed.

This approach was confirmed in *Saunderson v Secretary of State for Work and Pensions* [2012] CSIH 102; [2013] AACR 16, which concerned reg.51 of the JSA Regulations (the equivalent of reg.5). The claimant had worked as a self-employed golf caddie in St Andrews in the spring and summer months for a number of years. His authorisation to work as a caddie was withdrawn in October 2007 because the demand for caddies is reduced in the winter. There was no commitment that he would be able to work as a caddie in St Andrews the following or any future year. The Inner House of the Court of Session stated that the notion that a seasonal worker was, by dint of being a seasonal worker, engaged in an annual cycle of work, with the consequence that his hours or earnings fell to be averaged over 12 months, had its origin in the obiter observations in *R(JSA) 1/03* (see para.12). However, the concept of a "recognisable cycle of work" in reg.51(2) only came into play for the purpose of averaging the weekly hours of work *after* the primary question under reg.51(1) as to whether the claimant was "in work" at the time of his claim for JSA had been answered. That primary question was not determined by whether there was a recognisable cycle of work but was a matter of fact, giving "in work" its ordinary meaning. The Secretary of State had accepted this in relation to those who were employees in seasonal work (as held in *R (JSA) 1/07*) but contended that seasonal self-employment was an annual activity. The Court of Session, however, rejected this sharp distinction. While there may be many self-employed trading or professional activities in which the activity continues during an idle period, there are also many seasonally pursued activities, which, while treated as self-employment, are in substance little different from employment. What needed to be considered was the primary question of whether the person was "in work" when his seasonal activity came to an end.

See also *TC v Department for Social Development (JSA)* [2013] NI Com 65 (a decision of a Northern Ireland Commissioner). The claimant was a self-employed eel fisherman on Lough Neagh who claimed JSA following the breakdown of his boat towards the end of the eel fishing season. The Commissioner follows *Sanderson*, rather than the majority in the House of Lords in *Banks* (which was primarily concerned with the calculation of hours of a person in remunerative work and could be distinguished on its facts). The Commissioner considered that in the past the Great Britain Commissioners (as they then were) had taken different approaches to the question of seasonal employment and seasonally-based self-employment but, as stated by the Court of Session (see para.20), there was no textual warrant in the legislative definition of remunerative work for any distinction to be drawn between previously employed or self-employed claimants.

Paragraph (4)
See the notes to s.126 of the Contributions and Benefits Act (1986 Act s.23).   **2.90**

Paragraph (5)

2.91 Where payments in lieu of remuneration are paid or (within four weeks) holiday pay, the person is treated as in remunerative work for the period covered. See regs 29 and 31. Following the increased disregard of payments made on the termination of full-time employment that was introduced on October 1, 2007 (see para.1 of Sch.8 and the notes to that paragraph), this provision will only apply where a person's employment has been suspended.

Paragraph (7)

2.92 Paid meal or refreshment breaks count in the calculation of the hours for which a person is engaged in work.

Persons not treated as engaged in remunerative work

2.93 **6.**—[¹⁰(1)] A person shall not be treated as engaged in [² remunerative work in so far as—]

[³(a) [¹². . .]]]

(b) he is engaged in child minding in his home;

(c) he is engaged by a charity or [⁷voluntary organisation [⁸—],] or is a volunteer where the only payment received by him or due to be paid to him, is a payment which is to be disregarded under regulation 40(2) and paragraph 2 of Schedule 9 (sums to be disregarded in the calculation of income other than earnings) [²¹ and in this paragraph "volunteer" means a person who is engaged in voluntary work, otherwise than for a relative, where the only payment received, or due to be paid to the person by virtue of being so engaged, is in respect of any expenses reasonably incurred by the person in connection with that work];

(d) he is engaged on a scheme for which a training allowance is being paid; [⁴. . .]

[¹⁵(dd) he is receiving assistance under the self-employment route;]

(e) [¹². . .]

[⁹(f) [¹². . .]]

[⁶(g) [¹². . .]]

[⁴(h) he is engaged in any one of the employments mentioned in heads (a) to (d) of sub-paragraph (1) of paragraph 7 of Schedule 8 (which relates to persons serving as firemen, in coastal rescue activities etc); [⁵. . .]

(j) he is performing his duties as a councillor, and for this purpose "councillor" has the same meaning as in [¹²section 171F(2) of the Contributions and Benefits Act];] [⁵ or

(k) he is engaged in caring for a person who is accommodated with him by virtue of arrangements made under any of the provisions referred to in paragraph 26 [⁷ or in accordance with paragraph 27] of Schedule 9 (sums to be disregarded in the calculation of income other than earnings) and is in receipt of any payment specified in [⁷those paragraphs].]

[²³(ka) he is engaged in caring for a person who is provided with continuing care by a local authority by virtue of arrangements made under section 26A of the Children (Scotland) Act 1995 (duty to provide continuing care) and is in receipt of a payment made under that section of that Act;]

(l) *[Omitted]*

[¹⁰ (m)   he is engaged in an activity in respect of which—

      (i)   a sports award has been made, or is to be made, to him; and

      (ii)   no other payment is made or is expected to be made to him]

(2)–(3) [¹⁶. . .]

[¹² (4) The following persons shall not be treated as engaged in remunerative work—

  (a)   [²⁰ . . .]

  (b)   subject to regulation 5(4) and (5) (persons treated as engaged in remunerative work), a person to whom section 126 of the Contributions and Benefits Act (trade disputes) applies or in respect of whom section 124(1) of that Act (conditions of entitlement to income support) has effect as modified by section 127(b) of that Act (effect of return to work);

  (c)   a person to whom paragraph 4 of Schedule 1B applies;

[¹⁷ (d) [²⁰ . . .]]

[¹³(5) A person shall not be treated as engaged in remunerative work for the period specified in paragraph (6) in so far as—

  (a)   he or his partner is engaged in work which—

      (i)   is remunerative work; and

      (ii)   he, or his partner, is expected to be engaged in remunerative work for a period of no less than five weeks;

  (b)   he or his partner had, for a continuous period of 26 weeks ending on the day before the day on which he commenced the work referred to in sub-paragraph (a), been entitled to and in receipt of income support [¹⁹ , an income-based jobseeker's allowance or an income-related employment and support allowance];

  (c)   he or his partner had, as at the day before the day on which he commenced the work referred to in sub-paragraph (a), an applicable amount which included—

      (i)   an amount determined in accordance with Schedule 3 (housing costs) as applicable to him in respect of [¹⁸ housing costs which qualify [²² under paragraph 17]] of that Schedule; [¹⁹ . . .]

      (ii)   an amount determined in accordance with Schedule 2 to the Jobseeker's Allowance Regulations 1996 (housing costs) as applicable to him in respect of [¹⁸ housing costs which qualify [²² under paragraph 16]] of that Schedule; [¹⁹ or

      (iii)   an amount determined in accordance with Schedule 6 to the Employment and Support Allowance Regulations (housing costs) as applicable to him in respect of housing costs which qualify [²² under paragraph 18]] of that Schedule; and]

  (d)   he or his partner remain liable to make payments [¹⁸ in respect of such housing costs].

(6) A person referred to in paragraph (5) shall not be treated as engaged in remunerative work for—

  (a)   the period of four weeks commencing with the day on which he was first engaged in the work referred to in sub-paragraph (a) of that paragraph; [¹⁶. . .]

(7) In calculating the period of benefit entitlement referred to in paragraph [¹⁶. . .] (5)(b), no account shall be taken of entitlement arising by virtue of paragraph [¹⁶. . .] (6).

(8) In paragraph (5), a reference to the claimant or his partner being entitled to and in receipt of an income-based jobseeker's allowance or

to an amount being applicable to either of them under the Jobseeker's Allowance Regulations 1996 shall include a reference to the claimant and his partner being entitled to, and in receipt of, a joint-claim jobseeker's allowance and to an amount being applicable to that couple under those Regulations.]

AMENDMENTS

1. Income Support (General) Amendment Regulations 1988 (SI 1988/663) reg.5 (April 11, 1988).
2. Income Support (General) Amendment No.4 Regulations 1988 (SI 1988/1445) reg.4 (September 12, 1988).
3. Income Support (General) Amendment No.4 Regulations 1991 (SI 1991/1559) reg.4 (October 7, 1991).
4. Income Support (General) Amendment Regulations 1992 (SI 1992/468) reg.2 (April 6, 1992).
5. Income-related Benefits Schemes (Miscellaneous Amendments) (No.3) Regulations 1992 (SI 1992/2155) reg.13 (October 5, 1992).
6. Social Security Benefits (Miscellaneous Amendments) Regulations 1993 (SI 1993/518) reg.5 (April 1, 1993).
7. Income-related Benefits Schemes (Miscellaneous Amendments) (No.5) Regulations 1994 (SI 1994/2139) reg.23 (October 3, 1994).
8. Income-related Benefits Schemes (Miscellaneous Amendments) Regulations 1995 (SI 1995/516) reg.20 (April 10, 1995).
9. Income Support (General) (Jobseeker's Allowance Consequential Amendments) Regulations 1996 (SI 1996/206) reg.6 (October 7, 1996).
10. Social Security Amendment (Sports Award) Regulations 1999 (SI 1999/2165) reg.6(2) (August 23, 1999).
11. Social Security (Miscellaneous Amendments) (No.2) Regulations 1999 (SI 1999/2556 reg.2(3) (October 4, 1999).
12. Social Security (Miscellaneous Amendments) Regulations 2000 (SI 2000/681) reg.2(b)(i) (April 3, 2000).
13. Social Security (Miscellaneous Amendments) Regulations 2001 (SI 2001/488) reg.4 (April 9, 2001).
14. Social Security Amendment (Residential Care and Nursing Homes) Regulations 2001 (SI 2001/3767) reg.2 and Sch. Pt I para.2 (April 8, 2002).
15. Social Security (Income-Related Benefits Self-Employment Route Amendment) Regulations 2004 (SI 2004/963) reg.3 (May 4, 2004).
16. Social Security (Back to Work Bonus and Lone Parent Run-on) (Amendment and Revocation) Regulations 2003 (SI 2003/1589) reg.2(a) (October 25, 2004).
17. Social Security (Care Homes and Independent Hospitals) Regulations 2005 (SI 2005/2687) reg.2 and Sch.1 para.2 (October 24, 2005).
18. Social Security (Housing Costs and Miscellaneous Amendments) Regulations 2007 (SI 2007/3183) reg.3(2) (December 17, 2007).
19. Employment and Support Allowance (Consequential Provisions) (No.2) Regulations 2008 (SI 2008/1554) reg.2(1) and (3) (October 27, 2008).
20. Social Security (Miscellaneous Amendments) (No.5) Regulations 2009 (SI 2009/3228) reg.4(a)(i) (January 25, 2010).
21. Social Security (Miscellaneous Amendments) (No.2) Regulations 2010 (SI 2010/641) reg.2(1) and (4) (April 6, 2010).
22. Loans for Mortgage Interest Regulations 2017 (SI 2017/725) reg.18 and Sch.5 para.2 (April 6, 2018).
23. Social Security and Child Support (Care Payments and Tenant Incentive Scheme) (Amendment) Regulations 2017 (SI 2017/995), reg.10(1) and (2) (November 7, 2017).

DEFINITIONS

"the Act"—see reg.2(1).
"remunerative work"—*ibid.*
"training allowance"—*ibid.*
"voluntary organisation"—*ibid.*

GENERAL NOTE

Claimants and their partners must be deemed not to be in remunerative work   2.94
for the time engaged in these activities, although the "not" could be better placed.
The effect is that there is no automatic exclusion from entitlement under s.124(1)
(c) of the Contributions and Benefits Act (1986 Act s.20(3)(c)). Any earnings from
employment must still be taken into account as income. Most of the categories are
self-explanatory.
 Paragraph (1)(b) deems a person who is childminding in her own home not to be
in remunerative work. However, there is no specific provision in Sch.1B to enable
childminders to qualify for income support. If a claimant who is a childminder does
not come within any other paragraph of Sch.1B, it may be possible to argue that
para.3 applies (looking after a child whose parent is temporarily absent from home).
This would be along the lines that a parent who is out at work is absent from home
on a temporary basis. Paragraph 3 does not seem to require that the person should
be looking after the child all the time; as long as this is done on a regular basis this
should suffice.
 Under para.(1)(c), para.2 of Sch.9 refers to payments solely of expenses to volunteers or people working for charitable or voluntary bodies. A volunteer is someone
who without any legal obligation performs a service for another person without
expectation of payment (*R(IS)12/92*).
 Under para.(1)(d), training allowances are most commonly paid to people on   2.95
Work Based Learning for Young People (in Scotland "Skillseekers"), which has
replaced Youth Training, Modern Apprenticeships, etc.
 Under para (1)(dd) those receiving assistance under the "self-employment route"
are treated as not being in remunerative work. See the annotation to the definition
of "self-employment route" in reg.2(1) and the General Note to reg.39A.
 In addition, reg.2(2)(a) of the New Deal (Lone Parents) (Miscellaneous
Provisions) Order 2001 (SI 2001/2915), has the effect that from September 13,
2001, top-up payments made to those participating in the self-employment route
of the New Deal for Lone Parents and other payments made to assist with the
expenses of such participation are to be treated as a training allowance for the
purpose of reg.6(1)(d).
 Under para.(1)(j), the definition of "councillor" is—   2.96
  "(a) in relation to England and Wales, a member of a London borough
       council, a county council, a district council, a parish or community
       council, the Common Council of the City of London or the Council of
       the Isles of Scilly; and
   (b) in relation to Scotland, a member of a regional, islands or district
       council."
Under para.(1)(k) foster parents who receive statutory payments for fostering, or
people receiving payments for providing temporary care in their home, are deemed
not to be in remunerative work by reason of those payments.
 Paragraph (1)(m) provides that a person will be deemed not to be in remunerative
work while engaged in activity for which the only payment he is, or will be, receiving
is a "sports award" (defined in reg.2(1)). See also reg.37(2)(c) which ensures that
the sports award is not treated as self-employed earnings. A sports award is disregarded as income other than earnings under para.69 of Sch.9 except to the extent
that it has been made for any of the items listed in para.69(2). There is a similar
disregard where the sports award counts as capital (see para.56 of Sch.10) but in
this case the disregard only applies for 26 weeks from the date of receipt.

2.97   Paragraphs (2) and (3) *Lone-parent run-on*: The "lone-parent run-on" previously established by these paras was abolished on October 25, 2004. For details of the former run-on see p.262 of Vol.II of the 2004 edition.

      Paragraph (4) Until January 25, 2010, para.(4) treated disabled workers (subpara. (a)), certain claimants affected by a trade dispute (subpara.(b)), carers who fall within Sch.1B para.4 (subpara.(c)) and claimants living in care homes, Abbeyfield Homes and independent hospitals (subpara.(d)) as not being in remunerative work. On that date, paras 8 and 9 of Sch.1B (under which people within subparas (a) and (d) automatically fell within a prescribed category for the purposes of s.124(1)(e) of SSCBA) were revoked, as were subparas (a) and (d) themselves. The revocations are part of a broader policy that those who are unable to work fully by reason of a medical condition should claim ESA rather than IS. For further details, see the commentary to Sch.1B.

      Those revocations are subject to savings provisions in reg.4 of SI 2009/3228 (below). Those provisions apply where a claimants is entitled to income support for a period including January 24, 2010 (irrespective of when income support was claimed) and falls within subpara.(a) or (d) on that date. In those circumstances, subpara.(a) or (d)—and paras 8 or 9 of Sch.1B—continue to apply to the claimant until they cease to fall within subpara.(a) or (d) or they cease to be entitled to income support, whichever is earlier: see reg.4(3), (4), (7) and (8) of SI 2009/3228.

2.98   Paragraphs (5)–(8) *Housing costs run-on*: under paras (5)–(8), some claimants who have been receiving IS, JSA or ESA housing costs are treated as not in remunerative work (and hence still entitled to IS) for the first four weeks of full-time work (i.e., 16 hours for the claimant or 24 for the claimant's partner—see reg.5(1) and (1A)). Before October 25, 2004, those claimants who qualified for the "lone-parent run-on" under the former paras (2) and (3) were potentially entitled to what was then the mortgage interest run-on for two weeks after the end of the two-week lone-parent run-on period (under para.6(b)). However, with the abolition of the lone-parent run-on, para.(6)(b) was revoked, so that in all cases the mortgage interest (now housing costs) run-on lasts for the four-week period specified in para.(6)(a). To qualify, a claimant (or her/his partner) must have been in receipt of IS, income-based or income-related JSA for a continuous period of at least 26 weeks (not including any earlier run-on periods—see para.(7)) ending on the day before the commencement of full-time work and must have been entitled to housing costs on that day. In addition, the full-time work must be expected to last for a period of at least five weeks.

      During the run-on period, IS is paid at the lower of the weekly amount of housing costs which was payable immediately before the claimant or her/his partner commenced full-time work or the rate of IS, income-related ESA or income-based JSA which was being paid (or would have been paid but for the receipt of a training allowance) in the benefit week before full-time work commenced (see para.19A of Sch.7).

      Under para.9A of Sch.1B a person to whom para.(5) applies is in a prescribed category and therefore eligible for IS even if they were previously receiving JSA or ESA.

      It is not necessary for a claim to be made to qualify for the mortgage interest (now housing costs) run-on. When the claimant informs the DWP that he or his partner has started full-time work the run-on should be paid automatically.

Meaning of employment

2.99   7.—[¹. . .]

AMENDMENT

1. Income Support (General) (Jobseeker's Allowance Consequential Amendments) Regulations 1996 (SI 1996/206) reg.28 and Sch.3 (October 7, 1996).

Persons not required to be available for employment

8.—[¹. . .]   2.100

AMENDMENT

1. Income Support (General) (Jobseeker's Allowance Consequential Amendments) Regulations 1996 (SI 1996/206) reg.28 and Sch.3 (October 7, 1996).

Persons treated as available for employment

9.—[¹. . .]   2.101

AMENDMENT

1. Income Support (General) (Jobseeker's Allowance Consequential Amendments) Regulations 1996 (SI 1996/206) reg.28 and Sch.3 (October 7, 1996).

Circumstances in which claimants are not to be treated as available for employment

10.—[¹. . .]   2.102

AMENDMENT

1. Income Support (General) (Jobseeker's Allowance Consequential Amendments) Regulations 1996 (SI 1996/206) reg.28 and Sch.3 (October 7, 1996).

[¹Actively seeking employment

10A.   [². . .]   2.103

AMENDMENTS

1. Income Support (General) Amendment No.2 Regulations 1989 (SI 1989/1323) reg.6 (October 9, 1989).
2. Income Support (General) (Jobseeker's Allowance Consequential Amendments) Regulations 1996 (SI 1996/206) reg.28 and Sch.3 (October 7, 1996).

Registration for employment

11.—[¹. . .]   2.104

AMENDMENT

1. Income Support (General) (Jobseeker's Allowance Consequential Amendments) Regulations 1996 (SI 1996/206) reg.28 and Sch.3 (October 7, 1996).

[¹Relevant Education

[² 12.—For the purposes of these Regulations, a person is to be treated   2.105
as receiving relevant education if he is a qualifying young person within the meaning of section 142 of the Contributions and Benefits Act (child and qualifying young person).]]

AMENDMENTS

1. Income Support (General) Amendment Regulations 1990 (SI 1990/547) reg.5 (April 9, 1990).
2. Social Security (Young Persons) Amendment Regulations 2006 (SI 2006/718) reg.2(2) (April 10, 2006).

DEFINITIONS

"child"—see SSCBA s.137(1).
"qualifying young person"—see reg.14.

GENERAL NOTE

2.106   The general rule under s.124(1)(d) of the Contributions and Benefits Act is that if a claimant is receiving relevant education he is not entitled to income support. Reg.12, which provides when a person is to be treated as receiving relevant education, was recast following the commencement of the Child Benefit Act 2005 on April 10, 2006. The test under reg.12 is now whether the person is a qualifying young person within the meaning of s.142 of the Contributions and Benefits Act 1992 (s.142 was substituted by s.1(2) of the 2005 Act on April 10, 2006).

Qualifying young person

2.107   The Child Benefit Act 2005 changes the definition of "child" for the purposes of child benefit so that it is now divided into a "child", which means a person under 16, and a "qualifying young person" (see the substituted s.142 of the Contributions and Benefits Act in Vol.IV of this series). A "qualifying young person" is a person who is 16 or over but who has not attained a prescribed age and who satisfies prescribed conditions. Thus the upper age limit for child benefit and the conditions under which child benefit will be paid for a young person aged 16 or over are now all contained in secondary legislation (see regs 3–8 of the Child Benefit (General) Regulations 2006 (SI 2006/223) in Vol.IV). The Government stated that its intention in the first instance was to extend child benefit to young people who were undertaking "approved training" and to 19-year-olds who were completing such training or a course of full-time, non-advanced education; thus the increase in eligibility is relatively modest, at least at this point.

The substance of the definition of "qualifying young person" is in reg.3 of the 2006 Child Benefit Regulations. It applies to a person who is: (i) under 20; *and* (ii) undertaking a course of full-time, non-advanced education, which is not provided by virtue of his employment or any office held by him, but which is provided at a school or college, or elsewhere as approved by the Revenue (in the latter case he must have been receiving the approved education before he was 16); *or* (iii) in England (from June 4, 2014), receiving "appropriate full-time education" (commonly referred to as "16–19 study programmes") within s.4 Education and Skills Act 2008, which is not advanced education (see reg.3(2)(ab)(i) which reproduces the definition of "advanced education" in reg.1(3) of the 2006 Child Benefit Regulations), and which is not provided by virtue of his employment or any office held by him (there is no requirement as to where the education is provided); *or* (iv) undertaking approved training that is not provided by means of a contract of employment. "Approved training" covers various training programmes under "arrangements made by the Government" (see the definitions of both these terms in reg.1(3) of the 2006 Regulations). Note that from August 31, 2015 there are no programmes specified for the purposes of the definition of "approved training" in England (sub-para. (a) which used to list these programmes in England was omitted by reg.2(a) of the Child Benefit (General) (Amendment) Regulations 2015 (SI 2015/1512) with effect from August 31, 2015). The Explanatory Memorandum which accompanies SI 2015/1512 appears to take the view that such training will fall within s.4 of the Education and Skills Act 2008 since a study programme under s.4 also includes traineeship. In Scotland approved training includes Employability Fund activity and in Wales it includes Traineeships or Foundation Apprenticeships.

However, note that a person aged 19 can only be a qualifying young person if he began, or was enrolled on, or had been accepted to undertake, the full time education or approved training before he was 19 (although a person who was on such a course/training and has been accepted or enrolled to undertake another such course/training is also included). Furthermore, the new rules did not apply to anyone who became 19 before April 10, 2006; such a person cannot be a "qualifying young person".

"Full-time education" (defined in reg.1(3) of the 2006 Regulations; the defini- 2.108
tion is broadly similar to that which applied under the previous child benefit regulations) requires contact hours of at least 12 a week during term-time. *R(F) 1/93* held that "supervised study" (in reg.5 of the Child Benefit Regulations 1976) "would normally be understood to import the presence or close proximity of a teacher or tutor".

A 16 to 19-year-old is not a qualifying person if he is receiving in his own right income support, income-based JSA, incapacity benefit for people disabled in youth, ESA, tax credit or universal credit (reg.8 of the 2006 Regulations).

Ceasing to be a qualifying young person
A person continues to be a qualifying young person during temporary interruptions, 2.109
like school holidays, or by reason of illness, etc. When he ceases actually to receive relevant education or approved training he still counts as a qualifying young person (unless he is in remunerative work of 24 hours or more a week and in certain other circumstances) until: (i) in the case of a 16-year-old, the August 31 which follows his 16th birthday (reg.4 of the 2006 Regulations); or (ii) in the case of a person who leaves the education or training before he is 20, the first Sunday on or after the next "terminal date", or, if he reaches 20 before that date, the Sunday on or after his 20th birthday (unless his 20th birthday is on a Monday when he will count as a qualifying person until the Sunday before his birthday). The terminal dates are the last day in February, the last day in May, the last day in August and the last day in November (reg.7 of the 2006 Regulations). The terminal dates are no longer based on school terms as they now also apply to young people who leave approved training. In addition, reg.5 of the 2006 Regulations allows for a twenty week "extension period" for 16- and 17-year-olds who have left education or training (note that "education" and "training" are not defined in this context and so may refer to any kind of education or training) and who are registered for work, education or training, not in remunerative work of 24 hours or more a week and not in receipt of income support, income-based JSA, incapacity benefit for people disabled in youth, ESA, tax credit or universal credit. Provided that a written application for the extension is made within three months of the 16- or17-year-old ceasing education or training, he will continue to count as a qualifying young person during the extension period (or until he reaches 18). Note that this extension period begins on the first day of the week after that in which the 16- or 17-year-old left education or training. Thus it no longer follows on from but runs concurrently with the automatic extension period relevant in his case.

Note that the reg.12 question is one to which the assumption in reg.13(2) of the Decisions and Appeals Regulations 1999 (see Vol.III in this series) applies. If the Secretary of State considers that he does not have all the relevant information or evidence to decide whether the person should count as in relevant education, he will proceed on the basis that the child benefit decision would be adverse to the claimant in the income support sense.

Note also reg.13 and para.15A of Sch.1B which allow certain claimants to receive income support though in relevant education.

Circumstances in which persons in relevant education may be entitled to income support

13.—(1) Notwithstanding that a person is to be treated as receiving rel- 2.110
evant education under regulation 12 (relevant education) he shall, if paragraph (2) applies to him and he satisfies the other conditions of entitlement to income support, be entitled to income support.

(2) This paragraph applies to [³a person [⁷ who [⁸ (subject to paragraph (2A))] is a qualifying young person within the meaning of section 142 of the Contributions and Benefits Act (child and qualifying young person)] (hereinafter referred to as an eligible person)] who—

(a) is the parent of a child for whom he is treated as responsible under regulation 15 (circumstances in which a person is to be treated as responsible or not responsible for another) and who is treated as a member of his household under regulation 16 (circumstances in which a person is to be treated as being or not being a member of the household); or

[⁷ (b) [¹⁰ . . .]
 (bb) [¹⁰ . . .]
 (bc) [¹⁵ . . .]]

(c) has no parent nor any person acting in the place of his parents; or

[¹(d) of necessity has to live away from his [² parents and any] person acting in the place of his parents because—

(i) he is estranged from his [² parents and that person]; or
(ii) he is in physical or moral danger; or
(iii) there is a serious risk to his physical or mental health;] or

[⁴(dd) has ceased to live in accommodation provided for him by a local authority under Part III of the Children Act 1989 (local authority support for children and families) [¹¹ or Part II of the Children (Scotland) Act 1995 (promotion of children's welfare by local authorities and by children's hearings etc.)] [¹⁶ or Part 4 (meeting needs) or Part 6 (looked after and accommodated children) of the Social Services and Well-being (Wales) Act 2014] [¹⁴, or by virtue of any order or warrant made under the Children's Hearings (Scotland) Act 2011,] and is of necessity living away from his parents and any person acting in place of his parents;]

(e) is living away from his parents and any person acting in the place of his parents in a case where his parents are or, as the case may be, that person is unable financially to support him and—

(i) chronically sick or mentally or physically disabled; or
(ii) detained in custody pending trial or sentence upon conviction or under a sentence imposed by a court; or
(iii) prohibited from entering or re-entering Great Britain; or

(f) [⁶. . .]
(g) [⁶. . .]

[⁶(h) is a person to whom paragraph 18 of Schedule 1B (refugees) applies.]

[⁸ (2A) For the purposes of paragraph (2)—

(a) the eligible person shall be treated as satisfying the condition prescribed in regulation 8 of the Child Benefit (General) Regulations 2006 (child benefit not payable in respect of qualifying young person: other financial support);

(b) where sub-paragraphs (c) to (e) apply, the eligible person shall be treated as satisfying the condition prescribed in regulation 5(2)(e) and (f) of the Child Benefit (General) Regulations 2006 (extension period: 16 and 17 year olds).]

(3) In this regulation—

[⁵(a) any reference to a person acting in the place of an eligible person's parents includes—

    (i) for the purposes of paragraph (2)(c), (d) and (dd), a reference to a local authority or voluntary organisation where the eligible person is being looked after by them under a relevant enactment or where the eligible person is placed by the local authority or voluntary organisation with another person, that other person whether or not a payment is made to him;

    (ii) for the purposes of paragraph (2)(e), the person with whom the person is so placed;]

(b) "chronically sick or mentally disabled" means, in relation to a person to whom that expression refers, a person—

    (i) in respect of whom the condition specified in paragraph 12(1) of Schedule 2 (additional condition for the higher pensioner and disability premiums) is satisfied; or

    (ii) [9 . . .]

    (iii) who is substantially and permanently disabled [12 ; or

    (iv) who is entitled to an employment and support allowance which includes a work-related activity component or support component [13 or who would be entitled to an employment and support allowance including a work-related activity component but for the application of section 1A of the Welfare Reform Act (duration of contributory allowance)].]

AMENDMENTS

1. Family Credit and Income Support (General) Amendment Regulations 1989 (SI 1989/1034) reg.4 (July 10, 1989).

2. Income Support (General) Amendment Regulations 1991 (SI 1991/236) reg.5 (April 8, 1991).

3. Income Support (General) Amendment No.4 Regulations 1991 (SI 1991/1559) reg.6 August 5, 1991).

4. Income Support (General) Amendment Regulations 1992 (SI 1992/468) reg.3 (April 6, 1992).

5. Income Support (General) Amendment Regulations 1992 (SI 1992/468) Sch. para.2 (April 6, 1992).

6. Income Support (General) (Jobseeker's Allowance Consequential Amendments) Regulations 1996 (SI 1996/206) reg.7 (October 7, 1996).

7. Social Security (Young Persons) Amendment Regulations 2006 (SI 2006/718) reg.2(3) (April 10, 2006).

8. Social Security (Miscellaneous Amendments) Regulations 2008 (SI 2008/698) reg.2(4) (April 14, 2008).

9. Social Security (Miscellaneous Amendments) (No.4) Regulations 2009 (SI 2009/2655) reg.2(4) (October 26, 2009).

10. Income Support (Prescribed Categories of Person) Regulations 2009 (SI 2009/3152) reg.2 (December 30, 2009). Regulation 2(1)(a) revoked reg.13(2)(b) and (bb) with effect from December 30, 2009 but this was subject to the saving provisions in reg.2(2). See the 2015/16 edition of this volume for these Regulations and the notes to them.

11. Social Security (Miscellaneous Amendments) (No.2) Regulations 2010 (SI 2010/641 reg.2(5) (April 6, 2010).

12. Social Security (Miscellaneous Amendments) Regulations 2012 (SI 2012/757) reg.14 (April 1, 2012).

13. Employment and Support Allowance (Duration of Contributory Allowance) (Consequential Amendments) Regulations 2012 (SI 2012/913) reg.3(2) (May 1, 2012).

14. Children's Hearings (Scotland) Act 2011 (Consequential and Transitional

Provisions and Savings) Order 2013 (SI 2013/1465) art.17(1) and Sch.1 Pt 2 para.12(2) (June 24, 2013).

15. Social Security (Miscellaneous Amendments) (No.3) Regulations 2013 (SI 2013/2536) reg.4(4) (October 29, 2013).

16. Social Services and Well-being (Wales) Act 2014 and the Regulation and Inspection of Social Care (Wales) Act 2016 (Consequential Amendments) Order 2017 (SI 2017/901) art.2(1) and (2) (November 3, 2017).

DEFINITIONS

"child"—see SSCBA s.137(1).
"relevant enactment"—see reg.2(1) and reg.16(8)(a).

GENERAL NOTE

2.111   In the circumstances set out in para.(2) a claimant, if he satisfies the other conditions of entitlement, is entitled to income support, even though he is treated as in relevant education under reg.12. From April 10, 2006 a person counts as in relevant education if he is a "qualifying young person within the meaning of s.142 of the Contributions and Benefits Act" (see further the note to reg.12). Some 19-year-olds now come with the definition of "qualifying young person" as well as certain 16-to 18-year-olds.

See also para.15A of Sch.1B which extends eligibility for income support to a person who is under 21 and has enrolled on, been accepted for, or is undertaking a course of full-time, non-advanced education, or who reaches the age of 21 while undertaking such a course and who satisfy conditions that are the same as those in para.(2)(c),(d) and (e).

However the effect of regs 2(4) and 8 of the Child Benefit Regulations 2006 (SI 2006/223) (see Vol.IV in this series) is that for a person to be a qualifying young person he must not be in receipt of certain benefits, including income support. Paragraph (2A)(a) therefore provides that a qualifying young person who meets any of the conditions in para.(2) (and is therefore entitled to income support) will be treated as satisfying the condition in reg.8 of the 2006 Regulations.

If a claimant satisfies any of para.(2)(a) to (e), he will be eligible for income support under para.15 of Sch.1B. If he comes within para.(2)(h), he will qualify under para.18.

Paragraph (2)

2.112   *Sub-paragraph (a)*: A person of at least 16 who is the parent of a child who is in the same household can claim although in relevant education.

2.113   *Sub-paragraphs (b) and (bb)*: These sub-paragraphs covered a qualifying young person who was entitled to the disability or severe disability premium (sub-para. (b)), or who had been incapable of work, or treated as incapable of work, or treated as capable of work by virtue of reg.18 of the Incapacity for Work Regulations (disqualification for misconduct, etc.), or entitled to statutory sick pay, for at least 28 weeks (two or more periods separated by not more than eight weeks counted as continuous) (sub- para.(bb). However, as a consequence of the introduction of ESA, *new* claims for income support under sub-paras (b) and (bb) were no longer possible from October 27, 2008, except in certain circumstances. Sub-paragraphs (b) and (bb) were then revoked on December 30, 2009, subject to a saving provision. See pp.284–286 of the 2015/16 edition of this volume under "Consequences of the introduction of ESA", "Revocation of sub-paras (b) and (bb) on December 30, 2009" and "Migration to ESA" for further details.

2.114   *Sub-paragraph (bc)*: This covered a qualifying young person who had limited leave to enter or remain in the UK without recourse to public funds but who was temporarily without funds because remittances from abroad had been interrupted.

However, sub-para.(bc) was revoked on October 29, 2013 because entitlement to income support in those circumstances (under reg.2(1) of and para.1 of Pt I of the Schedule to the Social Security (Immigration and Asylum) Consequentional Amendments Regulations 2000 (SI 2000/636)) was abolished with effect from October 29, 2013.

Sub-paragraph (c): A parent presumably means a natural parent or an adoptive parent. A person acting in place of parents may include some informal relationships, for example, where a child's parents have died and the child is brought up by another member of the family. It did not include, however, the claimant's boyfriend's father in *NP v SSWP* [2009] UKUT 243 (AAC).The claimant was living with her boyfriend at the house of his father. The father provided shelter and some food but took no financial or parental responsibility for her and had not claimed child benefit or child tax credit in respect of her. Judge Wikeley, while accepting that a person acting in place of a parent need not formally hold parental responsibility in relation to the young person, confirms that the person must in practice be acting broadly in a way that a parent would. 2.115

If a person is claiming child benefit or child tax credit for the eligible person, this would be a relatively strong factor.

However, a sponsor under the Immigration Act 1971 is not a person acting in place of parents. A sponsor's duties are restricted to the maintenance and accommodation of the dependant without recourse to public funds and there is no responsibility for other aspects of the dependant's life (*R(IS) 9/94*).

Paragraph (3)(a)(i) specifically includes for this purpose local authorities and voluntary organisations who are looking after children (what used to be known as having them in care) under a relevant enactment (defined in reg.16(8)(a)), and foster parents with whom the eligible person has been placed by *the* local authority or voluntary organisation. Since head (1) refers to eligible persons placed by "the", not "a", local authority or voluntary organisation, it would seem that head (i) only applies where the eligible person is being looked after by the local authority or voluntary organisation under a relevant enactment. In *CIS 447/1994* the claimant was estranged from his parents. A local authority social worker gave him a list of approved accommodation and he went to lodge at an address on the list. The Commissioner decides that "placed" in the second limb of para.(3)(a)(i) referred to placement under the Children Act. But even if it did not, in the Commissioner's view, providing the claimant with a list of approved accommodation did not constitute "placing" him (even in a non-technical sense) with another person. This did not mean that the second limb was redundant. Its purpose was to make clear that where a claimant had been placed with a person by a local authority, it was estrangement, etc., from that person, not from the local authority, that was relevant. 2.116

CIS 11766/1996 concerned the position of a claimant who had continued to live with his ex-foster parents after his care order had ended. The Commissioner follows the approach of *CSB 325/1985* and holds that ex-foster parents cease to be acting in place of parents when their fostering contract comes to an end.

Note para.(2A)(b) which deems a 16- or 17-year old who is in the child benefit extension period to satisfy the conditions in reg.5(2)(e) and (f) of the Child Benefit Regulations 2006 (SI 2006/223) (these provisions require that the person responsible for the qualifying young person was entitled to child benefit in respect of him and has applied for payment of this during the child benefit extension period; they are therefore unlikely to be met by a person who comes within sub-para.(c)). This will allow the 16-or 17-year old to remain on income support during the child benefit extension period and avoid the need for him to claim income-based JSA for a short period if there is a gap between his terminal date and his return to education or training.

Sub-paragraph (d): See sub-para.(c) above for the meaning of parent and of person acting in place of a parent. The 1991 amendment to the effect that the eligible person must be living away from parents *and* substitutes (and see head (i) on 2.117

estrangement) was described by the DSS as technical. However, this was a change of substance. The previous form referred to living away from or estrangement from parents *or* substitutes. When the Conditions of Entitlement Regulations were in this form, *CSB 677/1983* decided that the eligible person qualified if estranged from his parents even though he was not estranged from a person acting in their place. Now the eligible person has to be living away from or estranged from both. See sub-para.(dd) on eligible persons leaving care.

If the eligible person is within the child benefit extension period note para.(2A)(b) (see the note to sub-para.(c)).

2.118   *Head (i)*: The 1989 form of sub-para.(d) is an attempt to provide a test of "genuine estrangement." It is in some respects stricter than the previous form because in addition to showing estrangement, the person in relevant education must also show that as a result, at least partly, of that he has of necessity to live away from his parents and any substitute. It is obviously a matter of judgment when estrangement is serious enough to necessitate that the young person leaves home. There is perhaps some widening in the addition of two extra categories which may lead to a need to leave home.

Estrangement has "connotations of emotional disharmony" (*R(SB) 2/87, R(IS) 5/05*), although *CH/117/2005* and *CH/3777/2007* (discussed in the note to para.4(b) of Sch.10) take a contrary view. Whether emotional disharmony is a necessary feature may depend on the context but it is suggested that it is relevant in the context of head (i). It seems that estrangement can exist even though financial support is being provided (see, for example, *CIS/11441/1995* below).

In *CIS/4096/2005* the claimant's partner, K, who was aged 16 and in full-time education, had come to live with him after her mother had asked her to leave the family home. The mother did not like the claimant and did not approve of her daughter's pregnancy. The tribunal accepted that K was estranged from her mother but concluded that head (i) did not apply because the alienation was not mutual. The Commissioner reviewed the authorities on estrangement and concluded that there was no requirement of mutuality of feeling for estrangement to exist (as had been suggested by the Commissioner in *CIS/4498/2001*). Disharmony could arise from one person's attitude to another even though the other person might not wish this to be the situation. The position had to be judged from the point of view of the claimant and not from the point of view of the parent(s) or any person acting in place of the parent(s). Since K was estranged from her mother she came within head (i).

2.119   *CIS 11441/1995* decides that estrangement from a local authority can exist. The claimant, aged 16, was in the care of a local authority but because of her violent and aggressive behaviour in a community home it had been decided that she should live in rented accommodation by herself. She was given help to find suitable accommodation and the authority met her liability for council tax and because income support had been refused provided her with a payment equivalent to her income support entitlement. Her rent was met through housing benefit. The care order remained in place as the claimant wished it to continue for "emotional" reasons. The Commissioner decides that sub-para.(dd) did not apply because the local authority were continuing to provide the claimant with accommodation by supervising and assisting in the arrangements for her rented accommodation (see s.23(2)(f) of the Children Act 1989). But sub-para.(d) did apply. The claimant was "living away" from the local authority because she was living away from the people who represented the authority, i.e. the community home (the terms of reg.13 were clearly intended to reverse *R(SB) 2/87* which had held that it was not possible for a person to live away from a local authority). Further it was "necessary" for her to do this because it had been accepted that it was not possible for the claimant to live in a community home or with foster parents. Moreover she was "estranged" from the local authority because she was estranged from the community home where the local authority had placed her. The fact that she continued to have some contact with and received some assistance from the local authority did not alter the fact of the estrangement.

See further the decisions on the meaning of "estrangement" discussed in the note to para.4 of Sch.10, although note that the meaning may depend, to some degree at least, on the context (see *CPC/683/2007*).

Head (ii): Under head (ii), the meaning of "physical or moral danger" is again a matter of judgment. It is not a term of art with an established meaning. Obvious points are that a person can be in danger from himself or from others and that a danger can exist before any harm has actually occurred (see *Kelly v Monklands DC* 1986 S.L.T. 169 on the phrase "at risk of sexual or financial exploitation" in the Code of Guidance on Homelessness). Nor is the danger specified to be immediate, but the test will no doubt be whether the danger is sufficient to necessitate living away from parents or their substitute. The danger does not have to emanate from the pupil's parents. In *R(IS) 9/94* the claimant's parents were in a refugee camp in Ethiopia, having fled there after civil war broke out in Somalia. It is held that he had to live away from his parents in view of the situation in Somalia, as otherwise he was in physical or moral danger; in addition, there was a serious risk to his physical or mental health under head (iii).

2.120

Head (iii): Under head (iii) there is an echo of the "serious risk to health" test of reg.30 of the Supplementary Benefit (Single Payments) Regulations. There was there some dispute about how closely a tribunal had to define the seriousness of the risk (compare *R(SB) 5/81* and *CSB 11/81* with *R(SB) 3/82* and *R(SB) 8/82*). The nature of the risk must no doubt be identified (as the danger must be under head (ii)) and some reason given why it is serious enough to necessitate living away from parents and any substitute. See *R(IS) 9/94* in the notes to head (ii).

2.121

Sub-paragraph (dd): This provision protects the entitlement of eligible persons leaving local authority care who need to live away from their parents and any substitute without the necessity of proving estrangement or moral danger or one of the other conditions in sub-para.(d). See the note to sub-para.(c) for the meaning of parent and person acting in place of a parent.

2.122

If the eligible person is within the child benefit extension period note para.(2A) (b) (see the note to sub-para.(c)).

Sub-paragraph (e): Here the eligible person must be living away from both parents and persons acting in place of parents, and they must be unable to provide financial support. The reason for this inability must be one of those listed. See para.(3) (b) for the definition of chronically sick or mentally or physically disabled. This includes (from April 1, 2012) a person who is entitled to ESA with either the work-related activity component or the support component. It also includes (from May 1, 2012) a person who would have been entitled to ESA with a work-related activity component but for the 365 days' limit on entitlement to contributory ESA for a person who is in the work-related activity group (this limit was introduced by s.1A of the Welfare Reform Act 2007 (inserted into the 2007 Act by s.51 of the Welfare Reform Act 2012 on May 1, 2012)).

2.123

See the note to sub-para.(c) for the meaning of parent and person acting in place of a parent.

If the eligible person is within the child benefit extension period note para.(2A) (b) (see the note to sub-para.(c)).

Head (iii): In *R(IS) 9/94* the claimant's parents who were in a refugee camp in Ethiopia had no leave to enter the UK at the date of the claim. Under s.3 of the Immigration Act 1971 (subject to certain exceptions) all persons who are not British citizens require leave to enter the UK. The claimant's parents were thus prohibited from entering Great Britain.

2.124

Sub-paragraph (h): This is a special case of refugees.

2.125

Paragraph (3)(a)
2.126   See the note to para.(2)(c).

[¹Persons under 18 years

2.127   **13A.**—[². . .],]

AMENDMENTS

1. Income Support (General) Amendment No.3 Regulations 1988 (SI 1988/1228) reg.4 (September 12, 1988).
2. Income Support (General) (Jobseeker's Allowance Consequential Amendments) Regulations 1996 (SI 1996/206) reg.28 and Sch.3 (October 7, 1996).

PART III

MEMBERSHIP OF THE FAMILY

Persons of a prescribed description

2.128   **14.**—(1) Subject to paragraph (2), a person of a prescribed description for the purposes of section 20(11) of the Act [SSCBA, s.137(1)] as it applies to income support (definition of the family) and section 23(1) [¹and (3)] of the Act [SSCBA, s.126(1) and (3)] is a person [⁵ who falls within the definition of qualifying young person in section 142 of the Contributions and Benefits Act (child and qualifying young person)], and in these Regulations such a person is referred to as a "young person".
    [³ (2) Paragraph (1) shall not apply to a person who is—
    (a) [⁵ . . .];
    (b) entitled to income support or would, but for section 134(2) (provision against dual entitlement of members of family) of the Contributions and Benefits Act, be so entitled; [⁶ . . .]
    (c) a person to whom section 6 of the Children (Leaving Care) Act 2000 (exclusion from benefits) applies.] [⁶ [⁷ . . .]
    (d) entitled to an employment and support allowance or would, but for paragraph 6(1)(d) of Schedule 1 to the Welfare Reform Act (conditions of entitlement to income-related employment and support allowance), be so entitled [⁷ ; or
    (e) entitled to universal credit].]
    [⁴ (3) A person of a prescribed description for the purposes of section 137(1) of the Contributions and Benefits Act as it applies to income support (definition of family) includes a child or young person in respect of whom section 145A of that Act applies for the purposes of entitlement to child benefit but only for the period prescribed under section 145A(1) of that Act.]

AMENDMENTS

1. Income Support (General) Amendment No.4 Regulations 1988 (SI 1988/1445) reg.5 (September 12, 1988).
2. Income Support (General) Amendment Regulation 1990 (SI 1990/547) reg.6 (April 9, 1990).
3. Children (Leaving Care) Act 2000 (Commencement No.2 and Consequential Provisions) Order 2001 (SI 2001/3070) art.3(2) and Sch.1 para.(b) (October 1, 2001).

4. Income-related Benefits and Jobseeker's Allowance (Working Tax Credit and Child Tax Credit) (Amendment) Regulations 2002 (SI 2002/2402) reg.2 and Sch.1 para.2 (April 6, 2003).

5. Social Security (Young Persons) Amendment Regulations 2006 (SI 2006/718), reg.2(4) (April 10, 2006).

6. Employment and Support Allowance (Consequential Provisions) (No.2) Regulations 2008 (SI 2008/1554) reg.2(1) and (4) (October 27, 2008).

7. Universal Credit (Consequential, Supplementary, Incidental and Miscellaneous Provisions) Regulations 2013 (SI 2013/630) reg.28(1) and (3) (April 29, 2013).

DEFINITION

"the Act"—see reg.2(1).

GENERAL NOTE

For the circumstances in which a person of 16 to 19 is treated as a qualifying young person for child benefit purposes, see reg.12. If such a person could be entitled to income support or ESA in his or her own right (see reg.13) (para.(2)(b) and (d)) or is a 16- or 17-year-old who has been looked after by a local authority in England or Wales on or after October 1, 2001 or a local authority in Scotland on or after April 1, 2004 and is excluded from income support, income-based JSA and housing benefit (see the notes to reg.2 of the Children (Leaving Care) Social Security Benefits Regulations 2001 (SI 2001/3074) (p.765) and to reg.2 of the Children (Leaving Care) Social Security Benefits (Scotland) Regulations 2004 (SI 2004/747) (p.770)) (para.(2)(c)), that person does not come within reg.14. Under s.145A of SSCBA 1992 and reg.20 of the Child Benefit (General) Regulations 2006 (see Vol I) a claimant who is entitled to child benefit for a child who dies continues to receive that benefit for the following eight weeks or until the end of the week which would have included the qualifying young person's 20th birthday (whichever is the shorter period). Paragraph (3), taken together with the amendment to reg.15(1), has the effect that such a claimant will also continue to get income support in respect of the dead child for the same period.

2.129

Circumstances in which a person is to be treated as responsible or not responsible for another

15.—[¹(1) Subject to the following provisions of this regulation, a person is to be treated as responsible for a child or young person for whom he is receiving child benefit [² and this includes a child or young person to whom paragraph (3) of regulation 14 applies].

2.130

(1A) In a case where a child ("the first child") is in receipt of child benefit in respect of another child ("the second child"), the person treated as responsible for the first child in accordance with the provisions of this regulation shall also be treated as responsible for the second child.

(2) In the case of a child or young person in respect of whom no person is receiving child benefit, the person who shall be treated as responsible for that child or young person shall be—

(a) except where sub-paragraph (b) applies, the person with whom the child or young person usually lives; or

(b) where only one claim for child benefit has been made in respect of the child or young person, the person who made that claim.]

(3) Where regulation 16(6) (circumstances in which a person is to be treated as being or not being a member of the household) applies in respect of a child or young person, that child or young person shall be treated as the responsibility of the claimant for that part of the week for which he is

under that regulation treated as being a member of the claimant's household.

(4) Except where paragraph (3) applies, for the purposes of these Regulations a child or young person shall be treated as the responsibility of only one person in any benefit week and any person other than the one treated as responsible for the child or young person under this regulation shall be treated as not so responsible.

AMENDMENTS

1. Income-related Benefits Schemes (Miscellaneous Amendments) (No.4) Regulations 1993 (SI 1993/2119) reg.5 (October 4, 1993).

2. Income-related Benefits and Jobseeker's Allowance (Working Tax Credit and Child Tax Credit) (Amendment) Regulations 2002 (SI 2002/2402) reg.2 and Sch.1 para.2 (April 6, 2003).

DEFINITIONS

"benefit week"—see reg.2(1).
"child"—see SSCBA s.137(1).
"claimant"—see reg.2(1).
"young person"—*ibid.*, and reg.14.

GENERAL NOTE

Paragraph (1)

2.131   This regulation sets out the circumstances in which a person is "responsible" for a child or young person for the purposes of income support. Before April 6, 2004 that question determined whether or not the claimant could claim an applicable amount for the child or young person under regs 17(b) or 18(c) and a family premium under regs 17(c) or 18(d) (because of the definition of "family" in s.137(1) of the Contributions and Benefits Act). Subject to exceptions in transitional cases (as to which see the note to reg.17), income support became an "adults only" benefit on April 6, 2004 with all support for the costs of bringing up children and young persons transferred to child tax credit and regs 17(b) and (c) and 18(c) and (d) were repealed. Regulation 15 has not, however, been repealed, because it continues to be of relevance to the issue of whether or not a claimant is a "lone parent" within para.1 of Sch.1B, for the purposes of housing costs (see Sch.3) and in the transitional cases referred to above.

The definition of family in s.137(1) of the Contributions and Benefits Act refers to a person being responsible for a child or young person (on which see reg.14). Regulation 15 makes the test of responsibility receipt of child benefit.

In *CIS/2317/2006*, the Commissioner confirmed that the person who is "receiving child benefit" for the purposes of para.(1) is the person who claimed and was awarded that benefit even when that person subsequently paid over a sum equal to the amount of that benefit to another person.

2.132   Similarly in *CJSA/2811/2006* a father who (before separating from the mother) had his name on the child benefit book as an alternative payee under reg.34(1) of the Child Benefit and Guardian's Allowance (Administration) Regulations 2003 and who—with the mother's consent—continued to receive child benefit under her claim following the separation was not "receiving child benefit" for the purpose of the equivalent provision of the JSA Regulations.

In *C2/01–02(IS)(T)*, a Tribunal of Commissioners in Northern Ireland rejected a challenge to the vires of the Northern Ireland equivalent of reg.15(1). The regulation was held not to conflict either with the requirement under art.3 of the Children Order (Northern Ireland) 1995 (equivalent to s.1 of the Children Act 1989) that where a court determines a question with respect to the upbringing of a child, that child's welfare is to be the paramount consideration or with the provisions of the

Northern Ireland Act 1998 which apply the European Convention on Human Rights within the province.

Paragraph (1A)

2.133

If a child (B) for whom a person (A) is responsible gets child benefit for another child (C), (A) is also treated as responsible for (C).

Paragraph (2)

2.134

If no one is receiving child benefit for the child, then if one claim only has been made, the person who made that claim is responsible. Otherwise the person responsible is the person with whom the child usually lives. Since para.(4) refers to consideration of responsibility on the basis of benefit weeks, the test of where a child usually lives should be applied week by week and not on some kind of overall assessment on a long-term basis (*CIS 49/1991*). In the vast majority of cases, however, the question of who is responsible for a child for the purposes of income support will now be determined by who is receiving child benefit. The rules for child benefit include methods of establishing priorities between claimants, and a child benefit claimant can agree that someone with lower priority should be paid it.

Paragraphs (3) and (4)

2.135

Paragraph (4) provides that only one person can be treated as responsible for a child in any one benefit week. There is no provision for dividing up income support where a child spends time in different households. The only exceptions are under para.(3), which allows a person to be treated as responsible for a child for the part of the week in which he is in the household, but only where the child is being looked after by a local authority or is in custody (reg.16(6)). The result of the new test is that if someone else is in receipt of child benefit for a child in any one benefit week, an income support claimant cannot be treated as responsible for that child even if the child spends most of, or even all, his time with the claimant. This may provide for even greater administrative simplicity than the previous test of primary responsibility but at a cost of a lack of justice in certain situations.

In this connection note *R. (Chester) v Secretary of State for Social Security* [2001] EWHC (Admin) 1119, HC, December 7, 2001. The claimant and her husband had separated and a contact order provided that the children should reside with her husband during the week in school term times and with the claimant over the weekends and for half of the school holidays. Both the claimant and her husband applied for child benefit. The Secretary of State awarded child benefit to the husband and the claimant applied for judicial review, relying largely on art.8 of the ECHR (right to respect for family life). Collins J held that the Secretary of State had erred in law because he could have made an award which reflected more closely the division of care (for example, a fairer result could have been achieved by awarding the claimant child benefit for one child for the whole period of the school holidays). Collins J also pointed to the power in reg.34 of the Claims and Payments Regulations under which benefit can be paid to a third party on behalf of a beneficiary. However, the question as to the effect that that would have on the claimant's JSA was left open. Although the actual decision in *Chester* remains good law, Collins J's suggestion that payment of child benefit to only one parent in shared care cases might be capable of amounting to a breach of art.8 of the European Convention on Human Rights (or, possibly, arts 8 and 14 taken together) is impossible to reconcile with the decision of the Court of Appeal in *Carson and Reynolds v Secretary of State for Work & Pensions* [2003] EWCA Civ 797. More recently, in CIS/4003/2001 and CIS/1616/2004, two different Commissioners have confirmed that the failure to make split payments of child benefit does not interfere with a claimant's Convention Rights. In *Hockenjos v Secretary of State for Social Security* [2004] EWCA Civ 1749, the Court of Appeal held (on appeal from CJSA/4890/1998) that reg.77(1)–(3) and (5) of the JSA Regulations (equivalent to paras (1)–(2) and (4)) discriminated against men contrary to art.4 of EC

Directive 79/7 (see Vol.III) and therefore could not be applied to Mr Hockenjos and, by implication, to any man within the personal scope of that Directive—see further the note to reg.77 of the JSA Regulations. Note, however, that although that decision applies to both income-based and contribution-based JSA—see the earlier decision of the Court of Appeal in the same case (*Hockenjos v Secretary of State for Social Security* [2001] EWCA Civ 624; [2001] 2 C.M.L.R. 51; [2001] I.C.R. 966)—it does not apply to income support because that benefit is not within the material scope of the Directive —see *Jackson and Cresswell v Chief Adjudication Officer* (C–63/91 and C–64/91) [1992] E.C.R. I-4737 (also reported as an appendix to *R(IS) 10/91*).

Although Dir.79/7 does not apply to income support, it could be argued—by analogy with *Hockenjos*—that the link between entitlement to IS and child benefit and the "one child one claimant" rule discriminate unlawfully against men contrary to ECHR art.14 and art.1 of Protocol 1. However, the point is probably academic because it has not been possible to make a fresh claim for the child elements of IS since September 7, 2005 (see the commentary to reg.17 below). If unusual circumstances were to occur in which it might benefit a man to make such a claim, it seems probable that any discrimination would be held to be objectively justified: see the decisions of the Supreme Court on the similar (but not identical) rule for child tax credit in *Humphreys v HMRC* [2012] UKSC 18, [2012] AACR 46 and of the Upper Tribunal on the similar (but not identical) rules for housing benefit and council tax benefit in *Camden LBC v NW and SSWP (HB)* [2011] UKUT 262 (AAC).

Circumstances in which a person is to be treated as being or not being a member of the household

2.136

16.—(1) Subject to paragraphs (2) and (5), the claimant and any partner and, where the claimant or his partner is treated as responsible under regulation 15 (circumstances in which a person is to be treated as responsible or not responsible for another) for a child or young person, that child or young person and any child of that child or young person shall be treated as members of the same household [¹notwithstanding that any of them] [⁷is temporarily living away from the other members of his family].

[⁷(2) Paragraph (1) shall not apply to a person who is living away from the other members of his family where—

    (a) that person does not intend to resume living with the other members of his family; or

    (b) his absence from the other members of his family is likely to exceed 52 weeks, unless there are exceptional circumstances (for example the person is in hospital or otherwise has no control over the length of his absence), and the absence is unlikely to be substantially more than 52 weeks.]

(3) Paragraph (1) shall not apply in respect of any member of a couple or of a polygamous marriage where—

    (a) one, both or all of them are patients detained in a hospital provided under section 4 of the National Health Service Act 1977 ([¹²high security psychiatric services]) or [¹⁰section 102 of the National Health Service (Scotland) Act 1978 (state hospitals)]; or

[⁹(b) one, both or all of them are—

      (i) detained in custody pending trial or sentence upon conviction or under a sentence imposed by a court; or

      (ii) on temporary release in accordance with the provisions of the Prison Act 1952 or the Prisons (Scotland) Act 1989;]

(c) [⁶. . .]
(d) the claimant is abroad and does not satisfy the conditions of regulation 4 (temporary absence from Britain); or
(e) one of them is permanently [¹¹ residing in a care home, an Abbeyfield Home or an independent hospital.]

(4) A child or young person shall not be treated as a member of the claimant's household where he is—

[⁵(a) placed with the claimant or his partner by a local authority under [¹⁵ section 22C(2)] of the Children Act 1989 or by a voluntary organisation under section 59(1)(a) of that Act; or

[¹⁴(aa) placed with the claimant or his partner by a local authority under section 81(2) of the Social Services and Well-being (Wales) Act 2014; or]

(b) placed with the claimant or his partner prior to adoption; or]

(c) placed for adoption with the claimant or his partner pursuant to a decision under the Adoption Agencies Regulations 1983 or the Adoption Agencies (Scotland) Regulations 1984.

(5) Subject to paragraph (6), paragraph (1) shall not apply to a child or young person who is not living with the claimant[¹ and who]—

(a) [⁴in a case which does not fall within sub-paragraph (aa),] has been continuously absent from Great Britain for a period of more than four weeks commencing—
  (i) [⁸ subject to paragraph (5A),] where he went abroad before the date of claim for income support, with that date;
  (ii) in any other case,[⁴on the day which immediately follows the day] on which he went abroad; or

[⁴(aa) where regulation 4(3) or paragraph 11A or 12A of Schedule 7 (temporary absence abroad for the treatment of a child or young person) applies, has been continuously absent from Great Britain for a period of more than eight weeks, that period of eight weeks commencing—
  (i) [⁸ subject to paragraph (5A),] where he went abroad before the date of the claim for income support, on the date of that claim;
  (ii) in any other case, on the day which immediately follows the day on which he went abroad; or]

(b) has been an in-patient or in [¹accommodation [¹¹ . . .]] for a continuous period of more than 12 weeks commencing—
  (i) [⁸ subject to paragraph (5A),] where he became an in-patient or, as the case may be, entered that accommodation, before the date of the claim for income support, with that date; or
  (ii) in any other case, with the date on which he became an in-patient or entered that accommodation,
  and, in either case, has not been in regular contact with either the claimant or any member of the claimant's household; or

[⁵(c) is being looked after by a local authority under a relevant enactment; or

(d) has been placed with a person other than the claimant prior to adoption; or]

(e) has been placed for adoption pursuant to a decision under the Adoption Agencies Regulations 1983 or the Adoption Agencies (Scotland) Regulations 1984; or

(f) is detained in custody pending trial or sentence upon conviction or under a sentence imposed by a court.

[⁸(5A) Sub-paragraphs (a)(i), (aa)(i) and (b)(i) of paragraph (5) shall not apply in a case where immediately before the date of claim for income support the claimant was entitled to an income-based jobseeker's allowance.]

(6) A child or young person to whom any of the circumstances mentioned in sub-paragraphs (c) or (f) of paragraph (5) applies shall be treated as being a member of the claimant's household only for that part of any benefit week where that child or young person lives with the claimant.

(7) Where a child or young person for the purposes of attending the educational establishment at which he is receiving relevant education is living with the claimant or his partner and neither one is treated as responsible for that child or young person that child or young person shall be treated as being a member of the household of the person treated as responsible for him and shall not be treated as a member of the claimant's household.

(8) In this regulation—

[¹¹ (za) "accommodation" means accommodation provided by a local authority in a home owned or managed by that local authority—

   (i) under sections 21 to 24 of the National Assistance Act 1948 (provision of accommodation),

   (ii) in Scotland, under section 13B or 59 of the Social Work (Scotland) Act 1968 (provision of residential or other establishment), [¹³ . . .]

   (iii) under section 25 of the Mental Health (Care and Treatment) (Scotland) Act 2003 (care and support services etc.), [¹³ [¹⁴ ...]

   (iv) under section 18 or 19 of the Care Act 2014 (duty and power to meet needs for care and support), [¹⁴ or

   (v) under section 35 or 36 of the Social Services and Well-being (Wales) Act 2014 (duty and power to meet care and support needs of an adult),

where the accommodation is provided for a person whose stay in that accommodation has become other than temporary;]

[⁵(a) "relevant enactment" means the Army Act 1955, the Social Work (Scotland) Act 1968, the Matrimonial Causes Act 1973, the Adoption (Scotland) Act 1978, the Family Law Act 1986 and [¹⁴, the Children Act 1989 and the Social Services and Well-being (Wales) Act 2014];]

   (b) "voluntary organisation" has the meaning assigned to it in the [⁵Children Act 1989] or, in Scotland, the Social Work (Scotland) Act 1968.

AMENDMENTS

1. Income Support (General) Amendment Regulations 1988 (SI 1988/663) reg.8 (April 11, 1988).

2. Income Support (General) Amendment Regulations 1989 (SI 1989/534) reg.3 (April 10, 1989).

3. Income Support (General) Amendment Regulations 1989 (SI 1989/534) Sch.1 para.3 (October 9, 1989).

4. Income Support (General) Amendment Regulations 1990 (SI 1990/547) reg.7 (April 9, 1990).

5. Income Support (General) Amendment Regulations 1992 (SI 1992/468) Sch. para.3 (April 6, 1992). *Note:* The previous form (see the 1991 edition) of sub-paras (4) (a) and (b), (5)(c) and (d) and (8)(a) and (b) remains in force in Scotland. The new form was introduced on April 6, 1992, as a consequence of the Children Act 1989.

6. Social Security Benefits (Amendments Consequential Upon the Introduction of Community Care) Regulations 1992 (SI 1992/3147) Sch.1 para.1 (April 1, 1993).

7. Income-related Benefits Schemes (Miscellaneous Amendments) (No.4) Regulations 1993 (SI 1993/2119) reg.6 (October 4, 1993).

8. Income Support (General) (Jobseeker's Allowance Consequential Amendments) Regulations 1996 (SI 1996/206) reg.8 (October 7, 1996).

9. Income-related Benefits Schemes and Social Fund (Miscellaneous Amendments) Regulations 1996 (SI 1996/1944) reg.6(5) (October 7, 1996).

10. Mental Health (Care and Treatment) (Scotland) Act 2003 (Modification of Subordinate Legislation) Order 2005 (SSI 2005/445) art.2 and Sch. para.3(2) (Scotland) and the Mental Health (Care and Treatment) (Scotland) Act 2003 (Consequential Provisions) Order 2005, (SI 2005/2078) art.15 and Sch.3 para.3(3) (England and Wales) (October 5, 2005).

11. Social Security (Care Homes and Independent Hospitals) Regulations 2005 (SI 2005/2687) reg.2 and Sch.1 para.3 (October 24, 2005).

12. Social Security (Miscellaneous Amendments) (No.4) Regulations 2006 (SI 2006/2378) reg.5(2) (October 2, 2006).

13. Care Act 2014 (Consequential Amendments) (Secondary Legislation) Order 2015 (SI 2015/643) art.2 and Sch. para.5(2) (April 1, 2015).

14. Social Services and Well-being (Wales) Act 2014 and the Regulation and Inspection of Social Care (Wales) Act 2016 (Consequential Amendments) Order 2017 (SI 2017/901) art.2(1) and (3) (November 3, 2017).

15. Social Services and Well-being (Wales) Act 2014 and the Regulation and Inspection of Social Care (Wales) Act 2016 (Consequential Amendments) Order 2017 (SI 2017/901) art.20(1) and (2) (November 3, 2017).

MODIFICATION

With effect from April 8, 2020, para.(3)(b)(ii) is modified by reg.3(1)(a) of the Social Security (Coronavirus) (Prisoners) Regulations 2020 (SI 2020/409). The modification provides that reg.16(3)(b)(ii) is to be read as if the words "the Prison Act 1952 or" were omitted. By reg.6 of SI 2020/409 (as amended by reg.2 of SI 2020/1156), the modification will expire at the end of May 12, 2021.

DEFINITIONS

"child"—see SSCBA s.137(1).
"claimant"—see reg.2(1).
"couple"—*ibid.*
"date of claim"—*ibid.*
"dwelling occupied as the home"—*ibid.*
"partner"—see reg.2(1).
"polygamous marriage"—*ibid.*
"young person"—*ibid.*, and reg.14.

GENERAL NOTE

Paragraph (1)

This provision does two things. The first is to provide that a claimant and partner are deemed to be members of the same household, notwithstanding that they are temporarily apart. Before October 4, 1993, the deeming applied notwithstanding one partner's absence from the dwelling occupied as the home (see below). Since a partner is one of a married or unmarried couple and it is an essential part of the definition of both kinds of couple that the parties should be members of the same household, para.(1) cannot subvert the general meaning of household referred to in the notes to s.137(1) of the Contributions and Benefits Act (see *CIS 671/1992*). Paragraph (1) must only mean that because one partner is temporarily living elsewhere this does not in itself mean that membership of the same household

2.137

ceases. This means that the exceptions in para.(3) perhaps do not achieve much, but probably indicate that those circumstances do terminate membership of the household.

The other thing done by para.(1) is to deem that where an adult is responsible for a child or young person under reg.15, the child or young person is to be treated as in the same household as the adult, notwithstanding that one of them is temporarily living elsewhere (again, before October 4, 1993, the test was absence from the home). After April 6, 2004, this deeming provision is only of relevance in relation to transitional cases (see the notes to reg.15 and reg.17). There are exceptions in paras (4) and (5).

Thus the test under para.(1) is now one of absence from other members of the family, rather than from the home. *CIS 209/1989* held that the old form of para.(1) only applied if there was a dwelling which could be regarded as the home of both partners. This is no longer required, but it is still necessary for the family to have previously lived as members of the same household. The Commissioner in *CIS 508/1992* seems to have accepted that the home need not have been in this country; how this applies to the new test of absence from other members of the family is not entirely clear. Temporarily is not defined and each case will need to be decided on its particular facts. However, adjudicating authorities still need to investigate whether either of the conditions in para.(2) applies. Note in particular *CIS 13805/1996* in the note to para.(2).

The difficulties which can arise when one member of a couple is living temporarily in a residential care home (or in any of the other types of accommodation listed in para.9 of Sch.7) while the other member continues to live at the couple's home were considered by the Commissioner in *CIS/1544/2001*. In those circumstances, para.9 provides that claimant's applicable amount is to be the higher of the applicable amount to which he would be entitled as a member of the couple or the aggregate of the applicable amounts to which he and his partner would be entitled as a single claimant or (in an appropriate case) as a lone parent. Previous DWP Guidance (now replaced—see *DMG Letter 05/02*) stated that for the purpose of carrying out this calculation, each member of the couple was to be treated as a non-dependent of the other. One consequence of this approach was that—under para.13(2)(a)(ii) of Sch.2—neither partner was entitled to the severe disability premium. The Commissioner held that there was no justification for such an approach. As long as the absence was only temporary, the claimant and his wife remained members of the same household by virtue of reg.16(1). Each therefore remained the partner of the other and could not be each other's non-dependant because of reg.3(2)(a). The notional calculation required by the second alternative in para.9 (which treated the couple as if they were single claimants and therefore did imply that they were to be treated as normally living apart) *only* applied for the purpose of calculating the applicable amount. Applying that approach, the claimant was entitled to have the severe disability premium to which his wife would have been entitled as a single claimant normally living on her own, included in her applicable amount.

Paragraph (2)

2.138   Paragraph (1) does not apply where the person living away does not intend to resume living together with the other members of the family or is likely to be away for more than 52 weeks (or longer in exceptional circumstances, provided it is not substantially longer). When either of these conditions applies membership of the same household immediately ceases.

In *CIS 13805/1996* the Commissioner points out that the "not" in para.(2)(a) relates to "intend" rather than "resume". This was significant because it was possible for a person to have no intention one way or the other. For example, where a couple had agreed to live apart for a couple of months, and neither had an intention to resume living with the other, but equally neither had an intention not to do so, para.(2)(a) could apply. This interpretation was further supported by the fact that once an intention not to resume living together had been formed, a separation was no longer temporary and so para.(1) ceased to apply in any event; thus para.(2)(a) would serve no function (other perhaps than to provide a partial definition of "temporary") if it was read as only operating when there was an intention not to resume living together. The facts in *CIS 13805/1996* were that the claimant's husband was in Pakistan. He had applied for permission to enter the UK but it had not yet been granted. They intended to resume living together, as long as permission was granted for the claimant's husband to join her. The Commissioner states that the question therefore was whether such intention counted for the purposes of para.(2)(a). *CIS 508/1992* and *CIS 484/1993* had held in relation to para.4(8) of the former Sch.3 (now para.3(10)) that the intention to return must not be a contingent one. In the Commissioner's view the same interpretation applied for the purposes of para.(2)(a), since there was no material distinction between that provision and para.(2)(a). Thus para.(2)(a) applied because the claimant's intention to resume living in the same household as her husband was not an unqualified one. Therefore the fact that the claimant's husband was in remunerative work did not bar her from entitlement to income support.

Paragraph (3)

Paragraph (1) does not apply in these circumstances, as between partners and polygamous marriages. The intention seems to be that the members of the couple or marriage cease to be partners in these circumstances, but para.(3) does not exactly say so. Under sub-para.(b) a person required to live in a bail hostel is not "detained in custody" pending trial (*R(IS) 17/93*); see Sch.7 para.9 as to how his applicable amount is calculated if he is a member of a couple. However, once a person has been charged, he is detained in custody pending trial, even if subsequently no trial takes place (*R(IS) 1/94*). In *Chief Adjudication Officer v Carr, The Times*, June 2, 1994, also reported as *R(IS) 20/95*, the Court of Appeal held that a person on home leave while serving a prison sentence was not "detained in custody" during the leave period. The definition of "prisoner" in reg.21(3) was amended with effect from April 10, 1995, so as to include periods of temporary release, and sub-para.(b) has now been similarly amended with effect from October 7, 1996.

Paragraph (4)

Children or young persons are not to be members of the household of their foster-parents or the people they are placed with for adoption. They therefore cannot be a member of the family.

Paragraph (5)

Paragraph (1) does not apply to a child or young person who is not living with the claimant when one of heads (a)–(f) applies. Again, the intention seems to be that in these circumstances the child or young person is to be treated as not a member of the household, but para.(5) does not expressly say so. It may be that the general test of membership of the household is relevant. See para.(8) for the meaning of "relevant enactment".

In *Secretary of State for Work & Pensions v Bobezes* [2005] EWCA Civ. 111 CA (Pill & Buxton LJJ and Lord Slynn of Hadley), February 16, 2005 (also reported as *R(IS) 6/05*), the claimant was denied an applicable amount for his 16-year-old step-daughter who was staying temporarily with her grandparents in Portugal. He argued that if he had been British it was probable that the grandparents would have been living in Great Britain with the consequence that para.(5)(a) would not have applied and the general rule in para.(1) would have treated his daughter as continuing to be a member of his household during her temporary absence. The issue before the Commissioner (*CIS/825/2001*) had been whether the fact that income support was a special non-contributory benefit within art.4(2)(a) of Council Regulation 1408/71 (see Vol.III) (and therefore, under art.10a payable "exclusively ... in accordance with the legislation of" Great Britain), prevented Mr Bobezes from arguing that para.(5)(a) therefore discriminated against him indirectly on the grounds of

2.139

2.140

2.141

his Portuguese nationality contrary to art.7 of Council Regulation 1612/68 (see Vol.III). The Commissioner held that it did not but, by the time the case reached the Court of Appeal, it was appreciated that nothing actually turned on this point because, even if Regulation 1408/71 applied to the exclusion of Regulation 1612/68, art.3 of the former Regulation had substantially the same effect as art.7 of the latter.

The issue before the Court of Appeal therefore became whether the jurisprudence of the ECJ required Mr Bobezes to produce detailed statistical evidence, which would not in practice be available, in order to establish discrimination. The Court held that it did not and that, in contrast to the position where discrimination on the ground of sex is alleged, "the Commissioners and the court are entitled to take a broad approach and to find that indirect discrimination is liable to affect a significant number of migrant workers on the ground of nationality without statistical proof being available."

In Mr Bobezes' case, the Court considered that:

> "the proper approach is to compare the children of migrant workers with British children whose families are normally resident here. It is intrinsically likely that significantly more of the former than the latter will be prejudiced by paragraph 16(5) of the Regulation. ..."

and therefore remitted the appeal to a tribunal to decide the question of whether such discrimination could be justified by the Secretary of State. The Tribunal decided that the discrimination could not be justified and the Secretary of State did not appeal against that decision.

Paragraph (6)

2.142   This provision provides a limited exception to para.(5), allowing a claimant to receive benefit for children or young persons being looked after by a local authority or in custody for the days on which they are in the claimant's home.

Paragraph (7)

2.143   This is a special rule where children live away from home while at school.

PART IV

APPLICABLE AMOUNTS

Applicable amounts

2.144   **17.**—Subject to regulations [⁸ 18 to 22A] [¹⁴ . . .] (applicable amounts in other cases and reductions in applicable amounts [¹⁴ . . .]), a claimant's weekly applicable amount shall be the aggregate of such of the following amounts as may apply in his case:

  (a) an amount in respect of himself or, if he is a member of a couple, an amount in respect of both of them, determined in accordance with paragraph 1(1), (2) or (3), as the case may be, of Schedule 2;

  (b) [¹¹ . . .]

  [⁶ (bb) [¹⁰ . . .]]

  (c) [¹¹ . . .]

  (d) the amount of any premiums which may be applicable to him, determined in accordance with Parts III and IV of Schedule 2 (premiums);

  (e) any amounts determined in accordance with Schedule 3 (housing costs) which may be applicable to him in respect of [¹⁵ housing costs as prescribed] in that Schedule.

[¹(f) any amounts determined in accordance with [²paragraphs (2) to (7)].

[² (g) [13 . . .]]

(2) Where—

(a) a claimant has throughout the period beginning on 11th April 1988 and ending immediately before the coming into force of paragraphs 25 to 28 of Schedule 10 (capital to be disregarded) failed to satisfy the capital condition in section 22(6) of the Act (no entitlement to benefit if capital exceeds prescribed amount); and

(b) as a consequence he is not entitled to any transitional addition, special transitional addition or personal expenses addition under Part II of the Transitional Regulations; and

(c) had those paragraphs been in force on 11th April 1988 he would have satisfied that condition and been entitled to any such addition,

the amount applicable under this paragraph shall, subject to paragraph (3) be equal to the amount of any transitional addition, special transitional addition and personal expenses addition to which he would be entitled under Part II of the Transitional Regulations had he been entitled to any such addition in the week commencing 11th April 1988.

(3) For the purposes of paragraph (2), in determining a claimant's total benefit income in his second benefit week for the purpose of calculating the amount of any transitional addition to which he would have been entitled, no account shall be taken of any payment referred to in paragraph (1)(j) of regulation 9 of the Transitional Regulations (total benefit income) which is made in respect of that week to compensate for the loss of entitlement to income support.

(4) Subject to paragraph (6), where—

(a) the claimant or any member of his family was temporarily absent from his home in the claimant's first or second benefit week (or both), because he was—

(i) a patient; or

(ii) outside Great Britain for the purpose of receiving treatment for any disease or bodily or mental disablement or for the purpose of accompanying a child or young person who is outside Great Britain for the purpose of receiving such treatment; or

[¹² (iii) in a care home, an Abbeyfield Home or an independent hospital; or]

(iv) in the care of a local authority under a relevant enactment; or

(v) staying with a person who was contributing to his maintenance; and

(b) as a result—

(i) in the claimant's first benefit week his requirements for the purpose of calculating his entitlement to supplementary benefit were increased or reduced or he was not entitled to that benefit; or

(ii) in the claimant's second benefit week his applicable amount was increased or reduced or he was not entitled to income support; and

(c) the period during which his requirements were, or his applicable amount was, increased or reduced, or he was not entitled to benefit, or any one or more of those circumstances existed, did not exceed eight weeks,

315

the amount applicable under this paragraph (4) shall be equal to the amount determined under paragraph (5).

(5) The amount for the purposes of paragraph (4) shall be an amount equal to the difference between—

(a) the amount that his total benefit income in his first benefit week would have been had he been entitled in respect of that week to supplementary benefit calculated on the basis that he or any member of his family had not been absent from the home; and, if less,

(b) the amount of his total benefit income in the first complete week after the period of temporary absence ends; but for the purpose of calculating his total benefit income in that week—

(i) no account shall be taken of any payment referred to in paragraph (l)(j) of regulation 9 of the Transitional Regulations which is made in respect of that week to compensate for the loss (in whole or in part) of entitlement to income support; and

(ii) if the period of temporary absence ends after the coming into force of paragraph (4), the amount of income support to be taken into account shall, notwithstanding regulation 9(6) of the Transitional Regulations, be calculated as if that paragraph were not in force.

(6) The amount under paragraph (4) shall cease to be applicable to a claimant if he ceases to be entitled to income support for a period exceeding [⁴the permitted period determined in accordance with regulation 3A (permitted period)].

[⁴(6A) For the purposes of paragraph (6), where a claimant has ceased to be entitled to income support because he or his partner is participating in arrangements for training made under section 2 of the Employment and Training Act 1973 [⁵or section 2 of the Enterprise and New Towns (Scotland) Act 1990] or attending a course at an employment rehabilitation centre established under that section [⁵of the 1993 Act], he shall be treated as if he had been entitled to income support for the period during which he or his partner is participating in such arrangements or attending such a course.]

(7) In this Regulation—

"first benefit week" and "second benefit week" have the meanings given to those expressions in regulations 2(1) of the Transitional Regulations and shall also include the week which would have been the claimant's "first benefit week" or, as the case may be, "second benefit week" had he been entitled to supplementary benefit or, as the case may be, income support in that week;

"total benefit income" has, subject to paragraphs (3) and (5)(b), the same meaning as in regulation 9 of the Transitional Regulations;

"Transitional Regulations" means the Income Support (Transitional Regulations 1987.]

AMENDMENTS

1. Income Support (General) Amendment No.2 Regulations 1988 (SI 1988/910) reg.2 (May 30, 1988).

2. Income Support (General) Amendment No.4 Regulations 1988 (SI 1988/1445) Sch.1 para.11 (April 10, 1989).

3. Income Support (General) Amendment Regulations 1989 (SI 1989/534) Sch.1 para.17 (October 9, 1989).

4. Income Support (General) Amendment No.3 Regulations 1989 (SI 1989/1678) reg.4 (October 9, 1989).

5. Enterprise (Scotland) Consequential Amendments Order 1991 (SI 1991/387) art.2 and 9 (April 1, 1991).

6. Social Security Benefits (Amendments Consequential Upon the Introduction of Community Care) Regulations 1992 (SI 1992/3147) reg.2(1) (April 1, 1993).

7. Income-related Benefits Schemes (Miscellaneous Amendments) (No.4) Regulations 1993 (SI 1993/2119) reg.7 (October 4, 1993).

8. Income Support (General) (Jobseeker's Allowance Consequential Amendments) Regulations 1996 (SI 1996/206) reg.9 (October 7, 1996).

9. Social Security Amendment (Residential Care and Nursing Homes) Regulations 2001 (SI 2001/3767) reg.2 and Sch. Pt I para.3 (April 8, 2002).

10. Social Security (Removal of Residential Allowance and Miscellaneous Amendments) Regulations 2003 (SI 2003/1121) reg.2 and Sch.1 para.2 (October 6, 2003).

11. Social Security (Working Tax Credit and Child Tax Credit) (Consequential Amendments) Regulations 2003 (SI 2003 No.455) reg.2 and Sch.1 para.2 (April 6, 2004, except in "transitional cases" and see further the note to reg.17 of the Income Support Regulations).

12. Social Security (Care Homes and Independent Hospitals) Regulations 2005 (SI 2005/2687) reg.2 and Sch.1 para.4 (October 24, 2005).

13. Social Security (Miscellaneous Amendments) Regulations 2006 (SI 2006/588) reg.2(4) (April 3, 2006).

14. Social Security (Miscellaneous Amendments) (No.5) Regulations 2009 (SI 2009/3228) reg.3(2)(a) (January 25, 2010).

15. Loans for Mortgage Interest Regulations 2017 (SI 2017/725) reg.18 and Sch.5 para.2 (April 6, 2018).

DEFINITIONS

"child"—see SSCBA s.137(1).
"claimant"—see reg.2(1).
"couple"—*ibid*.
"family"—see SSCBA s.137(1).
"young person"—see reg.2(1) and reg.14.

GENERAL NOTE

Regulation 17 sets out the individual amounts that are aggregated to calculate the applicable amount. Those amounts fall into four categories, namely: (1) personal allowances under reg.17(a); (2) premiums under reg.17(d); (3) housing costs under reg.17(e); and (4) certain transitional amounts under reg.17(2). There are special rules in regs 18, 21, 21AA and 22A and in Sch.7 for particular categories of claimant, including those in polygamous marriages, those detained in prison or hospital, persons from abroad and those appealing against decisions that they are capable of work.

2.145

Personal allowances

Regulation 17(a) establishes a personal allowance for the claimant, either as a single person or as a member of a couple. The amount of the allowance is specified in Sch.2 para.1 and varies according to the age of the claimant and/or any partner and on whether the claimant or partner is responsible for a child.

2.146

Before April 6, 2004, reg.17(b) and Sch.2 para.2 provided for a further personal allowance for each child or young person who was a member of the family (see s.137(1) of SSCBA 1992 and regs 14–16). On that date, the "child elements" (see below) of IS were withdrawn for all claimants other than those whom this book describes as "transitional cases", namely:

- those who were in receipt of the child elements on April 6, 2004 and have not subsequently been awarded CTC; and

- those claimants whose families included a child or young person on April 6, 2004, who have not been awarded CTC and who made a new claim for income support or income-based JSA after that date but before September 8, 2005.

See reg.1(2), (3) and (4) of the Social Security (Working Tax Credit and Child Tax Credit) (Consequential Amendments) Regulations 2003 (SI 2003/455), the text of which is analysed below and set out later in this volume.

That withdrawal was the start of a process, under which it was intended that all financial support for children and young persons would be transferred from IS or JSA to child tax credit ("CTC"). However, that process has yet to be completed and, it now seems, never will be. As a result, any claimant who is a transitional case continues to be entitled to the child elements when the applicable amount is calculated.

2.147   What this commentary describes as the "child elements" (and what legislation has taken to describing—incorrectly—as the "child premia") are:

- the additional personal allowance for each child or young person who is a member of the claimant's family (see above);

- the family premium (Sch.2 para.3);

- the enhanced disability premium in respect of a child or young person (Sch.2 para.13A); and

- the disabled child premium (Sch.2 para.14).

The use of the phrase "child premia" to describe those elements is incorrect because a personal allowance for a child or young person is not a "premium" and because, in any event, the plural of "premium" is "premiums", not "premia" (see, e.g. para.12 of Sch.2 to the Income Support Regulations where the correct word is used). The transitional text of Sch.2 paras 3, 13A and 14, and the current rates of the child elements are given in the commentary to Sch.2.

Section 1(3)(d) of the Tax Credits Act 2002 abolishes the child elements. It was originally intended to complete the process of transfer by April 6, 2005 (see art.2(5) of the Tax Credits Act 2002 (Commencement No.4, Transitional and Savings) Order 2003 (SI 2003/962) which brought s.1(3)(d) into force on that date) but that did not happen. The second target date of December 31, 2006 (SI 2005/1106) was also missed, as was the third target date of December 31, 2008 (SI 2006/3369), the fourth on December 31, 2011 (SI 2008/3151) and the fifth on December 31, 2014 (SI 2011/2910). On July 14, 2014, the Tax Credits Act 2002 (Commencement and Transitional Provisions)(Partial Revocation) Order 2014 (SI 2014/1848) revoked art.2(5) of SI 2003/962 with the result that there is no longer any date fixed for s.1(3)(d) to come into force. It appears (see, e.g. the explanatory note to SI 2014/1848) that it is no longer intended to complete the transfer. As part of the transition to universal credit, CTC was abolished (subject to savings) on February 1, 2019 (see s.33(1)(f) of the Welfare Reform Act 2012 and the Welfare Reform Act 2012 (Commencement No. 32 and Savings and Transitional Provisions) Order 2019 (SI 2019/167) in Vol.V) and IS and JSA are in the process of being abolished. The current position will eventually be resolved by that abolition or possibly—given the rate at which universal credit is being introduced—by the fact that all the children and young persons for whom transitional cases are responsible, have grown up.

In the meantime, the current position is governed by reg.1(2), (3) and (4) of SI 2003/455 and appears to be as follows:

- for claimants who did not have a child or young person who was a member of their family before April 6, 2004, para.(b) of reg.17 (and also reg.18(b) and paras 2, 14 and the relevant parts of para.13A of Sch.2) was revoked with effect from April 6, 2004 (reg.1(4) of SI 2003/455);

- for claimants who had a child or young person who was a member of their family and who were (or whose partners were) in receipt of CTC prior to April 6, 2004, para.(b) of reg.17 (and also reg.18(b) and paras 2, 14 and the relevant parts of para.13A of Sch.2) was revoked with effect from April 6, 2004 (reg.1(2) of SI 2003/455). From the first day of the first benefit week beginning on or after that date, such claimants are not entitled to the child elements;

- for claimants who have a child or young person who is a member of their family and who were not (and whose partners were not) in receipt of CTC prior to April 6, 2004 but who subsequently became (or whose partners subsequently became) entitled to CTC in respect of a period which precedes that date (i.e. under reg.7 of the Tax Credits (Claims and Notifications) Regulations 2002—see Vol.IV), reg.7 of SI 2003/455 (which provides that, subject to limited disregards, CTC counts as income for income support purposes between April 7, 2003 and April 6, 2004) applies from the first day of the first benefit week beginning on or after the commencement date of the CTC award. (This may mean that there will have been an overpayment for the period before CTC was awarded which, it would seem, would be recoverable under s.74(1) of the Administration Act.) For such claimants, para.(b) of reg.17 (and the other provisions referred to above) are revoked with effect from April 6, 2004 (reg.1(2) of SI 2003/455) with the same consequences as are set out in the previous paragraph;

- for claimants who have a child or young person who is a member of their family and who are in receipt of income support but have not been awarded (and whose partners have not been awarded) CTC as at April 6, 2004 and who do not subsequently become entitled to CTC for a period which begins before that date, para.(b) of reg.17 (and the other provisions referred to above) remain in force until CTC is awarded. They are then revoked with effect from the first day of the first benefit week beginning on or after the day on which the CTC award begins. Claimants in this category to whom a child is born (or otherwise becomes a member of the family) after April 6, 2017 may be affected by the "two-child limit" imposed by the Social Security (Restrictions on Amounts for Children and Qualifying Young Persons) Amendment Regulations 2017 (SI 2017/376), below;

- since September 8, 2005, claimants who have a child or young person who is a member of their family but who were not in receipt of income support before April 6, 2004 can no longer make a new claim for income support and be awarded the child elements on that claim (see the amendments to SI 2003/455 by SI 2005/2294 with effect from that date); and

- it is unclear whether such a claimant could have made a new claim for income support between April 7, 2004 and September 7, 2005 and be awarded the child elements on that claim (although the better view is that he or she would have been entitled to do so). For a discussion of this point, which is now of merely historical interest, see pp.275–276 of Vol.II of the 2005 edition.

Until October 5, 2003, claimants living in residential care homes or nursing homes also received a "residential allowance" under para.(bb) (for further details, see pp.486–488 of Vol.II of the 2003 edition). With effect from October 6, 2003, para.(bb) was revoked and residential allowances abolished. All financial help with the costs of care is now provided by local authority social services departments.

Premiums

The second main category covers premiums. The former family premium under paragraph (c) (payable if the claimant's family included a child or a young person) was also abolished with effect from April 6, 2004 subject to the same transitional provisions.

2.148

The other premiums are in Pts III and IV of Sch.2.

Housing Costs

2.149   The third category covers housing costs, set out in Sch.3. Note reg.13(1) of the Decisions and Appeals Regulations 1999 (see Vol.III of this series).

Transitional amounts

2.150   The fourth category, in sub-para.(f), covers transitional protection for a number of groups. Sub-para.(f) first deals with those assisted by paras 25–28 of Sch.10 on disregarded capital, which were inserted from May 30, 1988. The details are in paras (2) and (3). Sub-paragraph (f) secondly deals with groups who lost out on the ordinary transitional protection because of temporary absence from home around April 11, 1988. Here the details are in paras (4)–(6).

Paragraphs (2) and (3) apply where a person was continuously excluded from entitlement to income support by the capital rule before the additional disregards were added with effect from May 30, 1988. If the person would have satisfied the capital rule on April 11, 1988, if those disregards had been in the regulations and would have been entitled to some transitional protection, then the amount of that protection is applicable from May 30, 1988. There is no statutory provision for filling the gap between April 11 and May 30, but extra-statutory payments were made. The effect of para.(3) is that in doing the calculations of total benefit income in the second benefit week around April 11, any extra-statutory payment is to be ignored.

Paragraphs (4)–(6A): where the calculation of total benefit income in either the first or second benefit week is affected by a person's temporary absence from home (for one of the reasons set out in para.(4)(a)), then the calculation can be done as if the person was still at home. The absence must not exceed eight (or sometimes 12) weeks (para.(4)(c)) and the addition applied will cease if there is a subsequent break in entitlement of more than eight (or sometimes 12) weeks (para.(6)).

Polygamous marriages

2.151   **18.**—[¹(1) Subject to paragraph (2) and [⁹regulations 21] [⁸ to 22A] [¹³ . . .] (applicable amounts in other cases and reductions in applicable amounts [¹³ . . .]), where a claimant is a member of a polygamous marriage his weekly applicable amount shall be the aggregate of such of the following amounts as may apply in his case:

(a) the highest amount applicable to him and one of his partners determined in accordance with paragraph 1(3) of Schedule 2 as if he and that partner were a couple;

(b) an amount equal to the differences between the amounts specified in [⁸sub-paragraph (3)(d)] [⁴and (1)(e)] of paragraph 1 of Schedule 2 in respect of each of his other partners;

(c) [¹¹ . . .]

[⁶ (cc) [¹⁰ . . .]]

(d) [¹¹ . . .]

(e) the amount of any premiums which may be applicable to him determined in accordance with Parts III and IV of Schedule 2 (premiums);

(f) any amounts determined in accordance with Schedule 3 (housing costs) which may be applicable to him in respect of [¹⁵ housing costs as prescribed] in that Schedule.

[²(g) any amount determined in accordance with regulation 17(1)(f) (applicable amounts);]

[³(h) [¹² . . .]]

[¹(2) In the case of a partner who is aged less than 18, the amount which applies in respect of that partner shall be nil unless—

(a) that partner is treated as responsible for a child, or [⁸(b) that partner is a person who—

   (i) had he not been a member of a polygamous marriage would have qualified for income support under regulation 4ZA; or

   (ii) satisfies the requirements of section 3(1)(f)(iii) of the Jobseekers Act 1995 (prescribed circumstances for persons aged 16 but less than 18); or

   (iii) is the subject of a direction under section 16 of the Jobseekers Act 1995 (persons under 18: severe hardship).]

AMENDMENTS

1. Income Support (General) Amendment No.3 Regulations 1988 (SI 1988/1228) reg.5 (September 9, 1988).

2. Income Support (General) Amendment No.4 Regulations 1988 (SI 1988/1445) reg.6 (September 9, 1988).

3. Income Support (General) Amendment No.4 Regulations 1988 (SI 1988/1445) Sch.1 para.12 (April 10, 1989).

4. Family Credit and Income Support (General) Amendment Regulations 1989 (SI 1989/1034) reg.5 (July 10, 1989)

5. Income Support (General) Amendment Regulations 1989 (SI 1989/534) Sch.1 para.17 (October 9, 1989).

6. Social Security Benefits (Amendments Consequential Upon the Introduction of Community Care) Regulations 1992 (SI 1992/3147) reg.2(1) (April 1, 1993).

7. Income-related Benefits Schemes (Miscellaneous Amendments) (No.4) Regulations 1993 (SI 1993/2119) reg.8 (October 4, 1993).

8. Income Support (General) (Jobseeker's Allowance Consequential Amendments) Regulations 1996 (SI 1996/206) reg.10 (October 7, 1996).

9. Social Security Amendment (Residential Care and Nursing Homes) Regulations 2001 (SI 2001/3767) reg.2 and Sch. Pt I para.4 (April 8, 2002).

10. Social Security (Removal of Residential Allowance and Miscellaneous Amendments) Regulations 2003 (SI 2003/1121) reg.2 and Sch.1 para.3 (October 6, 2003).

11. Social Security (Working Tax Credit and Child Tax Credit) (Consequential Amendments) Regulations 2003 (SI 2003 No.455) reg.2 and Sch.1 para.3 (April 6, 2004, except in "transitional cases" and see further the note to reg.17 of the Income Support Regulations).

12. Social Security (Miscellaneous Amendments) Regulations 2006 (SI 2006/588) reg.2(4) (April 3, 2006).

13. Social Security (Miscellaneous Amendments) (No.5) Regulations 2009 (SI 2009/3228) reg.3(2)(b) (January 25, 2010).

14. Loans for Mortgage Interest Regulations 2017 (SI 2017/725) reg.18 and Sch.5 para.2 (April 6, 2018).

DEFINITIONS

"the Act"—see reg.2(1).
"child"—see SSCBA s.137(1).
"claimant"—see reg.2(1).
"couple"—*ibid.*
"partner"—*ibid.*
"polygamous marriage"—*ibid.*
"young person"—*ibid.*, and reg.14.

GENERAL NOTE

2.152   Regulation 18 contains special rules for polygamous marriages, but not for other kinds of relationships. There the ordinary living together as husband and wife rule in s.137(1) of the Contributions and Benefits Act (1986 Act s.20(11)) applies.

Applicable amounts for persons in residential care and nursing homes

2.153   **19.**—[¹ . . .]

AMENDMENT

1. Social Security Amendment (Residential Care and Nursing Homes) Regulations 2001 (SI 2001/3767) reg.2 and Sch. Pt I para.5 (April 8, 2002).

GENERAL NOTE

2.154   The revocation of reg.19 abolished the system of "preserved rights" for those who were resident in a nursing or residential care home on March 31, 1993 (i.e. immediately before the introduction of care in the community). For details of the operation of that system see pp.255–265 of Vol.II of the 2001 edition.

Applicable amounts for persons on board and lodging accommodation and hostels

2.155   **20.**—[¹. . .]

AMENDMENT

1. Income Support (General) Amendment Regulations 1989 (SI 1989/534) Sch.1 para.4 (October 9, 1989).

Special cases

2.156   **21.**—(1) Subject to [²⁷paragraph (1B)] [²¹[²⁵regulation 21ZB] (treatment of refugees) and][¹⁹regulation 22A] (reductions in applicable amounts) in the case of a person to whom any paragraph in column (1) of Schedule 7 applies (applicable amounts in special cases), the amount included in the claimant's weekly amount in respect of him shall be the amount prescribed in the corresponding paragraph in column (2) of that Schedule [³⁰ . . .].
      [⁶ (1A) [³⁷ . . .]]
      [²⁷(1B)[²⁹. . .[²⁸ . . .]]]
      (2) [³⁵ . . .]
      (3) [¹⁸ [³¹ ³⁶ In Schedule 7]
      [²⁵. . .]
      [²⁵"partner of a person subject to immigration control" means a person—
          (i)   who is not subject to immigration control within the meaning of section 115(9) of the Immigration and Asylum Act; or
         (ii)   to whom section 115 of that Act does not apply by virtue of regulation 2 of the Social Security (Immigration and Asylum) Consequential Amendments Regulations 2000; and
        (iii)   who is a member of a couple and [³⁴ the member's] partner is subject to immigration control within the meaning of section 115(9) of that Act and section 115 of that Act applies to [³⁴ the partner] for the purposes of exclusion from entitlement to income support;]
      [¹⁴ ³⁶ "person from abroad" has the meaning given in regulation 21AA;]
      "patient" means a person (other than a prisoner) who is regarded as receiv-

ing free in-patient treatment within the meaning of [[35] regulation 2(4) and (5) of the Social Security (Hospital In-Patients) Regulations 2005]; [[16]"prisoner" means a person who—

(a) is detained in custody pending trial or sentence upon conviction or under a sentence imposed by a court; or

(b) is on temporary release in accordance with the provisions of the Prison Act 1952 or the Prisons (Scotland) Act 1989,

other than a person [[23] who is detained in hospital under the provisions of the Mental Health Act 1983, or, in Scotland, under the provisions of the [[32] Mental Health (Care and Treatment) (Scotland) Act 2003] or the Criminal Procedure (Scotland) Act 1995;]]

[[38] (3ZA) In Schedule 7 "person serving a sentence of imprisonment detained in hospital" means a person ("P") who satisfies either of the following conditions.

(3ZB) The first condition is that—

(a) P is being detained under section 45A or 47 of the Mental Health Act 1983 (power of higher courts to direct hospital admission; removal to hospital of persons serving sentences of imprisonment etc.); and

(b) in any case where there is in relation to P a release date within the meaning of section 50(3) of that Act, P is being detained on or before the day which the Secretary of State certifies to be that release date.

(3ZC) The second condition is that P is being detained under—

(a) section 59A of the Criminal Procedure (Scotland) Act 1995 (hospital direction); or

(b) section 136 of the Mental Health (Care and Treatment) (Scotland) Act 2003 (transfer of prisoners for treatment of mental disorder).

[[33] . . .]
[[18 36] . . .]
[[31 36] . . .]
[[33] . . .]

(5) A claimant to whom paragraph 19 of Schedule 7 (disability premium) applies shall be entitled to income support for the period in respect of which that paragraph applies to him notwithstanding that his partner was also entitled to income support for that same period.

AMENDMENTS

1. Income Support (General) Amendment No.4 Regulations 1988 (SI 1988/1445) Sch.1 para.1 (April 10, 1989).

2. Income Support (General) Amendment Regulations 1989 (SI 1989/534) Sch.1 para.5 (October 9, 1989).

3. Income Support (General) Amendment Regulations 1990 (SI 1990/547) reg.8 (April 9, 1990).

4. Income Support (General and Transitional) Amendment Regulations 1990 (SI 1990/2324) reg.2 (December 17, 1990).

5. Income Support (General) Amendment Regulations 1991 (SI 1991/236) reg.7 (April 8, 1991).

6. Income Support (General) Amendment (No.3) Regulations 1991 (SI 1991/1033) reg.2 (May 20, 1991).

7. Income Support (General) Amendment (No.5) Regulations 1991 (SI 1991/1656) reg.2 (August 12, 1991).

8. Income-related Benefits Schemes (Miscellaneous Amendments) (No.3) Regulations 1992 (SI 1992/2155) reg.15 (October 5, 1992).

9. Social Security Benefits (Amendments Consequential Upon the Introduction of Community Care) Regulations 1992 (SI 1992/3147) Sch.1 para.3 (April 1, 1993).

10. Social Security Benefits (Miscellaneous Amendments) Regulations 1993 (SI 1993/518) reg.5 (April 1, 1993).

11. Income-related Benefits Schemes (Miscellaneous Amendments) Regulations 1993 (SI 1993/315) reg.4 (April 12, 1993).

12. Income-related Benefits Schemes (Miscellaneous Amendments) (No.4) Regulations 1993 (SI 1993/2119) reg.10 (October 4, 1993).

13. Income-related Benefits Schemes (Miscellaneous Amendments) Regulations 1994 (SI 1994/527) reg.3 (April 11, 1994).

14. Income-related Benefits Schemes (Miscellaneous Amendments) (No.3) Regulations 1994 (SI 1994/1807) reg.4(1) (August 1, 1994).

15. Income-related Benefits Schemes (Miscellaneous Amendments) (No.5) Regulations 1994 (SI 1994/2139) reg.25 (October 3, 1994).

16. Income-related Benefits Schemes (Miscellaneous Amendments) Regulations 1995 (SI 1995/516) reg.21 (April 10, 1995).

17. Social Security (Persons from Abroad) Miscellaneous Amendments Regulations 1996 (SI 1996/30) reg.8(2) (February 5, 1996).

18. Income-related Benefits (Montserrat) Regulations 1996 (SI 1996/2006) reg.4 (August 28, 1996).

19. Income Support (General) (Jobseeker's Allowance Consequential Amendments) Regulations 1996 (SI 1996/206) reg.12 (October 7,1996).

20. Income-related Benefits Schemes and Social Fund (Miscellaneous Amendments) Regulations 1996 (SI 1996/1944) reg.6(6) (October 7, 1996).

21. Income Support and Social Security (Claims and Payments) (Miscellaneous Amendments) Regulations 1996 (SI 1996/2431) reg.2 (October 15, 1996).

22. Income Support (General) Amendment (No.3) Regulations 1996 (SI 1996/2614) reg.2 (November 8, 1996).

23. Social Security (Miscellaneous Amendments) Regulations 1998 (SI 1998/563) reg.8(1) and (2)(c)(i) (April 6, 1998).

24. Social Security (Miscellaneous Amendments) Regulations 1998 (SI 1998/563) reg.18(3) and (4)(c) (April 6, 1998).

25. Social Security (Immigration and Asylum) Consequential Amendments Regulations 2000 (SI 2000/636) reg.3(4)(a) (April 3, 2000).

26. Income-related Benefits and Jobseeker's Allowance (Amendment) Regulations 2000 (SI 2000/979) reg.2 (May 2, 2000).

27. Social Security Amendment (Residential Care and Nursing Homes) Regulations 2001 (SI 2001/3767) reg.2 and Sch. Pt I para.6 (April 8, 2002).

28. Social Security (Removal of Residential Allowance and Miscellaneous Amendments) Regulations 2003 (SI 2003/1121) reg.2 and Sch.1 para.4 (October 6, 2003).

29. Social Security (Third Party Deductions and Miscellaneous Amendments) Regulations 2003 (SI 2003/2325) reg.3 (October 6, 2003).

30. Social Security (Working Tax Credit and Child Tax Credit) (Consequential Amendments) Regulations 2003 (SI 2003 No.455) reg.2 and Sch.1 para.4 (April 6, 2004), except in "transitional cases" and see further the note to reg.17 of the Income Support Regulations.

31. Social Security (Habitual Residence) Amendment Regulations 2004 (SI 2004/1232) reg.3 (May 1, 2004).

32. Mental Health (Care and Treatment) (Scotland) Act 2003 (Modification of Subordinate Legislation) Order 2005 (SSI 2005/445) art.2 and Sch. para.3(3) (Scotland); Mental Health (Care and Treatment) (Scotland) Act 2003 (Consequential Provisions) Order 2005 (SI 2005/2078) art.15 and Sch.2 para.3(4) (England and Wales) (October 5, 2005).

33. Social Security (Care Homes and Independent Hospitals) Regulations 2005 (SI 2005/2687) reg.2 and Sch.1 para.5 (October 24, 2005).

34 Civil Partnership (Pensions, Social Security and Child Support) (Consequential, etc. Provisions) Order 2005 (SI 2005/2877) art.2(3) and Sch.3 para.13(3) (December 5, 2005).

35. Social Security (Hospital In-Patients) Regulations 2005 (SI 2005/3360) reg.4 (April 10, 2006).

36. Social Security (Persons from Abroad) Amendment Regulations 2006 (SI 1026/2006) reg.6(2) (April 30, 2006).

37. Social Security (Miscellaneous Amendments) Regulations 2009 (SI 2009/583) reg.2(1) and (5) (April 6, 2009).

38. Social Security (Persons Serving a Sentence of Imprisonment Detained in Hospital) Regulations 2010 (SI 2010/442) reg.3(1) and (2) (March 25, 2010).

MODIFICATION

The definition of "prisoner" in para.(3) is modified with effect from April 8, 2020 by reg.2(1) and (2)(a) of the Social Security (Coronavirus) (Prisoners) Regulations 2020 (SI 2020/409). The modification provides that the IS Regulations "are to be read as if the definition of 'prisoner' did not include a person on temporary release in accordance with the provisions of the Prison Act 1952". By reg.6 of SI 2020/409 (as amended by reg.2 of SI 2020/1156), the modification will expire at the end of May 12, 2021.

DEFINITIONS

"child"—see SSCBA s.137(1).
"claimant"—see reg.2(1).
"local authority"—*ibid.*
"residential care home"—*ibid.*, and reg.19(3).
"young person"—*ibid.*, and reg.14.

GENERAL NOTE

Paragraph (1)
Applicable amounts in special cases are to be as prescribed in Sch.7. Regulation 21ZB was revoked with effect from June 14, 2007. However, the reference to that regulation in para.(1) has yet to be revoked.

2.157

Claimants without accommodation
Under para.6 of Sch.7 a person "without accommodation" is only entitled to a personal allowance for himself (or the allowance for a couple, if he is a member of a couple). In *R(IS) 23/98* the claimant had lived in his car for approximately two weeks. He was refused a disability premium as part of his income support. The Commissioner decides that a car could not be regarded as accommodation in the context of para.6. He approved of the following description of accommodation in para.29503 of the *Adjudication Officer's Guide*: "An effective shelter from the elements which is capable of being heated; and in which the occupants can sit, lie down, cook and eat; and which is reasonably suited for continuous occupation". While there is force in the Commissioner's reasoning in relation to a car, his (obiter) view that an ordinary tent or touring caravan may not constitute accommodation is more surprising (particularly in the light of the AO's concession to the contrary). It is suggested that the AO's distinction between a car as a means of transport and a tent (or caravan) as a means of shelter is correct. In this connection, note also para.17(1)(f) of Sch.3 under which payments in respect of a tent count as allowable housing costs (without any restriction as to the kind of tent).

2.158

In *R. (M) v Secretary of State for Work and Pensions* [2008] UKHL 63, (Lords Hope, Rodger, Walker, Mance and Neuberger) rejected an argument that the refusal of premiums to a person without accommodation constituted unlawful discrimination contrary to ECHR, art.14 and art.1 of the First Protocol ("A1P1") on the basis that:

"(a) RJM's claim that he has wrongfully been deprived of disability premium falls, in principle, within the ambit of A1P1, and therefore of article 14;

(b) The discrimination of which RJM claims is based on his homelessness, which is an "other status" for the purposes of article 14;

(c) However, the discrimination of which RJM complains has been justified by the Secretary of State".

The justification put forward by the Secretary of State and accepted by the House was as follows (per Lord Neuberger, with whom all their Lordships agreed):

"50. First, the Secretary of State takes the view that he should encourage the disabled homeless, who are "in a vulnerable position" to seek shelter, and therefore help, rather than rendering it easier, at least in financial terms, for them to remain without accommodation. It appears that 90% of those without accommodation in this country have problems connected with substance abuse and around 45% have mental health problems. Those who are disabled need, or at least would benefit from, accommodation, as indeed is reflected by the fact that they are included among those who are accorded priority need for housing under the Housing Acts (the 1985 Act when disability premium was introduced, and now the 1996 Act). As Mr Johnson [counsel for the Secretary of State] explains,

'In the government's view, helping homeless people into accommodation is a much more effective way of helping them than handing out money through the disability premium.'

"51. Secondly, the Secretary of State considers that the disabled are less likely to need a supplement if they are without accommodation than if they are not. This view is based on the proposition that, while the disability premium was not precisely calculated by reference to specific needs, much of it would be spent on heating and other household expenses, items which would not be required by someone without accommodation. Mr Johnson says that "claimants in accommodation have a range of expenses and financial pressures related to that accommodation that claimants without accommodation do not have".

The House of Lords also held that the Court of Appeal had not been bound to follow its earlier decision in *Campbell v South Northamptonshire DC* [2004] EWCA Civ 409 that income-related benefits did not constitute "possessions" within A1P1, given the subsequent decision to the contrary by the Grand Chamber of the European Court of Human Rights in *Stec v UK*.

Members of religious orders

2.159   Under para.7 of Sch.7 a claimant "who is a member of and fully maintained by a religious order" has an applicable amount of nil and is therefore not entitled to IS. In *CSPC/677/2007*, the Commissioner considered the position of 12 Carmelite nuns. The monastery in which they lived was "self-maintaining", i.e. the nuns paid all their income into a central account and their living expenses were met from that account. To the extent that a nun's living expenses were less than her contributions to the account, they were met by the contributions of the other nuns. There was no support from the wider Carmelite order and, if its members were unable to support each other, the monastery would have to close. It was held that the legislation did not draw any distinction between self-maintaining, and other, religious communities. Ministerial suggestions to the contrary were "unfortunate". Moreover, as the arrangements for the *maintenance* of the nuns were the same in each case, it was not possible to distinguish between those nuns who had income, and were therefore able to contribute that income to the community were to be ignored for the purpose of deciding whether a claimant was "fully maintained" by a religious order.

The issue whether the exclusion from benefit of those who are fully maintained by religious orders amounts to unlawful discrimination contrary to the ECHR has been reconsidered by a three-judge panel of the Upper Tribunal (Walker J, CP,

Judges Pacey and Jacobs) following the decision of the House of Lords in *M* (see above). (The issue had been considered in *CSPC/677/2007* but, at that time, the Commissioner was bound by the decisions of the Court of Appeal in the *Campbell* case and *M* ([2007] EWCA Civ 614) that that income-related benefits did not constitute "possessions" within A1P1: see above under *Claimants without accommodation*.) The Upper Tribunal held that the claimants were not "victims" within s.7(1) of the Human Rights Act 1998 because the discriminatory effect of the exclusion could be removed without conferring any advantage on them. As proceedings under the Act may only be brought by a "victim", it was unnecessary to consider any other Human Rights issues.

Temporarily separated couples
On para.9 of Sch.7 see *CIS 1544/2001* in the notes to reg.16(1). 2.160

Paragraph (1A)
Until it was revoked on April 6, 2009, this provision provided that, except where 2.161
the particular paragraph of Sch.7 expressly allows the payment of a premium, a person whose entitlement falls under Sch.7 does not qualify for the severe disability premium.

The effect of the revocation is not entirely clear. If para.(1A) ever performed a function, revocation would mean that some special cases have become entitled to a severe disability premium even though no such entitlement is conferred by Sch.7. However, the better view is that para.(1A) was always otiose. Regulations 17 and 18 are expressly subject to reg.21 and para.(1) makes it clear that for all special cases, the applicable amount "shall be" the amount specified in Sch.7 (i.e. that amount and no other).

Paragraph (3)
This paragraph contains some important definitions for Sch.7, which are also 2.162
referred to in other parts of the Regulations.

"Partner of a person subject to immigration control"
For a discussion of "person subject to immigration control" see the notes 2.163
to the Social Security (Immigration and Asylum) Consequential Amendments Regulations 2000 (SI 2000/636). In *CIS 1159/2004*, the claimant had been entitled to the severe disability premium under para.13(2)(a) of Sch.2. Subsequently his wife, who was a person subject to immigration control, came to live with him and he therefore became a "partner of a person subject to immigration control". The consequence was that whilst he retained his own personal allowance, he could not claim for his wife because, under para.16A of Sch.7, her personal allowance was nil. Ms Commissioner Fellner held that despite this circumstance, his wife was still the claimant's "partner" as defined by reg.2(1) with the effect that—as she herself was not entitled to the severe disability premium—para.13(2)(b) of Sch.2 disentitled the claimant to the premium. The Commissioner also rejected the claimant's argument that the SDP provisions were ultra vires.

"Patient"
See the commentary to the Social Security (Hospital In-Patients) Regulations 2.164
2005 in Vol.I.

"Prisoner"
A person is detained in custody pending trial once he has been charged. It does 2.165
not matter that in fact no trial takes place because the proceedings are discontinued. For the period he was in custody he was a prisoner (*R(IS) 1/94*). However, a person required to live in a bail hostel is not detained in custody pending trial (*R(IS) 17/93*); see Sch.7 para.9 as to how his applicable amount is calculated if he is a member of a couple.

Sub-paragraph (b) of the definition has been added to reverse the effect of *Chief Adjudication Officer v Carr, The Times*, June 2, 1994, also reported as *R(IS) 20/95*. A person on temporary release will now continue to count as a prisoner and will not be eligible for income support.

For the rules regarding prisoners who are detained in hospital under the Mental Health Act 1983, the Criminal Procedure (Scotland) Act 1995 or the Mental Health (Care and Treatment) (Scotland) Act 2003, see *Person serving a sentence of imprisonment detained in hospital* below.

Person serving a sentence of imprisonment detained in hospital

2.166   Paragraphs (3ZA)–(3ZC) were introduced to reverse the decision of the Court of Appeal (Waller, Carnwath and Patten LJJ) in *R(RD & PM) v SSWP* [2010] EWCA Civ 18. In that case, the appellants were "post-tariff lifers", i.e. prisoners serving a mandatory term of life imprisonment whose "tariff" sentences had expired but who had not been released on licence. By the time under consideration, they had been transferred to psychiatric hospitals under s.47 of the Mental Health Act 1983 and were prevented from applying to the Parole Board for release. Under the previous version of Sch.7 para.(2A), a s.47 patient had an applicable amount of nil "but not if his detention continues after ... *the earliest date on which he could have been released* in respect of, or from, the prison sentence if he had not been detained in hospital" (emphasis added). The Court of Appeal held that, in relation to those serving a life sentence, the italicised words referred to the date on which the prisoner's tariff expired and the Parole Board was first able to direct release and not, as the High Court had held ([2008] EWHC 2635 (Admin), para.48), the first date on which the prisoner was entitled to be released (which in the case of a prisoner serving a life sentence was never). The effect was that a post-tariff lifer who was compulsorily removed to a hospital under s.47 became eligible for income support at the normal rate applicable to him as soon as his tariff expired. The amendments from March 25, 2010, reverse that result by amending para.2A of Sch.7 to create a new category of *Person serving a sentence of imprisonment detained in hospital* with an applicable amount of nil. Paragraphs (3ZA)–(3ZC) then define that category in terms which include any claimant who is detained in hospital under either s.45A or s.47 of the Mental Health Act until his or her "release date" as defined by s.50(3) of that Act. That section is in the following terms:

"(3)   In this section, references to a person's release date are to the day (if any) on which he would be entitled to be released (whether unconditionally or on licence) from any prison or other institution in which he might have been detained if the transfer direction had not been given; and in determining that day there shall be disregarded—

(a)   any powers that would be exercisable by the Parole Board if he were detained in such a prison or other institution, and
(b)   any practice of the Secretary of State in relation to the early release under discretionary powers of persons detained in such a prison or other institution."

As prisoners serving a life sentence are never "entitled" to be released, the effect is to exclude them from entitlement to IS while they are detained in hospital.

Note, finally, that in *R(EM) v SSWP* [2010] EWCA Civ 18 (which was heard together with *RD & PM*) the Court of Appeal rejected an argument that to exclude those detained under ss.45A and 47 (who are detained in hospital in addition to a prison sentence) from benefit that was payable to claimants detained under s.37 (who are detained in hospital instead of a prison sentence) constituted unlawful discrimination contrary to art.14 of, and art.1 of the First Protocol to, ECHR taken together. Neither does the introduction of the exclusion with effect from April 10, 2006 (in the Social Security (Hospital In-Patients) Regulations 2005) amount to the deprivation of a possession contrary to art.1 of the First Protocol taken on its own: see *JB v SSWP (IS)* [2010] UKUT 263 (AAC).

[¹ Special cases: supplemental—persons from abroad

21AA.—(1) "Person from abroad" means, subject to the following provisions of this regulation, a claimant who is not habitually resident in the United Kingdom, the Channel Islands, the Isle of Man or the Republic of Ireland.

2.167

(2) No claimant shall be treated as habitually resident in the United Kingdom, the Channel Islands, the Isle of Man or the Republic of Ireland unless he has a right to reside in (as the case may be) the United Kingdom, the Channel Islands, the Isle of Man or the Republic of Ireland other than a right to reside which falls within paragraph (3) [¹² or (3A)].

(3) A right to reside falls within this paragraph if it is one which exists by virtue of, or in accordance with, one or more of the following—

  (a) regulation 13 of the [¹² Immigration (European Economic area Regulations 2016];
  (b) regulation 14 of those Regulations, but only in a case where the right exists under that regulation because the claimant is—
   (i) a jobseeker for the purpose of the definition of "qualified person" in regulation 6(1) of those Regulations, or
   (ii) a family member (within the meaning of regulation 7 of those Regulations) of such a jobseeker; [¹⁴ or]
[⁷ [¹² (bb) regulation 16 of those Regulations, but only in a case where the right exists under that regulation because the claimant satisfies the criteria in paragraph (5) of that regulation;]]
[¹⁴ (c)–(e) ...]
  [¹² (3A) A right to reside falls within this paragraph if it exists by virtue of a claimant having been granted limited leave to enter, or remain in, the United Kingdom under the Immigration Act 1971 by virtue of—
  (a) Appendix EU to the immigration rules made under section 3(2) of that Act; [¹⁵ ...]
  (b) being a person with a Zambrano right to reside as defined in Annex 1 of Appendix EU to the immigration rules made under section 3(2) of that Act.]
[¹⁵; or (c) having arrived in the United Kingdom with an entry clearance that was granted under Appendix EU (Family Permit) to the immigration rules made under section 3(2) of that Act.]
  [¹³ (3B) Paragraph (3A)(a) does not apply to a person who—
  (a) has a right to reside granted by virtue of being a family member of a relevant person of Northern Ireland; and
  (b) would have a right to reside under the [¹² Immigration (European Economic Area) Regulations 2016] if the relevant person of Northern Ireland were an EEA national, provided that the right to reside does not fall within paragraph (3).]
(4) A claimant is not a person from abroad if he is—
[¹⁰ (za) a qualified person for the purposes of regulation 6 of the Immigration (European Economic Area) Regulations 2006 as a worker or a self-employed person;
  (zb) a family member of a person referred to in sub-paragraph (za) [¹³ ...];
  (zc) a person who has a right to reside permanently in the United Kingdom by virtue of regulation 15(1)(c), (d) or (e) of those Regulations;]
[¹³ (zd) a family member of a relevant person of Northern Ireland, with a right to reside which falls within paragraph (3A)(a), provided that the

relevant person of Northern Ireland falls within sub-paragraph (za), or would do so but for the fact that they are not an EEA national;]

[¹⁴(ze) a frontier worker within the meaning of regulation 3 of the Citizens' Rights (Frontier Workers) (EU Exit) Regulations 2020;

  (zf) a family member, of a person referred to in sub-paragraph (ze), who has been granted limited leave to enter, or remain in, the United Kingdom by virtue of Appendix EU to the immigration rules made under section 3(2) of the Immigration Act 1971;]

  (g) a refugee within the definition in Article 1 of the Convention relating to the Status of Refugees done at Geneva on 28th July 1951, as extended by Article 1(2) of the Protocol relating to the Status of Refugees done at New York on 31st January 1967;

[³ [⁹ (h) a person who has been granted leave or who is deemed to have been granted leave outside the rules made under section 3(2) of the Immigration Act 1971 where that leave is—

    (i) discretionary leave to enter or remain in the United Kingdom;

    (ii) leave to remain under the Destitution Domestic Violence concession; or

    (iii) leave deemed to have been granted by virtue of regulation 3 of the Displaced Persons (Temporary Protection) Regulations 2005;]

  (hh) a person who has humanitarian protection granted under those rules;] [⁹ or]

  (i) a person who is not a person subject to immigration control within the meaning of section 115(9) of the Immigration and Asylum Act and who is in the United Kingdom as a result of his deportation, expulsion or other removal by compulsion of law from another country to the United Kingdom; [⁵. . .] [⁹ . . .]

[¹³ (5) In this regulation—

"EEA national" has the meaning given in regulation 2(1) of the Immigration (European Economic Area) Regulations 2016;

"family member" has the meaning given in regulation 7(1)(a), (b) or (c) of the Immigration (European Economic Area) Regulations 2016 except that regulation 7(4) of those Regulations does not apply for the purposes of paragraphs (3B) and (4)(zd);

"relevant person of Northern Ireland" has the meaning given in Annex 1 of Appendix EU to the immigration rules made under section 3(2) of the Immigration Act 1971.]

[¹⁴ (6) In this regulation references to the Immigration (European Economic Area) Regulations 2016 are to be read with Schedule 4 to the Immigration and Social Security Co-ordination (EU Withdrawal) Act 2020 (Consequential, Saving, Transitional and Transitory Provisions) Regulations 2020.]

AMENDMENTS

1. Social Security (Persons from Abroad) Amendment Regulations 2006 (SI 1026/2006) reg.6(3) (April 30, 2006).

2. Social Security (Lebanon) Amendment Regulations 2006 (SI 2006/1981) reg.2 (July 25, 2006). The amendment ceased to have effect from January 31, 2007.

3. Social Security (Persons from Abroad) Amendment (No.2) Regulations 2006 (SI 2006/2528) reg.2 (October 9, 2006).

4. Social Security (Bulgaria and Romania) Amendment Regulations 2006 (SI 2006/3341) reg.2 (January 1, 2007).

5. Social Security (Habitual Residence) (Amendment) Regulations 2009 (SI 2009/362) reg.2 (March 18, 2009).

6. Social Security (Miscellaneous Amendments) (No.3) Regulations 2011 (SI 2011/2425) reg.7(1) and (3) (October 31, 2011).

7. Social Security (Habitual Residence) (Amendment) Regulations 2012 (SI 2012/2587) reg.2 (November 8, 2012).

8. Social Security (Croatia) Amendment Regulations 2013 (SI 2013/1474) reg.2 (July 1, 2013).

9. Social Security (Miscellaneous Amendments) (No.3) Regulations 2013 (SI 2013/2536) reg.4(1) and (5) (October 29, 2013).

10. Social Security (Habitual Residence) (Amendment) Regulations 2014 (SI 2014/902) reg.2(1) (May 31, 2014).

11. Social Security (Updating of EU References) (Amendment) Regulations 2018 (SI 2018/1084) reg.4 and Sch. para.6 (November 15, 2018).

12. Social Security (Income-related Benefits) (Updating and Amendment) (EU Exit) Regulations 2019 (SI 2019/872) reg.2 (May 7, 2019).

13. Social Security (Income-Related Benefits) (Persons of Northern Ireland - Family Members) (Amendment) Regulations 2020 (SI 2020/683) reg.2 (August 24, 2020).

14. Immigration and Social Security Co-ordination (EU Withdrawal) Act 2020 (Consequential, Saving, Transitional and Transitory Provisions) (EU Exit) Regulations 2020 (SI 2020/1309) reg.53 (December 31, 2020 at 11.00 pm).

15. Immigration (Citizens' Rights etc.) (EU Exit) Regulations 2020 (SI 2020/1372) reg.8 (December 31, 2020 at 11.00 pm).

GENERAL NOTE   2.168

The UK left the EU at 11.00 pm on January 31, 2020: see the definition of "exit day" in s.20 of the European Union (Withdrawal) Act 2018 as amended by reg.2 of the European Union (Withdrawal) Act 2018 (Exit Day) (Amendment) (No. 3) Regulations 2019. However, those parts of this regulation that relate to the right to reside test continue to have effect as they relate to those with pre-settled status and who are awaiting a decision under EUSS: see SI 2020/1209 and SI 2020/1309 below.

Claimants who are "persons from abroad" are excluded from entitlement to IS because, under para.12 of Sch.7, they have an applicable amount of nil. They are to be distinguished from "persons subject to immigration control". The latter are also excluded from entitlement to IS but by virtue of s.115 Immigration and Asylum Act 1999 (see the commentary to SI 2000/636 in Vol.II).

Paragraph (1) defines "person from abroad" as a claimant who is not habitually resident in the Common Travel Area ("CTA") (i.e. the UK, the Channel Islands, the Isle of Man and the Republic of Ireland).

Paragraph (2) qualifies that definition by providing that no claimant should be treated as habitually resident in the CTA unless they have a right to reside in one of the CTA countries.

Paragraph (3) sets out the rights of residence that do not count for IS. In particular, a right to reside as a jobseeker (in the sense that that word is used in EU law), or as the family member of a jobseeker, does not count.

Paragraph (4) contains a list of categories of people who are deemed not to be "persons from abroad".

The practical effect of the regulation is therefore to create two tests, a habitual residence test and a right to reside test. Unless the claimant is exempt under para.(4), *both* tests need to be satisfied for entitlement to IS.

In practice, the right to reside test affects nationals of the European Economic Area ("EEA"). The relevant law is contained in the former Immigration (European Economic Area) Regulations 2016 ("the 2016 Regulations"), as preserved and modified by SI 2020/1209 and SI 2020/1309, are set out below.

The remainder of this note discusses the habitual residence test.

Habitual residence

2.169   Unless they are exempt under para.(4)(g)–(i), the following claimants must satisfy the habitual residence test in para.1:

- British nationals who have recently spent time outside the CTA in circumstances that do not engage their rights to free movement under EC law;
- nationals of the Channel Islands or the Isle of Man who have recently spent time outside the CTA;
- EEA nationals and their family members who have a right to reside but who do not fall within para.(4)(za)–(zc); and
- nationals of non-EEA states who are not family members of EEA nationals.

Who is exempt?

2.170   The following are deemed not to be persons from abroad and are therefore exempt from the habitual residence test:

- EEA nationals and their family members who have a right to reside that falls within para.4(za)–(zc).
- Refugees, and those who—outside the Immigration Rules—have been granted humanitarian protection or exceptional leave to enter, or to remain in, the UK are deemed not to be persons from abroad: see sub-paras (g)–(hh).

    In *R(IS) 9/98* the Commissioner confirms that a person counts as a refugee entitled to the protection of the 1951 Convention from the time he fulfils the criteria contained in the definition in the Convention. It is not necessary for his status as a refugee to have been recognised by the Home Office. Such recognition does not make the person a refugee but merely declares him one.

- People who have been deported, expelled or otherwise compulsorily removed from another country to the UK: see sub-para.(i). The exemption does not apply to those who are "persons subject to immigration control"—see the overview above.

- (For the period from August 28, 1996 to October 28, 2013) people from Montserrat who came to Great Britain after November 1, 1995 following the volcanic eruption in that territory: see the former sub-para.(j) (p.299 of Vol. II of the 2013/2014 edition).

- (For the period from July 25, 2006 to January 31, 2007 only) people from Lebanon who came to Great Britain on or after July 12, 2006 because of the armed conflict there: see the former sub-para.(k), temporarily inserted by the Social Security (Lebanon) Amendment Regulations 2006 (SI 2006/1981) as follows:

    "(k) a person in Great Britain who left Lebanon on or after 12th July 2006 because of the armed conflict there."

Habitual residence: overview

The requirement to be habitually resident only applies to the claimant, not to a   2.171
partner or dependant.

"Habitual residence" is not defined in the regulation but case law since 1994
has established that, except in cases where EU citizens are exercising their rights
as migrant workers (see *Swaddling*, below), to be habitually resident in the CTA, a
claimant must:

- have a settled intention to reside here; and

- have been "[resident] in fact for a period that shows that the residence has
  become 'habitual' and . . . will or is likely to continue to be habitual".

See *Nessa v Chief Adjudication Officer* [1999] 1 W.L.R. 1937; [1999] 4 All E.R.
677, HL (also reported as *R(IS) 2/00*). Whether that legal test is satisfied so that a
person is habitually resident is a question of fact to be decided by reference to all the
circumstances in each case (*Re J*).

The period of residence that is necessary is usually referred to as the "appreci-   2.172
able period" in accordance with the use of that phrase by Lord Bridge of Harwich in
Re J (A Minor) (Abduction: Custody Rights) [1990] 2 A.C. 562; [1990] 2 All E.R. 961
HL:

"In considering this issue it seems to me to be helpful to deal first with a
number of preliminary points. The first point is that the expression 'habitually
resident' . . . is nowhere defined. It follows, I think, that the expression is not to
be treated as a term of art with some special meaning, but is rather to be understood according to the ordinary and natural meaning of the two words which
it contains. The second point is that the question whether a person is or is not
habitually resident in a specified country is a question of fact to be decided by
reference to all the circumstances of any particular case. The third point is that
there is a significant difference between a person ceasing to be habitually resident
in country A, and his subsequently becoming habitually resident in country B. A
person may cease to be habitually resident in country A in a single day if he or
she leaves it with a settled intention not to return to it but to take up long-term
residence in country B instead. Such a person cannot, however, become habitually resident in country B in a single day. An appreciable period of time and a
settled intention will be necessary to enable him or her to become so. During
that appreciable period of time the person will have ceased to be habitually
resident in country A but not yet have become habitually resident in country B.
The fourth point is that, where a child of J.'s age is in the sole lawful custody of
the mother, his situation with regard to habitual residence will necessarily be the
same as hers."

Habitual residence is not the same as domicile (*R(U)8/88*). It is possible to be
habitually resident in more than one country although it is unusual (*R(IS) 2/00*,
para.20); it is also possible to be habitually resident in none.

Habitual residence can continue during absences of long or short duration.

"Settled intention" and "appreciable period of time"

The two limbs of the habitual residence test, a settled intention and an appreciable   2.173
period of time, are difficult to analyse separately. This is because the two are closely
linked: the overall question is whether "in all the circumstances, including the set-
tledness of the person's intentions as to residence, the residence has continued for a
sufficient period for it to be said to be habitual" (*R(IS) 2/00*). So, if there is a doubt
about the claimant's intention to reside in the UK, it may require a longer period of
residence to resolve that doubt. Similarly, where a person's circumstances are such
that s/he clearly intends to make a home in the UK, it may be possible to say that
s/he has become habitually resident after a relatively short period of time. There

is thus no minimum "appreciable period": the length of the period required will depend upon all the circumstances of the individual case.

The intention to reside here does not need to be permanent or indefinite. It can be for a limited period. To be resident a person had to be seen to be making a "genuine home for the time being" here but it need not be his only home or a permanent one (*R(IS) 6/96*). (Actual residence in two places is perfectly possible: *R(IS) 9/99*.) Some of the relevant factors in judging intention will include the reason for coming (or returning) here, the location of his/her possessions and family, where s/he has previously worked, the length and purpose of any absence from the UK, etc.

If the claimant's intention is conditional, e.g. on benefit being awarded, this is not a settled intention to stay (*CIS/12703/1996*).

2.174   The leading case on the requirement for an appreciable period is the decision of the House of Lords in *Nessa* [1999] 1 W.L.R. 1937. Mrs Nessa came to the UK in August 1994, aged 55. She had previously lived all her life in Bangladesh. Her father-in-law, in whose house she had been living, had died and she had come to the UK for the emotional support of her late husband's brother and his family. Her husband had lived and worked in the UK until his death in 1975 and she had a right of abode here. She claimed income support in September 1994.

The Commissioner (*R(IS) 2/00*) and a majority of the Court of Appeal followed *Re J* and held that in order to establish habitual residence it was necessary for a claimant not only to have been in the UK voluntarily, and for settled purposes, but also to have fulfilled those conditions for an appreciable period of time. However, the Court of Appeal considered that the appreciable period need not be particularly long. The dissenting judge (Thorpe LJ) considered that Lord Brandon's comments in *Re J* were clearly obiter and that an appreciable period was not an essential ingredient of habitual residence. In his view the adjective "habitual" ensured that "the connection [to the country] is not transitory or temporary but enduring and the necessary durability can be judged prospectively in exceptional cases".

Mrs Nessa appealed again to the House of Lords which unanimously upheld the majority in the Court of Appeal. Lord Slynn of Hadley, with whom all the other judges agreed, reviewed the authorities discussed above and stated:

> "With the guidance of these cases it seems to me plain that as a matter of ordinary language a person is not habitually resident in any country unless he has taken up residence and lived there for a period. . . . If Parliament had intended that a person seeking to enter the United Kingdom or such a person declaring his intention to settle here is to have income support on arrival, it could have said so. It seems to me impossible to accept the argument at one time advanced that a person who has never been here before who says on landing, 'I intend to settle in the United Kingdom' and who is fully believed is automatically a person who is habitually resident here. Nor is it enough to say I am going to live at X or with Y. He must show residence in fact for a period which shows that the residence has become 'habitual' and, as I see it, will or is likely to continue to be habitual."

Lord Slynn did accept that there might be "special cases where the person concerned is not coming here for the first time, but is resuming an habitual residence previously had . . . On such facts the Adjudication Officer may or of course may not be satisfied that the previous habitual residence has been resumed. This position is quite different from that of someone coming to the United Kingdom for the first time." Although *Swaddling* (see below) was cited by Lord Slynn as one example of this type of case the exception seems to be considerably narrower than the principle of Community law established by that case, namely that the length of residence in a Member State could not be regarded as an intrinsic element of the concept of habitual residence where a claimant comes within Regulation 1408/71. Lord Slynn appears to be saying no more than that in some cases it will be possible to say on the facts that a returning resident is merely resuming a habitual residence which has already been established. The reference to the possibility that the AO (now decision-maker) "may not be satisfied" clearly indicates that this will not always be the case and that some returning residents will need to re-establish habitual residence by living in the CTA for a period of time.

How long is the appreciable period?

Lord Slynn's opinion also contains interesting observations on how long the appreciable period of time should be. Whilst recognising that the period is not fixed and "may be longer where there are doubts", he also stated that "it may be short" and quoted with approval the statement of Butler Sloss LJ in *Re F (A Minor) (Child Abduction)* [1994] F.L.R. 548, at 555 that "A month can be . . . an appreciable period of time". He also agreed with the Commissioner that there were factors which indicated that habitual residence had been established in Mrs Nessa's case, "even by the date of the tribunal hearing *or as I see it, even earlier*" (emphasis added). At the date of her tribunal hearing on December 6, 1994, Mrs Nessa had been in the UK for 15 weeks.

It must be stressed that the House of Lords clearly regarded this issue as one to be determined by tribunals on the facts of individual cases; however the view of the Commissioner in *R(IS) 6/96* that the establishment of habitual residence would normally require residence of at least some months must now be read in the light of Lord Slynn's comments.

As the issue of what is an "appreciable period" is one of fact and degree, and the decisions highlighted by Commissioners for wider circulation normally concern issues of law, there are few public examples of how the Commissioners approach that issue when exercising their discretion under s.14(8)(a) of SSA 1998. However, post-*Nessa* examples can be found in *CIS/1304/1997* and *CJSA/5394/1998* and in *CIS/376/2002*, all of which involved returning residents.

2.175

In the former decision, guidance was given that in a typical case tribunals should conduct a three-stage enquiry into: (i) the circumstances in which the claimant's earlier habitual residence was lost; (ii) the links between the claimant and the UK while abroad; and (iii) the circumstances of his return to the UK. So, for example, if the claimant's departure from the UK was temporary (albeit long-term) or conditional or if habitual residence was lost only as a result of events which occurred after the claimant's departure, those would be factors favouring a resumption of habitual residence immediately on return. On the facts of those appeals, the Commissioner held that the claimants, both British nationals who—as was accepted—had previously been habitually resident here, but had lost that habitual residence during an extended period of absence abroad, nevertheless resumed their previous habitual residence on the very day of their return to Britain. The relevant extracts from *CIS/1304/1997* and *CJSA/5394/1998* were reissued as an Appendix to *CIS/4474/2003* (see below).

2.176

By contrast the claimant in *CIS/376/2002*, a naturalised British citizen who had worked in Britain for many years but had spent no more than 11 months here in the five years before the claims for benefit which were under consideration, was held not to have become habitually resident immediately. Commissioner Howell Q.C. accepted the tribunal's finding that although the claimant had been habitually resident in the past he had ceased to be so over that five-year period, but rejected the tribunal's doubts about whether he had a settled intention to remain here. On that basis, the Commissioner held that the claimant had not been resident for an appreciable period of time when his claim for IS was made (some three days after his arrival) but had become habitually resident by the date of the decision on that claim approximately five weeks later. In reaching his decision the Commissioner denied the possibility that a claimant who had lost his or her habitual residence could resume it immediately without first being present for an appreciable period of time. He stated (at para.12):

"Everything therefore depends on what counts as an 'appreciable period' of resumed residence in this context so that his residence in the United Kingdom can be said to have become established as habitual . . . As has been said many times in the cases where judges from the House of Lords down to more humble levels have had to struggle with the meaning of this expression, this is ultimately a question of fact and degree, depending on the individual circumstances of each case, and there are no hard and fast rules to apply. For a returning citizen of this country coming back to live here again after a period of residence overseas . . . the period may be short: as little as a month or so. But it is not zero or minimal, since even a returning expatriate may change his plans again and there is therefore at least some space of time after actual arrival when one simply has to wait and see."

The issue of the length of the appreciable period was also considered by the Commissioner in *CIS/4474/2003*. The Commissioner also noted that the approach taken by Commissioners to that issue had developed since *R(IS) 6/96* and gave the following guidance:

"19. What is an appreciable period depends on the circumstances of the particular case. But I agree with the Secretary of State that in the general run of cases the period will lie between one and three months. *I would certainly require cogent reasons from a tribunal to support a decision that a significantly longer period was required*" (emphasis added).

2.177   In *R(IS) 7/06*, the Commissioner indicated his broad agreement with *CIS/ 4474/2003*:

"I am content to accept that, where a claimant is likely to remain in the United Kingdom permanently or for a substantial period of time, the conventional period that must have elapsed between his arrival and his establishing habitual residence is between one month and three months. However, those are not rigid limits. In an exceptional case, a person with a right of abode in the United Kingdom who, although not falling within the scope of regulation 21(3)(d), has been forced to flee another country and is nonetheless able to show a settled intention to remain in the United Kingdom might be accepted as habitually resident after less than a month of residence. Perhaps less exceptionally, a person with no ties to the United Kingdom and making no effort to become established here despite a vague intention to remain might be found not to be habitually resident in the United Kingdom until considerably longer than three months had elapsed."

However, disagreement with that approach was expressed in *CIS/1972/2003* (at para.14):

"I comment only that I have seen tribunals decide on shorter periods than a month and longer periods than three months without being appealed, or appealed successfully. Too much should not be read into the facts of individual decisions or, I suggest, trends in the small number of—usually difficult—cases that Commissioners come to decide on the facts. It does not help when Commissioners' decisions are used to play a forensic game (for it is no more than that) of finding the longest, or the shortest, period endorsed by a Commissioner and then claiming some general rule from it. Parliament could have set a specific time limit. It did not. Advisors cannot seek certainty where it does not exist."

That disagreement was echoed by the Tribunal of Commissioners in *CIS/2559/2005*. The Commissioners stated that:

"The relevant period of residence required to support evidence of intention is not, in our view, something which can be reduced to a tariff. In so far as the decision of Mr Commissioner Jacobs in *CIS/4474/2003* can be interpreted to the contrary, we take a different view."

2.178   It is suggested that the approach in *CIS/4474/2003* and *R(IS) 7/06* (a reported decision that was subsequently upheld by the Court of Appeal) is to be preferred. Although it is accepted that no two cases are identical and that the decision must always be one of fact and degree in an individual case, justice as between claimants in similar situations requires that there should be some consistency in decision-making: that the appreciable periods of time required by different decision makers, tribunals and Commissioners should at least be "in the same ball park". In the early days of the test, the periods chosen varied wildly from case to case: at that time, many decision-makers—and some tribunals—would have required an appreciable period of at least a year and sometimes more on the facts of *Nessa*, whereas the Commissioner and Lord Slynn considered that Mrs Nessa had become habitually resident in approximately three months or less. In such circumstances, recognising the existence of a conventional period does not involve the imposition of a tariff as long as the period is applied flexibly in each individual case. As Commissioner Jacobs has subsequently said (in *CJSA/1223/2006* and *CJSA/1224/2006*):

> "I respectfully agree with the Tribunal of Commissioners in *CIS/2559/2005* . . . that: 'The relevant period of residence required to support evidence of intention is not, in our view, something which can be reduced to a tariff.' I do not understand why the Tribunal thought that my comments might be interpreted as setting a tariff and counsel could not suggest how they might have been so understood. I remain of the view that for most cases an appreciable period is likely to be between one and three months. [Counsel for the Secretary of State] told me that that was the experience of decision-makers and he was not instructed to argue otherwise".

It is suggested that Commissioner Jacobs was surely correct to express the point in *CIS/4474/2003* as being about reasoning: a tribunal may be justified in giving a decision that is outside the normal range of decisions given by tribunals generally, but if so, it should be prepared to explain why.

For an analysis of the process involved in fixing an appreciable period, see *CJSA/1223/2006* and *CJSA/1224/2006*. That decision emphasises the importance of looking at the steps taken by the claimant to integrate him- or herself into the UK during that period.

Viability

Another issue that has vexed the application of the habitual residence test over the years is that of viability. The starting point is *R(IS) 6/96*, the first Commissioner's decision on the habitual residence test. The Commissioner in that case held that the "appreciable period of time" should be a period which showed "a settled and viable pattern of living here as a resident". Thus the practicality of a person's arrangements for residence had to be considered. In determining whether the plans were viable, the possibility of claiming income support had to be left out of account (although this did not mean that there must be no conceivable circumstances in which a person might need to resort to income support). In reliance on that decision, some decision-makers and tribunals took the view that many people from abroad could never become habitually resident because the mere fact that they had claimed income support showed that their residence was not viable in the sense required by the Commissioner. The requirement of viability certainly contributed towards the phenomenon of very long appreciable periods in the early days of the test that has been referred to above.

However, the law has developed since *R(IS) 6/96*. The Commissioner in *Nessa* *(R(IS) 2/00)* disagreed with *R(IS) 6/96* to the extent that the viability of a person's residence in the UK, either generally or with or without assistance from public funds, was only one relevant factor among others, to be given the appropriate weight according to the circumstances. In his view *R(IS) 6/96* should not be read as imposing an additional condition that only residence without resort to IS or public assistance was relevant to the *Re J* test.

The approach that whether the claimant's residence in the UK is viable without recourse to public funds is only one factor and not by itself decisive was followed in *CIS/1459/1996* and *CIS/16097/1996*. And in *CIS/4474/2003*, the Commissioner warns against the danger of overemphasising viability as a factor:

2.179

"16. The danger of overemphasising viability is this. A claimant needs to establish habitual residence in order to claim an income-related benefit. A claim would not be necessary if the claimant has a guaranteed source of funds sufficient for survival. The danger is that the only claimants who can establish habitual residence will be those who have sufficient access to funds not to need it. That cannot be right. Habitual residence is a test of entitlement, not a bar to entitlement. It must be applied in a way that allows for the possibility of a claimant establishing both habitual residence and an entitlement to income support."

Habitual residence and EEA nationals

2.180   As explained above, for many EEA nationals, the habitual residence test is irrelevant. If they satisfy the right to reside test, then in most cases they are exempt from the habitual residence test. If they do not satisfy the right to reside test then they are not habitually resident for that reason. But there are a few categories of EEA nationals with the right to reside, in particular those nationals whose only right to reside is as a workseeker, who are not exempt from the habitual residence test and must therefore actually be habitually resident in order to receive benefit.

The habitual residence test differs in its application to some EEA nationals:

- Claimants who have been absent from the UK as migrant workers within the EEA can become habitually resident here immediately on their return and without first living here for an appreciable period of time (see *Swaddling v Adjudication Officer* (C–90/97), reported as *R(IS) 6/99*).

- For EEA workseekers who have not previously worked in the UK, the requirement for an appreciable period of residence must be applied having regard to the principles established in *Collins v Secretary of State for Work and Pensions* ((C–138/02) in the ECJ and [2006] EWCA Civ 376 in the Court of Appeal, both reported as *R(JSA) 3/06*).

Swaddling

2.181   Mr Swaddling was a British national who, until he was 23, had lived and worked in the UK. From 1980–1994 for the majority of the time he worked in France. In late 1994 he was made redundant. After failing to find further employment in France, he returned to the UK in January 1995 to live with his brother and in order to obtain work here. His claim for IS was made on January 9, 1995 (i.e. at a time when IS was a benefit claimed by workseekers as well as those currently entitled) and was refused on the ground that he was not habitually resident in the UK.

The Commissioner held that the appropriate appreciable period in all the circumstances was eight weeks from the date of his return to the UK. Under the terms of purely domestic law the claimant was thus not entitled to income support for the period January 9 through March 3, 1995. The Commissioner rejected an argument put forward by the claimant that under art.10a(2) of Regulation 1408/71 he could rely on his period of residence in France to satisfy the habitual residence condition. The Commissioner decided that art.10a(2) did not assist the claimant since the habitual residence test did not make entitlement to IS subject to completion of a period of employment, self-employment or residence (note that in Regulation 1408/71 "residence" means "habitual residence": art.1(h)) but went to whether habitual residence had been established initially.

But the Commissioner did refer to the ECJ the question whether the application of a habitual residence test (involving the requirement of an appreciable period of residence) to a person who had exercised his right to freedom of movement and had worked and been habitually resident in another Member State and then returned to the UK to seek work infringed art.48 of the Treaty of Rome. It was contended on behalf of the claimant that the test had the effect of deterring a person from exercising his Community rights since he had been made worse off by its application than if he had worked throughout in the UK. For the AO it was submitted that the principle in art.48 did not extend to conditions for acquiring entitlement to a non-contributory benefit like income support.

However, the ECJ did not answer the question as to whether there had been an   2.182
infringement of art.48 since it considered that the case could be dealt with under Regulation 1408/71. It was accepted that Mr Swaddling was a person covered by Regulation 1408/71 (as an employed person he had been subject to both the British and French social security schemes). Article 10a(1) provides that a person to whom the Regulation applies is to be granted certain special non-contributory benefits (which include IS) in the territory of the Member State in which s/he resides. "Reside" means "habitually reside": art.1(h). The Court stated that, in deciding where a person habitually resided, account had to be taken in particular of his/her family situation; the reasons which had led him/her to move; the length and continuity of his/her residence; the fact (where this was the case) that s/he was in stable employment; and his/her intention as it appeared from all the circumstances. However, the Court also held that the length of residence in the Member State in which payment of benefit was sought could not be regarded as an intrinsic element of the concept of residence within the meaning of art.10a.

The result of the ECJ's judgment would thus seem to be that a person covered by Regulation 1408/71 can be habitually resident in a Member State for the purposes of art.10a on the day of arrival if the circumstances as a whole, including the other factors referred to by the Court, lead to that conclusion. The Community meaning of "habitually resident" therefore differs from the interpretation that currently applies in a domestic context.

One question that arises is to whom does the ECJ's judgment apply? Clearly it covers returning British nationals who come within the scope of Regulation 1408/71 and, it is difficult to see how non-British EEA nationals in a similar position could be excluded without breaching art.7 of Regulation 1612/68.

For a detailed discussion of the personal scope of Regulation 1408/71 see *R(IS) 1/06*. The Commissioner in *R(IS) 1/06* also decided that—at least in the circumstances of that case—the habitual residence test did not discriminate against the claimant on the grounds of her nationality contrary to art.12 of the EC Treaty (see Vol.III) because even if that article were otherwise applicable, any discriminatory effect was objectively justified as a way of ensuring that a national of another Member State had a sufficient link to UK society (see also the decision of the ECJ in *R. (on the application of Bidar) v London Borough of Ealing* (C–209/03) [2005] E.C.R. I-2119.

Collins

Where the benefit claimed is JSA and the claimant is an EEA national, the   2.183
habitual residence test must now be applied in accordance with the decision of the Court of Justice of the European Union in *Collins v Secretary of State for Work and Pensions* (C–138/02) [2005] Q.B. 145 (ECJ, March 23, 2004) and the subsequent decisions of Commissioner Mesher in *CJSA/4065/1999* and the Court of Appeal [2006] EWCA Civ 376 (*R(JSA) 3/06*). Mr Collins was born and brought up in the USA and had American citizenship. He spent one semester studying in the UK in 1978 and had also spent 10 months doing part-time and casual work in London between 1980 and 1981. During that period he acquired Irish nationality. Since 1981 he had worked in the US and Africa but had not worked in the UK. In 1998 he returned to the UK for settlement and, on June 8, 1998, claimed JSA while he looked for work. On July 1, 1998 an adjudication officer decided that he was not habitually resident. Mr Collins' appeal against that decision was referred to the ECJ by the Commissioner. The Court held that the work which Mr Collins had done in the UK in 1980 and 1981 was not sufficiently closely connected to the work he was seeking in 1998 for him to have retained his former status as a "worker" and that he therefore was in the same position—from an EU/EEA law point of view—as someone who had never worked in the UK. On that basis the Court held that:

- Mr Collins was not a "worker" for the purposes of Title II of Part I of Regulation 1612/68; and

- Directive 68/630 only accords rights of residence to those already in employment and therefore Mr Collins did not have a right of residence under that provision.

Up to this point, the decision of the Court breaks no new ground. However, in its answer to the third question referred to it, the Court went on to hold that in the light of the establishment (by the Maastricht Treaty) of EU citizenship and of its previous decision in *Grzelczyk v Belgium* (C–184/99) [2005] E.C.R. I-6193, it was no longer possible to exclude from the scope of art.39(2) of the Treaty (now art.45(2) TFEU)—which abolishes discrimination based on nationality between workers of the Member States as regards employment, remuneration and other conditions of work and employment (see Vol.III)—a benefit of a financial nature intended to facilitate access to employment in the labour market of a Member State. As the habitual residence test could more easily be met by UK nationals, it disadvantaged nationals of other Member States who had exercised their rights of movement to seek employment and could only be justified if it was based on objective considerations which were independent of the nationality of the persons concerned and proportionate to the legitimate aim of the national provisions. Although Member States were entitled to ensure that there was a genuine link between the person seeking work and the employment market of that State before granting an allowance such as JSA, and although that link might be determined by the fact that the claimant had genuinely sought work in the Member State in question for a reasonable period, a residence requirement could not, if it was to be proportionate, go beyond what was necessary to obtain the objective of ensuring such a link:

"More specifically, its application by the national authorities must rest on clear criteria known in advance and provision must be made for the possibility of a means of redress of a judicial nature. In any event, if compliance with the requirement demands a period of residence, the period must not exceed what is necessary in order for the national authorities to be able to satisfy themselves that the person concerned is genuinely seeking work in the employment market of the host Member State."

Mr Collins' appeal therefore returned to the Commissioner to decide the issue of justification in accordance with the ruling of the Court. The Commissioner rejected the submissions of counsel for Mr Collins (which were along similar lines to the views expressed in a previous edition) that the answer to the question of whether the claimant was genuinely seeking work was provided by the satisfaction of the other conditions of entitlement to JSA so that there was no justifiable role left for a habitual residence test, or that, in the alternative, the habitual residence test as established by reg.85 and interpreted by the courts (including the ECJ) did not "rest on clear criteria known in advance" as the ECJ had required. Rather:

"The application of the residence requirement embodied in the habitual residence test in the JSA legislation and in Article 10a of Regulation 1408/71 is, subject to the proviso mentioned below, justified by objective considerations independent of the nationality of the claimant and proportionate to the legitimate aim in the making of the JSA legislation. The requirement meets the conditions as to proportionality set out in paragraph 72 of the ECJ's judgment in relation to the legitimate aim of establishing that a real or genuine link exists between a claimant and the UK employment market, such as by being satisfied of the genuineness of the claimant's search for work in that employment market."

2.184   The proviso referred to is that if, on any day, the answer to the question "has the point been reached on that day that the relevant national authority has become satisfied of the genuineness of the claimant's search for work [in the sense referred to in the next paragraph]?" is answered yes, the result of the normal habitual residence test can no longer be applied in his case.

An important part of the Commissioner's decision is that, for the purpose of assessing whether the habitual residence test is proportional, the genuineness of the claimant's search for work is not established on the basis that s/he satisfies the labour market conditions for entitlement to JSA for a particular week:

"32. I leave aside for the moment what was said in paragraph 72 of the ECJ's judgment about proportionality, clear criteria and means of redress. The crucial sentence is then this: 'In any event, if compliance with the [residence] requirement demands a period of residence, the period must not exceed what is necessary in order for the national authorities to be able to satisfy themselves that the person concerned is genuinely seeking work in the employment market of the host Member State.'
33. First, I have no doubt that that sentence does not have the effect that the sole legitimate question to be asked is whether the claimant was genuinely seeking work on any particular day, in the sense merely of taking active and appropriate steps to seek suitable work. The relevant legitimate aim in making the JSA legislation, as identified by the ECJ, is the wish to ensure that there is a genuine link (or in other words a real link) between the claimant and the UK employment market. That is the aim in relation to which proportionality must be tested.
34. Then, paragraph 69 of the judgment spells out that in pursuance of that aim it is legitimate to award benefit only after it has been possible to establish that such a link exists. And it is plainly accepted in paragraphs 69 and 70 that it is legitimate only to accept that there is such a link at any particular date if there has previously been some sufficiently concrete expression of a connection with the UK employment market. It also seems to me that the notion of a genuine link or a real link carries with it a sense that the link has to have some concrete expression. In that context, I conclude that the pivotal part of the final sentence of paragraph 72 is the reference to what period of residence is necessary for the national authorities to be able to satisfy themselves that the claimant is genuinely seeking work. To be consistent with what has been said earlier, it must be legitimate for the national authorities to say that they are not able to satisfy themselves about the genuineness of a search for work until a proper search has continued for some period. A person may actually take steps to search for work on a particular day and actually have on that day an intention to continue to search diligently for suitable vacancies, but national authorities can legitimately say that they have not been satisfied that the search is genuine until they have seen that the search has been sustained, and in a sufficiently diligent and well directed form, for some period. The condition of proportionality laid down by the final sentence of paragraph 72 is thus that a residence requirement, in principle appropriate, cannot be applied to deny entitlement to benefit beyond the date at which the relevant national authority has become satisfied of the genuineness of the claimant's search for work."

Applying those principles to Mr Collins' appeal the Commissioner held that Mr Collins had not been habitually resident from June 8, 1998 to July 1, 1998 and, on the assumption that *R(IS) 7/06* was correctly decided (as to which see the commentary under the heading *"Habitual residence" and "down to the date of decision"* below), would not have become so by July 31, 1998, shortly after which, Mr Collins found work.

The Court of Appeal dismissed Mr Collins' appeal against the Commissioner's decision. The reasoning of Jonathan Parker LJ, who gave the judgment of the court, mirrors that of the Commissioner except in relation to the proviso referred to above. On that point, he stated:

2.185

"86. The effect of the Commissioner's proviso, as I understand it, is that although the habitual residence test is to be applied in the ordinary way, it cannot be justified as laying down the sole test for establishing the existence of the requisite 'genuine link' between an applicant for JSA and the UK market; so that if the decision-maker can be satisfied on other grounds that such a link has been established, then the habitual residence requirement must fall away.

87. With respect to the Commissioner, I cannot see any basis in Community law for the introduction of such a proviso. Certainly, as I read the ECJ's judgments in this case and in *Swaddling*, there is nothing in those judgments which suggests the need for such a proviso. In my judgment the correct analysis is that under Community law it is a matter for the national legislature whether to require the existence of a 'genuine link' and (if so) to prescribe how that link may be established; and that the prescription of a habitual residence test for that purpose is both legitimate and justified. Had the ECJ taken a contrary view, I would have expected it to say so: the more so because, as I have already pointed out (see paragraph 81 above), the discussion which follows paragraph 66 of its judgment is clearly directed specifically at the habitual residence requirement prescribed by regulation 85(4), rather at the general concept of a residence requirement.

88. Accordingly I respectfully conclude that the Commissioner was in error in concluding that in order to render the habitual residence requirement compatible with Community law it was necessary to introduce the proviso in question; and that on the proper interpretation of the ECJ's judgment in this case a habitual residence test *simpliciter* as a means of establishing the requisite 'genuine link' between an applicant for JSA and the UK employment market is fully compatible with Community law."

The problem faced by decision makers and tribunals who must apply the Court of Appeal's approach (and the problem that the Commissioner's proviso was intended to help them address) is that the length of an appreciable period of time is a question of judgment to be made taking into account all the circumstances of the individual case. If the purpose of the test as applied to EEA nationals is that a Member State is entitled to require a genuine link between the person seeking work and its employment market before granting an allowance such as JSA, then whether or not a link has been forged must be a circumstance to be taken into account when fixing the length of the appreciable period. The question that divides the Court of Appeal and the Commissioner is whether it is possible to decide in an individual case that the genuine link exists but that the claimant has nevertheless not been resident for an appreciable period of time, and is therefore not habitually resident. On the approach required by the Court of Appeal such a decision is at least theoretically possible because the habitual residence test *simpliciter* satisfies EU law. However, it is difficult to think of circumstances in which such a decision would in fact be appropriate. If a genuine link with the UK employment market exists in an individual case, that is likely to be a compelling factor in favour of the conclusion that the claimant has been present for an appreciable period of time and has become habitually resident in the UK. On that basis, there is little practical difference between the approaches of the Court of Appeal and the Commissioner and the Commissioner's proviso, though not part of the legal test in the light of the Court of Appeal's decision, is a useful reminder to tribunals of the importance of the existence of the genuine link with the UK employment market as a factor in habitual residence decisions involving UK nationals.

The additional "three-months" requirement for jobseeker's allowance

2.186   From January 1, 2014, reg.85A of the Jobseeker's Allowance Regulations 1996 was amended to provide (in para.(2)(a)) that no claimant shall be treated as habitually resident in the UK, the Channel Islands, the Isle of Man or the Republic of Ireland unless s/he has been living in any of those places for the past three months. That "three-months" requirement was subsequently applied to child benefit and child tax credit with effect from July 1, 2014 by the Child Benefit (General) and the Tax Credits (Residence) (Amendment) Regulations 2014 (SI 2014/1511), subject to a number of exceptions: see further Vol.IV. For those affected, the requirement applies even if they have a right of residence and would satisfy the habitual residence test on the "settled intention" and "appreciable period of time" tests.

Not all those claiming JSA are affected. Although the drafting could be clearer—and, in particular, could say in as many words that reg.85A(2) is subject to reg.85A(4)—that is the effect of the regulation taken as a whole. It is categorically stated that a person who falls within para.(4) "is not a person from abroad". Under para.(1), the habitual residence test is a mechanism for determining whether a person is a "person from abroad". There is therefore no need to apply it in cases where it is known that the person is not a person from abroad because para.(4) says so. The "three-months" and right to reside tests are part of the habitual residence test and are therefore subject to para.(4) for the same reason.

The three-month requirement is that the claimant must have been "living in" the Common Travel Area for "the past three months". The use of "living in" rather than "residing in" suggests a factual rather than legal test. A JSA claimant who has in fact been living in the UK for the past three months (and who has become habitually resident as a mater of fact) but who only acquired a right of residence on the day when he first claims JSA appears to satisfy the test.

"Living in" is also to be distinguished from "present in". Whether a period of   2.187
absence abroad has the effect that the claimant is no longer "living in" the CTA on his/her return will be a question of fact for decision makers and tribunals to decide taking into account all the circumstances of the case: see *AEKM v Department for Communities (JA)* [2016] NICom 80 and *TC v SSWP (JSA)* [2017] UKUT 222 (AAC).

The three-month requirement is compatible with EU law: see *CL v SSWP* [2020] UKUT 146 (AAC).

The requirement is not that the claimant should have been living in the CTA for an *initial* period of three months, but rather that s/he should have been so living for *the past* three months. In other words the test is continuous. However long the claimant may have been living in the CTA, if at any time it can be said that s/he has not been doing so for the past three months, then s/he ceases to be habitually resident and becomes a person from abroad. Even a very brief period during which the claimant is not "living in" the CTA means that s/he must live here for a further period of three months before becoming entitled to benefit again. However, note the transitional protection in reg.3 of SI 2013/2196 (reproduced later in this volume) under which the three-months test does not apply "in relation to a claim for a jobseeker's allowance which is made or treated as made before" January 1, 2014.

The three-months test affects JSA claimants of all nationalities—including British   2.188
citizens—unless they are exempt under para.(4). However, issues arise in its application to EEA nationals who have exercised their rights to freedom of movement.

In the particular case of returning residents, it is difficult to reconcile the test with EU law as established in *Swaddling* (above). The ECJ in that case stated that the length of residence in the Member State in which payment of benefit was sought could *not* be regarded as an intrinsic element of habitual residence.

More generally, it will have to be decided whether the "habitual residence test *simpliciter*" continues to comply with EU law—as it was previously held to do in *Collins*—now that it effectively includes inflexible rules that a genuine link with the UK employment market cannot be established without having lived in the UK for at least three months and that, once established, such a link is invariably lost by ceasing to live in the UK.

Habitual residence and "down to the date of decision"

Until May 23, 2007, it was possible to make an advance award of benefit where   2.189
the a claimant failed the habitual residence test because s/he had not been resident for an appreciable period of time by the date of the Secretary of State's decision, but it was likely that habitual residence would be established within three months (see

Secretary of State for Work and Pensions v Bhakta [2006] EWCA Civ 65, reported as *R(IS) 7/06*).

However, the *Bhakta* case has now been reversed by legislation. For the position where the Secretary of State's decision was made before May 23, 2007, see pp.317–318 of Vol.II of the 2007 edition.

[¹ Treatment of refugees

2.190   [² **21ZB.**—[¹. . .]]

1. Asylum and Immigration (Treatment of Claimants, etc.) Act 2004 (c.19) s.12(2)(a)(i) (June 14, 2007).
2. Social Security (Immigration and Asylum) Consequential Amendments Regulations 2000 (SI 2000/636) reg.3 (5) (April 3, 2000).
3. Social Security (Working Tax Credit and Child Tax Credit) (Consequential Amendments) Regulations 2003 (SI 2003/455) reg.2 and Sch.1 para.5 (April 6, 2004), except in "transitional cases" and see further the note to reg.17 of the Income Support Regulations.

GENERAL NOTE

2.191   Backdated payments of income support to refugees under reg.21ZB and the former s.123 of the Immigration and Asylum Act 1999 have been abolished and replaced with discretionary "refugee integration loans" under s.13 of the Asylum and Immigration (Treatment of Claimants, etc.) Act 2004 (c.19) and the Integration Loans for Refugees and Others Regulations 2007 (SI 2007/1598).

By art.2(3) of the Asylum and Immigration (Treatment of Claimants, etc.) Act 2004 (Commencement No.7 and Transitional Provisions) Order 2007 (SI 2007/1602), the revocation of reg.21ZB "shall not apply to a person who is recorded as a refugee on or before 14th June 2007". For those purposes a person is recorded as a refugee on the day on which the Home Secretary notifies him that he has been recognised as a refugee and granted asylum in the UK (see art.2(4)).

For the text of, and commentary on, the former reg.21ZB see pp.318-320 of Vol. II of the 2007 edition. Note that *Tkachuk v Secretary of State for Work and Pensions* (which is referred to in that commentary) has now been reported as *R(IS) 3/07*.

2.192   The revocation of reg.21ZB did not offend against EU law or infringe the ECHR. Article 28 of Directive 2004/83/EC (the "Qualification Directive") does not require the UK to provide income support to a refugee for the period prior to the decision recognising refugee status even once such a decision has been made, and if the removal of the backdating rule did discriminate against the appellant (pursuant to art.14 of the European Convention on Human Rights when read with art.1 of the First Protocol to that Convention) it is justified: see the decision of the Court of Appeal in *Blakesley v Secretary of State for Work and Pensions* [2015] EWCA Civ 141, [2015] AACR 17, upholding the decision of the three-judge panel of the Upper Tribunal in *HB v Secretary of State for Work and Pensions (IS)* [2013] UKUT 433 (AAC).

No provision equivalent to reg.21ZB was ever made in relation to SPC. The effect was that between October 6, 2003 and June 13, 2007 backdated benefit was available to refugees under the age of 60 but not to those who were 60 or over (60 being the qualifying age for SPC at the time). In *CPC/3396/2006*, the Commissioner held that, even if that situation amounted to unlawful discrimination on the grounds of age contrary to art.14 ECHR (and no ruling was made on that point), the Human Rights Act 1998 did not permit him to remedy that discrimination.

2.193   ## [¹Reductions in applicable amounts in certain cases of failure to attend courses

21A.—[² . .].]

AMENDMENTS

1. Income Support (General and Transitional) Amendment Regulations 1990 (SI 1990/2324) reg.3 (December 17, 1990).
2. Income Support (General) (Jobseeker's Allowance Consequential Amendments) Regulations 1996 (SI 1996/206) reg.28 and Sch.3 (October 7, 1996).

[Reductions in applicable amounts in certain cases of actual or notional unemployment benefit disqualification

22.—[¹. . .]

2.194

AMENDMENT

1. Income Support (General) (Jobseeker's Allowance Consequential Amendments) Regulations 1996 (SI 1996/206) reg.28 and Sch.3 (October 7, 1996).

[¹Reduction in applicable amount where the claimant is appealing against a decision [²which embodies a determination] that he is not incapable of work

22A.—(1) Subject to paragraph (3), where a claimant falls within para-   2.195
graph 25 of Schedule 1B (persons appealing against a decision [²which embodies a determination] that they are not incapable of work under the [³personal capability assessment]), and none of the other paragraphs of that Schedule applies to him, his applicable amount shall be reduced by a sum equivalent to 20 per cent, of the following amount—

(a) in the case of a person to whom regulation 17 or 18 or paragraphs 6, 9 to 12 [⁶ . . .] of Schedule 7 applies—

  (i) where he is a single claimant aged less than 18 or a member of a couple or a polygamous marriage where all the members, in either case, are less than 18, the amount specified in paragraph 1(1)(a), (b) or (c), as the case may be, of Schedule 2 (applicable amounts);

  (ii) where he is a single claimant aged not less than 18 but less than 25 or a member of a couple or a polygamous marriage where one member is aged not less than 18 but less than 25 and the other member, or in the case of a polygamous marriage each other member, is a person under 18 who—

    (aa) does not qualify for income support under regulation 4ZA, or who would not so qualify if he were to make a claim; and

    (bb) does not satisfy the requirements of section 3(1)(f)(iii) of the Jobseekers Act 1995 (prescribed circumstances for persons aged 16 but less than 18); and

    (cc) is not the subject of a direction under section 16 of the Jobseekers Act 1995 (persons under 18: severe hardship), the amount specified in paragraph 1(1)(d) of that Schedule;

  (iii) where he is a single claimant aged not less than 25 or a member of a couple or a polygamous marriage (other than a member of a couple or a polygamous marriage to whom head (ii) of this sub-paragraph applies) at least one of whom is aged not less than 18, the amount specified in paragraph 1(1)(e) of that Schedule;

(b) [⁵. . .].

(2) A reduction under paragraph (1) shall, if it is not a multiple of 5p, be rounded to the nearest such multiple or, if it is a multiple of 2.5p but not of 5p, to the next lower multiple of 5p.

(3) Paragraph (1) shall not apply to a claimant who is appealing against a decision [²which embodies a determination] that he is not incapable of work under the [³personal capability assessment] where that [²determination] was [⁴the first determination made in accordance with, the all work test before 3rd April 2000 or, after that date, the personal capability assessment, in relation to the claimant], and the claimant was, immediately prior to 13th April 1995, either—

  (a) in receipt of invalidity pension under Part II of the Contributions and Benefits Act as then in force, or severe disablement allowance; or

  (b) incapable of work in accordance with paragraph 5 of Schedule 1 as in force on 12th April 1995 and had been so for a continuous period of 28 weeks.]

AMENDMENTS

1. Income Support (General) (Jobseeker's Allowance Consequential Amendments) Regulations 1996 (SI 1996/206) reg.13 (October 7, 1996).

2. Social Security Act 1998 (Commencement No.9 and Savings and Consequential and Transitional Provisions) Order 1999 (SI 1999/2422 (C.61)) art.3(7) and Sch.6 para.1 (September 6, 1999).

3. Social Security (Incapacity for Work) Miscellaneous Amendments Regulations 1999 (SI 1999/3109) reg.6 (April 3, 2000).

4. Social Security (Incapacity) Miscellaneous Amendments Regulations 2000 (SI 2000/590) reg.5 (April 3, 2000).

5. Social Security Amendment (Residential Care and Nursing Homes) Regulations 2001 (SI 2001/3767) reg.2(1) and Pt I of Sch. para.7 (April 8, 2002).

6. Social Security (Miscellaneous Amendments) (No.5) Regulations 2007 (SI 2007/2618) reg.5(4) (October 1, 2007).

DEFINITION

  "personal capability assessment"—SSCBA s.171C and Incapacity for Work Regulations reg.24.

GENERAL NOTE

2.196 This regulation is no longer of any practical application because it relates to the old incapacity for work regime. However, it has not been formally revoked and so is being retained, together with the note to it.

Paragraphs (1) and (2) of this regulation replace the provisions formerly in regs 8(2A) and 22 (now revoked). Paragraph (3) repeats the transitional protection in reg.19(5) of the Disability Working Allowance and Income Support (General) Amendment Regulations 1995 (see p.1754).

The regulation applies where a claimant is appealing against a decision that he is fit for work on the basis of the "personal capability assessment" (which replaced the "all work test" from April 3, 2000) and so is eligible for income support under para.25 of Sch.1B (and does not qualify under any of the other paragraphs in Sch.1B). See the 2010/11 edition of Vol.I of this series for full details of the personal capability assessment and when it applies. A claimant will be eligible for income support under para.25 until the appeal is determined (which means the final determination of the appeal, e.g. if it is taken to the Social Security Commissioner (now Upper Tribunal), confirmed in *CIS 2654/1999*, see further the notes to para.25 of Sch.1B). However, his income support will be reduced by 20 per cent of the appropriate personal allowance for a single claimant of his age (para.(1)). If the appeal is successful the reduction will be repaid—see further the note to paras 24–25 of Sch.1B. (Paragraph (3) allowed full income support to be paid where the claimant had appealed after failing his first all work test or personal capability assessment if he had been incapable of work for 28 weeks or in receipt of invalidity benefit or severe disablement allowance immediately before April 13, 1995. Note also reg.27(3) of the Income Support (General) (Jobseeker's Allowance Consequential Amendments) Regulations 1996 which provided for the reduction under para.(1) not to apply to people covered by reg.19(5) of the Disability Working Allowance and Income Support (General) Amendment Regulations 1995 as originally made (see the notes to reg.19(5) and (6) of those Regulations).)

In order to receive full benefit the person will have to sign on as available for work   2.197
and claim JSA while waiting for his appeal to be decided (or after the introduction of ESA on October 27, 2008 he could consider claiming ESA). The fact that a person has been available for employment will not prejudice the appeal about incapacity as it will be a change of circumstances that has occurred after the date of decision under appeal (s.12(8)(b), SSA 1998). See further the notes to para.25 of Sch.1B.

In *Smyth* (High Court of Northern Ireland, July 6, 2001) it was argued that the reduction under the equivalent Northern Ireland provision to para.(1) constituted "an impermissible clog" on the exercise of the right to appeal and was therefore a violation of art.6 of the European Convention on Human Rights. However, this was rejected by Kerr J. In his view, the reduction was "a proportionate means of discouraging unmeritorious or frivolous appeals" and was not such a disincentive that it destroyed the essence of the right to appeal. He considered that a claimant's art.6 rights were "sufficiently safeguarded by the existence of the right of appeal, the availability of income support (albeit at a reduced level) while the appeal is pending, and the backdated repayment of the full amount on a successful outcome for the appeal".

Note that following the introduction of ESA on October 27, 2008 most *new* claims for benefit on the basis of incapacity for work made on or after that date will be treated as claims for ESA. See further the note to para.7 of Sch.1B in the 2015/16 edition of this volume.

[¹ Period for which applicable amount is to be calculated where person not excluded from income support under section 115 of the Immigration and Asylum Act 1999

22B.—[² . . .]]   2.198

AMENDMENTS

1. Social Security (Miscellaneous Amendments) (No.5) Regulations 2009 (SI 2009/3228) reg.3(2)(c) (January 25, 2010).
2. Social Security (Miscellaneous Amendments) (No.3) Regulations 2013 (SI 2013/2536) reg.4(1) and (6) (October 29, 2013).

GENERAL NOTE

Until its revocation, reg.22B (taken together with reg.2 of, and para.1 of Pt 1   2.199
of the Schedule to, the Social Security (Immigration and Asylum) Consequential Amendments Regulations 2000 (SI 2000/636), which was also revoked with effect from October 29, 2009) allowed claimants with limited leave to enter or remain in the UK subject to a condition that they do not have recourse to public funds, to receive income support in some circumstances where they were temporarily without funds because remittances to them from abroad had been disrupted. Such people would otherwise have been—and are now—excluded from benefit under s.115 of the Immigration and Asylum Act 1999 as persons subject to immigration control.

For commentary on the law as it stood before October 29, 2013, see pp.375, 800–801 and 809–810 of Vol.II of the 2013/14 edition.

PART V

INCOME AND CAPITAL

Chapter I

General

Calculation of income and capital of members of claimant's family and of a polygamous marriage

2.200

23.—(1) [³Subject to paragraph (4), the income and capital of a claimant's partner which by virtue of section 136(1) of the Contributions and Benefits Act] is to be treated as income and capital of the claimant, shall be calculated in accordance with the following provisions of this Part in like manner as for the claimant; and any reference to the "claimant" shall, except where the context otherwise requires, be construed, for the purposes of this Part, as if it were a reference to his partner [³. . .].

[³(2) Subject to the following provisions of this Part, the income paid to, or in respect of, and capital of, a child or young person who is a member of the claimant's family shall not be treated as the income or capital of the claimant.]

(3) [¹Subject to paragraph (5)] where a claimant or the partner of a claimant is married polygamously to two or more members of his household—

(a) the claimant shall be treated as possessing capital and income belonging to each such member [³. . .]; and

(b) the income and capital of that member [³. . .] shall be calculated in accordance with the following provisions of this Part in like manner as for the claimant [³. . .].

[¹(4) Where at least one member of a couple is aged less than 18 and the applicable amount of the couple falls to be determined under [²paragraphs 1(3)(b), (c), (f) or (g)] of Schedule 2 (applicable amounts), the income of the claimant's partner shall not be treated as the income of the claimant to the extent that—

(a) in the case of a couple where both members are aged less than 18, the amount specified in paragraph 1(3)(a) of that Schedule exceeds the amount specified in [²paragraph 1(3)(c)] of that Schedule; and

(b) in the case of a couple where only one member is aged less than 18, the amount specified in paragraph 1(3)(d) of that Schedule exceeds the amount which applies in that case which is specified in [²paragraph 1(3)(f) or (g)] of that Schedule.

(5) Where a member of a polygamous marriage is a partner aged less than 18 and the amount which applies in respect of him under regulation 18(2) (polygamous marriages) is nil, the claimant shall not be treated as possessing the income of that partner to the extent that an amount in respect of him would have been included in the applicable amount if he had fallen within the circumstances set out in regulation 18(2)(a) or (b).]

AMENDMENTS

1. Income Support (General) Amendment No.3 Regulations 1988 (SI 1988/ 1228) reg.6 (September 12, 1988).

2. Income Support (General) (Jobseeker's Allowance Consequential Amendments) Regulations 1996 (SI 1996/206) reg.14 (October 7, 1996).

3. Social Security (Working Tax Credit and Child Tax Credit) (Consequential Amendments) Regulations 2003 (SI 2003/455) reg.2 and Sch.1 para.6 (April 6, 2004, except in "transitional cases" and see further the note to reg.17 of the Income Support Regulations).

DEFINITIONS

"child"—see SSCBA s.137(1).
"claimant"—see reg.2(1).
"couple"—*ibid.*
"family"—see SSCBA s.137(1).
"partner"—see reg.2(1).
"polygamous marriage"—*ibid.*
"young person"—*ibid.*, and reg.14.

GENERAL NOTE

Distinction between capital and income

Resources are to be either capital or income. There is nothing in between. That statement was cited with approval in *R(IS)) 3/93* and without disapproval in *R(IS) 9/08* below, which also confirms that advance payments (in that case made by a local authority to a foster parent) could not be taken into account, as either income or capital, before the period to which they related.

The distinction between capital and income is one which has given a good deal of trouble in the past, and in many other legal contexts. There is no attempt at any general definition in the Regulations, although there are some important deemings. Regulation 35(1) gives a wide meaning to earnings as an employed earner (any remuneration or profit derived from that employment—a test familiar from income tax law) and then provides a number of examples to be treated as so derived. Regulation 41 specifies categories of capital that are to be treated as income. In particular, para.(5) provides that any earnings to the extent that they are not a payment of income are to be treated as income. Thus in combination with reg.35, any payment derived from employment, in the sense of paid as a reward for past services or as an incentive to enter into employment and provide future services, whether on general principle to be regarded as capital or income, is to be treated as income. Regulation 48 specifies categories of income that are to be treated as capital.

The approach tends to be that around the borderlines a decision can go either way, and it is only if a decision is completely unreasonable that it embodies an error of law (*R. v W. London SBAT, Ex p. Taylor* [1975] 2 All E. R. 790). But ultimately the question is one of law (see *Lillystone v SBC* [1982] 3 F.L.R. 52 CA). However, note *CIS 2537/1997* in which the Commissioner queries whether the question is one of law. He points to *Gallagher v Jones* [1994] Ch. 107 CA and *Herbert Smith v Honour* [1999] S.T.C. 173 as authority for the proposition that for income tax and similar purposes the principal guide to whether something is income or capital is by reference to accounting principles. See also *CIS 5481/1997* below.

So far as general principle goes it has been said that the "essential feature of receipts by way of income is that they display an element of periodic recurrence. Income cannot include ad hoc receipts." (Bridge J in *R. v Supplementary Benefits Commission Ex p. Singer* [1973] 1 W.L.R. 713). That links the notion of recurrence (which may only be expected in the future) with the notion of a period to which the income is linked. Similar notions are applied by the Commissioner in *R(SB) 29/85* where the issue was the proper treatment of a £15 loan made to a striking miner by a local authority Social Work Department to meet arrears on hire purchase agreements. That was held to be a capital payment, since it was a "one-off" advance and there was no evidence that it was one of a series of payments. Earlier he had referred to income payments normally bearing a readily identifiable relationship

2.201

2.202

with a period. However, periodic recurrence alone is not enough. The nature of the obligation (if any) under which a payment is made must be looked at. As the Court of Appeal put it in *Minter v Kingston upon Hull CC* and *Potter v Secretary of State for Work and Pensions* [2011] EWCA Civ 1155; [2012] AACR 21, the "first task is to determine the true characteristics of the payment in the hands of the recipient" (see *R. v National Insurance Commissioner Ex p. Stratton* [1979] I.C.R. 209, Appendix II to *R(U) 1/79*). In determining the true characteristic of the payment (i.e. its substantive nature and purpose), the label that the parties attach to it was said to be irrelevant.

A capital payment may be made by instalments. Then in general each instalment is a capital payment, so that reg.41(1), probably to be interpreted as treating each instalment on receipt to be income if the amount of the outstanding instalments plus any other capital comes to more than £16,000, is necessary (see the notes to reg.41(1)). The general rule is supported by the Court of Appeal in *Lillystone v SBC* where the purchase price of a house was to be paid in monthly instalments over 10 years. It was agreed that each £70 instalment, when it was paid, was capital, not income. Another potential example might have been thought to be withdrawals by instalments from an "income drawdown" personal pension policy, where, because the initial investment had lost value, the instalments inevitably ate into capital funds (*SSWP v IG (SPC)* [2018] UKUT 228 (AAC), where *Lillystone* was relied on). However, on appeal by the SSWP the Court of Appeal rejected the Upper Tribunal's approach to the meaning of income in the specific context, so that this example should not be relied on (*Secretary of State for Work and Pensions v Goulding* [2019] EWCA Civ 839). See the notes to reg.42(2ZA)–(2CA).

A similar approach was taken by the Court of Appeal in *Morrell v Secretary of State for Work and Pensions* [2003] EWCA Civ 526, reported as *R(IS) 6/03*. Following her divorce, the claimant had been receiving regular sums of money from her mother, either paid to her to help her pay her rent and other living expenses, or paid directly to her landlord in respect of her rent. It was not in dispute that the payments were made to the claimant by way of loan, although the repayment terms were quite vague, the mother merely expecting reimbursement gradually as her daughter's problems decreased. The claimant argued that because the payments made by her mother were a loan, they were not income payments but should have been treated as capital. However, the Court rejected this argument. Referring to *Chief Adjudication Officer v Leeves*, CA, reported as *R(IS) 5/99* (see the note to reg.40), it said that the word "income" was to be given its ordinary and natural meaning. There was no general principle (in tax cases or elsewhere) that loans should be treated as capital rather than income. (On this see also *R(H) 8/08*.) The regular monthly receipts from her mother clearly had the character of income. The Court agreed with *Leeves* that a sum received under a certain and immediate obligation to repay did not amount to income. However, there was no such obligation in this case and so the payments counted as income.

2.203 See also *KW v Lancaster CC & SSWP (HB)* [2011] UKUT 266 (AAC) in which a large payment of arrears of child support accrued over many years was income, not capital.

DN v Leicester CC (HB) [2010] UKUT 253 (AAC) discusses the nature of annuity payments. In that case the claimant's annual annuity payment, which was derived from a personal pension plan and was subject to income tax, counted as income to be attributed over the whole year. In any event, however, reg.41(2) of the Housing Benefit Regulations 2006 (which is in the same terms as reg.41(2)) was there to ensure that all annuity payments, whatever their complexion, were taken into account as income.

See also *CIS 5481/1997* which concerned the assets of a business partnership. The Commissioner emphasised that some of the assets would be income, not capital; the distinction was to be drawn in accordance with accounting practice. This provided that the key principle was what the expenditure was calculated to effect from a practical and business point of view, and the same also applied to receipts (see *CIR v Wattie* [1998] S.T.C. 1160).

2.204 Particularly difficult problems have been raised by lump sum payments of compensation for breach of various employment rights calculated by reference to the difference between past wages or salary actually paid, and what should have been paid. The analysis now has to start with the decision of the Court of Appeal in *Minter v Kingston upon Hull CC* and *Potter v Secretary of State for Work and Pensions* [2011] EWCA Civ 1155; [2012] AACR 21.

Minter was the claimant's appeal from the decision of Judge Howell in *Kingston upon Hull CC v DLM (HB)* [2010] UKUT 234 (AAC). *Potter* was the claimant's appeal from the decision of Judge Jacobs in *SSWP v JP (JSA)* [2010] UKUT 90 (AAC). In *JP*, which was decided first, the claimant received a payment from her employer as part of an offer of a settlement of a claim under the Equal Pay Act 1970. The payment of 10 per cent of the amount of the offer was made on the basis that, if the claimant accepted the offer she would be paid the remaining 90 per cent, but that if she did not accept the offer (as she did not) she would keep the 10 per cent payment, which would be treated as paid on account of any award that might eventually be made by an employment tribunal. The judge applied the accepted principle that the classification of the payment depended on what it was made for. The Equal Pay Act claim against the employer was not for the loss of a capital asset, such as a job or the right to bring proceedings, but for the amount that the claimant would have been paid if her employer had honoured the terms of the equality clause that was part of her contract of employment. That essential nature as income was not changed by the fact that that amount was paid later and as a lump sum.

Judge Jacobs in *JP* was prepared to accept that there was a distinction from the result of *EM v London Borough of Waltham Forest* [2009] UKUT 245 (AAC), which concerned payments from an employer in settlement of a potential claim under the Part-time Workers (Prevention of Less Favourable Treatment) Regulations 2000 (SI 2000/1551) ("the PTWR 2000"). The payments were calculated on the basis of the additional amount of the bonus payments that would have been received over a three-year period if the conditions applying to full-time drivers had been applied to part-time drivers. Judge Wikeley considered that there was a difference from cases like *CIS/590/1993* (itself following *R(SB) 21/86*) on actual compensatory awards for loss of earnings made by employment tribunals (see further the notes to reg.35(1)(b)). The basis of compensation under the PTWR 2000 was what was just and equitable, so that there was no guarantee that any award actually made would be based on the difference in the amounts of the bonus payments. Nor was there an absolute contractual right to the bonus payments, since the Regulations did not operate by implying a statutory term into the contract of employment, as the equal pay legislation did. The judge therefore found the payments by way of settlement of a potential (and highly probable) legal liability to be capital.

In *DLM* Judge Howell took the same view as in *JP* of a payment received in settlement of an equal pay claim that had been calculated using average comparators over the period for which the claimant had been paid less than she should have been. He decided that the payment was clearly income in the form of earnings. But he disagreed with *JP* in concluding that there was no material distinction between such payments and those made in *EM*: both were "catch-up redress for past failure to recognise the existence of claims to equal treatment in the matter of remuneration" and so were income.

2.205

The appeals to the Court of Appeal of the claimants in *JP* and *DLM* were dismissed.

Thomas LJ, who gave the judgment of the court, stated that the first task was "to determine the true characteristic of the payment in the hands of the recipient" (see *R. v National Insurance Commissioner Ex p. Stratton* [1979] I.C.R. 209, Appendix II to *R(U) 1/79*). In determining the true characteristic of the payment, the label that the parties attach to it is irrelevant. Nor does it matter whether the payment is made as a lump sum or as a series of periodic payments. The size of the payment is also irrelevant, as is the fact that the sum may have accumulated over a prolonged period. The payments that the two claimants had received were compensation for the lower wages that had been paid in breach of equal pay provisions and as such were compensation for past lost income. Since the payments were payments of income that should have been paid as wages, they fell to be treated as earnings. Further, the effect of the equivalents of reg.41(5) was that, even if the payments were to be regarded as capital, as they were earnings within the meaning of reg.35(1) (remuneration or profit derived from employment) they were to be treated as income.

2.206 It is submitted that Thomas LJ went too far in saying that the label attached to the payment is irrelevant. Surely a label should be regarded as one out of many relevant considerations, but not decisive, as stated by Judge Jacobs in *JP*. That is more in line with Lord Denning MR's statement in *Stratton* that the matter depends on the true characteristic of the payment, not on the way it is described or calculated.

Unfortunately, although the Court was referred to the decision in *EM*, it dealt with the decision in a rather obscure way at para.30. It is submitted that the reason why the Court found it unnecessary to say whether the payment involved in *EM* should properly have been found to be capital or income was that even if it was capital (as Judge Wikeley had decided), it should have been treated as income under the equivalent of reg.41(5). The necessary implication is that *EM* was wrongly decided for failing to consider that provision. Even if that is not the proper view, it is submitted here that the approach to similar cases in the future must be to apply the general principles approved in *Minter and Potter* rather than to seek draw analogies with the circumstances of *EM*. If necessary, *EM* should be regarded as wrongly decided on the general principle. The nature of the payments made there appear different in their fundamental nature from. say, the elements of a compensatory sex discrimination award for injured feelings and the loss of a tax rebate, accepted as being capital in *CIS/590/1993*.

The *Minter and Potter* approach appears consistent with the principle established in *R(SB) 4/89* and *CH 1561/2005* that payments of arrears of social security benefits that would have been income if paid on the proper date retain their character as income, rather than capital. However, any money left after the end of the period to which the payments are attributed as income would become capital under the principles discussed at paras 2.208 and 2.209 below.

2.207 A further 2020 example might occur if an income support claimant or partner is "furloughed" (put on leave of absence) by their employer under the Coronavirus Job Retention Scheme, but is not paid by the employer until receipt of the grant under the Scheme, when a lump sum is paid for the period of furlough. Such a payment would retain its character as income, rather than capital. See the notes to reg.37 for discussion of the difficult questions whether grants under the Coronavirus Self-Employed Income Support Scheme ("SEISS") or from the Small Business Grant Fund or the Retail, Hospitality and Leisure Grant Fund are capital or income receipts for the purpose of calculating self-employed earnings. Also see those notes and the notes to reg.30 for discussion of the inadequacy of the guidance in Memo DMG 13/20 on treating SEISS grants as income receipts and as self-employed earnings for the three months from the date of payment, in relation to the existing form of the relevant regulations. A simple amendment to the regulations for the affected means-tested benefits could have avoided the difficulty.

See reg.31 below for the rules on the dates on which payments of earnings from an employed earner's employment and of income other than earnings are to be treated as paid. The general rule is to use the date on which the payment is due to be made, rather than to attribute the payment forward from the date of payment. However, see the notes to reg.31 for several complications and the difficulties in determining when some of the kinds of payments discussed above are due to be paid. See reg.30 for self-employed earnings.

The metamorphosis of income into capital

2.208 In *R(SB) 2/83* the Tribunal of Commissioners says "In most cases capital resources arise out of income resources. They represent savings out of past earnings. However, before they undergo the metamorphosis from income to capital all relevant debts, including, in particular, tax liabilities, are first deducted." In *R(SB) 35/83* the Commissioner holds that accumulated earnings will not become capital until all relevant liabilities are deducted. Since the "relevant liabilities" seems to mean the deductions appropriate under the benefit legislation, presumably for employed earners, it is only the categories mentioned in reg.36(3), if not already deducted, which can be considered, plus, it seems, expenses necessarily incurred in obtaining the earnings *(R(FC) 1/90* and *R(IS) 16/93*—see the note to reg.36(3)). *CIS 563/1991* decides that such expenses are not deductible in the case of income other than earnings (see the note to reg.40(1)). There is no provision for deducting amounts which are to be used for ordinary current expenditure *(R(IS) 3/93)*.

R(IS) 3/93 also confirms that a payment does not metamorphose into capital until the end of the period to which it is attributed as income. Thus, for example, payment of a month's salary, attributable for a forward period of a month from the date it was due to be paid, would retain its character as income until the end of that period. This principle should apply to other forms of income as it does to earnings. Thus if, for instance, arrears of a social security benefit are paid, then any amount of those arrears left after the end of the period to which the benefit is properly attributed as income comes into the category of capital. *R(SB) 4/89*, holding arrears of special hardship allowance to be income, did not deal with this point.

However, in *CIS/515/2006* the Commissioner took a rather different approach. He rejected the proposition that saved benefit left over at the end of each month becomes capital. He considered that a longer view had to be taken, possibly by looking at the situation after a year in line with the position he considered applied to arrears of benefits, and considering the reason for the accumulation of income and where it was held. There were several difficulties in working out the consequences of that approach, discussed fully in the 2016/17 and earlier editions.

The conflict between *R(IS) 3/93* and *CIS/515/2006* was considered in *R(IS) 9/08*.   **2.209**
The Commissioner states:

> "I prefer the authority of *R(IS) 3/93* for these reasons. First, it is a reported decision, which shows that the majority of the Commissioners at the time considered that it was at least broadly correct. Second, I consider that its reasoning is sound. Given that a resource has to be either income or capital, it must become capital when it is no longer income. Mr [Commissioner] Williams did not deal with that point. Third and particularly relevant to this case, the income support legislation failed to carry forward an express provision in supplementary benefit law that disregarded savings made out of income in order to meet personal living expenses and the expenses of the home. (It is quoted in *R(IS) 3/93* at paragraph 24.) Income support replaced supplementary benefit in April 1988 and was, of course, a new benefit. However, there is sufficient continuity in the income and capital provisions of the two schemes to make it significant that no equivalent disregard was adopted in income support. Fourth, the approach in *CIS/515/2006* draws on the Commissioner's experience in business and tax. In those contexts, it may be appropriate to identify capital on an annual basis. However, income support is a weekly benefit and a much shorter timescale is appropriate. The timescale fixed by *R(IS) 3/93* is consistent with the allocation of income to a particular period."

But note that the "metamorphosis" principle does not apply to self-employed earnings, as held by the Commissioner in *CIS/2467/2003* (although he confirmed that it did apply to income other than earnings, such as incapacity benefit and disability living allowance which were in issue in that case, as well as earnings from employment). This was because the calculation of earnings from self-employment did not turn on when particular receipts came in but was, under reg.30(1), to be calculated as average weekly earnings (net profit, subject to deductions for income tax and social security) over a period of normally a year. Those average weekly earnings are then taken into account for income support purposes for an equivalent period into the future. There was therefore no period of attribution to be attached to any particular business receipt and the basis of the *R(IS) 3/93* principle did not exist.

In the Commissioner's view it would be artificial and wrong to regard all business receipts as retaining the character of income until the expiry of the period for which earnings calculated over the whole period were taken into account. Instead the protection for self-employed earners in relation to the capital rules lay in the disregard of the value of business assets under para.6 of Sch.10. The Commissioner also held that the *R(IS) 3/93* principle did not apply to self-employed earnings covered by the special attribution rule in reg.30(2) (royalties, etc.). The claimant in *CIS/2467/2003* was a self-employed author who received advances on contracting to write a book and subsequent royalties on sales. His claim for income support was refused on the ground that he had capital in excess of the prescribed limit. The Commissioner rejected his argument that money paid by way of advances was not legally owned by him because the advances were repayable if he did not fulfill the contract. In his view the advances fully belonged to the claimant as soon as they were received. The Commissioner further concluded that the claimant's business receipts had the character of capital as soon as they were paid to him and that the disregard of business assets in para.6 of Sch.10 did not apply (for further discussion of this case see the note to reg.30 and the note to para.6 of Sch.10).

R(PC) 3/08 rejects the Secretary of State's argument that "capital" has a special meaning in the state pension credit scheme and the "metamorphosis" principle did not apply. The general rule as stated in *R(IS) 3/93* applied, despite the absence of an equivalent provision to reg.29(2)(a) in the State Pension Credit Regulations.

What constitutes income of the claimant?

2.210 On the meaning of "income" see *R(IS) 4/01*. The Commissioner decides, applying *Leeves* (see the note to reg.40), that the part of the claimant's occupational pension that was being paid to his former wife under an attachment of earnings order did not count as his income for the purposes of income support. He concluded that in the absence of a statutory definition, income meant "money paid regularly to the recipient or to his order but not money which is being paid and which he cannot prevent from being paid directly to a third party instead of him". The Commissioner also held that the notional income rule in reg.42(4)(a) did not apply: see the note to reg.42(4)(a). In *CH/1672/2007* the half of the claimant's pension that he was required to pay to his wife under the terms of a court order following a judicial separation did not count as his income. However, income subject to a direction which could be revoked at any time (in that case a pension signed over by a nun to a religious order under a deed of trust) remained the claimant's income (*C 10/06–07(IS)*, a Northern Ireland decision). So did the half of his annuities that the claimant in *CH/1076/2008* voluntarily paid to his wife from whom he was separated. In that case the Commissioner drew attention to the "further problem" that would need to be considered if the annuities were retirement annuity pensions in connection with a former employment, namely the conditions in s.91 of the Pension Schemes Act 1995 for assignment of such an annuity.

In addition see *CIS 5479/1997* in which an overpayment of an occupational pension was being recovered by the Italian authorities by withholding the monthly payments of the pension. The Commissioner refers to *Leeves* as confirming his own view that in the general context of the income support scheme income to be taken into account is income that is actually paid to a claimant. If a claimant who has not actually received income is to be treated as having that income, that has to be achieved by a specific provision in the legislation (but now see *BL v SSWP (SPC)* [2018] UKUT 4 (AAC) below). In *R(IS) 4/02* the same Commissioner applies this approach to conclude, contrary to the view taken in *CIS 212/1989*, para.9 (and followed with some hesitation in *CIS 295/1994*), that payments of the claimant's husband's annuity which had vested in his trustee in bankruptcy under s.306 of the Insolvency Act 1986 were not part of his income (and thus not part of the claimant's income) for the purposes of income support. See also *R(IS) 2/03*, which agrees with *R(IS) 4/02* (on the basis of the principle in *Re Landau* [1998] Ch. 223, affirmed in *Krasner v Dennison* [2001] Ch. 76) that *CIS 212/1989* should no longer be followed. Thus the payments under the claimant's self-employed pension annuity that were being applied entirely for the benefit of his creditors were not his actual income (see the note to reg.42(4) and (4ZA) for the position in relation to notional income). Note that the law has now changed on the exclusion of pension rights from a bankrupt's estate (Welfare Reform and Pensions Act 1999 s.11), but only for bankruptcy orders made on or after May 29, 2000. Regulation 42(4) and (4ZA) were also amended on November 9, 1999 to make specific provision for pensions paid to third parties (see the note to reg.42(4) and (4ZA) and in particular *R(IS) 4/01* discussed in that note). The general principle of the meaning of "income", however, will remain of significance.

See *BL v SSWP (SPC)* [2018] UKUT 4 (AAC) for a helpful illustration of the general principles. Payments of the claimant's personal pension to his ex-wife were his income because they were made at his order and he retained practical control over the money. Under a deed of separation he had undertaken to make maintenance payments of a specified amount. Once he started to draw the pension he directed the provider to pay those amounts to his ex-wife. It did not matter that the claimant never actually received those amounts from the pension provider. He was still free to deal with that money as he wished and retained not just legal, but also practical, control over it. The statement in *CIS/5479/1997* noted above about claimants who have not actually received income was distinguished as based on different facts. It is submitted that that statement should not be taken out of its context of a withholding of social security payments to recover a debt owed to the social security institution making the payments.

The question has also arisen in relation to overpaid working tax credit. *CIS/647/2007* points out that the Court of Appeal in *Leeves* had made it clear that the demand for repayment and the immediate obligation it gave rise to only affected the claimant's grant income that was to be attributed to the future. It did not have retrospective effect so as to remove the quality of income from the part of the grant that had already been attributed. The key date was the date of the demand for repayment. So up to the date that the Revenue decided that the claimant had to repay her working tax credit it counted as her income. This is confirmed by the same Upper Tribunal Judge in *CC v SSWP* [2009] UKUT 280 (AAC). The claimant's award of old style JSA had been reduced to take account of the working tax credit that he was being (wrongly) paid. Subsequently a decision was made retrospectively terminating his working tax credit. This provided grounds for a supersession of the decision awarding JSA so as to increase the amount payable. The claimant's appeal was treated as both an appeal against the decision awarding JSA at a reduced rate and the supersession decision. That did not, however, assist the claimant. That was because: (i) the removal of the working tax credit was not a circumstance obtaining at the date of the decision awarding JSA (at the date of that decision the claimant was receiving working tax credit) and so could not be taken into account by virtue of s.12(8)(b) SSA 1998; (ii) under reg.7(2) of the Decisions and Appeals Regulations the supersession decision took effect on the date the change occurred, i.e. the date HMRC made the change to the working tax credit award, not the date from which that change had effect. Judge Jacobs acknowledges that this meant that the claimant lost both part of his JSA and the tax credit but he could see no way to avoid this effect.

However, in *CIS/1813/2007* the Commissioner holds that payments of working tax credit made after the claimant had notified the Revenue that she had ceased work and had asked for the payments to stop did not count as income. Or, if that was wrong, the payments were voluntary payments which were to be disregarded under para.15(5A) (b) of Sch.9. Once the claimant had made proper disclosure, and even more so where she had asked not to be paid, it was entirely a matter for the Revenue whether to continue payment. The Commissioner distinguishes *CIS/647/2007* on the basis that the claimant in that case had not informed the Revenue of her change of circumstances. The Revenue had therefore continued to be under an obligation to make the payments and there was no question of the payments being voluntary. Similarly in *Leeves* there was no suggestion that the claimant had told the local authority before the grant was paid that it should not pay him or that there were grounds for revoking the award and so the question of whether the payments were voluntary had not arisen.

2.211

For a discussion of the meaning of "voluntary payment" see the notes to para.15 of Sch.9; note in particular *R(H) 5/05* which held that the loans in that case which had not created any legally enforceable rights or obligations and for which the lender had not obtained anything in return were voluntary payments. Thus loans made at regular intervals which do count as income because they do not satisfy the *Leeves* test of a certain and immediate obligation to repay may nevertheless be disregarded under para.15(5A)(b) of Sch.9, depending on the circumstances of the loan. If the loan is a one-off or the loans are irregular, note reg.48(9) which treats irregular voluntary payments as capital.

2.212   *R(H) 5/05* also considered the position in relation to bank overdrafts. The Commissioner referred to the fact that the standard terms of a bank overdraft were that it was repayable on demand, although the demand might not be made while the amount stayed within an agreed limit. Those terms brought the repayment obligation within the *Leeves* principle. The obligation was certain, as the amount overdrawn could be identified day by day, and was immediate, even though the bank choose not to enforce the immediate obligation. Thus the resources provided by the use of the claimant's overdraft facility did not amount to income. The Commissioner commented that that result was also in accord with the ordinary and natural meaning of "income". One would not naturally speak of a person having an income from incurring expenditure and running up an overdraft. (Note that the Commissioner did not refer to the Court of Appeal's decision in *R. v West Dorset DC, Ex p. Poupard* [1998] 28 R.V.R. 40 which had held that borrowings by way of a bank overdraft secured by capital and used for living expenses constituted income for the purposes of the housing benefit scheme as it then existed. But arguably this decision is no longer pertinent, bearing in mind that it concerned the former housing benefit scheme, and in the light of *Leeves*. And see *AR v Bradford Metropolitan DC* [2008] UKUT 30 (AAC), reported as *R(H) 6/09*, in which the judge states that *Poupard* never stood for any rigid rule that loans have to count as income and that the decision was not relevant to the current housing benefit and council tax benefit schemes, and should be confined to a historical footnote at most.) The Commissioner in *R(H) 5/05* left open the question of whether the same would apply to credit cards, although he did refer to *CH/3393/2003* in which it was accepted that the juggling of credit card balances, where there was no immediate liability to repay beyond the minimum monthly payment, created a regular funding facility to be taken into account as income; however in the circumstances of the case before him there was no need to decide whether or not *CH/3393/2003* was correctly decided or whether it depended on its particular facts. But note *R(H) 8/08* in which the Commissioner does voice his opinion that *CH/3393/2003* was wrong to treat credit card payments as income.

SH v SSWP [2008] UKUT 21 (AAC) concerned the weekly sums which the claimant was allowed to withdraw for living expenses from his bank account which was subject to a restraint order under s.77 of the Criminal Justice Act 1988. It is held that these sums were not income at the time of withdrawal but remained capital. Furthermore there was nothing in the JSA Regulations 1996 (or the equivalent provisions in the Income Support Regulations) which treated these payments of capital as income. They were not capital payable by instalments within the meaning of reg.104(1) of the JSA Regulations 1996 (the equivalent of reg.41(1)) as this provision only applied if there was a contractual or other obligation on the part of some other person to pay a capital sum to the claimant by instalments.

Drawings from a partnership (or a business) are not income other than earnings, nor are they earnings from self-employment (*AR v Bradford Metropolitan DC* [2008] UKUT 30 (AAC), reported as *R(H) 6/09*). Otherwise there would be an unfair double counting (see the notes to reg.37).

Paragraphs (1) and (2)

2.213   These provisions contain the basic rule on the aggregation of resources. With effect from April 6, 2004 (except in "transitional cases"—see the note to reg.17), only the income and capital of the claimant's partner is treated as the claimant's.

Note that the definition of partner refers on to a couple, also defined in reg.2(1) (and see para.(3) for polygamous marriages). It is an essential part of the definition of couple that the parties should be members of the same household, so that reg.16 may also be relevant. There are special rules for couples where at least one member is under 18 (paras (4) and (5)).

Under the form of reg.23 in force before April 6, 2004 (the old form continues to apply for "transitional cases"—see the note to reg.17) the income (but not the capital) of a child or young person who was a member of the clamaint's family was aggregated with the claimant's (see the 2003 edition of this volume for the old form of reg.23 and the notes to that regulation for further details of the former rules relating to treatment of a child or young person's income and capital). However, with effect from April 6, 2004 (except in "transitional cases"—see the note to reg.17) amounts for children and young persons have been removed from the income support scheme; financial assistance to help with the cost of bringing up a child or young person is now to be provided through the child tax credit system, see Vol.IV of this series. As a consequence the new form of para.(2) provides that income paid to, or in respect of, and the capital of, a child or young person does not count as that of the claimant. Note the new disregards of child benefit and child tax credit (see para.5B of Sch.9) (for income support claimants who had an award of child tax credit before April 6, 2004 see reg.7 of the Social Security (Working Tax Credit and Child Tax Credit) (Consequential Amendments) Regulations 2003 (SI 2003/455) (as amended) on p.1765 and the notes to that regulation).

References to "the claimant" in the following regulations are to be treated as references to any partner. However, see *R(IS) 3/03* discussed in the note to para.12 of Sch.10.

Paragraph (4)

This paragraph applies where a couple receives less than the ordinary couple's rate of personal allowance because of the ineligibility of one partner who is under 18 (this is the effect of the reference to para.1(3)(b), (c), (f) and (g) of Sch.2). The income of the ineligible partner is not treated as the claimant's except to the extent that it exceeds the difference between the reduced rate of personal allowance and the ordinary rate. The aggregation of capital is not affected.

2.214

Paragraph (5)

This makes similar provision for polygamous marriages.

2.215

[¹ Income of participants in the self-employment route [² . . .]

23A.—Chapters II, III, IV, V, VII and VIIA of this Part and regulations 62 to 66A, 68 and 69 shall not apply to any income which is to be calculated in accordance with Chapter IVA of this Part (participants in the self-employment route [² . . .]).]

2.216

AMENDMENTS

1. Social Security (Miscellaneous Amendments) (No.4) Regulations 1998 (SI 1998/1174) reg.6(2) (June 1, 1998).
2. Social Security Amendment (Employment Zones) (No.2) Regulations 2000 (SI 2000/2910) reg.5(1)(a) (November 27, 2000).

DEFINITION

"self-employment route"—see reg.2(1).

GENERAL NOTE

Regulation 23A takes any gross receipts from trading while on the "self-employment route" out of the categories of earnings, self-employed earnings and income

2.217

other than earnings for the purposes of any claim for income support. The rules for liable relative payments and student income (except reg.67) also do not apply. Any such receipts may only be taken into account in accordance with regs 39A–39D. For the definition of the "self-employment route", see reg.2(1).

Treatment of charitable or voluntary payments

2.218
    24.—[¹ . . .]

AMENDMENT

1. Income Support (General) Amendment No.5 Regulations 1988 (SI 1988/ 2022) reg.5 (December 12, 1988).

[² [⁴ . . .]] liable relative payments

2.219
    25.—Regulations 29 to [¹42], 46 to 52 and Chapter VIII of this Part shall not apply to any payment which is to be calculated in accordance with Chapter VII thereof ([³ [⁵ . . .] liable relative payments]).

AMENDMENTS

1. Social Security (Working Tax Credit and Child Tax Credit) (Consequential Amendments) Regulations 2003 (SI 2003/455) reg.2 and Sch.1 para.7 (April 6, 2004, except in "transitional cases" and see further the note to reg.17 of the Income Support Regulations).
2. Social Security (Child Maintenance Amendments) Regulations 2008 (SI 2008/2111) reg.2(2)(a) (October 27, 2008).
3. Social Security (Child Maintenance Amendments) Regulations 2008 (SI 2008/2111) reg.2(3) (October 27, 2008).
4. Social Security (Miscellaneous Amendments) (No.4) Regulations 2009 (SI 2009/2655) reg.2(5) (April 12, 2010).
5. Social Security (Miscellaneous Amendments) (No.4) Regulations 2009 (SI 2009/2655) reg.2(6) (April 12, 2010).

[¹Child support

2.220
    25A.—[² . . .]]

AMENDMENTS

1. Social Security (Miscellaneous Provisions) Amendment Regulations 1993 (SI 1993/846) reg.2 (April 19, 1993).
2. Social Security (Child Maintenance Amendments) Regulations 2008 (SI 2008/2111) reg.2(4)(a) (October 27, 2008).

Calculation of income and capital of students

2.221
    26.—The provisions of Chapters II to VI of this Part (income and capital) shall [¹ have effect in relation to students and their partners subject to the modifications set out in Chapter VIII thereof (students)].

AMENDMENT

1. Income Support (General) Amendment Regulations 2001 (SI 2001/721) reg.2(a) (March 29, 2001).

DEFINITIONS

"partner"—see reg.2(1).
"student"—*ibid.*, and reg.61(1).

[¹Rounding of fractions

27.—Where any calculation under this Part results in a fraction of a penny that fraction shall, if it would be to the claimant's advantage, be treated as a penny, otherwise it shall be disregarded.]

2.222

AMENDMENT

1. Income Support (General) Amendment Regulations 1988 (SI 1988/663) reg.13 (April 11, 1988).

CHAPTER II

INCOME

Calculation of income

28.—(1) For the purposes of section 20(3) of the Act [SSCBA, s.124(1)] (conditions of entitlement to income support), the income of a claimant shall be calculated on a weekly basis—
(a) by determining in accordance with this Part, other than Chapter VI, the weekly amount of his income; and
(b) by adding to that amount the weekly income calculated under regulation 53 (calculation of tariff income from capital).
[¹(2) For the purposes of paragraph (1) "income" includes capital treated as income under regulations 41 (capital treated as income) and income which a claimant is treated as possessing under regulation 42 (notional income).]

2.223

AMENDMENT

1. Income Support (General) Amendment No.4 Regulations 1991 (SI 1991/1559) reg.7 (October 7, 1991).

DEFINITIONS

"the Act"—see reg.2(1).
"claimant"—*ibid.*

GENERAL NOTE

Regulation 28 simply confirms that all resources which would come under the description of income, including resources specifically treated as earnings or income, are to be taken into account in the income calculation.

2.224

Calculation of earnings derived from employed earner's employment and income other than earnings

29.—(1) [¹. . .] Earnings derived from employment as an employed earner and income which does not consist of earnings shall be taken into account over a period determined in accordance with the following paragraphs and at a weekly amount determined in accordance with regulation 32 (calculation of weekly amount of income).
(2) Subject to [⁴the following provisions of this regulation], the period over which a payment is to be taken into account shall be—
[⁹ (a) where the payment is monthly, a period equal to the number of weeks from the date on which the payment is treated as paid to

2.225

the date immediately before the date on which the next monthly payment would have been so treated as paid whether or not the next monthly payment is actually paid;

(aa) where the payment is in respect of a period which is not monthly, a period equal to the length of the period for which payment is made;]

(b) in any other case, a period equal to such number of weeks as is equal to the number obtained (and any fraction shall be treated as a corresponding fraction of a week) by dividing the net earnings, or in the case of income which does not consist of earnings, the amount of that income [³less any amount paid by way of tax on that income which is disregarded under paragraph 1 of Schedule 9 (income other than earnings to be disregarded)] by the amount of income support which would be payable had the payment not been made plus an amount equal to the total of the sums which would fall to be disregarded from that payment under Schedule 8 [³(earnings to be disregarded) or, as the case may be, any paragraph of Schedule 9 other than paragraph 1 of that Schedule,] as is appropriate in the claimant's case;

and that period shall begin on the date on which the payment is treated as paid under regulation 31 (date on which income is treated as paid).

[⁴(2A) The period over which a Career Development Loan, which is paid pursuant to section 2 of the Employment and Training Act 1973, shall be taken into account shall be the period of education and training intended to be supported by that loan.

(2B) Where grant income as defined in Chapter VIII of this Part has been paid to a person who ceases to be a [⁸ full-time student] before the end of the period in respect of which that income is payable and, as a consequence, the whole or part of that income falls to be repaid by that person, that income shall be taken into account over the period beginning on the date on which that income is treated as paid under regulation 31 and ending—

(a) on the date on which repayment is made in full; or

[⁵(aa) where the grant is paid in instalments, on the day before the next instalment would have been paid had the claimant remained a [⁸ full-time student]; or]

(b) on the last date of the academic term or vacation during which that person ceased to be a [⁸ full-time student],

whichever shall first occur.]

[¹⁰ [¹¹(2C)(a) This paragraph applies where earnings are derived by a claimant as a member of a reserve force prescribed in Part 1 of Schedule 6 to the Contributions Regulations—

(i) in respect of a period of annual continuous training for a maximum of 15 days in any calendar year; or

(ii) in respect of training in the claimant's first year of training as a member of a reserve force for a maximum of 43 days in that year.

(b) Earnings, whether paid to the claimant alone or together with other earnings derived from the same source, are to be taken into account—

(i) in the case of a period of training which lasts for the number of days listed in column 1 of the table in sub-paragraph (c), over a period of time which is equal to the number of days set out in the corresponding row in column 2 of that table; or

(ii) in any other case, over a period of time which is equal to the number of days of the training period.

(c) This is the table referred to in sub-paragraph (b)(i)—

Column 1	Column 2
Period of training in days	*Period of time over which earnings are to be taken into account in days*
8 to 10	7
15 to 17	14
22 to 24	21
29 to 31	28
36 to 38	35
43	42]

(2D) The period over which earnings to which paragraph (2C) applies are to be taken into account shall begin on the date on which the payment is treated as paid under regulation 31.]

(3) Where earnings not of the same kind are derived from the same source and the periods in respect of which those earnings would, but for this paragraph, fall to be taken into account—
(a) overlap, wholly or partly, those earnings shall be taken into account over a period equal to the aggregate length of those periods;
(b) and that period shall begin with the earliest date on which any part of those earnings would otherwise be treated as paid under regulation 31 (date on which income is treated as paid).

[²(4) In a case to which paragraph (3) applies, earnings under regulation 35 (earnings of employed earners) shall be taken into account in the following order of priority—
(a) earnings normally derived from the employment;
(b) any payment to which paragraph (1)(b) or (c) of that regulation applies;
(c) any payment to which paragraph (1)(i) of that regulation applies;
(d) any payment to which paragraph (1)(d) of that regulation applies.]

[¹(4A) Where earnings to which regulation 35(1)(b) to (d) (earnings of employed earners) applies are paid in respect of part of a day, those earnings shall be taken into account over a period equal to a day.]

[²(4B) [¹⁰. . .]

(4C) Any earnings to which regulation 35(1)(i)(ii) applies which are paid in respect of or on the termination of part-time employment, shall be taken into account over a period equal to one week.

(4D) In this regulation—
(a) "part-time employment" means employment in which a person is not to be treated as engaged in remunerative work under regulation 5 or [⁶6(1)[⁷and (4)]] (persons treated, or not treated, as engaged in remunerative work);
(b) [⁹. . .].]

(5) For the purposes of this regulation the claimant's earnings and income which does not consist of earnings shall be calculated in accordance with Chapters III and V respectively of this Part.

AMENDMENTS

1. Income Support (General) Amendment No.5 Regulations 1988 (SI 1988/2022) reg.7 (December 12, 1988).
2. Income Support (General) Amendment No.2 Regulations 1989 (SI 1989/1323) reg.9 (October 9, 1989).
3. Income Support (General) Amendment Regulations 1990 (SI 1990/547) reg.10 (April 9, 1990).
4. Income-related Benefits and Jobseeker's Allowance (Miscellaneous Amendments) Regulations 1997 (SI 1997/65) reg.5 (April 7, 1997).
5. Social Security (Miscellaneous Amendments) Regulations 1998 (SI 1998/563) reg.12 (April 6, 1998).
6. Social Security (Miscellaneous Amendments) (No.2) Regulations 1999 (SI 1999/2556) reg.2(4) (October 4, 1999).
7. Social Security (Miscellaneous Amendments) Regulations 2000 (SI 2000/681) reg.2(c) (April 3, 2000).
8. Social Security Amendment (Students) Regulations 2000 (SI 2000/1981) reg.5(5) and Sch. (July 31, 2000).
9. Social Security (Miscellaneous Amendments) Regulations 2008 (SI 2008/698) reg.2(5) (April 14, 2008).
10. Social Security (Miscellaneous Amendments) (No.2) Regulations 2012 (SI 2012/2575) reg.2(3) (November 5, 2012).
11. Social Security (Members of the Reserve Forces) (Amendment) Regulations 2015 (SI 2015/389) reg.2(3) (April 6, 2015).

DEFINITIONS

"claimant"—see reg.2(1) and reg.23(1).
"employed earner"—see reg.2(1).
"first year of training"—*ibid.*
"full-time student"—see reg.61(1).
"grant income"—*ibid.*

GENERAL NOTE

Paragraphs (1)–(2)

2.226   This regulation applies to the earnings of employees and income other than earnings. Thus it covers other social security benefits. Earnings from self-employment are dealt with in reg.30. It defines the period over which income is to be taken into account and the date on which that period starts. The general rule is set out in para.(2).

The first part of para.(2) covers payments that are made in respect of a period. The form of para.(2)(a) and the new para.(2)(aa), introduced on April 14, 2008, distinguish between monthly and other payments. To avoid the need to reassess monthly income each month (because the length of a month varies), payments in respect of a month will be taken into account for a period equal to the number of weeks from the date on which the payment is treated as paid (see reg.31) to the date immediately before the date on which the next monthly payment would be treated as paid (even if it is not so paid).

The *Decision Makers Guide* (para.25056) gives the following example of the effect of the provision:

John claimed IS because he was absent from work due to an illness. His BWE [benefit week ending] day is Monday.

His employer pays him on the last day of each month. On 31 March 2008 John received three weeks SSP [statutory sick pay] of £217.65 (£72.55 × 3 weeks).

The DM decided that the payment should be taken into account for one month at the weekly rate of £50.22 (£217.65 × 12 ÷ 52).

The weekly amount is taken into account for the following period—

BWE 31.3.08 – £50.22

BWE 7.4.08 – £50.22
BWE 14.4.08 – £50.22
BWE 21.4.08 – £50.22
BWE 28.4.08 – £50.22

John's next payment from his employer would be due to be paid on 30 April 2008 (treated as paid on 29 April 2008) and the weekly amount would be taken into account for the period BWE 5 May 2008 to BWE 26 May 2008.

This example involves treating the claimant as receiving more income than actually received, but presumably the thinking is that in the following (four-week) month less may be attributed, so that the swings and roundabouts cancel out. See the discussion of *CIS/3737/2003* below for why the payment is to be treated as monthly.   2.227

If the payment is made in respect of a period which is other than monthly, it is taken into account for an equal period (para.(2)(aa)). Thus a fortnight's unemployment benefit was to be taken into account for a fortnight (*R(SB) 17/82*) and an annual covenant for a year (*R(SB) 25/86*, but see Chapter VIII for students).

There will be problems in determining the period in respect of which a payment is made in some cases. For instance, is holiday pay in terms of days, to be attributed to each of the seven days in a week (as done in *R(SB) 11/85* and *CSB 1004/1988*), or is it in terms of weeks, so that only five days' worth is attributed to each week? The Commissioner in *R(JSA) 1/06* adopts the former approach, preferring *CJSA/3438/1998* to *CJSA/4508/1998* (the latter decision had accepted that holiday pay should be attributed on the basis of "working days"). The claimant who had been contracted to work a three-day week was paid 11.115 days' holiday pay on the termination of his employment. The Commissioner holds that he was by virtue of that holiday pay (which counted as earnings: see reg.98(1)(c) of the JSA Regulations 1996) to be treated as being in remunerative work (see reg.52(3) of the JSA Regulations 1996) for 12 days (see reg.94(5) of the JSA Regulations 1996, the equivalent of para.(4A) where earnings are paid in respect of part of a day), and not for four weeks as the tribunal had decided. (Note that under the new form of para.1 of Sch.8 introduced on October 1, 2007, such holiday pay would now be disregarded.) A further example could be that of a supply teacher who works for a varying number of days in each month and is paid at the end of the month. Is that payment in respect of the month or in respect of the number of days worked? Much will turn on the precise contractual situation and the terms used by the parties, as confirmed by *R(IS) 3/93*. Decisions on the former reg.7(1)(g) of the Social Security (Unemployment, Sickness and Invalidity Benefit) Regulations 1983 (like *R(U) 3/84*) may be helpful.

The question in relation to supply teachers was specifically considered in *R(IS) 10/95*, decided in March 1992. The claimant had worked as a supply teacher for five days in the month of June. She was paid for work done in a month at the end of the following month. The Commissioner accepted that the claimant's contract with the local education authority was on a daily basis (see *R(U) 2/87*). However, he rejected her argument that the period for which payment was made was five days. He holds that since she was employed on a daily basis, she was in fact paid for five different periods in June. Paragraph (2)(a) clearly only envisaged payment in respect of a single period, since neither para.(2) nor reg.32(1) could operate satisfactorily if a single payment could be in respect of two or more periods. Thus the payment for the days worked in a particular month had to be attributed to the period of a month. *R(IS) 10/95* is followed with some reluctance in *CIS 167/1992*. The result of this approach is that the period is determined by the employer's administrative arrangements for payment, rather than the terms of the employment. But it is surely arguable that the period in respect of which the payment was payable was one day. The terms of the claimant's employment were that she was paid £42.23 per session (i.e. day). The Commissioner's approach equates the period in respect of which a payment is *payable* with the period for which payment is *due to be made*, which is not necessarily the same. Moreover, the Commissioner does not seem to have taken account of the fact that "payment" can include part of a payment (see reg.2(1)). Thus some of the   2.228

operational difficulties referred to by the Commissioner could be overcome by dividing the claimant's monthly payment by the number of days worked in that month and attributing this on a daily basis. However, this does not deal with the point that all the payments would be due on one day. If the payments were due before the date of the claim, reg.31(1)(a) would apply to attribute them all to that day; if they were paid during a claim see reg.32(5) and reg.31(1)(b). See also para.13 of Sch.8.

Despite the fact that "there appeared to be some force in this criticism", *R(IS) 10/95* is applied in *CIS/3737/2003*. The claimant, who worked three days a week, was paid in arrears on the 25th of each month. When she became ill her employer paid her statutory sick pay on a monthly basis. In calculating her entitlement to income support the Department took the monthly figure of SSP that her employer had paid her, multiplied that by 12 and then divided it by 52, and used the resulting figure in their assessment, rather than the standard weekly rate of SSP. As a consequence, the income figure it arrived at was some £10 above the actual weekly rate of SSP. Despite his initial doubts the Deputy Commissioner concludes that the SSP had been correctly attributed. *R(IS) 10/95* had made clear that a payment which is for days worked in a particular month is "payable in respect of that month" and that the period referred to in para.(2) had to be a single period. That decision had been followed and applied in *R(JSA) 2/03* and *CIS/2654/2000* and was therefore an established precedent which had stood the test of time. It was not possible to distinguish *R(IS) 10/95* on the facts because the claimant was paid monthly and the regulations prescribed how income was to be calculated for the purposes of income support when a claimant was paid monthly.

However, *R(IS) 10/95* is not followed in *CG/607/2008*, a decision which concerned the calculation of earnings for the purposes of carer's allowance.

2.229 If the payment is not in respect of a period then there is a mechanical rule in para.(2)(b) spreading it at the rate of income support which would otherwise be payable, taking account of any disregards. See *SSWP v JP (JSA)* [2010] UKUT 90 (AAC) (discussed in the notes to reg.31(1)) which concerned a payment made as part of an offer of settlement under the Equal Pay Act 1970. It was held that the payment was not in respect of a period and so came within reg.94(2)(b) of the JSA Regulations (the equivalent of para.(2)(b)). The appeal against this decision, which was dismissed by the Court of Appeal (*Minter v Kingston upon Hull CC* and *Potter v Secretary of State for Work and Pensions* [2011] EWCA Civ 1155; [2012] AACR 21) did not deal with this point.

Once the period is fixed, it begins on the date specified in reg.31.

In *Owen v Chief Adjudication Officer*, April 29, 1999, the Court of Appeal rejected the claimant's argument that reg.29(2) was ultra vires either as outside the power granted in s.136(5)(a) of the SSCBA 1992 (on the ground that the authorisation of treating claimants as possessing income that they did not possess could not extend to cases where actual income was possessed and was spread over an artificial period) or as irrational. See the notes to reg.35(2).

Paragraph (2A)

2.230 This relates to Career Development Loans.

Paragraph (2B)

2.231 Paragraph (2B), in force from April 7, 1997, concerns the situation where persons are due to repay part or all of a student grant because they leave or are dismissed from their course before it finishes. Note *CIS 4201/2003* which confirms that para.(2B) has no application if the claimant has already left the course by the time the grant (or instalment of the grant) is paid (see further below). If para.(2B) does apply, the grant income (defined in reg.61(1)) will be taken into account from the date it is treated as paid under reg.31 until full repayment has been made, or, where the grant is paid in instalments, the day before the next instalment would be due, or the last day of the term or vacation in which the person ceases to be a full-time student, whichever is earlier. See reg.32(6A) for calculation of the weekly amount to be taken into account and note reg.40(3B). Paragraph (2B) thus confirms the effect of the decision in *CIS 5185/1995*. The claimant, who had been a full-time student, left his course and claimed income support on January 10, 1994. The education authority did not inform him of the amount of the grant he had to repay until March 20, 1994. The Commissioner holds that the claimant was not entitled to income support because until the grant was repaid it was income that remained available to the claimant and had to be taken into account (see *R. v Bolton SBAT Ex p. Fordham* [1981] 1 All E.R. 50 and *CSB 1408/1988*) and it exceeded his applicable amount. Moreover, once the claimant had ceased to be a student, the disregards in reg.62 did not apply (but now see reg.32(6A)). The Commissioner rejects the argument that the grant income could be disregarded under the principle in *Barclays Bank v Quistclose Investments Ltd* [1970] A.C. 567. That principle did not apply because the education authority retained no beneficial interest in the grant. They merely reserved the right to demand repayment of a sum calculated in accordance with how much of the relevant term had expired when the claimant ceased to be a student.

A different view was taken by the Commissioner in *CIS 12263/1996*, who considered that a constructive trust arose in such circumstances, but on the Department's appeal against that decision (*Chief Adjudication Officer v Leeves*, reported as *R(IS) 5/99*) it was conceded on behalf of the claimant that there was no constructive trust in these circumstances, since no proprietary right had been retained by the education authority, nor had any fiduciary obligation been created. However, the Court of Appeal held that money that the claimant was under a "certain and immediate liability" to repay did not amount to income. Thus once the claimant had received a request for immediate repayment of a specified sum from the local education authority the grant ceased to count as his income (although it fell to be treated as such until that time, even though he had abandoned his course). The Court distinguished its decision in *Fordham* as the liability to repay in that case had been uncertain. The Court's approach in *Leeves* was affirmed in *Morrell v Secretary of State for Work and Pensions* [2003] EWCA Civ 526, reported as *R(IS) 6/03* (see the note to reg.23).

Thus in relation to periods before April 7, 1997, the repayable balance of a grant will not count as a claimant's income from the date that the liability to repay has "crystallised" (*Leeves*). As regards periods after April 6, 1997, para.(2B) will apply. However, it could be argued that this is subject to the preliminary question of whether the repayable grant counts as the claimant's income at all. If it does not do so because there is a "certain and immediate" liability to repay, it is arguable that para.(2B) will not (or will cease to) apply. That would be because neither para.(2B), nor reg.40(3B) or reg.32(6A), would seem to have the effect of deeming the grant to be income but simply provide for the period over which the grant is to be taken into account *if* it does count as income, and the method of calculating that income. Compare the wording of the former reg.40(3A) (in force until August 1, 2001; see *Social Security Legislation 2001*, Vol.II, p.337) (treatment of student loans where a claimant has ceased to be a full-time student): this required "a sum equal to the weekly amount" to be taken into account as income. On the other hand, the formula "shall be taken into account" can be seen as apt to deem claimants to have income that they do not possess for the period identified, as allowed by s.136(5)(a) of the SSCBA 1992.

Where para.(2B) is applicable (for example, where repayment is not required immediately, or the amount of the repayment has not been calculated), note that the disregards for grant income in reg.62 will apply (reg.32(6A)); see also reg.40(3B).

2.232

Note that para.(2B) will not apply if the claimant has already ceased to be a full-time student by the time the grant (or the instalment of the grant) is paid (*CIS 4201/2003*). In *CIS 4201/2003* the question of whether the third instalment of the claimant's dependants' grant for the year 2000/1 which had been paid to her after she left her course was income for the purposes of her income support claim therefore had to be determined in accordance with *Leeves*. The Commissioner analyses the relevant provisions of the Education (Student Support) Regulations 2000 and concludes that on the facts of that case there was no obligation to repay an ascertained amount until the request for repayment had been made by the Student Loan Company (which was almost a year later). The instalment therefore fell to be taken into account as income until the middle of June 2001 (presumably under reg.40(3AA) although the Commissioner does not refer to this provision).

Any grant or covenant income or student loan left over at the end of the person's course is disregarded as income (see para.61 of Sch.9).

Paragraphs (2C) and (2D)

2.233   Paragraph (2C), as substituted from April 6, 2015, provides that where a claimant (or any partner, see reg.23(1)) has earnings as a member of a reserve force from training (i) for a maximum of 43 days in the claimant's first year of training (see the definition of "first year of training" in reg.2(1)); *or* (ii) for a maximum of 15 days' annual continuous training in any calendar year, the earnings will be taken into account, where the training lasts for the number of days listed in column 1 of the table in sub-para.(c), for the number of days listed in column 2 of the table, or in any other case, for the number of days that the training lasts. The intention of the table in sub-para.(c) is apparently to ensure that claimants who undertake reservist training do not lose a disproportionate amount of benefit when training extends into a new benefit week for three days or less. The period begins on the date that the earnings are treated as paid under reg.31 (para.(2D)). Such earnings are disregarded to the extent that they would have the effect of reducing income support entitlement to less than 10p per week (see the disregard in para.15A of Sch.8).

Paragraphs (3) and (4)

2.234   Paragraph (3) establishes an exception in the case of earnings only, to the rule about the date from which a payment is to be taken into account. It is to deal mainly with the situation on the termination of employment when a claimant may be entitled to regular earnings, week in hand payments, pay in lieu of notice or compensation for breach of contract and holiday pay. The effect is that each payment which is not disregarded (Sch.8 paras 1–2) is to be taken into account for the appropriate period, and the periods are to be put together consecutively. Then the aggregate period starts on the earliest date which would be fixed for any of the periods under reg.31. Note that para.(3) only applies where the earnings are of different kinds, and derive from the same source. Thus it would not apply to payments from different employers.

Paragraph (4) deals with the order in which payments in lieu of notice, compensation payments and holiday pay are to be taken into account in conjunction with ordinary earnings.

Note that these provisions will be of less relevance following the increased disregard of payments made on the termination of full-time employment introduced on October 1, 2007 (see para.1 of Sch.8 and the notes to that paragraph). However they will still apply where part-time work ends while the claimant is claiming income support or where full-time employment has been suspended.

Paragraph (4A)

2.235   If these earnings are paid in respect of a part of a day they are taken into account for a day.

Paragraph (4C)

2.236   See the notes to reg.35(1)(i). Where a payment of compensation (defined in reg.35(3)(a)) is made on the termination of part-time employment (para.(4D)(a) and reg.35(3)(c)) it is to be taken into account for one week. See also reg.32(7).

Note however that earnings under reg.35(1)(i)(ii) paid on the cessation of part-time employment (whether or not the employment has terminated) are disregarded, except in the case of part-time work which ends while the claimant is claiming income support: see para.2 of Sch.8 and the notes to that paragraph.

Calculation of earnings of self-employed earners

30.—(1) Except where paragraph (2) applies, where a claimant's income 2.237
consists of earnings from employment as a self-employed earner the weekly
amount of his earnings shall be determined by reference to his average
weekly earnings from that employment—

(a) over a period of [¹one year]; or

(b) where the claimant has recently become engaged in that employment
or there has been a change which is likely to affect the normal pattern
of business, over such other period [¹. . .] as may, in any particular
case, enable the weekly amount of his earnings to be determined
more accurately.

(2) Where the claimant's earnings consist of [² any items to which paragraph (2A) applies] those earnings shall be taken into account over a period
equal to such number of weeks as is equal to the number obtained (and any
fraction shall be treated as a corresponding fraction of a week) by dividing
the earnings by the amount of income support which would be payable had
the payment not been made plus an amount equal to the total of the sums
which would fall to be disregarded from the payment under Schedule 8
(earnings to be disregarded) as is appropriate in the claimant's case.

[² [³ (2A) This paragraph applies to—

(a) royalties or other sums paid as a consideration for the use of, or the
right to use, any copyright, design, patent or trade mark; or

(b) any payment in respect of any—

    (i) book registered under the Public Lending Right Scheme 1982; or

    (ii) work made under any international public lending right scheme
that is analogous to the Public Lending Right Scheme 1982,

where the claimant is the first owner of the copyright, design, patent or
trade mark, or an original contributor to the book or work concerned.]]

(3) For the purposes of this regulation the claimant's earnings shall be
calculated in accordance with Chapter IV of this Part.

AMENDMENTS

1. Income-related Benefits Schemes (Miscellaneous Amendments) (No.4)
Regulations 1993 (SI 1993/2119) reg.11 (October 4, 1993).

2. Social Security (Miscellaneous Amendments) Regulations 2008 (SI 2008/698)
reg.2(6) (April 7, 2008).

3. Social Security (Miscellaneous Amendments) Regulations 2009 (SI 2009/583)
reg.2(6) (April 6, 2009).

DEFINITIONS

"claimant"—see reg.2(1) and reg.23(1).
"self-employed earner"—see reg.2(1).

GENERAL NOTE

Regulation 30 applies to earnings from self-employment. A person is a self- 2.238
employed earner if in "gainful employment", other than employed earner's
employment (SSCBA s.2(1)(b), imported by reg.2(1)). This is not the place for
any extensive discussion of how to distinguish between employed earners (i.e.
those employed under a contract of service (employees) or office-holders) and
self-employed earners. In most cases there will be no difficulty in identifying a
claimant or partner who falls within reg.30. There is a still helpful, although now
dated, summary of the traditional factors in Wikeley, Ogus and Barendt, *The Law*

of Social Security, 5th edn (London: Butterworths, 2002), pp.98–103. See also *CJSA/4721/2001*. There is perhaps a recent tendency to give particular significance to who takes the financial risk of operations as between the person doing the work and the employer/customer. Do not forget that someone who sets up a limited company of which they are the sole or main employee and who controls the company through being the sole or majority shareholder is nevertheless an employee. See the notes to s.7(8) of the old style Jobseekers Act 1995 for application of this definition to professional gamblers and the decisions in *Hakki v Secretary of State for Work and Pensions and another* [2014] EWCA Civ 530 and *French v Secretary of State for Work and Pensions and another* [2018] EWCA Civ 470; [2018] AACR 25.

The income support and old style JSA legislation has from the outset failed to provide a clear framework for determining the amount of earnings from self-employment to be attributed to any particular week, as pointed out by Commissioner Rowland in *R(JSA) 1/03* at para.11. It, and the rules on determining the hours test for remunerative work, have generated intensely confusing case law, but there has been no significant amendment.

In past editions it has been said that for self-employed earnings to be brought into account for any weeks under reg.30, the person concerned must be in gainful employment as a self-employed earner for the weeks in question. That is supported by para.15 of *CIS/166/1994* and by *TC v DSD (JSA)* [2013] NI Com 65 at para.57. It is now submitted that that is wrong and that the contrary view clearly stated and reasoned in *GM v SSWP (JSA)* [2010] UKUT 221, reported as [2011] AACR 9 at paras 18–21, should be followed. The opening words of reg.30(1) refer merely to a person having earnings from employment as a self-employed earner. It is in the nature of self-employment that a person may only actually receive the income due for work done in the past after they have ceased to trade. There appears no reason why that circumstance should fall outside the general ambit of reg.30. However, there are two very important qualifications on the practical effect of such a conclusion. The first is that, where there has been a change that is likely to affect the normal pattern of business, earnings are to be determined by reference, instead of to average earnings over a (past) year, by reference to such other period as may enable the weekly amount of earnings to be determined more accurately (para.(1)(b) and see the additional discretion in reg.38(10)). Ceasing to be gainfully employed may clearly be such a change (although it probably remains up for debate whether moving into a cyclical period of non-working, as for seasonal workers, has that effect: see *GM* at para.20) and para.(1)(b) is apparently directed primarily towards identifying the earnings to be expected from activities carried out after the change in question. See further below under "*Attribution of earnings*". But if a person is expecting after the change to receive significant income relating to work done before the change, there seems no reason why that should not be taken into account in setting the period under the very general discretion as to the period of assessment in para.(1)(b). Thus, the second qualification is equally, if not more, important, as stressed in *GM*. This is that under para.3 of Sch.8 if a person has ceased to be employed as a self-employed earner any earnings from that self-employment (apart from royalties, etc. under reg.30(2)) are disregarded. See the notes to para.3 for discussion of when self-employment has ceased. Note in particular that there may not need to be a permanent cessation. Thus, the practical effect of all these provisions in combination may be the same as that stated in previous editions, but that does not operate by reason of the terms of reg.30, but in particular by the terms of the disregard in para.3 of Sch.8.

Note also that reg.38(10) allows any item of income or expenditure to be assessed over a period other than that determined under reg.30, as enables the weekly amount of that item to be determined more accurately.

Attribution of earnings

2.239   As already stated, if the self-employment has ceased, earnings from that self-employment are ignored (para.3 of Sch.8). But note that this does not apply to royalty, copyright or public lending rights payments. For the treatment of those payments, see below. Note also the disregard as capital of business assets in para.6 of Sch.10, which will continue only for a limited period after the cessation of engagement in the business, and see *CIS/2467/2003* below.

Otherwise the earnings (calculated under regs 37–39) are generally to be averaged over a period of one year. The view previously expressed in this book was that it did not seem necessary that the period immediately precedes the benefit week in question and that any one-year period—normally the last year for which accounts are available—will do. However, *GM v SSWP (JSA)* [2010] UKUT 221 (AAC), reported as [2011] AACR 9 concludes that the relevant year is the year ending with the first week of the claim. The alternative period under para.(1)(b) can only be chosen if there has been a change likely to affect the normal pattern of business or if the self-employment has recently started. In *CIS 166/1994* the Commissioner accepts that where such a change had produced, or was likely to produce, a substantial reduction in the claimant's earnings, it was appropriate for the period to start from the date of the change (with the likely result that no earnings fell to be taken into account). See also *CIS 14409/1996*. Note also the more general exception hidden in reg.38(10), which allows the amount of any item of income or expenditure to be calculated over a different period if that will produce a more accurate figure.

It was suggested in *GM* (at para.20) that the move from an active period to a fallow period for a seasonal worker would not in itself trigger the application of an alternative period under para.(1)(b). Thus in the particular case of work etching registration numbers on car windows at clients' homes, that the person suspended between November and March, the primary period of a year was adopted. The position is thus in some confusion. In *Saunderson v Secretary of State for Work and Pensions* [2012] CSIH 102; [2013] AACR 16 (see the notes to reg.5(3) under the heading *Self-employment*), there was unfortunately no discussion of whether the claimant's earnings from self-employment might, when calculated under the equivalent of reg.30, be at a level to preclude entitlement to income-related JSA, although that point had featured before the First-tier Tribunal. The answer for the time being would be appear to be, given the vagueness of the test of a change that is likely to affect the normal pattern of business and the general discretion over items of income in reg.38(10), that everything depends on the particular facts of individual cases.

The general question may well be tested in 2020 and 2021. The coronavirus outbreak, the enforced closure of businesses and the accompanying economic disruption would seem in a great many cases to be a change likely to affect the normal pattern of business for the self-employed. Thus existing income support or old style ESA or JSA beneficiaries or their partners (where there would not be a need to claim universal credit) could apply for supersession on the ground of relevant change of circumstances, arguing that earnings should be determined by reference to an average over the period since that change. That might in many cases result in a figure of nil. Paragraph (1)(b) would appear to authorise the DWP's practice of performing a continuing recalculation over an extending period as and when circumstances developed and further evidence became available. The first grant under the Coronavirus Self-Employed Income Support Scheme ("SEISS") would not become payable until late May or June 2020. Any second or subsequent grant under any of the extensions to the scheme would be paid a few weeks after the claim. As discussed in the notes to reg.37 below (see those notes for more details of the terms of the SEISS and other coronavirus schemes), there is doubt whether such a grant is an income receipt that comes into the calculation of self-employed earnings, as the DWP considers, rather than being a capital receipt. The following discussion assumes that it would be an income receipt, but there are nonetheless problems in working out the application of reg.30. A self-employed claimant or partner might also have one or more employees who were furloughed and become entitled to payments under the Coronavirus Job Retention Scheme ("CJRS") in reimbursement of wage/salary costs, etc. Such payments would, as explained in the notes to reg.37, clearly be income receipts, but there are similar problems in the application of reg.30.

The circumstances of the coronavirus outbreak and the resulting disruption of

2.240

business could clearly be argued to constitute a change sufficient to displace the use of averaging over the previous year and to authorise the use of another period under para.(1)(b). Income receipts in the form of SEISS or CJRS grants could then come into the calculation, with allowable expenses and deductions to be set against their amount, for whatever period was appropriate starting with the date of the change. There could then be rolling recalculations as the period extended forward. However, it is to be noted that the period over which the average net earnings and profits are to be calculated would start with the date of the change triggering para. (1)(b), not with the date of receipt of the grants, so that the effect on entitlement at any particular date might be diluted.

That is not the view taken in the hopelessly inadequate guidance given in Memo DMG 13/20, para.12 of which says that SEISS and CJRS payments are to be taken into account as earnings "in the normal way" (with a reference to regs 30 and 35) and that SEISS payments "will be treated as self-employed earnings over three months from the date of payment" (with no supporting reference). To speak of "the normal way" in relation to self-employed earnings for the purposes of income support, old style ESA, old style JSA and state pension credit is so vague as to be useless when there is so much discretion as to the period over which an average is to be taken. The instruction on how to take SEISS payments into account (the same was presumably intended to apply to CJRS payments) seems not to take into account the averaging process under reg.30(1). The instruction could only be justified under reg.38(10), allowing a particular item of income or expenditure to be assessed over a different period from that determined under reg.30 if that enables the weekly amount of that item to be determined more accurately. That provision is not mentioned in the Memo. In principle, there ought to be an individual evaluation in each case of whether adopting the different period enables more accurate determination of the weekly amount, rather than a blanket instruction, but even apart from that it is hard to see just what the instruction has to do with accuracy. If a person's business had been disrupted from, say, the beginning of April 2020, why could not the receipt of a SEISS grant at the beginning of June 2020 not accurately be taken into account in relation to an expanding para.(1)(b) period starting in April 2020? If reg.38(10) is properly the basis for the instruction in the Memo, there may be difficult problems as to the period over which other items of income or items of expenditure or deductions are to be averaged.

Once the appropriate period has been identified under para.(1), the average must be taken including weeks in which there are no earnings, for whatever reason.

Paragraphs (2) and (2A) supply a special rule for payments of royalties or for copyright or public lending rights payments, which are to be spread in the same way as income of an employee not in respect of a period (reg.29(2)(b)). *CIS/731/2008* confirms that before specific provision for the treatment of public lending rights payments was made on April 7, 2008 such payments counted as earnings from self-employment under the general rule in para.(1). The April 2009 form of para. (2A) includes payments from abroad that are analogous to public lending rights payments.

2.241   *CIS/2467/2003* concerned a self-employed author who received advances on contracting to write a book and subsequent royalties on sales above the amount of the advance. However, he had not been able to undertake any writing for some months due to illness, although he intended to resume this activity as soon as he had recovered. His income support claim was refused on the ground that he had capital above the prescribed limit. The Commissioner rejected his argument that money paid by way of advances was not legally owned by him because the advances were repayable if he did not fulfill the contract. In his view the advances fully belonged to the claimant as soon as they were received. The Commissioner then went on to consider whether the principle in *R(IS) 3/93* that a payment does not metamorphose into capital until the end of the period to which it is attributed as income applied to self-employed earnings. He concluded that it did not. That was because the calculation of earnings from self-employment did not turn on when particular receipts came in but was, under para.(1), to be calculated as average weekly earnings (net profit, subject to deductions for income tax and social security) over a period of normally a year. Those average weekly earnings were then taken into account for an equivalent period into the future. There was therefore no period of attribution to be attached to any particular business receipt and the basis of the *R(IS) 3/93* principle did not exist. In the Commissioner's view it would be artificial and wrong to regard all business receipts as retaining the character of income until the expiry of the period for which earnings calculated over the whole period were taken into account. Instead the protection for self-employed earners in relation to the capital rules lay in the disregard of the value of business assets under para.6 of Sch.10. The Commissioner also held that the fact that para.(2) did provide a special rule for the attribution of the kind of self-employed earnings in issue in this case did not make a difference in relation to capital. First, there was still the protection of the disregard in para.6 of Sch.10. Secondly, the attribution rule in para.(2) (which was very difficult to apply) was an artificial one, not linked to any assessment of the period in respect of which any particular payment was made. The rationale for the operation of the *R(IS) 3/93* principle was therefore also missing in relation to these types of self-employed earnings. The Commissioner accordingly concluded that the claimant's business receipts had the character of capital as soon as they were paid to him (although he did accept that payments of VAT which the claimant had a liability to pay over to Customs and Excise did not form part of his capital). The Commissioner finally considered whether the disregard in para.6 applied but decided that it did not (see further the note to para.6 of Sch.10).

Note that the profit simply derived from a capital asset is not earnings, which must be derived from some employment or occupation. See *R(U) 3/77*. Thus, it is suggested that making a profit from one's own portfolio of shares on the stock market would probably not be self-employment. Note also *R(FC) 2/92* and *RM v Sefton Council (HB)* [2016] UKUT 357 (AAC), reported as [2017] AACR 5, and the other decisions in the note to para.6 of Sch.10 on the question of whether ownership of a tenanted house is a business.

Date on which income is treated as paid

31.—(1) Except where paragraph [8 (2) [9applies]], a payment of income to which regulation 29 (calculation of earnings derived from employed earner's employment and income other than earnings) applies shall be treated as paid—

(a) in the case of a payment which is due to be paid before the first benefit week pursuant to the claim, on the date on which it is due to be paid;

(b) in any other case, on the first day of the benefit week in which it is due to be paid or the first succeeding benefit week in which it is practicable to take it into account.

(2) Income support, [4jobseeker's allowance], [2maternity allowance,] [3short-term or long term incapacity benefit], [7 severe disablement allowance [10, employment and support allowance or universal credit]] [3. . .], shall be treated as paid [10 on any day] in respect of which [1it is payable].

[5[6(3)[9. . .]]]

[8(4)[9. . .]]

2.242

AMENDMENTS

1. Income Support (General) Amendment Regulations 1988 (SI 1988/663) reg.14 (April 11, 1988).

2. Income Support (General) Amendment No.4 Regulations 1988 (SI 1988/1445) reg.8 (September 12, 1988).

3. Disability Working Allowance and Income Support (General) Amendment Regulations 1995 (SI 1995/482) reg.10 (April 13, 1995).

4. Income Support (General) (Jobseeker's Allowance Consequential Amendments) Regulations 1996 (SI 1996/206) reg.15 (October 7, 1996).

5. Social Security (Miscellaneous Amendments) Regulations 2000 (SI 2000/681) reg.3(1) (April 3, 2000).

6. Social Security (Working Tax Credit and Child Tax Credit) (Consequential Amendments) (No.3) Regulations 2003 (SI 2003/1731) reg.2(2) (August 8, 2003).

7. Employment and Support Allowance (Consequential Provisions) (No.2) Regulations 2008 (SI 2008/1554) reg.2(5) (October 27, 2008).

8. Social Security (Miscellaneous Amendments) (No.6) Regulations 2008 (SI 2008/2767) reg.2(4) (November 17, 2008).

9. Social Security (Miscellaneous Amendments) Regulations 2011 (SI 2011/674) reg.3(2) (April 11, 2011).

10. Universal Credit (Consequential, Supplementary, Incidental and Miscellaneous Provisions) Regulations 2013 (SI 2013/630) reg.28(4) (April 29, 2013).

DEFINITIONS

"benefit week"—see reg.2(1).
"child tax credit"—*ibid.*
"working tax credit"—*ibid.*

GENERAL NOTE

Paragraph (1)

2.243   This provision applies to determine when the period of attribution of earnings from employment and income other than earnings (apart from the benefits specified in para.(2)) fixed in reg.29 begins. The crucial date is that on which the payment is due to be paid. This date may well be different from the date of actual payment. Legal obligations must be considered, e.g. the terms of a contract of employment *(R(SB) 33/83)*. If a claimant's contract of employment is terminated without due notice any deferred holiday pay and wages withheld under week-in-hand arrangements are due immediately. So are any agreed payments in lieu of notice *(R(SB) 23/84* and *R(SB) 11/85)*. Note the operation of reg.29(3) and (4) when different kinds of earnings are received for overlapping periods.

For an example of a case where payment was not due to be made when the claimant was laid off, see *CJSA/4261/2003*. The claimant was a "core casual" dock worker who was laid off and claimed JSA the next day. His employers said that six days' holiday pay was due to him and a decision-maker therefore treated him as in remunerative work for that period. However, evidence was provided by his union which confirmed that as a core casual worker his employment was not terminated when he was laid off. He could choose, but was not obliged, to take his holiday when he was laid off. Furthermore, if he did not take his holiday when laid off (or by agreement at other times), he could not receive payment for any accrued holiday entitlement until more than four weeks after the termination or interruption of his employment. Thus the terms of his contract clearly showed that no holiday pay was due when he was laid off and he was entitled to JSA from the day he claimed, subject to the then three waiting days rule.

If the payment is due before the first week pursuant to the claim (on which see Sch.7 to the Claims and Payments Regulations), it is treated as paid on the date it is due. This date then starts the period under reg.29. In other cases the payment is treated as paid on the first day of the benefit week in which it is due (or the next week if the main rule is impracticable).

2.244   A consequence of that principle is that if a payment is made late, either individually or combined with other payments in a lump sum, that retains the characteristic of income (see the notes to reg.23 under "*Distinction between capital and income*") it or they are to be treated as paid (and thus taken into account) when they were due to be paid rather than when they were actually received. The same applies to payments of compensation, including settlements of claims, for failure to pay income that was properly due.

An example of the first category is *McCorquodale v Chief Adjudication Officer*, reported as *R(SB) 1/88*. There was a County Court order for the claimant's ex-husband to make periodical payments of £78 per month to their son, who lived with the claimant. The first payment was made nearly two years later. In the interim the claimant had become entitled to supplementary benefit. On the supplementary benefit equivalent of reg.31(1) (in very similar terms, but using the word "payable" rather than "due to be paid"), the Court of Appeal held that in the absence of anything to indicate otherwise the payment was to be taken into account at the time when the first payment should have been paid, when the claimant was not in receipt of supplementary benefit, so that there could be no effect on her entitlement at the time the payment was made. But since the ex-husband had raised an argument that there had been an agreement not to enforce the order whilst he paid the son's school fees, which would if accepted have altered the payable date, that issue had to be remitted to a new tribunal for decision. The Court noted that the practical effect would have been different if the payment had been payable at a time when the claimant was in receipt of supplementary benefit, but did not say why. The answer lies in what is now s.74 of the SSAA 1992 (see Vol.III of this series). If a payment of prescribed income is paid after the prescribed date (first day of the period to which the payment relates), and as a result an amount of prescribed benefit was paid that would not have been paid if the prescribed income had been paid on the prescribed date, that amount is recoverable from the recipient. There does not have to have been any misrepresentation or failure to disclose.

Note that reg.59(2) now expressly applies a date of payment rule to periodical payments from liable relatives, including arrears, that *McCorquodale* held that the supplementary benefit legislation at the time failed to do.

An example of a payment of cumulative arrears in a lump sum is *R(SB) 4/89*.   **2.245**
In April 1986 the claimant was awarded special hardship allowance ("SHA") with effect from June 1984 and received a payment of about £2,200 representing the arrears. The Commissioner dismissed the claimant's argument on appeal that the payment should be treated as capital and confirmed that the SHA, being essentially compensation for loss of earnings due to an industrial accident or disease, had an income character whether paid in arrears or not. Then the payments were to be treated as income for the periods in which it would have been paid if the award had been made in June 1984. The Commissioner pointed out that if the claimant had been in receipt of supplementary benefit for the period covered by the arrears, the normal procedure would have been to abate the amount due in arrears by the amount of supplementary benefit that would not have been payable if the SHA had been paid on time (under what is now s.74(2) of the SSAA 1992). The claimant had not been in receipt of supplementary benefit for that period, so that such an abatement could not be carried out. However, it appears that the non-entitlement was based on a mistaken view of how much of the claimant's invalidity benefit was to be taken into account as an income resource. When that was sorted out by the adjudication officer, along with some other issues, as suggested by the Commissioner, the SHA could be taken into account in determining whether there was entitlement for all or part of the period.

It has long been established that compensation payments for loss of earnings retain an income character. Where the payment includes compensation for past loss of earnings, the general principle appeared to have been confirmed by *CIS/590/1993* (not currently on the UTAAC website). There the claimant had been dismissed from her employment in April 1991 because she was pregnant. In June 1992 she was awarded compensation by an industrial tribunal under the Sex Discrimination Act 1975 which included one month's loss of earnings. The tribunal had deducted the income support paid to the claimant for the month after her dismissal. It is held that the loss of earnings element of the award was to be taken into account as earnings under reg.35 (see the notes to reg.35). For the purpose of reg.31(1), the date on which it was due to be paid was the date when the lost earnings were due to be paid, not when the award was made. That was because the award was to be regarded as a payment in lieu of remuneration and the purpose of the sex discrimination legislation was to put the claimant in the position she would have been if the employer had not acted unlawfully. If the payment was treated as due at the date of the award this could produce unfairness. The result was that the earnings were to be attributed to a period of one month in April/May 1991 and she was to be treated as in remunerative work for that period. However, it was said that the income support that had been paid to the claimant for that period was not recoverable as there had been no failure to disclose or misrepresentation. It had in any event been recouped. It appears that the judge was mistaken about the possibility of recovery, by overlooking the effect of s.74 of the SSAA 1992, discussed above.

However, under the current legislation (the Employment Protection (Recoupment of Benefits) Regulations 1996 (SI 1996/2349) as amended (see Vol.III of this series)), employment tribunals are to make gross awards, payments of which are then to be postponed to allow the Secretary of State to serve a notice of recoupment of income support or other means-tested benefits on the employer requiring the employer to pay the recoupment amount to the Secretary of State and only the balance, if any, to the employee. If that process has been followed, it would seem that the amount of benefit covered by the recoupment notice could not be said to have been paid when it would not have been paid if the income had been paid on time within s.74.

2.246   In *SSWP v JP (JSA)* [2010] UKUT 90 (AAC) (see the notes to reg.23 under "*Distinction between capital and income*" for the facts and background) Judge Jacobs disagreed with *CIS/590/1993* on the basis that it confused the payment with what the payment was compensation was for. That took him into some convoluted (and it is submitted erroneous) reasoning leading to the conclusion that the payment that had been held to be earnings was to be taken into account from the date of its actual payment or the following benefit week. In past editions it has been said that the Court of Appeal in *Minter v Kingston upon Hull CC* and *Potter v SSWP* [2011] EWCA Civ 1155; [2012] AACR 21, which dismissed the claimants' appeals, did not deal with this point. It is now submitted that, although the dismissal of Miss Potter's appeal leaves doubts, the basis on which the Court rested its reasoning is incompatible with Judge Jacobs' approach.

First, it appears that the sole issue raised on behalf of the claimants on their appeals was whether the compensation payments were capital or income. The issue in the appeals was described at the outset of the judgment as whether the compensation payments were to be brought into account for a retrospective calculation of past entitlements to housing benefit and old style JSA. It was accepted that if the payments were income, they had to be brought into account and repayment of some past benefit would be required. It was common ground that there was no material difference between the legislative schemes for housing benefit and for old style JSA. Second, it was said in Miss Minter's case (at para.8) that it was accepted by all parties that if the payment was income it was to be attributed to a period in the past and that it was not necessary for the Court to concern itself with the detailed route to that conclusion (described as far from clear) because the sole issue in the appeal was income or capital. Then in the very short treatment (at para.31) of Miss Potter's case on the appeal from *JP* it was simply said that the same reasoning that applied to Miss Minter, and her housing benefit, applied to her and her JSA. Thus, although the matter was not the subject of argument before the Court, the basis of the judgment was that if Miss Potter's payment was income it was to attributed to the past, just as Miss Minter's had been by Judge Howell in *Kingston upon Hull CC v DLM (HB)* [2010] UKUT 234 (AAC). The dismissal of Miss Minter's appeal might have been expected to leave in place a decision by Judge Jacobs to the contrary effect, but what he had actually done was to confirm the Secretary of State's initial decision, which was not then described as doing anything more than declare the payment to be earnings, without saying anything about the dates on which the earnings were to be treated as paid. Thus, although Judge Jacob's reasoning was contrary to that accepted by the Court of Appeal, it could be said that his decision did not in fact implement his reasoning. It can therefore be argued that the dismissal of Miss Potter's appeal does not undermine the force of all parties in *Minter* and *Potter*, including the Secretary of State, agreeing that if the payment was income it should be treated as paid on the dates when she should have received the additional earnings under the equality clause implied in her contract of employment by the Equal Pay Act 1970.

Paragraph (2)

It seems that the effect of para.(2) is that all these benefits are treated as paid on a daily basis. This is made clearer by the April 2013 amendment. A proportion of the weekly rate is treated as paid for each day covered by the entitlement. This should avoid overlaps of the kind revealed in *R(SB) 15/82*. See regs 75(b) and 32(4). Other benefits are to be treated as paid on the day identified under the ordinary rules in para.(1).

2.247

Calculation of weekly amount of income

32.—(1) For the purposes of regulation 29 (calculation of earnings derived from employed earner's employment and income other than earnings) [⁹[¹⁰. . .]], subject to [³paragraphs (2) to (7)][¹. . .], where the period in respect of which a payment [⁹ of income or tax credit] is made—

2.248

  (a) does not exceed a week, the weekly amount shall be the amount of that payment;

  (b) exceeds a week, the weekly amount shall be determined—

    (i) in a case where that period is a month, by multiplying the amount of the payment by 12 and dividing the product by 52;

    (ii) in a case where that period is three months, by multiplying the amount of the payment by 4 and dividing the product by 52;

  [⁹ (iii) in a case where that period is a year and the payment is an award of working tax credit, by dividing the payment by the number of days in the year and multiplying the result by 7;

  (iiia) in a case where that period is a year and the payment is income other than an award of working tax credit, by dividing the amount of the payment by 52;]

    (iv) in any other case by multiplying the amount of the payment by 7 and dividing the product by the number equal to the number of days in the period in respect of which it is made.

(2) Where a payment for a period not exceeding a week is treated under regulation 31(1)(a) (date on which income is treated as paid) as paid before the first benefit week and a part is to be taken into account for some days only in that week (the relevant days), the amount to be taken into account for the relevant days shall be calculated by multiplying the amount of the payment by the number equal to the number of relevant days and dividing the product by the number of days in the period in respect of which it is made.

(3) Where a payment is in respect of a period equal to or in excess of a week and a part thereof is to be taken into account for some days only in a benefit week (the relevant days), the amount to be taken into account for the relevant days shall, except where paragraph (4) applies, be calculated by multiplying the amount of the payment by the number equal to the number of relevant days and dividing the product by the number of days in the period in respect of which it is made.

(4) In the case of a payment of—

(a) [⁵. . .] [²maternity allowance], [⁴short-term or long-term incapacity benefit], or severe disablement allowance [⁴. . .], the amount to be taken into account for the relevant days shall be the amount of benefit [¹payable] in respect of those days;

(b) income support[⁵[⁸, jobseeker's allowance or employment and support allowance]], the amount to be taken into account for the relevant days shall be calculated by multiplying the weekly amount of the benefit by the number of relevant days and dividing the product by seven.

(5) Except in the case of a payment which it has not been practicable to treat under regulation 31(1)(b) as paid on the first day of the benefit week in which it is due to be paid, where a payment of income from a particular source is or has been paid regularly and that payment falls to be taken into account in the same benefit week as a payment of the same kind and from the same source, the amount of that income to be taken into account in any one benefit week shall not exceed the weekly amount determined under paragraph (1)(a) or (b), as the case may be, of the payment which under regulation 31(1)(b) (date on which income is treated as paid) is treated as paid first.

(6) Where the amount of the claimant's income fluctuates and has changed more than once, or a claimant's regular pattern of work is such that he does not work every week, the foregoing paragraphs may be modified so that the weekly amount of his income is determined by reference to his average weekly income—

(a) if there is a recognisable cycle of work, over the period of one complete cycle (including, where the cycle involves periods in which the claimant does no work, those periods but disregarding any other absences);

(b) in any other case, over a period of five weeks or such other period as may, in the particular case, enable the claimant's average weekly income to be determined more accurately.

[⁶(6A) Where income is taken into account under paragraph (2B) of regulation 29 over the period specified in that paragraph, the amount of that income to be taken into account in respect of any week in that period shall be an amount equal to the amount of that income which would have been taken into account under regulation 62 had the person to whom that income was paid not ceased to be a[⁷ full-time student].]

[³(7) Where any payment of earnings is taken into account under paragraph (4C) of regulation 29 (calculation of earnings derived from employed earner's employment and income other than earnings), over the period specified in that paragraph, the amount to be taken into account shall be equal to the amount of the payment.]

AMENDMENTS

1. Income Support (General) Amendment Regulations 1988 (SI 1988/663) reg.15 (April 11, 1988).

2. Income Support (General) Amendment Regulations 1988 (SI 1988/1445) reg.8 (September 12, 1988).

3. Income Support (General) Amendment No.2 Regulations 1989 (SI 1989/1323) reg.10 (October 9, 1989).

4. Disability Working Allowance and Income Support (General) Amendment Regulations 1995 (SI 1995/482) reg.11 (April 13, 1995).

5. Income Support (General) (Jobseeker's Allowance Consequential Amendments) Regulations 1996 (SI 1996/206) reg.16 (October 7, 1996).

6. Income-related Benefits and Jobseeker's Allowance (Miscellaneous Amendments) Regulations 1997 (SI 1997/65) reg.6 (April 7, 1997).

7. Social Security Amendment (Students) Regulations 2000 (SI 2000/1981) reg.5(5) and Sch. (July 31, 2000).

8. Employment and Support Allowance (Consequential Provisions) (No.2) Regulations 2008 (SI 2008/1554) reg.2(6) (October 27, 2008).

9. Social Security (Miscellaneous Amendments) (No.6) Regulations 2008 (SI 2008/2767) reg.2(5) (November 17, 2008).

10. Social Security (Miscellaneous Amendments) Regulations 2011 (SI 2011/674) reg.3(3) (April 11, 2011).

DEFINITIONS

"benefit week"—see reg.2(1).
"claimant"—*ibid.*, and reg.23(1).
"full-time student"—see reg.61(1).

GENERAL NOTE

Paragraph(1)
This provision gives a straightforward method of converting payments to be taken 2.249
into account for various periods to a weekly equivalent. Regulation 75 deals with the calculation for part-weeks of entitlement.

The form of sub-para.(b)(iii) in force from November 17, 2008 was introduced to reflect the fact that the benefit computer systems were designed to produce a daily rate of working tax credit, which is then multiplied by seven to arrive at a weekly rate. This results in a slightly different weekly amount of WTC than by dividing the annual award by 52. Therefore, in order to reflect the computer process (which apparently results in a very small gain for claimants), the new form of sub-para.(b)(iii) contains a separate rule where the income to be taken into account is WTC.

Paragraphs (2)–(4)
These provisions establish the rules where the period for which a payment is to be 2.250
taken into account under regs 29 and 31 does not coincide with a benefit week and some odd days ("the relevant days") come into a benefit week.

Paragraph (5)
There are two different rules, according to whether two payments from the same 2.251
regular source fall into the same benefit week because of the rules of attribution or because of the operation of reg.31(1)(b). The general rule is the first one, under which the maximum amount to be taken into account in the benefit week is the weekly amount of the payment due first. The *Decision Makers Guide* (para.25081) gives an example of how this could arise. A claimant has been receiving statutory sick pay from his employer every two weeks on a Friday. He receives a payment for two weeks on May 15, 2009. This is attributed to the period May 15 to May 28 inclusive. The claimant is to return to work on June 1 and receives a final payment of two weeks' sick pay on May 26. The decision-maker treats this as paid on May 22 for the period May 22 to June 4. For the income support benefit week from May 22 to May 28 the amount of sick pay to be taken into account is limited to the weekly amount of the payment made on May 15. There is an exception to this rule in that if the first payment was due to be paid before the date of claim it is to be disregarded (Sch.8 para.13 and Sch.9 para.35). Then there will no longer be an overlap. The second rule applies where under reg.31(1)(b) it has not been practicable to take a payment into account in the benefit week in which it was due to be paid. The payment then is taken into account in the first practicable benefit week. In this situation both payments can be taken into account in the same week, although each payment can have the appropriate disregard applied (Sch.8 para.10 and Sch.9 para.37). The disregards in para.13 of Sch.8 and para.35 of Sch.9 (see above) may also apply.

Paragraph (6)

2.252   This paragraph is oddly placed because it only allows the preceding paragraphs to be modified, not any of the other regulations on the calculation or attribution of income.

In *MC v SSWP (IS)* [2013] UKUT 384 (AAC) the claimant worked as a football steward every other week when the club played at home. He received a payment for two home cup matches which for reasons that were not entirely clear the tribunal treated as an exceptional payment outside the normal pattern. The claimant argued that the payment should be treated as part of his 52-week cycle of work for the club and that his earnings should be averaged over 52 weeks under para.(6)(a).

Judge Wright points out that para.(6) mirrors reg.5(2)(b), albeit in the context of the income earned rather than hours of work. Thus in deciding whether the claimant did have a recognisable cycle of work, the case law under reg.5(2)(b), and the equivalent JSA provision, reg.51(2)(b), should be applied, in particular *R(JSA) 5/03* and *R(JSA) 1/07* (see the notes to reg.5(2)–(3A) for a discussion of these cases).

Judge Wright remitted the appeal to a fresh tribunal for it to decide whether the claimant did have a recognisable cycle of work, having regard to the nature of his agreement with the football club to work as a steward, how the off-season was treated, and whether he had to reapply (and if so, how) for the job of steward each August. (There was also the question of whether a six month period during which the claimant had not worked that year had broken any recognisable cycle.) The more casual the claimant's working relationship with the club was, the less likely it may be that he was in a recognisable cycle of work. The Secretary of State had accepted that para.(6) could apply in this case on the basis that the claimant's income fluctuated and had changed more than once. The new tribunal would therefore need to decide whether either para.(6)(a) or (b) applied (if neither applied, it would seem that para.(1) could not be modified and would apply to the payment). Judge Wright concluded by observing that this appeal had proceeded on the basis that the claimant was an employee (rather than self-employed)—if the claimant was self-employed, para.(6) would of course not apply.

Paragraph (6A)

2.253   Regulation 29(2B) deals with the period over which a student grant is to be taken into account in the case of a person who has left or been dismissed from his course before it finishes and so has to repay part or all of his grant. Paragraph (6A) provides that where reg.29(2B) applies, the weekly amount of the income to be taken into account is to be calculated in accordance with reg.62. That means that the grant income will be apportioned over the period of study (i.e. from the beginning of the academic year to the day before the summer vacation), except for those elements which are apportioned over 52 weeks, and the disregards in reg.62(2), (2A) and (2B) will apply. See further reg.62 and the notes to that regulation. See also reg.40(3B), which provides that the amount of the grant income to be taken into account is to be calculated on the basis that none of it has been repaid. However, note *Chief Adjudication Officer v Leeves*, reported as *R(IS) 5/99*, in the notes to reg.29(2B) and the argument discussed in those notes as to when reg.29(2B) applies.

Any grant or covenant income or student loan left over at the end of the person's course is disregarded as income (see para.61 of Sch.9).

Paragraph (7)

2.254   Where a payment of compensation (reg.35(3)(a)) is made on the termination of part-time employment (reg.29(4D)(a) and reg.35(3)(c)) it is taken into account for a week (reg.29(4C)). This provision confirms that the whole payment is taken into account for that week. Note the disregard in para.2 of Sch.8.

Weekly amount of charitable or voluntary payment

2.255   **33.**—(1)[¹ . . .]

AMENDMENT

1. Income Support (General) Amendment No.5 Regulations 1988 (SI 1988/2022) reg.8 (December 12, 1988).

Incomplete weeks of benefit

34.—[¹ . . .]   2.256

AMENDMENT

1. Income Support (General) Amendment Regulations 1988 (SI 1988/663) reg.16 (April 11, 1988).

CHAPTER III

EMPLOYED EARNERS

Earnings of employed earners

35.—(1) [²Subject to paragraphs (2) and (3),] "earnings" means in the   2.257
case of employment as an employed earner, any remuneration or profit
derived from that employment and includes—
  (a) any bonus or commission;
  (b) any payment in lieu of remuneration except any periodic sum paid
      to a claimant on account of the termination of his employment by
      reason of redundancy;
  (c) any payment in lieu of notice [². . .];
  (d) any holiday pay except any payable more than four weeks after the
      termination or interruption of employment but this exception shall
      not apply to a claimant to whom [¹section 23 of the Act [SSCBA,
      s.126] (trade disputes) applies or in respect of whom section
      20(3) of the Act [SSCBA, s.124(1)] (conditions of entitlement to
      income support) has effect as modified by section 23A(*b*) of the Act
      [SSCBA, s.127(b)] (effect to return to work)];
  (e) any payment by way of a retainer;
  (f) any payment made by the claimant's employer in respect of expenses
      not wholly, exclusively and necessarily incurred in the performance
      of the duties of the employment, including any payment made by the
      claimant's employer in respect of—
      (i) travelling expenses incurred by the claimant between his home
          and place of employment;
      (ii) expenses incurred by the claimant under arrangements made
           for the care of a member of his family owing to the claimant's
           absence from home;
  (g) any award of compensation made under section [¹¹112(4) or 117(3)
      (a) of the Employment Rights Act 1996 (the remedies: orders and
      compensation, enforcement of order and compensation)];
  [¹¹(gg) any payment or remuneration made under section 28, 34, 64,
      68 or 70 of the Employment Rights Act 1996 (right to guarantee
      payments, remuneration on suspension on medical or maternity
      grounds, complaints to employment tribunals);]
  (h) any such sum as is referred to in section [¹¹112(3) of the Contributions
      and Benefits Act [(certain sums to be earnings for social security pur-
      poses).

[²(i) where—
  (i) [¹² . . .]
  (ii) a payment of compensation is made in respect of employment which is part-time, the amount of the compensation.]
[⁶(j) the amount of any payment by way of a non-cash voucher which has been taken into account in the computation of a person's earnings in accordance with [¹⁰ Part 5 of Schedule 3 to the Social Security (Contributions) Regulations 2001].]
[²(1A) [¹² . . .].]
(2) "Earnings" shall not include—
  (a) [⁶ Subject to paragraph (2A),] any payment in kind;
  (b) any remuneration paid by or on behalf of an employer to the claimant [⁴in respect of a period throughout which the claimant is on maternity leave[⁹, paternity leave[¹⁵, adoption leave [¹⁶, shared parental leave or parental bereavement leave]]] or is absent from work because he is ill];
  (c) any payment in respect of expenses wholly, exclusively and necessarily incurred in the performance of the duties of the employment;
  (d) any occupational pension.
[⁵(e) any lump sum payment made under the Iron and Steel Re-adaptation Benefits Scheme].
[¹³(f) any payment in respect of expenses arising out of the [¹⁴ claimant participating as a service user].]
[⁶(2A) Paragraph (2)(a) shall not apply in respect of any non-cash voucher referred to in paragraph (1)(j).]
[²(3) In this regulation—
  (a) "compensation" means any payment made in respect of or on the termination of employment in a case where a person has not received or received only part of a payment in lieu of notice due or which would have been due to him had he not waived his right to receive it, other than—
    (i) any payment specified in paragraph (1)(a) to (h);
    (ii) any payment specified in paragraph (2)(a) to [⁵(e)];
    (iii) any redundancy payment within the meaning of section [¹¹135(1) of the Employment Rights Act 1996], and
    (iv) any refund of contributions to which that person was entitled under an occupational pension scheme within the meaning of section 66(1) of the Social Security Pensions Act 1975;
    [³(v) any compensation payable by virtue of section 173 or section 178(3) or (4) of the Education Reform Act 1988;]
  (b) [¹² . . .];
  (c) "part-time employment" means employment in which a person is not to be treated as engaged in remunerative work under regulation 5 or [⁷ 6(1) [⁸ and (4)]] (persons treated, or not treated, as engaged in remunerative work).]

AMENDMENTS

1. Income Support (General) Amendment Regulations 1988 (SI 1988/663) reg.17 (April 11, 1988).
2. Income Support (General) Amendment No.2 Regulations 1989 (SI 1989/1323) reg.11 (October 9, 1989).

3. Education (Inner London Education Authority) (Transitional and Supplementary Provisions) (No.2) Order 1990 (SI 1990/774) art.2 (April 1, 1990).

4. Income-related Benefits Schemes (Miscellaneous Amendments) (No.4) Regulations 1993 (SI 1993/2119) reg.12 (October 4, 1993).

5. Social Security (Miscellaneous Amendments) Regulations 1997 (SI 1997/454) reg.7 (April 7, 1997).

6. Social Security Amendment (Non-Cash Vouchers) Regulations 1999 (SI 1999/1509) reg.2(5) (July 1, 1999).

7. Social Security (Miscellaneous Amendments) (No.2) Regulations 1999 (SI 1999/2556) reg.2(4) (October 4, 1999).

8. Social Security (Miscellaneous Amendments) Regulations 2000 (SI 2000/681) reg.2(c) (April 3, 2000).

9. Social Security (Paternity and Adoption) Amendment Regulations 2002 (SI 2002/2689) reg.2(4) (December 8, 2002).

10. Social Security (Miscellaneous Amendments) (No.4) Regulations 2006 (SI 2006/2378) reg.5(3) (October 2, 2006).

11. Social Security (Miscellaneous Amendments) (No. 5) Regulations 2007 (SI 2007/2618) reg.5(6) (October 1, 2007).

12. Social Security (Miscellaneous Amendments) Regulations 2008 (SI 2008/698) reg.2(7) (April 14, 2008).

13. Social Security (Miscellaneous Amendments) (No.4) Regulations 2009 (SI 2009/2655) reg.2(7) (October 26, 2009).

14. Social Security (Miscellaneous Amendments) Regulations 2014 (SI 2014/591) reg.2(3) (April 28, 2014).

15. Shared Parental Leave and Statutory Shared Parental Pay (Consequential Amendments to Subordinate Legislation) Order 2014 (SI 2014/3255) art.5(4) (December 31, 2014).

16. Parental Bereavement Leave and Pay (Consequential Amendments to Subordinate Legislation) Regulations 2020 (SI 2020/354) reg.5(4) (April 6, 2020).

DEFINITIONS

"the Act"—see reg.2(1).
"adoption leave"—*ibid.*
"claimant"—*ibid.*, reg.23(1).
"claimant participating as a service user"—see reg.2(1B).
"employed earner"—see reg.2(1).
"family"—see SSCBA s.137(1).
"maternity leave"—see reg.2(1).
"occupational pension"—*ibid.*
"parental bereavement leave"—*ibid.*
"shared parental leave"—*ibid.*

GENERAL NOTE

Regulation 35 applies to earnings from employment as an employed earner. See the definition of "employed earner" in reg.2(1). On the tests for deciding whether a person is an employed earner or in self-employment, see *CJSA 4721/2001* and the notes to reg.30.

2.258

The category of office-holder includes holders of elective office, such as local councillors. Some payments made to councillors (e.g. for travelling expenses and subsistence allowances: *CIS 89/1989*) will be excluded under para.(2)(c), but attendance allowances, which are not paid to meet specific expenses, count as earnings (*R(IS) 6/92*). *CIS 77/1993* decides that basic allowances are also earnings, but applies the disregard in para.(2)(c), reg.40(4) (now reg.40(4)(a)) and Sch.9 para.3. The purpose of the basic allowance is to compensate councillors for their time and to cover the expenses incurred in the execution of their duties. The expenses may, as in that case, absorb the total allowance. See also *CJSA/2396/2002* and *SS v SSWP (JSA)* [2013] UKUT 233 (AAC).

Similarly, although payments of expenses to claimants participating as a service user (see reg.2(1B) for those to whom this refers) do not count as earnings (see para. (2)(f)) and are disregarded as income (see para.2A of Sch.9), any payment for taking part in a service user group (e.g. for attending meetings) will be taken into account as earnings. The notional income rules, however, do not apply (see reg.42(8ZA)).

2.259   See also the notes to reg.36(3) for discussion of the application of the principle of *Parsons v Hogg* [1985] 2 All E.R. 897, CA to the meaning of "gross earnings". This allows the deduction from earnings of necessary, etc., expenses incurred by the employee.

Note in addition *R(TC) 2/03* discussed below which concerned deductions for previously overpaid salary.

See Sch.8 for earnings that are disregarded. Note that the disregard that applies to payments made on the termination of full-time employment (i.e. 16 hours or more per week in the case of the claimant, 24 hours or more per week for a partner) was significantly extended with effect from October 1, 2007. See the new form of para.1 of Sch.8 and the notes to that paragraph.

CIS/1068/2006 holds that payments made to the claimant by his wife (from money she received from the local authority under s.57 of the Health and Social Care Act 2001) in consideration of the care services he provided to her were "earnings" and fell to be taken into account in calculating his income support. It did not matter whether the claimant was to be regarded as an employed or self-employed earner for these purposes—the issue was whether the claimant had been engaged by his wife to provide care services for reward, which on the facts of the case was the only possible inference. The Commissioner rejected the claimant's argument that the payments by his wife should be disregarded under para.58 of Sch.9 (see further the note to para.58). The claimant appealed to the Court of Appeal against this decision but his appeal was dismissed (*Casewell v Secretary of State for Work and Pensions* [2008] EWCA Civ 524, reported as *R(IS) 7/08*). The claimant contended that s.136 of the Contributions and Benefits Act requires that payments made to a member of the family are counted when they come into the family, and if at that point they are disregarded, they cannot be counted again if they are transferred from one member of the family to another. However the Court agreed with the Commissioner that the payments to the claimant by his wife were earnings in respect of the care he provided and in the claimant's hands they became his income under s.136(1). It should be noted that the payments to the claimant's wife in this case were made on the basis that she was instructed to pay the claimant the appropriate sum each week against a payslip. There was therefore a specific obligation for the claimant's wife to deal with the payments in a particular way, which had the result that the money paid to her husband was treated as earnings. Thus this was a somewhat different situation from the more usual informal transfer of resources between family members.

Paragraph (1)

2.260   This paragraph first provides a general definition of earnings from employment as an employee—any remuneration or profit derived from that employment—and then deems certain payments to be earnings. Paragraph (2) provides a number of exceptions and Sch.8 lists items which would otherwise count as earnings which are to be disregarded. See in particular paras 1 to 2 which concern the earnings that are ignored on the termination of employment or where hours of work are reduced (possibly to nil). The disregard that applies to payments made on the termination of full-time employment (i.e. 16 hours or more per week in the case of the claimant, 24 hours or more per week for a partner) was significantly extended with effect from October 1, 2007. See the new form of para.1 of Sch.8 and the notes to that paragraph.

Note that "furloughed" employees whose employers receive payments under the Coronavirus Job Retention Scheme (see the notes to reg.37 for details) continue to receive wages or salary, although the amount may be reduced. The CJRS payments are expressly made to employers in reimbursement of employment expenditure and are therefore income of the employer, not of the employee.

The general test covers straightforward wages or salary, but can extend to other remuneration derived from employment. According to *R(SB) 21/86*, these are wide words, which mean "having their origin in." Thus if it had been necessary to decide whether a compensatory award for unfair dismissal by an Industrial Tribunal was derived from employment, the Commissioner would have held that it did. *R(SB) 21/86* is followed in *CIS 590/1993*, which concerned the loss of earnings element in a compensation award for sex discrimination. In *Minter v Kingston upon Hull CC and Potter v Secretary of State for Work and Pensions* [2011] EWCA Civ 1155; [2012] AACR 21 the Court of Appeal held that payments in settlement of potential equal pay claims were "remuneration" within reg.35(1) of the Housing Benefit Regulations 2006 and reg.98(1) of the JSA Regulations 1996 (the equivalents of para.(1)), or, if not, were payments "in lieu of remuneration" within the equivalent housing benefit and JSA provisions of para.(1)(b). See the notes to reg.23 under the heading *The distinction between capital and income* for discussion of these cases and the effect of the principles laid down in *EM v London Borough of Waltham Forest* [2009] UKUT 245 (AAC). These cases also stress the important point that reg.41(5) deems any earnings, insofar as not payments of income, to be income. Thus capital payments, if derived from employment, count as earnings under reg.35.

Payments to a NCB employee in lieu of concessionary coal constituted remuneration derived from employment (*R(SB) 2/86*).

Tips and gratuities would be an example of payments from third parties which are nonetheless derived from employment (see Williams, *Social Security Taxation*, paras 4.21–4.22 for discussion of the income tax cases).   **2.261**

See also *CH 2387/2002*, a case on the then equivalent council tax benefit provision (reg.19(1) of the Council Tax Benefit Regulations). The company accounts showed that the claimant had drawn £6,400 for the year 1999/2000, whereas he had actually received less than half that amount, the remainder having been loaned by him to the company. The Commissioner rejects the claimant's contention that only the amount he received constituted earnings and confirms that for the purpose of council tax benefit his earnings were £6,400. But the repayment of a loan by a company to a director is not a profit derived from employment (*CCS 3671/2002*). The Commissioner in *CCS 3671/2002* and the judge in *GW v CMEC (CM)* [2012] UKUT 332 (AAC) refer to *Shilton v Wilmshurst (Inspector of Taxes)* [1991] 1 A.C. 684 in which the House of Lords stated that an emolument was not "from" employment if it was not paid as a reward for past services or as an inducement to enter into employment and provide future services, or in other words from being or becoming an employee. It was not enough on its own that the payment came from the employer. See also *CCS/3387/2006* (withdrawals from a director's current account were capital, not income).

Note *R(TC) 2/03* which concerned the meaning of "earnings" in reg.19(1) of the Family Credit Regulations (the working families' tax credit equivalent of this provision—see the 2002 edition of this volume for these Regulations). The claimant's partner's employer had made deductions from his current salary in order to recover an earlier overpayment. His payslips showed his "gross for tax" figure as £76 less than his usual salary. The Commissioner held that his gross earnings for the months the deduction was made was the reduced figure. The most likely analysis was that there had been a consensual variation of the contract of employment for those months, making the lower figure the remuneration or profit derived from that employment.

In *MH v SSWP and Rotherham MBC (HB)* [2017] UKUT 401 (AAC) Judge   **2.262** Wikeley adopted and applied the analysis in *R(TC) 2/03*. The claimant received a redundancy payment of nearly £15,000 in March 2016, which was used to pay off debts and make home improvements. In May 2016 he was offered his old job back on condition that he repaid the employer the amount of the redundancy payment by monthly deductions from salary within the 2016/17 tax year. The claimant accepted those terms. On his monthly payslips his basic salary was stated as £2,719.04 before overtime with deductions including income tax and national insurance and the sum of £1,222,22 described as "BS loan". On his claim for housing benefit the local authority (and the First-tier Tribunal) decided that under the equivalent of regs 35 and 36 the gross earnings had to be taken into account and there was nothing to allow the deduction or disregard of the £1,222.22 repayment. The judge held that the proper analysis was that the claimant's contract of employment had been varied by agreement so that he was only entitled to receive a salary reduced by the amount of the repayment and that that amount was his gross earnings. In fact, the case appears stronger than that of *R(TC) 2/03* because the initial terms on which the claimant was re-engaged incorporated the repayments of the redundancy payment. There was hardly a variation. It might also have been arguable that the principle of *Parsons v Hogg* [1985] 2 All E.R. 897, appendix to *R(FIS) 4/85* (see the notes to reg.36(1)) could have been applied, to the effect that the £1,222.22, as an expense necessarily incurred to win the salary, did not form part of the claimant's gross earnings.

The particular categories in sub-paras (a)–(j) are deemed to be earnings, whether they would in general count as earnings or not (*R(SB) 21/86*). Only a few categories require comment.

2.263   *Sub-paragraph (b)*: A payment in lieu of remuneration will in its nature be an income payment. Capital payments (e.g. for the loss of the job itself) are excluded, but see the effect of reg.41(5). *R(SB) 21/86* held that a compensatory award for unfair dismissal made by an industrial tribunal (now an employment tribunal) was a payment in lieu of remuneration, to be taken into account for the number of weeks specified in the award. Such an award is now expressly included in sub-para.(g) and so will fall to be taken into account on the termination of full-time employment, although since October 1, 2007 payments under sub-para.(b) on the termination of full-time employment have been disregarded (see para.1 of Sch.8 and the notes to that paragraph).

In *CIS/590/1993* the claimant's award of compensation under the Sex Discrimination Act included amounts for injured feelings, the loss of a tax rebate and one month's loss of earnings. It was accepted that the first two items counted as capital. The Commissioner follows *R(SB) 21/86* and holds that the loss of earnings element fell to be treated as earnings under sub-para.(b). There was no reason for drawing a distinction between a compensatory award for unfair dismissal and that part of a sex discrimination award that was for loss of earnings. The fact that only the former was referred to in sub-para.(g) did not imply that the loss of earnings elements in sex (or race) discrimination awards (or indeed awards made by county courts for breach of employment contracts) were excluded from para.(1), since the categories listed in sub-paras (a)–(i) were only included as examples. See the notes to reg.31(1) as to when the earnings were treated as due to be paid. However, the fact that the loss of earnings element in such awards comes within sub-para.(b), rather than sub-para.(g), means that from October 1, 2007 it will be disregarded (except where it is awarded in respect of employment which has been suspended or part-time work where the claimant was claiming income support, see paras 1–2 of Sch.8 and the notes to those paragraphs).

See also *Minter v Kingston upon Hull CC* and *Potter v Secretary of State for Work and Pensions* [2011] EWCA Civ 1155; [2012] AACR 21 in which payments in settlement of potential claims under the Equal Pay Act 1970 counted as earnings. (For a discussion of these decisions see the notes to reg.23 under "*Distinction between capital and income*").

2.264   *Sub-paragraph (c)*: This sub-paragraph is now confined to payments in lieu of notice, whether full or partial. Presumably, it covers payments expressly in lieu of notice (see *CIS 400/1994*). "Global" payments, i.e. payments not expressly broken down into elements, will fall under sub-para.(i). Note that from October 1, 2007 earnings received under this sub-paragraph are disregarded (except in the case of part-time work which ends while the claimant is claiming income support: see paras 1–2 of Sch.8 and the notes to those paragraphs).

Sub-paragraph (d): Holiday pay which is payable (i.e due to be paid, not received   **2.265**
or paid: *R(SB) 15/82, R(SB) 33/83, R(SB) 11/85*) within four weeks of termination or interruption of employment counts as earnings. In cases of termination, holiday pay will be due immediately, unless the contract of employment expressly provides otherwise. Therefore, whenever it is paid (and presumably it cannot count until it is actually paid) it will count as earnings to be taken into account for the benefit week in which it was due to be paid. Then s.74 of the SSAA 1992 might come into play. If employment is merely interrupted it is more likely that holiday pay will not be payable immediately. Note that from October 1, 2007 earnings received under this sub-paragraph are disregarded (except in the case of employment which has been suspended or where the holiday pay is paid in connection with part-time work undertaken while the claimant is claiming income support: see paras 1–2 of Sch.8 and the notes to those paragraphs).

Holiday pay outside this sub-paragraph is capital (reg.48(3)), but is then disregarded (Sch.9 para.32).

CIS 894/1994 holds that for a payment to be holiday pay there has to be entitlement to holidays under the contract of employment. The claimant worked on a North Sea oil rig. His contract of employment provided that there was no entitlement to holidays but that he would accrue 42 hours vacation pay per quarter. He could ask for this pay at any time and payment would be made at the end of the quarter. On the termination of his employment he was paid 100 days accrued vacation pay. The Commissioner decides that the vacation pay was not holiday pay in the ordinary sense of the word. It had nothing to do with the taking of holidays but was in reality compensation for the fact that there was no holiday entitlement. The consequence was that it fell to be disregarded under what was then para.1(a) (ii) (now para.1(1)(a)) of Sch.8.

Sub-paragraph (e): *R(IS) 9/95* decides that a guarantee payment under s.12 of   **2.266**
the Employment Protection (Consolidation) Act 1978 is a payment by way of a retainer. Presumably the same will apply to guarantee payments under the current provision, s.28 of the Employment Rights Act 1996.

See also the payments included under sub-para.(gg).

Note the amendments made to paras 1 and 2 of Sch.8 on October 26, 2009 which confirm that the disregards in those paragraphs do not apply to payments in the nature of a retainer (i.e. guarantee payments under s.28 of the Employment Rights Act 1996, and the right to remuneration while suspended on medical grounds under s.64 or while suspended on maternity grounds under s.68, together with awards under s.34 or 70, of that Act), as well as payments by way of a retainer.

Sub-paragraph (f): The conditions here are in line with those under which expenses   **2.267**
are deductible from earnings for income tax purposes. Payment for all items beyond those solely necessary for *the performance of* the duties of the employment are caught. It is not enough if the expenses are incurred in order to enable the person to perform those duties (*Smith v Abbott* [1994] 1 All E.R. 673). The express mention of the expenses of travel to and from work and of looking after a family member merely spells this out. (On child care expenses see *Jackson and Cresswell v Chief Adjudication Officer* (C-63/91 and C-64/91) [1992] E.C.R. I-4737, also reported as Appendix 2 to *R(IS) 10/91*, and *R(FC) 2/98 (Meyers)*, in the notes to reg.36(3).) The reimbursement of a local councillor's home telephone expenses in *CIS 38/1989* is an example. On the evidence, the expenses were necessarily incurred, but not wholly or exclusively, in the performance of his duties as a councillor. On other evidence, such expenses could be apportioned between personal and employment purposes (cf. *R(FC) 1/91, CFC 26/1989* and *R(FIS) 13/91* on reg.38(3)). See also *CFC 836/1995*

in the notes to reg.38(11) on apportionment of expenses between earnings as an employee and from self-employment. There is helpful guidance in *R(FIS) 4/85*.

2.268   *CIS 89/1989* holds that travel and subsistence allowances paid to a local council-lor, which included travel from home to the place of employment, were for necessary etc. expenses, because a councillor's home is also a place of employment. *R(IS) 6/92* confirms this result, because under s.174(1) of the Local Government Act 1972 pay-ments of travelling and subsistence allowances can only be made where the expenses have been necessarily incurred for the performance of any duty as a councillor. Therefore, such a payment must fall outside sub-para.(f) and within para.(2)(c).

In *CH/1330/2008* the claimant was a care worker who travelled to her clients from her home. The Commissioner finds that in these circumstances she did not have a place of employment within the meaning of reg.35(1)(f)(i) of the Housing Benefit Regulations 2006 (which is the equivalent of sub-para.(f)(i)) and that all her travel expenses from the moment she left home did not count as earnings.

2.269   But in *SS v St Edmundsbury BC (HB)* [2014] UKUT 172 (AAC) the travel allowance paid to the claimant following her employer's relocation which sub-stantially increased the distance she had to travel to work (which was taxable) was earnings.

See also the notes to reg.36(3).

2.270   *Sub-paragraph (g)*: Awards of compensation which come under this sub-paragraph, including "out of court" settlement payments, are taken into account on the termi-nation of full-time employment. They fall within the exception from the operation of the disregard in para.1 of Sch.8 in para.1(2)(b)(i), in relation to full-time employ-ment. But awards on the termination of part-time employment fall within the para.2 disregard.

2.271   *Sub-paragraph (gg)*: Section 28 of the Employment Rights Act 1996 provides a right to guarantee payments; s.64, a right to remuneration on suspension on medical grounds; and s.68, a right to remuneration on suspension on maternity grounds. Section 34 provides for a complaint to an employment tribunal in respect of an employer's failure to pay guarantee payments and s.70 for a complaint to an employment tribunal in respect of an employer's failure to pay under s.64 or 68.

Note the amendments made to paras 1 and 2 of Sch.8 on October 26, 2009 which have the effect that the disregards in those paragraphs do not apply to any of these payments.

2.272   *Sub-paragraph (h)*: The sums referred to in s.112(3) of the Contributions and Benefits Act are arrears of pay under an order for reinstatement or re-engagement under the Employment Rights Act 1996; a sum payable under an award for the continuation of a contract of employment; and remuneration under a protective award. Such payments, including "out of court" settlement payments, are taken into account on the termination of full-time employment (see para.1 of Sch.8 and the notes to that paragraph).

2.273   *Sub-paragraph (i)*: There was a significant change in 1989 in the treatment of lump sum payments made on the termination of employment, which was designed to simplify decision-making. It was along similar lines to the change in the UB rules, but intro-duced several differences. In *CIS 400/1994* the Commissioner drew attention to the different ways that termination payments at the end of a period of employment were treated by the income support and UB legislation. In particular, the definition of "com-pensation" was not the same (e.g. for UB purposes "compensation" could include pay-ments in lieu of notice; for income support it did not). For the position under old style JSA, see reg.98(1)(b) and (3) of the JSA Regulations 1996.

There were separate provisions depending whether it was full-time or part-time employment which was terminated. See para.(3)(c) and reg.29(4D)(a) which adopts the test of remunerative work in regs 5 and 6(1) and (4) for the dividing line.

However, since April 14, 2008, the provisions relating to compensation payments only apply where part-time employment is terminated (see the amendment to para.

(1)(i)). This is because the provisions were considered to be obsolete in relation to full-time employment following the increased disregard of payments made on the termination of full-time employment that was introduced on October 1, 2007 (see para.1 of Sch.8 and the notes to that paragraph). Where a compensation payment is made in respect of part-time employment that ceases before the claim for income support is made (whether or not the employment has terminated), it will continue to be ignored, as was the case before October 1, 2007 (see para.2 of Sch.8). However, a compensation payment will be taken into account in the case of part-time work which ends while the claimant is claiming income support: see the note to para.2 of Sch.8. The whole payment is taken into account in one week (reg.29(4C)), generally the week in which it is due to be paid (reg.31).

"Compensation" is defined in para.(3)(a). First, the person must not have received 2.274
a payment in lieu of all the notice to which he was legally entitled. If this has happened, no other payment can be "compensation" within sub-para.(i) (confirmed in *CIS 400/1994*). Second, all the payments already counted as earnings by para.(1)(a) to (h) or excluded from that category by para.(2), refunds of pension contributions and "any redundancy payment within the meaning of s.135(1) of the Employment Rights Act 1996" are excluded. On the meaning of "any redundancy payment . . .", see *CJSA 82/1998* (which concerned the same phrase in reg.98(2)(f) of the JSA Regulations 1996). In the Commissioner's view, a payment "within the meaning of . . ." was wider than a payment "made under . . .". He concludes that the exemption under reg.98(2)(f) applied to all payments genuinely made in lieu of a redundancy payment up to the level of entitlement that would arise under the statutory duty to make a redundancy payment (now contained in s.135 of the Employment Rights Act 1996). The same should apply to the exclusion under para.(3)(a)(iii).

Other payments made in respect of or on the termination of employment count as compensation. It does not particularly matter what the employer calls the payment, providing that it is connected to the termination (cf. *R(U) 4/92* and *R(U) 5/92*), so that merely calling the payment a capital payment (e.g. for loss of the job as a capital asset) does not take it outside sub-para.(i). The main categories will be payments from employers which are not precisely categorised (e.g. the ubiquitous "ex gratia" payment) and payments made in settlement of claims for unfair or wrongful dismissal (providing that a payment in lieu of full notice has not already been paid). But a payment solely in relation to racial discrimination during employment is not within the definition (*CU 88/1991*).

Note that although payments made on the termination of employment such as statutory redundancy payments, and (unless they count as "compensation" payments—see above) contractual redundancy payments and ex gratia payments are not earnings, they will count as capital. Periodic sums paid on account of the termination of employment due to redundancy do not count as earnings under para.(1)(b) but will be income other than earnings (or possibly capital payable by instalments, depending on the circumstances).

Sub-paragraph (j): The effect of this sub-paragraph, together with para.(2A), is 2.275
that non-cash vouchers liable for Class 1 national insurance contributions will be treated as earnings. This does not apply to non-cash vouchers that are not taken into account for national insurance purposes. As payments in kind they will count as other income (see reg.40(4)(a)) but note the disregard in para.21 of Sch.9.

Note that reg.2(2) of the Social Security Amendment (Non-Cash Vouchers) Regulations 1999 (SI 1999/1509) provides that where a claimant had an existing award of income support (or JSA) on June 30, 1999, sub-para.(j) and para.(2A) will not operate until the date that the first decision on review of that award after June 30, 1999 takes effect.

Paragraph (2)
These amounts—payments in kind; sick, maternity, paternity, shared parental or 2.276
adoption or parental bereavement leave pay; reimbursement of necessary expenses; payments of expenses that result from "a claimant participating as a service user"

(see reg.2(1B) for those to whom this refers); and occupational pensions—are not earnings, but do count as other income (reg.40(4)(a)). It is apparently intended that lump sum payments covered by subpara.(e) should count as capital (as their nature would indicate), although reg.40(4) (now reg.40(4)(a)) has not also been amended. But note that income in kind is disregarded (Sch.9 para.21); so are payments of necessary expenses (Sch.9 para.3) and payments of expenses in respect of a claimant participating as a service user (Sch.9 para.2A). Deductions from contractual or statutory sick, maternity, paternity, shared parental or adoption or parental bereavement leave pay for Class 1 NI contributions and one-half of any contribution by the claimant to an occupational or personal pension scheme are disregarded under paras 4 and 4A of Sch.9. There is no provision for the disregard of ill-health payments or occupational pensions (confirmed in *CIS 6/1989*). If a person is remunerated by payments in kind, there is the possibility of notional earnings being attributed to the person under reg.42(6). However, the notional income rules are specifically excluded in the case of expenses *and* earnings as a result of a claimant participating as a service user (see reg.42(2)(ga) and (8ZA)).

See the notes to para.(1)(f) for what are necessary, etc. expenses. In a decision on the equivalent provision in the Family Credit Regulations (reg.19(2)), the Commissioner suggested that its effect is that expenditure by the employee on necessary etc. expenses is to be deducted from the amount of his earnings (*CFC 2/1989*). This does not seem to be consistent with the pattern of reg.35, which is otherwise concerned with payments to the employee, and is rejected in *R(FC) 1/90, R(IS) 16/93* and *CIS 77/1993*. The payment can be by way of reimbursement to the employee for expenses initially met by him (*CIS 77/1993*). But the application of the principle of *Parsons v Hogg* to the meaning of "gross earnings" in reg.36 will, it seems, permit the deduction from earnings of necessary, etc. expenses incurred by the employee. See the notes to reg.36(3). *CJSA 2402/2003* confirms that a trade union subscription is not deductible as such an expense and that this does not infringe art.11 ECHR (right of assembly and association).

CIS 4317/1997 highlighted an anomaly in the legislation that results from sick or maternity pay, etc. not being treated as earnings. The claimant stopped work in September 1996 because of illness. He was paid four weeks' statutory and contractual sick pay on October 31, 1996 and his contract of employment was terminated on the same day. He claimed income support on November 1 but was treated as having income for four weeks from October 31 under regs 29(1) and (2) and 31(1). The Commissioner confirmed that this was correct. Although final earnings are disregarded under para.1 of Sch.8, there was no equivalent disregard in Sch.9 (or elsewhere) to enable final payments of sick pay to be ignored. He rejected the argument that reg.29(2) was ultra vires. This argument was renewed before the Court of Appeal but was dismissed (*Owen v Chief Adjudication Officer*, April 29, 1999). The claimant had contended that the power in s.136(5)(a) of the SSCBA 1992 (person can be treated as possessing income or capital which he does not possess) did not apply where the person in fact possessed the income; it therefore did not authorise a provision treating income received by the claimant at one time as available to him at another time. In addition, it was argued that reg.29(2) was outside the power in s.136(3) (income to be calculated or estimated in prescribed manner) because simply shifting income from one period to another was neither "calculation" nor "estimation". But the Court of Appeal held that reg.29(2) was within the power in s.136(5)(a). A deeming provision by its very nature had the effect of treating a fact or state of affairs as existing for a stated purpose when that fact or state of affairs did not in truth exist. Section 136(5)(a) was sufficiently widely framed to authorise a provision that spread or apportioned income to a stated period. The Court also rejected the contention that reg.29(2) was ultra vires on the ground of irrationality. However, the Court of Appeal (like the Commissioner and the tribunal) expressed disquiet at the anomalous result arising from the different treatment of sick pay and final earnings and voiced the hope that the operation of the regulations in these circumstances would be reconsidered. But this has not occurred despite the increased disregard of payments made on the termination of full-time employment introduced on October 1, 2007 (see para.1 of Sch.8 and the notes to that paragraph).

Calculation of net earnings of employed earners

36.—(1) For the purposes of regulation 29 (calculation of earnings of employed earners) the earnings of a claimant derived from employment as an employed earner to be taken into account shall, subject to paragraph (2), be his net earnings.

(2) There shall be disregarded from a claimant's net earnings, any sum specified in paragraphs 1 to 13 [²[³ or 15A]] of Schedule 8.

(3) For the purposes of paragraph (1) net earnings shall be calculated by taking into account the gross earnings of the claimant from that employment less—

    (a) any amount deducted from those earnings by way of—
        (i) income tax;
        (ii) primary Class 1 contributions under the Social Security Act; and

    (b) one-half of any sum paid by the claimant [¹in respect of a pay period] by way of a contribution towards an occupational or personal pension scheme.

2.277

AMENDMENTS

1. Income-related Benefits Schemes (Miscellaneous Amendments) (No.5) Regulations 1994 (SI 1994/2139) reg.26 (October 3, 1994).
2. Social Security (Miscellaneous Amendments) (No.2) Regulations 1999 (SI 1999/2556) reg.2(5) (October 4, 1999).
3. Social Security (Back to Work Bonus and Lone Parent Run-on) (Amendment and Revocation) Regulations 2003 (SI 2003/1589) reg.2(b) (October 25, 2004).

DEFINITIONS

"claimant"—see reg.2(1) and reg.23(1).
"employed earner"—see reg.2(1).
"occupational pension scheme"—see Pension Schemes Act 1993 s.1.
"pay period"—see reg.2(1).
"personal pension scheme"—*ibid.*
"Social Security Act"—*ibid.*

GENERAL NOTE

Paragraph (1)
Earnings defined in reg.35 are to be converted to net earnings before being taken into account. This is to be done according to para.(3).

2.278

Paragraph (2)
After the conversion to net earnings has been carried out, the amounts specified in paras 1–13 or 15A of Sch.8 are to be disregarded. (Paragraph (2) has not been updated to include a reference to para.15C of Sch.8.) For the position relating to earnings of a child or young person see the note to para.14 of Sch.8.

2.279

Paragraph (3)
Only this limited list of deductions for payments made by the employee may be made from gross earnings. Nothing is to be deducted for travel costs (see *CJSA 4721/2001*), child care expenses or meals at work. This leads to a much simpler calculation than under supplementary benefit. The compensation was an increase in the basic disregard to £5, but not changed since 1988.

2.280

R(FC) 1/90 holds that if the employee makes contributions to both an occupational and a personal pension scheme, half of both contributions can be deducted. See also *R(CS) 3/00* which decides that half of the contributions made under retirement annuity contracts by employed earners were to be deducted from gross earnings under para.1(3)(c) of Sch.1 to the Child Support (Maintenance Assessments and Special Cases) Regulations 1992. Such contracts came within the meaning of "personal pension scheme" for employed earners. The same definition of "personal pension scheme" was used for income support (see reg.2(1)) and the Commissioner's reasoning should apply to deductions under para.(3)(b). Now note that following the changes made by Pt 4 of the Finance Act 2004 retirement annuity contracts come within the definition of "personal pension scheme" (see further the notes to *"personal pension scheme"* in reg.2(1)).

There was, however, some doubt about the meaning of "gross earnings." In *R(FC) 1/90* the Commissioner refers to the principle adopted by the Court of Appeal in *Parsons v Hogg* [1985] 2 All E.R. 897, appendix to *R(FIS) 4/85*, and by the Commissioner in *R(FIS) 4/85*, that "earnings," even associated with the word "gross," in the Family Income Supplements (General) Regulations 1980 meant not the remuneration actually received, but the receipts after payment of expenses wholly and necessarily incurred in the course of winning those receipts. He applies this principle to the equivalent provision to reg.36 in the Family Credit Regulations (reg.20) (see the 2002 edition of this volume for the Family Credit Regulations) and holds that expenses necessarily wholly and exclusively incurred by the employee in the performance of the duties of employment are to be deducted from the gross receipts to produce a figure of gross earnings. The same Commissioner applies the principle to income other than earnings in *CIS 25/1989*, but this has not been followed in *CIS 563/1991* and *R(IS) 13/01* (see the note to reg.40(1)). In *R(FC) 1/90*, the claimant's expenditure on work equipment might be deducted, but not child care expenses (*R(FIS) 2/88*).

2.281   The wording of reg.36 is not the same as was considered in *Parsons v Hogg*, so that there was some doubt about the application of the principle. In *R(IS) 6/92* the Commissioner held that an attendance allowance paid to a local councillor had to be taken into account as earnings, subject only to the £5 disregard, although the councillor incurred necessary, etc. expenses on such things as stationery and telephone calls. However, the Commissioner referred only to reg.35 and not to reg.36 or any of the decisions cited in the previous paragraph. In *CIS 77/1993*, which concerned a local councillor's basic allowance, the same Commissioner considered that *Parsons v Hogg* did not apply, but decided that the allowance fell within reg.35(2)(c). However, the application of *Parsons v Hogg* does produce a result where only resources actually available to the person are counted. It is also the approach taken in para.26016 of the *Decision Makers Guide*. *R(IS) 16/93* has now expressly decided that the principle of *Parsons v Hogg* applies to reg.36. This has been followed in *CIS 507/1994*.

Parsons v Hogg has also been applied to "gross earnings" in para.1(3) of Sch.2 to the Child Support (Maintenance Assessments and Special Cases) Regulations 1992 (SI 1992/1815) in *R(CS) 2/96*. Moreover, *CCS 3882/1997* held that the principle of *Parsons v Hogg* is not restricted to expenses wholly, exclusively and necessarily incurred in the performance of the duties of the employment but can extend to subscriptions to professional bodies or learned societies which were tax-deductible under s.201 of the Income and Corporation Taxes Act 1988, provided that they have to be incurred in order to win the earnings in question. *CJSA 2402/2003* confirms that this would not apply to a trade union subscription since there was (as far as the Commissioner was aware) no specific provision of the income tax legislation under which the union subscription would be deductible in computing the amount of income for income tax purposes. However, arguably it could have been applied to the deduction for the repayment to the employer of a redundancy payment on the claimant's re-employment in *MH v SSWP and Rotherham MBC (HB)* [2017] UKUT 401 (AAC) where the analysis, following *R(TC) 2/03*, was that the contract of employment had been varied to make the claimant only entitled to earnings less that deduction (see the notes to reg.35(1)).

In calculating the amount of necessary, etc. expenses to be deducted the principle established in *R(FC) 1/91, CFC 26/1989* and *R(IS) 13/91* should be applied. That is that if items have a dual private and work use, and that use can be apportioned on a time basis, the appropriate proportion should be deducted. See the note to reg.38(3). See also *CFC 836/1995* in the notes to reg.38(11) on apportionment of expenses between two employments.

In *R(IS) 10/91*, a challenge to the inability to deduct child-care expenses from earnings as being discriminatory and therefore contrary to EC Directive 79/7 was rejected. On appeal, the Court of Appeal referred the question whether supplementary benefit and/or income support fall within art.3 of the Directive to the European Court of Justice (*Cresswell v Chief Adjudication Officer, Jackson v Chief Adjudication Officer*, reported as Appendix 1 to *R(IS) 10/91*).

2.282

A similar question in relation to housing benefit had been referred by the Divisional Court in *R. v Secretary of State for Social Security Ex p. Smithson* (June 26, 1990). The Advocate General's opinion in *Smithson* (delivered on November 20, 1991) was that the provisions on higher pensioner premium were part of the statutory scheme protecting against the risks of invalidity and old age, so that they came within art.3. The ECJ (February 4, 1992) (C-243/90) disagreed, finding that the higher pensioner premium was an inseparable part of the whole scheme of housing benefit, which was intended to compensate for the fact that the beneficiary's income was insufficient to meet housing costs and not to provide protection against one of the risks specified in art.3(1) (e.g. sickness, invalidity, old age). Although criteria concerning protection against old age and sickness were part of the criteria for determining the level against which the beneficiary's income was tested, that did not affect the purpose of the whole scheme.

Once that decision had been made, the ECJ's decision in *Cresswell and Jackson* (July 16, 1992) [1992] E.C.R. I-4737; [1993] 3 All E.R. 265, also reported as Appendix 2 to *R(IS) 10/91*, followed fairly inevitably. Benefits such as supplementary benefit and income support could be granted in a variety of personal situations to persons whose means are insufficient to meet their needs as defined by statute. Therefore, they did not come within art.3(1) of the Directive. In the particular cases the claimants' theoretical needs were set independently of any consideration of any of the risks specified in art.3(1). Nor did the fact that the conditions of entitlement to a benefit affected a single parent's ability to take up access to vocational training or part-time employment bring that benefit within EC Directive 76/207 on equal treatment for men and women as regards access to employment, vocational training and promotion, and working conditions. Benefit schemes only come within Directive 76/207 if their subject matter is access to employment, etc. or working conditions.

These decisions seem to rule out challenges to the income support scheme under either Directive, as accepted in *CIS 8/1990* and *CIS 375/1990*. (But the position is different under old style JSA. In *Hockenjos v Secretary of State;* [2001] EWCA Civ 624; [2001] 2 C.M.L.R. 51; [2001] I.C.R. 966, also reported as *R(JSA) 1/05*, the Court of Appeal held that the Jobseekers Act 1995 had set up a unitary statutory scheme to provide against the risk of unemployment which was covered by art.3(1)(a) of EC Directive 79/7. The result was that both contribution-based and income-based old style JSA were within the scope of Directive 79/7.)

Chapter IV

Self-Employed Earners

Earnings of self-employed earners

37.—(1) Subject to paragraph (2), "earnings", in the case of employment as a self-employed earner, means the gross receipts of the employment

2.283

and shall include any allowance paid under section 2 of the Employment and Training Act 1973 [¹or section 2 of the Enterprise and New Towns (Scotland) Act 1990] to the claimant for the purpose of assisting him in carrying on his business.

[²(2) "Earnings" shall not include—

(a) where a claimant is involved in providing board and lodging accommodation for which a charge is payable, any payment by way of such a charge;

[³(b) any payment to which paragraph [⁵26, 27 or 27A] of Schedule 9 refers (payments in respect of a person accommodated with the claimant under an arrangement made by a local authority or voluntary organisation [⁵, payments] made to the claimant by a health authority, local authority or voluntary organisation in respect of persons temporarily in the claimant's care) [⁵and any payments made to a claimant under section 73(1)(b) of the Children and Young People (Scotland) Act 2014 (kinship care assistance)].]]

[⁶(ba) any payment made in accordance with section 26A of the Children (Scotland) Act 1995 (duty to provide continuing care)—

(i) to a claimant; or

(ii) where paragraph (3) applies, to another person ("A") which A passes on to the claimant;]

[⁴(c) any sports award.]

[⁶(3) This paragraph applies only where A—

(a) was formerly in the claimant' s care;

(b) is aged 16 or over; and

(c) continues to live with the claimant.]

AMENDMENTS

1. Enterprise (Scotland) Consequential Amendments Order 1991 (SI 1991/ 387) art.2 (April 1, 1991).

2. Income-related Benefits Schemes (Miscellaneous Amendments) (No.3) Regulations 1992 (SI 1992/2155) reg.16 (October 5, 1992).

3. Income-related Benefits Schemes (Miscellaneous Amendments) (No.5) Regulations 1994 (SI 1994/2139) reg.27 (October 3, 1994).

4. Social Security Amendment (Sports Awards) Regulations 1999 (SI 1999/ 2165) reg.6(3) (August 23, 1999).

5. Social Security and Child Support (Care Payments and Tenant Incentive Scheme) (Amendment) Regulations 2017 (SI 2017/995) reg.2(2) (November 7, 2017).

6. Social Security and Child Support (Care Payments and Tenant Incentive Scheme) (Amendment) Regulations 2017 (SI 2017/995) reg.10(3) (November 7, 2017).

DEFINITIONS

"board and lodging accommodation"—see reg.2(1).
"claimant"—see reg.2(1) and reg.23(1).
"self-employed earner"—see reg.2(1).
"sports award"—*ibid.*
"voluntary organisation"—*ibid.*

GENERAL NOTE

Paragraph (1)

2.284   This is not the place for any extensive discussion of how to distinguish between employed earners (i.e. those employed under a contract of service: employees

or office-holders) and self-employed earners. In most cases there will be no difficulty in identifying a claimant or partner who falls within reg.37. There is a still
helpful, although now dated, summary of the traditional factors in Wikeley, Ogus
and Barendt, *The Law of Social Security*, 5th edn (London: Butterworths, 2002),
pp.98–103. See also *CJSA/4721/2001*. There is perhaps a recent tendency to give
particular significance to who takes the financial risk of operations as between the
person doing the work and the employer/customer. Do not forget that someone who
sets up a limited company of which they are the sole or main employee and who
controls the company through being the sole or majority shareholder is nevertheless
an employee.

On "professional" gambling, see *Hakki v Secretary of State for Work and Pensions*
[2014] EWCA Civ 530, followed and applied in *French v SSWP* [2018] EWCA Civ
470; [2018] AACR 25.

The starting point for the self-employed is the figure of gross receipts, to be
reduced to net profits under reg.38.

In *CFC 4/1991*, the claimant's husband had recently started a construction   2.285
business. He received a loan of £5,500 from a relative and made part repayment
of £4,000 not long afterwards. The Department and the Tribunal treated the loan
as part of the "gross receipts" of the self-employment. The repayment could not
be deducted from the gross receipts because of reg.22(5)(a) of the Family Credit
Regulations (the equivalent of reg.38(5)(a) below). (See the 2002 edition of this
volume for the Family Credit Regulations.) The result was that the net profit so
calculated took the claimant above family credit level. The Commissioner found
that the loan was a capital receipt, but concluded that the words of reg.21(1) of the
Family Credit Regulations (the equivalent of reg.37(1)) were unambiguous and
included capital receipts. On appeal under the name of *Kostanczwk*, an order of the
Registrar of the Court of Appeal (dated August 21, 1992) allowed the appeal by
consent and directed that capital receipts not generated by a claimant's business do
not form part of the gross receipts of that employment for the purposes of reg.21 of
the Family Credit Regulations. As *R(FC) 1/97* confirmed, since that direction was
contained in an Order made by consent and without argument it was not binding
on anyone other than the parties to the Order and the tribunal to whom the direction was made. That left *CFC/24/1989* as the only authoritative decision at the time.
There it was held that a grant of £900 from the Prince's Youth Business Trust
to assist in the setting up of a business did not form part of the claimant's gross
receipts. As a matter of principle, the argument that since reg.37 is placed within
the income section of the Regulations, gross receipts must mean "revenue receipts"
and exclude loans or the proceeds of sale of capital assets appeared compelling.
That approach was confirmed by the comprehensive decision in *R(FC) 1/97*, where
the Commissioner holds that neither a loan for business purposes nor the proceeds
of sale of capital assets (in that case a car and a computer printer) form part of the
gross receipts of the employment for the purposes of reg.21 of the Family Credit
Regulations (the equivalent of reg.37). It is, of course, different if the nature of the
business itself is the buying and selling of such things.

Those principles are reflected in the current guidance in para.27166 of the *DMG*,
which specifically mentions loans, injections of capital, grants from the Prince's
Trust and proceeds of sale of capital assets not part of the business's stock in trade
as capital receipts. It is particularly important to recall that injections of capital from
any source, but including from the personal resources of the person in question, do
not form part of gross receipts. Remember also that once an asset, including money,
becomes part of the fund employed and risked in the business, it is a business
asset whose capital value is disregarded under para.6 of Sch.10 while the person is
engaged in the business and for some time afterwards. By contrast, para.27138 says
that subsidies (as in agriculture) or compensation payments (as for BSE) should
be included in gross receipts. It is therefore apparent that in some cases there will
need to be reference to the general principles for distinguishing between capital and
income (see the notes to reg.23 under the "*Distinction between capital and income*").

Thus, compensation payments cannot all be lumped together. It depends what the compensation is for. If it is for loss or diminution in value of something that is a capital asset, it will be a capital receipt. If it is for the loss of income, it will be an income receipt and it does not lose that character because it comes in a lump sum on a one-off basis.

Drawings are not earnings from self-employment, because para.(1) confines consideration to the gross receipts of the self-employment. Nor are drawings to be taken into account as other income (*AR v Bradford Metropolitan DC* [2008] UKUT 30 (AAC), reported as *R(H) 6/09*). Otherwise there would be an unfair double counting.

Coronavirus payments

2.286   That principle may well be tested in 2020 and 2021 in relation to grants under the Coronavirus Self-Employed Income Support Scheme ("SEISS"). These grants, for those who meet the conditions, were described in the March 26, 2020 HMRC guidance as taxable grants of 80 per cent of taxable profits (as calculated by reference to an average over the previous three tax years, or fewer if that is all the evidence available) up to £2,500 per month. Note that the basis of the calculation is profits in the past years, not the revenue (income) receipts of the business in those years, which is what will have primarily been interrupted during the outbreak, while expenses might well continue. Two of the conditions for the grant are that the person's business has been adversely affected due to the coronavirus outbreak and that they intend to continue to trade in the tax year 2020/21. The amount of the grant does not, as confirmed in the Treasury Direction authorising the expenditure on the scheme (Coronavirus Act 2020 Functions of Her Majesty's Revenue and Customs (Self-Employment Income Support Scheme) Direction, signed on April 30, 2020), vary according to the degree of loss of current trading profits. Everyone who qualifies and applies gets the 80 per cent subject to the upper limit. The initial payment in late May and June 2020 (notionally to cover the months of May to July 2020) provided one quarter of the annual figure. The second grant (notionally to cover the months of August to October 2020) met only 70% of qualifying trading profits capped at £6,750 (see the Self-employed Income Support Scheme Extension Direction signed on July 1, 2020). The third and fourth tranches (notionally to cover the months of November 2020 to January 2021 and February to April 2021) went back to the original percentage and cap (see the Self-employed Income Support Scheme Grant Extension 3 Direction signed on November 21, 2020 and the Extension 4 Direction signed on April 6 and 7, 2021).

There are therefore factors pointing towards the grant being an income receipt, though on the most recent authority the label of "Income Support Scheme" is irrelevant or at least not decisive (see *Minter v Kingston upon Hull CC and Potter v Secretary of State for Work and Pensions* [2011] EWCA Civ 1155; [2012] AACR 21 in the notes to reg.23). The facts that the payment is a lump sum and limited to two payments do not necessarily point to the contrary, nor does the existence of a ceiling or the exclusion of the higher-paid or those whose main income in the past years was not from self-employment. However, the particularly crude method of calculation of the amount of the grant, not closely linked to the current level of trading profits and independent of how much current trading profit has been lost, could be argued to point in the other direction, i.e. towards a capital receipt. The Schedule to the Treasury Direction describes the purpose of the scheme simply as to provide payments to businesses adversely affected by the health, social and economic emergency resulting from coronavirus. That could be argued to suggest that the main aim is to allow self-employed businesses to keep going so as to be able to provide services once the worst of the emergency is over, rather than attempt to compensate for loss of personal income. It is understood that the position in income tax law is that an undifferentiated grant in the nature of compensation, one whose purpose is not stated, is treated as a revenue receipt. The HMRC statement in its guidance that the grant is taxable could be said necessarily to imply that at least one significant purpose is to replace what would have been revenue receipts for the period covered and that that is enough to exclude the conclusion of a capital receipt. But, is it enough in social security law for compensation for loss of income merely to be one purpose or does the essential characteristic of the payment have to be identified (otherwise you get different answers depending whether you ask about capital or income)? And is the nature of the SEISS payment far enough away from compensation for it simply being regarded as a capital receipt? The existence of the additional tranches of payment would tend to strengthen the argument that the payments are income receipts, not capital receipts.

Memo DMG 13/20 simply declares that, for the purposes of income support, old style ESA, old style JSA and state pension credit, SEISS payments are to be treated as self-employed earnings, and taken into account over three months from the date of payment (on which see the discussion in the notes to reg.30 indicating that that method of attribution cannot be right). There is no attempt at any reasoned justification for that conclusion and it has plainly been considered that no clarificatory amendments to the regulations, as have been carried out for universal credit, were necessary (see also para.20 of LA Welfare Direct 4/2020 on housing benefit). It may well be that the correct answer is that the grants are income receipts, but a simple amendment could have put the matter beyond doubt.

Self-employed claimants or partners who have employees and a PAYE scheme may also receive payments under the Coronavirus Job Retention Scheme ("CJRS") if they have one or more employees who have been "furloughed" under that scheme. Paragraph 2.1 of the Schedule to the Coronavirus Act 2020 Functions of Her Majesty's Revenue and Customs (Coronavirus Job Retention Scheme) Direction signed on May 20, 2020 (modifying the scheme in the direction signed on April 15, 2020) describes the purpose of the scheme as to provide for payments to be made to employers "incurring costs of employment in respect of furloughed employees arising from the health, social and economic emergency in the United Kingdom resulting from coronavirus and coronavirus disease" and para.2.2 says that it is integral that payments are only made in reimbursement of qualifying expenditure incurred or to be incurred by the employer. Any payment must be returned if the employer becomes unwilling or unable to use it for the specified purpose (para.2.4(b)). Those strict conditions showing the purpose of replacing (up to the initial limits of 80 per cent of qualifying expenditure and £2,500 per month, more limited assistance being available from August to the end of October 2020) what would otherwise have been revenue expenditure, indicates that CJRS payments should be regarded as income receipts. That is the outcome directed in Memo DMG 13/20, but there is a suspicion that it was thought that CJRS payments were relevant only to the earnings of employees. However, it is plain that the payments are made to employers. What furloughed employees within the scheme continue to receive is their remuneration from the employer, either in full or reduced (see the notes to reg.35).

The CJRS has been subject to a complicated series of extensions, currently taking the scheme down to September 30, 2021, the details of which do not need to be set out here (see the House of Commons Library Briefing Paper No.8847, *Coronavirus: Support for Businesses* (March 12, 2021) for these and other schemes). There have been varying levels of reimbursement of salary costs (reimbursement of employer's national insurance and pension contributions not having been available beyond July 21, 2020). As at April 1, 2021 the level of reimbursement of salary for full furlough was 80%. In the extensions announced in the March 2021 budget that level is to reduce to 70% in July 2021 and to 60% in August and September 2021. From July 1, 2020 "flexible furlough has been available. All such payments to self-employed claimants will be income receipts, as explained above. The same problem as identified above for the SEISS applies to the attribution of such earnings in accordance with reg.30.

Payments from the Small Business Grant Fund or the Retail, Hospitality and Leisure Fund seem also to be undifferentiated, but the conditions for payment are rather different from those for SEISS and the March 2020 Department for Business, Energy & Industrial Strategy guidance says nothing about taxability. They

2.287

can be made to business ratepayers who get certain forms of rate relief (one grant per property) and are to be paid at two rates: £10,000 if the rateable value of the property is up to £15,000 and £25,000 if the rateable value is over £15,000 up to £51,000. There is no condition that there has been any loss of trading income. It is therefore arguable that the nature of the grant is sufficiently far from that of compensation for loss of what would have been revenue receipts to be properly a capital receipt, akin to an injection of capital into the business. The same reasoning would apply to receipts from any of the Local Restrictions Support Grant or Additional Restrictions Grant schemes, administered through local authorities and available from autumn 2020 onwards (see Ch.10 of House of Commons Library Briefing Paper No.8847, above), or from a coronavirus Restart Grant.

Loans under the Business Interruption Loan Scheme or the Bounce Back Loan Scheme appear more likely to be capital receipts, although the terms of particular agreements may need to be considered. Memo DMG 13/20 accepts that what it calls business grants and loans to provide support during the coronavirus outbreak are to be treated as capital receipts.

Once a payment, either an income or capital receipt, is received and becomes part of the person's business assets, its amount is disregarded as capital under para.6 of Sch.10 while the person continues to trade and for some period after ceasing. Note in particular that if a person has ceased to trade, any self-employed earnings are to be disregarded as income under para.3 of Sch.8 (see the detailed notes to that provision).

Paragraph (2)

2.287.1 *CIS 55/1989* decided that the predecessor of sub-para.(a), which referred to a claimant "employed" in providing board and lodging accommodation (defined in reg.2(1)), applied whenever the claimant made a charge for providing the accommodation. It was not necessary for the claimant to provide it by way of business. The substitution of the word "involved" reinforces this conclusion. The payments received count as income under reg.40(4)(a), but subject to disregards.

Equally sub-para.(a) will apply where the claimant is engaged in a board and lodging business. In *CIS 521/2002* the claimant was one of four partners who ran a hotel providing board and lodging accommodation for the homeless. The consequence of sub-para.(a) was that rather than her share of the net partnership profits (after deducting income tax, NI contributions and half of any pension contributions) falling under reg.38(1)(b), the gross amount of the income from the boarders had to be taken into account under reg.40(4)(a), subject to any disregard in Sch.9. As the claimant lived in the hotel (and on the basis that she was to be regarded as living in the whole hotel as her home) para.20 of Sch.9 applied. The issue was how the claimant's income was to be calculated. The tribunal applied the disregard under para.20(b) to the total of the receipts from the boarders and then divided by four to obtain the claimant's share. The result of this calculation was that the claimant was not entitled to income support because her income exceeded her applicable amount. However, the Commissioner concluded that the disregard under para.20(b) fell to be applied *after* the claimant's gross income had been calculated. Her gross income was her partnership share, not the total of the board and lodging charges. Furthermore, as para.20 made no provision for partnerships or for taking into account only a proportion of the number of boarders, the disregard to be set against the claimant's quarter share under para.20(b) was £20 plus 50 per cent of any excess for each of the 16 boarders. On this basis, the claimant had no income to be taken into account for the purpose of income support.

Sub-paragraph (b) applies to payments to foster-parents and to people for providing temporary care in their home. Those payments are disregarded as income other than earnings under paras 26 and 27 of Sch.9. Sub-paragraph (b) ensures that they are not treated as earnings. See also reg.6(1)(k) (on not being treated as in remunerative work). Sub-paragraph (b) now also applies to kinship care assistance payments, available since April 2016 in Scotland to people who have applied or are at least considering applying for a kinship care order for a child who is at risk of going into care or was previously looked after by a local authority. However, there has been no amendment to reg.6(1)(k) to cover recipients of such payments. The payments are disregarded as income other than earnings by para.27A of Sch.9 and as capital by para.74 of Sch.10.

On sub-para.(ba), which has the limited application fixed by para.(3), see reg.6(1)(ka). 2.288

On sub-para.(c), see reg.6(1)(m) and the note to that provision. See also the disregards in para.69 of Sch.9 and para.56 of Sch.10.

Note also *CIS/1068/2006* which holds that payments made to the claimant by his wife (from money she received from the local authority under s.57 of the Health and Social Care Act 2001) in consideration of the care services he provided to her were "earnings" and fell to be taken into account in calculating his income support. It did not matter whether the claimant was to be regarded as an employed or self-employed earner for these purposes—the issue was whether the claimant had been engaged by his wife to provide care services for reward, which on the facts of the case was the only possible inference. The Commissioner rejected the claimant's argument that the payments by his wife should be disregarded under para.58 of Sch.9 (see further the note to para.58). The claimant appealed to the Court of Appeal against this decision but his appeal was dismissed (*Casewell v Secretary of State for Work and Pensions* [2008] EWCA Civ 524, reported as *R(IS) 7/08*). The claimant contended that s.136 of the Contributions and Benefits Act requires that payments made to a member of the family are counted when they come into the family, and if at that point they are disregarded, they cannot be counted again if they are transferred from one member of the family to another. However the Court agreed with the Commissioner that the payments to the claimant by his wife were earnings in respect of the care he provided and in the claimant's hands they became his income under s.136(1). It should be noted that the payments to the claimant's wife in this case were made on the basis that she was instructed to pay the claimant the appropriate sum each week against a payslip. There was therefore a specific obligation for the claimant's wife to deal with the payments in a particular way, which had the result that the money paid to her husband was treated as earnings. Thus this was a somewhat different situation from the more usual informal transfer of resources between family members.

Calculation of net profit of self-employed earners

38.—(1) For the purposes of regulation 30 (calculation of earnings of self-employed earners), the earnings of a claimant to be taken into account shall be— 2.289

(a) in the case of a self-employed earner who is engaged in employment on his own account, the net profit derived from that employment;

(b) in the case of a self-employed earner whose employment is carried on in partnership or is that of a share fisherman within the meaning of the Social Security (Mariners' Benefits) Regulations 1975, his share of the net profit derived from that employment less—

    (i) an amount in respect of income tax and of social security contributions payable under the Social Security Act [SSCBA] calculated in accordance with regulation 39 (deduction of tax and contributions for self-employed earners); and

    (ii) [¹one half of any premium paid [²in the period that is relevant under regulation 30] in respect of [⁷ . . .] a personal pension scheme].

(2) There shall be disregarded from a claimant's net profit any sum, where applicable, specified in paragraphs 1 to 13 [⁴ [⁶ . . .]] of Schedule 8.

(3) For the purposes of paragraph (1)(a) the net profit of the employment shall, except where paragraph (9) applies, be calculated by taking into account the earnings of the employment over the period determined under regulation 30 (calculation of earnings of self-employed earners) less—

    (a) subject to paragraphs (5) to (7), any expenses wholly and exclusively defrayed in that period for the purposes of that employment;

    (b) an amount in respect of—

        (i) income tax; and

        (ii) social security contributions payable under the Social Security Act [SSCBA],

    calculated in accordance with regulation 39 (deduction of tax and contributions for self-employed earners); and

    (c) [¹one half of any premium paid [² in the period that is relevant under regulation 30] in respect of [⁷ . . .] a personal pension scheme].

(4) For the purposes of paragraph (1)(b), the net profit of the employment shall be calculated by taking into account the earnings of the employment over the period determined under regulation 30 less, subject to paragraphs (5) to (7), any expenses wholly and exclusively defrayed in that period for the purposes of that employment.

(5) Subject to paragraph (6), no deduction shall be made under paragraph (3)(a) or (4) in respect of—

    (a) any capital expenditure;

    (b) the depreciation of any capital asset;

    (c) any sum employed or intended to be employed in the setting up or expansion of the employment;

    (d) any loss incurred before the beginning of the period determined under regulation 30 (calculation of earnings of self-employed earners);

    (e) the repayment of capital on any loan taken out for the purposes of the employment;

    (f) any expenses incurred in providing business entertainment.

(6) A deduction shall be made under paragraph (3)(a) or (4) in respect of the repayment of capital on any loan used for—

    (a) the replacement in the course of business of equipment or machinery; and

    (b) the repair of an existing business asset except to the extent that any sum is payable under an insurance policy for its repair.

(7) [⁵The Secretary of State] shall refuse to make a deduction in respect of any expenses under paragraph (3)(a) or (4) where he is not satisfied that the expense has been defrayed or, having regard to the nature of the expense and its amount, that it has been reasonably incurred.

(8) For the avoidance of doubt—

    (a) a deduction shall not be made under paragraph (3)(a) or (4) in respect of any sum unless it has been expended for the purposes of the business;

    (b) a deduction shall be made thereunder in respect of—

        (i) the excess of any VAT paid over VAT received in the period determined under regulation 30 (calculation of earnings of self-employed earners);

        (ii) any income expended in the repair of an existing asset except to the extent that any sum is payable under an insurance policy for its repair;

(iii) any payment of interest on a loan taken out for the purposes of the employment.

(9) Where a claimant is engaged in employment as a child minder the net profit of the employment shall be one-third of the earnings of that employment, less—

(a) an amount in respect of—

(i) income tax; and

(ii) social security contributions payable under the Social Security Act [SSCBA 1992],

calculated in accordance with regulation 39 (deduction of tax and contributions for self-employed); and

(b) [¹one half of any premium paid in respect of [⁷ . . .] a personal pension scheme].

(10) Notwithstanding regulation 30 (calculation of earnings of self-employed earners) and the foregoing paragraphs, [⁵the Secretary of State] may assess any item of a claimant's income or expenditure over a period other than that determined under regulation 30 as may, in the particular case, enable the weekly amount of that item of income or expenditure to be determined more accurately.

(11) For the avoidance of doubt where a claimant is engaged in employment as a self-employed earner and he is also engaged in one or more other employments as a self-employed or employed earner any loss incurred in any one of his employments shall not be offset against his earnings in any other of his employments.

(12)[³. . .].

AMENDMENTS

1. Income-related Benefits Schemes (Miscellaneous Amendments) (No.4) Regulations 1993 (SI 1993/2119) reg.13 (October 4, 1993).

2. Income-related Benefits Schemes (Miscellaneous Amendments) (No.5) Regulations 1994 (SI 1994/2139) reg.28 (October 3, 1994).

3. Income-related Benefits Schemes and Social Security (Claims and Payments) (Miscellaneous Amendments) Regulations 1995 (SI 1995/2303) reg.6(3) (October 2, 1995).

4. Social Security (Miscellaneous Amendments) (No.2) Regulations 1999 (SI 1999/2556) reg.2(6) (October 4, 1999).

5. Social Security Act 1998 (Commencement No.12 and Consequential and Transitional Provisions) Order 1999 (SI 1999/3178 (C.81)) art.3(5) and Sch.5 para.2 (November 29, 1999).

6. Social Security (Back to Work Bonus and Lone Parent Run-on) (Amendment and Revocation) Regulations 2003 (SI 2003/1589) reg.2(c) (October 25, 2004).

7. Social Security (Miscellaneous Amendments) (No.3) Regulations 2007 (SI 2007/1749) reg.2(3) (July 16, 2007).

DEFINITIONS

"claimant"—see reg.2(1) and reg.23(1).
"personal pension scheme"—see reg.2(1).
"self-employed earner"—*ibid*.
"Social Security Act"—*ibid*.

GENERAL NOTE

2.290   The structure is as follows:
(1) General rule.
(2) Disregards.
(3) Net profit of sole traders.
(4) Net profit of partners and share fishermen.
(5) Deductions not allowed.
(6) Deductions allowed.
(7) Tests for (3), (4) and (6).
(8) Tests for (3), (4) and (6).
(9) Child minders.
(10) Period of calculation to be adjusted.
(11) Two employments.

Paragraph (1)

2.291   This provision sets up two categories of the self-employed—

(a) those in employment on their own account ("sole traders"), and

(b) partners and share fishermen.

For both, the earnings to be taken into account under reg.30 are to be net profits. Under (b) the deductions for income tax, social security contributions and personal pension (see reg.2(1)) premiums are put under para.(1). For (a), these appear in para.(3).

A "net profit" of a business cannot be less than nil (*R(FC) 1/93*, para.10, *R(H) 5/08*). See further the note to para.(11).

Drawings are not earnings from self-employment because para.(1) confines earnings to the net profit of the employment, or in the case of a partnership to the person's share of the net profit. Nor are drawings to be taken into account as other income (*AR v Bradford Metropolitan DC* [2008] UKUT 30 (AAC), reported as *R(H) 6/09*). Otherwise there would be an unfair double counting.

Paragraph (2)

2.292   See the notes to reg.36(2). The difference is that para.(2) does not refer to the disregard in para.15A of Sch.8 as this is not relevant to self-employed earnings.

Paragraph (3)

2.293   For sole traders apart from child minders (para.(9)) the starting point in calculating net profit under para.(1) is earnings, i.e. gross receipts (see notes to reg.37(1) on the meaning of gross receipts). From that are deducted expenses. Any expenses wholly and exclusively defrayed may be deducted providing that they are reasonably incurred (para.(7)) and the rules of paras (5) and (6) are applied. The expenses must have been actually defrayed, so that unpaid liabilities cannot be deducted (*CIS 212/1988*). The difference between opening and closing stock is not an expense that has been defrayed in the accounting period (*SSWP v SK* [2014] UKUT 12 (AAC)).

There has been considerable doubt about whether the cost of items which have a dual use, for business and private purposes, can be apportioned. *The Adjudication Officer's Guide* originally suggested that the cost of telephone calls, units of gas or electricity consumption and petrol could be apportioned (because consumption can be identified as for business or private purposes), but not, for instance, standing charges or road fund tax or insurance for a car. In a series of appeals heard together, the Commissioner convincingly demolished this approach (*R(FC) 1/91, CFC 26/1989* and *R(IS) 13/91*). He holds that where expenses can be apportioned on a time basis, this can identify the amount wholly and exclusively defrayed on business expenses. There remain some expenses, like the cost of lunches for clients, which are not capable of apportionment. The Commissioner also holds that the apportionment made by the Inspector of Taxes is cogent evidence of the amounts wholly and exclusively incurred for the purposes of the business, which should be accepted in the absence of evidence to the contrary. The *Adjudication Officer's Guide* was subsequently amended to reflect this decision. Now see para.26029 of the *Decision Makers Guide*. See also *CFC 836/1995* in the note to para.(11).

The standard deductions for tax and social security contributions (see reg.39) and personal pension (see reg.2(1)) premiums are made.

Paragraph (4)

For partners and share fishermen the calculation is effectively the same apart 2.294 from the standard deductions already in para.(1)(b). The difference for partners is that the net profit of the partnership as a whole (para.(1)(b)) is to be identified by starting with the gross receipts and then deducting expenses and then the claimant's share of that net profit calculated according to the terms of the partnership.

Paragraph (5)

No deductions are allowed for these items, many of which will appear in profit 2.295 and loss accounts. But see para.(6) for exceptions to (e).

Paragraph (6)

Deductions can be made for the repayment of capital on loans for these repairs 2.296 or replacements. The interest on such a loan will be an allowable expense under the general test (and see para.(8)(b)(iii)).

R(H) 5/07, which concerned reg.31(6) of the Housing Benefit Regulations 1987 (the equivalent of para.(6)), holds that a car is capable of being "equipment" or "machinery" and therefore repayments of capital on a loan used to replace the car in the course of business were deductible. The Commissioner applied the principle in *R(FC) 1/91* (apportionment of expenses between business and personal use) to the capital (and interest—see paras (3)(a) and (8)(b)(iii)) repayments on the loan.

Paragraph (7)

This provision confirms that an expense must have been actually paid out (*CIS* 2.297 *212/1988*), and imposes a general test of reasonableness.

Paragraph (8)

The test of business purpose merely confirms the general requirement under 2.298 paras (3) and (4). It is useful to have the categories in (b) expressly confirmed.

Paragraph (9)

For child-minders the simple rule of taking profit as one third of gross receipts is 2.299 used. The standard deductions are then made. Child-minders who work at home are treated as not in remunerative work (reg.6(1)(b)). See the note to reg.6(1)(b).

Paragraph (10)

This provision gives a very general power to average items over different periods 2.300 from that set in reg.30, where the basic rule is to take the previous one year. But the different period must enable a "more accurate" determination of the weekly amount of the item in question. See the notes to reg.30 for further discussion, particularly related to payments under the various coronavirus schemes.

Paragraph (11)

R(FC) 1/93 applies the principle that a loss in one employment cannot be set off 2.301 against a profit or earnings in another separate employment. The claimant ran a sub-post office and a shop in the same premises. The Commissioner decides that

401

carrying out the office of sub-postmistress was employment as an employed earner, while running the shop was employment as a self-employed earner. The loss made by the shop could not be set off against the claimant's earnings as a sub-postmistress. *CFC 836/1995* concerned similar facts. However, the Commissioner there went on to consider the apportionment of expenses between the two employments. Applying by analogy *R(FC) 1/91* (apportionment of expenses between business and personal use), he held that expenses which were not solely attributable to the shop could be apportioned between the shop and the claimant's husband's employment as a sub-postmaster. The basis of the apportionment in that case was 75 per cent to the post office and 25 per cent to the shop, since the primary reason most customers visited the premises was for the post office services. Thus 75 per cent of the expenses relating to the general running of the premises and the two activities and the repayments on a loan to acquire the post office and shop could be deducted from the earnings as a sub-postmaster, as the Commissioner accepted that these had been wholly, exclusively and necessarily incurred in the performance of the duties of sub-postmaster (see *R(FC) 1/90*, applying *Parsons v Hogg*). See also *CFC 4238/1997*.

CPC/3373/2007 also confirms that under the equivalent state pension credit provision (see reg.17B of the State Pension Credit Regulations, which applies as modified reg.13 of the Social Security Benefit (Computation of Earnings) Regulations 1996) the loss from the claimant's self-employment could not be offset against his other income (retirement pension and an annuity). The Commissioner rejects the claimant's argument that because reg.13(12) (the equivalent of para.(11)) specifies particular circumstances in which losses may not be offset the implication was that in other circumstances offsetting of losses was possible. Regulation 13(12) (like para.(11)) stated that it had been made for the avoidance of doubt, that is, it was intended merely to clarify the law as it would exist even if the regulation had not been made. The calculation of state pension credit (like income support) was governed by a statutory scheme and in the absence of a regulation positively requiring an offset, either expressly or by necessary implication, that offset was not permitted. The Revenue permitted the offset of a loss from self-employment against other income because it was required to do this (for the current provision see s.64 of the Income Tax Act 2007) but the rules for state pension credit did not contain any equivalent provision.

In *R(H) 5/08* (which concerned reg.22 of the Council Tax Benefit Regulations 1992, the equivalent of reg.38) the claimant argued that the loss in his business should be deducted from his wife's earnings from her part-time employment (not in his business). The Commissioner accepted that reg.22(10) (the equivalent of para.(11)) did not apply because this only applied where the *claimant* was engaged in two or more employments. However, reg.22(1) (the equivalent of para.(1)) spoke of "net *profit*". A "net *profit*" of a business could not be less than nil (see also para.10 of *R(FC) 1/93* in which the Commissioner took the same approach). There was thus nothing to deduct.

Deduction of tax and contributions for self-employed earners

2.302 **39.**—(1) The amount to be deducted in respect of income tax under regulation 38(1)(b)(i), (3)(b)(i) or (9)(a)(i) (calculation of net profit of self-employed earners) shall be calculated on the basis of the amount of chargeable income and as if that income were assessable to income tax at [¹[⁶. . .] the basic rate [⁸, or in the case of a Scottish taxpayer, the Scottish basic rate,] of tax] less only the [⁸ personal reliefs to which the claimant is entitled under Chapters 2, 3 and 3A of Part 3 of the Income Tax Act 2007 as are] appropriate to his circumstances; but, if the period determined under regulation 30 (calculation of earnings of self-employed earners) is less than a year, [¹the earnings to which the [⁵ [⁶ basic] rate] [⁸, or the Scottish basic rate,] [³. . .] of tax is to be applied and] the amount of the [⁴ [⁸ personal reliefs]] deductible under this paragraph shall be calculated on a pro rata basis.

(2) The amount to be deducted in respect of social security contributions under regulation 38(1)(b)(i), (3)(b)(ii) or (9)(a)(ii) shall be the total of—

[²(a) the amount of Class 2 contributions payable under section [⁷ 11(2)] or, as the case may be, [⁷ 11(8)] of the Contributions and Benefits Act at the rate applicable at the date of claim except where the claimant's chargeable income is less than the amount specified in section 11(4) of that Act ([⁷ small profits threshold]) for the tax year in which the date of claim falls; but if the assessment period is less than a year, the amount specified for that tax year shall be reduced pro rata; and

(b) the amount of Class 4 contributions (if any) which would be payable under section 15 of that Act (Class 4 contributions recoverable under the Income Tax Acts) at the percentage rate applicable at the date of claim on so much of the chargeable income as exceeds the lower limit but does not exceed the upper limit of profits and gains applicable for the tax year in which the date of claim falls; but if the assessment period is less than a year, those limits shall be reduced pro rata.]

(3) In this regulation "chargeable income" means—

(a) except where sub-paragraph (b) applies, the earnings derived from the employment less any expenses deducted under paragraph (3)(a) or, as the case may be, (4) of regulation 38;

(b) in the case of employment as a child minder, one-third of the earnings of that employment.

AMENDMENTS

1. Income-related Benefits Schemes (Miscellaneous Amendments) (No.3) Regulations 1992 (SI 1992/2155) reg.17 (October 5, 1992).

2. Income-related Benefits Schemes (Miscellaneous Amendments) (No.4) Regulations 1993 (SI 1993/2119) reg.14 (October 4, 1993).

3. Income-related Benefits Schemes (Miscellaneous Amendments) (No.5) Regulations 1994 (SI 1994/2139) reg.29 (October 3, 1994).

4. Social Security (Miscellaneous Amendments) (No.3) Regulations 2007 (SI 2007/1749) reg.2(4) (July 16, 2007).

5. Social Security (Miscellaneous Amendments) (No.5) Regulations 2007 (SI 2007/2618) reg.5(7) (October 1, 2007).

6. Social Security (Miscellaneous Amendments) Regulations 2009 (SI 2009/583) reg.2(7) (April 6, 2009).

7. Social Security (Miscellaneous Amendments No.2) Regulations 2015 (SI 2015/478) reg.27 (April 6, 2015).

8. Social Security (Scottish Rate of Income Tax etc.) (Amendment) Regulations 2016 (SI 2016/233) reg. 2(3) (April 6, 2016).

DEFINITIONS

"claimant"—see reg.2(1) and reg.23(1).
"date of claim"—see reg.2(1).
"Scottish basic rate"—*ibid.*
"Scottish taxpayer"—*ibid.*

"Social Security Act"—*ibid.*
"starting rate"—*ibid.*

<small>General Note</small>

Paragraph (1)

2.303   The deduction for income tax from the amount of earnings calculated under reg.38 is to be made by applying the basic rate of tax (from April 6, 2008 the basic rate has been reduced to 20 per cent) or the Scottish basic rate, in the case of a Scottish taxpayer, and the personal relief as a single or married person. This figure may well be higher than the actual tax payable.

Paragraph (2)

2.304   Deductions are made for the Class 2 and Class 4 national insurance contributions payable on the amount calculated under reg.38.

[¹ *Chapter IVA*

Participants in the Self-Employment Route [² . . .]

Interpretation

2.305   **39A.**—In this Chapter—
"[² . . .]
"special account" means, where a person was carrying on a commercial activity in respect of which assistance is received under the self-employment route, the account into which the gross receipts from that activity were payable during the period in respect of which such assistance was received.]

<small>Amendments</small>

1. Social Security (Miscellaneous Amendments) (No.4) Regulations 1998 (SI 1998/1174) reg.6(3) (June 1, 1998).
2. Social Security Amendment (Employment Zones) (No.2) Regulations 2000 (SI 2000/2910) reg.5(1) (November 27, 2000).

<small>Definition</small>

"self-employment route"—see reg.2(1).

<small>General Note</small>

2.306   Regulations 39A–39D are the same in substance as regs 102A–102D of the JSA Regulations 1996 (apart from necessary differences in cross-references). They apply to the income from "test-trading" of people who have taken part in the "self-employment route" (defined in reg.2(1)). See the notes to reg.102C of the JSA Regulations 1996.

See also reg.23A, the effect of which is that the normal rules for the treatment of income do not apply to receipts from trading while on the self-employment route; such receipts are only to be taken into account as income in accordance with regs 39A–39D.

404

Note the disregards in para.64 of Sch.9 and para.6(3) and (4) and para.52 of Sch.10.

[¹ Treatment of gross receipts of participants in the self-employment route [² . . .]

39B.—The gross receipts of a commercial activity carried on by a person in respect of which assistance is received under the self-employment route, shall be taken into account in accordance with the following provisions of this Chapter.]

2.307

AMENDMENTS

1. Social Security (Miscellaneous Amendments) (No.4) Regulations 1998 (SI 1998/1174) reg.6(3) (June 1, 1998).
2. Social Security Amendment (Employment Zones) (No.2) Regulations 2000 (SI 2000/2910) reg.5(1)(c) (November 27, 2000).

DEFINITION

"self-employment route"—see reg.2(1).

GENERAL NOTE

See the note to reg.39A.

2.308

[¹ Calculation of income of participants in the self-employment route [² . . .]

39C.—(1) The income of a person who has received assistance under the self-employment route shall be calculated by taking into account the whole of the monies in the special account at the end of the last day upon which such assistance was received and deducting from those monies—

2.309

(a) an amount in respect of income tax calculated in accordance with regulation 39D (deduction in respect of tax for participants in the self-employment route [² . . .]); and
(b) any sum to which paragraph (4) refers.

(2) Income calculated pursuant to paragraph (1) shall be apportioned equally over a period which starts on the date the income is treated as paid under paragraph (3) and is equal in length to the period beginning with the day upon which assistance was first received under the self-employment route and ending on the last day upon which such assistance was received.

(3) Income calculated pursuant to paragraph (1) shall be treated as paid—

(a) in the case where it is due to be paid before the first benefit week in respect of which the participant or his partner first claims income support following the last day upon which assistance was received under the self-employment route, on the day in the week in which it is due to be paid which corresponds to the first day of the benefit week;
(b) in any other case, on the first day of the benefit week in which it is due to be paid.

(4) This paragraph refers, where applicable in each benefit week in respect of which income calculated pursuant to paragraph (1) is taken into account pursuant to paragraphs (2) and (3), to the sums which would have

405

been disregarded under paragraphs 4 to 6B and 9 of Schedule 8 had the income been earnings.]

AMENDMENTS

1. Social Security (Miscellaneous Amendments) (No.4) Regulations 1998 (SI 1998/1174) reg.6(3) (June 1, 1998).
2. Social Security Amendment (Employment Zones) (No.2) Regulations 2000 (SI 2000/2910) reg.5(1)(c) (November 27, 2000).

DEFINITION

"self-employment route"—see reg.2(1).

GENERAL NOTE

2.310   See the note to reg.39A.

[¹Deduction in respect of tax for participants in the self-employment route [². . .]

2.311   **39D.**—(1) The amount to be deducted in respect of income tax under regulation 39C(1)(a) (calculation of income of participants in the self-employment route [². . .]) in respect of the period determined under regulation 39C(2) shall be calculated as if—

(a) the chargeable income is the only income chargeable to tax:

[³[⁶(b) the personal reliefs applicable to the person receiving assistance under the self-employment route under Chapters 2, 3 and 3A of Part 3 of the Income Tax Act 2007 are allowable against that income;]]

(c) the rate at which the chargeable income less the personal [⁶reliefs] is assessable to income tax is [⁵. . .] the basic rate[⁶, or in the case of a Scottish tax payer, the Scottish basic rate,] of tax.

(2) For the purpose of paragraph (1), the [⁴ [⁵ basic] rate][⁶, or the Scottish basic rate,] of tax to be applied and the amount of the [³ [⁶personal reliefs]] deductible shall, where the period determined under regulation 39C(2) is less than a year, be calculated on a pro rata basis.

(3) In this regulation, "chargeable income" means the monies in the special account at the end of the last day upon which assistance was received under the self-employment route.]

AMENDMENTS

1. Social Security (Miscellaneous Amendments) (No.4) Regulations 1998 (SI 1998/1174) reg.6(3) (June 1, 1998).
2. Social Security Amendment (Employment Zones) (No.2) Regulations 2000 (SI 2000/2910) reg.5(1)(c) (November 27, 2000).
3. Social Security (Miscellaneous Amendments) (No.3) Regulations 2007 (SI 2007/1749) reg.2(5) (July 16, 2007).
4. Social Security (Miscellaneous Amendments) (No.5) Regulations 2007 (SI 2007/2618) reg.5(8) (October 1, 2007).
5. Social Security (Miscellaneous Amendments) Regulations 2009 (SI 2009/583) reg.2(8) (April 6, 2009).
6. Social Security (Scottish Rate of Income Tax etc.) (Amendment) Regulations 2016 (SI 2016/233) reg. 2(4) (April 6, 2016).

DEFINITIONS

"Scottish basic rate"—see reg.2(1).
"Scottish taxpayer"—*ibid.*

"self-employment route"—*ibid.*
"starting rate"—*ibid.*

General Note

See the note to reg.39A.   2.312

Chapter V

Other Income

Calculation of income other than earnings

40.—(1) For the purposes of regulation 29 (calculation of income other   2.313
than earnings) [¹³[¹⁴. . .]] the income of a claimant which does not consist of
earnings to be taken into account shall, subject to [⁶paragraphs (2) to (3B)],
be his gross income and any capital treated as income under [¹⁰regulation
41 (capital treated as income)].

(2) There shall be disregarded from the calculation of a claimant's gross
income under paragraph (1), any sum, where applicable, specified in Schedule 9.

(3) Where the payment of any benefit under the benefit Acts is subject
to any deduction by way of recovery the amount to be taken into account
under paragraph (1) shall be the gross amount payable.

[⁹ (3A) [¹¹ Paragraphs (3AA) and (3AAA) apply] where—
(a) a relevant payment has been made to a person in an academic
    year; and
(b) that person abandons, or is dismissed from, his course of study
    before the payment to him of the final instalment of the relevant
    payment.

[¹¹(3AA) Where a relevant payment is made quarterly, the] amount of a
relevant payment to be taken into account for the assessment period for the
purposes of paragraph (1) in respect of a person to whom paragraph (3A)
applies, shall be calculated by applying the formula—

$$\frac{A - (B \times C)}{D}$$

where—
  A = the total amount of the relevant payment which that person would
      have received had he remained a student until the last day of the aca-
      demic term in which he abandoned, or was dismissed from, his course,
      less any deduction under regulation 66A(5);
  B = the number of benefit weeks from the benefit week immediately
      following that which includes the first day of that academic year to the
      benefit week immediately before that which includes the day on which
      the person abandoned, or was dismissed from, his course;
  C = the weekly amount of the relevant payment, before the application
      of the £10 disregard, which would have been taken into account as
      income under regulation 66A(2) had the person not abandoned or
      been dismissed from, his course and, in the case of a person who was
      not entitled to income support immediately before he abandoned or

was dismissed from his course, had that person, at that time, been entitled to income support;

D = the number of benefit weeks in the assessment period.

(3AAA) Where a relevant payment is made by two or more instalments in a quarter, the amount of a relevant payment to be taken into account for the assessment period for the purposes of paragraph (1) in respect of a person to whom paragraph (3A) applies, shall be calculated by applying the formula in paragraph (3AA) but as if—

A = the total amount of relevant payments which that person received, or would have received, from the first day of the academic year to the day the person abandoned the course, or was dismissed from it, less any deduction under regulation 66A(5).]

(3AB) [[11] In this regulation]—

"academic year" and "student loan" shall have the same meanings as for the purposes of Chapter VIII of this Part;

[[11] "assessment period" means—

(a) in a case where a relevant payment is made quarterly, the period beginning with the benefit week which includes the day on which the person abandoned, or was dismissed from, his course and ending with the benefit week which includes the last day of the last quarter for which an instalment of the relevant payment was payable to that person;

(b) in a case where the relevant payment is made by two or more instalments in a quarter, the period beginning with the benefit week which includes the day on which the person abandoned, or was dismissed from, his course and ending with the benefit week which includes—
    (i) the day immediately before the day on which the next instalment of the relevant payment would have been due had the payments continued; or
    (ii) the last day of the last quarter for which an instalment of the relevant payment was payable to that person,

whichever of those dates is earlier;]

[[11] "quarter" in relation to an assessment period means a period in that year beginning on—

(a) 1st January and ending on 31st March;
(b) 1st April and ending on 30th June;
(c) 1st July and ending on 31st August; or
(d) 1st September and ending on 31st December;]

"relevant payment" means either a student loan or an amount intended for the maintenance of dependants referred to in regulation 62(3B) or both.]

[[4](3B) In the case of income to which regulation 29(2B) applies (calculation of income of former students), the amount of income to be taken into account for the purposes of paragraph (1) shall be the amount of that income calculated in accordance with regulation 32(6A) and on the basis that none of that income has been repaid.]

(4) [[7]Subject to paragraph (5)] for the avoidance of doubt there shall be included as income to be taken into account under paragraph (1)

[[7](a) any payment to which regulation 35(2) or 37(2) (payments not earnings) applies; or

(b) in the case of a claimant who is receiving support provided under section 95 or 98 of the Immigration and Asylum Act including support provided by virtue of regulations made under Schedule 9 to that Act, the amount of such support provided in respect of essential living needs of the claimant and his [[10] partner] (if any) as is specified in regulations made under paragraph 3 of Schedule 8 to the Immigration and Asylum Act;

(5) In the case of a claimant who is the partner of a person subject to immigration control and whose partner is receiving support provided under section 95 or 98 of the Immigration and Asylum Act including support provided by virtue of regulations made under Schedule 9 to that Act, there shall not be included as income to be taken into account under paragraph (1) the amount of support provided in respect of essential living needs of the partner of the claimant and his dependants (if any) as is specified in regulations made under paragraph 3 of Schedule 8 to the Immigration and Asylum Act.]

[[12] (6) Where the claimant—

(a) is a member of a couple;

(b) his partner is receiving a contributory employment and support allowance; and

(c) that benefit has been reduced under regulation 63 of the Employment and Support Allowance Regulations [[15] or section 11J of the Welfare Reform Act as the case may be],

the amount of that benefit to be taken into account is the amount as if it had not been so reduced.]

AMENDMENTS

1. Income Support (General) Amendment No.5 Regulations 1988 (SI 1988/2022) reg.9 (December 12, 1988).

2. Social Security Benefits (Student Loans and Miscellaneous Amendments) Regulations 1990 (SI 1990/1549) reg.5(4) (September 1, 1990).

3. Income Support (General) Amendment Regulations 1991 (SI 1991/236) reg.9 (March 13, 1991).

4. Income-related Benefits and Jobseeker's Allowance (Miscellaneous Amendments) Regulations 1997 (SI 1997/65) reg.7 (April 7, 1997).

5. Income-related Benefits and Jobseeker's Allowance (Amendment) (No.2) Regulations 1997 (SI 1997/2197) reg.5(3) (October 6, 1997).

6. Social Security (Miscellaneous Amendments) Regulations 1998 (SI 1998/563) reg.13(1)(a) (April 6, 1998).

7. Social Security (Immigration and Asylum) Consequential Amendments Regulations 2000 (SI 2000/636) reg.3(6) (April 3, 2000).

8. Social Security Amendment (Students) Regulations 2000 (SI 2000/1981) reg.5(5) and Sch. (July 31, 2000).

9. Social Security Amendment (Students and Income-related Benefits) Regulations 2001 (SI 2001/2319) reg.5(1) (August 1, 2001).

10. Social Security (Working Tax Credit and Child Tax Credit) (Consequential Amendments) Regulations 2003 (SI 2003/455) reg.2 and Sch.1 para.8 (April 6, 2004, except in "transitional cases" and see further the note to reg.17 of the Income Support Regulations).

11. Social Security (Students and Miscellaneous Amendments) Regulations 2008 (SI 2008/1599) reg.2(2) (September 1, 2008, or if the student's period of study begins between August 1 and August 31, 2008, the first day of the period).

12. Employment and Support Allowance (Consequential Provisions) (No.2) Regulations 2008 (SI 2008/1554) reg.2(7) (October 27, 2008).

13. Social Security (Miscellaneous Amendments) (No.4) Regulations 2009 (SI 2009/2655) reg.2(8) (October 26, 2009).

14. Social Security (Miscellaneous Amendments) Regulations 2011 (SI 2011/674) reg.3(4) (April 11, 2011).

15. Universal Credit (Consequential, Supplementary, Incidental and Miscellaneous Provisions) Regulations 2013 (SI 2013/630) reg.28(5) (April 29, 2013).

DEFINITIONS

"academic year"—see reg.61(1).
"the benefit Acts"—see reg.2(1).
"benefit week"—*ibid.*
"claimant"—see reg.2(1) and reg.23(1).
"couple"—see reg.2(1).
"full-time student"—see reg.2(1) and reg.61(1).
"Immigration and Asylum Act"—see reg.2(1).
"partner of a person subject to immigration control"—see reg.21(3).
"student"—see reg.61(1).
"student loan"—*ibid.*
"Welfare Reform Act"—see reg.2(1).

GENERAL NOTE

Paragraph (1)

2.314 This paragraph mainly confirms that all forms of income other than earnings fall into this category, and provides that the gross amount, subject in particular to the disregards in Sch.9, such as para.1 requiring the deduction of tax paid or due to be paid on the income, is to be taken into account.

Is it the claimant's or partner's income?

2.315 The first point is that the income must of course be the claimant's (or any partner's—as a consequence of the removal of amounts for children and young persons from income support (with effect from April 6, 2004, except in "transitional cases"—see the note to reg.17) the income of a child or young person who is a member of the claimant's family is no longer aggregated with the claimant's—see further the note to reg.23).

A loan can constitute income (*R(SB) 20/83, R(SB) 7/88, Morrell v Secretary of State for Work and Pensions* [2003] EWCA Civ 526, reported as *R(IS) 6/03, R(JSA) 4/04* (student loan paid (whether properly or otherwise) to part-time student), *R(H) 1/05* (wrongly obtained benefit), *R(H) 8/08*). However, note the disregard of regular voluntary payments in para.15(5A)(b) of Sch.9 (see the notes to para.15 of Sch.9). A loan may be a voluntary payment, depending on the circumstances of the loan (*R(H) 5/05*); if the loans are irregular, see reg.48(9) which treats irregular voluntary payments as capital.

However, money that a claimant is under a "certain and immediate liability" to repay does not amount to income after the date of the demand for repayment (see *Chief Adjudication Officer v Leeves*, reported as *R(IS) 5/99*) in the notes to reg.29(2B)). Thus resources provided by the use of an overdraft facility do not amount to income since the standard terms of a bank overdraft are that it is repayable on demand, even though that demand may not be made while the amount stays within an agreed limit (*R(H) 5/05*—see further the note to reg.23 under "*What constitutes income of the claimant*" and the discussion in that note as to whether the same applies to credit cards).

2.316 See also *R(IS) 4/01* which decides, applying *Leeves*, that the part of the claimant's occupational pension that was being paid to his former wife under an attachment of earnings order did not count as his income for the purposes of income support. The notional income rule in reg.42(4)(a) also did not apply: see the note to reg.42(4)(a). A similar approach was taken in *CIS 5479/1997* (where an overpayment of an occupational pension was being recovered by the Italian authorities by withholding the monthly payments of the pension) and in *R(IS) 4/02* (both decided by the same Commissioner). In *R(IS) 4/02* the Commissioner decides, contrary to the view taken in *CIS 212/1989*, para.9 (and followed with some hesitation in *CIS 295/1994*), that payments of the claimant's husband's annuity which had vested in his trustee in bankruptcy under s.306 of the Insolvency Act 1986 were not part of his income (and thus not part of the claimant's income) for the purposes of income support. In his view, in the general context of the income support scheme income to be taken into account is income that is actually paid to a claimant. Note also *R(IS) 2/03*, that concerned payments under the claimant's self-employed pension annuity that were being applied for the benefit of his creditors, which agrees with *R(IS) 4/02*. In *CH/1672/2007* the half of the claimant's pension that he was required to pay to his wife under the terms of a court order following a judicial separation did not count as his income. But income subject to a direction which could be revoked at any time (in that case, a pension signed over by a nun to a religious order under a deed of trust) remained the claimant's income (*C 10/06–07(IS)*, a Northern Ireland decision). So did the half of his annuities that the claimant in *CH/1076/2008* voluntarily paid to his wife from whom he was separated and the payments the claimant directed his pension provider to pay to his ex-wife out of his personal pension in satisfaction of his undertaking in a deed of separation to pay maintenance of a specified amount to her in *BL v SSWP (SPC)* [2018] UKUT 4 (AAC). See further the notes to reg.23 under "*What constitutes income of the claimant*".

The issue has also arisen in relation to overpaid working tax credit. *CIS/647/2007* holds that up to the date that the Revenue decided that the claimant had to repay her working tax credit it counted as her income, as the *Leeves* principle only applied to income after the date of the demand for repayment. It did not have retrospective effect so as to remove the quality of income from the working tax credit that had already been attributed. This is confirmed by the same Upper Tribunal Judge in *CC v SSWP* [2009] UKUT 280 (AAC) (see further the notes to reg.23 under "*What constitutes income of the claimant*"). However, in *CIS/1813/2007* the Commissioner holds that payments of working tax credit made after the claimant had notified the Revenue that she had ceased work and had asked for the payments to stop did not count as income. But if that was wrong, the payments were voluntary payments which were to be disregarded under para.15(5A)(b) of Sch.9 (see further the notes to reg.23 under "*What constitutes income of the claimant*").

In *SH v SSWP* [2008] UKUT 21 (AAC) the weekly sums that the claimant was allowed to withdraw for living expenses from his bank account which was subject to a restraint order under s.77 of the Criminal Justice Act 1988 were not income; furthermore there was nothing in the JSA Regulations 1996 (or the equivalent provisions in the Income Support Regulations) which treated these payments of capital as income.

Note also *AR v Bradford MDC* [2008] UKUT 30 (AAC), reported as *R(H) 6/09*, which holds that drawings from a partnership (or a business) are not income other than earnings (nor are they earnings from self-employment). Otherwise there would be an unfair double counting.

Meaning of "gross income"

Secondly, the amount of the gross income has to be calculated. *CIS 25/1989* held that, applying the principle of *Parsons v Hogg* [1985] 2 All E.R. 897, appendix to *R(FIS) 4/85*, expenditure necessary to produce the income is to be deducted to produce a figure of gross income. The claimant was entitled to £21.60 per month sickness benefit from the Ideal Benefit Society only while he continued to pay £60 annual payment to the Society. The monthly equivalent (£5) was to be deducted from the £21.60. However, in *CIS 563/1991* the Commissioner disagrees with *CIS 25/1989* and holds that gross income in para.(1) means without any deduction of the expenses incurred in gaining that income, except to the extent expressly allowed by Sch.9. He considers that the various provisions in Sch.9 relating to deduction of expenses incurred by the claimant would not be necessary if "gross income" meant

2.317

income after deducting the expenses of obtaining it. In his view *CIS 25/1989*, in applying *Parsons v Hogg* in this context, had not paid sufficient regard to the fact that that case was concerned with earnings of employed earners and involved different statutory provisions. The phrase "gross income" was an equivocal one, as indicated by the Court of Appeal's decision in *Parsons v Hogg*, and the statutory context had to be considered. The principle of *Parsons v Hogg* had been applied to earnings in *R(FC) 1/90* and *R(IS) 16/93*, (but apparently not to attendance and basic allowances paid to councillors, which are counted as earnings, in *R(IS) 6/92* and *CIS 77/1993*). (On the application of *Parsons v Hogg* to the meaning of "gross earnings", see further the notes to reg.36(3).) The Commissioner in *CIS 563/1991* considered that the statutory context of earnings of employed earners and income other than earnings was sufficiently different not to necessitate a uniform approach to the deduction of expenses.

This question was considered again in *R(IS) 13/01*. The Commissioner opined that arguably the principle in *Parsons v Hogg* should apply to income other than earnings in the light of the fact that so few of the paragraphs in Sch.9 were concerned with expenses. However, he followed *CIS 563/1991* rather than *CIS 25/1989* on the basis of *Colchester Estates (Cardiff) v Carlton Industries Plc* [1986] Ch. 80. In that case Nourse LJ had said that where there were two conflicting decisions of equal status and the earlier decision was fully considered in the later decision, the later decision should be followed unless the Judge was convinced that the later decision was wrong because, for instance, some binding or persuasive authority had not been cited in either of the two cases. The Commissioner considered that the same approach should be applied by Commissioners and therefore followed *CIS 563/1991* which had considered *CIS 25/1989* in detail and not followed it.

But on the issue of precedent, note *R(IS) 9/08* in which the Commissioner points out that *Colchester* had been disapproved in *Re Taylor (a bankrupt)* [2007] Ch.150. Thus a later decision of a Commissioner was not necessarily to be followed in preference to an earlier one but the question of which decision to follow had to be determined on the merits.

Certain kinds of income are disregarded under Sch.9 (para.(2)). In particular, para.1 requires the deduction of tax paid or due to be paid on the income. With the revocation of reg.24 there is now no special rule for charitable or voluntary payments, but note the now total disregard of these payments in para.15 of Sch.9. Note also reg.48 on income treated as capital.

Benefit income

2.318   A major form of income for income support claimants will be from other social security benefits. All benefits of an income nature (presumably benefits like bereavement payment and the initial lump sum bereavement support payment continue to be treated as capital although there is now no classification in the regulations (cf. *R(SB) 4/89*)) count in full as income unless disregarded under Sch.9. Benefits disregarded include housing benefit (para.5), the mobility component of disability living allowance, the mobility component of personal independence payment, and mobility supplement (paras 6 and 8), attendance allowance, the care component of disability living allowance and the daily living component of personal independence payment (para.9), armed forces independence payment (para.76A), social fund payments (para.31), local welfare provision (para.31A), payments under local council tax reduction schemes (para.46) and guardian's allowance (para.5A). In addition, with effect from April 6, 2004 (except in "transitional cases"—see the note to reg.17) child benefit and child tax credit are ignored (para.5B) (for income support claimants who had an award of child tax credit before April 6, 2004 see reg.7 of the Social Security (Working Tax Credit and Child Tax Credit) (Consequential Amendments) Regulations 2003 (SI 2003/455) (as amended) on p.1765 and the notes to that regulation).

Some benefits, such as income-related ESA, contribution-based JSA and state retirement pension, are paid gross, but are subject to income tax. Whether income tax is due depends on whether the total taxable income in the tax year exceeds the person's personal allowance and any other reliefs due. Paragraph 1 of Sch.9 requires the disregard of an amount of the gross income received equal to the amount of tax paid or due to be paid.

Benefits which count as income are income whether they are paid on time or in the form of arrears *(R(SB) 4/89)*. Then reg.31 defines the date on which the income is treated as paid. The fact that there is a partial disregard of some kinds of benefit arrears as capital in para.7 of Sch.10 does not affect this conclusion. That is because the conclusion, and *R(SB) 4/89*, must be subject to the principle of *R(SB) 2/83* and *R(SB) 35/83* that at some point accumulated income turns into capital. The sensible approach would be that if any amount of income is still possessed after the end of the period to which it is properly attributed as income under regs 29 and 31, then it becomes capital, subject to the deduction of relevant liabilities under *R(SB) 2/83* and *R(SB) 35/83*. See *R(IS) 3/93*. Thus there is still something for para.7 of Sch.10 to bite on. However, note *CIS/515/2006* discussed in the note to reg.23 in which the Commissioner takes a rather different approach.

Paragraph (2)

This paragraph authorises the disregards in Sch.9. See *CIS 563/1991* discussed in the note to para.22 of Sch.9 and *CIS 82/1993* and *CIS 13059/1996* in the notes to paras 19 and 30 where more than one disregard applies. *CIS 683/1993* confirms that income can only be disregarded to the extent allowed for by Sch.9. Therefore, no deduction could be made for the maintenance payments made by the claimant, whether under a court order or otherwise, or for his insurance premiums, in calculating his income. But see *R(IS) 4/01* (and also note the other decisions discussed above). If the maintenance payments are made under an attachment of earnings order rather than by the claimant out of his own income they will not count as his income. However, the deprivation of income rule in reg.42(1) might be applicable if the claimant has deliberately provoked an attachment of earnings order in order to secure benefit. 2.319

Paragraph (3)

If deductions are made from social security benefits for recovery of overpayments or social fund loans the gross amount of benefit is used in the calculation of income support. A deduction for child support maintenance is a deduction by way of recovery for the purposes of para.(3) (and reg.103(3) of the JSA Regulations 1996) (Social Security (Claims and Payments) Regulations 1987 Sch.9B para.8, see Vol.III in this series). 2.320

R(H) 2/09 confirms that if incapacity benefit is being reduced due to receipt of an occupational pension this is not a "deduction by way of recovery" for the purposes of para.(3). The income to be taken into account is the net amount of the incapacity benefit that the claimant actually receives.

Paragraphs (3A)–(3AB)

Paragraphs (3A)–(3AB) contain precise rules for calculating the amount of a student loan and/or any non-repayable amount for dependants to be taken into account as income where a student abandons or is dismissed from his course. Note the definitions in para.(3AB) and see the notes to reg.66A for a discussion of the current system for student support. For an example of how the provisions in paras (3A)–(3AB) work in practice see Annex D to HB/CTB Circular A31/2001. Note that the calculation can result in a nil income figure, depending on the point in the term at which the student abandoned or was dismissed from his course. The amendments made on September 1, 2008 clarify how student loans paid by two or more instalments in a quarter are to be taken into account when a student abandons or is dismissed from his course. 2.321

If the former student repays the loan this does not constitute a change of circumstances so as to provide grounds for supersession (see reg.6(6)(a) of the Decisions and Appeals Regulations 1999 in Vol.III of this series). The intention is that the amount calculated under para.(3AA) should still be taken into account as income. However the guidance to decision-makers does state that if the Student Loan Company demands immediate repayment (e.g. because the loan instalment should not have been paid because the student had abandoned or been dismissed from the course), no loan income should be taken into account from the date that demand is made (see *Decision Makers' Guide*, para.30470). This is on the basis that the student is under a "certain and immediate liability" to repay the loan and so it should not be treated as his income (see *Chief Adjudication Officer v Leeves*, reported as *R(IS) 5/99*, discussed in the notes to reg.29(2B)). But this would not apply if the former student voluntarily repaid the loan, as confirmed in *CJSA 549/2003*. The Commissioner considered that the particularly harsh effect of these provisions in such circumstances where no account was taken of any repayment and it was simply assumed that the loan could still be used for living expenses merited the attention of the Secretary of State (but so far the Commissioner's suggestion remains unheeded).

Note para.61 of Sch.9 under which any part of a student loan or grant left over at the end of a course is ignored.

See also para.(3B).

Paragraph (3B)

2.322   See the notes to regs 29(2B) and 32(6A). But note *Chief Adjudication Officer v Leeves*, reported as *R(IS) 5/99*) and the argument discussed in the notes to reg.29(2B) as to when that provision applies.

Note also para.61 of Sch.9 under which any grant or covenant income or student loan left over at the end of the person's course is disregarded.

Paragraph (4)(a)

2.323   These amounts, which do not count as earnings, do count as other income. However, note the disregards in paras 1, 2A, 3, 4, 4A, 18, 20, 21, 26, 27 and 69 of Sch.9. See also *CIS 521/2002* discussed in the note to reg.37(2).

Paragraphs (4)(b) and (5)

2.324   See the notes to reg.21(3).

Capital treated as income

2.325   **41.**—[8(1) Capital which is payable by instalments which are outstanding on—

    (a) the first day in respect of which income support is payable or the date of the determination of the claim, whichever is earlier; or

    (b) in the case of a supersession, the date of that supersession,

shall be treated as income if the aggregate of the instalments outstanding and the amount of the claimant's capital otherwise calculated in accordance with Chapter VI of this Part exceeds [13...] £16,000.]

(2) Any payment received under an annuity shall be treated as income.

(3) [12...]

[2(4) In the case of a person to whom section 20(3) of the Act [SSCBA, s.124(1)] (conditions of entitlement to income support) has effect as modified by section 23A(b) of that Act [SSCBA, s.127(b)] (effect of return to work), any amount by way of repayment of income tax deducted from his emoluments in pursuance of section 203 of the Income and Corporation Taxes Act 1988, shall be treated as income.]

[4(5) Any earnings to the extent that they are not a payment of income shall be treated as income.]

[7(6) Any Career Development Loan paid pursuant to section 2 of the Employment and Training Act 1973 shall be treated as income.]

414

[¹¹(7) Where an agreement or court order provides that payments shall be made to the claimant in consequence of any personal injury to the claimant and that such payments are to be made, wholly or partly, by way of periodical payments, any such periodical payments received by the claimant (but not a payment which is treated as capital by virtue of this Part), shall be treated as income.]

AMENDMENTS

1. Income Support (General) Amendment Regulations 1988 (SI 1988/663) reg.18 (April 11, 1988).
2. Income Support (General) Amendment No.4 Regulations 1988 (SI 1988/1445) reg.9 (September 12, 1988).
3. Family Credit and Income Support (General) Amendment Regulations 1989 (SI 1989/104) reg.7 (July 10, 1989).
4. Income Support (General) Amendment No.2 Regulations 1989 (SI 1989/1323) reg.13 (October 9, 1989).
5. Income-related Benefits (Miscellaneous Amendments) Regulations 1990 (SI 1990/671) reg.5 (April 9, 1990).
6. Income Support (General) Amendment Regulations 1992 (SI 1992/468) Sch. para.4 (April 6, 1992).
7. Income-related Benefits and Jobseeker's Allowance (Miscellaneous Amendments) Regulations 1997 (SI 1997/65) reg.3 (April 7, 1997).
8. Social Security Act 1998 (Commencement No.12 and Consequential and Transitional Provisions) Order 1999 (SI 1999/3178 (C.81)) art.3(5) and Sch.5 para.3 (November 29, 1999)
9. Social Security Amendment (Capital Limits and Earnings Disregards) Regulations 2000 (SI 2000/2545) reg.2(1)(a) (April 9, 2001).
10. Children (Leaving Care) Act 2000 (Commencement No.2 and Consequential Provisions) Order 2001 (SI 2001/3070) art.3(2) and Sch.1 para.(c) (October 1, 2001).
11. Social Security Amendment (Personal Injury Payments) Regulations 2002 (SI 2002/2442) reg.2 (October 28, 2002).
12. Social Security (Working Tax Credit and Child Tax Credit) (Consequential Amendments) Regulations 2003 (SI 2003/455) reg.2 and Sch.1 para.9 (April 6, 2004, except in "transitional cases" and see further the note to reg.17 of the Income Support Regulations).
13. Social Security (Miscellaneous Amendments) (No.2) Regulations 2005 (SI 2005/2465) reg.2(2) (April 10, 2006).

DEFINITIONS

"the Act"—see reg.2(1).
"claimant"—*ibid.*

GENERAL NOTE

Paragraph (1)
The value of the right to receive any outstanding instalments of capital payable by instalments is disregarded (Sch.10 para.16). See the notes to reg.23 on the line between capital and income. Normally each instalment, when it is paid, would add to the claimant's capital (*Lillystone v SBC* [1982] 3 F.L.R. 52). The literal effect of para.(1) is that if the amount of the instalments outstanding plus the claimant's (including partner's: reg.23) other capital comes to more than £16,000 (which has been the increased upper capital limit for income support (and income-based JSA) since April 10, 2006), the whole amount outstanding is to be treated as income. What para.(1) does not say is what this means. A capital sum cannot simply be treated as income. The common sense rule would be that each instalment, when

2.326

paid, was treated as a payment of income (as suggested in paras 28532 and 28536 of the *Decision Makers Guide*), but this is not expressed in para.(1). For an example of where the rule in para.(1) applied see *R(IS) 7/98* in the notes to para.15 of Sch.10 and see *R(IS) 10/01* referred to in the note to para.(2).

Weekly sums that the claimant was allowed to withdraw for living expenses from his bank account which was subject to a restraint order under s.77 of the Criminal Justice Act 1988 were not capital payable by instalments. Regulation 104(1) of the JSA Regulations 1996 (the equivalent of para.(1)) only applied if there was a contractual or other obligation on the part of some other person to pay a capital sum to the claimant by instalments (*SH v SSWP* [2008] UKUT 21 (AAC)).

Paragraph (2)

2.327   The value of the right to receive income under an annuity is disregarded as capital (Sch.10 para.11). The income under some "home income" schemes is disregarded under para.17 of Sch.9.

The general rule, however, is that payments under an annuity count as income. See *DN v Leicester CC (HB)* [2010] UKUT 253 (AAC) which discusses the nature of annuity payments.

In *R(IS) 10/01* part of the claimant's damages award following a road traffic accident was in the form of two structured settlement annuities. The monthly annuity payments were used for the claimant's substantial care needs. However, as these fell squarely within para.(2) they counted as income with the result that the claimant was not entitled to income support. The Commissioner also accepted that they came within para.(1). The claimant appealed but the Court of Appeal dismissed the appeal and upheld the decision of the Commissioner (*Beattie v Secretary of State for Social Security*, reported as part of *R(IS) 10/01*).

However, the problem highlighted by *Beattie* was ameliorated by the introduction on October 28, 2002 of a disregard for regular payments from annuities purchased from funds derived from personal injury awards to claimants (see the previous form of para.15 of Sch.9 in the 2006 edition of what was then Vol.II of this series). The disregard in para.15 of Sch.9 was changed to a total disregard on October 2, 2006.

Paragraph (3)

2.328   This paragraph was revoked with effect from April 6, 2004 by reg.2 of and para.9 of Sch.1 to the Social Security (Working Tax Credit and Child Tax Credit) (Consequential Amendments) Regulations 2003 (SI 2003/455), except in "transitional cases" (i.e. those cases in which the claimant is still receiving amounts for his children in his income support—see further the note to reg.17). For "transitional cases" para.(3) continues in force (see the 2003 edition of this volume for this provision). With effect from May 12, 2004, reg.5 of the Social Security (Miscellaneous Amendments) (No.2) Regulations 2004 (SI 2004/1141) substituted the words "section 12 of the Social Work (Scotland) Act 1968 or sections 29 or 30 of the Children (Scotland) Act 1995" for the words "section 12, 24 or 26 of the Social Work (Scotland) Act 1968" in para.(3). The effect of this amendment is simply to update the references to the Scottish legislation referred to in para.(3).

Paragraph (4)

2.329   In trade dispute cases repayments of PAYE tax, normally capital, are to be treated as income.

Paragraph (5)

2.330   In previous editions it has been said that this provision "merely" confirms that sums defined as earnings in reg.35 that might under the general law be categorised as capital are income. However, close analysis of the decision of the Court of Appeal in *Minter v Kingston upon Hull CC* and *Potter v Secretary of State for Work and Pensions* [2011] EWCA Civ 1155; [2012] AACR 21 (see the notes to reg.23 under "*Distinction between capital and income*" for the facts and the background) shows that that is far too narrow a view. It was common ground there that in the housing benefit and old style JSA equivalents of para.(5) "earnings" has the same meaning as in the equivalent of reg.35, but Thomas LJ emphasised (at para.29) the width of the phrase "any remuneration or profit derived from employment" (such that the specific categories in reg.35(1)(a)–(j) are merely examples). The essential issue was whether any payment was made in consideration of the employee's services, so as to be derived from the employment. If that test is met it does not matter that the payment might on general principle be regarded as having the true characteristic of capital. The payment is, if not in one of the excluded categories in reg.35(2), to be treated as income by virtue of para.(5). It is submitted that, although the treatment of *EM v London Borough of Waltham Forest* [2009] UKUT 245 (AAC) at para.30 of *Minter* and *Potter* is rather obscure, the reason why it was found unnecessary to say whether the payment involved in *EM* should on general principle have been found to be capital or income was that even if it was capital (as Judge Wikeley had decided), it should have been treated as income under the equivalent of para.(5). The necessary implication was that *EM* was wrongly decided for failing to consider that provision.

Paragraph (6)

This treats Career Development Loans, which are provided in order to help adults pay for vocational education or training, as income. However, the income will be disregarded under para.13 of Sch.9 (replacing the previous disregards in paras 59 and 60 of Sch.9 which were revoked on April 1, 2004), except any part of the loan that was intended to meet the cost of food, ordinary clothing or footwear, household fuel, rent for which housing benefit is payable, housing costs met by income support, council tax or water charges during the period of training or education. On "ordinary clothing or footwear" see paras 28671–2 of the *Decision Makers' Guide*. In addition, any part of the loan left over at the end of the course is ignored.

For treatment of career development loans before these rules were introduced on April 7, 1997, see *CIS 507/1997*.

Paragraph (7)

See the note to para.(2) above. Paragraph (7) provides that any periodical payments paid under an agreement or court order to a claimant in consequence of personal injury to him, other than payments that are treated as capital (see reg.48(4)), count as income. However, from October 2, 2006, such payments are totally ignored under para.15 of Sch.9. Note also that since the amendments to reg.48(4) on October 2, 2006, not only capital disregarded under para.12 (trusts of personal injury compensation) but also capital disregarded under paras 44 and 45 (funds held in court derived from compensation for personal injury or the death of a parent) are excepted from the rule in reg.48(4); thus regular payments from such sources will count as income in the normal way (and be disregarded under para.15 of Sch.9).

Notional income

42.—[[77] (1) A claimant is to be treated as possessing income of which the claimant has deprived themselves for the purpose of securing entitlement to income support or increasing the amount of that benefit, or for the purpose of securing entitlement to, or increasing the amount of a jobseeker's allowance or an employment and support allowance.]

(2) Except in the case of—

(a) a discretionary trust;

(b) a trust derived from a payment made in consequence of a personal injury;

[[23](c) jobseeker's allowance; or]

2.331

2.332

2.333

[²⁵(d) [⁵¹. . .]]
[⁸(e) [⁴⁸ working tax credit];
  (f) [⁴⁹ child tax credit],]
[²⁰(g) a personal pension scheme [⁵⁹, occupational pension scheme] [⁶³ [⁶⁵ . . .] or a payment made by the Board of the Pension Protection Fund] where the claimant [⁷⁴ has not attained the qualifying age for state pension credit],]
[⁷²(ga)any sum to which paragraph (8ZA) applies;]
[²⁴(h) [⁵⁴. . .]] [²⁶ or
[⁶⁴ (i) any sum to which paragraph 44(2)(a) of Schedule 10 (capital to be disregarded) applies which is administered in the way referred to in paragraph 44(1)(a);
  (ia) any sum to which paragraph 45(a) of Schedule 10 refers; or]
[³⁰ (j) rehabilitation allowance made under section 2 of the Employment and Training Act 1973],
income which would become available to the claimant upon application being made but which has not been acquired by him shall be treated as possessed by him but only from the date on which [¹it could be expected to be acquired were an application made.]

[²⁰ [⁶⁰ (2ZA) A claimant who has attained the [⁷⁴ qualifying age for state pension credit] shall be treated as possessing—
  (a) the amount of any income from an occupational pension scheme, [⁶³ a personal pension scheme [⁶⁵ . . .] or the Board of the Pension Protection Fund]—
    (i) for which no claim has been made, and
    (ii) to which he might expect to be entitled if a claim for it were made;
  (b) income from an occupational pension scheme which the claimant elected to defer,
but only from the date on which it could be expected to be acquired were an application for it to be made.

[⁶⁵ (2A) This paragraph applies where a person [⁷⁴ who has attained the qualifying age for state pension credit]—
  (a) is entitled to money purchase benefits under an occupational pension scheme or a personal pension scheme;
  (b) fails to purchase an annuity with the funds available in that scheme; and
  (c) either—
    (i) defers in whole or in part the payment of any income which would have been payable to him by his pension fund holder, or
    (ii) fails to take any necessary action to secure that the whole of any income which would be payable to him by his pension fund holder upon his applying for it, is so paid, or
    (iii) income withdrawal is not available to him under that scheme.

(2AA) Where paragraph (2A) applies, the amount of any income foregone shall be treated as possessed by that person, but only from the date on which it could be expected to be acquired were an application for it to be made.]]

(2B) The amount of any income foregone in a case [⁶⁵ where paragraph (2A)(c)(i) or (ii)] applies shall be the [⁸⁵rate of the annuity which may have been purchased with the fund] and shall be determined by the [³⁹ Secretary of State] who shall take account of information provided by the pension

418

fund holder in accordance with regulation 7(5) of the Social Security (Claims and Payments) Regulations 1987.

(2C) The amount of any income foregone in a case [65 where paragraph (2A)(c)(iii)] applies shall be the income that the [50 person] could have received without purchasing an annuity had the funds held under the [61 relevant occupational or personal pension scheme] [65 . . .] been held [61 under a scheme] where income withdrawal was available and shall be determined in the manner specified in paragraph (2B).]

[62 (2CA) In paragraph (2A), "money purchase benefits" has the meaning it has in the Pension Schemes Act 1993.]

[25(2D) [51 . . .]]]

(3) Except in the case of a discretionary trust, or a trust derived from a payment made in consequence of a personal injury, any income which is due to be paid to the claimant but—

(a) has not been paid to him;

(b) is not a payment prescribed in regulation [448 or 9] of the Social Security (Payments on Account, Overpayment and Recovery) Regulations [44 1988] (duplication and prescribed payments or maintenance payments) and not made on or before the date prescribed in relation to it,

shall [10except for any amount to which paragraph (3A) [41, (3B) or (3C)] applies] be treated as possessed by the claimant.

[10(3A) This paragraph applies to an amount which is due to be paid to the claimant under an occupational pension scheme but which is not paid because the trustees or managers of the scheme have suspended or ceased payments [13. . .] due to an insufficiency of resources.

(3B) This paragraph applies to any amount by which a payment made to the claimant from an occupational pension scheme falls short of the payment to which he was due under the scheme where the shortfall arises because the trustees or managers of the scheme have insufficient resources available to meet in full the scheme's liabilities [13. . .].]

[41(3C) This paragraph applies to any earnings which are due to an employed earner on the termination of his employment by reason of redundancy but which have not been paid to him.]

[2(4) [32 Any payment of income, other than a payment of income specified in [86paragraph (4ZA) or (4ZB)]], made—

(a) to a third party in respect of a single claimant or [51 his partner] (but not a member of the third party's family) shall be treated—

(i) in a case where the payment is derived from a payment of any benefit under the benefit Acts,[53 a payment from the Armed Forces and Reserve Forces Compensation Scheme,] a war disablement pension [21, war widow's pension [47 or war widower's pension] or a pension payable to a person as a [58 widow, widower or surviving civil partner] under [70. . .] any power of Her Majesty otherwise than under an enactment to make provision about pensions for or in respect of persons who have been disabled or have died in consequence of service as members of the armed forces of the Crown,] as possessed by that single claimant, if it is paid to him, [51 or by his partner, if it is paid to his partner];

[36(ia) in a case where that payment is a payment of an occupational pension [63, a pension or other periodical payment made under a personal pension scheme or a payment made by the Board of the Pension Protection Fund], as possessed by that single claimant or, as the case may be, by [51 the claimant's partner];]

(ii) in any other case, as possessed by that single claimant [51 or his partner] to the extent that it is used for the food, ordinary clothing or footwear, household fuel, rent [55. . .] for which housing benefit is payable, [16or] [7. . .] any housing costs to the extent that they are met under regulations 17(1)(e) or 18(1)(f) (housing costs) [16. . .] [4. . .] [3. . .] [4. . .], of that single claimant or, as the case may be, [51 of his partner] [7, or is used for any [12council tax] or water charges for which that claimant or [51 partner is liable]];

[51 (b) to a single claimant or his partner in respect of a third party (but not in respect of another member of his family) shall be treated as possessed by that single claimant or, as the case may be, his partner, to the extent that it is kept or used by him or used by or on behalf of his partner;]

but, except where sub-paragraph (a)(i) applies and in the case of a person to whom section 23 of the Act [SSCBA, s.126] (trade disputes) applies, this paragraph shall not apply to any payment in kind [56 to the third party].]

[32 (4ZA) Paragraph (4) shall not apply in respect of a payment of income made—

(a) under [75or by] the Macfarlane Trust, the Macfarlane (Special Payments) Trust, the Macfarlane (Special Payments) (No.2) Trust, the Fund, the Eileen Trust[73, MFET Limited][78, the Skipton Fund, the Caxton Foundation][82, the Scottish Infected Blood Support Scheme][84, an approved blood scheme[83, the London Emergencies Trust, the We Love Manchester Emergency Fund] [86, the National Emergencies Trust] or the Independent Living [68 Fund (2006)];

(b) pursuant to section 19(1)(a) of the Coal Industry Act 1994 (concessionary coal); or

(c) pursuant to section 2 of the Employment and Training Act 1973 in respect of a person's participation—

(i) in an employment programme specified in regulations 75(1)(a) (ii) of the Jobseeker's Allowance Regulations 1996;

(ii) in a training scheme specified in regulation 75(1)(b)(ii) of those Regulations; or

[45 (iia) in the Intensive Activity Period specified in regulation 75(1)(a) (iv) of those Regulations [67 . . .]; or]

(iii) in a qualifying course within the meaning specified in regulation 17A(7) of those Regulations.]

(iv) [*Omitted.*]

[76(ca) in respect of a person's participation in [79 a scheme prescribed in regulation 3 of the Jobseeker's Allowance (Schemes for Assisting Persons to Obtain Employment) Regulations 2013] or the Mandatory Work Activity Scheme; or]

[37(d) under an occupational pension scheme [63, in respect of a pension or other periodical payment made under a personal pension scheme or a payment made by the Board of the Pension Protection Fund] where—

(i) a bankruptcy order has been made in respect of the person in respect of whom the payment has been made or, in Scotland, the estate of that person is subject to sequestration or a judicial factor has been appointed on that person's estate under section 41 of the Solicitors (Scotland) Act 1980;

(ii) the payment is made to the trustee in bankruptcy or any other person acting on behalf of the creditors; and

(iii) the person referred to in (i) and [⁵¹ his partner (if any)] does not possess, or is not treated as possessing, any other income apart from that payment.]

[⁸⁶(4ZB) Paragraph (4) shall not apply in respect of a payment of income which is a Grenfell Tower payment.]

[¹⁶(4A) Where the claimant [⁵⁷ resides in a care home, an Abbeyfield Home or an independent hospital, or is temporarily absent from such a home or hospital], any payment made by a person other than the claimant or a member of his family in respect of some or all of the cost of maintaining the claimant [⁵¹ or his partner in that home [⁶⁹ or hospital] shall be treated as possessed by the claimant or his partner].]

(5) Where a claimant's earnings are not ascertainable at the time of the determination of the claim or of any [⁴⁰ revision or supersession the Secretary of State] shall treat the claimant as possessing such earnings as is reasonable in the circumstances of the case having regard to the number of hours worked and the earnings paid for comparable employment in the area.

[⁴³(5A) Where the amount of a subsistence allowance paid to a claimant in a benefit week is less than the amount of income-based jobseeker's allowance that person would have received in that benefit week had it been payable to him, less 50p, he shall be treated as possessing the amount which is equal to the amount of income-based jobseeker's allowance which he would have received in that week, less 50p.]

(6) [³³Subject to paragraph (6A),] where—

(a) a claimant performs a service for another person; and

(b) that person makes no payment of earnings or pays less than that paid for a comparable employment in the area,

the [³⁹Secretary of State] shall treat the claimant as possessing such earnings (if any) as is reasonable for that employment unless the claimant satisfies him that the means of that person are insufficient for him to pay or to pay more for the service [³³. . .].

[³³(6A) Paragraph (6) shall not apply—

(a) to a claimant who is engaged by a charitable or voluntary organisation or who is a volunteer if the [³⁸Secretary of State] is satisfied in any of those cases that it is reasonable for him to provide the service free of charge;

[⁴²(b) in a case where the service is performed in connection with—

(i) the claimant's participation in an employment or training programme in accordance with regulation 19(1)(q) of the Jobseeker's Allowance Regulations 1996 ,[⁴⁶, other than where the service is performed in connection with the claimant's participation in the Intensive Activity Period specified in regulation 75(1)(a)(iv) of those Regulations [⁶⁷ . . .]]; or

(ii) the claimant's or the claimant's partner's participation in an employment or training programme as defined in regulation 19(3) of those Regulations for which a training allowance is not payable or, where such an allowance is payable, it is payable for the sole purpose of reimbursement of travelling or meal

expenses to the person participating in that programme; or]
(c) to a claimant who is engaged in work experience whilst participating in—
   (i) the New Deal for Lone Parents; or
   (ii) a scheme which has been approved by the Secretary of State as supporting the objectives of the New Deal for Lone Parents [⁶⁶; or
(d) to a claimant who is participating in a work placement approved by the Secretary of State (or a person providing services to the Secretary of State) before the placement starts.

(6AA) In paragraph (6A)(d) "work placement" means practical work experience which is not undertaken in expectation of payment.]

   [⁵². . .].

(6B) [⁵². . .]

(6C) [⁵². . .]]

(6D) [*Omitted.*]

(7) Where a claimant is treated as possessing any income under any of [³¹ paragraphs (1) to (4A)] the foregoing provisions of this Part shall apply for the purposes of calculating the amount of that income as if a payment had actually been made and as if it were actual income which he does possess.

(8) Where a claimant is treated as possessing any earnings under paragraph (5) or (6) the foregoing provisions of this Part shall apply for the purposes of calculating the amount of those earnings as if a payment had actually been made and as if they were actual earnings which he does possess except that paragraph (3) of regulation 36 (calculation of net earnings of employed earners) shall not apply and his net earnings shall be calculated by taking into account the earnings which he is treated as possessing, less—

(a) an amount in respect of income tax equivalent to an amount calculated by applying to those earnings [¹¹ [⁷¹. . .] the basic rate [⁸¹, or in the case of a Scottish taxpayer, the Scottish basic rate,] of tax] in the year of assessment less only the [⁸¹ personal reliefs to which the claimant is entitled under Chapters 2, 3 and 3A of Part 3 of the Income Tax Act 2007 as are] appropriate to his circumstances; but, if the period over which those earnings are to be taken into account is less than a year, [¹¹the earnings to which the [⁶⁶ [⁷¹ basic] rate] [⁸¹, or the Scottish basic rate,] [¹⁸. . .] of tax is to be applied and] the amount of the [⁶⁵ [⁸¹ personal reliefs]] deductible under this paragraph shall be calculated on a pro rata basis;
[¹⁶(b) where the weekly amount of those earnings equals or exceeds the lower earnings limit, an amount representing primary Class 1 contributions under the Contributions and Benefits Act, calculated by applying to those earnings the initial and main primary percentages in accordance with sections 8(1) (a) and (b) of that Act; and]
(c) one-half of any sum payable by the claimant [¹⁷in respect of a pay period] by way of a contribution towards an occupational or personal pension scheme.

[⁷² (8ZA) Paragraphs (1), (2), (3), (4), (5) and (6) shall not apply in respect of any amount of income other than earnings, or earnings derived from employment as an employed earner, arising out of the [⁸⁰ claimant participating as a service user].]

[¹⁰(8A) In paragraphs (3A) and (3B) the expression "resources" has the same meaning as in the Social Security Pensions Act 1975 by virtue of section 66(1) of that Act.]

[²(9) In paragraph (4) the expression "ordinary clothing or footwear" means clothing or footwear for normal daily use, but does not include school uniforms, or clothing or footwear used solely for sporting activities.]

AMENDMENTS

1. Income Support (General) Amendment Regulations 1988 (SI 1988/663) reg.19 (April 11, 1988).
2. Income Support (General) Amendment (No.4) Regulations 1988 (SI 1988/1445) reg.10 (September 12, 1988).
3. Income Support (General) Amendment (No.4) Regulations 1988 (SI 1988/1445) Sch.1 para.4 (April 10, 1989).
4. Income Support (General) Amendment Regulations 1989 (SI 1989/534) Sch.1 para.7 (October 9, 1989).
5. Income-related Benefits Schemes Amendment Regulations 1990 (SI 1990/127) reg.3 (January 31, 1990).
6. Income-related Benefits Schemes and Social Security (Recoupment) Amendment Regulations 1991 (SI 1991/1175) reg.5 (May 11, 1991).
7. Income Support (General) Amendment No.4 Regulations 1991 (SI 1991/1559) reg.8 (October 7, 1991).
8. Income Support (General) Amendment Regulations 1992 (SI 1992/468) reg.4 (April 6, 1992).
9. Income-related Benefits Schemes and Social Security (Recoupment) Amendment Regulations 1992 (SI 1992/1101) reg.6 (May 7, 1992).
10. Income Support (General) Amendment (No.2) Regulations 1992 (SI 1992/1198) reg.2 (May 22, 1992).
11. Income-related Benefits Schemes (Miscellaneous Amendments) (No.3) Regulations 1992 (SI 1992/2155) reg.18 (October 5, 1992).
12. Income-related Benefits Schemes (Miscellaneous Amendments) Regulations 1993 (SI 1993/315) Sch. para.2 (April 1, 1993).
13. Income-related Benefits Schemes (Miscellaneous Amendments) Regulations 1993 (SI 1993/315) reg.6 (April 12, 1993).
14. Social Security Benefits (Miscellaneous Amendments) (No.2) Regulations 1993 (SI 1993/963) reg.2(3) (April 22, 1993).
15. Income-related Benefits Schemes and Social Security (Recoupement) Amendment Regulations 1993 (SI 1993/1249) reg.4(3) (May 14, 1993).
16. Income-related Benefits Schemes (Miscellaneous Amendments) Regulations 1994 (SI 1994/527) reg.4 (April 11, 1994).
17. Income-related Benefits Schemes (Miscellaneous Amendments) (No.5) Regulations 1994 (SI 1994/2139) reg.26 (October 3, 1994).
18. Income-related Benefits Schemes (Miscellaneous Amendments) (No.5) Regulations 1994 (SI 1994/2139) reg.29 (October 3, 1994).
19. Income-related Benefits Schemes (Miscellaneous Amendments) Regulations 1995 (SI 1995/516) reg.22 (April 10, 1995).
20. Income-related Benefits Schemes and Social Security (Claims and Payments) (Miscellaneous Amendments) Regulations 1995 (SI 1995/2303) reg.6(4) (October 2, 1995).
21. Income-related Benefits Schemes Amendment (No.2) Regulations 1995 (SI 1995/2792) reg.6(2) (October 28, 1995).
22. Income-related Benefits Schemes (Widows' etc. Pensions Disregards) Amendment Regulations 1995 (SI 1995/3282) reg.2 (December 20, 1995).
23. Income Support (General) (Jobseeker's Allowance Consequential Amendments) Regulations 1996 (SI 1996/206) reg.17 (October 7, 1996).
24. Income-related Benefits Schemes and Social Fund (Miscellaneous Amendments) Regulations 1996 (SI 1996/1944) reg.13 and Sch. para.3 (October 7, 1996).

25. Child Benefit, Child Support and Social Security (Miscellaneous Amendments) Regulations 1996 (SI 1996/1803) reg.37 (April 7, 1997).

26. Income-related Benefits and Jobseeker's Allowance (Amendment) (No.2) Regulations 1997 (SI 1997/2197) reg.5(4) (October 6, 1997).

27. Income-related Benefits and Jobseeker's Allowance (Amendment) (No.2) Regulations 1997 (SI 1997/2197) reg.7(3) and (4)(e) (October 6, 1997).

28. Social Security Amendment (New Deal) Regulations 1997 (SI 1997/ 2863) reg.17(1) and (2)(e) (January 5, 1998).

29. Social Security Amendment (New Deal) Regulations 1997 (SI 1997/ 2863) reg.17(3) and (4)(e) (January 5, 1998).

30. Social Security (Miscellaneous Amendments) Regulations 1998 (SI 1998/ 563) reg.6(1) and (2)(e) (April 6, 1998).

31. Social Security (Miscellaneous Amendments) Regulations 1998 (SI 1998/ 563) reg.13(1)(b) (April 6, 1998).

32. Social Security Amendment (New Deal) (No.2) Regulations 1998 (SI 1998/2117) reg.2(2) (September 24, 1998).

33. Income Support (General) Amendment Regulations 1999 (SI 1999/ 2554) reg.2(2)(a) and (b) (October 4, 1999).

34. Social Security and Child Support (Tax Credits) Consequential Amendments Regulations 1999 (SI 1999/2566) reg.2(1) and Sch.2 Pt I (October 5, 1999).

35. Social Security and Child Support (Tax Credits) Consequential Amendments Regulations 1999 (SI 1999/2566) reg.2(2) and Sch.2 Pt II (October 5, 1999).

36. Social Security Amendment (Notional Income and Capital) Regulations 1999 (SI 1999/2640) reg.2(1)(a) (November 15, 1999).

37. Social Security Amendment (Notional Income and Capital) Regulations 1999 (SI 1999/2640) reg.2(3)(c) (November 15, 1999).

38. Income Support (General) Amendment Regulations 1999 (SI 1999/ 2554) reg.2(2)(c) (November 29, 1999).

39. Social Security Act 1998 (Commencement No.12 and Consequential and Transitional Provisions) Order 1999 (SI 1999/3178 (C.81)) art.3(5) and Sch.5 para.4(a) (November 29, 1999).

40. Social Security Act 1998 (Commencement No.12 and Consequential and Transitional Provisions) Order 1999 (SI 1999/3178 (C.81)) art.3(5) and Sch.5 para.4(b) (November 29, 1999).

41. Income Support (General) and Jobseeker's Allowance Amendment (No.2) Regulations 1999 (SI 1999/3324) reg.2 (January 7, 2000).

42. Social Security (Approved Work) Regulations 2000 (SI 2000/678) reg.2(2) (April 3, 2000).

43. Social Security Amendment (Employment Zones) Regulations 2000 (SI 2000/724) reg.3(1) (April 3, 2000).

44. Social Security (Miscellaneous Amendments) (No.3) Regulations 2001 (SI 2001/859) reg.3(2) (April 9, 2001).

45. Social Security Amendment (New Deal) Regulations 2001 (SI 2001/ 1029) reg.15(4) and (5)(c) (April 9, 2001).

46. Social Security Amendment (New Deal) Regulations 2001 (SI 2001/ 1029) reg.15(6) and (7)(c) (April 9, 2001).

47. Social Security (Miscellaneous Amendments) Regulations 2002 (SI 2002/ 841) reg.2(2) (April 8, 2002).

48. Social Security (Working Tax Credit and Child Tax Credit) (Consequential Amendments) Regulations 2003 (SI 2003/455) reg.2 and Sch.1 para.10(b) (April 7, 2003).

49. Social Security (Working Tax Credit and Child Tax Credit) (Consequential Amendments) Regulations 2003 (SI 2003/455) reg.2 and Sch.1 para.10(c) (April 7, 2003).

50. State Pension Credit (Consequential, Transitional and Miscellaneous Provisions) Regulations 2002 (SI 2002/3019) reg.29(2) (October 6, 2003).

51. Social Security (Working Tax Credit and Child Tax Credit) (Consequential Amendments) Regulations 2003 (SI 2003/455) reg.2 and Sch.1 para.10 (except

sub-paras (b) and (c)) (April 6, 2004, except in "transitional cases" and see further the note to reg.17 of the Income Support Regulations).

52. Social Security (Miscellaneous Amendments) (No.3) Regulations 2004 (SI 2004/2308) reg.5(2) (October 4, 2004).

53. Social Security (Miscellaneous Amendments) Regulations 2005 (SI 2005/574) reg.2(5) (April 4, 2005).

54. Social Security (Miscellaneous Amendments) Regulations 2005 (SI 2005/574) reg.3(3)(a) (April 4, 2005).

55. Social Security (Miscellaneous Amendments) Regulations 2005 (SI 2005/574) reg.3(3)(b) (April 4, 2005).

56. Social Security (Miscellaneous Amendments) (No.2) Regulations 2005 (SI 2005/2465) reg.2(3)(e) (October 3, 2005).

57. Social Security (Care Homes and Independent Hospitals) Regulations 2005 (SI 2005/2687) reg.2 and Sch.1 para.6 (October 24, 2005).

58. Social Security (Civil Partnership) (Consequential Amendments) Regulations 2005 (SI 2005/2878) reg.4(2) (December 5, 2005).

59. Social Security (Miscellaneous Amendments) (No.2) Regulations 2005 (SI 2005/2465) reg.2(3)(a) (April 6, 2006).

60. Social Security (Miscellaneous Amendments) (No.2) Regulations 2005 (SI 2005/2465) reg.2(3)(b) (April 6, 2006).

61. Social Security (Miscellaneous Amendments) (No.2) Regulations 2005 (SI 2005/2465) reg.2(3)(c) (April 6, 2006).

62. Social Security (Miscellaneous Amendments) (No.2) Regulations 2005 (SI 2005/2465) reg.2(3)(d) (April 6, 2006).

63. Social Security (Miscellaneous Amendments) Regulations 2006 (SI 2006/588) reg.2(2) (April 6, 2006).

64. Social Security (Miscellaneous Amendments) Regulations 2007 (SI 2007/719) reg.2(3) (April 2, 2007).

65. Social Security (Miscellaneous Amendments) (No.3) Regulations 2007 (SI 2007/1749) reg.2(6) (July 16, 2007).

66. Social Security (Miscellaneous Amendments) (No.5) Regulations 2007 (SI 2007/2618) reg.5(9) (October 1, 2007).

67. Social Security (Miscellaneous Amendments) Regulations 2008 (SI 2008/698) reg.2(7)(a) (April 14, 2008).

68. Social Security (Miscellaneous Amendments) (No.6) Regulations 2008 (SI 2008/2767) reg.2(6) (November 17, 2008).

69. Social Security (Miscellaneous Amendments) (No.6) Regulations 2008 (SI 2008/2767) reg.2(7) (November 17, 2008).

70. Social Security (Miscellaneous Amendments) (No.7) Regulations 2008 (SI 2008/3157) reg.2(4) (January 5, 2009).

71. Social Security (Miscellaneous Amendments) Regulations 2009 (SI 2009/583) reg.2(7) (April 6, 2009).

72. Social Security (Miscellaneous Amendments) (No.4) Regulations 2009 (SI 2009/2655) reg.2(9) (October 26, 2009).

73. Social Security (Miscellaneous Amendments) (No.2) Regulations 2010 (SI 2010/641) reg.2(3)(b) (April 6, 2010).

74. Social Security (Miscellaneous Amendments) (No.2) Regulations 2010 (SI 2010/641) reg.2(6) (April 6, 2010).

75. Social Security (Miscellaneous Amendments) (No.2) Regulations 2010 (SI 2010/641) reg.2(7)(a) (April 6, 2010).

76. Social Security (Miscellaneous Amendments) (No.2) Regulations 2011 (SI 2011/1707) reg.4(4)(a) and (5) (August 5, 2011).

77. Social Security (Miscellaneous Amendments) (No.3) Regulations 2011 (SI 2011/2425) reg.7(4) (October 31, 2011).

78. Social Security (Miscellaneous Amendments) (No.3) Regulations 2011 (SI 2011/2425) reg.7(5) (October 31, 2011).

79. Jobseeker's Allowance (Schemes for Assisting Persons to Obtain Employment) Regulations 2013 (SI 2013/276) reg.13(b) (February 12, 2013).

80. Social Security (Miscellaneous Amendments) Regulations 2014 (SI 2014/591) reg.2(4) (April 28, 2014).

81. Social Security (Scottish Rate of Income Tax etc.) (Amendment) Regulations 2016 (SI 2016/233) reg. 2(5) (April 6, 2016).

82. Social Security (Scottish Infected Blood Support Scheme) Regulations 2017 (SI 2017/329) reg.3(3) (April 3, 2017).

83. Social Security (Emergency Funds) (Amendment) Regulations 2017 (SI 2017/689) reg.2(3)(a) (June 19, 2017).

84. Social Security (Infected Blood and Thalidomide) Regulations 2017 (SI 2017/870) reg.2(3)(a) (October 23, 2017).

85. Social Security (Miscellaneous Amendments No.4) Regulations 2017 (SI 2017/1015) reg.4 (November 16, 2017).

86. Social Security (Income and Capital) (Miscellaneous Amendments) Regulations 2020 (SI 2020/618) reg.2(3) (July 15, 2020).

DEFINITIONS

"Abbeyfield Home"—see reg.2(1).
"the Act"—*ibid.*
"approved blood scheme"—*ibid.*
"the Armed Forces and Reserve Forces Compensation Scheme"—*ibid.*
"the benefit Acts"—*ibid.*
"care home"—*ibid.*
"child tax credit"—*ibid.*
"claimant"—see reg.2(1), reg.23(1).
"claimant participating as a service user"—see reg.2(1B).
"earnings"—see reg.2(1).
"family"—see SSCBA s.137(1).
"Grenfell Tower Payment"—see reg.2(1)
"independent hospital"—*ibid.*
"Intensive Activity Period for 50 plus"—*ibid.*
"the London Emergencies Trust"—*ibid.*
"the Mandatory Work Activity Scheme"—*ibid.*
"MFET Limited"—*ibid.*
"occupational pension"—*ibid.*
"partner"—*ibid.*
"pay period"—*ibid.*
"payment"—*ibid.*
"pension fund holder"—*ibid.*
"personal pension scheme"—*ibid.*
"qualifying age for state pension credit"—see SSCBA s.137(1).
"Scottish basic rate"—see reg.2(1).
"Scottish Infected Blood Support Scheme"—*ibid.*
"Scottish taxpayer"—*ibid.*
"single claimant"—*ibid.*
"Social Security Act"—*ibid.*
"subsistence allowance"—*ibid.*
"the Caxton Foundation"—*ibid.*
"the Eileen Trust"—*ibid.*
"the Fund"—*ibid.*
"the Independent Living Fund (2006)"—*ibid.*
"the Macfarlane (Special Payments) Trust"—*ibid.*
"the Macfarlane (Special Payments) (No.2) Trust"—*ibid.*
"the Macfarlane Trust"—*ibid.*
"the National Emergencies Trust"—*ibid.*
"the Skipton Fund"—*ibid.*

"training allowance"—*ibid.*
"voluntary organisation"—*ibid.*
"war widow's pension"—*ibid.*
"war widower's pension"—*ibid.*
"water charges"—*ibid.*
"the We Love Manchester Emergency Fund"—*ibid.*
"working tax credit"—*ibid.*
"year of assessment"—*ibid.*

GENERAL NOTE

The structure is as follows: 2.334

(1) Deprivation of income.

(2)–(2CA) Income available on application and pensions and annuities not acquired.

(3) Income due.

(3A) and (3B) Income from occupational pension schemes not paid.

(3C) Unpaid earnings due on termination of employment by reason of redundancy.

(4)–(4A) Third parties.

(5) Earnings not ascertainable.

(5A) Subsistence allowances paid to people participating in employment zone programmes.

(6)–(6A) Underpaid services.

(7) Calculation.

(8) Deductions.

(8ZA) Service users.

(8A) and (9) Definitions.

Paragraph (1)—deprivation of income
  See notes to reg.51(1). A social security benefit is "income" which a claimant may   2.335
be treated as still possessing under para.(1) (*CSIS 57/1992*). But a refusal to take
up an offer of employment would not be a deprivation of income (*CCS 7967/1995*),
although leaving a job may be depending on the circumstances (*CCS/4056/2004*)
(both cases decided under the child support legislation).
  Note that until October 31, 2011, para.(1) only applied if the deprivation had
been for the purpose of securing entitlement to, or increasing the amount of, income
support. The question could therefore have arisen on a claimant transferring to
income support from JSA, or ESA, as to whether a deprivation which had only been
for the purposes of JSA or ESA could be caught by para.(1).
  Paragraph (1) has, however, been amended with effect from October 31, 2011 so
that it now applies if the person has deprived themself of income in order to secure
entitlement to, or increase the amount of, income support, JSA or ESA. A similar
amendment has been made to reg.105(1) of the JSA Regulations 1996, so that it
now also applies if the deprivation was for the purpose of securing entitlement to,
or increasing the amount of, ESA as well as income support or JSA. These provisions have not yet been extended to cover purposes relating to universal credit. In
the nature of things, one will normally be concerned with JSA and ESA in such
cases. However it is possible that a person could have been entitled to JSA or ESA,
but fall out of the scope of universal credit (e.g. by virtue for the moment of having
been entitled to the severe disability premium before transfer to universal credit)

and need to claim income support. The amount of a claimant's own earnings are relevant to entitlement to JSA and to ESA (together with some pension payments, but see para.2(g) below) so that deprivation of income for such purposes might conceivably be relevant.

2.336   According to the Explanatory Memorandum which accompanied the SI that made the 2011 amendments, the purpose of this "minor" change is to cover people who deprive themselves of income whilst claiming ESA and then move across to income support or JSA. The need for these amendments was apparently overlooked when ESA was introduced. However, the need for an amendment to para.(1) had also been overlooked when JSA was introduced in 1995. Furthermore, the change to para.(1) could have a significant effect in certain cases because a deprivation of income now counts for the purposes of all three benefits. Paragraph (1) arguably would not previously have applied where claimants have deprived themselves of income for the purposes of securing or increasing entitlement to ESA or JSA and then claimed income support. Equally reg.105(1) of the JSA Regulations 1996 would not have bitten if the deprivation had been for the purpose of securing, or increasing, entitlement to ESA.

Note that the income support deprivation of capital rule (reg.51(1)) has not been amended; it continues to apply only where the deprivation was for the purposes of securing entitlement to, or increasing the amount of, income support. The JSA deprivation of capital rule (reg.113(1) of the JSA Regulations 1996) has also not been amended and only applies where the deprivation was for the purpose of securing, or increasing, entitlement to JSA or income support.

Paragraph (2)(a)–(f)—income available on application

2.337   See notes to reg.51(2). There are some extra excluded categories here. The fact that a number of social security benefits are excluded suggests that social security benefits generally are caught by the rule. It is not at all clear that such benefits "would become available upon application being made" if an award has not already been made. Stages of the gathering of evidence and a decision by a decision-maker are necessary before a claimant becomes entitled to payment. The words "would become" may be broad enough to cover that process, but that could only possibly be the case where entitlement is straightforward. See *CIS 16271/1996*. The income available to be acquired by the claimant must be for their own benefit (and not, for example, rent under a sub-lease that had to be paid straight over to the head landlord) (*CIS 15052/1996*).

Note the exclusion of working tax credit (para.(2)(e)). Its various predecessors, working families' tax credit, disabled person's tax credit, family credit and disability working allowance had similarly been exempted. Child tax credit is also excluded (para.(2)(f)). Paragraph (2)(d) and para.(2D) (which exempted the additional amount of child benefit for a lone parent (if any)) were revoked with effect from April 6, 2004 (except in "transitional cases"—see the note to reg.17) as part of the amendments consequential on the removal of amounts for children and young persons from income support.

Paragraph (2)(g) and paras (2ZA)–(2CA)—income from pension schemes

2.338   Under para.(2)(g) income available on request from an occupational or a personal pension scheme (see reg.2(1)), or from the Board of the Pension Protection Fund ("PPF") is exempt from the notional income rules until a person reaches the qualifying age for state pension credit (defined in s.137(1) of the SSCBA 1992. The effect of that definition is that the qualifying age was 60 but from April 2010 it gradually rose in line with the staged increase in pensionable age for women until it reached 65 in November 2018. This equalisation of the state pension age for men and women was previously to have been completed by April 5, 2020 but the timetable for this in the Pensions Act 1995 was accelerated with effect from April 2016 so that women's state pension age became 65 in November 2018; in addition, the increase in state pension age to 66 for both men and women has been brought forward—it started to rise from 65 in December 2018 to reach 66 by October 2020 (see s.1 of the Pensions

Act 2011), and between 2026 and 2028 it will reach 67 (see s.26 of the Pensions Act 2014)). Occupational pensions have been included in this exemption from April 6, 2006 because, as a result of changes to income tax legislation made by the Finance Act 2004, which took effect on April 6, 2006, there is more scope for taking occupational pensions early (and for deferring entitlement). Payments from the PPF, which has been set up under the Pensions Act 2004 to provide protection for members of an occupational pension scheme in the event of their employer's insolvency, have also been included from this date as the earliest date such payments could be made is April 6, 2006.

If after reaching the qualifying age for state pension credit the "claimant" fails to claim income due from an occupational or personal pension scheme or the PPF, or elects to defer income from an occupational pension scheme, they will be treated as having that income (para.(2ZA)). Further, para.(2A) provides that if a person who has reached the qualifying age for state pension credit and who is entitled to "money purchase benefits" (defined in para.(2CA)) under an occupational or personal pension scheme fails to purchase an annuity with the money available from, and (if this is an option) does not draw the income from, any such pension fund, they will be assumed to have an amount of income determined in accordance with para.(2B) or (2C). On the 2017 amendment to para.(2B), the rate of annuity that could have been obtained with the fund can be ascertained by reference to tables issued by the Government Actuary's Department and available on the internet. The meaning of "money purchase benefits" in the Pensions Schemes Act 1993 is "in relation to a member of a personal or occupational pension scheme or the widow or widower of a member of such a scheme, . . . benefits the rate or amount of which is calculated by reference to a payment or payments made by the member or by any other person in respect of the member and which are not average salary benefits" (see s.181 of the 1993 Act). At first sight these provisions would not seem of particular relevance to income support since a person who has reached the qualifying age for state pension credit is not entitled to income support (s.124(1)(aa) of the SSCBA 1992). However, a claimant who has not yet reached the qualifying age for state pension credit may have a partner who has done so and who is entitled to income from an occupational or personal pension scheme or the PPF and thus these provisions could apply. But note that para.(2ZA) refers to a "claimant who has attained the qualifying age for state pension credit". It is not entirely clear why the draftsman has chosen to use the word "claimant" in this paragraph (which may be contrasted with para. (2A) which refers to a "person who has attained the qualifying age for state pension credit"). However, presumably the draftsman is relying on reg.23(1) which provides that a reference to the "claimant" in this Part of the regulations is to be treated as a reference to any partner.

The operation of para.(2A) is not completely straightforward, although the 2017 amendment has improved matters. Working through the conditions in sub-paras (a) to (c), all of which have to be met, the meaning of "money purchase benefits" in sub-para.(a) has been dealt with above. Under sub-para.(b), *BRG v SSWP (SPC)* [2014] UKUT 246 (AAC), a case about the broadly equivalent but not identical reg.18(2)–(5) of the State Pension Credit Regulations, holds that someone "fails" to purchase an annuity simply by not purchasing one in circumstances in which they could elect to do so. *BRG* also holds that funds are "available" to a person (who by definition has reached state pension age) although they have not yet reached the age originally selected under the scheme for taking benefits. That is because they have the option to purchase an annuity before reaching that age. *SSWP v IG (SPC)* [2018] UKUT 228 (AAC) follows that approach. Then, under sub-para.(c) the intention appears to be that it applies either if "income withdrawal" is not available under the scheme (head (iii)) or, if such withdrawal is available, it is deferred to any extent or the person fails to take the necessary action to secure the whole of income that would be available on application (heads (i) and (ii)). The assumption appears to be that what could be taken by way of income drawdown under such a scheme would be income in the person's hands. Paragraphs (2AA) to (2C) certainly proceed on the express assumption that where sub-para.(c) applies the result is that income has been foregone. However, the waters were temporarily muddied by the Upper Tribunal decision in *IG*. The judge there accepted the SSWP's general approach to the interpretation of the equivalent SPC provisions, but then decided the appeal by concluding that, since the value of the claimant's initial investment in the scheme had decreased, any amounts taken by way of income drawdown would inevitably come out of the capital of the fund and that they would then be capital in the claimant's hands. She held that there could then be no amount of income foregone to be calculated under reg.18(3) of the State Pension Credit Regulations as then in force, which supplied no mechanism for calculating that amount. On the SSWP's appeal, the Court of Appeal has rejected that approach (*Secretary of State for Work and Pensions v Goulding* [2019] EWCA Civ 839, [2019] 1 W.L.R. 5393). In the context of the provision as a whole, which had to include the relevant tax and pensions legislation, whatever was produced by way of income drawdown in a scheme regarded as an income drawdown scheme under that legislation would be income. Thus, deferral or failure to take action to secure available income drawdown would result in the foregoing of income.

2.339   Following the November 2017 amendment, para.(2B) now supplies a relatively simple rule as to the amount of notional income that is to be imputed under para.(2AA) in a para.(2A)(c)(i) or (ii) case. It is the rate of the annuity that could have been purchased with the fund, as at the date on which the income foregone could have been obtained (para.(2AA)). The rate can be ascertained from tables issued by the Government Actuary's Department and available on the internet. There may perhaps be scope for unfair double counting on a literal interpretation where there has been only a partial deferment or failure to secure income. Presumably in such a case "the fund" must refer only to the part of the original fund that has not been used in providing income. In para.(2A)(c)(iii) cases, where income drawdown is not available, para.(2C) simply deems there to have been income foregone in the form of what the person could have received, calculated as in para.(2B), if income drawdown had been available in the scheme.

No notional capital will be assumed (see reg.51(2)(d) and (da)), although in the case of an occupational pension or a PPF payment this only applies if the claimant has not reached the qualifying age for state pension credit (see reg.51(2)(da)). It is understood that the exemption under reg.51(2)(d) is not limited to claimants under the qualifying age for state pension credit because it would not be possible to predict in the case of a personal pension scheme how much capital a person might chose to take (and thus could be treated as having) from the scheme, whereas in relation to an occupational pension scheme there will be a default provision that can form the basis for the attribution of notional capital to the claimant under this rule.

In addition, the actual capital value of any funds held in a personal pension scheme is disregarded (para.23A of Sch.10); the value of the right to receive an occupational or personal pension is also ignored (para.23 of Sch.10). Note also the provisions in regs 7 and 32 of the Claims and Payments Regulations relating to the provision of information by pension fund holders (see Vol.III of this series).

For an illustration of the operation of the provisions in paras (2A)–(2C) in their then form, see *CIS 4080/2001*. In *CIS 4501/2002* para.(2A) applied even though the claimant was not drawing on her pension because it was a pension mortgage which she needed to retain in order to pay her mortgage. The argument that para.(2A) contravenes art.14, when read with art.1 of Protocol 1, ECHR because it interferes with a claimant's ability to leave funds in a pension scheme to accumulate was rejected in *R(IS)12/04*. The Commissioner holds that even if art.1 of Protocol 1 (or art.8) was engaged for the purposes of art.14 (which had not been established), the claimant had not shown a sufficient basis of comparison of his position with that of a woman for art.14 to be invoked.

Paragraph (2)(i)–(j)—miscellaneous

2.340   On para.(2)(i) and (ia), see the notes to paras 44 and 45 of Sch.10.

The purpose of para.(2)(j) was to enable a claimant who was on a full-time rehabilitation course and so eligible for rehabilitation allowance from the DfEE to choose whether to claim the allowance or remain on income support. Rehabilitation courses are designed to assist people who have been incapable of work for a prolonged period to return to the labour market. Anyone who claims the allowance is treated as capable of work and so would cease to be entitled to income support on the ground of incapacity for work (although they could claim JSA). From October 27, 2008 new claims for income support on the grounds of incapacity for work are not generally possible.

Paragraph (3)—income due but not paid
    Sub-paragraph (b) excludes almost all social security benefits from the operation of this paragraph (although abandoning entitlement might be a deprivation of income under para.(1)). The other exclusions are of income due, but not paid, under discretionary trusts and trusts of personal injury compensation, entitlements under occupational pension schemes covered by paras (3A) and (3B) and earnings due but not paid where employment has ended due to redundancy (para. (3C)).   **2.341**
    Outside these exclusions if income is due, i.e. legally due, it is to be treated as possessed by the claimant, and as income. The value of a debt would normally be a capital asset. Note that there is no discretion. An example would be of wages legally due but not paid but note the effect of para.(3C) where earnings are due but not paid on the termination of employment by reason of redundancy. However, the income that is due to be paid must be payable to the claimant for his own benefit (and not, for example, rent under a sub-lease that has to be paid straight over to the head landlord) (*CIS 15052/1996*).

Paragraphs (3A) and (3B) and (8A)—income from occupational pension schemes not paid
    Where a payment due from an occupational pension scheme is either not made or is not made in full because of a deficiency in the scheme's resources (defined in para.(8A)) the amount not paid does not fall within para.(3). The original form of the provisions applied only where the scheme stopped making payments to members of the scheme. The amendment puts beyond doubt that if payments to relatives or dependants of members are stopped, para.(3) does not apply.   **2.342**

Paragraph (3C)—unpaid earnings due on redundancy
    For the definition of earnings see reg.35. The intention is that when the earnings are paid any benefit that would not have been paid if the earnings had been paid at the right time will be recovered (see SSAA s.74 and Overpayments Regulations reg.7).   **2.343**

Paragraphs (4) and (4ZA)—third parties
    See the notes to reg.51(3) and (3A).   **2.344**
    The interpretation of paras (4) and (4ZA) has proved troublesome over the years. However, it must always be remembered that if a claimant is properly to be regarded as having actual income (on which see the notes to reg.23 under the heading "*What constitutes income of the claimant*"), there is no need to consider notional income. An example might be *BL v SSWP (SPC)* [2018] UKUT 4 (AAC), discussed in those notes, where payments of the claimant's personal pension by the pension provider to his ex-wife were his actual income because they were made at his order and he retained practical control over the money. The claimant argued that reg.24(1) of the State Pension Credit Regulations 2002 (with a much simpler general test of whether income was paid to a third party in respect of a claimant) meant that all payments of income to third parties should be discounted unless they were deployed for the alimentation of the claimant, adopting terms used by the Commissioner in *R(IS) 4/01* (see below). The judge rejected that argument, noting that the context of state pension credit, with which she was concerned, was not necessarily the same as that

of income support. But the basic proposition remains, that falling outside the terms of a provision as to notional income does not prevent actual income being taken into account. In *R(IS) 4/01*, the effect of an attachment of earnings order was that the payments made to the claimant's wife there did not form part of his actual income, so that notional income had to be considered.

In *R(FC) 4/98* (which concerned the similar provision in the Family Credit Regulations (reg.26(3)); see the 2002 edition of this volume for the Family Credit Regulations) the claimant's husband, from whom she was separated, was paying the mortgage payments on her home. They were joint owners of the property. The Commissioner held that only one half of the payments should be regarded as her notional income. Although the claimant and her husband were jointly and severally liable to the lender for the repayment of the mortgage, as between themselves they were each only responsible for repaying one half.

The words "to the third party" were added to the end of para.(4) on October 3, 2005 in order to close a potential loophole in the notional income rules revealed by the decision in *CJSA/3411/1998*.

2.345   In *CJSA 3411/1998* the claimant was on a one year residential training course. He was in receipt of an adult education bursary, part of which was paid directly to the college. The Commissioner decided that no notional income was to be attributed to the claimant under reg.105(10)(a)(ii) of the JSA Regulations 1996 (the equivalent of para.(4)(a)(ii)). Of the listed items only "food" was covered by the payment to the college (the power supplies used in the college did not constitute "household fuel"). But this was not caught by reg.105(10)(a)(ii) as the food provided by the college was a "payment in kind". These words referred to any payment to, or income of, the claimant in kind as well as any payment to the third party in kind. However, since many payments to third parties will result in the claimant receiving goods or services, it was felt that this could defeat the purpose of the "payments to third parties" rule because such payments would fall to be disregarded as payments in kind. Paragraph (4) (and reg.105(10) of the JSA Regulations 1996) were therefore amended to make it clear that the exemption for payments in kind only applies if the payment in kind is to the third party. See also the amendments to para.21 of Sch.9 and para.22 of Sch.7 to the JSA Regulations 1996, the effect of which is that income in kind disregarded under those provisions does not include a payment to a third party which is used by the third party to provide benefits in kind to the claimant.

Note also *SA v SSWP (IS)* [2010] UKUT 345 (AAC), reported as [2011] AACR 16, in the note to para.(4A) below.

R(IS) 4/01 considers the effect of head (ia) inserted into para.(4)(a) with effect from November 15, 1999 (note also para.(4ZA)(d) inserted at the same time). In that case virtually all of the claimant's occupational pension was paid over to his former wife under an attachment of earnings order. The Commissioner points out that before November 15, 1999 the effect of head (ii) was that payments of occupational pensions to third parties would be treated as the claimant's income only to the extent that the payments had been used for the support of the claimant. After that date head (ia) removed that limitation but it was still necessary to consider if the payments were made "in respect of" the claimant. In the Commissioner's view, the context of all three provisions in para.(4)(a) indicated that the payments caught by head (ia) were restricted to those payments which were made for the support of the claimant so as to reduce the need for him to be supported by income support. The payments in this case did nothing to support the claimant. The consequence was that the payments did not count as the claimant's income either before or after November 15, 1999. *R(IS) 2/03* agrees as to the effect of the phrase "in respect of" in the opening part of para.(4)(a). The result in that case was that payments under the claimant's self-employed pension annuity that were being applied entirely for the benefit of his creditors did not count as notional income (see further the note to reg.23 as to whether such payments count as actual income). *R(IS) 4/02* further refers to these somewhat problematic provisions, pointing out that even if heads (i) and (ii) of para.(4ZA)(d) are satisfied, head (iii) will not be if the claimant (or any member of his family, from April 6, 2004 (except in "transitional cases"—see the note to reg.17) only his partner) has, or is treated as having, any other income.

Paragraph (4A)

Where the claimant lives in a care home, an Abbeyfield Home or an independent hospital (for the definition of these terms see reg.2(1)), any payment made by a third party towards the cost of the claimant's or any partner's fees counts as the claimant's income (before April 6, 2004 the old form of this paragraph also applied to the cost of any other member of the claimant's family's fees—the old form remains in existence for "transitional cases"—see the note to reg.17). However, under paras 15, 30, 30A and 66 of Sch.9 certain payments to people in such accommodation are disregarded. "Person" in para.(4A) will include a local authority (Sch.1 to the Interpretation Act 1978).

2.346

In *SA v SSWP (IS)* [2010] UKUT 345 (AAC), reported as [2011] AACR 16, the claimant, who had learning difficulties, attended a residential college, the cost of which was funded, inter alia, by his local authority. The issue was whether part of the local authority's payment towards his college fees counted as notional income in respect of meals under para.(4)(a)(ii) or whether it fell within para.(4A), in which case it would be disregarded under para.66 of Sch.9. This hinged on whether the residential college was a care home. Judge Wikeley confirms that if an establishment satisfies the conditions in the definition of "care home" (see reg.2(1)), it falls to be treated as a care home even if it was also an educational establishment. The terms are not mutually exclusive. The consequence was that the payment in respect of meals counted as the claimant's notional income under para.(4A) but was then disregarded under para.66.

Paragraph (5)—earnings not ascertainable

This is a very general discretion, although no doubt it can only be invoked when the amount of earnings is unascertainable in some substantial way, not just because every last detail cannot be identified. The decision-maker (or tribunal) must have regard to the number of hours worked and the going rate locally for comparable employment in deciding what is reasonable, but is not prevented from considering all relevant circumstances (*R(SB) 25/83, R(SB) 15/86, R(SB) 6/88*). See the notes to para.(6). It would seem that if this provision is properly applied in relation to a week, the subsequent coming to light of accurate information could not ground a supersession for mistake or ignorance of material fact.

2.347

Paragraph (5A)—employment zone programme subsistence allowances

This concerns claimants who are participating in an "employment zone" (defined in reg.2(1)) programme established under s.60 of the Welfare Reform and Pensions Act 1999 and being paid a "subsistence allowance" (reg.2(1)). Employment zone programmes have not been in operation since September 1, 2011. See editions of this volume prior to 2018/19 for details of the operation of the provision.

2.348

Paragraphs (6)–(6A)—underpaid services

These paragraphs are concerned with what is commonly referred to as the "notional earnings" rule. Paragraph (6) was restructured in October 1999 so that it only contains the basic rule while the specific exceptions are now in para.(6A). Paragraph (6A)(a) and (b)(i) are simply a reordering of the exceptions that were previously set out in para.(6) itself but paras (6A)(c) and (b)(ii) (the latter was added on April 3, 2000) are new. In addition a further exception was introduced on October 1, 2007 (see para.(6A)(d)).

2.349

Paragraph (6)

If the two conditions in sub-paras (a) and (b) are met there is no discretion whether or not to apply the rule, unless the claimant comes within the proviso in

2.350

para.(6) itself or one of the exceptions in para.(6A). However, the application of both the rule and the exception in para.(6A)(a) involve a number of value judgments (e.g. in relation to "comparable employment", what earnings (if any) it is "reasonable" to treat the claimant as possessing and whether it is "reasonable" for the claimant to provide the service free of charge if they are a volunteer or working for a charitable or voluntary body). See *CIS 2916/1997* in which the claimant was spending time in her mother's shop to keep her mother company following recent bereavements. The Commissioner says that whether this amounted to a "service" was a question of fact and degree, having regard, inter alia, to the effort and time put in (see *Clear v Smith* [1981] 1 W.L.R. 399) but in particular to the advantage derived by the mother. If the help given was substantial, the claimant was providing a service. However, when deciding whether it was reasonable for her to provide this service free of charge, it was necessary to consider whether what the claimant was doing amounted to "work".

In *R(SB) 3/92* (on the supplementary benefit predecessor of this provision) the Commissioner held that the rule applied where a mother provided services to her disabled adult son out of love and affection. On appeal in *Sharrock v Chief Adjudication Officer* (March 26, 1991; appendix to *R(SB) 3/92*) the Court of Appeal agreed that such relationships came within the old provision, providing that the service provided was of a character for which an employer would be prepared to pay. In *CIS 93/1991* the Commissioner holds that the principle of *Sharrock* applies to reg.42(6), which thus covers services provided within informal family relationships without any contract. Under supplementary benefit there was no proviso exempting volunteers, etc. at the time. Now unpaid carers can be defined as volunteers (*CIS 93/1991*), so that there is a discretion not to apply the rule (see below). In *CIS 422/1992* (which again concerned Mrs Sharrock), the Commissioner held that she was a volunteer and that it was reasonable for her to provide her services free. The evidence was that her son made a substantial contribution to the household expenses. If she were to charge for her services the whole basis of the arrangement between them would have to change, which could have a deleterious effect on their relationship. (However, the part of the son's contribution that was not in respect of *his* living and accommodation costs could not be disregarded under para.18 of Sch.9.) It is difficult to see how in most cases it can be unreasonable for carers to look after a relative without payment. This is acknowledged by paras 26200–1 of the *Decision Makers Guide* which also lists factors to be considered in cases of doubt which are broadly in line with those suggested in *CIS 93/1991* (see below).

Under sub-para.(b) the "employer" must either make no payment or pay less than is paid for comparable employment in the area. Since the amount of notional earnings is set according to what is reasonable for that comparable employment, it seems that some comparable employment must exist in all cases.

2.351   Some of the points made in *R(SB) 13/86* on the previous supplementary benefit provision also apply to para.(6). It is necessary to identify the employer for whom the services were provided. "Person" includes a company or other corporate employer (Interpretation Act 1978 Sch.1). Thus in *R(IS) 5/95* where the claimant, who was an employee and director of a small company, was working unpaid because of the company's financial difficulties, and *CSJSA/23/2006* which concerned the sole director and majority shareholder of an unlimited company who was not paid for his part-time work for the company, it was necessary to consider whether para. (6) applied. See also *CCS 4912/1998* which holds that a similar child support rule applied where a person provided his services through a personal service company that he had set up himself and which was paying him a very low hourly rate and *R(CS) 9/08* where it was held that application of that rule had to be considered in the case of a salary sacrifice arrangement whereby an employer made contributions to an occupational pension scheme of the amount contractually agreed to be foregone by the employee.

Particulars of the services provided and any payments made must be ascertained.

See *CIS 701/1994* on the factors to consider when assessing comparable employment (the claimant in that case was again a carer) and the amount of notional earnings. In *CSJSA/23/2006* the tribunal had erred in simply adopting the decision-maker's use of the national minimum wage as the appropriate comparator for deciding the amount of the claimant's notional earnings. The test was what was paid for a comparable employment in the area and so relevant findings of fact needed to be made to establish local comparable earnings. In addition, in a case such as this where there was no actual or implied contract, the period over which the earnings were payable and when they were due to be paid also had to be established in accordance with what were the likely terms of employment in a similar job in the area.

It was suggested in earlier editions of the predecessor of this book that although payments of earnings in kind are disregarded in the calculation of income (reg.35(2)(a) and Sch.9 para.21), payments in kind should be considered in testing whether a claimant is paid at all or is paid less than the rate for comparable employment. However, *CIS 11482/1995* decides that this is not correct. The claimant's wife worked as a shop assistant for 12 hours a week for which she was paid £5 in cash and took goods to the value of £36 from the shelves. The Commissioner, after deciding that earnings in para.(6) meant earnings as defined in reg. 35 or 37 (see reg.2(1)), holds that since earnings in kind were ignored when considering whether any payment at all of earnings had been made, this must also be the case when deciding whether a person was paid less than the rate for comparable employment. Thus in considering whether the claimant's wife was paid less than the rate for comparable employment, the £36 that she received in goods was to be left out of account. But to avoid unfair double counting it was necessary to deduct any cash payments in the calculation of her notional earnings under para.(6). That was permissible because para.(6) allowed the amount of earnings which would be paid for comparable employment to be adjusted where circumstances made it reasonable. However, it would not be "reasonable" to deduct the earnings in kind because that did not involve a double counting as the actual value of the earnings in kind was disregarded.

Claimants can then escape if they prove (on the balance of probabilities) that the person to whom they have provided the services has insufficient means to pay more. That could well cause difficulties for claimants reluctant to make embarrassing enquiries. But there is an interest in preventing employers from economising at the expense of the income support budget. The Court of Appeal in *Sharrock v Chief Adjudication Officer* suggests that "means" refers simply to monetary resources and is a matter of broad judgment. No automatic test of ignoring certain benefits or regarding an income above income support level as available should be adopted. In *CIS 93/1991*, the claimant looked after his elderly and severely disabled father, but declined to give any information about the father's means. The Commissioner confirms that in such circumstances the basic rule of para.(6) must be applied, but subject to the exception for volunteers.

Paragraph (6A)

Paragraph (6A) specifies five situations in which the rule in para.(6) will not apply. First, sub-para.(a) allows volunteers or those engaged by charities or voluntary organisations not to have any notional earnings if it is reasonable for them to provide their services free of charge. Volunteer in this context means someone who without any legal obligation performs a service for another person without expectation of payment (*R(IS) 12/92*). Thus, it would seem that if any payment is made to the claimant, the proviso cannot apply. The Commissioner in *CIS 93/1991* holds that the means of the "employer" is a factor in assessing reasonableness here, but other factors are relevant too. *CSJSA/23/2006* emphasises that all the circumstances, not just the means of the employer, must be considered. There could be other factors making it reasonable for the claimant, who was the sole director and majority shareholder of an unlimited company who was not paid for his part-time work for the company, to undertake such gratuitous work, quite separate from the finances of the business.

2.352

It may be more reasonable for close relatives to provide services free of charge than for others to do so. The basis on which the arrangement was made, the expectations of the family members concerned, the housing arrangements and the reason why the carer gave up any paid work might need to be considered. Anomalies like the loss of invalid care allowance (now carer's allowance) if the carer accepted payment should be considered. So should the question of what alternatives would be available if the relative ceased to provide the care. If there was no realistic alternative to the relative continuing to provide the care and the person would not agree to make any payment, that would point to it being reasonable for the claimant to provide the services free of charge (*CIS 701/1994*). In *CIS 93/1991* the tribunal went wrong in not properly considering their discretion under the exception and concentrating on the legitimate inference that the "employer" could afford to pay the going rate. In *CIS 701/1994* the Commissioner expresses the view that if a person had substantial resources that were genuinely surplus to requirements, that would be different from the situation, for example, of a person saving towards the costs of future residential care. It should be noted that the test is whether it is reasonable for the person to provide their services free of charge, rather than whether it is reasonable for payment not to be made for the service, although this is a factor (*CIS 147/1993*). If the claimant was receiving training while, or by doing, the work, this may be relevant (*R(IS) 12/92*).

In *CIS 93/1991* the Commissioner points out that the aim of the rule is clearly to prevent an employer who has the means to pay the going rate profiting at the expense of the public purse. If, therefore, a claimant volunteers to undertake painting work (as in *CIS 147/1993*), which otherwise would have remained undone, there is no element of financial profit to the employer in the claimant doing the work. If, however, the employer would have paid the claimant if he had not said he did not wish to be paid, it may be concluded that it was not reasonable for the claimant to offer his services free of charge.

2.353　　Secondly, para.(6A)(b)(i) covers the situation where a person is on an employment programme or training scheme for three or more days in any benefit week and is not paid a training allowance. Sub-paragraph (b)(i) ensures that a person who is on such a programme or scheme will not be treated as possessing notional earnings by virtue of providing a service for which he is not being paid. (For income support purposes this provision will usually only be relevant to the claimant's partner rather than the claimant himself.) The third exception in para.(6A)(b)(ii) prevents the attribution of notional earnings where the claimant, or his partner, is taking part in an employment or training programme of any length, for which no training allowance, or one that only reimburses travelling or meal expenses, is payable.

The fourth exclusion from the notional earnings rule applies to lone parents who are on work experience while participating in the New Deal for Lone Parents (no longer in operation) or a similar scheme (para.(6A)(c)). The exemption originally only lasted for up to 150 hours, or six months, work with the same employer, but the October 2004 amendments meant that this exemption applied without limit.

The fifth (and new from October 1, 2007) exception provides that claimants are not to be treated as having notional earnings if they are undertaking an unpaid work placement (defined in para.(6AA)); the work placement must have been approved by the Secretary of State before it started.

Paragraphs (7)–(8)—calculations and deductions
2.354　　If notional income counts it is to be calculated as though it was actual income. Notional deductions are to be made from earnings to get a net figure.

Paragraph (8ZA)—service users
2.355　　The effect of this paragraph is that the notional income rules do not apply to either payments of expenses or earnings as a result of a "claimant participating as a service user" (see reg.2(1B) for those to whom this refers). Note that actual pay-

ments of such expenses are not earnings (see reg.35(2)(f)) and are disregarded as income (Sch.9 para.2A). However, earnings that result from a claimant participating as a service user other than expenses (e.g. for attending a meeting) will be taken into account in the normal way, subject to the appropriate disregard.

Paragraph (9)—ordinary clothing or footwear

The examples given in paras 28671–2 of the *Decision Makers Guide* suggest that football boots are not for "normal daily use", and that when applying the test of "for normal daily use" the wide needs of all claimants should be considered.   **2.356**

Notional earnings of seasonal workers

43.—[¹. . .].   **2.357**

AMENDMENT

1. Income Support (General) Amendment No.2 Regulations 1989 (SI 1989/1323) reg.14 (October 9, 1989).

GENERAL NOTE

When the special rules for seasonal workers were removed from the unemployment benefit scheme this was consequently also done for income support.   **2.358**

Modifications in respect of children and young persons

44.—[¹. . .]   **2.359**

AMENDMENT

1. Social Security (Working Tax Credit and Child Tax Credit) (Consequential Amendments) Regulations 2003 (SI 2003/455) reg.2 and Sch.1 para.11 (April 6, 2004, except in "transitional cases" and see further the note to reg.17 of the Income Support Regulations).

GENERAL NOTE

This regulation contained the special rules for treatment of the income of a child or young person who was a member of the claimant's family (see the 2003 edition of this volume for this regulation and the notes to it). However, with effect from April 6, 2004 (except in "transitional cases"—see the note to reg.17) amounts for children and young persons have been removed from the income support scheme; financial assistance to help with the cost of bringing up a child or young person is now to be provided through the child tax credit system, see Vol.IV of this series. As a consequence, the income of a child or young person is no longer aggregated with the claimant's (see the new form of reg.23 and the notes to that regulation) and therefore most of the modifications made by reg.44 are no longer needed (but see below). Regulation 44 does however remain in force for "transitional cases"—see the note to reg.17.   **2.360**

For income support claimants who had an award of child tax credit before April 6, 2004 see reg.7 of the Social Security (Working Tax Credit and Child Tax Credit) (Consequential Amendments) Regulations 2003 (SI 2003/455) (as amended) on p.1765 and the notes to that regulation.

Paragraph (2) of reg.44 was concerned with payments to residential schools for a child's or young person's maintenance. Since there is a continuing need to make provision for such payments, a new disregard (see para.25A of Sch.9) has been introduced with effect from April 6, 2004 (except in "transitional cases"—see the note to reg.17). This provides that payments to a boarding school for the maintenance of a child or young person who is a member of the claimant's family made by a third party or out of funds provided by a third party are ignored in full.

Chapter VI

Capital

[¹ Capital limit

2.361   **45.**—For the purposes of section 134(1) of the Contributions and Benefits Act as it applies to income support (no entitlement to benefit if capital exceeds prescribed amount), the prescribed amount is £16,000.]

AMENDMENT

1. Social Security (Miscellaneous Amendments) (No.2) Regulations 2005 (SI 2005/2465) reg.2(4) (April 10, 2006).

GENERAL NOTE

2.362   Under s.134(1) of the SSCBA 1992 there is no entitlement to income support if the claimant's capital exceeds the prescribed amount. From April 10, 2006 this is £16,000 for all claimants, thus bringing the limit into line with that which applies for housing benefit and until the abolition of council tax benefit on April 1, 2013 applied for that benefit. In addition, the amount above which the tariff income rule applies was increased to £6,000, except in the case of residents in a care home, Abbeyfield Home, Polish Resettlement home or independent hospital, for whom the tariff income rule continues to apply only to capital above £10,000 (see reg.53).

The capital of a claimant's partner is aggregated with the claimant's (reg.23(1)), but not that of children or young persons (reg.23(2), replacing the rule formerly in reg.47 with effect from April 6, 2004, except for "transitional cases"—see the note to reg.17).

In *CIS 127/1993* the Commissioner raises the question of where the burden of proof lies when considering whether the capital rule is satisfied. The Tribunal of Commissioners in *CIS 417/1992* (reported as part of *R(IS) 26/95*) treat that as part of what the claimant has to prove in showing entitlement to income support on a claim. However, the argument that the capital rule operates as an exception to the conditions of basic entitlement does not appear to have been put. See the sidenote to s.134 which is entitled "Exclusions from benefit". But once it has been shown that the claimant possesses an item of capital, it is for them to prove that one of the disregards in Sch.10 applies (*CIS 240/1992*) or that they have ceased to possess the item (*R(SB) 38/85* and see the notes to reg.46). Similarly, once it has been established that the claimant is the legal owner of a property, the burden is on them to show that they do not have any or all of the beneficial interest (*CIS 30/1993*). These decisions, however, need to be read in the light of the House of Lords' judgment in *Kerr v Department for Social Development* [2004] UKHL 23; [2004] 1 W.L.R. 1372, also reported as an appendix to *RI/04(SF)*, in which Baroness Hale emphasised that the process of adjudication for social security benefits is a co-operative one in which both the Department and the claimant should play their part and that normally it ought not to be necessary to resort to more formal concepts such as the burden of proof. In *MB v Royal Borough of Kensington & Chelsea (HB)* [2011] UKUT 321 (AAC) the claimant relied on *Chichester DC v B and SSWP* [2009] UKUT 34 (AAC) in which it was stated that it was for the Council to show that the claimant had a beneficial interest in the capital at issue (see para.28). Judge Wikeley, however, considered that the answer to this lay in the point made by Baroness Hale in *Kerr* that it was for each party (claimant or department) to provide such information as they reasonably can. The claimant in *MB v RB Kensington & Chelsea* was the one who had exclusive knowledge about the purchase of the property in issue and the mortgage payments and thus it was her responsibility to marshal what evidence she could to show that, although she was the legal owner, she was not the sole beneficial owner of the property. The same can be said of most, if not all, forms of capital.

Much will of course depend on context. The principles set out above cannot be allowed to dilute the position that if the Secretary of State is seeking to alter an existing award of income support to the detriment of the claimant the burden of showing a ground of revision or supersession and that the altered decision should be less favourable to the claimant lies on her. But see *AB v SSWP and Canterbury CC (IS and HB)* [2014] UKUT 212 (AAC) in the notes to reg.46.

Calculation of capital

46.—(1) For the purposes of Part II of the Act [SSCBA, Part VII] as it applies to income support, the capital of a claimant to be taken into account shall, subject to paragraph (2), be the whole of his capital calculated in accordance with this Part and any income treated as capital under [[1]regulation 48 (income treated as capital)].

(2) There shall be disregarded from the calculation of a claimant's capital under paragraph (1) any capital, where applicable, specified in Schedule 10.

2.363

AMENDMENT

1. Income Support (General) Amendment No.5 Regulations 1988 (SI 1988/2022) reg.10 (December 12, 1988).

DEFINITIONS

"the Act"—see reg.2(1).
"claimant"—*ibid.*, and reg.23(1).

GENERAL NOTE

All the claimant's (and partner's) capital, both actual and notional, counts towards the £16,000 limit, subject to the disregards in Sch.10. The disregards are to be applied before the value or the amount of the capital is calculated (*Guildford BC v MW (HB)* [2014] UKUT 49 (AAC), a case on the equivalent housing benefit provision). In *R(IS) 15/96*, followed in *R(IS) 5/07*, the Commissioner considered that claimants should be advised by the Benefits Agency of the existence of the disregards so that they can take advantage of them (the claimant had received a criminal injuries compensation award so that the trust disregard in para.12 of Sch.10 could have been relevant).

2.364

Distinguishing between actual and notional capital

AB v SSWP and Canterbury CC (IS and HB) [2014] UKUT 212 (AAC) emphasises the importance of decision-makers and tribunals making a clear distinction in their findings of fact as to whether the claimant has *actual* or *notional* capital. If it is found that the claimant has *actual* capital over £16,000, there will usually be no entitlement to income support. If the claimant shows that they possess capital of less than £16,000, because some of it has been spent or otherwise disposed of, it is usually necessary to consider whether they should be treated as possessing *notional* capital (see reg.51(1) and the notes to that regulation). In this case the claimant's wife had received an inheritance. On the DWP's discovery of this, supersession of the claimant's income support and housing benefit was sought. The burden therefore shifted to the claimant to show that his wife no longer possessed that capital. See *R(SB) 38/85* where Commissioner Hallett held at para.18:

2.365

"The claimant says that he expended this sum of £18,700 in repaying loans. It is for him to prove that this is so. Failing a satisfactory account of the way in which the money has been disposed of, it will be open to the tribunal, and a natural conclusion, to find that the claimant still has, in some form or other, that resource and consequently to conclude that his actual resources are above the prescribed limit."

The tribunal's statement of reasons in *AB* concluded that the claimant "should be deemed to still have, through his partner, capital in excess of £16,000". Judge Wikeley held that the ambiguity inherent in the use of the word "deemed" (or "treated") meant that it was not sufficiently clear whether the tribunal had found that the claimant, through his wife, still had the capital from the inheritance in some form or whether he had deprived himself of it for the purpose of obtaining benefit such as to be fixed with notional capital. In addition, the tribunal had failed to adequately explain why it did not accept the claimant's wife's explanation. In relation to this issue Judge Wikeley emphasises the importance of having a sound evidential basis for an adverse credibility finding against a claimant.

MS v DfC (JSA) [2020] NICom 42 holds that where a tribunal is not satisfied by a claimant's assertion that they have disposed of money, so that the amount remains part of their actual capital, it is not necessary for the tribunal to make a positive finding of fact about where the money was actually held. Submissions to the contrary were based on a misreading of remarks in *DMcC v DSD (IS)* [2012] NICom 326.

Actual capital

2.366   There is a good deal of law on actual capital.

The first condition is of course that the capital resource is the claimant's or their partner's. This is not as simple as it sounds.

In *CIS 634/1992* the claimant was made bankrupt on November 29, 1990. However, his trustee in bankruptcy was not appointed until April 1991. Between November 29 and December 28, 1990, when he claimed income support the claimant divested himself of most of his capital. Under the Insolvency Act 1986 (subject to certain exceptions) a bankrupt's property does not vest in his trustee in bankruptcy on the making of a bankruptcy order, but only when the trustee is appointed. The appointment does not have retrospective effect. It is held that since he had failed to give a satisfactory account of how he had disposed of his capital he was to be treated as still possessing it (*R(SB) 38/85* referred to in the notes to reg.51(1)). Thus the claimant was not entitled to income support prior to the appointment of the trustee in bankruptcy because until then he possessed actual capital over the income support limit.

2.367   *KS v SSWP (JSA)* [2009] UKUT 122 (AAC), reported as [2010] AACR 3, however, disagrees with *CIS/634/1992*. Judge Mark points out that a person cannot realise or use any part of his capital after a bankruptcy order has been made and that, subject to any order of the court, it will vest in his trustee in due course. Whether the capital remained the claimant's with a nil value or whether it ceased to be his capital at all (on which Judge Mark did not reach any firm conclusion), the result was that the claimant had no capital, or no capital of any value, after the bankruptcy order had been made.

In *SH v SSWP* [2008] UKUT 21 (AAC) Judge Turnbull also does not reach a final conclusion as to whether money in a bank account or other property that is subject to a restraint order under s.77 of the Criminal Justice Act 1988 (now the Proceeds of Crime Act 2002) or a freezing order ceases to be the claimant's capital. He was inclined to think that such assets remained the claimant's capital. However, their market value would be nil since the claimant was prohibited by court order from disposing of them. *CS v Chelmsford BC (HB)* [2014] UKUT 518 (AAC) takes the same view as *SH* but again without reaching a final conclusion on the point. In *CS*, which concerned assets subject to a restraint order under the Proceeds of Crime Act 2002, Judge Markus points out that not only is a restraint order under the Proceeds of Crime Act 2002 not expressed to deprive people of their interest in the property but also the terminology of the Act consistently presupposes that the person retains their interest in property that is subject to a restraint order. Its market value, however, would be nil.

See also *CIS 1189/2003* which concerned a claimant who was the sole residuary beneficiary under her mother's will. The estate had remained unadministered for several years so that her mother's property had not actually vested in the claimant. However, the property counted as the claimant's actual capital for the purposes of income support since, subject only to the formalities needed to perfect her title, she had for all practical purposes an entitlement in respect of the property that was equivalent to full beneficial ownership.

R(IS) 9/04 confirms that assets being administered on a patient's behalf either at the Court of Protection or by their receiver remain the patient's assets which have to be valued at their current market value (see reg.49) (following *CIS 7127/1995*). Such assets are held under a "bare trust" with the entire beneficial ownership remaining with the patient. The fact that the Court had discretionary powers of *control* over the management of the patient's property for their benefit did not mean that the patient's beneficial *ownership* had ceased.   **2.368**

However, capital that a claimant is under a "certain and immediate liability" to repay at the moment of its receipt by, or attribution to, the claimant, will not count as their capital (*CIS/2287/2008*). In *CIS/2287/2008* the Commissioner decides that the principle in *Chief Adjudication Officer v Leeves*, reported as *R(IS) 5/99* (see the note to reg.29(2B)) does apply to capital as well as income. However, it only applies at the moment of receipt or attribution and is relevant only to the issue of whether money or an asset should be classified as the claimant's capital. *Leeves* does not apply if the liability to repay arises after something has become capital in the claimant's hands. That issue continues to be governed by the principle in *R(SB) 2/83* that in calculating capital liabilities are not to be deducted, except those expressly provided for in the legislation. *SSWP v GF (ESA)* [2017] UKUT 333 (AAC), discussed later in this note under the heading "*Deduction of liabilities*", is a recent application of the principle of *R(SB) 2/83*. See also *JH v SSWP* [2009] UKUT 1 (AAC) which explains that *Leeves* only operates where, outside trust relationships, there is a certain obligation of immediate repayment or return of the asset to the transferor. It does not bite where the claimant is under some liability to a third party.

Beneficial ownership

The mere fact that an asset or a bank or building society account is in the claimant's sole name does not mean that it belongs to the claimant. It is the "beneficial ownership" which matters. It is only such an interest that has a market value. The claimant may hold the asset under a trust which means that they cannot simply treat the asset as theirs, but must treat it as if it belonged to the beneficiary or beneficiaries under the trust. It is they who are "beneficially entitled." A trustee may also be a beneficiary, in which case the rule in reg.52 may come into play, or may have no beneficial interest at all (see further below under "*Claimant holding as trustee*").   **2.369**

The basic principle was confirmed, as might have been thought unnecessary, by Judge Poynter in *SSWP v LB of Tower Hamlets and CT (IS & HB)* [2018] UKUT 25 (AAC) (see the notes under *Claimant holding as a trustee* for the details). However, it appeared that local authorities had routinely been submitting in housing benefit cases, wrongly taking a single sentence from the same judge's earlier decision in *CH/715/2006* out of context, that only legal interests were relevant.

These issues often arise in the context of attributing the beneficial ownership of former matrimonial assets. One example is *R(IS) 2/93*. The claimant had a building society account in her sole name, which she had had since before her marriage. Her husband deposited the bulk of the money in it, including his salary. On their separation, the AO and the SSAT treated the entire amount in the account as part of the claimant's capital. The Commissioner holds that she was not solely beneficially entitled to the money so that reg.52 had to operate. There is helpful guidance on the limited circumstances in which the "presumption of advancement" (i.e. that when a husband puts an asset into his wife's name he intends to make an outright gift of it) will operate in modern circumstances. (Note that the presumption of advancement was due to be abolished by s.199 of the Equality Act 2010 but this section has not yet been brought into force.) And see *CIS 982/2002* (which concerns the valuation of a share in a frozen joint bank account) in the notes to reg.52. Note also *R(IS) 10/99* below. In *CIS 553/1991* where a house was in the husband's sole name it is held that its valuation should take into account the wife's statutory right of occupation under the Matrimonial Homes Act 1967. See also *R(IS) 1/97*, in the note to para.5 of Sch.10.

2.370   In most cases of spouses or civil partners, in whoever's name the asset is, there will be some degree of joint ownership. But if an asset is in the sole name of one, the other should not be treated as having a half share as a beneficial tenant in common under reg.52 until it has been established that they do own at least part of it. On this see *R(IS) 1/03* which holds that a person's right to seek a lump sum payment or property transfer order under the Matrimonial Causes Act 1973 is not a capital asset. Moreover, *CIS 984/2002* should also be noted in this context. This holds that money held by the claimant's solicitor pending quantification of the statutory charge to the Legal Services Commission under s.10(7) of the Access to Justice Act 1999 was not part of the claimant's capital. Until that quantification had been carried out, it was not possible to identify any particular amount as the claimant's capital. Another way of looking at it was to treat the statutory charge as an incumbrance for the purpose of reg.49(a)(ii) (see *CIS 368/1993*). Nor was any part of the money available to the claimant on application for the purposes of reg.51(2). See also *CIS 7097/1995*, discussed in the notes to reg.52 (para.2.411).

In *LC v Bournemouth Borough Council (HB)* [2016] UKUT 175 (AAC), discussed in the note to reg.51(2), Judge White applies reg.49(2) of the Housing Benefit Regulations 2006 (the equivalent of reg.51(2)) in a case where the proceeds of sale of a former matrimonial home were being held in a solicitors' client account until the claimant's partner and his ex-wife agreed how the sum was to be split or the issue was resolved by a court order. In his view the value of the capital prior to agreement or an order of the court would be minimal.

Claimant holding as trustee

2.371   It would take many whole books to explore all the circumstances in which a trust relationship arises such that a person who holds the legal ownership of assets is subject to trust duties towards other people and so is a trustee and either has no beneficial interest in the assets or only a partial interest. The notes that follow concentrate on the social security case law, but only the barest outline of the general law can be given. In novel or complex cases there may need to be reference to specialist trust books. Sometimes the social security cases refer helpfully to the more general authorities. See, for recent examples, *SSWP v LB of Tower Hamlets and CT (IS & HB)* [2018] UKUT 25 (AAC) on resulting trusts and *VMcC v SSWP (IS)* [2018] UKUT 63 (AAC) on the *Quistclose* principle, both discussed further below.

The following notes first deal briefly with express trusts, where the existence and terms of the trust are stated or accepted, then with circumstances in which trusts arise by some form of implication, i.e implied, resulting or constructive trusts.

A trust can be created by declaration when assets are acquired (e.g. the familiar transfer of a house to a couple as beneficial joint tenants or tenants in common) or over assets already owned. In relation to assets other than land, no particular formality is required, although there must be certainty as to the assets covered by the trust and the beneficiaries as well as on the intention to create a trust. There may therefore be difficult questions in particular cases over whether there is sufficient persuasive evidence of the existence of a trust (as exemplified in several cases discussed below). It is in general for a claimant who has been shown to be the legal owner of an asset to show that they are not a beneficial owner (*MB v Royal Borough of Kensington and Chelsea (HB)* [2011] UKUT 321 (AAC) and *CT*, above).

2.372   In relation to trusts of land, *SB v SSWP (IS)* [2012] UKUT 252 (AAC) is a useful reminder that s.53(1)(b) of the Law of Property Act 1925 only requires a trust relating to land to be *evidenced* in writing. Absence of writing makes the trust unenforceable but not void. The tribunal had found that there was no trust of the property in question because there was no trust deed. This error of law had led the tribunal to fail to investigate and make findings on whether there had been a declaration of trust, whether the scope of the trust was certain, the subject matter of the trust, the objects/persons intended to benefit from any such trust and (in the absence of any documentation) whether the surrounding circumstances were consistent with the existence of a trust. It follows from the principle that the trust is merely unenforceable that the existence of later evidence in writing satisfies s.53(1) from the date of the original declaration. It is also said that the statute cannot be used as an instrument of fraud, so that a person who has taken the property knowing of the trust cannot be heard to deny the trust, despite there being no evidence in writing. Note also that s.53(1) does not apply to implied, resulting or constructive trusts.

In *R(IS) 1/90*, the claimant established a building society account in his own name which was to be used solely to finance his son's medical education. He executed no documents about the account. It was argued that there was sufficient evidence of a declaration of trust over the account, but the Commissioner holds that the claimant had not unequivocally renounced his beneficial interest in the sum in the account. Although he had earmarked the money for the son's education, the situation was like an uncompleted gift and there was insufficient evidence of a declaration of trust.

For the position under Scots law see *R(IS) 10/99*. The claimant agreed that he would pay his former wife (from whom he was separated) £22,250, representing a share of his pension. When he claimed income support, the claimant had £15,500 in his bank account that he said he was holding for his wife. The Commissioner decides that the £15,500 was not subject to a trust. That was because there had been no delivery of the subject of the trust, nor any satisfactory equivalent to delivery, "so as to achieve irrevocable divestiture of the truster [the equivalent of the settlor in English law] and investiture of the trustee in the trust estate", as required by Scots law (see *Clark Taylor & Co Ltd v Quality Site Development (Edinburgh) Ltd* 1981 S.C. 11). There was no separate bank account and had been no clear indication to the claimant's wife that the money was held on trust for her. In addition, as the truster would have been the sole trustee, the Requirements of Writing (Scotland) Act 1995 required the trust to be proved in writing. That had not been done. Nor was there an "incumbrance" within the meaning of reg.49(a)(ii) preventing the claimant disposing of the money. The consequence was that the £15,500 counted as the claimant's capital. No doubt the result would have been the same if the principles of trust law in England and Wales had been applied. Mere mental earmarking of an asset for a particular purpose is not enough to show the existence of a trust.

For a further case which considered whether a trust had been validly constituted for the purposes of Scots law, see *CSIS/639/2006*.

2.373

One particular instance of a resulting trust is where a person gives or loans some amount to another to be used for a particular purpose. In *R(SB) 53/83* the claimant's son had paid him £2,850 to be used for a holiday in India. The claimant died without taking the holiday or declaring the existence of the money to the DHSS. The Commissioner, applying the principle of *Barclays Bank Ltd v Quistclose Investments Ltd* [1970] A.C. 567, held that there was a trust to return the money to the son if the primary purpose of the loan was not carried out. Since the Commissioner held that there had been no overpayment while the claimant was alive, this must mean that the claimant held the money on trust to use it for the specified purpose or to return it. It was not part of the claimant's resources. This is an important decision, which overtakes some of the reasoning of *R(SB) 14/81* (see below). The actual decision in *R(SB) 53/83* was reversed (by consent) by the Court of Appeal, because the Commissioner had differed from the appeal tribunal on a point of pure fact. *R(SB) 1/85* holds that this does not affect its authority on the issue of principle. In *R(SB) 1/85*, the claimant's mother-in-law had some years previously provided the money for the purchase of the lease of a holiday chalet for the use of the claimant's mentally handicapped son, Keith. The lease was in the claimant's name and its current value was probably about

£5,000. The AO's initial statement of the facts was that the mother-in-law had bought the chalet in the claimant's name. The Commissioner holds that this would give rise to a presumption of a resulting trust in her favour, so that the claimant would have no beneficial interest in the chalet—nothing he could sell. The presumption could be rebutted if in fact the mother-in-law had made an outright gift to the claimant, or to Keith. In the second case the claimant again would have no beneficial interest. In the first, he would be caught, for even if he had said that he intended to use the chalet purely for Keith, he had not made the necessary written evidence of the trust (Law of Property Act 1925 s.53). Another possibility was that the mother-in-law had made a gift to the claimant subject to an express (but unwritten) trust in favour of Keith, when again the claimant clearly would not be the beneficial owner, as that would be a fraud. This is a very instructive decision, which will give valuable guidance in sorting out many family-type arrangements.

The dangers and difficulties of *Quistclose* were pointed out in *CSB/1137/1985*, particularly where family transactions are concerned. There, the claimant had received loans of £1,000 and £500, to fund a trip to India, from friends originally from the same village, who both later provided letters to say that, as the trip had not been taken, they had asked for, and received, their money back. Commissioner Rice held that the tribunal had gone wrong in law in concluding, following *R(SB) 53/83*, that the claimant did not have any beneficial interest in the funds, because the relationship between the lenders and the claimant indicated that nothing as sophisticated as the imposition of a trust had been intended. Rather, it had not been shown that there was any restriction on the claimant's use of the money.

2.374 Judge Wikeley in *VMcC v SSWP* [2018] UKUT 63 (AAC) has recently helpfully summarised the test required for the imposition of a *Quistclose* trust as set out in recent authority (in particular *Twinsectra Ltd v Yardley* [2002] 2 A.C. 164 and *Bellis v Challenor* [2015] EWCA Civ 59) and also discussed the distinction between *R(SB) 53/83* and *CSB/1137/1985*. The summary in para.42 is this:

> "The funds must be transferred on terms, typically for a stated purpose, which do not leave them at the free disposal of the transferee;
> There must be an intention to create what is, viewed objectively, a trust;
> A person creates a trust by their words or conduct, not their innermost thoughts;
> If such a trust is created, then the beneficial interest in the property remains in the transferor unless and until the purposes for which it has been transferred have been fulfilled;
> If such a trust is not created, then the ordinary consequence is that the money becomes the property of the transferee, who is free to apply it as they choose."

In addition, *Twinsectra* established that if there is a lack of clarity in identifying the stated purpose such that the funds cannot be applied the transferor's beneficial interest continues. Judge Wikeley acknowledged that there appeared to be a very thin line between the circumstances in *R(SB) 53/83* and *CSB/1137/1985*, but suggested in para.48 that, as well as the purpose being more specific, it might have been significant that the funds in *R(SB) 53/83* had been transferred, while the transaction in *CSB/1137/1985* was described in terms of a loan. With respect, it is hard to see why the transaction being a loan should point towards the claimant in *CSB/1137/1985* being subject to no trust obligations. It might be thought that the distinction, fine though it may be, was more in there not having been the necessary words or conduct, rather than innermost thoughts.

Cases in which *Quistclose* has been applied include the following. In *R(SB) 12/86*, £2,000 was lent to the claimant on condition that she did not touch the capital amount, but only took the interest, and repaid the £2,000 on demand. The £2,000 was not part of her capital, never having been at her disposal. The Commissioner in *CSB 975/1985* was prepared to apply the principle to a loan on mortgage from a Building Society for property renovation. But it would have to be found that the loan was made for no other purpose and was to be recoverable by the Building Society if for any reason the renovations could not be carried out. The furthest extension so far of the *Quistclose* principle is in *CFC 21/1989*. The claimant's father paid her each month an amount to meet her mortgage obligation to a building society. The Commissioner accepts that the money was impressed with a trust that it should be used only for that purpose and did not form part of her capital. The extension is that the purpose was to meet expenditure on an item that could be covered by income support.

The facts in *VMcC* were unusual. The claimant, who was a member of the Traveller community, had two accounts with TSB and Nationwide opened in her own name when she was a child (probably when she was about seven) for members of her family to put money in for her future education. When she became pregnant at the age of 19 she was disowned by her family and claimed income support in April 2015, disclosing two bank accounts, but not the TSB and Nationwide accounts. She said she only became aware of those accounts at a compliance interview in July 2015 and in August produced evidence that both accounts had been closed. She said that all the amounts in the accounts (some £13,000) had been returned to the family members by her mother, save for £2,000 that she was allowed to keep for her baby. The decision-maker treated all the amounts as the claimant's, generating a tariff income, and that was upheld on appeal. The tribunal found that as the claimant had opened the accounts she would have known of them and concluded that she could have used the money as she pleased. If her mother or the family had wanted to set aside money for her education they could have opened a trustee account. Judge Wikeley set the tribunal's decision aside because there was not evidence to support the finding that the claimant had opened the TSB and Nationwide accounts and gave some guidance to a new tribunal on rehearing. In para.44 he cited what had been said in the commentary in this volume, that there may well be evidential difficulties in establishing the components of a *Quistclose* trust in the context of family arrangements, not least because there is often no contemporary documentation, but stressed that the absence of a paper trail is not necessarily determinative. In principle a *Quistclose* trust can be created informally and by word of mouth, although very careful fact-finding is necessary. After comparing the outcomes of *R(SB) 53/83* and *CSB/1137/1995* (see above), he mentioned in para.47 two particular factors to be considered in family-type cases:

"The first is that in practice it is unusual for informal family arrangements to be *contemporaneously* evidenced in writing (whether within the Traveller community or elsewhere). The second is that if the Appellant's account about being cast out by the community is accepted, that in itself may explain the failure of witnesses to attend an oral hearing to support her."

The question was not what was objectively reasonable (or what a High Street solicitor would have advised) but whether the claimant's account could be accepted in the light of what was customary in the particular community (para.61). It should also be noted that the Secretary of State accepted that an account may contain funds subject to a trust mixed with funds that are not so subject (para.51).

Cases in which *Quistclose* has not been applied include the following, many 2.375
of which illustrate the thinness of the line between an outright gift or loan and one subject to an implied trust. *R(IS) 5/98* reached a similar outcome without any mention of *Quistclose*. The claimant had transferred her flat to her daughter partly on the condition that her daughter looked after her. It was held that the gift failed when this condition was not fulfilled and the daughter held the flat on trust for her mother. An appeal against this decision was dismissed by the Court of Appeal (*Ellis v Chief Adjudication Officer*, reported as part of *R(IS) 5/98*). The claimant had argued that the condition was void for uncertainty but this was rejected by the Court (and in accordance with the principles summarised in *VMcC* that would have led to the beneficial interest remaining with the mother from the outset).

In *YH v SSWP (IS)* [2015] UKUT 85 (AAC) the claimant raised a loan on his property and gave the money to his sons to establish a business. The sons used the money to set up the business and made the repayments on the loan. The *Quistclose* principle did not apply because there was no evidence to suggest that the lender had advanced the money on the condition that it was only to be used to establish the sons' business. A borrower does not create a trust in favour of the lender simply by having their own clear intention as to the application of the money. There was no separation between legal and beneficial interest so far as the sons were concerned, so that there was a question of whether the claimant had notional capital on the deprivation under reg.51.

A further example occurred in *CIS/5185/1995*, which held that *Quistclose* did not apply to a student grant which the claimant became liable to repay to the education authority when he left his course early (for the treatment of student grants in these circumstances now see reg.29(2B), but note the argument discussed in the notes to reg.29(2B) as to when that provision applies). The grant could not be disregarded under the *Quistclose* principle because the education authority retained no beneficial interest in the grant. The authority merely reserved the right to demand repayment of a sum calculated according to the unexpired balance of the relevant term when the person ceased to be a student. *CIS/12263/1996* (where a student was obliged to repay a grant immediately on abandoning the course), discussed in this context in past editions, does not now need mention because the Commissioner concluded that the circumstances fell outside *Quistclose* and on appeal (*Chief Adjudication Officer v Leeves*, reported as *R(IS) 5/99*) it was conceded on behalf of the claimant that there was no constructive trust in these circumstances, since no proprietary right had been retained by the education authority, nor had any fiduciary obligation been created.

2.376   In *MW v SSWP (JSA)* [2016] UKUT 469 (AAC), reported as [2017] AACR 15, a Scottish case, it was held that circumstances which would in England and Wales have given rise to a *Quistclose* trust did not do so as a matter of Scots law, because Scots law did not recognise a trust where the sole beneficiary was a trustee. The claimant had been lent money by his mother in order to buy his house. If it was not used for that purpose it was to be returned. Judge Gamble held that nevertheless the claimant was subject to a personal obligation to his mother to use the money only for the specified purpose, which in Scots law had a similar effect to a *Quistclose* trust, so that for the period in question the money lent did not form part of his capital. It is perhaps unclear to a non-Scots lawyer just why a trust could not be recognised (would not the mother also be a beneficiary?), but that appears not to matter as the essence of the decision is in the effect of the personal obligation identified by the judge.

So far as resulting trusts in general are concerned, the most authoritative statement is that of Lord Browne-Wilkinson, speaking for the majority of the House of Lords, in *Westdeutsche Landesbank Girozentrale v Islington LBC* [1996] AC 669 at 708:

"Under existing law a resulting trust arises in two sets of circumstances: (A) where A makes a voluntary payment to B or pays (wholly or in part) for the purchase of property which is vested either in B alone or in the joint names of A and B, there is a presumption that A did not intend to make a gift to B: the money or property is held on trust for A (if he is the sole provider of the money) or in the case of a joint purchase by A and B in shares proportionate to their contributions. It is important to stress that this is only a presumption, which presumption is easily rebutted either by the counter-presumption of advancement or by direct evidence of A's intention to make an outright transfer .... (B) [*Quistclose* cases]."

That statement was cited in para.48 of *SSWP v LB of Tower Hamlets and CT (IS & HB)* [2018] UKUT 25 (AAC), where it was also noted that in *R(SB) 49/83* Commissioner Hallett stated that "the principle that purchase of land in the name of another gives rise to a resulting trust for the true purchaser has been settled for centuries". The principle rests on giving effect to the common intention of the parties.

In *R(SB) 49/83* the claimant had bought a house, but said that this was on behalf of his son, who had not been able to obtain a loan in his own name but was paying off the loan. The Commissioner held that if this could be established, the claimant would hold the house on a resulting trust for his son. However, he stressed that the credibility of the claimant's evidence, in the light of any further documents that came forward, needed to be carefully tested. For instance why did the house have to be transferred into the claimant's name, rather than him guaranteeing a loan to his son?

2.377

In *CT* the claimant bought a house in her sole name with a buy-to-let mortgage, intending that the mortgage interest would be met by the rental income. The purchase price and expenses came to £377,728.09. The mortgage loan was for £310,215. The claimant only had £250 capital to contribute, so agreed with a friend, Mr G, for him to contribute the remaining £67,263.09. They could reach no agreement at the time about what interest that gave him in the property. On claims for income support and housing benefit the claimant was initially treated as having capital of the value of the house less the amount of the incumbrance of the mortgage and 10% for expenses of sale. A tribunal held that she held the property on a resulting trust for Mr G. That decision was upheld by the Upper Tribunal on the basis that the claimant's beneficial interest was only 0.04% of the value (£250 as against £67,362.09). That result would follow from the plain application of the general resulting trust principles, in that the payments of mortgage had no effect on the beneficial interests, as while the house was let they came out of the rent (to which the two would have been entitled in proportion to their beneficial interests). That was not affected by a period in which the claimant was forced to live in the house while her own home was uninhabitable and she paid the mortgage interest. That was equivalent to her paying an occupation rent.

The main submission made by the Secretary of State on the appeal to the Upper Tribunal was that the tribunal's approach was incompatible with that of the Supreme Court in *Jones v Kernott* [2011] UKSC 53; [2012] 1 A.C. 776, under which what was fair in the light of the whole course of dealings between the parties was determinative. Judge Poynter provides a helpful analysis of the effect of the decisions in *Stack v Dowden* [2007] UKHL 17; [2007] 2 A.C. 432 and *Jones v Kernott* in "family home" type cases. The principles applicable in such cases were summarised as follows in para.51 of the joint judgment of Lady Hale and Lord Walker in *Jones v Kernott* (the words in square brackets in sub-para.(1) were added by Judge Poynter when citing this passage in *CT*):

"*Conclusion*
51. In summary, therefore, the following are the principles applicable in a case such as this, where a family home is bought in the joint names of a cohabiting couple who are both responsible for any mortgage, but without any express declaration of their beneficial interests.
(1) The starting point is that equity follows the law and they are joint tenants both in law and in equity. [As this decision will be read by people who are not legally qualified, I should explain that the phrase "joint tenants" in this context has a technical legal meaning and is not a generic reference to any co-owner. To summarise, the distinction being drawn by the Supreme Court is between "joint tenants", who always own a property equally, and "tenants in common" who may own a property in equal shares but do not necessarily do so.]
(2) That presumption can be displaced by showing (a) that the parties had a different common intention at the time when they acquired the home, or (b) that they later formed the common intention that their respective shares would change.
(3) Their common intention is to be deduced objectively from their conduct:

"the relevant intention of each party is the intention which was reasonably understood by the other party to be manifested by that party's words and conduct notwithstanding that he did not consciously formulate that intention in his own mind or even acted with some different intention which he did not communicate to the other party" (Lord Diplock in *Gissing v Gissing* [1971] A.C. 886, 906).

Examples of the sort of evidence which might be relevant to drawing such inferences are given in *Stack v Dowden*, at para 69.

(4) In those cases where it is clear either (a) that the parties did not intend joint tenancy at the outset, or (b) had changed their original intention, but it is not possible to ascertain by direct evidence or by inference what their actual intention was as to the shares in which they would own the property, "the answer is that each is entitled to that share which the court considers fair having regard to the whole course of dealing between them in relation to the property": Chadwick LJ in *Oxley v Hiscock* [2005] Fam 211, para.69. In our judgment, "the whole course of dealing ... in relation to the property" should be given a broad meaning, enabling a similar range of factors to be taken into account as may be relevant to ascertaining the parties' actual intentions.

(5) Each case will turn on its own facts. Financial contributions are relevant but there are many other factors which may enable the court to decide what shares were either intended (as in case (3)) or fair (as in case (4))."

Judge Poynter took the view that, while the "family home" category has been expanded to some extent beyond the confines of cohabiting couples, it could not apply in *CT*, where the purchase of the house was intended as an investment, with no intention of the claimant and Mr G living together there or anywhere else. Therefore the traditional resulting trust approach was correct.

2.378   However, the important, but somewhat inconclusive, Privy Council case of *Marr v Collie* [2017] UKPC 17, [2018] A.C. 631 shows that things are not as simple as that, while not throwing doubt on the actual result in *CT*.

Mr Marr, a banker, and Mr Collie, a building contractor, were in a personal relationship in the Bahamas from 1991 to 2008. During that time a number of properties were acquired, not for them to live in, that were conveyed into their joint names. Mr Marr provided the purchase price and paid the mortgage instalments. According to Mr Marr, Mr Collie repeatedly assured him that he would make an equal contribution to the costs, but never did. According to Mr Collie, he was to carry out renovations and works on the properties, some of which he did. There were also purchases of a truck and a boat that were registered in joint names. After the relationship broke down Mr Marr brought proceedings claiming that he was entitled to full beneficial ownership of those properties and the truck and boat. At first instance, the judge, relying on *Laskar v Laskar* [2008] EWCA Civ 347, [2008] 1 W.L.R. 2695, held that the *Stack v Dowden* presumption that a conveyance into joint names indicated a legal and beneficial joint tenancy unless the contrary was proved applied only in the "domestic consumer context". So, as the properties were intended primarily as investments, that presumption did not apply even though there was a personal relationship between the parties and there was a presumption that there was a resulting trust in favour of Mr Marr unless Mr Collie could demonstrate that a gift to him had been intended, which the judge concluded he had failed to do. On appeal, the Court of Appeal of the Bahamas found that there was cogent evidence of Mr Marr having intended that the beneficial interest in the properties be shared equally, so that the presumption of a resulting trust was rebutted. However, that was in large part in reliance on a 2005 email from Mr Marr that he had not been given the opportunity to comment on. For that reason and because the Court of Appeal's conclusions on the common intention of the parties failed to address a number of factual findings by the first instance judge, the Privy Council allowed Mr Marr's appeal, but was unable to substitute a decision in view of the absence of a proper examination of the parties' intentions. Thus the discussion of the general principles noted below was not anchored in a concrete application to specific findings of fact.

Lord Kerr, giving the judgment of a Board that included both Lady Hale and Lord Neuberger, opined in para.40 that by stating in para.58 of *Stack v Dowden* that the starting point, at least in the domestic consumer context, was that conveyance into joint names indicates both legal and beneficial joint tenancy, unless and until the contrary is proved, Lady Hale did not intend that the principle be confined to the purely domestic setting. Nor was *Laskar*, a case of the purchase of the claimant's council house, for letting out, effectively funded by the claimant's daughter, to be regarded as an authority to the contrary. Thus where a property was bought in the joint names of a cohabiting couple, even if that was as an investment, the "resulting trust solution" did not provide the inevitable answer on beneficial ownership (para.49). However, "save perhaps where there is no evidence from which the parties' intentions can be identified", the answer was not to be provided by the triumph of one presumption over another (Lady Hale's starting point as against the resulting trust solution). Rather, the context of the parties' common intention, or lack of it, was crucial (para.54) and apparently (it is not entirely clear) it was accepted that that common intention could alter after the initial acquisition of the property (para.55).

Applying those principles to the facts of *CT*, it would seem that there was a lack of any common intention both at the time of acquisition of the property and subsequently about what beneficial interest the claimant and Mr G should have. Accordingly, either the case was one where the resulting trust solution should apply for that reason (most probable) or it was one where the lack of common intention in the context of an investment property was sufficient to displace the starting point of the beneficial interests following the legal ownership. 2.379

The main lesson to be taken from *Marr v Collie* is perhaps that great care needs to be taken in making findings of fact about the parties' intentions, common or otherwise, both at the time of acquisition of the property in question and subsequently. In addition it is noteworthy that the Privy Council apparently accepted that the same approach applied to the acquisition of chattels, in the form of the truck and boat, as to the acquisition of real property. What in particular is left unclear, even though the notion of a clash of presumptions was rejected, is on which party does the burden fall of showing that the common intention works in their favour. Or is the common intention to be identified on an objective analysis of the evidence, including the evaluation of credibility, without resort to propositions about burden of proof?

The same principle can apply to cases where a claimant has an account into which someone else's money is put either solely or mixed with the claimant's own money. In *R(IS) 9/08* payments of a boarding-out allowance which the foster parent had saved up over the years were not held on trust for the children in her care. However, *MC v SSWP (IS)* [2015] UKUT 600 (AAC) reaches the opposite conclusion where the claimant had saved up her daughters' disability living allowance in an account in the claimant's name. A tribunal accepted that in relation to an earlier period the claimant was holding the money on trust for her daughters. However, when she used a substantial part of the money to meet rent arrears, the tribunal considered that this suggested that what was previously held on trust had been subsequently "converted" into the claimant's capital by her actions. Judge Wikeley holds, however, that this was wrong in law. First, as the claimant had been made an appointee by DWP to act on behalf of her daughters in benefit matters, she was acting as a *de facto* trustee. Second, this was an obvious example of an informal trust over money, created without any legal formalities. Third, paying off rent arrears helped to keep a roof over the daughters' heads and was a perfectly reasonable use of their savings, consistent with the purposes of the trust. See also *DL v Southampton CC (CTB)* [2010] UKUT 453 (AAC) for a case where the tribunal failed to make adequate findings of fact about the circumstances in which the claimant's daughter had transferred funds into the claimant's savings account, so as to be able to decide whether there was a resulting trust or not.

2.380 *JK v SSWP (JSA)* [2010] UKUT 437 (AAC), reported as [2011] AACR 26, holds that by asking whether there was a trust the tribunal had posed the wrong question in relation to Scots law. It should have considered whether the presumption of ownership had been rebutted under Scots law. The claimant had contended that some of the money in his and his wife's joint account belonged to his mother-in-law. Applying the principle in *Cairns v Davidson* 1913 S.C. 1054, the tribunal should have considered, by way of such written or oral evidence available to it that it accepted, whether the presumption in favour of all the money in the joint account belonging to the claimant and his wife had been rebutted, so as to establish whether or not some of it belonged to his mother-in law.

It will sometimes be the case that the claimant's explanation as to why they are holding capital for someone else may involve some unlawful purpose, *e.g.* in order to conceal assets from the Revenue. In *MC v SSWP* [2010] UKUT 29 (AAC) the claimant had purchased a house for £26,000 in her own name. The money had come from her bank account. She asserted that £14,000 of the £26,000 had been paid into her account by her husband by way of a gift for their son and the remaining £12,000 was her son's money which had been paid into her bank account because he had no bank account of his own. The tribunal found that the only explanation for her son providing the £12,000 was to "deny monies obtained illicitly to the revenue or that the sums were obtained from some illegal sources" and that as a consequence her son was estopped from denying that the capital belonged to the claimant. Judge Turnbull points out, however, that this was wrong in law. As the House of Lords held in *Tinsley v Milligan* [1994] 1 A.C. 340, the principle that prevents a person putting forward evidence of his own wrongdoing in order to establish a resulting trust in his favour only applies where the person needs to put forward that evidence in order to *rebut* the presumption of advancement or of resulting trust. It does not apply where the person does not need to assert the illegality and only needs to show that he paid or contributed to the purchase price. In this case the claimant's son would be able to rely on the presumption of resulting trust without asserting any illegality. The question therefore was, in so far as it was accepted that the money was provided by her son, whether there was a resulting trust in his favour or whether he had intended to make a gift to the claimant.

DF v SSWP (ESA) [2015] UKUT 611 (AAC) concerns the question of whether the claimant could argue that he was not the beneficial owner of the funds in an Individual Savings Account ("ISA") that was in his name. One of the conditions for an ISA account is that money invested in the account is in the beneficial ownership of the account holder (see reg.4(6) of the Individual Savings Account Regulations 1998 (SI 1998/1870) (ISA Regulations 1998)). The claimant maintained that the money in his ISA account really belonged to his daughter. His daughter confirmed this, stating that the ISA was designed to keep her money away from an unreliable partner. The Secretary of State argued that a person in whose name an ISA is held has to be regarded as the beneficial owner of the money in the account, relying on the decision in *CIS/2836/2006*. While *CIS/2836/2006* concerned the Personal Equity Plan Regulations 1989 (SI 1989/469), the ISA Regulations 1998 were said to be identical.

2.381 Judge Mitchell, however, concludes that *CIS/2836/2006* is restricted to "presumption of advancement" cases, i.e. cases in which the money is given by someone standing in loco parentis to a child, or by a husband to a wife, where there is a presumption that a gift was intended (note that the presumption of advancement was due to be abolished by s.199 of the Equality Act 2010 but this section has not yet been brought into force). To the extent that *CIS/2836/2006* could be read as going further, in his view it was not consistent with the House of Lords' decision in *Tinsley v Milligan* [1994] 1 A.C. 34.

He also holds that *CIS/2836/2006* did not decide that ISA-type legislation operates to extinguish beneficial interests of third parties in ISA deposits. Neither the ISA Regulations 1998 nor the enabling power under which they were made (s.333(2) Income and Corporation Taxes Act 1988) had the effect of altering existing rights in relation to property. The legislation was only concerned with creating a special account with special tax advantages.

Judge Mitchell then goes on to reject the Secretary of State's argument that the law of illegality meant that, as a matter of public policy, the claimant could not rely on a beneficial interest that he had previously denied. This was inconsistent with the Supreme Court's decision in *Hounga v Allen* [2014] UKSC 47; [2014] 1 W.L.R. 2889 and the Court of Appeal's decision in *R. (Best) v Secretary of State for Justice* (Rev 1) [2015] EWCA Civ 17. In his view it was better for a First-tier Tribunal in an ISA case to ignore the role that may or may not be played by the law of illegality and simply focus on whether it accepted that the beneficial interest in the funds lay elsewhere.

He does, however, point out the risks that a claimant runs in arguing that a third party has a beneficial interest in the sums deposited in an ISA, namely, conceding that any ISA tax reliefs were improperly awarded and the possibility of criminal proceedings for a tax offence under s.106A of the Taxes Management Act 1970 (see para.17 of the decision).   **2.382**

An illustration of a constructive trust, which does not operate on the basis of a common intention but on it being unconscionable for the person with the legal interest to deny the beneficial interest of another, is *R(SB) 23/85*. The claimant's wife in a home-made and legally ineffective deed of gift purported to give an uninhabitable property to her son. He, as intended, carried out the works to make it habitable. The Commissioner holds that, although a court will not normally "complete" such an "uncompleted gift" in favour of someone who has not given valuable consideration, one of the situations in which a transfer of the property will be ordered is where the intended recipient is induced to believe that he has or will have an interest in the property and acts on that belief to his detriment. Thus in the meantime the claimant's wife held the property merely as a "bare trustee" and could not lawfully transfer it to anyone but the son. There is discussion of what kind of action might give rise to the right to complete the gift in *R(SB) 7/87*, where there was evidence of the claimant's intention to give a flat to her two sons, but all that one son had done in reliance was to redecorate the flat prior to its sale. See also *CIS/807/1991* on proprietary estoppel.

Note also the doctrine of secret trusts, under which a person who receives property under an intestacy when the deceased refrained from making a will in reliance on that person's promise to carry out their expressed intentions, holds the property on trust to carry out those intentions (*CSB/989/1985*). The doctrine also applies to property left by will where on the face of the will the property has been left to A but this is on the understanding that A is merely a trustee of it in favour of B.

For an example of where there may have been a secret trust, see *GK v SSWP (JSA)* [2012] UKUT 115 (AAC). In that case the claimant had inherited money from her aunt which she understood from conversations with her aunt was to be shared between her five children and herself. She used the money to purchase some land, which although in her sole name, she regarded as belonging to all six of them. Judge Mark held that the tribunal had erred in not considering whether there was a secret trust.   **2.383**

CIS/213/2004 and *CIS/214/2004* concerned the applicability of French law. A property in France had been purchased in the name of the claimant but the purchase price and renovation costs had been met by Ms V. Ms V was not the claimant's partner but they had a son and the purpose of putting the property in the claimant's name was so that their son and not Ms V's other children would inherit it (under French law all five of Ms V's children would otherwise have been entitled to an interest in the property). On the same day that the property was purchased the claimant executed a holograph will bequeathing a "usufruct" (the French equivalent of a life interest) in the property to Ms V. Applying the Recognition of Trusts Act 1987, which implements the Hague Convention of 1986 on the law applicable to trusts and their recognition, the Commissioner concludes that French law was the applicable law. But since French law does not recognise the concept of a trust, it followed that there was no resulting or constructive trust in favour of Ms V (although in the Commissioner's view if English law had been applicable the facts would have given rise to such a trust). The Commissioner directed the Secretary of State to obtain a further opinion as to the remedies available under French law to Ms V if the claimant decided to treat the property as his own, but after receiving this concluded that there was no reason under French law or otherwise why the value of the property should not be included in the claimant's capital. The claimant appealed against this decision to the Court of Appeal but the appeal was dismissed (*Martin v Secretary of State for Work and Pensions* [2009] EWCA Civ 1289; [2010] AACR 9).

It will be an error of law if a tribunal fails to consider the question of the applicable law in relation to property abroad (*MB v Royal Borough of Kensington & Chelsea (HB)* [2011] UKUT 321 (AAC)). The claimant in *MB* was an Irish national, who had, while domiciled and resident in Ireland, bought a property in Ireland with the assistance of a mortgage from an Irish bank. In those circumstances it was difficult to see how the applicable law could be other than Irish law but the tribunal had not referred to this issue at all, nor had it sought any evidence as to the nature and content of Irish law and the Irish law of trusts (foreign law is a question of fact (see *R(G) 2/00*, at para.20)).

Choses in action

2.384   There is also a remarkable range of interests in property which do have a present market value and so are actual capital resources. These are usually things in action (or choses in action), rights to sue for something. Debts, even where they are not due to be paid for some time, are things in action which can be sold. A good example is *R(SB) 31/83* where the claimant in selling a house allowed the purchaser a mortgage of £4,000, to be redeemed in six months. The debt conferred a right to sue and had to be valued at what could be obtained on the open market. In *CJSA 204/2002* the claimant had lent her son £8,500 for the deposit on a flat. The Commissioner holds that the legal debt owed by the son to the claimant had to be valued in order to decide whether the claimant had actual capital in excess of £8,000 (which was then the prescribed limit). The terms of the loan, including the rate of any interest and whether there was any security for the loan, as well as the terms of repayment, were clearly relevant to this valuation. Once the value of the loan had been determined, the question of deprivation of capital then had to be considered. To the extent that the value of the loan was less than £8,500, to that extent the claimant had deprived herself of capital. However, on the facts the Commissioner found that the claimant had not deprived herself of the capital for the purpose of securing entitlement to, or increasing the amount of, jobseeker's allowance (see further the note to reg.51(1)). See also *JC v SSWP* [2009] UKUT 22 (AAC) which points out that the value of the loan will depend on whether it is likely to be recoverable. If the claimant had lent the money with no expectation of getting it back he had in effect reduced the value of the *chose in action* to nil. The issue of deprivation of capital then arose. *R 2/09(IS)*, a Northern Ireland decision, gives further guidance on the approach to choses in action and their value.

In *GS v DSD (IS)* [2012] NI Com 284 (another Northern Ireland decision) the claimant agreed in June 2004 to buy a house (not yet built) from Mr McK in return for the transfer of ownership of the claimant's present house, plus £33,000. The £33,000 was paid by cheque in August 2006. However, the building work was delayed due to the illness of Mr McK's brother and the house was only eventually built during 2009. But by March 2010 (the date of the decision under appeal) the agreement still had not been fulfilled due to difficulties with Mr McK's title to the land. Mr McK accepted that the £33,000 deposit would be returned if these difficulties could not be resolved. Commissioner Stockman points out that a chose in action can only arise upon breach of contract, or possibly frustration of contract; the mere existence of the contract did not give rise to the right to sue for return of the deposit. The difficulty was determining whether there had been a breach of contract and in identifying when that occurred. In the circumstances of this case, where there was no date for the completion of the contract and the delay in completing the building work had been waived by the claimant because of the personal friendship between Mr McK and himself, the claimant would not have had a strong case for breach of contract for unreasonable delay. This would have a resultant effect on the value of the chose in action, for which there was unlikely to be a ready market. The Commissioner decides that the value of the chose in action was nil from August 2006 and £3,000 from November 2008 up to March 2010.

Similarly, a life interest in a trust fund or the right to receive income under a liferent in Scots law is a present asset which can be sold and has a market value (*R(SB) 2/84, R(SB) 43/84, R(SB) 15/86* and *R(SB) 13/87*). The practical effect is reversed by para.13 of Sch.10. An action for breach of fiduciary duty against an attorney appointed under the Enduring Powers of Attorney Act 1985 who had used the claimant's capital to repay her own debts also constitutes actual capital; so too would a claim against the attorney for misapplication of capital on the ground that she had made gifts outside the circumstances sanctioned by s.3(5) of the 1985 Act (this allows an attorney to make gifts (to herself or others) "provided that the value of each such gift is not unreasonable having regard to all the circumstances and in particular the size of the donor's estate") (*R(IS) 17/98*).

Bank or building society accounts

A more direct way of holding capital is in a bank or building society account. In *CSB 296/1985* the claimant's solicitor received £12,000 damages on behalf of the claimant and placed the money on deposit, presumably in the solicitor's client account. The Commissioner held that the £12,000 was an actual resource of the claimant, on the basis that there was no difference in principle between monies being held by a solicitor on behalf of a client and monies held by a bank or building society on behalf of a customer. This decision was upheld by the Court of Appeal in *Thomas v Chief Adjudication Officer* (reported as *R(SB) 17/87*). Russell LJ says "the possession of this money by the solicitors as the agent for the claimant was, in every sense of the term, possession by the claimant."

However, note *CIS 984/2002* which holds that money held by the claimant's solicitor pending quantification of the statutory charge to the Legal Services Commission under s.10(7) of the Access to Justice Act 1999 was not part of the claimant's capital. Until that quantification had been carried out, it was not possible to identify any particular amount as the claimant's capital. Another way of looking at it was to treat the statutory charge as an incumbrance for the purpose of reg.49(a)(ii) (see *CIS 368/1993*). Nor was any part of the money available to the claimant on application for the purposes of reg.51(2).

See also *LC v Bournemouth Borough Council (HB)* [2016] UKUT 175 (AAC), discussed in the notes to reg.51(2), where the proceeds of sale of a former matrimonial home were being held in a solicitors' client account until the claimant's partner and his ex-wife could agree how the sum was to be split or the issue was resolved by a court order. In Judge White's view the value of the capital prior to agreement or an order of the court would be minimal.

The approach taken in *Thomas* seems to involve valuing the amount of money directly, not as a technical chose in action. However, the importance of the legal relationship between a bank and a customer being one of debtor and creditor was revealed in *CSB 598/1987*. A large cheque was paid into the claimant's wife's bank account on October 9, 1987. The amount was credited to her account on that date, but the cheque was not cleared until October 15. The bank's paying-in slips reserved the bank's right to "postpone payment of cheques drawn against uncleared effects which may have been credited to the account." The effect was that the bank did not accept the relationship of debtor and creditor on the mere paying in of a cheque. Thus the amount did not become part of the claimant's actual resources until October 15. A person who deliberately refrains from paying in a cheque may be fixed with notional capital under reg.51.

CIS/255/2005 concerned the effect on capital of the issue of a cheque. The Commissioner holds that the claimant's capital was reduced from the date that the

2.385

2.386

cheque was issued (this would not apply if the cheque was postdated). After that time she could not honestly withdraw money from her bank account so as to leave insufficient funds to meet the cheque.

In *R(IS) 15/96* the Commissioner confirms that money in a building society or bank (or solicitor's client) account is an actual resource in the form of a chose in action. It is not, as the SSAT had decided, held in trust. If the money is in an account from which it can be withdrawn at any time, its value is the credit balance (less any penalties for early withdrawal, etc.). But if the money cannot be withdrawn for a specified term the value will be less (although the notional capital rules may come into play in respect of the difference in value: *CIS 494/1990*; see also *R(IS) 8/04*.

2.387   It was pointed out in *Q v SSWP (JSA)* [2020] UKUT 49 (AAC) that any joint bank or building society account involves a trust. In the simplest case the legal interest in the chose in action can be held as joint tenants in trust for the account-holders as joint tenants. The beneficial interest is not necessarily held as a joint tenancy. It depends on the source of the payments into the account and the intentions of the parties. The presumption that the beneficial interests follow the legal interests may not always be appropriate. Thus, in *Q*, funds derived from the claimant's personal injury compensation were held in joint accounts with one or other of her parents. Since there was no suggestion of any intention to make a gift to her parents there would be a resulting trust under which she and the parent would hold the funds for the claimant's benefit. See also *CIS/7097/1999*, detailed in the notes to reg.52, where the proceeds (£7,000) of the cashing-in of the claimant's husband's National Savings funds after he went into a nursing home were paid into their joint bank account. The intention was that the money should be used to meet the nursing home fees. Commissioner Howell held that the normal presumption of joint beneficial ownership between a husband and wife operating a joint bank account did not apply. The intention was plain that the £7,000 should remain the husband's sole property and it was only paid into the joint account for convenience. The beneficial interest was held under a tenancy in common reflecting that intention.

It may sometimes be necessary to consider the written terms governing the account, which may include an express declaration that the beneficial interest in the funds in the account is to be held under a joint tenancy. That would prevent the operation of any resulting trust arguments (see *Whitlock v Moree* [2017] UKPC 44)

Interests in trusts

2.388   The nature of interests in capital under trusts gives rise to several problems. It is clear that a person may have an absolute vested interest under a trust, although payment is deferred, e.g. until the age of 21. This was the case in *R(SB) 26/86*, where the resource was held to be the person's share of the fund. However, an interest may be contingent on reaching a particular age. This appears to have been one of the assumptions on which the Court of Appeal decided the unsatisfactory case of *Peters v Chief Adjudication Officer, R(SB) 3/89*. It was conceded that sums were held on trust to be paid over to each of three sisters on attaining the age of 18, with the power to advance up to 50 per cent of the capital before then. In the end, the Court of Appeal accepted the valuation of half of the full value for each sister under 18. The precise finding may depend on the supplementary benefit rule on discretionary trusts, which has not been translated into the income support legislation. But some statements about the general market value of such interests are made. May LJ says "in an appropriate market a discretionary entitlement of up to 50 per cent now and at least 50 per cent in, say, six months in a given case, or three to four years in another, could well be said to have a value greater than 50 per cent of the capital value of the trust." This clearly supports the view that a contingent interest has a market value and so is actual capital. See also *CTC 4713/2002* which concerned a similar trust in favour of the claimant's son to that in *Peters* (although in this case the trustees had power to advance the whole of the fund). The Commissioner notes that in *Peters* the Court of Appeal had accepted the valuation agreed by the parties without argument.

He acknowledged that each case must turn on its facts and that valuation of different interests would differ depending on such factors as the nature of the underlying investments (there was evidence in this case that due to lack of investor confidence the market value of the fund was much diminished); in addition in this case, unlike *Peters*, the whole of the fund could be advanced. However, he concluded that the Court of Appeal's approach in *Peters* led to a valuation of the claimant's son's equitable interest as being more or less equal to the whole net value of the trust fund (less 10 per cent for the expenses of sale).

All interests which can be sold or borrowed against will need to be considered. However, in the case of an interest under a discretionary trust, the DWP will normally only take payments of capital (or income) into account when they are actually made.

In *R(IS) 9/04* it was argued that funds held by the Court of Protection were analogous to those held by a discretionary trustee. Since neither the claimant nor her receiver could insist on the Court releasing any part of the funds it was contended that the market value of the claimant's actual interest was so small as to be negligible. However, the Commissioner followed *CIS 7127/1995* in holding that the entire beneficial interest in the funds administered by the Court remained with the claimant to whom alone they belonged. The fact the Court had discretionary powers of *control* over the management of a patient's property for his or her benefit did not mean that the patient's beneficial *ownership* had ceased. The funds therefore had to be valued at their current market value, less any appropriate allowance for sale expenses, in the normal way (see reg.49).

Realisation of assets

R(SB) 18/83 stresses that there are more ways of realising assets than sale. In particular, assets can be charged to secure a loan which can be used to meet requirements. In that case the asset was a minority shareholding in a family company. The Commissioner says that only a person prepared to lend money without security would do so in such circumstances. The articles of association of the company provided that if a shareholder wanted to sell shares they were first to be offered to the existing shareholders at the fair value fixed by the auditors. The Commissioner holds that the regulations do not require assets to be valued at a figure higher than anything the person would realise on them, i.e. the auditor's fair value. This is in line with the purpose of the capital cut-off that a claimant can draw on resources until they fall below the limit.

2.389

This approach to valuation can usefully deal with unrealisable assets. See the notes to reg.49. However, it is no part of the definition of capital that it should be immediately realisable, although its market value may be affected by such factors (see the notes to reg.49 on valuation). It remains possible for claimants to be fixed with large amounts of actual capital that are not immediately available to them by everyday means, but may have a value in some specialised market.

Deduction of liabilities

The general rule is that the whole of a capital resource is to be taken into account. Liabilities are not to be deducted from the value *(R(SB) 2/83)*. *SSWP v GF (ESA)* [2017] UKUT 333 (AAC) is an illustration of the application of that principle. For one part of the period in issue the claimant's brother-in-law had paid a costs order of some £48,000 made against the claimant in the expectation at least that he would be repaid once the 120-day notice period for withdrawal of funds in the claimant's building society bond with a balance of £75,000 had expired. On the evidence available the judge rightly concluded that there was no implied, resulting or constructive trust and that the claimant's debt did not change the beneficial ownership of the funds in the bond. However, there could in other similar cases be evidence of discussions or arrangements before the brother-in-law made his payment that could lead to a conclusion either that the debt had been secured on the claimant's rights in the bond or that the claimant had made a declaration of trust. In *GF* itself no such argument could have helped the claimant because even

2.390

if he had not been the beneficial owner of £48,000 of the balance in the bond, the value of the remainder (even subject to the 120-day notice provision) would no doubt have exceeded £16,000.

Otherwise, it is only if a debt is secured on the capital asset that it can be deducted, at the stage specifically required by reg.49 or 50 (*R(IS) 21/93*). See the notes to reg.49 and note *JRL v SSWP (JSA)* [2011] UKUT 63 (AAC), reported as [2011] AACR 30. There, the claimant had three accounts with the same bank, of which one was in credit, one was overdrawn and one had a nil balance. The three-judge panel pointed out that this meant that the claimant was both a creditor and a debtor of the same body. Under the bank's terms and conditions, the bank had a contractual right to debit at any time any of a customer's accounts which were in credit with sums sufficient to clear the customer's indebtedness to the bank. This created what was effectively a charge on the customer's credit balance(s). The market value of the account that was in credit was therefore its net value after deduction of the amount of the claimant's overdraft on his other account.

Disregard of capital of child or young person

2.391   **47.**—[¹. . .].

AMENDMENT

1. Social Security (Working Tax Credit and Child Tax Credit) (Consequential Amendments) Regulations 2003 (SI 2003/455) reg.2 and Sch.1 para.11 (April 6, 2004, except in "transitional cases" and see further the note to reg.17 of the Income Support Regulations).

GENERAL NOTE

2.392   This regulation provided that the capital of a child or young person who was a member of the claimant's family was not to be treated as the claimant's (see the 2003 edition of this volume for this regulation and the notes to it). However, with effect from April 6, 2004 (except in "transitional cases"—see the note to reg.17) amounts for children and young persons have been removed from the income support scheme; financial assistance to help with the cost of bringing up a child or young person is now to be provided through the child tax credit system (see Vol.IV of this series). As a consequence, under the new form of reg.23 (in force from April 6, 2004, except for "transitional cases"—see the note to reg.17) neither the income nor the capital of a child or young person counts as the claimant's (see the new form of reg.23(2) and the notes to that regulation). This regulation has therefore been revoked. It does however, remain in force for "transitional cases"—see the note to reg.17.

For income support claimants who had an award of child tax credit before April 6, 2004 see reg.7 of the Social Security (Working Tax Credit and Child Tax Credit) (Consequential Amendments) Regulations 2003 (SI 2003/455) (as amended) at p.1765 and the notes to that regulation.

Income treated as capital

2.393   **48.**—(1) Any [². . .] bounty derived from employment to which paragraph 7 of Schedule 8 applies [²and paid at intervals of at least one year] shall be treated as capital.

(2) Except in the case of an amount to which section 23(5)(a)(ii) of the Act [SSCBA, s.126(5)(a)(ii)] (refund of tax in trade dispute cases) [²or regulation 41(4) (capital treated as income)] applies, any amount by way of a refund of income tax deducted from profit or emoluments chargeable to income tax under Schedule D or E shall be treated as capital.

(3) Any holiday pay which is not earnings under regulation 35(1)(d) (earnings of employed earners) shall be treated as capital.

(4) Except any income derived from capital disregarded under paragraph 1, 2, 4, 6, [³12 [¹⁴25 to 28, 44 or 45] of Schedule 10, any income derived from capital shall be treated as capital but only from the date it is normally due to be credited to the claimant's account.

(5) Subject to paragraph (6), in the case of employment as an employed earner, any advance of earnings or any loan made by the claimant's employer shall be treated as capital.

[¹(6) Paragraph (5) shall not apply to a person to whom section 23 of the Act [SSCBA, s.126] (trade disputes) applies or in respect of whom section 20(3) of the Act [SSCBA, s.124(1)] (conditions of entitlement to income support) has effect as modified by section 23A(b) [SSCBA, s.127(b)] (effect of return to work).]

(7) Any payment under section 30 of the Prison Act 1952 (payments for discharged prisoners) or allowance under section 17 of the Prisons (Scotland) Act 1952 (allowances to prisoners on discharge) shall be treated as capital.

[¹¹(8) [¹³. . .]

(8A) [¹³. . .].]

[³(9) Any charitable or voluntary payment which is not made or not due to be made at regular intervals, other than one to which paragraph (10) applies, shall be treated as capital.

(10) This paragraph applies to a payment—

(a) which is made to a person to whom section 23 of the Act [SSCBA, s.126] (trade disputes) applies or in respect of whom section 20(3) of the Act [SSCBA, s.124(1)] (conditions of entitlement to income support) has effect as modified by section 23A(b) of the Act [SSCBA, s.127(b)] (effect of return to work) [¹³ or to the partner] of such a person;

(b) [¹³. . .].]

[²²(ab) which is a Grenfell Tower payment.]

(c) which is made under [¹⁷or by] the Macfarlane Trust[⁵, or the Macfarlane (Special Payments) Trust][⁶, the Macfarlane (Special Payments) (No.2) Trust][⁸, the Fund][¹⁰, the Eileen Trust][¹⁷, MFET Limited][¹⁸, the Skipton Fund, the Caxton Foundation] [¹⁹, the Scottish Infected Blood Support Scheme][²¹, an approved blood scheme][²⁰, the London Emergencies Trust, the We Love Manchester Emergency Fund][²², the National Emergencies Trust] or [⁹ the Independent Living [¹⁶ Fund (2006)]].]

[⁴(11) [¹⁵ . . .].]

[¹²(12) Any arrears of subsistence allowance which are paid to a claimant as a lump sum shall be treated as capital.]

AMENDMENTS

1. Income Support (General) Amendment Regulations 1988 (SI 1988/663) reg.21 (April 11, 1988).

2. Income Support (General) Amendment No.4 Regulations 1988 (SI 1988/1445) reg.11 (September 12, 1988).

3. Income Support (General) Amendment No.5 Regulations 1988 (SI 1988/2022) reg.11 (December 12, 1988).

4. Income Support (General) Amendment No.2 Regulations 1989 (SI 1989/1323) reg.15 (October 9, 1989).

5. Income-related Benefits Schemes Amendment Regulations 1990 (SI 1990/127) reg.33 (January 31, 1990).

6. Income-related Benefits Schemes and Social Security (Recoupment) Amendment Regulations 1991 (SI 1991/1175) reg.5 (May 11, 1991).

7. Income Support (General) Amendment Regulations 1992 (SI 1992/468) Sch. para.5 (April 6, 1992).

8. Income-related Benefits Schemes and Social Security (Recoupment) Amendment Regulations 1992 (SI 1992/1101) reg.6 (May 7, 1992).

9. Social Security Benefits (Miscellaneous Amendments) (No.2) Regulations 1993 (SI 1993/963) reg.2(3) (April 22, 1993).

10. Income-related Benefits Schemes and Social Security (Recoupment) Amendment Regulations 1993 (SI 1993/1249) reg.4(3) (May 14, 1993).

11. Social Security (Miscellaneous Amendments) Regulations 1998 (SI 1998/563) reg.4(1) (April 6, 1998).

12. Social Security Amendment (Employment Zones) Regulations 2000 (SI 2000/724) reg.3(2) (April 3, 2000).

13. Social Security (Working Tax Credit and Child Tax Credit) (Consequential Amendments) Regulations 2003 (SI 2003/455) reg.2 and Sch.1 para.12 (April 6, 2004, except in "transitional cases" and see further the note to reg.17 of the Income Support Regulations).

14. Social Security (Miscellaneous Amendments) (No.4) Regulations 2006 (SI 2006/2378) reg.5(4) (October 2, 2006).

15. Social Security (Miscellaneous Amendments) Regulations 2008 (SI 2008/698) reg.2(9) (April 14, 2008).

16. Social Security (Miscellaneous Amendments) (No.6) Regulations 2008 (SI 2008/2767) reg.2(6) (November 17, 2008).

17. Social Security (Miscellaneous Amendments) (No.2) Regulations 2010 (SI 2010/641 reg.2(3) (April 6, 2010).

18. Social Security (Miscellaneous Amendments) (No.3) Regulations 2011 (SI 2011/2425) reg.7(5) (October 31, 2011).

19. Social Security (Scottish Infected Blood Support Scheme) Regulations 2017 (SI 2017/329) reg.3(3) (April 3, 2017).

20. Social Security (Emergency Funds) (Amendment) Regulations 2017 (SI 2017/689) reg.2(3)(b) (June 19, 2017).

21. Social Security (Infected Blood and Thalidomide) Regulations 2017 (SI 2017/870) reg.2(3)(b) (October 23, 2017).

22. Social Security (Income and Capital) (Miscellaneous Amendments) Regulations 2020 (SI 2020/618) reg.2(4) (July 15, 2020).

DEFINITIONS

"the Act"—see reg.2(1).
"approved blood scheme"—*ibid.*
"claimant"—see SSCBA s.137(1) and reg.23(1).
"employed earner"—see reg.2(1).
"Grenfell Tower Payment"—*ibid.*
"MFET Limited"—*ibid.*
"Scottish Infected Blood Support Scheme"—*ibid.*
"subsistence allowance"—*ibid.*
"the Eileen Trust"—*ibid.*
"the Fund"—*ibid.*
"the Independent Living Funds"—*ibid.*
"the London Emergencies Trust"—*ibid.*
"the Macfarlane (Special Payments) Trust"—*ibid.*
"the Macfarlane (Special Payments) (No.2) Trust"—*ibid.*
"the Macfarlane Trust"—*ibid.*
"the National Emergencies Trust"—*ibid.*
"the We Love Manchester Emergency Fund"—*ibid.*

GENERAL NOTE

Most of these categories deemed to be capital are self-explanatory. They are then disregarded as income (Sch.9 para.32), although that seems unnecessary in view of the effect of reg.48 itself.

2.394

Paragraph (3)

Regulation 35(1)(d) makes holiday pay payable within four weeks of the termination or interruption of employment earnings (although such payments are disregarded under paras 1 and 2 of Sch.8 except in cases of suspension or part-time employment undertaken while on income support). Holiday pay outside reg.35(1)(d) would also count as earnings if it were not for reg.48(3) making it capital.

2.395

Paragraph (4)

The general rule is that the income from capital is not to be treated as income, but is added to the capital when it is credited. The excepted cases are premises and business assets plus trusts of personal injury compensation, and from October 2, 2006, funds held in court that derive from damages for personal injury or compensation for the death of a parent. In the case of such court funds (covered by paras 44 and 45 of Sch.10) and trust funds for personal injury compensation (covered by para.12 of Sch.10), it would appear that the income (not treated as capital) is disregarded as income under para.22 of Sch.9, despite it also apparently falling within para.15(1) and (5A)(c) or (e) of Sch.9. Income from the other excepted categories is only disregarded to the limited extent provided by para.22(2) of Sch.9. Income deemed to be capital by reg.48(4) does not need to be disregarded as income. If the process results in the amount of the claimant's capital exceeding the lower limit for the production of tariff income under reg.53 there is nothing to prevent the taking into account of that form of income.

2.396

For the rule in para.(4) to apply, the income must be derived from some capital asset of the claimant (*CIS 25/1989*). A 12-month assured shorthold tenancy is not a capital asset and income from the subletting of rooms is not "derived from" the tenancy (*CIS 82/1993*).

In *CIS 563/1991* the Commissioner considers that the effect of para.(4) is to treat a payment of income as capital for the same length of time as it would have been taken into account as income. So, for example, a payment of a month's rent from a property let out to tenants counts as capital for a month from the date that the claimant is due to receive it. After that, reg.48(4) ceases to have effect. Money spent during that month cannot form part of the claimant's actual capital at the end of the month (subject to the possible effect of the notional capital rule in reg.51(1)). Although saved-up income only metamorphoses into capital after deducting all relevant debts (see the notes to reg.23), the Commissioner considers that where para.(4) has effected a statutory metamorphosis, any unspent money at the end of the period covered by para.(4) continues to count as capital; it does not change into income and then immediately back into capital. Thus any outstanding debts will only reduce the amount of the capital if they are secured on the capital itself (reg.49(a)(ii)). *CIS 563/1991* also deals with the situation where more than one disregard in Sch.10 could apply. If a property was disregarded under para.26 (taking steps to dispose of premises) the rental income from it would count as income and would only be ignored to the extent allowed for by para.22(2) of Sch.9. But if the property was let by the claimant and the para.5 disregard also applied (as was possible under the form of para.5 in force before October 2, 1995: see the 1995 edition of J. Mesher and P. Wood, *Income-related Benefits: the Legislation*) the rental income would count as capital. The Commissioner concludes that considering reg.48(4) and para.22 of Sch.9 together, the primary rule was that income derived from capital was to be treated as capital. The disregard in para.5 therefore took precedence, and the rental income counted as capital, even during periods when the property could also be disregarded under one or more of the provisions listed in paras 22 and (4). Note that under the new form of para.5 a property let to

459

tenants by the claimant is no longer disregarded (see the note to para.5); the rent will still generally count as capital under the normal rule in para.(4) (unless one of the exceptions applies).

Paragraphs (8) and (8A)

2.397   These paragraphs provided that arrears of payments made by local authorities in Great Britain (para.(8)) and authorities in Northern Ireland (para.(8A)) towards the maintenance of children were treated as capital. For the disregard of current payments see para.25(1)(ba)–(d) of Sch.9. With effect from April 6, 2004 (except in "transitional cases"—see the note to reg.17) amounts for children and young persons have been removed from the income support scheme; financial assistance to help with the cost of bringing up a child or young person is now to be provided through the child tax credit system, see Vol.IV of this series. The revocation of paras (8) and (8A) is another of the consequential changes that apply from April 6, 2004 (except in "transitional cases"—see the note to reg.17) as a result of income support becoming an "adults only" benefit.

Paragraphs (9) and (10)

2.398   Regulations 24 and 33 on charitable or voluntary payments were revoked from December 1988. See the notes to para.15 of Sch.9 for the meaning of "charitable" and "voluntary." The general rule in para.(9) is that such payments not made or due to be made at regular intervals are to be treated as capital. This rule does not apply to the two kinds of payments set out in para.(10), but see the disregard as capital of payments of the kind covered by sub-para.(c) (Sch.10, para.22). However, there is nothing to say how such payments are to be treated. Presumably they must be treated as capital or income according to general legal principles (on which see the notes to reg.23). Similarly, there is nothing expressly to say how payments which are made or due to be made regularly are to be treated, but no doubt they will usually have the character of income and then be disregarded under para.15 of Sch.9.

In *CJSA/2336/2005* the claimant ceased work on September 3, 2004 and claimed JSA. Her mother lent her £200 to pay her rent on October 1, 2004, the agreement being that the money would be repaid on October 31, 2004. However, as no decision had been made on the claimant's claim for JSA her mother lent her a further £200 for the rent due on November 1, 2004. The claimant's claim for JSA was refused on November 11, 2004 on the grounds that her income (i.e. the £200 a month loan from her mother) exceeded her applicable amount. Her mother made a third payment for the rent due on December 1, 2004 but refused to make any further payments.

The Commissioner rejected the contention that the loans could be regarded as not part of the claimant's income under the principle in *Leeves v Adjudication Officer*, reported as *R(IS) 5/99*, and *Morrell v Secretary of State for Work and Pensions*, reported as *R(IS) 6/03*. That was because on the facts there was no intention to create legal relations and so it could not be said that the claimant was under a legal obligation to repay, let alone a certain and immediate obligation.

2.399   He considered whether the loan payments should be treated as capital, since the first payment was clearly intended to be a one-off when it was made. But did the character of the payments change after the second payment was made? The Commissioner did not reach a decision on this but instead went on to consider, if the loan payments were income, the effect of reg.110(9) of the JSA Regulations 1996 (the equivalent of para.(9)) in these circumstances.

He concludes that the loans were a voluntary payment and that, looking at the position at the date of the decision under appeal when only two payments had been made, the condition that the payments were not made at regular intervals was met. At that point there had not been payments at intervals in the plural and moreover the hope was that JSA and housing benefit would finally be awarded in time for the claimant to pay the December rent payment herself. The result was that the loan

payments were to be treated as capital under reg.110(9) and the claimant was entitled to JSA on the basis that her income was nil.

Note that since October 2, 2006 voluntary payments (such as the loans in
CJSA/2336/2005) which *are* made at regular intervals and so are not treated as
capital under para.(9) have in most cases been totally disregarded as income (see
para.15(5A)(b) of Sch.9).

Paragraph (12)

"Subsistence allowances" (reg.2(1)) were paid to claimants participating in an
employment zone programme. Such programmes have not been in operation since
September 1, 2011.

2.400

[¹ Calculation of capital in the United Kingdom

49.—Capital which a claimant possesses in the United Kingdom shall be
calculated at its current market or surrender value less—

    (a) where there would be expenses attributable to sale, 10 per cent; and

    (b) the amount of any incumbrance secured on it.]

2.401

AMENDMENT

1. Social Security (Miscellaneous Amendments) (No.5) Regulations 2007 (SI
2007/2618) reg.5(10) (October 1, 2007).

DEFINITION

"claimant"—see reg.2(1) and reg.23(1).

GENERAL NOTE

The form of reg.49 in force from October 1, 2007 no longer contains any
special provision for the valuation of National Savings Certificates (valuations of
National Savings and Investments were previously uprated annually on July 1 but
this no longer happens). See *CIS/1733/2008* on the valuation of National Savings
Certificates under the previous rule. Under the new form of reg.49 they will be
valued in the same way as other capital.

2.402

The general rule is that the market value of the asset is to be taken. The surrender value will be taken if appropriate (although the surrender value of life insurance
policies and of annuities is totally disregarded (Sch.10 paras 15 and 11)). The value
at this stage does not take account of any incumbrances secured on the assets, since
those come in under para.(b) (*R(IS) 21/93*). There is no definitive requirement that
there be a local market (*Reigate and Banstead BC v GB (HB)* [2018] UKUT 225
(AAC)), but the way in which markets work in practice in whatever asset is in question must be taken into account.

In *R(SB) 57/83* and *R(SB) 6/84* the test taken is the price that would be com-
manded between a willing buyer and a willing seller at a particular date. In *R(SB)
6/84* it is stressed that in the case of a house it is vital to know the nature and extent
of the interest being valued. Also, since what is required is a current market value,
the Commissioner holds that an estate agent's figure for a quick sale was closer to the
proper approach than the District Valuer's figure for a sale within three months. All
the circumstances must be taken into account in making the valuation. Arguments
have been raised that during the 2020 coronavirus outbreak, in the period when
estate agents' offices were closed and most viewings impossible, there was no market
in existence for domestic properties. In *CIS 553/1991* it is held that in valuing a former
matrimonial home the wife's statutory right of occupation under the Matrimonial
Homes Act 1967 has to be taken into account. See further the decisions discussed
under "*Valuation under reg.52*" in the notes to reg.52.

2.403   *Reigate and Banstead BC v GB* (above, and in detail in the notes to reg.52) is a helpful example of valuation of an interest as a tenant in common, in that case a deemed such interest, and of an acceptable District Valuer's report.

RM v Sefton Council (HB) [2016] UKUT 357 (AAC), reported as [2017] AACR 5, provides a good practical example of the valuation of a property with sitting shorthold tenants.

Similarly, if personal possessions are being valued, it is what the possessions could be sold for which counts, not simply what was paid for them (*CIS 494/1990, CIS 2208/2003*). See also *JJ v SSWP (IS)* [2012] UKUT 253 (AAC) which points out that where a sale of a chattel is by auction there are buyer's premiums added as well as seller's commission and that this could result in the seller being treated as having much more capital than he would realise on a sale. In the Judge's view this was not the object of the regulations and the valuation had to be based on the standard test of what the claimant could expect to realise on a transaction between a willing seller and a willing buyer.

Sometimes a detailed valuation is not necessary, such as where the value of an asset is on any basis clearly over the prescribed (which since April 10, 2006 has been £16,000) limit (*CIS/40/1989*). That, however, has the undesirable result that no baseline has been established for assessing the effects of future disposals of the assets.

Shares

2.404   It is accepted that the test of the willing buyer and the willing seller is the starting point for the valuation of shares (*R(SB) 57/83, R(SB) 12/89* and *R(IS) 2/90*). The latter case emphasises that in the income support context the value must be determined on the basis of a very quick sale, so that the hypothetical willing seller would be at a corresponding disadvantage. In the case of private companies there is often a provision in the articles of association that a shareholder wishing to sell must first offer the shares to other shareholders at a "fair value" fixed by the auditors (this was the case in *R(SB) 18/83* and *R(IS) 2/90*). Then the value of the shares ought not to be higher than the fair value, but for income support purposes may well be less. The possible complications are set out in *CSB 488/1982* (quoted with approval in *R(SB) 12/89* and *R(IS) 2/90*). In *R(IS) 8/92* it is suggested that the market value is what a purchaser would pay for the shares subject to the same restriction. Whether the shareholding gives a minority, equal or controlling interest is particularly significant. All the circumstances of the share structure of the company must be considered. For instance, in *R(SB) 12/89* shares could only be sold with the consent of the directors, which it was indicated would not be forthcoming. It seems to be agreed that valuation according to Revenue methods is not appropriate (*R(SB) 18/83* and *R(IS) 2/90*), although it is suggested in *R(SB) 12/89* that the Revenue Shares Valuation Division might be able to assist tribunals. It is not known if this is so. What is absolutely clear is that the total value of the company's shareholding cannot simply be divided in proportion to the claimant's holding (*R(SB) 18/83*).

However, in para.14 of *P v SSWP and P (CSM)* [2018] UKUT 60 (AAC) it was said, in a passage not necessary to the decision, that the tribunal in that child support case:

> "was correct in basing the value of the shares on the book value of the company's net assets, without making any discount to reflect the difficulty in selling part of the shareholding in a private company. In *Ebrahimi v Westbourne Galleries Limited* [1973] A.C. 360 it was held that in some circumstances a limited company could co-exist with a 'quasi-partnership' between those involved in the company, for example, if the shareholders were bound by personal relationships involving mutual confidence, if the shareholders were in practice involved in the conduct of the business, and if the transfer of the shares was restricted. In *re Bird Precision Bellows Ltd.* [1986] Ch. 658 Oliver LJ held

[674A] that in a 'quasi-partnership' case it was appropriate that: 'the shares of the company should be valued as a whole and that the petitioners should then simply be paid the proportionate part of that value which was represented by their shareholding, without there being made a discount for the fact that this was a minority shareholding'."

It is not though clear how far that approach should be translated to income support and old style JSA and ESA and how far it turns on the particular context of the child support variation provisions with their stress on a parent's control in practice over a company (see para.15 of *P*). But the application of reg.51(4) on notional capital would have to be considered in such circumstances. If that provision applies, reg.51(4)(a) expressly requires that the actual value of the claimant's shareholding be disregarded and the claimant is treated as owning the capital of the company, or the appropriate proportion of it (reg.51(4)(b) and see the notes to reg.51(4) for further discussion).

In the case of shares in companies quoted on the London Stock Exchange the Revenue method of valuation should be used (*R(IS) 18/95*). This involves looking at all the transactions relating to the relevant share during the previous day, taking the lowest figure and adding to this a quarter of the difference between the lowest and the highest figure. The Commissioner considered that decision-makers could use the valuation quoted in newspapers (which is the mean between the best bid and best offer price at the close of business the previous day) to obtain approximate valuations. However, where a completely accurate valuation was essential, the Revenue method would need to be adopted. See also *DW v SSWP (JSA)* [2012] UKUT 478 (AAC).

Valuation affected by difficulties in realisation

The proper approach to valuation can usefully deal with unrealisable assets. **2.405** Sometimes their market value will be nil (e.g. a potential interest under a discretionary trust: *R(SB) 25/83;* assets that are subject to a restraint or freezing order: *SH v SSWP* [2008] UKUT 21 (AAC); *CS v Chelmsford BC(HB)* [2014] UKUT 518 (AAC)); sometimes it will be very heavily discounted. However, if the asset will be realisable after a time, it may have a current value. The claimant may be able to sell an option to purchase the asset in the future (see *R(IS) 8/92*) or borrow, using the asset as security. But the valuation must reflect the fact that the asset is not immediately realisable. In *R(IS) 4/96* the claimant had on his divorce transferred his interest in the former matrimonial home to his wife in return for a charge on the property which could only be enforced if she died, remarried or cohabited for more than six months. The claimant's former wife was 46 and in good health. A discount had to be applied to the present day value of the charge to reflect the fact that it might not be realisable for as long as 40 years or more; consequently it was unlikely to be worth more than £3,000. See also *CIS 982/2002* in which the Commissioner sets out a number of detailed questions that had to be considered when valuing the claimant's share (if any) in a joint bank account that had been frozen following the claimant's separation from her husband. And note *LC v Bournemouth Borough Council (HB)* [2016] UKUT 175 (AAC), discussed in the notes to reg.51(2) and reg.52.

In *JC-W v Wirral MBC (HB)* [2011] UKUT 501 (AAC) Judge Mark concluded that nobody would be willing to purchase (for more than a nominal amount) the claimant's beneficial interest pending divorce in two heavily mortgaged properties, one of which was only partly built, in respect of which the claimant's parents-in-law claimed an interest in the proceeds of sale, and which the claimant's husband was unwilling to sell.

As the Tribunal of Commissioners in *R(SB) 45/83* point out, the market value (in that case of an interest in an entire trust fund) must reflect the outlay the purchaser would expect to incur in obtaining transfer of the assets and the profit he would expect as an inducement to purchase. If there might be some legal difficulty in obtaining the underlying asset (as there might have been in *R(SB) 21/83* and in

R(IS) 13/95, where shares were held in the names of the claimant's children) this must be taken into account.

2.406   See also *MB v Wychavon DC (HB)* [2013] UKUT 67 (AAC) which concerned the valuation of the claimant's beneficial interest under a declaration of trust made by his mother in relation to a property held in the mother's name. The claimant had contributed 10 per cent towards the purchase price. In the absence of a family member willing to purchase the claimant's share, Judge Mark finds that the market value of the claimant's interest was substantially less than the amount of his contribution to the purchase price (he decided it was less than half that amount). However, it was possible that there would be no market at all for the claimant's share, in which case its value would be nil.

   Where the property is jointly owned, see the decisions discussed under "*Valuation under reg.52*" in the notes to reg.52.

Deductions from market value

2.407   The general rule is that the whole of a capital resource is to be taken into account. Liabilities are not to be deducted from the value (*R(SB) 2/83* and *SSWP v GF (ESA)* [2017] UKUT 333 (AAC)). It is only where a debt is secured on the capital asset that it is deducted under para.(b).

   In this connection, note *JRL v SSWP (JSA)* [2011] UKUT 63 (AAC), reported as [2011] AACR 30. The claimant had three accounts with the same bank, of which one was in credit, one was overdrawn and one had a nil balance. The Three-Judge Panel pointed out that this meant that the claimant was both a creditor and a debtor of the same body. Under the bank's terms and conditions, the bank had a contractual right to debit at any time any of a customer's accounts which were in credit with sums sufficient to clear the customer's indebtedness to the bank. This created what was effectively a charge on the customer's credit balance(s). The market value of the account that was in credit was therefore its net value after deduction of the amount of the claimant's overdraft on his other account.

   The first deduction to be made is a standard 10 per cent if there would be *any* expenses attributable to sale, as there almost always will be. The second is the amount of any incumbrance secured on the asset. There is particularly full and helpful guidance on the nature of incumbrances on real property and the evidence which should be examined in *R(IS) 21/93*, and see below. In *R(IS) 10/99* the Commissioner points out that the word "incumbrance" is unknown to the law of Scotland, but goes on to interpret what is now para.(b) as meaning that there must be something attached to the capital in question that prevents the claimant from disposing of it.

2.408   The standard case of a debt being secured on a capital asset is a house that is mortgaged. The amount of capital outstanding will be deducted from the market value of the house. In *R(SB) 14/81* (see Sch.10 para.8) the claimant had been lent £5,000 for work on his bungalow, which was mortgaged to secure the debt. He had £3,430 left. Although he was obliged to make monthly repayments this liability could not be deducted from the £3,430, for the debt was not secured on the money. However, the principle of *R(SB) 53/83* (see the notes to reg.46) would make the money not part of the claimant's resources. In *JH v SSWP* [2009] UKUT 1 (AAC) the site owner's commission payable on the sale of a beach hut was not "an incumbrance secured on" the hut but a personal contractual obligation on the seller which could not be enforced against the asset itself.

   In *R(SB) 18/83* the Commissioner says that personal property such as shares (or money) can be charged by a contract for valuable consideration (e.g. a loan) without any writing or the handing over of any title documents. But this is not the case in Scots law (*R(SB) 5/88*). In *R(IS) 18/95* the claimant's brokers had a lien on his shares for the cost of acquisition and their commission which fell to be offset against the value of the shares. *CIS 368/1993* concerned money held under a solicitor's undertaking. £40,000 of the proceeds of sale of the claimant's house was retained by his solicitors in pursuance of an undertaking to his bank given because of a previous charge on the property. The Commissioner decides that the undertaking was an incumbrance within what is now para.(b). It was the equivalent of a pledge or lien and was secured on the proceeds of sale. Thus the £40,000 did not count as part of the claimant's resources. See also *CIS 984/2002* which concerned money held by the claimant's solicitor pending quantification of the statutory charge to the Legal Services Commission under s.10(7) of the Access to Justice Act 1999. The Commissioner holds that this was not part of the claimant's capital until the charge had been quantified, as until then it was not possible to identify any particular amount as the claimant's capital. He added that another way of looking at it was to treat the statutory charge as an incumbrance for the purpose of what is now para. (b).

In *R(IS) 5/98* the claimant transferred her flat to her daughter on the understanding that the daughter would care for her in the flat and pay off the mortgage. The daughter complied with the second condition, but evicted her mother from the flat. The Commissioner decides that the gift of the flat to the daughter had been subject to the condition that she looked after her mother. As that condition had not been fulfilled, the gift failed and the daughter held the property on trust for the claimant. In valuing the claimant's interest, the mortgage was to be deducted because the daughter was to be treated as subrogated to the rights of the mortgagee. In addition, the costs of the litigation to recover the property from the daughter also fell to be deducted. The claimant appealed against this decision to the Court of Appeal but her appeal was dismissed (*Ellis v Chief Adjudication Officer,* reported as part of *R(IS) 5/98*).

Calculation of capital outside the United Kingdom

50.—Capital which a claimant possesses in a country outside the United Kingdom shall be calculated— **2.409**

- (a) in a case in which there is no prohibition in that country against the transfer to the United Kingdom of an amount equal to its current market or surrender value in that country, at that value;
- (b) in a case where there is such a prohibition, at the price which it would realise if sold in the United Kingdom to a willing buyer,

less, where there would be expenses attributable to sale, 10 per cent. and the amount of any incumbrance secured on it.

<small>DEFINITION</small>

"claimant"—see reg.2(1) and reg.23(1).

<small>GENERAL NOTE</small>

There had been problems under supplementary benefit in valuing overseas assets. **2.410**
Now the standard rules about the deduction of 10 per cent. for sale expenses and the deduction of the amount of any incumbrance secured on the asset apply. But then there are two separate situations. Under para.(a), if there is no prohibition in the country where the asset is located against transferring to the UK an amount of money equal to the asset's value in that country, the market value there is the test. *CH 4972/2002* confirms that under para.(a) it is the local market value that is taken, not the value that could be obtained by marketing the asset in the UK. If there are merely restrictions or delays in transfer this does not seem to prevent the application of para.(a). If there is a prohibition, under para.(b) the value is the market value in the UK.

Notional capital

51.—(1) A claimant shall be treated as possessing capital of which he has **2.411**
deprived himself for the purpose of securing entitlement to income support or increasing the amount of that benefit [⁶ except—

    (a) where that capital is derived from a payment made in consequence of any personal injury and is placed on trust for the benefit of the claimant; or

    (b) to the extent that the capital which he is treated as possessing is reduced in accordance with regulation 51A (diminishing notional capital rule)] [¹⁵or

[³¹(c) any sum to which paragraph 44(2)(a) of Schedule 10 (capital to be disregarded) applies which is administered in the way referred to in paragraph 44(1)(a);

    (d) any sum to which paragraph 45(a) of Schedule 10 refers.]]

    (2) Except in the case of—

    (a) a discretionary trust;

    (b) a trust derived from a payment made in consequence of a personal injury; or

    (c) any loan which would be obtainable if secured against capital disregarded under Schedule 10, [¹³ or

    (d) a personal pension scheme [³³ . . .],] [¹⁵ or

[²⁹(da) an occupational pension scheme [³⁰ or a payment made by the Board of the Pension Protection Fund] where the claimant [³⁹ has not attained the qualifying age for state pension credit]; or]

[³²(e) any sum to which paragraph 44(2)(a) of Schedule 10 (capital to be disregarded) applies which is administered in the way referred to in paragraph 44(1)(a); or

    (f) any sum to which paragraph 45(a) of Schedule 10 refers,]]

any capital which would become available to the claimant upon application being made but which has not been acquired by him shall be treated as possessed by him but only from the date on which [¹ it could be expected to be acquired were an application made.]

    [²(3) [¹⁷ Any payment of capital, other than a payment of capital specified [⁴⁶paragraph (3A) or (3B)], made—

    (a) to a third party in respect of a single claimant or [²³ his partner] (but not a member of the third party's family) shall be treated—

        (i) in a case where that payment is derived from a payment of any benefit under the benefit Acts, [²⁵a payment from the Armed Forces and Reserve Forces Compensation Scheme,] a war disablement pension[¹⁴, war widow's pension [²² or war widower's pension] or a pension payable to a person as a [²⁷ widow, widower or surviving civil partner] under [³⁶ . . .] any power of Her Majesty otherwise than under an enactment to make provision about pensions for or in respect of persons who have been disabled or who have died in consequence of service as members of the armed forces of the Crown,] as possessed by that single claimant, if it is paid to him, [²³ or by his partner, if it is paid to his partner];

    [¹⁸(ia) in a case where that payment is a payment of an occupational pension or[³⁰, a pension or other periodical payment made under a personal pension scheme or a payment made by the Board of the Pension Protection Fund], as possessed by that single claimant or, as the case may be, by [²³ the claimant's partner];]

        (ii) in any other case, as possessed by that single claimant [²³ or his partner] to the extent that it is used for the food, ordinary clothing or footwear, household fuel, rent [²⁶. . .] for which housing benefit [²¹ is payable or] [⁸. . .] any housing costs to the extent that they are met under regulation 17(1)(e) and 18(1)(f) (housing costs) [²¹ . . .] of that single claimant or, as the case may be, [²³ of his partner] [⁸, or is used for any [¹⁰council tax] or water charges for which that claimant or [²³ partner is liable]];

[²³ (b) to a single claimant or his partner in respect of a third party (but not in respect of another member of his family) shall be treated as possessed by that single claimant or, as the case may be, his partner, to the extent that it is kept or used by him or used by or on behalf of his partner.]].

[¹⁷(3A) Paragraph (3) shall not apply in respect of a payment of capital made—

(a) under [³⁸or by] the Macfarlane Trust, the Macfarlane (Special Payments) Trust, the Macfarlane (Special Payments) (No.2) Trust, the Fund, the Eileen Trust [³⁷ , MFET Limited] [²⁴, the Independent Living [³⁵Fund (2006)][²⁸, the Skipton Fund[⁴¹, the Caxton Foundation][⁴³, the Scottish Infected Blood Support Scheme][⁴⁵, an approved blood scheme][⁴⁴, the London Emergencies Trust, the We Love Manchester Emergency Fund][⁴⁶, the National Emergencies Trust] or the London Bombings Relief Charitable Fund]];

(b) pursuant to section 2 of the Employment and Training Act 1973 in respect of a person's participation—

   (i) in an employment programme specified in regulation 75(1)(a) (ii) of the Jobseeker's Allowance Regulations 1996;

   (ii) in a training scheme specified in regulation 75(1)(b)(ii) of those Regulations; or

   [²⁰(iia) in the Intensive Activity Period specified in regulation 75(1)(a) (iv) of those Regulations [³⁴ . . .]; or]

   (iii) in a qualifying course within the meaning specified in regulation 17A(7) of those Regulations.]

   (iv) [*Omitted.*]

[⁴⁰(ba) in respect of a person's participation in [⁴² a scheme prescribed in regulation 3 of the Jobseeker's Allowance (Schemes for Assisting Persons to Obtain Employment) Regulations 2013] or the Mandatory Work Activity Scheme;]

[¹⁹(c) under an occupational pension scheme [³⁰, in respect of a pension or other periodical payment made under a personal pension scheme or a payment made by the Board of the Pension Protection Fund] where—

   (i) a bankruptcy order has been made in respect of the person in respect of whom the payment has been made or, in Scotland, the estate of that person is subject to sequestration or a judicial factor has been appointed on that person's estate under section 41 of the Solicitors (Scotland) Act 1980;

   (ii) the payment is made to the trustee in bankruptcy or any other person acting on behalf of the creditors; and

   (iii) the person referred to in (i) and [²³ his partner (if any)] does not possess, or is not treated as possessing, any other income apart from that payment.]

[46(3B) Paragraph (3) shall not apply in respect of a payment of capital which is a Grenfell Tower payment.]

(4) Where a claimant stands in relation to a company in a position analogous to that of a sole owner or partner in the business of that company, he shall be treated as if he were such sole owner or partner and in such a case—

(a) the value of his holding in that company shall, notwithstanding regulation 46 (calculation of capital), be disregarded; and

(b) he shall, subject to paragraph (5), be treated as possessing an amount of capital equal to the value or, as the case may be, his share of the value of the capital of that company and the foregoing provisions of this Chapter shall apply for the purposes of calculating that amount as if it were actual capital which he does possess.

(5) For so long as the claimant undertakes activities in the course of the business of the company, the amount which he is treated as possessing under paragraph (4) shall be disregarded.

(6) Where a claimant is treated as possessing capital under any of paragraphs (1) to (4), the foregoing provisions of this Chapter shall apply for the purposes of calculating its amount as if it were actual capital which he does possess.

[[1](7) For the avoidance of doubt a claimant is to be treated as possessing capital under paragraph (1) only if the capital of which he has deprived himself is actual capital.]

[[2](8) In paragraph (3) the expression "ordinary clothing or footwear" means clothing or footwear for normal daily use, but does not include school uniforms, or clothing or footwear used solely for sporting activities].

AMENDMENTS

1. Income Support (General) Amendment Regulations 1988 (SI 1988/663) reg.22 (April 11, 1988).

2. Income Support (General) Amendment No.4 Regulations 1988 (SI 1988/1445) reg.12 (September 12, 1988).

3. Income Support (General) Amendment No.4 Regulations (SI 1988/1445) Sch.1 para.4 (April 10, 1989).

4. Income Support (General) Amendment Regulations 1989 (SI 1989/534) Sch.1 para.7 (October 9, 1989).

5. Income-related Benefits Schemes Amendment Regulations 1990 (SI 1990/127) reg.3 (January 31, 1990).

6. Income Support (General) Amendment No.3 Regulations 1990 (SI 1990/1776) reg.5 (October 1, 1990).

7. Income-related Benefits Schemes and Social Security (Recoupment) Amendment Regulations 1991 (SI 1991/1175) reg.5 (May 11, 1991).

8. Income Support (General) Amendment No.4 Regulations 1991 (SI 1991/1559) reg.8 (August 5, 1991).

9. Income-related Benefits Schemes and Social Security (Recoupment) Amendment Regulations 1992 (SI 1992/1101) reg.6 (May 7, 1992).

10. Income-related Benefits Schemes (Miscellaneous Amendments) Regulations 1993 (SI 993/315) Sch. para.3 (April 1, 1993).

11. Social Security Benefits (Miscellaneous Amendments) (No.2) Regulations 1993 (SI 1993/963) reg.2(3) (April 22, 1993).

12. Income-related Benefits Schemes and Social Security (Recoupment) Amendment Regulations 1993 (SI 1993/1249) reg.4(3) (May 14, 1993).

13. Income-related Benefits Schemes and Social Security (Claims and Payments) (Miscellaneous Amendments) Regulations 1995 (SI 1995/2303) reg.6(5) (October 2, 1995).

14. Income-related Benefits and Jobseeker's Allowance (Miscellaneous Amendments) Regulations 1997 (SI 1997/65) reg.9 (April 7, 1997).

15. Income-related Benefits and Jobseeker's Allowance (Amendment) (No.2) Regulations 1997 (SI 1997/2197) reg.5(4) (October 6, 1997).

16. Social Security Amendment (New Deal) Regulations 1997 (SI 1997/2863) reg.17(5) and (6)(e) (January 5, 1998).

17. Social Security Amendment (New Deal) (No.2) Regulations 1998 (SI 1998/2117) reg.3(2) and (3)(c) (September 24, 1998).

18. Social Security Amendment (Notional Income and Capital) Regulations 1999 (SI 1999/2640) reg.2(1)(a) (November 15, 1999).

19. Social Security Amendment (Notional Income and Capital) Regulations 1999 (SI 1999/2640) reg.2(3)(c) (November 15, 1999).

20. Social Security Amendment (New Deal) Regulations 2001 (SI 2001/1029) reg.15(8) and (9)(c) (April 9, 2001).

21. Social Security Amendment (Residential Care and Nursing Homes) Regulations 2001 (SI 2001/3767) reg.2(1) and Pt I of Sch. para.8 (April 8, 2002).

22. Social Security (Miscellaneous Amendments) Regulations 2002 (SI 2002/841) reg.2(3) (April 8, 2002).

23. Social Security (Working Tax Credit and Child Tax Credit) (Consequential Amendments) Regulations 2003 (SI 2003/455) reg.2 and Sch.1 para.13 (April 6, 2004, except in "transitional cases" and see further the note to reg.17 of the Income Support Regulations).

24. Social Security (Miscellaneous Amendments) (No.3) Regulations 2004 (SI 2004/2308) reg.3(1) and (2)(a) (October 4, 2004).

25. Social Security (Miscellaneous Amendments) Regulations 2005 (SI 2005/574) reg.2(5) (April 4, 2005).

26. Social Security (Miscellaneous Amendments) Regulations 2005 (SI 2005/574) reg.3(4) (April 4, 2005).

27. Social Security (Civil Partnership) (Consequential Amendments) Regulations 2005 (SI 2005/2878) reg.4(3) (December 5, 2005).

28. Income-related Benefits (Amendment) (No.2) Regulations 2005 (SI 2005/3391) reg.2(3) (December 12, 2005).

29. Social Security (Miscellaneous Amendments) (No.2) Regulations 2005 (SI 2005/2465) reg.2(5) (April 6, 2006).

30. Social Security (Miscellaneous Amendments) Regulations 2006 (SI 2006/588) reg.2(3) (April 6, 2006).

31. Social Security (Miscellaneous Amendments) Regulations 2007 (SI 2007/719) reg.2(4)(a) (April 2, 2007).

32. Social Security (Miscellaneous Amendments) Regulations 2007 (SI 2007/719) reg.2(4)(b) (April 2, 2007).

33. Social Security (Miscellaneous Amendments) (No.3) Regulations 2007 (SI 2007/1749) reg.2(7) (July 16, 2007).

34. Social Security (Miscellaneous Amendments) Regulations 2008 (SI 2008/698) reg.2(7)(b) (April 14, 2008).

35. Social Security (Miscellaneous Amendments) (No.6) Regulations 2008 (SI 2008/2767) reg.2(6) (November 17, 2008).

36. Social Security (Miscellaneous Amendments) (No.7) Regulations 2008 (SI 2008/3157) reg.2(4) (January 5, 2009).

37. Social Security (Miscellaneous Amendments) (No.2) Regulations 2010 (SI 2010/641) reg.2(3)(d) (April 6, 2010).

38. Social Security (Miscellaneous Amendments) (No.2) Regulations 2010 (SI 2010/641) reg.2(7)(c) (April 6, 2010).

39. Social Security (Miscellaneous Amendments) (No.2) Regulations 2010 (SI 2010/641) reg.2(8) (April 6, 2010).

40. Social Security (Miscellaneous Amendments) (No.2) Regulations 2011 (SI 2011/1707) reg.4(6)(a) and (7) (August 5, 2011).

41. Social Security (Miscellaneous Amendments) (No.3) Regulations 2011 (SI 2011/2425) reg.7(6) (October 31, 2011).

42. Jobseeker's Allowance (Schemes for Assisting Persons to Obtain Employment) Regulations 2013 (SI 2013/276) reg.13(b) (February 12, 2013).

43. Social Security (Scottish Infected Blood Support Scheme) Regulations 2017 (SI 2017/329) reg.3(3) (April 3, 2017).

44. Social Security (Emergency Funds) (Amendment) Regulations 2017 (SI 2017/689) reg.2(3)(c) (June 19, 2017).

45. Social Security (Infected Blood and Thalidomide) Regulations 2017 (SI 2017/870) reg.2(3)(c) (October 23, 2017).

46. Social Security (Income and Capital) (Miscellaneous Amendments) Regulations 2020 (SI 2020/618) reg.2(5) (July 15, 2020).

DEFINITIONS

"approved blood scheme"—see reg.2(1).
"the Armed Forces and Reserve Forces Compensation Scheme"—*ibid*.
"the benefit Acts"—*ibid*.
"claimant"—see reg.2(1) and reg.23(1).
"family"—see SSCBA s.137(1).
"Grenfell Tower Payment"—see reg.2(1)
"Intensive Activity Period for 50 plus"—*ibid*.
"the London Bombings Relief Charitable Fund"—*ibid*.
"the London Emergencies Trust"—*ibid*.
"the Mandatory Work Activity Scheme"—*ibid*.
"MFET Limited"—*ibid*.
"occupational pension"—*ibid*.
"payment"—*ibid*.
"personal pension scheme"—*ibid*.
"Scottish Infected Blood Support Scheme"—*ibid*.
"the Caxton Foundation"—*ibid*.
"the Eileen Trust"—*ibid*.
"the Fund"—*ibid*.
"the Independent Living Funds"—see reg.2(1).
"the Macfarlane (Special Payments) Trust"—*ibid*.
"the Macfarlane (Special Payments) (No.2) Trust"—*ibid*.
"the Macfarlane Trust"—*ibid*.
"the National Emergencies Trust"—*ibid*.
"the Skipton Fund"—*ibid*.
"water charges"—see reg.2(1).
"the We Love Manchester Emergency Fund"—*ibid*.

GENERAL NOTE

2.412   See the note at the beginning of the annotation to reg.46 on distinguishing between actual and notional capital , and see below, under "*Deprivation*".

Paragraph (1)

2.413   In order for para.(1) to apply, only two elements must be proved by the decision-maker—that the person has deprived themself of actual capital (see para.(7)) and that their purpose was to secure entitlement to or increase the amount of income support. It is clear that the principles applied to these questions for supplementary benefit purposes are to be applied to para.(1) (*CIS 24/1988, CIS 40/1989* and *R(IS) 1/91*, although the first decision is in error in failing to note the crucial difference identified in the next sentence). There is now no discretion (the regulation says "shall," not "may"). That was thought to give rise to the problems mentioned at the end of the note to this paragraph under "*Diminishing capital*". Those problems led to the insertion of reg.51A, applying a diminishing capital rule. Capital subject to that rule is excluded from reg.51(1) by sub-para.(b).

Sub-paragraph (a) excludes the operation of reg.51(1) where money derived from compensation for personal injury is placed on trust for the claimant. Sub-paragraphs (c) and (d) do the same in respect of funds held in court on behalf of a person that derive from damages for personal injury to that person. See also the notes to para.12 and paras 44–45 of Sch.10.

Note *CIS/2540/2004* which confirms that a finding by a tribunal that a claimant is to be treated as having notional capital is not binding in relation to a subsequent claim. Section 17 of the SSA 1998 draws a distinction between a decision which by s.17(1) is made "final" and a finding of fact necessary to the decision which under s.17(2) is only conclusive for the purpose of further decisions to the extent that regulations so provide; no regulations providing for any such conclusive effect have been made in this context. A subsequent tribunal hearing an appeal against the refusal of income support when the claimant made a further claim was not therefore bound by the previous tribunal's finding on the issue of deprivation of capital but could consider the issue afresh.

Deprivation

Here the onus of proof is complicated by the relationship with the claimant's actual capital. Once it is shown that a person did possess, or received, an asset, the burden shifts to them to show that it has ceased to be a part of their actual capital, to be valued under reg.49 *(R(SB) 38/85)*, apparently whether on an initial claim or on revision or supersession by the SSWP *(LP v SSWP (ESA)* [2018] UKUT 389 (AAC) at para.13). Therefore, para.(1) can only come into play after these two stages have been passed, with the second stage depending on the claimant. If claimants cannot satisfactorily account for the way in which an asset or a sum of money which they say they no longer have was disposed of, the proper conclusion is that it remains a part of their actual capital. But if there is evidence as to where the money has gone, as there was in *WR v SSWP (IS)* [2012] UKUT 127 (AAC) where the claimant had made payments to each of her parents, the fact that the tribunal did not accept the claimant's explanations for the payments did not mean that the money remained the claimant's actual capital. Instead the claimant was to be treated as having notional capital and the diminishing capital rule in reg.51A applied from the date of the payments to her parents. It is important that tribunals should make it clear whether a decision is based on a claimant continuing to possess actual capital under this principle or on being treated as possessing notional capital under reg.51(1), and in particular should avoid the use of the word "deemed" if the first basis is relied on (see *AB v SSWP and Canterbury CC (IS and HB)* [2014] UKUT 212 (AAC) in the notes to reg.46).

MS v DfC (JSA) [2020] NICom 42 holds that where a tribunal is not satisfied by a claimant's assertion that he has disposed of money, so that the amount remains part of their actual capital, it is not necessary for the tribunal to make a positive finding of fact about where the money was actually held. Submissions to the contrary were based on a misreading of remarks in *DMcC v DSD (IS)* [2012] NICom 326.

In *CIS 634/1992* the claimant was made bankrupt on November 29, 1990. Between November 29 and December 28, 1990, when he claimed income support, the claimant divested himself of most of his capital. His trustee in bankruptcy was not appointed until April 1991. Under the Insolvency Act 1986 (subject to certain exceptions) a bankrupt's property does not vest in his trustee on the making of a bankruptcy order but only when the trustee is appointed. However, s.284 of the Insolvency Act 1986 makes any disposal of property or payment by a bankrupt between the presentation of a bankruptcy petition and the vesting of his estate in his trustee void (except with the consent or later ratification of the court). The claimant could not therefore in law deprive himself of any resources from November 29, onwards and para.(1) could not apply. However, since he had failed to give a satisfactory account of how he had disposed of his capital, he was to be treated as still possessing it *(R(SB) 38/85)*. Thus he was not entitled to income support prior to the appointment of the trustee in bankruptcy because until then he possessed actual capital over the income support limit. See however *KS v SSWP (JSA)* [2009] UKUT 122 (AAC), reported as [2010] AACR 3, in which Judge Mark agrees that the effect of s.284 of the Insolvency Act is that reg.51(1) cannot apply but disagrees that a bankrupt's capital remains his capital until the appointment of the trustee in

2.414

bankruptcy. Judge Mark points out that a bankrupt cannot realise or use any part of his capital after a bankruptcy order has been made and that, subject to any order of the court, it will vest in his trustee in due course. Whether the capital remains his capital with a nil value or whether it ceases to be his capital at all (on which the Judge did not reach any firm conclusion), the result was that the claimant in that case had no capital, or no capital of any value, after the bankruptcy order had been made. As a reported decision, *KS* is to be given more weight.

It is suggested that *R(SB) 38/85* should not be taken as sanctifying the Department's common practice of requiring claimants to produce receipts to substantiate their expenditure and of automatically treating them as still having the balance of their capital not covered by receipts. As the Commissioner in *CIS/515/2006* points out, it is inherently improbable that a claimant will be able to produce receipts for day to day expenditure, particularly in relation to a period sometimes several years in the past. Claimants should be asked to produce what records they do have and can be asked to explain any large or unusual payments. But to demand actual receipts for all expenditure, however small, particularly over a lengthy period is not reasonable. General conclusions should be drawn on the basis of the claimant's oral evidence and the documentary evidence that is available.

2.415 See also *KW v SSWP* [2012] UKUT 350 (AAC) in which lack of receipts for the claimant's alleged expenditure on sexual services was understandable, given the nature of that expenditure. The question as to whether this expenditure took place, and if so, how much, therefore came down to a question of credibility.

"Deprive" is an ordinary English word and is not to be given any special legal definition *(R(SB) 38/85, R(SB) 40/85)*. The result is that people deprive themselves of a resource if they cease to possess it, regardless of the reason for doing so or the fact that they receive some other resource in return. This is the clear assumption in *R(SB) 38/85* and is expressly decided in *R(SB) 40/85*. That decision holds that the approach in the *S Manual* (para.6042—set out on p.177 of the 2nd edition of J. Mesher, CPAG's *Supplementary Benefit and Family Income Supplement: the Legislation* (1985)), that a person had not deprived himself of a resource if he spent money or changed it into another form which is still available to him, was wrong. The effect is to put the main emphasis on the purpose of the deprivation.

However, this raises the question of the interaction of reg.51(1) with para.10 of Sch.10. Under para.10 the value of personal possessions is disregarded except those that have been acquired with the intention of reducing capital so as to gain entitlement to income support. This interaction was discussed in *CIS 494/1990* and *R(IS) 8/04*. Both cases concerned the use of capital to buy a vehicle, for the purpose of securing entitlement to income support. In *CIS 494/1990* the Commissioner points out that the value of the vehicle will be considerably less than the purchase price and treats only this "depreciation" as notional capital under reg.51(1). He proceeded on the assumption that there was an immediate depreciation of £1,000. The Commissioner in *R(IS) 8/04* agrees that where capital is used, for a purpose caught by reg.51(1), to buy personal possessions, the value of the assets as actual capital must be taken into account in calculating the amount of notional capital under reg.51(1). It would be unfair to treat a claimant as still having all the capital used to buy the possessions and also as having the market value of the possessions. He acknowledges that the mechanism for reaching this result was not entirely clear as reg.51(1) and the exception in para.10 of Sch.10 appear to operate independently. However, he was satisfied that the general principle that actual capital should be looked at before notional capital supported the approach taken in *CIS 494/1990*. But he did not agree with *CIS 494/1990* that as the value of the car further depreciated over time there was a corresponding increase in the claimant's notional capital. The amount of the capital of which the claimant had deprived himself had to be fixed at the date of the deprivation, since it was only that amount to which the prohibited purpose in reg.51(1) could be attached. Any future depreciation could only fairly be said to result from the operation of the market and not from the claimant's original purpose to gain entitlement to benefit. The Commissioner added that the same principles would apply to other factors which resulted in a difference between the amount of capital spent on an asset and the amount to be taken into account for the asset as actual capital (e.g. the effect of expenses that would be incurred in selling the asset). See also under *Diminishing capital*, below.

It is arguable that someone cannot deprive themselves of something which they have never possessed, but it may be that a deliberate failure to acquire an asset is also a deprivation. In *CSB 598/1987* it is suggested that a deliberate failure to pay a cheque into a bank account could be a deprivation. See also *CIS 1586/1997* which states that a sale at a known undervalue and the release of a debtor from a debt were capable of amounting to deprivation. However, the claimant in *R(IS) 1/03* did not deprive herself of an asset by failing to seek a lump sum payment or property transfer order under the Matrimonial Causes Act 1973, since the right to make an application under the Act is not a capital asset. Moreover, even if this had constituted deprivation, the claimant's reasons for not bringing proceedings (which included, inter alia, fear of her abusive husband) clearly indicated that her purpose had not been to secure entitlement to income support.

R(IS) 7/07 decides that the rule in para.(1) can apply to deprivations made by someone who only later becomes the claimant's partner. About a year before she became the claimant's partner, Ms H, who was unemployed and who had been in receipt of JSA, sold her house. She used the proceeds of sale to, among other things, repay her daughter's debts of £30,000 (incurred when the daughter was a student) and to take her family on holiday. The tribunal found that in disposing of her capital Ms H had acted with the purpose of securing entitlement to income support. Commissioner Jacobs considered that this conclusion was one that was open to the tribunal to make on the evidence before it. He then went on to decide that the claimant was caught by the rule in para.(1) even though Ms H was not his partner at the time of the deprivation.

In his view the combined effect of s.134(1) and the enabling provision in s.136(5)(a) of the SSCBA 1992 is to treat a partner's deprivation of capital as a deprivation by the claimant, even though they were not a couple at the time. The focus of reg.51(1) is on the purpose of a past disposal but reg.51(1) operates at the time when entitlement is in issue so the reference to the claimant (which by virtue of reg.23(1) includes a reference to his partner) is a reference to the person's status at that time. The Comissioner states:

> "Both in aggregating the capital of the members of a family and in taking account of notional capital, the legislation fulfils an anti-avoidance function. If notional capital were not aggregated, a future partner could dispose of capital before coming to live with the claimant or couples could separate in order to dispose of capital before reuniting. . . . The notional capital rule will only apply to a future partner where there has been conduct that is related to future entitlement to benefit either for the person alone or as a member of a family. That will limit the circumstances in which the rule applies and restrict it to those cases in which a course of conduct has been directed at future benefit entitlement."

The Commissioner further held that although he was prepared to assume that art.8 ECHR was engaged in respect of both the claimant's family life and home the interference was authorised by art.8(2).

Although it is not made explicit in the decision, it would seem that the Commissioner (and the tribunal) must have taken the view that Ms H was at least contemplating becoming the claimant's partner at the time of the disposals because otherwise there was no basis for the finding that Ms H had deprived herself of capital for the purpose of securing entitlement to *income support* (there is no indication that as a single person she would qualify for income support since before she received the proceeds of sale of her house she had been in receipt of JSA). Under para.(1) the deprivation has to be for the purpose of securing entitlement to income support; contrast the position under the corresponding old style JSA regulation (reg.113(1) of the JSA Regulations 1996) which applies if the person has deprived herself of capital in order to secure entitlement to or increase the amount of JSA *or* income support. It is suggested that the

2.416

2.417

decision should therefore be limited to such circumstances, that is where the parties may become a couple in the future. Moreover, this would seem to be in line with the Commissioner's view of when the rule will apply to a future partner (see above).

The decision in *R(IS)7/07* was a refusal of leave to appeal by the Commissioner. The claimant applied for judicial review of the Commissioner's decision but his application was dismissed (*R. (on the application of Hook) v Social Security Commissioner and Secretary of State for Work and Pensions* [2007] EWHC 1705 (Admin), reported as part of *R(IS)7/07*).

If the claimant's attorney appointed under the Enduring Powers of Attorney Act 1985 repays a loan or makes gifts of the claimant's capital this may amount to deprivation by the claimant, since the attorney is the agent of the claimant (*CIS 12403/1991*). In that case there was a question as to whether the loan was the responsibility of the claimant or the attorney and whether the gifts were allowable under s.3(5) of the 1985 Act which permitted the making of gifts "provided that the value of each such gift is not unreasonable having regard to all the circumstances and in particular the size of the donor's estate". The Commissioner states that the new tribunal would have to consider whether the payments were properly made; if not, there would be a claim against the attorney which would constitute actual capital; if they were properly made the question of deprivation would have to be considered. Under the Mental Capacity Act 2005, enduring powers of attorney have from October 1, 2007 been replaced by lasting powers of attorney, but existing powers continue in effect. Section 12(2) of the 2005 Act is in similar terms to s.3(5) of the 1985 Act.

Purpose
(i) Knowledge of the capital limit

2.418   *CIS/124/1990* held that it must be proved that the person actually knew of the capital limit rule, otherwise the necessary deliberate intention to obtain benefit could not have been present. It is not enough that the person ought to have known of the rule. The crunch comes, and the resolution with the approach in *R(SB) 40/85* (where it was suggested that the existence of some limit might be said to be common knowledge), in the assessment of the evidence about the person's knowledge. The Commissioner stresses that the person's whole background must be considered, including experience of the social security system and advice which is likely to have been received from the family and elsewhere. The burden of proof is on the Secretary of State, but in some circumstances a person's assertion that they did not know of the rule will not be credible. In *CIS/124/1990* itself the claimant was illiterate and spoke and understood only Gujerati. The Commissioner says that this should put her in no better or worse situation than a literate claimant whose mother tongue was English, but that the possibility of misunderstandings in interpretation should be considered. *CIS/124/1990* is followed in *R(SB) 12/91*, where the necessity of a positive finding of fact, based on sufficient evidence, that the person knew of the capital limit is stressed. Evidence that the person had been in receipt of supplementary benefit or income support for some years was not in itself enough. But information which the person has received, together with their educational standing and other factors, will be material in deciding whether actual knowledge exists or not. *CIS/30/1993* similarly holds that it is not possible to infer actual knowledge of the capital limit simply from the claimant signing a claim form which contained that information. The claimant there was partially sighted and had not completed the claim form herself but merely signed it. It was necessary for the tribunal to indicate what evidence satisfied it that the claimant did know of the capital limit.

Where a claimant has not previously claimed a means-tested benefit, nor made any inquiry about the conditions of entitlement, nor had any dealings with benefits, a specific finding that they knew of the capital limit is required (*LBC Waltham Forest v TM* [2009] UKUT 96 (AAC)).

However, in *RB v SSWP (ESA)* [2016] UKUT 384, Judge Markus, while accepting that normally a precise finding has to be made, said that there are some cases where there is no potentially credible alternative explanation for the payments made by the claimant and where the facts speak for themselves on both purpose and knowledge. So in the particular case the tribunal's statement that, after rejecting the claimant's explanations, it was left with only one conclusion that he had deprived himself of capital to continue to obtain old style ESA encompassed his knowledge of the effect of having the capital. It was also relevant that the claimant had never suggested at any stage of the case that he did not know of the capital limit. It may, though, when what is in issue is not whether the notional capital is above the £16,000 limit, but whether it would give rise to tariff income by exceeding £6,000, be necessary to consider whether the claimant knew of the tariff income rules. That point was unfortunately not explored in *RB*, although it potentially arose on the facts found by the tribunal (see the discussion in para.2.423 below).

(ii) The test for "purpose"

The decision-maker has to show that the person's purpose is one of those men-   2.419
tioned in para.(1). That approach was applied in *LP v SSWP (ESA)* [2018] UKUT 389 (AAC) at para.13, but see the discussion of *RB v SSWP (ESA)* [2016] UKUT 384 (AAC) below. There is unlikely to be direct evidence of purpose (although there might be contemporary letters or documents), so that primary facts must be found from which an inference as to purpose can be drawn (*CSB 200/1985, R(SB) 40/85*).See further discussion below.

The view put forward in *CSB 28/81* that the test is of the person's predominant purpose is rejected in *R(SB) 38/85* and *R(SB) 40/85*. In *R(SB) 38/85* it was suggested that it was enough that a subsidiary purpose was to obtain supplementary benefit. In *R(SB) 40/85* the Commissioner says that that must be a "significant operative purpose." If the obtaining of benefit was a foreseeable consequence of the transaction then, in the absence of other evidence, it could be concluded that that was the person's purpose. That would exclude some cases caught by the width of the approach to deprivation, e.g. where a resource is converted into another form in which it is still taken into account. For then there would be no effect on eligibility for benefit. But beyond that situation there remain great difficulties. The Commissioners mention a number of relevant factors, e.g. whether the deprivation was a gift or in return for a service, the personal circumstances of the person (e.g. age, state of health, employment prospects, needs), whether a creditor was pressing for repayment of a loan. It must be an issue of fact when these other factors indicate that the reasonably foreseeable consequence of obtaining benefit was not a significant operative factor. A tribunal is not entitled to infer that the claimant had the relevant purpose simply from rash and excessive expenditure with some knowledge of some sort of capital limit—it has to go further and consider whether on its assessment of the claimant's character and thinking this is what happened (*CH/264/2006*, a case on the equivalent housing benefit provision). As *R(H) 1/06* (another case on the equivalent housing benefit provision) confirms, the test is a subjective one, which depends upon the evidence about the particular claimant in question (the claimant in that case was a schizophrenic whose mental state was such that he was unlikely to fully appreciate the implications of his behaviour and had limited capacity to plan for the future). See also *KW v SSWP (IS)* [2012] UKUT 350 (AAC) in which the claimant spent £40 to £100 a day of his inheritance on "one or two females out of four doing some fetish things for me". The claimant had a personality disorder and may not have appreciated the potential implications of his behaviour.

R(H) 1/06 is followed in *CIS/218/2005*. The claimant in *CIS/218/2005* had made large gifts to her children from the proceeds of the sale of her former matrimonial home. The Commissioner states that whether a gift is reasonable or prudent, although relevant, does not answer the question of whether it was made for the purpose of securing or increasing entitlement to income support. The test is not one of reasonableness or prudence but what has to be considered is the claimant's purpose. On the other hand, in *CJSA/1425/2004* the fact that it was reasonable for the claimant to pay his credit card debts in order to avoid further liability for interest led to the conclusion that this had not been done for the purpose of obtaining or increasing entitlement to income-based JSA *(CJSA/1425/2004* is discussed further below).

2.420   The length of time since the disposal of the capital may be relevant (*CIS 264/1989*).

It has been held that where the claimant had been accurately warned about the consequences of a transaction by the local DSS office (i.e. that reg.51(1) would be applied) and still went ahead, this showed that he could not have had as any part of his purpose securing of entitlement, or continued entitlement, to income support (*CIS 621/1991*). But there must be limits to generalising from this decision. Can claimants, in cases not involving specific Departmental advice, be heard to say that because of their existing knowledge of the capital limits and the notional capital rules they anticipated that depriving themselves of some capital asset would not affect entitlement to benefit because they would be treated as having notional capital as a result, and thereby secure the very opposite result on the basis that their purpose could not have been to secure or increase entitlement? To admit the validity of such an argument would seem to involve internal contradictions in identifying claimants' purposes, not to mention ludicrous outcomes. That argument cannot be right.

An even more misguided suggestion, extraordinarily made on behalf of the Secretary of State, was rejected in *LP v SSWP (ESA)* [2018] UKUT 389 (AAC) at paras 8–11. This was that, since at the time of the deprivation (of amounts received as lump sums from a personal pension scheme) the claimant was in receipt of the maximum amount of income-related ESA she could aspire to, she could not have thought that spending the money could increase the amount of that benefit and securing or increasing benefit could not have been an operative purpose. The fundamental mistake in that suggestion was to ignore the potential purpose of securing entitlement for the weeks following the receipt of the capital if the DWP were informed or found out about the receipt. That could have been in her thoughts.

The effect of DWP advice on the claimant's intention is further considered in *LH v SSWP (IS)* [2014] UKUT 60 (AAC). The claimant received £54,000 from an endowment policy. She did not inform the DWP at the time because she thought that since the policy had been set up to pay the mortgage it did not count as capital. However, she was not required to use the money to pay off her mortgage and so she used part of it to pay other debts which charged a higher rate of interest. When she was later visited by a DWP officer, she sought advice from him about the impact on her income support entitlement of using the proceeds from the policy to pay off her debts before meeting her mortgage liability. He informed her that it was reasonable and acceptable to pay off outstanding loans and debts before using the remainder to pay off part of the mortgage, as long as she did not spend the money on, for example, exotic holidays. The officer did not advise the claimant that she would be able to secure entitlement to income support if she used the remaining excess capital in the way she was doing, nor was this the advice sought by the claimant. After the visit she continued to use the proceeds of the policy to pay her debts before paying off part of the mortgage.

2.421   Judge Wright emphasises that the effect of the advice depends on precisely what advice is sought, and given, and its context. He disagrees with the obiter remarks made in *CIS/307/1992* that advice given would of itself nullify any finding of adverse intention under para.(1) and thus insulate a claimant from being caught by para. (1). In his view (again obiter), if a claimant sought advice from the DWP in relation to disposal of capital, e.g. an inheritance, and was wrongly advised that it would not affect his entitlement, arguably securing or retaining entitlement to income support would have been the significant operative purpose behind the disposal of the capital. On the other hand, if the claimant was being taken to court over debts, the advice given would not change the position that staying on benefit was not a "significant operative purpose", the main motivation being to pay the debts.

Judge Wright concluded that the claimant's disposal of the capital after the DWP visit was not made with the "significant operative purpose" of securing entitlement to income support. In his view, it was reasonable for the claimant to use the proceeds of the policy to pay debts which she could not meet in any other way and which would avoid greater indebtedness than if they had not been paid off. Those were actions she had taken before the DWP officer's visit and planned to take after the visit, regardless of the consequences for her entitlement to income support, albeit that the remarks of the visiting officer reassured her that taking such steps was appropriate and either would not, or was unlikely to, affect her entitlement to income support. The tribunal had erred by failing to adequately investigate the effect of the DWP's advice and by focusing on whether the debts were immediately repayable, rather than the reasons *why* the claimant used the proceeds of the policy in the way that she did.

In effect, the test seems to be whether the person would have carried out the transaction at the same time if there had been no effect on eligibility for benefit. Similarly, where the transaction had no effect on the claimant's entitlement, as in *CJSA/3937/2002* where the property transferred was the house in which the claimant was living (which was therefore disregarded under para.1 of Sch.8 to the JSA Regulations 1996), an intention to secure entitlement to income-based JSA was not shown. The onus of proof on the Secretary of State may come into play in marginal cases.

A number of other decisions have firmed up the principles to be applied. **2.422**

The Commissioner in *R(SB) 9/91* stresses that a positive intention to obtain benefit must be shown to be a significant operative purpose. It is not enough for the AO merely to prove that the obtaining of benefit was a natural consequence of the transaction in question. The claimant had transferred her former home to her two daughters. Evidence was given that her sole intention was to make a gift to her daughters, as she intended to leave the property to them in her will and it was no longer of any use to her (she being permanently in need of residential nursing care). The Commissioner notes that this did not explain why the transfer was made when it was, why the proceeds of sale of the property would not have been of use to the claimant and what she thought she would live on if she gave the property away. She had been in receipt of supplementary benefit for several years. On the evidence the obtaining of benefit was a significant operative purpose. As *CJSA 1395/2002* confirms, *R(SB) 9/91* thus endorses the attribution of an intention to a claimant by implication from all the circumstances but the conclusion must be in terms of the claimant's purpose, not in terms of the natural consequences of the transaction in question. See *R(H) 1/06* (applied in *CIS/218/2005*) referred to above, which reiterates that it is necessary for a tribunal to determine the claimant's actual (i.e. subjective) intention.

In some circumstances the principles of *Kerr v Department for Social Development* [2004] UKHL 23; [2004] 1 W.L.R. 1372; *R 1/04 (SF)* may be relevant, even though the burden of showing a prohibited purpose lies on the Secretary of State, in that a failure by a claimant to come forward with evidence within his knowledge to support his explanations for the making of payments may support an inference that the purpose was to obtain benefit. That was the case in *RB v SSWP (ESA)* [2016] UKUT 384 (AAC). The claimant, who had been in receipt of income-related ESA since January 2013, received some £26,000 from a divorce settlement on March 7, 2014. On March 26, 2014 he made two payments of £6,000 each to his parents, which he said was to repay loans. On April 9, 2014 he paid £5,760 to his landlord by way of a year's rent in advance. The claimant supplied bank statements showing a number of cash withdrawals from his mother's account totalling £8,980 between June 2012 and April 2014, but no statements for his father's bank account. The tribunal confirmed the initial decision that all three payments had been made to reduce his capital below £16,000 and secure entitlement to ESA, so that the equivalent of reg.51(1) applied and entitlement to ESA ceased. It stated that it could not be "sure to the required standard" that the withdrawals from the mother's account, in the light of the pattern of amounts, were not merely to meet her own living expenses and that, with the absence of any contemporaneous evidence of the loans and of bank statements from the father's account, the claimant had not established that he had borrowed £12,000 from his parents. The advance payment of rent was said to be ridiculous in the absence of evidence that it was required by his tenancy agreement, so that it had to be concluded that it had been made to deprive himself of capital. Judge

Markus held that the tribunal had not erred in law in its approach to the burden and standard of proof. She took perhaps a generous view in reading the tribunal's statement of reasons as a whole, which in parts had given the appearance of requiring the claimant to disprove, to a level of sureness, that the payments were not made for the purpose of securing entitlement to ESA. Applying the *Kerr* principle that the claimant should supply as much information as he reasonably could, the state of the evidence was such that, the tribunal having rejected the claimant's credibility in general, there could have been no doubt that the finding as to the purpose of the payments was properly established.

2.423   It is unfortunate that the following conundrum was not addressed in *RB*. There was no mention of the claimant having other capital assets. On that basis, by the time that he paid the year's rent in advance his actual capital had been reduced below £16,000 by the two payments to his parents. Could it then be said that his purpose was to secure entitlement to ESA? If he had sufficient knowledge of the capital rules for the regulation to apply in the first place, it is plainly arguable that it could not. It would be odd to draw a line between claimants who knew that there was a capital rule, but not of the amount of the limit, and claimants who knew of the significance of the amount of £16,000. However, the question would then have to be asked whether the advance payment of rent was made for the purpose of increasing the amount of ESA, by reducing the amount of tariff income treated as produced by capital exceeding £6,000. In those circumstances, it might then be argued that a specific finding needed to be made as to the claimant's knowledge of the rules on tariff income from capital below £16,000 (see paragraph 2.418 above).

In *CIS 242/1993*, another case where the claimant had gone into residential care, the Commissioner reaches the opposite conclusion on the facts to that in *R(SB) 9/91*. The claimant's son had cared for his mother for 15 years. When she went into a residential care home, she gave her share of the proceeds of sale of their jointly owned home to her son to be used towards the purchase of his flat. The Commissioner accepts that she had relinquished her share in gratitude to her son and not to secure income support.

In *R(IS) 13/94* the claimant's capital was in excess of the statutory limit when he purchased his council house. The deposit used up enough of his capital to bring him below the limit. It was necessary to consider whether para.(1) applied to this use of the capital since the claimant was apparently dependent on income support to meet the mortgage interest. But in *R(IS) 15/96* using a criminal injuries compensation award to pay off part of a mortgage was not caught by para.(1). The SSAT had found that the claimant's purpose had been to secure his future and to reduce the burden on the DSS for his mortgage payments. This was a matter for the judgment of the tribunal.

2.424   A further example is *CJSA 204/2002*. The claimant had agreed to provide the deposit for a flat that she and her son would buy. In the event the claimant did not move into the new flat with her son and his girlfriend because of a disagreement but she still lent her son the deposit. The claimant did correspond with her solicitor about obtaining security for the loan but no formal agreement or legal charge was entered into. The Commissioner holds that the claimant clearly had reasons for keeping her promise to lend the deposit (for example, so as not to let her son down or sour relations further) and in his view there had been no deprivation within reg.51(1). See also *R(IS) 1/03* above. It may often be pertinent in similar cases to pose the question of what the claimant thought they would live on if the asset in question was disposed of.

In *CIS 109/1994* and *CIS 112/1994* the claimants had used their capital to purchase an annuity and a life insurance policy respectively. In *CIS 109/1994* the claimant was both physically and mentally frail and lived in a nursing home. The tribunal found that at the material time she had no knowledge of the income support capital and deprivation of capital rules, and entered into the transaction on her son's advice, who considered that this was the best use of her capital to enable her to stay in the nursing home. The Commissioner holds that the tribunal had not erred in concluding that she had not purchased the annuity in order to obtain income support. In

CIS 112/1994 the Commissioner decides that para.(1) did apply, but that para.15 of Sch.10 applied to disregard the life policy. The Commissioner also deals with "double counting" of notional and actual capital (see below under *"Diminishing capital"*). See also *R(IS) 7/98* where capital had been used to purchase an "investment bond". The Commissioner decides that the bond fell within the definition of "policy of life insurance" in reg.2(1) and so could be disregarded under para.15 of Sch.10. But the claimant's intention at the time of the investment had to be considered to see whether para.(1) applied.

In *R(SB) 12/91* Commissioner Rice held that if capital is used to repay debts which are immediately repayable, then that could not be said to be for the purpose of obtaining benefit (see para.13). In *R(SB) 12/91* there were doubts whether the alleged debts, to members of the family, were legally enforceable debts and whether they were owed by the claimant personally. But the fact that a debt is not legally enforceable and/or immediately repayable does not mean that repayment of it must be for the purpose of securing income support. As *CJSA 1395/2002* points out, what the Commissioner said in *R(SB) 12/91* at para.14 was that in such circumstances "the question will arise" of whether the securing of benefit or an increased amount was a significant operative purpose. It is still necessary to consider the claimant's purpose in repaying the debt (*CIS 2627/1995, Jones v Secretary of State for Work and Pensions* [2003] EWCA Civ 964). In *Jones* the Court of Appeal emphasises that the issue as to whether or not repayment of a debt was for the purpose of obtaining income support was a question of fact to be determined according to the circumstances in each case. Thus, even if a debt was not immediately repayable, that did not necessarily mean that its repayment was made in order to obtain income support. Conversely (and more rarely) there could be cases where repayment of an immediately repayable debt was for the purpose of securing entitlement to income support—an example might be where the debtor thought the creditor would not call in the debt for some time but still made immediate repayment. It was a question of fact in each case. *London Borough of Waltham Forest v TM* [2009] UKUT 96 (AAC) recognises that a claimant's financial predicament and possible insolvency may alone be the reason for the repayment.

The facts in *Jones* were unusual. The claimant and her husband had sold some land and used the money to pay off a number of their many debts. One of those debts was for £17,000 which was owed to a friend, Mr S. The claimant's husband and Mr S came to an arrangement whereby the claimant purchased a BMW car for £13,500 as security for this debt. The car was to be Mr S's property but he allowed the claimant and her husband full use of it on the basis that they paid all the running costs. The issue was whether the claimant's significant operative purpose in entering into this arrangement was the retention of entitlement to income support. 2.425

The Court of Appeal held that since the tribunal had accepted that the car belonged to Mr S, the effect of the transaction had been that the debt to Mr S had been repaid. The fact that Mr S was content for the money to be used to buy him a car was irrelevant, as was the fact that Mr S was content for the claimant and her husband to use the car. On the facts Mr S had been pressing for repayment of the debt and so the claimant had not deprived herself of capital for the purpose of securing entitlement to income support. However, even if the true position was that the claimant had not repaid Mr S and the car was hers, it was subject to a charge by way of security in favour of Mr S for £17,000 and so under reg.49(a)(ii) the charge had to be deducted from the value of the car (with the result that its value was nil). It could not be said that in creating the charge on the car the claimant had deprived herself of capital for the purpose of securing entitlement to income support since clearly this was the only way the claimant could secure use of the car and if the arrangement had not been made the claimant and her husband would have had to repay the £17,000 loan.

The question of whether a claimant who has used capital to repay debts is caught by para.(1) and in particular to what extent does it matter that the creditor is not pressing for payment, was revisited in *VW v SSWP (IS)* [2015] UKUT 51 (AAC), reported as [2015] AACR 39. The claimant had repaid her ex-partner £7,000 on the same day that she had been visited by a DWP compliance officer. She later supplied more details about the loan, together with a letter from her ex-partner stating that he had asked for the money to be returned because he himself had debts and his working hours had been reduced and there was a chance that he would lose his job altogether. Judge Rowland stated:

> "11. It is quite common for it to be argued that a debt is not immediately repayable if the creditor is not pressing for payment. However, it is clear from both *R(SB) 12/91* and from what Dyson LJ said in *Jones* that that is not terminologically accurate. All debts are immediately repayable unless there is a mutual agreement to the contrary, as in the examples given by Mr Commissioner Rice in paragraph 14 of *R(SB) 12/91*. On the other hand, as Dyson LJ makes clear, even where a debt is immediately repayable, a debtor who believes that the creditor will not call it in for some time is in the same position vis-à-vis regulation 51 as he or she would be if the debt were not immediately repayable.
>
> 12. Moreover, Dyson LJ also makes it clear that the fact that a debt *is not* immediately repayable or a creditor *is not* calling in an immediately repayable debt, is not decisive against the claimant for the purpose of regulation 51. Schiemann LJ mentioned the person who pays off a bank overdraft. In *CJSA/1425/2004*, I considered the position of a person who had paid off credit card debts and held that the payment had not been for the purpose of obtaining income-related jobseeker's allowance.
>
> 13. But, what if a creditor *is* calling for repayment of an immediately repayable debt? It is clear from the Court of Appeal's decision that it is a question of fact whether a claimant paying such a debt thereby deprives himself or herself of capital for the purpose of securing entitlement to income support or increasing the amount of that benefit, rather than it being an inevitable legal consequence that that is not the purpose of the deprivation. To that extent, the Court disagreed with Mr Commissioner Rice. However, this disagreement may be more one of legal theory than of practical significance. Dyson LJ said that "the fact-finder will not usually conclude that, in making the payment, the debtor's purpose was to secure an entitlement to income support, rather than simply to repay the debt" and none of the Judges suggested any circumstance in which it would be reasonable to say that a person who had no choice but to repay a debt was caught by regulation 51(1) as a result of the repayment."

Judge Rowland concluded that, although the compliance officer's visit may have precipitated the repayment of the loan, the debt had to be paid and the claimant had no *legitimate* choice but to repay it immediately; the repayment had not therefore been made for the purpose of obtaining income support.

2.426   *CJSA/1425/2004*, referred to in *VW v SSWP*, had concerned payment of credit card debts. The claimant had been made redundant and claimed JSA three months later. His claim was initially processed as a claim for contribution-based JSA only but was later "reviewed" and income-based JSA was awarded from the date of the initial claim. Between the date of the initial claim and the application for "review" the claimant paid £6,000 to three credit card accounts and £3,000 to his mother. The Commissioner accepts that the timing of the payments indicated that the claimant knew that this would reduce his capital to a level that would entitle him to benefit and that this was one purpose of the payments. However it did not follow that the claimant did not intend to pay the credit card bills in order to settle his debts and avoid the interest that would otherwise be charged on them. If the claimant had mixed motives, the question whether the purpose of obtaining benefit was a significant operative purpose had to be determined by deciding whether it was reasonable for the claimant to act in the way that he did. In the Commissioner's view, the threat of having to make high-interest payments was just as capable of making it reasonable to pay a debt as the threat of enforcement of a liability to pay. He considered that any other view would be contrary to public policy as expressed in s.94 of the Consumer Credit Act 1974 which entitles a debtor under a regulated consumer credit agreement to discharge his indebtedness at any time. The plain purpose of that provision was to allow a debtor to escape further interest payments. The Commissioner commented that it "would be anomalous if the benefit system were to require people to incur additional liability for interest. I can see no reason why the benefit system should treat differently a person who has just cleared his debts to avoid them growing and a person who never had any debts". He therefore concluded that payment of the credit cards debts was reasonable and was for the purpose of avoiding further substantial liabilities for interest payments and not for the purpose of obtaining or increasing entitlement to income-based JSA. However, the Commissioner did not find it reasonable for the claimant to have repaid his mother (the appellant's own evidence to the tribunal had been that "[i]t wasn't a loan but I felt obliged to give it back when she asked") and that this had been done for the purpose of increasing entitlement to income-based JSA.

However, in *CH/264/2006* the Commissioner disagrees with the approach of *CJSA/1425/2004* because in his view it "erroneously converts an evidentiary factor of reasonableness into a legal test and a subjective test of purpose into an objective test of reasonableness". Certainly as other decisions, for example *R(H) 1/06* and *CIS/218/2005*, have emphasised, correctly it is suggested, the test is one of the claimant's purpose, rather than whether the disposal/expenditure was reasonable or prudent, although reasonableness is a relevant factor. To the extent, therefore, that the Commissioner in *CJSA/1425/2004* considered that the reasonableness of the claimant's actions was determinative, his decision would seem to be out of step with the other authorities. He has, however, reiterated his view in *JM v SSWP* [2009] UKUT 145 (AAC). It was from the test of reasonableness of the expenditure that one inferred whether the claimant intended to gain entitlement to benefit or merely knew that that would be the consequence of the expenditure. A person who knows of the capital limit must be taken to realise that benefit may be payable if he disposes of capital above that limit and to intend that consequence if the expenditure was unreasonable.

SH v London Borough of Tower Hamlets (HB) [2011] UKUT 500 (AAC), however, agrees with the criticism of *CJSA/1425/2004* in *CH/264/2006*. In *SH* Judge Mark also disagrees with Judge Rowland's comments in *JM v SSWP*. In his view, such presumed intention is not the same as purpose. A person may act unreasonably in a way that could foreseeably lead to impoverishment but that did not mean that she acted "for the purpose of securing entitlement" to benefit. Making an unreasonable judgment or simply not thinking about the consequences did not mean that the person had acted for the purpose of obtaining benefit. The obtaining of benefit had to be a positive part of the person's planning.

CIS 40/1989 provides an interesting example on its facts of the securing or increase of benefit not being a significant operative purpose. The claimant had been on supplementary benefit and then income support since 1978. Her father died intestate. The estate consisted almost entirely of a house in which the claimant's sister had lived with the father. The claimant and her sister were the sole beneficiaries of the estate. Legal proceedings had to be taken to enforce a sale of the house. In March 1988 the claimant received £38,000 net of costs, which her solicitor divided equally between the claimant, her son, her daughter and her grand-daughter. After repaying a number of debts and buying a secondhand car, the amount possessed by the claimant quickly fell below £6,000. The tribunal found that she should be treated as still possessing the amounts given to her children and grandchild. The Commissioner, having heard the claimant give evidence and be cross-examined, accepted that her purpose was to carry out her father's wishes, which were that the house should be used to provide for his grandchildren and great-grandchildren. She had originally intended to take nothing, but had been encouraged by her children to take a quarter share. She knew of the capital limit, but did not know of the effect her actions would have on her benefit entitlement. On these particular facts, the Commissioner found that para. (1) did not apply. See also *CJSA 1395/2002* in which the claimant considered herself under a moral obligation to give £10,000 to her mother, brother and sister after her grandmother had made the claimant the sole beneficiary under her will, allegedly to spite the rest of the family.

2.427

In many cases of alleged deprivation of capital there will have been a course of spending, often on various items, and sometimes over a considerable period of time. In *R(H) 1/06* (a case on the equivalent housing benefit provision), the Commissioner emphasises the need to go through all the various items of expenditure, taking account of any explanations put forward by the claimant, and to reach a specific determination as to: (i) what amounts (if any) represent deprivation of capital in excess of a reasonable level of general expenditure in the claimant's circumstances; and as regards *those* (ii) what had been the claimant's purpose at the time and whether this included an intention to obtain benefit. The tribunal had erred in simply expressing its decision in generalised terms without attempting to analyse the movements on the claimant's account during the relevant period. *CIS/1775/2007* makes the same point. The tribunal had been wrong to treat all payments as having been made with the same motivation but should have considered each type of expenditure separately when applying the significant operative purpose test.

There was a problem on the transfer from the corresponding supplementary benefit provisions in 1988, discussed in previous editions. In short, it was whether claimants who deprived themselves of capital under the supplementary benefit regime, before income support existed, could be said to have done so for the purpose of securing entitlement to income support so as to be caught by reg.51(1) once the income support legislation had come into force. The decisions on the point do not now need to be examined in detail. There may, though, be a continuing relevance in the holding in *R(IS) 14/93* that the words "income support" in reg.51(1) cannot be taken to refer to means-tested benefits that previously went under the name of supplementary benefit. That is because, unlike reg.42(1) on the deprivation of income, reg.51(1) has not been amended to make it bite where the claimant's purpose is to secure entitlement to or increase the amount of JSA or ESA as well as when the purpose relates to income support. Thus, if a deprivation of capital occurs while a claimant is receiving, or contemplating a claim for, old style JSA or ESA, it may be arguable, depending on the exact circumstances, that the if claimant later claims income support the purpose of the deprivation was not to secure entitlement to income support.

Note that the corresponding regulation under old style JSA (reg.113(1) of the JSA Regulations 1996) applies if a person has deprived himself of capital in order to secure entitlement to or increase the amount of JSA *or income support*. That avoids the question that might otherwise have arisen on a claimant transferring from income support to JSA as to whether a deprivation which had only been for the purposes of income support could be caught by reg.113(1). Similarly the ESA deprivation rule (reg.115(1) of the ESA Regulations 2008—see Vol.I in this series) applies if a person has deprived himself of capital in order to secure entitlement to, or increase the amount of, ESA *or income support or JSA*.

Effect of bankruptcy on the notional capital rule

2.428   In *London Borough of Waltham Forest v TM* [2009] UKUT 96 (AAC) the claimant used the proceeds of sale of a property to repay loans to three family members three months before he was made bankrupt. The issue was whether any resulting notional capital that the claimant was found to have for the purposes of his housing benefit claim was part of his estate as a bankrupt. It is held that since by definition the claimant does not possess the capital but is only deemed to do so for the purposes of entitlement to benefit, notional capital is not part of a bankrupt's estate as defined in the Insolvency Act 1986. Thus the application of the notional capital rule was not affected by the claimant's bankruptcy. *KS v SSWP (JSA)* [2009] UKUT 122 (AAC), reported as [2010] AACR 3, agrees with *TM* where the deprivation occurs before a bankruptcy order is made. After the making of the order, however, claimants cannot deprive themselves of capital for the purposes of para.(1) (see under *"Deprivation"* at the beginning of this note). Judge Mark goes on to suggest that if a claimant presents a petition, or possibly fails to resist a petition presented by a creditor, and is declared bankrupt as a result, they may be found to have deprived themselves of capital if they have taken this step (or not opposed the petition) for the purpose of securing entitlement to benefit. The capital they would have deprived themselves of would be the capital they were entitled to after taking into account what they would have to pay to avoid bankruptcy. This is unlikely to be much in most circumstances.

Diminishing capital

There were problems from the removal of discretion in the shift to income support in 1998. Under the Supplementary Benefit (Resources) Regulations this was used in particular for two purposes. One was to avoid double counting with the rule about personal possessions, now contained in para.10 of Sch.10. The value of personal possessions is not disregarded if they were acquired with the intention of reducing capital so as to gain entitlement to benefit. With no discretion at either end a claimant could have the market value of the possessions counted as part of his actual capital and the money spent on them counted as notional capital under this paragraph. The Commissioner in *CIS 494/1990* avoided this problem by treating only the shortfall between the market value of the personal possessions from time to time and the purchase price (the "depreciation") as the notional capital to be imputed under reg.51(1). This is followed in part in *R(IS)8/04*. The Commissioner in *R(IS)8/04* agrees that only the shortfall should be treated as notional capital but does not agree that the notional capital should be deemed to increase over time in line with the reduction in the market value of the asset. In his view the amount of the capital of which the claimant had deprived himself had to be fixed at the date of the deprivation, since it was only that amount to which the prohibited purpose in reg.51(1) could be attached. Any future depreciation could only fairly be said to result from the operation of the market and not from the claimant's original purpose to gain entitlement to benefit. It would also seem to be difficult to combine such an increase with the diminishing capital rule under reg.51A.

In *CIS 112/1994* the Commissioner had also recognised the gross unfairness to a claimant if she were to be penalised twice because of the lack of discretion in reg.51(1). In the Commissioner's view this was not the intention of the regulation. But in that case double counting did not arise. The claimant had purchased a life insurance policy with a legacy. Although she was to be treated as still possessing the notional capital by virtue of reg.51(1), the actual capital (the life policy) could be disregarded under para.15 of Sch.10.

The second problem for which the use of discretion was useful was that it was unfair to fix claimants with an amount of notional capital for eternity. If they had still had the capital and not been entitled to benefit, they would have had to use up the capital for living expenses. Thus the figure of notional capital could be reduced by the equivalent of the weekly benefit lost by the capital counting (*R(SB) 38/85, R(SB) 40/85*). There had seemed no possibility of such a process applying to reg.51(1) until the decision of the Tribunal of Commissioners in *R(IS) 1/91*. The Tribunal concluded that the diminishing capital rule did apply. That was because para.(6) provides that regs 45–50 apply to the calculation of notional capital as if it was actual capital. If claimants have capital over the prescribed limit, reasonable expenditure on living and other sensible expenses (not necessarily limited to income support rates) will reduce the amount of capital until it falls below the limit. They will then be entitled to income support. The same situation is held to apply where it is notional capital, rather than actual, which is held initially. The decision is wrong in principle, because if actual capital is held, the actual amount, reduced by any expenditure, must be considered week by week. That is not a consequence of any of regs 45–50 and there is no analogy with the notional reduction of notional capital. Paragraph (6) is primarily concerned with the calculation of the market value of assets. Nonetheless, *R(IS) 1/91* must be followed in relation to weeks before October 1, 1990.

With effect from October 1, 1990, reg.51A provides an express diminishing notional capital rule. *R(IS) 9/92* decides that while the principles of *R(IS) 1/91*

2.429

apply up to that date, they do not apply thereafter. They are superseded by the rules laid down in reg.51A. See also *CIS 3268/2002*, discussed in the notes to reg.51A, as to the date when the rule in reg.51A comes into play and as to the position before that rule operates. *R(IS)8/04* confirms that reg.51A only applies if the claimant is not entitled to income support or entitled to a reduced amount of income support because of notional capital; it does not operate if for example their actual capital exceeds the prescribed limit (see further the notes to reg.51A). In that case their actual capital can reduce by the amount of their expenditure, using inferences in the fact-finding process if necessary (*CIS/2287/2008*).

Paragraph (2)

2.430   It is not at all clear what sort of capital would be caught by this rule. It must be available simply on application, with no other conditions, but not amount to actual capital (cf. *R(SB) 26/86* and *R(SB) 17/87*). Examples might be money held in court which would be released on application or arrears of employer's sick pay which needed to be applied for. Note the exclusions. Although discretionary trusts are specifically excluded, a potential beneficiary would not seem to be caught by para. (2) anyway. More than an application is needed for payment to be made: the discretion has to be exercised. On sub-paras (d) and (da) see the note to reg.42(2)(g) and (2ZA)–(2CA). On sub-paras (e) and (f) see the notes to paras 44 and 45 of Sch.10.

In *LC v Bournemouth Borough Council (HB)* [2016] UKUT 175 (AAC) Judge White applies reg.49(2) of the Housing Benefit Regulations 2006 (the equivalent of para.(2)) in a case where the proceeds of sale of a former matrimonial home were being held in a solicitors' client account until the claimant's partner and his ex-wife agreed how the sum was to be split. The claimant stated that it would be necessary to go to court to reach a settlement and that was likely to take between eight months and a year. The local authority had jumped the gun by treating the claimant as having capital in excess of £16,000 from the date that the proceeds of sale were placed in the client account. The local authority should make an assessment of the likely period it would take for a Financial Dispute Resolution hearing to be concluded and advise the claimant that the local authority would regard her as having capital above £16,000 from that date. Judge White also held that reg.51 of the Housing Benefit Regulations (the equivalent of reg.52) did not apply in these circumstances (see the notes to reg.52).

Paragraphs (3) and (3A)

2.431   Note that if the conditions are met, there is no discretion whether or not to apply para.(3). In this respect, as in others, *R(SB) 6/88* would be decided differently under income support.

Paragraph (3)(a) applies where payments are made to a third party in respect of the claimant or any partner. (The form of this provision in force before April 6, 2004, and which remains in force for "transitional cases"—see the note to reg.17, also applied if payments were made to a third party in respect of any child or young person who was a member of the claimant's family. However, with effect from April 6, 2004 (except in "transitional cases"—see the note to reg.17) amounts for children and young persons were removed from the income support scheme (financial support for children and young persons was from then on to be provided through the child tax credit system, see Vol. IV in this series) and income support became in effect an "adults only" benefit. Thus the current form of para.(3)(a) only applies to payments made to a third party in respect of the claimant or his partner, if any.)

If the payment is derived from a benefit or pension listed in head (i) it counts as the claimant's. From November 15, 1999 this also applies to a payment from an occupational or personal pension (head (ia)), but not if the payment is made to the trustee in bankruptcy (or other person acting on the creditors' behalf) of a person who is bankrupt (or the subject of sequestration) and he (and his partner (before April 6, 2004, and still in "transitional cases"—see the note to reg.17, his family)) has no other actual or notional income (para.(3A)(c)). See *R(IS) 4/01* in the note to reg.42(4) and (4ZA) on the effect of head (ia). From April 6, 2006 head (ia) and para.(3A)(c) also apply to payments from the Pension Protection Fund ("PPF"). The PPF has been set up under the Pensions Act 2004 to provide protection for members of an occupational pension scheme in the event of their employer's insolvency.

In other cases the payment counts as the claimant's in so far as it is actually used for food, ordinary clothing or footwear, fuel, housing costs met by income support or housing benefit, council tax or water charges (head (ii)). "Ordinary clothing or footwear" is defined in para.(8) in terms of normal daily use. Paragraph 29867 of the *Decision Makers Guide* suggests that wellington boots are not for "normal daily use", nor are special shoes needed because of a disability (as these are not worn by people in general on a daily basis).   2.432

If the payment is used for items or costs other than those listed in head (ii), it does not form part of the claimant's capital. However, *CJSA 1458/2002* holds that the exclusion from capital in head (ii) will not apply and money used for other items or costs will count as the claimant's if the money is paid to a third party at the claimant's own direction. The facts in *CJSA 1458/2002* were that the claimant had devised a scheme whereby rent from his tenant was paid into a particular account to be used "(either directly or indirectly) in respect of any of the landlords costs relating to the premises and (either directly or indirectly) in respect of any of the landlords mortgage capital repayments". The account into which the money was paid was a PEP (which the claimant had tried to open in the name of his mortgagee but had found this to be impossible in law). The Commissioner confirms the tribunal's decision that the claimant's deliberate failure to acquire an asset was a deprivation caught by para.(1). The claimant also contended that the payments into the PEP were excluded from his capital under head (ii) because they were being used for capital repayments on his mortgage. However, the tribunal had rejected this argument on the ground that the payments were not made to a third party but into an investment vehicle that was beneficially owned by the claimant. The Commissioner agreed with that analysis but stated that he would also reach the same result by another route, namely that the money was paid to the third party at the claimant's own direction and therefore the exclusion from capital in para.(3)(a) was not applicable. However, with respect to the Commissioner, it is suggested that there is nothing in the wording of para.(3)(a) that requires such an interpretation. Furthermore, it would seem to depart from the approach previously taken to this provision (and its income counterpart in reg.42(4)(a)(ii)), since it has long been recognised that the rules about payments to third parties do allow for some "benefit planning", as a means of meeting expenditure that is not covered by income support.

The operation of para.(3)(b) is clear. In these circumstances the payment would not form part of the claimant's actual capital in view of the obligation to use it for a third party.

Paragraph (3) does not apply to payments from the listed Trusts and Funds, nor to payments made in respect of an 18–25 year-old on a "New Deal" option or a person in the Intensive Activity Period ("IAP") of the New Deal (these schemes are no longer offered), nor to payments to a person aged 25 or over who is undertaking a "qualifying course" (see the note to reg.17A of the JSA Regulations 1996), or a person who is participating in the Mandatory Work Activity Scheme or a scheme listed in reg.3 of the Jobseeker's Allowance (Schemes for Assisting Persons to Obtain Employment) Regulations 2013 (para.(3A)). For the equivalent notional income disregard see reg.42(4ZA).

Paragraphs (4) and (5)

These two paragraphs establish an artificial method of dealing with one person companies or similar. The basic legal position is that if there is a company, the shareholders' assets are the value of the shares, not the value of the company's   2.433

assets (*R(SB) 57/83*). But under para.(4), if claimants are in a position analogous to a sole owner or partner in the business of the company (on which, see *R(IS) 8/92*), the value of their shareholding is disregarded, and they are treated as possessing a proportionate share of the capital of the company. The value is the net worth of the company's total assets taken together (*R(IS) 13/93*). The value of one particular asset within the total is not relevant in itself. However, as long as the claimant undertakes activities in the course of the business of the company, the amount produced by para.(4) is disregarded (para.(5)). Temporary interruptions in activity (e.g. holidays, short-term sickness) ought not to prevent para.(5) from applying. It is accepted in *R(IS) 13/93* that any activities which are more than de minimis satisfy para.(4). See also *R(IS) 14/98* discussed in the note to para.6 of Sch.10 (disregard of business assets for the self-employed).

This seems in many ways a generous provision, but there is a narrow line to be trodden for it to apply. To take the benefit of the disregard of the value of the notional capital (as with para.6 of Sch.10) the claimant must be undertaking activities in the course of the company's business, but to retain entitlement to income support must not be engaged in work for more than 16 hours a week (SSCBA s.124(1)(c) and reg.5). To count towards those hours under reg.5 payment must be made for the work or it must be done in expectation of payment. It is suggested that, even if the claimant was not taking a salary as an employee or director of the company, if the conditions of reg.51(4) were met, payment to the company or an expectation of payment to the company connected to the work of the claimant could be counted in determining whether the work was remunerative.

Note that reg.52 (capital jointly held) does not apply to notional capital under reg.51(4).

Paragraph (6)

2.434   One of the effects of para.(6) is that the disregards in Sch.10 can apply to notional capital. However, *CIS 30/1993* decides that the disregard in para.26 of Sch.10 (taking steps to dispose of premises) could not apply where the claimant had already disposed of the capital so as to trigger para.(1). Paragraph (6) did not provide any authority for altering the provisions of Sch.10 which could only apply where their conditions were met. This is a different view from that taken in some other decisions. See the note to para.26 of Sch.10.

CIS 231/1991 confirms that it is not necessary for the disregard under Sch.10 to have been applicable before the claimant deprived himself of the capital. The claimant had transferred his former home to his parents who were both over 60. When he claimed income support his parents were living in the home. The Commissioner holds that the former home fell to be disregarded under para.4(a) of Sch.10; the disregard in para.4 applied to notional, as well as actual, capital.

Paragraph (7)

2.435   The capital of which a person has deprived themselves must be actual capital. In *CIS 240/1992* and *CIS 30/1993* the Commissioner raises the question (without expressing a conclusion) as to whether para.(1) can apply when a claimant is deemed to possess an equal share in a capital asset under reg.52. In *CIS 240/1992* the claimant had a quarter share in a property, but the effect of reg.52 was thought (wrongly: *see Hourigan* below) to treat him as having a half-share. The claimant's parents (his mother owned the other three-quarters of the property) then bought his share for £5,000, out of which he repaid them loans of £3,883. The Commissioner points out that as reg.52 operated to treat the claimant as having a notional equal share in the property, his actual share should not also count, since otherwise there would be double counting. Therefore, when he sold his actual share to his parents, was there no disposal of *actual* capital at all, or no disposal to the extent that his notional share exceeded his actual share? Paragraph 29809 of the *Decision Makers Guide* assumes that the rule in para.(1) can only apply to the claimant's actual share of the capital, even though the effect of reg.52 is to deem him to own a larger share. But this does not entirely deal with the Commissioner's point. In fact in *CIS 240/1992*, since the property was subject to a tenancy, even if under para.(1) the claimant was treated as still possessing his actual interest, the disregard in para.5 of Sch.10 (as in force at that time) would result in him having no capital. The new tribunal would also have to consider whether para.(1) applied when the claimant repaid the loans (see *R(SB) 12/91* above). And note that the effect of the decision in *Hourigan v SSWP* [2002] EWCA Civ 1890, [2003] 1 W.L.R. 608, also reported as *R(IS) 4/03*, is that reg.52 is not applicable to what must have been a tenancy in common, not a joint tenancy.

[¹Diminishing notional capital rule

51A.—(1) Where a claimant is treated as possessing capital under regulation 51(1) (notional capital), the amount which he is treated as possessing—

    (a) in the case of a week that is subsequent to—

        (i) the relevant week in respect of which the conditions set out in paragraph (2) are satisfied, or

        (ii) a week which follows that relevant week and which satisfies those conditions,

    shall be reduced by an amount determined under paragraph (2);

    (b) in the case of a week in respect of which paragraph (1)(a) does not apply but where—

        (i) that week is a week subsequent to the relevant week, and

        (ii) that relevant week is a week in which the condition in paragraph (3) is satisfied,

    shall be reduced by the amount determined under paragraph (3).

(2) This paragraph applies to a benefit week or part week where the claimant satisfies the conditions that—

    (a) he is in receipt of income support; and

    (b) but for regulation 51(1), he would have received an additional amount of income support in that benefit week or, as the case may be, that part week;

and in such a case, the amount of the reduction for the purposes of paragraph (1)(a) shall be equal to that additional amount.

(3) Subject to paragraph (4), for the purposes of paragraph (1)(b) the condition is that the claimant would have been entitled to income support in the relevant week, but for regulation 51(1), and in such a case the amount of the reduction shall be equal to the aggregate of—

    (a) the amount of income support to which the claimant would have been entitled in the relevant week but for regulation 51(1); and for the purposes of this sub-paragraph if the relevant week is a part-week that amount shall be determined by dividing the amount of income support to which he would have been so entitled by the number equal to the number of days in the part-week and multiplying the quotient by 7;

    (b) the amount of housing benefit (if any) equal to the difference between his maximum housing benefit and the amount (if any) of housing benefit which he is awarded in respect of the benefit week, within the meaning of regulation 2(1) of [⁴ the Housing Benefit Regulations 2006] (interpretation), which includes the last day of the relevant week;

    (c) [⁶ . . .]

    [²(d) the amount of council tax benefit (if any) equal to the difference between his maximum council tax benefit and the amount (if any) of

2.436

council tax benefit which he is awarded in respect of the benefit week which includes the last day of the relevant week, and for this purpose "benefit week" [⁷ means a period of 7 consecutive days beginning on a Monday and ending on a Sunday].]

(4) The amount determined under paragraph (3) shall be redetermined under that paragraph if the claimant makes a further claim for income support and the conditions in paragraph (5) are satisfied, and in such a case—

- (a) sub-paragraphs [³(a) to (d)] of paragraph (3) shall apply as if for the words "relevant week" there were substituted the words "relevant subsequent week"; and
- (b) subject to paragraph (6), the amount as re-determined shall have effect from the first week following the relevant subsequent week in question.

(5) The conditions are that—

- (a) a further claim is made 26 or more weeks after—
  - (i) the date on which the claimant made a claim for income support in respect of which he was first treated as possessing the capital in question under regulation 51(1); or
  - (ii) in a case where there has been at least one re-determination in accordance with paragraph (4), the date on which he last made a claim for income support which resulted in the weekly amount being re-determined; or
  - (iii) the date on which he last ceased to be in receipt of income support;

  whichever last occurred; and
- (b) the claimant would have been entitled to income support but for regulation 51(1).

(6) The amount as re-determined pursuant to paragraph (4) shall not have effect if it is less than the amount which applied in that case immediately before the re-determination and in such a case the higher amount shall continue to have effect.

(7) For the purpose of this regulation—

- (a) "part-week" means a period to which sub-section (1A) of section 21 of the Act [SSCBA, s.124(5)] (amount etc. of income support) applies;
- (b) "relevant week" means the benefit week or part-week in which the capital in question of which the claimant has deprived himself within the meaning of regulation 51(1)—
  - (i) was first taken into account for the purpose of determining his entitlement to income support; or
  - (ii) was taken into account on a subsequent occasion for the purpose of determining or re-determining his entitlement to income support on that subsequent occasion and that determination or re-determination resulted in his beginning to receive, or ceasing to receive, income support;

  and where more than one benefit week or part-week is identified by reference to heads (i) and (ii) of this sub-paragraph the later or latest such benefit week or, as the case may be, the later or latest such part-week;
- (c) "relevant subsequent week" means the benefit week or part-week which includes the day on which the further claim or, if more than one further claim has been made, the last such claim was made.]

AMENDMENTS

1. Income Support (General) Amendment No.3 Regulations 1990 (SI 1990/1776) reg.6 (October 1, 1990).
2. Income-related Benefits Schemes (Miscellaneous Amendments) Regulations 1993 (SI 1993/315) Sch. para.4 (April 1, 1993).
3. Social Security (Miscellaneous Amendments) (No.3) Regulations 2001 (SI 2001/859) reg.6(2) (April 9, 2001).
4. Housing Benefit and Council Tax Benefit (Consequential Provisions) Regulations 2006 (SI 2006/217) reg.5 and Sch.2 para.1(3) (March 6, 2006).
5. Housing Benefit and Council Tax Benefit (Consequential Provisions) Regulations 2006 (SI 2006/217) reg.5 and Sch.2 para.1(4) (March 6, 2006).
6. Social Security (Miscellaneous Amendments) (No.6) Regulations 2008 (SI 2008/2767) reg.2(8) (November 17, 2008).
7. Council Tax Benefit Abolition (Consequential Provision) Regulations 2013 (SI 2013/458) reg.4 and Sch.2 para.1 (April 1, 2013).

DEFINITIONS

"benefit week"—see reg.2(1).
"claimant"—*ibid.*

GENERAL NOTE

See the note to reg.51(1) for the general background. Regulation 51A provides   **2.437**
for the reduction of the amount of notional capital fixed by reg.51(1). If the amount of notional capital remaining is not sufficient to remove entitlement to income support altogether, it is to be treated as reducing each week by the amount by which income support would be increased if it did not exist at all (paras (1)(a) and (2)). If the amount does remove entitlement it is to be treated as reducing each week by the amount of income support the person would receive if the notional capital had not been fixed plus the proportion of rent not met by housing benefit or council tax benefit (paras (1)(b) and (3)). It appears that since the replacement of council tax benefit by council tax reduction schemes there is now no scope for any reduction under para.(3)(d). There are complicated provisions for redetermination and recalculation.

Note that the reduction required by reg.51A does not start to operate until there is a week in which the claimant either would have been in receipt of income support (para.(3)) or would have been in receipt of an increased amount of income support (para.(2)) *but for* reg.51(1). Thus in *R(IS)8/04*, where the claimant had used capital to purchase a car for the purpose of securing entitlement to income support and it seemed likely that the value of the car (once this was established) would result in his actual capital exceeding the then prescribed limit of £8,000, reg.51A did not apply to reduce his notional capital. This was because it could not be said that "but for" the notional capital he would have been in receipt of income support.

The inter-relationship of this regulation, which ties the reduction in notional capital very much to income support rates, and *R(IS) 1/91* is of considerable difficulty. The Tribunal of Commissioners' diminishing capital rule worked on reasonable expenditure not necessarily limited to income support rates. Could a claimant take the benefit of this more generous rule, or was its implication from the regulations destroyed by the introduction of this express provision? *R(IS) 9/92* holds that the second alternative is correct.

Another pertinent issue is the date from which the diminishing notional capital rule applies. If reg.51A only operates from the date of the claim for income support, as its terms imply and as *CIS 3268/2002* confirms, it would seem unfair for some equivalent diminishing notional capital rule not to apply to amounts of notional capital during any gap between the date of the intentional deprivation and the claim for income support. This point is considered in *CIS 3268/2002*. However, the

Commissioner concludes that in many cases it is a "red herring". That is because expenses such as living and household expenses which could be taken into account in applying a diminishing notional capital rule will often have already been taken into account because the expenditure will have reduced the amount of the claimant's actual capital in the intervening period. If such expenses have already been taken into account there is no justification for making any further deduction from the amount of the notional capital. The Commissioner recognises that there may be a problem where a claimant has deprived himself of the entire amount of his actual capital in one transaction and then does not claim income support for some time. However, that did not arise on the facts of the case before him.

Capital jointly held

2.438   **52.**—Except where a claimant possesses capital which is disregarded under regulation 51(4) (notional capital), where a claimant and one or more persons are beneficially entitled in possession to any capital asset they shall be treated as if each of them were entitled in possession [¹to the whole beneficial interest therein in an equal share and the foregoing provisions of this Chapter shall apply for the purposes of calculating the amount of capital which the claimant is treated as possessing as if it were actual capital which the claimant does possess.]

AMENDMENT

1. Social Security Amendment (Capital) Regulations 1998 (SI 1998/2250) reg.2 (October 12, 1998).

DEFINITION

"claimant"—see reg.2(1) and reg.23(1).

GENERAL NOTE

2.439   Since this regulation has now been in its present form for more than 20 years, the detailed history of its amendment in 1995 and 1998 can be omitted. Readers who need to consider the state of the legislation prior to October 12, 1998 (possibly in relation to an alleged overpayment covering a very long past period) should consult the 2018/19 and earlier editions of what was then Vol.II of this series. In brief, the October 1995 amendment was intended to reverse the effect of the Court of Appeal's decision in *Chief Adjudication Officer v Palfrey*, reported as part of *R(IS) 26/95*, when reg.52 was in the same form as currently. That decision involved cases where the beneficial interest in property was held under a joint tenancy. The Court of Appeal rejected the argument that, once it was accepted that reg.52 in effect deemed the joint tenancy to have been severed so that the parties were to be treated as tenants in common in equal shares, the value of each share should be calculated by taking the market value of the whole property (less deductions for outstanding mortgage debt and expenses of sale) and dividing by the number of deemed tenants in common. It held that instead the market value of each deemed share should be identified. Where, as in *Palfrey* itself, the property was a dwelling house held for the purpose of accommodating the joint owners and that purpose still subsisted for the non-claimant(s) who should be taken as unwilling to sell (in *Palfrey* the daughter of the 81 year-old claimant who had moved into a residential care home), that value of the claimant's share might be a nominal amount. The 1995 amendment inserted a rule for valuation in accordance with the argument rejected in *Palfrey*. That amendment was held to be invalid by the Commissioner in *CIS/15963/1996*, *CIS/263/1997* and *CIS/3283/1997*. The Secretary of State decided not to appeal against that decision, but instead by the October 1998 amendment restored the text of reg.52 to its pre-1995 amendment form.

The decision in *Palfrey* thus remains a foundation stone in the interpretation of the current form of reg.52. The essence, according to Nourse LJ, is that, if the provision applies, the only entitlement known to the law under which the deemed circumstances of being entitled in possession to the whole beneficial interest and of the entitlement being to an equal share is a tenancy in common in equal shares. The phrase "in an equal share" is one long accepted as indicating a tenancy in common. Under such a tenancy each tenant is, while the asset is undivided, entitled to the whole in common with the other tenant(s) and, on division, to an equal share. (But do not forget that tenancies in common created in other ways can, and often do, have unequal shares). Problems of valuation are explored further below. The Court of Appeal noted that the sorts of capital assets covered are not limited to real property, but can extend to chattels or choses in action. Where the asset is easily divisible, such as a joint bank or building society account or a joint shareholding, there are likely to be fewer difficulties than in relation to real property. In relation to shares, note the exception to reg.52 where reg.51(4) applies, which disregards the value of a claimant's shareholding in a company in which they are in a position analogous to that of a sole owner or partner in the business and deems the claimant to possess capital equal to the value of the company's capital, or the appropriate share.

As mentioned above, the cases considered in *Palfrey* were all of real property held under a joint tenancy of the beneficial interest. There was a faint suggestion, particularly in Nourse LJ's judgment, that reg.52 might also apply to deem those holding the interest as tenants in common in unequal shares to have equal shares, but it was noted that no argument had been directed to that issue. The issue was expressly reserved for future decision in para.24 of the Tribunal of Commissioners' decision in *CIS/417/1992*, reported as part of *R(IS) 26/95*. The scope of reg.52 was certainly not determined by *Palfrey*. The DWP's view appears, however, to have remained that reg.52 could apply to tenancies in common. There had been support for that position in *CIS/204/1992*, where on brief consideration a claimant with a quarter-share of a property held with his mother as tenants in common was held by the Commissioner to be deemed to have a half-share.

However, doubt was thrown on that approach by the more detailed analysis in 2.440 *CIS 7097/1995*. The claimant's husband went to live in a nursing home on a permanent basis. In order to help finance the cost of this, £7,000 National Savings belonging to him was cashed in and paid into their joint bank account. It was never intended that this should thereby become part of the joint money in the account; it had simply been paid into the account so that the nursing home fees could be paid by direct debit. A separate tally was kept of this money which had been declared as the husband's own money for the purposes of his application to the local authority for help with the nursing home fees. The AO treated the claimant as entitled to half of the balance in the joint account (including the proceeds of her husband's National Savings) which when added to her other capital meant that she did not qualify for income support. However, the Commissioner holds that reg.52 did not apply to the proceeds of her husband's National Savings. Regulation 52 only operated where property was held in joint beneficial ownership because it was only then that two or more people were "beneficially entitled in possession" to a given capital asset. Regulation 52 was needed because of the special nature of joint beneficial ownership and deemed a joint beneficial owner to have the equal share that they would by law have if the joint ownership was severed. But cases where property was held in undivided shares fell outside reg.52 because under such an arrangement each co-owner was beneficially and individually entitled to their own share of the actual capital. Their share was a different asset from the shares belonging to the others; and in contrast to the joint right of a joint owner was an asset which was separately disposable. On the facts of this case, there was clear evidence that the normal presumption of joint beneficial ownership between a husband and wife operating a joint bank account did not apply. It was obviously intended that the proceeds of the husband's National Savings was to remain his sole property and that it had merely been paid into the joint account for convenience. The consequence was that the claimant was entitled to income support as her capital did not include any of her husband's National Savings. See also *JK v SSWP (JSA)* [2010] UKUT 437 (AAC), reported as [2011] AACR 26, in the note to reg.46 under "*Claimant holding as trustee*".

In *CIS/15936/1996*, *CIS/263/1997* and *CIS/3283/1997* the Commissioner expressly dissented from any statement in *CIS/7097/1995* that reg.52 was confined to joint tenancies and repeated his view that all kinds of co-ownership, including tenancies in common and joint tenancies, were covered by reg.52 (a view repeated in *CIS/2572/1997*). However, the position to the contrary has now been put beyond doubt by the decision of the Court of Appeal in *Hourigan v Secretary of State for Work and Pensions* [2002] EWCA Civ 1890, [2003] 1 W.L.R. 608, also reported as *R(IS) 4/03*. The claimant had purchased her home, which was conveyed into her sole name, from the local authority. Her son had contributed five-sixths of the purchase price and consequently she held the legal estate in trust for herself and her son as tenants in common in the proportions of one-sixth and five-sixths respectively. When she went into a residential care home her income support was stopped on the basis that she had capital in excess of the prescribed limit because she was deemed to be the beneficial owner of half the house under reg.52.

Brooke LJ accepted that the language of reg.52 lent itself naturally to the situation in which two or more people were jointly entitled to the equitable interest in the same capital asset since they did not each possess a separate share in the equitable interest. In that situation the effect of reg.52 was to treat the joint tenancy as severed and to deem the claimant to have an equal share (with the other joint tenants) of the whole beneficial interest. However, in relation to tenancies in common, there was no need for such a deemed severing as the beneficial interest that a tenant in common owned was a separately disposable asset. It was a misuse of language to say that the claimant and her son were beneficially entitled to the house within the meaning of reg.52 as they were not. To interpret the provision in the way contended for by the Secretary of State would require very much clearer words. The Court acknowledged that a crude deeming of equal apportionment where property is jointly-owned could produce unjust results, not only against claimants but also in some cases in their favour, as it could in the case of a tenancy in common. Its approach therefore was to restrict the manifest unfairness that could result from reg.52 to the situation where its wording clearly did apply, that is in relation to property held in joint beneficial ownership. The consequence was that it was the claimant's one-sixth share that fell to be valued with the result that she did not have capital in excess of the prescribed limit.

2.441   The Secretary of State decided not to apply for leave to appeal to the House of Lords against the decision in *Hourigan*. Thus the consequence is that it has now been authoritively established that reg.52 only applies to property held under a beneficial joint tenancy, not a tenancy in common. What reg.52 then deems is that the joint tenancy has been severed, so that the claimant becomes a deemed tenant in common of what, in the nature of the actual joint tenancy, must in any case be an equal share. Because there is only one interest (the so-called unity of interest) that is jointly owned, the interest of each tenant must be equal in extent, nature and duration, so that on severance the shares as tenants in common would have to be equal. *Goodman v Gallant* [1985] EWCA Civ 15, [1986] Fam. 106, mentioned in *Palfrey*, establishes that the sole exception could be where the terms of the trust establishing the joint tenancy expressly provided that on any severance the shares were not to be equal (which would be a vanishingly rare circumstance).

In the light of the limits on the scope of reg.52 established by *Palfrey* and *Hourigan*, arguments that the provision is invalid as being beyond the powers of s.136(5) of the SSCBA 1992 or as being irrational did not need to be addressed. The following question posed by Brooke LJ in *Hourigan* has been satisfactorily answered: "The intention of the statutory scheme is that people should be expected to dip into their capital rather than be reliant on the state for income support. Why should Parliament have expected people to dip into capital that they did not in fact possess?". The decisions secure that in substance claimants do not have to do that.

Former descriptions of the rule in reg.52 as extraordinary or draconian (see previous editions of this volume) can now only be applied to the original apparent policy intention and not to the effect of the rule on its proper interpretation.

Note that reg.52 only applies where the beneficial interest is jointly owned. It does not apply merely because there is a separation between legal and beneficial interests, for instance where one person holds assets on trust for another. But if an interest in a trust fund is jointly owned, then reg.52 may apply.

Former matrimonial assets

Thus reg.52 was held to apply in *R(IS)2/93*, where a building society account   2.442
in the claimant's sole name was in fact a joint asset of herself and her (separated) husband. She had to be treated as possessing half of the amount in the account, regardless of how it might be dealt with in matrimonial proceedings. But it is arguable that in the case of assets that are the subject of matrimonial (or other) dispute, reg.52 should not apply and their value should be disregarded, until ownership is resolved. See *Welfare Rights Bulletin* 108 p.5, referring to *CIS 298/1989* (a decision given without reasons). This should apply whether or not a couple were married. However, note *CIS 982/2002* which states that there is no general rule that property which is frozen or the subject of a dispute is to be disregarded or taken as having no value. The claimant and her husband, from whom she was separated, had a savings account in their joint names. The account was subject to a "matrimonial difficulties stop", the effect of which was that the claimant had no access to the funds without her husband's consent or an order from the court. The decision sets out a number of detailed questions that had to be considered in deciding whether the funds in the account were part of the claimant's capital and, if so, how her share was to be valued.

But in *LC v Bournemouth BC (HB)* [2016] UKUT 175 (AAC) Judge White holds that reg.51 of the Housing Benefit Regulations 2006 (the equivalent of reg.52) does not apply to the proceeds of sale held by a solicitor in a client account which could only be distributed with the agreement of the parties, or in accordance with an order of the court. That was because it could not be said that such funds constituted a capital asset to which the two parties were "beneficially entitled in possession". Judge White had doubts as to whether reg.51 applied to disputed matrimonial property at all.

Where the claimant had no legal title, joint or otherwise, to a property, but only a right to make a claim under the Matrimonial Causes Act 1973, she had no equitable interest unless and until a property adjustment order was made and before that her contingent right was not a capital asset at all (*R(IS) 1/03*). And note *R(IS) 1/97*, discussed in the note to para.5 of Sch.10, which decided that the claimant's wife, who had remained living in the former matrimonial home of which he was the sole legal owner, was a tenant for life under a constructive trust and so his interest could be disregarded under para.5.

Valuation under reg.52

The restoration of reg.52 to its original form on October 12, 1998 means that   2.443
it is the deemed equal share that has to be valued, *not* the proportionate share of the overall value that has to be taken (see the Court of Appeal's decision in *Chief Adjudication Officer v Palfrey*, reported as part of *R(IS) 26/95*, which had upheld the Tribunal of Commissioners' decisions in *CIS 391/1992* and *CIS 417/1992* (reported as part of *R(IS) 26/95*). The Tribunal of Commissioners gave detailed guidance as to the basis of a proper valuation of such a share (*CIS 391/1992*, paras 53 and 54). In both *CIS 391/1992* and *CIS 417/1992* ownership was shared with relatives who were unable or unwilling to sell the property or buy the claimant's interest. The Commissioners recognised, as did the Court of Appeal, that the market value in such cases may well be nil.

See J. Mesher and P. Wood, *Income-related Benefits: the Legislation* (1995) for a summary of the Tribunal of Commissioners' decision and the Court of Appeal's decision in *Palfrey*. See also *CIS 413/1992* which notes the differences that arise from the law of property in Scotland. In *Palfrey* the Tribunal of Commissioners state that the SSAT should have exercised its inquisitorial jurisdiction to call for the documents under which the property was acquired in order to sort out the beneficial ownership. But in *CIS 127/1993* the Commissioner did not find this necessary, since it was not disputed that the house had been conveyed into the names of the claimant and her daughter, and the method of valuation was the same whether the claimant and her daughter actually had equal shares or were deemed to do so by reg.52.

Note *R(IS) 3/96* which contains a useful discussion as to whether the District Valuer's opinion supplied in that case met the requirements of *CIS 391/1992*. The guidance to decision makers suggests that they should obtain an expert opinion on the market value of a deemed share in land/premises. In a case where the other owners will not buy the share or agree to a sale of the asset as a whole, the guidance states that the valuer should not simply assume that a court would order a sale but must consider the particular circumstances and take into account legal costs, length of time to obtain possession, etc. The guidance also says that the expert would need to explain whether on the facts of the case there was any market for the deemed share and indicate how the value of the deemed share had been calculated.

2.444 However, in practice, it seems that the valuations obtained do not always meet such criteria (as noted in *CIS 3197/2003*, see below). See, for example, *R(JSA) 1/02* which was concerned with valuing the claimant's interest in his former matrimonial home. His wife, from whom he was separated and who was in ill-health, continued to live there with their daughter, who had learning difficulties. The valuation obtained by the Jobcentre on a standard form (A64A/LA1) gave the open market value as £30,000 and the claimant's deemed undivided share as £9,200. No reasons were given for this conclusion. The property was leasehold but there was no evidence as to the remaining term of the lease, or as to the condition of the property. There was also no evidence as to the age of the daughter and no consideration as to whether a court would order a sale (which seemed very unlikely, given the purpose for which the property had been acquired and the purpose for which it was being used). The Commissioner, referring to *CIS 191/1994*, holds that there was no evidence that the claimant's capital exceeded the then prescribed limit of £8,000. He stated that everything depended on the facts and the evidence before the tribunal. In this case the valuation evidence was so unsatisfactory as to be worthless. He set out the following guidance on valuation:

"13. Proper valuation evidence should include details of the valuer's expertise, the basis on which he or she holds him or herself out as able to give expert evidence in relation to the property in question. Where it is the sale of a share in a property which is in issue, the evidence should deal with the valuer's experience in relation to such shares, and their sale. The property, and any leasehold interest, should be described in sufficient detail, including details of the length of any lease, of any special terms in it, and of the location, size and condition of the property, to show that the factors relevant to its value have been taken into account, and the reasons for the conclusion as to the value should be given. A similar approach should be applied to a share of a property, and an explanation should be given of the factors identified as relevant to the valuation, and how they affect it. The expert should also give evidence of any comparables identified, or of other reasons why it is concluded that the share could be sold at any particular price. If there is no evidence of actual sales of such interests, an acceptable explanation of the absence of such evidence should be given.
14. I appreciate that, in cases of this kind, this will on occasions be a counsel of perfection which cannot be realised. Where a valuer does not have relevant information, and proceeds upon assumptions, the report should state what is missing, and should also state the assumptions upon which it is based. This will normally give the claimant the opportunity to correct any mistaken assumptions or other errors of fact in the report."

See also *JC-W v Wirral MBC (HB)* [2011] UKUT 501 (AAC), paras 13–18, for Judge Mark's critical comments in relation to the District Valuer's valuation in that case, and *MN v LB Hillingdon (HB)* [2014] UKUT 427 (AAC) and *PE v SSWP (SPC)* [2014] UKUT 387 (AAC) noted below.

It will not always be the case that a deemed equal share in a property will be of minimal value, even if the other co-owners are unwilling to sell. As *Wilkinson v Chief Adjudication Officer*, CA, March 24, 2000, reported as *R(IS) 1/01*, illustrates, the purposes for which the joint ownership was established will need to be scrutinised in order to assess whether a court would order a sale. In *Wilkinson* the claimant's mother had died, leaving her home to the claimant and her brother "to do with as they wish". It was accepted that the mother had expressed the hope that the claimant's brother would live in the house with his son when his divorce proceedings in Australia were resolved (although there was nothing in the will to this effect). The claimant contended that the capital value of her half share in the property was of a nominal value only, because her brother was unwilling to leave the property and unwilling to sell his share in it. She maintained that a court would not order a sale under s.30 of the Law of Property Act 1925 (repealed with effect from January 1, 1998 and replaced by ss.14 and 15 of the Trusts of Land and Appointment of Trustees Act 1996). But the Court of Appeal, by a majority (Mummery and Potter LJJ), disagreed. This was not a case like *Palfrey* where property had been acquired by joint owners for a collateral purpose (e.g. for them to live in as long as they wished) and that purpose would be defeated by ordering a sale. On the contrary, this was a case where an order for sale would enable the claimant's mother's wishes, as expressed in her will, to be carried out. Her brother's unwillingness to sell or pay the claimant for the value of her share was in fact having the effect of defeating that testamentary purpose. Potter LJ said that the proper starting point for valuation of the claimant's half-share was half the market value of the house with vacant possession, with a discount for any factors materially affecting her ability to market the house on that basis. The tribunal's conclusion that in the circumstances the value of her half-share was half of the market value of the house less 10 per cent for expenses of sale and a charge to the testatrix's former husband was upheld. Evans LJ, however, took the opposite view. He considered that the claimant's share should be valued on the basis that a sale would not be ordered because this would defeat the mother's wish that her son and grandson be allowed to live in the property. As this case illustrates, much will depend on the circumstances in a particular case (and the view that is taken of those circumstances).

On very similar facts (a mother leaving a property to the claimant and his two sisters in equal shares, with no restriction or superadded purpose expressed in the will) the approach in *Wilkinson* was applied to the same effect in *JM v Eastleigh BC (HB)* [2016] UKUT 464 (AAC).

2.445

Those cases were ones where there was no obstacle to the sale of the property with vacant possession, even though there might have been some normal delay in the process during which the disregard in para.26 of Sch.10 could come into play. The approach of starting with the market value of the property as a whole and then dividing by the number of joint owners does not undermine the fundamental principle that under reg.52 it is the claimant's deemed severed share (i.e. as a deemed tenant in common) that must be valued. The following decisions illustrate some of problems of valuation in the more complicated cases where there is real doubt whether a court would order a sale if other joint owners were unwilling to agree.

In *CIS/3197/2003* the claimant owned a house with her daughter, who had a two-thirds share. (As we now know as a result of *Hourigan*, such circumstances do not fall within reg.52, but the approach to valuation is still relevant). The claimant went into a nursing home, leaving the house in the occupation of her daughter and the daughter's disabled child. The daughter would not agree to a sale of the house nor was she willing to buy out the claimant's share. It seemed unlikely that a court would order a sale. In view of the Secretary of State's failure to provide proper evidence of the value of the claimant's share the Commissioner found that the value of the claimant's interest was nil. However, he added that tribunals should not approach the matter in this way. If the evidence was incomplete they should adjourn with directions as to the ways in which the evidence should be supplemented and should not decide the case on the burden of proof. Clearly where there has been no attempt to obtain any valuation evidence this should apply. However, if such attempts have been made and the evidence remains inadequate, it is suggested that the burden of proof may need to come into play (and indeed this was the approach taken in both *R(IS) 3/96* and, in effect, in *R(JSA) 1/02*). For example, in *R(IS) 3/96* it was held that grounds for revising the claimant's award had not been shown in the light of the deficiencies in the District Valuer's report and in *R(JSA) 1/02* the Commissioner substituted his own decision on the existing evidence despite such deficiencies.

2.446   Despite the above case law, examples continue to crop up of a claimant's share in a property being wrongly valued simply as a proportion of the whole, rather than the claimant's actual or deemed share being properly valued, taking into account all the relevant circumstances. See, for instance, *R(IS) 5/07* and *AM v SSWP (SPC)* [2010] UKUT 134 (AAC).

As indeed do cases involving inadequate valuation evidence from the District Valuer. For a further example of a case where the valuation evidence from the District Valuer was wholly inadequate and the tribunal had erred in law in relying on it, see *MN v London Borough of Hillingdon (HB)* [2014] UKUT 427 (AAC). The claimant had been living in the jointly-owned matrimonial home with his wife, who had serious mental health problems, and their severely disabled son. However, it became necessary for the claimant and his son to leave, due to deterioration in his wife's health. Judge Ovey, after noting that the District Valuer appeared to have arrived at her valuation by halving the total value of the property and deducting just under 1 per cent, despite having been given details of the circumstances of the case, stated:

> "32. ... As a matter of common sense, it seems unlikely in the extreme that a purchaser would pay just under half the vacant possession value of a property for a half interest which would not enable him to occupy the property without first obtaining some form of court order against a defendant suffering from paranoid schizophrenia who was in occupation of a former matrimonial home, bought for the purpose of being a home, and who might be entitled to a property adjustment order. . . ."

See also *PE v SSWP (SPC)* [2014] UKUT 387 (AAC) which concerned the value of the claimant's interest in his former home, which remained occupied by his wife, son and step-son (the step-son had mental health problems). The District Valuer's valuation was based on an assumption that there had been a hypothetical application under the Trusts of Land and Appointment of Trustees Act 1996. The Secretary of State argued that in the circumstances of the case the District Valuer's assumption was unrealistic. Although no divorce proceedings were in place at the time, any application under the 1996 Act would be likely to generate such proceedings by the other party who was likely to obtain a more favourable outcome under the Matrimonial Causes Act 1973. Judge Jacobs accepted that the evidence relied on by the tribunal as to valuation was therefore flawed and decided, with the consent of the Secretary of State, that there were no grounds to supersede the decision awarding state pension credit.

There is a difficult balance between what might be a counsel of perfection (as in *R(JSA) 1/02*) and a realistic approach to what assumptions are acceptable in the inevitably imprecise exercise of valuing hypothetical interests. *Reigate and Banstead BC v GB (HB)* [2018] UKUT 225 (AAC) shows that tribunals should not go overboard in picking holes in a District Valuer's report. On the assumption (quite possibly inaccurate) that the claimant and his daughter were beneficial joint tenants and that there had not already been a severance, the tribunal went wrong in the reasons it relied on to find that the District Valuer had not properly valued the claimant's deemed equal share as a tenant in common and had not taken into account the possible need for an application to the court, as the property was occupied by the daughter and her son. In particular, the District Valuer did not need to provide evidence of a local market for an interest of the kind the claimant was deemed to have. There is undoubtedly a market for actual interests of the kind deemed to exist by reg.52 (see the many cases discussed above), often in specialist auctions, although that is no doubt not well-known to claimants. But there remains a question how much detail a District Valuer needs to give of the existence of such a market and of the prices fetched for comparable interests to validly underpin the valuation.

Calculation of tariff income from capital

53.—(1) [³Except where the circumstances prescribed in paragraph [¹⁰ . . .] (1B) apply to the claimant,] where the claimant's capital calculated in accordance with this Part exceeds [¹⁰£6,000] it shall be treated as equivalent to a weekly income of £1 for each complete £250 in excess of [¹⁰£6,000] but not exceeding [¹⁰£16,000]. [⁶(1ZA) [¹⁰ . . .]]

[³(1A) Where the circumstances prescribed in paragraph (1B) apply to the claimant and that claimant's capital calculated in accordance with this Part exceeds £10,000, it shall be treated as equivalent to a weekly income of £1 for each complete £250 in excess of £10,000 but not exceeding £16,000.

(1B) For the purposes of paragraph (1A) [¹⁰ . . .], the prescribed circumstances are that the claimant lives permanently in—

[⁹ (a) a care home or an independent hospital;
(b) an Abbeyfield Home;]
(c) accommodation provided under section 3 of, and Part II of the Schedule to, the Polish Resettlement Act 1947 (provision of accommodation in camps) where the claimant requires personal care [⁵ by reason of old age, disablement, past or present dependence on alcohol or drugs, past or present mental disorder or a terminal illness and the care is provided in the home].

[⁴(d) [⁹ . . .].]

(1C) For the purposes of paragraph (1B), a claimant shall be treated as living permanently in such home[⁹, hospital] or accommodation where he is absent—

(a) from a home[⁹, hospital] or accommodation referred to in sub-paragraph [⁴(a) [⁹ or (b)]] of paragraph (1B)—
  (i) [⁷ . . .] in the case of a person over pensionable age, for a period not exceeding 52 weeks, and
  (ii) in any other case, for a period not exceeding 13 weeks;
(b) from accommodation referred to in sub-paragraph (c) of paragraph (1B), where the claimant, with the agreement of the manager of the accommodation, intends to return to the accommodation in due course.]

(2) Notwithstanding [³paragraphs (1) [¹⁰ . . .] and (1A)], where any part of the excess is not a complete £250 that part shall be treated as equivalent to a weekly income of £1.

(3) For the purposes of [³paragraphs (1) [¹⁰ . . .] and (1A)], capital includes any income treated as capital under regulations [¹ . . .] 48 and 60 ([¹ . . .] income treated as capital and liable relative payments treated as capital).

[³(4) [⁹ . . .].]

2.447

AMENDMENTS

1. Income Support (General) Amendment No.5 Regulations 1988 (SI 1988/2022) reg.13 (December 12, 1988).

2. Income-Related Benefits (Miscellaneous Amendments) Regulations 1990 (SI 1990/671) reg.5 (April 9, 1990).

3. Income-related Benefits Schemes (Miscellaneous Amendments) Regulations 1996 (SI 1996/462) reg.12(1) (April 8, 1996).

4. Income-related Benefits and Jobseeker's Allowance (Miscellaneous Amendments) Regulations Regulations 1997 (SI 1997/65) reg.8 (April 7, 1997).

5. Income-related Benefits and Jobseeker's Allowance (Amendment) (No.2) Regulations 1997 (SI 1997/2197) reg.7(5) and (6)(a) (October 6, 1997).

6. Social Security Amendment (Capital Limits and Earnings Disregards) Regulations 2000 (SI 2000/2545) reg.2(1)(c) (April 9, 2001).

7. Social Security Amendment (Residential Care and Nursing Homes) Regulations 2001 (SI 2001/3767) reg.2(1) and Pt I of Sch. para.9 (April 8, 2002).

8. State Pension Credit (Consequential, Transitional and Miscellaneous Provisions) Regulations 2002 (SI 2002/3019) reg.29(3) (October 6, 2003).

9. Social Security (Care Homes and Independent Hospitals) Regulations 2005 (SI 2005/2687) reg.2 and Sch.1 para.7 (October 24, 2005).

10. Social Security (Miscellaneous Amendments) (No.2) Regulations 2005 (SI 2005/2465) reg.2(6) (April 10, 2006).

DEFINITIONS

"Abbeyfield Home"—see reg.2(1).
"care home"—*ibid.*
"claimant"—*ibid.*, and reg.23(1).
"independent hospital"—see reg.2(1).

GENERAL NOTE

2.448   On April 10, 2006 the overall capital limit for income support was raised to £16,000 for all claimants (reg.45) and the amount above which the tariff income rule applies was increased to £6,000 (para.(1)), except for claimants who live permanently in a care home, Abbeyfield Home or independent hospital (for the definitions of these terms see reg.2(1)) or a Polish resettlement home (para.(1B)). For these claimants the tariff income rule will continue to apply only to capital above £10,000 (para.(1A)). See the 2005 edition of this volume for the different upper capital limits that applied before April 10, 2006.

The effect of paras (1), (1A) and (2) is that if the claimant and partner (if any) have capital over £6,000 (£10,000 for claimants within para.(1B)) but not over £16,000, it is treated as producing an income of £1 per week for each complete £250 between the limits, and £1 per week for any odd amount left over. Thus if a claimant (other than one to whom para.(1B) applies) has exactly £9,000, that is treated as producing £12 per week. If they have £7,001, that is treated as producing £5 per week. The actual income from most forms of capital is disregarded under para.22 of Sch.9.

Paragraph (1B)

2.449   See the definitions of "Abbeyfield Home", "care home" and "independent hospital" in reg.2(1) and the notes to those definitions.

Paragraph (1C)

2.450   This deals with periods of temporary absence from the accommodation for claimants covered by para.(1B).

Chapter VII

[⁶ [⁸ . . .] Liable Relative Payments]

Interpretation

54.—In this Chapter, unless the context otherwise requires—
[⁷ [⁹ . . .]
"claimant" includes a young claimant;
[⁷ "claimant's family" shall be construed in accordance with section 137
of the Contributions and Benefits Act 1992 (interpretation of part 7
and supplementary provisions);]
[⁷ "housing costs" means those costs which may be met under regulation
17(1)(e) or 18(1)(f) (housing costs);]
"liable relative" means—

    (a) a spouse[³, former spouse, civil partner or former civil partner] of
a claimant or of a member of the claimant's family;

    (b) a parent of a child or young person who is a member of the claim-
ant's family or of a young claimant;

    (c) a person who has not been adjudged to be the father of a child
or young person who is a member of the claimant's family or of
a young claimant where that person is contributing towards the
maintenance of that child, young person or young claimant and
by reason of that contribution he may reasonably be treated as the
father of that child, young person or young claimant;

    (d) a person liable to maintain another person [¹ in the circumstances
set out in section 78(6)(c) of the Social Security Administration
Act 1992 (liability to maintain another person)] where the latter is
the claimant or a member of the claimant's family,

and, in this definition, a reference to a child's, young person's or young
claimant's parent includes any person in relation to whom the child,
young person or young claimant was treated as a child or a member of
the family;
[⁷"ordinary clothing and footwear" means clothing and footwear for
normal daily use but does not include school uniforms;]
"payment" means a periodical payment or any other payment made by
or derived from a liable relative [⁷ . . .] but it does not include any
payment—

    (a) arising from a disposition of property made in contemplation of,
or as a consequence of—

        (i) an agreement to separate; or

        (ii) any proceedings for judicial separation, divorce or nullity of
marriage;[⁴ or

        (iii) any proceedings for separation, dissolution or nullity in rela-
tion to a civil partnership;]

    (b) made after the death of the liable relative;

    (c) made by way of a gift but not in aggregate or otherwise exceed-
ing £250 in the period of 52 weeks beginning with the date on
which the payment, or if there is more than one such payment the
first payment, is made; and, in the case of a claimant who continues to be in receipt of income support at the end of the period of
52 weeks, this provision shall continue to apply thereafter with the

2.451

modification that any subsequent period of 52 weeks shall begin with the first day of the benefit week in which the first payment is made after the end of the previous period of 52 weeks;

(d) [² . . .]

[⁷ (e) made to a third party, or in respect of a third party, unless the payment is—

    (i) in relation to the claimant or the claimant's [⁹ partner or is made or derived from a person falling within sub-paragraph (d) of the definition of liable relative]; and

    (ii) [¹⁰ . . .] in respect of food, ordinary clothing or footwear, fuel,[¹⁰ rent for which housing benefit is payable, housing costs to the extent that they are met under regulation 17(1)(e) or 18(1))(f) (housing costs),] council tax or water charges;]

(f) in kind;

(g) to, or in respect of, a child or young person who is to be treated as not being a member of the claimant's household under regulation 16 (circumstances in which a person is to be treated as being or not being a member of the same household);

(h) which is not a periodical payment, to the extent that any amount of that payment—

    (i) has already been taken into account under this Part by virtue of a previous claim or determination; or

    (ii) has been recovered under section 27(1) of the Act [SSAA, s.74(1)] (prevention of duplication of payments) or is currently being recovered; or

    (iii) at the time the determination is made, has been used by the claimant except where he has deprived himself of that amount for the purpose of securing entitlement to income support or increasing the amount of that benefit;

[⁹ (i) to which paragraph 73 of Schedule 9 (sums to be disregarded in the calculation of income other than earnings) applies.]

"periodical payment" means—

(a) a payment which is made or is due to be made at regular intervals [⁷ . . .];

(b) in a case where the liable relative has established a pattern of making payments at regular intervals, any such payment;

(c) any payment [⁷[⁹. . .] that does not exceed] the amount of income support payable had that payment not been made;

(d) any payment representing a commutation of payments to which sub-paragraphs (a) or (b) of this definition applies whether made in arrears or in advance,

but does not include a payment due to be made before the first benefit week pursuant to the claim which is not so made;

"young claimant" means a person aged 16 or over but under [⁵ 20] who makes a claim for income support.

AMENDMENTS

1. Income Support (General) Amendment Regulations 1988 (SI 1988/663) reg.23 (April 11, 1988).

2. Social Security (Working Tax Credit and Child Tax Credit) (Consequential Amendments) Regulations 2003 (SI 2003/455) reg.2 and Sch.1 para.14 (April 6, 2004, except in "transitional cases" and see further the note to reg.17 of the Income Support Regulations).

3. Civil Partnership (Pensions, Social Security and Child Support) (Consequential, etc. Provisions) Order 2005 (SI 2005/2877) art.2(3) and Sch.3 para.13(4)(a) (December 5, 2005).

4. Civil Partnership (Pensions, Social Security and Child Support) (Consequential, etc. Provisions) Order 2005 (SI 2005/2877) art.2(3) and Sch.3 para.13(4)(b) (December 5, 2005).

5. Social Security (Young Persons) Amendment Regulations 2006 (SI 2006/718) reg.2(5) (April 10, 2006).

6. Social Security (Child Maintenance Amendments) Regulations 2008 (SI 2008/2111) reg.2(5) (October 27, 2008).

7. Social Security (Child Maintenance Amendments) Regulations 2008 (SI 2008/2111) reg.2(6) (October 27, 2008).

8. Social Security (Miscellaneous Amendments) (No.4) Regulations 2009 (SI 2009/2655) reg.2(6) (April 12, 2010).

9. Social Security (Miscellaneous Amendments) (No.4) Regulations 2009 (SI 2009/2655) reg.2(10) (April 12, 2010).

10. Social Security (Miscellaneous Amendments) Regulations 2013 (SI 2013/443) reg.2(3) (April 2, 2013).

DEFINITIONS

"the Act"—see reg.2(1).
"benefit week"—*ibid.*
"child"—see SSCBA s.137(1).
"claimant"—see reg.2(1) and reg.23(1).
"family"—see SSCBA s.137(1).
"young person"—see reg.2(1) and reg.14.

GENERAL NOTE

From October 27, 2008 regs 60A–60D, which contained separate rules for the treatment of child support maintenance, were revoked. Thereafter all liable relative and child maintenance payments were taken into account in accordance with this Chapter. However, as a consequence of the fact that payments of child maintenance are fully disregarded as income from April 12, 2010 (see para.73 of Sch.9), the special rules for the treatment of child maintenance have also been revoked from that date and this Chapter again only deals with liable relative payments. For the definition of "child maintenance" see para.73(2) of Sch.9. It would seem that a lump sum payment of child maintenance will count as capital.

2.452

"Liable relative"
Note that the definition for these purposes is not restricted to those who are obliged to maintain others under s.78(6)(c) of the SSAA 1992, but includes in particular, a former spouse (and from December 5, 2005) a civil partner or former civil partner, and a person who may reasonably be treated as the father of a child (by reason of contributing to the maintenance of the child).

2.453

"Payment"
The general definition is wide, but from October 27, 2008 no longer includes payments not yet acquired which would be made on application. The general category of "payment" is divided into "periodical payments" (further defined below) and "other payments". This division is important in the following regulations.

The list of exceptions is also very important—

(a) A payment arising from a disposition of property made in connection with an agreement to separate or matrimonial or civil partnership proceedings is not a liable relative payment (LRP). There had been great problems in construing the similar, but not identical, supplementary benefit provision, in particular in deciding when a payment "resulted from" a disposition of

2.454

property. Although the words here are "arising from," the authoritative settlement of the supplementary benefit problem in *R(SB)1/89* should apply. The claimant received a payment of £2,500 from her ex-husband pursuant to a county court order. This was a consent order made on the basis that the claimant gave up any claims against her ex-husband's houses. The Tribunal of Commissioners holds that there must be a chain of causation, however short, between the disposition and the payment, and that the prior disposition does not have to be by way of sale. Where a payment is made in discharge of a claimant's proprietary interest (or a claim to such an interest) it results from a disposition of property. Where it is made in discharge of maintenance obligations the payment stands alone and does not result from a disposition. *R(SB) 1/89* approves the result of *CSB 1160/1986* where a husband and wife had a joint building society account. On their separation they agreed to split the account and as a result the husband paid £2,500 to the wife, who was receiving supplementary benefit. It was held that the building society account was "property" and that the agreement to split it was a "disposition." The payment then resulted from a disposition of property. It was not a LRP, and had to be dealt with under the ordinary rules on resources.

(b) Payments made after the liable relative's death are not LRPs.

(c) Gifts up to £250 in 52 weeks do not count as LRPs. In view of para.(f), para. (c) must apply to gifts of money or property.

(d) This paragraph, which was revoked on April 6, 2004 (except in "transitional cases"—see the note to reg.17), excluded payments to which reg.44(2) (payments to residential schools for a child's or young person's maintenance) applied (reg.44(2) was also revoked with effect from April 6, 2004, except in "transitional cases"—see reg.17; see the 2003 edition of this volume for reg.44 and the notes to that regulation). The revocation of reg.44, and in turn this paragraph, are part of the consequential changes that apply from April 6, 2004 (except in "transitional cases"—see the note to reg.17) because of the removal of amounts for children and young persons from the income support scheme; financial assistance to help with the cost of bringing up a child or young person is now to be provided through the child tax credit system, see Vol.IV of this series.

Note that a new disregard has been introduced in place of the provisions formerly in reg.44(2) (see para.25A of Sch.9). Note also para.(e).

(e) Under the new form of para.(e) (substituted on October 27, 2008) payments from liable relatives to third parties in respect of the claimant or the claimant's family only count as liable relative payments if the payment is for the items listed in sub-para.(ii). The same applies if the payment is to the claimant or a member of the claimant's family for a third party. The test of reasonableness under the old form of para.(e) has gone. The April 12, 2010 amendment which replaces a reference to the claimant's family with a reference to the claimant's partner reflects the fact that payments of child maintenance are fully disregarded as income from that date (see para.73 of Sch.9).

The effect of the April 2, 2013 amendment is that third party payments for rent or housing costs are only taken into account where the payment is for rent for which housing benefit is payable or housing costs met by income support. The policy intention is that such payments should only count if they are in respect of items covered by benefit.

(f) Payments in kind are not LRPs. This could be an important factor in benefit planning.

(g) Payments to or in respect of a child or young person who would otherwise be a member of the claimant's household, but is treated as not being in the household by reg.16, do not count as LRPs. See reg.51(3).

(h) Where an "other payment" is being considered, its amount is to be reduced if any of the three categories listed apply. Category (iii) is likely to be particularly important where there is a significant gap between the date of receipt of the payment in question and the date on which the claim for income support is determined. See the notes to reg.51(1) for the difficulties of deciding when a claimant's purpose is to secure or increase entitlement to income support.

(i) From April 12, 2010, all payments of child maintenance are fully disregarded as income under para.73 of Sch.9.

"Periodical payment"

This definition is also wide, as the four categories are alternatives.　　　　2.455

Sub-paragraphs (a) and (b) are relatively straightforward, covering the standard cases where payments are due to be made at regular intervals or a regular pattern has been established.

The effect of sub-para.(d) is that a payment of arrears of payments under (a) and (b), or a payment in advance, also counts as a periodical payment (subject to the final exception). If, however, a regular pattern of payments has ceased to exist and there is no court order or agreement to make regular payments, such a payment cannot be a commutation of payments under sub-paras (a) or (b) (*Bolstridge v Chief Adjudication Officer* [1993] 2 F.L.R. 657). It will be a matter of fact in each case by what date a regular pattern of payments ceases to exist. In *Bolstridge* the claimant's ex-husband paid her maintenance of £40 per week on a voluntary basis up to July 31, 1986. He was then made redundant and ceased making payments. In September 1987 her ex-husband made her a payment of £10,500 "in lieu of future maintenance". In July 1988, she claimed income support. The Court of Appeal held that, in the absence of any subsisting contract or outstanding liability, it could not be said that by September 1987, there was an agreement for maintenance of any particular sum or any pattern of regular payment. Therefore, the £10,500 was not a periodical payment. It was an "other payment", to be taken into account under reg.57. Any part of the total amount which fell outside the definition of "payment" (above) would not be taken into consideration at all. In particular, amounts which the claimant had already spent for "legitimate" purposes would be excluded under sub-para.(h)(iii) of the definition.

The intention of sub-para.(c) seems to be that relatively small payments (i.e. up to the amount of one week's income support) are to be treated as periodical payments.

The final exception is crucial to the working of the LRP system. If a payment was due to be made before the first benefit week, pursuant to the claim, but is paid in or after that benefit week, it is an "other payment," not a periodical payment. Thus the treatment of arrears will vary according to whether the claimant was or was not in receipt of benefit during the period to which the arrears relate (on which see *McCorquodale v Chief Adjudication Officer*, reported as *R(SB) 1/88*).

Treatment of [²[⁴ . . .]] liable relative payments

55.—[¹Subject to regulation 55A] [⁵ . . . [³. . .]] a payment shall—　　　2.456
(a) to the extent that it is not a payment of income, be treated as income;
(b) be taken into account in accordance with the following provisions of this Chapter.

AMENDMENTS

1. Social Security Benefits (Maintenance Payments and Consequential Amendments) Regulations 1996 (SI 1996/940) reg.6(2) (April 19, 1996).

2. Social Security (Child Maintenance Amendments) Regulations 2008 (SI 2008/2111) reg.2(2)(b) (October 27, 2008).

3. Social Security (Child Maintenance Amendments) Regulations 2008 (SI 2008/2111) reg.2(7) (October 27, 2008).

4. Social Security (Miscellaneous Amendments) (No.4) Regulations 2009 (SI 2009/2655) reg.2(5) (April 12, 2010).

5. Social Security (Miscellaneous Amendments) (No.4) Regulations 2009 (SI 2009/2655) reg.2(11) (April 12, 2010).

DEFINITION

"payment"—see reg.54.

GENERAL NOTE

2.457   From April 12, 2010 reg.55 only applies to liable relative payments since all payments of child maintenance are fully disregarded from that date (see para.73 of Sch.9). The effect of reg.55 is that, subject to reg.55A, all liable relative payments that fall within reg.54 will be treated as and taken into account as income in accordance with regs 56–59.

[¹Disregard of payments treated as not relevant income

2.458   **55A.**—Where the Secretary of State treats any payment as not being relevant income for the purposes of section 74A of the Social Security Administration Act 1992 (payment of benefit where maintenance payments collected by Secretary of State), that payment shall be disregarded in calculating a claimant's income.]

AMENDMENT

1. Social Security Benefits (Maintenance Payments and Consequential Amendments) Regulations 1996 (SI 1996/940) reg.6(3) (April 19, 1996).

DEFINITIONS

"payment"—see reg.54.
"relevant income"—see reg.2(c), Social Security Benefits (Maintenance Payments and Consequential Amendments) Regulations 1996 (para.2.1154).

GENERAL NOTE

2.459   See the note to s.74A of the SSAA 1992 in Vol.III of this series.

Period over which periodical payments are to be taken into account

2.460   **56.**—(1) The period over which a periodical payment is to be taken into account shall be—
(a) in a case where the payment is made at regular intervals, a period equal to the length of that interval;
(b) in a case where the payment is due to be made at regular intervals but is not so made, such number of weeks as is equal to the number (and any fraction shall be treated as a corresponding fraction of a week) obtained by dividing the amount of that payment by the weekly amount of that periodical payment as calculated in accordance with regulation 58(4) (calculation of the weekly amount of a liable relative payment);
(c) in any other case, a period equal to a week.
(2) The period under paragraph (1) shall begin on the date on which

the payment is treated as paid under regulation 59 (date on which a liable relative payment is to be treated as paid).

DEFINITION

"periodical payment"—see reg.54.

GENERAL NOTE

If a periodical payment is actually paid at regular intervals, it is to be taken into account for the length of the interval. If it is due to be paid regularly but is not, each payment is spread at the weekly rate of proper payment. In other cases (e.g. some payments within sub-para.(c) of the definition of periodical payment) the payment is taken into account for a week.

2.461

The application of reg.56 to payments under sub-para.(d) of the definition of periodical payment is not straightforward. In *Bolstridge v Chief Adjudication Officer* [1993] 2 F.L.R. 657 it was accepted that reg.56(1)(b) can be given a sensible meaning only if the word "payment" in that regulation sometimes applies to the commutated payment and sometimes to the payment that was due to be made at regular intervals.

Payments are taken into account from the date on which they are treated as paid under reg.59.

[1 Period over which payments other than periodical payments are to be taken into account

57.—(1) The period over which a payment other than a periodical payment (a "non-periodical payment") is to be taken account shall be determined as follows.

2.462

(2) Except in a case where paragraph (4) applies, the number of weeks over which a non-periodical payment is to be taken into account shall be equal to the number obtained by dividing that payment by the amount referred to in paragraph (3).

(3) The amount is the aggregate of £2 and—

(a) the amount of income support that would be payable had no payment been made [2 . . .]

(b) [2 . . .].

(4) This paragraph applies in a case where a liable relative makes a periodical payment and a non-periodical payment concurrently and the weekly amount of the periodical payment (as calculated in accordance with regulation 58) is less than B.

(5) In a case where paragraph (4) applies, the non-periodical payment shall, subject to paragraphs (6) and (7), be taken into account over a period of the number of weeks equal to the number obtained by applying the formula—

$$\frac{A}{B-C}$$

(6) If the liable relative ceases to make periodical payments, the balance (if any) of the non-periodical payment shall be taken into account over the number of weeks equal to the number obtained by dividing that balance by the amount referred to in paragraph (3).

(7) If the amount of any subsequent periodical payment varies, the balance (if any) of the non-periodical payment shall be taken into account over a period of the number of weeks equal to the number obtained by applying the formula—

$$\frac{D}{B-E}$$

(8) The period under paragraph (2) or (4) shall begin on the date on which the payment is treated as paid under regulation 59 (date on which a liable relative payment is treated as paid) and the period under paragraph (6) and (7) shall begin on the first day of the benefit week in which the cessation or variation of the periodical payment occurred.

(9) Any fraction which arises by applying a calculation or formula referred to in this regulation shall be treated as a corresponding fraction of a week.

(10) In paragraphs (4) to (7)—

A = the amount of the non-periodical payment;

B = the aggregate of £2 and the amount of income support that would be payable had the periodical payment not been made [² . . .];

C = the weekly amount of the periodical payment;

D = the balance (if any) of the non-periodical payment;

E = the weekly amount of any subsequent periodical payment.]

AMENDMENTS

1. Social Security (Child Maintenance Amendments) Regulations 2008 (SI 2008/2111) reg.2(8) (October 27, 2008).

2. Social Security (Miscellaneous Amendments) (No.4) Regulations 2009 (SI 2009/2655) reg.2(12) (April 12, 2010).

DEFINITIONS

"benefit week"—see reg.2(1).
"liable relative"—see reg.54.
"payment"—*ibid.*
"periodical payment"—*ibid.*

GENERAL NOTE

2.463
This regulation deals with payments other than periodical payments (referred to in this regulation as "non-periodical payments"). The amendments made on April 12, 2010 reflect the fact that there is now a total disregard of child maintenance payments (see para.73 of Sch.9) and so this regulation once again only deals with liable relative payments. The basic rule under paras (2) and (3) is to spread non-periodical payments at the rate of income support that would have been payable if the payment had not been made, plus £2. Paragraphs (4)–(5) modify this rule where the non-periodical payment is in addition to periodical payments so as to spread the non-periodical payment at the rate of the difference between the amount identified under para.(3) and the periodical payment, as long as the periodical payments continue to be made. If the periodical payments cease, the balance of the non-periodical payment will be taken into account in accordance with paras (2) and (3) (see para.(6)). Paragraph (7) provides for an adaptation of the formula in para.(5) if the amount of any subsequent periodical payment varies. See para.(8) for when the period calculated under paras (2), (4), (6) or (7) begins and reg.58(5) for the weekly amount to be taken into account.

Note that the pre-April 6, 2004 form of this regulation which had been retained for "transitional cases" (i.e. where the claimant remains entitled to the child elements in income support and has not transferred to child tax credit, see further the note to reg.17) was omitted on October 27, 2008 (see reg.4 of the Social Security (Child Maintenance Amendments) Regulations 2008 (SI 2008/2111)).

Calculation of the weekly amount of a [¹[² . . .]] liable relative payment

58.—(1) Where a periodical payment is made or is due to be made at intervals of one week, the weekly amount shall be the amount of that payment.

    (2) Where a periodical payment is made or is due to be made at intervals greater than one week and those intervals are monthly, the weekly amount shall be determined by multiplying the amount of the payment by 12 and dividing the product by 52.

    (3) Where a periodical payment is made or is due to be made at intervals and those intervals are neither weekly nor monthly, the weekly amount shall be determined by dividing that payment by the number equal to the number of weeks (including any part of a week) in that interval.

    (4) Where a payment is made and that payment represents a commutation of periodical payments whether in arrears or in advance, the weekly amount shall be the weekly amount of the individual periodical payments so commutated, as calculated under paragraphs (1) to (3) as is appropriate.

    (5) The weekly amount of a payment to which regulation 57 applies (period over which payments other than periodical payments are to be taken into account) shall be equal to the amount of the divisor used in calculating the period over which the payment or, as the case may be, the balance is to be taken into account.

2.464

AMENDMENTS

    1. Social Security (Child Maintenance Amendments) Regulations 2008 (SI 2008/2111) reg.2(2)(c) (October 27, 2008).
    2. Social Security (Miscellaneous Amendments) (No.4) Regulations 2009 (SI 2009/2655) reg.2(5) (April 12, 2010).

DEFINITIONS

    "payment"—see reg.54.
    "periodical payment"—*ibid.*

GENERAL NOTE

    The weekly rate of periodical payments is normally calculated by dividing the payment into weekly bits depending on the intervals between payment dates (paras (1)–(3)). For a commutation of periodical payments, whether in arrears or in advance (which itself comes within the definition of periodical payment), the weekly rate is the appropriate one for the recurring payments.

2.465

Date on which a [¹[² . . .]] liable relative payment is to be treated as paid

59.—(1) A periodical payment is to be treated as paid—
  (a) in the case of a payment which is due to be made before the first benefit week pursuant to the claim, on the day in the week in which it is to be paid which corresponds to the first day of the benefit week;
  (b) in any other case, on the first day of the benefit week in which it is due to be paid unless, having regard to the manner in which income support is due to be paid in the particular case, it would be more

2.466

practicable to treat it as paid on the first day of a subsequent benefit week.

(2) Subject to paragraph (3), any other payment shall be treated as paid—

(a) in the case of a payment which is made before the first benefit week pursuant to the claim, on the day in the week in which it is paid which corresponds to the first day of the benefit week;

(b) in any other case, on the first day of the benefit week in which it is paid unless, having regard to the manner in which income support is due to be paid in the particular case, it would be more practicable to treat it as paid on the first day of a subsequent benefit week.

(3) Any other payment paid on a date which falls within the period in respect of which a previous payment is taken into account, not being a periodical payment, is to be treated as paid on the first day following the end of that period.

AMENDMENTS

1. Social Security (Child Maintenance Amendments) Regulations 2008 (SI 2008/2111) reg.2(2)(d) (October 27, 2008).
2. Social Security (Miscellaneous Amendments) (No.4) Regulations 2009 (SI 2009/2655) reg.2(5) (April 12, 2010).

DEFINITIONS

"benefit week"—see reg.2(1).
"payment"—see reg.54.
"periodical payment"—*ibid.*

GENERAL NOTE

Paragraph (1)

2.467 This provision effectively applies the ordinary rule for income (see reg.31) to periodical payments. Under sub-para.(a) for the payment still to be a periodical payment it must have been paid as well as been due before the first benefit week pursuant to the claim. Once the benefit week is determined under para.4 of Sch.7 to the Claims and Payments Regulations, prior weeks can be counted off and payments attributed to the first day of each week. Under sub-para.(b), for other periodical payments (which can include many payments of arrears) the crucial thing is the benefit week in which the payment is due, or, if it would be more practicable, a subsequent week. A payment of arrears within the definition of a periodical payment may well have been due in a large number of past weeks, for which benefit has already been paid on the assumption that no LRP had been received. This would seem to trigger the application of s.74(1) of the SSAA 1992. Paragraph 28834 of the *Decision Makers Guide* suggests that in such circumstances it is more practicable to take the payment into account from the next benefit week in which the amount of benefit can be adjusted, although the *Guide* does not really face the problem of payments of arrears. If continuing periodical payments are being made, the spreading of a payment of arrears over future benefit weeks could lead to more than one periodical payment being taken into account in the same benefit week. Whether this leaves the claimant better off than if recovery under s.74(1) had been triggered depends on the levels of payment in relation to income support entitlement. It is not at all clear that this solution is "more practicable" than spreading the payment of arrears over the past period to which the arrears related. The latter solution, with the recovery of any overpayment under s.74(1), may be better.

Paragraph (2)

This provision applies to all "other payments", including payments of   **2.468**
arrears identified in the final exception to the definition of "periodical payment",
i.e. where the due date fell before the first benefit week of the income support
claim. Here it is the date of actual payment, rather than the date on which
payment is due, which is crucial. Sub-paragraph (a) applies to payments made
before the first benefit week pursuant to the claim. Sub-paragraph (b) applies in
all other cases, and allows attribution to a later benefit week than that of payment
if that is more practicable.

The result for payments of arrears relating to a period before entitlement to
benefit, is that the payment is treated as income to be spread at the rate identified
in reg.58 from the date of actual payment. This reverses the result of *McCorquodale
v Chief Adjudication Officer* (reported as *R(SB) 1/88*). If this results in one "other
payment" being attributed to a benefit week to which another "other payment" has
already been attributed, the attribution of the later payment is deferred until the first
one runs out (para.(3)).

Liable relative payments to be treated as capital

   60.—[¹ . . .]   **2.469**

AMENDMENT

1. Social Security (Child Maintenance Amendments) Regulations 2008 (SI
2008/2111) reg.2(4)(b) (October 27, 2008).

[¹ *Chapter VIIA*

Child Support

Interpretation

   60A.—[² . . .]]   **2.470**

AMENDMENTS

1. Social Security (Miscellaneous Provisions) Amendment Regulations 1993 (SI
1993/846) reg.3 (April 19, 1993).
2. Social Security (Child Maintenance Amendments) Regulations 2008 (SI
2008/2111) reg.2(4)(c) (October 27, 2008).

[¹Treatment of child support maintenance

   60B.—[² . . .]]   **2.471**

AMENDMENTS

1. Social Security (Miscellaneous Provisions) Amendment Regulations 1993 (SI
1993/846) reg.3 (April 19, 1993).
2. Social Security (Child Maintenance Amendments) Regulations 2008 (SI
2008/2111) reg.2(4)(c) (October 27, 2008).

[¹Calculation of the weekly amount of payments of child support maintenance

2.472   **60C.**— [² . . .]]

AMENDMENTS

1. Social Security (Miscellaneous Provisions) Amendment Regulations 1993 (SI 1993/846) reg.3 (April 19, 1993).
2. Social Security (Child Maintenance Amendments) Regulations 2008 (SI 2008/2111) reg.2(4)(c) (October 27, 2008).

[¹Date on which child support maintenance is to be treated as paid

2.473   **60D.**— [² . . .]]

AMENDMENTS

1. Social Security (Miscellaneous Provisions) Amendment Regulations 1993 (SI 1993/846) reg.3 (April 19, 1993).
2. Social Security (Child Maintenance Amendments) Regulations 2008 (SI 2008/2111) reg.2(4)(c) (October 27, 2008).

[¹Disregard of payments treated as not relevant income

2.474   **60E.**—[² . . .]]

AMENDMENTS

1. Social Security Benefits (Maintenance Payments and Consequential Amendments) Regulations 1996 (SI 1996/940) reg.6(5) (April 19, 1996).
2. Social Security (Child Maintenance Amendments) Regulations 2008 (SI 2008/2111) reg.2(4)(c) (October 27, 2008).

Chapter VIII

[¹⁵ Students]

Interpretation

2.475   **61.**—[¹²(1)] In this Chapter, unless the context otherwise requires—
[¹⁸ "academic year" means the period of twelve months beginning on 1st January, 1st April, 1st July or 1st September according to whether the course in question begins in the winter, the spring, the summer or the autumn respectively but if students are required to begin attending the course during August or September and to continue attending through the autumn, the academic year of the course shall be considered to begin in the autumn rather than the summer;]
[¹³ "access funds" means—
    (a) grants made under section [²⁸68] of the Further and Higher Education Act 1992 [²⁸ . . .][³⁴ or section 74 of the Higher

Education and Research Act 2017] [18 for the purpose of providing funds on a discretionary basis to be paid to students];

(b) grants made under sections 73(a) and (c) and 74(1) of the Education (Scotland) Act 1980; [18 . . .]

(c) grants made under Article 30 of the Education and Libraries (Northern Ireland) Order 1993, or grants, or grants loans or other payments made under Article 5 of the Further Education (Northern Ireland) Order 1997 in each case being grants, or loans or other payments as the case may be, made for the purpose of assisting students in financial difficulties;] [18 [20 . . .]

(d) discretionary payments, known as "learner support funds", which are made available to students in further education by institutions out of funds provided by the [31 [32 Secretary of State under section 14 of the Education Act 2002] or [33 . . .] under sections 100 and 101 of [32 the Apprenticeships, Skills, Children and Learning Act 2009]];] [20 or

(e) Financial Contingency Funds made available by the [26Welsh Ministers];]

[8"college of further education" means a college of further education within the meaning of Part I of the Further and Higher Education (Scotland) Act 1992;]

[8 [27 "contribution" means—

(a) any contribution in respect of the income of a student or any person which the Secretary of State, the Scottish Ministers or an education authority takes into account in ascertaining the amount of a student's grant or student loan; or

(b) any sums, which in determining the amount of a student's allowance or bursary in Scotland under the Education (Scotland) Act 1980, the Scottish Ministers or education authority takes into account being sums which the Scottish Ministers or education authority consider that it is reasonable for the following persons to contribute towards the holder's expenses—

  (i) the holder of the allowance or bursary;
  (ii) the holder's parents;
  (iii) the holder's parent's spouse, civil partner or person ordinarily living with the holder's parent as if he or she were the spouse or civil partner of that parent; or
  (iv) the holder's spouse or civil partner;]]

[8"course of advanced education" means—

(a) a course leading to a postgraduate degree or comparable qualification, a first degree or comparable qualification, a diploma of higher education or a higher national diploma; or

(b) any other course which is of a standard above advanced GNVQ or equivalent, including a course which is of a standard above a general certificate of education (advanced level), [21a Scottish national qualification (higher or advanced higher)];]

"covenant income" means the income [8. . .] payable to a student under a Deed of Covenant by a person whose income is, or is likely to be, taken into account in assessing the student's grant or award;

"education authority" means a government department, [30 a local authority as defined in section 579 of the Education Act 1996 (interpretation)], [8a local education authority as defined in section 123 of

the Local Government (Scotland) Act 1973], an education and library board established under Article 3 of the Education and Libraries (Northern Ireland) Order 1986, any body which is a research council for the purposes of the Science and Technology Act 1965 or any analogous government department, authority, board or body, of the Channel Islands, Isle of Man or any other country outside Great Britain;
[¹⁶ . . .]
[⁸"full-time course of advanced education" means a course of advanced education which is [¹² . . .]—

(a) [¹² . . .] a full-time course of study which is not funded in whole or in part by [¹⁷ the [³¹[³² Secretary of State under section 14 of the Education Act 2002] [³³ or under section 100 of the Apprenticeships, Skills, Children and Learning Act 2009]] or by the [²³[²⁶ Welsh Ministers]]] or a full-time course of study which is not funded in whole or in part by the [¹⁹Scottish Ministers] at a college of further education or a full-time course of study which is a course of higher education and is funded in whole or in part by the [¹⁹Scottish Ministers];

[¹⁷(b) a course of study that is funded in whole or in part by the [³¹[³² Secretary of State under section 14 of the Education Act 2002] [³³ or under section 100 of the Apprenticeships, Skills, Children and Learning Act 2009]] or by the [²³[²⁶ Welsh Ministers]] if it involves more than 16 guided learning hours per week for the student in question, according to the number of guided learning hours per week for that student set out—

[³¹ (i) in the case of a course funded by the [³² Secretary of State [³³ . . .]], in the student's learning agreement signed on behalf of the establishment which is funded by [³³ the Secretary of State] for the delivery of that course; or]

(ii) in the case of a course funded by the [²³[²⁶ Welsh Ministers]], in a document signed on behalf of the establishment which is funded by that Council for the delivery of that course; or]

(c) [¹² . . .] a course of study (not being higher education) which is funded in whole or in part by the [¹⁹Scottish Ministers] at a college of further education if it involves—

(i) more than 16 hours per week of classroom-based or workshop-based programmed learning under the direct guidance of teaching staff according to the number of hours set out in a document signed on behalf of the college; or

(ii) 16 hours or less per week of classroom-based or workshop-based programmed learning under the direct guidance of teaching staff and it involves additional hours using structured learning packages supported by the teaching staff where the combined total of hours exceeds 21 per week, according to the number of hours set out in a document signed on behalf of the college;]

[⁸"full-time course of study" means a full-time course of study which—

(a) is not funded in whole or in part by [¹⁶ the [³¹[³² Secretary of State under section 14 of the Education Act 2002] [³³ or under section 100 of the Apprenticeships, Skills, Children and Learning Act 2009]] or by the [²³[²⁶ Welsh Ministers]]] or a full-time course of study which is not funded in whole or in part by the [¹⁹Scottish

Ministers] at a college of further education or a full-time course of study which is a course of higher education and is funded in whole or in part by the [¹⁹Scottish Ministers];

[¹⁶ (b) a course of study which is funded in whole or in part by the [³¹[³² Secretary of State under section 14 of the Education Act 2002] [³³ or under section 100 of the Apprenticeships, Skills, Children and Learning Act 2009]] or by the [²³[²⁶ Welsh Ministers]] if it involves more than 16 guided learning hours per week for the student in question, according to the number of guided learning hours per week for that student set out—

    [³¹ (i) in the case of a course funded by the [³² Secretary of State [³³. . .]], in the student's learning agreement signed on behalf of the establishment which is funded by [³³ the Secretary of State] for the delivery of that course; or]

    (ii) in the case of a course funded by the [²³[²⁶Welsh Ministers]], in a document signed on behalf of the establishment which is funded by that Council for the delivery of that course; or]

(c) is not higher education and is funded in whole or in part by the [¹⁹Scottish Ministers] at a college of further education if it involves—

    (i) more than 16 hours per week of classroom-based or workshop-based programmed learning under the direct guidance of teaching staff according to the number of hours set out in a document signed on behalf of the college; or

    (ii) 16 hours or less per week of classroom-based or workshop-based programmed learning under the direct guidance of teaching staff and it involves additional hours using structured learning packages supported by the teaching staff where the combined total of hours exceeds 21 per week, according to the number of hours set out in a document signed on behalf of the college;]

[¹² "full-time student" [²⁴means a person who is not a qualifying young person or child within the meaning of section 142 of the Contributions and Benefits Act (child and qualifying young person) and] who is—

(a) aged less than 19 and is attending or undertaking a full-time course of advanced education;

(b) aged 19 or over but under pensionable age and is attending or undertaking a full-time course of study at an educational establishment; or

(c) on a sandwich course;]

[¹³ "grant" (except in the definition of "access funds") means any kind of educational grant or award and includes any scholarship, studentship, exhibition, allowance or bursary but does not include a payment from access funds [²¹ or any payment to which paragraph 11 of Schedule 9 or paragraph 63 of Schedule 10 applies];]

"grant income" means—

(a) any income by way of a grant;

(b) in the case of a student other than one to whom sub-paragraph (c) refers, any contribution which has been assessed whether or not it has been paid;

(c) in the case of a student to whom [⁹ paragraph 1, 2 [²⁹10,] 11 [²⁷, [²⁹12] or 15A of Schedule 1B] applies (lone parent, disabled student or persons in education)], any contribution which has been assessed and which has been paid;

and any such contribution which is paid by way of a covenant shall be treated as part of the student's grant income;

[⁸"higher education" means higher education within the meaning of Part II of the Further and Higher Education (Scotland) Act 1992;]

[³"last day of the course" means the date on which the last day of the final academic term falls in respect of the course in which the student is enrolled;]

"period of study" means—

(a) in the case of a course of study for one year or less, the period beginning with the start of the course [³and ending with the last day of the course];

(b) in the case of a course of study for more than one year, in the first or, as the case may be, any subsequent year of the course, [³other than the final year of the course,] the period beginning with the start of the course or, as the case may be, that year's start and ending with either—

[¹⁴ (i) the day before the start of the next year of the course in a case where the student's grant or loan is assessed at a rate appropriate to his studying throughout the year or, if he does not have a grant or loan, where a loan would have been assessed at such a rate had he had one; or]

(ii) in any other case the day before the start of the normal summer vacation appropriate to his course;

[³ (c) in the final year of a course of study of more than one year, the period beginning with that year's start and ending with the last day of the course;]

[²⁰ "periods of experience" means periods of work experience which form part of a sandwich course;]

[³⁵"postgraduate loan" means a loan to a student undertaking a postgraduate master's degree course or a postgraduate doctoral degree course pursuant to regulations made under section 22 of the Teaching and Higher Education Act 1998;]

[¹³[²⁵ "sandwich course" has the meaning prescribed in regulation [2(9) of the Education (Student Support) Regulations 2008, regulation 4(2) of the Education (Student Loans) (Scotland) Regulations 2007, regulation 2(8) of the Education (Student Support) Regulations (Northern Ireland) 2007;]]

[⁸"standard maintenance grant" means—

(a) except where paragraph (b) or (c) applies, in the case of a student attending [¹² or undertaking] a course of study at the University of London or an establishment within the area comprising the City of London and the Metropolitan Police District, the amount specified for the time being in paragraph 2(2)(a) of Schedule 2 to the Education (Mandatory Awards) Regulations 1995 ("the 1995 Regulations") for such a student;

(b) except where paragraph (c) applies, in the case of a student residing at his parents' home, the amount specified in paragraph 3(2) thereof;

[¹⁸ (c) in the case of a student receiving an allowance or bursary under the Education (Scotland) Act 1980, the amount of money specified as the "standard maintenance allowance" for the relevant year appropriate for the student set out in the Student Support in Scotland

Guide issued by the Student Awards Agency for Scotland, or its nearest equivalent in the case of a bursary provided by a college of further education or a local education authority [^{25} . . .];]

(d) in any other case, the amount specified in paragraph 2(2) of Schedule 2 to the 1995 Regulations other than in sub paragraph (a) or (b) thereof;]

[^{12} "student" means a person, other than a person in receipt of a training allowance, who is attending or undertaking a course of study at an educational establishment;]

[^{11}"student loan" means a loan towards a student's maintenance pursuant to any regulations made under section 22 of the Teaching and Higher Education Act 1998, section 73 of the Education (Scotland) Act 1980 or Article 3 of the Education (Student Support) (Northern Ireland) Order 1998 [^{18} and shall include, in Scotland, a young student's bursary paid under regulation 4(1)(c) of the Students' Allowances (Scotland) Regulations 1999];

[^{18}. . .]

[^{12} (2) For the purposes of the definition of "full-time student" in paragraph (1), a person shall be regarded as attending or, as the case may be, undertaking a full-time course of study, a full-time course of advanced education or as being on a sandwich course—

(a) subject to paragraph (3), in the case of a person attending or undertaking a part of a modular course that would be a full-time course of study for the purposes of this Part, for the period beginning on the day on which that part of the course starts and ending—

   (i) on the last day on which he is registered with the educational establishment as attending or undertaking that part as a full-time course of study; or

   (ii) on such earlier date (if any) as he finally abandons the course or is dismissed from it;

(b) in any other case, throughout the period beginning on the date on which he starts attending or undertaking the course and ending on the last day of the course or on such earlier date (if any) as he finally abandons it or is dismissed from it.

(3) For the purpose of sub-paragraph (a) of paragraph (2), the period referred to in that sub-paragraph shall include—

(a) where a person has failed examinations or has failed to successfully complete a module relating to a period when he was attending or undertaking a part of the course as a full-time course of study, any period in respect of which he attends or undertakes the course for the purpose of retaking those examinations or that module;

(b) any period of vacation within the period specified in that paragraph or immediately following that period except where the person has registered with the educational establishment to attend or undertake the final module in the course and the vacation immediately follows the last day on which he is required to attend or undertake the course.

(4) In paragraphs (2), "modular course" means a course of study which consists of two or more modules, the successful completion of a specified number of which is required before a person is considered by the educational establishment to have completed the course.]

AMENDMENTS

1. Income Support (General) Amendments No.5 Regulations 1988 (SI 1988/2022) reg.14 (December 12, 1988).

2. Social Security Benefits (Student Loans and Miscellaneous Amendments) Regulations 1990 (SI 1990/1549) reg.5(5) (September 1, 1990).

3. Income Support (General) Amendment No.4 Regulations 1991 (SI 1991/1559) reg.10 (August 5, 1991).

4. Income Support (General) Amendment Regulations 1992 (SI 1992/468) reg.5 (April 6, 1992).

5. Income-related Benefits Schemes (Miscellaneous Amendments) (No.3) Regulations 1992 (SI 1992/2155) reg.19 (October 5, 1992).

6. Income-related Benefits Schemes (Miscellaneous Amendments) (No.4) Regulations 1993 (SI 1993/2119) reg.16 (October 4, 1993).

7. Social Security Benefits (Miscellaneous Amendments) Regulations 1995 (SI 1995/1742) reg.2 (August 1, 1995).

8. Income-related Benefits Schemes and Social Fund (Miscellaneous Amendments) Regulations 1996 (SI 1996/1944) reg.6(8) (October 7, 1996).

9. Income-related Benefits and Jobseeker's Allowance (Amendment) (No.2) Regulations 1997 (SI 1997/2197) reg.5(5) (October 6, 1997).

10. Social Security (Miscellaneous Amendments) Regulations 1998 (SI 1998/563) reg.4(1) and (2)(e) (April 6, 1998).

11. Social Security Amendment (Students) Regulations 1999 (SI 1999/1935) reg.3(2) (August 30, 1999, or if the student's period of study begins between August 1 and 29, 1999, the first day of the period).

12. Social Security Amendment (Students) Regulations 2000 (SI 2000/1981) reg.5(3) (July 31, 2000).

13. Social Security Amendment (Students and Income-related Benefits) Regulations 2000 (SI 2000/1922) reg.2(2) (August 28, 2000, or if the student's period of study begins between August 1 and 27, 2000, the first day of the period).

14. Social Security Amendment (Students and Income-related Benefits) Regulations 2000 (SI 2000/1922) reg.2(3) (August 28, 2000, or if the student's period of study begins between August 1 and 27, 2000, the first day of the period).

15. Income Support (General) Amendment Regulations 2001 (SI 2001/721) reg.2(b) (March 29, 2001).

16. Social Security (Miscellaneous Amendments) (No.2) Regulations 2001 (SI 2001/652) reg.3(1) and (2)(c) (April 1, 2001).

17. Social Security (Miscellaneous Amendments) (No.2) Regulations 2001 (SI 2001/652) reg.3(3) (April 1, 2001).

18. Social Security Amendment (Students and Income-related Benefits) Regulations 2001 (SI 2001/2319) reg.2(1) and (2)(c) (August 1, 2001).

19. Social Security Amendment (Students and Income-related Benefits) Regulations 2001 (SI 2001/2319) reg.2(3) (August 1, 2001).

20. Social Security Amendment (Students and Income-related Benefits) Regulations 2002 (SI 2002/1589) reg.2(1) (August 1, 2002).

21. Social Security (Students and Income-related Benefits) Amendment Regulations 2004 (SI 2004/1708) reg.5(1) (September 1, 2004, or if the student's period of study begins between August 1 and August 31, 2004, the first day of the period).

22. Civil Partnership (Pensions, Social Security and Child Support) (Consequential, etc. Provisions) Order 2005 (SI 2005/2877) art.2(3) and Sch.3 para.13(5) (December 5, 2005).

23. National Council for Education and Training for Wales (Transfer of Functions to the National Assembly for Wales and Abolition) Order 2005 (SI 2005/3238 (W.243)) art.9(2) and Sch.2 para.1(1) (April 1, 2006).

24. Social Security (Young Persons) Amendment Regulations 2006 (SI 2006/718) reg.2(6) (April 10, 2006).

25. Social Security (Miscellaneous Amendments) (No.6) Regulations 2008 (SI 2008/2767) reg.2(9) (November 17, 2008).

26. Social Security (Miscellaneous Amendments) (No.7) Regulations 2008 (SI 2008/3157) reg.2(5) (January 5, 2009).

27. Social Security (Miscellaneous Amendments) Regulations 2009 (SI 2009/583) reg.2(9) (April 6, 2009).

28. Social Security (Miscellaneous Amendments) (No.4) Regulations 2009 (SI 2009/2655) reg.2(13) (October 26, 2009).

29. Income Support (Prescribed Categories of Person) Regulations 2009 (SI 2009/3152) reg.3(2)(c) and 3(7) (December, 30, 2009). Regulation 3(2)(c) omits "10," and "12" in para.(c) of the definition of "grant income " with effect from December 30, 2009 but reg.3(7) provides that this does not apply in the case of a person who is subject to the saving provisions in reg.2(2) of those Regulations.

30. Local Education Authorities and Children's Services Authorities (Integration of Functions) (Local and Subordinate Legislation) Order 2010 (SI 2010/1172) art.5 and Sch.3 para.13 (May 5, 2010).

31. Apprenticeships, Skills, Children and Learning Act 2009 (Consequential Amendments to Subordinate Legislation) (England) Order 2010 (SI 2010/1941) art.3(3) (September 1, 2010).

32. Young People's Learning Agency Abolition (Consequential Amendments to Subordinate Legislation) (England) Order 2012 (SI 2012/956) art.3(3) (May 1, 2012).

33. Deregulation Act 2015 (Consequential Amendments) Order 2015 (SI 2015/971) art.2 and Sch.3 para.2(3) (May 26, 2015).

34. Higher Education and Research Act 2017 (Further Implementation etc.) Regulations 2019 (SI 2019/1027) reg.15 (August 1, 2019).

35. Social Security (Income and Capital) (Miscellaneous Amendments) Regulations 2020 (SI 2020/618) reg.2(6) (July 15, 2020).

DEFINITIONS

"training allowance"—see reg.2(1).
"course of study"—*ibid*.

GENERAL NOTE

"Academic year"
This definition is important for the purposes of calculating student loan income.   **2.476**
"Academic year" means a period of 12 months beginning on January 1, April 1, July 1 or September 1, depending on whether the course in question starts in the winter, the spring, the summer or the autumn respectively. For students who begin their course in August or September and continue to attend during the autumn (i.e. for most students) the academic year is treated as starting in the autumn—i.e. on September 1.

"Grant"
The definition of "grant" is in terms of any kind of educational grant or award.   **2.477**
The reasoning in *R(IS) 16/95* on the meaning of award is to be preferred to that in *R(SB) 20/83*. The everyday meaning, particularly in the educational context, was said to imply an outright gift with no liability to repay and so excludes a loan. Thus the education loan received from the Norwegian government by the claimant's partner did not fall within the definition of "grant" in reg.61. Nor would

it fall within the current definition of "student loan" and the provisions of reg.66A because it was not made under any of the UK legislative provisions specified there. Nevertheless the loan was to be treated as income under the ordinary rules in reg.40. The introduction of reg.66A treating certain student loans as income had been for the removal of doubt and did not indicate that such loans would otherwise have not counted as income. That approach is followed in *R(JSA) 4/04* where the receipts would on the ordinary tests be classified as income rather than capital. In that case the claimant was a part-time student and the equivalent of reg.66A at the time applied only to full-time students.

The September 2004 amendment ensures that education maintenance allowances (EMAs) are excluded from the definition of grant. EMAs (which now only apply in Wales and Scotland) are fully disregarded (see para.11 of Sch.9 for the income disregard and para.63 of Sch.10 for the capital disregard). In England, from September 2011, EMAs have been replaced by payments from the "16–19 Bursary Fund"; payments from this Fund are also disregarded under para.11 of Sch.9 and para.63 of Sch.10.

"Grant income"

2.478   Note that in most cases a contribution (e.g. from a parent) is included whether paid or not.

Where a person is due to repay part or all of a student grant because they leave or are dismissed from their course before it finishes, see regs 29(2B), 32(6A) and 40(3B). However, note *Chief Adjudication Officer v Leeves* reported as *R(IS) 5/99* in the notes to reg.29(2B) and the argument discussed in those notes as to when reg.29(2B) applies. Note also para.61 of Sch.9 under which any grant (or covenant income or student loan or contribution) left over at the end of a person's course is ignored.

"Student" and "Full-time student"

2.479   On July 31, 2000 the existing definition of "student" was substituted and a new definition of "full-time student" was inserted. The latter definition needs to be read in conjunction with paras (2)–(4) which expand upon it.

The aim of these new definitions was to reinforce the Government's policy intention that a full-time student should count as such throughout the duration of his course until he completes or is finally dismissed from or finally abandons it (but note the new provisions relating to "modular courses" (defined in para.(4)) in paras (2)(a) and (3)). It had been felt necessary to introduce these changes following the Court of Appeal's decisions in *Clarke and Faul* and *Webber* (see below). The Government's original proposals for change (first mooted in March 1998) were more extensive and were roundly rejected by the Social Security Advisory Committee (SSAC) in their report submitted in May 1998 (for SSAC's report and the Government's statement in reply see Cmnd. 4739 (2000)). SSAC's primary recommendation was that the proposed amendments should be withdrawn and replaced by regulations designed "to provide safety net support for people who are not currently engaged in full-time studies—either through social security (subject to the normal conditions of entitlement) or mandatory grants". Not surprisingly this did not find favour with the Government, although the Secretary of State's reply to SSAC's report did acknowledge "the need to ensure that the interaction of legislation underpinning [the Government's] overall policy on full-time students does not result in individual students being denied financial support in certain circumstances". Thus the final version of the amendments to the JSA Regulations 1996 included a provision enabling those full-time students who interrupted their studies because of illness or caring responsibilities but who have now recovered or whose caring responsibilities have ceased to claim old style JSA. They will be eligible until the earlier of the day before they rejoin their course or the day before the start of their next academic year, provided that they do not qualify for a student grant or loan in this period (see reg.1(3D) and (3E) of the JSA Regulations 1996).

(A similar provision was also introduced into the Housing Benefit and Council Tax Benefit Regulations). The Government did not, however, accept one of SSAC's other recommendations, namely, that lone parent students who had completed a substantial part of their full-time course should continue to be eligible for benefit after their youngest child reached 16. The response that "the Government believes that it is reasonable to expect a lone parent who wishes to study full-time to undertake and complete a course of full-time study before the youngest child reaches the age of 16" is not a particularly helpful one.

Note that the definitions of "student" and "full-time student" now encompass a person who is "undertaking" as well as "attending" a course. The stated purpose of the inclusion of the word "undertaking" is to indicate that it is not necessary for the person to be physically present at the relevant educational establishment in order to count as a student. Thus students operating through remote learning during the 2020 coronavirus outbreak will no doubt be covered.

"Full-time student"

The definition of full-time student is important not just for the purposes of this Chapter of the Regulations, but also because it feeds back in through the additional definition of "period of study" in reg.2(1) to remove most full-time students' entitlement (see reg.4ZA(2) and (3)). Note that those in receipt of a training allowance are excluded from the definition of student and hence full-time student. Further, from April 10, 2006 a person who is a "qualifying young person within the meaning of s.142 of the Contributions and Benefits Act 1992" is also excluded (see below).

2.480

Besides those on sandwich courses (see the definition of sandwich course later in para.(1)), there are two categories, depending on whether the person is under 19 or not. A person under 19 is a full-time student if attending or undertaking a full-time course of advanced education. Advanced education is defined earlier in para.(1).

A person of 19 or over (but under pensionable age) is a full-time student if attending or undertaking a full-time course of study at an educational establishment. It does not have to be any particular level. However, following the introduction of the new rules for child benefit on April 10, 2006, a person aged 19 who "falls within the definition of qualifying young person in s.142 of the Contributions and Benefits Act" can be in relevant education (see reg.12 and the notes to that regulation). An exception has therefore been added to the definition of full-time student for qualifying young persons.

"Course of study at an educational establishment"

The reference in the definition of full-time student (and student) is to a course of study, rather than of education, as it was in the Supplementary Benefit (Conditions of Entitlement) Regulations. Now that the reference is to "attending or undertaking" a course, there is clearly no scope for any argument that those pursuing degrees purely by research are not covered.

2.481

R(SB) 25/87 decides that a pupil barrister is not a student because pupillage is not a course of education, but an assimilation of specific vocational skills by attending on the pupil master. Presumably, a pupil barrister would be said not to be undertaking a "course of study" at an educational establishment (the phrase here) either. *CIS 50/1990* suggests that this approach is not lightly to be extended to other circumstances. The claimant was attending an intensive shorthand and typing course at a commercial training centre. There was little difficulty in deciding that this was a full-time course. The Commissioner holds that since there was active tuition, the claimant was engaged in study, regardless of the technical nature of the skills studied. The centre was within the ordinary meaning of "educational establishment." In *R(IS) 5/97* a person attending the Bar Vocational Course at the Council of Legal Education was a student. *R(SB) 25/87* was clearly distinguishable. See also *CIS 450/1997* which decides that a Project 2000 student nurse came within the definition of "student".

On the meaning of "course", see *R(IS) 1/96*. The claimant was training to be an architect. He had obtained his degree and had to find a year's placement with a firm before undertaking a further two years' study (to be followed by a further year's practical experience) in order to complete his professional training. The Commissioner holds that he was not a student during the year "out". In the Commissioner's view, a course was a "unified sequence of study, tuition and/or practical training ... intended to lead to one or more qualifications obtained on its completion". So if a profession required more than one qualification for which colleges did not provide a single sequence of tuition and/or experience, the person was not engaged on one continuous "course" throughout, but completed one "course" before moving onto another. Thus para.(a) of the then definition (see the 1995 edition of J. Mesher and P. Wood, *Income-related Benefits: the Legislation*) of student did not apply to him. Paragraph (b) also did not apply as the claimant was not on a "sandwich course", since any periods of outside practical experience were not "associated with" his full-time study within the meaning of the Education (Mandatory Awards) Regulations. See also *CIS 576/1994* in which the Commissioner similarly decides that the course is the whole course leading to the qualification and not a separate course each year. Note that a student who passes resits after a year's absence from his course is rejoining the same, not a different, course (*O'Connor v Chief Adjudication Officer* [1999] All E.R.(D) 220, also reported as *R(IS) 7/99* (see below)).

On the other hand, *R(JSA) 2/02* holds that where the course of training is separated from the course of examinations it is only the course of training that constitutes the course of study, not the course of examinations, nor some sort of amalgam of both. Thus where a University provided a course of training to prepare the claimant for a course of examinations set and marked by an outside professional institute, the claimant could abandon the University course and cease to be a student for the purposes of JSA, while still being able to pursue his professional qualification.

"Full-time course"

2.482   The question whether the course is full- or part-time is clearly important, since the exclusion from income support does not apply to part-time students who may be eligible for benefit if they fall within any of the categories in Sch.1B.

Note that it is the course which has to be full-time, rather than the claimant's hours of attendance on it (see *R(SB) 40/83, R(SB) 41/83, CSB 176/1987*). If a non-modular course (see below for the position of modular courses under the new rules introduced on July 31, 2000) is full-time, the effect of para.(2)(b) is that the definition of full-time student applies for the entire length of the course, unless the student finally abandons the course or is dismissed from it (see further below). Note *CIS 368/1992* which decided that a student who exercised the option of working in France for a year as part of her course remained a student throughout her four-year course. Her course was continuing, even if in a different form.

Although the distinction between full- and part-time courses is a crucial one, there continues to be no definition of "full-time course", with the exception of certain courses that are referred to in sub-paras (b) and (c) of the definitions of "full-time course of study" and "full-time course of advanced education". In England and Wales, for courses funded totally or partly by the Secretary of State under s.14 of the Education Act 2002 or the Welsh Ministers, the cut-off for a full-time course is 16 or more "guided learning hours" each week. The number of a person's "guided learning hours" will be set out in his learning agreement with his college (in Wales referred to simply as a document). Guided learning hours are "hours when a member of staff is present to guide learning on a programme including lectures, tutorials and supervised study", as opposed to time spent in private study (*Decision Makers Guide*, para.30077). Note the different definitions that apply in Scotland.

2.483   But for courses which are not so funded, whether or not a course is full-time remains to be determined by the circumstances in each case. The educational establishment's description of the course is not conclusive but should be accepted unless challenged by pertinent evidence *(R(SB) 40/83; R(SB) 41/83)*. An example of such evidence could be that the claimant is exempt from certain course requirements *(CG/3189/2004)*.

In *CIS 152/1994* the Commissioner recognised that recent developments in education, and in particular the advent of modular courses, have blurred the distinction between full-time and part-time courses, and that what is in essence the same course can often be accessed on either a full-time or a part-time basis. The claimant had begun a full-time course in 1992, studying 21 and three-quarters hours a week. In 1993 he reduced the number of modules he was taking from seven to five, so that his hours of study became 15 a week. The Commissioner states that it is no longer sufficient just to look at the course. The overall circumstances (e.g. the hours of study, number of modules, length of time it would take to obtain the qualification on the basis of five as opposed to seven modules at a time, correspondence from the college, fees payable and any relevant information in the college prospectus) therefore had to be examined to ascertain whether the course the claimant was *currently* attending was full or part-time. (But note that it now seems clear that whether a non-modular course is full-time is to be determined by the nature of the course at its start, not according to later changes, see *O'Connor* and *R(IS) 1/00* below. For the position of modular courses under the new rules introduced on July 31, 2000, see below.)

A similar approach was taken in *CIS 576/1994*. The claimant's modular degree course could be undertaken on a full-time or part-time basis. He attended on a full-time basis for the first year and then changed to part-time. He became full-time again for the last two terms of the third year. The Commissioner states that para.(a) of the then definition of "student" (see the 1995 edition of J. Mesher and P. Wood, *Income-related Benefits: the Legislation*) did not have the effect of turning a course, attendance on which was on a part-time basis, into a full-time course. Whether a person was, or was not, attending a full-time course depended on the facts at the material time. The factors suggested in *CIS 152/1994* were relevant; whether the person had a local authority grant or student loan might also be pertinent since these were not available to part-time students (see the Education (Mandatory Awards) Regulations). The claimant was not a student (as then defined) when he was attending part-time.

An appeal against this decision was dismissed by the Court of Appeal *(Chief Adjudication Officer v Webber* [1998] 1 W.L.R. 625, also reported as *R(IS) 15/98*, but for differing reasons. Hobhouse LJ stated that the definition of "course of study" presupposes that it is possible at the outset to categorise a course as full-time or part-time and that the same categorisation will apply from the start to the end of the course. However, that assumption did not accord with the practice of many educational institutions. Many courses allowed students the option of attending on a full- or part-time basis at different stages of the course, as was the case in this appeal. The consequence was that the claimant had *never* been a student (as then defined) because the course on which he was enrolled did not require full-time attendance and so could not be described as full-time. Such an interpretation clearly had significant implications and went considerably beyond that of the Commissioner. Evans LJ held that the deeming provision in para.(a) of the then definition of "student" could not be relied upon to confer the status of student when this did not in fact exist. In his view, if interpreted in that way the provision created "an anomalous class of people left to destitution without state support of any kind" and he would require "express words of the utmost clarity to persuade [him] that Parliament intended to produce that disgraceful result". Peter Gibson LJ's judgment was based on the fact that the definition of "student" at the time in question included the words "throughout any period of term or vacation within it" (which phrase was omitted from August 1, 1995 following the Court of Appeal's decision in *Clarke and Faul*, see below).

The result of these differing approaches was that the position was somewhat

2.484

unclear. However in *O'Connor v Chief Adjudication Officer* [1999] All E.R.(D) 220, also reported as *R(IS) 7/99*, the judges who were in the majority agreed with Hobhouse LJ that the status of student (as then defined) was determined by the nature of the course at its beginning and distinguished their own decision from that in *Webber* on that basis. Auld LJ stated that in Mr O'Connor's case his course was a full-time three year course, with no provision for part-time or modular or other flexible arrangements. Although he had been allowed a year's break in order to re-take exams that he had failed, this was not an option of the course when he started it. But if at its start a course could be followed full- or part-time according to the student's preference, the position was different for the reasons given by Hobhouse LJ in *Webber*.

The consequence therefore seemed to be that claimants on a course that could not be characterised as full-time at the outset because they could study full- or part-time for different periods of it would not come within the definition of "student" (as then defined). This was confirmed by *R(IS) 1/00*.

2.485   In *R(IS) 1/00* the claimant was undertaking a BTEC National Diploma course. When she claimed income support she was studying for 20 hours a week. The college stated that they did not designate courses as full-time or part-time, as students were able to take separate modules to build towards a final qualification. The Commissioner concluded that the express approval by Auld and Swinton LJJ in *O'Connor* of the view taken by Hobhouse LJ in *Webber* had been necessary to the decision in *O'Connor* and so authoritatively established the position. Thus the fundamental question was how the course was characterised at its outset. As Hobhouse LJ had stated, a course that did not have a fixed and determined character at its commencement and which could be followed on a full-time or part-time basis was not a full-time course. Moreover, in the Commissioner's view it inevitably followed from this approach that the result would be the same even if the claimant's actual attendance throughout had been on a full-time basis.

To determine whether the claimant's course should be treated as full-time, the Commissioner suggested that information would be needed about such matters as the structure of the course (modular or otherwise), the length of time over which it could be completed, whether a student was committed to any particular structure on initial registration and whether it was possible to change from full-time to part-time attendance or vice versa within the same course.

C5/98 (JSA) (a decision of a Northern Ireland Commissioner) also accepted that it was the nature of the course, as determined at the outset, that was relevant, as did *CJSA/836/1998*, although this was not the primary ground of the Commissioner's decision (see further below).

2.486   The Commissioner in *C5/98(JSA)* granted the claimant leave to appeal to the Court of Appeal in Northern Ireland but the appeal was dismissed (*McComb v Department for Social Development*, Northern Ireland Court of Appeal, reported as *R 1/01 (JSA)*). The claimant contended that the tribunal and the Commissioner, in classifying his course as full-time, had failed to take account of its modular nature. The Court agreed that a modular course was not readily distinguishable from a mixed mode one (the university concerned did not classify any course as mixed mode). It then continued: "The critical matter, however, is whether [the claimant] started out on a course of full-time study, even if he had the option of converting at a later stage to part-time by reducing the number of modules." But with respect to the Northern Ireland Court of Appeal this does not seem to fully accord with the approach of Hobhouse LJ in *Webber* (which has been followed in subsequent British cases, see above). If a claimant has the option of changing to studying on a part-time basis, how can it be said that the course requires full-time attendance, or that it has a fixed and determined character at its commencement? If it does not, then applying Hobhouse LJ's approach, it cannot be characterised as full-time at its outset.

On its facts, however, the decision in *McComb* that the claimant's course was full-time would seem correct. Mr McComb had enrolled on a full-time degree course for which he received an education authority grant for the first three years. When he failed to complete the final year's requirements he was allowed to register as an "examination only" student for a fourth year but he remained on the full-time course on which he had originally enrolled. Now see the new rules for modular courses introduced on July 31, 2000, although on the facts of Mr McComb's case the outcome is likely to be the same (see para.(3)(a)).

"Modular courses"

New rules were introduced on July 31, 2000 which were intended to clarify the position of modular courses. "Modular course" is defined in para.(4). To come within para.(4) a course must simply consist of two or more modules, the successful completion of a specific number of which is required in order for a student to finish the course.

2.487

A person attending or undertaking part of a modular course which would be classified as a full-time course will be treated as a full-time student for the period from the day that part of the course begins until the last day he is registered as attending or undertaking that part as a full-time course (subject to earlier final abandonment or dismissal) (para.(2)(a)). This includes any vacation in that period, or immediately following that part of the course, unless the vacation follows the last day on which he is required to attend or undertake the course (para.(3)(b)). It also includes any period that the person attends or undertakes the course in order to retake examinations or a module that he had previously taken on a full-time basis. It seems that this will apply even if the person is now registered as a part-time student.

It will be a question of fact whether a person is attending or undertaking a part of a modular course that counts as a full-time course. Relevant evidence might include the university or college's regulations and registration procedures, the course regulations and course handbook and any other relevant information given to the student about his status. As stated above, the educational establishment's description is not conclusive but should be accepted unless challenged by pertinent evidence *(R(SB) 40/83; R(SB) 41/83)*. It should be noted, however, that not all modular courses allow the option of full-time or part-time attendance. Some universities and colleges do not have mixed mode courses but only offer separate full-time and part-time courses, even though the courses are classed as modular. Disputes about whether the part of the modular course (or indeed the whole of the course) that the person is attending or undertaking counts as a full-time course may therefore still continue. If the modular course is a full-time course throughout it would seem to come within sub-para.(a) of para.(2) but may also be covered by sub-para.(b).

However, the importance of these new rules is that for modular courses the deeming of full-time student status only operates during the periods prescribed in paras (2) and (3). It does not apply outside these periods if the student's status has changed to part-time. A student on a part of a modular course which is not classed as full-time and who is not caught by para.(3) may thus be able to claim income support or old style JSA if he satisfies the normal condition of entitlement for one of these benefits. See *RVS v SSWP (ESA)* [2019] UKUT 102 (AAC), holding that a student on a modular course intermitting for a year was not undertaking a part of the course.

"Attending or undertaking [a course] . . . finally abandons . . . or is dismissed from it"

The deeming provision, whereby a person whose non-modular course is full-time (as determined at its start, see above under *"Full-time course"*) will count as a full-time student until the last day of the course or until he finally abandons or is dismissed from it is now contained in para.(2)(b). Note the separate deeming provision for those on a part of a modular course that is classed as full-time in para.(2)(a) (and note paras (3) and (4); see above for a discussion of these new rules for modular courses).

2.488

The predecessor of para.(2)(b) (para.(a) of the former definition of "student", see the 2000 edition of this book, and see the 1995 edition of J. Mesher and

P. Wood, *Income-related Benefits: the Legislation* for the form of para.(a) that was in force before August 1, 1995) came under close scrutiny in several cases, notably *Chief Adjudication Officer and Secretary of State for Social Security v Clarke and Faul* [1995] E.L.R. 259, *CIS 15594/1996* (appealed to the Court of Appeal as *O'Connor v Chief Adjudication Officer* [1999] All. E.R.(D) 220, also reported as *R(IS) 7/99*), *CIS 13986/1996* and *CIS 14255/1996*. For a discussion of these decisions see the 2000 edition of this book (pp.405–6). Note that one of the points decided in those cases, namely that "abandon" in this context meant "abandon permanently" has now received statutory endorsement in para.(2). Dismissal similarly means final dismissal (*CIS 15594/1996*). Note also *Driver v Chief Adjudication Officer* (Court of Appeal, December 12, 1996, reported as *R(IS) 6/97*) which held that a student on a sandwich course whose industrial placement ended prematurely nevertheless remained a student throughout the period of her intended placement.

As a result of those decisions, it seems fairly clearly established that a person whose non-modular course is full-time (as determined at its outset) will count as a full-time student until the last day of the course (subject to any earlier final abandonment or dismissal), regardless of non-attendance on the course for whatever reason. (But see above for the position of modular courses.) See also *MS v SSWP* [2009] UKUT 9 (AAC) which holds that the denial of JSA to a student who is not attending college for a year while he resits exams externally is not contrary to art.14, read with art.1 Prot.1 of the ECHR.

One other point should be made. Paragraph (2)(b) refers to "the course" that the full-time student is attending or undertaking. So if a student does finally abandon his full-time, non-modular course and then starts a separate part-time course he should not be caught by the deeming provision. In this connection it is interesting to note that para.12 of the Secretary of State's response to SSAC's report on the amendment regulations introduced on July 31, 2000 (Cmnd. 4739 (2000), see above under *"Student"* and *"Full-time Student"*) seems to accept that those changing from full-time to part-time courses are abandoning one course before starting another. Note, however, that this would not appear to assist a claimant who is not attending his course because he has failed exams and is only permitted to return if and when he successfully passes the resits. Although *CIS 13986/1996* decided that a claimant in that situation had been dismissed from his *original* course and if he passed the resit examinations a year later would be joining a *different* course, this was not followed in *CIS 15594/1996* (*O'Connor*). The Commissioner's view there was that if a person was readmitted after an interval to follow essentially the same programme, that person was returning to the same course. On appeal the Court of Appeal in *O'Connor* decided the substantive issue in *CIS 13986/1996* against the claimant (for further discussion see pp.405–6 of the 2000 edition of this volume). See also *MS v SSWP* [2009] UKUT 9 (AAC) above.

2.489   Until October 27, 2008 a full-time student who had been incapable of work for 28 weeks (or who qualified for a disability or severe disability premium or was receiving a disabled student's allowance on the grounds of deafness) was eligible for income support (reg.4ZA(3)(b) and paras 10 and 12 of Sch.1B). However, following the introduction of ESA on October 27, 2008, new claims for income support on these grounds were no longer possible, except in certain circumstances. Thus from October 27, 2008 full-time students who are sick or disabled and are making a new claim have to claim old style ESA. However they will not qualify for income-related ESA unless they are entitled to disability living allowance ("DLA") (at any rate), personal independence payment ("PIP") (at any rate) or armed forces independence payment—see further para.6(1)(g) of Sch.1 to the Welfare Reform Act 2007 and regs 14–18 of the ESA Regulations 2008 and the notes to those provisions. But a student who had an award of income support under paras 10 or 12 of Sch.1B when "migrated" to ESA will still be able to get old style ESA while a student, even though he is not entitled to DLA, PIP or armed forces independence payment (see Sch.1 para.2 and Sch.2 para.2 of the Employment and Support Allowance (Transitional Provisions, Housing Benefit and Council Tax Benefit)

(Existing Awards) (No.2) Regulations 2010 (SI 2010/1907) (as amended) ("the Migration Regulations")).

A further change took place on December 30, 2009 in relation to a student's eligibility for income support when paras 10 and 12 of Sch.1B were revoked, subject to a saving provision. See further the notes to reg.61 on pp.554–555 of the 2015/16 edition of what was then Vol.II of this series.

Note also that from July 31, 2000, a full-time student who has taken time out of his course with the consent of his university or college because of illness or caring responsibilities, and who has now recovered or whose caring responsibilities have ended, can claim old style JSA until the day before he rejoins his course or the first day of the following academic year, whichever is the earlier, provided that he is not eligible for a grant or student loan during this period (see reg.1(3D) and (3E) of the JSA Regulations 1996). Note that caring responsibilities in this context is not defined. For the position of pregnant students and old style JSA, see *Secretary of State for Social Security v Walter* [2001] EWCA Civ 1913, reported as *R(JSA) 3/02* (which overturned the decision in *CJSA 1920/1999*) and *CM v SSWP* [2009] UKUT 43 (AAC), reported as *R(IS) 7/09*, discussed in the notes to reg.130 of the JSA Regulations 1996. A pregnant student is excluded from income support (see reg.4ZA and Sch.1B; para.14 of Sch.1B which covers pregnant women is not one of the paragraphs applied to students by reg.4ZA(3)(b)). But once the child is born the student may be eligible under reg.4ZA(3)(b) and para.1 of Sch.1B if she is a lone parent. See further the note to reg.130 of the JSA Regulations 1996.

Differences between income support and old style JSA definition

The definitions applying to full-time students under the JSA Regulations 1996 take a slightly different form (see the notes to reg.130 of the JSA Regulations 1996).   **2.490**

Since the amendments made to both the Income Support and the JSA Regulations 1996 on July 31, 2000 by SI 2000 No.1981 the differences are less marked. However, in *CJSA 836/1998* (a decision on the pre-July 31, 2000 form) the Commissioner took the view that the differences between the then form of the JSA and income support definitions had a material effect. This was because for the purposes of old style JSA the provision deeming a person who had started a course to be attending or undertaking it until the last day of the course (or earlier abandonment or dismissal) was contained in the definition of "course of study" in reg.1(3) of the JSA Regulations 1996. Under income support the deeming provision was in the definition of "student" in reg.61. This defined a student as someone who was attending a full-time course and provided that a person who had started on "such a course" (i.e. a full-time course) was to be treated as attending it until the last day of the course or earlier abandonment or dismissal. The deeming under the definition of "course of study" in reg.1(3), on the other hand, did not necessarily refer to a full-time course. In the Commissioner's view, therefore, there was nothing in the JSA Regulations 1996 that required a person who had started a course on a full-time basis but changed to part-time to be treated as continuing to be a full-time student. Whether the course was full- or part-time was to be determined by looking at the situation at the time in question. But this approach was not followed in *C5/98 (JSA)*. The Commissioner in that case considered that the "it" in the definition of "course of study" in reg.1(3) referred to the course started. The fact that the "deeming" under old style JSA was contained in the definition of "course of study" rather than the definition of "student" was not material. This point was not dealt with by the Northern Ireland Court of Appeal in the appeal against *C5/98 (JSA)* (*McComb v Department for Social Development*, reported as *R 1/01 (JSA)*); see above).

But since the insertion of paras (3A)–(3C) into reg.1 of the JSA Regulations 1996 (which provisions parallel paras (2)–(4)) with effect from July 31, 2000 the Commissioner's reasoning in *CJSA 836/1998* no longer applies. That is because the deeming of full-time student status for the entire length of a course (subject to earlier final abandonment or dismissal) is now contained in reg.1(3A)(b) of the JSA Regulations 1996, rather than the definition of "course of study" in reg.1(3).

Note also paras (3D) and (3E) of reg.1 of the JSA Regulations 1996 (see the notes to reg.130 of the JSA Regulations 1996). There is no equivalent to these provisions in the Income Support Regulations.

Summary

2.491   The position for non-modular courses may thus be summarised as follows. Whether or not a person comes within the definition of "full-time student" depends on the nature of his course, as determined at its outset. If the course is not full-time so that the definition of full-time student does not apply, the fact that the person attends the course on a full-time basis throughout would seem to be immaterial (see *CIS 12823/1996*). On the other hand, if the person's course is classified as full-time at its beginning, he will count as a student for the duration of his course (subject to earlier abandonment or dismissal), regardless of his actual mode of attendance on the course.

If the course is a modular one (as defined in para.(4)), the rules in paras (2) and (3) will apply (see above under *"Modular courses"*). Under para.(2)(a), it will be a question of fact whether a student is attending or undertaking a part of a modular course that would be classified as a full-time course. If a modular course is a full-time course throughout it would seem to come within sub-para.(a) of para.(2) but may also be covered by sub-para.(b). However, the importance of these new rules is that for modular courses the deeming of full-time student status only operates during the periods prescribed in paras (2) and (3). It does not apply outside these periods if the student's status has changed to part-time. A student on a part of a modular course which is not classed as full-time and who is not caught by para.(3) may thus be able to claim income support or JSA if he satisfies the normal conditions of entitlement for one of these benefits.

As readers will be aware, the Human Rights Act 1998 came into force on October 2, 2000 (see Vol.III of this series). The claimant in *O'Connor* had relied on the right to education in art.2 of the First Protocol to the European Convention on Human Rights in support of his argument on irrationality. However, Auld LJ considered that there was no potential breach of the right to education. That was because, firstly, there were rulings of inadmissibility by the European Commission of Human Rights suggesting that art.2 was concerned primarily with school, not higher, education (although now see *R. (Douglas) v North Tyneside and MBC* [2003] EWCA Civ 1847 in which the Court of Appeal held that tertiary or higher education fell within the meaning of "education" in art.2). Secondly, art.2 did not require the state to subsidise a student in his exercise of his right to avail himself of education which it provided (see further *Douglas*). For further challenges to the treatment of students in social security legislation both under EC Directive 79/7 and the Human Rights Act, see *Secretary of State for Social Security v Walter* [2001] EWCA Civ 1913, reported as *R(JSA) 3/02*, and *CM v SSWP* [2009] UKUT 43 (AAC), reported as *R(IS) 7/09*, (discussed in the note to reg.130 of the JSA Regulations 1996) and *CJSA/2663/2006* (in the note to reg.15(a) of those Regulations).

"Postgraduate loan"

2.492   Under the Education (Postgraduate Master's Degree Loan) Regulations 2016 (SI 2016/606) a postgraduate master's degree loan is available for eligible full-time or part-time courses starting from the 2016/17 academic year. The loan (initially of up to £10,000, rising to £11,570 for 2020/21) is not paid specifically for tuition fees or maintenance costs. According to the Explanatory Memorandum for SI 2016/743, the average tuition fees for a full-time Master's degree course are £7,000, so that only the remaining 30 per cent (initially £3,000) would be taken into account as income for the purposes of income support, income-based JSA, income-related ESA, universal credit and housing benefit. That was to reflect the position that applies to undergraduates, for whom student income for daily living costs is taken into account and loans for tuition fees are ignored (reg.66C). This effect was achieved by adding postgraduate master's degree loans to student loans in the following regulations, so that in general such loans are to be treated as income (reg.66A(1)). A claimant is treated as possessing a postgraduate master's degree loan under reg.66A(3) as amended where a loan has actually been obtained or one could be acquired by taking reasonable steps, just as for an ordinary student loan. The disregard of fee loans under reg.66C would appear not to apply as a postgraduate master's degree loan, which the recipient can spend on anything, is not known as a fee loan or as a fee contribution loan. However, the new reg.66A(4A) restricts the amount to be taken into account as income to 30% of the maximum available loan.

There are further deductions under reg.66A(5) and a disregard of £10 per week under reg.66A(2).

In *CH/4429/2006* the claimant's partner had a religious objection to taking out a loan and it was argued that that made it unreasonable for him to do so. The Commissioner rejected that argument on the basis that "reasonable" only qualified the steps that could be taken to acquire a student loan. It is understood that that decision is under challenge in an appeal currently before the Upper Tribunal.

Postgraduate doctoral degree loans were introduced in 2018, at the same annual rate as for master's degree loans. With effect from July 2020 doctoral degree loans have been brought within the general definition of "postgraduate loan" so that they are subject to the same rules as previously applied only to master's degree loans. It would seem that prior to July 2020 postgraduate doctoral degree loans would have fallen within the definition of "student loan", since the relevant English regulations were made under s.22 of the Teaching and Higher Education Act 1998, meaning that the 30% rule would not have applied. It is not known if the 30% rule was applied in practice before the July 2020 amendments.

"Student loan"

Loans are not grants (see *R(IS) 16/95*, discussed in the note to the definition of "grant" above). Note that the definition applies only to loans towards a student's (very widely defined in reg.61) maintenance under the specified English and Welsh, Scottish and Northern Ireland legislation. Such loans are to be treated as income under reg.66A, with the maximum amounts deemed to be possessed whether actually acquired or merely available by taking reasonable steps, subject to small deductions. Loans to students that fall outside this definition can, if properly characterised as income, be taken into account as income under reg.40 (see *R(IS) 16/95*, where the education loan fell outside the definition because it came from the Norwegian government, and *R(JSA) 4/04*, where the student loan fell outside the definition because the claimant was a part-time student and the definition at the time applied only to full-time students). See reg.66C for the disregard of fee loans or fee contribution loans.

2.493

Calculation of grant income

62.—(1) The amount of a student's grant income to be taken into account shall, subject to [³paragraphs [⁷(2) and (2A)]], be the whole of his grant income.

2.494

(2) There shall be disregarded from the amount of a student's grant income any payment—

(a) intended to meet tuition fees or examination fees;

(b) [⁴...]

(c) intended to meet additional expenditure incurred by a disabled student in respect of his attendance on a course;

(d) intended to meet additional expenditure connected with term time residential study away from the student's educational establishment;

(e) on account of the student maintaining a home at a place other than that at which he resides during his course but only to the extent that his rent [²⁰...] is not met by housing benefit;

    (f) on account of any other person but only if that person is residing outside of the United Kingdom and there is no applicable amount in respect of him;

    (g) intended to meet the cost of books and equipment [⁴. . .] [⁶. . .];

    (h) intended to meet travel expenses incurred as a result of his attendance on the course.

[¹⁸(i) intended for the maintenance [¹⁹. . .] of a child dependant.]

[¹⁹(j) intended for the child care costs of a child dependant.]

[²⁵(k) of higher education bursary for care leavers made under Part III of the Children Act 1989 [²⁹or Part 6 of the Social Services and Well-being (Wales) Act 2014].]

    [⁶(2A) Where a student does not have a student loan [²⁸or a postgraduate [³⁰. . .] loan] and is not treated as possessing [²⁸ a student loan or a postgraduate [³⁰. . .] loan], there shall be excluded from the student's grant income—

    (a) the sum of [²³[²⁶ £303] per academic year] in respect of travel costs; and

[¹²(b) the sum of [²⁴[²⁷ £390] per academic year] towards the costs of books and equipment,]

whether or not any such costs are incurred.]

[¹³[¹⁸ (2B) [²¹[²². . .]]]]

    (3) [⁹ Subject to paragraph (3B), a student's grant income except any amount intended for the maintenance of [¹⁸ adult] dependants under Part III of Schedule 2 to the Education (Mandatory Awards) Regulations 1999 [¹⁸. . .]] shall be apportioned—

    (a) subject to paragraph (4), in a case where it is attributable to the period of study, equally between the weeks [¹⁶ in the period beginning with the benefit week, the first day of which coincides with, or immediately follows, the first day of the period of study and ending with the benefit week, the last day of which coincides with, or immediately precedes, the last day of the period of study];

    (b) in any other case, equally between the weeks in the period [¹⁶ beginning with the benefit week, the first day of which coincides with, or immediately follows, the first day of the period for which it is payable and ending with the benefit week, the last day of which coincides with, or immediately precedes, the last day of the period for which it is payable].

    [¹(3A) [¹⁴Any grant in respect of [¹⁸an adult dependant] paid under section 63(6) of the Health Services and Public Health Act 1968 (grants in respect of the provision of instruction to officers of hospital authorities) and] any amount intended for the maintenance of [¹⁸ an adult dependant] under the provisions referred to in paragraph (3) shall be apportioned equally over a period of 52 weeks or, if there are 53 benefit weeks (including part-weeks) in the year, 53.]

    [¹⁰(3B) [¹⁶ In a case where a student is in receipt of a student loan or where he could have acquired a student loan by taking reasonable steps but had not done so,] any amount intended for the maintenance of [¹⁸ an adult dependant] under provisions other than those referred to in paragraph (3) shall be apportioned over the same period as the student's loan is apportioned or[¹⁶, as the case may be, would have been apportioned].]

    (4) In the case of a student on a sandwich course, any periods of experi-

ence within the period of study shall be excluded and the student's grant income shall be apportioned equally between [¹⁶ the weeks in the period beginning with the benefit week, the first day of which immediately follows the last day of the period of experience and ending with the benefit week, the last day of which coincides with, or immediately precedes, the last day of the period of study].

AMENDMENTS

1. Income Support (General) Amendment Regulations 1988 (SI 1988/663) reg.24 (April 11, 1988).
2. Income Support (General) Amendment Regulations 1992 (SI 1992/468) reg.5 (April 6, 1992).
3. Income-related Benefits Schemes (Miscellaneous Amendments) (No.3) Regulations 1992 (SI 1992/2155) reg.20 (October 5, 1992).
4. Income-related Benefits Schemes and Social Fund (Miscellaneous Amendments) Regulations 1996 (SI 1996/1944) reg.6(9) (October 7, 1996).
5. Social Security (Student Amounts Amendment) Regulations 1998 (SI 1998/1379) reg.2 (August 31, 1998, or if the student's period of study begins between August 1, and 30, 1998, the first day of the period).
6. Social Security Amendment (Students) Regulations 1999 (SI 1999/1935) reg.3(3) (August 30, 1999, or if the student's period of study begins between August 1 and 29, 1999, the first day of the period).
7. Social Security Amendment (Students and Income-related Benefits) Regulations 2000 (SI 2000/1922) reg.2(4)(a) (August 28, 2000, or if the student's period of study begins between August 1 and 27, 2000, the first day of the period).
8. Social Security Amendment (Students and Income-related Benefits) Regulations 2000 (SI 2000/1922) reg.2(4)(b) (August 28, 2000, or if the student's period of study begins between August 1 and 27, 2000, the first day of the period).
9. Social Security Amendment (Students and Income-related Benefits) Regulations 2000 (SI 2000/1922) reg.2(4)(d) (August 28, 2000, or if the student's period of study begins between August 1 and 27, 2000, the first day of the period).
10. Social Security Amendment (Students and Income-related Benefits) Regulations 2000 (SI 2000/1922) reg.2(4)(e) (August 28, 2000, or if the student's period of study begins between August 1 and 27, 2000, the first day of the period).
11. Social Security Amendment (Students and Income-related Benefits) Regulations 2001 (SI 2001/2319) reg.3(1) and (3)(c) (August 27, 2001, or if the student's period of study begins between August 1 and 26, 2001, the first day of the period).
12. Social Security Amendment (Students and Income-related Benefits) Regulations 2001 (SI 2001/2319) reg.3(2) and (3)(c) (August 27, 2001, or if the student's period of study begins between August 1 and 26, 2001, the first day of the period).
13. Social Security Amendment (Students and Income-related Benefits) Regulations 2001 (SI 2001/2319) reg.3(4) (August 27, 2001, or if the student's period of study begins between August 1 and 26, 2001, the first day of the period).
14. Social Security Amendment (Students and Income-related Benefits) Regulations 2001 (SI 2001/2319) reg.6 (August 27, 2001, or if the student's period of study begins between August 1 and 26, 2001, the first day of the period).
15. Social Security Amendment (Students and Income-related Benefits) Regulations 2002 (SI 2002/1589) reg.3 (August 26, 2002, or if the student's period of study begins between August 1 and 25, 2002, the first day of the period).
16. Social Security Amendment (Students and Income-related Benefits) Regulations 2002 (SI 2002/1589) reg.4 (August 26, 2002, or if the student's period of study begins between August 1 and 25, 2002, the first day of the period).
17. Social Security Amendment (Students and Income-related Benefits) (No.2) Regulations 2002 (SI 2002/2207) reg.2 (September 2, 2002).

18. Social Security (Working Tax Credit and Child Tax Credit) (Consequential Amendments) Regulations 2003 (SI 2003/455) reg.2 and Sch.1 para.16 (April 6, 2004, except in transitional cases and see further the note to reg.17 of the Income Support Regulations), as amended by Social Security (Working Tax Credit and Child Tax Credit) (Consequential Amendments) (No.3) Regulations 2003 (SI 2003/1731) (August 8, 2003).

19. Social Security (Students and Income-related Benefits) Amendment Regulations 2004 (SI 2004/1708) reg.3(3) (September 1, 2004, or if the student's period of study begins between August 1 and August 31, 2004, the first day of the period).

20. Social Security (Miscellaneous Amendments) Regulations 2005 (SI 2005/574) reg.3(4) (April 4, 2005).

21. Social Security (Students and Income-related Benefits) Amendment Regulations 2005 (SI 2005/1807) reg.2(6) (September 1, 2005, or if the student's period of study begins between August 1 and August 31, 2005, the first day of the period).

22. Social Security (Students and Income-related Benefits) Amendment Regulations 2006 (SI 2006/1752) regs 4(3) and 6 (September 1, 2006, or if the student's period of study begins between August 1 and August 31, 2006, the first day of the period).

23. Social Security (Students and Income-related Benefits) Amendment Regulations 2007 (SI 2007/1632) reg.2(2)(a) (September 1, 2007, or if the student's period of study begins between August 1 and August 31, 2007, the first day of the period).

24. Social Security (Students and Income-related Benefits) Amendment Regulations 2007 (SI 2007/1632) reg.2(2)(b) (September 1, 2007, or if the student's period of study begins between August 1 and August 31, 2007, the first day of the period).

25. Social Security (Miscellaneous Amendments) Regulations 2009 (SI 2009/583) reg.2(10) (April 6, 2009).

26. Social Security (Students and Miscellaneous Amendments) Regulations 2009 (SI 2009/1575) reg.2(2) and (4)(a) (September 1, 2009, or if the student's period of study begins between August 1 and August 31, 2009, the first day of the period).

27. Social Security (Students and Miscellaneous Amendments) Regulations 2009 (SI 2009/1575) reg.2(3) and (4)(a) (September 1, 2009, or if the student's period of study begins between August 1 and August 31, 2009, the first day of the period).

28. Social Security (Treatment of Postgraduate Master's Degree Loans and Special Support Loans) (Amendment) Regulations 2016 (SI 2016/743) reg.2(3) (August 4, 2016).

29. Social Services and Well-being (Wales) Act 2014 and the Regulation and Inspection of Social Care (Wales) Act 2016 (Consequential Amendments) Order 2017 (SI 2017/901) art.2(4) (November 3, 2017).

30. Social Security (Income and Capital) (Miscellaneous Amendments) Regulations 2020 (SI 2020/618) reg.2(7) (July 15, 2020).

DEFINITIONS

    "grant"—see reg.61(1).
    "grant income"—*ibid.*
    "period of study"—*ibid.*
    "periods of experience"—*ibid.*
    "postgraduate loan"—*ibid.*
    "sandwich course"—*ibid.*
    "student"—*ibid.*
    "student loan"—*ibid.*

GENERAL NOTE

2.495   For students who started their course in or after the 1998/99 academic year, the main source of financial help is the student loan system (see the note to reg.66A). However, they may also be eligible for various additional allowances, which may be paid as grants (for example, if they have a child or a disability). Some of these grants will come under the rules in this regulation.

Paragraphs (2) and (2A)

A student's grant is first to be subject to the disregards listed in paras (2)–(2A).   **2.496**
Note that from August 30, 1999 the disregard in para.(2A) only applies if the
student does not, and is not deemed to, have a student loan or a postgraduate loan
(both defined in reg.61(1)). If the claimant is treated as possessing such a loan the
disregards that would otherwise have applied under para.(2A) apply to the amount
of loan deemed to be possessed (reg.66A(5)).

The disregard in para.(2)(i) is a general disregard of any payment intended for the
maintenance of a child and that in para.(2)(j) is a general disregard of any payment
intended for child care costs. They replaced the various disregards for students with
child care responsibilities previously contained in para.(2B). Paragraph (2B) had
gone through a number of forms and parts of the penultimate form of it remained
in force in "transitional cases" (i.e. those cases in which the claimant is still receiving amounts for his children in his income support—see the notes to reg.17) but
the one remaining sub-para.that was still in force for transitional cases (sub-para.
(e)) was revoked on September 1, 2006 (or if the student's period of study began
between August 1 and 31, 2006, on the first day of the period) by reg.4(3) of the
Social Security (Students and Income-related Benefits) Amendment Regulations
2006 (SI 2006/1752) (see further the notes to this regulation in the 2006 edition of
what was then Vol.II of this series and in the 2006/2007 Supplement to this series).

In *CIS 91/1994* the claimant argued that the disregard for books in para.(2)(g)
should be apportioned over 52 weeks. It would then reduce the dependants and
mature student elements of her grant that were taken into account in calculating her
income support during the summer vacation. But the Commissioner holds that the
deduction in sub-para.(g) could only be applied to the basic maintenance grant, as
this was clearly the part of the grant which contained provision for books.

R(IS) 7/95 confirms that it is the intention of the grant-making authority, not of   **2.497**
the student, that counts under sub-para.(h). *R(IS) 16/95* similarly holds that in the
case of the disregard for tuition fees under sub-para.(a), it is the intention of the provider of the payment that has to be considered. The fact that the claimant's partner
spent all his grants from the Norwegian Government on tuition fees was irrelevant.
Presumably the same approach would also be applied to the disregards in sub-paras
(c), (d), (g), (i) and (j).

In *SB v Oxford CC (HB)* [2014] UKUT 166 (AAC) Judge Rowland takes the
view that "to meet tuition fees" in reg.59(2)(a) of the Housing Benefit Regulations
2006 (the equivalent of sub-para.(a)) should be interpreted broadly so as to include
repayment of a loan which had been used to pay tuition fees. However, the evidence in this case suggested that the claimant's bursary was intended to be used
for living costs rather than tuition fees and so the repayment of the fee loan from
the bursary was not covered by sub-para.(a). But that did not prevent part of that
bursary being disregarded for other course-related costs, such as books and equipment and travel costs, since "living costs" may include course-related costs. On the
facts Judge Rowland concluded that the minimum amount of the bursary—£305 in
2007–2008—should be excluded from the claimant's grant income as the claimant
could legitimately expect this in accordance with published Government policy,
including DWP guidance to decision makers, at the time.

Paragraphs (3)–(4)

A grant is normally apportioned over the weeks of the period of study, i.e. from   **2.498**
the beginning of the academic year to the day before the summer vacation (para.
(3)(a)). (The August 2002 amendment to para.(3)(a) is to ensure that the grant
income is attributed to complete benefit weeks; see the similar amendments to
paras (3)(b) and (4)).

Elements of the grant for mature students or dependants under the Mandatory
Awards Regulations were apportioned over 52 weeks, but only while the person
remained a student. *CIS 7/1988* holds that these elements of grant would
ordinarily be attributable to the same period as the maintenance grant under the

Mandatory Awards Regulations. *CIS 7/1988* is followed (with some reservation) in *R(IS) 1/96*, where the Commissioner points out that under reg.15(1) of the Mandatory Awards Regulations an award comes to an end on the expiry of the course. This supported the conclusion that in the final year the dependants and mature student elements were, like the ordinary maintenance grant, to be treated as payable for the period up to the day before the summer vacation. After that date the person was no longer a student and reg.62 no longer applied. A grant or bursary for dependants paid to NHS-funded students is also apportioned over 52 weeks (para.(3A)). In relation to social work bursaries, see *SSWP v LB* [2009] UKUT 117 (AAC). The tribunal decided that because it was paid by three termly instalments (which was the only evidence before it) the bursary was to be taken into account during the claimant's period of study (43 weeks) under para.(3)(a). However, further evidence produced by the Secretary of State before the Upper Tribunal indicated that in other cases it might be appropriate to take a similar bursary into account over a 52-week period under para.(3)(b).

In *R(IS) 15/95* the claimant claimed income support for the summer vacation at the end of the first year of her course. Her grant included a dependants allowance and a single parent's allowance. The Commissioner decides that the single parent element had to be apportioned over 52 weeks. This was because the single parent's allowance was provided for in Sch.4 to the Mandatory Awards Regulations. The effect of Sch.4 was to increase in certain circumstances the amount awarded under Pt III of Sch.2 for the maintenance of dependants. Sch.4 on its own awarded nothing. Thus the single parent's allowance was in fact merely an increase of the amount intended for the maintenance of dependants and so fell to be apportioned in accord with para.(3A). Even if this was not the case, the allowance had to be apportioned equally between the weeks in the period in respect of which it was payable (para.(3)(b)). That period was 52 weeks (see paras 12(1) and 20 of Sch.2 to the Mandatory Awards Regulations).

2.499   However, if the student's course started on or after September 1, 1998 (August 1, 1998 for Scotland) the grant for dependants is taken into account for the same period as the student loan (this used to apply even if the claimant did not have a student loan but from August 2002 it only applies if the student has received such a loan or could get one by taking reasonable steps) (para.(3B)). This is because under the system for student support introduced from the start of the 1998/1999 academic year (see further the note to reg.66A), the non-repayable dependants element is payable on the same basis as the student loan.

Note that from September 1, 2003 grants for dependants have only been payable in respect of certain adult dependants or a spouse (Education (Student Support) (No.2) Regulations 2002 (SI 2002/3200) reg.15; the same applied to grants under the Education (Mandatory Awards) Regulations, see para.13(1) of Sch.2 to the 2003 Regulations (SI 2003/1994). "Partner" later replaced spouse and subsequently included, among others, a civil partner. Students with children are expected to apply for child tax credit for help with their costs

In addition, paras (3), (3A) and (3B) were amended with effect from April 6, 2004 (except in "transitional cases"—see reg.17) so that they only refer to grants in respect of adult dependants. This is as a consequence of the removal of amounts for children and young persons from the income support scheme with effect from April 6, 2004 (except in "transitional cases"). Financial assistance to help with the cost of bringing up a child or young person is to be provided through the child tax credit system, see Vol.IV of this series. The old form of these provisions (see the 2003 edition of this volume) continues in force for "transitional cases"—see the note to reg.17.

Current provisions for student support

2.500   The current provisions (as at April 2017) for support for students are in the Education (Student Support) Regulations 2011 (SI 2011/1986), as amended. Among the amending regulations note in particular the Educational (Student Support) (Amendment) Regulations 2015 (SI 2015/1951) which came into force on December 23, 2015. Regulation 57 and the Schedule to the Regulations contain the rates for student support in respect of an academic year beginning on or after August 1, 2016. See also the Education (Student Support) (Amendment) Regulations 2016 (SI 2016/270) (in force from March 25, 2016 and which apply in respect of an academic year beginning on or after August 1, 2016), the main effect of which is to increase the residence condition for a student who is an EU national (but not a UK national) from three to five years preceding the start of the course for which s/he seeks support.

A further amendment with effect from June 6, 2016 (by reg.7 of the Education (Student Fees, Awards and Support) (Amendment) Regulations 2016 (SI 2016/584) disapplies the increase in the length of the residence requirement where the student would have met the previous three-year requirement if an application for student support had been made before March 25, 2016 in relation to an academic year beginning before August 1, 2016.

Note that the 2015 Amendment Regulations also amended the 2011 Regulations so that from the start of the 2016/17 academic year new students who would previously have been entitled to a special support grant intended to meet the costs of books, equipment, travel expenses and child care will only be entitled to a special support loan for those purposes. Such a loan is to be disregarded as income under the new reg.66D.

Subject to reg.62, a student's grant will be taken into account as income under reg.40. Thus any relevant disregards in Sch.9 will apply (*R(IS) 16/95*).   2.501

For the disregard of any grant (or covenant income, student loan or contribution) left over after a student has completed his course, see para.61 of Sch.9.

Calculation of covenant income where a contribution is assessed

63.—(1) Where a student is in receipt of income by way of a grant during a   2.502
period of study and a contribution has been assessed, the amount of his covenant income to be taken into account for that period and any summer vacation immediately following shall be the whole amount of his covenant income less, subject to paragraph (3), the amount of the contribution.

(2) The weekly amount of the student's covenant income shall be determined—

(a) by dividing the amount of income which falls to be taken into account under paragraph (1) by 52 or, if there are 53 benefit weeks (including part weeks) in the year, 53; and

(b) by disregarding from the resulting amount, £5.

(3) For the purposes of paragraph (1), the contribution shall be treated as increased by the amount, if any, by which the amount excluded under [¹regulation 62(2)(h) (calculation of grant income) falls short of the amount for the time being specified in paragraph 7(4)(i) of Schedule 2 to the Education (Mandatory Awards) Regulations 1991 (travel expenditure).]

<small>AMENDMENT</small>

1. Income Support (General) Amendment Regulations 1992 (SI 1992/468) reg.5 (April 6, 1992).

<small>DEFINITIONS</small>

"benefit week"—see reg.2(1).
"contribution"—see reg.61(1).
"covenant income"—*ibid.*
"grant"—*ibid.*
"period of study"—*ibid.*
"student"—*ibid.*

2.503   Although the number of covenants dropped away following the 1988 Budget, some existing covenants may have continued running for a time, perhaps at inadequate levels.

If a student has a grant, with a parental contribution assessed, covenant income is only taken into account to the extent that it exceeds the assessed contribution (plus any addition under para.(3)). The definition of covenant income in reg.61 confines it to the payment net of tax. Any excess is spread over the whole year, with a £5 per week disregard.

Covenant income where no grant income or no contribution is assessed

2.504   **64.**—(1) Where a student is not in receipt of income by way of a grant the amount of his covenant income shall be calculated as follows—

(a) any sums intended for any expenditure specified in regulation 62(2) (a) to (f), (calculation of grant income) necessary as a result of his attendance on the course, shall be disregarded;

(b) any covenant income, up to the amount of the standard maintenance grant, which is not so disregarded, shall be apportioned equally between the weeks of the period of study and there shall be disregarded from the covenant income to be so apportioned the amount which would have been disregarded under [¹regulation 62(2)(g) and (h) and (2A)] (calculation of grant income) had the student been in receipt of the standard maintenance grant;

(c) the balance, if any, shall be divided by 52 or, if there are 53 benefit weeks (including part weeks) in the year, 53 and treated as weekly income of which £5 shall be disregarded.

(2) Where a student is in receipt of income by way of a grant and no contribution has been assessed, the amount of his covenant income shall be calculated in accordance with sub-paragraphs (a) to (c) of paragraph (1), except that—

(a) the value of the standard maintenance grant shall be abated by the amount of his grant income less an amount equal to the amount of any sums disregarded under regulation 62(2)(a) to (f); and

(b) the amount to be disregarded under paragraph (1)(b) shall be abated by an amount equal to the amount of any sums disregarded under [¹regulation 62(2)(g) and (h) and (2A)].

1. Income Support (General) Amendment Regulations 1992 (SI 1992/468) reg.5 (April 6, 1992).

"benefit week"—see reg.2(1).
"contribution"—see reg.61(1).
"covenant income"—*ibid.*
"grant"—*ibid.*
"grant income"—*ibid.*
"student"—*ibid.*

GENERAL NOTE

Paragraph (1)

If the student has no grant, first any sums earmarked for things listed in reg.62(2)   2.505
(a)–(f) are excluded. Then the amount of covenant income up to the rate of the
standard maintenance grant (less the items specified above) is spread over the weeks
of the period of study, disregarding items specified in reg.62(2)(g) and (h) and (2A).
Then any excess is spread over the whole year with a £5 p.w. disregard.

Paragraph (2)

If the student has a grant with no parental contribution, the effect is to spread the   2.506
covenant income, after topping up any deficiency from the standard maintenance
grant, over the whole year, as in para.(1).

Relationship with amounts to be disregarded under Schedule 9

65.—No part of a student's convenant income or grant income shall be   2.507
disregarded under paragraph 15 of Schedule 9 (charitable and voluntary
payments) [¹ . . .].

AMENDMENT

1. Social Security (Miscellaneous Amendments) (No.4) Regulations 2006 (SI
2006/2378) reg.5(5) (October 2, 2006).

DEFINITIONS

"covenant income"—see reg.61(1).
"grant income"—*ibid.*
"student"—*ibid*

Other amounts to be disregarded

66.—(1) For the purposes of ascertaining income [¹other than grant   2.508
income, covenant income and loans treated as income in accordance
with regulation 66A], any amounts intended for any expenditure specified in
regulation 62(2) (calculation of grant income) necessary as a result of his
attendance on the course shall be disregarded but only if, and to the extent
that, the necessary expenditure exceeds or is likely to exceed the amount of
the sums disregarded under regulation 62(2) [¹and (2A)], 63(3)[², 64(1)
(a) or (b) and 66A(5) (calculation of grant income, covenant income and
treatment of student loans)] on like expenditure.

(2) Where a claim is made in respect of any period in the normal summer
vacation and any income is payable under a Deed of Convenant which
commences or takes effect after the first day of that vacation, that income
shall be disregarded.

AMENDMENTS

1. Income-related Benefits Schemes (Miscellaneous Amendments) Regulations
1994 (SI 1994/527) reg.5 (April 11, 1994).
2. Social Security Amendment (Students) Regulations 1999 (SI 1999/1935)
reg.3(4) (August 30, 1999, or if the student's period of study begins between
August 1 and 29, 1999, the first day of the period).

DEFINITIONS

"covenant income"—see reg.61(1).

"grant income"—*ibid.*
"student loan"—*ibid.*

GENERAL NOTE

2.509   Paragraph (2) will not be of any practical effect, because new covenants are unlikely to be made now that the tax advantages have been removed in the 1988 Budget.

[¹Treatment of student loans [¹⁸and postgraduate [¹⁹...] loans]

2.510   **66A.**—[⁶(1) A student loan [¹⁸and a postgraduate [¹⁹...] loan] shall be treated as income [¹³. . .].

(1A) [¹³. . .].

(2) In calculating the weekly amount of the loan to be taken into account as income—

[¹⁰(a)   in respect of a course that is of a single academic year's duration or less, a loan which is payable in respect of that period shall be apportioned equally between the weeks in the period beginning with—

    (i)   except in a case where (ii) below applies, the benefit week, the first day of which coincides with, or immediately follows, the first day of the single academic year;

    (ii)   where the student is required to start attending the course in August or where the course is of less than an academic year's duration, the benefit week, the first day of which coincides with, or immediately follows, the first day of the course,

and ending with the benefit week, the last day of which coincides with, or immediately precedes, the last day of the course;]

[⁹(aa)   in respect of an academic year of a course which starts other than on 1st September, a loan which is payable in respect of that academic year shall be apportioned equally between the weeks in the period beginning with the benefit week [¹⁰ , the first day of which coincides with, or immediately follows, the first day of that academic year and ending with the benefit week, the last day of which coincides with, or immediately precedes,] the last day of that academic year but excluding any benefit weeks falling entirely within the quarter during which, in the opinion of the Secretary of State, the longest of any vacation is taken and for the purposes of this sub-paragraph, "quarter" shall have the same meaning as for the purposes of the Education (Student Support) Regulations 2001;]

  (b)   in respect of the final academic year of a course (not being a course of a single year's duration), a loan, which is payable in respect of that final academic year shall be apportioned equally between the weeks in the period beginning with [¹⁰. . .]—

    [¹⁰ (i)   except in a case where (ii) below applies, the benefit week, the first day of which coincides with, or immediately follows, the first day of that academic year;

    (ii)   where the final academic year starts on 1st September, the benefit week, the first day of which coincides with, or immediately follows, the earlier of 1st September or the first day of the autumn term;]

and ending with [¹⁰ the benefit week, the last day of which coincides with, or immediately precedes,] the last day of the course;

  (c)   in any other case, the loan shall be apportioned equally between the weeks in the period beginning with the earlier of—

(i) the first day of the first benefit week in September; or

[¹⁰ (ii) the benefit week, the first day of which coincides with, or immediately follows, the first day of the autumn term,]

and ending with [¹⁰ the benefit week, the last day of which coincides with, or immediately precedes, the last day of June],

and, in all cases, from the weekly amount so apportioned there shall be disregarded £10.]

[⁵(3) A student shall be treated as possessing a student loan [¹⁸or a postgraduate [¹⁹...] loan] in respect of an academic year where—

(a) a student loan [¹⁸or a postgraduate [¹⁹...] loan] has been made to him in respect of that year; or

(b) he could acquire [¹⁸a student loan or a postgraduate [¹⁹...] loan] in respect of that year by taking reasonable steps to do so.

(4) Where a student is treated as possessing a student loan under paragraph (3), the amount of the student loan to be taken into account as income shall be, subject to paragraph (5)—

(a) in the case of a student to whom a student loan is made in respect of an academic year, a sum equal to the maximum student loan he is able to acquire in respect of that year by taking reasonable steps to do so and either—

(i) in the case of a student other than one to whom head (ii) refers, any contribution whether or not it has been paid to him; or

(ii) in the case of a student to whom paragraph 1, 2, [¹⁷10,] 11[¹⁴, [¹⁷12] or 15A of Schedule 1B applies (lone parent, disabled student or persons in education)], any contribution which has actually been paid to him;

(b) in the case of a student to whom a student loan is not made in respect of an academic year, the maximum student loan that would be made to the student if—

(i) he took all reasonable steps to obtain the maximum student loan he is able to acquire in respect of that year; and

(ii) no deduction in that loan was made by virtue of the application of a means test.

[¹⁸(4A) Where a student is treated as possessing a postgraduate [¹⁹...] loan under paragraph (3) in respect of an academic year, the amount of that loan to be taken into account as income shall be, subject to paragraph (5), a sum equal to 30 per cent. of the maximum postgraduate master's degree loan the student is able to acquire in respect of that academic year by taking reasonable steps to do so.]

(5) There shall be deducted from the amount of income taken into account under paragraph (4) [¹⁸or (4A)]—

(a) the sum of [¹¹[¹⁵£303] per academic year] in respect of travel costs; and,

[⁸(b) the sum of [¹²[¹⁶£390] per academic year] towards the costs of books and equipment,]

whether or not any such costs are incurred.]]

AMENDMENTS

1. Social Security Benefits (Student Loans and Miscellaneous Amendments) Regulations 1990 (SI 1990/1549) reg.5(7) (September 1, 1990).

2. Income Support (General) Amendment Regulations 1991 (SI 1991/236) reg.9 (March 13, 1991).

3. Income Support (General) Amendment No.4 Regulations 1991 (SI 1991/1559) reg.12 (August 5, 1991).

4. Income-related Benefits Schemes (Miscellaneous Amendments) Regulations 1996 (SI 1996/462) reg.9 (April 8, 1996).

5. Social Security Amendment (Students) Regulations 1999 (SI 1999/1935) reg.3(5) (August 30, 1999, or if the student's period of study begins between August 1 and 29, 1999, the first day of the period).

6. Social Security Amendment (Students and Income-related Benefits) Regulations 2000 (SI 2000/1922) reg.2(5) (August 28, 2000, or if the student's period of study begins between August 1 and 27, 2000, the first day of the period).

7. Social Security Amendment (Students and Income-related Benefits) Regulations 2001 (SI 2001/2319) regs 3(1) and (3)(c) (August 27, 2001, or if the student's period of study begins between August 1 and 26, 2001, the first day of the period).

8. Social Security Amendment (Students and Income-related Benefits) Regulations 2001 (SI 2001/2319) reg.3(2) and (3)(c) (August 27, 2001, or if the student's period of study begins between August 1 and 26, 2001, the first day of the period).

9. Social Security Amendment (Students and Income-related Benefits) Regulations 2001 (SI 2001/2319) reg.4 (August 27, 2001, or if the student's period of study begins between August 1 and 26, 2001, the first day of the period).

10. Social Security Amendment (Students and Income-related Benefits) Regulations 2002 (SI 2002/1589) reg.5 (August 26, 2002, or if the student's period of study begins between August 1 and 25, 2002, the first day of the period).

11. Social Security (Students and Income-related Benefits) Amendment Regulations 2007 (SI 2007/1632) reg.2(3)(a) (September 1, 2007, or if the student's period of study begins between August 1 and August 31, 2007, the first day of the period).

12. Social Security (Students and Income-related Benefits) Amendment Regulations 2007 (SI 2007/1632) reg.2(3)(b) (September 1, 2007, or if the student's period of study begins between August 1 and August 31, 2007, the first day of the period).

13. Social Security (Miscellaneous Amendments) (No.6) Regulations 2008 (SI 2008/2767) reg.2(10) (November 17, 2008).

14. Social Security (Miscellaneous Amendments) Regulations 2009 (SI 2009/583) reg.2(11) (April 6, 2009).

15. Social Security (Students and Miscellaneous Amendments) Regulations 2009 (SI 2009/1575) reg.2(2) and (4)(a) (September 1, 2009, or if the student's period of study begins between August 1 and August 31, 2009, the first day of the period).

16. Social Security (Students and Miscellaneous Amendments) Regulations 2009 (SI 2009/1575) reg.2(3) and (4)(a) (September 1, 2009, or if the student's period of study begins between August 1 and August 31, 2009, the first day of the period).

17. Income Support (Prescribed Categories of Person) Regulations 2009 (SI 2009/3152) reg.3(2)(d) and 3(7) (December, 30, 2009). Regulation 3(2)(d) omitted "10," and "12" in reg.66A(4)(a)(ii) with effect from December 30, 2009 but reg.3(7) provided that this did not apply in the case of a person who was subject to the saving provisions in reg.2(2) of those Regulations. See the 2015/16 edition of this volume for these Regulations and the notes to them.

18. Social Security (Treatment of Postgraduate Master's Degree Loans and Special Support Loans) (Amendment) Regulations 2016 (SI 2016/743) reg.2(4) (August 4, 2016).

19. Social Security (Income and Capital) (Miscellaneous Amendments) Regulations 2020 (SI 2020/618) reg.2(8) (July 15, 2020).

DEFINITIONS

"academic year"—see reg.61(1).
"benefit week"—see reg.2(1).

"last day of the course"—see reg.61(1).
"postgraduate loan"—*ibid.*
"student"—*ibid.*
"student loan"—*ibid.*
"year"—*ibid.*

GENERAL NOTE

The changes made to this regulation on August 30, 1999, and the further changes made on August 28, 2000, reflected the introduction of the "new" system for student support from the start of the 1998/1999 academic year. The previous system of grants and non-means-tested loans continued for "existing" students (i.e. broadly those who started their course before September 1, 1998 (August 1, 1998 for Scotland)). However, "new" students received financial support by way of a loan.

The basic rule in para.(3) for student loans is that if a student is, exceptionally, not disqualified from entitlement to income support, the amount of the maximum student loan that could have been acquired by taking reasonable steps to do so is to be treated as income, attributed over the period identified in para.(2). That is so whether the student has been made a loan or not. The difference under para.(4) is that if a loan has been made, any assessed contribution (e.g. from a parent, a partner or from the student because of other income) whether paid or not counts as income, except for lone parents or foster carers, disabled students or certain students in non-advanced education under para.15A of Sch.1B, where only a contribution actually paid counts (sub-para.(a)). In those circumstances the maximum student loan that could have been acquired will have been reduced to take account of the assessed contribution. There are, though, immediately two practical exceptions. Under reg.67 a contribution from a partner is disregarded as part of the non-student's income and under reg.67A any part of the student's own income taken into account in the loan calculation is disregarded from the student's income. If no student loan has been made, then the maximum amount is to be treated as possessed, without any deductions that could have been made if the means test had been applied (sub-para.(b)). See reg.62(3B) for the treatment of grants for adult dependants. A deduction of £303 for travel costs and £390 for books and equipment will be made (para. (5)). Note that the amount of the travel disregard is now specified in the regulations as the DfEE has introduced one unified figure for travel costs rather than having differing amounts for those living in the parental home and elsewhere.

In *CH/4429/2006* the claimant's partner had a religious objection to taking out a loan and it was argued that that made it unreasonable for him to do so. The Commissioner rejected that argument on the basis that "reasonable" only qualified the steps that could be taken to acquire a student loan. It is understood that that decision is under challenge in an appeal currently before the Upper Tribunal.

Paragraph (3) also applies to postgraduate loans, where the amount to be taken into account is set by para.(4A). The amount to be treated as possessed is 30 per cent of the maximum loan available, subject to the same deductions under para.(5). That is because 70 per cent of the loan is regarded as covering fees, as explained in the notes to reg.61. Any amount of the student's own income taken into account in the calculation of the amount of the loan is disregarded under reg.67A.

With effect from July 2020 postgraduate doctoral degree loans have been brought within the general definition of "postgraduate loan", so that they are subject to the same rules as previously applied only to master's degree loans. Doctoral degree loans were introduced in 2018, at the same annual rate as for master's degree loans, with an overall cap of, for 2020/21, £27,265. It would seem that prior to July 2020 postgraduate doctoral degree loans would have fallen within the definition of "student loan", since the relevant English regulations were made under s.22 of the Teaching and Higher Education Act 1998, meaning that the 30% rule would not have applied. It is not known if the 30% rule was applied in practice before the July 2020 amendments.

The income so calculated is then apportioned in accordance with the rules in para. (2), with a £10 disregard. Note the definition of "academic year" in reg.61(1). If the

2.511

2.512

student is required to start attending their course during August or September (as will usually be the case) and to continue attending through the autumn, the academic year of the course will be the 12 months starting on September 1. Loans payable for courses of one year's duration or less, or for the final year of a course, are covered by sub-paras (a) and (b) respectively; sub-para.(aa) deals with courses in which the academic year starts other than in the autumn; and sub-para.(c) applies in other cases. The purpose of the amendments made to para.(2) in August 2002 is to ensure that a student loan is apportioned over and attributed to complete benefit weeks.

Under sub-para.(c), the loan is apportioned over the period from the first benefit week in September, or the benefit week, the first day of which coincides with, or immediately follows, the beginning of the autumn term (whichever is the earlier), to the benefit week, the last day of which coincides with, or immediately precedes the last day of June. In the first year of a course the effect of this rule could be to attribute loan income to a period before the actual start of the claimant's course. But since a claimant does not count as a student until he starts a course, it is suggested that any loan income should be ignored until the beginning of the term. This has now been confirmed by *CIS/3734/2004*. The Commissioner accepted the Secretary of State's submission that "a student loan can only have an existence for the purposes of the Income Support (General) Regulations 1987 where it is for the maintenance of a student. Until the claimant starts to attend or undertake the course of study . . . she is not a student. Until she is a student, whatever the point in its administrative path her student loan application has reached, it cannot meet the definition of student loan herein and so does not fall to be taken into account as income."

In the final year of the course the period for which the loan income is taken into account starts from the benefit week the first day of which coincides with, or immediately follows, the earlier of September 1 or the first day of the autumn term in a case where the final year begins on September 1; otherwise it starts from the benefit week, the first day of which coincides with, or immediately follows, the first day of that final year. It ends with the benefit week which coincides with, or immediately precedes, the last day of the course (sub-para.(b)).

2.513   In the case of courses of one year's duration or less, the period over which the loan is apportioned starts from the benefit week which coincides with, or immediately precedes, the first day of the course in a case where the course begins in August or is for less than one academic year; otherwise it starts from the benefit week, the first day of which coincides with, or immediately follows, the first day of the academic year. It ends with the benefit week, the last day of which coincides with, or immediately precedes, the last day of the course (sub-para.(a)).

2.514   Where the academic year starts other than in the autumn, the loan is apportioned over the period which begins with the benefit week, the first day of which coincides with, or immediately follows, the first day of that academic year and ends with the benefit week, the last day of which coincides with, or immediately precedes, the last day of that academic year but excluding any complete benefit weeks within the "quarter" during which the longest vacation falls (sub-para.(aa)). A quarter is one of the periods from January 1 to March 31, April 1 to June 30, July 1 to August 31 and September 1 to December 31 (see the Education (Student Support) Regulations 2011 (SI 2011/1986), as amended, which contain the current (as at April 2018) provisions for support for students).

For the apportionment of student loans under the previous form of para.(2) (in force until August 28, 2000), see the note to reg.66(2) in the 2000 edition of what was then Vol.II of this series.

2.515   See reg.40(3A)–(3B) for the position where a student ends the course prematurely.

For the disregard of any student loan (grant or covenant income or contribution) left over after the student has completed their course, see para.61 of Sch.9. This disregard does not apply to anything left over from a postgraduate loan.

For the treatment of access funds see regs 66B and 68(2) and (3).

[¹ Treatment of payments from access funds

66B.—(1) This regulation applies to payments from access funds that are not payments to which regulation 68(2) or (3) (income treated as capital) applies.

(2) A payment from access funds, other than a payment to which paragraph (3) of this regulation applies, shall be disregarded as income.

(3) Subject to paragraph (4) of this regulation and paragraph 36 of Schedule 9, any payments from access funds which are intended and used for food, ordinary clothing or footwear [⁴ . . .], household fuel, rent for which housing benefit is payable [² or any housing costs] to the extent that they are met under regulation 17(1)(e) or 18(1)(f) (housing costs) [² . . .], of a single claimant or, as the case may be, of [³ his partner], and any payments from access funds that are used for any council tax or water charges for which that claimant or [³ partner is liable] shall be disregarded as income to the extent of £20 per week.

[⁴ (3A) In paragraph (3) "ordinary clothing or footwear" means clothing or footwear for normal daily use, but it does not include—

(a) school uniforms, or

(b) clothing or footwear used solely for sporting activities.]

(4) Where a payment from access funds is made—

(a) on or after 1st September or the first day of the course, whichever first occurs, but before receipt of any student loan in respect of that year and that payment is intended for the purpose of bridging the period until receipt of the student loan; or

(b) before the first day of the course to a person in anticipation of that person becoming a student,

that payment shall be disregarded as income.]

2.516

AMENDMENTS

1. Social Security Amendment (Students and Income-related Benefits) Regulations 2000 (SI 2000/1922) reg.2(6) (August 28, 2000, or if the student's period of study begins between August 1 and 27, 2000, the first day of the period).

2. Social Security Amendment (Residential Care and Nursing Homes) Regulations 2001 (SI 2001/3767) reg.2(1) and Pt I of Sch. para.10 (April 8, 2002).

3. Social Security (Working Tax Credit and Child Tax Credit) (Consequential Amendments) Regulations 2003 (SI 2003/455) reg.2 and Sch.1 para.17 (April 6, 2004, except in "transitional cases" and see further the note to reg.17 of the Income Support Regulations).

4. Social Security (Miscellaneous Amendments) Regulations 2007 (SI 2007/719) reg.2(5) (April 2, 2007).

DEFINITIONS

"access funds"—see reg.61(1).
"claimant"—see reg.2(1).
"payment"—*ibid.*
"single claimant"—*ibid.*
"student"—see reg.61(1).
"student loan"—*ibid.*

GENERAL NOTE

Regulation 66B and the new paras (2) and (3) of reg.68 (added with effect from August 28, 2000) are concerned with the treatment of payments from access funds (defined in reg.61(1)). These funds are administered by individual colleges and uni-

2.517

versities. An access fund payment (for the definition of "payment" see reg.2(1)) that is paid as a single lump sum will be treated as capital (reg.68(2)). If such a payment of capital is intended and used for items other than food, ordinary clothing or footwear (defined in reg.68(4)), fuel, housing costs met by income support or housing benefit, council tax or water charges, it is disregarded for 52 weeks from the date of payment (reg.68(3)). Other payments from access funds are ignored as income unless they are intended and used for food, ordinary clothing or footwear (defined in para.(3A)), fuel, housing costs met by income support or housing benefit, council tax or water charges, in which case a disregard of up to £20 applies (this is subject to the overall limit of £20 for this and other payments in para.36 of Sch.9) (reg.66B(2) and (3)). But even if the payment is to cover the cost of food, etc. it will be totally ignored as income if it is intended to bridge a gap before the start of a course or receipt of a student loan (reg.66B(4)).

2.518   Note that the amendments made to this regulation (and to reg.68) with effect from April 6, 2004 (except in "transitional cases"—see the note to reg.17) are as a consequence of the removal of amounts for children and young persons from the income support scheme with effect from April 6, 2004 (except in "transitional cases"). Financial assistance to help with the cost of bringing up a child or young person is now to be provided through the child tax credit system, see Vol.IV of this series, and income support has in effect become an "adults only" benefit. The old form of this regulation (see the 2003 edition of this volume) continues in force for "transitional cases"—see the note to reg.17.

[¹ Treatment of fee loans

2.519   **66C.**—A loan for fees, known as a fee loan or a fee contribution loan, made pursuant to regulations made under Article 3 of the Education (Student Support) (Northern Ireland) Order 1998, section 22 of the Teaching and Higher Education Act 1998 or section 73(f) of the Education (Scotland) Act 1980, shall be disregarded as income.]

AMENDMENT

1. Social Security (Students and Income-related Benefits) Amendment Regulations 2006 (SI 2006/1752) reg.4(4) (September 1, 2006, or if the student's period of study begins between August 1 and August 31, 2006, the first day of the period).

GENERAL NOTE

2.520   Fee loans and fee-contribution loans were introduced as part of the student support system from the beginning of the academic year in 2006. Any such loan for tuition fees is to be disregarded. as income. As a matter of principle, the amount of the loan cannot be treated as capital during the period to which it relates.

[¹Treatment of special support loans

2.521   **66D.**—A special support loan within the meaning of regulation 68 of the Education (Student Support) Regulations 2011 is to be disregarded as income.]

AMENDMENT

1. Social Security (Treatment of Postgraduate Master's Degree Loans and Special Support Loans) (Amendment) Regulations 2016 (SI 2016/743) reg.2(5) (August 4, 2016).

General Note

A special support loan is the replacement (for new students from the start of the 2016/17 academic year) for the special support grant intended to meet the cost of books, equipment, travel expenses and child care, that had previously been available. See the notes to reg.62, under the heading *"Current provisions for student support"*. The amount of the loan is to be disregarded as income. As a matter of principle, the amount cannot be treated as capital during the period to which the loan relates.

2.522

Disregard of contribution

67.—Where the claimant or his partner is a student and[¹, for the purposes of assessing a contribution to the student's grant [²or student loan], the other partner's income has been taken into account, an account equal to that contribution shall be disregarded for the purposes of assessing that other partner's income.]

2.523

Amendments

1. Income-related Benefits Schemes (Miscellaneous Amendments) Regulations 1996 (SI 1996/462) reg.10 (April 8, 1996).
2. Social Security Amendment (Students) Regulations 1999 (SI 1999/1935) reg.3(6) (August 30, 1999, or if the student's period of study begins between August 1 and 29, 1999, the first day of the period).

Definitions

"claimant"—see reg.2(1) and reg 23(1).
"contribution"—see reg.61(1).
"grant"—*ibid.*
"partner"—see reg.2(1).
"student"—see reg.61(1).
"student loan"—*ibid.*

[¹ Further disregard of student's income

67A.—Where any part of a student's income has already been taken into account for the purposes of assessing his entitlement to a grant [²[³, student loan or postgraduate [⁴...] loan]], the amount taken into account shall be disregarded in assessing that student's income.]

2.524

Amendments

1. Social Security (Miscellaneous Amendments) Regulations 1998 (SI 1998/563) reg.4(3) and (4)(e) (April 6, 1998),
2. Social Security Amendment (Students) Regulations 1999 (SI 1999/1935) reg.3(7) (August 30, 1999, or if the student's period of study begins between August 1 and 29, 1999, the first day of the period).
3. Social Security (Treatment of Postgraduate Master's Degree Loans and Special Support Loans) (Amendment) Regulations 2016 (SI 2016/743) reg.2(6) (August 4, 2016).
4. Social Security (Income and Capital) (Miscellaneous Amendments) Regulations 2020 (SI 2020/618) reg.2(9) (July 15, 2020).

Definitions

"grant"—see reg.61(1).
"postgraduate loan"—*ibid.*

"student"—*ibid.*
"student loan"—*ibid.*

Income treated as capital

2.525   **68.**—[¹(1)] Any amount by way of a refund of tax deducted from a student's income shall be treated as capital.

[¹(2) An amount paid from access funds as a single lump sum shall be treated as capital.

(3) An amount paid from access funds as a single lump sum which is intended and used for an item other than food, ordinary clothing or foot-wear [⁴ . . .], household fuel, rent for which housing benefit is payable, [² or any housing costs] to the extent that they are met under regulation 17(1)(e) or 18(1)(f) (housing costs) [². . .], of a single claimant or, as the case may be, of [³ his partner], or which is used for an item other than any council tax or water charges for which that claimant or [³ partner is liable] shall be disregarded as capital but only for a period of 52 weeks from the date of the payment.]

[⁴(4) In paragraph (3) "ordinary clothing or footwear" means clothing or footwear for normal daily use, but it does not include—

(a) school uniforms, or

(b) clothing or footwear used solely for sporting activities.]

AMENDMENTS

1. Social Security Amendment (Students and Income-related Benefits) Regulations 2000 (SI 2000/1922) reg.2(7) (August 28, 2000, or if the student's period of study begins between August 1 and 27, 2000, the first day of the period).

2. Social Security Amendment (Residential Care and Nursing Homes) Regulations 2001 (SI 2001/3767) reg.2(1) and Pt I of Sch. para.11 (April 8, 2002).

3. Social Security (Working Tax Credit and Child Tax Credit) (Consequential Amendments) Regulations 2003 (SI 2003/455) reg.2 and Sch.1 para.17 (April 6, 2004, except in "transitional cases" and see further the note to reg.17 of the Income Support Regulations.

4. Social Security (Miscellaneous Amendments) Regulations 2007 (SI 2007/719) reg.2(6) (April 2, 2007).

DEFINITIONS

"access funds"—see reg.61(1).
"claimant"—see reg.2(1).
"payment"—*ibid.*
"single claimant"—*ibid.*
"student"—see reg.61(1).

GENERAL NOTE

2.526   On paras (2)–(4), see the note to reg.66A.

Disregard of changes occurring during summer vacation

2.527   **69.**—In calculating a student's income [¹ there shall be disregarded] any change in the standard maintenance grant occurring in the recognised summer vacation appropriate to the student's course, if that vacation does not from part of his period of study, from the date on which the change occurred up to the end of that vacation.

AMENDMENT

1. Social Security Act 1998 (Commencement No.12 and Consequential and Transitional Provisions) Order 1999 (SI 1999/3178 (C.81)) art.3(5) and Sch.5 para.7 (November 29, 1999).

DEFINITIONS

"period of study"—see reg.61(1).
"standard maintenance grant"—*ibid.*
"student"—*ibid.*

PART VI

URGENT CASES

GENERAL NOTE

For a detailed commentary on urgent cases payments, see pp.497–509 of Vol.II of the 2009/10 edition.   2.528

Part VI was revoked by the Social Security (Miscellaneous Amendments) (No.5) Regulations 2009 (SI 2009/3228) reg.2 with effect from January 25, 2010. That revocation was subject to savings, details of which are set out on pp.546–547 of Vol. II of the 2020/21 edition.

[¹PART VII

CALCULATION OF INCOME SUPPORT FOR PART-WEEKS

Amount of income support payable

73.—(1) Subject to regulations 75 (modifications in income) and 76 (reduction in certain cases), where a claimant is entitled to income support for a period (referred to in this Part as a part-week) to which subsection (1A) of section 21 of the Act [SSCBA, s.124(5)] (amount etc. of income-related benefit) applies, the amount of income support payable shall, except where paragraph (2) applies, be calculated in accordance with the following formulae—   2.529

(a) if the claimant has no income, $\dfrac{N \times A}{7}$;

(b) if the claimant has income, $\dfrac{N \times (A - I)}{7} - B$.

(2) [⁶. . .]

(3) In this Regulation—

"A", [⁶. . .] means the claimant's weekly applicable amount in the relevant week;

"B" means the amount of any income support, [⁵jobseeker's allowance], [²maternity allowance,] [⁴short-term or long-term incapacity benefit], or [⁷ severe disablement allowance or employment and support allowance] payable in respect of any day in the part-week;

"I" means his weekly income in the relevant week less B;

"N" means the number of days in the part-week;

"relevant week" means the period of 7 days determined in accordance with regulation 74.

(4) and (5) [⁶. . .]

AMENDMENTS

1. Income Support (General) Amendment Regulations 1988 (SI 1988/663) reg.27 (April 11, 1988).

2. Income Support (General) Amendment No.4 Regulations 1988 (SI 1988/1445) reg.17 (September 12, 1988).

4. Disability Working Allowance and Income Support (General) Amendment Regulations 1995 (SI 1995/482) reg.12 (April 13, 1995).

5. Income Support (General) (Jobseeker's Allowance Consequential Amendments) Regulations 1996 (SI 1996/206) reg.19 (October 7, 1996).

6. Social Security Amendment (Residential Care and Nursing Homes) Regulations 2001 (SI 2001/3767) reg.2 and Sch. Pt I para.13 (April 8, 2002).

7. Employment and Support Allowance (Consequential Provisions) (No.2) Regulations 2008 (SI 2008/1554) reg.2(1) and (9) (October 27, 2008).

DEFINITIONS

"the Act"—see reg.2(1).
"claimant"—*ibid.*

GENERAL NOTE

2.530   Although the rules set out in regs 73–77 do look very complex, they set out a relatively straightforward method of calculating benefit for part-weeks. See *CIS 706/1997* for an exposition of how these rules operate.

[¹Relevant week

2.531   **74.**—(1) Where the part-week—

(a) is the whole period for which income support is payable or occurs at the beginning of the claim, the relevant week is the period of 7 days ending on the last day of that part-week; or

(b) occurs at the end of the claim, the relevant week is the period of 7 days beginning on the first day of that part-week.

(2) Where during the currency of a claim the claimant makes a claim for a relevant social security benefit within the meaning of paragraph 4 of Schedule 7 to the Social Security (Claims and Payments) Regulations 1987 and as a result his benefit week changes, for the purpose of calculating the amount of income support payable—

(a) for the part-week beginning on the day after his last complete benefit week before the date from which he makes a claim for the relevant social security benefit and ending immediately before that date,

546

the relevant week is the period of 7 days beginning on the day after his last complete benefit week (the first relevant week);

(b) for the part-week beginning on the date from which he makes a claim for the relevant social security benefit and ending immediately before the start of his next benefit week after the date of that claim, the relevant week is the period of 7 days ending immediately before the start of his next benefit week (the second relevant week).

(3) Where during the currency of a claim the claimant's benefit week changes at the direction of the Secretary of State under paragraph 3 of Schedule 7 to the Social Security (Claims and Payments) Regulations 1987, for the purpose of calculating the amount of income support payable for the part-week beginning on the day after his last complete benefit week before the change and ending immediately before the change, the relevant week is the period of 7 days beginning on the day after the last complete benefit week.]

AMENDMENT

1. Income Support (General) Amendment Regulations 1988 (SI 1988/663) reg.27 (April 11, 1988).

DEFINITIONS

"benefit week"—see reg.2(1).
"claimant"—*ibid.*

[¹Modifications in the calculation of income

75.—For the purposes of regulation 73 (amount of income support payable for part-weeks), a claimant's income and the income of any person which the claimant is treated as possessing under section 22(5) of the Act [SSCBA, s.136(1)] or regulation 23(3) shall be calculated in accordance with Part V and, where applicable, VI subject to the following modifications—

    2.532

(a) any income which is due to be paid in the relevant week shall be treated as paid on the first day of that week;

(b) any income support, [⁴jobseeker's allowance], [²maternity allowance,] [³short-term or long-term incapacity benefit], [⁵ severe disablement allowance [⁶ , employment and support allowance or universal credit]] [³. . .] payable in the relevant week but not in respect of any day in the part-week shall be disregarded;

(c) where the part-week occurs at the end of the claim, any income or any change in the amount of income of the same kind which is first payable within the relevant week but not on any day in the part-week shall be disregarded;

(d) where the part-week occurs immediately after a period in which a person was treated as engaged in remunerative work) under regulation 5(5) (persons treated as engaged in remunerative work) any earnings which are taken into account for the purposes of determining that period shall be disregarded;

(e) where regulation 74(2) (relevant week) applies, any payment of income which—

    (i) is the final payment in a series of payments of the same kind or, if there has been an interruption in such payments, the last one before the interruption;

    (ii) is payable in respect of a period not exceeding a week; and

    (iii) is due to be paid on a day which falls within both the first and second relevant weeks,

shall be taken into account in either the first relevant week or, if it is impracticable to take it into account in that week, in the second relevant week; but this paragraph shall not apply to a payment of income support, [4jobseeker's allowance], [2maternity allowance,] [3short-term or long-term incapacity benefit] [5 severe disablement allowance or employment and support allowance], [3. . .];

  (f) where regulation 74(2) applies, any payment of income which—

    (i) is the final payment in a series of payments of the same kind or, if there has been an interruption in such payments, the last one before the interruption;

    (ii) is payable in respect of a period exceeding a week but not exceeding 2 weeks; and

    (iii) is due to be paid on a day which falls within both the first and second relevant weeks,

shall be disregarded; but this sub-paragraph shall not apply to a payment of income support, [4jobseeker's allowance], [2maternity allowance,] [3short-term or long term incapacity benefit], [5 severe disablement allowance or employment and support allowance] [3. . .]

  (g) where regulation 74(2) applies, if the weekly amount of any income which is due to be paid on a day which falls within both the first and second relevant weeks is more than the weekly amount of income of the same kind due to be paid in the last complete benefit week, the excess shall be disregarded;

  (h) where only part of the weekly amount of income is taken into account in the relevant week, the balance shall be disregarded.]

AMENDMENTS

1. Income Support (General) Amendment Regulations 1988 (SI 1988/663) reg.27 (April 11, 1988).

2. Income Support (General) Amendment No.4 Regulations 1988 (SI 1988/1445) reg.17 (September 12, 1988).

3. Disability Working Allowance and Income support (General) Amendment Regulations 1995 (SI 1995/482) reg.13 (April 13, 1995).

4. Income Support (General) (Jobseeker's Allowance Consequential Amendments) Regulations 1996 (SI 1996/206) reg.20 (October 7, 1996).

5. Employment and Support Allowance (Consequential Provisions) (No.2) Regulations 2008 (SI 2008/1554) reg.2(1) and (10) (October 27, 2008).

6. Universal Credit (Consequential, Supplementary, Incidental and Miscellaneous Provisions) Regulations 2013 (SI 2013/630) reg.28(1) and (6) (April 29, 2013).

DEFINITIONS

"claimant"—see reg.2(1).
"Social Security Act"—*ibid.*

[¹Reduction in certain cases

76.—There shall be deducted from the amount of income support which would, but for this regulation, be payable for a part-week—

2.533

    (a) [² in the case of a claimant to whom regulation 22A (reduction in applicable amount where the claimant is appealing against a decision [³ which embodies a determination] that he is not incapable of work) applies], the proportion of the relevant amount specified therein appropriate to the number of days in the part-week;

    (b) where regulation 75(f) (modifications in the calculation of income) applies, one-half of the amount disregarded under regulation 75(f) less the weekly amount of any disregard under Schedule 8 or 9 appropriate to that payment.]

AMENDMENTS

1. Income Support (General) Amendment Regulations 1988 (SI 1988/663) reg.27 (April 11, 1988).
2. Income Support (General) (Jobseeker's Allowance Consequential Amendments) Regulations 1996 (SI 1996/206) reg.21 (October 7, 1996).
3. Social Security Act 1998 (Commencement No.9 and Savings and Consequential and Transitional Provisions) Order 1999 (SI 1999/2422) art.3(7) and Sch.6 para.2.

DEFINITION

"claimant"—see reg.2(1).

[¹Modification of section 23(5) of the Act [SSCBA, s.126(5)]

77.—Where income support is payable for a part-week, section 23(5) of the Act [SSCBA, s.126(5)] (trade disputes) shall have effect as if the following paragraph were substituted for paragraph (b)—

2.534

        "(b) any payment by way of income support for a part-week which apart from this paragraph would be made to him, or to a person whose applicable amount if aggregated with his—

        (i) shall not be made if the payment for the part-week is equal to or less than the proportion of the relevant sum appropriate to the number of days in the part-week; or

        (ii) if it is more than that proportion, shall be made at a rate equal to the difference."

AMENDMENT

1. Income Support (General) Amendment Regulations 1988 (SI 1988/663) reg.27 (April 11, 1988).

DEFINITION

"the Act"—see reg.2(1).

SCHEDULES

SCHEDULE 1

2.535   *[Revoked by the Income Support (General) (Jobseeker's Allowance Consequential Amendments) Regulations 1996 (SI 1996/206), reg.28 and Sch.3 with effect from October 7, 1996.]*

SCHEDULE 1A

2.536   *[Revoked by the Income Support (General) (Jobseeker's Allowance Consequential Amendments) Regulations 1996 (SI 1996/206), reg.28 and Sch.3 with effect from October 7, 1996.]*

[¹ SCHEDULE 1B   **Regulation 4ZA**

PRESCRIBED CATEGORIES OF PERSON

2.537   [³²[³⁶[⁴⁶[⁵² **Lone Parents**
1.—(1) A lone parent who is responsible for, and a member of the same household as—
(a) a single child aged under 5, or
(b) more than one child where the youngest is aged under 5.
(2) A lone parent who is under the age of 18.]]]]

Single persons looking after foster children
2.538   [⁵⁵ **2.**—A single claimant or a lone parent with whom a child is placed—
(a) by a local authority or voluntary organisation within the meaning of the Children Act 1989;
(b) by a local authority or voluntary organisation within the meaning of the Children (Scotland) Act 1995;
(c) by virtue of any order or warrant made under the Children's Hearings (Scotland) Act 2011.]

[³⁸ **Single persons looking after children placed with them prior to adoption**
2.539   **2A.**—A single claimant or a lone parent with whom a child is placed for adoption by an adoption agency within the meaning of the Adoption and Children Act 2002 or the Adoption and Children (Scotland) Act 2007.]

Persons temporarily looking after another person
2.540   **3.**—A person who is—
(a) looking after a child because the parent of that child or the person who usually looks after him is [³⁵ temporarily] ill or is temporarily absent from his home; or
(b) looking after a member of his family who is temporarily ill.

Persons caring for another person   _see p 563_
2.541   **4.**—A person (the carer)—
(a) who is regularly and substantially engaged in caring for another person if—
  (i) the person being cared for is in receipt of attendance allowance [². . .] [⁵³ [⁵⁴, armed forces independence payment, the care component of disability living allowance at the highest or middle rate prescribed in accordance with section 72(3) of the Contributions and Benefits Act] or the daily living component of personal independence payment at the standard or enhanced rate in accordance with section 78(3) of the 2012 Act]; or
  (ii) the person being cared for has claimed attendance allowance [². . .] but only for the period up to the date of determination of that claim, or the period of 26 weeks from the date of that claim, whichever date is the earlier; or
  [²(iia) the person being cared for has claimed attendance allowance in accordance with section 65(6)(a) of the Contributions and Benefits Act (claims in advance of entitlement), an award has been made in respect of that claim under section 65(6)(b) of that Act and, where the period for which the award is payable has begun, that person in receipt of the allowance;] [¹⁶ or]
  (iii) the person being cared for has claimed entitlement to a disability living allowance [⁵⁴, armed forces independence payment] [⁵³or personal independence payment] but only for the period up to the date of determination of that claim,

550

or the period of 26 weeks from the date of that claim, whichever date is the earlier; or

[²(iiia) the person being cared for has claimed entitlement to the care component of a disability living allowance in accordance with regulation 13A of the Social Security (Claims and Payments) Regulations 1987 (advance claims and awards), an award at the highest or middle rate has been made in respect of that claim and, where the period for which the award is payable has begun, that person is in receipt of the allowance;] [⁵³ ; or

(iv) the person being cared for has claimed entitlement to the daily living component of personal independence payment in accordance with regulation 33 of the Universal Credit, Personal Independence Payment, Jobseeker's Allowance and Employment and Support Allowance (Claims and Payments) Regulations 2013 (advance claim for and award of personal independence payment), an award at the standard or enhanced rate has been made in respect of that claim and, where the period for which the award is payable has begun, that person is in receipt of the payment;]

(b) who is engaged in caring for another person and [¹⁰who is both entitled to, and in receipt of,] [¹⁸ a carer's allowance] [¹⁷ or would be in receipt of that allowance but for the application of a restriction under section [⁴⁴ 6B or] 7 of the Social Security Fraud Act 2001 (loss of benefit provisions)].

5.—A person to whom paragraph 4 applied, but only for a period of 8 weeks from the date on which that paragraph ceased to apply to him.

6.—A person who, had he previously made a claim for income support, would have fulfilled the conditions of paragraph 4, but only for a period of 8 weeks from the date on which he ceased to fulfil those conditions.

[⁴¹ Persons treated as capable of work and persons entitled to statutory sick pay]   2.542
7.—A person who—

[⁴⁰ (a) [⁴⁰ ...]

(b) [⁴⁰ ...]

(c) is treated as capable of work by virtue of regulations made under section 171E(1) of [⁴⁷the Contributions and Benefits Act] (disqualification etc); or

(d) is entitled to statutory sick pay.

[⁵⁸ Certain persons in receipt of the daily living component of personal independence payment
7A.—A person who is in receipt of the daily living component of personal independence   2.543
payment at the enhanced rate but only where, immediately before receiving that benefit, the person was entitled to and in receipt of income support because he or she was treated as incapable of work under regulation 10(2)(a)(i) of the Social Security (Incapacity for Work) (General) Regulations 1995.]

Disabled workers   2.544
8.—[⁴³ . . .]

Persons in employment living in residential care homes, nursing homes or residential accommodation   2.545
9.—[⁴³ . . .]

[¹⁵ Persons who have commenced remunerative work   2.546
9A.—A person to whom regulation 6(5) (persons not treated as engaged in remunerative work) applies.]

Disabled students   2.547
10.—[⁴⁰ . . .]

11.—A person who is a [¹¹ full-time student] and who—

(a) immediately before 1st September 1990 was in receipt of income support by virtue of paragraph 7 of Schedule 1 as then in force; or

(b) on or after that date makes a claim for income support and at a time during the period of 18 months immediately preceding the date of that claim was in receipt of income support either by virtue of that paragraph or regulation 13(2)(b),

but this paragraph shall not apply where for a continuous period of 18 months or more the person has not been in receipt of income support.

Deaf students

2.548   **12.**—[⁴⁰ . . .]

Blind persons

2.549   **13.**—[⁴⁰ . . .]

Pregnancy

2.550   **14.**—A woman who—

(a) is incapable of work by reason of pregnancy; or

(b) is or has been pregnant but only for the period commencing 11 weeks before her expected week of confinement and ending [⁴⁸. . .] [¹⁹ fifteen weeks after the date on which her pregnancy ends [⁴⁸ . . .]].

[⁶Parental leave

2.551   **14A.**—(1) A person who is—

(a) entitled to, and taking, parental leave by virtue of Part III of the Maternity and Parental Leave etc. Regulations 1999 in respect of a child who is a member of his household; and

(b) not entitled to any remuneration from his employer in respect of that leave for the period to which his claim for income support relates; and

(c) entitled [²². . .] [²¹ working tax credit, child tax credit payable at a rate higher than the family element,] housing benefit or council tax benefit on the day before that leave begins.

(2) In this paragraph "remuneration" means payment of any kind [²¹ and "family element" means in a case where any child in respect of whom child tax credit is payable is under the age of one year, the amount specified in regulation 7(3)(a) of the Child Tax Credit Regulations 2002 or in any other case, the amount specified in regulation 7(3)(b) of those Regulations] [²² but subject in any case to calculations of those amounts made in accordance with the Tax Credits (Income Thresholds and Determination of Rates) Regulations 2002.]]

[²⁰Paternity Leave

2.552   **14B.**— (1) A person who is entitled to, and is taking, [⁴⁹ [⁵⁶ . . .] paternity leave by virtue of section 80A or 80B of the Employment Rights Act 1996] and who satisfies either or both of the conditions set out in sub-paragraph (2) below.

(2) The conditions for the purposes of sub-paragraph (1) are—

(a) he is not entitled to [⁴⁹ [⁵⁶ . . .] statutory paternity pay] by virtue of Part 12ZA of the Contributions and Benefits Act, or to any remuneration from his employer in respect of that leave for the period to which his claim for income support relates;

(b) he is entitled to [²². . .] [²¹ working tax credit, child tax credit payable at a rate higher than the family element,] housing benefit or council tax benefit on the day before that leave begins.

(3) In this paragraph "remuneration" means payment of any kind [²¹ and "family element" means in a case where any child in respect of whom child tax credit is payable is under the age of one year, the amount specified in regulation 7(3)(a) of the Child Tax Credit Regulations 2002 or in any other case, the amount specified in regulation 7(3)(b) of those Regulations] [²² but subject in any case to calculations of those amounts made in accordance with the Tax Credits (Income Thresholds and Determination of Rates) Regulations 2002.]]

[⁵⁹ Parental Bereavement Leave

2.553   **14C.**—(1) A person who is entitled to, and is taking, parental bereavement leave by virtue of section 80EA of the Employment Rights Act 1996 and who satisfies either or both of the conditions set out in sub-paragraph (2) below.

(2) The conditions for the purposes of sub-paragraph (1) are that the person—

(a) is not entitled to statutory parental bereavement pay by virtue of Part 12ZD of the Contributions and Benefits Act, or to any remuneration from their employer in respect of that leave for the period to which the claim for income support relates;

(b) is entitled to working tax credit, child tax credit payable at a rate higher than the family element, housing benefit or council tax benefit on the day before that leave begins.

(3) In this paragraph "remuneration" means payment of any kind and "family element" means the amount specified in regulation 7(3) of the Child Tax Credit Regulations 2002(13) but subject in any case to calculations of that amount made in accordance with the Tax Credits (Income Thresholds and Determination of Rates) Regulations 2002.]

Persons in education

15.—A person to whom any provision of regulation 13(2)(a) to (e) (persons receiving relevant education who are parents, [27 disabled persons, persons with limited leave to enter or
remain], orphans and persons estranged from their parents or guardian) applies.

2.554

[35[39[50 **Certain persons who have enrolled on, been accepted for or are undertaking
full-time, non-advanced education]]**

15A.— [50 (1) A person ("P") who satisfies the following conditions.

2.555

(2) The first condition is that P has enrolled on, been accepted for or is undertaking a course
of full-time, non-advanced education.

(3) The second condition is that P is –

(a) under the age of 21; or

(b) 21 and attained that age whilst undertaking a course of full-time, non-advanced education.

(4) The third condition is that –

(a) P has no parent;

(b) of necessity P has to live away from P's parents because –

(i) P is estranged from P's parents,

(ii) P is in physical or moral danger, or

(iii) there is a serious risk to P's physical or mental health; or

(c) P is living away from P's parents because they are unable to support P financially and
are –

(i) chronically sick or mentally or physically disabled,

(ii) detained in custody pending trial or sentencing upon conviction or under a
sentence imposed by a court, or

(iii) prohibited from entering or re-entering Great Britain.]

(5) [50 . . .]

(6) In this paragraph—

"chronically sick or mentally or physically disabled" has the meaning given in regulation
13(3)(b);

[50 "course of full-time, non-advanced education" means a course of full-time education
which is not a course of advanced education and which is not provided to P by virtue of P's
employment or any office held by P, which is –

(a) provided at a school or college, or

(b) provided elsewhere but is approved by the Secretary of State as being such a course,
and for this purpose, "course of advanced education" has the same meaning as in regulation
61(1)];

"parent" includes a person acting in place of a parent which—

(a) for the purposes of sub-paragraph (5)(a) and (b) has the meaning given in regulation
13(3)(a)(i), and

(b) for the purposes of sub-paragraph (5)(c), has the meaning given in regulation 13(3)(a)(ii).]

Certain persons aged 50 who have not been in remunerative work for 10 years

16.—[28 . . .]

2.556

[14 **Certain persons aged between 55 and 60 whose spouse has died**

16A.—[26 . . .]]

2.557

Persons aged 60 or over

17.—[23. . .]

2.558

Refugees

18.—A person who is a refugee within the definition in Article 1 of the Convention relating
to the Status of Refugees done at Geneva on 28th July 1951 as extended by Article 1(2) of the
Protocol relating to the Status of Refugees done at New York on 31st January 1967 and who—

2.559

(a) is attending for more than 15 hours a week a course for the purpose of learning
English so that he may obtain employment; and

(b) on the date on which that course commenced, had been in Great Britain for not more
than 12 months.

but only for a period not exceeding nine months.

[8 18A.—[30 . . .]]

[²⁹ **Persons required to attend court or tribunal**

2.560   **19.**—(1) A person who is required to attend a court or tribunal as a justice of the peace, a party to any proceedings, a witness or a juror.

(2) In this paragraph, "tribunal" means any tribunal listed in Schedule 1 to the Tribunals and Inquiries Act 1992.]

Persons affected by a trade dispute

2.561   **20.**—A person to whom section 126 of the Contributions and Benefits Act (trade disputes) applies or in respect of whom section 124(1) of the Act (conditions of entitlement to income support) has effect as modified by section 127(b) of the Act (effect of return to work).

[⁴² **Persons from abroad**

2.562   **21.**—A person not excluded from entitlement to income support under section 115 of the Immigration and Asylum Act 1999 by virtue of regulation 2 of the Social Security (Immigration and Asylum) Consequential Amendments Regulations 2000 except for a person to whom paragraphs 2, 3 and 4 of Part 1 of the Schedule to those Regulations applies.]

Persons in custody

2.563   **22.**—A person remanded in, or committed in, custody for trial or for sentencing.

Member of couple looking after children while other member temporarily abroad

2.564   **23.**—A person who is a member of a couple and who is treated as responsible for a child who is a member of his household where the other member of that couple is temporarily not present in the United Kingdom.

Persons appealing against a decision [⁴ which embodies a determination] that they are not incapable of work

2.565   **24.**—A person—
- (a) in respect of whom it has been determined for the purposes of section 171B of the Contributions and Benefits Act (the own occupation test) that he is not incapable of work; and
- (b) whose medical practitioner continues to supply evidence of his incapacity for work in accordance with regulation 2 of the Social Security (Medical Evidence) Regulations 1976 (evidence of incapacity for work); and
- (c) who has made and is pursuing an appeal against the [⁴ decision which embodies a] determination that he is not so incapable.

but only for the period prior to the determination of his appeal.

    25.—A person—
- (a) in respect of whom it has been determined for the purposes of section 171C of the Contributions and Benefits Act ([⁷ personal capability assessment]) that he is not incapable of work; and
- (b) who has made and is pursuing an appeal against the [⁴ decision which embodies a] determination that he is not so incapable.

but only for the period [²⁴ beginning with the date on which that determination takes effect until] the determination of his appeal.

    26.—[³¹. . .]

    27.—[³¹. . .]

[²⁷ **Persons engaged in training**]

2.566   **28.**—A person who is [²⁷ not a qualifying young person or child within the meaning of section 142 of the Contributions and Benefits Act (child and qualifying young person) and who is] engaged in training, and for this purpose "training" means training for which persons aged under 18 are eligible and for which persons aged 18 to 24 may be eligible [¹³ secured by the [⁴⁵ [⁵¹ Secretary of State] [⁵⁷ . . .]] the Chief or by the [²⁵ [³³ Welsh Ministers]]] and, in Scotland, directly or indirectly by a Local Enterprise Company pursuant to its arrangement with, as the case may be, [³⁴ Skills Development Scotland,] Scottish Enterprise or Highlands and Islands Enterprise (whether that arrangement is known as an Operating Contract or by any other name).]

AMENDMENTS

    1. Income Support (General) (Jobseeker's Allowance Consequential Amendments) Regulations 1996 (SI 1996/206) reg.22 and Sch.1 (October 7, 1996).

2. Jobseeker's Allowance and Income Support (General) (Amendment) Regulations 1996 (SI 1996/1517) reg.33 (October 7, 1996).

3. Social Security and Child Support (Miscellaneous Amendments) Regulations 1997 (SI 1997/827) reg.5 (April 7, 1997).

4. Social Security Act 1998 (Commencement No.9 and Savings and Consequential and Transitional Provisions) Order 1999 (SI 1999/2422 (C.61)) art.3(7) and Sch.6 para.3 (September 6, 1999).

5. Social Security (Miscellaneous Amendments) (No.2) Regulations 1999 (SI 1999/2556) reg.2(7) (October 4, 1999).

6. Income Support (General) Amendment (No.2) Regulations 1999 (SI 1999/3329) reg.2 (January 5, 2000).

7. Social Security (Incapacity for Work) Miscellaneous Amendments Regulations 1999 (SI 1999/3109) reg.6 (April 3, 2000).

8. Social Security (Immigration and Asylum) Consequential Amendments Regulations 2000 (SI 2000/636) reg.3(9) (April 3, 2000).

9. Social Security (Miscellaneous Amendments) Regulations 2000 (SI 2000/681) reg.2(d) (April 3, 2000).

10. Social Security (Miscellaneous Amendments) Regulations 2000 (SI 2000/681) reg.4(1) (April 3, 2000).

11. Social Security Amendment (Students) Regulations 2000 (SI 2000/1981) reg.5(5) and Sch. (July 31, 2000).

12. Social Security Amendment (Students and Income-related Benefits) Regulations 2000 (SI 2000/1922) reg.2(8) (August 28, 2000, or if the student's period of study begins between August 1 and 27, 2000, the first day of the period).

13. Social Security (Miscellaneous Amendments) (No.2) Regulations 2001 (SI 2001/652) reg.4 (March 26, 2001).

14. Social Security Amendment (Bereavement Benefits) Regulations 2000 (SI 2000/2239) reg.2(2) (April 9, 2001).

15. Social Security (Miscellaneous Amendments) Regulations 2001 (SI 2001/488) reg.5 (April 9, 2001).

16. Social Security (Miscellaneous Amendments) (No.3) Regulations 2001 (SI 2001/859) reg.3(4) (April 9, 2001).

17. Social Security (Loss of Benefit) (Consequential Amendments) Regulations 2002 (SI 2002/490) reg.4 (April 1, 2002).

18. Social Security Amendment (Carer's Allowance) Regulations 2002 (SI 2002/2497) reg.3 and Sch.2 (April 1, 2003).

19. Social Security (Paternity and Adoption) Amendment Regulations 2002 (SI 2002/2689) reg.2(5)(a) (November 24, 2002).

20. Social Security (Paternity and Adoption) Amendment Regulations 2002 (SI 2002/2689) reg.2(5)(b) (December 8, 2002).

21. Social Security (Working Tax Credit and Child Tax Credit) (Consequential Amendments) Regulations 2003 (SI 2003/455) reg.2 and Sch.1 para.19 (April 7, 2003).

22. Social Security (Working Tax Credit and Child Tax Credit) (Consequential Amendments) (No.3) Regulations 2003 (SI 2003/1731) reg.2(3) (August 8, 2003).

23. State Pension Credit (Consequential, Transitional and Miscellaneous Provisions) Regulations 2002 (SI 2002/3019) reg.29(4) (October 6, 2003).

24. Social Security Child Support and Tax Credits (Miscellaneous Amendments) Regulations 2005 (SI 2005/337) reg.6 (March 18, 2005).

25. National Council for Education and Training for Wales (Transfer of Functions to the National Assembly for Wales and Abolition) Order 2005 (SI 2005/3238 (W.243)) art.9(2) and Sch.2 para.1(2) (April 1, 2006).

26. Social Security (Miscellaneous Amendments) Regulations 2006 (SI 2006/588) reg.2(4)(d) (April 10, 2006).

27. Social Security (Young Persons) Amendment Regulations 2006 (SI 2006/718) reg.2(7) (April 10, 2006).

28. Social Security (Miscellaneous Amendments) (No.4) Regulations 2006 (SI 2006/2378) reg.5(6) (October 7, 2006).

29. Social Security (Income Support and Jobseeker's Allowance) Amendment Regulations 2006 (SI 2006/1402) reg.3 (May 30, 2006).

30. Asylum and Immigration (Treatment of Claimants, etc.) Act 2004 (c.19) s.12(2)(a)(ii) (June 14, 2007).

31. Social Security (Miscellaneous Amendments) Regulations 2008 (SI 2008/698) reg.2(11) (April 14, 2008).

32. Social Security (Lone Parents and Miscellaneous Amendments) Regulations 2008 (SI 2008/3051) reg.2 (November 24, 2008).

33. Social Security (Miscellaneous Amendments) (No.7) Regulations 2008 (SI 2008/3157) reg.2(6) (January 5, 2009).

34. Social Security (Miscellaneous Amendments) Regulations 2009 (SI 2009/583) reg.2(3) (April 6, 2009).

35. Social Security (Miscellaneous Amendments) Regulations 2009 (SI 2009/583) reg.2(12) (April 6, 2009).

36. Social Security (Lone Parents and Miscellaneous Amendments) Regulations 2008 (SI 2008/3051) reg.3 (October 26, 2009).

37. Social Security (Miscellaneous Amendments) (No.4) Regulations 2009 (SI 2009/2655) reg.2(14)(a) (October 26, 2009).

38. Social Security (Miscellaneous Amendments) (No.4) Regulations 2009 (SI 2009/2655) reg.2(14)(b) (October 26, 2009).

39. Social Security (Miscellaneous Amendments) (No.4) Regulations 2009 (SI 2009/2655) reg.2(14)(c) (October 26, 2009).

40. Income Support (Prescribed Categories of Person) Regulations 2009 (SI 2009/3152) reg.2 (December, 30, 2009). Regulation 2(1)(b) revoked paras 7(a) and (b), 10, 12 and 13 with effect from December 30, 2009 but this was subject to the saving provisions in reg.2(2). See the 2015/16 edition of this volume for these Regulations and the notes to them.

41. Income Support (Prescribed Categories of Person) Regulations 2009 (SI 2009/3152) reg.3(2)(e) and 3(7) (December, 30, 2009). Regulation 3(2)(e) substitutes a new heading for the existing heading to para.7 with effect from December 30, 2009 but reg.3(7) provides that this does not apply in the case of a person who is subject to the saving provisions in reg.2(2) of those Regulations. For this reason the heading is in italics.

42. Social Security (Miscellaneous Amendments) (No .5) Regulations 2009 (SI 2009/3228) reg.3(2)(d) (January 25, 2010).

43. Social Security (Miscellaneous Amendments) (No. 5) Regulations 2009 (SI 2009/3228) reg.4(1)(a)(ii) (January 25, 2010).

44. Social Security (Loss of Benefit) Amendment Regulations 2010 (SI 2010/1160) reg.10(2) (April 1, 2010).

45. Apprenticeships, Skills, Children and Learning Act 2009 (Consequential Amendments to Subordinate Legislation) (England) Order 2010 (SI 2010/1941) art.3(4) (September 1, 2010).

46. Social Security (Lone Parents and Miscellaneous Amendments) Regulations 2008 (SI 2008/3051) reg.4 (October 25, 2010).

47. Social Security (Miscellaneous Amendments) (No. 5) Regulations 2010 (SI 2010/2429) reg.2(2)(a) (November 1, 2010).

48. Social Security (Miscellaneous Amendments) (No. 5) Regulations 2010 (SI 2010/2429) reg.2(2)(b) (November 1, 2010).

49. Social Security (Miscellaneous Amendments) Regulations 2012 (SI 2012/757) reg.3(3) (April 1, 2012).

50. Social Security (Miscellaneous Amendments) Regulations 2012 (SI 2012/757) reg.11 (April 1, 2012).

51. Young People's Learning Agency Abolition (Consequential Amendments to Subordinate Legislation) (England) Order 2012 (SI 2012/956) art.3(4) (May 1, 2012).

52. Social Security (Lone Parents and Miscellaneous Amendments) Regulations 2012 (SI 2012/874) reg.2 (May 21, 2012).

53. Personal Independence Payment (Supplementary Provisions and Consequential Amendments) Regulations 2013 (SI 2013/388) reg.8 and Sch. Pt 2 para.11(4) (April 8, 2013).

54. Armed Forces and Reserve Forces Compensation Scheme (Consequential Provisions: Subordinate Legislation) Order 2013 (SI 2013/591) art.7 and Sch. para.4(4) (April 8, 2013).

55. Children's Hearings (Scotland) Act 2011 (Consequential and Transitional Provisions and Savings) Order 2013 (SI 2013/1465) art.17(1) and Sch.1 Pt 2 para.12(3) (June 24, 2013).

56. Shared Parental Leave and Statutory Shared Parental Pay (Consequential Amendments to Subordinate Legislation) Order 2014 (SI 2014/3255) art.5(5) (April 5, 2015).

57. Deregulation Act 2015 (Consequential Amendments) Order 2015 (SI 2015/971) art.2 and Sch.3 para.2(4) (May 26, 2015).

58. Social Security (Miscellaneous Amendments No. 5) Regulations 2017 (SI 2017/1187) reg.2(1) and (2) (December 21, 2017).

59. Parental Bereavement Leave and Pay (Consequential Amendments to Subordinate Legislation) Regulations 2020 (SI 2020/354) reg.5(1) and (5) (April 6, 2020).

DEFINITIONS

"adoption leave"—see reg.2(1).
"armed forces independence payment"—*ibid.*
"attendance allowance"—*ibid.*
"child"—see SSCBA s.137(1).
"disability living allowance"—see reg.2(1).
"full-time student"—*ibid.*, reg.61(1).
"lone parent"—see reg.2(1).
"maternity leave"—*ibid.*
"paternity leave"—*ibid.*
"payment"—*ibid.*
"personal capability assessment"—SSCBA s.171C and Incapacity for Work Regulations reg.24.
"personal independence payment" —see reg.2(1).
"single claimant"—*ibid.*
"student"—*ibid.*, reg.61(1).
"voluntary organisation"—see reg.2(1).

GENERAL NOTE

As a consequence of the introduction of JSA on October 7, 1996, the income support scheme had to undergo a fundamental restructuring. Income support was no longer available to people who are claiming benefit because they are unemployed. People who have to be available for, and actively seeking, work as a condition of receiving benefit have to claim JSA. Since October 7, 1996, in order to qualify for income support a person has to fall within a "prescribed category" (see SSCBA s.124(1)(e) and reg.4ZA). Schedule 1B sets out these categories.

See the notes to reg.4ZA for discussion of the position of claimants who may be able to claim either income support or JSA; note also that the raising of the limit for remunerative work for partners to 24 hours a week from October 7, 1996 meant that some couples have to decide whether they will gain more by claiming working tax credit.

When Sch.1B was first introduced the categories broadly resembled most of those in the former Sch.1 (people not required to be available for employment) (revoked on October 7, 1996), but there were some differences. There was no equivalent to paras

2.567

12 (Open University students attending a residential course), 18 (discharged prisoners) or 23 (persons taking child abroad for medical treatment) of the former Sch.1. But if people in these circumstances claim JSA they will be treated as available for work (see sub-paras (f), (h) and (c) respectively of reg.14(1) of the JSA Regulations 1996). See the note to para.28 for people in receipt of a training allowance.

2.568 Schedule 1B provides an exhaustive list of the circumstances in which a person will be entitled to income support. There is no category of analogous circumstances or provision for a reduced rate of benefit on the ground of hardship for people who do not come within these categories (compare the former reg.8(3), see the 1996 edition of J. Mesher and P. Wood, *Income-related Benefits: the Legislation*). Moreover, the provision for hardship payments under JSA is considerably restricted (see regs 140–146 (regs 146A–146H in the case of joint-claim couples) of the JSA Regulations 1996 and the notes to those regulations). Part VI of the Income Support Regulations, which formerly contained some very limited provision for urgent cases outside the normal scope of the income support rules, was revoked (subject to three savings: see the note to Pt VI) with effect from January 25, 2010.

See the notes to reg.4ZA(1) for the subsequent major contraction in the coverage of the income support scheme that is a consequence of:

- on October 6, 2003 the introduction of state pension credit;

- starting from April 6, 2004 the removal of amounts for children and young persons from income support (except in "transitional cases"—see the note to reg.17);

- starting from November 24, 2008 the staged reduction of lone parents' entitlement to income support (see the note to para.1 below);

- on October 27, 2008 the introduction of ESA (see the notes to paras 7, 10, 12 and 13 below); and

- from February 28, 2011 the migration of claimants in receipt of income support on the grounds of incapacity or disability to ESA. It was intended that the conversion process to ESA would be completed by the end of March 2014 but it is not clear whether this was achieved.

Paragraph 1

2.569 See reg.15 for responsibility for a child and reg.16 for membership of the household. *CIS/43/2008* confirms that whether a person is "responsible for a child" is governed by reg.15. It is not sufficient for the purposes of para.1 that the claimant is caring for the child. However, para.3 may apply, depending on the circumstances. See further the note to para.3.

Before November 24, 2008 para.1 applied if a lone parent was responsible for a child (i.e. a person under 16) who was a member of her household. From that date, however, the staged reduction in the entitlement of lone parents under para.1 began. Subject to phasing-in provisions, from November 24, 2008 para.1 only applied if a lone parent was responsible for a sole or youngest child aged under 12; from October 26, 2009 only those lone parents with a sole or youngest child under 10 qualified; from October 25, 2010 the sole or youngest child had to be under seven; and from May 21, 2012 entitlement under para.1 has been limited to lone parents whose sole or youngest child is aged under five. Note subs.(1A) inserted into s.124 of the Contributions and Benefits Act on May 21, 2012 which provides that regulations must provide for income support to be available to a lone parent who has a child under five. Thus any further reduction in entitlement under para.1 will require an amendment to s.124(1A).

Note the additional change from May 21, 2012 which provides that a lone parent will be eligible for income support if she is under the age of 18 (regardless of the age of her child) (sub-para.(2)).

VL v SSWP (IS) [2011] UKUT 227 (AAC); [2012] AACR 10 holds that the reduced entitlement for lone parents, although indirectly discriminatory against women, was not in breach of art.14, read with art.1 Prot.1, ECHR because it was well within the wide margin of appreciation that the state has in the implementation of social policy and in economic matters. The claimant had also contended that the amending legislation was ultra vires s.7 of the Education Act 1996 because it prevented a lone parent from exercising the right to educate her children at home. Judge Levenson, however, rejected this argument, pointing out that s.7 does not confer a right to home educate but creates a duty to secure education (which may be fulfilled by home education). Permission to appeal against this decision was refused by the Court of Appeal on the papers on March 30, 2012.

Phasing-in provisions

In relation to the reductions in entitlement for lone parents which took effect on November 24, 2008, October 26, 2009 and October 25, 2010, there were special phasing-in provisions that applied to certain claimants who had an existing entitlement under para.1 at the respective date (and to whom no other paragraph in Sch.1B applied) (see the Schedule to the Social Security (Lone Parents and Miscellaneous Amendments) Regulations 2008 (SI 2008/3051)). These provisions did not, or ceased to, apply if the lone parent made a further claim for income support or while the transitional provisions for certain full-time students and full-time participants in the New Deal for Lone Parents in reg.13 of the 2008 Regulations applied to the claimant. For the effect of these phasing-in provisions see the notes to para.1 of Sch.1B in the 2009/10 edition of this volume; for reg.13 of the 2008 Regulations see the 2012/13 edition of this volume.

There were similar phasing-in provisions for certain claimants who were aged 18 or over and had an existing entitlement under para.1 immediately before May 21, 2012, and to whom no other paragraph in Sch.1B applied (see the Schedule to the Social Security (Lone Parents and Miscellaneous Amendments) Regulations 2012 (SI 2012/874)). Again these provisions did not, or ceased to, apply if the lone parent made a further claim for income support or while the transitional provisions for certain full-time students and those undertaking a full-time course of training or instruction under arrangements made, or approved, by the Secretary of State applied to the claimant.

For the effect of these phasing-in provisions, see the notes to para.1 of Sch.1B in the 2014/15 edition of this volume.

Transitional Provisions

As was the case under the 2008 Regulations (see the note to para.1 of Sch.1B in the 2012/13 edition of this volume), there is transitional protection for certain lone parents. The transitional protection under the 2012 Regulations applies to lone parents who: (i) immediately before May 21, 2012 were entitled to income support solely on the grounds of being a lone parent (and to whom no other paragraph in Sch.1B applies); (ii) immediately before, on and after May 21, 2012 are full-time students or undertaking a full-time course of training or instruction under arrangements made, or approved, by the Secretary of State; and (iii) on and after May 21, 2012 have an only or youngest child aged five or over (see reg.7 of the Social Security (Lone Parents and Miscellaneous Amendments) Regulations 2012 (SI 2012/874) (p.1779)).

The transitional protection does not apply (or ceases to apply) if the lone parent makes a further claim for income support on or after May 21, 2012.

A claimant to whom reg.7 applies will continue to be entitled to income support until the date she ceases attending the course or the date that her only or youngest child reaches the age at which her income support entitlement would have ended under the rules in force when she started her course, whichever is the earlier. The claimant will continue to be required to take part in work-focused interviews while reg.7 applies.

2.570

2.571

Requirement to take part in work-focused interviews

2.572   Since April 5, 2004 the requirement to attend work-focused interviews ("WFIs") has applied to all lone parents aged 18 or over and under 60 who are responsible for a child in their household and who are not subject to the Jobcentre Plus scheme (see the Social Security (Work-focused Interviews for Lone Parents) and Miscellaneous Amendments Regulations 2000 (SI 2000/1926) (as amended) in Vol.III of this series. Note that from April 6, 2010 the upper age limit has changed from "60" to "pensionable age" as a consequence of the staged equalisation of state pension age. This equalisation was to have taken place between April 6, 2010 and April 5, 2020 but the timetable for this in the Pensions Act 1995 has been accelerated with effect from April 2016 so that women's state pension age will now be 65 by November 2018; in addition, the increase in state pension age to 66 for both men and women has been brought forward—it will start to rise from 65 in December 2018 to reach 66 by October 2020 (see s.1 of the Pensions Act 2011, and between 2026 and 2028 it will rise to 67 (see s.26 of the Pensions Act 2014)). For the purposes of the 2000 Regulations and the Social Security (Jobcentre Plus Interviews) Regulations 2002 (SI 2002/1703) (as amended) (see Vol.III) "pensionable age" in the case of men born before April 6, 1955 is the age when a woman born on the same day as the man would attain that age.

A further amendment to the 2000 and 2002 Regulations was made on October 31, 2011 so that a lone parent who has a youngest child under one will not be required to attend a WFI (see reg.2(6)(b) of the Social Security (Work-focused Interviews for Lone Parents and Partners) (Amendment) Regulations 2011 (SI 2011/2428), which amends reg.4 of the 2000 Regulations and reg.3(9)(b) of the same Regulations which amends reg.8 of the 2002 Regulations). In addition, reg.7 of the 2000 Regulations was amended by reg.2(8) of the 2011 Regulations on October 31, 2011 so that under those regulations a lone parent who fails to take part in her initial WFI without good cause is no longer treated as not having made a claim for income support but instead will be subject to the same sanction that applies for failing to take part in subsequent WFIs.

Lone parents who were entitled to income support *solely* on the grounds of being a lone parent were required to take part in a WFI every 13 weeks under either the lone parents WFI scheme or the Jobcentre Plus scheme. From October 31, 2011 such a lone parent had to attend quarterly WFIs if she had a child of four, five or six—this change was made in anticipation of the lowering of the age threshold of the only or youngest child to under five that was due to come into force on May 21, 2012. From May 21, 2012 such a lone parent had to attend quarterly WFIs if she had a sole or youngest child aged four.

2.573   Since April 28, 2014 the requirement to take part in a WFI applies to such a lone parent whose only or youngest child is aged between one and four years and WFIs for such claimants will no longer take place at set intervals but their timing is to be at the discretion of the employment adviser. In addition, the requirement for such claimants to attend WFIs can no longer be waived but can still be deferred.

A lone parent who fails to take part in a WFI and who does not show good cause before the end of five working days following the date on which the Secretary of State gave notice of the failure (the five days can be extended to one month if the claimant provides new facts which could not reasonably have been provided within the five days) will be subject to a sanction. See reg.7(5) of the 2000 Regulations and reg.14 of the 2002 Regulations for a non-exclusive list of matters to be taken into account when determining whether the lone parent has shown good cause.

The sanction is that the lone parent's income support is reduced by 20 per cent of the applicable amount for a single claimant aged not less than 25 for the first failure, and for every subsequent failure (provided that it is not reduced below 10p). But no reduction will be made if a previous sanction under regs 7(3) and 8 of the 2000 Regulations, reg.12(2)(c) of the 2002 Regulations or reg.8(1) and (2) of the Income Support (Work-Related Activity) and Miscellaneous Amendments Regulations 2014 (see below) has been imposed in the two-week period before the date of the current failure. The sanction applies until the first day of the benefit week in which the claimant satisfies a "compliance condition" (i.e. a requirement to take part in a WFI or to undertake work-related activity (see below)).

Requirement for lone parents on income support to undertake work-related activity

From April 28, 2014 a lone parent who is entitled to income support solely on the grounds of being a lone parent and whose only or youngest child is aged three or four can also be required to undertake work-related activity as a condition of continuing to receive the full amount of income support (see Pt 2 of the Income Support (Work-Related Activity) and Miscellaneous Amendments Regulations 2014 (SI 2014/1097) (p.1782)).

2.574

"Work-related activity" is "activity which makes it more likely that the person will obtain or remain in work or be able to do so" (see s.2D(9)(d) SSAA 1992 in Vol.III of this series). The work-related activity that the lone parent is to carry out has to be notified in a written action plan, must be reasonable, having regard to her/his circumstances, and cannot include a requirement to apply for a job or undertake work (regs 2(3) and 3 of the 2014 Regulations). A requirement to undertake work-related activity can be deferred where it would be unreasonable to require the person to undertake it at, or by, that time (reg.4 of the 2014 Regulations).

The lone parent has to be available to undertake such work-related activity during her/his child's normal school hours or during any period when the child is in the care of a person over 18 (other than any form of health care for the child) but can otherwise restrict the times that s/he is available to undertake work-related activity (reg.10 of the 2014 Regulations).

If a lone parent fails to undertake the required work-related activity and does not show good cause for the failure before the end of five working days beginning with the date on which the Secretary of State gave notice of the failure (the five days can be extended to one month if new facts are provided which could not reasonably have been provided within the five days) s/he will be subject to a sanction (regs 6 and 8 of the 2014 Regulations). See reg.7 of the 2014 Regulations for a non-exclusive list of matters to be taken into account when determining whether the lone parent has shown good cause.

2.575

The sanction is that the lone parent's income support is reduced by 20 per cent of the applicable amount for a single claimant aged not less than 25 for the first failure, and for every subsequent failure (provided that it is not reduced below 10p). But no reduction will be made if a previous sanction under reg.8(1) and (2) of the 2014 Regulations, regs 7(3) and 8 of the 2000 Regulations or reg.12(2)(c) of the 2002 Regulations has been imposed in the two week period before the date of the current failure. The sanction applies until the lone parent is no longer required to carry out work-related activity or the first day of the benefit week in which s/he satisfies a "compliance condition" (i.e. a requirement to undertake work-related activity or take part in a WFI), whichever is earlier.

Following the Supreme Court's decision in *R (Reilly and Wilson) v Secretary of State for Work and Pensions* [2013] UKSC 68; [2014] AACR 9 (see in particular para.74), a lone parent may be able to argue that a sanction should not be imposed if she has not been given sufficient information about the work-related activity she will be required to undertake in order to make "informed and meaningful" representations before the requirement is imposed.

JSA and ESA claims by lone parents

Lone parents who are no longer eligible for income support will have to claim JSA (or ESA if they have limited capability for work). In recognition of the fact that "lone parents, parents and others with caring responsibilities for a child face circumstances that need special consideration" (to quote DMG Memo 45/08), when the reduction in entitlement to income support for lone parents was first introduced, amendments were made to the JSA rules governing availability for and actively seeking employment, good cause for refusing to carry out a jobseeker's direction or take up an offer of employment, and just cause for leaving a job voluntarily, in

2.576

order to introduce "additional flexibilities". See regs 5, 13, 14, 19 and 72 of the JSA Regulations 1996 and the notes to those Regulations. In addition, on April 26, 2010 a new reg.13A was inserted into the JSA Regulations 1996 by the JSA (Lone Parents) (Availability for Work) Regulations 2010 (SI 2010/837) which allows a lone parent who is responsible for, and a member of the same household as, a child aged under 13 to restrict her availability for work to the child's normal school hours.

A further amendment was made to the JSA Regulations 1996 on May 21, 2012 when the age threshold for the only or youngest child was reduced to under five. A new reg.17B was inserted to treat as available for employment, and a new reg.21B to treat as actively seeking employment, a lone parent whose sole or youngest child is aged five but who has not yet started (and who is not yet required by law to start) full-time education, where it would be unreasonable for the lone parent to make other arrangements for the care of the child.

Finally note that if a lone parent's income support included the disability premium when it came to an end under para.1, and she became entitled to ESA within 12 weeks of income support ceasing, her ESA will include the work-related activity or support component even though the ESA assessment period has not ended (see reg.7 of the ESA Regulations 2008 in Vol.1 in this series).

Paragraph 2

2.577   Special provision is necessary for foster children because they are not members of the foster-parent's household (reg.16(4)).

JS v SSWP (IS) [2015] UKUT 306 (AAC); [2016] AACR 13 discusses the meaning of "placed" in para.2. It concludes that "placed" within the meaning of the Children Act 1989 meant that the claimant must actually have a child living with her, or accommodated by her, in discharge of the local authority's functions under that Act. Paragraph 2 therefore did not apply when the claimant did not have a child staying with her, even though she continued to be on call as a foster carer, had a day care child and was providing support to other foster carers.

Paragraph 2A

2.578   With effect from October 26, 2009 a single claimant or a lone parent with whom a child is placed for adoption by an adoption agency prior to adoption can qualify for income support. Again, special provision is needed because such a child is not a member of the claimant's household (reg.16(4)).

Paragraph 3

2.579   This covers a person who is looking after a child (i.e. a person under 16: s.137(1) SSCBA) because his parent or the person who usually looks after him is (from April 6, 2009) temporarily ill or temporarily absent (sub-para.(a)); or who is looking after a member of the family (SSCBA s.137(1)) who is temporarily ill (sub-para.(b)).

The April 2009 amendment to para.3(a) so that it only applies where the parent of the child or the person who usually looks after him is *temporarily* ill reverses the effect of the decision in *R(IS) 11/08*. In that case the Commissioner had pointed out that it was only under sub-para.(b) that the illness of the other person (in that case the member of the family) must be temporary; under sub-para.(a) (in its then form) the illness of the parent or the person who usually looked after the child need not be. He therefore concluded that para.3 did not require that the claimant was only looking after the other person temporarily. The April 2009 amendment restores the policy intention.

In *CIS 866/2004* the claimant argued that she came within para.3(a) because her husband was unable to look after their young child due to his alcohol problems. The child had a long-term disability. However, the Deputy Commissioner holds that for para.3(a) to apply either the parent of the child who usually looked after the child or some other person who usually looked after the child had to be ill or temporarily absent. In his view it was only if read in this way that the use of the term "the parent" in para.3(a) rather than "a parent" made sense. On the facts it was the claimant who usually looked after the child, not her husband. Furthermore, para.3(b) did not apply.

This was because the child was not temporarily ill but had a long-term disability and the claimant was not looking after her husband. Since the husband could not claim because his application for asylum had been refused the consequence was that the claimant had no obvious means of state financial support other than child benefit.

CIS/4312/2007 also concerned a claimant who was looking after her husband who had no recourse to public funds and who was ill. He had kidney problems and underwent renal dialysis three times a week. He was on the waiting list for a kidney transplant and had been for three years. The Commissioner points out that it is possible for a person to have a permanent condition but not be ill except at particular times and that it did not necessarily follow that an *illness* could not be temporary because a *condition* would require long term treatment. It was common for people who need dialysis to feel better at times and worse at others. There was no doubt on the facts that the claimant was looking after her husband. Paragraph 3(b) therefore applied.

See also the note to reg.6(1)(b) on childminders.

Paragraphs 4–6

There is no requirement that alternative arrangements cannot be made. Under para.4(a) the fact of being substantially and regularly engaged in providing care for someone who receives or has been awarded attendance allowance, one of the two higher care components of disability living allowance, the daily living component of personal independence payment or armed forces independence payment, or who is waiting for a decision on entitlement is enough. In the last case, entitlement to income support under para.4(a) lasts for up to 26 weeks from the date of the claim for attendance allowance, disability living allowance, personal independence payment or armed forces independence payment, or until it is decided, whichever is the earlier.

For carer's allowance purposes "substantial" is 35 hours a week but *R(IS) 8/02* confirms that there is no such minimum requirement in order for para.4(a) to apply. Under para.4(a) it is simply a question of fact, having regard to the nature and amount of care provided, whether the claimant is "regularly and substantially engaged in caring". The Commissioner in *CSIS 1081/2001* also holds that care covers assistance or supervision arising out of the disabled person's needs and therefore will include domestic tasks that the person is unable to carry out themselves because of their disability, even if such tasks are not carried out in the person's presence. But it would not include travelling time to the person's home in order to provide the care as this is not in itself assistance to the disabled person. On the facts the claimant who went to her parents' home three times each weekday and provided care for 25–30 hours a week fell within para.4(a). It was irrelevant that she was also looking after her daughter (following a back injury) and her granddaughter.

Paragraph 4(b) covers anyone entitled to and in receipt of carer's allowance (or who would be but for the application of a sanction under s.7 of the Social Security Fraud Act 2001 (see Vol.III in this series)).

The effect of paras 5 and 6 is that the carer can qualify for income support in the eight weeks after ceasing to meet the conditions in para.4.

Paragraph 7

Paragraph 7 used to cover people who are incapable of work. However, from October 27, 2008, as a consequence of the start of the ESA scheme, *new* claims for income support under para.7(a) or (b) on the ground of incapacity or deemed incapacity for work were no longer possible, except in certain circumstances (see reg.2(2)(b)–(d) of the Employment and Support Allowance (Transitional Provisions) Regulations 2008 (SI 2008/795) (as amended) in Vol.I of this series for those circumstances).

Sub-paragraphs (a) and (b) of para.7 were then revoked with effect from December 30, 2009, subject to a savings provision for certain claimants (see the Income Support (Prescribed Categories of Person) Regulations 2009 (SI 2009/3152) at p.823 in the 2015/16 edition of this volume).

See the 2015/16 edition of this volume, pp.592–597, for details of who was previ-

2.580

2.581

2.582

ously covered by para.7(a) and (b) and for the consequences of the introduction of ESA and the revocation of para.7(a) and (b). See also under "*Migration to ESA*" on p.596 of the 2015/16 edition of this volume for the reassessment of claimants with existing awards of incapacity benefit, severe disablement allowance and/or income support on the grounds of incapacity or disability.

Sub-paragraphs (c) and (d) of para.7, however, remain in force. Sub-paragraph (c) covers people who are treated as capable of work under regulations made under s.171E(1) of the Social Security Contributions and Benefits Act 1992 (disqualification, etc.). The relevant regulation is reg.18 of the Social Security (Incapacity for Work) Regulations 1995 (SI 1995/311)—see the 2010/11 edition of Vol.I in this series for these provisions. As this relates to the incapacity for work scheme, it seems likely that sub-para.(c) will rarely, if ever, be applicable. Sub-paragraph (d), however, remains applicable as it covers people who are entitled to statutory sick pay.

"Fit notes, not sick notes"

2.583   Note also the amendments made to reg.2 of the Social Security (Medical Evidence Regulations) 1976 (SI 1976/615) on April 6, 2010 (see Vol.III of this series). These change the format of medical certificates and the rules for their completion to allow a doctor to consider not only whether the person is unfit for work but also whether he may be able to work with appropriate support if available. The Med 3 and Med 5 certificates are replaced by a new single certificate called "Statement of Fitness for Work" on which doctors are encouraged to provide more information on the functional effects of the person's condition and to suggest options that would facilitate a return to work, such as a phased return to work, altered hours, amended duties and workplace adaptations. Where the advice does not result in a return to work, the DWP's guidance to doctors ("*Statement of Fitness for Work: A Guide for General Practitioners and other doctors*" (February 2010)) stated that the person will be treated as if the doctor had advised that he was not fit for work. Furthermore, since reg.2(1) of the Medical Evidence Regulations (as amended) only requires the production of a "statement given by a doctor in accordance with the rules set out in Part 1 of Schedule 1 to these Regulations" as evidence of incapacity or limited capability for work, this would seem to include a statement that the claimant may be fit for work (as well as a statement that he is not fit for work). The new form of certificate may therefore have little effect on the payment of benefit.

Paragraphs 8 and 9

2.584   These paragraphs were revoked on January 25, 2010. Paragraph 8 covered a person to whom reg.6(4)(a) applied (disabled workers) and para.9 a person to whom reg.6(4)(d) applied (people in employment living in care homes, etc.). Regulation 6(4)(a) and (d) had treated such people as not engaged in remunerative work. See the 2009/10 edition of this volume for these provisions. According to the Explanatory Memorandum which accompanied the Social Security (Miscellaneous Amendments) (No.5) Regulations 2009 (SI 2009/3228), which abolished these provisions, they had "become obsolete, and the current more generous ESA and WTC regimes ensure the right level of support for this client group". The Memorandum also states that very few claimants currently receive benefit under these provisions. One wonders, however, if this was at least partly due to the fact that the necessary investigation in order to determine whether para.8 applied was not always carried out (for an analysis of reg.6(4)(a) and para.8 and when they were applicable see in particular *R(IS) 10/05* discussed in the notes to paras 7 and 8 of Sch.1B in the 2009/10 edition of this volume). *R(IS) 10/05* will still be of relevance where, e.g. there was an alleged overpayment of income support before January 25, 2010 because a person had failed to report that he was doing some work but the question as to whether he may have been eligible for income support as a disabled worker under para.8 has not been (fully) considered.

There is transitional protection for claimants to whom either of these paragraphs applied on January 24, 2010 which continues until the claimant ceases to fall within the relevant paragraph or ceases to be entitled to income support, whichever is the earlier (see reg.4 of the Social Security (Miscellaneous Amendments) (No.5) Regulations 2009 (SI 2009/3228) on p.1778).

Paragraph 9A
See the notes to reg.6(5)–(8).   2.585

Paragraphs 10–12
Paragraphs 10 and 12 covered full-time students (defined in reg.61) who contrary   2.586
to the normal rule could claim income support.

Paragraph 10 applied to a full-time student who qualified for the disability or severe disability premium or who had been incapable of work, or treated as incapable of work, or treated as capable of work by virtue of reg.18 of the Incapacity for Work Regulations (disqualification for misconduct, etc.) (see the 2010/11 edition of Vol.I in this series for these Regulations), or entitled to statutory sick pay, for at least 28 weeks (two or more periods of incapacity counted as one continuous period unless there was a break of more than eight weeks).

Paragraph 12 applied to full-time students who were within the definition of "deaf" for one of the listed grant purposes.

These paragraphs were revoked on December 30, 2009, subject to a saving provi-   2.587
sion. See under *"Introduction of ESA"*, *"Revocation of paras 10 and 12 on December 30, 2009"* and *"Migration to ESA"* on p.598 of the 2015/16 edition of this volume for further details.

Paragraph 11 continued to protect disabled full-time students who no longer fell under para.7 of the former Sch.1 following its amendment on September 1, 1990. See *CIS 276/1989* on the pre-September 1990 form of para.7, which held that in asking whether the student was unlikely to obtain employment within a reasonable period of time, the period started with the date of claim, not with the end of the course. It is no longer of any application.

Paragraph 13
Paragraph 13 covered people who were registered as blind and for 28 weeks after   2.588
they ceased to be registered if they regained their sight. Paragraph 13 was revoked on December 30, 2009, subject to a saving provision. See under *"Introduction of ESA"*, *"Revocation of para.13 on December 30, 2009"* and *"Migration to ESA"* on p.599 of the 2015/16 edition of this volume for further details.

Paragraph 14
Sub-paragraph (a) covers a person who is incapable of work because of pregnancy   2.589
and sub-para.(b) applies for 11 weeks before the expected week of confinement plus 15 weeks after the pregnancy ends. In *CIS 542/2001* the issue was the relationship, if any, between sub-para.(a) and para.7. Paragraph 7 covered, inter alia, a person who was incapable of work or treated as incapable of work in accordance with Pt XIIA SSCBA 1992 or regulations made thereunder. Those regulations included reg.14 of the Incapacity for Work (General) Regulations 1995, the effect of which was that a pregnant woman was to be treated as incapable of work during any period when, because of her pregnancy, there was a serious risk to her health or that of the unborn child if she continued to work. Sub-paragraph (a), on the other hand, simply requires the woman to be incapable of work due to her pregnancy. The Secretary of State argued that sub-para.(a) had to be read as incorporating the stricter test in reg.14(a). The Commissioner, however, holds that sub-para.(a) stands alone. In his view, if it had been intended that sub-para.(a) was to incorporate the reg.14(a) test, this could have been expressly stated. Furthermore, the provision in para.14 had been included in the Income Support Regulations since they first came into force in 1987 (it had formerly appeared as para.9 of Sch.1). This was several years before the introduction of incapacity benefit and thus supported the conclusion that sub-para. (a) was free-standing and not dependent on any other provision dealing with incapacity. The Secretary of State had relied on s.171A(1) SSCBA 1992 which provides

that whether a person is capable or incapable of work is to be determined in accordance with Pt XIIA of the Act (thus including reg.14(a)). In the Commissioner's opinion, however, s.171A(1) had to be read subject to the later provisions of the Jobseekers Act 1995 and associated regulations (including s.124(1)(e) SSCBA, inserted by the 1995 Act, which provides that a person is entitled to income support if they fall into a prescribed category, and s.40 of the 1995 Act which authorises the making of transitional, consequential and saving provisions). The result is that sub-para.(a) applies to any woman who is incapable of work by reason of pregnancy.

Paragraph 14A

2.590   This covers a member of a couple who is on unpaid parental leave to care for a child who is a member of his household (lone parents with a child under five are already eligible for income support, as are couples where one member is ill or temporarily absent, see paras 1, 3, and 23). The right to claim parental leave first came into effect on December 15, 1999 (for details see the Maternity and Parental Leave etc. Regulations 1999 (SI 1999/3312)). To come within para.14A the person not be getting any kind of payment from his employer during the parental leave (sub.para. (1)(b) and (2)) and must have been entitled to working tax credit, child tax credit ("CTC") payable at a rate higher than the family element, housing benefit or council tax benefit immediately before the leave began. (Note that para.14A has not been updated to reflect the fact that council tax benefit was abolished on April 1, 2013.)

Paragraph 14B

2.591   This applies to a person who is entitled to and is on paternity leave and who: (i) is not entitled to statutory paternity pay or any other pay from his employer in respect of the paternity leave, *or* (ii) was entitled to working tax credit, child tax credit ("CTC") payable at a rate higher than the family element, housing benefit or council tax benefit immediately before the paternity leave began.

The new rights to paternity leave and adoption leave introduced by the Employment Act 2002 applied where the expected week of confinement or birth was on or after April 6, 2003 (in the case of adoption leave and paternity leave for adopters this applied where a child was either matched or placed for adoption on or after April 6, 2003 (Paternity and Adoption Leave Regulations 2002 (SI 2002/2788 reg.3)). Such rights were further extended by the Work and Families Act 2006, which introduced additional paternity leave (of up to 26 weeks) from April 3, 2011.

Part 7 of the Children and Families Act 2014 makes provision for shared parental leave and statutory shared parental pay in place of additional paternity leave and additional statutory paternity pay. These new entitlements apply where the expected week of childbirth starts on or after April 5, 2015 or the adoption placement occurs on or after that date. As a consequence, from April 5, 2015 "ordinary paternity leave" and "ordinary statutory paternity pay" have become just "paternity leave" and "statutory paternity pay". (Note that para.14B has not been updated to reflect the fact that council tax benefit was abolished on April 1, 2013.)

Paragraph 14C

2.592   This applies to those who are entitled to, and taking, parental bereavement leave and who either:

- are not entitled either to remuneration from their employers or statutory parental bereavement pay; or

- were entitled to working tax credit, child tax credit payable at a rate higher than the family element, housing benefit or council tax benefit on the day before that leave began,

or both. As council tax benefit was abolished on April 1, 2013 and parental bereavement leave did not come into existence until nearly seven years later on March 10, 2020, it is not possible—whatever the paragraph may say—to fall within it by virtue of entitlement to council tax benefit on the day before parental bereavement leave began.

Paragraph 15

Since October 7, 1996 the lower age limit for income support is now 16 in all 2.593
cases (SSCBA s.124(1)(a)). However, the exclusion for those who are treated as
receiving relevant education (see reg.12 and the notes to that regulation) remains,
except for those who fall within reg.13(2). This paragraph enables "qualifying
young people" covered by reg.13(2)(a)–(e) to claim income support; a "qualifying
young person" to whom reg.13(2)(h) applies will be eligible under para.18. See the
notes to reg.13 for the circumstances in which reg.13(2) applies.

Paragraph 15A

A "qualifying young person" who comes within reg.13(2)(a)–(e) is eligible for 2.594
income support under para.15 even though he is in full-time, non-advanced education. However, it is part of the definition of "qualifying young person" that the
person is under 20. Paragraph 15A was therefore introduced on April 6, 2009 to
extend eligibility for income support to 20-year-olds in full-time, non-advanced
education (defined in sub-para.(6)) who meet conditions which are the same as
those in reg.13(2)(c), (d) and (e), provided that they were accepted to attend,
enrolled on, or began the course before reaching the age of 19.

With effect from April 1, 2012 para.15A has been extended so that it is no longer
a requirement that the person was accepted to attend, enrolled on, or began the
course before becoming 19. It is now sufficient if this occurred while he was under
the age of 21. In addition, para.15A also applies to a person who reaches the age
of 21 while undertaking a course of full-time, non-advanced education. This will
enable such a person to finish his course, even though he is aged 21 (or over). The
definition of "course of full-time, non-advanced education" has also been clarified
to make clear that it applies provided that the course is not a course of advanced
education, as defined in reg.61(1).

Note that the references in the definition of "parent" in sub-para.(6) have not
been updated and still refer to sub-paragraph (5)(a), (b) and (c). Following the
April 2012 amendments, the provisions that were in sub-para.(5) are now in sub-
para.(4). The Interpretation Act 1978 ss.17(2)(a) and 23(1) will apply.

Paragraph 16

This paragraph was revoked with effect from October 7, 2006 because it only 2.595
applied to people who were aged 50 or over on October 6, 1996. By October 7,
2006 such a person would be 60 or over and therefore would have reached the
qualifying age for state pension credit (which was 60 at that time) and so would no
longer be entitled to income support (SSCBA s.124(1)(aa)).

Paragraph 16A

This provision was a transitional provision introduced as part of the new system 2.596
of bereavement benefits that came into effect on April 9, 2001 (see the 2005 edition
of this volume for the details of this provision). It ceased to have effect on April 10,
2006 and has been revoked.

Paragraph 18A

Paragraph 18A covered asylum seekers who were allowed under reg.21ZB to claim 2.597
income support retrospectively if their refugee status was subsequently recognised
by the IND. It was revoked on June 14, 2007 (as was reg.21ZB). However under
art.2(3) of the Asylum and Immigration (Treatment of Claimants, etc.) Act 2004
(Commencement No.7 and Transitional Provisions) Order 2007 the revocation of
para.18A does not apply in the case of a person who is recorded as a refugee on or
before June 14, 2007. For these purposes a person is recorded as a refugee on the
day that the Secretary of State notifies him that he has been recognised as a refugee
(art.2(4) of the Order).

For people recorded as refugees or granted humanitarian protection after June
14, 2007 there is a new system of "refugee integration loans" under s.13 of the

2004 Act (as amended by s.45 of the Immigration, Asylum and Nationality Act 2006). Decisions in relation to these loans are made by the Home Office Border and Immigration Agency. See further the Integration Loans for Refugees and Others Regulations 2007 (SI 2007/1598) and the Social Security (Claims and Payments) Amendment (No.2) Regulations 2007 (SI 2007/1866) (the latter amends Sch.9 to the Claims and Payments Regulations to allow for deductions to repay integration loans—see Vol.III in this series).

Paragraph 19

2.598   The previous form of para.19 only applied to a person who had to attend court as a justice of the peace, a party to any proceedings, a witness or a juror. From May 30, 2006 this has been extended so that para.19 now also applies where a person is required to attend a tribunal in a relevant capacity.

Paragraph 21

2.599   A new form of this paragraph was introduced on January 25, 2010 as a consequence of the revocation of Pt VI (Urgent Cases) of the Income Support Regulations on that date (see the General Note to Pt VI). Claimants who first fell within reg.2(1) of and para.1 of Pt I of the Schedule to the Social Security (Immigration and Asylum) Consequential Amendments Regulations 2000 (SI 2000/636) after January 24, 2010 could claim income support at the full rate (as opposed to the urgent cases rate) under reg.22B. Paragraph 1 of Pt I of the Schedule to the 2000 Regulations related to claimants with limited leave to enter or remain in the UK (and who, but for that paragraph and reg.2 of the 2000 Regulations, would have been persons subject to immigration control) and who were temporarily without funds because remittances to them from abroad had been disrupted. Entitlement to income support lasted for a maximum of 42 days—or a number of periods not exceeding 42 days in total—within the same period of leave.

Paragraph 1 of Pt I of the Schedule to the 2000 Regulations was revoked with effect from October 29, 2013 by reg.9(3) of the Social Security (Miscellaneous Amendments) (No.3) Regulations 2013 (SI 2013/2536) on the basis that the provision was rarely used because people could use credit cards, etc. to tide them over. Regulation 22B (together with other income support provisions that involved entitlement under para.1 of Pt I of the Schedule to the 2000 Regulations) was also revoked. Paragraph 21, however, has not been revoked because it concerns possible entitlement to income support under reg.2 of the 2000 Regulations as a whole (see reg.2(4) and (5)) and is not restricted to entitlement under reg.2(1).

Paragraph 22

2.600   A person required to live in a bail hostel is not "detained in custody" (*R(IS) 17/93*; note the effect of Sch.7 para.9, if a person in a bail hostel is a member of a couple). However, once a person has been charged, he is detained in custody pending trial, even if subsequently no trial takes place (*R(IS) 1/94*). See the notes to "prisoner" in reg.21(3). The definition of prisoner was amended from April 10, 1995 to reverse the effect of *Chief Adjudication Officer v Carr* (reported as *R(IS) 20/95*) which held that a person serving a prison sentence was not "in custody" while on home leave.

Paragraph 23

2.601   Someone in this situation could not come within para.1 because they would not be a lone parent while the absence of the partner was only temporary, but clearly deserves the same treatment in these circumstances.

Paragraphs 24–25

2.602   These paragraphs are no longer of any practical application because they relate to the old incapacity for work regime. However, they have not been formally revoked and so are being retained, together with the note to them.

Paragraphs 24 and 25 cover those who are appealing against a decision that they are capable of work under the "own occupation test" (para.24) or the personal capability assessment" (para.25). See the 2010/11 edition of Vol.I of this series for full details of these tests and when they apply.

Under para.24, if the claimant's own doctor continues to certify that he is incapable of work while he is pursuing an appeal against the incapacity decision, he will be eligible for income support pending the determination of the appeal. This means the final determination of the appeal, e.g. if it is taken to the Social Security Commissioner, confirmed in *CIS 2654/1999*. The person does not have to have been in receipt of income support before the incapacity decision was made. If para.24 applies full income support is payable (compare para.25).

If the claimant is appealing against capacity for work on the basis of the personal capability assessment, there is no requirement under para.25 for him to continue to submit medical certificates from his own doctor. This is because they are no longer required once the personal capability assessment has been applied. Again it is not necessary for the person to have been in receipt of income support before the incapacity decision was made. But if para.25 applies, the claimant's income support is reduced by 20 per cent of the appropriate personal allowance for a single claimant of his age until the appeal is determined (reg.22A), unless he is appealing after failing his first all work test or personal capability assessment and immediately before April 13, 1995 he had been incapable of work for 28 weeks or in receipt of invalidity benefit or severe disablement allowance (reg.22A(3); and see the transitional protection in reg.27(3) of the Income Support (General) (Jobseeker's Allowance Consequential Amendments) Regulations 1996 referred to in the note to reg.22A(3)). (If the appeal is successful, the reduction will be repaid.) See above for when an appeal is determined. **2.603**

In order to receive full benefit, a claimant who is appealing against a failure to satisfy the personal capability assessment will have to sign on as available for work and claim JSA (unless any of the other paragraphs of Sch.1B apply; after the introduction of ESA on October 27, 2008 he could also consider claiming ESA). This could place the claimant in a dilemma if he is maintaining that he is unable to work. The best course may be for him to say to the Job Centre that he has been found capable of work and that he will accept any suitable work having regard to his limitations (see reg.13(3) of the JSA Regulations 1996). However, the fact that he has claimed JSA will not prejudice the appeal about incapacity as it will postdate the decision under appeal (s.12(8)(a) SSA 1998).

It will be noted that both paras 24 and 25 refer to a person who "has made and is pursuing an appeal" against an incapacity decision. There will usually be a gap between the date that the incapacity decision takes effect and the date the appeal is lodged. Can paras 24 or 25 apply during this gap? According to the Commissioner in *CIS 2075/2002* the legislation implies that benefit will be paid in respect of the period between such a decision being given and an appeal being brought, at least if the appeal is not late or is admitted despite its lateness (and moreover this also applied where an appeal had been rejected as not duly made but was later reinstated as had occurred in the case before him). He therefore agreed with the Secretary of State that the claimant had remained entitled to income support ever since the decision was made that he was not incapable of work. However, the difficulty was the procedural hurdles created by the Social Security Act 1998 and the Decisions and Appeals Regulations 1999. The question was, if lodging an appeal or having one reinstated retrospectively did affect entitlement to income support, what was the ground for backdating an income support claim or for revision or supersession and from what date was the supersession, if supersession was appropriate, effective? The Commissioner found a solution to this dilemma on the facts of the case before him but suggested that amendments to the Decisions and Appeals Regulations may be needed to adequately cater for decision-making under paras 24–25.

However, in *R(IS)2/05* the Commissioner disagreed with *CIS/2075/2002* as in his **2.604** view the legislation contained no such implication. He held that there was no entitlement to income support under para.25 in the period between the date of the decision that supersedes the award of benefit on the ground that the person is not incapable of work and the date of the appeal against that decision. On the Commissioner's reasoning the same would apply in relation to para.24.

The problems highlighted by these decisions lead to the amendment made to para.25 with effect from March 18, 2005. This provides that para.25 applies from the date that the determination that the claimant is not incapable of work takes effect. Associated amendments were also made to the Decisions and Appeals Regulations 1999 (see Vol.III of this series). Two new provisions were introduced into reg.3 of those regulations: reg.3(7C) which allows for revision of a decision to terminate income support entitlement where that entitlement was ended because the claimant was found capable of work and he appeals that decision (reg.3(7C) was further amended on April 10, 2006 to allow for revision of the income support decision where the incapacity determination is revised); and reg.3(7B) which provides that where the appeal against the incapacity decision is successful (or, from April 10, 2006, lapses) the decision to award reduced rate income support under reg.22A can be revised (in practice this has happened and the reduction has been repaid even in the absence of such an express provision). A further provision (reg.3(7F)), introduced on April 10, 2006, allows for revision of a decision to remove the disability premium (in a case where a claimant found capable of work had remained entitled to income support on another ground) and the claimant's appeal against the incapacity decision is subsequently successful or the incapacity decision is revised. In addition a new reg.6(2)(n) deals with the situation where income support has been disallowed as a result of the incapacity decision and the claimant appeals against that disallowance (as well as the incapacity decision). In the past, if the appeal against the income support disallowance was heard before the appeal against the incapacity decision (and assuming that the claimant did not qualify for income support on any other ground), the tribunal would (unless it adjourned that appeal pending the outcome of the incapacity appeal) be bound to uphold the disallowance decision. If the incapacity appeal subsequently succeeded, there was no provision that enabled the first tribunal's decision upholding the income support disallowance to be revised. However, reg.6(2)(n) of the 1999 Regulations now provides for supersession of the first tribunal's decision in these circumstances; in addition a new reg.7(34) provides that such a supersession takes effect from the date that income support was terminated as a result of the decision that the person was not incapable of work.

See *CIS/2445/2005* in the note to para.7 which highlights the problems that can occur in cases where a person who has been treated as capable of work because he failed to return the incapacity for work questionnaire (IB50) makes a (further) claim for income support which is refused and his appeal against the incapacity decision subsequently succeeds (note that paras 24 and 25 only apply while a person is appealing against a decision that he has failed the own occupation test/personal capability assessment; they do not apply in the case of a claimant who has been treated as capable of work because he has failed to return the IB50 (or attend a medical examination)).

Paragraph 28

2.605   Paragraph 11 of the former Sch.1 applied to a person in receipt of a training allowance. Paragraph 28 only covers a person under 25 who is on a training course provided by the Secretary of State, the Welsh Ministers, or, in Scotland, by a local enterprise company. However, under reg.170 of the JSA Regulations 1996 a person in receipt of a training allowance (in respect of training *other* than that covered by para.28) may qualify for income-based JSA without having to be available for, or actively seek, employment or enter into a jobseeker's agreement.

Note that as a result of the new child benefit rules introduced on April 10, 2006, a person under 20 who is on "approved training" can come within the definition of "qualifying young person within the meaning of s.142 of the Contributions and

Benefits Act" and so count as in relevant education (see reg.12 and the notes to that regulation). This paragraph has therefore been amended with effect from April 10, 2006 to exclude a qualifying young person or child.

SCHEDULE 2   Regulations 17 [³ (1)] and 18

A<small>PPLICABLE</small> A<small>MOUNTS</small>

[³⁵P<small>ART</small> I

Personal Allowances

1.—The weekly amounts specified in column (2) below in respect of each person or couple   **2.606**
specified in column (1) shall be the weekly amounts specified for the purposes of regulations
17(1) and 18(1) (applicable amounts and polygamous marriages).

Column (1)	*Column (2)*
Person or Couple	*Amount*
(1) Single claimant aged—	
(a) except where head (b) or (c) of this sub-paragraph applies, less than 18;	(1)(a) [⁸² £59.20];
[²⁸(b) less than 18 who falls within any of the circumstances specified in paragraph 1A;]	(b) [⁸² £59.20];
(c) less than 18 who satisfies the condition in [⁶⁵ paragraph 11(1)(a)]	(c) [⁸² £59.20];
(d) not less than 18 but less than 25;	(d) [⁸² £59.20];
(e) not less than 25.	(e) [⁸² £74.70].
(2) Lone parent aged—	(2)
(a) except where head (b) or (c) of this sub-paragraph applies, less than 18;	(a) [⁸² £59.20];
[²⁸(b) less than 18 who falls within any of the circumstances specified in paragraph 1A;]	(b) [⁸² £59.20];
(c) less than 18 who satisfies the condition in [⁶⁵ paragraph 11(1)(a)]	(c) [⁸² £59.20];
(d) not less than 18.	(d) [⁸² £74.70].
[²⁸(3) Couple—	(3)
(a) where both members are aged less than 18 and—	(a) [⁸² £89.45];
(i) at least one of them is treated as responsible for a child; or	
(ii) had they not been members of a couple, each would have qualified for income support under regulation 4ZA [⁷¹ or income-related employment and support allowance]; or	
(iii) the claimant's partner satisfies the requirement of section 3(1)(f)(iii) of the Jobseekers Act 1995 (prescribed circumstances for persons aged 16 but less than 18); or	
(iv) there is in force in respect of the claimant's partner a direction under section 16 of the Jobseekers Act 1995 (persons under 18: severe hardship);	
(b) where both members are aged less than 18 and head (a) does not apply but one member of the couple falls within any of the circumstances specified in paragraph 1A;	(b) [⁸² £59.20];
(c) where both members are aged less than 18 and heads (a) and (b) do not apply;	(c) [⁸² £59.20];
(d) where both members are aged not less than 18;	(d) [⁸² £117.40];
(e) where one member is aged not less than 18 and the	(e) [⁸² £117.40];

Column (1)	Column (2)
Person or Couple	*Amount*

other member is a person under 18 who—

   (i) qualifies for income support under regulation 4ZA [⁷¹ or income-related employment and support allowance], or who would so qualify if he were not a member of a couple; or

   (ii) satisfies the requirements of section 3(1)(f)(iii) of the Jobseekers Act 1995 (prescribed circumstances for persons aged 16 but less than 18); or

   (iii) is the subject of a direction under section 16 of the Jobseekers Act 1995 (persons under 18: severe hardship);

(f) where the claimant is aged not less than 18 but less than 25 and his partner is a person under 18 who—   (f) [⁸² £59.20];

   (i) would not qualify for income support under regulation 4ZA [⁷¹ or income-related employment and support allowance] if he were not a member of a couple; and

   (ii) does not satisfy the requirements of section 3(1)(f)(iii) of the Jobseekers Act 1995 (prescribed circumstances for persons aged 16 but less than 18); and

   (iii) is not the subject of a direction under section 16 of the Jobseekers Act 1995 (persons under 18: severe hardship);

(g)   where the claimant is aged not less than 25 and his partner is a person under 18 who—   (g) [⁸² £74.70].

   (i) would not qualify for income support under regulation 4ZA [⁷¹ or income-related employment and support allowance] if he were not a member of a couple; and

   (ii does not satisfy the requirements of section 3(1)(f)(iii) of the Jobseekers Act 1995 (prescribed circumstances for persons aged 16 but less than 18); and

   (iii) is not the subject of a direction under section 16 of the Jobseekers Act 1995 (persons under 18: severe hardship).]]

2.607   [²⁸ **1A.**—(1) The circumstances referred to in paragraph 1 are that—

   (a) the person has no parents nor any person acting in the place of his parents;

   (b) the person—

       (i) is not living with his parents nor any person acting in the place of his parents; and

       (ii) in England and Wales, was being looked after by a local authority pursuant to a relevant enactment who placed him with some person other than a close relative of his; or in Scotland, was in the care of a local authority under a relevant enactment and whilst in that care was not living with his parents or any close relative, or was in custody in any institution to which the Prison Act 1952 or the Prisons (Scotland) Act 1989 applied immediately before he attained the age of 16;

   (c) the person is in accommodation which is other than his parental home, and which is other than the home of a person acting in the place of his parents, who entered that accommodation—

       (i) as part of a programme of rehabilitation or resettlement, that programme being under the supervision of the probation service or a local authority; or

       (ii) in order to avoid physical or sexual abuse; or

       (iii) because of a mental or physical handicap or illness and needs such accommodation because of his handicap or illness;

   (d) the person is living away from his parents and any person who is acting in the place of his parents in a case where his parents are or, as the case may be, that person is, unable financially to support him and his parents are, or that person is—

       (i) chronically sick or mentally or physically disabled; or

       (ii) detained in custody pending trial or sentence upon conviction or under sentence imposed by a court; of

      (iii) prohibited from entering or re-entering Great Britain; or

  (e) the person of necessity has to live away from his parents and any person acting in the place of his parents because—

      (i) he is estranged from his parents and that person; or

      (ii) he is in physical or moral danger; or

      (iii) there is a serious risk to his physical or mental health.

(2) In this paragraph—

  (a) "chronically sick or mentally or physically disabled" has the same meaning it has in regulation 13(3)(b) (circumstances in which persons in relevant education are to be entitled to income support);

  (b) in England and Wales, any reference to a person acting in place of a person's parents includes a reference to—

      (i) where the person is being looked after by a local authority or voluntary organisation who place him with a family, a relative of his, or some other suitable person, the person with whom the person is placed, whether or not any payment is made to him in connection with the placement; or

      (ii) in any other case, any person with parental responsibility for the child, and for this purpose "parental responsibility" has the meaning it has in the Children Act 1989 by virtue of section 3 of that Act;

  (c) in Scotland, any reference to a person acting in place of a person's parents includes a reference to a local authority or voluntary organisation where the person is in their care under a relevant enactment, or to a person with whom the person is boarded out by a local authority or voluntary organisation whether or not any payment is made by them.]

[³⁵ **2.**—[⁵⁹ . . .]]   **2.608**

[¹⁷ **2A.**—[⁵⁵ . . .]]   **2.609**

PART II   **Regulations 17[³(1)(c)**
                                    [³and 18(1)](d)

Family Premium

3.—[⁵⁹ . . .]   **2.610**

PART III   **Regulations 17[³(1)](d)**
                                      [³and 18(1)](e)

Premiums

4.—Except as provided in paragraph 5, the weekly premiums specified in Part IV of this Schedule shall, for the purposes of regulations 17[³(1)](d)[³ and 18(1)](e), be applicable to a claimant who satisfies the condition specified in [⁴²paragraphs 8A] [¹⁰ to 14ZA] in respect of that premium.   **2.611**

5.—Subject to paragraph 6, where a claimant satisfies the conditions in respect of more than one premium in this Part of this Schedule, only one premium shall be applicable to him and, if they are different amounts, the higher or highest amount shall apply.

[⁵⁸ **6.**—(1) Subject to sub-paragraph (2), the following premiums, namely—

  (a) a severe disability to which paragraph 13 applies;

  (b) an enhanced disability premium to which paragraph 13A applies;

  (c) [⁵⁹ . . .]; and

  (d) a carer premium to which paragraph 14ZA applies,

may be applicable in addition to any other premium that may apply under this Schedule.

(2) An enhanced disability premium in respect of a person shall not be applicable in addition to—

  (a) a pensioner premium under paragraph 9 or 9A; or

  (b) a higher pension premium under paragraph 10.]

7.—[¹⁰(1) Subject to sub-paragraph (2)] for the purposes of this Part of this Schedule, once a premium is applicable to a claimant under this Part, a person shall be treated as being in receipt of any benefit—

  (a) in the case of a benefit to which the Social Security (Overlapping Benefits) Regulations 1979 applies, for any period during which, apart from the provisions of those Regulations, he would be in receipt of that benefit; and

(b) for any period spent by a claimant in undertaking a course of training or instruction provided or approved by the [¹² Secretary of State [⁶⁸ . . .]] under section 2 of the Employment and Training Act 1973 [¹¹, or by [⁶⁹ Skills Development Scotland,] Scottish Enterprise or Highlands and Islands Enterprise under section 2 of the Enterprise and New Towns (Scotland) Act 1990,] [⁷or for any period during which he is in receipt of a training allowance].

[¹⁰(2) For the purposes of the carer premium under paragraph 14ZA, a person shall be treated as being in receipt of [⁴⁹ carer's allowance] by virtue of sub-paragraph (1)(a) only if and for so long as the person in respect of whose care the allowance has been claimed remains in receipt of attendance allowance [¹⁵ , [⁷⁵ . . .] the care component of disability living allowance at the highest or middle rate prescribed in accordance with section 37ZB(3) of the Social Security Act [SSCBA, s.72(3)]] [⁷⁵ or the daily living component of personal independence payment at the standard or enhanced rate in accordance with section 78(3) of the 2012 Act] [⁷⁶ or armed forces independence payment].]

Lone Parent Premium

2.612   **8.**—[²⁹. . .].

[⁴² Bereavement Premium

2.613   **8A.**—[⁶⁷ . . .]]

[Pensioner premium for persons under 75

2.614   [⁵⁴ **9.**—The condition is that the claimant has a partner aged [⁷⁰ not less than the qualifying age for state pension credit] but less than 75.]

Pensioner premium for persons 75 and over

2.615   [⁵⁴ **9A.**—The condition is that the claimant has a partner aged not less than 75 but less than 80.]]

Higher Pensioner Premium

2.616   **10.**—[⁵⁴ (1) [⁶⁵ Subject to sub-paragraph (6), the] condition is that—

(a) the claimant's partner is aged not less than 80; or

(b) the claimant's partner is aged less than 80 but [⁷⁰ not less than the qualifying age for state pension credit] and either—

    (i) the additional condition specified in [⁵⁸ paragraph 12(1)(a), (c) or (d)] is satisfied; or

    (ii) the claimant was entitled to, or was treated as being in receipt of, income support and—

        (aa) the disability premium was or, as the case may be, would have been, applicable to him in respect of a benefit week within eight weeks of [⁷⁰ the day his partner attained the qualifying age for state pension credit]; and

        (bb) he has, subject to sub-paragraph (3), remained continuously entitled to income support since his partner attained [⁷⁰ the qualifying age for state pension credit].

(2) . . .]

(3) For the purposes of this paragraph and paragraph 12—

(a) once the higher pensioner premium is applicable to a claimant, if he then ceases, for a period of eight weeks or less, to be entitled to [⁴¹or treated as entitled to] income support, he shall, on becoming re-entitled to income support, thereafter be treated as having been continuously entitled thereto;

(b) in so far as [⁵⁴ sub-paragraph (1)(b)(ii) is] concerned, if a claimant ceases to be entitled to [⁴¹or treated as entitled to] income support for a period not exceeding eight weeks which includes [⁷⁰ the day his partner attained the qualifying age for state pension credit], he shall, on becoming re-entitled to income support, thereafter be treated as having been continuously entitled thereto.

[³³(4) In the case of a claimant who is a welfare to work beneficiary, references in sub-paragraphs (1)(b)(ii) [⁶⁵ . . .] and (3)(b) to a period of 8 weeks shall be treated as references to a period of [⁶⁴ 104 weeks].]

[⁴¹ (5) For the purposes of this paragraph, a claimant shall be treated as having been entitled to and in receipt of income support throughout any period which comprises only days on which he was participating in an employment zone programme and was not entitled to income support because, as a consequence of his participation in that programme, he was engaged in remunerative work or had income in excess of his applicable amount as prescribed in Part IV.]

[⁶⁵ (6) The condition is not satisfied if the claimant's partner to whom sub-paragraph (1) refers is a long-term patient.]

Disability Premium

11.—[[65] —(1) Subject to sub-paragraph (2), the] condition is that—

   (a) where the claimant is a single claimant or a lone parent, [[54] . . .] the additional condition specified in paragraph 12 is satisfied; or

   (b) where the claimant has a partner, either—

      [[54] (i) the claimant satisfies the additional condition specified in paragraph [[58] 12(1) (a), (b), (c) or (d)]; or]

      (ii) his partner [[70] has not attained the qualifying age for state pension credit] and the additional condition specified in [[58] paragraph 12(1)(a), (c) or (d)] is satisfied by his partner.

[[65] (2) The condition is not satisfied if—

   (a) the claimant is a single claimant or a lone parent and (in either case) is a long-term patient;

   (b) the claimant is a member of a couple or polygamous marriage and each member of the couple or polygamous marriage is a long-term patient; or

   (c) the claimant is a member of a couple or a polygamous marriage and a member of that couple or polygamous marriage is—

      (i) a long-term patient; and

      (ii) the only member of the couple or polygamous marriage to whom sub-paragraph (1)(b) refers.]

2.617

Additional condition for the Higher Pensioner and Disability Premiums

12.—(1) Subject to sub-paragraph (2) and paragraph 7 the additional condition referred to in paragraphs 10 and 11 is that either—

   (a) the claimant or, as the case may be, his partner—

      (i) is in receipt of one or more of the following benefits: attendance allowance, [[15]disability living allowance, [[76] armed forces independence payment,]][[75] personal independence payment,] [[50] the disability element or the severe disability element of working tax credit as specified in regulation 20(1)(b) and (f) of the Working Tax Credit (Entitlement and Maximum Rate) Regulations 2002], mobility supplement, [[25]long-term incapacity benefit] under [[22]Part II of the Contributions and Benefits Act or severe disablement allowance under Part III of that Act] [[1]but, in the case of [[25]long-term incapacity benefit] or severe disablement allowance only where it is paid in respect of him]; or

      (ii) is provided by the Secretary of State with an invalid carriage or other vehicle under section 5(2) of the National Health Service Act 1977 (other services) or, in Scotland, under section 46 of the National Health Service (Scotland) Act 1978 (provision of vehicles) or receives payments by way of grant from the Secretary of State under paragraph 2 of Schedule 2 to that 1977 Act (additional provisions as to vehicles) or, in Scotland, under that section 46; or

      [[77] (iii) is certified as severely sight impaired or blind by a consultant ophthalmologist; or]

   [[26](b) the claimant—

      (i) is entitled to statutory sick pay or [[27]is, or is treated as, incapable of work,] in accordance with the provisions of Part XIIA of the Contributions and Benefits Act and the regulations made thereunder (incapacity for work), and

      (ii) has been so entitled or so incapable [[27], or has been treated as so incapable,] for a continuous period of not less than—

         (aa) 196 days in the case of a claimant who is terminally ill within the meaning of section 30B(4) of the Contributions and Benefits Act; or

         (bb) [[63] subject to [[65] paragraph 2A] of Schedule 7] 364 days in any other case; and for these purposes any two or more periods of entitlement or incapacity separated by a break of not more than 56 days shall be treated as one continuous period; or]

   [[54] (c) the claimant's partner was in receipt of long-term incapacity benefit under Part II of the Contributions and Benefits Act when entitlement to that benefit ceased on account of the payment of a retirement pension under that Act [[81] or a state pension under Part 1 of the Pensions Act 2014] and—

      (i) the claimant has since remained continuously entitled to income support;

      (ii) the higher pensioner premium or disability premium has been applicable to the claimant; and

      (iii) the partner is still alive;

   (d) except where paragraph [[63] 2A [[65] . . .]] of Schedule 7 (patients) applies, the claimant

2.618

or, as the case may be, his partner was in receipt of attendance allowance [^{75} , disability living allowance or personal independence payment]—

    (i) but payment of that benefit has been suspended under the [^{60} Social Security (Attendance Allowance) Regulations 1991 [^{75} , the Social Security (Disability Living Allowance) Regulations 1991 or regulations made under section 86(1) (hospital in-patients) of the 2012 Act]] or otherwise abated as a consequence of the claimant or his partner becoming a patient within the meaning of regulation 21(3); and

    (ii) a higher pensioner premium or disability premium has been applicable to the claimant.]

[^{34}(1A) In the case of a claimant who is a welfare to work beneficiary, the reference in sub-paragraph (1)(b) to a period of 56 days shall be treated as a reference to a period of [^{64} 104 weeks].]

[^{77} (2) For the purposes of sub-paragraph (1)(a)(iii), a person who has ceased to be certified as severely sight impaired or blind on regaining his eyesight shall nevertheless be treated as severely sight impaired or blind, as the case may be, and as satisfying the additional condition set out in that sub-paragraph for a period of 28 weeks following the date on which he ceased to be so certified.]

    (3) [^{26} . . .]

    (4) For the purpose of [^{58} sub-paragraph (1)(c) and (d)], once the higher pensioner premium is applicable to the claimant by virtue of his satisfying the condition specified in that provision, if he then ceases, for a period of eight weeks or less, to be entitled to income support, he shall on again becoming so entitled to income support, immediately thereafter be treated as satisfying the condition in [^{58} sub-paragraph (1)(c) and (d)].

[^{4}(5) For the purposes of sub-paragraph (1)(b), once the disability premium is applicable to a claimant by virtue of his satisfying the additional condition specified in that provision, he shall continue to be treated as satisfying that condition for any period spent by him in undertaking a course of training provided under section 2 of the Employment and Training Act 1973 [^{7}or for any period during which he is in receipt of a training allowance].]

[^{25}(6) For the purposes of [^{58} sub-paragraph (1)(a)(i) and (c)], a reference to a person in receipt of long-term incapacity benefit includes a person in receipt of short-term incapacity benefit at a rate equal to the long-term rate by virtue of section 30B(4)(a) of the Contributions and Benefits Act (short-term incapacity benefit for a person who is terminally ill), or who would be or would have been in receipt of short-term incapacity benefit at such a rate but for the fact that the rate of short-term incapacity benefit already payable to him is or was equal to or greater than the long-term rate.]

    [^{40} [^{61} . . .]]

Severe Disability Premium

2.619   **13.**—(1) The condition is that the claimant is a severely disabled person.

    (2) For the purposes of sub-paragraph (1), a claimant shall be treated as being a severely disabled person if, and only if—

    (a) in the case of a single claimant[^{19}, a lone parent or a claimant who is treated as having no partner in consequence of sub-paragraph (2A)]—

        (i) he is in receipt of attendance allowance [^{15}[^{75} . . .] the care component of disability living allowance at the highest or middle rate prescribed in accordance with section 37ZB(3) of the Social Security Act [SSCBA, s.72(3)]] [^{75} or the daily living component of personal independence payment at the standard or enhanced rate in accordance with section 78(3) of the 2012 Act] [^{76} or armed forces independence payment], and

        (ii) subject to sub-paragraph (3), he has no non-dependants aged 18 or over [^{23}normally residing with him or with whom he is normally residing,] and

        (iii) [^{41}no person is entitled to, and in receipt of, [^{49} a carer's allowance] under section 70 of the Contributions and Benefits Act [^{80} or has an award of universal credit which includes the carer element] in respect of caring for him;]

    (b) [^{42} in the case of a claimant who] has a partner—

        (i) he is in receipt of attendance allowance [^{15}, [^{75} . . .] the care component of disability living allowance at the highest or middle rate prescribed in accordance with section 37ZB(3) of the Social Security Act [SSCBA, s.72(3)]] [^{75} or the daily living component of personal independence payment at the standard or enhanced rate in accordance with section 78(3) of the 2012 Act] [^{76} or armed forces independence payment]; and

        (ii) his partner is also in receipt of such an allowance or, if he is a member of a polygamous marriage, all the partners of that marriage are in receipt thereof; and

(iii) subject to sub-paragraph (3), he has no non-dependants aged 18 or over [²³nor-mally residing with him or with whom he is normally residing,]

and either [⁴¹a person is entitled to, and in receipt of, [⁴⁹ a carer's allowance] [⁸⁰ or has an award of universal credit which includes the carer element] in respect of caring for only one of the couple or, in the case of a polygamous marriage, for one or more but not all the partners of the marriage or, as the case may be, no person is entitled to, and in receipt of, such an allowance] [⁸⁰ or has such an award of universal credit] in respect of caring for either member of the couple or any partner of the polygamous marriage.

[¹⁹(2A) Where a claimant has a partner who does not satisfy the condition in sub-paragraph (2)(b)(ii), and that partner is [⁷⁷ severely sight impaired or blind or treated as severely sight impaired or blind] within the meaning of paragraph 12(1)(a)(iii) and (2), that partner shall be treated for the purposes of sub-paragraph (2) as if he were not a partner of the claimant.]

(3) For the purposes of sub-paragraph (2)(a)(ii) and (2)(b)(iii) no account shall be taken of—

(a) a person receiving attendance allowance [¹⁵, [⁷⁵ . . .] the care component of disability living allowance at the highest or middle rate prescribed in accordance with section 37ZB(3) of the Social Security Act [SSCBA, s.72(3)]] [⁷⁵ or the daily living compo-nent of personal independence payment at the standard or enhanced rate in accord-ance with section 78(3) of the 2012 Act] [⁷⁶ or armed forces independence payment]; or

(b) [²¹. . .]

(c) subject to sub-paragraph (4), a person who joins the claimant's household for the first time in order to care for the claimant or his partner and immediately before so joining the claimant or his partner was treated as a severely disabled person; [¹⁹ or

(d) a person who is [⁷⁷ severely sight impaired or blind or treated as severely sight impaired or blind] within the meaning of paragraph 12(1)(a)(iii) and (2).]

[¹(3A) For the purposes of sub-paragraph (2)(b) a person shall be treated [⁴¹. . .]

(a) [⁴¹ as being in receipt of] attendance allowance[¹⁵, or the care component of disability living allowance at the highest or middle rate prescribed in accordance with section 37ZB(3) of the Social Security Act [SSCBA, s.72(3)]] if he would, but for his being a patient for a period exceeding 28 days, be so in receipt;

(b) [⁴¹ as being entitled to and in receipt of [⁴⁹ a carer's allowance] [⁸⁰ or having an award of universal credit which includes the carer element] if he would, but for the person for whom he was caring being a patient in hospital for a period exceeding 28 days, be so entitled and in receipt [⁸⁰ of carer's allowance or have such an award of universal credit].]]

[⁷⁵ (c) as being in receipt of the daily living component of personal independence payment at the standard or enhanced rate in accordance with section 78(3) of the 2012 Act if he would, but for a suspension of benefit in accordance with regulations under section 86(1) (hospital in-patients) of the 2012 Act, be so in receipt.]

[²²(3ZA) For the purposes of sub-paragraph (2)(a)(iii) and (2)(b), no account shall be taken of an award of [⁴⁹ a carer's allowance] [⁸⁰ or universal credit which includes the carer element] to the extent that payment of such an award is back-dated for a period before [⁶⁶ the date on which the award is first paid].]

(4) Sub-paragraph (3)(c) shall apply only for the first 12 weeks following the date on which the person to whom that provision applies first joins the claimant's household.

[⁴⁵ (5) In sub-paragraph (2)(a)(iii) and (b), references to a person being in receipt of [⁴⁹ a carer's allowance] [⁸⁰ or as having an award of universal credit which includes the carer element] shall include references to a person who would have been in receipt of that allowance [⁸⁰ or had such an award] but for the application of a restriction under section [⁷² 6B or] 7 of the Social Security Fraud Act 2001 (loss of benefit provisions).]

[⁸⁰ (6) For the purposes of this paragraph, a person has an award of universal credit which includes the carer element if the person has an award of universal credit which includes an amount which is the carer element under regulation 29 of the Universal Credit Regulations 2013.]

[⁴³ Enhanced disability premium

13A.— [⁷⁵ ⁷⁶ (1) Subject to sub-paragraph (2), the condition is that—

(a) the claimant; or

(b) the claimant's partner, if any, who has not attained the qualifying age for state pension credit,

is a person to whom sub-paragraph (1ZA) applies.

2.620

(1ZA) This sub-paragraph applies to the person mentioned in sub-paragraph (1) where—

    (a) armed forces independence payment is payable to that person;

    (b) the care component of disability living allowance is, or would, but for a suspension of benefit in accordance with regulations under section 113(2) of the Contributions and Benefits Act or but for an abatement as a consequence of hospitalization, be payable to that person at the highest rate prescribed under section 72(3) of that Act; or

    (c) the daily living component of personal independence payment is, or would, but for regulations made under section 86(1) (hospital in-patients) of the 2012 Act, be payable to that person at the enhanced rate in accordance with section 78(2) of that Act.]

[73 (1A) Where the condition in sub-paragraph (1) ceases to be satisfied because of the death of a child or young person, the condition is that the claimant [74 or partner] is entitled to child benefit in respect of that person under section 145A of the Contributions and Benefits Act (entitlement after death of child or qualifying young person).]

    [65 (2) The condition is not satisfied if the person to whom sub-paragraph (1) refers is—

        (a) [50 . . .]

        (b) a single claimant or a lone parent and (in either case) is a long-term patient;

        (c) a member of a couple or polygamous marriage and each member of the couple or polygamous marriage is a long-term patient; or

        (d) a member of a couple or polygamous marriage who—

            (i) is a long-term patient; and

            (ii) is the only member of the couple or polygamous marriage to whom sub-paragraph (1) refers.]

Disabled Child Premium

2.621
    14.—[59 . . . 65]

[10Carer premium

2.622
    14ZA.—(1) [13Subject to sub-paragraphs (3) and (4),] the condition is that the claimant or his partner is, or both of them are, [41 entitled to [49 a carer's allowance] under section 70 of the Contributions and Benefits Act]

    (2) [57 . . .]

    [41 [48 (3) Where a carer premium is awarded but—

        (a) the person in respect of whose care the [49 carer's allowance] has been awarded dies; or

        (b) in any other case the person in respect of whom a carer premium has been awarded ceases to be entitled [57 . . .] to [49 a carer's allowance],

the condition for the award of the premium shall be treated as satisfied for a period of eight weeks from the relevant date specified in sub-paragraph (3A) below.

    (3A) The relevant date for the purposes of sub-paragraph (3) above shall be—

        (a) [57 where sub-paragraph (3)(a) applies,] the Sunday following the death of the person in respect of whose care [49 a carer's allowance] has been awarded or the date of death if the death occurred on a Sunday;

        (b) [57 . . .]

        (c) in any other case, the date on which the person who has been entitled to [46 a carer's allowance] ceases to be entitled to that allowance.]

    (4) Where a person who has been entitled to an invalid care allowance ceases to be entitled to that allowance and makes a claim for income support, the condition for the award of the carer premium shall be treated as satisfied for a period of eight weeks from the date on which—

        [48(a) the person in respect of whose care the [49 carer's allowance] has been awarded dies;

        (b) [57 . . .]

        [57 (c) in any other case, the person who has been entitled to a carer's allowance ceased to be entitled to that allowance.]]

[3Persons in receipt of concessionary payments

2.623
    14A.—For the purpose of determining whether a premium is applicable to a person [12 under paragraphs 12 to 14ZA], any concessionary payment made to compensate that person for the non-payment of any benefit mentioned in those paragraphs shall be treated as if it were a payment of that benefit.]

[⁸**Person in receipt of benefit**

14B.—For the purposes of this Part of this Schedule, a person shall be regarded as being in receipt of any benefit if, and only if, it is paid in respect of him and shall be so regarded only for any period in respect of which that benefit is paid.]

2.624

[³⁷ PART IV

Weekly Amounts of Premiums Specified in Part III

2.625

Column (1)	Column (2)
Premium	*Amount*
15.—(1)[²⁹. . .]	(1) [²⁹. . .].
[⁴²(1A) [⁶⁷ . . .]]	[⁴² (1A) [⁶⁷ . . .]]
[⁵⁴ (2) Pensioner premium for persons to whom paragraph 9 applies.	(2)
	[⁵⁴. . .]
	[⁸³ £152.90].
(2A) Pensioner premium for persons to whom paragraph 9A applies.	(2A)
	[⁵⁴. . .]
	[⁸³ £152.90].
(3) Higher pensioner premium for persons to whom paragraph 10 applies.]	(3)
	[⁵⁴. . .]
	[⁸³ £152.90].
(4) Disability Premium—	(4)
(a) where the claimant satisfies the condition in [⁶⁵ paragraph 11(1)(a)];	(a) [⁸³ £35.10];
(b) where the claimant satisfies the condition in [⁶⁵ paragraph 11(1)(b)].	(b) [⁸³ £50.05].
(5) Severe Disability Premium—	(5)
(a) where the claimant satisfies the condition in paragraph 13(2)(a);	(a) [⁸³ £67.30];
(b) where the claimant satisfies the condition in paragraph 13(2)(b).	(b)
(i) if there is someone in receipt of [⁴⁹ a carer's allowance] or if he or any partner satisfies that condition only by virtue of paragraph 13(3A);	(i) [⁸³ £67.30];
(ii) if no-one is in receipt of such an allowance.	(ii) [⁸³ £134.60].
(6) [⁵⁹ . . .]	(6) [⁵⁹ . . .]
(7) Carer Premium—	(7) [⁸³ £37.70] in respect of each person who satisfied the condition specified in paragraph 14ZA.]
[⁴³ (8) Enhanced disability premium where the conditions in paragraph 13A are satisifed—	(8) (a) [⁵⁹ . . .]
	(b) [⁸³ £17.20] in respect of each person who is neither—
	(i) a child or young person; nor
	(ii) a member of a couple or a polygamous

579

Column (1)	Column (2)
Premium	*Amount*
	marriage, in respect of whom the conditions specified in paragraph 13A are satisfied:
	(c) [⁸³ £24.60] where the claimant is a member of a couple or a polygamous marriage and the conditions specified in paragraph 13A are satisfied in respect of a member of that couple or polygamous marriage.]

PART V

Rounding of Fractions

2.626 **16.**—Where income support is awarded for a period which is not a complete benefit week and the applicable amount in respect of that period results in an amount which includes a fraction of a penny that fraction shall be treated as a penny.

AMENDMENTS

1. Income Support (General) Amendment Regulations 1988 (SI 1988/663) reg.29 (April 11, 1988).
2. Income Support (General) Amendment No.3 Regulations 1988 (SI 1988/1228) reg.9 (September 12, 1988).
3. Income Support (General) Amendment No.4 Regulations 1988 (SI 1988/1445) reg.19 (September 12, 1988).
4. Income Support (General) Amendment No.5 Regulations 1988 (SI 1988/2022) reg.17(b) (December 12, 1988).
5. Income Support (General) Amendment No.5 Regulations 1988 (SI 1988/2022) reg.17(a) (April 10, 1989).
6. Income Support (General) Amendment Regulations 1989 (SI 1989/534) reg.5 (October 9, 1989).
7. Income Support (General) Amendment No.3 Regulations 1989 (SI 1989/1678) reg.6 (October 9, 1989).
8. Income Support (General) Amendment Regulations 1990 (SI 1990/547) reg.17 (April 9, 1990).
9. Income Support (General) Amendment No.2 Regulations 1990 (SI 1990/1168) reg.2 (July 2, 1990).
10. Income Support (General) Amendment No.3 Regulations 1990 (SI 1990/1776) reg.8 (October 1, 1990).

11. Enterprise (Scotland) Consequential Amendments Order 1991 (SI 1991/3870 art.9 (April, 1991).

12. Income Support (General) Amendment Regulations 1991 (SI 1991/236) reg.2 (April 8, 1991).

13. Income Support (General) Amendment No.4 Regulations 1991 (SI 1991/236) reg.15 (August 5, 1991).

14. Income Support (General) Amendment No.4) Regulations 1991 (SI 1991/1559) reg.15 (October 7, 1991).

15. Disability Living Allowance and Disability Working Allowance (Consequential Provisions) Regulations 1991 (SI 1991/2742) reg.11(4) (April 6, 1992).

16. Income Support (General) Amendment Regulations 1992 (SI 1992/468) reg.6 (April 6, 1992).

17. Social Security Benefits (Amendments Consequential Upon the Introduction of community Care) Regulations 1992 (SI 1992/3147) reg.2 (April 1, 1993).

18. Social Security Benefits (Miscellaneous Amendments) Regulations 1993 (SI 1993/518) reg.5 (April 1, 1993).

19. Income-related Benefits Schemes (Miscellaneous Amendments) (No.2) Regulations 1993 (SI 1993/1150) reg.3 (May 25, 1993).

[20.]

21. Income-related Benefits Schemes (Miscellaneous Amendments) (No.4) Regulations 1993 (SI 1993/2119) reg.18 (October 4, 1993).

22. Income-related Benefits Schemes (Miscellaneous Amendments) (No.5) Regulations 1994 (SI 1994/2139) reg.30 (October 3, 1994).

23. Income-related Benefits Schemes (Miscellaneous Amendments) (No.6) Regulations 1994 (SI 1994/3061) reg.2(3) (December 2, 1994).

24. Income-related Benefits Schemes (Miscellaneous Amendments) Regulations 1995 (SI 1995/516) reg.24 (April 10, 1995).

25. Disability Working Allowance and Income Support (General) Amendment Regulations 1995 (SI 1995/482) reg.16 (April 13, 1995).

26. Disability Working Allowance and Income Support (General) Amendment Regulations 1995 (SI 1995/482) reg.17 (April 13, 1995).

27. Income-related Benefits Schemes and Social Security (Claims and Payments) (Miscellaneous Amendments) Regulations 1995 (SI 1995/2303) reg.6(8) (October 2, 1995).

28. Income Support (General) (Jobseeker's Allowance Consequential Amendments) Regulations 1996 (SI 1996/206) reg.23 and Sch.2 (October 7, 1996).

29. Child Benefit, Child Support and Social Security (Miscellaneous Amendments) Regulations 1996 (SI 1996/1803) reg.39 (April 7, 1997).

30. Income-related Benefits and Jobseeker's Allowance (Personal Allowances for Children and Young Persons) (Amendment) Regulations 1996 (SI 1996/2545) reg.2 (April 7, 1997).

31. Income-related Benefits and Jobseeker's Allowance (Amendment) (No.2) Regulations 1997 (SI 1997/2197) regs 7(5) and (6)(a) (October 6, 1997).

32. Social Security Amendment (Lone Parents) Regulations 1998 (SI 1998/766) reg.12 (April 6, 1998).

33. Social Security (Welfare to Work) Regulations 1998 (SI 1998/2231) reg.13(3)(a) (October 5, 1998).

34. Social Security (Welfare to Work) Regulations 1998 (SI 1998/2231) reg.13(3)(b) (October 5, 1998).

35. Social Security Benefits Up-rating Order 1999 (SI 1999/264) art.18(3) and Sch.4 (April 12, 1999).

36. Social Security Benefits Up-rating Order 1999 (SI 1999/264) art.18(4)(b) (April 12, 1999).

37. Social Security Benefits Up-rating Order 1999 (SI 1999/264) art.18(5) and Sch.5 (April 12, 1999).

38. Social Security Amendment (Personal Allowances for Children and Young Persons) Regulations 1999 (SI 1999/2555) reg.2(1)(b) and (2)(April 10, 2000).

39. Social Security and Child Support (Tax Credits) Consequential Amendments Regulations 1999 (SI 1999/2566) reg.2(2) and Sch.2 Pt II (October 5, 1999).

40. Social Security (Miscellaneous Amendments) (No.2) Regulations 1999 (SI 1999/2556) reg.2(8) (October 4, 1999).

41. Social Security (Miscellaneous Amendments) Regulations 2000 (SI 2000/681) reg.4 (April 3, 2000).

42. Social Security Amendment (Bereavement Benefits) Regulations 2000 (SI 2000/2239) reg.2(3) (April 9, 2001).

43. Social Security Amendment (Enhanced Disability Premium) Regulations 2000 (SI 2629) reg.2(c) (April 9, 2001).

44. Social Security Amendment (Residential Care and Nursing Homes) Regulations 2001 (SI 2001/3767) reg.2 and Sch. Pt I para.14 (April 8, 2002).

45. Social Security (Loss of Benefit) (Consequential Amendments) Regulations 2002 (SI 2002/490) reg.2 (April 1, 2002).

46. Social Security Amendment (Residential Care and Nursing Homes) Regulations 2001 (SI 2001/3767) reg.2 and Sch. Pt I para.14 (as amended by Social Security Amendment (Residential Care and Nursing Homes) Regulations 2002 (SI 2002/398) reg.4(2)) (April 8, 2002).

47. Social Security Amendment (Personal Allowances for Children and Young Persons) Regulations 2002 (SI 2002/2019) reg.2 (October 14, 2002).

48. Social Security Amendment (Carer Premium) Regulations 2002 (SI 2002/2020) reg.2 (October 28, 2002).

49. Social Security Amendment (Carer's allowance) Regulations 2002 (SI 2002/2497) reg.3 and Sch.2 (April 1, 2003).

50. Social Security (Working Tax Credit and Child Tax Credit) (Consequential Amendments) Regulations 2003 (SI 2003/455) regs 1(5) and 2 and Sch.1 para.20(b) (April 7, 2003).

51. Social Security Benefits Up-Rating Order 2003 (SI 2003/526) art.17(3) and Sch.2 (April 7, 2003).

52. Social Security Benefits Up-Rating Order 2003 (SI 2003/526) art.17(5) and Sch.3 (April 7, 2003).

53. Social Security Benefits Up-Rating Order 2003 (SI 2003/526) art.17(4) (April 7, 2003).

54. State Pension Credit (Consequential, Transitional and Miscellaneous Provisions) Regulations 2002 (SI 2002/3019) reg.29(5) (October 6, 2003).

55. Social Security (Removal of Residential Allowance and Miscellaneous Amendments) Regulations 2003 (SI 2003/1121) reg.2 and Sch.1 para.6 (October 6, 2003).

56. Social Security (Hospital In-Patients and Miscellaneous Amendments) Regulations 2003 (SI 2003/1195) reg.3 (May 21, 2003).

57. Social Security (Miscellaneous Amendments) (No.2) Regulations 2003 (SI 2003/2279 reg.2(3) (October 1, 2003).

58. Income Support (General) Amendment Regulations 2003 (SI 2003/2379) reg.2 (October 6, 2003).

59. Social Security (Working Tax Credit and Child Tax Credit) (Consequential Amendments) Regulations 2003 (SI 2003/455) reg.2 and Sch.1 para.20 (April 6, 2004, except in "transitional cases" and see further the note to reg.17 of the Income Support Regulations).

60. Social Security (Miscellaneous Amendments) (No.2) Regulations 2004 (SI 2004/1141) reg.6 (May 12, 2004).

61. Social Security (Back to Work Bonus and Lone Parent Run-on) (Amendment and Revocation) Regulations 2003 (SI 2003/1589) reg.2(d) (October 25, 2004).

62. Civil Partnership (Pensions, Social Security and Child Support) (Consequential, etc. Provisions) Order 2005 (SI 2005/2877) art.2(3) and Sch.3 para.13(3) (December 5, 2005).

63. Social Security (Hospital In-Patients) Regulations 2005 (SI 2005/3360) reg.4 (April 10, 2006).

64. Social Security (Miscellaneous Amendments) (No.4) Regulations 2006 (SI 2006/2378) reg.5(7) (October 2, 2006).

65. Social Security (Miscellaneous Amendments) Regulations 2007 (SI 2007/719) reg.2(7) (April 9, 2007). As it relates to paras 13A(2)(a) and 14, the amendment only affects "transitional cases". See further the note to reg.17 of the Income Support Regulations and the commentary below.

66. Social Security (Miscellaneous Amendments) Regulations 2007 (SI 2007/719) reg.2(7)(e) (April 2, 2007).

67. Social Security (Miscellaneous Amendments) (No. 5) Regulations 2007 (SI 2007/2618) reg.2 and Sch. (October 1, 2007).

68. Social Security (Miscellaneous Amendments) Regulations 2008 (SI 2008/698) reg.2(12) (April 14. 2008).

69. Social Security (Miscellaneous Amendments) Regulations 2009 (SI 2009/583) reg.2(1) and (3) (April 6, 2009).

70. Social Security (Equalisation of State Pension Age) Regulations 2009 (SI 2009/1488) reg.3 (April 6, 2010).

71. Social Security (Miscellaneous Amendments) (No.2) Regulations 2010 (SI 2010/641) reg.2(1) and (9) (April 13, 2010).

72. Social Security (Loss of Benefit) Amendment Regulations 2010 (SI 2010/1160) reg.10(1) and (3) (April 1, 2010).

73. Social Security (Miscellaneous Amendments) Regulations 2011 (SI 2011/674) reg.3(5) (April 11, 2011).

74. Social Security (Miscellaneous Amendments) (No. 3) Regulations 2011 (SI 2011/2425) reg.7(1) and (7) (October 31, 2011).

75. Personal Independence Payment (Supplementary Provisions and Consequential Amendments) Regulations 2013 (SI 2013/388) reg.8 and Sch. para.11(1) and (5) (April 8, 2013).

76. Armed Forces and Reserve Forces Compensation Scheme (Consequential Provisions: Subordinate Legislation) Order 2013 (SI 2013/591) art.7 and Sch. para.4(1) and (5) (April 8, 2013).

77. Universal Credit and Miscellaneous Amendments (No.2) Regulations 2014 (SI 2014/2888) reg.3(2)(a) (November 26, 2014).

78. Welfare Benefits Up-rating Order 2015 (SI 2015/30) art.6 and Sch.1 (April 6, 2015).

79. Social Security Benefits Up-rating Order 2015 (SI 2015/457) art.14(5) and Sch.3 (April 6, 2015).

80. Universal Credit and Miscellaneous Amendments Regulations 2015 (SI 2015/1754) reg.14 (October 28, 2015).

81. Pensions Act 2014 (Consequential, Supplementary and Incidental Amendments) Order 2015 (SI 2015/1985) art.8(1) and (3) (April 6, 2016).

82. Social Security Benefits Up-rating Order 2021 (SI 2021/162) art.21(1) and (3), and Sch.2 (April 12, 2021).

83. Social Security Benefits Up-rating Order 2021 (SI 2021/162) art.21(1) and (5), and Sch.3 (April 12, 2021).

DEFINITIONS

"attendance allowance"—see reg.2(1).
"benefit week"—*ibid.*
"child"—see SSCBA s.137(1).
"claimant"—see reg.2(1).
"close relative"—*ibid.*
"couple"—*ibid.*
"disability living allowance"—*ibid.*
"family"—see SSCBA s.137(1).
"invalid carriage or other vehicle"—see reg.2(1).
"lone parent"—*ibid.*
"mobility supplement"—*ibid.*

"non-dependent"—see reg.3.
"partner"—see reg.2(1).
"polygamous marriage"—*ibid.*
"preserved right"—see reg.2(1) and reg.19.
"single claimant"—see reg.2(1).
"Social Security Act"—*ibid.*
"welfare to work beneficiary"—*ibid.*
"young person"—*ibid.*, reg.14.

GENERAL NOTE

Up-rating

2.627   Until April 6, 2015, the amounts specified in para.1 were up-rated each year under s.150(1)(h) SSAA 1992. However, on March 16, 2016, s.11 and Sch.1 of the Welfare Reform and Work Act 2016 came into force. As a result, all the amounts specified in para.1 were frozen at their 2015/16 levels for four tax years and were not up-rated again until April 6, 2020, when they were increased to the rates shown in the text.

The amounts of the pensioner premiums and higher pensioner premium in para.15 continued to be up-rated as a consequence of the so-called "triple lock" under which the state pension increases each year by the higher of inflation, the increase in average earnings or 2.5 per cent.

The other amounts in para.15 were not subject to the four-year freeze. They were not up-rated for 2016/17 as the Secretary of State decided that they had maintained their value in relation to prices as measured by the Consumer Prices Index over the 12-month period ending September 2015 (which had showed negative inflation of 0.1 per cent): see para.4.2 of the Explanatory Memorandum to SI 2016/230. However, they were uprated for 2017/18, for 2018/19, for 2019/20, for 2020/21 and, to the rates shown in the text, for 2021/22.

Personal Allowances

Paragraph 1

2.628   This paragraph was amended (and para.1A was introduced) in October 1996 as a consequence of the changes to income support following the introduction of JSA.

The lower age limit for income support is now 16 (SSCBA s.124(1)(a)) but a person is only eligible if he falls into one of the categories prescribed by reg.4ZA and Sch.1B (s.124(1)(e)). (Note too that a person aged 16–18 in relevant education is still only entitled to income support in certain circumstances (s.124(1)(d) and reg.13)). However, the age-break of 18 remains significant as regards the rate of the personal allowance (and so the immense complexity of sub-para.(3) is retained), with another very significant break at 25 for single claimants.

For couples, where both partners are aged less than 18, the lower couple rate is only paid if either a child is a member of the family, or both partners are eligible for income support, or the non-claiming partner is either eligible for JSA or the subject of a severe hardship direction under s.16 of the Jobseekers Act 1995 (sub-para.(3)(a)). If this does not apply but one member of the couple comes within para.1A (person living away from parents and anyone acting in place of parents in specified circumstances), the personal allowance is the same as the higher rate for a single claimant under 18 (sub-para.(3)(b)), but otherwise only the equivalent of the lower rate for a single claimant under 18 is paid (sub-para.(3)(c)). Where one partner is 18 or over and the other is under 18, the higher couple rate is only paid if the partner under 18 is eligible for income support or income-based JSA or the subject of a JSA severe hardship direction (sub-para.(3)(e)). If this is not the case, the personal allowance is the same as for a single claimant (sub-para.(3)(f)), with another age-break at 25 (sub-para.(3)(g)).

2.629   The crucial age for lone parents is 18 (sub-para.(2)(d)). Lone parents of 16 and 17 are always eligible (para.1 of Sch.1B) but are paid at a higher rate if they fall within para.1A (person living away from parents and any substitute in certain circumstances) or qualify for a disability premium (sub-para.(2)(b) and (c)).

Single claimants under 18 qualify for the 18–24-year-old rate if they fall within para.1A (sub-para.(1)(b)) or qualify for a disability premium (sub-para.(1)(c)). But for single claimants there is another very significant break at the age of 25 (para.1(1) (e)). This is connected to the absence of any distinction in the personal allowances between householders and non-householders. Instead, the assumptions are made that most single people of 25 and over are responsible for their own households and that most single people under 25 are not responsible for independent households, typically living with parents. Thus a higher rate is paid to those of 25. Both these assumptions are correct, looking at the entire age-groups involved, but clearly have no direct applicability to the needs and circumstances of individuals. Young single claimants were one of the losing groups in the 1988 reforms.

In *Reynolds v SSWP* [2002] EWHC 426 (Admin), QBD (Wilson J), (March 7, 2002) a challenge to the lower rates for those under 25 on the basis that they infringed various provisions of the European Convention on Human Rights (including art.14 and art.1 of the First Protocol taken together) was rejected. That decision was upheld by the Court of Appeal and by the House of Lords in *Carson and Reynolds v SSWP* ([2003] EWCA Civ 797 (CA), [2005] UKHL 37 (HL)).

See Sch.7 for special cases, such as hospital patients. From April 1989 there are no special rules for people in board and lodging accommodation and from October 1989 no special rules for residents in most hostels. Special rules for the residents of residential care and nursing homes were abolished on October 6, 2003. For details of the position before that date, see pp.486–488 of Vol.II of the 2003 edition.

Paragraph 1A

This paragraph lists those categories of 16- and 17-year-olds who qualify for the higher rate of personal allowance under para.1(1)(b), (2)(b) and (3)(b). The categories replicate those formerly in paras 6–9A of Pt II of Sch.1A (Sch.1A was revoked on October 7, 1996 as a consequence of the changes to income support following the introduction of JSA).   **2.630**

See sub-para.(2) for definitions. On heads (a), (d) and (e) of sub-para.(1), see the notes to reg.13(2)(c), (e) and (d) respectively. Head (b) is similar to reg.13(2)(dd) but there are some important differences in the wording. Those covered by head (c) are expected to be particularly vulnerable.

Paragraph 2

Until April 5, 2004, IS, IBJSA, IRESA included allowances and premiums to provided financial help with the cost of supporting and bringing up a child or young person (see p.486 of Vol.II of the 2003 edition). From April 6, 2004 except in transitional cases (as to which see the note to reg.17)—such help was provided through child tax credit (see Vol.IV), which is itself now in the process of being replaced by universal credit (see Vol.II).   **2.631**

In transitional cases, the personal allowance for a child or young person was increased to £68.60 from the beginning of the first benefit week after April 12, 2021 by art.21(3)(b) of the Social Security Benefits Uprating Order 2021 (SI 2021/162).

Paragraph 2A

The system of special payments of IS, known as "residential allowances", to people in private or voluntary sector residential care or nursing homes were abolished with effect from October 6, 2003. For details of the position before that date, see pp.486–488 of Vol.II of the 2003 edition.   **2.632**

Premiums

Paragraph 3

The family premium was also abolished with effect from April 6, 2004. For details of the position before April 6, 2004, see pp.488–489 of Vol.II of the 2003   **2.633** edition and see the note to reg.17 for details of the transitional provisions. For those still entitled to the premium on a transitional basis, the text of para.3 is as follows:

"3.—(1) The weekly amount for the purposes of regulations 17(1)(c) and 18(1)(d) in respect of a family of which at least one member is a child or young person shall be—

(a) where the claimant is a lone parent to whom the conditions in both sub-paragraphs (2) and (3) apply and no premium is applicable under paragraph 9, 9A, 10 or 11, £17.65

(b) in any other case, £17.65.

(2) The first condition for the purposes of sub-paragraph (1)(a) is that the claim-ant—

(a) was both a lone parent and entitled to income support on 5th April 1998; or

(b) does not come within head (a) above but—

    (i) was both a lone parent and entitled to income support on any day during the period of 12 weeks ending on 5th April 1998;

    (ii) was both a lone parent and entitled to income support on any day during the period of 12 weeks commencing on 6th April 1998; and

    (iii) the last day in respect of which (i) above applied was no more than 12 weeks before the first day in respect of which (ii) above applied.

(3) The second condition for the purposes of sub-paragraph (1)(a) is that as from the appropriate date specified in sub-paragraph (4), the claimant has continued, subject to sub-paragraph (5), to be both a lone parent and entitled to income support.

(4) The appropriate date for the purposes of sub-paragraph (3) is—

(a) in a case to which sub-paragraph (2)(a) applies, 6th April 1998;

(b) in a case to which sub-paragraph (2)(b) applies, the first day in respect of which sub-paragraph (2)(b)(ii) applied.

(5) For the purposes of sub-paragraph (3), where the claimant has ceased, for any period of 12 weeks or less, to be—

(a) a lone parent; or

(b) entitled to income support; or

(c) both a lone parent and entitled to income support,

the claimant shall be treated, on again becoming both a lone parent and entitled to income support, as having continued to be both a lone parent and entitled to income support throughout that period.

(6) In determining whether the conditions in sub-paragraphs (2) and (3) apply, entitlement to an income-based jobseeker's allowance shall be treated as entitlement to income support for the purposes of any requirement that a person is entitled to income support.

(7) For the purposes of this paragraph, a claimant shall be treated as having been entitled to income support throughout any period which comprises only days on which he was participating in an employment zone programme and was not entitled to income support because, as a consequence of his participation in that programme, he was engaged in remunerative work or had income in excess of his applicable amount as prescribed in Part IV."

The rate of the premium (which had not been increased in April 2011, April 2012 or April 2013) was increased by 5 pence to £17.45 from the beginning of the first benefit week after April 7, 2014 by SI 2014/516, to £17.60 from the first benefit week after April 6, 2020 (SI 2020/234, and again to £17.65 from the first benefit week after April 12, 2021 by art.21(4) of the Social Security Benefits Uprating Order 2021 (SI 2021/162).

Paragraphs 4–7

2.634   These provisions establish the general framework for the other premiums, in paras 9–14. Paragraph 4 provides that in each case the premium is applicable to the claimant, although the condition will sometimes relate to the claimant's partner and, in the cases of the pensioner, enhanced pensioner and higher pensioner premiums, can only relate to, the claimant's partner since—with effect from October 6, 2003— people aged 60 or over can no longer be the claimant for income support (see note to s.124(1)(aa) of the Contributions and Benefits Act). The general rule is that only one of these premiums is applicable. If the claimant satisfies the conditions for more than one, the highest is applicable (para.5). However, a number of exceptions appear in para.6. The severe disability premium is allowed in addition to any other premium, as is the carer premium; so too is the enhanced disability premium in some cases.

Many of the conditions for premiums are based on the receipt of other social security benefits. Paragraph 7(1) deals with two situations where, once a premium has been allowed, the person concerned ceases actually to receive the other benefit. It allows entitlement to the premium to continue if the person has only ceased to receive the relevant benefit because of another, overlapping, benefit or is on a government training course or in receipt of a training allowance (the main example being Work Based Learning for Young People, which has replaced Youth Training and other training provision focussed on 16–17-year-olds). See para.14B on the meaning of receipt of benefit.

Under para.7(2), the above rules do not allow the carer premium to continue unless the person cared for continues to receive attendance allowance or one of the two higher rates of the care component of disability living allowance.

Paragraph 8A

The bereavement premium was introduced with effect from April 9, 2001 as 2.635 part of the overall reforms of the former widow's benefits. By reg.6 of the Social Security Amendment (Bereavement Benefits) Regulations 2000 (SI 2000/2239), the premium ceased to apply from April 10, 2006. For further details see pp.527–8 of the 2007 edition.

Paragraphs 9 and 9A

These provisions, together with the increases in the higher pensioner premium 2.636 under para.15(3), implemented the Government's commitment to give increased help to needy pensioners in October 1989. The ordinary pensioner premium under para.9 was limited to people aged 60–74. Paragraph 9A provided a separate premium for those aged 75–79, with a small differential over the ordinary pensioner premium. The effect of reg.14(1D) of the Transitional Regulations was that these increases did not affect any transitional addition in payment. Although from April 2001 the differential has been removed. From October 6, 2003, the premium can only be paid where a claimant who has not reached the qualifying age for state pension credit has a partner who has reached that age (or, in the case of the enhanced pensioner premium, is 75 or older) and who is not entitled to state pension credit. Many couples in this position will be better off by claiming state pension credit and the importance of the pensioner premium and enhanced pensioner premium is therefore likely to decline.

Paragraph 10

From October 6, 2003, the first qualification for the HPP is that the claimant's 2.637 partner is aged 80 or over. If that is not satisfied, there are another two alternatives, provided that the claimant's partner has reached the qualifying age for state pension credit. The first is that the claimant's partner satisfies the disability test in para.12(1)(a), (c), or (d). The second is that the claimant was entitled to, or treated as entitled to, the income support disability premium within eight weeks of the day on which the partner reached the qualifying age for state pension credit and has remained continuously entitled to income support since that birthday. The requirement that the disability premium was, or would have been applicable to the claimant presumably now means applicable in respect of his or her partner rather than in his or her own right, although sub-para.(1)(b)(ii)(aa) does not actually spell that out. Further, *CIS 458/1992* decides that a premium is not "applicable" unless it actually forms part of the claimant's applicable amount (but see *CIS 11293/1996* in the notes to para.12).

The second alternative is subject to a number of extensions which may assist claimants:

- first, entitlement to income-based JSA is treated as entitlement to income support—see reg.32 of the Income Support (General) (Jobseeker's Allowance Consequential Amendments) Regulations 1996;

- secondly, sub-para.(5) treats claimants who were participating in an employment zone programme and who were not entitled to income support because, as a result of that participation, they were in remunerative work (see regs 5 and 6) or had income in excess of their applicable amounts as being entitled to income support;

- thirdly, claimants who cease to be entitled to income support for a period of up to eight weeks which includes the day on which the partner reaches the qualifying age for state pension credit are treated by sub-para.(3)(b) as having been continuously entitled to income support when they become re-entitled. Whilst an eight week linking period is better than no linking period at all, this rule is entirely arbitrary. There are many circumstances in which a claimant might cease to be entitled to income support at the time his or her partner reaches the qualifying age for state pension credit (for example, receipt of capital from the proceeds of an endowment or retirement annuity policy or an occupational pension) which have nothing to do with the future disability needs of the claimant's partner;

- fourthly, if the claimant is a "welfare to work beneficiary" (as defined in reg.2(1)) the eight week period is extended to 104 weeks by sub-para.(4); and

- finally, sub-para.(3)(a) provides that once a claimant has become entitled to the HPP, breaks in entitlement to income support of up to eight weeks will not affect entitlement to the premium, despite the concluding words of sub-para.(1)(b)(ii).

Paragraph 11

2.638   The qualification for the DP can be for the claimant personally to satisfy one of the conditions in para.12. If it is the claimant's partner who might qualify, then only para.12(1)(a), (c) or (d), not (b), will do. If the condition is to be satisfied by the claimant's *partner*, s/he must be under 60. If s/he is over 60 then there will be entitlement to the HPP under para.10(1)(b)(i). Following the introduction of state pension credit on October 6, 2003, all income support claimants must be under 60 (see notes to s.124(1)(aa) of the Contributions and Benefits Act).

Paragraph 12

2.639   Sub-paragraph (1) prescribes four alternative conditions for HPP and DP. Heads (a) and (d) may be satisfied by either the claimant or his or her partner, head (b) may only be satisfied by the claimant. Head (c) contains some criteria which must be satisfied by the claimant's partner and some which must be satisfied by the claimant. As far as possible the conditions are made to depend on decisions already taken by other authorities, so that decision-making here should be routine.

Head (a) applies to receipt of the benefits listed in head (i), provision of or grant towards an invalid carriage, or being registered blind. From April 1990, para.14B defines receipt of benefit in terms of payment, reversing the effect of *R(SB) 12/87*. Long-term incapacity benefit requires 52 weeks of incapacity for work, and has a contribution test. (Previously invalidity pension required only 28 weeks of incapacity.) Note sub-para.(6), the effect of which is to treat a person who is terminally ill as in receipt of long-term incapacity benefit after 28 weeks. Severe disablement allowance is non-contributory, but has an additional (and tough) test of disablement. The extension to all levels of disability living allowance brought in some previously excluded claimants. See sub-para.(2) for blindness, and the notes to para.13 of Sch.1B.

Entitlement to HPP is affected by the discriminatory age limit for claims for long-term incapacity benefit (previously invalidity benefit) that results from the UK's different pensionable ages for men and women (i.e. 65 for men, between 60 and 65 for women (depending when they were born); full equalisation of pensionable age will not be achieved until November, 2018) (but see *CIB 13368/1998* below where the entitlement to incapacity benefit derives from an industrial injury or a prescribed industrial disease). (As a result of the ECJ's decision in *Secretary of State for Social Security v Thomas* [1993] E.C.R. I-1247, [1993] 4 All E.R. 556, also reported as *R(G) 2/94*, the discriminatory age limit for initial claims for severe disablement allowance was finally changed on October 28, 1994 (see Social Security (Severe Disablement Allowance and Invalid Care Allowance) Amendment Regulations 1994 (SI 1994/2556)). In *Secretary of State for Social Security and Chief Adjudication Officer v Graham* (C-92/94), [1995] 3 C.M.L.R. 169, [1995] All E.R. (EC) 865, also reported as *R(S) 2/95*) the ECJ held that the different treatment of men and women in relation to invalidity benefit was not in breach of EC Directive 79/7 on equal treatment for men and women in matters of social security. The discrimination in the rules for invalidity benefit was permitted under art.7(1)(a) of the Directive as it was "necessarily and objectively linked" to the UK's different pension ages (see *Thomas*). The Court's reasoning is scanty (compare the Advocate General's Opinion delivered on June 15, 1995). But the judgment has put an end to the argument that a discriminatory link to pensionable age for *contributory* (as opposed to non-contributory: see *Thomas*) benefits is unlawful. See the 1995 edition of J. Mesher and P. Wood, *Income-related Benefits: the Legislation* for further details of *Graham* (and associated issues) and related European case law on the scope of Directive 79/7. Long-term incapacity benefit is not payable to people over pensionable age (the transitional protection given to those who were over pensionable age before April 13, 1995 having expired). The consequence of the ECJ's judgment in *Graham* is that this discrimination against women (and its effect on entitlement to HPP) remains (until the pensionable age differential is finally abolished). Note, however, that in *CIB 13368/1996* Commissioner Levenson held that for women who were getting invalidity benefit because of industrial injury or prescribed disease, and who transferred to transitional incapacity benefit (being deemed to satisfy the contribution conditions), the discriminatory age limit was unlawful. Regulation 17(4) of the Social Security (Incapacity Benefit) (Transitional) Regulations 1995) fell on the *Thomas*, rather than the *Graham* side of the line. But Commissioner Levenson's decision was, by concession, reversed by the Court of Appeal in *CAO v Rowlands* on June 27, 2000, following the ECJ's decision in *Hepple*.

The current form of head (b) is a consequence of the changes associated with the introduction of incapacity benefit (which replaced sickness benefit and invalidity benefit from April 13, 1995). It is no longer linked to what is now para.7 of Sch.1B (see the 1994 edition of J. Mesher and P. Wood, *Income-related Benefits: the Legislation* for notes on the previous form of head (b)), although it employs the same criteria as heads (a), (b) and (d) of para.7. See the notes to para.7 of Sch.1B. The test must now be satisfied for a continuous period of at least 52 weeks before a disability or higher pensioner premium can be awarded under head (b), unless the claimant is terminally ill when the period is 28 weeks. Two or more periods separated by not more than eight weeks (from October 5, 1998, 104 weeks in the case of a "welfare to work beneficiary" (sub-para.(1A)); see the notes to reg.2(1) for when a person counts as a welfare to work beneficiary) count as one continuous period. A person is defined as terminally ill if he is expected to die from a progressive disease within six months. If the person has been incapable of work (or entitled to statutory sick pay) for 28 weeks by the time a decision-maker decides he is terminally ill, head

2.640

(b) will immediately apply. Before April 13,1995 the qualifying period under head (b) was 28 weeks. There is some transitional protection, see below. In the case of a couple, head (b) can only be satisfied by the claimant.

A person is entitled to statutory sick pay from the first day of incapacity (even though it is not paid for the first three "waiting days"). Otherwise it is only days on which it is accepted that the claimant is, or is to be treated as, incapable of work in accordance with the rules for determining incapacity for work (see Vol.I of this series) that count. A claimant does not have to be in receipt of income support during the qualifying period, so if a person has been incapable of work for 52 weeks before claiming income support head (b) will immediately apply.

Any days when the claimant is treated as capable of work under the incapacity rules (see Vol.I of this series) will not count, but note the linking rule. A person may be treated as capable of work for a maximum of 6 weeks under reg.18 of the Social Security (Incapacity for Work) (General) Regulations; or indefinitely in other cases. Thus the effect of a decision to treat a claimant as capable of work may (depending on the circumstances) only result in that period not counting towards establishing entitlement to a disability or higher pensioner premium, rather than necessitate a return to square one. If the claimant has already been awarded a premium it will not be payable while he is treated as capable of work. But if this is for eight weeks or less it will apply again immediately after the break. Note also the 52-week linking rule from October 5, 1998 for a claimant who is a "welfare to work beneficiary" (see reg.2(1) and the notes to that regulation).

2.641   Note *CIS 15611/1996* which decides that a claimant who had been entitled to a disability premium before going into prison and who continued to be incapable of work while in prison did not have to re-serve the 52-week qualifying period on his release. Although days of disqualification from incapacity benefit during a period of imprisonment did not count as days of incapacity for work under reg.4(1)(b) of the Incapacity Benefit Regulations 1994, this only applied for the purposes of incapacity benefit. The Incapacity for Work (General) Regulations 1995 contained no such provision and so subject to the claimant providing evidence of his incapacity for work throughout his period in prison he was entitled to a disability premium when he reclaimed income support on his release.

If a claimant makes a late claim for a benefit on the grounds of incapacity for work, the days on which it is accepted that he was, or was to be treated as, incapable of work should count under head (b). It does not matter that there is no entitlement to the benefit because the claim is late. See *R(IS) 8/93* (but note the amendments to reg.2(1) of the Social Security (Medical Evidence) Regulations 1976 (SI 1976/615) from April 13, 1995).

In *CIS/2699/2001* Commissioner Mesher considered whether the requirement that a claimant should have been incapable of work for a continuous period of 364 days (or 196 days if terminally ill) could be satisfied on the basis of retrospective medical evidence. He concluded that this was permitted by reg.28(2)(a) of the Social Security (Incapacity for Work) (General) Regulations 1995 and reg.2(1)(d) of the Social Security (Medical Evidence) Regulations 1976. However, by virtue of s.12(8)(b) of the Social Security Act 1998 (which prohibits a tribunal from considering circumstances arising after the date of the decision under appeal), such medical evidence had to be provided *before* the date of the Secretary of State's decision. This was because under reg.28(2)(a), the production of medical evidence was *itself* a circumstance relevant to the claimant's entitlement and not merely evidence related to some relevant circumstance. In so holding, Commissioner Mesher differed from the decision of Commissioner Rowland in *CIS/4772/2000* in which the point about s.12(8)(b) had not been raised.

2.642   There is transitional protection for claimants entitled to a disability premium on April 12, 1995 under head (b) as then in force. See reg.19(2) to (4) of the Disability Working Allowance and Income Support (General) Amendment Regulations 1995 (p.1754). The premium will continue to be paid as long as they remain incapable of work (in accordance with the new rules, including the transitional protection). Note the linking rule. In addition, any period immediately before April 13, 1995 during which a claimant satisfied para.5 of Sch.1 as then in force (see the 1994 edition of J. Mesher and P. Wood, *Income-related Benefits: the Legislation*) counts towards the qualifying period under head (b).

Heads (c) and (d) apply where receipt of some benefits specified in (a) only ceased because of age limits or going into hospital. The claimant has to remain continuously entitled to income support (or income-based JSA: reg.32 of the Income Support (General) (Jobseeker's Allowance Consequential Amendments) Regulations 1996 (see p.1758) under which entitlement to income-based JSA counts as entitlement to income support for the purpose of satisfying any condition that the person is or has been entitled to income support) and if it is his partner who has ceased to receive long-term incapacity benefit she must still be alive. Note the linking rule in sub-para.(4). Note also sub-para.(6) in relation to incapacity benefit, the effect of which is to treat a person who is terminally ill as in receipt of long-term incapacity benefit after 28 weeks. There is transitional protection for claimants entitled to a higher pensioner premium under the old form of head (c)(i) at any time in the eight weeks before April 12, 1995 (i.e. those who transferred to retirement pension from invalidity benefit): see reg.20(4) of the Disability Working Allowance and Income Support (General) Amendment Regulations 1995 (p.1753).

CIS 587/1990 exposes a gap in the legislation which has not yet been closed. The claimant transferred from invalidity benefit to retirement pension in 1982. He could not qualify under the old form of head (c) because he had not been continuously entitled to income support since the transfer. If he had delayed the transfer until after April 10, 1988, he would have qualified. The extent of his need at the relevant date (April 1990) was identical under either alternative. See sub-para.(4) for linking rules. Another gap is highlighted by *CIS 458/1992* which holds that the condition that a premium has been applicable requires that it should have been part of the claimant's applicable amount. So where a claimant had been in a residential care home he could not use head (c), because Sch.4 has no provision for premiums. But see *CIS 11293/1996* in the notes to para.4(6) of Sch.3 where the Commissioner holds that housing costs were "applicable" under para.5A(3) of the former Sch.3 if they were potentially applicable.

Paragraph 13

The presence of this category is required by s.22(3) of the 1986 Act, now s.135(5)   **2.643** of the Contributions and Benefits Act. The concern which prompted the inclusion of that subsection was that a severely disabled claimant on supplementary benefit might be getting high additional requirements for a range of extra needs (e.g. heating, laundry, diet, wear and tear on clothes, etc.), which the ordinary disability premium would go nowhere near matching. However, the conditions for the severe disability premium (SDP) are so tight that very few will qualify. The Independent Living Fund was set up to provide further cash help to the very severely disabled, but its budget was usually fully spent part way through its financial year. The Fund was suspended in 1992. On April 1, 1993, it was replaced by two funds, the Independent Living (Extension) Fund which took over payments to existing beneficiaries and the Independent Living (1993) Fund for new applications.

First note that the SDP can only apply to the claimant, not to his partner. But since a couple has a free choice as to which of them should be the claimant (Claims and Payments Regulations reg.4) this should not be a problem.

If the claimant has no partner, he first must either be in receipt of one of the two higher rates of the care component of disability living allowance, or of either rate of the daily living component of personal independence payment, or of armed forces independence payment: see sub-para.(2)(a)(i). That sub-paragraph also contemplates that a claimant might qualify for the premium through entitlement to attendance allowance. However, that appears to be a historical anomaly: anyone entitled to attendance allowance will have attained the qualifying age for state pension credit and therefore be disentitled to IS altogether by SSCBA 1992 s.124(1)(aa). Then there must be no non-dependants of 18 or over residing with him (sub-para. (2)(a)(ii)). The addition of the words "with whom he is normally residing" from December 2, 1994 is to reverse the effect of the Court of Appeal's decision in *Bate v Chief Adjudication Officer and Secretary of State for Social Security* [1995] 3 F.C.R. 145; *The Times*, December 12, 1994 (subsequently overturned by the House of Lords [1996] 1 W.L.R. 814: see the notes to reg.3).

2.644   The fact that the non-dependant is not lawfully resident in the UK does not prevent him or her from "normally residing" with the claimant. For the purposes of para.(2), whether one person "normally resides with" another is a purely factual question of their living arrangements and involves no judgment on the quality of his or her residence: see *ST v SSWP* [2009] UKUT 269 (AAC). In that case, Upper Tribunal Judge Jacobs explained the structure of para.13 as follows:

> "22. In the narrow context of paragraph 13, the emphasis is on a person who is living with the claimant and who is, therefore, able to provide some care for the claimant. The exclusion in paragraph 13(2)(a)(ii) is integral to the scope of the premium. It is reserved for claimants who (i) are disabled and (ii) have nobody available to provide care for them. (i) is shown by an appropriate award of a disability living allowance or an attendance allowance. (ii) is shown by the absence of an award of carer's allowance and of anyone resident with the claimant to help. Paragraph 13(3)(c) and (4) provides what Mr Brown conveniently called a bedding-in period. This allows a carer to move in with the claimant for a period of 12 weeks in order to see if the relationship works before the premium is removed."

The effect of sub-para.(3) is that adults in receipt of attendance allowance or one of the two higher rates of care component of disability living allowance or who are registered as blind or treated as blind or carers for the first 12 weeks of residence do not count for this purpose. "Non-dependant" is defined in reg.3. See the notes to that regulation for the intricacies of the definition. Care must be taken to apply the particular form of reg.3 in force at the relevant time. The current version makes it very diffcult for the parents, or other "close relatives", with whom an adult claimant is living not to be regarded as non-dependants. In *R(IS)12/06* the Commissioner holds that the refusal of the SDP to a claimant who lives with a close relative on a commercial basis in circumstances (i.e. where it would be paid if the claimant lived on the same terms with someone who was not a close relative) did not amount to unlawful discrimination contrary to art.14 of the ECHR. Finally, no one must be receiving carer's allowance (formerly invalid care allowance (ICA)) or the carer element of universal credit for caring for the claimant (sub-para.(2)(a)(iii)). Sub-para.(3ZA) provides that where an award of carer's allowance or the carer element of UC is made which includes arrears, entitlement to the SDP only ceases from the date the award of is actually made. So such an award does not lead to an overpayment of the SDP. This reverses the decision of the Commissioner in *R(IS) 14/94*.

If the claimant has a partner, the assumption is that the partner can care for the claimant. So there is an additional qualification that the partner is also in receipt of a qualifying allowance (sub-para.(2)(b)(ii)) or, if not, is registered as blind or treated as blind (sub-para.(2A)). There must be no eligible non-dependants in residence (see above), and at least one of the couple must not have a carer receiving carer's allowance or the carer element of universal credit.

2.645   In *R(IS) 22/93* and a number of associated appeals, the Commissioner held that sub-para.(2)(a)(ii) and (iii) were not validly made, since s.22(4) of the Social Security Act 1986 (now s.135(6) of the Contributions and Benefits Act) only gave power to prescribe conditions relating to a claimant's disability. Section 22(3) (SSSCBA s.135(5)) requires a severely disabled person's applicable amount to include a special premium. Heads (ii) and (iii) are concerned with the presence of others in the household and the benefit entitlement of other people, which are not connected to the claimant's disability. This cogently argued decision was reversed by the Court of Appeal in *Chief Adjudication Officer v Foster* [1992] Q.B.

31; [1991] 3 All E.R. 846, which held by a majority that the provisions were valid. The House of Lords confirmed this part of the Court of Appeal's decision (*Foster v Chief Adjudication Officer* [1993] A.C. 754, [1993] 1 All E.R. 705, also reported as part of *R(IS) 22/93*). Therefore, the full conditions of para.13 must be applied at all points of its history. See the notes to s.135 of the Contributions and Benefits Act for more details, and see Vol.III of this series for the power of the Social Security Commissioners and others to determine whether regulations have been validly made.

The premium is high, since it is in addition to DP or HPP (para.6(1)). For a claimant without a partner it is £65.85. For a couple (where both partners have to qualify) it is £65.85 for each of them who does not have a carer with carer's allowance (para.15(5)).

It was argued in *Rider v Chief Adjudication Officer*, reported as *R(IS) 10/94*, that for periods before April 1990, (when para.14B was introduced) where a lone parent received attendance allowance in respect of a child under 16, para.13(2)(a)(i) was satisfied. Regulation 6(4) of the Social Security (Attendance Allowance) (No.2) Regulations 1975 made the parent entitled to the attendance allowance in these circumstances. But if the parent, and not the child, were treated as in receipt of attendance allowance, that would mean that a child could never have satisfied the conditions of para.14(b) on the DCP. *R(IS) 10/94* decides that in the context of para.14(b) a child is in receipt of attendance allowance when the child satisfies the prescribed conditions and the meaning must be the same in para.13(2)(a)(i). The introduction of para.14B in April 1990, providing that a person is to be regarded as in receipt of any benefit only where it is paid in respect of that person was to clarify the law, not to change it. The decision in *R(IS) 10/94* was confirmed by the Court of Appeal which held that on an overall comparison of the words "in receipt of" in paras 13(2)(a)(i) and 14(b) (and also para.12(1)(a)(i) in relation to the disability premium), it could be seen that the words were not to be read just as they stood but as importing the additional requirement that the attendance allowance should be payable in respect of the recipient's own needs. Paragraph 13 (and para.12) was concerned only with the needs of claimants and their partners; para.14 only with the needs of children and young persons.

Note that entitlement to a severe disability premium is a question to which the assumption in reg.13(2) of the Decisions and Appeals Regulations 1999 applies (relevant information not in possession of decision-maker deemed to be adverse to claimant).

Paragraph 13A

With effect from April 9, 2001, this paragraph establishes an enhanced disability premium for claimants who (or whose partners or, in transitional cases (see the note to reg.17), family members) have not reached the qualifying age for state pension credit and are entitled to the highest rate of the care component of disability living allowance. By para.6(2) above the premium may be paid in addition to any other premium except the pensioner, enhanced pensioner and higher pensioner premiums payable under paras 9, 9A and 10. **2.646**

In transitional cases, the text of sub-para.(1)(b) reads as follows:

"(b) a member of the claimant's family who is aged less than 60."

and sub-para.(2)(a) remains in force in the following terms:

"(2) The condition is not satisfied if the person to whom sub-paragraph (1) refers is—
   (a) a child or young person—
      (i) whose capital if calculated in accordance with Part 5 of these Regulations in like manner as for the claimant, except as provided in regulation 44(1), would exceed £3,000; or
      (ii) who is a long-term patient;"

The premium is payable for the first 52 weeks of any stay in a hospital or similar institution even if payment of disability living allowance has been suspended because of the hospitalisation. If the claimant is a member of a couple or a polygamous marriage, the premium is payable unless both members of the couple or all members of the marriage have been hospitalised for 52 weeks.

In transitional cases, the enhanced disability premium for a child was increased to £26.60 from the beginning of the first benefit week after April 6, 2020 by art.21(5) of, and Sch.3 to, the Social Security Benefits Uprating Order 2020 (SI 2020/234).

Paragraph 14

2.647   Except in transitional cases (as to which see the note to reg.17), the disabled child premium was abolished with effect from April 6, 2004. For details of the position before that date, see p.496 of Vol.II of the 2003 edition. In transitional cases the disabled child premium was increased to £65.52 from the beginning of the first benefit week after April 6, 2020 by art.21(5) of, and Sch.3 to, the Social Security Benefits Uprating Order 2020 (SI 2020/234). The transitional text of para.14 (as substituted with effect from April 9, 2007 by reg.2(7)(g) of SI 2007/719 and amended with effect from April 11, 2011 by reg.3(5) of SI 2011/674, with effect from April 8, 2013 by reg.8 and Sch. para.11(5)(d) of SI 2013/388 and reg.7 and Sch. para.4(5)(e) of SI SI 2013/591, with effect from April 28, 2014 by reg.2(1) and (5) of SI 2014/591, and with effect from November 26, 2014 by reg.3(2)(a)(iii) of SI 2014/2888) is as follows:

"Disabled Child Premium

14.—(1) Subject to sub-paragraph (2), the condition is that where the child or young person for whom the claimant or a partner of his is responsible and who is a member of the claimant's household is—

> (a) in receipt of disability living allowance or is no longer in receipt of that allowance because he is a patient provided that the child or young person continues to be a member of the family; [. . .]
>
> (b) [severely sight impaired or blind or treated as severely sight impaired or blind] within the meaning of paragraph 12(1)(a)(iii) and (2)[; or
>
> (c) a child or young person in respect of whom section 145A of the Contributions and Benefits Act (entitlement after death of child or qualifying young person) applies for the purposes of entitlement to child benefit but only for the period prescribed under that section, and in respect of whom a disabled child premium was included in the claimant's applicable amount immediately before the death of that child or young person, or ceased to be included in the claimant's applicable amount because of that child or young person's death] [; or
>
> (d) a young person who is in receipt of personal independence payment or who would, but for regulations made under section 86(1) (hospital in-patients) of the 2012 Act, be so in receipt provided that the young person continues to be a member of the family] [; or
>
> (e) in receipt of armed forces independence payment.]
>
> (2) The condition [in sub-paragraph (1)(a) [, (b), (d) or (e)]] is not satisfied in respect of a child or young person —
>
> (a) whose capital, if calculated in accordance with Part.5 of these Regulations in like manner as for the claimant, except as provided in regulation 44(1), would exceed £3,000; or
>
> (b) who is a long-term patient."

Paragraph 14ZA

2.648   The carer premium (CP) is part of the Government's shift of resources amongst the disabled. It goes to a person who is entitled to carer's allowance. The CP may encourage the claiming of carer's allowance (formerly called "invalid care allowance" ("ICA")) against which must be balanced the possible loss of SDP for the disabled person being cared for. See *R(IS) 14/94* above and para.13(3ZA). Under sub-paras (3) and (4) entitlement to the premium continues for eight weeks after ceasing to receive carer's allowance. In cases where carer's allowance is not payable because of the overlapping benefits rules, one of the conditions of entitlement is that the claim for carer's allowance should have been made on or after October 1, 1990. Whether this means the original claim or can also encompass any later claim is not entirely clear. DWP Policy is now that those who established an underlying entitlement to ICA (as it then was) before October 1, 1990 can be paid the premium with effect from April 3, 2000 (see Memo DMG JSA/IS 32). For the legal basis for the advice given in the Memo see *CIS/367/2003*.

Paragraph 14ZA (as it was worded in July 1999) was considered by Commissioner Jacobs in *CIS 4267/2001*. In that case, the claimant had been entitled to ICA and hence—under sub-para.(1)—to a carer permium (CP) immediately before he reached the age of 65. He then ceased to receive ICA because of the operation of the Overlapping Benefits Regulations (i.e. presumably because he had begun to receive his state retirement pension) but nevertheless continued to be *treated as* receiving that benefit—and therefore to be entitled to the CP—under sub-para.(2), as then in force. Subsequently, the person for whom he was caring ceased to be entitled to disability living allowance ("DLA"). If the Overlapping Benefits Regulations had not applied, the claimant would have continued to be entitled to ICA even though he was no longer caring for a severely disabled person (see SSCBA 1992 s.70(6) and reg.11 of the Invalid Care Allowance Regulations) and would therefore have continued to be entitled to a CP under sub-para.(1). However, sub-para.(2) provided that a person who was not *actually* in receipt of ICA could only be *treated as* in receipt of that benefit for as long as the person cared for was in receipt of attendance allowance or the middle or highest rates of the care component of DLA. The Commissioner rejected the argument by the claimant's representative that the income support legislation was in conflict with the ICA legislation and that the latter should be given priority. The legislation simply established different rules for different benefits and there was nothing inconsistent in providing differently for the carer premium and for ICA itself.

The wording of para.14ZA has been clarified by the amendments made by SI 2002/2020 with effect from October 28, 2002.

Paragraph 14A

In paras 12–14ZA receipt of a concessionary (i.e. extra-statutory) payment to compensate for non-payment of a benefit is to be equated with actual payment of that benefit.   **2.649**

Paragraph 14B

This important definition of receipt of benefit in terms of payment, not entitlement, reverses the effect of *R(SB) 12/87*. It makes for a further simplification of decision-making. It also ended the argument that it was the parent of a child under 16 who qualified for attendance allowance who received the benefit. See the note to para.13.   **2.650**

[¹SCHEDULE 3   **Regulations 17(1)(e)
and 18(1)(f)**

HOUSING COSTS

Housing costs

1.—(1) Subject to the following provisions of this Schedule, the housing costs applicable to a claimant are those costs—   **2.651**
    (a) which he or, where he is a member of a family, he or any member of that family is, in

accordance with paragraph 2, liable to meet in respect of the dwelling occupied as the home which he or any other member of his family is treated as occupying, and

  (b) which qualify [⁷⁹ under paragraph 17].

(2) In this Schedule—

"housing costs" means those costs to which sub-paragraph (1) refers;

[⁷⁴ . . .]

[⁷⁴ . . .]

[⁷⁹ . . .]

(3) For the purposes of this Schedule a disabled person is a person—

  (a) in respect of whom a disability premium, a disabled child premium, a pensioner premium for persons aged 75 or over or a higher pensioner premium is included in his applicable amount or the applicable amount of a person living with him; or

  (b) [². . .] who, had he in fact been entitled to income support, would have had included in his applicable amount a disability premium, a disabled child premium, a pensioner premium for persons aged 75 or over or a higher pensioner premium [³⁸ ; or

  (c) who is disabled or severely disabled for the purposes of section 9(6) (maximum rate) of the Tax Credits Act 2002.]

[⁴⁹[⁶⁵(d) who-

    (i) is in receipt of an employment and support allowance which includes an amount under section 2(2) [⁷⁵ . . .] or 4(4) [⁷⁵ . . .] of the Welfare Reform Act [⁷⁵ . . .] [⁷⁵ (component) or is a member of the work-related activity group]; or

    (ii) would be entitled to an employment and support allowance [⁷⁵ . . .], but for the application of section 1A of the Act (duration of contributory allowance)]] [⁷⁰ ; or

  (e) who is entitled to an award of universal credit [⁷⁶ and has limited capability for work or limited capability for work and work-related activity as construed in accordance with regulations 39 and 40 of the Universal Credit Regulations 2013.]]

(4) For the purposes of sub-paragraph (3), a person shall not cease to be a disabled person on account of his being disqualified for receiving benefit or treated as capable of work by virtue of the operation of section 171E of the Contributions and Benefits Act (incapacity for work, disqualification etc.) [⁴⁹ or disqualified for receiving employment and support allowance or treated as not having limited capability for work in accordance with regulations made under section 18 of the Welfare Reform Act (disqualification)].

[⁶ [⁴⁴ Previous entitlement to income-based jobseeker's allowance [⁴⁹, income-related employment and support allowance] or state pension credit]

2.652   **1A.**—(1) Where a claimant or his partner was in receipt of or was treated as being in receipt of income-based jobseeker's allowance [⁴⁹ or income-related employment and support allowance] not more than 12 weeks before one of them becomes entitled to income support or, where the claimant or his partner is a person to whom paragraph 14(2) or (8) (linking rules) refers, not more than 26 weeks before becoming so entitled and—

  (a) the applicable amount for that allowance included an amount in respect of housing costs [⁷⁹ under [⁴⁴ ...] paragraph 16 of Schedule 2] to the Jobseeker's Allowance Regulations 1996 [⁴⁹ or [⁷⁹ paragraph 18 of Schedule 6] to the Employment and Support Allowance Regulations]; and

  (b) the circumstances affecting the calculation of those housing costs remain unchanged since the last calculation of those costs,

the applicable amount in respect of housing costs for income support shall be the applicable amount in respect of those costs current when entitlement to income-based jobseeker's allowance [49 or income-related employment and support allowance] was last determined.

[⁴⁴ (1A) Where a claimant or his partner was in receipt of state pension credit not more than 12 weeks before one of them becomes entitled to income support or, where the claimant or his partner is a person to whom paragraph 14(2) or (8) (linking rules) refers, not more than 26 weeks before becoming so entitled, and—

  (a) the appropriate minimum guarantee included an amount in respect of housing costs under [⁷⁹ paragraph 13 of Schedule II] to the State Pension Credit Regulations 2002; and

  (b) the circumstances affecting the calculation of those housing costs remain unchanged since the last calculation of those costs,

the applicable amount in respect of housing costs for income support shall be the amount applicable in respect of those costs current when entitlement to state pension credit was last determined.]

(2) Where, in the period since housing costs were last calculated for income-based job-

seeker's allowance [[49] or income-related employment and support allowance] [[44] or (as the case may be) state pension credit], there has been a change of circumstances, other than a reduction in the amount of an outstanding loan, which increases or reduces those costs, the amount to be met under this Schedule shall, for the purposes of the claim for income support, be recalculated so as to take account of that change.]

Circumstances in which a person is liable to meet housing costs

2.653

   2.—(1) A person is liable to meet housing costs where—
     (a) the liability falls upon him or his partner but not where the liability is to a member of the same household as the person on whom the liability falls;
     (b) because the person liable to meet the housing costs is not meeting them, the claimant has to meet those costs in order to continue to live in the dwelling occupied as the home and it is reasonable in all the circumstances to treat the claimant as liable to meet those costs;
     (c) he in practice shares the housing costs with other members of the household none of whom are close relatives either of the claimant or his partner, and
        (i) one or more of those members is liable to meet those costs, and
        (ii) it is reasonable in the circumstances to treat him as sharing responsibility.
   (2) Where any one or more, but not all, members of the claimant's family are affected by a trade dispute, the housing costs shall be treated as wholly the responsibility of those members of the family not so affected.

Circumstances in which a person is to be treated as occupying a dwelling as his home

2.654

   3.—(1) Subject to the following provisions of this paragraph, a person shall be treated as occupying as his home the dwelling normally occupied as his home by himself or, if he is a member of a family, by himself and his family and he shall not be treated as occupying any other dwelling as his home.
   (2) In determining whether a dwelling is the dwelling normally occupied as the claimant's home for the purposes of sub-paragraph (1) regard shall be had to any other dwelling occupied by the claimant or by him and his family whether or not that other dwelling is in Great Britain.
   (3) Subject to sub-paragraph (4), where a single claimant or a lone parent is a [[15] full-time student] or is on a training course and is liable to make payments (including payments of mortgage interest or, in Scotland, payments under heritable securities or, in either case, analogous payments) in respect of either (but not both) the dwelling which he occupies for the purpose of attending his course of study or his training course or, as the case may be, the dwelling which he occupies when not attending his course, he shall be treated as occupying as his home the dwelling in respect of which he is liable to make payments.
   (4) A full-time student shall not be treated as occupying a dwelling as his home for any week of absence from it, other than an absence occasioned by the need to enter hospital for treatment, outside the period of study, if the main purpose of his occupation during the period of study would be to facilitate attendance on his course.
   (5) Where a claimant has been required to move into temporary accommodation by reason of essential repairs being carried out to the dwelling normally occupied as his home and he is liable to make payments (including payments of mortgage interest or, in Scotland, payments under heritable securities or, in either case, analogous payments) in respect of either (but not both) the dwelling normally occupied or the temporary accommodation, he shall be treated as occupying as his home the dwelling in respect of which he is liable to make those payments.
   (6) Where a person is liable to make payments in respect of two (but not more than two) dwellings, he shall be treated as occupying both dwellings as his home only—
     (a) where he has left and remains absent from the former dwelling occupied as the home through fear of violence in that dwelling or by a former member of his family and it is reasonable that housing costs should be met in respect of both his former dwelling and his present dwelling occupied as the home; or
     (b) in the case of a couple or a member of a polygamous marriage where a partner is [[15] full-time student] or is on a training course and it is unavoidable that he or they should occupy two separate dwellings and reasonable that housing costs should be met in respect of both dwellings; or
     (c) in the case where a person has moved into a new dwelling occupied as the home, except where sub-paragraph (5) applies, for a period not exceeding four benefit weeks [[43] from the first day of the benefit week in which the move occurs] if his liability to make payments in respect of two dwellings is unavoidable.
   (7) Where—

    (a) a person has moved into a dwelling and was liable to make payments in respect of that dwelling before moving in, and

    (b) he had claimed income support before moving in and either that claim has not yet been determined or it has been determined but an amount has not been included under this Schedule and if the claim has been refused a further claim has been made within four weeks of the date on which the claimant moved into the new dwelling occupied as the home; and

    (c) the delay in moving into the dwelling in respect of which there was liability to make payments before moving in was reasonable and—

        (i) that delay was necessary in order to adapt the dwelling to meet the disablement needs of the claimant or any member of his family; or

     [^{39} (ii) the move was delayed pending [^{66} local welfare provision or] the outcome of an application under Part 8 of the Contributions and Benefits Act for a social fund payment to meet a need arising out of the move or in connection with setting up the home in the dwelling, and—

        (aa) a member of the claimant's family is aged five or under,

        (bb) the claimant's applicable amount includes a premium under paragraph 9, 9A, 10, 11, 13 or 14 of Schedule 2 (applicable amounts), or

        (cc) a child tax credit is paid for a member of the claimant's family who is disabled or severely disabled for the purposes of section 9(6) (maximum rate) of the Tax Credits Act 2002; or]

       (iii) the person became liable to make payments in respect of the dwelling while he was a patient or was in residential accommodation,

he shall be treated as occupying the dwelling as his home for any period not exceeding four weeks immediately prior to the date on which he moved into the dwelling and in respect of which he was liable to make payments.

  (8) This sub-paragraph applies to a person who enters residential accommodation—

    (a) for the purpose of ascertaining whether the accommodation suits his needs; and

    (b) with the intention of returning to the dwelling which he normally occupies as his home should, in the event, the residential accommodation prove not to suit his needs,

and while in the accommodation, the part of the dwelling which he normally occupies as his home is not let, or as the case may be, sub-let to another person.

  (9) A person to whom sub-paragraph (8) applies shall be treated as occupying the dwelling he normally occupies as his home during any period (commencing with the day he enters the accommodation) not exceeding 13 weeks in which the person is resident in the accommodation, but only in so far as the total absence from the dwelling does not exceed 52 weeks.

  (10) A person, other than a person to whom sub-paragraph (11) applies, shall be treated as occupying a dwelling as his home throughout any period of absence not exceeding 13 weeks, if, and only if—

    (a) he intends to return to occupy the dwelling as his home; and

    (b) the part of the dwelling normally occupied by him has not been let or, as the case may be, sub-let to another person; and

    (c) the period of absence is unlikely to exceed 13 weeks.

  (11) This sub-paragraph applies to a person whose absence from the dwelling he normally occupies as his home is temporary and—

    (a) he intends to return to occupy the dwelling as his home; and

    (b) while the part of the dwelling which is normally occupied by him has not been let or, as the case may be, sub-let; and

    (c) he is—

     [^{30} (i) detained in custody on remand pending trial or, as a condition of bail, required to reside—

        (aa) in a dwelling, other than the dwelling he occupies as his home; or

        (bb) in premises approved under [^{53} section 13 of the Offender Management Act 2007],

      or, detained pending sentence upon conviction, or]

      (ii) resident in a hospital or similar institution as a patient, or

      (iii) undergoing or, as the case may be, his partner or his dependent child is undergoing, in the United Kingdom or elsewhere, medical treatment, or medically approved convalescence, in accommodation other than residential accommodation, or

      (iv) following, in the United Kingdom or elsewhere, a training course, or

      (v) undertaking medically approved care of a person residing in the United Kingdom or elsewhere, or

(vi) undertaking the care of a child whose parent or guardian is temporarily absent from the dwelling normally occupied by that parent or guardian for the purpose of receiving medically approved care or medical treatment, or

(vii) a person who is, whether in the United Kingdom or elsewhere, receiving medically approved care provided in accommodation other than residential accommodation, or

(viii) a [15 full-time student] to whom sub-paragraph (3) or (6)(b) does not apply, or

(ix) a person other than a person to whom sub-paragraph (8) applies, who is receiving care provided in residential accommodation; or

(x) a person to whom sub-paragraph (6)(a) does not apply and who has left the dwelling he occupies as his home through fear of violence in that dwelling [2, or by a person] who was formerly a member of his family; and

(d) the period of his absence is unlikely to exceed a period of 52 weeks or, in exceptional circumstances, is unlikely substantially to exceed that period.

(12) A person to whom sub-paragraph (11) applies is to be treated as occupying the dwelling he normally occupies as his home during any period of absence not exceeding 52 weeks beginning with the first day of that absence.

(13) In this paragraph—

(a) "medically approved" means certified by a medical practitioner;

(b) "patient" means a person who is undergoing medical or other treatment as an in-patient in a hospital or similar institution;

[56 (ba) "period of study" has the meaning given in regulation 61(1) (interpretation);]

[32 (c) "residential accommodation" means accommodation which is a care home, an Abbeyfield Home or an independent hospital;]

(d) "training course" means such a course of training or instruction provided wholly or partly by or on behalf of or in pursuance of arrangements made with, or approved by or on behalf of, [55 Skills Devolopment Scotland,] Scottish Enterprise, Highlands and Islands Enterprise, a government department or the Secretary of State.

Housing costs not met

4.—(1) No amount may be met under the provisions of this Schedule—   2.655

(a) in respect of housing benefit expenditure; or

(b) where the claimant is [32 living in care home, an Abbeyfield Home or an independent hospital except where he is living in such a home or hospital] during a temporary absence from the dwelling he occupies as his home and in so far as they relate totemporary absences, the provisions of paragraph 3(8) to (12) apply to him during that absence.

(2)–(12) [79 . . .]

Apportionment of housing costs

5.—(1) Where the dwelling occupied as the home is a composite hereditament and—   2.656

(a) before 1st April 1990 for the purposes of section 48(5) of the General Rate Act 1967 (reduction of rates on dwellings), it appeared to a rating authority or it was determined in pursuance of subsection (6) of section 48 of that Act that the hereditament, including the dwelling occupied as the home, was a mixed hereditament and that only a proportion of the rateable value of the hereditament was attributable to use for the purpose of a private dwelling; or

(b) in Scotland, before 1st April 1989 an assessor acting pursuant to section 45(1) of the Water (Scotland) Act 1980 (provision as to valuation roll) has apportioned the net annual value of the premises including the dwelling occupied as the home between the part occupied as a dwelling and the remainder,

the amounts applicable under this Schedule shall be such proportion of the amounts applicable in respect of the hereditament or premises as a whole as is equal to the proportion of the rateable value of the hereditament attributable to the part of the hereditament used for the purposes of a private tenancy or, in Scotland, the proportion of the net annual value of the premises apportioned to the part occupied as a dwelling house.

(2) Subject to sub-paragraph (1) and the following provisions of this paragraph, where the dwelling occupied as the home is a composite hereditament, the amount applicable under this Schedule shall be the relevant fraction of the amount which would otherwise be applicable under this Schedule in respect of the dwelling occupied as the home.

(3) For the purposes of sub-paragraph (2), the relevant fraction shall be obtained in accordance with the formula—

$$\frac{A}{A+B}$$

where—

"A" is the current market value of the claimant's interest in that part of the composite hereditament which is domestic property within the meaning of section 66 of the Act of 1988;

"B" is the current market value of the claimant's interest in that part of the composite hereditament which is not domestic property within that section.

(4) In this paragraph—

"composite hereditament" means—
  (a) as respects England and Wales, any hereditament which is shown as a composite hereditament in a local non-domestic rating list;
  (b) as respects Scotland, any lands and heritages entered in the valuation roll which are part residential subjects within the meaning of section 26(1) of the Act of 1987;
"local non-domestic rating list" means a list compiled and maintained under section 41(1) of the Act of 1988;
"the Act of 1987" means the Abolition of Domestic Rates Etc. (Scotland) Act 1987;
"the Act of 1988" means the Local Government Finance Act 1988.

(5) Where responsibility for expenditure which relates to housing costs met under this Schedule is shared, the amounts applicable shall be calculated by reference to the appropriate proportion of that expenditure for which the claimant is responsible.

Existing housing costs

2.657   **6.**—[74 . . .]

Transitional Protection

2.658   **7.**—[74 . . .]

[74 Housing costs]

2.659   **8.**—(1) Subject to the provisions of this Schedule, the [74 . . .] housing costs to be met in any particular case are—
  (a) where the claimant has been [2 entitled to] income support for a continuous period of 39 weeks or more, an amount—
      (i) [79 . . .]
      (ii) equal to any payments which qualify under paragraph 17(1)(a) to (c);
  (b) in any other case, nil.
  [2 (1A) [79 ...]]
  [6 (1B) [79 ...]]
  (2) [74 . . .]
  (3) [74 . . .]
  (4) [74 . . .]
  (5) [74 . . .]

General exclusions from [74 paragraph 8]

2.660   **9.**—(1) [74 Paragraph 8] shall not apply where—
  [25 (a) the claimant's partner has attained the qualifying age for state pension credit;]
  (b) the housing costs are payments—
      (i) under a co-ownership agreement;
      (ii) under or relating to a tenancy or licence of a Crown tenant; or
      (iii) where the dwelling occupied as the home is a tent, in respect of the tent and the site on which it stands.
  (2) In a case falling within sub-paragraph (1), the housing costs to be met are—
  (a) where head (a) of sub-paragraph (1) applies, an amount—
      (i) [79 . . .]
      (ii) equal to the payments which qualify under paragraph 17;
  (b) where head (b) of sub-paragraph (1) applies, an amount equal to the payments which qualify under paragraph 17(1)(d) to (f).

[20 The calculation for loans

2.661   **10.**—[79 ...]]

General provisions applying to [74 . . .] housing costs

2.662   **11.**—[79 ...]

The standard rate
  12.—[⁷⁹ ...]   **2.663**

Excessive Housing Costs
  13.—[⁷⁹ ...]   **2.664**

Linking rule
  14.—(1) [⁶²...] for the purposes of this Schedule—   **2.665**
  (a) a person shall be treated as being in receipt of income support during the following
       periods—
       (i)   any period in respect of which it was subsequently [¹³determined] that he was
             entitled to income support; and
       (ii) any period of 12 weeks or less [¹⁶ or, as the case may be, 52 weeks or less,] in
             respect of which he was not in receipt of income support and which fell imme-
             diately between periods in respect of which
             [⁴(aa) he was, or was treated as being, in receipt of income support,
                (bb) he was treated as entitled to income support for the purpose of subpara-
                      graph (5) or (5A), or
                (cc) (i) above applies;]
  (b) a person shall be treated as not being in receipt of income support during any period
       other than a period to which (a)(ii) above applies in respect of which it is subsequently
       [¹³determined] that he was not so entitled;
  (c) where—
       (i)   the claimant was a member of a couple or a polygamous marriage; and
       (ii) his partner was, in respect of a past period, in receipt of income support for
             himself and the claimant; and
       (iii) the claimant is no longer a member of that couple or polygamous marriage;
             and
       (iv) the claimant made his claim for income support within twelve weeks [¹⁶ or,
             as the case may be, 52 weeks,] of ceasing to be a member of that couple or
             polygamous marriage,
       he shall be treated as having been in receipt of income support for the same period as
       his former partner had been or had been treated, for the purposes of this Schedule, as
       having been;
  (d) where the claimant's partner's applicable amount was determined in accordance
       with paragraph 1(1) (single claimant) or paragraph 1(2) (lone parent) of Schedule
       2 (applicable amounts) in respect of a past period, provided that the claim was made
       within twelve weeks [¹⁶ or, as the case may be, 52 weeks,] of the claimant and his partner
       becoming one of a couple or polygamous marriage, the claimant shall be treated as
       having been in receipt of income support for the same period as his partner had been or
       had been treated, for the purposes of this Schedule, as having been;
  (e) where the claimant is a member of a couple or a polygamous marriage and his partner
       was, in respect of a past period, in receipt of income support for himself and the claim-
       ant, and the claimant has begun to receive income support as a result of an election
       by the members of the couple or polygamous marriage, he shall be treated as having
       been in receipt of income support for the same period as his partner had been or had
       been treated, for the purposes of this Schedule, as having been;
  [⁷(ee) where the claimant—
       (i)   is a member of a couple or a polygamous marriage and the claimant's partner
             was, immediately before the participation by any member of that couple or polyg-
             amous marriage in an employment programme specified in regulation 75(1)(a)
             (ii) of the Jobseeker's Allowance Regulations 1996 [¹⁹, in the Intensive Activity
             Period specified in regulation 75(1)(a)(iv) of those Regulations [⁴⁷ . . .]], in
             receipt of income support and his applicable amount included an amount for the
             couple or for the partners of the polygamous marriage; and
       (ii) has, immediately after that participation in that programme, begun to receive
             income support as a result of an election under regulation 4(3) of the Social
             Security (Claims and Payments) Regulations 1987 by the members of the
             couple or polygamous marriage,
       the claimant shall be treated as having been in receipt of income support for the same
       period as his partner had been or had been treated, for the purposes of this Schedule,
       as having been;]
  (f) where—
       (i)   the claimant was a member of a family of a person (not being a former partner)

entitled to income support and at least one other member of that family was a child or young person; and

   (ii) the claimant becomes a member of another family which includes that child or young person; and

   (iii) the claimant made his claim for income support within 12 weeks 1996[¹⁶ or, as the case may be, 52 weeks,] of the date on which the person entitled to income support mentioned in (i) above ceased to be so entitled,

the claimant shall be treated as being in receipt of income support for the same period as that person had been or had been treated, for the purposes of this Schedule, as having been.

(2) [⁶³ . . .]

(3) For the purposes of this Schedule, where a claimant has ceased to be entitled to income support because he or his partner is participating in arrangements for training made under section 2 of the Employment and Training Act 1973 or attending a course at an employment rehabilitation centre established under that section [⁵³ or under the Enterprise and New Towns (Scotland) Act 1990], he shall be treated as if he had been in receipt of income support for the period during which he or his partner was participating in such arrangements or attending such a course.

[⁷(3ZA) For the purposes of this Schedule, a claimant who has ceased to be entitled to income support because—

   (a) that claimant or his partner was participating in an employment programme specified in reglation 75(1)(a)(ii) of the Jobseeker's Allowance Regulations 1996 [¹⁹ , in the Intensive Activity Period specified in regulation 75(1)(a)(iv) of those Regulations [⁴⁸ . . .]] [¹⁴or in an employment zone scheme]; and

   (b) in consequence of such participation the claimant or his partner was engaged in remunerative work or had an income in excess of the claimant's applicable amount as prescribed in Part IV,

shall be treated as if he had been in receipt of income support for the period during which he or his partner was participating in that programme [¹⁹or activity].]

[²(3A) Where, for the purposes of sub-paragraphs [⁷(1), (3) and (3ZA)], a person is treated as being in receipt of income support, for a certain period, he shall [¹², subject to sub-paragraph (3AA),] be treated as being entitled to income support for the same period.]

[¹²(3AA) [⁷⁹ ...]]

[⁷(3B) For the purposes of this Schedule, in determining whether a person is entitled to or to be treated as entitled to income support, entitlement to a contribution-based jobseeker's allowance immediately before a period during which that person or his partner is participating in an employment programme specified in regulation 75(1)(a)(ii) of the Jobseeker's Allowance Regulations 1996 [¹⁹, in the Intensive Activity Period specified in regulation 75(1)(a)(iv) of those Regulations [⁴⁷ . . .]] shall be treated as entitlement to income support for the purposes of any requirement that a person is, or has been, entitled to income support for any period of time.]

(4) For the purposes of this Schedule, sub-paragraph (5) applies where a person is not entitled to income support by reason only that he has—

   (a) capital exceeding [³⁶£16,000]; or

   (b) income [⁶¹equal to or] exceeding the applicable amount which applies in his case, or

   (c) both capital exceeding [³⁶£16,000] and income exceeding the applicable amount which applies in his case.

(5) A person to whom sub-paragraph (4) applies shall be treated as entitled to income support throughout any period of not [²more] than 39 weeks which comprises only days—

   (a) on which he is entitled to unemployment benefit, [³a contribution-based jobseeker's allowance,] statutory sick pay [⁴⁹ , incapacity benefit or contributory employment and support allowance]; or

   (b) on which he is, although not entitled to any of the benefits mentioned in head (a) above, entitled to be credited with earnings equal to the lower earnings limit for the time being in force in accordance with [¹¹regulation 8A or 8B] of the Social Security (Credits) Regulations 1975; or

   (c) in respect of which the claimant is treated as being in receipt of income support.

[²(5A) Subject to sub-paragraph (5B), a person to whom sub-paragraph (4) applies and who is either a person to whom [³paragraph 4 or 5 of Schedule 1B (persons caring for another person) applies] or a lone parent shall, for the purposes of this Schedule, be treated as entitled to income support throughout any period of not more than 39 weeks following the refusal of a claim for income support made by or on behalf of that person.

(5B) Sub-paragraph (5A) shall not apply in relation to a person mentioned in that sub-paragraph who, during the period referred to in that sub-paragraph—

(a) is engaged in, or is treated as engaged in, remunerative work or whose partner is engaged in, or is treated as engaged in, remunerative work;

[³(b) is a [¹⁵ full-time student], other than one who would qualify for income support under regulation 4ZA(3) (prescribed categories of person);]

(c) is temporarily absent from Great Britain, other than in the circumstances specified in regulation 4(2) and (3)(c) (temporary absence from Great Britain).]

(6) In a case where—

(a) [²sub-paragraphs (5) and (5A) apply] solely by virtue of sub-paragraph (4)(b); and

(b) the claimant's income includes payments under a policy taken out to insure against the risk that the policy holder is unable to meet [⁷⁹ any payment which qualifies under paragraph 17],

[²sub-paragraphs (5) and (5A)] shall have effect as if for the words "throughout any period of not [²more] than 39 weeks" there shall be substituted the words "throughout any period that payments made in accordance with the terms of the policy".

(7) [². . .]

(8) This sub-paragraph applies—

(a) to a person who claims income support, or in respect of whom income support is claimed, and who—

(i) received payments under a policy of insurance taken out to insure against loss of employment, and those payments are exhausted; and

(ii) had a previous award of income support where the applicable amount included an amount by way of housing costs; and

(b) where the period in respect of which the previous award of income support was payable ended not more than 26 weeks before the date the claim was made.

(9) Where sub-paragraph (8) applies, in determining—

(a) [⁷⁴ . . .]

(b) for the purposes of paragraph 8(1) whether a claimant has been [²entitled to] income support for a continuous period of 39 weeks or more,

any week falling between the date of the termination of the previous award and the date of the new claim shall be ignored.

[¹⁰(10) In the case of a person who is a welfare to work beneficiary, the references in sub-paragraphs (1)(a)(ii), [¹⁷ (1)(c)(iv),] (1)(d) and (1)(f)(iii) to a period of 12 weeks shall be treated as references to a period of [⁴² 104] weeks.]

[¹⁸ (11) For the purposes of sub-paragraph (1)(a)(ii), (1)(c)(iv), (1)(d) and (1)(f)(iii), the relevant period shall be—

(a) 52 weeks in the case of a person to whom sub-paragraph (12) applies;

(b) subject to sub-paragraph (10), 12 weeks in any other case.

(12) This sub-paragraph applies, subject to sub-paragraph (13), in the case of a person who, on or after 9th April 2001, has ceased to be entitled to income support because he or his partner—

(a) has commenced employment as an employed earner or as a self-employed earner or has increased the hours in which he is engaged in such employment;

(b) is taking active steps to establish himself in employment as an employed earner or as a self-employed earner under any scheme for assisting persons to become so employed which is mentioned in regulation 19(1)(r)(i) to (iii) of the Jobseeker's Allowance Regulations 1996; or

(c) is participating in—

(i) a New Deal option;

(ii) an employment zone programme; or

(iii) the self-employment route; [¹⁹ or

(iv) the Intensive Activity Period specified in regulation 75(1)(a)(iv) of the Jobseeker's Allowance Regulations 1996 [⁴⁷ . . .],]

and, as a consequence, he or his partner was engaged in remunerative work or had income [⁶¹ equal to or] in excess of the applicable amount as prescribed in Part IV.

(13) Sub-paragraph (12) shall only apply to the extent that immediately before the day on which the person ceased to be entitled to income support, his housing costs were being met in accordance with paragraph [⁷⁴ . . .] 8(1)(a) or would have been so met but for any non-dependant deduction under paragraph 18.]

[²⁵ (14) For the purpose of determining whether the linking rules set out in this paragraph apply in a case where a claimant's former partner was entitled to state pension credit, any reference to income support in this Schedule shall be taken to include also a reference to state pension credit.]

[⁴⁹ (15) For the purpose of determining whether the linking rules set out in this paragraph apply in a case where [^{50} a claimant, a claimant's partner or] a claimant's former partner was entitled to income-related employment and support allowance, any reference to income support in this Schedule shall be taken to include also a reference to income-related employment and support allowance.]

Loans on residential property

2.666   **15.**—[^{79} ...]

Loans for repairs and improvements to the dwelling occupied as the home

2.667   **16.**—[^{79} ...]

[^{79} Housing costs]

2.668   **17.**—(1) Subject to the deduction specified in sub-paragraph (2) and the reductions applicable in sub-paragraph (5), there shall be met under this paragraph the amounts, calculated on a weekly basis, in respect of the following housing costs—

  (a) payments by way of rent or ground rent relating to a long tenancy [^{41} ...];
  (b) service charges;
  (c) payments by way of rentcharge within the meaning of section 1 of the Rentcharges Act 1977;
  (d) payments under a co-ownership scheme;
  (e) payments under or relating to a tenancy or licence of a Crown tenant;
  (f) where the dwelling occupied as the home is a tent, payments in respect of the tent and the site on which it stands.

(2) Subject to sub-paragraph (3), the deductions to be made from the weekly amounts to be met under this paragraph are—

  (a) where the costs are inclusive of any of the items mentioned in [^{33} paragraph 6(2) of Schedule 1 to the Housing Benefit Regulations 2006] (payment in respect of fuel charges), the deductions prescribed in that paragraph unless the claimant provides evidence on which the actual or approximate amount of the service charge for fuel may be estimated, in which case the estimated amount;
  (b) where the costs are inclusive of ineligible service charges within the meaning of [^{34} paragraph 1 of Schedule 1 to the Housing Benefit Regulations 2006] (ineligible service charges) the amounts attributable to those ineligible service charges or where that amount is not separated from or separately identified within the housing costs to be met under this paragraph, such part of the payments made in respect of those housing costs which are fairly attributable to the provision of those ineligible services having regard to the costs of comparable services;
  (c) any amount for repairs and improvements, and for this purpose the expression "repairs and improvements" has [^{79} the meaning in sub-paragraph (6)].

(3) Where arrangements are made for the housing costs, which are met under this paragraph and which are normally paid for a period of 52 weeks, to be paid instead for a period of 53 weeks, or to be paid irregularly, or so that no such costs are payable or collected in certain periods, or so that the costs for different periods in the year are of different amounts, the weekly amount shall be the amount payable for the year divided by 52.

(4) Where the claimant or a member of his family—

  (a) pays for reasonable repairs or redecorations to be carried out to the dwelling they occupy; and
  (b) that work was not the responsibility of the claimant or any member of his family; and
  (c) in consequence of that work being done, the costs which are normally met under this paragraph are waived,

then those costs shall, or a period not exceeding 8 weeks, be treated as payable.

(5) Where in England and Wales an amount calculated on a weekly basis in respect of housing costs specified in sub-paragraph (1)(e) (Crown tenants) includes water charges, that amount shall be reduced—

  (a) where the amount payable in respect of water charges is known, by that amount;
  (b) in any other case, by the amount which would be the likely weekly water charge had the property not been occupied by a Crown tenant.

[^{79}(6) For the purposes of sub-paragraph (2)(c), "repairs and improvements" means any of the following measures undertaken with a view to maintaining the fitness of the dwelling for human habitation or, where the dwelling forms part of a building, any part of a building containing that dwelling—

  (a) provision of a fixed bath, shower, wash basin, sink or lavatory, and necessary associated plumbing, including the provision of hot water not connected to a central heating system;

(b) repairs to existing heating system;
(c) damp proof measures;
(d) provision of ventilation and natural lighting;
(e) provision of drainage facilities;
(f) provision of facilities for preparing and cooking food;
(g) provision of insulation of the dwelling occupied as the home;
(h) provision of electric lighting and sockets;
(i) provision of storage facilities for fuel or refuse;
(j) repairs of unsafe structural defects;
(k) adapting a dwelling for the special needs of a disabled person; or
(l) provision of separate sleeping accommodation for persons of different sexes aged 10 or over but under the age of 20 who live with the claimant and for whom the claimant or the claimant's partner is responsible.]

Non-dependant deductions

18.—(1) Subject to the following provisions of this paragraph, the following deductions **2.669** from the amount to be met under the preceding paragraphs of this Schedule in respect of housing costs shall be made—

[31(a) in respect of a non-dependant aged 18 or over who is engaged in any remunerative work, [82 £102.85];
(b) in respect of a non-dependant aged 18 or over to whom paragraph (a) does not apply, [82 £15.95].]

(2) In the case of a non-dependant aged 18 or over to whom sub-paragraph (1)(a) applies because he is in [2 remunerative] work, where the claimant satisfies the [13 Secretary of State] that the non-dependant's gross weekly income is—

(a) less than [82 £149.00], the deduction to be made under this paragraph shall be the deduction specified in sub-paragraph (1)(b);
(b) not less than [82 £149.00] but less than [82 £217.00], the deduction to be made under this paragraph shall be [82 £36.65];
(c) not less than [82 £217.00] but less than [82 £283.00], the deduction to be made under this paragraph shall be [82 £50.30];
(d) not less than [82 £283.00] but less than [82 £377.00], the deduction to be made under this paragraph shall be [82 £82.30];
(e) not less than [82 £377.00] but less than [82 £469.00], the deduction to be made under this paragraph shall be [82 £93.70]].

[79 (2A) Where a non-dependant deduction is being made under the Loans for Mortgage Interest Regulations 2017, the amount of the deduction under sub-paragraph (1) or (2) is to be reduced by an amount equal to that non-dependant deduction.]

(3) Only one deduction shall be made under this paragraph in respect of a couple or, as the case may be, the members of a polygamous marriage, and where, but for this sub-paragraph, the amount that would fall to be deducted in respect of one member of a couple or polygamous marriage is higher than the amount (if any) that would fall to be deducted in respect of the other, or any other, member, the higher amount shall be deducted.

(4) In applying the provisions of sub-paragraph (2) in the case of a couple or, as the case may be, a polygamous marriage, regard shall be had, for the purpose of sub-paragraph (2), to the couple's or, as the case may be, all the members of the polygamous marriage's, joint weekly income.

(5) Where a person is a non-dependant in respect of more than one joint occupier of a dwelling (except where the joint occupiers are a couple or members of a polygamous marriage), the deduction in respect of that non-dependant shall be apportioned between the joint occupiers (the amount so apportioned being rounded to the nearest penny) having regard to the number of joint occupiers and the proportion of the housing costs in respect of the dwelling occupied as the home payable by each of them.

(6) No deduction shall be made in respect of any non-dependants occupying the dwelling occupied as the home of the claimant, if the claimant or any partner of his is—

(a) [73 severely sight impaired or blind or treated as severely sight impaired or blind] by virtue of paragraph 12 of Schedule 2 (additional condition for the higher pensioner and disability premiums); or
(b) receiving in respect of himself either—
  (i) an attendance allowance; [68. . .]
  (ii) the care component of the disability living allowance [68 ; [69 . . .]

     (iii) the daily living component of personal independence payment] [⁶⁹ or

     (iv) armed forces independence payment].

(7) No deduction shall be made in respect of a non-dependant—

  (a) if, although he resides with the claimant, it appears to the [¹³ Secretary of State] that the dwelling occupied as his home is normally elsewhere; or

  (b) if he is in receipt of a training allowance paid in connection with [⁵³ youth training] established under section 2 of the Employment and Training Act 1973 or section 2 of the Enterprise and New Towns (Scotland) Act 1990; or

  (c) if he is a full-time student during a period of study or, if he is not in remunerative work, during a recognised summer vacation appropriate to his course; or

  (d) if he is aged under 25 and in receipt of income support [⁵or an income-based jobseeker's allowance]; or

  (e) in respect of whom a deduction in the calculation of a rent rebate or allowance falls to be made under [³⁵ regulation 74 of the Housing Benefit Regulations 2006] (non-dependant deductions); or

  (f) to whom, but for paragraph (2C) of regulation 3 (definition of non-dependant) paragraph (2B) of that regulation would apply; or

  (g) if he is not residing with the claimant because he has been a patient for a period in excess of [²⁴ 52] weeks, or is a prisoner, and for these purposes—

     [³⁷ (i) "patient" has the meaning given in paragraph 3(13)(b) and "prisoner" has the meaning given in regulation 21(3); and

     (ii) in calculating a period of 52 weeks as a patient, any two or more distinct periods separated by one or more intervals each not exceeding 28 days shall be treated as a single period; or]

[³¹(h) if he is in receipt of state pension credit.]

[⁴⁹ (i) he is aged less than 25 and is in receipt of [⁶⁷ income–related] employment and support allowance [⁷⁵ and is not a member of the work-related activity group or a member of the support group; or]

[⁷¹ (j) if he is aged less than 25 and is entitled to an award of universal credit which is calculated on the basis that he does not have any earned income].

(8) In the case of a non-dependant to whom sub-paragraph (2) applies because he is in [²remunerative] work, there shall be disregarded from his gross income—

  (a) [⁸¹ any Grenfell Tower payment, or] any attendance allowance [⁶⁸ , disability living allowance or personal independence payment] [⁶⁹ or armed forces independence payment] received by him;

  (b) any payment made under [⁵⁸ or by] the Macfarlane Trust, the Macfarlane (Special Payments) Trust, the Macfarlane (Special Payments) (No.2) Trust, the Fund, the Eileen Trust [⁵⁷, MFET Limited] [⁶⁴, the Skipton Fund, the Caxton Foundation] [⁷⁷, the Scottish Infected Blood Support Scheme] [⁷⁹, an approved blood scheme] [⁷⁸, the London Emergencies Trust, the We Love Manchester Emergency Fund] [⁸¹, the National Emergencies Trust] or the Independent Living [⁵² Fund (2006)] which, had his income fallen to be calculated under regulation 40 (calculation of income other than earnings), would have been disregarded under paragraph 21 of Schedule 9 (income in kind); and

  (c) any payment which, had his income fallen to be calculated under regulation 40 would have been disregarded under paragraph 39 of Schedule 9 (payments made under certain trusts and certain other payments).

[¹⁰⁶ (d) any payment made under or by a trust, established for the purpose of giving relief and assistance to disabled persons whose disabilities were caused by the fact that during their mother's pregnancy she had taken a preparation containing the drug known as Thalidomide, and which is approved by the Secretary of State.]

[⁷¹ (9) For the purposes of sub-paragraph (7)(j), "earned income" has the meaning given in regulation 52 of the Universal Credit Regulations 2013.]

Rounding of fractions

2.670   **19.**—Where any calculation made under this Schedule results in a fraction of a penny, that fraction shall be treated as a penny.]

Amendments

1. Social Security (Income Support and Claims and Payments) Amendment Regulations 1995 (SI 1995/1613) reg.2 and Sch.1 (October 2, 1995).

2. Social Security (Income Support, Claims and Payments and

Adjudication) Amendment Regulations 1995 (SI 1995/2927) reg.5 (December 12, 1995).

3. Income Support (General) (Jobseeker's Allowance Consequential Amendments) Regulations 1996 (SI 1996/206) reg.24 (October 7, 1996).

4. Income-related Benefits Schemes and Social Fund (Miscellaneous Amendments) Regulations 1996 (SI 1996/1944) reg.6(10) (October 7, 1996).

5. Social Security and Child Support (Miscellaneous Amendments) Regulations 1997 (SI 1997/827) reg.6 (April 7, 1997).

6. Social Security (Miscellaneous Amendments) (No.4) Regulations 1997 (SI 1997/2305) reg.2 (October 22, 1997).

7. Social Security Amendment (New Deal) Regulations 1997 (SI 1997/2863) reg.16 (January 5, 1998).

8. Social Security (Non-Dependant Deductions) Regulations 1996 (SI 1996/2518) reg.4 (April 6, 1998).

9. Social Security (Welfare to Work) Regulations 1998 (SI 1998/2231) reg.13(4)(a) (October 5, 1998).

10. Social Security (Welfare to Work) Regulations 1998 (SI 1998/2231) reg.13(4)(b) (October 5, 1998).

11. Social Security Benefits (Miscellaneous Amendments) Regulations 1999 (SI 1999/714) reg.3 (April 5, 1999).

12. Income Support (General) and Jobseeker's Allowance Amendment Regulations 1999 (SI 1999/1921) reg.2(1) (August 2, 1999).

13. Social Security Act 1998 (Commencement No.12 and Consequential and Transitional Provisions) Order 1999 (SI 1999/3178 (C.81)) art.3(5) and Sch.5 para.9 (November 29, 1999)

14. Social Security Amendment (Employment Zones) Regulations 2000 (SI 2000/724) reg.4(3)(c) (April 3, 2000).

15. Social Security Amendment (Students) Regulations 2000 (SI 2000/1981) reg.5(5) and Sch. (July 31, 2000).

16. Social Security (Miscellaneous Amendments) Regulations 2001 (SI 2001/488) reg.6(a) (April 9, 2001).

17. Social Security (Miscellaneous Amendments) Regulations 2001 (SI 2001/488) reg.6(b) (April 9, 2001).

18. Social Security (Miscellaneous Amendments) Regulations 2001 (SI 2001/488) reg.6(c) (April 9, 2001).

19. Social Security Amendment (New Deal) Regulations 2001 (SI 2001/1029) reg.14 (April 9, 2001).

20. Income Support (General) and Jobseeker's Allowance Amendment Regulations 2001 (SI 2001/3651) reg.2(1) (December 10, 2001).

21. Social Security Amendment (Residential Care and Nursing Homes) Regulations 2001 (SI 2001/3767) reg.2(1) and Pt I of Sch. para.15 (April 8, 2002).

22. Social Security (Miscellaneous Amendments) Regulations 2002 (SI 2002/841) reg.6 (April 8, 2002).

23. Child Support (Consequential Amendments and Transitional Provisions) Regulations 2001 (SI 2001/158) reg.6(3) (in force in relation to any particular case on the day on which s.1 of the Child Support, Pensions and Social Security Act 2000 comes into force in relation to that type of case).

24. Social Security (Hospital In-Patients and Miscellaneous Amendments) Regulations 2003 (SI 2003/1195) reg.3(4) (May 21, 2003).

25. State Pension Credit (Consequential, Transitional and Miscellaneous Provisions) Regulations 2002 (SI 2002/3019) reg.29(6) (October 6, 2003).

26. Social Security (Housing Costs Amendments) Regulations 2004 (SI 2004/2825) reg.2(2) (November 28, 2004).

27. Social Security (Housing Costs Amendments) Regulations 2004 (SI 2004/2825) reg.2(3) (November 28, 2004).

28. Social Security (Housing Costs Amendments) Regulations 2004 (SI 2004/2825) reg.2(4) (November 28, 2004).

29. Social Security (Housing Costs Amendments) Regulations 2004 (SI 2004/2825) reg.2(5) (November 28, 2004).

30. Social Security (Housing Benefit, Council Tax Benefit, State Pension Credit and Miscellaneous Amendments) Regulations 2004 (SI 2004/2327) reg.5(a) (April 4, 2005).

31. Social Security (Housing Benefit, Council Tax Benefit, State Pension Credit and Miscellaneous Amendments) Regulations 2004 (SI 2004/2327) reg.5(b) (April 4, 2005).

32. Social Security (Care Homes and Independent Hospitals) Regulations 2005 (SI 2005/2687) reg.2 and Sch.1 para.8 (October 24, 2005).

33. Housing Benefit and Council Tax Benefit (Consequential Provisions) Regulations 2006 (SI 2006/217) reg.5 and Sch.2 para.1(5)(a) (March 6, 2006).

34. Housing Benefit and Council Tax Benefit (Consequential Provisions) Regulations 2006 (SI 2006/217) reg.5 and Sch.2 para.1(5)(b) (March 6, 2006).

35. Housing Benefit and Council Tax Benefit (Consequential Provisions) Regulations 2006 (SI 2006/217) reg.5 and Sch.2 para.1(5)(c) (March 6, 2006).

36. Social Security (Miscellaneous Amendments) (No.2) Regulations 2005 (SI 2005/2465) reg.2(7) (April 10, 2006).

37. Social Security (Hospital In-Patients) Regulations 2005 (SI 2005/3360) reg.4(4) (April 10, 2006).

38. Social Security (Miscellaneous Amendments) (No.4) Regulations 2006 (SI 2006/2378) reg.5(8)(a) (October 2, 2006).

39. Social Security (Miscellaneous Amendments) (No.4) Regulations 2006 (SI 2006/2378) reg.5(8)(b) (October 2, 2006).

40. Social Security (Miscellaneous Amendments) (No.4) Regulations 2006 (SI 2006/2378) reg.5(8)(c) (October 2, 2006).

41. Social Security (Miscellaneous Amendments) (No.4) Regulations 2006 (SI 2006/2378) reg.5(8)(d) (October 2, 2006).

42. Social Security (Miscellaneous Amendments) (No.4) Regulations 2006 (SI 2006/2378) reg.5(7)(b) (October 9, 2006).

43. Social Security (Miscellaneous Amendments) (No.5) Regulations 2006 (SI 2006/3274) reg.2 (January 8, 2007).

44. Social Security (Housing Costs and Miscellaneous Amendments) Regulations 2007 (SI 2007/3183) reg.3(3)(a) (December 17, 2007).

45. Social Security (Housing Costs and Miscellaneous Amendments) Regulations 2007 (SI 2007/3183) reg.3(3)(b) (December 17, 2007).

46. Social Security (Housing Costs and Miscellaneous Amendments) Regulations 2007 (SI 2007/3183) reg.3(3)(c) (December 17, 2007).

47. Social Security (Miscellaneous Amendments) Regulations 2008 (SI 2008/698) reg.2(8)(c) (April 14, 2008).

48. Social Security (Miscellaneous Amendments) Regulations 2008 (SI 2008/698) reg.2(13) (April 14, 2008).

49. Employment and Support Allowance (Consequential Provisions) (No.2) Regulations 2008 (SI 2008/1554) reg.2(11) (October 27, 2008).

50. Employment and Support Allowance (Miscellaneous Amendments) Regulations 2008 (SI 2008/2428) reg.41(2)(a) (October 27, 2008).

51. Employment and Support Allowance (Miscellaneous Amendments) Regulations 2008 (SI 2008/2428) reg.41(2)(b) (October 27, 2008).

52. Social Security (Miscellaneous Amendments) (No.6) Regulations 2008 (SI 2008/2767) reg.2(6) (November 17, 2008).

53. Social Security (Miscellaneous Amendments) (No.6) Regulations 2008 (SI 2008/2767) reg.2(11) (November 17, 2008).

54. Social Security (Housing Costs Special Arrangements) (Amendment and Modification) Regulations 2008 (SI 2008/3195) reg.2(1)(b) and (2) (January 5, 2009).

55. Social Security (Miscellaneous Amendments) Regulations 2009 (SI 2009/583) reg.2(3) (April 6, 2009).

56. Social Security (Miscellaneous Amendments) (No.4) Regulations 2009 (SI 2009/2655) reg.2(15)(a) (October 26, 2009).

57. Social Security (Miscellaneous Amendments) (No.2) Regulations 2010 (SI 2010/641) reg.2(3)(e) (April 6, 2010).

58. Social Security (Miscellaneous Amendments) (No.2) Regulations 2010 (SI 2010/641) reg.2(7)(d) (April 6, 2010).

59. Social Security (Miscellaneous Amendments) (No.4) Regulations 2009 (SI 2009/2655) reg.2(15)(b) (April 12, 2010).

60. Social Security (Housing Costs) (Standard Interest Rate) Amendment Regulations 2010 (SI 2011/1811) reg.2(1)(a) and (2) (October 1, 2010).

61. Social Security (Miscellaneous Amendments) Regulations 2011 (SI 2011/674) reg.3(6)(a) (April 11, 2011).

62. Social Security (Miscellaneous Amendments) Regulations 2011 (SI 2011/674) reg.3(6)(b) (April 11, 2011).

63. Social Security (Miscellaneous Amendments) Regulations 2011 (SI 2011/674) reg.3(6)(c) (April 11, 2011).

64. Social Security (Miscellaneous Amendments) (No.3) Regulations 2011 (SI 2011/2425) reg.7(5) (October 31, 2011).

65. Employment and Support Allowance (Duration of Contributory Allowance) (Consequential Amendments) Regulations 2012 (SI 2012/913) reg.3(3) (May 1, 2012).

66. Social Security (Miscellaneous Amendments) Regulations 2013 (SI 2013/443) reg.2(4)(a) (April 2, 2013).

67. Social Security (Miscellaneous Amendments) Regulations 2013 (SI 2013/443) reg.2(4)(b) (April 2, 2013).

68. Personal Independence Payment (Supplementary Provisions and Consequential Amendments) Regulations 2013 (SI 2013/388) reg. 8 and Sch. Pt 2 para.11(6) (April 8, 2013).

69. Armed Forces and Reserve Forces Compensation Scheme (Consequential Provisions: Subordinate Legislation) Order 2013 (SI 2013/591) art.7 and Sch. para.4(6) (April 8, 2013).

70. Universal Credit (Consequential, Supplementary, Incidental and Miscellaneous Provisions) Regulations 2013 (SI 2013/630) reg.28(7)(a) (April 29, 2013).

71. Universal Credit (Consequential, Supplementary, Incidental and Miscellaneous Provisions) Regulations 2013 (SI 2013/630) reg.28(7)(b) (April 29, 2013).

72. Social Security (Miscellaneous Amendments) Regulations 2014 (SI 2014/591) reg.2(6) (April 28, 2014).

73. Universal Credit and Miscellaneous Amendments (No.2) Regulations 2014 (SI 2014/2888) reg.3(2)(b) (November 26, 2014).

74. Social Security (Housing Costs Amendments) Regulations 2015 (SI 2015/1647) reg.2(2) (April 1, 2016).

75. Employment and Support Allowance and Universal Credit (Miscellaneous Amendments and Transitional and Savings Provisions) Regulations 2017 (SI 2017/204) reg.7(1) and Sch.1, Pt.1, para.1(1) and (3) (April 3, 2017).

76. Employment and Support Allowance and Universal Credit (Miscellaneous Amendments and Transitional and Savings Provisions) Regulations 2017 (SI 2017/204) reg.7(1) and Sch.1, Pt.2, para.10 (April 3, 2017).

77. Social Security (Scottish Infected Blood Support Scheme) Regulations 2017 (SI 2017/329) reg.3(1) and (3)(d) (April 3, 2017).

78. Social Security (Emergency Funds) (Amendment) Regulations 2017 (SI 2017/689) reg.2(1) and (3) (June 19, 2017).

79. Loans for Mortgage Interest Regulations 2017 (SI 2017/725) reg.18 and Sch.5 para.2(d) (April 6, 2018).

80. Social Security (Infected Blood and Thalidomide) Regulations 2017 (SI 2017/870) reg.2 (October 23, 2017).

81 Social Security (Income and Capital) (Miscellaneous Amendments) Regulations 2020 (SI 2020/618) reg.2(1) and (10) (July 15, 2020).

82 Social Security Benefits Up-rating Order 2021 (SI 2021/162) art.21(7) (April 12, 2021).

DEFINITIONS

"Abbeyfield Home"—see reg.2(1).
"armed forces independence payment"—*ibid.*
"attendance allowance"—*ibid.*
"benefit week"—*ibid.*
"care home"—*ibid.*
"claimant"—*ibid.*
"close relative"—*ibid.*
"couple"—*ibid.*
"course of study"—*ibid.*
"co-ownership scheme"—*ibid.*
"Crown tenant"—*ibid.*
"disability living allowance"—*ibid.*
"dwelling occupied as the home"—*ibid.*
"employment zone"—*ibid.*
"family"—see SSCBA s.137(1).
"full-time student"—see reg.61(1).
"housing benefit expenditure"—see reg.2(1).
"independent hospital"—*ibid.*
"Intensive Activity Period for 50 plus"—*ibid.*
"local welfare provision" —*ibid.*
"lone parent"—*ibid.*
"MFET Limited"—*ibid.*
"non-dependant"—see reg.3.
"partner"—see reg.2(1).
"period of study"—*ibid.*
"personal independence payment"—*ibid.*
"polygamous marriage"—*ibid.*
"remunerative work"—see reg.5.
"self-employment route"—see reg.2(1).
"single claimant"—*ibid.*
"the Caxton Foundation"—*ibid.*
"the Eileen Trust"—*ibid.*
"the Fund"—*ibid.*
"the Independent Living Funds"—*ibid.*
"the Macfarlane (Special Payments) Trust"—*ibid.*
"the Macfarlane (Special Payments) (No.2) Trust"—*ibid.*
"the Macfarlane Trust"—*ibid.*
"the Skipton Fund"—*ibid.*
"training allowance"—*ibid.*
"universal credit"—*ibid.*
"water charges"—*ibid.*
"Welfare Reform Act"—*ibid.*
"welfare to work beneficiary"—*ibid.*
"year of assessment"—*ibid.*

GENERAL NOTE

Introduction

2.671   Schedule 3 sets out the circumstances in which an amount in respect of housing costs is to be included in a claimant's applicable amount under reg.17(1)(e). Until April 5, 2018 the Schedule allowed for certain payments of mortgage interest and interest on loans taken out for repairs or improvements to a property to be met by

IS. However, from April 6, 2018 (subject to transitional provisions) those parts of the Schedule were revoked by the Loans for Mortgage Interest Regulations 2017 (SI 2017/725): see Vol.II. As a result, the Schedule now only covers service charges, payments of rent under a long tenancy, rentcharges, payments under a co-owner-ship scheme, payments by Crown tenants and payments in respect of a tent and the site on which it stands.

Housing costs

Paragraph 1: Sub-paras (1) and (2) provide that, to be entitled to a sum for   2.672
housing costs, the claimant, or another member of the family, must be liable—in respect of a dwelling that the claimant (or family member) is occupying as his or her home—to meet at least one of the types of costs that are eligible under para.17. For liability to meet costs, see para.2; for occupation as a home, see para.3.

Sub-paras (3) and (4) define the circumstances in which a person is a "disa-bled person" for the purposes of the Schedule. That definition is exhaustive: see *CIS/13661/1996*.

Paragraph 1A sets out rules to ensure continuity in certain circumstances where the   2.673
claimant (or partner) had previously been awarded housing costs as part of an award of income-based JSA, income-related ESA or SPC. There are parallel provisions in para.1A of Sch.2 to the JSA Regulations 1996, para.3 of Sch.6 to the ESA Regulations 2008 and para.7(4A)-(5) of Sch.II to the State Pension Credit Regulations.

Paragraph 2 deals with when a person is "liable to meet housing costs". Three situ-   2.674
ations are specified, to satisfy para.1(1):

(A) Where the claimant, or any partner, has a liability for housing costs, it must not be to a member of the same household. See *R(SB) 13/82*, *R(SB) 4/83*, *CSB 145/1984* and *CSB 463/1986*, and the notes to s.137(1) of the Contributions and Benefits Act 1992.

(B) This may apply, e.g. in the case of separated couples. It must be reasonable in all the circumstances to treat the claimant as liable where the person liable is not paying the housing costs, which will probably be the case for most separated couples.
   It is not necessary for the claimant to have continuously lived in the home since the person liable to meet the housing costs failed to meet, or stopped meeting, them. What is required is that the claimant is living in the home and has to meet the housing costs in order to continue to do so when she claims income support. See *Ewens v Secretary of State for Social Security*, reported as *R(IS) 8/01*.

(C) Only sharing with another member of the same household will do, but see the definition of close relative. This enables sharers to get their proportionate share of housing costs. See para.5(5).

Paragraph 3—occupying a dwelling as the home

Generally a claimant can only have one home—the one normally occupied   2.675
(sub-paras (1) and (2)), although in some circumstances two separate units of accommodation may constitute one dwelling (see notes to reg.2(1)). *R(SB) 7/86* holds that premises cannot be "normally occupied as the home" if the claimant has never actually resided in them. However, doubts were expressed about this rule in *CSB/524/1985* and *CIS/4/1990* and it is suggested that the issue will be one of fact in each case. See *CH/2521/2002* and *R(H) 9/05* (which concerned reg.5(1) of the Housing Benefit Regulations 1987, the equivalent provision to sub-para.(1)) and the other cases referred to in the note to the definition of "*dwelling occupied as the home*" in reg.2(1) for further discussion of this question.

Sub-paragraphs (3) and (4) give special rules for choosing the home of full-time   2.676
students (defined in reg.61(1)) with a term-time and a vacation base.

2.677   *Sub-paragraph (5)* covers moving into temporary accommodation while repairs are done.

2.678   *Sub-paragraph (6)* allows payments in three cases where there is an overlap of liability. One is fear of violence in the former home or by a former member of the family; the second is where one of a couple is a full-time student or on a training course and the double expenditure is unavoidable and the third is an unavoidable overlap of liability on moving home. What is unavoidable is a matter of fact.

2.679   *Sub-paragraph (7)* is an important provision allowing a person in certain circumstances to be treated as occupying a dwelling as his home for up to four weeks before moving in.

2.680   *Sub-paragraphs (8)–(12)* deal with temporary absences from home. See also the definitions in sub-para.(13).

2.681   *Paragraph 4* sets out the circumstances in which housing costs are ineligible to be met. Since the April 6, 2018 amendments, there are only two such circumstances. The first is where the costs are "housing benefit expenditure": see sub-para.(a). The second is where the claimant is living in a care home, Abbeyfield Home or independent hospital, except where the absence from home is only temporary, in which case paras 3(8)-(12) apply: see sub-para.(b).

2.682   *Paragraph 5* provides for housing costs to be apportioned in cases where the dwelling is a "composite hereditament" (i.e. mixed residential and commercial accommodation) and where residential accommodation is shared.

2.683   *Paragraph 8* establishes the 39-week rule: except where para.9 applies, housing costs are met under para.17 where the claimant has been entitled to income support for a continuous period of at least 39 weeks, but not otherwise.

2.684   *Paragraph 9.* The 39-week waiting period does not apply where the claimant's partner has reached the qualifying age for state pension credit or to payments under a co-ownership agreement, payments by Crown tenants, or—where the claimant is living in a tent—to payments for the site on which the tent stands.

2.685   *Paragraph 14* establishes linking rules. The basic linking period is 12 weeks but note the extended linking periods of 52 weeks where sub-paras (11)–(13) apply and 104 weeks in the case of a welfare to work beneficiary.

     Regulation 32 of the Income Support (General) (Jobseeker's Allowance Consequential Amendments) Regulations 1996 (see p.1759) should also be noted. This provides that entitlement to income-based JSA counts as entitlement to income support for the purpose of satisfying any condition that the person is or has been entitled to income support for any period of time. It also has the same effect where the requirement is that the person is or has been treated as being in receipt of income support. See para.18(1)(c) of Sch.2 to the JSA Regulations for the converse provision under the JSA rules. Where the claimant's former partner was entitled to state pension credit, see sub-para.(14). See also sub-para.(15), inserted with effect from October 27, 2008, where the claimant, his partner or his former partner was entitled to income-related ESA.

Paragraph 17—Housing costs

2.686   This provision lists the miscellaneous housing costs covered by income support (sub-para.(1)(a)–(f)) and contains the conditions for meeting these costs.

Service charges

2.687   Of these items, the category of "service charges" (sub-para.(1)(b)) is probably of most interest. This phrase is given no special definition. (It does not include an administration fee charged by a lender where mortgage payments are in arrears (*CIS*

392/1994).) *CIS 157/1989* suggested that it means charges in respect of a service rendered to a tenant by the landlord. The Tribunal of Commissioners in *R(IS) 3/91* and *R(IS) 4/91* decides that the category can extend to owner-occupiers as well. The essence is the determination and arranging of what would otherwise be left for the occupier to do for himself, on the basis of an arrangement which the terms of occupation of the property make binding on all those with the same interest in the property.

In *R(IS) 4/91* the claimant, an owner-occupier, had to pay £93 a year to have his cess-pit emptied. The appeal had to be returned to the SSAT for further findings of fact, but it was suggested that if the service was carried out by an outside contractor engaged by the claimant, the cost would not be a service charge.

However, things within the housing benefit definition of ineligible service charges are excluded (sub-para.(2)(b)). This list covers charges in respect of day-to-day living expenses, a number of personal services and other services "not connected with the provision of adequate accommodation" (see *CIS 1460/1995* and the other decisions discussed below under "*Sheltered accommodation*"). *CJSA 5493/1999* expresses the view that "adequate" has a looser meaning than fitness for human habitation but is not to be equated with what is desirable; nor is a provision for bad debt connected with the adequacy of accommodation (although see *CH/3548/2006*). But a provision for future repairs could be: see *CIS 667/2002* and *R(IS) 2/07* below.

In *R(IS) 3/91* a leaseholder's share of the cost of roof repairs was a service charge. The obligation was imposed on the claimant by the conditions of her occupation and the service was connected with the provision of adequate accommodation, so that the exclusion in sub-para.(2)(b) did not bite. In the light of *CIS/2132/1998* and *R(IS) 2/07* (see below) it would seem that the exclusion in sub-para.(2)(c) also did not apply.

2.688

Under sub-para.(2)(c) charges for the cost of repairs and improvements, as defined in sub-para.(6), are also deducted. *CIS/488/2008* highlights a very common difficulty with appeals concerning sub-para.(2)(c), namely a dearth of evidence in relation to the nature of the repairs and improvements for which the service charges are being levied. The Commissioner holds that since the claimant could be expected to have some information as to the state of repair of the building and where the SoS had failed to ask the right questions, the tribunal should have directed an oral hearing nd had erred in not doing so.

Sub-paragraph (2)(a) provides that if a charge includes fuel charges, deductions are also made (except for charges in respect of communal areas: para.4 of Sch.1 to the Housing Benefit Regulations, confirmed in *CIS 1460/1995*). The standard amounts to be deducted under sub-para.(2)(a) are (from April 2015, not increased in April 2016): heating (apart from hot water), £28.80; hot water, £3.35; lighting, £2.30; cooking, £3.35. The standard amounts can be altered on evidence of the actual or estimated charge.

Insurance charges: In *R(IS) 4/92* it was held that sums required to be paid by a tenant under the terms of the lease to reimburse the landlord for the cost of property insurance were a service charge within the principles set out in *R(IS) 3/91* and *R(IS) 4/91*. The Commissioner also found that the landlord's obligation to use any money paid out under the insurance policy as a result of fire on reinstatement of the property meant that the charge was connected with the provision of adequate accommodation. The Commissioner in *CSIS 4/1990* doubted that building insurance was so connected (referring to the earlier decision in *CIS 17/1988* where there was a suggestion to the contrary). The Court of Session in the *McSherry* case (which is the appeal in *CSIS 4/1990*) does not deal with this point. However, in *R(IS) 19/93* the Commissioner agrees with *R(IS) 4/92* and dissents from the suggestion in *CIS 17/1988*. The weight of authority would therefore seem to favour the interpretation taken in *R(IS) 4/92* in relation to payments by tenants to reimburse landlords for the cost of building insurance. But note the effect of para.4(1)(a). In *R(IS) 4/92* the Commissioner made his award subject to enquiries whether the reimbursement of the landlord's insurance premiums would be included in the claimant's rent for housing benefit purposes.

2.689

In *Dunne v Department of Health and Social Security* (September 10, 1993), the

Court of Appeal in Northern Ireland decided that the building insurance premium paid by the claimant as an owner occupier was not a service charge. Although the claimant was obliged to take out such insurance under the terms of both his building lease and his mortgage, it did not fulfill the test laid down in *R(IS) 3/91* and *R(IS) 4/91*. Such a premium was to be distinguished from payment required to be made to the landlord for building insurance by occupiers of a block of flats which clearly was a service charge. In *Secretary of State for Social Security v McSherry* (March 17, 1994) the property insurance premium at issue was mandatory under the terms of the claimant's mortgage. The Court of Session agrees with the decision in *Dunne*, holding that the omission of insurance premiums from para.1 of the former Sch.3 (in contrast to the express provision for routine maintenance and insurance in the supplementary benefit scheme) was deliberate. (*R(SB) 1/90* holds that although decisions of the Court of Appeal of Northern Ireland are not binding on Commissioners in Great Britain, identically worded provisions operating in both Northern Ireland and Great Britain are to be interpreted uniformly. Decisions of the Court of Session are binding.)

R(IS) 19/93 had come to a similar conclusion. The Commissioner states that the claimant's obligation to pay the insurance premium to his building society was not an obligation arising from his interest or estate in the property, but from his mortgage. It was a consequence of the claimant's financial arrangements, not his ownership of the property itself, and thus was not a service charge. In essence, the payment was no different from a house insurance premium paid under an ordinary contract between an owner/occupier and his insurance company (which had been held in *CIS 17/1988* not to constitute a service charge).

The result is that whether the obligation to pay insurance charges or to reimburse a landlord for the payment of insurance premiums constitutes a service charge depends upon it coming within the principles set out in *R(IS) 3/91* and *R(IS) 4/91*. It seems clear that payments required to be made to the landlord from occupiers of a block of flats to cover insurance for the building are a service charge, whereas a building insurance premium payable under the terms of a claimant's mortgage is not. An insurance charge of the kind concerned in *R(IS) 4/92* also constitutes a service charge. On the other hand, an obligation on the claimant to effect insurance under the terms of a lease would not qualify.

2.690 *Reserve funds*: *CIS 667/2002* considered payments into a reserve fund. The Commissioner referred to *CCS 5242/1995* (a child support case) which had decided that payments into a reserve fund could be eligible as housing costs, although there might have to be an apportionment for any relevant deductions under sub-para.(2). The only relevant deductions in this context were those that were not connected with the provision of adequate accommodation and any amounts for repairs and improvements as defined in para.16(2). The Commissioner acknowledges that because the works for which the reserve fund will eventually be used are not yet known an element of speculation is required. But this could be informed by the following factors: (i) the terms governing the use of the reserve fund or the scope of the landlord's powers under the service charge; (ii) information on how the reserve fund has been used in the past; and (iii) details of any work that is planned or anticipated. In this case the only evidence available related to (iii). Future works were to cover roof recovering, repair of a lift, external repointing and redecoration and improvements of the common parts. The Commissioner concluded that none of those constituted a repair or improvement under para.16(2) (see *CIS 2132/1998* in the notes to para.16 in relation to roof renewal) and all related to the provision of adequate accommodation. The consequence was that the whole of the current payment into the reserve fund was an eligible service charge (although in future years the available evidence might justify a different conclusion).

Payments for future maintenance was also one of the issues in *R(IS) 2/07*. The Secretary of State had argued that the cost of replacement windows and roof repairs provided for in the reserve fund were deductible from the service charge under sub-para.(2)(c) as being in respect of the provision of insulation, natural light, damp proofing or the repair of unsafe structural defects. However, this is rejected by the Commissioner who points out that the purpose of a reserve fund is to avoid the need for the repair of unsafe structural defects and that the repeated use of the word "provision" in para.16(2) implies the furnishing of something not already in existence or the replacement of something which no longer functions. He agrees with *CIS/2132/1998* that damp proofing is not the predominant purpose of a roof. However, he goes on to state that in his view "damp proofing" and "insulation" are terms of art in the building trade which have found their way into ordinary language. As used in para.16(2), he considered that the former was limited to measures taken to prevent rising damp or damp from condensation in an existing building, and the latter to such things as the installation of double-glazing, loft insulation and cavity wall insulation to reduce heat loss in an existing building. Furthermore, the contribution to the reserve fund in respect of future window repairs in the claimant's own flat came within the definition of service charge in *R(IS) 4/91*, para.15. The Commissioner also made the more general observation that even if any of the contingencies itemised in a reserve fund do correspond to the para.16(2) list, what is deductible under sub-para.(2)(c) is the current or recent capital cost of works referred to in para.16(2) incurred within the time prescribed by para.16(1), not the claimant's current contributions to a reserve against such capital costs in the future.

Sheltered accommodation: *CIS 1460/1995* concerned a service charge for residents of sheltered accommodation for the elderly. The claimant lived in a self-contained bungalow and had the use of communal areas (pathways and gardens) and a communal lounge; the service charge covered the costs of broadly the maintenance of the common areas and the structure of the buildings, as well as a resident warden. The Commissioner accepts that the terms of the appendix to *R(IS) 3/91* and *R(IS) 4/91* as a whole (as opposed to the headnote) made it clear that a service charge was only to be excluded under sub-para.(2)(b) to the extent it related to matters specified as ineligible in para.1 of Sch.1 to the Housing Benefit Regulations; there was no over-riding test of connection with the adequacy of the accommodation (see para.1(g) of Sch.1). Where an element of a service charge was not dealt with in sub-paras (a)–(f) of para.1 of Sch.1 so that sub-para.(g) had to be considered, a common sense view had to be taken. In general, where a claimant had a right to use a communal lounge, gardens, etc. services related to those communal areas should be accepted as related to the provision of adequate accommodation. Paragraph 1 as a whole did contemplate that charges for communal areas could be eligible (see, for example, sub-para. (a)(ii) (laundry facilities), (iii) (children's play area) and (iv) (cleaning of communal areas)). Moreover, if service charges were thought to be excessive, the appropriate control mechanism was para.10 (now see para.13). (See also *CP v Aylesbury Vale DC* [2011] UKUT 22 (AAC) which confirms that charges for maintaining a communal garden are eligible service charges.) On the meaning of para.1(g) itself, although it excluded services which related purely to meeting the personal needs of residents, this did not mean that in considering whether a service was related to the provision of adequate accommodation the question of suitability for the personal needs of the residents was not relevant (see Sedley J in *R. v North Cornwall DC, Ex p. Singer* (High Court, November 26, 1993, 11–12 of the transcript). Paragraph 1 of Sch.1 did envisage that the personal needs of the claimant could be considered (see sub-para. (a)(iv) on window-cleaning and sub-para.(c) on emergency alarm systems where the eligibility of a service charge depended on the claimant's personal circumstances). What was connected to the provision of adequate accommodation, including how far the personal needs of residents should be taken into account, was a question of fact in each case (para.17 of the appendix to *R(IS) 3/91* and *R(IS) 4/91*).

The Commissioner also deals with the meaning of "sheltered accommodation" (see the definition of "communal area" in what was then para.7 (now para.8) of Sch.1 to the Housing Benefit Regulations which includes rooms of common use in sheltered, but not non-sheltered, accommodation). He suggests that the characteristics of such accommodation were the grouping together of individual dwellings,

2.691

which were offered primarily to those with some special housing need, and where some communal facilites, the employment of a warden and an emergency alarm system, were included. But accommodation could still be sheltered accommodation even without some of these features.

The meaning of "sheltered accommodation" is further considered in *JB v Oxford CC and SSWP (HB)* [2011] UKUT 136 (AAC). The claimant had severe learning difficulties; he had his own bedroom and shared a kitchen, bathroom, toilet, sitting rooms etc. with four other tenants, who had similar difficulties. Care, support and supervision was provided on a 24-hour basis. Judge Levenson held that "sheltered accommodation" clearly meant "something more than ordinary accommodation or shelter . . . this can only really mean that it is accommodation provided for people who are in some way (and probably for some defined reason) more vulnerable than most people are, or are vulnerable in a particular kind of way". There was no need, as the LA had argued, for the accommodation to be self-contained and if there were resident staff, there was no reason for the purposes of the definition for there to be a warden or alarm system (he otherwise agreed with the Commissioner's comments in *CIS/1460/1995*). Although some types of accommodation, such as residential care homes, standard student accommodation and accommodation which was not designed for any kind of vulnerable person, were clearly not "sheltered accommodation", it should be given a broad meaning and clearly encompassed the claimant's accommodation.

2.692 This decision was upheld by the Court of Appeal in *Oxford CC v Basey* [2012] EWCA Civ 115; [2012] AACR 38. Sullivan LJ concluded:

"Parliament did not choose to define sheltered accommodation and the Court should not impose a prescriptive definition upon an inherently flexible concept which can take many different forms, and which now includes very sheltered or extra care sheltered accommodation."

In *Liverpool CC v (1) NM, (2) WD (HB)* [2015] UKUT 523 (AAC) M was a licensee of a room in a supported housing scheme for 16-25 year olds. D was an assured tenant in a sheltered housing scheme for those over 55 and for younger people with disabilities. In both cases their service charges for water rates were broken down into communal water charges, which were stated to be "eligible for HB", and charges for personal use of water (in their room/flat), which were stated to be "not eligible for HB". The local authority disallowed housing benefit in respect of the communal water charges, contending that all water charges, whether for personal or communal use, fell to be deducted under reg.12(B)(5) of the Housing Benefit Regulations 2006. It also contended that communal water charges were ineligible service charges in accordance with Sch.1 to the Housing Benefit Regulations 2006 because they were either for "day-to-day living expenses" within the meaning of para.1(a) or charges which were not connected with the provision of adequate accommodation within the meaning of para.1(g).

Judge Knowles firstly rejected the Council's submission that the accommodation occupied by M was not "sheltered accommodation". Applying *Basey*, "sheltered accommodation" was "an inherently flexible concept" and included accommodation, such as in M's case, where the accommodation was provided on the basis that the licensee accepted support services. She then went on to hold that reg.12(B)(5) was only concerned with the deduction of water charges for personal use when the claimant was not separately billed. It had no application to communal water charges. She also rejected the contention that communal water charges were "day-to-day living expenses" and found that they were clearly charges related to the provision of adequate accommodation, applying *CIS/1460/1995*. The result was that the service charges for the supply of water for communal areas were eligible for housing benefit (and thus are not excluded under para.17(2)(b)), except for water used for the provision of laundry which is ineligible under para.1(a)(ii) of Sch.1. But water charges for the cleaning of a communal laundry are eligible (see para.1(a)(iv)(aa) of Sch.1); this would include the cleaning of laundry equipment (see para.1(a)(ii)).

In *R(IS) 2/07* the claimant owned a leasehold property in a sheltered accommodation complex. Under the terms of her lease she had to pay a service charge which covered services in respect of the buildings, gardens and other ground that formed the complex (but not the insides of any dwelling), as well as personal and communal services for herself and the other owners. One of the issues was the proportion of staff salaries and associated administrative costs that were to be attributed to housing related services (and therefore eligible for income support), as opposed to personal care services (which would be met under the "Supporting People" programme). The tribunal had simply accepted the estimate provided by the company that managed the complex. However, the Commissioner set the tribunal's decision aside, stating that it was necessary to make findings on how many hours the staff actually spent providing accommodation-related services (as opposed to personal services). This ratio should then be applied to the other staff-related costs, such as staff advertising. See also *ET v Rossendale BC* [2010] UKUT 222 (AAC) which concerned whether an allowance for management and administrative costs as part of a concierge charge was excessive (it also considered whether a provision for bad debts and voids included in the charge was excessive).

In *R(PC) 1/07*, which concerned para.13(2)(b) of Sch.II to the State Pension Credit Regulations (the equivalent of sub-para.(2)(b)), the Commissioner recognises that the "gold standard" process for assessing what proportion of service charges are eligible or ineligible put forward in *R(IS) 2/07*, para.28, may not always be necessary or possible and concurs with *CPC/968/2005* that a broad approach is needed. In his view, given, e.g. the terms of the lease relating to the services and service charges, a breakdown of the service charges, details of what service charges (if any) are met by the Supporting People programme and a statement from the warden (or scheme manager as he was referred to in this case) as to how his working hours are usually divided up, it should be possible to make a reasoned estimate of how much of the service charges are accommodation-related. However, each case will depend on its own facts and evidential requirements will vary.   **2.693**

R(PC) 1/07 had also taken a different approach to that of *R(IS) 2/07* on the attribution of general administrative costs (e.g. management fees, telephones, audit, accountancy charges, etc.). *R(IS) 2/07* had stated that these should be apportioned in the same ratio as the staff costs (see para.28). *R(PC) 1/07*, however, concluded that general administrative costs had to be apportioned on the same basis as the ratio of eligible to ineligible costs for the rest of the overall budget (see para.8) (following *CPC/968/2005*). This inconsistency is dealt with in *SSWP v DL (SPC)* [2013] UKUT 29 (AAC); [2013] AACR 22, which decides that *R(PC) 1/07* is to be preferred on this point. *SSWP v DL* also contains a useful summary of the general propositions arising from the case law on the eligibility/non-eligibility of service charges (see paras 24–28).

R(PC) 2/08 discusses the provisions for supersession in a case where the claimant was awarded housing costs based on an estimate of his service charges for the year and then later (a considerable time later in that case) submits the invoice for his actual service charges for the year in question.

Other miscellaneous housing costs

Sub-paragraph (a) concerns payments of rent or ground rent relating to a long tenancy (for the definition of "long tenancy" see reg.2(1)). See *SSWP v UP (JSA)* [2010] UKUT 262 (AAC); [2011] AACR 12 which refers to the fact, as *R(H) 3/07* had pointed out, that a lease of more than seven years of registered land "does not operate at law until the relevant registration requirements are met" (see s.27 of the Land Registration Act 2002). Thus until the claimant's tenancy (which was part of a home financing scheme designed to be compliant with Shari'a principles, i.e. not involving the payment of any interest), had been registered at the Land Registry a long tenancy did not exist and so no payments of rent made by the claimant could be payments relating to a long tenancy.   **2.694**

On the meaning of "long tenancy" under Scots law see *NR v SSWP (SPC)* [2013] UKUT 647 (AAC); [2014] AACR 22.

On sub-para.(1)(d) (payments under a co-ownership scheme), see *CJSA 5493/1999*.

2.695   *Sub-paragraph (6)*: To qualify, both repairs and improvements must be under-taken with a view to "maintaining the fitness of the dwelling for human habitation …", *and* be one of the measures listed in heads (a)-(l).

In general, the criterion of fitness for human habitation focusses the test on an "objective" standard rather than on the particular needs of individual claimants.

However, head (k) (adapting the dwelling for the special needs of a disabled person) will inevitably involve consideration of the needs of the disabled person concerned). As Upper Tribunal Judge Mark stated in *FJ v SSWP* [2009] UKUT 207 (AAC):

> "It is plain that a dwelling is fit for human habitation as a matter of ordinary English if able bodied persons can live there without a problem, even if it is not adapted for the special needs of a disabled person. It is also plain that it is fit for human habitation in that sense even if it does not provide separate sleeping accommodation for children of different sexes who are part of the claimant's family. It is clear therefore that in the context of this provision, and to make sense of [paragraph 17(6)(k and (l)], maintaining the fitness of the home for human habitation means so maintaining it for human habitation by the claimant and her family living there. Further, if the expression has that meaning in relation to (k) and (l), it must also have the same meaning in relation to the remainder of [paragraph 17(6)], including sub-paragraph [(6)(a)]."

2.696   The same judge emphasises in *JT v SSWP (JSA)* [2013] UKUT 184 (AAC) that the test is *maintaining* fitness for habitation, not making fit for habitation. He refers to the Department for Communities and Local Government's publication "*A Decent Home: Definition and guidance for implementation*" (June 2006). While the test of what is a decent home is not the same as whether a home is fit for human habitation, he considered that he could have some regard to the definition as an indication of what a person can reasonably expect in respect of a home.

SSWP v AR (IS) [2010] UKUT 308 (AAC) decides that the test for deciding whether repairs and improvements have been undertaken "with a view to maintaining the fitness of the dwelling for human habitation" was whether they would have been carried out by a sensible and prudent householder properly advised as to the reasonable necessity of the repairs/improvements and the likely consequences if they were not undertaken (as opposed to measures that are undertaken principally out of choice or preference).

"Provision of" would not seem to be limited to initial installation, but could cover repairs to, or replacement of, an existing facility (see *R. v Social Fund Inspector, Ex p. Tuckwood* (High Court, April 27, 1995). *CJSA/5439/1999* confirmed that provision includes replacement in this context and note *DC v SSWP (JSA)* [2010] UKUT 459 (AAC). See also *R(IS) 2/07* in which the Commissioner states that, in the context of what is now para.17(6), "provision" means providing something not already in existence or the replacement of something which no longer functions. However, as *JT v SSWP (JSA)* [2013] UKUT 184 (AAC) points out, *R(IS) 2/07* must be read in the light of para.32 of *SSWP v AR (IS)* [2010] UKUT 308 (AAC) which stated that "the reference to 'maintaining' the fitness of the dwelling implies that it is not necessary that the property has fallen in some respect below the standard of fitness before the costs can be allowed".

On the meaning of "adapt a dwelling" in head (k), see *R. (on the application of Mahmoudi) v London Borough of Lewisham* [2014] EWCA Civ 284; [2014] AACR 14. The question to be asked is whether the process which the dwelling has undergone is a change that makes it more suitable for the needs of the disabled person.

Separate sleeping accommodation

2.697   On head (l) see *CIS/14657/1996*. The Commissioner points out that the loan has to be taken out "for the purpose" of the relevant improvements. The claimant's loan could therefore fall within head (l) where his daughter was aged 10 but her brother would not reach that age for another year or so because the money was being used for something that was bound to happen in the near future. The Commissioner also decides that the cost of a survey could come within head (j) as reasonably incidental to the carrying out of the work covered by that head. *CIS/1678/1999* goes further than *CIS/14657/1996* in holding that it was not necessary for the provision of separate sleeping accommodation to have been the sole or even the main purpose in taking out the loan. It was enough if it was one of two or more purposes (the claimant had wanted her children to have separate bedrooms from the beginning so as not to disturb each other's sleep). Furthermore, it did not matter how long a time had elapsed between the taking out of the loan and the children's attainment of the age of 10 (the loan in question had been incurred while the claimant was expecting her second child). This was because if there were children of different sexes their need for separate sleeping accommodation was a foreseeable and inevitable future need that was likely to have been in the mind of a claimant extending her house. The Commissioner in *CIS/1678/1999* expressly does not follow *CIS/16936/1996* which had decided that the relevant children must all have been at least 10 years old at the date on which the loan was taken out. However, in *CIS/5119/2001* the Commissioner declines to follow *CIS/1678/1999*. In his view it conflicted with *CIS/14657/1998*. But in any event it conflicted with *CIS/2711/1999* (decided by the same Commissioner as *CIS/14657/1998*).

In *CIS 2711/1999* the Commissioner had stated that in deciding whether the conditions in head (l) were met it was the circumstances as they stood at the time the loan was taken out and the money was used in carrying out the repairs and improvements that had to be considered, not any later date when a claim for income support was made, or some still later date when during the continuation of a claim a child reached 10. The Commissioner in *CIS/5119/2001* was in complete agreement that the focus had to be on the nature and purpose of the loan at the time when it was taken out rather than any later date.

There is therefore a conflict between these various decisions, although the weight of authority would seem to be that the relevant children must be approaching 10 or within a year or two of doing so when the loan is taken out. This conflict was considered in *HMRC v CA* [2009] UKUT 13 (AAC) which concludes that a loan taken out in advance of a child reaching 10 can come within head (l) but how far in advance will depend on the circumstances of the case (preferring *CIS/14657/1996* and *CIS/5119/2001* to *CIS/1678/1999*).

Provision of hot water not connected to a central heating system

In *KW v SSWP (IS)* [2012] UKUT 180 (AAC) the claimant was refused housing costs in respect of interest on a loan that he had taken out in order to install solar panels. The claimant had an existing gas central heating system with a boiler, storage tank and hot water cylinder, which provided both heating and hot water. The solar panels were installed to provide hot water only via the cylinder; the gas system would still "kick-in" to heat the water, should the solar panels not provide sufficient energy. The tribunal therefore concluded that the solar panels were providing hot water as part of the whole central heating system and that the loan for the solar panels did not fall within head (a).   **2.698**

Judge Ward upheld the tribunal's decision. The words "not connected to a central heating system" must have some purpose and were intended to have an exclusionary effect in relation to the provision of hot water that *is* connected to a central heating system. Judge Ward also held that "necessary associated plumbing" referred to plumbing associated with one of the listed five items, such as connecting the appliance to a water supply or a drain; it did not cover such plumbing when one of the five items was not being provided.

Heating systems

On the meaning of "repairs to existing heating systems" in head (b), see *CIS/781/2002*. The claimant had two storage radiators in her home. She replaced these with a boiler and ten radiators. The Commissioner considered that repairing an existing system meant changing a part of the system that did not work or putting   **2.699** it back into working order. A repair could have as an incidental effect an improvement in the system. But in the circumstances of this case there had clearly been a replacement of the system, not a repair of the existing system.

Note also *CIS 15036/1996* which concerned whether replacement of a central heating boiler came within para.8(3)(h) of the former Sch.3 ("provision of heating, including central heating"). The Commissioner decides that the installation of the new boiler was an improvement which had been undertaken with a view to "improving fitness for occupation" and so came within para.8(3) (it was not contended that it constituted a major repair necessary to maintain the fabric of the home). The fact that the boiler had merely been replaced by its modern equivalent did not matter. The Commissioner refers to *Morcom v Campbell-Johnson* [1956] 1 Q.B. 106 in which Denning LJ had drawn a distinction between the provision of something new which would constitute an improvement and the replacement of something worn out, albeit with a modern equivalent, which would come within the category of repairs, not improvement. Presumably on the basis of this dictum the replacement of a boiler would also fall within head (b) as it would seem to fulfil the test of maintaining fitness for human habitation. The consequence for the claimant in *CIS/15036/1996* was that the element of her service charge attributable to the new boiler had to be deducted under what is now para.17(2)(c).

Damp proofing; insulation

2.700   In *CIS 2132/1998* the claimant had been billed for the cost of renewing a roof over one of the other flats in her block. The Commissioner decides that this did not come within any of the relevant heads in sub-para.(2). Head (g) did not apply as the roof was not part of the dwelling occupied by the claimant as her home. Head (j) was also not applicable, as there was no evidence that the roof had been renewed because of an unsafe structural defect. In addition, although a repair to a roof could, depending on its nature, be a damp-proofing measure, the renewal of a roof did not fall within head (c). In *R(IS) 2/07* the Commissioner stated that in his view "damp proofing" and "insulation" were terms of art in the building trade which have found their way into ordinary language. As used in head (c), he considered that "damp proofing" was limited to measures taken to prevent rising damp or damp from condensation, and "insulation" in head (g) was similarly restricted to such things as the installation of double-glazing, loft insulation and cavity wall insulation.

SSWP v AR (IS) [2010] UKUT 308 (AAC) did not consider that the reference to "rising damp or damp from condensation" in *R(IS) 2/07* was intended to be an exhaustive list of the causes of damp and that work undertaken for the purpose of curing penetrating damp, such as rendering or re- rendering walls, could constitute damp proof measures, as could internal plastering, depending on the circumstances. Equally the replacement of barge boards and fascias, if they were rotten and their replacement was a necessary accompaniment to the replacement of gutters and downpipes, could also be part of damp proofing (although they might also fall within head (e) (provision of drainage facilities)).

JT v SSWP (JSA) [2013] UKUT 184 (AAC) accepts that the replacement of the claimant's windows was needed to provide adequate insulation for her home.

Provision of facilities for preparing and cooking food

2.701   In *DC v SSWP (JSA)* [2010] UKUT 459 (AAC) the work undertaken was a kitchen extension and modernisation because the previous kitchen was very small and in a bad state of repair. Judge Turnbull considered that the provision of facilities for preparing and cooking food was not necessarily limited to the provisions of items such as cookers and worktops but could include the construction or adaptation of the part of the building containing them. Thus, if the previous kitchen was too small and poorly located so that some reconstruction was necessary to render the house habitable, that would amount to the provision of facilities for cooking, notwithstanding that there had previously been a kitchen. However, storage facilities (such as kitchen cupboards) and facilities for eating (such as a "breakfast room") would not be included.

A similar approach was taken in *JT v SSWP (JSA)* [2013] UKUT 184 (AAC). The cost of the new sink, cooker, hobs, hood and work surfaces (and associated building and electrical work) was allowed as housing costs but not the base units and cupboards, washing machine, drier and fridge freezer.

Paragraph 18—non-dependent deductions

Non-dependent is defined in reg.3. The standard deductions depend on whether   **2.702** the non-dependent is in remurative work or not, and the level of earnings (sub-paras (1) and (2)). The same deduction is made for a couple as for a single person (sub-paras (3) and (4)). Note that no deduction is made from the benefit of a claimant who (or whose partner) is severely sight impaired or blind or who is in receipt of attendance allowance, the care component of disability living allowance, the daily living component of personal independence payment or armed forces independence payment for himself (sub-para.(6)). Note also the list in sub-para.(7) of non-dependants for whom no deduction is made. Those covered include those getting a training allowance while on youth training (head (b)); students (head (c)); under-25s on income support or income-based JSA (head (d)); those for whom a deduction has already been made from housing benefit (head (e)); people who would not count as non-dependents under reg.3(2B) but for reg.3(2C) (e.g. co-owners who are close relatives or their partners, where the co-ownership arose after April 11, 1988) (head (f)); patients absent from home for more than 52 weeks (note that with effect from April 10, 2006 the definition of "patient" for the purposes of this provision is to be found in para.3(13)(b); this definition is wide enough to include a person who is in hospital as a private patient) or prisoners (head (g)); people in receipt of state pension credit (head (h)); under 25s who are in receipt of income-related ESA at the assessment phase rate (head (i)); and under 25s whose award of universal credit is calculated on the basis that they do not have any earned income (as defined in reg.52 of the Universal Credit Regulations (sub-para.(9); see Vol.V in this series for the Universal Credit Regulations) (head (j)). See also sub-para.(8).

In *CH/48/2006* (a case concerning the calculation of a non-dependent's earnings for the purposes of council tax benefit) the local authority had applied the highest rate of the non-dependent deduction in respect of the claimant's daughter in the absence of any actual evidence as to what she was earning. She had refused to provide this information. The claimant's evidence was that his daughter was 19-years-old and worked for 20 hours a week in a clothes shop. She occasionally worked overtime. The Commissioner recognised that the local authority was entitled to require evidence from claimants and that, in the absence of such evidence, it could make adverse inferences. However, any such adverse inference had to be based on some sense of reality. The claimant's daughter was only 19 and working in a junior role in an occupation that was not known for paying high wages. It was inherently unlikely that she would have been paid much above the minimum wage. The local authority and the tribunal had a duty to assess, on the evidence available and drawing *reasonable* adverse assumptions where no evidence was available, what was the likely level of the daughter's earnings. On this basis the Commissioner concluded on the balance of probabilities, and drawing the most adverse inferences that could sensibly be taken in the circumstances, that the claimant's daughter's pay was £5 per hour and that she did 10 hours paid overtime a week.

SCHEDULE 3A

[Revoked by the Social Security (Miscellaneous Amendments) Regulations 2006 (SI 2006/588),   **2.703** *reg.2(4)(e) with effect from April 3, 2006]*

SCHEDULE 3B

[Revoked by the Social Security (Miscellaneous Amendments) Regulations 2006 (SI 2006/588),   **2.704** *reg.2(4)(f) with effect from April 3, 2006]*

SCHEDULE 3C

2.705 *[Revoked by the Social Security (Removal of Residential Allowance and Miscellaneous Amendments) Regulations 2003 (SI 2003/1121), reg.2 and Sch.1, para.7 with effect from October 6, 2003.]*

SCHEDULE 4

2.706 *[Revoked by Social Security Amendment (Residential Care and Nursing Homes) Regulations 2001 (SI 2001/3767), reg.2 and Sch. Pt I para.16 with effect from April 8, 2002.]*

2.707 SCHEDULE 7 [³⁵ **Regulations 21 and 21AA**]

APPLICABLE AMOUNTS IN SPECIAL CASES

Column (1)	*Column (2)*
Patients **1.**—[³⁴ . . .]	**1.**—[³⁴ . . .]
[³⁴ ³⁹ **Persons serving a sentence of imprisonment detained in hospital** **2A.**—A person serving a sentence of imprisonment detained in hospital.]	**2A.**—[³⁸ Nil.
2B.—[³⁶. . .]	**2B.**—[³⁶. . .]
3.—[³¹ ³⁷. . .]	**3.**—[³¹ ³⁷. . .]
4.—[⁶. . .]	
5.—[⁶. . .].	
Claimants without accommodation **6.**—A claimant who is without accommodation.	**6.**—The amount applicable to him under regulation 17[³(1)](a) only.
Members of religious orders **7.**—A claimant who is a member of and fully maintained by a religious order.	**7.**—Nil.
Prisoners **8.**—A person— (a) except where sub-paragraph (b) applies, who is a prisoner; (b) who is detained in custody pending trial or sentence following conviction by a court.	**8.**— (a) Nil; (b) only such amount, if any, as may be applicable under regulation 17[³(1)](e).
9.—A claimant who is a member of a couple and who is temporarily separated from his partner [¹⁰where— (a) one member of the couple is— [³³ (i) not a patient but is residing in a care home, an Abbeyfield Home or an independent hospital, or] (ii) resident in premises used for the rehabilitation of alcoholics or drug addicts, or	**9.**—Either— (a) the amount applicable to him as a member of a couple under regulation 17; or

Column (1)	Column (2)

(iii) resident in accommodation provided under section 3 of and Part II of the Schedule to, the Polish Resettlement Act 1947 (provision of accommodation in camps), or
(iv) participating in arrangements for training made under section 2 of the Employment and Training Act 1973 [¹² or section 2 of the Enterprise and New Towns (Scotland) Act 1990] or attending a course at an employment rehabilitation centre established under that section [¹² of the 1973 Act], where the course requires him to live away from the dwelling occupied as the home, or
(v) in a probation or bail hostel approved for the purpose by the Secretary of State; and
(b) the other member of the couple is—
  (i) living in the dwelling occupied as the home, or
  (ii) a patient, or
[³³ (iii) residing in a care home, an Abbeyfield Home or an independent hospital.]
	(b) the aggregate of his applicable amount and that of his partner assessed under the provisions of these Regulations as if each of them were a single claimant, or a lone parent, whichever is the greater.

Column (1)	Column (2)
Polygamous marriages where one or more partners are temporarily separated **10.**—A claimant who is a member of a polygamous marriage and who is temporarily separated from a partner of his, where one of them is living in the home while the other member is— [³³ (a) not a patient but is residing in a care home, an Abbeyfield Home or an independent hospital, or] (b) [³³ . . .] (c) [¹ . . .] (d) resident in premises used for the rehabilitation of alcoholics or drug addicts; or (e) attending a course of training or instruction provided or approved by the [¹²Secretary of State for Employment] where the course requires him to live away from home; or (f) in a probation or bail hostel approved for the purpose by the Secretary of State.	**10.**—Either— (a) the amount applicable to the members of the polygamous marriage under regulation 18; or (b) the aggregate of the amount applicable for the members of the polygamous marriage who remain in the home under regulation 18 and the amount applicable in respect of those members not in the home calculated as if each of them were a single claimant, or a lone parent, whichever is the greater.

Column (1)	Column (2)
[²⁴**Single claimants temporarily in local authority accommodation** **10A.**—[³⁰ . . .]	**10A.**—[³⁰ . . .]

Column (1)	Column (2)

Couples and members of polygamous marriages where one member is or all are temporarily in local authority accommodation
    10B.—[³⁰ . . .]
Lone parents who are in residential accommodation temporarily
    10C.—[³⁰. . .]
	10B.—[³⁰ . . .]
	
	10C.—[³⁰ . . .]]

10D.—[¹⁵ . . .]	**10D.**—[¹⁵ . . .]
Couples where one member is abroad **11.**—[¹¹Subject to paragraph 11A] a claimant who is a member of a couple and whose partner is temporarily not present in [³United Kingdom].	**11.**—For the first four weeks of that absence, the amount applicable to them as a couple under regulation 17, [²⁷. . .] [⁹ or 21] as the case may be and thereafter the amount applicable to the claimant in Great Britain under regulation 17 [²⁷. . .] or [⁹ or 21] as the case may be as if the claimant were a single claimant or, as the case may be, a lone parent.

[¹¹**Couple or member of couple taking child or young person abroad for treatment**
    11A.—[¹⁵—(1)] A claimant who is a member of a couple where either—
    (a) he or his partner is, or,
    (b) both he and his partner are absent from the United Kingdom [¹⁴in the circumstances specified in paragraph (2).
    (2) For the purposes of sub-paragraph (1), the specified circumstances are—
    (a) in respect of a claimant, those in regulation 4(3)(a) to (d);
    (b) in respect of a claimant's partner as if regulation 4(3)(a) to (d) applies to that partner.]
	11A.—For the first eight weeks of that absence, the amount applicable to the claimant under regulation 17(1) [²⁷. . .] or 21, as the case may be, and, thereafter, if the claimant is in Great Britain the amount applicable to him under regulation 17(1) [²⁷. . .] or 21, as the case may be, as if the claimant were a single claimant, or, as the case may be, a lone parent.

Polygamous marriages where any member is abroad
    12.—Subject to paragraph 12A, a claimant who is a member of a polygamous marriage where—
    (a) he or one of his partners is, or
    (b) he and one or more of his partners are, or
    (c) two or more of his partners are, temporarily absent from the United Kingdom.
	12.—For the first four weeks of that absence, the amount applicable to the claimant under regulations 17 to 21, as the case may be, and thereafter, if the claimant is in Great Britain the amount applicable to him under regulations 18 to 21, as the case may be, as if any member of the polygamous marriage not in the United Kingdom were not a member of the marriage.

Polygamous marriage: taking child or young person abroad for treatment
    12A.—[¹⁵—(1)] A claimant who is a member of a polygamous marriage where—
    (a) he or one of his partners is,
    (b) he and one or more of his partners are, or
	12A.—For the first 8 weeks of that absence the amount applicable to the claimant under regulations 18 to 21, as the case may be, as if any member of the polygamous marriage

Column (1)	Column (2)
(c) two or more of his partners are, absent from the United Kingdom [¹⁴in the circumstances specified in paragraph (2).	not in the United Kingdom were not a member of the marriage.]
(2) For the purposes of subparagraph (1), the specified circumstances are—	
(a) in respect of a claimant, those in regulation 4(3)(a) to (d);	
(b) in respect of a claimant's partner or partners, as the case may be, as if regulation	
4(3)(a) to (d) applied to that partner or those partners.]	
[²⁴**Persons in residential accommodation.** **13.**—(1) [²⁹ . . .] [³⁰ . . .] (2) [²⁹ . . .]	**13.**—(1) [³⁰ . . .] **13A.**—[³⁰ . . .]
Polish Resettlement (2) [²⁹ . . .]	**13A.**—[³⁰ . . .]
[¹⁸**Polish resettlement: Persons temporarily absent from accommodation** **13B.**—[³⁰ . . .]	**13B.**—[³⁰ . . . [²⁹ . . .]]]
Polish resettlement **14.**—[⁹. . .]	**14.**—[⁹ . . .]
Resettlement units **15.**—[⁹. . .]	**15.**—[⁹ . . .]
Persons temporarily absent from a hostel, residential care or nursing home **16.**—[²⁷. . .]	**16.**—[²⁷. . .]
[²⁵**Partner of a person subject to immigration control** **16A.**—(a) A claimant who is the partner of a person subject to immigration control. (b) Where regulation 18 (polygamous marriages) applies and the claimant is a person— (i) who is not subject to immigration control within the meaning of section 115(9) of the Immigration and Asylum Act; or (ii) to whom section 115 of that Act does not apply by virtue of regulation 2 of the Social Security (Immigration and Security (Immigration and Asylum) Consequential Amendments Regulations 2000; and	[³¹ **16A.**—[³¹. . .](a) The amount applicable in respect of the claimant only under regulation 17(1)(a), any amount which may be applicable to him under regulation 17(1)(d) plus the amount applicable to him under regulation 17(1)(e), (f) and (g) or, as the case may be, regulation 21. (b) The amount determined in accordance with that regulation or regulation 21 in respect of the claimant and any partners of his who are not subject to immigration control within the meaning of section 115(9) of the Immigration and Asylum Act and to whom section 115 of that Act does not apply for the purposes of exclusion from entitlement to income

Column (1)	Column (2)
(iii) who is a member of a couple and one or more of his partners is subject to immigration control within the meaning of section 115(9) of that Act and section 115 of that Act applies to her for the purposes of exclusion from entitlement to income support.]	support.]
17.—[²⁵**Person from abroad**]	17.—[³⁸ nil]
[²⁴**Persons in residential care or nursing homes who become patients**] 18.—[²⁷. . .]	18.—[²⁷. . .]

Claimants entitled to the disability premium for a past period
19.—A claimant—
  (a) whose time for claiming ncome support has been
    extended under regulation 19(2) of the Social Security (Claims and Payments) Regulations 1987 (time for claiming benefit); and
  (b) whose partner was entitled to income support in respect of the period beginning with the day on which the claimant's
    claim is treated as made under [¹⁹regulation 6(3) of those Regulations] and [¹⁹ending with the day before the day] on which the claim is actually made; and
  (c) who satisfied the condition in [³⁶ paragraph 11(1)(b)] of Schedule 2 and the additional condition referred to in that paragraph and specified in paragraph 12(1)(b) of that Schedule in respect of that period.
	19.—The amount only of the disability premium applicable by virtue of [³⁶ paragraph 11(1)(b)] of Schedule 2
	as specified in paragraph 15(4)(b) of that Schedule.

[²⁶**Persons who have commenced remunerative work**
19A.—(1) A person to whom regulation 6(5) (persons not treated as in remunerative work) applies.]
 	
(i) Schedule 3 (housing costs); [³⁸ . . .]
	[²⁶19A.—(1) Subect to sub-paragraph (2), the lowest of either—
	  (a) the amount determined in accordance with—
	    (i) Schedule 3 (housing costs); [³⁸ . . .]
	    (ii) as the case may be, Schedule 2 to the Jobseeker's Allowance Regulations 1996 (housing costs), [³⁸ or
	    (iii) as the case may be, Schedule 6 to the Employment and Support Allowance Regulations (housing costs),]

Column (1)	Column (2)
	which was applicable to the claimant or his partner immediately before he or his partner commenced the remunerative work referred to in regulation 6(5)(a); or
	(b) the amount of income support [38 , income-related employment and support allowance] or, as the case may be, income-based jobseeker's allowance which the claimant or his partner was entitled to in the benefit week immediately before the benefit week in which he or his partner commenced the remunerative work referred to in regulation 6(5) (a) or, where he or his partner was in receipt of a training allowance in that benefit week, the amount of income support or income-based jobseeker's allowance which he would have been entitled to in that week had he not been in receipt of a training allowance.
	(2) Nothing in sub-paragraph (1) shall prevent any adjustment being made to the amount referredto in (a) or, as the case may be, (b) of that sub-paragraph during the period referred to in regulations 6(6), in order to reflect changes during that period to the amounts prescribed in Schedule 2 [28. . .] or 4 or in this Schedule or to reflect changes in circumstances during that period relating to the matters specified to in sub-paragraph (3).
	(3) The changes in circumstances referred to in sub-paragraph (2) are changes to the amount of housing costs to be met in accordance with Schedule 3 in the claimant's case occasioned by—
	(a) the claimant becoming entitled to income support for a continuous period of 26 weeks or more;
	(b) a change to the standard interest rate; or
	(c) any non-dependant deduction becoming applicable, or ceasing to be applicable.
	(4) In sub-paragraph (1), a reference to the claimant or his partner being entitled to and in receipt or an income-based jobseeker's allowance or to an amount being applicable to either of them under the Jobseeker's Allowance Regulations 1996 shall include a reference to the claimant and his partner being entitled to, and in

Column (1)	Column (2)
	receipt of, a joint-claim jobseeker's allowance and to an amount being applicable to that couple under those Regulations.]
Rounding of fractions **20.**—Where any calculation under this Schedule or as a result of income support being awarded for a period less than one complete benefit week results in a fraction of a penny that fraction shall be treated as a penny.	

AMENDMENTS

1. Income Support (General) Amendment Regulations 1988 (SI 1988/663) reg.33 (April 11, 1988).

2. Employment Act 1988 s.24(3) (May 26, 1988).

3. Income Support (General) Amendment No.4 Regulations 1988 (SI 1988/1445) reg.23 (September 12, 1988).

4. Income Support (General) Amendment No.5 Regulations 1988 (SI 1988/2022) reg.21 (December 12, 1988).

5. Income Support (General) Amendment No.4 Regulations 1988 (SI 1988/1445) Sch.1 para.1 (April 10, 1989).

6. Income Support (General) Amendment No.4 Regulations 1988 (SI 1988/1445) Sch.1 para.1 (April 10, 1989).

7. Income Support (General) Amendment No.4 Regulations 1988 (SI 1988/1445) Sch.1 para.15 (April 10, 1989).

8. Income Support (General) Amendment Regulations 1989 (SI 1989/534) reg.9 (April 10, 1989).

9. Income Support (General) Amendment Regulations 1989 (SI 1989/534) Sch.1 para.13 (October 9, 1989).

10. Income Support (General) Amendment No.3 Regulations 1989 (SI 1989/1678) reg.11 (October 9, 1989).

11. Income Support (General) Amendment Regulations 1990 (SI 1990/547) reg.21 (April 9, 1990).

12. Enterprise (Scotland) Consequential Amendments Order 1991 (SI 1991/387) art.2 (April 1, 1991).

13. Income Support (General) Amendment Regulations 1991 (SI 1991/236) reg.2(1) (April 8, 1991).

14. Income Support (General) Amendment Regulations 1991 (SI 1991/236) reg.13 (April 8, 1991).

15. Income Support (General) Amendment No.4 Regulations 1991 (SI 1991/1559) reg.19 (October 7, 1991).

16. Social Security Benefits (Amendments Consequential Upon the Introduction of Community Care) Regulations 1992 (SI 1992/3147) Sch.1 para.6 (April 1, 1993).

17. Income-related Benefits Schemes (Miscellaneous Amendments) (No.4) Regulations 1993 (SI 1993/2119) reg.21 (October 4, 1993).

18. Income-related Benefits Schemes (Miscellaneous Amendments) (No.5) Regulations 1994 (SI 1994/2139) reg.31 (October 3, 1994).

19. Income-related Benefits Schemes (Miscellaneous Amendments) Regulations 1995 (SI 1995/516) reg.26 (April 10, 1995).

20. Child Benefit, Child Support and Social Security (Miscellaneous Amendments) Regulations 1996 (SI 1996/1803) reg.40 (April 7, 1997).

21. Income-related Benefits and Jobseeker's Allowance (Amendment) (No.2) Regulations 1977 (SI 1997/2197) reg.5(7) (October 6, 1997).

22. Social Security (Miscellaneous Amendments) Regulations 1998 (SI 1998/563) reg.8(1) and (2)(c)(ii) (April 6, 1998).

23. Social Security (Miscellaneous Amendments) Regulations 1998 (SI 1998/563) reg.8(3) (April 6, 1998).

24. Social Security Benefits Up-rating Order 2003 (SI 2003/526) art.17(7) and Sch.4 (April 8, 2002).

25. Social Security (Immigration and Asylum) Consequential Amendments Regulations 2000 (SI 2000/636) reg.3 (April 3, 2000).

26. Social Security (Miscellaneous Amendments) Regulations 2001 (SI 2001/488) reg.7 (April 9, 2001).

27. Social Security Amendment (Residential Care and Nursing Homes) Regulations 2001 (SI 2001/3767) reg.2 and Sch. Pt I para.17 (April 8, 2002).

28. Social Security Amendment (Residential Care and Nursing Homes) Regulations 2001 (SI 2001/3767) reg.2 and Sch. Pt I para.17 (as amended by Social Security Amendment (Residential Care and Nursing Homes) Regulations 2002 (SI 2002/398) reg.4(2)) (April 8, 2002).

29. Social Security (Hospital In-Patients and Miscellaneous Amendments) Regulations 2003 (SI 2003/1195) reg.3 (May 21, 2003).

30. Social Security (Removal of Residential Allowance and Miscellaneous Amendments) Regulations 2003 (SI 2003/1121) reg.2 and Sch.1 para.8 (October 6, 2003).

31. Social Security (Working Tax Credit and Child Tax Credit) (Consequential Amendments) Regulations 2003 (SI 2003/455) reg.2 and Sch.1 para.21 (April 6, 2004, except in "transitional cases"—see further the note to reg.17 of the Income Support Regulations).

32. Mental Health (Care and Treatment) (Scotland) Act 2003 (Modification of Subordinate Legislation) Order 2005 (SSI 2005/445) art.2 and Sch. para.3(4) (Scotland); Mental Health (Care and Treatment) (Scotland) Act 2003 (Consequential Provisions) Order 2005 (SI 2005/2078) art.15 and Sch.2 para.3(5) (England and Wales) (October 5, 2005).

33. Social Security (Care Homes and Independent Hospitals) Regulations 2005 (SI 2005/2687) reg.2 and Sch.1 para.10 (October 24, 2005).

34. Social Security (Hospital In-Patients) Regulations 2005 (SI 2005/3360) reg.4 (April 10, 2006).

35. Social Security (Miscellaneous Amendments) Regulations 2007 (SI 2007/719) reg.2(8)(a) (April 2, 2007).

36. Social Security (Miscellaneous Amendments) Regulations 2007 (SI 2007/719) reg.2(8)(b) (April 9, 2007).

37. Social Security (Miscellaneous Amendments) Regulations 2007 (SI 2007/719) reg.2(8)(c) (April 8, 2007).

38. Employment and Support Allowance (Consequential Provisions) (No.2) Regulations 2008 (SI 2008/1554) reg.2(1) and (12) (October 27, 2008).

39. Social Security (Persons Serving a Sentence of Imprisonment Detained in Hospital) Regulations 2010 (SI 2010/442) reg.3(1) and (3) (March 25, 2010).

DEFINITIONS

"Abbeyfield Home"—see reg.2(1).
"care home"—*ibid.*
"child"—see SSCBA s.137(1).
"claimant"—see reg.2(1).
"couple"—*ibid.*
"family"—see SSCBA s.137(1).
"independent hospital"—see reg.2(1).
"lone parent"—see reg.2(1).
"partner"—*ibid.*
"patient"—see reg.21(3).

"partner of a person subject to immigration control"—*ibid.*
"person from abroad"—*ibid.*
"polygamous marriage"—see reg.2(1).
"prisoner"—see reg.21(3).
"relative"—see reg.2(1).
"single claimant"—*ibid.*
"young person"—*ibid.*, reg.14.

GENERAL NOTE

2.708   See the notes to regs 21 and 6(5)–(8).

SCHEDULE 8   **Regulations 36(2), 38(2) and 44(6)**

SUMS TO BE DISREGARDED IN THE CALCULATION OF EARNINGS

2.709   [²⁷ **1.**—(1) In the case of a claimant who has been engaged in remunerative work as an employed earner or, had the employment been in Great Britain, would have been so engaged—

   (a) any earnings, other than items to which sub-paragraph (2) applies, paid or due to be paid from that employment which terminated before the first day of entitlement to income support;

   (b) any earnings, other than a payment of the nature described in [²⁹ sub-paragraph (2) (a) or (b)(ii)], paid or due to be paid from that employment which has not been terminated where the claimant is not-

       (i) engaged in remunerative work, or

       (ii) suspended from his employment.

   (2) This sub-paragraph applies to—

[²⁹ (a) any payment of the nature described in—

       (i)   regulation 35(1)(e), or

       (ii) section 28, 64 or 68 of the Employment Rights Act 1996 (guarantee payments, suspension from work on medical or maternity grounds); and]

   (b) any award, sum or payment of the nature described in—

       (i)   regulation 35(1)(g) or (h), or

       (ii) section 34 or 70 of the Employment Rights Act 1996 (guarantee payments and suspension from work: complaints to employment tribunals),

       including any payment made following the settlement of a complaint to an employment tribunal or of court proceedings.]

[²⁰ **1A.**—If the claimant's partner has been engaged in remunerative work as an employed earner or, had the employment been in Great Britain, would have been so engaged, any earnings paid or due to be paid on termination of that employment by way of retirement but only if the partner has attained the qualifying age for state pension credit on retirement.]

[²⁷ **2.**—(1) In the case of a claimant to whom this paragraph applies, any earnings (other than a payment of the nature described in [²⁹ paragraph 1(2)(a) or (b)(ii)]) which relate to employment which ceased before the first day of entitlement to income support whether or not that employment has terminated.

   (2) This paragraph applies to a claimant who has been engaged in part-time employment as an employed earner or, had the employment been in Great Britain, would have been so engaged; but it does not apply to a claimant who has been suspended from his employment.]

   3.—In the case of a claimant who has been engaged in remunerative work or part-time employment as a self-employed earner [¹or, had the employment been in Great Britain would have been so engaged] and who has ceased to be so employed, from the date of the cessation of his employment any earnings derived from that employment except earnings to which regulation 30(2) (royalties etc.) applies.

   [⁴**4.**—(1) In a case to which this paragraph applies, [¹⁶£20]; but notwithstanding regulation 23 (calculation of income and capital of members of claimant's family and of a polygamous marriage), if this paragraph applies to a claimant it shall not apply to his partner except where, and to the extent that, the earnings of the claimant which are to be disregarded under this paragraph are less than [¹⁶£20].

   (2) This paragraph applies where the claimant's applicable amount includes, or but for his being an in-patient [¹⁸. . .] [²⁵ . . .] would include, an amount by way of a disability premium under Schedule 2 (applicable amounts).

   (3) This paragraph applies where—

    (a) the claimant is a member of a couple, and—

         (i) his applicable amount would include an amount by way of the disability premium under Schedule 2 but for the higher pensioner premium under that Schedule being applicable; or

        (ii) had he not been an in-patient [[18] . . .] [[25] . . .] his applicable amount would include the higher pensioner premium under that Schedule and had that been the case he would also satisfy the condition in (i) above; and

    (b) [[20] . . .]

(4) This paragraph applies where—

    (a) the claimant's applicable amount includes, or but for his being an in-patient [[18] . . .] [[25] . . .] would include, an amount by way of the higher pensioner premium under Schedule 2; and

[[20] (b) the claimant's partner has attained the qualifying age for state pension credit;]

    (c) immediately before attaining that age [[20] . . .] his partner was engaged in part-time employment and the claimant was entitled by virtue of sub-paragraph (2) [[20] . . .] to a disregard of [[16]£20]; and

    (d) he or, as the case may be, he or his partner has continued in part-time employment.

(5) [[15] . . .].

(6) [[15] . . .].

[[6](7) For the purposes of this paragraph—

    (a) except where head (b) or (c) applies, no account shall be taken of any period not exceeding eight consecutive weeks occurring—

        [[20] (i) on or after the date on which the claimant's partner attained the qualifying age for state pension credit during which the partner was not engaged in part-time employment or the claimant was not entitled to income support [[28] or employment and support allowance]; or]

        (ii) immediately after the date on which the claimant or his partner ceased to participate in arrangements for training made under section 2 of the Employment and Training Act 1973 [[7]or section 2 of the Enterprise and New Towns (Scotland) Act 1990] or to attend a course at an employment rehabilitation centre established under that section [[7]of the 1973 Act];

    (b) in a case where the claimant has ceased to be entitled to income support [[28] or employment and support allowance] because he, or if he is a member of a couple, he or his partner becomes engaged in remunerative work, no account shall be taken of any period, during which he was not entitled to income support [[28] or employment and support allowance], not exceeding the permitted period determined in accordance with regulation 3A (permitted period) occurring on or after the date on which [[20] the claimant's partner attains the qualifying age for state pension credit];

    (c) no account shall be taken of any period occurring on or after the date on which [[20] the claimant's partner, if he is a member of a couple, attained the qualifying age for state pension credit] during which the claimant was not entitled to income support [[28] or employment and support allowance] because he or his partner was participating in arrangements for training made under section 2 of the Employment and Training Act 1973 [[7]or section 2 of the Enterprise and New Towns (Scotland) Act 1990] or attending a course at an employment rehabilitation centre established under that section [[7]of the 1973 Act].]]

[[13]5.—In a case where the claimant is a lone parent and paragraph 4 does not apply, [[16]£20].]

[[11]6.—Where the claimant is a member of a couple—

    (a) in a case to which none of paragraphs 4, 6A, 6B, 7 and 8 applies, £10; but notwithstanding regulation 23 (calculation of income and capital of members of claimant's family and of a polygamous marriage), if this paragraph applies to a claimant it shall not apply to his partner except where, and to the extent that, the earnings of the claimant which are to be disregarded under this sub-paragraph are less than £10;

    (b) in a case to which one or more of paragraphs 4, 6A, 6B, 7 and 8 applies and the total amount disregarded under those paragraphs is less than £10, so much of the claimant's earnings as would not in aggregate with the amount disregarded under those paragraphs exceed £10.]

[[9]6A.—(1) In a case to which none of paragraphs 4 to 6 applies to the claimant, and subject to sub-paragraph (2), where the claimant's applicable amount includes an amount by way of the carer premium under Schedule 2 (applicable amounts), [[16]£20] of the earnings of the person who is, or at any time in the preceding eight weeks was, in receipt of [[19] carer's allowance] or treated in accordance with paragraph 14ZA(2) of that Schedule as being in receipt of [[19] carer's allowance].

(2) Where the carer premium is awarded in respect of the claimant and of any partner of his, their earnings shall for the purposes of this paragraph be aggregated, but the amount to be disregarded in accordance with paragraph (1) shall not exceed [16£20] of the aggregated amount.

6B.—Where the carer premium is awarded in respect of a claimant who is a member of a couple and whose earnings are less than [16£20], but is not awarded in respect of the other member of the couple, and that other member is engaged in an employment—

(a) specified in paragraph 7(1), so much of the other member's earnings as would not when aggregated with the amount disregarded under paragraph 6A exceed [16£20];

(b) other than one specified in paragraph 7(1), so much of the other member's earnings from such other employment up to £5 as would not when aggregated with the amount disregarded under paragraph 6A exceed [16£20].]

7.—(1) In a case to which none of paragraphs [9 4 to 6B] applies to the claimant, [16£20] of earnings derived from one or more employments as—

[32 (a) a part-time fire-fighter employed by a fire and rescue authority under the Fire and Rescue Services Act 2004 or by the Scottish Fire and Rescue Service established under section 1A of the Fire (Scotland) Act 2005;]

[23 (aa) [32 . . .]]

[24 (ab) [32 . . .]]

(b) an auxiliary coastguard in respect of coast rescue activities;

(c) a person engaged part time in the manning or launching of a life boat;

(d) a member of any [33 . . .] reserve force prescribed in Part I of [26 Schedule 6 to the Social Security (Contributions) Regulations 2001];

but, notwithstanding regulation 23 (calculation of income and capital of members of claimant's family and of a polygamous marriage), if this paragraph applies to a claimant it shall not apply to his partner except to the extent specified in sub-paragraph (2).

(2) If the claimant's partner is engaged in employment—

(a) specified in sub-paragraph (1) so much of his earnings as would not in aggregate with the amount of the claimant's earnings disregarded under this paragraph exceed [16£20];

(b) other than one specified in sub-paragraph (1) so much of his earnings from that employment up to £5 as would not in aggregate with the claimant's earnings disregarded under this paragraph exceed [16£20].

8.—Where the claimant is engaged in one or more employments specified in paragraph 7(1) but his earnings derived from such employments are less than [16£20] in any week and he is also engaged in any other part-time employment so much of his earnings from that other employment up to £5 as would not in aggregate with the amount of his earnings disregarded under paragraph 7 exceed [16£20].

9.—In a case to which none of paragraphs 4 to 8 applies to the claimant, £5.

[11**10.**—Notwithstanding the foregoing provisions of this Schedule, where two or more payments of the same kind and from the same source are to be taken into account in the same benefit week, because it has not been practicable to treat the payments under regulation 31(1)(b) (date on which income treated as paid) as paid on the first day of the benefit week in which they were due to be paid, there shall be disregarded from each payment the sum that would have been disregarded if the payment had been taken into account on the date on which it was due to be paid.]

11.—Any earnings derived from employment which are payable in a country outside the United Kingdom for such period during which there is a prohibition against the transfer to the United Kingdom of those earnings.

12.—Where a payment of earnings is made in a currency other than sterling, any banking charge or commission payable in converting that payment into sterling.

13.—Any earnings which are due to be paid before the date of claim and which would otherwise fall to be taken into account in the same benefit week as a payment of the same kind and from the same source.

14.—Any earnings of a child or young person [21 . . .].

15.—[21 . . .].

[11[30 **15A.**—(1) Where earnings to which sub-paragraph (2) applies (in aggregate with the claimant's other income (if any) calculated in accordance with this Part) exceed the applicable amount (as specified in Part IV and Schedule 2) less 10 pence, the amount of those earnings corresponding to that excess.

(2) This sub-paragraph applies to earnings, in so far as they exceed the amount disregarded under paragraph 7, derived by the claimant from employment as a member of any [33 . . .] reserve force prescribed in Part 1 of Schedule 6 to the Contributions Regulations in respect of

a period of annual continuous training for a maximum of 15 days in any calendar year [[33] or in respect of training in the claimant's first year of training as a member of a reserve force for a maximum of 43 days in that year.]]]

[[14]**15B.**—[[22] . . .]]

[[17]**15C.**—In the case of a person to whom paragraph (5) of regulation 6 (persons not treated as in remunerative work) applies, any earnings.]

16.—In this Schedule "part-time employment" means employment in which the person is not to be treated as engaged in remunerative work under regulation 5 or 6 (persons treated, or not treated, as engaged in remunerative work).

AMENDMENTS

1. Income Support (General) Amendment Regulations 1988 (SI 1988/663) reg.34 (April 11, 1988).

2. Income Support (General) Amendment No.4 Regulations 1988 (SI 1988/ 1445) reg.24 (September 12, 1988).

3. Income Support (General) Amendment No.4 Regulations 1988 (SI 1988/ 1445) Sch.1 para.8 (April 10, 1989).

4. Income Support (General) Amendment Regulations 1989 (SI 1989/534) reg.10 and Sch.1 (October 9, 1989).

5. Income Support (General) Amendment No.2 Regulations 1989 (SI 1989/ 1323) reg.18 (October 9, 1989).

6. Income Support (General) Amendment No.3 Regulations 1989 (SI 1989/ 1678) reg.12 (October 9, 1989).

7. Enterprise (Scotland) Consequential Amendments Order 1991 (SI 1991/ 387) art.2 and 9 (April 1, 1991).

8. Income Support (General) Amendment Regulations 1992 (SI 1992/468) reg.7 (April 6, 1992).

9. Income-related Benefits Schemes (Miscellaneous Amendments) Regulations 1993 (SI 1993/315) reg.8 (April 12, 1993).

10. Income-related Benefits Schemes (Miscellaneous Amendments) (No.4) Regulations 1993 (SI 1993/2119) reg.22 (October 4, 1993).

11. Income-related Benefits Schemes and Social Fund (Miscellaneous Amendments) Regulations 1996 (SI 1996/1944) reg.6(11) (October 7,1996).

12. Child Benefit, Child Support and Social Security (Miscellaneous Amendments) Regulations 1996 (SI 1996/1803) reg.41 (April 7, 1997).

13. Social Security Amendment (Lone Parents) Regulations 1998 (SI 1998/ 766) reg.13 (April 6, 1998).

14. Social Security (Miscellaneous Amendments) (No.2) Regulations 1999 (SI 1999/2556) reg.2(9) (October 4, 1999).

15. Social Security (Miscellaneous Amendments) Regulations 2000 (SI 2000/ 681) reg.12(a) (April 3, 2000).

16. Social Security Amendment (Capital Limits and Earnings Disregards) Regulations 2000 (SI 2000/2545) reg.3 and Sch. para.2 (April 9, 2001).

17. Social Security (Miscellaneous Amendments) Regulations 2001 (SI 2001/ 488) reg.8 (April 9, 2001).

18. Social Security Amendment (Residential Care and Nursing Homes) Regulations 2001 (SI 2001/3767) reg.2(1) and Pt I of Sch. para.18 (April 8, 2002).

19. Social Security Amendment (Carer's Allowance) Regulations 2002 (SI 2002/2497) reg.3 and Sch.2 (April 1, 2003).

20. State Pension Credit (Consequential, Transitional and Miscellaneous Provisions) Regulations 2002 (SI 2002/3019) reg.29(7) (October 6, 2003).

21. Social Security (Working Tax Credit and Child Tax Credit)(Consequential Amendments) Regulations 2003 (SI 2003/455) reg.2 and Sch.1 para.22 (April 6, 2004, except in "transitional cases" and see further the note to reg.17 of the Income Support Regulations).

22. Social Security (Back to Work Bonus and Lone Parent Run-on) (Amendment and Revocation) Regulations 2003 (SI 2003/1589) reg.2(d) (October 25, 2004).

23. Fire and Rescue Services Act 2004 (Consequential Amendments) (England) Order 2004 (SI 2004/3168) art.14 (December 30, 2004) (in relation to England); Fire and Rescue Services Act 2004 (Consequential Amendments) (Wales) Order 2005 (SI 2005/2929 (W.214)) art.15 (October 25, 2005) (in relation to Wales). The amendment does not extend to Scotland.

24. Fire (Scotland) Act 2005 (Consequential Provisions and Modifications) Order 2005 (SI 2005/2060 (S.7)) art.3 and Sch. para.5 (August 2, 2005) (in relation to Scotland only; this amendment also revokes head (a) of para.7(1), again in relation to Scotland only).

25. Social Security (Care Homes and Independent Hospitals) Regulations 2005 (SI 2005/2687) reg.2 and Sch.1 para.11 (October 24, 2005).

26. Social Security (Miscellaneous Amendments) (No.4) Regulations 2006 (SI 2006/2378) reg.5(9) (October 2, 2006).

27. Social Security (Miscellaneous Amendments) (No.5) Regulations 2007 (SI 2007/2618) reg.5(11) (October 1, 2007).

28. Employment and Support Allowance (Consequential Provisions) (No.2) Regulations 2008 (SI 2008/1554) reg.2(13) (October 27, 2008).

29. Social Security (Miscellaneous Amendments) (No.4) Regulations 2009 (SI 2009/2655) reg.2(16) (October 26, 2009).

30. Social Security (Miscellaneous Amendments) (No.2) Regulations 2012 (SI 2012/2575) reg.2(4) (November 5, 2012).

31. Police and Fire Reform (Scotland) Act 2012 (Consequential Provisions and Modifications) Order 2013 (SI 2013/602) art.26 and Sch.2 para.69 (April 1, 2013).

32. Social Security (Miscellaneous Amendments) (No.3) Regulations 2013 (SI 2013/2536) reg.4(7) (October 29, 2013).

33. Social Security (Members of the Reserve Forces) (Amendment) Regulations 2015 (SI 2015/389) reg.2(4) (April 6, 2015).

DEFINITIONS

"benefit week"—see reg.2(1).
"child"—see SSCBA s.137(1).
"claimant"—see reg.2(1).
"couple"—*ibid.*
"date of claim"—*ibid.*
"employed earner"—*ibid.*
"family"—see SSCBA s.137(1).
"first year of training"—see reg.2(1).
"partner"—see reg.2(1).
"polygamous marriage"—*ibid.*
"remunerative work"—*ibid.*
"Social Security Act"—*ibid.*
"supplementary benefit"—*ibid.*
"young person"—*ibid.*, reg.14.

GENERAL NOTE

2.710   Before April 6, 2004 the income (but not the capital) of a child or young person who was a member of the claimant's family was aggregated with the claimant's, subject to the modifications in reg.44. Under the form of this Schedule in force at that time paras 1–10 did not apply to children or young persons (see the form of reg.23(2) then in force) and paras 14 and 15 only applied to children and young persons (see the 2003 edition of this volume for the old form of reg.23 and of paras 14 and 15 of this Schedule). However, with effect from April 6, 2004 (except in "transitional cases"— see the note to reg.17), amounts for children and young persons have been removed from the income support scheme; financial assistance to help with the cost of bringing up a child or young person is now to be provided through the child tax credit system, see Vol.IV of this series. As a consequence, the income of a child or young person is no longer aggregated with the claimant's (see the new form of reg.23 and the notes to that regulation) and so the disregards that applied to such income are no longer needed (although note that part of para.14 has been retained). The former disregards do however remain in force for "transitional cases"—see the note to reg.17.

For income support claimants who had an award of child tax credit before April 6, 2004 see reg.7 of the Social Security (Working Tax Credit and Child Tax Credit) (Consequential Amendments) Regulations 2003 (SI 2003/455) (as amended) on p.1763 and the notes to that regulation.

The categories of disregards of earnings are as follows (* indicates no further note below):

Para.1	final earnings on termination of full-time employment;
Para.1A	final earnings on retirement of claimant's partner;
Para.2	final earnings on termination of part-time employment;
Para.3	earnings on termination of self-employment;
Para.4	£20 disregard where disability premium or higher pensioner premium;
Para.5	lone parent £20 disregard;
Para.6	couple's disregard;
Para.6A	£20 disregard where carer premium;
Para.6B	£20 disregard where carer premium – rules for partners;
Para.7	default £20 disregard for particular employments;
Para.8	default £20 disregard – additional part-time employment;
Para.9	default £5 disregard;
Para.10	payments taken into account in same week;
Para.11	prohibition on transfer of earnings from outside the UK*;
Para.12	charges for conversion to sterling*;
Para.13	earnings due before date of claim and overlap;
Para.14	earnings of child or young person;
Para.15A	annual continuous training for reserve forces;
Para.15C	persons treated as not in remunerative work by reg.6(5).

Paragraph 1

This disregard is crucial to entitlement following the termination of full-time employment as an employed earner (i.e. 16 hours or more per week in the case of the claimant, 24 hours or more per week for a partner: reg.5(1) and (1A); references to the "claimant" in Pt V of the Income Support Regulations include a partner (if any), unless the context otherwise requires (reg.23(1))).

2.711

For the disregard of a partner's earnings paid on the termination of full-time (24 hours plus a week) employment due to retirement see para.1A.

The effect of the new form of para.1 introduced on October 1, 2007, is to significantly extend the disregard that applies to payments made on the termination of full-time work. The new rules are as follows.

- Where the full-time employment terminated before the first day of entitlement to income support, all payments (except those referred to below) made on its cessation, including final earnings, payments in lieu of wages, or in lieu of notice, holiday pay and compensation payments (as defined in reg.35(3)) are ignored (sub-para.(1)(a)). (Note that from April 14, 2008 the definition of "compensation" in reg.35(1)(i) and (3) is amended so that it no longer applies to payments made in respect of full-time employment.) This means that entitlement to income support can begin immediately (subject to the other conditions of entitlement being met). Note, however, that holiday pay that is payable more than four weeks after the termination (or interruption) of employment counts as capital (see reg.48(3)), as may redundancy payments or ex gratia payments, depending on their nature. See further the notes to reg.35(1)(i).

- However, any retainer (reg.35(1)(e)), and the employment protection payments referred to in reg.35(1)(g) or (h), or ss.34 or 70 of the Employment

Rights Act 1996 (including any payment made in settlement of an employment tribunal claim or court action), will be taken into account (sub-para.
(2)). But note that these payments are not listed in reg.5(5) (which treats a
person who receives earnings of the kind listed in reg.5(5) as in full-time work
for the period covered by such earnings (see reg.29(3) and (4)). Thus if any
of these payments are made they will not lead to complete disentitlement,
although they will, subject to the relevant earnings disregard, be taken into
account in calculating the amount of income support (if any) that is payable.
See reg.31(1) for the date on which the earnings will be treated as paid; note
also reg.29(3) and (4).

R(IS) 9/95 decided that a guarantee payment under s.12 of the
Employment Protection (Consolidation) Act 1978 counted as a retainer,
and presumably the same would apply to guarantee payments under the
current provision, s.28 of the Employment Rights Act 1996. That is confirmed by the amendment to para.1(2)(a) on October 26, 2009 which has
the effect that payments of that nature (i.e. guarantee payments under s.28
of the Employment Rights Act 1996, and the right to remuneration while
suspended on medical grounds under s.64 of that Act or while suspended on
maternity grounds under s.68), as well as payments by way of a retainer (i.e.
those covered by reg.35(1)(e)), are not disregarded.

Section 34 of the Employment Rights Act 1996 provides for a complaint
to an employment tribunal if an employer fails to pay under s.28 of the Act;
and s.70 similarly so provides if an employer fails to pay under s.64 or s.68,
or under s.67 fails to offer alternative suitable work where this is available
before suspending on maternity grounds.

Regulation 35(1)(g) applies to compensation awards for unfair dismissal
and reg.35(1)(h) to arrears of pay under an order for reinstatement or re-
engagement; any sum payable under an award for the continuation of a
contract of employment; and remuneration under a protective award.

- Where the employment has not terminated but the claimant is working less
  than 16 hours a week (or none at all), only payment of any retainer, and (from
  October 26, 2009) awards under ss.34 or 70 of the Employment Rights Act
  1996 (including any payment made in settlement of an employment tribunal
  claim or court action) are taken into account (sub-para.(1)(b)). See above
  for the meaning of "retainer", which from October 26, 2009 includes payments in the nature of, as well as by way of, a retainer. The employment
  protection payments referred to in reg.35(1)(g) or (h) will not be applicable
  if the employment has not terminated. Thus from October 26, 2009 the
  disregard in these circumstances is no longer more extensive than in the case
  of termination of full-time employment before the first day of entitlement to
  income support.

  However, if the person has been suspended from his employment the disregard does not apply and earnings will be taken into account in the normal way.

Note that payments of sick pay, maternity pay, paternity pay, shared parental
pay or adoption or parental bereavement leave pay are taken into account. That
is because they do not count as earnings (reg.35(2)) but are taken into account as
income (reg.40(4)(a); note the disregards in paras 1, 4 and 4A of Sch.9).

Paragraph 1A

2.712   Since the commencement of the state pension credit scheme on October 6, 2003,
claimants who have reached the qualifying age for state pension credit (defined in
s.137(1) of the Contributions and Benefits Act 1992) or whose partner is entitled
to state pension credit are not entitled to income support (Contributions and
Benefits Act s.124(1)(aa) and (g)). The effect of the definition in s.137(1) is that
the qualifying age was 60 but from April 2010 it gradually rose in line with the staged

increase in pensionable age for women until it reached 65 in November 2018 (this equalisation of the state pension age for men and women was previously to have been completed by April 5, 2020 but the timetable for this in the Pensions Act 1995 was accelerated with effect from April 2016 so that women's state pension age became 65 in November 2018; in addition, the increase in state pension age to 66 for both men and women has been brought forward—it started to rise from 65 in December 2018 to reach 66 by October 2020, see s.1 of the Pensions Act 2011); between 2026 and 2028 it will reach 67 (see s.26 of the Pensions Act 2014)). There is thus no need for a disregard of a claimant's earnings paid on termination of employment due to retirement at pensionable age (before October 6, 2003 such earnings had been totally disregarded for the purposes of income support). However, provision still needs to be made in relation to a partner's earnings paid on termination of full-time (24 hours plus a week) employment due to retirement in cases where the claimant has not reached pensionable age and so is still eligible for income support. Under para.1A such earnings will be disregarded in full, provided that the partner has reached the qualifying age for state pension credit.

Paragraph 2

The disregard where a person's part-time (i.e. less than 16 hours per week (24 hours in the case of a partner): reg.5(1) and (1A)) work as an employed earner has stopped before the claim (provided that he has not been suspended) is also extensive (as was the case before October 1, 2007; the new form of para.2 introduced on October 1, 2007 appears to be merely a recasting of the previous form). But note that with effect from October 26, 2009 not only payments by way of a retainer but also payments in the nature of a retainer (i.e. guarantee payments under s.28 of the Employment Rights Act 1996, and the right to remuneration while suspended on medical grounds under s.64 or while suspended on maternity grounds under s.68, together with awards under ss.34 or 70, of that Act; see further the note to para.1), will be taken into account. However, if the person has been suspended from his employment the disregard does not apply and earnings will be taken into account in the normal way.

2.713

It is not necessary for the part-time employment to have ended. On this, see *R(JSA)8/03* which concerned a part-time supply teacher who claimed JSA during the school summer holidays. The Commissioner decides that because she did not have a recognisable cycle of work the equivalent disregard in para.2 of Sch.6 to the JSA Regulations 1996 applied. However, if a cycle of work has been established, *R(JSA) 2/03* holds that a person is to be regarded as engaged in employment (whether remunerative or part-time) during the whole of the cycle and so the disregard in para.2 will not apply. See further the notes to para.2 of Sch.6 to the JSA Regulations 1996.

Payments of sick pay, maternity pay, paternity pay, shared parental pay or adoption or parental bereavement leave pay are however taken into account. That is because they do not count as earnings (reg.35(2)) but are taken into account as income (reg.40(4)(a); note the disregards in paras 1, 4 and 4A of Sch.9).

If the part-time work ends while the claimant is claiming income support, termination payments are taken into account as earnings in the usual way.

Paragraph 3

When a previously self-employed person ceases to be so employed, only royalties or payments for copyright or public lending rights continue to be counted as earnings. This is an important and potentially quite generous disregard.

2.714

Note that there is nothing in the context of para.3 to displace the provision in reg.23(1) that a reference to the claimant includes the claimant's partner. Although paras 1A and 4 make separate provision for claimants and partners, that does not affect the specific self-contained context of para.3.

There will be difficult issues of judgment as to whether and when a person has ceased to be employed as a self-employed earner. There is a good deal of case law

from which it is difficult to extract a consistent approach. In *R(JSA) 1/09* Judge
Rowland took the view that there is a distinction between whether a person is
employed as a self-employed earner, which he took to mean trading, and whether
the person, if so employed, is engaged in remunerative work or part-time work as a
self-employed earner (in particular for the purposes of the equivalent of reg.5 and
the condition of entitlement of not being engaged in remunerative work). That
distinction has sometimes been summarised as the difference between being <u>in</u>
work and being <u>at</u> work (see *R(JSA) 1/07* at para.18, in the context of employed
earners). He also took the view that a person ceased to be so employed only on
no longer being employed in the former sense. Although some of the reasoning
in that case has been doubted in subsequent decisions, it is submitted that the
basic distinction remains. In *TC v DSD (JSA)* [2013] NI Com 65 at para.64, a
Northern Ireland Commissioner expressed the view that it is possible to cease self-
employment with an intention of resumption at a later date. There is no need for
a permanent cessation. That element of the decision seems consistent with Judge
Rowland's views.

2.715   Paragraph 27037 of the *DMG* suggests that the employment must have ceased
"outright", whatever that means (although the term was endorsed in *GM v SSWP
(JSA)* [2010] UKUT 221, reported as [2011] AACR 9), at para.19, but it would be
submitted, even in the absence of authority, that that is an impermissible gloss on
the statutory word "ceased". Since the suggestion is inconsistent with *R(JSA) 1/09*
and *TC*, it is submitted that it should not be accepted. It seems that para.27020
of the *DMG* is more to the point in suggesting nine factors potentially relevant to
whether a person is still trading, rather than there merely being an interruption in
the person's activities in a continuing employment. The substance of that approach
(although then directed to whether the claimant was in gainful employment within
the definition of self-employment) was approved in *CIS/166/1994*. The nine factors
overlap somewhat and it is recognised that not all will be relevant in a particular
case, but represent a sensible approach. In summary, they are whether the person
has reasonable prospects of work in the near future; whether the business is a going
concern and regarded as such by others; whether the person is genuinely available
for and seeking alternative work; whether the person hopes or intends to resume
work when conditions improve; whether the person is undertaking any activities in
connection with the self-employment; whether there is any work in the pipeline;
whether the person is regarded as self-employed by HMRC; whether the person is
making it known that the business can take on work; and whether the interruption
is part of the normal pattern of the business.

There should be reference to the case law discussed in the notes to regs 5 and
30, including *TC*, mentioned above, and *Saunderson v Secretary of State for Work
and Pensions* [2012] CSIH 102; [2013] AACR 16 as the most recent authorities.
See those notes for the facts and background. It appears that the question of
whether a person is "in work" in the ordinary meaning of the word, as applied in
Saunderson for the purposes of reg.5, involves essentially the same factors as the
question of whether the person has ceased trading. In *Saunderson*, although the
issue of the attribution of earnings to periods when no work was actually being
done had been raised at an earlier stage, the Inner House of the Court of Session
restricted its consideration to the reg.5 issue. The earnings issue was addressed in
TC. The Commissioner held, in applying the equivalent of the para.3 disregard
when substituting a decision, that the claimant had ceased employment as an
eel-fisherman when he made his claim in September 2011, although he hoped
to resume fishing in May 2012. For the months of January to April, statutory
rules prohibited fishing and it was not economically worthwhile to fish from
October to December. In the particular year the gearbox of his engine broke in
early August and he could not afford a repair or source a replacement in time to
resume fishing that season. Some further discussion of the weighing-up of the
factors considered relevant would have been helpful. In particular, the steps that
the claimant was taking and intended to take in the months before May 2012 to

get his boat in a condition to resume fishing and possibly to recruit helpers could have been said to point to his continuing to be in work, i.e. still trading. However, the uncertainty of the outcome of such steps as at the date of decision perhaps outweighed that factor in the context of the length of the break and the test not requiring a permanent cessation of employment. What was clear was that the mere fact that the claimant had fished only during the restricted season for several years did not automatically lead to a conclusion that the self-employment had not ceased in August 2011.

There may be further testing of the scope of para.3 and its equivalents for other benefits in 2020 and 2021 in the context of the treatment of grants paid to self-employed claimants or partners under the Coronavirus Self-Employed Income Support Scheme ("SEISS") in late May or June 2020, in the second round claimable from August 17, 2020, and in further rounds. These grants are described in the HMRC guidance as a taxable grant of 80 per cent of taxable profits (as calculated by reference to previous tax years) up to £2,500 per month, initially to cover the three months from March to May 2020. The second grant was of 70 per cent and capped at £6,570 for another three months. See the notes to regs 30 and 37 for the further tranches of SEISS down to April 2021 and discussion of whether a SEISS grant (and other grants and loans) are properly capital receipts and so not to be taken into account as income receipts and, if not, how the receipt fits into the process of calculation of net profits from the date of payment onwards. However, if the receipt does go into that calculation, there may well be cases where existing income support claimants or their partners have had to close down their self-employed activities during the COVID-19 outbreak for an unknown duration and will have real doubts about their ability to resume activities even though they hope to. There may well then be arguments, in the absence of any specific amending provisions, that even if they have self-employed earnings enhanced by the grants, those earnings are to be disregarded under para.3. The view of the DWP expressed in housing benefit guidance in para.37 of *LA Welfare Direct 4/2020*, is that a SEISS grant is income from self-employment and that no changes in housing benefit legislation are necessary.

Note also the disregard of business assets in para.6 of Sch.10.

Paragraph 4

This provision allows a disregard of £20 between the claimant and any partner if the claimant meets the basic conditions for a disability premium or if the conditions for the higher pensioner premium are met with the restrictive extra conditions of sub-para.(4). Note that there appears to be a spare "and" at the end of sub-para. (3) as a result of the amendments made on October 6, 2003 consequent upon the introduction of state pension credit.

See the saving provision in reg.4 of the Social Security Amendment (Capital Limits and Earnings Disregards) Regulations 2000 (SI 2000/2545) at para.6.28 to enable claimants who were entitled to the previous £15 disregard under sub-paras (2) and (3) to meet the condition in sub-para.(4)(c). The saving provision also applies to para.5(4)(c) of Sch.6 to the JSA Regulations 1996.

2.716

Paragraph 5

If the claimant is a lone parent the first £20 of net earnings are disregarded. Since April 6, 1998 it had not been necessary for the claimant to be receiving the lone parent rate of the now abolished family premium under para.3(1)(a) of Sch.2 for this disregard to apply; *all* lone parents qualify for a disregard under this paragraph, unless they are entitled to a £20 disregard under para.4.

2.717

Paragraph 6

From October 7, 1996 the previous £15 disregard for long-term unemployed couples aged less than 60 which applied under this paragraph has been replaced by a £10 earnings disregard that applies to all couples. This is the same as the disregard that applies for old style JSA.

2.718

Paragraphs 6A and 6B

2.719   Where the carer premium is payable, the first £20 of the earnings of the carer are disregarded. If the carer does not use up the disregard, what is spare may be applied to a (non-carer) partner's earnings under para.6B. Only £5 may be disregarded in this way, except for the employment mentioned in para.7(1).

Paragraph 7

2.720   Earnings from these activities attract a £20 disregard, but a couple cannot have a total disregard of more than £20.

The insertion of a new sub-para.(1)(a) (and the omission of the previous form of sub-para.(1)(a) and of sub-para.(1)(aa)–(ab)) on October 29, 2013 were intended to reflect the policy intention that sub-para.(1)(a) applies to part-time fire-fighters who live in Scotland but are employed by a fire and rescue authority in England and Wales (and those who live in England or Wales but are employed by the Scottish Fire and Rescue Service), as well as those who live and are employed as part-time fire-fighters in the same country.

Paragraph 9

2.721   The basic disregard of net earnings from part-time work is £5.

Paragraph 10

2.722   See notes to reg.32(5).

Paragraph 13

2.723   Where earnings are due before the date of claim, overlaps with payments of the same kind are avoided. See notes to reg.32(5).

Paragraph 14

2.724   See the note at the beginning of the Schedule. The old forms of paras 14 and 15 continue in force for "transitional cases"—see the note to reg.17. It is not entirely clear why this disregard is being retained.

Paragraph 15A

2.725   Under para.15A, as amended from April 6, 2015, earnings as a member of a reserve force from training (i) for a maximum of 43 days in the first year of training (see the definition of "first year of training" in reg.2(1)); or (ii) for a maximum of 15 days' annual continuous training in any calendar year, are disregarded to the extent that, together with any other income, they would have the effect of reducing income support entitlement to less than 10p per week. This disregard is in addition to the £20 disregard of earnings as a member of a reserve force in para.7(1)(d).

The purpose of the disregard is to enable entitlement to income support to continue while a claimant (or partner) is attending such training (note that a person is not treated as in remunerative work for the purposes of income support when engaged in employment as a member of a reserve force: see reg.6(1)(h)). See also reg.29(2C) which provides that earnings from such reservist training will be taken into account, where the training lasts for the number of days listed in column 1 of the table in reg.29(2C)(c), for the number of days listed in column 2 of the table; or in any other case, for the number of days that the training lasts. The period begins on the date that the earnings are treated as paid under reg.31 (see reg.29(2D)).

Paragraph 15C

2.726   From April 9, 2001 a claimant who, or whose partner, starts remunerative work (i.e. 16 hours or more a week in the case of a claimant, 24 hours in the case of the claimant's partner) after either of them has been in receipt of income support or income-based JSA for at least six months was allowed a four-week "mortgage interest run-on" (see further reg.6(5)–(8) and the notes to those provisions). From December 17, 2007 this was extended so that it applied to all housing costs that can be met by income support. From October 27, 2008 it also applies where the claimant or partner had been in receipt of income-related ESA for at least six months before starting remunerative work. Note that periods when the run-on applies cannot count towards the required six months' continuous entitlement to benefit. Payment of the run-on was made direct to the claimant, not the lender. The purpose of the run-on is to tackle some of the hurdles (such as the gap between starting work and receiving wages and the wait for in-work benefits) that face people when they begin full-time work. The amount of benefit paid during the run-on period will be the lower of the amount for housing costs that was being met or the income support/income-based JSA/income-related ESA that was in payment before the claimant or his partner started work (see further the new para.19A of Sch.7). Paragraph 15C provides that all of the person's earnings in the run-on period will be disregarded. See also the disregards in para.74 of Sch.9 and para.62 of Sch.10.

Since the coming into force of the Loans for Mortgage Interest Regulations 2017 on April 6, 2018 income support housing costs have no longer covered interest on loans. However, a similar provision for run-on is provided in those regulations, but the para.15C disregard has remained limited to situations where the claimant had income support, JSA or ESA housing costs in their applicable amount.

Regulation 36(2) has not been amended to give effect to the insertion of para.15C into Sch.8, but presumably no one will object to claimants being given the benefit of the disregard.

SCHEDULE 9   **Regulation 40(2)**

SUMS TO BE DISREGARDED IN THE CALCULATION OF INCOME OTHER THAN EARNINGS

1.—Any amount paid by way of tax on income which is taken into account under regulation 40 (calculation of income other than earnings).   2.727

[[144] **1A.**—Any payment in respect of any travel or other expenses incurred, or to be incurred, by the claimant in respect of that claimant's participation in [[149] a scheme prescribed in regulation 3 of the Jobseeker's Allowance (Schemes for Assisting Persons to Obtain Employment) Regulations 2013] or the Mandatory Work Activity Scheme.]

2.—Any payment in respect of any expenses incurred[[77], or to be incurred,] by a claimant who is—
 (a) engaged by a charitable or [[32]voluntary organisation]; or
 (b) a volunteer,
if he otherwise derives no remuneration or profit from the employment and is not to be treated as possessing any earnings under regulation 42(6) (notional income).

[[133] **2A.**—Any payment in respect of expenses arising out of the [[159] claimant participating as a service user].]

3.—In the case of employment as an employed earner, any payment in respect of expenses wholly, exclusively and necessarily incurred in the performance of the duties of the employment.

4.—In the case of a payment [[122] under Parts 11 to] 12ZB [[180] or under Part 12ZD] of the Contributions and Benefits Act] or any remuneration paid by or on behalf of an employer to the claimant who for the time being is unable to work due to illness or maternity [[86] or who is taking paternity leave [[161] , adoption leave or [[180], shared parental leave or parental bereavement leave]]]—
 (a) any amount deducted by way of primary Class 1 contributions under the Social Security Act [SSCBA];
 (b) one-half of any sum paid by the claimant by way of a contribution towards an occupational or personal pension scheme.

[[1]**4A.**—In the case of the payment of statutory sick pay under Part II of the Social Security (Northern Ireland) Order 1982 [[86], statutory maternity pay under Part XII of the Social Security Contributions and Benefits (Northern Ireland) Act 1992 or a payment under any enactment having effect in Northern Ireland corresponding to a payment of [[148] [[163] ...] statutory paternity pay][[162] , statutory adoption pay or statutory shared parental pay]]—
 (a) any amount deducted by way of primary Class 1 contributions under the Social Security (Northern Ireland) Act 1975;

(b) one-half of any sum paid by way of a contribution towards an occupational or personal pension scheme.]

[¹³¹ **5.**—Any housing benefit to which the claimant is entitled.]

[⁸⁸ **5A.**—(1) Any guardian's allowance.]

[⁹⁴ **5B.**—(1) Any child tax credit.

(2) Any child benefit.]

[¹⁴⁰ (3) Any increase in respect of a dependent child or dependent young person under section 80 or 90 of the Contributions and Benefits Act where—

(a) the claimant has a child or young person who is a member of the claimant's family for the purposes of the claimant's claim for income support, and

(b) the claimant, or that claimant's partner, has been awarded a child tax credit.]

[¹³⁰ **5C.** ...].

6.—[¹³¹The] mobility component of disability living allowance [¹⁵³ or the mobility component of personal independence payment].

7.—Any concessionary payment made to compensate for the non-payment of—

(a) any payment specified in [¹⁸paragraph 6 [⁴⁸ or 9]];

[¹³¹ (b) income support;

(c) an income-based jobseeker's allowance; [¹⁵⁷ ...]

(d) an income-related employment and support allowance [¹⁵⁷; or

(e) universal credit].]

8.—Any mobility supplement or any payment intended to compensate for the non payment of such a supplement.

[²⁵ **9.**—Any attendance allowance[¹⁵⁴ , the care component of disability living allowance or the daily living component of personal independence payment][⁹⁰ . . .].]

[²⁹**9A.**—. . .]

10.—Any payment to the claimant as holder of the Victoria Cross or George Cross or any analogous payment.

[⁹⁷ **11.**—(1) Any payment—

(a) by way of an education maintenance allowance made pursuant to—

(i) regulations made under section 518 of the Education Act 1996;

(ii) regulations made under section 49 or 73(f) of the Education (Scotland) Act 1980;

[¹³¹ (iii) directions made under section 73ZA of the Education (Scotland) Act 1980 and paid under section 12(2)(c) of the Further and Higher Education (Scotland) Act 1992; [¹⁴⁷ . . .]]

(b) corresponding to such an education maintenance allowance, made pursuant to—

(i) section 14 or section 181 of the Education Act 2002; or

(ii) regulations made under section 181 of that Act[¹⁴⁷; or

(c) in England, by way of financial assistance made pursuant to section 14 of the Education Act 2002.]

(2) Any payment, other than a payment to which sub-paragraph (1) applies, made pursuant to—

(a) regulations made under section 518 of the Education Act 1996;

(b) regulations made under section 49 of the Education (Scotland) Act 1980; or

[¹³¹ (c) directions made under section 73ZA of the Education (Scotland) Act 1980 and paid under section 12(2)(c) of the Further and Higher Education (Scotland) Act 1992,]

in respect of a course of study attended by a child or a young person or a person who is in receipt of an education maintenance allowance [¹⁴⁷ or other payment] made pursuant to any provision specified in sub-paragraph (1).]

[⁸³ **11A.**—Any payment made to the claimant by way of a repayment under regulation 11(2) of the Education (Teacher Student Loans) (Repayment etc) Regulations 2002.]

12.—[⁶⁴ . . .].

[⁹³ **13.**—(1) Any payment made pursuant to section 2 of the Employment and Training Act 1973 (functions of the Secretary of State) or section 2 of the Enterprise and New Towns (Scotland) Act 1990 (functions in relation to training for employment etc.) except a payment—

(a) made as a substitute for income support, a jobseeker's allowance, incapacity benefit [¹²⁶ , severe disablement allowance or an employment and support allowance];

(b) of an allowance referred to in section 2(3) of the Employment and Training Act 1973 or section 2(5) of the Enterprise and New Towns (Scotland) Act 1990;

(c) intended to meet the cost of living expenses which relate to any one or more of the items specified in sub-paragraph (2) whilst a claimant is participating in an education, training or other scheme to help him enhance his employment prospects unless the payment is a Career Development Loan paid pursuant to section 2 of the Employment and Training Act 1973 and the period of education or training or the scheme, which is supported by that loan, has been completed; or

    (d)   made in respect of the cost of living away from home to the extent that the payment relates to rent for which housing benefit is payable in respect of accommodation which is not normally occupied by the claimant as his home.

(2) The items specified in this sub-paragraph for the purposes of sub-paragraph (1)(c) are food, ordinary clothing or footwear, household fuel, rent for which housing benefit is payable, or any housing costs to the extent that they are met under regulation 17(1)(e) or 18(1)(f) (housing costs), of the claimant or, where the claimant is a member of a family, any other member of his family, or any council tax or water charges for which that claimant or member is liable.

(3) For the purposes of this paragraph, "ordinary clothing or footwear" means clothing or footwear for normal daily use, but does not include school uniforms, or clothing or footwear used solely for sporting activities.]

    14.—[³⁴ . . .]

[¹⁰**15.**—[²⁹[¹¹³ (1) Subject to sub-paragraph (3) and paragraph 39, any relevant payment made or due to be made at regular intervals.]

    (2) [¹¹³. . .]

    (3) [¹¹³ Sub-paragraph (1)] shall not apply—

    (a)   to a payment which is made by a person for the maintenance of any member of his family or of his former partner or of his children;

    (b)   in the case of a person to whom section 23 of the Act [SSCBA, s.126] (trade disputes) applies or in respect of whom section 20(3) of the Act [SSCBA, s.124(1)] (conditions of entitlement to income support) has effect as modified by section 23A(b) of the Act [SSCBA, s.127(b)] (effect of return to work).

    (4) [¹¹³. . .]

    (5) [¹¹³. . .]]

[⁸⁴ (5A) In this paragraph, "relevant payment" means—

    (a)   a charitable payment;

    (b)   a voluntary payment;

    (c)   a payment (not falling within sub-paragraph (a) or (b) above) from a trust whose funds are derived from a payment made in consequence of any personal injury to the claimant;

    (d)   a payment under an annuity purchased—

        (i)   pursuant to any agreement or court order to make payments to the claimant; or

        (ii)   from funds derived from a payment made,

    in consequence of any personal injury to the claimant; or

    (e)   a payment (not falling within sub-paragraphs (a) to (d) above) received by virtue of any agreement or court order to make payments to the claimant in consequence of any personal injury to the claimant.]

[²⁹(6) [⁷⁹. . .].]

[²⁵**15A.**—[¹¹⁴. . .]]

[³⁸ **15B.**—[⁹⁰ . . .].]

[³⁵**16.**—Subject to paragraphs 36 and 37, £10 of any of the following, namely—

    (a)   a war disablement pension (except insofar as such a pension falls to be disregarded under paragraph 8 or 9);

    (b)   a war widow's pension [⁸¹ or war widower's pension];

    (c)   a pension payable to a person as a [¹⁰⁷ widow, widower or surviving civil partner] under [¹³¹. . .] any power of Her Majesty otherwise than under an enactment to make provision about pensions for or in respect of persons who have been disabled or have died in consequence of service as members of the armed forces of the Crown;

[¹⁰²(cc)   a guaranteed income payment [¹³¹ and, if the amount of that payment has been abated to less than £10 by a [¹³⁴ pension or payment falling within article 31(1)(a) or (b) of the Armed Forces and Reserve Forces (Compensation Scheme) Order 2005], so much of [¹³⁴ that pension or payment] as would not, in aggregate with the amount of [¹³⁴ any] guaranteed income payment disregarded, exceed £10];]

    (d)   a payment made to compensate for the non-payment of such a pension [¹⁰² or payment] as is mentioned in any of the preceding sub-paragraphs;

    (e)   a pension paid by the government of a country outside Great Britain which is analogous to any of the [¹⁰² pensions or payments mentioned in sub-paragraphs (a) to (cc) above];

[¹⁶⁶(f)   a pension paid by a government to victims of National Socialist persecution;]

643

[⁷⁰(g) any widowed mother's allowance paid pursuant to section 37 of the Contributions and Benefits Act;

(h) any widowed parent's allowance paid pursuant to section 39A of the Contributions and Benefits Act.]

17.—Where a person receives income under an annuity purchased with a loan which satisfies the following conditions—

(a) that the loan was made as part of a scheme under which not less than 90 per cent. of the proceeds of the loan were applied to the purchase by the person to whom it was made of an annuity ending with his life or with the life of the survivor of two or more persons (in this paragraph referred to as "the annuitants") who include the person to whom the loan was made;

(b) that the interest on the loan is payable by the person to whom it was made or by one of the annuitants;

(c) that at the time the loan was made the person to whom it was made or each of the annuitants had attained the age of 65 [¹⁷⁷or, if it was higher at that time, pensionable age];

(d) that the loan was secured on a dwelling in Great Britain and the person to whom the loan was made or one of the annuitants owns an estate or interest in that dwelling; and

(e) that the person to whom the loan was made or one of the annuitants occupies the accommodation on which it was secured as his home at the time the interest is paid,

the amount, calculated on a weekly basis equal to—

[³¹(i) where, or insofar as, section 369 of the Income and Corporation Taxes Act 1988 (mortgage interest payable under deduction of tax) applies to the payments of interest on the loan, the interest which is payable after deduction of a sum equal to income tax on such payments at the applicable percentage of income tax within the meaning of section 369(1A) of that Act;]

(ii) in any other case the interest which is payable on the loan without deduction of such a sum.

[³²**18.**—Any payment made to the claimant by a person who normally resides with the claimant, which is a contribution towards that person's living and accommodation costs, except where that person is residing with the claimant in circumstances to which paragraph 19 or 20 refers.]

[³⁰**19.**—Where the claimant occupies a dwelling as his home and the dwelling is also occupied by [³²another person], and there is a contractual liability to make payments to the claimant in respect of the occupation of the dwelling by that person or a member of his family—

[¹²¹ (a) where the aggregate of any payments made in respect of any one week in respect of the occupation of the dwelling by that person or a member of his family, or by that person and a member of his family, is less than £20, the whole of that amount; or

(b) where the aggregate of any such payments is £20 or more per week, £20.]]

[³⁰**20.**—Where the claimant occupies a dwelling as his home and he provides in that dwelling board and lodging accommodation, an amount, in respect of each person for whom such accommodation is provided for the whole or any part of a week, equal to—

(a) where the aggregate of any payments made in respect of any one week in respect of such accommodation provided to such person does not exceed £20.00, 100% of such payments; or

(b) where the aggregate of any such payments exceeds £20.00, £20.00 and 50% of the excess over £20.00.]

[¹**21.**—(1) [⁶¹Subject to sub-paragraphs (2) and (3)], except where [⁶¹regulation 40(4)(b) (provision of support under section 95 or 98 of the Immigration and Asylum Act including support provided by virtue of regulations made under Schedule 9 to that Act in the calculation of income other than earnings) or] regulation 42(4)(a)(i) (notional income) applies or in the case of a person to whom section 23 of the Act [SSCBA, s.126] (trade disputes) applies and for so long as it applies, any income in kind;

(2) The exception under sub-paragraph (1) shall not apply where the income in kind [¹⁸¹is a Grenfell Tower payment or] is received from the Macfarlane Trust[⁸, the Macfarlane (Special Payments) Trust] [¹⁵, the Macfarlane (Special Payments) (No.2) Trust][²¹, the Fund][²⁷, the Eileen Trust] [¹³⁶, MFET Limited][¹⁴⁵, the Skipton Fund, the Caxton Foundation][¹⁶⁷, the Scottish Infected Blood Support Scheme][¹⁷⁰, an approved blood scheme][¹⁶⁹, the London Emergencies Trust, the We Love Manchester Emergency Fund] [¹⁸¹, the National Emergencies Trust] [² or [²⁶ the Independent Living [¹²⁸ Fund (2006)]]].]

[⁶¹(3) The first exception under sub-paragraph (1) shall not apply where the claimant is the partner of a person subject to immigration control and whose partner is receiving support provided under section 95 or 98 of the Immigration and Asylum Act including support provided by virtue of regulations made under Schedule 9 to that Act and the income in kind is support provided in respect of essential living needs of the partner of the claimant and his dependants (if any) as is specified in regulations made under paragraph 3 of Schedule 8 to the Immigration and Asylum Act.]

[¹⁰⁴ (4) The reference in sub-paragraph (1) to "income in kind" does not include a payment to a third party made in respect of the claimant which is used by the third party to provide benefits in kind to the claimant.]

22.—(1) Any income derived from capital to which the claimant is or is treated under regulation 52 (capital jointly held) as beneficially entitled but, subject to sub-paragraph (2), not income derived from capital disregarded under paragraph 1, 2, 4, 6 [³12 or 25 to 28] of Schedule 10.

(2) Income derived from capital disregarded under paragraph 2 [³4 or 25 to 28] of Schedule 10 but [²⁴only to the extent of—

(a) any mortgage repayments made in respect of the dwelling or premises in the period during which that income accrued; or

(b) any council tax or water charges which the claimant is liable to pay in respect of the dwelling or premises and which are paid in the period during which that income accrued.

(3) The definition of "water charges" in regulation 2(1) shall apply to sub-paragraph (2) with the omission of the words "in so far as such charges are in respect of the dwelling which a person occupies as his home".]

23.—Any income which is payable in a country outside the United Kingdom for such period during which there is a prohibition against the transfer to the United Kingdom of that income.

24.—Where a payment of income is made in a currency other than sterling, any banking charge or commission payable in converting that payment into sterling.

25.—(1) Any payment made to the claimant in respect of a child or young person who is a member of his family—

[²⁰(a) [¹⁰⁹ pursuant to regulations under section 2(6)(b), 3 or 4 of the Adoption and Children Act 2002 or in accordance] with a scheme approved by the [¹³¹ Scottish Ministers under section 51A] of the Adoption (Scotland) Act 1978 (schemes for payment of allowances to adopters) [¹⁴³ or in accordance with an adoption allowance scheme made under section 71 of the Adoption and Children (Scotland) Act 2007 (adoption allowances schemes)];

[⁴⁹(b) [¹³¹ . . .]

[¹³⁵(ba) which is a payment made by a local authority in Scotland in pursuance of section 50 of the Children Act 1975 (payments towards maintenance of children);]

(c) which is a payment made by a local authority in pursuance of section 15(1) of, and paragraph 15 of Schedule 1 to, the Children Act 1989 (local authority contribution to a child's maintenance where the child is living with a person as a result of a [¹⁵⁸ child arrangements] order);

(d) which is a payment made by an authority, as defined in Article 2 of the Children Order, in pursuance of Article 15 of, and paragraph 17 of Schedule 1 to, that Order (contribution by an authority to child's maintenance);]]

[¹⁰⁰(e) in accordance with regulations made pursuant to section 14F of the Children Act 1989 (special guardianship support services);]

[⁹⁴ . . .].

[¹¹⁰ (1A) Any payment, other than a payment to which sub-paragraph (1)(a) applies, made to the claimant pursuant to regulations under section 2(6)(b), 3 or 4 of the Adoption and Children Act 2002.]

(2) [⁹⁴ . . .].

[⁹⁴ **25A.**—In the case of a claimant who has a child or young person—

(a) who is a member of his family, and

(b) who is residing at an educational establishment at which he is receiving relevant education,

any payment made to that educational establishment, in respect of that child or young person's maintenance by or on behalf of a person who is not a member of the family or by a member of the family out of funds contributed for that purpose by a person who is not a member of the family.]

[¹⁴¹ **26.**—Any payment made to the claimant with whom a person is accommodated by virtue of arrangements made—

(a) by a local authority under—

[¹⁷²(i) section 22C(2) of the Children Act 1989 (ways in which looked after children are to be accommodated and maintained),]

[¹⁷¹(ia) section 81(2) of the Social Services and Well-being (Wales) Act 2014 (ways in which looked after children are to be accommodated and maintained);]

   (ii) section 26 of the Children (Scotland) Act 1995 (manner of provision of accommodation to child looked after by local authority), or

   (iii) regulations 33 or 51 of the Looked After Children (Scotland) Regulations 2009 (fostering and kinship care allowances and fostering allowances); or

(b) by a voluntary organisation under section 59(1)(a) of the Children Act 1989 (provision of accommodation by voluntary organisations).]

27.—[⁴⁶ Any payment made to the claimant or his partner for a person ("the person concerned"), who is not normally a member of the claimant's household but is temporarily in his care, by—

(a) a health authority;

(b) a local authority [¹⁰³ but excluding payments of housing benefit made in respect of the person concerned];

(c) a voluntary organisation; or

(d) the person concerned pursuant to section 26(3A) of the National Assistance Act 1948] [⁷³ [¹³¹ . . .]

[¹⁰³ (dza) the person concerned where the payment is for the provision of accommodation in respect of the meeting of that person's needs under section 18 or 19 of the Care Act 2014 (duty and power to meet needs for care and support);]

[¹⁷¹(dzb) the person concerned where the payment is for the provision of accommodation to meet that person's need for care and support under section 35 or 36 of the Social Services and Well-being (Wales) Act 2014 (duty and power to meet care and support needs of an adult);]

[¹⁵⁶ (da)a clinical commissioning group established under section 14D of the National Health Service Act 2006;

(db) the National Health Service Commissioning Board; or]

(e) [¹⁵⁶ . . .]]

[¹³¹ (f) a Local Health Board established under section 16BA of the National Health Service Act 1977 or established by an order made under section 11 of the Health Service (Wales) Act.]

[¹⁷³**27A.**—Any payment made to a claimant under section 73(1)(b) of the Children and Young People (Scotland) Act 2014 (kinship care assistance).]

[¹²³ **28.**—(1) Any payment made by a local authority in accordance with—

(a) section 17, 23B, 23C or 24A of the Children Act 1989,

(b) section 12 of the Social Work (Scotland) Act 1968, [¹⁷¹ . . .]

(c) section [¹⁴² 22,] [¹⁶⁵26A, 29] 30 of the Children (Scotland) Act [¹⁷¹1995, or

(d) the following sections of the Social Services and Well-being (Wales) Act 2014—

   (aa) section 37 or 38, but excluding any direct payment made in accordance with regulations made under section 51 of that Act; or

   (bb) section 109.110, 114 or 115.]

(2) Any payment (or part of a payment) made by a local authority in accordance with section 23C of the Children Act 1989 or section [142 22 [165, 26A or 29 of the Children (Scotland) Act 1995 (local authorities' duty to promote welfare of children, duty to provide continuing care and provision of advice and assistance for certain young persons)] to a person ("A") which A passes on to the claimant.

(3) Sub-paragraphs (1) and (2) are subject to the following provisions.

(4) Neither of those sub-paragraphs applies where the claimant is a person—

(a) to whom section 126 of the Contributions and Benefits Act (trade disputes) applies, or

(b) in respect of whom section 124(1) of the Contributions and Benefits Act (conditions of entitlement to income support) has effect as modified by section 127 of that Act (effect of return to work).

(5) Sub-paragraph (2) applies only where A—

(a) was formerly in the claimant's care, and

[¹⁶⁵(b) is aged 18 or over or, in the case of a payment or part of a payment made in accordance with section 26A of the Children (Scotland) Act 1995, aged 16 or over, and]

(c) continues to live with the claimant.]

[¹⁷⁴**29.** Any payment received under an insurance policy taken out to insure against the risk of being unable to maintain repayments on a loan which qualifies under Part 1 of Schedule 1 to the Loans for Mortgage Interest Regulations 2017 (legacy benefit claimants and SPC claimants) and used to meet such repayments.]

30.—(1) Except where paragraph 29 [⁵⁰or 30ZA] applies, and subject to sub-paragraph (2), any payment made to the claimant which is intended to be used and is used as a contribution towards—

(a) any payment due on a loan if secured on the dwelling occupied as the home which does not qualify under [¹⁷⁴Part 1 of Schedule 1 to the Loans for Mortgage Interest Regulations];

[¹⁷⁴(b) any charge which qualifies in accordance with paragraph 17 of Schedule 3 (housing costs) to these Regulations or any interest payment on a loan which qualifies under Part 1 of Schedule 1 to the Loans for Mortgage Interest Regulations, to the extent that the charge or payment is not met under these Regulations or by loan payments (as the case may be)];

(c) any payment due on a loan which qualifies under [¹⁷⁴Part 1 of Schedule 1 to the Loans for Mortgage Interest Regulations] attributable to the payment of capital;

(d) any amount due by way of premiums on—

(i) [³⁶ an insurance policy taken out to insure against the risk of being unable to make the payments referred to in (a) to (c) above;] or

(ii) a policy of insurance taken out to insure against loss or damage to any building or part of a building which is occupied by the claimant as his home.

(e) his rent in respect of the dwelling occupied by him as his home but only to the extent that it is not met by housing benefit; or his accommodation charge but only to the extent that the actual charge [⁷⁹ exceeds] the amount payable by a local authority in accordance with Part III of the National Assistance Act 1948 [¹⁶³ or Part 1 of the Care Act 2014 (care and support).]

(2) This paragraph shall not apply to any payment which is treated as possessed by the claimant by virtue of regulation 42(4)(a)(ii) (notional income).]

[¹⁷⁴(3) In this paragraph—

(a) "Loans for Mortgage Interest Regulations" means the Loans for Mortgage Interest Regulations 2017;

(b) "loan payments" has the meaning given in the Loans for Mortgage Interest Regulations.]

[⁵⁰**30ZA.**—(1) Subject to sub-paragraph (2), any payment received under an insurance policy, other than an insurance policy referred to in paragraph 29, taken out to insure against the risk of being unable to maintain repayments under a regulated agreement as defined for the purposes of the Consumer Credit Act 1974 or under a hire-purchase agreement or a conditional sale agreement as defined for the purposes of Part III of the Hire-Purchase Act 1964.

(2) A payment referred to in sub-paragraph (1) shall only be disregarded to the extent that the payment received under that policy does not exceed the amounts, calculated on a weekly basis, which are used to—

(a) maintain the repayments referred to in sub-paragraph (1); and

(b) meet any amount due by way of premiums on that policy.]

[²⁹**30A.**—(1) Subject to sub-paragraphs (2) and (3), in the case of a claimant [¹⁰⁶ residing in a care home, an Abbeyfield Home or an independent hospital], any payment, [¹¹⁸ except a charitable or voluntary payment disregarded under paragraph 15], [¹¹⁶. . .] made to the claimant which is intended to be used and is used to meet the cost of maintaining the claimant in that home [¹⁰⁶ or hospital].

(2) This paragraph shall not apply to a claimant for whom accommodation in a [¹⁰⁶ care home, an Abbeyfield Home or an independent hospital] is provided by

[¹⁶³ (a) a local authority under section 26 of the National Assistance Act 1948 [⁷⁹. . .]; or

(b) a person other than a local authority under arrangements made with the person by a local authority in the exercise of the local authority's functions under section 18 or 19 of the Care Act 2014 (duty and power to meet needs for care and support).]

(3) The amount to be disregarded under this paragraph shall not exceed the difference between—

[⁷⁹(a) the claimant's applicable amount; and]

(b) the weekly charge for the accommodation.]

[¹⁹**31.**—Any social fund payment made pursuant to [¹³¹ Part 8 of the Contributions and Benefits Act].]

[¹⁵¹ **31A.**—Any local welfare provision.]

32.—Any payment of income which under regulation 48 (income treated as capital) is to be treated as capital.

33.—Any payment under [¹³¹ Part 10 of the Contributions and Benefits Act] (pensioners' Christmas bonus).

34.—In the case of a person to whom section 23 of the Act [SSCBA, s.126] (trade disputes) applies and for so long as it applies, any payment up to the amount of the relevant sum within the meaning of sub-section (6) of that section made by a trade union; but, notwithstanding regulation 23 (calculation of income and capital of members of claimant's family and of a polygamous marriage) if this paragraph applies to a claimant it shall not apply to his partner except where, and to the extent that, the amount to be disregarded under this paragraph is less than the relevant sum.

35.—Any payment which is due to be paid before the date of claim which would otherwise fall to be taken into account in the same benefit week as a payment of the same kind and from the same source.

36.—The total of a claimant's income or, if he is a member of a family, the family's income and the income of any person which he is treated as possessing under regulation 23(3) (calculation of income and capital of members of claimant's family and of a polygamous marriage) to be disregarded under regulation 63(2)(b) and 64(1)(c) (calculation of covenant income where a contribution assessed)[¹¹, regulation 66A(2) (treatment of student loans)][⁶⁷, regulation 66B(3) (treatment of payments from access funds)] and [¹¹⁷ paragraph 16] shall in no case exceed [³⁹£20] per week.

37.—Notwithstanding paragraph 36 where two or more payments of the same kind and from the same source are to be taken into account in the same benefit week, there shall be disregarded from each payment the sum which would otherwise fall to be disregarded under this Schedule; but this paragraph shall only apply in the case of a payment which it has not been practicable to treat under regulation 31(1)(b) (date on which income treated as paid) as paid on the first day of the benefit week in which it is due to be paid.

[¹**38.**—[¹¹² . . .]]

[¹⁵**39.**—(1) Any payment made under [¹³⁷ or by] the Macfarlane Trust, the Macfarlane (Special Payments) Trust, the Macfarlane (Special Payments) (No.2) Trust ("the Trusts"), [²¹the Fund][²⁷, the Eileen Trust][¹³⁶, MFET Limited][¹⁴⁵, the Skipton Fund, the Caxton Foundation][¹⁶⁷, the Scottish Infected Blood Support Scheme][¹⁷⁰, an approved blood scheme][¹⁶⁹, the London Emergencies Trust, the We Love Manchester Emergency Fund][¹⁸¹, the National Emergencies Trust] or [²⁶the Independent Living [¹²⁸ Fund (2006)]].

[¹⁸¹(1A) Any Grenfell Tower payment.]

(2) Any payment by or on behalf of a person who is suffering or who suffered from haemophilia [²¹or who is or was a qualifying person], which derives from a payment made under [¹³⁷ or by] any of the Trusts to which sub-paragraph (1) refers[¹⁸¹, or from a Grenfell Tower payment,] and which is made to or for the benefit of—

(a) that person's partner or former partner from whom he is not, or where that person has died was not, estranged or divorced [¹⁰⁷ or with whom he has formed a civil partnership that has not been dissolved or, where that person has died, had not been dissolved at the time of that person's death];

(b) any child who is a member of that person's family or who was such a member and who is a member of the claimant's family; or

(c) any young person who is a member of that person's family or who was such a member and who is a member of the claimant's family.

(3) Any payment by or on behalf of the partner or former partner of a person who is suffering or who suffered from haemophilia [²¹or who is or was a qualifying person] provided that the partner or former partner and that person are not, or if either of them has died were not, estranged or divorced [¹⁰⁷ or, where the partner or former partner and that person have formed a civil partnership, the civil partnership has not been dissolved or, if either of them has died, had not been dissolved at the time of the death], which derives from a payment made under [¹³⁷ or by] any of the Trusts to which sub-paragraph (1) refers[¹⁸¹, or from a Grenfell Tower payment,] and which is made to or for the benefit of—

(a) the person who is suffering from haemophilia [²¹or who is a qualifying person];

(b) any child who is a member of that person's family or who was such a member and who is a member of the claimant's family; or

(c) any young person who is a member of that person's family or who was such a member and who is a member of the claimant's family.

(4) Any payment by a person who is suffering from haemophilia [²¹or who is a qualifying person], which derives from a payment under [¹³⁷ or by] any of the Trusts to which sub-paragraph (1) refers,[¹⁸¹ or from a Grenfell Tower payment,] where—

(a) that person has no partner or former partner from whom he is not estranged or divorced [¹⁰⁷ or with whom he has formed a civil partnership that has not been dissolved], nor any child or young person who is or had been a member of that person's family; and

(b) the payment is made either—

(i) to that person's parent or step-parent, or

(ii) where that person at the date of the payment is a child, a young person or a

[⁶⁶ full-time student] who has not completed his full-time education and has no
parent or step-parent, to his guardian,
but only for a period from the date of the payment until the end of two years from that person's
death.

(5) Any payment out of the estate of a person who suffered from haemophilia [²¹or who was
a qualifying person], which derives from a payment under [¹³⁷ or by] any of the Trusts to which
sub-paragraph (1) refers, [¹⁸¹or from a Grenfell Tower payment,], where—

  (a) that person at the date of his death (the relevant date) had no partner or former
      partner from whom he was not estranged or divorced [¹⁰⁷ or with whom he had
      formed a civil partnership that had not been dissolved], nor any child or young person
      who was or had been a member of his family; and
  (b) the payment is made either—
       (i) to that person's parent or step-parent, or
      (ii) where that person at the relevant date was a child, a young person or a [⁶⁶ full-
           time student] who had not completed his full-time education and had no parent
           or step-parent, to his guardian,
but only for a period of two years from the relevant date.

(6) In the case of a person to whom or for whose benefit a payment referred to in this paragraph is made, any income which derives from any payment of income or capital made under
or deriving from any of the Trusts [¹⁸¹or from a Grenfell Tower payment].]

[²¹(7) For the purposes of sub-paragraphs (2) to (6), any reference to the Trusts shall be con-
strued as including a reference to the Fund[⁹⁹, the Eileen Trust[¹³⁶, MFET Limited][¹⁰⁸, the
Skipton Fund[¹⁴⁶, the Caxton Foundation][¹⁶⁷, the Scottish Infected Blood Support Scheme]
[¹⁷⁰, an approved blood scheme][¹⁶⁹, the London Emergencies Trust, the We Love Manchester
Emergency Fund][¹⁸¹, the National Emergencies Trust,] and the London Bombings Relief
Charitable Fund]].]]

[³**40.**—Any payment made by the Secretary of State to compensate for the loss (in whole or
in part) of entitlement to housing benefit.]

[⁴**41.**—[¹²⁴ . . .]

42.—[¹²⁴ . . .]

43.—Any payment made to a juror or a witness in respect of attendance at a court other
than compensation for loss of earnings or for the loss of a benefit payable under the benefit Acts.

44.—[²³ . . .].]

[⁹**45.**—[¹²⁹ . . .]

[¹²⁵ **46.**—Any payment in consequence of a reduction of council tax under section 13 [¹⁵²,
13A]or 80 of the Local Government Finance Act 1992 (reduction of liability for council tax).]]

47.—[¹³¹ . . .].]

[¹² [¹³¹ **48.**—(1) Any payment or repayment made—

  (a) as respects England, under regulation 5, 6 or 12 of the National Health Service
      (Travel Expenses and Remission of Charges) Regulations 2003 (travelling expenses
      and health service supplies);
  (b) as respects Wales, under regulation 5, 6 or 11 of the National Health Service
      (Travelling Expenses and Remission of Charges) (Wales) Regulations 2007 (travel-
      ling expenses and health service supplies);
  (c) as respects Scotland, under regulation 3, 5 or 11 of the National Health Service
      (Travelling Expenses and Remission of Charges) (Scotland) (No.2) Regulations 2003
      (travelling expenses and health service supplies).

(2) Any payment or repayment made by the Secretary of State for Health [¹⁷⁵and Social
Care], the Scottish Ministers or the Welsh Ministers which is analogous to a payment or
repayment mentioned in sub-paragraph (1).

49.—Any payment made to such persons entitled to receive benefits as may be determined
by or under a scheme made pursuant to section 13 of the Social Security Act 1988 in lieu of
vouchers or similar arrangements in connection with the provision of those benefits (including
payments made in place of healthy start vouchers, milk tokens or the supply of vitamins).]

50.—Any payment made either by the Secretary of State for [¹²⁰ Justice] or by the [¹³¹ Scottish
Ministers] under a scheme established to assist relatives and other persons to visit persons in
custody.]

[¹⁹**51.**—Any payment (other than a training allowance) made, whether by the Secretary of
State or by any other person, under the Disabled Persons (Employment) Act 1944 [⁹³. . .] to
assist disabled persons to obtain or retain employment despite their disability.]

[¹³¹ **52.**—[¹⁵⁰. . .]

53.—(1) If the claimant is in receipt of any benefit under Part 2, 3 or 5 of the Contributions
and Benefits Act, any increase in the rate of that benefit arising under Part 4 (increases for

dependants) or section 106(a) (unemployability supplement) of that Act, where the dependant in respect of whom the increase is paid is not a member of the claimant's family.

(2) If the claimant is in receipt of any pension or allowance under Part 2 or 3 of the Naval, Military and Air Forces Etc. (Disablement and Death) Service Pensions Order 2006, any increase in the rate of that pension or allowance under that Order, where the dependant in respect of whom the increase is paid is not a member of the claimant's family.]

54.—Any supplementary pension under article 23(2) of the Naval, Military and Air Forces Etc. (Disablement and Death) Service Pensions Order 2006 (pensions to surviving spouses and surviving civil partners) and any analogous payment made by the Secretary of State for Defence to any person who is not a person entitled under that Order.]

55.—In the case of a pension awarded at the supplementary rate under article 27(3) of the Personal Injuries (Civilians) Scheme 1983 (pensions to [¹⁰⁷ widows, widowers or surviving civil partners]), the sum specified in paragraph 1(c) of Schedule 4 to that Scheme.

56.—(1) Any payment which is—

> (a) made under any of the Dispensing Instruments to a [¹⁰⁷ widow, widower or surviving civil partner] of a person—
>> (i) whose death was attributable to service in a capacity analogous to service as a member of the armed forces of the Crown; and
>> (ii) whose service in such capacity terminated before 31st March 1973; and

[¹³¹ (b) equal to the amount specified in article 23(2) of the Naval, Military and Air Forces Etc. (Disablement and Death) Service Pensions Order 2006.]

(2) In this paragraph "the Dispensing Instruments" means the Order in Council of 19th December 1881, the Royal Warrant of 27th October 1884 and the Order by His Majesty of 14th January 1922 (exceptional grants of pay, non-efective pay and allowances).]

[⁴¹**57.**—[¹¹⁹ [¹³¹ . . .]]]

[⁴²**58.**—Any payment made [¹³² . . .] under section 12B of the Social Work (Scotland) Act 1968 [¹³⁸, or under sections 12A to 12D of the National Health Service Act 2006 (direct payments for health care)] [¹⁶³ or under sections 31 to 33 of the Care Act 2014 (direct payments),] [⁸⁸ᵃ or under regulations made under section 57 of the Health and Social Care Act 2001 (direct payments)[¹⁷¹, or in accordance with regulations made under section 50 or 52 of the Social Services and Well-being (Wales) Act 2014 (direct payments)]].

59.—[⁹³ . . .]

60.—[⁹³ . . .]

61.—(1) Any payment specified in sub-paragraph (2) to a claimant who was formerly a [⁶⁹student] and who has completed the course in respect of which those payments were made.

(2) The payments specified for the purposes of sub-paragraph (1) are—

> (a) any grant income and covenant income as defined for the purposes of Chapter VIII of Part V;
> [⁵⁷(b) any student loan as defined in Chapter VIII of Part V;
> (c) any contribution as defined in Chapter VIII of Part V which—
>> (i) is taken into account in ascertaining the amount of a student loan referred to in head (b); and
>> (ii) has been paid.]]

[⁷⁵ **62.**—[⁹³. . .].]

[⁸² **62A.**—[⁹³. . .].]

[⁴⁵**63.**—[⁹³. . .].]

[⁵¹**64.**—(1) Subject to sub-paragraph (2), in the case of a person who is receiving, or who has received, assistance under [⁶⁸ "the self-employment route"] , any payment to the person—

> (a) to meet expenses wholly and necessarily incurred whilst carrying on the commercial activity;
> (b) which is used or intended to be used to maintain repayments on a loan taken out by that person for the purpose of establshing or carrying on the commercial activity, in respect of which such assistance is or was received.

(2) Sub-paragraph (1) shall apply only in respect of payments which are paid to that person from the special account as defined for the purposes of Chapter IVA of Part V.]

[⁵³**65.**—[⁹³. . .].]

[⁵⁴**66.**—Any payment made with respect to a person on account of the provision of after-care under section 117 of the Mental Health Act 1983 or [¹⁰⁵ section 25 of the Mental Health (Care and Treatment) (Scotland) Act 2003] or the provision of accommodation or welfare services to which [⁶³ Part III of the National Assistance Act 1948 refers or to which the Social Work (Scotland) Act 1968 refers, [¹⁶³ or the provision of care and support under Part 1 of the Care Act 2014 (care and support) [¹⁷¹, or the provision of care and support in respect of an adult under Part 4 of the Social Services and Well-being (Wales) Act 2014 (meeting needs)],] which falls to be treated as notional income under paragraph (4A) of regulation 42 above (payments made in respect of a person [¹⁰⁶ living in a care home, an Abbeyfield Home or an independent hospital]).]

67.—*[Omitted]*

68.—*[Omitted]*

[⁵⁶**69.**—(1) Any payment of a sports award except to the extent that it has been made in respect of any one or more of the items specified in sub-paragraph (2).

(2) The items specified for the purposes of sub-paragraph (1) are food, ordinary clothing or footwear, household fuel, rent for which housing benefit is payable or any housing costs to the extent that they are met under regulation 17(1)(e) or 18(1)(f) (housing costs) [⁷⁹. . .], of the claimant or, where the claimant is a member of a family, any other member of his family, or any council tax or water charges for which that claimant or member is liable.

(3) For the purposes of sub-paragraph (2)—

"food" does not include vitamins, minerals or other special dietary supplements intended to enhance the performance of the person in the sport in respect of which the award was made;

"ordinary clothing and footwear" means clothing or footwear for normal daily use but does not include school uniforms or clothing or footwear used solely for sporting activities.]

[⁵⁹**70.**—[¹⁰¹ . . .]]

[⁶⁵**71.**—Where the amount of a subsistence allowance paid to a person in a benefit week exceeds the amount of income-based jobseeker's allowance that person would have received in that benefit week had it been payable to him, less 50p, that excess amount.

72.—In the case of a claimant participating in an employment zone programme, any discretionary payment made by an employment zone contractor to the claimant, being a fee, grant, loan or otherwise.]

[⁸⁵ [⁹²[¹³⁹**73.**—(1) Any payment of child maintenance made or derived from a liable relative where the child or young person in respect of whom the payment is made is a member of the claimant's family, except where the person making the payment is the claimant or the claimant's partner.

(2) In paragraph (1)—

"child maintenance" means any payment towards the maintenance of a child or young person, including any payment made voluntarily and payments made under—

(a) the Child Support Act 1991;

(b) the Child Support (Northern Ireland) Order 1991;

(c) a court order;

(d) a consent order;

(e) a maintenance agreement registered for execution in the Books of Council and Session or the sheriff court books;

"liable relative" means a person listed in regulation 54 (interpretation) other than a person falling within sub-paragraph (d) of that definition.]]]

[⁷¹**74.**—In the case of a person to whom paragraph (5) of regulation 6 (persons not treated as in remunerative work) applies, the whole of his income.]

[⁷⁶**75.**—Any discretionary housing payment paid pursuant to regulation 2(1) of the Discretionary Financial Assistance Regulations 2001.]

[⁸⁷ [⁸⁹**76.**—(1) Any payment made by a local authority, or by the [¹³¹Welsh Ministers], to or on behalf of the claimant or his partner relating to a service which is provided to develop or sustain the capacity of the claimant or his partner to live independently in his accommodation.]

(2) For the purposes of sub-paragraph (1) "local authority" includes, in England, a county council.]

[¹⁵⁵**76A.**—Armed forces independence payment.]

[⁸⁹**77.**—[⁹³ . . .].]

[⁹¹**78.**—[⁹³ . . .].]

[¹⁶⁰**79.**—Any payments to a claimant made under section 49 of the Children and Families Act 2014 (personal budgets and direct payments).]

[¹⁶⁸**80.**—Any bereavement support payment under section 30 of the Pensions Act 2014 (bereavement support payment) except any such payment which is disregarded as capital under paragraph 7(1)(f) or 72 of Schedule 10.]

[¹⁷⁶**81.**—Any payment of carer's allowance supplement made under section 81 of the Social Security (Scotland) Act 2018.]

[¹⁷⁸**82.**—Any early years assistance given in accordance with section 32 of the Social Security (Scotland) Act 2018.]

[¹⁷⁹**83.**—Any funeral expense assistance given in accordance with section 34 of the Social Security (Scotland) Act 2018.]

[¹⁸²**84.**—Any Scottish child payment assistance given in accordance with section 79 of the Social Security (Scotland) Act 2018.]

[¹⁸³**85.**—Any short-term assistance given in accordance with regulations made under section 36 of the Social Security (Scotland) Act 2018.]

1. Income Support (General) Amendment Regulations 1988 (SI 1988/663) reg.35 (April 11, 1988).

2. Family Credit and Income Support (General) Amendment Regulations 1988 (SI 1988/999) reg.5 (June 9, 1988).

3. Income Support (General) Amendment No.4 Regulations 1988 (SI 1988/1445) reg.25 (September 12, 1988).

4. Income Support (General) Amendment No.5 Regulations 1988 (SI 1988/2022) reg.22 (December 12, 1988).

5. Income Support (General) Amendment No.4 Regulations 1988 (SI 1988/1445) Sch.1 para.9 (April 10, 1989).

6. Family Credit and Income Support (General) Amendment Regulations 1989 (SI 1989/1034) reg.12 (July 10, 1989).

7. Income Support (General) Amendment Regulations 1989 (SI 1989/534) Sch.1 para.15 (October 9, 1989).

8. Income-related Benefits Schemes Amendment Regulations 1990 (SI 1990/127) reg.3 (January 31, 1990).

9. Income Support (General) Amendment Regulations 1990 (SI 1990/547) reg.22(e) (April 1, 1990).

10. Income Support (General) Amendment Regulations 1990 (SI 1990/547) reg.22 (April 1, 1990).

11. Income-related Benefits Amendment Regulations 1990 (SI 1990/1657) reg.5(4) (September 1, 1990).

12. Income Support (General) Amendment No.3 Regulations 1990 (SI 1990/1776) reg.10 (October 1, 1990).

13. Enterprise (Scotland) Consequential Amendments Order 1991 (SI 1991/387) arts 2 and 9 (April 1, 1991).

14. Income Support (General) Amendment Regulations 1991 (SI 1991/236) reg.14 (April 8, 1991).

15. Income-related Benefits Schemes and Social Security (Recoupment) Amendment Regulations 1991 (SI 1991/1175) reg.5 (May 11, 1991).

16. Income Support (General) Amendment No.4 Regulations 1991 (SI 1991/1559) reg.20 (October 7, 1991).

17. Social Security Benefits Up-rating (No.2) Order 1991 (SI 1991/2910) art.13(13) (April 6, 1992).

18. Disability Living Allowance and Disability Working Allowance (Consequential Provisions) Regulations 1991 (SI 1991/2742) reg.11(6) (April 6, 1992).

19. Income Support (General) Amendment Regulations 1992 (SI 1992/468) reg.8 (April 6, 1992).

20. Income Support (General) Amendment Regulations 1992 (SI 1992/468) Sch. para.9 (April 6, 1992).

21. Income-related Benefits Schemes and Social Security (Recoupment) Amendment Regulations 1992 (SI 1992/1101) reg.6 (May 7, 1992).

22. Social Security Benefits (Amendments Consequential Upon the Introduction of Community Care) Regulations 1992 (SI 1992/3147) Sch.1 para.7 (April 1, 1993).

23. Income-related Benefits Schemes (Miscellaneous Amendments) Regulations 1993 (SI 1993/315) Sch. para.5 (April 1, 1993).

24. Income-related Benefits Schemes (Miscellaneous Amendments) Regulations 1993 (SI 1993/315) reg.9 (council tax and council tax benefit: April 1 1993; otherwise April 12, 1993).

25. Social Security Benefits (Miscellaneous Amendments) Regulations 1993 (SI 1993/518) reg.5 (April 1, 1993).

26. Social Security Benefits (Miscellaneous Amendments) (No.2) Regulations 1993 (SI 1993/963) reg.2(3) (April 22, 1993).

27. Income-related Benefits Schemes and Social Security (Recoupment) Amendment Regulations 1993 (SI 1993/1249) reg.4(4) (May 14, 1993).

28. Income Support (General) Amendment No.3 Regulations 1993 (SI 1993/1679) reg.6 (August 2, 1993).

29. Income-related Benefits Schemes (Miscellaneous Amendments) (No.4) Regulations 1993 (SI 1993/2119) reg.23 (October 4, 1993).

30. Income-related Benefits Schemes (Miscellaneous Amendments) Regulations 1994 (SI 1994/527) reg.9 (April 11, 1994).

31. Income-related Benefits Schemes (Miscellaneous Amendments) (No.5) Regulations 1994 (SI 1994/2139) reg.32 (October 3, 1994).

32. Income-related Benefits Schemes (Miscellaneous Amendments) Regulations 1995 (SI 1995/516) reg.27 (April 10, 1995).

33. Social Security (Income Support and Claims and Payments) Amendment Regulation 1995 (SI 1995/1613) reg.4 and Sch.3 (October 2, 1995).

34. Income-related Benefits Schemes and Social Security (Claims and Payments) (Miscellaneous Amendments) Regulations 1995 (SI 1995/2303) reg.6(9) (October 2, 1995).

35. Income-related Benefits Schemes Amendment (No.2) Regulations 1995 (SI 1995/2792) reg.6(3) (October 28, 1995).

36. Social Security (Income Support, Claims and Payments and Adjudication) Amendment Regulations 1995 (SI 1995/2927) reg.6 (December 12, 1995).

37. Income-related Benefits Schemes (Widows, etc. Pensions Disregards) Amendment Regulations 1995 (SI 1995/3282) reg.2 (December 20, 1995).

38. Income Support (General) Amendment Regulations 1996 (SI 1996/606) reg.2 (April 8, 1996).

39. Income-related Benefits Schemes (Miscellaneous Amendments) Regulations 1996 (SI 1996/462) reg.8 (April 8, 1996).

40. Social Security Benefits Up-rating Order 1996 (SI 1996/599) reg.18(13) (April 8, 1996).

41. Income Support and Social Security (Claims and Payments) (Miscellaneous Amendments) Regulations 1996 (SI 1996/2431) reg.5 (October 15, 1996).

42. Income-related Benefits and Jobseeker's Allowance (Miscellaneous Amendments) Regulations 1997 (SI 1997/65) reg.2(3) (April 7, 1997).

43. Income-related Benefits and Jobseeker's Allowance (Amendment) (No.2) Regulations 1997 (SI 1997/2197) reg.7(7) and (8)(e) (October 6, 1997).

44. Social Security Amendment (New Deal) Regulations 1997 (SI 1997/2863) reg.17(7) and (8)(e) (January 5, 1998).

45. Social Security Amendment (New Deal) Regulations 1997 (SI 1997/2863) reg.17(9) and (10)(e) (January 5, 1998).

46. Social Security (Miscellaneous Amendments) Regulations 1998 (SI 1998/563) reg.7(3) and (4)(e) (April 6, 1998).

47. Social Security (Miscellaneous Amendments) Regulations 1998 (SI 1998/563) reg.13(1)(c) (April 6, 1998).

48. Social Security (Miscellaneous Amendments) Regulations 1998 (SI 1998/563) reg.15(1) (April 6, 1998).

49. Social Security (Miscellaneous Amendments) Regulations 1998 (SI 1998/563) reg.15(2) (April 6, 1998).

50. Social Security (Miscellaneous Amendments) (No.3) Regulations 1998 (SI 1998/1173) reg.4 (June 1, 1998).

51. Social Security (Miscellaneous Amendments) (No.4) Regulations 1998 (SI 1998/1174) reg.6(4) (June 1, 1998).

52. Social Security (Miscellaneous Amendments) (No.4) Regulations 1998 (SI 1998/1174) reg.7(3) and (4)(e) (June 1, 1998).

53. Social Security Amendment (New Deal) (No.2) Regulations 1998 (SI 1998/2117) reg.4(4) (September 24, 1998).

54. Social Security Amendment (New Deal) (No.2) Regulations 1998 (SI 1998/2117) reg.6(2) (September 24, 1998).

55. Social Security Amendment (Educational Maintenance Allowance) Regulations 1999 (SI 1999/1677) reg.2(1) and (2)(e) (August 16, 1999).

56. Social Security Amendment (Sports Awards) Regulations 1999 (SI 1999/2165) reg.6(4) (August 23, 1999).

57. Social Security Amendment (Students) Regulations 1999 (SI 1999/1935) reg.3(8) (August 30, 1999, or if the student's period of study begins between August 1 and 29, 1999, the first day of the period).

58. Income Support (General) Amendment Regulations 1999 (SI 1999/ 2554) reg.2(3) (October 4, 1999).

59. Social Security (Miscellaneous Amendments) (No.2) Regulations 1999 (SI 1999/2556) reg.2(10) (October 4, 1999).

60. Social Security Amendment (Education Maintenance Allowance) Regulations 2000 (SI 2000/55) reg.2(1) and (2)(c) (February 7, 2000).

61. Social Security (Immigration and Asylum) Consequential Amendments Regulations 2000 (SI 2000/636) reg.3(12) (April 3, 2000).

62. Social Security (Immigration and Asylum) Consequential Amendments Regulations 2000 (SI 2000/636) reg.3(13) (April 3, 2000).

63. Social Security (Miscellaneous Amendments) Regulations 2000 (SI 2000/ 681) reg.7 (April 3, 2000).

64. Social Security (Miscellaneous Amendments) Regulations 2000 (SI 2000/ 681) reg.12(a) (April 3, 2000).

65. Social Security Amendment (Employment Zones) Regulations 2000 (SI 2000/724) reg.3(3) (April 3, 2000).

66. Social Security Amendment (Students) Regulations 2000 (SI 2000/1981) reg.5(5) and Sch. (July 31, 2000).

67. Social Security Amendment (Students and Income-related Benefits) Regulations 2000 (SI 2000/1922) reg.2(9) (August 28, 2000, or if the student's period of study begins between August 1 and 27, 2000, the first day of the period).

68. Social Security Amendment (Employment Zones) (No.2) Regulations 2000 (SI 2000/2910) reg.4(1) and (2)(c)(i) (November 27, 2000).

69. Income Support (General) Amendment Regulations 2001 (SI 2001/721) reg.2(c) (March 29, 2001).

70. Social Security Amendment (Bereavement Benefits) Regulations 2000 (SI 2000/2239) reg.2(4) (April 9, 2001).

71. Social Security (Miscellaneous Amendments) Regulations 2001 (SI 2001/ 488) reg.9 (April 9, 2001).

72. Social Security (Miscellaneous Amendments) (No.3) Regulations 2001 (SI 2001/859) reg.3(5) (April 9, 2001).

73. Social Security (Miscellaneous Amendments) (No.3) Regulations 2001 (SI 2001/859) reg.6(3)(c) (April 9, 2001).

74. Social Security Amendment (New Deal) Regulations 2001 (SI 2001/ 1029) reg.15(10) and (11)(c) (April 9, 2001).

75. Social Security Amendment (New Deal) Regulations 2001 (SI 2001/ 1029) reg.15(12) and (13)(c) (April 9, 2001).

76. Social Security Amendment (Discretionary Housing Payments) Regulations 2001 (SI 2001/2333) reg.2(1)(c) (July 2, 2001).

77. Social Security Amendment (Volunteers) Regulations 2001 (SI 2001/ 2296) reg.2(1) and (2)(c) (September 24, 2001).

78. Children (Leaving Care) Act 2000 (Commencement No.2 and Consequential Provisions) Order 2001 (SI 2001/3070) art.3(2) and para.(c) of Sch.1 (October 1, 2001).

79. Social Security Amendment (Residential Care and Nursing Homes) Regulations 2001 (SI 2001/3767) reg.2(1) and Pt I of Sch. para.19 (April 8, 2002).

80. Social Security Benefits Up-rating Order 2002 (SI 2002/668) art.16(9) (April 8, 2002).

81. Social Security (Miscellaneous Amendments) Regulations 2002 (SI 2002/ 841) reg.2(4) (April 8, 2002).

82. Social Security Amendment (Employment Programme) Regulations 2002 (SI 2002/2314) reg.3(3) (October 14, 2002).

83. Social Security (Miscellaneous Amendments) (No.2) Regulations 2002 (SI 2002/2380) reg.2(a) ((October 14, 2002).

84. Social Security Amendment (Personal Injury Payments) Regulations 2002 (SI 2002/2442) reg.3(1)(d) and (2)(c) (October 28, 2002).

85. Social Security (Child Maintenance Premium and Miscellaneous Amendments) Regulations 2000 (SI 2000/3176) reg.2(1)(b) (in force in relation to any particular case on the day on which s.23 CSPSSA 2000 comes into force in relation to that type of case).

86. Social Security (Paternity and Adoption) Amendment Regulations 2002 (SI 2002/2689) reg.2(6) (December 8, 2002).

87. Social Security (Miscellaneous Amendments) Regulations 2003 (SI 2003/511) reg.2(2) (April 1, 2003)

88. Social Security (Working Tax Credit and Child Tax Credit) (Consequential Amendments) Regulations 2003 (SI 2003/455) reg.2 and Sch.1 para.23(a) (April 7, 2003).

88a. Community Care, Services for Carers and Children's Services (Direct Payments) (England) Regulations 2003 (SI 2003/762) reg.11(2) and Sch.2 (April 8, 2003).

89. Social Security (Miscellaneous Amendments) (No.2) Regulations 2003 (SI 2003/2279) reg.2(4) (October 1, 2003).

90. Social Security (Removal of Residential Allowance and Miscellaneous Amendments) Regulations 2003 (SI 2003/1121) reg.2 and Sch.1 para.9 (October 6, 2003).

91. Social Security (Incapacity Benefit Work-focused Interviews) Regulations 2003 (SI 2003/2439) reg.13(a) (October 27, 2003).

92. Social Security (Child Maintenance Premium) Amendment Regulations 2004 (SI 2004/98) reg.2 (in force on: (i) February 16, 2004 in relation to any particular case in respect of which s.23 CSPSSA 2000 has come into force before February 16, 2004; (ii) where this does not apply, the day on which s.23 comes into force in relation to that type of case; (iii) February 16, 2004 in relation to a person who is entitled to income support/income-based JSA on that date and who receives her first payment of child maintenance made voluntarily whilst entitled to income support/income-based JSA on that date; (iv) in such a case where the day that the first voluntary payment is received is after February 16, 2004, the day the payment is received; and (v) February 16, 2004 in relation to a person who makes a claim for income support/income-based JSA on or after that date and receives a payment of child maintenance made voluntarily on or after the date of that claim).

93. Social Security (Miscellaneous Amendments) Regulations 2004 (SI 2004/565) reg.2(3) (April 1, 2004).

94. Social Security (Working Tax Credit and Child Tax Credit) (Consequential Amendments) Regulations 2003 (SI 2003/455) reg.2 and Sch.1 para.23 (except sub-para.(a) (April 6, 2004, except in "transitional cases" and see further the note to reg.17 of the Income Support Regulations).

95. Social Security (Miscellaneous Amendments) (No.2) Regulations 2004 (SI 2004/1141) reg.4(1) and (2)(c) (May 12, 2004).

96. Social Security (Miscellaneous Amendments) (No.2) Regulations 2004 (SI 2004/1141) reg.4(3) and (4)(c) (May 12, 2004).

97. Social Security (Students and Income-related Benefits) Amendment Regulations 2004 (SI 2004/1708) reg.5(2) (September 1, 2004, or if the student's period of study begins between August 1 and August 31, 2004, the first day of the period).

98. Social Security (Miscellaneous Amendments) (No.3) Regulations 2004 (SI 2004/2308) reg.2(1) and (2)(a) (October 4, 2004).

99. Social Security (Miscellaneous Amendments) (No.3) Regulations 2004 (SI 2004/2308) reg.3(3) and (4)(a) (October 4, 2004).

100. Social Security (Miscellaneous Amendments) (No.3) Regulations 2004 (SI 2004/2308) reg.4(3) and (4)(a) (October 4, 2004).

101. Social Security (Back to Work Bonus and Lone Parent Run-on) (Amendment and Revocation) Regulations 2003 (SI 2003/1589) reg.2(d) (October 25, 2004).

102. Social Security (Miscellaneous Amendments) Regulations 2005 (SI 2005/574) reg.2(7) and (8)(a) (April 4, 2005).

103. Social Security (Miscellaneous Amendments) Regulations 2005 (SI 2005/574) reg.3(5) (April 4, 2005).

104. Social Security (Miscellaneous Amendments) (No.2) Regulations 2005 (SI 2005/2465) reg.2(8)(a) (October 3, 2005).

105. Mental Health (Care and Treatment) (Scotland) Act 2003 (Modification of Subordinate Legislation) Order 2005 (SSI 2005/445) art.2 and Sch., para.3(5) (Scotland); Mental Health (Care and Treatment) (Scotland) Act 2003 (Consequential Provisions) Order 2005 (SI 2005/2078) art.15 and Sch.2 para.3(6) (England and Wales) (October 5, 2005).

106. Social Security (Care Homes and Independent Hospitals) Regulations 2005 (SI 2005/2687) reg.2 and Sch.1 para.12 (October 24, 2005).

107. Civil Partnership (Pensions, Social Security and Child Support) (Consequential, etc. Provisions) Order 2005 (SI 2005/2877) art.2(3) and Sch.3 para.13(8) (December 5, 2005).

108. Income-related Benefits (Amendment) (No.2) Regulations 2005 (SI 2005/3391) reg.2(3) (December 12, 2005).

109. Social Security (Miscellaneous Amendments) (No.2) Regulations 2005 (SI 2005/2465) reg.2(8)(b) (December 30, 2005).

110. Social Security (Miscellaneous Amendments) (No.2) Regulations 2005 (SI 2005/2465) reg.2(8)(c) (December 30, 2005).

111. Housing Benefit and Council Tax Benefit (Consequential Provisions) Regulations 2006 (SI 2006/217) reg.5 and Sch.2 para.1(8) (March 6, 2006).

112. Social Security (Hospital In-Patients) Regulations 2005 (SI 2005/3360) reg.4(6) (April 10, 2006).

113. Social Security (Miscellaneous Amendments) (No.4) Regulations 2006 (SI 2006/2378) reg.5(10)(a) (October 2, 2006).

114. Social Security (Miscellaneous Amendments) (No.4) Regulations 2006 (SI 2006/2378) reg.5(10)(b) (October 2, 2006).

115. Social Security (Miscellaneous Amendments) (No.4) Regulations 2006 (SI 2006/2378) reg.5(10)(c) (October 2, 2006).

116. Social Security (Miscellaneous Amendments) (No.4) Regulations 2006 (SI 2006/2378) reg.5(10)(d) (October 2, 2006).

117. Social Security (Miscellaneous Amendments) (No.4) Regulations 2006 (SI 2006/2378) reg.5(10)(e) (October 2, 2006).

118. Social Security (Miscellaneous Amendments) Regulations 2007 (SI 2007/719) reg.2(9) (April 2, 2007).

119. Asylum and Immigration (Treatment of Claimants, etc.) Act 2004 (c.19) s.12(2)(a)(iii) (June 14, 2007).

120. Secretary of State for Justice Order 2007 (SI 2007/2128) Sch. para.13(2) (August 22, 2007).

121. Social Security (Miscellaneous Amendments) (No.5) Regulations 2007 (SI 2007/2618) reg.5(12) (April 7, 2008).

122. Social Security (Miscellaneous Amendments) Regulations 2008 (SI 2008/698) reg.2(14)(a) (April 14, 2008).

123. Social Security (Miscellaneous Amendments) Regulations 2008 (SI 2008/698) reg.2(14)(b) (April 7, 2008).

124. Social Security (Miscellaneous Amendments) Regulations 2008 (SI 2008/698) reg.2(14)(c) (April 14, 2008).

125. Social Security (Miscellaneous Amendments) Regulations 2008 (SI 2008/698) reg.2(14)(d) (April 14, 2008).

126. Employment and Support Allowance (Consequential Provisions) (No.2) Regulations 2008 (SI 2008/1554) reg.2(14) (October 27, 2008).

127. Social Security (Child Maintenance Amendments) Regulations 2008 (SI 2008/2111) reg.2(9) (October 27, 2008).

128. Social Security (Miscellaneous Amendments) (No.6) Regulations 2008 (SI 2008/2767) reg.2(6) (November 17, 2008).

129. Social Security (Miscellaneous Amendments) (No.6) Regulations 2008 (SI 2008/2767) reg.2(12) (November 17, 2008).

130. Social Security (Child Benefit Disregard) Regulations 2008 (SI 2008/3140) reg.2 (January 5, 2009; this regulation ceases to have effect on April 6, 2009).

131. Social Security (Miscellaneous Amendments) (No.7) Regulations 2008 (SI 2008/3157) reg.2(7) (January 5, 2009).

132. Social Security (Miscellaneous Amendments) Regulations 2009 (SI 2009/583) reg.2(13) (April 6, 2009).

133. Social Security (Miscellaneous Amendments) (No.4) Regulations 2009 (SI 2009/2655) reg.2(17)(a) (October 26, 2009).

134. Social Security (Miscellaneous Amendments) (No.4) Regulations 2009 (SI 2009/2655) reg.2(17)(b) (October 26, 2009).

135. Social Security (Miscellaneous Amendments) (No.4) Regulations 2009 (SI 2009/2655) reg.2(17)(c) (October 26, 2009).

136. Social Security (Miscellaneous Amendments) (No.2) Regulations 2010 (SI 2010/641) reg.2(3)(f) (April 6, 2010).

137. Social Security (Miscellaneous Amendments) (No.2) Regulations 2010 (SI 2010/641) reg.2(7)(e) (April 6, 2010).

138. Social Security (Miscellaneous Amendments) (No.2) Regulations 2010 (SI 2010/641) reg.2(10) (April 6, 2010).

139. Social Security (Miscellaneous Amendments) (No.4) Regulations 2009 (SI 2009/2655) reg.2(17)(d) (April 12, 2010).

140. Social Security (Miscellaneous Amendments) (No.5) Regulations 2010 (SI 2010/2429) reg.2(3)(a) (November 1, 2010).

141. Social Security (Miscellaneous Amendments) (No.5) Regulations 2010 (SI 2010/2429) reg.2(3)(b) (November 1, 2010).

142. Social Security (Miscellaneous Amendments) (No. 5) Regulations 2010 (SI 2010/2429) reg.2(3)(c) (November 1, 2010).

143. Adoption and Children (Scotland) Act 2007 (Consequential Modifications) Order 2011 (SI 2011/1740) art.2 and Sch.1 para.9(3) (July 15, 2011).

144. Social Security (Miscellaneous Amendments) (No.2) Regulations 2011 (SI 2011/1707) reg.4(8)(a) and (9) (August 5, 2011).

145. Social Security (Miscellaneous Amendments) (No.3) Regulations 2011 (SI 2011/2425) reg.7(5) (October 31, 2011).

146. Social Security (Miscellaneous Amendments) (No.3) Regulations 2011 (SI 2011/2425) reg.7(6) (October 31, 2011).

147. Social Security (Miscellaneous Amendments) (No.3) Regulations 2011 (SI 2011/2425) reg.7(8) (October 31, 2011).

148. Social Security (Miscellaneous Amendments) Regulations 2012 (SI 2012/757) reg.3(4) (April 1, 2012).

149. Jobseeker's Allowance (Schemes for Assisting Persons to Obtain Employment) Regulations 2013 (SI 2013/276) reg.13(b) (February 12, 2013).

150. Council Tax Benefit Abolition (Consequential Provision) Regulations 2013 (SI 2013/458) reg.3 and Sch.1 (April 1, 2013).

151. Social Security (Miscellaneous Amendments) Regulations 2013 (SI 2013/443) reg.2(5)(a) (April 2, 2013).

152. Social Security (Miscellaneous Amendments) Regulations 2013 (SI 2013/443) reg.2(5)(b) (April 2, 2013).

153. Personal Independence Payment (Supplementary Provisions and Consequential Amendments) Regulations 2013 (SI 2013/388) reg.8 and Sch. Pt 2 para.11(7)(a) (April 8, 2013).

154. Personal Independence Payment (Supplementary Provisions and

Consequential Amendments) Regulations 2013 (SI 2013/388) reg.8 and Sch. Pt 2 para.11(7)(b) (April 8, 2013).

155. Armed Forces and Reserve Forces Compensation Scheme (Consequential Provisions: Subordinate Legislation) Order 2013 (SI 2013/591) art.7 and Sch. para.4(7) (April 8, 2013).

156. National Treatment Agency (Abolition) and the Health and Social Care Act 2012 (Consequential, Transitional and Saving Provisions) Order 2013 (SI 2013/235) art.11 and Sch.2 Pt I para.10(3) (April 1, 2013).

157. Universal Credit (Consequential, Supplementary, Incidental and Miscellaneous Provisions) Regulations 2013 (SI 2013/630) reg.28(8) (April 29, 2013).

158. Child Arrangements Order (Consequential Amendments to Subordinate Legislation) Order 2014 (SI 2014/852) art.2 (April 22, 2014).

159. Social Security (Miscellaneous Amendments) Regulations 2014 (SI 2014/591) reg.2(7) (April 28, 2014).

160. Special Educational Needs (Consequential Amendments to Subordinate Legislation) Order 2014 (SI 2014/2103) art.3(2) (September 1, 2014).

161. Shared Parental Leave and Statutory Shared Parental Pay (Consequential Amendments to Subordinate Legislation) Order 2014 (SI 2014/3255) art.5(6)(a) (December 31, 2014).

162. Shared Parental Leave and Statutory Shared Parental Pay (Consequential Amendments to Subordinate Legislation) Order 2014 (SI 2014/3255) art.5(6)(b) (ii) (December 31, 2014).

163. Care Act 2014 (Consequential Amendments) (Secondary Legislation) Order 2015 (SI 2015/643) art.2 and Sch. para.5(3) (April 1, 2015).

164. Shared Parental Leave and Statutory Shared Parental Pay (Consequential Amendments to Subordinate Legislation) Order 2014 (SI 2014/3255) art.5(6)(b) (i) (April 5, 2015).

165. Children and Young People (Scotland) Act 2014 (Consequential Modifications) Order 2016 (SI 2016/732) art.2(2) (August 5, 2016).

166. Social Security (Income-Related Benefits) Amendment Regulations 2017 (SI 2017/174) reg.2 (March 20, 2017).

167. Social Security (Scottish Infected Blood Support Scheme) Regulations 2017 (SI 2017/329) reg.3(3) (April 3, 2017).

168. Pensions Act 2014 (Consequential, Supplementary and Incidental Amendments) Order 2017 (SI 2017/422) art.9(3) (April 6, 2017).

169. Social Security (Emergency Funds) (Amendment) Regulations 2017 (SI 2017/689) reg.2(3)(e) (June 19, 2017).

170. Social Security (Infected Blood and Thalidomide) Regulations 2017 (SI 2017/870) reg.2(3)(e) (October 23, 2017).

171. Social Services and Well-being (Wales) Act 2014 and the Regulation and Inspection of Social Care (Wales) Act 2016 (Consequential Amendments) Order 2017 (SI 2017/901) art.2(5) (November 3, 2017).

172. Social Services and Well-being (Wales) Act 2014 and the Regulation and Inspection of Social Care (Wales) Act 2016 (Consequential Amendments) Order 2017 (SI 2017/901) art.20(3) (November 3, 2017).

173. Social Security and Child Support (Care Payments and Tenant Incentive Scheme) (Amendment) Regulations 2017 (SI 2017/995) reg.2(3) (November 7, 2017).

174. Loans for Mortgage Interest Regulations 2017 (SI 2017/725) Sch.5, as amended by Loans for Mortgage Interest and Social Fund Maternity Grant (Amendment) Regulations 2018 (SI 2018/307) reg.2(18)(c) (April 6, 2018).

175. Secretaries of State for Health and Social Care and for Housing, Communities and Local Government and Transfer of Functions (Commonhold Land) Order 2018 (SI 2018/378) Sch., para.21(a) (April 11, 2018).

176. Social Security (Scotland) Act 2018 (Consequential Modifications) Order 2018 (SI 2018/872) art.2 (September 3, 2018).

177. Social Security (Miscellaneous Amendments No.5) Regulations 2017 (SI 2017/1187) reg.2(3) (December 6, 2018).

178. Social Security (Scotland) Act 2018 (Best Start Grants) (Consequential Modifications and Saving) Order 2018 (SI 2018/1138) art.5(2) (December 10, 2018).

179. Social Security (Scotland) Act 2018 (Funeral Expense Assistance and Early Years Assistance) (Consequential Modifications and Savings) Order 2019 (SI 2019/1060) art.7(2) (September 16, 2019).

180. Parental Bereavement Leave and Pay (Consequential Amendments to Subordinate Legislation) Regulations 2020 (SI 2020/354) reg.5(6) (April 6, 2020).

181. Social Security (Income and Capital) (Miscellaneous Amendments) Regulations 2020 (SI 2020/618) reg.2(11) (July 15, 2020).

182. Social Security (Scotland) Act 2018 (Information-sharing and Scottish Child Payment) (Consequential Provision and Modifications) Order 2020 (SI 2020/482) art.3(2) (November 9, 2020).

183. Social Security (Scotland) Act 2018 (Young Carer Grants, Short-Term Assistance and Winter Heating Assistance) (Consequential Provision and Modifications) Order 2020 (SI 2020/989) art.9(2) (November 9, 2020).

DEFINITIONS

"Abbeyfield Home"—see reg.2(1).
"access funds"—see reg.61(1).
"the Act"—see reg.2(1).
"adoption leave"—*ibid.*
"approved blood scheme"—*ibid.*
"armed forces independence payment"—*ibid.*
"attendance allowance"—*ibid.*
"the benefit Acts"—*ibid.*
"benefit week"—*ibid.*
"care home"—*ibid.*
"child"—see SSCBA s.137(1).
"the Children Order"—see reg.2(1).
"claimant"—*ibid.*
"claimant participating as a service user"—see reg.2(1B).
"contribution"—see reg.61.
"course of study"—see reg.2(1).
"disability living allowance"—*ibid.*
"dwelling occupied as the home"—*ibid.*
"employed earner"—*ibid.*
"employment zone contractor"—*ibid.*
"employment zone programme"—*ibid.*
"family"—see SSCBA s.137(1).
"full-time student"—see reg.61(1).
"Grenfell Tower payment"—see reg.2(1).
"a guaranteed income payment"—*ibid.*
"Immigration and Asylum Act"—*ibid.*
"independent hospital"—*ibid.*
"Intensive Activity Period for 50 plus"—*ibid.*
"loan payments"—see para.30(3)(b) and reg.2(1) of the Loans for Mortgage Interest Regulations 2017.
"local welfare provision"—see reg.2(1).
"the London Bombings Relief Charitable Fund"—*ibid.*
"the London Emergencies Trust"—*ibid.*
"MFET Limited"—*ibid.*
"the Mandatory Work Activity Scheme"—*ibid.*

"maternity leave"—*ibid.*
"mobility allowance"—see reg.2(1).
"mobility supplement"—*ibid.*
"occupational pension"—*ibid.*
"occupational pension scheme"—see Pension Schemes Act 1993 s.1.
"parental bereavement leave"—see reg.2(1).
"partner of a person subject to immigration control"—see reg.21(3).
"paternity leave"—see reg.2(1).
"payment"—*ibid.*
"personal independence payment"—*ibid.*
"personal pension scheme"—*ibid.*
"qualifying person"—*ibid.*
"remunerative work"—see reg.2(1) and reg.5.
"Scottish Infected Blood Support Scheme"—see reg.2(1).
"self-employment route"—see reg.2(1).
"shared parental leave"—*ibid.*
"Social Security Act"—*ibid.*
"special account"—see reg.39A.
"sports award"—see reg.2(1).
"student"—see reg.61.
"student loan"—*ibid.*
"subsistence allowance"—see reg.2(1).
"the Caxton Foundation"—*ibid.*
"the Eileen Trust"—*ibid.*
"the Fund"—*ibid.*
"the Independent Living Funds"—*ibid.*
"the Macfarlane (Special Payments) Trust"—*ibid.*
"the Macfarlane (Special Payments) (No.2) Trust"—*ibid.*
"the Macfarlane Trust"—*ibid.*
"the National Emergencies Trust"—*ibid.*
"the Skipton Fund"—*ibid.*
"training allowance"—*ibid.*
"universal credit" —*ibid.*
"voluntary organisation"—*ibid.*
"war disablement pension"—*ibid.*
"the We Love Manchester Emergency Fund"—*ibid.*
"young person"—*ibid.*, and reg.14.

GENERAL NOTE

2.728   The categories of disregards of income other than earnings are as follows (* indicates no further note below):

Para.1	tax paid;
Para.1A	payments of travel expenses for certain schemes;
Para.2	payments of expenses to volunteers etc;
Para.2A	payments of expenses to service users:
Para.3	payments of necessary etc expenses to employees;
Para.4	social security and pension contributions on sick, maternity, paternity, shared parental or adoption leave pay;
Para.4A	rules for Northern Ireland pay of that kind;
Para.5	housing benefit;
Para.5A	guardian's allowance;
Para.5B	child tax credit, child benefit and dependency increases for children and young persons;
Para.6	mobility component of DLA or PIP;
Para.7	concessionary payments to compensate for non-payment of certain benefits*;
Para.8	mobility supplement or compensation for non-payment*;

660

Para.9	attendance allowance, care component of DLA or daily living component of PIP;
Para.10	VC or GC payments or analogous*;
Para.11	educational maintenance allowances or similar;
Para.11A	repayments of student loans under teachers' schemes;
Para.13	payments under New Deal schemes etc;
Para.15	charitable and voluntary payments etc made at regular intervals;
Para.16	£10 of various war pension and widows' benefits etc;
Para.17	annuities under equity release schemes so far as applied to mortgage interest;
Para.18	contributions towards living and accommodation expenses by person residing with claimant;
Para.19	£20 of payments under contractual liability by another occupier of claimant's home;
Para.20	payments for board and lodging in claimant's home;
Para.21	income in kind, with exceptions;
Para.22	income derived from capital, with exceptions;
Para.23	income payable outside UK where prohibition on transfer*;
Para.24	charges for conversion to sterling;
Para.25	payments in respect of child or young person;
Para.25A	payments to educational establishments in respect of child or young person;
Para.26	payments to foster-parents;
Para.27	payments for person temporarily accommodated by claimant;
Para.27A	kinship care assistance payments;
Para.28	statutory payments to prevent child going into care or to support a care-leaver;
Para.29	proceeds of mortgage protection policies so far as used for certain purposes not covered by housing costs;
Para.30	payments intended to be used for certain purposes not covered by housing costs;
Para.30ZA	payments received under creditor insurance policies;
Para.30A	certain payments towards cost of maintenance in Abbeyfield Home or independent hospital;
Para.31	social fund payments*;
Para.31A	local welfare provision;
Para.32	income treated as capital by reg.48*;
Para.33	pensioners' Christmas bonus*;
Para.34	payments by trade unions during trade disputes, with limits;
Para.35	payments due to be paid before date of claim where overlap;
Para.36	£20 limit on disregards under regs.63(2)(b), 64(1)(c), 66A(2), 66B(3) and para.16*;
Para.37	overlap of two or more payments of same kind;
Para.39	payments from certain funds for haemophiliacs, contaminated blood products, various victims etc;
Para.40	compensation payments for loss of entitlement to housing benefit*;
Para.43	payments to jurors or witnesses, with exceptions*;
Para.46	payments under council tax reduction schemes;
Para.48	NHS travel expenses*;
Para.49	payments in lieu of certain vouchers*;
Para.50	prison visiting payments*;
Para.51	certain payment to disabled persons to obtain or retain employment;
Para.53	certain increases for dependants not residing with claimant;
Para.54	certain armed forces surviving spouse pensions;
Para.55	certain surviving spouse pensions under civilians' scheme;
Para.56	certain other payments to surviving spouses under armed forces schemes;

Para. 58	payments by local authorities in lieu of community care services;
Para. 61	student income left over at end of course;
Para. 64	certain payment to persons on the "self-employment route";
Para. 66	certain payments in relation to care or notional income under reg.42(4A);
Para. 69	sports awards, with exceptions;
Para. 71	subsistence allowances from employment zone contractors;
Para. 72	discretionary payments from employment zone contractors;
Para. 73	child maintenance from liable relatives;
Para. 74	persons treated as not in remunerative work by reg.6(5);
Para. 75	discretionary housing payments;
Para. 76	payments for service charges in supported accommodation;
Para. 76A	armed forces independence payments★;
Para. 79	payments under s.49 of the Children and Families Act 2014;
Para. 80	bereavement support payments;
Para. 81	Scottish carer's allowance supplement★;
Para. 82	Scottish early years assistance;
Para. 83	Scottish funeral expense assistance.
Para. 84	Scottish child payments
Para. 85	Scottish short-term assistance

With effect from May 29, 2020, reg.26(1)(a) of the Victims' Payments Regulations 2020 (SI 2020/103) (see later in this Part) provides that a victims' payment or a lump sum under those Regulations is to be disregarded as income or capital. Under the Regulations payments are to be made to those injured in a "Troubles-related incident", which is defined in s.10(11) of the Northern Ireland (Executive Formation etc) Act 2019 as "an incident involving an act of violence or force carried out in Ireland, the United Kingdom or anywhere in Europe for a reason related to the constitutional status of Northern Ireland or to political or sectarian hostility between people there".

The taxable £500 payment, administered by local authorities, to be made to those in England entitled to a qualifying income-related benefit (including income support, income-related ESA and income-based JSA) who are required by NHS Test and Trace on or after September 28, 2020 (down at least to summer 2021) to self-isolate for 14 (or 10) days, are unable to work from home and will lose income from employment or self-employment as a result was said in the guidance on scheme eligibility not to affect entitlement to other benefits. The same was to apply to the discretionary payment available to those not entitled to a qualifying benefit. However, there has been no amendment to Sch.9 or its equivalents, or elsewhere, to disregard such payments (or payments under the very similar, but not identical, schemes available in Wales, Scotland and Northern Ireland (a discretionary scheme only)) as income (in contrast to the position in universal credit: see the notes to reg.66(1) of the Universal Credit Regulations in Vol.II of this series). The payments would appear to be in the nature of income because, with the eligibility condition that income will be lost, they constitute compensation for loss of the income that would otherwise have been received (see the notes to reg.23 above). But it is strongly arguable that the payments constitute "local welfare provision", disregarded as income under para.31A (see the notes to that provision below). That is the view taken in Memo DMG 18/20. In addition, could a discretionary payment possibly be regarded as a voluntary payment not made or due to be made at regular intervals and so to be treated as capital under reg.48(9)?

The intention was also expressed that the £500 payments were not to be taken into account as capital. If the suggestion above is correct, they are not as such payments of capital. But there is nothing in the legislation to prevent any amount remaining out of the £500 at the end of the required days of self-isolation from being treated as capital under the usual principles. If the payments are local welfare provision, there would be a disregard as capital under para.18A of Sch.10.

It was announced in the March 2021 budget that an automatic £500 payment would be made by HMRC to those in receipt of working tax credit (or child tax credit alone if eligible for WTC but income too high for payability), in view of the withdrawal in April 2021 of the temporary uplift to WTC rates during the coronavirus pandemic. The payment is due to be made in April 2021 without the need for any claim and apparently under powers in the Coronavirus Act 2020. It will therefore not be a payment of WTC and would appear to be in the nature of a capital receipt, rather than income. According to LA Welfare Direct 3/2021, the payment is to be disregarded for housing benefit and universal credit purposes, but there has been no amendment of the legislation for the purposes of income support, income-related ESA or income-based JSA.

Paragraph 1

There is no provision in Ch.V itself for deducting tax. So if taxable payments are treated as income under reg.40 a disregard is needed.   2.729

R(IS) 4/05 decides that "any amount paid by way of tax" includes tax that is to be paid. The claimant's income support claim had been rejected because her state retirement pension exceeded her applicable amount. Her retirement pension was paid gross, with any tax due being payable by her in a lump sum following the end of the tax year. The claimant produced a forecast from the Inland Revenue, which estimated her likely tax liability for the current year. She contended that this amount should be deducted from her retirement pension. The Commissioner agreed. He held that the disregard in para.1 is not concerned with the time at which tax is paid. It applies to tax which at the date of the benefit decision either has been, or is to be, paid, the only condition being that it is tax on income which is being taken into account under reg.40. The tax to be disregarded is the tax paid or due on the income attributable to the benefit weeks in question, not the tax payable in respect of earlier tax years. Where the tax payable is an annual sum, reg.32(1) provides a method for calculating the weekly amount.

As a consequence of this decision guidance was issued to decision-makers (DMG Letter 04/05) which stated that if claimants provide evidence, such as a forecast from the Inland Revenue, which shows the tax due on income other than earnings paid to them for the current year, the amount of the estimated tax should be disregarded and the net amount taken into account (now see DMG para.28010).

Paragraph 1A

Any payment of expenses in relation to participation in the Mandatory Work Activity Scheme (discontinued after April 2016) or a scheme listed in reg.3 of the Jobseeker's Allowance (Schemes for Assisting Persons to Obtain Employment) Regulations 2013 is ignored. See para.1A of Sch.10 for the disregard as capital.   2.730

Paragraph 2

A payment purely of expenses to a volunteer or someone working for a charity or a voluntary organisation is disregarded unless the person is caught by reg.42(6) on underpaid services. The September 2001 amendment allows an advance payment of expenses to be disregarded. A volunteer is someone who without any legal obligation performs a service for another person without expectation of payment *(R(IS) 12/92)*.   2.731

Paragraph 2A

Payments of expenses in respect of a "claimant participating as a service user" (see reg.2(1B) for those to whom this refers) are ignored. This disregard is needed because if those who come within reg.2(1B) are paid for their involvement as well as receiving expenses the disregard under para.2 does not apply. Payments of expenses in respect of a claimant participating as a service user are excluded from the definition of "earnings" by reg.35(2)(f). But any payment (e.g. for attending meetings) that results from a claimant participating as a service user will count as earnings,   2.732

subject to the appropriate disregard. Note, however, that the notional income rules do not apply to either expenses *or* earnings as a result of a claimant participating as a service user (see reg.42(2)(ga) and reg.42(8ZA)).

Paragraph 3

2.733 Such payments of necessary, etc. expenses are not earnings (reg.35(2)), but are income (reg.40(4)). See the notes to reg.35(1)(f) for "wholly, exclusively and necessarily." *CFC/2/1989* might suggest that payments made by the employee for necessary, etc. expenses out of such income are to be deducted from that income. But that is not consistent with the scheme of the legislation and is rejected in *R(FC) 1/90*, *R(IS) 16/93* and *CIS/77/1993*. See the notes to reg.35(2). However, note the effect of the application of the principle in *Parsons v Hogg* to the meaning of "gross earnings" (see the notes to reg.36(3)).

Paragraphs 4 and 4A

2.734 The standard deductions are to be made from contractual or statutory sick, maternity, paternity, shared parental or adoption or parental bereavement leave pay, which are not earnings (reg.35(2)), but are income (reg.40(4)).

Paragraph 5

2.735 See also paras 40, 42, 45, 46 and 52.

In *CIS/521/2002* the claimant was one of four partners who ran a hotel providing board and lodging accommodation for the homeless. Under reg.37(2)(a) payments received for providing board and lodging accommodation do not count as earnings from self-employment. They count as income under reg.40(4)(a) and thus any appropriate disregard in Sch.9 may apply. The board and lodging charges were primarily met by housing benefit which was paid direct to the partnership. The Commissioner raises the point that such payments would seem to come within para.5 (although he did not have to reach a conclusion on the issue). However, to apply the disregard to direct payments of housing benefit to landlords would draw a line between such landlords and those receiving rent from tenants who had housing benefit paid to them and there seemed to be no reason for such a distinction. For further discussion of *CIS/521/2002* see the note to para.20 below.

The inclusion from January 5, 2009 of the words "to which the claimant is entitled" is intended to make clear that it is only payments of housing benefit to which the claimant is entitled that are ignored under para.5 and that the disregard does not extend to housing benefit paid direct to the claimant as a landlord. This amendment was made as a result of the Commissioner's decision in *CH/2321/2002* on the ambit of the disregard in para.27(b) (see the note to para.27) but it also deals with the point raised by the Commissioner in *CIS/521/2002*.

Paragraph 5A

2.736 A new disregard of guardian's allowance was introduced as part of the changes associated with the start of child tax credit in April 2003.

Paragraph 5B

2.737 With effect from April 6, 2004 (except in "transitional cases"—see the note to reg.17), amounts for children and young persons have been removed from the income support scheme; financial assistance to help with the cost of bringing up a child or young person is now provided through the child tax credit system, see Vol. IV of this series. As part of the changes associated with the introduction of child tax credit, child tax credit is ignored, as is child benefit (except in "transitional cases—see the note to reg.17).

For income support claimants who had an award of child tax credit before April 6, 2004 see reg.7 of the Social Security (Working Tax Credit and Child Tax Credit) (Consequential Amendments) Regulations 2003 (SI 2003/455) (as amended) on p.1763 and the notes to that regulation.

The effect of the new sub-para.(3) inserted in November 2010 is that any child dependency increase paid with another benefit, such as incapacity benefit or carer's allowance, is disregarded if the claimant has been awarded child tax credit. The disregard does not apply to those claimants who continue to receive amounts for their children as part of their income support.

Paragraph 6

The mobility component of disability living allowance and the mobility component of personal independence payment is disregarded. See also paras 7 and 8.

2.738

Paragraph 9

The general rule is that attendance allowance, the care component of disability living allowance and the daily living component of personal independence payment is disregarded.

2.739

Paragraph 11

Education maintenance allowances ("EMAs") (which now only apply in Wales and Scotland) are disregarded in full.

A national scheme for the payment of EMAs was originally introduced from the start of the 2004/5 academic year (this replaced the previous pilot project). EMAs are payable for up to three years to 16–19-year-olds who remain in non-advanced education after the age of 16. Under the national scheme they include weekly payments (depending on income), together with periodic bonuses. The allowance is fully disregarded when calculating entitlement to income support, old style JSA, old style ESA, working tax credit and child tax credit (as well as housing benefit and, until its abolition on April 1, 2013, council tax benefit). For the capital disregard see para.63 of Sch.10.

The October 31, 2011 amendments to para.11 allow for payments made from the "16–19 Bursary Fund" to be disregarded in the same way as EMAs. The bursary scheme was introduced in September 2011 to help vulnerable 16–19 year olds continue in full-time education and replaces the EMA in England.

2.740

Paragraph 11A

As part of the Government's strategy to recruit and retain teachers, s.186 of the Education Act 2002 and the Education (Teacher Student Loans) (Repayment, etc.) Regulations 2002 provide for the reduction/extinguishment of the amount owing on student loans for newly qualified teachers in shortage subjects working in England and Wales. The scheme operates differently depending on where the student loan was originally incurred. For those teachers who took out student loans while living in England and Wales the Department for Education and Skills will simply waive repayment. However, for those who took out their loans while living in Scotland, Northern Ireland or another EEA country, annual payments will be made to the teacher over a number of years to enable them to repay the Student Loan Company. Under the new para.11A any such payments are disregarded.

2.741

Paragraph 13

The new form of para.13 in force from April 1, 2004 was introduced in order to provide a single disregard of the various allowances, grants and other payments made under s.2 of the Employment and Training Act 1973 or s.2 of the Enterprise and New Towns (Scotland) Act 1990 to people participating in New Deals and other training and welfare to work schemes. Before April 1, 2004 separate disregards had existed in respect of such payments under a number of the provisions in this Schedule. As a consequence of this change, those provisions have been revoked or amended. The revoked paragraphs are paras 59, 60, 62, 62A, 63, 65, 77 and 78; the two paragraphs that have been amended are paras 51 and 70.

Sub-paragraph (1) provides that payments under s.2 of the 1973 Act or s.2 of the 1990 Act are ignored *unless* they are: (i) paid instead of income support, old style

2.742

JSA, incapacity benefit, old style ESA or severe disablement allowance (sub-para. (1)(a)); (ii) payments of a "bridging allowance" to a young person under s.2(3) of the 1973 Act (s.2(5) of the 1990 Act) (sub-para.(1)(b)); (iii) intended to cover food, ordinary clothing or footwear (defined in sub-para.(3)), fuel, housing costs met by income support or rent for which housing benefit is payable, council tax or water charges while the claimant is on an education, training or other scheme to help "enhance his employment prospects", but not if the payment is a Career Development Loan and the period of education or training in respect of which the loan was paid has ended (sub-paras (1)(c) and (2)); or (iv) paid for living away from home costs which overlap with housing benefit (sub-para.(1)(d)).

A single capital disregard of such payments has also been introduced at the same time. See para.30 of Sch.10. If these payments do count as capital they are only ignored for 52 weeks from the date of receipt.

Paragraph 15

2.743   With effect from October 2, 2006, charitable and voluntary payments and payments from funds derived from a personal injury award to the claimant, made or due to be made at regular intervals, are totally disregarded. Paragraph 15A became unnecessary as a result. Note the payments to which the disregard does not apply in sub-para.(3) and para.39, which makes special provision for the disregard of payments from various trusts as income whether made at regular intervals or not.

This provision assumes that such regular charitable, voluntary or personal injury payments amount to income. Irregular charitable or voluntary payments count as capital (reg.48(9)), but that rule does not apply to payments from the trusts falling within para.39 (reg.48(10)(c)). See reg.41(7) which treats any periodical payments paid under an agreement or court order to a claimant in consequence of personal injury to him, other than payments deemed to be capital under reg.48(4), as income. Since the amendments to reg.48(4) on October 2, 2006, not only capital disregarded under para.12 (trusts of personal injury compensation) but also capital disregarded under paras 44 and 45 (funds held in court derived from compensation for personal injury or the death of a parent) are excepted from the rule in reg.48(4); thus regular payments from such sources will count as income in the normal way.

In the case of personal injury payments, the disregard is applicable whether the payments are made from a trust fund, or under an annuity, or by virtue of an agreement or court order. This thus ameliorates the problem highlighted by *Beattie v Secretary of State for Social Security*, reported as part of *R(IS) 10/01* (see the note to reg.41(2)).

2.744   A monthly NHS pension payable as a result of an injury the claimant had suffered in the course of his employment did not, however, come within sub-para.(5A)(e) (*Malekout v Secretary of State for Work and Pensions* [2010] EWCA Civ 162; [2010] AACR 28). The claimant argued that the pension fell within the words "received by virtue of any agreement" in head (e) because he had a contract of employment with the NHS; the NHS Pension Scheme and the regulations governing it were to be read into his contract of employment; and so he was entitled to the pension by virtue of that agreement. The Court of Appeal, however, disagreed. The word "agreement" in head (e) had to be read in context. One element of that context was that heads (c) and (d) relate to the situation where a claimant has been injured and the consequential damages are put into a trust or used to purchase an annuity. This suggested that head (e) was there to deal with the situation where a similar payment was made, but not via a trust or an annuity. A second piece of context was that the word "agreement" appeared in the phrase "agreement or court order". This indicated an agreement that was reached instead of a court order after the injury had occurred. Thus the proper construction of head (e) was that it was the agreement or court order that had to be "in consequence of any personal injury" and so had to postdate the personal injury. The result was that the claimant's pension could not be disregarded under head (e).

In *Lloyd v London Borough of Lewisham and Secretary of State for Work and*

Pensions [2013] EWCA Civ 923; [2013] AACR 28 the claimant had been assaulted while working as a traffic warden and under the terms of her employment became entitled to an income loss award of £15,000 a year. The Court of Appeal found the reasoning in *Malekout* highly persuasive and concluded that payments made under "pre-injury" agreements (as in Ms Lloyd's case) are not disregarded under para.14(1)(e) of Sch.5 to the Housing Benefit Regulations 2006 (the equivalent provision to head (e)). Paragraph 14(1)(e) only applies to sums paid under agreements (or court orders) which are made *after* the injury occurs.

Note that the payment must derive from an award for personal injury *to the claimant*. Compare the capital disregards of payments for personal injury and of trust funds of personal injury compensation in paras 12 and 12A of Sch.10 which (since October 2, 2006) also apply where the injury was to the claimant's partner (and note the exemptions from the notional capital rules in reg.51(1) and (2) for trusts of personal injury compensation which simply refer to trusts of payments made in consequence of "personal injury"). See *R(IS) 3/03*, discussed in the notes to para.12 of Sch.10 in the 2006 edition of what was then Vol.II of this series, in which the Commissioner considered that, at least on the facts of that case, the reference to "the claimant" in para.12 before the October 2, 2006 amendment did not, by virtue of reg.23(1), include the claimant's partner. See also *CP v SSWP (IS)* [2011] UKUT 157 (AAC) discussed in the notes to paras 12 and 44 of Sch.10. It is not clear why the wording of the income disregard of personal injury payments has not been amended to include payments in respect of an injury to the claimant's partner in line with the change to the capital disregard.

There is no special definition of "charitable" or "voluntary". The words must be applied to whoever makes the payment. In *R. v Doncaster BC ex p. Boulton*, (1993) 25 H.L.R. 195, on the equivalent provision in housing benefit, Laws J holds that the word "charitable" appearing in a statute providing for the distribution and calculation of legal rights must refer only to payments under a charitable trust, rather than referring to acts done for some generous motive. He finds the legislative purpose to be to allow charities to make payments to claimants knowing that they will not simply reduce the amount of benefit. That decision must be highly persuasive, but does not preempt the income support position. 2.745

Laws J also takes a different view from that expressed in the 1992 edition of J. Mesher, *Income-related Benefits: the Legislation*, on the meaning of "voluntary." He holds that it does not refer to a payment which is not compulsory or not legally enforceable, but to a payment for which the person making the payment gets nothing in return. It does not matter that in voluntarily undertaking the payment the person comes under an obligation. The legislative purpose would then be consistent with that for charitable payments. He then had to apply that principle to payments by the National Coal Board in lieu of concessionary coal to a miner's widow. The concessionary coal scheme and the conditions for the payment of cash in lieu, including to widows, were contained in a collective agreement which was incorporated into miners' contracts of employment. Laws J holds that neither he nor the Housing Benefit Review Board had sufficient evidence of the particular contractual arrangements to be able to conclude that under the principle of *Beswick v Beswick* [1968] A.C. 58 the widow could as administratrix of her husband's estate obtain specific performance of the contract to make payments to his widow. However, he was satisfied that the NCB did receive something in return for payments made under the collective agreement, in the promotion of the efficient running of the coal industry. An element of this purpose was seeing that employees, ex-employees and their spouses were properly looked after. Therefore, he finds that the payments were not voluntary and the disregard did not apply. On this point also, the *Boulton* case cannot be conclusive for income support purposes, but is cogently argued and persuasive. But the reasoning was accepted and applied to *R(IS) 4/94* (at para.15), another case about payments in lieu of concessionary coal.

It must though be noted that the Commissioner went too far in saying in *R(IS)*

4/94 (at para.6) that Laws J had stated that legal enforceability was wholly irrelevant. In *LG v SSWP (ESA)* [2019] UKUT 220 (AAC), reported as [2020] AACR 5, Judge Poole QC shows that Laws J had left the door open to legal enforceability being one relevant consideration in deciding whether a payment of income was voluntary. The case concerned a liferent trust created in the claimant's favour under Scots law in her mother's will, a liferent being the right to receive for life the benefits of property or assets, without the right to dispose of the property or assets. The will gave the trustees power to make advancements of capital to the claimant or other beneficiaries. Thus the claimant was entitled to receive any income of the trust funds, and the trustees were under an absolute obligation to pay that income over to her. The fact that the trustees could decide the timing and frequency of the payments of liferent income did not make the trust discretionary. There was no discretion as to the making of those payments at all, in contrast to the position on distributions out of capital.

Applying the test in *Boulton*, the payments of liferent income were not "voluntary". The trustees received something in return for making those payments: the discharge of their legal obligation under the trust to make those payments. Thus in so far as the payments were made or due at regular intervals they could not be disregarded under the old style ESA equivalent of para.15 and were to count in full as income. Nor, in so far as such payments were not made or due at regular intervals, could they be treated as capital under the old style ESA equivalent of reg.48(9), so would also be taken into account as income. By contrast, payments made under the trustees' power to advance capital (i.e. payments beyond the amount of liferent income) were voluntary. Since there was no obligation to make such payments, merely a discretion to do so or not, there could be no discharge received in return for making the payments. Such payments made or due at regular intervals were to be disregarded under the equivalent of para.15 and those not so paid were to be treated as capital under the equivalent of reg.48(9). Presumably, that would apply to payments to be regarded on general principle as income in the hands of the claimant. Payments that would be regarded as capital in her hands (e.g. payments to buy some capital asset), though voluntary, would count as capital, where no disregard is available in Sch.10.

SM v SSWP (ESA) [2020] UKUT 265 (AAC) has followed *LG* in finding that payments made by trustees under discretionary powers were voluntary and so fell within the equivalent IRESA disregard. The decision also held that payments made by trustees of the claimant's parents' wills were not "made by a person for the maintenance of any member of his family or of his former partner or of his children", so as to fall within the exception in the equivalent of para.(3)(a). The payments made by the trustees were not to be regarded as having been made by the parents.

In *CIS 702/1991* an annuity had been purchased for the claimant under the terms of her friend's will. It was argued that the payments under the annuity were "voluntary" as in essence there was a gift of them from the friend under the will. It is held that the disregard in para.15 did not apply since the payments under the annuity were contractual in nature. That was consistent with the decision of Laws J in the *Boulton* case. See also *CIS 492/1992*.

However, the irregular payments received by the claimant in *R(H) 5/05* from a friend and his parents following his inability to work after a stroke were "voluntary". The friend had written a letter which indicated that the payments from her were by way of a loan to be repaid at some unspecified date. But in the Commissioner's view the payments were made without any clear thought about their legal nature. The overall circumstances showed that no legally enforceable rights or obligations were created by the payments to the claimant and that she obtained nothing in return for the payments. The Commissioner commented that "if something like the maintenance of a relationship of affection or of familial duty on the part of the payer or the creation of a merely moral obligation on the part of the payee, dependent on undefined future developments, takes a case out of the category of "voluntary payment" nothing significant would be left". Thus, applying *Boulton*, since the friend had obtained nothing in return for the payments she made to the claimant by way of loan, they were voluntary payments within the meaning of reg.40(6) of the Housing Benefit Regulations (the equivalent of reg.48(9); it was accepted that the payments were not regular and therefore fell to be treated as capital. The payments from the claimant's parents, where the presumption of gift applied in the absence of evidence to the contrary, also fell within reg.40(6).

In *CIS/1813/2007* payments of working tax credit made to the claimant after she had notified the Revenue that she had ceased work and had asked for the payments to stop were "voluntary" payments. This was because once the claimant had made proper disclosure, and even more so where she had asked not to be paid, it was entirely a matter for the Revenue whether to continue payment. For further discussion of *CIS/1813/2007* see the note to reg.23 under "*What constitutes income?*"

2.746

See also *CJSA/2336/2005* discussed in the note to reg.48(9) which held that the loans from the claimant's mother to pay her rent pending the outcome of her benefit claims were voluntary payments. *R(H) 8/08* also concerned loans to pay rent while a claim for housing benefit was being determined. The Commissioner concludes that just because there was no immediate obligation to repay the loans it did not automatically follow that they were properly to be considered income. It was necessary to examine all the facts before reaching such a conclusion in relation to all or some of the loans. He does not refer to *CJSA/2336/2005* or go on to deal with the question of whether the loans were voluntary payments.

If regular payments are not charitable or voluntary or made from funds derived from a personal injury award to the claimant, they count as ordinary income with no disregard.

Paragraph 16

The £10 disregard under sub-para.(a) only applies if the payment is not fully disregarded under para. 8 or 9.

2.747

"War disablement pension" is now defined in reg.2(1) to cover retired pay or pension or allowance payable in respect of disablement under legislation specified in s.639(2) of the Income Tax (Earnings and Pensions) Act 2003. The relevant legislation is set out in Appendix 1 to Ch.28 of the *Decision Makers' Guide*. That legislation applies to disablements caused by service prior to April 6, 2005. See sub-para.(cc) for the schemes in force in relation to service from April 6, 2005 onwards.

The claimant in *CIS 276/1998* was discharged from the RAF on medical grounds and was awarded a service invaliding pension. This pension was exempt from income tax under s.315 of the Income and Corporation Taxes Act 1988 (as referred to in the pre-2009 definition). The Department treated the pension as an occupational pension. But the Commissioner holds that the concepts of occupational pension and war disablement pension were not mutually exclusive. The claimant's pension clearly fell within the pre-2009 definition and so it was also a war disablement pension. He was thus entitled to a £10 disregard under sub-para. (a). The result would be the same under the current definition.

Under sub-para.(b), the definitions of war widows' and widowers' pensions refer to the same legislation as mentioned above, which applies to deaths due to service prior to April 6, 2005.

2.748

On sub-para.(cc), see the note to the definition of "the Armed Forces and Reserve Forces Compensation Scheme" in reg.2(1).

Under sub-para.(f), the extension of the £10 disregard by the amendment from March 2017 to pensions paid by any government to victims of National Socialist persecution, not just by the German or Austrian governments, was a rather belated response to the decision in April 2014 of Judge Williams in *MN v Bury Council and SSWP (HB)* [2014] UKUT 187 (AAC). That case was concerned with para.15(g) of Sch.5 to the Housing Benefit Regulations 2006, the equivalent of para.16(f). The judge held, after a meticulous examination of the issues, that the failure to extend the disregard to people receiving a pension as a victim of such persecution under the Netherlands WUV scheme was discriminatory in breach of art.1 Protocol 1, read with art.14, ECHR, and that such discrimination was manifestly without reasonable justification (see *Humphreys v Her Majesty's Revenue and Customs* [2012] UKSC 18; [2012] 1 W.L.R. 1545, also reported as [2012] AACR 46). Judge Williams directed the Council to treat the claimant in *MN* as if the disregard extended to him, but declined to redraft or read down the terms of para.15(g) so as to remove the discrimination that he had identified. Instead, he referred the matter to the Secretary of State. The Secretary of State has apparently eventually accepted the need for amendment for there to be compliance with the ECHR and has amended all the relevant regulations so as to extend the disregard not merely to the Dutch scheme but to similar pensions paid by any government. The delay in the amendment may not be as serious as it appears because presumably any individual claimant could in relation to periods prior to March 20, 2017 have demanded of the SSWP or of a housing authority that they take the same action as Bury Council were directed to take in *MN* and, if refused, been successful on appeal.

Paragraph 17

2.749   If a person takes out one of these schemes for converting the capital value of the home into income, then so much of the annuity as goes to the mortgage interest is disregarded. The conditions are complicated. Only schemes entered by those aged at least 65 or over pensionable age count, which will exclude most income support claimants.

Paragraph 18

2.750   The inter-relationship of this and the following two paragraphs is now much clearer. The new form of this paragraph, together with the amendment to para.19, was introduced in April 1995, following the decision in *CIS 82/1993*. The Commissioner held that on the previous wording the dividing line between paras 18 and 19 was not whether a payment for accommodation was made under a contractual obligation, but whether or not the payment was made by a person who normally resided with the claimant. Paragraph 19 only applied where the person did not normally reside with the claimant. (See the 1994 Supplement to J. Mesher and P. Wood, *Income-related Benefits: the Legislation* for a summary of the Commissioner's reasoning.) "Normally resides" in para.18 had no special meaning (cf. reg.3) and could include someone who was liable to make payments to the claimant for his occupation of the claimant's home. On the facts, the two "lodgers" who shared the claimant's flat, and each paid him £70 per week, did reside with him. The result was that para.18, not para.19, applied. "Payment" could include part of a payment (see reg.2(1)), so the proportion of each payment that went to meeting the "lodger's" living and accommodation costs could be disregarded under para.18 (*CIS 422/1992* followed). The evidence was that the benefit of the outgoings on the flat was shared more or less equally between the three occupants, so the Commissioner divided the rent, water rates and fuel costs by three and added to this the cost of the services provided by the claimant (e.g. laundry, routine repairs and replacements). This led to a much larger proportion of each payment (£47) being disregarded, than would have been the case if para.19 applied.

The new form of para.18, and the amendment to para.19, have dealt with most of the difficulties exposed in *CIS 82/1993* regarding the inter-relationship of these two paragraphs. Paragraphs 18, 19 and 20 can now all apply where the person is residing with the claimant, so the problem identified in the 1994 edition of J. Mesher and P. Wood, *Income-related Benefits: the Legislation* no longer exists. If para.18 applies, payments by someone who normally resides with the claimant towards their own living and accommodation costs continue to be wholly disregarded. The new wording confirms, as decided in *CIS 422/1992* and *CIS 82/1993*, that it is only payments towards the "lodger's" living expenses that are disregarded (see above). However, para.18 does not apply in the circumstances covered by paras 19 and 20, so that those provisions must be looked at first. The intention is that payments from sub-tenants and licensees should fall within para.19, not para.18 (see below).

If the person making the payment is a non-dependant (see reg.3), note that standard deductions are made from housing costs for the presence of a non-dependant in the household (see para.18 of Sch.3).

Paragraph 19

Whenever the person occupying the claimant's home has a contractual liability   2.751
to make payments (an oral agreement will suffice: *CIS 1501/2002*), this paragraph applies. This is certainly wide enough to cover income from sub-tenants and licensees. People referred to in paras 18 and 20 are no longer excluded, but para.18 does not apply if the circumstances come within para.19 (see above). Although some payments could fall within both para.19 and para.20, it does not matter that there is no provision for choosing between them, for a claimant can simply take advantage of the more generous disregard in para.20 when the conditions of that paragraph are met (*CIS 82/1993*).

In *CIS 82/1993* the Commissioner raised the possibility of whether the disregard in para.30(d) (now para.30(1)(e)) (contribution intended and used towards rent) might apply to payments by a sub-tenant or licensee of a tenant. He accepted the Department's submission that in view of the specific provisions in paras 18, 19 and 20, para.30(d) (now (1)(e)) did not cover such payments, but did consider that legislative clarification of the relationship between para.30 and para.18, 19 and 20 would be useful. It is not clear on the wording of para.30(1)(e) why payments from a sub-tenant or licensee should be excluded, provided that they are intended and used as a contribution towards rent not met by housing benefit. Payments may be disregarded under more than one paragraph of Sch.9, provided this is not specifically proscribed. Paragraph 30(1)(e) does not refer to payments under paras 18, 19 or 20; the only payments that are specifically excluded from para.30 are those covered by para.29. Indeed this was the approach taken by the Commissioner in *CIS 13059/1996*, who declined to follow *CIS 82/1993* on this point. He decides that para.30 can apply at the same time as any of paras 18 to 20 because paras 18 to 20 are not concerned with the same sort of payments as para.30. Paragraph 30 makes provision for disregarding payments designed to help meet certain elements of a claimant's housing expenditure, whereas this is not the specific purpose of paras 18 to 20. See further the notes to para.30.

In April 1994 the wording of para.19 was tightened up so that only one disregard per week applies to payments for each licence or subtenancy. On the pre-April 1994 form a separate disregard could have applied to each payment regardless of the period covered by it (e.g. daily).

A further change was made on April 7, 2008 when the previous two-tier disregard in para.19 (see the 2007 edition of what was then Vol.II of this series) was replaced by a single disregard of £20 per week per sub-tenancy or licence. If the income is less than £20 per week the whole of it will be ignored.

Paragraph 20

This disregard (and not para.18) applies when people provide board and lodging   2.752
accommodation in their home. The post-April 1994 form makes it clear that only one disregard is allowed per week per boarder (see the notes to para.19).

Under reg.37(2)(a) payments received for providing board and lodging accommodation do not count as earnings from self-employment. They count as income under reg.40(4)(a) and thus any appropriate disregard in Sch.9 may apply. In *CIS 521/2002* the claimant was a partner in a board and lodging business run in what was formerly a fully-fledged hotel. As the claimant lived in the hotel (and on the basis that she was to be regarded as living in the whole hotel as her home) para.20 applied. The issue was how her income was to be calculated. The Commissioner holds that the full disregard under sub-para.(b) in respect of each boarder was to be applied to her share of the weekly board and lodging payments. As the Commissioner points out, there is no provision in para.20 for cases of partnerships or for taking into account only a proportion of the total number of persons being provided with board and lodging. The consequence was that the claimant had no income to be taken into account for the purposes of income support. For further discussion of *CIS 521/2002* see the note to reg.37(2). See also the note to para.5 above.

Paragraph 21

2.753   Income in kind is normally disregarded but note the exceptions. Earnings in kind are not earnings (reg.35(2)), but are income. There is some scope for benefit planning here, but note *R(IS) 2/98* in the notes to reg.42(6) (notional earnings). On the first exception in sub-para.(1) and on sub-para.(3) see the notes to reg.21(3).

Sub-paragraph (4), added with effect from October 3, 2005, provides that the disregard of income in kind under para.21 does not apply to payments to a third party which are used by the third party to provide benefits in kind to the claimant. See further the note to reg.42(4).

Paragraph 22

2.754   The general rule is that the actual income derived from capital is disregarded as income. It can go to increase the amount of capital under reg.48(4). But income in the categories specified—premises, business assets and trusts of, and funds held in court that derive from, personal injury compensation (see the note to reg.48(4))—is not disregarded. Where this income is from premises whose capital value is disregarded, any mortgage repayments, water charges and council tax can be set off against it. Mortgage repayments in sub-para.(2)(a) include capital and interest, buildings insurance, and if an endowment policy is a condition of the mortgage, premiums on that policy (*CFC 13/1993*). *CIS 563/1991* deals with the situation where both a disregard in the excepted categories and a disregard under some other paragraph of Sch.10 apply. See the notes to reg.48(4).

Paragraph 24

2.755   In *CIS 627/1995* the Commissioner puts forward the view that since para.24 disregards the *cost* of converting a payment into sterling, it was the *gross* sterling equivalent of the claimant's Canadian pension that had to be taken into account (i.e. the cost of conversion had to be added back to the net amount paid to the claimant). However, it is respectfully suggested that the purpose of para.24 is not to disregard any banking charge or commission *as a cost*, but simply to ensure that the amount of any banking charge or commission is not included in the income taken into account. Although the wording of para.24 could be clearer, it seems unlikely that the Commissioner's interpretation is the intended one. It is also not the approach taken in the *Decision Makers Guide* (see para.28415).

Paragraph 25

2.756   With effect from April 6, 2004 (except in "transitional cases"—see the note to reg.17) amounts for children and young persons have been removed from the income support scheme; financial assistance to help with the cost of bringing up a child or young person is now to be provided through the child tax credit system, see Vol.IV of this series. As a consequence the disregard in para.25 has been amended with effect from April 6, 2004 (except in "transitional cases"—see the note to reg.17) so that payments made to adopters in respect of a child or young person who is a member of the claimant's family are fully disregarded. The same applies to payments from local authorities towards the maintenance of children by subparas (ba)–(d). Subparagraph (e) covers payments by local authorities to special guardians (s.115 of the Adoption and Children Act 2002 amended the Children Act 1989 to introduce from December 30, 2005 a new special guardianship order, which is intended to provide permanence for children for whom adoption is not appropriate; the special guardian has parental responsibility for the child but the child's legal relationship with his birth parents is not severed). For the capital disregard of such payments see para.68A of Sch.10.

The old form of para.25(1) and (2) (see the 2003 edition of this volume), but as amended on October 4, 2004, remains in force for "transitional cases"—see the note to reg.17.

In addition, any payment, other than one that falls under sub-para.(1)(a), that is made in accordance with regulations under ss.2(6)(b), 3 or 4 of the Adoption and Children Act 2002 (see the Adoption Support Services Regulations 2005 (SI 2005/691) and the Adoption Support Services (Local Authorities) (Wales) Regulations 2005 (SI 2005/1512)) that is not in respect of a child or young person who is a member of the claimant's family is ignored in full (sub-para.(1A)). This could apply, for example, to payments made before placing the child with the family. Note that *any* payment made under ss.2(6), 3 or 4 of the Adoption and Children Act 2002 that counts as capital is fully disregarded (see para.68 of Sch.10). But there appears to be no capital disregard for payments from the Scottish scheme referred to in sub-para.(a).

Paragraph 25A

With effect from April 6, 2004 (except in "transitional cases"—see the note to reg.17) amounts for children and young persons have been removed from the income support scheme; financial assistance to help with the cost of bringing up a child or young person is now to be provided through the child tax credit system, see Vol.IV of this series. Income support has in effect become an "adults only" benefit. Accordingly the income (as well as the capital) of a child or young person who is a member of the claimant's family is not aggregated with the claimant's (see the new form of reg.23(2)) and the income support applicable amount no longer includes any personal allowance for a child or young person, the family premium, the disabled child premium or an enhanced disability premium for a child or young person. 2.757

This new disregard is another of the consequential changes that apply from April 6, 2004 (except in "transitional cases"—see the note to reg.17) as a result of the new system. Under this paragraph payments to a boarding school for the maintenance of a child or young person, who is a member of the claimant's family, made by a third party or out of funds provided by a third party are ignored in full (compare the previous form of this provision in reg.44(2) (now revoked, except in "transitional cases"—see the note to reg.17; see the 2003 edition of what was then Vol.II of this series for reg.44 and the notes to that regulation) which applied when the income of a child or young person who was a member of the claimant's family was, subject to the modifications in reg.44, aggregated with the claimant's (see the old form of reg.23 in the 2003 edition)).

Paragraph 26

Payments to foster-parents are disregarded completely. Foster-children are not members of the family (reg.16(4)). 2.758

Paragraph 27

CIS 17020/1996 concerned a local authority scheme for placing disabled people in the carers' own homes. In order to attempt to take advantage of the disregard in para.27 the local authority sent the disabled person a bill for his care and accommodation and then paid the money to the claimant, instead of the disabled person paying the claimant directly. However, the Commissioner decides that para.27 only applied to payments made by a local authority from its own resources. The appropriate disregard was in para.20. He also discusses the meaning of the words "not normally a member of the claimant's household but is temporarily in his care". In his view the word "normally" referred to the period of the membership, not the manner of it. The question of whether the disabled person was temporarily in the claimant's care was one of fact, having regard to the intention of the parties and the length of the stay. 2.759

In *CH/2321/2002* (which concerned para.25 of Sch.4 to the Housing Benefit Regulations, the equivalent of para.27), the Commissioner decided that the disregard could apply to payments of housing benefit paid direct to the claimant in respect of a person in their care. However this was not the policy intention; in addition it was felt that this interpretation created an anomaly since the full disregard under sub-para.(b) would not apply where the housing benefit was paid to the tenant, who then used it to pay for board and lodging; in that case only the more limited disregard in para.20 would apply. Sub-paragraph (b) was therefore amended with effect from April 4, 2005 to exclude payments of housing benefit from the disregard. See also the amendment to para.5.

Paragraph 27A

2.760   Payments under s.73 of the Children and Young People (Scotland) Act 2014 have been available in Scotland since April 2016 to people who have applied or are at least considering applying for a kinship care order for a child who is at risk of going into care or was previously looked after by a local authority. They are disregarded as income other than earnings by para.27A, as earnings from self-employment by reg.37(2)(b) and as capital by para.74 of Sch.10.

Paragraph 28

2.761   This disregard does not apply in trade dispute cases (sub-para.(4)). Outside that special situation payments under the legislation (broadly to prevent children going into care, or to support certain care leavers) can be capital or income (*R(SB) 29/85*). Income is disregarded here and capital under para.17 of Sch.10.

The disregard under para.28 has been extended with effect from April 7, 2008 so that it also applies where a person who was formerly in the care of the claimant continues to live with the claimant after he reaches 18 and pays the money to the claimant.

Paragraph 29

2.762   From October 1995 to April 5, 2018 the proceeds of mortgage protection policies were disregarded in so far as they did not exceed the aggregate of payments in respect of any interest on a loan that qualified under paras 15 or 16 of Sch.3 as then in force that was not met by income support, capital repayments due on a qualifying loan and any premiums due on the policy or on a building insurance policy. Any excess counted as income (*KS v SSWP* [2009] UKUT 202 (AAC)). If the loan protected by the policy was not a qualifying loan, para.30 could apply, as also where the policy was a general income protection policy (*R(IS) 13/01*). See the notes in earlier editions of what was then Vol.II of this series for further details of the pre-2018 form of para.29.

With effect from April 6, 2018, the position under reg.29 is simpler. The link is now to loans that qualify under Part 1 of Sch.1 to the Loans for Mortgage Interest Regulations 2017 for the offer of a loan to cover the interest payable (see Vol.II of this series, *Universal Credit, State Pension Credit and the Social Fund*). The conditions for a loan to qualify are much the same as previously under Sch.3 to the Income Support Regulations. Only loans secured on the home qualify. Then any payments from the policy are disregarded but only to the extent that they are used to meet the repayments of interest on the qualifying loan. Any excess counts as income unless falling within para.30. In particular, payments intended and used to cover repayments of capital on a qualifying loan are disregarded under para.30(1)(c). Paragraph 30 may also apply if the loan does not qualify under the 2017 Regulations.

Paragraph 30

2.763   Payments other than those disregarded under para.29 or, from June 1, 1998, para.30ZA, earmarked for these elements of housing expenditure, are ignored (sub-para.(1)). There has been some restructuring with effect from April 6, 2018 to take account of the introduction of the Loans for Mortgage Interest Regulations 2017. Note that payments from liable relatives are dealt with in reg.54.

If payments are made for purposes within sub-para.(1)(a) to (e), it should be assumed, in the absence of clear evidence to the contrary, that they are made out of income "intended to be used" for those purposes (*R(IS) 13/01*). See also *CIS 13059/1996* below.

However, *CIS 4255/2002* holds that the disregard under sub-para.(1) does not extend to payments from social security benefits. Benefits such as incapacity benefit, child benefit and invalid care allowance (now carer's allowance) were no more closely connected with or referable to housing costs than to a claimant's expenses generally and thus could not be said to be "intended to be used . . . as a contribution towards" the expenses in sub-para.(1). The necessary connection that had been found to exist in *CIS 13059/1996* (see below) and in *R(IS) 13/01* (because in that case the income protection policy had been taken out a few days after the mortgage from which it could be inferred that there was an intention that income from the policy would be used, if necessary, to pay the mortgage) was not present. A similar approach was taken in *CIS 3911/1998* which held that payments from an occupational pension scheme could not be disregarded under sub-para.(1).

From October 1995 to April 5, 2018, the disregard extended to payments intended and used towards meeting payments on *any* loan secured on the home that was not a qualifying loan under Sch.3 (e.g. a loan for business purposes) (head (a)); any housing cost that was eligible under Sch.3 to the extent that it was not met by income support (head (b)); capital repayments on a qualifying loan (head c)), and premiums on any buildings insurance policy and (since December 1995) any policy taken out to insure against the risk of not being able to make the payments in heads (a)–(c) (head (d)).

2.764

The changes with effect from April 6, 2018, by inserting new forms of sub-para. (1)(a)–(c), maintain the substance of the previous provisions. Head (a) covers payments intended and used for a contribution towards meeting payments on any loan secured on the home that does not qualify under the 2017 Regulations. Head (b) covers payments towards meeting any charge under para.17 of Sch.3 or any interest payments on a 2017 Regulations qualifying loan to the extent that the charge is not met under the Income Support Regulations or the interest covered by a loan under the 2017 Regulations. Head (c) covers payments towards meeting capital repayments on a qualifying loan. Heads (d) and (e) are unaffected.

CIS 13059/1996 decides (contrary to the view taken in *CIS 82/1993*, see the note to para.19) that sub-para.(1) can apply to payments made by a tenant (or licensee) of the claimant who lives in her home. The claimant's mortgage interest was met by income support but only to the extent of the interest on £125,000 (there was about £160,000 owing on her mortgage). There were two tenants living in her flat. The AO decided that the rent received from the tenants had to be taken into account in calculating the claimant's income support, subject only to the disregard in para.19. However, the Commissioner concludes that para.30 could apply at the same time as para.19 (or paras 18 or 20) because these paragraphs were not concerned with the same sort of payments. Paragraphs 18 to 20 were not intended to make specific provision for disregarding payments designed to help meet a claimant's housing costs, whereas para.30 was so intended. Moreover, there was no reason why para.30 should not apply to payments made under a contractual liability. The Commissioner also deals with the meaning of the phrase "payment . . . which is intended to be used and is used as a contribution towards" in para.(1). He rejects the argument that it was only necessary to look at the intention of the claimant. But he holds that it was possible to infer from a tenancy agreement that the tenant intended the landlord to use the rent, so far as necessary, to pay the landlord's own liabilities on the property so that the tenant could continue to occupy it. "Intended" in para.(1) was used in the sense of "designed" or "calculated" and it was necessary to look at the general context in which payments were made in order to ascertain the intention of the parties. The Commissioner also confirms that there was no reason why part of a payment could not be disregarded under para.30 in addition to part being disregarded under any of paras 18–20. (See reg.2(1): "payment" includes part of a payment). Thus in addition to the para.19 disregard, a further amount to cover the claimant's mortgage interest that was not met under paras 7 and 8 of Sch.3 as then in force could be disregarded from the rent payments.

The same Commissioner again considered the operation of the para.30 disregard in *R(IS) 13/01*. The claimant had an income protection policy, not a mortgage protection policy, so para.29 did not apply. The Commissioner holds that the difference between the amount the claimant was "due to pay" his building society (rather than

2.765

the amount actually debited from his mortgage account—see *CIS 632/1992* upheld by the Court of Appeal in *Brain v Chief Adjudication Officer*, December 2, 1993) and the amount of mortgage interest met by income support, to the extent that the claimant actually made up that difference, could be deducted from the income he received under the income protection policy under heads (a) and (b) of sub-para.(1). In addition, head (c) covered the premiums on his endowment policy because the premiums were "due on a loan attributable to the payment of capital" (following *CIS 642/1992* rather than the approach he had taken in *CIS 13059/1996*). The claimant's building insurance premiums also fell within head (d)(ii). However, the premiums on the income protection policy itself could not be disregarded under para.30. Head (d)(i) did not apply as the policy had not been *taken out* to insure against the risk of being unable to maintain his mortgage payments.

Again, sub-para.(2) seems merely declaratory as the disregard under para.(1) only applies to elements of housing expenditure that are not met by income support.

Paragraph 30ZA

2.766   This provides for a disregard of payments received under so-called "creditor insurance" policies. It will apply to payments received under an insurance policy to cover, for example, hire-purchase payments or loan or similar payments. But any excess above the amount of the payment due, plus any premiums on the policy concerned, counts as income.

Paragraph 30A

2.767   Where a claimant is in a care home, Abbeyfield Home or independent hospital (for the definitions of these terms see reg.2(1)) and the accommodation has not been arranged by a local authority, payments towards the cost of the home's fees are disregarded. The amount ignored is the difference between the claimant's applicable amount and the weekly charge for the accommodation. However, if the payment is a charitable or voluntary payment (which may well be the case), it is fully disregarded under para.15 (see the notes to para.15 for what counts as a charitable or voluntary payment).

Paragraph 31A

2.768   This disregard was introduced in April 2013 on the abolition of social fund community care and crisis loans, which had been disregarded as income under para.31. In replacement, local authorities in England and the devolved administrations in Wales and Scotland were able, at their discretion, to set up local schemes for financial and other assistance. Paragraph 31A and the definition of "local welfare provision" in reg.2(1) were intended to ensure the disregard as income of payments under such a scheme (income in kind is already disregarded under para.21). But the definition is capable of covering a wider variety of payments from those authorities, providing that they are "occasional" and (a) to meet an immediate short-term need arising out of an exceptional event or circumstances, to avoid a risk to an individual's welfare, or (b) to aid the provision of a settled home to certain categories. For instance, it is strongly arguable that NHS Test and Trace payments (see the beginning of the notes to Sch.9) fall within para.31A. That is the view taken in Memo DMG 18/20. The Guidance to English local authorities on the administration of the Covid Winter Grant scheme December 2020, para.12, specifically says that outlay has been classified as local welfare provision. That scheme has been continued until September 2021 under the name of the Local Support Grant.

Paragraph 34

2.769   This is the compensation for the automatic counting of the "relevant sum" as part of the family's income under s.126(5)(b) of the Contributions and Benefits Act. The relevant sum was increased in April 2020 to £41.00, from £40.50, where it had stood since April 2015.

Paragraph 35

2.770   See notes to reg.32(5).

Paragraph 37
See notes to reg.32(5).   2.771

Paragraph 39
The disregard now extends to payments to haemophiliacs from the three trusts,   2.772
and to non-haemophiliacs from the Fund, the Eileen Trust, MFET Limited, the
Skipton Fund, the Caxton Foundation, the Scottish Infected Blood Support Scheme
and other contaminated blood schemes, the London Emergencies Trust and the We
Love Manchester Emergency Fund, the National Emergencies Trust, funds giving
rise to a Grenfell Tower payment and the Independent Living Fund, and to distributions of income payments to the close family, or to a slightly wider class for the
two years following such a person's death. Such distribution of income payments
are also ignored if they derive from a payment from the London Bombings Relief
Charitable Fund (it is understood that no disregard under sub-para.(1) is considered necessary because these funds only provide lump sum payments).
   Sub-paragraphs (4)(b)(i) and (ii) and (5)(b)(i) and (ii) include references to step-
parents. Note that from December 5, 2005, references to "step" relationships and
"in laws" are to be read as including relationships arising through civil partnership
in any provision to which s.246 of the Civil Partnership Act 2004 applies. Section
246 is applied to sub-paras (4)(b)(i) and (ii) and (5)(b)(i) and (ii) by art.3 of and
para.22 of the Schedule to the Civil Partnership Act 2004 (Relationships Arising
Through Civil Partnership) Order 2005 (SI 2005/3137).

Paragraph 46
The reference to s.13A of the Local Government Act 1992 (inserted on April 2,   2.773
2013) should cover any payment (probably only arising from transitional reliefs)
under local council tax reduction schemes which have replaced council tax benefit
from April 2013.

Paragraph 51
Payments to disabled persons to assist them to obtain or retain employment   2.774
under the Disabled Persons (Employment) Act 1994 are ignored. The previous
form of this paragraph also referred to payments for this purpose under s.2 of the
Employment and Training Act 1973. However from April 1, 2004 a single disregard
has been introduced in relation to payments under all s.2 schemes. See para.13.

Paragraph 53
Increases for dependants who are not residing with the claimant paid with certain   2.775
benefits (e.g. retirement pension) or war pensions are disregarded. Such increases
are only paid if the claimant is contributing at least that amount to the maintenance
of the dependant.

Paragraphs 54–56
See para.47. These new disregards arose from the transfer of responsibility for   2.776
the payment of most pre-1973 war widows' (and widowers') pensions from the
Ministry of Defence to the DSS from October 1994. From December 5, 2005 these
paragraphs also apply to pensions payable under the relevant provisions to surviving
civil partners.

Paragraph 58
Payments by local authorities in lieu of community care services are to be ignored.   2.777
   In *CIS/1068/2006* the claimant's wife paid the community care payments that
she received to her husband in consideration of the care services he provided to
her. The Commissioner held that these payments counted as "earnings" because
the claimant had been engaged by his wife to provide care services for reward.
They therefore fell to be taken into account in calculating his income support.
The Commissioner rejected the claimant's argument that the payments should be

disregarded under para.58. In his view the policy that underlaid the exemption for direct payments in para.58 was that the direct payments were intended to be spent in purchasing from a third party care services which would otherwise have had to be provided by the local authority. Thus the payments *to the claimant's wife* were disregarded under para.58 but not to take her payments *to the claimant* into account would have been to put them in a more advantageous position than they would have been had she paid a third party for care services.

The claimant's appeal to the Court of Appeal against this decision was dismissed (*Casewell v SSWP* [2008] EWCA Civ 524, reported as *R(IS) 7/08*). The claimant contended that s.136 of the Contributions and Benefits Act requires that payments made to a member of the family are counted when they come into the family, and if at that point they are disregarded, they cannot be counted again if they are transferred from one member of the family to another. However the Court agreed with the Commissioner that the payments to the claimant by his wife were earnings in respect of the care he provided and in the claimant's hands they became his income under s.136(1). It should be noted that the payments to the claimant's wife in this case were made on the basis that she was instructed to pay the claimant the appropriate sum each week against a payslip. There was therefore a specific obligation for the claimant's wife to deal with the payments in a particular way, which had the result that the money paid to her husband was treated as earnings. Thus this was a somewhat different situation from the more usual informal transfer of resources between family members.

Modification of para.58

2.778   With effect from April 1, 2014, the disregard in para.58 is modified by art.2 of, and para.1 of the Schedule to, the Social Care (Self-directed Support) (Scotland) Act 2013 (Consequential Modifications and Savings) Order 2014 (SI 2014/513) so that the words "as a direct payment as defined in section 4(2) of the Social Care (Self-directed Support) (Scotland) Act 2013" are substituted for the words "under section 12B of the Social Work (Scotland) 1968". However, under art.3 of the Order, this modification does not apply if a payment is made under s.12B of the 1968 Act on or after April 1, 2014.

Paragraph 61

2.779   Any grant or covenant income, student loan or contribution (for definitions see reg.61) left over at the end of a person's course , when the person is no longer within the reg.61 meaning of "student", is ignored. See regs 29(2B), 32(6A) and 40(3B) for the position where part or all of a student's grant is repayable because they have left or been dismissed from their course before it finishes.

Paragraph 64

2.780   (*Note*: this is a new para.64; the previous para.64 is now para.66).

This disregards any payment to a person, who is on, or has left, the "self-employment route" (defined in reg.2(1)), from his "special account" (defined in reg.39A) if it is: (i) to meet expenses wholly and necessarily incurred in his business while on the self-employment route; or (ii) used, or intended to be used, to make repayments on a loan taken out for the purposes of that business. For the treatment of a person's income from "test-trading" while on the self-employment route, see regs 39A to 39D and the note to reg.102C of the JSA Regulations 1996.

See also the disregard in para.13.

Paragraph 66

2.781   This is the renumbered para.64. See the note to reg.42(4A).

Paragraph 69

2.782   A "sports award" (defined in reg.2(1)) is ignored, except to the extent that it has been made for any of the items listed in sub-para.(2) (note the definitions in sub-para.(3)). For the disregard where the sports award counts as capital see para.56 of Sch.10 but note that under para.56 the disregard only applies for 26 weeks from the date of receipt. See also reg.6(1)(m) under which a person will be deemed not to be in remunerative work while engaged in activity for which the only payment he is, or will be, receiving is a sports award and reg.37(2)(c) which ensures that the award is not treated as self-employed earnings.

Paragraphs 71 and 72
See the note to reg.42(5A).   2.783

Paragraph 73
The disregard under this paragraph was originally introduced as part of the child   2.784
support reforms under the Child Support, Pensions and Social Security Act 2000.
It replaced the child maintenance bonus scheme under s.10 of the Child Support
Act 1995 which allowed income support and income-based JSA claimants receiving
child maintenance to build up a "child maintenance bonus" (see the 2008/2009
edition of what was then Vol.II of this series for s.10 and the Social Security (Child
Maintenance Bonus) Regulations 1996 (SI 1996/3195)). Section 23 of the Child
Support, Pensions and Social Security Act 2000 which repealed s.10 was brought
fully into force by the Child Support, Pensions and Social Security Act 2000
(Commencement No.14) Order 2008 (SI 2008/2545) (c.109) art.4, with effect
from October 27, 2008. The result was that from October 27, 2008 it was no longer
possible for any person to accrue a child maintenance bonus.
The disregard was initially a partial disregard but from April 12, 2010 any
payment of child maintenance from a liable relative is fully disregarded as income.
For the definition of "child maintenance" see sub-para.(2) and note also the definition of "liable relative" for the purposes of para.73. The special rules for the treatment of child maintenance in Ch.VII of these Regulations have also been revoked
from April 12, 2010. It would seem that a lump sum payment of child maintenance
other than arrears of income payments will count as capital.

Paragraph 74
This provides for the whole of a claimant's income to be disregarded during any   2.785
"mortgage run-on" period. See the notes to reg.6(5)–(8) as to when this applies
(note that from December 17, 2007 it was extended so that it now applies to all
housing costs that can be met by income support). However, since the coming into
force of the Loans for Mortgage Interest Regulations 2017 on April 6, 2018 income
support housing costs have no longer covered interest on loans (so the name should
now more properly be a "housing costs run-on"). A similar provision for run-on is
provided in those regulations, but the para.74 disregard has remained limited to
situations where the claimant had income support, old style JSA or old style ESA
housing costs in their applicable amount. See also the disregards in para.15C of
Sch.8 and para.62 of Sch.10 and the note to para.15C.

Paragraph 75
Discretionary housing payments can be made by a local authority to claimants   2.786
who need extra help with the cost of their housing liability. They replaced the previous system of exceptional circumstances payments and exceptional hardship payments with effect from July 2, 2001. Any such payments are ignored as income; for
the capital disregard see para.7 of Sch.10.

Paragraph 76
From April 1, 2003 the responsibility for meeting the cost of housing-related   2.787
services for people in supported accommodation passed to local authorities
under the "Supporting People" programme (between April 2000 and April 2003
under the "Transitional Housing Benefit Scheme" certain service charges for claimants in supported accommodation had been met by housing benefit (see Sch.1B to
the Housing Benefit Regulations which ceased to have effect on April 7, 2003)).

This paragraph provides for payments under this programme to be ignored. The previous form of the disregard (see the 2003 edition of this volume) referred to payments from a local authority in respect of "welfare services" within the meaning of s.93(1) or (2) of the Local Government Act 2000 (in Scotland "housing support services" under s.91(1) of the Housing (Scotland) Act 2001). However the form in force from October 1, 2003 has been reworded to remove those legislative references in order to ensure that the disregard covers all payments made under the Supporting People programme.

For the indefinite capital disregard of such payments see para.66 of Sch.10.

Paragraph 79

2.788　　This provides for an income disregard of payments under s.49 of the Children and Families Act 2014. Under s.49, parents of a child/young person with an education, health and care plan ("an EHC plan") will have the option of a personal budget, through which they will have control over how some of the provision in the EHC plan will be delivered. EHC plans will gradually replace special educational needs statements and learning disability assessments in England. For the capital disregard of payments under s.49, see para.71 of Sch.10.

Paragraph 80

2.789　　The initial one-off lump sum payment of the new (from April 2017) and controversial bereavement support payment and any arrears of monthly payments included in the first monthly payment are disregarded as capital under paras 7(1) and 72 of Sch.10 for 52 weeks from the date of receipt. Paragraph 80 disregards other monthly payments as income other than earnings for so long as they continue. In so far as arrears retain their character as income rather than capital (see the notes to para.7 of Sch.10) they would be disregarded under para.80.

Paragraph 82

2.790　　Scottish early years assistance, constituted initially (from December 10, 2018) by best start grants replacing the Sure Start Maternity grants still available to those living in England and Wales, is to be disregarded as income. Since such assistance will take the form of lump sum payments, it would probably not constitute income in any event. It is disregarded as capital by para.75 of Sch.10.

Paragraph 83

2.791　　Funeral expense assistance, disregarded as income by this paragraph, is implemented by the Funeral Expense Assistance (Scotland) Regulations 2019 (SSI 2019/292) (see Vol.IV of this series). See para.76 of Sch.10 for the disregard as capital.

Paragraph 84

2.792　　The regulations referred to in para.84 are the Scottish Child Payment Regulations 2020 (SSI 2020/351) (see Vol.IV of this series), which provide for a payment of £10 per week (paid four-weekly in arrears) to claimants in receipt of a UK income-related benefit who are responsible for a child under the age of six. Applications and initial payments could not have effect before mid-February 2021. See para.7(1)(a) of Sch.10 for the disregard as capital of payments of arrears.

Paragraph 85

2.793　　The regulations referred to in para.85 have not yet been made. The introduction of a scheme was originally planned for 2020, providing for payments to be made to claimants who have appealed against or requested redetermination of a determination to reduce or stop paying another form of assistance (initially in relation to the new child disability payments to replace DLA for the under-18s) under the 2018 Act. The plans were deferred until summer 2021 for a pilot of the child disability payment and the autumn for a full roll-out. It appears that the pilot scheme will be implemented in July 2021 and presumably regulations will be made to set up the short-term assistance scheme at the same time. See para.7(1)(a) of Sch.10 for the disregard as capital of payments of arrears.

SCHEDULE 10   **Regulation 46(2)**

CAPITAL TO BE DISREGARDED

1.—The dwelling occupied as the home but, notwithstanding regulation 23 (calculation of income and capital of members of claimant's family and of a polygamous marriage), only one dwelling shall be disregarded under this paragraph.   **2.794**

[⁹⁶ **1A.**—Any payment in respect of any travel or other expenses incurred, or to be incurred, by the claimant in respect of that claimant's participation in [¹⁰⁰ a scheme prescribed in regulation 3 of the Jobseeker's Allowance (Schemes for Assisting Persons to Obtain Employment) Regulations 2013] or the Mandatory Work Activity Scheme, but only for 52 weeks beginning with the date of receipt of the payment.]

2.—Any premises acquired for occupation by the claimant which he intends to occupy [⁴as his home] within 26 weeks of the date of acquisition or such longer period as is reasonable in the circumstances to enable the claimant to obtain possession and commence occupation of the premises.

3.—Any sum directly attributable to the proceeds of sale of any premises formerly occupied by the claimant as his home which is to be used for the purchase of other premises intended for such occupation within 26 weeks of the date of sale or such longer period as is reasonable in the circumstances to enable the claimant to complete the purchase.

4.—Any premises occupied in whole or in part by—
  (a) a partner or relative of [¹²a single claimant or any member of] the family [⁴as his home] where that person [⁹² has attained the qualifying age for state pension credit] or is incapacitated;
  (b) the former partner of a claimant [² . . .] as his home; but this provision shall not apply where the former partner is a person from whom the claimant is estranged or divorced [⁷¹ or with whom he formed a civil partnership that has been dissolved].

[²⁶**5.**—Any future interest in property of any kind, other than land or premises in respect of which the claimant has granted a subsisting lease or tenancy, including sub-leases or sub-tenancies.]

6.—[¹²(1)] The assets of any business owned in whole or in part by the claimant and for the purposes of which he is engaged as a self-employed earner or, if he has ceased to be so engaged, for such period as may be reasonable in the circumstances to allow for disposal of any such asset.

[¹²(2) The assets of any business owned in whole or in part by the claimant where—
  (a) he is not engaged as a self-employed earner in that business by reason of some disease or bodily or mental disablement; but
  (b) he intends to become engaged (or, as the case may be, re-engaged) as a self-employed earner in that business as soon as he recovers or is able to become engaged, or re-engaged, in that business;
for a period of 26 weeks from the date on which the claim for income support is made, or is treated as made, or, if it is unreasonable to expect him to become engaged or re-engaged in that business within that period for such longer period as is reasonable in the circumstances to enable him to become so engaged or re-engaged.]

[³³(3) In the case of a person who is receiving assistance under [⁴⁴ the self-employment route], the assets acquired by that person for the purpose of establishing or carrying on the commercial activity in respect of which such assistance is being received.

(4) In the case of a person who has ceased carrying on the commercial activity in respect of which assistance was received as specified in sub-paragraph (3), the assets relating to that activity for such period as may be reasonable in the circumstances to allow for disposal of any such asset.]

7.—[⁵⁵—(1) Subject to sub-paragraph (2),] any arrears of, or any concessionary payment made to compensate for arrears due to the non-payment of—
  (a) any payment specified in paragraph [¹²⁰6, 8, [¹²¹9, 76A, 84 or 85] of Schedule 9] (other income to be disregarded);
  [⁸² (b) an income-related benefit[⁸⁷, an income-related employment and support allowance] or an income-based jobseeker's allowance, child tax credit or working tax credit under Part 1 of the Tax Credits Act 2002;]

[²⁹(c) [⁶⁸ . . .]]
[⁵⁰(d) any discretionary housing payment paid pursuant to regulation 2(1) of the Discretionary Financial Assistance Regulations 2001] [¹⁰³ ; or
   (e) universal credit]
[¹⁰⁸(f) bereavement support payment under section 30 of the Pensions Act 2014,]
[¹¹⁸(g) maternity allowance under section 35 of the Contributions and Benefits Act (state maternity allowance for employed or self-employed earner).]
but only for a period of 52 weeks from the date of the receipt of the arrears or of the concessionary payment.

[⁵⁵(2) In a case where the total of any arrears and, if appropriate, any concessionary payment referred to in sub-paragraph (1) relating to any one of the specified payments, benefits or allowances amounts to £5,000 or more (referred to in this sub-paragraph and in sub-paragraph (3) as the "relevant sum") and is—
[¹¹⁵(a) paid in order to rectify, or to compensate for—
       (i) an official error as defined in regulation 1(2) of the Social Security and Child Support (Decisions and Appeals) Regulations 1999, or
      (ii) an error on a point of law; and]
   (b) received by the claimant in full on or after 14th October 2001,
sub-paragraph (1) shall have effect in relation to such arrears or concessionary payment either for a period of 52 weeks from the date of receipt, or, if the relevant sum is received in its entirety during the award of income support, for the remainder of that award if that is a longer period.

(3) For the purposes of sub-paragraph (2), "the award of income support" means—
   (a) the award [¹⁰³ of any of] income support[⁸⁷, an income-related employment and support allowance] [¹⁰³ , an income-based jobseeker's allowance or universal credit] in which the relevant sum (or first part thereof where it is paid in more than one instalment) is received, and
   (b) where that award is followed by one or more further awards which in each case may be [¹⁰³ any] of income support[⁸⁷, an income-related employment and support allowance] [¹⁰³ , an income-based jobseeker's allowance or universal credit] and which, or each of which, begins immediately after the end of the previous award, such further awards until the end of the last such award, provided that for any such further awards the claimant—
       (i) is the person who received the relevant sum, or
      (ii) is the partner of the person who received the relevant sum, or was that person's partner at the date of his death, or
     (iii) in the case of a joint-claim jobseeker's allowance, is a joint-claim couple either member or both members of which received the relevant sum] [¹⁰³ , or
      (iv) in a case where universal credit is awarded to the claimant and another person as joint claimants, either the claimant or the other person, or both of them, received the relevant sum].

8.—Any sum—
   (a) paid to the claimant in consequence of damage to, or loss of the home or any personal possession and intended for its repair or replacement; or
   (b) acquired by the claimant (whether as a loan or otherwise) on the express condition that it is to be used for effecting essential repairs or improvements to the home,
and which is to be used for the intended purpose, for a period of 26 weeks from the date on which it was so paid or acquired or such longer period as is reasonable in the circumstances to enable the claimant to effect the repairs, replacement or improvements.

9.—Any sum—
   (a) deposited with a housing association as defined in section 189(1) of the Housing Act 1985 or section 338(1) of the Housing (Scotland) Act 1987 as a condition of occupying the home;
   (b) which was so deposited and which is to be used for the purchase of another home, for the period of 26 weeks of such longer period as is reasonable in the circumstances to complete the purchase.

10.—Any personal possessions except those which had or have been acquired by the claimant with the intention of reducing his capital in order to secure entitlement to [⁸³ . . .] income support or to increase the amount of that benefit.

11.—The value of the right to receive any income under an annuity and the surrender value (if any) of such an annuity.

[¹²**12.**—Where the funds of a trust are derived from a payment made in consequence of any personal injury to the claimant [⁷⁶ or the claimant's partner], the value of the trust fund and the value of the right to receive any payment under that trust.]

[[77]12A.— (1) Any payment made to the claimant or the claimant's partner in consequence of any personal injury to the claimant or, as the case may be, the claimant's partner.

(2) But sub-paragraph (1)—

   (a) applies only for the period of 52 weeks beginning with the day on which the claimant first receives any payment in consequence of that personal injury;
   (b) does not apply to any subsequent payment made to him in consequence of that injury (whether it is made by the same person or another);
   (c) ceases to apply to the payment or any part of the payment from the day on which the claimant no longer possesses it;
   (d) does not apply to any payment from a trust where the funds of the trust are derived from a payment made in consequence of any personal injury to the claimant.

(3) For the purposes of sub-paragraph (2)(c), the circumstances in which a claimant no longer possesses a payment or a part of it include where the claimant has used a payment or part of it to purchase an asset.

(4) References in sub-paragraphs (2) and (3) to the claimant are to be construed as including references to his partner (where applicable).]

13.—The value of the right to receive any income under a life interest or from a liferent.

14.—The value of the right to receive any income which is disregarded under paragraph 11 of Schedule 8 or paragraph 23 of Schedule 9 (earnings or other income to be disregarded).

15.—The surrender value of any policy of life insurance.

16.—Where any payment of capital falls to be made by instalments, the value of the right to receive any outstanding instalments.

[[84] **17.**—(1) Any payment made by a local authority in accordance with—

   (a) section 17, 23B, 23C or 24A of the Children Act 1989,
   (b) section 12 of the Social Work (Scotland) Act 1968, or
   (c) section [[106] 26A,] 29 or 30 of the Children (Scotland) Act [[112]1995, or
   (d) the following sections of the Social Services and Well-being (Wales) Act 2014—
      (aa) section 37 or 38, but excluding any direct payment made in accordance with regulations made under section 51 of that Act; or
      (bb) section 109, 110, 114 or 115.]

(2) Any payment (or part of a payment) made by a local authority in accordance with section 23C of the Children Act 1989 [[106] or section 26A or 29 of the Children (Scotland) Act 1995 (local authorities' duty to promote welfare of children, duty to provide continuing care and provision of advice and assistance for certain young persons)] to a person ("A") which A passes on to the claimant.

(3) Sub-paragraphs (1) and (2) are subject to the following provisions.

(4) Neither of those sub-paragraphs applies where the claimant is a person—

   (a) to whom section 126 of the Contributions and Benefits Act (trade disputes) applies, or
   (b) in respect of whom section 124(1) of the Contributions and Benefits Act (conditions of entitlement to income support) has effect as modified by section 127 of that Act (effect of return to work).

(5) Sub-paragraph (2) applies only where A—

   (a) was formerly in the claimant's care, and
   [[106](b) is aged 18 or over or, in the case of a payment or part of a payment made in accordance with section 26A of the Children (Scotland) Act 1995, aged 16 or over, and]
   (c) continues to live with the claimant.]

[[17]**18.**—Any social fund payment made pursuant to [[90] Part 8 of the Contributions and Benefits Act].]

[[101]**18A.**—Any local welfare provision.]

19.—Any refund of tax which fell to be deducted under [[90]section 369 of the Income and Corporation Taxes Act 1988 (mortgage interest payable under deduction of tax)] on a payment of relevant loan interest for the purpose of acquiring an interest in the home or carrying out repairs or improvements in the home.

20.—Any capital which under [[11]regulation 41 [[61] . . .] or 66A (capital treated as income [[61] . . .] or treatment of student loans)] is to be treated as income.

21.—Where a payment of capital is made in a currency other than sterling, any banking charge or commission payable in converting that payment into sterling.

[[1]**22.**—[[14](1) Any payment made under [[94] or by] the Macfarlane Trust, the Macfarlane (Special Payments) Trust, the Macfarlane (Special Payments) (No.2) Trust ("the Trusts"), [[19]the Fund][[23], the Eileen Trust][[93], MFET Limited][[63], the Independent Living [[88] Fund (2006)][[72], the Skipton Fund[[98], the Caxton Foundation][[107], the Scottish Infected Blood Support Scheme][[111], an approved blood scheme][[109], the London Emergencies Trust, the

We Love Manchester Emergency Fund][[119], the National Emergencies Trust] or the London Bombings Relief Charitable Fund]].

[[119](1A) Any Grenfell Tower payment or any payment made by the Child Migrants Trust (registered charity number 1171479) under the scheme for former British child migrants.]

(2) Any payment by or on behalf of a person who is suffering or who suffered from hae-mophilia [[19]or who is or was a qualifying person], which derives from a payment made under [[94] or by] any of the Trusts to which sub-paragraph (1) refers[[119], or from a Grenfell Tower payment,] and which is made to or for the benefit of—

- (a) that person's partner or former partner from whom he is not, or where that person has died was not, estranged or divorced [[71] or with whom he has formed a civil partnership that has not been dissolved or, where that person has died, had not been dissolved at the time of that person's death];
- (b) any child who is a member of that person's family or who was such a member and who is a member of the claimant's family; or
- (c) any young person who is a member of that person's family or who was such a member and who is a member of the claimant's family.

(3) Any payment by or on behalf of the partner or former partner of a person who is suffering or who suffered from haemophilia [[19]or who is or was a qualifying person] provided that the partner or former partner and that person are not, or if either of them has died were not, estranged or divorced [[71] or, where the partner or former partner and that person have formed a civil partnership, the civil partnership has not been dissolved or, if either of them has died, had not been dissolved at the time of the death], which derives from a payment made under [[94] or by] any of the Trusts to which sub-paragraph (1) refers[[119], or from a Grenfell Tower payment,] and which is made to or for the benefit of—

- (a) the person who is suffering from haemophilia [[19]or who is a qualifying person];
- (b) any child who is a member of that person's family or who was such a member and who is a member of the claimant's family; or
- (c) any young person who is a member of that person's family or who was such a member and who is a member of the claimant's family.

(4) Any payment by a person who is suffering from haemophilia [[19]or who is a qualify-ing person], which derives from a payment under [[94]or by] any of the Trusts to which sub-paragraph (1) refers, [[119]or from a Grenfell Tower payment,] where—

- (a) that person has no partner or former partner from whom he is not estranged or divorced [[71]or with whom he has formed a civil partnership that has not been dissolved], nor any child or young person who is or had been a member of that person's family; and
- (b) the payment is made either—
  - (i) to that person's parent or step-parent, or
  - (ii) where that person at the relevant date was a child, a young person or a [[43] full-time student] who had not completed his full-time education and had no parent or step-parent, to his guardian,

but only for a period of two years from the date of the payment until the end of two years from that person's death.

(5) Any payment out of the estate of a person who suffered from haemophilia [[19]or who was a qualifying person], which derives from a payment under [[94] or by] any of the Trusts to which sub-paragraph (1) refers, [[119]or from a Grenfell Tower payment,] where—

- (a) that person at the date of his death (the relevant date) had no partner or former partner from whom he was not estranged or divorced [[71] or with whom he had formed a civil partnership that had not been dissolved], nor any child or young person who was or had been a member of his family; and
- (b) the payment is made either—
  - (i) to that person's parent or step-parent, or
  - (ii) where that person at the relevant date was a child, a young person or a [[43] full-time student] who had not completed his full-time education and had no parent or step-parent, to his guardian,

but only for a period of two years from the relevant date.

(6) In the case of a person to whom or for whose benefit a payment referred to in this para-graph is made, any capital resource which derives from any payment of income or capital made under or deriving from any of the Trusts [[119]or from a Grenfell Tower payment].]

[[19](7) For the purposes of sub-paragraphs (2) to (6), any reference to the Trusts shall be construed as including a reference to the Fund[[64], the Eileen Trust [[93], MFET Limited] [[72], the Skipton Fund[[98], the Caxton Foundation][[107], the Scottish Infected Blood Support Scheme][[111], an approved blood scheme][[109], the London Emergencies Trust, the We

Love Manchester Emergency Fund][[119], the National Emergencies Trust] and the London Bombings Relief Charitable Fund]].]

[[69] **22A.**—[[72] . . .]]

23.—The value of the right to receive an occupational [[15]or personal] pension.

[[26]**23A.**—The value of any funds held under a personal pension scheme [[79] . . .].]

24.—The value of the right to receive any rent [[26]except where the claimant has a reversionary interest in the property in respect of which rent is due.]]

[[2]**25.**—Where a claimant has ceased to occupy what was formerly the dwelling occupied as the home following his estrangement or divorce from[[71], or dissolution of his civil partnership with,] his former partner, that dwelling for a period of 26 weeks from the date on which he ceased to occupy that dwelling [[56] or, where that dwelling is occupied as the home by the former partner who is a lone parent, for as long as it is so occupied].

26.—Any premises where the claimant is taking reasonable steps to dispose of those premises, for a period of 26 weeks from the date on which he first took such steps, or such longer period as is reasonable in the circumstances to enable him to dispose of those premises.

[[5]**27.**—Any premises which the claimant intends to occupy as his home, and in respect of which he is taking steps to obtain possession and has sought legal advice or has commenced legal proceedings, with a view to obtaining possession, for a period of 26 weeks from the date on which he first sought such advice or first commenced such proceedings whichever is earlier, or such longer period as is reasonable in the circumstances to enable him to obtain possession and commence occupation of those premises.]

28.—Any premises which the claimant intends to occupy as his home to which essential repairs or alterations are required in order to render them fit for such occupation, for a period of 26 weeks from the date on which the claimant first takes steps to effect those repairs or alterations, or such longer period as is reasonable in the circumstances to enable those repairs or alterations to be carried out and the claimant to commence occupation of the premises.]

[[4]**29.**—Any payment in kind [[119]which is a Grenfell Tower payment or] made by a charity [[8]or under [[94] or by] the Macfarlane (Special Payments) Trust][[19], the Macfarlane (Special Payments) (No.2) Trust][[22], [[81] the Fund [[89]. . .][[96], MFET Limited][[97], the Skipton Fund, the Caxton Foundation][[107], the Scottish Infected Blood Support Scheme][[111], an approved blood scheme] or the Independent Living Fund (2006)]].

[[60]**30.**—Any payment made pursuant to section 2 of the Employment and Training Act 1973 or section 2 of the Enterprise and New Towns (Scotland) Act 1990, but only for the period of 52 weeks beginning on the date of receipt of the payment.]

31.—Any payment made by the Secretary of State to compensate for the loss (in whole or in part) of entitlement of housing benefit.]

[[5]**32.**—[[85] . . .]

33.—[[85] . . .]

34.—Any payment made to a juror or a witness in respect of attendance at a court other than compensation for loss of earnings or for the loss of a benefit payable under the benefit Acts.

35.—[[20] . . .].]

[[9]**36.**—Any payment in consequence of a reduction of [[20] [[86] . . .] council tax under section 13 [[102], 13A] or, as the case may be, section 80 of the Local Government Finance Act 1992 (reduction of liability for council tax)] but only for a period of 52 weeks from the date of the receipt of the payment.]

[[10]**37.**—Any grant made to the claimant in accordance with a scheme made under section 129 of the Housing Act 1988 or section 66 of the Housing (Scotland) Act 1988 (schemes for payments to assist local housing authority and local authority tenants to obtain other accommodation) which is to be used—

    (a) to purchase premises intended for occupation as his home; or

    (b) to carry out repairs or alterations which are required to render premises fit for occupation as his home

for a period of 26 weeks from the date on which he received such a grant or such longer period as is reasonable in the circumstances to enable the purchase, repairs or alterations to be completed and the claimant to commence occupation of those premises as his home.]

[[12] [[90] **38.**—(1) Any payment or repayment made—

    (a) as respects England, under regulation 5, 6 or 12 of the National Health Service (Travel Expenses and Remission of Charges) Regulations 2003 (travelling expenses and health service supplies);

    (b) as respects Wales, under regulation 5, 6 or 11 of the National Health Service (Travelling Expenses and Remission of Charges) (Wales) Regulations 2007 (travelling expenses and health service supplies);

(c) as respects Scotland, under regulation 3, 5 or 11 of the National Health Service (Travelling Expenses and Remission of Charges) (Scotland) (No.2) Regulations 2003 (travelling expenses and health service supplies),

but only for a period of 52 weeks from the date of receipt of the payment or repayment.

(2) Any payment or repayment made by the Secretary of State for Health [¹¹⁴and Social Care], the Scottish Ministers or the Welsh Ministers which is analogous to a payment or repayment mentioned in sub-paragraph (1), but only for a period of 52 weeks from the date of receipt of the payment or repayment.

39.—Any payment made to such persons entitled to receive benefits as may be determined by or under a scheme made pursuant to section 13 of the Social Security Act 1988 in lieu of vouchers or similar arrangements in connection with the provision of those benefits (including payments made in place of healthy start vouchers, milk tokens or the supply of vitamins), but only for a period of 52 weeks from the date of receipt of the payment.]

[⁹¹ **39A.**—Any payment made under Part 8A of the Contributions and Benefits Act (entitlement to health in pregnancy grant).]

40.—Any payment made either by the Secretary of State for [⁸⁰ Justice] or by the [⁹⁰ Scottish Ministers] under a scheme established to assist relatives and other persons to visit persons in custody, but only for a period of 52 weeks from the date of receipt of the payment.

[⁹⁰ **41.**—Any arrears of supplementary pension which is disregarded under paragraph 54 of Schedule 9 (sums to be disregarded in the calculation of income other than earnings) or of any amount which is disregarded under paragraph 55 or 56 of that Schedule, but only for a period of 52 weeks from the date of receipt of the arrears.]]

[¹⁷**42.**—Any payment (other than a training allowance[⁶⁰ . . .]) made, whether by the Secretary of State or by any other person, under the Disabled Persons (Employment) Act 1944 [⁶⁰ . . .] to assist disabled persons to obtain or retain employment despite their disability.

43.—Any payment made by a local authority under section 3 of the Disabled Persons (Employment) Act 1958[¹¹²or under Part 4 of the Social Services and Well-being (Wales) Act 2014] to homeworkers under the Blind Homeworkers' Scheme.]

[²⁵[⁷⁸**44.**—(1) Any sum of capital to which sub-paragraph (2) applies and—
  (a) which is administered on behalf of a person by the High Court or the County Court under Rule 21.11(1) of the Civil Procedure Rules 1998 or by the Court of Protection;
  (b) which can only be disposed of by order or direction of any such court; or
  (c) where the person concerned is under the age of 18, which can only be disposed of by order or direction prior to that person attaining age 18.

(2) This sub-paragraph applies to a sum of capital which is derived from—
  (a) an award of damages for a personal injury to that person; or
  (b) compensation for the death of one or both parents where the person concerned is under the age of 18.]]

45.—Any sum of capital administered on behalf of a person [³¹. . .] in accordance with an order made under [⁵⁸ section 13 of the Children (Scotland) Act 1995], or under Rule 36.14 of the Ordinary Cause Rules 1993 or under Rule 128 of the Ordinary Cause Rules, where such sum derives from—
  (a) an award of damages for a personal injury to that person; or
  (b) compensation for the death of one or both parents [³¹ where the person concerned is under the age of 18].]

[²⁷**46.**—Any payment to the claimant as holder of the Victoria Cross or George Cross.]

[³⁰**47.**—[⁹⁰ . . .]

48.—[⁹⁰. . .]

49.—[⁹⁰ . . .]]

[⁴⁸ **50.**—[⁶⁰. . .].]

[⁵⁴ **50A.**—[⁶⁰. . .].]

[³² **51.**—[⁶⁰. . .].]

[³⁵ **52.**—In the case of a person who is receiving, or who has received, assistance under [⁴⁴ the self-employment route], any sum of capital which is acquired by that person for the purpose of establishing or carrying on the commercial activity in respect of which such assistance is or was received but only for a period of 52 weeks from the date on which that sum was acquired.]

[³⁶**53.**—[⁶⁰. . .].]

54.—*[Omitted.]*

55.—*[Omitted.]*

[³⁷**56.**—(1) Any payment of a sports award for a period of 26 weeks from the date of receipt of that payment except to the extent that it has been made in respect of any one or more of the items specified in sub-paragraph (2).

(2) The items specified for the purposes of sub-paragraph (1) are food, ordinary clothing or footwear, household fuel, rent for which housing benefit is payable or any housing costs to the extent that they are met under regulation 17(1)(e) or 18(1)(f) (housing costs) [53. . .], of the claimant or, where the claimant is a member of a family, any other member of his family, or any council tax or water charges for which that claimant or member is liable.

(3) For the purposes of sub-paragraph (2)—

"food" does not include vitamins, minerals or other special dietary supplements intended to enhance the performance of the person in the sport in respect of which the award was made;

"ordinary clothing and footwear" means clothing or footwear for normal daily use but does not include school uniforms or clothing or footwear used solely for sporting activities.]

[38**57.**—[67. . .]]

[42**58.**—In the case of a claimant participating in an employment zone programme, any discretionary payment made by an employment zone contractor to the claimant, being a fee, grant, loan or otherwise, but only for the period of 52 weeks from the date of receipt of the payment.

59.—Any arrears of subsistence allowance paid as a lump sum but only for the period of 52 weeks from the date of receipt of the payment.]

60.—*[Omitted.]*

[45 **61.**—Where an ex-gratia payment of £10,000 has been made by the Secretary of State on or after 1st February 2001 in consequence of the imprisonment or internment of—

(a)   the claimant;

(b)   the claimant's partner;

(c)   the claimant's deceased spouse [71 or deceased civil partner]; or

(d)   the claimant's partner's deceased spouse [71 or deceased civil partner],

by the Japanese during the Second World War, £10,000.]

[46**62.**—In the case of a person to whom paragraph (5) of regulation 6 (persons not treated as in remunerative work) applies, the whole of his capital.]

[65 **63.**—(1) Any payment—

(a)   by way of an education maintenance allowance made pursuant to—

(i)   regulations made under section 518 of the Education Act 1996;

(ii)   regulations made under section 49 or 73(f) of the Education (Scotland) Act 1980;

[90 (iii)   directions made under section 73ZA of the Education (Scotland) Act 1980 and paid under section 12(2)(c) of the Further and Higher Education (Scotland) Act 1992; [99 . . .]]

(b)   corresponding to such an education maintenance allowance, made pursuant to—

(i)   section 14 or section 181 of the Education Act 2002; or

(ii)   regulations made under section 181 of that Act[99; or

(c)   in England, by way of financial assistance made pursuant to section 14 of the Education Act 2002.]

(2) Any payment, other than a payment to which sub-paragraph (1) applies, made pursuant to—

(a)   regulations made under section 518 of the Education Act 1996;

(b)   regulations made under section 49 of the Education (Scotland) Act 1980; or

[90 (c)   directions made under section 73ZA of the Education (Scotland) Act 1980 and paid under section 12(2)(c) of the Further and Higher Education (Scotland) Act 1992,]

in respect of a course of study attended by a child or a young person or a person who is in receipt of an education maintenance allowance [99 or other payment] made pursuant to any provision specified in sub-paragraph (1)].

[49**64.**—(1) Subject to sub-paragraph (2), the amount of any trust payment made to a claimant or a member of a claimant's family who is—

(a)   a diagnosed person;

(b)   the diagnosed person's partner or the person who was the diagnosed person's partner at the date of the diagnosed person's death;

(c)   a parent of a diagnosed person, a person acting in the place of the diagnosed person's parents or a person who was so acting at the date of the diagnosed person's death; or

(d)   a member of the diagnosed person's family (other than his partner) or a person who was a member of the diagnosed person's family (other than his partner) at the date of the diagnosed person's death.

(2) Where a trust payment is made to—

(a)   a person referred to in sub-paragraph (1)(a) or (b), that sub-paragraph shall apply for the period beginning on the date on which the trust payment is made and ending on the date on which that person dies;

(b) a person referred to in sub-paragraph (1)(c), that sub-paragraph shall apply for the period beginning on the date on which the trust payment is made and ending two years after that date;

(c) a person referred to in sub-paragraph (1)(d), that sub-paragraph shall apply for the period beginning on the date on which the trust payment is made and ending—

    (i) two years after that date; or

    (ii) on the day before the day on which that person—

        (aa) ceases receiving full-time education; or

        (bb) attains the age of [[75] 20],

whichever is the latest.

(3) Subject to sub-paragraph (4), the amount of any payment by a person to whom a trust payment has been made, or of any payment out of the estate of a person to whom a trust payment has been made, which is made to a claimant or a member of a claimant's family who is—

(a) the diagnosed person's partner or the person who was the diagnosed person's partner at the date of the diagnosed person's death;

(b) a parent of a diagnosed person, a person acting in the place of the diagnosed person's parents or a person who was so acting at the date of the diagnosed person's death; or

(c) a member of the diagnosed person's family (other than his partner) or a person who was a member of the diagnosed person's family (other than his partner) at the date of the diagnosed person's death,

but only to the extent that such payments do not exceed the total amount of any trust payments made to that person.

(4) Where a payment as referred to in sub-paragraph (3) is made to—

(a) a person referred to in sub-paragraph (3)(a), that sub-paragraph shall apply for the period beginning on the date on which that payment is made and ending on the date on which that person dies;

(b) a person referred to in sub-paragraph (3)(b), that sub-paragraph shall apply for the period beginning on the date on which that payment is made and ending two years after that date;

(c) a person referred to in sub-paragraph (3)(c), that sub-paragraph shall apply for the period beginning on the date on which that payment is made and ending—

    (i) two years after that date; or

    (ii) on the day before the day on which that person—

        (aa) ceases receiving full-time education; or

        (bb) attains the age of [[75] 20],

    whichever is the latest.

(5) In this paragraph, a reference to a person—

(a) being the diagnosed person's partner;

(b) being a member of the diagnosed person's family; or

(c) acting in the place of the diagnosed person's parents,

at the date of the diagnosed person's death shall include a person who would have been such a person or a person who would have been so acting, but for the diagnosed person [[70] residing in a care home, an Abbeyfield Home or an independent hospital] on that date.

(6) In this paragraph—

"diagnosed person" means a person who has been diagnosed as suffering from, or who, after his death, has been diagnosed as having suffered from, variant Creutzfeldt-Jakob disease;

"relevant trust" means a trust established out of funds provided by the Secretary of State in respect of persons who suffered, or who are suffering, from variant Creutzfeldt-Jakob disease for the benefit of persons eligible for payments in accordance with its provisions;

"trust payment" means a payment under a relevant trust.]

[[52]**65.**—The amount of a payment, other than a war pension [[90]. . .], to compensate for the fact that the claimant, the claimant's partner, the claimant's deceased spouse [[71] or deceased civil partner] or the claimant's partner's deceased spouse [[71] or deceased civil partner]—

(a) was a slave labourer or a forced labourer;

(b) had suffered property loss or had suffered personal injury; or

(c) was a parent of a child who had died,

during the Second World War.]

[[56][[58] **66.**—(1) Any payment made by a local authority, or by the [[90] Welsh Ministers], to or on behalf of the claimant or his partner relating to a service which is provided to develop or sustain the capacity of the claimant or his partner to live independently in his accommodation.]

(2) For the purposes of sub-paragraph (1) "local authority" includes, in England, a county council.]

[⁵⁸ **67.**—Any payment made under [⁹¹. . .] [¹⁰⁵ sections 31 to 33 of the Care Act 2014 (direct payments) or under] regulations made under section 57 of the Health and Social Care Act 2001 or under section 12B of the Social Work (Scotland) Act 1968 [⁹⁵ , or under sections 12A to 12D of the National Health Service Act 2006 (direct payments for health care)[¹¹², or in accordance with regulations made under section 50 or 52 of the Social Services and Well-being (Wales) Act 2014 (direct payments)]].

[⁷³ **68.**—Any payment made to the claimant pursuant to regulations under section 2(6)(b), 3 or 4 of the Adoption and Children Act 2002.]

[⁶⁶ **68A.**—Any payment made to the claimant in accordance with regulations made pursuant to section 14F of the Children Act 1989 (special guardianship support services).]

69.—[⁶⁰. . .].]

[⁵⁹ **70.**—[⁶⁰. . .].]

[¹⁰⁴ **71.**—Any payments to a claimant made under section 49 of the Children and Families Act 2014 (personal budgets and direct payments).]

[¹⁰⁸**72.** Any bereavement support payment in respect of the rate set out in regulation 3(2) or (5) of the Bereavement Support Payment Regulations 2017 (rate of bereavement support payment), but only for a period of 52 weeks from the date of receipt of the payment.]

[¹¹⁰**73.**—Any payment made under or by a trust, established for the purpose of giving relief and assistance to disabled persons whose disabilities were caused by the fact that during their mother's pregnancy she had taken a preparation containing the drug known as Thalidomide, and which is approved by the Secretary of State.]

[¹¹³**74.**—Any payment made to a claimant under section 73(1)(b) of the Children and Young People (Scotland) Act 2014 (kinship care assistance).]

[¹¹⁶**75.**—Any early years assistance given in accordance with section 32 of the Social Security (Scotland) Act 2018.]

[¹¹⁷**76.**—Any funeral expense assistance given in accordance with section 34 of the Social Security (Scotland) Act 2018.]

[¹²⁰**77.**—Any assistance given in accordance with the Carer's Assistance (Young Carer Grants) (Scotland) Regulations 2019.]

[¹²¹**78.**—Any winter heating assistance given in accordance with regulations made under section 30 of the Social Security (Scotland) Act 2018.]

AMENDMENTS

1. Income Support (General) Amendment Regulations 1988 (SI 1988/663) reg.36 (April 11, 1988).

2. Income Support (General) Amendment No.2 Regulations 1988 (SI 1988/910) reg.3 (May 30, 1988).

3. Family Credit and Income Support (General) Amendment Regulations 1988 (SI 1988/999) reg.5 (June 9, 1988).

4. Income Support (General) Amendment No.4 Regulations 1988 (SI 1988/1445) reg.26 (September 12, 1988).

5. Income Support (General) Amendment No.5 Regulations 1988 (SI 1988/2022) reg.23 (December 12, 1988).

6. Family Credit and Income Support (General) Amendment Regulations 1989 (SI 1989/1034) reg.12 (July 10, 1989).

7. Income Support (General) Amendment Regulations 1989 (SI 1989/534) Sch.1 para.18 (October 9, 1989).

8. Income-related Benefits Schemes Amendment Regulations 1990 (SI 1990/127) reg.3 (January 31, 1990).

9. Income Support (General) Amendment Regulations 1990 (SI 1990/547) reg.23(*a*) (April 1, 1990).

10. Income Support (General) Amendment Regulations 1990 (SI 1990/547) reg.23(*b*) (April 9, 1990).

11. Social Security Benefits (Student Loans and Miscellaneous Amendments) Regulations 1990 (SI 1990/1549) reg.5(9) (September 1, 1990).

12. Income Support (General) Amendment No.3 Regulations 1990 (SI 1990/1776) reg.11 (October 1, 1990).

13. Enterprise (Scotland) Consequential Amendments Order 1991 (SI 1991/387) arts 2 and 9 (April 1, 1991).

14. Income-related Benefits Schemes and Social Security (Recoupment) Amendment Regulations 1991 (SI 1991/1175) reg.5 (May 11, 1991).

15. Income Support (General) Amendment No.4 Regulations 1991 (SI 1991/1559) reg.21 (October 7, 1991).

16. Disability Living Allowance and Disability Working Allowance (Consequential Provisions) Regulations 1991 (SI 1991/2742) reg.11(7) (April 6, 1992).

17. Income Support (General) Amendment Regulations 1992 (SI 1992/468) reg.9 (April 6, 1992).

18. Income Support (General) Amendment Regulations 1992 (SI 1992/468) Sch. para.10 (April 6, 1992).

19. Income-related Benefits Schemes and Social Security (Recoupment) Amendment Regulations 1992 (SI 1992/1101) reg.6(8) (May 7, 1992).

20. Income-related Benefits Schemes (Miscellaneous Amendments) Regulations 1993 (SI 1993/315) Sch. para.6 (April 1, 1993).

21. Social Security Benefits (Miscellaneous Amendments) (No.2) Regulations 1993 (SI 1993/963) reg.2(3) (April 22, 1993).

22. Social Security Benefits (Miscellaneous Amendments) (No.2) Regulations 1993 (SI 1993/963) reg.2(5) (April 22, 1993).

23. Income-related Benefits Schemes and Social Security (Recoupment) Amendment Regulations 1993 (SI 1993/1249) reg.4(5) (May 14, 1993).

24. Income-related Benefits Schemes (Miscellaneous Amendments) (No.4) Regulations 1993 (SI 1993/2119) reg.24 (October 4, 1993).

25. Income-related Benefits Schemes (Miscellaneous Amendments) (No.5) Regulations 1994 (SI 1994/2139) reg.33 (October 3, 1994).

26. Income-related Benefits Schemes and Social Security (Claims and Payments) (Miscellaneous Amendments) Regulations 1995 (SI 1995/2303) reg.6(10) (October 2, 1995).

27. Income-related Benefits Schemes (Miscellaneous Amendments) Regulations 1996 (SI 1996/462) reg.11(1) (April 8, 1996).

28. Income Support (General) (Jobseeker's Allowance Consequential Amendments) Regulations 1996 (SI 1996/206) reg.26 (October 7, 1996).

29. Income-related Benefits Schemes and Social Fund (Miscellaneous Amendments) Regulations 1996 (SI 1944) reg.13 and Sch. para.7 (October 7, 1996).

30. Income Support and Social Security (Claims and Payments) (Miscellaneous Amendments) Regulations 1996 (SI 1996/2431) reg.6 (October 15, 1996).

31. Income-related Benefits and Jobseeker's Allowance (Amendment) (No.2) Regulations 1997 (SI 1997/2197) reg.7(9) and (10)(e) (October 6, 1997).

32. Social Security Amendment (New Deal) Regulations 1997 (SI 1997/ 2863) reg.17(11) and (12)(e) (January 5, 1998).

33. Social Security (Miscellaneous Amendments) (No.4) Regulations 1998 (SI 1998/1174) reg.7(7) and (8)(e) (June 1, 1998).

34. Social Security (Miscellaneous Amendments) (No.4) Regulations 1998 (SI 1998/1174) reg.7(9) and (10)(e) (June 1, 1998).

35. Social Security (Miscellaneous Amendments) (No.4) Regulations 1998 (SI 1998/1174) reg.7(11) and (12)(e) (June 1, 1998).

36. Social Security Amendment (New Deal) (No.2) Regulations 1998 (SI 1998/2117) reg.5(2) and (3)(c) (September 24, 1998).

37. Social Security Amendment (Sports Awards) Regulations 1999 (SI 1999/2165) reg.6(5) (August 23, 1999).

38. Social Security (Miscellaneous Amendments) (No.2) Regulations 1999 SI 1999/2556) reg.2(11) (October 4, 1999).

39. Social Security Amendment (Education Maintenance Allowance) Regulations 2000 (SI 2000/55) reg.2(3) and (4)(c) (February 7, 2000).

40. Social Security (Miscellaneous Amendments) Regulations 2000 (SI 2000/681) reg.9 (April 3, 2000).

41. Social Security (Immigration and Asylum) Consequential Amendments Regulations 2000 (SI 2000/636) reg.3(13) (April 3, 2000).

42. Social Security Amendment (Employment Zones) Regulations 2000 (SI 2000/724) reg.3(4) (April 3, 2000).

43. Social Security Amendment (Students) Regulations 2000 (SI 2000/1981) reg.5(5) and Sch. (July 31, 2000).

44. Social Security Amendment (Employment Zones) (No.2) Regulations 2000 (SI 2000/2910) reg.4(1) and (2)(c)(ii) (November 27, 2000)

45. Social Security Amendment (Capital Disregards) Regulations 2001 (SI 2001/22) reg.2(a) (February 1, 2001).

46. Social Security (Miscellaneous Amendments) Regulations 2001 (SI 2001/488) reg.10 (April 9, 2001).

47. Social Security (Miscellaneous Amendments) (No.3) Regulations 2001 (SI 2001/859) reg.3(6) (April 9, 2001).

48. Social Security Amendment (New Deal) Regulations 2001 (SI 2001/1029) reg.15(14) and (15)(c) (April 9, 2001).

49. Social Security Amendment (Capital Disregards and Recovery of Benefits) Regulations 2001 (SI 2001/1118) reg.2(1) (April 12, 2001).

50. Social Security Amendment (Discretionary Housing Payments) Regulations 2001 (SI 2001/2333) reg.2(2)(c) (July 2, 2001).

51. Children (Leaving Care) Act 2000 (Commencement No.2 and Consequential Provisions) Order 2001 (SI 2001/3070) art.3(2) and para.(c) of Sch.1 (October 1, 2001).

52. Social Security Amendment (Capital Disregards) (No.2) Regulations 2001 (SI 2001/3481) reg.2 (November 19, 2001).

53. Social Security Amendment (Residential Care and Nursing Homes) Regulations 2001 (SI 2001/3767) reg.2(1) and Pt I of Sch. para.20 (April 8, 2002).

54. Social Security Amendment (Employment Programme) Regulations 2002 (SI 2002/2314) reg.3(4) (October 14, 2002).

55. Social Security (Miscellaneous Amendments) (No.2) Regulations 2002 (SI 2002/2380) reg.2(b) (October 14, 2002).

56. Social Security (Miscellaneous Amendments) Regulations 2003 (SI 2003/511) reg.2(3) (April 1, 2003).

57. Social Security (Working Tax Credit and Child Tax Credit) (Consequential Amendments) Regulations 2003 (SI 2003/455) reg.2 and Sch.1 para.24(a) (April 7, 2003).

58. Social Security (Miscellaneous Amendments) (No.2) Regulations 2003 (SI 2003/2279) reg.2(5) (October 1, 2003).

59. Social Security (Incapacity Benefit Work-focused Interviews) Regulations 2003 (SI 2003/2439) reg.13(b) (October 27, 2003).

60. Social Security (Miscellaneous Amendments) Regulations 2004 (SI 2004/565) reg.2(4) (April 1, 2004).

61. Social Security (Working Tax Credit and Child Tax Credit) (Consequential Amendments) Regulations 2003 (SI 2003/455) reg.2 and Sch.1 para.24(b) (April 6, 2004, except in "transitional cases" and see further the note to reg.17 of the Income Support Regulations).

62. Social Security (Miscellaneous Amendments) (No.2) Regulations 2004 (SI 2004/1141) reg.3(1) and (2)(c) (May 12, 2004).

63. Social Security (Miscellaneous Amendments) (No.2) Regulations 2004 (SI 2004/1141) reg.3(3) and (4)(c) (May 12, 2004).

64. Social Security (Miscellaneous Amendments) (No.2) Regulations 2004 (SI 2004/1141) reg.3(5) and (6)(c) (May 12, 2004).

65. Social Security (Students and Income-related Benefits) Amendment Regulations 2004 (SI 2004/1708) reg.5(3) (September 1, 2004, or if the student's period of study begins between August 1 and August 31, 2004, the first day of the period).

66. Social Security (Miscellaneous Amendments) (No.3) Regulations 2004 (SI 2004/2308) reg.4(5) (October 4, 2004).

67. Social Security (Back to Work Bonus and Lone Parent Run-on) (Amendment and Revocation) Regulations 2003 (SI 2003/1589) reg.2(d) (October 25, 2004).

68. Social Security (Miscellaneous Amendments) Regulations 2005 (SI 2005/574) reg.3(6) (April 4, 2005).

69. Income-related Benefits (Amendment) Regulations 2005 (SI 2005/2183) reg.2 (August 5, 2005).

70. Social Security (Care Homes and Independent Hospitals) Regulations 2005 (SI 2005/2687) reg.2 and Sch.1 para.13 (October 24, 2005).

71. Civil Partnership (Pensions, Social Security and Child Support) (Consequential, etc. Provisions) Order 2005 (SI 2005/2877) art.2(3) and Sch.3 para.13(9) (December 5, 2005).

72. Income-related Benefits (Amendment) (No.2) Regulations 2005 (SI 2005/3391) reg.2(5) (December 12, 2005).

73. Social Security (Miscellaneous Amendments) (No.2) Regulations 2005 (SI 2005/2465) reg.2(9) (December 30, 2005).

74. Housing Benefit and Council Tax Benefit (Consequential Provisions) Regulations 2006 (SI 2006/217) reg.5 and Sch.2 para.1(9) (March 6, 2006).

75. Social Security (Young Persons) Amendment Regulations 2006 (SI 2006/718) reg.2(9) (April 10, 2006).

76. Social Security (Miscellaneous Amendments) (No.4) Regulations 2006 (SI 2006/2378) reg.5(11)(a) (October 2, 2006).

77. Social Security (Miscellaneous Amendments) (No.4) Regulations 2006 (SI 2006/2378) reg.5(11)(b) (October 2, 2006).

78. Social Security (Miscellaneous Amendments) (No.4) Regulations 2006 (SI 2006/2378) reg.5(11)(c) (October 2, 2006).

79. Social Security (Miscellaneous Amendments) (No.3) Regulations 2007 (SI 2007/1749) reg.2(8) (July 16, 2007).

80. Secretary of State for Justice Order 2007 (SI 2007/2128) Sch. para.13(3) (August 22, 2007).

81. Independent Living Fund (2006) Order 2007 (SI 2007/2538) reg.2(3) (October 1, 2007).

82. Social Security (Miscellaneous Amendments) Regulations 2008 (SI 2008/698) reg.2(15)(a) (April 14, 2008).

83. Social Security (Miscellaneous Amendments) Regulations 2008 (SI 2008/698) reg.2(15)(b) (April 14, 2008).

84. Social Security (Miscellaneous Amendments) Regulations 2008 (SI 2008/698) reg.2(15)(c) (April 7, 2008).

85. Social Security (Miscellaneous Amendments) Regulations 2008 (SI 2008/698) reg.2(15)(d) (April 14, 2008).

86. Social Security (Miscellaneous Amendments) Regulations 2008 (SI 2008/698) reg.2(15)(e) (April 14, 2008).

87. Employment and Support Allowance (Consequential Provisions) (No.2) Regulations 2008 (SI 2008/1554) reg.2(15) (October 27, 2008).

88. Social Security (Miscellaneous Amendments) (No.6) Regulations 2008 (SI 2008/2767) reg.2(6) (November 17, 2008).

89. Social Security (Miscellaneous Amendments) (No.6) Regulations 2008 (SI 2008/2767) reg.2(13) (November 17, 2008).

90. Social Security (Miscellaneous Amendments) (No.7) Regulations 2008 (SI 2008/3157) reg.2(8) (January 5, 2009).

91. Social Security (Miscellaneous Amendments) Regulations 2009 (SI 2009/583) reg.2(14) (April 6, 2009).

92. Social Security (Equalisation of State Pension Age) Regulations 2009 (SI 2009/1488) reg.4 (April 6, 2010).

93. Social Security (Miscellaneous Amendments) (No.2) Regulations 2010 (SI 2010/641 reg.2(3)(g) (April 6, 2010).

94. Social Security (Miscellaneous Amendments) (No.2) Regulations 2010 (SI 2010/641 reg.2(7)(f) (April 6, 2010).

95. Social Security (Miscellaneous Amendments) (No.2) Regulations 2010 (SI 2010/641 reg.2(10) (April 6, 2010).

96. Social Security (Miscellaneous Amendments) (No.2) Regulations 2011 (SI 2011/1707) reg.4(10)(a) and (11) (August 5, 2011).

97. Social Security (Miscellaneous Amendments) (No.3) Regulations 2011 (SI 2011/2425) reg.7(5) (October 31, 2011).

98. Social Security (Miscellaneous Amendments) (No.3) Regulations 2011 (SI 2011/2425) reg.7(6) (October 31, 2011).

99. Social Security (Miscellaneous Amendments) (No.3) Regulations 2011 (SI 2011/2425) reg.7(8) (October 31, 2011).

100. Jobseeker's Allowance (Schemes for Assisting Persons to Obtain Employment) Regulations 2013 (SI 2013/276) reg.13(b) (February 12, 2013).

101. Social Security (Miscellaneous Amendments) Regulations 2013 (SI 2013/443) reg.2(6)(a) (April 2, 2013).

102. Social Security (Miscellaneous Amendments) Regulations 2013 (SI 2013/443) reg.2(6)(b) (April 2, 2013).

103. Universal Credit (Consequential, Supplementary, Incidental and Miscellaneous Provisions) Regulations 2013 (SI 2013/630) reg.28(9) (April 29, 2013).

104. Special Educational Needs (Consequential Amendments to Subordinate Legislation) Order 2014 (SI 2014/2103) art.3(3) (September 1, 2014).

105. Care Act 2014 (Consequential Amendments) (Secondary Legislation) Order 2015 (SI 2015/643) art.2 and Sch. para.5(4) (April 1, 2015).

106. Children and Young People (Scotland) Act 2014 (Consequential Modifications) Order 2016 (SI 2016/732) art.2(3) (August 5, 2016).

107. Social Security (Scottish Infected Blood Support Scheme) Regulations 2017 (SI 2017/329) reg.3(3) (April 3, 2017).

108. Pensions Act 2014 (Consequential, Supplementary and Incidental Amendments) Order 2017 (SI 2017/422) art.9(4) (April 6, 2017).

109. Social Security (Emergency Funds) (Amendment) Regulations 2017 (SI 2017/689) reg.2(3)(f) (June 19, 2017).

110. Social Security (Emergency Funds) (Amendment) Regulations 2017 (SI 2017/689) reg.2(5) (June 19, 2017).

111. Social Security (Infected Blood and Thalidomide) Regulations 2017 (SI 2017/870) reg.2(3)(f) (October 23, 2017).

112. Social Services and Well-being (Wales) Act 2014 and the Regulation and Inspection of Social Care (Wales) Act 2016 (Consequential Amendments) Order 2017 (SI 2017/901) art.2(6) (November 3, 2017).

113. Social Security and Child Support (Care Payments and Tenant Incentive Scheme) (Amendment) Regulations 2017 (SI 2017/995) reg.2(4) (November 7, 2017).

114. Secretaries of State for Health and Social Care and for Housing, Communities and Local Government and Transfer of Functions (Commonhold Land) Order 2018 (SI 2018/378) Sch., para.21(a) (April 11, 2018).

115. Social Security (Treatment of Arrears of Benefit) Regulations 2018 (SI 2018/932) reg.2 (September 11, 2018).

116. Social Security (Scotland) Act 2018 (Best Start Grants) (Consequential Modifications and Saving) Order 2018 (SI 2018/1138) art.5(3) (December 10, 2018).

117. Social Security (Scotland) Act 2018 (Funeral Expense Assistance and Early Years Assistance) (Consequential Modifications and Savings) Order 2019 (SI 2019/1060) art.7(3) (September 16, 2019).

118. Social Security (Capital Disregards) (Amendment) Regulations 2019 (SI 2019/1314) reg.2(2) (October 31, 2019).

119. Social Security (Income and Capital) (Miscellaneous Amendments) Regulations 2020 (SI 2020/618) reg.2(12) (July 15, 2020).

120. Social Security (Scotland) Act 2018 (Young Carer Grants, Short-Term Assistance and Winter Heating Assistance) (Consequential Provision and Modifications) Order 2020 (SI 2020/989) art.2 (November 9, 2020).

121. Social Security (Scotland) Act 2018 (Young Carer Grants, Short-Term Assistance and Winter Heating Assistance) (Consequential Provision and Modifications) Order 2020 (SI 2020/989) art.15 (November 9, 2020).

DEFINITIONS

"Abbeyfield Home"—see reg.2(1).
"the Act"—*ibid.*
"approved blood scheme"—*ibid.*
"the benefit Acts"—*ibid.*
"care home"—*ibid.*
"child"—see SSCBA s.137(1).
"civil partnership"—see Interpretation Act 1978 Sch.1.
"claimant"—see reg.2(1).
"dwelling occupied as the home"—*ibid.*
"employment zone contractor"—*ibid.*
"employment zone programme"—*ibid.*
"family"—see SSCBA s.137(1).
"full-time student"—see reg.61(1).
"Grenfell Tower payment"—see reg.2(1).
"income-related benefit"—see SSCBA s.123(1).
"income-related employment and support allowance"—see reg.2(1).
"independent hospital"—*ibid.*
"Intensive Activity Period for 50 plus"—*ibid.*
"local welfare provision"—*ibid.*
"the London Bombings Relief Charitable Fund"—*ibid.*
"the London Emergencies Trust"—*ibid.*
"lone parent"—*ibid.*
"the Mandatory Work Activity Scheme"—*ibid.*
"MFET Limited"—*ibid.*
"occupational pension"—*ibid.*
"partner"—*ibid.*
"payment"—*ibid.*
"personal pension scheme"—*ibid.*
"policy of life insurance"—*ibid.*
"qualifying age for state pension credit"—see SSCBA s.137(1).
"qualifying person"—see reg.2(1).
"relative"—*ibid.*
"remunerative work"—*ibid.*
"Scottish Infected Blood Support Scheme"—*ibid.*
"self-employed earner"—*ibid.*
"self-employment route"—*ibid.*
"sports award"—*ibid.*
"subsistence allowance"—*ibid.*
"supplementary benefit"—*ibid.*
"the Caxton Foundation"—*ibid.*
"the Eileen Trust"—*ibid.*
"the Independent Living Funds"—*ibid.*
"the Macfarlane (Special Payments) Trust"—*ibid.*
"the Macfarlane (Special Payments) (No.2) Trust"—*ibid.*

"the Macfarlane Trust"—*ibid.*
"the National Emergencies Trust"—*ibid.*
"the Skipton Fund"—*ibid.*
"training allowance"—*ibid.*
"universal cerdit"—*ibid.*
"the We Love Manchester Emergency Fund"—*ibid.*
"young person"—*ibid.*, reg.14.

GENERAL NOTE

The categories of disregards of capital are as follows (* indicates no further note below):

2.795

Para.1	dwelling occupied as the home (one dwelling only);
Para.1A	payments of travel expenses for certain schemes;
Para.2	premises acquired for occupation, for 26 weeks or longer if reasonable;
Para.3	proceeds of sale of former home to be used for purchase of new home within 26 weeks or longer if reasonable;
Para.4	premises occupied by incapacitated or aged partner or relative or by former partner, except where estranged or divorced;
Para.5	any future interest in property;
Para.6	assets of a claimant's business as a self-employed person;
Para.7	payments of arrears of most benefits and of concessionary payments to compensate for non-payment of such arrears;
Para.8	sums paid for repair or replacement of loss or damage to home or personal possessions or acquired for essential repairs or improvements to home;
Para.9	certain deposits with housing associations;
Para.10	personal possessions not acquired to reduce capital to secure entitlement to income support;
Para.11	value of right to receive income under annuity and surrender value*;
Para.12	value of trusts derived from payments in consequence of personal injury to claimant or partner;
Para.12A	payments in consequence of personal injury to claimant or partner, for 52 weeks;
Para.13	value of right to receive income under life interest or liferent;
Para.14	value of right to receive income disregarded under para.11 of Sch.8 or para.23 of Sch.9;
Para.15	surrender value of life insurance policies;
Para.16	value of right to receive outstanding instalments of capital;
Para.17	local authority payments under children's legislation;
Para.18	social fund payments*;
Para.18A	local welfare provision;
Para.19	income tax refunds relating to mortgage loan interest*;
Para.20	capital treated as income by reg.41 or 66A;
Para.21	charges for conversion to sterling*;
Para.22	payments from certain funds for haemophiliacs, contaminated blood products, various victims etc;
Para.23	value of right to receive occupational or personal pension;
Para.23A	value of funds in personal pension scheme;
Para.24	value of right to receive rent;
Para.25	home claimant ceased to occupy on divorce, estrangement etc;
Para.26	premises up for sale;
Para.27	premises intended to be occupied by claimant as home;
Para.28	premises intended to be occupied by claimant as home: essential repairs or alterations needed;
Para.29	payments in kind by charities or certain trusts;

Para.30	payments under New Deal schemes etc;
Para.31	compensation for loss of entitlement to housing benefit*;
Para.34	payments to jurors or witnesses, with exceptions*;
Para.36	council tax reduction payments, for 52 weeks;
Para.37	certain housing grants*;
Para.38	certain NHS payments*;
Para.39	payments in lieu of certain vouchers*;
Para.39A	health in pregnancy grants*;
Para.40	prison visiting payments*;
Para.41	arrears disregarded under para.54, 55 or 56 of Sch.9*;
Para.42	certain payments to disabled persons to obtain or retain employment;
Para.43	capital payments under blind homeworkers' scheme;
Para.44	capital deriving from personal injury compensation administered by court;
Para.45	capital deriving from personal injury compensation administered by court (Scotland);
Para.46	payments to holders of VC or GC*;
Para.52	certain payment to persons on the "self-employment route";
Para.56	sports awards, with exceptions;
Para.58	discretionary payments from employment zone contractors;
Para.59	lump sum arrears of subsistence payments;
Para.61	ex gratia payments to WWII prisoners and internees of Japan;
Para.62	persons treated as not in remunerative work by reg.6(5);
Para.63	educational maintenance allowances etc;
Para.64	payments from variant Creutsfeldt-Jakob disease trusts;
Para.65	compensation for WWII losses etc;
Para.66	local authority payments for independent living;
Para.67	direct payments for health care;
Para.68	payments under regulations under s.2(6)(b), 3 or 4 of the Adoption and Children Act 2002;
Para.68A	special guardianship support payments;
Para.71	payments under s.49 of the Children and Families Act 2014;
Para.72	bereavement support payments;
Para.73	payments from Thalidomide trusts;
Para.74	kinship care assistance payments;
Para.75	Scottish early years assistance;
Para.76	Scottish funeral expense assistance;
Para.77	Scottish young carer grants;
Para.78	Scottish winter heating assistance.

2.795.1   With effect from May 29, 2020, reg.26(1)(a) of the Victims' Payments Regulations 2020 (SI 2020/103) (see later in this Part) provides that a victims' payment or a lump sum under those Regulations is to be disregarded as capital or income. Under the Regulations payments are to be made to those injured in a "Troubles-related incident", which is defined in s.10(11) of the Northern Ireland (Executive Formation etc) Act 2019 as "an incident involving an act of violence or force carried out in Ireland, the United Kingdom or anywhere in Europe for a reason related to the constitutional status of Northern Ireland or to political or sectarian hostility between people there".

See the notes to Sch.9 for the taxable £500 payment, administered by local authorities, to be made to those in England entitled to a qualifying income-related benefit (including income support, income-related ESA and income-based JSA) who are required by NHS Test and Trace on or after September 28, 2020 (down at least to summer 2021) to self-isolate for 14 (or 10) days, are unable to work from home and will lose income from employment or self-employment and the discretionary payments available to those not entitled to a qualifying benefit. It is suggested there that the payments are in the nature of income, subject to the possible argument that a discretionary payment could be regarded as a voluntary payment not made or due to be made at regular intervals and so to be treated as capital under reg.48(9). Also, any amount remaining out of the £500 at the end of the required days of self-isolation could be treated as capital under the usual principles.

The intention was expressed in the guidance on scheme eligibility that the £500 payments were not to be taken into account as capital for benefit purposes. There has been no specific amendment to the legislation to secure that result. But the payments, being made by local authorities, appear to constitute "local welfare provision" within the capital disregard in para.18A (see the notes to para.31A of Sch.9 for discussion of the definition of that phrase and the income disregard).

It was announced in the March 2021 budget that an automatic £500 payment would be made by HMRC to those in receipt of working tax credit (or child tax credit alone if eligible for WTC but income too high for payability), in view of the withdrawal in April 2021 of the temporary uplift to WTC rates during the coronavirus pandemic. The payment is due to be made in April 2021 without the need for any claim and apparently under powers in the Coronavirus Act 2020. It will therefore not be a payment of WTC and would appear to be in the nature of a capital receipt, rather than income. According to LA Welfare Direct 3/2021, the payment is to be disregarded for housing benefit and universal credit purposes, but there has been no amendment of the legislation for the purposes of income support, income-related ESA or income-based JSA.

Capital may be disregarded under more than one paragraph of Sch.10 at the same time, or in succession. There is no provision in reg.46(2) or Sch.10 for establishing any order of priority if different paragraphs of Sch.10 are applicable, so the claimant will be entitled to the benefit of the most favourable disregard (this is also the case for Sch.9). The disregards in Sch.10 apply to notional capital (*CIS 25/1990*, *CIS 81/1991*, *CIS 562/1992* and *CIS 30/1993*), provided that their conditions are met (*CIS 30/1993*). See the note to para.26 and to reg.51(6).

In *R(IS) 15/96*, followed in *R(IS) 5/07*, the Commissioner expresses the view that claimants should be advised by the Benefits Agency of the existence of relevant disregards so that they can take advantage of them. In that case the claimant had received a criminal injuries compensation award so he could have taken steps to utilise the disregard in para.12.

A number of the provisions in Sch.10 allow for a disregard to apply for a set period "or such longer period as is reasonable in the circumstances". In *Guildford BC v MW (HB)* [2014] UKUT 49 (AAC) (a case on Sch.6 to the Housing Benefit Regulations 2006, the equivalent to Sch.10), Judge Wright confirms that whether a capital disregard is to be extended is a matter for a tribunal on appeal to determine entirely afresh and by assessing reasonableness for itself.

Paragraph 1

The value of the home is disregarded. Paragraph 3 of Sch.3 contains rules about when a person is or is not to be treated as occupying a dwelling as their home. The fact that Sch.10 did not originally contain paras 25–28 gave rise to a number of problems (for which see p.178 of J. Mesher, *Income Support, the Social Fund and Family Credit: the Legislation* (1988)). The introduction of, in particular, a disregard of the value of premises which are for sale will solve, or at least postpone, many of the problems. See reg.17(f) and (2)–(7) for transitional protection for those excluded from income support from April 11, 1988 to May 29, 1988, and the now revoked Sch.9 para.41 and Sch.10 para.32.

On the meaning of "dwelling occupied as the home", see notes to reg.2(1). Paragraph 1 can apply to notional capital (*CIS 81/1991* (although it was not necessary to the decision) and *CIS 30/1993*).

Paragraph 1A

Any payment of expenses in relation to participation in the Mandatory Work Activity Scheme or a scheme listed in reg.3 of the Jobseeker's Allowance (Schemes

2.796

2.797

for Assisting Persons to Obtain Employment) Regulations 2013 is ignored if it counts as capital, only for 52 weeks from the date of receipt. See also para.1A of Sch.9 for the disregard as income.

Paragraph 2

2.798   In *JH v SSWP* [2009] UKUT 1 (AAC) Judge Mesher points out that the form of para.2 of Sch.8 to the JSA Regulations 1996 (which is the same as this paragraph) is different from that of the disregard of the value of premises in some of the other paragraphs in Sch.8 (and in this Schedule). It does not provide that it applies for a period of 26 weeks or such longer period as is reasonable. Instead, it makes it a condition of its application week by week that the claimant intends to occupy the premises as his home within 26 weeks of its acquisition or such longer period as is reasonable. Thus the commentary to this paragraph in the 2008/09 edition (and previous editions) of what was then Vol.II of this series was wrong in saying that the value of the premises must be disregarded for the first 26 weeks after the acquisition (and had been wrong since he originally wrote that in 1988!). There is no such automatic disregard.

All the circumstances must be looked at in deciding whether a longer period is reasonable. There must be some realistic prospect of occupation starting.

It might be thought that the requirement that the premises have been "acquired for occupation by the claimant" would exclude some forms of acquisition (e.g. inheritance). But according to para.29553 of the *Decision Makers Guide*, a person may acquire premises by purchase, gift or inheritance.

"Premises" is to be given a reasonably wide meaning; thus acquiring land on which a person intends to build a home is covered by the disregard (see *CIS 8475/1995* in the note to para.3). But the disregard under para.2 does not extend to money in the claimant's bank account, even though it is intended for use for the purchase of premises (*GS v Department for Social Development (IS)* [2012] NI Com 284, a decision of a Northern Ireland Commissioner).

The income from premises whose value is disregarded under this provision counts as income (Sch.9 para.22), but mortgage repayments, water charges and council tax can be set off against it.

Paragraph 3

2.799   The sum must be directly attributable to the actual (*R(IS) 4/96*) proceeds of sale of a home, and must be intended for the purchase of another home (not repairs or refurbishment: *R(SB) 14/85; CIS 368/1993*). Money paid out on the surrender of endowment policies that had not been used to repay the claimant's mortgage on his former home was not "directly attributable to the proceeds of sale" of that home (*CFC 2493/1997*). *R(IS) 6/95* decides that para.3 is not restricted to circumstances where a claimant is free to sell to a third party but can apply where a statutory tenancy of a home has been surrendered to the landlord. The claimant had sold his home, albeit technically by a surrender rather than a sale, and it was irrelevant to whom he had sold it.

As well as the purpose of using the proceeds for the purchase of a home that is already erected, the disregard also covers buying land and building a house on it (*CIS 8475/1995*). There the claimant decided to use the proceeds of sale of his former home to buy a plot of land and build a bungalow on it. When he made his claim for income support the sale proceeds were held on deposit. By the date of the tribunal hearing the claimant had used the majority of the proceeds to purchase and clear the land. He had about £10,000 left for materials and labour to build the bungalow. The Commissioner decides that the claimant's intended use of the proceeds of sale fell within para.3. The words "purchase of other premises" in para.3 were to be given a reasonably wide meaning and included the outlay of money in stages to acquire land and build a house on it. This approach was consistent with that adopted in *R(IS) 11/94* in relation to housing costs met by income support; the Commissioner also agrees with *R(IS) 3/96* that the word "premises" in the first four paragraphs of this Schedule has a similar meaning (see the note to para.4). But the disregard in para.3 only applied to sums of money. Once the claimant had acquired the plot of land, the land and the partly-built bungalow as the work progressed fell to be disregarded under para.2. On the facts of this case it was reasonable for the period of the disregard under paras 2 and 3 to be extended to 18 months from the date of the claim for income support. The Commissioner comments that in self-build cases a disregard of 12 months rather than six will normally be reasonable.

In *CIS 8475/1995* the Commissioner also makes the point that there is a difference between the wording "is to be used" in para.3 and the tests of intended occupation in, for example, paras 2, 27 and 28. In his view, para.3 required an element of practical certainty as well as subjective intent. This could be shown, for example, by a binding contract for purchase which had not yet been completed, or an agreement "subject to contract" in circumstances where it seemed likely that the money would not be diverted to other purposes. On the facts of that case the Commissioner found obtaining planning permission, placing the purchase in the hands of solicitors and accepting a builder's quote to be sufficient. *CIS 685/1992*, however, decides that it is not necessary, in order for there to be an extension of the primary 26-week period, that an intention to occupy specific premises should have been formed before the end of that period. If the proceeds of sale had not been used at the end of the 26 weeks there was a general discretion for the Department (or tribunal) to allow a longer period for the finding of another home and the completion of its purchase. However, a mere hope that the proceeds might be used at some future date for another home was not sufficient. In *R(IS) 7/01* the Commissioner considers that these two decisions are not irreconcilable and, adopting the approach of *CIS 15984/1996* to the words "to be used", concludes that the test under para.3 is that there must not only be an intention to use the capital to buy another home but also reasonable certainty that it will be used within 26 weeks or such further period as may be reasonable. In *CIS/4757/2003*, the same Commissioner confirms that personal circumstances (such as illness, as in that case, or awaiting the outcome of job applications that might determine the location of the new home as in *CIS/15984/1996*) can justify an extension beyond the 26 weeks. If the claimant can still demonstrate an intention to use the proceeds of sale to purchase another home, and it is reasonably certain that a property will be purchased within a further identifiable period, an extension of time will generally be appropriate.

2.800

In *EAM v SSWP (UC)* [2020] UKUT 247 (AAC), Judge Poynter has declined to follow *R(IS) 7/01* and the other decisions referred to there as being inconsistent with the principle conclusively confirmed in *In re B (Children)* [2008] UKHL 35, [2009] A.C. 11 that there is only one civil standard of proof and that is proof that the fact in issue more probably occurred than not. His view was that to apply a test to the equivalent provision in para.13 of Sch.10 to the Universal Credit Regulations in terms of any kind of certainty was to place a higher burden on the claimant than the balance of probabilities. Although he agreed with the proposition in *R(IS) 7/01* that a mere genuine intention to use the sum to purchase a new home is not enough, he continued in para.33 that the phrase "is to be used for the purchase of premises" is about "what in all the circumstances of the case (including the claimant's intentions) is likely to happen in practice." Then he said in para.34 that to the extent that the *R(IS) 7/01* test requires a claimant to prove any fact to any standard other than the balance of probabilities he declined to follow that decision.

There are at least two problems in applying *EAM* in the context of income support, income-related ESA and income-based JSA. One is that it was not necessary to the decision for the judge to reach a definite conclusion on the correctness of *R(IS) 7/01*. On the facts as found by the First-tier Tribunal, the remaining amount attributable to the proceeds of sale of the claimant's home (£37,000) was not enough to buy a new home for her and her partner, so that they would need a mortgage, which on the balance of probabilities they would be unable to secure because of the level of their indebtedness. Accordingly, although the tribunal had been inconsistent on the nature of the test and had seemed to apply a test of practical certainty in concluding that the sum was not to be disregarded, its decision was not set aside because the same result would have followed if Judge Poynter's suggested test had been used. That undermines the basis for not following a reported decision that might otherwise have existed if a First-tier Tribunal or the Secretary of State considered Judge Poynter's reasoning, especially as supported by House of Lords' authority, to be persuasive.

The second problem is that the judge's reasoning appears dubious. There is a slight uncertainty about whether the disagreement with *R(IS) 7/01* extends only to the burden of proving facts necessary to the application of the legislative test or whether it extends also to the burden of showing that that test is met in all the circumstances as established by findings of fact. On balance, the latter seems to be intended. But then the result in accordance with para.33 is that the test to be applied is whether it is more likely than not that the sum will be used for the purchase of premises. Such a test appears, as a matter of the ordinary use of language, to be significantly different from and less restrictive than the legislative test in terms of "is to be used". Arguably, Judge Poynter's approach conflates the nature of the burden of proving that the legislative test is met with the true meaning of that test.

Unless and until *EAM* is taken to the Court of Appeal or is given the status of a reported decision or there is some further decision clarifying the issue (which may well take some years), tribunals may wish to hedge their bets by applying both approaches in the alternative, but only if properly satisfied that the outcome would be the same whichever was applied. If not so satisfied, a choice will have to be made as to whether the reasoning in *EAM* is sufficiently persuasive to be preferred to the approach approved in *R(IS) 7/01*.

2.801 Note also *CIS/4269/2003* which confirms that there is nothing in para.3 which says that the proceeds of sale must be of the property that was occupied immediately before the property which is to be purchased. The disregard in para.3 can still apply if a claimant who has a sum directly attributable to the proceeds of sale of home A is currently living in home B, providing that the condition that the sum is to be used to purchase home C within 26 weeks (or reasonable longer period) of the sale of home A is met. But the disregard in para.3 does not apply if the claimant has already purchased a new home prior to the sale of the former home and at the time of the purchase it was not intended that the former home would be sold (*WT v DSD (IS)* [2011] NI Com 203, a decision of the Northern Ireland Chief Commissioner).

In *CIS 222/1992* the claimant intended to use her share of the proceeds of sale of her deceased mother's house to purchase her own council house. The claimant had lived in her mother's house for a short time some 10 years before. The Commissioner rejects the argument that the claimant was entitled to the benefit of the disregard in para.3 because she formerly occupied her mother's home as her home. He finds that the conditions for a purposive construction of para.3 were satisfied (see Lord Diplock at 105 in *Jones v Wrotham Park Settled Estates Ltd* [1980] A.C. 74), and holds that para.3 only applied where the claimant had owned the property when she had lived there.

Paragraph 4

2.802 In *R(IS) 3/96* the Commissioner rejects a submission from the Secretary of State (said to reflect the policy intention) that para.4 applied to disregard premises of any kind and extent. He decides that "premises" in para.4 was to be interpreted in accordance with the definition of "dwelling occupied as the home" in reg.2(1). The first four paragraphs of Sch.10 were all concerned with disregarding the claimant's home or what would be the home if the claimant was in actual occupation, and thus it was entirely consistent for "premises" in paras 2, 3 and 4 to be given a similar interpretation. Thus when the claimant went to live in a residential care home the farmhouse she jointly owned with her husband could be ignored under para.4(b), but not the farmland which had its own access and could have been sold separately.

Sub-paragraph (a)

Sub-paragraph (a) applies where the premises, as construed above, are occupied   2.803
in whole or in part by a partner or relative of a single claimant (or of any member of the family) as their home and the occupant is over state pension age or is incapacitated. "Relative" is quite widely defined in reg.2(1), where the list can be read (and see also the definition there of "close relative"), as is "single claimant". "Family" is defined in s.137(1) of the SSCBA 1992. "Incapacitated" is not defined anywhere. Paragraph 29434 of the *DMG* suggests that the test is met by receipt of, or qualification on the relevant disability or illness conditions for, attendance allowance, constant attendance allowance, DLA, the disability element of working tax credit, incapacity benefit, severe disablement allowance, statutory sick pay or a similar benefit. The list of specific benefits is now rather dated, so that the category of "similar benefit" must now be taken to include invalidity benefit, ESA, PIP, armed forces independence payments, etc. as well as satisfaction of the test of having limited capability for work under universal credit. It must also be open to argument that a person is incapacitated in the ordinary meaning of the word although not within para.29434.

There is difficulty in working out how sub-para.(a) can ever apply to a partner of the claimant when a person who has a partner cannot satisfy the definition of "single claimant". The definition of "family" in s.137(1) of the SSCBA 1992 includes a couple, so one of them could be said to be a partner of the claimant as another member of the family. But to be a partner the person must be sharing a household with the claimant. And a person with whom the claimant no longer shares a household is not a partner but a former partner. It is therefore difficult to see how a person could still be a member of the claimant's household and occupy other premises as their home. As discussed below in the notes to sub-para.(b), a partner who is temporarily living away from the other members of the family remains a member of the claimant's household (see reg.16) and remains a partner, e.g. while being looked after elsewhere by a friend or relative during a temporary illness. However, can it be held that while so temporarily away the person occupies the other premises as their home? Normally, only one dwelling can be the dwelling occupied as the home with its value disregarded under para.1, but could the partner in at least some circumstances of merely temporary absence be said to have two homes? If so, then if either the claimant or partner had an interest in that other dwelling, its capital value would be disregarded under sub-para.(a) if the partner met the age or incapacity condition. The ordinary case of a partner looking after the sick relative comes under sub-para.(a) if the relative meets either of those conditions.

Under supplementary benefit, occupation was held to connote occupation as a residence, not merely as a holiday home (*R(SB) 1/85*). That conclusion would now follow from the requirement of occupation by the partner or relative as the home.

Sub-paragraph (b)

Sub-paragraph (b) applies where the premises are occupied by a former partner   2.804
as their home, but not where the claimant is estranged from the former partner or there has been a divorce or the dissolution of a civil partnership. See the potential disregard in para.25 for 26 weeks from the estrangement/divorce/dissolution or longer for lone parents.

Divorce or dissolution of a civil partnership is easy to identify and pinpoint to a particular date. Estrangement is a much more slippery concept that has generated case law from which it is difficult to take clear guidance, not least because it is hard to see just what policy objective is served by preventing the application of the disregard when the claimant is estranged from the former partner. It is easy to say that the overall purpose is to identify property that it is unreasonable to require a claimant to sell or raise money on to meet living expenses. It is another thing to work out why, if that is so when the property is occupied by any non-divorced, etc. former partner, no matter from how far in the past, the factor of estrangement should be the one to screen out cases where the disregard is not justified. In the absence of any definition in the legislation, estrangement must be given its ordinary meaning in context. Some difference in expression among decisions, none of which purport to give definitions, is therefore to be expected and too much attention should not be given to such differences that may simply stem from the circumstances of the particular case in which the question was addressed (*CIS/4096/2005* and *AC v SSWP (IS)* [2015] UKUT 49 (AAC)). The discussion below attempts to concentrate on principles on which there is general agreement without citing all the decisions mentioned in past editions.

First, it is well established that estrangement is not the same as separation (*CIS/4843/2002, R(IS) 5/07*) and that separation does not necessarily imply estrangement (*R(IS) 5/05*). By definition, to be a former partner (outside the cases of divorce or dissolution of a civil partnership) the person must at least no longer be a member of the same household as the claimant. It must be remembered that, as pointed out in *R(IS) 5/05*, a person may temporarily be living away from a claimant and yet still be a member of the household. That is so on the general meaning of the term and in accordance with the special rules in reg.16, which give significance to whether the person intends to resume living with the claimant. Examples might be where a spouse or partner is in a care or nursing home or hospital or caring for a sick relative or friend in another place for a time that is realistically hoped to be temporary. In such circumstances, the two remain a couple as defined in reg.2(1) and partners, so that the person cannot claim income support separately from the claimant. But the value of the premises where the person is staying (if the claimant happened to have an interest in them) could not be disregarded under para.1 (because only one dwelling occupied as the home is covered) or sub-para.(b) (because the person is not a *former* partner). Sub-paragraph 4(a) could possibly apply as discussed above. If the separation has been permanent or open-ended from the outset (so as not to be merely temporary) or becomes non-temporary after a change of circumstances (including the time that it has continued), the person will be a former partner.

2.805 If there is separation such as to make the person a former partner, "estrangement" must entail something further in order to give some force to the use of the term in the exception. *R(IS) 5/05* agrees with *R(SB) 2/87* that estrangement has a "connotation of emotional disharmony". That has been accepted in subsequent decisions, but the important matter is the context in which such disharmony is to be assessed. There can be friendly relations between the claimant and former partner although they are estranged for the purposes of sub-para.(b) (*R(IS) 5/05* at para.12, *CPC/683/2007, CH/377/2007* and *Bristol CC v SJP (HB)* [2019] UKUT 360 (AAC) at paras 34–37, where there is a helpful summary of the earlier decisions). The way that Commissioner Rowland stated it in *R(IS) 5/05* was that the question was whether the parties had ceased to consider themselves a couple, as has been accepted and applied in later cases. This description needs some unpacking because "couple" has a particular meaning within the legislation that by definition cannot be met where the person is a former partner. So the word must be used in a more general everyday sense.

In *CPC/683/2007* (at para.13), Commissioner Jacobs said this:

"It seems to me that the proper analysis of the relationship between the claimant and his wife is this. They remain married and have no plans to divorce. He would like to resume living with her, but she is opposed to the idea. The reality is that they will never resume living as husband and wife; the claimant accepts that. However, they are not hostile to each other on a personal level and he feels a continuing responsibility towards her. This leads him to help her when she cannot manage on account of her ill-health. In other words, there is no emotional disharmony between the claimant and his wife as adults, but there is emotional disharmony between them as partners. That is a key distinction, because the language used in the legislation is attempting to identify those cases in which the relationship between the parties is such that it is appropriate for their finances to be treated separately for the purposes of benefit entitlement. Once the facts of the case are set out, they seem to me to allow of only one interpretation, which is that the couple are estranged."

The distinction between disharmony as partners and disharmony as adults is a useful one. It is no doubt going too far to say, as the same judge did in *CH/117/2005*, that two people are not estranged if they retain all the indicia of partners apart from physical presence in the same household, at least if that were to be taken out of context to represent a test that separation equals estrangement unless that condition is met. That would not be compatible with a proper consideration of the circumstances of particular cases and an application of the ordinary meaning of estrangement. But it perhaps illustrates one end of the continuum, where although the person is a former partner, because the separation is non-temporary, they and the claimant would be members of the same household if it were not for the circumstances enforcing the separation. At the other end of the continuum are cases where a relationship has broken down such that there is no current prospect of a resumption of living together. Then, no matter how amicable and co-operative the parties might be about, say children, finances and other practical matters, there is estrangement. There is an emotional disharmony between them as partners.

In *CIS/4096/2005*, Commissioner Jupp, in a different context, indicated that estrangement does not require mutuality of feeling. Disharmony can arise from one person's attitude to another, even though the other party may not wish the situation to be as it is. There has been some suggestion that because the test in sub-para.(b) is whether the claimant is estranged from the former partner the matter should be looked at from the point of view of the claimant. However, the approach in general has been to look at whether a state of estrangement exists between the parties. If the realistic position is that the attitude of one party prevents any resumption of a relationship as partners, the fact that the other party did not wish the situation to be as it was or hoped that the estrangement might not be permanent (*CH/377/2007*) does not on its own point against a conclusion that the other party is estranged from the first.

Renewed contact does not necessarily end estrangement; it is question of fact in each case (*R 1/02(SF)*, *AC v SSWP (IS)* [2015] UKUT 49 (AAC)).

In *CIS 231/1991* the claimant had transferred his former home to his parents who were both over 60 (which was the age limit in para.4(a) at that time). When he claimed income support they were living in the home. The Commissioner decides that para.4(a) applied to the former home; the disregard applied to notional, as well as actual, capital.

Note that from April 6, 2010, as a result of the start of the equalisation of state pension age, the age limit in para.4(a) is "the qualifying age for state pension credit" (defined in s.137(1) of the Contributions and Benefits Act 1992—the effect of that definition is that the qualifying age was 60 but from April 2010 it gradually rose in line with the staged increase in pensionable age for women until it reached 65 in November 2018 (this equalisation of the state pension age for men and women was previously to have been completed by April 5, 2020 but the timetable for this in the Pensions Act 1995 was accelerated with effect from April 2016 so that women's state pension age became 65 in November 2018; in addition, the increase in state pension age to 66 for both men and women has been brought forward—it started to rise from 65 in December 2018 to reach 66 by October 2020, see s.1 of the Pensions Act 2011), and between 2026 and 2028 it will reach 67 (see s.26 of the Pensions Act 2014)).

2.806

Paragraph 5

2.807   Before October 2, 1995 the disregard in para.5 applied to "any reversionary interest". The amendment was in response to the Court of Appeal's decision in *Chief Adjudication Officer v Palfrey*, reported as part of *R(IS) 26/95*, which upheld the Tribunal of Commissioners' decision in *CIS 85/1992* that property subject to a tenancy was a reversionary interest and so was to be disregarded. The Commissioners had held that *R(SB) 3/86* (which decided that a reversionary interest was "something which does not afford any present enjoyment but carries a vested or contingent right to enjoyment in the future" and that a landlord's interest in a freehold property was not merely such an interest) was not to be followed. In *CIS 85/1992* the rented property was freehold, but *CIS 563/1991* and *CIS 615/1993* confirmed that the disregard under the previous form of para.5 applied to leasehold property as well.

It was considered that the effect of these decisions was to create an easy loophole which could enable a claimant to have the capital value of property disregarded simply by letting it, and so the new form of para.5 was introduced. Under the new form, the disregard applies to future interests in property but not land or premises which have been let by the claimant. A future interest in property is one that does not take effect immediately. An example would be where the claimant's entitlement only arises on the death of a person who has a life interest in the particular fund or property. Note that for the exception to operate, the lease, etc. has to be granted by the claimant. So, if the tenancy was granted by someone else (e.g. before the claimant owned the property) the disregard should still apply.

CIS 635/1994 suggests that the disregard could also apply if the property was subject to an irrevocable licence (rather than a lease or tenancy). The Commissioner expressed doubts as to whether a freehold or leasehold interest in a property subject to a tenancy could be said to be a future interest, but considered that the way the exception was put appeared to assume that it was. This meant that the new disregard might not be limited (as at first sight it seemed to be) to future interests in the sense of interests where there was no right at all until the future event happened. If the consequence is that the new form of para.5 covers situations where the claimant's interest affords no present enjoyment (and is a future interest in that sense) then, leaving aside the exception, the disregard itself may not be significantly different. Indeed it could be argued that a future interest is wider than a reversionary interest as it could include not only an interest that will revert to the claimant but also one that will only take effect in the future. (Note that in *Palfrey* both the Court of Appeal and the Commissioners considered that the capital value of the element of possession involved in a tenanted property fell to be disregarded under para.24 (in its previous form); it was the right to regain possession of the property at the end of the term which was a purely reversionary right that was covered by the old form of para.5.)

2.808   See also *R(IS) 1/97*. The claimant on separating from his wife had agreed that she could remain in the former matrimonial home (which was in his sole name) for her lifetime. There was no written agreement. The Commissioner decides that in the circumstances an irrevocable licence had been granted or could be inferred which gave rise to a constructive trust which in turn made the wife a tenant for life for the purposes of the Settled Land Act 1925. The Commissioner decides that the test laid down in *Ashburn Anstalt v Arnold* [1989] Ch. 1 for imposing a constructive trust, that is, that the owner of the property had so conducted himself that it would be inequitable to allow him to deny the beneficiary an interest in the property, was satisfied. The result was that the claimant's interest in the former matrimonial home was a reversionary one as it did not afford any present enjoyment. If the claimant's interest can similarly be ignored under the new form of para.5 (see above), this decision may have potentially wide implications for separating couples. See *R(IS) 5/07* in which the Commissioner stated that further information about the terms on which the claimant's husband continued to live in the former matrimonial home was needed but clearly considered that the disregard in para.5 might be applicable.

Note also *R(IS) 4/96* which decides that a charge on a former matrimonial home which was not to be enforced until the claimant's ex-wife died, remarried or cohabited for longer than six months was not a reversionary interest but gave the claimant a secured debt payable at a future date (see *Re Fisher* [1943] Ch. 377).

See also the amendment to para.24.

Rent from tenanted property, as and when it is received, will generally count as capital, not income (Sch.9 para.22), under reg.48(4). But note the excepted cases, e.g. if the property is up for sale (and so disregarded under para.26). See the notes to reg.48(4) and para.22 of Sch.9 and note *CIS 563/1991* discussed in the note to reg.48(4).

Paragraph 6

The business assets of a self-employed person are primarily disregarded under sub-para.(1) if they are engaged in the business. Paragraph 29371 of the *Decision Makers Guide* states that people should be treated as engaged in a business for as long as they perform some work in it in a practical sense. **2.809**

Business assets have to be distinguished from personal assets by asking if they are "part of the fund employed and risked in the business" (*R(SB) 4/85*). The income tax and accounting position are factors to be taken into account, but are not conclusive (*CFC 10/1989*), although see *CIS 5481/1997* which emphasises the relevance of accounting practice. The Commissioner in *R(SB) 4/85* notes that, while people in a business partnership owe a duty to the other partner(s) to keep business assets severed from and not mixed with their own assets, the same does not apply to sole traders. They can mix their own and business assets together and can freely transfer items from business to personal assets and vice versa. Although so far as money is concerned it is much more straightforward if a self-employed person maintains a business account separate from any personal accounts and keeps receipts and expenditure to the appropriate account, many of those in small-scale self-employment will not maintain any separate bank or building society account. The account may even be a joint account with a person not involved in the business. That in itself is not fatal to the identification of some sums in the mixed account as employed and risked in the business. It becomes a matter of whether there is sufficient evidence (and no doubt it falls to the claimant to come forward with the evidence if there is no separate business account) to be able to identify such an asset (but see the discussion of *CIS/2467/2003* below). Thus, for instance, if claimants can show that they have a sum of money in a mixed account that is set aside to meet income tax due for payment in the future on their self-employed earnings, that would seem to fall within the scope of this disregard.

In *JJ v SSWP (IS)* [2012] UKUT 253 (AAC) the Aston Martin which the claimant had purchased with the intention of starting a classic car rental business was a business asset and not a personal possession, even though the claimant did not proceed with his project. The new tribunal would need to decide whether the claimant could be regarded as engaged in the business so that the disregard in sub-para. (1) applied, and if so, for what period.

CIS/2467/2003 concerned a self-employed author who received advances on contracting to write a book and subsequent royalties on sales. The Commissioner rejected his argument that money paid by way of advances was not legally owned by him because the advances were repayable if he did not fulfill the contract. In his view the advances fully belonged to the claimant as soon as they were received. He further concluded that the receipts from the claimant's business were capital (see further the note to reg.30) and that they could not be disregarded under para.6. This was because, applying the test in *R(SB) 4/85*, the money was not employed in and risked in the business. The Commissioner rejected the claimant's argument that the ISA into which advances had been paid constituted a long-term reserve fund that underwrote and underpinned his business. It was a Maxi ISA; these were designed for personal savings by investment on a medium and long-term basis. The money in it was thus not employed in the business but in the personal sphere as the proceeds of the business. As the claimant was the business, if things went wrong he might need to draw on the value of the investment but this would represent a **2.810** putting back into the business of resources from the claimant's personal sphere. The claimant also had a joint account with his wife into which some business receipts were paid and which was used for domestic purposes. The Commissioner stated that claimants who wished to benefit from the para.6 disregard in relation to money that was not in a separate business account would have to show a clear demarcation between the assets of the business and personal assets. However, it is submitted that that should be taken more as an explanation of why, on the circumstances of the particular case, the claimant had failed to show that he could benefit from the disregard than as a rule of thumb to be applied in place of the principle laid down in *R(SB) 4/85*. Everything depends on the assessment of the evidence in individual cases.

R(FC) 2/92 holds that the ownership by an individual of a tenanted house is not in itself a business, although there may come a point, depending on the circumstances, at which the amount of administration and/or activity involved even in the letting out of a single property could amount to self-employment (*CCS 2128/2001; CIB 1595/2000* and *CIB 2114/2000*). See also *CFC 4238/1997*. In *CH/4258/2004*, which concerned para.7(1) of Sch.5 to the Housing Benefit Regulations (the equivalent of para.6(1)), the claimant ran a retail business from the ground floor and basement of a building which also included three flats on the upper floors. She purchased the freehold of the whole building (as the owner was not prepared to sell the retail part separately). The Comissioner concludes that the flats (which were let to tenants) were not used for the retail business (the fact that one business loan had been used to purchase the whole building did not affect this). Nor, applying *R(FC) 2/92*, were they assets of another business. As a consequence their value counted as the claimant's capital. Note that since October 2, 1995 a property that the claimant has let to tenants is not ignored as a reversionary interest (see the notes to para.5).

In *R(IS) 14/98* although the claimant was only a sleeping partner, the Commissioner decides that she continued to be gainfully employed and so a self-employed earner (s.2(1)(b) of the Contributions and Benefits Act 1992) in the farm business she owned with her son. The claimant had ceased to take an active role, having gone to live permanently in a residential care home, but she remained entitled to a share of the profits and capital and jointly and severally liable for the partnership's losses. Thus he held that her share of the partnership assets, including the farm, fell to be disregarded under para.6. See also *CG 19/1994* where the claimant who had become a partner in her husband's business solely for tax purposes was held to be gainfully employed in the business. But the decision in *R(IS) 14/98* was appealed to the Court of Appeal, which allowed the appeal (*Chief Adjudication Officer v Knight*, reported as part of *R(IS) 14/98*). The Court held that for the disregard in para.6 to apply, a financial commitment to a business on its own was insufficient. The claimant had to be involved or engaged in the business in some practical sense as an earner. Thus a sleeping partner in a business managed and worked exclusively by others could not benefit from para.6.

2.811   That conclusion seems to involve a similar distinction to that discussed in the notes to para.3 of Sch.8, between being in work and being at work. An issue there is whether a person has ceased to be "so employed" as a self-employed earner for the purposes of disregarding earnings from self-employment. It is argued in those notes that the better view is that for para.3 to apply self-employment does not have to have ceased permanently or outright. Thus, for the purposes of para.6 it appears that for a person to be "engaged in self-employment" it is not enough still to be in self-employment in the broader sense of being in work, of continuing to trade, but there must be some practical engagement in the business in the sense laid down in *Knight*. That also appears consistent with the provision in para.6(2) for interruptions due to illness, etc. It would be convenient (but probably not the case) if ceasing to be engaged in para.6 meant the same as ceasing to be so employed in para.3 of Sch.8.

If the claimant ceases to be engaged in the business, the value of the assets is disregarded for a period which is reasonable to allow them to be disposed of. In

CIS 5481/1997 the partnership that the claimant had been involved in had ceased trading. The Commissioner points out that a partnership did not cease to exist when it stopped trading. It ceased to exist when it was dissolved (which might or might not be the same time as it stopped trading). The assets remained business assets until the partnership was dissolved. However, the disregard in para.6 operated while a person was engaged as a self-employed earner for the purposes of the business and for such further time as was reasonable to allow for the disposal of the business's assets. The point when a person ceased to be engaged as a self-employed earner might be at the same time as a partnership ceased trading, or when it was dissolved, or at some other time (e.g. see *Knight* above). Thus in considering what was a reasonable time for disposal of assets under para.6 account had to be taken of the obligation on partners to sort out the partnership debts before distributing the assets. This would depend on the terms of any partnership deed or agreement or the Partnership Act 1890, and what was a reasonable period of time might alter if the circumstances changed. It may be useful for a tribunal dealing with a case of this kind to include a financially qualified member in view of the nature of the issues involved.

Where the self-employed person is temporarily not engaged in the business because of illness, there is a disregard under sub-para.(2). The reference to engagement or re-engagement clearly contemplates that the person may not previously have been engaged in the business (*JJ v SSWP (IS)* [2012] UKUT 253 (AAC)).

There may well be many applications of this provision during the 2020 and 2021 coronavirus outbreak, probably involving the extension beyond 26 weeks. Is it arguable that a temporary ceasing to trade due to government instruction or the adverse economic situation, although the self-employed person has not personally been infected, is nonetheless "by reason of some disease or bodily or mental disablement"? The terms of head (a) would appear to allow this, but head (b), referring to the person intending to engage in the business "as soon as he recovers", point in the opposite direction. Thus, in those circumstances to claim the benefit of the disregard it would have to be argued under sub-para.(1) that the person had ceased to be engaged in the business (in the sense suggested above) and that a generous view of "such period as may be reasonable in the circumstances to allow for disposal" of the asset should be taken. It is easy enough if there has been a permanent cessation. But can the words cover a period when the person does not know if their intention to resume the business when external factors improve can be fulfilled and does not know whether disposal of assets would be wise?

2.812

Sub-paragraphs (3) and (4) disregard any assets of a business carried on while a person is participating in the "self-employment route" (defined in reg.2(1)), and, if the person later ceases to be engaged in that business, for a period which is reasonable to allow them to be disposed of. See also para.52 under which any capital acquired for the purposes of such a business is ignored for 52 weeks from the date of receipt.

Note in addition the general disregard of payments made under s.2 of the Employment and Training Act 1973 or s.2 of the Enterprise and New Towns (Scotland) Act 1990 for 52 weeks from the date of receipt in para.30.

Income derived from capital disregarded under para.6 is not disregarded (Sch.9 para.22) and is not treated as capital (reg.48(4)).

Paragraph 7

Arrears of benefit which would be income when paid on the proper date retain their character as income (*R(SB) 4/89*). However, if any money is left after the end of the period to which the benefit is attributed as income then this will be capital (see notes to regs 23 and 40(1)).

2.813

Paragraph 7 applies, under sub-para.(1)(a), to mobility allowance or supplement, attendance allowance, any care or mobility component of disability living allowance, the daily living component or mobility component of personal independence payment and (from October 31, 2019, correcting an accidental omission to implement the policy intention earlier) armed forces independence payment; and under sub-para.(1)(b), to income support, income-based JSA, income-related ESA, child tax credit, working tax credit, housing benefit and council tax benefit (note that council tax benefit was abolished on April 1, 2013). From July 2, 2001 it also applies under sub-para.(1)(d) to discretionary housing payments. These are payments that can be made by a local authority to claimants who need extra help with their housing liability. They replaced the previous system of exceptional circumstances payments and exceptional hardship payments with effect from July 2, 2001. Under sub-para.(1)(e), added with effect from April 29, 2013, it applies to universal credit. With effect from April 6, 2017, arrears of regular monthly payments of the new and controversial bereavement support payments, in so far as they are characterised as capital, come within this disregard (sub-para.(1)(f)). In so far as they retain their character as income, they are disregarded under para.80 of Sch.9. Sub-paragraph (1)(g) adds, with effect from October 31, 2019, a disregard of arrears of maternity allowance (but only if payable under s.35 of the SSCBA 1992, not s.35B). In so far as such payments retain their character as income there is no disregard.

For all of the benefits listed in sub-para.(1)(a)–(g), there is a disregard for 52 weeks from the date of receipt under sub-para.(1), unless the more extensive disregard in sub-para.(2) applies.

2.814 The effect of sub-para.(2) is that if, on or after October 14, 2001, as a consequence of an official error (as defined in reg.1(3) of the Decisions and Appeals Regulations 1999, see Vol.III of this series), a claimant receives arrears and/or concessionary payment(s) totalling £5,000 or more in relation to any one of the benefits listed in sub-para.(1) ("the relevant sum"), this will be ignored indefinitely while any award during which the payment(s) are made continues, or for 52 weeks from the date of receipt, whichever is the longer. Award for this purpose means the award of income support, income-related ESA, income-based JSA or universal credit during which the arrears/concessionary payment (or first instalment thereof) was received and includes subsequent awards of income support, income-related ESA, income-based JSA or universal credit, provided that such awards are continuous and that the claimant is either the person who received the relevant sum or the partner of that person, or was their partner at the date of his death, or in the case of joint-claim JSA is a joint-claim couple, either or both of whom received the relevant sum (sub-para.(3)). Thus the sub-para.(2) disregard will not apply and a claimant will be restricted to the 52-week disregard under sub-para.(1) if the relevant sum (or part thereof) was paid before income support/income-based JSA/income-related ESA/universal credit was claimed. It also seems that £5,000 or more must have been paid in respect of one of the listed benefits for the indefinite disregard to apply; payments in relation to more than one of these benefits cannot be aggregated for this purpose. Further, the requirement that a subsequent award should begin immediately after the end of the previous award for the indefinite disregard to continue to apply may cause difficulties, since there can often be a gap between claims when a claimant moves between benefits and the limited circumstances in which claims can be backdated may not apply.

The December 2018 amendment extends the effect of sub-para.(2) to arrears paid because there has been an error of law as well as those where there has been an official error. Errors of law revealed by a decision of the courts or the Upper Tribunal are excluded from the definition of official error in the Decisions and Appeals Regulations. The same has been done for the equivalent old style ESA and JSA provisions. Remember that, as pointed out at the beginning of this note, payments of arrears of a benefit that would have been income if paid on time will retain their character as income in relation to the period from the date on which they were due to be paid or in respect of which they were payable. Amounts left over after that period of attribution will be capital and therefore come within the potential scope of the para.7 disregard.

MK v SSWP (IS) [2013] UKUT 629 (AAC) confirms that the disregard in para.7 only applies to the arrears of benefit that are paid and not to a sum equivalent to the arrears.

2.815 *CIS/2448/2006*, followed in *R(IS)5/08*, decides that a refund of charges by a local authority to a claimant because the claimant had been wrongly charged for after-care services under s.117 of the Mental Health Act 1983 (see *R. v Manchester CC, Ex p.*

Stennett [2002] UKHL 34, [2002] 2 A.C. 1127 in which the House of Lords held that a local authority was not entitled to charge for such after-care) was not "arrears of income support" and therefore could not be disregarded under para.7. The fact that the charges had been paid out of the claimant's income support did not turn the repayment of charges wrongly made into a payment of arrears of income support.

Note also the disregards in paras 38–41.

Paragraph 8

This meets the problems in *R(SB) 14/81* and para.8(2) of *R(SB) 14/85*. Such sums may not be part of the claimant's capital anyway (see *CSB 975/1985* and the notes to reg.46).

R(IS) 6/95 decides that sub-para.(a) only applies where the claimants have suffered damage to, or the loss of, their property against their will, not where they have deliberately brought this about. Thus it did not cover payment received for the surrender of a statutory tenancy of the claimant's home. *JM v SSWP* [2009] UKUT 87 (AAC) holds that the case law on the meaning of "to be used" in para.3 is equally applicable to para.8 (see the note to para.3 for this case law). In *JM* the claimant had received compensation some five years earlier for the destruction of his home in a gas explosion. He had not yet bought another property as he was caring for his disabled cousin but he intended to do so once his caring role ended (the date of which was uncertain). In these circumstances his intention to use the money to purchase a replacement home was no more than an aspiration and the disregard in sub-para.(a) did not apply from the outset. The claimant had also received a further sum for the sale of the land on which his house had stood. In the Upper Tribunal Judge's view this did not fall within sub-para.(a) which relates to sums paid for damage to, or loss of, the *home*; it could fall within para.3 but again the disregard in that paragraph did not apply because the claimant did not have a sufficient intention to use the money for the purpose envisaged by para.3.

CIS/368/1993 rejects the argument that money (in that case proceeds of sale of a previous home) ear-marked for the renovation of the claimant's home came within sub-para.(b). The Commissioner decides that the money had not been "acquired on the express condition" that it was to be used for the renovation, but as a consequence of the sale.

Paragraph 9

Sub-paragraph (b) gets round the problem in *R(SB) 4/87*.

Paragraph 10

Only personal possessions acquired with the intention of reducing capital so as to gain income support count. Otherwise their value is disregarded by para.10. See the notes to reg.51(1) for "purpose". But here the word is "intention". Does that indicate that the disregard is only excluded where the person's predominant purpose was securing entitlement to income support or increasing its amount?

Note that the corresponding paragraph under old style JSA (para.15 of Sch.8 to the JSA Regulations 1996) applies if a person has bought possessions with the intention of reducing capital in order to secure entitlement to or increase the amount of old style JSA *or income support*. That avoids the question that might otherwise have arisen on a claimant transferring from income support to old style JSA as to whether possessions that had been bought only for the purpose of income support could be caught by para.15 of Sch.8. Similarly para.14 of Sch.9 to the ESA Regulations 2008 applies if a person has acquired possessions with the intention of reducing capital in order to secure entitlement to or increase the amount of old style ESA *or income support or JSA*. However, para.10 has not been amended along those lines.

If the value of personal possessions does count, it is their current market value, i.e. their second hand value, not what was paid for them (*CIS/494/1990, CIS/2208/2003*), which must be included, less 10 per cent if there would be *any* expenses in selling. For the possible problems of double counting and the interac-

2.816

2.817

2.818

tion of this paragraph if personal possessions are not ignored and reg.51(1), see *CIS 494/1990* and *R(IS)8/04*, discussed under *"Deprivation"* in the notes to reg.51(1).

2.819 Presumably, in general, anything which is not real property is a personal posses-sion, providing that it is an object and not a right to sue for something, like a debt. But hard lines might have to be drawn between ordinary coins and bank-notes (obviously capital) and investments like paintings, stamps, furniture (apparently disregarded). What about gold bars?

In *R(H) 7/08* the Commissioner concludes that "personal possessions" means any physical assets other than land and assets used for business purposes (on which, see para.6). Thus the claimant's caravan was a personal possession and fell to be disregarded under this paragraph. In *JH v SSWP* [2009] UKUT 1 (AAC) a beach hut was a personal possession to which the disregard in para.15 of Sch.8 to the JSA Regulations 1996 (the equivalent of this paragraph) applied. But the right under a contractual licence to put the hut on the site was not a personal possession, did count as capital and had a market value.

That approach would seem to require that the actual value of items acquired mainly, or even solely, as investments be disregarded, but does that necessarily follow? Might it still be argued that, as Commissioner Jacobs was not directly concerned in *R(H) 7/08* with any line between personal possessions and investments, the decision does not exclude a conclusion that the adjective "personal" is an indication that some-thing has to be used at least partly for personal or domestic or household purposes, not solely for investment? Prior to its amendment in October 2014 by s.3(1) of the Inheritance and Trustees' Powers Act 2014, the definition of "personal chattels" in s.55(1)(x) of the Administration of Estates Act 1925 (for the purposes of identifying how an estate is to be distributed on intestacy and set out in para.35 of *R(H) 7/08*), as well as setting out a long list of specific items, included "articles of household or personal use or ornament". The courts, bearing in mind the test in terms of the use made of the article at the time of death, took quite a generous approach to when that use had a personal element. In one case, *Re Reynolds Will Trusts* [1966] 1 W.L.R. 19, the aptly named Stamp J, having held the intestate's valuable stamp collection, built up since childhood as his main hobby, to be part of his personal chattels, suggested that if he had gone into a shop and bought a similar collection that he then installed in his flat it could hardly be said that that was an article of personal use. Paragraph 10 makes no express reference to the use made of any possession, but it may be arguable that the word "personal" entails the exclusion of items with no element of personal enjoyment or cherishing (such as collections of jewellery, art work, stamps etc. locked away in a safe or bank vault and never inspected). However, such an approach would again involve the drawing of difficult lines after careful investigation that it may be thought that the legislation was intended to avoid. Perhaps the most telling point in Commissioner Jacobs' analysis in *R(H) 7/08* was that the supplementary benefit legislation in force prior to April 1988 expressly excluded possessions in the nature of an investment from the disregard of personal possessions, and that that exception was not taken over into the income support legislation.

No doubt, whatever the general answer, the more evidence there is that an item was acquired by a person for investment, the stronger the argument would be for the intention having been to reduce the amount of capital to gain income support, so that the disregard would not apply. It is the intention at the time of acquistion that matters, not the intention behind retention at the date of claim. And if the possibility of having to claim income support was not on the horizon at the time of acquisition, the prohibited intention could only be found in a most unusual case.

Paragraph 12

2.820 There is an unlimited disregard of the value of a trust fund deriving from a payment made in consequence of personal injury to the claimant or (from October 2, 2006) the claimant's partner. This seems particularly generous compared to the treatment of other forms of capital.

Note that "personal injury" includes a disease and any injuries suffered as a result of a disease (e.g. amputation of both legs following meningitis and septicaemia), as well as any accidental or criminal injury (*R(SB) 2/89*).

Compensation for personal injury includes all heads of an award for personal injury (*Peters v East Midlands Strategic Health Authority* [2009] EWCA Civ 145, [2010] Q.B. 48, a decision on the meaning of "an award of damages for a personal injury" in para.44(2)(a) but the same reasoning will apply). In particular, it is not restricted to general damages for pain, suffering and loss of amenity, but can include other heads of loss, such as loss of earnings and any sum awarded by a court in respect of the cost of providing accommodation and care. See also *R(IS) 15/96* (para.18).

KQ v SSWP (IS) [2011] UKUT 102 (AAC), reported as [2011] AACR 43, holds that a compensation payment received from negligent solicitors, which purely related to what should have been claimed from the negligent surgeon, was in consequence of the personal injury to the claimant. Judge Levenson accepts that the chain of causation does not go on for ever and so damages for the stress caused by the negligent solicitors or an element of punitive damages might not come within the disregard in para.12 (or para.12A). But there was no such element in the compensation in this case.

2.821

From October 2, 2006 the disregard applies where the injury was to the claimant *or* the claimant's partner. Before that date para.12 had simply referred to a trust derived from a payment made in compensation of any personal injury to the claimant. See *R(IS) 3/03* (discussed in the notes to para.12 of the 2006 edition of what was then Vol.II of this series) in which the Commissioner considered, at least on the facts of that case, that the reference to "the claimant" in para.12 did not include, by virtue of reg.23(1), a reference to the claimant's partner.

The disregard does not apply where the compensation is an award under the Fatal Accidents Act 1976 (*CP v SSWP (IS)* [2011] UKUT 157 (AAC)). There, the claimant, who had Down's syndrome, received substantial compensation under the 1976 Act after her mother (and primary carer) was killed in a road traffic accident. Paragraph 12 did not bite on such an award where the personal injury (or rather the fatality) was suffered by the claimant's mother, not the claimant.

Q v SSWP (JSA) [2020] UKUT 49 (AAC) shows that the trust under para.12 does not have to be in any particular form. It does not have to be an express personal injury trust or an express trust at all. It is enough that there is a trust in existence over assets including funds derived from a payment covered by para.12 and the value of the claimant or partner's beneficial interest under the trust would otherwise have counted as part of their capital. So where funds derived from personal injury compensation paid to the claimant were held in joint bank accounts with either of her parents, the disregard applied. The legal right to payment of the funds in the account (a chose in action) was held by the claimant and the parent jointly, but since the funds remained the claimant's (there was nothing to suggest any intention to make a gift to the parent) there was a resulting trust under which they held the funds for the benefit of the claimant. Presumably this will be the case even if the joint account is with the claimant's partner.

2.822

Before October 2, 2006, if there was no trust, the compensation counted as capital. But now see para.12A, inserted with effect from October 2, 2006, which provides a general capital disregard of payments made in consequence of personal injury either to the claimant or the claimant's partner for 52 weeks from the date that the claimant first receives any payment in respect of the injury. Paragraph 12A thus introduces a "grace period" during which a trust fund can be set up (which, as *Q* above shows, can occur very simply by putting the funds into a joint account with another person), or an annuity purchased (see the disregard in para.11), or the money spent. See further the notes to para.12A.

If para.12A does not, or has ceased to, apply, and there is no trust, etc. the compensation counts as capital, even though it is in a solicitor's hands (*Thomas v Chief Adjudication Officer*, reported as (*R(SB) 17/87*; see also *R(IS) 15/96* in the notes to reg.46. But note *CIS 984/2002* which holds that money held by the claimant's solicitor pending quantification of the statutory charge to the Legal Services Commission under s.10(7) of the Access to Justice Act 1999 was not part of the claimant's capital: see further the note to reg.46).

2.823   If the claimant then transfers the compensation to trustees in some way that does not just produce a resulting trust back to the claimant, the exception in reg.51(1)(a) operates so that they will not be treated as having deprived themself of the capital placed on trust. Although putting money into a trust would normally count as deprivation, to do so in the case of trusts of personal injury compensation would defeat the purpose of para.12. It is not necessary for the trust to be set up before the compensation is received. Furthermore, since para.12 refers to funds "derived" from personal injury compensation, it is certainly arguable that the disregard should also apply even if the compensation was initially used for other purposes before being placed on trust. An example could be if the compensation was used to buy a home but this was later sold and the proceeds of sale put on trust. If the money placed on trust derived (in the sense of "originated") from personal injury compensation, there would seem to be no policy reason why the disregard in para.12 should not apply. The purpose of the disregard is presumably to allow such compensation payments to be used for the person's disablement needs that have arisen as a result of the injury. The fact that the funds have been employed elsewhere for an intermediate period would not seem to affect this policy intention.

CIS 368/1994 decides that the disregard in para.12 applied where the compensation was held and administered by a combination of the Public Trustee and the Court of Protection. In the Commissioner's view, the word "trust" was used to cover the situation where the legal estate was in one person and the beneficial interest in another. It did not matter for the purposes of para.12 whether a particular trust had been set up or whether there was in operation a statutory scheme involving, for example, the Court of Protection. The effect of this decision would seem to be that the disregard in para.12 can apply whether the money is administered by the Court of Protection itself or held in the name of the receiver or the Public Trustee. For further discussion of the position of funds held by the Court of Protection, see *R(IS) 9/04* in the note to reg.46.

Now see paras 44 and 45 which have introduced a specific disregard for funds held in court that derive from damages for personal injury, or compensation for the death of a parent, where the person for whom the funds are held is under 18. See the notes to paras 44 and 45.

Any payment from the trust will be income or capital depending on the nature of the payment (income from trusts disregarded under this paragraph is one of the excepted cases from the general rule in reg.48(4) that income from capital counts as capital). But note that from October 2, 2006, income payments, made or due to be made at regular intervals, from a trust fund derived from a payment made in consequence of any personal injury to the claimant is fully disregarded under para.15 of Sch.9. For reasons that are not entirely clear that income disregard has not been amended to include payments in respect of an injury to the claimant's partner in line with the disregard under this paragraph and para.12A. See further the notes to para.15 of Sch.9. Note also the rules for payments to third parties in regs 42(4) and 51(3). The notional income rule in reg.42(2) (income available on application) and the notional capital rules in reg.51(1) (deprivation of capital) and reg.51(2) (capital available on application) do not apply to trusts of personal injury compensation.

Paragraph 12A

2.824   Paragraph 12A provides for a general capital disregard of payments for personal injury (for the disregard where the personal injury payment is held on trust, see para.12 or where it is being administered by a court for a minor, see paras 44 and 45). The disregard applies to a payment made in consequence of a personal injury to *either* the claimant *or* the claimant's partner. It does not apply to payments from a trust fund. But note that the disregard only applies for 52 weeks from the date that the claimant *first* receives any payment in respect of the injury; it does not apply to any subsequent payment (even if made by another person). This is because the purpose of the disregard is to introduce a "grace period" during which a trust fund can be set up (the disregard in para.12 will then apply), or an annuity purchased (see the disregard in para.11), or the money spent.

The disregard under para.12A will cease to apply to the payment or any part of it when the claimant no longer possesses it. See sub-para.(3) which specifically provides that this includes the situation where the claimant has used the payment or part of it to purchase an asset. Unless any of the other disregards in Sch.10 apply (e.g. para.10), it will then be taken into account as capital.

Note also that from October 2, 2006, regular income payments from funds derived from a personal injury award to the claimant are fully disregarded (see para.15 of Sch.9 and the notes to that paragraph). For reasons that are not at all clear that income disregard has not been amended to include payments in respect of an injury to the claimant's partner in line with the disregard under para.12 and this paragraph.

Paragraph 13

This disregard of the value of the right to receive any income under a life interest (under a trust) or from a liferent in Scots law reverses the consequence of *R(SB) 43/84*, where it was pointed out that such a right had a capital value. The nature of a liferent, i.e. the right to receive for life the benefits of property or assets, without the right to dispose of the property or assets, is explained in *LG v SSWP (ESA)* [2019] UKUT 220 (AAC), reported as [2020] AACR 5 (see the notes to para.15 of Sch.9).   **2.825**

Paragraph 14

The provisions mentioned deal with situations where foreign income or earnings cannot be transmitted to the United Kingdom.   **2.826**

Paragraph 15

The surrender value of all life insurance policies is disregarded. In supplementary benefit there was a limit of £1,500.   **2.827**

In *R(IS) 7/98* the claimant had placed her capital in an "investment bond". This provided for a low guaranteed minimum death benefit if the investment had not been fully cashed in before death. But it also included, among other surrender options, a "monthly withdrawal plan", under which the claimant received a sum of £75.20 a month by way of partial encashment until the value of the investment was exhausted. The Commissioner decides that the bond fell within the definition of "policy of life insurance" in reg.2(1). For this definition to apply, it was not necessary for death of the investor to be the only contingency under which money was payable (see *CIS 122/1991*), nor was the relative size of the death benefits on one hand, and the investment benefits on the other, relevant (see *Gould v Curtis* [1913] 3 K.B. 84). The value of the bond therefore fell to be disregarded under para.15 (even though its full investment value was obtainable on demand and so would have come within reg.51(2) (capital available on demand), except for para.15). However, in relation to the original decision to purchase the bond, the deprivation rule in reg.51(1) would have to be considered (see *CIS 112/1994* (and *CIS 109/1994*) in the notes to reg.51). Moreover, since the £75.20 monthly payments represented payments of capital by instalments, for as long as the total outstanding under the policy together with any other capital belonging to the claimant exceeded £8,000 (the then capital limit), such payments would count as income for the period they were paid under reg.41. (See para.16 as regards the right to receive these payments.)

Paragraph 16

See reg.41(1) and *R(IS) 7/98* in the note to para.15.   **2.828**

Paragraph 17

See the notes to para.28 of Sch.9.   **2.829**

Paragraph 18A

2.830 See the note to para.31A of Sch.9.

Paragraph 20

2.831 This is to avoid double counting. Note that the amendments made to this provision on April 6, 2004 do not apply in "transitional cases"—see the note to reg.17. The amendments were made because with effect from April 6, 2004 (except in "transitional cases"—see the note to reg.17) amounts for children and young persons were removed from the income support scheme (financial support for children and young persons is now to be provided through the child tax credit system, see Vol.IV in this series) and income support became in effect an "adults only" benefit. See the 2003 edition of this volume for the old form of para.20.

Paragraph 22

2.832 The disregard now extends to payments to haemophiliacs from the three trusts and to non-haemophiliacs from the Fund, the Eileen Trust, MFET Limited, the Skipton Fund, the Caxton Foundation, the Scottish Infected Blood Support Scheme and other contaminated blood schemes, the London Emergencies Trust and the We Love Manchester Emergency Fund, and the London Bombings Relief Charitable Fund, the National Emergencies Trust, funds giving rise to a Grenfell Tower payment, the Child Migrants Trust and to distributions of capital payments to the close family, or a slightly wider class for the two years following such a person's death. Any payments from the Independent Living Fund are ignored.

Sub-paragraphs (4)(b)(i) and (ii) and (5)(b)(i) and (ii) include references to step-parents. Note that from December 5, 2005, references to "step" relationships and "in laws" are to be read as including relationships arising through civil partnership in any provision to which s.246 of the Civil Partnership Act 2004 applies. Section 246 is applied to sub-paras (4)(b)(i) and (ii) and (5)(b)(i) and (ii) by art.3 of and para.23 of the Schedule to the Civil Partnership Act 2004 (Relationships Arising Through Civil Partnership) Order 2005 (SI 2005/3137).

Paragraph 23

2.833 Accrued rights to receive an occupational or personal pension in the future are often amongst a person's most valuable assets, but they are not capable of being bought or sold, and so have no market value anyway.

Paragraph 23A

2.834 See the notes to reg.42(2)(g) and (2ZA) to (2CA).

Paragraph 24

2.835 This paragraph was amended on October 2, 1995 at the same time as the new form of para.5 was introduced. See the notes to para.5. Since the annual amount of the rent due can be used to calculate the value of a tenanted property the amendment will prevent the annual rent (and thus the capital value of the property) from being reduced to nil because of the disregard.

Paragraph 25

2.836 This paragraph applies where a claimant has ceased to be part of a couple (so that there is a "former partner") following an estrangement or divorce, or dissolution of a civil partnership, and has left what was formerly the home. In these circumstances the claimant may well have an actual or deemed (see reg.52) interest in the dwelling, but no longer be able to get within para.1. But see the notes to reg.52 under "*Former matrimonial assets*" and "*Valuation under regulation 52*" and *R(IS) 1/97* in the notes to para.5.

Divorce or the dissolution of a civil partnership is an easily proved event, but estrangement is a less hard-edged concept. See the note to para.4 for a discussion of the meaning of "estrangement". It seems plain that the meaning should be the same in paras 4 and 25.

The disregard used to be limited to 26 weeks from the date on which the claimant left the dwelling, with no extension. However, with effect from April 1, 2003 it applies without limit if the former partner who occupies the home is a lone parent. This brings the disregard into line with that which applies for the purpose of housing benefit and, until its abolition on April 1, 2013, applied for council tax benefit.

Paragraph 26

This provision restores some of the effect of the similar supplementary benefit disregard. It eases some of the problems noted on p.178 of J. Mesher, *Income Support, the Social Fund and Family Credit: the Legislation* (1988), but not all of them. It applies if reasonable steps are being taken to dispose of premises. "Premises" in para.26 is to be construed widely and includes land without buildings (*R(IS)* 4/97, preferring *CSB 222/1986* to *CIS 673/1993*). See also *R(IS) 3/96* and *CIS 8475/1995* in the notes to paras 3 and 4. What are reasonable steps must be a question of fact. The Commissioner in *R(IS)* 4/97 considers that the test is an objective one. So, if the sale price was totally unrealistic, that attempt at sale should be disregarded and the period of the disregard would not start to run until reasonable steps to dispose of the premises were *first* taken. In his view the period of the disregard must be continuous. *CIS 6908/1995* also confirms that the disregard starts when the claimant first takes steps to dispose of the premises, which may well be before a property is put on the open market. Making a genuine approach to the other tenant in common to agree to a sale, or reaching agreement on an auctioneer and a conveyancer, could constitute taking reasonable steps (*JH v SSWP* [2009] UKUT 1 (AAC)). In *JT v Leicester CC (CTB)* [2012] UKUT 445 (AAC) obtaining a solicitor's quotation for charges associated with a sale and a written valuation from an estate agent were undoubtedly "steps". They were also reasonable steps up to the point when the claimant stopped taking steps to dispose of the property, at which point the disregard in para.26 ceased to apply.

In *R(IS) 5/05* the Commissioner points out that the bringing of ancillary relief proceedings within a divorce suit may have been a necessary preliminary step before a former matriomonial home was put on the market; there also seemed no reason why the para.26 disregard should not apply while arrangements were being made for a former partner to buy the interest of the claimant, which avoided putting the home on the market at all. He added that if the claimant was proposing to buy out the former partner and move back into the matrimonial home herself, the disregard in para.27 might be applicable instead.

CIS/1915/2007 confirms that bringing divorce proceedings could constitute reasonable steps. But the Commissioner also emphasises that a flexible approach had to be taken to the question of reasonableness. If there was a temporary suspension of the divorce proceedings and the resulting disposal of the property, because of family pressures, or threats of violence, or to see if a reconciliation could be achieved, all the circumstances had to be considered to determine whether the claimant was still taking reasonable steps. By putting her divorce proceedings on hold until she had moved to other accommodation and so was in a position where she could safely proceed the claimant was continuing to take such steps. See also *JC-W v Wirral MBC (HB)* [2011] UKUT 501 (AAC) (paras 26–27) decided by the same Commissioner (now Judge).

The initial disregard is for 26 weeks, but can be extended where reasonable to enable the disposal to be carried out.

In *CIS 562/1992* it is held that the 26 weeks does not run from the beginning of each fresh claim for income support, but from the day on which the claimant first took steps to dispose of the property. On its particular facts (it was several years since the property was first put on the market and the claimant had transferred ownership of it to his son for some time but then taken it back) this decision seems right. However,

2.837

2.838

if a property is up for sale, then is genuinely taken off the market and put up for sale again later, it must be arguable that the time under para.26 starts running afresh from the second occasion of taking steps to dispose of the property. This approach is supported by *CIS/2668/1998* and *CJSA/2379/1998* (see in particular para.9). As the Commissioner in those cases confirms, it will depend on the circumstances of each case. See also *SP v SSWP* [2009] UKUT 255 (AAC) which states that para.29585 of the *Decision Makers Guide*, in taking the view that the disregard always runs from the date the person first took steps, does not properly reflect the law on this point. (Note that the current version of para.29585 does acknowledge that there may be exceptional circumstances where the first date may change due to a break in attempts to market the property.)

A further question is for how long the disregard should apply. This again is pre-eminently a question of fact (*SP v SSWP* [2009] UKUT 255 (AAC); *CIS/6908/1995*). In *CIS/6908/1995* the Commissioner suggests some of the factors that might be relevant in deciding whether the 26 weeks should be extended. Besides the efforts made by the claimant to dispose of the property, other factors might be the state of the housing market, the claimant's intentions as regards the proceeds of sale, the value of his interest in the property and his ability to borrow money on the strength of that interest. *SP v SSWP* suggests that a person's state of health may also be a relevant consideration (see *CIS/4757/2003* decided in the context of the disregard under para.3 of this Schedule).

2.839   *CIS/6908/1995* accepts that the 26 weeks could run while the property was being disregarded under some other paragraph of Sch.10. But it would often be right to extend the period to a date (at least) 26 weeks after the property had ceased to be disregarded under that other paragraph (because otherwise the effect could be to deprive a claimant of the benefit of para.26).

CIS 30/1993 decides that this disregard cannot apply to notional capital if the claimant has already disposed of the same capital so as to trigger reg.51(1). This is because para.26 is only applicable where the *claimant* is taking steps to dispose of premises. The Commissioner in *CIS 30/1993* acknowledges that this view is different from that taken in some other decisions, but having reviewed these (*R(SB) 9/91*, *CIS 25/1990*, *CIS 81/1991* and *CIS 562/1992*) concludes that the only one in which this question had been central to the appeal was *CIS 25/1990* and in that case the point had not been argued in any detail. He was therefore not bound by it (*R1/92 (IS)*, a decision of the Chief Commissioner in Northern Ireland, had come to the same conclusion as he had done). It had been argued on behalf of the claimant that if the property was put up for sale by the actual possessor of it, para.26 should apply. The Secretary of State had submitted, first, that the wording of para.26 made it clear that the disregard only applied if the claimant was taking steps to dispose of the premises; second, that the purpose of the disregard in para.26 was to allow the claimant a reasonable time to liquidate assets to provide money to live on. There could be no guarantee that the third party would allow the proceeds of sale to be used to support the claimant and thus there was no reason to delay counting the notional capital. The Commissioner holds that the words of para.26 were plain and unambiguous and could not apply because the claimant could not be taking steps to dispose of what she had already disposed of. This seems unfair in that a claimant deemed to have notional capital may suffer an additional penalty through not being able to benefit from the disregard in para.26. But the Commissioner's conclusion is cogently argued.

Paragraph 27

2.840   In these circumstances the claimant will have an interest in the premises, but it would be unfair to count the value of the interest. The initial disregard is for 26 weeks from the date of first seeking legal advice or commencing proceedings with a view to obtaining possession, with an extension as reasonable.

In *CIS 240/1992* the legal advice given to the claimant was that he could not obtain possession of the premises until the end of the current tenancy. The

Commissioner states that for para.27 to apply the claimant must be taking steps to obtain possession and rejects a submission that a failure to take steps that were bound to be unsuccessful did not preclude the application of para.27. But in seeking legal advice was not the claimant taking such steps? Paragraph 27 does not require claimants to have commenced legal proceedings for the disregard to apply; it is sufficient if they have sought legal advice with a view to obtaining possession. Provided that a claimant is willing to commence proceedings immediately the tenancy ends (which did not appear to be the case in *CIS 240/1992*) it is difficult to see what other steps they could take in such circumstances.

Paragraph 28

Since the value of the home is disregarded, this is a limited extension, to cover premises needing work to be fit for human habitation and which the claimant intends to occupy as the home. Then the disregard is for 26 weeks from first taking steps to effect the works, with an extension as reasonable.   **2.841**

The scope of the similar disregard in para.27 of Sch.5 to the Housing Benefit Regulations was considered in *R. v Tower Hamlets LBC Housing Benefit Review Board, Ex p. Kapur, The Times*, June 28, 2000, HC. The claimant, who was in receipt of housing and council tax benefit, owned a house valued at £240,000 which was vacant and unfit for human habitation. He wanted to move into the property and made several unsuccessful attempts to obtain finance to effect repairs to it. The local authority decided that the value of the property could not be disregarded because the steps taken by the applicant to raise finance were merely preparatory and were not steps taken to effect repairs. Scott Baker J held that this was the wrong approach. He referred to the *Adjudication Officer's Guide* which stated, in relation to the income support disregard in para.28, that steps could include getting a grant or loan to pay for repairs or alterations, employing an architect, getting planning permission or finding someone to do the work, and the date that a person first took such steps could be the date he first started making these inquiries. It was a question of fact as to when the first steps were taken but the Board's approach had been too narrow. Now see paras 29572–6 of the *Decision Makers Guide*.

Paragraph 29

Payments of earnings or other income in kind are disregarded as income (see regs 35(2) and 40(4) and Sch.9 para.21). Most payments of capital in kind would be personal possessions (see the disregard in para.10). Note that the trusts covered by this provision are now not quite the same as those covered by para.22(1) and (7).   **2.842**

Paragraph 30

The new form of this paragraph in force from April 1, 2004 provides a blanket capital disregard of the various allowances, grants and other payments made under s.2 of the Employment and Training Act 1973 or s.2 of the Enterprise and New Towns (Scotland) Act 1990 to people participating in New Deals and other training and welfare to work schemes. However if these payments do count as capital they are only ignored for 52 weeks from the date of receipt.   **2.843**

Before April 1, 2004 separate disregards had existed in respect of such payments under a number of the provisions in this Schedule. As a consequence of this change, those provisions have been revoked or amended. The revoked paragraphs are paras 50, 50A, 51, 53, 69 and 70; the amended paragraph is para.42.

For the income disregard of payments under s.2 of the 1973 Act and s.2 of the 1990 Act see para.13 of Sch.9.

Paragraph 36

See the note to para.46 of Sch.9 but if any such payment does count as capital the disregard only applies for 52 weeks from the date of receipt of the payment.   **2.844**

Paragraph 42

2.845   These are capital payments from special Department of Employment schemes to assist disabled people, such as the "business on own account' scheme and the "personal reader service."

Paragraph 43

2.846   Start-up capital payments under the Blind Homeworkers' Scheme are disregarded, but payments of income are taken into account.

Paragraphs 44–45

2.847   These paragraphs were amended in October 1997 so that the disregard of funds held in court that derive from damages for personal injury is no longer restricted to under 18-year-olds but now applies without age limit. However, where the compensation was awarded for the death of a parent (or parents), the person concerned must be under 18 for the disregard to apply. Death benefits under a pension or insurance policy are not compensation, since this implies the replacement of something lost, whereas such benefits are paid on the basis of a contract made by the deceased (*McAuley v Department for Social Development*, Court of Appeal of Northern Ireland, reported as *R 3/01(IS)*).

See para.12 for the disregard of compensation payments for personal injury held on trust. *CIS 368/1994* decided that the disregard in para.12 applied to compensation for personal injury that was held and administered by the Court of Protection, since in the circumstances such an arrangement amounted to a "trust". (For further discussion of the position of funds held by the Court of Protection, see *R(IS) 9/04* in the note to reg.46.) The disregard in para.44(2)(a) will now apply to damages for personal injury held by the Court of Protection (and also the High Court and the County Court, and, under para.45(a), the equivalent Scottish courts).

The term "Court of Protection" in para.44 is apt to refer to the current Court of Protection (established under the Mental Capacity Act 2005 with effect from October 1, 2007) which replaced the former Court of Protection (which was an office of the Supreme Court constituted under the Mental Health Act 1983) (*R(ZYN) v Walsall MBC* [2014] EWHC 1918 (Admin)).

2.848   Note that the award must be for injury "to that person". The disregard under para.44(2)(a) does not apply where the award was under the Fatal Accidents Act 1976 (*CP v SSWP (IS)* [2011] UKUT 157 (AAC)). There, the claimant, who had Down's syndrome, received substantial compensation under the 1976 Act after her mother (and primary carer) was killed in a road traffic accident. Paragraph 44(2)(a) did not apply because the personal injury (or rather the fatality) was suffered by the claimant's mother, not the claimant. Furthermore, the fact that it did not apply was not contrary to ECHR.

CP v SSWP also decides that the disregard in para.44(2)(b) only applies while the person concerned is under 18. As the claimant was 22 when she first claimed income support, para.44(2)(b) did not apply.

A new form of para.44 was substituted with effect from October 2, 2006, so that it applies not only to capital administered by a court but also to capital "which can only be disposed of by order or direction of [a] court" (see sub-para.(1)(b) and (c)). This amendment is apparently to allow for the contracting-out of the administering of court funds to the private sector, which the DCA, now the Ministry of Justice, was apparently contemplating.

2.849   "Personal injury" includes a disease and any injuries suffered as a result of a disease (e.g. amputation of both legs following meningitis and septicaemia), as well as any accidental or criminal injury (*R(SB) 2/89*).

"An award of damages for a personal injury" covers all heads of an award of damages for personal injury (*Peters v East Midland Strategic Heath Authority* [2009] EWCA Civ 145; [2010] Q.B.48). In particular, it is not restricted to general damages for pain, suffering and loss of amenity, but can include other heads of loss, such as loss of earnings and any sum awarded by a court in respect of the cost of providing accommodation and care. See also *R(IS) 15/96* (para.18).

Note that with effect from October 2, 2006, paras 44 and 45 have been added to the list of exceptions from the general rule in reg.48(4) that income from capital counts as capital. Payments to a claimant from funds disregarded under para.44 or 45 will therefore count as income or capital depending on the nature of the payments. The intention is to align the treatment of payments from funds held in court that derive from personal injury with that of payments from trusts of personal injury compensation, and that the disregard in para.15 of Sch.9, which from October 2, 2006 is a total disregard, should equally apply to regular payments from personal injury funds held in court. Presumably it is considered that, applying *CIS/368/1994*, payments from such court funds are covered by para.15(5A)(c) (payments from a trust fund derived from a payment made in consequence of any personal injury to the claimant). In addition, they may fall within para.15(5A)(e) (payments "received by virtue of any agreement or court order to make payments to the claimant in consequence of any personal injury to the claimant"). Note that the income disregard in para.15 of Sch.9 only applies to payments made as a consequence of personal injury to the claimant (see further the notes to para.15 of Sch.9). The disregard in para.15 would not normally seem to apply where the funds held in court are derived from compensation for the death of one or both parents.

2.850

Note also that funds disregarded under para.44(2)(a) and para.45(a) are excluded from the notional income rule in reg.42(2) (income available on application) and the notional capital rules in reg.51(1)(c) and (2)(e) (deprivation of capital and capital available on application).

2.851

Paragraph 52

Any capital acquired for the purposes of a business carried on while a person is participating in the "self-employment route" (defined in reg.2(1)) is ignored for 52 weeks from the date of receipt.

2.852

See also the disregard of business assets for people participating in the self-employment route in para.6(3) and (4) and the general disregard of payments made under s.2 of the Employment and Training Act 1973 or s.2 of the Enterprise and New Towns (Scotland) Act 1990 in para.30.

Paragraph 56

See the note to para.69 of Sch.9. Note that if a sports award (or part of it) counts as capital, the payment will only be disregarded for 26 weeks from the date of receipt.

2.853

Paragraphs 58 and 59

See the note to reg.42(5A).

2.854

Paragraph 60

This paragraph has not been reproduced as it only related to a pilot scheme to reduce under-occupation operating in three London boroughs (Croydon, Haringey and Newham) from April 3, 2000. It was added by reg.12 of the Social Security (Payments to Reduce Under-occupation) Regulations 2000 (SI 2000/637) on April 3, 2000 and provided that a payment made under the scheme would be ignored for 52 weeks from the date of payment. The pilot scheme lasted for three years and the Payments to Reduce Under-occupation Regulations ceased to have effect on March 31, 2003.

2.855

Paragraph 61

This allows ex-gratia payments of £10,000, made to former Japanese prisoners of war or internees or to their surviving spouse or civil partner, on or after February 1, 2001, to be disregarded indefinitely.

2.856

Paragraph 62

2.857   This provides for the whole of a claimant's capital to be disregarded during any "housing costs run-on" period. See the notes to reg.6(5)–(8) as to when this applies (note that from December 17, 2007 it was extended so that it applies to all housing costs that can be met by income support). See also the disregards in para.15C of Sch.8 and para.74 of Sch.9 and the note to para.15C.

Paragraph 63

2.858   See the note to para.11 of Sch.9. Note that the new form of para.63 in force from the start of the national scheme of education maintenance allowances (EMAs) provides for an indefinite disregard of any part of the EMA that counts as capital.

The October 31, 2011 amendments to para.63 allow for payments made from the "16–19 Bursary Fund" to be disregarded in the same way as EMAs. The bursary scheme was introduced in September 2011 to help vulnerable 16–19 year olds continue in full-time education and replaces the education maintenance allowance in England.

Paragraph 64

2.859   This refers to payments from, or derived from, the government-funded trust funds set up to help those who have contracted variant Creutsfeldt-Jakob disease. The disregard extends to distribution of capital to the partner of the "diagnosed person" (defined in sub-para.(6)), to any child for two years from the date of the payment, or until he leaves full-time education or becomes 20, if this is later, or to any parent for two years from the date of the payment.

Paragraph 65

2.860   This provides for an indefinite disregard as capital of compensation paid because the claimant, partner, deceased spouse or deceased civil partner or partner's deceased spouse or deceased civil partner was forced to work, lost property or suffered personal injury, or was the parent of a child who died, during the Second World War.

Paragraph 66

2.861   See the note to para.76 of Sch.9.

Paragraph 67

2.862   This disregard has been introduced to ensure that if payments for community care services which a local authority makes direct to the person concerned do count as capital they are not taken into account. For the income disregard see para.58 of Sch.9.

Modification of para.67

2.863   With effect from April 1, 2014, the disregard in para.67 is modified by art.2 of, and para.1 of the Schedule to, the Social Care (Self-directed Support) (Scotland) Act 2013 (Consequential Modifications and Savings) Order 2014 (SI 2014/513) so that the words "as a direct payment as defined in section 4(2) of the Social Care (Self-directed Support) (Scotland) Act 2013" are substituted for the words "under section 12B of the Social Work (Scotland) 1968". However, under art.3 of the Order, this modification does not apply if a payment is made under s.12B of the 1968 Act on or after April 1, 2014.

Paragraph 68

2.864   For the regulations under ss.2(6)(b), 3 or 4 of the Adoption and Children Act 2002 see the Adoption Support Services Regulations 2005 (SI 2005/691) and the Adoption Support Services (Local Authorities) (Wales) Regulations 2005 (SI 2005/1512). Any payments to adopters or potential adopters made under these provisions are fully disregarded as capital. For the disregard as income see para.25(1)(a) of Sch.9. There appears to be no capital disregard for payments under the corresponding Scottish scheme (see the Adoption Services and Allowances

(Scotland) Regulations 2009 (SSI 2009/152)), although there is an income disregard.

Paragraph 68A

Section 115 of the Adoption and Children Act 2002 amended the Children Act **2.865** 1989 to introduce a new special guardianship order, which is intended to provide permanence for children for whom adoption is not appropriate; the special guardian has parental responsibility for the child but the child's legal relationship with his birth parents is not severed. The special guardianship provisions came into force on December 30, 2005. Payments made by local authorities to special guardians are ignored. For the income disregard see para.25(1)(e) of Sch.9.

Paragraph 71

This provides for a capital disregard of payments under s.49 of the Children and **2.866** Families Act 2014. See further the annotation to para.79 of Sch.9, under which payments under s.49 are disregarded as income.

Paragraph 72

The initial one-off lump sum payment of the new (from April 2017) and contro- **2.867** versial bereavement support payment is disregarded as capital under this provision for 52 weeks from the date of receipt. The insertion of sub-para.(f) into para.7(1) secures the disregard as capital of payments of arrears of monthly payments, also for 52 weeks from the date of receipt. In so far as arrears of monthly payments retain their character as income rather than capital (see the notes to para.7 above) they would be disregarded under para.80 of Sch.9.

Paragraph 73

Any capital payments from trusts to do with the effects of thalidomide are dis- **2.868** regarded as capital by this provision. There is no special provision in Sch.9 for payments of income from such trusts. Thus in so far as payments of income from such trusts are not made or due to be made at regular intervals they would appear as charitable or voluntary payments to be treated as capital (reg.48(9)) and then disregarded by this provision. In so far as such payments are not treated as capital in that way they would be disregarded as income under para.15 of Sch.9.

Paragraph 74

Payments under s.73 of the Children and Young People (Scotland) Act 2014 **2.869** have been available in Scotland since April 2016 to people who have applied or are at least considering applying for a kinship care order for a child who is at risk of going into care or was previously looked after by a local authority. They are disregarded as income other than earnings by para.27A of Sch.9, as earnings from self-employment by reg.37(2)(b) and as capital by the present provision.

Paragraph 75

Scottish early years assistance, constituted initially (from December 10, 2018) **2.870** by best start grants replacing the Sure Start Maternity grants still available to those living in England and Wales, is to be disregarded as capital. It is disregarded as income by para.82 of Sch.9, if the lump sum payments could constitute income.

Paragraph 76

Funeral expense assistance, disregarded as capital by this paragraph, is imple- **2.871** mented by the Funeral Expense Assistance (Scotland) Regulations 2019 (SSI 2019/292) (see Vol.IV of this series). See para.83 of Sch.9 for the disregard as income.

Paragraph 77

Under the specified regulations (SSI 2019/324, in operation from October 21, **2.872** 2019: see Vol.IV of this series), young carer grants of (from April 2021) £308.15, limited to one a year, are payable in Scotland to carers aged 16 to 18 who care for at least 16 hours a week over a 13-week period for a person who normally receives a disability benefit. There appears to have been a gap during which grants were not disregarded as capital, since para 77 did not come into force until November 9, 2020. No disregard as income has been introduced, but no doubt the grants are in their nature payments of capital.

Paragraph 78

2.873   The relevant regulations under s.30 of the Social Security (Scotland) Act 2018 are the Winter Heating Assistance for Children and Young People (Scotland) Regulations 2020 (SSI 2020/352, in operation from November 9, 2020: see Vol.IV of this series), which initially provide an automatic annual grant in November 2020 to a family of £200 (£202 for 2021) for each child entitled to the highest rate of the care component of DLA in the week of September 21–27, 2020. No disregard as income has been introduced, as the grant plainly constitutes capital.

The Income Support (Liable Relatives) Regulations 1990

(SI 1990/1777) (AS AMENDED)

Made by the Secretary of State under s.166(1) to (3A) of the Social Security Act 1975 and ss.24A(1), 24B(5) and 84(1) of the Social Security Act 1986

Citation, commencement and interpretation

2.874   **1.**—(1) These Regulations may be cited as the Income Support (Liable Relatives) Regulations 1990 and shall come into force on 15th October 1990.
(2) In these Regulations—
"the Act" means the Social Security Act 1986; and
"the Income Support Regulations" means the Income Support (General) Regulations 1987.

Prescribed amounts for the purposes of section 24A of the Act [SSAA, s.107]

2.875   **2.**—(1) For the purposes of section 24A of the Act [SSAA, s.107] (recovery of expenditure on income support: additional amounts and transfer of orders) the amount which may be included in the sum which the court may order the other parent to pay under section 24(4) of the Act [SSAA, s.106(2)] shall be the whole of the following amounts which are payable to or for the claimant—
(a) any personal allowance under paragraph 2 of Part I of Schedule 2 to the Income Support Regulations for each of the children whom the other parent is liable to maintain;
(b) any family premium under paragraph 3 of Part II of that Schedule;
(c) any lone parent premium under paragraph 8 of Part III of that Schedule;
(d) any disabled child premium under paragraph 14 of Part III of that Schedule in respect of a child whom the other parent is liable to maintain; and
(e) any carer premium under paragraph 14ZA of Part III of that Schedule if, but only if, that premium is payable because the claimant is in receipt, or is treated as being in receipt, of [¹ carer's allowance] by reason of the fact that he is caring for a severely disabled child or young person whom the other parent is liable to maintain.

(2) If the court is satisfied that in addition to the amounts specified in paragraph (1) above the liable parent has the means to pay, the sum which the court may order him to pay under section 24 of the Act [SSAA, s.106] may also include all or some of the amount of any personal allowance payable to or for the claimant under paragraph 1 of Part I of Schedule 2 to the Income Support Regulations.

<small>AMENDMENT</small>

1. Social Security Amendment (Carer's Allowance) Regulations 2002 (SI 2002/2497) reg.3 and Sch.2 (April 1, 2003).

Notice to the Secretary of State of applications to alter etc. maintenance orders

3.—(1) For the purposes of section 24B(5) of the Act [SSAA, s.108(5)]   2.876
(prescribed person in prescribed circumstances to notify the Secretary of State of application to alter etc. a maintenance order) the prescribed person is, and in paragraph (2) below that expression means,—
(a) in England and Wales—
    (i) in relation to the High Court, where the case is proceeding in the deputy principal registry the senior registrar of that registry, and where the case is proceeding in a district registry the district registrar;
    (ii) in relation to a county court, the proper officer of that court within the meaning of Order 1, Rule 3 of the County Court Rules 1981; and
    (iii) in relation to a magistrates' court, the clerk to the justices of that court; and
(b) in Scotland—
    (i) in relation to the Court of Session, the deputy principal clerk of session; and
    (ii) in relation to a sheriff court, the sheriff clerk.
(2) For the purposes of that subsection the prescribed circumstances are that before the final determination of the application the Secretary of State has made a written request to the prescribed person that he be notified of any such application, and has not made a written withdrawal of that request.

<small>GENERAL NOTE</small>

See the notes to ss.107 and 108 of the Administration Act in Vol.III of   2.877
this series.

The Social Security (Restrictions on Amounts for Children and Qualifying Young Persons) Amendment Regulations 2017

(SI 2017/376)

[IN FORCE APRIL 6, 2017]

The Secretary of State, in exercise of the powers conferred by sections 123(1)(a)   2.878
*and (d), 135(1), 136(3) and (5)(b), 137 and 175(1), (3) and (4) of the Social
Security Contributions and Benefits Act 1992, sections 4(5), 12(1) and (4)(b), 35*

and 36(2) of the Jobseekers Act 1995, sections 4(5)(b), 10(4), 11(3)(b) and (c), 12(1) and (4)(b), 19(2)(d), 20(1)(b), 24(5), 40 and 42(1), (2) and (3) of, and paragraphs 4(1)(a) and (3)(a) and 5(1) of Schedule 1 and paragraphs 1(1) and 3(1)(b) of Schedule 6 to, the Welfare Reform Act 2012 and sections 14(6) and 34 of the Welfare Reform and Work Act 2016, makes the following Regulations.

REGULATIONS REPRODUCED

5. Restrictions on amounts for children and young persons – consequential changes to the Income Support (General) Regulations 1987
6. Restrictions on amounts for children and young persons – consequential changes to the Jobseeker's Allowance Regulations 1996

GENERAL NOTE

2.879   The effect of the main amending provisions of these Regulations, which restrict the amount of the child element of universal credit payable in cases where the claimant (or claimants) are responsible for more than two children or young persons, are shown in Pt IIA of Vol.II of this series, *Universal Credit etc*, and readers are referred to the detailed commentary in that volume.

Since April 6, 2004, IS and income-based JSA have been adults only benefits except in what this volume calls "transitional cases": see the commentary to reg.17 of the Income Support Regulations. In such cases, regs 5 and 6 impose the two-child limit if a child is born (or a child or young person joins the claimant's household) after April 6, 2017.

Note that where the effect of reg.5 or reg.6 is that no IS or JSA personal allowance for a particular child or young person is included in the claimant's applicable amount, child benefit for that child or young person is disregarded when calculating the claimant's income: see regs 5(3) and 6(3).

Restrictions on amounts for children and young persons – consequential changes to the Income Support (General) Regulations 1987

2.880   **5.**—(1) Subject to paragraph (2) where, in relation to an award of income support, an amount in respect of one or more children or young persons is included in the applicable amount because regulation 2 of, and Schedule 1 to, the Social Security (Working Tax Credit and Child Tax Credit) (Consequential Amendments) Regulations 2003 do not have effect, no amount is to be included in respect of a child or young person who is born after 6th April 2017 if—

(a) when that child or young person is born or (if later) becomes a member of the claimant's family, there are two or more children or young persons in respect of whom an amount is already included in the claimant's applicable amount; and

(b) two or more of those children or young persons remain members of the claimant's family.

(2) Paragraph (1) does not prevent an amount being included in respect of a child or young person in respect of whom [¹ the child element specified in regulation 24(1) of the Universal Credit Regulations 2013 would be payable] if the claimant were entitled to an award of universal credit.

(3) Where an amount may not be included in the applicable amount in respect of a child or young person by virtue of paragraph (1), any child benefit in respect of that child or young person is to be disregarded in the calculation of the claimant's gross income for the purposes of regulation 40 of the Income Support (General) Regulations 1987.

(4) In this regulation—

(a) "claimant" has the meaning prescribed in regulation 2(1) of the Income Support (General) Regulations 1987;

(b) "young person" has the meaning prescribed in regulation 14 of the Income Support (General) Regulations 1987.

AMENDMENT

1. Universal Credit and Jobseeker's Allowance (Miscellaneous Amendments) Regulations 2018 (SI 2018/1129) reg.5(a) (November 28, 2018).

Restrictions on amounts for children and young persons – consequential changes to the Jobseeker's Allowance Regulations 1996

6.—(1) Subject to paragraph (2) where, in relation to an award of jobseeker's allowance, an amount in respect of one or more children or young persons is included in the applicable amount because regulation 3 of, and Schedule 2 to, the Social Security (Working Tax Credit and Child Tax Credit) (Consequential Amendments) Regulations 2003 do not have effect, no amount is to be included in respect of a child or young person who is born after 6th April 2017 if—   **2.881**

(a) when that child or young person is born or (if later) becomes a member of the claimant's family, there are two or more children or young persons in respect of whom an amount is already included in the claimant's applicable amount; and

(b) two or more of those children or young persons remain members of the claimant's family.

(2) Paragraph (1) does not prevent an amount being included in respect of a child or young person in respect of whom [¹ the child element specified in regulation 24(1) of the Universal Credit Regulations 2013 would be payable] if the claimant were entitled to an award of universal credit.

(3) Where an amount may not be included in the applicable amount in respect of a child or young person by virtue of paragraph (1), any child benefit in respect of that child or young person is to be disregarded in the calculation of the claimant's gross income for the purposes of regulation 103 of the Jobseeker's Allowance Regulations 1996.

(4) In this regulation, "young person" has the meaning prescribed in regulation 76 of the Jobseeker's Allowance Regulations 1996.

AMENDMENT

1. Universal Credit and Jobseeker's Allowance (Miscellaneous Amendments) Regulations 2018 (SI 2018/1129) reg.5(b) (November 28, 2018).

The Social Security (Persons from Abroad) Miscellaneous Amendments Regulations 1996

(SI 1996/30)

The saving provisions in reg.12 of these Regulations (which was the only regulation previously reproduced here) have now been omitted because it is unlikely that they are still relevant to any cases. The full text of reg.12 appears in all edi-   **2.882** *tions of Vol.II from 2000 to 2018/19. See also the note to Part VI (Urgent Cases) of the IS Regulations on pp.497–509 of Vol.II of the 2009/10 edition.*

The Social Security (Habitual Residence) Amendment Regulations 2004

(SI 2004/1232)

Made by the Secretary of State under ss.123(1)(a), (d) and (e), 131(3) (b), 135(1) and (2), 137(1) and (2)(i) and 175(1), (3) and (4) of the Social Security Contributions and Benefits Act 1992, ss.4(5), 35(1) and 36(2) and (4) of the Jobseekers Act 1995 and ss.1(5)(a) and 17(1) of the State Pension Credit Act 2002

[In force May 1, 2004]

GENERAL NOTE

2.883   See the commentary to reg.21AA of the Income Support Regulations.

These regulations were completely revoked by reg.11(1)(d) of SI 2006/1026 with effect from April 30, 2006 but with a saving (in reg.11(2)(b)) for the transitional protection in reg.6 below.

Transitional arrangements and savings

2.884   **6.**—(1) Paragraph (2) shall apply where a person—

(a) is entitled to a specified benefit in respect of a period which includes 30th April 2004;

(b) claims a specified benefit on or after 1 May 2004 and it is subsequently determined that he is entitled to that benefit in respect of a period which includes 30 April 2004;

(c) claims a specified benefit on or after 1 May 2004 and it is subsequently determined that he is entitled to such a benefit in respect of a period which is continuous with a period of entitlement to the same or another specified benefit which includes 30 April 2004;

[¹ (ca) to whom sub-paragraph (c) applied, claims an employment and support allowance and it is subsequently determined that he is entitled to that benefit, and this entitlement is linked to a previous period of entitlement by virtue of regulation 145(1) of the Employment and Support Allowance Regulations (linking rules);]

(d) claims jobseeker's allowance on or after 1 May 2004 and it is subsequently determined that he is entitled to jobseeker's allowance in respect of a period of entitlement to that benefit which is linked to a previous period of entitlement which includes 30 April 2004 by virtue of regulations made under paragraph 3 of Schedule 1 to the Jobseekers Act 1995.

(2) Where this paragraph applies—

(a) *[Omitted]*;

(b) regulation 21 of the Income Support Regulations shall continue to have effect as if regulation 3 had not been made;

(c) regulation 85 of the Jobseeker's Allowance Regulations shall continue to have effect as if regulation 4 had not been made; [¹ . . .]
(d) regulation 2 of the State Pension Credit Regulations shall continue to have effect as if regulation 5 had not been made. [¹ ; and
(e) regulation 70(2) to (4) of the Employment and Support Allowance Regulations (special cases: supplemental – persons from abroad) does not apply.]

(3) The provisions saved by paragraph (2) shall continue to have effect until the date on which entitlement to a specified benefit for the purposes of paragraph (1) ceases, and if there is more than one such specified benefit, until the last date on which such entitlement ceases.

[¹ (4) In this regulation—
(a) "the Employment and Support Allowance Regulations" means the Employment and Support Allowance Regulations 2008; and
(b) "specified benefit" means income support, housing benefit, council tax benefit, jobseeker's allowance, state pension credit and employment and support allowance.]

AMENDMENT

1. Social Security (Miscellaneous Amendments) (No.3) Regulations 2011 (SI 2011/2425) reg.17 (October 31, 2011).

MODIFICATION

Regulation 6 is modified by Sch.2 para.27 of the Employment and Support Allowance (Transitional Provisions, Housing Benefit and Council Tax Benefit) (Existing Awards) (No.2) Regulations 2010 (SI 2010/1907) (as amended) for the purposes specified in reg.16(1). For details of the modification, see the text of those Regulations in Vol.I.

The Social Security (Persons from Abroad) Amendment Regulations 2006

(2006/1026)

Made by the Secretary of State under sections 123(1)(a), (d) and (e), 131(3) (b), 135(1) and (2), 137(1) and (2), 138(1)(a) and (4) and 175(1), (3) and (4) of the Social Security Contributions and Benefits Act 1992, sections 4(5) and (12), 35(1) and 36(2) and (4) of, and paragraph 11 of Schedule 1 to, the Jobseekers Act 1995 and sections 1(5)(a) and 17(1) of the State Pension Credit Act 2002, after agreement by the Social Security Advisory Committee that proposals to make these Regulations should not be referred to it;

ARRANGEMENT OF REGULATIONS

2.885

[30th April 2006]

Citation and commencement

2.886   **1.**—These Regulations shall be cited as the Social Security (Persons from Abroad) Amendment Regulations 2006 and shall come into force on 30th April 2006.

[Regulations 2–5 omitted as relating solely to housing benefit and council tax benefit]

[Regulations 6–9 noted at the appropriate places in the text of the amended regulations]

Nationals of Norway, Iceland, Liechtenstein and Switzerland

2.887   **10.**—The following provisions shall apply in relation to a national of Norway, Iceland, Liechtenstein or Switzerland or a member of his family (within the meaning of Article 2 of Council Directive No. 2004/38/EC) as if such a national were a national of a member State—

(a)–(d) *[Omitted as relating solely to housing benefit and council tax benefit]*

   (e) regulation 21AA(4)(a) to (e) of the Income Support (General) Regulations 1987;

   (f) regulation 85A(4)(a) to (e) of the Jobseeker's Allowance Regulations 1996;

   (g) regulation 7(10) of the Social Fund Maternity and Funeral Expenses (General) Regulations 2005; and

   (h) regulation 2(4)(a) to (e) of the State Pension Credit Regulations 2002.

Revocations and savings

2.888   **11.**—(1) The following Regulations are revoked—

(a)–(d) *[Noted at the appropriate places in the text of the revoked regulations]*

   (2) Nothing in these Regulations shall affect the continued operation of the transitional arrangements and savings provided for in—

   (a) regulation 12 of the Social Security (Persons From Abroad) Miscellaneous Amendments Regulations 1996;

   (b) regulation 6 of the Social Security (Habitual Residence) Amendment Regulations 2004; or

   (c) *[Omitted as applying solely to housing benefit and council tax benefit]*

The Community Charges (Deductions from Income Support) (No.2) Regulations 1990

(SI 1990/545) (AS AMENDED)

Made by the Secretary of State under ss.22(3) and 146(6) and Sch.4 para.6 of the Local Government Finance Act 1988

The first version of these Regulations (SI 1990/107) was defective and was **2.889**
replaced.

The Community Charges (Deductions from Income Support) (Scotland) Regulations 1989 (SI 1989/507) made provision for Scotland from April 10, 1989. They have been amended by SI 1990/113 to bring them into line with these Regulations, but are not reproduced.

Citation, commencement and interpretation

1.—(1) These Regulations may be cited as the Community Charges **2.890**
(Deductions from Income Support) (No.2) Regulations 1990 and shall come into force on 1 April 1990.

(2) In these Regulations, unless the context otherwise requires—

[³. . .];

"the 1986 Act" means the Social Security Act 1986;

[³. . .];

[⁴"the 1998 Act" means the Social Security Act 1998;]

"appropriate social security office" means an office of the Department of Social Security which is normally open to the public for the receipt of claims for income support and includes an office of the [¹Department for Education and Employment] which is normally open to the public for the receipt of claims for [¹jobseeker's allowance and income support];

[⁸ "assessment period" means the period prescribed by regulation 21 of the UC Regulations;]

[⁵"Commissioner" has the meaning it bears in section 39(1) of the 1998 Act;]

[²"contribution-based jobseeker's allowance", except in a case to which paragraph (b) of the definition of income-based jobseeker's allowance applies, means a contribution-based jobseeker's allowance under Part I of the Jobseekers Act 1995, but does not include any back to work bonus under section 26 of the Jobseekers Act which is paid as jobseeker's allowance;]

"couple" means a married or unmarried couple;

"debtor" means a person against whom a liability order has been obtained;

"5 per cent. of the personal allowance for a single claimant aged not less than 25" and

"5 per cent. of the personal allowance for a couple where both members are aged not less than 18" means, in each case, where the percentage is not a multiple of 5 pence, the sum obtained by rounding that 5 per cent. to the next higher such multiple;

"income support" means income support within the meaning of the 1986 Act [¹but does not include any back to work bonus under section 26 of the Jobseekers Act which is paid as income support;]

[²"income-based jobseeker's allowance" means—

(a) an income-based jobseeker's allowance under Part I of the Jobseekers Act 1995; and

(b) in a case where, if there was no entitlement to contribution-based jobseeker's allowance, there would be entitlement to income-based jobseeker's allowance at the same rate, contribution-based jobseeker's allowance;]

but does not include any back to work bonus under section 26 of the Jobseekers Act which is paid as jobseeker's allowance;]

[¹"Jobseekers Act" means the Jobseekers Act 1995;

"jobseeker's allowance" means an allowance under Part I of the Jobseekers Act but does not include any back to work bonus under section 26 of that Act which is paid as jobseeker's allowance;]

"liability order" means an order under regulation 29 of the Community Charges (Administration and Enforcement) Regulations 1989;

"married couple" has the meaning ascribed to it in section 20(11) of the 1986 Act [SSCBA, s.137(1)];

"payments to third parties" means direct payments to third parties in accordance with Schedule 9 to the Social Security (Claims and Payments) Regulations 1987 [⁸ or Schedule 6 to the UC etc. Claims and Payments Regulations,];

"polygamous marriage" means a marriage to which section 22B of the Social Security Act 1986 [SSCBA, s.133] refers;

"single debtor" means a debtor who is not a member of a couple;

[⁷ "state pension credit" means the benefit of that name payable under the State Pension Credit Act 2002;]

[⁶"tribunal" means an appeal tribunal constituted under Chapter I of Part I of the 1998 Act;]

[⁸ "the UC Regulations" means the Universal Credit Regulations 2013; and

"the UC etc. Claims and Payments Regulations" means the Universal Credit, Personal Independence Payment, Jobseeker's Allowance and Employment and Support Allowance (Claims and Payments) Regulations 2013;

"universal credit" means universal credit under Part 1 of the Welfare Reform Act 2012;]

"unmarried couple" has the meaning ascribed to it in section 20(11) of the 1986 Act [SSCBA, s.137(1)].

(3) Unless the context otherwise requires, any reference in these Regulations to a numbered regulation or Schedule is a reference to the regulation and Schedule bearing that number in the Regulations and any reference in a regulation or Schedule to a numbered paragraph is a reference to the paragraph of that regulation or Schedule having that number.

AMENDMENTS

1. Social Security (Jobseeker's Allowance Consequential Amendments) (Deductions) Regulations 1996 (SI 1996/2344) reg.6 (October 7, 1996).

2. Social Security (Miscellaneous Amendments) Regulations 1998 (SI 1998/563) regs 3(1) and (2)(a) (April 1, 1998). (Note that the commencement date for this provision was amended by Social Security (Miscellaneous Amendments) (No.2) Regulations 1998 (SI 1998/865) reg.2 (March 20, 1998).)

3. Social Security Act 1998 (Commencement No.12, and Consequential and Transitional Provisions) Order 1999 (SI 1999/3178 (C.81)) art.3(11) and Sch.11 para.1(a).

4. Social Security Act 1998 (Commencement No.12, and Consequential and Transitional Provisions) Order 1999 (SI 1999/3178 (C.81)) art.3(11) and Sch.11 para.1(b) (November 29, 1999).

5. Social Security Act 1998 (Commencement No.12, and Consequential and Transitional Provisions) Order 1999 (SI 1999/3178 (C.81)) art.3(11) and Sch.11 para.1(c) (November 29, 1999).

6. Social Security Act 1998 (Commencement No.12, and Consequential and Transitional Provisions) Order 1999 (SI 1999/3178 (C.81)) art.3(11) and Sch.11 para.1(d) (November 29, 1999).

7. State Pension Credit (Consequential, Transitional and Miscellaneous Provisions) Regulations 2002 (SI 2002/3019) reg.35 (October 6, 2003).

8. Fines, Council Tax and Community Charges (Deductions from Universal Credit and Other Benefits) Regulations 2013 (SI 2013/612) regs 13 and 14 (April 29, 2013). (The extraneous comma at the end of the amended definition of "payments to third parties" is required by reg.14(3) and is not an editorial error.)

MODIFICATION

Regulation 1 is modified by Sch.2 para.23 of the Employment and Support Allowance (Transitional Provisions, Housing Benefit and Council Tax Benefit) (Existing Awards) (No.2) Regulations 2010 (SI 2010/1907) (as amended) for the purposes specified in reg.16(1). For details of the modification, see the text of those Regulations in Vol.I.

[3[4Application for deductions] from income support, [8 universal credit,] [6, state pension credit] [7, jobseeker's allowance or employment and support allowance]]

2.—(1) Where a debtor is entitled to income support [6, state pension credit] [3or jobseeker's allowance], an authority may apply to the Secretary of State by sending an application in respect of the debtor or, where a liability order is made against a couple in respect of both of the couple, to an appropriate social security office asking the Secretary of State to deduct sums from any amount payable to the debtor, or as the case may be either of the couple by way of income support [3[7, jobseeker's allowance or employment and support allowance]].

[8 (1A) Subject to paragraphs (1B), (1C) and (4A) and regulation 4, where the Secretary of State receives an application from an authority in respect of a debtor who is entitled to universal credit, the Secretary of State may deduct an amount from the universal credit payable to the debtor which is equal to 5 per cent. of the appropriate universal credit standard allowance and pay that sum to the authority towards satisfaction of any outstanding sum which is, or forms part of, the amount in respect of which the liability order was made.

(1B) No amount may be deducted under paragraph (1A) where it would reduce the amount of universal credit payable to the debtor to less than 1 penny.

(1C) For the purpose of paragraph (1A), where 5 per cent. of the appropriate universal credit standard allowance results in a fraction of a penny, that fraction is to be disregarded if it is less than half a penny and otherwise it is to be treated as a penny.

(1D) In paragraphs (1A) and (1C), "appropriate universal credit standard allowance" means the appropriate universal credit standard allowance for the debtor for the assessment period in question under regulation 36 of the UC Regulations.]

(2) An application from an authority shall be in writing and shall contain the following particulars—

(a) the name and address of the debtor or where the liability order is made against a couple, the names and address of both of them;

2.891

731

(b) the name and place of the court which made the liability order;
(c) the date when the liability order was made;
(d) the total amount of the arrears specified in the liability order;
(e) the total amount which the authority wishes to have deducted from income support [⁶, state pension credit] [³[⁷, jobseeker's allowance or employment and support allowance]].

(3) Where it appears to the Secretary of State that an application from an authority gives insufficient particulars to enable the debtor to be identified he may require the authority to furnish such further particulars as may reasonably be required.

(4) [⁵. . .].

[⁸(4A) Before making a deduction under paragraph (1A), the Secretary of State must make any deduction which falls to be made in respect of a liability mentioned in paragraph 5(2)(a) to (c) of Schedule 6 to the UC etc. Claims and Payments Regulations.]

(5) [⁵. . .].

(6) [⁵. . .].

AMENDMENTS

1. Social Security (Claims and Payments) Amendment Regulation 1992 (SI 1992/1026) reg.7 (May 25, 1992).
2. Social Security (Claims and Payments) Amendment (No.3) Regulations 1993 (SI 1993/2113) reg.5 (September 27, 1993).
3. Social Security (Jobseeker's Allowance Consequential Amendments) (Deductions) Regulations 1996 (SI 1996/2344) reg.7 (October 7, 1996).
4. Social Security Act 1998 (Commencement No.12, and Consequential and Transitional Provisions) Order 1999 (SI 1999/3178 (C.81)) art.3(11) and Sch.11 para.2(1) (November 29, 1999).
5. Social Security Act 1998 (Commencement No.12, and Consequential and Transitional Provisions) Order 1999 (SI 1999/3178 (C.81)) art.3(11) and Sch.11 para.2(2) (November 29, 1999).
6. State Pension Credit (Consequential, Transitional and Miscellaneous Provisions) Regulations 2002 (SI 2002/3019) reg.35 (October 6, 2003).
7. Employment and Support Allowance (Consequential Provisions) (No.2) Regulations 2008 (SI 2008/1554) reg.53(1) and (2) (October 27, 2008).
8. Fines, Council Tax and Community Charges (Deductions from Universal Credit and Other Benefits) Regulations 2013 (SI 2013/612) regs 13 and 15 (April 29, 2013).

DEFINITIONS

"adjudication officer"—see reg.1(2).
"authority"—see Local Government Finance Act 1988 s.144.
"appropriate social security officer"—see reg.1(2).
"couple"—*ibid.*
"debtor"—*ibid.*
"5 per cent. of the personal allowance for a single claimant aged not less than 25"—*ibid.*
"5 per cent. of the personal allowance for a couple where both members are aged not less than 18"—*ibid.*
"income support"—*ibid.*
"Jobseekers Act"—*ibid.*
"jobseeker's allowance"—*ibid.*
"liability order"—*ibid.*

"payments to third parties"—*ibid.*
"polygamous marriage"—*ibid.*

GENERAL NOTE

R(IS) 3/92 held that if the Secretary of State accepted the validity (i.e. the form and   2.892
content) of an application under para.(2), the AO or SSAT also had to accept it. But
where there is an issue as to whether the claimant is a "debtor" (defined in reg.1(2))
at all, the tribunal must satisfy itself that the basic conditions for the operation of the
procedure exist: namely that there *is* a subsisting liability order, properly obtained,
under which there *is* outstanding a sum due of the amount sought to be deducted from
income support (*R(IS) 1/98*). In that case neither the alleged liability order nor any evidence from the local authority confirming that an amount was still due from the claimant had been produced, whereas the claimant had produced evidence which appeared
to substantiate that she was in fact in credit on her community charge account. The
Commissioner therefore decided that there was no jurisdiction to make any deduction
from the claimant's income support in respect of the community charge.

[¹ Deductions from debtor's income support [², [⁴ universal credit,] state pension credit] or [³, jobseeker's allowance or employment and support allowance]

3.—(1) Subject to paragraph (4) and regulation 4, where the Secretary of   2.893
State receives an application from an authority in respect of a debtor who
is entitled to income support [², state pension credit] [³, income-based jobseeker's allowance or income-related employment and support allowance]
and the amount payable by way of that benefit, after any deduction under
this paragraph, is 10 pence or more, the Secretary of State may deduct a sum
from that benefit which is equal to 5 per cent. of the personal allowance—
  (a) set out in paragraph 1(1)(e) of Schedule 2 to the Income Support
      (General) Regulations 1987 or, as the case may be, of Schedule 1 to
      the Jobseeker's Allowance Regulations 1996 for a couple where—
        (i) a liability order is made; and
        (ii) that benefit is payable, in respect of both members of a couple
             both of whom are aged not less than 18; and
  (b) in any other case, for a single claimant aged not less than 25 set out
      in paragraph 1(3)(c) of Schedule 2 to the Income Support (General)
      Regulations 1987 or, as the case may be, paragraph 1(3)(e) of
      Schedule 1 to the Jobseeker's Allowance Regulations 1996,
and pay that sum to the authority towards satisfaction of any outstanding
sum which is or forms part of the amount in respect of which the liability
order was made.
    [⁴ (1A) Subject to paragraphs (1B), (1C) and (4A) and regulation 4,
where the Secretary of State receives an application from an authority in
respect of a debtor who is entitled to universal credit, the Secretary of State
may deduct an amount from the universal credit payable to the debtor
which is equal to 5 per cent. of the appropriate universal credit standard
allowance and pay that sum to the authority towards satisfaction of any
outstanding sum which is, or forms part of, the amount in respect of which
the liability order was made.
    (1B) No amount may be deducted under paragraph (1A) where it would
reduce the amount of universal credit payable to the debtor to less than 1
penny.
    (1C) For the purpose of paragraph (1A), where 5 per cent. of the appro-

priate universal credit standard allowance results in a fraction of a penny, that fraction is to be disregarded if it is less than half a penny and otherwise it is to be treated as a penny.

(1D) In paragraphs (1A) and (1C), "appropriate universal credit standard allowance" means the appropriate universal credit standard allowance for the debtor for the assessment period in question under regulation 36 of the UC Regulations.]

(2) Subject to paragraph (3) and regulation 4, where—

(a) the Secretary of State receives an application from an authority in respect of a debtor who is entitled to contribution-based job-seeker's allowance; and

(b) the amount of contribution-based jobseeker's allowance payable before any deduction under this paragraph is equal to or more than one-third of the age-related amount applicable to the debtor under section 4(1)(a) of the Jobseekers Act,

the Secretary of State may deduct a sum from that benefit which is equal to one-third of the age-related amount applicable to the debtor under section 4(1)(a) of the Jobseekers Act and pay that sum to the authority towards satisfaction of any outstanding sum which is or forms part of the amount in respect of which the liability order was made.

(3) Where the sum that would otherwise fall to be deducted under paragraph (2) includes a fraction of a penny, the sum to be deducted shall be rounded down to the next whole penny.

(4) Before making a deduction under paragraph (1) the Secretary of State shall make any deduction which falls to be made in respect of a liability mentioned in any of the following provisions of the Social Security (Claims and Payments) Regulations 1987—

(a) regulation 34A (mortgage interest);

(b) paragraph 3 (housing costs) of Schedule 9;

(c) paragraph 5 (rent and certain service charges for fuel) of Schedule 9;

(d) paragraph 6 (fuel costs) of Schedule 9; and

(e) paragraph 7 (water charges) of Schedule 9.

[⁴ (4A) Before making a deduction under paragraph (1A), the Secretary of State must make any deduction which falls to be made in respect of a liability mentioned in paragraph 5(2)(a) to (c) of Schedule 6 to the UC etc. Claims and Payments Regulations.]

(5) Subject to regulations 5 and 6, a decision of the Secretary of State under this regulation shall be final.

(6) The Secretary of State shall notify the debtor in writing of a decision to make a deduction under this regulation as soon as is practicable and at the same time shall notify the debtor of his right of appeal.]

AMENDMENTS

1. Social Security Act 1998 (Commencement No.12, and Consequential and Transitional Provisions) Order 1999 (SI 1999/3178 (C.81)) art.3(11) and Sch.11 para.3 (November 29, 1999).

2. State Pension Credit (Consequential, Transitional and Miscellaneous Provisions) Regulations 2002 (SI 2002/3019) reg.35 (October 6, 2003).

3. Employment and Support Allowance (Consequential Provisions) (No.2) Regulations 2008 (SI 2008/1554) reg.53(1) and (3) (October 27, 2008).

4. Fines, Council Tax and Community Charges (Deductions from Universal Credit and Other Benefits) Regulations 2013 (SI 2013/612) regs 13 and 16 (April 29, 2013).

Circumstances, time of making and termination of deductions

4.—[²(1) The Secretary of State—   2.894
  (a) shall make deductions under [⁵ regulation 3(1) or (2)] only where the debtor is entitled to income support [³ , state pension credit] [⁴, jobseeker's allowance or employment and support allowance] throughout any benefit week; and
  (b) shall not determine any application under regulation 2 which relates to a debtor in respect of whom—
      (i) he is making deductions; or
      (ii) deductions fall to be made,
pursuant to an earlier application under regulation 3 until no deductions pursuant to that earlier application fall to be made.]
  [⁵ (1A) The Secretary of State may make deductions from universal credit under regulation 3(1A) only if—
  (a) the debtor is entitled to universal credit throughout any assessment period; and
  (b) no deductions are being made in respect of the debtor under any other application.]
  (2) The Secretary of State shall make deductions from income support [³, [⁵ universal credit,] state pension credit] [¹[⁴, jobseeker's allowance or employment and support allowance] at a time which corresponds to the payment of income support [³, [⁵ universal credit,] state pension credit] [¹[⁴, jobseeker's allowance or employment and support allowance]] to the debtor and he shall cease making deductions when—
  (a) a payment to a third party has priority;
  (b) there is insufficient entitlement to income support [³, [⁵ universal credit,] state pension credit] [¹[⁴, jobseeker's allowance or employment and support allowance]] to enable him to make the deduction;
  (c) entitlement to income support [³, [⁵ universal credit,] state pension credit] [¹[⁴, jobseeker's allowance or employment and support allowance]] ceases;
  (d) an authority withdraws its application for deductions to be made; or
  (e) the debt in respect of which he was making the deductions is discharged.
  (3) Payments shall be made to the authority at such intervals as the Secretary of State may decide.

AMENDMENTS

1. Social Security (Jobseeker's Allowance Consequential Amendments) (Deductions) Regulations 1996 (SI 1996/2344) reg.9 (October 7, 1996).
2. Social Security Act 1998 (Commencement No.12, and Consequential and Transitional Provisions) Order 1999 (SI 1999/3178 (C.81)) art.3(11) and Sch.11 para.4 (November 29, 1999).
3. State Pension Credit (Consequential, Transitional and Miscellaneous Provisions) Regulations 2002 (SI 2002/3019) reg.35 (October 6, 2003).
4. Employment and Support Allowance (Consequential Provisions) (No.2) Regulations 2008 (SI 2008/1554) reg.53(1) and (4) (October 27, 2008).
5. Fines, Council Tax and Community Charges (Deductions from Universal Credit and Other Benefits) Regulations 2013 (SI 2013/612) regs 13 and 17 (April 29, 2013).

"adjudication officer"—see reg.1(2).
"authority"—see Local Government Finance Act 1988 s.144.
"debtor"—see reg.1(2).
"income support"—*ibid.*
"jobseeker's allowance"—*ibid.*

[¹Revision and supersession

2.895   **5.**—Any decision of the Secretary of State under regulation 3 may be revised under section 9 of the 1998 Act or superseded under section 10 of that Act as though the decision were made under section 8(1)(c) of that Act.]

AMENDMENT

1. Social Security Act 1998 (Commencement No.12, and Consequential and Transitional Provisions) Order 1999 (SI 1999/3178 (C.81)) art.3(11) and Sch.11 para.5 (November 29, 1999).

[¹ Appeal

2.896   **6.**—Any decision of the Secretary of State under regulation 3 (whether as originally made or as revised under regulation 5) may be appealed to a tribunal as though the decision were made on an award of a relevant benefit (within the meaning of section 8(3) of the 1998 Act) under section 8(1)(c) of the 1998 Act.]

AMENDMENT

1. Social Security Act 1998 (Commencement No.12, and Consequential and Transitional Provisions) Order 1999 (SI 1999/3178 (C.81)) art.3(11) and Sch.11 para.5 (November 29, 1999).

Correction of accidental errors

2.897   **7.**—[¹ . . .]

AMENDMENT

1. Social Security Act 1998 (Commencement No.12, and Consequential and Transitional Provisions Order 1999 (SI 1999/3178 (C.81)) art.3(11) and Sch.11 para.6 (November 29, 1999).

Setting aside decisions on certain grounds

2.898   **8.**—[¹ . . .]

AMENDMENT

1. Social Security Act 1998 (Commencement No.12, and Consequential and Transitional Provisions) Order 1999 (SI 1999/3178 (C.81)) art.3(11) and Sch.11 para.6 (November 29, 1999).

Provisions common to regulations 7 and 8

2.899   **9.**—[¹ . . .]

AMENDMENT

1. Social Security Act 1998 (Commencement No.12, and Consequential and Transitional Provisions) Order 1999 (SI 1999/3178 (C.81)) art.3(11) and Sch.11 para.6 (November 29, 1999).

The Fines (Deductions from Income Support) Regulations 1992

(SI 1992/2182) (AS AMENDED)

Made by the Secretary of State under ss.24 and 30 of the Criminal Justice Act 1991

Citation, commencement and interpretation

1.—(1) These Regulations may be cited as the Fines (Deductions from Income Support) Regulations 1992 and shall come into force on 1 October 1992.

2.900

(2) In these Regulations, unless the context otherwise requires—

"the 1971 Act" means the Vehicles (Excise) Act 1971;

"the 1973 Act" means the Powers of the Criminal Courts Act 1973;

[4 "the 1998 Act" means the Social Security Act 1998;]

[9 "the 2012 Act" means the Welfare Reform Act 2012;]

[4 . . .];

"application" means an application made under regulation 2 [6 . . .] containing the information specified in regulation 3(1);

[4 . . .];

[9 "assessment period" means the period prescribed by regulation 21 of the UC Regulations;]

"benefit week" has the meaning prescribed in regulation 2(1) of the Income Support Regulations [2 or, as the case may be, [7 regulation 1(2) of the State Pension Credit Regulations 2002 or] regulation 1(3) of the Jobseeker's Allowance Regulations 1996 [8 or regulation 2(1) of the Employment and Support Allowance Regulations];]

"the Claims and Payments Regulations" means the Social Security (Claims and Payments) Regulations 1987;

[4 "Commissioner" has the meaning it bears in section 39(1) of the 1998 Act;]

[3 "contribution-based jobseeker's allowance", except in a case to which paragraph (b) of the definition of income-based jobseeker's allowance applies, means a contribution-based jobseeker's allowance under Part I of the Jobseekers Act 1995 [9 as amended by the provisions of Part 1 of Schedule 14 to the 2012 Act that remove references to an income-based allowance or under Part 1 of the Jobseekers Act 1995 as it has effect apart from those amendments], but does not include any back to work bonus under section 26 of the Jobseekers Act which is paid as jobseeker's allowance;]

[8 "contributory employment and support allowance" means a contributory allowance under Part 1 of the Welfare Reform Act [9 as amended by the provisions of Schedule 3, and Part 1 of Schedule 14, to the 2012 Act that remove references to an income-related allowance or under Part 1 of the Welfare Reform Act as it has effect apart from those amendments];]

"court" means in England and Wales a magistrates' court and in Scotland a court;

[⁸ "the Employment and Support Allowance Regulations" means the Employment and Support Allowance Regulations 2008;]

"5 per cent. of the personal allowance for a single claimant aged not less than 25" means, where the percentage is not a multiple of 5 pence, the sum obtained by rounding that 5 per cent. to the next higher such multiple;

[² "income support" means income support under Part VII of the Social Security Contributions and Benefits Act 1992, but does not include any back to work bonus under section 26 of the Jobseekers Act which is paid as income support;]

"Income Support Regulations" means the Income Support (General) Regulations 1987;

[³ "income-based jobseeker's allowance" means—

(a) an income-based jobseeker's allowance under Part I of the Job-seekers Act 1995; and

(b) in a case where, if there was no entitlement to contribution-based jobseeker's allowance, there would be entitlement to income-based jobseeker's allowance at the same rate, contribution-based jobseeker's allowance,

but does include any back to work bonus under section 26 of the Jobseekers Act which is paid as jobseeker's allowance;]

[⁸ "income-related employment and support allowance" means—

(a) an income-related allowance under Part 1 of the Welfare Reform Act; and

(b) in a case where, if there was no entitlement to contributory employment and support allowance, there would be entitlement to income-related employment and support allowance at the same rate, contributory employment and support allowance;]

[² "Jobseekers Act" means the Jobseekers Act 1995;

"jobseeker's allowance" means an allowance under Part I of the Jobseekers Act but does not include any back to work bonus under section 26 of that Act which is paid as jobseeker's allowance;]

"payments to third parties" means direct payments to third parties in accordance with Schedules 9 and 9A to the Claims and Payments Regulations [⁹ Schedule 6 to the Universal Credit, Personal Independence Payment, Jobseeker's Allowance and Employment and Support Allowance (Claims and Payments) Regulations 2013,], regulation 2(4) of the Community Charges (Deductions from Income Support) (No.2) Regulations 1990 and regulation 2(4) of the Community Charges (Deductions from Income Support) (Scotland) Regulations 1989 [¹and regulation 2 of the Council Tax (Deductions from Income Support) Regulations 1993];

[⁷ "personal allowance for a single claimant aged not less than 25" means—

(a) in the case of a person who is entitled to either income support or state pension credit, the amount for the time being specified in paragraph 1(1)(e) of column (2) of Schedule 2 to the Income Support Regulations; or

(b) in the case of a person who is entitled to an income-based job-seeker's allowance, the amount for the time being specified in paragraph 1(1)(e) of column (2) of Schedule 1 to the Jobseeker's Allowance Regulations 1996;]

[⁸ (c) in the case of a person who is entitled to an income-related employment and support allowance, the amount specified for the time being in paragraph 1(1)(b) of column 2 of Schedule 4 to the Employment and Support Allowance Regulations;]

"social security office" means an office of the [⁵ Department for Work and Pensions which is open to the public for the receipt of claims for income support or a [⁸ , jobseeker's allowance or an employment and support allowance]].

[⁷ "state pension credit" means the benefit of that name payable under the State Pension Credit Act 2002]

[⁴ "tribunal" means an appeal tribunal constituted under Chapter 1 of Part I of the 1998 Act.]

[⁹ "the UC Regulations" means the Universal Credit Regulations 2013; "universal credit" means universal credit under Part 1 of the 2012 Act;]

[⁸ "the Welfare Reform Act" means the Welfare Reform Act 2007;]

(3) Unless the context otherwise requires, any reference in these Regulations to a numbered regulation, Part or Schedule bearing that number in these Regulations and any reference in a regulation or Schedule to a numbered paragraph is a reference to the paragraph of that regulation or Schedule having that number.

AMENDMENTS

1. Deductions from Income Support (Miscellaneous Amendment) Regulations 1993 (SI 1993/495) reg.3 (April 1, 1993).

2. Social Security (Jobseeker's Allowance Consequential Amendments) (Deductions) Regulations 1996 (SI 1996/2344) reg.10 (October 7, 1996).

3. Social Security (Miscellaneous Amendments) Regulations 1998 (SI 1998/563) reg.3(1) and (2)(d) (April 1, 1998). (Note that the commencement date for this provision was amended by Social Security (Miscellaneous Amendments) (No.2) Regulations 1998 (SI 1998/865) reg.2 (March 20, 1998).)

4. Social Security Act 1998 (Commencement No.12, and Consequential and Transitional Provisions) Order 1999 (SI 1999/3178 (C.81)) art.3(12) and Sch.12 para.1 (November 29, 1999).

5. Secretaries of State for Education and Skills and for Work and Pensions Order 2002 (SI 2002/1397) art.12 and Sch. para.22 (June 27, 2002).

6. Fines (Deductions from Income Support) (Amendment) Regulations 2003 (SI 2003/1360) reg.2(a) (June 20, 2003).

7. State Pension Credit (Consequential, Transitional and Miscellaneous Provisions) Regulations 2002 (SI 2002/3019) reg.32 (October 6, 2003).

8. Employment and Support Allowance (Consequential Provisions) (No.2) Regulations 2008 (SI 2008/1554) reg.54(1) and (2) (October 27, 2008).

9. Fines, Council Tax and Community Charges (Deductions from Universal Credit and Other Benefits) Regulations 2013 (SI 2013/612) regs 2 and 3 (April 29, 2013). (The double comma in the definition of "payments to third parties" is required by reg.3(6) and is not an editorial error.)

MODIFICATION

Regulation 1 is modified by Sch.2 para.24 of the Employment and Support Allowance (Transitional Provisions, Housing Benefit and Council Tax Benefit)

(Existing Awards) (No.2) Regulations 2010 (SI 2010/1907) (as amended) for the purposes specified in reg.16(1). For details of the modification, see the text of those Regulations in Vol.I.

[¹Application for deductions from support [², [⁴ universal credit,] state state pension credit] or [³, jobseeker's allowance or employment and support allowance]]

2.901   **2.**—(1) Where a fine has been imposed on an offender by a court or a sum is required to be paid by a compensation order which has been made against an offender by a court and (in either case) the offender is entitled to income support [², [⁴ universal credit,] state pension credit] [¹[³, jobseeker's allowance or employment and support allowance]], the court may, subject to paragraph (2), apply to the Secretary of State asking him to deduct sums from any amounts payable to the offender by way of income support [², [⁴ universal credit,] state pension credit] [¹[³, jobseeker's allowance or employment and support allowance]], in order to secure the payment of any sum which is or forms part of the fine or compensation.

(2) Before making an application the court shall make an enquiry as to the offender's means.

AMENDMENTS

1. Social Security (Jobseeker's Allowance Consequential Amendments) (Deductions) Regulations 1996 (SI 1996/2344) reg.11 (October 7, 1996).
2. State Pension Credit (Consequential, Transitional and Miscellaneous Provisions) Regulations 2002 (SI 2002/3019) reg.32 (October 6, 2003).
3. Employment and Support Allowance (Consequential Provisions) (No.2) Regulations 2008 (SI 2008/1554) reg.54(1) and (3) (October 27, 2008).
4. Fines, Council Tax and Community Charges (Deductions from Universal Credit and Other Benefits) Regulations 2013 (SI 2013/612) regs 2 and 4 (April 29, 2013).

DEFINITIONS

"court"—see reg.1(2).
"income support"—*ibid.*
"jobseeker's allowance"—*ibid.*

[¹ Information that the court may require

2.902   **2A.**—(1) Where an application is made the court may require the offender to provide his full name, full address, date of birth, national insurance number and the name of any benefits to which he is entitled.

(2) For the purposes of this regulation "benefits" means income support, state pension credit [² , a jobseeker's allowance or an employment and support allowance].]

AMENDMENTS

1. Fines (Deductions from Income Support)(Amendment) Regulations 2004 reg.2(a) (December 18, 2004).
2. Employment and Support Allowance (Consequential Provisions) (No.2) Regulations 2008 (SI 2008/1554) reg.54(1) and (4) (October 27, 2008).

Contents of application

3.—(1) An application [¹. . .] shall contain the following information   2.903

- (a) the name and address of the offender, and, if it is known, his date of birth;
- (b) the date when the fine was imposed or the compensation order made;
- (c) the name and address of the court imposing the fine or making the compensation order;
- (d) the amount of the fine or the amount payable by the compensation order as the case may be;
- (e) the date on which the application is made;
- (f) the date on which the court enquired into the offender's means;
- (g) whether the offender has defaulted in paying the fine, compensation order or any instalment of either.

(2) A court making an application shall serve it on the Secretary of State by sending or delivering it to a social security office.

(3) Where it appears to the Secretary of State that an application from a court gives insufficient information to enable the offender to be identified, he may require the court to furnish such further information as he may reasonably require for that purpose.

AMENDMENT

1. Fines (Deductions from Income Support) (Amendment) Regulations 2003 (SI 2003/1360) reg.2(b) (June 20, 2003).

DEFINITIONS

"application"—see reg.1(2).
"court"—*ibid.*
"social security office"—*ibid.*

[¹Deductions from offender's income support [², [⁵ universal credit,] state pension credit] or jobseeker's allowance

4.—(1) Subject to regulation 7, where—   2.904
- (a) the Secretary of State receives an application from a court in respect of an offender who is entitled to income support [² , state pension credit] [⁴, income-based jobseeker's allowance or income-related employment and support allowance];
- (b) the amount payable by way of that benefit, after any deduction under this paragraph, is 10 pence or more; and
- (c) the aggregate amount payable under one or more of the following provisions, namely, paragraphs 3(2)(a), 5(6), 6(2)(a) and 7(3)(a) and (5)(a) of Schedule 9 to the Claims and Payments Regulations, and regulation 2 of the Council Tax (Deductions from Income Support) Regulations 1993, together with the amount to be deducted under this paragraph does not exceed an amount equal to 3 times 5 per cent. of the personal allowance for a single claimant aged not less than 25 years,

the Secretary of State may deduct a sum from that benefit which is equal to 5 per cent. of the personal allowance for a single claimant aged not less than 25 [³ or £5, whichever is the greater amount allowed by sub-paragraphs

(b) and (c)] and pay that sum to the court towards satisfaction of the fine or the sum required to be paid by compensation order.

[⁵ (1A) Subject to paragraphs (1C) and (1D) and regulation 7, where the Secretary of State receives an application from a court in respect of an offender who is entitled to universal credit, the Secretary of State may deduct from the universal credit payable to the offender an amount permitted by paragraph (1B) and pay that amount to the court towards satisfaction of the fine or the sum required to be paid by compensation order.

(1B) The amount that may be deducted under paragraph (1A) is any sum which is no less than 5 per cent. of the appropriate universal credit standard allowance for the offender for the assessment period in question under regulation 36 of the UC Regulations but no greater than £108.35.

(1C) No amount may be deducted under paragraph (1A) where it would reduce the amount of universal credit payable to the offender to less than 1 penny.

(1D) For the purpose of paragraph (1B), where 5 per cent. of the appropriate universal credit standard allowance results in a fraction of a penny, that fraction is to be disregarded if it is less than half a penny and otherwise it is to be treated as a penny.]

[⁵(2) Subject to paragraph (3) and regulation 7, where—

(a) the Secretary of State receives an application from a court in respect of an offender who is entitled to contribution-based jobseeker's allowance or contributory employment and support allowance; and

(b) the amount of that allowance payable, before any deduction under this paragraph, is 10 pence or more,

the Secretary of State may deduct a sum from that allowance, up to the appropriate maximum specified in paragraph (2A), and pay that sum to the court towards satisfaction of the fine or the sum required to be paid by compensation order.

(2A) The appropriate maximum is 40 per cent. of the appropriate age-related amount for the offender specified—

(a) where the offender is entitled to contribution-based jobseeker's allowance, in regulation 79 of the Jobseeker's Allowance Regulations 1996 or, as the case may be, regulation 49 of the Jobseeker's Allowance Regulations 2013;

(b) where the offender is entitled to contributory employment and support allowance, in paragraph 1(1) of Schedule 4 to the Employment and Support Allowance Regulations or, as the case may be, regulation 62(1)(b) of the Employment and Support Allowance Regulations 2013.]

(3) No deduction shall be made under paragraph (2) where a deduction is being made from the offender's contribution-based jobseeker's allowance under the Community Charges (Deductions from Income Support) (No.2) Regulations 1990, the Community Charges (Deductions from Income Support) (Scotland) Regulations 1989 or the Council Tax (Deductions from Income Support) Regulations 1993.

[⁵ . . .]

(5) The Secretary of State shall notify the offender and the court in writing of a decision to make a deduction under this regulation so far as is practicable within 14 days from the date on which he made the decision and at the same time shall notify the offender of his right of appeal.]

AMENDMENTS

1. Social Security Act 1998 (Commencement No.12, and Consequential and Transitional Provisions) Order 1999 (SI 1999/3178 (C.81)) art.3(12) and Sch.12 para.2 (November 29, 1999).
2. State Pension Credit (Consequential, Transitional and Miscellaneous Provisions) Regulations 2002 (SI 2002/3019) reg.32 (October 6, 2003).
3. Fines (Deductions from Income Support) (Amendment) Regulations 2004 reg.2(b) (December 18, 2004).
4. Employment and Support Allowance (Consequential Provisions) (No.2) Regulations 2008 (SI 2008/1554) reg.54(1) and (5) (October 27, 2008).
5. Fines, Council Tax and Community Charges (Deductions from Universal Credit and Other Benefits) Regulations 2013 (SI 2013/612) regs 2 and 5 (April 29, 2013).

GENERAL NOTE

The replacement of para.(2) with paras (2) and (2A) by regs 2 and 5(4) of SI   **2.905**
2013/612 does not have effect in respect of an application received by the Secretary of State from the court in respect of an offender before April 29, 2013: see reg.5(6) of SI 2013/612.

Notification of decision

5.—[¹ . . .]   **2.906**

AMENDMENT

1. Social Security Act 1998 (Commencement No.12, and Consequential and Transitional Provisions) Order 1999 (SI 1999/3178 (C.81)) art.3(12) and Sch.12 para.2 (November 29, 1999).

[¹Deductions from offender's income support or income-based jobseeker's allowance]

6.—[² . . .]   **2.907**

AMENDMENTS

1. Social Security (Jobseeker's Allowance Consequential Amendments) (Deductions) Regulations 1996 (SI 1996/2344) reg.13 (October 7, 1996).
2. Social Security Act 1998 (Commencement No.12, and Consequential and Transitional Provisions) Order 1999 (SI 1999/3178 (C.81)) art.3(12) and Sch.12 para.2 (November 29, 1999).

DEFINITIONS

"adjudication officer"—see reg.1(2).
"court"—*ibid.*
"5 per cent. of the personal allowance for a single claimant aged not less than 25"—*ibid.*

[¹Deductions from offender's contribution-based jobseeker's allowance

6A.—[² . . .]   **2.908**

AMENDMENTS

1. Social Security (Jobseeker's Allowance Consequential Amendments) (Deductions) Regulations 1996 (SI 1996/2344) reg.14 (October 7, 1996).

2. Social Security Act 1998 (Commencement No.12, and Consequential and Transitional Provisions) Order 1999 (SI 1999/3178 (C.81)) art.3(12) and Sch.12 para.2 (November 29, 1999).

Circumstances, time of making and termination of deductions

2.909

7.—(1) The Secretary of State may make deductions from income support [⁴, state pension credit] [¹[⁵, jobseeker's allowance or employment and support allowance]] under [² under [⁶ regulation 4(1) or (2)]] only if—

(a) the offender is entitled to income support [⁴, state pension credit] [¹[⁵, jobseeker's allowance or employment and support allowance]] throughout any benefit week; and

(b) no deductions are being made in respect of the offender under any other application.

[⁶ (1A) The Secretary of State may make deductions from universal credit under regulation 4(1A) only if—

(a) the offender is entitled to universal credit throughout any assessment period; and

(b) no deductions are being made in respect of the offender under any other application.]

(2) The Secretary of State shall not make a deduction unless—

(a) the offender at the date of application by the court is aged not less than 18;

(b) the offender is entitled to income support [⁴, [⁶ universal credit,] state pension credit] [¹[⁵, jobseeker's allowance or employment and support allowance]]; and

(c) the offender has defaulted in paying the fine, compensation order or any instalment of either.

(3) The Secretary of State shall make deductions from income support [⁴, [⁶ universal credit,] state pension credit] [¹[⁵, jobseeker's allowance or employment and support allowance]] by reference to the times at which payment of income support [⁴ , state pension credit] [¹[⁵, jobseeker's allowance or employment and support allowance]] is made to the offender.

(4) The Secretary of State shall cease making deductions from income support [⁴, [⁶ universal credit,] state pension credit] [¹[⁵, jobseeker's allowance or employment and support allowance]] if—

(a) there is no longer sufficient entitlement to income support [⁴, state pension credit][¹[⁵, jobseeker's allowance or employment and support allowance]] to enable him to make the deduction;

(b) entitlement to income support [⁴, [⁶ universal credit,] state pension credit] [¹[⁵, jobseeker's allowance or employment and support allowance]] ceases;

(c) a court withdraws its application for deductions to be made; or

(d) the liability to make payment of the fine or under the compensation order as the case may be has ceased.

[³ (5) The Secretary of State shall not determine any application under regulation 2 which relates to an offender in respect of whom—

(a) he is making deductions; or

(b) deductions fall to be made,

pursuant to an earlier application under that regulation until no deductions pursuant to that earlier application fall to be made.]

(6) Payments of sums deducted from income support [⁴, [⁶ universal

credit,] state pension credit] [¹ [⁵ , jobseeker's allowance or employment and support allowance]] by the Secretary of State under these Regulations shall be made to the court at intervals of 13 weeks.

(7) Where the whole of the amount to which the application relates has been paid, the court shall so far as is practicable give notice of that fact within 21 days to the Secretary of State.

(8) The Secretary of State shall notify the offender in writing of the total of the sums deducted by him under any application—

(a) on receipt of a written request for such information from the offender; or

(b) on the termination of deductions made under any such application.

AMENDMENTS

1. Social Security (Jobseeker's Allowance Consequential Amendments) (Deductions) Regulations 1996 (SI 1996/2344) reg.15 (October 7, 1996).

2. Social Security Act 1998 (Commencement No.12, and Consequential and Transitional Provisions) Order 1999 (SI 1999/3178 (C.81)) art.3(12) and Sch.12 para.3(a) (November 29, 1999).

3. Social Security Act 1998 (Commencement No.12, and Consequential and Transitional Provisions) Order 1999 (SI 1999/3178 (C.81)) art.3(12) and Sch.12 para.3(b) (November 29, 1999).

4. State Pension Credit (Consequential, Transitional and Miscellaneous Provisions) Regulations 2002 (SI 2002/3019) reg.32 (October 6, 2003).

5. Employment and Support Allowance (Consequential Provisions) (No.2) Regulations 2008 (SI 2008/1554) reg.54(1) and (6) (October 27, 2008).

6. Fines, Council Tax and Community Charges (Deductions from Universal Credit and Other Benefits) Regulations 2013 (SI 2013/612) regs 2 and 6 (April 29, 2013).

DEFINITIONS

"adjudication officer"—see reg.1(2).
"authority"—*ibid.*
"benefit week"—*ibid.*
"court"—*ibid.*
"income support"—*ibid.*
"jobseeker's allowance"—*ibid.*

Withdrawal of application

8.—A court may withdraw an application at any time by giving notice in writing to the social security office to which the application was sent or delivered.   2.910

DEFINITIONS

"application"—see reg.1(2).
"court"—*ibid.*
"social security office"—*ibid.*

[¹Revision and supersession

9.—Any decision of the Secretary of State under regulation 4 may be revised under section 9 of the 1998 Act or superseded under section 10 of that Act as though the decision were made under section 8(1)(c) of that Act.]   2.911

AMENDMENT

1. Social Security Act 1998 (Commencement No.12, and Consequential and Transitional Provisions) Order 1999 (SI 1999/3178 (C.81)) art.3(12) and Sch.12 para.4 (November 29, 1999).

[¹Appeal

2.912   **10.**—Any decision of the Secretary of State under regulation 4 (whether as originally made or as revised under regulation 9) may be appealed to a tribunal as though the decision were made on an award of a relevant benefit (within the meaning of section 8(3) of the 1998 Act) under section 8(1)(c) of the 1998 Act.]

AMENDMENT

1. Social Security Act 1998 (Commencement No.12, and Consequential and Transitional Provisions) Order 1999 (SI 1999/3178 (C.81)) art.3(12) and Sch.12 para.4 (November 29, 1999).

Correction of accidental errors

2.913   **11.**—[¹ . . .]

AMENDMENT

1. Social Security Act 1998 (Commencement No.12, and Consequential and Transitional Provisions) Order 1999 (SI 1999/3178 (C.81)) art.3(12) and Sch.12 para.5 (November 29, 1999).

Setting aside decisions on certain grounds

2.914   **12.**—[² . . .]

AMENDMENTS

1. Deductions from Income Support (Miscellaneous Amendment) Regulations 1993 (SI 1993/495) reg.3 (April 1, 1993).
2. Social Security Act 1998 (Commencement No.12, and Consequential and Transitional Provisions) Order 1999 (SI 1999/3178 (C.81)) art.3(12) and Sch.12 para.5 (November 29, 1999).

Provisions common to regulations 11 and 12

2.915   **13.**—[¹ . . .]

AMENDMENT

1. Social Security Act 1998 (Commencement No.12, and Consequential and Transitional Provisions) Order 1999 (SI 1999/3178 (C.81)) art.3(12) and Sch.12 para.5 (November 29, 1999).

Manner of making applications or appeals and time limits

2.916   **14.**—[¹ . . .]

AMENDMENT

1. Social Security Act 1998 (Commencement No.12, and Consequential and Transitional Provisions) Order 1999 (SI 1999/3178 (C.81)) art.3(12) and Sch.12 para.5 (November 29, 1999).

Manner and time for the service of notices etc.

15.—[² . . .]   2.917

AMENDMENTS

1. Deductions from Income Support (Miscellaneous Amendment) Regulations 1993 (SI 1993/495) reg.3 (April 1, 1993).

2. Social Security Act 1998 (Commencement No.12, and Consequential and Transitional Provisions) Order 1999 (SI 1999/3178 (C.81)) art.3(12) and Sch.12 para.5 (November 29, 1999).

SCHEDULE 1

TIME LIMITS FOR MAKING APPLICATIONS OR APPEALS

[¹ . . .]   2.918

AMENDMENT

1. Social Security Act 1998 (Commencement No.12, and Consequential and Transitional Provisions) Order 1999 (SI 1999/3178 (C.81)) art.3(12) and Sch.12 para.5 (November 29, 1999).

SCHEDULE 2

CONDUCT AND PROCEDURE IN RELATION TO APPEALS AND APPLICATIONS

[¹ . . .]   2.919

AMENDMENT

1. Social Security Act 1998 (Commencement No.12, and Consequential and Transitional Provisions) Order 1999 (SI 1999/3178 (C.81)) art.3(12) and Sch.12 para.5 (November 29, 1999).

SCHEDULE 3

FORM

APPLICATION TO SECRETARY OF STATE UNDER THE FINES (DEDUCTIONS FROM INCOME SUPPORT) REGULATIONS 1992

[¹ . . .]   2.920

AMENDMENT

1. Fines (Deductions from Income Support) (Amendment) Regulations 2003 (SI 2003/1360) reg.2(c) (June 20, 2003).

The Council Tax (Deductions from Income Support) Regulations 1993

(SI 1993/494) (AS AMENDED)

Made by the Secretary of State under ss.14(3), 97(5), 113 and 116(1) of and Schs 4, paras 1 and 6, and 8, para.6, to the Local Government Finance Act 1992

Citation, commencement and interpretation

2.921   **1.**—(1) These Regulations may be cited as the Council Tax (Deductions from Income Support) Regulations 1993 and shall come into force on 1st April 1993.

(2) In these Regulations, unless the context otherwise requires—

[³ "the 1998 Act" means the Social Security Act 1998;]

[⁷ "the 2012 Act" means the Welfare Reform Act 2012;]

[³ . . .]

"application means an application made under regulation 2 or regulation 3 containing the information specified in regulation 4;

[³ . . .]

[⁷ "assessment period" means the period prescribed by regulation 21 of the UC Regulations;]

"authority" means—

(a) in relation to England and Wales, a billing authority, and

(b) in relation to Scotland, a levying authority;

"benefit week" has the meaning prescribed in regulation 2(1) of the Income Support (General) Regulations 1987 [¹or, as the case may be, [⁵ regulation 1(2) of the State Pension Credit Regulations 2002 [⁶ , regulation 2(1) of the Employment and Support Allowance Regulations 2008] or] regulation 1(3) of the Jobseeker's Allowance Regulations 1996;]

"Claims and Payments Regulations" means the Social Security (Claims and Payments) Regulations 1987;

[³ "Commissioner" has the meaning it bears in section 39(1) of the 1998 Act;]

[² "contribution-based jobseeker's allowance", except in a case to which paragraph (b) of the definition of income-based jobseeker's allowance applies, means a contribution-based jobseeker's allowance under Part I of the Jobseekers Act 1995 [⁷ as amended by the provisions of Part 1 of Schedule 14 to the 2012 Act that remove references to an income-based allowance or under Part 1 of the Jobseekers Act 1995 as it has effect apart from those amendments], but does not include any back to work bonus under section 26 of the Jobseekers Act which is paid as jobseeker's allowance;]

[⁶ "contributory employment and support allowance" means a contributory allowance under Part 1 of the Welfare Reform Act (employment and support allowance) [⁷ as amended by the provisions of Schedule 3, and Part 1 of Schedule 14, to the 2012 Act that remove references to an income-related allowance or under Part 1 of the Welfare Reform Act as it has effect apart from those amendments];]

"debtor"—
- (a) in relation to England and Wales, has the same meaning as in paragraph 6 of Schedule 4 to the Local Government Finance Act, and
- (b) in relation to Scotland, has the same meaning as in paragraph 6 of Schedule 8 to that Act;

"5 per cent. of the personal allowance for a single claimant aged not less than 25" means, where the percentage is not a multiple of 5 pence, the sum obtained by rounding that 5 per cent. to the next higher such multiple;

"income support" means income support within the meaning of the Social Security Contributions and Benefits Act 1992 [¹but does not include any back to work bonus under section [26 of the Jobseekers Act which is paid as income support;]

[² "income-based jobseeker's allowance" means—
- (a) an income-based jobseeker's allowance under Part I of the Jobseekers Act 1995; and
- (b) in a case where, if there was no entitlement to contribution-based jobseeker's allowance, there would be entitlement to income-based jobseeker's allowance at the same rate, contribution-based jobseeker's allowance,

but does not include any back to work bonus under section 26 of the Jobseekers Act which is paid as jobseeker's allowance;]

[⁶ "income-related employment and support allowance" means—
- (a) an income-related allowance under Part 1 of the Welfare Reform Act; and
- (b) in a case where, if there was no entitlement to contributory employment and support allowance, there would be entitlement to income-related employment and support allowance at the same rate, contributory employment and support allowance;]

[¹ "Jobseekers Act" means the Jobseekers Act 1995;

"jobseeker's allowance" means an allowance under Part I of the Jobseekers Act but does not include any back to work bonus under section 26 of that Act which is paid as jobseeker's allowance;]

"the Local Government Finance Act" means the Local Government Finance Act 1992;

[⁵ "personal allowance for a single claimant aged not less than 25" means—
- (a) in the case of a person who is entitled to either income support or state pension credit, the amount for the time being specified in paragraph 1(1)(e) of column (2) of Schedule 2 to the Income Support Regulations; [⁶ . . .]
- (b) in the case of a person who is entitled to an income-based jobseeker's allowance, the amount for the time being specified in paragraph 1(1)(e) of column (2) of Schedule 1 to the Jobseeker's Allowance Regulations 1996;] [⁶ or
- (c) in the case of a person who is entitled to income-related employment and support allowance, the amount specified for the time being in paragraph 1 of column 2 of Schedule 4 to the Employment and Support Allowance Regulations 2008;]

"social security office" means an office of the [⁴ Department for Work and Pensions which is open to the public for the receipt of claims for income support [⁶ , a jobseeker's allowance or an employment and support allowance].]

[⁵ "state pension credit" means the benefit of that name payable under the State Pension Credit Act 2002;]

[³ "tribunal" means an appeal tribunal constituted under Chapter 1 of Part I of the 1998 Act.]

[⁷ "the UC Regulations" means the Universal Credit Regulations 2013; "universal credit" means universal credit under Part 1 of the 2012 Act;]

[⁶ "the Welfare Reform Act" means the Welfare Reform Act 2007.]

(3) Unless the context otherwise requires, any reference in these Regulations to a numbered regulation or Schedule is a reference to the regulation or Schedule bearing that number in these Regulations and any reference in a regulation or Schedule to a numbered paragraph is a reference to the paragraph of that regulation or Schedule having that number.

Amendments

1. Social Security (Jobseeker's Allowance Consequential Amendments) (Deductions) Regulations 1996 (SI 1996/2344) reg.17 (October 7, 1996).

2. Social Security (Miscellaneous Amendments) Regulations 1998 (SI 1998/563) reg.3(1) and (2)(c) (April 1, 1998). (Note that the commencement date for this provision was amended by Social Security (Miscellaneous Amendments) (No.2) Regulations 1998 (SI 1998/865) reg.2 (March 20, 1998).)

3. Social Security Act 1998 (Commencement No.12, and Consequential and Transitional Provisions) Order 1999 (SI 1999/3178) art.3(13) and Sch.13 para.1 (November 29, 1999).

4. Secretaries of State for Education and Skills and for Work and Pensions Order 2002 (SI 2002/1397) art.12 and Sch. para.23 (June 27, 2002).

5. State Pension Credit (Consequential, Transitional and Miscellaneous Provisions) Regulations 2002 (SI 2002/3019) reg.33 (October 6, 2003).

6. Employment and Support Allowance (Consequential Provisions) (No.2) Regulations 2008 (SI 2008/1554) reg.55(1) and (2) (October 27, 2008).

7. Fines, Council Tax and Community Charges (Deductions from Universal Credit and Other Benefits) Regulations 2013 (SI 2013/612) regs 7 and 8 (April 29, 2013).

Modification

Regulation 1 is modified by Sch.2 para.25 of the Employment and Support Allowance (Transitional Provisions, Housing Benefit and Council Tax Benefit) (Existing Awards) (No.2) Regulations 2010 (SI 2010/1907) (as amended) for the purposes specified in reg.16(1). For details of the modification, see the text of those Regulations in Vol.I.

[¹Application for deductions from income support [², [⁴ universal credit,] state pension credit] or [³ , jobseeker's allowance or employment and support allowance]: England and Wales]

2.922   **2.**—Where a liability order has been made against a debtor by a magistrates' court and the debtor is entitled to income support [², [⁴ universal credit,] state pension credit] [¹ [³, a jobseeker's allowance or an employment and support allowance]] the billing authority concerned may apply to the Secretary of State asking him to deduct sums from any amounts payable to the debtor by way of to income support [², [⁴ universal credit,] state pension credit] [¹ [³ , a jobseeker's allowance or an employment and support allowance]] in order to secure the payment of any outstanding sum which is or forms part of the amount in respect of which the liability order was made.

AMENDMENTS

1. Social Security (Jobseeker's Allowance Consequential Amendments) (Deductions) Regulations 1996 (SI 1996/2344) reg.18 (October 7, 1996).
2. State Pension Credit (Consequential, Transitional and Miscellaneous Provisions) Regulations 2002 (SI 2002/3019) reg.33 (October 6, 2003).
3. Employment and Support Allowance (Consequential Provisions) (No.2) Regulations 2008 (SI 2008/1554) reg.55(1) and (3) (October 27, 2008).
4. Fines, Council Tax and Community Charges (Deductions from Universal Credit and Other Benefits) Regulations 2013 (SI 2013/612) regs 7 and 9 (April 29, 2013).

DEFINITIONS

"debtor"—see reg.1(2).
"income support"—*ibid.*
'jobseeker's allowance"—*ibid.*

[²Application for deductions from income support [², [⁵ universal credit,] state pension credit] [⁴ , jobseeker's allowance or employment and support allowance]: Scotland]

3.—(1) Where a levying authority has obtained a summary warrant or a decree against a debtor in respect of arrears of sums payable under paragraph 1(1) of Schedule 8 to the [¹Local Government Finance Act] and the debtor is entitled to income support [², [⁵ universal credit,] state pension credit] [² [⁴ , a jobseeker's allowance or an employment and support allowance]] the levying authority may, without prejudice to its right to pursue any other means of recovering such arrears, apply to the Secretary of State asking him to deduct sums from any amounts payable to the debtor by way of income support [², [⁵ universal credit,] state pension credit] [² [⁴ , a jobseeker's allowance or an employment and support allowance]] in order to secure the payment of any outstanding sum which is or forms part of the amount in respect of which the summary warrant or decree was granted.

2.923

AMENDMENTS

1. Social Security (Claims and Payments) Amendment (No.3) Regulations 1993 (SI 1993/2113) reg.6 (September 27, 1993).
2. Social Security (Jobseeker's Allowance Consequential Amendments) (Deductions) Regulations 1996 (SI 1996/2344) reg.19 (October 7, 1996).
3. State Pension Credit (Consequential, Transitional and Miscellaneous Provisions) Regulations 2002 (SI 2002/3019) reg.33 (October 6, 2003).
4. Employment and Support Allowance (Consequential Provisions) (No.2) Regulations 2008 (SI 2008/1554) reg.55(1) and (4) (October 27, 2008).
5. Fines, Council Tax and Community Charges (Deductions from Universal Credit and Other Benefits) Regulations 2013 (SI 2013/612) regs 7 and 10 (April 29, 2013).

DEFINITIONS

"debtor"—see reg.1(2).

"income support"—*ibid.*
"jobseeker's allowance"—*ibid.*
"Local Government Finance Act"—*ibid.*

Contents of application

2.924

4.—(1) An application shall contain the following particulars—
  (a) the name and address of the debtor;
  (b) the name and address of the authority making the application;
  (c) the name and place of the court which made the liability order or granted the summary warrant, or decree as the case may be;
  (d the date on which the liability order was made or the summary warrant or decree granted as the case may be;
  (e) the amount specified in the liability order, summary warrant or decree as the case may be;
  (f) the total sum which the authority wishes to have deducted from income support [² , state pension credit] [¹ [³ , a jobseeker's allowance or an employment and support allowance]].

(2) An authority making application shall serve it on the Secretary of State by sending or delivering it to a social security office.

(3) Where it appears to the Secretary of State that an application from an authority gives insufficient particulars to enable the debtor to be identified he may require the authority to furnish such further particulars as may reasonably be required for that purpose.

AMENDMENTS

1. Social Security (Jobseeker's Allowance Consequential Amendments) (Deductions) Regulations 1996 (SI 1996/2344) reg.20 (October 7, 1996).
2. State Pension Credit (Consequential, Transitional and Miscellaneous Provisions) Regulations 2002 (SI 2002/3019) reg.33 (October 6, 2003).
3. Employment and Support Allowance (Consequential Provisions) (No.2) Regulations 2008 (SI 2008/1554) reg.55(1) and (5) (October 27, 2008).

DEFINITIONS

"application"—see reg.1(2).
"authority"—*ibid.*
"debtor"—*ibid.*
"jobseeker's allowance"—*ibid.*
"social security office"—*ibid.*

GENERAL NOTE

2.925

On regs 2, 3 and 4 see *R(IS) 3/92* and *R(IS) 1/98* in the notes to reg.2 of the Community Charges (Deductions from Income Support) (No.2) Regulations 1990. *CIS 1725/1997* confirms that *R(IS) 1/98* applies to deductions for council tax arrears as well as those for arrears of the community charge.

[¹Deductions from debtor's income support [², [⁴ universal credit,] state pension credit] [³ , jobseeker's allowance or employment and support allowance]

2.926

5.—(1) Subject to regulation 8, where—
  (a) the Secretary of State receives an application from an authority in respect of a debtor who is entitled to income support [² , state pension credit] [³ , a jobseeker's allowance or an employment and support allowance];

(b) the amount payable by way of that benefit, after any deduction under this paragraph, is 10 pence or more; and

(c) the aggregate amount payable under one or more of the following provisions, namely, paragraphs 3(2)(a), 5(6), 6(2)(a) and 7(3)(a) and (5)(a) of Schedule 9 to the Claims and Payments Regulations together with the amount to be deducted under this paragraph does not exceed an amount equal to 3 times 5 per cent. of the personal allowance for a single claimant aged not less than 25 years,

the Secretary of State may deduct a sum from that benefit which is equal to 5 per cent. of the personal allowance for a single claimant aged not less than 25 and pay that sum to the authority towards satisfaction of any outstanding sum which is or forms part of the amount in respect of which the liability order was made or the summary warrant or the decree was granted.

[⁴ (1A) Subject to paragraphs (1B) and (1C) and regulation 8, where the Secretary of State receives an application from an authority in respect of a debtor who is entitled to universal credit, the Secretary of State may deduct from the universal credit payable to the debtor an amount equal to 5 per cent. of the appropriate universal credit standard allowance and pay that sum to the authority towards satisfaction of any outstanding sum which is, or forms part of, the amount in respect of which the liability order was made or the summary warrant or decree was granted.

(1B) No amount may be deducted under paragraph (1A) where it would reduce the amount of universal credit payable to the debtor to less than 1 penny.

(1C) For the purpose of paragraph (1A), where 5 per cent. of the appropriate universal credit standard allowance results in a fraction of a penny, that fraction is to be disregarded if it is less than half a penny and otherwise it is to be treated as a penny.

(1D) In paragraphs (1A) and (1C), "appropriate universal credit standard allowance" means the appropriate universal credit standard allowance for the debtor for the assessment period in question under regulation 36 of the UC Regulations.]

[⁴ (2) Subject to regulation 8, where—

(a) the Secretary of State receives an application from an authority in respect of a debtor who is entitled to contribution-based jobseeker's allowance or contributory employment and support allowance; and

(b) the amount of that allowance payable, before any deduction under this paragraph, is 10 pence or more,

the Secretary of State may deduct a sum from that allowance, up to the appropriate maximum specified in paragraph (2A), and pay that sum to the authority towards satisfaction of any outstanding sum which is, or forms part of, the amount in respect of which the liability order was made or the summary warrant or decree was granted.

(2A) The appropriate maximum is 40 per cent. of the appropriate age-related amount for the debtor specified—

(a) where the debtor is entitled to contribution-based jobseeker's allowance, in regulation 79 of the Jobseeker's Allowance Regulations 1996 or, as the case may be, regulation 49 of the Jobseeker's Allowance Regulations 2013;

(b) where the debtor is entitled to contributory employment and support allowance, in paragraph 1(1) of Schedule 4 to the Employment and Support Allowance Regulations 2008 or, as the case may be, regulation

62(1)(b) of the Employment and Support Allowance Regulations 2013.]
[⁴ . . .]
(4) The Secretary of State shall notify the debtor and the authority concerned in writing of a decision to make a deduction under this regulation so far as is practicable within 14 days from the date on which he made the decision and at the same time shall notify the debtor of his right of appeal.]

AMENDMENTS

1. Social Security Act 1998 (Commencement No.12, and Consequential and Transitional Provisions) Order 1999 (SI 1999/3178 (C.81)) art.3(13) and Sch.13, para.2 (November 29, 1999).
2. State Pension Credit (Consequential, Transitional and Miscellaneous Provisions) Regulations 2002 (SI 2002/3019) reg.33 (October 6, 2003).
3. Employment and Support Allowance (Consequential Provisions) (No.2) Regulations 2008 (SI 2008/1554) reg.55(1) and (6) (October 27, 2008).
4. Fines, Council Tax and Community Charges (Deductions from Universal Credit and Other Benefits) Regulations 2013 (SI 2013/612) regs 7 and 11 (April 29, 2013).

GENERAL NOTE

2.927   The replacement of para.(2) with paras (2) and (2A) by regs 2 and 11(4) of SI 2013/612 does not have effect in respect of an application received by the Secretary of State from the court in respect of an offender before April 29, 2013: see reg.11(6) of SI 2013/612.

Notification of decision

2.928   **6.**—[¹ . . .]

AMENDMENT

1. Social Security Act 1998 (Commencement No.12, and Consequential and Transitional Provisions) Order 1999 (SI 1999/3178 (C.81)) art.3(13) and Sch.13 para.2 (November 29, 1999).

[¹Deductions from debtor's income support or income-based jobseeker's allowance]

2.929   **7.**—[² . . .]

AMENDMENTS

1. Social Security (Jobseeker's Allowance Consequential Amendments) (Deductions) Regulations 1996 (SI 1996/2344) reg.22 (October 7, 1996).
2. Social Security Act 1998 (Commencement No.12, and Consequential and Transitional Provisions) Order 1999 (SI 1999/3178 (C.81)) art.3(13) and Sch.13 para.2 (November 29, 1999).

[¹Deductions from debtor's contribution-based jobseeker's allowance]

2.930   **7A.**—[² . . .]

AMENDMENTS

1. Social Security (Jobseeker's Allowance Consequential Amendments) (Deductions) Regulations 1996 (SI 1996/2344) reg.23 (October 7, 1996).

2. Social Security Act 1998 (Commencment No.12 and Consequential and Transitional Provisions) Order 1999 (SI 1999/3178 (C.81)) art.3(13) and Sch.13 para.2 (November 29, 1999).

Circumstances, time of making and termination of deductions

8.—(1) The Secretary of State may make deductions from [¹income support [³, state pension credit] [⁴, jobseeker's allowance or employment and support allowance] under [⁴ [⁵ regulation 5(1) or (2)]] only if—

    (a) the debtor is entitled to income support [³, state pension credit] [¹ [⁴, jobseeker's allowance or employment and support allowance]] throughout any benefit week;

    (b) no deductions are being made in respect of the debtor under any other application; and

    (c) no payments are being made under regulation 2 of the Community Charge (Deductions from Income Support) (Scotland) Regulations 1989 or regulation 2 of the Community Charge (Deductions from Income Support) (No.2) Regulations 1990.

[⁵ (1A) The Secretary of State may make deductions from universal credit under regulation 5(1A) only if—

    (a) the debtor is entitled to universal credit throughout any assessment period;

    (b) no deductions are being made in respect of the debtor under any other application; and

    (c) no payments are being made under regulation 2 of the Community Charge (Deductions from Income Support)(Scotland) Regulations 1989(12) or regulation 2 of the Community Charge (Deductions from Income Support)(No.2) Regulations 1990.]

(2) The Secretary of State shall make deductions from income support [³, [⁵ universal credit,] state pension credit] [¹ [⁴, jobseeker's allowance or employment and support allowance]] by reference to the times at which payment of income support [³, [⁵ universal credit,] state pension credit] [¹ [⁴, jobseeker's allowance or employment and support allowance]] is made to the debtor.

(3) The Secretary of State shall cease making deductions from income support [³, [⁵ universal credit,] state pension credit] [¹[⁴, jobseeker's allowance or employment and support allowance]] if—

    (a) there is no longer sufficient entitlement to income support [³, [⁵ universal credit,] state pension credit] [¹ [⁴, jobseeker's allowance or employment and support allowance]] to enable him to make the deduction;

    (b) an authority withdraws its application for deductions to be made; or

    (c) the debt in respect of which he was making deductions is discharged.

[²(4) The Secretary of State shall not determine any application under regulation 2 or 3 which relates to a debtor in respect of whom—

    (a) he is making deductions; or

    (b) deductions fall to be made,

pursuant to an earlier application under either of those regulations until no deductions pursuant to that earlier application fall to be made.]

(5) Payments of sums deducted from income support [³, [⁵ universal credit,] state pension credit] [¹ [⁴, jobseeker's allowance or employment and support allowance]] by the Secretary of State under these Regulations

shall be made to the authority concerned, as far as is practicable, at intervals not exceeding 13 weeks.

(6) Where the whole of the amount to which the application relates has been paid, the authority concerned shall, so far as is practicable, give notice of that fact within 21 days to the Secretary of State.

(7) The Secretary of State shall notify the debtor in writing of the total of the sums deducted by him under any application—

(a) on receipt of a written request for such information from the debtor; or

(b) on the termination of deductions made under any such application.

AMENDMENTS

1. Social Security (Jobseeker's Allowance Consequential Amendments) (Deductions) Regulations 1996 (SI 1996/2344) reg.24 (October 7, 1996).

2. Social Security Act 1998 (Commencement No.12, and Consequential and Transitional Provisions) Order 1999 (SI 1999/3178 (C.81)) art.3(13) and Sch.13 para.3 (November 29, 1999).

3. State Pension Credit (Consequential, Transitional and Miscellaneous Provisions) Regulations 2002 (SI 2002/3019) reg.33 (October 6, 2003).

4. Employment and Support Allowance (Consequential Provisions) (No.2) Regulations 2008 (SI 2008/1554) reg.55(1) and (7) (October 27, 2008).

5. Fines, Council Tax and Community Charges (Deductions from Universal Credit and Other Benefits) Regulations 2013 (SI 2013/612) regs 7 and 12 (April 29, 2013).

Withdrawal of application

2.932   **9.**—An authority may withdraw an application at any time by giving notice in writing to the social security office to which the application was sent or delivered.

[¹Revision and supersession

2.933   **10.**—Any decision of the Secretary of State under regulation 5 may be revised under section 9 of the 1998 Act or superseded under section 10 of that Act as though the decision were made under section 8(1)(c) of that Act.]

AMENDMENT

1. Social Security Act 1998 (Commencement No.12, and Consequential and Transitional Provisions) Order 1999 (SI 1999/3178 (C.81)) art.3(13) and Sch.13 para.4 (November 29, 1999).

[¹Appeal

2.934   **11.**—Any decision of the Secretary of State under regulation 5 (whether as originally made or as revised under regulation 10) may be appealed to a tribunal as though the decision were made on an award of a relevant benefit (within the meaning of section 8(3) of the 1998 Act) under section 8(1)(c) of the 1998 Act.]

AMENDMENT

1. Social Security Act 1998 (Commencement No.12, and Consequential and Transitional Provisions) Order 1999 (SI 1999/3178 (C.81)) art.3(13) and Sch.13 para.4 (November 29, 1999).

Correction of accidental errors

12.—[¹ . . .]   2.935

AMENDMENT

1. Social Security Act 1998 (Commencement No.12, and Consequential and Transitional Provisions) Order 1999 (SI 1999/3178 (C.81)) art.3(13) and Sch.13 para.5 (November 29, 1999).

Setting aside decisions on certain grounds

13.—[¹ . . .]   2.936

AMENDMENT

1. Social Security Act 1998 (Commencement No.12, and Consequential and Transitional Provisions) Order 1999 (SI 1999/3178 (C.81)) art.3(13) and Sch.13 para.5 (November 29, 1999).

Provisions common to regulations 12 and 13

14.—[¹ . . .]   2.937

AMENDMENT

1. Social Security Act 1998 (Commencement No.12, and Consequential and Transitional Provisions) Order 1999 (SI 1999/3178 (C.81)) art.3(13) and Sch.13 para.5 (November 29, 1999).

Manner of making applications or appeals and time limits

15.—[¹ . . .]   2.938

AMENDMENT

1. Social Security Act 1998 (Commencement No.12, and Consequential and Transitional Provisions) Order 1999 (SI 1999/3178 (C.81)) art.3(13) and Sch.13 para.5 (November 29, 1999).

Manner and time for the service of notices etc.

16.—[¹ . . .]   2.939

AMENDMENT

1. Social Security Act 1998 (Commencement No.12, and Consequential and Transitional Provisions) Order 1999 (SI 1999/3178 (C.81)) art.3(13) and Sch.13 para.5 (November 29, 1999).

SCHEDULE 1

TIME LIMITS FOR MAKING APPLICATIONS OR APPEALS

2.940   [¹ . . .]

AMENDMENT

1. Social Security Act 1998 (Commencement No.12, and Consequential and Transitional Provisions) Order 1999 (SI 1999/3178 (C.81)) art.3(13) and Sch.13 para.5 (November 29, 1999).

SCHEDULE 2

CONDUCT AND PROCEDURE IN RELATION TO APPEALS AND APPLICATIONS

2.941   [¹ . . .]

AMENDMENT

1. Social Security Act 1998 (Commencement No.12, and Consequential and Transitional Provisions) Order 1999 (SI 1999/3178 (C.81)) art.3(13) and Sch.13 para.5 (November 29, 1999).

The Social Security Benefits (Maintenance Payments and Consequential Amendments) Regulations 1996

(SI 1996/940) (AS AMENDED)

Made by the Secretary of State under ss.74A(5) and (6), 189(1) and (3)–(5) and 191 of the Social Security Administration Act 1992 and ss.136(5)(b), 137(1) and 175(1)–(4) of the Social Security Contributions and Benefits Act 1992

[In force April 19, 1996]

Interpretation for the purposes of section 74A of the Act

2.942   2.—In section 74A of the Act (payment of benefit where maintenance payments collected by Secretary of State)—
   (a) "child maintenance" means any payment towards the maintenance of a child or young person, including payments made—
       (i) under a court order;
       (ii) under a maintenance [¹ calculation] made under the Child Support Act 1991;
       (iii) under an agreement for maintenance; or
       (iv) voluntarily,
       and for this purpose a "young person" is a person referred to in regulation 3 of these Regulations (persons of a prescribed description);
   (b) "spousal maintenance" means any payment made by a person towards the maintenance of that person's spouse [² or civil partner], including payments made—
       (i) under a court order;

    (ii) under an agreement for maintenance; or

    (iii) voluntarily;

  (c) "relevant income" means—

    (i) any income which is taken into account under Part V of the Income Support Regulations for the purposes of calculating the amount of income support to which the claimant is entitled; or

    (ii) any income which is taken into account under Part VIII of the Jobseeker's Allowance Regulations for the purposes of calculating the amount of jobseeker's allowance to which the claimant is entitled [³ or

    (iii) any income which is taken into account under Part 10 of the Employment and Support Allowance Regulations for the purposes of calculating the amount of employment and support allowance to which the claimant is entitled.]

AMENDMENTS

1. Child Support (Consequential Amendments and Transitional Provisions) Regulations 2001 (SI 2001/158) reg.8 (in force in relation to a particular case from the date on which CSPSSA 2000 s.1 comes into force in relation to that type of case).

2. Civil Partnership (Pensions, Social Security and Child Support) (Consequential, etc. Provisions) Order 2005 (SI 2005/2877) art.2(3) and Sch.3 para.27 (December 5, 2005).

3. Employment and Support Allowance (Consequential Provisions) (No.2) Regulations 2008 (SI 2008/1554) reg.59(3) (October 27, 2008).

Persons of a prescribed description

3.—For the purposes of the definition of "family" in section 74A(5) of the Act, a person of a prescribed description is any person who—   **2.943**

  (a) is referred to as a "young person" in the Income Support Regulations by virtue of regulation 14 of those Regulations; or

  (b) is referred to as a "young person" in the Jobseeker's Allowance Regulations by virtue of regulation 76 of those Regulations [¹ or

  (c) is referred to as a "young person" in the Employment and Support Allowance Regulations by virtue of regulation 2(1) of those Regulations.]

AMENDMENT

1. Employment and Support Allowance (Consequential Provisions) (No.2) Regulations 2008 (SI 2008/1554) reg.59(4) (October 27, 2008).

Circumstances in which a person is to be treated as responsible for another

4.—A person shall be treated as responsible for another for the purposes of section 74A of the Act if he is treated as responsible for that other person under either regulation 15 of the Income Support Regulations or regulation 77 of the Jobseeker's Allowance Regulations.   **2.944**

Circumstances in which persons are to be treated as being members of the same household

5.—Persons shall be treated as members of the same household for the purposes of section 74A of the Act if they are treated as members of the same household under [¹. . .] regulation 16 of the Income Support   **2.945**

Regulations or regulation 78 of the Jobseeker's Allowance Regulations [¹ or regulation 156 of the Employment and Support Allowance Regulations].

AMENDMENT

1. Employment and Support Allowance (Consequential Provisions) (No.2) Regulations 2008 (SI 2008/1554) reg.59(5) (October 27, 2008).

GENERAL NOTE

2.946   For s.74A of the Social Security Administration Act, see Vol.III of this series. See the note to para.73 of Sch.9 to the Income Support Regulations.

The Care Planning, Placement and Case Review (England) Regulations 2010

(SI 2010/959)

Made by the Secretary of State for Children, Schools and Families under ss.22C(11), 23ZA(3) and (4), 23ZB(1)(a), 23D(2), 23E(1) and (2), 25A(4), 25B(1)(b) and (2)(a), 26(1) and (2), 31A(3), 34(8) and 104(4) of, and paras 12A–12E, 12F(1)(a), 12G and 19B(2)(b), (3), (7) and (8) of Sch.2 to, the Children Act 1989

[In force April 1, 2011]

REGULATIONS REPRODUCED

GENERAL NOTE

2.948   See the notes to reg.2 of the Children (Leaving Care) Social Security Benefits Regulations 2001.

Eligible children

Meaning of eligible child

2.949   **40.**—(1) For the purposes of paragraph 19B(2)(b) of Schedule 2 to the 1989 Act (meaning of eligible child), the prescribed period is 13 weeks and the prescribed age is 14.

(2) For the purposes of paragraph 19B(3)(b) of that Schedule, if C is a child to whom regulation 48 applies, C is not an eligible child despite falling within paragraph 19B(2) of that Schedule.

Application of these Regulations with modifications to short breaks

2.950   **48.**—(1) In the circumstances set out in paragraph (2) these Regulations apply with the modifications set out in paragraph (3).

(2) The circumstances are that—

(a) C is not in the care of the responsible authority,

(b) the responsible authority have arranged to place C in a series of short-term placements with the same person or in the same accommodation ("short breaks"), and

(c) the arrangement is such that—

(i) no single placement is intended to last for longer than 17 days,

(ii) at the end of each such placement, C returns to the care of C's parent or a person who is not C's parent but who has parental responsibility for C, and

(iii) the short breaks do not exceed 75 days in total in any period of 12 months.

(3) *[Omitted].*

The Care Leavers (England) Regulations 2010

(SI 2010/2571)

Made by the Secretary of State for Education under ss.23A(3), 23B(8)(c) and (10), 23D(2), 23E(1), (1B), (1C) and (2), 24B(6) and 104(4) of, and para.19B(2), (3), (7) and (8) of Sch.2 to, the Children Act 1989
[In force April 1, 2011]

GENERAL NOTE

See the note to reg.2 of the Children (Leaving Care) Social Security Benefits Regulations 2001.   2.951

Relevant children

3.—(1) For the purposes of section 23A(3), children falling within paragraph (2) are an additional category of relevant children.   2.952

(2) Subject to paragraph (3), a child falls within this paragraph if—

(a) the child is aged 16 or 17,

(b) the child is not subject to a care order, and

(c) on attaining the age of 16 the child was detained, or in hospital, and immediately before being detained or admitted to hospital had been looked after by a local authority for a period or periods amounting in total to at least 13 weeks, which began after the child attained the age of 14.

(3) In calculating the period of 13 weeks referred to in paragraph (2) (b), no account is to be taken of any period in which the child was looked after by a local authority in the course of a pre-planned series of short-term placements, none of which individually exceeded four weeks, where at the end of each such placement the child returned to the care of their parent, or a person who is not a parent but who has parental responsibility for them.

(4) For the purposes of this regulation—

(a) "detained" means detained in a remand centre, a young offender institution or a secure training centre, or any other institution pursuant to an order of a court [¹, but excludes remand to youth detention accommodation], and

(b) "hospital" has the meaning given in section 275(1) of the National Health Service Act 2006

[¹ (c) "remand to youth detention accommodation" has the meaning given in section 102(1) of the Legal Aid, Sentencing and Punishment of Offenders Act 2012.]

(5) Subject to paragraph (6), a child who has lived for a continuous period of six months or more (whether that period commenced before or after they ceased to be looked after) with—

(a) their parent,

(b) someone who is not their parent but who has parental responsibility for them, or

(c) where they were in care and there was a [² child arrangements] order in force immediately before the care order was made, a person [² named in the child arrangements order as a person with whom they were to live],

is not a relevant child despite falling within section 23A(2).

[² (5A) For the purposes of paragraph (5), a child arrangements order is one that consists of, or includes, arrangements relating to either or both of the following—

(i) with whom the child is to live, and

(ii) when the child is to live with any person.]

(6) Where living arrangements described in paragraph (5) break down and the child ceases to live with the person concerned, the child is a relevant child.

AMENDMENTS

1. Care Planning, Placement and Case Review (England) (Miscellaneous Amendments) Regulations 2013 (SI 2013/706) reg.12 (April 19, 2013).

2. Child Arrangements Order (Consequential Amendments to Subordinate Legislation) Order 2014 (SI 2014/852) art.19 (April 22, 2014).

The Care Planning, Placement and Case Review (Wales) Regulations 2015

(SI 2015/1818)

Made by the Welsh Ministers under ss. 81(6)(d), 83(5), 84, 87, 97(4)(a), 97(5), 98(1)(a), 100(1)(b), 100(2)(a), 102(1), 102(2), 104(2)(c), 104(6), 106(4), 107(7)(c), 107(8), 107(9), 108(6) and 196(2) of the Social Services and Well-being (Wales) Act 2014 and ss. 31A and 34(8) of the Children Act 1989

[In force April 6, 2016]

REGULATIONS REPRODUCED

Title, commencement and application

2.954   **1.**—(1) The title of these Regulations is the Care Planning, Placement and Case Review (Wales) Regulations 2015 and they come into force on 6 April 2016.

(2) These Regulations apply in relation to Wales.

Meaning of category 1 young person

47.—(1) For the purposes of section 104(2) of the 2014 Act the pre- scribed period is 13 weeks and the prescribed age is 14.

(2) For the purposes of section 104(6)(b) of the 2014 Act, if C is a child to whom regulation 62 applies, C is not a category 1 young person despite falling within section 104(2) of that Act.

2.955

Application of these Regulations with modifications to short breaks

62.—(1) In the circumstances set out in paragraph (2), these Regulations apply with the modifications set out in paragraph (3).

(2) The circumstances are that—

(a) C is not in the care of the responsible authority,

(b) the responsible authority has arranged to place C in a series of short- term placements with the same person or in the same accommoda- tion ("short breaks"), and

(c) the arrangement is such that—

(i) no single placement is intended to last for more than 4 weeks,

(ii) at the end of each such placement C returns to the care of C's parent or a person who is not C's parent but who has parental responsibility for C, and

(iii) the short breaks do not exceed 120 days in total in any period of 12 months.

(3) *[Omitted]*

2.956

The Care Leavers (Wales) Regulations 2015

(SI 2015/1820)

Made by the Welsh Ministers under ss. 104(2) and (6), 106(4), 107(7)(c) and (8), 108(6), 109(1) and (3), 116(2) and 196(2) of the Social Services and Well-being (Wales) Act 2014

[In force April 6, 2016]

REGULATIONS REPRODUCED

Title, commencement and application

1.—(1) The title of these Regulations is the Care Leavers (Wales) Regulations 2015 and they come into force on 6 April 2016.

(2) These Regulations apply in relation to Wales.

2.958

Category 2 young persons

3.—(1) For the purposes of section 104(6)(a) of the Act, children falling within paragraph (2) are an additional category of category 2 young person.

2.959

(2) Subject to paragraph (3), a child falls within this paragraph if—

(a) the child is aged 16 or 17,

(b) the child is not subject to a care order, and

(c) on attaining the age of 16 the child was detained, or in hospital, and immediately before being detained or admitted to hospital had been looked after by a local authority for a period or periods amounting in total to at least 13 weeks, which began after the child attained the age of 14.

(3) In calculating the period of 13 weeks referred to in paragraph (2) (c), no account is to be taken of any period in which the child was looked after by a local authority or a local authority in England in the course of a pre-planned series of short-term placements, none of which individually exceeded four weeks, where at the end of the each such placement the child returned to the care of their parent or a person who is not a parent but who has parental responsibility for them.

(4) Subject to paragraph (5), a child who has lived for a continuous period of six months or more (whether that period commenced before or after they ceased to be looked after) with—

(a) their parent,

(b) someone who is not their parent but who has parental responsibility for them, or

(c) where they were in care and there was a child arrangements order in force immediately before the care order was made, a person named in the child arrangements order as the person with whom they were to live, is not to be treated as a category 2 young person despite falling within the definition set out in section 104(2) of the Act.

(5) Where living arrangements described in paragraph (4) break down and the child ceases to live with the person concerned, the child is to be treated as a category 2 young person.

(6) For the purposes of paragraph (4), a child arrangements order is one that consists of, or includes, arrangements relating to either or both of the following—

(a) with whom the child is to live, and

(b) when the child is to live with any person.

(7) For the purposes of this regulation—

"child arrangements order" has the meaning given in section 8(1) of the Children Act 1989; and

"hospital" has the same meaning as in the Mental Health Act 1983.

The Children (Leaving Care) Social Security Benefits Regulations 2001

(SI 2001/3074) (AS AMENDED)

Made by the Secretary of State for Work and Pensions under s.6(3), (5), (6) and (7) of the Children (Leaving Care) Act 2000

[In force October 1, 2001]

REGULATIONS REPRODUCED

2.960   2.   Entitlement to Benefits

Entitlement to Benefits

2.—(1) Section 6 (exclusion from benefits) shall not apply for the purposes of entitlement to income support [² , income-based jobseeker's allowance or income-related employment and support allowance] where a person—

    (a) falls within subsection (2)(a) or (b) of that section; and

    (b) falls within a category of person prescribed in—

        (i) provided the person is a lone parent, regulation 13(2)(a) (circumstances in which persons in relevant education may be entitled to income support) of; [³ or]

        (ii) [³ . . .]

        (iii) paragraph 1, 2, 7, 8, [³ . . .] 11, [³ . . .] [³ . . .] 24 or 25 of Schedule 1B (prescribed categories of person) to,

the Income Support (General) Regulations 1987 ("the Income Support Regulations").

(2) Section 6 shall not apply to a person who falls within subsection (2) (a) or (b) of that section who has not been looked after by a local authority for the purposes of paragraph 19B of Schedule 2 to the Children Act 1989 on or after 1st October 2001.

(3) Where a person who falls within subsection (2)(a) or (b) of section 6 is residing in Scotland but is not supported by a local authority in England or Wales then, notwithstanding that he has been looked after by such a local authority for the purposes of paragraph 19B of Schedule 2 to the 1989 Act on or after 1st October 2001, section 6 shall not apply to that person [¹ provided that he ceased to be so looked after before 1st April 2004].

(4) In paragraph (1)(b)(i) above, "lone parent" has the meaning it bears in regulation 2(1) of the Income Support Regulations.

2.961

AMENDMENTS

    1. Social Security (Miscellaneous Amendments) Regulations 2004 (SI 2004/565) reg.12 (April 1, 2004).
    2. Employment and Support Allowance (Consequential Provisions) (No.2) Regulations 2008 (SI 2008/1554) reg.70 (October 27, 2008).
    3. Income Support (Prescribed Categories of Person) Regulations 2009 (SI 2009/3152) reg.3(3) and 3(7) (December, 30, 2009). Regulation 3(3) amended reg.2(1)(b) with effect from December 30, 2009 but reg.3(7) provided that this did not apply in the case of a person who was subject to the saving provisions in reg.2(2) of those Regulations. See the 2015/16 edition of this volume for these Regulations and the notes to them.

GENERAL NOTE

This regulation deals with the exceptions to the exclusion from benefit in s.6(2) (a) and (b) of the Children (Leaving Care) Act 2000 (see the note to the Children (Leaving Care) Act 2000). See the Children (Leaving Care) Social Security Benefits (Scotland) Regulations 2004 (SI 2004/747) below which provide for similar exceptions to the exclusion under s.6(2)(c) of the 2000 Act (as well as defining the scope of the exclusion under that provision).

Note that s.6 of the 2000 Act has not been amended following the introduction of ESA on October 27, 2008 so as to also exclude entitlement to income-related ESA. This would appear to be an oversight as a purported amendment to reg.2(1) has been made to include a reference to income-related ESA. However, in view of the fact that s.6 has not been amended to exclude an "eligible child" or a "relevant

2.962

child" from entitlement to ESA, such an amendment is not necessary (and is ultra vires).

Note also that this regulation has not been amended to include a person who falls within subs.(2)(ba) or (bb) of s.6 of the Children (Leaving Care) Act 2000. Subsection (2)(ba) and (bb) came into force on April 6, 2016 and refer to a "category 1 young person" and a "category 2 young person" respectively within the meaning of s.104(2) of the Social Services and Well-being (Wales) Act 2014. A "category 1 young person" is the equivalent in Wales of an "eligible child" and a "category 2 young person" is the equivalent in Wales of a "relevant child". It is not known why this regulation has not been amended to include a person who falls within subs.(2) (ba) or (bb). However, the result, at least for the time being, is that category 1 and category 2 young people would not seem to be covered by the exceptions in this regulation to the exclusion from benefit in s.6(2) of the 2000 Act.

Eligible and relevant children

2.963   Under s.6, an "eligible child" (defined in para.19B of Sch.2 to the Children Act 1989) or a "relevant child" (defined in s.23A of the 1989 Act) is not entitled to income-based JSA, income support or housing benefit (subss.(1), (2)(a) and (2) (b)). (Nor is a category 1 or category 2 young person.) See also the consequential amendments to reg.4ZA of the Income Support Regulations and reg.57 of the JSA Regulations 1996 made by the Children (Leaving Care) Act 2000 (Commencement No.2 and Consequential Provisions) Order 2001 (SI 2001/ 3070) with effect from October 1, 2001.

Paragraph 19B of Sch.2 to, and s.23A of, the Children Act 1989 were inserted by ss.1 and 2 respectively of the Children (Leaving Care) Act 2000 (p.148).

Under para.19B, together with regs 40 and 48 of the Care Planning, Placement and Case Review (England) Regulations 2010 (SI 2010/959) ("the English Regulations (eligible children)"), an "eligible child" is a 16-or 17-year-old who is being looked after by a local authority and who has, since the age of 14, been looked after by a local authority for a period of at least 13 weeks, or periods totalling at least 13 weeks, which ended after he became 16. However, periods of respite care are excluded. Thus the child will not be an eligible child if he is not in the care of the responsible authority and has been/is placed by the responsible authority in a series of short-term placements with the same person or in the same accommodation, none of which are intended to exceed 17 days and which do not total more than 75 days in any 12-month period and the child returns to the care of his parent or the person who has parental responsibility for him at the end of each placement (see reg.48 of the English Regulations).

A "relevant child" is a 16- or 17-year-old who was an eligible child but who is no longer being looked after by a local authority (s.23A(2) of the 1989 Act). It also includes a 16- or 17-year-old (not subject to a care order) who at the age of 16 was in hospital or detained in a remand centre, a young offenders institution, a secure training centre, or any other institution pursuant to an order of a court (other than remand to youth detention accommodation), and who immediately before he was in hospital or detained, had, since the age of 14, been looked after by a local authority for a period or periods totalling at least 13 weeks (reg.3(2) of the Care Leavers (England) Regulations 2010 (SI 2010/2571) ("the English Regulations (relevant children)"). In calculating the 13 weeks any pre-planned short-term placement which does not exceed four weeks and at the end of which the child returns to the care of his parent or the person who has parental responsibility for him is ignored (reg.3(3) of the English Regulations (relevant children)). However, a child who has lived with his parent, the person who has parental responsibility for him or, in the case of a child subject to a care order, the person in whose favour a child arrangements order had been made before the care order was made for at least six months, whether or not the six months started before or after the child stopped being looked after by a local authority, does not count as a relevant child (reg.3(5) of the English Regulations (relevant children)) but will do so if the living arrangements break down and the child ceases to live with the person concerned (reg.3(6) of the English Regulations (relevant children)).

Once an eligible or relevant child becomes 18 he ceases to count as such and the exclusion from benefit in s.6 will not apply.

If there is a dispute over whether the s.6 exclusion applies, it may be necessary for decision-makers (and appeal tribunals) to decide whether a child falls within either definition. For this reason the text of the relevant parts of both the English and the Welsh Regulations has been included (see pp.950–955, but note what is said above about the fact that this regulation has not been amended to include a person who falls within subs.(2)(ba) or (bb) of s.6 of the Children (Leaving Care) Act 2000). Clearly information from the relevant social services department will be useful in determining these issues. But if, for example, a local authority has decided that living arrangements have broken down with the result that the person concerned is again treated as a relevant child, is a tribunal bound by the local authority decision or can it reach a different conclusion? As this will be largely a question of fact, there seems to be no reason why the tribunal cannot consider this issue in deciding whether the s.6 exclusion applies.

See also the amendments to reg.14 of the Income Support Regulations and reg.76(2) of the JSA Regulations 1996 made by the Children (Leaving Care) Act 2000 (Commencement No.2 and Consequential Provisions) Order 2001 (SI 2001/3070) with effect from October 1, 2001. The result of these amendments is that a person to whom the s.6 exclusion applies cannot form part of a claimant's family for the purposes of income support and income-based JSA.

Category 1 and Category 2 young persons

The definition of a category 1 young person in s.104(2) of the Social Services and Well-being (Wales) Act 2014 is to all intents and purposes the same as the definition of "eligible child" in para.19B of Sch.2 to the Children Act 1989. Similarly, the definition of a category 2 young person in s.104(2) replicates the definition of "relevant child" in s.23A(2) of the 1989 Act.   2.964

In addition, the provisions of regs 47 and 62 of the Care Planning, Placement and Case Review (Wales) Regulations 2015 (SI 2015/1818), which relate to category 1 young persons, are the same as those in regs 40 and 48 of the Care Planning, Placement and Care Review (England) Regulations 2010, which relate to eligible children, except that in Wales the limit for the intended length of a short-term placement is four weeks (as opposed to 17 days) and the overall limit on the length of time the child can spend in such short breaks is 120 (as opposed to 75) days. As regards category 2 young persons, reg.3 of the Care Leavers (Wales) Regulations 2015 (SI 2015/1820) is the same as reg.3 of the Care Leavers (England) Regulations 2010, which concerns relevant children.

The s.6 exclusion

The circumstances in which the s.6 exclusion will not apply are set out in reg.2.   2.965

Note firstly that the exclusion only applied to an eligible or relevant child who had been looked after by a local authority on or after October 1, 2001 (para.(2)) (i.e. it did not apply to a 16- or 17-year-old who left local authority care before that date). It also did not originally apply if an eligible or relevant child who would otherwise be caught by s.6 was living in Scotland, provided that he was not being supported by an English or Welsh local authority (para.(3)). However, this now only applies if the person ceased to be so looked after before April 1, 2004. This is because, with the exception of s.6, the Children (Leaving Care) Act 2000 did not apply to Scotland and so 16- or 17-year-olds who left Scottish local authority care remained potentially entitled to income support, income-based JSA and housing benefit, whether they were in Scotland, England or Wales. However, with effect from April 1, 2004 equivalent legislation came into force in Scotland and so 16- or 17-year-olds leaving Scottish local authority care then came within s.6. See the Support and Assistance of Young People Leaving Care (Scotland) Regulations 2003 (SSI SI 2003/608).

In addition to these general exceptions, para.(1) provides that an eligible child or a relevant child can still qualify for income support or income-based JSA if he is: (i) in relevant education and a lone parent (as defined in reg.2(1) of the Income Support Regulations (para.(4))); or (ii) a lone parent, a single foster parent, incapable of work or appealing against a decision that he is capable of work, or a disabled worker within the meaning of para.8 of Sch.1B to the Income Support Regulations (but note that para.8 was revoked on January 25, 2010, although there is some transitional protection: see the note to para.8). (Paragraph 11 of Sch.1B is also listed in para.(1)(b)(iii) but is no longer of any application). But note that there is no exception under para.(1) to the exclusion from housing benefit even if the person does fall within any of these categories.

Note the amendments made to para.(1)(b) by the Income Support (Prescribed Categories of Person) Regulations 2009 (SI 2009/3152) with effect from December 30, 2009. However, the amendments did not apply to claimants to whom the savings provisions in reg.2(2) of the 2009 Regulations applied. See the 2015/16 edition of this volume for the 2009 Regulations and the notes to those Regulations. It is not known why sub-paras (a) and (b) of para.7 of Sch.1B (incapacity for work) have not also been omitted.

As pointed out at the beginning of this note, however, an eligible child, relevant child, category 1 young person or category 2 young person can claim ESA as the s.6 exclusion does not include ESA. But note, as has also already been pointed out, reg.2 has not been amended to take account of the changes in Wales made by the Social Services and Well-being (Wales) Act 2014. Thus, as things stand at the moment, the exceptions to the s.6 exclusion do not apply in Wales with effect from April 6, 2016.

The Children (Leaving Care) Social Security Benefits (Scotland) Regulations 2004

(SI 2004/747)

Made by the Secretary of State for Work and Pensions under ss.6(4), (6) and (7) of the Children (Leaving Care) Act 2000

[In force April 1, 2004]

REGULATIONS REPRODUCED

2.966   2.   Entitlement to Benefits (Scotland)

Entitlement to Benefits (Scotland)

2.967   **2.**—(1) For the purposes of section 6(2)(c) of the Children (Leaving Care) Act 2000 (exclusion from benefits of persons of a prescribed description)—

    (a) a person of the description set out in paragraph (2) is hereby prescribed unless he is a person to whom paragraph (3)(b) applies; and

    (b) a person of the description set out in paragraph (3) is hereby prescribed in relation only to entitlement to housing benefit.

    (2) The description of person mentioned in paragraph (1)(a) is a person—

    (a) who is less than 18 years of age,

[³ (b) to whom a local authority in Scotland is obliged to provide—
  (i) continuing care in accordance with section 26A of the Children (Scotland) Act 1995 (duty of local authorities to provide accommodation and assistance to persons who were, but are no longer, looked after by a local authority), or
  (ii) advice, guidance and assistance in accordance with section 29(1) of the Children (Scotland) Act 1995 (duty of local authorities to provide after-care to persons who were, but are no longer, looked after by a local authority),]
  (c) who ceased to be looked after on or after 1st April 2004 and since the age of 14 has been looked after and accommodated for a period of, or periods totaling, 13 weeks or more, and
  (d) who either—
  (i) is not living with his family, or
  (ii) is living with his family and is provided with regular financial assistance [³ under that section 29(1)].

(3) The description of person mentioned in paragraph (1)(b) is a person—
  (a) who falls within the description set out in paragraph (2)(a) to (d), and
  (b) who also falls within a category of person prescribed in—
  (i) provided the person is a lone parent, regulation 13(2)(a) (circumstances in which persons in relevant education may be entitled to income support) of; [¹ or]
  (ii) [¹ . . .]
  (iii) paragraph 1, 2, 7, 8, [¹ . . .] 11, [¹ . . .] [¹ . . .] 24 or 25 of Schedule 1B (prescribed categories of person) to,
  the Income Support (General) Regulations 1987 ("the Income Support Regulations").

(4) In this regulation—
  (a) in calculating the period of, or periods, totaling 13 weeks referred to in paragraph (2)(c) no account shall be taken of any pre-planned series of short-term placements, of 4 weeks or less where the person returns to his family at the end of each such placement,
  (b) "accommodated" means provided with accommodation by a local authority pursuant to its duties under section 25 of the Children (Scotland) Act 1995 or [² by giving effect to a compulsory supervision order and a requirement within that order of the type mentioned in section 83(2)(a) of the Children's Hearings (Scotland) Act 2011,] but does not include circumstances where a person has been placed with his family either under arrangements made under section 26(1)(c) of [² the Children (Scotland) Act 1995 or by giving effect to a requirement within a compulsory supervision order under the Children's Hearings (Scotland) Act 2011,]
  (c) "family" includes any person who has parental responsibility for another person who is less than 18 years of age and any person with whom that other person was living prior to being looked after by a local authority, but does not include a local authority,
  (d) "lone parent" has the meaning assigned to it in regulation 2(1) of the Income Support Regulations,
  (e) "looked after" has the meaning assigned to it in section 17(6) of the Children (Scotland) Act 1995.

AMENDMENTS

1. Income Support (Prescribed Categories of Person) Regulations 2009 (SI 2009/3152) reg.3(5) and 3(7) (December, 30, 2009). Regulation 3(5) amended reg.2(3)(b) with effect from December 30, 2009 but reg.3(7) provided that this did not apply in the case of a person who was subject to the saving provisions in reg.2(2) of those Regulations. See the 2015/16 edition of this volume for these Regulations and the notes to them.

2. Children's Hearings (Scotland) Act 2011 (Consequential and Transitional Provisions and Savings) Order 2013 (SI 2013/1465) art.17(1) and Sch.1 Pt 2 para.20 (June 24, 2013).

3. Children and Young People (Scotland) Act 2014 (Consequential Modifications) Order 2016 (SI 2016/732) art.5 (August 5, 2016).

GENERAL NOTE

2.968   See the note to the Children (Leaving Care) Act 2000 and the Children (Leaving Care) Social Security Benefits Regulations 2001. The effect of these regulations and s.6 of the 2000 Act is to remove entitlement to income support, income-based JSA and housing benefit for most 16- or 17-year-old Scottish care-leavers with effect from April 1, 2004, thus bringing the rules in Scotland broadly into line with those that already existed in England and Wales. Note that the rules only apply to 16- or 17-year-olds who stop being looked after by a Scottish local authority on or after April 1, 2004 (i.e. they do not apply to a 16- or 17-year-old who left Scottish local authority care before that date). Note also that in Scotland the s.6 exclusion does not apply if the care leaver is living with his family (unless he is receiving regular financial assistance from the local authority under s.29(1) of the Children (Scotland) Act 1995). The exceptions to the s.6 exclusion in para.(3)(b) are the same as in reg. 2(1) (b) of the Children (Leaving Care) Social Security Benefits Regulations 2001 (again there is no exception to the exclusion from housing benefit).

Note the amendments made to para.(3)(b) by the Income Support (Prescribed Categories of Person) Regulations 2009 (SI 2009/3152) with effect from December 30, 2009. However, the amendments did not apply to claimants to whom the savings provisions in reg.2(2) of the 2009 Regulations applied. See the 2015/16 edition of this volume for the 2009 Regulations and the notes to those Regulations. It is not known why para.7 (or at least sub-paras (a) and (b) of para.7) of Sch.1B (incapacity for work) has not also been omitted.

As pointed out at the beginning of the note to the Children (Leaving Care) Social Security Benefits Regulations 2001, however, an eligible child, relevant child, category 1 young person or category 2 young person can claim ESA as the s.6 exclusion does not include ESA.

The Child Support (Maintenance Calculations and Special Cases) Regulations 2000

(SI 2001/155) (AS AMENDED)

Made by the Secretary of State under various provisions of the Child Support Act 1991

REGULATIONS REPRODUCED

PART II

CALCULATION OF CHILD SUPPORT MAINTENANCE

2.969   4.   Flat rate.

GENERAL NOTE

See the note to s.43 of the Child Support Act 1991.   2.970

Flat rate

4.—(1) The following benefits, pensions and allowances are prescribed   2.971
for the purposes of paragraph 4(1)(b) of Schedule 1 to the Act—
  (a) under the Contributions and Benefits Act—
      (i) [¹⁰ . . .];
      (ii) category A retirement pension under section 44;
      (iii) category B retirement pension under section 48C;
      (iv) category C and category D retirement pensions under section 78;
      (v) incapacity benefit under section 30A;
      (vi) [¹ carer's allowance] under section 70;
      (vii) maternity allowance under section 35 [⁸ or 35B];
     (viii) severe disablement allowance under section 68;
      (ix) industrial injuries benefit under section 94;
      (x) widowed mother's allowance under section 37;
      (xi) widowed parent's allowance under section 39A; and
      (xii) widow's pension under section 38;
  (b) contribution-based jobseeker's allowance under section 1 of the
      Jobseekers Act;
  (c) a social security benefit paid by a country other than the United
      Kingdom;
  (d) a training allowance (other than work-based training for young
      people or, in Scotland, Skillseekers training); [⁴ . . .]
  (e) a war disablement pension [³ . . .] within the meaning of section
      150(2) of the Contributions and Benefits Act or a pension which is
      analogous to such a pension paid by the government of a country
      outside Great Britain [³ [⁴ . . .]
[⁵ (f) a war widow's pension, war widower's pension or surviving civil
      partner's war pension;]] [⁴ [⁶ . . .]
  (g) a payment under a scheme mentioned in section 1(2) of the Armed
      Forces (Pensions and Compensation) Act 2004 (compensation
      schemes for armed and reserve forces);] [⁶ [⁹ . . .]
  (h) contributory employment and support allowance under section 2 of
      the Welfare Reform Act] [⁹ ; and
  (i) a state pension under Part 1 of the Pensions Act 2014.]
  (2) The benefits prescribed for the purposes of paragraph 4(1)(c) of
Schedule 1 to the Act are—
  (a) income support under section 124 of the Contributions and Benefits
      Act; and
  (b) income-based jobseeker's allowance under section 1 of the Jobseekers
      Act [² and
  (c) state pension credit] [⁶[⁷ . . .]
  (d) income-related employment and support allowance under section 4
      of the Welfare Reform Act] [⁷ ; and
  (e) universal credit under Part 1 of the Welfare Reform Act 2012, where
      the award of universal credit is calculated on the basis that the non-
      resident parent does not have any earned income].
  (3) Where the non-resident parent is liable to a pay a flat rate by virtue of
paragraph 4(2) of Schedule 1 to the Act—

(a) if he has one partner, then the amount payable by the non-resident parent shall be half the flat rate; and

(b) if he has more than one partner, then the amount payable by the non-resident parent shall be the result of apportioning the flat rate equally among him and his partners.

[⁷ (4) For the purposes of paragraph (2)(e) and regulation 5(d), "earned income" has the meaning given in regulation 52 of the Universal Credit Regulations 2013 (earned income).]

AMENDMENTS

1. Social Security Amendment (Carer's Allowance) Regulations 2002 (SI 2002/2497) reg.3 and Sch.2 (April 1, 2003).

2. State Pension Credit (Consequential, Transitional and Miscellaneous Provisions) Regulations 2002 (SI 2002/3019) reg.27(3) (October 6, 2003).

3. Child Support (Miscellaneous Amendments) (No.2) Regulations 2003 (SI 2003/2779) reg.6(3) (November 5, 2003).

4. Child Support (Miscellaneous Amendments) Regulations 2005 (SI 2005/785) reg.6(2) (March 16, 2005).

5. Civil Partnership (Pensions, Social Security and Child Support) (Consequential, etc. Provisions) Order 2005 (SI 2005/2877) art.2(4) and Sch.4 para.7(3) (December 5, 2005).

6. Employment and Support Allowance (Consequential Provisions) (No.2) Regulations 2008 (SI 2008/1554) reg.61(3) (October 27, 2008).

7. Universal Credit (Consequential, Supplementary, Incidental and Miscellaneous Provisions) Regulations 2013 (SI 2013/630) reg.43(3) (April 29, 2013).

8. Social Security (Maternity Allowance) (Miscellaneous Amendments) Regulations 2014 (SI 2014/884) reg.3(2) (May 18, 2014).

9. Pensions Act 2014 (Consequential, Supplementary and Incidental Amendments) Order 2015 (SI 2015/1985) art.19 (April 6, 2016).

10. Pensions Act 2014 (Consequential, Supplementary and Incidental Amendments) Order 2017 (SI 2017/422) art.17 (April 6, 2017).

The Child Support Maintenance Calculation Regulations 2012

(SI 2012/2677) (AS AMENDED)

Made by the Secretary of State under various provisions of the Child Support Act 1991

REGULATIONS REPRODUCED

PART 4

THE MAINTENANCE CALCULATION RULES

2.972   44. Flat Rate

GENERAL NOTE

2.973   See the note to s.43 of the Child Support Act 1991.

Flat rate

2.974   **44.**—(1) The following benefits, pensions or allowances are prescribed for the purposes of paragraph 4(1)(b) of Schedule 1 to the 1991 Act (that is the benefits, pensions or allowances that qualify the non-resident parent for the flat rate)—

(a) under the Social Security Contributions and Benefits Act 1992—
   (i) [⁴ . . .],
   (ii) category A retirement pension under section 44,
   (iii) category B retirement pension under section 48C,
   (iv) category C and category D retirement pension under section 78,
   (v) incapacity benefit under section 30A,
   (vi) carer's allowance under section 70,
   (vii) maternity allowance under section 35 [² or 35B],
   (viii) severe disablement allowance under section 68,
   (ix) industrial injuries benefit under section 94,
   (x) widowed mother's allowance under section 37,
   (xi) widowed parent's allowance under section 39A, and
   (xii) widow's pension under section 38;
(b) contribution-based jobseeker's allowance under the Jobseekers Act 1995;
(c) a social security benefit paid by a country other than the United Kingdom;
(d) a training allowance (other than work-based training for young people or, in Scotland, Skillseekers training);
(e) a war disablement pension within the meaning of section 150(2) of the Social Security Contributions and Benefits Act 1992 or a pension which is analogous to such a pension paid by the government of a country outside Great Britain;
(f) a war widow's pension, war widower's pension or surviving civil partner's war pension within the meaning of that section;
(g) a payment under a scheme mentioned in section 1(2) of the Armed Forces (Pensions and Compensation) Act 2004 (compensation schemes for armed and reserve forces); [³ . . .]
(h) contributory employment and support allowance [; and
(i) a state pension under Part 1 of the Pensions Act 2014.]

(2) The following benefits are prescribed for the purposes of paragraph 4(1)(c) of Schedule 1 to the 1991 Act (that is the benefits that qualify the non-resident parent for the flat rate if received by the non-resident parent or their partner)—

(a) income support;
(b) income-based jobseeker's allowance;
(c) income-related employment and support allowance; [¹ . . .]
(d) state pension credit [¹ and
(e) universal credit under Part 1 of the Welfare Reform Act 2012, where the award of universal credit is calculated on the basis that the non-resident parent does not have any earned income].

(3) Where the conditions referred to in paragraph 4(2) of Schedule 1 to the 1991 Act are satisfied (that is where an income-related benefit is payable to the non-resident parent or their partner and a maintenance calculation is in force in respect of each of them) the flat rate of maintenance payable is half the flat rate that would otherwise apply.

(4) In paragraph (1)(d) "training allowance" means a payment under section 2 of the Employment and Training Act 1973 or section 2 of the Enterprise and New Towns (Scotland) Act 1990 which is paid to a person for their maintenance while they are undergoing training.

[¹ (5) For the purposes of paragraph (2)(e) and regulation 45(1)(c), "earned income" has the meaning given in regulation 52 of the Universal Credit Regulations 2013.]

AMENDMENTS

1. Universal Credit (Consequential, Supplementary, Incidental and Miscellaneous Provisions) Regulations 2013 (SI 2013/630) reg. 44(3) (April 29, 2013).
2. Social Security (Maternity Allowance) (Miscellaneous Amendments) Regulations 2014 (SI 2014/884) reg.3(3) (May 18, 2014).
3. Pensions Act 2014 (Consequential, Supplementary and Incidental Amendments) Order 2015 (SI 2015/1985) art.38 (April 6, 2016).
4. Pensions Act 2014 (Consequential, Supplementary and Incidental Amendments) Order 2017 (SI 2017/422) art.40 (April 6, 2017).

The Victims' Payments Regulations 2020

SI 2020/103

2.975   *The Secretary of State, Northern Ireland Office, makes these Regulations in exercise of the powers conferred by sections 10 and 11 of the Northern Ireland (Executive Formation etc) Act 2019.*

The Secretary of State has had regard to advice given by the Commission for Victims and Survivors for Northern Ireland in accordance with section 10(10) of that Act.

PART 1

PRELIMINARY

Citation and commencement and extent

2.976   **1.**—(1) These Regulations may be cited as the Victims' Payments Regulations 2020.

(2) The following provisions come into force on the 24th February 2020—

(a) regulation 1;
(b) regulation 3;
(c) Schedule 1;
(d) paragraph 4(1) of Schedule 2, and regulation 15(8) so far as it relates to that   paragraph;
(e) paragraphs 1, 4 and 5 of Schedule 3, and regulation 53 so far as it relates to that paragraph.

(3) The remaining provisions of these Regulations come into force on 29th May 2020.

(4) Except as provided by paragraphs (5) to (7), these Regulations extend to Northern Ireland only.

(5) Regulations 1, 2, 26, 28, 29 and 31 extend to England and Wales, Scotland and Northern Ireland.

(6) The amendments made by paragraph 2 of Schedule 3 extend to England and Wales only.

(7) Any other amendment made by these Regulations has the same extent as the provision it amends.

Disregard of payments and lump sums for certain purposes

26.—(1) A payment of victims' payments or a lump sum is to be disre-garded—

    2.977

(a) from the calculation of a person's income or capital when determin-ing entitlement to a relevant social security benefit;

(b) for the purposes of an assessment of a person's ability to pay under regulations made under Article 36(6) or 99(5) (cost of providing res-idential accommodation) of the Health and Personal Social Services (Northern Ireland) Order 1972;

(c) for the purposes of determining whether a person should repay (either fully or in part) an award of criminal injuries compensation where the application for that award was determined before these Regulations come into force.

(2) In paragraph (1)—

"criminal injuries compensation" means compensation under a scheme established under the Criminal Injuries Compensation Act 1995 or the Criminal Injuries Compensation (Northern Ireland) Order 2002;

"relevant social security benefit" means any of the following—

(a) employment and support allowance under—

    (i) Part 1 of the Welfare Reform Act 2007 as it has effect apart from the amendments made by Schedule 3, and Part 1 of Schedule 14, to the Welfare Reform Act 2012 (to remove refer-ences to an income-related allowance);

    (ii) Part 1 of the Welfare Reform Act (Northern Ireland) 2007 as it has effect apart from the amendments made by Schedule 3, and Part 5 of Schedule 12, to the Welfare Reform Order (Northern Ireland) 2015 (to remove references to an income related allow-ance);

(b) housing benefit under—

    (i) Part 7 of the Social Security Contributions and Benefits Act 1992, or

    (ii) Part 7 of the Social Security Contributions and Benefits (Northern Ireland) Act 1992;

(c) income support under—

    (i) Part 7 of the Social Security Contributions and Benefits Act 1992, or

    (ii) Part 7 of the Social Security Contributions and Benefits (Northern Ireland) Act 1992;

(d) jobseeker's allowance under—

    (i) the Jobseekers Act 1995 as it has effect apart from the amend-ments made by Part 1 of Schedule 14 to the Welfare Reform Act 2012 (to remove references to an income-based allowance);

    (ii) the Jobseekers (Northern Ireland) Order 1995 as it has effect apart from the amendments made by Part 1 of Schedule 12 to the Welfare Reform Order (Northern Ireland) 2015 (to remove references to an income-based allowance);

(e) state pension credit under—

    (i) section 1 of the State Pension Credit Act 2002, or

(ii)   section 1 of the State Pension Credit Act (Northern Ireland) 2002;
(f)   universal credit under—
(i)   Part 1 of the Welfare Reform Act 2012, or
(ii)   Part 2 of the Welfare Reform (Northern Ireland) Order 2015.

GENERAL NOTE

2.978   The relevant provisions for income support purposes are reg.26(1)(a) and para. (c) of the definition of "relevant social security benefit in reg.26(2). Under the Regulations payments are to be made to those injured in a "Troubles-related incident", which is defined in s.10(11) of the Northern Ireland (Executive Formation etc) Act 2019 as "an incident involving an act of violence or force carried out in Ireland, the United Kingdom or anywhere in Europe for a reason related to the constitutional status of Northern Ireland or to political or sectarian hostility between people there". The disregard as capital would apply whether the original payment constituted a capital receipt or whether payments of income have metamorphosed into capital by not being spent.

The relevant provisions for IRESA and IBJSA purposes are reg.26(1)(a) and paras (a) and (d) respectively of the definition of "relevant social security benefit".

PART III

OLD STYLE JOBSEEKER'S ALLOWANCE

The Jobseeker's Allowance Regulations 1996

(SI 1996/207) (AS AMENDED)

Made by the Secretary of State for Education and Employment and the Secretary of State for Social Security under various powers in the Jobseekers Act 1995, the Social Security Administration Act 1992 and the Social Security Contributions and Benefits Act 1992

ARRANGEMENT OF REGULATIONS

PART I

GENERAL

PART IA

JOINT-CLAIM COUPLES

PART II

JOBSEEKING

Chapter I

Interpretation

Chapter II

Availability for employment

Chapter III

Actively seeking employment

Chapter IV

Attendance, information and evidence

PART VIII

INCOME AND CAPITAL

Chapter I

General

Chapter II

Income

Chapter III

Employed earners

Chapter IV

Self-employed earners

Chapter VIII

Child support

Chapter IX

Students

PART IX

HARDSHIP

PART IXA

HARDSHIP FOR JOINT-CLAIM COUPLES

PART X

URGENT CASES

PART XI

PART-WEEKS

PART XII

SPECIAL CATEGORIES

Omitted

PART XIII

MISCELLANEOUS

Recovery of maintenance

Training allowance

Trade disputes

SCHEDULES

A1. Categories of members of a joint-claim couple who are not required to satisfy the conditions in s.1(2B)(b)
1. Applicable amounts
2. Housing costs
3. *Revoked*
4. *Revoked*
4A. *Revoked*
5. Applicable amounts in special cases
5A. Applicable amounts of joint-claim couples in special cases
6. Sums to be disregarded in the calculation of earnings
6A. Sums to be disregarded in the calculation of earnings of members of joint-claim couples
7. Sums to be disregarded in the calculation of income other than earnings
8. Capital to be disregarded

GENERAL NOTE

The regulations set out here are those that still apply after April 2021 to income-based JSA (IBJSA), in cases where a claimant has a continuing award of that benefit, originally made at a date when for that claimant it was not possible to make a claim for universal credit. See the introductory notes to the old style Jobseekers Act 1995. It is not now for nearly all practical purposes possible to make a new claim for JSA that is for anything other than new style JSA, which is subject to contribution conditions (see Vol.I of this series). For someone who needs to make a new claim for an income-related benefit the only option now is universal credit.

3.2

PART I

GENERAL

[⁸¹ Citation, commencement, interpretation and application]

1.—(1) These Regulations may be cited as the Jobseeker's Allowance Regulations 1996.
(2) These Regulations shall come into force on 7th October 1996.
[⁸¹ (2A) These Regulations do not apply to a particular case on any day on which section 33(1)(a) of the 2012 Act (abolition of income-based job-seeker's allowance) is in force and applies in relation to that case.]
(3) In these Regulations—
[⁷⁹ "the 2012 Act" means the Welfare Reform Act 2012;]
[⁴⁰ "Abbeyfield Home" means an establishment run by the Abbeyfield Society including all bodies corporate or incorporate which are affiliated to that Society;]
"the Act" means the Jobseekers Act 1995;
[³¹ "adoption leave" means a period of absence from work on ordinary or additional adoption leave by virtue of section 75A or 75B of the Employment Rights Act 1996;]
[⁹⁹ "approved blood scheme" means a scheme established or approved by the Secretary of State, or trust established with funds provided by the Secretary of State, for the purpose of providing compensation in respect of a person having been infected from contaminated blood products;]

3.3

[⁸⁰ "armed forces independence payment" means armed forces independence payment under the Armed Forces and Reserve Forces (Compensation Scheme) Order 2011;]

"attendance allowance" means—

(a) an attendance allowance under section 64 of the Benefits Act;

(b) an increase of disablement pension under section 104 or 105 of the Benefits Act (increases where constant attendance needed and for exceptionally severe disablement);

(c) a payment under regulations made in accordance with section 111 of, and paragraph 7(2) of Schedule 8 to, the Benefits Act (payments for constant attendance in workmen's compensation cases);

(d) an increase in allowance which is payable in respect of constant attendance under section 111 of, and paragraph 4 of Schedule 8 to, the Benefits Act (industrial diseases benefit schemes);

(e) a payment by virtue of article 14, 15, 16, 43 or 44 of the Personal Injuries (Civilians) Scheme 1983 or any analogous payment;

(f) any payment based on the need for attendance which is paid as an addition to a war disablement pension;

[⁵⁶ "Back to Work Session" means a seminar or appointment referred to as "a Back to Work Session" arranged by or on behalf of the Secretary of State, the purpose of which is to provide a person who attends with information, support and advice with a view to assisting him to find employment or to improve his chances of finding employment;]

[⁵⁷ "basic rate", where it relates to the rate of tax, has the same meaning as in the Income Tax Act 2007 (see section 989 of that Act).]

[⁵⁵ "the Benefit Acts" means the Act, the Benefits Act [⁷⁹ , Part 1 of the Welfare Reform Act 2007 [⁹³, Part 4 of the 2012 Act and the Pensions Act 2014]];]

[⁵⁹ "benefit week" means—

(a) a period of 7 days ending with a day determined in accordance with paragraph (b) unless, in any particular case or class of case, the Secretary of State arranges otherwise;

(b) the day specified for the purposes of paragraph (a) is the day in column (2) which corresponds to the series of numbers in column (1) which includes the last 2 digits of the person's national insurance number—

(1)	*(2)*
00 to 19	Monday
20 to 39	Tuesday
40 to 59	Wednesday
60 to 79	Thursday
80 to 99	Friday;]

"board and lodging accommodation" means—

(a) accommodation provided to a person or, if he is a member of a family, to him or any other member of his family, for a charge which is inclusive of the provision of that accommodation and at least some cooked or prepared meals which both are cooked or prepared (by a person other than the person to whom the accommodation is provided or a member of his family) and are consumed in that accommodation or associated premises; or

(b) accommodation provided to a person in a hotel, guest house, lodging house or some similar establishment,

except accommodation provided by a close relative of his or of any other member of his family, or other than on a commercial basis;

[40"care home" in England [101 ...] has the meaning assigned to it by section 3 of the Care Standards Act 2000, [101 in Wales means a care home service within the meaning of Part 1 of the Regulation and Inspection of Social Care (Wales) Act 2016 which is provided wholly or mainly to persons aged 18 or over] and in Scotland means a care home service within the meaning assigned to it by [20 paragraph 2 of schedule 12 to the Public Services Reform (Scotland) Act 2010];]

[71 "the Caxton Foundation" means the charitable trust of that name established on 28th March 2011 out of funds provided by the Secretary of State for the benefit of certain persons suffering from hepatitis C and other persons eligible for payment in accordance with its provisions;]

[32 "child tax credit" means a child tax credit under section 8 of the Tax Credits Act 2002;]

[7"the Children Order" means the Children (Northern Ireland) Order 1995;]

"Claims and Payments Regulations" means the Social Security (Claims and Payments) Regulations 1987;

"close relative" means, except in Parts II [4 . . .] and V, a parent, parent-in-law, son, son-in-law, daughter, daughter-in-law, step parent, step-son, step-daughter, brother, sister, [41or, if any of the preceding persons is one member of a couple, the other member of that couple];

"college of further education" means a college of further education within the meaning of Part I of the Further and Higher Education (Scotland) Act 1992;

"concessionary payment" means a payment made under arrangements made by the Secretary of State with the consent of the Treasury which is charged either to the National Insurance Fund or to a Departmental Expenditure Vote to which payments of benefit [55 or tax credits under the benefit Acts or the Tax Credits Act 2002] are charged;

[75 "the Contributions Regulations" means the Social Security (Contributions) Regulations 2001;]

[81 "contributory employment and support allowance" means an allowance under Part 1 of the Welfare Reform Act as amended by the provisions of Schedule 3, and Part 1 of Schedule 14, to the 2012 Act that remove references to an income-related allowance, and a contributory allowance under Part 1 of the Welfare Reform Act as that Part has effect apart from those provisions;]

"co-ownership scheme" means a scheme under which a dwelling is let by a housing association and the tenant, or his personal representative, will, under the terms of the tenancy agreement or of the agreement under which he became a member of the association, be entitled, on his ceasing to be a member and subject of any condition stated in either agreement, to a sum calculated by reference directly or indirectly to the value of the dwelling;

[⁴¹ [⁸³ ⁸⁵ "couple" means—

(a) two people who are married to, or civil partners of, each other and are members of the same household; or

(b) two people who are not married to, or civil partners of, each other but are living together [¹⁰² as if they were a married couple or civil partners];]]

"course of advanced education" means—

  (a) a course leading to a postgraduate degree or comparable qualification, a first degree or comparable qualification, a diploma of higher education or a higher national diploma; or

  (b) any other course which is of a standard above advanced GNVQ or equivalent, including a course which is of a standard above a general certificate of education (advanced level), [³⁶ a Scottish national qualification (higher or advanced higher)]

[¹⁶ "course of study" means any course of study, whether or not it is a sandwich course and whether or not a grant is made for attending or undertaking it;]

[⁸⁹ "Crown servant" means a person holding an office or employment under the Crown;]

"Crown tenant" means a person who occupies a dwelling under a tenancy or licence where the interest of the landlord belongs to Her Majesty in right of the Crown or to a government department or is held in trust for Her Majesty for the purposes of a government department, except (in the case of an interest belonging to Her Majesty in right of the Crown) where the interest is under the management of the Crown Estate Commissioners [⁹⁷ or a relevant person];

"date of claim" means the date on which the claimant makes, or is treated as making, a claim for a jobseeker's allowance for the purposes of regulation 6 of the Claims and Payments Regulations;

"disability living allowance" means a disability living allowance under section 71 of the Benefits Act;

[³² . . .]

"dwelling occupied as the home" means the dwelling together with any garage, garden and outbuildings, normally occupied by the claimant as his home including any premises not so occupied which it is impracticable or unreasonable to sell separately, in particular, in Scotland, any croft land on which the dwelling is situated;

"earnings" has the meaning specified, in the case of an employed earner, in regulation 98, or in the case of a self-employed earner, in regulation 100;

[³⁹ . . .]

"the Eileen Trust" means the charitable trust of that name established on 29th March 1993 out of funds provided by the Secretary of State for the benefit of persons eligible for payment in accordance with its provisions;

[⁵³ "the Employment and Support Allowance Regulations" means the Employment and Support Allowance Regulations 2008;]

"employment-related course" means a course the purpose of which is to assist persons to acquire or enhance skills required for employment, for seeking employment or for a particular occupation;

[⁶⁹ "the Employment, Skills and Enterprise Scheme" means a scheme under section 17A (schemes for assisting persons to obtain employment:

"work for your benefit" schemes etc.) of the Jobseekers Act 1995 known by that name and provided pursuant to arrangements made by the Secretary of State that is designed to assist claimants to obtain employment, including self-employment, and which may include for any individual work-related activity (including work experience or job search);]

[[12] "employment zone" means an area within Great Britain designated for the purposes of section 60 of the Welfare Reform and Pensions Act 1999 and an "employment zone programme" means a programme established for such an area or areas designed to assist claimants for a jobseeker's allowance to obtain sustainable employment;

"employment zone contractor" means a person who is undertaking the provision of facilities in respect of an employment zone programme on behalf of the Secretary of State [[52] . . .];]

[[61] "enactment" includes an enactment comprised in, or in an instrument made under, an Act of the Scottish Parliament [[82] or the National Assembly for Wales];]

[[35] . . .]

[[24] . . .]

[[91] "first year of training" means a period of one year beginning with a person's first day of training.]

[[60] "the Flexible New Deal" means the employment programme specified in regulation 75(1)(a)(v);]

"full-time course of advanced education" means a course of advanced education which is [[16]. . .]—

(a) [[16] . . .] a full-time course of study which is not funded in whole or in part by [[24] the [[65] [[74] Secretary of State under section 14 of the Education Act 2002] [[92] or under section 100 of the Apprenticeships, Skills, Children and Learning Act 2009]] or by the [[45] [55] Welsh Ministers]] or a full-time course of study [[1] . . .] which is not funded in whole or in part by the Secretary of State for Scotland at a college of further education [[1] or a full-time course of study which is a course of higher education and is funded in whole or in part by the Secretary of State for Scotland;]

[[24](b) a course of study which is funded in whole or in part by the [[65] [[74] Secretary of State under section 14 of the Education Act 2002] [[92] or under section 100 of the Apprenticeships, Skills, Children and Learning Act 2009]] or by the [[45] [55] Welsh Ministers] if it involves more than 16 guided hours per week for the student in question, according to the number of guided learning hours per week for that student set out—

    [[65] (i) in the case of a course funded by the [[74] Secretary of State [[92] . . .]] [[92] . . .], in the student's learning agreement signed on behalf of the establishment which is funded by [[92] the Secretary of State] for the delivery of that course; or]

    (ii) in the case of a course funded by the [[45] [55] Welsh Ministers], in a document signed on behalf of the establishment which is funded by the National Council for Education and Training for Wales for the delivery of that course; or,]

(c) [[16] . . .] a course of study (not being higher education) which is funded in whole or in part by the Secretary of State for Scotland at a college of further education if it involves—

    (i) more than 16 hours per week of classroom-based or

workshop-based programmed learning under the direct guidance of teaching staff according to the number of hours set out in a document signed on behalf of the college; or

(ii) 16 hours or less per week of classroom-based or workshop-based programmed learning under the direct guidance of teaching staff and it involves additional hours using structured learning packages supported by the teaching staff where the combined total of hours exceeds 21 per week, according to the number of hours set out in a document signed on behalf of the college;

"full-time student" means a person, other than a person in receipt of a training allowance [⁴⁴ or a person who is a qualifying young person or child within the meaning of section 142 of the Benefits Act (child and qualifying young person)], who is—

(a) aged less than 19 and [⁶³ attending or undertaking] a full-time course of advanced education or

(b) aged 19 or over but under pensionable age and—

(i) attending [⁶³ or undertaking] a full-time course of study which is not funded in whole or in part by [²⁴ the [⁶⁵ [⁷⁴ Secretary of State under section 14 of the Education Act 2002] [⁹² or under section 100 of the Apprenticeships, Skills, Children and Learning Act 2009]] or by the [⁴⁵ ⁵⁵ Welsh Ministers]] or a full-time course of study [¹ . . .] which is not funded in whole or in part by the Secretary of State for Scotland at a college of further education [¹ or a full-time course of study which is a course of higher education and is funded in whole or in part by the Secretary of State for Scotland;]

[²⁴(ii) [⁶³ attending or undertaking] a course of study which is funded in whole or in part by the [⁶⁵ [⁷⁴ Secretary of State under section 14 of the Education Act 2002] [⁹² or under section 100 of the Apprenticeships, Skills, Children and Learning Act 2009]] or by the [⁴⁵ ⁵⁵ Welsh Ministers] if it involves more than 16 guided hours per week for the student in question, according to the number of guided learning hours per week for that student set out—

[⁶⁵ (aa) in the case of a course funded by the [⁷⁴ Secretary of State [⁹² . . .]] [⁹² . . .], in the student's learning agreement signed on behalf of the establishment which is funded by [⁹² the Secretary of State] for the delivery of that course; or,]

(bb) in the case of a course funded by the National Council for Education and Training for Wales, in a document signed on behalf of the establishment which is funded by the [⁴⁵ ⁵⁵ Welsh Ministers] for the delivery of that course; or]

(iii) [⁶³ attending or undertaking] a course of study (not being higher education) which is funded in whole or in part by the Secretary of State for Scotland at a college of further education if it involves—

(aa) more than 16 hours per week of classroom-based or workshop-based programmed learning under the direct guidance of teaching staff according to the number of hours set out in a document signed on behalf of the college; or

(bb) 16 hours or less per week of classroom or workshop based programmed learning under the direct guidance of teaching staff and it involves additional hours using structured learning packages supported by the teaching staff where the combined total of hours exceeds 21 per week, according to the number of hours set out in a document signed on behalf of the college;

"the Fund" means moneys made available from time to time by the Secretary of State for the benefit of persons eligible for payment in accordance with the provisions of a scheme established by him on 24th April 1992 or, in Scotland, on 10th April 1992;

[104 "Grenfell Tower payment" means a payment made to a person because that person was affected by the fire on 14th June 2017 at Grenfell Tower, or a payment to the personal representative of such a person—

(a) from the £5 million fund announced on 16th June 2017 for the benefit of certain persons affected by the fire on 14th June 2017 at Grenfell Tower and known as the Grenfell Tower Residents' Discretionary Fund;

(b) by the Royal Borough of Kensington and Chelsea; or

(c) by a registered charity;]

[38 "a guaranteed income payment" means a payment made under article 14(1)(b) or article 21(1)(a) of the Armed Forces and Reserve Forces (Compensation Scheme) Order 2005;]

[89 "Her Majesty's forces" has the meaning in the Armed Forces Act 2006;]

[54 "Health Service Act" means the National Health Service Act 2006; "Health Service (Wales) Act" means the National Health Service (Wales) Act 2006;]

"higher education" means higher education within the meaning of Part II of the Further and Higher Education (Scotland) Act 1992;

"housing association" has the meaning assigned to it by section 1(1) of the Housing Associations Act 1985;

[5"housing benefit expenditure" means expenditure in respect of which housing benefit is payable as specified in [43 regulation 12(1) of the Housing Benefit Regulations 2006] but does not include any such expenditure in respect of which an amount is applicable under regulation 83(f) or 84(1)(g) (housing costs);]

[14 "Immigration and Asylum Act" means the Immigration and Asylum Act 1999;]

"Income Support Regulations" means the Income Support (General) Regulations 1987;

[40 [66 "independent hospital"—

(a) in England, means a hospital as defined by section 275 of the National Health Service Act 2006 that is not a health service hospital as defined by that section;

(b) in Wales, has the meaning assigned to it by section 2 of the Care Standards Act 2000; and

[72 (c) in Scotland, means an independent health care service as defined in section 10F(1)(a) and (b) of the National Health Service (Scotland) Act 1978;]

[54 . . .]
[49 "the Independent Living Fund (2006)" means the Trust of that name
    established by a deed dated 10th April 2006 and made between the
    Secretary of State for Work and Pensions of the one part and Margaret
    Rosemary Cooper, Michael Beresford Boyall and Marie Theresa
    Martin of the other part;]
[54 . . .]
[23 52 . . .]
"invalid carriage or other vehicle" means a vehicle propelled by a petrol
    engine or by electric power supplied for use on the road and to be
    controlled by the occupant;
"jobseeking period" means the period described in regulation 47 [8except
    where otherwise provided];
"last day of the course" has the meaning prescribed in regulation 130 for
    the purposes of the definition of "period of study" in this paragraph;
"liable relative" has the meaning prescribed in regulation 117;
[78 "local welfare provision" means occasional financial or other assist-
    ance given by a local authority, the Scottish Ministers or the Welsh
    Ministers, or a person authorised to exercise any function of, or
    provide a service to, them, to or in respect of individuals for the
    purpose of—
(a) meeting, or helping to meet, an immediate short term need—
        (i) arising out of an exceptional event, or exceptional circum-
             stances; and
        (ii) that requires to be met in order to avoid a risk to the well-being
             of an individual; or
(b) enabling individuals to establish or maintain a settled home, where
     those individuals have been or, without the assistance, might other-
     wise be—
        (i) in prison, hospital, a residential care establishment or other
             institution; or
        (ii) homeless or otherwise living an unsettled way of life;]
[42"the London Bombings Relief Charitable Fund" means the company
    limited by guarantee (number 5505072) and registered charity of
    that name established on 11th July 2005 for the purpose of (amongst
    other things) relieving sickness, disability or financial need of victims
    (including families or dependants of victims) of the terrorist attacks
    carried out in London on 7th July 2005;]
[98 "the London Emergencies Trust" means the company of that name
    (number 09928465) incorporated on 23rd December 2015 and the
    registered charity of that name (number 1172307) established on 28th
    March 2017;]
"lone parent" means a person who has no partner and who is responsible
    for, and a member of the same household as, a child or young person;
"long tenancy" means a tenancy granted for a term of years certain
    exceeding twenty one years, whether or not the tenancy is, or may
    become, terminable before the end of that term by notice given by or
    to the tenant or by re-entry, forfeiture (or, in Scotland, irritancy) or
    otherwise and includes a lease for a term fixed by law under a grant
    with a covenant or obligation for perpetual renewal unless it is a lease
    by subdemise from one which is not a long tenancy;
[47 "long-term patient" means a person who—

(a) is a patient within the meaning of regulation 85(4); and

(b) has been such a patient for a continuous period of more than 52 weeks;]
[51 . . .]

"the Macfarlane (Special Payments) Trust" means the trust of that name, established on 29th January 1990 partly out of funds provided by the Secretary of State for the benefit of certain persons suffering from haemophilia;

"the Macfarlane (Special Payments) (No.2) Trust" means the trust of that name, established on 2nd May 1991 partly out of funds provided by the Secretary of State, for the benefit of certain persons suffering from haemophilia and other beneficiaries;

"the Macfarlane Trust" means the charitable trust, established partly out of funds provided by the Secretary of State to the Haemophilia Society, for the relief of poverty or distress among those suffering from haemophilia;

"making a claim" includes treated as making a claim;

[68 "the Mandatory Work Activity Scheme" means a scheme within section 17A (schemes for assisting persons to obtain employment: "work for your benefit" schemes etc.) of the Jobseekers Act 1995 known by that name and provided pursuant to arrangements made by the Secretary of State that is designed to provide work or work-related activity for up to 30 hours per week over a period of four consecutive weeks with a view to assisting claimants to improve their prospects of obtaining employment;]

"maternity leave" means a period during which a woman is absent from work because she is pregnant or has given birth to a child, and at the end of which she has a right to return to work either under the terms of her contract of employment or under [50 Part VIII of the Employment Rights Act 1996];

[95 "member of the work-related activity group" means a claimant who has or is treated as having limited capability for work under either—

(a) Part 5 of the Employment and Support Allowance Regulations 2008 other than by virtue of regulation 30 of those Regulations; or

(b) Part 4 of the Employment and Support Allowance Regulations 2013 other than by virtue of regulation 26 of those Regulations;]

[63 MFET Limited" means the company limited by guarantee (number 7121661) of that name, established for the purpose in particular of making payments in accordance with arrangements made with the Secretary of State to persons who have acquired HIV as a result of treatment by the NHS with blood or blood products;]

"mobility supplement" means any supplement under [55 article 20 of the Naval, Military and Air Forces Etc. (Disablement and Death) Service Pensions Order 2006] including such a supplement by virtue of any other scheme or order or under article 25A of the Personal Injuries (Civilians) Scheme 1983;

[104 "the National Emergencies Trust" means the registered charity of that name (number 1182809) established on 28th March 2019;]

"net earnings" means such earnings as are calculated in accordance with regulation 99;

"net profit" means such profit as is calculated in accordance with regulation 101;

[15 "the New Deal options" means the employment programmes specified in regulation 75(1)(a)(ii) and the training scheme specified in regulation 75(1)(b)(ii);]

"non-dependant" has the meaning prescribed in regulation 2;

"non-dependant deduction" means a deduction that is to be made under regulation 83(f) and paragraph 17 of Schedule 2;

[⁴⁰ . . .]

"occupational pension" means any pension or other periodical payment under an occupational pension scheme but does not include any discretionary payment out of a fund established for relieving hardship in particular cases;

[¹⁰³ "parental bereavement leave" means leave under section 80EA of the Employment Rights Act 1996;]

"partner" means where a claimant—

    (a) is a member of [⁴¹ a couple], the other member of that couple;

    (b) is married polygamously to two or more members of his household, any such member;

[¹⁹but in so far as this definition applies to a member of a joint-claim couple, it shall only apply to such a member specified in regulation 3E(2)].

"part-time student" means a person who is attending or undertaking a course of study and who is not a full-time student;

[³¹ ⁷³ "paternity leave" means a period of absence from work on [⁸⁷ . . .] paternity leave by virtue of section 80A or 80B of the Employment Rights Act 1996 [⁸⁷ . . .];]

"payment" includes a part of a payment;

"pay period" means the period in respect of which a claimant is, or expects to be, normally paid by his employer, being a week, a fortnight, four weeks, a month or other longer or shorter period as the case may be;

"period of study" except in Parts II, IV and V means—

(a) in the case of a course of study for one year or less, the period beginning with the start of the course and ending with the last day of the course;

(b) in the case of a course of study for more than one year, in the first or, as the case may be, any subsequent year of the course, other than the final year of the course, the period beginning with the start of the course or, as the case may be, that year's start and ending with either —

    [¹⁷(i) the day before the start of the next year of the course in a case where the student's grant or loan is assessed at a rate appropriate to his studying throughout the year, or, if he does not have a grant or loan, where a loan would have been assessed at such a rate had he had one; or]

    (ii) in any other case the day before the start of the normal summer vacation appropriate to his course;

    (c) in the final year of a course of study of more than one year, the period beginning with that year's start and ending with the last day of the course;

[⁷⁹ "personal independence payment" means personal independence payment under Part 4 of the 2012 Act;]

"policy of life insurance" means any instrument by which the payment of money is assured on death (except death by accident only) or the happening of any contingency dependent on human life, or any instrument evidencing a contract which is subject to payment of premiums for a term dependent on human life;

"polygamous marriage" means any marriage during the subsistence of which a party to it is married to more than one person and the ceremony of marriage took place under the law of a country which permits polygamy;

[[25] . . .]

[[62] "qualifying age for state pension credit" means—

(a) in the case of a woman, pensionable age; or

(b) in the case of a man, the age which is pensionable age in the case of a woman born on the same day as the man;]

[[61] "public authority" includes any person certain of whose functions are functions of a public nature;]

"qualifying person" means a person in respect of whom [[104] a Grenfell Tower payment has been made or] payment has been made from the Fund [[37], the Eileen Trust [[63], MFET Limited] [[42], the Skipton Fund [[71], the Caxton Foundation] [[96], the Scottish Infected Blood Support Scheme] [[99], an approved blood scheme] [[98], the London Emergencies Trust, the We Love Manchester Emergency Fund][[104], the National Emergencies Trust] or the London Bombings Relief Charitable Fund]];

"relative" means close relative, grand-parent, grand-child, uncle, aunt, nephew or niece;

"relevant enactment" has the meaning prescribed in [[2] regulation 78(9) (a)];

[[97] "relevant person", in relation to any property, rights or interests to which section 90B(5) of the Scotland Act 1998 applies, means the person who manages that property or those rights or interests;]

"remunerative work" has the meaning prescribed in regulation 51(1);

[[40] . . .]

[[33] . . .]

[[40] . . .]

[[17 54] "sandwich course" has the meaning prescribed in regulation 2(9) of the Education (Student Support) Regulations 2008, regulation 4(2) of the Education (Student Loans) (Scotland) Regulations 2007, regulation 2(8) of the Education (Student Support) Regulations (Northern Ireland) 2007;]

[[94] "Scottish basic rate" means the rate of income tax of that name calculated in accordance with section 6A of the Income Tax Act 2007;

[[96] "Scottish Infected Blood Support Scheme" means the scheme of that name administered by the Common Services Agency (constituted by section 10 of the National Health Service (Scotland) Act 1978);]

"Scottish taxpayer" has the same meaning as in Chapter 2 of Part 4A of the Scotland Act 1998;]

"self-employed earner" has the meaning it has in Part I of the Benefits Act by virtue of section 2(1)(b) of that Act;

[[18 30 36] "self-employment route" means assistance in pursuing self-employed earner's employment whilst participating in—

(a) an employment zone programme; [[69] . . .]

(b) a programme provided or other arrangements made pursuant to section 2 of the Employment and Training Act 1973 (functions of the Secretary of State) or section 2 of the Enterprise and New

Towns (Scotland) Act 1990 (functions in relation to training for employment etc.)] [[69 76] ; or
   (c) a scheme prescribed in regulation 3 of the Jobseeker's Allowance (Schemes for Assisting Persons to Obtain Employment) Regulations 2013;]
[[61] [[84] . . .]
[[86] "shared parental leave" means leave under section 75E to 75G of the Employment Rights Act 1996;]
"single claimant" means a claimant who neither has a partner nor is a lone parent;
[[37] "the Skipton Fund" means the ex-gratia payment scheme administered by the Skipton Fund Limited, incorporated on 25th March 2004, for the benefit of certain persons suffering from hepatitis C and other persons eligible for payment in accordance with the scheme's provisions;]
[[11] "sports award" means an award made by one of the Sports Councils named in section 23(2) of the National Lottery etc. Act 1993 out of sums allocated to it for distribution under that section;]
[[50 57] . . .]
[[13] "subsistence allowance" means an allowance which an employment zone contractor has agreed to pay to a person who is participating in an employment zone programme;]
"terminal date" in respect of a claimant means the terminal date in his case for the purposes of regulation 7 of the Child Benefit (General) Regulations 1976;
"training allowance" means an allowance (whether by way of periodical grants or otherwise) payable—
   (a) out of public funds by a Government department or by or on behalf of the Secretary of State [[52] . . .], [[58] Skills Development Scotland,] Scottish Enterprise or Highlands and Islands Enterprise [[21] , [[74] . . . [[65] . . .] [[92] . . .] or the [[55] Welsh Ministers]]; and
   (b) to a person for his maintenance or in respect of a member of his family; and
   (c) for the period, or part of the period, during which he is following a course of training or instruction provided by, or in pursuance of arrangements made with, that department or approved by that department in relation to him or so provided or approved by or on behalf of the Secretary of State [[52] . . .], [[58] Skills Development Scotland,] Scottish Enterprise or Highlands and Islands Enterprise [[22] or the [[55] Welsh Ministers]],
but it does not include an allowance paid by any Government department to or in respect of a person by reason of the fact that he is following a course of full-time education, other than under arrangements made under section 2 of the Employment and Training Act 1973 [[3] or section 2 of the Enterprise and New Towns (Scotland) Act 1990,] or is training as a teacher;
[[90] "traineeship" means a course which—
(a) is funded (in whole or in part) by, or under arrangements made by, the—
   (i) Secretary of State under section 14 of the Education Act 2002, or
   (ii) Chief Executive of [[100] Education and Skills Funding]
(b) lasts no more than 6 months;

(c) includes training to help prepare the participant for work and a work experience placement; and

(d) is open to persons who on the first day of the course have attained the age of 16 but not 25;]

[[81] "universal credit" means universal credit under Part 1 of the 2012 Act;]

[[79] "the Universal Credit etc. Claims and Payments Regulations" means the Universal Credit, Personal Independence Payment, Jobseeker's Allowance and Employment and Support Allowance (Claims and Payments) Regulations 2013;]

"voluntary organisation" means a body, other than a public or local authority, the activities of which are carried on otherwise than for profit;

[[55] "war disablement pension" means any retired pay or pension or allowance payable in respect of disablement under an instrument specified in section 639(2) of the Income Tax (Earnings and Pensions) Act 2003;

"war pension" means a war disablement pension, a war widow's pension or a war widower's pension;

"war widow's pension" means any pension or allowance payable to a woman as a widow under an instrument specified in section 639(2) of the Income Tax (Earnings and Pensions) Act 2003 in respect of the death or disablement of any person;

"war widower's pension" means any pension or allowance payable to a man as a widower or to a surviving civil partner under an instrument specified in section 639(2) of the Income Tax (Earnings and Pensions) Act 2003 in respect of the death or disablement of any person;]

"water charges" means—

(a) as respects England and Wales, any water and sewerage charges under Chapter 1 of Part V of the Water Industry Act 1991;

(b) as respects Scotland, any water and sewerage charges under Schedule 11 to the Local Government Finance Act 1992;

in so far as such charges are in respect of the dwelling which a person occupies as his home;

[[98] "the We Love Manchester Emergency Fund" means the registered charity of that name (number 1173260) established on 30th May 2017;]

"week" in [[6] the definitions of "full-time course of advanced education" and of "full-time student" and] [[3] Parts III, VI, VII, VIII, IX, X, XI, XII and XIII] means a period of 7 days;

[[53] "the Welfare Reform Act" means the Welfare Reform Act 2007;]

[[9]"welfare to work beneficiary" means a person—

(a) to whom regulation 13A(1) of the Social Security (Incapacity for Work) (General) Regulations 1995 applies; and

(b) who again becomes incapable of work for the purposes of Part XIIA of the Contributions and Benefits Act 1992;]

[[67] "Work Experience" means the employment programme specified in regulation 75(1)(a)(vi);]

[[32] "working tax credit" means a working tax credit under section 10 of the Tax Credits Act 2002;]

[[32] . . .]

"year of assessment" has the meaning prescribed in section 832(1) of the Income and Corporation Taxes Act 1988;

"young person" except in Part IV has the meaning prescribed in regulation 76.

[[16] (3A) For the purposes of the definition of "full-time student" in paragraph (3) but subject to paragraph (3D), a person shall be regarded as attending or, as the case may be, undertaking a course of study or as being on a sandwich course—

(a) subject to paragraph (3B), in the case of a person attending or undertaking a part of a modular course which would be a full-time course of study, for a period beginning on the day on which that part of the course starts and ending—

    (i) on the last day on which he is registered with the educational establishment as attending or undertaking that part as a full-time course of study; or

    (ii) on such earlier date (if any) as he finally abandons the course or is dismissed from it;

(b) in any other case, throughout the period beginning on the date on which he starts attending or undertaking the course and ending on the last day of the course or on such earlier date (if any) as he finally abandons it or is dismissed from it.

(3B) For the purpose of sub-paragraph (a) of paragraph (3A), the period referred to in that sub-paragraph shall include—

(a) where a person has failed examinations or has failed to successfully complete a module relating to a period when he was attending or undertaking a part of the course as a full-time course of study, any period in respect of which he attends or undertakes the course for the purpose of retaking those examinations or that module;

(b) any period of vacation within the period specified in that paragraph or immediately following that period except where the person has registered with the educational establishment to attend or undertake the final module in the course and the vacation immediately follows the last day on which he is required to attend or undertake the course.

(3C) In paragraph (3A), "modular course" means a course of study which consists of two or more modules, the successful completion of a specified number of which is required before a person is considered by the educational establishment to have completed the course.

(3D) A full-time student shall not be regarded as undertaking a full-time course of advanced education or a full-time course of study for the period specified in paragraph (3E) if—

(a) at any time during an academic year, with the consent of the relevant educational establishment, he ceases to attend or undertake a course because he is—

    (i) engaged in caring for another person; or

    (ii) ill;

(b) he has subsequently ceased to be engaged in caring for that person or, as the case may be, he has subsequently recovered from that illness; and

(c) he is not eligible for a grant or a student loan (as defined in regulation 130) in respect of the period specified in paragraph (3E).

(3E) The period specified for the purposes of paragraph (3D) is the period, [[29], not exceeding one year,] beginning on the day on which he ceased to be engaged in caring for that other person or, as the case may be, the day on which he recovered from that illness and ending on the day before—

    (a) the day on which he resumes attending or undertaking the course; or

[²⁹(b) the day from which the relevant educational establishment has agreed that he may resume attending or undertaking the course,

whichever shall first occur.]

[²⁵ (3F) For the purposes of these Regulations, where a person's principal place of residence is a [⁴⁰care home, an Abbeyfield Home or an independent hospital and he is temporarily absent from that home or hospital, he shall be regarded as continuing to reside in that home or hospital]—

    (a) where he is absent because he is a patient, for the first [³⁴ 52] weeks of any such period of absence and for this purpose—

        (i) "patient" has the meaning it has in Schedule 5 by virtue of regulation 85; and

       (ii) periods of absence separated by not more than 28 days shall be treated as a single period of absence equal in duration to all those periods; and

    (b) for the first three weeks of any other period of absence.]

[⁸⁴ (3G) References in these Regulations to a claimant participating as a service user are to—

    (a) a person who is being consulted by or on behalf of—

        (i) a body which has a statutory duty to provide services in the field of health, social care or social housing; or

       (ii) a body which conducts research or undertakes monitoring for the purpose of planning or improving such services, in their capacity as a user, potential user, carer of a user or person otherwise affected by the provision of those services;

[⁸⁸ (ab) a person who is being consulted by or on behalf of—

        (i) the Secretary of State in relation to any of the Secretary of State's functions in the field of social security or child support or under section 2 of the Employment and Training Act 1973; or

       (ii) a body which conducts research or undertakes monitoring for the purpose of planning or improving such functions,

      in their capacity as a person affected or potentially affected by the exercise of those functions or the carer of such a person;] or

    (b) the carer of a person consulted under [⁸⁸ sub-paragraphs (a) or (ab)].]

(4) In these Regulations, unless the context otherwise requires, a reference—

    (a) to a numbered section is to the section of the Act bearing that number;

    (b) to a numbered Part is to the Part of these Regulations bearing that number;

    (c) to a numbered regulation or Schedule is to the regulation in or Schedule to these Regulations bearing that number;

    (d) in a regulation or Schedule to a numbered paragraph is to the paragraph in that regulation or Schedule bearing that number;

    (e) in a paragraph to a lettered or numbered sub-paragraph is to the sub-paragraph in that paragraph bearing that letter or number.

(5) Unless the context requires otherwise, any reference to the claimant's family or, as the case may be, to a member of his family, shall be construed for the purposes of these Regulations as if it included in relation to a

polygamous marriage a reference to any partner and to any child or young person who is treated as the responsibility of the claimant or his partner, where that child or young person is a member of the claimant's household.

[[70] (6) In such cases and subject to such conditions or requirements as the Secretary of State may specify by means of a direction, any requirement imposed by or under these Regulations for a signature may be satisfied by means of an electronic signature (within the meaning given in section 7(2) of the Electronic Communications Act 2000.)]

AMENDMENTS

1. Jobseeker's Allowance (Amendment) Regulations 1996 (SI 1996/1516) reg.2 (October 7, 1996).
2. Jobseeker's Allowance (Amendment) Regulations 1996 (SI 1996/1516) reg.20 and Sch. (October 7, 1996).
3. Jobseeker's Allowance and Income Support (General) (Amendment) Regulations 1996 (SI 1996/1517) reg.2 (October 7, 1996).
4. Social Security and Child Support (Jobseeker's Allowance) (Miscellaneous Amendments) Regulations 1996 (SI 1996/2538) reg.2(2) (October 28, 1996).
5. Income-related Benefits and Jobseeker's Allowance (Miscellaneous Amendments) Regulations 1997 (SI 1997/65) reg.4(2) (April 7, 1997).
6. Social Security (Miscellaneous Amendments) Regulations 1997 (SI 1997/454) reg.2(2) (April 7, 1997).
7. Social Security (Miscellaneous Amendments) Regulations 1998 (SI 1998/563) reg.5(1) and (2)(f) (April 6, 1998).
8. Social Security Amendment (New Deal) Regulations 1998 (SI 1998/1274) reg.2 (June 1, 1998).
9. Social Security (Welfare to Work) Regulations 1998 (SI 1998/2231) reg.14(2) (October 5, 1998).
10. Social Security and Child Support (Tax Credits) Consequential Amendments Regulations 1999 (SI 1999/2566) reg.2(3) and Sch.2 Pt III (October 5, 1999).
11. Social Security Amendment (Sports Award) Regulations 1999 (SI 1999/2165) reg.2(1) and (2)(e) (August 23, 1999).
12. Social Security Amendment (Employment Zones) Regulations 2000 (SI 2000/724) reg.2(1) (April 3, 2000).
13. Social Security Amendment (Employment Zones) Regulations 2000 (SI 2000/724) reg.2(1) (April 3, 2000).
14. Social Security (Immigration and Asylum) Consequential Amendments Regulations 2000 (SI 2000/636) reg.4(2) (April 3, 2000).
15. Jobseeker's Allowance (Amendment) Regulations 2000 reg.2(2) (March 6, 2000).
16. Social Security Amendment (Students) Regulations 2000 (SI 2000/1981) reg.6(2) (July 31, 2000).
17. Social Security Amendment (Students and Income-related Benefits) Regulations 2000 (SI 2000/1922) reg.3(2) (August 28, 2000, or if the student's period of study begins between August 1 and 27, 2000, the first day of the period).
18. Social Security Amendment (Employment Zones) (No.2) Regulations 2000 (SI 2000/2910) reg.2(3) (November 27, 2000).
19. Jobseeker's Allowance (Joint Claims) Regulations 2000 (SI 2000/1978) reg.2(5) and Sch.2 para.(1) (March 19, 2001).
20. Social Security (Miscellaneous Amendments) (No.2) Regulations 2001 (SI 2001/652) reg.2(a) (March 26, 2001).
21. Social Security (Miscellaneous Amendments) (No.2) Regulations 2001 (SI 2001/652) reg.2(b)(i) (March 26, 2001).
22. Social Security (Miscellaneous Amendments) (No.2) Regulations 2001 (SI 2001/652) reg.2(b)(ii) (March 26, 2001).

23. Social Security Amendment (New Deal) Regulations 2001 (SI 2001/1029) reg.2 (April 9, 2001).

24. Jobseeker's Allowance (Amendment) Regulations 2001 (SI 2001/1434) reg.2(2)(a) (April 1, 2001).

25. Social Security Amendment (Residential Care and Nursing Homes) Regulations 2001 (SI 2001/3767) reg.2 and Sch. Pt II para.1 (April 8, 2002).

26. Social Security (Miscellaneous Amendments) Regulations 2002 (SI 2002/841) reg.3 (April 8, 2002).

27. Income Support (General) and Jobseeker's Allowance Amendment Regulations 2002 (SI 2002/1411) reg.2 (June 17, 2002).

28. Social Security Amendment (Students and Income-related Benefits) Regulations 2002 (SI 2002/1589) reg.2(3) (August 1, 2002).

29. Social Security Amendment (Intercalating Students) Regulations 2002 (SI 2002/1763) reg.2 (August 1, 2002).

30. Social Security Amendment (Employment Programme) Regulations 2002 (SI 2002/2314) reg.2(2) (October 14, 2002).

31. Social Security (Paternity and Adoption) Amendment Regulations 2002 (SI 2002/2689) reg.3 (December 8, 2002).

32. Income-related Benefits and Jobseeker's Allowance (Working Tax Credit and Child Tax Credit) (Amendment) Regulations 2002 (SI 2002/2402) reg.3 and Sch.2 para.1 (April 6, 2003).

33. Social Security (Removal of Residential Allowance and Miscellaneous Amendments) Regulations 2003 (SI 2003/1121) reg.4 and Sch.2 para.1 (October 6, 2003).

34. Social Security (Hospital In-Patients and Miscellaneous Amendments) Regulations 2003 (SI 2003/1195) reg.6 (May 21, 2003).

35. Social Security (Miscellaneous Amendments) Regulations 2004 (SI 2004/565) reg.5(2) (April 1, 2004).

36. Social Security (Income-Related Benefits Self-Employment Route Amendment) Regulations 2004 (SI 2004/963) reg.2 (May 4, 2004).

37. Social Security (Miscellaneous Amendments) (No.2) Regulations 2004 (SI 2004/1141) reg.2(a) (May 12, 2004).

38. Social Security (Miscellaneous Amendments) Regulations 2005 (SI 2005/574) reg.2 (April 4, 2005).

39. Social Security (Miscellaneous Amendments) Regulations 2005 (SI 2005/574) reg.6 (April 4, 2005).

40. Social Security (Care Homes and Independent Hospitals) Regulations 2005 (SI 2005/2687) reg.3 and Sch.2 para.2 (October 24, 2005).

41. Civil Partnership (Pensions, Social Security and Child Support) (Consequential, etc. Provisions) Order 2005 (SI 2005/2877) art.2(3) and Sch.3 para.26(2) (December 5, 2005).

42. Income-related Benefits (Amendment) (No.2) Regulations 2005 reg.5 (December 12, 2005).

43. Housing Benefit and Council Tax Benefit (Consequential Provisions) Regulations 2006 (SI 2006/217) reg.5 and Sch.3 para.8 (March 6, 2006).

44. Social Security (Young Persons) Amendment Regulations 2006 (SI 2006/718) reg.3(2) (April 10, 2006).

45. National Council for Education and Training for Wales (Transfer of Functions to the National Assembly for Wales and Abolition) Order 2005 art.9(2) and Sch.2 para.8 (April 1, 2006).

46. Social Security (Miscellaneous Amendments) (No.4) Regulations 2006 (SI 2006/2378) reg.13(2) (October 2, 2006).

47. Social Security (Miscellaneous Amendments) Regulations 2007 (SI 2007/719) reg.3(2) (April 9, 2007).

48. Social Security (Miscellaneous Amendments) (No.3) Regulations 2007 (SI 2007/1749) reg.3(2) (July 17, 2007).

49. Independent Living Fund (2006) Order 2007 (SI 2007/2538) reg.4 (October 1, 2007).

50. Social Security (Miscellaneous Amendments) (No.5) Regulations 2007 (SI 2007/2618) reg.8(2) (October 1, 2007).

51. Social Security (Miscellaneous Amendments) (No.5) Regulations 2007 (SI 2007/2618) reg.2 and Sch.1 (October 1, 2007).

52. Social Security (Miscellaneous Amendments) Regulations 2008 (SI 2008/698) reg.4(2) (April 14, 2008).

53. Employment and Support Allowance (Consequential Provisions) (No.2) Regulations 2008 (SI 2008/1554) reg.3(1) and (2) (October 27, 2008).

54. Social Security (Miscellaneous Amendments) (No.6) Regulations 2008 (SI 2008/2767) reg.4(1) and (2) (November 17, 2008).

55. Social Security (Miscellaneous Amendments) (No.7) Regulations 2008 (SI 2008/3157) reg.3(1) and (2) (January 5, 2009).

56. Social Security (Flexible New Deal) Regulations 2009 (SI 2009/480) reg.2(2) (a) (April 6, 2009).

57. Social Security (Miscellaneous Amendments) Regulations 2009 (SI 2009/583) reg.4(1) and (2) (April 6, 2009).

58. Social Security (Miscellaneous Amendments) Regulations 2009 (SI 2009/583) reg.4(1) and (3) (April 6, 2009).

59. Social Security (Claims and Payments) Amendment Regulations 2009 (SI 2009/604) reg.3 (April 6, 2009).

60. Social Security (Flexible New Deal) Regulations 2009 (SI 2009/480) reg.2(2) (b) (October 5, 2009).

61. Social Security (Miscellaneous Amendments) (No.4) Regulations 2009 (SI 2009/2655) reg.4(1) and (2) (October 26, 2009).

62. Social Security (Equalisation of State Pension Age) Regulations 2009 (SI 2009/1488) reg.10 (April 6, 2010). That the definition is not in alphabetical order is required by the amending legislation and is not a publishing error.

63. Social Security (Miscellaneous Amendments) (No.2) Regulations 2010 (SI 2010/641) reg.4 (April 6, 2010).

64. Housing and Regeneration Act 2008 (Consequential Provisions) (No.2) Order 2010 art.4 and Sch.1 para.15 (April 1, 2010).

65. Apprenticeships, Skills, Children and Learning Act 2009 (Consequential Amendments to Subordinate Legislation) (England) Order 2010 (SI 2010/1941) reg.5(1) and (2) (September 1, 2010).

66. Health and Social Care Act 2008 (Miscellaneous Consequential Amendments) Order 2010 (SI 2010/1881) regs 2 and 8 (October 1, 2010).

67. Jobseeker's Allowance (Work Experience) (Amendment) Regulations 2011 (SI 2011/798) reg.2(2) (April 5, 2011).

68. Jobseeker's Allowance (Mandatory Work Activity Scheme) Regulations 2011 (SI 2011/688) reg.11 (April 25, 2011).

69. Jobseeker's Allowance (Employment, Skills and Enterprise Scheme) Regulations 2011 (SI 2011/917) reg.11 (May 20, 2011).

70. Social Security (Electronic Communications) Order 2011 (SI 2011/1498) art.3(2) (June 20, 2011)

71. Social Security (Miscellaneous Amendments) (No. 3) Regulations 2011 (SI 2011/2425) reg.10(1) and (2) (October 31, 2011).

72. Public Services Reform (Scotland) Act 2010 (Consequential Modifications of Enactments) Order 2011 (SI 2011/2581) art.2 and Sch.2 para.20 (October 28, 2011).

73. Social Security (Miscellaneous Amendments) Regulations 2012 (SI 2012/757) reg.4(1) and (2) (April 1, 2012).

74. Young People's Learning Agency Abolition (Consequential Amendments to Subordinate Legislation) (England) Order 2012 (SI 2012/956) reg.5(2) (May 1, 2012).

75. Jobseeker's Allowance (Members of the Reserve Forces) Regulations 2012 (2012/1616) reg.2(1) and (2) (July 30, 2012).

76. Jobseeker's Allowance (Schemes for Assisting Persons to Obtain Employment) Regulations 2013 (SI 2013/276) reg.8(1)(c) and (2) (February 12, 2013). (The former para.(c) in the definition of "self-employment route"—see p.882 of Vol II of the 2012/13 edition—was inserted by SI 2011/917 (see point 69 above). Section 1(14) of the Jobseekers (Back to Work Schemes) Act 2013 provides that SI 2011/917 (which was held to be ultra vires by the Court of Appeal in R. *(Reilly and Wilson) v Secretary of State for Work and Pensions* [2013] EWCA Civ 66) is to be treated as having been revoked by SI 2013/276 upon the coming into force of the latter instrument).

77. National Treatment Agency (Abolition) and the Health and Social Care Act 2012 (Consequential, Transitional and Saving Provisions) Order 2013 (SI 2013/235) art.9 and Sch.1 para.27(1) and (2) (April 1, 2013).

78. Social Security (Miscellaneous Amendments) Regulations 2013 (SI 2013/443) reg.4(1) and (2) (April 2, 2013).

79. Personal Independence Payment (Supplementary Provisions and Consequential Amendments) Regulations 2013 (SI 2013/388) reg.8 and Sch. para.16(1) and (2) (April 8, 2013).

80. Armed Forces and Reserve Forces Compensation Scheme (Consequential Provisions: Subordinate Legislation) Order 2013 (SI 2013/591) art.7 and Sch. para.10(1) and (2) (April 8, 2013).

81. Universal Credit (Consequential, Supplementary, Incidental and Miscellaneous Provisions) Regulations 2013 (SI 2013/630) reg.30(1) and (2) (April 29, 2013).

82. Social Security (Miscellaneous Amendments) (No.3) Regulations 2013 (SI 2013/2536) reg.6(1) and (2) (October 29, 2013).

83. Marriage (Same Sex Couples) Act 2013 (Consequential Provisions) Order 2014 (SI 2014/107) reg.2 and Sch.1 para.16 (March 13, 2014). The amendment extends to England and Wales only (see SI 2014/107 art.1(4)).

84. Social Security (Miscellaneous Amendments) Regulations 2014, (SI 2014/591) reg.4(1) and (2) (April 28, 2014).

85. Marriage and Civil Partnership (Scotland) Act 2014 and Civil Partnership Act 2004 (Consequential Provisions and Modifications) Order 2014 (SI 2014/3229) art.29 and Sch.6 para.11 (December 16, 2014). The amendment relates only to Scotland (see SI 2014/3229 art.3(4)) but is in the same terms as the amendments made in relation to England and Wales by SI 2014/107 (see point 83 above).

86. Shared Parental Leave and Statutory Shared Parental Pay (Consequential Amendments to Subordinate Legislation) Order 2014 (SI 2014/3255) art.7(1) and (2)(c) (December 31, 2014).

87. Shared Parental Leave and Statutory Shared Parental Pay (Consequential Amendments to Subordinate Legislation) Order 2014 (SI 2014/3255) art.7(1) and (2)(a) and (b) (April 5, 2015). The amendment is subject to the transitional provision in art.35 of SI 2014/3255, which is reproduced below.

88. Social Security (Miscellaneous Amendments) Regulations 2015 (SI 2015/67) reg.2(1)(b) and (2) (February 23, 2015).

89. Jobseeker's Allowance (Habitual Residence) Amendment Regulations 2014 (SI 2014/2735) reg.2 (November 9, 2014).

90. Social Security (Traineeships and Qualifying Young Persons) Amendment Regulations 2015 (SI 2015/336) reg.2(1) and (2) (March 27, 2015).

91. Social Security (Members of the Reserve Forces) (Amendment) Regulations 2015 (SI 2015/389) reg.3(1) and (2) (April 6, 2015).

92. Deregulation Act 2015 (Consequential Amendments) Order 2015 (SI 2015/971) art.2 and Sch.3 para.4(1) and (2) (May 26, 2015).

93. Pensions Act 2014 (Consequential, Supplementary and Incidental Amendments) Order 2015 (SI 2015/1985) art.16(1) and (2) (April 6, 2016).

94. Social Security (Scottish Rate of Income Tax etc.) (Amendment) Regulations 2016 (SI 2016/233) reg.3(1) and (2) (April 6, 2016).

95. Employment and Support Allowance and Universal Credit (Miscellaneous Amendments and Transitional and Savings Provisions) Regulations 2017 (SI 2017/204) reg.7(1) and Sch.1, Pt.1, para.3(1) and (2) (April 3, 2017).

96. Social Security (Scottish Infected Blood Support Scheme) Regulations 2017 (SI 2017/329) reg.3(1) and (2) (April 3, 2017).

97. Crown Estate Transfer Scheme 2017 (SI 2017/524) para.8 and Sch.5, Pt 3, para.74 (April 1, 2017).

98. Social Security (Emergency Funds) (Amendment) Regulations 2017 (SI 2017/689) reg.3(1) and (2) (June 19, 2017).

99. Social Security (Infected Blood and Thalidomide) Regulations 2017 (SI 2017/870) reg.3(1) and (2) (October 23, 2017).

100. Social Security (Qualifying Young Persons Participating in Relevant Training Schemes) (Amendment) Regulations 2017 (SI 2017/987) reg.2 (November 6, 2017).

101. Social Security and Child Support (Regulation and Inspection of Social Care (Wales) Act 2016) (Consequential Provision) Regulations 2018 (SI 2018/228) reg.5 (April 2, 2018).

102. Civil Partnership (Opposite-sex Couples) Regulations 2019 (SI 2019/1458) reg.41 and Sch.3 Pt.2 para.47 (December 2, 2019).

103. Parental Bereavement Leave and Pay (Consequential Amendments to Subordinate Legislation) Regulations 2020 (SI 2020/354) reg.8(1) and (2) (April 6, 2020).

104. Social Security (Income and Capital) (Miscellaneous Amendments) Regulations 2020 (SI 2020/618) reg.3(1) and (2) (July 15, 2020).

DEFINITIONS

"Benefits Act"—see Jobseekers Act 1995 s.35(1).
"child"—*ibid.*
"claimant"—*ibid.*
"family"—*ibid.*
"occupational pension scheme"—*ibid.*

GENERAL NOTE

3.4
See the notes to reg.2(1) of the Income Support Regulations for points on some of these definitions, namely, "board and lodging accommodation", "close relative", "couple", "dwelling occupied as the home", "occupational pension", "self-employed earner", "self-employment route", "the Skipton fund", "training allowance" and "welfare to work beneficiary". Otherwise, the significance of particular definitions is dealt with in the notes to the regulations in which they occur.

Note also the additional definitions in reg.3 and the definitions in reg.4 for the purposes of Pt II (jobseeking), Pt IV (young persons), Pt V (sanctions) and various sections of the Jobseekers Act.

On the definitions relating to students and on paras (3A)–(3E), see the note to reg.130.

Definition of non-dependant

3.5
2.—(1) In these Regulations, "non-dependant" means any person, except a person to whom paragraph (2), (3) or (4) applies, who normally resides with the claimant or with whom the claimant normally resides.

(2) This paragraph applies to—

(a) any member of the claimant's family;

(b) a child or young person who is living with the claimant but who is not a member of his household by virtue of regulation 78 (circumstances in which a person is to be treated as being or not being a member of the household);

(c) a person who lives with the claimant in order to care for him or for the claimant's partner and who is engaged for that purpose by a charitable or voluntary organisation (other than a public or local authority) which makes a charge to the claimant or the claimant's partner for the care provided by that person;

(d) the partner of a person to whom sub-paragraph (c) applies.

(3) This paragraph applies to a person, other than a close relative of the claimant or the claimant's partner,—

(a) who is liable to make payments on a commercial basis to the claimant or the claimant's partner in respect of his occupation of the claimant's dwelling;

(b) to whom the claimant or the claimant's partner is liable to make payments on a commercial basis in respect of his occupation of that person's dwelling;

(c) who is a member of the household of a person to whom subparagraph (a) or (b) applies.

(4) Subject to paragraph (5), this paragraph applies to—

(a) a person who jointly occupies the claimant's dwelling and who is either—

(i) a co-owner of that dwelling with the claimant or the claimant's partner (whether or not there are other co-owners); or

(ii) jointly liable with the claimant or the claimant's partner to make payments to a landlord in respect of his occupation of that dwelling; or

(b) a partner of a person to whom sub-paragraph (a) applies.

(5) Where a person is a close relative of the claimant or the claimant's partner, paragraph (4) shall apply to him only if the claimant's, or the claimant's partner's, co-ownership, or joint liability to make payments to a landlord in respect of his occupation, of the dwelling arose either before 11th April 1988, or, if later, on or before the date upon which the claimant or the claimant's partner first occupied the dwelling in question.

(6) For the purposes of this regulation a person resides with another only if they share any accommodation except a bathroom, a lavatory or a communal area but not if each person is separately liable to make payments in respect of his occupation of the dwelling to the landlord.

(7) In this regulation "communal area" means any area (other than rooms) of common access (including halls and passageways) and rooms of common use in sheltered accommodation.

DEFINITIONS

"child"—see Jobseekers Act 1995 s.35(1).
"claimant"—*ibid.*
"close relative"—see reg.1(3).
"family"—see s.35(1).
"partner"—see reg.1(3).
"voluntary organisation"—*ibid.*

GENERAL NOTE

See the notes to reg.3 of the Income Support Regulations.

3.6

[¹Disapplication of section 1(1A) of the Administration Act

3.7   **2A.**—Section 1(1A) of the Administration Act (requirement to state national insurance number) shall not apply—

(a) [² . . .]

(b) to any claim for jobseeker's allowance made or treated as made before 5th October 1998].

[³ (c) to a person who—

(i) is a person in respect of whom a claim for jobseeker's allowance is made;

(ii) is subject to immigration control within the meaning of section 115(9)(a) of the Immigration and Asylum Act;

(iii) is not entitled to any jobseeker's allowance for the purposes of section 1 of the Act; and

(iv) has not previously been allocated a national insurance number.]

AMENDMENTS

1. Social Security (National Insurance Number Information: Exemption) Regulations 1997 (SI 1997/2676) reg.12 (December 1, 1997).

2. Social Security (Working Tax Credit and Child Tax Credit) (Consequential Amendments) Regulations 2003 (SI 2003/455) reg.3 and Sch.2 para.1 (April 6, 2004, except in "transitional cases" and see further the note to reg.83 and to reg.17 of the Income Support Regulations).

3. Social Security (National Insurance Number Information: Exemption) Regulations 2009 (SI 2009/471) reg.7 (April 6, 2009).

DEFINITIONS

"child"—see Jobseekers Act 1995 s.35(1).
"young person"—see reg.76.

GENERAL NOTE

3.8   See the notes to s.1(1A)–(1C) of the Administration Act and reg.2A of the Income Support Regulations. Note that in the case of jobseeker's allowance, unlike income support, the requirement to have, or apply for, a national insurance number as a condition of entitlement to benefit does not apply to any claim made or treated as made before October 5, 1998 (para.(b)).

Meanings of certain expressions used in the Jobseekers Act 1995

3.9   **3.**—For the purposes of the Act and of these Regulations—

"employed earner" has the meaning it has in Part I of the Benefits Act by virtue of section 2(1)(a) of that Act;

[¹"employment", except as provided in regulations 4 and 75, includes any trade, business, profession, office or vocation;]

"pensionable age" has the meaning it has in Parts I to VI of the Benefits Act by virtue of section 122(1) of that Act.

AMENDMENT

1. Social Security Amendment (New Deal) Regulations 1997 (SI 1997/2863) reg.2 (January 5, 1998).

DEFINITION

"the Benefits Act"—see Jobseekers Act 1995 s.35(1).

GENERAL NOTE

"*Employed earner*". See the note to reg.2(1) of the Income Support Regulations.　　**3.10**

"*Employment*". The 1998 amendments to this definition and to the definition of "employment" in reg.4 were made as a consequence of the introduction of the "New Deal" for 18–24- year olds. The amendments removed Pt V of these Regulations and s.19 of the Jobseekers Act 1995 from the list of provisions in reg.4 in which employment only refers to work as an employee and does not include self-employment (unless otherwise stated); employment for the purposes of Pt V and s.19 was then defined in reg.75. The intention behind the amendments was that the fixed term sanctions of two or four weeks would apply to all people taking part in the New Deal, regardless of whether they were employed or in receipt of an allowance. The New Deal programmes no longer exist.

The definition of "employment" in reg.75 was further amended (and other amendments were made to reg.75) as a result of the new JSA sanctions regime that came into force in October 2012.

Note also the definition of employment in s.7(8) of the Act for the purposes of regs 18–22.

"*Pensionable age*". Pensionable age is currently 65 for men and 60 for women born before April 6, 1950. Women born between April 6, 1950 and November 6, 1953 will reach pensionable age at a date between their sixtieth and sixty-fifth birthday (the exact days are set out in Pt I of Sch.4 to the Pensions Act 1995). In addition, the increase in state pension age for both men and women will start to rise from 65 in December 2018 to reach 66 by October 2020; it will rise to 67 between 2026 and 2028.

[¹ PART IA

JOINT-CLAIM COUPLES

Prescribed description of a joint-claim couple for the purposes of section 1(4)

3A.—(1) For the purposes of section 1(4), a joint-claim couple shall　　**3.11** include any joint-claim couple within the meaning given in section 1(4) of the Act where at least one member [² is aged 18 or over and] was born after [³28th October [⁴1947]], unless a member of the couple is treated as responsible for a child or young person under regulation 77(3), or the couple has care of a child or young person in one or more of the circumstances mentioned in regulation 78(4), or a child or young person is living with either member of the couple in the circumstances mentioned in regulation 78(8).

(2) In a case where a person would (but for these Regulations) be a member of more than one joint-claim couple, a joint-claim couple means the couple of which he is a member which that person nominates (or in default of such nomination, which the Secretary of State nominates), to the exclusion of any other couple of which he is a member.]

AMENDMENTS

1. Jobseeker's Allowance (Joint Claims) Regulations 2000 (SI 2000/1978) reg.2(2) (March 19, 2001).

2. Social Security Amendment (Joint Claims) Regulations 2001 (SI 2001/518) reg.2(2) (March 19, 2001).

3. Jobseeker's Allowance (Joint Claims) Amendment Regulations 2002 (SI 2002/1701) reg.2(a) (October 28, 2002).

4. Jobseeker's Allowance (Joint Claims) Amendment Regulations 2008 (SI 2008/13) reg.2(2) (February 25, 2008).

DEFINITIONS

"the Act"—see reg.2(1).
"child"—see Jobseekers Act 1995 s.35(1).
"joint-claim couple"—see Jobseekers Act 1995 s.1(4).
"young person"—see regs 1(3) and 76.

GENERAL NOTE

3.12   The standard old style JSA picture had been one of claimants claiming in their own right a contribution-based jobseeker's allowance and claiming income-based jobseeker's allowance (IBJSA) for themselves, and any partner and/or children, with consequent aggregation of needs and resources. From March 19, 2001, a new dimension was added: the requirement that a "joint-claim couple" make a joint claim for JSA (what in reality is a joint-claim IBJSA) (s.1(2B)–(2D)). This aspect of the scheme goes beyond the familiar notion of aggregation of needs and resources (although "joint-claim jobseeker's allowance" embodies that too (see ss.3A and 4)) since that traditional model embodies the notion of one partner in a couple being dependent on the other, the latter being the claimant having to fulfil the conditions of entitlement. The "joint-claim couple" aspect goes further than this in that each partner is party to the claim and each must satisfy the conditions of entitlement in s.1(2)(a)–(c) and (e)–(i). In other words, each partner of a joint-claim couple must: (i) be available for employment; (ii) have entered into a jobseeker's agreement; (iii) be actively seeking employment; (iv) not be engaged in remunerative work; (v) be capable of work; (vi) not be receiving relevant education; (vii) be under pensionable age; and (viii) be in Great Britain.

The "joint-claim" scheme has, legislatively speaking, required the adaptation of rules designed for a single claimant to deal instead with two people. Of particular note are the provisions for entitlement notwithstanding that one member of the couple does not meet the "labour market conditions" (see JSA Regulations 1996 reg.3D) and the provisions enabling one member of the couple to receive a reduced rate jobseeker's allowance where the other is caught by a sanction.

The old style Jobseekers Act 1995 s.1(4) defines "joint-claim couple" as a couple, of a prescribed description, who are not members of any family that includes someone for whom one of the members of the couple is entitled to child benefit. Regulation 3A, as amended from February 25, 2008, gives the prescribed description: where one of the members of the couple is aged 18 or over and was born after October 28, 1947. Such a couple, however, will not be of a prescribed description if:

(a) under reg.77(3), one of its members is treated as responsible for a child or young person;

(b) the couple has care of a child or young person in one or more of the circumstances mentioned in reg.78(4) (where they are fosterers or the child has been placed with them for adoption); or

(c) a child or young person is living with the couple in the circumstances mentioned in reg.78(8) (a child living with the couple when he is away from home while at school).

[¹Entitlement of a former joint-claim couple to a jobseeker's allowance

3.13   **3B.**—(1) Where a joint-claim couple cease to be a joint-claim couple because they become, or are treated as, responsible for one or more children—

(a) any claim made by both members of that couple for a jobseeker's allowance may be treated as a claim for a jobseeker's allowance made by either member of that couple;

(b) any award of a joint-claim jobseeker's allowance in respect of that couple may be terminated and may be replaced by a replacement award,

where the conditions specified in paragraph (2) have been complied with.

(2) The conditions specified in this paragraph are that a member of the couple—

(a) provides such evidence as the Secretary of State may require confirming that the couple are responsible for one or more children; and

(b) advises the Secretary of State as to which member of the couple is to be the claimant.

(3) The claim by a member of the couple for a jobseeker's allowance referred to in paragraph (1)(a) shall be treated as made on the date on which he and his partner were treated as having claimed a jobseeker's allowance as a joint-claim couple as determined in accordance with regulation 6 of the Claims and Payments Regulations.

(4) In this regulation, "replacement award" shall have the meaning ascribed to it by paragraph 9A of Schedule 1 to the Act.]

AMENDMENT

1. Jobseeker's Allowance (Joint Claims) Regulations 2000 (SI 2000/1978) reg.2(2) (March 19, 2001).

DEFINITIONS

"the Act"—see reg.1(3).
"child"—see Jobseekers Act 1995 s.35(1).
"Claims and Payments Regulations"—see reg.1(3).
"joint-claim couple"—see Jobseekers Act 1995 s.1(4).

GENERAL NOTE

This regulation sets out what happens if a joint-claim couple become responsible for a child (and therefore cease to be a joint-claim couple—see the definition in reg.3A(1)). Although the regulation refers only to children (where there is a specific definition in the old style Jobseekers Act 1995), presumably it must also be taken as applying when a member of the couple becomes responsible for a young person. The existing joint claim can be treated as a claim by either member of the couple and the joint award of benefit is terminated and replaced by a "replacement award". If the couple wish this to happen, they must provide the Secretary of State with evidence that they have become responsible for a child and notify him as to which member of the couple is to be the claimant.

3.14

[¹Entitlement of a new joint-claim couple to a jobseeker's allowance

3C.—(1) Paragraph (2) shall apply where a couple become a joint-claim couple because the child, or all the children, for which they were responsible have—

(a) died;

(b) ceased to be a child or children for whom they are responsible; or

(c) reached the age of 16 and are [² not qualifying young persons within

3.15

the meaning of section 142 of the Benefits Act (child and qualifying young person)].

(2) In a case to which this paragraph applies—

(a) any claim made by either member of that couple for a jobseeker's allowance may be treated as a claim made by both members of the couple;

(b) any award of an income-based jobseeker's allowance, or a replacement award, in respect of either member of that couple may be terminated and may be replaced by a new award in respect of the couple,

where the conditions specified in paragraph (3) have been complied with.

(3) The conditions specified in this paragraph are that the Secretary of State—

(a) has sufficient evidence to decide whether a new award should be made; and

(b) is informed as to which member of the couple is to be the nominated member for the purposes of section 3B.

(4) The claim by both members of the joint-claim couple for a jobseeker's allowance referred to in paragraph (2)(a) shall be treated as made on the date on which the claim by a member of that couple was treated as made in accordance with regulation 6 of the Claims and Payments Regulations.

(5) For the purposes of paragraphs 6 and 7 of Schedule 2 (housing costs), any award of an income-based jobseeker's allowance which related to the day before the day on which the relevant event specified in paragraph (1) occurred and any new award referred to in paragraph (2)(b) shall be treated as a continuous award of an income-based jobseeker's allowance.

(6) In this regulation, "new award" shall have the meaning ascribed to it by paragraph 9C of Schedule 1 to the Act.]

AMENDMENTS

1. Jobseeker's Allowance (Joint Claims) Regulations 2000 (SI 2000/1978) reg.2(2) (March 19, 2001).

2. Social Security (Young Persons) Amendment Regulations 2006 (SI 2006/718) reg.3(3) (April 10, 2006).

DEFINITIONS

"the Act"—see reg.1(3).
"the Benefits Act"—see Jobseekers Act 1995, s.35(1).
"Claims and Payments Regulations"—see reg.1(3).
"child"—see Jobseekers Act 1995 s.35(1).
"an income-based jobseeker's allowance"—see Jobseekers Act 1995 s.1(4)
"joint-claim couple"—*ibid*.

GENERAL NOTE

3.16 Regulation 3C is the mirror image of reg.3B. The latter regulation sets out what happens when a couple become responsible for a child (or young person?) and therefore cease to be a joint-claim couple whereas reg.3C sets out what happens when a couple becomes a joint-claim couple because they are no longer responsible for a child or a qualifying young person. In the circumstances listed in para.(1), any claim by either member of the couple may be treated as a joint claim and any award in favour of either may be terminated and replaced with a joint award.

[¹Further circumstances in which a joint-claim couple may be entitled to a joint-claim jobseeker's allowance

3D.—(1) Subject to paragraph (2), a joint-claim couple are entitled to a   3.17
joint-claim jobseeker's allowance where—
  (a) the members of that couple claim a jobseeker's allowance jointly;
  (b) one member satisfies the conditions set out in section 1(2)(a) to (c)
     and (e) to (i); and
  [² (c) the other member satisfies the condition in section 1(2)(e) and (h)
     but is not required to satisfy the other conditions in section 1(2B)
     (b) because, subject to paragraph (3), he is a person to whom any
     paragraph in Schedule A1 applies; and]
  (d) the conditions set out in section 3A are satisfied in relation to the
     couple.
  (2) A member of a joint-claim couple who falls within any paragraph in
Schedule A1 for the purposes of this regulation for any day in a benefit week
shall fall within that category for the whole of that week.
  (3) Subject to paragraph (4), paragraph 2 of Schedule A1 (students) may
only apply to a member of a joint-claim couple in respect of one claim for a
jobseeker's allowance made jointly by that couple in respect of a jobseeking
period applying to the other member of that couple.
  (4) Notwithstanding paragraph (3), paragraph 2 of Schedule A1 may
apply to a member of a joint-claim couple in respect of a further claim for a
jobseeker's allowance made jointly by the couple where the couple's previous entitlement to a joint-claim jobseeker's allowance ceased because one
member of the couple—
  (a) was engaged in remunerative work;
  (b) had been summoned to jury service; or
  (c) was within a linked period as prescribed in regulation 48(2).]

AMENDMENTS

  1. Jobseeker's Allowance (Joint Claims) Regulations 2000 (SI 2000/1978)
reg.2(2) (March 19, 2001).
  2. Social Security Amendment (Joint Claims) Regulations 2001 (SI 2001/518)
reg.2(3) (March 19, 2001).

DEFINITIONS

  "benefit week"—see reg.1(3).
  "jobseeking period"—see regs 1(3) and 47.
  "joint-claim couple"—see Jobseekers Act 1995 s.1(4).
  "a joint-claim jobseeker's allowance"—*ibid.*

GENERAL NOTE

  In the circumstances set out in reg.3D, a joint-claim couple can be entitled to   3.18
income-based JSA even though only one of them satisfies the labour market conditions. This applies if one member is in Great Britain, under pensionable age,
capable of, available for and actively seeking work, has a jobseeker's agreement, and
is neither in remunerative work nor receiving relevant education. The other member
must be under pensionable age and not in remunerative work and must fall into one
of the prescribed categories listed in Sch.A1.
  Note that this regulation only dispenses the "failing" member from compliance
with the labour market conditions. It is still necessary for the couple to make a joint

claim, except where reg.3E applies, and to meet the requirements of s.3A of the old style Jobseekers Act 1995.

[¹Entitlement of a member of a joint-claim couple to a jobseeker's allowance without a claim being made jointly by the couple

3.19

3E.—(1) A member of a joint-claim couple is entitled to a jobseeker's allowance if, without making a claim jointly for that allowance with the other member of the couple—

(a) he satisfies the conditions set out in section 1(2) (a) to (c) and (e) to (i);

(b) he satisfies the conditions set out in section 3; and

(c) the other member of that couple fails to meet the conditions of entitlement set out in section 1(2B)(b) and is a person to whom paragraph (2) applies.

(2) This paragraph applies to a member of a joint-claim couple—

(a) who has failed to attend at the time and place specified by the employment officer for the purposes of regulation 6 of the Claims and Payments Regulations;

(b) in respect of whom it has been determined by the Secretary of State that the conditions in section 1(2)(a) to (c) have not been satisfied but only for so long as it has been so determined in respect of that member;

(c) who is temporarily absent from Great Britain;

(d) who is a person from abroad as defined for the purposes of regulation [⁴85A] and Schedule 5;

(e) who is subject to immigration control within the meaning of section 115(9) of the Immigration and Asylum Act;

(f) who is over pensionable age;

(g) who is engaged, or has agreed to be engaged, in remunerative work for [² 16 hours or more] per week but less than 24 hours per week;

(h) who has claimed a maternity allowance payable in accordance with section 35 [⁷ or 35B] of the Benefits Act or who has claimed statutory maternity pay payable in accordance with Part XII of that Act;

(i) who is or has been pregnant and to whom sub-paragraph (h) does not apply but only for the period commencing 11 weeks before the expected week of confinement and ending [⁶twenty eight weeks after the date on which the pregnancy ends];

(j) in respect of whom there is an Order in Council under section 179 of the Administration Act giving effect to a reciprocal agreement which, for the purposes of jobseeker's allowance, has effect as if a payment made by another country is to be treated as a payment of a jobseeker's allowance; [³ . . .]

(k) who is in receipt of statutory sick pay and who, immediately before he became incapable of work, was engaged in remunerative work for 16 hours or more per week; [³ or

(l) where the other member was entitled to an income-based jobseeker's allowance on [⁵24th February 2008], save that this sub-paragraph shall apply only until the day on which he is required to attend at a place specified by an employment officer in a notification given or sent to him.]]

AMENDMENTS

1. Jobseeker's Allowance (Joint Claims) Regulations 2000 (SI 2000/1978) reg.2(2) (March 19, 2001).
2. Social Security Amendment (Joint Claims) Regulations 2001 (SI 2001/518) reg.2(4) (March 19, 2001).
3. Jobseeker's Allowance (Joint Claims) Amendment Regulations 2002 (SI 2002/1701) reg.2(b) (October 28, 2002).
4. Social Security (Miscellaneous Amendments) Regulations 2007 (SI 2007/719) reg.3(3) (April 2, 2007).
5. Jobseeker's Allowance (Joint Claims) Amendment Regulations 2008 (SI 2008/13) reg.2(3) (February 25, 2008).
6. Social Security (Miscellaneous Amendments) (No.2) Regulations 2010 (SI 2010/641) reg.4(4) (April 6, 2010).
7. Social Security (Maternity Allowance) (Miscellaneous Amendments) Regulations 2014 (SI 2014/884) reg. 4(2) (May 18, 2014).

DEFINITIONS

"the Administration Act"—see Jobseekers Act 1995 s.35(1).
"the Benefits Act"—*ibid.*
"Claims and Payments Regulations"—see reg.1(3).
"employment officer"—see Jobseekers Act 1995 s.35(1).
"Great Britain"—*ibid.*
"the Immigration and Asylum Act"—see reg.1(3).
"an income-based jobseeker's allowance"—see Jobseekers Act 1995 s.1(4)
"joint-claim couple"—*ibid.*
"making a claim"—see reg.1(3).

GENERAL NOTE

In the circumstances set out in reg.3E, one member of a joint-claim couple   3.20
can make a standard claim for old style JSA (i.e. not jointly with the other member) as long as s/he meets the labour market conditions and the conditions in s.3 of the old style Jobseekers Act 1995. The circumstances in which this is possible are listed in para.(2) and are self-explanatory.

[¹Transitional case couples: prescribed circumstances and period for the purposes of paragraph 8A(2) of Schedule 1

3F.—[² . . .]]   3.21

AMENDMENTS

1. Jobseeker's Allowance (Joint Claims) Regulations 2000 (SI 2000/1978) reg.2(2) (March 19, 2001).
2. Jobseeker's Allowance (Joint Claims) Amendment Regulations 2008 (SI 2008/13) reg.2(4) (February 25, 2008).

[¹ Supply of information

3G.—Where a claim for a jobseeker's allowance has been made jointly   3.22
by a joint-claim couple, information relating to that claim may be supplied by the Secretary of State to either or both members of that couple for any purpose connected with that claim.]

AMENDMENT

1. Jobseeker's Allowance (Joint Claims) Regulations 2000 (SI 2000/1978) reg.2(2) (March 19, 2001).

GENERAL NOTE

3.23   This regulation is self-explanatory. Normally information provided in connection with a claim is confidential to the claimant. With a joint claim, the Secretary of State may discuss the claim with either or both claimants.

PART II

JOBSEEKING

Chapter I

Interpretation

Interpretation of Parts II, IV and V

3.24   **4.**—In Parts II, IV and V and, as provided below, the Act—

"appropriate office" means the office of the Department for [6 Work and Pensions] which the claimant is required to attend in accordance with a notice under regulation 23, or any other place which he is so required to attend;

"caring responsibilities" means responsibility for caring for a child or for an elderly person or for a person whose physical or mental condition requires him to be cared for, who is either in the same household or a close relative;

"casual employment" means employment from which the employee can be released without his giving any notice [3except where otherwise provided];

"close relative" means [1, except in Part IV] [5a member of a couple], parent, step-parent, grandparent, parent-in-law, son, step-son, son-in-law, daughter, step-daughter, daughter-in-law, brother, sister, grandchild, [5or if any of the preceding persons is one member of a couple, the other member of that couple];

"elderly person" means a person of over pensionable age;

"employment" in sections 1, 3, 6, 8, 14 [2 . . .] and 20 and paragraph 8 of Schedule 1 to the Act and in [2Parts II and IV] means employed earner's employment except where otherwise provided;

[8 . . . ;]

[3"examination" in relation to a qualifying course means an examination which is specified as an examination related to the qualifying course in a document signed on behalf of the establishment at which the qualifying course is being undertaken;

"made a claim for a jobseeker's allowance" includes treated as having made a claim for the allowance and treated as having an award of the allowance in accordance with regulation 5, 6 or 7 of the Jobseeker's Allowance (Transitional Provisions) Regulations 1996;]

"Outward Bound course" means any course or programme for personal development which is made available to persons who are not in employment by the charitable trust known as the Outward Bound Trust Limited;

"part-time member of a fire brigade" means a person who is a part-time member of a fire brigade maintained in pursuance of the Fire Services Acts 1947–1959;

"pattern of availability" has the meaning given in regulation 7;

[⁴ "period of study" means—

(a) the period during which the student is regarded as attending or undertaking the course of study; and

(b) any period of attendance by the student at his educational establishment or any period of study undertaken by the student, in connection with the course, which occurs before or after the period during which he is to be regarded as undertaking the course of study;]

"a person who is kept on short-time" means a person whose hours of employment have been reduced owing to temporary adverse industrial conditions;

"a person who is laid off " means a person whose employment has been suspended owing to temporary adverse industrial conditions;

[³"qualifying course" has the meaning given in regulation 17A;

"term-time" in relation to a qualifying course means the period specified as term-time in relation to a person to whom regulation 17A(2) applies in a document signed on behalf of the establishment at which the qualifying course is being undertaken;

"vacation" in relation to a qualifying course means any period falling within the period of study, which is not term-time;]

"voluntary work" means work for an organisation the activities of which are carried on otherwise than for profit, or work other than for a member of the claimant's family, where no payment is received by the claimant or the only payment due to be made to him by virtue of being so engaged is a payment in respect of any expenses reasonably incurred by him in the course of being so engaged;

"week" in sections 6 and 7 and in Parts II and IV means benefit week except where provided otherwise in Parts II and IV;

"work camp" means any place in Great Britain where people come together under the auspices of a charity, a local authority or a voluntary organisation to provide a service of benefit to the community or the environment.

AMENDMENTS

1. Social Security and Child Support (Jobseeker's Allowance) (Miscellaneous Amendments) Regulations 1996 (SI 1996/2538) reg.2(3) (October 28, 1996).

2. Social Security Amendment (New Deal) Regulations 1997 (SI 1997/2863) reg.3 (January 5, 1998).

3. Social Security Amendment (New Deal) Regulations 1998 (SI 1998/1274) reg.3 (June 1, 1998).

4. Social Security Amendment (Students) Regulations 2000 (SI 2000/1981) reg.6(3) (July 31, 2000).

5. Civil Partnership (Pensions, Social Security and Child Support) (Consequential, etc. Provisions) Order 2005 (SI 2005/2877) art.2(3) and Sch.3 para.26 (December 5, 2005).

6. Social Security (Miscellaneous Amendments) Regulations 2008 (SI 2008/698) reg.4(3) (April 14, 2008).

7. Jobseeker's Allowance (Sanctions for Failure to Attend) Regulations 2010 (SI 2010/509) reg.2(2) (April 6, 2010).

8. Jobseeker's Allowance (Sanctions) (Amendment) Regulations 2012 (SI 2012/2568) reg.5(2) (October 22, 2012).

DEFINITIONS

"benefit week"—see reg.1(3).
"child"—see Jobseekers Act 1995 s.35(1).
"couple"—*ibid*.
"course of study"—*ibid*.
"payment"—*ibid*.
"pensionable age"—see reg.3.
"voluntary organisation"—see reg.1(3).

GENERAL NOTE

3.25   *"Close relative"*. See the note to reg.2(1) of the Income Support Regulations, except that in relation to Parts II and V partners count as close relatives.

"Employment". See the note to the definition of "employment" in reg.3.

"Part-time member of a fire brigade": as regards Wales, with effect from October 25, 2005, the definition was modified by the Fire and Rescue Services Act 2004 (Consequential Amendments) (Wales) Order 2005 (SI 2005/2929) art.36(2) to read as follows:

"*'Part-time member of a fire brigade'* means a person who is a part-time member of a fire brigade maintained in pursuance of the Fire Services Acts 1947–1959 [or, in England or Wales, a part-time fire-fighter employed by a fire and rescue authority]."

As regards Scotland, the definition was modified with effect from August 5, 2005 by the Fire (Scotland) Act 2005 (Consequential Provisions and Modifications) Order 2005 (SI 2005/2060 (S7)) art.3 and Sch. para.10(2) to read as follows:

"*'Part-time member of a fire brigade'* means a person who is a part-time [fire-fighter employed by a fire and rescue authority (as defined in section 1 of the Fire (Scotland) Act 2005 (asp 5)) or a joint fire and rescue board constituted by an amalgamation scheme made under section 2(1) of that Act]."

"Period of study". See R(JSA) 2/02.

Chapter II

Availability for employment

Exceptions to requirement to be available immediately: carers, voluntary workers, persons providing a service and persons under an obligation to provide notice

3.26   **5.**—[¹(1) [⁴ Subject to paragraph (1A),] in order to be regarded as available for employment—
    (a) [². . .];
    (b) a person who is engaged in voluntary work [²or who has caring responsibilities] is not required to be able to take up employment immediately, providing he is willing and able—

(i) to take up employment on being given one week's notice; and

(ii) to attend for interview in connection with the opportunity of any such employment on being given 48 hours' notice.]

[[4](1A) In order to be regarded as available for employment, a person who has caring responsibilities in relation to a child is not required to take up employment or attend for interview within the periods referred to in paragraph (1) if those responsibilities make it unreasonable for him to do so, providing he is willing and able—

(a) to take up employment on being given 28 days notice; and

(b) to attend for interview in connection with the opportunity of any such employment on being given 7 days notice.

(1B) For the purposes of paragraph (1A), it is for the claimant to show that it is unreasonable for him to take up employment or attend for interview within the periods referred to in paragraph (1).]

(2) In order to be regarded as available for employment, a person who is engaged, whether by contract or otherwise, in providing a service with or without remuneration, other than a person who has caring responsibilities or who is engaged in voluntary work, is not required to be able to take up employment immediately, providing he is willing and able to take up employment on being given 24 hours' notice.

(3) In order to be regarded as available for employment, a person who is in employed earner's employment and is not engaged in remunerative work and who is required by [[3](section 86 of the Employment Rights Act 1996] to give notice to terminate his contract is not required to be able to take up employment immediately, providing he is willing and able to take up employment immediately he is able to do so in accordance with his statutory obligations.

(4) Where in accordance with regulation 7, 13[[5](, 13A] or 17 a person is only available for employment at certain times, he is not required to be able to take up employment at a time at which he is not available, but he must be willing and able to take up employment immediately he is available.

(5) Where in accordance with paragraph[[4]((1), (1A) or (2)] a person is not required to be able to take up employment immediately, the [[4](. . .] periods referred to in those paragraphs include periods when in accordance with regulation 7[[5](, 13 or 13A] he is not available.

[[1](6) In this regulation "week" means any period of seven consecutive days.]

AMENDMENTS

1. Jobseeker's Allowance (Amendment) Regulations 2002 (SI 2002/3072) reg.3 (January 1, 2003).

2. Social Security (Income Support and Jobseeker's Allowance) Amendment Regulations 2006 (SI 2006/1402) reg.2(2) (May 30, 2006).

3. Social Security (Miscellaneous Amendments) (No.5) Regulations 2007 (SI 2007/2618) reg.8(3) (October 1, 2007).

4. Social Security (Lone Parents and Miscellaneous Amendments) Regulations 2008 (SI 2008/3051) reg.11(2) (November 4, 2008).

5. Jobseeker's Allowance (Lone Parents) (Availability for Work) Regulations 2010 (SI 2010/837) reg.2(2) (April 26, 2010).

DEFINITIONS

"caring responsibilities"—see reg.4.
"child"—see Jobseekers Act 1995 s.35(1).

"claimant"—*ibid.*

"employed eamer's employment"—see Jobseekers Act 1995 s.6(9); SSCBA 1992 s.2(1)(a).

"employment"—see reg.4.

"remunerative work"—see regs 1(3) and 51(1).

"voluntary work"—see reg.4.

GENERAL NOTE

3.27   The general rule on availability set out in s.6(1) of the old style Jobseekers Act 1995 requires that a claimant be willing and able to take up *immediately* any employed earner's employment (on which see s.6(9) of that Act and SSCBA 1992 ss.2(1)(a) and 122(1)). The reasoning in *GP v SSWP (JSA)* [2015] UKUT 476 (AAC), reported as [2016] AACR 14 (discussed in the notes to s.7(1) of the old style Jobseekers Act 1995), indicates that only availability for employed earner's employment in Great Britain can be required. This regulation provides qualifications of and exceptions to that general rule.

Paragraph (4) qualifies the "immediately" condition by requiring that it be related to the claimant's "pattern of availability" (the times at which he is available to take up employment) permitted by regs 7 (enabling restriction of hours to 40 or more), 13 (enabling carers to restrict hours of availability to between 16 and 40 hours to suit caring responsibilities, and the sick/disabled to restrict times and/or hours of availability so far as reasonable in light of physical or mental condition), 13A (certain lone parents) and 17 (treating as available persons laid off from employment or put on short-time). Paragraph (4) stipulates that a claimant, available only at certain times in accordance with any of those provisions, is not required to be able to take up employment during one of their permitted periods of non-availability, but must be willing and able to take up employment immediately in one of their periods of availability. In addition, paras (1)–(3) give varying periods of grace within which they must be willing and able to take up employment to carers, voluntary workers, to other service-providers, and to persons employed for less than 16 hours per week and under a specific statutory obligation to provide notice. These provisions are discussed further below.

Temporary Coronavirus Provisions

3.28   Regulation 7 of the Social Security (Coronavirus) (Further Measures) Regulations 2020 (SI 2020/371) provided that for the three months beginning with March 30, 2020 anyone with an award of old style JSA was to be treated as available for employment, as well as actively seeking employment. It is arguable that, by virtue of reg.15(5) of the JSA Regulations 1996 the deeming of non-availability in reg.15 trumps the effect of reg.7 except where modified by reg.4 of the Social Security (Coronavirus) (Prisoners) Regulations 2020 (SI 2020/409) (temporary release of English and Welsh prisoners: see the notes to reg.15). The effect of reg.7 of the Further Measures Regulations expired at the end of November 12, 2020 (reg.10(2)). The power to extend the three-month period was not exercised before it expired.

It is not clear whether the restriction of the effect of reg.7 to those who had an award of old style JSA meant that on a new claim (insofar as a claim for old style JSA, as opposed to new style JSA and universal credit, was still possible) the availability condition was to be applied in determining initial entitlement. The mechanism suggested for new style JSA in the notes to s.6E of the new style Jobseekers Act 1995 (Vol.I of this series) cannot work for old style JSA because the availability and actively seeking work conditions are imposed directly by the legislation as conditions of entitlement. It appears that in practice little if any attention was given to "conditionality" during the period affected.

Carers (paras (1), (1A), (1B) and (5))

3.29   A carer (someone "who has caring responsibilities", defined as discussed below) has from May 30, 2006 the benefit of an enhanced relaxation of the rules on immediate availability. Such persons are from that date exempt from the requirement to be immediately available provided that they are willing and able to take up employed earner's employment on being given one week's notice (meaning any seven days: para.(6)) so long as they are also willing and able to attend for interview in connection with the opportunity of any such employment on being given 48 hours' notice. In *CIS 142/1993* the Commissioner decided that the same phrase (except that the required notice was only 24 hours) in reg.12(1) of the Unemployment, Sickness and Invalidity Benefit Regulations 1983 meant that the notice should only start to run when the claimant would receive notification of the job (in that case by a telephone call from his parents in the evening as he was doing voluntary work during the day). See also para.21236 of the *DMG*. From November 24, 2008, carers for children were given a further concession: if they can establish that complying with the one week or 48 hours requirement in para.(1) is unreasonable because of their caring responsibilities, they will not be required to comply with those limits so long as they are willing and able to take up employment on being given 28 days' notice or to attend for interview for such employment on being given seven days' notice (see paras (1A) and (1B)).

Paragraph (5) makes clear that the one week or 48-hour notice periods include periods of non-availability in accordance with regs 7, 13 or 13A. Regulation 7 enables restriction of hours to 40 or more in an pattern of employment recorded in the current jobseeker's agreement. Under reg.13, so long as they have reasonable prospects of employment despite the restriction, carers can restrict availability to such hours between 16 and 40 hours per week as their caring responsibilities allow, and for the specific hours those responsibilities allow (reg.13(4), (5), and 8). Reg.13 also permits anyone to restrict their times and/or hours of availability so far as reasonable in light of their physical or mental condition (reg.13(3)). Regulation 13A allows a lone parent, who is both responsible for and a member of the same household as a child under 13, to restrict their availability to the child's normal school hours.

A carer (a person "who has caring responsibilities") is someone who has responsibility for caring for a child or for an elderly person or for a person whose physical or mental condition requires them to be cared for. But the child, the elderly person and the person whose condition requires being cared for must either be a close relative or in the same household (reg.4). "Close relative" means a spouse, civil partner or other member of a couple, parent, step-parent, grandparent, parent-in-law, son, step-son, son-in-law, daughter, step-daughter, daughter-in-law, brother, sister, grandchild or the spouse of any of these persons or, if that person is one of a couple, the other member of that couple (*ibid.*). On "couple" see the notes to reg.2(1) of the Income Support Regulations and the note thereto.

Voluntary workers (paras (1) and (5))

A voluntary worker ("a person who is engaged . . . in voluntary work", discussed below) is exempt from the requirement to be immediately available, subject to being willing and able to take up employed earner's employment on being given one week's notice, and to attend for interview in connection with the opportunity of any such employment on being given 48 hours' notice. The one week and 48-hour periods include periods when in accordance with regs.7, 13 or 13A the claimant is not available (para.(5)).

"Voluntary work" covers work for an organisation, the activities of which are carried on otherwise than for profit, or work other than for a member of the claimant's family, where no payment is received by the claimant or the only payment due to be made by virtue of being so engaged is one in respect of any expenses reasonably incurred in the course of being engaged in the work (reg.4). On "family", see old style Jobseekers Act 1995 s.35(1) and regs 76–78.

See also reg.12 on cases where claimants have restricted the number of hours for which they are available. Time engaged in voluntary work and the extent to which it may have improved prospects of employment is to be taken into account in determining whether in any week the claimant has taken all the steps that are reasonable for the purposes of the actively seeking employment test (reg.18(2)(g)).

3.30

Others providing a service (paras (2) and (5))

3.31   These paragraphs cover those engaged in providing a service, other than carers or voluntary workers, who are, in any event, more generously treated under para.(1), examined above. It is irrelevant whether the service is provided by contract or not. Nor is it material whether the service is or is not remunerated. Those engaged in providing a service do not have to be available immediately. It suffices that they are available on being given 24 hours' notice. That 24-hour period includes periods when, in accordance with regs 7, 13 or 13A, the service-provider is not available (para.(5)).

The provision is similar to, but wider than, its UB predecessor (USI Regulations reg.12(1)), which was interpreted in *CU/96/1994*. There Commissioner Skinner considered the phrase "providing a service with or without remuneration" found both in USI Regulations reg.12(1) and in the old style JSA provision now under consideration. The claimant had been found not to be available for work because he was not in a position to accept a job offer at once, but would require 24 hours' notice in order to make arrangements for his wife and two teenage children to be able to make their way to college and school and return from there to home. In setting aside the tribunal decision as erroneous in law, Commissioner Skinner opined that the phrase was "a wide one", capable of embracing the necessary help given to members of one's own family: "The service provided does not have to be for the public, it does not have to arise under a contract of employment" (para.5). The contrast between the wording of paras (1) and (1A) (the same contrast as between paras (1) and (2) of this regulation) reinforced his view, as did the *Shorter Oxford English Dictionary* definition of "service" as "the action of serving, helping or benefiting: conduct tending to the welfare or advantage of another: an act of helping or benefiting". That was the sense in which the word was used in para.(1) of the regulation:

> "So consequently if the claimant does an act which helps or benefits a member of his family or does something which tends to their welfare or advantage, he can be said to be rendering a service. However it must be necessary service not some fanciful help. No doubt many unemployed people may be able to satisfy that [criterion]". (para.5)

But the claimant taking his children to school could not be a "service" in the sense of the regulation; it was merely an exercise of parental responsibility, fulfilling a parental duty rather than rendering a service to his children. Transporting his wife to and from her nursing course, however, was in law capable of amounting to a "service":

> "It was something done for the wife's benefit and it does not seem that the claimant had any duty or responsibility so to transport her. No doubt it was a worthwhile and kindly thing to do, but he did not have to do it, and I accept that he could in law provide a service". (para.7)

Commissioner Skinner thought the real restriction on the operation of USI Regulations reg.12(1) to be the requirement therein that the circumstances be such that it would not be reasonable to expect the claimant to be ready for suitable employment on less than 24 hours' notice. That restriction is not embodied in the old style JSA provision now under consideration.

Those working less than 16 hours per week and under an obligation to provide notice (para.(3))

3.32   This provision covers claimants, employed in employed earner's employment, who are not "engaged in remunerative work" and so not precluded from old style JSA. In short, it embraces those working but for less than 16 hours a week, who are statutorily obliged to give notice (i.e. those continuously employed for one month or more) (s.86 of the Employment Rights Act 1996 requires a minimum of one week's notice). Such persons are not required to be available to take up employment immediately, provided they are willing to and can do so immediately their statutory obligations permit. Should that occur during a permitted spell of non-availability under regs.7, 13 or 13A, they will not be ruled out by the "immediately" requirement, so long as they are willing and able to take up employment immediately that spell of non-availability ends (para.(4)).

The effect of para.(5)

In calculating the expiry of the 48-hour period allowed to carers and voluntary workers and also the 24-hour period allowed to other service providers (the groups embraced by paras (1) and (2)), there must be included any period of permitted non-availability under regs 7, 13 or 13A. See further the notes on those groups.
3.33

Employment of at least 40 hours per week

6.—(1) In order to be regarded as available for employment, a person must be willing and able to take up employment of at least 40 hours per week, unless he has restricted his availability in accordance with paragraph [[1](3), (3A) or (4)] of regulation [[2] 13, regulation 13A or] paragraph (2) of regulation 17 or two or more of those provisions.
3.34

(2) In order to be regarded as available for employment, a person must be willing and able to take up employment of less than 40 hours per week but not for a greater number of hours per week than the number for which he is available in accordance with paragraph [[1](3), (3A) or (4)] of regulation [[2]13, regulation 13A] or paragraph (2) of regulation 17 or two or more of those provisions.

AMENDMENTS

1. Social Security (Lone Parents and Miscellaneous Amendments) Regulations 2008 (SI 2008/3051) reg.11(3) (November 4, 2008).
2. Jobseeker's Allowance (Lone Parents) (Availability for Work) Regulations 2010 (SI 2010/837) reg.2(3) (April 26, 2010).

DEFINITIONS

"employment"—see reg.4.
"week"—*ibid.*

GENERAL NOTE

Under the previous regime of benefits for the unemployed, being available for part-time work only did not of itself necessarily preclude availability (*CU 109/48(KL); CU22/91*, paras 9 and 10). Under the old style Jobseekers Act 1995, the general rule is different. Section 6(1) states simply that someone is available for employment if willing and able to take up immediately *any* employed earner's employment. But that is subject to qualification and modification by regulations. This regulation stipulates that, normally, in order to be regarded as available for employment, a person must be willing and able to take up employment for a minimum of 40 hours per week (and see reg.7(1)), but also be willing to take up employment of less than 40 hours per week. In other words, being available merely for part-time employment (less than 40 hours per week) does not suffice, but to be available one must not only be available for full-time employment (40 or more hours per week) but be willing and able to accept part-time employment (less than 40 hours per week), if offered.
3.35

The general rule stated in this regulation is itself subject to exceptions for those in certain protected groups—those covered by reg.13(3), (3A) or (4), reg.13A or reg.17(2)—who are permitted to reduce their hours of availability to a level below 40 per week (e.g. to 26 because of caring responsibilities) and cannot be required to take up work for a number of hours below 40 but above that permitted level. The first protected group is the sick/disabled, who can impose *any* restrictions on availability which are reasonable in light of their physical or mental condition (reg.13(3)). Carers (the second protected group) can restrict their hours to between 16 and 40 per week, so long as they are available for as many hours as their caring responsibilities allow and for the specific hours those responsibilities permit so long as there are reasonable prospects of employment despite the restriction (reg.13(4)). A lone parent, who is both responsible for and a member of the same household as a child under 13, can restrict their availability to the child's normal school hours (reg.13A). Those in employment but currently kept on short time (defined in reg.4) (the fourth group) are treated as available for up to 13 weeks so long as they are willing and able to resume that employment (it is obviously beneficial for all concerned to aid their ultimate return to full-time working in that job) and are available for casual employment so that the total number of hours for which they work and are available for casual employment is at least 40 per week (reg.17).

For availability purposes, "week" means "benefit week": generally the period of seven days ending with the day corresponding to the claimant's "signing"/attendance day (regs 4 and 1(3)).

In *CJSA/1434/00*, Commissioner Bano held that reg.6 was not contrary to EC Council Directive 79/7 as indirectly discriminatory on grounds of sex.

Restriction of hours for which a person is available to 40 hours per week

3.36

7.—(1) Except as provided in [¹ regulations 13, 13A and 17(2)], a person may not restrict the total number of hours for which he is available for employment to less than 40 hours in any week.

(2) A person may restrict the total number of hours for which he is available for employment in any week to 40 hours or more providing—

(a) the times at which he is available to take up employment (his"pattern of availability") are such as to afford him reasonable prospects of securing employment;

(b) his pattern of availability is recorded in his jobseeker's agreement and any variations in that pattern are recorded in a varied agreement and

(c) his prospects of securing employment are not reduced considerably by the restriction imposed by his pattern of availability.

(3) A person who has restricted the total number of hours for which he is available in accordance with paragraph (2) and who is not available for employment, and is not to be treated as available for employment in accordance with regulation 14, for one day or more in a week in accordance with his pattern of availability shall not be regarded as available for employment even if he was available for employment for a total of 40 hours or more during that week.

AMENDMENT

1. Jobseeker's Allowance (Lone Parents) (Availability for Work) Regulations 2010 (SI 2010/837) reg.2(4) (April 26, 2010).

DEFINITIONS

"employment"—see reg.4.
"week"—*ibid.*

GENERAL NOTE

3.37

For availability purposes, "week" means "benefit week": generally the period of seven days ending with the day corresponding to the claimant's "signing"/attendance day (regs 4 and 1(3)).

Paragraph (1)

This paragraph reinforces the general rule, stated in reg.6(1), that, save for those   3.38
in the groups protected by regs.13 (the sick/disabled, carers), 13A (lone parents
responsible for a child under 13 in the same household) and 17(2) (those working
short time), in order to be available for employment, one must be willing and able
to take up employment of at least 40 hours per week: this paragraph stipulates that a
person not in a protected group may not restrict the total number of hours for which
he is available to less than 40 hours in any week.

Paragraph (2)

Section 6(1) of the old style Jobseekers Act 1995 stipulates that a person is avail-   3.39
able for employment if willing and able to take up immediately *any employed earner's
employment*. This paragraph qualifies the rigour of that by enabling claimants to set
a ceiling at or above 40 hours on the total number of hours, and on what days, for
which they are available in any week. This involves the claimant and an employment officer agreeing a "pattern of availability"—the times at which the claimant
is available to take up employment (sub-para.(a))—which must be recorded in
the jobseeker's agreement (sub-para.(b)). On the jobseeker's agreement, see old
style Jobseekers Act 1995 s.9. Any variation in that pattern must be agreed with an
employment officer and recorded in a varied agreement (on variation see old style
Jobseekers Act 1995 s.10). A ceiling on total hours of availability can only be set
in this way if the pattern of availability is such as to afford the claimant reasonable
prospects of securing employment and those prospects are not reduced considerably by the restriction imposed by the pattern of availability (sub-paras (a) and
(c)). The burden of establishing reasonable prospects of employment rests on the
claimant (reg.10(2)). In deciding that issue, regard must be had in particular to: the
claimant's skills, qualifications and experience; the type and number of vacancies
within daily travelling distance of their home; how long they have been unemployed;
what job applications they have made and their outcome (reg.10(1)(a)–(d)). If the
claimant also wishes to place restrictions on the nature of the employment they are
prepared to accept (under reg.8 or 13(2)), regard must also be had to whether they
are willing to move home to take up employment (reg.10(1)(e)).

To make proper sense, para.(2) needs to be read by looking at the whole of the
regulation (*R(JSA) 2/07*, para.12). "[R]egulation 7 covers cases of restrictions not
just on the total hours to be worked in a week or on the start and finish times on a
day, but also restrictions on the days of the week on which a claimant is available.
The phrase "the times at which he is available" in regulation 7(2)(a) has a broad
enough meaning to cover such cases. There is then also a neat fit with regulation
8, which deals with restrictions on the nature, terms and conditions or locality of
employment (para.13). Paragraph (2)(b) accordingly requires that to be available
the claimant must adhere in practice to the pattern of availability (either strictly
or by following an even less restrictive pattern) embodied in the jobseeker's agreement unless and until that agreement is varied pursuant to old style Jobseekers
Act 1995 s.10 (*ibid.*, para.14). So, in *R(JSA) 2/07*, the claimant who had agreed
to Saturday working in his jobseeker's agreement, but adopted an actual pattern
which excluded Saturday, was not protected by reg.7(2) and so was not available.
Claimants who are unhappy about the pattern proposed for the agreement have a
number of choices. First, they can refuse to sign and ask for the agreement to be
referred to the Secretary of State, hoping that the Secretary of State will agree with
them about its terms and will also backdate the agreement so that the claimant,
without benefit until the matter is decided, will not have lost but merely postponed
benefit. Alternatively, they can sign under protest and immediately seek a variation
of the agreement. But if they do so, they must, if they are to retain benefit pending
the variation adhere to the "agreed" pattern set out in the agreement.

In *CJSA 1279/98* and *R(JSA) 3/01* (considered in the notes to para.(3), below),
Commissioner Levenson, taking a "whole week" approach to this regulation (as
now endorsed by subsequent case law) seems to take the view that if the claimant

has not expressly restricted their hours to less than 40 hours per week they must be taken to have restricted them to 40 hours or more so that this paragraph and para. (3) interact, unless some other exception applies, so that non-availability even for one day in a week will preclude availability throughout the benefit week. It may even apply where others effect the restriction (e.g. the police taking the claimant into custody). In *R(JSA) 3/01*, however, the Commissioner held that the claimant was saved by reg.13(3): the restriction was reasonable in view of his physical condition (incarceration). That "saving" was rejected as erroneous in law by the Court of Appeal in *Secretary of State for Social Security v David* (reported in *R(JSA) 3/01*) (see notes to para.(3), below). *David* was applied in *CJSA/5944/99*, another case of someone detained in police custody. See further commentary to reg.14.

Paragraph (3)

3.40   This at first sight baffling provision stresses that claimants must ensure availability each week in accordance with their agreed pattern of availability; failure to be available on one or more days in a week in accordance with the agreed pattern will preclude entitlement even though the claimant was available for a total of 40 hours or more in that week unless, with respect to the day(s) of non-availability the claimant is protected by a "deemed availability" rule in reg.14. So, if a claimant with an agreed pattern of availability under para.(2) goes away on a holiday which includes one of their agreed days of availability without informing an employment officer and agreeing a revised pattern in accordance with para.(2), this paragraph precludes availability for the whole of that benefit week, despite the claimant's being available for 40 or more hours spread over the other days of that week (see also *DMG* 21231); similarly (until May 30, 2006) if the day of non-availability arose because the claimant was in custody. From that date, a degree of deemed availability is afforded those in police custody (reg.14(1)(s)).

But what of persons not available on a particular day(s) for similar reasons, but who do not have a para.(2) pattern of availability (e.g. because they are willing to do any job, for whatever hours at any time)? *DMG* 21233 advises decision-makers to treat them as not available throughout that week, despite their being available in the rest of the week for 40 hours or more, unless there has been a variation of the jobseeker's agreement, as discussed below (if action took them below 40 hours availability reg.6(1) would, of course, rule them non-available). That preclusion throughout the week clearly cannot be founded on para.(3) which only applies where a claimant "has *restricted* the total number of hours for which he is available *in accordance with paragraph (2)*" (emphasis supplied). Someone away on holiday may have de facto "restricted" their hours but, not having sought or obtained a revision of their jobseeker's agreement, has not done so "in accordance with paragraph (2)"; nor has someone in custody who might in any event not properly be regarded as having restricted their hours as opposed to having them restricted for them by the action of others which may or may not have been warranted. Clearly such claimants are not available on the particular days of non-availability (unless the day(s) can be brought within one of the situations of deemed availability in reg.14). Despite the degree of anomaly identified above and the doubts expressed in previous editions of what was then Vol.II of this series, the Departmental view appears to have been accepted. See the discussion in the notes to s.6(1) and in particular the decisions in *AT v SSWP (JSA)* [2013] UKUT 73 (AAC) and *R(JSA) 2/07*. Those decisions do, though, indicate a way out in certain circumstances through a variation, retrospective if necessary, of the jobseeker's agreement to render the claimant's restrictions in accord with para.(2).

Commissioner Levenson has considered the approach to reg.7 in two decisions. In *R(JSA) 3/01* he thought it clear that—

"there is no provision (other than for exceptions that do not apply in this case) to award jobseeker's allowance for parts of the week or to find that a claimant was available for employment during part of a week but not during the rest of the week. The claimant is either available for employment during a particular week or he is not so available". (para.4)

In consequence, as regards holidays, Commissioner Levenson has supported   3.41
the Department's approach. In *CJSA 1279/98*, the claimant's signing-on day was Tuesday, so that his benefit week ran from Wednesday to Tuesday. He went on holiday, having informed the Jobcentre, from Saturday to Saturday for one week, stating that in that period he would not be available for work. Commissioner Levenson upheld the finding that pursuant to paras (2) and (3) of this regulation, his non-availability even for one day in each of the benefit weeks meant he was not entitled to benefit in either of those weeks. Judge Rowland took the same approach in *AT*, which concerned the two benefit weeks ending on December 31, 2009 and January 7, 2010 and a London-based JSA claimant whose jobseeker's agreement contained no restrictions on days or times of availability. After the Jobcentre had closed on December 31 the claimant decided to go away on holiday to Yorkshire. Bad weather delayed his planned return to January 8, 2010, so that he missed signing on on January 7. The judge agreed that the claimant had not been available for the benefit week ending on January 7, but accepted the Secretary of State's submission that, as he had been available for all of the week down to the evening of December 31, his travelling to Yorkshire did not significantly affect his prospects of employment and that there should be a retrospective variation of his jobseeker's agreement to accord with the actual restriction on availability in that week. Accordingly, he could take advantage of reg.7(2) and was not disentitled for non-availability in that week. The claimant had also no doubt done enough in that week to satisfy the condition of actively seeking employment.

In *R(JSA) 3/01* the Commissioner dealt with someone in police custody for two days of his benefit week. He held that, even though someone else imposed the restrictions, that is the police, reg.13(3) protected the claimant from the preclusive effect of reg.7: the restriction (two days in police custody) was reasonable (indeed inevitable) in light of his physical condition which was such that he was not free, legally or practically to leave (para.6). On appeal, however, the Court of Appeal held that Commissioner Levenson had erred in law (*Secretary of State for Social Security v David*, reported in *R(JSA) 3/01*: see the notes to reg.13(3) below). Simon Brown LJ expressed some concerns about the justice of the result, saying in paras 25 and 26:

"The first of these relates to the jobseeker's agreement itself. Section 6 of the Act, as noted, requires the claimant to be willing and able to take up employment 'immediately'. That 'immediately' means within a very short space of time indeed is clear not only from the word itself but also from regulation 5 which provides for exceptions to this requirement in the case of those with caring responsibilities or engaged in voluntary work (who need only be willing and able to take up employment on 48 hours' notice) and certain others engaged in providing a service (who get 24 hours' notice). No doubt the requirement for immediate availability allows the claimant time to wash, dress and have his breakfast, but strictly it would seem inconsistent with, say, a claimant's stay overnight with a friend or relative, or attendance at a weekend cricket match, or even an evening at the cinema (unless perhaps he had left a contact number and had not travelled far).

In these circumstances, claimants ought clearly to be wary of entering into an agreement which offers unrestricted availability throughout the entire week, day and night, weekdays and weekends."

The judge was also concerned, particularly in view of the presumption of innocence, that mere detention by the police for some part of one day should lead to loss of entitlement to JSA for a whole benefit week and suggested that some amendment should be considered. Regulation 14(1)(s) now contains a deeming of availability in circumstances like those of *David*, limited to 96 hours.

Other restrictions on availability

3.42   **8.**—Subject to regulations 6, 7 and 9, any person may restrict his availability for employment by placing restrictions on the nature of the employment for which he is available, the terms or conditions of employment for which he is available (including the rate of remuneration) and the locality or localities within which he is available, providing he can show that he has reasonable prospects of securing employment notwithstanding those restrictions and any restrictions on his availability in accordance with regulations 7(2), [¹13(2), (3), (3A) or (4)][², 13A] or 17(2).

AMENDMENTS

1. Social Security (Lone Parents and Miscellaneous Amendments) Regulations 2008 (SI 2008/3051) reg.11(4) (November 4, 2008).
2. Jobseeker's Allowance (Lone Parents) (Availability for Work) Regulations 2010 (SI 2010/837) reg.2(5) (April 26, 2010).

DEFINITION

"employment"—see reg.4.

GENERAL NOTE

3.43   Section 6(1) of the old style Jobseekers Act 1995 states that a claimant is available for employment if he is willing and able to take up immediately *any employed earner's employment*. This regulation mitigates the rigour of that by enabling claimants to restrict their availability by placing restrictions on the nature of the employment for which they are available, on its terms and conditions (including rate of remuneration) and on the locality or localities within which they are available. The regulation is subject to regs 6, 7 and 9, so the apparent width of this regulation cannot be used to circumvent the limitations imposed by those regulations. That means that claimants cannot under this regulation restrict hours of work to below 40 (reg.6), the pattern of availability (the times at which he is available to take up employment) must conform to the criteria in reg.7, and no remuneration restrictions are permissible after six months from the date of claim (reg.9). Moreover, restrictions are only allowable under this regulation to claimants who can establish that they have reasonable prospects of securing employment despite these restrictions and any other restrictions imposed under other availability regulations (namely, regs 7(2), 13(2), (3) or (4), 13A and 17(2)). Regulation 10(2) emphasises that the burden of establishing this lies on the claimant. In determining whether they have reasonable prospects of employment, regard must be had in particular to: their skills, qualifications and experience; the type and number of vacancies within daily travelling distance of their home; how long they have been unemployed; what job applications they have made and their outcome (reg.10(1)(a)–(d)). If the restrictions include ones on the nature of the employment claimants are prepared to accept (both regs 8 and 13(2) enable such restrictions), regard must also be had to whether they are willing to move home to take up employment (reg.10(1)(e)). Note that the standard is "reasonable prospects" of employment, not the higher standard of "good prospects" (see Commissioner Levenson in *CJSA/4435/1998*).

Note that claimants who are allowed by some of the provisions of reg.13 to impose restrictions on the nature of the employment for which they are available (in particular where the restrictions are reasonable in the light of the claimant's physical or mental condition: reg.13(3); and where a person with caring responsibilities for a child is subject to a parenting order or a parenting contract: reg.13(3A)) do not have to meet the condition of having reasonable prospects of employment subject to those restrictions to take the benefit of reg.13. Nor does a lone parent responsible for a child under the age of 13 who is allowed by reg.13A to restrict availability to that child's normal school hours. The reasonable prospects condition is built in to reg.13(2) (religious belief or conscientious objection) and (4) (caring responsibilities and available for less than 40 hours but at least 16 per week). Note also the categories of deemed availability in regs 14 and 14A and 16–17B and the special rules about what availability means in reg.5.

No restrictions on pay after six months

9.—After the expiry of the six month period beginning with the date of claim, a person may not restrict his availability for employment by placing restrictions on the level of remuneration in employment for which he is available.

3.44

DEFINITIONS

"date of claim"—see reg.1(3).
"employment"—see reg.4.

GENERAL NOTE

Regulation 8 (and possibly reg.13(3)) allow restrictions as to remuneration in the employment for which a claimant is available. This regulation stipulates that restrictions on the level of remuneration in the employment for which a claimant is available are allowable, if at all, only for maximum of six months beginning with the date the claim for old style JSA is made or treated as made (see reg.6 of the Social Security (Claims and Payments) Regulations 1987).

3.45

Reasonable prospects of employment

10.—(1) For the purposes of regulations 7 and 8 and paragraphs (2) and (4) of regulation 13, in deciding whether a person has reasonable prospects of securing employment, regard shall be had, in particular, to the following matters—
  (a) his skills, qualifications and experience;
  (b) the type and number of vacancies within daily travelling distance from his home;
  (c) the length of time for which he has been unemployed;
  (d) the job applications which he has made and their outcome;
  (e) if he wishes to place restrictions on the nature of the employment for which he is available, whether he is willing to move home to take up employment.
  (2) It shall be for the claimant to show that he has reasonable prospects of securing employment if he wishes to restrict his availability in accordance with regulation 7 or 8 or paragraph (2) or (4) of regulation 13.

3.46

DEFINITION

"employment"—see reg.4.

GENERAL NOTE

A number of regulations enabling claimants to restrict their availability make the permissibility of restrictions depend on whether, despite all the restrictions they impose, they have reasonable prospects of securing employment (see regs 7, 8, 13(2), (4)). Paragraph (2) of this regulation places on the claimant the burden of showing that such is the case. Paragraph (1) of this regulation requires that in deciding the matter of "reasonable prospects", regard must be had *in particular* (the list is thus not exhaustive) to: the claimant's skills, qualifications and experience;

3.47

the type and number of vacancies within daily travelling distance of their home; how long they have been unemployed; what job applications they have made and their outcome (sub-paras (a)–(d)). If the restrictions include ones on the nature of the employment they are prepared to accept (both regs 8 and 13(2) enable such restrictions), regard must also be had to whether they are willing to move home to take up employment (sub-para.(e)). Note that the standard is "reasonable prospects" of employment, not the higher standard of "good prospects" (see Commissioner Levenson in *CJSA/4435/1998*).

Part-time students

3.48   **11.**—(1) If in any week a person is a part-time student and—
  (a) he falls within paragraph (2)
  (b) he has restricted the total number of hours for which he is available in accordance with regulation 7(2), [¹ [⁵ 13(3), (3A) or (4)]] [⁶, 13A] or 17(2); and
  (c) the hours of his course of study fall in whole or in part within his pattern of availability,
in determining whether he is available for employment no matter relating to his course of study shall be relevant providing he is willing and able to re-arrange the hours of his course in order to take up employment at times falling within his pattern of availability, to take up such employment immediately or, if he falls within paragraph [⁵ (1), (1A), (2) or (3)] of regulation 5, at the time specified in that paragraph and providing he complies with the requirements of regulation 6.
  (2) A person falls within this paragraph if—
  (a) for a continuous period of not less than 3 months falling immediately before the date on which he first attended the course of study he was in receipt of jobseeker's allowance[⁴, incapacity benefit or employment and support allowance] or was on a course of training or he was in receipt of income support and he fell within paragraph 7 of Schedule 1B to the Income Support Regulations or
  (b) during the period of 6 months falling immediately before the date on which he first attended the course of study he was—
      (i) for a period, or periods in the aggregate, of not less than 3 months in receipt of jobseeker's allowance[⁴, incapacity benefit or employment and support allowance] or on a course of training or he was in receipt of income support and he fell within paragraph 7 of Schedule 1B to the Income Support Regulations and
      (ii) after the period referred to in (i), or in the case of periods in the aggregate, after the first such period and throughout the remainder of the 6 months for which that sub-paragraph did not apply to him, engaged in remunerative work or other work the emoluments of which are such as to disentitle him from receipt of jobseeker's allowance[⁴, incapacity benefit or employment and support allowance] or from receipt of income support which would have been payable because he fell within paragraph 7 of Schedule 1B to the Income Support Regulations
      and the period of 3 months referred to in sub-paragraph (i) or, as the case may be, the period of 6 months referred to in sub-paragraph (ii), fell wholly after the terminal date.
  (3) In this regulation, "training" means training for which persons aged

under 18 are eligible and for which persons aged 18 to 24 may be eligible [³ secured in England and Wales by the Learning and Skills Council for England or by the National Council for Education and Training for Wales, and in Scotland, provided] directly or indirectly by a Local Enterprise Company pursuant to its arrangement with, as the case may be, Scottish Enterprise or Highlands and Islands Enterprise (whether that arrangement is known as an Operating Contract or by any other name).

AMENDMENTS

1. Jobseeker's Allowance and Income Support (General) (Amendment) Regulations 1996 (SI 1996/1517) reg.3 (October 7, 1996).

2. Jobseeker's Allowance (Amendment) (No.2) Regulations 1999 (SI 1999/3087) reg.2 (November 30, 1999).

3. Jobseeker's Allowance (Amendment) Regulations 2001 (SI 2001/1434) reg.2(3) (March 26, 2001).

4. Employment and Support Allowance (Consequential Provisions) (No.2) Regulations 2008 (SI 2008/1554) reg.3(3) (October 27, 2008).

5. Social Security (Lone Parents and Miscellaneous Amendments) Regulations 2008 (SI 2008/3051) reg.11(5) (November 24, 2008).

6. Jobseeker's Allowance (Lone Parents) (Availability for Work) Regulations 2010 (SI 2010/837) reg.2(6) (April 26, 2010).

DEFINITIONS

"course of study"—see reg.1(3).
"employment"—see reg.4.
"Income Support Regulations"—see reg.1(3).
"part-time student"—see reg.1(3).
"pattern of availability"—see regs 4 and 7(2)(a).
"terminal date"—see reg.1(3).
"week"—see reg.4.

GENERAL NOTE

The effect of this provision, broadly, is to disregard part-time students' course of study when deciding whether they are available for employment, as long as they are prepared and able to re-arrange the hours of the course in order to take up employment, to start work immediately, or on notice if reg.5(1), (1A), (2) or (3) applies, and they comply with reg.6. However, it only applies to part-time students who satisfy the conditions in para.(2) and who have restricted the hours for which they are available under regs 7(2), 13(3), (3A) or (4), 13A or 17(2). Note that if a part-time student's hours of study fall completely outside the times they have agreed to be available for work they will not need to rely on this provision as their availability will not be affected.

A part-time student is a person who is undertaking a course of study who is not a full-time student (reg.1(3)). See reg.1(3) for the definitions of "full-time student" and "course of study" and the notes to reg.130.

This regulation does not apply to a person in relevant education (defined in reg.54(1) and (2); see the notes to reg.54) because such a person is excluded from old style JSA (s.1(2)(g) of the old style Jobseekers Act 1995). But note that under reg.54(3) a young person (i.e. under 19: reg.76) who is a part-time student on a course other than one of advanced education or of a kind within para.(b) of the definition of full-time student in reg.1(3) and who satisfies para.(2) of this regulation does not count as in relevant education (and will not do so after he finishes or leaves his part-time course (reg.54(4))). Thus para.(1) may apply to such a young person.

3.49

A part-time student (except a person whose course does not conflict with their permitted pattern of availability) who does not satisfy the conditions in this regulation will probably not be treated as available unless prepared to abandon the course in order to take up employment. But note reg.17A, in force from June 1, 1998, under which a claimant aged 25 or over may be able to attend a full-time employment-related course while continuing to receive old style JSA, and the more limited deeming of availability in reg.14(1)(a), (aa) and (f).

Paragraph (2)

3.50 The main condition (sub-para.(a)) is that for the whole three months immediately before the course the claimant was either in receipt of JSA, incapacity benefit, ESA or income support while sick or on Work Based Training for Young People (see the definition of training in para.(3)). Receipt of benefit means entitlement to benefit, whether benefit is actually in payment or not (*R(SB) 12/87*). The intention is that the claimant should be primarily unemployed and not simply wishing to continue to study on benefit. A person who leaves school in the summer will not be entitled to old style JSA until the first Monday in September (see reg.54(2)) and thus will not have had three months on benefit in time to start a course before January.

The three months (or the six months in sub-para.(b), see below) cannot begin until after the "terminal date", that is, after the person has ceased to be treated as in relevant education. If the claimant starts (say in September) a course whose contact hours are below 12, so as to be outside the definition of relevant education (see the notes to reg.54), and after three months on benefit increases the hours, it may be difficult to decide when the claimant first attended "the" course. The official view in the previous edition of the *Adjudication Officer's Guide* (para.25529) (in relation to the 21-hour rule in the former reg.9 of the Income Support Regulations, see J. Mesher and P. Wood, *Income-Related Benefits: The Legislation* (1996)) was that a mere change in hours did not mean that a new course was starting, so that the three months' benefit would have been at the wrong time, but that if the subjects taken had changed there would have been a new course.

Under sub-para.(b) a claimant can mix receipt of a relevant benefit, Work Based Training and work over the six months, provided that the relevant benefit and the Work Based Training add up to at least three months.

3.51 *The transition from new style JSA*

In para.(2)(a) the reference to jobseeker's allowance is, where art.13(1) and (2) of the Welfare Reform Act 2012 (Commencement No.9 and Transitional and Transitory Provisions and Commencement No.8 and Savings and Transitional Provisions (Amendment)) Order 2013 (as amended and set out in Pt V of this volume) applies, to be read as if it included a reference to new style JSA (art.13(3) (za) of that Order, in force from June 16, 2014).

Volunteers

3.52 [¹ **12.**—(1) Paragraph (2) applies if in any week a person is engaged in voluntary work and—

(a) he has restricted the total number of hours for which he is available in accordance with regulation 7(2),[² 13(3), (3A) or (4)][³, 13A] or 17(2); and

(b) the hours in which he is engaged in voluntary work fall in whole or in part within his pattern of availability.

(2) In determining whether a person to whom this paragraph applies is available for employment no matter relating to his voluntary work shall be relevant providing—

(a) on being given one week's notice, he is willing and able to re-arrange the hours in which he is engaged in voluntary work in order to take up employment at times falling within his pattern of availability; and

(b) on being given 48 hours' notice, he is willing and able to re-arrange the hours in which he is engaged in voluntary work in order to attend for interview at times falling within his pattern of availability in connection with the opportunity of any such employment; and

(c) he complies with the requirements of regulation 6.

(3) In paragraph (2) "week" means any period of seven consecutive days.]

AMENDMENTS

1. Jobseeker's Allowance (Amendment) Regulations 2002 (SI 2002/3072) reg.4 (January 1, 2003).

2. Social Security (Lone Parents and Miscellaneous Amendments) Regulations 2008 (SI 2008/3051) reg.11(6) (November 4, 2008).

3. Jobseeker's Allowance (Lone Parents) (Availability for Work) Regulations 2010 (SI 2010/837) reg.2(7) (April 26, 2010).

DEFINITIONS

"employment"—see reg.4.
"pattern of availability"—*ibid.*, and reg.7(2)(a).
"voluntary work"—see reg.4.

GENERAL NOTE

Section 6(1) of the old style Jobseekers Act 1995 stipulates that a claimant is available for employment if willing and able to take up *immediately* any employed earner's employment. This regulation mitigates the rigour of that section as regards determining the availability of a claimant engaged in voluntary work (defined below).   3.53

If claimants have restricted their hours of availability under regs.7(2), 13(3) or (4), 13A or 17(2), any voluntary work (defined in reg.4) that they do which coincides with the times they have agreed to be available for work will be disregarded when deciding whether they are available for work, as long as they are prepared and able, on one week's notice (meaning any seven days: para.(3)), to re-arrange the hours in which they are engaged in voluntary work in order to take up employment at times falling within their pattern of availability, and, on 48 hours' notice, to re-arrange the hours in which they are engaged in voluntary work in order to attend for interview at times falling within their pattern of availability in connection with the opportunity of any such employment. They must, however, comply with reg.6. If a person's voluntary work falls outside the hours of agreed availability this regulation does not apply as availability will not be affected.

See also reg.5(1)(b) under which a person doing voluntary work only has to be available to take up employment on one week's notice and to attend for interview for such employment on 48 hours' notice.

Claimants are engaged in voluntary work when working for an organisation the activities of which are carried on otherwise than for profit, or for someone other than a member of their family, where they receive no payment by virtue of such engagement or the only payment due for it is one in respect of their reasonable expenses of such engagement (reg.4). For availability purposes, "week" means "benefit week": generally the period of seven days ending with the day corresponding to the claimant's "signing"/attendance day (regs 4 and 1(3)).   3.54

Note also that reg.18(3)(g) requires time engaged in voluntary work and the extent to which it may have improved prospects of employment to be taken into account in determining for the purposes of the actively seeking employment test whether a claimant has taken all reasonably expected steps to have the best prospects of securing employment.

Additional restrictions on availability for certain groups

3.55   **13.**—(1) In any week a person may restrict his availability for employment in the following ways, if the circumstances set out apply.

(2) Subject to regulations 6, 7 and 9, a person may impose restrictions on the nature of the employment for which he is available by reason of a sincerely held religious belief, or a sincerely held conscientious objection providing he can show that he has reasonable prospects of employment notwithstanding those restrictions and any restrictions on his availability in accordance with regulation 7(2), 8, paragraph [¹(3), (3A) or (4)] of this regulation[², regulation 13A or] or regulation 17(1) or (2).

(3) A person may restrict his availability in any way providing the restrictions are reasonable in the light of his physical or mental condition.

[¹ (3A) A person who has caring responsibilities in relation to a child and who—

(a) is the subject of a parenting order concerning that child under section 8 of the Crime and Disorder Act 1998, section 20 of the Anti-social Behaviour Act 2003("the 2003 Act") [³or Chapter 4 of Part 11 of the Sentencing Code], or in relation to Scotland, under section 102 of the Antisocial Behaviour etc. (Scotland) Act 2004, or

(b) has entered into a parenting contract concerning that child under section 19 of the 2003 Act,

may restrict his availability in any way providing the restrictions are reasonable in the light of the terms of the order or contract.]

(4) A person with caring responsibilities may restrict the total number of hours for which he is available for employment to less than 40 hours in any week providing—

(a) in that week he is available for employment for as many hours as his caring responsibilities allow and for the specific hours that those responsibilities allow and

(b) he has reasonable prospects of securing employment notwithstanding that restriction and

(c) he is available for employment of at least 16 hours in that week.

(5) In deciding whether a person satisfies the conditions in paragraph (4)(a), regard shall be had, in particular, to the following matters—

(a) the particular hours and days spent in caring;

(b) whether the caring responsibilities are shared with another person;

(c) the age and physical and mental condition of the person being cared for.

[¹(6) This paragraph applies to a person who has caring responsibilities in relation to a child if an employment officer determines that, due to the type and number of employment vacancies within daily travelling distance of the person's home, he would not satisfy the condition in paragraph (4)(b).

(7) Paragraph (4) has effect in relation to a person to whom paragraph (6) applies as if sub-paragraph (b) were omitted.]

AMENDMENTS

1. Social Security (Lone Parents and Miscellaneous Amendments) Regulations 2008 (SI 2008/3051) reg.11(7) (November 4, 2008).
2. Jobseeker's Allowance (Lone Parents) (Availability for Work) Regulations 2010 (SI 2010/837) reg.2(8) (April 26, 2010).
3. Sentencing Act 2020 Sch.24 para.318 (December 1, 2020).

DEFINITIONS

"caring responsibilities"—see reg.4.
"child"—see Jobseekers Act 1995 s.35(1).
"employment"—see reg.4.
"employment officer"—see Jobseekers Act 1995 s.35(1).
"the Sentencing Code"—see Interpretation Act 1978 Sch.1 and Sentencing Act 2020 s.1(1).
"week"—see reg.4.

GENERAL NOTE

Section 6(1) of the old style Jobseekers Act 1995 stipulates that a claimant   3.56
is available for employment if he is willing and able to take up immediately *any employed earner's employment*. This regulation mitigates the rigour of that by enabling certain claimants to impose restrictions on availability without thereby precluding entitlement to old style JSA. For availability purposes, "week" means "benefit week": generally the period of seven days ending with the day corresponding to the claimant's "signing"/attendance day (regs 4 and 1(3)).

Paragraph (1)
This makes clear that in any week a claimant may be able to impose restrictions   3.57
under more than one of the other paragraphs in this regulation; this paragraph reads "may restrict his availability for employment in the following *ways*" (emphasis added by annotator).

Paragraph (2)
Claimants complying with the dictates of regs 6, 7 and 9 can impose restric-   3.58
tions on the nature of the employment for which they are available because of a sincerely held religious belief or conscientious objection, so long as they can show that they have reasonable prospects of employment despite those and any other restrictions imposed under other availability regulations (namely, regs 7(2); 8, paras (3) and (4) of this regulation, reg.13A and regs 17(1) and (2)). Regulation 10(2) provides that the burden of establishing this proviso lies on the claimant. In determining whether they have reasonable prospects of employment, regard must be had in particular to: their skills, qualifications and experience; the type and number of vacancies within daily travelling distance of their home; how long they have been unemployed; what job applications they have made and their outcome (reg.10(1)(a)–(d)). Since the restrictions include ones on the nature of the employment they are prepared to accept, regard must also be had to whether they are willing to move home to take up employment (reg.10(1)(e)).
The restrictions themselves do not need to be reasonable provided that they stem from a religious belief or a conscientious objection that is sincerely held. There is obviously a good deal of judgment involved in identifying what is a conscientious objection. But no doubt it must be founded on some coherent and serious belief as to some substantial aspect of human life or behaviour and not be incompatible with human dignity or the fundamental rights of others.

Paragraph (3)
This provides protection for the sick/disabled: those who are in some way phys-   3.59
ically or mentally affected and who are unable or unwilling (especially in the light of

regs 55, 55ZA and 55A allowing an old style JSA claimant to be treated as capable of work or as not having limited capability for work during short and shortish periods of actual inability to work) to claim ESA. Where and for so long as any of regs 55, 55ZA or 55A apply a claimant is deemed by reg.14(1)(l) to be available for employment and by reg.19(1)(l), (lzl) or (ll), as the case may be, to be actively seeking employment. Thus for those periods what restrictions are permissible under reg.13(3) is less important, although it appears that any restrictions should still be recorded in the claimant's jobseeker's agreement (reg.31(c)) as well as the general pattern of availability. Regulation 13(3) becomes more important where the deeming mentioned above does not apply and provides a general protection to take reasonable account of the particular nature of the claimant's physical or mental condition. Regard must also be had to a claimant's physical or mental limitations when determining under the actively seeking employment condition whether all reasonably expected steps have been taken to secure employment (reg.18(3)(b)).

Under this paragraph, claimants can restrict their availability *in any way*. This can therefore include restrictions on the rate of pay acceptable as well as on the nature or location of employment, terms and conditions, hours and days of availability etc. The essential test is that such restrictions are reasonable in light of their physical or mental condition. If all the restrictions imposed can be so justified, no issue of "reasonable prospects of employment" arises. If, however, restrictions are imposed which require justification under certain other provisions (regs 7, 8 or para.(2) of this regulation), then claimants have to show that they have reasonable prospects of employment despite the totality of restrictions imposed (including those justified under this paragraph). In such a case, reg.10(2) requires that the burden of establishing this lies on the claimant. In determining whether they have reasonable prospects of employment, regard must be had in particular to: their skills, qualifications and experience; the type and number of vacancies within daily travelling distance of their home; how long they have been unemployed; what job applications they have made and their outcome (reg.10(1)(a)–(d)). If the restrictions include ones on the nature of the employment they are prepared to accept (this and regs 8 and 13(2) enable such restrictions), regard must also be had to whether they are willing to move home to take up employment (reg.10(1)(e)). If, however, the only other restrictions imposed are those as a carer on hours and pattern of availability justifiable under para.(4), the reasonable prospects issue focuses only on the restrictions imposed under that paragraph. Note that, in contrast to para.(4), this paragraph sets no minimum on hours of availability; the touchstone is reasonableness in light of physical or mental condition.

This provision is potentially quite wide. It permits *any* restrictions on availability that are reasonable because of the claimant's physical or mental condition. Indeed, in *R(JSA) 3/01*, Commissioner Levenson held that, even though someone else imposed the restrictions, that is the police, reg.13(3) protected the claimant from the preclusive effect of reg.7: the restriction (two days in police custody) was reasonable (indeed inevitable) in light of his physical condition which was such that he was not free, legally or practically, to leave (para.6). On appeal, however, the Court of Appeal held that Commisioner Levenson had erred in law (*Secretary of State for Social Security v David*, reported in *R(JSA) 3/01*). Simon Brown LJ said:

"In short, the Commissioner took the view, first that the expression in regulation 13(3) 'physical or mental condition' is apt to refer not only to some disability on the claimant's part but also to any extraneous physical constraints that may be placed upon him; and second that it is unnecessary under this regulation for the claimant himself to have invoked his 'condition' so as to justify restricting his availability in advance of the week in question; rather the claimant's non-availability can retrospectively be overlooked under this provision.

I have to say that to my mind both limbs of this construction are impossible. The reference to the claimant's 'physical or mental condition' seems to me clearly confined to some personal disability. And it seems to me no less clear that the provision applies prospectively only and specifically with regard to the completion of the jobseeker's agreement. That this is so is surely demonstrated also by regulation 55 which deals with short periods of sickness ... .

On the Commissioner's approach there would be no need for regulation 55: such a person could instead invoke regulation 13(3) and, notwithstanding his jobseeker's agreement, assert that his availability was restricted by his temporary physical incapacity.

It follows that in my judgment the Commissioner was wrong in his decision and that, so far from resolving the appeal in favour of the claimant (who had not appealed), he should have decided it in favour of the adjudication officer (who had)". (paras 19–22 of the judgment)

Note that para.(3) is not made subject to any other provisions. Thus, for example, although restrictions on the rate of pay may only be imposed for six months under reg.9, it is apparently accepted that restrictions under para.(3) can include limits on the rate of pay the claimant will accept *after* six months, as long as the restriction is reasonable in the light of his condition, e.g. because of additional transport costs (see *Welfare Rights Bulletin* 138, p.4).

Paragraph (3A)

Since November 24, 2008, carers with responsibilities for caring for a child, who are subject in respect of that child to parenting orders under the anti-social behaviour legislation, or who have entered in respect of that child into a parenting contract under that legislation, can restrict availability in any way so long as the restrictions are reasonable in the light of the terms of that order or contract.   **3.60**

Paragraphs (4) and (5)

These paragraphs provide assistance to claimants who are carers ("a person with caring responsibilities", discussed below), enabling them to restrict their total hours of availability in any week to below 40 hours but not less than 16 hours per week, provided that in that week they are available for employment for as many hours as their caring responsibilities permit and for the specific hours they allow, and provided that they have reasonable prospects of employment notwithstanding that restriction (para.(4)). In determining whether in any week they are available for as many hours as their caring responsibilities allow and for the specific hours they allow ("the conditions in paragraph (4)(a)"), regard must be had, in particular (the list is not exhaustive), to: the particular hours and days spent in caring; whether the caring responsibilities are shared with someone else; and the age, physical and mental condition of the person being cared for by the claimant (para.(5)). In determining whether they have reasonable prospects of employment (and the burden of establishing this lies on the claimant: reg.10(2)), regard must be had in particular to: their skills, qualifications and experience; the type and number of vacancies within daily travelling distance of their home; how long they have been unemployed; what job applications they have made and their outcome (reg.10(1)(a)–(d)). If the claimants have placed other restrictions on their availability under regs 7, 8 or para.(2) of this regulation, the matter of "reasonable prospects" must be looked at in the context of the totality of restrictions imposed, although that flows from those other provisions rather than this. If those restrictions include ones on the nature of the employment they are prepared to accept (reg.8 and para.(2) of this regulation enable such restrictions), regard must also be had to whether they are willing to move home to take up employment (reg.10(1)(e)). If, however, the only restrictions imposed apart from those under para.(4) are ones justified under para.(3) of this regulation (reasonable in light of physical or mental condition), the "reasonable prospects" issue would fall to be decided only with regard to the total hours and pattern of availability restrictions imposed under para.(4).   **3.61**

A carer (a person "who has caring responsibilities") is someone who has responsibility for caring for a child or for an elderly person or for a person whose physical or mental condition requires them to be cared for. But the child, the elderly person and the person whose conditions requires being cared for must either be a close relative or in the same household (reg.4). "Close relative" means a spouse, civil partner or other member of a couple, parent, step-parent, grandparent, parent-in-law, son, step-son, son-in-law, daughter, step-daughter, daughter-in-law, brother, sister, grandchild or the spouse of any of these persons or, if that person is one of a couple, the other member of that couple (*ibid.*). On "couple", see the notes to reg.2(1) of the Income Support Regulations.

[¹ Additional restrictions on availability for lone parents

3.62   **13A.**—A lone parent who in any week is responsible for, and a member of the same household as, a child under the age of 13 may restrict his availability for employment to the child's normal school hours.]

Amendment

1. Jobseeker's Allowance (Lone Parents) (Availability for Work) Regulations 2010 (SI 2010/837) reg.2(9) (April 26, 2010).

Definitions

"lone parent"—see reg.1(3).
"week"—see reg.4.

General note

3.63   From April 26, 2010, this allows a lone parent, who in any week is both responsible for (see regs 77 and 78) and a member of the same household as a child under 13, to restrict their hours of availability to that child's normal school hours, without any added condition as to reasonable prospects of employment. Note the deemed availability under reg.17B for certain lone parents of children aged five who are not required to be in full-time education.

Circumstances in which a person is to be treated as available

3.64   **14.**—(1) A person [¹⁶. . .] shall be treated as available for employment in the following circumstances for as long as those circumstances apply, subject to any maximum period specified in this paragraph—

    (a) notwithstanding regulation [⁸15(1)(a)], if he is participating as a full-time student in an employment-related course where participation by him has been approved before the course started by an employment officer, for a maximum of 2 weeks and one such course in any period of 12 months;

[¹⁶(aa) notwithstanding regulation 15(1)(a), if he is participating in a traineeship;]

    (b) if he is attending a residential work camp, for a maximum of 2 weeks and one such occasion in any period of 12 months;

    (c) if he is temporarily absent from Great Britain because he is taking a member of his family who is a child or young person abroad for treatment, for a maximum of 8 weeks;

    (d) if he is engaged in the manning or launching of a lifeboat or in the performance of duty as a part-time member of a fire brigade or engaged during an emergency in duties for the benefit of others;

    (e) if he is a member of a couple and is looking after a member of his family who is a child while the other member is temporarily absent from the United Kingdom, for a maximum of 8 weeks;

(f) if he is following an Open University course and is attending, as a requirement of that course, a residential course, for a maximum of one week per course;

(g) if he is temporarily looking after a child full-time because the person who normally looks after the child is ill or temporarily absent from home or the person is looking after a member of the family who is ill, for a maximum of 8 weeks;

(h) if he has been discharged from detention in a prison, remand centre or youth custody institution [¹²and he is not given notice to participate in [¹³a scheme prescribed in regulation 3 of the Jobseeker's Allowance (Schemes for Assisting Persons to Obtain Employment) Regulations 2013]], for one week commencing with the date of his discharge;

[²(i) if the period beginning on the date of claim and ending on the day before the beginning of the first week after the date of claim is less than 7 days and the circumstances in paragraph (2A) apply, for any part of that period when he is not treated as available for employment under any other provision of this regulation;]

[¹(j) if the award is terminated other than on the last day of a week, for the period beginning with the beginning of the week in which the award is terminated and ending on the day on which the award is terminated;]

(k) notwithstanding regulation [⁸15(1)(a)], if he is participating in a programme provided by the Venture Trust in pursuance of an arrangement made by [⁷ the Scottish Ministers], for a maximum of 4 weeks and one such programme in any period of 12 months;

(l) if he is treated as capable of work [¹⁰or as not having limited capability for work] in accordance with regulation 55, [¹⁷55ZA or 55A], for the period determined in accordance with that regulation;

[⁵(ll) [¹⁷···]

(m) if he is temporarily absent from Great Britain to attend an interview for employment and has given notice to an employment officer, in writing if so required by the employment officer, that he will be so absent for a maximum of one week;

(n) if he is a member of a couple [⁴ other than a joint-claim couple] and he and his partner are both absent from Great Britain and a premium referred to in paragraph 10, 11, 12, 13 or 15 of Schedule 1 (applicable amounts) is applicable in respect of his partner, for a maximum of 4 weeks.

[⁴(nn) if he is a member of a joint-claim couple and he and his partner are both absent from Great Britain and a premium referred to in paragraph 20E, 20F, 20G or 20I of Schedule 1 (applicable amounts) is applicable in respect of his partner, for a maximum of 4 weeks;]

[³(o) if—
  (i) he is available for employment, or is treated as such, on the day he makes his claim for a jobseeker's allowance; and
  (ii) the Secretary of State has directed that the prescribed time for claiming a jobseeker's allowance be extended under regulation 19(6) of the Claims and Payments Regulations where the circumstances specified in regulation 19(7)(d) of those Regulations applied in relation to an entitlement to incapacity

benefit[[10], employment and support allowance] or an entitlement to income support by virtue of paragraph 7 of Schedule
1B to the Income Support Regulations,
for the period of that extension.]

[[4](p) if he is temporarily absent from Great Britain in the circumstances
prescribed in regulation 50(6B)(a) or (c) for the period of any such
temporary absence.]

[[5](q) if he is temporarily absent from Great Britain in the circumstances
prescribed in regulation 50(6AA) or, as the case may be, (6C).]

[[6](r) if he is required to attend a court or tribunal as a justice of the peace,
a party to any proceedings, a witness or a juror;

  (s) if, for a maximum of 96 hours before being released, he is in—

    (i) police detention within the meaning in section 118(2) of the
Police and Criminal Evidence Act 1984 (general interpretation),
or

    (ii) legal custody within the meaning in section 295 of the Criminal
Procedure (Scotland) Act 1995 (legal custody in Scotland) but
is not a prisoner as defined by regulation 85(4) (special cases).]

[[9](t) he is looking after a child for whom he has caring responsibilities
during the child's school holidays or another similar vacation period
and it would be unreasonable for him to make other arrangements
for the care of that child;

  (u) he is looking after a child for whom he has caring responsibilities at
a time when the child—

    (i) is excluded from school or another educational establishment,
and

    (ii) is not receiving education pursuant to arrangements made by a
local education authority or (in Scotland) an education authority, and

there are no other arrangements for the care of that child it would be
reasonable for him to make.]

[[18](v) if he is a member of a reserve force prescribed in Part I of Schedule
6 to the Contributions Regulations, either—

    (i) if he is engaged in his first year of training, for a maximum of
43 days in that year; or

    (ii) if he is engaged in annual continuous training, for a maximum
of 15 days in any calendar year.]

(2) [[9]Subject to [[14]paragraphs (2ZB), (2ZC) and (2ZD)] a person [[16]. . .]
shall be treated as available for employment in the following circumstances—

  (a) if there is a death or serious illness of a close relative or close friend
of his;

  (b) if there is a domestic emergency affecting him or a close relative or
close friend of his;

  (c) if there is a funeral of a close relative or close friend of his;

  (d) if he has caring responsibilities and the person being cared for has
died;

for the time required to deal with the emergency or other circumstance
and for a maximum of one week on the occurrence of any of the circumstances set out in sub-paragraphs (a) to (d), or any combination of those
circumstances, and on no more than 4 such periods in any period of 12
months.

[⁹(2ZA) A person who has caring responsibilities in relation to a child may be treated as available for employment for more than one week, but for no more than 8 weeks, on the occurrence of any of the circumstances set out in paragraph (2)(a) or (b), or any combination of those circumstances, but on no more than one occasion in any period of 12 months.

(2ZB) Where a claimant has been treated as available for employment under paragraph (2ZA) in any period of 12 months, the first week in which he is so treated shall count towards the 4 periods allowable under paragraph (2).]

[¹⁵(2ZC) A person who has recently become homeless shall be treated as available for employment under paragraph (2)(b) only where he takes such steps as are reasonable for him to take to find living accommodation.

(2ZD) A person to whom paragraph (2ZC) applies may be treated as available for employment under paragraph (2)(b) for periods of longer than one week and on more than 4 occasions in any 12 months.]

[²(2A) A person shall be treated as available for employment under paragraph (1)(i) only if—

(a) where a pattern of availability is recorded in his jobseeker's agreement, or where he has restricted the hours for which he is available in accordance with regulations [⁹ 13(3), (3A) or (4)] [¹¹, 13A] or 17(2) and that restriction has been agreed with an employment officer, he is available for employment during such of the period referred to in paragraph (1)(i) as he is not treated as available for employment under any other provision of this regulation, in accordance with—

    (i) his pattern of availability or, as the case may be, the hours to which he has restricted his availability in accordance with regulations [⁹13(3), (3A) or (4)][¹¹, 13A] or 17(2), and

    (ii) any other restrictions he has placed on his availability for employment which will apply in the first week after the date of claim, provided those restrictions have been agreed with an employment officer, and

    (iii) if he falls within regulation 5, that regulation;

(b) where no pattern of availability is recorded in his jobseeker's agreement, he is available for employment during such of the period referred to in paragraph (1)(i) as he is not treated as available for employment under any other provision of this regulation—

    (i) in accordance with any restrictions he has placed on his availability for employment which will apply in the first week after the date of claim, provided those restrictions have been agreed with an employment officer, and

    (ii) for 8 hours on each day falling within that period on which he is not treated as available for employment to any extent under any other provision of this regulation, and

    (iii) if he falls within regulation 5, in accordance with that regulation.]

[⁶ (2B) A person shall not be treated as available for employment under paragraph (1)(r)—

(a) for more than eight weeks,

(b) where he does not, before the period during which he is required to attend the court or tribunal, give an employment officer notice, in writing where requested by the employment officer, that he is so required, or

(c) where he is a prisoner as defined by regulation 85(4) (special cases).]

(3) If any of the circumstances set out in paragraph (1), except those in sub-paragraphs (i) and (j), or any of those set out in paragraph (2) apply to a person for part of a week, he shall for the purposes of regulation 7(1) be treated as available for 8 hours on any day on which those circumstances applied subject to the maximum specified in paragraph (1) or (2), unless he has restricted the total number of hours for which he is available in a week in accordance with regulation 7(2), [¹ 13(4)] or 17(2). If he has so restricted the total number of hours for which he is available, he shall, for the purposes of regulation [¹ 7(1), 13(4) or 17(2)], be treated as available for the number of hours for which he would be available on that day in accordance with his pattern of availability recorded in his jobseeker's agreement, if any of the circumstances set out in paragraph (1) except those in sub-paragraphs (i) and (j) or any of those set out in paragraph (2) applied on that day, subject to the maximum specified in paragraph (1) or (2).

(4) In paragraph (1)(c), "treatment" means treatment for a disease or bodily or mental disablement by or under the supervision of a person qualified to provide medical treatment, physiotherapy or a form of treatment which is similar to, or related to, either of those forms of treatment.

(5) For the purposes of paragraph (1)(d),
(a) a person is engaged in duties for the benefit of others while—
   (i) providing assistance to any person whose life may be endangered or who may be exposed to the risk of serious bodily injury or whose health may be seriously impaired,
   (ii) protecting property of substantial value from imminent risk of serious damage or destruction, or
   (iii) assisting in measures being taken to prevent a serious threat to the health of the people,
   as a member of a group of persons organised wholly or partly for the purpose of providing such assistance or, as the case may be, protection;
(b) events which may give rise to an emergency include—
   (i) a fire, a flood or an explosion,
   (ii) a natural catastrophe,
   (iii) a railway or other transport accident,
   (iv) a cave or mountain accident,
   (v) an accident at sea,
   (vi) a person being reported missing and the organisation of a search for that person.

(6) In paragraph (1), except in sub-paragraphs (i) and (j), and in paragraph (2), "week" means any period of 7 consecutive days.

[⁶ (7) In this regulation, "tribunal" means any tribunal listed in Schedule 1 to the Tribunals and Inquiries Act 1992.]

AMENDMENTS

1. Jobseeker's Allowance and Income Support (General) (Amendment) Regulations 1996 (SI 1996/1517) reg.5 (October 7, 1996).

2. Social Security (Jobseeker's Allowance and Mariners' Benefits) (Miscellaneous Amendments) Regulations 1997 (SI 1997/563) reg.2 (March 11, 1997).

3. Jobseeker's Allowance (Amendment) (No.2) Regulations 1999 (SI 1999/3807) reg.3 (November 30, 1999).

4. Jobseeker's Allowance (Joint Claims: Consequential Amendments) Regulations 2000 (SI 2000/3336) reg.2 (March 19, 2001).

5. Social Security (Income Support and Jobseeker's Allowance) Amendment Regulations 2004 (SI 2004/1869) reg.3(2) (October 4, 2004).

6. Social Security (Income Support and Jobseeker's Allowance) Amendment Regulations 2006 (SI 2006/1402) reg.2(3) (May 30, 2006).

7. Social Security (Miscellaneous Amendments) Regulations 2008 (SI 2008/698) reg.4(4) (April 14, 2008).

8. Social Security (Students Responsible for Children or Young Persons) Amendment Regulations 2008 (SI 2008/1826) reg.3(5) (July 9, 2008).

9. Social Security (Lone Parents and Miscellaneous Amendments) Regulations 2008 (SI 2008/3051) reg.11(8) (November 4, 2008).

10. Employment and Support Allowance (Consequential Provisions) (No.2) Regulations 2008 (SI 2008/1554) reg.4(4) (October 27, 2008).

11. Jobseeker's Allowance (Lone Parents) (Availability for Work) Regulations 2010 (SI 2010/837) reg.2(10) (April 26, 2010).

12. Jobseeker's Allowance (Jobseeking and Work for Your Benefit) (Amendment and Revocation) Regulations 2012 (SI 2012/397) reg.2 (March 1, 2012).

13. Jobseeker's Allowance (Schemes for Assisting Persons to Obtain Employment) Regulations 2013 (SI 2013/276) reg.14 (February 12, 2013 at 6.45 pm).

14. Jobseeker's Allowance (Homeless Claimants) Amendment Regulations 2014 (SI 2014/1623) reg.2(2) (July 21, 2014).

15. Jobseeker's Allowance (Homeless Claimants) Amendment Regulations 2014 (SI 2014/1623) reg.2(3) (July 21, 2014).

16. Social Security (Traineeships and Qualifying Young Persons) Amendment Regulations 2015 (SI 2015/336) reg.2(3) (March 27, 2015).

17. Jobseeker's Allowance (Extended Period of Sickness) Amendment Regulations 2015 (SI 2015/339) reg.2(2) (March 30, 2015).

18. Social Security (Members of the Reserve Forces) (Amendment) Regulations 2015 (SI 2015/389) reg.3(3) (April 6, 2015).

DEFINITIONS

"a joint-claim couple"—see Jobseekers Act 1995 s.1(4).
"capable of work"—see Jobseekers Act 1995 s.35(2) and Sch.1 para.2; reg.55.
"caring responsibilities"—see reg.4.
"child"—see Jobseekers Act 1995 s.35(1).
"close relative"—see reg.4.
"Contributions Regulations"—see reg.1(3).
"couple"—*ibid.*
"date of claim"—*ibid.*
"employment"—see reg.4.
"employment officer"—see Jobseekers Act 1995 s.35(1).
"employment-related course"—see reg.1(3).
"family"—see Jobseekers Act 1995 s.35(1).
"first year of training"—see reg.1(3).
"full-time student"—*ibid.*
"Great Britain"—see Jobseekers Act 1995 s.35(1).
"partner"—see reg.1(3).
"part-time member of a fire brigade"—see reg.4.
"traineeship"—see reg.1(3).
"week" (except in paras (1)(i) and (j) and (2))—see para.(6).
"week" (in paras (1)(i) and (j) and (2))—see reg.4.
"work camp"—see reg.4.
"young person"—see regs 1(3) and 76.

GENERAL NOTE

3.65　　This regulation sets out in paras (1) and (2) a diverse range of specific situations in which, for the periods specified, someone is to be treated as available for employment even though the person might otherwise fail to satisfy the test of availability in s.6(1) of the old style Jobseekers Act 1995 as modified by these Regulations. The previous express exception at the beginning of para.(1) where reg.15(1)(a), (b), (bc) or (c) applied was removed with effect from March 30, 2015. The specific provision in para.(1)(a), (aa) and (k) for those sub-paras to apply notwithstanding reg.15(1)(a) would suggest the intention that, apart from those circumstances, a person deemed under reg.15(1) not to be available cannot take advantage of reg.14. However, that result is expressly achieved by the new reg.15(5). See the notes to reg.15 for the treatment of full-time students, to which para.(1)(a) and (k) is relevant.

　　The categories set out in para.(1) need to be examined carefully. They cannot apply for longer than the circumstances prescribed last. However, some categories contain more stringent limits. Sub-paragraph (l) is an important element of the protection given to those who are treated as capable of work or as not having limited capability for work under regs 55, 55ZA or 55A, by deeming such persons to be available for employment (and see reg.19(1)(l), (lzl) and (ll) on deemed actively seeking employment). However, claimants who fall outside those regulations but who restrict their availability as reasonable in the light of their physical or mental condition (reg.13(3)) still have to meet the s.6(1) test in relation to whatever is left after applying those restrictions.

　　The remainder of the categories specified in para.(1) fall into four main groups (sometimes overlapping): those taking part in certain educational or training activities (sub-paras (a), (aa), (b), (f), (k) and (v)); those involving temporary absence from Great Britain (sub-paras (c), (e), (m), (n), (nn), (p) and (q)); those involving caring for others (sub-paras (e), (g), (t) and (u)); and those involving some public service (sub-paras (d), with para.(5), (r) and (v)). The remaining miscellaneous categories, often to do with the beginning or end of a period of entitlement, are in sub-paras (h), (i), (j), (o) and (s).

3.66　　In *Secretary of State for Social Security v David* (reported as *R(JSA)3/01* alongside the decision of Commissioner Levenson, whose reasoning the Court rejected)(see further the commentary to reg.13(3)), the Court of Appeal thought that the scheme of deemed availability should be extended to cover those, like Mr David, unavailable through circumstances beyond their control (detention in police custody). This was effected by para.(1)(s) from May 30, 2006. *David* was applied in *CJSA/5944/99*, another case of someone detained in police custody. Commissioner Angus held that reg.14(1)(h) did not aid the claimant, as the establishments mentioned in it were all places to which a person could be committed by a court to await further procedures or serve a sentence and its scope could not extend to the normally temporary detention in a police cell.

　　Paragraph (2), unless any of the contrary rules in reg.15(1) apply (see reg.15(5)), requires claimants to be treated as available for employment when affected by various adverse personal circumstances, such as the death or serious illness of a close relative (defined) or close friend (not defined) (sub-para.(a)) or the funeral of such a person (sub-para.(c)). However, the deeming lasts only for the time required to deal with the circumstance up to a maximum of one week for each occurrence, subject to the potential extensions mentioned below. There can ordinarily only be four periods of such deeming within any 12-month period. There is a more general category of deeming under para.(2)(b) covering a domestic emergency (not defined) affecting the claimant or a close relative or close friend. In *RR v SSWP (UC)* [2017] UKUT 459 (AAC) it was suggested, in relation to reg.95(2)(b) of the Universal Credit Regulations 2013 (see Vol.II of this series), that having to deal with the fall-out from divorce or other family proceedings could amount to a domestic emergency or other temporary circumstances. Since July 21, 2014 there has, under para.(2ZC), been a limitation on the application of para.(2)(b) if the claimant has recently become homeless (not defined), when the claimant must take such steps as are reasonable to find living accommodation (not defined) to benefit from the deeming. However, if that condition is met, both the one-week limit and the four occasions rule do not apply (para.(2ZD)). Paragraph (2)(d) applies to a person with caring responsibilities (defined in reg.4 to require the person cared for to be a close relative or a member of the same household) when the person cared for has died, subject to the ordinary limits. Paragraph (2ZA) allows the one-week limit in relation to para.(2)(a) or (b) to be extended to eight weeks where the claimant has caring responsibilities for a child (and see para.(1)(t) and (u)). The mere death of a child for whom the claimant has caring responsibilities but who is not a close relative (see para.(2)(a)) cannot trigger the extension in para.(2ZA) except on the rather artificial basis either that the child was a "close friend" or that there is a domestic emergency.

Paragraph (3) concerns the situation in which para.(1) protections (other than those in sub-paras (i) and (j)) and para.(2) protections apply only in respect of part of a benefit week (generally the period of seven days ending with the day corresponding to the claimant's "signing"/attendance day; see regs 4 and 1(3)). The protection offered by para.(1)(i) only extends to claimants meeting the conditions in para.(2A). The protection offered by para.(1)(r) only extends to claimants meeting the conditions in para.(2B).The remainder of the regulation contains relevant definitions.

In applying this regulation, careful note should be taken of the specific definition of certain terms (listed under "Definitions", above), in particular the different meanings of "week". One must also remember and maintain the distinction between Great Britain (England, Scotland and Wales) on the one hand, and the United Kingdom (of Great Britain and Northern Ireland) on the other.   3.67

Note that where it has been decided that a person is to be treated as available for employment in any benefit week, a subsequent revision or supersession of that decision can embrace also the question whether in that week the person was actually available for employment (old style Jobseekers Act 1995 s.6(6)). Note further that unlike the position with UB, where full benefit remained in payment pending resolution of the issue, under old style JSA if there remains an unresolved issue as to the claimant's availability for work there will be no entitlement to benefit, although the person excluded may be eligible for a hardship payment (see regs 140–146 ("standard" cases) and regs 146A–146H ("joint-claim" couples, below).

[¹14A.—(1) Paragraph (2) applies where a person (V) notifies the   3.68
Secretary of State, in such manner as the Secretary of State specifies, that—
(a) domestic violence has been inflicted on or threatened against V by V's partner or former partner or a family member, during the period of 26 weeks ending on the date of the notification; and
(b) at the time of the notification, V is not living at the same address as the person who inflicted domestic violence on or threatened it against V.
(2) Where this paragraph applies V is to be treated as being available for employment for a period of 4 weeks ("the 4 week exemption period") beginning on the date of V's notification to the Secretary of State under paragraph (1).
(3) V is to be treated as available for employment under paragraph (2)—
(a) whether or not V is entitled to a jobseeker's allowance for the whole or part of the 4 week exemption period; and
(b) on only one occasion in any 12 month period.
(4) Paragraph (6) applies where domestic violence has been inflicted on or threatened against V by V's partner or former partner or a family member.

(5) Domestic violence is only to be regarded as having been inflicted on or threatened against V for the purpose of paragraph (4) if V provides relevant evidence to the Secretary of State during the 4 week exemption period.

(6) Where this paragraph applies, V is to be treated as being available for employment for a period of 13 weeks ("the 13 week exemption period") beginning on the date of V's notification to the Secretary of State under paragraph (1).

(7) Subject to paragraphs (8) and (9), the 13 week exemption period shall apply for 13 consecutive weeks, whether or not V is entitled to a jobseeker's allowance for the whole or part of that period.

(8) After the first 4 weeks of the 13 week exemption period, V may notify the Secretary of State that V no longer wishes to be treated as available for employment by virtue of paragraph (6).

(9) Where V gives such a notification to the Secretary of State, the 13 week exemption period—

    (a) shall be suspended from the date of the notification until the date on which V gives a further notification to the Secretary of State that V wishes again to be treated as available for employment by virtue of paragraph (6); and

    (b) shall not apply at any time after the expiry of 12 months from the date of the notification referred to in paragraph (1).

(10) For the purpose of this regulation—

[2 "coercive behaviour" means an act of assault, humiliation or intimidation or other abuse that is used to harm, punish or frighten V;

"controlling behaviour" means an act designed to make V subordinate or dependent by isolating them from sources of support, exploiting their resources and capacities for personal gain, depriving them of the means needed for independence, resistance or escape or regulating their everyday behaviour;

"domestic violence" means any incident or pattern of incidents of controlling behaviour, coercive behaviour, violence or abuse including but not limited to—

    (a) psychological abuse;

    (b) physical abuse;

    (c) sexual abuse;

    (d) financial abuse; and

    (e) emotional abuse;

regardless of the gender or sexuality of V;]

"family member" means the following members of the family of V, V's partner or V's former partner – grandparent, grandchild, parent, parent-in-law, son, son-in-law, daughter, daughter-in-law, step-parent, step-son, step-daughter, brother, brother-in-law, sister, sister-in-law, or, if any of the preceding persons is a member of a couple, the other member of that couple,

"health care professional" means a person who is a member of a profession regulated by a body mentioned in section 25(3) of the National Health Service Reform and Health Care Professions Act 2002,

"person acting in an official capacity" means a health care professional, a police officer, a registered social worker, V's employer or a representative of V's trade union and any public, voluntary or charitable body which has had direct contact with V in connection with domestic violence, "registered social worker" means a person registered as a social worker in a register maintained by—

[⁴(a) Social Work England,]

[³(b) Social Care Wales,]

(c) the Scottish Social Services Council, or

(d) the Northern Ireland Social Care Council,

"relevant evidence" means written evidence from a person acting in an official capacity showing that—

(a) V's circumstances are consistent with those of a person who has had domestic violence inflicted on or threatened against them during the period of 26 weeks ending on the date of the notification referred to in paragraph (1); or

(b) V has made contact with the person acting in an official capacity in relation to such an incident, which occurred during that period.]

AMENDMENTS

1. Jobseeker's Allowance (Domestic Violence) (Amendment) Regulations 2012 (SI 2012/853) reg.2(2) (April 23, 2012).

2. Jobseeker's Allowance (Domestic Violence) (Amendment) Regulations 2013 (SI 2013/2722) reg.2 (October 29, 2013).

3. Social Services and Well-being (Wales) Act 2014 and the Regulation and Inspection of Social Care (Wales) Act 2016 (Consequential Amendments) Order 2017 (SI 2017/901) art.19 (November 3, 2017).

4. Children and Social Work Act 2017 (Consequential Amendments) (Social Workers) Regulations 2019 (SI 2019/1094) reg.2(c) and Sch.3 para.1 (July 9, 2019).

DEFINITIONS

"couple"—see reg.1(3).

"employment"—see reg.4.

"partner"—see reg.1(3).

"week"—see reg.4.

GENERAL NOTE

This regulation operates in combination with reg.19(1)(x) and reg.34(g). In combination they provide that an old style JSA claimant (V) who has been a victim of domestic violence is, if the conditions of this regulation are met, to be treated both as available for employment (this reg.) and actively seeking work (reg.19(1)(x)), and also as having a jobseeker's agreement if they do not already have one (reg.34(g)). V can be so treated for a set 13-week "exemption period" commencing with V's notification to the Secretary of State if they provide relevant evidence during the initial four weeks of the period.

3.69

Victims remain entitled to old style JSA provided they meet the other conditions of entitlement. The 13 weeks run consecutively—unless suspended in accordance with paras (8) and (9)—and whether or not V is entitled to old style JSA for all or only part of that period (para.(7))

Initially, the definition of "domestic violence" in para.(10) was in terms of abuse as specified on a particular page of the December 2005 Department of Health document *Responding to domestic abuse: a handbook for health professionals*. It was not very satisfactory for an important definition not only not to be set out in the Regulations, but to be in a publication that was difficult to find (the text was reproduced in the note to reg.98 of the Universal Credit Regulations in Vol.V, *Universal Credit*, 2013/14 ed), and its terms were perhaps not well-suited to the particular benefits context. The new definition in para.(10), expanded into various forms of abuse and into further definitions of coercive and controlling behaviour, is still very wide. It uses the terms of the government's official approach to the meaning of domestic violence across departments, which had not previously been used as a statutory definition. Note that the new criminal offence of controlling or coercive behaviour in intimate or familial relationships under s.76 of the Serious Crime Act 2015, while using the terms of controlling and coercive behaviour (the meaning of which is discussed in Home Office Statutory Guidance of December 2015) contains conditions that are different from those in reg.14A. While the definition here expressly includes coercive behaviour and controlling behaviour (both given their own definitions in para.(10)), any other incident of abuse of any kind can come within the ambit of domestic violence. Thus, although the specific definition of "coercive behaviour" requires the act or abuse to be used to harm, punish or frighten the victim and the specific definition of "controlling behaviour" is restricted to acts designed to make the victim subordinate or dependant by particular means (as taken to extremes by the vile Rob Titchener in *The Archers*), abuse of similar kinds where that specific form of intention or purpose is not present or is difficult to prove can nonetheless be domestic violence. The width of that approach makes the specification in para.(1) of the circumstances in which reg.14A applies more important. Victims can be of any gender and their sexuality is immaterial. The person perpetrating or threatening the domestic violence must be V's partner, former partner or a family member (defined in para.(10) to cover a wide range of members of the family of V, V's partner or V's former partner).

3.70   The regulation applies only if V notifies the Secretary of State in the specified manner and at that time V is not living at the same address as the perpetrator of the domestic violence or the person threatening it (para.(1)). It covers domestic violence perpetrated or threatened in the 26 weeks prior to the notification (*ibid.*). There is under para.(2) an initial deeming of availability (called an "exemption period") for four weeks, designed to enable V to gather "relevant evidence" (see para.(10)) of the domestic violence. The 13-week exemption period under para.(6) (also running from the date of notification to the Secretary of State) can only apply if V does provide relevant evidence within the four weeks (para.(5)). The initial period also allows V time to deal with pressing issues resulting from leaving an abusive relationship such as getting new accommodation, legal advice or children settled in new schools. "Relevant evidence" is written evidence from someone in an official capacity (as quite widely defined in para.(10)) showing either: (i) that V has contacted that person in relation to an incident of domestic violence during the 26-week period prior to V's notification to the Secretary of State, or (ii) that V's circumstances are consistent with those of someone who has in that period had domestic violence threatened against them or inflicted on them. The evidence must be furnished to the Secretary of State within four weeks of V's initial notification (para.(5)).

Note that there can only be one four-week evidence-gathering period and 13-week "exemption period" (of which the four-week period forms part) in any 12-month period (para.(3)). After four weeks of being treated as available, V can by notifying the Secretary of State suspend the remainder of the 13-week period of deemed availability and actively seeking work and resurrect it within a year from the initial notification setting the exemption period regulation in motion (paras (8) and (9)).

The transition from new style JSA

3.71   Paragraph (3)(b) is, where art.13(1) and (2) of the Welfare Reform Act 2012 (Commencement No.9 and Transitional and Transitory Provisions and Commencement No. 8 and Savings and Transitional Provisions (Amendment)) Order 2013 (as amended and set out in Part V of this volume) applies, to be read as if para.(2) had applied where the person had been treated as available for employment under reg.15 of the JSA Regulations 2013 (art.13(3)(a) of that Order).

Circumstances in which a person is not to be regarded as available

3.72   **15.**—[² (1)] A person shall not be regarded as available for employment in the following circumstances—

[² (a) [⁴. . .] if he is full-time student during the period of study];

(b) if he is a prisoner on temporary release in accordance with the provisions of the Prison Act 1952 or rules made under section 39(6) of the Prisons (Scotland) Act 1989;

[¹(bb) if the period beginning on the date of claim and ending on the day before the beginning of the first week after the date of claim is less than 7 days, for that period, unless he is treated as available for employment for that period in accordance with regulation 14;]

[⁵(bc) if that person is on ordinary or additional adoption leave, shared parental leave, paternity leave, or parental bereavement leave by virtue of section 75A, 75B, or 80EA of the Employment Rights Act 1996;]

[³(c) if she is in receipt of a maternity allowance under section 35 or 35B of the Benefits Act or maternity pay in accordance with sections 164–171 of that Act.]

[²(2) [⁷ Paragraph (1)(a) shall not apply to a full-time student] during the period of the summer vacation appropriate to his course, but only if the first and second conditions are satisfied.

(3) The first condition is satisfied if—

(a) in the case of a student with a partner, the partner is also a full-time student and either of them is treated as responsible for a child or a young person; or

(b) in any other case, the student is treated as responsible for a child or young person.

(4) The second condition is satisfied if the student is—

(a) available for employment in accordance with this Chapter; or

(b) treated as available for employment in accordance with regulation 14(1)(a) or (k).]

[⁴(5) Any provision of these Regulations under which a person is treated as available for employment is subject to paragraph (1) except to the extent that these Regulations expressly provide otherwise.]

AMENDMENTS

1. Social Security (Jobseeker's Allowance and Mariners' Benefits) (Miscellaneous Amendments) Regulations 1997 (SI 1997/563) reg.3 (March 11, 1997).

2. Social Security (Students Responsible for Children or Young Persons) Amendment Regulations 2008 (SI 2008/1826) reg.3(2)–(4) (July 9, 2008).

3. Social Security (Maternity Allowance) (Miscellaneous Amendments) Regulations 2014 (SI 2914/884) reg.4(3) (May 18, 2014).

4. Social Security (Traineeships and Qualifying Young Persons) Amendment Regulations 2015 (SI 2015/336) reg.2(4) (March 27, 2015).

5. Parental Bereavement Leave and Pay (Consequential Amendments to Subordinate Legislation) Regulations 2020 (SI 2020/354) reg.8(3) (April 6, 2020).

MODIFICATION

With effect from April 8, 2020 to May 21, 2021, reg.15(1)(b) is modified by reg.4 of the Social Security (Coronavirus) (Prisoners) Regulations 2020 (SI 2020/409) so as to be read as if the words "the provisions of the Prison Act 1952 or" were omitted. The end date of the modification was extended from November 12, 2020 to May 21, 2021 by reg.2 of the Social Security (Coronavirus) (Prisoners) Amendment Regulations 2020 (SI 2020/1156). There is to be a further extension to August 31, 2021 (reg.4 of the Social Security (Coronavirus) (Miscellaneous Amendments) Regulations 2021 (SI 2021/476)). See the notes to para.(1)(b) below for the purpose of the modification.

DEFINITIONS

"adoption leave"—see reg.1(3).
"child"—see Jobseekers Act 1995 s.35(1).
"date of claim"—see reg.1(3).
"employment"—see reg.4.
"full-time student"—reg.1(3).
"parental bereavement leave"—*ibid.*
"paternity leave"—*ibid.*
"partner"—*ibid.*
"period of study"—see reg.4.
"shared parental leave"—see reg.1(3).
"week"— see reg.4.
"young person"—see regs 1(3) and 76.

GENERAL NOTE

Temporary Coronavirus Provisions

3.73   In addition to the modification recorded above, reg.7 of the Social Security (Coronavirus) (Further Measures) Regulations 2020 (SI 2020/371) provided that for the three months beginning with March 30, 2020 anyone with an award of old style JSA was to be treated as available for employment (and as actively seeking employment). It is arguable that, by virtue of reg.15(5) the deeming of non-availability in reg.15 trumps the effect of reg.7, except where modified as identified above. The effect of reg.7 of the Further Measures Regulations expired at the end of November 12, 2020 (reg.10(2)). The power to extend the three-month period was not exercised before it expired.

It is not clear whether the restriction of the effect of reg.7 to those who had an award of old style JSA meant that on a new claim (insofar as a claim for old style JSA, as opposed to new style JSA and universal credit, was still possible) the availability condition was to be applied in determining initial entitlement. The mechanism suggested for new style JSA in the notes to s.6E of the new style Jobseekers Act 1995 (Vol.I of this series) cannot work for old style JSA because the availability and actively seeking work conditions are imposed directly by the legislation as conditions of entitlement. It appears that in practice little if any attention was given to "conditionality" during the period affected.

3.74   This regulation excludes certain groups from entitlement to old style JSA by treating them (whatever would be the reality of the situation applying the standard availability test) as not available for employment. Paragraph (5) now confirms that the exclusionary effect of para.(1) trumps any other provision in these Regulations unless it contains something expressly to the contrary, as some of the entries in regs 14 and 17A do. The excluded groups (and the circumstances of their exclusion) are set out below.

(1) Full-time students (paras (1)(a), (2), (3) and (4)).

With two exceptions, any claimant who is a full-time student (defined in reg.1(3)) is treated as not available for employment throughout the "period of study": the period beginning with the start of the claimant's course of study and ending on its last day or on such earlier date as he abandons it or is dismissed from it (reg.4). Note that the "period of study" includes any period of attendance at the student's educational establishment, or any period of study undertaken, in connection with his course whether occurring before or after the period of the course (*ibid.*, and see further *CJSA/1457/1999*). The fact that this includes students who are not attending college for a year while they resit exams externally is not contrary to art.14, read with art.1 Prot.1 of the ECHR (*MS v SSWP* [2009] UKUT 9 (AAC)).

The first exception covers claimants falling within reg.17A (employment-related courses for certain over-25s). The second exception covers the situation where both claimant and partner are full-time students and one is treated for child benefit

purposes as responsible for a child or young person. Following the decision in
CJSA/2663/2006, from July 9, 2008 it also covers the situation where a single
student is treated as responsible for a child or young person. In either case, the
exception only applies, however, during the summer vacation of the claimant's
course, and only then if actually available for work in accordance with the usual
rules on availability or treated as available under reg.14(1)(a) (when participating
in an approved employment-related course) or reg.14(1)(k) (when participating
in a Venture Trust programme). See also *MB v SSWP (JSA)* [2013] UKUT 535
(AAC), in which Judge Wikeley discusses the case of a lone parent mature student.

(2) Prisoners on temporary release (para.(1)(b)).

The modification recorded above is to avoid English and Welsh prisoners on temporary release on licence because of the COVID-19 outbreak being excluded from
effective access to old style JSA by being deemed not to be available for employment.
The authority for such temporary release is in rule 9A of the Prison Rules 1999 (SI
1999/728), made under s.47(5) of the Prison Act 1952, as added by rule 2 of the
Prison and Young Offender Institution (Coronavirus) (Amendment) Rules 2020
(SI 2020/400). However, the modification goes wider and removes any prisoner on
temporary release, e.g. under rule 9, from the deeming of non-availability. Although
reg.7 of the Social Security (Coronavirus) (Further Measures) Regulations 2020
provided that for the three months beginning with March 30, 2020 anyone with an
award of old style JSA was to be treated as available for employment, the effect of
reg.15(5) would arguably have been to negate that deeming without the operation
of this modification.

There was no need to modify the effect of para.(1)(b) in respect of Scotland
because the provisions actually used there to authorise temporary release were not
the rules specified in para.(1)(b).

*(3) Women receiving maternity allowance (see SSCBA 1992 ss.35 or 35B) or statutory
maternity pay (see SSCBA 1992 ss.164–171) (para.(1)(c)).*

(4) Claimants in respect of part weeks at the beginning of a claim (para.(1)(bb))

This provides that a claimant is not to be regarded as available for employment
(and is therefore excluded from old style JSA) for a part-week at the beginning of
a claim unless he is treated as available for that period by one of the provisions in
reg.14, above.

*(5) Persons on paternity leave or shared parental leave, ordinary, additional adoption
leave or parental bereavement leave (para.(1)(bc)).*

Further circumstances in which a person is to be treated as available: permitted period

16.—(1) A person who is available for employment—   3.75
(a) only in his usual occupation;
(b) only at a level of remuneration not lower than that which he is accustomed to receive, or
(c) only in his usual occupation and at a level of remuneration not lower
than that which he is accustomed to receive
may be treated for a permitted period as available for employment in that
period.
(2) Whether a person should be treated as available for a permitted
period and if so, the length of that permitted period shall be determined
having regard to the following factors—
(a) the person's usual occupation and any relevant skills or qualifications
which he has;

(b) the length of any period during which he has undergone training relevant to that occupation;

(c) the length of the period during which he has been employed in that occupation and the period since he was so employed;

(d) the availability and location of employment in that occupation.

(3) A permitted period shall be for a minimum of one week and a maximum of 13 weeks and shall start on the date of claim and in this paragraph "week" means any period of 7 consecutive days.

Definitions

"date of claim"—see reg.1(3).
"employment"—see reg.4.

General Note

3.76 Section 6(1) of the old style Jobseekers Act 1995 stipulates that a claimant is available for employment if willing and able to take up immediately *any employed earner's employment*. This regulation mitigates the rigour of that by enabling claimants who have a usual occupation to be treated, for a permitted period of between one and 13 weeks, as available for employment even though only available for employment in their usual occupation and/or at their accustomed level of remuneration (paras (1), (3)). Here "week" in para.(3) means any period of seven days, not a benefit week, and the permitted period begins on the date of claim (para.(3)). Whether claimants should be so treated and for how long is to be determined having regard to: their usual occupation and any of their relevant skills and qualifications; the length of any period of training, relevant to that occupation, which they have undergone; how long they were employed in that occupation and the length of time elapsed since they were last employed in it; and the location and availability of employment in that occupation. Note also that under reg.20(1), such a claimant can be treated as actively seeking employment for a corresponding period. Furthermore, under reg.20(2), someone who has at any time in the 12 months prior to the date of claim for old style JSA been engaged in self-employment in their usual occupation, can be treated as actively seeking employment during the "permitted period" even though they confine their jobsearch to employment, self-employment, or both, only in their usual occupation, or only at their accustomed rate of remuneration, or only in their usual occupation and at their accustomed rate. But under the terms of this regulation, they must still be available for *employment* as opposed to *self-employment*. Whether claimants have a usual occupation will be a question of fact looking at their employment history and the time for which they have followed a particular occupation.

For limitations on the application of this regulation in the case of a claimant laid-off from employment or working short-time, see reg.17(4).

Laid off and short-time workers

3.77 **17.**—(1) A person who is laid off shall be treated as available for employment providing he is willing and able to resume immediately the employment from which he has been laid off and to take up immediately any casual employment which is within daily travelling distance of his home or, if he falls within paragraph [²(1), (1A) or (2)] of regulation 5, at the time specified in that regulation.

(2) [¹(a)] A person who is kept on short-time shall be treated as available for employment, providing he is willing and able to resume immediately the employment in which he is being kept on short-time and to take up immediately any casual employment which is within daily travelling distance of his home or, if he falls within paragraph (1)

or (2) of regulation 5, at the time specified in that regulation in the hours in which he is not working short-time but the total number of hours for which he works and is available for casual employment must be at least 40 in any week [¹unless paragraph (b) or (c) applies.

(b) The total number of hours for which a person kept on short-time works and is available for casual employment may be less than 40 in any week if that person has imposed restrictions on his availability which are reasonable in the light of his physical or mental condition;

(c) The total number of hours for which a person kept on short-time works and is available for casual employment may be less than 40 in any week if he has caring responsibilities providing the total number of hours for which he works and is available for casual employment is as many as his caring responsibilities allow and for the specific hours those responsibilities allow and is at least 16 in any week;]

(3) A person shall not be treated as available for employment in accordance with this regulation for more than 13 weeks, starting with the day after the day he was laid off or first kept on short-time.

(4) A person who is laid off or kept on short-time may not be treated as available for employment for a permitted period in accordance with regulation 16, unless he ceases to be laid off or kept on short-time within 13 weeks of the day on which he was laid off or first kept on short time, in which case he may be treated as available for employment for a permitted period ending a maximum of 13 weeks after the date of claim.

(5) In paragraphs (3) and (4), "week" means any period of 7 consecutive days.

AMENDMENTS

1. Jobseeker's Allowance and Income Support (General) (Amendment) Regulations 1996 (SI 1996/1517) reg.6 (October 7, 1996).

2. Social Security (Lone Parents and Miscellaneous Amendments) Regulations 2008 (SI 2008/3051) reg.11(9) (November 4, 2008).

DEFINITIONS

"casual employment"—see reg.4.
"employment"—*ibid.*
"permitted period"—see reg.16(3).
"a person who is kept on short-time"—see reg.4.
"a person who is laid off "—*ibid.*
"week" (in paras (3), (4))—see para.(5).
"week" (in para.(2))—see reg.4.

GENERAL NOTE

Temporary Coronavirus Provisions

Regulation 7 of the Social Security (Coronavirus) (Further Measures) Regulations 2020 (SI 2020/371) provided that for the three months beginning with March 30, 2020 anyone with an award of old style JSA was to be treated as available for employment (and as actively seeking employment). The effect of reg.7 expired at the end of November 12, 2020 (reg.10(2)). The power to extend the three-month period was not exercised. It is not clear whether the restriction of the effect of reg.7 to those who had an award of old style JSA meant that on a new claim (insofar as a claim for old style JSA, as opposed to new style JSA and universal credit, was still possible) the availability condition was to be applied in determining initial entitlement. The mechanism suggested for new style JSA in the notes to s.6E of the new

3.78

style Jobseekers Act 1995 (Vol.I of this series) cannot work for old style JSA because the availability and actively seeking work conditions are imposed directly by the legislation as conditions of entitlement. It appears that in practice little if any attention was given to "conditionality" during the period affected.

Thus, anyone falling within this temporary provision will not need the assistance of reg.17. Employees "furloughed" under the Coronavirus Job Retention Scheme could be argued to come within the meaning of a "person who is laid off", their employment having been suspended owing to temporary adverse industrial conditions. The Scheme only prohibits employment by the furloughing employer, so that they would be able to take up casual employment, as well as being willing to resume the previous employment. But there would be a problem in using reg.17 after the effect of reg.7 of the Further Measures Regulations ran out, in that reg.17(3) limits its effect to the 13 weeks immediately after the first day of lay-off. Employees who are not furloughed but have earnings cut will only count as persons kept on short-time, with the same consequences, if their working hours have been reduced.

3.79   For up to 13 weeks from the day after being laid off or put on short time, as the case may be, this regulation enables a claimant who is laid off or kept on short time to be treated as available for employment (paras (1)–(3)). It also sets limitations on treating such a claimant as available for employment during the permitted period under reg.16 (para.(4)). Its aim is to assist for a short period claimants whose employment has been affected by temporary adverse industrial conditions in the hope that before the end of that period a recovery will mean that they can return to working or to usual hours of working in that employment and thus cease to need old style JSA.

A claimant who is laid off (para.(1))

3.80   A person is laid off when their employment has been suspended owing to temporary adverse industrial conditions (reg.4). Claimants who are laid off must be treated as available for employment provided (1) that they are willing and able to resume immediately the employment from which they have been laid off, and (2) that they are willing and able to take up, immediately or, if a carer, voluntary worker or person providing a service, within the period of grace afforded by reg.5(1), (1A) or (2), any casual employment within daily travelling distance of their home (para.(1)). "Casual employment" means employment from which the employee can be released without giving notice (reg.4).

A claimant who is kept on short-time (para.(2))

3.81   A person is kept on short time when their hours of employment have been reduced owing to temporary adverse industrial conditions (reg.4). Given that the remunerative work exclusion precludes claims by those working 16 or more hours per week (old style Jobseekers Act 1995 s.1(2)(e); regs 51–53), the reduction must take the claimant below that threshold. Nor must their earnings exceed the prescribed amount (old style Jobseekers Act 1995 s.2(1)(c); reg.56), since that also precludes entitlement. Claimants who are kept on short time in an employment must be treated as available for employment, provided they are willing and able to resume immediately that employment and to take up, generally immediately, any casual employment within daily travelling distance of their home in the hours they are not working short time. Usually, however, the total number of hours for which they work and are available for casual employment must be at least 40 in any [benefit] week (para.(2)(a), regs 4 and 1(3)). "Casual employment" is employment from which the employee can be released without giving notice (reg.4). As regards willingness and ability to take up casual employment, the general requirement "immediately" does not apply to carers, voluntary workers, and those providing a service, who are afforded the appropriate period of grace in reg.5(1) and (2): 48 hours for carers and voluntary workers; 24 hours for those providing a service (para.(2)(a)). The total hours rule (at least 40) does not apply to claimants who have imposed restrictions on their availability which are reasonable in the light of their physical or mental condition (para.(2)(b)). Nor does it apply to a claimant who is a carer (a person with caring responsibilities as defined in reg.4): in any week in such a case the total of hours worked and those of availability for casual employment can be as many hours between 16 and 40 as their caring responsibilities allow (para.(2)(c)).

Paragraph (3)

Some claimants will only experience lay off, others only being kept on short time. For others, short time may be followed by lay-off. This paragraph stipulates that, whichever of these situations is the case, a claimant can only be treated as available under this regulation for up to 13 weeks from the day after the day he was laid off or first kept on short time.   **3.82**

Paragraph (4)

The effect of this is that a claimant who is laid off or kept on short time for 13 weeks cannot then take advantage of the one to 13 weeks permitted period afforded by reg.16 during which, for example, a claimant can confine availability to employment in his usual occupation. A claimant, laid off or kept on short time, can only be eligible for protection under reg.16 if they cease to be laid off or kept on short time within the 13-week period afforded by this regulation. If they do so, in reality by becoming wholly unemployed, they can be treated as available under reg.16 for a permitted period ending no more than 13 weeks from the date of claim. The date of claim is the date the claimant makes, or is treated as making, a claim for old style JSA for the purposes of reg.6 of the Claims and Payments Regulations (reg.1(3)). In many (but not necessarily all) cases that will be immediately after the day he was first laid off or put on short time, so that in such a case, for example, a claimant who has had 10 weeks' protection under this regulation, could get no more than three weeks' protection under reg.16.   **3.83**

[¹Further circumstances in which a person is to be treated as available: full-time students participating in a qualifying course

17A.—(1) A person to whom paragraph (2) applies shall, notwith-standing regulation [⁵15(1)(a)], be treated as available for employment in accordance with paragraph (3).   **3.84**

(2) This paragraph applies to a person—

(a) who is aged 25 years or over; and

(b) [²subject to paragraph (2A),] who has made a claim for a jobseek-er's allowance and has been receiving benefit within a jobseeking period for not less than 2 years as at the date he started, or is due to start, the qualifying course and for the purposes of this paragraph the linking provision set out in regulation 48 shall apply.

[²(2A) A person who has been receiving benefit in accordance with paragraph (b) of the definition of "receiving benefit" in paragraph (7) shall, for the purposes of paragraph (2)(b), be treated as having received benefit within a jobseeking period.]

(3) Subject to paragraph (4), where an employment officer has determined, having regard to the factors specified in paragraph (5), that a person to whom paragraph (2) applies may undertake a qualifying course, that person shall be treated as available for employment in any week in which he is undertaking the qualifying course as a full-time student and—

(a) which falls wholly or partly in term-time, providing he—

(i) provides evidence, as often as may be required by an employ-ment officer, within 5 days of being so required by the employ-ment officer, consisting of a document signed by him and on behalf of the establishment at which he is undertaking the qualifying course, confirming that he is attending the establishment when required to attend, in such form as may be required by the employment officer; and

(ii) provides evidence, as often as may be required by an employment officer, within 5 days of being so required by the employment officer, consisting of a document signed by him and on behalf of the establishment at which he is undertaking the qualifying course, confirming that he is making satisfactory progress on the course, in such form as may be required by the employment officer;

(b) in which he is taking examinations relating to the qualifying course; or

(c) which falls wholly in a vacation from the qualifying course, if he is willing and able to take up immediately any casual employment.

(4) In a case where the combined duration of—

(a) any qualifying course, other than one falling within paragraph (6), which a person to whom paragraph (2) applies has previously undertaken in respect of which he was, for any part of such qualifying course, treated as available for employment in accordance with paragraph (3); and

(b) the qualifying course which he is currently undertaking

is more than 1 year, the person shall only be treated as available for employment in accordance with paragraph (3) if he has been receiving benefit within a jobseeking period for not less than 2 years since the last day of the most recent such qualifying course in respect of which he was, for any part, treated as available in accordance with paragraph (3), and for the purposes of this paragraph the linking provision set out in regulation 48 shall apply.

(5) The factors which an employment officer must take into account when determining whether a person may undertake a qualifying course are—

(a) the skills, qualifications and abilities of that person;

(b) whether the course would assist him to acquire new skills and qualifications;

(c) whether he would have to give up a course of study in order to undertake this course;

(d) any needs arising from his physical or mental condition;

(e) the time which has elapsed since he was last engaged in employment as an employed earner or as a self-employed earner;

(f) his work experience;

(g) the number of jobs in the labour market and, if relevant, the local labour market, which require the skills and qualifications which he would acquire on the course; and

(h) any evidence about whether this course or this type of course has facilitated the obtaining by persons of work.

(6) A qualifying course falls within this paragraph if the person had [⁶ a good reason] for any act or omission for the purposes of section [⁶ 19A(2) (d), (e) or (f)] in relation to that course.

(7) In this regulation—

[³ "benefit" means—

(a) income support, unemployment benefit, a jobseeker's allowance or any earnings credited to a person in accordance with regulation 8A or 9A of the Social Security (Credits) Regulations 1975 or which would be credited to a person in accordance with paragraph (1) of that regulation 9A but are not so credited by reason only of the fact that no further earnings are in his case required for the purpose mentioned in that paragraph; or

(b) any earnings credited to a person for unemployment in accordance with regulation 9 of the Social Security (Credits) Regulations 1975 as it applied before 7th October 1996 and]

"receiving benefit" means [²receiving—

(a) benefit which that person has claimed and received as an unemployed person or in accordance with Part I of the Act [⁴ or in accordance with regulation 9A of the Social Security (Credits) Regulations 1975] or

(b) income support which that person has claimed and received as an asylum seeker pursuant to regulation 70(3A) of the Income Support Regulations but only to the extent that—

   (i) any periods in respect of which he was in receipt of income support as an asylum seeker pursuant to regulation 70(3A) of the Income Support Regulations link with the jobseeking period which includes the date on which he started, or is due to start, the qualifying course and for this purpose, such periods shall link where they are separated by a period of 12 weeks or less in respect of which he was not in receipt of income support; and

   (ii) he is, at the date he started, or is due to start, the qualifying course, a person to whom paragraph (7A) applies;]

"casual employment" means employment from which the employee can be released without his giving any notice or, if he is required to give notice, employment from which he can be released before the end of the vacation;

"duration" in relation to a qualifying course means the period beginning with the start of the course and ending with the last day of the course;

"jobseeking period" means the period described in regulation 47 and any period treated as a jobseeking period pursuant to regulation 47A;

"last day" in relation to a qualifying course means the date on which the last day of the course falls, or the date on which the final examination relating to that course is completed, whichever is the later;

"qualifying course" means a course which—

(a) is an employment-related course;

(b) lasts no more than 12 consecutive months; and

(c) except where it falls within paragraph (8), is either—

   (i) a course of a description falling within Schedule 2 to the Further and Higher Education Act 1992; or

   (ii) a programme of learning falling within section 6 of the Further and Higher Education (Scotland) Act 1992.

[²(7A) Subject to paragraph (7B), this paragraph shall apply in the case of a person—

(a) who—

   (i) is a refugee within the definition of Article 1 of the Convention relating to the Status of Refugees done at Geneva on 28th July 1951, as extended by Article 1(2) of the Protocol relating to the Status of Refugees done at New York on 31st January 1967; or

   (ii) has been granted exceptional leave—

      (aa) to enter the United Kingdom by an immigration officer appointed for the purposes of the Immigration Act 1971; or (bb) to remain in the United Kingdom by the Secretary of State; and

(b) who was in receipt of income support as an asylum seeker pursuant to regulation 70(3A) of the Income Support Regulations at any time during the period of 12 weeks immediately preceding the beginning of the jobseeking period which includes the date on which he started, or is due to start, the qualifying course.

(7B) Paragraph (7A) shall include a person who has been recorded as a refugee by the Secretary of State within the definition in sub-paragraph (a) of that paragraph and whose claim for income support was determined in accordance with regulation 21ZA(2) or (3) of the Income Support Regulations (treatment of refugees).]

(8) A course or a programme of learning which is of a standard above that of a course or programme of learning falling within paragraph (c) of the definition of "qualifying course" falls within this paragraph if an employment officer so determines in a particular case.]

AMENDMENTS

1. Social Security Amendment (New Deal) Regulations 1998 (SI 1998/1274) reg.4 (June 1, 1998).

2. Jobseeker's Allowance Amendment (New Deal) Regulations 1998 (SI 1998/2874) reg.2 (November 24, 1998).

3. Jobseeker's Allowance Amendment (New Deal) Regulations 1999 (SI 1999/3083) reg.2(2) (November 30, 1999).

4. Jobseeker's Allowance Amendment (New Deal) Regulations 1999 (SI 1999/3083) reg.2(3) (November 30, 1999).

5. Social Security (Students Responsible for Children or Young Persons) Amendment Regulations 2008 (SI 2008/1826) reg.3(5) (July 9, 2008).

6. Jobseeker's Allowance (Sanctions) (Amendment) Regulations 2012 (SI 2012/2568) reg.7(3) (October 22, 2012).

DEFINITIONS

"course of study"—see reg.1(3).
"employed earner"—see reg.3 and SSCBA 1992 s.2(1)(a).
"employment"—see reg.4.
"employment officer"—see Jobseekers Act 1995 s.35(1).
"employment-related course"—see reg.1(3).
"examination"—see reg.4.
"full-time student"—see reg.1(3).
"made a claim for jobseeker's allowance"—see reg.4.
"self-employed earner"—see reg.1(3) and SSCBA 1992 s.2(1)(b).
"term-time"—see reg.4.
"vacation"—*ibid.*
"week"—*ibid.*

GENERAL NOTE

3.85   One element of equipping people for work is that of encouraging education in terms of following an employment-related course to acquire new or better skills.

This regulation allows a claimant doing so, in certain limited circumstances, to be treated as available for employment (and see reg.21A for actively seeking employment). The claimant must be 25 or over, have made a claim for old style JSA and been "receiving benefit" (see below) for at least two years within a jobseeking period (the linking provision in reg.48 applies) as at the start date for the course, and must be undertaking a qualifying course with the agreement of an employment officer. A qualifying course is one meeting the criteria set out in para.(7) read with para.(8): in essence a course of further or higher education (or one at a level superior to that if an employment officer so determines in a particular case) which is employment related and lasts no more than 12 months. In determining whether to agree that a claimant can undertake such a course, an employment officer must take into account the factors listed in para.(5). Basically, such claimants must be treated as available for employment in any week in which they are undertaking such a course which falls: (i) wholly or partly within term-time (note the evidence requirements in para.(3)(a) including one with respect to "satisfactory progress"), (ii) which is one in which they are taking examinations relating to the course, or (iii) which falls wholly in a vacation from the course provided in this third case that they are willing and able to take up immediately any casual employment (defined for these purposes in para.(7) rather than according to the general definition in reg.4 (para.(3)). Note, however, that para. (3) is expressed to be "subject to paragraph (4)". Paragraph (4) deals with the situation where the claimant has already been treated as available with respect to one qualifying course and is now undertaking another. If the combined duration of the two courses is more than a year, then claimants cannot be treated as available under this regulation unless they have been receiving benefit within a jobseeking period for at least two years (the linking provision in reg.48 applies) since the last day of the most recent qualifying course in respect of which they were for any part of that course treated as available by para.(3) of this regulation. In short, claimants can only be treated as available under this regulation for up to one year without having to serve a two-year requalification period in receipt of benefit. Note, however, when looking to the combined duration of qualifying courses that one ignores any course where the claimant had a good reason for the purposes of s.19A(2)(d), (e) or (f) (neglect to avail himself of a place on a course, refusing to apply for a vacant place or accept it when offered, giving up such a place or failing to attend the course) with respect to any act or omission in relation to that course (para.(6)).

These rules became effective on June 1, 1998. "Receiving benefit" is not just confined to receiving benefit (income support or JSA) as an unemployed person or in accordance with Pt I of the old style Jobseekers Act 1995 (para.7). However, note in relation to paras (7A) and (7B) that both reg.70 and reg.21ZA of the Income Support Regulations have been revoked, the former with effect from January 25, 2000 and the latter with effect from April 3, 2000. The revocations were subject to savings, which now seem very unlikely to have any scope for operation. With effect from November 30, 1999, "benefit" and "receiving benefit" also includes receipt of earnings credited for contributions purposes in respect of unemployment and for men born before October 6, 1954 but who have not yet attained 65.

Note, finally, that during any week in which someone is treated as available under this regulation they will be treated also as actively seeking work (reg.19(1)(a)). Where the week is during a vacation from the course, they must however show that during that week they have taken such steps as they can reasonably be expected to have to take to have the best prospects of securing the casual employment for which reg.17A requires them to be available (see reg.21A below).

The transition from new style JSA

In para.(a) of the definition of "benefit" in para.(7), the reference to job-seeker's allowance is, where art.13(1) and (2) of the Welfare Reform Act 2012 (Commencement No.9 and Transitional and Transitory Provisions and Commencement No.8 and Savings and Transitional Provisions (Amendment)) Order 2013 (as amended and set out in Part V of this volume) applies, to be read as if it included a reference to new style JSA (art.13(3)(aa) of that Order, in force from June 16, 2014). **3.86**

[¹Further circumstances in which a person is to be treated as available: lone parents with children aged 5 not in full-time education

3.87   **17B.**—A lone parent shall be treated as available for employment in any week where—

    (a) the lone parent is responsible for, and a member of the same household as, a child who is aged 5;

    (b) the child—

        (i) is not receiving full-time education by regular attendance at school or otherwise; and

        (ii) is not required by law to receive full-time education; and

    (c) it would be unreasonable for the lone parent to make other arrangements for the care of that child.]

AMENDMENT

1. Social Security (Lone Parents and Miscellaneous Amendments) Regulations 2012 (SI 2012/874) reg.3(2) (May 21, 2012, subject to special commencement provisions in the Sch. to this amending instrument).

DEFINITIONS

"child"—see Jobseekers Act 1995 s.35(1).
"lone parent"—see reg.1(3).
"week"—see reg.4.

GENERAL NOTE

3.88   There is no rule automatically treating all lone parents of children under the age of five as available for employment, although some categories in reg.14(1) may apply in particular circumstances. A lone parent whose sole or youngest child is under five is eligible for income support (Income Support Regulations Sch.1B para.1). Regulation 17B applies to lone parents who have a child aged exactly five in the household. They are then treated as available for employment (and as actively seeking employment: reg.21B) if the child is not and is not required to be at school. Compulsory school age is reached at the beginning of the school term following 1 January, 1 April or 1 September, according to which date first follows the child's fifth birthday.

Chapter III

Actively seeking employment

Steps to be taken by persons actively seeking employment

3.89   **18.**—[¹(1) For the purposes of section 7(1) (actively seeking employment) a person shall be expected to have to take more than two steps in any week unless taking one or two steps is all that is reasonable for that person to do in that week.]

(2) Steps which it is reasonable for a person to be expected to have to take in any week include—

    (a) oral or written applications (or both) for employment made to persons—

        (i) who have advertised the availability of employment; or

        (ii) who appear to be in a position to offer employment;

    (b) seeking information on the availability of employment from—

    (i) advertisements;

    (ii) persons who have placed advertisements which indicate the availability of employment;

    (iii) employment agencies and employment businesses;

    (iv) employers;

(c) registration with an employment agency or employment business;

(d) appointment of a third party to assist the person in question in finding employment;

(e) seeking specialist advice, following referral by an employment officer, on how to improve the prospects of securing employment having regard to that person's needs and in particular in relation to any mental or physical limitations of that person;

(f) drawing up a curriculum vitae;

(g) seeking a reference or testimonial from a previous employer;

(h) drawing up a list of employers who may be able to offer employment to him with a view to seeking information from them on the availability of employment;

(i) seeking information about employers who may be able to offer employment to him;

(j) seeking information on an occupation with a view to securing employment in that occupation.

(3) In determining whether, in relation to any steps taken by a person, the requirements of section 7(1) are satisfied in any week, regard shall be had to all the circumstances of the case, including—

(a) his skills, qualifications and abilities;

(b) his physical or mental limitations;

(c) the time which has elapsed since he was last in employment and his work experience;

(d) the steps which he has taken in previous weeks and the effectiveness of those steps in improving his prospects of securing employment;

(e) the availability and location of vacancies in employment;

(f) any time during which he was—

    (i) engaged in the manning or launching of a lifeboat or in the performance of duty as a part-time member of a fire brigade or engaged during an emergency in duties for the benefit of others.

    (ii) attending an Outward Bound course,

    (iii) in the case of a blind person, participating in a course of training in the use of guide dogs,

    (iv) participating in training in the use of aids to overcome any physical or mental limitations of his in order to improve his prospects of securing employment,

    [²(v) engaged in duties as a member of any territorial or reserve force prescribed in Part I of [Schedule 6 to the Social Security (Contributions) Regulations 2001,]

    (vi) participating as a part-time student in an employment-related course,

    (vii) participating for less than 3 days in an employment or training programme for which a training allowance is not payable;

(g) any time during which he was engaged in voluntary work and the extent to which it may have improved his prospects of securing employment;

(h) whether he is treated as available for employment under regulation 14;
(i) whether he has applied for, or accepted, a place on, or participated in, a course or programme the cost of which is met in whole or in part out of central funds or by the European Community and the purpose of which is to assist persons to select, train for, obtain or retain employed earner's employment or self-employed earner's employment; and
(j) where he had no living accommodation in that week the fact that he had no such accommodation and the steps which he needed to take and has in fact taken to seek such accommodation.

(4) Any act of a person which would otherwise be relevant for purposes of section 7 shall be disregarded in the following circumstances—
(a) where, in taking the act, he acted in a violent or abusive manner,
(b) where the act comprised the completion of an application for employment and he spoiled the application,
(c) where by his behaviour or appearance he otherwise undermined his prospects of securing the employment in question,
unless those circumstances were due to reasons beyond his control.

(5) In this regulation—
"employment agency" and "employment business" mean an employment agency or (as the case may be) employment business within the meaning of the Employment Agencies Act 1973;
"employment or training programme" means a course or programme the person's participation in which is attributable to arrangements made by the Secretary of State under section 2 of the Employment and Training Act 1973 for the purpose of assisting persons to select, train for, obtain or retain employed earner's employment.

AMENDMENTS

1. Jobseeker's Allowance (Amendment) Regulations 2004 (SI 2004/1008) reg.2(2) (April 19, 2004 [new claimants]; October 18, 2004 [existing claimants and existing recipients of jobseeking credits]).
2. Social Security (Miscellaneous Amendments) (No.4) Regulations 2006 (SI 2006/2378) reg.13(3)(a) (October 2, 2006).

DEFINITIONS

"employment"—see Jobseekers Act 1995 s.7(8).
"employment officer"—see Jobseekers Act 1995 s.35(1).
"employment-related course"—see reg.1(3).
"engaged during an emergency in duties for the benefit of others"—see reg.22.
"Outward Bound course"—see reg.4.
"part-time member of a fire brigade"—*ibid*.
"part-time student"—see reg.1(3).
"training allowance"—*ibid*.
"voluntary work"—see reg.4.
"week"—*ibid*.

GENERAL NOTE

Temporary Coronavirus Provisions
3.90   Regulation 7 of the Social Security (Coronavirus) (Further Measures) Regulations 2020 (SI 2020/371) provided that for the three months beginning with March 30, 2020 anyone with an award of old style JSA was to be treated as actively seeking employment (see the notes to s.1(2)), as well as available for employment. The effect of reg.7 expired at the end of November 12, 2020 (reg.10(2)). The power to extend the three-month period was not exercised before it expired.

It is not clear whether the restriction of the effect of reg.7 to those who had an award of old style JSA meant that on a new claim (insofar as a claim for old style JSA, as opposed to new style JSA and universal credit, was still possible) the actively seeking employment condition was to be applied in determining initial entitlement. The mechanism suggested for new style JSA in the notes to s.6D of the new style Jobseekers Act 1995 (Vol.I of this series) cannot work for old style JSA because the availability and actively seeking work conditions are imposed directly by the legislation as conditions of entitlement. It appears that in practice little if any attention was given to "conditionality" during the period affected.

For the purposes of the old style Jobseekers Act 1995, in any week a person is **3.91** actively seeking employment if during that week they take such steps as they can reasonably be expected to have to take in order to have the best prospects of securing employment (s.7(1)). The reasoning in *GP v SSWP (JSA)* [2015] UKUT 476 (AAC), reported as [2016] AACR 14, (discussed in the notes to s.7(1)) indicates that steps to search for employment outside Great Britain do not count for these purposes (though see reg.19(2)(m), not mentioned in the decision). See regs 19–21B below for circumctances in which a claimant is deemed to be actively seeking employment. In its original form, para.(1) of this regulation amplified that "touchstone test" by stipulating that a person would be expected to take more than one step on one occasion in any week unless taking one step on a single occasion in the week is all that it is reasonable for that person to do in that week (see *CJSA/2162/2001*, noted in the commentary to old style Jobseekers Act 1995 ss.7 and 9). A new version was substituted with effect from April 19, 2004 for new claimants and from October 18, 2004 for those who were existing claimants at April 19 or then in receipt of jobseeking credits. The substitution increased the minimum number of steps that a jobseeker must take to be actively seeking employment from at least two to at least three in a week, unless taking one or two steps is all that it is reasonable to do in that week. The qualification is an important one. A claimant's responsibility has, in the past at least, been misstated in jobseekers' agreements in terms of a declaration that "I know that I must take at least three steps each week".

Concerns were expressed by the SSAC (see Cmd.6145) about the lack of need for and the effect of the change at a time of national low unemployment, and against a background of personnel cuts at Jobcentres. Despite this, the change was made. The Secretary of State was of the view that tailored support was an important way to help people return to work but that, in addition to special provision, it was reasonable in a buoyant labour market to increase expectations of the claimant unemployed through measures designed to be adapted to the individual to increase prospects of getting a job more quickly. There was no change to reduce the minimum number of steps in the more recent periods of high unemployment.

In deciding whether the "touchstone" test is met, the focus should be on what the claimant did in the week in question rather than on whether each of the steps set out in the jobseeker's agreement were performed (*CJSA/1814/2007*, noted in more detail in the commentary to old style Jobseekers Act 1995 s.7, above). In para.25 of *PG v SSWP (JSA)* [2017] UKUT 388 (AAC) (see the notes to s.9 of the old style Jobseekers Act 1995) the judge suggested (in a passage not necessary to the decision), in response to a tribunal's statement that there was no objection in principle to requiring a claimant to engage in actively seeking work as a full time task, that it might take very cogent reasoning to justify a person having to take very well in excess of the three steps per week that are the starting point under reg.18(1). However, that seems to overlook the fundamental nature of the "touchstone test" in s.7(1) of how many steps are reasonably to be expected, with reg.18(1) merely fixing a minimum of three steps per week (or one or two if reasonable). Thus cogent reasoning for a considerable excess over three steps may not be too difficult to find. That is especially so if, as seems to be correct (see below), taking the same step five days a week (e.g. checking a website) counts as five steps.

In past editions it has been suggested, relying in part on Commissioner's decision **3.92**

CJSA/2162/2001 (see above), that there might be circumstances in which the application of the "touchstone test" would result in a conclusion that there were no steps that it was reasonable for the claimant to take in a particular week, so that the test in s.7(1) could be satisfied by taking no steps. It is now submitted that that is wrong. Despite the view expressed there by Commissioner Williams that reg.18 read as a whole did not preclude such a conclusion, it is hard to read reg.18(1) as requiring anything less than an absolute minimum of one step in any week to satisfy s.7(1). It must also be remembered that reg.19 sets out a wide variety of deserving circumstances in which a claimant is to be treated as actively seeking employment, whether or not s.7(1) would otherwise be satisfied, and that regs 20–21B cover some more specific circumstances.

In determining the number of steps taken in any week it is now accepted that doing the same type of act (e.g. looking in a local newspaper for job advertisements) on three different occasions during a week counts as three steps. That was decided in Commissioner's decision *CJSA/3146/2009*, as followed in *CSJSA/548/2014*. By the same token, applying for three vacancies or making enquiries to three employers on the same day would count as three steps. However, those decisions rightly stress that that would only get a claimant over the normal minimum limit in reg.18(1) and it still has to be asked, however many steps over the minimum have been taken, whether the claimant has taken such steps as can reasonably be expected.

CJSA/3146/2009 also contains some helpful guidance about the significance of the contents of a jobseeker's agreement to the actively seeking employment test. The plain (although not uncommonly forgotten) basis is that the test is not that the claimant must carry out all the activities as specified in the jobseeker's agreement. The test is the "touchstone test" of reasonableness in all the circumstances, as modified by reg.18. However, the jobseeker's agreement can set the context for a claimant's job search activities in forming a starting point in identifying the sorts of things that the claimant might reasonably be expected to do (see para.33 of the decision).

3.93   The remainder of the regulation supplies further detail to flesh out that "touchstone test" in terms of providing a partial definition of "steps" (para.(2)), stipulating circumstances to be taken into account in determining whether the test is met in any week (para.(3)) and, most controversially, setting out the circumstances in which otherwise relevant acts are to be disregarded (para.(4)). Paragraph (5) provides definitions of certain terms used in this regulation: "employment agency", "employment business" and "employment or training programme". "Week" means "benefit week" (reg.4); that is, generally, the period of seven days ending with the day corresponding to the claimant's "signing"/attendance day (reg.1(3)).

Paragraph (2) provides a partial definition of "steps" and thus gives a general indication of the type of action claimants must take in order not to fall foul of the actively seeking work test. The list is not exhaustive: the provision reads "steps which it is reasonable to expect a person to have to take in any week *include*" (emphasis supplied by annotator). Regard must still be had to all the steps taken by the claimant to try to get employment: the "touchstone test" remains that in the statute: "such steps as he can reasonably be expected to have to take in order to have the best prospects of securing employment". To determine whether in a particular week any steps taken by a particular claimant satisfy that test, para.(3) requires that regard must be had to all the circumstances of the case, including those specifically there listed. In para.(2) the specifically listed "steps" are:

(a) written and/or oral applications for employment to those who have advertised its availability or who appear to be in a position to offer it;

(b) seeking information on the availability of employment from advertisements, advertisers and employers, or from employment agencies and employment businesses within the meaning of the Employment Agencies Act 1973;

(c) registration with an employment agency or employment business within the meaning of the Employment Agencies Act 1973;

(d) the appointment of a third party to assist the claimant in finding employment (an actor appointing an agent might be an example);

(e) seeking specialist advice, after referral by an employment officer, on how to improve prospects of securing employment having regard to the claimant's needs and in particular any of his physical or mental limitations;

(f) drawing up a curriculum vitae (CV);

(g) seeking a testimonial or reference from a former employer;

(h) drawing up a list of possible employers with a view to seeking information from them on the availability of employment;

(i) seeking information about possible employers; and

(j) seeking information on an occupation with a view to securing employment in it.

To determine whether in a particular week any steps taken by a particular claimant (whether listed in para.(2) or not—that list not being exhaustive) satisfy the touchstone test, para.(3) requires that regard must be had to all the circumstances of claimants' cases, including those specifically listed. The listed circumstances are:

(a) their skills, qualifications and abilities;

(b) their physical or mental limitations (something important to those once on ESA who have been found capable of work and therefore have to look to JSA);

(c) their work experience and how long they have been unemployed;

(d) what they have done in previous weeks to find employment and the effectiveness of that in improving their prospects of finding it;

(e) what jobs are available and where they are;

(f) time spent in certain worthwhile activities as listed in sub-para.(f) (noting some definitions in para.(5) and regs 1(3) and 22);

(g) engagement in voluntary work and the extent to which it may have improved their prospects of securing employment;

(h) whether they are treated as available for work under reg.14 (para.(1)(d) of which is in identical terms to para.(f)(i) of this regulation);

(i) whether they have applied for, or accepted a place on, or participated in, a wholly or partially centrally or European Union-funded course or programme designed to help people select, train for, obtain and retain employment or self-employment; and

(j) the fact that they are homeless, the steps taken and those that they needed to take to find somewhere to live.

It must, however, be stressed again that this list of particular factors is not exhaustive; regard must be had to all the circumstances of the claimant's case to decide whether they meet the touchstone test, the hallmark of which is flexibility and adaptability to different claimants and different labour markets by setting a general target and allowing flexibility of interpretation and application to the individual case, to decide what should be the appropriate extent of job search for a particular individual at a particular time and place. For instance, since it is possible for a claimant to satisfy the condition in s.1(2)(e) of the old style Jobseekers Act 1995 of not being in remunerative work while working for less than 16 hours a week on average or while, say, being on a zero hours contract currently producing few or no hours but likely to produce more in the future, it is arguable that it would be relevant to consider how reasonable it is to expect the claimant to take steps to seek alternative employment. **3.94**

The aim of the controversial provision in para.(4) was to "enable a person's jobseeking activity to be disregarded if he behaves or presents himself in such a way as deliberately to reduce or extinguish his chance of receiving offers of employment" (DSS, *Notes on Clauses* [with respect to the Jobseekers Bill]). It provides that an otherwise relevant act of a person is to be disregarded in a number of circumstances unless the circumstances were due to reasons beyond their control: (i) where in taking the act they acted in a violent or abusive manner; (ii) where the act comprised the completion of an application for employment and they spoiled the application; and (iii) where, by their behaviour or appearance, they otherwise undermined their prospects of securing the employment in question. Arguably, the provision is unnecessary, because in any circumstances that it covers the claimant will not have taken such steps as they could reasonably have been expected to take to have the best prospects of securing employment.

The paragraph, particularly in head (iii) thus involves a more explicit "policing" of behaviour, appearance and, possibly, form-filling competence by Jobcentre Plus personnel, decision-makers and tribunals. The concept of "spoiled the application" in head (ii) is by no means crystal clear. The saving for circumstances beyond one's control will presumably protect the dyslexic and the illiterate, but what about the semi-literate? Electoral law, of course, has the concept of the "spoilt ballot paper", which covers the situation in which the voter has, in that context inadvertently, dealt with his ballot paper in such a manner that it cannot conveniently be used as a ballot paper, but whether that in any way provides a valid analogy for "spoiled" in this regulation remains to be seen. On "spoiled", see the remarks of Commissioner Howell in *CJSA/4665/01*, noted in the commentary to old style Jobseekers Act 1995 s.19(2)(c). Given the aim of the provision, it might have been better for the sake of clarity to have worded it "deliberately spoiled". A further sanction for some such behaviour lies in the preclusion of payment of benefit under s.19(2)(c) in respect of the person having, without a good reason, neglected to avail himself of a reasonable opportunity of employment; the equivalent provision in the unemployment benefit regime enabled disqualification of a claimant who had attended an interview for a job as a parcel porter in a "dirty and unshaven state" (*R(U)28/55*). Care will have to be taken to avoid applying the provision in a manner discriminatory on grounds of sex or race (e.g. to penalise men with long hair or Rastafarians with dreadlocks). Many other difficult cases can be envisaged, like those of claimants with visible tattoos or who wish to wear overt symbols of religious faith or political affiliation.

For an interesting consideration of para.(4) and old style Jobseekers Act 1995 s.7(3), see N. Wikeley, "What the Unemployed Need is a Good Haircut . . ." in [1996] 25 I.L.J. 71.

[¹Actively seeking employment in the period at the beginning of a claim

3.95

18A.—(1) Paragraph (2) applies in any case [²other than a case which falls within regulation 19(1)(i) or (s),] where the period beginning on the date of claim and ending on the day before the beginning of the first week after the date of claim is less than 7 days.

(2) Where this paragraph applies, a person is actively seeking employment in the period referred to in paragraph (1) if he takes in that period such steps as he can reasonably be expected to have to take in order to have the best prospects of securing employment and in determining whether a person has taken such steps—

(a) the steps which it is reasonable for him to be expected to have to take include those referred to in regulation 18(2); and

(b) regard shall be had to all the circumstances of the case, including those matters referred to in regulation 18(3).]

AMENDMENTS

1. Social Security (Jobseeker's Allowance and Mariners' Benefits) (Miscellaneous Amendments) Regulations 1997 (SI 1997/563) reg.4 (March 11, 1997).

2. Jobseeker's Allowance (Amendment) (No.2) Regulations 1999 (SI 1999/3087) reg.4 (November 30, 1999).

DEFINITIONS

"date of claim"—see reg.1(3).
"employment"—see Jobseekers Act 1995 s.7(8).
"week"—see reg.4.

GENERAL NOTE

The actively seeking employment test in old style Jobseekers Act 1995 s.7 is **3.96**
expressed in terms of each week. This regulation, inserted with effect from March
11, 1997, adapts that test to cover a part-week at the beginning of a claim, so that
claimants will satisfy the test if in that part-week period they take such steps as they
can reasonably be expected to have to take in order to have the best prospects of
securing employment, having regard to all the circumstances of the case including
the matters set out in reg.18(3), above. "Steps" include, but are not restricted to,
those referred to in reg.18(2), above.

The practical application of reg.18A will be limited by the extension to seven from
October 27, 2014 of the number of "waiting days" under para.4 of Sch.1 to the old
style Jobseekers Act 1995, but there may not necessarily be waiting days to serve at
the beginning of each claim (see reg.46 and the meaning of "jobseeking period").

Circumstances in which a person is to be treated as actively seeking employment

19.—(1) A person shall be treated as actively seeking employment in the **3.97**
following circumstances, subject to [⁷paragraphs (2) and (2A)] and to any
maximum period specified in this paragraph—

  (a) in any week during which he is participating for not less than 3
        days as a full-time student in an employment-related course where
        participation by him has been approved before the course started
        by an employment officer, for a maximum of 2 weeks and one such
        course in any period of 12 months;
[¹⁵(aa) for any period for which he is treated as available for employment
        under regulation 14(1)(aa) (traineeships);]
  (b) in any week during which he is attending for not less than 3 days
        a residential work camp, for a maximum of 2 weeks and one such
        occasion in any period of 12 months;
  (c) in any week during which he is temporarily absent from Great Britain
        for not less than 3 days because he is taking a member of his family
        who is a child or young person abroad for treatment, for a maximum
        of 8 weeks;
  (d) in any week during which he is engaged for not less than 3 days in the
        manning or launching of a lifeboat or in the performance of duty as a
        part-time member of a fire brigade or engaged during an emergency
        in duties for the benefit of others;
  (e) if he is a member of a couple, in any week during which he is for
        not less than 3 days looking after a member of his family who is a
        child while the other member is temporarily absent from the United
        Kingdom, for a maximum of 8 weeks;
  (f) if he is following an Open University course, in any week during
        which he is attending for not less than 3 days, as a requirement of that
        course, a residential course, for a maximum of one week per course;
  (g) in any week during which he is for not less than 3 days temporarily
        looking after a child full-time because the person who normally looks
        after the child is ill or temporarily absent from home or the person is
        looking after a member of the family who is ill, for a maximum of 8
        weeks;
  (h) in the first week after the date of claim if he is treated as available for
        employment to any extent in that week under regulation 14(1)(h);

[³(i) for any period if he is treated as available for employment to any extent in that period under regulation 14(1)(h);]

[¹(j) if the award is terminated other than on the last day of a week, for the period beginning with the beginning of the week in which the award is terminated and ending on the day on which the award is terminated;]

(k) in any week during which he is participating for not less than 3 days in a programme provided by the Venture Trust in pursuance of an arrangement made by [⁸ the Scottish Ministers], for a maximum of 4 weeks and one such programme in any period of 12 months;

(l) in any week during which he is for not less than 3 days treated as capable of work [¹²or as not having limited capability for work] in accordance with regulation 55;

[¹⁶(lzl) in any week during which he is treated as capable of work or as not having limited capability for work under regulation 55ZA unless it would be reasonable for him to take steps in that week to seek employment and he has not taken such steps.]

[⁶(ll) in any week during which he is for not less than 3 days treated as capable of work [¹²or as not having limited capability for work] in accordance with regulation 55A;]

(m) in any week during which he is temporarily absent from Great Britain for not less than 3 days in order to attend an interview for employment and has given notice to an employment officer, in writing if so required by the employment officer, that he will be so absent, for a maximum of 1 week;

(n) if he is a member of a couple [⁵ other than a joint-claim couple], in any week during which he and his partner are both absent from Great Britain for not less than 3 days and in which a premium referred to in paragraph 10, 11, 12, 13 or 15 of Schedule 1 (applicable amounts) is applicable in respect of his partner for a maximum of 4 weeks;

[⁵(nn) if he is a member of a joint-claim couple, in any week during which he and his partner are both absent from Great Britain for not less than 3 days and in which a premium referred to in paragraph 20E, 20F, 20G or 20I of Schedule 1 (applicable amounts) is applicable in respect of his partner, for a maximum of 4 weeks;]

(o) in any week during which he is treated as available for employment on not less than 3 days under regulation [⁹ 14(2)or (2ZA)];

(p) in any week in respect of which he has given notice to an employment officer, in writing if so required by the employment officer, that—
    (i) he does not intend to be actively seeking employment, but
    (ii) he does intend to reside at a place other than his usual place of residence for at least one day;

(q) in any week during which he is participating for not less than 3 days in an employment or training programme [¹³(other than Work Experience)] for which a training allowance is not payable;

[²(r) in any week, being part of a single period not exceeding 8 weeks falling within a period of continuous entitlement to a jobseeker's allowance, during which he is taking active steps to establish himself in self-employed earner's employment under any scheme for assisting persons to become so employed—
    (i) where, in Wales, his participation under the scheme is attributable to arrangements made by the Secretary of State under section 2 of the Employment and Training Act 1973,

      (ii) where, in Scotland, the scheme—
         (aa) is established by virtue of arrangements made by [¹⁰ Skills Development Scotland,] Scottish Enterprise or Highlands and Islands Enterprise under section 2(3) of the Enterprise and New Towns (Scotland) Act 1990 or
         (bb) is directly or indirectly provided by, or with financial assistance from, the Secretary of State,
      (iii) where, in England, the scheme is directly or indirectly provided by, or with financial assistance from, the Secretary of State, the [¹¹ Homes and Communities Agency] an urban development corporation or a housing action trust,
and the single period referred to above shall begin with the week in which he is accepted on a place under the scheme.]

[⁴(s) for any period if he is treated as available for employment to any extent in that period under regulation 14(1)(o).]

[⁵(t) if he is temporarily absent from Great Britain in the circumstances prescribed in regulation 50(6B)(a) or (c), for the period of any such temporary absence.]

[⁶(u) if he is temporarily absent from Great Britain in the circumstances prescribed in regulation 50(6AA) or, as the case may be (6C).]

[⁷(v) in any week during which he is, for not less than three days, required to attend a court or tribunal as a justice of the peace, a party to any proceedings, a witness or a juror;

  (w) if, for a maximum of 96 hours before being released, he is in—
      (i) police detention within the meaning in section 118(2) of the Police and Criminal Evidence Act 1984 (general interpretation), or
      (ii) legal custody within the meaning in section 295 of the Criminal Procedure (Scotland) Act 1995 (legal custody in Scotland) but is not a prisoner as defined by regulation 85(4) (special cases).]

[¹⁴(x) in any week during which he is treated as available for employment under regulation 14A;]

[¹⁷(y) in any week during which he is engaged for not less than 3 days in training as a member of a reserve force prescribed in Part I of Schedule 6 to the Contributions Regulations, either—
      (i) if he is engaged in his first year of training, for a maximum of 43 days in that year; or
      (ii) if he is engaged in annual continuous training, for a maximum of 15 days in any calendar year.]

(2) In any period of 12 months a person shall be treated as actively seeking employment under paragraph (1)(p) only for the number of weeks specified in one of the following subparagraphs—
  (a) a maximum of 2 weeks; or
  (b) a maximum of 3 weeks during which he is attending for at least 3 days in each such week an Outward Bound course; or
  (c) if he is a blind person, a maximum of 6 weeks during which, apart from a period of no more than 2 weeks, he participates for a maximum period of 4 weeks in a course of training in the use of guide dogs of which at least 3 days in each such week is spent in that training.

[⁷(2A) A person shall not be treated as actively seeking employment under paragraph (1)(v)—
  (a) for more than eight weeks,
  (b) where he does not, before the period during which he is required

to attend the court or tribunal, give an employment officer notice, in writing where requested by the employment officer, that he is so required, or

(c) where he is a prisoner as defined by regulation 85(4) (special cases).]

(3) In this regulation—

"employment or training programme" means a course or programme the person's participation in which is attributable to arrangements made by the Secretary of State under section 2 of the Employment and Training Act 1973 for the purpose of assisting persons to select, train for, obtain or retain employment;

"housing action trust" means a corporation established by an order of the Secretary of State pursuant to section 62(1) of the Housing Act 1988;

"treatment" means treatment for a disease or bodily or mental disablement by or under the supervision of a person qualified to provide medical treatment, physiotherapy or a form of treatment which is similar to, or related to, either of those forms of treatment;

[⁷"tribunal" means any tribunal listed in Schedule 1 to the Tribunals and Inquiries Act 1992;]

"urban development corporation" means a corporation established by an order of the Secretary of State pursuant to section 135(1) of the Local Government, Planning and Land Act 1980;

[¹¹ . . .]

Amendments

1. Jobseeker's Allowance and Income Support (General) (Amendment) Regulations 1996 (SI 1996/1517) reg.7 (October 7, 1996).

2. Social Security Amendment (New Deal) Regulations 1998 (SI 1998/1274) reg.5 (June 1, 1998).

3. Jobseeker's Allowance (Amendment) (No.2) Regulations 1999 (SI 1999/3087) reg.5(2) (November 30, 1999).

4. Jobseeker's Allowance (Amendment) (No.2) Regulations 1999 (SI 1999/3087) reg.5(3) (November 30, 1999).

5. Jobseeker's Allowance (Joint Claims: Consequential Amendments) Regulations 2000 (SI 2000/3336) reg.2 (March 19, 2001).

6. Social Security (Income Support and Jobseeker's Allowance) Amendment Regulations 2004 (SI 2004/1869) reg.3(3) (October 4, 2004).

7. Social Security (Income Support and Jobseeker's Allowance) Amendment Regulations 2006 (SI 2006/1402) reg.2(4) (May 30, 2006).

8. Social Security (Miscellaneous Amendments) Regulations 2008 (SI 2008/698) reg.4(6) (April 14, 2008).

9. Social Security (Lone Parents and Miscellaneous Amendments) Regulations 2008 (SI 2008/3051) reg.11(10) (November 4, 2008).

10. Social Security (Miscellaneous Amendments) Regulations 2009 (SI 2009/583) reg.4(3) (April 6, 2009).

11. The Housing and Regeneration Act 2008 (Consequential Provisions) (No.2) Order 2008 (SI 2008/2831) Sch.1 para.7 (December 1, 2008).

12. Employment and Support Allowance (Consequential Provisions) (No.2) Regulations 2008 (SI 2008/1554) reg.3(5) (October 27, 2008).

13. Jobseeker's Allowance (Work Experience) (Amendment) Regulations 2011 (SI 2011/789) reg.2(3) (April 5, 2011).

14. Jobseeker's Allowance (Domestic Violence) (Amendment) Regulations 2012 (SI 2012/853) reg.2(3) (April 23, 2012).

15. Social Security (Traineeships and Qualifying Young Persons) Amendment Regulations 2015 (SI 2015/336) reg.2(5) (March 27, 2015).

16. Jobseeker's Allowance (Extended Period of Sickness) Amendment Regulations 2015 (SI 2015/339) reg.2(3) (March 30, 2015).

17. Social Security (Members of the Reserve Forces) (Amendment) Regulations 2015 (SI 2015/389) reg.3(4) (April 6, 2015).

DEFINITIONS

"a joint-claim couple"—see Jobseekers Act 1995 s.1(4).

"capable of work"—see Jobseekers Act 1995 s.35(2) and Sch.1 para.2; reg.55.

"child"— see Jobseekers Act 1995 s.35(1).

"the Contributions Regulations"—see reg.1(3).

"couple"—*ibid.*

"date of claim"—*ibid.*

"employed earner's employment"—see Jobseekers Act 1995 s.7(8); SSCBA 1992 s.2(1)(a).

"employment"—see Jobseekers Act 1995 s.7(8).

"employment officer"—see Jobseekers Act 1995 s.35(1).

"employment-related course"—see reg.1(3).

"engaged during an emergency in duties for the benefit of others"—see reg.22.

"family"—see Jobseekers Act 1995 s.35(1).

"first year of training"—see reg.1(3).

"full-time student"—*ibid.*

"Great Britain"—see Jobseekers Act 1995 s.35(1).

"partner"—see reg.1(3).

"part-time member of a fire brigade"—see reg.4.

"self-employed earner's employment"—see Jobseekers Act 1995 s.7(8); SSCBA 1992 s.2(1)(b).

"training allowance"—see reg.1(3).

"week"—see reg.4.

"work camp"—*ibid.*

"young person"—see regs 1(3) and 76.

GENERAL NOTE

Temporary Coronavirus Provisions

Regulation 7 of the Social Security (Coronavirus) (Further Measures) Regulations 2020 (SI 2020/371) provided that for the three months beginning with March 30, 2020 anyone with an award of old style JSA was to be treated as actively seeking employment (see the notes to s.1(2)), as well as available for employment. The effect of reg.7 expired at the end of November 12, 2020 (reg.10(2)). The power to extend the three-month period was not exercised before it expired. **3.98**

It is not clear whether the restriction of the effect of reg.7 to those who had an award of old style JSA meant that on a new claim (insofar as a claim for old style JSA, as opposed to new style JSA and universal credit, was still possible) the actively seeking employment condition was to be applied in determining initial entitlement. The mechanism suggested for new style JSA in the notes to s.6D of the new style Jobseekers Act 1995 (Vol.I of this series) cannot work for old style JSA because the availability and actively seeking work conditions are imposed directly by the legislation as conditions of entitlement. It appears that in practice little if any attention was given to "conditionality" during the period affected.

This regulation sets out in para.(1) a range of situations in which, for the periods specified therein or in para.(2), someone is to be treated as actively seeking employment, even though, were it applied to them, they might fail to satisfy the touchstone test of actually actively seeking employment set out in old style Jobseekers Act 1995 **3.99** s.7(1) as amplified by reg.18. Note, however, that where it has been decided that a person is to be treated as actively seeking employment in any week, a subsequent revision and supersession of that decision can embrace also the question whether in that week the person was actually actively seeking employment (old style Jobseekers Act 1995 s.7(7)). In applying the regulation, careful note should be taken of the specific definition of certain terms (listed in "Definitions", above and in para.(3)). One must also remember the distinction between *Great Britain* (England, Scotland and Wales) and the *United Kingdom* (of Great Britain and Northern Ireland).

The categories set out in para.(1) need to be examined carefully. They cannot apply for longer than the circumstances prescribed last. However, some categories contain more stringent limits. Sub-paragraphs (l), (lza) and (ll) are an important element of the protection given to those who are treated as capable of work or as not having limited capability for work under regs 55, 55ZA or 55A, by deeming such persons to be actively seeking employment (and see reg.14(1)(l) on deemed availability). Another particularly interesting category, in the light of the state of the rules on potential availability for employment while claimants are on holiday (see the notes to s.6 of the old style Jobseekers Act 1995), is sub-para.(p), covering weeks in respect of which a claimant has given (advance) notice to an employment officer of the absence of an intention to be actively seeking employment and an intention to reside for at least a day in that week at a place other than the claimant's usual place of residence. Under para.(2) advantage can generally only be taken of sub-para.(p) for two weeks in any 12 months, although there are specific extensions for Outward Bound courses and guide dog training for the blind. In para.(1)(m) (temporary absence from Great Britain for at least three days to attend an interview for employment) it would be ludicrous if "employment" were restricted to employment in Great Britain, despite the decision in *GP v SSWP (JSA)* [2015] UKUT 476 (AAC), reported as [2016] AACR 14, (discussed in the notes to s.7(1)).

The remainder of the categories specified in para.(1) fall into four main groups (sometimes overlapping): those taking part in certain educational or training activities (sub-paras (a), (aa), (b), (f), (k), (q) and (y)); those involving temporary absence from Great Britain (sub-paras (c), (e), (m), (n), (nn), (t) and (u)); those involving caring for others (sub-paras (e), (g), (t) and (u)); and those involving some public service (sub-paras (d), (v) and (y)). The remaining miscellaneous categories, often to do with the beginning or end of a period of entitlement, are in sub-paras (h), (i), (j), (o), (r), (s), (w) and (x).

The transition from new style JSA

3.100   In para.(1)(r) the reference to jobseeker's allowance is, where art.13(1) and (2) of the Welfare Reform Act 2012 (Commencement No.9 and Transitional and Transitory Provisions and Commencement No.8 and Savings and Transitional Provisions (Amendment)) Order 2013 (as amended and set out in Part V of this volume) applies, to be read as if it included a reference to new style JSA (art.13(3)(ab) of that Order, in force from June 16, 2014).

Further circumstances in which a person is to be treated as actively seeking employment: permitted period

3.101   **20.**—(1) A person to whom paragraph (2) does not apply shall be treated as actively seeking employment in any week during any permitted period determined in his case in accordance with regulation 16, if he is actively seeking employment in that week—

(a) only in his usual occupation,
(b) only at a level of remuneration not lower than that which he is accustomed to receive, or
(c) only in his usual occupation and at a level of remuneration not lower than that which he is accustomed to receive.

(2) A person to whom this paragraph applies shall be treated as actively seeking employment in any week during any permitted period determined in his case in accordance with regulation 16, if he is actively seeking employment, self-employed earner's employment, or employment and self-employed earner's employment in that week—

    (a) only in his usual occupation,

    (b) only at a level of remuneration not lower than that which he is accustomed to receive, or

    (c) only in his usual occupation and at a level of remuneration not lower than that which he is accustomed to receive.

(3) Paragraph (2) applies to a person who has, at any time during the period of 12 months immediately preceding the date of claim, been engaged in his usual occupation in self-employed earner's employment.

DEFINITIONS

> "employment"—see Jobseekers Act 1995 s.7(8).
> "employed earner's employment"—see Jobseekers Act 1995 s.7(8); SSCBA 1992 s.2(1)(a).
> "self-employed earner's employment"—see Jobseekers Act 1995 s.7(8); SSCBA 1992 s.2(1)(b).
> "week"—see reg.4.

GENERAL NOTE

Under the old style Act, all claimants must be available for employment (as opposed to self-employment). For a "permitted period" of up to 13 weeks, claimants can be treated as available even though only available for employment in their usual occupation and/or at their accustomed level of remuneration (reg.16). Paragraph (1) of this regulation enables such a person to be treated as actively seeking employment for that period. Under para.(2), someone who has at any time in the 12 months prior to their date of claim for old style JSA been engaged in self-employment in their usual occupation can be treated as actively seeking employment during the "permitted period", even though they confine their jobsearch to employment, self-employment or both, only in their usual occupation, or only at their accustomed rate of remuneration, or only in their usual occupation and at their accustomed rate. But they must, of course, still be available for employment as an employed earner. On determining whether a particular claimant can have such a "permitted period" and, if so, its length, see reg.16(2). For limitations on the application of the period in the case of a claimant laid of from, or kept on short time in, his employment, see reg.17(4).

    3.102

Further circumstances in which a person is to be treated as actively seeking employment: laid off and short time workers

21.—A person who has restricted his availability for employment in accordance with regulation 17(1) or, as the case may be, regulation 17(2), shall in any week in which he has so restricted his availability for not less than 3 days be treated as actively seeking employment in that week if he takes such steps as he can reasonably be expected to have to take in order to have the best prospects of securing employment for which he is available under regulation 17.

    3.103

DEFINITIONS

> "employment"—see reg.4.
> "week"—*ibid.*

GENERAL NOTE

3.104   Under reg.17, claimants laid off from employment or put on short time owing to temporary adverse industrial conditions can, for up to 13 weeks, be treated as available for employment, provided they are willing and able to resume immediately the employment from which, as the case may be, they are laid off or kept on short time, and to take up immediately any casual employment within daily travelling distance of their home. The requirement of immediacy is modified for carers and volunteers (48 hours' notice) and those providing a service (24 hours' notice), protected by reg.5(1) and (2). See the notes to reg.17 for the effect of temporary coronavirus provisions.

This regulation stipulates that claimants who have restricted their availability in that way for not less than three days in a particular week are to be treated as actively seeking employment in that week, provided they take such steps as they can reasonably be expected to have to take in order to have the best prospects of securing the employment for which, under reg.17, they are available. In short, for up to 13 weeks of short time or lay off, they can confine their jobsearch to the job with respect to which they have been laid off or kept on short time and casual employment within daily travelling distance of their home.

[¹Further circumstances in which a qualifying person is to be treated as actively seeking employment: full-time students participating in a qualifying course

3.105   **21A.**—A person who is treated as available for employment in accordance with regulation 17A(3) shall be treated as actively seeking employment in any week—

(a) which, in relation to the qualifying course, falls wholly or partly in term-time;

(b) in which he is taking examinations relating to the qualifying course; or

(c) which falls wholly in a vacation from the qualifying course, if in that week he takes such steps as he can reasonably be expected to have to take in order to have the best prospects of securing employment for which he is available under regulation 17A(3)(c).]

AMENDMENT

1. Social Security Amendment (New Deal) Regulations 1998 (SI 1998/1274) reg.6 (June 1, 1998).

DEFINITIONS

"employment"—see Jobseekers Act 1995 s.7(8).
"employed earner's employment"—see Jobseekers Act 1995 s.7(8); SSCBA 1992 s.2(1)(a).
"examination"—see reg.4.
"qualifying course"—*ibid.*, reg.17A(7).
"term-time"—see reg.4.
"vacation"—*ibid.*
"week"—*ibid.*

GENERAL NOTE

3.106   Complementing reg.17A, reg.21A provides that during any week in which a person is treated as available under reg.17A, they will be treated also as actively seeking employment. Where the week is during a vacation from the course, they must however show that during that week they have taken such steps as they can reasonably be expected to have to take to have the best prospects of securing the casual employment for which reg.17A requires them to be available.

[¹Further circumstances in which a person is to be treated as actively seeking employment: lone parents with children aged 5 not in full-time education

21B.—A lone parent who is treated for any period as being available for employment under regulation 17B shall be treated as actively seeking employment for the same period.]

3.107

AMENDMENT

1. Social Security (Lone Parents and Miscellaneous Amendments) Regulations 2012 (SI 2012/874) reg.3(2) (May 21, 2012, subject to special commencement provisions in the Sch. to this amending instrument).

Interpretation of certain expressions for the purposes of regulations 18(3)(f)(i) and 19(1)(d)

22.—For the purposes of regulations 18(3)(f)(i) and 19(1)(d)—

3.108

(a) a person is engaged in duties for the benefit of others while—
  (i) providing assistance to any person whose life may be endangered or who may be exposed to the risk of serious bodily injury or whose health may be seriously impaired,
  (ii) protecting property of substantial value from imminent risk of serious damage or destruction, or
  (iii) assisting in measures being taken to prevent a serious threat to the health of the people,
  as a member of a group of persons organised wholly or partly for the purpose of providing such assistance or, as the case may be, protection;
(b) events which may give rise to an emergency include—
  (i) a fire, a flood or an explosion,
  (ii) a natural catastrophe,
  (iii) a railway or other transport accident,
  (iv) a cave or mountain accident,
  (v) an accident at sea,
  (vi) a person being reported missing and the organisation of a search for that person.

GENERAL NOTE

Regulation 18(3)(f)(i) provides that in applying the touchstone test of actively seeking employment to a claimant's jobseeking activity in a week, the fact that a claimant was engaged during an emergency in duties for the benefit of others is one of the circumstances to be taken into account. Under reg.19(1)(d) a claimant so engaged for at least three days in a week is treated as actively seeking work in that week. For the purposes of those provisions, this regulation provides in para.(1) a complete definition of when "a person is engaged in duties for the benefit of others" and in para.(b) an indication of what events can give rise to an "emergency". Paragraph (b) is not, however, exhaustive; it reads "events which may give rise to an emergency *include*" (emphasis supplied by annotator). See further reg.14, where the same definitions are deployed, and the annotations to that provision.

3.109

Chapter IV

Attendance, information and evidence

Attendance

3.110   **23.**—[¹A claimant shall [²participate in an interview in such manner, time and place] as an employment officer may specify by a notification which is given or sent to the claimant and which may be in writing, by telephone or by electronic means.]

AMENDMENTS

1. Jobseeker's Allowance (Amendment) (No.3) Regulations 2000 (SI 2000/ 2194) reg.2(2) (September 11, 2000).
2. Jobseeker's Allowance (Sanctions) (Amendment) Regulations 2012 (SI 2012/2568) reg.5(4) (October 22, 2012).

DEFINITIONS

"claimant"—see Jobseekers Act 1995 s.35(1).
"employment officer"—*ibid.*
"writing"—see Interpretation Act 1978 Sch.1.

GENERAL NOTE

3.111   *"Sent"*: In *R(JSA)1/04*, the claimant had been sent a notice, dated October 8, 2001 calling him for interview on October 25, 2001, but, Commissioner Turnbull accepted, had probably not received it. The Commissioner held that the proper interpretation of "sent" in reg.23 in accordance with s.7 of the Interpretation Act 1978, as applied by s.23 of that Act to subordinate legislation, meant that the claimant was entitled to prove non-receipt in order to say it had not been "sent" with the consequence that his entitlement to JSA could not be terminated since he had not "failed to attend" the interview. It appears to have been accepted by the Supreme Court in *Newcastle upon Tyne Hospitals Trust NHS Foundation v Haywood* [2018] UKSC 22; [2018] 1 W.L.R. 2073 that the presumption of receipt under s.7 is rebuttable.

No particular period of notification is required by reg.23, but it must necessarily be implied that the notification is given in time for the claimant to attend the appointment (as confirmed in *R(JSA) 1/04*). Non-receipt by such a time would undermine the validity of any action in purported reliance on a failure to participate in the interview. In the case of unreasonably short notice, the claimant's remedy appears to lie in contacting the employment officer within five days after the notified date and thus avoiding the ending of entitlement (reg.25(1)(a) and (b)). Unreasonably short notice would also be relevant to a good reason for failing to comply with reg.23 and to the possibility of a sanction under s.19A(2)(a) of the Act (see the notes to reg.25 below).

The Interpretation Act presumption only applies where the letter containing the notice was properly addressed. The decisions in *CJSA/4720/2014* (not at present on the AAC website) and *DD v SSWP (JSA)* [2015] UKUT 318 (AAC) arose under the SAPOE Regulations (below), where reg.2(2) provides that where a notice is sent by post it is to be taken to have been received on the second working day after posting. The judges in both cases held that that provision only applied if the letter was correctly addressed, and that outside any presumption the question was whether the Secretary of State had shown on the balance of probabilities that the notice had been received. The cases concerned the same claimant and the same mistake in the address, but different letters and notices to participate in schemes and it is evident that neither Upper Tribunal judge knew of the existence of the other appeal. The first line and the postcode was correct, but the address included the name of an estate some miles away from the estate on which the claimant lived. The claimant denied receiving the letters in question. In *CJSA/4720/2014*, the First-tier Tribunal decided that, in the light of the claimant's history of non-attendance at Work Programme appointments and of sending back letters from the provider unopened, she did in fact receive the letter in question so that the sanction (presumably under s.19A(2)(b) of the old style Jobseekers Act 1995, as only Mandatory Work Activity is prescribed for the purposes of s.19(2)(e)) was upheld. Judge West set that decision aside on the basis (perhaps only doubtfully made out on the extracts cited) that the tribunal had regarded it as crucial that the correct postcode had been used and that, as asserted on behalf of the Secretary of State, that would have enabled delivery to the correct address before the appointment. However, there was a reference to a new tribunal to give the Secretary of State the opportunity to produce evidence from the Royal Mail in support of the assertion that use of the correct postcode would enable the correct delivery of a letter when other parts of the address are incorrect. By contrast, in *DD* Judge Mark, on the material before him, while accepting that the Royal Mail would have had little difficulty in identifying the correct address, considered that the doubt about how long that process would take meant that on the balance of probabilities it had not been shown that a letter said to have been posted on January 9, 2014 (a Thursday) had been received by Wednesday January 15, 2014 in time for the claimant to know that she was required to attend on that day. He substituted a decision setting aside the sanction imposed on the claimant. The judge also queried whether evidence that a letter had been issued on a particular date was necessarily evidence of posting on that day, given common office practice of post put in an out-tray after mid-afternoon not in fact being posted until the following working day.

There is some doubt, as was raised in *CS v SSWP (JSA)* [2015] UKUT 61 (AAC), whether the provision that the notification of the manner, time and place of the interview "may" be in writing, by telephone or by electronic means is exhaustive or merely illustrative. The issue potentially raised in that case was whether an oral notification given in the course of face to face contact between the claimant and the employment officer qualified. In the event, Judge Wikeley did not have to decide that point of interpretation, because the Secretary of State conceded that, in the absence of any entry in the claimant's Action Plan for the date on which it was said that the employment officer had told him orally that he was to sign on in seven days' time rather than on the previous fortnightly basis, the First-tier Tribunal erred in law by accepting the DWP's assertion that notification had been given in preference to the claimant's evidence that he had not been told that he had to attend on any particular date and time different from his previous pattern. Judge Wikeley accepted that concession, suggesting that, just as in sanctions cases (see *DL v SSWP (JSA)* [2013] UKUT 295 (AAC)), the legislation should be construed strictly, giving the claimant the benefit of any doubt that might reasonably arise. The Secretary of State's submission in *CS* had been that the provision is purely illustrative, so that a properly proved oral notification comes within reg. 23. The contrary argument is that there would appear to be little point in specifying the particular means of communication if the intention was to be purely illustrative and that "may be" can often properly be construed as setting out the permissible means of doing something. It is of course to be implied that the notification is in a form that the particular claimant is reasonably to be known to be capable of comprehending.

DC v SSWP (JSA) [2020] UKUT 257 (AAC) has decided the issue of interpretation left open in *CS*, holding that reg. 23 allows the oral notification of the manner, time and place of an interview in the course of face to face contact. That was because of the use of the permissive "may" in the regulation and of the lack of any apparent reason for not accepting such notification if oral notification by telephone is accepted. But the tribunal had erred in upholding the decision that the claimant's entitlement to old style JSA terminated on the day of the interview that

3.112

he had failed to participate in, because he had on the previous day posted a letter to the DWP saying that he would no longer attend for daily signing until he had been given formal notification of the purpose of that requirement. Thus, as accepted by the Secretary of State before the Upper Tribunal, the claimant had made contact with an employment officer within the period ending five working days after the day of the interview, so that entitlement could not cease under reg.25(1)(a). The claimant was, though, subject to a four-week sanction under s.19A(2)(a) of the old style Jobseekers Act 1995 and reg.69A because the judge found that he did not have good reason for failing to participate in the interview. A refusal to attend by way of ultimatum could not amount to good reason. That conclusion must have been reached on the basis that the claimant had been given a sufficient explanation of the purpose orally.

Judge West also noted, in explaining why permission to appeal had been refused on a particular point, that, although the work coach had apparently expressed the requirement as being to sign daily, the daily visit for evidence of daily jobsearch to be seen entailed an interview as well. The Secretary of State did not rely in the Upper Tribunal on any failure under reg.24(6) and (10) to provide a signed declaration, but that failure could not have led to the termination of entitlement under regs 25(1)(c) and 26(c) because the making of contact with an employment officer within the time limit prevented that result under reg.27. As explained in the notes to reg.27, despite the words of reg.27, there is no requirement for the claimant also to show a good reason for failing to provide the declaration. On the four-week sanction, the prohibition on a reduction in benefit in reg.23 cases (reg.70A(2)(b)) would have been excluded by reg.70A(3). The prohibition in reg.24 cases has no exceptions.

It was accepted in *CS* that a proper notification would have to specify the time (including date) and place of the interview. It appears, because the obligation to participate in the interview arises by the force of reg.23 merely on specification of those matters, that the notification need not itself say that the claimant is required to attend, although it would plainly be good practice for it to do so (and a failure to do so would plainly be relevant to "good reason" for failure to comply with the regulation: s.19A(2)(a) of the old style Jobseekers Act 1995). It remains unclear just what has to be specified about the manner in which the claimant is to participate in the interview. Regulation 25 makes it a condition for terminating entitlement on a failure to comply with regs 23, 23A or 24(6) and (10) that the claimant has failed to make contact with an employment officer "in the manner set out in [a reg.23 or 23A] notification" before the end of the period of five working days from the failure to comply. Thus, the notification should tell the claimant by what means contact can be made with an employment officer if the day or time of the interview is missed and/or if a signed declaration was not provided on the notified day. It may be arguable, applying the strict interpretation principle suggested in *CS*, that if the notification fails to provide that information, reg.25 cannot be applied.

In *CJSA/1080/2002*, Commissioner Rowland held that the requirement to attend as a condition of entitlement to old style JSA lapses once the claimant has been informed that his claim for JSA has been rejected. In that case, the letter so informing the claimant may have been meant to refer only to IBJSA but was so worded that a reasonable claimant would understand it to reject her claim for both IBJSA and CBJSA. Accordingly, the tribunal had erred in not considering title to CBJSA: the requirement to attend having lapsed, regs 25 and 26 were inapplicable, so that there was no limit to the period for which the tribunal could have awarded CBJSA on the appeal.

3.113 Judge Rowland followed *CJSA/1080/2002*, with the apparent agreement of the Secretary of State, in *GM v SSWP (JSA)* [2014] UKUT 57 (AAC). The principle therefore seems to be accepted, although the technical mechanism to implement it is not entirely clear. Perhaps the requirement under reg.23 (or 23A) is simply to be regarded as of no effect in such circumstances.

Note that the test has now become, in line with universal credit and new style JSA, not merely attendance at an interview at the notified date and time, but participation in the interview. This would appear to mean that a claimant can be required to participate in an interview over the telephone, providing that notification has been given of that manner of conducting it. However, in an ambiguous Parliamentary answer on November 24, 2015 (UIN 17005), the Minister of State, Priti Patel, said:

> "Under JSA, claimants are not sanctioned for failing to answer their telephone. In Universal Credit, claimants who have a prearranged telephone interview with their Work Coach, and who fail to participate without good reason, can be referred for a sanction decision."

There is no further provision about what participation means. It must at least entail turning up at the place and time specified, although the decision of Judge Knowles in *SA v SSWP (JSA)* [2015] UKUT 454 (AAC) (see the notes to s.19A(2) (c) of the old style Jobseekers Act 1995 for full discussion) would indicate that tribunals should consider, in cases where the claimant arrives not very late, whether it is proportionate to the nature of all the circumstances to regard that as a failure to participate in an interview. There were all sorts of mitigating circumstances in *SA*, that may well not be present in other cases. See *SN v SSWP (JSA)* [2018] UKUT 279 (AAC), detailed in the notes to s.19(2)(a) of the old style Jobseekers Act 1995, for discussion of what might amount to a failure to participate (in that case in a mandatory work activity scheme) and the expression in para.45 of some doubt about the result in *SA*. Also, there is specific provision in reg.25(1)(b) for cases where a claimant makes contact with an employment officer on the right day, but does not participate in an interview at the right time, which may provide a significantly different context. As discussed further below, it is relatively easy for claimants to avoid a ceasing of entitlement under reg.25, but they may still be subject to a sanction under s.19A(2)(a). The approach in *SA* might be more relevant in that context.

Participation must also extend to making some meaningful contribution to the interview, but the limits will probably not be established until some more appeals have reached the Upper Tribunal. Behaviour that leads to the premature termination of the interview may well amount to a failure to participate (see the facts of *DM v SSWP (JSA)* [2015] UKUT 67 (AAC) in the notes to s.19A(2)(c)). There may, though, in cases of uncooperative claimants or heavy-handed officials or a combination, be difficult questions about when an interview has ceased to exist, so that subsequent behaviour cannot be relevant to whether there has been a failure to participate (see *PH v SSWP (ESA)* [2016] UKUT 119 (AAC) on failing to submit to a medical examination). **3.114**

It was recognised in *CS v SSWP (JSA)* [2019] UKUT 218 (AAC), detailed in the notes to s.19A(2)(b) of the old style Jobseekers Act 1995, that it was legitimate for a scheme provider to require a person attending to verify their identity before starting a scheme, so that a refusal to do so would usually amount to a failure to participate in the scheme. The same principle could apply to an interview, but the particular issues that arose in *CS*, to do with a scheme provider external to the DWP, are unlikely to arise in an interview with an employment officer that has been notified.

A failure to comply with a requirement under s.8(1) can lead to the ceasing of entitlement under regs 25–27 below, as authorised by s.8(2), and also to a sanction under s.19A(2)(a) of the old style Jobseekers Act 1995. Regulation 25(1) specifies in sub-paras (a) and (b) that a failure to participate in a notified interview and to contact the employment officer within five working days after the notified date leads to the ceasing of entitlement. Sub-paragraph.(c) specifies that result where a claimant fails to provide a signed declaration on the day required under reg.24(10). See the notes to reg.25 for the details.

In relation to reg.25(1)(a) and (b), as exemplified in *DC* above, on failing to comply with a requirement under regs 23 or 23A, the cessation of entitlement cannot be applied where the claimant has made contact with an employment officer within the appropriate five-day period, however feeble the reason for not participating in the interview on the right day or at the right time. In those circumstances, the claimant will still have failed to comply with a requirement under either reg.23 or 23A, by failing to participate in an interview on the right date or at the right time.

That is a sanctionable failure under s.19A(2)(a) of the old style Jobseekers Act 1995 if the claimant does not have a good reason for the failure to comply, which reg.70A(2)(b), (3) and (4) allows to lead to a reduction in benefit for the appropriate fixed period under reg.69A. If the claimant has not made contact within the five-day period, the cessation of entitlement under reg.25(1)(a) or (b) must follow. However, in those circumstances there can be no reduction in benefit following the sanctionable failure. Regulation 70A(2)(b), (3)(b) and (4)(d) requires that result in regs 23 or 23A cases, except where the claimant has made contact with an employment officer within the prescribed period. The sanctionable failure then does not count as a previous failure for the purpose of calculating the period of reduction of benefit on any subsequent "offence" (reg.69A(2)(a)).

[¹Attendance by members of a joint-claim couple

3.115   **23A.**—Each member of a joint-claim couple shall [²participate in an interview in such manner, time and place] as the employment officer may specify by a notification which is given or sent to that member and which may be in writing, by telephone or by electronic means.]

AMENDMENTS

1. Jobseeker's Allowance (Joint Claims) Regulations 2000 (SI 2000/1978) Sch.2 para.2 (March 19, 2001).
2. Jobseeker's Allowance (Sanctions) (Amendment) Regulations 2012 (SI 2012/2568) reg.5(4) (October 22, 2012).

DEFINITIONS

"employment officer"—see Jobseekers Act 1995 s.35(1).
"joint claim couple"—see Jobseekers Act 1995 ss.35(1) and 1(4).

GENERAL NOTE

3.116   This makes the same provision as in reg.23 for both members of a joint-claim couple. See the notes to reg.23.

Provision of information and evidence

3.117   **24.**—(1) A claimant shall provide such information as to his circumstances, his availability for employment and the extent to which he is actively seeking employment as may be required by the Secretary of State in order to determine the entitlement of the claimant to a jobseeker's allowance, whether that allowance is payable to him and, if so, in what amount.
    [¹(1A) A member of a joint-claim couple shall provide such information as to the circumstances of each or either member of a couple, the availability for employment of each or either member of the couple and the extent to which each or either member of the couple is actively seeking employment as may be required by the Secretary of State in order to determine the entitlement of the couple to a jobseeker's allowance, whether that allowance is payable to the couple and, if so, in what amount.]
    (2) A claimant shall furnish such other information in connection with the claim, or any question arising out of it, as may be required by the Secretary of State.
    (3) Where—
        (a) a jobseeker's allowance may be claimed by either member of a couple, or
        (b) entitlement to a jobseeker's allowance or whether that allowance

is payable and, if so, in what amount, is or may be affected by the circumstances of either member of a couple or any member of a polygamous marriage,

the Secretary of State may require the member of the couple other than the claimant to certify in writing whether he agrees to the claimant's making the claim, or that he, or any member of a polygamous marriage, confirms the information given about his circumstances[¹, and in this paragraph "couple" does not include a joint-claim couple.

(3A) Where entitlement to a joint-claim jobseeker's allowance or whether that allowance is payable and, if so, in what amount, is or may be affected by the circumstances of any member of a polygamous marriage, the Secretary of State may require either member of the joint-claim couple to certify in writing that any member of the polygamous marriage confirms the information given about that member's circumstances.]

(4) A claimant shall furnish such certificates, documents and other evidence as may be required by the Secretary of State for the determination of the claim.

(5) A claimant shall furnish such certificates, documents and other evidence affecting his continuing entitlement to a jobseeker's allowance, whether that allowance is payable to him and, if so, in what amount as the Secretary of State may require.

[¹(5A) A member of a joint-claim couple shall furnish such certificates, documents and other evidence affecting the continuing entitlement of the couple to a jobseeker's allowance, whether that allowance is payable to the couple and, if so, in what amount as the Secretary of State may require.]

(6) A claimant shall, if the Secretary of State requires him to do so, provide a signed declaration to the effect that—

(a) since making a claim for a jobseeker's allowance or since he last provided a declaration in accordance with this paragraph he has either been available for employment or satisfied the circumstances to be treated as available for employment, save as he has otherwise notified the Secretary of State.

(b) since making a claim for a jobseeker's allowance or since he last provided a declaration in accordance with this paragraph he has either been actively seeking employment to the extent necessary to give him his best prospects of securing employment or he has satisfied the circumstances to be treated as actively seeking employment, save as he has otherwise notified the Secretary of State, and

(c) since making a claim for a jobseeker's allowance or since he last provided a declaration in accordance with this paragraph there has been no change to his circumstances which might affect his entitlement to a jobseeker's allowance or the amount of such an allowance, save as he has notified the Secretary of State.

(7) A claimant shall notify the Secretary of State—

(a) of any change of circumstances which has occurred which he might reasonably be expected to know might affect his entitlement to a jobseeker's allowance [¹or, in the case of a joint-claim couple, the entitlement of the couple to a joint-claim jobseeker's allowance] or the payability or amount of such an allowance; and

(b) of any such change of circumstances which he is aware is likely so to occur,

and shall do so as soon as reasonably practicable after its occurrence or, as the case may be, after he becomes so aware, by giving notice [³of the change to an office of the Department for Work and Pensions specified by the Secretary of State—

    (i) in writing or by telephone (unless the Secretary of State determines in any particular case that notice must be in writing or may be given otherwise than in writing or by telephone); or

    (ii) in writing if in any class of case he requires written notice (unless he determines in any particular case to accept notice given otherwise than in writing).]

(8) Where, pursuant to paragraph (1) [¹(1A)] or (2), a claimant is required to provide information he shall do so [⁵at the time he is required to participate in an interview] in accordance with a [²notification] under regulation 23 [¹or 23A], if so required by the Secretary of State, or within such period as the Secretary of State may require.

(9) Where, pursuant to paragraph (4) [⁴ . . .], a claimant is required to provide certificates, documents or other evidence he shall do so within seven days of being so required or such longer period as the Secretary of State may consider reasonable.

[⁴(9A) Where, pursuant to paragraph (5) or (5A), a claimant is required to provide certificates, documents or other evidence, he shall do so within the period applicable under regulation 17(4) of the Social Security and Child Support (Decisions and Appeals) Regulations 1999.]

(10) Where, pursuant to paragraph (6), a claimant is required to provide a signed declaration he shall provide it [⁵on the day on which he is required to participate in an interview] in accordance with a [²notification] under regulation 23 [¹or 23A] or on such other day as the Secretary of State may require.

AMENDMENTS

1. Jobseeker's Allowance (Joint Claims) Regulations 2000 (SI 2000/1978) Sch.2 para.3 (March 19, 2001).

2. Jobseeker's Allowance (Amendment) (No.3) Regulations 2000 (SI 2000/2194) reg.2(3) (September, 11, 2000).

3. Social Security (Miscellaneous Amendments) (No.2) Regulations 2006 (SI 2006/832) reg.4 (April 10, 2006).

4. Social Security (Suspension of Payment of Benefits and Miscellaneous Amendments) Regulations 2012 (SI 2012/824) reg.3 (April 17, 2012).

5. Jobseeker's Allowance (Sanctions) (Amendment) Regulations 2012 (SI 2012/2568) reg.5(5) (October 22, 2012).

DEFINITIONS

    "claimant"—see Jobseekers Act 1995 s.35(1).
    "couple"—*ibid.*
    "employment"—see reg.4.
    "a joint-claim couple"—see Jobseekers Act 1995 ss.35(1) and 1(4).
    "polygamous marriage"—see reg.1(3).
    "writing"—see Interpretation Act 1978 Sch.1.

GENERAL NOTE

3.118   A failure to provide a signed declaration in accordance with reg.24(6) and (10) means loss of entitlement to old style JSA (see reg.25(1)(c), subject to reg.27). The mere non-furnishing of the evidence contemplated by the other provisions in reg.24 has no such automatic preclusive effect, but could lead to a sanction under s.19A(2)

(a) of the old style Jobseekers Act 1995 if there was no good reason for the failure to comply, if it were not for the prohibition in reg.70A(2)(a) on any reduction in benefit under s.19A for any failure to comply with reg.24. It, may also, of course, cause a decision-maker or tribunal to doubt assertions about actively seeking work (see Commissioner Brown in the Northern Ireland decisions *C1/00–01 (JSA)* and *C2/00–01 (JSA)*, para.35).

[¹Alternative means of notifying changes of circumstances

24A.—(1) In such cases and subject to such conditions as the Secretary of State may specify, the duty in regulation 24(7) to notify a change of circumstances may be discharged by notifying the Secretary of State as soon as reasonably practicable—

    (a) where the change of circumstances is a birth or death, through a relevant authority, or a county council in England, by personal attendance at an office specified by that authority or county council, provided the Secretary of State has agreed with that authority or county council for it to facilitate such notification; or

    (b) where the change of circumstances is a death, by telephone to a telephone number specified for that purpose by the Secretary of State.

(2) In this regulation "relevant authority" has the same meaning as in the Housing Benefit Regulations 2006 [². . .].]

3.119

AMENDMENTS

1. Inserted by the Social Security (Notification of Change of Circumstances) Regulations 2010 (SI 2010/444) reg.3 (April 5, 2010).
2. Council Tax Benefit Abolition (Consequential Provision) Regulations 2013 (SI 2013/458) reg.3 and Sch.1 (April 1, 2013).

GENERAL NOTE

This allows the Secretary of State to enable a broadening of the routes by which the duty to notify changes of circumstances imposed by reg.24(7) may be discharged. "Relevant authority" is defined in reg.2(1) of the Housing Benefit Regulations 2006 as an authority administering housing benefit.

3.120

[¹Information given electronically

24B.—(1) A person may give any certificate, notice, information or evidence required to be given and in particular may give notice of a change of circumstances required to be notified under regulation 24 by means of an electronic communication, in accordance with the provisions set out in Schedule 9ZC to the Claims and Payments Regulations.

(2) In this regulation, "electronic communication" has the meaning given in section 15(1) of the Electronic Communications Act 2000.]

3.121

AMENDMENT

1. Social Security (Electronic Communications) Order 2011 (SI 2011/1498) art.3(3) (June 20, 2011).

DEFINITION

"Claims and Payments Regulations"—see reg.1(3).

Entitlement ceasing on a failure to comply

3.122   **25.**—(1) [⁴Entitlement] to a jobseeker's allowance shall cease in the following circumstances—

[⁴(a) if a claimant fails to [⁸ participate in an interview] on the day specified in a relevant notification, and fails to make contact with an employment officer in the manner set out in that notification before the end of the period of five working days beginning with the first working day after the day on which the claimant failed to [⁸participate in an interview;]]

(b) if—

[¹(i) [⁸that claimant makes contact with an employment officer on the day specified in the relevant notification but fails to participate in an interview at the time specified in that notification, and the Secretary of State has informed that claimant in writing that a failure to participate in an interview, on the next occasion on which he is required to participate in an interview], at the time specified in such a [²notification] may result in his entitlement to a jobseeker's allowance ceasing [⁴or the benefit not being payable for a period], and

(ii) he fails to [⁸ participate in an interview] at the time specified in such a [²notification] on the next occasion; [⁴and

(iii) that claimant fails to make contact with an employment officer in the manner set out in such a notification before the end of the period of five working days beginning with the first working day after the day on which that claimant failed to [⁸ participate in an interview] at the time specified;]

(c) [⁴subject to regulation 27,] if [³that claimant] was required to provide a signed declaration as referred to in regulation 24(6) and he fails to provide it on the day on which he ought to do so in accordance with regulation 24(10).]

[⁴(1A) In this regulation and in regulations 27A, 28 and 30—

"relevant notification" means a notification under regulation 23 or 23A, other than a notification requiring attendance under an employment programme or a training scheme[⁷, under a scheme prescribed in regulation 3 of the Jobseeker's Allowance (Schemes for Assisting Persons to Obtain Employment) Regulations 2013][⁹, under a scheme prescribed in regulation 3 of the Jobseeker's Allowance (18–21 Work Skills Pilot Scheme) Regulations 2014][⁶, under the Employment, Skills and Enterprise Scheme] [⁵or under the Mandatory Work Activity Scheme];

"working day" means any day on which the appropriate office is not closed.]

(2) In this regulation, "an employment programme" and "a training scheme" have the meaning given in regulation 75.

AMENDMENTS

1. Jobseeker's Allowance (Amendment Regulations) 1999 (SI 1999/530) reg.2 (March 25, 1999).

2. Jobseeker's Allowance (Amendment) (No.3) Regulations 2000 (SI 2000/2194) reg.2(4) (September 11, 2000).

3. Jobseeker's Allowance (Joint Claims) Regulations 2000 (SI 2000/1978) Sch.2 para.4 (March 19, 2001).

4. Jobseeker's Allowance (Sanctions for Failure to Attend) Regulations 2010 (SI 2010/509) reg.2 (April 6, 2010).

5. Jobseeker's Allowance (Mandatory Work Activity Scheme) Regulations 2011 (SI 2011/688) reg.16(a) (April 25, 2011).

6. Jobseeker's Allowance (Employment, Skills and Enterprise Scheme) Regulations 2011 (SI 2011/917) reg.16(a) (May 20, 2011).

7. Jobseeker's Allowance (Schemes for Assisting Persons to Obtain Employment) Regulations 2013 (SI 2013/276) reg.14(b) (February 12, 2013 at 6.45 pm).

8. Social Security (Miscellaneous Amendments) Regulations 2013 (SI 2013/443) reg.4(3) (April 2, 2013).

9. Jobseeker's Allowance (18–21 Work Skills Pilot Scheme) Regulations 2014 (SI 2014/3117) reg.19 (November 25, 2014).

DEFINITIONS

"claimant"—see Jobseekers Act 1995 s.35(1).
"employment officer"—*ibid.*
"an employment programme"—see reg.75(1).
"a training scheme"—see reg.75(1).

GENERAL NOTE

Sub-paragraphs (a) and (b) of para.(1) specify that a failure to participate in a notified interview and to contact the employment officer within five working days after the notified date leads to the ceasing of entitlement, on the day specified in reg.26. Sub-paragraph (c) specifies that result where a claimant fails to provide a signed declaration on the day required under reg.24(10), but not where there is a failure to comply with any other requirement under reg.24. Under all of sub-paras (a), (b) and (c) it is irrelevant, if the claimant has not made contact with an employment officer within the relevant five-day period, how good the reasons might have been for not participating in the interview or for not providing the signed declaration. The claimant's basic remedy is to make a new claim and possibly apply for the backdating of the claim (available only in restricted circumstances under reg.19 of the Claims and Payments Regulations). See further the notes to reg.26 below.

If the claimant has made contact within the five-day period there cannot be a termination of entitlement. Although sub-para.(c) is subject to reg.27, which purports to make it an extra condition in such cases that the claimant shows, within that period, a good reason for failing to comply, the reasoning of Commissioner Stockman in the Northern Ireland decision in *LDG v DSD (JSA)* [2015] NICom 16, reported as [2016] AACR 37, indicates that that condition is not valid, having been imposed outside the power given by s.8(2) of the old style Jobseekers Act 1995. Section 8(2) only allows regulations to provide for entitlement to cease if the claimant does not make the prescribed contact within a prescribed period. It does not allow the addition of the extra condition that, as well as making contact in the way prescribed, the claimant must also do something different in showing a good reason. In *KH v SSWP (JSA)* [2015] UKUT 497 (AAC) Judge Hemingway applied the exception to reg.25(1)(c) in reg.27 without consideration of the convincing reasoning of Commissioner Stockman in *LDG*. As the judge had not been referred to *LDG*, the decision in *KH* cannot be taken as undermining the force of the reasoning in *LDG* in any way. See the notes to reg.27 for further details. If the extra condition were valid, it appears that the good reason has to be shown within the five-day period (see the reasoning in paras 255–268 of *SSWP v TJ (JSA)* [2015] UKUT 56 (AAC)). See the notes to reg.23 for what must be specified in a reg.23 or 23A notification.

Sub-paragraph (a) is relatively straightforward in its terms. It appears to apply where the claimant does not turn up at all on the day, or at least makes no contact with an employment officer on that day, specified in a notification under regs 23 or 23A. See the notes to reg.23 for what a failure to participate in an interview might entail. Sub-paragraph (b) is much more convoluted and there is some difficulty, stemming partly from the conventional use of the present tense in legislation, in

3.123

working out the order in which things have to happen and at what point the duty to bring an end to entitlement is triggered. It appears to work in the following way. First, a claimant who has been notified to participate in an interview on a particular day turns up on the right day but at the wrong time and sees an employment officer, who gives a written warning that a failure to participate in an interview on the next day on which he is notified to participate may result in the ceasing of entitlement or a sanction (sub-para.(b)(i)). Those circumstances do not fall within sub-para. (a) because, although the claimant has failed to participate in an interview on the notified day, there has been contact with an employment officer. Then, if heads (ii) and (iii) of sub-para.(b) are both satisfied, requiring the expiry of five working days without contact with an employment officer in the manner set out in the latest notification and a failure to participate in an interview at the right time on the next notified day, the duty to bring an end to entitlement is triggered. Under reg.26(b), the day on which the claimant was required to participate in an interview must presumably refer, in the case of sub-para.(b) of reg.25(1), to that final day on which the operation of the provision was triggered. See further the notes to reg.26.

3.124   In relation to sub-paras (a) and (b), the cessation of entitlement cannot be applied where the claimant has made contact with an employment officer within the appropriate five-day period in the manner set out in the relevant notification, however feeble the reason for not participating in the interview on right day or at the right time. In those circumstances, the claimant will still have failed to comply with a requirement under regs 23 or 23A, by failing to participate in an interview on the right date or at the right time. That is a sanctionable failure under s.19A(2)(a) of the old style Jobseekers Act 1995 if the claimant does not have a good reason for the failure to comply, which reg.70A(2)(b), (3) and (4) allows to lead to a reduction in benefit for the appropriate fixed period under reg.69A. If the claimant has not made contact within the five-day period, the cessation of entitlement under reg.25(1)(a) or (b) must follow. However, in those circumstances there can be no reduction in benefit following the sanctionable failure. Regulation 70A(2)(b), (3)(b) and (4)(d) requires that result in regs 23 or 23A cases except where the claimant has made contact with an employment officer within the prescribed period. The sanctionable failure then does not count as a previous failure for the purpose of calculating the period of reduction of benefit on any subsequent "offence" (reg.69A(2)(a)).

In relation to sub-para.(c), reg.27 provides that entitlement is not to cease if the claimant not only contacts an employment officer within five working days in the manner set out in the notification to participate in an interview on the day on which the declaration was to be signed but also shows a good reason for the failure to provide the signed declaration. On the basis, discussed above, that that extra condition is not valid, where the claimant makes contact within the relevant period, there would still have been a sanctionable failure under s.19A(2)(a) of the old style Jobseekers Act 1995, unless there was a good reason for the failure. However, reg.70A(2)(a) prevents there being any reduction in benefit as a result and reg.69A(2)(a) applies as above. If entitlement ceases under sub-para.(c), there may be such a sanctionable failure. However, there can, for the same reason, be no reduction of benefit as a result (which in any case could only bite on entitlement under a new claim). See the notes to reg.26 for the date from which entitlement ceases.

In *CJSA/3139/2001*, Commissioner Rowland held that someone who attended on the right day but failed to sign the required declaration, could not lose entitlement because of reg.25(1)(a) or (b) but was instead caught by reg.25(1)(c). Here the claimant knew he had to sign on, but left the Jobcentre rather than waiting for a member of staff to return to the enquiries desk. Accordingly, he did not have good cause for the failure to sign.

Time at which entitlement is to cease

3.125   **26.**—Entitlement to a jobseeker's allowance shall cease in accordance with regulation 25 on whichever is the earlier of—

(a) the day after the last day in respect of which [⁴ that claimant] has provided information or evidence which [² shows that he continues to be entitled] to a jobseeker's allowance,

(b) if [¹ regulation 25(1)(a) or (b)] applies, the day on which he was required to [⁵ participate in an interview], and

(c) if [¹ regulation 25(1)(c)] applies, the day on which he ought to have provided the signed declaration,

provided that it shall not cease earlier than the day after he last [⁵ participated in an interview] in compliance with a [³notification] under regulation 23 [⁴or 23A].

AMENDMENTS

1. Jobseeker's Allowance (Amendment) Regulations 1996 (SI 1996/1516) reg.8 and Sch. (October 7, 1996).

2. Jobseeker's Allowance and Income Support (General) (Amendment) Regulations 1996 (SI 1996/1517) reg.9 (October 7, 1996).

3. Jobseeker's Allowance (Amendment) (No.3) Regulations 2000 (SI 2000/2194) reg.2(5) (September 11, 2000).

4. Jobseeker's Allowance (Joint Claims) Regulations 2000 (SI 2000/1978) Sch.2 para.5 (March 19, 2001).

5. Social Security (Miscellaneous Amendments) Regulations 2013 (SI 2013/443) reg.4(4) (April 2, 2013).

GENERAL NOTE

In *CJSA/2652/2001*, Commissioner Williams approved the approach in *CJSA/3139/2001*, noted in the commentary to reg.25, above. It did not, however, apply to his case. He attempted in the case to elucidate regs 23–26 and, in particular, to make some sense of reg.26. His approach was, however, overturned on appeal by the Court of Appeal in *Ferguson v Secretary of State for Work and Pensions* [2003] EWCA Civ 536, reported as *R(JSA)6/03*. Arden LJ, giving the judgment of the Court, stated:

    3.126

"**38.** I turn to the first of the substantial issues, which I would call the devoid issue. I accept, for the reasons I have already given, the submission of the Secretary of State that there is a clear distinction between regulations 25 and 26. They reflect the enabling power and deal separately with cessation events and the effective date for cessation of a benefit. When we examine regulation 26(a) it is clear that that is directed to ensuring that the claimant only receives benefit for the period in respect of which he fulfils all the conditions of entitlement, otherwise there would be no point in having paragraph 26(a). It is necessary, of course, to fix a date other than that of the cessation event, and regulation 26 has that object because it refers, as I have said, to the earlier of certain events. The purpose of regulation 26(a), in contrast to 26(b) and (c), seems to me clearly to be to fix the date so that the claimant only receives benefit for the period in which he fulfils all the conditions of entitlement and has demonstrated that. As I have said, the proviso confirms that. It is also important to note that, contrary to the conclusion of the Commissioner, regulation 26(a) is dealing with a factual situation; namely, it is establishing the date as the day after the last day in respect of which the claimant provided information or evidence of the requisite kind. It is not dealing in terms with a failure to provide information or evidence; it is directed simply to a factual situation. Had it been intended to deal with a failure to comply with a requirement to produce information or evidence, as it seems to me, it would necessarily have been differently worded.

39. As I see it, the answer to the devoid issue must be that 26(a) does not render 26(b) and (c) devoid of meaning. Circumstances can arise in which no declaration is required, in which case 26(b) and (c) will become operative. Circumstances can also arise where there is a failure to attend and reasonable cause for non-attendance is not shown but the claimant does produce satisfactory evidence of compliance with the conditions. On this point I would turn to the evidence of Mr Anthony Booth, an administrator in the Department for Work and Pensions responsible for certain policy aspects of the JSA. His witness statement is dated 13th November 2002. He says this:

'3. JSA claimants are normally required to attend the Jobcentre each fortnight. They lose entitlement if they fail to do so, unless they can show good cause for the failure within the next five working days. In the second quarter of 2002, about 180,000 JSA claims were terminated in these circumstances.

4. Most of those failing to attend make no contact with the Jobcentre during the five days. Consequently in terminating their entitlement, the Jobcentre has no information as to whether the JSA conditions were satisfied during the preceding fortnight. Entitlement is therefore terminated indefinitely with effect from the day after their last correct attendance.

5. Of those whose entitlement is terminated on a failure to attend, a minority make contact during the next five days but are found not to have good cause for their failure. They can, however, usually show that they satisfied the JSA conditions during the previous fortnight. Their entitlement is therefore terminated with effect from the date of failure only. They are also in a position to make an immediate new claim, so that their period of disentitlement lasts only from the date of failure to the date of renewal. About 30,000 people fell into this category in the second quarter of 2002.'

40. Pausing there, as Keene L.J. pointed out, the date of failure to which Mr Booth referred is the date of failure to attend. So circumstances can arise in which a person fails to attend but produces subsequently, and is accepted as producing, evidence of entitlement, so that paragraph (a) of regulation 26 would not apply.
41. Before I leave Mr Booth's statement on this point, I note that in the next paragraph he draws the conclusion that, although it cannot be substantiated, it is probable that a significant proportion of the people who fail to attend and make no contact with the Jobcentre have in fact ceased to satisfy the JSA entitlement conditions at some point between their last attendance and the date of failure. He adds:

'Paying JSA to them for that period therefore risks making an overpayment.'

42. Therefore, this evidence illustrates that section 26(a) does not render the subsequent paragraphs of that regulation inoperative or ineffective. Regulation 26(a) does not, moreover, provide that the necessary information can only be provided on the specified date for interview or in the window of opportunity permitted by regulation 27.
43. I therefore turn to the next substantial issue of construction, which I will call the analogue issue. That is the question which much concerned the Commissioner. It is as to whether there was a sanction for failure to comply with a requirement under regulation 24(5) to produce information or evidence. As I see it, the answer to this issue has been provided by the Secretary of State's reference to the Social Security and Child Support (Decisions and Appeals) Regulations 1999, from which I have read extracts. Accordingly, there is separate statutory machinery which comes into operation if there is a failure to provide information or evidence and therefore it is not significant, in my judgment, that the failure to provide information or evidence is not a cessation event for the purpose of regulation 25."

Although, since this decision, the regulation was amended from April 2, 2013 substituting "failure to participate in an interview" for "failure to attend", this does not affect the interpretation given in the judgment with regard to the consequences of the relevant "failure"; one simply reads its references to "failure to attend" as "failure to participate in an interview".

The Court also held that the term "evidence" in para.(a) includes the declaration required by regs 24(6) and 25(1)(c) (para.44). Regulation 26(c) is not limited to "postal signers" (para.48). Arden LJ considered the conclusion the court had reached to be a "logical one" (para.50). Commissioner Williams had erred in failing

"to give appropriate weight in his conclusion to two important textual points from these Regulations. The first point is that regulations 25 and 26 cover different subject matters. They have a different scope. Regulation 25 deals with cessation events; regulation 26 deals with the effective date of cessation of benefit. In addition, the Commissioner failed, in my judgment, to give appropriate weight to the 'earlier' point. As I see it, regulation 26 compels reference to the earlier of two dates. The court must give effect to those words and apply the regulation so that benefit terminates on whichever of those dates first occurs. It seems to me that the regulation was probably correct to say 'earlier' rather than 'earliest', since only one of the cessation events in paragraphs (b) and (c) of regulation 26 will occur. Once it occurs, the benefit terminates and any subsequent event is irrelevant. Contrary to Mr Ferguson's submission, I cannot treat as subsumed within a failure to attend a failure to provide information or to sign a declaration with which a requirement to attend was coupled. It seems to me that those two matters must be decoupled in order to apply the regulation properly in accordance with its wording.

50. The conclusion which I reach is, in my judgment, a logical one. Entitlement to JSA depends on eligibility. Eligibility depends for one of its requirements on showing entitlement at the end of the 14-day period. On the interpretation which I prefer, benefit will cease as at the date immediately following the last date for which the necessary proof was given if there is a failure to attend in accordance with regulation 25(a) or (b) or a failure to sign a declaration. As Mr Forsdick put it, the Commissioner's construction gives the claimant who is in default an additional two-week period of grace for which he cannot in fact prove eligibility. That seems to me to be contrary to the scheme of the Regulations. In addition, it seems to me to undermine regulations 27 and 28, which give a window of opportunity for five days only provided that the claimant can establish a reasonable cause for nonattendance. As I see it, the Commissioner's construction, with respect to him, was inconsistent with and undermined those regulations. Accordingly, on the main issue of construction I would allow the appeal". (paras 49 and 50)

In *R(JSA)2/04*, Commissioner Rowland considered *Ferguson* and noted that, as the Secretary of State submitted in *Ferguson* at para.18: 3.127

"regulation 26(a) is intended to avoid overpayments by allowing the Secretary of State to terminate promptly an award of jobseeker's allowance in a case where a claimant has failed to 'sign on' and has not shown continued entitlement during the previous fortnight. However, I am satisfied that the language used does not prevent the Secretary of State's decision from being adjusted on revision or appeal if the claimant takes appropriate action within the time allowed under the Social Security and Child Support (Decisions and Appeals) Regulations 1999 and provides the information or evidence before a further decision is made".

The Commissioner had accepted that if a claimant fails to make contact with an employment officer within the relevant five working days it is proper for a decision-maker to make a decision that entitlement ceased from the date identified in reg.26(a). Since JSA is paid fortnightly in arrears and most claimants are required to attend fortnightly and sign a declaration as to their availability and actively seeking employment in the days since their previous signing day, the earliest day for cessation of entitlement will usually be the day after that previous signing day when the last declaration under reg.24(10) had been provided (reg.26(a)). However, he went on to hold that, if the claimant later (for instance on turning up at the next fortnightly signing day having missed the previous one) came forward with evidence and information to show that they had satisfied the conditions of entitlement to JSA throughout the previous four weeks, that would indicate that the original reg.26(a) date was now wrong, so that the date in either (b) or (c) as appropriate was to be taken as the date of cessation of entitlement. Thus the Secretary of State should revise the original decision. If the claimant had made a new claim for JSA and asked for backdating to the day after the last day of entitlement under the previous award which was refused, any appeal would encompass an appeal against the decision terminating entitlement, on which the approach above could be taken into account. Although that result was apparently supported by the Secretary of State in *R(JSA) 2/04*, there remains some doubt about the reasoning. If reg.26(a) cannot be interpreted as referring to anything other than the last day that the claimant provided information or evidence showing entitlement before the day on which the failure to comply occurred, then the chain appears to be broken. A subsequent provision of such information or evidence could then not alter the reg.26(a) date.

[¹Where entitlement is not to cease under regulation 25(1)(c)

3.128   **27.**—Entitlement to a jobseeker's allowance is not to cease by virtue of regulation 25(1)(c) if, before the end of the period of five working days beginning with the first working day after the day on which a claimant ("C") failed to provide a signed declaration in accordance with regulation 24(10), C makes contact with an employment officer in the manner set out in a notification under regulation 23 or 23A and shows that C had [²a good reason] for the failure.]

AMENDMENTS

1. Jobseeker's Allowance (Sanctions for Failure to Attend) Regulations 2010 (SI 2010/509) reg.2(4) (April 6, 2010).
2. Jobseeker's Allowance (Sanctions) (Amendment) Regulations 2012 (SI 2012/2568) reg.5(6) (October 22, 2012).

GENERAL NOTE

3.129   See the annotations to reg.25.
Note in particular that the decision of Commissioner Stockman in the Northern Ireland decision in *LDG v DSD (JSA)* [2015] NICom 16, reported as [2016] AACR 37, indicates that the condition that the claimant is to show a good reason for failing to provide a signed declaration under reg.24(10) within the five working days after the failure is not valid, having been imposed outside the power given by s.8(2) of the old style Jobseekers Act 1995. Section 8(2) only allows regulations to provide for entitlement to cease if the claimant does not make the prescribed contact within a prescribed period. It does not allow the addition of the extra condition that to escape the cessation of employment the claimant, as well as making contact in the way prescribed in reg.27 (by making contact with an employment officer in the manner set out in the regs 23 or 23A notification), must also do something different in showing a good reason.
In *KH v SSWP (JSA)* [2015] UKUT 497 (AAC) Judge Hemingway set aside a decision of a First-tier Tribunal for failing to give proper consideration to whether a letter received from the claimant within five days of failing to provide a signed

declaration under reg.24(6) and (10) might have contained information relevant to whether she had a good reason for the failure, so as, according to the terms of reg.27, to prevent the termination of entitlement under reg.25(1)(c). However, he had not been referred to and did not take into account the convincing reasoning in *LDG* that the requirement in reg.27 for a claimant to show a good reason for the failure to provide the signed declaration, in addition to making contact with an employment officer within the five days, is not valid. The judge was inclined to say that the claimant's letter (which was not in the papers before him) was, in the absence of any submission to the contrary from the Secretary of State, a making of contact in the manner set out in the relevant notification under reg.23. Thus, if the reasoning in *LDG* had been adopted, he might well have been able to substitute a decision in the claimant's favour, rather than remit the case to a new tribunal for rehearing. In view of the complete lack of any reference to *LDG*, the decision in *KH* should not be taken as in any way undermining the force and authority of the reasoning in *LDG*.

Judge Hemingway rightly criticised the apparent lack of care in the decision-making process and in the presentation of the case to the First-tier Tribunal, in failing to provide copies of potentially relevant documents or of a decision under appeal. He stressed that "decisions which result in a claimant ceasing to have income can have potentially very serious consequences such that considerable care ought to be taken at all stages in the decision-making process and the explanation of that process once an appeal is lodged."

DEFINITIONS

"claimant"—see Jobseekers Act 1995 s.35(1).
"employment officer"—*ibid*.

Regulations 27A – 30 revoked by Jobseeker's Allowance (Sanctions) (Amendment) Regulations 2012 (SI 2012/2568) reg.5(7) (October 22, 2012).

Chapter V

Jobseeker's Agreement

GENERAL NOTE

The terms and effects of the regulations in this Chapter (regs 31–40) are noted in the annotations to ss.9 and 10 of the Jobseekers Act 1995 as follows: **3.130**
Section 9 (the jobseeker's agreement): regs 31–36.
Section 10 (variation of jobseeker's agreement): regs 37–40.

Contents of Jobseeker's Agreement

31.—The prescribed requirements for a jobseeker's agreement are that it   **3.131**
shall contain the following information—
  (a) the claimant's name;
  (b) where the hours for which the claimant is available for employment are restricted in accordance with regulation 7, the total number of hours for which he is available and any pattern of availability;
  (c) any restrictions on the claimant's availability for employment, including restrictions on the location or type of employment, in accordance with regulations 5, 8, 13[³, or 13A] and 17;
  (d) a description of the type of employment which the claimant is seeking;

(e) the action which the claimant will take—
    (i) to seek employment; and
    (ii) to improve his prospects of finding employment;
(f) the dates of the start and of the finish of any permitted period in his case for the purposes of sections 6(5) and 7(5);
(g) a statement of the claimant's right—
    (i) to have a proposed jobseeker's agreement referred to [¹the Secretary of State];
    (ii) to seek a [² revision or supersession] of any determination of, or direction given by, [¹ the Secretary of State]; and
    (iii) to appeal to [²an appeal tribunal] against any determination of, or direction given by [¹the Secretary of State] [² following a revision or supersession];
(h) the date of the agreement.

AMENDMENTS

1. Social Security Act 1998 (Commencement No.11, and Savings and Consequential and Transitional Provisions) Order 1999 Sch.12 para.2 (SI 1999/2860) (C.75)) (October 18, 1999).
2. Social Security Act 1998 (Commencement No.11, and Savings and Consequential and Transitional Provisions) Order 1999 Sch.12 para.1 (SI 1999/2860) (C.75)) (October 18, 1999).
3. Jobseeker's Allowance (Lone Parents) (Availability for Work) Regulations 2010 (SI 2010/837) reg.2(11) (April 26, 2010).

DEFINITIONS

"claimant"—see Jobseekers Act 1995 s.35(1).
"employment"—see reg.4.
"pattern of availability"—see regs 4 and 7(2)(a).

Back-dating of a Jobseeker's Agreement [¹ . . .]

3.132   **32.**—In giving a direction under section 9(7)(c), the [² Secretary of State] shall take into account all relevant matters including—
(a) where the claimant refused to accept the agreement proposed by the employment officer, whether he was reasonable in so refusing;
(b) where the claimant has signified to the employment officer or to the [² Secretary of State] that the claimant is prepared to accept an agreement which differs from the agreement proposed by the employment officer, whether the terms of the agreement which he is prepared to accept are reasonable;
(c) where the claimant has signified to the employment officer or to the [² Secretary of State] that the claimant is prepared to accept the agreement proposed by the employment officer, that fact;
(d) the date on which, in all the circumstances, he considers that the claimant was first prepared to enter into an agreement which the [² Secretary of State] considers reasonable; and
(e) where the date on which the claimant first had an opportunity to sign a jobseeker's agreement was later than the date on which he made a claim, that fact.

AMENDMENTS

1. Social Security Act 1998 (Commencement No.11, and Savings and Consequential and Transitional Provisions) Order 1999 Sch.12 para.3 (SI 1999/2860) (C.75)) (October 18, 1999).
2. Social Security Act 1998 (Commencement No.11, and Savings and Consequential and Transitional Provisions) Order 1999 Sch.12 para.2 (SI 1999/2860) (C.75)) (October 18, 1999).

DEFINITIONS

"claimant"—see Jobseekers Act 1995 s.35(1).
"employment officer"—*ibid.*

Notification of Determinations and Directions under Section 9

33.—The claimant shall be notified of—   3.133
  (a) any determination of the [¹ Secretary of State] under section 9;
  (b) any direction given by the [¹ Secretary of State] under section 9;

AMENDMENT

1. Social Security Act 1998 (Commencement No.11, and Savings and Consequential and Transitional Provisions) Order 1999 Sch.12 para.2 (SI 1999/2860) (C.75)) (October 18, 1999).

DEFINITION

"claimant"—see Jobseekers Act 1995 s.35(1).

Jobseeker's Agreement treated as having been made

34.—A claimant is to be treated as having satisfied the condition men-   3.134
tioned in section 1(2)(b)—
  (a) where he is permitted to make a claim for a jobseeker's allowance without attending at an office of the [³Department for Work and Pensions], for the period beginning with the date of claim and ending on the date on which he has an interview with an employment officer for the purpose of drawing up a jobseeker's agreement;
  (b) where, after the date of claim, the claim is terminated before he has an interview with an employment officer for the purpose of drawing up a jobseeker's agreement;
  (c) as long as he is treated as available for employment in accordance with regulation 14 where the circumstances set out in that regulation arise after the date of claim and before he has an interview with an employment officer for the purpose of drawing up a job-seeker's agreement;
  (d) as long as there are circumstances not peculiar to the claimant which make impracticable or unduly difficult the normal operation of the provisions governing, or the practice relating to, the claiming, awarding or payment of jobseeker's allowance;
  [¹(e) where the claimant was in receipt of a training allowance and was, in accordance with regulation 170, entitled to an income-based jobseeker's allowance without being available for employment, having entered into a jobseeker's agreement or actively seeking employment, for the period beginning with the date on which regu-

lation 170 ceased to apply to him and ending on the date on which he has an interview with an employment officer for the purpose of drawing up a jobseeker's agreement.]

[² (f) if he is temporarily absent from Great Britain in the circumstances prescribed in regulation 50(6B)(a) or (c), for the period of any such temporary absence.]

[⁴(g) in any period during which he is treated as available for employment under regulation 14A if the claimant has not entered into a jobseeker's agreement before that period begins.]

AMENDMENTS

1. Jobseeker's Allowance (Amendment) Regulations 1996 (SI 1996/1516) reg.3 (October 7, 1996).
2. Jobseeker's Allowance (Joint Claims) Regulations 2000 (SI 2000/1978) Sch.2 para.9 (March 19, 2001).
3. Secretaries of State for Education and Skills and for Work and Pensions Order 2002 (SI 2002/1397) art.12 and Sch. para.26 (June 27, 2002).
4. Jobseeker's Allowance (Domestic Violence) (Amendment) Regulations 2012 (SI 2012/853) reg.2(4) (April 23, 2012).

DEFINITIONS

"date of claim"—see reg.1(3).
"employment"—see reg.4.
"employment officer"—see Jobseekers Act 1995 s.35(1).
"training allowance"—see reg.1(3).

Automatic Back-dating of Jobseeker's Agreement

3.135 **35.**—Where a jobseeker's agreement is signed on a date later than the date of claim and there is no reference of that agreement to [¹the Secretary of State] under section 9(6), the agreement shall be treated as having effect on the date of claim.

AMENDMENT

1. Social Security Act 1998 (Commencement No.11, and Savings and Consequential and Transitional Provisions) Order 1999 Sch.12 para.2 (SI 1999/2860) (C.75)) (October 18, 1999).

DEFINITION

"date of claim"—see reg.1(3).

Jobseeker's Agreement to remain in effect

3.136 **36.**—A jobseeker's agreement entered into by a claimant shall not cease to have effect on the coming to an end of an award of a jobseeker's allowance made to him—

(a) where a further claim for a jobseeker's allowance is made within a period not exceeding 14 days; or
(b) in respect of any part of a period of suspension, where—
   (i) the Secretary of State has directed under regulation 37(1A) of the Claims and Payments Regulations that payment under an award be suspended for a definite or indefinite period on the ground that

a question arises whether the conditions for entitlement to that allowance are or were fulfilled or the award ought to be revised,

(ii) subsequently that suspension expires or is cancelled in respect of a part only of the period for which it has been in force, and

(iii) it is then determined that the award should be revised to the effect that there was no entitlement to the allowance in respect of all or any part of the period between the start of the period over which the award has been suspended and the date when the suspension expires or is cancelled; or

(c) for as long as the claimant satisfies the conditions of entitlement to national insurance credits, other than any condition relating to the existence of a jobseeker's agreement, in accordance with the Social Security (Credits) Regulations 1975.

DEFINITIONS

"claimant"—see Jobseekers Act 1995 s.35(1).
"Claims and Payments Regulations"—see reg.1(3).

Variation of Jobseeker's Agreement

37.—The prescribed manner for varying a jobseeker's agreement shall be in writing and signed by both parties in accordance with section 10(2) on the proposal of the claimant or the employment officer.

3.137

DEFINITIONS

"claimant"—see Jobseekers Act 1995 s.35(1).
"employment officer"—*ibid.*

Direction to vary Agreement: time for compliance

38.—The prescribed period for the purposes of section 10(6)(c) shall be the period of 21 days beginning with the date on which the direction was issued.

3.138

Variation of Agreement: matters to be taken into account

39.—In giving a direction under section 10(6)(b) or (d) [¹the Secretary of State] shall take into account the preference of the claimant if he considers that both the claimant's proposals and those of employment officer satisfy the requirements of section 10(5).

3.139

AMENDMENT

1. Social Security Act 1998 (Commencement No.11, and Savings and Consequential and Transitional Provisions) Order 1999 Sch.12 para.2 (SI 1999/2860) (C.75)) (October 18, 1999).

DEFINITIONS

"claimant"—see Jobseekers Act 1995 s.35(1).
"employment officer"—*ibid.*

Notification of Determinations and Directions under Section 10

3.140   **40.**—The claimant shall be notified of—
(a) any determination of [¹ the Secretary of State] under section 10;
(b) any direction of [¹ the Secretary of State] under section 10.

AMENDMENT

1. Social Security Act 1998 (Commencement No.11, and Savings and Consequential and Transitional Provisions) Order 1999 Sch.12 para.2 (SI 1999/2860) (C.75)) (October 18, 1999).

DEFINITION

"claimant" —see Jobseekers Act 1995 s.35(1).

[Regulations 41–45 were revoked by Social Security Act 1998 (Commencement No.11, and Savings and Consequential and Transitional Provisions) Order 1999 Sch.12 para.4 (SI 1999/2860) (October 18, 1999).]

PART III

OTHER CONDITIONS OF ENTITLEMENT

The contribution-based conditions and relevant earnings

3.141   **45A.** *[Omitted as not relevant to income-based JSA].*

Relaxation of the first set of conditions

3.142   **45B.** *[Omitted as not relevant to income-based JSA]*

Waiting days

3.143   **46.**—(1) Paragraph 4 of Schedule 1 to the Act shall not apply in a case where—
(a) a person's entitlement to a jobseeker's allowance commences within 12 weeks of an entitlement of his to income support, incapacity benefit[³, employment and support allowance] or [²carer's allowance] coming to an end; or
(b) a claim for a jobseeker's allowance falls to be determined by reference to section 3(1)(f)(ii) (persons under the age of 18);[¹or
(c) a joint-claim couple are entitled to a joint-claim jobseeker's allowance in respect of themselves and that paragraph of that Schedule has already applied to one member of that couple in respect of a jobseeking period which is linked to a jobseeking period relating to that member which has commenced by virtue of his having claimed a jobseeker's allowance as a member of that couple;
(d) a joint-claim couple have claimed a jobseeker's allowance jointly within 12 weeks of either member of that couple being entitled to a jobseeker's allowance, income support, incapacity benefit [³, employment and support allowance] or [² carer's allowance];

(e) a member of a joint-claim couple is both in receipt of a training allowance and the nominated member for the purposes of section 3B.]

(2) In the case of a person to whom paragraph 4 of Schedule 1 to the Act applies, the number of days is [⁴7].

AMENDMENTS

1. Jobseeker's Allowance (Joint Claims) Regulations 2000 (SI 2000/1978) Sch.2 para.10 (March 19, 2001).
2. Social Security (Miscellaneous Amendments) Regulations 2003 (SI 2003/511) reg.3(5) (April 1, 2003).
3. Employment and Support Allowance (Consequential Provisions) (No.2) Regulations 2008 (SI 2008/1554) reg.3(6) (October 27, 2008).
4. Social Security (Jobseeker's Allowance and Employment and Support Allowance) (Waiting Days) Amendment Regulations 2014 (SI 2014/2309) reg.2(1) (October 27, 2014).

DEFINITION

"the Act"—see reg.1(3).
"couple"—see Jobseekers Act 1995 s.35(1).
"jobseeking period"—see reg.1(3).
"a joint-claim couple"—see Jobseekers Act 1995 ss.35(1) and 1(4).
"a joint-claim jobseeker's allowance"—*ibid.*
"training allowance"—see reg.1(3).

GENERAL NOTE

Unemployment benefit was a daily benefit payable in respect of a six-day week. **3.144** JSA is a weekly benefit. Nonetheless, through para.4 of Sch.1 to the old style Jobseekers Act 1995, as amplified by this regulation, it deploys the traditional concept of "waiting days".

There is no entitlement to old style JSA for a number of days (initially three, but extended to seven with effect from October 27, 2014 (see para.(2)) at the start of a jobseeking period. The amendment to increase the number of waiting days to seven does not apply where the relevant jobseeking period began before October 27, 2014 (reg.4(1) of the amending regulations). Seven days' worth of benefit is a substantial amount, so that the provision in the Social Security (Payments on Account of Benefit) Regulations 2013 (Vol.III of this series) for the making of payments on account of benefit, in certain cases of financial need (restrictively defined), has become more important. However, the claimant has to repay the "advance" out of future payments of JSA. On "jobseeking period" and the effect of "linking", see notes to regs 47 and 48 below.

Note further that the "waiting days" rule does not apply where the claimant's entitlement to old style JSA begins within 12 weeks of the ending of entitlement to income support, incapacity benefit or carer's allowance, nor where the claim for income-based JSA has to be determined by reference to s.3(1)(f)(ii) (i.e. the person is 16 or 17, registered for training but is not being provided with any, severe hardship will result to him if JSA is not paid, and the Secretary of State directs that s.16 is to apply to him) (para.(1)(a), (b)).

As regards a "joint-claim couple", the waiting days will not have to be served **3.145** again where the jobseeking period commenced because of a claim as a "joint claim couple" links to a jobseeking period in which one of the members had already served the waiting days (para.(1)(c)). Nor will they need to be served where the joint-claim is within 12 weeks of either member's entitlement to JSA, income support, incapacity benefit, ESA or carer's allowance (para.(1)(d)). Nor do the waiting days have to be served if the nominated member (see Jobseekers Act 1995 s.3B) of the couple is receiving a training allowance (para.(1)(e)).

A sanction imposed under ss.19 or 19A of the Act (see Pt V of these Regulations) will not begin until after any waiting days have been served. But a claimant who is entitled to IBJSA will qualify for maximum housing benefit during any waiting days (see reg.2(3)(b) of the Housing Benefit Regulations 2006).

The transition from new style JSA

3.146   In para.(1)(a) and (d) the references (second reference in sub-para.(d)) to job-seeker's allowance are, where art.13(1)(a) and (2)(b) of the Welfare Reform Act 2012 (Commencement No.9 and Transitional and Transitory Provisions and Commencement No.8 and Savings and Transitional Provisions (Amendment)) Order 2013 (as amended and set out in Part V of this volume, *Universal Credit*) applies and the claimant was entitled to new style JSA under reg.36(1) of the JSA Regulations 2013 during what would otherwise have been waiting days when that award continued as an award of old style JSA, to be read as if it included a reference to the new style JSA award (art.13(3)(b) of that Order).

Jobseeking period

3.147   **47.**—(1) For the purposes of the Act, but subject to paragraphs (2) and (3), the "jobseeking period" means any period throughout which the claimant satisfies or is treated as satisfying the conditions specified in paragraphs (a) to (c) and (e) to (i) of subsection (2) of section 1 (conditions of entitlement to a jobseeker's allowance).

(2) Any period in which—

(a) a claimant does not satisfy any of the requirements in section 1(2)(a) to (c), and

(b) a jobseeker's allowance is payable to him in accordance with Part IX (Hardship), [³or, where the claimant is a member of a joint-claim couple, a jobseeker's allowance is payable in accordance with Part IXA (hardship)]

shall, for the purposes of paragraph (1), be treated as a period in which the claimant satisfies the conditions specified in paragraphs (a) to (c) of subsection (2) of section 1.

[¹(2A) Any period in which a claimant is entitled to a jobseeker's allowance in accordance with regulation 11(3) of the Jobseeker's Allowance (Transitional Provisions) Regulations 1995 shall, for the purposes of paragraph (1), be treated as a period in which he satisfies the conditions specified in paragraphs (a) to (c) and (e) to (i) of subsection (2) of section 1.]

(3) The following periods shall not be, or be part of, a jobseeking period—

(a) any period in respect of which no claim for a jobseeker's allowance has been made or treated as made;

(b) such period as falls before the day on which a claim for a jobseeker's allowance is made or treated as made [². . .];

(c) where a claim for a jobseeker's allowance has been made or treated as made but no entitlement to benefit arises in respect of a period before the date of claim by virtue of section 1(2) of the Administration Act (limits for backdating entitlement), that period;

(d) where—

(i) a claimant satisfies the conditions specified in paragraphs (a) to (c) and (e) to (i) of subsection (2) of section 1; and

(ii) entitlement to a jobseeker's allowance ceases in accordance with regulation 25 (entitlement ceasing on a failure to comply), the period beginning with the date in respect of which, in accordance with regulation 26, entitlement ceases and ending with the day before the date in respect of which the claimant again becomes entitled to a jobseeker's allowance; or

(e) any week in which a claimant is not entitled to a jobseeker's allowance in accordance with section 14 (trade disputes).

[²(f) subject to regulation 2A, any period in respect of which the claimant is not entitled to a jobseeker's allowance because section 1(1A) of the Administration Act (requirement to state national insurance number) applies.]

(4) For the purposes of section 5 (duration of a contribution-based jobseeker's allowance) any day—

(a) which falls within a jobseeking period; [⁰and either

(b) (i) on which the claimant satisfies the conditions specified in section 2 (the contribution-based conditions) other than the conditions specified in subsection (1)(c) and (d) of that section; and

(ii) on which a contribution–based jobseeker's allowance is not payable to the claimant by virtue of [¹⁰section 19 or 19A or regulation 69B] [⁴or on which the claimant is a member of a joint-claim couple and a joint-claim jobseeker's allowance is not payable or is reduced because he is subject to sanctions by virtue of [¹⁰section 19 or 19A or regulation 69B]][⁵or by virtue of a restriction imposed pursuant [⁷ . . .] [⁶to section [⁹6B], 7, 8 or 9 of the Social Security Fraud Act 2001 (loss of benefit provisions)]]];

shall be treated as if it was a day in respect of which he was entitled to a contribution-based jobseeker's allowance.

AMENDMENTS

0. Jobseeker's Allowance and Income Support (General) (Amendment) Regulations 1996 (SI 1996/1517) reg.14(3) (October 7, 1996).

1. Social Security and Child Support (Jobseeker's Allowance) (Miscellaneous Amendments) Regulations 1996 (SI 1996/2538) reg.2(4) (October 28, 1996).

2. Social Security (Incapacity Benefit and Jobseeker's Allowance) Amendment Regulations 1999 (SI 1999/2226) reg.3 (September 6, 1999).

3. Jobseeker's Allowance (Joint Claims) Regulations 2000 (SI 2000/1978) Sch.2 para.11 (March 19, 2001).

4. Social Security Amendment (Joint Claims) Regulations 2001 (SI 2001/ 518) reg.2(5) (March 19, 2001).

5. Social Security (Breach of Community Order) (Consequential Amendments) Regulations 2001 (SI 2001/1711) reg.2(4) (October 15, 2001).

6. Social Security (Loss of Benefit) (Consequential Amendments) Regulations 2002 (SI 2002/490) reg.7 (April 1, 2002).

7. Welfare Reform Act 2009 (Section 26) (Consequential Amendments) Regulations 2010 (SI 2010/424) reg.3(2) (March 22, 2010, but where someone is subject to a restriction under ss.62 or 63 of the Child Support, Pensions and Social Security Act 2000 immediately before that date, on the first day of the first benefit week to commence for that person on or after March 22, 2010).

8. Jobseekers Allowance (Sanctions for Failure to Attend) Regulations 2010 (SI 2010/509) reg.2(7) (April 6, 2010).

9. Social Security (Loss of Benefit) (Amendment) Regulations 2010 (SI 2010/1160) reg.11(2) (April 1, 2010).

10. Jobseeker's Allowance (Sanctions) (Amendment) Regulations 2012 (SI 2012/2568) reg.5(8) (October 22, 2012).

DEFINITIONS

"the Administration Act"—see Jobseekers Act 1995 s.35(1).
"the Act"—see reg.1(3).
"claimant"—see Jobseekers Act 1995 s.35(1).
"contribution-based jobseeker's allowance"—see ss.35(1) and 1(4).
"jobseeking period"—see para.(1).

GENERAL NOTE

Paragraphs (1)–(3)

3.148   This regulation, read with regs 48 and 49 below and para.3 of Sch.1 to the old style Jobseekers Act 1995, provides some relief to those whose unemployment is intermittent, interspersed with, say, periods of employment, of incapacity for work, of training for work or periods when pregnant. It uses, somewhat after the fashion of unemployment benefit and its notion of "period of interruption of employment" ("PIE"), the concept of "linking" and "linked periods" where what would otherwise be separate jobseeking periods are fused into one and certain periods ("linked periods") do not "break" a jobseeking period.

There are three particular purposes for which the concept of the jobseeking period was relevant: (a) in the identification of the tax years in which the two contribution conditions in s.2(1)(a) and (b) of the Act must be satisfied; (b) in the application of the waiting days rule in para.4 of Sch.1 to the Act only once in each jobseeking period; and (c) in the possibly redundant provisions in para.(3) about days which count towards the 182-day limit on a period of entitlement under s.5 of the Act. Only (b) is now relevant to IBJSA.

Regulation 47 provides the general definition of "jobseeking period" and some important exceptions. Regulation 47A deals with cases going back into the unemployment benefit regime. Regulations 48 and 49 deal with linking.

3.149   A "jobseeking period" is under para.(1) any period throughout which the claimant satisfies (or is treated as satisfying) the conditions of entitlement to JSA set out in the old style Jobseekers Act 1995 s.1(2)(a)–(c) and (e)–(i): available for employment; a current jobseeker's agreement; actively seeking employment; not in remunerative work; not receiving relevant education; under pensionable age; and in Great Britain (para.(1)) (note that reg.49, below, treats certain days as ones meeting those conditions in respect of men over 60 but under pensionable age). Where a hardship payment under Pts IX or IXA (joint-claim couple) of these Regulations is paid to a claimant who does not satisfy a labour market condition (any of the conditions in the old style Jobseekers Act 1995 s.1(2)(a)–(c): availability; actively seeking; jobseeker's agreement), he is to be treated as satisfying them for purposes of applying the above definition of jobseeking period (para.(2)). Note that Transitional Reg.11(3) in para.(2A) is now reg.13(3) of the JSA (Transitional) Regs 1996.

Certain periods listed in para.(3) cannot constitute, or be part of, a jobseeking period: (i) any period in which no claim for JSA has been made or treated as made; (ii) any period before the day on which a claim is made; (iii) a period caught by the 12-month limit on backdating entitlement under s.1(2) of the SSAA 1992; (iv) a period of disentitlement under regs 25 and 26; (v) any week of disentitlement because the claimant is caught by the trade dispute rule in old style Jobseekers Act 1995 s.14; and (vi) any period for which the claimant is not entitled to JSA because he has not provided the required information or evidence about his national insurance number or that of any adult dependant included in his claim (para.(3)). Paragraph (3)(f) will apply to days falling on or after September 6, 1999 but not to any period before that date. The amendment was considered necessary to avoid a possible advantage being gained by a person who makes a further claim to JSA that links to the earlier disallowed claim. Without this provision the jobseeking period formed by the earlier claim would determine what tax years were used to decide entitlement to CBJSA and the claimant would not need to serve the three waiting days on the second claim.

Under para.(4), for the purpose only of the rules in s.5 of the Act limiting the duration of entitlement to 182 days, a day which would otherwise fall within a jobseeking period, but on which someone satisfying the two contribution conditions in s.2 is subject to an old style JSA sanction or a fraud sanction so that JSA is not payable, is nonetheless to be treated as a day of entitlement to JSA, so that it will count as one of the 182 days. This provision is arguably unnecessary because sanctions under ss.19 and 19A of the Act and restrictions under the Social Security Fraud Act 2001 only affect the payability of benefit or the amount payable, not entitlement.

The transition from new style JSA

Regulation 47 as a whole is, where art.13(1) and (2) of the Welfare Reform Act 2012 (Commencement No.9 and Transitional and Transitory Provisions and Commencement No.8 and Savings and Transitional Provisions (Amendment)) Order 2013 (as amended and set out in Part V of this volume, *Universal Credit*) applies, to be read as if a jobseeking period includes any period that formed part of a jobseeking period under reg.37 of the JSA Regulations 2013 and in para.(4) as if the reference to a day treated as a day on which the claimant was entitled to contribution-based JSA included a reference to a day treated under reg.37(3) of the JSA Regulations 2013 as a day of entitlement to new style JSA (art.13(3)(c) of that Order).

3.150

[¹ Jobseeking periods: periods of interruption of employment

[³ **47A.**—(1)] For the purposes of section 2(4)(b)(i) and for determining any waiting days—

[²(za) where a linked period commenced before 7th October 1996 [³. . .], any days of unemployment which form part of a period of interruption of employment where the last day of unemployment in that period of interruption of employment was no more than 8 weeks before the date upon which that linked period commenced;]

(a) where a jobseeking period or a linked period commences on 7th October 1996, any period of interruption of employment ending within the 8 weeks preceding that date; or

(b) where a jobseeking period or a linked period commences after 7th October 1996, any period of interruption of employment ending within the 12 weeks preceding the day the jobseeking period or linked period commenced,

shall be treated as a jobseeking period [²and, for the purposes of paragraph (za), a day shall be treated as being, or not being, a day of unemployment in accordance with section 25A of the Social Security Contributions and Benefits Act 1992 and with any regulations made under that section, as in force on 6th October 1996].]

[³(2) In paragraph (1) "period of interruption of employment" in relation to a period prior to 7th October 1996 has the same meaning as it had in the Benefits Act by virtue of section 25A of that Act (determination of days for which unemployment benefit is payable) as in force on 6th October 1996.]

3.151

AMENDMENTS

1. Social Security and Child Support (Jobseeker's Allowance) (Miscellaneous Amendments) Regulations 1996 (SI 1996/2538) reg.2(5) (October 28, 1996).

2. Jobseeker's Allowance (Amendment) (No.2) Regulations 1997 (SI 1997/2677) reg.2 (December 1, 1997).

3. Social Security (Miscellaneous Amendments) Regulations 1998 (SI 1998/563) reg.16 (April 1, 1998).

"the Benefits Act"—see Jobseekers Act 1995 s.35(1).
"jobseeking period"—see reg.47(1).
"linked period"—see reg.48(2).

GENERAL NOTE

3.152 Some spells of unemployment are continuous, others intermittent. A jobseeking period can consist of a long chain of such spells, interspersed with spells of work or entitlement to certain other benefits. This regulation enables such a chain to go back to the benefits regime before October 7, 1996, when JSA was introduced, for the purposes of the contribution conditions and the waiting days rule. Then the relevant concept was "period of interruption of employment" (PIE) and the regime worked on an eight-week linking rule where two or more ostensibly separate PIEs were fused into a single one where they were not more than eight weeks apart. Old style JSA works on a 12-week linking period (see reg.48(1) and (3)), as does new style JSA.

Linking periods

3.153 **48.**—(1) For the purposes of the Act, two or more jobseeking periods shall be treated as one jobseeking period where they are separated by a period comprising only—

(a) any period of not more than 12 weeks;

(b) a linked period;

(c) any period of not more than 12 weeks falling between—
   (i) any two linked periods; or
   (ii) a jobseeking period and a linked period;

[¹(d) a period in respect of which the claimant is summoned for jury service and is required to attend court.]

(2) Linked periods for the purposes of the Act are any of the following periods—

(a) to the extent specified in paragraph (3), any period throughout which the claimant is entitled to [⁸ a carer's allowance] under section 70 of the Benefits Act;

(b) any period throughout which the claimant is incapable of work, or is treated as incapable of work, in accordance with Part XIIA of the Benefits Act;

[¹⁰(bb)any period throughout which the claimant has, or is treated as having, limited capability for work for the purposes of Part 1 of the Welfare Reform Act;]

(c) any period throughout which the claimant was entitled to a maternity allowance under section 35[¹¹or 35B] of the Benefits Act;

(d) any period throughout which the claimant was engaged in training for which a training allowance is payable.

[²(e) a period which includes 6th October [³1996] during which the claimant attends court in response to a summons for jury service and which was immediately preceded by a period of entitlement to unemployment benefit.]

[⁴(f) any period throughout which the claimant was participating—
   (i) in the [⁷ Self-Employed] Employment Option of the New Deal as specified in regulation 75(1)(a)(ii)(aa);
   [⁶(ii) in the Voluntary Sector Option of the New Deal specified in regulation 75(1)(a)(ii)(bb), in the Environment Task Force

Option of the New Deal specified in regulation 75(1)(a)(ii)
(cc), [⁹ or in the Intensive Activity Period specified in regulation
75(1)(a)(iv)] and was not entitled to a jobseeker's allowance
because, as a consequence of his participation, the claimant was
engaged in remunerative work or failed to satisfy the condition
specified either in section 2(1)(c) or in section 3(1)(a).]

[⁵(g) any period throughout which the claimant was participating in an
employment zone programme and was not entitled to a job-seeker's
allowance because, as a consequence of his participation in that
programme, he was engaged in remunerative work or failed to satisfy
the condition specified in section 2(1)(c) or in section 3(1)(a).]

[²(2A) A period is a linked period for the purposes of section 2(4)(b)(ii)
of the Act only where it ends within 12 weeks or less of the commencement
of a jobseeking period or of some other linked period.]

(3) A period of entitlement to [⁸carer's allowance] shall be a linked period
only where it enables the claimant to satisfy contributions for entitlement
to a contribution-based jobseeker's allowance which he would otherwise be
unable to satisfy.

AMENDMENTS

1. Jobseeker's Allowance and Income Support (General) (Amendment)
Regulations 1996 (SI 1996/1517) reg.15 (October 7, 1996).

2. Social Security and Child Support (Jobseeker's Allowance) (Miscellaneous
Amendments) Regulations 1996 (SI 1996/2538) reg.2(6) (October 28, 1996).

3. Social Security (Miscellaneous Amendments) Regulations 1997 (SI 1997/
454) reg.2(4) (April 7, 1997).

4. Social Security Amendment (New Deal) Regulations 1997 (SI 1997/2863)
reg.4 (January 5, 1998).

5. Social Security Amendment (Employment Zones) Regulations 2000 (SI
2000/724) reg.4(4)(a) (April 3, 2000).

6. Social Security Amendment (New Deal) Regulations 2001 (SI 2001/1029)
reg.3 (April 9, 2001).

7. Social Security Amendment (Employment Programme) Regulations 2002 (SI
2002/2314) reg.2(3) (October 14, 2002).

8. Social Security (Miscellaneous Amendments) Regulations 2003 (SI 2003/511)
reg.3(5) (April 1, 2003).

9. Social Security (Miscellaneous Amendments) Regulations 2008 (SI 2008/698)
reg.4(7) (April 14, 2008).

10. Employment and Support Allowance (Consequential Provisions) (No.2)
Regulations 2008 (SI 2008/1554) reg.3(7) (October 27, 2008).

11. Social Security (Maternity Allowance) (Miscellaneous Amendments)
Regulations 2014 (SI 2914/884) reg.4(4) (May 18, 2014).

DEFINITIONS

"the Act"—see reg.1(3).
"the Benefits Act"—see Jobseekers Act 1995 s.35(1).
"claimant"—*ibid.*
"employment zone programme"—see reg.1(3).
"jobseeking period"—see reg.47(1)–(3).
"linked period"—see paras (2) and (3).
"training allowance"—see reg.1(3).
"week"—*ibid.*

GENERAL NOTE

3.154 Under para.(1), two or more jobseeking periods as defined in reg.47 must be fused into a single jobseeking period where separated by no more than 12 weeks, by a linked period (defined in para.(2)), by any period of not more than 12 weeks falling between any two linked periods or a jobseeking period and a linked period, or by a period in respect of which the claimant is summoned for jury service and is required to attend court. Thus, through the list of categories in para.(2), are the intermittently unemployed protected, while oscillating between unemployment and work or training, or unemployment and sickness/disability related inability to work, or unemployment and maternity or performing jury service, or caring, or any combination of these. Not all linked periods count as such for all purposes. Thus, a period of entitlement to a carer's allowance (para.(2)(a)) counted only to enable the old style JSA claimant to satisfy the JSA contribution conditions (old style Jobseekers Act 1995 s.2(1)(a) and (b)) that otherwise would not be satisfied (para.(3)). Also, para. (2A) contains a condition relevant only to the contribution conditions.

Note that linked periods or intervening periods of 12 weeks or less cannot themselves form part of a jobseeking period.

Persons approaching retirement and the jobseeking period

3.155 **49.**—(1) [² Subject to paragraph (5),] the provisions of this regulation apply only to days which fall—
   (a) after 6th October 1996; and
   (b) within a tax year in which the claimant has attained [⁴ the qualifying age for state pension credit] but is under pensionable age;
and in respect of which a jobseeker's allowance is not payable because the decision of the determining authority is that the claimant—
   (i) has exhausted his entitlement to a contribution-based job-seeker's allowance; or
   (ii) fails to satisfy one or both the contribution conditions specified in section 2(1)(a) and (b); or
   (iii) is entitled to a contribution-based jobseeker's allowance but the amount payable is reduced to Nil by virtue of deductions made in accordance with regulation 81 for pension payments.
   [¹(2) For the purposes of paragraph (1) of regulation 47 (jobseeking period) but subject to paragraphs [³3, 4 and 4A], any days to which paragraph (1) applies and in respect of which the person does not satisfy or is not treated in accordance with regulation 14, 16, 17, 19, 20, 21 or 34 as satisfying the conditions specified in paragraphs (a) to (c) of subsection (2) of section (1) (conditions of entitlement to a jobseeker's allowance), shall be days on which the person is treated as satisfying the condition in paragraphs (a) to (c) and (e) to (i) of subsection (2) of section (1).]
   (3) Where a person—
   (a) [¹. . .]
   (b) is employed as an employed earner or a self-employed earner for a period of more than 12 weeks,
then no day which falls within or follows that period shall be days on which the person is treated as satisfying those conditions so however that this paragraph shall not prevent paragraph (2) from again applying to a person who makes a claim for a jobseeker's allowance after that period.
   (4) Any day which is, for the purposes of section 30C of the Benefits Act, a day of incapacity for work falling within a period of incapacity for work

shall not be a day on which the person is treated as satisfying the conditions referred to in paragraph (2).

[³(4A) Any day which, for the purposes of Part 1 of the Welfare Reform Act, is a day where the person has limited capability for work falling within a period of limited capability for work shall not be a day on which the person is treated as satisfying the conditions referred to in paragraph (2).]

[²(5) This regulation shall not apply in respect of any days in respect of which a joint-claim jobseeker's allowance has been claimed.]

AMENDMENTS

1. Jobseeker's Allowance and Income Support (General) (Amendment) Regulations 1996 (SI 1996/1517) reg.16 (October 7, 1996).
2. Jobseeker's Allowance (Joint Claims) Regulations 2000 (SI 2000/1978) Sch.2 para.12 (March 19, 2001).
3. Employment and Support Allowance (Consequential Provisions) (No.2) Regulations 2008 (SI 2008/1554) reg.3(8) (October 27, 2008).
4. Social Security (Equalisation of State Pension Age) Regulations 2009 (SI 2009/1488) reg.11 (April 6, 2010).

DEFINITIONS

"the Benefits Act"—see Jobseekers Act 1995 s.35(1).
"claimant"—*ibid.*
"a contribution-based jobseeker's allowance"—see Jobseekers Act 1995 ss.35(1) and 1(4).
"employed earner"—see reg.3.
"a joint-claim jobseeker's allowance"—see Jobseekers Act 1995 ss.35(1) and 1(4).
"pensionable age"—see reg.3.
"qualifying age for state pension credit"—see reg.1(3).
"self-employed earner"—*ibid.*
"tax year"—see Jobseekers Act 1995 s.35(1).
"the Welfare Reform Act"—see reg.1(3).

GENERAL NOTE

This provision benefits persons (in practice only men: para.(1)(b)) for some days 3.156 falling after October 6, 1996 during the tax year in which they reach the qualifying age for SPC. The days are ones in that tax year prior to actual attainment of pensionable age on which old style JSA is not payable because of exhaustion of entitlement, failure to satisfy one or both contribution conditions (old style Jobseekers Act 1995 s.2(1)(a) and (b)), or because the JSA amount has been reduced to nil under reg.81 because of pension payments. Any such days (other than those excluded by any of paras (3)–(5)) are to be days in a jobseeking period notwithstanding that the claimant is not available for and actively seeking work and has not entered into a jobseeker's agreement.

Days which were ones of incapacity for work within a period of incapacity for work cannot form part of a jobseeking period in this way (para.(4)). Nor can days of limited capability for work forming part of a period of limited capability for work (para.(4A)). But both such situations rank as linked periods under reg.48(2)(b). Further, where someone works in employment or self-employment for more than 12 weeks, no day within or after that period can be treated as part of a jobseeking period in this way, but the protection afforded by paras (1) and (2) of the regulation can apply again after such a period when the person makes a claim for old style JSA (para.(3)).

Note that this regulation cannot apply to days which are the subject of a claim for joint-claim JSA (para.(5)).

Persons temporarily absent from Great Britain

3.157   **50.**—(1) For the purposes of the Act, a claimant shall be treated as being in Great Britain during any period of temporary absence from Great Britain—

(a) not exceeding 4 weeks in the circumstances specified in paragraphs (2), (3) and (4);

(b) not exceeding 8 weeks in the circumstances specified in paragraph (5).

(2) The circumstances specified in this paragraph are that—

(a) the claimant is in Northern Ireland and satisfies the conditions of entitlement to a jobseeker's allowance; and

(b) immediately preceding the period of absence from Great Britain the claimant was entitled to a jobseeker's allowance; and

(c) the period of absence is unlikely to exceed 52 weeks.

(3) The circumstances specified in this paragraph are that—

(a) immediately preceding the period of absence from Great Britain the claimant was entitled to a jobseeker's allowance; and

(b) the period of absence is unlikely to exceed 52 weeks; and

(c) while absent from Great Britain, the claimant continues to satisfy, or be treated as satisfying, the other conditions of entitlement to a jobseeker's allowance; and

(d) is one of a couple, both of whom are absent from Great Britain, where a premium referred to in paragraphs 10, 11, 12, 13 or 15 of Schedule 1 (applicable amounts) is applicable in respect of the claimant's partner.

(4) The circumstances of this paragraph are that—

(a) while absent from Great Britain the person is in receipt of a training allowance; and

(b) regulation 170 (person in receipt of training allowance) applies in his case; and

(c) immediately preceding his absence from Great Britain, he was entitled to a jobseeker's allowance.

(5) The circumstances specified in this paragraph are that—

(a) immediately preceding the period of absence from Great Britain, the claimant was entitled to a jobseeker's allowance; and

(b) the period of absence is unlikely to exceed 52 weeks; and

(c) the claimant continues to satisfy or be treated as satisfying the other conditions of entitlement to a jobseeker's allowance; and

(d) the claimant is, or the claimant and any other member of his family are, accompanying a member of the claimant's family who is a child or young person solely in connection with arrangements made for the treatment of that child or young person for a disease or bodily or mental disablement; and

(e) those arrangements related to treatment—

(i) outside Great Britain;

(ii) during the period whilst the claimant is, or the claimant and any member of his family are, temporarily absent from Great Britain; and

(iii) by, or under the supervision of, a person appropriately qualified to carry out that treatment.

(6) A person shall also be treated, for the purposes of the Act, as being in Great Britain during any period of temporary absence from Great Britain where—

(a) the absence is for the purpose of attending an interview for employment; and

(b) the absence is for 7 consecutive days or less; and

(c) notice of the proposed absence is given to the employment officer before departure, and is given in writing if so required by the officer; and

(d) on his return to Great Britain the person satisfies the employment officer that he attended for the interview in accordance with his notice.

[¹(6A) A member of a joint-claim couple shall be treated, for the purposes of the Act, as being in Great Britain where he is a member of a transitional case couple as defined for the purposes of paragraph 8A(2) of Schedule 1 to the Act and, as at the date on which Schedule 7 to the Welfare Reform and Pensions Act 1999 comes into force—

(a) he is temporarily absent from Great Britain; or

(b) he has made definite arrangements to be temporarily absent from Great Britain from some future date,

and that member shall be so treated during any such period of temporary absence from Great Britain.

[²(6AA) For the purposes of the Act a claimant shall be treated as being in Great Britain during any period of temporary absence from Great Britain if—

(a) he was entitled to a jobseeker's allowance immediately before the beginning of that period of temporary absence; and

(b) that period of temporary absence is for the purpose of the claimant receiving treatment at a hospital or other institution outside Great Britain where that treatment is being provided—

(i) under section 3 of the National Health Service Act 1977 (services generally);

(ii) pursuant to arrangements made under section 23 of that Act (voluntary organisations and other bodies); or

(iii) pursuant to arrangements made under paragraph 13 of Schedule 2 to the National Health Service and Community Care Act 1990 (National Health Service Trusts—specific powers).]

(6B) A member of a joint-claim couple shall be treated, for the purposes of the Act, as being in Great Britain during any period of temporary absence from Great Britain—

(a) not exceeding 4 weeks where he is in Northern Ireland and the period of absence is unlikely to exceed 52 weeks;

(b) not exceeding 4 weeks where he is in receipt of a training allowance during the period of absence and regulation 170 applies in his case; or

(c) not exceeding 7 days where the absence is for the purpose of attending an interview for employment,

where that member is so temporarily absent as at the date of claim by the other member of that couple.]

[²(6C) For the purposes of the Act a member of a joint-claim couple ("the first member") shall be treated as being in Great Britain during any period of temporary absence if—

(a) he and the other member of that couple were entitled to a joint-claim jobseeker's allowance immediately before the beginning of that period of temporary absence; and

(b) that period of temporary absence is for the purpose of the first member receiving treatment at a hospital or other institution outside Great Britain where that treatment is being provided—

    (i) under section 3 of the National Health Service Act 1977;

    (ii) pursuant to arrangements made under section 23 of that Act; or

    (iii) pursuant to arrangements made under paragraph 13 of Schedule 2 to the National Health Service and Community Care Act 1990.]

[³(6D) For the purposes of the Act, a person ("P") shall be treated as being in Great Britain during any period of temporary absence from Great Britain not exceeding 15 days where—

(a) P's absence is for the purpose of taking part in annual continuous training as a member of any territorial or reserve force prescribed in Part 1 of Schedule 6 to the Contributions Regulations; and

(b) P or P's partner was entitled to a jobseeker's allowance immediately before the period of absence began.]

(7) In this regulation—

"appropriately qualified" means qualified to provide medical treatment, physiotherapy or a form of treatment which is similar to, or related to, either of those forms of treatment;

"employment officer" means a person who is an employment officer for the purposes of sections 9 and 10.

AMENDMENTS

1. Jobseeker's Allowance (Joint Claims) Regulations 2000 (SI 2000/1978) Sch.2 para.13 (March 19, 2001).

2. Social Security (Income Support and Jobseeker's Allowance) Amendment Regulations 2004 (SI 2004/1869) reg.3(4) (October 4, 2004).

3. Social Security (Miscellaneous Amendments) (No 2) Regulation 2012 (SI 2012/2575) reg.3 (November 5, 2012).

DEFINITIONS

"the Act"—see reg.1(3).
"child"—see Jobseekers Act 1995 s.35(1).
"claimant"—*ibid.*
"employment"—see reg.3.
"employment officer"—see para.(7); Jobseekers Act 1995 s.9(13).
"entitled"—see Jobseekers Act 1995 s.35(1).
"family"—*ibid.*
"joint-claim couple"—see Jobseekers Act 1995 s.1(4).
"Great Britain"—see Jobseekers Act 1995 s.35(1).
"training allowance"—see reg.1(3).
"week"—*ibid.*
"young person"—see regs 1(3) and 76.

GENERAL NOTE

Paragraph (1)

3.158   Entitlement to JSA is dependent on the claimant being in Great Britain (old style Jobseekers Act 1995 s.1(2)(i)). This regulation treats a claimant as being in Great Britain during a range of periods of temporary absence from Great Britain, thus rendering him eligible for JSA. On "temporary absence", see notes on Persons Abroad Regulations 1975 reg.2 in D. Bonner, I. Hooker and R. White, *Social Security Legislation 2002: Vol.I. Non-Means Tested Benefits*. Note, however, that in contrast to that regulation, some of the paragraphs defining the circumstances in which someone is to be treated as if in Great Britain themselves set a requirement that the absence must be unlikely to exceed a specified number of weeks.

Paragraph (2) read with para. (1) (a)

A claimant entitled to old style JSA immediately prior to the absence can be treated as being in Great Britain for up to four weeks of temporary absence from Great Britain where the period of absence is unlikely to exceed 52 weeks, he is in Northern Ireland, and satisfies the conditions of entitlement to JSA.

3.159

Paragraph (3) read with para. (1) (a)

A claimant entitled to old style JSA immediately prior to the absence can be treated as being in Great Britain for up to four weeks of temporary absence from Great Britain where the period of absence is unlikely to exceed 52 weeks, and during the absence he continues to satisfy or be treated as satisfying the other conditions of entitlement to JSA, provided that the claimant is one of a couple and a premium is applicable to his partner under any of paras 10–13 or 15 of Sch.1. The relevant premiums are: pensioner premium for persons over 60; pensioner premium for a partner 75 or over; higher pensioner premium; disability premium; and severe disability premium.

3.160

Paragraph (4) read with para. (1) (a)

A claimant entitled to old style JSA immediately prior to the absence can be treated as being in Great Britain for up to four weeks of temporary absence from Great Britain provided that while absent he is entitled to a training allowance but training is not being provided so that reg.170 applies to him. This would appear to limit this provision to claimants under 25.

3.161

Paragraph (5) read with para. (1) (b)

A claimant entitled to old style JSA immediately prior to the absence can be treated as being in Great Britain for up to eight weeks of temporary absence from Great Britain where the period of absence is unlikely to exceed 52 weeks, and during the absence he continues to satisfy or be treated as satisfying the other conditions of entitlement to JSA, provided that the claimant (or the claimant and another family member) is (are) accompanying a child or young person of the claimant's family solely in connection with arrangements made for the treatment of that child or young person for a disease or bodily or mental disablement outside Great Britain and during the period of absence, by or under the supervision of someone appropriately qualified to carry out that treatment. "Appropriately qualified" means qualified to provide medical treatment, physiotherapy or a similar or related form of treatment (para.(7)).

3.162

Paragraph (6)

A person must also be treated as being in Great Britain during a period of temporary absence of up to seven days where the absence is for the purpose of attending an interview for employment, notice (in writing if required) of the absence was given to an employment officer before his departure, and on return he satisfies an employment officer that he attended for the interview in accordance with the notice. An "employment officer" is an officer of the Secretary of State or any other person designated as employment officer by the Secretary of State (para.(7), old style Jobseekers Act 1995 ss.9(13) and 35(1): see the notes to the definition in s.35(1)).

3.163

Paragraphs (6A)–(6C)

These apply only to members of a joint-claim couple.

3.164

Paragraph (6D)
This establishes a special rule for partners of members of the territorial or reserve forces temporarily absent from Great Britain for training of the specified kind.

The transition from new style JSA

3.165 In paras (2)(b), (3)(a) and (c), (5)(a) and (c), (6AA)(a) and (6D)(b) the references to entitlement to jobseeker's allowance are, where art.13(1)(b) of the Welfare Reform Act 2012 (Commencement No.9 and Transitional and Transitory Provisions and Commencement No.8 and Savings and Transitional Provisions (Amendment)) Order 2013 (as amended and set out in Vol.V of this series, *Universal Credit*) applies, to be read as if they included a reference to entitlement under a new style JSA award (art.13(3)(d) of that Order).

Remunerative work

3.166 **51.**—(1) For the purposes of the Act "remunerative work" means—

(a) in the case of [5 a claimant], work in which he is engaged or, where his hours of work fluctuate, is engaged on average, for not less than 16 hours per week; and

(b) in the case of any partner of the claimant, work in which he is engaged or, where his hours of work fluctuate, is engaged on average, for not less than 24 hours per week; [1 and

(c) in the case of a non-dependant, or of a child or young person to whom paragraph 18 of Schedule 6 refers, work in which he is engaged or, where his hours of work fluctuate, is engaged on average, for not less than 16 hours per week,]

and for those purposes, [3 "work" is work] for which payment is made or which is done in expectation of payment.

(2) For the purposes of paragraph (1), the number of hours in which [5 a claimant] or his partner is engaged in work shall be determined—

(a) where no recognisable cycle has been established in respect of a person's work, by reference to the number of hours or, where those hours are likely to fluctuate, the average of the hours, which he is expected to work in a week;

(b) where the number of hours for which he is engaged fluctuate, by reference to the average of hours worked over—

(i) if there is a recognisable cycle of work, and sub-paragraph (c) does not apply, the period of one complete cycle (including, where the cycle involves periods in which the person does not work, those periods but disregarding any other absences);

(ii) in any other case, the period of five weeks immediately before the date of claim or the date of [4 supersession], or such other length of time as may, in the particular case, enable the person's average hours of work to be determined more accurately;

(c) [7 . . .]

(3) In determining in accordance with this regulation the number of hours for which a person is engaged in remunerative work—

(a) that number shall include any time allowed to that person by his employer for a meal or for refreshments, but only where the person is, or expects to be, paid earnings in respect of that time;

(b) no account shall be taken of any hours in which the person is engaged in an employment or scheme to which any one of paragraphs (a) to (h) of regulation 53 (person treated as not engaged in remunerative work) applies;

(c) no account shall be taken of any hours in which the person is engaged otherwise than in an employment as an earner in caring for—

    (i) a person who is in receipt of attendance allowance [¹ . . .] [⁹ , the care component of disability living allowance at the highest or middle rate [¹⁰ , armed forces independence payment] or the daily living component of personal independence payment at the standard or enhanced rate]; or

    (ii) a person who has claimed an attendance allowance [¹ . . .] [⁹, disability living allowance [¹⁰ , armed forces independence payment] or personal independence payment], but only for the period beginning with the date of claim and ending on the date the claim is determined or, if earlier, on the expiration of the period of 26 weeks from the date of claim; or

    (iii) another person [² and] is in receipt of [⁶ carer's allowance] under Section 70 of the [¹Benefits Act; or

    (iv) a person who has claimed either attendance allowance or disability living allowance and has an award of attendance allowance or the care component of disability living allowance at one of the two higher rates prescribed under section 72(4) of the Benefits Act for a period commencing after the date on which that claim was made] [⁹ ; or

    (v) a person who has claimed personal independence payment and has an award of the daily living component at the standard or enhanced rate under section 78 of the 2012 Act for a period commencing after the date on which that claim was made] [¹⁰ ; or

    (vi) a person who has claimed and has an award of armed forces independence payment for a period commencing after the date on which that claim was made.]

[⁸ ...]

AMENDMENTS

1. Jobseekers's Allowance (Amendment) Regulations 1996 (SI 1996/15160) reg.9 (October 7, 1996).

2. Jobseekers's Allowance (Amendment) Regulations 1996 (SI 1996/1516) reg.20 and Sch. (October 7, 1996).

3. Social Security (Miscellaneous Amendments) Regulations 1997 (SI 1997/454) reg.2(5) (April 7, 1997).

4. Social Security Act 1998 (Commencement No.11, and Savings and Consequential and Transitional Provisions) Order 1999 (SI 1999/2860 (C.75)) art.3(1) and (12) and Sch.12 para.5 (October 18, 1999)

5. Jobseeker's Allowance (Joint Claims) Regulations 2000 (SI 2000/1978) reg.2(5) and Sch.2 para.14 (March 19, 2001).

6. Social Security (Miscellaneous Amendments) Regulations 2003 (SI 2003/511) reg.3(4) and (5) (April 1, 2003).

7. Social Security (Miscellaneous Amendments) Regulations 2009 (SI 2009/583) reg.4(1) and (4) (April 6, 2009).

8. Social Security (Miscellaneous Amendments) (No.3) Regulations 2011 (SI 2011/2425) reg.10(1) and (3) (October 31, 2011).

9. Personal Independence Payment (Supplementary Provisions and Consequential Amendments) Regulations 2013 (SI 2013/388) reg.8 and Sch. para.16(1) and (3) (April 8, 2013).

10. Armed Forces and Reserve Forces Compensation Scheme (Consequential Provisions: Subordinate Legislation) Order 2013 (SI 2013/591) art.7 and Sch. para.10(1) and (3) (April 8, 2013).

Definitions

"the Act"—see reg.1(3).
"attendance allowance"—*ibid.*
"the Benefits Act"—see Jobseekers Act s.35(1).
"child"—*ibid.*
"claimant"—*ibid.*
"date of claim"—see reg.1(3).
"disability living allowance"—*ibid.*
"earnings"—*ibid.*
"employment"—see reg.3.
"partner"—see reg.1(3).
"payment"—*ibid.*
"week"—*ibid.*
"young person"—*ibid.*, reg.76.

General Note

3.167   A person who is in remunerative work is not entitled to JSA (s.1(2)(e) of the old style Jobseekers Act). This applies to both contribution-based and income-based JSA. For income-based JSA there is also no entitlement if a person is a member of a couple whose partner is engaged in remunerative work (s.3(1)(e) of the Jobseekers Act).

Paragraph (1) contains the basic rule. Remunerative work is work for 16 hours or more on average a week in the case of the claimant (sub-para.(a)), or a non-dependent (see reg.2) or (in "transitional cases"—see notes to reg.83 and reg.17 of the Income Support Regulations) a child or young person who has left school and is treated as in relevant education until the next terminal date (sub-para.(c)). (Whether a non-dependent or such a child or young person is in remunerative work is relevant to income-based JSA: see para.17 of Sch.2 (non-dependent deductions from housing costs) and para.18 of Sch.6 (earnings of a child or young person not disregarded)). But in the case of a partner remunerative work is 24 hours or more a week (sub-para.(b)). Work is remunerative if payment is made for it, or it is done in the expectation of payment. See further the notes to reg.5 of the Income Support Regulations.

Paragraph (2) is similar to reg.5(2) and (3B) and para.(3)(a) and (b) to reg.5(7) and (6) respectively of the Income Support Regulations. On para.(3)(c) see the note to reg.53 below. Like reg.5(2) of the Income Support Regulations, the opening words of para.(2) suggest a mechanism for determining the hours worked in all cases but sub-paras (a), (b) and (c) do not cover all situations. In particular, a person who works for a regular number of contracted hours seems to fall outside para.(2) and inside para.(1).

3.168   The notes to reg.5 of the IS Regulations must, however, be read subject to the decision of the Tribunal of Commissioners in *R(JSA) 4/03*, which held that reg.51(2)(c) of the JSA Regulations (which is in similar terms to reg.5(3B) of the Income Support Regulations) discriminated indirectly against women and could not be objectively justified by reference to factors other than sex and therefore was inconsistent with EC Directive 79/7 (see Vol.III). In consequence reg.51(2)(c) was to be regarded as being of no effect. It has now been revoked with effect from April 6, 2009.

For an example of the application of the principles in *R(JSA) 5/03* (and, in particular, the treatment of paid public or extra-statutory holidays falling outside term-time) see the decision of Commissioner Mesher in *CJSA 1638/2003*.

It is important to note that the above decisions were all concerned with JSA, *not* IS. The Government conceded that, as had been held by the Court of Appeal in *Hockenjos v Secretary of State for Social Security* [2001] EWCA Civ 624 (CA), JSA was within the material scope of Directive 79/7. By contrast the ECJ held in *Jackson and Cresswell v Chief Adjudication Officer* (C-63/91 and C-64/91) [1992] E.C.R. I-4737 (also reported as an appendix to *R(IS) 10/91*) that IS was *not* within the material scope of the Directive because it provided protection against poverty rather than against any of the risks listed in art.3 of the Directive. Therefore reg.5(3B) of the Income Support Regulations (as interpreted by the HL in *Stafford and Banks*) remains good law even though the equivalent JSA Regulation is of no effect.

Note also that all those who stand to benefit from the disapplication of reg.51(2)(c) will ex hypothesi be workers and will therefore inevitably come within the personal scope of the Directive as defined by art.2.

Paragraphs (4) and (5)

Regulations 22–24 of the Income Support (General) Amendment No.4 Regulations 1991 (SI 1991/1559) provided transitional protection for existing income support claimants when the limit for remunerative work for income support was reduced from 24 to 16 hours per week in April 1992. The effect of paras (4) and (5) was to continue that protection for claimants on the transfer to jobseeker's allowance. They were revoked by SI 2011/2425 with effect from October 31, 2011. **3.169**

Persons treated as engaged in remunerative work

52.—(1) Except in the case of a person on maternity leave [[6], paternity leave, adoption leave] [[10], shared parental leave [[11], parental bereavement leave]] or absent from work through illness, a person shall be treated as engaged in remunerative work during any period for which he is absent from work referred to in regulation 51(1) (remunerative work) where the absence is either without [[9] a good reason] or by reason of a recognised, customary or other holiday. **3.170**

(2) For the purposes of an income-based jobseeker's allowance, [[3] but not a joint-claim jobseeker's allowance] the partner of a claimant shall be treated as engaged in remunerative work where—

(a) the partner is or was involved in a trade dispute; and

(b) had the partner claimed a jobseeker's allowance, section 14 (trade disputes) would have applied in his case; and

(c) the claimant was not entitled to an income-based jobseeker's allowance when the partner became involved in the trade dispute;

and shall be so treated for a period of 7 days beginning on the date the stoppage of work at the partner's place of employment commenced, or if there was no stoppage of work, the date on which the partner first withdrew his labour in furtherance of the trade dispute.

[[4](2A) For the purposes of a joint-claim jobseeker's allowance, a member of a joint-claim couple shall be treated as engaged in remunerative work where—

(a) he is or was involved in a trade dispute;

(b) had the joint-claim couple of which he is a member claimed a jobseeker's allowance jointly, section 14 (trade disputes) would have applied in the case of one or both members of that couple; and

(c) the joint-claim couple were not entitled to a joint-claim jobseeker's allowance when that member of the joint-claim couple became involved in the trade dispute,

and shall be so treated for a period of 7 days beginning on the date the stoppage of work commenced at that member's place of employment or, if there was no stoppage of work, the date on which that member first withdrew his labour in furtherance of the trade dispute.]

(3) [[7] Subject to paragraph (3A), a person] who was, or was treated as being, engaged in remunerative work and in respect of that work earnings

to which [¹⁸ regulation 98(1)(c)] (earnings of employed earners) applies are paid, shall be treated as engaged in remunerative work for the period for which those earnings are taken into account in accordance with Part VIII.

[⁷ (3A) Paragraph (3) shall not apply to earnings disregarded under paragraph 1 of Schedule 6 to these regulations.]

[⁵(4)–(6) . . .]

AMENDMENTS

1. Jobseekers's Allowance (Amendment) Regulations 1996 (SI 1996/1516) reg.20 and Sch. (October 7, 1996).
2. Social Security (Miscellaneous Amendments) (No.2) Regulations 1999 (SI 1999/2556) reg.3 (October 4, 1999).
3. Jobseeker's Allowance (Joint Claims) Regulations 2000 (SI 2000/1978) reg.2(5) and Sch.2 para.15(a) (March 19, 2001).
4. Jobseeker's Allowance (Joint Claims) Regulations 2000 (SI 2000/1978) reg.2(5) and Sch.2 para.15(b) (March 19, 2001).
5. Social Security (Miscellaneous Amendments) Regulations 2001 (SI 2001/488) reg.12(a) (April 9, 2001).
6. Social Security (Paternity and Adoption) Amendment Regulations 2002 (SI 2002/2689) reg.3 (December 8, 2002).
7. Social Security (Miscellaneous Amendments) (No.5) Regulations 2007 (SI 2007/2618) reg.8(4) (October 1, 2007).
8. Social Security (Miscellaneous Amendments) Regulations 2008 (SI 2008/698) reg.4(8) (April 14, 2008).
9. Jobseeker's Allowance (Sanctions) (Amendment) Regulations 2012 (SI 2012/2568) reg.5(9) (October 22, 2012).
10. Shared Parental Leave and Statutory Shared Parental Pay (Consequential Amendments to Subordinate Legislation) Order 2014 (SI 2014/3255) art.7(1) and (4) (December 31, 2014).
11. Parental Bereavement Leave and Pay (Consequential Amendments to Subordinate Legislation) Regulations 2020 (SI 2020/354) reg.8(1) and (4) (April 6, 2020).

DEFINITIONS

"maternity leave"—see reg.1(3).
"partner"—*ibid.*
"remunerative work"—see reg.51(1).
"trade dispute"—see Jobseekers Act s.35(1).

GENERAL NOTE

3.171   This provision deems people to be in remunerative work in certain circumstances.

Paragraph (1)
3.172   See reg.5(3) and (3A) of the Income Support Regulations and the notes to those paragraphs. See also the discussion under the heading "Term-time only workers" in the notes to reg.5.

Paragraph (2)
3.173   See the notes to s.15 of the Jobseekers Act.

Paragraph (3)
3.174   Where (within four weeks) holiday pay is paid, the person is treated as in remunerative work for the period covered. See regs 94 and 96. Following the increased disregard of payments made on the termination of full-time employment that was introduced on October 1, 2007 (see para.1 of Sch.6 and the notes to that

paragraph) this provision will only apply where a person's employment has been suspended.

Persons treated as not engaged in remunerative work

53.—A person shall be treated as not engaged in remunerative work in   3.175
so far as—

  (a) he is engaged by a charity or a voluntary organisation or is a volunteer where the only payment received by him or due to be paid to him is a payment which is to be disregarded under regulation 103(2) and paragraph 2 of Schedule 7 (sums to be disregarded in the calculation of income other than earnings)[¹² and in this paragraph "volunteer" means a person who is engaged in voluntary work, otherwise than for a relative, where the only payment received, or due to be paid to the person by virtue of being so engaged, is in respect of any expenses reasonably incurred by the person in connection with that work];

  (b) he is engaged on a scheme for which a training allowance is being paid;

[³(bb) he is receiving assistance [⁷under the self-employment route]

[⁵⁹(c) [¹¹ . . .]]

  (d) he is engaged in employment as—
        [⁸ ¹⁸ . . .]
      [¹⁸ (i) a part-time fire-fighter employed by a fire and rescue authority under the Fire and Rescue Services Act 2004 or by the Scottish Fire and Rescue Service established under section 1A of the Fire (Scotland) Act 2005;]

    [⁶(ia) [¹⁸ . . .]]
    [⁸(ib) [¹⁸ [¹⁷]. . .]]

       (ii) an auxiliary coastguard in respect of coastal rescue activities;
      (iii) a person engaged part-time in the manning or launching of a lifeboat;
       (iv) a member of any [¹⁹ . . .] reserve force prescribed in Part I of [¹⁰ Schedule 6 to the Social Security (Contributions) Regulations 2001];

  (e) he is performing his duties as a councillor, and for this purpose "councillor" has the same meaning as in section 171F(2) of the Benefits Act;

  (f) he is engaged in caring for a person who is accommodated with him by virtue of arrangements made under any of the provisions referred to in paragraph 27 or 28 of Schedule 7 (sums to be disregarded in the calculation of income other than earnings), and is in receipt of any payment specified in that paragraph;

[²⁰(fa) he is engaged in caring for a person who is provided with continuing care by a local authority by virtue of arrangements made under section 26A of the Children (Scotland) Act 1995 and is in receipt of a payment made under that section of that Act;".]

  (g) he is—
        (i) the partner of the claimant; and
       (ii) involved in a trade dispute; and
      (iii) not a person to whom regulation 52(2) applies,
            and had he claimed a jobseeker's allowance, section 14 (trade disputes) would have applied in his case;

[⁴(gg) he is—

(i) a member of a joint-claim couple; and
(ii) involved in a trade dispute; and
(iii) not a person to whom regulation 52(2A) applies,
        and had the joint-claim couple of which he is a member claimed
        a jobseeker's allowance jointly, section 14 (trade disputes) would
        have applied in the case of one or both members of that couple;]
(h) [^{11} . . .]
[^{2}(i) he is engaged in an activity in respect of which—
        (i) a sports award has been made, or is to be made, to him; and
        (ii) no other payment is made or is expected to be made to him].
(j) [*Omitted.*]
[^{13} (k) he is engaged in the programme known as Work Experience.]
[^{14} (l) he is participating in the Mandatory Work Activity Scheme.]
[$^{15\ 16}$ (m) he is participating in a scheme prescribed in regulation 3 of the
        Jobseeker's Allowance (Schemes for Assisting Persons to Obtain
        Employment) Regulations 2013.]

AMENDMENTS

1. Jobseekers's Allowance (Amendment) Regulations 1996 (SI 1996/1516) reg.20 and Sch. (October 7, 1996).

2. Social Security Amendment (Sports Awards) Regulations 1999 (SI 1999/2165) reg.7(2) (August 23, 1999).

3. Social Security Amendment (Employment Zones) (No.2) Regulations 2000 (SI 2000/2910) reg.3 (November 27, 2000).

4. Jobseeker's Allowance (Joint Claims) Regulations 2000 (SI 2000/1978) reg.2(5) and Sch.2 para.16 (March 19, 2001).

5. Social Security Amendment (Residential Care and Nursing Homes) Regulations 2001 (SI 2001/3767) reg.2 and Sch. Pt II para.2 (April 8, 2002).

6. Fire and Rescue Services Act 2004 (Consequential Amendments) (England) Order 2004 (SI 2004/3168) reg.36(3) (December 30, 2004) (in relation to England); Fire and Rescue Services Act 2004 (Consequential Amendments) (Wales) Order 2005 (WSI 2005/2929 (W.214)) reg.33(6) (October 25, 2005) (in relation to Wales). The amendment does not extend to Scotland.

7. Social Security (Income-Related Benefits Self-Employment Route Amendment) Regulations 2004 (SI 2004/963) reg.4 (May 4, 2004).

8. Fire (Scotland) Act 2005 (Consequential Provisions and Modifications) Order 2005 (SI 2005/2060) art.3 and Sch. para.10(3) (August 2, 2005).

9. Social Security (Care Homes and Independent Hospitals) Regulations 2005 (SI 2005/2687) reg.3 and Sch.2 para.2 (October 24, 2005).

10. Social Security (Miscellaneous Amendments) (No.4) Regulations 2006 (SI 2006/2378) reg.13(3) (October 2, 2006).

11. Social Security (Miscellaneous Amendments) (No.5) Regulations 2009 (SI 2009/3228) reg.4(b)(i) (January 25, 2010).

12. Social Security (Miscellaneous Amendments) (No.2) Regulations 2010 (SI 2010/641) reg.4(1) and (5) (April 6, 2010).

13. Jobseeker's Allowance (Work Experience) (Amendment) Regulations 2011 (SI 2011/798) reg.2(4) (April 5, 2011).

14. Jobseeker's Allowance (Mandatory Work Activity Scheme) Regulations 2011 (SI 2011/688) reg.16(c) (April 25, 2011).

15. Jobseeker's Allowance (Employment, Skills and Enterprise Scheme) Regulations 2011 (SI 2011/917) reg.16(b) (May 20, 2011).

16. Jobseeker's Allowance (Schemes for Assisting Persons to Obtain Employment) Regulations 2013 (SI 2013/276) reg.14(c) (February 12, 2013).

17. Police and Fire Reform (Scotland) Act 2012 (Consequential Provisions and

Modifications) Order 2013 (SI 2013/602) art.26 and Sch.2 para.74(1) and (3) (April 1, 2013).

18 Social Security (Miscellaneous Amendments) (No.3) Regulations 2013 (SI 2013/2536) reg.6(1) and (5) (October 29,2013).

19. Social Security (Members of the Reserve Forces) (Amendment) Regulations 2015 (SI 2015/389) reg.3(1) and (7)(c) (April 6, 2015).

20. Social Security and Child Support (Care Payments and Tenant Incentive Scheme) (Amendment) Regulations 2017 (SI 2017/995), reg.11(1) and (2) (November 7, 2017).

DEFINITIONS

"Abbeyfield Home"—see reg.1(3).
"the Benefits Act"—see Jobseekers Act s.35(1).
"care home"—see reg.1(3).
"earnings"—*ibid.*
"employment"—see reg.3.
"independent hospital"—see reg.1(3).
"partner"—*ibid.*
"remunerative work"—see reg.51(1).
"trade dispute"—see Jobseekers Act s.35(1).
"training allowance"—see reg.1(3).
"voluntary organisation"—*ibid.*

GENERAL NOTE

See the notes to reg.6 of the Income Support Regulations. The categories are similar to those in paras (1) and (4) of reg.6 but there are slight differences. On para. (g), see the notes to s.15 of the Jobseekers Act.

3.176

Unlike income support (see reg.6(4)(c)), carers are not covered by reg.53. Instead, unless they are "employed as an earner", no account is taken of the hours they spend in caring in deciding whether they are engaged in remunerative work (see reg.52(3)(c)).

There is no equivalent to reg.6(b). So a childminder working 16 or more hours a week (or 24 if she is the partner of a claimant) may count as in remunerative work.

The revocations of paras (c) and (h) with effect from January 25, 2010 are subject to savings provisions in reg.4 of SI 2009/3228 (above). Those provisions apply where a claimant is entitled to jobseeker's allowance for a period including January 24, 2010 (irrespective of when jobseeker's allowance was claimed) and falls within paras (c) or (h) on that date. In those circumstances, para.(c) or (h)—and also para.7 or 8 of Sch.A1 (which were revoked on the same date)—continue to apply to the claimant until either they cease to fall within para.(c) or (h) or they cease to be entitled to jobseeker's allowance, whichever is earlier: see reg.4(3), (5), (7) and (8) of SI 2009/3228.

Relevant education

54.—(1) Only full-time education which is undertaken by a child or young person and which is not a course of advanced education shall be treated as relevant education for the purposes of the Act.

3.177

[² (2) A child or young person shall be treated as receiving full-time education where he is a qualifying young person or child within the meaning of section 142 of the Benefits Act (child and qualifying young person).]

(3) A young person who—

(a) is a part-time student; and

(b) before he became a part-time student fulfilled the requirements specified for a person falling within paragraph (2) of regulation 11 (part-time students); and

(c) is undertaking a course of study, other than a course of advanced education or a course of study of a kind specified in head (i), (ii) or (iii) of the definition of "full-time student" in regulation 1(3),

shall not be treated as receiving relevant education.

(4) A young person to whom paragraph (3) applied and who has completed or terminated his course of part-time study shall not be treated as receiving relevant education.

[³ (4A) A young person who is participating in a traineeship shall not be treated as receiving relevant education.]

[¹(5) [³ . . .]]

AMENDMENTS

1. Social Security Amendment (New Deal) Regulations 1997 (SI 1997/2863) reg.5 (January 5, 1998).
2. Social Security (Young Persons) Amendment Regulations 2006 (SI 2006/718) reg.3(4) (April 10, 2006).
3. Social Security (Traineeships and Qualifying Young Persons) Amendment Regulations 2015 (SI 2015/336) reg.2(6) (March 27, 2015).

DEFINITIONS

"the Benefits Act"—see Jobseekers Act s.35(1).
"child"—*ibid.*
"course of advanced education"—see reg.1(3).
"course of study"—*ibid.*
"part-time student"—*ibid.*
"traineeship" – *ibid.*
"young person"—*ibid.*, reg.76.

GENERAL NOTE

Paragraphs (1) and (2)

3.178   Under s.1(2)(g) of the old style Jobseekers Act 1995 a person is excluded from old style JSA if he is in relevant education.

Paragraphs (1) and (2) provide an exhaustive test of when a person is to be treated as receiving relevant education. On para.(2), see the note to reg.12 of the Income Support Regulations.

Note that some claimants may be able to receive income support though in relevant education (see reg.13 of, and paras 15 and 15A of Sch.IB to, the Income Support Regulations), in which case some may also be eligible for old style JSA (see regs 57(1) (meaning of "young person"), 57(2) and (4)(a) and 61(1)(c)). It will normally be better for most young people to claim income support in these circumstances, so as to avoid the risk of being sanctioned for not complying with the JSA labour market conditions.

Paragraphs (3) and (4)

3.179   Under para.(3) a young person (as defined in reg.76) who is a part-time student (see the definitions of full-time and part-time student in reg.1(3); note also reg.1(3A)–(3E)) undertaking a course other than one of advanced education or of a kind within para.(b) of the definition of "full-time student" in reg.1(3) who satisfies the conditions in sub-para. (b) does not count as in relevant education (and will not so count after he finishes or leaves his part-time course (para.(4)). The conditions in para.(3)(b) are that for the three months before he started his course he was in receipt of JSA, ESA, incapacity benefit or income support while sick or on a course of "training" (see reg.11(3)) or in the six months before the course was in receipt of any of these benefits or on a course of "training" for a total of three months and for the remainder of the time was in remunerative work (see reg.51) or earning too much to be entitled to benefit (in both cases the three and the six months must be after the young person has ceased to be in relevant education).

See reg.11 which may enable such a part-time student to be accepted as available for work even though his hours of study coincide with the times he is required to be available for employment.

Paragraph (4A)

This provision ensures that a young person who is on a "traineeship" is not treated as in relevant education. A "traineeship" is a course of up to six months which helps 16–24 year olds to prepare for work and is funded by, or under arrangements made by, the Secretary of State under s.14 of the Education Act 2002 (see the definition in reg.1(3)). A person who is on a traineeship is treated as available for, and actively seeking, work (see regs 14(1)(aa) and 19(1)(aa)) and so may be eligible for JSA.

3.180

Short periods of sickness

55.—(1) Subject to the following provisions of this regulation, a person who—

3.181

(a) [¹ has been awarded a jobseeker's allowance] [¹⁰ . . .]; and

(b) proves to the satisfaction of [² the Secretary of State] that he is unable to work on account of some specific disease or disablement; and

(c) [¹² during the period of his disease or disablement, satisfies] the requirements for entitlement to a jobseeker's allowance other than those specified in section 1(2)(a), (c) and (f) (available for and actively seeking employment, and capable of work [⁵or not having limited capability for work]),

shall be treated for a period of not more than 2 weeks as capable of work [⁵ or as not having limited capability for work], except where the claimant states in writing that for the period of his disease or disablement he proposes to claim or has claimed incapacity benefit, [⁵ employment and support allowance,] [¹² universal credit,] severe disablement allowance or income support.

(2) The evidence which is required for the purposes of paragraph (1)(b) is a declaration made by the claimant in writing, in a form approved for the purposes by the Secretary of State, that he has been unfit for work from a date or for a period specified in the declaration.

(3) [¹² Paragraph (1) does] not apply to a claimant on more than two occasions in any one jobseeking period or where a jobseeking period exceeds 12 months, in each successive 12 months within that period and for the purposes of calculating any period of 12 months, the first 12 months in the jobseeking period commences on the first day of the jobseeking period.

[¹¹(4) [¹² Paragraph (1) does] not apply to any person where the first day in respect of which they are unable to work falls within eight weeks beginning with the day the person ceased to be entitled to statutory sick pay.]

[⁴(5) [¹² Paragraph (1) does] not apply to a claimant who is temporarily absent from Great Britain in the circumstances prescribed by regulation 50(6AA) or, as the case may be, (6C).]

[¹² (6) Paragraph (1) does not apply to any person—

(a) during any period where the person is treated as capable of work or as not having limited capability for work under regulation 55ZA (extended period of sickness); or

(b) where the first day in respect of which that person would, apart from this sub-paragraph, have been treated as capable of work or as not having limited capability for work under this regulation falls immediately after the last day on which the person is so treated under regulation 55ZA.]

[[13](7) For the purposes of calculating the number of occasions under paragraph (3), any occasion on which regulation 55ZA applies to the claimant is to be disregarded.]

AMENDMENTS

1. Jobseeker's Allowance and Income Support (General) (Amendment) Regulations 1996 (SI 1996/1517) reg.17 (October 7, 1996).

2. Social Security Act 1998 (Commencement No.11, and Savings and Consequential and Transitional Provisions) Order 1999 (SI 1999/2860) art.3(12) and Sch.12 para.2 (October 18, 1999).

3. Jobseeker's Allowance (Joint Claims) Regulations 2000 (SI 2000/1978) reg.2(5) and Sch.2 para.17 (March 19, 2001).

4. Social Security (Income Support and Jobseeker's Allowance) Amendment Regulations 2004 (SI 2004/1869) reg.3(5) (October 4, 2004).

5. Employment and Support Allowance (Consequential Provisions) (No.2) Regulations 2008 (SI 2008/1554) reg.3(9) (October 27, 2008).

6. Jobseeker's Allowance (Sanctions for Failure to Attend) Regulations 2010 (SI 2010/509) reg.2(8) (April 6, 2010).

7. Employment and Support Allowance (Transitional Provisions, Housing Benefit and Council Tax Benefit) (Existing Awards) (No.2) Regulations 2010 (SI 2010/1907) as amended by the Employment and Support Allowance (Transitional Provisions, Housing Benefit and Council Tax Benefit) (Existing Awards) (No. 2) (Amendment) Regulations 2010 (SI 2010/2430) reg.26 and Sch.4 para.1A(1) (January 31, 2011).

8. Social Security (Miscellaneous Amendments) Regulations 2011 (SI 2011/674) reg.7(2) (April 11, 2011).

9. Jobseeker's Allowance (Mandatory Work Activity Scheme) Regulations 2011 (SI 2011/688) reg.16(d) (April 25, 2011).

10. Jobseeker's Allowance (Sanctions) (Amendment) Regulations 2012 (SI 2012/2568) reg.5(10) (October 22, 2012).

11. Social Security (Miscellaneous Amendments) (No.3) Regulations 2013 (SI 2013/2536) reg.6(6) (October 29, 2013).

12. Jobseeker's Allowance (Extended Period of Sickness) Amendment Regulations 2015 (SI 2015/339) reg. 2(4) (March 30, 2015).

13. Jobseeker's Allowance (Extended Period of Sickness) Amendment Regulations 2016 (SI 2016/502) reg.2(2) (May 23, 2016).

DEFINITIONS

"claimant"—see Jobseekers Act s.35(1).
"jobseeking period"—see regs 1(3) and 47(1)–(3).
"limited capability for work"—see Jobseekers Act s.35(2) and Sch.1, para.2.

GENERAL NOTE

Temporary Coronavirus Provisions

3.182   Note that by virtue of reg.8(2) of the Social Security (Coronavirus) (Further Measures) Regulations 2020 (SI 2020/371), as in effect down to at least August 31,

2021, any period during which a claimant is deemed to be capable of work or not to have limited capability for work under reg.8(1) (see the notes to s.1(2)(f) of the old Style Jobseekers Act 1995) does not count in determining under para.(3) the number of occasions within 12 months that advantage can be taken of reg.55.

Paragraph (1) (along with regs 14(1)(l) and 19(1)(l)—see below) allows an old style JSA award to continue for up to two weeks while a claimant is unable to work due to illness or disablement by treating them as capable of work, or as not having limited capability for work, for that period. However, this does not apply if the claimant has stated in writing that they propose to claim, or have claimed, ESA or universal credit (it is no longer possible to make a claim for severe disablement allowance, incapacity benefit or income support on the grounds of incapacity for work). Presumably the intention is to avoid claimants having to chop and change between benefits where their period of unfitness is only likely to be short.

3.183

This provision is subject to a limit of two such periods in one jobseeking period or, if the jobseeking period lasts longer than 12 months, in each successive 12-month period—see para.(3). Paragraph (7) confirms, if confirmation was needed, that in applying this limit, occasions when reg.55ZA (extended periods of sickness) applied do not count.

Note that under para.(1)(b) claimants only have to show that they are unable to work on account of some specific disease or disablement (not further defined). This is achieved by claimants providing a written declaration in a form approved by the Secretary of State that they have been unfit for work from a certain date or for a specified period (para.(2)).

There has been some discussion of whether reg.55 could apply immediately at the beginning of the period covered by a claim for old style JSA, e.g. where a claimant previously entitled to old style ESA has lost entitlement on being found not to have limited capability for work and is challenging that decision. It is not now possible, except in very rare cases, to make a new claim for IBJSA, but discussion of the problem has been retained for interest. Could new claimants of IBJSA in the past, take advantage of regs 55 and 55ZA immediately, so as to be able to maintain the contention of incapacity for work while claiming JSA and to maintain a continuity of benefit entitlement without falling between the two stools of ESA and JSA? In some circumstances a claimant who appeals against the decision terminating ESA entitlement can be awarded old style ESA pending the determination of the appeal (see reg.147A of the ESA Regulations 2008). However, even where that is so, there may well be some delay while the mandatory reconsideration process is completed, so that potential entitlement to old style JSA is of practical importance. The difficulty lies mainly in the terms of regs 55(1)(a) and 55ZA(1)(a). The reference to an award in the past tense (in contrast to the normal use of the present tense in legislation) appears to require that there has already been a decision that the claimant is entitled to old style JSA (even if no benefit is payable, e.g because of a sanction) under the normal conditions of entitlement (without modification under reg.55 or 55ZA) before those provisions can operate. The terms of regs 55(1)(c) and 55ZA(1)(d) are perhaps neutral.

3.184

It might be thought that, even if that is correct, a claimant disputing an ESA decision could have avoided more than a short-term disadvantage by claiming and being awarded old style JSA on the ordinary conditions and then immediately applying for a supersession in reliance on the rules in reg.55 or 55ZA as appropriate. The immediate difficulty, though, is that claimants then have to satisfy the condition of entitlement of not having limited capability for work (old style Jobseekers Act 1995 s.1(2)(f)) when they are maintaining that they *do* have limited capability for work. However, it is arguable that reg.10 of the Decisions and Appeals Regulations (in contrast to reg.40 of the Universal Credit etc. (Decisions and Appeals) Regulations 2013 on new style ESA and JSA: both regulations in Vol.III of this series) applies to make the old style ESA determination that the claimant does not have limited capability for work conclusive for the purposes of a subsequent old style JSA decision. Thus the claimant, being forced at that point to accept that conclusive effect, may legitimately claim to satisfy all the ordinary conditions of entitlement, if the conditions other than s.1(2)(f) are met. Then there would be no inconsistency in substance in the claimant's immediately maintaining an application for supersession on the basis of a relevant change of circumstances (having been awarded JSA) and in fact being unable to work on account of some specific disease or disablement (in any event a different test from that for limited capability for work in ESA), relying on the terms of reg.55 or 55ZA. If those terms apply, the claimant does not have to satisfy the conditions of entitlement of being available for and actively seeking employment or of not having limited capability for work (so that the conclusive effect of the ESA determination becomes irrelevant). The claimant would still have to have entered into a jobseeker's agreement under s.1(2)(b), but arguably would be treated as meeting that condition by virtue of regs 14(1)(l) (deemed to be available for employment where treated as not having limited capability for work under reg.55, 55ZA or 55A) and 34(c) (deemed to satisfy s.1(2)(b) so long as deemed available under reg.14).

It must be stressed that the above arguments do not reflect any accepted Departmental views and have not been tested before the Upper Tribunal. However, elementary considerations of fairness require that some way must be found of preventing claimants being denied entitlement to ESA on the basis that they do not have limited capability for work and also being denied entitlement to JSA on the basis that they maintain that they do have limited capability for work. It may therefore be necessary to consider a more direct route beyond the 13 weeks allowed by reg.55ZA and perhaps as an alternative to the above argument. This would involve first submitting that the claimant satisfies s.1(2)(b) by virtue of the conclusive effect of the ESA determination, regardless of what he says himself about his capability for work. Then the claimant would have to assert that under reg.13(3) his availability could be restricted to nil or something minimal in the light of his actual physical and mental condition and that it was not reasonable to expect him to take more than one or a few simple steps each week under the actively seeking employment test, plus persuade an employment officer that those restrictions should be incorporated into his jobseeker's agreement in a way that complies with s.9(5) of the old style Jobseekers Act 1995.

3.185   Regulation 55 does not apply if the first day that the claimant is unable to work falls within eight weeks of the day on which they ceased to be entitled to statutory sick pay (para.(4)) or if they are temporarily absent from Great Britain for the purpose of receiving NHS treatment abroad (para.(5)). On para.(5), see the note to reg.55A.

Under para.(6), inserted with effect from March 30, 2015, this provision does not apply during any period when reg.55ZA applies (sub-para.(a)); or if the two-week period would follow *immediately* after the last day of a period to which reg.55ZA applied (sub-para.(b)).

While someone is treated as not having limited capability for work under this regulation, they are treated as available for work (see reg.14(1)(l)); they are also treated as actively seeking work in any week in which they are covered by this regulation for at least three days in that week (see reg.19(1)(l)).

3.186   However, someone can still choose to claim old style or new style ESA or universal credit (as available) on the ground of limited capability for work in the circumstances to which this regulation applies if they wish to do so.

See further reg.55ZA and the notes to that regulation.

In *CIS 2107/1998* the claimant, who had been in receipt of income-based JSA, was advised to claim incapacity benefit when he became unfit for work. This was refused but income support was awarded from a later date. The claimant appealed against the refusal to backdate his income support. The Commissioner states that when a claimant appeals against a gap in benefit, that should be taken as an appeal against *all* the decisions that gave rise to that gap (in this case potentially JSA, incapacity benefit and income support). He also held that the proviso at the end of para.(1) should be construed narrowly in order not to defeat the primacy of the rule in reg.55. In his view the proviso meant that there had to be some written statement by the claimant, other than the claim form for incapacity benefit; moreover, the statement had to make it clear that it applied to the whole period of sickness. The result was that the proviso did not operate in this case and the claimant was entitled to JSA for the two week period after he became ill (which period coincided with the gap in his claim).

[¹ Extended period of sickness

55ZA.—(1) This regulation applies to a person who— 3.187
(a) has been awarded a jobseeker's allowance;
(b) proves to the satisfaction of the Secretary of State that he is unable to work on account of some specific disease or disablement [²("the initial condition")];
(c) either—
    (i) declares that he has been unable to work, or [²expects] to be unable to work, on account of [²the initial condition or any other disease or disablement] for more than 2 weeks but [²not] more than 13 weeks; or
    (ii) is not a person to whom regulation 55(1) (short periods of sickness) applies by virtue of paragraph (3) of that regulation[², and declares that he has been unable to work or expects to be unable to work, on account of the initial condition or any other disease or disablement, for two weeks or less];
(d) during the period of his disease or disablement, satisfies the requirements for entitlement to a jobseeker's allowance other than those specified in section 1(2)(a), (c) and (f) (availability for and actively seeking employment and capable of work or not having limited capability for work); and
(e) has not stated in writing that for the period of his disease or disablement he proposes to claim or has claimed an employment and support allowance or universal credit.
(2) The evidence which is required for the purposes of paragraph (1)(b) in a case where paragraph (1)(c)(i) applies is—
(a) evidence of incapacity for work or limited capability for work in accordance with the Social Security (Medical Evidence) Regulations 1976 (which prescribe the form of a doctor's statement or other evidence required in each case); and
(b) any such additional information as the Secretary of State may request.
(3) [²Subject to paragraph (3A),] the evidence which is required for the purposes of paragraph (1)(b) in a case where paragraph (1)(c)(ii) applies is a declaration made by the person in writing, in a form approved for the purposes by the Secretary of State, that the person has been unfit for work from a date or for a period specified in the declaration.
[²(3A) In a case where paragraph (1)(c)(ii) applies, but the period in which the person has been unable to work or expects to be unable to work exceeds 2 weeks, the evidence that is required for the purposes of paragraph (1)(b) is the evidence that is required in a case where paragraph (1)(c)(i) applies.]
(4) Subject to the following paragraphs, a person to whom this regulation applies is to be treated as capable of work or as not having limited capability for work for the continuous period beginning on the first day on which

he is unable to work on account of [² . . .] disease or disablement ("the first day") and ending on—

(a) the last such day; or

(b) if that period would otherwise exceed 13 weeks, the day which is 13 weeks after the first day.

(5) This regulation does not apply to a person on more than one occasion in any one period of 12 months starting on the first day applying for the purpose of paragraph (4).

(6) Paragraphs (4) and (5) of regulation 55 apply for the purposes of this regulation as they apply for the purposes of paragraph (1) of regulation 55.]

AMENDMENTS

1. Jobseeker's Allowance (Extended Period of Sickness) Amendment Regulations 2015 (SI 2015/339) reg.2(5) (March 30, 2015).

2. Jobseeker's Allowance (Extended Period of Sickness) Amendment Regulations 2016 (SI 2016/502) reg.2(3) (May 23, 2016).

DEFINITION

"limited capability for work"—see Jobseekers Act s.35(2) and Sch.1 para.2.

GENERAL NOTE

Temporary Coronavirus Provisions

3.188   Note that by virtue of reg.8(2) of the Social Security (Coronavirus) (Further Measures) Regulations 2020 (SI 2020/371), as in effect down to at least August 31, 2021, any period during which a claimant is deemed to be capable of work or not to have limited capability for work under reg.8(1) (see the notes to s.1(2)(f) of the old Style Jobseekers Act 1995) does not count in determining under para.(5) the number of occasions within 12 months that advantage can be taken of reg.55ZA.

3.189   This provision allows an old style JSA claimant to remain on JSA despite being unable to work due to illness or disablement for up to 13 weeks (referred to by the DWP as an extended period of sickness ("EPS")). The intention is apparently to keep claimants more engaged with the labour market and to support a return to work more quickly, as well as reducing the administrative burden of requiring claimants to switch from JSA to ESA for a short period of time. See the notes to reg.55 for how far reg.55ZA can apply at or near the beginning of a claim.

This regulation applies in addition to the two periods of two weeks' sickness that are allowed under reg.55. If therefore a claimant has already had two periods of two weeks' sickness in their jobseeking period (or, if the jobseeking period lasts longer than 12 months, in each successive 12 month period—see reg.55(3)), this regulation may apply in the case of a third period of sickness. It may also apply if a claimant's sickness turns out to last more than two weeks (although it seems that any days covered by reg.55 will count towards the 13-week limit under this regulation—see para.(4) which states that the 13-week period starts on the first day on which the claimant is unable to work due to illness or disablement). However, in such a case it seems that reg.55 could still apply for two periods of two weeks in the jobseeking period/successive 12-month period—see reg.55(6)(a) which provides that reg.55 does not apply during any period when a person is covered by reg.55ZA. Note also that claimants cannot start a two-week period under reg.55 *immediately* after the last day of a period in which they were treated as not having limited capability for work under this regulation (see reg.55(6)(b)).

Regulation 55ZA can only apply on one occasion in any period of 12 months (para.(5)); the 12-month period starts on the first day that the person is unable to work due to illness or disablement (see the definition of "the first day" in para.

(4))—presumably this means the first day on which the claimant's inability to work is accepted by the Secretary of State. Note that this 12-month period is therefore not the same 12-month period as that which applies under reg.55(3); the 12-month period under reg.55(3) starts from the beginning of the claimant's jobseeking period (or, if the jobseeking period lasts longer than 12 months, from the start of each successive 12-month period).

Note that for reg.55ZA to apply, someone only has to show that they are unable to work on account of some specific disease or disablement (not further defined). In addition, claimants must either declare that due to that illness or disablement they have been unable to work or expect to be unable to work, for more than two weeks but not more than 13 weeks; *or* be a person who has already had two periods of up to two weeks' sickness within their jobseeking period (or, if the jobseeking period lasts longer than 12 months, within each successive 12-month period—see reg.55(3)); *and* satisfy the conditions for an award of old style JSA (other than the requirements of being available for, and of actively seeking, work and of not having limited capability for work); *and* not have stated in writing that he proposes to claim ESA or universal credit (para.(1)).   3.190

Regulation 55ZA does not apply if the first day that the claimant is unable to work falls within eight weeks of the day on which they ceased to be entitled to statutory sick pay or if they are temporarily absent from Great Britain for the purpose of receiving NHS treatment abroad (para.(6)).

If the claimant declares that they are unable to work for more than two but not more than 13 weeks, they have to provide a doctor's statement or other evidence in accordance with the Social Security (Medical Evidence) Regulations 1976 (see Vol.III in this series), together with any other information the Secretary of State may require (para.(2)). If someone has already had two periods of up to two weeks sickness (i.e. this is in effect a third period of short sickness), they have to provide a written declaration in a form approved by the Secretary of State that they have been unfit for work from a certain date or for a specified period, except where the latest period of unfitness extends beyond two weeks, when a doctor's statement is required (paras (3) and (3A)).

If the conditions in reg.55ZA are met, claimants are treated as capable of work or as not having limited capability for work, for a continuous period from the first day on which they are unable to work due to the illness or disablement to the last such day, or for 13 weeks after the first day, if the period is longer than 13 weeks (para.(4)).   3.191

It remains possible for claimants still to claim benefit on the ground of limited capability for work in the circumstances to which reg.55ZA applies if they wish to do so.

While claimants are treated as not having limited capability for work under reg.55ZA, they are treated as available for work (see reg.14(1)(l)). They are also treated as actively seeking work in any week to which reg.55ZA applies, provided that there are no steps that it would be reasonable for them to take to seek employment in that week (see reg.19(1)(lzl)).

[¹Periods of sickness and persons receiving treatment outside Great Britain

55A.—(1) A person—   3.192

   (a) who has been awarded a jobseeker's allowance, a joint-claim jobseeker's allowance [⁶. . .]; and

   (b) who is temporarily absent from Great Britain in the circumstances prescribed by regulation 50(6AA) or, as the case may be, (6C); and

   (c) who proves to the satisfaction of the Secretary of State that he is unable to work on account of some specific disease or disablement; and

(d) but for his disease or disablement, would satisfy the requirements for entitlement to a jobseeker's allowance other than those specified in section 1(2)(a), (c) and (f) (available for and actively seeking employment and capable of work [² or not having limited capability for work]),

shall be treated during that period of temporary absence abroad as capable of work [²or as not having limited capability for work], except where that person has stated in writing before that period of temporary absence abroad begins that immediately before the beginning of the period of that temporary absence abroad he has claimed [⁴ . . .] [² employment and support allowance] [⁴ . . .].

(2) The evidence which is required for the purposes of paragraph (1)(c) is a declaration made by that person in writing, in a form approved for the purposes by the Secretary of State, that he will be unfit for work from a date or for a period specified in the declaration.]

AMENDMENTS

1. Social Security (Income Support and Jobseeker's Allowance) Amendment Regulations 2004 (SI 2004/1869) reg.3(6) (October 4, 2004).
2. Employment and Support Allowance (Consequential Provisions) (No.2) Regulations 2008 (SI 2008/1554) reg.3(10) (October 27, 2008).
3. Jobseeker's Allowance (Sanctions for Failure to Attend) Regulations 2010 (SI 2010/509) reg.2(9) (April 6, 2010).
4. Employment and Support Allowance (Transitional Provisions, Housing Benefit and Council Tax Benefit) (Existing Awards) (No.2) Regulations 2010 (SI 2010/1907) as amended by the Employment and Support Allowance (Transitional Provisions, Housing Benefit and Council Tax Benefit) (Existing Awards) (No. 2) (Amendment) Regulations 2010 (SI 2010/2430) reg.26 and Sch.4 para.1A(2) (January 31, 2011).
5. Jobseeker's Allowance (Mandatory Work Activity Scheme) Regulations 2011 (SI 2011/688) reg.16(e) (April 25, 2011).
6. Jobseeker's Allowance (Sanctions) (Amendment) Regulations 2012 (SI 2012/2568) reg.5(11) (October 22, 2012).

DEFINITIONS

"joint-claim jobseeker's allowance"—see Jobseekers Act 1995 s.35(1) and s.1(4).
"limited capability for work"—see Jobseekers Act s.35(2) and Sch.1 para.2.

GENERAL NOTE

3.193   The purpose of this provision, together with the amendments that have been made to regs 14, 19, 50 and 55, is to enable entitlement to old style JSA to continue during any period that the claimant (including a member of a joint-claim couple) goes abroad temporarily for the purpose of receiving treatment funded by the NHS. Regulation 55A treats such a person as capable of work, or as not having limited capability for work, provided that he supplies a written declaration on an approved form that he is unfit for work from a stated date or for a specified period and satisfies the conditions for an award of old style JSA (other than the requirements of being available for, and of actively seeking, work and of not having limited capability for work). However, he will not be treated as capable of work, or as not having limited capability for work, if he has stated in writing before the absence abroad begins that he has claimed ESA. Thus a person in these circumstances can choose to remain in receipt of old style JSA or to claim benefit on the ground of limited capability for work if he wishes to do so.

Prescribed amount of earnings

56. [*Omitted as not relevant to income-based JSA*]   3.194

PART IV

YOUNG PERSONS

Interpretation of Part IV

57.—(1) In this Part—   3.195
[¹⁴ ...]
[⁷ "child benefit extension period" means the extension period within the
  meaning of regulation 5(3) of the Child Benefit (General) Regulations
  2006 (extension period: 16 and 17 year olds).]
"chronically sick or mentally or physically disabled" has the same
  meaning as in regulation 13(3)(b) of the Income Support Regulations
  (circumstances in which persons in relevant education may be entitled
  to income support);
[⁴ [¹² [¹⁴ ...]]]
"full-time education" has the same meaning as in regulation 1 of the
  Child Benefit (General) Regulations 1976;
"suitable training" means training which is suitable for that young person
  in vocationally relevant respects, namely his personal capacity, aptitude, his preference, the preference of the training provider, the level
  of approved qualification aimed at, duration of the training, proximity
  and prompt availability of the training;
"training" in sections 3, 16 and 17 and in this Part except in regulation 65
  read with section 7 and except in the phrase "suitable training", means
  training for which persons aged under 18 are eligible and for which
  persons aged 18 to 24 may be eligible [⁵ secured by the [¹³ [¹⁵ Secretary
  of State] [¹⁶ . . .]] or by the [⁸ ⁹ Welsh Ministers] and, in Scotland, pro-
  vided] directly or indirectly by a Local Enterprise Company pursuant
  to its arrangement with, as the case may be, [¹⁰ Skills Development,
  Scotland] Scottish Enterprise or Highlands and Islands Enterprise
  (whether that arrangement is known as an Operating Contract or by
  any other name);
"treatment" means treatment for a disease or bodily or mental disablement by or under the supervision of a person qualified to provide
  medical treatment, physiotherapy or a form of treatment which is
  similar to, or related to, either of those forms of treatment;
[¹ "young person" means a person—
  (a) who has reached the age of 16 but not the age of 18;
  (b) who does not satisfy the conditions in section 2 or whose entitle-
      ment to a contribution-based jobseeker's allowance has ceased as
      a result of section 5(1); and
  (c) who is not a person to whom section 6 of the Children (Leaving
      Care) Act 2000 (exclusion from benefits) applies.]
(2) A young person falls within this paragraph if he is—   3.196

(a) a member of a married couple [⁶ or of a civil partnership] where the other member of that couple [⁶ or civil partnership]—
  (i) has reached the age of 18 or
  (ii) is a young person who has registered for employment and training in accordance with regulation 62 or
  (iii) is a young person to whom paragraph (4) applies;
(b) a person who has no parent nor any person acting in the place of his parents;
(c) a person who—
  (i) is not living with his parents nor any person acting in the place of his parents; and
  (ii) immediately before he attained the age of 16 was—
    (aa) [² in England and Wales] being looked after by a local authority pursuant to a relevant enactment which placed him with some person other than a close relative of his [² . . .]
    (bb) in custody in any institution to which the Prison Act 1952 applies or under [² the Prisons (Scotland) Act 1989; or]
    [²(cc) in Scotland, in the care of a local authority under a relevant enactment and whilst in that care was not living with his parents or any close relative.]
(d) a person who is in accommodation which is other than his parental home and which is other than the home of a person acting in the place of his parents, who entered that accommodation—
  (i) as part of a programme of rehabilitation or resettlement, that programme being under the supervision of the probation service or a local authority; or
  (ii) in order to avoid physical or sexual abuse; or
  (iii) because of a mental or physical handicap or illness and he needs such accommodation because of his handicap or illness;
(e) a person who is living away from his parents and any person who is acting in the place of his parents in a case where his parents are or, as the case may be, that person is, unable financially to support him and his parents are, or that person is—
  (i) chronically sick or mentally or physically disabled; or
  (ii) detained in custody pending trial or sentence upon conviction or under a sentence imposed by a court; or
  (iii) prohibited from entering or re-entering Great Britain;
(f) a person who of necessity has to live away from his parents and any person acting in the place of his parents because—
  (i) he is estranged from his parents and that person; or
  (ii) he is in physical or moral danger; or
  (iii) there is a serious risk to his physical or mental health.
[²(3)(a) In England and Wales, any reference in this regulation to a person acting in place of a person's parents includes a reference to—
  (i) where the person is being looked after by a local authority or voluntary organisation which places him with a family, a relative of his, or some other suitable person, the person with whom the person is placed, whether or not any payment is made to him in connection with the placement; or
  (ii) in any other case, any person with parental responsibility for the child, and for this purpose "parental responsibility" has the

meaning it has in the Children Act 1989 by virtue of section 3 of that Act; and

(b) in Scotland, any reference in this regulation to a person acting in place of a person's parents includes a reference to a local authority or voluntary organisation where the person is in its care under a relevant enactment, or to a person with whom the person is boarded out by a local authority or voluntary organisation whether or not any payment is made by it.]

(4) This paragraph applies to—

(a) a person who falls under any of the following paragraphs of Schedule 1B to the Income Support Regulations—

Paragraph 1	(lone parents)
Paragraph 2	(single person looking after foster children)
Paragraph 3	(persons temporarily looking after another person)
Paragraph 4	(persons caring for another person)
[¹¹ . . .]	
Paragraph 11	
[¹¹ . . .]	
[¹¹ . . .]	
Paragraph 14	(pregnancy)
Paragraph 15	(persons in education)
Paragraph 18	(refugees)
Paragraph 21	(persons from abroad)
Paragraph 23	(member of couple looking after children while other member temporarily abroad)
Paragraph 28	(persons in receipt of a training allowance);

(b) a person who is a member of a couple and is treated as responsible for a child who is a member of his household;

(c) a person who is laid off or kept on short-time, who is available for employment in accordance with section 6 and Chapter II of Part II read with regulation 64 and who has not been laid off or kept on short-time for more than 13 weeks;

(d) a person who is temporarily absent from Great Britain because he is taking a member of his family who is a child or young person abroad for treatment, and who is treated as being in Great Britain in accordance with regulation 50(1)(b) or whose entitlement to income support is to continue in accordance with regulation 4(3) of the Income Support Regulations and who is not claiming a jobseeker's allowance or income support;

(e) a person who is incapable of work and training by reason of some disease or bodily or mental disablement if, in the opinion of a medical practitioner, that incapacity is unlikely to end within 12 months because of the severity of that disease or disablement.

AMENDMENTS

1. Children (Leaving Care) Act 2000 (Commencement No. 2 and Consequential Provisions) Order 2001 (SI 2001/3070) art.3(5) and Sch.4.

2. Jobseeker's Allowance and Income Support (General) (Amendment) Regulations 1996 (SI 1996/1517) reg.11 (October 7, 1996).

3. Jobseeker's Allowance (Amendment) (No. 2) Regulations 1998 (SI 1998/1698) reg.2 (August 4, 1998).

4. Social Security (Miscellaneous Amendments) (No. 2) Regulations 2001 (SI 2001/652) reg.5(a) (April 1, 2001).

5. Social Security (Miscellaneous Amendments) (No. 2) Regulations 2001 (SI 2001/652) reg.5(c) (March 26, 2001).

6. Civil Partnership (Pensions, Social Security and Child Support) (Consequential, etc. Provisions) Order 2005 (SI 2005/2877) art.2(3) and Sch.3 para.26(4) (December 5, 2005).

7. Social Security (Young Persons) Amendment Regulations 2006 (SI 2006/718) reg.3(5) (April 10, 2006).

8. National Council for Education and Training for Wales (Transfer of Functions to the National Assembly for Wales and Abolition) Order 2005 (SI 2005/3238) art.9(2) and Sch.2 para.8 (April 1, 2006).

9. Social Security (Miscellaneous Amendments) (No.7) Regulations 2008 (SI 2008/3157) reg.3(1) and (4) (January 5, 2009).

10. Social Security (Miscellaneous Amendments) Regulations 2009 (SI 2009/583) reg.4(1) and (3) (April 6, 2009).

11. Social Security (Miscellaneous Amendments) (No.2) Regulations 2010 (SI 2010/641) reg.4(1) and (6) (April 6, 2010).

12. Education and Inspections Act 2006 and Education and Skills Act 2008 (Consequential Amendments to Subordinate Legislation) (England) Regulations 2010 (SI 2010/1939) reg.2 (September 1, 2010).

13. Apprenticeships, Skills, Children and Learning Act 2009 (Consequential Amendments to Subordinate Legislation) (England) Order 2010 (SI 2010/1941) reg.5(1) and (4) (September 1, 2010).

14. Social Security (Miscellaneous Amendments) (No. 3) Regulations 2011 (SI 2011/2425) reg.10(1) and (4) (October 31, 2011).

15. Young People's Learning Agency Abolition (Consequential Amendments to Subordinate Legislation) (England) Order 2012 (SI 2012/956) reg.5(4) (May 1, 2012).

16. Deregulation Act 2015 (Consequential Amendments) Order 2015 (SI 2015/971) art.2 and Sch.3 para.4(1) and (4) (May 26, 2015).

DEFINITIONS

"the Benefits Act"—see Jobseekers Act s.35(1).
"child"—*ibid*.
"close relative"—see reg.4.
"couple"—see reg.1(3).
"employment"—see reg.4.
"married couple"—see Jobseekers Act s.35(1).
"a person who is kept on short-time"—see reg.4.
"a person who is laid off "—*ibid*.
"relative"—see reg.1(3).
"voluntary organisation"—*ibid*.

GENERAL NOTE

Paragraph (1)
3.197   "*Young person*". To be entitled to income-based JSA, a person must in general be 18 (s.3(1)(f)(i) of the Jobseekers Act). This Part of the Regulations deals with the exceptions to this general exclusion (see s.3(1)(f)(ii) and (iii) of the Jobseekers Act). The lower age limit does not apply to contribution-based JSA, although in practice

people below 18 will be unlikely to satisfy the contribution conditions (see s.2(1) of the Jobseekers Act). If a 16- or 17-year-old does qualify for contribution-based JSA, he does not count as a young person for the purposes of this Part.

The categories of 16- and 17-year-olds who under regs 58–61 are entitled to income-based JSA are similar (but not identical) to those who qualified for income support before October 7, 1996. (16- and 17-year-olds who are entitled to benefit while in relevant education can still claim income support under reg.13 of the Income Support Regulations, see para.15 of Sch.1B to those Regulations.) In *some* cases (see reg.61), a 16- or 17-year-old who is eligible for income-based JSA will also be eligible for income support. Because of the stricter benefit regime associated with JSA, it will usually be better for such a young person to claim income support. If the claimant does not come within one of the prescribed circumstances for JSA there is still the possibility of a severe hardship direction being made by the Secretary of State under s.16 of the Jobseekers Act, which then exempts the young person from the lower age limit (see s.3(1)(f)(ii)).

It is important to remember that satisfying an exception only gets the young person past the age condition for income-based JSA. All the other conditions of entitlement (see ss.1 and 3 of the Jobseekers Act) must be met. In order to meet the labour market conditions the young person will have to: (i) register for work and training (reg.62); (ii) be available for work, although if he has not been "sanctioned" for a training-related "offence" or refusing a job opportunity or voluntary unemployment or losing a job through misconduct, laid off or put on short-time or accepted an offer to enlist in the armed forces within the next eight weeks, he can restrict his availability to employment where the employer provides "suitable training" (defined in reg.57(1)) (reg.64); (iii) actively seek work and training (reg.65); and (iv) enter into a jobseeker's agreement (reg.66).

Paragraphs (2)–(4)

See the notes to regs 58–61.   3.198

The amendments made to para.(4) by SI 2010/641 (which consisted in the deletion of the references to paras 10 (disabled students), 12 (which relates to deaf students) and 13 (blind persons) of Sch.1B to the Income Support Regulations) do not apply to young people who fall within reg.2(2) of the Income Support (Prescribed Categories of Person) Regulations (SI 2009/3152) (see the *Transitional, Savings and Modifications* section, above).

[¹Young persons to whom section 3(1)(f)(iii) or 3A(1)(e)(ii) applies

58.—For the period specified in relation to him, a young person to whom   3.199 regulation 59, 60 or 61 applies shall be regarded as a person within prescribed circumstances for the purposes of section 3(1)(f)(iii) or section 3A(1)(e)(ii) (conditions of entitlement for certain persons under the age of 18).]

AMENDMENT

1. Jobseeker's Allowance (Joint Claims) Regulations 2000 (SI 2000/1978) reg.2(5) and Sch.2 para.18 (March 19, 2001).

DEFINITION

"young person"—see reg.57(1).

GENERAL NOTE

3.200   This regulation, together with regs 59, 60 and 61, prescribes the circumstances in which, and the periods for which, 16- and 17-year-olds can be exempted from the lower age limit of 18 imposed by s.3(1)(f)(i) of the Jobseekers Act. See the notes to regs 59, 60 and 61.

Young persons in the child benefit extension period

3.201   **59.**—(1) For the period specified in paragraph (2), this regulation applies to a young person who falls within paragraph (2) of regulation 57.

(2) The period in the case of any person falling within paragraph (1) is the child benefit extension period, except where regulation 61(1)(d) or (e) applies.

DEFINITIONS

"child benefit extension period"—see reg.57(1).
"young person"—*ibid.*

GENERAL NOTE

3.202   A 16- or 17-year-old who comes within any of the categories in reg.57(2) is exempt from the ordinary lower age limit for income-based JSA imposed by s.3(1)(f)(i) of the Jobseekers Act until the end of the child benefit extension period, unless reg.61(1)(d) or (e) applies (see below). See reg.57(1) for the definition of the "child benefit extension period" and the notes to reg.54. Note that reg.59 only gets the young person past the age condition for income-based JSA. All the other conditions of entitlement must be met (see the note to the definition of "young person" in reg.57(1)).

The categories in reg.57(2) are broadly the same as those in the former Pt II of Sch.1A to the Income Support Regulations (revoked on October 7, 1996) (16- or 17-year-olds exempt from the age test for income support during the child benefit extension period). Note, however, the slightly different conditions in reg.57(2)(a)(ii) (the young person must have registered for employment *and* training), and in reg.57(4)(c) and (d).

If, in the circumstances set out in reg.62, the young person registers for employment and training with Jobcentre Plus, rather than the person specified by the Secretary of State under that regulation, then reg.61(1)(d) or (e) will apply to him. In that case, he will be exempt from the lower age limit for JSA for the (normally shorter) periods specified in, respectively, reg.61(2)(c) or (d) (see below) rather than for the whole of the child benefit extension period. He must therefore register with the specified person before the expiry of those time limits if he is to continue to receive JSA.

See also regs 60 and 61.

Young persons at the end of the child benefit extension period

3.203   **60.**—(1) For the period specified in relation to him in paragraph (2), this regulation applies to a young person who is—

[² (a) a person who has ceased to live in accommodation provided for him by a local authority under—

    (i) Part 3 of the Children Act 1989 (local authority support children and families), or

    (ii) Part 4 (meeting needs) or 6 (looked after and accommodated children) of the Social Services and Well-being (Wales) Act 2014, and

is of necessity living away from his parents and any person acting in place of his parents;]

  (b) a person who has been discharged from any institution to which the Prison Act 1952 applies or from custody under the Criminal Procedure (Scotland) Act 1975 after the child benefit extension period and who is a person falling within paragraph (2) of regulation 57.

(2)(a) Except where regulation 61(1)(d) or (e) applies, the period in the case of a person falling within paragraph 1(a) is the period which begins on the day on which that paragraph first applies to that person and ends on the day before the day on which that person attains the age of 18 or the day at the end of a period of 8 weeks immediately following the day on which paragraph 1(a) first had effect in relation to him, whichever is the earlier; and this period may include any week in which regulation 7 of the Child Benefit (General) Regulations 1976 (circumstances in which a person who has ceased to receive full-time education is to continue to be treated as a child) also applies to that person;

  (b) except where regulation 61(1)(d) or (e) applies, the period in the case of any person falling within paragraph 1(b) is the period beginning on the day [¹ . . .] he was discharged, and ends on the last day of the period of 8 weeks beginning with the date on which the period began or on the day before the date on which that person attains the age of 18, whichever first occurs.

  (3) In this regulation, "week" means any period of 7 consecutive days.

AMENDMENT

1. Social Security (Miscellaneous Amendments) (No.4) Regulations 2009 (SI 2009/2655) regs 4(1) and (3) (October 29, 2009).

2. Social Services and Well-being (Wales) Act 2014 and the Regulation and Inspection of Social Care (Wales) Act 2016 (Consequential Amendments) Order 2017 (SI 2017/901) art.6(1) and (2) (November 3, 2017).

DEFINITIONS

"child benefit extension period"—see reg.57(1).
"young person"—*ibid.*

GENERAL NOTE

This provision is similar to the former reg.13A(4)(c) and (d) of the Income Support Regulations (now revoked). The effect, with reg.58, is to exempt 16- and 17-year-olds from the ordinary lower age limit for income-based JSA (see s.3(1)(f)(i) of the Jobseekers Act) if they leave local authority care and have to live away from their parents and any substitute (para.(1)(a)), or if they have been discharged from custody after the end of the child benefit extension period and one of the conditions in reg.57(2) applies (para.(1)(b)). Except where reg.61(1) (d) or (e) applies (see the note to reg.59 above as to when these apply), the exemption lasts for eight weeks, or until the person reaches 18, if sooner (para. (2)). If the exemption is under para.(1)(a), any week in the child benefit extension period can count in the eight weeks (it is understood that this is the intended

3.204

meaning, although para.(2)(a) refers to reg.7, not reg.7D, of the Child Benefit Regulations).

Note that there is no equivalent to the former reg.13A(4)(a) (incapacity for work and training which is likely to end within 12 months). Such a young person could claim income support: see para.7 of Sch.1B to the Income Support Regulations.

It is important to remember that reg.60 only gets the young person past the age condition for income-based JSA. All the other conditions of entitlement must be met (see the note to the definition of "young person" in reg.57(1)).

See also reg.61.

Other young persons in prescribed circumstances

3.205   **61.**—(1) For the period specified in relation to him in paragraph (2), this regulation applies to a young person—

   (a) who is a person who is laid off or kept on short-time and is available for employment in accordance with section 6 and Chapter II of Part II read with regulation 64;

   (b) who is a member of a couple and is treated as responsible for a child who is a member of his household;

   (c) who falls within a prescribed category of persons for the purposes of section 124(1)(e) of the Benefits Act and who is not claiming income support;

   [6 (d) to whom section 3(1)(f)(ii) or section 3A(1)(e)(i) does not apply, who is a person falling within paragraph (2) of regulation 57, sub-paragraph (a) or (b) of paragraph (1) of regulation 60, or sub-paragraph (b) or (c) of this paragraph, and who registers with Jobcentre Plus in accordance with regulation 62(2)(a); and

   (e) to whom section 3(1)(f)(ii) or section 3A(1)(e)(i) does not apply, who is a person falling within paragraph (2) of regulation 57, sub-paragraph (a) or (b) of paragraph (1) of regulation 60, or sub-paragraph (b) or (c) of this paragraph, and who registers with Jobcentre Plus in accordance with regulation 62(2)(b).]

   (f) who has accepted a firm offer of enlistment by one of the armed forces with a starting date not more than 8 weeks after the offer was made who was not in employment or training at the time of that offer and whose jobseeker's allowance has never been reduced in accordance with regulation 63 or [7 section 19(2)(c) or (d) or section 19A(2)(d), (e), (f) or (g)] read with regulation 68 or [7 reduced in accordance with section 19(2)(a) or (b)] read with Part V.

   [5 (g) who has limited capability for work for the purposes of Part 1 of the Welfare Reform Act.]

   (2)(a) The period in the case of any person falling within paragraph (1)(a) is the period starting with the date on which he was laid off or first kept on short-time and ending on the date on which he ceases to be laid off or kept on short-time or the day before the day he attains the age of 18 or at the expiry of the 13 week period starting with the date of the lay off, or date he was first kept on short-time, whichever first occurs;

   (b) except where paragraph (1)(d) or (e) applies, the period in the case of any person falling within paragraph [5 1(b), (c) or (g)] is the period until the day before that person attains the age of 18 or until paragraph [5 1(b), (c) or (g)] ceases to apply, whichever first occurs;

   (c) the period in the case of any person falling within paragraph (1)(d) is the period starting with the date of registration with [⁶ Jobcentre Plus] and ending on the day on which the person is next due to attend in accordance with regulation 23 [³ or regulation 23A] or on the date on which the period calculated in accordance with regulation 59(2) or 60(2) or sub-paragraph (b) would have expired, whichever first occurs;

(d) the period in the case of any person falling within paragraph 1(e) is the period starting on the date of registration with [⁶ Jobcentre Plus] and ending five days after that date or on the day after the day on which he registered with [⁶ a person other than Jobcentre Plus specified by the Secretary of State for the purposes of regulation 62(1)], or on the date on which the period calculated in accordance with regulation 59(2) or 60(2) or sub-paragraph (b) would have expired, whichever first occurs;

(e) the period in the case of any person falling within paragraph 1(f) is the period starting with the date of claim and ending with the day before the day on which he is due to enlist or the day before he attains the age of 18, whichever first occurs.

(3) In this regulation "week" means a period of 7 consecutive days.

AMENDMENTS

1. Jobseeker's Allowance (Joint Claims) Regulations 2000 (SI 2000/1978) reg.2(5) and Sch.2 para.19(a) (March 19, 2001).
2. Jobseeker's Allowance (Joint Claims) Regulations 2000 (SI 2000/1978) reg.2(5) and Sch.2 para.19(b) (March 19, 2001).
3. Jobseeker's Allowance (Joint Claims) Regulations 2000 (SI 2000/1978) reg.2(5) and Sch.2 para.19(c) (March 19, 2001).
4. Social Security (Miscellaneous Amendments) (No.2) Regulations 2001 (SI 2001/652) reg.5(b) (April 1, 2001).
5. Employment and Support Allowance (Consequential Provisions) (No.2) Regulations 2008 (SI 2008/1554) reg.3(1) and (11) (October 27, 2008).
6. Social Security (Miscellaneous Amendments) (No.3) Regulations 2011 (SI 2011/2425) reg.10(1) and (5) (October 31, 2011).
7. Jobseeker's Allowance (Sanctions) (Amendment) Regulations 2012 (SI 2012/2568) reg.5(12) (October 22, 2012).

DEFINITIONS

"the Benefits Act"—see Jobseekers Act s.35(1).
"child"—see Jobseekers Act s.35(1).
"couple"—see reg.1(3).
"a person who is kept on short-time"—see reg.4.
"a person who is laid off"—*ibid.*

GENERAL NOTE

This sets out additional circumstances in which a 16- or 17-year-old will be exempt from the lower age limit imposed by s.3(1)(f)(i) of the Jobseekers Act. Paragraph.(1) defines the categories covered and para.(2) the length of the exemption. **3.206**

> *Paragraph (1)(a).* A person who is laid off or on short-time working and who is available for work (see reg.64) will be exempt for up to 13 weeks (para.(2) (a)).

> *Paragraph (1)(b).* A person who is a member of a couple and responsible for a child (see regs 77 and 78) is exempt until 18 (except where para.(1)(d) or (1)(e) applies, see below) (para.(2)(b)).

Paragraph (1)(c). A person who falls within para.4ZA of, and Sch.1B to, the Income Support Regulations (which prescribe the categories of people entitled to income support under s.124(1)(e) of the SSCBA), and who is not claiming income support, is exempt until 18 (except where para.(1)(d) or (e) applies, see below) (para.(2)(b)). As the age limit for income support is now 16 (see s.124(1)(a) of the SSCBA, amended with effect from October 7, 1996), it will be better for most young people who come within Sch.1B to claim income support so as to avoid the risk of being sanctioned for not complying with the JSA labour market conditions.

Paragraph (1)(d) and (e). These sub-paras do not apply if a severe hardship direction has been made. Except for a young person who is laid off or on short-time (sub-para.(a)) or has accepted an offer to enlist in the armed forces in the next eight weeks (sub-para.(f)), a 16-or 17-year-old who is eligible for income-based JSA must register for employment and training with "such person as the Secretary of State may specify". However, if s/he is unable to do so because of "an emergency affecting that person such as a strike or fire" (reg.62(2))(a)) or because s/he "would suffer hardship because of the extra time it would take to register with that person" (reg.62(2)(b)), the young person must register with Jobcentre Plus instead. If he does so, the young person will be exempt from the lower age limit for JSA for the period until his next signing on day (normally two weeks) if reg.61(1)(d) applies (see reg.61(2)(c)), or five days if reg.61(1)(e) applies (see reg.61(2)(d)) (or until he ceases to be eligible for JSA under regs. 59 or 60 or reaches 18, if that is earlier).

Paragraph (1)(f). This applies to a person who has accepted an offer (made when he was not employed or in training) to enlist in the armed forces within the next eight weeks and who has never been sanctioned for a training-related "offence" or refusing a job opportunity or voluntary unemployment or losing a job through misconduct. The exemption lasts until he enlists (para.(2)(e)).

Note that reg.61 only gets the young person past the age condition for income-based JSA. All the other conditions of entitlement must be met (see the note to the definition of "young person" in reg.57(1)).

Registration

3.207

62.—(1) Except in the circumstances set out in paragraphs (2) and (3) a young person to whom section 3(1)(f)(ii) or (iii) [¹ or section 3A(1)(e)(i) or (ii)] applies other than one falling within regulation 61(1)(a) or (f), must register with [³ such person as the Secretary of State may specify [² ...]] for both employment and training.

[³ (2) A young person must register with Jobcentre Plus for both employment and training where the Secretary of State has specified a person other than Jobcentre Plus for the purposes of paragraph (1) and—

(a) the young person is unable to register with that person because of an emergency affecting that person such as a strike or fire, or

(b) the young person would suffer hardship because of the extra time it would take to register with that person.]

AMENDMENTS

1. Jobseeker's Allowance (Joint Claims) Regulations 2000 (SI 2000/1978), reg.2(5) and Sch.2 para.20 (March 19, 2001).
2. Social Security (Miscellaneous Amendments) (No.2) Regulations 2001 (SI 2001/652) reg.5(b) (April 1, 2001).
3. Social Security (Miscellaneous Amendments) (No.3) Regulations 2011 (SI 2011/2425) reg.10(1) and (6) (October 31, 2011).

DEFINITIONS

"employment"—see reg.4.
"training"—see reg.57(1).
"young person"—*ibid.*

GENERAL NOTE

Except for a young person who is laid off or on short-time, or who has never been   3.208
sanctioned for a training-related "offence" or refusing a job opportunity or voluntary unemployment or losing a job through misconduct and has accepted an offer
to enlist in the armed forces within the next eight weeks, a 16- or 17-year-old who
is exempt from the lower age limit for income-based JSA has to register with "such
person as the Secretary of State may specify" (para.(1)). For para.(2) see the commentary to reg.61(1)(d) and (e) above.

While paras (2) or (3) apply, he will be deemed to have entered into a jobseeker's
agreement (reg.66(2)).

See also regs 64–66.

Reduced payments under section 17

63.—(1) Except as provided in paragraph (3), the amount of an   3.209
income-based jobseeker's allowance which would otherwise be payable
to a young person shall be reduced by[¹, if he is a single person or a lone
parent,] a sum equal to 40 per cent of the amount applicable in his case by
way of a personal allowance determined [¹ in accordance with paragraph
1(1) or 1(2) of Schedule 1 (as the case may be) or, if he is a member of
a couple, a sum equal to 40 per cent of the amount which would have
been applicable in his case if he had been a single person determined in
accordance with paragraph 1(1) of Schedule 1] for the period set out in
paragraph (2) if—

(a) he was previously entitled to an income-based jobseeker's
   allowance and that entitlement ceased by virtue of the revocation of a direction under section 16 because he had failed to
   pursue an opportunity of obtaining training or rejected an offer
   of training;

(b) his allowance has at any time in the past been reduced in accordance
   with this regulation or in accordance with regulation 68 because
   he has done an act or omission falling within [⁷ section 19(2)(a) or
   (b) or section 19A(2)(c) to (g)] and he has—
   (i) failed to pursue an opportunity of obtaining training without
      showing [⁷ a good reason] for doing so,
   (ii) rejected an offer of training without showing [⁷ a good reason]
      for doing so or
   (iii) failed to complete a course of training and no certificate has
      been issued to him under subsection (4) of section 17 with
      respect to that failure;

(c) he has—
   (i) done an act or omission falling within section 16(3)(b)(i) or (ii)
      and has not shown [⁷ a good reason] for doing so or done an act
      or omission falling within [⁷ section 19A(2)(d) or (e) or failed
      to attend a training scheme or employment programme] [⁴ ⁷
      . . .] without [⁷ a good reason] or done an act or omission falling
      within [⁷ section 19A(2)(d) or (e) or failed to attend a training
      scheme or employment programme] [⁴ ⁷ . . .] for which he was

regarded as having [⁷ a good reason] in accordance with regulation 67(1) and

(ii) after that act or omission failed to complete a course of training and no certificate has been issued to him under subsection (4) of section 17 with respect to that failure and at the time he did the act or omission falling within subparagraph (i) he was a new jobseeker;

(d) he has—

(i) failed to complete a course of training and no certificate has been issued to him under subsection (4) of section 17 with respect to that failure or [⁷ given up a place on a training scheme or employment programme] [⁵ ⁷ . . .] without [⁷ a good reason] or [⁷ given up a place on a training scheme or employment programme] [⁵ ⁷ . . .] for which he was regarded as having [⁷ a good reason] in accordance with regulation 67(1) and

(ii) after that failure he has failed to complete a course of training and no certificate has been issued to him under subsection (4) of section 17 with respect to that failure and on the day before the day he first attended the course referred to in sub-paragraph (i) he was a new jobseeker; or

(e) he has failed to complete a course of training and no certificate has been issued to him under subsection (4) of section 17 with respect to that failure and on the day before he first attended the course he was not a new jobseeker; or

(f) he has failed to complete a course of training and no certificate has been issued to him under subsection (4) of section 17 with respect to that failure and he lost his place on the course through his misconduct.

(2) The period shall start with the date on which the first severe hardship direction is made under section 16 after the act or acts referred to in paragraph (a), (b), (c), (d), (e) or (f) of paragraph (1) have taken place and shall end fourteen days later.

(3) In the case of a young person who is pregnant or seriously ill who does an act falling within sub-paragraphs (a)–(f) of paragraph (1), the reduction shall be [¹ if he is a single person or a lone parent] of 20 per cent of the amount applicable in his case by way of a personal allowance [¹ determined in accordance with paragraph 1(1) or 1(2) of Schedule 1 (as the case may be) or, if he is a member of a couple, of 20 per cent of the amount which would have been applicable in his case if he had been a single person determined in accordance with paragraph 1(1) of Schedule 1].

(4) For the purposes of this regulation, "new jobseeker" means a young person who has not since first leaving full-time education been employed or self-employed for 16 or more hours per week or completed a course of train in or failed to complete a course of training and no certificate has been issued to him to show [⁷ a good reason] for that failure under subsection (4) of section 17 or [⁷ given up a place on a training scheme or employment programme [⁶ ⁷ . . .] without [⁷ a good reason] or done an act or omission falling within [⁷ section 19A(2)(g)] [⁶ ⁷ . . .]].

(5) A reduction under paragraph (1) or (3) shall, if it is not a multiple of 5p, be rounded to the nearest such multiple or, if it is a multiple of 2.5p but not of 5p, to the next lower multiple of 5p.

AMENDMENTS

1. Social Security and Child Support (Miscellaneous Amendments) Regulations 1997 (SI 1997/827) reg.2 (April 7, 1997).

2. Jobseeker's Allowance (Joint Claims) Regulations 2000 (SI 2000/1978) reg.2(5) and Sch.2 para.21(a)(i)(aa) (March 19, 2001).

3. Jobseeker's Allowance (Joint Claims) Regulations 2000 (SI 2000/1978) reg.2(5) and Sch.2 para.21(a)(i)(bb) (March 19, 2001).

4. Jobseeker's Allowance (Joint Claims) Regulations 2000 (SI 2000/1978) reg.2(5) and Sch.2 para.21(a)(ii) (March 19, 2001).

5. Jobseeker's Allowance (Joint Claims) Regulations 2000 (SI 2000/1978) reg.2(5) and Sch.2 para.21(a)(iii) (March 19, 2001).

6. Jobseeker's Allowance (Joint Claims) Regulations 2000 (SI 2000/1978) reg.2(5) and Sch.2 para.21(b) (March 19, 2001).

7. Jobseeker's Allowance (Sanctions) (Amendment) Regulations 2012 (SI 2012/2568) reg.5(13) (October 22, 2012).

DEFINITIONS

"full-time education"—see reg.57(1).
"income-based jobseeker's allowance"—see Jobseekers Act s.1(4).
"training"—see reg.57(1).
"young person"—*ibid.*

GENERAL NOTE

Paragraph (1)

Section 20(2) of the Act provides that where a severe hardship direction is in force   **3.210**
and the young person has without a good reason failed to pursue an opportunity, or rejected an offer, of training or failed to complete a training course, a s.19A sanction will not be applied. Instead, the circumstances in which income-based JSA payable under a severe hardship direction will be paid at a reduced rate are set out in this regulation. The reduction is 40 per cent of the appropriate single person or lone parent personal allowance under para.1 of Sch.1, or 20 per cent if the young person is pregnant or seriously ill (not defined) (para.(3)), and lasts for two weeks (para. (2)). If the person is a member of a couple, the same reduction is applied as if he was a single claimant.

The effect of para.(1) is that in some cases, e.g. where the person was previously a "new jobseeker," the reduction will only be applied where it is a "second offence". The detailed rules provide for the reduction to be imposed if:

(i) a previous severe hardship direction was revoked because the person failed to pursue an opportunity, or rejected an offer, of training without a good reason (sub-para.(a));

(ii) at any time in the past the person's JSA has been subject to a reduction under this regulation, or reg.68 for a training-related "offence" or stopped because of voluntary unemployment or losing a job through misconduct, and then without a good reason he fails to pursue an opportunity, or rejects an offer, or fails to complete a course, of training (sub-para.(b));

(iii) while he was a new jobseeker (defined in para.(4)) he failed to pursue an opportunity, or rejected an offer, of training without a good reason while a severe hardship direction was in force, or did not avail himself of, or failed to apply for or accept after having been notified of, or failed to attend, a place on a training scheme or employment programme either without a good reason, or only with a deemed good reason under reg.67(1), and then fails without a good reason to complete a course of training (sub-para.(c));

(iv) he has failed to complete a course of training without a good reason while a severe hardship direction was in force, or given up a training scheme or employment programme place either without a good reason or only with a deemed good reason under reg.67(1), and was a new jobseeker (defined in para.(4)) on the day before he started the course, and then fails to complete a course of training without a good reason (sub-para.(d));

(v) he has failed to complete a course of training without a good reason and was not a new jobseeker on the day before he started the course (sub-para.(e)); or

(vi) he has lost his training place through misconduct before finishing the course (sub-para.(f)).

The above is a summary of the very detailed rules in para.(1) but the reader is advised to check the text of the regulation where there is any doubt as to whether a particular sub-paragraph applies.

Paragraph (4)

3.211   A new jobseeker is a 16- or 17-year-old who since leaving full-time education (see reg.57(1)) has not been employed or self-employed for 16 hours or more a week, or finished a training course, or failed to finish a training course without a good reason or given up without a good reason or lost through misconduct a training scheme or employment programme place.

Availability for employment

3.212   **64.**—(1) A young person is required to be available for employment in accordance with section 6 and Chapter II of Part II except as provided in paragraphs (2) and (3).

(2) A young person whose jobseeker's allowance has not been reduced in accordance with regulation 63 or in accordance with regulation 68 because he has done an act or omission falling within [² section 19A(2)(d), (e), (f) or (g) or section 19(2)(c) or (d) or in accordance with section 19(2)(a) or (b)] read with Part V and who does not fall within regulation 61(1)(a) or (f) may restrict his availability for employment to employment where suitable training is provided by the employer.

(3) A young person who places restrictions on the nature of employment for which he is available as permitted by paragraph (2) does not have to show that he has reasonable prospects of securing employment notwithstanding those restrictions.

AMENDMENTS

1. Jobseeker's Allowance (Joint Claims: Consequential Amendments) Regulations 2000 (SI 2000/3336) reg.2(8) (March 19, 2001).
2. Jobseeker's Allowance (Sanctions) (Amendment) Regulations 2012 (SI 2012/2568) reg.5(14) (October 22, 2012).

DEFINITIONS

"employment"—see reg.4.
"suitable training"—see reg.57(1).

GENERAL NOTE

3.213   In order to be entitled to JSA, a young person has to be available for work under the normal rules (see s.6 of the Jobseekers Act and regs 5–17) (para.(1)). However, provided that he is not subject to a sanction under reg.63 or under reg.68 for a training-related "offence" or refusing a job opportunity or voluntary unemployment or losing a job through misconduct, a 16- or 17-year-old can restrict his availability to employment where the employer provides "suitable training" (para.(2)). See reg.57(1) for the definition of suitable training. This does not apply to a young person who has been laid off or is on short-time working, or who has never been sanctioned for a training-related "offence" or refusing a job opportunity or voluntary unemployment or losing a job through misconduct and has accepted an offer to join the armed forces in the next eight weeks. Presumably this is because such a young person is only expected to be unemployed for a short time and so it would not be reasonable to require an employer to provide him with training. The young person does not have to show that he still has reasonable prospects of obtaining work (para.(3)). Note also reg.67(2).

In addition, see regs 62 and 65–66.

Active seeking

65.—(1) Subject to the following paragraphs, Section 7 and Chapter III of Part II shall have effect in relation to a young person as if "employment" included "training".

(2) Subject to paragraphs (4) and (5), in order to have the best prospects of securing employment or training a young person can be expected to have to take more than one step on one occasion in any week unless taking one step on one occasion is all that it is reasonable for that person to do in that week, and unless it is reasonable for him to take only one step on one occasion, he can be expected to have to take at least one step to seek training and one step to seek employment in that week.

(3) Subject to paragraph (4), steps which it is reasonable for a young person to be expected to have to take include, in addition to those set out in regulation 18(2)—

(a) seeking training and

(b) seeking full-time education.

(4) Paragraphs (1), (2) and (3) do not apply to a young person falling within regulation 61(1)(a) or (f).

(5) Paragraphs (1) and (2) do not apply to a young person [² [³ . . .]] who has had his jobseeker's allowance reduced in accordance with regulation 63 or regulation 68 because he has done an act or omission falling within [³ section 19A(2)(a), (d), (e), (f) or (g) or section 19(2)(c) or (d) or in accordance with section 19(2)(a) or (b)] read with Part V but paragraph (3) does apply to such a young person.

(6) "Training" in section 7 and in this regulation means suitable training.

AMENDMENTS

1. Jobseeker's Allowance (Joint Claims: Consequential Amendments) Regulations 2000 (SI 2000/3336) reg.2(9) (March 19, 2001).

2. Jobseeker's Allowance (Sanctions for Failure to Attend) Regulations 2010 (SI 2010/509) reg.2(10) (April 6, 2010).

3. Jobseeker's Allowance (Sanctions) (Amendment) Regulations 2012 (SI 2012/2568) reg.5(15) (October 22, 2012).

DEFINITIONS

"employment"—see reg.4.
"full-time education"—see reg.57(1).
"suitable training"—*ibid.*
"young person"—*ibid.*

GENERAL NOTE

The normal rules in relation to actively seeking work apply to young people (see s.7 of the Jobseekers Act and regs 18–22) but they must seek training (which

3.214

3.215

means suitable training (para.(6)) as well as work (para.(1)). See reg.57(1) for the definition of "suitable training". They are expected to take more than one step (see reg.18(2)) each week, including at least one step to find work and one to find training, unless it is reasonable to take only one step that week (para.(2)). In the case of a young person, "steps" include, as well as those referred to in reg.18(2), seeking training and seeking full-time education (para.(3)).

These special rules do not apply to a young person who is laid off or on short-time working or who has never been sanctioned for a training-related "offence" or refusing a job opportunity or voluntary unemployment or losing a job through misconduct and has accepted an offer to join the armed forces within the next eight weeks (para.(4)). Presumably this is because they are only expected to be unemployed for a short time and so it would not be reasonable to require them to seek training or education in that time, only work.

Paragraph (5) appears to provide that a young person whose JSA is subject to a sanction under reg.63 or under reg.68 for a training-related "offence" or refusing a job opportunity or voluntary unemployment or losing a job through misconduct is not required to seek training as well as work, since it states that paras (1) and (2) do not apply to such a person. But this is followed by the somewhat contradictory statement that para.(3) does apply; that is, such a young person *is* required to seek training and full-time education. The policy intention apparently is that a 16- or 17-year-old who has been sanctioned should only be seeking training (and education) with a view to finding work and not as an end in itself.

See also regs 62, 64, 65A and 66.

[¹Attendance, information and evidence

3.216   **65A.**—A young person who does not fall within regulation 61(1)(a) or (f) shall, if the Secretary of State requires him to do so, provide, in addition to the declaration specified in regulation 24(6), a declaration to the effect that since making a claim for a jobseeker's allowance or since he last provided a declaration in accordance with this regulation he has been actively seeking suitable training to the extent necessary to give him his best prospects of securing suitable training save as he has otherwise notified the Secretary of State.]

AMENDMENT

1. Jobseeker's Allowance and Income Support (General) (Amendment) Regulations 1996 (SI 1996/1517) reg.12 (October 7, 1996).

DEFINITIONS

"suitable training"—see reg.57(1).
"young person"—*ibid.*

GENERAL NOTE

3.217   This regulation provides that a 16- or 17-year-old may be required to declare that he has been actively seeking suitable training as well as work when he signs on. There is the usual exception from this rule for a young person who has been laid off or is on short-time working, or who has never been sanctioned for a training-related "offence" or refusing a job opportunity or voluntary unemployment or losing a job through misconduct and has accepted an offer to join the armed forces within the next eight weeks.

See also regs 62, 64, 65 and 66.

The jobseeker's agreement

66.—(1) In a jobseeker's agreement with a young person, other than one falling within regulation 61(1)(a) or (f), the following information is required in addition to that prescribed in Chapter V of Part II: a broad description of the circumstances in which the amount of the person's benefit may be reduced in accordance with section 17 and regulation 63, or [⁴ section 19(2)(a), (b), (c) or (d) or section 19A(2)(a), (c), (d), (e), (f) or (g)] and regulation 68.

(2) A young person is to be treated as having entered into a jobseeker's agreement and as having satisfied the condition mentioned in section 1(2)(b) as long as the circumstances set out in [¹regulation 62(2) or 62(3) apply.]

3.218

AMENDMENTS

1. Jobseekers's Allowance (Amendment) Regulations 1996 (SI 1996/1516) reg.8 and Sch. (October 7, 1996).
2. Jobseeker's Allowance (Joint Claims) Regulations 2000 (SI 2000/1978) reg.2(5) and Sch.2 para.22 (March 19, 2001).
3. Jobseeker's Allowance (Sanctions for Failure to Attend) Regulations 2010 (SI 2010/509) reg.2(11) (April 6, 2010).
4. Jobseeker's Allowance (Sanctions) (Amendment) Regulations 2012 (SI 2012/2568) reg.5(16) (October 22, 2012).

DEFINITIONS

"jobseeker's agreement"—see Jobseekers Act s.9(1).
"young person"—see reg.57(1).

GENERAL NOTE

See the notes to ss.9–11 of the Jobseekers Act and regs 31–45 for the rules relating to jobseeker's agreements.

3.219

Paragraph (1)
A 16- or 17-year-old has to enter into a jobseeker's agreement as a condition of receiving JSA in the normal way. But the agreement must contain additional information as to the sanctions that can be applied. There is the usual exception from this rule for a young person who has been laid off or is on short-time working, or who has never been sanctioned for a training-related "offence" or refusing a job opportunity or voluntary unemployment or losing a job through misconduct and has accepted an offer to join the armed forces within the next eight weeks.

3.220

Paragraph (2)
A young person will be deemed to have entered into a jobseeker's agreement while he has to register with Jobcentre Plus for work and training instead of the person specified by the Secretary of State under reg.62(1) due to an emergency or because the extra time involved in registering with the Careers Service would cause him hardship.

Regulation 62(3) was revoked by reg.10(6)(b) of SI 2011/2425 with effect from October 31, 2011. However, the reference to it in para.(2) has not been revoked.

3.221

Sanctions

67.—(1) Without prejudice to any other circumstances in which a person may be regarded as having [⁹ a good reason] for any act or omission for the

3.222

purposes of [⁹ section 19A(2)(d), (e) or (f)] and in addition to the circumstances listed in regulation 73, a young person is to be regarded as having [⁹ a good reason] for any act or omission for the purposes of [⁹ section 19A(2) (d), (e) or (f)] where—

(a) this is the first occasion on which he has done an act or omission falling within [⁹ section 19A(2)(d), (e) or (f)] and he has not while claiming a jobseeker's allowance failed to pursue an opportunity of obtaining training without [⁹ a good reason] or rejected an offer of training without [⁹ a good reason] or failed to complete a course of training and no certificate has been issued to him under subsection (4) of section 17 with respect to that training; and

(b) at the time he did the act or omission falling within [⁹ section 19A(2) (d) or (e) or failed to attend a training scheme or employment programme] he was [¹. . .] a new jobseeker or, [⁹ in the case where he has given up a place on a training scheme or employment programme] at the time he first attended the scheme or programme he was [¹. . .] a new jobseeker.

(2) Without prejudice to any other circumstances in which a person may be regarded as having [⁹ a good reason] for any act or omission for the purposes of [⁹ [¹⁰ section 19(2)(c) or (d)]] a young person is to be regarded as having [⁹ a good reason] for any act or omission for the purposes of [⁹ [¹⁰ section 19(2)(c) or (d)]] where the employer did not offer suitable training unless he falls within regulation 61(1)(a) or (f) or his jobseeker's allowance has been reduced in accordance with regulation 63 or in accordance with regulation 68 because he has done an act or omission falling within [⁹ section 19A(2)(d), (e), (f) or (g)] or [⁹ section 19A(2)(c) or (d)] [⁹] [¹⁰ section 19(2)(a), (b), (c) or (d) read with Part V].

(3) For the purposes of this regulation, "new jobseeker" means a young person who has not since first leaving full-time education been employed or self-employed for 16 or more hours per week or completed a course of training or failed to complete a course of training and no certificate has been issued to him to show [⁹ a good reason] for that failure under subsection (4) of section 17 or [⁹ given up a place on a training scheme or employment programme] without [⁹ a good reason] or done an act or omission falling within [⁹ section 19A(2)(g)].

AMENDMENTS

1. Jobseeker's Allowance and Income Support (General) (Amendment) Regulations 1996 (SI 1996/1517) reg.13 (October 7, 1996).

2. Jobseeker's Allowance (Joint Claims) Regulations 2000 (SI 2000/1978) reg.2(5) and Sch.2 para.23(a)(i) (March 19, 2001).

3. Jobseeker's Allowance (Joint Claims) Regulations 2000 (SI 2000/1978) reg.2(5) and Sch.2 para.23(a)(ii) (March 19, 2001).

4. Jobseeker's Allowance (Joint Claims) Regulations 2000 (SI 2000/1978) reg.2(5) and Sch.2 para.23(b)(i) (March 19, 2001).

5. Jobseeker's Allowance (Joint Claims) Regulations 2000 (SI 2000/1978) reg.2(5) and Sch.2 para.23(b)(ii) (March 19, 2001).

6. Jobseeker's Allowance (Joint Claims) Regulations 2000 (SI 2000/1978) reg.2(5) and Sch.2 para.23(b)(iii) (March 19, 2001).

7. Jobseeker's Allowance (Joint Claims) Regulations 2000 (SI 2000/1978) reg.2(5) and Sch.2 para.23(c)(i) (March 19, 2001).

8. Jobseeker's Allowance (Joint Claims) Regulations 2000 (SI 2000/1978) reg.2(5) and Sch.2 para.23(c)(ii) (March 19, 2001).

9. Jobseeker's Allowance (Sanctions) (Amendment) Regulations 2012 (SI 2012/2568) reg.5(17) (October 22, 2012).

10. Social Security (Miscellaneous Amendments) Regulations 2013 (SI 2013/443) reg.4(1) and (5) (April 2, 2013).

DEFINITIONS

"full-time education"—see reg.57(1).
"suitable training"—*ibid.*
"training"—*ibid.*
"young person"—*ibid.*

GENERAL NOTE

See the notes to ss.19–19B of the Jobseekers Act and Pt V of the JSA Regulations for the circumstances in which sanctions may be applied.

3.223

Paragraph (1)

The broad effect of paragraph (1) is to give a "new jobseeker" (see para.(3)) a second chance in certain circumstances where a sanction might otherwise be imposed. He will be deemed to have a good reason for the purposes of s.19A(2)(d), (e) or (f) if this is the first time he has refused or given up, etc. a training scheme or employment programme opportunity.

3.224

Paragraph (2)

This provides that unless a young person has been sanctioned under reg.63 or under reg.68 for a training-related "offence" or refusing a job opportunity or voluntary unemployment or losing a job through misconduct, he will have a good reason for failing to apply for or accept a notified job, or for not taking advantage of a reasonable opportunity of employment if the employer does not offer suitable training (defined in reg.57(1)). There is the usual exception from this rule for a young person who has been laid off or is on short-time working, or who has never been sanctioned for a training-related "offence" or refusing a job opportunity or voluntary unemployment or losing a job through misconduct and has accepted an offer to join the armed forces within the next eight weeks. See also s.64 which provides that a 16- or 17-year-old may limit his availability to employment where the employer provides suitable training.

3.225

Paragraph (3)

See the note to reg.63(4).

3.226

Reduced amount of allowance

68.—(1) Subject to paragraphs (2) and (4), the amount of an income-based jobseeker's allowance which would otherwise be payable to a young person shall be reduced by [¹, if he is a single person or a lone parent,] a sum equal to 40 per cent of the amount applicable in his case by way of a peronal allowance determined [¹in accordance with paragraph 1(1) or 1(2) of Schedule 1 (as the case may be) or, if he is a member of a couple [³(including a joint-claim couple)], sum equal to 40 per cent of the amount which would have been applicable in his case if he had been a single person determined in accordance with paragraph 1(1) of Schedule 1] for a period of two weeks from the beginning of the first week after [²the Secretary of State]'s decision where the young person [⁴ ⁵ . . .] has done any act or omission falling within [⁵ section 19(2)(c) or (d) or section 19A(2)(a), (c), (d), (e), (f) or (g)] unless the young person reaches the

3.227

age of 18 before that two week period expires, in which case the allowance shall be payable at the full rate applicable in his case from the date he reaches the age of 18.

(2) Subject to paragraph (4), in a case where the young person or any member of his family is pregnant or seriously ill the amount of an income-based job-seeker's allowance which would otherwise be payable to the young person shall be reduced by [¹, if he is a single person or a lone parent,] a sum equal to 20 per cent of the amount applicable in his case by way of a personal allowance determined [¹ in accordance with paragraph 1(1) or 1(2) of Schedule 1 (as the case may be) or, if he is a member of a couple, a sum equal to 20 per cent of the amount which would have been applicable in his case if he had been a single person determined in accordance with paragraph 1(1) of Schedule 1] for a period of two weeks from the beginning of the first week after [² the Secretary of State]'s decision where the young person [⁴ ⁵ . . .] has done any act or omission falling within [⁵ section 19(2)(c) or (d) or section 19A(2)(a), (c), (d), (e), (f) or (g)] unless the young person reaches the age of 18 before that two week period expires, in which case the allowance shall be payable at the full rate applicable in his case from the date he reaches the age of 18.

(3) A reduction under paragraph (1) or (2) shall, if it is not a multiple of 5p, be rounded to the nearest such multiple or if it is a multiple of 2.5p but not of 5p, to the next lower multiple of 5p.

(4) If a young person's claim for an income-based jobseeker's allowance is terminated before the expiry of the period determined in accordance with paragraphs (1) and (2), and he makes a fresh claim for the allowance, it shall be payable to him at the reduced rate determined in accordance with paragraph (1) or (2) for the balance of the time remaining of that two weeks, unless the young person reaches the age of 18 before that two week period expires, in which case the allowance shall be payable at the full rate applicable in his case from the date he reaches the age of 18.

(5) An income-based jobseeker's allowance shall be payable to a young person at the full rate applicable in his case after the expiry of the two week period referred to in paragraphs (1) and (2).

AMENDMENTS

1. Social Security and Child Support (Miscellaneous Amendments) Regulations 1997 (SI 1997/827) reg.3 (April 7, 1997).
2. Social Security Act 1998 (Commencement No.11, and Savings and Consequential and Transitional Provisions) Order 1999 (SI 1999/2860 (C.75)) art.3(1) and (12) and Sch.12 para.2 (October 18 1999).
3. Jobseeker's Allowance (Joint Claims) Regulations 2000 (SI 2000/1978) reg.2(5) and Sch.2 para.24 (March 19, 2001).
4. Jobseeker's Allowance (Sanctions for Failure to Attend) Regulations 2010 (SI 2010/509) reg.2(12) (April 6, 2010).
5. Jobseeker's Allowance (Sanctions) (Amendment) Regulations 2012 (SI 2012/2568) reg.5(18) (October 22, 2012).

DEFINITIONS

"income-based jobseeker's allowance"—see Jobseekers Act s.1(4).
"young person"—see reg.57(1).

GENERAL NOTE

See the notes to ss.19–19B of the Jobseekers Act and Pt V of the JSA Regulations   **3.228**
as to the circumstances in which sanctions may be applied.

The rules as to the amount and duration of a benefit sanction are different from
those for adults. A person aged 18 or over who is sanctioned will only be paid
JSA (at a reduced rate) if he is in hardship; see regs 140–146. If a young person
is "sanctioned" under s.19(2)(c) or (d) or s.19A(2)(a), (c), (d),(e), (f) or (g), his
income-based JSA will continue to be paid but at a reduced rate. (Note that this
does not apply if the sanction is imposed under s.19(2)(a) or (b), or s.19A(2)(b),
in such a case the young person will only qualify for JSA if he can show hardship.)
The reduction is 40 per cent of the appropriate single person or lone parent personal allowance under para.1 of Sch.1 or 20 per cent if the young person or any
member of the family is pregnant or seriously ill. If the person is a member of a
couple the same reduction is applied as if he was a single claimant. It lasts for two
weeks but will cease if the young person becomes 18 within that time. If the young
person stops receiving JSA before the end of the two weeks but then claims JSA
again, the reduction will be applied for the unexpired balance of the two-week
period or until the person reaches 18.

PART V

SANCTIONS

[¹The period of a reduction under section 19: higher-level sanctions

69.— [²(1) Subject to paragraphs (3) and (4), a reduction under section   **3.229**
19 (higher-level sanctions) in the circumstances described in the first
column of the following table is to have effect for the period set out in the
second column.

Circumstances in which reduction period applies	Reduction Period
Where there has been no previous sanctionable failure by the claimant that falls within paragraph (2)	13 weeks
Where there have been one or more previous sanctionable failures by the claimant that fall within paragraph (2) and the date of the most recent previous sanctionable failure is not within 52 weeks beginning with the date of the current sanctionable failure	13 weeks
Where there have been one or more previous sanctionable failures by the claimant that fall within paragraph (2) and the date of the most recent previous sanctionable failure is within 52 weeks, but not within 2 weeks, beginning with the date of the current sanctionable failure and the period of reduction applicable to the most recent previous sanctionable failure is or, but for paragraph (4), would have been—	
(a) 13 weeks	26 weeks
(b) 26 weeks	[³26 weeks]

Circumstances in which reduction period applies	Reduction Period
(c) [³...]	
Where there have been one or more previous sanctionable failures by the claimant that fall within paragraph (2) and the date of the most recent previous sanctionable failure is within 2 weeks beginning with the date of the current sanctionable failure and the period of reduction applicable to the most recent previous sanctionable failure is or, but for paragraph (4), would have been—	
(a) 13 weeks	13 weeks
(b) 26 weeks	26 weeks
(c) [³...]]	[³...]]

(2) A previous sanctionable failure referred to in paragraph (1) falls within this paragraph if—
    (a) the failure resulted in a decision to reduce the claimant's award in accordance with section 19; [²and]
    (b) in the case of a joint-claim couple, the failure was by the same claimant; [² . . .]

(3) Where a claimant's award has been reduced in relation to a sanctionable failure which is specified in section 19(2)(a), (b) or (d) and which occurred before the date of claim for a jobseeker's allowance, any such failure must not be counted for the purpose of determining the period of a reduction for a subsequent sanctionable failure under section 19.

(4) Where a sanctionable failure which is specified in section 19(2)(a), (b) or (d) occurs on or before the date on which a claim for a jobseeker's allowance is made—
    (a) except where sub-paragraph (b) applies, the reduction relating to that failure is to have effect for the period set out in paragraph (1) that applies in the claimant's case (the "applicable sanction period") minus the period beginning with the day after the date of the sanctionable failure and ending with the day before the date of claim;
    (b) if—
        (i) the failure was in relation to employment which was due to last for a limited period,
        (ii) the limited period ends on or before the end of the applicable sanction period, and
        (iii) the date of claim is on or before the last day of the limited period,
the reduction relating to that failure is to have effect for the period beginning with the day after the date of the sanctionable failure and ending with the last day of the limited period minus the period beginning with the day after the date of the sanctionable failure and ending with the day before the date of claim.

(5) In paragraph (4)(b), "limited period" means a specific term which is fixed, or which can be ascertained, before it begins, by reference to some relevant circumstance.

(6) The period of a reduction under section 19 begins—
    (a) on the first day of the benefit week in which the sanctionable failure

occurred where, on the date of the determination to reduce the award, the claimant has not been paid a jobseeker's allowance since the sanctionable failure occurred; or

(b) in any other case, on the first day of the benefit week after the end of the benefit week in respect of which the claimant was last paid a jobseeker's allowance.]

AMENDMENTS

1. Jobseeker's Allowance (Sanctions) (Amendment) Regulations 2012 (SI 2012/2568) reg.2(2) (October 22, 2012).

2. Social Security (Jobseeker's Allowance, Employment and Support Allowance and Universal Credit) (Amendment) Regulations 2016 (SI 2016/678) reg.3(2) (July 25, 2016).

3. Jobseeker's Allowance and Universal Credit (Higher-Level Sanctions) (Amendment) Regulations 2019 (SI 2019/1357) reg.2 (November 27, 2019).

DEFINITIONS

"claimant"—see Jobseekers Act 1995 s.35(1).
"current sanctionable failure"—see reg.75(5).
"sanctionable failure"—*ibid.*

GENERAL NOTE

Higher-level sanctions are applicable to failures under s.19 of the old style **3.230** Jobseekers Act 1995. No failures under s.19A can come within the present regulation. If the circumstances fall within both sections only the s.19 sanction can apply (s.19A(3)). There is a distinction between certain sanctionable failures that occurred on or before the date of claim and other failures within s.19. The pre-claim failures identified in para.(4) are losing employment through misconduct, without a good reason voluntarily leaving employment and without a good reason neglecting to avail oneself of a reasonable opportunity of employment. There seems to be no good reason why refusing or failing to apply or accept if offered a situation in employment that the claimant has been informed is vacant or about to become vacant (s.19(2)(c)) should not, if it occurs before the date of the claim for old style JSA, be treated in the same way. However, the omission of s.19(2)(c) from the list in para.(4) (and para.(3)) is clear.

The general rule in para.(1)(a) for all cases prior to November 27, 2019 was that the reduction period was 13 weeks if there had been no other higher-level sanctionable failures in the previous 52 weeks, 26 weeks if there had been one other such failure in that period and 156 weeks (three years) if there had been two or more such failures in that previous 52 weeks. The amendment with effect from that date in effect secures that in the third category the length of the sanction is 26 weeks rather than 156. That is in fulfilment of the undertaking by the then Secretary of State (Amber Rudd) in her written statement to Parliament on May 9, 2019 (HCWS 1545) to remove three-year sanctions for third and subsequent failures and reduce the maximum sanction length to six months by the end of the year. Because of the cumulative nature of old style JSA sanctions (see below), the result is that a claimant can never have an outstanding period of sanction of more than 26 weeks, no matter how many have been imposed. The position is different in new style JSA and universal credit.

Regulation 5(1) of the amending regulation made the transitional provision **3.231** that, where an award of old style JSA was subject to a 156-week reduction under s.19 as at November 27, 2019, that reduction was to be terminated where the award had been reduced for at least 26 weeks. That appears to apply whether the 26 weeks expired before, on or after November 27, 2019, provided that the award was subject to the 156-week reduction on that date. It then appears that, once the 156-week reduction has been terminated, the reduction period "applicable" to the previous sanctionable failure becomes 26 weeks, so that the case would fall within the new form of para.(b) of the third part of the table.

A previous failure must be by the same person concerned, even in the case of a joint-claim couple (para.(2)(b)). The general rule is subject first to the rule in para.(2)(a) that only a sanctionable failure that resulted in a reduction in benefit counts for this purpose as a previous failure. Secondly, under the terms of the table in para.(1) any sanctionable failure occurring within the two weeks before the date of claim, or of a relevant previous sanctionable failure, is disregarded. This provision was, before the 2016 amendments, contained in para.(2)(c) and appeared not to extend to previous sanctionable failures.

There are two further equally important qualifications to the simple application of the table in para.(1). First, para.(3) provides that pre-claim sanctionable failures of the kind specified cannot count at all as previous sanctionable failures for the purposes of subs.(1). That seems to render irrelevant the references in the table in para.(1) to "but for paragraph (4)". If a previous sanctionable failure could have come within the special rules for pre-claim failures in para.(4) it must also fall within para.(3) and so not count at all.

3.232
Second, the operation of reg.70(2) on the cumulative effect of a number of reductions of any kind must be taken into account, in conjunction with the provision in para.(6) about the date on which each particular period of reduction under s.19 is to start. The mechanism is different from that in new style JSA where reduction periods run consecutively (JSA Regulations 2013 reg.18(2)). Regulation 70(2) provides that if, for any particular day, a claimant's award of old style JSA is already reduced for any level of sanction, there cannot be a reduction for that day under a new sanction decision. Take as an example a single existing JSA claimant who receives a first s.19 sanction of 13 weeks and then six weeks later commits another s.19 failure. That leads straightforwardly to the imposition of a further sanction, this time for 26 weeks. The period of the new sanction will in most cases begin with the benefit week in which the new sanctionable failure occurred (para.(6)(a)). However, for the first seven weeks of that reduction period no reduction can be applied by virtue of reg.70(2). The new sanction can therefore only start to bite after the expiry of those seven weeks and run for a further 19 weeks. If during that 19 weeks the claimant were to commit another s.19 sanctionable failure, the resulting 26-week sanction could not bite until the expiry of the 19 weeks, with a corresponding reduction in the period covered after the end of the 19 weeks. One consequence of this structure is that a claimant can never be faced with a prospective reduction period of more than 26 weeks.

For pre-claim sanctionable failures under para.(4)(a) the number of days between the date of the failure and the date of the relevant claim is deducted from the number of days in the reduction period calculated as under para.(1). That is subject to the further rule that if the sanctionable failure relates to paid work that was due to last only for a limited period, the period down to the date when the work was due to end is substituted for the para.(4)(a) period in the calculation. Presumably that is to give an incentive to people to take such work. See also reg.70A(1) (removing the possibility of a reduction of benefit if the JSA claim is made outside the period of reduction that would otherwise have applied to such a pre-claim failure).

Paragraph (6) stipulates when the period of reduction under a s.19 sanction starts. If the claimant has not been paid (i.e., it seems, actually paid) old style JSA since the date of the sanctionable failure in question, the reduction period starts from the beginning of the benefit week in which the sanctionable failure occurred (sub-para.(a)). These circumstances will occur, for example, if a single claimant (or both members of a joint-claim couple) is already subject to a reduction period for a previous sanctionable failure of any kind or where a pre-claim failure is in issue on the initial determination of a claim, unless hardship payments were made. In all other cases the reduction period starts from the beginning of the benefit week following the last week in respect of which the claimant was paid old style JSA (sub-para.(b)). Regulation 70 sets the amount of the reduction at 100% of the amount otherwise payable in cases of single claimants or joint-claim couples where both members are subject to a sanction, with a smaller reduction where only one member of a joint-claim couple is sanctioned.

[¹The period of a reduction under section 19A: Other sanctions

69A.—[²(1) A reduction under section 19A (other sanctions) in the cir- cumstances described in the first column of the following table is to have effect for the period set out in the second column.

3.233

Circumstances in which reduction period applies	Reduction Period
Where there has been no previous sanctionable failure by the claimant that falls within paragraph (2)	4 weeks
Where there have been one or more previous sanctionable failures by the claimant that fall within paragraph (2) and the date of the most recent previous sanctionable failure is not within 52 weeks beginning with the date of the current sanctionable failure	4 weeks
Where there have been one or more previous sanctionable failures by the claimant that fall within paragraph (2) and the date of the most recent previous sanctionable failure is within 52 weeks, but not within 2 weeks, beginning with the date of the current sanctionable failure and the period of reduction applicable to the most recent previous sanctionable failure is—	
(a) 4 weeks	13 weeks
(b) 13 weeks	13 weeks
Where there have been one or more previous sanctionable failures by the claimant that fall within paragraph (2) and the date of the most recent previous sanctionable failure is within 2 weeks beginning with the date of the current sanctionable failure and the period of reduction applicable to the most recent previous sanctionable failure is—	
(a) 4 weeks	4 weeks
(b) 13 weeks	13 weeks.]

(2) A previous sanctionable failure falls within this paragraph if—
  (a) the failure resulted in a decision to reduce the claimant's award in accordance with section 19A; [²and]
  (b) in the case of a joint-claim couple, the failure was by the same claimant; [² . . .]
(3) The period of a reduction under section 19A begins—
  (a) on the first day of the benefit week in which the sanctionable failure occurred where, on the date of the determination to reduce the award, the claimant has not been paid a jobseeker's allowance since the sanctionable failure occurred; or
  (b) in any other case, on the first day of the benefit week after the end of the benefit week in respect of which the claimant was last paid a jobseeker's allowance.]

AMENDMENTS

1. Jobseeker's Allowance (Sanctions) (Amendment) Regulations 2012 (SI 2012/2568) reg.2(2) (October 22, 2012).
2. Social Security (Jobseeker's Allowance, Employment and Support Allowance and Universal Credit) (Amendment) Regulations 2016 (SI 2016/678) reg.3(3) (July 25, 2016).

DEFINITIONS

"benefit week"—see reg.1(3).
"claimant"—see Jobseekers Act 1995 s.35(1).
"current sanctionable failure"—see reg.75(5).
"a joint-claim couple"—see Jobseekers Act 1995 ss.35(1) and 1(4).
"sanctionable failure"—see reg.75(5).
"week"—see reg.75(3).

GENERAL NOTE

3.234   Made under s.19A, which sets out other conduct ranking as a sanctionable failure in respect of which an award of old style JSA is to be reduced, this provision sets the period for which the reduction is to apply. Basically, looking at things over a 52-week period and looking at the same person (whether single or the defaulting member in a joint couple), the period is four weeks for a first "offence" and 13 weeks for a subsequent offence (paras (1) and (2)). Under the terms of the table in para.(1) any sanctionable failure occurring within the two weeks before the date of claim, or of a relevant previous sanctionable failure, is disregarded. This provision was, before the 2016 amendments, contained in para.(2)(c) and appeared not to extend to previous sanctionable failures. Paragraph (3) stipulates when the period of reduction under s.19A begins (see the notes to reg.69(6) above). Regulation 70 first sets the amount of the reduction at 100% of the amount otherwise payable in cases of single claimants or joint-claim couples where both members are subject to a sanction, with a smaller reduction where only one member of a joint-claim couple is sanctioned. Regulation 70(2) has an important effect in dealing with the cumulative effect if more than one reduction, of any kind, is applicable to the same day or days. See the discussion in the notes to regs 69 and 70.

Note that reg.70A(2)–(5) prevents a reduction in benefit following from certain s.19A sanctionable failures.

[¹The period of a reduction under section 19B: Claimants ceasing to be available for employment etc.

3.235   **69B.**—(1) Subject to paragraph (5), the amount of an award of a jobseeker's allowance, other than a joint-claim jobseeker's allowance, is to be reduced in accordance with this regulation and regulation 70 (amount of a reduction) if the claimant—

(a) was previously entitled to a jobseeker's allowance, or was a member of a couple entitled to a joint-claim jobseeker's allowance; and
(b) ceased to be so entitled by failing to comply with the condition in section 1(2)(a) or (c) (availability for employment and actively seeking employment).

(2) Subject to paragraph (5), the amount of an award of a joint-claim jobseeker's allowance is to be reduced in accordance with this regulation and regulation 70 (amount of a reduction) if the case falls within either paragraph (3) or (4).

(3) A case falls within this paragraph if—

(a) one of the claimants was previously entitled to a jobseeker's allowance, other than a joint-claim jobseeker's allowance; and

(b) ceased to be so entitled by failing to comply with the condition in
    section 1(2)(a) [²or (c)] .
(4) A case falls within this paragraph if—
(a) the couple were previously entitled to a joint-claim jobseeker's allow-
    ance but ceased to be so entitled by either or both of them failing to
    comply with the condition in section 1(2)(a) or (c); or
(b) either member of the couple was a member of another couple previ-
    ously entitled to such an allowance and that couple ceased to be so
    entitled by that person failing to comply with the condition in section
    1(2)(a) or (c).
(5) This regulation does not apply where—
(a) the claimant had been treated as available for work under regulation
    14 (circumstances in which a person is to be treated as available), or
    as actively seeking employment under regulation 19 (circumstances
    in which a person is to be treated as actively seeking employment);
(b) the claimant ceased to be so treated due to no longer falling within
    regulation 14 or 19;
(c) as a result of (b), the claimant's award was terminated for failing to
    comply with the conditions in section 1(2)(a) or (c) (availability for
    employment and actively seeking employment); and
(d) the Secretary of State considers that a reduction is not appropriate in
    the claimant's circumstances.
[³(6) Subject to paragraph (7), a reduction under this regulation in the
circumstances described in the first column of the following table is to have
effect for the period set out in the second column.

Circumstances in which reduction period applies	Reduction Period
Where there has been only one occasion on which the claimant's previous entitlement ceased	4 weeks
Where there have been two or more occasions on which the claimant's previous entitlement ceased and the date of the most recent occasion is not within 52 weeks beginning with the date of the next most recent occasion	4 weeks
Where there have been two or more occasions on which the claimant's previous entitlement ceased and the date of the most recent occasion is within 52 weeks, but not within 2 weeks, beginning with the date of the next most recent occasion and the period of reduction applicable on that occasion is, or but for paragraph (7), would have been—	
(a) 4 weeks	13 weeks
(b) 13 weeks	13 weeks
Where there have been two or more occasions on which the claimant's previous entitlement ceased and the date of the most recent occasion is within 2 weeks beginning with the date of the next most recent occasion and the period of reduction applicable on that occasion is or, but for paragraph (7), would have been—	
(a) 4 weeks	4 weeks
(b) 13 weeks	13 weeks.]

(7) The period specified in paragraph (6) is to be reduced by the period beginning with the first day of the benefit week following the benefit week in which the claimant was last paid an award of jobseeker's allowance and ending with the day before the date of claim [² or where regulation 3(g) of the Claims and Payments Regulations applies, the day before the suspension ends].

(8) The period of a reduction under this regulation begins on the date of claim] [² or where regulation 3(g) of the Claims and Payments Regulations applies, the date on which the suspension ends.]

AMENDMENTS

1. Jobseeker's Allowance (Sanctions) (Amendment) Regulations 2012 (SI 2012/2568) reg.2(2) (October 22, 2012).
2. Social Security (Miscellaneous Amendments) Regulations 2013 (SI 2013/443) reg.4(8) (April 2, 2013).
3. Social Security (Jobseeker's Allowance, Employment and Support Allowance and Universal Credit) (Amendment) Regulations 2016 (SI 2016/678) reg.3(4) (July 25, 2016).

DEFINITIONS

"claimant"—see Jobseekers Act 1995 s.35(1).
"Claims and Payments Regulations"—see reg.1(3).
"couple"—*ibid.*
"a joint-claim jobseeker's allowance"—see Jobseekers Act 1995 ss.35(1) and 1(4).
"week"—see reg.75(3).

GENERAL NOTE

3.236   Section 19B of the old style Jobseekers Act 1995 enables regulations to provide for an award of old style JSA to be reduced in respect of a claim for a period not exceeding 13 weeks where a previous JSA entitlement had ended because of failing to be available for or actively seeking employment. When a reduction is to apply is set out in paras (1)–(5) of this regulation. Paragraph (1) deals with JSA claims other than joint claims. Paragraphs (2)–(4) deal with joint claims, differentiating situations: (i) where one of the joint-claim couple had previously been entitled to non-joint-claim JSA terminated because of non-availability (para.(3)); and (ii) where a previous joint-claim award of JSA ended because one or both had not complied with availability and/or actively seeking employment requirements (para. (4)). The regulation does not apply in cases covered by para.(5). This deals with the situation where the claimant's award of old style JSA had been terminated because of no longer being being treated as available or actively seeking employment under regs 14 or 19 (paras (5)(a)–(c)). In such a case this regulation will not apply where the Secretary of State considers that a reduction is not appropriate to the claimant's circumstances (para.(5)(d)).

The period of reduction is set by paras (6) and (7) (broadly speaking four weeks for a first offence and 13 weeks if there was a previous "offence" within 52 weeks of (but earlier than two weeks before) the most recent one. If the previous "offence" (or offences) was or were within that two weeks the period is four weeks unless the starting period imposed for the most recent offence was 13 weeks, in which case the period is 13 weeks again. Note the operation of para.(7) in deducting from the reduction period the days between the last day for which payment was made under the terminated award and the date of the new claim for old style JSA. The start of the period of reduction is stipulated as the date of claim (reg.69(8)). Regulation 70 first sets the amount of the reduction at 100% of the amount otherwise payable in cases of single claimants or joint-claim couples where both members are subject to a sanction, with a smaller reduction where only one member of a joint-claim couple is sanctioned. Regulation 70(2) has an important effect in dealing with the cumulative effect if more than one reduction, of any kind, is applicable to the same day or days. See the discussion in the notes to regs 69 and 70.

Regulation 70A does not apply to reductions under s.19B.

[¹The amount of a reduction under section 19 and 19A and regulation 69B

70.—(1) Subject to paragraph (2), the amount of a reduction under section 19 or 19A or regulation 69B is—

3.237

(a) 100% of the allowance payable to the claimant; or

(b) in the case of a joint-claim couple—

    (i) 100% of the allowance payable to the couple, where the reduction relates to a sanctionable failure by each member of the couple, or

    (ii) an amount calculated in accordance with paragraph (3), where the reduction relates to a sanctionable failure by only one member of the couple.

(2) In a case where the following circumstances apply —

(a) a claimant's award is already reduced in accordance with section 19 or 19A or regulation 69B; or

(b) in the case of a joint-claim couple, an award of a joint-claim jobseeker's allowance is already reduced in accordance with section 19 or 19A or regulation 69B as a result of a sanctionable failure by one or each member of the couple and the current sanctionable failure is by the same claimant,

no reduction is to be made for any days when those circumstances apply.

(3) The amount referred to in paragraph (1)(b)(ii) is such amount which, after its deduction from the full amount of the award of a joint-claim jobseeker's allowance, leaves the following amount—

(a) in any case in which the member of the couple, who is not the member whose sanctionable failure led to the reduction, satisfies the conditions set out in section 2 of the Act (contribution based conditions), a rate equal to the amount calculated in accordance with section 4(1) (amount payable by way of a jobseeker's allowance);

(b) in any case where the couple are a couple in hardship for the purposes of Part IXA, a rate equal to the amount calculated in accordance with regulation 146G (applicable amount in hardship cases for joint-claim couples);

(c) in any other case, a rate calculated in accordance with section 4(3A) (5) (amount payable by way of a joint-claim jobseeker's allowance) save that the applicable amount shall be the amount determined by reference to paragraph 1(1) of Schedule 1 which would have been the applicable amount had the member of the couple who is not subject to sanctions been a single claimant.

AMENDMENT

1. Jobseeker's Allowance (Sanctions) (Amendment) Regulations 2012 (SI 2012/2568) reg.2(3) (4) (October 22, 2012).

DEFINITIONS

"the Act"—see reg.1(3).
"claimant"—see Jobseekers Act 1995 s.35(1).

"current sanctionable failure"—see reg.75(5).
"a joint-claim couple"—see Jobseekers Act 1995 ss.35(1) and 1(4).
"a joint-claim jobseeker's allowance"—*ibid.*
"sanctionable failure"—see reg.75(5).

GENERAL NOTE

3.238   This sets the amount of the reduction under ss.19 or 19A of the Act and under reg.69B. Basically, this means a reduction of 100 per cent for a single claimant and where each member of a joint-claim couple commits a sanctionable failure (para.(1) (a) and (b)(i)), with a lesser reduction where the sanctionable failure is only by one member of such a couple (paras (1)(b)(ii), (3)). However, note the highly restricted provisions in regs 140 – 146H below allowing the payment of a limited amount of income-based JSA in cases of hardship.

Paragraph (2) provides an important element of the structure of sanctions under old style JSA, and a contrast with the new style JSA structure where reduction periods run consecutively subject to an overall limit of 1095 days (JSA Regulations 2013 reg.18(2)). The effect of regs 69(6), 69A(3) and 69B(8) in specifying the start date for the reduction period attached to each sanctionable failure is independent of the existence of any other reduction periods. And the length of the reduction period is fixed under regs 69(1), 69A(1) and 69B(1). Thus a number of reduction periods (each normally requiring a reduction of 100% of the amount otherwise payable) can overlap in relation to any particular day or days. Paragraph (2) provides that no reduction is to be made in relation to any particular sanctionable failure for any day or days where a reduction under any of ss.19 or 19A or reg.69B already applies. However, there is nothing to take such days out of counting towards the expiry of the affected reduction period. Some of the consequences of those rules are discussed in the notes to reg.69.

[¹Cases in which no reduction is to be made under section 19 or 19A

3.239   **70A.**—(1) No reduction is to be made under section 19 (higher-level sanctions) where—

(a) the sanctionable failure is listed in section 19(2)(a), (b), or (d);
(b) the sanctionable failure occurs before a claim to a jobseeker's allowance is made; and
(c) the period of the reduction as calculated under sub-paragraph (a) or (b) of regulation 69(4) is the same as, or shorter than, the period between the date of the sanctionable failure and the date of claim.

(2) No reduction is to be made under section 19A (other sanctions) where the sanctionable failure is specified in section 19A(2)(a) (failure to comply with regulations under section 8(1) or (1A)) and—

(a) is a failure to comply with regulation 24 (provision of information and evidence); or
(b) unless paragraph (3) or (4) applies, is a failure to comply with regulation 23 (attendance) or 23A (attendance by members of a joint-claim couple)(6).

(3) This paragraph applies where the claimant—

(a) fails to [²participate] on the day specified in a relevant notification;
(b) makes contact with an employment officer in the manner set out in a relevant notification before the end of the period of five working days beginning with the first working day after the day on which the claimant failed to [²participate] on the day specified; and
(c) fails to show a good reason for that failure to [²participate].

(4) This paragraph applies where—

[²(a) the claimant fails to participate in an interview at the time specified in a relevant notification, but makes contact with an employment officer in the manner set out in the notification on the day specified in the notification;]

[²(b) the Secretary of State has informed the claimant in writing that a failure to participate in an interview at the time specified in a relevant notification, on the next occasion on which a claimant is required to participate in an interview] may result in the claimant's entitlement to a jobseeker's allowance or a joint-claim jobseeker's allowance ceasing or the award being subject to a reduction;

(c) the claimant fails to [²participate in an interview at the time specified] in a relevant notification on the next occasion;

(d) the claimant makes contact with an employment officer in the manner set out in a relevant notification before the end of the period of five working days after the day on which the claimant failed to [²participate in an interview at the time specified]; and

(e) the claimant fails to show a good reason for that failure to [²participate in an interview at the time specified].

(5) In this regulation, "relevant notification" has the meaning given in regulation 25.]

AMENDMENTS

1. Jobseeker's Allowance (Sanctions) (Amendment) Regulations 2012 (SI 2012/2568) reg.2(3) and (4) (October 22, 2012).

2. Social Security (Miscellaneous Amendments) Regulations 2013 (SI 2013/443) reg.4(7) (April 2, 2013).

DEFINITIONS

"claimant"—see Jobseekers Act 1995 s.35(1).
"date of claim"—see reg.1(3).
"employment officer"—see Jobseekers Act 1995 s.35(1).
"a joint-claim jobseeker's allowance"—see Jobseekers Act 1995 ss.35(1) and 1(4).
"relevant notification"—see para.(5); reg.25.
"sanctionable failure"—see reg.75(5).

GENERAL NOTE

Paragraph (1)

This sets out the situations in which no reduction is to be made in respect of 3.240
certain sanctionable failures in s.19 (higher-level sanctions). The potentially relevant failures are those under s.19(2)(a) (misconduct), (b) (voluntarily leaving) or (d) (neglect to avail) which occurred before the old style JSA claim was made. In such a case, no reduction of JSA is to be made where the otherwise applicable period of the reduction under reg.69 is the same as or shorter than the period of no-claim after the date of the sanctionable failure.

Paragraphs (2)–(4)

This stipulates that no reduction is to be made in respect of sanctionable failures 3.241
under s.19A(2)(a) (failure to comply with regulations made under s.8(1) or (1A) of the Act) where the failure is failure to comply with reg.24 (provision of information or evidence). Nor is one to be made in respect of failure to comply with regs 23 or 23A (attendance, i.e. participation in an interview, by single claimant or joint-claim couple), unless either para.(3) or (4) applies. See the annotations to regs 23 and 24 for the interactions.

[¹Sanctionable failures under section 19: schemes under section 17A(1)

3.242   **70B.**—(1) Mandatory Work Activity is a prescribed scheme for the purposes of section 19(2)(e) (higher level sanctions).

(2) In paragraph (1) "Mandatory Work Activity" means a scheme under section 17A(1) (schemes for assisting persons to obtain employment; "work for your benefit" schemes etc) designed to provide work or work-related activity for up to 30 hours per week over a period of four consecutive weeks with a view to assisting claimants to improve their prospects of obtaining employment.]

AMENDMENT

1. Jobseeker's Allowance (Sanctions) (Amendment) Regulations 2012 (SI 2012/2568) reg.2(3) and (4) (October 22, 2012).

GENERAL NOTE

3.243   This makes Mandatory Work Activity (as defined in para.(2)) a prescribed scheme for the purposes of the sanctionable failure set out in s.19(2)(e), applying a higher level sanction in respect of failure to participate in a scheme within s.17A designed to assist in obtaining employment, which is prescribed for purposes of s.19.

Mandatory Work Activity was a scheme under s.17A(1) by virtue of the Jobseeker's Allowance (Mandatory Work Activity Scheme) Regulations 2011, which were found to be validly made by the Court of Appeal in *Smith v Secretary of State for Work and Pensions* ([2015] EWCA Civ 229, affirming the decision of Hickinbottom J ([2014] EWHC 843 (Admin)) on essentially the same reasoning. See further the annotations to s.17A and to the MWAS Regulations. The scheme ceased to operate after April 2016.

[¹Application of a reduction to a new award

3.244   **70C.**—(1) Subject to paragraph (4), this regulation applies where—
  (a) the amount of an award is reduced in accordance with section 19 or 19A or regulation 69B;
  (b) that award ("the previous award") is terminated;
  (c) the reduction period had either not yet begun or not ended when the previous award was terminated;
  (d) a new award is made to the claimant who had been entitled to the previous award; and
  (e) in the case of an award of a joint-claim jobseeker's allowance, the reduction to the previous award was made in relation to a sanctionable failure by the claimant who is entitled to the new award.

(2) Where this regulation applies, the reduction period that would have applied to the previous award but for the award having terminated applies to the new award from the first day of the benefit week in which the claim for the new award is made for the outstanding period.

(3) In this regulation—
"outstanding period" means the period determined under regulation 69, 69A or 69B in relation to the previous award minus—
  (a) the benefit weeks in respect of which the previous award was reduced; and
  (b) the period beginning with the first day of the benefit week after the benefit week in which the previous award was terminated and ending with the first day of the benefit week in which entitlement to the new award begins;

"reduction period" means the period determined under regulation 69, 69A or 69B in relation to the previous award.

(4) This regulation does not apply where the Secretary of State is satisfied that, since the date of the most recent sanctionable failure, the claimant has been in employment for a period of, or more than one period where the total of those periods amounts to, at least 26 weeks.]

AMENDMENT

1. Jobseeker's Allowance (Sanctions) (Amendment) Regulations 2012 (SI 2012/2568) reg.2(3) and (4) (October 22, 2012).

DEFINITIONS

"benefit week"—see reg.1(3).
"claimant"—see Jobseekers Act 1995 s.35(1).
"a joint-claim jobseeker's allowance"—see Jobseekers Act 1995 ss.35(1) and 1(4).
"sanctionable failure"—see reg.75(5).
"week"—see reg.75(3).

GENERAL NOTE

This deals with the situation where a reduction of old style JSA has been made under ss.19 or 19A or reg.69B, but the award was terminated before the reduction period began or before it had ended. In such a case, the unexpired part of the reduction period (eroded by the intervening weeks before the beginning of the new award: head (b) of definition of "outstanding period" in para.(3)) is carried over into a new award of JSA to the person entitled to the previous award subject to the sanction. Note that under para.(4) this does not apply where the Secretary of State is satisfied that since the date of the most recent sanctionable failure the claimant has been in work for a period of 26 weeks or combined periods totalling 26 weeks. 3.245

Voluntary redundancy

71.—(1) A claimant is to be treated as not having left his employment voluntarily— 3.246
(a) where he has been dismissed by his employer by reason of redundancy after volunteering or agreeing to be so dismissed, [¹ ...]
(b) where he has left his employment on a date agreed with his employer without being dismissed, in pursuance of an agreement relating to voluntary redundancy, [¹ or
(c) where he has been laid-off or kept on short-time to the extent specified in [² section 148 of the Employment Rights Act 1996], and has complied with the requirements of that section.]

(2) In paragraph (1) "redundancy" means one of the facts set out in paragraphs (a) and (b) of section [² 139(1) of the Employment Rights Act 1996].

AMENDMENTS

1. Jobseeker's Allowance (Amendment) Regulations 1996 (SI 1996/1516) reg.5 (October 7, 1996).
2. Social Security (Miscellaneous Amendments) (No.5) Regulations 2007 (SI 2007/2618) reg.8(5) (October 1, 2007).

DEFINITIONS

"claimant"—see Jobseekers Act s.35(1).
"employment"—see reg.75(4).

GENERAL NOTE

3.247   Section 19(7) of the old style Jobseekers Act 1995 enables the making of regulations setting out circumstances in which a person who might otherwise be regarded, under the normal rules discussed in the notes to s.19(6), as having left employment voluntarily, is to be treated as not having left voluntarily. This regulation is the result, covering a number of instances of voluntary redundancy.

Regulation 71 provides that a claimant is not to be treated as having left voluntarily in three situations. First, it protects claimants who have been dismissed by their employer by reason of redundancy after volunteering or agreeing to be so dismissed. The reference to "dismissal" might be thought unfortunate if it were to perpetuate or risk reopening old controversies on its precise meaning. Were it the sole protective limb, *R(U)3/91* ought probably to be followed to give it a wide meaning. But in any event the narrower meaning cannot, given the wording and structure of the new provision, have the same detrimental consequences, since the second limb of reg.71(1) now protects claimants who have left their employment on a date agreed with their employer *without being dismissed*, in pursuance of an agreement relating to voluntary redundancy. "Redundancy", rather than dismissal, is thus the key limiting factor in these protective limbs. It means one of the facts set out in s.139(1) of the Employment Rights Act 1996 (reg.71(2)). That subsection provides two facts: (a) the fact that the employer has ceased, or intends to cease, to carry on the business in the place where the employee [the JSA claimant] was employed; and (b) the fact that the requirements of that business for employees to carry out work of a particular kind, or for employees to carry out work of a particular kind in the place where [the claimant] was employed, have ceased or diminished or are expected to cease or diminish.

The third situation of protection afforded by reg.71 embraces the claimant who has been laid off or kept on short-time to the extent specified in s.148 of the Employment Rights Act 1996 and has complied with the requirements of that section, thus protecting claimants like the one in *CU/71/1994* and thereby going wider than the range of protections previously afforded by SSCBA 1992 s.28(4), even when that section was interpreted broadly. Section 148 of the 1996 Act enables a person laid off or kept on short time to claim a redundancy payment if he serves on his employer written notice of his intention to do so. He must have been laid off or kept on short time either for four or more consecutive weeks or for a series of six or more weeks within a period of 13 weeks prior to service of the notice. To get the s.148 payment, the employee must terminate the contract of employment and not be dismissed by the employer.

[¹Good reason for the purpose of section 19(2)(c) and (d) and 19A(2) (c)

3.248   **72.**—A person is not to be regarded as having a good reason for any act or omission for the purposes of section 19(2)(c) and (d) and section 19A(2)(c) if, and to the extent that, the reason for that act or omission relates to the time it took, or would normally take, for the person to travel from his home to the place of the employment, or a place mentioned in the jobseeker's direction, and back to his home where that time was or is normally less than [²one hour and thirty minutes either way,] by a route and means appropriate to his circumstances and to the employment, or to the carrying out of the jobseeker's direction, unless, in view of the health of the person or any caring responsibilities of his, that time was or is unreasonable.]

AMENDMENTS

1. Jobseeker's Allowance (Sanctions) (Amendment) Regulations 2012 (SI 2012/2568) reg.2(5) (October 22, 2012)

2. Social Security (Miscellaneous Amendments) (No.2) Regulations 2012 (SI 2012/2575) reg.3(3) (November 5, 2012).

Regulations 73 and 73A revoked by Jobseeker's Allowance (Sanctions) (Amendment) Regulations 2012 (SI 2012/2568) reg. 2(6) from October 22, 2012.

Person of prescribed description for the purpose of section 20(3)

74.—(1) Subject to paragraph (2), a person shall be of a prescribed   **3.249** description for the purposes of section 20(3) [¹. . .] (exemption from non-payment of jobseeker's allowance) and shall not fall within [¹section 19(2) (b) or (d)] [¹. . .] if he has neither worked in employed earner's employment, nor has been a self-employed earner, nor been a full-time student nor been in relevant education, during the period of 13 weeks preceding the day of the commencement of the employment.

(2) For the purposes of paragraph (1), a person shall not be regarded as having—

(a) worked in employed earner's employment; or

(b) been a self-employed earner; or

(c) been a full-time student or been in relevant education;

by reason only of any engagement in an activity referred to in paragraph (3) or by his attendance for a period of up to 14 days at a work camp.

(3) The activities referred to in this paragraph are—

(a) the manning or launching of a lifeboat; or

(b) the performance of duty as a part-time member of a fire brigade.

(4) A trial period in section 20(3) [¹. . .] means a period of 8 weeks beginning with the commencement of the fifth week of the employment in question and ending at the end of the twelfth week of that employment and for the purposes of this definition in determining the time at which the fifth week of the employment in question commences or at which the twelfth week of that employment ends, any week in which a person has not worked in the employment for at least 16 hours shall be disregarded.

AMENDMENT

1. Jobseeker's Allowance (Sanctions) (Amendment) Regulations 2012 (SI 2012/2568) reg.2(7) (October 22, 2012).

DEFINITIONS

"employed earner"—see regs 3 and 75(4); SSCBA 1992 s.2(1)(a).

"employment"—see reg.75(4).

"full-time student"—see reg.1(3).

"part-time member of a fire brigade"—see reg.4.

"relevant education"—see Jobseekers Act 1995 s.35(2) and Sch.1 para.14 and reg.54.

"self-employed earner"—see reg.1(3); SSCBA 1992 s.2(1)(b).

"week"—see reg.75(3).

"work camp"—see reg.4.

GENERAL NOTE

Taken together, s.20(3) of the old style Jobseekers Act 1995 and this regulation   **3.250** protect from preclusion from JSA under the voluntarily leaving employment without good reason head of s.19(2)(b) or under s.19(2)(d) (neglect without a good reason to avail oneself of a reasonable opportunity of employment) certain persons who leave employment voluntarily without a good reason at any time during a trial period.

These provisions are designed to encourage people to enter or re-enter employment who may be apprehensive about taking up work, fearful that they might not be able to handle it or that it might prove unsuitable and they might have to leave it. The encouragement is afforded by reducing the fear of preclusion from benefit should their fears be realised and they have to give up the job. An example of such people might be carers who have been out of the job market caring for sick or elderly relatives, but the provisions are by no means so limited. Specifically, the persons protected by the provisions are those who have neither worked in employed earner's employment nor been a self-employed earner, nor a full-time student or in relevant education during the 13-week period preceding the day of commencement of the employment. It is specifically stated that engagement in certain activities does not constitute working in employed earner's employment, being a self-employed earner or having been a full-time student or in relevant education: the manning or launching of a lifeboat; the performance of duty as a part-time member of a fire brigade; or attendance for a period of up to 14 days at a work camp (paras (2) and (3)).

"Trial period" is a period of eight weeks beginning with the commencement of the fifth week of the employment in question and ending at the end of the 12th week of that employment. In determining when the fifth week commences or when the 12th week ends, one disregards any week in which the claimant worked in the employment for less than 16 hours.

3.251   Note that there appears to be no requirement that the claimant has taken up the employment on a "trial basis". Note also that protection is afforded those persons "who leave that employment voluntarily *and without good reason*" (subs.(3), emphasis supplied by annotator). In some circumstances those who leave employment taken on a trial basis because it proves unsuitable may well have good reason for voluntarily leaving, thus obviating the need to rely on this subsection, being protected from preclusion under s.19(2)(b) by the terms of that provision, if interpreted in the light of case law on "just cause" from the comparable UB context. Since establishing "just cause" may be more difficult to establish than "good reason" (see further the notes to s.19(2)(b)), such persons would surely also have "good reason" so as to protect them from the "neglect to avail" preclusion in s.19(2)(d).

"Week" is defined for the purposes of this regulation as any period of seven consecutive days (reg.75(3)). That differs from the predecessor "trial period" provisions where week then meant a period of seven days beginning with a Sunday. But even had the new definition then been applicable, it would not have assisted the unfortunate claimant in *R(U)1/92*, since he had only completed the requisite number of "working" as opposed to "seven day" weeks.

3.252   *Regulation 74A revoked by Social Security (Miscellaneous Amendments) (No.2) Regulations 2012 (SI 2012/2575) reg.3 from November 5, 2012.*

3.253   *Regulation 74B revoked by Jobseeker's Allowance (Sanctions) (Amendment) Regulations 2012 (SI 2012/2568) reg.2(8) from October 22, 2012.*

Interpretation

3.254   **75.**—(1) For the purposes of [² section 19A] and of this Part:
[² (a) "an employment programme" means a programme or scheme which is designed to assist a claimant to prepare for or move into work;
   (b) "a training scheme" means a scheme or course which is designed to assist a claimant to gain the skills, knowledge or experience that will make it more likely, in the opinion of the Secretary of State, that the claimant will obtain work or be able to do so;
   (2) [² . . .]
[²(3) In section 19A and in this Part, "week" means any period of 7 consecutive days.]

[³(4) In section 19 and 19A][³ and in this Part, "employment" means employed earner's employment other than such employment in which a person is employed whilst participating in an employment programme falling within paragraph (1)(a) and "employed earner" shall be construed accordingly; and for the purposes of paragraph (4) of regulation 70C includes self-employment where the claimant's income as calculated under Part VIII exceeds his applicable amount as calculated under sections 4(1), 12 and 13 of the Act.]

(5) [² In this Part,

"current sanctionable failure" means a failure which is sanctionable under section 19 (higher-level sanctions), 19A (other sanctions) or 19B (claimants ceasing to be available for employment etc) in relation to which the Secretary of State has not yet determined whether the amount of an award is to be reduced in accordance with section 19 or 19A or regulation 69B;]

[³ . . .];

[²"sanctionable failure" means a failure which is sanctionable under section 19 (higher-level sanctions), 19A (other sanctions) or 19B (claimants ceasing to be available for employment etc).]

AMENDMENTS

1. Social Security (Miscellaneous Amendments) Regulations 2008 (SI 2008/698) reg.4(9) (April 14, 2008).

2. Jobseeker's Allowance (Sanctions) (Amendment) Regulations 2012 (SI 2012/2568) reg.2(9) (October 22, 2012).

3. Social Security (Miscellaneous Amendments) Regulations 2013 (SI 2013/443) reg.4(6) (April 2, 2013).

DEFINITIONS

"the Act"—see reg.1(3).
"claimant"—see Jobseekers Act 1995 s.35(1).
"employed earner"—see reg.3.

PART VI

MEMBERSHIP OF THE FAMILY

Persons of a prescribed description

76.—(1) Subject to paragraph (2), a person of a prescribed description   3.255
for the purposes of the definition of "family" in section 35(1) of the Act is a person [³ who falls within the definition of qualifying young person in section 142 of the Benefits Act (child and qualifying young person)], and in these Regulations, except in Part IV, such a person is referred to as a "young person".

(2) Paragraph (1) shall not apply to a person who is—

(a) [³ . . .]
(b) entitled to a jobseeker's allowance or would, but for section 3(1)(d) of the Act (provision against dual entitlement) be so entitled; or
(c) entitled to income support or would, but for section 134(2) of the Benefits Act (exclusion from benefit) be [² so entitled; or
(d) a person to whom section 6 of the Children (Leaving Care) Act 2000 (exclusion from benefits) applies.] [⁴ or

(e) entitled to an income-related employment and support allowance or would, but for paragraph 6(1)(d) of Schedule 1 to the Welfare Reform Act (conditions of entitlement to income-related employment and support allowance), be entitled [⁵ ; or
(f) entitled to universal credit].]

[¹(3) A person of a prescribed description for the purposes of the definition of "family" in section 35(1) of the Act includes a child or young person in respect of whom section 145A of the Benefits Act applies for the purposes of entitlement to child benefit but only for the period prescribed under section 145A(1) of that Act.]

DEFINITIONS

"the Act"—see reg.1(3).
"course of advanced education"—*ibid.*

AMENDMENTS

1. Income-related Benefits and Jobseeker's Allowance (Working Tax Credit and Child Credit) (Amendment) Regulations 2002 (SI 2002/2402) reg.3 and Sch.2 para.2 (April 6, 2003).
2. Children (Leaving Care) Act 2000 (Commencement No.2 and Consequential Provisions) Order 2001 (SI 2001/3070) art.3(5) and Sch.4.
3. Social Security (Young Persons) Amendment Regulations 2006 (SI 2006/718) reg.3(6) (April 10, 2006).
4. Employment and Support Allowance (Consequential Provisions) (No.2) Regulations 2008 (SI 2008/1554) reg.3(1) and (12) (October 27, 2008).
5. Universal Credit (Consequential, Supplementary, Incidental and Miscellaneous Provisions) Regulations 2013 (SI 2013/630) reg.30(1) and (3) (April 29, 2013).

GENERAL NOTE

3.256   This regulation is very similar to reg.14 of the Income Support Regulations, except that para.(2) contains an additional exception that the person must not be entitled to income support in their own right (sub-para.(c)). Note that para.(1) expressly provides that this definition of "young person" does not apply for the purposes of Pt IV (entitlement of 16- and 17-year-olds to JSA).
See the note to reg.14 of the Income Support Regulations.

Circumstances in which a person is to be treated as responsible or not responsible for another

3.257   77.—(1) Subject to the following provisions of this regulation, a person is to be treated for the purposes of the Act as responsible for a child or young person for whom he is receiving child benefit [¹and this includes a child or young person to whom paragraph (3) of regulation 76 applies.]
(2) In a case where a child ("the first child") is in receipt of child benefit in respect of another child ("the second child"), the person treated as responsible for the first child in accordance with the provisions of this regulation shall also be treated as responsible for the second child.
(3) In the case of a child or young person in respect of whom no person is receiving child benefit, the person who shall be treated as responsible for that child or young person shall be—
(a) except where sub-paragraph (b) applies, the person with whom the child or young person usually lives; or
(b) where only one claim for child benefit has been made in respect of the child or young person, the person who made that claim.

(4) Where regulation 78(7) (circumstances in which a person is to be treated as being or not being a member of the household) applies in respect of a child or young person, that child or young person shall be treated as the responsibility of the claimant for that part of the week for which he is under that regulation treated as being a member of the claimant's household.

(5) Except where paragraph (4) applies, a child or young person shall be treated as the responsibility of only one person in any benefit week and any person other than the one treated as responsible for the child or young person under this regulation shall be treated as not so responsible.

AMENDMENT

1. Income-related Benefits and Jobseeker's Allowance (Working Tax Credit and Child Tax Credit) (Amendment) Regulations 2002 (SI 2002/2402) reg. and Sch.2 para.3 (April 6, 2003).

DEFINITIONS

"the Act"—see reg.1(3).
"benefit week"—*ibid.*
"child"—see Jobseekers Act s.35(1).
"claimant"—*ibid.*
"week"—*ibid.*
"young person"—see reg.76.

GENERAL NOTE

The definition of family in s.35(1) of the Jobseekers Act refers to a person being responsible for a child or young person (on which see reg.76). This provision mirrors that in reg.15 of the Income Support Regulations and makes the test of responsibility for a child or young person receipt of child benefit. See the notes to reg.15.

Note however, the decision of the Court of Appeal in *Hockenjos v Secretary of State for Social Security* [2004] EWCA Civ 1749 (on appeal from *CJSA 4890/1998*) that paras (1)–(3) and (5) of this regulation discriminated against men contrary to art.4 of Directive 79/7 (see Vol.III) and that such discrimination was not objectively justifiable. Those provisions therefore could not be applied to Mr Hockenjos or, by implication, any man within the personal scope of that Directive. In such a case, whether or not a child or young person was a member of the claimant's "family" was to be decided by applying the definition in s.35 of the Jobseekers Act as if reg.77 did not exist, i.e. by asking whether that child or young person was a member of the same household for whom the claimant or any partner was responsible. Applying that test to Mr Hockenjos (who had shared parental responsibility and whose daughters lived with him for substantial parts, though not the majority, of each week under a joint residence order made by a court) there was no doubt that it was satisfied. The effect was that Mr Hockenjos was entitled to JSA for his children on the same basis as if they lived with him full time and, as the "one claimant per child" rule in reg.77(5) was indirectly discriminatory, the fact the Secretary of State might also have to pay income support or JSA for the children to their mother on the same basis did not affect that conclusion. The Secretary of State petitioned the House of Lords for leave to appeal, but leave was refused.

CJSA/2507/2002 decides that a woman who is the substantial minority carer of her children cannot rely on *Hockenjos* because she cannot establish direct or indirect discrimination against her *as a woman*. The decision also holds that reg.77 does not infringe such a woman's Convention Rights.

For an example where, on somewhat unusual facts, a man could not claim the benefit of *Hockenjos* see *CJSA/2811/2006*. That decision leaves open the possibility that the rules might discriminate unlawfully against a man who, following a period

3.258

3.259

of joint care, becomes a child's sole carer in comparison with a woman in the same position (see para.12).

For the reasons given in the note to reg.15 of the IS Regulations, the *Hockenjos* decision does not apply to income support.

Circumstances in which a person is to be treated as being or not being a member of the household

3.260

78.—(1) Subject to paragraphs (2) to (5), the claimant and any partner and, where the claimant or his partner is treated as responsible under regulation 77 (circumstances in which a person is to be treated as responsible or not responsible for another) for a child or young person, that child or young person and any child of that child or young person shall be treated for the purposes of the Act as members of the same household notwithstanding that any of them is temporarily living away from the other members of his family.

[³(1A) Subject to paragraphs (2) and (3), the members of a joint-claim couple shall be treated for the purposes of the Act as members of the same household notwithstanding that they are temporarily living away from each other.]

(2) [⁴Paragraphs (1) and (1A)] shall not apply to a person who is living away from the other members of his family where—

(a) that person does not intend to resume living with the other members of his family; or

(b) his absence from the other members of his family is likely to exceed 52 weeks, unless there are exceptional circumstances (for example the person is in hospital or otherwise has no control over the length of his absence), and the absence is unlikely to be substantially more than 52 weeks.

(3) [⁵Paragraphs (1) and (1A)] shall not apply in respect of any member of a couple or of a polygamous marriage where—

(a) one, both or all of them are patients detained in a hospital provided under section 4 of the National Health Service Act 1977 ([⁹ high security psychiatric services]) or [⁸ section 102 of the National Health Service (Scotland) Act 1978[24] (state hospitals)]; or

[²(b) one, both or all of them are—

(i) detained in custody pending trial or sentence upon conviction or under a sentence imposed by a court; or

(ii) on temporary release in accordance with the provisions of the Prison Act 1952 or rules made under section 39(6) of the Prisons (Scotland) Act 1989]

(c) [⁶ a claimant] is abroad and does not satisfy the conditions of regulation 50 (persons absent from Great Britain); or

(d) one of them is permanently [⁷ residing in a care home, an Abbeyfield Home or an independent hospital].

(4) A child or young person shall not be treated as a member of the claimant's household where he is—

(a) placed with the claimant or his partner by a local authority under [¹³ section 22C(2)] of the Children Act 1989 or by a voluntary organisation under section 59(1)(a) of that Act; or

[¹²(aa) placed with the claimant or his partner by a local authority under section 81(2) of the Social Services and Well-being (Wales) Act 2014; or]

(b) placed with the claimant or his partner prior to adoption; or

(c) in accordance with a relevant Scottish enactment, boarded out with the claimant or his partner, whether or not with a view to adoption; or

(d) placed for adoption with the claimant or his partner pursuant to a decision under the Adoption Agencies Regulations 1983 or the Adoption Agencies (Scotland) Regulations 1984.

(5) Subject to paragraphs (6) and (7), paragraph (1) shall not apply to a child or young person who is not living with the claimant and who—

(a) in a case which does not fall within sub-paragraph (b), has been continuously absent from Great Britain for a period of more than four weeks commencing—

(i) where he went abroad before the date of the claim for a jobseeker's allowance, with that date;

(ii) in any other case, on the day which immediately follows the day on which he went abroad; or

(b) where [¹regulation 50(5)] or paragraph 11 or 13 of Schedule 5 (temporary absence abroad for the treatment of a child or young person) applies, has been continuously absent from Great Britain for a period of more than 8 weeks, that period of 8 weeks commencing—

(i) where he went abroad before the date of the claim for a jobseeker's allowance, on the date of that claim;

(ii) in any other case, on the day which immediately follows the day on which he went abroad; or

(c) has been an in-patient or in accommodation [⁷ . . .] for a continuous period of more than 12 weeks commencing—

(i) where he became an in-patient or, as the case may be, entered that accommodation before the date of the claim for a jobseeker's allowance, with that date; or

(ii) in any other case, with the date on which he became an in-patient or entered that accommodation,

and, in either case, has not been in regular contact with either the claimant or any member of the claimant's household; or

(d) is being looked after by a local authority under a relevant enactment; or

(e) has been placed with a person other than the claimant prior to adoption, or

(f) is in the care of a local authority under a relevant Scottish enactment; or

(g) has been boarded out under a relevant Scottish enactment with a person other than the claimant prior to adoption; or

(h) has been placed for adoption pursuant to a decision under the Adoption Agencies Regulations 1983 or the Adoption Agencies (Scotland) Regulations 1984; or

(i) is detained in custody pending trial or sentence upon conviction or under a sentence imposed by a court.

(6) In the case of a person who was entitled to income support [¹⁰ or an income-related employment and support allowance] immediately before his entitlement to a jobseeker's allowance commenced, sub-paragraphs (a), (b) and (c) of paragraph (5) [¹shall] each have effect as if head (i) was omitted.

(7) A child or young person to whom any of the circumstances mentioned in [¹sub-paragraphs (d), (f) or (i)] of paragraph (5) applies shall be

treated as being a member of the claimant's household only for that part of any benefit week where that child or young person lives with the claimant.

(8) Where a child or young person for the purposes of attending the educational establishment at which he is receiving relevant education is living with the claimant or his partner and neither one is treated as responsible for that child or young person that child or young person shall be treated as being a member of the household of the person treated as responsible for him and shall not be treated as a member of the claimant's household.

(9) In this regulation—

[⁷ (za) "accommodation" means accommodation provided by a local authority in a home owned or managed by that local authority—

    (i) under sections 21 to 24 of the National Assistance Act 1948 (provision of accommodation),

    [¹¹ (ia) under section 18 or 19 of the Care Act 2014 (duty and power to meet needs for care and support); or]

    (ii) in Scotland, under section 13B or 59 of the Social Work (Scotland) Act 1968 (provision of residential or other establishment), or

    (iii) under section 25 of the Mental Health (Care and Treatment) (Scotland) Act 2003 (care and support services etc.), [¹² or

    (iv) in Wales, under section 35 or 36 of the Social Services and Well-being (Wales) Act 2014 (duty and power to meet care and support needs of an adult);]

where the accommodation is provided for a person whose stay in that accommodation has become other than temporary;]

(a) "relevant enactment" means the Army Act 1955, the Social Work (Scotland) Act 1968, the Matrimonial Causes Act 1973, the Adoption (Scotland) Act 1978, the Family Law Act 1986 and [¹², the Children Act 1989 and the Social Services and Well-being (Wales) Act 2014];

(b) "relevant Scottish enactment" means the Army Act 1955, the Air Force Act 1955, the Naval Discipline Act 1957, the Adoption Act 1958, the Matrimonial Proceedings Children Act 1958, the Children Act 1958, the Social Work (Scotland) Act 1968, the Family Law Reform Act 1969, the Children and Young Persons Act 1969, the Matrimonial Causes Act 1973, the Guardianship Act 1973, the Children Act 1975, the Domestic Proceedings and Magistrates' Courts Act 1978, the Adoption (Scotland) Act 1978, the Child Care Act 1980, and the Foster Children Act 1980;

(c) "voluntary organisation" has the meaning assigned to it in the Children Act 1989 or, in Scotland, the Social Work (Scotland) Act 1968.

AMENDMENTS

1. Jobseeker's Allowance (Amendment) Regulations 1996 (SI 1996/1516) reg.20 and Sch. (October 7, 1996).

2. Jobseeker's Allowance and Income Support (General) (Amendment) Regulations 1996 (SI 1996/1517) reg.18 (October 7, 1996).

3. Jobseeker's Allowance (Joint Claims) Regulations 2000 (SI 2000/1978) reg.2(5) and Sch.2 para.33(a) (March 19, 2001).

4. Jobseeker's Allowance (Joint Claims) Regulations 2000 (SI 2000/1978) reg.2(5) and Sch.2 para.33(b) (March 19, 2001).

5. Jobseeker's Allowance (Joint Claims) Regulations 2000 (SI 2000/1978) reg.2(5) and Sch.2 para.33(c)(i) (March 19, 2001).

6. Jobseeker's Allowance (Joint Claims) Regulations 2000 (SI 2000/1978) reg.2(5) and Sch.2 para.33(c)(ii) (March 19, 2001).

7. Social Security (Care Homes and Independent Hospitals) Regulations 2005 (SI 2005/2687) reg.3 and Sch.2 para.3 (October 24, 2005).

8. Social Security (Miscellaneous Amendments) Regulations 2006 (SI 2006/588) reg.3 (April 1, 2006).

9. Social Security (Miscellaneous Amendments) (No.4) Regulations 2006 (SI 2006/2378) reg.13(4) (October 2, 2006).

10. Employment and Support Allowance (Consequential Provisions) (No.2) Regulations 2008 (SI 2008/1554) reg.3(1) and (13) (October 27, 2008).

11. Care Act 2014 (Consequential Amendments) (Secondary Legislation) Order 2015 (SI 2015/643) art.2 and Sch. para.9(2) (April 1, 2015).

12. Social Services and Well-being (Wales) Act 2014 and the Regulation and Inspection of Social Care (Wales) Act 2016 (Consequential Amendments) Order 2017 (SI 2017/901) art.6(1) and (3) (November 3, 2017).

13. Social Services and Well-being (Wales) Act 2014 and the Regulation and Inspection of Social Care (Wales) Act 2016 (Consequential Amendments) Order 2017 (SI 2017/901) art.22(1) and (2) (November 3, 2017).

MODIFICATION

With effect from April 8, 2020, para.(3)(b)(ii) is modified by reg.3(2) of the Social Security (Coronavirus) (Prisoners) Regulations 2020 (SI 2020/409). The modification provides that reg.78(3)(b)(ii) is to be read as if the words "the provisions of the Prison Act 1952 or" were omitted. By reg.6 of SI 2020/409 (as amended by reg.2 of SI 2020/1156), the modification will expire at the end of May 12, 2021.   3.261

DEFINITIONS

"Abbeyfield Home"—see reg.1(3).
"the Act"—*ibid.*
"care home"—*ibid.*
"claimant"—see Jobseekers Act s.35(1).
"child"—*ibid.*
"couple"—see reg.1(3).
"date of claim"—*ibid.*
"family"—see Jobseekers Act s.35(1).
"independent hospital"—see reg.1(3).
"partner"—*ibid.*
"polygamous marriage"—*ibid.*
"young person"—see reg.76.

GENERAL NOTE

This regulation is very similar to reg.16 of the Income Support Regulations. Unlike the Income Support Regulations, the JSA Regulations make separate reference to the Scottish legislation in the case of provisions that were amended in the Income Support Regulations as a consequence of the Children Act 1989 (see para. (4)(c), para.(5)(f) and (g) and (9)(b)).   3.262

See the notes to reg.16 of the Income Support Regulations.

PART VII

AMOUNTS

Weekly amounts of contribution-based jobseeker's allowance

79. [*Omitted as not relevant to income-based JSA*]   3.263

Deductions in respect of earnings

3.264   **80.** [*Omitted as not relevant to income-based JSA*]

Payments by way of pensions

3.265   **81.** [*Omitted as not relevant to income-based JSA*]

[¹ Income-based jobseeker's allowance

3.266   **82.**—(1) Regulations 83 to [² 85] and 87 apply in the case of an income-based jobseeker's allowance but not a joint-claim jobseeker's allowance.

(2) Regulations 86A to [² 86C] only apply in the case of a joint-claim jobseeker's allowance.]

AMENDMENTS

1. Jobseeker's Allowance (Joint Claims) Regulations 2000 (SI 2000/1978) reg.2(5) and Sch.2 para.34 (March 19, 2001).
2. Social Security Amendment (Residential Care and Nursing Homes) Regulations 2001 (SI 2001/3767) reg.2 and Sch. Pt II para.3 (April 8, 2002).

Applicable amounts

3.267   **83.**—Except in the case of a claimant to whom regulation 84, 85, [¹ . . .] [⁴ . . .] (applicable amounts in other cases [⁴ . . .]) applies, a claimant's weekly applicable amount shall be the aggregate of such of the following amounts as may apply in this case—

(a) an amount in respect of himself or if he is a member of a couple, an amount in respect of both of them, determined in accordance with sub-paragraph (1), (2) or (3), as the case may be, of paragraph 1 of Schedule 1;
(b) [³ . . .]
(c) [² . . .]
(d) [³ . . .]
(e) the amount of any premiums which may be applicable to him, determined in accordance with Parts III and IV of Schedule 1 (premiums); and
(f) any amounts determined in accordance with Schedule 2 (housing costs) which may be applicable to him in respect of [⁵ housing costs as prescribed] in that Schedule.

AMENDMENTS

1. Social Security Amendment (Residential Care and Nursing Homes) Regulations 2001 (SI 2001/3767) reg.2 and Sch. Pt II para.4 (April 8, 2002).
2. Social Security (Removal of Residential Allowance and Miscellaneous Amendments) Regulations 2003 (SI 2003/1121) reg.4 and Sch.2 para.2 (October 6, 2003).
3. Social Security (Working Tax Credit and Child Tax Credit) (Consequential Amendments) Regulations 2003 (SI 2003/455) reg.3 and Sch.2 para.2 (April 6, 2004, except in "transitional cases" and see further the note to this regulation and to reg.17 of the Income Support Regulations).
4. Social Security (Miscellaneous Amendments) (No.5) Regulations 2009 (SI 2009/3228) reg.3(3)(a) (January 25, 2010).
5. Loans for Mortgage Interest Regulations 2017 (SI 2017/725) reg.18 and Sch.5 para.3(a) (April 6, 2018).

DEFINITIONS

"child"—see Jobseekers Act s.35(1).
"claimant"—*ibid.*
"couple"—see reg.1(3).
"family"—see Jobseekers Act s.35(1).
"young person"—see reg.76.

GENERAL NOTE

Income-based JSA uses the same formula as income support for calculating the amount of a claimant's benefit, that is, by setting his "applicable amount" against his income. Regulation 83 sets out the categories which go towards the total applicable amount which are the same as those in reg.17 of the Income Support Regulations. See the notes to reg.17. There is no equivalent to reg.17(1)(f) and (g) and (2) to (7) which contain various transitional protection provisions. But note the rules for "transitional supplement" to income-based JSA in reg.87 which preserve the effect of these and other income support transitional protection provisions for JSA claimants who would have been covered by them had they been entitled to claim income support after October 6, 1996 (for claimants entitled to a special transitional addition or transitional addition under the Income Support (Transitional) Regulations before October 7, 1996, see para.(1) of reg.87).   **3.268**

As with income support there are special rules for particular categories, see regs 84–86D.   **3.269**

Subject to exceptions in "transitional cases", JSA became an "adults only" benefit on April 6, 2004 with all support for the costs of bringing up children and young persons transferred to child tax credit and regs 83(b) and 84(c) (personal allowances for children and young persons), regs 383(d) and 84(e) (family premium) and para.16 of Sch.1 (disabled child premium) were revoked from that date. At the same time para.15A(1)(b) of Sch.1 was amended to remove the possibility of claiming the enhanced disability premium for a child. For JSA the rules which create "transitional cases" are contained in reg.1(6)–(8) of SI 2003/455 (p.1763) and are the same as the rules for income support in reg.1(2)–(4). For a detailed discussion, see the note to reg.17 of the Income Support Regulations.   **3.270**

Polygamous marriages

84.—(1) Except in the case of a claimant to whom regulation 83, [²or 85] (applicable amounts in special cases) [². . .] [⁵. . .] or paragraph (2) applies, where a claimant is a member of a polygamous marriage his weekly applicable amount shall be the aggregate of such of the following amounts as may apply in his case—   **3.271**
  (a) the highest amount applicable to him and one of his partners determined in accordance with sub-paragraph (3) of paragraph 1 of Schedule 1 as if he and that partner were a couple;
  (b) an amount equal to the difference between the amounts specified in [¹sub-paragraph (3)(e)] and (1)(e) of paragraph 1 of Schedule 1 in respect of each of his other partners;
  (c) [⁴. . .]
  (d) [³. . .]
  (e) [⁴. . .]
  (f) the amount of any premiums which may be applicable to him determined in accordance with Parts III and IV of Schedule 1 (premiums); and
  (g) any amounts determined in accordance with Schedule 2 (housing costs) which may be applicable to him in respect of [⁵ housing costs as prescribed] in that Schedule.

3.272   (2) In the case of a partner who is aged less than 18 the amount which applies in respect of that partner shall be Nil unless that partner—

(a) is treated as responsible for a child; or

(b) is a person who, had he not been a member of a polygamous marriage, would have qualified for a jobseeker's allowance by virtue of section 3(1)(f)(ii) or section 3(1)(f)(iii) and the regulations made thereunder (jobseeker's allowance for persons aged 16 or 17).

AMENDMENTS

3.273   1. Jobseeker's Allowance (Amendment) Regulations 1996 (SI 1996/1516) reg.20 and Sch. (October 7, 1996).

2. Social Security Amendment (Residential Care and Nursing Homes) Regulations 2001 (SI 2001/3767) reg.2 and Sch. Pt II para.5 (April 8, 2002).

3. Social Security (Removal of Residential Allowance and Miscellaneous Amendments) Regulations 2003 (SI 2003/1121) reg.4 of and Sch.2 para.3 (October 6, 2003).

4. Social Security (Working Tax Credit and Child Tax Credit) (Consequential Amendments) Regulations 2003 (SI 2003/455) reg.3 and Sch.2 para.3 (April 6, 2004, except in "transitional cases" and see further the note to regs 83 and to 17 of the Income Support Regulations).

5. Social Security (Miscellaneous Amendments) (No.5) Regulations 2009 (SI 2009/3228) reg.3(3)(b) (January 25, 2010).

6. Loans for Mortgage Interest Regulations 2017 (SI 2017/725) reg.18 and Sch.5 para.3(b) (April 6, 2018).

DEFINITIONS

3.274   "child"—see Jobseekers Act s.35(1).
"claimant"—*ibid.*
"couple"—see reg.1(3).
"family"—see Jobseekers Act s.35(1).
"young person"—see reg.76.

GENERAL NOTE

3.275   Regulation 84 contains the special rules for polygamous marriages but not for other kinds of relationships. There the ordinary living together as husband and wife rule in s.35(1) of the Jobseekers Act applies.

This provision only applies to income-based JSA (reg.82).

Special cases

3.276   **85.**—(1) [⁹ [¹⁸. . .]] in the case of a person to whom any paragraph in column (1) of Schedule 5 applies (applicable amounts in special cases) the amount included in the claimant's weekly applicable amount in respect of him shall be the amount prescribed in the corresponding paragraph in column (2) of that Schedule [¹¹. . .].

(2) [¹⁹. . .]

[⁹(2A) [¹⁰. . .]]

(3) [¹⁶ . . .]

(4) [³ [¹² ¹⁷ In this regulation] and Schedule 5—

[⁷. . .]

[⁷ "partner of a person subject to immigration control" means a person—

(i) who is not subject to immigration control within the meaning of section 115(9) of the Immigration and Asylum Act; or

(ii) to whom section 115 of that Act does not apply by virtue of regulation 2 of the Social Security (Immigration and Asylum) Consequential Amendments Regulations 2000; and

(iii) who is a member of a couple and [¹⁵ the member's] partner is subject to immigration control within the meaning of section 115(9) of that Act and section 115 of that Act applies to [¹⁵ the partner] for the purposes of exclusion from entitlement to jobseeker's allowance;]

[¹⁷ "person from abroad" has the meaning given in regulation 85A]

"patient" means a person (other than a prisoner) who is regarded as receiving free in-patient treatment within the meaning of [¹⁶ regulation 2(4) and (5) of the Social Security (Hospital In-Patients) Regulations 2005];

"prisoner" means a person who—

(a) is detained in custody pending trial or sentence upon conviction or under a sentence imposed by a court; or

(b) is on temporary release in accordance with the provisions of the Prison Act 1952 or the Prisons (Scotland) Act 1989,

other than a person [⁵who is detained in hospital under the provisions of the Mental Health Act 1983, or, in Scotland, under the provisions of the [¹³ Mental Health (Care and Treatment) (Scotland) Act 2003] or the Criminal Procedure (Scotland) Act 1995;]

[¹⁴ . . .]

(4A) [³ ¹⁷ . . .]

(4B) [¹² ¹⁷ . . .]

(5) [¹⁴ . . .]

(6) [¹⁴ . . .]

AMENDMENTS

1. Jobseeker's Allowance (Amendment) Regulations 1996 (SI 1996/1516) reg.10(1) (October 7, 1996).

2. Jobseeker's Allowance (Amendment) Regulations 1996 (SI 1996/1516) reg.20 and Sch. (October 7, 1996).

3. Social Security and Child Support (Jobseeker's Allowance) (Miscellaneous Amendments) Regulations 1996 (SI 1996/2538) reg.2(7) (October 28, 1996).

4. Social Security (Miscellaneous Amendments) Regulations 1997 (SI 1997/454) reg.2(10) (April 7, 1997).

5. Social Security (Miscellaneous Amendments) Regulations 1998 (SI 1998/563) reg.8(1) and (2)(d) (April 6, 1998).

6. Social Security (Miscellaneous Amendments) Regulations 1998 (SI 1998/563) reg.18(3) and (4)(d) (April 6, 1998).

7. Social Security (Immigration and Asylum) Consequential Amendments Regulations 2000 (SI 2000/636) reg.4(3)(a) (April 3, 2000).

8. Income-related Benefits and Jobseeker's Allowance (Amendment) Regulations 2000 (SI 2000/979) reg.3 (May 2, 2000).

9. Social Security Amendment (Residential Care and Nursing Homes) Regulations 2001 (SI 2001/3767) reg.2 and Sch. Pt II para.6 (April 8, 2002).

10. Social Security (Removal of Residential Allowance and Miscellaneous Amendments) Regulations 2003 (SI 2003/1121) reg.4 and Sch.2 para.4 (October 6, 2003).

11. Social Security (Working Tax Credit and Child Tax Credit) (Consequential Amendments) Regulations 2003 (SI 2003/455) reg.3 and Sch.4 para.1 (April 6, 2004, except in "transitional cases" and see further the note to regs 83 and to 17 of the Income Support Regulations).

12. Social Security (Habitual Residence) Amendment Regulations 2004 (SI 2004/1232) reg.4 (May 1, 2004).

13. Mental Health (Care and Treatment) (Scotland) Act 2003 (Modification of Subordinate Legislation) Order 2005 (SSI 2005/445) art.2 and Sch. para.23(2) (Scotland); Mental Health (Care and Treatment) (Scotland) Act 2003 (Consequential Provisions) Order 2005 (SI 2005/2078) art.15 and Sch.2 para.17(3) (England and Wales) (October 5, 2005).

14. Social Security (Care Homes and Independent Hospitals) Regulations 2005 (SI 2005/2687) reg.3 and Sch.2 para.4 (October 24, 2005).

15. Civil Partnership (Pensions, Social Security and Child Support) (Consequential, etc. Provisions) Order 2005 (SI 2005/2877) art.2(3) and Sch.3 para.26(5) (December 5, 2005).

16. Social Security (Hospital In-Patients) Regulations 2005 (SI 2005/3360) reg.6 (April 10, 2006).

17. Social Security (Persons from Abroad) Amendment Regulations 2006 (SI 1026/2006) reg.7(2) (April 30, 2006).

18. Social Security (Miscellaneous Amendments) (No.5) Regulations 2007 (SI 2007/2618) reg.8(6) (October 1, 2007).

19. Social Security (Miscellaneous Amendments) Regulations 2009 (SI 2009/583) reg.4(1) and (5) (April 6, 2009).

MODIFICATION

The definition of "prisoner" in para.(4) is modified with effect from April 8, 2020 by reg.2(1) and (2)(b) of the Social Security (Coronavirus) (Prisoners) Regulations 2020 (SI 2020/409). The modification provides that the JSA Regulations 1996 "are to be read as if the definition of 'prisoner' did not include a person on temporary release in accordance with the provisions of the Prison Act 1952". By reg.6 of SI 2020/409 (as amended by reg.2 of SI 2020/1156), the modification will expire at the end of May 12, 2021.

DEFINITIONS

"child"—see Jobseekers Act s.35(1).
"claimant"—*ibid.*
"Income Support Regulations"—see reg.1(3).
"young person"—see reg.76.

GENERAL NOTE

3.277   This regulation only applies to income-based JSA (reg.82).
Applicable amounts in special cases are to be as prescribed in Sch.5.
This provision is similar to reg.21 of the Income Support Regulations. See the notes to that regulation.

[¹ Special cases: supplemental – persons from abroad

3.278   **85A.**—(1) "Person from abroad" means, subject to the following provisions of this regulation, a claimant who is not habitually resident in the United Kingdom, the Channel Islands, the Isle of Man or the Republic of Ireland.

[¹⁰ (2) No claimant shall be treated as habitually resident in the United Kingdom, the Channel Islands, the Isle of Man or the Republic of Ireland unless—

(a) [¹² subject to the exceptions in paragraph (2A),] the claimant has been living in any of those places for the past three months; and
(b) the claimant has a right to reside in any of those places, other than a right to reside which falls within paragraph (3) [¹³ or (3A)].]

[¹² (2A) The exceptions are where the claimant has at any time during the period referred to in paragraph (2)(a)—

(a) paid either Class 1 or Class 2 contributions by virtue of regulation 114, 118, 146 or 147 of the Social Security (Contributions) Regulations 2001 or by virtue of an Order in Council having effect under section 179 of the Social Security Administration Act 1992; or

(b) been a Crown servant posted to perform overseas the duties of a Crown servant; or

(c) been a member of Her Majesty's forces posted to perform overseas the duties of a member of Her Majesty's forces.]

(3) A right to reside falls within this paragraph if it is one which exists by virtue of, or in accordance with, one or more of the following—

(a) regulation 13 of the [¹³ Immigration (European Economic Area) Regulations 2016]; [¹⁵ or]

[⁷ [¹³ (aa) regulation 16 of those Regulations, but only in a case where the right exists under that regulation because the claimant satisfies the criteria in paragraph (5) of that regulation;]

(b) [¹⁵ ...]

(c) [¹⁵ ...]

[¹³ (3A) A right to reside falls within this paragraph if it exists by virtue of a claimant having been granted limited leave to enter, or remain in, the United Kingdom under the Immigration Act 1971 by virtue of—

(a) Appendix EU to the immigration rules made under section 3(2) of that Act; [¹⁶ ...]

(b) being a person with a Zambrano right to reside as defined in Annex 1 of Appendix EU to the immigration rules made under section 3(2) of that Act.] [¹⁶; or

(c) having arrived in the United Kingdom with an entry clearance that was granted under Appendix EU (Family Permit) to the immigration rules made under section 3(2) of that Act.]

[¹⁴ (3B) Paragraph (3A)(a) does not apply to a person who—

(a) has a right to reside granted by virtue of being a family member of a relevant person of Northern Ireland; and

(b) would have a right to reside under the Immigration (European Economic Area) Regulations 2016 if the relevant person of Northern Ireland were an EEA national, provided that the right to reside does not fall within paragraph (3A).]

(4) A claimant is not a person from abroad if he is—

[¹¹ (za) a qualified person for the purposes of regulation 6 of the [¹³ Immigration (European Economic Area) Regulations 2016] as a worker or a self-employed person;

(zb) a family member of a person referred to in sub-paragraph (za) [¹⁴ ...];

(zc) a person who has a right to reside permanently in the United Kingdom by virtue of regulation 15(1)(c), (d) or (e) of those Regulations;]

[¹⁴ (zd) a family member of a relevant person of Northern Ireland, with a right to reside which falls within paragraph (3A)(a), provided that the relevant person of Northern Ireland falls within sub-paragraph (za), or would do so but for the fact that they are not an EEA national;]

[¹⁵ (ze) a frontier worker within the meaning of regulation 3 of the Citizens' Rights (Frontier Workers) (EU Exit) Regulations 2020;

(zf) a family member, of a person referred to in sub-paragraph (ze), who has been granted limited leave to enter, or remain in, the United

Kingdom by virtue of Appendix EU to the immigration rules made
under section 3(2) of the Immigration Act 1971;]
(g) a refugee within the definition in Article 1 of the Convention relating to the Status of Refugees done at Geneva on 28th July 1951,
as extended by Article 1(2) of the Protocol relating to the Status of
Refugees done at New York on 31st January 1967;
[³ [⁹ (h) a person who has been granted leave or who is deemed to have
been granted leave outside the rules made under section 3(2) of the
Immigration Act 1971 where that leave is—
  (i) discretionary leave to enter or remain in the United Kingdom;
  (ii) leave to remain under the Destitution Domestic Violence concession; or
  (iii) leave deemed to have been granted by virtue of regulation 3
  of the Displaced Persons (Temporary Protection) Regulations
  2005(19);]]
(hh) a person who has humanitarian protection granted under those rules;]
  [⁹ or]
(i) a person who is not a person subject to immigration control within
the meaning of section 115(9) of the Immigration and Asylum Act
and who is in the United Kingdom as a result of his deportation,
expulsion or other removal by compulsion of law from another
country to the United Kingdom; [⁵ . . .]
[⁹ . . .]
[¹⁴ (5) In this regulation—
"EEA national" has the meaning given in regulation 2(1) of the
Immigration (European Economic Area) Regulations 2016;
"family member" has the meaning given in regulation 7(1)(a), (b) or
(c) of the Immigration (European Economic Area) Regulations 2016
except that regulation 7(4) of those Regulations does not apply for the
purposes of paragraphs (3B) and (4)(zd);
"relevant person of Northern Ireland" has the meaning given in Annex 1
of Appendix EU to the immigration rules made under section 3(2) of
the Immigration Act 1971.]
[¹⁵ (6) In this regulation references to the Immigration (European
Economic Area) Regulations 2016 are to be read with Schedule 4 to
the Immigration and Social Security Co-ordination (EU Withdrawal)
Act 2020(Consequential, Saving, Transitional and Transitory Provisions)
Regulations 2020.]

AMENDMENTS

1. Social Security (Persons from Abroad) Amendment Regulations 2006 (SI
1026/2006) reg.7(3) (April 30, 2006).
2. Social Security (Lebanon) Amendment Regulations 2006 (SI 2006/1981) reg.3
(July 25, 2006). The amendment ceased to have effect from January 31, 2007.
3. Social Security (Persons from Abroad) Amendment (No.2) Regulations 2006
(SI 2006/2528) reg.3 (October 9, 2006).
4. Social Security (Bulgaria and Romania) Amendment Regulations 2006 (SI
2006/3341) reg.3 (January 1, 2007).
5. Social Security (Habitual Residence) (Amendment) Regulations 2009 (SI
2009/362) reg.3 (March 18, 2009).
6. Social Security (Miscellaneous Amendments) (No.3) Regulations 2011 (SI
2011/2425) reg.10(1) and (7) (October 31, 2011).

7. Social Security (Habitual Residence) (Amendment) Regulations 2012 (SI 2012/2587) reg.3 (November 8, 2012).

8. Social Security (Croatia) Amendment Regulations 2013 (SI 2013/1474) reg.3 (July 1, 2013).

9. Social Security (Miscellaneous Amendments) (No.3) Regulations 2013 (SI 2013/2536) reg.6(1) and (8) (October 29,2013).

10. Jobseeker's Allowance (Habitual Residence) Amendment Regulations 2013 (SI 3196/2013) reg.2 (January 1, 2014).

11. Social Security (Habitual Residence) (Amendment) Regulations 2014 (SI 2014/902) reg.3 (May 31, 2014).

12. Jobseeker's Allowance (Habitual Residence) Amendment Regulations 2014 (SI 2014/2735) reg.3 (November 9, 2014).

13. Social Security (Income-related Benefits) (Updating and Amendment) (EU Exit) Regulations 2019 (SI 2019/872) reg.3 (May 7, 2019).

14. Social Security (Income-Related Benefits) (Persons of Northern Ireland – Family Members) (Amendment) Regulations 2020 (SI 2020/683) reg.3 (August 24, 2020).

15. Immigration and Social Security Co-ordination (EU Withdrawal) Act 2020 (Consequential, Saving, Transitional and Transitory Provisions) (EU Exit) Regulations 2020 (SI 2020/1309) reg.55 (December 31, 2020 at 11.00 pm).

GENERAL NOTE

See the commentary to reg.21AA of the IS Regulations and the Immigration (European Economic Area) Regulations 2016. Note, in particular, the difference in wording between reg.21AA(3) and reg.85A(3), the effect of which was that, from April 30, 2006 until new claims for JSA became impossible because of the transition to universal credit, any claimant seeking to establish a right to reside as a workseeker for social security purposes must claim JSA rather than IS if his or her claim is not to be defeated by reg.21AA.

3.279

From April 30, 2006, subparas (a)–(e) of para.(4) applied to nationals of Switzerland as well as to nationals of Iceland, Liechtenstein and Norway—and to members of their families as defined by art.2 of the Rights of Residence Directive—as if those nationals were EU nationals (see reg.10(f) of SI 1026/2006). Paragraph 4 has been amended many times, so that sub-paras (a)–(e) are now sub-paras (za) to (i)—without reg.10 of SI 2006/1026 being changed to refer to the amended law. However, ss.17(2) and 23 of the Interpretation Act 1978 had the effect that reg.10 must be interpreted as referring to para.(4) in its current form.

Applicable amounts for persons in residential care and nursing homes

86.—[¹. . .]

3.280

AMENDMENT

1. Social Security Amendment (Residential Care and Nursing Homes) Regulations 2001 (SI 2001/3767) reg.2 and Sch. Pt II para.7 (April 8, 2002).

[¹Applicable amounts for joint-claim couples

86A.—Except in the case of a joint-claim couple where regulation 86B (polygamous marriages), [²or 86C] (special cases) [². . .] [⁵. . .] applies, the applicable amount of a joint-claim couple who are jointly claiming a jobseeker's allowance shall be the aggregate of such of the following amounts as may apply in their case—

3.281

    (a) an amount in respect of the joint-claim couple determined in accordance with sub-paragraph (3) of paragraph 1 of Schedule 1;

(b) [³. . .]

(c) the amount of any premiums which may be applicable to either or both members of the joint-claim couple, determined in accordance with Parts IVA and IVB of Schedule 1 (premiums); and

(d) any amounts determined in accordance with Schedule 2 (housing costs) which may be applicable to the joint-claim couple in respect of [⁶ housing costs as prescribed] in that Schedule.]

AMENDMENTS

1. Jobseeker's Allowance (Joint Claims) Regulations 2000 (SI 2000/1978) reg.2(5) and Sch.2 para.35 (March 19, 2001).

2. Social Security Amendment (Residential Care and Nursing Homes) Regulations 2001 (SI 2001/3767) reg.2 and Sch. Pt II para.8 (April 8, 2002).

3. Social Security (Removal of Residential Allowance and Miscellaneous Amendments) Regulations 2003 (SI 2003/1121) reg.4 and Sch.2 para.5 (October 6, 2003).

4. Social Security (Hospital In-Patients) Regulations 2005 (SI 2005/3360) reg.6 (April 10, 2006).

5. Social Security (Miscellaneous Amendments) (No.5) Regulations 2009 (SI 2009/3228) reg.3(3)(c) (January 25, 2010).

6. Loans for Mortgage Interest Regulations 2017 (SI 2017/725) reg.18 and Sch.5 para.3(c) (April 6, 2018).

GENERAL NOTE

3.282   This regulation applies to income-based JSA only (see reg.82). It makes provision corresponding to reg.83 for joint-claim couples.

[¹Applicable amounts for joint-claim couples: polygamous marriages

3.283   **86B.**—Except in the case of a joint-claim couple where regulation 86A, [²or 86C] (special cases) [². . .] [⁴. . .] applies, the applicable amount of a joint-claim couple who are jointly claiming a jobseeker's allowance where either or both members of that couple are members of a polygamous marriage, shall be the aggregate of such of the following amounts as may apply in their case—

(a) the highest amount applicable to a member of the joint-claim couple and one other member of that marriage determined in accordance with sub-paragraph (3) of paragraph 1 of Schedule 1 as if those members were a couple;

(b) an amount equal to the difference between the amounts specified in sub-paragraphs (3)(e) and (1)(e) of paragraph 1 of Schedule 1 in respect of each of the other members of the polygamous marriage who are members of that household;

(c) [³ . . .]

(d) the amount of any premiums which may be applicable to a member of the joint-claim couple determined in accordance with Parts IVA and IVB of Schedule 1 (premiums); and

(e) any amounts determined in accordance with Schedule 2 (housing costs) which may be applicable to the joint-claim couple in respect of [⁵ housing costs as prescribed] in that Schedule.]

AMENDMENTS

1. Jobseeker's Allowance (Joint Claims) Regulations 2000 (SI 2000/1978) reg.2(5) and Sch.2 para.35 (March 19, 2001).
2. Social Security Amendment (Residential Care and Nursing Homes) Regulations 2001 (SI 2001/3767) reg.2 and Sch. Pt II para.8 (April 8, 2002).
3. Social Security (Removal of Residential Allowance and Miscellaneous Amendments) Regulations 2003 (SI 2003/1121) reg.4 and Sch.2 para.6 (October 6, 2003).
4. Social Security (Miscellaneous Amendments) (No.5) Regulations 2009 (SI 2009/3228) reg.3(3)(d) (January 25, 2010).
5. Loans for Mortgage Interest Regulations 2017 (SI 2017/725) reg.18 and Sch.5 para.3(d) (April 6, 2018).

GENERAL NOTE

This regulation applies to income-based JSA only (see reg.82). It makes provision corresponding to reg.84 for joint-claim couples.

3.284

[¹Joint-claim couples: special cases

86C.—(1) [²[³Where]] a member of a joint-claim couple is a person to whom any paragraph in column (1) of Schedule 5A applies (applicable amounts in special cases for joint-claim couples), the amount included in the joint-claim couple's weekly applicable amount shall be the amount prescribed in the corresponding paragraph in column (2) of that Schedule.

(2) Except where the amount prescribed in Schedule 5A in respect of a joint-claim couple includes an amount applicable under regulation 86A(c) or 86B(d), a person to whom paragraph (1) applies shall be treated as not falling within the conditions specified in paragraph 20I of Schedule 1 (severe disability premium).

[²(2A) [³. . .]

(3) [⁴ . . .]

(4) Expressions used in this regulation and in Schedule 5A shall have the same meaning as those expressions have for the purposes of regulation 85 and Schedule 5 save that for the purposes of this regulation and of Schedule 5A, the definition of "person from abroad" in regulation 85(4) shall have effect as if after the words "a claimant" there were inserted the words ",other than a member of a joint-claim couple who is not the nominated member for the purposes of section 3B,".]

3.285

AMENDMENTS

1. Jobseeker's Allowance (Joint Claims) Regulations 2000 (SI 2000/1978) reg.2(5) and Sch.2 para.35 (March 19, 2001).
2. Social Security Amendment (Residential Care and Nursing Homes) Regulations 2001 (SI 2001/3767) reg.2 and Sch. Pt II para.9 (April 8, 2002).
3. Social Security (Miscellaneous Amendments) Regulations 2004 (SI 2004/565) reg.6 (April 1, 2004).
4. Social Security (Hospital In-Patients) Regulations 2005 (SI 2005/3360) reg.6 (April 10, 2006).

GENERAL NOTE

This regulation applies to income-based JSA only (see reg.82). It makes provision corresponding to reg.85 for joint-claim couples.

3.286

[¹Applicable amount for a joint-claim couple where a member is in residential care or a nursing home

3.287   **86D.**—[². . .]]

AMENDMENTS

1. Jobseeker's Allowance (Joint Claims) Regulations 2000 (SI 2000/1978) reg.2(5) and Sch.2 para.35 (March 19, 2001).
2. Social Security Amendment (Residential Care and Nursing Homes) Regulations 2001 (SI 2001/3767) reg.2 and Sch. Pt II para.10 (April 8, 2002).

GENERAL NOTE

3.288   This regulation applied to income-based JSA only (see reg.82). It made provision corresponding to reg.86 for joint-claim couples.

Transitional supplement to income-based jobseeker's allowance

3.289   **87.**—(1) In the case of a person who, before 7th October 1996 was entitled to a special transitional addition or transitional addition in accordance with the Income Support (Transitional) Regulations 1987, the amount of any income-based jobseeker's allowance payable to him shall be increased by an amount equal to those additions, but the increase shall continue to be payable only for so long as the claimant continues to satisfy the requirements imposed in those Regulations for payment of the addition.

(2) A claimant's weekly applicable amount shall include an amount (the "protected sum") equal to any protected sum which would have been applicable in his case under regulation 17(1)(g) or 18(1)(h) of, and Schedules 3A and 3B to, the Income Support Regulations had he been entitled to income support and not a jobseeker's allowance.

(3) In the case of any person who had he been entitled to income support and not a jobseeker's allowance, would in any week have had a higher applicable amount, in accordance with regulation 17(2) to (6A) of the Income Support Regulations, than the amount applicable to him in accordance with regulation 82 or, as the case may be, 83 then that amount shall be substituted for the applicable amount determined under that regulation.

(4) [⁴ . . .]

(5) [⁴ . . .]

(6) In determining for the purposes of this regulation whether, if the claimant were entitled to income support—

(a) an amount would be applicable;

(b) an amount would be payable; or

(c) if an amount was payable, the rate at which it would be payable,

any requirement that the person be entitled to income support, or to income support for any period of time, shall be treated as if the reference to income support included also a reference to an income-based jobseeker's allowance.

(7) [²For the purposes of applying paragraph (1), regulation 2A of the Income Support (Transitional) Regulations, and for the purposes of paragraph (6), regulation 3A of the Income Support Regulations shall have effect in accordance with the following sub-paragraphs]—

(a) as if in paragraph (1)(a), after the words "permitted period", there was included the words "subject to paragraph 2A"; and

(b) with the addition after paragraph (1) of the following paragraphs—

"(2A) Subject to paragraph (2B) where the claimant or his partner has ceased to be engaged in remunerative work, the permitted period shall be 8 weeks if—

(a) a jobseeker's allowance [²is not payable] to the claimant in the circumstances mentioned in [³ section 19(2)(a) or (b)] of the Jobseekers Act 1995 (employment left voluntarily or lost through misconduct); or

(b) the claimant or his partner has ceased to be engaged in that work within 4 weeks of beginning it; or

(c) at any time during the period of 13 weeks immediately preceding the beginning of that work, the person who has ceased to be engaged in it—

(i) was engaged in remunerative work; or

(ii) was in relevant education; or

(iii) was a student.

(2B) [¹Paragraph (2A)(b) or (2A)(c)] shall not apply in the case of a person who, by virtue of regulation 74 of the Jobseeker's Allowance Regulations 1996, is a person to whom [³ section 19(2)(b)] of the Jobseekers Act 1995 does not apply.

(2C) In this regulation, 'remunerative work' means remunerative work for the purposes of the Jobseekers Act 1995."

AMENDMENTS

1. Jobseeker's Allowance (Amendment) Regulations 1996 (SI 1996/1516) reg.20 and Sch. (October 7, 1996).

2. Jobseeker's Allowance and Income Support (General) (Amendment) Regulations 1996 (SI 1996/1517) reg.20 (October 7, 1996).

3. Jobseeker's Allowance (Sanctions) (Amendment) Regulations 2012 (SI 2012/2568) reg.5(19) (October 22, 2012).

4. Loans for Mortgage Interest Regulations 2017 (SI 2017/725) reg.18 and Sch.5 para.3(e) (April 6, 2018).

DEFINITIONS

"claimant"—see Jobseekers Act s.35(1).
"Income Support Regulations"—*ibid.*
"remunerative work"—see reg.51(1).

GENERAL NOTE

This provision only applies to income-based JSA (reg.82). 3.290

Paragraphs (2)–(5) preserve the effect of various income support transitional protection provisions for JSA claimants who would have been covered by them had they been entitled to claim income support after October 6, 1996. Paragraph (1) concerns those who were entitled to a special transitional addition or transitional addition under the Income Support (Transitional) Regulations before October 7, 1996. For the regulations referred to in para.(4) see pp.800 and 803. The effect of those Regulations is explained in the notes to para.11((4)–(11) of Sch.3 to the Income Support Regulations.

[¹Minimum amount of a jobseeker's allowance

87A.—Where the amount of a jobseeker's allowance is less than 10 pence a week that allowance shall not be payable.] 3.291

AMENDMENT

1. Jobseeker's Allowance and Income Support (General) (Amendment) Regulations 1996 (SI 1996/1517) reg.21 (October 7, 1996).

PART VIII

INCOME AND CAPITAL

Chapter I

General

Calculation of income and capital of members of claimant's family and of a polygamous marriage

3.292   **88.**—(1) Subject to [³ paragraph] (3) [²and [³regulation] 88ZA (calculation of income and capital of a joint-claim couple)] [³ . . .], the income and capital of a claimant's partner [³. . .] which by virtue of section 13(2) is to be treated as the income and capital of the claimant, shall be calculated in accordance with the following provisions of this Part in like manner as for the claimant; and any reference to the "claimant" shall, except where the context otherwise requires, be construed, for the purposes of this Part, as if it were a reference to his partner [³. . .].

[³(2) Subject to the following provisions of this Part, the income paid to, or in respect of, and capital of, a child or young person who is a member of the claimant's family shall not be treated as the income or capital of the claimant.]

(3) Where at least one member of a couple is aged less than 18 and the applicable amount of the couple falls to be determined under [¹paragraph 1(3)(b), (c), (g) or (h)] of Schedule 1 (applicable amounts), the income of the claimant's partner shall not be treated as the income of the claimant to the extent that—

(a) in the case of a couple where both members are aged less than 18, the amount specified in paragraph 1(3)(a) of that Schedule exceeds the amount specified in paragraph 1(3)(c) of that Schedule; and

(b) in the case of a couple where only one member is aged less than 18, the amount specified in paragraph 1(3)(e) of that Schedule exceeds the amount which applies in that case which is specified in [¹paragraph 1(3)(g) or (h)] of that Schedule.

(4) Subject to paragraph (5), where a claimant is married polygamously to two or more members of his household—

(a) the claimant shall be treated as possessing capital and income belonging to each such member [³. . .]; and

(b) the income and capital of that member [³. . .] shall be calculated in accordance with the following provisions of this Part in like manner as for the claimant [³. . .].

(5) Where a member of a polygamous marriage is a partner aged less than 18 and the amount which applies in respect of him under regulation 84(2)

(polygamous marriages) is nil, the claimant shall not be treated as possessing the income of that partner to the extent that an amount in respect of him would have been included in the applicable amount if he had fallen within the circumstances set out in regulation 84(2)(a) or (b).

AMENDMENTS

1. Jobseeker's Allowance (Amendment) Regulations 1996 (SI 1996/1516) reg.20 and Sch. (October 7, 1996).
2. Jobseeker's Allowance (Joint Claims) Regulations 2000 (SI 2000/1978) reg.2(5) and Sch.2 para.36 (March 19, 2001).
3. Social Security (Working Tax Credit and Child Tax Credit) (Consequential Amendments) Regulations 2003 (SI 2003/455) reg.3 and Sch.2 para.6 (April 6, 2004, except in "transitional cases" and see further the note to reg.83 and to reg.17 of the Income Support Regulations).

DEFINITIONS

"child"—see Jobseekers Act s.35(1).
"claimant"—*ibid.*
"couple"—see reg.1(3).
"family—see Jobseekers Act s.35(1).
"joint-claim couple"—see Jobseekers Act s.1(4).
"partner"—see reg.1(3).
"polygamous marriage"—*ibid.*
"young person"—see reg.76.

GENERAL NOTE

This regulation contains the basic rule on aggregation of resources which is the same as that in reg.23 of the Income Support Regulations. With effect from April 6, 2004 (except in "transitional cases"—see the note to reg. 83 and to reg.17 of the Income Support Regulations), only the income and capital of the claimant's partner is treated as the claimant's.   **3.293**

Under the form of reg.88 in force before April 6, 2004 (the old form continues to apply for "transitional cases"—see the note to reg.83 and to reg.17 of the Income Support Regulations) the income (but not the capital) of a child or young person who was a member of the claimant's family was aggregated with the claimant's (see the 2003 edition of this volume for the old form of reg.88 and the notes to that regulation for further details of the former rules relating to treatment of a child or young person's income and capital). However, with effect from April 6, 2004 (except in "transitional cases") amounts for children and young persons have been removed from income-based JSA; financial assistance to help with the cost of bringing up a child or young person is now to be provided through the child tax credit system, see Vol.IV of this series. As a consequence the new form of para.(2) provides that income paid to, or in respect of, and the capital of, a child or young person does not count as that of the claimant. Note the new disregards of child benefit and child tax credit (see para.6B of Sch.7) (for income-based JSA claimants who had an award of child tax credit before April 6, 2004 see reg.8 of the Social Security (Working Tax Credit and Child Tax Credit) (Consequential Amendments) Regulations 2003 (SI 2003/455) (as amended) on p.1766 and the notes to that regulation).

See further the notes to reg.23 of the Income Support Regulations.

[¹ Calculation of income and capital of a joint-claim couple

88ZA.—(1) Subject to paragraphs (2) and (4), the income and capital of a joint-claim couple shall be calculated by—   **3.294**

(a) determining the income and capital of each member of that couple in accordance with this Part; and

(b) aggregating the amount determined in respect of each member in accordance with sub-paragraph (a) above.

(2) Where—

(a) a member of a joint-claim couple is aged less than 18;

(b) the other member is aged over 18; and

(c) the applicable amount of the couple falls to be determined under paragraph 1(3)(g) or (h) of Schedule 1 (applicable amounts),

the income of the joint-claim couple shall not be aggregated to the extent that the amount specified in paragraph 1(3)(e) of that Schedule exceeds the amount which applies in that case which is specified in paragraph 1(3)(g) or (h) of that Schedule.

(3) Where a member of a joint-claim couple is married polygamously to two or more members of his household, the joint-claim couple shall be treated as possessing income and capital belonging to each such member and the income and capital of that member shall be calculated in accordance with the following provisions of this Part in like manner as for each member of the joint-claim couple.

(4) Regulations 99(2) and 101(2) in so far as they relate to paragraphs 5,7, 8 and 11 of Schedule 6 (earnings to be disregarded) shall not apply to a member of a joint-claim couple but there shall instead be disregarded from the net earnings of a member of a joint-claim couple any sum, where applicable, specified in—

(a) paragraphs 1 to 4 and 13 to 16 of Schedule 6; and

(b) paragraphs 1 to 6 of Schedule 6A.]

AMENDMENT

1. Jobseeker's Allowance (Joint Claims) Regulations 2000 (SI 2000/1978) reg.2(5) and Sch.2, para.37 (March 19, 2001).

DEFINITIONS

"joint-claim couple"—see JSA s.1(4).
"polygamous marriage"—see reg.1(3).

[¹ Income of participants in the self-employment route [². . .]

3.295   **88A.**—Chapters II, III, IV, V, VII and VIII of this Part and regulations 131 to 136, 138 and 139 shall not apply to any income which is to be calculated in accordance with Chapter IVA of this Part (participants in the self-employment route [². . .]).]

AMENDMENTS

1. Social Security (Miscellaneous Amendments) (No.4) Regulations 1998 (SI 1998/1174) reg.3(3) (June 1, 1998).
2. Social Security Amendment (Employment Zones) (No.2) Regulations 2000 (SI 2000/2910) reg.5(2)(a) (November 27, 2000).

DEFINITION

"self-employment route"—see reg.1(3).

Regulation 88A takes any gross receipts from trading while on the self-employment   **3.296**
route (defined in reg.1(3)) out of the categories of earnings, self-employed earnings
and income other than earnings. The rules for liable relative payments and student
income (except reg.137) also do not apply. Any such receipts may only be taken into
account in accordance with regs 102A–102D.

[²[⁴. . .]] liable relative payments

89.—Regulations 94 to [¹ 105], 108 to 115 and Chapter IX of this Part   **3.297**
shall not apply to any payment which is to be calculated in accordance with
Chapter VII thereof ([³ [⁵ . . .] liable relative payments]).

AMENDMENTS

1. Social Security (Working Tax Credit and Child Tax Credit) (Consequential
Amendments) Regulations 2003 (SI 2003/455) reg.3 and Sch.2 para.7 (April 6,
2004, except in "transitional cases" and see further the note to reg.83 and to reg.17
of the Income Support Regulations).
2. Social Security (Child Maintenance Amendments) Regulations 2008 (SI
2008/2111) reg.3(2) (October 27, 2008).
3. Social Security (Child Maintenance Amendments) Regulations 2008 (SI
2008/2111) reg.3(3) (October 27, 2008).
4. Social Security (Miscellaneous Amendments) (No.4) Regulations 2009 (SI
2009/2655) reg.4(4) (April 12, 2010).
5. Social Security (Miscellaneous Amendments) (No.4) Regulations 2009 (SI
2009/2655) reg.4(5) (April 12, 2010).

GENERAL NOTE

See reg.25 of the Income Support Regulations.   **3.298**

Child support

90.—[¹ . . .]   **3.299**

AMENDMENT

1. Social Security (Child Maintenance Amendments) Regulations 2008 (SI
2008/2111) reg.3(4)(a) (October 27, 2008).

Calculation of income and capital of full-time students

91.—The provisions of Chapters II to VI of this Part (income and   **3.300**
capital) shall have effect in relation to full-time students and their partners subject to the modifications set out in Chapter IX thereof (full-time
students).

DEFINITIONS

"full-time student"—see reg.1(3).
"partner"—*ibid.*

GENERAL NOTE

See reg.26 of the Income Support Regulations.   **3.301**

Rounding of fractions

3.302   **92.**—Where any calculation under this Part results in a fraction of a penny that fraction shall, if it would be to the claimant's advantage, be treated as a penny, otherwise it shall be disregarded.

CHAPTER II

INCOME

Calculation of income

3.303   **93.**—(1) For the purposes of [¹sections 3(1) (the income-based conditions) and 3A(1) (the conditions for claims by joint-claim couples)] (the income-based conditions) the income of a claimant shall be calculated on a weekly basis—

(a) by determining in accordance with this Part, other than Chapter VI, the weekly amount of his income; and

(b) by adding to that amount the weekly income calculated under regulation 116 (calculation of tariff income from capital).

(2) For the purposes of paragraph (1) "income" includes capital treated as income under regulation 104 and income which a claimant is treated as possessing under regulation 105 (notional income).

AMENDMENT

1. Jobseeker's Allowance (Joint Claims) Regulations 2000 (SI 2000/1978) reg.2(5) and Sch.2 para.38 (March 19, 2001).

DEFINITIONS

"claimant"—see Jobseekers Act 1995 s.35(1).
"joint-claim couple"—see Jobseekers Act 1995 s.1(4).

GENERAL NOTE

3.304   This confirms that for the purposes of income-based JSA all resources which come under the description of income, including resources specifically treated as earnings or income, are to be taken into account in the income calculation.

Calculation of earnings derived from employed earner's employment and income other than earnings

3.305   **94.**—(1) Earnings derived from employment as an employed earner and income which does not consist of earnings shall be taken into account over a period determined in accordance with the following paragraphs and at a weekly amount determined in accordance with regulation 97 (calculation of weekly amount of income).

(2) Subject to the following provisions of this regulation, the period over which a payment is to be taken into account shall be—

[⁶ (a) where the payment is monthly, a period equal to the number of weeks from the date on which the payment is treated as paid to the date immediately before the date on which the next monthly payment would have been so treated as paid whether or not the next monthly payment is actually paid;

(aa) where the payment is in respect of a period which is not monthly, a period equal to the length of the period for which payment is made;]

[⁹(b) in any other case, a period equal to such number of weeks as is equal to the number obtained by applying the formula—

$$\frac{E}{J+D}$$

where—

E is the amount of net earnings, or in the case of income which does not consist of earnings, the amount of that income less any amount paid by way of tax on that income which is disregarded under paragraph 1 of Schedule 7 (sums to be disregarded in the calculation of income other than earnings);

J is the amount of jobseeker's allowance which would be payable had the payment not been made;

D is an amount equal to the total of the sums which would fall to be disregarded from that payment under Schedule 6 and Schedule 6A (sums to be disregarded in the calculation of earnings) or, as the case may be, any paragraph of Schedule 7 other than paragraph 1 of that Schedule, as is appropriate in the claimant's case,]

and that period shall begin on the date on which the payment is treated as paid under regulation 96.

[¹(2A) The period over which a Career Development Loan, which is paid pursuant to section 2 of the Employment and Training Act 1973, shall be taken into account shall be the period of education and training intended to be supported by that loan.

(2B) Where grant income as defined in Chapter IX of this Part has been paid to a person who ceases to be a full-time student before the end of the period in respect of which that income is payable and, as a consequence, the whole or part of that income falls to be repaid by that person, that income shall be taken into account over the period beginning on the date on which that income is treated as paid under regulation 96 and ending—

(a) on the date on which repayment is made in full; or

[²(aa) where the grant is paid in instalments, on the day before the next instalment would have been paid had the claimant remained a student; or]

(b) on the last date of the academic term or vacation during which that person ceased to be a full-time student

whichever shall first occur.]

[⁷ [¹⁰(2C)(a) This paragraph applies where earnings are derived by a claimant as a member of a reserve force prescribed in Part 1 of Schedule 6 to the Contributions Regulations—

(i) in respect of a period of annual continuous training for a maximum of 15 days in any calendar year; or

(ii) in respect of training in the claimant's first year of training as a member of a reserve force for a maximum of 43 days in that year.

987

(b) Earnings, whether paid to the claimant alone or together with other earnings derived from the same source, are to be taken into account—

  (i) in the case of a period of training which lasts for the number of days listed in column 1 of the table in sub-paragraph (c), over a period of time which is equal to the number of days set out in the corresponding row in column 2 of that table; or

  (ii) in any other case, over a period of time which is equal to the number of days of the training period.

(c) This is the table referred to in sub-paragraph (b)(i)—

Column 1 Period of training in days	Column 2 Period of time over which earnings are to be taken into account in days
8 to 10	7
15 to 17	14
22 to 24	21
29 to 31	28
36 to 38	35
43	42]

(2D) The period referred to in paragraph (2C) over which earnings are to be taken into account shall begin on the date on which they are treated as paid under regulation 96.]

(3) Where earnings not of the same kind are derived from the same source and the periods in respect of which those earnings would, but for this paragraph, fall to be taken into account—

(a) overlap, wholly or partly, those earnings shall be taken into account over a period equal to the aggregate length of those periods;

(b) and that period shall begin with the earliest date on which any part of those earnings would otherwise be treated as paid under regulation 96 (date on which income is treated as paid).

(4) In a case to which paragraph (3) applies, earnings under regulation 98 (earnings of employed earners) shall be taken into account in the following order of priority—

(a) earnings normally derived from the employment;

(b) any compensation payment;

(c) any holiday pay.

(5) Where earnings to which regulation 98(1)(b) or (c) (earnings of employed earners) applies are paid in respect of part of a day, those earnings shall be taken into account over a period equal to a day.

(6) Subject to paragraph (7), the period over which a compensation payment is to be taken into account shall be the period beginning on the date on which the payment is treated as paid under regulation 96 (date on which income is treated as paid) and ending—

(a) subject to sub-paragraph (b), where the person who made the payment represents that it, or part of it, was paid in lieu of notice of termination of employment or on account of the early termination of a contract of employment for a term certain, on the expiry date;

(b) in a case where the person who made the payment represents that it, or part of it, was paid in lieu of consultation under section 188 of the

Trade Union and Labour Relations (Consolidation) Act 1992, on the later of—

    (i) the date on which the consultation period under that section would have ended;

    (ii) in a case where sub-paragraph (a) also applies, the expiry date; or

    (iii) the standard date;

(c) in any other case, on the standard date.

(7) The maximum length of time over which a compensation payment may be taken into account under paragraph (6) is 52 weeks from the date on which the payment is treated as paid under regulation 96.

(8) In this regulation—

(a) "compensation payment" means any payment to which paragraph (3) of regulation 98 (earnings of employed earners) applies;

(b) "the expiry date" means in relation to the termination of a person's employment—

    (i) the date on which the period of notice applicable to the person was due to expire, or would have expired had it not been waived; and for this purpose "period of notice" means the period of notice of termination of employment to which a person is entitled by statute or by contract, whichever is the longer, or, if he is not entitled to such notice, the period of notice which is customary in the employment in question; or

    (ii) subject to paragraph (9), where the person who made the payment represents that the period in respect of which that payment is made is longer than the period of notice referred to in head (i) above, the date on which that longer period is due to expire; or

    (iii) where the person had a contract of employment for a term certain, the date on which it was due to expire;

(c) "the standard date" means the earlier of—

    (i) the expiry date; and

    (ii) the last day of the period determined by dividing the amount of the compensation payment by the maximum weekly amount which, on the date on which the payment is treated as paid under regulation 96, is specified in [⁵ section 227(1) of the Employment Rights Act 1996], and treating the result (less any fraction of a whole number) as a number of weeks.

(9) For the purposes of paragraph (8), if it appears to [³the Secretary of State] in a case to which sub-paragraph (b)(ii) of that paragraph applies that, having regard to the amount of the compensation payment and the level of remuneration normally received by the claimant when he was engaged in the employment in respect of which the compensation payment was made, it is unreasonable to take the payment into account until the date specified in that sub-paragraph, the expiry date shall be the date specified in paragraph (8)(b)(i).

(10) For the purposes of this regulation the claimant's earnings and income which does not consist of earnings shall be calculated in accordance with Chapters III and V respectively of this Part.

[⁹(11) For the purposes of the number obtained as referred to in paragraph (2)(b), any fraction is to be treated as a corresponding fraction of a week.]

AMENDMENTS

1. Income-related Benefits and Jobseeker's Allowance (Miscellaneous Amendments) Regulations 1997 (SI 1997/65) reg.5(2) (April 7, 1997).

2. Social Security (Miscellaneous Amendments) Regulations 1998 (SI 1998/563) reg.12 (April 6, 1998).

3. Social Security Act 1998 (Commencement No.11, and Savings and Consequential and Transitional Provisions) Order 1999 (SI 1999/2860 (C.75)) art.3(12) and Sch.12 para.2 (October 18, 1999).

4. Jobseeker's Allowance (Joint Claims) Regulations 2000 (SI 2000/1978) reg.2(5) and Sch.2 para.39 (March 19, 2001).

5. Social Security (Miscellaneous Amendments) (No.5) Regulations 2007 (SI 2007/2618) reg.8(7) (October 1, 2007).

6. Social Security (Miscellaneous Amendments) Regulations 2008 (SI 2008/698) reg.4(10) (April 14, 2008).

7. Jobseeker's Allowance (Members of the Reserve Forces) Regulations 2012 (SI 2012/1616) reg.2(6) (July 30, 2012).

8. Social Security (Miscellaneous Amendments) (No.2) Regulations 2012 (SI 2012/2575) reg.3(5) (November 5, 2012).

9. Social Security (Miscellaneous Amendments) (No.3) Regulations 2013 (SI 2013/2536) reg.6(9) (October 29, 2013).

10. Social Security (Members of the Reserve Forces) (Amendment) Regulations 2015 (SI 2015/389) reg.3(5) (April 6, 2015).

DEFINITIONS

"claimant"—*ibid.*, reg.88(1)
"earnings"—see reg.1(3).
"employed earner"—see reg.3 and SSCBA s.2(1)(a).
"first year of training"—see reg.1(3).
"full-time student"—see reg.1(3).
"grant income"—see reg.130.

GENERAL NOTE

3.306   On paras (1)–(5) see the notes to reg.29(1)–(4A) of the Income Support Regulations. In relation to paras (2C) and (2D) note the disregard in para.19 of Sch.6. Claimants are treated as available for employment while engaged in such reservist training (see reg.14(1)(v)) and as actively seeking employment in any week in which they are taking part in such training for three or more days a week (see reg.19(1)(y)).

Paragraphs (3) and (4) will be of less relevance following the increased disregard of payments made on the termination of full-time employment introduced on October 1, 2007 (see para.1 of Sch.6 and the notes to that paragraph). However they will still apply where part-time work ends while the claimant is claiming old style JSA, or where full-time employment has been suspended.

Note that para.(2)(b) was rewritten and a new para.(11) was added on October 29, 2013 so as to match the equivalent provisions for new style JSA (see reg.54(2)(c) and (13) of the JSA Regulations 2013 in Vol.I of this series) but the substance remains the same.

Paragraphs (6)–(9)

3.307   These provisions define the length of the period for which a "compensation payment" (defined in reg.98(3)) is to be taken into account. Note that from October 1, 2007 such compensation payments are ignored except in the case of part-time work which ends while the person is claiming old style JSA (paras 1–3 of Sch.6). There is no equivalent to reg.29(4C) of the Income Support Regulations so it seems that a compensation payment made on the termination of such part-time employment will be taken into account as earnings for the period covered by the payment. The "maximum weekly amount" referred to in para.(8)(c)(ii) is the amount specified at the relevant time as the amount to be used in calculating the basic award for unfair dismissal and redundancy payments. The figure in effect from April 6, 2021 is £544.

Note *CJSA 5529/1997* in which the effect of para.(6) was that the period to which the claimant's compensation payment was to be attributed ended before it started. On October 1, 1996 the claimant agreed with her employer that her employment would end on December 31, 1996 by way of voluntary redundancy. She was to receive a payment of £41,500 on January 4, 1997, which would not include any sum in lieu of notice. She claimed JSA with effect from January 1, 1997. The Commissioner states that the period for which the compensation period was to be taken into account under para.(6) ended on the "standard date". Under para.(8)(c) the standard date was the earlier of the "expiry date" and what might be termed the "apportionment date". The expiry date in this case was no later than December 31, 1996 because the claimant was entitled to 12 weeks' (or three months') notice and the agreement for redundancy had been made on October 1, 1996 (see para.(8)(b)(i)). The result was that there was no period in respect of which the compensation payment was to be taken into account and thus no period during which she was to be treated as in remunerative work after December 31, 1996.

Calculation of earnings of self-employed earners

95.—(1) Except where paragraph (2) applies, where a claimant's income consists of earnings from employment as a self-employed earner the weekly amount of his earnings shall be determined by reference to his average weekly earnings from that employment— 3.308

(a) over a period of one year; or

(b) where the claimant has recently become engaged in that employment or there has been a change which is likely to affect the normal pattern of business, over such other period as may, in any particular case, enable the weekly amount of his earnings to be determined more accurately.

(2) Where the claimant's earnings consist of [2 any items to which paragraph (2A) applies] those earnings shall be taken into account over a period equal to such number of weeks as is equal to the number obtained (and any fraction shall be treated as a corresponding fraction of a week) by dividing the earnings by the amount of jobseeker's allowance which would be payable had the payment not been made plus an amount equal to the total of the sums which would fall to be disregarded from the payment under Schedule 6 [1 and Schedule 6A] (earnings to be disregarded) as is appropriate in the claimant's case.

[2 [3 (2A) This paragraph applies to—

(a) royalties or other sums paid as a consideration for the use of, or the right to use, any copyright, design, patent or trade mark; or

(b) any payment in respect of any—

(i) book registered under the Public Lending Right Scheme 1982; or

(ii) work made under any international public lending right scheme that is analogous to the Public Lending Right Scheme 1982,

where the claimant is the first owner of the copyright, design, patent or trade mark, or an original contributor to the book or work concerned.]]

(3) For the purposes of this regulation the claimant's earnings shall be calculated in accordance with Chapter IV of this Part.

AMENDMENTS

1. Jobseeker's Allowance (Joint Claims) Regulations 2000 (SI 2000/1978) reg.2(5) and Sch.2 para.40 (March 19, 2001).
2. Social Security (Miscellaneous Amendments) Regulations 2008 (SI 2008/698) reg,.4(11) (April 7, 2008).
3. Social Security (Miscellaneous Amendments) Regulations 2009 (SI 2009/583) reg.4(6) (April 6, 2009).

DEFINITIONS

"claimant"—see Jobseekers Act s.35(1) and reg.88(1).
"earnings"—see reg.1(3).
"self-employed earner"—*ibid.*, SSCBA s.2(1)(b).

GENERAL NOTE

3.309   See the notes to reg.30 of the Income Support Regulations, including on the proper treatment of payments under Coronavirus Self-Employed Income Support Scheme.

Note the more general exception to the rule in para.(1)(a) that is hidden in reg.101(11) which allows the amount of any item of income or expenditure to be calculated over a different period if that will produce a more accurate figure.

Date on which income is treated as paid

3.310   **96.**—(1) Except where paragraph [⁵ [(2) [⁶ applies]], a payment of income to which regulation 94 (calculation of earnings derived from employed earner's employment and income other than earnings) applies shall be treated as paid—

(a) in the case of a payment which is due to be paid before the first benefit week pursuant to the claim, on the date on which it is due to be paid;

(b) in any other case, on the first day of the benefit week in which it is due to be paid or the first succeeding benefit week in which it is practicable to take it into account.

(2) Income support, maternity allowance, short-term or long-term incapacity benefit, severe disablement allowance [⁴ , jobseeker's allowance [⁷, employment and support allowance or universal credit]] shall be treated as paid [⁷ on any day] in respect of which it is payable.

[³ (3) [⁶ . . .]]
[⁵ (4) [⁶ . . .]]

AMENDMENTS

1. Social Security (Miscellaneous Amendments) Regulations 2000 (SI 2000/681) reg.3(2) (April 3, 2000).
2. Income-related Benefits and Jobseeker's Allowance (Working Tax Credit and Child Tax Credit) (Amendment) Regulations 2002 (SI 2002/2402) reg.3 and Sch.2 para.4 (April 6, 2003).
3. Social Security (Working Tax Credit and Child Tax Credit) (Consequential Amendments) (No.3) Regulations 2003 (SI 2003/1731) reg.4 (August 8, 2003).
4. Employment and Support Allowance (Consequential Provisions) (No.2) Regulations 2008 (SI 2008/1554) reg.3(14) (October 27, 2008).

5. Social Security (Miscellaneous Amendments) (No.6) Regulations 2008 (SI 2008/2767) reg.4(4) (November 17, 2008).

6. Social Security (Miscellaneous Amendments) Regulations 2011 (SI 2011/674) reg.7(3) (April 11, 2011).

7. Universal Credit (Consequential, Supplementary, Incidental and Miscellaneous Provisions) Regulations 2013 (SI 2013/630) reg.30(4) (April 29, 2013).

DEFINITIONS

"benefit week"—see reg.1(3).
"child tax credit"—*ibid.*
"universal credit"—*ibid.*
"working tax credit"—*ibid.*

GENERAL NOTE

See the notes to reg.31 of the Income Support Regulations.   3.311

Calculation of weekly amount of income

97.—(1) For the purposes of regulation 94 (calculation of earnings   3.312
derived from employed earner's employment and income other than earnings) [⁴[⁵ . . .]], subject to paragraphs (2) to [²(7)], where the period in
respect of which a payment [⁴ of income or tax credit] is made—
  (a) does not exceed a week, the weekly amount shall be the amount of
      that payment;
  (b) exceeds a week, the weekly amount shall be determined—
        (i) in a case where that period is a month, by multiplying the
            amount of the payment by 12 and dividing the product by 52;
       (ii) in a case where that period is three months, by multiplying the
            amount of the payment by 4 and dividing the product by 52;
  [⁴ (iii) in a case where that period is a year and the payment is an award
            of working tax credit, by dividing the payment by the number of
            days in the year and multiplying the result by 7;
     (iiia) in a case where that period is a year and the payment is income
            other than an award of working tax credit, by dividing the
            amount of the payment by 52;]
       (iv) in any other case by multiplying the amount of the payment by
            7 and dividing the product by the number equal to the number
            of days in the period in respect of which it is made.
  (2) Where a payment for a period not exceeding a week is treated under
regulation 96(1)(a) (date on which income is treated as paid) as paid before
the first benefit week and a part is to be taken into account for some days only
in that week ("the relevant days"), the amount to be taken into account for the
relevant days shall be calculated by multiplying the amount of the payment by
the number equal to the number of relevant days and dividing the product by
the number of days in the period in respect of which it is made.
  (3) Where a payment is in respect of a period equal to or in excess of a
week and a part thereof is to be taken into account for some days only in a
benefit week ("the relevant days"), the amount to be taken into account for
the relevant days shall, except where paragraph (4) applies, be calculated by
multiplying the amount of the payment by the number equal to the number
of relevant days and dividing the product by the number of days in the
period in respect of which it is made.

(4) In the case of a payment of—

(a) maternity allowance, short-term or long-term incapacity benefit or severe disablement allowance, the amount to be taken into account for the relevant days shall be the amount of benefit payable in respect of those days;

(b) jobseeker's allowance[³, income support or employment and support allowance], the amount to be taken into account for the relevant days shall be calculated by multiplying the weekly amount of the benefit by the number of relevant days and dividing the product by seven.

(5) Except in the case of a payment which it has not been practicable to treat under regulation 96(1)(b) as paid on the first day of the benefit week in which it is due to be paid, where a payment of income from a particular source is or has been paid regularly and that payment falls to be taken into account in the same benefit week as a payment of the same kind and from the same source, the amount of that income to be taken into account in any one benefit week shall not exceed the weekly amount determined under paragraph (1)(a) or (b), as the case may be, of the payment which under regulation 96(1)(b) (date on which income is treated as paid) is treated as paid first.

(6) Where the amount of the claimant's income fluctuates and has changed more than once, or a claimant's regular pattern of work is such that he does not work every week, the foregoing paragraphs may be modified so that the weekly amount of his income is determined by reference to his average weekly income—

(a) if there is a recognisable cycle of work, over a period of one complete cycle (including, where the cycle involves periods in which the claimant does no work, those periods but disregarding any other absences);

(b) in any other case, over a period of five weeks or such other period as may, in the particular case, enable the claimant's average weekly income to be determined more accurately.

[¹(7) Where income is taken into account under paragraph (2B) of regulation 94 over the period specified in that paragraph, the amount of that income to be taken into account in respect of any week in that period shall be an amount equal to the amount of that income which would have been taken into account under regulation 131 had the person to whom that income was paid not ceased to be a full-time student.]

AMENDMENTS

1. Income-related Benefits and Jobseeker's Allowance (Miscellaneous Amendments) Regulations 1997 (SI 1997/65) reg.6(2) (April 7, 1997).

2. Social Security (Miscellaneous Amendments) Regulations 1997 (SI 1997/454) reg.2(11) (April 7, 1997).

3. Employment and Support Allowance (Consequential Provisions) (No.2) Regulations 2008 (SI 2008/1554) reg.3(15) (October 27, 2008).

4. Social Security (Miscellaneous Amendments) (No.6) Regulations 2008 (SI 2008/2767) reg.4(5) (November 17, 2008).

5. Social Security (Miscellaneous Amendments) Regulations 2011 (SI 2011/674) reg.7(4) (April 11, 2011).

DEFINITIONS

"benefit week"—see reg.1(3).
"claimant"—see Jobseekers Act s.35(1) and reg.88(1).
"full-time student"—see reg.1(3).

See the notes to reg.32 of the Income Support Regulations. In relation to para.   **3.313**
(5), the old style JSA disregards corresponding to the income support disregards
referred to in those notes are in Sch.6 para.13, Sch.7 para.39, Sch.6 para.16 and
Sch.7 para.37.

Note that there is no equivalent of reg.32(7) as the JSA rules for the treatment
of compensation payments made on the termination of part-time employment are
different from those under the income support scheme (see reg.98(1)(b) and (3)
and the note to reg.94(6)–(9)).

On calculation of entitlement to income-based JSA for part-weeks, see reg.150.

Chapter III

Employed Earners

Earnings of employed earners

98.—(1) Subject to paragraphs (2) and (3), "earnings" means in the case   **3.314**
of employment as an employed earner, any remuneration or profit derived
from that employment and includes—

(a) any bonus or commission;

(b) any compensation payment;

(c) any holiday pay except any payable more than four weeks after the
termination or interruption of employment but this exception shall
not apply to a person who is, or would be, prevented from being
entitled to a jobseeker's allowance by section 14 (trade disputes);

(d) any payment by way of a retainer;

(e) any payment made by the claimant's employer in respect of expenses
not wholly, exclusively and necessarily incurred in the performance
of the duties of the employment, including any payment made by the
claimant's employer in respect of—

   (i) travelling expenses incurred by the claimant between his home
   and place of employment;

   (ii) expenses incurred by the claimant under arrangements made
   for the care of a member of his family owing to the claimant's
   absence from home;

[¹(f) any payment or award of compensation made under section [⁶
112(4), 113, 117(3)(a), 128, [⁸131 or 132] of the Employment
Rights Act 1996 (the remedies: orders and compensation, the
orders, enforcement of order and compensation, interim relief)];

(ff) any payment or remuneration made under section [⁶ 28, 34, 64,
68 or 70 of the Employment Rights Act 1996 (right to guarantee
payments, remuneration on suspension on medical or maternity
grounds, complaints to employment tribunals)]:]

(g) any award of compensation made under section 156, [⁶ . . .] 161 to
166, 189 or 192 of the Trade Union and Labour Relations (Consolidation) Act 1992 (compensation for unfair dismissal or redundancy
on grounds of involvement in trade union activities, and protective
awards).

[³(h) the amount of any payment by way of a non-cash voucher which has
been taken into account in the computation of a person's earnings

in accordance with [⁵ Part 5 of Schedule 3 to the Social Security (Contributions) Regulations 2001].]

(2) "Earnings" shall not include—

(a) [³ Subject to paragraph (2A),] any payment in kind;

(b) any periodic sum paid to a claimant on account of the termination of his employment by reason of redundancy;

(c) any remuneration paid by or on behalf of an employer to the claimant in respect of a period throughout which the claimant is on maternity leave[⁴, paternity leave, adoption leave][¹⁰, shared parental leave][¹¹, parental bereavement leave] or is absent from work because he is ill;

(d) any payment in respect of expenses wholly, exclusively and necessarily incurred in the performance of the duties of the employment;

(e) any occupational pension;

(f) any redundancy payment within the meaning of [⁶ section 135(1) of the Employment Rights Act 1996];

[²(g) any lump sum payment made under the Iron and Steel Re-adaptation Benefits Scheme].

[⁷ (h) any payment in respect of expenses arising out of the [⁹ claimant participating as a service user].]

[³(2A) Paragraph (2)(a) shall not apply in respect of any non-cash voucher referred to in paragraph (1)(h).]

(3) In this regulation "compensation payment" means any payment made in respect of the termination of employment other than—

(a) any remuneration or emolument (whether in money or in kind) which accrued in the period before the termination;

(b) any holiday pay;

(c) any payment specified in paragraphs (1)(f)[,¹(ff),] or (g) or (2);

(d) any refund of contributions to which that person was entitled under an occupational pension scheme.

AMENDMENTS

1. Jobseeker's Allowance and Income Support (General) (Amendment) Regulations 1996 (SI 1996/1517) reg.22 (October 7, 1996).

2. Social Security (Miscellaneous Amendments) Regulations 1997 (SI 1997/454) reg.2(12) (April 7, 1997).

3. Social Security Amendment (Non-Cash Vouchers) Regulations 1999 (SI 1999/1509) reg.2(6) (July 1, 1999).

4. Social Security (Paternity and Adoption) Amendment Regulations 2002 (SI 2002/2689) reg.3(5) (December 8, 2002).

5. Social Security (Miscellaneous Amendments) (No.4) Regulations 2006 (SI 2006/2378) reg.13(5) (October 2, 2006).

6. Social Security (Miscellaneous Amendments) (No.5) Regulations 2007 (SI 2007/2618) reg.8(8) (October 1, 2007).

7. Social Security (Miscellaneous Amendments) (No.4) Regulations 2009 (SI 2009/2655) reg.4(6) (October 26, 2009).

8. Social Security (Miscellaneous Amendments) (No.3) Regulations 2013 (SI 2013/2536) reg.6(10) (October 29, 2013).

9. Social Security (Miscellaneous Amendments) Regulations 2014 (SI 2014/591) reg.4(3) (April 28, 2014).

10. Shared Parental Leave and Statutory Shared Parental Pay (Consequential Amendments to Subordinate Legislation) Order 2014 (SI 2014/3255) art.7(5) (December 31, 2014).

11. Parental Bereavement Leave and Pay (Consequential Amendments to Subordinate Legislation) Regulations 2020 (SI 2020/354) reg.8(5) (April 6, 2020).

DEFINITIONS

"adoption leave"—see reg.1(3).
"claimant"—see Jobseekers Act s.35(1) and reg.88(1).
"claimant participating as a service user"—see reg.1(3G).
"employed earner"—see reg.3 and SSCBA s.2(1)(a).
"family"—see Jobseekers Act, s.35(1).
"maternity leave"—see reg.1(3).
"occupational pension"—*ibid.*
"parental bereavement leave"—*ibid.*
"paternity leave"—*ibid.*
"shared parental leave"—*ibid.*

GENERAL NOTE

Regulation 98 applies to earnings from employment as an employed earner. It is   **3.315**
similar to reg.35 of the Income Support Regulations but there are some differences
which are referred to below. Otherwise see the notes to reg.35.

Like reg.35(1), para.(1) first provides a general definition of earnings from
employment as an employee—any remuneration or profit derived from that employment—and then deems certain payments to be earnings. Paragraph (2) provides a
number of exceptions and Sch.6 lists items which would otherwise count as earnings which are to be disregarded.

See in particular paras 1–3 of Sch.6 which concern the earnings that are ignored
on the termination of employment or where hours of work are reduced (possibly to
nil). The disregard that applies to payments made on the termination of full-time
employment (i.e. 16 hours or more per week in the case of the claimant, 24 hours or
more per week for a partner) was significantly extended with effect from October 1,
2007. See the new form of para.1 of Sch.6 and the notes to that paragraph.

Paragraph (1)

Note that the particular categories that are deemed to be earnings are the same   **3.316**
as for income support, except that there is no equivalent of reg.35(1)(b), (c) and
(i); instead sub-para.(b) refers to "any compensation payment" (defined in para.
(3)). In addition, sub-paras (f), (ff) and (g) slightly expand on the list of awards of
compensation or pay made by an employment tribunal and other payments under
the employment protection legislation that are specifically deemed to count as earnings (compare reg.35(1)(g), (gg) and (h)). Holiday pay outside the period in sub-
para.(c) is capital (reg.110(3)).

See the notes to reg.35(1) for further discussion.

Paragraph (2)

Sub-paragraphs (b) and (f) contain two additions to the list of payments that   **3.317**
do not count as earnings, which otherwise are the same as for income support.
Sub-paragraph (b) in fact contains the same provision that in the Income Support
Regulations is expressed as an exception to reg.35(1)(b). But by placing it in the
para.(2) list the old style JSA rules make it clear that such periodic redundancy
payments, although not earnings, will count as income (see below). Sub-paragraph
(f) expressly states that redundancy payments "within the meaning of s.135(1) of
the Employment Rights Act 1996" are not earnings, nor are lump sum payments
under the Iron and Steel Re-adaptation Benefits Scheme (sub-para.(g)). On the
meaning of redundancy payment under sub-para.(f) see *CJSA 82/1998* in the notes
to reg.35(1) of the Income Support Regulations.

Note that although the payments listed in para.(2)(a)–(e) are deemed not to be
earnings they do count as other income (reg.103(6)). However, income in kind is disregarded (Sch.7 para.22) and so are payments of necessary expenses (Sch.7 para.3).
Payment of expenses that result from a "claimant participating as a service user" (sub-
para.(h)—see reg.1(3G) for those to whom this refers) are also ignored (para.2A of

Sch.7). Under sub-paras (f) and (g) redundancy payments and lump sum payments under the Iron and Steel Re-adaptation Benefits Scheme will count as capital.

See the notes to reg.35(2) for further discussion.

Paragraph (3)

3.318
This provision is different from reg.35(1)(i) and (3) of the Income Support Regulations but is based on the previous unemployment benefit rule. It provides a broad definition of a "compensation payment" as "any payment made in respect of the termination of employment" but then lists those payments which are not to count as compensation payments.

If a payment is a compensation payment it counts as earnings under para.(1)(b). However from October 1, 2007 such earnings are disregarded (except in the case of part-time work which ends while the person is claiming old style JSA: see paras 1–2 of Sch.6 and the notes to those paragraphs). The consequence of the different definition of compensation payment for old style JSA is that contractual redundancy payments, ex gratia payments and other kinds of compensation (other than employment tribunal awards and "out of court" settlements) are ignored (for income support they count as capital).

Calculation of net earnings of employed earners

3.319
99.—(1) For the purposes of regulation 94 (calculation of earnings of employed earners) the earnings of a claimant derived from employment as an employed earner to be taken into account shall, subject to paragraph (2), be his net earnings.

(2) Subject to paragraph (3), there shall be disregarded from a claimant's net earnings, any sum, where applicable, specified in paragraphs 1 to 16 and 19 of Schedule 6.

(3) For the purposes of calculating the amount to be deducted in respect of earnings under regulation 80 (contribution-based jobseeker's allowance: deductions in respect of earnings) the disregards specified in paragraphs 5 to 8 and 11 of Schedule 6 shall not apply.

(4) For the purposes of paragraph (1) net earnings shall be calculated by taking into account the gross earnings of the claimant from that employment less—

    (a) any amount deducted from those earnings by way of—

        (i) income tax;

        (ii) primary Class 1 contributions payable under the Benefits Act; and

    (b) one-half of any sum paid by the claimant in respect of a pay period by way of a contribution towards an occupational or personal pension scheme.

DEFINITIONS

    "the Benefits Act"—see Jobseekers Act s.35(1).
    "claimant"—*ibid.*, reg.88(1).
    "employed earner"—see reg.3 and SSCBA s.2(1)(a).
    "occupational pension scheme"—see Jobseekers Act s.35(1).
    "pay period"—see reg.1(3).
    "personal pension scheme"—see Jobseekers Act s.35(1).

GENERAL NOTE

3.320
See the notes to reg.36 of the Income Support Regulations. Paragraph (3) has no equivalent in reg.36, but only operated for the purposes of CBJSA. However, the default £5 disregard in para.12 of Sch.6 does seem to apply.

Chapter IV

Self-Employed Earners

Earnings of self-employed earners

100.—(1) Subject to paragraph (2), "earnings", in the case of employment as a self-employed earner, means the gross receipts of the employment and shall include any allowance paid under any scheme referred to in regulation 19(1)(r) (circumstances in which a person is to be treated as actively seeking employment: schemes for assisting persons to become self-employed earners) to the claimant for the purpose of assisting him in carrying on his business.

3.321

(2) "Earnings" shall not include—

(a) where a claimant is involved in providing board and lodging accommodation for which a charge is payable, any payment by way of such a charge;

(b) any payment to which paragraph [²27, 28 or 28A] of Schedule 7 refers (payments in respect of a person accommodated with the claimant under an arrangement made by a local authority or voluntary organisation, [², payments] made to the claimant by a health authority, local authority or voluntary organisation in respect of persons temporarily in the claimant's care [²and any payments made to a claimant under section 73(1)(b) of the Children and Young People (Scotland) Act 2014 (kinship care assistance)]).

[³(ba) any payment made in accordance with section 26A of the Children (Scotland) Act 1995 (duty to provide continuing care)—

  (i) to a claimant; or

  (ii) where paragraph (3) applies, to another person ("A") which A passes on to the claimant;]

[¹(c) any sports award.]

[³(3) This paragraph applies only where A—

(a) was formerly in the claimant's care;

(b) is aged 16 or over; and

(c) continues to live with the claimant.]

AMENDMENTS

1. Social Security Amendment (Sports Awards) Regulations 1999 (SI 1999/2165) reg.7(3) (August 23, 1999).

2. Social Security and Child Support (Care Payments and Tenant Incentive Scheme) (Amendment) Regulations 2017 (SI 2017/995) reg.3(2) (November 7, 2017).

3. Social Security and Child Support (Care Payments and Tenant Incentive Scheme) (Amendment) Regulations 2017 (SI 2017/995) reg.11(3) (November 7, 2017).

DEFINITIONS

"board and lodging accommodation"—see reg.1(3).
"claimant"—see Jobseekers Act s.35(1) and reg.88(1).
"employment"—see reg.3.
"self-employed earner"—see reg.1(3), SSCBA s.2(1)(b).

"sports award"—see reg.1(3).
"voluntary organisation"—*ibid.*

GENERAL NOTE

3.322 See the notes to reg.37 of the Income Support Regulations, including on the proper treatment of payments under the Coronavirus Self-Employed Income Support Scheme.

The payments in para.(2)(a) count as income under reg.103(6) but subject to disregards.

Paragraph (2)(b) applies to payments to foster-parents and to people for providing temporary care in their home. These payments are disregarded as income other than earnings under paras 27 and 28 of Sch.7. Paragraph (2)(b) ensures that they are not treated as earnings. See also reg.53(f) on deeming not to be in remunerative work. Sub-paragraph (b) now also applies to kinship care assistance payments, available since April 2016 in Scotland to people who have applied or are at least considering applying for a kinship care order for a child who is at risk of going into care or was previously looked after by a local authority. However, there has been no amendment to reg.53(f) to cover recipients of such payments. The payments are disregarded as income other than earnings by para.28A of Sch.7 and as capital by para.66 (though it should be 67) of Sch.8.

On sub-para.(ba), which has the limited application fixed by para.(3), see reg.53(fa).

In relation to para.(2)(c), see the disregard in para 67 of Sch.7 and para.51 of Sch.8. See also reg.53(i).

Calculation of net profit of self-employed earners

3.323 **101.**—(1) For the purposes of regulation 95 (calculation of earnings of self-employed earners), the earnings of a claimant to be taken into account shall be—

(a) in the case of a self-employed earner who is engaged in employment on his own account, the net profit derived from that employment;

(b) in the case of a self-employed earner whose employment is carried on in partnership, or is that of a share fisherman within the meaning of regulation 156, his share of the net profit derived from that employment less—

(i) an amount in respect of income tax and of [²national insurance contributions] payable under the Benefits Act calculated in accordance with regulation 102 (deduction of tax and contributions for self-employed earners); and

(ii) one half of any premium paid in the period that is relevant under regulation 95 in respect of a personal pension scheme.

(2) Subject to paragraph (3), there shall be disregarded from a claimant's net profit any sum, where applicable, specified in paragraphs 1 to 16 of Schedule 6.

(3) For the purposes of calculating the amount to be deducted in respect of earnings under regulation 80 (contribution-based jobseeker's allowance: deductions in respect of earnings) the disregards in paragraphs 5 to 8 and 11 of Schedule 6 shall not apply.

(4) For the purposes of paragraph (1)(a) the net profit of the employment shall, except where paragraph (10) applies, be calculated by taking into account the earnings of the employment over the period determined under regulation 95 (calculation of earnings of self-employed earners) less—

(a) subject to paragraphs (6) to (8), any expenses wholly and exclusively defrayed in that period for the purposes of that employment;

(b) an amount in respect of—

   (i) income tax; and

   (ii) [²national insurance contributions] payable under the Benefits Act, calculated in accordance with regulation 102 (deductions of tax and contributions for self-employed earners); and

(c) one-half of any premium paid in the period that is relevant under regulation 95 in respect of a personal pension scheme.

(5) For the purposes of paragraph (1)(b), the net profit of the employment shall be calculated by taking into account the earnings of the employment over the period determined under regulation 95 less, subject to paragraphs (6) to (8), any expenses wholly and exclusively defrayed in that period for the purposes of that employment.

(6) Subject to paragraph (7), no deduction shall be made under paragraph (4)(a) or (5) in respect of—

(a) any capital expenditure;

(b) the depreciation of any capital asset;

(c) any sum employed or intended to be employed in the setting up or expansion of the employment;

(d) any loss incurred before the beginning of the period determined under regulation 95;

(e) the repayment of capital on any loan taken out for the purposes of the employment;

(f) any expenses incurred in providing business entertainment.

(7) A deduction shall be made under paragraph (4)(a) or (5) in respect of the repayment of capital on any loan used for—

(a) the replacement in the course of business of equipment or machinery; and

(b) the repair of an existing business asset except to the extent that any sum is payable under an insurance policy for its repair.

(8) [¹The Secretary of State] shall refuse to make a deduction under paragraph (4)(a) or (5) in respect of any expenses where he is not satisfied that the expense has been defrayed or, having regard to the nature of the expense and its amount, that it has been reasonably incurred.

(9) For the avoidance of doubt—

(a) a deduction shall not be made under paragraph (4)(a) or (5) in respect of any sum unless it has been expended for the purposes of the business;

(b) a deduction shall be made there under in respect of—

   (i) the excess of any VAT paid over VAT received in the period determined under regulation 95;

   (ii) any income expended in the repair of an existing asset except to the extent that any sum is payable under an insurance policy for its repair;

   (iii) any payment of interest on a loan taken out for the purposes of the employment.

(10) Where a claimant is engaged in employment as a child-minder the net profit of the employment shall be one-third of the earnings of that employment, less—

(a) an amount in respect of—

   (i) income tax; and

(ii) [² national insurance contributions] payable under the Benefits Act, calculated in accordance with regulation 102 (deductions of tax and contributions for self-employed earners); and

(b) one half of any premium paid in the period that is relevant under regulation 95 in respect of a personal pension scheme.

(11) Notwithstanding regulation 95 and the foregoing paragraphs, [¹the Secretary of State] may assess any item of a claimant's income or expenditure over a period other than that determined under regulation 95 such as may, in the particular case, enable the weekly amount of that item of income or expenditure to be determined more accurately.

(12) For the avoidance of doubt where a claimant is engaged in employment as a self-employed earner and he is engaged in one or more other employments as a self-employed or employed earner, any loss incurred in any one of his employments shall not be offset against his earnings in any other of his employments.

AMENDMENTS

1. Social Security Act 1998 (Commencement No.11, and Savings and Consequential and Transitional Provisions) Order 1999 (SI 1999/2860 (c.75)) art.3(12) and Sch.12 para.2 (October 18, 1999).

2. Social Security (Miscellaneous Amendments) (No.3) Regulations 2013 (SI 2013/2536) reg.6(11) (October 29, 2013).

DEFINITIONS

"the Benefits Act"—see Jobseekers Act s.35(1).
"claimant"—*ibid.*, and reg.88(1).
"earnings"—see reg.1(3) and reg.100.
"employment"—see reg.3.
"personal pension scheme"—see Jobseekers Act s.35(1).
"self-employed earner"—see reg.1(3) and SSCBA s.2(1)(b).

GENERAL NOTE

3.324   See the notes to reg.38 of the Income Support Regulations, including on the proper treatment of payments under the Coronavirus Self-Employed Income Support Scheme. Paragraph (3) has no equivalent in reg.38, but only operated for the purposes of CBJSA.

[¹ Deduction of tax and contributions for self-employed earners

3.325   **102.**—(1) Subject to paragraph (2), the amount to be deducted in respect of income tax under regulation 101(1)(b)(i), (4)(b)(i) or (10)(a)(i) (calculation of net profit of self-employed earners) is to be calculated—

(a) on the basis of the amount of chargeable income; and

[³ (b) as if that income was assessable to income tax at the basic rate, or in the case of a Scottish taxpayer, the Scottish basic rate, of tax less only the personal reliefs to which the claimant is entitled under Chapters 2, 3 and 3A of Part 3 of the Income Tax Act 2007 as are appropriate to their circumstances.]

(2) If the period determined under regulation 95 is less than a year, the earnings to which the basic rate[³ , or the Scottish basic rate,] of tax is to be applied and the amount of the [³ personal reliefs deductible under paragraph (1) are] to be calculated on a pro rata basis.

(3) Subject to paragraph (4), the amount to be deducted in respect of national insurance contributions under regulation 101(1)(b)(i), (4)(b)(ii) or (10)(a)(ii) is to be the total of—

(a) the amount of Class 2 contributions payable under section [^{2} 11(2)] or, as the case may be, [^{2} 11(8)] of the Benefits Act at the rate applicable at the date of claim except where the claimant's chargeable income is less than the amount specified in section 11(4) of that Act ([^{2} small profits threshold]) for the tax year in which the date of claim falls; and

(b) the amount of Class 4 contributions (if any) which would be payable under section 15 of that Act (Class 4 contributions recoverable under the Income Tax Acts) at the percentage rate applicable at the date of claim on so much of the chargeable income as exceeds the lower limit but does not exceed the upper limit of profits and gains applicable for the tax year in which the date of claim falls.

(4) If the period determined under regulation 95 is less than a year—

(a) the amount specified for the tax year referred to in paragraph (3)(a) is to be reduced pro rata; and

(b) the limits referred to in paragraph (3)(b) are to be reduced pro rata.

(5) In this regulation "chargeable income" means—

(a) except where sub-paragraph (b) applies, the earnings derived from the employment less any expenses deducted under regulation 101(4)(a) or, as the case may be, (5); and

(b) in the case of employment as a child minder, one-third of the earnings of that employment.]

AMENDMENTS

1. Social Security (Miscellaneous Amendments) (No.3) Regulations 2013 (SI 2013/2536) reg.6(12) (October 29, 2013).

2. Social Security (Miscellaneous Amendments No.2) Regulations 2015 (SI 2015/478) reg.29 (April 6, 2015).

3. Social Security (Scottish Rate of Income Tax etc.) (Amendment) Regulations 2016 (SI 2016/233) reg.3(3) (April 6, 2016).

DEFINITIONS

"the Benefits Act"—see Jobseekers Act s.35(1).
"claimant"—*ibid.*, reg.88(1).
"date of claim"—see reg.1(3).
"earnings"—*ibid.*, reg.100.
"Scottish basic rate"—see reg.1(3).
"Scottish taxpayer"—*ibid.*

GENERAL NOTE

See the notes to reg.39 of the Income Support Regulations.   **3.326**

Regulation 102 was rewritten on October 29, 2013 so as to match the equivalent provision for new style JSA (see reg.62 of the JSA Regulations 2013 in Vol.I of this series) but the substance remains the same.

[¹Chapter IVA

Participants in the self-employment route [² . . .]

Interpretation

3.327   **102A.**—In this Chapter—
[² . . .]
"special account" means, where a person was carrying on a commercial
activity in respect of which assistance was received under the self-
employment route, the account into which the gross receipts from that
activity were payable during the period in respect of which such assistance was received.]

AMENDMENTS

1. Social Security (Miscellaneous Amendments) (No.4) Regulations 1998
(SI 1998/1174) reg.3(4) (June 1, 1998).
2. Social Security Amendment (Employment Zones) (No.2) Regulations 2000
(SI 2000/2910) reg.5(2) (November 27, 2000).

DEFINITION

"self-employment route"—see reg.1(3).

GENERAL NOTE

3.328   For the definition of the "self-employment route" see reg.1(3).
See the note to reg.102C.

[¹ Treatment of gross receipts of participants in the self-employment route [² . . .]

3.329   **102B.**—The gross receipts of a commercial activity carried on by a
person in respect of which assistance is received under the self-employment
route, shall be taken into account in accordance with the following provisions of this Chapter.]

AMENDMENTS

1. Social Security (Miscellaneous Amendments) (No.4) Regulations 1998
(SI 1998/1174) reg.3(4) (June 1, 1998).
2. Social Security Amendment (Employment Zones) (No.2) Regulations 2000
(SI 2000/2910) reg.5(2)(c) (November 27, 2000).

DEFINITION

"self-employment route"—see reg.1(3).

[¹ Calculation of income of participants in the self-employment route [² . . .]

3.330   **102C.**—(1) The income of a person who has received assistance under the
self-employment route shall be calculated by taking into account the whole
of the monies in the special account at the end of the last day upon which
such assistance was received and deducting from those monies—
(a) an amount in respect of income tax calculated in accordance with

regulation 102D (deduction in respect of tax for participants in the self-employment route [² . . .]).

(b) any sum to which paragraph (4) refers.

(2) Income calculated pursuant to paragraph (1) shall be apportioned equally over a period which starts on the date the income is treated as paid under paragraph (3) and is equal in length to the period beginning with the day upon which assistance was first received under the self-employment route and ending on the last day upon which such assistance was received.

(3) Income calculated pursuant to paragraph (1) shall be treated as paid—

(a) in the case where it is due to be paid before the first benefit week in respect of which the participant or his partner [³ or, in the case of a joint-claim couple, the participant and the other member of the couple of which the participant is a member,] first claims a job-seeker's allowance following the last day upon which assistance was received under the self-employment route, on the day in the week in which it is due to be paid which corresponds to the first day of the benefit week;

(b) in any other case, on the first day of the benefit week in which it is due to be paid.

(4) This paragraph refers, where applicable in each benefit week in respect of which income calculated pursuant to paragraph (1) is taken into account pursuant to paragraphs (2) and (3), to the sums which would have been disregarded under paragraphs 5 to 8, 11 and 12 of Schedule 6 [³ or paragraphs 1, 2, 5 and 6 of Schedule 6A] had the income been earnings.]

AMENDMENTS

1. Social Security (Miscellaneous Amendments) (No.4) Regulations 1998 (SI 1998/1174) reg.3(4) (June 1, 1998).

2. Social Security Amendment (Employment Zones) (No.2) Regulations 2000 (SI 2000/2910) reg.5(2)(c) (November 27, 2000).

3. Jobseeker's Allowance (Joint Claims) Regulations 2000 (SI 2000/1978) reg.2(5) and Sch.2 para.41 (March 19, 2001).

DEFINITIONS

"benefit week"—see reg.1(3).
"joint-claim couple"—see JSA s.1(4).
"self-employment route"—see reg.1(3).
"special account"—*ibid*.
"week"—see reg.1(3).

GENERAL NOTE

This regulation, together with reg.102D, applies to the income from "test-trading" of people who have taken part in the "self-employment route" (defined in reg.1(3)). See also reg.88A which takes any gross receipts from trading while on the self-employment route out of the categories of earnings, self-employed earnings and income other than earnings. The rules for liable relative payments and student income (except reg.137) also do not apply. Any such receipts may only be taken into account in accordance with regs 102A–102D. For an example of a case in which regs 102A–102D applied, see *JL v SSWP (JSA)* [2012] UKUT 72 (AAC).

There are several issues raised by reg.102C that need clarifying. The intention seems to be that, after deducting an amount for income tax in accordance with reg.102D and applying the relevant earnings disregard under paras 5–8, 11 or 12

3.331

of Sch.6 in each benefit week that would have been applicable if the income had been earnings, the balance of the money in the person's "special account" (defined in reg.102A) at the end of the day on which he ceases to receive "assistance" (not defined) under the self-employment route is to be spread over a period equal in length to the period that the person received such assistance. The period starts on the date that the income is treated as paid under para.(3). Under para.(3)(a), if the income is due to be paid before the first benefit week pursuant to the claimant's (or his partner's) first old style JSA claim after assistance under the self-employment route finishes, it is treated as paid on the day in the week in which it was due that corresponds to the first day of the benefit week. In any other case it is treated as paid on the first day of the benefit week in which it is due (para.(3)(b)).

But when is this income due to be paid and what or who determines this? According to the guidance (see para.27484 of the DMG), it is due to be paid on the day after: (i) the person leaves the self-employment route if he is not entitled to old style JSA or income support immediately after leaving the self-employment route; (ii) his entitlement to JSA or income support ends if that entitlement stops within 13 weeks of the day after he left the self-employment route; or (iii) the expiry of 13 weeks starting on the day after he left the self-employment route if he is entitled to JSA or income support throughout that period. These rules are presumably part of the terms of the New Deal, since such provisions do not appear in the old style JSA (or Income Support) Regulations themselves. The 13-week "period of grace" in (iii) may perhaps be related to the fact that according to Employment Service guidance a person can continue to receive assistance in connection with trying to establish himself in self-employment for a further 13 weeks after his participation in the self-employment route ends. Presumably the intention is that any profit from his "test-trading" should not affect his benefit entitlement until after that period.

3.332   Note also that para.(1) refers to "the whole of the monies" in the person's special account but reg.102B refers to the "gross receipts" of the activity carried on while on the self-employment route. The normal rules for the calculation of earnings of self-employed earners (see regs 100–102) do not apply (see reg.88A), although presumably the case law on the meaning of "gross receipts" for self-employed earners will be relevant (see the notes to reg.37 of the Income Support Regulations). However, certain sums are ignored in calculating the person's income in his "special account". Thus any payment to him from this account (whether before or after he leaves the self-employment route) will disregarded if it is: (i) to meet expenses wholly and necessarily incurred in his business while on the self-employment route; or (ii) used, or intended to be used, to make repayments on a loan taken out for the purposes of that business (see para.62 of Sch.7). See also para.11(3) and (4) of Sch.8, which disregard any assets of the business while the person is participating in the self-employment route and, if the person later ceases to be engaged in that business, for a period which is reasonable to allow them to be disposed of. In addition, any capital acquired for the purposes of the business is ignored for 52 weeks from the date of receipt (para.47 of Sch.8).

See also regs 23A and 39A–39D of, and para.64 of Sch.9 and paras 6(3) and (4) and 52 of Sch.10 to, the Income Support Regulations which introduce similar provisions for the treatment of income from "test-trading" while on the self-employment route when the person or his partner claims income support.

[¹ Deduction in respect of tax for participants in the self-employment route [² . . .]

3.333   **102D.**—(1) The amount to be deducted in respect of income tax under regulation 102C(1)(a) (calculation of income of participants in the self-employment route [². . .]) in respect of the period determined under regulation 102C(2) shall be calculated as if—

(a) the chargeable income is the only income chargeable to tax;

[⁶(b) the personal reliefs applicable to the person receiving assistance under the self-employment route under Chapters 2, 3 and 3A of Part 3 of the Income Tax Act 2007 are allowable against that income; and

(c) the rate at which the chargeable income less the personal reliefs is assessable to income tax is the basic rate, or in the case of a Scottish taxpayer, the Scottish basic rate, of tax.]

(2) For the purpose of paragraph (1), the [⁴[⁵basic] rate][⁶ , or the Scottish basic rate,] of tax to be applied and the amount of the [³ [⁶personal reliefs]] deductible shall, where the period determined under regulation 102C(2) is less than a year, be calculated on a pro rata basis.

(3) In this regulation, "chargeable income" means the monies in the special account at the end of the last day upon which assistance was received under the self-employment route.]

AMENDMENTS

1. Social Security (Miscellaneous Amendments) (No.4) Regulations 1998 (SI 1998/1174) reg.3(4) (June 1, 1998).

2. Social Security Amendment (Employment Zones) (No.2) Regulations 2000 (SI 2000/2910) reg.5(2)(c) (November 27, 2000).

3. Social Security (Miscellaneous Amendments) (No.3) Regulations 2007 (SI 2007/1749) reg.3(3) (July 16, 2007).

4. Social Security (Miscellaneous Amendments) (No.5) Regulations 2007 (SI 2007/2618) reg.8(10) (October 1, 2007).

5. Social Security (Miscellaneous Amendments) Regulations 2009 (SI 2009/583) reg.4(8) (April 6, 2009).

6. Social Security (Scottish Rate of Income Tax etc.) (Amendment) Regulations 2016 (SI 2016/233) reg.3(4) (April 6, 2016).

DEFINITIONS

"Scottish basic rate"—see reg.1(3).
"Scottish taxpayer"—*ibid.*
"self-employment route"—*ibid.*
"special account"—*ibid.*

GENERAL NOTE

See the note to reg.102C above.   3.334

Chapter V

Other Income

Calculation of income other than earnings

103.—(1) For the purposes of regulation 94 (calculation of income   3.335
other than earnings) [¹⁰ [¹¹ . . .]] the income of a claimant which does not consist of earnings to be taken into account shall, subject to the following provisions of this regulation, be his gross income and any capital treated as income under [⁶ regulation 104 (capital treated as income)].

(2) There shall be disregarded from the calculation of a claimant's

gross income under paragraph (1) any sum, where applicable, specified in Schedule 7.

(3) Where the payment of any benefit under the Act or under the Benefits Act is subject to any deduction by way of recovery, the amount to be taken into account under paragraph (1) shall be the gross amount to which the beneficiary is entitled.

(4) [⁷ . . .]

[⁵ (5) [⁸ Paragraphs (5ZA) and (5AZA) apply] where—

(a) a relevant payment has been made to a person in an academic year; and

(b) that person abandons, or is dismissed from, his course of study before the payment to him of the final instalment of the relevant payment.

(5ZA) [⁸ Where a relevant payment is made quarterly, the] amount of a relevant payment to be taken into account for the assessment period for the purposes of paragraph (1) in respect of a person to whom paragraph (5) applies, shall be calculated by applying the formula—

$$\frac{A - (B \times C)}{D}$$

where—

A = the total amount of the relevant payment which that person would have received had he remained a student until the last day of the academic term in which he abandoned, or was dismissed from, his course, less any deduction under regulation 136(5);

B = the number of benefit weeks from the benefit week immediately following that which includes the first day of that academic year to the benefit week immediately before that which includes the day on which the person abandoned, or was dismissed from, his course;

C = the weekly amount of the relevant payment, before the application of the £10 disregard, which would have been taken into account as income under regulation 136(2) had the person not abandoned or been dismissed from, his course and, in the case of a person who was not entitled to a jobseeker's allowance immediately before he abandoned or was dismissed from his course, had that person, at that time, been entitled to a jobseeker's allowance;

D = the number of benefit weeks in the assessment period.

[⁸ (5AZA) Where a relevant payment is made by two or more instalments in a quarter, the amount of a relevant payment to be taken into account for the assessment period for the purposes of paragraph (1) in respect of a person to whom paragraph (5) applies, shall be calculated by applying the formula in paragraph (5ZA) but as if—

A = the total amount of relevant payments which that person received, or would have received, from the first day of the academic year to the day the person abandoned the course, or was dismissed from it, less any deduction under regulation 136(5).]

(5ZB) [⁸ In this regulation]—

"academic year" and "student loan" shall have the same meanings as for the purposes of Chapter IX of this Part;

[⁸ "assessment period" means—

(a) in a case where a relevant payment is made quarterly, the period beginning with the benefit week which includes the day on which the person abandoned, or was dismissed from, his course and ending with the benefit week which includes the last day of the last quarter for which an instalment of the relevant payment was payable to that person;

(b) in a case where the relevant payment is made by two or more instalments in a quarter, the period beginning with the benefit week which includes the day on which the person abandoned, or was dismissed from, his course and ending with the benefit week which includes—

    (i) the day immediately before the day on which the next instalment of the relevant payment would have been due had the payments continued; or

    (ii) the last day of the last quarter for which an instalment of the relevant payment was payable to that person ,

    whichever of those dates is earlier;]

[8 "quarter" in relation to an assessment period means a period in that year beginning on—

(a) 1st January and ending on 31st March;

(b) 1st April and ending on 30th June;

(c) 1st July and ending on 31st August; or

(d) 1st September and ending on 31st December;]

"relevant period" means either a student loan or an amount intended for the maintenance of dependants referred to in regulation 131(5A) or both.]

[2(5A) In the case of income to which regulation 94(2B) applies (calculation of income of former full-time students), the amount of income to be taken into account for the purposes of paragraph (1) shall be the amount of that income calculated in accordance with regulation 97(7) and on the basis that none of that income has been repaid.]

[9 (5B) Where the claimant—

(a) is a member of a couple;

(b) his partner is receiving a contributory employment and support allowance; and

(c) that benefit has been reduced under regulation 63 of the Employment and Support Allowance Regulations [12 or section 11J of the Welfare Reform Act as the case may be],

the amount of that benefit to be taken into account is the amount as if it had not been reduced.]

(6) For the avoidance of doubt there shall be included as income to be taken into account under paragraph (1)—

[4(a) any payment to which regulation 98(2)(a) to (e) or 100(2) (payments not earnings) applies; or

(b) in the case of a claimant who is receiving support under section 95 or 98 of the Immigration and Asylum Act including support provided by virtue of regulations made under Schedule 9 to that Act, the amount of such support provided in respect of essential living needs of the claimant and his [6 parter] (if any) as is specified in regulations made under paragraph 3 of Schedule 8 to the Immigration and Asylum Act.]

AMENDMENTS

1. Jobseeker's Allowance and Income Support (General) (Amendment) Regulations 1996 (SI 1996/1517) reg.23 (October 7, 1996).

2. Income-related Benefits and Jobseeker's Allowance (Miscellaneous Amendments) Regulations 1997 (SI 1997/65) reg.7(2) (April 7, 1997).

3. Social Security (Miscellaneous Amendments) Regulations 1997 (SI 1997/454), reg.2(13) April 7, 1997).

4. Social Security (Immigration and Asylum) Consequential Amendments Regulations 2000 (SI 2000/636) reg.4(4) (April 3, 2000).

5. Social Security Amendment (Students and Income-related Benefits) Regulations 2001 (SI 2001/2319) reg.5(2) (August 1, 2001).

6. Social Security (Working Tax Credit and Child Tax Credit) (Consequential Amendments) Regulations 2003 (SI 2003/455) reg.3 and Sch.2 para.8 (April 6, 2004, except in "transitional cases" and see further the note to reg.83 and to reg.17 of the Income Support Regulations).

7. Social Security (Miscellaneous Amendments) Regulations 2005 (SI 2005/574) reg.6(3) (April 4, 2005).

8. Social Security (Students and Miscellaneous Amendments) Regulations 2008 (SI 2008/1599) reg.4(2) (September 1, 2008, or if the student's period of study begins between August 1 and 31, 2008, the first day of the period).

9. Employment and Support Allowance (Consequential Provisions) (No.2) Regulations 2008 (SI 2008/1554) reg.3(16) (October 27, 2008).

10. Social Security (Miscellaneous Amendments) (No.4) Regulations 2009 (SI 2009/2655) reg.4(7) (October 26, 2009).

11. Social Security (Miscellaneous Amendments) Regulations 2011 (SI 2011/674) reg.7(5) (April 11, 2011).

12. Universal Credit (Consequential, Supplementary, Incidental and Miscellaneous Provisions) Regulations 2013 (SI 2013/630) reg.30(5) (April 29, 2013).

DEFINITIONS

"academic year"—see reg.130.
"the Act"—see reg.1(3).
"the Benefits Act"—see Jobseekers Act s.35(1).
"benefit week"—see reg.1(3).
"claimant"—see Jobseekers Act s.35(1) and reg.88(1).
"earnings"—see reg.1(3).
"full-time student"—*ibid.*
"Immigration and Asylum Act"—*ibid.*
"student loan"—see reg.130.
"Welfare Reform Act"—see reg.1(3).

GENERAL NOTE

3.336   On paras (1)–(3) and (5)–(6), see the notes to reg.40 of the Income Support Regulations but in relation to para.(6)(b) note that there is no equivalent to reg.40(5).

Capital treated as income

3.337   **104.**—(1) Any capital payable by instalments which are outstanding on the first day in respect of which an income-based jobseeker's allowance is payable, or, in the case of a [³supersession], the date of that [³supersession], shall, if the aggregate of the instalments outstanding and the amount of the claimant's capital otherwise calculated in accordance with Chapter VI of this Part exceeds [⁸ . . .] [¹£16,000], be treated as income.

(2) Any payment received under an annuity shall be treated as income.

(3) [⁷ . . .]

(4) Any earnings to the extent that they are not a payment of income shall be treated as income.

[²(5) Any Career Development Loan paid pursuant to section 2 of the Employment and Training Act 1973 shall be treated as income.]

[⁶ (6) Where an agreement or court order provides that payments shall be made to the claimant in consequence of any personal injury to the claimant and that such payments are to be made, wholly or partly, by way of periodical payments, any such periodical payments received by the claimant (but not a payment which is treated as capital by virtue of this Part), shall be treated as income.]

AMENDMENTS

1. Income-related Benefits and Jobseeker's Allowance (Miscellaneous Amendments) Regulations 1997 (SI 1997/65) reg.3(2) (April 7, 1997).

2. Income-related Benefits and Jobseeker's Allowance (Miscellaneous Amendments) Regulations 1997 (SI 1997/65) reg.3(3) (April 7, 1997).

3. Social Security Act 1998 (Commencement No.11, and Savings and Consequential and Transitional Provisions) Order 1999 (SI 1999/2860 c.75)) art.3(12) and Sch.12 para.5 (October 18, 1999).

4. Social Security Amendment (Capital Limits and Earnings Disregards) Regulations 2000 (SI 2000/2545) reg.2(2)(a) (April 9, 2001).

5. Children (Leaving Care) Act 2000 (Commencement No.2 and Consequential Provisions) Order 2001 (SI 2001/3070) art.3(5) and Sch.4 para.(c) (October 1, 2001).

6. Social Security Amendment (Personal Injury Payments) Regulations 2002 (SI 2002/2442) reg.2 (October 28, 2002).

7. Social Security (Working Tax Credit and Child Tax Credit) (Consequential Amendments) Regulations 2003 (SI 2003/455) reg.3 and Sch.2 para.9 (April 6, 2004, except in "transitional cases" and see further the note to reg.83 and to reg.17 of the Income Support Regulations).

8. Social Security (Miscellaneous Amendments) (No.2) Regulations 2005 (SI 2005/2465) reg.3(2) (April 10, 2006).

DEFINITIONS

"claimant"—see Jobseekers Act s.35(1) and reg.88(1).
"payment"—see reg.1(3).

GENERAL NOTE

See the notes to reg.41 of the Income Support Regulations.   3.338

Paragraph (3) was revoked with effect from April 6, 2004 by reg.3 of and para.9 of Sch.2 to the Social Security (Working Tax Credit and Child Tax Credit) (Consequential Amendments) Regulations 2003 (SI 2003/455), except in "transitional cases" (i.e. those cases in which the claimant is still receiving amounts for his children in his income-based JSA—see further the notes to reg.83 and reg.17 of the Income Support Regulations). For "transitional cases" para.(3) continues in force (see the 2003 edition of this volume for this provision). With effect from May 12, 2004, reg.5 of the Social Security (Miscellaneous Amendments) (No.2) Regulations 2004 (SI 2004/1141) substituted the words "section 12 of the Social Work (Scotland) Act 1968 or sections 29 or 30 of the Children (Scotland) Act 1995" for the words "section 12, 24 or 26 of the Social Work (Scotland) Act 1968" in para.(3). The effect of this amendment is simply to update the references to the Scottish legislation referred to in para.(3).

Notional income

3.339

105.—[⁴⁷(1) A claimant is to be treated as possessing income of which the claimant has deprived themselves for the purpose of securing entitlement to a jobseeker's allowance or increasing the amount of that allowance, or for the purpose of securing entitlement to, or increasing the amount of income support or an employment and support allowance.]

(2) Except in the case of—

    (a) a discretionary trust;

    (b) a trust derived from a payment made in consequence of a personal injury;

[¹(c) [¹⁹ . . .]]

    (d) [¹⁸ working tax credit or child tax credit];

    (e) a jobseeker's allowance;

    (f) [²¹ . . .]

    (g) a personal pension scheme [²⁴ [²⁹, occupational pension scheme or a payment made by the Board of the Pension Protection Fund]] where the claimant [⁴³ has not attained the qualifying age for state pension credit]; [² or

[⁴¹(ga) any sum to which paragraph (15A) applies;]

[³⁰(h) any sum to which paragraph 42(2)(a) of Schedule 8 (capital to be disregarded) applies which is administered in the way referred to in paragraph 42(1)(a);

    (ha) any sum to which paragraph 43(a) of Schedule 8 refers; or]]

[⁵ (i) rehabilitation allowance made under section 2 of the Employment and Training Act 1973],

income which would become available to the claimant upon application being made but which has not been acquired by him shall be treated as possessed by him but only from the date on which it could be expected to be acquired were an application made.

[¹ (2A) [¹⁹ . . .]]

[²⁵(2B) A claimant who has attained the [⁴³qualifying age for state pension credit] shall be treated as possessing—

    (a) the amount of any income from an occupational pension scheme [²⁹ a personal pension scheme or the Board of the Pension Protection Fund]—

        (i) for which no claim has been made, and

        (ii) to which he might expect to be entitled if a claim for it were made;

    (b) income from an occupational pension scheme which the claimant elected to defer,

but only from the date on which it could be expected to be acquired were an application for it to be made.]

[³² (3) This paragraph applies where a person [⁴³ who has attained the qualifying age for state pension credit]—

    (a) is entitled to money purchase benefits under an occupational pension scheme or a personal pension scheme;

    (b) fails to purchase an annuity with the funds available in that scheme; and

    (c) either—

        (i) defers in whole or in part the payment of any income which would have been payable to him by his pension fund holder, or

        (ii) fails to take any necessary action to secure that the whole of any income which would be payable to him by his pension fund holder upon his applying for it, is so paid, or

(iii) income withdrawal is not available to him under that scheme.

(3A) Where paragraph (3) applies, the amount of any income foregone shall be treated as possessed by that person, but only from the date on which it could be expected to be acquired were an application for it to be made.]

(4) The amount of any income foregone in a case [³² where paragraph (3) (c)(i) or (ii)] applies shall be the [⁵⁶rate of the annuity which may have been purchased with the fund] and shall be determined by [⁹ the Secretary of State] who shall take account of information provided by the pension fund holder in accordance with regulation 7(5) of the Social Security (Claims and Payments) Regulations 1987.

(5) The amount of any income foregone in a case [³² where paragraph (3) (c)(iii)] applies shall be the income that the claimant could have received without purchasing an annuity had the fund held under the relevant [²⁷ occupational or personal pension scheme been held under a scheme] where income withdrawal was available and shall be determined in the manner specified in paragraph (4).

[²⁸ (5A) In paragraph (3), "money purchase benefits" has the meaning it has in the Pension Schemes Act 1993.]

(6) Subject to paragraph (7), any income which is due to be paid to the claimant but has not been paid to him, shall be treated as possessed by the claimant.

(7) Paragraph (6) shall not apply to—

(a) any amount to which paragraph (8) or (9) applies;

(b) a payment to which section 74(2) or (3) of the Administration Act applies (abatement of prescribed payments from public funds which are not made before the prescribed date, and abatement from prescribed benefits where maintenance not paid); and

(c) a payment from a discretionary trust, or a trust derived from a payment made in consequence of a personal injury.

[¹²(d) any earnings which are due to an employed earner on the termination of his employment by reason of redundancy but which have not been paid to him.]

(8) This paragraph applies to an amount which is due to be paid to the claimant under an occupational pension scheme but which is not paid because the trustees or managers of the scheme have suspended or ceased payment due to an insufficiency of resources.

(9) This paragraph applies to any amount by which a payment made to the claimant from an occupational pension scheme falls short of the payment to which he was due under the scheme where the shortfall arises because the trustees or managers of the scheme have insufficient resources available to them to meet in full the scheme's liabilities.

(10) [⁶Any payment of income, other than a payment of income specified in paragraph (10A)], made—

(a) to a third party in respect of a single claimant or in respect of a single claimant or [¹⁹ his partner] shall be treated—

(i) in a case where that payment is derived from a payment of any benefit under the [³⁸ benefit Acts, a payment from the Armed Forces and Reserve Forces Compensation Scheme, a war disablement pension, war widow's pension or war widower's pension or a pension payable to a person as a widow, widower or surviving civil partner under any power of Her Majesty otherwise than under an enactment to make provision about pensions for or in respect of persons who have been disabled or have died in consequence of service as members of the armed forces of the Crown] as possessed by that single claimant, if it would normally be paid to him, or as possessed [¹⁹ by his partner, if it would normally be paid to his partner];

[¹⁰ (ia) in a case where that payment is a payment of an occupational pension[²⁹, a pension or other periodical payment made under a personal pension scheme or a payment made by the Board of the Pension Protection Fund], as possessed by that single claimant or, as the case may be, by [¹⁹ the claimant's partner];]

    (ii) in any other case, as possessed by that single claimant [¹⁹ or his partner] to the extent that it is used for the food, ordinary clothing or footwear, household fuel, rent for which housing benefit is payable, or any housing costs to the extent that they are met under regulation 83(f)[¹⁵, 84(1)(g), 86A(d) or 86B(e)], of that single claimant or, as the case may be, [¹⁹ of his partner], or is used for any council tax or water charges for which that claimant or [¹⁹ partner is liable];

[¹⁹ (b) to a single claimant or his partner in respect of a third party (but not in respect of another member of his family) shall be treated as possessed by that single claimant or, as the case may be, his partner, to the extent that it is kept or used by him or used by or on behalf of his partner;]

but, except where sub-paragraph (a)(i) applies and in the case of a person who is, or would be, prevented from being entitled to a jobseeker's allowance by section 14 (trade disputes), this paragraph shall not apply to any payment in kind [²² to the third party].

[⁶(10A) Paragraph (10) shall not apply in respect of a payment of income made—

(a) under [⁴⁴or by] the Macfarlane Trust, the Macfarlane (Special Payments) Trust, the Macfarlane (Special Payments) (No.2) Trust, the Fund, the Eileen Trust[⁴², MFET Limited] [⁴⁸, the Skipton Fund, the Caxton Foundation][⁵³, the Scottish Infected Blood Support Scheme][⁵⁵, an approved blood scheme][⁵⁴, the London Emergencies Trust, the We Love Manchester Emergency Fund][⁵⁷, the National Emergencies Trust] or the Independent Living [³⁷ Fund (2006)];

[⁵⁷(ab) which is a Grenfell Tower payment;]

(b) pursuant to section 19(1)(a) of the Coal Industry Act 1994 (concessionary coal); or

(c) pursuant to section 2 of the Employment and Training Act 1973 in respect of a person's participation—

    (i) in an employment programme specified in regulation 75(1)(a)(ii);

    (ii) in a training scheme specified in regulation 75(1)(b)(ii); or

[¹⁶ (iia) [³⁶ . . .] in the Intensive Activity Period specified in regulation 75(1)(a)(iv); or]

    (iii) in a qualifying course within the meaning specified in regulation 17A(7)] [⁴⁰ ; or

    (iv) in the Flexible New Deal.]

(ca) [*Omitted*]

[⁴⁵(cb)in respect of a person's participation in the Mandatory Work Activity Scheme;]

[⁴⁶(cc) [⁵⁰ . . .]]

[⁴⁹(cc) in respect of a claimant's participation in a scheme prescribed in regulation 3 of the Jobseeker's Allowance (Schemes for Assisting Persons to Obtain Employment) Regulations 2013;]

(cd) *[Omitted]*

(ce) *[Omitted]*

[¹¹(d) under an occupational pension scheme [²⁹, in respect of a pension or other periodical payment made under a personal pension scheme or a payment made by the Board of the Pension Protection Fund] where—

   (i) a bankruptcy order has been made in respect of the person in respect of whom the payment has been made or, in Scotland, the estate of that person is subject to sequestration or a judicial factor has been appointed on that person's estate under section 41 of the Solicitors (Scotland) Act 1980;

  (ii) the payment is made to the trustee in bankruptcy or any other person acting on behalf of the creditors; and

 (iii) the person referred to in (i) and [¹⁹ his partner (if any)] does not possess, or is not treated as possessing, any other income apart from that payment.]

(11) Where the claimant [²³ resides in a care home, an Abbeyfield Home or an independent hospital, or is temporarily absent from such a home or hospital], any payment made by a person other than the claimant or a member of his family in respect of some or all of the cost of maintaining the claimant [¹⁹ or his partner in that home [³⁷ or hospital] shall be treated as possessed by the claimant or his partner].

[¹⁴(11A) Where the amount of a subsistence allowance paid to a claimant in a benefit week is less than the amount of income-based jobseeker's allowance that person would have received in that benefit week had it been payable to him, less 50p, he shall be treated as possessing the amount which is equal to the amount of income-based jobseeker's allowance which he would have received in that week, less 50p.]

(12) Where a claimant's earnings are not ascertainable at the time of the determination of the claim or of any [⁹ review or supersession] [⁹the Secretary of State] shall treat the claimant as possessing such earnings as is reasonable in the circumstances of the case having regard to the number of hours worked and the earnings paid for comparable employment in the area.

(13) [¹³ Subject to paragraph (13A),] where—

(a) a claimant performs a service for another person; and

(b) that person makes no payment of earnings or pays less than that paid for a comparable employment in the area,

[⁹ the Secretary of State] shall treat the claimant as possessing such earnings (if any) as is reasonable for that employment unless the claimant satisfies him that the means of that person are insufficient for him to pay or to pay more for the service [¹³ . . .].

[¹³(13A) Paragraph (13) shall not apply—

(a) to a claimant who is engaged by a charitable or voluntary organisation or who is a volunteer if the Secretary of State is satisfied in any of those cases that it is reasonable for him to provide those services free of charge;

(b) in a case where the service is performed in connection with—
    (i) the claimant's participation in an employment or training programme in accordance with regulation 19(1)(q) [¹⁶, other than where the service is performed in connection with the claimant's participation [³⁶ . . .] in the Intensive Activity Period specified in regulation 75(1)(a)(iv)]; or
    (ii) the claimant's or the claimant's partner's participation in an employment or training programme as defined in regulation 19(3) for which a training allowance is not payable or, where such an allowance is payable, it is payable for the sole purpose of reimbursement of travelling or meal expenses to the person participating in that programme] [³³; or
(c) to a claimant who is participating in a work placement approved by the Secretary of State (or a person providing services to the Secretary of State) before the placement starts.]

(14) Where a claimant is treated as possessing any income under any of paragraphs (1) to (11) the foregoing provisions of this Part shall apply for the purposes of calculating the amount of that income as if a payment had actually been made and as if it were actual income which he does possess.

(15) Where a claimant is treated as possessing any earnings under paragraphs (12) or (13) the foregoing provisions of this Part shall apply for the purposes of calculating the amount of those earnings as if a payment had actually been made and as if they were actual earnings which he does possess, except that paragraph (4) of regulation 99 (calculation of net earnings of employed earners) shall not apply and his net earnings shall be calculated by taking into account the earnings which he is treated as possessing, less—

(a) an amount in respect of income tax equivalent to an amount calculated by applying to those earnings [³⁹ . . .] the basic rate [⁵², or in the case of a Scottish taxpayer, the Scottish basic rate,] of tax in the year of assessment less only the [⁵² personal reliefs to which the claimant is entitled under Chapters 2, 3 and 3A of Part 3 of the Income Tax Act 2007 as are] appropriate to his circumstances; but, if the period over which those earnings are to be taken into account is less than a year, the earnings to which the [³⁴ [³⁹ basic] rate] [⁵², or the Scottish basic rate,] of tax is to be applied and the amount of the [⁵² personal reliefs] deductible under this paragraph shall be calculated on a pro rata basis;
(b) where the weekly amount of those earnings equals or exceeds the lower earnings limit, an amount representing primary Class 1 contributions under the Benefits Act, calculated by applying to those earnings the initial and main primary percentages in accordance with section 8(1)(a) and (b) of that Act; and
(c) one-half of any sum payable by the claimant in respect of a pay period by way of a contribution towards an occupational or personal pension scheme.

[⁴¹ (15A) Paragraphs (1), (2), (6), (10), (12) and (13) shall not apply in respect of any amount of income other than earnings, or earnings derived from employment as an employed earner, arising out of the [⁵¹ claimant participating as a service user].]

(16) In this regulation—
"ordinary clothing or footwear" means clothing or footwear for normal

daily use, but does not include school uniforms, or clothing or foot-wear used solely for sporting activities;

"pension fund holder" means with respect to a personal pension scheme [[32] or an occupational pension scheme] the trustees, managers or scheme administrators, as the case may be, of the scheme concerned;

"resources" has the same meaning as in section 181 of the Pension Schemes Act 1993;

[[35] "work placement" means practical work experience which is not undertaken in expectation of payment.]

AMENDMENTS

1. Child Benefit, Child Support and Social Security (Miscellaneous Amendments) (Regulation 1996 (SI 1996/1803) reg.42 (April 7, 1997).

2. Income-related Benefits and Jobseeker's Allowance (Amendment) (No.2) Regulations 1997 (SI 1997/2197) reg.6 (October 6, 1997).

3. Income-related Benefits and Jobseeker's Allowance (Amendment) (No.2) Regulations 1997 (SI 1997/2197) reg.7(3) and (4)(f) (October 6, 1997).

4. Social Security Amendment (New Deal) Regulations 1997 (SI 1997/2863) reg.9 (January 5, 1998).

5. Social Security (Miscellaneous Amendments) Regulations 1998 (SI 1998/563) reg.6(1) and (2)(f) (April 6, 1998).

6. Social Security Amendment (New Deal) (No.2) Regulations 1998 (SI 1998/2117) reg.2(1) (September 24, 1998).

7. Social Security and Child Support (Tax Credits) Consequential Amendments Regulations 1999 (SI 1999/2566) reg.2(1) and Sch.2 Pt I (October 5, 1999).

8. Social Security and Child Support (Tax Credits) Consequential Amendments Regulations 1999 (SI 1999/2566) reg.2(2) and Sch.2 Pt II (October 5, 1999).

9. Social Security Act 1998 (Commencement No.11, and Savings and Consequential and Transitional Provisions) Order 1999 (SI 1999/2860 (C.75)) art.3(12) and Sch.12 (October 18, 1999).

10. Social Security Amendment (Notional Income and Capital) Regulations 1999 (SI 1999/2640) reg.2(1)(b) (November 15, 1999).

11. Social Security Amendment (Notional Income and Capital) Regulations 1999 (SI 1999/2640) reg.2(3)(d) (November 15, 1999).

12. Income Support (General) and Jobseeker's Allowance Amendment (No.2) Regulations 1999 (SI 1999/3324) reg.2 (January 7, 2000).

13. Social Security (Approved Work) Regulations 2000 (SI 2000/678) reg.2(1) (April 3, 2000).

14. Social Security Amendment (Employment Zones) Regulations 2000 (SI 2000/724) reg.3(1) (April 3, 2000).

15. Jobseeker's Allowance (Joint Claims) Regulations 2000 (SI 2000/1978) reg.2(5) and Sch.2 para.42 (March 19, 2001).

16. Social Security Amendment (New Deal) Regulations 2001 (SI 2001/1029) reg.7 (April 9, 2001).

17. Social Security (Miscellaneous Amendments) Regulations 2002 (SI 2002/841) reg.3(2) (April 8, 2002).

18. Social Security (Working Tax Credit and Child Tax Credit) (Consequential Amendments) Regulations 2003 (SI 2003/455) reg.3 and Sch.2 para.10(b) (April 7, 2003).

19. Social Security (Working Tax Credit and Child Tax Credit) (Consequential Amendments) Regulations 2003 (SI 2003/455) reg.3 and Sch.2 para.10 (except sub-para.(b)) (April 6, 2004, except in "transitional cases" and see further the note to reg.83 and to reg.17 of the Income Support Regulations).

20. Social Security (Miscellaneous Amendments) Regulations 2005 (SI 2005/574) reg.2(6) (April 4, 2005).

21. Social Security (Miscellaneous Amendments) Regulations 2005 (SI 2005/574) reg.6(4) (April 4, 2005).

22. Social Security (Miscellaneous Amendments) (No.2) Regulations 2005 (SI 2005/2465) reg.3(3)(f) (October 3, 2005).

23. Social Security (Care Homes and Independent Hospitals) Regulations 2005 (SI 2005/2687) reg.3 and Sch.2 para.5 (October 24, 2005).

24. Social Security (Miscellaneous Amendments) (No.2) Regulations 2005 (SI 2005/2465) reg.3(3)(a) (April 6, 2006).

25. Social Security (Miscellaneous Amendments) (No.2) Regulations 2005 (SI 2005/2465) reg.3(3)(b) (April 6, 2006).

26. Social Security (Miscellaneous Amendments) (No.2) Regulations 2005 (SI 2005/2465) reg.3(3)(c) (April 6, 2006).

27. Social Security (Miscellaneous Amendments) (No.2) Regulations 2005 (SI 2005/2465) reg.3(3)(d) (April 6, 2006).

28. Social Security (Miscellaneous Amendments) (No.2) Regulations 2005 (SI 2005/2465) reg.3(3)(e) (April 6, 2006).

29. Social Security (Miscellaneous Amendments) Regulations 2006 (SI 2006/588) reg.3(3) (April 6, 2006).

30. Social Security (Miscellaneous Amendments) Regulations 2007 (SI 2007/719) reg.3(4) (April 2, 2007).

31. Social Security (Miscellaneous Amendments) (No.3) Regulations 2007 (SI 2007/1749) reg.3(3) (July 16, 2007).

32. Social Security (Miscellaneous Amendments) (No.3) Regulations 2007 (SI 2007/1749) reg.3(4) (July 16, 2007).

33. Social Security (Miscellaneous Amendments) (No.5) Regulations 2007 (SI 2007/2618) reg.8(11)(a) (October 1, 2007).

34. Social Security (Miscellaneous Amendments) (No.5) Regulations 2007 (SI 2007/2618) reg.8(11)(b) (October 1, 2007).

35. Social Security (Miscellaneous Amendments) (No.5) Regulations 2007 (SI 2007/2618) reg.8(11)(c) (October 1, 2007).

36. Social Security (Miscellaneous Amendments) Regulations 2008 (SI 2008/698) reg.4(12)(a) (April 14, 2008).

37. Social Security (Miscellaneous Amendments) (No.6) Regulations 2008 (SI 2008/2767) reg.4(6) (November 17, 2008).

38. Social Security (Miscellaneous Amendments) (No.7) Regulations 2008 (SI 2008/3157) reg.3(6) (January 5, 2009).

39. Social Security (Miscellaneous Amendments) Regulations 2009 (SI 2009/583) reg.4(7) (April 6, 2009).

40. Social Security (Flexible New Deal) Regulations 2009 (SI 2009/480) reg.2(6) (October 5, 2009).

41. Social Security (Miscellaneous Amendments) (No.4) Regulations 2009 (SI 2009/2655) reg.4(8) (October 26, 2009).

42. Social Security (Miscellaneous Amendments) (No.2) Regulations 2010 (SI 2010/641) reg.4(3)(b) (April 6, 2010).

43. Social Security (Miscellaneous Amendments) (No.2) Regulations 2010 (SI 2010/641) reg.4(7) (April 6, 2010).

44. Social Security (Miscellaneous Amendments) (No.2) Regulations 2010 (SI 2010/641) reg.4(8)(a) (April 6, 2010).

45. Jobseeker's Allowance (Mandatory Work Activity Scheme) Regulations 2011 (SI 2011/688) reg.12(1)(d) and (2) (April 25, 2011).

46. Jobseeker's Allowance (Employment, Skills and Enterprise Scheme) Regulations 2011 (SI 2011/917) reg.12(1)(d) and (2) (May 20, 2011).

47. Social Security (Miscellaneous Amendments) (No.3) Regulations 2011 (SI 2011/2425) reg.10(8) (October 31, 2011).

48. Social Security (Miscellaneous Amendments) (No.3) Regulations 2011 (SI 2011/2425) reg.10(9) (October 31, 2011).

49. Jobseeker's Allowance (Schemes for Assisting Persons to Obtain Employment) Regulations 2013 (SI 2013/276) reg.9(1)(d) and (2) (February 12, 2013).

50. Jobseekers (Back to Work Schemes) Act 2013 s.1(14) (March 26, 2013).

51. Social Security (Miscellaneous Amendments) Regulations 2014 (SI 2014/591) reg.4(4) (April 28, 2014).

52. Social Security (Scottish Rate of Income Tax etc.) (Amendment) Regulations 2016 (SI 2016/233) reg.3(5) (April 6, 2016).

53. Social Security (Scottish Infected Blood Support Scheme) Regulations 2017 (SI 2017/329) reg.4(3) (April 3, 2017).

54. Social Security (Emergency Funds) (Amendment) Regulations 2017 (SI 2017/689) reg.3(3)(a) (June 19, 2017).

55. Social Security (Infected Blood and Thalidomide) Regulations 2017 (SI 2017/870) reg.3(3)(a) (October 23, 2017).

56. Social Security (Miscellaneous Amendments No.4) Regulations 2017 (SI 2017/207) reg.8 (November 16, 2017).

57. Social Security (Income and Capital) (Miscellaneous Amendments) Regulations 2020 (SI 2020/618) reg.3(3) (July 15, 2020).

DEFINITIONS

"Abbeyfield Home"—see reg.1(3).
"the Act"—*ibid.*
"approved blood scheme"—*ibid.*
"the Armed Forces and Reserve Forces Compensation Scheme"—*ibid.*
"the Benefits Act"—see Jobseekers Act s.35(1).
"care home"—see reg.1(3).
"the Caxton Foundation"—*ibid.*
"child tax credit"—*ibid.*
"civil partner"—see Interpretation Act 1978 Sch.1.
"claimant"—see regs 1(3) and 88(1).
"claimant participating as a service user"—see reg.1(3G).
"earnings"—see reg.1(3).
"the Employment, Skills and Enterprise Scheme"—*ibid.*
"family"—Jobseekers Act s.35(1).
"Grenfell Tower Payment"—see reg.1(3)
"independent hospital"—*ibid.*
"Intensive Activity Period for 50 plus"—*ibid.*
"the London Emergencies Trust"—*ibid.*
"the Mandatory Work Activity Scheme"—*ibid.*
"MFET Limited"—*ibid.*
"occupational pension"—*ibid.*
"occupational pension scheme"—see Jobseekers Act s.35(1).
"partner"—see reg.1(3).
"pay period"—*ibid.*
"payment"—*ibid.*
"personal pension scheme"—see Jobseekers Act s.35(1).
"qualifying age for state pension credit"—see reg.1(3).
"Scottish basic rate"—*ibid.*
"Scottish Infected Blood Support Scheme"—*ibid.*
"Scottish taxpayer" —*ibid.*
"single claimant"—*ibid.*
"the Skipton Fund"—*ibid.*
"subsistence allowance"—*ibid.*
"the Eileen Trust"—*ibid.*
"the Fund"—*ibid.*
"the Independent Living Funds"—*ibid.*

"the Macfarlane (Special Payments) Trust"—*ibid.*
"the Macfarlane (Special Payments) (No.2) Trust"—*ibid.*
"the Macfarlane Trust"—*ibid.*
"the National Emergencies Trust"—*ibid.*
"the Skipton Fund"—*ibid.*
"training allowance"—*ibid.*
"voluntary organisation"—*ibid.*
"war disablement pension"—*ibid.*
"war widow's pension"—*ibid.*
"war widower's pension"—*ibid.*
"water charges"—*ibid.*
"the We Love Manchester Emergency Fund"—*ibid.*
"working tax credit"—*ibid.*
"year of assessment"—*ibid.*

GENERAL NOTE

3.340   See the notes to reg.42 of the Income Support Regulations. There are some differences which are mainly related to the different nature of the two benefits (for example, there is no equivalent in reg.105 to reg.42(6A)(c) as this relates to lone parents).

See also the new head (iv) inserted in para.(10A)(c) on October 5, 2009 which has not been reproduced in reg.42(4ZA)(c) of the Income Support Regulations.

Note that a new para.(10A)(cc) was inserted with effect from February 12, 2013 and the original para.(10A)(cc) (which related to a claimant's participation in the Employment, Skills and Enterprise Scheme) has been treated as revoked from that date as a result of s.1(14) of the Jobseekers (Back to Work Schemes) Act 2013. The Jobseeker's Allowance (Employment, Skills and Enterprise Scheme) Regulations 2011 (SI 2011/917) were held to be ultra vires by the Court of Appeal in *R (Reilly and Wilson) v Secretary of State for Work and Pensions* [2013] EWCA Civ 66, [2013] 1 W.L.R. 2239. The appeal against this decision was allowed by the Supreme Court on October 30, 2013 (*R (on the application of Reilly) v Secretary of State for Work and Pensions* [2013] UKSC 68, [2014] 1 A.C. 453) but "on the basis only that the Jobseekers (Back to Work Schemes) Act 2013 has come into force" (the 2013 Act came into force on March 26, 2013).

Sub-paragraphs (ca), (cd) and (ce) of para.(10A) have not been included. This is because they only apply to pilot schemes in certain areas of the country under provisions that have ceased to have effect. See previous editions of what was then Vol.II of this series for details.

Paragraph (1)
3.341   Until October 31, 2011 para.(1) applied if the deprivation had been for the purpose of securing entitlement to, or increasing the amount of, old style JSA *or income support*. This avoided the question that might otherwise have arisen on a claimant transferring from income support to old style JSA whether a deprivation which had only been for the purposes of income support was caught by para.(1). But para.(1) was not amended immediately on the introduction of ESA to include a reference to a deprivation for the purposes of ESA. The question could therefore have arisen on a claimant transferring from ESA to old style JSA as to whether a deprivation which had only been for the purposes of old style ESA was caught by para.(1).

Paragraph (1) was, however, amended with effect from October 31, 2011 so that it now applies to people who have deprived themselves of income in order to secure entitlement to, or increase the amount of, old style JSA, income support or old style ESA. A similar amendment was made to reg.42(1) of the Income Support Regulations, so that it now also applies if the deprivation was for the purpose of securing entitlement to, or increasing the amount of, income support, old style JSA or old style ESA. The Explanatory Memorandum which accompanied the SI that made these amendments describes this as a "minor" change, the need for which was apparently overlooked when ESA was introduced. However, the change to para.(1) could have a significant effect in certain cases because a deprivation of income now counts for the purposes of all three benefits. It is suggested that para.(1) would not previously have bitten if the deprivation had been for the purpose of securing, or increasing, entitlement to old style ESA.

Note that the old style JSA deprivation of capital rule (reg.113(1)) has not been amended; it continues to apply only where the deprivation was for the purposes of securing entitlement to, or increasing the amount of, old style JSA or income support.

Modifications in respect of children and young persons

106.—[¹. . .]   3.342

AMENDMENT

1. Social Security (Working Tax Credit and Child Tax Credit) (Consequential Amendments) Regulations 2003 (SI 2003/455) reg.3 and Sch.2 para.11 (April 6, 2004, except in "transitional cases" and see further the note to reg.83 and to reg.17 of the Income Support Regulations).

GENERAL NOTE

See the notes to reg.44 of the Income Support Regulations.   3.343

Chapter VI

Capital

[¹Capital limit

107.—For the purposes of section 13(1) and (2A) (no entitlement to   3.344
an income-based jobseeker's allowance if capital exceeds a prescribed
amount), the prescribed amount is £16,000.]

AMENDMENT

1. Social Security (Miscellaneous Amendments) (No.2) Regulations 2005 (SI 2005/2465) reg.3(4) (April 10, 2006).

DEFINITION

"claimant"—see Jobseekers Act s.35(1) and reg.88(1).

GENERAL NOTE

Under s.13(1) of the old style Jobseekers Act 1995 there is no entitlement to   3.345
income-based JSA if the claimant's capital exceeds the prescribed amount. The limit
is the same as it is for income support, that is from April 10, 2006 it is £16,000 for
all claimants, thus bringing income-based JSA and income support into line with
housing benefit and, until its abolition on April 1, 2013, council tax benefit. In addition, the amount above which the tariff income rule applies was increased to £6,000,
except in the case of residents in a care home, Abbeyfield Home, Polish Resettlement
home or independent hospital, for whom the tariff income rule will continue to apply
only to capital above £10,000 (see reg.116).

The capital of a claimant's partner is aggregated with the claimant's (reg.88(1)),
but not that of children and young persons (reg.88(2)).

See the notes to reg.45 of the Income Support Regulations.

Calculation of capital

3.346   **108.**—(1) Subject to paragraph (2), the capital of a claimant to be taken into account shall be the whole of his capital calculated in accordance with this Part and any income treated as capital under regulation 110.

(2) There shall be disregarded from the calculation of a claimant's capital under paragraph (1) any capital, where applicable, specified in Schedule 8.

DEFINITION

"claimant"—see Jobseekers Act s.35(1) and reg.88(1).

GENERAL NOTE

3.347   See the notes to reg.46 of the Income Support Regulations.

Disregard of capital of child or young person

3.348   **109.**—[¹. . .]

AMENDMENT

1. Social Security (Working Tax Credit and Child Tax Credit) (Consequential Amendments) Regulations 2003 (SI 2003/455) reg.3 and Sch.2 para.11 (April 6, 2004, except in "transitional cases" and see further the note to reg.83 and to reg.17 of the Income Support Regulations).

GENERAL NOTE

3.349   See the notes to reg.47 of the Income Support Regulations.

Income treated as capital

3.350   **110.**—(1) Any bounty derived from employment to which paragraph 9 of Schedule 6 applies and paid at intervals of at least one year shall be treated as capital.

(2) Except in the case of an amount to which section 15(2)(c)(i) (refund of tax in trade dispute cases) applies, any amount by way of a refund of income tax deducted from profits or emoluments chargeable to income tax under Schedule D or E shall be treated as capital.

(3) Any holiday pay which is not earnings under regulation 98(1)(c) (earnings of employed earners) shall be treated as capital.

(4) Except any income derived from capital disregarded under paragraphs 1, 2, 4 to 8, 11 [⁴, 17, 42 or 43] of Schedule 8, any income derived from capital shall be treated as capital but only from the date it is normally due to be credited to the claimant's account.

(5) Subject to paragraph (6), in the case of employment as an employed earner, any advance of earnings or any loan made by the claimant's employer shall be treated as capital.

(6) Paragraph (5) shall not apply to a person who is, or would be, prevented from being entitled to a jobseeker's allowance by section 14 (trade disputes).

(7) Any payment under section 30 of the Prison Act 1952 (payments for discharged prisoners) or allowance under section 17 of the Prisons (Scotland) Act 1989 (allowances to prisoners on discharge) shall be treated as capital.

(8) [³. . .]

(9) Any charitable or voluntary payment which is not made or not due to be made at regular intervals, other than one to which paragraph (10) applies, shall be treated as capital.

(10) This paragraph applies to a payment—

(a) which is made to a person who is, or would be, prevented from being entitled to a jobseeker's allowance by section 14 (trade disputes);

[¹²(ab) which is a Grenfell Tower payment;]

(b) [³ . . .]

(c) which is made under [⁷ or by] the Macfarlane Trust, the Macfarlane (Special Payments) Trust, the Macfarlane (Special Payments) (No.2) Trust, the Fund, the Eileen Trust[⁶ , MFET Limited][⁸ , the Skipton Fund, the Caxton Foundation][⁹, the Scottish Infected Blood Support Scheme][¹¹, an approved blood scheme][¹⁰, the London Emergencies Trust, the We Love Manchester Emergency Fund][¹², the National Emergencies Trust] or the Independent Living [⁵ Fund (2006)].

[²(11) Any arrears of subsistence allowance which are paid to a claimant as a lump sum shall be treated as capital.]

AMENDMENTS

1. Social Security (Miscellaneous Amendments) Regulations 1998 (SI 1998/563) reg.14(2) (April 6, 1998).

2. Social Security Amendment (Employment Zones) Regulations 2000 (SI 2000/724) reg.3(2) (April 3, 2000).

3. Social Security (Working Tax Credit and Child Tax Credit) (Consequential Amendments) Regulations 2003 (SI 2003/455) reg.3 and Sch.2 para.12 (April 6, 2004, except in "transitional cases" and see further the note to reg.83 and to reg.17 of the Income Support Regulations).

4. Social Security (Miscellaneous Amendments) (No.4) Regulations 2006 (SI 2006/2378) reg.13(6) (October 2, 2006).

5. Social Security (Miscellaneous Amendments) (No.6) Regulations 2008 (SI 2008/2767) reg.4(7) (November 17, 2008).

6. Social Security (Miscellaneous Amendments) (No.2) Regulations 2010 (SI 2010/641) reg.4(3)(c) (April 6, 2010).

7. Social Security (Miscellaneous Amendments) (No.2) Regulations 2010 (SI 2010/641) reg.4(8)(b) (April 6, 2010).

8. Social Security (Miscellaneous Amendments) (No.3) Regulations 2011 (SI 2011/2425) reg.10(9) (October 31, 2011).

9. Social Security (Scottish Infected Blood Support Scheme) Regulations 2017 (SI 2017/329) reg.4(3) (April 3, 2017).

10. Social Security (Emergency Funds) (Amendment) Regulations 2017 (SI 2017/689) reg.3(3)(b) (June 19, 2017).

11. Social Security (Infected Blood and Thalidomide) Regulations 2017 (SI 2017/870) reg.3(3)(b) (October 23, 2017).

12. Social Security (Income and Capital) (Miscellaneous Amendments) Regulations 2020 (SI 2020/618) reg.3(4) (July 15, 2020).

DEFINITIONS

"approved blood scheme"—see reg.1(3).
"child"—see Jobseekers Act 1995 s.35(1).
"the Caxton Foundation"—see reg.1(3).
"the Children Order"—*ibid.*
"claimant"—Jobseekers Act 1995, s.35(1) and reg.88(1).
"earnings"—see reg.1(3).

"employed earner"—see reg.3 and SSCBA s.2(1)(a).
"the Eileen Trust"—see reg.1(3).
"family"—see Jobseekers Act 1995 s.35(1).
"the Fund"—see reg.1(3).
"Grenfell Tower Payment"—*ibid.*
"the Independent Living Funds"—*ibid.*
"the London Emergencies Trust"—*ibid.*
"the Macfarlane (Special Payments) Trust"—*ibid.*
"the MacFarlane (Special Payments) (No.2) Trust"—*ibid.*
"the Macfarlane Trust"—*ibid.*
"MFET Limited"—*ibid.*
"the National Emergencies Trust"—*ibid.*
"Scottish Infected Blood Support Scheme"—*ibid.*
"the Skipton Fund"—*ibid.*
"subsistence allowance"—*ibid.*
"the We Love Manchester Emergency Fund"—*ibid.*

GENERAL NOTE

3.351   See the notes to reg.48 of the Income Support Regulations. Most of the categories deemed to be capital are self-explanatory. They are then disregarded as income (Sch.7 para.34).

[¹ Calculation of capital in the United Kingdom

3.352   **111.**—Capital which a claimant possesses in the United Kingdom shall be calculated at its current market or surrender value less—
   (a) where there would be expenses attributable to sale, 10 per cent ; and
   (b) the amount of any incumbrance secured on it.]

AMENDMENT

1. Social Security (Miscellaneous Amendments) (No.5) Regulations 2007 (SI 2007/2618) reg.8(12) (October 1, 2007).

DEFINITION

"claimant"—see Jobseekers Act 1995 s.35(1) and reg.88(1).

GENERAL NOTE

3.353   See the notes to reg.49 of the Income Support Regulations.

Calculation of capital outside the United Kingdom

3.354   **112.**—Capital which a claimant possesses in a country outside the United Kingdom shall be calculated—
   (a) in a case in which there is no prohibition in that country against the transfer to the United Kingdom of an amount equal to its current market or surrender value in that country, at that value;
   (b) in a case where there is such a prohibition, at the price which it would realise if sold in the United Kingdom to a willing buyer,
less, where there would be expenses attributable to sale, 10 per cent, and the amount of any incumbrance secured on it.

DEFINITION

"claimant"—see Jobseekers Act 1995 s.35(1) and reg.88(1).

GENERAL NOTE

See the note to reg.50 of the Income Support Regulations. 3.355

Notional capital

113.—(1) A claimant shall be treated as possessing capital of which he 3.356
has deprived himself for the purpose of securing entitlement to a jobseeker's
allowance or increasing the amount of that allowance, or for the purpose
of securing entitlement to or increasing the amount of income support,
except—

  (a) where that capital is derived from a payment made in consequence of
        a personal injury and is placed on trust for the benefit of the claim-
        ant; or
  (b) to the extent that the capital he is treated as possessing is reduced in
        accordance with regulation 114 (diminishing notional capital rule);
        [¹or
[¹⁶(c) any sum to which paragraph 42(2)(a) of Schedule 8 (capital to be
        disregarded) applies which is administered in the way referred to in
        paragraph 42(1)(a); or
  (d) any sum to which paragraph 43(a) of Schedule 8 refers.]]
  (2) Except in the case of—
  (a) a discretionary trust;
  (b) a trust derived from a payment made in consequence of a personal
        injury;
  (c) any loan which would be obtainable only if secured against capital
        disregarded under Schedule 8; or
  (d) a personal pension scheme; [¹or
[¹⁴(da) an occupational pension scheme [¹⁵or a payment made by the Board
        of the Pension Protection Fund] where the claimant [²⁴has not
        attained the qualifying age for state pension credit]; or]
[¹⁷(e) any sum to which paragraph 42(2)(a) of Schedule 8 (capital to be
        disregarded) applies which is administered in the way referred to in
        paragraph 42(1)(a); or
  (f) any sum to which paragraph 43(a) of Schedule 8 refers,]]
any capital which would become available to the claimant upon application
being made but which has not been acquired by him shall be treated as
possessed by him but only from the date on which it could be expected to
be acquired were an application made.
  (3) [³Any payment of capital, other than a payment of capital specified in
[³³ paragraph (3A) or (3B)]], made—
  (a) to a third party in respect of a single claimant or [¹⁰ his partner] shall
        be treated—
        (i) in a case where that payment is derived from a payment of
             any benefit under the [²⁰ benefit Acts, a payment from the
             Armed Forces and Reserve Forces Compensation Scheme, a
             war disablement pension, war widow's pension or war wid-
             ower's pension or a pension payable to a person as a widow,
             widower or surviving civil partner under any power of Her

Majesty otherwise than under an enactment to make provision about pensions for or in respect of persons who have been disabled or have died in consequence of service as members of the armed forces of the Crown], as possessed by that single claimant, if it would normally be paid to him, or as possessed [¹⁰ by his partner, if it would normally be paid to his partner];

[⁴(ia) in a case where that payment is a payment of an occupational pension[¹⁵, a pension or other periodical payment made under a personal pension scheme or a payment made by the Board of the Pension Protection Fund], as possessed by that single claimant or, as the case may be, by [¹⁰ the claimant's partner];]

(ii) in any other case, as possessed by that single claimant [¹⁰ or his partner] to the extent that it is used for the food, ordinary clothing or footwear, household fuel, rent for which housing benefit [⁸ is payable] or any housing costs to the extent that they are met under regulation 83(f) [⁶84(1)(g), 86A(d) or 86B(e)] [⁸ . . .], of that single claimant or, as the case may be, [¹⁰ of his partner], or is used for any council tax or water charges for which that claimant or [¹⁰ partner is liable];

[¹⁰ (b) to a single claimant or his partner in respect of a third party (but not in respect of another member of his family) shall be treated as possessed by that single claimant or, as the case may be, his partner, to the extent that it is kept or used by him or used by or on behalf of his partner.]

[³(3A) Paragraph (3) shall not apply in respect of a payment of capital made—

(a) under [²³or by] the Macfarlane Trust, the Macfarlane (Special Payments) Trust, the Macfarlane (Special Payments) (No.2) Trust, the Fund, the Eileen Trust[²², MFET Limited][¹¹, the Independent Living [¹⁹ Fund (2006)][¹³, the Skipton Fund[²⁷, the Caxton Foundation][³⁰, the Scottish Infected Blood Support Scheme][³², an approved blood scheme][³¹, the London Emergencies Trust, the We Love Manchester Emergency Fund] [³³, the National Emergencies Trust] or the London Bombings Relief Charitable Fund]]; or

(b) pursuant to section 2 of the Employment and Training Act 1973 in respect of a person's participation—

(i) in an employment programme specified in regulation 75(1)(a)(ii);

(ii) in a training scheme specified in regulation 75(1)(b)(ii); or

[⁷(iia) [¹⁸ . . .] in the Intensive Activity Period specified in regulation 75(1)(a)(iv); or]

(iii) in a qualifying course within the meaning specified in regulation 17A(7)] [²¹; or

(iv) in the Flexible New Deal.]

(ba) [*Omitted*]

[²⁵(bb) in respect of a person's participation in the Mandatory Work Activity Scheme;]

[²⁶(bc) [²⁹ . . .]]

[²⁸(bc) in respect of a claimant's participation in a scheme prescribed in regulation 3 of the Jobseeker's Allowance (Schemes for Assisting Persons to Obtain Employment) Regulations 2013;]

(bd) *[Omitted]*

(be) *[Omitted]*

[[5](c) under an occupational pension scheme[[15], in respect of a pension or other periodical payment made under a personal pension scheme or a payment made by the Board of the Pension Protection Fund] where—

    (i) a bankruptcy order has been made in respect of the person in respect of whom the payment has been made or, in Scotland, the estate of that person is subject to sequestration or a judicial factor has been appointed on that person's estate under section 41 of the Solicitors (Scotland) Act 1980;

    (ii) the payment is made to the trustee in bankruptcy or any other person acting on behalf of the creditors; and

    (iii) the person referred to in (i) and [[10] his partner (if any)]does not possess, or is not treated as possessing, any other income apart from that payment.]

[[33](3B) Paragraph (3) shall not apply in respect of a payment of capital which is a Grenfell Tower payment.]

(4)Where a claimant stands in relation to a company in a position analogous to that of a sole owner or a partner in the business of that company, he shall be treated as if he were such sole owner or partner and in such a case—

    (a) the value of his holding in that company shall, notwithstanding regulation 108 (calculation of capital), be disregarded; and

    (b) he shall, subject to paragraph (5), be treated as possessing an amount of capital equal to the value or, as the case may be, his share of the value of the capital of that company and the foregoing provisions of this Chapter shall apply for the purposes of calculating that amount as if it were actual capital which he does possess.

(5) For so long as the claimant undertakes activities in the course of the business of the company, the amount which he is treated as possessing under paragraph (4) shall be disregarded.

(6) Where a claimant is treated as possessing any capital under any of paragraphs (1) to (4) the foregoing provisions of this Chapter shall apply for the purposes of calculating the amount of that capital as if it were actual capital which he does possess.

(7) For the avoidance of doubt a claimant is to be treated as possessing capital under paragraph (1) only if the capital of which he has deprived himself is actual capital.

(8) In paragraph (3) the expression "ordinary clothing or footwear" means clothing or footwear for normal daily use, but does not include school uniforms, or clothing or footwear used solely for sporting activities.

AMENDMENTS

1. Income-related Benefits and Jobseeker's Allowance (Amendment) (No.2) Regulations 1997 (SI 1997/2197) reg.6 (October 6, 1997).

2. Social Security Amendment (New Deal) Regulations 1997 (SI 1997/2863) reg.10 (January 5, 1998).

3. Social Security Amendment (New Deal) (No.2) Regulations 1998 (SI 1998/2117) reg.3(1) (September 24, 1998).

4. Social Security Amendment (Notional Income and Capital) Regulations 1999 (SI 1999/2640) reg.2(1)(b) (November 15, 1999).

5. Social Security Amendment (Notional Income and Capital) Regulations 1999 (SI 1999/2640) reg.2(3)(d) (November 15, 1999).

6. Jobseeker's Allowance (Joint Claims) Regulations 2000 (SI 2000/1978) reg.2(5) and Sch.2 para.44 (March 19, 2001).

7. Social Security Amendment (New Deal) Regulations 2001 (SI 2001/1029) reg.8 (April 9, 2001).

8. Social Security Amendment (Residential Care and Nursing Homes) Regulations 2001 (SI 2001/3767) reg.2(2) and Pt II of Sch. para.11 (April 8, 2002).

9. Social Security (Miscellaneous Amendments) Regulations 2002 (SI 2002/841) reg.3(3) (April 8, 2002).

10. Social Security (Working Tax Credit and Child Tax Credit) (Consequential Amendments) Regulations 2003 (SI 2003/455) reg.3 and Sch.2 para.13 (April 6, 2004, except in "transitional cases" and see further the note to regs 83 and 17 of the Income Support Regulations).

11. Social Security (Miscellaneous Amendments) (No.3) Regulations 2004 (SI 2004/2308) reg.3(1) and (2)(d) (October 4, 2004).

12. Social Security (Miscellaneous Amendments) Regulations 2005 (SI 2005/574) reg.2(6) (April 4, 2005).

13. Income-related Benefits (Amendment) (No.2) Regulations 2005 (SI 2005/3391) reg.5(3) (December 12, 2005).

14. Social Security (Miscellaneous Amendments) (No.2) Regulations 2005 (SI 2005/2465) reg.3(5) (April 6, 2006).

15. Social Security (Miscellaneous Amendments) Regulations 2006 (SI 2006/588) reg.3(4) (April 6, 2006).

16. Social Security (Miscellaneous Amendments) Regulations 2007 (SI 2007/719) reg.3(5)(a) (April 2, 2007).

17. Social Security (Miscellaneous Amendments) Regulations 2007 (SI 2007/719) reg.3(5)(b) (April 2, 2007).

18. Social Security (Miscellaneous Amendments) Regulations 2008 (SI 2008/698) reg.4(12)(b) (April 14, 2008).

19. Social Security (Miscellaneous Amendments) (No.6) Regulations 2008 (SI 2008/2767) reg.4(7) (November 17, 2008).

20. Social Security (Miscellaneous Amendments) (No.7) Regulations 2008 (SI 2008/3157) reg.3(6) (January 5, 2009).

21. Social Security (Flexible New Deal) Regulations 2009 (SI 2009/480) reg.2(7) (October 5, 2009).

22. Social Security (Miscellaneous Amendments) (No.2) Regulations 2010 (SI 2010/641) reg.4(3)(d) (April 6, 2010).

23. Social Security (Miscellaneous Amendments) (No.2) Regulations 2010 (SI 2010/641) reg.4(8)(c) (April 6, 2010).

24. Social Security (Miscellaneous Amendments) (No.2) Regulations 2010 (SI 2010/641) reg.4(9) (April 6, 2010).

25. Jobseeker's Allowance (Mandatory Work Activity Scheme) Regulations 2011 (SI 2011/688) reg.13(1)(d) and (2) (April 25, 2011).

26. Jobseeker's Allowance (Employment, Skills and Enterprise Scheme) Regulations 2011 (SI 2011/917) reg.13(1)(d) and (2) (May 20, 2011).

27. Social Security (Miscellaneous Amendments) (No.3) Regulations 2011 (SI 2011/2425) reg.10(10) (October 31, 2011).

28. Jobseeker's Allowance (Schemes for Assisting Persons to Obtain Employment) Regulations 2013 (SI 2013/276) reg.10(1)(d) and (2) (February 12, 2013).

29. Jobseekers (Back to Work Schemes) Act 2013 s.1(14) (March 26, 2013).

30. Social Security (Scottish Infected Blood Support Scheme) Regulations 2017 (SI 2017/329) reg.4(3) (April 3, 2017).

31. Social Security (Emergency Funds) (Amendment) Regulations 2017 (SI 2017/689) reg.3(3)(c) (June 19, 2017).

32. Social Security (Infected Blood and Thalidomide) Regulations 2017 (SI 2017/870) reg.3(3)(c) (October 23, 2017).

33. Social Security (Income and Capital) (Miscellaneous Amendments) Regulations 2020 (SI 2020/618) reg.3(5) (July 15, 2020).

DEFINITIONS

"the Act"—see reg.1(3).
"approved blood scheme"—*ibid.*
"the Armed Forces and Reserve Forces Compensation Scheme"—*ibid.*
"the Benefits Act"—see Jobseekers Act s.35(1).
"the Caxton Foundation"—see reg.1(3).
"civil partner"—see Interpretation Act 1978 Sch.1.
"claimant"—see Jobseekers Act s.35(1) and reg.88(1).
"the Employment, Skills and Enterprise Scheme"—see reg.1(3).
"family"—see Jobseekers Act s.35(1).
"occupational pension"—see reg.1(3).
"payment"—*ibid.*
"personal pension scheme"—see Jobseekers Act s.35(1).
"the Eileen Trust"—see reg.1(3).
"the Fund"—*ibid.*
"Grenfell Tower Payment"—*ibid.*
"the Independent Living Funds"—*ibid.*
"the London Bombings Relief Charitable Fund"—*ibid.*
"the London Emergencies Trust"—*ibid.*
"the Macfarlane (Special Payments) Trust"—*ibid.*
"the Macfarlane (Special Payments) (No.2) Trust"—*ibid.*
"the Macfarlane Trust"—*ibid.*
"the Mandatory Work Activity Scheme"—*ibid.*
"MFET Limited"—*ibid.*
"the National Emergencies Trust"—*ibid.*
"qualifying age for state pension credit"—*ibid.*
"Scottish Infected Blood Support Scheme"—*ibid.*
"the Skipton Fund"—*ibid.*
"single claimant"—*ibid.*
"war disablement pension"—*ibid.*
"war widow's pension"—*ibid.*
"war widower's pension"—*ibid.*
"water charges"—*ibid.*
"the We Love Manchester Emergency Fund"—*ibid.*

GENERAL NOTE

See the notes to reg.51 of the Income Support Regulations. Note that para.(3A) **3.357** (b)(iv), (bb) and (bc) have no equivalent in reg.51.

In relation to para.(3A)(bc), note that a further para.(3A)(bc) was inserted on February 12, 2013, and the original para.(3A)(bc) has been treated as revoked from that date as a result of s.1(14) of the Jobseekers (Back to Work Schemes) Act 2013. The original para.(3A)(bc) related to a claimant's participation in the Employment, Skills and Enterprise Scheme. The Jobseeker's Allowance (Employment, Skills and Enterprise Scheme) Regulations 2011 (SI 2011/917) were held to be ultra vires by the Court of Appeal in *R (Reilly and Wilson) v Secretary of State for Work and Pensions* [2013] EWCA Civ 66; [2013] 1 W.L.R. 2239. The appeal against this decision was allowed by the Supreme Court on October 30, 2013 (*R (on the application of Reilly) v Secretary of State for Work and Pensions* [2013] UKSC 68; [2014] 1 A.C. 453) but "on the basis only that the Jobseekers (Back to Work Schemes) Act 2013 has come into force" (the 2013 Act came into force on March 26, 2013).

Sub-paragraphs (ba), (bd) and (be) of para.(3A) have not been included. That is because they only apply to pilot schemes in certain areas of the country under provisions that have ceased to have effect. See previous editions of what was then Vol.II of this series for details.

Paragraph (1)

Under para.(1) people who have deprived themselves of capital will be caught by **3.358** this rule if the purpose of the deprivation was to secure entitlement to or increase the amount of old style JSA *or income support*. This avoids the question that might otherwise have arisen on a claimant transfering from income support to old style JSA whether a deprivation which had only been for the purposes of income support could be caught by para.(1). But note that para.(1) has not been amended to include a reference to a deprivation for the purposes of obtaining old style ESA. Such an amendment, however, was made to para.(1) of reg.105 on October 31, 2011.

Diminishing notional capital rule

3.359   **114.**—(1) Where a claimant is treated as possessing capital under regulation 113(1) (notional capital), the amount which he is treated as possessing—

(a) in the case of a week that is subsequent to—
  (i) the relevant week in respect of which the conditions set out in paragraph (2) are satisfied, or
  (ii) a week which follows that relevant week and which satisfies those conditions,
  shall be reduced by an amount determined under paragraph (2);

(b) in the case of a week in respect of which paragraph (1)(a) does not apply but where—
  (i) that week is a week subsequent to the relevant week, and
  (ii) that relevant week is a week in which the condition in paragraph (3) is satisfied,
  shall be reduced by an amount determined under paragraph (3).

(2) This paragraph applies to a benefit week or part week where the claimant satisfies the conditions that—

(a) he is in receipt of a jobseeker's allowance; and

(b) but for regulation 113(1), he would have received an additional amount of jobseeker's allowance in that benefit week or, as the case may be, that part week;

and in such a case, the amount of the reduction for the purposes of paragraph (1)(a) shall be equal to that additional amount.

(3) Subject to paragraph (4), for the purposes of paragraph (1)(b) the condition is that the claimant would have been entitled to an income-based jobseeker's allowance in the relevant week but for regulation 113(1), and in such a case the amount of the reduction shall be equal to the aggregate of—

(a) the amount of jobseeker's allowance to which the claimant would have been entitled in the relevant week but for regulation 113(1); and for the purposes of this sub-paragraph if the relevant week is a part-week that amount shall be determined by dividing the amount of jobseeker's allowance to which he would have been entitled by the number equal to the number of days in the part-week and multiplying the quotient by 7;

(b) the amount of housing benefit (if any) equal to the difference between his maximum housing benefit and the amount (if any) of housing benefit which he is awarded in respect of the benefit week which includes the last day of the relevant week, and for this purpose "benefit week" has the same meaning as in regulation 2(1) of [¹ the Housing Benefit Regulations 2006] (interpretation);

(c) the amount of council tax benefit (if any) equal to the difference between his maximum council tax benefit and the amount (if any) of council tax benefit which he is awarded in respect of the benefit week which includes the last day of the relevant week, and for this purpose "benefit week" [² means a period of 7 consecutive days beginning on a Monday and ending on a Sunday].

(4) The amount determined under paragraph (3) shall be re-determined under that paragraph if the claimant makes a further claim for a jobseeker's allowance and the conditions in paragraph (5) are satisfied, and in such a case—

(a) sub-paragraphs (a), (b) and (c) of paragraph (3) shall apply as if for the words "relevant week" there were substituted the words "relevant subsequent week"; and

(b) subject to paragraph (6), the amount as re-determined shall have effect from the first week following the relevant subsequent week in question.

(5) The conditions referred to in paragraph (4) are that—

(a) a further claim is made 26 or more weeks after—

   (i) the date on which the claimant made a claim for a jobseeker's allowance in respect of which he was first treated as possessing the capital in question under regulation 113(1); or

   (ii) in a case where there has been at least one re-determination in accordance with paragraph (4), the date on which he last made a claim for a jobseeker's allowance which resulted in the weekly amount being re-determined; or

   (iii) the date on which he last ceased to be in receipt of a jobseeker's allowance;

   whichever last occurred; and

(b) the claimant would have been entitled to a jobseeker's allowance but for regulation 113(1).

(6) The amount as re-determined pursuant to paragraph (4) shall not have effect if it is less than the amount which applied in that case immediately before the re-determination and in such a case the higher amount shall continue to have effect.

(7) For the purposes of this regulation—

(a) "part-week" has the same meaning as in regulation 150(3);

(b) "relevant week" means the benefit week or part-week in which the capital in question of which the claimant has deprived himself within the meaning of regulation 113(1)—

   (i) was first taken into account for the purposes of determining his entitlement to a jobseeker's allowance or income support; or

   (ii) was taken into account on a subsequent occasion for the purposes of determining or re-determining his entitlement to a jobseeker's allowance or income support on that subsequent occasion and that determination or re-determination resulted in his beginning to receive, or ceasing to receive, a jobseeker's allowance or income support;

   and where more than one benefit week or part-week is identified by reference to heads (i) and (ii) of this sub-paragraph, the later or latest such benefit week or part-week;

(c) "relevant subsequent week" means the benefit week or part-week which includes the day on which the further claim or, if more than one further claim has been made, the last such claim was made.

AMENDMENTS

1. Housing Benefit and Council Tax Benefit (Consequential Provisions) Regulations 2006 (SI 2006/217) reg.5 and Sch.2 para.8(3) (March 6, 2006).

2. Council Tax Benefit Abolition (Consequential Provision) Regulations 2013 (SI 2013/458) reg.4 and Sch.2 para.3 (April 1, 2013).

DEFINITIONS

"benefit week"—see reg.1(3).
"claimant"—see Jobseekers Act s.35(1) and reg.88(1).
"week"—see Jobseekers Act s.35(1).

GENERAL NOTE

3.360   See the notes to reg.51A of the Income Support Regulations.

Capital jointly held

3.361   **115.**—Except where a claimant possesses capital which is disregarded under regulation 113(4) (notional capital), where a claimant and one or more persons are beneficially entitled in possession to any capital asset, they shall be treated as if each of them were entitled in possession [¹to the whole beneficial interest therein in an equal share and the foregoing provisions of this Chapter shall apply for the purposes of calculating the amount of capital which the claimant is treated as possessing as if it were actual capital which the claimant does possess.]

AMENDMENT

1. Social Security Amendment (Capital) Regulations 1998 (SI 1998/2250) reg.2 (October 12, 1998).

DEFINITION

"claimant"—see Jobseekers Act s.35(1) and reg.88(1).

GENERAL NOTE

3.362   See the notes to reg.52 of the Income Support Regulations.

Calculation of tariff income from capital

3.363   **116.**—(1) [¹Except in a case to which paragraph [⁷ . . .] (1B) applies,] where the claimant's capital calculated in accordance with this Part exceeds [⁷£6,000] it shall be treated as equivalent to a weekly income of £1 for each complete £250 in excess of [⁷£6,000] but not exceeding [⁷£16,000].
[⁴ (1ZA) [⁷ . . .]]
[¹(1A) In the case of a claimant to whom paragraph (1B) applies and whose capital calculated in accordance with Chapter VI of Part VIII exceeds £10,000, it shall be treated as equivalent to a weekly income of £1 for each complete £250 in excess of £10,000 but not exceeding £16,000.

(1B) This paragraph applies where the claimant lives permanently in—
[⁶ (a) a care home or an independent hospital;
(b) an Abbeyfield Home;]
(c) accommodation provided under section 3 of, and Part II of the Schedule to, the Polish Resettlement Act 1947 (provision of accommodation in camps) where the claimant requires personal care [³by reason of old age, disablement, past or present dependence on alcohol or drugs, past or present mental disorder or a terminal illness and the care is provided in the home];
[²(d) [⁶ . . .].]
(1C) For the purpose of paragraph (1B), a claimant shall be treated as living permanently in such home [⁶, hospital] or accommodation where he is absent—
[⁵(a) from a home [⁶, hospital] or accommodation referred to in sub-paragraph (a) [⁶ or (b)] of paragraph (1B) for a period not exceeding 13 weeks;]
(b) from accommodation referred to in sub-paragraph (c) of paragraph (1B), but intends, with the agreement of the manager of the accommodation, to return to the accommodation in due course.]
(2) Notwithstanding [¹paragraphs (1) [⁷ . . .] and (1A)], where any part of the excess is not a complete £250 that part shall be treated as equivalent to a weekly income of £1.
(3) For the purposes of [¹paragraphs (1) [⁷ . . .] and (1A)], capital includes any income treated as capital under regulations 110 and 124 (income treated as capital and liable relative payments treated as capital).
[¹(4) [⁶ . . .].]

AMENDMENTS

1. Jobseeker's Allowance (Amendment) Regulations 1996 (SI 1996/1516) reg.12 (October 7, 1996).
2. Income-related Benefits and Jobseeker's Allowance (Miscellaneous Amendments) Regulations 1997 (SI 1997/65) reg.8 (April 7, 1997).
3. Income-related Benefits and Jobseeker's Allowance (Amendment) (No.2) Regulations 1997 (SI 1997/2197) reg.7(5) and (6)(b) (October 6, 1997).
4. Social Security Amendment (Capital Limits and Earnings Disregards) Regulations 2000 (SI 2000/2545) reg.2(2)(c) (April 9, 2001).
5. Social Security Amendment (Residential Care and Nursing Homes) Regulations 2001 (SI 2001/3767) reg.2(2) and Pt II of Sch. para.12 (April 8, 2002).
6. Social Security (Care Homes and Independent Hospitals) Regulations 2005 (SI 2005/2687) reg.3 and Sch.2 para.6 (October 24, 2005).
7. Social Security (Miscellaneous Amendments) (No.2) Regulations 2005 (SI 2005/2465) reg.3(6) (April 10, 2006).

DEFINITIONS

"Abbeyfield Home"—see reg.1(3).
"care home"—*ibid.*
"claimant"—see Jobseekers Act s.35(1) and reg.88(1).
"independent hospital"—see reg.1(3).

GENERAL NOTE

See the notes to reg.53 of the Income Support Regulations.

3.364

Chapter VII

[⁴[⁶ . . .] Liable Relative Payments]

Interpretation

3.365   **117.**—In this Chapter, unless the context otherwise requires—
[⁵ [⁷. . .]]
"claimant" includes a young claimant;
[⁵ "claimant's family" shall be construed in accordance with section
35(1) of the Jobseekers Act 1995 (interpretation);]
[⁵ "housing costs" means those costs which may be met under regulation
83(f) or 84(1)(g) (housing costs);]
"liable relative" means—
(a) a spouse [², former spouse, civil partner or former civil partner] of
a claimant or of a member of the claimant's family;
(b) a parent of a young claimant or of a child or young person who is a
member of a claimant's family;
(c) a person who has not been adjudged to be the father of a young
claimant or of a child or young person who is a member of a
claimant's family, where that person is contributing to the maintenance of that young claimant, child or young person and by reason
of that contribution he may reasonably be treated as the father of
that young claimant, child or young person;
(d) a person liable to maintain another person by virtue of section
78(6)(c) of the Administration Act where the latter is the claimant
or a member of the claimant's family,
and, in this definition, a reference to a child's, young person's or
young claimant's parent includes any person in relation to whom
the child, young person or young claimant was treated as a child or
a member of the family;
[⁵ "ordinary clothing and footwear" means clothing and footwear for
normal daily use but does not include school uniforms;]
"payment" means a periodical payment or any other payment made by
or derived from a liable relative [⁵ . . .]; but it does not include any
payment—
(a) arising as a consequence of a disposition of property made in contemplation of, or as a consequence of—
(i) an agreement to separate; or
(ii) any proceedings for judicial separation, divorce or nullity of
marriage; [² or
(iii) any proceedings for separation, dissolution or nullity in relation
to a civil partnership;]
(b) made after the death of the liable relative;
(c) made by way of a gift but not in aggregate or otherwise exceeding
£250 in the period of 52 weeks beginning with the date on which
the payment, or if there is more than one such payment the first
payment, is made; and in the case of a claimant who continues to
be in receipt of an income-based jobseeker's allowance at the end
of the period of 52 weeks, this provision shall continue to apply
thereafter with the modification than any subsequent period of
52 weeks shall begin with the first day of the benefit week in

which the first payment is made after the end of the previous period of 52 weeks;

(d) [¹ . . .]

[⁵(e) made to a third party, or in respect of a third party, unless the payment is—

  (i) in relation to the claimant or the claimant's [⁷ partner or is made or derived from a person falling within sub-paragraph (d) of the definition of liable relative]; and

  (ii) [⁸ . . .] in respect of food, ordinary clothing or footwear, fuel, [⁸ rent for which housing benefit is payable, housing costs to the extent that they are met under regulations 83(f) or 84(1) (g) (housing costs),] council tax or water charges;]

(f) in kind;

(g) to or in respect of a child or young person who is to be treated as not being a member of the claimant's household under regulation 78;

(h) which is not a periodical payment, to the extent that any amount of that payment—

  (i) has already been taken into account under this Part by virtue of a previous claim or determination; or

  (ii) has been recovered under section 74(1) of the Administration Act (prevention of duplication of payments) or is currently being recovered; or

  (iii) at the time the determination is made, has been used by the claimant except where he has deprived himself of that amount for the purpose of securing entitlement to a job-seeker's allowance or increasing the amount of that allowance;

[⁷ (i) to which paragraph 70 of Schedule 7 (sums to be disregarded in the calculation of income other than earnings) applies;]

"periodical payment" means—

(a) a payment which is made or is due to be made at regular intervals [⁵ . . .];

(b) in a case where the liable relative has established a pattern of making payments at regular intervals, any such payment;

(c) any payment [⁵ [⁷ . . .] that does not exceed] the amount of jobseeker's allowance payable had that payment not been made;

(d) any payment representing a commutation of payments to which subparagraph (a) or (b) of this definition applies whether made in arrears or in advance,

but does not include a payment due to be made before the benefit week in which the claimant first became entitled to an income-based jobseeker's allowance, which was not so made;

"young claimant" means a person aged 16 or over but under [³ 20] who makes a claim for a jobseeker's allowance.

AMENDMENTS

1. Social Security (Working Tax Credit and Child Tax Credit) (Consequential Amendments) Regulations 2003 (SI 2003/455) reg.3 and Sch.2 para.14 (April 6, 2004, except in "transitional cases" and see further the note to reg.83 and to reg.17 of the Income Support Regulations).

2. Civil Partnership (Pensions, Social Security and Child Support) (Consequential, etc. Provisions) Order 2005 (SI 2005/2877) art.2(3) and Sch.3 para.26(6) (December 5, 2005).

3. Social Security (Young Persons) Amendment Regulations 2006 (SI 2006/718) reg.3(7) (April 10, 2006).

4. Social Security (Child Maintenance Amendments) Regulations 2008 (SI 2008/2111) reg.3(5) (October 27, 2008).

5. Social Security (Child Maintenance Amendments) Regulations 2008 (SI 2008/2111) reg.3(6) (October 27, 2008).

6. Social Security (Miscellaneous Amendments) (No.4) Regulations 2009 (SI 2009/2655) reg.4(5) (April 12, 2010).

7. Social Security (Miscellaneous Amendments) (No.4) Regulations 2009 (SI 2009/2655) reg.4(9) (April 12, 2010).

8. Social Security (Miscellaneous Amendments) Regulations 2013 (SI 2013/443) reg.4(9) (April 2, 2013).

DEFINITIONS

"benefit week"—see reg.1(3).
"child"—see Jobseekers Act s.35(1).
"claimant"—*ibid.*, and reg.88(1).
"family"—see Jobseekers Act s.35(1).
"young person"—see reg.76.

GENERAL NOTE

3.366   See the notes to reg.54 of the Income Support Regulations.

Treatment of [¹ [³ . . .]] liable relative payments

3.367   **118.**—Subject to regulation 119 [⁴ . . .[² . . .]] a payment shall—
   (a) to the extent that it is not a payment of income, be treated as income;
   (b) be taken into account in accordance with the following provisions of this Chapter.

AMENDMENTS

1. Social Security (Child Maintenance Amendments) Regulations 2008 (SI 2008/2111) reg.3(2)(b) (October 27, 2008).

2. Social Security (Child Maintenance Amendments) Regulations 2008 (SI 2008/2111) reg.3(7) (October 27, 2008).

3. Social Security (Miscellaneous Amendments) (No.4) Regulations 2009 (SI 2009/2655) reg.4(4) (April 12, 2010).

4. Social Security (Miscellaneous Amendments) (No.4) Regulations 2009 (SI 2009/2655) reg.4(10) (April 12, 2010).

DEFINITION

"payment"—*ibid.*

GENERAL NOTE

3.368   See the note to reg.55 of the Income Support Regulations.

Disregard of payments treated as not relevant income

3.369   **119.**—Where the Secretary of State treats any payment as not being relevant income for the purposes of section 74A of the Administration Act (payment of benefit where maintenance payments collected by Secretary of State), that payment shall be disregarded in calculating a claimant's income.

DEFINITIONS

"the Administration Act"—see Jobseekers Act 1995 s.35(1).
"payment"—see reg.117.
"relevant income"—see reg.2(c), Social Security Benefits (Maintenance Payments and Consequential Amendments) Regulations 1996 (SI 1996/940) (p.758).

GENERAL NOTE

See reg.55A of the Income Support Regulations and the note to s.74A of the Administration Act in Vol.III of this series.

3.370

Period over which periodical payments are to be taken into account

120.—(1) The period over which a periodical payment is to be taken into account shall be—

3.371

(a) in a case where the payment is made at regular intervals, a period equal to the length of that interval;

(b) in a case where the payment is due to be made at regular intervals but is not so made, such number of weeks as is equal to the number obtained (and any fraction shall be treated as a corresponding fraction of a week) by dividing the amount of that payment by the weekly amount of that periodical payment as calculated in accordance with regulation 122(4);

(c) in any other case, a period equal to a week.

(2) The period under paragraph (1) shall begin on the date on which the payment is treated as paid under regulation 123.

DEFINITION

"periodical payment"—see reg.117.

GENERAL NOTE

See the note to reg.56 of the Income Support Regulations.

3.372

[¹ Period over which payments other than periodical payments are to be taken into account

121.—(1) The period over which a payment other than a periodical payment (a "non-periodical payment") is to be taken account shall be determined as follows.

3.373

(2) Except in a case where paragraph (4) applies, the number of weeks over which a non-periodical payment is to be taken into account shall be equal to the number obtained by dividing that payment by the amount referred to in paragraph (3).

(3) The amount is the aggregate of £2 and—

(a) the amount of jobseeker's allowance that would be payable had no payment been made [² . . .]

(b) [² . . .].

(4) This paragraph applies in a case where a liable relative makes a

periodical payment and a non-periodical payment concurrently and the weekly amount of the periodical payment (as calculated in accordance with regulation 122) is less than B.

(5) In a case where paragraph (4) applies, the non-periodical payment shall, subject to paragraphs (6) and (7), be taken into account over a period of the number of weeks equal to the number obtained by applying the formula—

$$\frac{A}{B-C}$$

(6) If the liable relative ceases to make periodical payments, the balance (if any) of the non-periodical payment shall be taken into account over the number of weeks equal to the number obtained by dividing that balance by the amount referred to in paragraph (3).

(7) If the amount of any subsequent periodical payment varies, the balance (if any) of the non-periodical payment shall be taken into account over a period of the number of weeks equal to the number obtained by applying the formula—

$$\frac{D}{B-E}$$

(8) The period under paragraph (2) or (4) shall begin on the date on which the payment is treated as paid under regulation 123 (date on which a liable relative payment is treated as paid) and the period under paragraph (6) and (7) shall begin on the first day of the benefit week in which the cessation or variation of the periodical payment occurred.

(9) Any fraction which arises by applying a calculation or formula referred to in this regulation shall be treated as a corresponding fraction of a week.

(10) In paragraphs (4) to (7)—

A = the amount of the non-periodical payment;
B = the aggregate of £2 and the amount of jobseeker's allowance that would be payable had the periodical payment not been made [2 . . .];
C = the weekly amount of the periodical payment;
D = the balance (if any) of the non-periodical payment;
E = the weekly amount of any subsequent periodical payment.]

AMENDMENTS

1. Social Security (Child Maintenance Amendments) Regulations 2008 (SI 2008/2111) reg.3(8) (October 27, 2008).
2. Social Security (Miscellaneous Amendments) (No.4) Regulations 2009 (SI 2009/2655) reg.4(11) (April 12, 2010).

DEFINITIONS

"benefit week"—see reg.1(3).
"liable relative"—see reg.117.
"payment"—*ibid.*
"periodical payment"—*ibid.*

GENERAL NOTE

3.374   See the note to reg.57 of the Income Support Regulations.

Calculation of the weekly amount of a [¹[² . . .]] liable relative payment

122.—(1) Where a periodical payment is made or is due to be made at intervals of one week, the weekly amount shall be the amount of that payment.

3.375

(2) Where a periodical payment is made or is due to be made at intervals greater than one week and those intervals are monthly, the weekly amount shall be determined by multiplying the amount of the payment by 12 and dividing the product by 52.

(3) Where a periodical payment is made or is due to be made at intervals and those intervals are neither weekly or monthly, the weekly amount shall be determined by dividing that payment by the number equal to the number of weeks (including any part of a week) in that interval.

(4) Where a payment is made and that payment represents a commutation of periodical payments whether in arrears or in advance, the weekly amount shall be the weekly amount of the individual periodical payments so commuted as calculated under paragraphs (1) to (3) as appropriate.

(5) The weekly amount of a payment to which regulation 121 applies (period over which payments other than periodical payments are to be taken into account) shall be equal to the amount of the divisor used in calculating the period over which the payment or, as the case may be, the balance is to be taken into account.

AMENDMENTS

1. Social Security (Child Maintenance Amendments) Regulations 2008 (SI 2008/2111) reg.3(2)(c) (October 27, 2008).
2. Social Security (Miscellaneous Amendments) (No.4) Regulations 2009 (SI 2009/2655) reg.4(4) (April 12, 2010).

DEFINITIONS

"payment"—*ibid.*
"periodical payment"—*ibid.*

GENERAL NOTE

See the note to reg.58 of the Income Support Regulations.

3.376

Date on which a [¹[² . . .]] liable relative payment is to be treated as paid

123.—(1) A periodical payment is to be treated as paid—

3.377

(a) in the case of a payment which is due to be made before the benefit week in which the claimant first became entitled to an income-based jobseeker's allowance, on the day in the week in which it is due to be paid which corresponds to the first day of the benefit week;

(b) in any other case, on the first day of the benefit week in which it is due to be paid unless, having regard to the manner in which jobseeker's allowance is due to be paid in the particular case, it would be more practicable to treat it as paid on the first day of a subsequent benefit week.

(2) Subject to paragraph (3), any other payment shall be treated as paid—

(a) in the case of a payment which is made before the benefit week in which the claimant first became entitled to an income-based job-seeker's allowance, on the day in the week in which it is paid which corresponds to the first day of the benefit week;

(b) in any other case, on the first day of the benefit week in which it is paid unless, having regard to the manner in which jobseeker's allowance is due to be paid in the particular case, it would be more practicable to treat it as paid on the first day of a subsequent benefit week.

(3) Any other payment paid on a date which falls within the period in respect of which a previous payment is taken into account, not being a periodical payment, is to be treated as paid on the first day following the end of that period.

AMENDMENTS

1. Social Security (Child Maintenance Amendments) Regulations 2008 (SI 2008/2111) reg.3(2)(d) (October 27, 2008).
2. Social Security (Miscellaneous Amendments) (No.4) Regulations 2009 (SI 2009/2655) reg.4(4) (April 12, 2010).

DEFINITIONS

"benefit week"—see reg.1(3).
"payment"—*ibid.*
"periodical payment"—*ibid.*

GENERAL NOTE

3.378   See the notes to reg.59 of the Income Support Regulations.

Liable relative payments to be treated as capital

3.379   **124.**—[¹ . . .]

AMENDMENT

1. Social Security (Child Maintenance Amendments) Regulations 2008 (SI 2008/2111) reg.3(4)(b) (October 27, 2008).

Chapter VIII

Child Support

Interpretation

3.380   **125.**—[¹ . . .]

AMENDMENT

1. Social Security (Child Maintenance Amendments) Regulations 2008 (SI 2008/2111) reg.3(4)(c) (October 27, 2008).

Treatment of child support maintenance

126.—[¹ . . .]   3.381

AMENDMENT

1. Social Security (Child Maintenance Amendments) Regulations 2008 (SI 2008/2111) reg.3(4)(c) (October 27, 2008).

Disregard of payments treated as not relevant income

127.—[¹ . . .]   3.382

AMENDMENT

1. Social Security (Child Maintenance Amendments) Regulations 2008 (SI 2008/2111) reg.3(4)(c) (October 27, 2008).

Calculation of the weekly amount of child support maintenance

128.—[¹ . . .]   3.383

AMENDMENT

1. Social Security (Child Maintenance Amendments) Regulations 2008 (SI 2008/2111) reg.3(4)(c) (October 27, 2008).

Date on which child support maintenance is to be treated as paid

129.—[¹ . . .]   3.384

AMENDMENT

1. Social Security (Child Maintenance Amendments) Regulations 2008 (SI 2008/2111) reg.3(4)(c) (October 27, 2008).

Chapter IX

[⁴Students]

Interpretation

130.—In this Chapter, unless the context otherwise requires—   3.385
[⁷ "academic year" means the period of twelve months beginning on 1st January, 1st April, 1st July or 1st September according to whether the course in question begins in the winter, the spring, the summer or the autumn respectively but if students are required to begin attending the course during August or September and to continue attending through the autumn, the academic year of the course shall be considered to begin in the autumn rather than the summer;]
[⁵ "access funds" means—
    (a) grants made under section [¹⁴ 68] of the Further and Higher Education Act 1992 [¹⁴ . . .] [²⁰or section 74 of the Higher Education and Research Act 2017] [⁷ for the purpose of providing funds on a discretionary basis to be paid to students];

    (b) grants made under sections 73(a) and (c) and 74(1) of the Education (Scotland) Act 1980; [⁷ . . .]

    (c) grants made under Article 30 of the Education and Libraries (Northern Ireland) Order 1993, or grants, loans or other payments made under Article 5 of the Further Education (Northern Ireland) Order 1997 in each case being grants, or grants, loans or other payments as the case may be, made for the purpose of assisting students in financial difficulties;] [⁷ [⁸ . . .]

    (d) discretionary payments, known as "learner support funds", which are made available to students in further education by institutions out of funds provided by the [¹⁷ [¹⁸ Secretary of State under section 14 of the Education Act 2002] or [¹⁹ . . .] under sections 100 and 101 of [¹⁸ the Apprenticeships, Skills, Children and Learning Act 2009]];] [⁸ or

    (e) Financial Contingency Funds made available by the [¹² Welsh Ministers];]

[¹³ "contribution" means—

    (a) any contribution in respect of the income of a student or any person which the Secretary of State, the Scottish Ministers or an education authority takes into account in ascertaining the amount of a student's grant or student loan; or

    (b) any sums, which in determining the amount of a student's allowance or bursary in Scotland under the Education (Scotland) Act 1980, the Scottish Ministers or education authority takes into account being sums which the Scottish Ministers or education authority consider that it is reasonable for the following persons to contribute towards the holder's expenses—

       (i) the holder of the allowance or bursary;

       (ii) the holder's parents;

       (iii) the holder's parent's spouse, civil partner or person ordinarily living with the holder's parent as if he or she were the spouse or civil partner of that parent; or

       (iv) the holder's spouse or civil partner;]

"covenant income" means the income payable to a student under a deed of covenant by a person whose income is, or is likely to be, taken into account in assessing the student's grant or award;

"education authority" means a government department, [¹⁶a local authority as defined in section 579 of the Education Act 1996], a local education authority as defined in section 123 of the Local Government (Scotland) Act 1973, an education and library board established under article 3 of the Education and Libraries (Northern Ireland) Order 1986, any body which is a research council for the purposes of the Science and Technology Act 1965 or any analogous government department, authority, board or body, of the Channel Islands, Isle of Man or any other country outside Great Britain;

[⁵ "grant" (except in the definition of "access funds") means any kind of educational grant or award and includes any scholarship, studentship, exhibition, allowance or bursary but does not include a payment from access funds [⁹ or any payment to which paragraph 12 of Schedule 7 or paragraph 52 of Schedule 8 applies];]

"grant income" means—

   (a) any income by way of a grant;
   (b) in the case of a student other than one to whom sub-paragraph (c)
        refers, any contribution that has been taken into account whether
        or not it has been paid;
   (c) in the case of a student who satisfies the additional conditions for
        a disability premium in paragraph 14 of Schedule 1 (applicable
        amounts), any contribution which has been taken into account
        and which has been paid,

and any such contribution which is paid by way of a covenant shall be
treated as part of the student's grant income;

[³ . . .]

[¹⁵ "last day of the course" means the date on which the last day of the
final academic term falls in respect of the course in which the student
is enrolled;]

[⁸ "periods of experience" means periods of work experience which form
part of a sandwich course;]

[²¹"postgraduate loan" means a loan to a student undertaking a postgraduate master's degree course or a postgraduate doctoral degree
course pursuant to regulations made under section 22 of the Teaching
and Higher Education Act 1998;]

"standard maintenance grant" means—

   (a) except where paragraph (b) or (c) applies, in the case of a student
        attending [³or undertaking] a course of study at the University
        of London or an establishment within the area comprising the
        City of London and the Metropolitan Police District, the amount
        specified for the time being in paragraph 2(2)(a) of Schedule 2 to
        the Education (Mandatory Awards) Regulations 1995 ("the 1995
        regulations") for such a student;
   (b) except where paragraph (c) applies, in the case of a student resid-
        ing at his parents' home, the amount specified in paragraph 3(2)
        thereof;
   [⁷ (c) in the case of a student receiving an allowance or bursary under the
        Education (Scotland) Act 1980, the amount of money specified as
        the "standard maintenance allowance" for the relevant year appro-
        priate for the student set out in the Student Support in Scotland
        Guide issued by the Student Awards Agency for Scotland, or its
        nearest equivalent in the case of a bursary provided by a college of
        further education or a local education authority [¹¹ . . .];]
   (d) in any other case, the amount specified in paragraph 2(2) of the
        1995 regulations other than in sub-paragraph (a) or (b) thereof;

[⁶ . . .]

[² "student loan" means a loan towards a student's maintenance pursuant
to any regulations made under section 22 of the Teaching and Higher
Education Act 1998, section 73 of the Education (Scotland) Act 1980
or Article 3 of the Education (Student Support) (Northern Ireland)
Order 1998 [⁷ and shall include, in Scotland, a young student's bursary
paid under regulation 4(1)(c) of the Students' Allowances (Scotland)
Regulations 1999];

[⁷ . . .]

AMENDMENTS

1. Social Security (Miscellaneous Amendments) Regulations 1998 (SI 1998/563) reg.4(1) and (2)(f) (April 6, 1998).

2. Social Security Amendment (Students) Regulations 1999 (SI 1999/1935) reg.2(2) (August 30, 1999, or if the student's period of study begins between August 1 and 29, 1999, the first day of the period).

3. Social Security Amendment (Students) Regulations 2000 (SI 2000/1981) reg.6(4) (July 31, 2000).

4. Social Security Amendment (Students and Income-related Benefits) Regulations 2000 (SI 2000/1922) reg.3(3) (August 28, 2000, or if the student's period of study begins between August 1 and 27, 2000, the first day of the period).

5. Social Security Amendment (Students and Income-related Benefits) Regulations 2000 (SI 2000/1922) reg.3(4) (August 28, 2000, or if the student's period of study begins between August 1 and 27, 2000, the first day of the period).

6. Social Security Amendment (Students and Income-related Benefits) Regulations 2000 (SI 2000/1922) reg.3(5) (August 28, 2000, or if the student's period of study begins between August 1 and 27, 2000, the first day of the period).

7. Social Security Amendment (Students and Income-related Benefits) Regulations 2001 (SI 2001/2319) reg.2(1)(a) and (2)(d) (August 1, 2001).

8. Social Security Amendment (Students and Income-related Benefits) Regulations 2002 (SI 2002/1589) reg.2(3)(b) (August 1, 2002).

9. Social Security (Students and Income-related Benefits) Amendment Regulations 2004 (SI 2004/1708) reg.6(2) (September 1, 2004, or if the student's period of study begins between August 1 and August 31, 2004, the first day of the period).

10. Civil Partnership (Pensions, Social Security and Child Support) (Consequential, etc. Provisions) Order 2005 (SI 2005/2877) art.2(3) and Sch.3 para.26(7) (December 5, 2005).

11. Social Security (Miscellaneous Amendments) (No.6) Regulations 2008 (SI 2008/2767) reg.4(8) (November 17, 2008).

12. Social Security (Miscellaneous Amendments) (No.7) Regulations 2008 (SI 2008/3157) reg.3(7) (January 5, 2009).

13. Social Security (Miscellaneous Amendments) Regulations 2009 (SI 2009/583) reg.4(9) (April 6, 2009).

14. Social Security (Miscellaneous Amendments) (No.4) Regulations 2009 (SI 2009/2655) reg.4(12) (October 26, 2009).

15. Social Security (Miscellaneous Amendments) (No.2) Regulations 2010 (SI 2010/641) reg.4(10) (April 6, 2010).

16. Local Education Authorities and Children's Services Authorities (Integration of Functions) (Local and Subordinate Legislation) Order 2010 (SI 2010/1172) art.5 and Sch.3 para.27(3) (May 5, 2010).

17. Apprenticeships, Skills, Children and Learning Act 2009 (Consequential Amendments to Subordinate Legislation) (England) Order 2010 (SI 2010/1941) art.5(6) (September 1, 2010).

18. Young People's Learning Agency Abolition (Consequential Amendments to Subordinate Legislation) (England) Order 2012 (SI 2012/956) art.5(6) (May 1, 2012).

19. Deregulation Act 2015 (Consequential Amendments) Order 2015 (SI 2015/971) art.2 and Sch.3 para.4(5) (May 26, 2015).

20. Higher Education and Research Act 2017 (Further Implementation etc.) Regulations 2019 (SI 2019/1027) reg.18 (August 1, 2019).

21. Social Security (Income and Capital) (Miscellaneous Amendments) Regulations 2020 (SI 2020/618) reg.3(6) (July 15, 2020).

DEFINITIONS

"full-time student"—see reg.1(3).
"sandwich course"—*ibid.*

GENERAL NOTE

See the notes to reg.61 of the Income Support Regulations.   3.386

Under old style JSA the definitions applying to full-time students are in a slightly different form. The main definitions for the purpose of defining full-time student status are in reg.1(3) (namely "course of advanced education", "course of study", "full-time course of advanced education", "full-time student" and "part-time student"); see also paras (3A)–(3E) of reg.1 which apply for the purposes of the definition of "full-time student". Since the amendments made to both the Income Support Regulations and the JSA Regulations 1996 on July 31, 2000 by SI 2000/1981 the differences from income support are less marked.

On the pre-July 31, 2000 form, see *CJSA 836/1996*, discussed in the notes to reg.61 of the Income Support Regulations under *"Difference between income support and JSA definition"*. The Commissioner in that case took the view that the differences between the then form of the JSA and income support definitions were material. In his view the result was that for the purposes of JSA the question whether a person was attending or undertaking a full- or part-time course had to be determined by looking at the situation at the time in question (rather than at the commencement of the course, as was the case for income support). (Note that *CJSA 836/1996* was not followed in *C5/98(JSA)* (a Northern Ireland decision)). However, since the insertion of paras (3A)–(3C) into reg.1 (which provisions parallel reg.61(2)–(4) of the Income Support Regulations) with effect from July 31, 2000, the Commissioner's reasoning in *CJSA 836/1998* no longer applies. This is because the deeming of full-time student status for the entire length of a course (subject to earlier final abandonment or dismissal) is now contained in reg.1(3A)(b), rather than the definition of "course of study" in reg.1(3).

Note paras (3D) and (3E) inserted into reg.1 at the same time. (There is no   3.387 equivalent to these provisions in the Income Support Regulations.) The effect of these provisions is to allow full-time students who have taken time out of their course with the consent of their university or college because of illness or caring responsibilities (not defined), and who have now recovered or whose caring responsibilities have ended, to claim old style JSA until the earlier of the day before they rejoin their course or the date the relevant educational establishment has agreed that they can rejoin (subject to a maximum of one year). This does not apply if the person is eligible for a grant or student loan during this period.

In *CJSA 1920/1999* the claimant was a full-time student who had applied for a fixed term leave of absence from her course because she was pregnant. Her claim for JSA was refused because she was deemed to be a full-time student. The Commissioner decided (disagreeing with *CJSA 4890/1998*) that JSA was a single benefit and was within the scope of EC Directive 79/7 (on equal treatment in social security). He also concluded that discrimination against a pregnant student was direct discrimination against women in breach of art.4 of Directive 79/7, that there was such discrimination under the JSA Regulations 1996 and that no justification for that discrimination had been established.

The Commissioner in *CJSA 1920/1999* granted the Secretary of State leave to appeal to the Court of Appeal. But in the meantime on May 2, 2001 the Court of Appeal allowed the claimant's appeal against the decision in *CJSA 4890/1998* (*Hockenjos v Secretary of State*, [2001] EWCA Civ 624; [2001] 2 C.M.L.R. 51; [2001] I.C.R. 966, also reported as *R(JSA) 1/05*). The Court of Appeal held that the Jobseekers Act 1995 had set up a unitary statutory scheme to provide against the risk of unemployment which was covered by art.3(1)(a) of the Directive. Thus both contribution-based and income-based JSA were within the scope of Directive 79/7.

However, the Court of Appeal allowed the Secretary of State's appeal against   3.388 the decision in *CJSA 1920/1999* (*Secretary of State for Social Security v Walter* [2001] EWCA Civ 1913, reported as *R(JSA) 3/02*). The Court disagreed with the Commissioner's conclusion that the JSA Regulations 1996 directly discriminate against pregnant women, although the question of whether they may indirectly discriminate was left open.

The argument that refusal of JSA to a pregnant student constituted indirect discrimination contrary to Directive 79/7 was raised in *CJSA/825/2004* but the Commissioner considered that evidence that women were disproportionately affected was needed.

In *CM v SSWP* [2009] UKUT 43 (AAC), reported as *R(IS) 7/09*, the Upper Tribunal Judge accepted that statistical evidence was not necessary to establish indirect discrimination in this situation since only women could become pregnant and this was the only difference between female and male intercalating students that was being argued before him. The Secretary of State conceded that pregnancy was an "other status" for the purposes of art.14 ECHR. However, the discrimination against pregnant students who are intercalating was justified because the Government's policy was that students who intercalate for essentially transient reasons should not be supported by benefits. Students in the later stages of pregnancy were thus being treated in a similar way to those who were ill or had caring responsibilities and the inclusion of pregnant students within that policy was objectively justifiable. There was therefore no breach of art.14, read with art.1 Prot.1 of the ECHR. It had also been argued that the denial of income support meant that pregnant students were more likely to be forced to abandon their course so as to have a means of subsistence. However, the Upper Tribunal Judge held that this did not bring this case within art.2 Prot.1 (right to education) because the claimant had not in fact abandoned her course but had chosen to intercalate.

Note also *MS v SSWP* [2009] UKUT 9 (AAC), which holds that the denial of JSA to a student who is not attending college for a year while he resits exams externally is not contrary to art.14, read with art.1 Prot.1 of the ECHR.

Calculation of grant income

3.389   **131.**—(1) The amount of a student's grant income to be taken into account shall, subject to paragraphs [⁴(2) and (3)], be the whole of his grant income.

(2) There shall be disregarded from the amount of a student's grant income any payment—

(a) intended to meet tuition fees or examination fees;
(b) intended to meet additional expenditure incurred by a disabled student in respect of his attendance on a course;
(c) intended to meet additional expenditure connected with term time residential study away from the student's educational establishment;
(d) on account of the student maintaining a home at a place other than that at which he resides while attending his course but only to the extent that his rent is not met by housing benefit;
(e) on account of any other person but only if that person is residing outside the United Kingdom and there is no applicable amount in respect of him;
(f) intended to meet the cost of books and equipment [¹ . . .] [³ . . .];
(g) intended to meet travel expenses incurred as a result of his attendance on the course.
[¹²(h) intended for the maintenance [¹³. . .] of a child dependent].
[¹³(i) intended for the child care costs of a child dependant.]
[¹⁸(j) of higher education bursary for care leavers made under Part III of the Children Act 1989 [²²or Part 6 of the Social Services and Well-being (Wales) Act 2014].]

[³(3) Where a student does not have a student loan [²¹or a postgraduate [²³...] loan] and is not treated as possessing [²¹a student loan or a postgraduate [²³...] loan], there shall be excluded from the student's grant income—

(a) the sum of [¹⁶[¹⁹£303] per academic year] in respect of travel costs; and

[⁶(b) the sum of [¹⁷[²⁰£390] per academic year] towards the costs of books and equipment,]

whether or not any such costs are incurred.]

[⁷[¹² (3A) [¹⁴[¹⁵. . .]]]]

(4) [⁴ Subject to paragraph (5A), a student's grant income except for any amount intended for the maintenance of [¹² adult] dependants under Part III of Schedule 2 to the Education (Mandatory Awards) Regulations 1999 [¹² . . .]] shall be apportioned—

(a) subject to paragraph (6), in a case where it is attributable to the period of study, equally between the weeks [¹⁰ in the period beginning with the benefit week, the first day of which coincides with, or immediately follows, the first day of the period of study and ending with the benefit week, the last day of which coincides with, or immediately precedes, the last day of the period of study];

(b) in any other case, equally between the weeks in the period [¹⁰beginning with the benefit week, the first day of which coincides with, or immediately follows, the first day of the period for which it is payable and ending with the benefit week, the last day of which coincides with, or immediately precedes, the last day of the period for which it is payable].

(5) [⁸Any grant paid under section 63(6) of the Health Services and Public Health Act 1968 (grants in respect of the provision of instruction to officers of hospital authorities) and] any amount intended for the maintenance of [¹² an adult dependant] under the provisions referred to in paragraph (4) shall be apportioned equally over a period of 52 weeks, or if there are 53 weeks (including part-weeks) in the year, 53.

[⁴(5A) [¹⁰ In a case where a student is in receipt of a student loan or where he could have acquired a student loan by taking reasonable steps but had not done so,] any amount intended for the maintenance of [¹²an adult dependant] under provisions other than those referred to in paragraphs (4) and (5), shall be apportioned over the same period as the student's loan is apportioned or[¹⁰, as the case may be, would have been apportioned]].

(6) In the case of a student on a sandwich course, any periods of experience within the period of study shall be excluded and the student's grant income shall be apportioned equally between [¹⁰the weeks in the period beginning with the benefit week, the first day of which immediately follows the last day of the period of experience and ending with the benefit week, the last day of which coincides with, or immediately precedes, the last day of the period of study].

AMENDMENTS

1. Jobseeker's Allowance (Amendment) Regulations 1996 (SI 1996/1516) reg.20 and Sch. (October 7, 1996).

2. Social Security (Student Amounts Amendment) Regulations 1998 (SI 1998/1379) reg.2 (August 31, 1998, or if the student's period of study begins between August 1, and 30, 1998, the first day of the period).

3. Social Security Amendment (Students) Regulations 1999 (SI 1999/1935) reg.2(3) (August 30, 1999, or if the student's period of study begins between August 1 and 29, 1999, the first day of the period).

4. Social Security Amendment (Students and Income-related Benefits)

Regulations 2000 (SI 2000/1922) reg.3(6) (August 28, 2000, or if the student's period of study begins between August 1 and 27, 2000, the first day of the period).

5. Social Security Amendment (Students and Income-related Benefits) Regulations 2001 (SI 2001/2319) reg.3(1) and (3)(d) (August 27, 2001, or if the student's period of study begins between August 1 and 26, 2001, the first day of the period).

6. Social Security Amendment (Students and Income-related Benefits) Regulations 2001 (SI 2001/2319) reg.3(2) and (3)(d) (August 27, 2001, or if the student's period of study begins between August 1 and 26, 2001, the first day of the period).

7. Social Security Amendment (Students and Income-related Benefits) Regulations 2001 (SI 2001/2319) reg.3(4) (August 27, 2001, or if the student's period of study begins between August 1 and 26, 2001, the first day of the period).

8. Social Security Amendment (Students and Income-related Benefits) Regulations 2001 (SI 2001/2319) reg.6 (August 27, 2001, or if the student's period of study begins between August 1 and 26, 2001, the first day of the period).

9. Social Security Amendment (Students and Income-related Benefits) Regulations 2002 (SI 2002/1589) reg.3 (August 26, 2002, or if the student's period of study begins between August 1 and 25, 2002, the first day of the period).

10. Social Security Amendment (Students and Income-related Benefits) Regulations 2002 (SI 2002/1589) reg.4 (August 26, 2002, or if the student's period of study begins between August 1 and 25, 2002, the first day of the period).

11. Social Security Amendment (Students and Income-related Benefits) (No.2) Regulations 2002 (SI 2002/2207) reg.2 (September 2, 2002).

12. Social Security (Working Tax Credit and Child Tax Credit) (Consequential Amendments) Regulations 2003 (SI 2003/455) reg.3 and Sch.2 para.16 (April 6, 2004, except in "transitional cases" and see further the note to regs 83 and 17 of the Income Support Regulations), as amended by Social Security (Working Tax Credit and Child Tax Credit) (Consequential Amendments) (No.3) Regulations 2003 (SI 2003/1731), reg.6(5)(a) (August 8, 2003).

13. Social Security (Students and Income-related Benefits) Amendment Regulations 2004 (SI 2004/1708) reg.3(4) (September 1, 2004, or if the student's period of study begins between August 1 and August 31, 2004, the first day of the period).

14. Social Security (Students and Income-related Benefits) Amendment Regulations 2005 (SI 2005/1807) reg.2(7) (September 1, 2005, or if the student's period of study begins between August 1 and August 31, 2005, the first day of the period).

15. Social Security (Students and Income-related Benefits) Amendment Regulations 2006 (SI 2006/1752) regs 5(3) and 6 (September 1, 2006, or if the student's period of study begins between August 1 and August 31, 2006, the first day of the period).

16. Social Security (Students and Income-related Benefits) Amendment Regulations 2007 (SI 2007/1632) reg.3(2)(a) (September 1, 2007, or if the student's period of study begins between August 1 and 31, 2007, the first day of the period).

17. Social Security (Students and Income-related Benefits) Amendment Regulations 2007 (SI 2007/1632) reg.3(2)(b) (September 1, 2007, or if the student's period of study begins between August 1 and 31, 2007, the first day of the period).

18. Social Security (Miscellaneous Amendments) Regulations 2009 (SI 2009/583) reg.4(10) (April 6, 2009).

19. Social Security (Students and Miscellaneous Amendments) Regulations 2009 (SI 2009/1575) reg.2(2) and (4)(b) (September 1, 2009, or if the student's period of study begins between August 1 and 31, 2009, the first day of the period).

20. Social Security (Students and Miscellaneous Amendments) Regulations 2009 (SI 2009/1575) reg.2(3) and (4)(b) (September 1, 2009, or if the student's period of study begins between August 1 and 31, 2009, the first day of the period).

21. Social Security (Treatment of Postgraduate Master's Degree Loans and Special Support Loans) (Amendment) Regulations 2016 (SI 2016/743) reg.3(3) (August 4, 2016).

22. Social Services and Well-being (Wales) Act 2014 and the Regulation and Inspection of Social Care (Wales) Act 2016 (Consequential Amendments) Order 2017 (SI 2017/901) art.6(4) (November 3, 2017).

23. Social Security (Income and Capital) (Miscellaneous Amendments) Regulations 2020 (SI 2020/618) reg.3(7) (July 15, 2020).

DEFINITIONS

"grant"—see reg.130.
"grant income"—*ibid.*
"period of study"—see reg.1(3).
"periods of experience"—see reg.130.
"postgraduate loan"—*ibid.*
"sandwich course"—see reg.1(3).
"student loan"—see reg.130.

GENERAL NOTE

See the notes to reg.62 of the Income Support Regulations.   3.390

The disregard in para.(2)(h) is a general disregard of any payment intended for the maintenance of a child and that in para.(2)(i) is a general disregard of any payment intended for child care costs. They replaced the various disregards for students with child care responsibilities previously contained in para.(3A). Paragraph (3A) had gone through a number of forms and parts of the penultimate form of it remained in force in "transitional cases" (i.e. those cases in which the claimants are still receiving amounts for their children in their income-based JSA—see the note to reg.83 and to reg.17 of the Income Support Regulations) but the one remaining sub-para. that was still in force for transitional cases (sub-para.(e)) was omitted on September 1, 2006 (or if the student's period of study begins between August 1 and 31, 2006, on the first day of the period) by reg.5(3) of the Social Security (Students and Income-related Benefits) Amendment Regulations 2006 (SI 2006/1752) (see further the notes to this regulation in the 2006 edition of what was then Vol.II and in the 2006/2007 Supplement to this series).

Calculation of covenant income where a contribution is assessed

132.—(1) Where a student is in receipt of income by way of a grant   3.391
during a period of study and a contribution has been assessed, the amount of his covenant income to be taken into account for that period and any summer vacation immediately following shall be the whole amount of his covenant income less, subject to paragraph (3), the amount of the contribution.

(2) The weekly amount of the student's covenant income shall be determined—

(a) by dividing the amount of income which falls to be taken into account under paragraph (1) by 52 or, if there are 53 benefit weeks (including part-weeks) in the year, 53; and

(b) by disregarding £5 from the resulting amount.

(3) For the purposes of paragraph (1), the contribution shall be treated as increased by the amount, if any, by which the amount excluded under regulation 131(2)(g) falls short of the amount for the time being specified in paragraph 7(4)(i) of Schedule 2 to the Education (Mandatory Awards) Regulations 1995 (travel expenditure).

DEFINITIONS

"benefit week"—see reg.1(3).
"contribution"—see reg.130.

"covenant income"—*ibid.*
"grant"—*ibid.*
"period of study"—see reg.1(3).

GENERAL NOTE

3.392   See the note to reg.63 of the Income Support Regulations.

Covenant income where no grant income or no contribution is assessed

3.393   **133.**—(1) Where a student is not in receipt of income by way of a grant the amount of his covenant income shall be calculated as follows—

(a) any sums intended for any expenditure specified in regulation 131(2) (a) to (e), necessary as a result of his attendance on the course, shall be disregarded;

(b) any covenant income, up to the amount of the standard maintenance grant, which is not so disregarded, shall be apportioned equally between the weeks of the period of study and there shall be disregarded from the covenant income to be so apportioned the amount which would have been disregarded under regulation 131(2)(f) and (g) and (3) had the student been in receipt of the standard maintenance grant;

(c) the balance, if any, shall be divided by 52 or, if there are 53 benefit weeks (including part-weeks) in the year, 53 and treated as weekly income of which £5 shall be disregarded.

(2) Where a student is in receipt of income by way of a grant and no contribution has been assessed, the amount of his covenant income shall be calculated in accordance with paragraph (1), except that—

(a) the value of the standard maintenance grant shall be abated by the amount of his grant income less an amount equal to the amount of any sums disregarded under regulation 131(2)(a) to (e); and

(b) the amount to be disregarded under paragraph (1)(b) shall be abated by an amount equal to the amount of any sums disregarded under regulation 131(2)(f) and (g) and (3).

DEFINITIONS

"benefit week"—see reg.1(3).
"contribution"—see reg.130.
"covenant income"—*ibid.*
"grant income"—*ibid.*

GENERAL NOTE

3.394   See the note to reg.64 of the Income Support Regulations.

Relationship with amounts to be disregarded under Schedule 7

3.395   **134.**—No part of a student's covenant income or grant income shall be disregarded under paragraph 15 of Schedule 7 (charitable and voluntary payments) [¹. . .].

AMENDMENT

1. Social Security (Miscellaneous Amendments) (No.4) Regulations 2006 (SI 2006/2378) reg.13(7) (October 2, 2006).

DEFINITIONS

"covenant income"—see reg.130.
"grant income"—*ibid.*

GENERAL NOTE

See reg.65 of the Income Support Regulations.   3.396

Other amounts to be disregarded

135.—(1) For the purposes of ascertaining income other than grant   3.397
income, covenant income, and loans treated as income in accordance
with regulation 136, any amounts intended for any expenditure specified in regulation 131(2) (calculation of grant income) necessary as a
result of the student's attendance on the course shall be disregarded but
only if, and to the extent that, the necessary expenditure exceeds or is
likely to exceed the amount of the sums disregarded under regulation
131(2) and (3), 132(3)[¹, 133(1)(a) or (b) and 136(5) (calculation of
grant income, covenant income and treatment of student loans)] on like
expenditure.

(2) Where a claim is made in respect of any period in the normal summer
vacation and any income is payable under a deed of covenant which commences or takes effect after the first day of that vacation, that income shall
be disregarded.

AMENDMENT

1. Social Security Amendment (Students) Regulations 1999 (SI 1999/1935)
reg.2(4) (August 30, 1999, or if the student's period of study begins between
August 1 and 29, 1999, the first day of the period).

DEFINITIONS

"covenant income"—see reg.130.
"grant income"—*ibid.*
"student loan"—*ibid.*

GENERAL NOTE

See the note to reg.66 of the Income Support Regulations.   3.398

Treatment of student loans [¹³and postgraduate [¹⁴...] loans]

136.—[²(1) A student loan [¹³and a postgraduate [¹⁴...] loan] shall be   3.399
treated as income [¹⁰ . . .].

(1A) [¹⁰ . . .]

(2) In calculating the weekly amount of the loan to be taken into account
as income—

[⁷(a) in respect of a course that is of a single academic year's duration or less,
a loan which is payable in respect of that period shall be apportioned
equally between the weeks in the period beginning with—

    (i) except in a case where (ii) below applies, the benefit week, the
first day of which coincides with, or immediately follows, the
first day of the single academic year;

    (ii) where the student is required to start attending the course in
August or where the course is of less than an academic year's

duration, the benefit week, the first day of which coincides with, or immediately follows, the first day of the course, and ending with the benefit week, the last day of which coincides with, or immediately precedes, the last day of the course;]

[⁵(aa) in respect of an academic year of a course which starts other than on 1st September, a loan which is payable in respect of that academic year shall be apportioned equally between the weeks in the period beginning with the benefit week [⁷, the first day of which coincides with, or immediately follows, the first day of that academic year and ending with the benefit week, the last day of which coincides with, or immediately precedes,] the last day of that academic year but excluding any benefit weeks falling entirely within the quarter during which, in the opinion of the Secretary of State, the longest of any vacation is taken and for the purposes of this sub-paragraph, "quarter" shall have the same meaning as for the purposes of the Education (Student Support) Regulations 2001;]

(b) in respect of the final academic year of a course (not being a course of a single year's duration), a loan which is payable in respect of that final academic year shall be apportioned equally between the weeks in the period beginning with [⁷. . .]—

[⁷(i) except in a case where (ii) below applies, the benefit week, the first day of which coincides with, or immediately follows, the first day of that academic year;

(ii) where the final academic year starts on 1st September, the benefit week, the first day of which coincides with, or immediately follows, the earlier of 1st September or the first day of the autumn term;]

and ending with [⁷the benefit week, the last day of which coincides with, or immediately precedes,] the last day of the course;

(c) in any other case, the loan shall be apportioned equally between the weeks in the period beginning with the earlier of—

(i) the first day of the first benefit week in September; or

[⁷(ii) the benefit week, the first day of which coincides with, or immediately follows, the first day of the autumn term,]

and ending with [⁷the benefit week, the last day of which coincides with, or immediately precedes, the last day of June],

and, in all cases, from the weekly amount so apportioned there shall be disregarded £10.]

[¹(3) A student shall be treated as possessing a student loan [¹³or a post-graduate [¹⁴...] loan] in respect of an academic year where—

(a) a student loan [¹³or a postgraduate [¹⁴ ...] loan] has been made to him in respect of that year; or

(b) he could acquire [¹³a student loan or a postgraduate [¹⁴...] loan] in respect of that year by taking reasonable steps to do so.

(4) Where a student is treated as possessing a student loan under paragraph (3), the amount of the student loan to be taken into account as income shall be, subject to paragraph (5)—

(a) in the case of a student to whom a student loan is made in respect of an academic year, a sum equal to the maximum student loan he is able to acquire in respect of that year by taking reasonable steps to do so and either—

(i) in the case of a student other than one to whom head (ii) refers, any contribution whether or not it has been paid to him; or

    (ii) in the case of a student who satisfies the additional conditions for a disability premium specified in paragraph 14 of Schedule 1 (applicable amounts), any contribution which has actually been paid to him;

(b) in the case of a student to whom a student loan is not made in respect of an academic year, the maximum student loan that would be made to the student if—

    (i) he took all reasonable steps to obtain the maximum student loan he is able to acquire in respect of that year; and

    (ii) no deduction in that loan was made by virtue of the application of a means test.

[¹³(4A) Where a student is treated as possessing a postgraduate [¹⁴...] loan under paragraph (3) in respect of an academic year, the amount of that loan to be taken into account as income shall be, subject to paragraph (5), a sum equal to 30 per cent. of the maximum postgraduate [¹⁴...] loan the student is able to acquire in respect of that academic year by taking reasonable steps to do so.]

(5) There shall be deducted from the amount of income taken into account under paragraph (4) [¹³or (4A)]—

(a) the sum of [⁸[¹¹ £303] per academic year] in respect of travel costs; and

[⁴(b) the sum of [⁹[¹² £390] per academic year] towards the costs of books and equipment,]

whether or not any such costs are incurred.]

AMENDMENTS

1. Social Security Amendment (Students) Regulations 1999 (SI 1999/1935) reg.2(5) (August 30, 1999, or if the student's period of study begins between August 1 and 29, 1999, the first day of the period).
2. Social Security Amendment (Students and Income-related Benefits) Regulations 2000 (SI 2000/1922) reg.3(7) (August 28, 2000, or if the student's period of study begins between August 1 and 27, 2000, the first day of the period).
3. Social Security Amendment (Students and Income-related Benefits) Regulations 2001 (SI 2001/2319) reg.3(1) and (3)(d) (August 27, 2001, or if the student's period of study begins between August 1 and 26, 2001, the first day of the period).
4. Social Security Amendment (Students and Income-related Benefits) Regulations 2001 (SI 2001/2319) reg.3(2) and (3)(d) (August 27, 2001, or if the student's period of study begins between August 1 and 26, 2001, the first day of the period).
5. Social Security Amendment (Students and Income-related Benefits) Regulations 2001 (SI 2001/2319) reg.4 (August 27, 2001, or if the student's period of study begins between August 1 and 26, 2001, the first day of the period).
6. Social Security Amendment (Students and Income-related Benefits) Regulations 2002 (SI 2002/1589) reg.3 (August 26, 2002, or if the student's period of study begins between August 1 and 25, 2002, the first day of the period).
7. Social Security Amendment (Students and Income-related Benefits) Regulations 2002 (SI 2002/1589) reg.5 (August 26, 2002, or if the student's period of study begins between August 1 and 25, 2002, the first day of the period).
8. Social Security (Students and Income-related Benefits) Amendment

Regulations 2007 (SI 2007/1632) reg.3(3)(a) (September 1, 2007, or if the student's period of study begins between August 1 and 31, 2007, the first day of the period).

9. Social Security (Students and Income-related Benefits) Amendment Regulations 2007 (SI 2007/1632) reg.3(3)(b) (September 1, 2007, or if the student's period of study begins between August 1 and 31, 2007, the first day of the period).

10. Social Security (Miscellaneous Amendments) (No.6) Regulations 2008 (SI 2008/2767) reg.4(9) (November 17, 2008).

11. Social Security (Students and Miscellaneous Amendments) Regulations 2009 (SI 2009/1575) reg.2(2) and (4)(b) (September 1, 2009, or if the student's period of study begins between August 1 and 31, 2009, the first day of the period).

12. Social Security (Students and Miscellaneous Amendments) Regulations 2009 (SI 2009/1575) reg.2(3) and (4)(b) (September 1, 2009, or if the student's period of study begins between August 1 and 31, 2009, the first day of the period).

13. Social Security (Treatment of Postgraduate Master's Degree Loans and Special Support Loans) (Amendment) Regulations 2016 (SI 2016/743) reg.3(4) (August 4, 2016).

14. Social Security (Income and Capital) (Miscellaneous Amendments) Regulations 2020 (SI 2020/618) reg.3(8) (July 15, 2020).

DEFINITIONS

"academic year"—see reg.130.
"postgraduate loan"—*ibid.*
"student loan"—*ibid.*

GENERAL NOTE

3.400   See the note to reg.66A of the Income Support Regulations.

[¹ Treatment of payments from access funds

3.401   **136A.**—(1) This regulation applies to payments from access funds that are not payments to which regulation 138(2) or (3) (income treated as capital) applies.

(2) A payment from access funds, other than a payment to which paragraph (3) of this regulation applies, shall be disregarded as income.

(3) Subject to paragraph (4) of this regulation and paragraph 38 of Schedule 7, any payments from access funds which are intended and used for food, ordinary clothing or footwear [⁴. . .], household fuel, rent for which housing benefit is payable [² or any housing costs] to the extent that they are met under regulation 83(f) or 84(1)(g) (housing costs) [². . .], of a single claimant or, as the case may be, of [³ his partner], and any payments from access funds which are used for any council tax or water charges for which that claimant or [³partner is liable] shall be disregarded as income to the extent of £20 per week.

[⁴ (3A) In paragraph (3) "ordinary clothing or footwear" means clothing or footwear for normal daily use, but it does not include—
(a) school uniforms, or
(b) clothing or footwear used solely for sporting activities.]
(4) Where a payment from access funds is made—
(a) on or after 1st September or the first day of the course, whichever first occurs, but before receipt of any student loan in respect of that

year and that payment is intended for the purpose of bridging the period until receipt of the student loan; or

(b) before the first day of the course to a person in anticipation of that person becoming a student,

that payment shall be disregarded as income.]

AMENDMENTS

1. Social Security Amendment (Students and Income-related Benefits) Regulations 2000 (SI 2000/1922) reg.3(8) (August 28, 2000, or if the student's period of study begins between August 1 and 27, 2000, the first day of the period).
2. Social Security Amendment (Residential Care and Nursing Homes) Regulations 2001 (SI 2001/3767) reg.2(2) and Pt II of Sch. para.13 (April 8, 2002).
3. Social Security (Working Tax Credit and Child Tax Credit) (Consequential Amendments) Regulations 2003 (SI 2003/455) reg.3 and Sch.2 para.17 (April 6, 2004, except in "transitional cases" and see further the note to reg.83 and reg.17 of the Income Support Regulations).
4. Social Security (Miscellaneous Amendments) Regulations 2007 (SI 2007/719) reg.3(6) (April 2, 2007).

DEFINITIONS

"access funds"—see reg.130.
"payment"—see reg.1(3).
"single claimant"—*ibid.*
"student loan"—see reg.1(3).

GENERAL NOTE

See the note to reg.66B of the Income Support Regulations.   3.402

[¹ Treatment of fee loans

136B.—A loan for fees, known as a fee loan or a fee contribution loan,   3.403
made pursuant to regulations made under article 3 of the Education (Student Support) (Northern Ireland) Order 1998, section 22 of the Teaching and Higher Education Act 1998 or section 73(f) of the Education (Scotland) Act 1980, shall be disregarded as income.]

AMENDMENT

1. Social Security (Students and Income-related Benefits) Amendment Regulations 2006 (SI 2006/1752) reg.5(4) (September 1, 2006, or if the student's period of study begins between August 1 and August 31, 2006, the first day of the period).

GENERAL NOTE

See the note to reg.66C of the Income Support Regulations.   3.404

[¹Treatment of special support loans

136C.—A special support loan within the meaning of regulation 68 of   3.405
the Education (Student Support) Regulations 2011 is to be disregarded as income.]

AMENDMENT

1. Social Security (Treatment of Postgraduate Master's Degree Loans and Special Support Loans) (Amendment) Regulations 2016 (SI 2016/743) reg.3(5) (August 4, 2016).

GENERAL NOTE

3.406 See the notes to reg.66D of the Income Support Regulations. The amount of a special support loan is to be disregarded as income. As a matter of principle, the amount cannot be treated as capital during the period to which the loan relates.

Disregard of contribution

3.407 **137.**—Where the claimant or his partner is a student and, for the purposes of assessing a contribution to the student's grant [¹ or student loan], the other partner's income has been taken into account, an amount equal to that contribution shall be disregarded for the purposes of assessing that other partner's income.

AMENDMENT

1. Social Security Amendment (Students) Regulations 1999 (SI 1999/1935) reg.2(6) (August 30, 1999, or if the student's period of study begins between August 1 and 29, 1999, the first day of the period).

DEFINITIONS

"claimant"—see Jobseekers Act 1995 s.35(1) and reg.88(1).
"contribution"—see reg.130.
"grant"—*ibid.*
"partner"—see reg.1(3).
"student loan"—see reg.130.

GENERAL NOTE

3.408 See reg.67 of the Income Support Regulations.

[¹Further disregard of student's income

3.409 **137A.**—Where any part of a student's income has already been taken into account for the purposes of assessing his entitlement to a grant[², student loan or postgraduate [³...] loan], the amount taken into account shall be disregarded in assessing that student's income.]

AMENDMENTS

1. Social Security (Miscellaneous Amendments) Regulations 1998 (SI 1998/563) reg.4(3) and (4)(f) (April 6, 1998).
2. Social Security (Treatment of Postgraduate Master's Degree Loans and Special Support Loans) (Amendment) Regulations 2016 (SI 2016/743) reg.3(6) (August 4, 2016).
3. Social Security (Income and Capital) (Miscellaneous Amendments) Regulations 2020 (SI 2020/618) reg.3(9) (July 15, 2020).

DEFINITIONS

"grant"—see reg.130.
"postgraduate loan"—*ibid.*
"student loan"—*ibid.*

Income treated as capital

3.410 **138.**—[¹(1)] Any amount by way of a refund of tax deducted from a student's income shall be treated as capital.

[¹(2) An amount paid from access funds as a single lump sum shall be treated as capital.

(3) An amount paid from access funds as a single lump sum which is intended and used for an item other than food, ordinary clothing or footwear [⁴. . .], household fuel, rent for which housing benefit is payable [²or any housing costs] to the extent that they are met under regulation 83(f) or 84(1)(g) (housing costs) [². . .], of a single claimant or, as the case may be, of [³his partner], or which is used for an item other than any council tax or water charges for which that claimant or [³partner is liable] shall be disregarded as capital but only for a period of 52 weeks from the date of the payment.]

[⁴ (4) In paragraph (3) "ordinary clothing or footwear" means clothing or footwear for normal daily use, but it does not include-

(a) school uniforms, or

(b) clothing or footwear used solely for sporting activities.]

AMENDMENTS

1. Social Security Amendment (Students and Income-related Benefits) Regulations 2000 (SI 2000/1922) reg.3(9) (August 28, 2000, or if the student's period of study begins between August 1 and 27, 2000, the first day of the period).

2. Social Security Amendment (Residential Care and Nursing Homes) Regulations 2001 (SI 2001/3767) reg.2(2) and Pt II of Sch. para.14 (April 8, 2002).

3. Social Security (Working Tax Credit and Child Tax Credit) (Consequential Amendments) Regulations 2003 (SI 2003/455) reg.3 and Sch.2 para.17 (April 6, 2004, except in "transitional cases" and see further the note to reg.83 and to reg.17 of the Income Support Regulations).

4. Social Security (Miscellaneous Amendments) Regulations 2007 (SI 2007/719) reg.3(7) (April 2, 2007).

DEFINITIONS

"access funds"—see reg.130.
"partner"—see reg.1(3).
"payment"—*ibid*.
"single claimant"—*ibid*.
"water charges"—*ibid*.

GENERAL NOTE

On paras (2) and (3), see the note to reg.66B of the Income Support Regulations.

3.411

Disregard of changes occurring during summer vacation

139.—In calculating a student's income [¹the Secretary of State] shall disregard any change in the standard maintenance grant occurring in the recognised summer vacation appropriate to the student's course, if that vacation does not form part of his period of study, from the date on which the change occurred up to the end of that vacation.

3.412

AMENDMENT

1. Social Security Act 1998 (Commencement No.11, and Savings and Consequential and Transitional Provisions) Order 1999 (SI 1999/2860 (C.75)) art.3(12) and Sch.12 para.2 (October 18, 1999).

DEFINITIONS

DEFINITIONS

"period of study"—see reg.1(3).
"standard maintenance grant"—see reg.130.

GENERAL NOTE

3.413   See reg.69 of the Income Support Regulations.

PART IX

HARDSHIP

GENERAL NOTE

3.414   This Part deals with the circumstances in which a hardship payment of JSA will be made. A hardship payment can only be paid if a sanction has been imposed; or the claimant is waiting for a decision at the beginning of his claim as to whether he satisfies the labour market conditions in s.1(2)(a)–(c) of the Jobseekers Act; or payment of JSA has been suspended because a question has arisen as to whether the claimant satisfies the labour market conditions; or, in the case of a claimant who is in a "vulnerable group" (see reg.140(1)) only, a decision-maker has decided that he does not satisfy the labour market conditions. Hardship payments are not available in any other circumstances.

See reg.140 for the meaning of "hardship". Unless the claimant falls into a vulnerable group (see reg.140(1)), no hardship payment will be made for the first two weeks, however severe the person's hardship. If a hardship payment is made, it will be subject to a 40 per cent or 20 per cent reduction of the appropriate personal allowance for a single claimant (see reg.145). While hardship payments are being paid the claimant must continue to satisfy the other conditions of entitlement for income-based JSA and in addition will be required to sign a declaration of hardship (see reg.143).

See also the notes to s.20(4)–(6) of the Jobseekers Act on hardship payments where a sanction has been imposed.

Meaning of "person in hardship"

3.415   **140.**—(1) In this Part of these Regulations, a "person in hardship" means for the purposes of regulation 141 a claimant, other than a claimant to whom paragraph (3) or (4) applies [⁷or a member of a joint-claim couple and regulation 3E does not apply], who—

(a) is a single woman—
    (i) who is pregnant; and
    (ii) in respect of whom [⁵the Secretary of State] is satisfied that, unless a jobseeker's allowance is paid to her, she will suffer hardship; or

(b) is a single person who is responsible for a [¹⁴ child or young person], and [⁵the Secretary of State] is satisfied that, unless a jobseeker's allowance is paid to the single person, the [¹⁴ child or young person] will suffer hardship; or

(c) is a member of [¹² a couple], where—
    [¹² (i) at least one member of the couple is a woman who is pregnant; and]

    (ii) [⁵the Secretary of State] is satisfied that, unless a jobseeker's allowance is paid, the woman will suffer hardship; or

(d) is a member of a polygamous marriage and—

    (i) one member of the marriage is pregnant; and

    (ii) [⁵the Secretary of State] is satisfied that, unless a jobseeker's allowance is paid, that woman will suffer hardship; or

(e) is a member of [¹² a couple] or of a polygamous marriage where—

    (i) one or both members of the couple, or one or more members of the polygamous marriage, are responsible for a child or young person; and

    (ii) [⁵the Secretary of State] is satisfied that, unless a jobseeker's allowance is paid, the child or young person will suffer hardship; or

(f) has an award of a jobseeker's allowance which includes or would, if a claim for a jobseeker's allowance from him were to succeed have included, in his applicable amount a disability premium and—

    (i) where the person has an award, a jobseeker's allowance is not payable [²⁰ . . .] because it is suspended [²⁰ or the award is reduced in accordance with section 19 or 19A or regulation 69B]; and

    (ii) [⁵the Secretary of State] is satisfied that, unless a jobseeker's allowance is paid, the person who would satisfy the conditions of entitlement to that premium would suffer hardship; or

(g) suffers, or whose partner suffers from a chronic medical condition which results in functional capacity being limited or restricted by physical [²⁴ or mental] impairment and [⁵ the Secretary of State] is satisfied that—

    (i) the suffering has already lasted, or is likely to last, for not less than 26 weeks; and

    (ii) unless a jobseeker's allowance is paid to the claimant the probability is that the health of the person suffering would, within 2 weeks of [⁵the Secretary of State] making his decision, decline further than that of a normally healthy adult and that person would suffer hardship; or

(h) does, or whose partner does, or in the case of a claimant who is married to more than one person under a law which permits polygamy, at least one of those persons do, devote a considerable portion of each week to caring for another person who—

    (i) is in receipt of an attendance allowance [²² , the care component of disability living allowance at one of the two higher rates prescribed under section 72(4) of the Benefits Act or the daily living component of personal independence payment at the standard or enhanced rate in accordance with section 78 of the 2012 Act] [²³ or armed forces independence payment]; or

    (ii) has claimed either attendance allowance [²² , disability living allowance [²³ armed forces independence payment] or personal independence payment] but only for so long as the claim has not been determined, or for, 26 weeks from the date of claiming, [¹ whichever is the earlier; or

    (iii) has claimed either attendance allowance or disability living allowance and has an award of either attendance allowance or the care component of disability living allowance at one of the two higher rates prescribed under section 72(4) of the Benefits Act for a

period commencing after the date on which that claim was made,]
[²² or

(iv) has claimed personal independence payment and has an award of the daily living component of personal independence payment at the standard or enhanced rate in accordance with section 78 of the 2012 Act for a period commencing after the date on which that claim was made,] [²³ ; or

(v) has claimed and has an award of armed forces independence payment for a period commencing after the date on which that claim was made,]

and [⁵the Secretary of State] is satisfied, after taking account of the factors set out in [²paragraph (5)] in so far as they are appropriate to the particular circumstances of the case, that the person providing the care will not be able to continue doing so unless a jobseeker's allowance is paid to the claimant; or

(i) is a person or is the partner of a person to whom section 16 applies by virtue of a direction issued by the Secretary of State, except where the person to whom the direction applies does not satisfy the requirements of section 1(2)(a) to (c); or

(j) is a person—

(i) to whom section 3(1)(f)(iii) (persons under the age of 18) applies, or is the partner of such a person; and

(ii) in respect of whom [⁵the Secretary of State] is satisfied that the person will, unless a jobseeker's allowance is paid, suffer [²⁴ hardship; or]

[⁶(k) is a person—

(i) who, pursuant to the Children Act 1989, [²⁵ or the Social Services and Well-being (Wales) Act 2014] was being looked after by a local authority;

(ii) with whom the local authority had a duty, pursuant to [²⁵ either of those Acts], to take reasonable steps to keep in touch; or

(iii) who, pursuant to [²⁵ either of those Acts], qualified for advice and assistance from a local authority,

but in respect of whom (i), (ii) or, as the case may be, (iii) above had not applied for a period of three years or less as at the date on which he complies with the requirements of regulation 143; and

(iv) as at the date on which he complies with the requirements of regulation 143, is under the age of 21] [²⁴; or]

[²⁴(l) is a person who is homeless within the meaning of Part 7 of the Housing Act 1996, Part 2 of the Housing (Wales) Act 2014 or Part 2 of the Housing (Scotland) Act 1987, as the case may be.]

(2) Except in a case to which paragraph (3) [² ...] [⁴ ...] [¹⁵ ...] [¹⁹ [²⁰ ...]] applies [⁸ or where the person in hardship is a member of a joint-claim couple and regulation 3E does not apply] a "person in hardship" means for the purposes of regulation 142, a claimant where [⁵the Secretary of State] is satisfied that he or his partner will suffer hardship unless a jobseeker's allowance is paid to him.

(3) In paragraphs (1) and (2) a "person in hardship" does not include a claimant who is entitled, or whose partner is entitled, to income support [¹³ or an income-related employment and support allowance] or [³ a claim-

ant or a partner of a claimant] who falls within a category of persons prescribed for the purpose of section 124(1)(e) of the Benefits Act.

(4) Paragraph (1)(h) shall not apply in a case where the person being
cared for resides in a [¹¹ care home, an Abbeyfield Home or an independent hospital].

[⁴(4A) [²⁰ . . .]]

[¹⁵(4B) [²⁰ . . .]]

[¹⁹ (4C) [²⁰ . . .]]

(5) Factors which, for the purposes of paragraphs (1) and (2), [⁵the
Secretary of State] is to take into account in determining whether a person
will suffer hardship are—

(a) the presence in the claimant's family of a person who satisfies the
requirements for a disability premium specified in paragraphs 13 and
14 of Schedule 1 [¹or [¹⁰an element of child tax credit in respect of
a child or young person who is disabled or severely disabled within
the meaning of regulation 8 of the Child Tax Credit Regulations
2002]];

(b) the resources which, without a jobseeker's allowance, are likely
to be available to the claimant's family, the amount by which these
resources fall short of the amount applicable in his case in accordance with regulation 145 (applicable amount in hardship cases), the
amount of any resources which may be available to members of the
claimant's family from any person in the claimant's household who
is not a member of his family, and the length of time for which those
factors are likely to persist;

(c) whether there is a substantial risk that essential items, including
food, clothing, heating and accommodation, will cease to be available to the claimant or to a member of the claimant's family, or will
be available at considerably reduced levels and the length of time
those factors are likely to persist.

[²¹ (6) In paragraph (5)(b), "resources" does not include any sum, where
applicable, specified in paragraph 6B(1) and (2) of Schedule 7 (sums to
be disregarded in the calculation of income other than earnings—child tax
credit and child benefit).]

AMENDMENTS

1. Jobseeker's Allowance (Amendment) Regulations 1996 (SI 1996/1516) reg.13
(October 7, 1996).

2. Jobseeker's Allowance (Amendment) Regulations 1996 (SI 1996/1516) reg.20
and Sch. (October 7, 1996).

3. Jobseeker's Allowance and Income Support (General) (Amendment)
Regulations 1996 (SI 1996/1517) reg.25 (October 7, 1996).

4. Social Security Amendment (New Deal) Regulations 1997 (SI 1997/2863)
reg.11 (January 5, 1998).

5. Social Security Act 1998 (Commencement No.11, and Savings and
Consequential and Transitional Provisions) Order 1999 (SI 1999/2860 (C.75))
Arts 3(1) and (12) and Sch.12 para.2 (October 18 1999).

6. Jobseeker's Allowance (Amendment) Regulations 2000 (SI 2000/239) reg.2(4)
(March 6, 2000).

7. Jobseeker's Allowance (Joint Claims) Regulations 2000 (SI 2000/1978)
reg.2(5) and Sch.2 para.45(a) (March 19, 2001).

8. Jobseeker's Allowance (Joint Claims) Regulations 2000 (SI 2000/1978) reg.2(5) and Sch.2 para.45(b) (March 19, 2001).

9. Social Security Amendment (New Deal) Regulations 2001 (SI 2001/1029) reg.9(1) (April 9, 2001).

10. Social Security (Working Tax Credit and Child Tax Credit) (Consequential Amendments) Regulations 2003 (SI 2003/455) reg.3 and Sch.2 para.18 (April 6, 2004, except in "transitional cases" and see further the note to reg.83 and to reg.17 of the Income Support Regulations).

11. Social Security (Care Homes and Independent Hospitals) Regulations 2005 (SI 2005/2687) reg.3 and Sch.2 para.7 (October 24, 2005).

12. Civil Partnership (Pensions, Social Security and Child Support) (Consequential, etc. Provisions) Order 2005 (SI 2005/2877) art.2(3) and Sch.3 para.26(8) (December 5, 2005).

13. Employment and Support Allowance (Consequential Provisions) (No.2) Regulations 2008 (SI 2008/1554) reg.3(1) and (17) (October 27, 2008).

14. Social Security (Lone Parents and Miscellaneous Amendments) Regulations 2008 (SI 2008/3051) reg.11(14) (November 24, 2008).

15. Social Security (Flexible New Deal) Regulations 2009 (SI 2009/480) reg.2(8) (April 6, 2009).

16. Social Security (Flexible New Deal) Regulations 2009 (SI 2009/480) reg.2(8)(b) (October 5, 2009).

17. Jobseeker's Allowance (Sanctions for Failure to Attend) Regulations 2010 (SI 2010/509) reg.2(14) (April 6, 2010).

18. Jobseeker's Allowance (Mandatory Work Activity Scheme) Regulations 2011 (SI 2011/688) reg.16(f) (April 25, 2011).

19. Jobseeker's Allowance (Employment, Skills and Enterprise Scheme) Regulations 2011 (SI 2011/917) reg.9 (May 20, 2011).

20. Jobseeker's Allowance (Sanctions) (Amendment) Regulations 2012 (SI 2012/2568) reg.3 (October 22, 2012).

21. Social Security (Miscellaneous Amendments) Regulations 2013 (SI 2013/443) reg.4(1) and (10) (April 2, 2013).

22. Personal Independence Payment (Supplementary Provisions and Consequential Amendments) Regulations 2013 (SI 2013/388) reg.8 and Sch. para.16(1) and (4) (April 8, 2013).

23. Armed Forces and Reserve Forces Compensation Scheme (Consequential Provisions: Subordinate Legislation) Order 2013 (SI 2013/591) art.7 and Sch. para.10(1) and (4) (April 8, 2013).

24. Jobseeker's Allowance (Hardship) (Amendment) Regulations 2017 (SI 2018/760) reg.2(1) and (2) (October 23, 2017).

25. Social Services and Well-being (Wales) Act 2014 and the Regulation and Inspection of Social Care (Wales) Act 2016 (Consequential Amendments) Order 2017 (SI 2017/901) art.6(1) and (5) (November 3, 2017).

DEFINITIONS

"Abbeyfield Home"—see reg.1(3).
"attendance allowance"—*ibid*.
"care home"—*ibid*.
"child"—see Jobseekers Act s.35(1).
"claimant"—*ibid*.
"couple"—see reg.1(3).
"independent hospital"—*ibid*.
"partner"—*ibid*.
"polygamous marriage"—*ibid*.
"week"—*ibid*.
"young person"—see reg.76.

G ENERAL N OTE

Paragraph (1)
This lists those claimants who are eligible for hardship payments without any   3.416
waiting period (the "vulnerable groups"). Note the exclusion in para.(3) of claimants who (or whose partners) are in a category who can claim income support
(claimants who, or whose partners, are entitled to income support would in any
event be excluded from JSA under s.3(1)(b) or (c) of the Jobseekers Act).
The categories are:
  (i) a single claimant who is pregnant whom the decision-maker accepts will
       suffer hardship if no payment is made (sub-para.(a));
 (ii) a single claimant who is responsible for (see reg.77) a child or a young
       person (see regs 1(3) and 76(3)) where the decision maker accepts that the
       child or young person will suffer hardship if no payment is made (sub-para.
       (b)). Note however, that where claimant is responsible for a child under the
       age of five, the claimant will be entitled to IS and therefore ineligible for a
       hardship payment under para.(3);
(iii) a member of a couple, or of a polygamous marriage, where the/a woman is
       pregnant and the decision-maker accepts that the woman will suffer hard-
       ship if no payment is made (sub-paras (c) and (d));
(iv) a member of a couple, or of a polygamous marriage, who is/are responsible
       (see reg.77) for a child or young person (see reg.76) and the decision- maker
       accepts that the child or young person will suffer hardship if no payment is
       made (sub-para.(e));
  (v) people eligible for a disability premium in their income-based JSA and
       the decision-maker accepts that the person who qualifies for the disability
       premium would suffer hardship if no payment is made (sub-para.(f)). In
       contrast to the other sub-paragraphs, sub-para.(f) refers to a person who
       "has an award of " JSA which includes a disability premium (or whose
       claim, if successful, would include a disability premium). The intention
       would seem to be that this category does not apply if the reason for the non-
       payment of JSA is that the claimant has failed to satisfy the labour market
       conditions (in such a case the person would not have an award of JSA and
       see head (i)). But if such a person having failed to satisfy the labour market
       conditions then makes a further claim for JSA, arguably he falls within sub-
       para.(f) because he has made a claim for JSA which were it to succeed would
       include a disability premium;
(vi) a claimant who, or whose partner, has a chronic medical condition result-
       ing in his functional capacity being restricted by physical impairment which
       has lasted, or is likely to last, for at least 26 weeks and the decision-maker
       accepts that in the next two weeks the person's health is likely to "decline
       further than that of a normally healthy adult" and that that person will suffer
       hardship if no payment is made (sub-para.(g)). If such a person is incapable
       of work he will be eligible for income support and so will not qualify for a
       hardship payment (see para.(3));
(vii) a claimant who, or whose partner, "devotes a considerable portion of
       each week" to caring for someone (not in a residential care or nursing home,
       see para.(4)) who is in receipt of, or (in certain circumstances) has claimed
       attendance allowance, or the higher or middle rate care component of disa-
       bility living allowance, or the daily living component of PIP, or armed forces
       independence payment, and the decision-maker accepts that the person will
       not be able to continue caring if no payment is made (sub-para.(h)). (*Note*:
       a person in this situation may well be eligible for income support, see paras
       4–6 of Sch.1B to the Income Support Regulations.);
(viii) a claimant who, or whose partner, is under 18, the subject of a severe hard-
       ship direction and who satisfies the labour market conditions (sub-para.(i));
(ix) a claimant who, or whose partner, is under 18, but eligible for JSA and the

decision-maker accepts that that person will suffer hardship if no payment is made (sub-para.(j)). (*Note*: a 16- or 17-year-old who is being sanctioned for an "offence" under s.19(2)(c) or (d) or s.19A(2)(a), (c), (d),(e), (f) or (g) of the Jobseekers Act will automatically be paid a reduced rate of JSA and will not need to rely on this provision: see reg.68.); and

(x) a person under the age of 21 who was being looked after by a local authority under the Children Act 1989 (or was the subject of certain other local authority duties under that Act) within the past three years (sub-para.(k)).

See para.(5) for the factors the decision-maker must consider when deciding whether a person will suffer hardship.

Note the requirement under reg.143 for the claimant to sign a written declaration as to why he will suffer hardship if no payment is made.

Paragraph (2)

3.417   If a person does not come within one of the categories listed in para.(1) he will only be entitled to a hardship payment after two weeks (reg.142(2), (4) and (5)) and if the decision-maker accepts that he or his partner will suffer hardship if no payment is made. Note the exclusions in para.(3). As regards para.(3), claimants who, or whose partners, are entitled to income support would in any event be excluded from JSA under s.3(1)(b) or (c) of the Jobseekers Act. See para.(5) for the factors the decision-maker must consider when deciding whether hardship will occur and reg.143 for the declaration the claimant will be required to sign.

Paragraph (5)

3.418   This lists factors that the decision-maker must consider when deciding whether a person will suffer hardship. The list is not exhaustive and the decision-maker should consider all the circumstances of the claimant and his family (if any). "Hardship" is not defined. The *Decision Makers Guide* suggests that it means "severe suffering or privation", and that "privation means a lack of the necessities of life" (para.35155).

The factors that the decision-maker must consider are whether a member of the claimant's family qualifies for a disability or (in "transitional cases" only—see the note to regs 83 and 17 of the Income Support Regulations) a disabled child premium, or the disabled child, or severely disabled child, element of child tax credit (sub-para.(a)); other available resources, including those which may be available to the claimant's family from anyone else in the claimant's household (sub-para.(b)); and whether there is a "substantial risk" that the claimant or a member of his family will go without essential items such as food, clothing, heating and accommodation, or that they will be available at "considerably reduced" levels, and if so, for how long (sub-para.(c)).

Sub-paragraph (a) is straightforward. Under sub-para.(b) the decision-maker has to take into account other resources that are likely to be available to the claimant or his family. Thus income and capital that is normally disregarded (e.g. disability living allowance) will be taken into account under sub-para.(b). But note that para.35181 of the *Decision Makers Guide* considers that JSA paid for an earlier period should not be taken into account. (Note that if the decision-maker does decide that the person is in hardship the normal income and capital rules will be applied when calculating the amount of a hardship payment; unlike urgent cases payments there are no special rules for the calculation of income and capital. However, the payment will be reduced by 40 or 20 per cent of the appropriate personal allowance for a single person of the claimant's age: see reg.145.) In addition, if there are any non-dependents (for example, a grown-up son or daughter) living in the claimant's household, any contribution that they might be expected to make will be considered. But the resources have to be available to the claimant. So, for example, if a payment from a pension fund will only be available in four weeks' time, or savings can only be cashed after a period of notice has been given, a hardship payment can be made until these resources become available (see paras 35185–35195 of *DMG*).

Moreover, money that might be obtainable from credit facilities (e.g. a credit card or overdraft) should not be taken into account as such facilities are not resources but only increase the claimant's indebtedness (see para.35196 of *DMG*). The decision-maker also has to consider the length of time for which any other resources are likely to be available. Clearly the longer the period of time that JSA will not be payable (e.g. if a sanction of several weeks or months' duration has been imposed) the more likely it is that hardship will occur. Sub-paragraph (c) gives examples of essential items that the decision-maker should take into account but this does not exclude consideration of other items that may be essential to the particular claimant or a member of his family.

If the claimant is not in hardship when the claim is first made but the decision-maker decides that hardship will be established by a later date, the decision to impose the sanction (i.e. that JSA is payable at a nil rate for the sanction period) can be superseded with effect from that later date on the basis that it is anticipated that a relevant change of circumstances will occur under reg.6(1)(a)(ii) of the Social Security and Child Support (Decisions and Appeals) Regulations 1999 (see Vol.III).

[¹Period when a person is not a person in hardship

140A.—[⁷ . . .]]   3.419

AMENDMENTS

1. Social Security Amendment (New Deal) Regulations 1997 (SI 1997/2863) reg.12 (January 5, 1998).
2. Jobseeker's Allowance (Amendment) Regulations 2000 (SI 2000/239) reg.2(5)(a) (March 6, 2000).
3. Jobseeker's Allowance (Amendment) Regulations 2000 (SI 2000/239) reg.2(5)(b) (March 6, 2000).
4. Social Security Amendment (New Deal) Regulations 2001 (SI 2001/1029) reg.10(1) (April 9, 2001).
5. Social Security Amendment (New Deal) Regulations 2001 (SI 2001/1029) reg.10(2) (April 9, 2001).
6. Social Security (Flexible New Deal) Regulations 2009 (SI 2009/480) reg.2(9) (October 5, 2009).
7. Jobseeker's Allowance (Sanctions) (Amendment) Regulations 2012 (SI 2012/2568) reg.3 (October 22, 2012).

Circumstances in which an income-based jobseeker's allowance is payable to a person in hardship

141.—(1) This regulation applies to persons in hardship within the   3.420
meaning of regulation 140(1), and is subject to the provisions of regulations 143 and 144.

(2) Subject to paragraph (3) a person in hardship [¹, other than a person to whom regulation 46(1) (waiting days) applies, shall be treated as entitled to an income-based jobseeker's allowance for the period beginning with the [⁷ 8th] day of the jobseeking period or,] if later, from the day he first becomes a person in hardship and ending on the day before the claim is determined where [²the sole reason for the delay] in determining the claim is that a question arises as to whether the claimant satisfies any of the conditions of entitlement specified in section 1(2)(a) to (c) [²provided he satisfies the conditions of entitlement specified in [⁸ paragraph (b) of subsection (2A)] of section 1.]

(3) A person in hardship to whom paragraph (2) applies may be treated as entitled to an income-based jobseeker's allowance for a period after the date [¹ . . .] referred to in that paragraph [¹which is applicable

in his case] but before the date the statement mentioned in regulation 143(1) is furnished where [³the Secretary of State] is satisfied that the claimant suffered hardship because of a lack of resources during that period.

(4) A person in hardship, except where the person has been treated as not available for employment in accordance with regulations under section 6(4) of the Act shall, subject to the conditions specified in regulation 143 (conditions for hardship payments), be entitled to an income-based jobseeker's allowance without satisfying the requirements of section 1(2)(a) to (c) of the Act provided he satisfies the other conditions of entitlement to that benefit.

(5) An income-based jobseeker's allowance shall be payable to a person in hardship even though payment to him of a jobseeker's allowance has been suspended in accordance with [⁴regulation 16 of the Social Security and Child Support (Decisions and Appeals) Regulations 1999] on the ground that a doubt has arisen as to whether he satisfies the requirements of section 1(2)(a) to (c), but the allowance shall be payable only if and for so long as the claimant satisfies the other conditions of entitlement to an income-based jobseeker's allowance.

(6) An income-based jobseeker's allowance shall be payable to a person in hardship even though [⁵ [⁶ his award of jobseeker's allowance has been reduced in accordance with section 19 or 19A or regulation 69B] but the allowance shall be payable only if and for so long as he satisfies the conditions of entitlement to an income-based jobseeker's allowance.

AMENDMENTS

1. Jobseeker's Allowance and Income Support (General) (Amendment) Regulations 1996 (SI 1996/1517) reg.26 (October 7, 1996).
2. Social Security and Child Support (Jobseeker's Allowance) (Miscellaneous Amendments) Regulations 1996 (SI 1996/2538) reg.2(9) (October 28, 1996).
3. Social Security Act 1998 (Commencement No.11, and Savings and Consequential and Transitional Provisions) Order 1999 (SI 1999/2860 (C.75)) Arts 3(1) and (12) and Sch.12 para.2 (October 18 1999).
4. Social Security Act 1998 (Commencement No.11, and Savings and Consequential and Transitional Provisions) Order 1999 (SI 1999/2860 (C.75)) arts 3(1) and (12) and Sch.12 para.8 (October 18, 1999).
5. Jobseeker's Allowance (Sanctions for Failure to Attend) Regulations 2010 (SI 2010/509) reg.2(15) (April 6, 2010).
6. Jobseeker's Allowance (Sanctions) (Amendment) Regulations 2012 (SI 2012/2568) reg.3 (October 22, 2012).
7. Social Security (Jobseeker's Allowance and Employment and Support Allowance) (Waiting Days) Amendment Regulations 2014 (SI 2014/2309) reg.3(1) and (2) (October 27, 2014).
8. Jobseeker's Allowance (Hardship) (Amendment) Regulations 2017 (SI 2018/760) reg.2(1) and (3) (October 23, 2017).

DEFINITIONS

"claimant"—see Jobseekers Act s.35(1).
"entitled"—*ibid.*

GENERAL NOTE

3.421   The circumstances in which hardship payments can be made are set out in this regulation for claimants who can be paid immediately and in reg.142 for claimants who have to wait two weeks. No payment will be made under this regulation or reg.142 unless the claimant has signed the declaration required by reg.143 (but note para.(3) below) and provided information about the person in hardship (see reg.144).

Paragraph (2) applies where a question arises as to whether the claimant satisfies the labour market conditions in s.1(2)(a)–(c) of the Jobseekers Act (availability for work, signing a jobseeker's agreement, actively seeking work) when a claim is made. This has to be the only reason for the delay in deciding the claim; hardship payments will not be available if the delay is for some other reason (e.g. because there is a question whether the person has too much capital or income). If hardship is established a payment will be made until the claim is decided, except for the first three— or if the claimant's jobseeking period began on or after October 27, 2014 (see SI 2014/2309 regs 3 and 4(1))—seven waiting (see para.4 of Sch.1 to the Jobseekers Act and reg.46) if these apply. The claimant must continue to satisfy the other conditions of entitlement for income-based JSA in s.3 of the Jobseekers Act. A payment under para.(2) may also be made for the period before the claimant has completed a reg.143 declaration if the decision-maker accepts that he suffered hardship because of "a lack of resources" during that period (para.(3)). Once the decision-maker has decided the claim this paragraph no longer applies but the claimant may be eligible for hardship payments under para.(4).

Paragraph (4) covers a person who is not entitled to JSA because a decision-maker has decided that he does not satisfy the labour market conditions in s.1(2) (a)–(c) of the Jobseekers Act. But it does not apply if the person is treated as not available for work under reg.15 (full-time students, prisoners on temporary release, women in receipt of maternity pay or allowance, people treated as not available at the start of a claim). The person must be in hardship and continue to satisfy the other conditions of entitlement for income-based JSA. Hardship payments can start from the date of the decision-maker's decision and continue for as long as the person remains in hardship. There is no requirement that the claimant has appealed against the decision-maker's decision. Note that there is no equivalent of this provision in reg.142 (persons eligible for hardship payments after waiting period).

Paragraph (5) applies where payment of a person's JSA has been suspended because a question has arisen as to whether he satisfies the labour market conditions. The person must be in hardship and continue to satisfy the other conditions of entitlement for income-based JSA. Hardship payments can be made until the suspension is lifted or the decision-maker decides that the claimant does not satisfy the labour market conditions. If the decision goes against the claimant he may be eligible for hardship payments under para.(4).

3.422

Under para.(6) a person can be paid hardship payments if a sanction has been applied, provided that he is in hardship and that he continues to satisfy the other conditions of entitlement for income-based JSA (including the labour market conditions). Payments under para.(6) can last as long as the sanction lasts.

See reg.145 for the amount of a hardship payment.

Further circumstances in which an income-based jobseeker's allowance is payable to a person in hardship

142.—(1) This regulation applies to a person in hardship who falls within paragraph (2) but not paragraph (1) of regulation 140 and is subject to the provisions of regulations 143 and 144.

3.423

(2) A person in hardship shall be treated as entitled to an income-based jobseeker's allowance for a period commencing on whichever is the later of—

[¹(a) the 15th day following the date of claim disregarding any waiting days; or]

(b) [¹. . .]

    (c) the day the claimant complies with the requirements of regulation 143,

and ending on the day before the claim is determined where [¹the sole reason for the delay] in determining the claim is that a question arises as to whether the claimant satisfies any of the conditions of entitlement specified in section 1(2)(a) to (c) [¹provided he satisfies the conditions of entitlement specified in paragraph (d)(ii) of subsection (2) of section 1.]

(3) An income-based jobseeker's allowance shall be payable subject to paragraph (4) to a person in hardship even though payment to him of a jobseeker's allowance has been suspended in accordance with regulations made by virtue of [²section 21 of the Social Security Act 1998] (suspension of benefit) on the ground that a doubt has arisen as to whether he satisfies the requirements of section 1(2)(a) to (c) but the allowance shall be payable only if and for so long as the claimant satisfies the other conditions of entitlement to an income-based jobseeker's allowance.

(4) An income-based jobseeker's allowance shall not be payable in respect of the first 14 days of the period of suspension.

(5) An income-based jobseeker's allowance shall be payable to a person in hardship even though [³ his award of jobseeker's allowance has been reduced in accordance with section 19 or 19A or regulation 69B], but the allowance—

    (a) shall not be payable under this paragraph in respect of the first 14 days of the period to which [³ the reduction] applies; and

    (b) shall be payable thereafter only where the conditions of entitlement to an income-based jobseeker's allowance are satisfied.

AMENDMENTS

1. Social Security and Child Support (Jobseeker's Allowance) (Miscellaneous Amendments) Regulations 1996 (SI 1996/2538) reg.2(10) (October 28, 1996).

2. Social Security Act 1998 (Commencement No.11, and Savings and Consequential and Transitional Provisions) Order 1999 (SI 1999/2860 (c.75)) arts 3(1) and (12) and Sch.12 para.9 (October 18 1999).

3. Jobseeker's Allowance (Sanctions) (Amendment) Regulations 2012 (SI 2012/2568) reg.3 (October 22, 2012).

DEFINITION

    "claimant"—see Jobseekers Act s.35(1).

GENERAL NOTE

3.424   See the notes to reg.141. This regulation applies to claimants who do not come within any of the categories listed in reg.140(1) and so have to wait for two weeks before any hardship payments can be made.

The circumstances in which hardship payments can be made under this regulation are similar to those in reg.141 (the differences are noted below), *except* that there is no provision for payment to claimants who have failed to satisfy the labour market conditions in s.1(2)(a)–(c) (compare reg.141(4)); there is only provision in para.(2) for payment where a question arises when a claim is made as to whether a claimant satisfies the labour market conditions and in para.(3) where a claimant's benefit has been suspended because of doubt as to whether these conditions are satisfied. Once a decison-maker has decided that the person does not satisfy the labour market conditions he will not be eligible for hardship payments if he is not in a "vulnerable group". This is the case even if the claimant is appealing against the decision-maker's decision.

Paragraphs (3) and (5) correspond to paras (5) and (6) in reg.141, except that in each case a hardship payment under this regulation is not payable for the first two weeks (see para.(4) and para.(5)(a)). Paragraph (2) is the equivalent of reg.141(2) except that under this regulation a hardship payment can only be made from the 15th day after the date of claim, or the 18th day if the "waiting days" apply (see para.4 of Sch.1 to the Jobseekers Act and reg.46) or from the day the claimant makes the declaration required by reg.143, whichever is the later. There is thus no discretion in the case of hardship payments under para.(2) of this regulation to make any payment for the period before a reg.143 declaration is signed (compare para.(3) of reg.141).

Conditions for hardship payments

143.—(1) A jobseeker's allowance shall not be payable in accordance with regulation 141 or, as the case may be, 142, except where the claimant has—

3.425

(a) furnished on a form approved for the purpose by the Secretary of State or in such other form as he may in any particular case approve a statement of the circumstances he relies upon to establish entitlement under regulation 141 or as the case may be regulation 142; and
(b) signed the statement.

(2) The completed and signed form shall be delivered by the claimant to such office as the Secretary of State may specify.

DEFINITION

"claimant"—see Jobseekers Act s.35(1).

Provision of information

144.—For the purposes of [¹section 20(5) of and] paragraph 10(3) of Schedule 1 to the Act, a claimant shall provide to the Secretary of State information as to the circumstances of the person alleged to be in hardship.

3.426

AMENDMENT

1. Jobseeker's Allowance (Amendment) Regulations 1996 (SI 1996/1516) reg.14 (October 7, 1996).

DEFINITION

"claimant"—see Jobseekers Act s.35(1).

Applicable amount in hardship cases

145.—[¹(1) The weekly applicable amount of a person to whom an income-based jobseeker's allowance is payable in accordance with this Part of these Regulations shall be reduced by a sum equivalent to 40% or, in a case where the claimant or any other member of his family is either pregnant or is seriously ill, 20% of the following amount]—

3.427

(a) where he is a single claimant aged less than 18 or a member of a couple or a polygamous marriage where all the members, in either case, are less than 18, the amount specified in paragraph 1(1)(a), (b) or (c), as the case may be, of Schedule 1 (applicable amounts);
(b) where he is a single claimant aged not less than 18 but less than 25 or a member of a couple or polygamous marriage where one member is aged not less than 18 but less than 25 and the other member or, in the case of a polygamous marriage each other

member, is a person under 18 who is not eligible for an income-based jobseeker's allowance under section 3(1)(f)(iii) or is not subject to a direction under section 16, the amount specified in paragraph 1(1)(d) of Schedule 1;

(c) where he is a single claimant aged not less than 25 or a member of a couple or a polygamous marriage (other than a member of a couple or polygamous marriage to whom sub-paragraph (b) [²applies]) at least one of whom is aged not less than 18, the amount specified in paragraph 1(1)(e) of Schedule 1.

(2) [¹. . .]

(3) A reduction under paragraph (1) or (2) shall, if it is not a multiple of 5p, be rounded to the nearest such multiple or, if it is a multiple of 2.5p but not of 5p, to the next lower multiple of 5p.

AMENDMENTS

1. Jobseeker's Allowance (Amendment) Regulations 1996 (SI 1996/1516) reg.15 (October 7, 1996).
2. Jobseeker's Allowance and Income Support (General) (Amendment) Regulations 1996 (SI 1996/1517) reg.28 (October 7, 1996).

DEFINITIONS

"claimant"—see Jobseekers Act s.35(1).
"couple"—see reg.1(3).
"polygamous marriage"—*ibid.*
"single claimant"—*ibid.*

GENERAL NOTE

3.428
Hardship payments of JSA are paid at a reduced rate. The reduction in benefit is 40 per cent of the appropriate personal allowance for a single claimant of that age, or 20 per cent if a member of the claimant's family is pregnant or seriously ill (not defined).

Payments made on account of suspended benefit

3.429
146.—(1) This regulation applies to a person to whom—
(a) payments of a jobseeker's allowance have been suspended in accordance with regulations made under [¹section 21 of the Social Security Act 1998];
(b) an income-based jobseeker's allowance is paid under regulation 141 or 142.

(2) In the case of a person to whom—
(a) this regulation applies; and
(b) payments in respect of the benefit suspended fall to be made, any benefit paid or payable by virtue of regulation 141(5) or 142(3) shall be treated as having been paid on account of the suspended benefit and only the balance of the suspended benefit (if any) shall be payable.

AMENDMENT

1. Social Security Act 1998 (Commencement No.11, and Savings and Consequential and Transitional Provisions) Order 1999 (SI 1999/2860 (C.75)) arts 3(1) and (12) and Sch.12 para.9 (October 18, 1999).

This provides that hardship payments made while payment of a claimant's JSA **3.430** was suspended will be taken into account if it is later decided that the suspension should be lifted, and only the balance of the benefit owing will be paid. In other cases (e.g. where hardship payments have been made because of a delay in deciding the claim for JSA) offsetting will be applied under the normal rules (see reg.5 of the Payments on Account, Overpayments and Recovery Regulations).

[¹ PART IXA

HARDSHIP FOR JOINT-CLAIM COUPLES

Meaning of "couple in hardship"

146A.—(1) In this Part of these Regulations, a "couple in hardship" **3.431** means for the purposes of regulation 146C, a joint-claim couple who are claiming a jobseeker's allowance jointly, other than a couple which includes a member to whom paragraph (3) or (4) applies, where—

(a) [⁴, at least one member of the joint-claim couple is a woman who is pregnant] and the Secretary of State is satisfied that, unless a joint-claim jobseeker's allowance is paid, she will suffer hardship; or

(b) one or both members of the couple are members of a polygamous marriage, one member of the marriage is pregnant and the Secretary of State is satisfied that, unless a joint-claim jobseeker's allowance is paid, she will suffer hardship; or

(c) the award of a joint-claim jobseeker's allowance includes, or would, if a claim for a jobseeker's allowance from the couple were to succeed, have included in their applicable amount a disability premium and—

   (i) where the couple have an award, a joint-claim jobseeker's allowance is not payable [¹⁰ . . .] because it is suspended [¹⁰ or the award is reduced in accordance with section 19 or 19A or regulation 69B]; and

   (ii) the Secretary of State is satisfied that, unless a joint-claim jobseeker's allowance is paid, the member of the couple who would have caused the disability premium to be applicable to the couple would suffer hardship; or

(d) either member of the couple suffers from a chronic medical condition which results in functional capacity being limited or restricted by physical [¹³ or mental] impairment and the Secretary of State is satisfied that—

   (i) the suffering has already lasted or is likely to last, for not less than 26 weeks; and

   (ii) unless a joint-claim jobseeker's allowance is paid, the probability is that the health of the person suffering would, within two weeks of the Secretary of State making his decision, decline further than that of a normally healthy adult and the member of the couple who suffers from that condition would suffer hardship; or

(e) either member of the couple, or where a member of that couple is married to more than one person under a law which permits polygamy, one member of that marriage, devotes a considerable portion of each week to caring for another person who—

    (i) is in receipt of an attendance allowance [^{11} , the care component of disability living allowance at one of the two higher rates prescribed under section 72(4) of the Benefits Act [^{12} , armed forces independence payment] or the daily living component of personal independence payment at the standard or enhanced rate in accordance with section 78 of the 2012 Act]; or

    (ii) has claimed either attendance allowance [^{11} , disability living allowance [^{12} , armed forces independence payment] or personal independence payment], but only for so long as the claim has not been determined, or for 26 weeks from the date of claiming, whichever is the earlier; or

    (iii) has claimed either attendance allowance or disability living allowance and has an award of either attendance allowance or the care component of disability living allowance at one of the two higher rates prescribed under section 72(4) of the Benefits Act for a period commencing after the date on which that claim was made, [^{11} ; or

    (iv) has claimed personal independence payment and has an award of the daily living component of personal independence payment at the standard or enhanced rate in accordance with section 78 of the 2012 Act for a period commencing after the date on which that claim was made] [^{12} ; or

    (v) has claimed and has an award of armed forces independence payment for a period commencing after the date on which that claim was made,]

and the Secretary of State is satisfied, after taking account of the factors set out in paragraph (6) in so far as they are appropriate to the particular circumstances of the case, that the person providing the care will not be able to continue doing so unless a joint-claim jobseeker's allowance is paid; or

(f) section 16 applies to either member of the couple by virtue of a direction issued by the Secretary of State, except where the member of the joint-claim couple to whom the direction applies does not satisfy the requirements of section 1(2)(a) to (c); or

(g) section 3A(1)(e)(ii) (member of joint-claim couple under the age of 18) applies to either member of the couple and the Secretary of State is satisfied that unless a joint-claim jobseeker's allowance is paid, the couple will suffer hardship; [^{13} or]

(h) one or both members of the couple is a person—

    (i) who, pursuant to the Children Act 1989[^{14} or the Social Services and Well-being (Wales) Act 2014], was being looked after by a local authority;

    (ii) with whom the local authority had a duty, pursuant to [^{14} either of those Acts], to take reasonable steps to keep in touch; or

    (iii) who, pursuant to [^{14} either of those Acts], qualified for advice or assistance from a local authority,

but in respect of whom head (i), (ii) or, as the case may be, (iii) above had not applied for a period of three years or less as at the date on which the requirements of regulation 146F are complied with; and

(iv) as at the date on which the requirements of regulation 146F are complied with, that member is, or both of those members are, under the age of 21 [¹³; or]

[¹³(i) either member of the couple is a person who is homeless within the meaning of Part 7 of the Housing Act 1996, Part 2 of the Housing (Wales) Act 2014 or Part 2 of the Housing (Scotland) Act 1987, as the case may be.]

(2) Except in a case to which paragraph (3), (4) [⁶ [¹⁰ . . .]] applies, a "couple in hardship" means for the purposes of regulation 146D, a joint-claim couple where the Secretary of State is satisfied, after taking account of the factors set out in paragraph (6) in so far as they are appropriate to the particular circumstances of the case, that the couple will suffer hardship unless a joint-claim jobseeker's allowance is paid.

(3) In paragraph (1) and (2), a "couple in hardship" does not include a couple one of whose members is entitled to income support [⁵ or an income-related employment and support allowance] or who falls within a category of persons prescribed for the purposes of section 124(1)(e) of the Benefits Act.

(4) Paragraph (1)(e) shall not apply in a case where the person being cared for resides in a [³ care home, an Abbeyfield Home or an independent hospital].

(5) [¹⁰ . . .]

[⁶ (5A) [¹⁰ . . .]]

[⁹ (5B) [¹⁰ . . .]]

(6) Factors which, for the purposes of paragraphs (1) and (2), the Secretary of State is to take into account in determining whether a joint-claim couple will suffer hardship are—

(a) the presence in the joint-claim couple of a person who satisfies the requirements for a disability premium specified in paragraphs 20H and 20I of Schedule 1;

(b) the resources which, without a joint-claim jobseeker's allowance, are likely to be available to the joint-claim couple, the amount by which these resources fall short of the amount applicable in their case in accordance with regulation 146G (applicable amount in hardship cases for joint-claim couples), the amount of any resources which may be available to the joint-claim couple for any person in the couple's household who is not a member of the family and the length of time for which those factors are likely to persist;

(c) whether there is a substantial risk that essential items, including food, clothing, heating and accommodation, will cease to be available to the joint-claim couple, or will be available at considerably reduced levels, the hardship that will result and the length of time those factors are likely to persist.]

AMENDMENTS

1. Jobseeker's Allowance (Joint Claims) Regulations 2000 (SI 2000/1978) reg.2(3) (March 19, 2001).

2. Social Security Amendment (New Deal) Regulations 2001 (SI 2001/1029) reg.9(2) (April 9, 2001).

3. Social Security (Care Homes and Independent Hospitals) Regulations 2005 (SI 2005/2687) reg.3 and Sch.2 para.8 (October 24, 2005).

4. Civil Partnership (Pensions, Social Security and Child Support) (Consequential, etc. Provisions) Order 2005 (SI 2005/2877) art.2(3) and Sch.3 para.26(9) (December 5, 2005).

5. Employment and Support Allowance (Consequential Provisions) (No.2) Regulations 2008 (SI 2008/1554) reg.3(1) and (18) (October 27, 2008).

6. Social Security (Flexible New Deal) Regulations 2009 (SI 2009/480) reg.2(10) (April 6, 2009).

7. Social Security (Flexible New Deal) Regulations 2009 (SI 2009/480) reg.2(10) (b) (October 5, 2009).

8. Jobseeker's Allowance (Sanctions for Failure to Attend) Regulations 2010 (SI 2010/509) reg.2(16) (April 6, 2010).

9. Jobseeker's Allowance (Employment, Skills and Enterprise Scheme) Regulations 2011 (SI 2011/917) reg.10 (May 20, 2011).

10. Jobseeker's Allowance (Sanctions) (Amendment) Regulations 2012 (SI 2012/2568) reg.4 (October 22, 2012).

11. Personal Independence Payment (Supplementary Provisions and Consequential Amendments) Regulations 2013 (SI 2013/388) reg.8 and Sch. para.16(1) and (5) (April 8, 2013).

12. Armed Forces and Reserve Forces Compensation Scheme (Consequential Provisions: Subordinate Legislation) Order 2013 (SI 2013/591) art.7 and Sch. para.10(1) and (5) (April 8, 2013).

13. Jobseeker's Allowance (Hardship) (Amendment) Regulations 2017 (SI 2018/760) reg.2(1) and (4) (October 23, 2017).

14. Social Services and Well-being (Wales) Act 2014 and the Regulation and Inspection of Social Care (Wales) Act 2016 (Consequential Amendments) Order 2017 (SI 2017/901) art.6(1) and (6) (November 3, 2017).

GENERAL NOTE

3.432   This regulation makes provision corresponding to reg.140 for joint-claim couples.

[¹Period when a joint-claim couple is not in hardship

3.433   **146B.**—[⁴ . . .]]

AMENDMENTS

1. Jobseeker's Allowance (Joint Claims) Regulations 2000 (SI 2000/1978) reg.2(3) (March 19, 2001).

2. Social Security Amendment (New Deal) Regulations 2001 (SI 2001/1029) reg.10(1) (April 9, 2001).

3. Social Security Amendment (New Deal) Regulations 2001 (SI 2001/1029) reg.10(2) (April 9, 2001).

4. Jobseeker's Allowance (Sanctions) (Amendment) Regulations 2012 (SI 2012/2568) reg.4 (October 22, 2012).

[¹Circumstances in which a joint-claim jobseeker's allowance is payable where a joint-claim couple is a couple in hardship

3.434   **146C.**—(1) This regulation applies where a joint-claim couple is a couple in hardship within the meaning of regulation 146A(1) and is subject to the provisions of regulations 146E and 146F.

(2) Subject to paragraph (3), a couple in hardship referred to in paragraph (1), other than a couple in hardship where either or both members are persons to whom regulation 46(1) (waiting days) applies,

shall be treated as entitled to a joint-claim jobseeker's allowance for the period—

(a) beginning with the [⁴ eighth] day of the jobseeking period or, if later, from the day the couple first becomes a couple in hardship; and

(b) ending on the day before the claim is determined,

where the sole reason for the claim being determined on that day and not earlier is that a question arises as to whether either or both members satisfy the conditions of entitlement in section 1(2)(a) to (c) provided the joint-claim couple satisfy the conditions set out in section 1(2B)(c).

(3) A couple in hardship to whom paragraph (2) applies may be treated as entitled to a joint-claim jobseeker's allowance for a period after the date referred to in that paragraph which is applicable in their case but before the date of the statement referred to in regulation 146E(1) is furnished where the Secretary of State is satisfied that that couple suffered hardship because of a lack of resources during that period.

(4) A couple in hardship, except where either or both members have been treated as not available for employment in accordance with regulations under section 6(4) shall, subject to the conditions specified in regulation 146E (conditions for hardship payments), be entitled to a joint-claim jobseeker's allowance without both members satisfying the requirements of section 1(2)(a) to (c) provided the joint-claim couple satisfy the other conditions of entitlement to that benefit.

(5) A joint-claim jobseeker's allowance shall be payable to a joint-claim couple who are a couple in hardship even though payment to the couple of a joint-claim jobseeker's allowance has been suspended in accordance with regulations made under section 21 of the Social Security Act 1998 on the ground that a doubt has arisen as to whether either joint-claimant satisfies the requirements of section 1(2)(a) to (c), but the allowance shall be payable only if and for so long as—

(a) the joint-claim couple satisfy the other conditions of entitlement to a joint-claim jobseeker's allowance; or

(b) one member satisfies those conditions and the other member comes within any paragraph in Schedule A1 (categories of members not required to satisfy conditions in section 1(2B)(b)).

(6) A joint-claim jobseeker's allowance shall be payable to a couple in hardship even though [²³ the award of joint-claim jobseeker's allowance has been reduced in accordance with section 19 or 19A or regulation 69B] but the allowance shall be payable only if and for so long as—

(a) the joint-claim couple satisfy the other conditions of entitlement to a joint-claim jobseeker's allowance; or

(b) one member satisfies those conditions and the other member comes within any paragraph in Schedule A1 (categories of members not required to satisfy conditions in section 1(2B)(b)).]

AMENDMENTS

1. Jobseeker's Allowance (Joint Claims) Regulations 2000 (SI 2000/1978) reg.2(3) (March 19, 2001).

2. Jobseeker's Allowance (Sanctions for Failure to Attend) Regulations 2010 (SI 2010/509) reg.2(17) (April 6, 2010).

3. Jobseeker's Allowance (Sanctions) (Amendment) Regulations 2012 (SI 2012/2568) reg.4 (October 22, 2012).

4. Social Security (Jobseeker's Allowance and Employment and Support Allowance) (Waiting Days) Amendment Regulations 2014 (SI 2014/2309) reg.3(1) and (3) (October 27, 2014).

GENERAL NOTE

3.435   This regulation makes provision corresponding to reg.141 for joint-claim couples.

The increase from three to seven in the number of days at the beginning of a jobseeking period during which no hardship payment can be made (see para.(2)(a)) only applies where the claimant's jobseeking period began on or after October 27, 2014 (see SI 2014/2309 regs 3 and 4(1)).

[¹Further circumstances in which a joint-claim jobseeker's allowance is payable to a couple in hardship

3.436   **146D.**—(1) This regulation applies to a couple in hardship falling within paragraph (2) but not paragraph (1) of regulation 146A and is subject to the provisions of regulations 146E and 146F.

(2) A couple in hardship shall be treated as entitled to a joint-claim jobseeker's allowance for a period commencing on whichever is the later of—

(a) the 15th day following the date of claim disregarding any waiting days; or

(b) the day on which regulation 146E is complied with,

and ending on the day before the claim is determined where the sole reason for the claim being determined on that day and not earlier is that a question arises as to whether either or both members of that couple satisfy the conditions of entitlement in section 1(2)(a) to (c) provided the joint-claim couple satisfy the conditions set out in section 1(2B)(c).

(3) A joint-claim jobseeker's allowance shall be payable, subject to paragraph (4), to a couple in hardship even though payment to them of a joint-claim jobseeker's allowance has been suspended in accordance with regulations made under section 21 of the Social Security Act 1998 (suspension of benefit) on the ground that a doubt has arisen as to whether either or both members of that couple satisfy the requirements of section 1(2)(a) to (c) of the Act but the allowance shall be payable only if and for so long as—

(a) the joint-claim couple satisfy the other conditions of entitlement to a joint-claim jobseeker's allowance; or

(b) one member satisfies those conditions and the other member comes within any paragraph in Schedule A1 (categories of members not required to satisfy conditions in section 1(2B)(b)).

(4) A joint-claim jobseeker's allowance shall not be payable in respect of the first 14 days of the period of suspension.

(5) A joint-claim jobseeker's allowance shall be payable to a couple in hardship even though [² the award of joint-claim jobseeker's allowance has been reduced in accordance with section 19 or 19A or regulation 69B] but the allowance—

(a) shall not be payable under this paragraph in respect of the first 14 days of the period to which [² the reduction] applies; and

(b) shall be payable thereafter only where the conditions of entitlement to a joint-claim jobseeker's allowance are satisfied or where one member satisfies those conditions and the other member comes within any paragraph in Schedule A1 (categories of members not required to satisfy conditions in section 1(2B) (b)).]

AMENDMENTS

1. Jobseeker's Allowance (Joint Claims) Regulations 2000 (SI 2000/1978) reg.2(3) (March 19, 2001).
2. Jobseeker's Allowance (Sanctions) (Amendment) Regulations 2012 (SI 2012/2568) reg.4 (October 22, 2012).

GENERAL NOTE

This regulation makes provision corresponding to reg.142 for joint-claim couples.   **3.437**

[¹Conditions for hardship payments to a joint-claim couple

146E.—(1) A joint-claim jobseeker's allowance shall not be payable in   **3.438**
accordance with regulation 146C or, as the case may be, 146D, except where either member of the joint-claim couple has—
(a) furnished on a form approved for the purpose by the Secretary of State or in such other form as he may in any particular case approve, a statement of the circumstances he relies upon to establish entitlement under regulation 146C or, as the case may be, regulation 146D; and
(b) signed the statement.
(2) The completed and signed form shall be delivered by either member to such office as the Secretary of State may specify.]

AMENDMENT

1. Jobseeker's Allowance (Joint Claims) Regulations 2000 (SI 2000/1978) reg.2(3) (March 19, 2001).

GENERAL NOTE

This regulation makes provision corresponding to reg.143 for joint-claim   **3.439**
couples.

[¹Provision of information

146F.—For the purposes of section 20B(5) and paragraph 10(3) of   **3.440**
Schedule 1 to the Act, a member of a joint-claim couple shall provide to the Secretary of State information as to the circumstances of the alleged hardship of that couple.]

AMENDMENT

1. Jobseeker's Allowance (Joint Claims) Regulations 2000 (SI 2000/1978) reg.2(3) (March 19, 2001).

GENERAL NOTE

3.441   This regulation makes provision corresponding to reg.144 for joint-claim couples.

[¹Applicable amount in hardship cases for joint-claim couples

3.442   **146G.**—[² (1) The weekly applicable amount of the joint-claim couple to whom a joint-claim jobseeker's allowance is payable in accordance with this Part of these Regulations shall be reduced by a sum equivalent to—
>   (a) 20% of the amount specified in paragraph 1(1)(e) of Schedule 1 in a case where a member of a joint-claim couple is—
>>   (i) either pregnant or seriously ill, or
>>   (ii) a member of a polygamous marriage and one of the members of that marriage is pregnant or seriously ill, or
>   (b) 40% of the amount specified in paragraph 1(1)(e) of Schedule 1 in all other cases.]

(2) A reduction under paragraph (1) shall, if it is not a multiple of 5p, be rounded to the nearest such multiple or, if it is a multiple of 2.5p but not of 5p, to the next lower multiple of 5p.]

AMENDMENTS

1. Jobseeker's Allowance (Joint Claims) Regulations 2000 (SI 2000/1978) reg.2(3) (March 19, 2001).
2. Social Security (Miscellaneous Amendments) (No.2) Regulations 2010 (SI 2010/641) reg.4(1) and (11) (April 13, 2010).

GENERAL NOTE

3.443   This regulation makes provision corresponding to reg.145 for joint-claim couples.

[¹Payments made on account of suspended benefit

3.444   **146H.**—(1) This regulation applies to a joint-claim couple to whom—
>   (a) payments of a joint-claim jobseeker's allowance have been suspended in accordance with regulations made under section 21 of the Social Security Act 1998;
>   (b) a joint-claim jobseeker's allowance is paid under regulation 146C or 146D.

(2) In the case of a joint-claim couple to whom—
>   (a) this regulation applies; and
>   (b) payments in respect of the benefit suspended fall to be made,

any benefit paid or payable by virtue of regulation 146C(5) or 146D(3) shall be treated as having been paid on account of the suspended benefit and only the balance of the suspended benefit, if any, shall be payable.]

AMENDMENT

1. Jobseeker's Allowance (Joint Claims) Regulations 2000 (SI 2000/1978) reg.2(3) (March 19, 2001).

GENERAL NOTE

3.445   This regulation makes provision corresponding to reg.146 for joint-claim couples.

PART X

URGENT CASES

GENERAL NOTE

Part X (regs 147–149), which provided for "urgent cases" payments of JSA was **3.446**
revoked by the Social Security (Miscellaneous Amendments) (No.5) Regulations
2009 (SI 2009/3228) reg.2 with effect from January 25, 2010.
For the abolition of urgent cases payments generally, see the commentary to Pt
VI of the Income Support Regulations.

PART XI

PART-WEEKS

Amount of a jobseeker's allowance payable

150.—(1) Subject to the following provisions of this Part, the amount **3.447**
payable by way of an income-based jobseeker's allowance in respect of part-
week shall be calculated by applying the formula—
  (a) where the claimant has no income—

$$\frac{(N \times A)}{7}; \text{ or}$$

  (b) where the claimant has an income—

$$\frac{(N \times (A - I))}{(7)} - B,$$

where—
  A is the claimant's weekly applicable amount in the relevant week;
  B is the amount of any jobseeker's allowance, income support,
     maternity allowance, incapacity benefit [³ , severe disablement
     allowance or employment and support allowance] payable to
     any member of the claimant's family other than the claimant in
     respect of any day in the part-week;
  I is the claimant's weekly income in the relevant week less B;
  N is the number of days in the part-week.
  [¹ (1A) In relation to a joint-claim couple jointly claiming a joint-claim
jobseeker's allowance, paragraph (1) shall have effect as if the references to
the claimant were references to the joint-claim couple.
  (1B) Where a joint-claim couple become, or cease to be, a joint-claim
couple on any day other than on the first day of a benefit week, the amount
payable by way of a joint-claim jobseeker's allowance in respect of that
benefit week shall be calculated by applying the formula in paragraph (1).]

(2) Subject to the following provisions of this Part, the amount payable by way of a contribution-based jobseeker's allowance in respect of a part-week shall be calculated by applying the formula—

$$\frac{(N \times X) - Y}{(7)}$$

where—

X is the personal rate determined in accordance with section 4(1);

Y is the amount of any widow's benefit, [2 carer's allowance], training allowance and any increase in disablement pension payable in accordance with Part I of Schedule 7 to the Benefits Act (Unemployment Supplement) payable in respect of any day in the part-week;

N is the number of days in the part-week

(3) In this Part—

"part-week" means an entitlement to a jobseeker's allowance in respect of any period of less than a week;

"relevant week" means the period of 7 days determined in accordance with regulation 152.

AMENDMENTS

1. Jobseeker's Allowance (Joint Claims) Regulations 2000 (SI 2000/1978) reg.2(5) and Sch.2 para.48 (March 19, 2001).

2. Social Security (Miscellaneous Amendments) Regulations 2003 (SI 2003/511) reg.3(4) and (5) (April 1, 2003).

3. Employment and Support Allowance (Consequential Provisions) (No.2) Regulations 2008 (SI 2008/1554) reg.3(1) and (20) (October 27, 2008).

DEFINITION

"claimant"—see Jobseekers Act s.35(1).

Amount of a jobseeker's allowance payable where a person is in a residential care or nursing home

3.448   **151.**—[¹ . . .]

AMENDMENT

1. Social Security Amendment (Residential Care and Nursing Homes) Regulations 2001 (SI 2001/3767) reg.2 and Sch. Pt II para.17 (April 8, 2002).

Relevant week

3.449   **152.**—(1) Where the part-week—

(a) is the whole period for which a jobseeker's allowance is payable or occurs at the beginning of an award, the relevant week is the period of 7 days ending on the last day of that part-week; or

(b) occurs at the end of an award, the relevant week is the period of 7 days beginning on the first day of the part-week; or

(c) occurs because a jobseeker's allowance [7 is reduced for any period in accordance with regulations 69, 69A or 69B], the relevant week is the 7 days ending immediately before the start of the next benefit week to commence for that claimant [² or the joint-claim couple].

(2) [³ Except in a case to which paragraph (3) applies,] where a person has an award of a jobseeker's allowance and his benefit week changes, for the purpose of calculating the amounts of a jobseeker's allowance payable for the art-week beginning on the day after his last complete benefit week before the change and ending immediately before the change, the relevant week is the period of 7 days beginning on the day after the last complete benefit week.

[⁴ (3) Where a joint-claim couple have an award of a joint-claim job-seeker's allowance and their benefit week changes, for the purpose of calculating the amounts of a joint-claim jobseeker's allowance payable for the part-week beginning on the day after their last complete benefit week before the change and ending immediately before the change, the relevant week is the period of 7 days beginning on the day after the last complete benefit week.]

AMENDMENTS

1. Jobseeker's Allowance (Joint Claims) Regulations 2000 (SI 2000/1978) reg.2(5) and Sch.2 para.50(a)(i) (March 19, 2001).
2. Jobseeker's Allowance (Joint Claims) Regulations 2000 (SI 2000/1978) reg.2(5) and Sch.2 para.50(a)(ii) (March 19, 2001).
3. Jobseeker's Allowance (Joint Claims) Regulations 2000 (SI 2000/1978) reg.2(5) and Sch.2 para.50(b) (March 19, 2001).
4. Jobseeker's Allowance (Joint Claims) Regulations 2000 (SI 2000/1978) reg.2(5) and Sch.2 para.50(c) (March 19, 2001).
5. Jobseeker's Allowance (Sanctions for Failure to Attend) Regulations 2010 (SI 2010/509) reg.2(18) (April 6, 2010).
6. Jobseeker's Allowance (Mandatory Work Activity Scheme) Regulations 2011 (SI 2011/688) reg.16(g) (April 25, 2011).
7. Jobseeker's Allowance (Sanctions) (Amendment) Regulations 2012 (SI 2012/2568) reg.5(20) (October 22, 2012).

DEFINITION

"benefit week"—see reg.1(3).

Modification in the calculation of income

153.—For the purposes of regulation 150 (amount of jobseeker's allow-   3.450
ance payable for part-weeks) a claimant's income and, in determining the amount payable by way of an income-based jobseeker's allowance, the income of any person which the claimant is treated as possessing under section 12(4) or [¹ regulation 88(4) or 88ZA(3)], shall be calculated in accordance with Parts VIII, and, where applicable, IX and X subject to the following changes—

(a) any income which is due to be paid in the relevant week shall be treated as paid on the first day of that week;

(b) in determining the amount payable by way of an income-based jobseeker's allowance, any jobseeker's allowance, income support, maternity allowance, incapacity benefit or severe disablement allowance under the Benefits Act [⁴ , universal credit] [³ or employment and support allowance] payable in the relevant week but not in respect of any day in the part-week shall be disregarded;

(c) in determining the amount payable by way of a contribution-based jobseeker's allowance, any widow's benefit, [² carer's allowance], training allowance or any increase in disablement pension payable in accordance with Part I of Schedule 7 to the Benefits Act (Unemployment Supplement) which is payable in the relevant week but not in respect of any day in the part-week shall be disregarded;

(d) where the part-week occurs at the end of the claim, any income or any change in the amount of income of the same kind which is first payable within the relevant week but not on any day in the part-week shall be disregarded;

(e) where the part-week occurs immediately after a period in which a person was treated as engaged in remunerative work under regulation 52 (persons treated as engaged in remunerative work) any earnings which are taken into account for the purposes of determining that period shall be disregarded;

(f) where only part of the weekly amount of income is taken into account in the relevant week, the balance shall be disregarded.

AMENDMENTS

1. Jobseeker's Allowance (Joint Claims) Regulations 2000 (SI 2000/1978) reg.2(5) and Sch.2 para.51 (March 19, 2001).
2. Social Security (Miscellaneous Amendments) Regulations 2003 (SI 2003/511) reg.3(4) and (5) (April 1, 2003).
3. Employment and Support Allowance (Consequential Provisions) (No.2) Regulations 2008 (SI 2008/1554) reg.3(1) and (21) (October 27, 2008).
4. Universal Credit (Consequential, Supplementary, Incidental and Miscellaneous Provisions) Regulations 2013 (SI 2013/630) reg.30(1) and (6) (April 29, 2013).

DEFINITIONS

"the Benefits Act"—see Jobseekers Act s.35(1).
"claimant"—*ibid.*

Reduction in certain cases

3.451   **154.**—The reduction to be made in accordance with Part IX (Hardship) in respect of an income based jobseeker's allowance shall be an amount equal to one seventh of the reduction which would be made under that Part for a week multiplied by the number of days in the part-week.

Modification of section 15(2) of the Act

3.452   **155.**—[¹ (1)] In its application to an income-based jobseeker's allowance [² but not a joint-claim jobseeker's allowance] payable for a part-week, section 15(2)(d) shall have effect subject to the following modification—

"(d) any payment by way of an income-based jobseeker's allowance for that period or any part of it which apart from this paragraph would be made to the claimant—
(i) shall not be made, if the amount of an income-based jobseeker's allowance which would be payable for a period of less than a week is equal to or less than the proportion of the prescribed sum appropriate to the number of days in the part-week;
(ii) shall be at a rate equal to the difference between the amount which would be payable for a period of less than a week and the prescribed sum where that amount would be more than the prescribed sum."

[³ (2) In its application to a joint-claim jobseeker's allowance payable for a part-week, section 15(2)(d) shall have effect subject to the following modification—

"(d) any payment by way of a joint-claim jobseeker's allowance for that period or any part of it which apart from this paragraph would be made to the nominated member for the purposes of section 3B—
(i) shall not be made, if the amount of joint-claim jobseeker's allowance which would be payable for less than a week is equal to or less than the proportion of the prescribed sum appropriate to the number of days in the part-week;
(ii) shall be at a rate equal to the difference between the amount which would be payable for a period of less than a week and the prescribed sum where that amount would be more than the prescribed sum."]

AMENDMENTS

1. Jobseeker's Allowance (Joint Claims) Regulations 2000 (SI 2000/1978) reg.2(5) and Sch.2 para.52 (March 19, 2001).
2. Jobseeker's Allowance (Joint Claims) Regulations 2000 (SI 2000/1978) reg.2(5) and Sch.2 para.52(a) (March 19, 2001).
3. Jobseeker's Allowance (Joint Claims) Regulations 2000 (SI 2000/1978) reg.2(5) and Sch.2 para.52(b) (March 19, 2001).

PART XII

SPECIAL CATEGORIES

GENERAL NOTE

The text of the regulations in Pt XII, which mainly amend other regulations, has been omitted. The major special category for which the ordinary rules are altered is of share fishermen. These provisions have not been reproduced in previous editions. The substance is the same as Pt 9 of the JSA Regulations 2013 in Pt VI below, with some differences of drafting and arrangement and to take account of the specific nature of old style and new style JSA. Thus, regs 156–158 of the JSA Regulations 1996 equate to regs 67–69 of the JSA Regulations 2013 and regs 160–164 equate to regs 70–74. Regulation 159 of the JSA Regulations 1996, deeming work as a share fisherman to be employed earner's employment for the purposes of ss.19 and 20 of the old style Jobseekers Act 1995 has no equivalent in the JSA Regulations 2013. Anyone dealing with an actual old style JSA case involving a share fisherman, rather than merely seeking general information, should take care to consult the text of the JSA Regulations 1996.

Regulation 163 of the JSA Regulations 1996 has the same effect as reg.75 of the JSA Regulations 2013, but the modification it makes is not incorporated into the text of s.2 of the old style Jobseekers Act 1995 in Pt I as it is into the new style Jobseekers Act 1995 in Pt VI.

PART XIII

MISCELLANEOUS

Recovery of Maintenance

Recovery orders

169.—(1) Where an award of income-based jobseeker's allowance has been made to a person ("the claimant"), the Secretary of State may apply

3.453

3.454

to the court for a recovery order against the claimant's spouse [¹ or civil partner] ("the liable person").

(2) On making a recovery order the court may order the liable person to pay such amount at such intervals as it considers appropriate, having regard to all the circumstances of the liable person and in particular his income.

(3) Except in Scotland, a recovery order shall be treated for all purposes as if it were a maintenance order [² made by the family court].

(4) Where a recovery order requires the liable person to make payments to the Secretary of State, the Secretary of State may, by giving notice in writing to the court which made the order, the liable person, and the claimant, transfer to the claimant the right to receive payments under the order and to exercise the relevant rights in relation to the order.

(5) In this regulation—

the expressions "the court" and "recovery order" have the same meanings as in section 23 of the Act; and

"the relevant rights" means, in relation to a recovery order, the right to bring any proceedings, take any steps or do any other thing under or in relation to the order.

AMENDMENTS

1. Civil Partnership (Pensions, Social Security and Child Support) (Consequential, etc. Provisions) Order 2005 (SI 2005/2877) art.2(3) and Sch.3 para.26(10) (December 5, 2005).

2. Crime and Courts Act 2013 (Family Court: Consequential Provision) (No.2) Order 2014 (SI 2014/879) art.74 (April 22, 2014).

DEFINITION

"the Act"—see reg.1(3).
"claimant"—see Jobseekers Act 1995 s.35(1).
"income-based jobseeker's allowance"—see Jobseekers Act 1995 ss.35(1) and 1(4).

GENERAL NOTE

3.455   See the note to s.23 of the old style Jobseekers Act 1995.

Training Allowance

Persons in receipt of a training allowance

3.456   **170.**—[³(1) A person who is not receiving training falling within paragraph (2) [⁵and is not a qualifying young person or child within the meaning of section 142 of the Benefits Act (child and qualifying young person)] may be entitled to an income-based jobseeker's allowance without—

(a) being available for employment;

(b) having entered into a jobseeker's agreement; or

(c) actively seeking employment,

if he is in receipt of a training allowance [⁸ . . .].]

(2) Training falls within this paragraph if it is training for which persons aged under 18 are eligible and for which persons aged 18 to 24 may be

eligible [² secured by the [⁹ [¹⁰ Secretary of State] [¹¹ . . .]] or by the [⁴ [⁶ Welsh Ministers]] and, in Scotland, provided] directly or indirectly by a Local Enterprise Company pursuant to its arrangement with, as the case may be, [⁷ Skills Development Scotland,] Scottish Enterprise or Highlands and Islands Enterprise (whether that arrangement is known as an Operating Contract or by any other name).

AMENDMENTS

1. Jobseeker's Allowance (Amendment) (No.2) Regulations 1998 (SI 1998/1698) reg.5 (August 4, 1998).
2. Social Security (Miscellaneous Amendments) (No.2) Regulations 2001 (SI 2001/652) reg.5(c) (March 26, 2001).
3. Social Security (Breach of Community Order) (Consequential Amendments) Regulations 2001 (SI 2001/1711) reg.2(4)(b) (October 15, 2001).
4. National Council for Education and Training for Wales (Transfer of Functions to the National Assembly for Wales and Abolition) Order 2005 (SI 2005/3238 (W.243)) art.9(2) and Sch.2 para.8(5) (April 1, 2006).
5. Social Security (Young Persons) Amendment Regulations 2006 (SI 2006/718) reg.3(8) (April 10, 2006).
6. Social Security (Miscellaneous Amendments) (No.7) Regulations 2008 (SI 2008/3157) reg.3(8) (January 5, 2009).
7. Social Security (Miscellaneous Amendments) Regulations 2009 (SI 2009/583) reg.4(3) (April 6, 2009).
8. Welfare Reform Act 2009 (Section 26) (Consequential Amendments) Regulations 2010 (SI 2010/424) reg.3(3) (March 22, 2010).
9. Apprenticeships, Skills, Children and Learning Act 2009 (Consequential Amendments to Subordinate Legislation) (England) Order 2010 (SI 2010/1941) art.5(5) (September 1, 2010).
10. Young People's Learning Agency Abolition (Consequential Amendments to Subordinate Legislation) (England) Order 2012 (SI 2012/956) art.5(7) (May 1, 2012).
11. Deregulation Act 2015 (Consequential Amendments) Order 2015 (SI 2015/971) art.2 and Sch.3 para. 4(6) (May 26, 2015).

DEFINITIONS

"the Benefits Act"—see Jobseekers Act 1995 s.35(1).
"employment"—see reg.4.
"income-based jobseeker's allowance"—see Jobseekers Act 1995 ss.35(1) and 1(4).
"training allowance"—see reg.1(3).

GENERAL NOTE

See the note to para.28 of Sch.1B to the Income Support Regulations. 3.457

Trade Disputes

Trade disputes: exemptions from section 15 of the Act

171.—Section 15(2) (trade disputes: effect on other claimants) shall not 3.458
apply to a claimant during any period where—
  (a) a member of the claimant's family is, or would be, prevented by section 14 from being entitled to a jobseeker's allowance; and
  (b) that member is—

    (i) a child or young person; [² . . .]
    (ii) [¹incapable of work] or within the maternity period, and for this purpose "the maternity period" means the period commencing at the beginning of the 6th week before the expected week of confinement and ending at the end of the 7th week after the week in which confinement takes place [² or
    (iii) has limited capability for work.]

AMENDMENTS

1. Jobseeker's Allowance (Amendment) Regulations 1996 (SI 1996/1516) reg.20 and Sch. (October 7, 1996).
2. Employment and Support Allowance (Consequential Provisions) (No.2) Regulations 2008 (SI 2008/1554) reg.3(22) (October 27, 2008).

DEFINITIONS

"child"—see Jobseekers Act s.35(1).
"claimant"—*ibid.*
"family"—*ibid.*
"trade dispute"—*ibid.*
"young person"—see reg.76.

GENERAL NOTE

3.459   See the note to s.15 of the old style Jobseekers Act.

Trade disputes: prescribed sum

3.460   **172.**—The prescribed sum for the purposes of section 15(2)(d) is [¹£41.00].

AMENDMENT

1. Social Security Benefits Up-rating Order 2020 (SI 2020/234) art.29 (April 6, 2020).

GENERAL NOTE

3.461   The April 2020 up-rating is the first since April 2015.

[¹ SCHEDULE A1

CATEGORIES OF MEMBERS OF A JOINT-CLAIM COUPLE WHO ARE NOT REQUIRED TO SATISFY THE CONDITIONS IN SECTION 1(2B)(b)

Interpretation
3.462   **1.**—In this Schedule, "member" means a member of a joint-claim couple.

Member studying full-time
3.463   [² **2.**—(1) A member—
    (a) who, at the date of claim, is [⁶ a qualifying young person within the meaning of] section 142 of the Benefits Act;
    (b) who, at the date of claim, is a full-time student; or

   (c) to whom (a) or (b) does not apply but to whom sub-paragraph (1A) or (2) does apply.

(1A) This sub-paragraph applies to a member who—
   (a) as at the date of claim—
      (i) had applied to an educational establishment to commence a full-time course of study commencing from the beginning of the next academic term or, as the case may be, the next academic year after the date of claim and that application has not been rejected; or
     (ii) had been allocated a place on a full-time course of study commencing from the beginning of the next academic term or, as the case may be, the next academic year; and
   (b) is either—
      (i) [[6] a qualifying young person within the meaning of] section 142 of the Benefits Act; or
     (ii) a full-time student.

(2) This sub-paragraph applies to a member who has applied to an educational establishment to commence a full-time course of study (other than a course of study beyond a first degree course or a comparable course)—
   (a) within one month of—
      (i) the last day of a previous course of study; or
     (ii) the day on which the member received examination results relating to a previous course of study; and
   (b) who is either—
      (i) [[6] a qualifying young person within the meaning of] section 142 of the Benefits Act; or
     (ii) a full-time student.]

(3) A member to whom any provision of regulation 13(2)(b) to (e) of the Income Support Regulations (persons receiving relevant education who are severely handicapped, orphans and persons estranged from their parents or guardian) applies.

Member caring for another person
3.—A member (the carer)—   3.464
   (a) who is regularly and substantially engaged in caring for another person if—
      (i) the person being cared for is in receipt of attendance allowance [[19], the care component of disability living allowance at the highest or middle rate prescribed in accordance with section 72(3) of the Benefits Act [[20] , armed forces independence payment] or the daily living component of personal independence payment at the standard or enhanced rate in accordance with section 78(3) of the 2012 Act]; or
     (ii) the person being cared for has claimed attendance allowance but only for the period up to the date of determination of that claim, or the period of 26 weeks from the date of that claim, whichever date is the earlier; or
    (iii) the person being cared for has claimed attendance allowance in accordance with section 65(6)(a) of the Benefits Act (claims in advance of entitlement), an award has been made in respect of that claim under section 65(6)(b) of that Act and, where the period for which the award is payable has begun, that person is in receipt of the allowance;
     (iv) the person being cared for has claimed entitlement to a disability living allowance [[20] , armed forces independence payment] [[19] or personal independence payment] but only for the period up to the date of determination of that claim, or the period of 26 weeks from the date of that claim, whichever date is the earlier; or
     (v) the person being cared for has claimed entitlement to the care component of a disability living allowance in accordance with regulation 13A of the Claims and Payments Regulations (advance claims and awards), an award at the highest or middle rate has been made in respect of that claim and, where the period for which the award is payable has begun, that person is in receipt of the allowance; [[19] [[20] . . .]
     (vi) the person being cared for has claimed entitlement to the daily living component of personal independence payment in accordance with regulation 33 of the Universal Credit etc. Claims and Payments Regulations (advance claim for and award of personal independence payment), an award of the standard or enhanced rate of the daily living component has been made in respect of that

claim and, where the period for which the award is payable has begun, that person is in receipt of that payment;] [20] or

(vii) the person being cared for has claimed entitlement to armed forces independence payment and an award has been made in respect of that claim and, where the period for which the award is payable has begun, that person is in receipt of that payment;]

(b) who is engaged in caring for another person and who is both entitled to, and in receipt of, [4] a carer's allowance].

4. A member to whom paragraph 3 applied, but only for a period of 8 weeks from the date on which that paragraph ceased to apply to him.

5. A member who, had he previously made a claim for, and had been entitled to, a jobseeker's allowance, would have fulfilled the conditions of paragraph 3, but only for a period of 8 weeks from the date on which he ceased to fulfil those conditions.

[15] Member treated as capable of work, or member entitled to statutory sick pay]

3.465   6.—A member who—
    (a) [14] . . .]
    (b) [14] . . .]
    (c) is treated as capable of work by virtue of regulations made under section 171E(1) of [16] the Benefits Act] (disqualification etc.); or
    (d) is entitled to statutory sick pay.

[8] Member has limited capability for work

3.466   6A.—A person who—
    (a) has limited capability for work under section 8 of the Welfare Reform Act; or
    (b) is treated as having limited capability for work under regulations made under paragraph 1 of Schedule 2 to that Act; or
    (c) is treated as not having limited capability for work under regulations made under section 18(1) of that Act (disqualification).]

[17] 6B.—(1) Subject to sub-paragraph (2), a person who provides-
    (a) a statement which complies with the rules in Part 1 of Schedule 1 to the Social Security (Medical Evidence) Regulations 1976,
    (b) a self-certificate for a period of limited capability for work which lasts less than 8 days or in respect of any of the first 7 days of limited capability for work, or
    (c) where it would be unreasonable to require a person to provide a statement in accordance with paragraph (a), such other evidence as the Secretary of State considers to be sufficient to show that the person has limited capability for work.

(2) Sub-paragraph (1) applies to a person for the period covered by evidence falling within that sub-paragraph.

(3) For the purposes of this paragraph-
    (a) "limited capability for work" has the meaning given by section 1(4) of the Welfare Reform Act 2007; and
    (b) "self-certificate" means a declaration made by the person in writing on a form approved for the purpose by the Secretary of State that the person has been unfit for work on a date or for a period specified in the declaration and may include a statement that the person expects to continue to be unfit for work on days subsequent to the date on which it is made.]

Members in employment living in residential care homes, nursing homes or residential accommodation

3.467   7.—[11] . . .]

Disabled workers

3.468   8.—[11] . . .]

Disabled students

3.469   9.—[14] . . .]

Deaf students

3.470   10.—[14] . . .]

Blind members
    11.—[¹⁴ . . .]   3.471

Pregnancy
    12.—A member who is a woman and who is incapable of work [⁸ or who has limited capabil-   3.472
ity for work] by reason of pregnancy.

[¹²Members who have attained the qualifying age for state pension credit
    13.—A member who has attained the qualifying age for state pension credit.]   3.473

Refugees
    14.—A member who is a refugee within the definition in Article 1 of the Convention relating   3.474
to the Status of Refugees done at Geneva on 28th July 1951 as extended by Article 1(2) of the
Protocol relating to the Status of Refugees done at New York on 31st January 1967 and who—
    (a) is attending for more than 15 hours a week a course for the purpose of learning
        English so that he may obtain employment; and
    (b) on the date on which that course commenced, had been in Great Britain for not more
        than 12 months,
but only for a period not exceeding nine months.

[⁷ Members required to attend a court or tribunal
    15.—(1) A member who is required to attend a court or tribunal as a justice of the peace, a   3.475
party to any proceedings, a witness or a juror.
    (2) In this paragraph, "tribunal" means any tribunal listed in Schedule 1 to the Tribunals
and Inquiries Act 1992.]

Young persons in training
    16.—A member who [⁶ is not a qualifying young person or child within the meaning of   3.476
section 142 of the Benefits Act (child and qualifying young person) and who] is engaged in
training and for this purpose "training" means training for which persons aged under 18 are
eligible and for which persons aged 18 to 24 may be eligible [³ secured by the [¹³ [¹⁸Secretary
of State [²¹ . . .]] or by the [⁵[⁹ Welsh Ministers]]] and, in Scotland, directly or indirectly by
a Local Enterprise Company pursuant to its arrangements with, as the case may be, [¹⁰ Skills
Development Scotland,] Scottish Enterprise or Highlands and Islands Enterprise (whether
that arrangement is known as an Operating Contract or by any other name).

Trade disputes
    17.—A member who is or would be prevented from being entitled to a jobseeker's allowance   3.477
by virtue of section 14 (trade disputes) but only where that section does not prevent the other
member from being so entitled.]

AMENDMENTS

    1. Jobseeker's Allowance (Joint Claims) Regulations 2000 (SI 2000/1978)
reg.2(4) and Sch.1 (March 19, 2001).
    2. Social Security Amendment (Joint Claims) Regulations 2001 (SI 2001/518)
reg.2(6) (March 19, 2001).
    3. Social Security (Miscellaneous Amendments) (No.2) Regulations 2001 (SI
2001/652) reg.4 (March 26, 2001).
    4. Social Security (Miscellaneous Amendments) Regulations 2003 (SI 2003/
511) reg.3(4) and (5) (April 1, 2003).
    5. National Council for Education and Training for Wales (Transfer of Functions
to the National Assembly for Wales and Abolition) Order 2005 (SI 2005/3238
(W.243)) art.9(2) and Sch.2 para.8(6) (April 1, 2006).
    6. Social Security (Young Persons) Amendment Regulations 2006 (SI 2006/718)
reg.3(9) (April 10, 2006).
    7. Social Security (Income Support and Jobseeker's Allowance) Amendment
Regulations 2006 (SI 2006/1402) reg.2(6) (May 30, 2006).
    8. Employment and Support Allowance (Consequential Provisions) (No.2)
Regulations 2008 (SI 2008/1554) reg.3(23) (October 27, 2008).
    9. Social Security (Miscellaneous Amendments) (No.7) Regulations 2008 (SI
2008/3157) reg.3(9) (January 5, 2009).

10. Social Security (Miscellaneous Amendments) Regulations 2009 (SI 2009/583) reg.4(3) (April 6, 2009).

11. Social Security (Miscellaneous Amendments) (No.5) Regulations 2009 (SI 2009/3228) reg.4(1)(b)(ii) (January 25, 2010).

12. Social Security (Equalisation of State Pension Age) Regulations 2009 (SI 2009/1488) reg.12 (April 6, 2010).

13. Apprenticeships, Skills, Children and Learning Act 2009 (Consequential Amendments to Subordinate Legislation) (England) Order 2010 (SI 2010/1941) art.5(5) (September 1, 2010).

14. Social Security (Miscellaneous Amendments) (No.5) Regulations 2010 (SI 2010/2429) reg.4(2)(a) (November 1, 2010).

15. Social Security (Miscellaneous Amendments) (No.5) Regulations 2010 (SI 2010/2429) reg.4(2)(b) (November 1, 2010).

16. Social Security (Miscellaneous Amendments) (No.5) Regulations 2010 (SI 2010/2429) reg.4(2)(c) (November 1, 2010).

17. Social Security (Miscellaneous Amendments) (No.3) Regulations 2011 (SI 2011/2425) reg.10(11) (October 31, 2011).

18. Young People's Learning Agency Abolition (Consequential Amendments to Subordinate Legislation) (England) Order 2012 (SI 2012/956) art.5(8) (May 1, 2012).

19. Personal Independence Payment (Supplementary Provisions and Consequential Amendments) Regulations 2013 (SI 2013/388) reg.8 and Sch. Pt 2 para.16(6) (April 8, 2013).

20. Armed Forces and Reserve Forces Compensation Scheme (Consequential Provisions: Subordinate Legislation) Order 2013 (SI 2013/591) art.7 and Sch. para.10(6) (April 8, 2013).

21. Deregulation Act 2015 (Consequential Amendments) Order 2015 (SI 2015/971) art.2 and Sch.3 para.4(7) (May 26, 2015).

DEFINITIONS

"armed forces independence payment"—see reg.1(3).
"attendance allowance"—*ibid.*
"the Benefits Act"—see Jobseekers Act s.35(1).
"course of study"—see reg.1(3).
"date of claim"—*ibid.*
"disability living allowance"—*ibid.*
"full-time student"—*ibid.*
"joint-claim couple"—see JSA s.1(4).
"personal independence payment"—see reg.1(3).
"qualifying age for state pension credit"—*ibid.*
"remunerative work"—reg.51(1).
"single claimant"—see reg.1(3).
"student"—see reg.130.
"the Universal Credit etc. Claims and Payments Regulations"—see reg.1(3).
"young person"—see regs 1(3) and 76.

GENERAL NOTE

3.478 See the note to reg.3D.

Many of the categories are similar to those in Sch.1B to the Income Support Regulations (people eligible for income support). See the notes to that Schedule.

In order to mirror the changes to Sch.1B to the Income Support Regulations made as a result of the introduction of ESA, paras 6(a) and (b), 9, 10 and 11 were revoked with effect from November 1, 2010. This will not, however, apply to joint-claim claimants who immediately before November 1, 2010 were entitled to JSA and to whom one of those provisions applied (reg.4(3) of the Social Security (Miscellaneous Amendments) (No.5) Regulations 2010 (SI 2010/2429)). This savings provision ceases to apply when the JSA award to which the couple were entitled before November 1, 2010 ends (reg.4(4) of the 2010 Regulations).

The new para.6B inserted on October 31, 2011 covers a member of a JSA joint-claim couple who provides evidence of his limited capability for work, without the need for that member to make a claim for ESA. Paragraph 6B will apply for the period covered by the evidence (see sub-para.(2)). Such evidence can take the form of a self-certificate for up to seven days, a medical certificate, or, where it would be unreasonable to require the person to provide the latter, such other evidence as the Secretary of State considers sufficient.

SCHEDULE 1   **Regulations 83 and 84(1)**

APPLICABLE AMOUNTS

[⁹*Part I*

Personal Allowances

1.—The weekly amounts specified in column (2) below in respect of each person or couple specified in column (1) shall be the weekly amounts specified for the purposes of regulations 83 [²⁸ 84(1), 86A and 86B] (applicable amounts and polygamous marriages).   **3.479**

(1)	(2)
Person or Couple	*Amount*
(1) Single claimant aged—	
(a) except where head (b) or (c) of this sub-paragraph applies, less than 18;	1. (a) [⁵² £59.20];
(b) less than 18 who falls within paragraph (2) of regulation 57 and who—	(b) [⁵² £59.20];
(i) is a person to whom regulation 59, 60 or 61 applies [¹. . .]; or	
(ii) is the subject of a direction under section 16;	
(c) less than 18 who satisfies the condition in [³³ paragraph 13(1)(a)] of Part 3;	(c) [⁵² £59.20];
(d) not less than 18 but less than 25;	(d) [⁵² £59.20];
(e) not less than 25.	(e) [⁵² £74.70].
(2) Lone parent aged—	
(a) except where head (b) or (c) of this sub-paragraph applies, less than 18;	2. (a) [⁵² £59.20];
(b) less than 18 who falls within paragraph (2) of regulation 57 and who—	(b) [⁵² £59.20];
(i) is a person to whom regulation 59, 60 or 61 applies [¹. . .]; or	
(ii) is the subject of a direction under section 16;	
(c) less than 18 who satisfies the condition in [³³ paragraph 13(1)(a)] [²of Part 3];	(c) [⁵² £59.20];
(d) not less than 18.	(d) [⁵² £74.70].
(3) Couple—	
(a) where both members are aged less than 18 and—	3. (a) [⁵² £89.45];
(i) at least one of them is treated as responsible for a child; or	
(ii) had they not been members of a couple, each would have been a person to whom regulation 59, 60 or 61 (circumstances in which a person aged 16 or 17 is eligible for a jobseeker's allowance) applied or	
(iii) had they not been members of a couple, the claimant would have been a person to whom regulation 59, 60 or 61 (circumstances in which a person aged 16 or 17 is eligible for a jobseeker's allowance) applied and his partner satisfies the requirements for entitlement to income support	

(1)	(2)
Person or Couple	Amount

[³⁶ or an income-related employment and support allowance]
    other than the requirement to make a claim for it; or

[¹(iv) they are married [³¹ or civil partners]and one member a
    of the couple is person to whom regulation 59, 60 or 61
    applies and the other member is registered in accordance
    with regulation 62; or

  (iva) they are married [³¹ or civil partners] and each member
    of the couple is a person to whom regulation 59, 60 or
    61 applies; or]

  (v) there is a direction under section 16 (jobseeker's
    allowance in cases of severe hardship) in respect
    of each member; or

  (vi) there is a direction under section 16 in respect of one of
    them and the other is a person to whom regulation 59,
    60 or 61 applies [¹. . .], or

  (vii) there is a direction under section 16 in respect of one
    of them and the other satisfies requirements for
    entitlement to income support [³⁶ or an income-related
    employment and support allowance] other than the
    requirement to make a claim for it;

(b) where both members are aged less than 18 and sub-
    paragraph (3)(a) does not apply but one
    member of the couple falls within paragraph (2)
    of regulation 57 and either—
    (i) is a person to whom regulation 59, 60 or 61
      applies [¹. . .]; or
    (ii) is the subject of a direction under section 16 of the Act;
                                (b) [⁵² £59.20];

(c) where both members are aged less than 18 and neither
    head (a) nor (b) of sub-paragraph (3) applies but one
    member of the couple—
    (i) is a person to whom regulation 59, 60 or
      61 applies [1. . .]; or
    (ii) is the subject of a direction under section 16;
                                 (c) [⁵² £59.20];

(d) where both members are aged less than 18 and none of
    heads (a), (b) or (c) of sub-paragraph (3) apply but one
    member of the couple is a person who satisfies the
    requirements of [³³ paragraph 13(1)(a)];
                                 (d) [⁵¹ £59.20];

[³⁵ (e) where—   (e) [⁵² £117.40];
      (i) both members are aged not less than 18; or
      (ii) one member is aged not less than 18 and the
    other member is a person who is—
    (aa)under 18, and
    (bb)treated as responsible for a child;]

(f) where [³⁵ paragraph (e) does not apply and] one   (f) [⁵² £117.40];
    member is aged not less than 18 and the
    other member is a person under 18 who—
    (i) is a person to whom regulation 59, 60 or
      61 applies [1. . .]; or
    (ii) is the subject of a direction under section 16; [³⁸ or
    (iii) satisfies requirements for entitlement to income
      support or who would do so if he were not a
      member of a couple, other than the
      requirement to make a claim for it; or
    (iv) satisfies requirements for entitlement to an
      income-related employment and support allowance
      other than the requirement to make a claim for it;]

(g) where one member is aged not less than 18 but less than 25 (g) [⁵¹ £59.20];
    and the other member is a person under 18—
    (i) to whom none of the regulations 59 to 61applies; or

(1)	(2)
Person or Couple	*Amount*
(ii) who is not the subject of a direction under section 16; and (iii) does not satisfy requirements for entitlement to income support [³⁶ or an income-related employment and support allowance] disregarding the requirement to make a claim for it;	
(h) where one member is aged not less than 25 and the other member is a person under 18— (i) to whom none of the regulations 59 to 61 applies; or (ii) is not the subject of a direction under section 16; and (iii) does not satisfy requirements for entitlement to income support [³⁶ or an income-related employment and support allowance] disregarding the requirement to make a claim for it.	(h) [⁵² £74.70].

2.—[³⁰ . . .]
3.—[²⁹ . . .]

PART II

Family Premium

4.—[³⁰ . . .]   3.480

PART III

Premiums

5.—Except as provided in paragraph 6, the weekly premiums specified in Part IV of this   3.481
Schedule shall for the purposes of regulations 83(e) and 84(1)(f), be applicable to a claimant
who satisfies the condition specified in [⁴ ¹⁵ paragraphs 9A] to 17 in respect of that premium.
    6.—Subject to paragraph 7, where a claimant satisfies the conditions in respect of more than
one premium in this Part of this Schedule, only one premium shall be applicable to him and,
if they are different amounts, the higher or highest amount shall apply.
    [¹⁶ **7.**—(1) Subject to sub-paragraph (2), the following premiums, namely—
    (a) a severe disability premium to which paragraph 15 applies;
    (b) an enhanced disability premium to which paragraph 15A applies;
    (c) [³⁰ . . .]; and
    (d) a carer premium in which paragraph 17 applies,
        may be applicable in addition to any other premium which may apply under this Part
        of this Schedule.
    (2) An enhanced disability premium in respect of a person shall not be applicable in addition
to—
    (a) a pensioner premium under paragraph 10 or 11; or
    (b) a higher pensioner premium under paragraph 12.]
    8.—(1) Subject to sub-paragraph (2) for the purposes of this Part of this Schedule, once
a premium is applicable to a claimant under this Part, a person shall be treated as being in
receipt of any benefit—
    (a) in the case of a benefit to which the Social Security (Overlapping Benefits)
        Regulations 1979 applies, for any period during which, apart from the provisions of
        those Regulations, he would be in receipt of that benefit; and
    [³(b) for any period spent by a claimant in undertaking a course of training or instruc-
        tion provided or approved by the Secretary of State [³⁵ . . .] under section 2 of the
        Employment and Training Act 1973, or by [³⁷ Skills Development Scotland,] Scottish
        Enterprise or Highlands and Islands Enterprise under section 2 of the Enterprise and
        New Towns (Scotland) Act 1990 or for any period during which he is in receipt of a
        training allowance.]
    (2) For the purposes of the carer premium under paragraph 17, a person shall be treated as
being in receipt of [²⁴ carer's allowance] by virtue of sub-paragraph (1)(a) only if and for so
long as the person in respect of whose care the allowance has been claimed remains in receipt

of attendance allowance, [⁴⁶ the care component of disability living allowance at the highest or middle rate prescribed in accordance with section 72(3) of the Benefits Act [⁴⁷ , armed forces independence payment] or the daily living component of personal independence payment at the standard or enhanced rate prescribed in accordance with section 78(3) of the 2012 Act].

Lone parent premium

3.482   **9.**—[⁴. . .]

[¹⁵ Bereavement Premium

3.483   **9A.**—[³⁴ . . .]]

Pensioner premium for persons [⁴⁰over the qualifying age for state pension credit]

3.484   **10.**—The condition is that the claimant—
    (a) is a single claimant or lone parent who has attained [⁴⁰ the qualifying age for state pension credit]; or
    (b) has attained [⁴⁰ the qualifying age for state pension credit] and has a partner; or
    (c) has a partner and the partner has attained [⁴⁰ the qualifying age for state pension credit] but not the age of 75.

Pensioner premium where claimant's partner has attained the age of 75

3.485   **11.**—The condition is that the claimant has a partner who has attained the age of 75 but not the age of 80.

Higher pensioner premium

3.486   **12.**—(1) [³³ Subject to sub-paragraph (5), the] condition is that—
    (a) the claimant is a single claimant or lone parent who has attained [⁴⁰ the qualifying age for state pension credit] and either—
        (i) satisfies one of the additional conditions specified in paragraph 14(1)(a), (c), [⁵¹ (ca), (cb),] (e), (f) [⁵¹, (fa)] or (h); or
        (ii) was entitled to either income support or income-based jobseeker's allowance [¹², or was treated as being entitled to either of those benefits and the disability premium was or, as the case may be, would have been,] applicable to him in respect of a benefit week within 8 weeks of [⁴⁰ the date he attained the qualifying age for state pension credit] and he has, subject to sub-paragraph (2), remained continuously entitled to one of those benefits since attaining that age; or
    (b) the claimant has a partner and—
        (i) the partner has attained the age of 80; or
        (ii) the partner has attained [⁴⁰ the qualifying age for state pension credit] but not the age of 80, and the additional conditions specified in paragraph 14 are satisfied in respect of him; or
    (c) the claimant—
        (i) has attained [⁴⁰ the qualifying age for state pension credit];
        [³(ii) satisfies the requirements of either sub-head (i) or (ii) of paragraph 12(1)(a); and]
        (iii) has a partner.
    (2) For the purposes of this paragraph and paragraph 14—
    (a) once the higher pensioner premium is applicable to a claimant, if he then ceases, for a period of eight weeks or less, to be entitled to either income support or income-based jobseeker's allowance [¹² or ceases to be treated as entitled to either of those benefits], he shall, on becoming re-entitled to either of those benefits, thereafter be treated as having been continuously entitled thereto;
    (b) in so far as sub-paragraphs (1)(a)(ii) and (1)(c)(ii) are concerned, if a claimant ceases to be entitled to either income support or an income-based jobseeker's allowance [¹² or ceases to be treated as entitled to either of those benefits] for a period not exceeding eight weeks which includes [⁴⁰ the date he attained the qualifying age for state pension credit], he shall, on becoming re-entitled to either of those benefits, thereafter be treated as having been continuously entitled thereto.
    [⁸(3) In this paragraph where a claimant's partner is a welfare to work beneficiary, sub-paragraphs (1)(a)(ii) and (2)(b) shall apply to him as if for the words "8 weeks" there were substituted the words "[³² 104 weeks]".]
    [¹² (4) For the purposes of this paragraph, a claimant shall be treated as having been entitled to income support or to an income-based jobseeker's allowance throughout any period which comprises only days on which he was participating in an employment zone programme and was not entitled to—

(a) income support because, as a consequence of his participation in that programme, he was engaged in remunerative work or had income in excess of the claimant's applicable amount as prescribed in Part IV of the Income Support Regulations; or

(b) a jobseeker's allowance because, as a consequence of his participation in that programme, he was engaged in remunerative work or failed to satisfy the condition specified in section 2(1)(c) or in section 3(1)(a).]

[³³ (5) The condition is not satisfied if—

(a) the claimant is a single claimant or a lone parent and (in either case) is a long-term patient;

(b) the claimant is a member of a couple or polygamous marriage and each member of the couple or polygamous marriage is a long-term patient; or

(c) the claimant is a member of a couple or a polygamous marriage and a member of that couple or polygamous marriage is—
   (i) a long-term patient; and
   (ii) the only member of the couple or polygamous marriage to whom sub-paragraph (1)(b) or (c) refers.]

Disability premium

13. [³³ —(1) Subject to sub-paragraph (2), the] condition is that the claimant—   3.487

(a) is a single claimant or lone parent who has not attained [⁴⁰ the qualifying age for state pension credit] and satisfies any one of the additional conditions specified in paragraph 14(1)(a), (c), [⁵¹ (ca), (cb),] (e), (f) [⁵¹, (fa)] or (h); or

(b) has not attained [⁴⁰ the qualifying age for state pension credit], has a partner and the claimant satisfies any one of the additional conditions specified in paragraph 14(1)(a), (c), [⁵¹ (ca), (cb),] (e), (f) [⁵¹, (fa)] or (h); or

(c) has a partner and the partner has not attained [⁴⁰ the qualifying age for state pension credit] and also satisfies any one of the additional conditions specified in paragraph 14.

[³³ (2) The condition is not satisfied if—

(a) the claimant is a single claimant or a lone parent and (in either case) is a long-term patient;

(b) the claimant is a member of a couple or polygamous marriage and each member of the couple or polygamous marriage is a long-term patient; or

(c) the claimant is a member of a couple or polygamous marriage and a member of that couple or polygamous marriage—
   (i) is a long-term patient; and
   (ii) is the only member of the couple or polygamous marriage to whom the condition in sub-paragraph (1)(b) or (c) refers.]

Additional conditions for higher pensioner and disability premium

14.—(1) The additional conditions specified in this paragraph are that—   3.488

(a) the claimant or, as the case may be, his partner, is in receipt [²⁵ the disability element or the severe disability element of working tax credit as specified in regulation 20(1)(b) and (f) of the Working Tax Credit (Entitlement and Maximum Rate) Regulations 2002] or mobility supplement;

(b) the claimant's partner is in receipt of severe disablement allowance;

(c) the claimant or, as the case may be, his partner, is in receipt of attendance allowance or disability living allowance or is a person whose disability living allowance is payable, in whole or in part, to another in accordance with regulation 44 of the Claims and Payments Regulations (payment of disability living allowance on behalf of third party);

[⁴⁶ (ca) the claimant or, as the case may be, his partner, is in receipt of personal independence payment or is a person whose personal independence payment is payable, in whole or in part, to another in accordance with regulation 58(2) of the Universal Credit etc. Claims and Payments Regulations (payment to another person on the claimant's behalf);]

[⁴⁷ (cb) the claimant or, as the case may be, the claimant's partner, is in receipt of armed forces independence payment or is a person whose armed forces independence payment is payable, in whole or in part, to another in accordance with article 24D of the Armed Forces and Reserve Forces (Compensation Scheme) Order 2011;]

(d) the claimant's partner is in receipt of long-term incapacity benefit or is a person to whom section 30B(4) of the Benefits Act (long term rate of incapacity benefit payable to those who are terminally ill) applies;

(e) the claimant or, as the case may be, his partner, has an invalid carriage or other vehicle provided to him by the Secretary of State under section 5(2)(a) of and Schedule 2 to the National Health Service Act 1977 or under section 46 of the National Health Service (Scotland) Act 1978 or provided by the Department of Health and Social Services for Northern Ireland under article 30(1) of the Health and Personal Social Services (Northern Ireland) Order 1972, or receives payments by way of grant from the Secretary of State under paragraph 2 of Schedule 2 to the Act of 1977 (additional provisions as to vehicles) or, in Scotland, under section 46 of the Act of 1978;

(f)   the claimant or, as the case may be, his partner, is a person who is entitled to the mobility component of disability living allowance but to whom the component is not payable in accordance with regulation 42 of the Claims and Payments Regulations (cases where disability living allowance not payable);

[⁴⁶ (fa)   the claimant or, as the case may be, his partner, is a person who is entitled to the mobility component of personal independence payment but to whom the component is not payable in accordance with regulation 61 of the Universal Credit etc. Claims and Payments Regulations (cases where mobility component of personal independence payment not payable);]

(g)   the claimant's partner was either—
(i)   in receipt of long term incapacity benefit under section 30A(5) of the Benefits Act immediately before attaining pensionable age and he is still alive;
(ii)   entitled to attendance allowance or disability living allowance but payment of that benefit was suspended in accordance with regulations under section 113(2) of the Benefits Act or otherwise abated as a consequence of [²the partner] becoming a patient within the meaning of regulation 85(4) (special cases), [⁴⁶ ; or
(iii)   entitled to personal independence payment but no amount is payable in accordance with regulations made under section 86(1) (hospital in-patients) of the 2012 Act]
and in either case the higher pensioner premium or disability premium had been applicable to the claimant or his partner;

[⁴⁸ (h)   the claimant or, as the case may be, his partner, is certified as severely sight impaired or blind by a consultant ophthalmologist.]

[⁴⁸ (2) For the purposes of sub-paragraph (1)(h), a person who has ceased to be certified as severely sight impaired or blind on regaining his eyesight shall nevertheless be treated as severely sight impaired or blind, as the case may be, and as satisfying the additional condition set out in that sub-paragraph for a period of 28 weeks following the date on which he ceased to be so certified.]

Severe disability premium

3.489   **15.**—(1) In the case of a single claimant, a lone parent or a claimant who is treated as having no partner in consequence of sub-paragraph (3), the condition is that—

(a)   he is in receipt of attendance allowance [⁴⁶ , the care component of disability living allowance at the highest or middle rate in accordance with section 72(3) of the Benefits Act [⁴⁷ , armed forces independence payment] or the daily living component of personal independence payment at the standard or enhanced rate in accordance with section 78(3) of the 2012 Act]; and

(b)   subject to sub-paragraph (4), there are no non-dependants aged 18 or over normally residing with him or with whom he is normally residing; and

[¹¹(c)   no person is entitled to, and in receipt of, [²⁴ a carer's allowance] under section 70 of the Benefits Act [⁵⁰ or has an award of universal credit which includes the carer element] in respect of caring for him;]

(2) Where the claimant has a partner, the condition is that—

(a)   the claimant is in receipt of attendance allowance [⁴⁶ , the care component of disability living allowance at the highest or middle rate prescribed in accordance with section 72(3) of the Benefits Act [⁴⁷ , armed forces independence payment] or the daily living component of personal independence payment at the standard or enhanced rate in accordance with section 78(3) of the 2012 Act]; and

(b)   the partner is also in receipt of a qualifying benefit, or if he is a member of a polygamous marriage, all the partners of that marriage are in receipt of a qualifying benefit; and

(c)   subject to sub-paragraph (4), there is no non-dependant aged 18 or over normally residing with him or with whom he is normally residing; and

(d)   either—

    (i) [¹¹no person is entitled to, and in receipt of, [²⁴ a carer's allowance] under section 70 of the Benefits Act [⁵⁰ or has an award of universal credit which includes the carer element] in respect of] caring for either member of the couple or all the members of the polygamous marriage; or

    (ii) a person is engaged in caring for one member (but not both members) of the couple, or one or more but not all members of the polygamous marriage, and in consequence is [¹¹entitled to] [²⁴ a carer's allowance] under section 70 of the Benefits Act [⁵⁰ or has an award of universal credit which includes the carer element].

(3) Where the claimant has a partner who does not satisfy the condition in subparagraph (2) (b), and that partner is [⁴⁸ severely sight impaired or blind or treated as severely sight impaired or blind] within the meaning of paragraph 14(1)(h) and (2), that partner shall be treated for the purposes of sub-paragraph (2) as if he were not a partner of the claimant.

(4) The following persons shall not be regarded as a non-dependant for the purposes of sub-paragraphs (1)(b) and (2)(c)—

    (a) a person in receipt of attendance allowance [⁴⁶ , the care component of disability living allowance at the highest or middle rate prescribed in accordance with section 72(3) of the Benefits Act [⁴⁷ , armed forces independence payment] or the daily living component of personal independence payment at the standard or enhanced rate in accordance with section 78(3) of the 2012 Act];

    (b) subject to sub-paragraph (6), a person who joins the claimant's household for the first time in order to care for the claimant or his partner and immediately before so joining the claimant or his partner satisfied the condition in sub-paragraph (1) or, as the case may be, (2);

    (c) a person who is [⁴⁸ severely sight impaired or blind or treated as severely sight impaired or blind] within the meaning of paragraph 14(1)(h) and (2).

(5) For the purposes of sub-paragraph (2), a person shall be treated [¹¹ . . .]

    (a) [¹¹as being in receipt of] attendance allowance, or the care component of disability living allowance at the highest or middle rate prescribed in accordance with section 72(3) of the Benefits Act if he would, but for his being a patient for a period exceeding 28 days, be so in receipt;

[⁴⁶ (aa) as being in receipt of the daily living component of personal independence payment at the standard or enhanced rate in accordance with section 78 of the 2012 Act if he would, but for regulations made under section 86(1) (hospital in-patients) of the 2012 Act, be so in receipt;]

[¹¹(b) as being entitled to and in receipt of [²⁴ a carer's allowance] [⁵⁰ or having an award of universal credit which includes the carer element] if he would, but for the person for whom he was caring being a patient in hospital for a period exceeding 28 days, be so entitled and in receipt [⁵⁰ of carer's allowance or have such an award of universal credit].]

(6) Sub-paragraph (4)(b) shall apply only for the first 12 weeks following the date on which the person to whom that provision applies first joins the claimant's household.

(7) For the purposes of sub-paragraph (1)(c) and (2)(d), no account shall be taken of an award of [²⁴ carer's allowance] [⁵⁰ or universal credit which includes the carer element] to the extent that payment of such an award is backdated for a period before [³⁴ the date on which the award is first paid].

(8) A person shall be treated as satisfying this condition if he would have satisfied the condition specified for a severe disability premium in income support in paragraph 13 of Schedule 2 to the Income Support Regulations by virtue only of regulations 4 to 6 of the Income Support (General) Amendment (No.6) Regulations 1991 (savings provisions in relation to severe disability premium) and for the purposes of determining whether in the particular case regulation 4 of those Regulations had ceased to apply in accordance with regulation 5(2)(a) of those Regulations, a person who is entitled to an income-based jobseeker's allowance shall be treated as entitled to income support.

[²⁰ (9) In sub-paragraphs (1)(c) and (2)(d), references to a person being in receipt of [²⁴ a carer's allowance] [⁵⁰ or as having an award of universal credit which includes the carer element] shall include references to a person who would have been in receipt of that allowance [⁵⁰ or had such an award] but for the application of a restriction under section [³⁹ 6B or] 7 of the Social Security Fraud Act 2001 (loss of benefit provisions).]

[⁵⁰ (10) For the purposes of this paragraph, a person has an award of universal credit which includes the carer element if the person has an award of universal credit which includes an amount which is the carer element under regulation 29 of the Universal Credit Regulations 2013.]

[^{16} **Enhanced disability premium**

3.490   **15A.**—[^{46} (1)   Subject to sub-paragraph (2), the condition is that—

(a) the claimant; or

(b) the claimant's partner (if any),

is a person who has not attained the qualifying age for state pension credit and is a person to whom sub-paragraph (1ZA) applies.

(1ZA) This sub-paragraph applies to the person mentioned in sub-paragraph (1) where—

(a) the care component of disability living allowance is, or would, but for a suspension of benefit in accordance with regulations under section 113(2) of the Benefits Act or but for an abatement as a consequence of hospitalisation, be payable to that person at the highest rate prescribed under section 72(3) of the Benefits Act; or

(b) the daily living component of personal independence payment is, or would, but for a suspension of benefits in accordance with regulations under section 86(1) (hospital in-patients) of the 2012 Act, be payable to that person at the enhanced rate in accordance with section 78(2) of the 2012 Act][^{47} ; or

(c) armed forces independence payment is payable to that person.]

[^{42} (1A) Where the condition in sub-paragraph (1) ceases to be satisfied because of the death of a child or young person, the condition is that the claimant is entitled to child benefit in respect of that person under section 145A of the Benefits Act (entitlement after death of child or qualifying young person).]

[^{33} (2) The condition is not satisfied where the person to whom sub-paragraph (1) refers is—

(a) a child or young person—

(i) whose capital if calculated in accordance with Part 8 of these Regulations in like manner as for the claimant, except as provided in regulation 106(1), would exceed £3,000; or

(ii) who is a long-term patient;

(b) a single claimant or a lone parent and (in either case) is a long-term patient;

(c) a member of a couple or polygamous marriage and each member of the couple or polygamous marriage is a long-term patient; or

(d) a member of a couple or polygamous marriage who is—

(i) a long-term patient; and

(ii) the only member of the couple or polygamous marriage to whom sub-paragraph (1) refers.]]

Disabled child premium

3.491   **16.**—[^{30} . . . ^{33}]

Carer premium

3.492   **17.**—(1) Subject to sub-paragraphs (3) and (4), the condition is that the claimant or his partner is, or both of them are, [^{11}entitled to] [^{24} a carer's allowance] under section 70 of the Benefits Act.

(2) [^{28} . . .]

[^{23} (3) Where a carer premium is awarded but—

(a) the person in respect of whose care the [^{24} carer's allowance] has been awarded dies; or

(b) in any other case the person in respect of whom a carer premium has been awarded ceases to be entitled [^{28} . . .] to [^{24} a carer's allowance],

the condition for the award of the premium shall be treated as satisfied for a period of eight weeks from the relevant date specified in sub-paragraph (3A) below.

(3A) The relevant date for the purposes of sub-paragraph (3) above shall be—

(a) [^{28} where sub-paragraph (3)(a) applies,] the Sunday following the death of the person in respect of whose care [^{24} a carer's allowance] has been awarded or the date of death if the death occurred on a Sunday;

(b) [^{28} . . .]

(c) in any other case, the date of which the person who has been entitled to [^{24} a carer's allowance] ceases to be entitled to that allowance.]

(4) Where a person who has been entitled to an invalid care allowance ceases to be entitled to that allowance and makes a claim for a jobseeker's allowance, the condition for the award of the carer premium shall be treated as satisfied for a period of eight weeks from the date on which—

[^{23}(a) the person in respect of whose care the [^{24} carer's allowance] has been awarded dies;

(b) [^{28} . . .]

[^{28} (c) in any other case, the person who has been entitled to a carer's allowance ceased to be entitled to that allowance.]

Persons in receipt of concessionary payments

18.—For the purpose of determining whether a premium is applicable to a person under paragraphs 14 to 17, any concessionary payment made to compensate that person for the non-payment of any benefit mentioned in those paragraphs shall be treated as if it were a payment of that benefit.

3.493

Person in receipt of benefit

19.—For the purposes of this Part of this Schedule, a person shall be regarded as being in receipt of any benefit if, and only if, it is paid in respect of him and shall be so regarded only for any period in respect of which that benefit is paid.

3.494

PART IV

Weekly Amounts of Premiums Specified in Part III

3.495

Premium	Amount
20.—(1) [⁴. . .]	(1) [⁴ . . .]
(1A) [³⁴ . . .]	(1A) [³⁴ . . .];
(2) Pensioner premium for persons [⁴⁰ who have attained the qualifying age for state pension credit]—	
(a) where the claimant satisfies the condition in paragraph 10(a);	(2) (a) [⁵³ £102.40];
(b) where the claimant satisfies the condition in paragraph 10(b).	(b) [⁵³ £152.90];
(c) where the claimant satisfies the condition in paragraph 10(c).	(c) [⁵³ £152.90];
(3) Pensioner premium for claimants whose partner has attained the age of 75 where the claimant satisfies the condition in paragraph 11;	(3) [⁵³ £152.90];
(4) Higher Pensioner Premium—	
(a) where the claimant satisfies the condition in paragraph 12(1)(a);	(4) (a) [⁵³ £102.40];
(b) where the claimant satisfies the condition in paragraph 12(1)(b) or (c).	(b) [⁵³ £152.90];
(5) Disability Premium—	
(a) where the claimant satisfies the condition in [³³ paragraph 13(1)(a)];	(5) (a) [⁵³ £35.10];
(b) where the claimant satisfies the condition in [³³ paragraph 13(1)(b) or (c)].	(b) [⁵³ £50.05].
(6) Severe Disability Premium—	
(a) where the claimant satisfies the condition in paragraph 15(1);	(6) (a) [⁵³ £67.30];
(b) where the claimant satisfies the condition in paragraph 15(2)—	(b)
(i) if there is someone in receipt of [²⁴ a carer's allowance] or [²if any partner of the claimant] satisfies that condition by virtue of paragraph 15(5);	(i) [⁵³ £67.30];
(ii) if no-one is in receipt of such an allowance.	(ii) [⁵³ £134.60].
(7) [³⁰ . . .]	(7) [³⁰ . . .]
(8) Carer Premium.	(8) [⁵³ £37.70] in respect of each person who satisfied the condition specified in paragraph 17.]
[¹⁶ (9) Enhanced disability premium where the conditions in paragraph 15A are satisfied.]	[¹⁶ (9)(a)[³⁰ . . .] (b) [⁵³ £17.20] in respect of each person who is neither— (i) a child or young person; nor

Premium	Amount
	(ii) a member of a couple or a polygamous marriage, respect of whom the in conditions specified in paragraph 15A are satisfied; (c) [⁵³ £24.60] where the claimant is a member of a couple or a polygamous marriage and the conditions specified in paragraph 15A are satisfied in respect of a member of that couple or polygamous marriage.]

3.496

[¹⁴ PART IVA

Premiums for Joint-claim Couples

3.497 **20A.**—Except as provided in paragraph 20B, the weekly premium specified in Part IVB of this Schedule shall, for the purposes of regulations 86A(c) and 86B(d), be applicable to a joint-claim couple where either or both members of a joint-claim couple satisfy the condition specified in paragraphs 20E to 20J in respect of that premium.

20B.—Subject to paragraph 20C, where a member of a joint-claim couple satisfies the conditions in respect of more than one premium in this Part of this Schedule, only one premium shall be applicable to the joint-claim couple in respect of that member and, if they are different amounts, the higher or highest amount shall apply.

[¹⁶ **20C.**—(1) Subject to sub-paragraph (2), the following premiums, namely—
    (a) a severe disability premium to which paragraph 20I applies;
    (b) an enhanced disability premium to which paragraph 20IA applies; and
    (c) a carer premium to which paragraph 20J applies,
        may be applicable in addition to any other premium which may apply under this Part of this Schedule.

(2) An enhanced disability premium in respect of a person shall not be applicable in addition to—
    (a) a pensioner premium under paragraph 20E; or
    (b) a higher pensioner premium under paragraph 20F.]

20D.—(1) Subject to sub-paragraph (2) for the purposes of this Part of this Schedule, once a premium is applicable to a joint-claim couple under this Part, a person shall be treated as being in receipt of any benefit—
    (a) in the case of a benefit to which the Social Security (Overlapping Benefits) Regulations 1979 applies, for any period during which, apart from the provisions of those Regulations, he would be in receipt of that benefit; and
    (b) for any period spent by a person in undertaking a course of training or instruction provided or approved by the Secretary of State under section 2 of the Employment and Training Act 1973, or by [³⁷ Skills Development Scotland,] Scottish Enterprise or Highlands and Islands Enterprise under section 2 of the Enterprise and New Towns (Scotland) Act 1990, or for any period during which he is in receipt of a training allowance.

(2) For the purposes of the carer premium under paragraph 20J, a person shall be treated as being in receipt of [²⁴ carer's allowance] by virtue of sub-paragraph (1)(a) only if and for so long as the person in respect of whose care the allowance has been claimed remains in receipt of attendance allowance, [⁴⁶ the care component of disability living allowance at the highest or middle rate prescribed in accordance with section 72(3) of the Benefits Act or the daily living component of personal independence payment at the standard or enhanced rate in accordance with section 78(3) of the 2012 Act [⁴⁷ or armed forces independence payment]].

Pensioner premium where one member of a joint-claim couple has attained [⁴⁰ the qualifying age for state pension credit]

3.498 **20E.**—The condition is that one member of a joint-claim couple has attained [⁴⁰ the qualifying age for state pension credit]but not the age of 75.

Higher pensioner premium

20F.—(1) [³³ Subject to sub-paragraph (5), the] condition is that one member of a joint-claim couple—

    (a) has attained [⁴⁰ the qualifying age for state pension credit] but not the age of 80, and either the additional conditions specified in paragraph 20H are satisfied in respect of him; or

    (b) has attained [⁴⁰ the qualifying age for state pension credit] and—

        (i) was entitled to or was treated as entitled to either income support or an income-based jobseeker's allowance and the disability premium was or, as the case may be, would have been applicable to him in respect of a benefit week within 8 weeks of [⁴⁰ the date he attained the qualifying age for state pension credit] and he has, subject to sub-paragraph (2), remained continuously entitled to one of those benefits since attaining that age; or

        (ii) was a member of a joint-claim couple who had been entitled to, or who had been treated as entitled to, a joint-claim jobseeker's allowance and the disability premium was or, as the case may be, would have been applicable to that couple in respect of a benefit week within 8 weeks of [⁴⁰ the date either member of that couple attained the qualifying age for state pension credit] and the couple have, subject to that sub-paragraph (2), remained continuously entitled to a joint-claim jobseeker's allowance since that member attained that age.

    (2) For the purpose of this paragraph and paragraph 20H—

    (a) once the higher pensioner premium is applicable to a joint-claim couple, if that member then ceases, for a period of 8 weeks or less, to be entitled or treated as entitled to either income support or income-based jobseeker's allowance or that couple cease to be entitled to or treated as entitled to a joint-claim jobseeker's allowance, he shall or, as the case may be, that couple shall, on becoming re-entitled to any of those benefits, thereafter be treated as having been continuously entitled thereto;

    (b) in so far as sub-paragraph (1)(b)(i) or (ii) is concerned, if a member of a joint-claim couple ceases to be entitled or treated as entitled to either income support or an income-based jobseeker's allowance or that couple cease to be entitled to or treated as entitled to a joint-claim jobseeker's allowance for a period not exceeding 8 weeks which includes [⁴⁰ the date either member of that couple attained the qualifying age for state pension credit], he shall or, as the case may be, the couple shall, on becoming re-entitled to either of those benefits, thereafter be treated as having been continuously entitled thereto.

    (3) In this paragraph, where a member of a joint-claim couple is a welfare to work beneficiary, sub-paragraphs (1)(b)(i) and (2)(b) shall apply to him as if for the words "8 weeks" there were substituted the words "[³²104 weeks]".

    (4) For the purposes of this paragraph, a member of a joint-claim couple shall be treated as having been entitled to income support or to an income-based jobseeker's allowance or the couple of which he is a member shall be treated as having been entitled to a joint-claim jobseeker's allowance throughout any period which comprises only days on which a member was participating in an employment zone scheme and was not entitled to—

    (a) income support because, as a consequence of his participation in that scheme, he was engaged in remunerative work or had income in excess of the claimant's applicable amount as prescribed in Part IV of the Income Support Regulations; or

    (b) a jobseeker's allowance because, as a consequence of his participation in that scheme, he was engaged in remunerative work or failed to satisfy the condition specified in section 2(1)(c) or the couple of which he was a member failed to satisfy the condition in section 3A(1)(a).

[³³ (5) The condition is not satisfied if the member of the joint-claim couple to whom sub-paragraph (1) refers is a long-term patient.]

[³³ Disability Premium

20G.—(1) Subject to sub-paragraph (2), the condition is that a member of a joint-claim couple has not attained [⁴⁰ the qualifying age for state pension credit] and satisfies any one of the additional conditions specified in paragraph 20H.

    (2) The condition is not satisfied if—

    (a) paragraph (1) only refers to one member of a joint-claim couple and that member is a long-term patient; or

    b) paragraph (1) refers to both members of a joint-claim couple and both members of the couple are long-term patients]

3.499

3.500

Additional conditions for higher pensioner and disability premium

3.501   **20H.**—(1) The additional conditions specified in this paragraph are that a member of a joint-claim couple—

(a) is in receipt of [²⁶ the disability element or the severe disability element of working tax credit as specified in regulation 20(1)(b) and (f) of the Working Tax Credit (Entitlement and Maximum Rate) Regulations 2002] or mobility supplement;

(b) is in receipt of severe disablement allowance;

(c) is in receipt of attendance allowance or disability living allowance or is a person whose disability living allowance is payable, in whole or in part, to another in accordance with regulation 44 of the Claims and Payments Regulations (payment of disability living allowance on behalf of third party);

[⁴⁶ (ca) is in receipt of personal independence payment or is a person whose personal independence payment is payable, in whole or in part, to another in accordance with regulation 58(2) of the Universal Credit etc. Claims and Payments Regulations (payment to another person on the claimant's behalf);]

[⁴⁷ (cb) is in receipt of armed forces independence payment or is a person whose armed forces independence payment is payable, in whole or in part, to another in accordance with article 24D of the Armed Forces and Reserve Forces (Compensation Scheme) Order 2011;]

(d) is in receipt of long-term incapacity benefit or is a person to whom section 30B(4) of the Benefits Act (long-term rate of incapacity benefit payable to those who are terminally ill) applies;

(e) has been entitled to statutory sick pay, has been incapable of work or has been treated as incapable of work for a continuous period of not less than—

(i) 196 days in the case of a member of a joint-claim couple who is terminally ill within the meaning of section 30B(4) of the Benefits Act; or

(ii) 364 days in any other case,

and for these purposes, any two or more periods of entitlement or incapacity separated by a break of not more than 56 days shall be treated as one continuous period;

[³⁶ (ee) has had limited capability for work or has been treated as having limited capability for work for a continuous period of not less than—

(i) 196 days in the case of a member of a joint-claim couple who is terminally ill within the meaning of regulation 2(1) of the Employment and Support Allowance Regulations; or

(ii) 364 days in any other case,

and for these purposes any two or more periods of limited capability for work separated by a break of not more than 12 weeks is to be treated as one continuous period;]

(f) has an invalid carriage or other vehicle provided to him by the Secretary of State under section 5(2)(a) of, and Schedule 2 to, the National Health Service Act 1977 or under section 46 of the National Health Service (Scotland) Act 1978 or provided by the Department of Health and Social Services for Northern Ireland under article 30(1) of the Health and Personal Social Services (Northern Ireland) Order 1972, or receives payments by way of grant from the Secretary of State under paragraph 2 of Schedule 2 to the Act of 1977 (additional provisions as to vehicles) or, in Scotland, under section 46 of the Act of 1978;

(g) is a person who is entitled to the mobility component of disability living allowance but to whom the component is not payable in accordance with regulation 42 of the Claims and Payments Regulations (cases where disability living allowance not payable);

[⁴⁶ (ga) is a person who is entitled to the mobility component of personal independence payment but to whom the component is not payable in accordance with regulation 61 of the Universal Credit etc. Claims and Payments Regulations (cases where mobility component of personal independence payment not payable);]

(h) was either—

(i) in receipt of long-term incapacity benefit under section 30A(5) of the Benefits Act immediately before attaining pensionable age and he is still alive; or

(ii) entitled to attendance allowance or disability living allowance but payment of that benefit was suspended in accordance with regulations under section 113(2) of the Benefits Act or otherwise abated as a consequence of either member of the joint-claim couple becoming a patient within the meaning of regulation 85(4) (special cases), [⁴⁶ or

(iii) entitled to personal independence payment but no amount is payable in accordance with regulations under section 86(1) (hospital in-patients) of the 2012 Act,]

and in either case, the higher pensioner premium or disability premium had been
applicable to the joint-claim couple; or

[⁴⁸ (l) is certified as severely sight impaired or blind by a consultant ophthalmologist.]

(2) [⁴¹ . . . [³² . . .]]

[⁴⁸ (3) For the purposes of sub-paragraph (1)(i), a person who has ceased to be certified
as severely sight impaired or blind on regaining his eyesight shall nevertheless be treated as
severely sight impaired or blind, as the case may be, and as satisfying the additional condition
set out in that sub-paragraph for a period of 28 weeks following the date on which he ceased
to be so certified.]

Severe disability premium

20I.—(1) The condition is that—   3.502

(a) a member of a joint-claim couple is in receipt of attendance allowance [⁴⁶ , the care
component of disability living allowance at the highest or middle rate prescribed in
accordance with section 72(3) of the Benefits Act [⁴⁷ , armed forces independence
payment] or the daily living component of personal independence payment at the
standard or enhanced rate in accordance with section 78(3) of the 2012 Act] ; and

(b) the other member is also in receipt of such an allowance, or if he is a member of a
polygamous marriage, all the partners of that marriage are in receipt of a qualifying
benefit; and

(c) subject to sub-paragraph (3), there is no non-dependant aged 18 or over normally
residing with the joint-claim couple or with whom they are normally residing; and

(d) either—

(i) no person is entitled to, and in receipt of, [²⁴ a carer's allowance] under section
70 of the Benefits Act [⁵⁰ or has an award of universal credit which includes the
carer element] in respect of caring for either member or the couple or all the
members of the polygamous marriage; or

(ii) a person is engaged in caring for one member (but not both members) of the
couple, or one or more but not all members of the polygamous marriage, and
in consequence is entitled to [²⁴ a carer's allowance] under section 70 of the
Benefits Act [⁵⁰ or has an award of universal credit which includes the carer
element].

(2) Where the other member does not satisfy the condition in sub-paragraph (1)(b), and
that member is [⁴⁸ severely sight impaired or blind or treated as severely sight impaired or
blind] within the meaning of paragraph 20H(1)(i) and (2), that member shall be treated for
the purposes of sub-paragraph (1) as if he were not a member of the couple.

(3) The following persons shall not be regarded as non-dependant for the purposes of sub-
paragraph (1)(c)—

(a) a person in receipt of attendance allowance [⁴⁶ , the care component of disability
living allowance at the highest or middle rate prescribed in accordance with section
72(3) of the Benefits Act [⁴⁷ , armed forces independence payment] or the daily living
component of personal independence payment at the standard or enhanced rate in
accordance with section 78(3) of the 2012 Act];

(b) subject to sub-paragraph (5), a person who joins the joint-claim couple's household
for the first time in order to care for a member of a joint claim couple and immediately
before so joining, that member satisfied the condition in sub-paragraph (1);

(c) a person who is [⁴⁸ severely sight impaired or blind or treated as severely sight
impaired or blind] within the meaning of paragraph 20H(1)(i) and (2).

(4) For the purposes of sub-paragraph (1), a member of a joint-claim couple shall be
treated—

(a) as being in receipt of attendance allowance, or the care component of disability living
allowance at the highest or middle rate prescribed in accordance with section 72(3) of
the Benefits Act if he would, but for his being a patient for a period exceeding 28 days,
be so in receipt;

(b) as being entitled to and in receipt of [²⁴ a carer's allowance] [⁵⁰ or having an award
of universal credit which includes the carer element] if he would, but for the person
for whom he was caring being a patient in hospital for a period exceeding 28 days, be
so entitled and in receipt [⁵⁰ of carer's allowance or have such an award of universal
credit].

[⁴⁶ (c) as being in receipt of the daily living component of personal independence payment
at the standard or enhanced rate in accordance with section 78 of the 2012 Act if he
would, but for regulations made under section 86(1) (hospital in-patients) of the 2012
Act, be so in receipt.]

(5) Sub-paragraph (3)(b) shall apply only for the first 12 weeks following the date on which the person to whom that provision applies first joins the joint-claim couple's household.

(6) For the purposes of sub-paragraph (1)(d), no account shall be taken of an award of [²⁴ carer's allowance] [⁵⁰ or universal credit which includes the carer element] to the extent that payment of such an award is back-dated for a period before [³⁴ the date on which the award is first paid].

[²⁰ (7) In sub-paragraph (1)(d), the reference to a person being in receipt of [²⁴ a carer's allowance] [⁵⁰ or as having an award of universal credit which includes the carer element] shall include a reference to a person who would have been in receipt of that allowance [⁵⁰ or had such an award] but for the application of a restriction under section [³⁹ 6B or] 7 of the Social Security Fraud Act 2001 (loss of benefit provisions).]

[⁵⁰ (8) For the purposes of this paragraph, a person has an award of universal credit which includes the carer element if the person has an award of universal credit which includes an amount which is the carer element under regulation 29 of the Universal Credit Regulations 2013.]

[¹⁶ Enhanced disability premium

3.503 **20IA.**—[⁴⁶ (1) Subject to sub-paragraph (2), the condition is that in respect of a member of a joint-claim couple who has not attained the qualifying age for state pension credit—
- (a) the care component of disability living allowance is, or would, but for a suspension of benefit in accordance with regulations under section 113(2) of the Benefits Act or but for an abatement as a consequence of hospitalisation, be payable at the highest rate prescribed under section 72(3) of the Benefits Act; or
- (b) the daily living component of personal independence payment is, or would, but for regulations made under section 86(1) (hospital in-patients) of the 2012 Act, be payable at the enhanced rate in accordance with section 78(2) of the 2012 Act [⁴⁷ or armed forces independence payment is payable].]

[³³ (2) The condition is not satisfied if—
- (a) paragraph (1) only refers to one member of a joint-claim couple and that member is a long-term patient; or
- (b) paragraph (1) refers to both members of a joint-claim couple and both members of the couple are long-term patients.]]

Carer premium

3.504 **20J.**—(1) Subject to sub-paragraphs (3) and (4), the condition is that either or both members of a joint-claim couple are entitled to [²⁸ . . .] [²⁴ a carer's allowance] under section 70 of the Benefits Act.

(2) [²⁸ . . .]

[²³ (3) Where a carer premium is awarded but—
- (a) the person in respect of whose care the [²⁴ carer's allowance] has been awarded dies: or
- (b) in any other case the member of the joint-claim couple in respect of whom a carer premium has been awarded ceases to be entitled [²⁸ . . .] to [²⁴ a carer's allowance],

the condition for the award of the premium shall be treated as satisfied for a period of eight weeks from the relevant date specified in sub-paragraph (3A) below.

(3A) The relevant date for the purposes of sub-paragraph (3) above shall be—
- (a) [²⁸ where sub-paragraph (3)(a) applies,] the Sunday following the death of the person in respect of whose care [²⁴ a carer's allowance] has been awarded or beginning with the date of death if the death occurred on a Sunday;
- (b) [²⁸ . . .]
- (c) in any other case, the date on which that member ceased to be entitled to [²⁴ a carer's allowance].]

(4) Where a member of a joint-claim couple who has been entitled to an invalid care allowance ceases to be entitled to that allowance and makes a claim for a jobseeker's allowance jointly with the other member of that couple, the condition for the award of the carer premium shall be treated as satisfied for a period of eight weeks from the date on which—
- [²³(a) the person in respect of whose care the [²⁴ carer's allowance] has been awarded dies;
- (b) [²⁸ . . .]
- (c) [²⁸ (c) in any other case, the person who has been entitled to a carer's allowance ceased to be entitled to that allowance.]

Member of a joint-claim couple in receipt of concessionary payments
   20K.—For the purpose of determining whether a premium is applicable to a joint-claim   3.505
couple under paragraphs 20H to 20J, any concessionary payment made to compensate a
person for the non-payment of any benefit mentioned in those paragraphs shall be treated as
if it were a payment of that benefit.

Person in receipt of benefit
   20L.—For the purposes of this Part of this Schedule, a member of a joint-claim couple shall   3.506
be regarded as being in receipt of any benefit if, and only if, it is paid in respect of him and shall
be so regarded only for any period in respect of which that benefit is paid.

PART IVB

Weekly Amounts of Premiums Specified in Part IVA   3.507

Premium	Amount
20M.—	(1) [⁵⁴ £152.90].
(1) Pensioner premium where one member of a joint-claim couple [⁴⁰ has attained the qualifying age for state pension credit] and the condition in paragraph 20E is satisfied.	
(2) Higher Pensioner Premium where one member of a joint-claim couple satisfies the condition in paragraph 20F.	(2) [⁵⁴ £152.90].
(3) Disability Premium where one member of a joint-claim couple satisfies the condition in paragraph [³³ 20G(1)].	(3) [⁵⁴ £50.05].
(4) Severe Disability Premium where one member of a joint-claim couple satisfies the condition in paragraph 20I(1)—	
(i) if there is someone in receipt of [²⁴ a carer's allowance] or if either member satisfies that condition only by virtue of paragraph [¹⁶ 20I(4)];	(4) (i) [⁵⁴ £67.30];
(ii) if no-one is in receipt of such an allowance.	(ii) [⁵⁴£152.90].
(5) Carer Premium.	(5) [⁵⁴ £37.70] in respect of each person who satisfied the condition specified in paragraph 20J.]
[¹⁶ (6) Enhanced disability premium where the conditions in paragraph 20IA are satisfied.	(6) [⁵⁴ £24.60]] where the conditions specified in paragraph 20IA are satisfied in respect of a member of a joint-claim couple.]

PART V

Rounding of Fractions

   21.—Where an income-based jobseeker's allowance is awarded for a period which is   3.508
not a complete benefit week and the applicable amount in respect of that period results in
an amount which includes a fraction of one penny that fraction shall be treated as one penny.

AMENDMENTS

   1. Jobseeker's Allowance (Amendment) Regulations 1996 (SI 1996/1516) reg.18
(October 7, 1996).
   2. Jobseeker's Allowance (Amendment) Regulations 1996 (SI 1996/1516) reg.20
and Sch. (October 7, 1996).

1105

3. Social Security and Child Support (Jobseeker's Allowance) (Miscellaneous Amendments) Regulations 1996 (SI 1996/2538) reg.2(11) (October 28, 1996).

4. Child Benefit, Child Support and Social Security (Miscellaneous Amendments) Regulations 1996 (SI 1996/1803) reg.44 (April 7, 1997).

5. Income-related Benefits and Jobseeker's Allowance (Personal Allowances for Children and Young Persons) (Amendment) Regulations 1996 (SI 1996/2545) reg.2 (April 7, 1997).

6. Income-related Benefits and Jobseeker's Allowance (Amendment) (No.2) Regulations 1997 (SI 1997/2197) reg.7(5) and (6)(b) (October 6, 1997).

7. Social Security Amendment (Lone Parents) Regulations 1998 (SI 1998/ 766) reg.14 (April 6, 1998).

8. Social Security (Welfare to Work) Regulations 1998 (SI 1998/2231) reg.14(3) (October 5, 1998).

9. Social Security Amendment (Personal Allowances for Children and Young Persons) Regulations 1999 (SI 1999/2555) reg.2(1)(b) and (2) (April 10, 2000).

10. Social Security and Child Support (Tax Credits) Consequential Amendments Regulations 1999 (SI 1999/2566) reg.2(2) and Sch.2 Pt III (October 5, 1999).

11. Social Security (Miscellaneous Amendments) Regulations 2000 (SI 2000/ 681) reg.4(3) (April 3, 2000)

12. Social Security Amendment (Employment Zones) Regulations 2000 (SI 2000/724) reg.4 (April 3, 2000)

13. Social Security Amendment (Personal Allowances for Children) Regulations 2000 (SI 2000/1993) reg.2 (October 23, 2000).

14. Jobseeker's Allowance (Joint Claims) Regulations 2000 (SI 2000/1978) reg.2(5) and Sch.2 para.53 (March 19, 2001).

15. Social Security Amendment (Breavement Benefits) Regulations 2000 (SI 2000/2239) reg.3(2) (April 9, 2001).

16. Social Security Amendment (Enhanced Disability Premium) Regulations 2000 (SI 2629) reg.5(c) (April 9, 2001).

17. Social Security Amendment (Joint Claims) Regulations 2001 (SI 2001/518) reg.2(7) (March 19, 2001).

18. Social Security Amendment (Bereavement Benefits) Regulations 2000 (SI 2000/2239) reg.3(2)(c) (April 9, 2001).

19. Social Security Amendment (Residential Care and Nursing Homes) Regulations 2001 (SI 2001/3767) reg.2 and Sch. Pt II para.18 (April 8, 2002).

20. Social Security (Loss of Benefit) (Consequential Amendments) Regulations 2002 (SI 2002/490) reg.2 (April 1, 2002).

21. Social Security Amendment (Residential Care and Nursing Homes) Regulations 2001 (SI 2001/3767) reg.2 and Sch. Pt II para.18 (as amended by Social Security Amendment (Residential Care and Nursing Homes) Regulations 2002 (SI 2002/398) reg.4(3)) (April 8, 2002).

22. Social Security Amendment (Personal Allowances for Children and Young Persons) Regulations 2002 (SI 2002/2019) reg.2 (October 14, 2002).

23. Social Security Amendment (Carer Premium) Regulations 2002 (SI 2002/2020) reg.3 (October 28, 2002).

24. Social Security (Miscellaneous Amendments) Regulations 2003 (SI 2003/ 511) reg.3(4) and (5) (April 1, 2003).

25. Social Security (Working Tax Credit and Child Tax Credit) (Consequential Amendments) Regulations 2003 (SI 2003/455) regs 1(9), 3 and Sch.2 para.20(b) (April 7, 2003).

26. Social Security (Working Tax Credit and Child Tax Credit) (Consequential Amendments) Regulations 2003 (SI 2003/455) regs 1(9), 3 and Sch.2 para.20(e) (April 7, 2003).

27. Social Security (Hospital In-Patients and Miscellaneous Amendments) Regulations 2003 (SI 2003/1195) reg.6 (May 21, 2003).

28. Social Security (Miscellaneous Amendments) (No.2) Regulations 2003 (SI 2003/2279) reg.3(3) (October 1, 2003).

29. Social Security (Removal of Residential Allowance and Miscellaneous Amendments) Regulations 2003 (SI 2003/1121) reg.4 and Sch.2 para.9 (October 6, 2003).

30. Social Security (Working Tax Credit and Child Tax Credit) (Consequential Amendments) Regulations 2003 (SI 2003/455) reg.3 and Sch.2 para.20 (April 6, 2004, except in "transitional cases" and see further the note to regs 83 and to 17 of the Income Support Regulations).

31. Civil Partnership (Pensions, Social Security and Child Support) (Consequential, etc. Provisions) Order 2005 (SI 2005/2877) art.2(3) and Sch.3 para.26(11) (December 5, 2005).

32. Social Security (Miscellaneous Amendments) (No.4) Regulations 2006 (SI 2006/2378) reg.13(10) (October 1, 2006).

33. Social Security (Miscellaneous Amendments) Regulations 2007 (SI 2007/719) reg.3(8) (April 9, 2007). As it relates to paras 15(2)(a) and 16, the amendment only affects "transitional cases". See further the note to reg.17 of the Income Support Regulations and the commentary below.

34. Social Security (Miscellaneous Amendments) (No.5) Regulations 2007 (SI 2007/2618) reg.2 and Sch. (October 1, 2007).

35. Social Security (Miscellaneous Amendments) Regulations 2008 (SI 2008/698) reg.4(14) (April 14, 2008).

36. Employment and Support Allowance (Consequential Provisions) (No.2) Regulations 2008 (SI 2008/1554) reg.3(1) and (24) (October 27, 2008).

37. Social Security (Miscellaneous Amendments) Regulations 2009 (SI 2009/583) reg.4(1) and (3) (April 6, 2009).

38. Social Security (Students and Miscellaneous Amendments) Regulations 2009 (SI 2009/1575) reg.3 (August 1, 2009).

39. Social Security (Loss of Benefit) Amendment Regulations 2010 (SI 2010/1160) reg.11(1) and (3) (April 1, 2010).

40. Social Security (Equalisation of State Pension Age) Regulations 2009 (SI 2009/1488) reg.13 (April 6, 2010).

41. Employment and Support Allowance (Transitional Provisions, Housing Benefit and Council Tax Benefit) (Existing Awards) (No.2) Regulations 2010 (SI 2010/1907) reg.26(1) and Sch.4 para.1A(3) (as amended by the Employment and Support Allowance (Transitional Provisions, Housing Benefit and Council Tax Benefit) (Existing Awards) (No.2) (Amendment) Regulations 2010 (SI 2010/2430) reg.15) (November 1, 2010).

42. Social Security (Miscellaneous Amendments) Regulations 2011 (SI 2011/674) reg.7(7) (April 11, 2011).

43. Social Security Benefits Up-rating Order 2012 (SI 2012/780) art.25(3) and Sch.13 (April 9, 2012).

44. Social Security Benefits Up-rating Order 2012 (SI 2012/780) art.25(5) and Sch.14 (April 9, 2012).

45. Social Security Benefits Up-rating Order 2012 (SI 2012/780) art.25(6) and Sch.15 (April 9, 2012).

46. Personal Independence Payment (Supplementary Provisions and Consequential Amendments) Regulations 2013 (SI 2013/388) reg.8 and Sch. para.16(1) and (7) (April 8, 2013).

47. Armed Forces and Reserve Forces Compensation Scheme (Consequential Provisions: Subordinate Legislation) Order 2013 (SI 2013/591) art.7 and Sch. para.10(1) and (7) (April 8, 2013).

48. Universal Credit and Miscellaneous Amendments (No.2) Regulations 2014 (SI 2014/2888) reg.3(3) (November 26, 2014).

49. Welfare Benefits Up-rating Order 2015 (SI 2015/30) art.9 and Sch.3 (April 6, 2015).

50. Universal Credit and Miscellaneous Amendments Regulations 2015 (SI 2015/1754) reg.15 (October 28, 2015).

51. Universal Credit and Jobseeker's Allowance (Miscellaneous Amendments) Regulations 2018 (SI 2018/1129) reg.2 (November 28, 2018).

52. Social Security Benefits Up-rating Order 2021 (SI 2021/0162) art 27(1) and (3)(a) and Sch.8 (April 12, 2021).

53 Social Security Benefits Up-rating Order 2021 (SI 2021/0162) art 27(1) and (5) and Sch.9 (April 12, 2021).

54 Social Security Benefits Up-rating Order 2021 (SI 2021/0162) art 27(1) and (6) and Sch.10 (April 12, 2021).

DEFINITIONS

"attendance allowance"—see reg.1(3).
"the Benefits Act"—see Jobseekers Act s.35(1).
"child"—*ibid.*
"claimant"—*ibid.*
"couple"—see reg.1(3).
"disability living allowance"—*ibid.*
"family"—see Jobseekers Act s.35(1).
"invalid carriage or other vehicle"—see reg.1(3).
"lone parent"—*ibid.*
"mobility supplement"—*ibid.*
"non-dependent"—see reg.2.
"partner"—see reg.1(3).
"polygamous marriage"—*ibid.*
"preserved right"—*ibid.*
"single claimant"—*ibid.*
"welfare to work beneficiary"—*ibid.*
"young person"—see reg.76.

GENERAL NOTE

3.509   Here the details of the personal allowances and premiums for income-based JSA are set out. They follow a similar pattern to those for income support. But there are some differences. These are in relation to the qualifying conditions for the different rates of personal allowance paid where one or both members of a couple are under 18 (see para.1(3)) and the conditions for the pensioner and disability premiums.

See the notes to Sch.2 to the Income Support Regulations for discussion of the personal allowances and premiums where the rules are the same for JSA and income support. The note below just refers to the main differences.

Up-rating

3.510   Until April 6, 2015, the amounts specified in para.1 were up-rated each year under s.150(1)(k) SSAA 1992. However, on March 16, 2016, s.11 and Sch.1 of the Welfare Reform and Work Act 2016 came into force. As a result, the age-related amounts of contribution-based JSA and all the amounts specified in para.1 were frozen at their 2015/16 levels for four tax years and were not up-rated again until April 6, 2020. They were then uprated again from April 12, 2021 to the rates shown in the text.

The amounts of the pensioner premiums and higher pensioner premium in paras 20 and 20M continued to be up-rated as a consequence of the so-called "triple lock" under which the state pension increases each year by the higher of inflation, the increase in average earnings, or 2.5 per cent.

The other amounts in paras 20 and 20M were not subject to the four-year freeze. They were not up-rated for 2016/17 as the Secretary of State decided that they had maintained their value in relation to prices as measured by the Consumer Prices Index over the 12-month period ending September 2015 (which had showed negative inflation of 0.1 per cent): see para.4.2 of the Explanatory Memorandum to SI 2016/230. However, they were uprated for 2017/18, for 2018/19, for 2019/20, for 2020/21 and, to the rates shown in the text, for 2021/22.

Paragraph 1

The conditions for the lower and higher rate of personal allowance for 16- or 17-year-olds who are single or lone parents match those that applied under income support before October 7, 1996 (see the 1996 edition of J. Mesher and P. Wood, *Income-related Benefits: the Legislation*). Similarly JSA, like income support, is paid at a lower rate for single people who are under 25.

But in relation to couples there are some additional categories so that para.1(3) is even more complex than the pre-October 7, 1996 form of para.1(3) of Sch.2 to the Income Support Regulations. See heads (a)(iii), (a)(vii), (f)(iii), (g)(iii) and (h)(iii) where the fact that the other member of the couple would or would not be eligible for income support is an additional means of the couple qualifying or not qualifying for a higher rate. For an example of the potential unfairness caused by this see *CJSA/3009/2006* (where, at para.10, the Commissioner rejects an argument similar to the tentative suggestion in previous editions that the "and" at the end of head (f)(ii) should perhaps be read as if it were an "or"). Note also the new categories in heads (a)(iv) and (d).

3.511

Paragraphs 2–4

For a discussion of when the provisions abolishing JSA personal allowances for children and young persons, and the family premium, come into effect—and the "transitional cases" thereby created—see the notes to reg.83 and to reg.17 of the Income Support Regulations. In transitional cases, the personal allowance for a child or young person was increased to £68.60, and the family premium was increased to £17.65, from the beginning of the first benefit week after April 12, 2021 by art.27(3)(b) and (4) of the Social Security Benefits Uprating Order 2021 (SI 2021/162).

3.512

Paragraph 9A

This paragraph established a bereavement premium with effect from April 9, 2001. By reg.6 of the Social Security Amendment (Bereavement Benefits) Regulations 2000 (SI 2000/2239), it ceased to have effect from April 10, 2006.

3.513

Paragraphs 10 and 11

The conditions for qualifying for a pensioner premium (for the rates see para.20; the premiums are paid at the same rate as the pensioner premiums for income support) differ from the income support rules to reflect the fact that income support claimants must be under 60, whereas JSA claimants must be below pensionable age (which for men is 65) (cf. s.124(1)(aa) of the Contributions and Benefits Act 1992 and s.1(2)(h) of the Jobseekers Act 1995). For the premium under para.10 to be payable the claimant must be 60 or over, or have a partner aged 60–74. If his partner is aged 75–79 the claimant will qualify for the premium under para.11.

3.514

Paragraphs 12–14

Similarly, the rules for the higher pensioner and disability premiums differ from those for income support to reflect the fact that to be entitled to JSA the claimant has to be capable of work (s.1(2)(f) of the Jobseekers Act). Thus severe disablement allowance and long-term incapacity benefit (or short-term incapacity benefit at the higher rate payable to people who are terminally ill) remain qualifying benefits for the purpose of these premiums but only where it is the claimant's partner that receives them (see para.14(1)(b) and (d)). See also para.14(1)(g) (and note the differences from para.12(1)(c) of the Income Support Regulations). In addition, there is (obviously) no equivalent to para.12(1)(b) of Sch.2 to the Income Support Regulations (claimant incapable of work for at least 52 weeks or 28 weeks in the case of terminal illness).

3.515

Paragraph 15

Note the saving provision in sub-para.(8). Regulations 4–6 of the Income Support (General) Amendment (No.6) Regulations 1991 are on p.1749.

3.516

Paragraph 15A

In transitional cases (as to which see the note to reg.17 of the Income Support Regulations), the enhanced disability premium is also available for children who

3.517

satisfy the conditions in para.15A. From the first benefit week after April 12, 2021, the weekly amount of the premium is £26.67 for each child or young person who meets the conditions: see Social Security Benefits Up-rating Order 2021 (SI 2021/162), art.27(5) and Sch.9.

Paragraph 16

3.518   Except in transitional cases (as to which, see the note to reg.17 of the Income Support Regulations), the disabled child premium was abolished with effect from April 6, 2004. For details of the position before that date see p.496 of Vol.II of the 2003 edition. In transitional cases the disabled child premium was increased to £65.94 from the beginning of the first benefit week after April 12, 2021 by art.27(5) of, and Sch.9 to, the Social Security Benefits Uprating Order 2021 (SI 2021/162).

The transitional text of para.16 (as substituted with effect from April 9, 2007 by reg.3(8)(f) of SI 2007/719 and amended with effect from April 11, 2011 by reg.7(6) of SI 2011/674), and with effect from April 8, 2013 by reg.8 and Sch. para.16(7)(e) of SI 2013/388 and reg.7 and Sch. para.10(7)(e) of SI 2013/591, and with effect from November 26, 2014 by reg.3(3)(a)(iii) of SI 2014/2888) is as follows:

"Disabled Child Premium

16.—(1) Subject to sub-paragraph (2), the condition is that where the child or young person for whom the claimant or a partner of his is responsible and who is a member of the claimant's household is—

(a) in receipt of disability living allowance or is no longer in receipt of that allowance because he is a patient provided that the child or young person continues to be a member of the family;

[(aa) a young person who is in receipt of personal independence payment or who would, but for regulations made under section 86(1) (hospital in-patients) of the 2012 Act, be so in receipt, provided that the young person continues to be a member of the family;]

[(ab) a young person who is in receipt of armed forces independence payment;]

(b) [severely sight impaired or blind or treated as severely sight impaired or blind] within the meaning of paragraph 14(1)(h) and (2). [; or

(c) a child or young person in respect of whom section 145A of the Benefits Act (entitlement after death of child or qualifying young person) applies for the purposes of entitlement to child benefit but only for the period prescribed under that section, and in respect of whom a disabled child premium was included in the claimant's applicable amount immediately before the death of that child or young person, or ceased to be included in the claimant's applicable amount because of that child or young person's death.]

(2) The condition [in sub-paragraph (1)(a) [, (aa)] [, (ab)] or (b)] is not satisfied in respect of a child or young person—

(a) whose capital, if calculated in accordance with Part 8 of these Regulations in like manner as for the claimant, except as provided in regulation 106(1), would exceed £3,000; or

(b) who is a long-term patient."

SCHEDULE 2   **Regulations 83(f) and 84(1)(g)**

HOUSING COSTS

Housing costs

3.519   **1.**—(1) Subject to the following provisions of this Schedule, the housing costs applicable to a claimant are those costs—

(a) which he or, where he is a member of a family, he or any member of that family is, in accordance with paragraph 2, liable to meet in respect of the dwelling occupied as the home which he or any other member of his family is treated as occupying; and

(b) which qualify [⁷² under paragraph 16].

(2) In this Schedule—

"housing costs" means those costs to which sub-paragraph (1) refers;
[⁶⁶ . . .]

[^{66}...]
[^{72}...]

(3) For the purposes of this Schedule a disabled person is a person—

    (a) in respect of whom a disability premium, a disabled child premium, a pensioner premium where the claimant's partner has attained the age of 75 or a higher pensioner premium is included in his applicable amount or the applicable amount of a person living with him; or

    (b) who, had he in fact been entitled to a jobseeker's allowance or to income support, would have had included in his applicable amount a disability premium, a disabled child premium, a pensioner premium where the claimant's partner has attained the age of 75 or a higher pensioner premium; or

    (c) who satisfies the requirements of paragraph 9A of Schedule 2 to the Income Support [^{1}Regulations] (pensioner premium for person aged 75 or over) [^{32}; [^{42}...]

    (d) who is disabled or severely disabled for the purposes of section 9(6) (maximum rate) of the Tax Credits Act 2002] [^{42} or

[^{57} (e) who-

        (i) is in receipt of an employment and support allowance which includes an amount under section 2(2) [^{67}...] or 4(4) [^{67}...]of the Welfare Reform Act ([^{67} component]) [^{70} or who is a member of the work-related activity group]; or

        (ii) would be entitled to an employment and support allowance [^{67}...], but for the application of section 1A of the Act (duration of contributory allowance)]] [^{62}; or

    (f) who is entitled to an award of universal credit [^{68} and has limited capability for work or limited capability for work and work-related activity as construed in accordance with regulations 39 and 40 of the Universal Credit Regulations 2013.]].

(4) For the purposes of sub-paragraph (3), a person shall not cease to be a disabled person on account of his being disqualified for receiving benefit or treated as capable of work by virtue of the operation of section 171E of the Benefits Act (incapacity for work, disqualification etc.) [^{42} or disqualified for receiving employment and support allowance or treated as not having limited capability for work in accordance with regulations made under section 18 of the Welfare Reform Act (disqualification)].

[^{5} [^{37} Previous entitlement to income support [^{42}, income-related employment and support allowance] or state pension credit]

1A.—(1) Where a claimant or his partner was in receipt of or was treated as being in receipt of income support [^{42} or income-related employment and support allowance] not more than 12 weeks before one of them becomes entitled to income-based jobseeker's allowance or, where the claimant or his partner is a person to whom paragraph 13(2) or (10) (linking rules) refers, not more than 26 weeks before becoming so entitled and—   **3.520**

    (a) the applicable amount for income support [^{42} or income-related employment and support allowance] included an amount in respect of housing costs [^{72} under paragraph 17 of Schedule 3] to the Income Support Regulations [^{41} or [^{72} under paragraph 18 of Schedule 6] to the Employment and Support Allowance Regulations]; and

    (b) the circumstances affecting the calculation of those housing costs remain unchanged since the last calculation of those costs,

the applicable amount in respect of housing costs for income-based jobseeker's allowance shall be the applicable amount in respect of those costs current when entitlement to income support [^{42} or income-related employment and support allowance] was last determined.

[^{37} (1ZA) Where a claimant or his partner was in receipt of state pension credit not more than 12 weeks before one of them becomes entitled to income-based jobseeker's allowance or, where the claimant or his partner is a person to whom paragraph 13(2) or (10) (linking rules) refers, not more than 26 weeks before becoming so entitled, and—

    (a) the appropriate minimum guarantee included an amount in respect of housing costs [^{72} under paragraph 13 of Schedule II] to the State Pension Credit Regulations 2002; and

    (b) the circumstances affecting the calculation of those housing costs remain unchanged since the last calculation of those costs,

the applicable amount in respect of housing costs for income-based jobseeker's allowance shall be the amount applicable in respect of those costs current when entitlement to state pension credit was last determined.]

[^{16} (1A) Where either member of a joint-claim couple was in receipt of or treated as being in receipt of income support [^{41} or income-related employment and support allowance] not more than 12 weeks before the couple becomes entitled to a joint-claim jobseeker's allowance, or, where either member is a person to whom paragraph 13(2) or (10) (linking rules) refers, not more than 26 weeks before becoming so entitled and—

(a) the applicable amount for income support [⁴¹ or income-related employment and support allowance] included an amount in respect of housing costs [⁷² under paragraph 17 of Schedule 3] to the Income Support Regulations [⁴² or [⁷² under paragraph 18 of Schedule 6] to the Employment and Support Allowance Regulations]; and

(b) the circumstances affecting the calculation of those housing costs remain unchanged since the last calculation of those costs,

the applicable amount in respect of housing costs for joint-claim jobseeker's allowance shall be the applicable amount in respect of those costs current when entitlement to income support [⁴¹ or income-related employment and support allowance] was last determined.]

[³⁷ (1B) Where either member of a joint-claim couple was in receipt of state pension credit not more than 12 weeks before the couple becomes entitled to a joint-claim jobseeker's allowance, or, where either member is a person to whom paragraph 13(2) or (10) (linking rules) refers, not more than 26 weeks before becoming so entitled, and—

(a) the appropriate minimum guarantee included an amount in respect of housing costs [⁷² under paragraph 13 of Schedule II] to the State Pension Credit Regulations 2002; and

(b) the circumstances affecting the calculation of those housing costs remain unchanged since the last calculation of those costs,

the applicable amount in respect of housing costs for joint-claim jobseeker's allowance shall be the amount applicable in respect of those costs current when entitlement to state pension credit was last determined.]

(2) Where, in the period since housing costs were last calculated for income support [⁴¹ or income-related employment and support allowance] [³⁷ or (as the case may be) state pension credit], there has been a change of circumstances, other than a reduction in the amount of an outstanding loan, which increases or reduces those costs, the amount to be met under this Schedule shall, for the purposes of the claim for income-based jobseeker's allowance, be recalculated so as to take account of that change.]

Circumstances in which a person is liable to meet housing costs

3.521   **2.**—(1) A person is liable to meet housing costs where—

(a) the liability falls upon him or his partner [¹⁶ or, where that person is a member of a joint-claim couple, the other member of that couple,] but not where the liability is to a member of the same household as the person on whom the liability falls;

(b) because the person liable to meet the housing costs [¹is not meeting them], the claimant has to meet those costs in order to continue to live in the dwelling occupied as the home and it is reasonable in all the circumstances to treat the claimant as liable to meet those costs;

(c) he in practice shares the housing costs with other members of the household none of whom are close relatives either of the claimant or his partner, [¹⁶ or, where that person is a member of a joint-claim couple, the other member of that couple,] and—

(i) one or more of those members is liable to meet those costs, and

(ii) it is reasonable in the circumstances to treat him as sharing responsibility.

(2) Where any one or more, but not all, members of the claimant's family are affected by a trade dispute, the housing costs shall be treated as wholly the responsibility of those members of the family not so affected.

Circumstances in which a person is to be treated as occupying a dwelling as his home

3.522   **3.**—(1) Subject to the following provisions of this paragraph, a person shall be treated as occupying as his home the dwelling normally occupied as his home by himself or, if he is a member of a family, by himself and his family and he shall not be treated as occupying any other dwelling as his home.

(2) In determining whether a dwelling is the dwelling normally occupied as the claimant's home for the purposes of sub-paragraph (1) regard shall be had to any other dwelling occupied by the claimant or by him and his family whether or not that other dwelling is in Great Britain.

(3) Subject to sub-paragraph (4), where a single claimant or a lone parent is a full-time student or is on a training course and is liable to make payments (including payments of mortgage interest or, in Scotland, payments under heritable securities or, in either case, analogous payments) in respect of either (but not both) the dwelling which he occupies for the purpose of attending his course of study or his training course or, as the case may be, the dwelling which he occupies when not attending his course, he shall be treated as occupying as his home the dwelling in respect of which he is liable to make payments.

(4) A full-time student shall not be treated as occupying a dwelling as his home for any week

of absence from it, other than an absence occasioned by the need to enter hospital for treatment, outside the period of study, if the main purpose of his occupation during the period of study would be to facilitate attendance on his course.

(5) Where a claimant has been required to move into temporary accommodation by reason of essential repairs being carried out to the dwelling normally occupied as his home and he is liable to make payments (including payments of mortgage interest or, in Scotland, payments under heritable securities or, in either case, analogous payments) in respect of either (but not both) the dwelling normally occupied or the temporary accommodation, he shall be treated as occupying as his home the dwelling in respect of which he is liable to make those payments.

(6) Where a person is liable to make payments in respect of two (but not more than two) dwellings, he shall be treated as occupying both dwellings as his home only—

(a) where he has left and remains absent from the former dwelling occupied as the home through fear of violence in that dwelling or by a former member of his family and it is reasonable that housing costs should be met in respect of both his former dwelling and his present dwelling occupied as the home; or

(b) in the case of a couple or a member of a polygamous marriage where a partner is a full-time student or is on a training course and it is unavoidable that he or they should occupy two separate dwellings and reasonable that housing costs should be met in respect of both dwellings; or

(c) in the case where a person has moved into a new dwelling occupied as the home, except where sub-paragraph (5) applies, for a period not exceeding four benefit weeks [36 from the first day of the benefit week in which the move occurs] if his liability to make payments in respect of two dwellings is unavoidable.

(7) Where—

(a) a person has moved into a dwelling and was liable to make payments in respect of that dwelling before moving in; and

(b) he had claimed a jobseeker's allowance before moving in and either that claim has not yet been determined or it has been determined but an amount has not been included under this Schedule and if the claim has been refused a further claim has been made within four weeks of the date on which the claimant moved into the new dwelling occupied as the home; and

(c) the delay in moving into the dwelling in respect of which there was liability to make payments before moving in was reasonable and—

(i) that delay was necessary in order to adapt the dwelling to meet the disablement needs of the claimant or any member of his family; or

[33 (ii) the move was delayed pending [58 local welfare provision or] the outcome of an application under Part 8 of the Benefits Act for a social fund payment to meet a need arising out of the move or in connection with setting up the home in the dwelling, and—

(aa) a member of the claimant's family is aged five or under,

(bb) the claimant's applicable amount includes a premium under paragraph 10, 11, 12, 13, 15 or 16 of Schedule 1 (applicable amounts), or

(cc) a child tax credit is paid for a member of the claimant's family who is disabled or severely disabled for the purposes of section 9(6) (maximum rate) of the Tax Credits Act 2002; or]

(iii) the person became liable to make payments in respect of the dwelling while he was a patient or was in residential accommodation,

he shall be treated as occupying the dwelling as his home for any period not exceeding four weeks immediately prior to the date on which he moved into the dwelling and in respect of which he was liable to make payments.

(8) This sub-paragraph applies to a person who enters residential accommodation—

(a) for the purpose of ascertaining whether the accommodation suits his needs; and

(b) with the intention of returning to the dwelling which he normally occupies as his home should, in the event, the residential accommodation prove not to suit his needs,

and while in the accommodation, the part of the dwelling which he normally occupies as his home is not let, or as the case may be, sub-let to another person.

(9) A person to whom sub-paragraph (8) applies shall be treated as occupying the dwelling he normally occupies as his home during any period (commencing with the day he enters the accommodation) not exceeding 13 weeks in which the person is resident in the accommodation, but only in so far as the total absence from the dwelling does not exceed 52 weeks.

(10) A person, other than a person to whom sub-paragraph (11) applies, shall be treated as occupying a dwelling as his home throughout any period of absence not exceeding 13 weeks, if, and only if—

(a) he intends to return to occupy the dwelling as his home; and

(b) the part of the dwelling normally occupied by him has not been let or, as the case may be, sub-let to another person; and

(c) the period of absence is unlikely to exceed 13 weeks.

(11) This sub-paragraph applies to a person whose absence from the dwelling he normally occupies as his home is temporary and—

(a) he intends to return to occupy the dwelling as his home; and

(b) while the part of the dwelling which is normally occupied by him has not been let or, as the case may be, sub-let; and

(c) he is—

[²⁷ (i) required, as a condition of bail, to reside—

(aa) in a dwelling, other than the dwelling he occupies as his home; or

(bb) in premises approved under [⁴⁵ section 13 of the Offender Management Act 2007], or]

(ii) resident in a hospital or similar institution as a patient and is treated under regulation 55 as capable of work, or

(iii) undergoing or, as the case may be, his partner or his dependent child is undergoing, in the United Kingdom or elsewhere, medical treatment, or medically approved convalescence, in accommodation other than residential accommodation, or

(iv) following, in the United Kingdom or elsewhere, a training course, or

(v) undertaking medically approved care of a person residing in the United Kingdom or elsewhere, or

(vi) undertaking the care of a child whose parent or guardian is temporarily absent from the dwelling normally occupied by that parent or guardian for the purpose of receiving medically approved care or medical treatment, or

(vii) a person who is, whether in the United Kingdom or elsewhere, receiving medically approved care provided in accommodation other than residential accommodation, or

(viii) a full-time student to whom sub-paragraph (3) or (6)(b) does not apply, or

(ix) a person other than a person to whom sub-paragraph (8) applies, who is receiving care provided in residential accommodation, or

(x) a person to whom sub-paragraph (6)(a) does not apply and who has left the dwelling he occupies as his home through fear of violence in that dwelling or by a person who was formerly a member of [¹ his] family, and

(d) the period of his absence is unlikely to exceed a period of 52 weeks or, in exceptional circumstances, is unlikely substantially to exceed that period.

(12) A person to whom sub-paragraph (11) applies is to be treated as occupying the dwelling he normally occupies as his home during any period of absence not exceeding 52 weeks beginning with the first day of that absence.

(13) In this paragraph—

(a) "medically approved" means certified by a registered medical practitioner;

(b) "patient" means a person who is undergoing medical or other treatment as an in-patient in a hospital or similar institution;

[²⁹ (c) "residential accommodation" means accommodation which is a care home, an Abbeyfield Home or an independent hospital;]

(d) "training course" means such a course of training or institution provided wholly or partly by or on behalf of or in pursuance of arrangements made with, or approved by or on behalf of, [⁴⁷ Skills Development Scotland,] Scottish Enterprise, Highlands and Islands Enterprise, a government department or the Secretary of State.

Housing costs not met

3.523   **4.**—(1) No amount may be met under the provisions of this Schedule—

(a) in respect of housing benefit expenditure; or

(b) where [¹⁶ a claimant] is [²⁹ living in a care home, an Abbeyfield Home or an independent hospital except where he is living in such a home or hospital] during a temporary absence from the dwelling he occupies as his home and in so far as they relate to temporary absences, the provisions of paragraph 3(8) to (12) apply to him during that absence.

(2)–(12) [⁷² …]

Apportionment of housing costs

3.524   **5.**—(1) Where the dwelling occupied as the home is a composite hereditament and—

(a) before 1st April 1990 for the purposes of section 48(5) of the General Rate Act 1967 (reduction of rates on dwellings), it appeared to a rating authority or it was determined in pursuance of sub-section (6) of section 48 of that Act that the hereditament, including the dwelling occupied as the home, was a mixed hereditament and that only a proportion of the rateable value of the hereditament was attributable to use for the purpose of a private dwelling; or

(b) in Scotland, before 1st April 1989 an assessor acting pursuant to section 45(1) of the Water (Scotland) Act 1980 (provision as to valuation roll) has apportioned the net annual value of the premises including the dwelling occupied as the home between the part occupied as a dwelling and the remainder,

the amounts applicable under this Schedule shall be such proportion of the amounts applicable in respect of the hereditament or premises as a whole as is equal to the proportion of the rateable value of the hereditament attributable to the part of the hereditament used for the purposes of a private tenancy or, in Scotland, the proportion of the net annual value of the premises apportioned to the part occupied as a dwelling house.

(2) Subject to sub-paragraph (1) and the following provisions of this paragraph, where the dwelling occupied as the home is a composite hereditament, the amount applicable under this Schedule shall be the relevant fraction of the amount which would otherwise be applicable under this Schedule in respect of the dwelling occupied as the home.

(3) For the purposes of sub-paragraph (2), the relevant fraction shall be obtained in accordance with the formula—

$$\frac{A}{A + B}$$

where—

"A" is the current market value of the claimant's interest in that part of the composite hereditament which is domestic property within the meaning of section 66 of the Act of 1988;

"B" is the current market value of the claimant's interest in that part of the composite hereditament which is not domestic property within that section.

(4) In this paragraph—

"composite hereditament" means—
   (a) as respects England and Wales, any hereditament which is shown as a composite hereditament in a local non-domestic rating list;
   (b) as respects Scotland, any lands and heritages entered in the valuation roll which are part residential subjects within the meaning of section 26(1) of the Act of 1987;

"local non-domestic rating list" means a list compiled and maintained under section 41(1) of the Act of 1988;
"the Act of 1987" means the Abolition of Domestic Rates Etc. (Scotland) Act 1987;
"the Act of 1988" means the Local Government Finance Act 1988.

(5) Where responsibility for expenditure which relates to housing costs met under this Schedule is shared, the amounts applicable shall be calculated by reference to the appropriate proportion of that expenditure for which the claimant is responsible.

Existing housing costs
   6.—[^{66} . . .]   3.525

[^{66} Housing Costs]
   7.—(1) Subject to the provisions of this Schedule, the [^{66} . . .] housing costs to be met in   3.526
any particular case are—
   (a) where the claimant has been entitled to a jobseeker's allowance for a continuous period of 39 weeks or more, an amount—
      (i) [^{72} ...]
      (ii) equal to any payments which qualify under paragraph 16(1)(a) to (c);
   (b) in any other case, nil.
   (2) [^{72} . . .]
   [^{5} (2A)[^{72} ...]]
   [^{16}(2B) [^{72} . . .]]
   (3) [^{66} . . .]
   (4) [^{66} . . .]
   (5) [^{66} . . .]
   (6) [^{66} . . .]
   (7) [^{66} . . .]

General exclusions from [⁶⁶ paragraph 7]

3.527   **8.**—(1) [⁶⁶ Paragraph] shall not apply where—
   (a) the claimant or his partner [¹⁶ or either member of a joint-claim couple] [⁴⁹ has attained the qualifying age for state pension credit];
   (b) the housing costs are payments—
      (i)   under a co-ownership agreement;
      (ii) under or relating to a tenancy or licence of a Crown tenant; or
      (iii) where the dwelling occupied as the home is a tent, in respect of the tent and the site on which it stands.
   (2) In a case falling within sub-paragraph (1), the housing costs to be met are—
   (a) where head (a) of sub-paragraph (1) applies, an amount—
      (i)   [⁷² ...]
      (ii) equal to the payments which qualify under paragraph 16;
   (b) where head (b) of sub-paragraph (1) applies, an amount equal to the payments which qualify under paragraph 16(1)(d) to (f).

[¹⁸ The calculation for loans

3.528   **9.**—[⁷² ...]

General provisions applying to [⁶⁶ . . .] housing costs

3.529   **10.**—[⁷² . . .]

The standard rate

3.530   **11.**— [⁷² . . .]

Excessive housing costs

3.531   **12.**—[⁷² . . .]

Linking rule

3.532   **13.**—(1) Subject to [¹⁶ [⁵⁴ sub-paragraph (2A)]] for the [¹purposes] of this Schedule—
   (a) a person shall be treated as being in receipt of a jobseeker's allowance during the following periods—
      (i)   any period in respect of which it was subsequently held, on appeal or [¹¹revision], that he was so entitled to a jobseeker's allowance; and
      (ii) any period of 12 weeks or less [¹³ or, as the case may be, 52 weeks or less,] in respect of which he was not in receipt of a jobseeker's allowance and which fell immediately between periods in respect of which
      [²(aa) he was, or was treated as being, in receipt of a jobseeker's allowance,
         (bb) he was treated as entitled to a jobseeker's allowance for the purposes of sub-paragraphs (5), (6) and (7), or
         (cc) (i) above applies;]
   (b) a person shall be treated as not being in receipt of a jobseeker's allowance during any period other than a period to which (a)(ii) above applies in respect of which it is subsequently held on appeal [¹¹, revision or supersession] that he was not so entitled;
   (c) where—
      (i)   the claimant was a member of a couple or a polygamous marriage; and
      (ii) his partner was, in respect of a past period, in receipt of a jobseeker's allowance for himself and the claimant; and
      (iii) the claimant is no longer a member of that couple or polygamous marriage; and
      (iv) the claimant made his claim for a jobseeker's allowance within twelve weeks [¹³ or, as the case may be, 52 weeks,] of ceasing to be a member of that couple or polygamous marriage,
      he shall be treated as having been in receipt of a jobseeker's allowance for the same period as his former partner had been or had been treated, for the purposes of this Schedule, as having been;
   (d) where the claimant's partner's applicable amount was determined in accordance with paragraph 1(1) (single claimant) or paragraph 1(2) (lone parent) of Schedule 1 (applicable amounts) in respect of a past period, provided that the claim was made within twelve weeks [¹³ or, as the case may be, 52 weeks,] of the claimant and his partner becoming one of a couple or polygamous marriage, the claimant shall be treated as having been in receipt of a jobseeker's allowance for the same period as his partner had been or had been treated, for the purposes of this Schedule, as having been;
   [¹⁶(dd) where the applicable amount of a member of a joint-claim couple was determined in

accordance with paragraph 1(1) (single claimant) or paragraph 1(2) (lone parent) of Schedule 1 (applicable amounts) in respect of a past period, provided that the claim was made within twelve weeks of the joint-claimant becoming a member of the joint-claim couple, the joint-claim couple shall be treated as having been in receipt of a jobseeker's allowance for the same period as that member of the joint-claim couple had been treated, for the purposes of this Schedule, as having been;]

(e) where the claimant is a member of a couple or a polygamous marriage and his partner was, in respect of a past period, in receipt of a jobseeker's allowance for himself and the claimant, and the claimant has begun to receive a jobseeker's allowance as a result of an election by the members of the couple or polygamous marriage, he shall be treated as having been in receipt of a jobseeker's allowance for the same period as his partner had been or had been treated, for the purposes of this Schedule, as having been;

[6(ee) where the claimant—

  (i) is a member of a couple or a polygamous marriage and the claimant's partner was, immediately before the participation by any member of that couple or polygamous marriage in an employment programme specified in regulation 75(1)(a)(ii) [17, in the Intensive Activity Period specified in regulation 75(1) (a)(iv) [48 or in the Flexible New Deal] [41 . . .]], in receipt of income-based jobseeker's allowance and his applicable amount included an amount for the couple or for the partners of the polygamous marriage; and

  (ii) has, immediately after that participation in that programme, begun to receive income-based jobseeker's allowance as a result of an election under regulation 4(3B) of the Claims and Payments Regulations by the members of the couple or polygamous marriage,

the claimant shall be treated as having been in receipt of a jobseeker's allowance for the same period as his partner had been or had been treated, for the purposes of this Schedule, as having been;]

(f) where—

  (i) the claimant was a member of a family of a person (not being a former partner) entitled to a jobseeker's allowance and at least one other member of that family was a child or young person; and

  (ii) the claimant becomes a member of another family which includes that child or young person; and

  (iii) the claimant made his claim for a jobseeker's allowance within 12 weeks [13 or, as the case may be, 52 weeks,] of the date on which the person entitled to a jobseeker's allowance mentioned in head (i) above ceased to be so entitled,

the claimant shall be treated as being in receipt of a jobseeker's allowance for the same period as that person had been or had been treated, for the purposes of this Schedule, as having been.

(2) [54 . . .]

[16(2A) Where a joint-claim jobseeker's allowance is payable to one member of a joint-claim couple in accordance with section 3B, both members of the couple shall be treated as receiving, or having received, a jobseeker's allowance for the purpose of this paragraph.

(2B) Where both joint-claimants claiming a jobseeker's allowance in respect of themselves have not been in receipt of a jobseeker's allowance for a period before they became a joint-claim couple, sub-paragraph (1) shall have effect in respect of that couple in relation to the period which is most favourable to the couple for the purposes of this Schedule.]

[4(3) For the purposes of this Schedule, where a claimant has ceased to be entitled to a jobseeker's allowance because he or his partner [16 or, where a claimant is a member of a joint-claim couple, the other member of that couple] is participating in arrangements for training made under section 2 of the Employment and Training Act 1973 or attending a course at an employment rehabilitation centre established under that section [45 or under the Enterprise and New Towns (Scotland) Act 1990], he shall be treated as if he had been in receipt of a jobseeker's allowance for the period during which he or his partner [16 or, where a claimant is a member of a joint-claim couple, the other member of that couple] was participating in such a course.]

[6(3A) For the purposes of this Schedule, a claimant who has ceased to be entitled to a jobseeker's allowance because—

(a) that claimant or his partner [16 or, where a claimant is a member of a joint-claim couple, the other member of that couple] was participating in an employment programme specified in regulation 75(1)(a)(ii) [17 in the Intensive Activity Period specified in regulation 75(1)(a)(iv) [40 . . .]] [12or in an employment zone programme] [48 or in the Flexible New Deal], and

(b) in consequence of such participation the claimant or his partner [16 or, where a claimant is a member of a joint-claim couple, the other member of that couple] was engaged in renumerative work or failed to satisfy the condition specified either in section 2(1)(c) [¹⁶, 3(1)(a) or 3A(1)(a)],

shall be treated as if he had been in receipt of a jobseeker's allowance for the period during which he or his partner [¹⁶ or, where a claimant is a member of a joint-claim couple, the other member of that couple] was participating in that programme [¹⁷ or activity].]

(4) Where, for the purposes of sub-paragraphs [⁶(1), (3) and (3A)], a person is treated as being in receipt of a jobseeker's allowance, for a certain period, he shall [¹⁰, subject to sub-paragraph (4A),] be treated as being entitled to a jobseeker's allowance for the same period.

[¹⁰ (4A) [⁷² . . .]]

(5) For the purposes of this Schedule, sub-paragraph (6) applies where a person is not entitled to an income-based jobseeker's allowance by reason only that he has—

    (a) capital exceeding £8,000; or

    (b) income [⁵⁴ equal to or] exceeding the applicable amount which applies in his case; or

[³(bb) a personal rate of contribution-based jobseeker's allowance that is equal to, or exceeds, the applicable amount in his case; or]

    (c) both capital exceeding £8,000 and income exceeding the applicable amount which applies in his case.

(6) A person to whom sub-paragraph (5) applies shall be treated as entitled to a jobseeker's allowance throughout any period of not more than 39 weeks which comprises only days—

    (a) on which he is entitled to a contribution-based jobseeker's allowance, statutory sick pay [⁴² , incapacity benefit or contributory employment and support allowance]; or

    (b) on which he is, although not entitled to any of the benefits mentioned in head (a) above, entitled to be credited with earnings equal to the lower earnings limit for the time being in force in accordance with [⁹regulation 8A or 8B of the Social Security (Credits) Regulations 1975].

(7) Subject to sub-paragraph (8), a person to whom sub-paragraph (5) applies and who is either a person to whom regulation 13(4) applies (persons with caring responsibilities) or a lone parent shall, for the purposes of this Schedule, be treated as entitled to a jobseeker's allowance throughout any period of not more than 39 weeks following the refusal of a claim for a jobseeker's allowance made by or on behalf of that person.

(8) Sub-paragraph (7) shall not apply in relation to a person mentioned in that sub-paragraph who, during the period referred to in that sub-paragraph—

    (a) is engaged in, or is treated as engaged in, remunerative work or whose partner is engaged in, or is treated as engaged in, remunerative work;

    (b) is treated as not available for employment by virtue of regulation [⁴¹ 15(1)(a)] (circumstances in which students are not treated as available for employment);

    (c) is temporarily absent from Great Britain, other than in the circumstances specified in regulation 50 (temporary absence from Great Britain).

(9) In a case where—

    (a) sub-paragraphs (6) and (7) apply solely by virtue of sub-paragraph (5)(b), and

    (b) the claimant's income includes payments under a policy taken out to insure against the risk that the policy holder is unable to meet [⁷² any payment which qualifies under paragraph 16],

sub-paragraphs (6) and (7) shall have effect as if for the words "throughout any period of not more than 39 weeks" there are substituted the words "throughout any period that payments are made in accordance with the terms of the policy".

(10) This sub-paragraph applies—

    (a) to a person who claims a jobseeker's allowance, or in respect of whom a jobseeker's allowance is claimed, and who—

        (i) received payments under a policy of insurance taken out to insure against loss of employment, and those payments are exhausted; and

        (ii) had a previous award of a jobseeker's allowance where the applicable amount included an amount by way of housing costs; and

    (b) where the period in respect of which the previous award of jobseeker's allowance was payable ended not more than 26 weeks before the date the claim was made.

(11) Where sub-paragraph (10) applies, in determining—

    (a) [⁶⁶ . . .]

    (b) for the purposes of paragraph 7(1) whether a claimant has been entitled to a jobseeker's allowance for a continuous period of 39 weeks or more,

any week falling between the date of the termination of the previous award and the date of the new claim shall be ignored.

[⁸(12) Where the claimant's partner to whom this paragraph applies is a welfare to work beneficiary, sub-paragraphs (1)(a)(ii), [¹⁴ (1)(c)(iv),] (1)(d) and (1)(f)(iii) shall apply to him as if for the words "twelve weeks" there were substituted the words "[³⁵ 104 weeks]".]

[¹⁵ (13) For the purposes of sub-paragraph (1)(a)(ii), (1)(c)(iv), (1)(d) and (1)(f)(iii), the relevant period shall be—

    (a) 52 weeks in the case of a person to whom sub-paragraph (14) applies;

    (b) subject to sub-paragraph (12), 12 weeks in any other case.

(14) This sub-paragraph applies, subject to sub-paragraph (15), in the case of a person who, on or after 9th April 2001, has ceased to be entitled to a jobseeker's allowance because he or his partner or, where that person is a member of a joint-claim couple, the other member of that couple—

    (a) has commenced employment as an employed earner or as a self-employed earner or has increased the hours in which he is engaged in such employment;

    (b) is taking active steps to establish himself in employment as an employed earner or as a self-employed earner under any scheme for assisting persons to become so employed which is mentioned in regulation 19(1)(r)(i) to (iii); or

    (c) is participating in—

        (i) a New Deal option;

        (ii) an employment zone programme;

        (iii) the self-employment route; [¹⁷ or

        (iv) the Intensive Activity Period specified in regulation 75(1)(a)(iv) [⁴¹ . . .]]

and, as a consequence, [⁵⁶ that person, their partner or, where that person is a member of a joint-claim couple, the other member of that couple, was engaged in remunerative work or had income equal to or in excess of the amount of earnings calculated under regulation 56 or the applicable amount determined in accordance with regulations 83 to 86C, whichever applies].

(15) Sub-paragraph (14) shall only apply to the extent that immediately before the day on which the person ceased to be entitled to an income-based jobseeker's allowance or the joint-claim couple of which he was a member ceased to be entitled to a joint-claim jobseeker's allowance, his housing costs were being met in accordance with paragraph [⁶⁶ . . .] 7(1)(a) or would have been so met but for any non-dependant deduction under paragraph 17.]

[²² (16) For the purpose of determining whether the linking rules set out in this paragraph apply in a case where a claimant's former partner was entitled to state pension credit, any reference to income-based jobseeker's allowance in this Schedule shall be taken to include also a reference to state pension credit.]

Loans on residential property
    14.—[⁷² ...]   3.533

Loans for repairs and improvements to the dwelling occupied as the home
    15.—[⁷² ...]   3.534

[⁷² Housing costs]
    16.—(1) Subject to the deduction specified in sub-paragraph (2) and the reductions applicable in sub-paragraph (5), there shall be met under this paragraph the amounts, calculated on a weekly basis, in respect of the following housing costs—   3.535

    (a) payments by way of rent or ground rent relating to a long tenancy [³⁴ . . .];

    (b) service charges;

    (c) payments by way of the rentcharge within the meaning of section 1 of the Rentcharges Act 1977;

    (d) payments under a co-ownership scheme;

    (e) payments under or relating to a tenancy or licence of a Crown tenant;

    (f) where the dwelling occupied as the home is a tent, payments in respect of the tent and the site on which it stands.

(2) Subject to sub-paragraph (3), the deductions to be made from the weekly amounts to be met under this paragraph are—

    (a) where the costs are inclusive of any of the items mentioned in [³⁰ paragraph 6(2) of Schedule 1 to the Housing Benefit Regulations 2006] (payment in respect of fuel charges), the deductions prescribed in that paragraph unless the claimant provides evidence on which the actual or approximate amount of the service charge for fuel may be estimated, in which case the estimated amount;

    (b) where the costs are inclusive of ineligible service charges within the meaning of [³⁰ paragraph 1 of Schedule 1 to the Housing Benefit Regulations 2006] (ineligible service charges) the amounts attributable to those ineligible service charges or where that amount is not separated from or separately identified within the housing costs to be met under this paragraph, such part of the payments made in respect of those housing costs which are fairly attributable to the provision of those ineligible services having regard to the costs of comparable services;

 (c) any amount for repairs and improvements, and for this purpose the expression "repairs and improvements" has [72 the meaning in sub-paragraph (6)].

(3) Where arrangements are made for the housing costs, which are met under this paragraph and which are normally paid for a period of 52 weeks, to be paid instead for a period of 53 weeks, or to be paid irregularly, or so that no such costs are payable or collected in certain periods, or so that the costs for different periods in the year are of different amounts, the weekly amount shall be the amount payable for the year divided by 52.

(4) Where the claimant or a member of his family—

 (a) pays for reasonable repairs or redecoration to be carried out to the dwelling they occupy; and

 (b) that work was not the responsibility of the claimant or any member of his family; and

 (c) in consequence of that work being done, the costs which are normally met under this paragraph are waived,

then those costs shall, for a period not exceeding 8 weeks, be treated as payable.

(5) Where in England and Wales an amount calculated on a weekly basis in respect of housing costs specified in sub-paragraph (1)(e) (Crown tenants) includes water charges, that amount shall be reduced—

 (a) where the amount payable in respect of water charges is known, by that amount;

 (b) in any other case, by the amount which would be the likely weekly water charge had the property not been occupied by a Crown tenant.

[72(6) For the purposes of sub-paragraph (2)(c), "repairs and improvements" means any of the following measures undertaken with a view to maintaining the fitness of the dwelling for human habitation or, where the dwelling forms part of a building, any part of a building containing that dwelling—

 (a) provision of a fixed bath, shower, wash basin, sink or lavatory, and necessary associated plumbing, including the provision of hot water not connected to a central heating system;

 (b) repairs to existing heating system;

 (c) damp proof measures;

 (d) provision of ventilation and natural lighting;

 (e) provision of drainage facilities;

 (f) provision of facilities for preparing and cooking food;

 (g) provision of insulation of the dwelling occupied as the home;

 (h) provision of electric lighting and sockets;

 (i) provision of storage facilities for fuel or refuse;

 (j) repairs of unsafe structural defects;

 (k) adapting a dwelling for the special needs of a disabled person; or

 (l) provision of separate sleeping accommodation for persons of different sexes aged 10 or over but under the age of 20 who live with the claimant and for whom the claimant or the claimant's partner is responsible.]

Non-dependant deductions

3.536 17.—(1) Subject to the following provisions of this paragraph, the following deductions from the amount to be met under the preceding paragraphs of this Schedule in respect of housing costs shall be made—

 [28 (a) in respect of a non-dependant aged 18 or over who is engaged in any remunerative work, [75 £102.83];

 (b) in respect of a non-dependant aged 18 or over to whom paragraph (a) does not apply, [75 £15.95].]

(2) In the case of a non-dependant aged 18 or over to whom sub-paragraph (1)(a) applies because he is in remunerative work, where the claimant satisfies [11 the Secretary of State] that the non-dependant's gross weekly income is—

 (a) less than [75 £149.00], the deduction to be made under this paragraph shall be the deduction specified in sub-paragraph (1)(b);

 (b) not less than [75 £149.00] but less than [75 £217.00], the deduction to be made under this paragraph shall be [75 £36.65];

 (c) not less than [75 £217.00] but less than [75 £283.00], the deduction to be made under this paragraph shall be [75 £50.30];

 [1 (d) not less than [75 £283.00] but less than [75 £377.00], the deduction to be made under this paragraph shall be [75 £82.30];

(e) not less than [^{75} £377.00] but less than [^{75} £469.00], the deduction to be made under this paragraph shall be [^{75} £93.70]].

[^{72} (2A) Where a non-dependant deduction is being made under the Loans for Mortgage Interest Regulations 2017, the amount of the deduction under sub-paragraph (1) or (2) is to be reduced by an amount equal to that non-dependant deduction.]

(3) Only one deduction shall be made under this paragraph in respect of a couple or, as the case may be, the members of a polygamous marriage, and where, but for this sub-paragraph, the amount that would fall to be deducted in respect of one member of a couple or polygamous marriage is higher than the amount (if any) that would fall to be deducted in respect of the other, or any other member, the higher amount shall be deducted.

(4) In applying the provisions of sub-paragraph (2) in the case of a couple or, as the case may be, a polygamous marriage, regard shall be had, for the purpose of sub-paragraph (2), to the couple's or, as the case may be, all the members of the polygamous marriage's, joint weekly income.

(5) Where a person is a non-dependant in respect of more than one joint occupier of a dwelling (except where the joint occupiers are a couple or members of a polygamous marriage), the deduction in respect of that non-dependant shall be apportioned between the joint occupiers (the amount so apportioned being rounded to the nearest penny) having regard to the number of joint occupiers and the proportion of the housing costs in respect of the dwelling occupied as the home payable by each of them.

(6) No deduction shall be made in respect of any non-dependants occupying the dwelling occupied as the home of the claimant, if the claimant or any partner of his is—

(a) [^{65} severely sight impaired or blind or treated as severely sight impaired or blind] within the meaning of paragraph 14(1)(h) and (2) of Schedule 1 (additional condition for the higher pensioner and disability premiums); or

(b) receiving in respect of himself either—
    (i) an attendance allowance, or
    (ii) the care component of the disability living allowance [^{60} , [^{61} . . .]
    (iii) the daily living component of personal independence payment] [^{61} , or
    (iv) armed forces independence payment].

(7) No deduction shall be made in respect of a non-dependant—

(a) if, although he resides with the claimant, it appears to [^{11} the Secretary of State] that the dwelling occupied as his home is normally elsewhere; or

[^{2}(b) if he is in receipt of [^{3}a training allowance paid in connection with [^{45} youth training] established under section 2 of the Employment and Training Act 1973 or section 2 of the Enterprise and New Towns (Scotland) Act 1990; or]]

(c) if he is a full-time student during a period of study or, if he is not in remunerative work, during a recognised summer vacation appropriate to his course; or

(d) if he is aged under 25 and in receipt of [^{4}an income-based jobseeker's allowance] or income support; or

(e) in respect of whom a deduction in the calculation of a rent rebate or allowance falls to be made under [^{30} regulation 74 of the Housing Benefit Regulations 2006] (non-dependant deductions); or

(f) to whom, but for paragraph (5) of regulation 2 (definition of non-dependant) paragraph (4) of that regulation would apply; or

(g) if he is not residing with the claimant because he has been a patient for a period in excess of [^{21} 52] weeks, or is a prisoner, and for these purposes—
    [^{31} (i) "patient" has the meaning given in paragraph 3(13)(b) and "prisoner" has the meaning given in regulation 85(4), and
    (ii) in calculating any period of 52 weeks as a patient, any two or more distinct periods separated by one or more intervals each not exceeding 28 days shall be treated as a single period; [^{42} . . .]]

(h) if he is in receipt of state pension credit] [^{42} or

(i) he is aged less than 25 and is in receipt of [^{59} income–related] employment and support allowance which does not include an amount under section [^{43} . . .] 4(4) [^{67} . . .] of the Welfare Reform Act [^{67} (component) and is not a member of the work-related activity group]] [^{63}; or

(j) if he is aged less than 25 and is entitled to an award of universal credit which is calculated on the basis that he does not have any earned income].

(8) In the case of a non-dependant to whom sub-paragraph (2) applies because he is in remunerative work, there shall be disregarded from his gross income—

(a) any attendance allowance [^{60} , disability living allowance [^{61} , armed forces independence payment] or personal independence payment] received by him;

(b) [⁷⁴ any Grenfell Tower payment or] any payment made under [⁵¹ or by] the Macfarlane Trust, the Macfarlane (Special Payments) Trust, the Macfarlane (Special Payments) (No.2) Trust, the Fund, the Eileen Trust [⁵⁰ , MFET Limited] [⁵⁵ , the Skipton Fund, the Caxton Foundation] [⁶⁹, the Scottish Infected Blood Support Scheme] [⁷³, an approved blood scheme] [⁷¹, the London Emergencies Trust, the We Love Manchester Emergency Fund] [⁷⁴, the National Emergencies Trust] or the Independent Living [⁴⁴ Fund (2006)] which, had his income fallen to becalculated under regulation 103 (calculation of income other than earnings), would have been disregarded under paragraph 22 of Schedule 7 (income in kind); and

(c) any payment which, had his income fallen to be calculated under regulation 103 would have been disregarded under paragraph 41 of Schedule 7 (payments made under certain trusts and certain other payments).

[⁷³ (d) any payment made under or by a trust, established for the purpose of giving relief and assistance to disabled persons whose disabilities were caused by the fact that during their mother's pregnancy she had taken a preparation containing the drug known as Thalidomide, and which is approved by the Secretary of State.]

[⁶³ (9) For the purposes of sub-paragraph (7)(j), "earned income" has the meaning given in regulation 52 of the Universal Credit Regulations 2013.]

Continuity with income support [⁴² or income-related employment and support allowance]

3.537   **18.**—(1) For the purpose of providing continuity between income support and a job-seeker's allowance—

(a) [⁶⁶ . . .]

(b) had the award of a jobseeker's allowance been an award of income support and the housing costs which would then have been met would have included an additional amount met in accordance with paragraph 7 of Schedule 3 to the Income Support Regulations (add back), an amount equal to that additional amount shall be added to the housing costs to be met under this Schedule, but that amount shall be subject to the same qualifications and limitations as it would have been had the award been of income support; and

(c) for the purposes of any linking rule [²or for determining whether any qualifying or other period is satisfied], any reference to a jobseeker's allowance in this Schedule shall be taken also to include a reference to income support [⁴² or income-related employment and support allowance].

(2) [⁷² . . .]

Rounding of Fractions

3.538   **19.**—Where any calculation made under this Schedule results in a fraction of a penny, that fraction shall be treated as a penny.

Amendments

1. Jobseeker's Allowance (Amendment) Regulations 1996 (SI 1996/1516) reg.20 and Sch. (October 7, 1996).

2. Jobseeker's Allowance and Income Support (General) (Amendment) Regulations 1996 (SI 1996/1517) reg.29 (October 7, 1996).

3. Social Security and Child Support (Jobseeker's Allowance) (Miscellaneous Amendments) Regulations 1996 (SI 1996/2538) reg.2(12) (October 28, 1996).

4. Social Security and Child Support (Miscellaneous Amendments) Regulations 1997 (SI 1997/827) reg.4 (April 7, 1997).

5. Social Security (Miscellaneous Amendments) (No.4) Regulations 1997 (SI 1997/2305) reg.3 (October 22, 1997).

6. Social Security Amendment (New Deal) Regulations 1997 (SI 1997/2863) reg.13 (January 5, 1998).

7. Social Security (Non-Dependant Deductions) Regulations 1996 (SI 1996/2518) reg.4 (April 6, 1998).

8. Social Security (Welfare to Work) Regulations 1998 (SI 1998/2231) reg.14(4) (October 5, 1998).

9. Social Security Benefits (Miscellaneous Amendments) Regulations 1999 (SI 1999/714) reg.2(2) (April 5, 1999).

10. Income Support (General) and Jobseeker's Allowance Amendment Regulations 1999 (SI 1999/1921) reg.2(2) (August 2, 1999).

11. Social Security Act 1998 (Commencement No.11, and Savings and Consequential and Transitional Provisions) Order 1999 (SI 1999/2860 (C.75)) art.3(12) and Sch.12 (October 18, 1999).

12. Social Security Amendment (Employment Zones) Regulations 2000 (SI 2000/724) reg.4(4)(d) (April 3, 2000).

13. Social Security (Miscellaneous Amendments) Regulations 2001 (SI 2001/488) reg.12(b)(i) (April 9, 2001).

14. Social Security (Miscellaneous Amendments) Regulations 2001 (SI 2001/488) reg.12(b)(ii) (April 9, 2001).

15. Social Security (Miscellaneous Amendments) Regulations 2001 (SI 2001/488) reg.12(b)(iii) (April 9, 2001).

16. Jobseeker's Allowance (Joint Claims) Regulations 2000 (SI 2000/1978) reg.2(5) and Sch.2 para.54 (March 19, 2001).

17. Social Security Amendment (New Deal) Regulations 2001 (SI 2001/1029) reg.11 (April 9, 2001).

18. Income Support (General) and Jobseeker's Allowance Amendment Regulations 2001 (SI 2001/3651) reg.2(2) (December 10, 2001).

19. Social Security (Miscellaneous Amendments) Regulations 2002 (SI 2002/841) reg.6 (April 8, 2002).

20. Child Support (Consequential Amendments and Transitional Provisions) Regulations 2001 (SI 2001/158) reg.7(3) (in force in relation to any particular case on the day on which s.1 of the Child Support, Pensions and Social Security Act 2000 comes into force in relation to that type of case).

21. Social Security (Hospital In-Patients and Miscellaneous Amendments) Regulations 2003 (SI 2003/1195) reg.6(4) (May 21, 2003).

22. State Pension Credit (Consequential, Transitional and Miscellaneous Provisions) Regulations 2002 (SI 2002/3019) reg.30 (October 6, 2003).

23. Social Security (Housing Costs Amendments) Regulations 2004 (SI 2004/2825) reg.2(2) (November 28, 2004).

24. Social Security (Housing Costs Amendments) Regulations 2004 (SI 2004/2825) reg.2(3) (November 28, 2004).

25. Social Security (Housing Costs Amendments) Regulations 2004 (SI 2004/2825) reg.2(4) (November 28, 2004).

26. Social Security (Housing Costs Amendments) Regulations 2004 (SI 2004/2825) reg.2(5) (November 28, 2004).

27. Social Security (Housing Benefit, Council Tax Benefit, State Pension Credit and Miscellaneous Amendments) Regulations 2004 (SI 2004/2327) reg.6(a) (April 4, 2005).

28. Social Security (Housing Benefit, Council Tax Benefit, State Pension Credit and Miscellaneous Amendments) Regulations 2004 (SI 2004/2327) reg.6(b) (April 4, 2005).

29. Social Security (Care Homes and Independent Hospitals) Regulations 2005 (SI 2005/2687) reg.3 and Sch.2 para.9 (October 24, 2005).

30. Housing Benefit and Council Tax Benefit (Consequential Provisions) Regulations 2006 (SI 2006/217) reg.5 and Sch.2 para.8(4) (March 6, 2006).

31. Social Security (Hospital In-Patients) Regulations 2005 (SI 2005/3360) reg.6(4) (April 10, 2006).

32. Social Security (Miscellaneous Amendments) (No.4) Regulations 2006 (SI 2006/2378) reg.13(11)(a) (October 2, 2006).

33. Social Security (Miscellaneous Amendments) (No.4) Regulations 2006 (SI 2006/2378) reg.13(11)(b) (October 2, 2006).

34. Social Security (Miscellaneous Amendments) (No.4) Regulations 2006 (SI 2006/2378) reg.13(11)(c) (October 2, 2006).

35. Social Security (Miscellaneous Amendments) (No.4) Regulations 2006 (SI 2006/2378) reg.13(10)(b) (October 9, 2006).

36. Social Security (Miscellaneous Amendments) (No.5) Regulations 2006 (SI 2006/3274) reg.3 (January 8, 2007).

37. Social Security (Housing Costs and Miscellaneous Amendments) Regulations 2007 (SI 2007/3183) reg.4(2)(a) (December 17, 2007).

38. Social Security (Housing Costs and Miscellaneous Amendments) Regulations 2007 (SI 2007/3183) reg.4(2)(b) (December 17, 2007).

39. Social Security (Housing Costs and Miscellaneous Amendments) Regulations 2007 (SI 2007/3183) reg.4(2)(c) (December 17, 2007).

40. Social Security (Miscellaneous Amendments) Regulations 2008 (SI 2008/698) reg.4(15) (April 14, 2008).

41. Social Security (Students Responsible for Children or Young Persons) Amendment Regulations 2008 (SI 2008/1826) reg.3(5) (July 9, 2008).

42. Employment and Support Allowance (Consequential Provisions) (No.2) Regulations 2008 (SI 2008/1554) reg.3(25) (October 27, 2008).

43. Employment and Support Allowance (Miscellaneous Amendments) Regulations 2008 (SI 2008/2428) reg.41(3) (October 27, 2008).

44. Social Security (Miscellaneous Amendments) (No.6) Regulations 2008 (SI 2008/2767) reg.4(7) (November 17, 2008).

45. Social Security (Miscellaneous Amendments) (No.6) Regulations 2008 (SI 2008/2767) reg.4(10) (November 17, 2008).

46. Social Security (Housing Costs Special Arrangements) (Amendment and Modification) Regulations 2008 (SI 2008/3195) reg.2(1)(c) and (2) (January 5, 2009).

47. Social Security (Miscellaneous Amendments) Regulations 2009 (SI 2009/583) reg.4(3) (April 6, 2009).

48. Social Security (Flexible New Deal) Regulations 2009 (SI 2009/480) reg.2(12) (October 5, 2009).

49. Social Security (Equalisation of State Pension Age) Regulations 2009 (SI 2009/1488) reg.14 (April 6, 2010).

50. Social Security (Miscellaneous Amendments) (No.2) Regulations 2010 (SI 2010/641) reg.4(3)(e) (April 6, 2010).

51. Social Security (Miscellaneous Amendments) (No.2) Regulations 2010 (SI 2010/641) reg.4(8)(d) (April 6, 2010).

52. Social Security (Miscellaneous Amendments) (No.4) Regulations 2009 (SI 2009/2655) reg.4(13) (April 12, 2010).

53. Social Security (Housing Costs) (Standard Interest Rate) Amendment Regulations 2010 (SI 2010/1811) reg.2(1)(b) and (2) (October 1, 2010).

54. Social Security (Miscellaneous Amendments) Regulations 2011 (SI 2011/674) reg.7(7) (April 11, 2011).

55. Social Security (Miscellaneous Amendments) (No.3) Regulations 2011 (SI 2011/2425) reg.10(9) (October 31, 2011).

56. Social Security (Miscellaneous Amendments) (No.3) Regulations 2011 (SI 2011/2425) reg.10(13) (October 31, 2011).

57. Employment and Support Allowance (Duration of Contributory Allowance) (Consequential Amendments) Regulations 2012 (SI 2012/913) reg.4 (May 1, 2012).

58. Social Security (Miscellaneous Amendments) Regulations 2013 (SI 2013/443) reg.4(11)(a) (April 2, 2013).

59. Social Security (Miscellaneous Amendments) Regulations 2013 (SI 2013/443) reg.4(11)(b) (April 2, 2013).

60. Personal Independence Payment (Supplementary Provisions and Consequential Amendments) Regulations 2013 (SI 2013/388) reg.8 and Sch. Pt 2 para.16(8) (April 8, 2013).

61. Armed Forces and Reserve Forces Compensation Scheme (Consequential Provisions: Subordinate Legislation) Order 2013 (SI 2013/591) art.7 and Sch. para.10(8) (April 8, 2013).

62. Universal Credit (Consequential, Supplementary, Incidental and Miscellaneous Provisions) Regulations 2013 (SI 2013/630) reg.30(7)(a) (April 29, 2013).

63. Universal Credit (Consequential, Supplementary, Incidental and Miscellaneous Provisions) Regulations 2013 (SI 2013/630) reg.30(7)(b) (April 29, 2013).

64. Social Security (Miscellaneous Amendments) Regulations 2014 (SI 2014/591) reg.4(5) (April 28, 2014).

65. Universal Credit and Miscellaneous Amendments (No.2) Regulations 2014 (SI 2014/2888) reg.3(3)(b) (November 26, 2014).

66. Social Security (Housing Costs Amendments) Regulations 2015 (SI 2015/1647) reg.3 (April 1, 2016).

67. Employment and Support Allowance and Universal Credit (Miscellaneous Amendments and Transitional and Savings Provisions) Regulations 2017 (SI 2017/204) reg.7(1) and Sch.1, Pt.1, para.3(1) and (3) (April 3, 2017).

68. Employment and Support Allowance and Universal Credit (Miscellaneous Amendments and Transitional and Savings Provisions) Regulations 2017 (SI 2017/204) reg.7(1) and Sch.1, Pt.2, para.12 (April 3, 2017).

69. Social Security (Scottish Infected Blood Support Scheme) Regulations 2017 (SI 2017/329) reg.3(1) and (3)(d) (April 3, 2017).

70. Employment and Support Allowance (Miscellaneous Amendments and Transitional and Savings Provision) Regulations 2017 (SI 2017/581) reg.3 (June 23, 2017, subject to the transitional and savings provision in reg.10).

71. Social Security (Emergency Funds) (Amendment) Regulations 2017 (SI 2017/689) reg.3(1) and (3) (June 19, 2017).

72. Loans for Mortgage Interest Regulations 2017 (SI 2017/725) reg.18 and Sch.5 para.3(f) April 6, 2018).

73. Social Security (Infected Blood and Thalidomide) Regulations 2017 (SI 2017/870) reg.3 (October 23, 2017).

74. Social Security (Income and Capital) (Miscellaneous Amendments) Regulations 2020 (SI 2020/618) reg.3(1) and (10) (July 15, 2020).

75. Social Security Benefits Up-rating Order 2021 (SI 2021/0162) art 27(1) and (8) (April 12, 2021).

DEFINITIONS

"Abbeyfield Home"—see reg.1(3).
"armed forces independence payment"—*ibid.*
"attendance allowance"—*ibid.*
"the Benefits Act"—see Jobseekers Act s.35(1).
"benefit week"—see reg.1(3).
"care home"—*ibid.*
"the Caxton Foundation"—*ibid.*
"claimant"—see Jobseekers Act s.35(1).
"close relative"—see reg.1(3).
"couple"—*ibid.*
"course of study"—*ibid.*
"co-ownership scheme"—*ibid.*
"Crown tenant"—*ibid.*
"disability living allowance"—*ibid.*
"dwelling occupied as the home"—*ibid.*
"the Eileen Trust"—*ibid.*
"employment zone programme"—*ibid.*
"family"—see Jobseekers Act s.35(1).
"the Fund"—see reg.1(3).
"housing benefit expenditure"—*ibid.*
"independent hospital"—*ibid.*
"the Independent Living Funds"—*ibid.*
"local welfare provision"—*ibid.*
"lone parent"—*ibid.*
"the Macfarlane (Special Payments) Trust"—*ibid.*

"the Macfarlane (Special Payments) (No.2) Trust"—*ibid.*
"the Macfarlane Trust"—*ibid.*
"MFET Limited"—*ibid.*
"non-dependant"—see reg.2.
"partner"—see reg.1(3).
"period of study"—*ibid.*
"personal independence payment"—*ibid.*
"polygamous marriage"—*ibid.*
"qualifying age for state pension credit"—*ibid.*
"remunerative work"—see reg.51(1).
"single claimant"—see reg.1(3).
"the Skipton Fund"—*ibid.*
"student"—see reg.130 and reg.1(3).
"training allowance"—see reg.1(3).
"universal credit"—*ibid.*
"water charges"—*ibid.*
"welfare to work beneficiary"—*ibid.*
"year of assessment"—*ibid.*

GENERAL NOTE

3.539 Most of this Schedule is very similar to Sch.3 to the Income Support Regulations, subject to some minor differences in the wording. See the notes to Sch.3. There are a few differences which reflect the fact that a claimant must satisfy the labour market conditions in order to be entitled to JSA. Thus there was no equivalent of para.8(2)(b) of Sch.3 in para.7 (note that para.8(2)–(5) of Sch.3 and para.7(3)–(7) were revoked on April 1, 2016, subject to a saving provision (see p.1776)). See also the differences in para.3(11)(c)(i) and (ii) (person treated as occupying his home during temporary absences of up to 52 weeks). Note also in para.13 (linking rules) the additional category (from October 28, 1996) in sub-para.(5)(bb): person who is not entitled to income-based JSA because his contribution-based JSA equals or exceeds his applicable amount for income-based JSA; and that a carer in sub-para.(7) is defined by reference to reg.13(4) (person with caring responsibilities, see reg.4 for the definition of "caring responsibilities") rather than being restricted to a person who cares for someone receiving attendance allowance or disability living allowance, etc.

Note that in relation to, for example, satisfying the waiting periods for housing costs (from April 1, 2016, there is only one waiting period of 39 weeks, subject to a saving provision (see p.1776)), periods during which hardship payments are being made will count, since hardship payments are payments of JSA. In addition, periods when a claimant is sanctioned will count towards the waiting period, since entitlement to JSA continues during the sanction, even though JSA is not paid. This will be so whether or not a hardship payment is made. But "waiting days" at the beginning of a JSA claim are not days of entitlement. The amendments made on March 19, 2001 are necessary because of the introduction of joint-claim jobseeker's allowance (see the notes at the beginning of the Jobseekers Act 1995 and to s.1(4) of the Act). Obviously there is no equivalent to these amendments in Sch.3 to the Income Support Regulations.

The transitional protection provisions in para.7 of Sch.3 to the Income Support Regulations have been omitted, but note the effect of para.18(1)(b) (para.7 of Sch.3 was revoked on April 1, 2016). Paragraph 18 is important for claimants transferring from income support or income-related ESA to jobseeker's allowance. For the equivalent of para.18(1)(c) where the transfer is to income support, see reg.32 of the Income Support (General) (Jobseeker's Allowance Consequential Amendments) Regulations 1996 (p.1759) and para.20 of Sch.6 to the ESA Regulations 2008 in Vol.I of this series where the transfer is to ESA. See p.1757 for reg.3 of the Income Support (General) Amendment and Transitional Regulations 1995 referred to in para.18(2) and see the note to para.7 of Sch.3. Note also the further transitional provisions in reg.87(4)–(6). For the linking rule where the claimant's former partner was entitled to state pension credit, see para.13(16), inserted with effect from October 6, 2003.

Note also that entitlement to either contribution-based or income-based JSA counts towards the waiting periods in paras 6 and 7 (there is now only one waiting period of 39 weeks, as para.6 has been revoked and para.7 has been amended with effect from April 1, 2016, subject to a saving provision (see p.1776)). As the Commissioner points out in *CJSA 2028/2000* the words used are "a jobseeker's allowance" and so refer to either element of JSA.   **3.540**

From April 3, 2017, ss.18–19 and 21 of the Welfare Reform & Work Act 2016 (see Vol.V) has conferred power on the Secretary of State to make regulations replacing the payments made to owner occupiers under this Schedule, and Sch.3 to the Income Support Regulations, with loans. At the time of going to press, no such regulations have been made and it is not known what, if any, transitional protection there will be for existing claimants.

SCHEDULE 3

[Revoked by the Social Security (Removal of Residential Allowance and Miscellaneous Amendments) Regulations 2003 (SI 2003/1121), reg.4 and Sch.2, para.10 with effect from October 6, 2003.]   **3.541**

SCHEDULE 4

APPLICABLE AMOUNTS OF PERSONS IN RESIDENTIAL CARE AND NURSING HOMES

[Revoked by Social Security Amendment (Residential Care and Nursing Homes) Regulations 2001 (SI 2001/3767) reg.2 and Sch. Pt II para.19 with effect from April 8, 2002.]   **3.542**

SCHEDULE 4A

APPLICABLE AMOUNT OF A JOINT-CLAIM COUPLE WHERE A MEMBER IS IN A RESIDENTIAL CARE OR NURSING HOME

[Inserted by Jobseeker's Allowance (Joint Claims) Regulations 2000 (SI 2000/1978) reg.2(5) and Sch.2, para.55 with effect from March 19, 2001 and revoked by Social Security Amendment (Residential Care and Nursing Homes) Regulations 2001 (SI 2001/3767) reg.2 and Sch. Pt II para.19 with effect from April 8, 2002.]   **3.543**

SCHEDULE 5   [¹⁵ Regulations 85 and 85A]

APPLICABLE AMOUNTS IN SPECIAL CASES

Column (1)	Column (2)
1.—[¹⁴ . . .]	1.—[¹⁴ . . .]
[¹⁴ **Claimant who is a patient** **1A.**—[¹⁶ . . .]	**1A.**—[¹⁶ . . .]
2.—[¹² ¹⁷ . . .] **2.**—[¹² ¹⁷ . . .]	
Claimants Without Accommodation **3.**—A claimant who is without accommodation.	**3.**—The amount applicable to him under regulation 83(a) (personal allowance) only.
Members of Religious Orders **4.**—A claimant who is a member of and fully maintained by a religious order.	**4.**—Nil

*(Column (2) for the table above appears at right, marked **3.544**.)*

Column (1)	Column (2)
Specified Cases of Temporarily Separated Couples	
5.—A claimant who is a member of a couple and who is temporarily separated from his partner, where—	**5.**—Either—
(a) one member of the couple is—	(a) the amount applicable to him as a member of a couple under regulation 83; or
[¹³ (i) not a patient but is residing in a care home, an Abbeyfield Home or an independent hospital, or]	
(ii) [¹³ . . .]	
(iii) resident in premises used for the rehabilition of alcoholics or drug addicts, or	
(iv) resident in accommodation provided under section 3 of and Part II of the Schedule to, the Polish Resettlement Act 1947 (provision of accommodation in camps),	
(v) or participating in arrangements for training made under section 2 of the Employment and Training Act 1973, or section 2 of the Enterprise and New Towns (Scotland) Act 1990 or participating in an employment rehabilitation programme established under that section of the Act of 1973, where the course requires him to live away from the dwelling occupied as the home, or	
(vi) in a probation or bail hostel approved for the purpose by the Secretary of State, and	
(b) the other member of the couple is—	(b) the aggregate of his applicable amount and that of his partner assessed under the provisions of these Regulations as if each of them were a single claimant, or a lone parent. whichever is the greater.
(i)living in the dwelling occupied as the home, or	
(ii)a patient, or	
[¹³ (iii)residing in a care home, an Abbeyfield Home or an independent hoptial.]	
Polygamous Marriages where one or more partners are temporarily separated 6. Either—	
6.—A claimant who is a member of a polygamous marriage and who is temporarily separated from a partner of his, where one of them is living in the home while the other member is—	
[¹³ (a) not a patient but is residing in a care home, an Abbeyfield Home or or an independent hospital, or]	(a) the amount applicable to the members of the polygamous marriage under regulation 84; or
(b) resident in premises used for the rehabilitation of alcoholics or drug addicts; or	(b) the aggregate of the amount applicable for the members of the polygamous marriage

Column (1)	Column (2)
(c) attending a course of training or instruction provided or approved by the Secretary of State where the course requires him to live away from home; or (d) in a probation or bail hostel approved for the purpose by the Secretary of State.	who remain in the home under regulation 84 and the amount applicable in respect of those members not in the home calculated as if each of them were a single claimant, or a lone parent, whichever is the greater.
Single claimants temporarily in local authority accommodation 7.—[¹¹ . . .]	7.—[¹¹ . . .]
Couples and members of polygamous marriages where one member is or all are temporarily in local authority accommodation 8.—[¹¹ . . .]	8.—[¹¹ . . .]
Lone parents who are in residential accommodation temporarily 9.—[¹¹ . . .]	9.—[¹¹ . . .]
Couples where one member is absent from the United Kingdom 10.—[⁷(1)] Subject to paragraph 11, a claimant who is a member of a couple and whose partner is temporarily absent from the United Kingdom. applicable to the claimant in Great Britain under regulation 83 [⁹ . . .] as the case may be as if the claimant were a single claimant or, as the case may be, a lone parent. [⁷ (2) A claimant who is a member of a joint-claim couple and whose partner is temporarily absent from the United Kingdom— (a) in the circumstances prescribed in regulation 50(6A); (b) in any other circumstances.]	10.—[⁷(1)] For the first four weeks of that absence, the amount applicable to them as a couple under regulation 83 [⁹ . . .] as the case may be and thereafter the amount [⁷ (2) (a) For the first four weeks of that absence, the amount applicable to them as a couple under regulation 83 [⁹ . . .] and thereafter the amount applicable to the claimant in Great Britain under regulation 83 [⁹ . . .] as if the claimant were a single claimant; (b) The amount which would be applicable to the claimant under regulation 83 [⁹ . . .] if that claimant was a single claimant for the period commencing on the date of claim and ending on the day after the day on which the partner returns to the United Kingdom.]
Couple or member of couple taking child or young person abroad for treatment 11.—(1) A claimant who is a member of a couple where either— (a) he or his partner is, or (b) both he and his partner are absent from [¹United Kingdom] in the circumstances specified in	11.—For the first 8 weeks of that absence, the amount applicable to the claimant under regulation 83 [⁸ . . .], as the case may be, and, thereafter, if the claimant is in Great Britain the amount applicable to him under regulation 83 [⁸ . . .], as the

Column (1)	Column (2)
sub-paragraph (2), (2) For the purpose of sub-paragraph (1), the specified circumstances are— (a) the claimant is absent from the United Kingdom but is treated as [⁵available for and actively seeking] employment in accordance with regulations 14(1) and 19(1); (b) the claimant's partner is absent from the United Kingdom and regulation 50(5) would have applied to him if he had claimed a jobseeker's allowance.	case may be, as if the claimant were a single claimant, or, as the case may be, a lone parent

Polygamous marriages where any member is abroad

12.—Subject to paragraph 13 a claimant who is a member of a polygamous marriage where— (a) he or one of his partners is, or (b) he and one or more of his partners are, or (c) two or more of his partners are, temporarily absent from the United Kingdom.	**12.**—For the first four weeks of that absence, the amount applicable to the claimant under regulations 84 to 87, as the case may be, and thereafter, if the claimant is in Great Britain the amount applicable to him under regulations 84 to 87, as the case may be, as if any member of the polygamous marriage not in the United Kingdom were not a member of the marriage.

Polygamous marriage: taking child or young person abroad for treatment

13.—(1) A claimant who is a member of a polygamous marriage where— (a) he or one of his partners is, (b) he and one of his partners are, or [¹(c) two or more of his partners are, absent from the United Kingdom in the circumstances specified in sub-paragraph (2).] (2) For the purposes of sub-paragraph (1) the specified circumstances are— (a) in respect of the claimant, [³ . . .] he is absent from the United Kingdom but is treated as available for and actively seeking employment in accordance with regulations 14(1) and 19(1); or [³(b)] one or more of the members of the polygamous marriage is absent from the United Kingdom and regulation 50(5) would have applied to the absent partner [¹if he had claimed a jobseeker's allowance.]	**13.**—For the first 8 weeks of that absence, the amount applicable to the claimant under regulations 84 to 87, as the case may be, and thereafter, if the claimant is in Great Britain the amount applicable to him under regulations 84 to 87, as the case may be, as if any member of the polygamous marriage not in the United Kingdom were not a member of the marriage.

[⁶Partner of a person subject to immigration control

13A.—	[¹² **13A.—**

Column (1)	Column (2)
(a) A claimant who is the partner of a person subject to immigration control.	(a) the amount applicable in respect of the claimant only under regulation 83(a), plus any amount which may be applicable to him under regulation 83(e) or (f) plus the amount applicable to him under regulation 87(2) or (3) or, as the case may be, regulation 85;
(b) Where regulation 84 (polygamous marriages) applies and the claimant is a person— (i) who is not subject to immigration control within the meaning of section 115(9) of the Immigration and Asylum Act; or (ii) to whom section 115 of that Act does not apply by virtue of regu- lation 2 of the Social Security (Immigration and Asylum) Consequential Amendments Regulations 2000; and (iii) who is a member of a couple and one or more of his partners is subject to immigration control within the meaning of section 115(9) of that Act and section 115 of that Act applies to her for the purposes of exclusion frwom entitlement to income-based jobseeker's allowance.]	(b) the amount determined in accordance with that regulation or regulation 85 in respect of the claimant and any partners of his who are not subject to immigration control within the meaning of section 115(9) of the Immigration and Asylum Act and to whom section 115 of that Act does not apply for the purposes of exclusion from entitlement to jobseeker's allowance;]

Persons from abroad **14.**—[⁶ person from abroad]	**14.**—[¹⁸ . . . nil]

[⁶**Persons in residential accommodation** **15.**—(1) [¹¹ . . .] (2) [¹⁰ . . .]	**15.**—(1) [¹¹ . . .] (2) [¹⁰ . . .]]
Persons temporarily absent from a hostel, residential care or nursing home **16.**—[⁸ . . .]	**16.**—[⁸ . . .]

Persons in residential care or nursing homes who become patients **17.**—[⁸ . . .]	**17.**—[⁸ . . .]

[⁷ **Joint-claim couples where a claim is made other than jointly by both members** **17A.**—A joint claim couple and one member— (a) is a person to whom regulation 3E(2)(a) applies; (b) is a person to whom regulation 3E(2)(b) applies.]	[⁷ (a) The amount which would be applicable to the claimant under regulation 83 [¹⁰ . . .] if that claimant was a single claimant for the period commencing on the day on which the member of the couple who is not the claimant fails to attend at the time and place specified by the Secretary of State for the purposes of regulation 6

Column (1)	Column (2)
	of the Claims and Payments Regulations and ending on the day on which that member does so attend;
	(b) The amount which would be applicable to the claimant under regulation 83 [^{10} . . .] if that claimant was a single claimant.]

Rounding of fractions

3.545   **18.**—Where any calculation under this Schedule or as a result of a jobseeker's allowance being awarded for a period less than one complete benefit week results in a fraction of a penny that fraction shall be treated as a penny.

AMENDMENTS

1. Jobseeker's Allowance (Amendment) Regulations 1996 (SI 1996/1516) reg.20 and Sch. (October 7, 1996).

2. Jobseeker's Allowance and Income Support (General) (Amendment) Regulations 1996 (SI 1996/1517) reg.30 (October 7, 1996).

3. Social Security and Child Support (Jobseeker's Allowance) (Miscellaneous Amendments) Regulations 1996 (SI 1996/2538) reg.2(13) (October 28, 1996).

4. Child Benefit, Child Support and Social Security (Miscellaneous Amendments) Regulations 1996 (SI 1996/1803) reg.45 (April 7, 1997).

5. Social Security (Miscellaneous Amendments) Regulations 1997 (SI 1997/454) reg.2(15) (April 7, 1997).

6. Social Security (Immigration and Asylum) Consequential Amendments Regulations 2000 (SI 2000/636) reg.4 (April 3, 2000).

7. Jobseeker's Allowance (Joint Claims) Regulations 2000 (SI 2000/1978) reg.2(5) and Sch.2 para.56 (March 19, 2001).

8. Social Security Amendment (Residential Care and Nursing Homes) Regulations 2001 (SI 2001/3767) reg.2 and Sch. Pt II para.20 (April 8, 2002).

9. Social Security Amendment (Residential Care and Nursing Homes) Regulations 2001 (SI 2001/3767) reg.2 and Sch. Pt II para.20 (as amended by Social Security Amendment (Residential Care and Nursing Homes) Regulations 2002 (SI 2002/398) reg.4(3)) (April 8, 2002).

10. Social Security (Hospital In-Patients and Miscellaneous Amendments) Regulations 2003 (SI 2003/1195) reg.6 (May 21, 2003).

11. Social Security (Removal of Residential Allowance and Miscellaneous Amendments) Regulations 2003 (SI 2003/1121) reg.4 and Sch.2 para.11 (October 6, 2003).

12. Social Security (Working Tax Credit and Child Tax Credit) (Consequential Amendments) (SI 2003/455) reg.3 and Sch.2 para.20 (April 6, 2004, except in "transitional cases" and see further the note to reg.83 and to reg.17 of the Income Support Regulations).

13. Social Security (Care Homes and Independent Hospitals) Regulations 2005 (SI 2005/2687) reg.3 and Sch.2 para.10 (October 24, 2005).

14. Social Security (Hospital In-Patients) Regulations 2005 (SI 2005/3360) reg.6 (April 10, 2006).

15. Social Security (Miscellaneous Amendments) Regulations 2007 (SI 2007/719) reg.3(9)(a) (April 2, 2007).

16. Social Security (Miscellaneous Amendments) Regulations 2007 (SI 2007/719) reg.3(9)(b) (April 9, 2007).

17. Social Security (Miscellaneous Amendments) Regulations 2007 (SI 2007/719) reg.3(9)(c) (April 8, 2007).

18. Social Security Benefits Up-rating Order 2007 (SI 2007/688) art.24(8) and Sch.17 (April 9, 2007).

DEFINITIONS

"Abbeyfield Home"—see reg.1(3).
"care home"—*ibid.*
"child"—see Jobseekers Act s.35(1).
"claimant"—*ibid.*
"couple"—see reg.1(3).
"family"—see Jobseekers Act s.35(1).
"independent hospital"—see reg.1(3).
"lone parent"—*ibid.*
"partner"—*ibid.*
"patient"—see reg.85(4).
"person from abroad"—*ibid.*
"polygamous marriage"—see reg.1(3).
"prisoner"—see reg.85(4).
"relative"—see reg.1(3).
"single claimant"—*ibid.*
"young person"—see reg.76.

GENERAL NOTE

See the note to reg.85.   3.546
There are some differences between this Schedule and Sch.7 to the Income Support Regulations, mainly due to the different conditions of entitlement for JSA (see, e.g. paras 1 and 2).

[¹ SCHEDULE 5A   **Regulation 86C**

APPLICABLE AMOUNTS OF JOINT-CLAIM COUPLES IN SPECIAL CASES

Column (1)	*Column (2)*	
Patients **1.**—[⁸ . . . **1A.**—[⁹ . . .]	**1.**—[⁸ . . . **1A.**—[⁹ . . .]	3.547
Joint-claim couple without accommodation **2.**—A joint-claim couple who are without accommodation.	**2.**—The amount applicable to the couple under regulation 86A(a) (personal allowance) only.	
Members of religious orders **3.**—A joint-claim couple who are both members of and fully maintained by a religious order.	**3.**—Nil.	

Specified cases of temporarily separated joint-claim couples
4.—A joint-claim couple who are temporarily separated where—
  (a) one member is—
    [⁷ (i) not a patient but is residing in a care home, an Abbeyfield Home or an independent hospital, or]
    (ii) [⁷ . . .
    (iii) resident in premises used for
	4.—Either—
	  (a) the amount applicable to the joint-claim couple under	

Column (1)	Column (2)
the rehabilitation of alcoholics or drug addicts;	
(iv) resident in accommodation provided under section 3 of, and Part II of the Schedule to, the Polish Resettlement Act 1947 (provision of accommodation in camps);	
(v) participating in arrangements for training made under section 2 of the Employment and Training Act 1973, or section 2 of the Enterprise and New Towns (Scotland) Act 1990 or participating in an employment rehabilitation programme established under that section of the Act of 1973, where the course requires him to live away from the dwelling occupied as the home; or	
(vi) in a probation or bail hostel approved for the purpose by the Secretary of State, and	
(b) the other member is—	(b) the aggregate of the applicable amounts of both claimants assessed under the provisions of these Regulations as if each of them were a single claimant, whichever is the greater.
(i) living in the dwelling occupied as the home;	
(ii) a patient;	
[⁷ (iii) residing in a care home, an Abbeyfield Home or an independent hospital.]	

Polygamous Marriages where one or more members of the marriage are temporarily separated

Column (1)	Column (2)
5.—A joint-claim couple where one member is a member of a polygamous marriage and is temporarily separated from a partner of his, where one of them is living in the home while the other member is—	5.—Either—
[⁷ (a) not a patient but is residing in a care home, an Abbeyfield Home or an independent hospital, or]	(a) the amount applicable to the joint-claim couple under regulation 86B; or
(b) [⁷ . . .]	(b) the aggregate of the amount applicable for the joint-claim couple in respect of the members of the polygamous marriage who remain in the home under regulation 86B and the amount applicable in respect of those members not in the home calculated as if each of them were a single claimant, whichever is the greater.
(c) resident in premises used for the rehabilitation of alcoholics or drug addicts;	
(d) attending a course of training or instruction provided or approved by the Secretary of State where the course requires him to live away from home; or	
(e) in a probation or bail hostel approved for the purpose by the Secretary of State.	

Joint-claim couples and members of polygamous marriages where one member is, or all are, temporarily in local authority accommodation

Column (1)	Column (2)
6.—[⁶ . . .]	6.—[⁶ . . .]

Column (1)	Column (2)
Joint-claim couples where one member is absent from the United Kingdom 7.—A joint-claim couple where one member is temporarily absent from the United Kingdom— (a) in the circumstances prescribed in regulation 50(6B); (b) in any other circumstances.	7.— (a) The amount applicable to them as a couple under regulation 86A [² . . .] for the relevant period prescribed in regulation 50(6B). (b) For the first four weeks of that absence, the amount applicable to them as a couple under regulation 86A [² . . .] as the case may be and thereafter the amount applicable to the claimant in Great Britain under regulation 83 [² . . .] as the case may be as if that claimant were a single claimant.
Polygamous marriages where any member of the marriage is abroad 8.—A joint-claim couple where one member is a member of a polygamous marriage and— (a)he, the other member or one of his partners is; (b) he, the other member and one or more of his partners are; or (c) the other member and one or more of his partners or two or more of his partners are, temporarily absent from the United Kingdom.	8.—For the first four weeks of that absence, the amount applicable to the joint-claim couple under regulations 86B to [² 86C], as the case may be, and thereafter, if the joint-claim couple are in Great Britain the amount applicable to them under regulations 86B to [² 86C], as the case may be, as if any member of the polygamous marriage not in the United Kingdom were not a member of the marriage.
Members of joint-claim couples in residential accommodation 9.—[⁴ . . .]	9.—[⁴ . . .]
Members of joint-claim couples temporarily absent from a hostel, residential care or nursing home 10.—[² . . .]	10.—[² . . .]
Members of joint-claim couples in residential care or nursing homes who become patients 11.—[² . . .]	11.—[² . . .]

Rounding of fractions

12.—Where any calculation under this Schedule or as a result of a joint-claim jobseeker's allowance being awarded for a period of less than one complete benefit week results in a fraction of a penny, that fraction shall be treated as a penny.]   **3.548**

AMENDMENTS

1. Jobseeker's Allowance (Joint Claims) Regulations 2000 (SI 2000/1978) reg.2(5) and Sch.2 para.57 (March 19, 2001).

2. Social Security Amendment (Residential Care and Nursing Homes) Regulations 2001 (SI 2001/3767) reg.2 and Sch. Pt II para.21 (April 8, 2002).

3. Social Security Benefits Up-Rating Order 2003 (SI 2003/526) art.23(9) and Sch.14 (April 7, 2003).

4. Social Security (Removal of Residential Allowance and Miscellaneous Amendments) Regulations 2003 (SI 2003/1121) reg.4 and Sch.2 para.12 (October 6, 2003).

5. Social Security (Hospital In-Patients and Miscellaneous Amendments) Regulations 2003 (SI 2003/1195) reg.6 (May 21, 2003).

6. Social Security (Miscellaneous Amendments) Regulations 2004 (SI 2004/565) reg.6 (April 1, 2004).

7. Social Security (Care Homes and Independent Hospitals) Regulations 2005 (SI 2005/2687) reg.3 and Sch.2 para.10 (October 24, 2005).

8. Social Security (Hospital In-Patients) Regulations 2005 (SI 2005/3360) reg.6 (April 10, 2006).

9. Social Security (Miscellaneous Amendments) Regulations 2007 (SI 2007/719) reg.3(10) (April 9, 2007).

GENERAL NOTE

3.549   This regulation makes provision corresponding to Sch.5 for joint-claim couples.

SCHEDULE 6   **Regulations 99(2), 101(2)**
                                          and 106(6)

SUMS TO BE DISREGARDED IN THE CALCULATION OF EARNINGS

3.550   [^{15} 1.—(1) In the case of a claimant who has been engaged in remunerative work as an employed earner or, had the employment been in Great Britain, would have been so engaged—
  (a) any earnings, other than items to which sub-paragraph (2) applies, paid or due to be paid from that employment which terminated before the first day of entitlement to a jobseeker's allowance;
  (b) any earnings, other than a payment of the nature described in [^{17} sub-paragraph (2) (a) or (b)(ii)] paid or due to be paid from that employment which has not been terminated where the claimant is not—
       (i)   engaged in remunerative work, or
       (ii) suspended from his employment.
  (2) This sub-paragraph applies to—
  [^{17} (a) any payment of the nature described in—
       (i)   regulation 98(1)(d), or
       (ii) section 28, 64 or 68 of the Employment Rights Act 1966 (guarantee payments, suspension from work on medical or maternity grounds); and]
  (b) any award, sum or payment of the nature described in—
       (i)   regulation 98(1)(f) or (g), or
       (ii) section 34 or 70 of the Employment Rights Act 1996 (guarantee payments and suspension from work: complaints to employment tribunals),
       including any payment made following the settlement of a complaint to an employment tribunal or of court proceedings.
  1A.—If the claimant's partner has been engaged in remunerative work as an employed earner or, had the employment been in Great Britain, would have been so engaged, any earnings paid or due to be paid on termination of that employment by way of retirement but only if—
  (a) on retirement the partner is entitled to a retirement pension under the Benefits Act, or
  (b) the only reason the partner is not entitled to a retirement pension under the Benefits Act is because the contribution conditions are not satisfied.
  [^{23} **1B.** If the claimant's partner has been engaged in remunerative work as an employed earner or, had the employment been in Great Britain, would have been so engaged, any earnings paid or due to be paid on termination of that employment by way of retirement but only if—
  (a) on retirement the partner is entitled to a state pension under Part 1 of the Pensions Act 2014, or

(b) the only reason the partner is not entitled to a state pension under Part 1 of the Pensions Act 2014 is because the partner does not have the minimum number of qualifying years.]

2.—(1) In the case of a claimant to whom this paragraph applies, any earnings (other than items to which paragraph 1(2) applies) which relate to employment which ceased before the first day of entitlement to a jobseeker's allowance whether or not that employment has terminated.

(2) This paragraph applies to a claimant who has been engaged in part-time employment as an employed earner or, had the employment been in Great Britain, would have been so engaged; but it does not apply to a claimant who has been suspended from his employment.]

3.—Any payment to which regulation 98(1)(f) applies—
(a) which is due to be paid more than 52 weeks after the date of termination of the employment in respect of which the payment is made; or
(b) which is a compensatory award within the meaning of section [15118(1)(b) of the Employment Rights Act 1996] for so long as such an award remains unpaid and the employer is insolvent within the meaning of section 127 of that Act.

4.—In the case of a claimant who has been engaged in remunerative work or part-time employment as a self-employed earner or, had the employment been in Great Britain, would have been so engaged and who has ceased to be so employed, from the date of the cessation of his employment any earnings derived from that employment except earnings to which regulation 95(2) (royalties etc.) applies.

5.—(1) In a case to which this paragraph applies, [7£20.00] but notwithstanding regulation 88 (calculation of income and capital of members of claimant's family and of a polygamous marriage), if this paragraph applies to a claimant it shall not apply to his partner except where, and to the extent that, the earnings of the claimant which are to be disregarded under this paragraph are less than [7£20.00].

(2) This paragraph applies where the claimant's applicable amount includes, or but for his being an in-patient [8 . . .] [13 . . .] would include, an amount by way of a disability premium under Schedule 1 (applicable amounts).

(3) This paragraph applies where—
(a) the claimant is a member of a couple, and—
  (i) his applicable amount would include an amount by way of the disability premium under Schedule 1 but for the higher pensioner premium under that Schedule being applicable; or
  (ii) had he not been an in-patient [8 . . .] [13 . . .] his applicable amount would include the higher pensioner premium under that Schedule and had that been the case he would also satisfy the condition in (i) above; and
(b) he or his partner [18 has not attained the qualifying age for state pension credit] and at least one is engaged in part-time employment.

(4) This paragraph applies where—
(a) the claimant's applicable amount includes, or but for his being an in-patient [8 . . .] [13 . . .] would include, an amount by way of the higher pensioner premium under Schedule 1; and
(b) the claimant or, if he is a member of a couple, either he or his partner has attained [18 the qualifying age for state pension credit]; and
(c) immediately before attaining that age he or, as the case may be, he or his partner was engaged in part-time employment and the claimant was entitled by virtue of sub-paragraph (2) or (3) to a disregard of [7£20.00]; and
(d) he or, as the case may be, he or his partner has continued in part-time employment.

(5) [6 . . .].
(6) [6 . . .].

(7) For the purposes of this paragraph—
(a) except where head (b) or (c) applies, no account shall be taken of any period not exceeding eight consecutive weeks occurring—
  (i) on or after the date on which the claimant or, if he is a member of a couple, he or his partner attained [18 the qualifying age for state pension credit] during which either was or both were not engaged in part-time employment or the claimant was not entitled to a jobseeker's allowance [16 , income support or an employment and support allowance]; or
  (ii) immediately after the date on which the claimant or his partner ceased to participate in arrangements for training made under section 2 of the Employment and Training Act 1973 or section 2 of the Enterprise and New Towns (Scotland) Act 1990 or to participate in an employment rehabilitation programme established under that section of the 1973 Act;

(b) in a case where the claimant has ceased to be entitled to a jobseeker's allowance [¹⁶ , income support or an employment and support allowance] because he, or if he is a member of a couple, he or his partner becomes engaged in remunerative work, no account shall be taken of any period, during which he was not entitled to a jobseeker's allowance [¹⁶ , income support or an employment and support allowance], not exceeding the permitted period, occurring on or after the date on which the claimant or, as the case may be, his partner attained [¹⁸ the qualifying age for state pension credit];

(c) no account shall be taken of any period occurring on or after the date on which the claimant or, if he is a member of a couple, he or his partner attained [¹⁸ the qualifying age for state pension credit] during which the claimant was not entitled to a jobseeker's allowance [¹⁶ , income support or an employment and support allowance] because he or his partner was participating in arrangements for training made under section 2 of the Employment and Training Act 1973 or section 2 of the Enterprise and New Towns (Scotland) Act 1990 or participating in an employment rehabilitation programme established under that section of the 1973 Act;

[⁵6.—In a case where the claimant is a lone parent and paragraph 5 does not apply, [⁷£20.00].

7.—(1) In a case to which neither paragraph 5 or 6 applies to the claimant, and subject to sub-paragraph (2), where the claimant's applicable amount includes an amount by way of the carer premium under Schedule 1 (applicable amounts), [⁷£20.00] of the earnings of the person who is, or at any time in the preceding eight weeks was, in receipt of [⁹ carer's allowance] or treated in accordance with paragraph 17(2) of that Schedule as being in receipt of [⁹ carer's allowance].

(2) Where the carer premium is awarded in respect of the claimant and of any partner of his, their earnings shall for the purposes of this paragraph be aggregated, but the amount to be disregarded in accordance with sub-paragraph (1) shall not exceed [⁷£20.00] of the aggregated amount.

8.—Where the carer premium is awarded in respect of a claimant who is a member of a couple and whose earnings are less than [⁷£20.00], but is not awarded in respect of the other member of the couple, and that other member is engaged in an employment—

(a) specified in paragraph 9(1), so much of the other member's earnings as would not when aggregated with the amount disregarded under paragraph 7 exceed [⁷£20.00];

(b) other than one specified in paragraph 9(1), so much of the other member's earnings from such other employment up to £5 as would not when aggregated with the amount disregarded under paragraph 7 exceed [⁷£20.00].

9.—(1) In a case to which none of paragraphs 5 to 8 applies to the claimant, [⁷£20.00] of earnings derived from one or more employments as—

(a) [²¹. . .]

[¹¹ (aa) [²¹. . .]]

[¹² (ab) [²¹. . .]]

[²¹ (a) a part-time fire-fighter employed by a fire and rescue authority under the Fire and Rescue Services Act 2004 or by the Scottish Fire and Rescue Service established under section 1A of the Fire (Scotland) Act 2005;]

(b) an auxiliary coastguard in respect of coast rescue activities;

(c) a person engaged part-time in the manning or launching of a lifeboat;

(d) a member of any [²² . . .] reserve force prescribed in Part I of [¹⁴ Schedule 6 to the Social Security (Contributions) Regulations 2001];

but, notwithstanding regulation 88 (calculation of income and capital of members of claimant's family and of a polygamous marriage), if this paragraph applies to a claimant it shall not apply to his partner except to the extent specified in sub-paragraph (2).

(2) If the claimant's partner is engaged in employment—

(a) specified in sub-paragraph (1), so much of his earnings as would not in aggregate with the amount of the claimant's earnings disregarded under this paragraph exceed [⁷£20.00];

(b) other than one specified in sub-paragraph (1), so much of his earnings from that employment up to £5 as would not in aggregate with the claimant's earnings disregarded under this paragraph exceed [⁷£20.00].

10.—Where the claimant is engaged in one or more employments specified in paragraph 9(1) but his earnings derived from such employments are less than [⁷£20.00] in any week and he is also engaged in any other part-time employment, so much of his earnings from that other employment up to £5 as would not in aggregate with the amount of his earnings disregarded under paragraph 9 exceed [⁷£20.00].

11.—Where the claimant is a member of a couple [¹ . . .]—

(a) in a case to which none of paragraphs 5 to 10 applies, £10; but, notwithstanding regulation 88 (calculation of income and capital of members of a claimant's family and of a polygamous marriage), if this paragraph applies to a claimant it shall not apply to his partner except where, and to the extent that, the earnings of the claimant which are to be disregarded under this sub-paragraph are less than £10;

(b) in a case to which one or more of paragraphs 5 to 10 applies and the total amount disregarded under those paragraphs is less than £10, so much of the claimant's earnings as would not in aggregate with the amount disregarded under paragraphs 5 to 10 exceed £10.

12.—In a case to which none of paragraphs 5 to 11 applies to the claimant, £5.

13.—Notwithstanding the foregoing provisions of this Schedule, where two or more payments of the same kind and from the same source are to be taken into account in the same benefit week, because it has not been practicable to treat the payments under regulation 96(1)(b) (date on which income treated as paid) as paid on the first day of the benefit week in which they were due to be paid, there shall be disregarded from each payment the sum that would have been disregarded if the payment had been taken into account on the date on which it was due to be paid.

14.—Any earnings derived from employment which are payable in a country outside the United Kingdom for such period during which there is a prohibition against the transfer to the United Kingdom of those earnings.

15.—Where a payment of earnings is made in a currency other than sterling, any banking charge or commission payable in converting that payment into sterling.

16.—Any earnings which are due to be paid before the date of claim and which would otherwise fall to be taken into account in the same benefit week as a payment of the same kind and from the same source.

17.—Any earnings of a child or young person [¹⁰ . . .].

18.—[¹⁰ . . .]

[¹⁹ **19.**—(1) In the case of a contribution-based jobseeker's allowance, where by reason of earnings to which sub-paragraph (3) applies (in aggregate with the claimant's other earnings (if any) calculated in accordance with this Part) the claimant would (apart from this paragraph) have a personal rate of less than 10 pence, the amount of such earnings but only to the extent that that amount exceeds the claimant's personal rate less 10 pence.

(2) In the case of an income-based jobseeker's allowance, where earnings to which sub-paragraph (3) applies (in aggregate with the claimant's other income (if any) calculated in accordance with this Part) exceed the applicable amount less 10 pence, the amount of those earnings corresponding to that excess.

(3) This sub-paragraph applies to earnings, in so far as they exceed the amount disregarded under paragraph 9, derived by the claimant from employment as a member of any [²² . . .] reserve force prescribed in Part 1 of Schedule 6 to the Contributions Regulations in respect of a period of annual continuous training for a maximum of 15 days in any calendar year [²² or in respect of training in the claimant's first year of training as a member of a reserve force for a maximum of 43 days in that year.]

(4) In sub-paragraph (1), "personal rate" means the rate for the claimant calculated as specified in section 4(1) of the Act.]

20.—In this Schedule "part-time employment" means employment in which the person is not to be treated as engaged in remunerative work under regulation 52 or 53 (persons treated as engaged, or not engaged, in remunerative work).

21.—In paragraph 5(7)(b) "permitted period" means a period determined in accordance with regulation 3A of the Income Support Regulations, as it has effect by virtue of regulation 87(7) of these Regulations.

AMENDMENTS

1. Jobseeker's Allowance (Amendment) Regulations 1996 (SI 1996/1516) reg.19 (October 7, 1996).

2. Jobseeker's Allowance (Amendment) Regulations 1996 (SI 1996/1516) reg.20 and Sch. (October 7, 1996).

3. Jobseeker's Allowance and Income Support (General) (Amendment) Regulations 1996 (SI 1996/1517) reg.31 (October 7, 1996).

4. Child Benefit, Child Support and Social Security (Miscellaneous Amendments) Regulations 1996 (SI 1996/1803) reg.46 (April 7, 1997).

5. Social Security Amendment (Lone Parents) Regulations 1998 (SI 1998/766) reg.15 (April 6, 1998).

6. Social Security (Miscellaneous Amendments) Regulations 2000 (SI 2000/681) reg.12(b) (April 3, 2000).

7. Social Security Amendment (Capital Limits and Earnings Disregards) Regulations 2000 (SI 2000/2545) reg.3 and Sch. para.3 (April 9, 2001).

8. Social Security Amendment (Residential Care and Nursing Homes) Regulations 2001 (SI 2001/3767) reg.2(2) and Pt II of Sch. para.22 (April 8, 2002).

9. Social Security (Miscellaneous Amendments) Regulations 2003 (SI 2003/511) reg.3(4) and (5) (April 1, 2003).

10. Social Security (Working Tax Credit and Child Tax Credit) (Consequential Amendments) Regulations 2003 (SI 2003/455) reg.3 and Sch.2 para.22 (April 6, 2004, except in "transitional cases" and see further the note to regs 83 and to 17 of the Income Support Regulations).

11. Fire and Rescue Services Act 2004 (Consequential Amendments) (England) Order 2004 (SI 2004/3168) art.36(4) (December 30, 2004) (in relation to England); Fire and Rescue Services Act 2004 (Consequential Amendments) (Wales) Order 2005 (SI 2005/2929 (W.214)) art.36(4) (October 25, 2005) (in relation to Wales). The amendment does not extend to Scotland.

12. Fire (Scotland) Act 2005 (Consequential Provisions and Modifications) Order 2005 (SI 2005/2060 (S.7)) art.3 and Sch. para.10(4) (August 2, 2005) (in relation to Scotland only; this amendment also revokes head (a) of para.9(1), again in relation to Scotland only).

13. Social Security (Care Homes and Independent Hospitals) Regulations 2005 (SI 2005/2687) reg.3 and Sch.2 para.12 (October 24, 2005).

14. Social Security (Miscellaneous Amendments) (No.4) Regulations 2006 (SI 2006/2378) reg.13(3)(c) (October 2, 2006).

15. Social Security (Miscellaneous Amendments) (No.5) Regulations 2007 (SI 2007/2618) reg.8(14) (October 1, 2007).

16. Employment and Support Allowance (Consequential Provisions) (No.2) Regulations 2008 (SI 2008/1554) reg.3(26) (October 27, 2008).

17. Social Security (Miscellaneous Amendments) (No.4) Regulations 2009 (SI 2009/2655) reg.4(14) (October 26, 2009).

18. Social Security (Equalisation of State Pension Age) Regulations 2009 (SI 2009/1488) reg.15 (April 6, 2010).

19. Jobseeker's Allowance (Members of the Reserve Forces) Regulations 2012 (SI 2012/1616) reg.2(7) (July 30, 2012).

20. Police and Fire Reform (Scotland) Act 2012 (Consequential Provisions and Modifications) Order 2013 (SI 2013/602) art.26 and Sch.2 para.74(4) (April 1, 2013).

21. Social Security (Miscellaneous Amendments) (No.3) Regulations 2013 (SI 2013/2536) reg.6(14) (October 29, 2013).

22. Social Security (Members of the Reserve Forces) (Amendment) Regulations 2015 (SI 2015/389) reg.3(6) (April 6, 2015).

23. Pensions Act 2014 (Consequential, Supplementary and Incidental Amendments) Order 2015 (SI 2015/1985) art.16(3) (April 6, 2016).

DEFINITIONS

"the Benefits Act"—see Jobseekers Act s.35(1).
"benefit week"—see reg.1(3).
"child"—see Jobseekers Act s.35(1).
"claimant"—*ibid.*, and reg.88(1).
"couple"—see reg.1(3).
"date of claim"—*ibid.*
"employment"—see reg.3
"employed earner"—see reg.3 and SSCBA s.2(1)(a).
"first year of training"—see reg.1(3).
"Great Britain"—see Jobseekers Act s.35(1).
"family"—*ibid.*
"partner"—see reg.1(3).

"polygamous marriage"—*ibid.*
"qualifying age for state pension credit"—*ibid.*
"remunerative work"—*ibid.*, and reg.51(1).
"self employed earner"—see reg.1(3) and SSCSA s.2(1)(b).
"young person"—see regs 1(3) and 76.

GENERAL NOTE

Before April 6, 2004 the income (but not the capital) of a child or young person   3.551
who was a member of the claimant's family was aggregated with the claimant's,
subject to the modifications in reg.106. Under the form of this Schedule in force
at that time paras 1–13 and 19 did not apply to children or young persons (see the
form of reg.88(2) then in force) and paras 17 and 18 only applied to children and
young persons (see the 2003 edition of this volume for the old form of reg.88 and of
paras 17 and 18 of this Schedule). However, with effect from April 6, 2004 (except
in "transitional cases"—see the note to reg.83 and to reg.17 of the Income Support
Regulations), amounts for children and young persons have been removed from
income-based JSA; financial assistance to help with the cost of bringing up a child
or young person is now provided through the child tax credit system, see Vol.IV of
this series. As a consequence, the income of a child or young person is no longer
aggregated with the claimant's (see the new form of reg.88 and the notes to that
regulation) and so the disregards that applied to such income are no longer needed
(although note that part of para.17 has been retained). The former disregards do
however remain in force for "transitional cases"—see the note to reg.83 and to
reg.17 of the Income Support Regulations.

For income-based JSA claimants who had an award of child tax credit before
April 6, 2004 see reg.8 of the Social Security (Working Tax Credit and Child
Tax Credit) (Consequential Amendments) Regulations 2003 (SI 2003/455) (as
amended) on p.1763 and the notes to that regulation.

The disregards in this Schedule are similar to those in Sch.8 to the Income
Support Regulations but there are some differences, the main ones being the slight
difference in the treatment of earnings where part-time employment has stopped
(para.2) and the disregard in para.3. See the notes to Sch.8.

Note that where the claimant is a member of a couple, unless the £20 disregard
in paras 5–10 applies (para.6 cannot in fact apply as it only applies to lone parents)
the earnings disregard is £10 (para.11). Since October 7, 1996 this has also been
the case for income support (replacing the previous £15 earnings disregard for long-
term unemployed couples aged less than 60). For a single claimant the earnings
disregard is £5 (unless the £20 disregard in paras 5–10 applies) (para.12).

Paragraphs 1, 1A, 1B and 2
See the notes to paras 1 and 2 of Sch.8 to the Income Support Regulations.   3.552
However, note that in the case of old style JSA the disregard is slightly less extensive
where part-time work has ceased before the first day of entitlement to benefit (see
para.2). Under para.2 any employment protection payments referred to in reg.98(1)
(f) (but see para.3 if the payment is due to be made more than 52 weeks after the
termination of the employment) or (g) (including any payment made in settlement
of an employment tribunal claim or court action) are taken into account, which is
not the case for income support. It is not entirely clear why this different rule for old
style JSA is being maintained (although the difference is of less significance since the
October 2009 changes to paras 1 and 2 of Sch.8 to the Income Support Regulations
and to para.1 of this Schedule), since the stated intention behind the October 2007
changes was to align the treatment of termination payments on all new claims to
benefit.

Paragraphs 1A and 1B apply to a claimant's partner's earnings paid on termination of employment due to retirement. Such earnings will be disregarded in full,
provided that the partner is retiring at pensionable age. For the equivalent income
support provision see para.1A of Sch.8 to the Income Support Regulations. Under

that provision the disregard applies if the partner has reached the qualifying age for state pension credit. The difference between the two provisions reflects the fact that it is possible for a person to claim old style JSA up to pensionable age (i.e. currently 65 in the case of a man), whereas a person who has reached the qualifying age for state pension credit is not entitled to income support. "Qualifying age for state pension credit" is defined in reg.1(3)—the effect of that definition is that the qualifying age was 60 but from April 2010 it gradually rose in line with the staged increase in pensionable age for women until it reached 65 in November 2018 (this equalisation of the state pension age for men and women was previously to have been completed by April 5, 2020 but the timetable for this in the Pensions Act 1995 was accelerated with effect from April 2016 so that women's state pension age became 65 in November 2018; in addition, the increase in state pension age to 66 for both men and women has been brought forward—it started to rise from 65 in December 2018 to reach 66 by October 2020 (see s.1 of the Pensions Act 2011) and between 2026 and 2028 it will reach 67 (see s.26 of the Pensions Act 2014)).

In *R(JSA) 8/03* the claimant, a supply teacher who worked part-time, claimed JSA at the beginning of the school summer holidays. The Commissioner accepts that unless it could be shown that the claimant had a cycle of work she had ceased to be engaged in employment at the time of her claim for JSA and so her earnings fell to be disregarded under para.2. Since she worked odd days with a number of schools on an irregular basis a cycle of work could not be established. See also *CIS 914/1997* and *CJSA 2759/1998* in the note to reg.5 of the Income Support Regulations under the heading "*Term-time only workers*" for other examples of circumstances in which a cycle of work had not, or had not yet, been established.

But when a part-time worker does have a recognisable cycle of work, *R(JSA) 2/03* holds that they are to be treated as engaged in part-time work for the whole of the cycle. The Commissioner considered that it would be odd if "engaged in . . . employment" had a different meaning in para.2 from the meaning in para.1 and that although para.20 (definition of "part-time work") was not well-drafted, the reference to reg.52 in his view made it plain that a person was to be regarded as engaged in part-time work in circumstances where they would be engaged in remunerative work if a greater number of hours per week were worked. [Note that in *R(JSA) 2/03* the Commissioner held that the claimant was to be regarded as engaged in part-time employment during the whole of the cycle by virtue of reg.51(2)(c) in accordance with the House of Lords' decision in *Banks v Chief Adjudication Officer* [2001] UKHL 33, [2001] 1 W.L.R. 1411 (reported as *R(IS) 15/01*). In relation to JSA (although not income support) *R(JSA) 4/03* has since held that reg.51(2)(c) is inconsistent with EC Directive 79/7 and should be regarded as being of no effect (see the note to reg.51). The consequence is that reg.51(2)(b)(i) applies instead (see *R(JSA) 5/03* in the note to reg.51). However, this does not affect the reasoning in *R(JSA) 2/03* that a part-time worker with a recognisable cycle of work is to be regarded as engaged in employment during the whole of the cycle.] Thus the disregard in para.2 did not apply because the claimant had not ceased to be engaged in part-time employment. The claimant in *R(JSA) 2/03* was paid monthly for a 12-hour working week during term-time only. The Commissioner holds, under reg.80(1) and applying *R(IS) 10/95*, that her earnings were paid "in respect of a month" and that under the form of reg.94(2)(a) as then in force they were to be taken into account for the period of a month beginning with the first day of the benefit week in which the earnings were due to be paid. The result was that the claimant was not entitled to JSA during the half-term holiday as her earnings exceeded her JSA applicable amount.

Paragraph 3

3.553   Under old style JSA, any payment of compensation for unfair dismissal under ss.112(4), 113, 117(3)(a), 128, 131 and 132 of the Employment Rights Act 1996 is disregarded if it is due to be paid more than 52 weeks after the end of the employment to which it relates (sub-para.(a)). In addition, any unpaid compensatory award under s.118(1)(b) of the 1996 Act where the employer is insolvent is also disregarded (sub-para.(b)).

Paragraph 19

The effect of para.19, as amended from April 6, 2015, is that earnings as a member of a reserve force from training (i) for a maximum of 43 days in the first year of training (see the definition of "first year of training" in reg.1(3)); or (ii) for a maximum of 15 days' annual continuous training in any calendar year, are disregarded to the extent that they would have the effect of reducing old style JSA entitlement to less than 10p per week. This disregard is in addition to the £20 disregard of earnings as a member of a reserve force in para.9(1)(d).

3.554

Note that a claimant is treated as available for employment while engaged in such reservist training (see reg.14(1)(v)) and as actively seeking employment in any week in which he is taking part in such training for three or more days a week (see reg.19(1)(y)).

The purpose of these amendments is to enable entitlement to old style JSA to continue while a claimant (or any partner: see reg.88(1)) is attending such training. Note also that reg.2 of the Social Security (Benefit) (Members of the Forces) Regulations 1975 (SI 1975/493) has been amended by reg.2(3) of the Social Security (Benefit) (Members of the Forces) (Amendment) Regulations 2012 (SI 2012/1656) with effect from July 30, 2012, in order to remove the prohibition on entitlement to old style JSA for serving members of the armed forces.

See reg.94(2C) which provides that earnings from such reservist training will be taken into account, where the training lasts for the number of days listed in column 1 of the table in reg.94(2C)(c), for the number of days listed in column 2 of the table; or in any other case, for the number of days that the training lasts. The period begins on the date that the earnings are treated as paid under reg.96 (see reg.94(2D)).

Paragraph 20

See *R(JSA) 2/03* in the note to para.2 above.

3.555

[¹ SCHEDULE 6A

SUMS TO BE DISREGARDED IN THE CALCULATION OF EARNINGS OF MEMBERS OF JOINT-CLAIM COUPLES

1.—(1) In a case to which this paragraph applies, [² £20]; but notwithstanding regulation 88ZA (calculation of income and capital of members of a joint-claim couple), if this paragraph applies to one member of a joint-claim couple, it shall not apply to the other member except where, and to the extent that, the earnings of the member which are to be disregarded under this paragraph are less than [² £20].

3.556

(2) This paragraph applies where the joint-claim couple's applicable amount includes, or but for one member being an in-patient [³ . . .] [⁵ . . .] would include, an amount by way of a disability premium under Schedule 1 (applicable amounts).

(3) This paragraph applies where—
  (a) the joint-claim couple's applicable amount would include—
    (i) an amount by way of the disability premium under Schedule 1 but for the higher pensioner premium under that Schedule being applicable; or
    (ii) had a member of that couple not been an in-patient [³ . . .] [⁵ . . .], the higher pensioner premium under that Schedule and had that been the case, the joint-claim couple would also satisfy the condition in (i) above; and
  (b) either member [⁸ has not attained the qualifying age for state pension credit] and at least one is engaged in part-time employment.

(4) This paragraph applies where—
  (a) the joint-claim couple's applicable amount includes, or but for a member being an inpatient [³ . . .] [⁵ . . .] would include, an amount by way of the higher pensioner premium under Schedule 1; and

(b) either member has attained [8 the qualifying age for state pension credit]; and

(c) immediately before attaining that age either, or as the case may be both, members were engaged in part-time employment and the joint-claimant was entitled by virtue of sub-paragraph (2) or (3) to a disregard of [2 £20]; and

(d) either, or as the case may be both, members have continued in part-time employment.

(5) For the purposes of this paragraph—

(a) except where paragraph (b) or (c) applies, no account shall be taken of any period not exceeding eight consecutive weeks occurring—

(i) on or after the date on which either member attained [8 the qualifying age for state pension credit] during which either member was, or both members were, not engaged in part-time employment or either member was, or both members were, not entitled to a jobseeker's allowance or [7 , income support or an employment and support allowance]; or

(ii) immediately after the date on which either member ceased to participate in arrangements for training made under section 2 of the Employment and Training Act 1973 or section 2 of the Enterprise and New Towns (Scotland) Act 1990 or ceased to participate in an employment rehabilitation programme established under that section of the 1973 Act;

(b) in a case where either or both members have ceased to be entitled to a jobseeker's allowance or [7 , income support or an employment and support allowance] because either member becomes engaged in remunerative work, no account shall be taken of any period during which either or both members were not entitled to a jobseeker's allowance or [7 , income support or an employment and support allowance], not exceeding the permitted period, occurring on or after the date on which either member attained [8 the qualifying age for state pension credit];

(c) no account shall be taken of any period occurring on or after the date on which either member attained [8 the qualifying age for state pension credit] during which either or both members were not entitled to a jobseeker's allowance or [7 , income support or an employment and support allowance] because either or both members were participating in arrangements for training made under section 2 of the Employment and Training Act 1973 or section 2 of the Enterprise and New Towns (Scotland) Act 1990 or participating in an employment rehabilitation programme established under that section of the 1973 Act.

2.—(1) In a case where paragraph 1 does not apply to a member of a joint-claim couple and subject to sub-paragraph (2), where the joint-claim couple's applicable amount includes an amount by way of the carer premium under Schedule 1 (applicable amounts), [2 £20] of the earnings of the person who is, or at any time in the preceding eight weeks was, in receipt of [4 a carer's allowance] or treated in accordance with paragraph 20J(2) of that Schedule as being in receipt of [4 a carer's allowance].

(2) Where the carer premium is awarded in respect of a joint-claim couple, the earnings of each member shall for the purposes of this paragraph be aggregated but the amount to be disregarded in accordance with sub-paragraph (1) shall not exceed [2 £20] of the aggregated amount.

3.—(1) In the case to which neither paragraph 1 nor 2 applies to a member of a joint-claim couple ("the first member"), [2 £20] of earnings derived from one or more employments to which paragraph 9 of Schedule 6 applies but, notwithstanding regulation 88ZA (calculation of income and capital of a joint-claim couple), if this paragraph applies to one member of a joint-claim couple it shall not apply to the other member except to the extent specified in sub-paragraph (2).

(2) If the other member is engaged in employment—

(a) specified in sub-paragraph (1), so much of his earnings as would not in aggregate with the amount of the first member's earnings disregarded under this paragraph exceed [2 £20];

(b) other than one specified in sub-paragraph (1), so much of his earnings from that employment up to £5 as would not in aggregate with the first member's earnings disregarded under this paragraph exceed [2 £20] .

4.—Where a member of a joint-claim couple is engaged in one or more employments specified in paragraph 3(1) but his earnings derived from such employments are less than [2 £20] in any week and he is also engaged in any other part-time employment, so much of his earnings from that other employment up to £5 as would not in aggregate with the amount of his earnings disregarded under paragraph 3 exceed [2 £20].

5.—[9 . . .]

6.—(1) In a case where none of paragraphs 1 to 5 apply, £10 but, notwithstanding regulation 88ZA (calculation of income and capital of joint-claim couples), if this paragraph applies to one member of a joint-claim couple, it shall not apply to the other member except where, and to the extent that, the earnings of the member which are to be disregarded under this sub-paragraph are less than £10.

(2) In a case where one or more of paragraphs 1 to 5 apply and the total amount disregarded under those paragraphs is less than £10, so much of the earnings of the member of a joint-claim couple as would not in aggregate with the amount disregarded under paragraphs 1 to 5 exceed £10.

7.—In this Schedule, "part-time employment" and "permitted period" shall bear the meanings prescribed respectively in paragraphs 20 and 21 of Schedule 6.]

AMENDMENTS

1. Jobseeker's Allowance (Joint Claims) Regulations 2000 (SI 2000/1978) reg.2(5) and Sch.2 para.58 (March 19, 2001).
2. Social Security Amendment (Capital Limits and Earnings Disregards) Regulations 2000 (SI 2000/2545) reg.3 and Sch. para.3 (April 9, 2001).
3. Social Security Amendment (Residential Care and Nursing Homes) Regulations 2001 (SI 2001/3767) reg.2(2) and Pt II of Sch. para.23 (April 8, 2002).
4. Social Security (Miscellaneous Amendments) Regulations 2003 (SI 2003/511) reg.3(4) and (5) (April 1, 2003).
5. Social Security (Care Homes and Independent Hospitals) Regulations 2005 (SI 2005/2687) reg.3 and Sch.2 para.13 (October 24, 2005).
6. Social Security (Miscellaneous Amendments) (No.4) Regulations 2006 (SI 2006/2378) reg.13(3)(d) (October 2, 2006).
7. Employment and Support Allowance (Consequential Provisions) (No.2) Regulations 2008 (SI 2008/1554) reg.3(27) (October 27, 2008).
8. Social Security (Equalisation of State Pension Age) Regulations 2009 (SI 2009/1488) reg.16 (April 6, 2010).
9. Jobseeker's Allowance (Members of the Reserve Forces) Regulations 2012 (SI 2012/1616) reg.2(8) (July 30, 2012).

DEFINITIONS

"employment"—see reg.3.
"joint-claim couple"—see Jobseekers Act 1995 s.1(4).
"joint-claim jobseeker's allowance"—*ibid.*
"qualifying age for state pension credit"—see reg.1(3).
"remunerative work"—see reg.1(3) and reg.51(1).

SCHEDULE 7   **Regulation 103(2)**

SUMS TO BE DISREGARDED IN THE CALCULATION OF INCOME OTHER THAN EARNINGS

A1.—[*Omitted*]   3.557
[[88]**A2.**—Any payment made to the claimant in respect of any travel or other expenses incurred, or to be incurred, by him in respect of his participation in the Mandatory Work Activity Scheme.]
[[89] [[96] **A3.** . . .]]
[[95]**A3.**—Any payment made to the claimant in respect of any travel or other expenses incurred, or to be incurred, by him in respect of his participation in a scheme prescribed in regulation 3 of the Jobseeker's Allowance (Schemes for Assisting Persons to Obtain Employment) Regulations 2013.]
A4.—[*Omitted*]
A5.—[*Omitted*]
1.—Any amount paid by way of tax on income which is taken into account under regulation 103 (calculation of income other than earnings).

1145

2.—Any payment in respect of any expenses incurred [²⁷, or to be incurred,] by a claimant who is—

    (a) by a charitable or voluntary organisation; or

    (b) a volunteer,

if he otherwise derives no remuneration or profit from the employment and is not to be treated as possessing any earnings under regulation 105(13) (notional income).

[⁷⁶²**2A.**—Any payment in respect of expenses arising out of the [¹⁰⁶ claimant participating as a service user].]

3.—In the case of employment as an employed earner, any payment in respect of expenses wholly, exclusively and necessarily incurred in the performance of the duties of the employment.

4.—In the case of a payment of [³⁶ [⁹⁴ [¹¹⁰ statutory paternity pay]] by virtue of Part 12ZA of the Benefits Act, statutory adoption pay by virtue of Part 12ZB of the Benefits Act,] [¹⁰⁸ statutory shared parental pay by virtue of Part 12ZC of the Benefits Act,] [¹²⁶statutory parental bereavement pay by virtue of Part 12ZD of the Benefits Act,] statutory sick pay or statutory maternity pay or any remuneration paid by or on behalf of an employer to the claimant who for the time being is unable to work due to illness or maternity [³⁶ or who is taking paternity leave[¹⁰⁸, adoption leave [¹²⁶, shared parental leave or parental bereavement leave.]]]—

    (a) any amount deducted by way of primary Class 1 contributions under the Benefits Act;

    (b) one-half of any sum paid by the claimant by way of a contribution towards an occupational or personal pension scheme.

5.—In the case of the payment of statutory sick pay or statutory maternity pay under Parts XI or XII of the Social Security Contributions and Benefits (Northern Ireland) Act 1992 [³⁶, or a payment under any enactment having effect in Northern Ireland corresponding to a payment of [¹¹⁰ statutory paternity pay] [¹⁰⁸ statutory shared parental pay or statutory adoption pay]]—

    (a) any amount deducted by way of primary Class 1 contributions under that Act;

    (b) one-half of any sum paid by way of a contribution towards an occupational or personal pension scheme.

6.—Any housing benefit [⁵¹ to which the claimant is entitled].

[³⁸ **6A.**—(1) Any guardian's allowance.]

[⁴³ **6B.**—(1) Any child tax credit.

    (2) Any child benefit.]

[⁸⁵ (3) Any increase in respect of a dependent child or dependent young person under section 80 or 90 of the Benefits Act where—

    (a) the claimant has a child or young person who is a member of the claimant's family for the purposes of the claimant's claim for income-based jobseeker's allowance, and

    (b) the claimant, or that claimant's partner, has been awarded a child tax credit.]

[⁷³ **6C.**—(1) £1.20 in relation to each week in which child benefit is payable to the claimant at the enhanced rate in respect of a child or qualifying young person for whom the claimant is treated as responsible.

    (2) 65 pence in relation to each week in which child benefit is payable to the claimant other than at the enhanced rate in respect of a child or qualifying young person for whom the claimant is treated as responsible (and if there is more than one, 65 pence in relation to each such child or young person).

    (3) This paragraph does not apply to a claimant in relation to whom regulation 3 of, and Schedule 2 to, the Social Security (Working Tax Credit and Child Tax Credit) (Consequential Amendments) Regulations 2003 have effect.

    (4) In this paragraph—

"child" and "qualifying young person" have the meanings given in section 142 of the Contributions and Benefits Act;

"treated as responsible" is to be construed in accordance with section 143 of that Act;

"the enhanced rate" has the meaning given in regulation 2(1)(a) of the Child Benefit (Rates) Regulations 2006.]

[⁷⁴ **7.**—The mobility component of disability living allowance [¹⁰⁰ or the mobility component of personal independence payment].]

8.—Any concessionary payment made to compensate for the non-payment of—

    (a) any payment specified in paragraph 7 or 10;

[⁷⁴ (b) income support;

    (c) an income-based jobseeker's allowance; [¹⁰⁴. . .]

    (d) an income-related employment and support allowance] [¹⁰⁴ ; or

    (e) universal credit].

9.—Any mobility supplement or any payment intended to compensate for the non-payment of such a supplement.

10.—Any attendance allowance[[101] , the care component of disability living allowance or the daily living component of personal independence payment] [[29] . . .].

11.—Any payment to the claimant as holder of the Victoria Cross or George Cross or any analogous payment.

[[46] **12.**—(1) Any payment—
   (a) by way of an education maintenance allowance made pursuant to—
      (i) regulations made under section 518 of the Education Act 1996;
      (ii) regulations made under section 49 or 73(f) of the Education (Scotland) Act 1980;
      [[74] (iii) directions made under section 73ZA of the Education (Scotland) Act 1980 and paid under section 12(2)(c) of the Further and Higher Education (Scotland) Act 1992; [[93] . . .]]
   (b) corresponding to such an education maintenance allowance, made pursuant to—
      (i) section 14 or section 181 of the Education Act 2002; or
      (ii) regulations made under section 181 of that Act [[93] ; or
   (c) in England, by way of financial assistance made pursuant to section 14 of the Education Act 2002.]

(2) Any payment, other than a payment to which sub-paragraph (1) applies, made pursuant to—
   (a) regulations made under section 518 of the Education Act 1996;
   (b) regulations made under section 49 of the Education (Scotland) Act 1980; or
   [[74] (c) directions made under section 73ZA of the Education (Scotland) Act 1980 and paid under section 12(2)(c) of the Further and Higher Education (Scotland) Act 1992,]
in respect of a course of study attended by a child or a young person or a person who is in receipt of an education maintenance allowance [[93] or other payment] made pursuant to any provision specified in sub-paragraph (1).]

[[33] **12A.**—Any payment made to the claimant by way of repayment under regulation 11(2) of the Education (Teacher Student Loans) (Repayment, etc.) Regulations 2002.]

13.—In the case of a claimant to whom regulation 11 (part-time students) applies, any sums intended for any expenditure specified in paragraph (2) of regulation 131 (calculation of grant income) necessary as a result of his attendance on his course.

[[42] **14.**—(1) Any payment made pursuant to section 2 of the Employment and Training Act 1973 or section 2 of the Enterprise and New Towns (Scotland) Act 1990 except a payment—
   (a) made as a substitute for income support, a jobseeker's allowance, incapacity benefit [[69] , severe disablement allowance or employment and support allowance];
   (b) of an allowance referred to in section 2(3) of the Employment and Training Act 1973 or section 2(5) of the Enterprise and New Towns (Scotland) Act 1990;
   (c) intended to meet the cost of living expenses which relate to any one or more of the items specified in sub-paragraph (2) whilst a claimant is participating in an education, training or other scheme to help him enhance his employment prospects unless the payment is a Career Development Loan paid pursuant to section 2 of the Employment and Training Act 1973 and the period of education or training or the scheme, which is supported by that loan, has been completed; or
   (d) made in respect of the cost of living away from home to the extent that the payment relates to rent for which housing benefit is payable in respect of accommodation which is not normally occupied by the claimant as his home.

(2) The items specified in this sub-paragraph for the purposes of sub-paragraph (1)(c) are food, ordinary clothing or footwear, household fuel, rent for which housing benefit is payable, or any housing costs to the extent that they are met under regulation 83(f) or 84(1)(g) (housing costs), of the claimant or, where the claimant is a member of a family, any other member of his family, or any council tax or water charges for which that claimant or member is liable.

(3) For the purposes of this paragraph, "ordinary clothing or footwear" means clothing or footwear for normal daily use, but does not include school uniforms, or clothing or footwear used solely for sporting activities.]

15.—[[59] (1) Subject to sub-paragraph (3) and paragraph 41, any relevant payment made or due to be made at regular intervals.]

(2) [[59] . . .]

(3) [[59] Sub-paragraph (1)] shall not apply—
   (a) to a payment which is made by a person for the maintenance of any member of his family or of his former partner or of his children;

    (b) to a payment made—
        (i) to a person who is, or would be, prevented from being entitled to a jobseeker's allowance by section 14 (trade disputes); or
        (ii) to a member of the family of such a person where the payment is made by virtue of that person's involvement in the trade dispute.

(4) [^{59} . . .]

(5) [^{59} . . .]

[^{34} (5A) In this paragraph, "relevant payment" means—
    (a) a charitable payment;
    (b) a voluntary payment;
    (c) a payment (not falling within sub-paragraph (a) or (b) above) from a trust whose funds are derived from a payment made in consequence of any personal injury to the claimant;
    (d) a payment under an annuity purchased—
        (i) pursuant to any agreement or court order to make payments to the claimant; or
        (ii) from funds derived from a payment made,
    in consequence of any personal injury to the claimant; or
    (e) a payment (not falling within sub-paragraphs (a) to (d) above) received by virtue of any agreement or court order to make payments to the claimant in consequence of any personal injury to the claimant.]

(6) [^{29} . . .].

16.—[^{60} . . .]

[^{2}**16A.**—[^{29} . . .].]

[^{74} **17.**—Subject to paragraphs 38 and 39, £10 of any of the following, namely—
    (a) a war disablement pension (except insofar as such a pension falls to be disregarded under paragraph 9 or 10);
    (b) a war widow's pension or war widower's pension;
    (c) a pension payable to a person as a widow, widower or surviving civil partner under any power of Her Majesty otherwise than under an enactment to make provision about pensions for or in respect of persons who have been disabled or have died in consequence of service as members of the armed forces of the Crown;
    (d) a guaranteed income payment and, if the amount of that payment has been abated to less than £10 by a [^{77} pension or payment falling within article 31(1)(a) or (b) of the Armed Forces and Reserve Forces (Compensation Scheme) Order 2005], so much of [^{77} that pension or payment] as would not, in aggregate with the amount of [^{77} any] guaranteed income payment disregarded, exceed £10;
    (e) a payment made to compensate for the non-payment of such a pension or payment as is mentioned in any of the preceding sub-paragraphs;
    (f) a pension paid by the government of a country outside Great Britain which is analogous to any of the pensions or payments mentioned in sub-paragraphs (a) to (d) above;
[^{112}(g) a pension paid by a government to victims of National Socialist persecution;]
    (h) any widowed mother's allowance paid pursuant to section 37 of the Benefits Act;
    (i) any widowed parent's allowance paid pursuant to section 39A of the Benefits Act.]

18.—Where a claimant receives income under an annuity purchased with a loan which satisfies the following conditions—
    (a) that the loan was made as part of a scheme under which not less than 90 per cent. of the proceeds of the loan were applied to the purchase by the person to whom it was made of an annuity ending with his life or with the life of the survivor of two or more persons (in this paragraph referred to as "the annuitants") who include the person to whom the loan was made;
    (b) that the interest on the loan is payable by the person to whom it was made or by one of the annuitants;
    (c) that at the time the loan was made the person to whom it was made or each of the annuitants had attained the age of 65 [^{123}or, if it was higher at that time, pensionable age];
    (d) that the loan was secured on a dwelling in Great Britain and the person to whom the loan was made or one of the annuitants owns an estate or interest in that dwelling; and
    (e) that the person to whom the loan was made or one of the annuitants occupies the accommodation on which it was secured as his home at the time the interest is paid,
the amount, calculated on a weekly basis equal to—
    (i) where, or in so far as, section 369 of the Income and Corporation Taxes Act 1988

(mortgage interest payable under deduction of tax) applies to the payments of interest on the loan, the interest which is payable after deduction of a sum equal to income tax on such payments at the applicable percentage of income tax within the meaning of section 369(1A) of that Act;

(ii) in any other case the interest which is payable on the loan without deduction of such a sum.

19.—Any payment made to the claimant by a person who normally resides with the claimant, which is a contribution towards that person's living and accommodation costs, except where that person is residing with the claimant in circumstances to which paragraph 20 or 21 refers.

20.—Where the claimant occupies a dwelling as his home and the dwelling is also occupied by another person and there is a contractual liability to make payments to the claimant in respect of the occupation of the dwelling by that person or a member of his family—

[⁶⁶ (a) where the aggregate of any payments made in respect of any one week in respect of the occupation of the dwelling by that person or a member of his family, or by that person and a member of his family, is less than £20, the whole of that amount; or

(b) where the aggregate of any such payments is £20 or more per week, £20.]

21.—Where the claimant occupies a dwelling as his home and he provides in that dwelling board and lodging accommodation, an amount, in respect of each person for whom such accommodation is provided for the whole or any part of a week, equal to—

(a) where the aggregate of any payments made in respect of any one week in respect of such accommodation provided to such person does not exceed £20, 100% of such payments; or

(b) where the aggregate of any such payments exceeds £20, £20 and 50% of the excess over £20.

22.—(1) [¹⁹ Subject to sub-paragraphs (2) and (3)], except where [¹⁹ regulation 103(6)(b) (provision of support under section 95 or 98 of the Immigration and Asylum Act including support provided by virtue of regulations made under Schedule 9 to that Act in the calculation of income other than earnings) or] regulation 105(10)(a)(i) (notional income) applies or in the case of a payment made—

(a) to a person who is, or would be, prevented from being entitled to a jobseeker's allowance by section 14 (trade disputes); or

(b) to a member of the family of such a person where the payment is made by virtue of that person's involvement in the trade dispute,

any income in kind.

(2) The exceptions under sub-paragraph (1) shall not apply where the income in kind [¹²⁷ is a Grenfell Tower payment or] is received from the Macfarlane Trust, the Macfarlane (Special Payments) Trust, the Macfarlane (Special Payments) (No.2) Trust, the Fund, the Eileen Trust[⁸⁰, MFET Limited][⁹¹, the Skipton Fund, the Caxton Foundation][¹¹³, the Scottish Infected Blood Support Scheme][¹¹⁶, an approved blood scheme][¹¹⁵, the London Emergencies Trust, the We Love Manchester Emergency Fund] [¹²⁷, the National Emergencies Trust] or the Independent Living [⁷¹ Fund (2006)].

[¹⁹ (3) The first exception under sub-paragraph (1) shall not apply where the claimant is the partner of a person subject to immigration control and whose partner is receiving support provided under section 95 or 98 of the Immigration and Asylum Act including support provided by virtue of regulations made under Schedule 9 to that Act and the income in kind is support provided in respect of essential living needs of the partner of the claimant and his dependants (if any) as is specified in regulations made under paragraph 3 of Schedule 8 to the Immigration and Asylum Act.]

[⁵³ (4) The reference in sub-paragraph (1) to "income in kind" does not include a payment to a third party made in respect of the claimant which is used by the third party to provide benefits in kind to the claimant.]

23.—(1) Any income derived from capital to which the claimant is, or is treated under regulation 115 (capital jointly held) as, beneficially entitled but, subject to sub-paragraph (2), not income [¹ derived] from capital disregarded under paragraph 1, 2, 4 to 8, 11 or 17 of Schedule 8.

(2) Income derived from capital disregarded under paragraph 2 or 4 to 8 of Schedule 8 but only to the extent of—

(a) any mortgage repayments made in respect of the dwelling or premises in the period during which that income accrued; or

(b) any council tax or water charges which the claimant is liable to pay in respect of the dwelling or premises and which are paid in the period during which that income accrued.

(3) The definition of "water charges" in regulation 1(3) shall apply to sub-paragraph (2) with the omission of the words "in so far as such charges are in respect of the dwelling which a person occupies as his home".

24.—Any income which is payable in a country outside the United Kingdom for such period during which there is prohibition against the transfer to the United Kingdom of that income.

25.—Where a payment of income is made in a currency other than sterling, any banking charge or commission payable in converting that payment into sterling.

26.—(1) Any payment made to the claimant in respect of a child or young person who is a member of his family—

(a) [⁵⁷ pursuant to regulations under section 2(6)(b), 3 or 4 of the Adoption and Children Act 2002 or in accordance] with a scheme approved by the [⁷⁴ Scottish Ministers under section 51A] of the Adoption (Scotland) Act 1978 (schemes for payment of allowances to adopters) [⁹⁰ or in accordance with an adoption allowance scheme made under section 71 of the Adoption and Children (Scotland) Act 2007 (adoption allowances schemes)];

(b) [⁷⁴ . . .]

[⁷⁸ (ba) which is a payment made by a local authority in Scotland in pursuance of section 50 of the Children Act 1975 (payments towards maintenance of children);]

(c) which is a payment made by a local authority in pursuance of section 15(1) of, and paragraph 15 of Schedule 1 to, the Children Act 1989 (local authority contribution to a child's maintenance where the child is living with a person as a result of a [¹⁰⁵ child arrangements] order);

[⁷ (d) which is a payment made by an authority, as defined in Article 2 of the Children Order, in pursuance of Article 15 of, and paragraph 17 of Schedule 1 to, that Order (contribution by an authority to child's maintenance);]

[⁴⁹ (e) in accordance with regulations made pursuant to section 14F of the Children Act 1989 (special guardianship support services);]

[⁴³ . . .]

[⁵⁸ (1A) Any payment, other than a payment to which sub-paragraph (1)(a) applies, made to the claimant pursuant to regulations under section 2(6)(b), 3 or 4 of the Adoption and Children Act 2002.]

(2) [⁴³ . . .]

[⁴³ **26A.**—In the case of a claimant who has a child or young person—

(a) who is a member of his family, and

(b) who is residing at an educational establishment at which he is receiving relevant education,

any payment made to that educational establishment, in respect of that child or young person's maintenance by or on behalf of a person who is not a member of the family or by a member of the family out of funds contributed for that purpose by a person who is not a member of the family.]

[⁸⁶ **27.**—Any payment made to the claimant with whom a person is accommodated by virtue of arrangements made—

(a) by a local authority under—

[¹¹⁸(i) section 22C(2) of the Children Act 1989 (ways in which looked after children are to be accommodated and maintained),]

[¹¹⁷(ia) section 81(2) of the Social Services and Well-being (Wales) Act 2014 (ways in which looked after children are to be accommodated and maintained;]

(ii) section 26 of the Children (Scotland) Act 1995 (manner of provision of accommodation to child looked after by local authority), or

(iii) regulations 33 or 51 of the Looked After Children (Scotland) Regulations 2009 (fostering and kinship care allowances and fostering allowances); or

(b) by a voluntary organisation under section 59(1)(a) of the Children Act 1989 (provision of accommodation by voluntary organisations).]

28.—[⁸Any payment made to the claimant or his partner for a person ("the person concerned"), who is not normally a member of the claimant's household but is temporarily in his care, by—

(a) a health authority;

(b) a local authority [⁵¹ but excluding payments of housing benefit made in respect of the person concerned];

(c) a voluntary organisation; or

(d) the person concerned pursuant to section 26(3A) of the National Assistance Act 1948 [²⁴ [⁷⁴ . . .]

[¹⁰⁹(dza) the person concerned where the payment is for the provision of accommodation in respect of the meeting of that person's needs under section 18 or 19 of the Care Act 2014 (duty and power to meet needs for care and support);]

[¹¹⁷(dzb) the person concerned where the payment is for the provision of accommodation to meet that person's need for care and support under section 35 or 36 of the Social

Services and Well-being (Wales) Act 2014 (duty and power to meet care and support needs of an adult);]
[^{103}(da) a clinical commissioning group established under section 14D of the National Health Service Act 2006;
(db) the National Health Service Commissioning Board; or]
(e) [^{103} ...]]
[^{74} (f) a Local Health Board established under section 16BA of the National Health Service Act 1977 or established by an order made under section 11 of the Health Service (Wales) Act.]]
[^{119}**28A.**—Any payment made to a claimant under section 73(1)(b) of the Children and Young People (Scotland) Act 2014 (kinship care assistance).]
[^{67} **29.**—(1) Any payment made by a local authority in accordance with—
(a) section 17, 23B, 23C or 24A of the Children Act 1989,
(b) section 12 of the Social Work (Scotland) Act 1968, [^{117} ...]
(c) section [^{87} 22,] [^{111}26A, 29] or 30 of the Children (Scotland) Act [^{117}1995, or
(d) the following sections of the Social Services and Well-being (Wales) Act 2014—
  (aa) section 37 or 38, but excluding any direct payment made in accordance with regulations made under section 51 of that Act; or
  (bb) section 109.110, 114 or 115.].
(2) Any payment (or part of a payment) made by a local authority in accordance with section 23C of the Children Act 1989 or section [^{87} 22][^{111}, 26A or 29 of the Children (Scotland) Act 1995 (local authorities' duty to promote welfare of children, duty to provide continuing care and provision of advice and assistance for certain young persons)].
(3) Sub-paragraphs (1) and (2) are subject to the following provisions.
(4) Neither of those sub-paragraphs applies where the claimant is a person who is, or would be, prevented from being entitled to a jobseeker's allowance by section 14 (trade disputes).
(5) Sub-paragraph (2) applies only where A—
(a) was formerly in the claimant's care, and
[^{111}(b) is aged 18 or over or, in the case of a payment or part of a payment made in accordance with section 26A of the Children (Scotland) Act 1995, aged 16 or over, and]
(c) continues to live with the claimant.]
[^{120}**30.** Any payment received under an insurance policy taken out to insure against the risk of being unable to maintain repayments on a loan which qualifies under Part 1 of Schedule 1 to the Loans for Mortgage Interest Regulations 2017 (legacy benefit claimants and SPC claimants) and used to meet such repayments.]
31.—(1) Except where paragraph 30 [^{10}or 31A] applies, and subject to sub-paragraph (2), any payment made to the claimant which is intended to be used and is used as a contribution towards—
(a) any payment due on a loan if secured on the dwelling occupied as the home which does not qualify under [^{120}Part 1 of Schedule 1 to the Loans for Mortgage Interest Regulations];
[^{120}(b) any charge which qualifies in accordance with paragraph 16 of Schedule 2 (housing costs) to these Regulations or any interest payment on a loan which qualifies under Part 1 of Schedule 1 to the Loans for Mortgage Interest Regulations, to the extent that the charge or payment is not met under these Regulations or by loan payments (as the case may be)];
(c) any payment due on a loan which qualifies under [^{120}Part 1 of Schedule 1 to the Loans for Mortgage Interest Regulations] attributable to the payment of capital;
(d) any amount due by way of premiums on—
  (i) an insurance policy taken out to insure against the risk of being unable to make the payments referred to in (a) to (c) above, or
  (ii) an insurance policy taken out to insure against loss or damage to any building or part of a building which is occupied by the claimant as his home;
(e) his rent in respect of the dwelling occupied by him as his home but only to the extent that it is not met by housing benefit; or his accommodation charge but only to the extent that the actual charge [^{29} exceeds] the amount payable by a local authority in accordance with Part III of the National Assistance Act 1948 [^{109} or Part 1 of the Care Act 2014 (care and support) [^{117}or Part 4 of the Social Services and Well-being (Wales) Act 2014 (meeting needs) other than any direct payment made in accordance with regulations made under section 50 or 52 of that Act].]
(2) This paragraph shall not apply to any payment which is treated as possessed by the claimant by virtue of regulation 105(10)(a)(ii) (notional income).
[^{120}(3) In this paragraph—

(a) "Loans for Mortgage Interest Regulations" means the Loans for Mortgage Interest Regulations 2017;

(b) "loan payments" has the meaning given in the Loans for Mortgage Interest Regulations.]

[¹⁰**31A.**—(1) Subject to sub-paragraph (2), any payment received under an insurance policy, other than an insurance policy referred to in paragraph 30, taken out to insure against the risk of being unable to maintain repayments under a regulated agreement as defined for the purposes of the Consumer Credit Act 1974 or under a hire-purchase agreement or a conditional sale agreement as defined for the purposes of Part III of the Hire-Purchase Act 1964.

(2) A payment referred to in sub-paragraph (1) shall only be disregarded to the extent that the payment received under that policy does not exceed the amounts, calculated on a weekly basis, which are used to—

(a) maintain the repayment referred to in sub-paragraph (1); and

(b) meet any amount due by way of premiums on that policy.]

32.—(1) Subject to sub-paragraphs (2) and (3), in the case of a claimant [⁵⁴ residing in a care home, an Abbeyfield Home or an independent hospital], any payment, [⁶⁴ except a charitable or voluntary payment disregarded under paragraph 15] [⁶² . . .], made to the claimant which is intended to be used and is used to meet the cost of maintaining the claimant in that home [⁵⁴ or hospital].

(2) This paragraph shall not apply to a claimant for whom accommodation in a [⁵⁴ care home, an Abbeyfield Home or an independent hospital] is provided by

[¹⁰⁹(a) a local authority under section 26 of the National Assistance Act 1948 or section 59 of the Social Work (Scotland) Act 1968 [²⁹. . .]; or

(b) a person other than a local authority under arrangements made with the person by a local authority in the exercise of the local authority's functions under section 18 or 19 of the Care Act 2014 (duty and power to meet needs for care and support)[¹¹⁷or under section 35 or 36 of the Social Services and Well-being (Wales) Act 2014 (duty and powers to meet care and support needs of an adult)].]

(3) The amount to be disregarded under this paragraph shall not exceed the difference between—

[²⁹(a) the claimant's applicable amount; and]

(b) the weekly charge for the accommodation.

33.—Any social fund payment made pursuant to Part VIII of the Benefits Act.

[⁹⁸ **33A.**—Any local welfare provision.]

34.—Any payment of income which under regulation 110 (income treated as capital) is in to be treated as capital.

35.—Any payment under Part X of the Benefits Act (pensioner's Christmas bonus).

36.—In the case of a person who is, or would be, prevented from being entitled to a jobseeker's allowance by section 14 (trade disputes), any payment up to the amount of the prescribed sum within the meaning of section 15(2)(d) made by a trade union.

37.—Any payment which is due to be paid before the date of claim which would otherwise fall to be taken into account in the same benefit week as a payment of the same kind and from the same source.

38.—The total of a claimant's income or, if he is a member of a family, the family's income and the income of any person which he is treated as possessing under regulation 88(4) (calculation of income and capital of members of claimant's family and of a polygamous marriage) to be disregarded under regulations 132(2)(b) and 133(1)(c) (calculation of covenant income where a contribution assessed), regulation 136(2) (treatment of student loans) [²¹, regulation 136A(3) (treatment of payments from access funds)] and [⁶³ paragraph 17] shall in no case exceed £20 per [⁴benefit week].

39.—Notwithstanding paragraph 38, where two or more payments of the same kind and from the same source are to be taken into account in the same benefit week, there shall be disregarded from each payment the sum which would otherwise fall to be disregarded under this Schedule; but this paragraph shall only apply in the case of a payment which it has not been practicable to treat under regulation 96(1)(b) (date on which income treated as paid) as paid on the first day of the benefit week in which it is due to be paid.

40.—[⁷⁴ . . .]

41.—(1) Any payment made under [⁸¹ or by] the Macfarlane Trust, the Macfarlane (Special Payments) Trust, the Macfarlane (Special Payments) (No.2) Trust, the Fund, the Eileen Trust ("the Trusts")[⁸² , MFET Limited][⁹¹ , the Skipton Fund, the Caxton Foundation] [¹¹³, the Scottish Infected Blood Support Scheme] [¹¹⁶, an approved blood scheme][¹¹⁵, the London Emergencies Trust, the We Love Manchester Emergency Fund][¹²⁷, the National Emergencies Trust] or the Independent Living [⁷⁴ Fund (2006)].

[¹²⁷(1A) Any Grenfell Tower payment.]

(2) Any payment by or on behalf of a person who is suffering or who suffered from haemophilia or who is or was a qualifying person, which derives from a payment made under [⁸¹ or by] any of the Trusts to which sub-paragraph (1) refers[¹²⁷, or from a Grenfell Tower payment,] and which is made to or for the benefit of—

    (a) that person's partner or former partner from whom he is not, or where that person has died was not, estranged or divorced [⁵⁵ or with whom he has formed a civil partnership that has not been dissolved or, where that person has died, had not been dissolved at the time of that person's death];

    (b) any child or young person who is a member of that person's family or who was such a member and who is a member of the claimant's family.

(3) Any payment by or on behalf of the partner or former partner of a person who is suffering or who suffered from haemophilia or who is or was a qualifying person, provided that the partner or former partner and that person are not, or if either of them has died were not, estranged or divorced, [⁵⁵ or, where the partner or former partner and that person have formed a civil partnership, the civil partnership has not been dissolved or, if either of them has died, had not been dissolved at the time of the death], which derives from a payment made under [⁸¹ or by] any of the Trusts to which sub-paragraph (1) refers[¹²⁷, or from a Grenfell Tower payment,] and which is made to or for the benefit of—

    (a) the person who is suffering from haemophilia or who is a qualifying person;

    (b) any child or young person who is a member of that person's family or who was such a member and who is a member of the claimant's family.

(4) Any payment by a person who is suffering from haemophilia or who is a qualifying person, which derives from the payment under [⁸¹or by] any of the Trusts to which sub-paragraph (1) refers, [¹²⁷ or from a Grenfell Tower payment,] where

    (a) that person has no partner or former partner from whom he is not estranged or divorced, [⁵⁵ or with whom he has formed a civil partnership that has not been dissolved], nor any child or young person who is or had been a member of that person's family; and

    (b) the payment is made either—

        (i) to that person's parent or step-parent, or

        (ii) where that person at the date of the payment is a child, a young person or a student who has not completed his full-time education, and had no parent or step-parent, to his guardian,

but only for a period from the date of the payment until the end of two years from that person's death.

(5) Any payment out of the estate of a person who suffered from haemophilia or who was a qualifying person, which derives from a payment under [⁸¹ or by] any of the Trusts to which sub-paragraph (1) refers, [¹²⁷ or from a Grenfell Tower payment,] where—

    (a) that person at the date of his death (the relevant date) had no partner or former partner from whom he was not estranged or divorced [⁵⁵ or with whom he had formed a civil partnership that had not been dissolved], nor any child or young person who was or had been a member of his family; and

    (b) the payment is made either—

        (i) to that person's parent or step-parent, or

        (ii) where that person at the relevant date was a child, a young person or a student who had not completed his full-time education, and had no parent or step-parent, to his guardian,

but only for a period of two years from the relevant date.

(6) In the case of a person to whom or for whose benefit a payment referred to in this paragraph is made, any income which derives from any payment of income or capital made under or deriving from any of the Trusts [¹²⁷ or from a Grenfell Tower payment].

[⁴⁸ (7) For the purposes of paragraphs (2) to (6), any reference to the Trusts shall be construed as including a reference to the Skipton Fund[⁹² , the Caxton Foundation] [¹¹³, the Scottish Infected Blood Support Scheme][¹¹⁶, an approved blood scheme][¹¹⁵, the London Emergencies Trust, the We Love Manchester Emergency Fund] [⁸², MFET Limited][¹²⁷, the National Emergencies Trust] [⁵⁶ and the London Bombings Relief Charitable Fund].]

42.—Any payment made by the Secretary of State to compensate for the loss (in whole or in part) of entitlement to housing benefit.

43.—Any payment made to a juror or a witness in respect of attendance at a court other than compensation for loss of earnings or for the loss of a benefit payable under the [⁷⁴ benefit Acts].

44.—[⁷² . . .]

[⁶⁸ **45.**—Any payment in consequence of a reduction of council tax under section 13[⁹⁹,

13A]or 80 of the Local Government Finance Act 1992 (reduction of liability for council tax).]

46.—[[74] . . .]

[[74] **47.**—(1) Any payment or repayment made—

    (a) as respects England, under regulation 5, 6 or 12 of the National Health Service (Travel Expenses and Remission of Charges) Regulations 2003 (travelling expenses and health service supplies);

    (b) as respects Wales, under regulation 5, 6 or 11 of the National Health Service (Travelling Expenses and Remission of Charges) (Wales) Regulations 2007 (travelling expenses and health service supplies);

    (c) as respects Scotland, under regulation 3, 5 or 11 of the National Health Service (Travelling Expenses and Remission of Charges) (Scotland) (No.2) Regulations 2003 (travelling expenses and health service supplies).

(2) Any payment or repayment made by the Secretary of State for Health [[121]and Social Care], the Scottish Ministers or the Welsh Ministers which is analogous to a payment or repayment mentioned in sub-paragraph (1).

48.—Any payment made to such persons entitled to receive benefits as may be determined by or under a scheme made pursuant to section 13 of the Social Security Act 1988 in lieu of vouchers or similar arrangements in connection with the provision of those benefits (including payments made in place of healthy start vouchers, milk tokens or the supply of vitamins).]

49.—Any payment made either by the Secretary of State for [[65] Justice] or by the [[74] Scottish Ministers] under a scheme established to assist relatives and other persons to visit persons in custody.

50.—Any payment (other than a training allowance) made, whether by the Secretary of State or by any other person, under the Disabled Persons (Employment) Act 1944 [[42] . . .] to assist disabled persons to obtain or retain employment despite their disability.

51.—[[97] . . .]

[[74] **52.**—(1) If the claimant is in receipt of any benefit under Part 2, 3 or 5 of the Benefits Act, any increase in the rate of that benefit arising under Part 4 (increases for dependants) or section 106(a) (unemployability supplement) of that Act, where the dependant in respect of whom the increase is paid is not a member of the claimant's family.

(2) If the claimant is in receipt of any pension or allowance under Part 2 or 3 of the Naval, Military and Air Forces Etc. (Disablement and Death) Service Pensions Order 2006, any increase in the rate of that pension or allowance under that Order, where the dependant in respect of whom the increase is paid is not a member of the claimant's family.

53.—Any supplementary pension under article 23(2) of the Naval, Military and Air Forces Etc. (Disablement and Death) Service Pensions Order 2006 (pensions to surviving spouses and surviving civil partners) and any analogous payment made by the Secretary of State for Defence to any person who is not a person entitled under that Order.]

54.—In the case of a pension awarded at the supplementary rate under article 27(3) of the Personal Injuries (Civilians) Scheme 1983 (pensions to [[55] widows, widowers or surviving civil partners]), the sum specified in paragraph 1(c) of Schedule 4 to that Scheme.

55.—(1) Any payment which is—

    (a) made under any of the Dispensing Instruments to a [[55] widow, widower or surviving civil partner] of a person—

        (i) whose death was attributable to service in a capacity analogous to service as a member of the armed forces of the Crown; and

        (ii) whose service in such capacity terminated before 31st March 1973; and

[[74] (b) equal to the amount specified in article 23(2) of the Naval, Military and Air Forces Etc. (Disablement and Death) Service Pensions Order 2006.]

(2) In this paragraph "the Dispensing Instruments" means the Order in Council of 9th December 1881, the Royal Warrant of 27th October 1884 and the Order by His Majesty of 14th January 1922 (exceptional grants of pay, non-effective pay and allowances).

[[3]**56.**—Any payment made [[75] . . .] under section 12B of the Social Work (Scotland) Act 1968 [[83] , or under sections 12A to 12D of the National Health Service Act 2006 (direct payments for health care)] [[109] or under sections 31 to 33 of the Care Act 2014 (direct payments)] [[39a] or under regulations made under section 57 of the Health and Social Care Act 2001 (direct payments) [[117]or in accordance with regulations made under section 50 or 52 of the Social Services and Well-being (Wales) Act 2014 (direct payments)]].

57.—[[42]. . .]

58.—[[42]. . .]

59.—(1) Any payment specified in sub-paragraph (2) to a claimant who was formerly a full-time student and who has completed the course in respect of which those payments were made.

(2) The payments specified for the purposes of sub-paragraph (1) are—
  (a) any grant income and covenant income as defined for the purposes of Chapter IX of Part VIII;
[¹⁷(b) any student loan as defined in Chapter IX of Part VIII;
  (c) any contribution as defined in Chapter IX of Part VIII which—
    (i) is taken into account in ascertaining the amount of a student loan referred to in head (b); and
    (ii) has been paid.]]

[²⁵ **60.**—[⁴². . .]].

[³² **60A.**—[⁴². . .].]

[⁶ **61.**—[⁴². . .].]

[¹²**62.**—(1) Subject to sub-paragraph (2), in the case of a person who is receiving, or who has received, assistance under [²² the self-employment route], any payment to that person—
  (a) to meet expenses wholly and necessarily incurred whilst carrying on the commercial activity;
  (b) which is used or intended to be used to maintain repayments on a loan taken out by that person for the purpose of establishing or carrying on the commercial activity,
in respect of which such assistance is or was received.
(2) Sub-paragraph (1) shall apply only in respect of payments which are paid to that person from the special account as defined for the purposes of Chapter IVA of Part VIII.]

[¹³**63.**—[⁴². . .].]

[¹⁴**64.**—Any payment [⁷⁹ made with respect to a person on account of the provision of after-care under section 117 of the Mental Health Act 1983 or section 25 of the Mental Health (Care and Treatment) (Scotland) Act 2003 or the provision of accommodation or welfare services to which Part III of the National Assistance Act 1948 refers or to which the Social Work (Scotland) Act 1968 refers,] [¹⁰⁹ or the provision of care and support under Part 1 of the Care Act 2014 [¹¹⁷or the provision of care and support in respect of an adult under Part 4 of the Social Services and Well-being (Wales) Act 2014 (meeting needs)],] which falls to be treated as notional income made under paragraph (11) of regulation 105 above (payments made in respect of a person [⁵⁴ residing in a care home, an Abbeyfield Home or an independent hospital]).]

  65.—[*Omitted.*]
  66.—[*Omitted.*]

[¹⁶**67.**—(1) Any payment of a sports award except to the extent that it has been made in respect of any one or more of the items specified in sub-paragraph (2).
(2) The items specified for the purposes of sub-paragraph (1) are food, ordinary clothing or footwear, household fuel, rent for which housing benefit is payable or any housing costs to the extent that they are met under regulation 83(f) or 84(1)(g) (housing costs) [²⁹ . . .], of the claimant or, where the claimant is a member of a family, any other member of his family, or any council tax or water charges for which that claimant or member is liable.
(3) For the purposes of sub-paragraph (2)—

"food" does not include vitamins, minerals or other special dietary supplements intended to enhance the performance of the person in the sport in respect of which the award was made;
"ordinary clothing and footwear" means clothing or footwear for normal daily use but does not include school uniforms or clothing or footwear used solely for sporting activities.]

[²⁰ **68.**—Where the amount of a subsistence allowance paid to a person in a benefit week exceeds the amount of income-based jobseeker's allowance that person would have received in that benefit week had it been payable to him, less 50p, that excess amount.
  69.—In the case of a claimant participating in an employment zone programme, any discretionary payment made by an employment zone contractor to the claimant, being a fee, grant, loan or otherwise.]

[³⁵[⁴¹[⁸⁴**70.**—(1) Any payment of child maintenance made or derived from a liable relative where the child or young person in respect of whom the payment is made is a member of the claimant's family, except where the person making the payment is the claimant or the claimant's partner.
(2) In paragraph (1)—
"child maintenance" means any payment towards the maintenance of a child or young person, including any payment made voluntarily and payments made under—
  (a) the Child Support Act 1991;
  (b) the Child Support (Northern Ireland) Order 1991;
  (c) a court order;

(d) a consent order;

(e) a maintenance agreement registered for execution in the Books of Council and Session or the sheriff court books;

"liable relative" means a person listed in regulation 117 (interpretation) other than a person falling within sub-paragraph (d) of that definition.]]]

[²⁶**71.**—Any discretionary housing payment paid pursuant to regulation 2(1) of the Discretionary Financial Assistance Regulations 2001.]

[³⁷ [³⁹ **72.**—(1) Any payment made by a local authority, or by the [⁷⁴ Welsh Ministers], to or on behalf of the claimant or his partner relating to a service which is provided to develop or sustain the capacity of the claimant or his partner to live independently in his accommodation.]]

(2) For the purposes of sub-paragraph (1) "local authority" means—

(a) in relation to England, a county council, a district council, a London borough council, the Common Council of the City of London or the Council of the Isles of Scilly;

(b) in relation to Wales, a county council or a county borough council;

(c) in relation to Scotland, a council constituted under section 2 of the Local Government etc. (Scotland) Act 1994.]

[¹⁰² **72A.**—Armed forces independence payment.]

[³⁹ **73.**—[⁴². . .].]

[⁴⁰ **74.**—[⁴². . .].]

[¹⁰⁷ **75.**—Any payments to a claimant made under section 49 of the Children and Families Act 2014 (personal budgets and direct payments).]

[¹¹⁴**76.**—Any bereavement support payment under section 30 of the Pensions Act 2014 (bereavement support payment) except any such payment which is disregarded as capital under paragraph 12(1)(e) or 65 of Schedule 8.]

[¹²²**77.**—Any payment of carer's allowance supplement made under section 81 of the Social Security (Scotland) Act 2018.]

[¹²⁴**78.**—Any early years assistance given in accordance with section 32 of the Social Security (Scotland) Act 2018.]

[¹²⁵**79.**—Any funeral expense assistance given in accordance with section 34 of the Social Security (Scotland) Act 2018.]

[¹²⁸**80.**—Any Scottish child payment assistance given in accordance with section 79 of the Social Security (Scotland) Act 2018.]

[¹²⁹**81.**—Any short-term assistance given in accordance with regulations made under section 36 of the Social Security (Scotland) Act 2018.]

AMENDMENTS

1. Jobseeker's Allowance (Amendment) Regulations 1996 (SI 1996/1516) reg.20 and Sch. (October 7, 1996).

2. Jobseeker's Allowance and Income Support (General) (Amendment) Regulations 1996 (SI 1996/1517) reg.32 (October 7, 1996).

3. Income-related Benefits and Jobseeker's Allowance (Miscellaneous Amendments) Regulations 1997 (SI 1997/65) reg.2(4) (April 7, 1997).

4. Social Security (Miscellaneous Amendments) Regulations 1997 (SI 1997/454) reg.2(16) (April 7, 1997).

5. Income-related Benefits and Jobseeker's Allowance (Amendment) (No.2) Regulations 1997 (SI 1997/2197) reg.7(7) and (8)(f) (October 6, 1997).

6. Social Security Amendment (New Deal) Regulations 1997 (SI 1997/2863) reg.14 (January 5, 1998).

7. Social Security (Miscellaneous Amendments) Regulations 1998 (SI 1998/563) reg.7(1) and (2)(e) (April 6, 1998).

8. Social Security (Miscellaneous Amendments) Regulations 1998 (SI 1998/563) reg.7(3) and (4)(f) (April 6, 1998).

9. Social Security (Miscellaneous Amendments) Regulations 1998 (SI 1998/563) reg.13(2), (April 6, 1998).

10. Social Security (Miscellaneous Amendments) (No.3) Regulations 1998 (SI 1998/1173) reg.5 (June 1, 1998).

11. Social Security (Miscellaneous Amendments) (No.4) Regulations 1998 (SI 1998/1174) reg.4(a) (June 1, 1998).

12. Social Security (Miscellaneous Amendments) (No.4) Regulations 1998 (SI 1998/1174) reg.4(b) (June 1, 1998).

13. Social Security Amendment (New Deal) (No.2) Regulations 1998 (SI 1998/2117) reg.4(1) (September 24, 1998).

14. Social Security Amendment (New Deal) (No.2) Regulations 1998 (SI 1998/2117) reg.6(1) (September 24, 1998).

15. Social Security Amendment (Educational Maintenance Allowance) Regulations 1999 (SI 1999/1677) reg.2(1) and (2)(f) (August 16, 1999).

16. Social Security Amendment (Sports Awards) Regulations 1999 (SI 1999/2165) reg.6(4) (August 23, 1999).

17. Social Security Amendment (Students) Regulations 1999 (SI 1999/1935) reg.3(8) (August 30, 1999, or if the student's period of study begins between August 1 and 29, 1999, the first day of the period).

18. Social Security Amendment (Education Maintenance Allowance) Regulations 2000 (SI 2000/55) reg.2(1) and (2)(d) (February 7, 2000).

19. Social Security (Immigration and Asylum) Consequential Amendments Regulations 2000 (SI 2000/636) reg.4(9) (April 3, 2000).

20. Social Security Amendment (Employment Zones) Regulations 2000 (SI 2000/724) reg.3(3) (April 3, 2000).

21. Social Security Amendment (Students and Income-related Benefits) Regulations 2000 (SI 2000/1922) reg.3(10) (August 28, 2000, or if the student's period of study begins between August 1 and 27, 2000, the first day of the period).

22. Social Security Amendment (Employment Zones) (No.2) Regulations 2000 (SI 2000/2910) reg.4(1) and (2)(d)(i) (November 27, 2000).

23. Social Security Amendment (Bereavement Benefits) Regulations 2000 (SI 2000/2239) reg.3(3) (April 9, 2001).

24. Social Security (Miscellaneous Amendments) (No.3) Regulations 2001 (SI 2001/859) reg.6(3) (April 9, 2001).

25. Social Security Amendment (New Deal) Regulations 2001 (SI 2001/1029) reg.12 (April 9, 2001).

26. Social Security Amendment (Discretionary Housing Payments) Regulations 2001 (SI 2001/2333) reg.2(1) (July 2, 2001).

27. Social Security Amendment (Volunteers) Regulations 2001 (SI 2001/2296) reg.2 (September 24, 2001).

28. Children (Leaving Care) Act 2000 (Commencement No.2 and Consequential Provisions) Order 2001 (SI 2001/3070) art.3(5) and Sch.4 para.(c) (October 1, 2001).

29. Social Security Amendment (Residential Care and Nursing Homes) Regulations 2001 (SI 2001/3767) reg.2(2) and Pt II of Sch. para.24 (April 8, 2002).

30. Social Security Benefits Up-rating Order 2002 (SI 2002/668) art.22(10) (April 8, 2002).

31. Social Security (Miscellaneous Amendments) Regulations 2002 (SI 2002/841) reg.3(4) (April 8, 2002).

32. Social Security Amendment (Employment Programme) Regulations 2002 (SI 2002/2314) reg.2(5) (October 14, 2002).

33. Social Security (Miscellaneous Amendments) (No.2) Regulations 2002 (SI 2002/2380) reg.3(b) (October 14, 2002).

34. Social Security Amendment (Personal Injury Payments) Regulations 2002 (SI 2002/2442) reg.3 (October 28, 2002)

35. Social Security (Child Maintenance Premium and Miscellaneous Amendments) Regulations 2000 (SI 2000/3176) reg.2(2)(b) (in force in relation to any particular case on the day on which s.23 of the Child Support, Pensions and Social Security Act 2000 comes into force in relation to that type of case).

36. Social Security (Paternity and Adoption) Amendment Regulations 2002 (SI 2002/2689) reg.3(6) (December 8, 2002).

37. Social Security (Miscellaneous Amendments) Regulations 2003 (SI 2003/511) reg.3(2) (April 1, 2003).

38. Social Security (Working Tax Credit and Child Tax Credit) (Consequential Amendments) Regulations 2003 (SI 2003/455) reg.3 and Sch.2 para.23(a) (April 7, 2003).

39. Social Security (Miscellaneous Amendments) (No.2) Regulations 2003 (SI 2003/2279) reg.3(4) (October 1, 2003).

39a. Community Care, Services for Carers and Children's Services (Direct Payments) (England) Regulations 2003 (SI 2003/762) reg.11(2) and Sch.2 (April 8, 2003).

40. Social Security (Incapacity Benefit Work-focused Interviews) Regulations 2003 (SI 2003/2439) reg.16(a) (October 27, 2003).

41. Social Security (Child Maintenance Premium) Amendment Regulations 2004 (SI 2004/98) reg.3 (in force on: (i) February 16, 2004 in relation to any particular case in respect of which s.23 CSPSSA 2000 has come into force before February 16, 2004; (ii) where this does not apply, the day on which s.23 comes into force in relation to that type of case; (iii) February 16, 2004 in relation to a person who is entitled to income support/income-based JSA on that date and who receives her first payment of child maintenance made voluntarily whilst entitled to income support/income-based JSA on that date; (iv) in such a case where the day that the first voluntary payment is received is after February 16, 2004, the day that payment is received; and (v) February 16, 2004 in relation to a person who makes a claim for income support/income-based JSA on or after that date and receives a payment of child maintenance made voluntarily on or after the date of that claim).

42. Social Security (Miscellaneous Amendments) Regulations 2004 (SI 2004/565) reg.5(3) (April 1, 2004).

43. Social Security (Working Tax Credit and Child Tax Credit) (Consequential Amendments) Regulations 2003 (SI 2003/455) reg.3 and Sch.2 para.23 (except sub-para.(a)) (April 6, 2004, except in "transitional cases" and see further the note to reg.83 and to reg.17 of the Income Support Regulations).

44. Social Security (Miscellaneous Amendments) (No.2) Regulations 2004 (SI 2004/1141) reg.4(1) and (2)(d) (May 12, 2004).

45. Social Security (Miscellaneous Amendments) (No.2) Regulations 2004 (SI 2004/1141) reg.4(3) and (4)(d) (May 12, 2004).

46. Social Security (Students and Income-related Benefits) Amendment Regulations 2004 (SI 2004/1708) reg.6(3) (September 1, 2004, or if the student's period of study begins between August 1 and August 31, 2004, the first day of the period).

47. Social Security (Miscellaneous Amendments) (No.3) Regulations 2004 (SI 2004/2308) reg.2(1) and (2)(b) (October 4, 2004).

48. Social Security (Miscellaneous Amendments) (No.3) Regulations 2004 (SI 2004/2308) reg.3(5) (October 4, 2004).

49. Social Security (Miscellaneous Amendments) (No.3) Regulations 2004 (SI 2004/2308) reg.4(3) and (4)(b) (October 4, 2004).

50. Social Security (Miscellaneous Amendments) Regulations 2005 (SI 2005/574) reg.2(9) (April 4, 2005).

51. Social Security (Miscellaneous Amendments) Regulations 2005 (SI 2005/574) reg.6(5) (April 4, 2005).

52. Mental Health (Care and Treatment) (Scotland) Act 2003 (Modification of Subordinate Legislation) Order 2005 (SSI 2005/445) art.2 and Sch. para.23(3) (Scotland); Mental Health (Care and Treatment) (Scotland) Act 2003 (Consequential Provisions) Order 2005 (SI 2005/2078) art.15 and Sch.2 para.17(4) (England and Wales) (October 5, 2005).

53. Social Security (Miscellaneous Amendments) (No.2) Regulations 2005 (SI 2005/2465) reg.3(8)(a) (October 3, 2005).

54. Social Security (Care Homes and Independent Hospitals) Regulations 2005 (SI 2005/2687) reg.3 and Sch.2 para.14 (October 24, 2005).

55. Civil Partnership (Pensions, Social Security and Child Support) (Consequential, etc. Provisions) Order 2005 (SI 2005/2877) art.2(3) and Sch.3 para.26(12) (December 5, 2005).

56. Income-related Benefits (Amendment) (No.2) Regulations 2005 (SI 2005/3391) reg.5(4) (December 12, 2005).

57. Social Security (Miscellaneous Amendments) (No.2) Regulations 2005 (SI 2005/2465) reg.3(8)(b) (December 30, 2005).

58. Social Security (Miscellaneous Amendments) (No.2) Regulations 2005 (SI 2005/2465) reg.3(8)(c) (December 30, 2005).

59. Social Security (Miscellaneous Amendments) (No.4) Regulations 2006 (SI 2006/2378) reg.13(12)(a) (October 2, 2006).

60. Social Security (Miscellaneous Amendments) (No.4) Regulations 2006 (SI 2006/2378) reg.13(12)(b) (October 2, 2006).

61. Social Security (Miscellaneous Amendments) (No.4) Regulations 2006 (SI 2006/2378) reg.13(12)(c) (October 2, 2006).

62. Social Security (Miscellaneous Amendments) (No.4) Regulations 2006 (SI 2006/2378) reg.13(12)(d) (October 2, 2006).

63. Social Security (Miscellaneous Amendments) (No.4) Regulations 2006 (SI 2006/2378) reg.13(12)(e) (October 2, 2006).

64. Social Security (Miscellaneous Amendments) Regulations 2007 (SI 2007/719) reg.3(11) (April 2, 2007).

65. Secretary of State for Justice Order 2007 (SI 2007/2128) Sch. para.16(2) (August 22, 2007).

66. Social Security (Miscellaneous Amendments) (No.5) Regulations 2007 (SI 2007/2618) reg.8(15) (April 7, 2008).

67. Social Security (Miscellaneous Amendments) Regulations 2008 (SI 2008/698) reg.4(16)(a) (April 7, 2008).

68. Social Security (Miscellaneous Amendments) Regulations 2008 (SI 2008/698) reg.4(16)(b) (April 14, 2008).

69. Employment and Support Allowance (Consequential Provisions) (No.2) Regulations 2008 (SI 2008/1554) reg.3(28) (October 27, 2008).

70. Social Security (Child Maintenance Amendments) Regulations 2008 (SI 2008/2111) reg.3(9) (October 27, 2008).

71. Social Security (Miscellaneous Amendments) (No.6) Regulations 2008 (SI 2008/2767) reg.4(7) (November 17, 2008).

72. Social Security (Miscellaneous Amendments) (No.6) Regulations 2008 (SI 2008/2767) reg.4(11) (November 17, 2008).

73. Social Security (Child Benefit Disregard) Regulations 2008 (SI 2008/3140) reg.3 (January 5, 2009; this regulation ceases to have effect on April 6, 2009).

74. Social Security (Miscellaneous Amendments) (No.7) Regulations 2008 (SI 2008/3157) reg.3(10) (January 5, 2009).

75. Social Security (Miscellaneous Amendments) Regulations 2009 (SI 2009/583) reg.4(12) (April 6, 2009).

76. Social Security (Miscellaneous Amendments) (No.4) Regulations 2009 (SI 2009/2655) reg.4(15)(a) (October 26, 2009).

77. Social Security (Miscellaneous Amendments) (No.4) Regulations 2009 (SI 2009/2655) reg.4(15)(b) (October 26, 2009).

78. Social Security (Miscellaneous Amendments) (No.4) Regulations 2009 (SI 2009/2655) reg.4(15)(c) (October 26, 2009).

79. Social Security (Miscellaneous Amendments) (No.4) Regulations 2009 (SI 2009/2655) reg.4(15)(d) (October 26, 2009).

80. Social Security (Miscellaneous Amendments) (No.2) Regulations 2010 (SI 2010/641) reg.4(3)(f) (April 6, 2010).

81. Social Security (Miscellaneous Amendments) (No.2) Regulations 2010 (SI 2010/641) reg.4(8)(e) (April 6, 2010).

82. Social Security (Miscellaneous Amendments) (No.2) Regulations 2010 (SI 2010/641) reg.4(12) (April 6, 2010).

83. Social Security (Miscellaneous Amendments) (No.2) Regulations 2010 (SI 2010/641) reg.4(13) (April 6, 2010).

84. Social Security (Miscellaneous Amendments) (No.4) Regulations 2009 (SI 2009/2655) reg.4(15)(e) (April 12, 2010).

85. Social Security (Miscellaneous Amendments) (No.5) Regulations 2010 (SI 2010/2429) reg.4(5)(a) (November 1, 2010).

86. Social Security (Miscellaneous Amendments) (No.5) Regulations 2010 (SI 2010/2429) reg.4(5)(b) (November 1, 2010).

87. Social Security (Miscellaneous Amendments) (No.5) Regulations 2010 (SI 2010/2429) reg.4(5)(c) (November 1, 2010).

88. Jobseeker's Allowance (Mandatory Work Activity Scheme) Regulations 2011 (SI 2011/688) reg.14(1)(d) and (2) (April 25, 2011).

89. Jobseeker's Allowance (Employment, Skills and Enterprise Scheme) Regulations 2011 (SI 2011/917) reg.14(1)(d) and (2) (May 20, 2011).

90. Adoption and Children (Scotland) Act 2007 (Consequential Modifications) Order 2011 (SI 2011/1740) art.2 and Sch.1 para.19(3) (July 15, 2011).

91. Social Security (Miscellaneous Amendments) (No.3) Regulations 2011 (SI 2011/2425) reg.10(9) (October 31, 2011).

92. Social Security (Miscellaneous Amendments) (No.3) Regulations 2011 (SI 2011/2425) reg.10(10) (October 31, 2011).

93. Social Security (Miscellaneous Amendments) (No.3) Regulations 2011 (SI 2011/2425) reg.10(14) (October 31, 2011).

94. Social Security (Miscellaneous Amendments) Regulations 2012 (SI 2012/757) reg.4(3) (April 1, 2012).

95. Jobseeker's Allowance (Schemes for Assisting Persons to Obtain Employment) Regulations 2013 (SI 2013/276) reg.11(1)(d) and (2) (February 12, 2013).

96. Jobseekers (Back to Work Schemes) Act 2013 s.1(14) (March 26, 2013).

97. Council Tax Benefit Abolition (Consequential Provision) Regulations 2013 (SI 2013/458) reg.3 and Sch.1 (April 1, 2013).

98. Social Security (Miscellaneous Amendments) Regulations 2013 (SI 2013/443) reg.4(12)(a) (April 2, 2013).

99. Social Security (Miscellaneous Amendments) Regulations 2013 (SI 2013/443) reg.4(12)(b) (April 2, 2013).

100. Personal Independence Payment (Supplementary Provisions and Consequential Amendments) Regulations 2013 (SI 2013/388) reg.8 and Sch. Pt 2 para.16(9)(a) (April 8, 2013).

101. Personal Independence Payment (Supplementary Provisions and Consequential Amendments) Regulations 2013 (SI 2013/388) reg.8 and Sch. Pt 2 para.16(9)(b) (April 8, 2013).

102. Armed Forces and Reserve Forces Compensation Scheme (Consequential Provisions: Subordinate Legislation) Order 2013 (SI 2013/591) art.7 and Sch. para.10(9) (April 8, 2013).

103. National Treatment Agency (Abolition) and the Health and Social Care Act 2012 (Consequential, Transitional and Saving Provisions) Order 2013 (SI 2013/235) art.11 and Sch.2 para.27(3) (April 1, 2013).

104. Universal Credit (Consequential, Supplementary, Incidental and Miscellaneous Provisions) Regulations 2013 (SI 2013/630) reg.30(8) (April 29, 2013).

105. Child Arrangements Order (Consequential Amendments to Subordinate Legislation) Order 2014 (SI 2014/852) art.6 (April 22, 2014).

106. Social Security (Miscellaneous Amendments) Regulations 2014 (SI 2014/591) reg.4(6) (April 28, 2014).

107. Special Educational Needs (Consequential Amendments to Subordinate Legislation) Order 2014 (SI 2014/2103) art.4(1) (September 1, 2014).

108. Shared Parental Leave and Statutory Shared Parental Pay (Consequential Amendments to Subordinate Legislation) Order 2014 (SI 2014/3255) art.7(6) (December 31, 2014).

109. Care Act 2014 (Consequential Amendments) (Secondary Legislation) Order 2015 (SI 2015/643) art.2 and Sch. para.9(3) (April 1, 2015).

110. Shared Parental Leave and Statutory Shared Parental Pay (Consequential

Amendments to Subordinate Legislation) Order 2014 (SI 2014/3255) art.7(6) (April 5, 2015).

111. Children and Young People (Scotland) Act 2014 (Consequential Modifications) Order 2016 (SI 2016/732) art.3(2) (August 5, 2016).

112. Social Security (Income-Related Benefits) Amendment Regulations 2017 (SI 2017/174) reg.3 (March 20, 2017).

113. Social Security (Scottish Infected Blood Support Scheme) Regulations 2017 (SI 2017/329) reg.4(3) (April 3, 2017).

114. Pensions Act 2014 (Consequential, Supplementary and Incidental Amendments) Order 2017 (SI 2017/422) art.14(2) (April 6, 2017).

115. Social Security (Emergency Funds) (Amendment) Regulations 2017 (SI 2017/689) reg.3(3)(e) (June 19, 2017).

116. Social Security (Infected Blood and Thalidomide) Regulations 2017 (SI 2017/870) reg.3(3)(e) (October 23, 2017).

117. Social Services and Well-being (Wales) Act 2014 and the Regulation and Inspection of Social Care (Wales) Act 2016 (Consequential Amendments) Order 2017 (SI 2017/901) art.6(7) (November 3, 2017).

118. Social Services and Well-being (Wales) Act 2014 and the Regulation and Inspection of Social Care (Wales) Act 2016 (Consequential Amendments) Order 2017 (SI 2017/901) art.21(3) (November 3, 2017).

119. Social Security and Child Support (Care Payments and Tenant Incentive Scheme) (Amendment) Regulations 2017 (SI 2017/995) reg.3(3) (November 7, 2017).

120. Loans for Mortgage Interest Regulations 2017 (SI 2017/725) Sch.5, as amended by Loans for Mortgage Interest and Social Fund Maternity Grant (Amendment) Regulations 2018 (SI 2018/307) reg.2(18)(c) (April 5, 2018).

121. Secretaries of State for Health and Social Care and for Housing, Communities and Local Government and Transfer of Functions (Commonhold Land) Order 2018 (SI 2018/378) Sch., para.21(d) (April 11, 2018).

122. Social Security (Scotland) Act 2018 (Consequential Modifications) Order 2018 (SI 2018/872) art.3 (September 3, 2018).

123. Social Security (Miscellaneous Amendments No.5) Regulations 2017 (SI 2017/1187) reg.3 (December 6, 2018).

124. Social Security (Scotland) Act 2018 (Best Start Grants) (Consequential Modifications and Saving) Order 2018 (SI 2018/1138) art.6(2) (December 10, 2018).

125. Social Security (Scotland) Act 2018 (Funeral Expense Assistance and Early Years Assistance) (Consequential Modifications and Savings) Order 2019 (SI 2019/1060) art.9(2) (September 16, 2019).

126. Parental Bereavement Leave and Pay (Consequential Amendments to Subordinate Legislation) Regulations 2020 (SI 2020/354) reg.8(6) (April 6, 2020).

127. Social Security (Income and Capital) (Miscellaneous Amendments) Regulations 2020 (SI 2020/618) reg.3(11) (July 15, 2020).

128. Social Security (Scotland) Act 2018 (Information-sharing and Scottish Child Payment) (Consequential Provision and Modifications) Order 2020 (SI 2020/482) art.4(2) (November 9, 2020).

129. Social Security (Scotland) Act 2018 (Young Carer Grants, Short-Term Assistance and Winter Heating Assistance) (Consequential Provision and Modifications) Order 2020 (SI 2020/989) art.10(2) (November 9, 2020).

DEFINITIONS

"Abbeyfield Home"—see reg.1(3).
"access funds"—*ibid.*
"approved blood scheme"—*ibid.*
"armed forces independence payment"—*ibid.*
"attendance allowance"—see reg.1(3).

"the Benefits Act"—see Jobseekers Act s.35(1).
"benefit week"—see reg.1(3).
"board and lodging accommodation"—*ibid.*
"care home"—*ibid.*
"the Caxton Foundation"—*ibid.*
"child"—see Jobseekers Act s.35(1).
"the Children Order"—see reg.1(3).
"claimant"—see Jobseekers Act s.35(1) and reg.88(1).
"claimant participating as a service user"—see reg.1(3G).
"concessionary payment"—see reg.1(3).
"contribution"—see reg.130.
"course of study"—see reg.1(3).
"disability living allowance"—*ibid.*
"dwelling occupied as the home"—*ibid.*
"the Eileen Trust"—*ibid.*
"employed earner"—see reg.3 and SSCBA s.2(1)(a).
"the Employment, Skills and Enterprise Scheme"—see reg.1(3).
"employment zone contractor"—*ibid.*
"employment zone programme"—*ibid.*
"family"—see Jobseekers Act s.35(1).
"the Fund"—see reg.1(3).
"Grenfell Tower payment"—*ibid.*
"a guaranteed income payment"—*ibid.*
"Immigration and Asylum Act"—*ibid.*
"independent hospital"—*ibid.*
"the Independent Living Fund (2006)"—*ibid.*
"Intensive Activity Period for 50 plus"—*ibid.*
"loan payments"—see para.31(3)(b) and reg.2(1) of the Loans for Mortgage Interest Regulations 2017.
"local welfare provision"—see reg.1(3).
"the London Bombings Relief Charitable Fund"—*ibid.*
"the London Emergencies Trust"—*ibid.*
"the Macfarlane (Special Payments) Trust"—*ibid.*
"the Macfarlane (Special Payments) (No.2) Trust"—*ibid.*
"the Macfarlane Trust"—*ibid.*
"the Mandatory Work Activity Scheme"—*ibid.*
"MFET Limited"—*ibid.*
"mobility supplement"—*ibid.*
"the National Emergencies Trust"—*ibid.*
"occupational pension scheme"—see Jobseekers Act s.35(1).
"parental bereavement leave"—see reg.1(3).
"partner"—*ibid.*
"partner of a person subject to immigration control"—see reg.85(4).
"payment"—see reg.1(3).
"personal independence payment"—*ibid.*
"personal pension scheme"—see Jobseekers Act s.35(1).
"qualifying person"—see reg.1(3).
"Scottish Infected Blood Support Scheme"—*ibid.*
"self-employment route"—*ibid.*
"shared parental leave"—*ibid.*
"the Skipton Fund"—*ibid.*
"sports award"—*ibid.*
"subsistence allowance"—*ibid.*
"student loan"—see reg.130.
"training allowance"—see reg.1(3).
"universal credit"—*ibid.*
"voluntary organisation"—*ibid.*

"war disablement pension"—*ibid.*
"war widow's pension"—*ibid.*
"war widower's pension"—*ibid.*
"the We Love Manchester Emergency Fund"—*ibid.*
"young person"—see reg.76.

GENERAL NOTE

Most of the disregards in Sch.7 are the same as those in Sch.9 to the Income   **3.558**
Support Regulations (with minor adjustments in the wording). See the notes to
Sch.9.

The only paragraphs in Sch.9 that were not reproduced in the original Sch.7 were
paras 41 and 42 which related to compensation payments made as a consequence
of the 1988 benefit changes and so were not relevant. In addition, there was no
equivalent to para.57 of Sch.9 (backdated payments under reg.21ZB of the Income
Support Regulations) (now revoked), but the disregard in para.12 of Sch.8 should
have applied to such payments.

On para.62, see the note to reg.102C.

Paragraphs 41(4)(b)(i) and (ii) and 41(5)(b)(i) and (ii) include references to step-   **3.559**
parents. Note that from December 5, 2005, references to "step" relationships and
"in laws" are to be read as including relationships arising through civil partnership
in any provision to which s.246 of the Civil Partnership Act 2004 applies. Section
246 is applied to paras 41(4)(b)(i) and (ii) and 41(5)(b)(i) and (ii) by art.3 of and
para.63 of the Schedule to the Civil Partnership Act 2004 (Relationships Arising
Through Civil Partnership) Order 2005 (SI 2005/3137).

The amendment to para.64 on October 26, 2009 brings it into line with the
corresponding income support and old style ESA provisions (see para.66 of Sch.9
to the Income Support Regulations and para.56 of Sch.8 to the ESA Regulations
2008 respectively). Where a claimant lives in a care home, an Abbeyfield Home
or an independent hospital, under reg.105(11) any payment made by a third party
towards the cost of the claimant's or any partner's fees, counts as the claimant's
income. The effect of the previous form of para.64 was that all such payments
were then disregarded. The intention, however, was that only certain payments
made by a health or local authority should be disregarded, hence the amendment.

With effect from May 29, 2020, reg.26(1)(a) of the Victims' Payments Regulations   **3.560**
2020 (SI 2020/103) (see Part II) provides that a victims' payment or a lump sum
under those Regulations is to be disregarded as income or capital. Under the
Regulations payments are to be made to those injured in a "Troubles-related incident", which is defined in s.10(11) of the Northern Ireland (Executive Formation
etc) Act 2019 as "an incident involving an act of violence or force carried out in
Ireland, the United Kingdom or anywhere in Europe for a reason related to the constitutional status of Northern Ireland or to political or sectarian hostility between
people there".

See the notes to Sch.9 to the Income Support Regulations for the status of the   **3.561**
£500 payment from local authorities to certain people who are required by NHS
Test and Trace to self-isolate and the automatic April 2021 payment to recipients
of WTC. If, as suggested there, the former constitute "local welfare provision" (on
which see the notes to para.31A of Sch.9 to the Income Support Regulations), the
disregard for IBJSA purposes is in para.33A. The payments to WTC recipients
appear to be capital, not income (see the notes to Sch.8 below).

Paragraphs A2–A3

Paragraph A2 provides for an income disregard of payments of expenses in   **3.562**
respect of a person's participation in the Mandatory Work Activity Scheme (now
discontinued). The original para.A3 contained the same disregard in relation to the
Employment, Skills and Enterprise Scheme. However, a further para.A3 was inserted

on February 12, 2013, and the original para.A3 has been treated as revoked from that date as a result of s.1(14) of the Jobseekers (Back to Work Schemes) Act 2013. This was because the Jobseeker's Allowance (Employment, Skills and Enterprise Scheme) Regulations 2011 (SI 2011/917) were held to be ultra vires by the Court of Appeal in *R (Reilly and Wilson) v Secretary of State for Work and Pensions* [2013] EWCA Civ 66, [2013] 1 W.L.R. 2239. The appeal against this decision was allowed by the Supreme Court on October 30, 2013 (*R (on the application of Reilly and another) v Secretary of State for Work and Pensions* [2013] UKSC 68, [2014] 1 A.C. 453) but "on the basis only that the Jobseekers (Back to Work Schemes) Act 2013 has come into force" (the 2013 Act came into force on March 26, 2013). The new para.A3 provides that payments of expenses in respect of a person's participation in a scheme listed in reg.3 of the Jobseeker's Allowance (Schemes for Assisting Persons to Obtain Employment) Regulations 2013 (SI 2013/276) are ignored as income.

Paragraphs A1, A4 and A5
3.563   These paragraphs have not been included. This is because they only apply to pilot schemes in certain areas of the country under provisions that have ceased to have effect. See previous editions of this Volume for details.

Paragraph 56
3.564   With effect from April 1, 2014, the disregard in para.56 is modified by art.2 of, and para.5 of the Schedule to, the Social Care (Self-directed Support) (Scotland) Act 2013 (Consequential Modifications and Savings) Order 2014 (SI 2014/513) so that the words "as a direct payment as defined in section 4(2) of the Social Care (Self-directed Support) (Scotland) Act 2013" are substituted for the words "under section 12B of the Social Work (Scotland) 1968". However, under art.3 of the Order, this modification does not apply if a payment is made under s.12B of the 1968 Act on or after April 1, 2014.

SCHEDULE 8   **Regulation 108(2)**

CAPITAL TO BE DISREGARDED

3.565   **A1.**—[*Omitted*]
[⁵⁴**A2.**—Any payment made to the claimant in respect of any travel or other expenses incurred, or to be incurred, by him in respect of his participation in the Mandatory Work Activity Scheme but only for 52 weeks beginning with the date of receipt of the payment.]
[⁵⁵ [⁶⁰ **A3.**— . . .]]
[⁵⁹**A3.**—Any payment made to the claimant in respect of any travel or other expenses incurred, or to be incurred, by him in respect of his participation in a scheme prescribed in regulation 3 of the Jobseeker's Allowance (Schemes for Assisting Persons to Obtain Employment) Regulations 2013 but only for 52 weeks beginning with the date of receipt of the payment.]
A4.—[*Omitted*]
A5.—[*Omitted*]
1.—The dwelling occupied as the home but, notwithstanding regulation 88, (calculation of income and capital of members of claimant's family and of a polygamous marriage), only one dwelling shall be disregarded under this paragraph.
2.—Any premises acquired for occupation by the claimant which he intends to occupy as his home within 26 weeks of the date of acquisition or such longer period as is reasonable in the circumstances to enable the claimant to obtain possession and commence occupation of the premises.
3.—Any sum directly attributable to the proceeds of sale of any premises formerly occupied by the claimant as his home which is to be used for the purchase of other premises intended for such occupation within 26 weeks of the date of sale, or such longer period as is reasonable in the circumstances to enable the claimant to complete the purchase.
4.—Any premises occupied in whole or in part by—
 (a) a partner or relative of a single claimant or of any member of the family as his home where that person [⁵⁰ has attained the qualifying age for state pension credit] or is incapacitated;
 (b) the former partner of a claimant as his home; but this provision shall not apply where

the former partner is a person from whom the claimant is estranged or divorced [³⁵ or with whom he formed a civil partnership that has been dissolved].

5.—Where a claimant has ceased to occupy what was formerly the dwelling occupied as the home following his estrangement or divorce from [³⁵ or dissolution of a civil partnership with] his former partner, that dwelling for a period of 26 weeks from the date on which he ceased to occupy that dwelling [²² or, where that dwelling is occupied as the home by the former partner who is a lone parent, for as long as it is so occupied].

6.—Any premises where the claimant is taking reasonable steps to dispose of those premises, for a period of 26 weeks from the date on which he first took such steps, or such longer period as is reasonable in the circumstances to enable him to dispose of those premises.

7.—Any premises which the claimant intends to occupy as his home, and in respect of which he is taking steps to obtain possession and has sought legal advice or has commenced legal proceedings with a view to obtaining possession, for a period of 26 weeks from the date on which he first sought such advice or first commenced such proceedings, whichever is earlier, or such longer period as is reasonable in the circumstances to enable him to obtain possession and commence occupation of those premises.

8.—Any premises which the claimant intends to occupy as his home to which essential repairs or alterations are required in order to render them fit for such occupation, for a period of 26 weeks from the date on which the claimant first takes steps to effect those repairs or alterations, or such longer period as is reasonable in the circumstances to enable those repairs or alterations to be carried out and the claimant to commence occupation of the premises.

9.—Any grant made to the claimant in accordance with a scheme made under section 129 of the Housing Act 1988 or section 66 of the Housing (Scotland) Act 1988 (schemes for payments to assist local housing authority and local authority tenants to obtain other accommodation) which is to be used—

    (a) to purchase premises intended for occupation as his home; or

    (b) to carry out repairs or alterations which are required to render premises fit for occupation as his home,

for a period of 26 weeks from the date on which he received such a grant or such longer period as is reasonable in the circumstances to enable the purchase, repairs or alterations to be completed and the claimant to commence occupation of those premises as his home.

10.—Any future interest in property of any kind, other than land or premises in respect of which the claimant has granted a subsisting lease or tenancy, including sub-leases or sub-tenancies.

11.—(1) The assets of any business owned in whole or in part by the claimant and for the purposes of which he is engaged as a self-employed earner or, if he has ceased to be so engaged, for such period as may be reasonable in the circumstances to allow for disposal of any such asset.

    (2) The assets of any business owned in whole or in part by the claimant where—

    (a) he is not engaged as a self-employed earner in that business by reason of some disease or bodily or mental disablement; but

    (b) he intends to become engaged (or, as the case may be, re-engaged) as a self-employed earner in that business as soon as he recovers or is able to become engaged or re-engaged in that business,

for a period of 26 weeks from the date on which the claim for a jobseeker's allowance is made, or is treated as made, or if it is unreasonable to expect him to become engaged or re-engaged in that business within that period, for such longer period as is reasonable in the circumstances to enable him to become so engaged or re-engaged.

[⁴(3) In the case of a person who is receiving assistance under [¹² the self-employment route], the assets acquired by that person for the purpose of establishing or carrying on the commercial activity in respect of which such assistance is being received.

(4) In the case of a person who has ceased carrying on the commercial activity in respect of which assistance was received as specified in sub-paragraph (3), the assets relating to that activity for such period as may be reasonable in the circumstances to allow for disposal of any such asset.]

12.—[²¹—(1) Subject to sub-paragraph (2),] any arrears of, or any concessionary payment made to compensate for arrears due to the non-payment of—

    (a) any payment specified in paragraph [⁷9⁷, 9, [⁸¹10, 72A, 80 or 81] of Schedule 7] (other income to be disregarded);

    (b) [⁴⁸ an income-based jobseeker's] allowance or an income-related benefit under Part VII of the Benefits Act [²³, [⁴³ . . .] child tax credit, working tax credit[⁶³ , universal credit], [⁴⁶ or an income-related employment and support allowance]];

    [¹(c) [³² . . .]]

[16(d) any discretionary housing payment paid pursuant to regulation 2(1) of the Discretionary Financial Assistance Regulations 2001;]

[68(e) bereavement support payment under section 30 of the Pensions Act 2014,]

[77(f) maternity allowance under section 35 of the Contributions and Benefits Act (state maternity allowance for employed or self-employed earner).]

but only for a period of 52 weeks from the date of receipt of the arrears of the concessionary payment.

[21 (2) In a case where the total of any arrears and, if appropriate, any concessionary payment referred to in sub-paragraph (1) relating to any one of the specified payments, benefits or allowances amounts to £5,000 or more (referred to in this sub-paragraph and in sub-paragraph (3) as the "relevant sum") and is—

[74(a) paid in order to rectify, or to compensate for—
    (i) an official error as defined in regulation 1(3) of the Social Security and Child Support (Decisions and Appeals) Regulations 1999, or
    (ii) an error on a point of law; and]
(b) received by the claimant in full on or after 14th October 2001,

sub-paragraph (1) shall have effect in relation to such arrears or concessionary payment either for a period of 52 weeks from the date of receipt, or, if the relevant sum is received in its entirety during the award of an income-based jobseeker's allowance, for the remainder of that award if that is a longer period.

(3) For the purposes of sub-paragraph (2), "the award of an income-based jobseeker's allowance" means—
(a) the award either of an income-based jobseeker's allowance [46, income support or of an income-related employment and support allowance] in which the relevant sum (or first part thereof where it is paid in more than one instalment) is received, and
(b) where that award is followed by one or more further awards which in each case may be either of an income-based jobseeker's allowance [46, income support or of an income-related employment and support allowance] and which, or each of which, begins immediately after the end of the previous award, such further awards until the end of the last such award, provided that for any such further awards the claimant—
    (i) is the person who received the relevant sum, or
    (ii) is the partner of the person who received the relevant sum, or was that person's partner at the date of his death, or
    (iii) in the case of a joint-claim jobseeker's allowance, is a joint-claim couple either member or both members of which received the relevant sum.]

13.—Any sum—
(a) paid to the claimant in consequence of damage to, or loss of, the home or any personal possession and intended for its repair or replacement; or
(b) acquired by the claimant (whether as a loan or otherwise) on the express condition that it is to be used for effecting essential repairs or improvements to the home,

and which is to be used for the intended purpose, for a period of 26 weeks from the date on which it was so paid or acquired or such longer period as is reasonable in the circumstances to enable the claimant to effect the repairs, replacement or improvements.

14.—Any sum—
(a) deposited with a housing association as defined in section 1(1) of the Housing Associations Act 1985 as a condition of occupying the home;
(b) which was so deposited and which is to be used for the purchase of another home, for the period of 26 weeks or such longer period as is reasonable in the circumstances to complete the purchase.

15.—Any personal possessions except those which have or had been acquired by the claimant with the intention of reducing his capital in order to secure entitlement to a jobseeker's allowance or to income support or to increase the amount of those benefits.

16.—The value of the right to receive any income under an annuity and the surrender value (if any) of such an annuity.

17.—Where the funds of a trust are derived from a payment made in consequence of any personal injury to the claimant [39 or the claimant's partner], the value of the trust fund and the value of the right to receive any payment under that trust.

[40 **17A.**—(1) Any payment made to the claimant or the claimant's partner in consequence of any personal injury to the claimant or, as the case may be, the claimant's partner.

(2) But sub-paragraph (1)—
(a) applies only for the period of 52 weeks beginning with the day on which the claimant first receives any payment in consequence of that personal injury;

    (b)   does not apply to any subsequent payment made to him in consequence of that injury (whether it is made by the same person or another);

    (c)   ceases to apply to the payment or any part of the payment from the day on which the claimant no longer possesses it;

    (d)   does not apply to any payment from a trust where the funds of the trust are derived from a payment made in consequence of any personal injury to the claimant.

(3) For the purposes of sub-paragraph (2)(c), the circumstances in which a claimant no longer possesses a payment or a part of it include where the claimant has used a payment or part of it to purchase an asset.

(4) References in sub-paragraphs (2) and (3) to the claimant are to be construed as including references to his partner (where applicable).]

18.—The value of the right to receive any income under a life interest or from a liferent.

19.—The value of the right to receive any income which is disregarded under paragraph 14 of Schedule 6 or paragraph 24 of Schedule 7 (earnings or other income payable in a country outside the United Kingdom).

20.—The surrender value of any policy of life insurance.

21.—Where any payment of capital falls to be made by instalments, the value of the right to receive any outstanding instalments.

[⁴⁴ **22.**—(1) Any payment made by a local authority in accordance with—

    (a)   section 17, 23B, 23C or 24A of the Children Act 1989,

    (b)   section 12 of the Social Work (Scotland) Act 1968, [⁷¹ . . .]

    (c)   section [⁶⁶ 26A,] 29 or 30 of the Children (Scotland) Act [⁷¹1995, or

    (d)   the following sections of the Social Services and Well-being (Wales) Act 2014—

        (aa)   section 37 or 38, but excluding any direct payment made in accordance with regulations made under section 51 of that Act; or

        (bb)   section 109, 110, 114 or 115.]

(2) Any payment (or part of a payment) made by a local authority in accordance with section 23C of the Children Act 1989 [⁶⁶or section 26A or 29 of the Children (Scotland) Act 1995 (local authorities' duty to promote welfare of children, duty to provide continuing care and provision of advice and assistance for certain young persons)] to a person ("A") which A passes on to the claimant.

(3) Sub-paragraphs (1) and (2) are subject to the following provisions.

(4) Neither of those sub-paragraphs applies where the claimant is a person who is, or would be, prevented from being entitled to a jobseeker's allowance by section 14 (trade disputes).

(5) Sub-paragraph (2) applies only where A—

    (a)   was formerly in the claimant's care, and

[⁶⁶(b)   is aged 18 or over or, in the case of a payment or part of a payment made in accordance with section 26A of the Children (Scotland) Act 1995, aged 16 or over, and]

    (c)   continues to live with the claimant.]

23.—Any social fund payment made pursuant to Part VIII of the Benefits Act.

[⁶¹ **23A.**—Any local welfare provision.]

24.—Any refund of tax which falls to be deducted under section 369 of the Income and Corporation Taxes Act 1988 (deductions of tax from certain loan interest) on a payment of relevant loan interest for the purpose of acquiring an interest in the home or carrying out repairs or improvements in the home.

25.—Any capital which under regulation 104 [²⁵ . . .] or 136 (capital treated as income [²⁵ . . .] and treatment of student loans) is to be treated as income.

26.—Where a payment of capital is made in a currency other than sterling, any banking charge or commission payable in converting that payment into sterling.

27.—(1) Any payment made under [⁵² or by] the Macfarlane Trust, the Macfarlane (Special Payments) Trust, the Macfarlane (Special Payments) (No.2) Trust, the Fund, the Eileen Trust[⁵¹, MFET Limited][²⁹, the Skipton Fund][⁵⁷, the Caxton Foundation][⁶⁷, the Scottish Infected Blood Support Scheme][⁷⁰, an approved blood scheme][⁶⁹, the London Emergencies Trust, the We Love Manchester Emergency Fund][³⁶, the London Bombings Relief Charitable Fund][⁷⁸, the National Emergencies Trust] ("the Trusts") or the Independent Living [⁴⁷Fund (2006)].

[⁷⁸(1A) Any Grenfell Tower payment or any payment made by the Child Migrants Trust (registered charity number 1171479) under the scheme for former British child migrants.]

(2) Any payment by or on behalf of a person who is suffering or who suffered from haemophilia or who is or was a qualifying person, which derives from a payment made under [⁵² or by] any of the Trusts to which sub-paragraph (1) refers[⁷⁸, or from a Grenfell Tower payment,] and which is made to or for the benefit of—

(a) that person's partner or former partner from whom he is not, or where that person had died was not, estranged or divorced [³⁵ or with whom he has formed a civil partnership that has not been dissolved or, where that person has died, had not been dissolved at the time of that person's death];

(b) any child or young person who is a member of that person's family or who was such a member and who is a member of the claimant's family.

(3) Any payment by or on behalf of the partner or former partner of a person who is suffering or who suffered from haemophilia or who is or was a qualifying person, provided that the partner or former partner and that person are not, or if either of them has died were not, estranged or divorced [³⁵ or, where the partner or former partner and that person have formed a civil partnership, the civil partnership has not been dissolved or, if either of them has died, had not been dissolved at the time of the death], which derives from a payment made under [⁵² or by] any of the Trusts to which sub-paragraph (1) refers[⁷⁸, or from a Grenfell Tower payment,] and which is made to or for the benefit of

(a) the person who is suffering from haemophilia or who is a qualifying person;

(b) any child or young person who is a member of that person's family or who was such a member and who is a member of the claimant's family.

(4) Any payment by a person who is suffering from haemophilia or who is a qualifying person, which derives from a payment made under [⁵² or by] any of the Trusts to which sub-paragraph (1) refers,[⁷⁸ or from a Grenfell Tower payment,] where—

(a) that person has no partner or former partner from whom he is not estranged or divorced [³⁵ or with whom he has formed a civil partnership that has not been dissolved], nor any child or young person who is or had been a member of that person's family; and

(b) the payment is made either—

(i) to that person's parent or step-parent, or

(ii) where that person at the date of payment is a child, a young person or a student who has not completed his full-time education, and has no parent or step-parent, to his guardian,

but only for a period from the date of the payment until the end of two years from that person's death.

(5) Any payment out of the estate of a person who suffered from haemophilia or who was a qualifying person, which derives from a payment made under [⁵² or by] any of the Trusts to which sub-paragraph (1) refers,[⁷⁸ or from a Grenfell Tower payment,] where—

(a) that person at the date of his death (the relevant date) had no partner or former partner from whom he was not estranged or divorced [³⁵ or with whom he had formed a civil partnership that had not been dissolved], nor any child or young person who was or had been a member of his family; and

(b) the payment is made either—

(i) to that person's parent or step-parent, or

(ii) where that person at the relevant date was a child, a young person or a student who had not completed his full-time education, and had no parent or step-parent, to his guardian,

but only for a period of two years from the relevant date.

(6) In the case of a person to whom or for whose benefit a payment referred to in this paragraph is made, any capital resource which derives from any payment of income or capital made under or deriving from any of the Trusts [⁷⁸ or from a Grenfell Tower payment].

[³³ **27A.**—[³⁶ . . .]]

28.—The value of the right to receive an occupational or personal pension.

29.—The value of any funds held under a personal pension scheme.

30.—The value of the right to receive any rent except where the claimant has a reversionary interest in the property in respect of which rent is due.

31.—Any payment in kind [⁷⁸which is a Grenfell Tower payment or] made by a charity or under [⁵² or by] the Macfarlane Trust, the Macfarlane (Special Payments) Trust, the Macfarlane (Special Payments) (No.2) Trust, the Fund, the Eileen Trust[⁵¹, MFET Limited][⁵⁶, the Skipton Fund, the Caxton Foundation][⁶⁷, the Scottish Infected Blood Support Scheme][⁷⁰, an approved blood scheme] or the Independent Living [⁴⁷ Fund (2006)].

[²⁶ **32.**—Any payment made pursuant to section 2 of the Employment and Training Act 1973 or section 2 of the Enterprise and New Towns (Scotland) Act 1990, but only for the period of 52 weeks beginning on the date of receipt of the payment.]

33.—Any payment made by the Secretary of State to compensate for the loss (in whole or in part) of entitlement to housing benefit.

34.—Any payment made to a juror or a witness in respect of attendance at a court other than compensation for loss of earnings or for the loss of a benefit payable under the [48 benefit Acts].

35.—Any payment in consequence of a reduction [45 . . .] of council tax under section 13[62 , 13A] or, as the case may be, section 80 of the Local Government Finance Act 1992 (reduction of liability for council tax), but only for a period of 52 weeks from the date of the receipt of the payment.

[48 **36.**—(1) Any payment or repayment made—

(a) as respects England, under regulation 5, 6 or 12 of the National Health Service (Travel Expenses and Remission of Charges) Regulations 2003 (travelling expenses and health service supplies);

(b) as respects Wales, under regulation 5, 6 or 11 of the National Health Service (Travelling Expenses and Remission of Charges) (Wales) Regulations 2007 (travelling expenses and health service supplies);

(c) as respects Scotland, under regulation 3, 5 or 11 of the National Health Service (Travelling Expenses and Remission of Charges) (Scotland) (No.2) Regulations 2003 (travelling expenses and health service supplies),

but only for a period of 52 weeks from the date of receipt of the payment or repayment.

(2) Any payment or repayment made by the Secretary of State for Health [73and Social Care], the Scottish Ministers or the Welsh Ministers which is analogous to a payment or repayment mentioned in sub-paragraph (1), but only for a period of 52 weeks from the date of receipt of the payment or repayment.

37.—Any payment made to such persons entitled to receive benefits as may be determined by or under a scheme made pursuant to section 13 of the Social Security Act 1988 in lieu of vouchers or similar arrangements in connection with the provision of those benefits (including payments made in place of healthy start vouchers, milk tokens or the supply of vitamins), but only for a period of 52 weeks from the date of receipt of the payment.]

[49 **37A.**—Any payment made under Part 8A of the Benefits Act (entitlement to health in pregnancy grant).]

38.—Any payment made either by the Secretary of State for [42 Justice] or by the [48 Scottish Ministers] under a scheme established to assist relatives and other persons to visit persons in custody, but only for a period of 52 weeks from the date of receipt of the payment.

[48 **39.**—Any arrears of supplementary pension which is disregarded under paragraph 53 of Schedule 7 (sums to be disregarded in the calculation of income other than earnings) or of any amount which is disregarded under paragraph 54 or 55 of that Schedule, but only for a period of 52 weeks from the date of receipt of the arrears.]

40.—Any payment (other than a training allowance [26 . . .]) made, whether by the Secretary of State or by any other person, under the Disabled Persons (Employment) Act 1944 [26 . . .] to assist disabled persons to obtain or retain employment despite their disability.

41.—Any payment made by a local authority under section 3 of the Disabled Persons (Employment) Act 1958 [71or under Part 4 of the Social Services and Well-being (Wales) Act 2014] to homeworkers assisted under the Blind Homeworkers Scheme.

[41 **42.**—(1) Any sum of capital to which sub-paragraph (2) applies and—

(a) which is administered on behalf of a person by the High Court or the County Court under rule 21.11(1) of the Civil Procedure Rules 1998 or by the Court of Protection;

(b) which can only be disposed of by order or direction of any such court; or

(c) where the person concerned is under the age of 18, which can only be disposed of by order or direction prior to that person attaining age 18.

(2) This sub-paragraph applies to a sum of capital which is derived from—

(a) an award of damages for a personal injury to that person; or

(b) compensation for the death of one or both parents where the person concerned is under the age of 18.]

43.—Any sum of capital administered on behalf of a person [2. . .] in accordance with an order made under [24 section 13 of the Children (Scotland) Act 1995], or under Rule 36.14 of the Ordinary Cause Rules 1993 or under Rule 128 of the Ordinary Cause Rules, where such sum derives from—

(a) an award of damages for a personal injury to that person; or

(b) compensation for the death of one or both parents [2where the person concerned is under the age of 18].

44.—Any payment to the claimant as holder of the Victoria Cross or George Cross.

[14 **45.**—[26 . . .].]

[20 **45A.**—[26 . . .].]

[3**46.**—[26 . . .].]

[6**47.**—In the case of a person who is receiving, or who has received, assistance under [12 the self-employment route], any sum of capital which is acquired by that person for the purpose of establishing or carrying on the commercial activity in respect of which such assistance is or was received but only for a period of 52 weeks from the date on which that sum was acquired.]

[⁷**48.**—[²⁶ . . .].]

49.—[*Omitted.*]

50.—[*Omitted.*]

[⁸ **51.**—(1) Any payment of a sports award for a period of 26 weeks from the date of receipt of that payment except to the extent that it has been made in respect of any one or more of the items specified in sub-paragraph (2).

(2) The items specified for the purposes of sub-paragraph (1) are food, ordinary clothing or footwear, household fuel, rent for which housing benefit is payable or any housing costs to the extent that they are met under regulation 83(f) or 84(1)(g) (housing costs) [¹⁹ . . .], of the claimant or, where the claimant is a member of a family, any other member of his family, or any council tax or water charges for which that claimant or member is liable.

(3) For the purposes of sub-paragraph (2)—

"food" does not include vitamins, minerals or other special dietary supplements intended to enhance the performance of the person in the sport in respect of which the award was made;

"ordinary clothing and footwear" means clothing or footwear for normal daily use but does not include school uniforms or clothing or footwear used solely for sporting activities.]

[³⁰ **52.**—(1) Any payment—

(a) by way of an education maintenance allowance made pursuant to—

(i) regulations made under section 518 of the Education Act 1996;

(ii) regulations made under section 49 or 73(f) of the Education (Scotland) Act 1980;

[⁴⁸ (iii) directions made under section 73ZA of the Education (Scotland) Act 1980 and paid under section 12(2)(c) of the Further and Higher Education (Scotland) Act 1992; [⁵⁸ . . .]]

(b) corresponding to such an education maintenance allowance, made pursuant to—

(i) section 14 or section 181 of the Education Act 2002; or

(ii) regulations made under section 181 of that Act [⁵⁸ ; or

(c) in England, by way of financial assistance made pursuant to section 14 of the Education Act 2002.]

(2) Any payment, other than a payment to which sub-paragraph (1) applies, made pursuant to—

(a) regulations made under section 518 of the Education Act 1996;

(b) regulations made under section 49 of the Education (Scotland) Act 1980; or

[⁴⁸ (c) directions made under section 73ZA of the Education (Scotland) Act 1980 and paid under section 12(2)(c) of the Further and Higher Education (Scotland) Act 1992,]

in respect of a course of study attended by a child or a young person or a person who is in receipt of an education maintenance allowance [⁵⁸ or other payment] made pursuant to any provision specified in sub-paragraph (1).]

[¹¹ **53.**—In the case of a claimant participating in an employment zone programme, any discretionary payment made by an employment zone contractor to the claimant, being a fee, grant, loan or otherwise, but only for the period of 52 weeks from the date of receipt of the payment.

54.—Any arrears of subsistence allowance paid as a lump sum but only for the period of 52 weeks from the date of receipt of the payment.]

55.—[*Omitted.*]

[¹³ **56.**—Where an ex-gratia payment of £10, 000 has been made by the Secretary of State on or after 1st February 2001 in consequence of the imprisonment or internment of—

(a) the claimant;

(b) the claimant's partner;

(c) the claimant's deceased spouse [³⁵ or deceased civil partner]; or

(d) the claimant's partner's deceased spouse [³⁵ or deceased civil partner],

by the Japanese during the Second World War, £10, 000.]

[¹⁵ **57.**—(1) Subject to sub-paragraph (2), the amount of any trust payment made to a claimant or a member of a claimant's family who is—

(a) a diagnosed person;

(b) the diagnosed person's partner or the person who was the diagnosed person's partner at the date of the diagnosed person's death;

(c) a parent of a diagnosed person, a person acting in the place of the diagnosed person's

parents or a person who was so acting at the date of the diagnosed person's death; or
- (d) a member of the diagnosed person's family (other than his partner) or a person who was a member of the diagnosed person's family (other than his partner) at the date of the diagnosed person's death.

(2) Where a trust payment is made to—
- (a) a person referred to in sub-paragraph (1)(a) or (b), that sub-paragraph shall apply for the period beginning on the date on which the trust payment is made and ending on the date on which that person dies;
- (b) a person referred to in sub-paragraph (1)(c), that sub-paragraph shall apply for the period beginning on the date on which the trust payment is made and ending two years after that date;
- (c) a person referred to in sub-paragraph (1)(d), that sub-paragraph shall apply for the period beginning on the date on which the trust payment is made and ending—
    - (i) two years after that date; or
    - (ii) on the day before the day on which that person—
        - (aa) ceases receiving full-time education; or
        - (bb) attains the age of [38 20],
    whichever is the latest.

(3) Subject to sub-paragraph (4), the amount of any payment by a person to whom a trust payment has been made, or of any payment out of the estate of a person to whom a trust payment has been made, which is made to a claimant or a member of a claimant's family who is—
- (a) the diagnosed person's partner or the person who was the diagnosed person's partner at the date of the diagnosed person's death;
- (b) a parent of a diagnosed person, a person acting in the place of the diagnosed person's parents or a person who was so acting at the date of the diagnosed person's death; or
- (c) a member of the diagnosed person's family (other than his partner) or a person who was a member of the diagnosed person's family (other than his partner) at the date of the diagnosed person's death,

but only to the extent that such payments do not exceed the total amount of any trust payments made to that person.

(4) Where a payment as referred to in sub-paragraph (3) is made to—
- (a) a person referred to in sub-paragraph (3)(a), that sub-paragraph shall apply for the period beginning on the date on which that payment is made and ending on the date on which that person dies;
- (b) a person referred to in sub-paragraph (3)(b), that sub-paragraph shall apply for the period beginning on the date on which that payment is made and ending two years after that date;
- (c) a person referred to in sub-paragraph (3)(c), that sub-paragraph shall apply for the period beginning on the date on which that payment is made and ending—
    - (i) two years after that date; or
    - (ii) on the day before the day on which that person—
        - (aa) ceases receiving full-time education; or
        - (bb) attains the age of [38 20],
    whichever is the latest.

(5) In this paragraph, a reference to a person—
- (a) being the diagnosed person's partner;
- (b) being a member of the diagnosed person's family; or
- (c) acting in the place of the diagnosed person's parents,

at the date of the diagnosed person's death shall include a person who would have been such a person or a person who would have been so acting, but for the diagnosed person [34 residing in a care home, an Abbeyfield Home or an independent hospital] on that date.

(6) In this paragraph—
"diagnosed person" means a person who has been diagnosed as suffering from, or who, after his death, has been diagnosed as having suffered from, variant Creutzfeldt-Jakob disease;
"relevant trust" means a trust established out of funds provided by the Secretary of State in respect of persons who suffered, or who are suffering, from variant Creutzfeldt-Jakob disease for the benefit of persons eligible for payments in accordance with its provisions;
"trust payment" means a payment under a relevant trust.]

[18 **58.**—The amount of a payment, other than a war pension [48 . . .], to compensate for the fact that the claimant, the claimant's partner, the claimant's deceased spouse [35 or deceased civil partner] or the claimant's partner's deceased spouse [35 or deceased civil partner]—
- (a) was a slave labourer or a forced labourer;

(b)　had suffered property loss or had suffered personal injury; or

(c)　was a parent of a child who had died, during the Second World War.]

[²² [²⁴ **59.**—(1) Any payment made by a local authority, or by the [⁴⁸ Welsh Ministers], to or on behalf of the claimant or his partner relating to a service which is provided to develop or sustain the capacity of the claimant or his partner to live independently in his accommodation.]

(2) For the purposes of sub-paragraph (1) "local authority" means—

(a)　in relation to England, a county council, a district council, a London borough council, the Common Council of the City of London or the Council of the Isles of Scilly;

(b)　in relation to Wales, a county council or a county borough council;

(c)　in relation to Scotland, a council constituted under section 2 of the Local Government etc. (Scotland) Act 1994.]

[²⁴**60.**—Any payment made under [⁴⁹ . . .] [⁶⁵ sections 31 to 33 of the Care Act 2014 (direct payments) or under] regulations made under section 57 of the Health and Social Care Act 2001 or under section 12B of the Social Work (Scotland) Act 1968[⁵³ , or under sections 12A to 12D of the National Health Service Act 2006 (direct payments for health care)[⁷¹, or in accordance with regulations made under section 50 or 52 of the Social Services and Well-being (Wales) Act 2014 (direct payments)]].

[³⁷ **61.**—Any payment made to the claimant pursuant to regulations under section 2(6)(b), 3 or 4 of the Adoption and Children Act 2002.]

[³¹ **61A.**—Any payment made to the claimant in accordance with regulations made pursuant to section 14F of the Children Act 1989 (special guardianship support services).]

　　62.—[²⁶. . .].]

[²⁵ **63.**—[²⁶. . .].]

[⁶⁴ **64.**—Any payments to a claimant made under section 49 of the Children and Families Act 2014 (personal budgets and direct payments).]

[⁶⁸**65.**—Any bereavement support payment in respect of the rate set out in regulation 3(2) or (5) of the Bereavement Support Payment Regulations 2017 (rate of bereavement support payment), but only for a period of 52 weeks from the date of receipt of the payment.]

[⁷⁰**66.**—Any payment made under or by a trust, established for the purpose of giving relief and assistance to disabled persons whose disabilities were caused by the fact that during their mother's pregnancy she had taken a preparation containing the drug known as Thalidomide, and which is approved by the Secretary of State.]

[⁷²**66.**—Any payment made to a claimant under section 73(1)(b) of the Children and Young People (Scotland) Act 2014 (kinship care assistance).]

[⁷⁵**68.**—Any early years assistance given in accordance with section 32 of the Social Security (Scotland) Act 2018.]

[⁷⁶**69.**—Any funeral expense assistance given in accordance with section 34 of the Social Security (Scotland) Act 2018.]

[⁸⁰**70.**—Any assistance given in accordance with the Carer's Assistance (Young Carer Grants) (Scotland) Regulations 2019.]

[⁸⁰**71.**—Any winter heating assistance given in accordance with regulations made under section 30 of the Social Security (Scotland) Act 2018.]

AMENDMENTS

1. Social Security and Child Support (Jobseeker's Allowance) (Miscellaneous Amendments) Regulations 1996 (SI 1996/2538) reg.2(14) (October 28, 1996).

2. Income-related Benefits and Jobseeker's Allowance (Amendment) (No.2) Regulations 1997 (SI 1997/2197) reg.7(9) and (10)(f) (October 6, 1997).

3. Social Security Amendment (New Deal) Regulations 1997 (SI 1997/2863) reg.15 (January 5, 1998).

4. Social Security (Miscellaneous Amendments) (No.4) Regulations 1998 (SI 1998/1174) reg.5(a) (June 1, 1998).

5. Social Security (Miscellaneous Amendments) (No.4) Regulations 1998 (SI 1998/1174) reg.5(b) (June 1, 1998).

6. Social Security (Miscellaneous Amendments) (No.4) Regulations 1998 (SI 1998/1174) reg.5(c) (June 1, 1998).

7. Social Security Amendment (New Deal) (No.2) Regulations 1998 (SI 1998/2117) reg.5(1) (September 24, 1998).

8. Social Security Amendment (Sports Awards) Regulations 1999 (SI 1999/2165) reg.7(5) (August 23, 1999).

9. Social Security Amendment (Education Maintenance Allowance) Regulations 2000 (SI 2000/55) reg.2(3) and (4)(d) (February 7, 2000).

10. Social Security (Miscellaneous Amendments) Regulations 2000 (SI 2000/681) reg.9 (April 3, 2000).

11. Social Security Amendment (Employment Zones) Regulations 2000 (SI 2000/724) reg.3(4) (April 3, 2000).

12. Social Security Amendment (Employment Zones) (No.2) Regulations 2000 (SI 2000/2910) reg.4(1) and (2)(d)(ii) (November 27, 2000).

13. Social Security Amendment (Capital Disregards) Regulations 2001 (SI 2001/22) reg.2 (February 1, 2001).

14. Social Security Amendment (New Deal) Regulations 2001 (SI 2001/1029) reg.13 (April 9, 2001).

15. Social Security Amendment (Capital Disregards and Recovery of Benefits) Regulations 2001 (SI 2001/1118) reg.2(1) (April 12, 2001).

16. Social Security Amendment (Discretionary Housing Payments) Regulations 2001 (SI 2001/2333) reg.2(2)(d) (July 2, 2001).

17. Children (Leaving Care) Act 2000 (Commencement No.2 and Consequential Provisions) Order 2001 (SI 2001/3070) art.3(5) and Sch.4 para.1(c) of (October 1, 2001).

18. Social Security Amendment (Capital Disregards) (No.2) Regulations 2001 (SI 2001/3481) reg.2 (November 19, 2001).

19. Social Security Amendment (Residential Care and Nursing Homes) Regulations 2001 (SI 2001/3767) reg.2(2) and Sch.1 Pt II of para.25 (April 8, 2002).

20. Social Security Amendment (Employment Programme) Regulations 2002 (SI 2002/2314) reg.2(6) (October 14, 2002).

21. Social Security (Miscellaneous Amendments) (No.2) Regulations 2002 (SI 2002/2380) reg.3(c) (October 14, 2002).

22. Social Security (Miscellaneous Amendments) Regulations 2003 (SI 2003/511) reg.3(3) (April 1, 2003).

23. Social Security (Working Tax Credit and Child Tax Credit) (Consequential Amendments) Regulations 2003 (SI 2003/455) reg.3 and Sch.2 para.24(a) (April 7, 2003).

24. Social Security (Miscellaneous Amendments) (No.2) Regulations 2003 (SI 2003/2279) reg.3(5) (October 1, 2003).

25. Social Security (Incapacity Benefit Work-focused Interviews) Regulations 2003 (SI 2003/2439) reg.16(b) (October 27, 2003).

26. Social Security (Miscellaneous Amendments) Regulations 2004 (SI 2004/565) reg.5(4) (April 1, 2004).

27. Social Security (Working Tax Credit and Child Tax Credit) (Consequential Amendments) Regulations 2003 (SI 2003/455) reg.3 and Sch.2 para.24(b) (April 6, 2004, except in "transitional cases" and see further the note to reg.83 and to reg.17 of the Income Support Regulations).

28. Social Security (Miscellaneous Amendments) (No.2) Regulations 2004 (SI 2004/1141) reg.3(1) and (2)(d) (May 12, 2004).

29. Social Security (Miscellaneous Amendments) (No.2) Regulations 2004 (SI 2004/1141) reg.3(7) and (8)(b) (May 12, 2004).

30. Social Security (Students and Income-related Benefits) Amendment Regulations 2004 (SI 2004/1708) reg.6(4) (September 1, 2004, or if the student's period of study begins between August 1 and August 31, 2004, the first day of the period).

31. Social Security (Miscellaneous Amendments) (No.3) Regulations 2004 (SI 2004/2308) reg.4(7) (October 4, 2004).

32. Social Security (Miscellaneous Amendments) Regulations 2005 (SI 2005/574) reg.6(6) (April 4, 2005).

33. Income-related Benefits (Amendment) Regulations 2005 (SI 2005/2183) reg.5 (August 5, 2005).

34. Social Security (Care Homes and Independent Hospitals) Regulations 2005 (SI 2005/2687) reg.3 and Sch.2 para.15 (October 24, 2005).

35. Civil Partnership (Pensions, Social Security and Child Support) (Consequential, etc. Provisions) Order 2005 (SI 2005/2877) art.2(3) and Sch.3 para.26(13) (December 5, 2005).

36. Income-related Benefits (Amendment) (No.2) Regulations 2005 (SI 2005/3391) reg.5(5) (December 12, 2005).

37. Social Security (Miscellaneous Amendments) (No.2) Regulations 2005 (SI 2005/2465) reg.3(9) (December 30, 2005).

38. Social Security (Young Persons) Amendment Regulations 2006 (SI 2006/718) reg.3(11) (April 10, 2006).

39. Social Security (Miscellaneous Amendments) (No.4) Regulations 2006 (SI 2006/2378) reg.13(13)(a) (October 2, 2006).

40. Social Security (Miscellaneous Amendments) (No.4) Regulations 2006 (SI 2006/2378) reg.13(13)(b) (October 2, 2006).

41. Social Security (Miscellaneous Amendments) (No.4) Regulations 2006 (SI 2006/2378) reg.13(13)(c) (October 2, 2006).

42. Secretary of State for Justice Order 2007 (SI 2007/2128) Sch. para.16(3) (August 22, 2007).

43. Social Security (Miscellaneous Amendments) Regulations 2008 (SI 2008/698) reg.4(17)(a) (April 14, 2008).

44. Social Security (Miscellaneous Amendments) Regulations 2008 (SI 2008/698) reg.4(17)(b) (April 7, 2008).

45. Social Security (Miscellaneous Amendments) Regulations 2008 (SI 2008/698) reg.4(17)(c) (April 14, 2008).

46. Employment and Support Allowance (Consequential Provisions) (No.2) Regulations 2008 (SI 2008/1554) reg.3(29) (October 27, 2008).

47. Social Security (Miscellaneous Amendments) (No.6) Regulations 2008 (SI 2008/2767) reg.4(7) (November 17, 2008).

48. Social Security (Miscellaneous Amendments) (No.7) Regulations 2008 (SI 2008/3157) reg.3(11) (January 5, 2009).

49. Social Security (Miscellaneous Amendments) Regulations 2009 (SI 2009/583) reg.4(13) (April 6, 2009).

50. Social Security (Equalisation of State Pension Age) Regulations 2009 (SI 2009/1488) reg.17 (April 6, 2010).

51. Social Security (Miscellaneous Amendments) (No.2) Regulations 2010 (SI 2010/641) reg.4(3)(g) (April 6, 2010).

52. Social Security (Miscellaneous Amendments) (No.2) Regulations 2010 (SI 2010/641) reg.4(8(f) (April 6, 2010).

53. Social Security (Miscellaneous Amendments) (No.2) Regulations 2010 (SI 2010/641) reg.4(13) (April 6, 2010).

54. Jobseeker's Allowance (Mandatory Work Activity Scheme) Regulations 2011 (SI 2011/688) reg.15(1)(d) and (2) (April 25, 2011).

55. Jobseeker's Allowance (Employment, Skills and Enterprise Scheme) Regulations 2011 (SI 2011/917) reg.15(1)(d) and (2) (May 20, 2011).

56. Social Security (Miscellaneous Amendments) (No.3) Regulations 2011 (SI 2011/2425) reg.10(9) (October 31, 2011).

57. Social Security (Miscellaneous Amendments) (No.3) Regulations 2011 (SI 2011/2425) reg.10(10) (October 31, 2011).

58. Social Security (Miscellaneous Amendments) (No.3) Regulations 2011 (SI 2011/2425) reg.10(14) (October 31, 2011).

59. Jobseeker's Allowance (Schemes for Assisting Persons to Obtain Employment) Regulations 2013 (SI 2013/276) reg.12(1)(d) and (2) (February 12, 2013).

60. Jobseekers (Back to Work Schemes) Act 2013 s.1(14) (March 26, 2013).

61. Social Security (Miscellaneous Amendments) Regulations 2013 (SI 2013/443) reg.4(13)(a) (April 2, 2013).

62. Social Security (Miscellaneous Amendments) Regulations 2013 (SI 2013/443) reg.4(13)(b) (April 2, 2013).

63. Universal Credit (Consequential, Supplementary, Incidental and Miscellaneous Provisions) Regulations 2013 (SI 2013/630) reg.30(9) (April 29, 2013).

64. Special Educational Needs (Consequential Amendments to Subordinate Legislation) Order 2014 (SI 2014/2103) art.4(2) (September 1, 2014).

65. Care Act 2014 (Consequential Amendments) (Secondary Legislation) Order 2015 (SI 2015/643) art.2 and Sch. para.9(4) (April 1, 2015).

66. Children and Young People (Scotland) Act 2014 (Consequential Modifications) Order 2016 (SI 2016/732) art.3(3) (August 5, 2016).

67. Social Security (Scottish Infected Blood Support Scheme) Regulations 2017 (SI 2017/329) reg.4(3) (April 3, 2017).

68. Pensions Act 2014 (Consequential, Supplementary and Incidental Amendments) Order 2017 (SI 2017/422) art.14(3) (April 6, 2017).

69. Social Security (Emergency Funds) (Amendment) Regulations 2017 (SI 2017/689) reg.3(3)(f) (June 19, 2017).

70. Social Security (Infected Blood and Thalidomide) Regulations 2017 (SI 2017/870) reg.3(3)(f) (October 23, 2017).

71. Social Services and Well-being (Wales) Act 2014 and the Regulation and Inspection of Social Care (Wales) Act 2016 (Consequential Amendments) Order 2017 (SI 2017/901) art.6(8) (November 3, 2017).

72. Social Security and Child Support (Care Payments and Tenant Incentive Scheme) (Amendment) Regulations 2017 (SI 2017/995) reg.3(4) (November 7, 2017).

73. Secretaries of State for Health and Social Care and for Housing, Communities and Local Government and Transfer of Functions (Commonhold Land) Order 2018 (SI 2018/378) Sch., para.21(d) (April 11, 2018).

74. Social Security (Treatment of Arrears of Benefit) Regulations 2018 (SI 2018/932) reg.3 (September 11, 2018).

75. Social Security (Scotland) Act 2018 (Best Start Grants) (Consequential Modifications and Saving) Order 2018 (SI 2018/1138) art.5(3) (December 10, 2018).

76. Social Security (Scotland) Act 2018 (Funeral Expense Assistance and Early Years Assistance) (Consequential Modifications and Savings) Order 2019 (SI 2019/1060) art.9(3) (September 16, 2019).

77. Social Security (Capital Disregards) (Amendment) Regulations 2019 (SI 2019/1314) reg.3(2) (October 31, 2019).

78. Social Security (Income and Capital) (Miscellaneous Amendments) Regulations 2020 (SI 2020/618) reg.3(12) (July 15, 2020).

79. Social Security (Scotland) Act 2018 (Information-sharing and Scottish Child Payment) (Consequential Provision and Modifications) Order 2020 (SI 2020/482) art.4(3) (November 9, 2020).

80. Social Security (Scotland) Act 2018 (Young Carer Grants, Short-Term Assistance and Winter Heating Assistance) (Consequential Provision and Modifications) Order 2020 (SI 2020/989) arts 3 and 16 (November 9, 2020).

81. Social Security (Scotland) Act 2018 (Young Carer Grants, Short-Term Assistance and Winter Heating Assistance) (Consequential Provision and Modifications) Order 2020 (SI 2020/989) art.10(3) (November 9, 2020).

DEFINITIONS

"Abbeyfield Home"—see reg.1(3).
"approved blood scheme"—*ibid.*
"the Benefits Act"—see Jobseekers Act s.35(1).
"care home"—see reg.1(3).
"the Caxton Foundation"—*ibid.*

"child"—see Jobseekers Act s.35(1).

"claimant"—*ibid.,* and reg.88(1).

"concessionary payment"—see reg.1(3).

"dwelling occupied as the home"—*ibid.*

"the Eileen Trust"—*ibid.*

"the Employment, Skills and Enterprise Scheme"—*ibid.*

"employment zone contractor"—*ibid.*

"employment zone programme"—*ibid.*

"family"—see Jobseekers Act s.35(1).

"the Fund"—see reg.1(3).

"Grenfell Tower payment"—*ibid.*

"independent hospital"—*ibid.*

"the Independent Living Funds"—*ibid.*

"the London Bombings Relief Charitable Fund"—*ibid.*

"the London Emergencies Trust"—*ibid.*

"the Macfarlane (Special Payments) Trust"—*ibid.*

"the Macfarlane (Special Payments) (No.2) Trust"—*ibid.*

"the Macfarlane Trust"—*ibid.*

"the Mandatory Work Activity Scheme"—*ibid.*

"the National Emergencies Trust"—*ibid.*

"the Skipton Fund"—*ibid.*

"MFET Limited"—*ibid.*

"occupational pension"—*ibid.*

"partner"—*ibid.*

"payment"—*ibid.*

"personal pension scheme"—see Jobseekers Act s.35(1).

"policy of life insurance"—see reg.1(3).

"qualifying age for state pension credit"—*ibid.*

"qualifying person"—*ibid.*

"relative"—*ibid.*

"Scottish Infected Blood Support Scheme"—*ibid.*

"self-employed earner"—*ibid.,* and SSCBA s.2(1)(b).

"sports award"—see reg.1(3).

"subsistence allowance"—*ibid.*

"training allowance"—*ibid.*

"universal credit"—*ibid.*

"the We Love Manchester Emergency Fund"—*ibid.*

"young person"—see reg.76.

GENERAL NOTE

3.566   Most of the disregards in Sch.8 are the same as those in Sch.10 to the Income Support Regulations (subject to some reordering and minor adjustments in the wording). See the notes to Sch.10.

Paragraphs 32 and 33 of Sch.10 were not reproduced in the original Sch.8 as they are no longer relevant. There was also no equivalent of paras 47–49 of Sch.10, but see para.12 of this Schedule.

Note that in para.15 the disregard of the value of personal possessions does not apply if they have been acquired in order to reduce capital so as to gain jobseeker's allowance *or income support*. This avoids the question that might otherwise have arisen on a claimant transferring from income support to jobseeker's allowance whether if the acquisition had only been for the purposes of income support the disregard in para.15 applies. However, para.15 has not been amended to include an acquisition for the purposes of income-related ESA.

3.567   On paras 11(3) and (4) and 47, see the note to reg.102C and on paras 53 and 54, see the note to reg.42(5A) of the Income Support Regulations.

Paragraphs 27(4)(b)(i) and (ii) and 27(5)(b)(i) and (ii) include references to step-parents. Note that from December 5, 2005, references to "step" relationships and "in laws" are to be read as including relationships arising through civil partnership in any provision to which s.246 of the Civil Partnership Act 2004 applies. Section 246 is applied to paras 27(4)(b)(i) and (ii) and 27(5)(b)(i) and (ii) by art.3 of and para.64 of the Schedule to the Civil Partnership Act 2004 (Relationships Arising Through Civil Partnership) Order 2005 (SI 2005/3137).

With effect from May 29, 2020, reg.26(1)(a) of the Victims' Payments Regulations **3.568** 2020 (SI 2020/103) (see Part II of this volume) provides that a victims' payment or a lump sum under those Regulations is to be disregarded as capital or income. Under the Regulations payments are to be made to those injured in a "Troubles-related incident", which is defined in s.10(11) of the Northern Ireland (Executive Formation etc) Act 2019 as "an incident involving an act of violence or force carried out in Ireland, the United Kingdom or anywhere in Europe for a reason related to the constitutional status of Northern Ireland or to political or sectarian hostility between people there".

See the notes to Sch.9 to the Income Support Regulations for the taxable £500 payment, administered by local authorities, to be made to those in England entitled to a qualifying income-related benefit (including income support, income-related ESA and income-based JSA) who are required by NHS Test and Trace on or after September 28, 2020 (down at least to summer 2021) to self-isolate for 14 (or 10) days, are unable to work from home and will lose income from employment or self-employment and the discretionary payments available to those not entitled to a qualifying benefit. It is suggested there that the payments are in the nature of income, subject to the possible argument that a discretionary payment could be regarded as a voluntary payment not made or due to be made at regular intervals and so to be treated as capital under reg.48(9). Also, any amount remaining out of the £500 at the end of the required days of self-isolation could be treated as capital under the usual principles. But the payment appears to constitute "local welfare provision", to be disregarded as capital under para.23A (see the notes to para.31A of Sch.9 to the Income Support Regulations).

See the notes to Sch.10 to the Income Support Regulations for the automatic **3.569** April 2021 £500 payments under powers in the Coronavirus Act 2020 to recipients of WTC. Those payments appear to be in the nature of a capital receipt, rather than income. According to LA Welfare Direct 3/2021, the payment is to be disregarded for housing benefit and universal credit purposes, but there has been no amendment of the legislation for the purposes of income support, income-related ESA or income-based JSA.

Paragraph 55

This paragraph has not been reproduced as it only related to a pilot scheme to **3.570** reduce under-occupation operating in three London boroughs (Croydon, Haringey and Newham) from April 3, 2000, which ceased to have effect after three years.

Paragraphs A2–A3

Paragraph A2 provides for a capital disregard of payments of expenses in respect **3.571** of a person's participation in the Mandatory Work Activity Scheme (now discontinued) for 52 weeks from the date the payment was received. The original para.A3 contained the same disregard in relation to the Employment, Skills and Enterprise Scheme. However, a further para.A3 was inserted on February 12, 2013, and the original para.A3 has been treated as revoked from that date as a result of s.1(14) of the Jobseekers (Back to Work Schemes) Act 2013. This was because the Jobseeker's Allowance (Employment, Skills and Enterprise Scheme) Regulations 2011 (SI 2011/917) were held to be ultra vires by the Court of Appeal in *R (Reilly and Wilson) v Secretary of State for Work and Pensions* [2013] EWCA Civ 66, [2013] 1 W.L.R. 2239. The appeal against this decision was allowed by the Supreme Court on October 30, 2013 (*R (on the application of Reilly) v Secretary of State for Work and Pensions* [2013] UKSC 68; [2014] 1 A.C. 453) but "on the basis only that the

Jobseekers (Back to Work Schemes) Act 2013 has come into force" (the 2013 Act came into force on March 26, 2013). The new para.A3 provides that payments of expenses in respect of a person's participation in a scheme listed in reg.3 of the Jobseeker's Allowance (Schemes for Assisting Persons to Obtain Employment) Regulations 2013 are ignored as capital but only for 52 weeks from the date of receipt.

Paragraphs A1, A4 and A5

3.572　These paragraphs have not been included. This is because they only apply to pilot schemes in certain areas of the country under provisions that have ceased to have effect. See previous editions of this Volume for details.

Paragraph 12

3.573　In relation to the April 2013 amendment to para.12, this only amends para.12(1)(b). It is not clear why para.12(3) has not been amended in the same way as para.7(3) of Sch.10 to the Income Support Regulations.

Paragraph 60

3.574　With effect from April 1, 2014, the disregard in para.60 is modified by art.2 of, and para.5 of the Schedule to, the Social Care (Self-directed Support) (Scotland) Act 2013 (Consequential Modifications and Savings) Order 2014 (SI 2014/513) so that the words "as a direct payment as defined in section 4(2) of the Social Care (Self-directed Support) (Scotland) Act 2013" are substituted for the words "under section 12B of the Social Work (Scotland) 1968". However, under art.3 of the Order, this modification does not apply if a payment is made under s.12B of the 1968 Act on or after April 1, 2014.

Paragraph 66 bis

3.575　Although the amending regulation clearly labels this new provision as "66", it appears to have been overlooked that a new para.66 had already been inserted. The plain mistake can be corrected to regard this provision as para.67. See the notes to para.74 0f Sch.10 to the Income Support Regulations for s.73(1)(b) of the Children and Young People (Scotland) Act 2014 and kinship care assistance.

The Jobseeker's Allowance (Transitional Provisions) Regulations 1996

(SI 1996/2567)

3.576　*For the text of these regulations, omitted here for reasons of space and relative infrequency of use, see Social Security: Legislation 2000: Vol.II: Income Support, Jobseeker's Allowance, Tax Credits and the Social Fund, pp.1054—83.*

The Social Security (Miscellaneous Amendments) (No. 5) Regulations 2010

(SI 2010/2429)

Made by the Secretary of State under ss.123(1)(a), (d) and (e), 124(1)(e), 136(3) and (5)(b), 136A(3), 137(1) and 175(1), (3) and (4) of the Social Security Contributions and Benefits Act 1992, ss.2A(1), (3)(e), (4)(b) and (5), 15A(2)(a) and (4), 189(1), (4) and (5) and 191 of the Social Security Administration Act 1992, ss.12(1) and (4)(b), 35(1) and 36(2) and (4)(a) of, and para.8A(1) of Sch.1 to, the Jobseekers Act 1995, s.16 of the Employment Tribunals Act 1996, ss.15(3) and (6) (b) and 17(1) of the State Pension Credit Act 2002 and ss.17(1) and (3)(a) and (b), 24(1) and 25(3),(4) and (5)(a) of the Welfare Reform Act 2007

[In force November 1, 2010]

Amendments to the Jobseeker's Allowance Regulations 1996

4.—(1) The Jobseeker's Allowance Regulations 1996 are amended as follows.

(2) In Schedule A1 (categories of members of a joint-claim couple who are not required to satisfy the conditions in section 1(2B)(b)), subject to paragraph (3) below—

  (a) the following provisions are revoked—

      (i) paragraph 6(a) and (b) (member incapable of work),

      (ii) paragraph 9 (disabled students),

      (iii) paragraph 10 (deaf students), and

      (iv) paragraph 11 (blind members);

  (b) *[Omitted.]*

  (c) *[Omitted.]*

(3) A provision revoked or amended by paragraph (2) continues to have effect in relation to a joint-claim couple as if that revocation or amendment had not been made where, immediately before 1st November 2010—

  (a) the couple were entitled to a jobseeker's allowance, and

  (b) that provision applied to a member of that couple.

(4) Paragraph (3) ceases to apply to a joint-claim couple upon termination of the jobseeker's allowance award that they were entitled to immediately before 1st November 2010.

GENERAL NOTE

See the note to Sch.A1 to the JSA Regulations.

3.577

3.578

The Jobseeker's Allowance (Mandatory Work Activity Scheme) Regulations 2011

(SI 2011/688)

The text of these Regulations is omitted here because the Mandatory Work Activity Scheme ceased operation after April 2016. The Regulations are set out in the 2017/18 edition of this Volume and earlier editions. The introductory general note has been retained to aid understanding of the history.

GENERAL NOTE

The present Regulations (the MWAS Regulations), made under s.17A of the old style Jobseekers Act 1995, were not directly considered in *R (Reilly and Wilson) v Secretary of State for Work and Pensions* [2013] EWCA Civ 66; [2013] 1 W.L.R. 2239. If a claimant has been selected to participate in the scheme under reg.3 and been given a valid notice under reg.4 requiring participation in the scheme, a failure without good reason to participate in the scheme is a higher-level sanctionable failure under s.19(2)(e) of the old style Jobseekers Act 1995 (and see reg.70B of the JSA Regulations 1996). See the notes to s.19(2) for "good reason". Note that the

3.579

scheme has ceased to operate after April 2016.

The Jobseekers (Back to Work Schemes) Act 2013 was designed to validate retrospectively the ESES Regulations that had been declared ultra vires by the Court of Appeal in *Reilly and Wilson* on the ground that the regulations failed to describe, rather than merely name, the schemes they purported to bring within s.17A. The Act was passed on the day on which the Secretary of State sought permission to appeal to the Supreme Court. On the day of the Court of Appeal's judgment (February 12, 2013) the ESES Regulations were replaced by the SAPOE Regulations, which set out the details of the schemes that had been named in the ESES Regulations.

The 2013 Act also sought to protect the operation of the MWAS Regulations from challenge on the basis that notices given to claimants under reg.4 were invalid in the same way as notices under reg.4 of the ESES Regulations in *Reilly and Wilson*, on which now see the decision of the Supreme Court ([2013] UKSC 68; [2014] 1 A.C. 453) and the decision of the three-judge panel of the Upper Tribunal in *SSWP v TJ (JSA)* [2015] UKUT 56 (AAC), discussed in detail in the introductory note to the 2013 Act. The Upper Tribunal rejected the argument that in Mr Wilson's case the notice to participate in the scheme was vitiated by a failure to give him adequate information about the scheme in advance of the notice so as to allow him the opportunity to make meaningful representations about whether the notice should be issued. That conclusion was overturned by the Court of Appeal in Appeal in *SSWP v Reilly and Hewstone* and *SSWP v Jeffrey and Bevan* [2016] EWCA Civ 413, [2017] Q.B. 657, [2017] AACR 14. See the notes to the 2013 Act for extensive citations from the illuminating judgment on the nature of the prior information duty or requirement, which was found to be potentially relevant both at the stage of initial referral to the scheme involved in that case and at the stage at which specific requirements were imposed. The duty rested on the requirements of fairness.

3.580   The Jobseekers (Back to Work Schemes Act 2013) (Remedial) Order 2020 (SI 2020/1085) came into effect on October 3, 2020, inserting new ss.1A and 1B (s.1B dealing specifically with the MWAS) into the 2013 Act. See the introductory notes to the Act at para.1.454. The primary aim is to remedy the breach of the right to a fair trial caused by the retrospective effect of the 2013 Act, as accepted by the Court of Appeal, of a group of claimants who had commenced appeal or judicial review proceedings before March 13, 2013. A group of MWAS appeal cases has been added, attention having been drawn to the existence of that group by an Upper Tribunal judge (see *SSWP v DM (rule 17) (JSA)* [2018] UKUT 424 (AAC) at para.7).

NM v SSWP (JSA) [2016] UKUT 351 (AAC) shows that the "prior information duty", as elucidated by the Court of Appeal, may be relevant both to whether a claimant has validly been referred to a scheme and to whether there was a good reason for not participating in it. Judge Wright held, as eventually conceded by the Secretary of State, that the inability to show that relevant DWP guidance had been considered before the claimant was given notice to participate in a Mandatory Work Activity scheme meant either that the claimant should not have been referred to the scheme (because the officer either would have followed the guidance or could have been persuaded to do so on representations from the claimant) or that he had good reason for not participating in the scheme. The appeal related to a sanction for failing to participate, through behaviour on the scheme. The guidance, in something called *Mandatory Work Activity Guidance* or *Operational Instructions – Procedural Guidance – Mandatory Work Activity – January 2012*, was relevant because at the time it instructed that claimants should not be considered for referral to Mandatory Work Activity if, among other circumstances, they were currently working (paid or voluntary). The claimant had been volunteering in a Sue Ryder shop, which activity he had to give up to attend the required scheme as a volunteer in a Salvation Army shop. The Secretary of State submitted that the guidance had since been changed to introduce an element of discretion about referral of claimants doing voluntary work.

Judge Wright held that this would not excuse a failure by an officer of the Secretary of State to consider his own guidance or, on any appeal, a failure to provide the guidance to a First-tier Tribunal in accordance with the principles of natural justice.

SSWP v DM (rule 17) (JSA) [2018] UKUT 424 (AAC), a decision merely recording consent to the withdrawal of the Secretary of State's appeal to the Upper Tribunal, contains details of the Department's Operational Guidance (as in force in April 2012) about identifying when claimants were suitable for the MWAS, that had wrongly not been produced to the First-tier Tribunal. The Secretary of State accepted that, if that guidance had been properly applied, the claimant in *DM* should not, because of his complex barriers to employment, have been referred to the scheme.

AW v SSWP (JSA) [2016] UKUT 387 (AAC) confirms that a requirement to participate in a Mandatory Work Activity scheme is not invalidated by the fact that the claimant's jobseeker's agreement restricts his availability for employment to work that paid at least the national minimum wage. Participation in the scheme was not employment, and satisfaction of the conditions of entitlement in paras (a) to (g) of s.1(2) of the old style Jobseekers Act 1995 did not prevent the imposition of requirements under s.17A, as s.1(2) is subject to the provisions of the Act as a whole. Note that the decision quotes an out-of-date version of s.19(2)(e) referring to good cause instead of a good reason.

3.581

The 2013 Act gave no protection to the MWAS Regulations against a vires challenge on the same grounds as in *Reilly and Wilson*. Such a challenge was rejected by Hickinbottom J in *R (Smith) v Secretary of State for Work and Pensions* [2014] EWHC 843 (Admin). He held that there was sufficient description of the scheme to meet the standard required by the Supreme Court. The reasons included that the prescription of the period of the scheme was relevant to its description under s.17A(1) and was not relevant only to subs.(2). The Court of Appeal in *Smith v Secretary of State for Work and Pensions* [2015] EWCA Civ 229 has affirmed that decision on essentially the same reasoning.

The Jobseeker's Allowance (Employment, Skills and Enterprise Scheme) Regulations 2011

(SI 2011/917)

The text of these Regulations is omitted here because they were revoked with effect from 1845 on February 12, 2013. The Regulations are set out in the 2017/18 edition of what was then Vol.II and earlier editions. The introductory general note has been retained to aid understanding of the history.

GENERAL NOTE

In *R (Reilly and Wilson) v Secretary of State for Work and Pensions* [2013] EWCA Civ 66; [2013] 1 W.L.R. 2239, the Court of Appeal quashed as unlawful these Regulations (SI 2011/917) ("the ESES Regulations") because the Secretary of State acted ultra vires in failing to provide sufficient detail about the various schemes in the Regulations to satisfy s.17A of the old style Jobseekers Act 1995. The Court also held that notices sent to claimants advising them that they were required to take part in a programme within the ESE Scheme did not comply with the requirements of reg.4 of these Regulations. The effect of the decision was that the DWP had no right to impose a sanction on claimants who had failed to meet their requirements. That decision was confirmed by the Supreme Court ([2013] UKSC 68; [2014]1 A.C. 453), which is now the authoritative basis for the principle involved.

3.582

The DWP immediately on the handing down of the Court of Appeal's decision issued the Jobseeker's Allowance (Schemes for Assisting Persons to Obtain Employment) Regulations 2013, SI 2013/276 ("the SAPOE Regulations"), which came into effect at 1845 on February 12, 2013 so that sanctions could be applied from the date those new Regulations came into force.

The Jobseekers Allowance (Back to Work) Act 2013 is designed retrospectively to validate the impugned ESES Regulations making actions which related to participation in these employment programmes effective, and providing that notices served under those Regulations informing claimants of requirements as to participation, and about consequences of failing to meet requirements, were effective. The provisions affect claimants where sanctions have been applied for failures to comply with the ESES Regulations and cases where the claimant has failed to comply with a requirement of the ESES Regulations but a decision to impose a sanction has not yet been taken. It aims to ensure that any such decisions cannot be challenged on the grounds that the ESES Regulations were invalid or the notices inadequate, notwithstanding the Court of Appeal's judgment, so that benefit sanctions already imposed or to be imposed stand, saving the public purse some £130 million which would otherwise have to be paid to claimants who had been, if the Court of Appeal decision had stood, treated unlawfully. The Act also aims to protect from challenge on the basis of the reasoning in *Reilly and Wilson* notices given under the MWAS Regulation (see the notes to those Regulations).

3.583   See the introductory note to the 2013 Act for the state of the case law current as at the date of publication on whether that Act has in law retrospectively validated these Regulations and notices issued under them prior to February 12, 2013 in relation to sanctioned claimants who had lodged appeals prior to March 26, 2013 as well as to other categories of claimant. The Court of Appeal in *SSWP v Reilly and Hewstone* and *SSWP v Jeffrey and Bevan* [2016] EWCA Civ 413; [2017] Q.B. 657; [2017] AACR 14 has decided that the 2013 Act was to be construed as having that effect, whether as "read down" under s.3 of the Human Rights Act 1998 or not, contrary to the view of the majority of the three-judge panel of the Upper Tribunal in *SSWP v TJ (JSA)* [2015] UKUT 56 (AAC). The Court of Appeal gave a declaration of incompatibility with art.6 of the ECHR in respect of claimants who had lodged appeals, but that does not affect the validity or continuing operation of the Act, including in its effect on the ESES Regulations (s.4(6) of the Human Rights Act 1998).

Section 1(14) of the 2013 Act also treats these Regulations as revoked by the SAPOE Regulations with effect from the day and time those SPAOE Regulations came into force: 18.45 on February 12, 2013. It does so in order that two sets of Regulations covering the same ground were not in force simultaneously. However, s.1(10) of the Act means that the original penalty provisions (on which see the text of those Regulations in the 2012/13 edition of this volume) continue to apply to failures occurring before the entry into force of the Jobseeker's Allowance (Sanctions) (Amendment) Regulations 2012 (SI 2012/2568), namely October 22, 2012, even if the penalty was imposed after that date.

One of the appeals in *MH v SSWP (JSA)* [2016] UKUT 199 (AAC), CJSA/3093/2014, concerned a notice to attend an interview issued by a Work Programme provider purportedly under reg.4(2) of the ESES Regulations on February 12, 2013 itself. This was the very day on which the Court of Appeal in *Reilly and Wilson* quashed the ESES Regulations and the notice must have been issued before the SAPOE Regulations came into force at 1845 on that day. The Secretary of State submitted in the Upper Tribunal that, regardless of the outcome of the litigation on the question of whether the 2013 Act did retrospectively validate the ESES Regulations (which has for the time being been determined by the Court of Appeal in *Reilly, Hewstone, Jeffrey and Bevan*), no sanction could be imposed under s.19A(2)(b) of the old style Jobseekers Act 1995 for a failure to comply with the requirement to participate in the scheme in accordance with the notice. That was because on February 12, 2013 the DWP had contacted all Work Programme providers to tell them that they no longer had delegated authority (under reg.17(2)) to issue "mandatory activity notices" such as the appointment letter in question. The category of cases covered by this reasoning is obviously exceptionally narrow. The validity of notices issued before February 12, 2013 will depend on the outcome of the litigation on the effect of the 2013 Act. For notices issued after 18.45 on February 12, 2013, see the notes to the SAPOE Regulations.

The Jobseeker's Allowance (Schemes for Assisting Persons to Obtain Employment) Regulations 2013

(SI 2013/276)

Made by the Secretary of State for Work and Pensions under the powers conferred by sections 123(1)(d) and (e), 136(3) and (5)(a) and (b), 137(1) and 175(1), (3) and (4) of the Social Security Contributions and Benefits Act 1992, section 113(1) and (2) of, and paragraph 4 of Schedule 1A to, the Local Government Finance Act 1992, sections 12(1), (4)(a) and (b), 17A(1), (2) and (5)(a) and (b), 20E(3)(a), 35(1) and 36(2) and (4) of the Jobseekers Act 1995 and sections 30 and 146(1) and (2) of the Housing Grants, Construction and Regeneration Act 1996 and sections 17(1) and (3)(a) and (b), 24(1) and 25(2) and (3) of the Welfare Reform Act 2007, the Social Security Advisory Committee having agreed that by reason of the urgency of the matter it was not expedient to refer the proposal in respect of these Regulations to it.

ARRANGEMENT OF REGULATIONS

PART 1

SCHEMES FOR ASSISTING PERSONS TO OBTAIN EMPLOYMENT

PART 2

CONSEQUENTIAL AMENDMENTS

PART 3

CONTRACTING OUT

17. Contracting out certain functions

GENERAL NOTE

3.585   See the annotations to the Jobseekers (Back to Work) Act 2013 and to s.17A of the old style Jobseekers Act 1995. It would seem that the schemes prescribed below are validly described for the purposes of s.17A within the principles laid down by the Supreme Court in *R (Reilly and Wilson) v Secretary of State for Work and Pensions* [2013] UKSC 68, [2014] 1 A.C. 453 and applied to the MWAS Regulations by Hickinbottom J in *R (Smith) v Secretary of State for Work and Pensions* [2014] EWHC 843 (Admin), as confirmed on appeal ([2015] EWCA Civ 229).

One of the appeals in *MH v SSWP (JSA)* [2016] UKUT 199 (AAC), CJSA/3094/2014, concerned a notice to attend an interview issued by a Work Programme provider on March 4, 2013, after the SAPOE Regulations had come into force. On some date from February 13–17, 2013, Jobcentre Plus on behalf of the Secretary of State had sent the claimant a WP05(C) letter to replace the WP05 letter originally sent in June 2011. Judge Wright accepted that there was no issue over the claimant having received the WP05(C) letter and held that, despite some clumsy use of words in references to revision of earlier notices, it evidenced a fresh decision to select the claimant for participation in the Work Programme scheme under reg.4(1). Then, through the combination of the WP05(C) letter and the appointment letter of March 4, 2013 (as allowed in the Upper Tribunal decision in *SSWP v TJ (JSA)* [2015] UKUT 56 (AAC): see the notes to the 2013 Act), sufficient notice had been given to meet the requirements of reg.5(2) in substance. Accordingly, the First-tier Tribunal's finding that the claimant had not shown a good reason for failing to comply with the requirement to participate in the scheme being accepted, a sanction under s.19A(2)(b) of the old style Jobseekers Act 1995 had to be imposed, but with the period adjusted because of the setting aside in CJSA/3093/2014 (see the notes to the ESES Regulations) of a previous sanction.

In *SN v SSWP (JSA)* [2018] UKUT 279 (AAC), para.91, it was confirmed that, despite the failure to issue the claimant with a MWA05 letter, he had been sufficiently notified of the requirement to participate in a mandatory work activity scheme within reg.4 of the Jobseeker's Allowance (Mandatory Work Activity Scheme) Regulations 2011 by a combination of information given in an interview with an adviser and a letter from the programme provider about the specific placement as a retail assistant in a charity shop.

3.586   The points decided in *MH v SSWP* were confirmed in *DH v SSWP (JSA)* [2016] UKUT 355 (AAC). In addition it was held that the First-tier Tribunal erred in law in apparently dismissing the claimant's objections to attending a Work Programme run by a particular provider (on the grounds that staff of the company concerned had lied in a police statement and in court about whether travel expenses had been refunded to him and had bullied him) as, even if true, irrelevant to whether he had a good reason for failing to comply with requirements to attend. The tribunal had said that the claimant's remedies were to contact the police and to use appropriate complaints procedures, not to refuse to attend interviews or courses. The judge asked the rhetorical question in para.20 what could amount to good reason if such matters did not. The circumstances are to be distinguished from those in *R(JSA) 7/03*, not mentioned in *DH*, where the claimant's objection was a generalised one to the involvement of private companies in the provision of such schemes.

SSWP v DC (JSA) [2017] UKUT 464 (AAC); [2018] AACR 16 concerned two sanctions imposed in August 2013 for failures, without good cause, to participate in a Scheme as required under reg.4 of the ESES Regulations in June and August 2012. By August 2013 the Regulations had been revoked, but continued to apply in relation to failures to participate that occurred while they were in force. For the same reason, the sanctions provisions in reg.8 (revoked with effect from October 22, 2012) applied in *DC*, rather than s.19A of the old style Jobseekers Act 1995. The principles are relevant to the questions of whether an effective notice has been given under reg.5 of the present Regulations and whether there has been authorisation under reg.17 of other people to exercise functions of the Secretary of State.

The first appeal (in relation to August 2012) raised the issue of the effect of the Secretary of State being unable to provide to the First-tier Tribunal, as directed, a copy of the appointment letter known as a Mandatory Activity Notification (MAN) sent or handed to the claimant in respect of the appointment that he failed to attend. The tribunal had allowed the claimant's appeal on the basis that the Secretary of State had failed to show that the claimant had been properly notified in accordance with the conditions in reg.4(2). In concluding that there was no error of law in that, Judge Rowland held that this was not a matter of the drawing of adverse inferences, but of the Secretary of State simply having failed to come forward with evidence on a matter on which the burden of proof was on him. Although there was evidence before the tribunal that the claimant had been given an appointment letter, that evidence did not go beyond showing the date and time of the appointment. It did not show where the claimant was to attend or what other information was provided and how it was expressed. The judge rejected the Secretary of State's submission relying on the presumption of regularity and the "inherent probabilities". Although the tribunal could, using its specialist experience, properly have concluded that the letter had contained enough information to make it effective, it was not bound to do so, given that it is not unknown for documents to be issued in an unapproved form or to use language that is not intelligible to an uninitiated recipient. The judge agreed with the tribunal that a copy of the appointment letter should have been in the tribunal bundle: a decision-maker might be able to rely on the presumption of regularity, but on an appeal (where it is not known what issues may eventually emerge) a copy of the letter should be provided. Much the same approach was taken by the Chief Commissioner in Northern Ireland in *PO'R v DFC (JSA)* [2018] NI Com 1, where it was said that the tribunal there should not have decided against the claimant without having adjourned to obtain a copy of the appointment letter.

If a copy of the appointment letter was not in the bundle, then Judge Rowland's view was that a tribunal, exercising its inquisitorial jurisdiction in an area where unrepresented claimants in particular could not be expected to identify such technical points, could properly exercise its discretion under s.12(8)(a) of the SSA 1998 to direct that a copy be provided. It would not be fair to decide the case against the Secretary of State without giving that opportunity to provide the evidence. But where, as in *DC*, the evidence directed was not provided, the tribunal could properly conclude that the Secretary of State had failed to come forward with evidence on a matter on which the burden of proof was on him. There is therefore no formal incompatibility in the decision of Judge Wright in *SSWP v CN (JSA)* [2020] UKUT 26 (AAC), discussed in the introductory note to the Jobseekers (Back to Work Schemes) Act 2013, although there was less emphasis there on the inquisitorial role of the tribunal.

The judge accepted that the tribunal had erred in law in deciding against the Secretary of State on the authorisation point (discussed below) without giving him an opportunity to provide relevant evidence, but that error was not material as, even

3.587

if there was evidence that the provider was authorised to issue reg.4 notices, the tribunal would have been entitled to allow the claimant's appeal on the basis of the lack of necessary evidence that an effective notice had been given.

The second appeal (in relation to June 2012) raised the issue of whether the tribunal had been entitled to conclude that the Secretary of State had not shown that the Scheme provider in question had been authorised under reg.18 to give reg.4 notices when he was unable to produce a copy of a letter of authorisation. Judge Rowland held that the tribunal had gone wrong in law. Regulation 18 did not specify the form in which authorisation had to be given, so that it was a matter of fact and degree. Authority could thus be found to exist in evidence as to the conduct of those concerned, including what they have said and written over a period. The tribunal did not consider that possibility, raised by the provider acting as though authorised and the Secretary of State asserting that authority had been given. The judge went on to re-make the decision on the appeal. It had emerged that, by an administrative mistake, no formal letter of authority had ever been issued, but the existence of a contract between the Secretary of State and the main contractor for the sub-contractor to act in the area in question and a draft authorisation letter was sufficient to satisfy reg.18. He found that the claimant had been properly notified and had not shown good cause for his failure to participate, so that a sanction was to be imposed. On close analysis of reg.8 the sanction was to be for four weeks, rather than the 26 that had originally been imposed.

Citation and commencement

3.588   **1.**—These Regulations may be cited as the Jobseeker's Allowance (Schemes for Assisting Persons to Obtain Employment) Regulations 2013 and come into force on 12th February 2013 at 6.45pm.

Interpretation

3.589   **2.**—(1) In these Regulations—
"the Act" means the Jobseekers Act 1995;
"claimant" means a person who claims a jobseeker's allowance, except that in relation to a joint-claim couple claiming a joint-claim jobseeker's allowance, it means either or both of the members of the couple;
"the Council Tax Benefit Regulations" means the Council Tax Benefit Regulations 2006;
"the Housing Benefit Regulations" means the Housing Benefit Regulations 2006;
"the Housing Renewal Grants Regulations" means the Housing Renewal Grants Regulations 1996;
"the Jobseeker's Allowance Regulations" means the Jobseeker's Allowance Regulations 1996;
"working day" means any day except for a Saturday, Sunday, Christmas Day, Good Friday or bank holiday under the Banking and Financial Dealings Act 1971 in England and Wales or in Scotland.

(2) For the purpose of these Regulations where a written notice is given by sending it by post it is taken to have been received on the second working day after posting.

Schemes for Assisting Persons to Obtain Employment

3.590   **3.**—(1) The schemes described in the following paragraphs are prescribed for the purposes of section 17A(1) (schemes for assisting persons to obtain employment: "work for your benefit" schemes etc) of the Act.

(2) [³...].

(3) [³...].

(4) Full-time Training Flexibility is a scheme comprising training of 16 to 30 hours per week, for any claimant who has been receiving jobseeker's allowance for a continuous period of not less than 26 weeks ending on the first required entry date to the scheme.

(5) New Enterprise Allowance is a scheme designed to assist a claimant into self-employed earner's employment comprising guidance and support provided by a business mentor, access to a loan to help with start-up costs (subject to status) and a weekly allowance for a period of 26 weeks once the claimant starts trading.

(6) The sector-based work academy is a scheme which provides, for a period of up to 6 weeks, training to enable a claimant to gain the skills needed in the work place and a work experience placement for a period to be agreed with the claimant, and either a job interview with an employer or support to help participants through an employer's application process.

(7) Skills Conditionality is a scheme comprising training or other activity designed to assist a claimant to obtain skills needed to obtain employment.

(8) The Work Programme is a scheme designed to assist a claimant at risk of becoming long-term unemployed in which, for a period of up to 2 years, the claimant is given such support as the provider of the Work Programme considers appropriate and reasonable in the claimant's circumstances, subject to minimum levels of support published by the provider, to assist the claimant to obtain and sustain employment which may include work search support, provision of skills training and work placements for the benefit of the community.

[¹(8A) [³...].

(8B)[².. .]].

[³(8C) The Work and Health Programme is a scheme designed to assist a claimant who is long-term unemployed in which, for a period of up to 456 calendar days, the claimant is given such support, and required to participate in such activity, as the provider of the Work and Health Programme considers appropriate and reasonable in the claimant's circumstances to assist the claimant to obtain and sustain employment.]

(9) In this regulation—

[³ . . .];

[³ . . .];

"self-employed earner" has the same meaning as in section 2(1)(b) of the Social Security Contributions and Benefits Act 1992; and

[³ . . .].

AMENDMENTS

1. Jobseeker's Allowance (Schemes for Assisting Persons to Obtain Employment) (Amendment) Regulations 2013 (SI 2013/2584) reg.2 (November 5, 2013).

2. Social Security (Traineeships and Qualifying Young Persons) Amendment Regulations 2015 (SI 2015/336) reg.3 (March 27, 2015).

3. Jobseeker's Allowance (Schemes for Assisting Persons to Obtain Employment) (Amendment) Regulations 2017 (SI 2017/1020) reg.2(2) (November 20, 2017).

GENERAL NOTE

The 2017 amendments are in the main to remove references to schemes that no longer operate. The Work and Health Programme (WHP) is newly prescribed

3.591

in para.(8C). There may perhaps be some doubt whether para.(8C) provides sufficient description of the scheme to satisfy the test for validity under s.17A of the old style Jobseekers Act 1995 as laid down in *R (Reilly and Wilson) v Secretary of State for Work and Pensions* [2013] UKSC 68; [2014] 1 A.C. 453 (that a description is prescribed, not merely a label), since the nature of the support and activity in which participation can be required is left to the provider to identify in the light of a claimant's particular circumstances. On the other hand, the statements of the aim of assisting a claimant to obtain and sustain employment and of a maximum length indicating long-term assistance may point towards satisfaction of the test. Paragraph (8C) also leaves open who might count as long-term unemployed and what the "health" part of the name of the scheme might imply.

The revised Explanatory Memorandum to the amending regulations reveals (para.7.3) that the great majority of participants in the scheme will be those with disabilities (75%) or within an Early Access Disadvantaged Group (up to 10%), who can volunteer to take part. The mandatory process under s.17A is restricted to the long-term unemployed, regarded as covering claimants who have not moved into employment within 24 months of their claim. There may be further doubt whether a description in the SAPOE Regulations that is restricted to the mandatory part of a scheme rather than of the scheme as a whole is sufficient and how far there could be reference to the Explanatory Memorandum to flesh out the statutory description in determining validity or otherwise under s.17A.

The Explanatory Memorandum says (para.4.6) that a Designation Order will be made designating employees of WHP providers as "employment officers" for the purposes of s.19(2)(c) of the old style Jobseekers Act 1995 in relation to informing a claimant of an existing or imminent employment vacancy, with the consequence of a higher-level sanction for, without a good reason, failing or refusing to apply for such a vacancy or accept an offer. See the notes to the definition of "employment officer" in s.35(1) of the old style Jobseekers Act 1995. The Jobseeker's Allowance (Work and Health Programme) (Employment Officers) Designation Order 2018 (available in the Deposited Papers section of the UK Parliament website) carries out the designation with effect from April 1, 2018. The list of prime contractors, and the areas covered (which do not cover Scotland) set out in the Schedule to the Order is reproduced in Memo DMG 06/18.

Selection for participation in a Scheme

3.592   **4.**—(1) The Secretary of State may select a claimant for participation in a scheme described in regulation 3.

(2) The scheme in which the claimant is selected to participate is referred to in these Regulations as "the Scheme".

Requirement to participate and notification

3.593   **5.**—(1) Subject to regulation 6, a claimant selected under regulation 4 is required to participate in the Scheme where the Secretary of State gives the claimant a notice in writing complying with paragraph (2).

(2) The notice must specify—

(a) that the claimant is required to participate in the Scheme;
(b) the day on which the claimant's participation will start;
(c) details of what the claimant is required to do by way of participation in the Scheme;
(d) that the requirement to participate in the Scheme will continue until the claimant is given notice by the Secretary of State that the claimant's participation is no longer required, or the claimant's award of jobseeker's allowance terminates, whichever is earlier; and

(e) information about the consequences of failing to participate in the Scheme.

(3) Any changes made to the requirements mentioned in paragraph (2)(c) after the date on which the claimant's participation starts must be notified to the claimant in writing.

Circumstances in which requirement to participate in the Scheme is suspended or ceases to apply

6.—(1) Paragraph (2) applies where a claimant is—   3.594
  (a) subject to a requirement to participate in the Scheme; and
  (b) while the claimant is subject to such a requirement, the Jobseeker's Allowance Regulations apply so that the claimant is not required to meet the jobseeking conditions.

(2) Where this paragraph applies the claimant's requirement to participate in the Scheme is suspended for the period during which the claimant is not required to meet the jobseeking conditions.

(3) A requirement to participate in the Scheme ceases to apply to a claimant if—
  (a) the Secretary of State gives the claimant notice in writing that the claimant is no longer required to participate in the Scheme; or
  (b) the claimant's award of jobseeker's allowance terminates,
whichever is earlier.

(4) If the Secretary of State gives the claimant a notice in writing under paragraph (3)(a), the requirement to participate in the Scheme ceases to apply on the day specified in the notice.

Exemptions from requirement to meet the jobseeking conditions

7.—(1) A claimant who is participating in the New Enterprise Allowance   3.595
scheme described in regulation 3(5) is not required to meet the condition set out in section 1(2)(c) of the Act (conditions for entitlement to a jobseeker's allowance: actively seeking employment).

(2) A claimant who is participating in the Scheme is not required to meet the conditions set out in section 1(2)(a) and (c) of the Act (conditions for entitlement to a jobseeker's allowance: available for and actively seeking employment) if the claimant is a full-time student.

(3) A claimant who is participating in the Scheme is not required to meet the conditions set out in section 1(2)(a) and (c) of the Act if the claimant has been discharged from detention in a prison, remand centre or youth custody institution, for one week commencing with the date of that discharge.

(4) In this regulation, "full-time student" has the same meaning as in regulation 1(3) of the Jobseeker's Allowance Regulations.

Definitions

8.—*The amendments effected by this regulation have been taken into account*   3.596
in the text of the Jobseekers Allowance Regulations elsewhere in this volume.

Notional income

9.—*The amendments effected by this regulation have been taken into account*   3.597
in the text of the Jobseekers Allowance Regulations elsewhere in this volume.

Notional capital

3.598   **10.**—*The amendments effected by this regulation have been taken into account in the text of the Jobseekers Allowance Regulations elsewhere in this volume.*

Income to be disregarded

3.599   **11.**—*The amendments effected by this regulation have been taken into account in the text of the Jobseekers Allowance Regulations elsewhere in this volume.*

Capital to be disregarded

3.600   **12.**—*The amendments effected by this regulation have been taken into account in the text of the Jobseekers Allowance Regulations elsewhere in this volume.*

Amendments to the Income Support (General) Regulations 1987

3.601   **13.**—*The amendments effected by this regulation have been taken into account in the text of the Jobseekers Allowance Regulations elsewhere in this volume.*

Further amendments to the Jobseeker's Allowance Regulations

3.602   **14.**—*The amendments effected by this regulation have been taken into account in the text of the Jobseekers Allowance Regulations elsewhere in this volume.*

Amendments to the Employment and Support Allowance Regulations 2008

3.603   **15.**—*The amendments effected by this regulation have been taken into account in the text of the Employment and Support Allowance Regulations elsewhere in this volume*

Amendments to the Council Tax Reduction Schemes (Default Scheme) (England) Regulations 2012

3.604   **16.**—[*Omitted.*]

Contracting out certain functions

3.605   **17.**—(1) Any function of the Secretary of State specified in paragraph (2) may be exercised by, or by employees of, such person (if any) as may be authorised by the Secretary of State.

(2) The functions are any function under—

(a) regulation 5 (requirement to participate and notification); and

(b) regulation 6(3)(a) (notice that requirement to participate ceases).

The Jobseeker's Allowance (Habitual Residence) Amendment Regulations 2013

(SI 2013/3196)

The Secretary of State for Work and Pensions makes the following Regulations in exercise of the powers conferred by sections 4(5) and (12), 35(1) and 36(2) of the Jobseekers Act 1995.

The Secretary of State has not referred proposals in respect of these Regulations to the Social Security Advisory Committee, as it appears to him that by reason of the urgency of the matter it is inexpedient to do so.

[In force January 1, 2014]

REGULATION REPRODUCED

3. Saving   **3.606**

GENERAL NOTE

See the commentary to reg.85A of the Jobseeker's Allowance Regulations 1996   **3.607**
and reg.21AA of the Income Support Regulations

Saving

3.—The amendment in regulation 2 does not apply in relation to a claim for a   **3.608**
jobseeker's allowance which is made or treated as made before these Regulations
come into force.

The Jobseeker's Allowance (Supervised Jobsearch Pilot Scheme) Regulations 2014

(SI 2014/1913)

The text of these regulations is omitted here because they were only in force down   **3.609**
to April 29, 2015. The regulations are set out in the Supplement to the 2014/15
edition.

The Jobseeker's Allowance (18–21 Work Skills Pilot Scheme) Regulations 2014

(SI 2014/3117)

[In force November 25, 2014]   **3.610**
The text of these regulations is omitted here because they only apply to claimants
registered at Jobcentres in the Black Country, Devon, Somerset and Cornwall,
Kent and Mercia. The regulations are set out in the Supplement to the 2014/15
edition.

The Jobseeker's Allowance and Universal Credit (Higher-Level Sanctions) (Amendment) Regulations 2019

(SI 2019/1357)

Made by the Secretary of State for Work and Pensions under the powers con-
ferred by sections 6J(5)(b) and (6), 19(4)(b) and (5), 35(1) and 36(4)(a) of
the Jobseekers Act 1995 and sections 26(6)(b) and (7) and 42(1) and (3)(a)

of the Welfare Reform Act 2012, the Social Security Advisory Committee having agreed that the proposals in respect of these Regulations should not be referred to it.

ARRANGEMENT OF REGULATIONS

Citation and commencement

3.612   **1.** These Regulations may be cited as the Jobseeker's Allowance and Universal Credit (Higher-Level Sanctions) (Amendment) Regulations 2019 and come into force on 27th November 2019.

Amendment of the Jobseeker's Allowance Regulations 1996

3.613   **2.** (*Amendment incorporated into the text of the JSA Regulations 1996 in this Part of this volume*)

Amendment of the Universal Credit Regulations 2013

3.614   **3.** (*Amendment incorporated into the text of the Universal Credit Regulations 2013 in Vol.II of this series*)

Amendment of the Jobseeker's Allowance Regulations 2013

3.615   **4.** (*Amendment incorporated into the text of the JSA Regulations 2013 in Vol.I of this series*)

Transitional provision

3.616   **5.**—(1) Where, on the date that these Regulations come into force, the amount of an award of jobseeker's allowance is subject to a reduction under section 19 of the Jobseekers Act 1995 for a period of 156 weeks, the reduction is to be terminated where, since the date that the reduction took effect, the award has been reduced for a period of at least 26 weeks.

(2) Where, on the date that these Regulations come into force, the amount of an award of jobseeker's allowance is subject to a reduction under section 6J of the Jobseekers Act 1995 for a period of 1095 days, the reduction is to be terminated where, since the date that the reduction took effect, the award has been reduced for a period of at least 182 days.

(3) Where, on the date that these Regulations come into force, the amount of an award of universal credit is subject to a reduction under section 26 of the Welfare Reform Act 2012, or which is treated as a reduction under section 26 of that Act by virtue of regulation 32(3) of the Universal Credit (Transitional Provisions) Regulations 2014(**c**), for a period of 1095 days, the reduction is to be terminated where, since the date that the reduction took effect, the award has been reduced for a period of at least 182 days.

The Social Security (Coronavirus) (Further Measures) Regulations 2020

(SI 2020/371)

Made by the Secretary of State for Work and Pensions under sections 70(8), 123(1)(d), 136(1), (3) and (5)(b), 137(1), 171D, 171G(2) and 175(1) and (3) to (5) of the Social Security Contributions and Benefits Act 1992, sections 6(4), 6E(5), 6F(1), 7(4), 35(1) and 36(2) and (4) of the Jobseekers Act 1995, sections 122(1) and (6) of the Housing Act 1996 and sections 9(2), 18(5), 22(2), 37(6), 40 and 42(1) to (3) and (5) of, and paragraph 4(4) of Schedule 1 and paragraphs 1(1) and 4(1), (2)(a), (c) and (d) and (3) of Schedule 6 to, the Welfare Reform Act 2012, it appearing to the Secretary of State inexpedient, by reason of urgency, to refer the proposals in respect of these Regulations to the Social Security Advisory Committee or to consult with representative bodies.

Citation, commencement and interpretation

1.—(1) These Regulations may be cited as the Social Security (Coronavirus) (Further Measures) Regulations 2020 and come into force on 30th March 2020.

3.617

(2) In these Regulations—

"coronavirus" means severe acute respiratory syndrome coronavirus 2 (SARS-CoV-2);

"coronavirus disease" means COVID-19 (the official designation of the disease which can be caused by coronavirus);

"isolation" in relation to a person, means the separation of that person from any other person in such a manner as to prevent infection or contamination with coronavirus disease;

"universal credit" means universal credit under Part 1 of the Welfare Reform Act 2012;

"Universal Credit Regulations" means the Universal Credit Regulations 2013.

Universal credit – minimum income floor

2. [*Omitted as applying only to universal credit – see Vol.II of this series*]

3.618

Universal credit – standard allowance modification

3. [*Omitted as applying only to universal credit – see Vol.II of this series*]

3.619

Local housing allowance

4. [*Omitted as applying only to housing benefit and universal credit – see Vol.II of this series*]

3.620

Housing benefit – disregards from income modification

5. [*Omitted as applying only to housing benefit*]

3.621

Universal credit and new style JSA – work-related requirements

6. [*Omitted as applying only to new style JSA—see Vol.I of this series*]

3.622

Old style JSA – availability for employment and actively seeking employment

3.623   7.—(1) As a consequence of the outbreak of coronavirus disease, a person who has an award of old style JSA is to be treated as—

(a) available for employment; and

(b) actively seeking employment,

for the purposes of the Jobseekers Act 1995.

(2) This regulation applies for a period of 3 months beginning with the date that these Regulations come into force and the Secretary of State may extend that period for all cases or any class of case where it appears expedient as a consequence of the continuation of the outbreak of coronavirus disease.

(3) In this regulation, "old style JSA" means a jobseeker's allowance under the Jobseekers Act 1995 as that Act has effect apart from the amendments made by Part 1 of Schedule 14 to the Welfare Reform Act 2012 that remove references to an income-based allowance.

Jobseeker's Allowance – periods of sickness

3.624   8.—(1) A person who has an award of jobseeker's allowance and who is—

(a) infected or contaminated with coronavirus disease;

(b) in isolation; or

(c) caring for a child or qualifying young person who is a member of the person's household and who falls within sub-paragraph (a) or (b),

and who satisfies the requirements for entitlement to a jobseeker's allowance other than those specified in section 1(2)(f) of the Jobseekers Act 1995 (not having limited capability for work) is to be treated as capable of work or as not having limited capability for work.

(2) Any period during which this regulation applies to the person is to be disregarded for the purposes of calculating the number of occasions for the purposes of—

(a) regulation 55(3) or 55ZA(5) of the Jobseeker's Allowance Regulations 1996;

(b) regulation 46(3) or 46A(5) of the Jobseeker's Allowance Regulations 2013.

(3) In this regulation, "jobseeker's allowance" means an allowance under the Jobseekers Act 1995.

Carer's allowance

3.625   9. [*Omitted as applying only to carer's allowance – see Vol.I of this series*]

Expiry

3.626   10.—(1) The Secretary of State must keep the operation of these Regulations under review.

(2) Regulations [¹6 and 7] cease to have effect at the end of the period of eight months beginning on 13th March 2020.

[¹(2A) Regulation 2 ceases to have effect on [²31st July].

(2B) Regulations 8 and 9 cease to have effect on 12th May 2021.]

(3) Regulation 3 (treating a person as having limited capability for work) and regulation 4 (suspension of the minimum income floor) of the

Employment and Support Allowance and Universal Credit (Coronavirus Disease) Regulations 2020 no longer have effect in so far as they apply to universal credit.

AMENDMENTS

1. Social Security (Coronavirus) (Further Measures) (Amendment) and Miscellaneous Amendment Regulations 2020 (SI 2020/1201) reg.2 (November 12, 2020).

2. Universal Credit (Extension of Coronavirus Measures) Regulations 2021 (SI 2021/313) reg.3 (April 6, 2021).

GENERAL NOTE

Note that reg.3 of the Social Security (Coronavirus) (Miscellaneous Amendments) Regulations 2021 (SI 2021/476) has, with effect from May 12, 2021, amended the date in para.(2B) to August 31, 2021.

PART IV

"OLD STYLE" EMPLOYMENT AND SUPPORT ALLOWANCE

The Employment and Support Allowance Regulations 2008

(SI 2008/794) (*as amended*)

PART 1

GENERAL

PART 2

THE ASSESSMENT PHASE

PART 3

CONDITIONS OF ENTITLEMENT—CONTRIBUTORY ALLOWANCE

PART 4

CONDITIONS OF ENTITLEMENT—INCOME-RELATED ALLOWANCE

PART 5

LIMITED CAPABILITY FOR WORK

PART 6

LIMITED CAPABILITY FOR WORK-RELATED ACTIVITY

PART 7

EFFECT OF WORK ON ENTITLEMENT TO AN EMPLOYMENT AND SUPPORT ALLOWANCE

PART 8

CONDITIONALITY

CHAPTER 1

WORK-FOCUSED HEALTH-RELATED ASSESSMENT

CHAPTER 2

WORK-FOCUSED INTERVIEWS

CHAPTER 3

REDUCTION OF EMPLOYMENT AND SUPPORT ALLOWANCE

CHAPTER 3

STATUTORY PAYMENTS

PART 10

INCOME AND CAPITAL

CHAPTER 1

GENERAL

CHAPTER 2

INCOME

CHAPTER 3

EMPLOYED EARNERS

CHAPTER 4

SELF-EMPLOYED EARNERS

CHAPTER 5

PARTICIPANTS IN THE SELF-EMPLOYMENT ROUTE

CHAPTER 6

OTHER INCOME

CHAPTER 7

CAPITAL

CHAPTER 8

LIABLE RELATIVES

CHAPTER 9

CHILD SUPPORT

CHAPTER 10

STUDENTS

PART 13

URGENT CASES

PART 14

PERIODS OF LESS THAN A WEEK

SCHEDULE 1   4.2

HER MAJESTY'S FORCES

PART 1

PRESCRIBED ESTABLISHMENTS AND ORGANISATIONS

PART 2

ESTABLISHMENTS AND ORGANISATIONS OF WHICH HER MAJESTY'S FORCES DO NOT CONSIST

SCHEDULE 2

ASSESSMENT OF WHETHER A CLAIMANT HAS LIMITED CAPABILITY FOR WORK

PART 1

PHYSICAL DISABILITIES

PART 2

MENTAL, COGNITIVE AND INTELLECTUAL FUNCTION ASSESSMENT

SCHEDULE 3

ASSESSMENT OF WHETHER A CLAIMANT HAS LIMITED CAPABILITY FOR WORK-RELATED ACTIVITY

SCHEDULE 4

AMOUNTS

PART 1

PRESCRIBED AMOUNTS

PART 2

PREMIUMS

PART 3

WEEKLY AMOUNT OF PREMIUMS SPECIFIED IN PART 2

PART 4

THE COMPONENTS

SCHEDULE 5

SPECIAL CASES

PART 1

AMOUNTS PRESCRIBED FOR THE PURPOSES OF SECTION 4(2) OF THE ACT

PART 2

AMOUNTS PRESCRIBED FOR THE PURPOSES OF SECTIONS 2(1) AND 4(2) OF THE ACT

SCHEDULE 6

HOUSING COSTS

SCHEDULE 7

SUMS TO BE DISREGARDED IN THE CALCULATION OF EARNINGS

SCHEDULE 8

Sᴜᴍꜱ ᴛᴏ ʙᴇ Dɪꜱʀᴇɢᴀʀᴅᴇᴅ ɪɴ ᴛʜᴇ Cᴀʟᴄᴜʟᴀᴛɪᴏɴ ᴏꜰ Iɴᴄᴏᴍᴇ Oᴛʜᴇʀ ᴛʜᴀɴ
Eᴀʀɴɪɴɢꜱ

SCHEDULE 9

Cᴀᴘɪᴛᴀʟ ᴛᴏ ʙᴇ Dɪꜱʀᴇɢᴀʀᴅᴇᴅ

The Secretary of State for Work and Pensions, in exercise of the powers conferred by sections 2(1)(a) and (c), (4)(a) and (c), 3(1)(c), (2)(b) and (d) and (3)(1), 4(2)(a), (3), (6)(a) and (c), 5(2) and (3), 8(1) to (3), (4)(a) and (b), (5) and (6), 9(1) to (3) and (4)(a) and (b), 11(1), (2) (a) to (g), (3) to (5), (6)(a) and (7)(c), 12(1), (2)(a) to (h), (3) to (7), 14(1) and (2)(a) and (b), 16(2)(a) and (4), 17, 18(1), (2) and (4), 20(2) to (7), 22(2), 23(1) and (3), 24(1)(3), (2) (b) and (3), 25(1) to (5) and 26(2) of, and paragraphs 1(4), 3(2), 4(1)(a) and (c), (3) and (4) and 6(1)(b), (2) to (5)(4), (7) and (8) of Schedule 1 to, and paragraphs 1 to 7, 8(1), 9, 10, 12 and 14 of Schedule 2 to, the Welfare Reform Act 2007, section 5(1) of the Social Security Administration Act 1992 and section 21(1)(a) of the Social Security Act 1998(7) makes the following Regulations, which are made by virtue of, or consequential on, the provisions of the Welfare Reform Act 2007 and which are made before the end of a period of 6 months beginning with the coming into force of those provisions:

Pᴀʀᴛ 1

Gᴇɴᴇʀᴀʟ

[¹ Citation, commencement and application]

1. These Regulations may be cited as the Employment and Support   4.3
Allowance Regulations 2008 and shall come into force—
(a) subject to paragraphs (b) and (c), on 27th October 2008;
(b) in relation to regulation 128(6)(a) and paragraph 15(2) of Schedule 6, so far as it applies to a maintenance calculation, in relation to a particular case, on the day on which paragraph 11(20)(d) of Schedule 3 to the 2000 Act comes into force for the purposes of that type of case;
(c) [² . . .]
[¹ (2) These Regulations do not apply to a particular case on any day on which section 33(1)(b) of the 2012 Act (abolition of income-related employment and support allowance) is in force and applies in relation to that case.]

Aᴍᴇɴᴅᴍᴇɴᴛꜱ

1. Universal Credit (Consequential, Supplementary, Incidental and Miscellaneous Provisions) Regulations 2013 (SI 2013/630) reg.37(1) and (2) (April 29, 2013).
2. Shared Parental Leave and Statutory Shared Parental Pay (Consequential Amendments to Subordinate Legislation) Order 2014 art.20(2) (April 5, 2014).

Interpretation

2.—(1) In these Regulations—   4.4
[²³ "the 2012 Act" means the Welfare Reform Act 2012;]

"Abbeyfield Home" means an establishment run by the Abbeyfield Society including any body corporate or incorporate which is affiliated to that Society;

"the Act" means the Welfare Reform Act 2007;

[[12] ...]

"adoption leave" means a period of absence from work on ordinary or additional adoption leave under section 75A or 75B of the Employment Rights Act 1996;

"aircraft worker" means a person who is, or has been, employed under a contract of service either as a pilot, commander, navigator or other member of the crew of any aircraft, or in any other capacity on board any aircraft where—

  (a) the employment in that other capacity is for the purposes of the aircraft or its crew or of any passengers or cargo or mail carried on that aircraft; and

  (b) the contract is entered into in the United Kingdom with a view to its performance (in whole or in part) while the aircraft is in flight, but does not include a person who is in employment as a member of Her Majesty's forces;

[[40] "approved blood scheme" means a scheme established or approved by the Secretary of State, or trust established with funds provided by the Secretary of State, for the purpose of providing compensation in respect of a person having been infected from contaminated blood products;]

"Armed Forces and Reserve Forces Compensation Scheme" means the scheme established under section 1(2) of the Armed Forces (Pensions and Compensation) Act 2004;

[[24] "armed forces independence payment" means armed forces independence payment under the Armed Forces and Reserve Forces (Compensation Scheme) Order 2011;]

"attendance allowance" means—

  (a) an attendance allowance under section 64 of the Contributions and Benefits Act;

  (b) an increase of disablement pension under section 104 or 105 of that Act;

  (c) [[26] ...]

  (d) [[26] ...]

  (e) a payment by virtue of article 14, 15, 16, 43 or 44 of the Personal Injuries (Civilians) Scheme 1983 or any analogous payment;

  (f) any payment based on the need for attendance which is paid as an addition to a war disablement pension;

[[1] "basic rate" has the same meaning as in the Income Tax Act 2007 (see section 989 of that Act);]

"benefit Acts" means the Contributions and Benefits Act, Jobseekers Act [[35], Part 1 of the Act and the Pensions Act 2014];

"benefit week" means a period of 7 days ending on such day as the Secretary of State may direct but for the purposes of calculating any payment of income "benefit week" means the period of 7 days ending on the day before the first day of the first benefit week following the date of claim or the last day on which an employment and support allowance is paid if it is in payment for less than a week;

"board and lodging" means—
  (a) accommodation provided to a person or, if the person is a member of a family, to that person or any other member of that person's family, for a charge which is inclusive of the provision of that accommodation and at least some cooked or prepared meals which both are cooked or prepared (by a person other than the person to whom the accommodation is provided or a member of that person's family) and are consumed in that accommodation or associated premises; or
  (b) accommodation provided to a person in a hotel, guest house, lodging house or some similar establishment, except accommodation provided by a close relative of the person or any other member of the person's family, or other than on a commercial basis;

"care home" in England [42 . . .] has the meaning assigned to it by section 3 of the Care Standards Act 2000, [42 in Wales means a care home service within the meaning of Part 1 of the Regulation and Inspection of Social Care (Wales) Act 2016 which is provided wholly or mainly to persons aged 18 or over] and in Scotland means a care home service within the meaning assigned to it by [16 paragraph 2 of schedule 12 to the Public Services Reform (Scotland) Act 2010];

"carer's allowance" means an allowance under section 70 of the Contributions and Benefits Act;

"child" means a person under the age of 16;

[14 "the Caxton Foundation" means the charitable trust of that name established on 28th March 2011 out of funds provided by the Secretary of State for the benefit of certain persons suffering from hepatitis C and other persons eligible for payment in accordance with its provisions;]

"child tax credit" means a child tax credit under section 8 of the Tax Credits Act;

"close relative" means a parent, parent-in-law, son, son-in-law, daughter, daughter-in-law, step-parent, step-son, step-daughter, brother, sister, or if any of the preceding persons is one member of a couple, the other member of that couple;

"college of further education" means a college of further education within the meaning of Part 1 of the Further and Higher Education (Scotland) Act 1992;

"concessionary payment" means a payment made under arrangements made by the Secretary of State with the consent of the Treasury which is charged [3 . . .] to a Departmental Expenditure Vote to which payments of benefit or tax credits under the benefit Acts or the Tax Credits Act are charged;

"confinement" has the meaning given to it by section 171(1) of the Contributions and Benefits Act;

[25 "contribution-based jobseeker's allowance" means an allowance under the Jobseekers Act as amended by the provisions of Part 1 of Schedule 14 to the 2012 Act that remove references to an income-based allowance, and a contribution-based allowance under the Jobseekers Act as that Act has effect apart from those provisions;]

"co-ownership scheme" means a scheme under which a dwelling is let by a housing association and the tenant, or the tenant's personal representative, will, under the terms of the tenancy agreement or of the agreement under which the tenant became a member of the association, be entitled, on that tenant ceasing to be a member and subject to any condition stated in either agreement, to a sum calculated by reference directly or indirectly to the value of the dwelling and "co-ownership agreement" will be construed accordingly;

"councillor" means—

(a) in relation to England and Wales, a member of a London borough council, a county council, [26 a county borough council,] a district council, a parish or community council, the Common Council of the City of London or the Council of the Isles of Scilly; and

(b) in relation to Scotland, a member of a council constituted under section 2 of the Local Government etc. (Scotland) Act 1994;

"councillor's allowance" means—

(a) in England [26 ...], an allowance under or by virtue of—

(i) section 173 or 177 of the Local Government Act 1972; or

(ii) a scheme made by virtue of section 18 of the Local Government and Housing Act 1989, other than such an allowance as is mentioned in section 173(4) of the Local Government Act 1972; or

(b) in Scotland, an allowance or remuneration under or by virtue of—

(i) a scheme made by virtue of section 18 of the Local Government and Housing Act 1989; or

(ii) [26 section 11] of the Local Governance (Scotland) Act 2004; [26 or

(c) in Wales, an allowance under or by virtue of a scheme made by virtue of section 18 of the Local Government and Housing Act 1989 other than such an allowance as is mentioned in section 173(4) of the Local Government Act 1972;]

[27 29 "couple" means—

(a) two people who are married to, or civil partners of, each other and are members of the same household; or

(b) two people who are not married to, or civil partners of, each other but are living together [43 as if they were a married couple or civil partners];]

"Crown tenant" means a person who occupies a dwelling under a tenancy or licence where the interest of the landlord belongs to Her Majesty in right of the Crown or to a government department or is held in trust for Her Majesty for the purposes of a government department, except (in the case of an interest belonging to Her Majesty in right of the Crown) where the interest is under the management of the Crown Estate Commissioners;

[23 "daily living component" means the daily living component of personal independence payment under section 78 of the 2012 Act;]

"dependent child" means any child or qualifying young person who is treated as the responsibility of the claimant or the claimant's partner, where that child or young person is a member of the claimant's household;

"descriptor" means, in relation to an activity specified in column (1) of Schedule 2, a descriptor in column (2) of that Schedule which describes a person's ability to perform that activity;

"disability living allowance" means a disability living allowance under section 71 of the Contributions and Benefits Act;

"doctor" means a registered medical practitioner, or in the case of a medical practitioner practising outside the United Kingdom of whom the Secretary of State may request a medical opinion, a person registered or recognised as such in the country in which the person undertakes medical practice;

"dwelling" means any residential accommodation, whether or not consisting of the whole or part of a building and whether or not comprising separate and self-contained premises;

"dwelling occupied as the home" means the dwelling together with any garage, garden and outbuildings, normally occupied by the claimant as the claimant's home including any premises not so occupied which it is impracticable or unreasonable to sell separately, in particular, in Scotland, any croft land on which the dwelling is situated;

"Eileen Trust" means the charitable trust of that name established on 29th March 1993 out of funds provided by the Secretary of State for the benefit of persons eligible for payment in accordance with its provisions;

"employed earner" is to be construed in accordance with section 2(1)(a) of the Contributions and Benefits Act;

"employment" includes any trade, business, profession, office or vocation and "employed" has a corresponding meaning;

[13 "the Employment, Skills and Enterprise Scheme" means a scheme within section 17A (schemes for assisting persons to obtain employment: "work for your benefit" schemes etc.) of the Jobseekers Act 1995, known by that name and provided pursuant to arrangements made by the Secretary of State that is designed to assist claimants to obtain employment or self-employment, and which may include for any individual work-related activity (including work experience or job search);]

"employment zone" means an area within Great Britain designated for the purposes of section 60 of the Welfare Reform and Pensions Act 1999 and an "employment zone programme" means a programme established for such an area or areas designed to assist claimants for a jobseeker's allowance to obtain sustainable employment;

[5 "enactment" includes an enactment comprised in, or in an instrument made under, an Act of the Scottish Parliament [26 or the National Assembly for Wales];]

"failure determination" has the meaning given by regulation 63(1);

"family" means—
    (a) a couple;
    (b) a couple and a member of the same household for whom one of them is or both are responsible and who is a child or a young person;
    (c) a person who is not a member of a couple and a member of the same household for whom that person is responsible and who is a child or a young person;

"first contribution condition" means the condition set out in paragraph 1(1) of Schedule 1 to the Act;

[11 "First-tier Tribunal" has the meaning given by section 3(1) of the Tribunals, Courts and Enforcement Act 2007;]

[33 "first year of training" means a period of one year beginning with a person's first day of training.]

"full-time student" has the meaning prescribed in regulation 131 (students: interpretation);

"the Fund" means monies made available from time to time by the Secretary of State for the benefit of persons eligible for payment in accordance with the provisions of a scheme established by the Secretary of State on 24th April 1992 or, in Scotland, on 10th April 1992;

[[45] "Grenfell Tower payment" means a payment made to a person because that person was affected by the fire on 14th June 2017 at Grenfell Tower, or a payment to the personal representative of such a person—

    (a) from the £5 million fund announced on 16th June 2017 for the benefit of certain persons affected by the fire on 14th June 2017 at Grenfell Tower and known as the Grenfell Tower Residents' Discretionary Fund;

    (b) by the Royal Borough of Kensington and Chelsea; or

    (c) by a registered charity;]

"guaranteed income payment" means a payment made under article 14(1)(b) or 21(1)(a) of the Armed Forces and Reserve Forces (Compensation Scheme) Order 2005;

[[20] "hardship payment" means an income-related employment and support allowance payable at a reduced rate in accordance with the provisions of regulation 64D;]

"health care professional" means—

    (a) a registered medical practitioner;

    (b) a registered nurse; or

    (c) an occupational therapist or physiotherapist registered with a regulatory body established by an Order in Council under section 60 of the Health Act 1999;

"Health Service Act" means the National Health Service Act 2006;

"Health Service (Wales) Act" means the National Health Service (Wales) Act 2006;

"housing association" has the meaning given to it by section 1(1) of the Housing Associations Act 1985;

"housing benefit expenditure" means expenditure in respect of which housing benefit is payable as specified in regulation 12(1) of the Housing Benefit Regulations 2006 but does not include any such expenditure in respect of which an additional amount is applicable under regulation 67(1)(c) or 68(1)(d)(housing costs);

"Immigration and Asylum Act" means the Immigration and Asylum Act 1999;

"income-related benefits" means the benefits listed in section 123(1) of the Contributions and Benefits Act;

"Income Support Regulations" means the Income Support (General) Regulations 1987;

[[9] "independent hospital"—

(a) in England, means a hospital as defined by section 275 of the National Health Service Act 2006 that is not a health service hospital as defined by that section;

(b) in Wales, has the meaning assigned to it by section 2 of the Care Standards Act 2000; and

[[16] (c) in Scotland, means an independent health care service as defined in section 10F(1)(a) and (b) of the National Health Service (Scotland) Act 1978;]]

[[1] ...]

"the Independent Living Fund (2006)" means the Trust of that name
established by a deed dated 10th April 2006 and made between the
Secretary of State for Work and Pensions of the one part and Margaret
Rosemary Cooper, Michael Beresford Boyall and Marie Theresa
Martin of the other part;

[¹ ...]

"Jobseekers Act" means the Jobseekers Act 1995;

"Jobseeker's Allowance Regulations" means the Jobseeker's Allowance
Regulations 1996;

"last day of the course" means the last day of the final academic term of
the course in which the student is enrolled;

"limited capability for work assessment" means the assessment of
whether a person has limited capability for work as set out in regulation
19(2) and in Schedule 2;

[²² "local welfare provision" means occasional financial or other assistance
given by a local authority, the Scottish Ministers or the Welsh Ministers,
or a person authorised to exercise any function of, or provide a service
to, them, to or in respect of individuals for the purpose of—

(a) meeting, or helping to meet, an immediate short term need—

    (i) arising out of an exceptional event, or exceptional circum-
stances; and

    (ii) that requires to be met in order to avoid a risk to the well-being
of an individual; or

(b) enabling individuals to establish or maintain a settled home, where
those individuals have been or, without the assistance, might otherwise be—

    (i) in prison, hospital, a residential care establishment or other
institution; or

    (ii) homeless or otherwise living an unsettled way of life;]

"London Bombings Relief Charitable Fund" means the company limited
by guarantee (number 5505072) and registered charity of that name
established on 11th July 2005 for the purpose of (amongst other things)
relieving sickness, disability or financial need of victims (including
families or dependants of victims) of the terrorist attacks carried out in
London on 7th July 2005;

[³⁹ "the London Emergencies Trust" means the company of that name
(number 09928465) incorporated on 23rd December 2015 and the
registered charity of that name (number 1172307) established on 28th
March 2017;]

[¹⁵ ...]

"long tenancy" means a tenancy granted for a term of years certain
exceeding twenty one years, whether or not the tenancy is, or may
become, terminable before the end of that term by notice given by or
to the tenant or by re-entry, forfeiture (or, in Scotland, irritancy) or
otherwise and includes a lease for a term fixed by law under a grant
with a covenant or obligation for perpetual renewal unless it is a lease
by sub-demise from one which is not a long tenancy;

"Macfarlane (Special Payments) Trust" means the trust of that name,
established on 29th January 1990 partly out of funds provided by the
Secretary of State, for the benefit of certain persons suffering from
haemophilia;

"Macfarlane (Special Payments) (No. 2) Trust" means the trust of that name, established on 3rd May 1991 partly out of funds provided by the Secretary of State, for the benefit of certain persons suffering from haemophilia and other beneficiaries;

"Macfarlane Trust" means the charitable trust, established partly out of funds provided by the Secretary of State to the Haemophilia Society, for the relief of poverty or distress among those suffering from haemophilia;

"main phase employment and support allowance" means an employment and support allowance where the calculation of the amount payable in respect of the claimant includes a component under section 2(1)(b) or 4(2)(b) of the Act [38 or where the claimant is a member of the work-related activity group];

[13 "the Mandatory Work Activity Scheme" means a scheme within section 17A of the Jobseekers Act 1995, known by that name and provided pursuant to arrangements made by the Secretary of State that is designed to provide work or work-related activity for up to 30 hours per week over a period of four consecutive weeks with a view to assisting claimants to improve their prospects of obtaining employment;]

"mariner" means a person who is or has been in employment under a contract of service either as a master or member of the crew of any ship or vessel, or in any other capacity on board any ship or vessel where—

    (a) the employment in that other capacity is for the purposes of that ship or vessel or her crew or any passengers or cargo or mails carried by the ship or vessel; and

    (b) the contract is entered into in the United Kingdom with a view to its performance (in whole or in part) while the ship or vessel is on her voyage; but does not include a person who is in employment as a member of Her Majesty's forces;

[28 ...]

"medical evidence" [11, except in regulation 32A,] means—

    (a) evidence from a health care professional approved by the Secretary of State; and

    (b) evidence (if any) from any health care professional or a hospital or similar institution, or such part of such evidence as constitutes the most reliable evidence available in the circumstances;

"Medical Evidence Regulations" means the Social Security (Medical Evidence) Regulations 1976;

[8 ...]

"medical treatment" means medical, surgical or rehabilitative treatment (including any course or diet or other regimen), and references to a person receiving or submitting to medical treatment are to be construed accordingly;

"member of Her Majesty's forces" means a person, other than one mentioned in Part 2 of Schedule 1 who is—

    (a) over 16 years of age; and

    (b) a member of an establishment or organisation specified in Part 1 of that Schedule who gives full pay service, but does not include any such person while absent on desertion;

[38 "member of the work-related activity group" means a claimant who has or is treated as having limited capability for work under Part 5 of these Regulations other than by virtue of regulation 30 of these

Regulations;]

[⁷ "MFET Limited" means the company limited by guarantee (number 7121661) of that name, established for the purpose in particular of making payments in accordance with arrangements made with the Secretary of State to persons who have acquired HIV as a result of treatment by the NHS with blood or blood products;]

"mobility supplement" means any supplement under article 20 of the Naval, Military and Air Forces Etc. (Disablement and Death) Service Pensions Order 2006 including such a supplement by virtue of any other scheme or order or under article 25A of the Personal Injuries (Civilians) Scheme 1983;

[⁴⁵ "the National Emergencies Trust" means the registered charity of that name (number 1182809) established on 28th March 2019;]

[¹¹ "National Minimum Wage" means the rate of the national minimum wage specified in regulation 11 of the National Minimum Wage Regulations 1999 (rate of the national minimum wage);]

"net earnings" means such earnings as are calculated in accordance with regulation 96;

"net profit" means such profit as is calculated in accordance with regulation 98;

"New Deal options" means the employment programmes specified in regulation 75(1)(a)(ii) of the Jobseeker's Allowance Regulations and the training scheme specified in regulation 75(1)(b)(ii) of those Regulations;

[²⁵ "new style ESA" means an allowance under Part 1 of the Act as amended by the provisions of Schedule 3, and Part 1 of Schedule 14, to the 2012 Act that remove references to an income-related allowance;]

"non-dependant" has the meaning prescribed in regulation 71;

"non-dependant deduction" means a deduction that is to be made under regulation 67(1)(c) (prescribed amounts) and paragraph 19 of Schedule 6 (housing costs);

"occupational pension" means any pension or other periodical payment under an occupational pension scheme but does not include any discretionary payment out of a fund established for relieving hardship in particular cases;

"occupational pension scheme" has the meaning given by section 1 of the Pension Schemes Act 1993;

"ordinary clothing or footwear" means clothing or footwear for normal daily use, but does not include school uniforms, or clothing or footwear used solely for sporting activities;

[⁴⁴ "parental bereavement leave" means leave under section 80EA of the Employment Rights Act 1996;]

"partner" means where a claimant—

    (a) is a member of a couple, the other member of that couple;

    (b) is a husband or wife by virtue of a polygamous marriage, the other party to the marriage or any spouse additional to either party to the marriage;

"passenger" means any person carried on a ship except—

    (a) a person employed or engaged in any capacity on board the ship on the business of the ship; or

    (b) a person on board the ship either in pursuance of the obligation to carry shipwrecked, distressed or other persons, or by reason of any circumstance that neither the master nor the owner nor the charterer (if any) could have prevented or forestalled;

[[17] "paternity leave" means a period of absence from work on [[31] ...] paternity leave by virtue of section 80A or 80B of the Employment Rights Act 1996 [[31] ...];]

"payment" includes a part of a payment;

"pay period" means the period in respect of which a claimant is, or expects to be, normally paid by the claimant's employer, being a week, a fortnight, four weeks, a month or other shorter or longer period as the case may be;

"pension fund holder" means in relation to a personal pension scheme or an occupational pension scheme, the trustees, managers or scheme administrators, as the case may be, of the scheme concerned;

"pensionable age" has the meaning given by the rules in paragraph 1 of Schedule 4 to the Pensions Act 1995;

"period of limited capability for work" means [[8] except in paragraph (5), a period throughout which a person has, or is treated as having, limited capability for work, and does not include a period which is outside the prescribed time for claiming as specified in regulation 19 of the Social Security (Claims and Payments) Regulations 1987];

"period of study" means the period beginning with the date on which a person starts attending or undertaking a course of study and ending with the last day of the course or such earlier date (if any) as that person finally abandons it or is dismissed from it;

[[23] "personal independence payment" means personal independence payment under Part 4 of the 2012 Act;]

"personal pension scheme" means—

    (a) a personal pension scheme as defined by section 1 of the Pension Schemes Act 1993;

    (b) an annuity contract or trust scheme approved under section 620 or 621 of the Income and Corporation Taxes Act 1988 or a substituted contract within the meaning of section 622(3) of that Act which is treated as having become a registered pension scheme by virtue of paragraph 1(1)(f) of Schedule 36 to the Finance Act 2004;

    (c) a personal pension scheme approved under Chapter 4 of Part 14 of the Income and Corporation Taxes Act 1988 which is treated as having become a registered pension scheme by virtue of paragraph 1(1)(g) of Schedule 36 to the Finance Act 2004;

"policy of life insurance" means any instrument by which the payment of money is assured on death (except death by accident only) or the happening of any contingency dependent on human life, or any instrument evidencing a contract which is subject to payment of premiums for a term dependent on human life;

"polygamous marriage" means any marriage entered into under a law which permits polygamy where—

    (a) either party has for the time being any spouse additional to the other party; and

    (b) the claimant, the other party to the marriage and the additional spouse are members of the same household;

[[5] "public authority" includes any person certain of whose functions are functions of a public nature;

"the qualifying age for state pension credit" means—

    (a) in the case of a woman, pensionable age, and

    (b) in the case of a man, the age which is pensionable age in the case of a woman born on the same day as the man;]

"qualifying person" means a person in respect of whom [45 a Grenfell Tower payment has been made or] payment has been made from the Fund, the Eileen Trust, [7 MFET Limited] the Skipton Fund [14, the Caxton Foundation] [37, the Scottish Infected Blood Support Scheme] [40, an approved blood scheme] [39, the London Emergencies Trust, the We Love Manchester Emergency Fund] [45, the National Emergencies Trust] or the London Bombings Relief Charitable Fund;

"qualifying remunerative work" has the meaning given by Part 1 of the Tax Credits Act;

"qualifying young person" has the meaning given by section 142 of the Contributions and Benefits Act (child and qualifying young person);

"relative" means close relative, grand-parent, grand-child, uncle, aunt, nephew or niece;

[14 ...]

"relevant enactment" means the Army Act 1955, the Air Force Act 1955, the Naval Discipline Act 1957, the Matrimonial Proceedings Children Act 1958, the Social Work (Scotland) Act 1968, the Family Law Reform Act 1969, the Children and Young Persons Act 1969, the Matrimonial Causes Act 1973, the Domestic Proceedings and Magistrates' Courts Act 1978, the Adoption (Scotland) Act 1978, the Family Law Act 1986, the Children Act 1989 and the Adoption and Children Act 2002;

[14 [26 ...]]

"remunerative work" has the meaning prescribed in regulations 41 and 42 except in relation to Schedules 6 and 7;

[36 "Scottish basic rate" means the rate of income tax of that name calculated in accordance with section 6A of the Income Tax Act 2007;

[37 "Scottish Infected Blood Support Scheme" means the scheme of that name administered by the Common Services Agency (constituted by section 10 of the National Health Service (Scotland) Act 1978);]

"Scottish taxpayer" has the same meaning as in Chapter 2 of Part 4A of the Scotland Act 1998;]

"second contribution condition" means the condition set out in paragraph 2(1) of Schedule 1 to the Act;

"self-employed earner" is to be construed in accordance with section 2(1)(b) of the Contributions and Benefits Act;

"self-employment route" means assistance in pursuing self-employed earner's employment whilst participating in—

    (a) an employment zone programme; or

    (b) a programme provided or other arrangements made under section 2 of the Employment and Training Act 1973 (functions of the Secretary of State) or section 2 of the Enterprise and New Towns (Scotland) Act 1990 (functions in relation to training for employment etc.);

[5 [26 ...[21]]]]

[30 "shared parental leave" means leave under section 75E or 75G of the Employment Rights Act 1996;]

"single claimant" means a claimant who neither has a partner nor is a lone parent [15 or a person who has no partner and who is responsible for and a member of the same household as a young person];

"Skipton Fund" means the ex-gratia payment scheme administered by the Skipton Fund Limited, incorporated on 25th March 2004, for the benefit of certain persons suffering from hepatitis C and other persons eligible for payment in accordance with the scheme's provisions;

"sports award" means an award made by one of the Sports Councils named in section 23(2) of the National Lottery etc. Act 1993 out of sums allocated to it for distribution under that section;
[1 ...]

[1 "state pension credit" means a state pension credit under the State Pension Credit Act 2002;]

"subsistence allowance" means an allowance which an employment zone contractor has agreed to pay to a person who is participating in an employment zone programme;

"the Tax Credits Act" means the Tax Credits Act 2002;

"terminally ill", in relation to a claimant, means the claimant is suffering from a progressive disease and death in consequence of that disease can reasonably be expected within 6 months;

[41 "traineeship" means a course which—

    (a) is funded (in whole or in part) by, or under arrangements made by, the—

        (i) Secretary of State under section 14 of the Education Act 2002, or

        (ii) Chief Executive of Education and Skills Funding;

    (b) lasts for no more than 6 months;

    (c) includes training to help prepare the participant for work and a work experience placement, and

    (d) is open to persons who on the first day of the course have reached the age of 16 but not the age of 25;]

"training" means—

    (a) training in pursuance of arrangements made under section 2(1) of the Employment and Training Act 1973 or section 2(3) of the Enterprise and New Towns (Scotland) Act 1990; or

    (b) any training received on a course which a person attends for 16 hours or more a week, the primary purpose of which is the teaching of occupational or vocational skills;

"training allowance" means an allowance, (whether by way of periodical grants or otherwise) payable—

    (a) out of public funds by a Government department or by or on behalf of the Secretary of State for Work and Pensions, [4 Skills Development Scotland] or Highlands and Islands Enterprise, the [19 ...], [10 [34 ...]] or the Welsh Ministers;

    (b) to a person for that person's maintenance or in respect of a member of that person's family; and

    (c) for the period, or part of the period, during which the person is following a course of training or instruction provided by, or in pursuance of arrangements made with, that department or approved by that department in relation to that person or so provided or approved by or on behalf of the Secretary of State for Work and Pensions, [⁴ Skills Development Scotland] or Highlands and Islands Enterprise, or the Welsh Ministers, but does not include an allowance paid by any Government department to or in respect of a person by reason of the fact that that person is following a course of full-time education, other than under arrangements made under section 2 of the Employment and Training Act 1973 or section 2 of the Enterprise and New Towns (Scotland) Act 1990, or is training as a teacher;

[²⁵ "universal credit" means universal credit under Part 1 of the 2012 Act;]

"voluntary organisation" means a body, other than a public or local authority, the activities of which are carried on otherwise than for profit;

"war disablement pension" means [³ retired pay or pension or allowance payable] in respect of disablement under an instrument specified in section 639(2) of the Income Tax (Earnings and Pensions) Act 2003;

"war widow's pension" [³ means any pension or allowance] payable to a woman as a widow under an instrument specified in section 639(2) of the Income Tax (Earnings and Pensions) Act 2003 in respect of the death or disablement of any person;

"war widower's pension" [³ means any pension or allowance] payable to a man as a widower or to a surviving civil partner under an instrument specified in section 639(2) of the Income Tax (Earnings and Pensions) Act 2003 in respect of the death or disablement of any person;

"water charges" means—

    (a) as respects England and Wales, any water and sewerage charges under Chapter 1 of Part 5 of the Water Industry Act 1991;

    (b) as respects Scotland, any water and sewerage charges under Part 2 of the Local Government etc. (Scotland) Act 1994, in so far as such charges are in respect of the dwelling which a person occupies as the home;

[³⁹ "the We Love Manchester Emergency Fund" means the registered charity of that name (number 1173260) established on 30th May 2017;]

"week" means a period of 7 days except in relation to regulation 26;
[¹⁸ ...]

"working day" means any day except for a Saturday, Sunday, Christmas Day, Good Friday or bank holiday under the Banking and Financial Dealings Act 1971 in England, Wales or Scotland;

"working tax credit" means a working tax credit under section 10 of the Tax Credits Act;

"young person" is a person who, except where section 6 of the Children (Leaving Care) Act 2000 (exclusion from benefits) applies, falls within the definition of qualifying young person in section 142 of the Contributions and Benefits Act (child and qualifying young person).

(2) In [² ...] paragraph 15(2) of Schedule 6 (housing costs—linking rule)—

"child support maintenance" means such periodical payments as are referred to in section 3(6) of the Child Support Act 1991 and includes any payments made by the Secretary of State in lieu of such payments;

"the 1991 Act" means the Child Support Act 1991;

"the 2000 Act" means the Child Support, Pensions and Social Security Act 2000;

"maintenance assessment" has the same meaning as in the 1991 Act by virtue of section 54 of that Act as it has effect apart from the 2000 Act;

"maintenance calculation" has the same meaning as in the 1991 Act by virtue of section 54 of that Act as amended by the 2000 Act.

(3) Any reference to the claimant's family is to be construed as if it included in relation to a polygamous marriage a reference to any partner and any child or young person who is a member of the claimant's household.

(4) For the purposes of paragraph 5 of Schedule 1 to the Act, "week" means a period of 7 days.

[⁸ (5) For the purposes of paragraph 4 of Schedule 1 to the Act (condition relating to youth) "period of limited capability for work" means a period throughout which a person has, or is treated as having, limited capability for work.]

[¹⁵ (6) Subject to paragraph (7), for the purposes of section 24(3A)(b) of the Act, a lone parent is to be treated as responsible for, and a member of the same household as, a person under the age of 16 only where the circumstances set out in regulation 156 apply.

(7) For the purposes of sections 12 and 13 of the Act, and regulations made under those sections, a lone parent is to be treated as responsible for, and a member of the same household as a child only where the lone parent would be treated as responsible for and a member of the same household as such a child under regulations 15 and 16 of the Income Support (General) Regulations 1987, if references in those Regulations to income support were to employment and support allowance.]

[²⁶ (8) References in these Regulations to a person or claimant participating as a service user are to—

    (a) a person who is being consulted by or on behalf of—

        (i) a body which has a statutory duty to provide services in the field of health, social care or social housing; or

        (ii) a body which conducts research or undertakes monitoring for the purpose of planning or improving such services, in their capacity as a user, potential user, carer of a user or person otherwise affected by the provision of those services; or

[³² (ab) a person who is being consulted by or on behalf of—

        (i) the Secretary of State in relation to any of the Secretary of State's functions in the field of social security or child support or under section 2 of the Employment and Training Act 1973; or

        (ii) a body which conducts research or undertakes monitoring for the purpose of planning or improving such functions,

    in their capacity as a person affected or potentially affected by the exercise of those functions or the carer of such a person;]

    (b) the carer of a person consulted under [³² sub-paragraphs (a) or (ab)].]

AMENDMENTS

1. Employment and Support Allowance (Miscellaneous Amendments) Regulations 2008 (SI 2008/2428) reg.3 (October 27, 2008).

2. Employment and Support Allowance (Miscellaneous Amendments) Regulations 2008 (SI 2008/2428) reg.20(1) (October 27, 2008).

3. Social Security (Miscellaneous Amendments) (No.7) Regulations 2008 (SI 2008/3157) reg.11(2) (January 5, 2009).

4. Social Security (Miscellaneous Amendments) Regulations 2009 (SI 2009/583) reg.10(2) (April 6, 2009).

5. Social Security (Miscellaneous Amendments) (No.4) Regulations 2009 (SI 2009/2655) reg.11(1) and (2) (October 26, 2009).

6. Housing and Regeneration Act 2008 (Consequential Provisions) (No.2) Order 2010 (SI 671/2010) reg.4 and Sch.1 para.70 (April 1, 2010).

7. Social Security (Miscellaneous Amendments) (No.2) Regulations 2010 (SI 2010/641) reg.12(2) (April 6, 2010).

8. Social Security (Miscellaneous Amendments) (No.3) Regulations 2010 (SI 2010/840) reg.9(1) and (2) (June 29, 2010).

9. Health and Social Care Act 2008 (Miscellaneous Consequential Amendments) Order 2010 (SI 2010/1881) regs 2 and 25 (September 1, 2010).

10. Apprenticeships, Skills, Children and Learning Act 2009 (Consequential Amendments to Subordinate Legislation) (England) Order 2010 (SI 2010/1941) regs 28(1) and (2) (September 1, 2010).

11. Social Security (Miscellaneous Amendments) Regulations 2011 (SI 2011/674) reg.16(2) (April 11, 2011).

12. Employment and Support Allowance (Work-Related Activity) Regulations 2011 (SI 2011/1349) reg.10 (June 1, 2011).

13. Social Security (Miscellaneous Amendments) (No.2) Regulations 2011 (SI 2011/1707) reg.4(2)(b) and (3) (August 5, 2011).

14. Social Security (Miscellaneous Amendments) (No.3) Regulations 2011 (SI 2011/2425) reg.23(2) (October 30, 2011).

15. Social Security (Work-focused Interviews for Lone Parents and Partners) (Amendment) Regulations 2011 (SI 2011/2428) reg.5(2) (October 30, 2011).

16. Public Services Reform (Scotland) Act 2010 (Consequential Modifications of Enactments) Order 2011 (SI 2011/2581) art.2 and Sch.2 para.58 (October 28, 2011).

17. Social Security (Miscellaneous Amendments) Regulations 2012 (SI 2012/757) reg.6 (April 1, 2012).

18. Employment and Support Allowance (Amendment of Linking Rules) Regulations 2012 (SI 2012/919), reg.5(2) (May 1, 2012).

19. Young People's Learning Agency Abolition (Consequential Amendments to Subordinate Legislation) (England) Order 2012 (SI 2012/956) reg.22(1) and (2) (May 1, 2012). (The fact that the amended text does not make grammatical sense, reflects the wording of the amending instrument and is not an editorial error).

20. Employment and Support Allowance (Sanctions) (Amendment) Regulations 2012 (SI 2012/2756) reg.2 (December 3, 2012).

21. National Treatment Agency (Abolition) and the Health and Social Care Act 2012 (Consequential, Transitional and Saving Provisions) Order 2013 (SI 2013/235) art.9 and Sch.1 para.116(1) and (2) (April 1, 2013).

22. Social Security (Miscellaneous Amendments) Regulations 2013 (SI 2013/443) reg.9(1) and (2) (April 2, 2013).

23. Personal Independence Payment (Supplementary Provisions and Consequential Amendments) Regulations 2013 (SI 2013/388) reg.8 and Sch. para.40(1) and (2) (April 8, 2013).

24. Armed Forces and Reserve Forces Compensation Scheme (Consequential Provisions: Subordinate Legislation) Order 2013 (SI 2013/591) art.7 and Sch. para.37(1) and (2) (April 8, 2013).

25. Universal Credit (Consequential, Supplementary, Incidental and Miscellaneous Provisions) Regulations 2013 (SI 2013/630) reg.37(1) and (3) (April 29, 2013).

26. Social Security (Miscellaneous Amendments) (No.3) Regulations 2013 (SI 2013/2536) reg.13(1)-(3) (October 29, 2013).

27. Marriage (Same Sex Couples) Act 2013 (Consequential Provisions) Order

2014 (SI 2014/107) reg.2 and Sch.1, para.45 (March 13, 2014). The amendment extends to England and Wales only (see SI 2014/107, art.1(4)).

28. Social Security (Maternity Allowance) (Miscellaneous Amendments) Regulations 2014 (SI 2014/884) reg.5(2) (May 18, 2014).

29. Marriage and Civil Partnership (Scotland) Act 2014 and Civil Partnership Act 2004 (Consequential Provisions and Modifications) Order 2014 (SI 2014/3229) art.29 and Sch.6, para.32 (December 16, 2014). The amendment relates only to Scotland (see SI 2014/3229, art.3(4)) but is in the same terms as the amendment made in relation to England and Wales by SI 2014/107 (see note 27 above).

30. Shared Parental Leave and Statutory Shared Parental Pay (Consequential Amendments to Subordinate Legislation) Order 2014 art.20(3)(c) (December 31, 2014).

31. Shared Parental Leave and Statutory Shared Parental Pay (Consequential Amendments to Subordinate Legislation) Order 2014 art.20(3)(a) and (b) (April 5, 2015).

32. Social Security (Miscellaneous Amendments) Regulations 2015 (SI 2015/67) reg.2(1)(f) and (2) (February 23, 2015).

33. Social Security (Members of the Reserve Forces) (Amendment) Regulations 2015 (SI 2014/389) reg.4(2) (April 6, 2015).

34. Deregulation Act 2015 (Consequential Amendments) Order 2015 (SI 2015/971) art.2 and Sch.3, para.14(1) and (2) (May 26, 2015).

35. Pensions Act 2014 (Consequential, Supplementary and Incidental Amendments) Order 2015 (SI 2015/1985) art.31(1) and (2) (April 6, 2016).

36. Social Security (Scottish Rate of Income Tax etc.) (Amendment) Regulations 2016 (SI 2016/233) reg.6(1) and (2) (April 6, 2016).

37. Social Security (Scottish Infected Blood Support Scheme) Regulations 2017 (SI 2017/329) reg.8(1) and (2) (April 3, 2017).

38. Employment and Support Allowance (Miscellaneous Amendments and Transitional and Savings Provision) Regulations 2017 (SI 2017/581) reg.7(1) and (2) (June 23, 2017, subject to the transitional and savings provision in reg.10).

39. Social Security (Emergency Funds) (Amendment) Regulations 2017 (SI 2017/689) reg.8(1) and (2) (June 19, 2017).

40. Social Security (Infected Blood and Thalidomide) Regulations 2017 (SI 2017/870) reg.8(1) and (2) (October 23, 2017).

41. Social Security (Qualifying Young Persons Participating in Relevant Training Schemes) (Amendment) Regulations 2017 (SI 2017/987) reg.3(1) and (2) (November 6, 2017).

42. Social Security and Child Support (Regulation and Inspection of Social Care (Wales) Act 2016) (Consequential Provision) Regulations 2018 (SI 2018/228) reg.11(1) and (2) (April 2, 2018).

43. Civil Partnership (Opposite-sex Couples) Regulations 2019 (SI 2019/1458) reg.41(b) and Sch.3, para.90 (December 2. 2019).

44. Parental Bereavement Leave and Pay (Consequential Amendments to Subordinate Legislation) Regulations 2020 (SI 2020/354) reg.19(1) and (2) (April 6, 2020).

45. Social Security (Income and Capital) (Miscellaneous Amendments) Regulations 2020 (SI 2020/618) reg.7(1) and (2) (July 15, 2020).

GENERAL NOTE

4.5   Most of these definitions are either self-explanatory, or references to definitions in other regulations or are similar to those in reg.2(1) of the IS Regs and reg.1(2) of the JSA Regs. See the notes to those Regulations above. The following merit comment

"*aircraft worker*": The definition is used in reg.11 (Condition relating to youth—residence or presence). By para.4 of Sch.1 to the Welfare Reform Act, those under 20 (or in prescribed cases 25) may, if they satisfy certain conditions (set out in reg.11), be entitled to contributory ESA even though they do not satisfy the second contribution condition. For the purposes of reg.11, the claimant is treated as being resident and present in Great Britain while absent "abroad in the capacity of being an aircraft worker or mariner". The definition covers all those employed on an aircraft while in flight under a contract that was entered into in the UK, other than members of the armed forces.

"confinement": The definition in s.171 of the Contributions and Benefits Act reads as follows:

"confinement" means—

    (a) labour resulting in the issue of a living child, or

    (b) labour after 24 weeks of pregnancy resulting in the issue of a child whether alive or dead,

and "confined" shall be construed accordingly; and where a woman's labour begun on one day results in the issue of a child on another day she shall be taken to be confined on the day of the issue of the child or, if labour results in the issue of twins or a greater number of children, she shall be taken to be confined on the day of the issue of the last of them;"

"dependent child": This definition (which does not appear in the IS Regulations or the JSA Regs) refers to any child or qualifying young person who a member of the claimant's household and is treated as the responsibility of the claimant or the claimant's partner (i.e., under reg.156(10)).

"mariner": See the commentary on "aircraft worker" above. The definition is similar except that the reference to "aircraft" is to "ship or vessel".

"member of Her Majesty's forces": Members of the armed forces and their families are, in certain circumstances, treated as being in Great Britain while abroad. The definition is supplemented by Sch.1 below.

"National Minimum Wage" is defined as the rate of the national minimum wage specified in regulation 11 of the National Minimum Wage Regulations 1999. However, those Regulations were revoked and replaced by the National Minimum Wage Regulations 2015. In those circumstances, the reference in the definition to the 1999 Regulations is to be taken to be to the 2015 Regulations (Interpretation Act 1978 ss.17 and 23). Since reg.11 of the 1999 Regulations originally specified the single hourly rate of the national minimum wage, the equivalent must presumably be taken as being reg.4 of the current form of the 2015 Regulations. Regulation 4 now specifies the single hourly rate (i.e. the rate applicable to workers aged at least 25) and reg.4A specifies lower rates for workers of younger ages, so that for old style ESA purposes the over-25 rate is to be used regardless of the age of the person concerned.

[¹Disapplication of section 1(1A) of the Social Security Administration Act 1992

2A. Section 1(1A) of the Social Security Administration Act 1992 (requirement to state a national insurance number) shall not apply to a person who—   **4.6**

    (a) is a person in respect of whom a claim for employment and support allowance is made;

    (b) is subject to immigration control within the meaning of section 115(9)(a) of the Immigration and Asylum Act;

    (c) does not satisfy the basic conditions of entitlement to employment and support allowance for the purposes of section 1(3) of the Act; and

    (d) has not previously been allocated a national insurance number.]

AMENDMENT

1. Social Security (National Insurance Number Information: Exemption) Regulations 2009 (SI 2009/471) reg.13 (April 6, 2009).

4.7   See the commentary to reg.2A(c) of the Income Support Regulations.

Rounding of fractions

4.8   **3.** For the purposes of these Regulations—
  (a) where any calculation under these Regulations results in a fraction of a penny that fraction is, if it would be to the claimant's advantage, to be treated as a penny, otherwise it must be disregarded;
  (b) where an employment and support allowance is awarded for a period which is not a complete benefit week and the applicable amount in respect of the period results in an amount which includes a fraction of a penny that fraction is to be treated as a penny.

GENERAL NOTE

4.9   Fractions are always rounded in the claimant's favour.

PART 2

THE ASSESSMENT PHASE

MODIFICATION

4.10   Note that for the purpose of making "conversion decisions" under the "Migration Regulations" from October 1, 2010, Pt 2 (the assessment phase) does not apply. See reg.6(1) and Sch.1 para.8 to those Regulations: the Employment and Support Allowance (Transitional Provisions, Housing Benefit and Council Tax Benefit) (Existing Awards) (No. 2) Regulations 2010 (SI 2010/1907) (as amended), below.

The end of the assessment phase

4.11   **4.**—(1) Subject to [²paragraphs (2) and (3)] and [¹regulation 5], the assessment phase in relation to a claimant ends on the last day of [³ the relevant period].
  [²(2) Where paragraph (3) applies, the assessment phase is to end when it is determined whether the claimant has limited capability for work.
  (3) This paragraph applies where, at the end of [³ the relevant period]—
  (a) the claimant has not been assessed in accordance with a limited capability for work assessment; and
  (b) the claimant has not been treated as having limited capability for work in accordance with regulations 20, 25, 26, 29 or 33(2) (persons to be treated as having limited capability for work).]
  [³(4) In this regulation, "the relevant period" means the period of 13 weeks beginning with—
  (a) the first day of the assessment phase as determined under section 24(2)(a) of the Act; or
  (b) where that day immediately follows an extended period of sickness, the first day of the extended period of sickness.
  (5) In paragraph (4), "extended period of sickness" means a period in which the claimant was—
  (a) entitled to a jobseeker's allowance; and
  (b) treated as capable of work or as not having limited capability for work under regulation 55ZA of the Jobseeker's Allowance Regulations 1996 or regulation 46A of the Jobseeker's Allowance Regulations 2013 (extended period of sickness).]

AMENDMENTS

1. Social Security (Miscellaneous Amendments) (No.3) Regulations 2010 (SI 2010/840) reg.9(3) (June 28, 2010).

2. Social Security (Miscellaneous Amendments) (No.3) Regulations 2013 (SI 2013/2536) reg.13(4) (October 29, 2013).

3. Jobseeker's Allowance (Extended Period of Sickness) Amendment Regulations 2015 (SI 2015/339) reg.4 (March 30, 2015).

DEFINITIONS

"the assessment phase"—see WRA 2007 s.24(2).
"claimant"—see WRA 2007 s.24(1).
"extended period of sickness"—see para.(5).
"limited capability for work"—see WRA 2007 s.1(4).
"limited capability for work assessment"—see reg.2(1).
"the relevant period"—see para.(4).
"week"—see reg.2(1).

GENERAL NOTE

During an initial "assessment phase", generally (reg.7, below, affords exceptions)   **4.12**
a claimant can only be entitled to "basic allowance" ESA; entitlement to the appropriate additional component (support or work-related) only arises after the end of
that phase (WRA 2007 s.2(2), (3)). The assessment phase ends on the last day of
the "relevant period" (para.(1)). That period is one of 13 weeks beginning either
with the first day of the assessment phase determined by WRA 2007 s.24(2)(a) or
if that day followed an extended period of sickness in which the claimant remained
entitled to JSA under the specified regulations, with the first day of that extended
period of sickness (paras(4), (5)). Section 24(2)(a) of the WRA 2007 stipulates that
the "assessment phase" begins on the first day of entitlement to ESA, i.e. the first
day of limited capability for work after service of the "waiting days" (these are days
of non-entitlement: see WRA 2007 Sch.2, para.2 and reg.144). This regulation in
contrast sets out when the "assessment phase" ends. It ends after 13 weeks, unless
at that time it still has not been determined whether the claimant has, or is to be
treated under the regulations enumerated in para.(3) as having, limited capability
for work. In that case the "assessment phase" lasts longer than the 13-week period
and ends when the limited capability for work determination is made, that is, when
it is decided whether or not the person has, or is to be treated as having, limited
capability for work.

In short, the assessment phase ends after the later of 13 weeks or the decision on whether the claimant has (or is to be treated as having) limited capability for work. Where, however, the claimant appeals a decision embodying an
adverse determination on limited capability for work, the assessment phase ends
only when the appeal is determined by an appeal tribunal (see regs 5(4) and
147A).

In *SSWP v NC (ESA)* [2013] UKUT 477 (AAC), Judge Bano held that, despite
poor wording, the effect of the then reg.4(2) (now reg.4(2), (3)) was that "subject to
exceptions in cases involving appeals, the assessment phase lasts until the end of the
three month period, or until a determination that a claimant has (or is to be treated
as having) limited capability for work, whichever is the later" (para.9). In *SSWP v
RM* [2014] UKUT 42 (AAC), Judge Jacobs agreed with Judge Bano both as to the
result of a proper reading of reg.4 and that reg.4(2) as worded before the October
2013 amendments was poorly worded, but considered that it could be rendered
coherent by inserting "by" at the beginning of the then para.(2)(a). Fortunately, the
October 2013 amendment makes things much clearer and with the same effect as
in these two decsions.

The assessment phase—previous claimants

4.13   **5.**—(1) Where the circumstances in paragraph (2) apply in relation to a claimant the assessment phase —

(a) begins on the first day of the period for which the claimant was previously entitled to an employment and support allowance; and

(b) subject to [³ paragraphs (3), (3A) and (4)], ends on the day when the sum of the period for which the claimant was previously entitled to an employment and support allowance and the period for which the claimant is currently entitled to such an allowance is 13 weeks.

[⁴(1A) For the purposes of paragraph (1), any period when the claimant was—

(a) entitled to a jobseeker's allowance; and

(b) treated as capable of work or as not having limited capability for work under regulation 55ZA of the Jobseeker's Allowance Regulations 1996 or regulation 46A of the Jobseeker's Allowance Regulations 2013,

is to be treated as a period when the claimant was previously entitled to an employment and support allowance.]

(2) The circumstances are that—

(a)   (i) the claimant's current period of limited capability for work is to be treated as a continuation of an earlier period of limited capability for work under regulation 145(1) [²...];

(ii) the claimant was entitled to an employment and support allowance in the earlier period of limited capability for work;

(iii) the assessment phase had not ended in the previous period for which the claimant was entitled to an employment and support allowance; and

(iv) the period for which the claimant was previously entitled was no more than 13 weeks; or

[²(b) (i) the claimant's current period of limited capability for work is to be treated as a continuation of an earlier period of limited capability for work under regulation 145(1),

(ii) the claimant was entitled to an employment and support allowance in the earlier period of limited capability for work,

(iii) the previous period of limited capability for work was terminated by virtue of a determination that the claimant did not have limited capability for work,

(iv) the period for which the claimant was previously entitled was no more than 13 weeks, and

(v) a determination is made in relation to the current period of limited capability for work that the claimant has or is treated as having limited capability for work, other than under regulation 30; or

(c) (i) the claimant's current period of limited capability for work is to be treated as a continuation of an earlier period of limited capability for work under regulation 145(1),

(ii) the claimant was entitled to an employment and support allowance in the earlier period of limited capability for work,

(iii) in relation to the previous award of an employment and support allowance, a determination was made that the claimant had limited capability for work or was treated as having limited capability for work, other than under regulation 30, and

(iv) the period for which the claimant was previously entitled was no more than 13 weeks.]

[³(3) Where paragraph (3A) applies, the assessment phase is to end when it is determined whether the claimant has limited capability for work.

(3A) This paragraph applies where on the day referred to in paragraph (1)(b)—

(a) the claimant has not been assessed in accordance with a limited capability for work assessment; and

(b) the claimant has not been treated as having limited capability for work in accordance with regulations 20, 25, 26, 29 or 33(2) (persons to be treated as having limited capability for work).]

[¹(4) Where a person has made and is pursuing an appeal against a decision of the Secretary of State that embodies a determination that the claimant does not have limited capability for work—

(a) [³ paragraphs (3) and (3A) do] not apply; and

(b) paragraph (1) does not apply to any period of limited capability for work to which regulation 147A(2) applies until a determination of limited capability for work has been made following the determination of the appeal by the First-tier Tribunal.]

AMENDMENTS

1. Social Security (Miscellaneous Amendments) (No.3) Regulations 2010 (SI 2010/840) reg.9(4) (June 28, 2010).

2. Employment and Support Allowance (Amendment of Linking Rules) Regulations 2012 (SI 2012/919) reg.5(3) (May 1, 2012).

3. Social Security (Miscellaneous Amendments) (No.3) Regulations 2013 (SI 2013/2536) reg.13(5) (October 29, 2013).

4. Jobseeker's Allowance (Extended Period of Sickness) Amendment Regulations 2015 (SI 2015/339) reg.4 (March 30, 2015).

DEFINITIONS

"the assessment phase"—see WRA 2007 s.24(2).
"claimant"—see WRA 2007 s.24(1).
"entitled"—see WRA 2007 s.24(1).
"limited capability for work"—see WRA 2007 s.1(4).
"limited capability for work assessment"—see reg.2(1).
"week"—see reg.2(1).

GENERAL NOTE

This regulation deals with determining the end of the "assessment phase" in cases of intermittent limited capability for work (where spells of limited capability for work are interspersed with spells in which capability for work is not limited), where the ostensibly separate spells of limited capability are fused into one by the operation of the "linking rule" in reg.145. As noted in the commentary to that regulation, this will happen where the two spells are not separated by more than 12 weeks. Until May 1, 2012, in some cases the permissible separation period could have been as long as 104 weeks, but that date saw the abolition of the 104 week linking rule for work or training beneficiaries, that abolition itself being the result of time-limiting entitlement to CESA for those not in the support group to 365 days (see WRA 2007 s.1A, above). A period in which a claimant remained entitled to JSA during an extended period of sickness under the specified JSA Regs counts as a period of previous entitlement to ESA (paras (1), (1A)). The effect of reg.5 is that the weeks of entitlement to ESA in each period thus linked are added together and the assessment phase ends when their sum reaches 13, unless no limited capability for work determination (see commentary to reg.4) has by then been made, in which case, as with continuous periods of limited capability for work under reg.4, it ends when that determination

4.14

has been made. In short, the assessment phase ends after the later of 13 weeks (in two or more linked spells of limited capability) or the decision on whether the claimant has (or is to be treated as having) limited capability for work. Where, however, the claimant appeals a decision embodying an adverse determination on limited capability for work, the assessment phase ends only when the appeal is determined by an appeal tribunal (see reg.147A).

The assessment phase—claimants appealing against a decision

4.15   [¹6. *Omitted.*]

AMENDMENT

1. Social Security (Miscellaneous Amendments) (No.3) Regulations 2010 (SI 2010/840) reg.9(5) (June 28, 2010).

Circumstances where the condition that the assessment phase has ended before entitlement to the support component [⁶ . . .] arises does not apply

4.16   **7.**—(1) Subject to paragraph (2), [⁶ sections 2(2)(a) and 4(4)(a)] of the Act do not apply where—

(a) a claimant is terminally ill and has either—
  (i) made a claim expressly on the ground of being terminally ill; or
  (ii) made an application for supersession or revision in accordance with the Social Security and Child Support (Decisions and Appeals) Regulations 1999 which contains an express statement that the claimant is terminally ill; [¹ . . .]

(b) [⁴ the case is a relevant linked case;]

[¹(c) (i) the claimant's entitlement to an employment and support allowance commences within 12 weeks of the claimant's entitlement to income support coming to an end;
  (ii) in relation to that entitlement to income support, immediately before it ended the claimant's applicable amount included the disability premium by virtue of satisfying the conditions in paragraphs 11 and 12 of Schedule 2 to the Income Support Regulations; and
  (iii) that entitlement to income support ended solely by virtue of the coming into force, in relation to the claimant, of the Social Security (Lone Parents and Miscellaneous Amendments) Regulations] [⁵2012] [³; or

(d) a claimant is entitled to an employment and support allowance by virtue of section 1B of the Act (further entitlement after time-limiting).]

[⁴(1A) For the purposes of paragraph (1)(b) a relevant linked case is a case mentioned in paragraph (1B) where a period of limited capability for work is to be treated as a continuation of an earlier period of limited capability for work under regulation 145(1).

(1B) Paragraph (1A) applies to the following cases—

(a) case 1 is where—
  (i) the claimant was entitled to an employment and support allowance (including entitlement to a component under sections [⁶ 2(2) or 4(4)] of the Act [⁷ or the claimant was a member of the work-related activity group]) in the earlier period of limited capability for work, and

    (ii) the previous period for which the claimant was entitled to an employment and support allowance was terminated other than by virtue of a determination that the claimant did not have limited capability for work;

(b) case 2 is where—

    (i) the claimant was entitled to an employment and support allowance in the earlier period of limited capability for work,

    (ii) the previous period for which the claimant was entitled to an employment and support allowance was 13 weeks or longer,

    (iii) the previous period for which the claimant was entitled to an employment and support allowance was terminated by virtue of a determination that the claimant did not have, or was treated as not having, limited capability for work, and

    (iv) it is determined in relation to the current period of limited capability for work that the claimant has limited capability for work or is treated as having limited capability for work, other than under regulation 30;

(c) case 3 is where—

    (i) the claimant was entitled to an employment and support allowance in the earlier period of limited capability for work,

    (ii) the previous period for which the claimant was entitled to an employment and support allowance was 13 weeks or longer,

    (iii) the previous period for which the claimant was entitled to an employment and support allowance was terminated before it could be determined whether the claimant had limited capability for work or was treated as having limited capability for work, other than under regulation 30, and

    (iv) it is determined in relation to the current period of limited capability for work that the claimant has limited capability for work or is treated as having limited capability for work, other than under regulation 30; and

(d) case 4 is where—

    (i) the claimant was entitled to an employment and support allowance (including entitlement to a component under sections [6 2(2) or 4(4)] of the Act [7 or the claimant was a member of the work-related activity group]) in the earlier period of limited capability for work,

    (ii) the previous period for which the claimant was entitled to an employment and support allowance was terminated because it was determined that the claimant did not have limited capability for work or was treated as not having limited capability for work, and

    (iii) it is determined in relation to the current period of limited capability for work that the claimant has limited capability for work or is treated as having limited capability for work, other than under regulation 30.]

(2) Paragraph (1)(b) does not apply to [2any period of limited capability for work to which regulation 147A(2) applies until the determination of limited capability for work has been made following the determination of the appeal by the First-tier Tribunal].

AMENDMENTS

1. Social Security (Lone Parents and Miscellaneous Amendments) Regulations 2008 (SI 2008/3051) reg.12(2) (November 24, 2008).

2. Social Security (Miscellaneous Amendments) (No.3) Regulations 2010 (SI 2010/840) reg.9(6) (June 28, 2010).

3. Employment and Support Allowance (Duration of Contributory Allowance) (Consequential Amendments) Regulations 2012 (SI 2012/913) reg.9(2) (May 1, 2012).

4. Employment and Support Allowance (Amendment of Linking Rules) Regulations 2012 (SI 2012/919) reg.5(4) (May 1, 2012 immediately after amendment 3, above—see reg.1(2)).

5. Social Security (Lone Parents and Miscellaneous Amendments) Regulations 2012 (SI 2012/874) reg.6 (May 21, 2012).

6. Employment and Support Allowance and Universal Credit (Miscellaneous Amendments and Transitional and Savings Provisions) Regulations 2017 (SI 2017/204) reg.2(2) (April 3, 2017).

7. Employment and Support Allowance (Miscellaneous Amendments and Transitional and Savings Provision) Regulations 2017 (SI 2017/581) reg.7(3) (June 23, 2017).

DEFINITIONS

"claimant"—see WRA 2007 s.24(1).
"entitled"—see WRA 2007 s.24(1).
"limited capability for work"—see WRA 2007 s.1(4).
"period of limited capability for work"—see reg.2(1).
"relevant linked case"—see paras (1)(b), (1A), (1B).
"terminally ill"—see reg.2(1).
"the assessment phase"—see WRA 2007 s.24(2).

GENERAL NOTE

4.17   WRA 2007 ss.2 and 4 provide that until the "assessment phase" ends there can be no entitlement other than to basic allowance ESA; entitlement to the support component normally cannot arise until the assessment phase has ended (on which see WRA 2007 s.24(2) and ESA Regs regs 4–6). This regulation provides that the general rule precluding entitlement does not apply in four situations. First of all it does not apply to someone terminally ill who has claimed ESA expressly on that basis or has sought supersession or revision expressly stating that he is terminally ill (para.(1)(a)). Note that someone is terminally ill where he is suffering from a progressive disease and death as a consequence of it can reasonably be expected within six months (reg.2(1)). The second situation where the general preclusive rule is disapplied is where the claimant's entitlement to ESA arises within 12 weeks of entitlement to IS which had included the disability premium, ending solely because of the entry into force in relation to him of the Social Security (Lone Parents and Miscellaneous Amendments) Regulations 2012 (para.(1)(c)). The third situation of disapplication of the general preclusive rule is where the claimant is entitled to ESA because of the further entitlement after time-limiting provisions in WRA 2007 s.1B (para.(1)(d)).

The fourth situation in which the general preclusive rule is disapplied is where the claimant's position falls within one of the four cases each constituting "a relevant linked case" (paras (1)(b), (1A), (1B)). A "relevant linked case" is one of those in para.(1B) in which a period of limited capability for work is to be treated as a continuation of an earlier one under reg.145(1) (the 12 week rule) (paras (1)(b), (1A)). Case 1 covers the situation in which the previous entitlement to ESA was one in which there was entitlement to the support component and that entitlement to ESA ended other than by virtue of it being determined that the claimant did not have limited capability for work (para.(1B)(a))). Case 2 embraces the situation in which the previous period of entitlement to ESA lasted 13 weeks or more, was ended because of a determination that the claimant did not have, or was treated as not having, limited capability for work and in the current period of ESA entitlement it has been decided that the claimant has limited capability for work or is to be treated as having it other than through reg.30 (treating someone as having limited capability for work pending an actual determination) (para.(1B)(b)). Case 3 covers the situation in which the previous period of ESA entitlement lasted 13 weeks or more but was ended before a determination of actual or deemed limited capability for work had been made (other than under reg.30), and in the current period of ESA entitlement it has been decided that the claimant has limited capability for work or is to be treated as having it other than through reg.30 (treating someone as having limited capability for work pending an actual determination) (para.(1B)(c)). Case 4 embraces the situation where the claimants previous period of entitlement to ESA included a component, was ended because it was decided the claimant did not have limited capability for work or was to be treated as not having it, and in the current period of ESA entitlement it has been decided that the claimant has limited capability for work or is to be treated as having it other than through reg.30 (para.(1B)(d)).

PART 3

CONDITIONS OF ENTITLEMENT—CONTRIBUTORY ALLOWANCE

[¹Conditions relating to national insurance and relevant earnings

7A.—(1) A claimant's relevant earnings for the purposes of paragraph 1(2)(a) of Schedule 1 to the Act (employment and support allowance: conditions relating to national insurance) are the total amount of the claimant's earnings at the lower earnings limit for the base tax year.   **4.18**

(2) For the purposes of paragraph (1), earnings which exceed the lower earnings limit are to be disregarded.]

AMENDMENT

1. Social Security (Contribution Conditions for Jobseeker's Allowance and Employment and Support Allowance) Regulations 2010 (SI 2010/2446) reg.3(1) (November 1, 2010).

GENERAL NOTE

As noted in the General Note to Sch.1, para.1 to the Welfare Reform Act 2007, the changes effected by s.13 of the Welfare Reform Act 2009 and this regulation made in consequence significantly tighten the contribution conditions for CESA. Together they mean that the requisite level of "relevant earnings" in the tax year relied on for the first contribution condition is now 26 times that year's lower earnings limit, rather than 25. This new regulation defines "relevant earnings" to cover only earnings at that lower earnings limit, so that new claimants will have to have worked for at least 26 weeks in one of the last two tax years (April 6–April 5) complete before the start of the benefit year (beginning in early January) which includes the first day of claim in the relevant period of limited capability for work.   **4.19**

Relaxation of the first contribution condition

8. [*Omitted as not applying to income-related ESA*]   **4.20**

Condition relating to youth—claimants aged 20 or over but under 25

9. [*Omitted as not applying to income-related ESA*]   **4.21**

Condition relating to youth—previous claimants

4.22   **10.**[*Omitted as not applying to income-related ESA*]

Condition relating to youth—residence or presence

4.23   **11.**—[*Omitted as not applying to income-related ESA*]

Condition relating to youth—full-time education

4.24   **12.**[*Omitted as not applying to income-related ESA*]

[¹Modification of the relevant benefit year

4.25   **13.**[*Omitted as not applying to income-related ESA*]

PART 4

CONDITIONS OF ENTITLEMENT—INCOME-RELATED ALLOWANCE

Meaning of education

4.26   **14.**—(1) Subject to regulations 15 and 16, for the purposes of paragraph 6 of Schedule 1 to the Act, "education" means a course of study to which paragraph (2) applies which is being undertaken at an educational establishment.

4.27   (2) This paragraph applies to a course of study which is—
　　(a) a full-time course which is not funded in whole or in part by—
　　　　[¹ (i) the [³ Secretary of State under section 14 of the Education Act 2002] [⁵ or section 100 of the Apprenticeships, Skills, Children and Learning Act 2009];
　　　　(ia) [⁵ . . .];]
　　　　(ii) the Welsh Ministers; or
　　　　(iii) the Scottish Ministers at a college of further education;
　　(b) a full-time course of higher education which is funded in whole or in part by the Scottish Ministers;
　　(c) funded in whole or in part by the [¹[³ Secretary of State under section 14 of the Education Act 2002], [⁵ or section 100 of the Apprenticeships, Skills, Children and Learning Act 2009]] or by the Welsh Ministers if it involves more than 16 guided learning hours per week for the student in question, according to the number of guided learning hours per week for that student set out—
　　　　[¹ (i) in the case of a course funded by the [³ Secretary of State [⁵ . . .]], in the student's learning agreement signed on behalf of the establishment which is funded by [⁵ the Secretary of State] for the delivery of that course;]
　　　　(ii) in the case of a course funded by the Welsh Ministers, in a document signed on behalf of the establishment which is funded by those Ministers for the delivery of that course;
　　(d) not a course of higher education and which is funded in whole or in part by the Scottish Ministers at a college of further education and involves—

(i) more than 16 hours per week of classroom-based or workshop-based programmed learning under the direct guidance of teaching staff according to the number of hours set out in a document signed on behalf of the college; or

(ii) 16 hours or less per week of classroom-based or workshop-based programmed learning under the direct guidance of teaching staff and it involves additional hours using structured learning packages supported by the teaching staff where the combined total of hours exceeds 21 per week according to the number of hours set out in a document signed on behalf of the college; or

(e) a sandwich course within the meaning prescribed in regulation 2(9) of the Education (Student Support) Regulations 2007, regulation 4(2) of the Education (Student Loans) (Scotland) Regulations 2007 or regulation 2(8) of the Education (Student Support) Regulations (Northern Ireland) 2007.

[² (2A) Paragraph (2) does not apply to any course of study which the claimant is required to attend for the purpose of meeting a requirement to undertake work-related activity.]   **4.28**

[⁶ (2B) Paragraph (2) does not apply to a traineeship.]

(3) In this regulation "higher education" means higher education within the meaning of Part 2 of the Further and Higher Education (Scotland) Act 1992.   **4.29**

AMENDMENTS

1. Apprenticeships, Skills, Children and Learning Act 2009 (Consequential Amendments to Subordinate Legislation) (England) Order 2010 (SI 2010/1941), reg.28(3) (September 1, 2010).

2. Social Security (Miscellaneous Amendments) Regulations 2012 (SI 2012/757) reg.20(3) (April 1, 2012).

3. Young People's Learning Agency Abolition (Consequential Amendments to Subordinate Legislation) (England) Order 2012 (SI 2012/956), art.22(3)(a) (May 1, 2012).

4. Young People's Learning Agency Abolition (Consequential Amendments to Subordinate Legislation) (England) Order 2012 (SI 2012/956), art.22(3)(b) (May 1, 2012).

5. Deregulation Act 2015 (Consequential Amendments) Order 2015 (SI 2015/971), art.2 and Sch.3 para.14(3) (May 26, 2015).

6. Social Security (Qualifying Young Persons Participating in Relevant Training Schemes) (Amendment) Regulations 2017 (SI 2017/987) reg.3(3) (November 6, 2017).

GENERAL NOTE

It is a condition of entitlement to income-related ESA that a claimant is not receiving education (see para.6(1)(g) of Sch.1 to the Welfare Reform Act 2007). But see reg.18 below which exempts claimants who are entitled to disability living allowance ("DLA"), personal independence payment ("PIP") or armed forces independence payment (see reg.2(1) for the definition of "armed forces independence payment") from this requirement.   **4.30**

Note that para.6(1)(g) of Sch.1 does not apply in the case of claimants who had an existing award of income support by virtue of reg.13(2)(b) or (bb) (persons in relevant education who are ill or disabled) of, or paras 10 or 12 (disabled or deaf students) of Sch.1B to, the Income Support Regulations (see the   **4.31**

2015/16 edition of Vol.II in this series for these provisions) and who have been transferred to ESA as a result of a conversion decision under the Employment and Support Allowance (Transitional Provisions, Housing Benefit and Council Tax Benefit) (Existing Awards) (No.2) Regulations 2010 (SI 2010/1907) (as amended) (see p.1577 for these Regulations). The modifications to s.1(2) of the 2007 Act made by Sch.1, para.2 and Sch.2, para.2 of the 2010 Regulations mean that such claimants will be able to get ESA 1329 while in education even if they do not get DLA, PIP or armed forces independence payment.

4.32 "Education" for these purposes means a course of study that comes within para. (2) that is being undertaken at an educational establishment. Paragraph (2) is in the same terms as the definitions of "full-time course of study" and "sandwich course" in reg.131(1) (which in turn reproduces the definitions of these terms in reg.61(1) of the Income Support Regulations; see also the definitions of "full-time student" and "sandwich course" in reg.1(3) of the JSA Regulations 1996). Regulation 17 provides when a person will count as undertaking a course of study. It is in the same terms as reg.131(2)–(4) (which in turn reproduces the provisions in reg.61(2)–(4) of the Income Support Regulations and reg.1(3A)–(3C) of the JSA Regulations 1996). The combined effect of regs 14 and 17 is to exclude full-time students from income-related ESA (except those who are entitled to DLA, PIP or armed forces independence payment: see reg.18 and the note to that regulation). But note that in the case of a person aged under 19 this will only apply if he is attending a course of advanced education (reg.16).

4.33 Paragraph (2A), inserted with effect from April 1, 2012, confirms that a claimant will not be treated as receiving education in relation to any course of study that he is required to attend as part of his work-related activity.

In addition, a "qualifying young person", unless he is entitled to DLA, PIP or armed forces independence payment, is to be treated as receiving education (see reg.15).

See also *RVS v SSWP (ESA)* [2019] UKUT 102 (AAC), discussed in the note to reg.17 below.

Claimants to be treated as receiving education

4.34 **15.** [¹ (1)] Subject to regulation 18 [¹ and paragraph (2)], a qualifying young person is to be treated as receiving education for the purposes of paragraph 6(1)(g) of Schedule 1 to the Act.

[¹ (2) A qualifying young person is not to be treated as receiving education if they are participating in a traineeship.]

AMENDMENTS

1. Social Security (Qualifying Young Persons Participating in Relevant Training Schemes) (Amendment) Regulations 2017 (SI 2017/987) reg.3(4) (November 6, 2017).

DEFINITION

"qualifying young person"—reg.2(1), s.142 SSCBA.

GENERAL NOTE

4.35 A qualifying young person (other than one who is entitled to disability living allowance ("DLA"), personal independence payment ("PIP") or armed forces independence payment (see reg.2(1) for the definition of "armed forces independence payment"): see reg.18) is to be treated as receiving education and so is excluded from income-related ESA. A "qualifying young person" (as defined in s.142 of the Contributions and Benefits Act) is a person who is 16 or over but who has not attained a prescribed age and who satisfies prescribed conditions.

The substance of the definition of "qualifying young person" is in reg.3 of the   **4.36**
Child Benefit Regulations 2006 (see Vol.IV in this series). It applies to a person who
is (i) under 20; *and* (ii) undertaking a course of full-time, non-advanced education,
which is not provided by virtue of his employment or any office held by him, but
which is provided at a school or college, or elsewhere as approved by the Revenue
(in the latter case he must have been receiving the approved education before he
was 16); *or* (iii) undertaking approved training that is not provided by means of a
contract of employment. "Approved training" covers various training programmes
under "arrangements made by the Government" (see the definition of both these
terms in reg.1(3) of the 2006 Regulations). "Full-time education" (also defined in
reg.1(3)) requires contact hours of at least 12 a week during term-time. Note that a
person aged 19 can only be a qualifying young person if he began, or was enrolled
on, or had been accepted to undertake, the full-time, non-advanced education or
approved training before he was 19 (although a person who was on such a course/
training and has been accepted or enrolled to undertake another such course/train-
ing is also included).

Claimants not to be treated as receiving education

16. Where a claimant is under 19 but not a qualifying young person, that   **4.37**
claimant is not to be treated as receiving education where the course of
study is not—
- (a) a course leading to a postgraduate degree or comparable qualification, a first degree or comparable qualification, a diploma of higher
education or a higher national diploma; or
- (b) any other course which is of a standard above advanced GNVQ or
equivalent, including a course which is of a standard above a general
certificate of education (advanced level) or above a Scottish national
qualification (higher or advanced higher).

<small>DEFINITION</small>

"qualifying young person"—see reg.2(1), s.142 SSCBA.

<small>GENERAL NOTE</small>

The effect of this regulation is that if the claimant is aged less than 19 and is not a   **4.38**
qualifying young person (see the note to reg.15), he will not count as receiving education unless he is undertaking a course of advanced education (see the definition
of "course of advanced education" in reg.131(1) which is in the same terms as paras
(a) and (b), and which in turn reproduces the definition of "course of advanced
education" in reg.61(1) of the Income Support Regulations and reg.1(3) of the JSA
Regulations 1996). See further the note to reg.14.

Courses of study

17.—(1) For the purposes of the definition of "education" in regulation   **4.39**
14, a person is to be regarded as undertaking a course of study—
- (a) subject to paragraph (2), in the case of a person undertaking a part
of a modular course that would be a course of study for the purposes
of these Regulations, for the period beginning on the day on which
that part of the course starts and ending—
  - (i) on the last day on which the person is registered with the educational establishment as attending or undertaking that part as
a full-time course of study; or
  - (ii) on such earlier date (if any) as the person finally abandons the
course or is dismissed from it;

(b) in any other case, throughout the period beginning on the date on which the person starts undertaking the course and ending on the last day of the course or on such earlier date (if any) as the person finally abandons it or is dismissed from it.

(2) For the purpose of sub-paragraph (a) of paragraph (1), the period referred to in that sub-paragraph includes—

(a) where a person has failed examinations or has failed to successfully complete a module relating to a period when the person was attending or undertaking a part of the course as a course of study, any period in respect of which the person attends or undertakes the course for the purpose of retaking those examinations or that module;

(b) any period of vacation within the period specified in that paragraph or immediately following that period except where the person has registered with the educational establishment to attend or undertake the final module in the course and the vacation immediately follows the last day on which the person is required to attend or undertake the course.

(3) In paragraph (1), "modular course" means a course of study which consists of two or more modules, the successful completion of a specified number of which is required before a person is considered by the educational establishment to have completed the course.

GENERAL NOTE

4.40 Regulation 14 defines "education" as a course of study undertaken at an educational establishment while reg.17 sets out when a person is to be regarded as undertaking a course of study. In *RVS v SSWP (ESA)* [2019] UKUT 102 (AAC) the claimant was enrolled on a modular University course, of which he had completed two years. He then "intermitted" (suspended) his studies for the final 2017/18 academic year for reasons of ill-health. His claim for ESA in November 2017 was refused on the basis that he was receiving education and so not entitled (WRA 2007, s.1(2)(b) and Sch.1 para. 6(1)(g)). The FTT dismissed his appeal. Allowing his appeal to the Upper Tribunal, Judge Poynter held the FTT had erred by applying the standard test for non-modular courses (see reg.17(1)(b)) rather than investigating the facts to see if the claimant had the benefit of the potentially more favourable rules for modular courses in reg.17(1)(a). Remaking the decision to the effect that the claimant was not receiving education, and so was not excluded from entitlement to ESA, the judge held that (a) each year of study amounted to a "part" of a modular course and (b) the claimant had completed his second year successfully and never embarked on the next "part" of that course, namely the third and final year. Accordingly, when the claimant applied for ESA, having intermitted, he was not undertaking part of a modular course as the previous part had ended on the last day of his second year of study (see reg.17(1)(a)(i)).

Circumstances in which the condition that the claimant is not receiving education does not apply

4.41 **18.** Paragraph 6(1)(g) of Schedule 1 to the Act does not apply where the claimant is entitled to a disability living allowance [² , armed forces independence payment] [¹ or personal independence payment].

AMENDMENTS

1. Personal Independence Payment (Supplementary Provisions and Consequential Amendments) Regulations 2013 (SI 2013/388) reg.8 and Sch., Pt II, para.40(3) (April 8, 2013).

2. Armed Forces and Reserve Forces Compensation Scheme (Consequential Provisions: Subordinate Legislation) Order 2013 (SI 2013/591) art.7 and Sch. para.37(3) (April 8, 2013).

DEFINITIONS

"armed forces independence payment"—see reg.2(1).
"disability living allowance"—*ibid.*
"personal independence payment"—*ibid.*

GENERAL NOTE

Paragraph 6(1)(g) of Sch.1 to the Welfare Reform Act 2007 provides that it is a condition of entitlement to income-related ESA that the claimant is not receiving education—this effectively excludes full-time students and qualifying young persons from income-related ESA: see regs 14–17. However the effect of reg.18 is that such claimants will not be excluded if they are entitled to disability living allowance ("DLA") (either component at any rate), personal independence payment ("PIP") (either component at either rate) or armed forces independence payment. **4.42**

See also reg.33(2) which treats a claimant who is receiving education but who is entitled to DLA, PIP or armed forces independence payment as having limited capability for work for the purposes of income-related ESA. But this does not apply in the case of a qualifying young person (reg.33(2)(a)). A qualifying young person who is entitled to DLA, PIP or armed forces independence payment and who claims income-related ESA will have to satisfy the limited capability for work test (as will any claimant who counts as receiving education who claims contributory ESA, even though he is entitled to DLA, PIP or armed forces independence payment).

See *MW v SSWP (ESA)* [2018] UKUT 304 (AAC), confirming that although there is a general entitlement condition that a claimant "is not receiving education" (see Welfare Reform Act 2007, Sch.1, para. 6(1)(g)) this regulation disapplies that requirement to a claimant entitled to PIP, DLA or armed forces independence payment. Moreover, reg.33(2) provides that, for the purposes of income-related ESA, a claimant is to be treated as having limited capability for work where they are (a) not a qualifying young person, (b) receiving education and (c) not subject to Sch.1, para.6(1)(g) in accordance with reg.18.

Note that para.6(1)(g) of Sch.1 does not apply in the case of claimants who had an existing award of income support by virtue of reg.13(2)(b) or (bb) (persons in relevant education who are ill or disabled) of, or paras 10 or 12 (disabled or deaf students) of Sch.1B to, the Income Support Regulations (see the 2015/16 edition of Vol.II in this series for these provisions) and who have been transferred to ESA as a result of a conversion decision under the Employment and Support Allowance (Transitional Provisions, Housing Benefit and Council Tax Benefit) (Existing Awards) (No. 2) Regulations 2010 (SI 2010/1907) (as amended) (see p.1577 for these Regulations). The modifications to s.1(2) of the 2007 Act made by Sch.1, para.2 and Sch.2, para.2 of the 2010 Regulations mean that such claimants will be able to get ESA while in education even if they do not get DLA, PIP or armed forces independence payment.

PART 5

LIMITED CAPABILITY FOR WORK

Determination of limited capability for work

19.—(1) For the purposes of Part 1 of the Act, whether a claimant's capability for work is limited by the claimant's physical or mental condition and, **4.43**

if it is, whether the limitation is such that it is not reasonable to require the claimant to work is to be determined on the basis of a limited capability for work assessment of the claimant in accordance with this Part.

(2) The limited capability for work assessment is an assessment of the extent to which a claimant who has some specific disease or bodily or mental disablement is capable of performing the activities prescribed in Schedule 2 or is incapable by reason of such disease or bodily or mental disablement of performing those activities.

(3) Subject to paragraph (6), for the purposes of Part 1 of the Act a claimant has limited capability for work if, by adding the points listed in column (3) of Schedule 2 against [² each descriptor] listed in that Schedule [² which applies in the claimant's case], the claimant obtains a total score of at least—

    (a) 15 points whether singly or by a combination of descriptors specified in Part 1 of that Schedule;

    (b) 15 points whether singly or by a combination of descriptors specified in Part 2 of that Schedule; or

    (c) 15 points by a combination of descriptors specified in Parts 1 and 2 of that Schedule.

[¹(4) In assessing the extent of a claimant's capability to perform any activity listed in Part 1 of Schedule 2, the claimant is to be assessed as if—

    (a) fitted with or wearing any prosthesis with which the claimant is normally fitted or normally wears; or, as the case may be,

    (b) wearing or using any aid or appliance which is normally, or could reasonably be expected to be, worn or used.

(5) In assessing the extent of a claimant's capability to perform any activity listed in Schedule 2, it is a condition that the claimant's incapability to perform the activity arises—

    (a) in respect of any descriptor listed in Part 1 of Schedule 2, from a specific bodily disease or disablement;

    (b) in respect of any descriptor listed in Part 2 of Schedule 2, from a specific mental illness or disablement; or

    (c) in respect of any descriptor or descriptors listed in—

        (i) Part 1 of Schedule 2, as a direct result of treatment provided by a registered medical practitioner for a specific physical disease or disablement; [² or]

        (ii) Part 2 of Schedule 2, as a direct result of treatment provided by a registered medical practitioner for a specific mental illness or disablement.]

(6) Where more than one descriptor specified for an activity [² applies] to a claimant, only the descriptor with the highest score in respect of each activity which applies is to be counted.

(7) Where a claimant—

    (a) has been determined to have limited capability for work; or

    (b) is to be treated as having limited capability for work under regulations 20, 25, 26, 29 or 33(2),

the Secretary of State may, if paragraph (8) applies, determine afresh whether the claimant has or is to be treated as having limited capability for work.

(8) This paragraph applies where—

    (a) the Secretary of State wishes to determine whether there has been a relevant change of circumstances in relation to the claimant's physical or mental condition;

(b) the Secretary of State wishes to determine whether the previous determination of limited capability for work or that the claimant is to be treated as having limited capability for work, was made in ignorance of, or was based on a mistake as to, some material fact; or

(c) at least 3 months have passed since the date on which the claimant was determined to have limited capability for work or to be treated as having limited capability for work.

AMENDMENTS

1. Employment and Support Allowance (Amendment) Regulations 2012 (SI 2012/3096) reg.3(2) (January 28, 2013, subject to application, transitional and savings provisions in reg.2 of this amending instrument, below, para.9.614).

2. Social Security (Miscellaneous Amendments) (No. 3) Regulations 2013 (SI 2013/2536) reg.13(7) (October 29, 2013).

DEFINITIONS

"claimant"—see WRA 2007 s.24(1).
"descriptor"—see reg.2(1).
"limited capability for work"—see WRA 2007 s.1(4).
"limited capability for work assessment"—see para.(2).

GENERAL NOTE

Entitlement to ESA requires that the claimant has limited capability for work **4.44** (WRA 2007, s.1(3)(a)). Whether his capability for work is limited by his physical or mental condition such that it is not reasonable to require him to work is to be determined in accordance with regulations (WRA 2007 s.8(1)). This regulation, setting out how "actual" limited capability to work is to be determined through the limited capability for work assessment is the product. The remainder of this Part (regs 20–33), deal with situations in which someone, whatever the reality, is to be treated as having limited capability for work, and also with aspects of the decision-making process.

Paragraph (1)

ESA is a benefit designed to help people with a limiting health condition over- **4.45** come barriers, and where appropriate move into work and improve their lives. The Work Capability Assessment (WCA) seeks more accurately to relate to modern context than the IB/IS system, and to focus more on what people can do, rather on what they are unable to do. The matter of whether the claimant's capability for work is limited by his physical or mental condition, and, if so, whether the limitation is to such an extent that it is not reasonable to require him to work, is to be decided on the basis of the "limited capability for work assessment" (WCAt or LCWA). This is the first element in a new three-part "work capability assessment" (WCA), developed out of the review of the IB "personal capability assessment" (PCA), which governs entitlement to the basic allowance and the additional components of ESA. The new WCA underpinning ESA was devised by the DWP's Health Work and Wellbeing Directorate with input from two technical working groups, one focusing on mental health and learning difficulties, the other on physical function and conditions (hereinafter "review group"). The review group consisted of medical and other relevant experts. It examined how the IB Personal Capability Assessment (PCA) (characterized by them as "the best assessment of its type in the world" could nonetheless be improved and updated so as to reflect the many changes since its inception:

"in the prevalence of disabling conditions; in advances in medical science resulting in the availability of new and more effective medical interventions; and in the
workplace environment. The Disability Discrimination Act, introduced after the
PCA had been developed, has influenced the ability of employers to make reasonable adjustments to accommodate people with long term disabilities. It has also
raised the expectations of disabled people that adjustments should be made to
enable them to work."

The three-element WCA is not merely an incapacity-based tool for determining
entitlement to ESA. That remains true of its first element the subject of this regulation. However, its second element is rather a more positive assessment considering
ability to benefit from work-related activity with a view to promoting capacity for
work. The assessment has two aspects: an assessment of limited capability to work
(WCAt) and an assessment of limited capacity to engage in work-related activity
(WRAAt). Both assessments will generally be conducted at the same time. The
WCAt is a more rigorous test than the PCA and far fewer groups are exempted
from it.

Paragraphs (2) and (5)

4.46   This defines the "limited capability for work assessment" (WCAt). Like the IB
"personal capability assessment" (PCA) and its predecessor, the "all work" test, the
ESA WCAt is an assessment of the extent to which someone with a specific disease
or bodily or mental disablement is (despite that) capable of performing the activities set out in Sch.2 or is because of it incapable of performing them. Since the test
is thus so similar to that in IB (see Incapacity for Work Regs, reg.24 and Sch.), the
position taken here is that case authorities (whether Commissioner or court) on the
PCA will also apply to the WCAt. As with the IB PCA, the tasks involved in applying
the WCAt are twofold:

1. ascertaining from all the evidence in the case which descriptors apply (paras
   (2), (5) and Sch.2);
2. computing the scores (paras (3), (6)).

The terms of para.(2) require the incapacity to perform the Sch.2 activities to arise
by reason of "some specific disease or bodily or mental disablement". This is further
stressed in paras (5)(a) and (b), the latter of which specifically also brings in "mental
illness", while para.(5)(c) in effect adds that the rubric will also cover incapability
as a direct result of treatment provided by a registered medical practitioner for such
a disease, illness or disablement. Para.(5) was introduced with effect from January
28, 2013 and was not explicitly subject to the transitional protection afforded by
reg.2 of the amending instrument to claimants who had completed an ESA questionnaire issued to them based on the pre-January 28, 2013 versions of Schs 2 and
3; that reg on its face appeared only to give protection in respect of the changes to
the Schs themselves, effected by reg.5 of the amending instrument, whereas the
para.(5) amendment was effected by reg.3 (see, below, para.9.614). In *FR v SSWP
(ESA)* [2015] UKUT 175 (AAC), however, Judge Ward accepted the Secretary of
State's submission that the tribunal had erred in law in applying the para.(5) "split"
to this claimant who had completed such a questionnaire. Judge Ward interpreted
the Secretary of State's concession "as being that the requirement for the provisions
of Schedule 2 "to continue to apply. . .*as they had effect* immediately before the commencement date" [Judge Ward's emphasis] is sufficient [in a case such as this] to
maintain the pre-2013 position of no physical/mental split as part of how Schedule
2 "had effect"" (para.2). This "specific disease or bodily or mental disablement"
phraseology was found in the sickness/invalidity benefits statutory test and in both
the "own occupation" test and the IB PCA, so decisions on this phraseology from
those regimes will still be authoritative here. In *VT v SSWP (ESA)* [2016] UKUT
241 (AAC) Judge Ward subsequently rejected an attempt by the Secretary of State
to resile from the concession made in *FR v SSWP (ESA)*.

1242

"Specific" means "of a kind identified by medical science" (*CS/57/82*, noted in [1983] J.S.W.L. 306). "Specific" is designed to keep out conditions that may in some ordinary sense be said to be mental illness or disablement but which are not (as yet) recognised, or accounted for, as physical or mental conditions by medical science" (*JG v SSWP (ESA)* [2013] UKUT 37 (AAC); [2013] AACR 23 (a decision of a three judge panel of Upper Tribunal Judges, para.38, citing to similar effect (*R(IB)2/98*, para.7). A "specific mental illness" is a mental disease and also falls within the term "mental disablement" (*JG*, paras 36, 37). "Disease" has been described as "a departure from health capable of identification by its signs and symptoms, an abnormality of some sort", and sickness falls within the definition (*CS/221/49*, para.3; *CS/7/82*, noted in [1983] J.S.W.L. 306). "Disablement"—which may be bodily or mental—constitutes a state of deprivation or incapacitation of ability measured against the abilities of a normal person (*CS/7/82, ibid.*).

In most cases there will be little problem, given the medical evidence, as to whether the claimant's condition amounts to disease or disablement; disagreement will generally centre on whether it prevents him carrying out the activities in Sch.2. However, a number of areas can be identified where difficult lines may have to be drawn on whether or not the condition comes within the rubric "disease or . . . disablement" at all. Pregnancy alone does not, but a disease or disablement associated with, but going beyond the normal incidents of, pregnancy does, as in *CS/221/49* where the certified incapacity, "sickness of pregnancy", was suffered throughout the day. See also *R(S) 4/93*. But note now that certain pregnant women are to be treated as incapable of work (see reg.20(e)). Alcoholism can come within the rubric, but in some circumstances might bring about a period of disqualification from benefit (see reg.157).Whether certain conditions constitute a disease of the mind or a mental disablement can be problematical in that the line between a recognisable mental illness or disablement, on the one hand, and states of malingering or being workshy on the other, can be fine and uncertain. The difficulty is to decide from the available evidence whether the claimant is genuinely ill or disabled and thereby incapacitated for work in the sense understood above, or whether his is a voluntary attitude of work shyness where he could but will not work. The problem will be compounded where the outward symptoms of these alternative states are the same. What will be crucial will be the terms in which the medical (psychiatric) evidence is cast, and the inevitable value judgments about whether a particular claimant's attitudes to doing work are voluntary or involuntary. Perhaps here the appellate authorities' jurisdiction to seek further medical (in this case psychiatric) reports at public expense could prove valuable. In *R(S) 6/59*, the Commissioner considered a particular case of Munchausen's syndrome, under which condition a person repeatedly presents himself for treatment to a hospital or series of hospitals recounting symptoms of a particular disease or disability from which he is not in fact suffering, which the Commissioner there described as a strange condition in the nature of malingering. The Commissioner in that case was not satisfied on the evidence that the claimant believed the symptoms actually to exist, and felt unable to regard the condition as a psychosis, which would have come within the statutory rubric. The claim for benefit failed, the Commissioner stating as an additional ground for the decision his view that the syndrome in any event did not affect that particular claimant's capacity to work since he had driven from hospital to hospital in his lorry. In effect, the condition was treated as a defect of character. In *CS/1/81* (noted in [1982] J.S.W.L. 48), the dispute initially centred on whether the claimant, suffering from what the RMO (now a DWP MS doctor) and his own doctor described as an anxiety state, was as a result incapable of work. The consultant psychiatrist to whom the claimant was referred considered him an inadequate personality by reason of his total self-indulgence and extreme degree of sheltering behind psychiatric symptoms to avoid responsibility. His condition resulted from a dismal personality structure rather than illness. Accordingly the Commissioner held that he was incapable of work but not by reason of disease or disablement, so the claim failed. Mesher (now

Commissioner Mesher) suggests in [1982] J.S.W.L. 48 that the Commissioner there gave inadequate consideration to whether the defect (clearly on the evidence not an illness) could nevertheless be a mental disablement. In contrast, *CS 7/82* (noted in [1983] J.S.W.L. 306) dealt with a situation in which the claimant was said to have a severe personality disorder but not to be mentally ill. "Personality disorder" is a term sometimes used as a euphemism for workshy. The Commissioner held that its use in the particular case conveyed a notion of disability of mind sufficient to bring the claimant within the statutory rubric. It is submitted that one should avoid using euphemisms which may confuse; the loser in the case is entitled to know why he has lost. If he is thought workshy, that should be stated and reasons given for that conclusion. Sheltering behind euphemisms may also cloud the steps in reasoning which go towards good adjudication and decision-making.

In *DMcK v SSWP (ESA)* [2014] UKUT 45 (AAC), having allowed the appeal on other grounds, Judge Wikeley went on to consider the fact that the tribunal had found that the appellant had exhibited "illness behaviour" so that it did not find credible the level of her claimed physical disabilities. Judge Wikeley gave some guidance for the new tribunal to which the case was remitted. He thought it unclear whether the tribunal's rejection of the claimant's appeal "was indeed a recognition that she was displaying genuine but abnormal responses or whether it was a polite way of suggesting that she was malingering" (para.18). Citing para.43(ii) of the panel of three Upper Tribunal Judges in *JG*, below, an adjournment would have enabled the claimant to deal with a new point not taken by the Secretary of State, namely whether she had a recognized disease or disablement. On "illness behaviour" itself, Judge Wikeley referred the new tribunal to two unreported cases, one from the industrial injuries area, the other on incapacity benefit. In *CSI/1180/2001*, Commissioner (now Judge) Parker observed

> "The new tribunal, if it considers that there is an insufficient organic basis for all of the claimant's problems, must decide if he is consciously exaggerating or if he is genuine and his complaints form part of an abnormal illness behaviour linked to his accident. In the latter situation, it can form part of the relevant loss of faculty. The courts have long recognised there can be compensation for an unconscious reaction to physical injury sustained, provided the latter remains a material cause of the former" (para.8).

In *CIB/4841/2002*, Commissioner (now Judge) Jacobs gave this guidance:

> "10. The Secretary of State's medical advice, which I accept, is in summary this. Abnormal illness behaviour is one of a number of terms used to describe symptoms which are caused by the influence of psychological makeup and social environment on the perception of the disabling effects of a medical condition. This phenomenon is reflected by more modern approaches to treatment, which address the psychosocial as well as the medical factors. The symptoms are subjective in the sense that they depend on an experience of pain or fatigue. In order to distinguish between claimants who genuinely experience a particular disability from those who merely claim to do so, it is helpful to consider the history of their daily activity and unobtrusive observations. This can identify consistency or inconsistency.
> 11. In this case, the examining doctor detected resistance on examination and exaggeration of response to the testing of the reflexes. The claimant was also observed to walk normally and to be able to stand erect, albeit briefly. The claimant's performance on examination and the observations recorded by the doctor are not consistent with a genuine experience of illness behaviour. This was confirmed by the tribunal, who observed the claimant to walk differently at the beginning and end of the hearing. All of this was in conflict with the Surgeon's evidence, which accepted that the claimant was genuinely experiencing the symptoms he exhibited. In view of the actual observations of the examining doctor and the tribunal, the Surgeon's opinion could obviously not be accepted."

What has to be established, to what standard of proof, and by what evidence, is **4.47**
analysed well by Commissioner Jacobs in *CIB/26/2004*. There must be established,
on the civil standard of balance of probabilities, that the claimant has a recognised
medical condition (paras 18, 25, citing *R2/99 (IB)*, para.8; *CSDLA/552/2001*,
para.27; and *CDLA/944/2001*, paras 9 and 10). A medical diagnosis is useful evidence, but is not decisive in that an appeal tribunal, giving appropriate reasons,
can refuse to accept it. The cogency of a diagnosis varies according to a number
of factors: the nature of the condition (some being easier to diagnose than others);
how well qualified in the relevant area of medicine the doctor is who makes the
diagnosis; the range of information and material on which the diagnosis is based;
and the degree of certainty with which it is made (e.g. is the diagnosis "firm", or
qualified as "working", "presumptive" or "provisional") (para.22). If there is general
consensus among medical authorities as to the existence of a particular condition, a
tribunal (even one containing a medical member) will normally err in law if, being
sceptical, it denies its existence (para.21, citing a Northern Ireland Tribunal of
Commissioners in *C38/03–04 (DLA)*, para.20(3)). If a medical diagnosis is not necessarily decisive, nor is the lack of one necessarily fatal; in appropriate circumstances
a tribunal can make a diagnosis without medical evidence (para.19). While agreeing to some extent with Commissioner Brown's view *(R 2/99 (IB)*, para.11) that a
tribunal should be cautious of making a diagnosis of mental disease or disablement
in the absence of supportive medical evidence, Commissioner Jacobs qualified that
by noting that at the time of that decision there was no medical member on the
tribunal—it merely then had advice from an assessor—that change in composition
rendering it easier now for a tribunal to make a diagnosis on the evidence available
(para.20).

In *AD v SSWP (ESA)* [2011] UKUT 307 (AAC), Judge Levenson considered
a case where the First-tier tribunal had upheld a decision that the claimant did not
have limited capability for work on the basis that the claimant's abuse of alcohol and
drugs were "a lifestyle choice" rather than coming about because of a specific physical or mental illness or disability. He held that it had erred in law. Alcohol or drug
dependence, whether for DLA, incapacity benefit or ESA, constitutes a "mental
condition". That was decided as regards DLA by a tribunal of Commissioners in *R
(DLA) 6/06 (T)* and correctly applied to incapacity benefit by Commissioner Jacobs
in *CIB/1296/2007*. Judge Levenson thought mistaken Judge May's decision in *RA
v SSWP (ESA)* [2010] UKUT 301 (AAC) to disapprove Commissioner Jacob's
decision on incapacity benefit and to seek there to confine *R (DLA) 6/06(T)* to the
effects of the wording in ss.72 and 73 of the SSCBA 1992. In *RA*, Judge May stated
that a "mental condition" is not necessarily the same as "specific disease or bodily
or mental disablement" (para.13), but had already held that the claimant could not
succeed under Activity 11 of the original ESA Regs, Sch.2 because that required a
link to a *physical* disease or disablement.

In *JG v SSWP (ESA)* [2013] UKUT 37 (AAC); [2013] AACR 23 a three judge
panel of Upper Tribunal Judges held that Parliament clearly intended that alcohol
dependency falls within the phrase "specific disease or bodily or mental disablement". Were that not so, WRA 2007 s.15A and Sch.1A would have nothing to bite
on. WRA 2007 s.18 and ESA Regs reg.157 on disqualification indicate that self-
induced or self-inflicted physical or mental conditions can still amount to a "specific disease or bodily or mental disablement" (paras 18–20). Moreover, the three
judge panel held that the summary of the expert evidence on alcohol dependence
in *R(DLA)6/06*, itself a decision of a tribunal of Commissioners, "can and should
be adopted by decision makers and tribunals in ESA cases as representing the currently accepted and mainstream medical view in respect of alcohol dependence"
(para.47). That expert evidence is summarised in paras 16–19 of *R(DLA)6/)06*
and set out in para.44 of *JG v* SSWP *(ESA)*. The three judge panel thus disapproved Judge May's rejection of this approach in *RA v SSWP (ESA)*, above, and
saw nothing wrong with Judge Jacobs's direction in *CIB/1296/2007* that alcohol
dependence was a mental condition rather than a physical one. See further, on drug

dependency, *SD v SSWP (ESA)* [2016] UKUT 100 (AAC); [2016] AACR 35, discussed in the ESA commentary.

The current version of para.(5) entered into force on January 28, 2013, subject to application, transitional and savings provisions in reg.2 of the amending instrument (see, below, para.9.614). It brings in the requirement—familiar from the IB regime—that Pt 1 of Sch.2 must be linked to incapacity arising from a specific bodily disease or disablement or as a direct result of treatment provided by a registered medical practitioner for such a disease or disablement. Similarly it introduces the requirement that Pt 2 of Sch.2 must be linked to incapacity arising from a specific mental illness or disablement or as a direct result of treatment provided by a registered medical practitioner for such an illness or disablement. Commenting on the new wording, Judge Rowland in *MC v SSWP (ESA)* [2015] UKUT 646 (AAC) has observed as follows:

> "the correct approach, best giving effect to the purpose behind the legislation – is that the claimant's "specific mental illness or disablement" had to be an *effective* cause of her inability to go out unaccompanied. That is not the same as being the root cause or the primary cause. In my judgement, where a specific mental illness or disablement would not by itself have been sufficiently serious to enable a claimant to satisfy a descriptor, it is enough for the purposes of regulation 19(5)(b) that it has made the difference between the claimant being able to satisfy a descriptor and not being able to do so even though there may have been another, perhaps more important, cause" (at para.9).

Under the previous wording of the paragraph (still applicable to some cases after January 28, 2013—see reg.2 of the amending instrument, below, para.9.614), there was no such link (*JG v SSWP (ESA)* [2013] UKUT 37 (AAC); [2013] AACR 23 (a decision of a three judge panel of Upper Tribunal Judges, disapproving Judge May's decision in *RA v SSWP*, above, which should not be followed on this issue); *KP v SSWP (ESA)* [2011] UKUT 216 (AAC); *KN v SSWP (ESA)* [2011] UKUT 229 (AAC); *RM v SSWP (ESA)* [2011] UKUT 454 (AAC); *AH v SSWP (ESA)* [2011] UKUT 333 (AAC)).

See also *NC v SSWP (ESA)* [2016] UKUT 401 (AAC) (Judge Gray) for confirmation that the term 'mental illness or disablement' in reg.19(5)(b) as amended "encompasses not merely mental ill-health in the form of conditions such as depression or schizophrenia but mental disablement of all kinds, for example learning difficulties and cognitive deficiency whether that be by reason of age or acquired brain injury" (at para.13).

Paragraph (4)

4.48 The current version of para.(4) entered into force on January 28, 2013, subject to application, transitional and savings provisions in reg.2 of the amending instrument (see, below, para.9.614). In *RP v SSWP* (ESA) [2011] UKUT 449 (AAC), Judge Levenson had thought the approach now embodied in sub-para.(b) was implicit in the previous wording. In addition, however, he thought that there had to be some "explanation of how the aid or appliance could help the particular claimant . . ..The degree of detail is a matter for the tribunal on the facts of each particular case, but in my view, in the absence of actual use or prescription, there does need to be some explanation" (para.16). See also *TM v SSWP (ESA)* [2018] UKUT 9 (AAC), where Judge Wikeley accepted a concession by the Secretary of State that reg.19(4) limits consideration of aids and appliances to the *physical health* descriptors in Part 1 of Sch.2. and so in the context of activity 15 (getting about) the FTT should not have considered the claimant's ability to navigate by a mobile phone app.

Paragraphs (3) and (6)

4.49 *Computing the scores:* Achievement of a particular score is required before the claimant can be found to have limited capability for work. Under ESA, the scoring system is simpler. The score attained must be at least 15 points whether from Sch.2, Pt 1 alone (physical disabilities), Pt 2 alone (mental, cognitive and intellectual function assessment), or from a combination of the descriptors in both parts. In each case, where more than one descriptor for an activity applies, only the highest scoring one counts (para.(6)). Following the approach to the IB PCA), it is submitted that there are no implied limits on simply adding together the highest scores from each activity (*R(IB) 3/98*).

Paragraphs (7), (8)
These make clear that the matters of whether someone actually has limited capability for work, or whether he is to be treated as having it under regs 20, 25, 26, 29 or 33(2), are ones that can be revisited where one or more of the situations in para. (8) arise: **4.50**

a desire to determine whether there has been a relevant change of circumstances in relation to the claimant's health condition (is he getting better or worse?) (sub-para.(a));

● a wish to determine whether the prior determination of actual or deemed limited capability was made in ignorance of, or was based on a mistake as to, a material fact (sub-para.(b));

● at least three months have elapsed since the previous decision on actual or deemed limited capability (sub-para.(c)).

Certain claimants to be treated as having limited capability for work

20.—[²(1)] A claimant is to be treated as having limited capability for work if—   **4.51**
(a) the claimant is terminally ill;
(b) the claimant is—
    (i) receiving treatment for cancer by way of chemotherapy or radiotherapy;
    (ii) likely to receive such treatment within six months after the date of the determination of capability for work; or
    (iii) recovering from such treatment,
and the Secretary of State is satisfied that the claimant should be treated as having limited capability for work];
(c) the claimant is—
    (i) excluded or abstains from work [²...] pursuant to a request or notice in writing lawfully made [²or given] under an enactment; or
    (ii) otherwise prevented from working pursuant to an enactment, by reason of it being known or reasonably suspected that the claimant is infected or contaminated by, or has been in contact with a case of, a relevant infection or contamination;
(d) in the case of a pregnant woman, there is a serious risk of damage to her health or to the health of her unborn child if she does not refrain from work;
(e) in the case of a pregnant woman, she—
    (i) is within the maternity allowance period [²(which has the meaning it has in [³ . . .] the Contributions and Benefits Act)]; and
    (ii) is entitled to a maternity allowance under [³section 35(1) or 35B(1)] of the Contributions and Benefits Act;

(f) in the case of a pregnant woman whose expected or actual date of confinement has been certified in accordance with the Medical Evidence Regulations, on any day in the period—

    (i) beginning with the first date of the 6th week before the expected week of her confinement or the actual date of her confinement, whichever is earlier; and

    (ii) ending on the 14th day after the actual date of her confinement,

if she would have no entitlement to a maternity allowance or statutory maternity pay were she to make a claim in respect of that period.

(g) [²the claimant meets] [¹any of the descriptors at paragraph 15 or 16 of Schedule 3] [²in accordance with regulation 34(2), (3) and (6) where applicable].

[²(2) In this regulation, "relevant infection or contamination" means—

(a) in England and Wales—

    (i) any incidence or spread of infection or contamination, within the meaning of section 45A(3) of the Public Health (Control of Disease) Act 1984 in respect of which regulations are made under Part 2A of that Act (public health protection) for the purpose of preventing, protecting against, controlling or providing a public health response to, such incidence or spread; or

    (ii) tuberculosis or any infectious disease to which regulation 9 of the Public Health (Aircraft) Regulations 1979 (powers in respect of persons leaving aircraft) applies or to which regulation 10 of the Public Health (Ships) Regulations 1979 (powers in respect of certain persons on ships) applies; and

(b) in Scotland, any—

    (i) infectious disease within the meaning of section 1(5) of the Public Health etc (Scotland) Act 2008, or exposure to an organism causing that disease; or

    (ii) contamination within the meaning of section 1(5) of that Act, or exposure to a contaminant,

to which sections 56 to 58 of that Act (compensation) apply.]

AMENDMENTS

1. Employment and Support Allowance (Limited Capability for Work and Limited Capability for Work-Related Activity) (Amendment) Regulations 2011 (SI 2011/228) reg.3(2) (March 28, 2011).

2. Social Security (Miscellaneous Amendments) (No. 3) Regulations 2013 (SI 2013/2536) reg.13(8) (October 29, 2013).

3. Social Security (Maternity Allowance) (Miscellaneous Amendments) Regulations 2014/884 reg.5(3) (May 18, 2014).

DEFINITIONS

"claimant"—see WRA 2007 s.24(1).
"confinement"—see reg.2(1).
"Contributions and Benefits Act"—see WRA 2007 s.65.
"limited capability for work"—see WRA 2007 s.1(4).
"maternity allowance period"—see para. (1)(e)(i).
"Medical Evidence Regulations"—see reg.2(1).
"relevant infection or contamination"—see para. (2).
"terminally ill"—see reg.2(1).
"week"—see reg.2(1).

GENERAL NOTE

This regulation—the parent power for which is WRA 2007 s.22 and Sch.2,   4.52
para.9—sets out the situations in which a claimant is to be treated as having
limited capability for work. This is important because such claimants will be
exempt from the WCA and its information gathering processes (see reg.21). Those
exempt are:

- the terminally ill (para.(1)(a))—"suffering from a progressive disease and
  death in consequence of that disease can reasonably be expected within 6
  months" (reg.2(1));

- provided that the Secretary of State is satisfied that the claimant should be
  treated as having limited capability for work (note the discretion), the claimant is receiving treatment for cancer by way of chemotherapy or radiotherapy;
  likely to receive such treatment within six months from the date of the determination of capability for work; or recovering from such treatment (para.(1)(b));

- those excluded or prevented from working by reason of it being known or
  reasonably suspected that the claimant is infected or contaminated by, or has
  been in contact with a case of, a relevant infection or contamination covered
  by a variety of public health enactments) (paras (1)(c), (2));

- pregnant women where there is a serious risk of damage to their or their
  unborn child's health if they do not refrain from work (para.(1)(d));

- pregnant women at a certain stage in pregnancy (paras (1)(e), (f)). Paragraph
  (1)(e) covers the pregnant woman during the maternity allowance period
  (see reg.2(1) and SSCBA 1992, s.35(2)) entitled to a maternity allowance
  under SSCBA 1992, s.35. Para.(1)(f) in contrast deals with the pregnant
  woman whose expected or actual date of confinement has been duly certified
  in accordance with the Medical Evidence Regulations. It covers her during a
  period beginning with the earlier of the actual date of confinement or the first
  day of the sixth week before the expected week of confinement and ending on
  the 14th day after the actual date of confinement. But it does so only where she
  would not be entitled to maternity allowance or SMP if she were to claim in
  respect of that period.

- in accordance with reg.34(2), (3) and (6), where applicable, those to whom
  there applies any of the descriptors in para.15 or 16 of Sch.2 operable from
  that date (para.(1)(g)).

*Paragraph (1)(b): "recovering" from treatment for cancer by way of chemotherapy or
    radiotherapy*

In *W Da-C v SSWP (ESA)* [2015] UKUT 158 (AAC), Judge Markus considered   4.53
that, since "recovering" was not defined in the legislation, it had to bear its ordinary
meaning. She had no doubt

> "that, when used in a health context, "recovering" refers to a process of getting
> better. It may not result in a person's condition reverting to the way it was before
> the treatment in question, but it denotes a process of some improvement or, at the
> very least, hoped-for improvement. Thus the Shorter Oxford English Dictionary
> defines the word, in so far as it relates to health, as "restoration or return to health
> from sickness". At some stage a person will cease to recover. This may occur when
> they are completely better. Or it may occur when they have reached a point when
> no further recovery will take place" (para.12).

Looking at the wider legislative context confirmed her view that this was "the only
sensible way" in which the term could be understood; other ESA Regulations (e.g.
regs 25, 26) suggested a period of recovery was time-limited. Moreover, interpret-

ing para.(1)(b) to be without limit of time would jar with the underlying policy with respect to ESA that it should not simply be assumed that someone with a significant health condition or disability must be incapable of work.

The case concerned recovery from radiotherapy. Judge Markus accepted the Secretary of State's argument that

> "the normal recovery period following the immediate side effects of radiotherapy is up to six months and that the evidence in this case indicates that after six months the appellant had [completely] recovered from the short term effects of radiotherapy . . . [so] that where the long-term effects of radiotherapy are chronic it cannot be said that the appellant is recovering. The treatment has caused a separate health condition from which she has not recovered" (para.10).

In essence in this case, since there was no prospect of recovery, the claimant could not be said to be "recovering" (para.16).

Information required for determining capability for work

4.54 **21.**—(1) Subject to paragraphs (2) and (3), the information or evidence required to determine whether a claimant has limited capability for work is—

(a) evidence of limited capability for work in accordance with the Medical Evidence Regulations (which prescribe the form of doctor's statement or other evidence required in each case);

(b) any information relating to a claimant's capability to perform the activities referred to in Schedule 2 as may be requested in the form of a questionnaire; and

(c) any such additional information as may be requested.

(2) Where the Secretary of State is satisfied that there is sufficient information to determine whether a claimant has limited capability for work without the information specified in paragraph (1)(b), that information [¹ must] not be required for the purposes of making the determination.

(3) Paragraph (1) does not apply in relation to a determination whether a claimant is to be treated as having limited capability for work under any of regulations 20 (certain claimants to be treated as having limited capability for work), 25 (hospital in-patients), 26 (claimants receiving certain regular treatment) and 33(2) (additional circumstances in which a claimant is to be treated as having limited capability for work).

AMENDMENT

1. Social Security (Miscellaneous Amendments) (No.3) Regulations 2013 (SI 2013/2536) reg.13(9) (October 29, 2013).

DEFINITIONS

"claimant"—see WRA 2007 s.24(1).
"doctor"—see reg.2(1).
"limited capability for work"—see WRA 2007 s.1(4).
"Medical Evidence Regulations"—see reg.2(1).

GENERAL NOTE

4.55 This regulation deals with the information required for determining whether someone has limited capability for work. It is designed to give the decision-maker sufficient information to decide that matter for himself (the minority of cases), or whether to seek advice from a health care professional on the basis of the papers in respect of that decision, or to refer the claimant for a face to face WCAt, including a medical examination (see reg.23).

Unless para.(3) operates, the claimant will have to supply: (i) evidence of his incapacity for work in accordance with the Medical Evidence Regs (para.(1)(a)); and (ii) such additional information relating to the relevant test as the Secretary of State asks for (para.(1)(c)). Furthermore, he must generally complete and return the appropriate questionnaire (para.(1)(b)), unless para.(3) operates or the Secretary of State decides that completion of the questionnaire is not necessary because without it he has sufficient information to determine whether the claimant does or does not have limited capability for work (para.(2)). Note that where the claimant is requested by the Secretary of State to complete and return the question-naire, failure to do so can result in his being treated as capable of work (and thus not entitled to ESA) (reg.22).

The impact on claimants with mental health problems (MHP) of the information collecting and assessment process originally administered by Atos Healthcare, the medical services provider for the DWP (although Atos was subsequently replaced by MAXIMUS Health and Human Services Ltd from March 2015) was the subject of challenge by way of the Upper Tribunal's judicial review jurisdiction, as constituting disability discrimination under the Equality Act 2010. The decision of a three judge tribunal in favour of the applicants in *MM & DM v SSWP* [2013] UKUT 259 (AAC) was appealed to the Court of Appeal by the Secretary of State.

On December 4, 2013, that Court rejected the appeal as to several matters and upheld it as to another in *Secretary of State for Work and Pensions v The Queen on the application of MM and DM (as respondents) and MIND, the National Autistic Society, Rethink Mental Illness and the Equality and Human Rights Commission (as interveners)* [2013] EWCA Civ 1565; [2016] AACR 11. The Court held that the Upper Tribunal was correct in holding that it had jurisdiction to deal with the matter of discrimination contrary to the Equality Act 2010 by way of judicial review, and that the applicants and the interveners had the requisite standing to maintain the application for judicial review. The Court also found that the Upper Tribunal's declaration that the infor-mation and examination process caused substantial disadvantage to claimants with mental health problems (and was thus discriminatory) was not erroneous in law nor, in the light of the evidence, was it perverse or irrational. However, the Court held that the Upper Tribunal had misunderstood the scope of its powers and should not have directed the Secretary of State to carry out an investigation or assessment within a specified time to see how the "Evidence Seeking Recommendation" (see below) could be implemented. Rather it was for the applicants to advance a reasonable adjustment proposal, leaving "the Secretary of State to adduce such evidence and advance such arguments as he thinks appropriate in order to discharge the burden now falling on him" of showing that such adjustment cannot reasonably be made (para.83).

The "Evidence Seeking Recommendation" was a less rigorous one than the pro-posal that in every case involving a mental health patient the decision-maker should always be required to seek further medical evidence (FME) before a decision was reached thus in many cases obviating the need for the ESA50 questionnaire and/or the face to face interview, both of which substantially disadvantaged mental health patients. The Upper Tribunal had rejected that as unduly onerous. Instead, the "Evidence Seeking Recommendation", seen by the Upper Tribunal as a prima facie "reasonable adjustment", proposes that "the decision-maker should at least be required to consider obtaining FME in the case of MHP claimants and if FME was not sought, should explain why it was thought to be unnecessary" (para.2).

It should be noted that the need for this change was also supported as part of the independent review undertaken by Professor Harrington (see para.40 of his third report, cited in para.21 of the Court of Appeal judgment).

The judicial review challenge then returned to the Upper Tribunal for a renewed hearing on remedies (*R (MM and DM) v SSWP* [2015] UKUT 107 (AAC); [2016] AACR 11). The three judge panel disallowed the applications, holding that it was clear from the Court of Appeal's decision that ss.20 and 21 of the Equality Act created a two stage approach to determining whether an individual applicant could establish discrimination, namely: (i) has there been a failure to comply with a duty to make reasonable adjustments; and (ii) has the individual applicant shown a failure to comply with that duty in relation him or her. At the second stage, the individual applicant has to show that he or she was put at such a disadvantage by the failure to comply with the duty to make reasonable adjustments (paragraphs 49 and 51). The Upper Tribunal ruled that the individual applicants could not show that the alleged failure of the Secretary of State to comply with his anticipatory duty by making the adjustments said to be reasonable had caused (or indeed was causing or would cause) them any substantial disadvantage or had, was or would subject them to any detriment that caused them an unreasonably adverse experience. This was fatal to the applicants' claims for judicial review (para.58). Thus, despite proceeding on the assumption that the Secretary of State had failed to establish that the adjustments suggested by the applicants were not reasonable, the applicants had failed to establish that there had been an individual breach, and so discrimination, as required by s.21(2) of the Equality Act 2010 (paragraphs 60 to 62, 78 and 90).

Following the Upper Tribunal decision, the Secretary of State subsequently issued new guidance in the form of Memo DMG 13/17 about the circumstances in which further medical evidence (FME) for assessing limited capability for work should be obtained. This circular states that additional medical evidence should be gathered at the scrutiny (or "filework") stage "where the HCP considers that further information would be helpful to the assessing HCP and Decision Maker. This is FME to inform the assessment." It adds that "there MUST be a reasonable expectation that the FME would assist the assessing HCP and subsequently the Decision Maker."

Failure to provide information in relation to limited capability for work

4.56   **22.**—(1) Where a claimant fails without good cause to comply with the request referred to in regulation 21(1)(b), that claimant is, subject to paragraph (2), to be treated as not having limited capability for work.

(2) Paragraph (1) does not apply unless—
(a) [²(a) the claimant was sent a further request at least three weeks after the date of the first request;]
(b) [². . .] at least [¹1 week has] passed since the further request was sent.

AMENDMENT

1. Social Security (Miscellaneous Amendments) (No.3) Regulations 2011 (SI 2011/2425) reg.23(5), (6) (October 31, 2011).
2. Social Security (Miscellaneous Amendments) (No.3) Regulations 2013 (SI 2013/2536) reg.13(10) (October 29, 2013).

DEFINITIONS

"claimant"—see WRA 2007 s.24(1).
"limited capability for work"—see WRA 2007 s.1(4).
"week"—see reg.2(1)

GENERAL NOTE

4.57   If a claimant fails without good cause (on which more, below) to comply with the requirement to complete and return a limited capability for work questionnaire, he must be treated as not having limited capability for work, that is, as having no entitlement to ESA. This can only happen, however, if a further request for information was sent at least three weeks after the first and at least one week has gone by since the second request was sent. Commissioners' decisions on IB establish that as regards calculating a period before the end of which something cannot be done (e.g. "at least six weeks have passed"—para.(2)(a)), one must ignore the day from which the period runs as well as the day on which it expires (per Commissioner Jacobs in *R(IB) 1/00)*. "Week" here means any period of seven days (reg.2(1)). But note that the para refers, like the IB provision, to a request being "sent" rather than "received" (as stressed by Commissioner Rowland in *CIB/3512/1998)*. Non-receipt has, however, an important bearing on "good cause". "Good cause" is not exhaustively defined in legislation, although reg.24 non-exhaustively prescribes certain matters which must be taken into account in determining the issue. Some guidance may be found in authorities on the corresponding area in unemployment benefit (see USI Regs regs 7(1)(i), (j)—see pp.720–21 of Bonner, Hooker and White, *Non Means Tested Benefits: The Legislation* (1996)), the matter of relief from disqualification from sickness and invalidity benefit under the now revoked USI Regs reg.17 (see pp.737–740 of the 1994 edition of *Non Means Tested Benefits, The Legislation)*, and that from disqualification/being treated as incapable under Incapacity for Work Regs reg.18 or, in time, reg.157 of these ESA Regs.

Determining when a request/reminder was "sent"   **4.58**
In *CT* v *SSWP (ESA)* [2013] UKUT 414 (AAC), Judge Mark (following his decision in *CIB/4012/2004)* stressed the need for very careful appraisal of the evidence to determine exactly when requests and reminders were sent and their exact nature. However, it appears that elsewhere in this decision Judge Mark arguably set the bar too high for the Secretary of State and those acting on his behalf. Three other Upper Tribunal decisions have adopted a rather more pragmatic approach to the evidential requirements imposed on the Secretary of State. In *AL v SSWP (ESA)* [2011] UKUT 512 (AAC), Judge May QC held that a tribunal was entitled to make a finding that an appointment letter had been sent on the basis of a computer generated letter history log. In particular, he accepted (at para.27) the Secretary of State's submission that the fact that the word "triggered" was used in the log did not mean it was uncertain whether that letter was actually posted. Similarly, in *SH v SSWP (ESA)* [2014] UKUT 574 (AAC), Judge Ward expressed the view that "printouts of the type in issue are capable of providing evidence from which a tribunal may draw inferences that a document was 'sent'. It is then for the tribunal of fact to decide what weight to put on it" (at para.36). Both those decisions were approved and followed by Judge Wright in *DW v SSWP (ESA)* [2016] UKUT 179 (AAC), a decision which contains a useful review of the authorities.

Claimant may be called for a medical examination to determine whether the claimant has limited capability for work

23.—(1) Where it falls to be determined whether a claimant has limited   **4.59**
capability for work, that claimant may be called by or on behalf of a health care professional approved by the Secretary of State to attend for a medical examination [²in person, by telephone or by video].

(2) Subject to paragraph (3), where a claimant fails without good cause to attend for or to submit to an examination [¹mentioned] in paragraph (1), the claimant is to be treated as not having limited capability for work.

[¹(3) Paragraph (2) does not apply unless—
(a) written notice of the date, time and place for the examination was sent to the claimant at least seven days in advance; or
(b) that claimant agreed to accept a shorter period of notice whether given in writing or otherwise.]

AMENDMENTS

1. Social Security (Miscellaneous Amendments) (No.3) Regulations 2013 (SI 2013/2536) reg.13(11) (October 29, 2013).

2. Social Security (Claims and Payments, Employment and Support Allowance, Personal Independence Payment and Universal Credit) (Telephone and Video Assessment) (Amendment) Regulations 2021 (SI 2021/230) reg.3(2) (March 25, 2021).

DEFINITIONS

> "claimant"—see WRA 2007 s.24(1).
> "health care professional"—see reg.2(1).
> "limited capability for work"—see WRA 2007 s.1(4).

GENERAL NOTE

Introduction

4.60   This regulation enables the DWP to have a claimant medically examined by a health care professional (technically any health service professional approved by the Secretary of State) when a question arises as to the claimant's capability for work (see para.(1)). Failure without good cause to attend for or submit to such an examination (see para.(2)), of which he was given proper written notice (see para.(3)), will result in the claimant being treated as not having limited capability for work and not entitled to ESA.

An appeal against a decision under reg.23 is heard by a judge sitting alone: *CH v SSWP (ESA)* [2017] UKUT 6 (AAC). See also the annotation to regulation 21, above, on the judicial review challenge under the Equality Act 2010 with regard to the system of medical examinations and its impact on those with mental health problems.

Para.(1)

4.61   Paragraph (1) vests the Secretary of State with a discretion – where a question as to limited capability for work arises, a claimant "*may* be called ... to attend for a medical examination" (emphasis added). In principle, and probably only in exceptional cases, if it was unreasonable of the Secretary of State to arrange a medical examination, the claimant can argue that he had good cause for refusing to submit to it (*CIB/2645/99*; *CIB/2011/2001*, para.16). But since, as Commissioner Rowland stressed, "the integrity of the system depends upon their being appropriate tests in place" (*CIB/2011/2001*, para.16), establishing unreasonableness in that context is unlikely to be easy.

Para.(2)
"where a claimant fails..."

4.62   The question of what is meant by the phrase "where a claimant *fails*..." (emphasis added) was examined by Judge Poynter in *PPE v SSWP (ESA)* [2020] UKUT 59 (AAC), where he held (at para.56) that "regulation 23(2) does not permit the Secretary of State to treat a claimant as not having limited capability for work unless: (a) she was under a legal obligation to attend for and submit to a medical examination; (b) in breach of that obligation she did not do so; and (c) she did not have good cause for her breach of that obligation." Moreover, there was "a clear line of authority in the case law of the Social Security Commissioners, the Upper Tribunal and the higher courts that, before the Secretary of State can subject a claimant to adverse consequences for failing to do something—whether that something is to provide information, notify a change of circumstances, or to attend a specified place and undertake a specified activity—she must tell the claimant in the most unambiguous terms: (a) that it must be done; and (b) what it is that must be done. In short, there needs to be "the language of clear and unambiguous mandatory requirement" and there needs to be "crystal clarity" (para.57). Judge Poynter accordingly concluded as follows:

> "76. If the Secretary of State has the power to impose a legal obligation on claimants to do something, she can impose that obligation on a particular claimant

simply by telling that claimant unambiguously that she must do it.

77. However, the Secretary of State must use "the language of clear and unambiguous mandatory requirement". No legal obligation is imposed if either:

(a) the Secretary of State merely invites, advises, or encourages the claimant to do the thing, as opposed to telling her she must do it; or

(b) it is unclear whether the Secretary of State has told the claimant that she must do the thing, as opposed to merely inviting, advising, or encouraging her to do it.

78. Moreover, the requirement to use "clear and unambiguous language" is to be applied strictly. The Secretary of State must be "crystal clear"."

On the evidence in that case, there were only two sentences that "could even arguably be read as imposing a legal obligation on the claimant to attend the examination rather than merely inviting her to do so". One was the statement that "It is very important you go to your assessment on [date]." The other was that "**You could lose your ESA payments and/or National Insurance credits if you don't go to your Work Capability Assessment**" (original emphasis) (at paras 92-95). Judge Poynter concluded that "the wording of the standard letter that was sent to the claimant did not include anything that unambiguously expressed the element of compulsion to that was necessary to impose a legal requirement on the claimant to attend the medical examination" (at para.100). It followed that the claimant "did not fail to attend for examination because she was never under any legal obligation to do so" (para.124). In terms of the proper approach in such appeals, Judge Poynter held that tribunals should "allow the appeal and reinstate the claimant's benefit unless both: (a) the papers before it include either: (i) a copy of the letter that was sent to the claimant calling him or her for examination; or (ii) a specimen of the standard letter that would have been sent and evidence from the relevant computer system that a letter in that form was generated and despatched; and (b) that letter imposes a legal obligation on the claimant to attend for the examination, as opposed to merely inviting, advising, or encouraging her to do so" (at para.6).

"without good cause"

The notion of "good cause" (see also reg.24) will necessarily be fact and context-specific, as reinforced by Judge Church in *SA v SSWP (ESA)* [2019] UKUT 118 (AAC). There the claimant, who had epilepsy, had a seizure on the day of his appointment and did not attend. The DWP argued that, having also missed previous appointments due to seizures, the claimant should have anticipated the possibility that he might have a seizure on the day and should therefore have requested a home visit. Judge Church held that the FTT's findings that the claimant did not act reasonably when he failed to ask in advance for a home visit, and that his state of health at the relevant time did not amount to good cause for his failure to attend, fell outside the range of reasonable decisions open to it on the facts. See also *JS v SSWP (ESA)* [2019] UKUT 303 (AAC) on the significance to be attached to previously missed appointments (see note to reg.24).

Several decisions have involved cases which have involved some form of 'stand-off' between the claimant and the HCP. If a claimant makes it clear that he or she will not be medically examined, then that arguably constitutes failure to "submit to" an examination. Going to the medical examination but refusing to be examined, constitutes attendance but also a failure to submit. In *CIB/849/2001*, Commissioner Turnbull stated:

"The purpose of the medical examination was of course to enable the adjudication officer, with the benefit of the doctor's report, to determine whether the Claimant passed the all work test. The condition which the Claimant wished to impose on his submitting to an examination—i.e. that the doctor's report should not be passed to any layman, including an adjudication officer—rendered an examination useless for the purpose for which it was required. I have no doubt that, by imposing such a condition, the Claimant was failing to submit himself to a medical examination within the meaning of reg.8(2) [by analogy ESA Regs, reg.23(2)]. A person 'fails' to submit himself to an examination not only if he absolutely refuses to be examined, but also if he seeks to impose as a condition of being examined a term which would render the examination useless for the purpose for which it is required" (para.11).

The importance of careful fact-finding in such cases is demonstrated by *PH v SSWP (ESA)* [2016] UKUT 119 (AAC). In that case the claimant (Mr H) attended the examination centre and entered the examination room with the HCP, who asked him to sign an audio-recording agreement. Mr H could not take in its contents so signed the form but added "unread". The HCP informed him this was not acceptable, but added he could take the agreement away to read and another examination would be arranged for another date. On the day Mr H could not agree a new date as he did not have his diary with him. After having remonstrated with staff at the reception desk, security guards were called and he then left the centre. A tribunal dismissed his appeal against the Secretary of State's decision that he had "failed to participate" without good cause in a medical examination. As Judge Mitchell notes, reg.23 does not use the concept of "participating". Rather, it deals with failing to (a) "attend for" or (b) "submit to" a medical examination: "To put it in more everyday terms, (a) refers to a person who fails to turn up for an examination of which s/he has been duly notified and (b) refers to a person who fails to co-operate with the examination process so as to thwart its purpose" (at para.22). On the undisputed facts of the case, Mr H had plainly attended for a medical examination but the examination itself had never started, so he could not have failed to "submit to" such an examination:

"32. On this case's undisputed facts, Mr H's medical examination did not begin. The evidence cannot support a contrary finding. The planned medical examination was abandoned or cancelled once it became clear to the healthcare professional that Mr H would not, on the day, complete the audio-recording form in the way the centre's management thought he should. If Mr H's refusal was in the circumstances unreasonable, in the light of the examination's purpose, he could properly be said to have failed to submit to the examination. However, it was not viewed as unreasonable by the assessment staff as is shown, in my view, by the staff informing Mr H that another examination could be arranged. For that reason, I conclude that Mr H's conduct before the planned examination was cancelled was not unreasonable. And what happened afterwards is not relevant to the question whether he failed to submit to the medical examination."

The decision in *PH v SSWP (ESA)* may be usefully contrasted with that in *JW v SSWP (ESA)* [2016] UKUT 207 (AAC), where the assessment interview did actually commence, only to be abandoned when the claimant began cross- examining the HCP about her qualifications and insisted on recording the interview on his mobile phone. Judge Hemingway held "that if a claimant seeks to impose an unreasonable condition and, absent that unreasonable condition's fulfilment, withholds consent to the examination taking place, then he does not submit to the examination" (at para.13). However, in that case the tribunal's failure to find sufficient facts resulted in the decision being set aside and the appeal remitted for rehearing. See also *JW v SSWP (ESA)* [2016] UKUT 208 (AAC), where the claimant had sought to insist on e.g. knowing the details of the HCP's experience as a nurse, the history of her nursing career and the qualifications she had over and above the fact that she was a qualified general nurse. Judge Hemingway upheld the tribunal's decision that the appellant had failed without good cause to submit to a medical examination:

"38. It seems to me that, given my acceptance that, as a matter of law, a person can fail to submit by imposing unreasonable conditions and given the tribunal's findings it was clearly open to it to conclude that the additional information he was seeking, as a condition of allowing the examination to proceed, was being unreasonably required and did amount to a failure to submit. He already knew he was to be examined by a person whose name he was aware of and he knew that she was qualified as a registered general nurse. He also knew that she was authorised to carry out the examination for the purpose for which it was required. That ought to have been sufficient to reassure him as to any genuine concerns he might have had. It was open to the tribunal to conclude his insistence on more than that, even absent the intimidating behaviour it found him guilty of, amounted to a failure to submit."

Judge Hemingway's decision in *JW v SSWP (ESA)* [2016] UKUT 208 (AAC) was followed by Judge Mitchell in *RO v SSWP (ESA)* [2016] UKUT 402 (AAC), in which the claimant insisted on proof that the HCP (who was not wearing a name badge) was a registered nurse. The claimant (Mr O) was offered access to the relevant website but declined that offer in the absence of photographic evidence and left the examination centre. The First-tier Tribunal decided he did not have good cause for failing to participate in the medical examination. Judge Mitchell, having referred to the terms of the statutory provisions defining who is qualified to be a HCP, ruled that "a claimant is entitled to make a reasonable request for proof that a purported healthcare professional is in fact a health care professional" (at para.17), not least because a medical examination is an invasion of privacy (at para.22). However, the claimant's appeal failed on the facts.

RO v SSWP (ESA) was followed by Judge Gray in *CH v SSWP (ESA)* [2017] UKUT 6 (AAC), where she expressed the view (obiter on the facts) that "it is for the Secretary of State to decide on the type of health care professional who will conduct the examination, and for a claimant to refuse to submit to the examination on the basis that the healthcare professional chosen was not a doctor, or to insist as a precondition of attendance that it must be a doctor conducting the examination, would amount to a failure to attend" (para.22). The nature and extent of the medical examination to which the claimant must submit is a matter for the examining health care professional rather than the claimant, tribunal or Commissioner, "fundamentally a medical matter and for the judgment of the clinician in each individual case" (*C1/07–08(IB)*, para.12). The health care professional's demands of the claimant must, however, fall within the bounds of a "medical examination" and there remains the issue of whether a claimant has good cause for refusing to submit to the examination (*C1/07–08(IB)*, para.15).

A health care professional can insist on the presence of a suitable chaperone (e.g. a DWP employee bound by confidentiality not to broadcast details to the world at large), and unreasonable refusal to allow such a chaperone to be present constitutes refusing to submit to the examination (*CIB/2645/99*; *CIB/2011/2001*, para.15). Claimants cannot expect their medical details to be kept from those who must determine their claims; those who insist on strict medical confidentiality can do so, but only at the cost of foregoing their rights to benefit or credits (*CIB/2011/2001*, para.15).

The effect of a finding of lack of good cause precludes benefit until a new claim is submitted and a new period of incapacity for work begins. It may also prevent the claimant being treated under reg.30 as incapable of work pending a limited capability for work assessment. However, if the claimant is found to have limited capability for work in that assessment, benefit can be backdated to the beginning of the period covered by the new claim or application. See also on this aspect *R(IB)2/01* and para.8 of *CIB/3512/1998*. On "good cause", see also the commentary to reg.22 and note the non-exhaustive prescription in reg.24 of matters which must be taken into account in determining good cause.

Para. (3)

Paragraph (3) imposes a due notice requirement. If this condition is not met, then whether the claimant has good cause or not becomes irrelevant. Note that proper

4.64

written notice means written notice of the date, time and place of the examination, sent to the claimant at least seven days beforehand, unless the person agreed to accept a shorter period of notice, whether given in writing or otherwise. On determining whether and when a written notice was sent, see also the commentary to reg.22, above. Interpreted by analogy with the approach to another time period issue in *R(IB)2/00*, para.(3) requires at least seven days' clear notice so that neither the day of sending nor that of receipt count in determining that period (*CIB/2576/2007*, para.6). The notice may be given by or on behalf of the approved (generally DWPMS) health care professional concerned (para.(1)). The notice must, however, be written. So, where an appointment had been made over the telephone by leaving a message with the claimant's sister, which the claimant asserted was not passed on, he could not properly be treated as capable of work for not having attended without good cause, since the regulation's clear requisite of written notice had not been satisfied (see *CIB/969/97*). In *R(IB) 1/01*, Commissioner Rowland considered that where, when a claimant stated that he would not be able to attend a medical examination, the Department in consequence said they would cancel it, the claimant cannot be held not to have attended it.

As to the meaning of "sent", in *CIB/1381/2003* Deputy Commissioner Wikeley declined, after reviewing a range of authority on analogous provisions in child support and jobseeker's allowance, to determine whether "sent" meant "despatched" or "delivered", since a failure to attend because of not receiving the notice could in any event constitute "good cause" as the tribunal had held. In *CSIB/721/2004*, however, Commissioner Parker was of the view that where the claimant proved that the notification duly despatched (a matter for the Secretary of State to establish) had not in fact been received by him, in the ordinary course of post or at all, then it had not been "sent" within the meaning of para.(3), thus precluding treating the claimant as capable of work for "failure to attend or submit to examination" so that the issue of "good cause" never arose. She there took account of a Secretary of State concession on the point noted in *CIB/4512/2002* (not on the Commissioners' website), to which the Secretary of State's representative referred her. But in contrast note that Commissioner Rowland in *CIB/3512/1998*, dealing with an analogous Incapacity for Work Reg., stressed that it said "sent" rather than "received", albeit that non-receipt would be a matter as regards "good cause".

The Northern Ireland decision *C11/03–04(IB)* is a useful reminder of the need to ascertain the precise facts and be careful in applying to them the concept of "good cause". The case concerned a common "defence", where the claimant alleged he had never received a particular letter sent by the Department, a typical case of conflict of evidence. Deputy Commissioner Powell thought that sometimes it is right to reject such allegations in a robust manner, for example, where the excuse extends to a number of letters, or is coupled with suspicious circumstances, or if the non-receipt of mail is selective so that only certain letters are not received. The case before him, however, concerned a rather different situation—the uncontradicted evidence of the claimant, who did not attend the appeal hearing, of the non-receipt of a single letter in plausible circumstances, namely, a communal delivery of mail to particular premises and the possibility that another went through it before the claimant had a chance to do so. The Commissioner could not see how an effective challenge could be mounted to the claim and that, in these circumstances, the claimant had established good cause. The Secretary of State bears the burden of proof in establishing that the requirements of para.(3) have been met, a precondition for being able to find the claimant capable of work for non-attendance etc.

In *CIB/4012/2004*, Deputy Commissioner Mark, considering the cases noted above, found that the burden had not been discharged. Computer records showing that a letter had been issued were not sufficient evidence of it being "sent" on the facts of that case. However, in other respects it appears that Judge Mark arguably set the bar too high for the Secretary of State and those acting on his behalf. Three other Upper Tribunal decisions have adopted a rather more pragmatic approach to the evidential requirements imposed on the Secretary of State. See further *AL v*

SSWP (ESA) [2011] UKUT 512 (AAC), *SH v SSWP (ESA)* [2014] UKUT 574 (AAC) and *DW v SSWP (ESA)* [2016] UKUT 179 (AAC)—the last a decision which contains a useful review of the authorities—all discussed in the commentary to reg.22 above.

Matters to be taken into account in determining good cause in relation to regulations 22 or 23

24. The matters to be taken into account in determining whether a claimant has good cause under regulations 22 (failure to provide information in relation to limited capability for work) or 23 (failure to attend a medical examination to determine limited capability for work) include—

    (a) whether the claimant was outside Great Britain at the relevant time;

    (b) the claimant's state of health at the relevant time; and

    (c) the nature of any disability the claimant has.

4.65

DEFINITION

    "claimant"—see WRA 2007 s.24(1).

GENERAL NOTE

    This regulation, made pursuant to WRA 2007 s.8(4), stipulates that in determining whether someone had good cause for failing to provide information (under reg.22) or for failing to attend for or submit to a medical examination (under reg.23) decision-makers and appellate bodies must take into account (i) whether the person was outside Great Britain at the relevant time, (ii) his state of health at the relevant time, and (iii) the nature of his disability. This list is not, however, exhaustive (the regulation says "shall include"). On "good cause", see further the commentary to regs 22 and 23.

4.66

    On the relevance of previously missed appointments when assessing whether a claimant has shown good cause for not attending an HCP appointment, see *JS v SSWP (ESA)* [2019] UKUT 303 (AAC), where Judge Jacobs held as follows:

"16. Take first a claimant whose explanations refer to the same condition. Much will depend on the nature of that condition. It should come as no surprise if there are repeated failures to attend on account of agoraphobia. There would be no cause for suspicion. Quite the contrary, an ability to attend sometimes but not others could call into question the claimant's asserted disability. In contrast, if the claimant's condition is variable, chronic fatigue syndrome say, variation is to be expected and not of itself a cause for suspicion.

17. The position may be more complicated if the claimant gives different reasons for not attending on successive occasions. By definition, the decisionmaker will have accepted good cause on the earlier occasions. There is no question of changing those decisions, but a later decision-maker may conclude, looking back at the history of the case and taking account of evidence now available, that there has been a pattern of avoidance by the claimant. Even then, it is important to focus on the current failure. The previous conduct may justify careful scrutiny of the current failure, with perhaps a request for supporting evidence. But even a claimant with a lengthy history of failing to attend for what appear, in hindsight, to be highly dubious reasons may still be delayed by inclement weather or have a domestic emergency. And a claimant who has more than one disabling condition may be prevented from attending for different reasons on different occasions.

18. In short, it all depends, which means that tribunals need to take care in their reasoning to show whether they took any account of a claimant's previous failures and, if so, how in order to demonstrate that their relevance was assessed rationally, taking account of points both for and against the claimant."

A judicial review claim challenging the legality of the DWP's safeguarding policies for vulnerable claimants was brought in *R (on the application of Turner) v Secretary of State for Work and Pensions* [2021] EWHC 465 (Admin). Ms Turner brought the proceedings following the inquest into the death of her relative Errol Graham, who had starved to death after his benefits (including ESA) had been stopped when he had failed to attend a fitness for work assessment and not responded to other communications. The grounds of challenge related to the lawfulness of both the DWP's safeguarding policy and the decision to stop Mr Graham's benefits respectively. Bourne J dismissed both grounds of judicial review.

As to the former, Bourne J rejected the argument that putting the burden of proof on the claimant to show good cause under reg.24 was unlawful. However, the judge ruled that "Where the issue is 'good cause' for a claimant's failure to attend an assessment, it is logical and reasonable to look to the claimant for the explanation. However, cases such as *Kerr* are a reminder that the claimant is not the only possible source of an explanation and, moreover, that the Defendant's officials must consider any relevant information which is reasonably available to them" (para.71). Moreover, "The point being made under regulation 24 is straightforward. That regulation, quoted above, requires decision makers to have regard to matters including the claimant's state of health and any disability he may have. A public law decision maker must in general ask himself the right question and 'take reasonable steps to acquaint himself with the relevant information to enable him to answer it correctly': *Secretary of State for Education and Science v Tameside MBC* [1977] AC 1014 at 1065B per Lord Diplock" (at para.76). Furthermore, s.149 of the Equality Act 2010 did not materially affect the interpretation of that duty (para.88).

As to the latter, Bourne J held that while the DWP was aware of some of Mr Graham's circumstances it did not know of the acute illness he had suffered more recently or of any individual other than his GP (who was contacted by the DWP but had little to report) who might have been expected to provide relevant information. In all the circumstances the DWP was not bound to make further inquiries into Mr Graham's health.

[¹Hospital patients

4.67   **25.**—(1) A claimant is to be treated as having limited capability for work on any day on which that claimant is undergoing medical or other treatment as a patient in a hospital or similar institution, or on any day which is a day of recovery from that treatment.

(2) The circumstances in which a claimant is to be regarded as undergoing treatment falling within paragraph (1) include where the claimant is attending a residential programme of rehabilitation for the treatment of drug or alcohol addiction.

(3) For the purposes of this regulation, a claimant is to be regarded as undergoing treatment as a patient in a hospital or similar institution only if that claimant has been advised by a health care professional to stay in a hospital or similar institution for a period of 24 hours or longer.

(4) For the purposes of this regulation, "day of recovery" means a day on which a claimant is recovering from treatment as a patient in a hospital or similar institution and the Secretary of State is satisfied that the claimant should be treated as having limited capability for work on that day.]

AMENDMENT

1. Employment and Support Allowance (Amendment) Regulations 2012 (SI 2012/3096), reg.3(4) (January 28, 2013, subject to application, transitional and savings provisions in reg.2 of this amending instrument, below, para.9.614).

DEFINITIONS

"claimant"—see WRA 2007 s.24(1).
"day of recovery"—see para.(4).
"limited capability for work"—see WRA 2007 s.1(4).
"medical treatment"—see reg.2(1).

GENERAL NOTE

Paragraphs (1), (3)

This regulation stipulates that those undergoing medical or other treatment as a **4.68** patient in a hospital or other institution, must be treated as having limited capability for work on any day on which they are undergoing that treatment, or on any day of recovery from that treatment.

The notion of "undergoing treatment as a patient in a hospital or similar institution" was initially not defined at all and was the subject of criticism and guidance by Judge Williams in *CJ v SSWP (ESA)* [2012] UKUT 201 (AAC) which still has application to those cases still subject, after the amended version of reg.25 inserted from January 28, 2013, to the previously worded reg.25.

The current wording was subject to analysis by Judge Mitchell in *SJ v SSWP (ESA)* [2015] UKUT 180 (AAC). He regarded himself as bound in several respects by the Court of Appeal decision in *Secretary of State for Work and Pensions* v *Slavin* [2012] AACR 30, interpreting similar terms in the DLA Regs 1991 reg.9, the appeal from Judge Turnbull's decision in *AS v SSWP (DLA)* [2010] UKUT 482 (AAC) (see, above, para.4.53) (hereinafter "*Slavin*").

Judge Mitchell considered that the regulation has to be "read as a whole". Para.(1) read with para.(3) sets out four elements all of which must be fulfilled for a day to be treated as one of limited capability for work:

"(a) the claimant must be undergoing medical or other treatment; and

(b) the treatment must be as a patient; and

(c) the treatment must be in a hospital or similar institution; and

(d) the claimant must have been advised by a health care professional to stay in the hospital or other institution for a period of 24 hours or longer" (para.15).

If any element is absent, the claim based on para.(1) must fail. Therefore, a tribunal can reject an argument founded on para.(1) "simply by reference to the non-satisfaction of any one element" (para.16).

"*Hospital or similar institution*": this is not defined in the ESA Regs, but features in a number of social security legislative contexts and its meaning has been elucidated by case law on them and is to be applied to the term in this regulation (para.52). Essentially, a hospital is any institution for the reception and treatment of persons suffering from illness, with "illness" being defined as including mental illness and any injury or disability requiring medical or dental treatment or nursing (para.38).

"*Medical or other treatment*": "medical treatment" is defined in reg.2(1), above, as

"medical, surgical or rehabilitative treatment (including any course or diet or other regimen), and references to a person receiving or submitting to medical treatment are to be construed accordingly".

Judge Mitchell considered that *Slavin* (binding on him) held that "medical or other treatment is confined to medical treatment, dental treatment or nursing care" (para.42). He also approved Judge Turnbull's view in para.88 of *AS*, noting that nothing in the Court of Appeal's decision in *Slavin* upholding that of Judge Turnbull in *AS* indicated disapproval of it. Judge Turnbull accepted counsel's view that "nursing" and "treatment" could not be confined to "care and skill exercised by doctors and nurses", but had to extend to that administered by other health care professionals (e.g. physiotherapy or occupational therapy) (paras 46-48, 60). Para.(2) of reg.25 (see further, below) stipulates that treatment falling within para.(1) includes attendance at "a residential programme of rehabilitation for the treatment of drug or alcohol addiction".

Accordingly, Judge Mitchell upheld the tribunal's decision that the refuge in which the claimant was staying as a victim of domestic violence did not fall within para.(1) because she was not undergoing medical or other treatment there. Nor had she been advised by a health care professional to stay in the refuge for a period of at least 24 hours so that the condition in para.(3) was not met. Judge Mitchell considered that his decision did not mean that all refuges would fall outside reg.25; labels "are of no intrinsic significance. . . What matters is whether the facts of a particular case come within regulation 25" (para.67), but stated, by way of general guidance, that he "would not be surprised if most refuge placements have characteristics matching, in material respects, [this claimant's] so that their residents fall outside regulation 25(1)" (para.68).

Paragraphs (1), (4)

4.69   The regulation protects not only those "undergoing medical or other treatment as a patient in a hospital or other institution" but also their days of "recovery from that treatment". "Day of recovery" is defined in para.(4). Note the discretion given to the Secretary of State—the day on which the former in-patient is recovering from that treatment will only count if the Secretary of State is satisfied that the claimant should on that day be treated as having limited capability for work. In *SI v SSWP (ESA)* [2013] UKUT 453 (AAC), Judge Mark was not satisfied

> "that the tribunal did properly consider the question whether the claimant was still recovering from the treatment. It does not follow just because the wound had scarred over and he had restricted movement back in his joint that he was fully recovered. The remaining limitations could in part still be due to the fact that he had not fully recovered. There does not appear to have been any investigation of the extent of his limitation previously or the nature of the operation or of his prognosis or the reasons for his continuing therapies and consultations or of the expected period within which recovery from the operation was to be expected" (para.10).

This lapse did not assist the claimant because the tribunal on the facts was entitled to conclude that there was no good ground for treating him as incapable of work.

Paragraphs (1), (2)

4.70   Attendance at a residential programme of rehabilitation for the treatment of drug or alcohol addiction counts as undergoing "treatment falling within paragraph (1)". This statutory stipulation is exhaustive and does not permit extension by analogy so as to cover other rehabilitation programmes (*SJ v SSWP (ESA)* [2015] UKUT 180 (AAC), paras 65, 66).

Regulation 21(1) (information gathering requirements) does not apply to a determination under this regulation (see reg.21(3)).

Claimants receiving certain regular treatment

4.71   **26.**—(1) Subject to paragraph (2), a claimant receiving—
    (a) regular weekly treatment by way of haemodialysis for chronic renal failure;
    (b) treatment by way of plasmapheresis [². . .]; or

(c) regular weekly treatment by way of total parenteral nutrition for gross impairment of enteric function,

is to be treated as having limited capability for work during any week in which that claimant is engaged in [³receiving] that treatment or has a day of recovery from that treatment.

[¹(2) A claimant who receives the treatment referred to in paragraph (1) is only to be treated as having limited capability for work from the first week of treatment in which the claimant undergoes no fewer than—

(a) two days of treatment;

(b) two days of recovery from any of the forms of treatment listed in paragraph 1(a) to (c); or

(c) one day of treatment and one day of recovery from that treatment,

but the days of treatment or recovery from that treatment or both need not be consecutive.]

(3) For the purpose of this regulation "day of recovery" means a day on which a claimant is recovering from any of the forms of treatment listed in paragraph (1)(a) to (c) and the Secretary of State is satisfied that the claimant should be treated as having limited capability for work on that day.

AMENDMENTS

1. Employment and Support Allowance (Miscellaneous Amendments) Regulations 2008 (SI 2008/2428) reg.5(1) (October 27, 2008).

2. Employment and Support Allowance (Amendment) Regulations 2012 (SI 2012/3096) reg.3(5) (January 28, 2013, subject to application, transitional and savings provisions in reg.2 of this amending instrument, below, para.9.614).

3. Social Security (Miscellaneous Amendments) (No.3) Regulations 2013 (SI 2013/2536) reg.13(12) (October 29, 2013).

DEFINITIONS

"claimant"—see WRA 2007 s.24(1).
"day of recovery"—see para.(3).
"limited capability for work"—see WRA 2007 s.1(4).
"week"—see WRA 2007 s.24(1); reg.2(1).

GENERAL NOTE

Someone undergoing certain treatments is treated as having limited capability   4.72
for work on during any week in which he is engaged in that treatment or has a day of recovery from that treatment (para.(1)). The treatments concerned are: regular weekly treatment by way of haemodialysis for chronic renal failure (para.(1)(a)); treatment by way of plasmapheresis (para.(1)(b); or regular weekly treatment by way of total parenteral nutrition for gross impairment of enteric function (para. (1)(c)). "Day of recovery" is defined in para.(3) as one on which the claimant is recovering from any of the forms of treatment so long as the Secretary of State (note the discretion) is satisfied that the claimant should be treated as having limited capability for work on that day. Paragraph (2) deals with the first week of any such treatment. During that week, the claimant can only be treated as having limited capability for work if in that week he undergoes no fewer than two days of treatment, or two days of recovery from such treatment or one day of treatment and one day of recovery. The days of treatment or recovery from it need not be consecutive.

Regulation 21(1) (information gathering requirements) does not apply to a determination under this regulation (see reg.21(3)).

Claimant to be treated as having limited capability for work throughout a day

4.73   **27.** A claimant who at the commencement of any day has, or thereafter develops, limited capability for work as determined in accordance with the limited capability for work assessment is to be treated as having limited capability for work throughout that day.

DEFINITIONS

"claimant"—see WRA 2007 s.24(1).
"limited capability for work"—see WRA 2007 s.1(4).
"limited capability for work assessment"—see reg.2(1).

GENERAL NOTE

4.74   The situation encompassed here in which someone is to be treated as having limited capability for work, confers no exemption from the information gathering processes for the limited capability for work assessment (reg.21(3)).

The effect of this regulation is that those with limited capability for work at the start of a day or who thereafter develop it on that day are to be treated as having limited capability for work throughout that day. In *CIB/6244/1997*, Commissioner Jacobs considered the application of the IB regulation to intermittent and variable conditions. He considered that the provision must be read in the light that, under the all work test/PCA and its descriptors, one cannot confine consideration merely to a particular time on a particular day—otherwise a claimant could always satisfy the "cannot" descriptors and the "sometimes" ones (not in any event in the ESA limited capability for work assessment activities and descriptors) would never apply. The "cannot" and "sometimes" descriptors inevitably require a focus over a period and not at a specific moment in time. Thus he thought that Incapacity for Work Regs, reg.15 "does not operate to ensure that a claimant with a variable condition that incapacitates him for a part of each day must be considered as incapable throughout the whole of every day" (para.23). However, it will "apply where there is a sudden onset of or recovery from an incapacitating condition, including an intermittent incapacitating condition or the incapacitating intermittent features of a condition" (*ibid.* and see also *CIB/15482/1996*, paras 7–9). In *CIB/243/1998*. Deputy Commissioner Mark considered that a claimant who suffered an asthma attack for part of a day had to be treated as incapable of work throughout that day under this regulation, provided that the effect of the attack when ongoing was such that he would score at least 15 points for more than a minimal period on that day. In *CIB/399/2003*, Commissioner Mesher very firmly rejected that approach of Deputy Commissioner Mark in *CIB/243/1998* and preferred the approach taken by Commissioner Jacobs in *CIB/6244/1997* and by Deputy Commissioner Ramsay in *CIB/15482/1996*, thus establishing a strong line of authority against Deputy Commissioner Mark's view of the application of Incapacity for Work Regs, reg.15. Commissioner Mesher thought the rejected approach to be inconsistent with the concept of "reasonable regularity" applicable to the "cannot" descriptors and out of tune with the tenor of *R(IB)2/99(T)* (on which see further the commentary to Sch.2).

Night workers

4.75   **28.**—(1) Where a claimant works for a continuous period which extends over midnight into the following day, that claimant is to be treated as having limited capability for work on the day on which the lesser part of that period falls if that claimant had limited capability for work for the remainder of that day.

(2) Where, in relation to a period referred to in paragraph (1), the number of hours worked before and after midnight is equal—

(a) if the days in question fall at the beginning of a period of limited capability for work, the claimant is to be treated as having limited capability on the second day; and

(b) if the days in question fall at the end of a period of limited capability for work, the claimant is to be treated as having limited capability for work on the first day.

DEFINITIONS

"claimant"—see WRA 2007 s.24(1).
"limited capability for work"—see WRA 2007 s.1(4).
"period of limited capability for work"—see reg.2(1).

GENERAL NOTE

Although unlike IB, ESA is a weekly rather than a daily benefit, there is still need to be able to attribute limited capability for work to a particular day, where the person doing nightwork has a shift spanning midnight and thus covering two days. The ESA scheme in some circumstances permits awards for periods of less than a week (the amount payable being determined under regs 165–169) (e.g. the period at the start or end of a claim; persons receiving certain regular treatments). Although the ESA scheme neither in Act or Regs defines "day", the general rule for benefit purposes has been that a day is the period midnight to midnight, and performance of work on a day will generally preclude the week in which it is done ranking as one of entitlement to ESA (see reg.40(1)). But there are exceptions to that preclusive rule (regs 40(4), 46) where the preclusion is only to affect the day(s) actually worked. There is thus a need to attribute a nightshift spanning two days to one day or the other. Otherwise, the application of the rules to nightworkers whose shifts span midnight could cause hardship since they would, without this regulation, be regarded as working on two days and thus be treated less favourably than their day worker counterparts whose shift of exactly the same length (period of work) would be attributed to one day. Equally, even though the nightworker suffered the same degree of limited capability for work on one of those days, the day could not count as one of limited capability for work This regulation attempts some easing of the position of nightworkers in this regard.

4.76

Paragraph (1) provides that where someone works for a continuous period beginning one day and spanning midnight into the following day, the day on which there falls the lesser part of the period worked will be treated as one of limited capability for work if the claimant has limited capability for work for the rest of that day. To put it another way, the day with the longer period worked is to be treated for the purpose of the exceptions to the preclusive rules noted above as the day of work. Paragraph (2) deals with the situation in which the hours worked each side of midnight are equal. If the two days in question fall at the beginning of a period of limited capability for work, the second day is to be treated as one of incapacity and the first as the one of work. If the two days fall at the end of a period of incapacity for work, the first day is the one to be regarded as a day of limited capability for work and the second as the one of work.

Exceptional circumstances

29.—(1) A claimant who does not have limited capability for work as determined in accordance with the limited capability for work assessment is to be treated as having limited capability for work if paragraph (2) applies to the claimant.

4.77

(2) [¹ Subject to paragraph (3)] this paragraph applies if—

(a) the claimant is suffering from a life threatening disease in relation to which—

(i) there is medical evidence that the disease is uncontrollable, or uncontrolled, by a recognised therapeutic procedure; and

(ii) in the case of a disease that is uncontrolled, there is a reasonable cause for it not to be controlled by a recognised therapeutic procedure; or

(b) the claimant suffers from some specific disease or bodily or mental disablement and, by reasons of such disease or disablement, there would be a substantial risk to the mental or physical health of any person if the claimant were found not to have limited capability for work.

[¹(3) Paragraph (2)(b) does not apply where the risk could be reduced by a significant amount by—

(a) reasonable adjustments being made in the claimant's workplace; or

(b) the claimant taking medication to manage the claimant's condition where such medication has been prescribed for the claimant by a registered medical practitioner treating the claimant.]

[²(4) In this regulation "medical evidence" means—

(a) evidence from a health care professional approved by the Secretary of State; and

(b) evidence (if any) from any health care professional or a hospital or similar Institution,

or such part of such evidence as constitutes the most reliable evidence available in the circumstances.]

AMENDMENTS

1. Employment and Support Allowance (Amendment) Regulations 2012 (SI 2012/3096) reg.3(6) (January 28, 2013, subject to application, transitional and savings provisions in reg.2 of this amending instrument, below, para.9.614).

2. Social Security (Miscellaneous Amendments) (No.3) Regulations 2013 (SI 2013/2536) reg.13(13) (October 29, 2013).

DEFINITIONS

"claimant"—see WRA 2007 s.24(1).
"limited capability for work"—see WRA 2007 s.1(4).
"limited capability for work assessment"—see reg.2(1).
"medical evidence"—see para.(4).

GENERAL NOTE

Paragraph (1): background and role

4.78   Like reg.27 in the IB scheme, this regulation reflects the fact that functional assessment systems like the IB PCA or the ESA LCWA would not properly measure the incapacitating effect of certain conditions, and so would "fail" some people who properly ought to be regarded as being incapable of work (IB) or having limited capability for work (ESA). Headed "exceptional circumstances", the regulation can only come into play where the claimant has been found *not* to have limited capability for work under reg.19 and Sch.2; where s/he has attained an insufficient score (less than 15 points) applying those descriptors.

The regulation envisages two classes of case in which someone assessed as not having limited capability for work can nonetheless be treated as having it.

Paragraph (2)(a): claimant suffering from a life threatening disease uncontrolled or uncontrollable by a recognised therapeutic procedure

4.79   The first class of case is where the claimant suffers from a life threatening disease (the IB requirement that it be "severe" is not continued into ESA) which *medical evidence establishes* is uncontrollable by a recognized therapeutic procedure or (but only with reasonable cause) is uncontrolled by such a procedure.

Dealing with the substantially similarly worded IB provision in *CIB/4506/01*, Commissioner Howell stated that here:

> "the question is only whether the nature of [the claimant's] condition is such that it is capable of being controlled by medical science, or not. Consequently the tribunal were right in taking account not only of the inhalers and adrenaline injector she is able to use for herself, but also the hospital treatment which unhappily she finds also has to be used on occasions as a means of bringing the condition under control. On the tribunal's findings the claimant's condition is thus controllable in the relevant sense, and their reasons are clearly and adequately given" (para.10).

The tribunal had not erred in law.

What level of "control" does the provision envisage? In *CIB/155/2004*, Commissioner Jacobs thought it inappropriate to deploy as a test whether the level of control would suffice to allow the claimant to work; since that test would always be satisfied. Rather, he thought that IB reg.27 [ESA reg.29] comes into play where a claimant is capable of work but has a condition that makes it inappropriate that he be expected to work. Since, as regards para.(2)(a) what makes that inappropriate is the fact that the condition is a threat to the claimant's life, the threshold for control should be whether the control is sufficient to remove the threat to the claimant's life. In the case at hand, while the evidence disclosed that the claimant's diabetes was poorly controlled, it was nonetheless sufficiently controlled that para.(2)(a) was inapplicable. While there were longer-term complications to which the Consultant referred, they were not yet present, and not currently threatening the claimant's life.

"Reasonable cause for it not to be controlled by a recognised therapeutic procedure": **4.80** even where a tribunal with the assistance of its medical member considers that a procedure would be of benefit, a claimant had reasonable cause for not taking advantage of it where two cardiologists had advised him not to do so and it had not been offered to him *(KR v SSWP (ESA)* [2013] UKUT 637 (AAC), para.6).

There must be "medical evidence" that the disease is uncontrollable or uncontrolled. The term "medical evidence" embraces (i) evidence from a health care professional approved by the Secretary of State, (ii) evidence (if any) from any other health care professional, hospital or similar institution, or such part of evidence in (i) or (ii) as constitutes the most reliable evidence available in the circumstances (para.(4)). "Health care professional" covers a registered medical practitioner, a registered nurse or an occupational therapist or physiotherapist registered with a regulatory body established by an Order in Council under section 60 of the Health Act 1999 (reg.2(1)). In a Northern Ireland decision *C5/00–01(IB)* Commissioner Brown stressed that the evidence "must relate to the claimant himself, it is not constituted by extracts from medical textbooks unless the doctor relates them to the claimant" (para.16). The medical evidence must have been issued before the Secretary of State's decision in the case. In *GC v SSWP (ESA)* [2013] UKUT 271 (AAC), the claimant sought to rely on medical evidence issued after the Secretary of State had made his decision, on the evidence then before him, that the claimant's disease (bladder cancer) was controlled. Judge Jacobs considered reg.29 in the context of SSA 1998 s.12(8)(b) (an appeal tribunal shall not take into account any circumstances not obtaining at the time when the decision appealed against was made). He held that this was not the same situation as that in *R(DLA) 2 & 3/01* where later evidence could properly be adduced to show the circumstances prevailing at the date of decision:

> "Regulation 29([2])(a)(i) is different. It does not refer to the claimant having a disease that is uncontrolled or uncontrollable. It refers to the need for *medical*

evidence that that is so. In applying section 12(8)(b), the relevant circumstance is the existence of the evidence of the state of the claimant's condition. In Mr C's case, the evidence that his cancer had returned and required surgery did not exist until after the Secretary of State made the decision under appeal. In such a case, it makes no sense to say that later evidence shows that there was evidence at the time of the decision. Such talk is entirely inconsistent with the requirements of [regulation 29(2)(a)] as it renders the requirement for contemporaneous evidence redundant" (para.12).

Paragraph (2)(b), (3): "by reasons of [the claimant's health condition or disability] there would be a substantial risk to the mental or physical health of any person if the claimant were found not to have limited capability for work"

4.81   The second class of case in which someone not assessed as having limited capability for work can nonetheless be treated as having it, concerns a claimant, suffering from some specific disease or bodily or mental disablement, and by reasons of such there would be substantial risk to the mental or physical health of any person if the claimant were found not to have limited capability for work. The scheme thus carries into ESA something the Department had tried unsuccessfully to remove as regards IB in 1997.

With effect from January 28, 2013, para.(2) was made "subject to paragraph (3)", so that the "substantial risk" provision in para.(2)(b) does not apply if the risk could be reduced by a "significant amount" by reasonable adjustments being made in the claimant's workplace or by the claimant taking medication prescribed by a registered medical practitioner treating the patient (para.(3)). "Significant amount" unfortunately is not defined but, given the protective purpose of para. (2)(b) should preferably be interpreted as one reducing the risk to a level describable as less than "substantial". The *Explanatory Memorandum* to the amending instrument refers to the risk being "greatly reduced" (See para.7.14) (*http:// www. legislation.gov.uk/uksi/2012/3096/pdfs/uksiem_20123096_en.pdf*). In contrast the two examples given in para.7.15 of Memo *DMG 1/13* to the *Decision Makers Guide* (*http://www.dwp.gov.uk/docs/m-1-13.pdf*) rather confusingly refer respectively to "the risk to his health could be alleviated" and "the risk could be substantially reduced". It is to be expected that the proper interpretation will be a matter appealed to the Upper Tribunal in due course.

Note that the old wording of para.(2) will still apply to some cases after January 28, 2013 (see reg.2 of the amending instrument, below, para.9.614).

On "specific disease or bodily or mental disablement", see the commentary to reg.19.

4.82   *The "substantial risk" must arise "by reasons of" a specific disease or bodily or mental disablement:* In *DR v SSWP (ESA)* [2014] UKUT 188 (AAC); [2014] AACR 38, Judge May held erroneous in law a tribunal decision that the claimant satisfied reg.29 because it had not made the necessary connection between the risk and the disease or disablement (see para.3). Alcohol misuse in itself is not such a disablement. To rank as disablement the misuse of alcohol must rank as "alcohol dependency" in terms of the "constellation of markers" found in quotations from *R(DLA) 6/06* in the Three-Judge Panel's decision in *JG v SSWP (ESA)* [2013] UKUT 37 (AAC); [2013] AACR 23 (see paras 5-7, 10 of *DR*). Para.45 of the panel decision sets out the constellation of markers as follows:

"A maladaptive pattern of substance use, leading to clinically significant impairment or distress, as manifested by three (or more) of the following, occurring at any time in the same 12-month period

(1) tolerance, as defined by either of the following:
    (a) a need for markedly increased amounts of the substance to achieve intoxication or desire effect

(b) markedly diminished effect with continued use of the same amount of the substance

(2) withdrawal, as manifested by either of the following:

(a) the characteristic withdrawal syndrome for the substance . . .
(b) the same (or a closely related) substance is taken to relieve or avoid withdrawal symptoms

(3) the substance is often taken in larger amounts or over a longer period than was intended

(4) there is a persistent desire or unsuccessful efforts to cut down or control substance use

(5) a great deal of time is spent in activities necessary to obtain the substance (e.g. visiting multiple doctors or driving long distances), use the substance (eg chain-smoking), or recover from its effects

(6) important social, occupational, or recreational activities are given up or reduced because of substance use

(7) the substance use is continued despite knowledge of having a persistent or recurrent physical or psychological problem that is likely to have been caused or exacerbated by the substance (e.g. current cocaine use despite recognition of cocaine-induced depression, or continued drinking despite recognition that an ulcer was made worse by alcohol consumption)."

These various factors were adopted from those listed in the category of Substance Dependence contained in the Diagnostic and Statistical Manual of Mental Disorders of the American Psychiatric Association (DSM IV). In *SD v SSWP (ESA)* [2016] UKUT 100 (AAC); [2016] AACR 35, in which the claimant used street heroin (an opoid), Judge Knowles QC held that the factors pointing towards alcohol dependence as set out in *JG v SSWP (ESA)* (above) also have application in the case of drug dependency:

"31. I note that the factors listed in the category of Substance Dependence in DSM-IV are not alcohol specific [see (vii) above for example] and thus, as a matter of logic, they must apply to other substances such as heroin and cocaine. I find that the constellation of markers set out in paragraph 45 is therefore equally applicable to drug dependence (such as that probably seen in this particular case)."

Judge Knowles QC observed that DSM-IV has now been superseded by DSM-5, in which substance-related/addictive disorders are divided into two categories, namely substance use disorders (including opioid use disorder) and substance induced disorders. Judge Knowles QC concluded as follows:

"37. The diagnostic criteria for opioid use disorder (heroin being an opioid) are as follows:

"*a problematic pattern of opioid use leading to clinically significant impairment or distress as manifested by at least two of the following occurring within a 12 month period:*

i) *opioids are often taken in larger amounts or over a longer period than was intended;*
ii) *a persistent desire or unsuccessful attempts to cut down or control opiate use;*
iii) *a great deal of time is spent in activities necessary to obtain the opioid, use the opioid or recover from its effects;*
iv) *craving or a strong desire to use opioids;*
v) *recurrent opioid use resulting in a failure to fulfil major role obligations at work, school or home;*
vi) *continued opioid use despite having persistent or recurrent social or interpersonal problems caused or exacerbated by the use of opioids;*
vii) *important social, occupational or recreational activities are given up or their*

> *engagement is reduced because of opioid use;*
>
> viii) *recurrent opioid use in situations in which it is physically hazardous;*
>
> ix) *continued opioid use despite knowledge of having a persistent or recurrent physical of psychological problem that is likely to have been caused or exacerbated by the substance;*
>
> x) *tolerance as defined by either a need for markedly increased amounts of opioids to achieve intoxication/desired effect or a markedly diminished effect with continued use of the same amount of opioid;*
>
> xi) *and withdrawal as manifested by either the characteristic opioid withdrawal syndrome or opioids (or a closely related substance) being taken to relieve or avoid withdrawal symptoms."*

38. Severity is specified as follows: mild substance use disorder is the presence of 2-3 of the above symptoms; moderate is the presence of 4-5 symptoms; and severe is the presence of six or more symptoms.

39. The category of opioid induced disorders includes opioid intoxication, opioid withdrawal; opioid induced anxiety disorder and opioid induced depressive disorder.

40. *JG* concluded that a diagnosis of alcohol dependence or alcohol dependency syndrome plainly brought that condition within regulation 19(5) of the Regulations [paragraph 48]. The position now is rather more complex given the adjustments made by DSM-5 to the category of substance related disorders.

41. I have come to the conclusion that a diagnosis of mild substance abuse disorder in accordance with DSM-5 would not bring that condition within regulation 19(5) or 29(2)(b) of the Regulations. I consider that, in order to fall within the ambit of the relevant regulations, the substance abuse disorder must fall within either the moderate or severe categories. My reasons for so concluding are as follows.

42. A DSM-IV diagnosis of alcohol dependency required three or more symptoms from the list occurring at any time in the same 12 month period. It is clear that all of the factors listed in DSM-IV are incorporated into the factors for substance abuse disorder listed in paragraph 37. The presence of three or more factors in a twelve month period from the DSM-5 list would establish a diagnosis of mild substance use disorder. However a DSM-5 diagnosis of substance use disorder equivalent to DSM-IV substance dependency requires, in my view, the presence of, at least 4-5 symptoms from the eleven listed, thus bringing it within the moderately severe category of substance use disorder. This is because the distinction between abuse and dependence In DSM-IV was based on the concept of substance abuse as a mild or early phase and substance dependence as the more severe manifestation."

4.83   *"Substantial risk to the mental or physical health of any person":* "Substantial" does not only refer to the likelihood of the risk occurring: "a risk may be 'substantial' if the harm would be serious, even though it was unlikely to occur and, conversely, may not be 'substantial' if the harm would be insignificant, even though the likelihood of some such harm is great. Paragraph (b) must be viewed in the light of the other paragraphs of regulation 27 [now ESA Regs reg.29] and the general scheme of the Regulations" (*CIB/3519/2002*, para.7). Commissioner Fellner accepted this as "probably right" in *CIB/2767/2004*, but added that:

> "invocation of the other paragraphs of regulation 27 as guides to interpretation suggests that the interpretation should be rather narrow. . . . the other paragraphs refer to more or less factual medical questions—presence of life-threatening or severe uncontrolled or uncontrollable disease, need for an identified major medical procedure within a short time" (para.6).

In *MW v SSWP (ESA)* [2012] UKUT 31 (AAC) Judge Parker was of the opinion that the question of "substantial risk" is an objective one and, as regards physical health, one to which the claimant's personal belief system and subjective views are not likely to be pertinent. In contrast, the position may well be different as regards mental health:

"while the determination of the point is still an objective one, what are the subjective beliefs of a claimant must form part of the background to the question whether, looked at objectively, she might suffer a significant deterioration in mental health, faced with the thought that, in work, she could not follow out her preferred therapeutic regime. The tribunal erred in concentrating only on a reaction mentally to the distressing news of a cancer diagnosis or on whether the state of her cancer was at the relevant date physically harmful. It ought also to have applied an objective test in consideration of the question whether, in all her circumstances, the prospect of having to give up her daily time-consuming regime which she believed was the right and only way to combat her cancer, could constitute the necessary substantial risk" (para. 3).

In relation to which employment contexts must the "substantial risk to health" be **4.84** *evaluated? Charlton and its application:* Whether "substantial risk to health" had to be evaluated against specific employments or in the abstract generated a number of conflicting Commissioners' decisions on IFW Regs, reg. 27(b), but its meaning and the approach to take to its application was resolved by the Court of Appeal in *Charlton v Secretary of State for Work and Pensions* [2009] EWCA Civ 42 (the appeal from the decision of Commissioner Williams in *CIB/143/2007*) in judgments that make it clear that they apply also to the same terms in the relevant ESA Regulations.

Regulation 29(2)((b) requires (as noted above) a decision firstly that a person suffers as a consequence of some specific disease or bodily or mental disablement which does not of itself cause such functional limitation as to justify a total score warranting a finding of limited capability for work; it can only come into play where it has been found that the claimant does not have limited capability for work under the LCWA. It requires, secondly, a decision on whether because of the disease or disablement there would be a substantial risk to the mental or physical health of *any person* if the claimant were found capable of work (*Charlton*, para. 30). The risk to be assessed must arise as a consequence of work the claimant would be found capable of undertaking, but for reg. 29 (*Charlton*, para. 33). Paragraph 2(b) might be satisfied

"where the very finding of capability might create a substantial risk to a claimant's health or that of others, for example when a claimant suffering from anxiety or depression might suffer a significant deterioration on being told that the benefit claimed was being refused. Apart from that, probably rare, situation, the determination must be made in the context of the journey to or from work or in the workplace itself" (*Charlton*, para. 34).

Although the regulation is headed "exceptional circumstances" and the wording of para. (2)(b) refers to the the health of "any person", in *HR v SSWP (ESA)* [2013] UKUT 55 (AAC), Judge Wikeley rightly pointed out that its coverage is in law determined by the words used in the body of the regulation. It cannot cover any circumstance describable as "exceptional". There was no evidence before the tribunal to enable it to conclude that the claimant being found capable of work posed any substantial risk to her. She did have an adult daughter recently diagnosed with terminal cancer, but again there was no evidence to show that the claimant being found capable of work would put the daughter's health at substantial risk. Indeed the claimant's regular visits to her daughter of about two hours a day were maintainable if having to claim JSA or being in full or part-time work. He thought the tribunal entitled to proceed and not adjourn to seek more evidence on that. ESA was not designed to cover a difficult case such as this. The more appropriate benefits might be DLA for the daughter and carer's allowance for the mother.

On one view the "proper approach" to para. (2)(b)—accepted as such in *CF v SSWP (ESA)* [2012] UKUT 29 (AAC) (Judge Parker); *SP v SSWP (ESA)* [2014] UKUT 522 (AAC) (Judge Parker); *SD v SSWP (ESA)* [2014] UKUT 240 (AAC)

(Judge Mark); *GS v SSWP (ESA)* [2014] UKUT 16 (AAC) (Judge Mark)—is to start with the statement of Judge Mark in *IJ v SSWP (IB)* [2010] UKUT 408 (AAC):

> "the test is not limited to whether there would be a substantial risk to the claimant from any work he may undertake. *The test is as to the risk as a result of being found capable of work.* If he was found capable of work, he would lose his incapacity benefit, and would very possibly need to seek work and apply for jobseeker's allowance. That would involve his attending interviews, and going through all the other steps that would be needed to obtain and keep jobseeker's allowance. In the present economic climate, a claimant who is 62 years old with mental health problems, and who has not worked since the early 1990's is unlikely to find work quickly and would very possibly never find it. His GP's assessment that it is inconceivable that he would ever be able to earn his living may be right. The tribunal would then have to determine how this change from his being in receipt of incapacity benefit would affect the claimant's mental health, looking not at some work he may do, but at the effect on his mental health of fruitless and repeated interviews and the possibly hopeless pursuit of jobs until he reached retirement age. These factors were not considered by the tribunal, and indeed they did not elicit the information necessary to enable them to be considered, such as whether he had in fact applied for jobseeker's allowance and if not, how he was coping or would cope" (para.10, emphasis supplied by commentator).

Such cases will be rare (*Charlton*, para.34; *MB v SSWP (ESA)* [2012] UKUT 228 (AAC), para.14 (Judge Jacobs)), so that in most cases the key task is to identify the nature of the relevant work and workplace and to consider the nature of the risk to the health of the claimant or another person in the context of that work, that workplace, and the journey to and from it.

The passage from Judge Mark's decision in *IJ v SSWP (IB)* [2010] UKUT 408 (AAC) (at para.10) cited immediately above was approved by Judge White in *NS v SSWP (ESA)* [2014] UKUT 115 (AAC); [2014] AACR 33, with the observation that reg.29(2)(b) "is not just about whether there is any work or type of work which a claimant can do without substantial risk to the mental or physical health of any person. It is about whether a substantial risk would arise from a claimant's being found not to have limited capability for work" (para.45). The same passage in *IJ v SSWP (IB)* was criticised by Judge Lane in *MW v SSWP (ESA)* [2015] UKUT 665 (AAC); however, Judge Lane's decision makes no reference to the previous reported decision of *NS v SSWP (ESA)*, which would appear to settle the point that e.g. conditionality issues *may* be relevant to the regulation 29 assessment. See further *JT v SSWP (ESA)* [2018] UKUT 124 (AAC). See also *ET v SSWP (UC)* [2021] UKUT 47 (AAC), not following *MW v SSWP (ESA)* and confirming that journeys to the Jobcentre or for job interviews are relevant to the reg.29 risk assessment.

Be that as it may, the Court in *Charlton* held that the correct approach to identifying the nature of the relevant work and workplace for the claimant was that identified with respect to IFW Regs, reg.27(b) in paras 17-18 of Deputy Commissioner Paines' decision in *CIB/360/2007*. It rejected the view that decision-makers and tribunals had to speculate as to the type of job which would have been set out for purposes of a JSA claim in a hypothetical Jobseeker's Agreement. Rather (reading Personal Capability Assessment as LCWA):

> "The decision-maker must assess the range or type of work which a claimant is capable of performing sufficiently to assess the risk to health either to himself or to others.
>
> Sufficient information may be elicited by reference to the claimant's completion of the initial questionnaire, questioning during his medical examination, or by any evidence he may choose to give on an appeal to the Tribunal. The process to be adopted by the decision-maker or Tribunal is to be regarded as inquisitorial and not adversarial. It is a process described by Diplock J. in *R. v Medical*

Appeal Tribunal (North Midland Region ex-parte Hubble) 1958 2 QB 228 at 240 as a fact gathering exercise in which there is no formal burden of proof on either side. There should be no difficulty provided the decision-maker or Tribunal recall that the essential question is whether there is an adequate range of work which the claimant could undertake without creating a substantial risk to himself or to others. This conclusion is consistent with the practical application of these regulations. Any interpretation must bear in mind that the regulations are designed to provide a fair and effective system for assessing entitlement to incapacity benefit and to allied benefits when a claimant has passed the Personal Capability Assessment. It would not be possible to achieve the aim of those regulations were the decision-maker to be required to make findings of the particularity for which the claimant contends. The decision-maker, it must be recalled, will be provided only with the report of the doctor based upon the doctor's interview with the claimant and the claimant's completion of the questionnaire. It is quite impossible for the decision-maker to identify actual positions of employment or the nature of the duties and location of any job which the claimant might undertake, not least because the decision-maker may often be based in Belfast, or elsewhere, and can have no possible means of discovering employment circumstances throughout the country. The conclusion which requires no more than that the decision-maker or Tribunal assess the range of work of which the claimant is capable for the purposes of assessing risk to health has the merit of achieving the objective of the regulations" (*Charlton*, paras 45-47).

The Court upheld Commissioner Williams' finding that Mr Charlton was capable of performing the kind of work:—

"... to which a person with no physical limitations, no qualifications, no skills and no experience might be directed ([section] 48) and that he could undertake straightforward and unstructured, unskilled work."

There is undoubtedly a tension between the approach of Judge Mark in *IJ v SSWP (IB)* and that of Judge Lane in *MW v SSWP (ESA)*, as recognised by Judge Bano in *JT v SSWP (ESA)* [2018] UKUT 124 (AAC). In the circumstances of that case, Judge Bano did not find it necessary to resolve that tension, although the tenor of his decision is more in keeping with the approach in *IJ v SSWP (IB)*. Thus Judge Bano held that "in the case of claimants with fragile mental health the possible effects on a claimant of any compulsion to perform a particular type of work may have to be taken into account when considering regulation 29(2)(b)." Furthermore, the inquiry necessary under reg.29(2)(b):

"can only be sensibly undertaken if full account is taken of risks to a particular claimant resulting from any compulsion to undertake the work because of an element of 'conditionality' in the relevant benefits regime. Regulation 29(2)(b) is intended to protect third parties as well as claimants, and there is no indication in the legislation that any matter which is relevant to an assessment of the risks resulting from a claimant carrying out a particular type of work should not be taken into account."

The tension between *IJ v SSWP (IB)* and *MW v SSWP (ESA)* was tackled head on by Judge Wright in *ET v SSWP (UC)* [2021] UKUT 47 (AAC), who held that consideration of the question of substantial risk (in that context under para.4 of Sch. 8 to the United Credit Regulations) can include travel to and from the Jobcentre and job interviews as well as to and from work. Furthermore, Judge Wright held (at paras.25-30) that *MW v SSWP (ESA)* was itself wrongly decided, given both the statutory language and the reasoning in *Charlton* and *NS v SSWP (ESA)*:

"29. Therefore, the statutory language does not provide any statutory restriction or fetter against taking into account, where relevant, travelling to and from the Jobcentre and job interviews (and engaging with others in so doing and at the

Jobcentre or job interview). In the context of income-replacement benefits, it will very often be the inevitable consequence of claimants being found not to have limited capability for work that they will have to take such steps in order to satisfy the conditions of entitlement to jobseeker's allowance or universal credit. Indeed, I struggle to understand the basis on which the statutory language could be taken as importing such a restriction in a context where, per *Charlton*, the reaction to the 'fit for work' decision itself and being in, and travelling to and from, work **are** to be taken as relevant consequences of the decision. To exclude what will in all likelihood be the more immediate or proximate consequences of the decision – for example, attending at the Jobcentre – but include what may perhaps be a remoter consequence of being found work, seems in my judgment to lack rationality, and is not justified on the statutory language alone."

Should a tribunal consider whether a claimant could work from home? It is submitted that the better view is that it should *not* do so, save perhaps in one rare case.

In *SM v SSMP (ESA)* [2014] UKUT 241 (AAC), Judge Wikeley held that a tribunal erred in law by looking at work from home That approach is supported by references in *Charlton* to travelling to and from a workplace and by the amendment to the regulation about taking account of an employer's reasonable adjustments to the workplace. Although working from home is more common that in the past it is entirely dependent on an employer's discretion and to take it into account would deprive the regulation of any real purpose for large number of cases and defeat the legislative purpose of protecting exceptionally vulnerable people, especially those with mental health problems (paras 7–11). He cited in support of his interpretation the tenor of Judge Ward's decision in *PD v SSWP (ESA)* [2014] UKUT 148. Judge Wikeley noted that Judge Ward there

"identified the central issue in that appeal as being the impact of regulation 29 "on persons who by reason of mental ill-health have an impaired ability to get to places, such as a hypothetical workplace" (at paragraph 1). If claimants could not avail themselves of regulation 29 simply because they could get a home-working job, then the whole premise of Judge Ward's analysis was flawed. I do not accept that it was" (para.11).

It should be noted, however, that later in *PD*, Judge Ward seemed to indicate that a tribunal *could* look at the viability and suitability of work from home before looking at ability to travel to a workplace. Judge Ward stated

"The tribunal may wish to explore types of work which the person could do from home. Even if the traditional fields for such activity have declined, information technology must bring with it a number of such opportunities for some people. But if such work is not appropriate to the particular claimant, the tribunal will have to conduct the assessment of risk, which is the primary purpose of regulation 29, as best it can in relation to the sort of range of work mandated by *Charlton*, outside the home. If someone has been found to be unable to do something, I find it hard to see how it might be possible to hold that there would be no substantial risk to their health on an assumption that they were effectively made to do that which had been found to be impossible for them (i.e. go to work unaccompanied), though I do not intend to lay that down as a proposition of law. Far more likely is it that what is required is an evaluation of their circumstances when making the hypothetical journey, in particular in relation to being accompanied, in order to see whether the conditions could be satisfied which would alleviate or avoid the risk to health" (para.16).

Agreeing that Judge Wikeley was correct on the facts of *SM*, in *CL v SSWP (ESA)* [2015] UKUT 375 (AAC), Judge Jacobs declined to find in *SM* an absolute prohibition on considering home working under this regulation, stating that it was possible, albeit rare, "that the only type of work for which the claimant is suitable might be in an industry where home working is possible, even encouraged" (para.12).

Where the claimant has an existing job to go back to but is as yet unable to do so, the **4.85**
relevance of that job to the reg.29(2) question lies solely in the reasons why the claimant
cannot return to that job. In *AJ v SSWP (ESA)* [2013] UKUT 279 (AAC), Judge
Wright stated:

> "For example, and these are no more than examples, if the appellant was not then
> doing the job because the police had in place a temporary cleaner whose contract
> still had a month to run and they did not want to have the appellant back at the
> same time, that may have little or nothing relevant to say about risk in terms of
> the appellant carrying out such a job. On the other hand, if the police had made
> its own assessment and found that the appellant needed until, say, the end of
> August 2010 before she could safely work as a cleaner then that would have been
> very relevant to regulation 29(2)(b) risk assessment. That may then have ruled
> out dexterous manual work as relevant work and would have needed the tribunal
> to look elsewhere for work the appellant was suited both as a matter of training
> and aptitude" (para.13).

Regulation 29(2)(b) looks to risk and not to more remote matters such as the ultimate
or longer-term benefit to the claimant. What is at issue is not the claimant's positive
attitude to work but rather whether there is a substantial risk to health if he were
found not to have limited capability for work; if that risk exists it is not altered by the
claimant's attitude to it (*JW v SSWP* (ESA) [2011] UKUT 416 (AAC), para.12).
Similarly, whether work would be good for the claimant is not the correct test (*CH
v SSMP) (ESA)* [2014] UKUT 11 (AAC)).

In terms of timescale, the claimant being found not to have limited capability for
work occurs when the Secretary of State makes his decision and tribunals must look
at the risk as at that date. But that decision has to look to the future, at what will be
the effect of the finding given that *Charlton* widened the scope of the enquiry to take
account of how the claimant would function in work (*CH v SSWP (ESA)* [2014]
UKUT 11 (AAC), paras11-13). As Judge Mark put it in *GS v SSWP (ESA)* [2014]
UKUT 16 (AAC):

> "the job of the tribunal was to assess . . ., as at the date of the decision, the risk to
> the claimant's health of her being found not to have limited capability for work.
> As pointed out repeatedly, this does not prevent tribunals from having regard to
> evidence coming into existence after the date of the decision, or of events after the
> decision under appeal, so long as it is relevant to the prognosis at that date. Thus
> in *R(DLA) 3/01* the actual rate of recovery of a claimant from a health problem
> was held to be relevant to the question whether as at the date of the decision the
> claimant was likely to satisfy the relevant conditions for benefit for 6 months after
> the date of the decision. So too, in the present case, the tribunal needed to assess
> whether there was a deterioration in the claimant's health following the decision,
> the extent of the deterioration, and the extent to which it was as a result of her
> being found not to have limited capability for work. This includes the stress from
> an appeal, successful or otherwise, the stress of dealing with the Jobcentre and
> possible interviews, the prospects of employment, and the ways in which it is said
> that the claimant's mental health can be kept stabilised bearing in mind, if the
> evidence is accepted, that it appears to have deteriorated even without seeking or
> obtaining work and without both the pressures of work and the additional pres-
> sures on daily life if she did spend part of it working" (paras 16, 17).

In *MB v SSWP (ESA)* [2012] UKUT 228 (AAC), Judge Jacobs was concerned
with the case of a claimant (Mr B) addicted to drugs and taking part in a drug
recovery programme. The argument was made that since wages from work which
were higher than benefit income would enable him to buy more drugs than when
on benefit, this would increase the risk to his health and so reg.29(2)(b) should
apply. Judge Jacobs identified the issue as: what connection does there have to
be between the risk and being found capable of work? Must the risk arise from

the work itself or is it enough that it arises from some consequence (in this case increased income) that follows from the work but is unrelated to the nature of the work? Applying *Charlton*, he accepted the Secretary of State's argument (see para.10) that the provision did not embrace the claimant's argument. As Judge Jacobs saw it, *Charlton*

> "decided that the trigger for the risk had to be found in the work the claimant would be undertaking. It had to arise from: (i) the decision that the claimant had capability for work; (ii) the work that the claimant might do; or (iii) travelling to and from work. (i) will be rare.
>
> The argument for Mr B is that the wages he would receive for the work would put more money in his pocket than he would spend on drugs. That is not a risk that arises from the work. The work is merely the circumstance that gives rise to it. It would not arise if his wages were so low that he would have been better off on benefit. Nor would it arise if the street price for the drugs increased in line with his income so that he could not afford any more drugs than previously. In other words, the risk arises from the comparative value of Mr B's benefit and the wages he might receive relative to the price of drugs" (paras 14, 15).

4.86 *Where travelling to work unaccompanied is the potential risk, a question arises as to whether third party assistance can be considered as alleviating it.* In *PD v SSWP (ESA)* [2014] UKUT 148 (AAC), Judge Ward considered that the risk with respect to travelling to work arising from physical elements was likely to be rare; the traveller contemplated by the Court of Appeal in *Charlton* was "the person whose mental health problems cause difficulties with the journey to work" (para.15). Judge Ward's starting point was that where there was appropriate evidence third party help could be taken into account, that line of argument was open to the Secretary of State (paras 23, 26):

> "There will be cases, for instance where a partner is not working, there is no one else at home who uses the car and where the evidence shows a pattern of the partner driving the claimant to wherever s/he wants or needs to go, that it may be open to a tribunal to infer that such help would similarly be available to get a claimant to the *Charlton*-mandated hypothetical workplace. If a scheme such as Access to Work were available on a sufficiently reliable basis, it is hard to see why it should not be taken into account. Such are ultimately conclusions of fact and not matters on which I need say more, except to observe that this may be, par excellence, a field in which tribunals can look to the principles of *Kerr v Department for Social Development* [2004] UKHL 23; [2004] 1 WLR 1372" (para.26).

Judge Ward also stated that

> "What is difficult in relation to transport is yet harder in relating to accompaniment within the workplace. Such a setup would be highly unusual, even if only to help with the first few days. I did not hear argument on whether that, unlike the provision of transport, could constitute a reasonable adjustment for Equality Act purposes" (para.27).

Judge Hemingway in *HT v SSWP (ESA)* [2018] UKUT 174 (AAC) has agreed with Judge Ward in *PD v SSWP (ESA)* [2014] UKUT 148 (AAC) that the risk within reg.29 with respect to travelling to work is likely to be "rare (though not impossible)" in the context of "physical health difficulties in circumstances where those same difficulties do not lead to the risk arising in the workplace itself" (at para.19). Likewise, "the prospect of third party assistance on the journey will be a potentially relevant consideration though the availability of such cannot simply, without evidence, be assumed. Where the arguments as to risk relate to falling the use of such as walking sticks and walking frames will need to be considered."

Where someone satisfies descriptor 15(c) in Sch.2 (needs assistance to get to an unfamiliar place), third party assistance might be a possibility of avoiding the risk to health for an initial period until the journey to and from the workplace became familiar *(EJ v SSWP (ESA)* [2014] UKUT 551 (AAC) paras 19, 21 (Judge Wikeley)). But practicalities need to be looked at *(SS v SSWP (ESA)* [2015] UKUT 101 (AAC), para.5 (Judge Rowland)) and a sound evidential basis shown for relevant findings of fact *(ET v SSWP (UC)* [2021] UKUT 47 (AAC)). In another context, the three-judge panel in *JC v SSWP (ESA)* [2014] UKUT 352 (AAC); [2015] AACR 6, did not consider that a person could properly be regarded "as able to engage in social contact if she or he can do so only if accompanied by someone, *at least without further explanation as to how it is envisaged that that might be realistic in the workplace*" (para.45, emphasis supplied by commentator).

It should also be noted that in stark contrast in *MT v SSWP (ESA)* [2013] UKUT 545 (AAC), in the context of reg.35(2), Judge Gray firmly rejected looking at capacity to perform activities with third party assistance, observing:

"I do need to deal however with the observation of the FTT in its statement of reasons that the appellant could take another person with her to any work-related activities. It may be that the Secretary of State would be facilitative in any matter which helped a claimant engage so as to improve their ultimate prospects of retaining work. I do not know. Whether or not that is so, is not relevant. As a matter of law any work-related activity which could only be accomplished because of the presence of another person must be looked upon as not being an activity that the claimant can carry out. *The issue under regulation 35 (2) (b) as to whether there would be a substantial risk to the mental or physical health of any person if the claimant were found not to have limited capability for work-related activity cannot be assessed as if the claimant under consideration had somebody else by their side.* There will be claimants who have a need for the personal reassurance of another person, but who do not have anybody available to perform that role. Even if they did, it would not be reasonable for such an assessment to be made on the basis of reliance on another's goodwill. Legal tests cannot depend upon that. Where an appellant who is found to have limited capability for work-related activities wishes to engage voluntarily, it may be that they choose to do so with the help of another person, and it may (or may not, I do not know) be possible for them to do so, but the capacity to engage only with that assistance cannot be part of the test of capability" (para.34, emphasis added by commentator).

In *PD*, Judge Ward agreed with the italicised passage insofar as it meant "without consideration as to whether the third party's presence would be made out in fact" (para.21), but otherwise distinguished the passage as focussing on the claimant's capability to perform activities (agreeing that there third party assistance should be ignored) rather than the different question of what risks would ensue (where, with respect to travelling, at least, third party assistance available in fact might obviate the risk). See also *SP v SSWP (ESA)* [2014] UKUT 522 (AAC), where Judge Parker did not categorically reject as inadmissible the Secretary of State's submission that the claimant could be accompanied (at least initially) to some interviews, but instead concluded that "this would not address some of the potential stress to which Judge Mark referred [in *IJ v SSWP (IB)* [2010] UKUT 408 (AAC)" (para.7).

As the foregoing discussion makes clear Charlton *must be applied in the light of all the available evidence.* In *LD v SSWP (ESA)* [2014] UKUT 131 (AAC), Judge Ward held that retirement on health grounds 17 years earlier could be of probative value and ongoing relevance since it had involved an assessment by experts that at that time the claimant was permanently incapable of doing a particular type of job and other evidence before the tribunal had indicated a deterioration rather than an improvement in the claimant's condition since that time. In *GS v SSWP (ESA)* [2014] UKUT 16 (AAC), Judge Mark held:

4.87

"It was the duty of the decision maker in relation to the present appeal, under rule 24(4)(b) of the Tribunal Procedure (First-tier Tribunal) (SEC) Rules 2008, to provide with the response to the appeal copies of all documents relevant to the case in the decision maker's possession. It was also the duty of the Secretary of State, under rule 2(4) of the same Rules, to help the tribunal to deal with the case fairly and justly. Under one head or the other, if not both, the tribunal ought to have been provided with copies of the evidence before the previous tribunal which had heard the appeal only 7 months before the new decision now under appeal. It is a duty which the new tribunal [to which he remitted the case] ought to have enforced" (para.5).

The effect of failure to follow the steps required by Charlton: Generally failing to follow the steps approved in *Charlton* will mean that the tribunal errs in law as in *JW v SSWP (ESA)* [2011] UKUT 416 (AAC). In *SSWP v Cattrell* [2011] EWCA Civ 572; [2011] AACR 35, however, the Court of Appeal held that while tribunals should normally identify the range of work that a claimant might be capable of, in this particular case because the first-tier tribunal had accepted evidence that there was no prospect of this claimant finding any suitably safe work, adopting the approach in *Charlton* and speculating about a range of possible work was not appropriate. But so doing was not here an error of law and the decision that this claimant was entitled to IB on the basis of "substantial risk" (there IFW Regs, reg.27(b), the equivalent of ESA Regs, reg.29(2)(b)) should stand. In contrast, in *RB v SSWP (ESA)* [2012] UKUT 431 (AAC), the tribunal merely stated that there was no evidence to suggest that reg.29 applied. Judge Ward held that it had erred in law in not identifying in its reasons that it had considered the range of work the claimant might be expected to do; given his knee problem and work background the answer was not self-evident (paras 4–7).

4.88 *A question which has troubled tribunals at both levels is whether reg.29(2)(b) must always be considered where the claimant has failed to achieve a sufficient score on the LCWA?* It need not be considered as a matter of routine, but whether it should be considered in any particular case depends on all the circumstances of that case (*PC v SSWP (ESA)* [2014] UKUT 1 (AAC); *SP v SSWP (ESA)* [2014] UKUT 10 (AAC); *DB v SSWP (ESA)* [2014] UKUT 41 (AAC); *NS v SSWP (ESA)* [2014] UKUT 115 (AAC); [2014] AACR 33). If a competent representative chooses not to raise it, then, absent unusual circumstances, a tribunal need not consider it. However, the more narrowly focused the descriptors in the LCWA become, the more likely it is that reg.29(2)(b) will be put in issue (*RB v SSWP (ESA)* [2012] UKUT 431 (AAC), para.7; *NS v SSWP (ESA)* [2014] UKUT 115 (AAC); [2014] AACR 33, para.50). It is likely particularly to be relevant where mental health issues are involved. In *NS v SSWP (ESA)* [2014] UKUT 115 (AAC); [2014] AACR 33, Judge White proffered the following useful guidance to tribunals:

"There will be some cases in which a tribunal need say nothing about regulation 29(2)(b). I give one clear example. Where a claimant is represented, claims only problems with physical functions, is found to score no points under Part 1 of Schedule 2 to the Employment and Support Allowance Regulations 2008, and where the representative does not put regulation 29(2)(b) in issue, a tribunal can safely leave out any mention of regulation 29(2)(b). However, in such a case a wise tribunal would seek confirmation from the representative that no issue is raised under regulation 29(2)(b) if they were to find that no points are scored under the Part 1 descriptors.

There will be some cases in which a tribunal must address regulation 29(2)(b). Clearly, if it is put in issue by a claimant, it must be fully and properly addressed. This will not require repetition of the findings of fact made in respect of the descriptors in Schedule 2, but that will be the obvious starting point for the explanation of why regulation 29(2)(b) does or does not apply.

In cases in which the descriptors relating to mental, cognitive and intellectual functions are in issue, it is more likely that regulation 29(2)(b) will be relevant.

After all, in cases which come before the tribunal, more often than not the claimant's GP has issued a certificate that the claimant is incapable of work (though I accept that the GP may not be making that judgment against the Schedule 2 assessment). If the GP has submitted a letter in support of the claimant's appeal, that will often indicate why the GP considers that the claimant is incapable of work" (paras 47–49).

That guidance was followed by Judge Gray in *KB v SSWP (ESA)* [2014] UKUT 303 (AAC).

Although reg.29(2)(b) can only come into play where the person has failed to achieve a sufficient score in the LCWA, the question of which descriptors a claimant satisfies is relevant to the application of the paragraph because one is determining the matter taking due account of the claimant's disabilities (*CF v SSWP (ESA)* [2012] UKUT 29 (AAC), paras 14, 15). Indeed, a claimant's satisfaction of descriptor 15(b) (9 points) must inevitably raise the question of the applicability of reg.29 since that means that the claimant has been found to be "unable to get to a particular place with which the claimant is familiar, without being accompanied by another person", thus raising issues about substantial risk to the claimant's health in terms of the journey to work (*SS v SSWP (ESA)* [2015] UKUT 101 (AAC), para.4 (Judge Rowland)).

While a Med 3 issued by the claimant's GP is not conclusive on the issue under reg.29(2), the implications of the certificate must be addressed and facts found to the extent possible (*SP v SSWP (ESA)* [2014] UKUT 278 (AAC), para.16). In *RU v SSWP (ESA)* [2014] UKUT 77 (AAC), Judge Ward held that:

> "if the claimant's GP was advising his or her patient to refrain from work for 6 months by a Med 3 issued more or less contemporaneously with the decision under appeal, it was incumbent on the tribunal to consider the implications of that. The work capability assessment is an artificial construct, which looks at certain activities only, and there is no necessary correlation between a doctor's views as to what the patient can manage and the outcome of the WCA applied to that person, or vice versa. Regulation 29 has the function of a safety valve addressing that lack of correlation, protecting claimants (and others) from the effect of determinations which in the circumstances set out in that regulation would otherwise result in substantial risk to health" (para.6).

In addition, the existence of a recent DLA award on the ground of day supervision is likely to be material evidence and required to be addressed (*NA (by ST) v SSWP (ESA)* [2012] UKUT 428 (AAC), para.3).

The standard of tribunal decision-making and giving of reasons as the applicability or otherwise of reg.29(2)(b) has caused concern among Upper Tribunal Judges.   If a tribunal chooses to address the provision, whether at the request of the claimant, representative or of its own volition, "it must do so properly . . . and an inadequate analysis" will not suffice (*EJ v SSWP (ESA)* [2014] UKUT 551 (AAC), para.18). Its findings on reg.29(2)(b) must be consistent with those it has made on the application of the Sch.2 descriptors (*CC v SSWP (ESA)* [2015] UKUT 62 (AAC), para.22; *SS v SSWP (ESA)* [2015] UKUT 101 (AAC), para.4). In *NS v SSWP (ESA)* [2014] UKUT 115 (AAC); [2014] AACR 33, Judge White proffered the following useful guidance to tribunals:

4.89

> "I do not consider that the level of detail required for proper reasons on the application of regulation 29(2)(b) is high. The more obvious it is that regulation 29(2)(b) does not apply, the easier it should be to give reasons why that is so.
>
> What is frequently missing from brief statements that regulation 29(2)(b) does not apply is the addition of a statement as to why it does not apply. This is exemplified by the statement in the appeal before me, where the tribunal said:

Regulation 29 does not apply as the Tribunal was not satisfied that there was a substantial risk to the appellant or to any person if he were not found to have limited capability for work.

What is needed is for that sentence to end in a comma and to be followed by the word "because" and then a phrase or two explaining why regulation 29(2) (b) does not apply. After all, if the tribunal has done a proper job in considering regulation 29(2)(b) they must have considered why the regulation did not apply. Otherwise, this is a mere formulaic response to the issue. A tribunal which embarks upon a consideration of regulation 29(2)(b) must do a proper job of considering it" (paras 50–53).

For a further example of a case in which the Upper Tribunal followed the same approach, namely that the more obvious it is that reg.29 does not apply, the easier it is to say why that is so, see *JH(S) v Secretary of State for Work and Pensions (ESA)* [2015] UKUT 567 (AAC). The following observation was made by Judge Hemingway in *RK v Secretary of State for Work and Pensions (ESA)* [2015] UKUT 549 (AAC), allowing an appeal on the reg.29 point:

"16. I would just wish to add one brief final comment. It seems to me that a consideration of the type or range of work a claimant might reasonably be expected to undertake is something which is often (though by no means always) missed by a tribunal. Often that will not be fatal. Indeed, as was made clear in *NS*, cited above, it will sometimes not be fatal even if regulation 29 is not referred to at all. However, there will be cases, as here, and it seems to me they are not infrequent, where there are indications that the range might be limited for various reasons, perhaps a lack of experience of or aptitude for certain categories of work, perhaps a difficulty with written or spoken English, perhaps an established physical or mental disablement, perhaps something else, such that a proper consideration of this aspect is needed. Of course, the test does not require anything like the sort of detailed analysis which might be involved in, say, testing the degree of risk to health by reference to specific jobs or job descriptions. A short assessment, perhaps only a couple of sentences or so, will often be enough. A tribunal will often already have some background information in the documents before it and will be able to ask questions about the sorts of matters referred to above if an oral hearing is held. Where competent representatives are involved it may well assist a tribunal if any written submission lodged in advance of a hearing can specify whether and on what basis regulation 29 is relied upon and can deal with, if thought to be relevant, the question of the range or type of work."

Merely reiterating the statutory test in negative form will not suffice. As Judge Bano rightly stressed in *PH v SSWP (ESA)* [2014] UKUT 502 (AAC)

"[t]he difficult issues which may arise under regulation 29 will often require detailed findings of fact to be made by the tribunal, rather than mantra-like recitations of the terms of the legislation and unparticularised references to adjustments in the workplace" (para.5).

In *MF v SSWP (ESA)* [2014] UKUT 523 (AAC), Judge Mark allowed the appeal stating that

"...The tribunal does not indicate what occupation or range of occupations it had in mind. More seriously it totally failed to deal with the points actually made in the written submissions. It was dealing with a claimant who had not worked for 20 years, whose appearance was described by the disability analyst as unkempt, and whose behaviour was described as restless with reduced facial expression, and whom it had found was prone to episodes of depression when he may lack the motivation to do things.

The tribunal needed to address how he would have coped not just with an interview and with some unspecified job when not having a depressive episode, but with all the matters identified by the claimant's representative in his written submissions and then determine whether there was a substantial risk to his mental or physical health (or that of anybody else) if he were found not to have limited capability for work. There have also been raised, at least before me, issues as to the extent to which the claimant can use public transport or travel at busy times and the tribunal may need to consider this both in connection with any requirements imposed in connection with jobseeker's allowance and in connection with any employment he may obtain. In failing to identify the correct issues and to make appropriate reasoned findings, the tribunal was in error of law. Its decision must be set aside and the matter remitted for rehearing by a new tribunal" (paras 7–8).

Similarly, Judge Wikeley in *CC v SSWP (ESA)* [2015] UKUT 62 (AAC) held erroneous in law a tribunal decision which inadequately explained why reg.29(2)(b) failed to apply. It had awarded the claimant 9 points under descriptor 8(c): "unable to navigate around unfamiliar surroundings, without being accompanied by another person, due to sensory impairment". The tribunal's finding that the claimant could "get about safely and see right in front of him at a short distance" was not, without further explanation, consistent with its decision on that descriptor (para.22).

Ultimately the adequacy of reasons required is going to be context-specific. For example, in *DB v SSWP (ESA)* [2016] UKUT 493 (AAC) Judge Gray, in dismissing the claimant's appeal, observed as follows:

"21. Regulation 29 whilst relevant at the outset of the appeal, really ceased to be so in view of the findings of the tribunal that the somewhat extreme difficulties the appellant put forward as being caused by her continuing chronic pain were not made out. The tribunal ... simply did not accept that she would have either the problems that she said she had, or, indeed, any problems at all under the descriptors. In those factual circumstances there could be no question of substantial risk. It would not have been inappropriate for the tribunal, having made its findings, to have decided not to formally consider regulation 29, or, to put it perhaps more accurately, to consider it only in order to confirm that it was not, or was not any longer, an applicable consideration in the light of those findings. In any event read as a whole the explanation satisfied the test set out by the Court of Appeal in *Charlton*."

In *DB v Secretary of State for Work and Pensions (ESA)* [2017] UKUT 251 (AAC) Judge Bano gave the following guidance on the application of reg.29:

"9. It is clear from the judgment of the Court of Appeal in *Charlton* that the question of whether regulation 29 applies to a claimant is fact-specific and that a tribunal's findings in relation to the Regulation must therefore be based specifically on a claimant's individual circumstances. That is not to say that the reasons for a tribunal's decision on whether regulation 29 applies to a claimant need necessarily be long or elaborate, and in many cases the tribunal's findings in relation to matters such as the nature and extent of a claimant's disablement will also provide a basis for their conclusions in relation to regulation 29. However, in carrying out the risk assessment required by the Regulation, it is in my view necessary that it should be reasonably apparent from the reasons, read as a whole, that the individual circumstances of the particular claimant have been fully and properly taken into account when deciding whether the Regulation applies."

The (in)applicability of the Equality Act 2010: the Equality Act 2010 has been mentioned and subject to varying degrees of consideration in a number of Upper Tribunal decisions in a number of contexts. But its specific applicability in the context of reg.29(2)(b) was most fully argued before Judge Wright in *JS v SSWP (ESA)* [2014] UKUT 428; [2015] AACR 12, a case in which an oral hearing was held, and the matter analysed in a judgment running to 78 paragraphs. His conclusion was that "the assessment of risk under regulation 29(2)(b) of the ESA Regs does not require or involve the decision maker (be that the Secretary of State's delegate or the First-tier Tribunal) in making an assessment as to whether employers would owe a duty under the Equality Act 2010 to make reasonable adjustments in respect of the individual claimant whose case falls for decision, and in my judgment the tribunal therefore erred in law in relying on the Equality Act 2010 to that effect" (para.5).

It is submitted that his conclusion that the Equality Act 2010 is not applicable is the correct approach to the matter, for the reasons he gave (summarised below). His decision has been reported, and is accepted as the correct approach by the Secretary of State; in *SB v SSWP (ESA)* [2015] UKUT 88 (AAC), Judge Ward accepted as "properly made" the concession by the Secretary of State in the appeal. The Secretary of State considered that in *JS*

"Judge Wright held that:

- it is not sufficient for the First-tier Tribunal (FtT) to assume that because the Equality Act 2010 will require an employer not to discriminate against and make reasonable adjustments in the work place to accommodate a disabled person, there will be no risk arising from the person being found fit for work;
- the assessment of risk under regulation 29(2)(b) of the ESA Regs 2008 however does <u>not</u> require or involve the SSWP or FtT in making an assessment as to whether employers would owe a duty under the Equality Act to make reasonable adjustments in respect of the individual claimant (specifically disagreeing with Judge Mark in *JB v SSWP (ESA)* [2013] UKUT 518 AAC.)"

The Secretary of State conceded that in practical terms, this meant "that in assessing [any] reg.29 risk, SSWP [and the First-tier Tribunal] must make a claimant specific risk assessment". While this includes the matter of what steps could reasonably and realistically be taken on the facts of the specific case to avoid substantial risk (a requirement now statutorily set by reg.29(3)(a)), it does not require evidence of what a potential employer would or might do by way of reasonable adjustments in compliance with any Equality Act duties the employer might be subject to.

Judge Wright supported his conclusion with a number of lines of reasoning which he saw as "incremental" (para.46).

He argued, firstly, that the Equality Act 2010 and employment and support allowance schemes have different statutory aims and materially different statutory contents. That the ESA Regs are not to be divorced from the real world (see *AS* and *SI*, above) points to the 2010 Act having potential relevance to the ESA Regs. But, as regards "statutory intendment", against that must be set the plain fact that the ESA Regs (and their predecessors for IB) have never on their face made any express link to the Equality Act 2010 or its predecessor, the Disability Discrimination Act 1995. Indeed, even where as now, para.(3)(a) requires consideration in applying para.(2)(b) to be given to "reasonable adjustments being made in the claimant's workplace" no link was made, pointing to para.(2)(b) "being intended to embody a test separate to the tests under the Equality Act 2010" (para.48). In addition, the ESA scheme applies to persons not in employment and unable to work, whereas the duties under the Equality Act 2010 apply only to employees or applicants for employment who have made known to the employer their disability. Moreover key elements for assessing disability are different, and noticeably different, under the two schemes (paras 53, 54).

Secondly, the Equality Act 2010 test sits uneasily with *Charlton*. That case eschewed an "actual employment" test which is essentially the test embodied in that Act (para.51). *Charlton* embraces the impact in respect of travelling to work; the 2010 Act does not (para.55). In addition, *Charlton* took account of the test under para (2)(b) "having to be applied practicably". Requiring a decision-maker to consider whether "the claimant would be likely to be owed a duty by an employer or employers to make reasonable adjustments under the statutory machinery contained within the Equality Act 2010" would be likely to render impracticable "a timeous decision" (para. 58).

Thirdly, the First-tier Tribunal is ill-equipped to make proper assessments under the Equality Act 2010, which matters are vested in the specialist employment tribunal. While the First-tier tribunal is also specialist in its sphere of operation, "on its face it is not concerned with assessing whether an employer will in fact owe a duty to make reasonable adjustments in respect of an individual disabled person" (para.57).

Finally, *recourse to the Equality Act 2010 is simply unnecessary*. The matter of applying the para.(2)(b) test in the light of reasonable adjustments which might be made in the envisaged range of workplaces is now explicit in para.(3)(a), but has also always been inherent in the risk assessment required by para.(2)(b),as interpreted in *Charlton*; as Judge Wright put it the wording is:

> "wide enough and flexible enough to encompass reasonable steps that realistically on the evidence may be taken by, or in respect of, the [specific individual] claimant, including by prospective employers. But that does not require an assessment to be made of employers' duties under the Equality Act 2010" (para.61).

There must first be analysis of the range and types of work which as a matter of training or aptitude the claimant is suited to do "and which his or her disabilities do not render him [or her] incapable of performing". There must then be assessed the risk the individual's disease(s) or disablement(s) would, on the balance of probabilities, give rise to

> "if the claimant was travelling to and from, and working in, employments he or she was otherwise suited to do. Part of that risk assessment will involve consideration of the steps that, on the evidence and having regard to the individual claimant's health conditions and other circumstances, could reasonably and realistically be taken to avoid any substantial risk to health" (para.62).

SB v SSWP (ESA) [2015] UKUT 88 (AAC) has been considered and followed in *SP v SSWP (ESA)* [2018] UKUT 205 (AAC), where the claimant had a latex allergy and appealed a refusal to award ESA on the basis of reg.29(2)(b). The tribunal dismissed her appeal, noting the duty of an employer to make adjustments under the Equality Act 2010, the claimant's responsibility to also consider making adjustments at work to minimise risk, and the claimant's failure to check for latex the chair she sat on at the tribunal hearing. Judge Poole QC held that the tribunal had made adequate findings of fact to support its conclusion under reg.29(2)(b). These included identifying the gravity of risk to health from the potential effects of allergic reactions to latex, the likelihood of the risk occurring, and risk mitigation measures (such as the claimant's use of medication and her experience in monitoring the environment around her to check for latex).

Paragraph (3)(a): reasonable adjustments in the claimant's workplace
See *SP v SSWP (ESA)* [2018] UKUT 205 (AAC), where the claimant had a   **4.90**
latex allergy and had appealed a refusal to award ESA on the basis of reg.29(2)(b) (discussed above). Judge Poole QC held as follows (at para.11):

> "The wording of regulation 29(3)(a) refers to reasonable adjustments in the claimant's workplace, without confining its application to adjustments made only by an employer. It is normal in the workplace to expect both employer and employee to play their parts in keeping the working environment as risk free as practicable. In my view both employer and employee can be expected to take reasonable measures. Accordingly, measures that a claimant may reasonably take to reduce risk are relevant either under the reasonable adjustment wording in regulation 29(3)(a), or even if that was wrong to the general consideration of whether a risk is substantial under regulation 29(2)(b)."

Conditions for treating a claimant as having limited capability for work until a determination about limited capability for work has been made

4.91   **30.**—(1) A claimant is, if the conditions set out in paragraph (2) are met, to be treated as having limited capability for work until such time as it is determined—

(a) whether or not the claimant has limited capability for work;

(b) whether or not the claimant is to be treated as having limited capability for work otherwise than in accordance with this regulation; or

(c) whether the claimant falls to be treated as not having limited capability for work in accordance with regulation 22 (failure to provide information in relation to limited capability for work) or 23 (failure to attend a medical examination to determine limited capability for work).

(2) The conditions are—

(a) that the claimant provides evidence of limited capability for work in accordance with the Medical Evidence Regulations; and

[³(b) in relation to the claimant's entitlement to any benefit, allowance or advantage which is dependent on the claimant having limited capability for work, it has not been determined—

(i) in the last determination preceding the date of claim for an employment and support allowance, that the claimant does not have limited capability for work; or

(ii) within the 6 months preceding the date of claim for an employment and support allowance, that the claimant is to be treated as not having limited capability for work under regulation 22 or 23,

unless paragraph (4) applies;]

(c) [²*omitted*].

[³(3) Paragraph 2(b) does not apply where a claimant has made and is pursuing an appeal against a relevant decision of the Secretary of State, and that appeal has not yet been determined by the First-tier Tribunal.]

[²(4) This paragraph applies where—

(a) the claimant is suffering from some specific disease or bodily or mental disablement from which the claimant was not suffering at the time of that determination;

(b) a disease or bodily or mental disablement from which the claimant was suffering at the time of that determination has significantly worsened; or

(c) in the case of a claimant who was treated as not having limited capability for work under regulation 22 (failure to provide information), the claimant has since provided the information requested under that regulation.]

[³(5) In this regulation a "relevant decision" means—

(a) a decision that embodies the first determination by the Secretary of State that the claimant does not have limited capability for work; or

(b) a decision that embodies the first determination by the Secretary of State that the claimant does not have limited capability for work since a previous determination by the Secretary of State or appellate authority that the claimant does have limited capability for work.

(6) In this regulation, "appellate authority" means the First-tier Tribunal,

the Upper Tribunal, the Court of Appeal, the Court of Session, or the Supreme Court.]

AMENDMENTS

1. Social Security (Miscellaneous Amendments) Regulations 2011 (SI 2011/674) reg.16(3) (April 11, 2011).
2. Social Security (Miscellaneous Amendments) (No.3) Regulations 2013 (SI 2013/2536) reg.13(14) (October 29, 2013).
3. Employment and Support Allowance (Repeat Assessments and Pending Appeal Awards) (Amendment) Regulations 2015 (SI 2015/437) reg.3 (March 30, 2015).

MODIFICATION

Regulation 30 is modified by Sch.1 para.10 of the Employment and Support Allowance (Transitional Provisions, Housing Benefit and Council Tax Benefit) (Existing Awards) (No.2) Regulations 2010 (SI 2010/1907) (as amended) for the purposes specified in reg.6(1). For details of the modification, pp.1410-1452 of Vol.1 of the 2020/21 edition.

DEFINITIONS

"appellate authority"—see para.(6).
"claimant"—see WRA 2007 s.24(1).
"limited capability for work"—see WRA 2007 s.1(4).
"Medical Evidence Regulations"—see reg.2(1).
"relevant decision"—see para.(5).

GENERAL NOTE

This regulation deals with the position of claimants for ESA pending a decision on eligibility. As amended with effect from March 30, 2015, it applies (a) where the claimant makes, or is treated as making a claim for ESA on or after that date, and (b) where, in respect of such a claim, the claimant makes and pursues an appeal against a Secretary of State's decision that s/he does not have limited capability for work (see reg.2 of the amending Regs). Claims made before March 30, 2015 and appeals in respect of them are instead regulated by the previous version of this regulation (for which see the 2014/15 edition of this book and the detailed analysis by Judge Wright in *EI v SSWP (ESA)* [2016] UKUT 397 (AAC))).

The March 2015 amendments were made to rectify an unintended consequence of the previous version of this regulation whereby someone whose entitlement had ended because of a finding that s/he did not have limited work could make a repeat claim after six months and gain a further period of entitlement to ESA pending a decision on eligibility even where the claimant could provide no evidence to suggest that their condition had significantly worsened or that they had a new health condition to be considered. One unwanted effect was that even where a First-tier Tribunal had upheld a fit for work decision, if the appeal process had taken longer than six months, a claimant could immediately make a repeat claim for ESA on the basis of exactly the same condition, and would be entitled to receive ESA at the assessment phase rate (the same rate as JSA) pending a new LCWA. The cycle between ESA claim, LCWA and disallowance would begin again.

As amended, the regulation provides that on a "repeat claim" for ESA (see below) the claimant will *not* be treated as having limited capability for work (and thus ESA entitlement at assessment rate pending determination of the claim) unless they can demonstrate either a significant deterioration in their health condition or that a new health condition has developed.

Note that *R (Connor) v SSWP* [2020] EWHC 1999 (Admin) holds that the requirement to undertake the mandatory reconsideration process before appealing

4.92

is unlawful in its application to ESA claimants who meet the conditions for payment while an appeal is pending. Swift J concluded "that regulation 3ZA of the Decisions and Appeals Regulations is a disproportionate interference with the right of access to court, so far as it applies to claimants to ESA who, once an appeal is initiated, meet the conditions for payment pending appeal under regulation 30(3) of the ESA Regulations" (at [28]). Swift J explained his reasoning as follows (at [31]):

> "when it comes to ESA claimants such as Mr Connor who, were an appeal to be in progress would meet the conditions for payment pending appeal under regulation 30(2) of the ESA Regulations, the requirement under regulation 3ZA is disproportionate having regard to the combined effect of (a) the period of time the benefits claimant will now need to wait before the right of appeal arises; and (b) the unexplained absence of any provision for payment of ESA during that period equivalent to the payment pending appeal arrangements that arise once an appeal has been started."

Swift J accordingly made "a declaration to the effect that regulation 3ZA of the Decisions and Appeals Regulations is unlawful insofar as it is applied to ESA claimants who would, if pursuing an appeal to the First-tier Tribunal, subject to compliance with the condition at regulation 30(2) of the ESA Regulations, be entitled to receive payment pending appeal pursuant to regulation 30(3)" (at [35]).

Paragraphs (1), (2)

4.93   If the conditions in para.(2) are met, this treats the claimant as having limited capability for work (thus grounding eligibility for ESA) until:

(a) the matter of actual capability is determined in accordance with the work capability assessment (LCWA) under reg.19 and Sch.2;

(b) it is decided whether some other "treated as having limited capability for work" regulation applies (e.g. person receiving certain regular treatment); or

(c) a decision is made that, as a sanction for non-compliance with information gathering or medical examination aspects of the assessment process under regs 22 and 23, he is to be treated as not having limited capability for work and thus disentitled to ESA (para.(1)).

Since the regulation only applies until the claimant has been "assessed", it cannot apply where the claimant is immediately assessed (*CIB/1959/1997 and CIB/2198/1997*, paras 28, 29).

Clearer analysis is afforded if one distinguishes between "a new claim" and a "repeat claim".

The position in respect of a "new claim": by "new claim" is envisaged the situation where there has never been a "determination" that the claimant does not have, or cannot be treated as having, limited capability for work. For example, this is the first ever claim for ESA. In such a case this regulation applies to treat the claimant as having that limited capability, provided that the claimant continues to provide a doctor's statement in accordance with the Medical Evidence Regs (paras (1), (2) (a)). "Determination" here is not confined to one on ESA eligibility but encompasses one on entitlement to any benefit, allowance or advantage dependent on the claimant having limited capability for work (para.(2)(b)).

4.94   *The position in respect of a "repeat claim":* by "repeat claim is here envisaged a situation in which there has been a previous "determination" that the claimant does not have limited capability for work, or was treated as not having such limited capability because of non-compliance with the medical examination aspect of assessment. On such a claim, the claimant can only be treated as having limited capability for work under this regulation in two situations (paras (2)(b), (4)(a), (b)):-

(i) if suffering from some specific disease or bodily or mental disablement from which he was not suffering at the time of that "determination" (a "new health condition"); or

(ii) there has been significant worsening of the disease or bodily or mental disablement suffered at the time of that "determination".

Similarly, if within the six months prior to the ESA claim, there has been a determination that the claimant is to be treated as not having limited capability for work under reg.22 (in effect one thereby applying a sanction for non-compliance with information gathering aspect of the assessment process), the claimant can nonetheless be treated as having limited capability for work (i) if s/he has since provided the information requested (paras (2)(b), (4)); or (ii) if they have a "new health condition" or their existing condition has significantly worsened. In addition, the claimant treated as not having limited capability for work under reg. 22 who reclaims more than six months after that determination can again be treated as having limited capability for work pending assessment (para.(2)(b)(ii)).

The words "significantly worsened", as regards the claimant's condition, must be related to the limited capability for work assessment (LCWA), so that it will only have significantly worsened if it has done so to an extent that it is fair to assume the claimant would satisfy that test of limited capability for work if he were subjected to it (see *EI v SSWP (ESA)* [2016] UKUT 397 (AAC) at paragraphs 34-42). If there is actual evidence that he would fail to satisfy that test, the Secretary of State can proceed on the basis that the condition has not significantly worsened (*CIB/1959/1977* and *CIB/2198/1997*, para.30). See further *EI v SSWP (ESA)* [2016] UKUT 397 (AAC) at paras 34–42 (but query whether this applies in relation to the period from the date of the repeat claim to the date of the assessment). That decision is also noteworthy because of the detailed but obiter consideration of whether there should be a right of appeal regarding whether a person's consideration has "significantly worsened" (see at paras 43–59). For the approach of decision-makers, see *Memo DMG 10/15*, paras 24–28.

In *CM v SSWP (ESA)* [2019] UKUT 284 (AAC) Judge Wright has revisited his decision in *EI v SSWP* (ESA) [2016] UKUT 397 (AAC). In particular, Judge Wright was asked to find that the decision in *EI v SSWP* (ESA) was wrong in two respects. First, if the DWP has decided a repeat claim on the basis that the claimant does not have limited capability for work (and cannot be treated as having limited capability for work under regulations other than regulation 30) then, on any appeal against such a decision, the sole issue for the FTT to decide was whether the claimant has limited capability for work under reg.19 and Sch.2 to the ESA Regs (or can be treated as having limited capability for work under the ESA Regs other than under reg.30). Second, once the determination as to limited capability for work in fact was made on a repeat claim, it always took effect from the date of the repeat claim (whether the determination finds the claimant has limited capability for work or not).

In *CM v SSWP (ESA)* Judge Wright and the Secretary of State agreed with submissions on behalf of the claimant by CPAG that (1) the decision on entitlement to ESA on a repeat claim will typically include determinations (a) on whether the claimant can be treated as having limited capability for work under reg.30 and (b) whether the claimant in fact had limited capability for work under reg.19 (or could be treated as having limited capability for work under reg.29); and (2) following *R(IB) 2/04*, on an appeal against such an entitlement decision, the FTT can give any decision that the decision maker could have made on the repeat claim.

As a result, the FTT is not in any sense bound by the Secretary of State's decision on that claim, even where the DWP's decision was to the effect that the claimant did not have limited capability for work in fact at the date of the repeat claim. Accordingly, in the instant appeal Judge Wright found the FTT was in error of law in not considering whether the claimant could have had an award of ESA on her repeat claim as a result of satisfying reg.30. Moreover, that error of law was material because it ought to have led to her at least being awarded ESA from the date of her repeat claim down to the date of the decision on that claim (subject to any waiting days).

For further discussion of *CM v SSWP (ESA)*, see Vol.III.

On "specific disease or bodily or mental disablement", see commentary to reg.19.

Those making a "repeat claim" who do not satisfy these conditions will not be treated as having limited capability for work pending assessment, and will thus not be entitled to ESA. Instead, if they wish to obtain a benefit they would have to resort to JSA (paid at the same rate as the assessment rate in ESA) and be subject to the JSA conditionality regime. The Government was not prepared to accept the SSAC's recommendation that, in such cases, claimants "should be offered back to work support on a voluntary basis but exempted from conditionality beyond attendance at a work-focused interview". The Government took the view that the recently introduced "extended period of sickness" changes and the flexibility of availability and actively seeking work rules afforded sufficient protection.

Paragraph (3): Continued entitlement to ESA pending appeal

4.95   This paragraph, when read with paras (2) and (4), has the effect that the supply of medical certificates will ground continued ESA entitlement pending an appeal against a "relevant decision", as defined in para.(5). This covers only appeals against the first ever decision that the claimant does not have limited capability for work, either in the context of a decision on a wholly new claim or on an ongoing claim where previous determinations (whether by the Secretary of State or an appellate authority) had found limited capability for work. In such cases, no claim is required (see Claims and Payments Regs 1987, reg.3(1)(l)) and ESA Regs. 2008, reg.147A applies.

Where, however, one is dealing with a "repeat claim", the position is different. By "repeat claim is here envisaged a situation in which there *has been* a previous "determination" that the claimant does not have limited capability for work, or was treated as not having such limited capability. Where the claimant appeals in such a case, para. (3) does not operate to disapply para. (2)(b) since this appeal is not one against a "relevant decision", and the condition for continued entitlement in para.(2) cannot be met. For the approach of decision-makers, see *Memo DMG 10/15*, paras 31–35. The intention of this as the DWP explained in the *Explanatory Memorandum* to the amending Regs, is

> "to align ESA with what happens for all other social security benefits where if a claimant is found not to be entitled, no benefit is paid whilst awaiting the outcome of the appeal. We believe this is reasonable because in their previous claim, the claimant will have had the opportunity to appeal to a tribunal if they disagreed with the decision. Claimants will instead be signposted to JSA as it is the appropriate benefit for someone who has been found fit for work. JSA provides claimants with personalised support to return to work taking into account their health condition or disability. It is acknowledged that not all ESA claimants will be eligible for JSA because they may not meet the conditions of entitlement" (para.7.5).

See also *R (Connor) v SSWP* [2020] EWHC 1999 (Admin) (discussed above), holding that the requirement to undertake the mandatory reconsideration process before appealing is unlawful in its application to ESA claimants who meet the conditions for payment while an appeal is pending.

Claimant who claims jobseeker's allowance to be treated as not having limited capability for work

4.96   **31.** [¹ *Revoked.*]

AMENDMENT

1. Employment and Support Allowance (Transitional Provisions, Housing Benefit and Council Tax Benefit) (Existing Awards) (No. 2) Regulations 2010 (SI 2010/1907) reg.25(1) (October 1, 2010).

Certain claimants to be treated as not having limited capability for work

32. [¹(1)] A claimant [²who is or has been a member of Her Majesty's Forces] is to be treated as not having limited capability for work on any day which is recorded by the Secretary of State [⁴. . .] as a day of sickness absence from duty.

[³(2) A claimant is to be treated as not having limited capability for work on any day on which the claimant attends a training course in respect of which the claimant is paid a training allowance or premium pursuant to arrangements made under section 2 of the Employment and Training Act 1973 or section 2(3) of the Enterprise and New Towns (Scotland) Act 1990.

(3) Paragraph (2) is not to apply—
(a) for the purposes of any claim to employment and support allowance for a period commencing after the claimant ceased attending the training course in question; or
(b) where any training allowance or premium paid to the claimant is paid for the sole purpose of travelling or meal expenses incurred or to be incurred under the arrangement made under section 2 of the Employment and Training Act 1973 or section 2(3) of the Enterprise and New Towns (Scotland) Act 1990.]

4.97

AMENDMENTS

1. Employment and Support Allowance (Miscellaneous Amendments) Regulations 2008 (SI 2008/2428) reg.5(2)(a) (October 27, 2008).
2. Employment and Support Allowance (Miscellaneous Amendments) Regulations 2008 (SI 2008/2428) reg.5(2)(b) (October 27, 2008).
3. Employment and Support Allowance (Miscellaneous Amendments) Regulations 2008 (SI 2008/2428) reg.5(2)(c) (October 27, 2008).
4. Social Security (Miscellaneous Amendments) (No.3) Regulations 2013 (SI 2013/2536) reg.13(15) (October 29, 2013).

DEFINITIONS

"claimant"—see WRA 2007 s.24(1).
"limited capability for work"—see WRA 2007 s.1(4).

GENERAL NOTE

Paragraph (1)
This draws a boundary between ESA and the sickness payment scheme operated by the Ministry of Defence. Days recorded by the Secretary of State as ones of sickness absence from duty are to be treated for ESA purposes as ones on which the person concerned does not have limited capability for work.

4.98

[¹Claimants to be treated as not having limited capability for work at the end of the period covered by medical evidence

32A. [²(1)] Where the Secretary of State is satisfied that it is appropriate in the circumstances of the case [³ . . .] a claimant may be treated as not

4.99

having limited capability for work if—

    (a) the claimant has supplied medical evidence [² . . .];

    (b) the period for which medical evidence was supplied has ended;

    (c) the Secretary of State has requested further medical evidence; and

    (d) the claimant has not, before whichever is the later of either the end of the period of 6 weeks beginning with the date of the Secretary of State's request or the end of 6 weeks beginning with the day after the end of the period for which medical evidence was supplied—

        (i) supplied further medical evidence, or

        (ii) otherwise made contact with the Secretary of State to indicate that they wish to have the question of limited capability for work determined.]

[²(2) In this regulation "medical evidence" means evidence provided under regulation 2 or 5 of the Medical Evidence Regulations.]

AMENDMENTS

1. Social Security (Miscellaneous Amendments) (No. 3) Regulations 2010 (SI 2010/840) reg.9(9) (June 28, 2010).

2. Social Security (Miscellaneous Amendments) Regulations 2011 (SI 2011/674) reg.16(4) (April 11, 2011).

3. Social Security (Miscellaneous Amendments) (No.3) Regulations 2013 (SI 2013/2536) reg.13(16) (October 29, 2013).

Additional circumstances where claimants are to be treated as having limited capability for work

4.100   **33.**—(1) For the purposes of paragraph 4(1)(d)(ii) of Schedule 1 to the Act, a claimant is to be treated as having limited capability for work on any day in respect of which that claimant is entitled to statutory sick pay.

(2) For the purposes of an income-related allowance, a claimant is to be treated as having limited capability for work where—

    (a) that claimant is not a qualifying young person;

    (b) that claimant is receiving education; and

    (c) paragraph 6(1)(g) of Schedule 1 to the Act does not apply in accordance with regulation 18.

DEFINITIONS

"claimant"—see WRA 2007 s.24(1).
"income-related allowance"—see WRA 2007 s.1(7).
"limited capability for work"—see WRA 2007 s.1(4).
"qualifying young person"—see reg.2(1).

GENERAL NOTE

Paragraph (1)

4.101   Like WRA 2007, s.20(1), this regulation deals with the relationship between ESA and employer paid statutory sick pay (SSP). Days of entitlement to SSP cannot rank as ones of entitlement to ESA. However, para.(1) of this regulation stipulates that such days are to be treated as ones of limited capability for work for the purposes of computing the 196 consecutive days of limited capability for work essential if someone is to qualify through the "condition relating to youth route" to CESA (WRA 2007, Sch.1, para.4(1)(d)(ii)). Being so treated confers no exemption from the information gathering requirements in reg.21 (see para.(3) of that regulation).

Paragraph (2)

This deals only with IRESA. It treats certain disabled students as having limited capability for work. It covers someone receiving education (sub-para.(b)) but not debarred from IRESA on account of that because he is receiving PIP, DLA or armed forces independence payment (sub-para.(c) [WRA 2007, Sch.1, para.6(1) (g) disapplied by reg.18]). If this person is not a qualifying young person, he is to be treated as having limited capability for work. A qualifying young person bears the same meaning as in SSCBA 1992, s.142 (see reg.2(1)): someone aged 16–19 inclusive undergoing a full-time course of non-advanced education or approved training which commenced before he attained 19 (see Child Benefit Regs, reg.3). See also *MW v SSWP (ESA)* [2018] UKUT 304 (AAC), confirming that although there is a general entitlement condition that a claimant "is not receiving education" (see Welfare Reform Act 2007, Sch.1, para. 6(1)(g) this is disapplied to a claimant entitled to PIP, DLA or armed forces independence payment by virtue of reg.18.

4.102

Being treated as having limited capability for work in this way confers exemption from the information gathering requirements in reg.21 (see para.(3) of that regulation).

PART 6

LIMITED CAPABILITY FOR WORK-RELATED ACTIVITY

Determination of limited capability for work-related activity

34.—(1) For the purposes of Part 1 of the Act, where, by reason of a claimant's physical or mental condition, at least one of the descriptors set out in Schedule 3 applies to the claimant, the [² claimant has limited] capability for work-related activity [² . . .] and the limitation [² must] be such that it is not reasonable to require that claimant to undertake such activity.

4.103

(2) A descriptor applies to a claimant if that descriptor applies to the claimant for the majority of the time or, as the case may be, on the majority of the occasions on which the claimant undertakes or attempts to undertake the activity described by that descriptor.

[¹(3) In determining whether a descriptor applies to the claimant, the claimant is to be assessed as if—

   (a) the claimant were fitted with or wearing any prosthesis with which the claimant is normally fitted or normally wears; or, as the case may be,

   (b) wearing or using any aid or appliance which is normally, or could reasonably be expected to be, worn or used.]

(3A) [² *Omitted.*]

(4) Where a determination has been made about whether a claimant—

   (a) has limited capability for work-related activity;

   (b) is to be treated as having limited capability for work-related activity; or

   (c) is to be treated as not having limited capability for work-related activity,

the Secretary of State may, if paragraph (5) applies, determine afresh whether the claimant has or is to be treated as having limited capability for work-related activity.

(5) This paragraph applies where—

   (a) the Secretary of State wishes to determine whether there has been a relevant change of circumstances in relation to the claimant's physical or mental condition;

(b) the Secretary of State wishes to determine whether the previous determination about limited capability for work-related activity or about treating the claimant as having or as not having limited capability for work-related activity, was made in ignorance of, or was based on a mistake as to, some material fact; or
(c) at least 3 months have passed since the date of the previous determination about limited capability for work-related activity or about treating the claimant as having or as not having limited capability for work-related activity.

[²(6) In assessing the extent of a claimant's capability to perform any activity listed in Schedule 3, it is a condition that the claimant's incapability to perform the action arises—

(a) in respect of descriptors 1 to 8, 15(a), 15(b), 16(a) and 16(b)—
    (i) from a specific bodily disease or disablement; or
    (ii) as a direct result of treatment provided by a registered medical practitioner for a specific physical disease or disablement; or
(b) in respect of descriptors 9 to 14, 15(c), 15(d), 16(c) and 16(d)—
    (i) from a specific mental illness or disablement; or
    (ii) as a direct result of treatment provided by a registered medical practitioner for a specific mental illness or disablement.]

AMENDMENTS

1. Employment and Support Allowance (Amendment) Regulations 2012 (SI 2012/3096) reg.4(2) (January 28, 2013, subject to application, transitional and savings provisions in reg.2 of this amending instrument, below, para.9.614).
2. Social Security (Miscellaneous Amendments) (No.3) Regulations 2013 (SI 2013/2536) reg.13(17) (October 29, 2013).

DEFINITIONS

"the Act"—see reg.2(1).
"claimant"—see WRA 2007 s.24(1).
"descriptor"—see reg.2(1).
"limited capability for work-related activity"—see WRA 2007 s.2(5).
"work-related activity"—see WRA 2007 ss.24(1), 13(7).

GENERAL NOTE

4.104   Establishing limited capability for work is the central condition governing entitlement to ESA. Establishing limited capacity for work related activity is, in contrast, the core condition of entitlement to support component, the more generous of the two components (support or work-related activity) only one of which can be added to ESA basic allowance. This regulation, read with WRA 2007, s.9 and Sch.3 to these Regs, sets out how limited capacity for work related activity is assessed and determined.

The assumption behind ESA is that the vast majority of claimants, if given the right support, are in fact capable of some work. Government anticipated that only some 10 per cent of claimants (those with more severe health conditions) will be entitled to the support allowance and so not be subject to work-related activity conditionality requirements (DWP, *Employment and Support Allowance Regulations 2008: Equality Impact Assessment* in *Explanatory Memorandum to Employment and Support Allowance Regulations 2008 (SI 2008/794)* and the *Employment and Support Allowance (Transitional Provisions) Regulations 2008 (SI 2008/795)*, p.19). Recent statistics indicate, however, that some 27 per cent of new claimants are put into the support group (DWP Press Release, April 24, 2012: see *http://www.dwp.gov.uk/news-*

room/press-releases/2012/apr-2012/dwp042-12.shtml). Entry to this protected support group depends on it being established—generally through a work-related activity assessment (WRAAt) of a more stringent nature than the WCAt—that the claimant has limited capacity for work related activity. The WRAAt is the second element in the new Work Capability Assessment (WCA) which will eventually replace the IB PCA. Establishing limited capability for work related activity is based on someone demonstrating that they have a severe level of functional limitation. This is established when by reason of the claimant's physical or mental condition, at least one of the ranges of descriptors in Sch.3 applies to the claimant (WRA 2007, s.9; para.(1)).

There is no scoring system (it is a matter of the descriptor being applicable that counts) and the criteria are deliberately more stringent than in the WCAt:

"The levels of functional limitation used in the descriptors for determining limited capability for work-related activity are greater because we intend to place in the support group only the minority of customers who are so severely impaired that it would not be reasonable to require them to undertake work-related activity . . . People with less severe functional limitations across a range of descriptors might score highly and be inappropriately included in the support group when they might benefit from work-related activity. . . . A number of case studies were provided in the background information, which hon. Members will find helpful [see DWP, *Welfare Reform Bill: Draft Regulations and Supporting Material* (January 2007), pp.13–17]. Under the revised PCA, someone with a moderate learning disability would score 50 points. They would be significantly above the 15-point threshold, but we clearly would not wish to put even someone with 50 points into the support group automatically, because we are determined to ensure that the new system does not write off people with learning disabilities. The technical groups considered all the options. A crude points-based system would have unintended consequences." (*Hansard*, Standing Committee A, October 19, 2006 (afternoon), col.120 (Mr Jim Murphy MP, Minister for Employment and Welfare Reform)).

Paragraph (2)

Paragraph (2) makes clear (as indeed does the expected transposition to the WRAAt of central elements in existing case law on approaching the PCA) that a descriptor applies to a claimant if it applies to him for the majority of the time or, as the case may be, on the majority of the occasions on which he undertakes or attempts to undertake the relevant activity. Moreover, as is the case with the IB PCA and the ESA WCAt, in matching claimant to descriptor, the claimant is to be assessed as if fitted with or wearing any prosthesis with which the claimant is normally fitted or normally wears; or wearing or using any aid or appliance which is normally, or could reasonably be expected to be, worn or used (para.(3), and see commentary to reg.19(4)). The interrelationship of para.(2) with descriptors in Sch.3 deploying differing wording on periodicity ("at least once a week" [activity/descriptor 8], "always" [activity/descriptor 13], "on a daily basis" [activity/descriptor 14],) has been explored in a number of cases. 4.105

In *KB v SSWP (ESA)* [2013] UKUT 152 (AAC), Judge Parker considered the relationship between this wording (the requisite of "always") and the stipulation in reg.34(2) that "a descriptor applies to a claimant if that descriptor applies to the claimant for the majority of the time or, as the case may be, on the majority of the occasions on which the claimant undertakes or attempts to undertake the activity described by that descriptor". Having looked at definitions of "always" in the Concise Oxford Dictionary, Judge Parker concluded that neither this activity and descriptor, nor its counterpart in Activity 16 of Sch.2 set out an "all or nothing test". Rather "always" here "means 'repeatedly' or 'persistent' or 'often':

"A 'majority' may be constituted by events which happen only on 50.1 per cent of the possible occasions, but a greater frequency is required by the use of the word 'always'. It is a question of degree, but a fact finding tribunal is eminently suited to applying these subtle nuances of difference in a common sense way. It suffices to say in the present case, that because a claimant attends one tribunal hearing, and his GP accepts that he comes to the surgery very occasionally, does not necessarily entail the conclusion, as the tribunal clearly considered that it did, that it 'cannot be said that engagement in social contact is always precluded'" (para.14).

Judge Fordham took much the same approach in *CH v SSWP (ESA)* [2013] UKUT 207 (AAC) (para.8).

In *LM v SSWP (ESA)* [2013] UKUT 552 (AAC) (see update to p. 1076), however, Judge Mark agreed that "always" meant repeatedly or "persistent" but considered it did not mean "often" or "for the majority of the time".

In *WT v SSWP (ESA)* [2013] UKUT 556 (AAC), Judge Gray was more definitive than Judge Parker on the relationship between reg.34(2) and activity/descriptor 14, stating that "the terminology of the descriptor in question excludes the application of regulation 34 (2), in that it cannot apply to qualify the meaning of the words "on a daily basis" to mean "the majority of the time" or, "on the majority of occasions that the claimant undertakes or tries to undertake the activity", which would in logic lead to satisfaction of the test if it was satisfied on more than half of the days or attempts. That would drive a coach and horses through the descriptor, rendering the inclusion of any reference to the word "daily" pointless. That cannot be what was intended. Regulation 34(2) does not apply to a schedule 3 descriptor where the "majority of the time" approach would be inconsistent with the actual wording of the descriptor" (para.36).

Judge Parker's decision was appealed to the Court of Session. In *SSWP v Brade* [2014] CSIH 39 XA81/13 (May 1, 2014); [2014] AACR 29, the Court held that the wording cannot have been intended to mean "always" in the sense of the claimant never, at any time, whatever the circumstances, being able to engage in "social contact " (para. 35). Instead, the provision required a purposive construction:

> "descriptor 13 must apply if a claimant suffers from a mental disorder which has the consequence that, for the majority of the time, he cannot engage in social contact. That construction properly embraces regulation 34(1), 34(2) and the terms of descriptor 13 and accords with their evident intention. Such a person is not likely to have labour market potential and, moreover, if, for the majority of the time, that person cannot engage in social contact, requiring participation in the work focused interview would be not only unreasonable but pointless. Further, that construction avoids the fact finder being necessarily driven to the absurd conclusion that descriptor 13 is not satisfied if, for instance, on a single occasion, a claimant has given instructions to a representative for the purposes of a tribunal hearing. The question of whether or not a person is wholly precluded from engagement in social contact for the majority of the time is one of fact having regard to the statutory provisions as understood by the guidance we have sought to provide. That question is not answered by the application of any precise mathematical approach but by the fact finding tribunal having regard to the evidence in the particular case of the effects of the claimant's condition in a realistic way whilst bearing in mind the purpose of the legisation" (para.37).

Activities in Sch.3

4.106   There are now 16 activities in Sch.3: mobilising unaided; transferring from one seated position to another; reaching; picking up and moving or transferring; manual dexterity; making self understood; understanding communication; absence or loss of control leading to extensive evacuation of the bowel and/or voiding of the bladder; learning tasks; awareness of hazard; initiating and completing personal action; coping with change; coping with social engagement; appropriateness of behaviour; conveying food or drink to the mouth; chewing or swallowing food or drink. The terms of the descriptors are also more stringent than in the WCAt, to avoid removing too many people from the group which affords incentive to engage in work-related activity and thus denying them the opportunity to take steps to make real their fundamental right to work. Thus, as regards walking, the single descriptor can only be met where a claimant cannot "mobilise" more than 50 metres on level ground without stopping to avoid significant discomfort or exhaustion (or cannot "repeatedly mobilise 50 metres...(etc)"). Most, with counterparts in the WCAt, are couched in terms equivalent to the more difficult of their 15 point descriptors. With effect from January 28, 2013, in deciding which descriptor applies, incapability must arise in respect of descriptors 1 to 8, 15(a), 15(b), 16(a) and 16 (b), from a specific bodily disease or disablement or as a direct result of treatment provided by a registered medical practitioner for such a disease or disablement (para.(3A) (a), (c)(i)). Similarly, as regards descriptors 9 to 14, 15(c), 15(d), 16(c) and 16 (d), incapability must arise from a specific mental illness or disablement; or as a direct result of treatment provided by a registered medical practitioner for such an illness or disablement (para.(3A)(b), (c)(i)). Note that for some cases after January 28, 2013, for a six month period, the previous version of reg.34 can be applicable (see reg.2 of the amending instrument, below, para.9.614).

Those meeting the WRAAt test will be placed in the support group and receive support component without having to satisfy work-related activity conditions, although they can voluntarily participate in those programmes. Their position can be reviewed periodically or where there has been a change of circumstances in the claimant's physical or mental condition or it is thought that a previous determination was made in ignorance of or a mistake as to some material fact (paras (4), (5)) The threshold for membership of the support group is high; CPAG consider that "many claimants in receipt of the middle and higher rates of Disability Living Allowance (DLA) may not meet the eligibility criteria". Those who fail to establish limited capability for work-related activity will instead be in the work-related activity group, which has stringent conditions attached in terms of appropriate behaviour (participation in work focussed health related assessments, work focused interviews and, eventually, specified work-related activity (see regs 47–60), involving the private and voluntary sector as well as JobCentre Plus).

Certain claimants to be treated as having limited capability for work-related activity

35.—(1) A claimant is to be treated as having limited capability for work-related activity if—

  (a) the claimant is terminally ill;

  [¹(b) the claimant is—

      (i) receiving treatment for cancer by way of chemotherapy or radiotherapy;

     (ii) likely to receive such treatment within six months after the date of the determination of capability for work-related activity; or

    (iii) recovering from such treatment,

and the Secretary of State is satisfied that the claimant should be treated as having limited capability for work-related activity; or]

  (c) in the case of a woman, she is pregnant and there is a serious risk of damage to her health or to the health of her unborn child if she does not refrain from work-related activity.

(2) A claimant who does not have limited capability for work-related activity as determined in accordance with regulation 34(1) is to be treated as having limited capability for work-related activity if—

  (a) the claimant suffers from some specific disease or bodily or mental disablement; and

  (b) by reasons of such disease or disablement, there would be a substantial risk to the mental or physical health of any person if the claimant were found not to have limited capability for work-related activity.

4.107

1. Employment and Support Allowance (Amendment) Regulations 2012 (SI 2012/3096) reg.4(3) (January 28, 2013, subject to application, transitional and savings provisions in reg.2 of this amending instrument, below, para.9.614).

DEFINITIONS

"claimant"—see WRA 2007 s.24(1).
"limited capability for work-related activity"—see WRA 2007 s.2(5).
"terminally ill"—see reg.2(1).
"work-related activity"—see WRA 2007 ss.24(1), 13(7).

GENERAL NOTE

Paragraph (1)

4.108
This has affinities with reg.20 (treating someone as having limited capability for work). Regulation 35 (1) treats someone as having limited capability for work-related activity but the range of groups so treated is much narrower. The terminally ill (para.(1)(a)) and those undergoing or (as amended from March 28, 2011) likely to undergo within six months, or recovering from chemotherapy (para.(1)(b)) are so treated, as is a pregnant woman where there is a serious risk of damage to her health or that of her unborn child if she does not refrain from work-related activity (para. (1)(c). Unlike reg.20 there is no protection for other pregnant women or for those receiving hospital treatment or certain regular treatments such as dialysis.

Paragraph (2)

4.109
This is a partial equivalent of the "exceptional circumstances" provision (reg.29) applicable to the limited capability for work question, considered above. *A claimant who does not pass the LCWRA* can nonetheless be treated as having the requisite limited capability for work-related activity grounding membership of the support group where, by reasons of the specific disease or bodily or mental disablement from which s/he suffers, "there would be a substantial risk to the mental or physical health of any person if the claimant were found not to have limited capability for work-related activity". Given the structure of the ESA legislative scheme, it is axiomatic that reg.35(2) can only come into play where the claimant has been found to have limited capability for work (either under the LCWA scoring 15 or more in terms of Sch.2 descriptors or through the operation of reg.29) and has also failed to satisfy any of the Sch.3 descriptors, thus being found not to have limited capability for work-related activity (*LH v SSWP (ESA)* [2015] UKUT 154 (AAC)). In such a case, reg.35(2) becomes that claimant's last hope of being placed in the support group by being treated as having limited capability for work-related activity. On "specific disease or bodily or mental disablement", see commentary to reg.19(2).

For an extreme example of reg.35(2) being found to apply, see *JL v SSWP (ESA)* [2018] UKUT 346 (AAC). The claimant had previously been placed in the support group. The evidence of two ESA medical assessments and the claimant's own GP showed that the claimant's blood pressure was indisputably high and uncontrolled. Moreover, the DWP's own guidance to decision-makers (Memo DMG 17/15, paragraph 25(3)) gives the example of a claimant with hypertension which is uncontrolled despite medication as an instance of "immediate substantial risk" in the context of reg.35(2). The FTT's decision (upholding the conclusion that reg.35(2) did not apply, despite the HCP terminating the assessment and advising the claimant to attend A&E forthwith) was set aside for inadequate reasoning and the decision re-made.

On "substantial risk to the mental or physical health of any person if the claimant were found not to have limited capability for work-related activity", see the commentary to reg.29, but note that there is in reg.35(2) no statutory counterpart to the modification effected by reg.29(3) (medication and reasonable adjustments to the claimant's workplace). As with reg. 29(2)(b), the key case is *Charlton v Secretary of State for Work and Pensions* [2009] EWCA Civ. 42.

The application of Charlton *to reg. 35(2)*: in *AH v SSWP (ESA)* [2013] UKUT 118   **4.110**
(AAC); [2013] AACR 32 Judge Jacobs considered how (if at all) the approach in
Charlton on the predecessor of reg.29 should be applied to the differently worded
context of reg.35 dealing as it does not with "work" but "work-related activity".
He thought the Court of Appeal's conclusion on reg.29(2)(b) equally applicable to
reg.35(2) so that the paragraph applies both to the effect of work-related activity
and not just to the effect of being found capable of it; so that it applies (i) not only
to the immediate effects of the decision on capability, but (ii) to the consequences of
having to undertake work-related activity and (iii) to having to travel to and from it.
Translating the Court's language on the range of work to be contemplated to fit this
analogous context of "work-related activity" means that the

> "decision-maker must assess the range or type of work-related activity which a
> claimant is capable of performing and might be expected to undertake sufficiently
> to assess the risk to health either to himself or to others" (para.26).

The Secretary of State ought in such cases to provide some evidence of the range
of "work- related activity" in contemplation. The tribunal should then assess that in
light of evidence on the claimant's conditions and limitations for it. It would need to
be able to consider, for example, what type of adjustments might be reasonable in
the claimant's case, and what type of support the Advisor might provide (para.32).
KB v SSWP (ESA) [2013] UKUT 152 (AAC) also took this approach to the applicability of *Charlton* reasoning to para.(2):

> "it is necessary, under regulation 35, to make the evaluation of substantial risk,
> not just an exercise limited to the ability to cope with the work related interview at
> the Job Centre, but also "in the context of the journey to or from" such an inter-
> view. This point has particular relevance to a claimant arguing under activity 13 of
> Schedule 3. The tribunal therefore went wrong in applying too narrow a statutory
> test, saying only "he should be able to cope with a work related interview at the
> Jobcentre" (para.18).

In *MN v SSWP (ESA)* [2013] UKUT 262 (AAC); [2014] AACR 6, Judge Wright
endorsed Judge Jacobs's point in *AH* on the Secretary of State and evidence, but
added two slight caveats. First, it might be enough in most cases to give a general
indication of what is involved in work-related activity. Secondly, where the claimant's grounds of appeal specifically raise reg.35(2), r.24(2)(e) of the Tribunal
Procedure Rules mandates the Secretary of State to say whether he opposed the
appellant's case on reg.35(2) and state "any grounds for such opposition which are
not set out in documents which are before the Tribunal" (paras 16, 17).

In *ML v SSWP (ESA)* [2013] UKUT 174 (AAC); [2013] AACR 33, a follow-
up decision to *AH*, Judge Jacobs stressed the need for the Secretary of State to
go beyond general formulaic statements to make effective the statutory right of
appeal by providing the necessary information to enable claimants to participate in
the appeal and the tribunal to make a decision" (para.15). He also considered the
relationship between regs 29 and 35. He accepted that a paragraph in the DWP,
Medical Services Handbook for ESA was merely guidance but also incorrect in
stating that someone found to be "at substantial risk for work" would be extremely
unlikely to be found not to be at "substantial risk for work-related activity". Instead
Judge Jacobs stated that it all depends on the precise circumstances of each case:

> "Regulations 29 and 35 use similar wording, but they do so for different pur-
> poses. The claimant's condition is a constant for both provisions. But the activi-
> ties to which the provisions apply differ. The former is concerned with the risk
> of work; the latter is concerned with the risk of work-related activity. There is no
> reason why the former should automatically be determinative of the latter. This
> will depend on: (i) the nature of the claimant's condition; (ii) its effects; and (iii)
> the nature of the work-related activity. It may be that the condition will give rise

to the same risk whether the claimant undertakes work or work-related activity. Or it may give rise to different risks. Or it may give rise to risk in respect of one but not the other" (para.14).

4.111   *What evidence of work-related activity must be provided by the Secretary of State and what can a tribunal do where no such evidence is supplied?*   How to deal with the practical difficulties posed for tribunals by the decisions in *AH*, *MN* and *ML* produced divergent views from Upper Tribunal judges (see *AK v SSWP (ESA)* [2013] UKUT 435 (AAC); *MT v SSWP (ESA)* [2013] UKUT 545 (AAC); *DH v SSWP (ESA)* [2013] UKUT (ESA) 573 (AAC); *HS v SSWP (ESA)* [2013] UKUT 591 (AAC); *AP v SSWP (ESA)* [2014] UKUT 35 (AAC); *AP v SSWP (ESA)* [2013] UKUT 553 (AAC); *PF v SSWP (ESA)* [2013] UKUT 634 (AAC); and *NA v SSWP (ESA)* [2014] UKUT 305 (AAC)). Those difficulties relate to avoiding the need for adjournments clogging up the adjudication system in a context in which the decision appealed against will have been made *before* the claimant has had an initial consultation with an adviser on appropriate work-related activity and in which there is generally no representative of the Secretary of State present at First-tier tribunals to be questioned as to what activity might be appropriate. In *NA*, Judge Gray deprecated the Secretary of State's failure to provide sufficient information to the tribunal; had the "action plan" seen by Judge Gray on appeal, and which predated the hearing before the First-tier tribunal, been made available to that tribunal the further appeal to the Upper Tribunal might well have been avoided (presumably because that tribunal would then have applied the regulation in the claimant's favour).

Fortunately, this divisive issue has now been dealt with authoritatively by a panel of three Upper Tribunal judges. In *IM v SSWP (ESA)* [2014] UKUT 412 (AAC); [2015] AACR 10, the panel dealt with the question of "the amount of detail the regulation 35(2) decision-makers should have of the possible results of the work-focused interview" to which those found not to be incapable of work-related activity will be subject.

The panel considered that the problem with decision-making on reg.35(2) arises because at the stage the decision maker (Secretary of State or First-tier tribunal) has to decide the matter of "substantial risk" exactly what will be required of this particular claimant at any such work-focused interview is unknown, a matter of conjecture, and the decision-maker must perforce engage in a degree of "crystal ball gazing" (para.75), with "substantial risk" bearing the commonly agreed meaning of a risk "that cannot sensibly be ignored having regard to the nature and gravity of the feared harm in the particular case" (para.65).

Having considered the range of case law on the provision noted above, the panel rightly held that a purposive approach, reflecting practicalities apparent in *Charlton*, must be taken to the regulation (para.83). In the view of the panel,

"the absence of any system for ensuring that relevant information obtained, and findings made, in the course of carrying out a work capability assessment and applying regulation 35(2) and the reasoning behind the decision made on regulation 35(2) are made available to a person considering whether a requirement to engage in work-related activity should be imposed on the claimant effectively destroys the Secretary of State's argument that only generalised information about some types of work-related activity need be taken into account by the regulation 35(2) decision-maker when considering the possible consequences of a particular claimant being found not to have limited capability for work-related activity. The purpose underlying regulation 35(2) requires that those applying it make predictions about the consequences to the particular claimant of him being found not to have limited capability for work-related activity. In a few cases, the risks of an inappropriate requirement to engage in work-related activity being imposed will be too great to be ignored" (para.101).

Given the present system of administering the legislation, the First-tier tribunal needs to know "not only what the least demanding types of work-related activity are but also what the most demanding types are in the area where the claimant lives.

. . . .

[O]n an appeal in which regulation 35(2) is in issue, [the Secretary of State] cannot be expected to anticipate exactly what work-related activity a particular claimant would in fact be required to do. This is axiomatic.

But what the Secretary of State can and should provide is evidence of the types of work-related activity available in each area [Wolverhampton in this claimant's case] and by reference thereto what the particular claimant may be required to undertake and those which he considers it would be reasonable for the provider to require the claimant to undertake. The First-tier Tribunal would then be in a position to assess the relevant risks.

[T]he types of work-related activity available may vary from provider to provider, but it should not be beyond the wit of the Department and providers to produce and maintain a list, perhaps for each of the regions into which the First-tier Tribunal is organised, of what is available in each area within the region. The relevant information could then be included in submissions in individual cases. The First-tier Tribunal would be able to assess the evidential force of such a submission.

. . .

Being unable to carry out an activity does not necessarily imply that there will be a substantial risk to anyone's health if the claimant is required to engage in the activity. Nor does the risk of being sanctioned. Therefore, it may be fairly obvious in most cases that the claimant does not have any realistic argument under regulation 35 and indeed, if made aware of the issues, the claimant may often accept that that is so. But where there turns out to be a serious argument in relation to regulation 35, the provision of the basic information about the more demanding types of work-related activity would enable the First-tier Tribunal to make the necessary predictions by reference to possible outcomes for the particular claimant" (paras.104-107, 110).

The panel considered that where the Secretary of State has accepted that the claimant has limited capability for work, the Secretary of State will be able to aid the tribunal with a more focused submission on why, given the claimant's disablement, reg. 35(2) does not apply. It noted that in some cases (see e.g. *CMcC v SSWP (ESA)* [2014] UKUT 176 (AAC); [2015] AACR 9) the work-focused interview will have taken place before the tribunal hears the appeal and its outcome and basis should be provided to it where possible, thereby reducing the element of prediction required, but always remembering that, because of SSA 1998 s.12(8)(b) any such evidence "should only be taken into account so far as it is relevant to the position at the time of the decision of the Secretary of State" (para.113).

The panel held that merely identifying that there is some work-related activity that a claimant could do is insufficient to ground a finding

"that there would not be risk to someone's health if the claimant were found not to have limited capability for work-related activity. That is because it does not wholly answer the statutory question" (para.116).

In *CL v SSWP (ESA)* [2015] UKUT 375 (AAC), Judge Jacobs considered it permissible to take into account work-related activity that the claimant could carry out at home (para.17).

But what if the Secretary of State fails to provide the required evidence? In such a case, **4.112** the panel considered that the First-tier Tribunal has a number of options as to how to proceed. It can use its own knowledge, if it is confident that it is up-to-date and complete as to the more demanding types of work-related activity. It may instead adjourn to obtain that evidence or decide that it can properly determine the case one way or the other without it. The right approach depends on the circumstances and, in particular, on how vulnerable the claimant is (para. 118).

Interestingly, the panel also made clear that there were ways in which the reg.35(2) risk could be greatly reduced or even eliminated by a change of practice in the way in which the scheme is administered (paras 98-100). But, unless and until the scheme of decision-making and the legislation is changed the approach in *IM* must be followed (see *EH v SSWP (ESA)* [2014] UKUT 473 (AAC); *KW v SSWP (ESA)* [2015] UKUT 131 (AAC); *GB v SSWP (ESA)* [2015] UKUT 200 (AAC)). Problems of decision-making are likely to be exacerbated where the claimant is unlikely to be able to engage in social contact with the provider so as explain their difficulties (*IM, GB*).

4.113   Thus the decision of the three-judge panel in *IM* highlighted:

> "that, because the results of work capability assessments are not routinely passed to providers who determine what work-related activity a claimant should be required to do, there may a risk of a provider requiring a person with, say, mental health problems to perform unsuitable work-related activity, due to the provider's ignorance of the those problems or their extent. This difficulty is liable to be exacerbated if, as in both *IM* and the present case, the claimant is, or is likely to be, unable to engage in social contact with the provider and so explain her difficulties herself" (see also *GB v SSWP (ESA)* [2015] UKUT 200 (AAC), *per* Judge Rowland).

This point was further emphasised by Judge Gray in *XT v SSWP (ESA)* [2015] UKUT 581 (AAC). There the First-tier Tribunal had decided that the appellant could undertake all likely work-related activities with the exception of work placements and work experience (because of her fragile mental health). The tribunal found she did not qualify for the support group, working on the assumption that its reservations would be communicated to the relevant provider of work-related activity. That assumption was misplaced in the light of *IM v SSWP (ESA)*. Judge Gray accordingly held the tribunal's decision to be in error of law; she went ahead to re-make the decision in the appellant's favour, explaining why there was a substantial risk within the terms of reg.35(2).

For another helpful example of a case in which the Upper Tribunal allowed the claimant's appeal and re-made the decision under reg.35, finding and explaining its reasoning as to why the claimant qualified on mental health grounds for the support group, see *SL v SSWP (ESA)* [2016] UKUT 170 (AAC). In that case Judge Sutherland Williams also approved of the DWP's guidance since *IM* (Memo ADM 7/16), which encourages decision makers to make better and more informed decisions in relation to reg.35 and LCRWA:

> "80. I might go further. If the Secretary of State can provide a tribunal with the types of work-related activity available in each area after the DM's decision is made, then it does not appear to me to be overly onerous on the DWP to provide HCP's with similar information before the decision is made, assuming that is not happening already. The HCP should then be able to provide a more reasoned statement in relation to regulation 35(2) in appropriate cases; and in turn the decision-maker could make a more informed decision in terms of predicative risk or otherwise, without that function being essentially passed onto the FTT."

The DWP's guidance since *IM* (both in its original format in Memo DMG 17/15 and its subsequent form in Memo ADM 7/16) was critiqued in more detail in *KC and MC v SSWP (ESA)* [2017] UKUT 94 (AAC). Judge Wright expressed the opinion that the DWP guidance for the most part accurately reflected the ruling in *IM*, subject to two notable exceptions.

The first was the erroneous suggestion in Memo DMG 17/15 that *IM* does not require a list of the most and least demanding types of work-related activity to be produced in appeals against whether a claimant even has limited capability for work (see paragraphs 87-90).

The second was in relation to para.36 of Memo DMG 17/15, which stated that tribunals should be provided with "examples of the most and last demanding WRA which it is considered the claimant *could* undertake" (emphasis added) rather than the whole list. Judge Wright took the view that "might be required to" was a better form of words than "could", which elided the two-stage approach required by *IM*. The first stage was to compile a list of work related activities in a given area, identifying the most and least demanding activities. The second stage was to explain the range of such activities that the particular appellant was capable of doing and might have been expected to undertake (see paragraphs 111-114).

The decision in *KC and MC v SSWP (ESA)* is also significant for the light it sheds on the DWP's provision of work-related activity through the so-called 'Jobcentre Plus Offer', a process which remarkably had not been properly disclosed to, and clarified before, the three-judge panel in *IM*. It transpired that the key distinction was between work-related activity delivered via an external work programme provider and such activity organised internally through the Jobcentre Plus Offer. Between June 2011 and April 2013, if the claimant's reassessment was scheduled for more than 6 months, then the Jobcentre Plus Offer applied. In April 2013 the prognosis criterion for the Jobcentre Plus Offer to apply increased to 12 months. The detailed arrangements under this internal form of provision are explained in Judge Wright's decision (at para.48), which also noted that the Jobcentre Plus Offer applied to all contributory ESA claimants living elsewhere in the EU (see para.95). The 'information gap' identified by the three-judge panel in *IM* still existed, at least until September 2016 (para.102). Judge Wright criticised the fact that the Jobcentre Plus Offer appeared to be unknown to large parts of the DWP responsible for applying regulation 35(2) (para.103). The judge also criticised the deficiencies in external work provider lists (paragraphs 104-110) relating to regulation 35(2).

In *RP v SSWP (ESA)* [2020] UKUT 148 Upper Tribunal Judge Wright further considered three main issues. The first was the progress the Secretary of State had made in providing a claimant's ESA 'adjudication history' with the appeal response to the FTT (paras 34-39). The second was the role of the 'Work Coach' in Jobcentre Plus in setting work-related activity for an individual claimant (paras 16-28). The third was the provision by the Secretary of State of the appellant's ESA 'action plan' to the First-tier Tribunal in an appeal where reg.35(2) was in issue (paras 29-33). It was held that the Secretary of State's appeals responses in ESA work capability appeals ought, where relevant, to include the claimant's ESA adjudication history and action plan since July 2018. Allowing the claimant's appeal, the Judge highlighted two main errors on the part of the FTT:

"14. First, the tribunal's lack of curiosity or concern about the mangled and adjudication history it was provided with in the Secretary of State's appeal response meant that it failed properly to appraise itself of the decision the appellant was seeking to have superseded and changed. . . .

15. Second, as is now rightly accepted by the Secretary of State, if the 'Work Coach' (or 'Job Coach', the titles appear to be used interchangeably) had advised the appellant to seek placement in the support group then that was plainly relevant evidence, and so the First-tier Tribunal's apparent lack of interest in this evidential area was a further material error of law. . . ."

The Secretary of State's failure to provide accurate lists of work-related activity in appeals which concerned the assessment of 'substantial risk' under reg.35(2) was revisited again in *MR v SSWP (ESA)* [2020] UKUT 210 (AAC). The FTT in that case, which had been provided with a list of 'soft skills' (e.g. setting an alarm clock, getting out of bed and leaving the house), had concluded that the claimant did not meet the terms of reg.35(2) as he could manage those 'soft skills'. However, on appeal to the Upper Tribunal, Judge Wright held that the FTT "was misled in so concluding because the 'soft skills' of work-related activities was a not a true reflection of the extent of the work-related activities claimants may have been expected to undertake in March 2017. Perhaps most critically (and worryingly), the list being of soft skills, it did not contain the more, or most, onerous forms of work-related activities." Judge Wright further explored in detail why it was that the Secretary of State's responses to such FTT appeals failed to comply with the relevant legal requirements. Having reviewed that sorry saga, Judge Wright concluded as follows:

> "42. The 'soft skills' list, therefore, ought not in fact have appeared in any ESA work capability appeal after January 2018, and in any event was irrelevant as accurate lists of the most and least onerous types of available work-related activity even before that date. In consequence, First-tier Tribunals will need to investigate with conspicuous care any work capability assessment appeals in which the 'soft skills' list is put forward as evidence of the available work-related activity."

See, to similar effect, *MD v SSWP (UC)* [2020] UKUT 215 (AAC).

Proper application of reg.35(2) requires "a determination to be made as to *the extent to which* a person has met Schedule 2 [the LCWA] at the date of the decision under appeal as that informs the factors to be take into account in assessing the regulation 35(2) risk" (*KW v SSWP (ESA)* [2015] UKUT 131 (AAC), para.8 (Judge Wright), emphasis in the original).

The burgeoning case law on this regulation covers five more issues, dealt with in turn, below.

4.114   *Issue 1: how does reg.35(2) apply if the claimant could never work again or if there is no work-related activity that could reasonably be required of him?* Here Judge Mark and Judge Jacobs take diametrically opposed positions, the former arguing that in such circumstances the provision can have no application, the latter arguing that it can and must in order to protect the most vulnerable by affording them an opportunity to be placed in the support group in circumstances in which their condition has not met the tailored specifics of ESA Regs 2008, Sch. 3. It is submitted that Judge Jacobs' approach is the better one in that promotes the purpose behind reg.35(2) and thus sits better with the purposive approach taken to the provision by the panel in *IM*, above.

Both judges rightly see the position as involving consideration of the WRA 2007, the ESA Regs 2008 and the Employment and Support Allowance (Work-Related Activity) Regulations 2011 (SI 2011/1349) ("the W-RA Regs"). Both note the definition of "work-related activity" in WRA 2007, s.13(7): "activity which makes it more likely that the person will obtain or remain in work or be able to do so". Although s.13(8) was not in force at the date of the decisions concerned, both judges noted its stipulation that such activity "includes work experience or a work placement". Similarly both took on board, reg. 3 of the W-RA Regs (see para.9.590) giving the Secretary of State discretion on whether or not to require a person in the work-related activity group actually to undertake any such activity, and providing that any such requirement imposed "must be reasonable in the view of the Secretary of State, having regard to the person's circumstances", and may not require him/her to undergo medical treatment or to apply for a job or undertake work, whether as an employee or otherwise.

In *JS v SSWP (ESA)* [2013] UKUT 635 (AAC), followed by him in *RV v SSWP (ESA)* [2014] UKUT 56 (AAC), Judge Mark held that the initial work-focused interview cannot constitute work-related activity since work-related activities can only be required once it has taken place (para.16). Moreover, the work-focused health assessment was also separate from such activity being an assessment, dealt with separately, and not meeting the s.13(7) definition, above (para.16). Given that definition, he considered "that if a person is patently not going to be able to obtain work at any stage, it is difficult to see how they could be required to carry out work-related activities" (para.15). Accordingly in his judgment, in this case reg.35(2) could not assist this claimant:

> "On the basis of the tribunal's finding as to his health problems, there would seem to be no real possibility of his resuming work and it is difficult to see how

any interview could come within the definition of work-focused interview in section 12(7) of the 2007 Act since, due to his ill health, there would seem to be no prospect of his getting into work. For the same reason, there would not seem to be any work-related activity that the claimant could be required to do, in that, because of his health problems, there would be no activity which would make it even arguably more likely that he would be able to obtain work.

It follows that, on the basis of the tribunal's findings of fact, there are no work-focused interviews or work-related activities that the Secretary of State could lawfully require the claimant to attend or undertake and that, in the absence of any other issue, there is no risk to his health as a result of not being found to have limited capability for work-related activity. Accordingly he does not fall within regulation 35(2)." (paras 27–28).

Judge Mark reiterated this in *GS v SSWP (ESA)* [2014] UKUT 16 (AAC), para.26.

In marked contrast, in *NS v SSWP (ESA)* [2014] UKUT 149 (AAC), Judge Jacobs rejected this way of looking at reg.35(2). Nor, in that case, did the Secretary of State support Judge Mark's analysis. There, Ms Wilkinson, appearing for the Secretary of State, argued that his analysis could not be right because it would remove from the most vulnerable claimants "who will not work again and for whom any WRA [work-related activity] will pose a substantial risk to their health" their final chance of being placed in the support group, final, of course, because reg.35(2) can only be applied where the claimant was not regarded as having limited capability for work-related activity, applying reg.34(1) and Sch.3 (para.23). Her suggested approach, based on s.13(7) requiring only that the activity make it "more likely" that the claimant will be able to obtain work and the chance that circumstances might change (e.g. "through a new form of treatment or medication"), was not accepted by Judge Jacobs as enough to cover the claimant who would clearly never work again. The approach, he thought, required a tribunal to make contradictory findings and, viewed as a statement that there was *at present* no work the claimant could do, left unresolved the question of whether reg.35(2) applied for the time being (para.24). The provision had to be applied effectively, whether before or after consideration had been given to the sort of work-related activity appropriate for a claimant (para.25). For him, it was critical to see reg.35(2) as being a *hypothesis* requiring the identification of "the possible consequences of a particular postulate (the *if* bit)" (para.26). The flaw in Judge Mark's analysis was to ignore the postulate. Judge Jacobs explained further:

"If a possible consequence would be a substantial risk to health, the provision is satisfied and the claimant qualifies for the support group. As I have already said, the postulate cannot be read literally. The tribunal does not simply have to postulate the claimant being found not to have limited capability for work-related activity. It also has to postulate the claimant actually undertaking such activity.

It does not have to identify that activity with precision. That is a separate stage that will only be reached if the tribunal decides that the claimant does not qualify for the support group. If and when that stage is reached, it is a matter for the Secretary of State, not the tribunal. The tribunal's task is preliminary to and necessarily more speculative and more general than the actual application of regulation 3 of the 2011 Regulations. The tribunal has to apply the hypothesis embodied in regulation 35(2). In doing so, it cannot deny the postulate. That, with respect to Judge Mark, is what he did. He denied that the postulate (the *if* bit) could ever apply in certain circumstances. But that is the very foundation of the provision. It is what the tribunal is required to accept. It cannot reject the basis of the hypothesis that forms the structure of regulation 35(2).

In doing so, the tribunal has to limit itself to applying regulation 35(2) and avoid trespassing into the Secretary of State's decision-making under regulation 3 of the 2011 Regulations. ... The way to remain properly within the tribunal's jurisdiction lies in the level of generality at which the tribunal has to consider work-related activity. Ms Wilkinson accepted that my decision in *AH* was correct. What the tribunal has to do is to identify in a general way 'the range and type of work-related activity which a claimant is capable of performing and might be expected to undertake' (to quote *AH*); and it must do so regardless of whether the Secretary of State would actually require the claimant to undertake any activity and regardless of whether any such activity would have any effect on the claimant's ability to 'obtain or remain in work' (to quote section 13(7))" (paras 26-28).

Judge Jacobs, in effect, requires the tribunal to ignore what might be done under reg.3 of the W-RA Regs. Judge Ward calls this a "thought experiment" and in *KB v SSWP (ESA)* [2015] UKUT 179 (AAC) applied it to require to be ignored in the application of reg. 35(2) the fact that this claimant, a carer entitled to carer's allowance, could not lawfully under the W-RA Regs be required to undertake work-related activity. This approach chimes well with the answer given by the three-judge panel in *IM* to the question in Issue 2, which must now be examined

4.115   *Issue 2: given that reg. 3 of the Employment and Support Allowance (Work-Related Activity) Regulations 2011 (SI 2011/1349) ("the W-RA Regs") stipulates that the work-related activity required must be "reasonable ..., having regard to the person's circumstances", does this mean that the condition in reg.35(2) cannot be met?* In *IM v SSWP (ESA)* [2014] UKUT 412 (AAC); [2015] AACR 10), the panel of three Upper Tribunal judges answered this in the negative since an affirmative answer would undermine the purpose of the provision. In so deciding they endorsed the decisions on this point given by Judge Jacobs in *NS v SSWP (ESA)* [2014] UKUT 149 (AAC) (paras 30, 34) and Judge Bano in *CMcC v SSWP (ESA)* [2014] UKUT 176 (AAC); [2015] AACR 9. As Judge Bano put it (in a passage endorsed by Judge Jacobs as consonant with his own view in *NS*):

"If regulation 35(2) is to have any real meaning, it is not open to a tribunal to find that work-related activity does not present a risk of harm to a claimant on the basis that the claimant will not actually be required to undertake *any* meaningful activity if it turns out to be harmful. I therefore consider that the action of the employment adviser of effectively bringing the claimant's action plan to an end out of concern for her health was evidence which the tribunal should have taken into account when evaluating the risk of harm to the claimant if she were not found to have limited capability for work-related activity" (para.12).

Judge Gray's decision in *YA and SA v SSWP (ESA)* [2017] UKUT 80 (AAC) is authority for two propositions in this context. First, the duty under s.26(6) of the Equality Act 2010 to make reasonable adjustments added nothing to the duty under regulation 3 of the W-RA Regs that the WRA activity is reasonable (paragraphs 49-53). Second, subject to safeguards, the WRA requirements made between the date of the decision under appeal and the FTT hearing may be considered. In particular, tribunals cannot simply assume that a claimant will not be required to undertake any more onerous types of WRA than those already stipulated (paragraphs 39-48).

Issue 3: the "substantial risk" must arise "by reasons of" a specific disease or bodily or mental disablement: in *DR v SSWP (ESA)* [2014] UKUT 188 (AAC); [2014] AACR 38, Judge May held erroneous in law a tribunal decision that the claimant satisfied reg.29 because it had not made the necessary connection between the risk and the disease or disablement (see para.3). He considered the same principle applied to reg.35 (para.10). Alcohol misuse in itself is not such a disablement. To rank as disablement the misuse of alcohol must rank as "alcohol dependency" in terms of the "constellation of markers" found in quotations from *R(DLA) 6/06* in the Three-Judge Panel's decision in *JG v SSWP (ESA)* [2013] UKUT 37 (AAC); [2013] AACR 23 (see paras 5-7, 10 of *DR*). See further, commentary to reg.29(2)(b), above.

Issue 4: can the availability of third party assistance be taken into account? In *MT v*   **4.116**
SSWP (ESA) [2013] UKUT 545 (AAC), in the context of reg.35(2) Judge Gray firmly rejected looking at capacity to perform activities with third party assistance, observing:

> "I do need to deal however with the observation of the FTT in its statement of reasons that the appellant could take another person with her to any work-related activities. It may be that the Secretary of State would be facilitative in any matter which helped a claimant engage so as to improve their ultimate prospects of retaining work. I do not know. Whether or not that is so, is not relevant. As a matter of law any work-related activity which could only be accomplished because of the presence of another person must be looked upon as not being an activity that the claimant can carry out. *The issue under regulation 35 (2) (b) as to whether there would be a substantial risk to the mental or physical health of any person if the claimant were found not to have limited capability for work-related activity cannot be assessed as if the claimant under consideration had somebody else by their side.* There will be claimants who have a need for the personal reassurance of another person, but who do not have anybody available to perform that role. Even if they did, it would not be reasonable for such an assessment to be made on the basis of reliance on another's goodwill. Legal tests cannot depend upon that. Where an appellant who is found to have limited capability for work-related activities wishes to engage voluntarily, it may be that they choose to do so with the help of another person, and it may (or may not, I do not know) be possible for them to do so, but the capacity to engage only with that assistance cannot be part of the test of capability" (para.34, emphasis added by commentator).

In *PD v SSWP (ESA)* [2014] UKUT 148 (AAC), in the context of the similarly worded reg. 29(2)(b), Judge Ward agreed with the italicised passage insofar as it meant "without consideration as to whether the third party's presence would be made out in fact" (para.21), but otherwise distinguished the passage as focussing on the claimant's capability to perform activities (agreeing that there third party assistance should be ignored) rather than the different question of what risks would ensue (where, with respect to travelling, at least, third party assistance available in fact might obviate the risk). See further commentary to reg.29(2)(b), above, substituting for "in the workplace" the different context of "the places where work-related activities might be performed".

Insofar as there is a difference of view between the two decisions in *MT v SSWP (ESA)* [2013] UKUT 545 (AAC) and *PD v SSWP (ESA)* [2016] UKUT 148 (AAC), Judge Hemingway in *MP v SSWP (ESA)* [2016] UKUT 502 (AAC) expressed a preference for the latter approach, noting that he could not:

> "see any reason why a third party's assistance ought not to be taken into account, in principle, when assessing whether or not the risk envisaged by the regulation would arise. There is nothing within the legislation which suggests that third party assistance cannot be relevant. The language of the test focuses upon risk. It would be artificial to approach the question of risk in a vacuum and without having regard to the prevailing circumstances. Such circumstances might include the availability of assistance" (at para.22).

See also *KN v SSWP (ESA)* [2016] UKUT 521 (AAC). In addition, Judge Gray in *YA and SA v SSWP (ESA)* [2017] UKUT 80 (AAC) accepted that third-party assistance may be considered, but "the circumstances need to be closely investigated and assessed prior to a finding that such assistance is reasonably available" (para.54). Thus "what should not be assumed is regular and open ended input from another person" (para.58). See also, on the importance of appropriate fact-finding in such cases, *ET v SSWP (UC)* [2021] UKUT 47 (AAC) (paras 6-12).

4.117   In *NN-K v Secretary of State for Work and Pensions (ESA)* [2015] UKUT 385 (AAC) Judge Jacobs reminded tribunals that, as a result of the decision in *IM v Secretary of State for Work and Pensions* [2014] UKUT 412 (AAC), a tribunal applying reg.35 must have regard to the type of work-related activity that the claimant might be expected to undertake in her area; in doing so, the tribunal must consider whether the activity would "be reasonable ... having regard to the person's circumstances" (reg.3(4)(a)). In that context the compatibility of any such activity with a claimant's existing education course would be one of those circumstances (para.9). However:

> "10. But such factors are only relevant in so far as they relate to the existence of a substantial risk to health. The tribunal should ignore any factor that is not relevant to that. If the tribunal does not have, and is not to be treated as having, limited capability for work-related activity, any issues such as the reasonableness of the activity would arise subsequently. In particular, the issue might arise whether to give a direction on work-related activity or whether she had good cause for not undertaking it or whether to reduce her benefit for failing to comply with the direction."

Issue 5: how does reg.35(2) operate if the claimant lives outside the UK? In *BB v Secretary of State for Work and Pensions (ESA)* [2015] UKUT 545 (AAC) the claimant lived in Spain and later in the Republic of Ireland. Following a conversion decision, he was found to qualify for ESA without the support component. A tribunal dismissed his appeal, finding that reg.35(2) was not satisfied. On appeal to the Upper Tribunal, the Secretary of State's representative confirmed that there were no arrangements in place to provide work-related activities in countries outside the UK and argued that the reg. 35(2) test has to be applied on a hypothetical basis, namely "what could happen if a claimant were required to undertake work-related activity, not what would happen" (para.14(b)). Judge Mitchell allowed the claimant's appeal, as he had not had "a fair opportunity to put forward a case in relation to regulation 35(2) because he was unaware of the type of work-related activity by reference to which regulation 35(2) would be applied" (para.20). The Secretary of State's representative further argued that "Where the claimant lives outside the UK and elects to have a paper hearing (as in this case) the hearing is almost always going to take place in Newcastle. However if the claimant chooses to attend in person they can choose a venue suitable to them. Thus, in such cases the relevant WRA evidence will be from the Newcastle area, or the area in which the tribunal was that the claimant attended" (para.17). Remitting the appeal to a new tribunal, Judge Mitchell observed as follows:

> "22. I acknowledge the conceptual difficulties raised by the application of regulation 35(2), given the existing authorities, in foreign cases such as this. The Secretary of State's proposed solution has the benefit of levelling, to an extent, the playing field. It reduces the chances of different reg. 35(2) outcomes solely by reason of a person's country of residence. If an appellant does not object, the First-tier Tribunal ought to adopt the course suggested by the Secretary of State. If the appellant does object, the Tribunal will need to decide for itself how to proceed taking into account the reasons for the objection and any submissions of the Secretary of State" (para.22).

[¹Relevant linked cases—limited capability for work-related activity

4.118   **35A.**—A claimant is to be treated as having limited capability for work-related activity where–

(a) they fall within case 1, as defined in regulation 7(1B)(a); and
(b) in respect of the earlier period of limited capability for work referred to in regulation 7(1B)(a)(i), they had been entitled to a support component under sections 2(2) or 4(4) of the Act.]

AMENDMENT

1. Employment and Support Allowance (Amendment of Linking Rules) Regulations 2012 (SI 2012/919) reg.5(5) (May 1, 2012).

Information required for determining capability for work-related activity

36.—(1) Subject to paragraph (2), the information or evidence required to determine whether a claimant has limited capability for work-related activity is—   4.119
(a) any information relating to the descriptors set out in Schedule 3 as may be requested in the form of a questionnaire; and
(b) any such additional information as may be requested.
(2) Where the Secretary of State is satisfied that there is sufficient information to determine whether a claimant has limited capability for work-related activity without the information specified in paragraph (1)(a), that information [¹must] not be required for the purposes of making the determination.

AMENDMENT

1. Social Security (Miscellaneous Amendments) (No.3) Regulations 2013 (SI 2013/2536) reg.13(18) (October 29, 2013).

DEFINITIONS

"claimant"—see WRA 2007 s.24(1).
"limited capability for work-related activity"—see WRA 2007 s.2(5).
"work-related activity"—see WRA 2007 ss.24(1), 13(7).

GENERAL NOTE

This regulation deals with the information required for determining whether someone has limited capability for work-related activity. It is designed to give the decision-maker sufficient information to decide that matter for himself (the minority of cases), or whether to seek advice from a health care professional on the basis of the papers in respect of that decision, or to refer the claimant for a face to face WRAAt, including a medical examination (see reg.38).   4.120
    Unless para.(2) operates, the claimant will have to supply (i) any information relating to the descriptors set out in Sch.3 as may be requested in the form of a questionnaire (para.(1)(a)), and (ii) such additional information relating to the relevant test as the Secretary of State asks for (para.(1)(b)). He must generally complete and return the appropriate questionnaire (para.(1)(a)), unless the Secretary of State decides that completion of the questionnaire is not necessary because without it he has sufficient information to determine whether the claimant does or does not have limited capability for work-related activity (para.(2)). Note that where the claimant is requested by the Secretary of State to complete and return the questionnaire, failure to do so can result in his being treated as not having limited capability for work-related activity (and thus not entitled to support component) (reg.37).

Failure to provide information in relation to work-related activity

37.—(1) Where a claimant fails without good cause to comply with the request referred to in regulation 36(1)(a), the claimant is, subject to paragraph   4.121

(2), to be treated as not having limited capability for work-related activity.

(2) Paragraph (1) does not apply unless—

(a) at least [¹4] weeks have passed since the claimant was sent the first request for the information; and

(b) [². . .] at least [¹1 week has] passed since the further request was sent.

AMENDMENTS

1. Social Security (Miscellaneous Amendments) (No. 3) Regulations 2011 (SI 2011/2425) reg.23(5), (6) (October 31, 2011).

2. Social Security (Miscellaneous Amendments) (No.3) Regulations 2013 (SI 2013/2536) reg.13(19) (October 29, 2013).

DEFINITIONS

"claimant"—see WRA 2007 s.24(1).
"limited capability for work-related activity"—see WRA 2007 s.2(5).
"week"—see reg.2(1).
"work-related activity"—see WRA 2007 ss.24(1), 13(7).

GENERAL NOTE

4.122   If a claimant fails without good cause (on which more, below) to comply with the requirement in reg.36(1)(a) to complete and return a limited capability for work-related activity questionnaire, he must be treated as not having limited capability for work-related activity, that is, as having no entitlement to support component. This can only happen, however, if a further request for information was sent at least three weeks after the first and at least one week has gone by since the second request was sent.

On applicable IB case law on calculating periods and on the matter of good cause, see further the commentary to the analogous reg.22, applicable in respect of similar processes with respect to determination of limited capability for work questions.

Claimant may be called for a medical examination to determine whether the claimant has limited capability for work-related activity

4.123   **38.**—(1) Where it falls to be determined whether a claimant has limited capability for work-related activity, that claimant may be called by or on behalf of a health care professional approved by the Secretary of State to attend for a medical examination [²in person, by telephone or by video].

(2) Subject to paragraph (3), where a claimant fails without good cause to attend for or to submit to an examination [¹mentioned] in paragraph (1), the claimant is to be treated as not having limited capability for work-related activity.

[¹(3) Paragraph (2) does not apply unless—

(a) written notice of the date, time and place for the examination was sent to the claimant at least seven days in advance; or

(b) the claimant agreed to accept a shorter period of notice whether given in writing or otherwise.]

AMENDMENTS

1. Social Security (Miscellaneous Amendments) (No.3) Regulations 2013 (SI 2013/2536) reg.13(20) (October 29, 2013).

2. Social Security (Claims and Payments, Employment and Support Allowance, Personal Independence Payment and Universal Credit) (Telephone and Video Assessment) (Amendment) Regulations 2021 (SI 2021/230) reg.3(3) (March 25, 2021).

DEFINITIONS

> "claimant"—see WRA 2007 s.24(1).
> "health care professional"—see reg.2(1).
> "limited capability for work-related activity"—see WRA 2007 s.2(5).
> "work-related activity"—see WRA 2007 ss.24(1), 13(7).

GENERAL NOTE

This regulation enables the DWP to have a claimant medically examined by a DWP Medical Service (DWPMS) health service professional (technically any health service professional approved by the Secretary of State) when a question arises as to the claimant's capability for work-related activity. Failure without good cause to attend for or submit to such an examination, of which he was given proper written notice (see para.(3)), will result in the claimant being treated as not having limited capability for work-related activity and thus be excluded from the support group. **4.124**

This regulation is a direct analogue of reg.23 with respect to medical examination as regards the matter of limited capability for work. The points, including the application of relevant IB case law, made in the commentary to reg.23 are equally applicable here.

Matters to be taken into account in determining good cause in relation to regulations 37 or 38

39. The matters to be taken into account in determining whether a claimant has good cause under regulations 37 (failure to provide information in relation to work-related activity) or 38 (failure to attend a medical examination to determine limited capability for work-related activity) include— **4.125**
  (a) whether the claimant was outside Great Britain at the relevant time;
  (b) the claimant's state of health at the relevant time; and
  (c) the nature of any disability the claimant has.

DEFINITION

> "claimant"—see WRA 2007 s.24(1).

GENERAL NOTE

This regulation, made pursuant to WRA 2007 s.9(4), stipulates that in determining whether someone had good cause for failing to provide information (under reg.37) or for failing to attend for or submit to a medical examination (under reg.38) decision-makers and appellate bodies must take into account: (i) whether the person was outside Great Britain at the relevant time; (ii) his state of health at the relevant time; and (iii) the nature of his disability. This list is not, however, exhaustive (the regulation says "shall include"). On "good cause", see further the commentary to regs 22 and 23. **4.126**

PART 7

EFFECT OF WORK ON ENTITLEMENT TO AN EMPLOYMENT AND SUPPORT ALLOWANCE

A claimant who works to be treated as not entitled to an employment and support allowance

40.—(1) Subject to the following paragraphs, a claimant is to be treated as not entitled to an employment and support allowance in any week in which that claimant does work. **4.127**
  (2) Paragraph (1) does not apply to—
  (a) work as a councillor;

(b) duties undertaken on either one full day or two half-days a week
as—
  (i) a member of the Disability Living Allowance Advisory Board; or
  [²(ii) a member of the First-tier Tribunal where the member is eligi-
    ble for appointment to be such a member in accordance with
    article 2(3) of the Qualifications for Appointment of Members
    to the First-tier Tribunal and Upper Tribunal Order 2008.]
(c) domestic tasks carried out in the claimant's own home or the care of
a relative;
(d) duties undertaken in caring for another person who is accommodated
with the claimant by virtue of arrangements made under any of the
provisions referred to in paragraphs [⁴28, 29 or 29A] of Schedule
8 (sums to be disregarded in the calculation of income other than
earnings) [³or] where the claimant is in receipt of any payment specified in those paragraphs;
[⁴ (da) duties undertaken in caring for another person who is provided with
continuing care by a local authority by virtue of arrangements made
under section 26A of the Children (Scotland) Act 1995 and is in
receipt of a payment made under that section of that Act;]
(e) any activity the claimant undertakes during an emergency to protect
another person or to prevent serious damage to property or livestock;
or
(f) any of the categories of work set out in regulation 45 (exempt work).
  (3) This regulation is subject to regulation 46 (effect of work on entitlement to contributory allowance where claimant is receiving certain regular
treatment).
  (4) A claimant who does work to which this regulation applies in a week
which is—
(a) the week in which the claimant first becomes entitled to a benefit,
allowance or advantage on account of the claimant's limited capability for work in any period; or
(b) the last week in any period in which the claimant has limited capability for work or is treated as having limited capability for work,
is to be treated as not entitled to an employment and support allowance by
virtue of paragraph (1) only on the actual day or days in that week on which
the claimant does that work.
  (5) Regulation 145 (linking rules) does not apply for the purposes of
calculating the beginning or end of any period of limited capability for work
under paragraph (4).
  (6) The day or days in a week on which a night worker works, for the
purposes of [¹paragraph (4)] above, are to be calculated by reference to
regulation 28 (night workers).
  (7) In this regulation—
"week" means a week in respect of which a claimant is entitled to an
employment and support allowance;
"work" means any work which a claimant does, whether or not that
claimant undertakes it in expectation of payment;
"work as a councillor" is to be taken to include any work which a claimant undertakes as a member of any of the bodies referred to in section
177(1) of the Local Government Act 1972 or sub-sections 49(1) or
49(1A) of the Local Government (Scotland) Act 1973, of which the
claimant is a member by reason of being a councillor.

AMENDMENTS

1. Employment and Support Allowance (Miscellaneous Amendments) Regulations 2008 (SI 2008/2428) reg.6(1) (October 27, 2008).

2. Tribunals, Courts and Enforcement Act 2007 (Transitional and Consequential Provisions) Order 2008 (SI 2008/2683) art.6(1), Sch1 para.342 (November 3, 2008).

3. Social Security (Miscellaneous Amendments) (No.3) Regulations 2013 (SI 2013/2536) reg.13(20) (October 29, 2013).

4. Social Security and Child Support (Care Payments and Tenant Incentive Scheme) (Amendment) Regulations 2017 (SI 2017/995) regs.7(2) and 13(2) (November 7, 2017).

DEFINITIONS

"claimant"—see WRA 2007 s.24(1).
"entitled"—see WRA 2007 s.24(1).
"relative"—see reg.2(1).
"week"—see para.(7) and reg.2(1).
"work"—see para.(7).
"work as a councillor"—see para.(7).

GENERAL NOTE

This regulation needs to be read in conjunction with regs 44–46. **4.128**

To find in any incapacity regime a general rule that working (whether or not for payment) negatives incapacity for work is unsurprising since, in principle, it is a strong indication of ability to work. This regulation contains just such a rule, precluding entitlement to ESA in any week in which a claimant does work. Moreover, in that period of non-entitlement, he or she will be treated as not having limited capability for work, unless the work done only negatives entitlement to IRESA (reg.44). That can happen in that work done in a week when someone, entitled to CESA, is receiving or recovering from certain regular treatments, does not negative title to CESA, but can to IRESA (regs 46 (to which para.(3) makes this regulation subject) and 44(3)). But like the incapacity benefit regime, the general preclusive rule is modified to permit engagement in a range of work without loss of benefit ("subject to the following paragraphs", one of which para.(2)(f) links this regulation to reg.45 and the concept of "exempt work"). These modifications recognize that work can assist recovery or help the claimant into thinking about work and a possibility to return to work, or merely not wanting to exclude the sick and disabled from participation in civic office or a range of voluntary or charitable work.

Although, unlike its IB comparator (Incapacity for Work Regs, reg.16) the point is no longer explicit, it is submitted that the regulation can operate despite the fact that, applying the limited capability for work assessment (WCAt), the person in fact has limited capability for work, or is someone treated as having such limited capability by virtue of other regs.

Paragraph (1) sets out the general preclusive rule: a person must be treated as capable of work on each day of any week during which he does work. "Work" for the purposes of the regulation is defined in para.(7) as any work done whether or not undertaken in expectation of payment. "Week" is a period of seven days beginning with Sunday (para.(7)).

Note, however, that this ostensibly very wide general preclusive rule is subject to the partial relief afforded by para.(4) and by reg.46 (see para.(3)) and the complete relief afforded by para.(2). Execution of some de minimis tasks can also be ignored as not constituting "work". Discussion is divided accordingly.

Partial relief

Paras (4), (5): Together these afford some relief from the general preclusive rule **4.129** set out in para.(1). Paragraph (4) contains an obviously necessary one, it covers the worker who initially falls sick part way through his working week and/or the period in which he is incapable of work finishes part way through a week in the course of which he returns to work. Here, the preclusive effect of the regulation is confined to ruling out only the days actually worked in that or those weeks.

Note that the linking rules in reg.145 do not apply for determining when, for the purposes of this relieving rule, a period of limited capability for work begins and ends (para.(5)). In effect, each "spell" of limited capability for work" is treated separately, thus helping those whose limited capability for work is intermittent and removing a disincentive to trying work for a while.

Para.(3): This regulation is "subject to regulation 46". That provides that those treated under reg.26 as having limited capability for work on days when receiving or recovering from certain regular treatments (e.g. chemotherapy), who work on other days of the week in which they receive or are recovering from such treatment such treatment, will not have their entitlement to CESA affected by doing that work. For the impact of such work on entitlement to IRESA, see the exclusionary "remunerative work" rules (WRA 2007 Sch.1, para.6(1)(e); reg.41) and, in terms of the IRESA "balance sheet", the impact of earnings on entitlement.

Complete relief

4.130   *Para.(2)* prevents the general preclusive rule in para.(1) applying to:
(i)   any of the categories of work in reg.45 (para.(2)(f));
(ii)   work as a councillor (see para.(7) for its breadth and see reg.88 for the abating effect on CESA of amounts of councillor's allowance over a specified weekly amount) (para.(2)(a);
       The scheme, as before, seeks to encourage sick and disabled people to participate in civic office by enabling them to receive CESA reduced or abated by the amount by which their councillor's allowance applicable to that week exceeds a specified amount.
(iii) care of a relative or domestic tasks carried out in his own home (para.(2)(c);
(iv)   work as a foster parent or other specified carer in respect of someone accommodated in one's home or where the claimant is in receipt of any payment specified in Sch.8, paras. 28, 29;
(v)   limited duties (one full day or two half days per week) as a member of a the DLA Advisory Board or as First-tier Tribunal member with a disability qualification (para.(2)(b)) (i.e. someone other than a registered medical practitioner, who is experienced in dealing with the physical or mental needs of disabled persons because they work with disabled persons in a professional or voluntary capacity, or are themselves disabled (see art.2(3) of the Qualifications for Appointment of Members to the First-tier Tribunal and Upper Tribunal Order 2008 (SI 2008/2692));
(vi)   any activity undertaken during an emergency solely to protect another person or to prevent serious damage to property or livestock (para.(2)(e)).
This exemption is essential to protect the benefit position of the rescuer; of the good neighbour who looks after his/her neighbour's children when she is rushed to hospital; of the person who helps round up livestock which have strayed into a busy road; or of the good neighbour who helps fight a fire until the emergency services arrive; or the husband on ESA who is compelled to drive to rush his pregnant wife in labour to hospital because the ambulance has not arrived. These can be but speculative examples.

"Emergency" is not defined. However, note it is not qualified by terms such as "severe" or "serious" or "great", so it ought not to be construed too narrowly. By way of comparison, in the industrial injuries context, case law dealing with "in the course of employment" has brought within that phrase persons responding to emergency. There "emergency" was construed broadly to encompass a wide range of unexpected occurrences (see commentary to SSCBA 1992, s.100). A broad approach ought to be taken, similarly, to the notion of "any activity to protect another person".

Applying the de minimis principle to ignore trivial or negligible amounts of work

It is submitted that this long-standing principle, which has applied to previous   **4.131**
inpacity for work regimes, is equally applicable to ESA and that previous case law
applies here.

CIB/5298/1997 supports the view (then found in AOG, paras 18782 and 18783)
that the de minimis principle applies to enable trivial or negligible amounts of work
to be ignored (paras 5–12), recognising as a practical proposition something seen
as a theoretical one in *CIB/14656/96*. Deputy Commissioner Wikeley's decision in
CIB/6777/1999 contains a thorough review of the authorities on this matter. He
notes that the rule here can apply irrespective of whether the work might in any
event be treated as exempt under Incapacity for Work Regs reg.17 (and thus ESA
Regs regs 40, 45). Whether work done is trivial or negligible is a matter of fact
and degree. Like Commissioner Williams in *CIB/5298/1997*, who had approved
guidance in the AOG, the Deputy Commissioner supported as illustrative but not
exhaustive, relevant factors, those set out in DMG para.13867:

> "whether work on a day is negligible depends on its proportion to the normal
> working hours, the type of work and the effort required in relation to normal
> working duties."

Stressing the role of incapacity benefit as "an earnings replacement . . . benefit
for those with the appropriate contributions record who cannot work in the
labour market" he (rightly in the opinion of this commentator) disagreed with
Commissioner Williams in *CIB/5298/1997* who took the view that the amount of
remuneration earned was always wholly irrelevant since para.(6) states that work
is "work" whether or not undertaken in expectation of payment. That means, of
course, that the lack of remuneration or of the expectation of it is irrelevant. The
key question is really what the tasks performed tell one about the person's capacity
for work. But, in contrast to the irrelevance of lack of remuneration, this author, like
the Deputy Commissioner, believes that the amount of remuneration received for
a relatively small degree of work-like activity, when contrasted with the weekly rate
of incapacity benefit (and now ESA), surely *is* a relevant factor in deciding whether
work done should be disregarded as trivial or negligible—it brings into play the
"anti-abuse" element of the rules here, which arguably takes one into the realm of
when the public (including other recipients of benefit) might view as inappropriate
receipt of incapacity benefit or ESA by someone with what looks like a source of
income from "employment", albeit only in that one week. Is that not one purpose
behind the earnings limits on exempt work in Incapacity for Work Regs, reg.17
(ESA Regs reg.45)? However, that Incapacity for Work Regs reg.16 (ESA Regs
reg.40) stipulates particular worthy tasks as ones to be disregarded seems to cast
doubt on the Deputy Commissioner's view that the identity of the person for whom
the task is performed may be a material factor in applying the de minimis rule.

CIB/3507/2002 affords another illustration of work being disregarded as de   **4.132**
minimis. The work in question was described by the Commissioner as follows:

> "On 28th November 2001, DW Windows wrote a letter in which they said:
> 'In July of this year we approached [the claimant] to see if he would like to do
> a couple of hours each week at [DW Windows] doing various light duties. i.e.
> Making coffees, emptying bins etc and occasionally driving a vehicle to transport
> [Mr S. E.] the Manager who holds no driving license. There is no dispute about
> what DW Windows say. Nor is there any dispute about the fact that the claim-
> ant was paid £3.85 per hour and that he worked between one and three hours
> per week. A schedule of his weekly hours and earnings between the beginning of
> July and the first week of October 2001 has been produced by DW Windows. He
> never worked for more than three hours and consequently never earned more
> than £11.55, in any one week. The period covered is one of 14 weeks. During
> three of those weeks he worked for 1 hour only. He worked for two hours for five
> of those weeks and for three hours for the remaining six weeks. The average is a
> little above two hours per week'" (paras 6, 7).

In marked contrast, in *CIB/4684/2003*, Commissioner Jacobs found the work done by the claimant was not so minimal that it could be disregarded. He did so, however, for a different reason to the tribunal which had so found on the basis that the claimant's contribution to the earnings from the post office was significant when compared to his wife's. Instead Commissioner Jacobs approached the matter thus:

> "For 8 hours a week, spread over 2 mornings, the claimant manned the post office. He was not there merely to summon his wife if a customer arrived. He was there to serve any customer who wanted any of the services offered by the office. Covering the office in those circumstances amounted to work, even if there were no customers at all. He was in exactly the same position as a stallholder on a market who had no customers. Surely that stallholder would be working, even if no one bought from, or even visited, the stall? How the claimant spent his time when he was not actually serving customers is irrelevant. It would be just as irrelevant whether a market stallholder at a market spent the time trying to entice customers to the stall or merely sat reading a book" (paras 10, 11).

PART 7

EFFECT OF WORK ON ENTITLEMENT TO AN EMPLOYMENT AND SUPPORT ALLOWANCE

Meaning of "remunerative work" for the purposes of paragraph 6(1)(e) of Schedule 1 to the Act

4.133
41.—(1) For the purposes of paragraph 6(1)(e) of Schedule 1 to the Act (conditions of entitlement to an income-related allowance), "remunerative work" means any work which a claimant does for which payment is made or which is done in expectation of payment, other than work listed in paragraph (2) of regulation 40.

(2) Subject to paragraph (3), a claimant who was, or who was being treated as—

(a) engaged in remunerative work; and

(b) in respect of that work earnings to which regulation 95(1)(b) and (d) applies are paid, is to be treated as being engaged in remunerative work for the period for which those earnings are taken into account in accordance with Part 10 of these Regulations.

(3) Paragraph (2) does not apply to earnings disregarded under paragraph 1 of Schedule 7 (sums to be disregarded in the calculation of earnings).

DEFINITIONS

"claimant"—Welfare Reform Act 2007 s.24(1).
"earnings"—regs 95 and 97.

GENERAL NOTE

4.134
Under para.6 of Sch.1 to the Welfare Reform Act, it is a condition of entitlement to income-related ESA that (among other things) the claimant is not engaged in remunerative work (para.6(1)(e)) and that, where the claimant is a member of a couple, neither is the other member of the couple (para.6(1)(f)). The meaning of the phrase "remunerative work" differs according to whether it is the claimant or her/his partner that is being considered. Regulation 41 sets out the test for the claimant and reg.42 (below), the test for the partner.

ESA is a benefit for those with limited capability for work and the general principle is that a claimant who does any work will normally not be entitled to ESA for that week (see reg.40 above). That is subject to the exceptions set out in reg.40(2). Paragraph (1) defines remunerative work as any work other than that specified in reg.40(2) with the additional requirement that it should be work "for which payment is made or which is done in expectation of payment". It is difficult to see what purpose this serves. The reg.41(1) definition is narrower than the reg.40 definition and therefore anyone falling within reg.41(1) will already have been disentitled by reg.40.

Perhaps more importantly, some claimants who are not actually working (and are not therefore disentitled by reg.40) are nevertheless *treated as* being in remunerative work (and therefore not entitled to income-related ESA) under powers conferred by para.6(3) of Sch.1 to the Act. Paragraphs (2) and (3) provide that where a claimant's employment is interrupted or comes to an end and he or she receives payment in lieu of remuneration (other than a redundancy payment) or holiday pay (unless it is payable more than four weeks after the termination or interruption of employment) then, except where those earnings are disregarded under para.1 of Sch.7, s/he is treated as engaged in remunerative work for the period during which those earnings are taken into account under Pt 10.

Meaning of "remunerative work" for the purposes of paragraph 6(1) (f) of Schedule 1 to the Act

42.—(1) For the purposes of paragraph 6(1)(f) of Schedule 1 to the Act, (conditions of entitlement to an income-related allowance where a claimant must not be a member of a couple the other member of which is engaged in remunerative work), "remunerative work" means work in which the claimant's partner is engaged or, where the partner's hours of work fluctuate, the partner is engaged on average, for not less than 24 hours a week, being work for which payment is made or which is done in expectation of payment.

4.135

(2) In calculating the number of hours for which a claimant's partner is engaged in work so as to determine whether that partner is engaged in remunerative work, the number of hours are to be determined in accordance with paragraphs (8) and (9) of regulation 45 and those paragraphs are to be read as though they referred to the claimant's partner.

(3) The claimant's partner is to be treated as engaged in remunerative work during any period for which that partner is absent from work referred to in paragraph (1) if the absence is either without good cause or by reason of a recognised, customary or other holiday.

(4) Subject to paragraph (5), a claimant's partner who was, or who was being treated as—

(a) engaged in remunerative work; and

(b) in respect of that work earnings to which regulation 95(1)(b) and (d) applies are paid, is to be treated as being engaged in remunerative work for the period for which those earnings are taken into account in accordance with Part 10 of these Regulations.

(5) Paragraph (4) does not apply to earnings disregarded under paragraph 1 of Schedule 7 (sums to be disregarded in the calculation of earnings).

(6) For the purposes of this regulation, in determining the number of hours in which a claimant's partner is engaged or treated as engaged in remunerative work, no account is to be taken of any hours in which the claimant's partner is engaged in an employment or a scheme to which regulation 43(1) or (2) (claimants' partners not treated as engaged in remunerative work) applies.

DEFINITIONS

"claimant"—Welfare Reform Act 2007 s.24(1).
"couple"—reg.2(1).

"earnings"—regs 95 and 97.
"partner"—reg.2(1).

GENERAL NOTE

4.136 In contrast to the position for ESA claimants, it is not a condition of entitlement that their partners should also have limited capability for work. Regulation 42 therefore defines "remunerative work" for the claimant's partner in terms that are similar to reg.5 of the IS Regulations and reg.51 of the JSA Regulations.

Circumstances under which partners of claimants entitled to an income-related allowance are not to be treated as engaged in remunerative work

4.137 **43.**—(1) A claimant's partner is not to be treated as engaged in remunerative work in so far as—

(a) the partner is engaged in child minding in the partner's home;

(b) the partner is engaged by a charity or voluntary organisation, or is a volunteer, where the only payment received by the partner or due to be paid to the partner, is a payment which is to be disregarded under regulation 104(2) (calculation of income other than earnings) and paragraph 2 of Schedule 8 (sums to be disregarded in the calculation of income other than earnings);

(c) the partner is engaged on a scheme for which a training allowance is being paid;

(d) the partner is receiving assistance under the self-employment route;

(e) the partner is engaged in employment as any one of the following—

    [³ (i) a part-time fire-fighter employed by a fire and rescue authority under the Fire and Rescue Services Act 2004 or by the Scottish Fire and Rescue Service established under section 1A of the Fire (Scotland) Act 2005;]

    (ii) [³ ...]

    (iii) [³ ...[²]]

    (iv) an auxiliary coastguard in respect of coast rescue activities;

    (v) a person engaged part-time in the manning or launching of a life boat;

    (vi) a member of any [⁵ ...] reserve force prescribed in Part 1 of Schedule 6 to the Social Security (Contributions) Regulations 2001; or

(f) the partner is undertaking work as a councillor;

(g) the partner is engaged in caring for a person who is accommodated with the partner by virtue of arrangements made under any of the provisions referred to in paragraphs 28 or 29 of Schedule 8 (sums to be disregarded in the calculation of income other than earnings) and the partner is in receipt of any payment specified in those paragraphs;

(h) the partner is engaged in an activity in respect of which—

    (i) a sports award has been made, or is to be made, to the partner; and

    (ii) no other payment is made or is expected to be made to the partner.

(2) A claimant's partner is not to be treated as engaged in remunerative work, where the partner is—

(a) [¹ ...]

1316

(b) subject to regulation 42(4) (partners treated as engaged in remunerative work), a person who would otherwise have satisfied section
126(1) of the Contributions and Benefits Act (trade disputes) or in
respect of whom section 124(1) of that Act (conditions of entitlement to income support) would otherwise have had effect as modified by section 127(b) of that Act (effect of return to work);
(c) a person who would otherwise satisfy the conditions set out in paragraph 4 of Schedule 1B to the Income Support Regulations;
(d) [¹ . . .]
(3) The claimant's partner is not to be treated as engaged in remunerative
work on any day on which that partner is on maternity leave, paternity leave
[⁴ , shared parental leave] [⁶, parental bereavement leave] or adoption leave
or is absent from work because the partner is ill.
(4) In this regulation—
"work as a councillor" has the same meaning as in regulation 40;
"volunteer" means a person who is engaged in voluntary work otherwise
than for a relative, where the only payment received or due to be paid
to the person by virtue of being so engaged is in respect of any expenses
reasonably incurred by the person in connection with that work.

AMENDMENTS

1. Social Security (Miscellaneous Amendments) (No.5) Regulations 2009 (SI
2009/3228) reg.4(1)(c) (January 25, 2010).
2. Police and Fire Reform (Scotland) Act 2012 (Consequential Provisions and
Modifications) Order 2013 (SI 2013/602) art.26 and Sch.2 Pt 3 para.91 (April 1,
2013).
3. Social Security (Miscellaneous Amendments) (No.3) Regulations 2013 (SI
2013/2536) reg.13(1) and (22) (October 29, 2013).
4. Shared Parental Leave and Statutory Shared Parental Pay (Consequential
Amendments to Subordinate Legislation) Order 2014 art.20(4) (December 31,
2014).
5. Social Security (Members of the Reserve Forces) (Amendment) Regulations
2015 (SI 2014/389) reg.4(5) (April 6, 2015).
6. Parental Bereavement Leave and Pay (Consequential Amendments to
Subordinate Legislation) Regulations 2020 (SI 2020/354) reg.19(1) and (3) (April
6, 2020).

DEFINITIONS

"Abbeyfield Home"—reg.2(1).
"adoption leave"—*ibid.*
"claimant"—WRA Act 2007 s.24(1).
"Contributions and Benefits Act"—WRA 2007 s.65.
"councillor"—reg.2(1).
"employment"—*ibid.*
"Income Support Regulations"—*ibid.*
"independent hospital"—*ibid.*
"maternity leave" "—*ibid.*
"parental bereavement leave"—*ibid.*
"partner"—*ibid.*
"remunerative work"—regs 2(1), 41 and 42.
"self-employment route"—reg.2(1).
"sports award"—*ibid.*
"training allowance"—*ibid.*
"work as a councillor"—reg.40.

GENERAL NOTE

4.138   This regulation is similar to reg.6 of the IS Regs and reg.52 of the JSA Regs.

The revocation of paras (2)(a) and (d) with effect from January 25, 2010 is subject to a savings provision for those entitled to ESA in respect of January 24, 2010: see regs 4(3), (6) and (7) of SI 2009/3228 in Vol.II.

Claimants who are treated as not entitled to any allowance at all by reason of regulation 40(1) are to be treated as not having limited capability for work

4.139   **44.**—(1) Where a claimant is treated as not entitled to an employment and support allowance by reason of regulation 40(1), subject to paragraph (2), the claimant is to be treated as not having limited capability for work.

(2) Paragraph (1) does not apply where the claimant remains entitled to a contributory allowance, but is not entitled to an income-related allowance by reason of regulation 40(1).

(3) Paragraph (1) applies even if—

(a)   it has been determined that the claimant has or is to be treated as having, under any of regulations 20 (certain claimants to be treated as having limited capability for work), 25 (hospital in-patients), 26 (claimants undergoing certain regular treatment) or 29 (exceptional circumstances), limited capability for work; or

(b)   the claimant meets the conditions set out in regulation 30(2) for being treated as having limited capability for work until a determination is made in accordance with the limited capability for work assessment.

DEFINITION

"claimant"

GENERAL NOTE

4.140   Regulation 40(1) precludes entitlement to ESA in any week in which a claimant does work. In the light of that, this regulation provides, moreover, that in that period of non-entitlement, he or she will be treated as not having limited capability for work (para.(1), unless the work done only negatives entitlement to IRESA (para. (2)). Such a situation can arise where reg.46 applies in that work done in a week when someone, entitled to CESA, is receiving or recovering from certain regular treatments, does not negative title to CESA, but can to IRESA. Paragraph (3) makes clear that the regulation can operate despite the fact that, applying the limited capability for work assessment (WCAt), the person in fact has limited capability for work incapable of work, or is someone treated as having such limited capability by virtue of certain other regs: 20 (certain claimants to be treated as having limited capability for work); 25 (hospital in-patients); 26 (claimants undergoing certain regular treatment); or 29 (exceptional circumstances). This suggests that this rule on treating the person as not having limited capability for work will not operate in other cases where regs treat someone (whatever the reality) as having limited capability for work: regs 30 (treated as having limited capability pending assessment) and 33(2) (certain disabled students). In those cases there will be no entitlement to ESA where the person is caught by reg.40, but the days might still rank as ones of limited capability for work.

Exempt work

4.141   **45.**—(1) The categories of work referred to in regulation 40(2)(f) are set out in the following paragraphs.

(2) Work for which the earnings in any week do not exceed £20.00.

(3) Work for which the earnings in any week do not exceed [¹16 x National Minimum Wage, subject to paragraph (9A),] and which—

    (a) is part of the claimant's treatment programme and is done under medical supervision while the claimant is an in-patient, or is regularly attending as an out-patient, of a hospital or similar institution; or

    (b) is supervised by a person employed by a public or local authority or [²a] voluntary organisation [²or community interest company] engaged in the provision or procurement of work for persons who have disabilities.

(4) Work which is done for less than 16 hours a week, for which earnings in any week do not exceed [¹16 x National Minimum Wage, subject to paragraph (9A)] [⁴ . . .].

(4A) [⁴ . . .]

(5) Work done in the course of receiving assistance in pursuing self-employed earner's employment whilst participating in a programme provided or other arrangements made under section 2 of the Employment and Training Act 1973 (functions of the Secretary of State) or section 2 of the Enterprise and New Towns (Scotland) Act 1990(functions in relation to training for employment etc.).

(6) Work done where the claimant receives no payment of earnings and where the claimant—

    (a) is engaged by a charity or voluntary organisation; or

    (b) is a volunteer,

where the Secretary of State is satisfied in any of those cases that it is reasonable for the claimant to provide the service free of charge.

(7) Work done in the course of participating in a work placement approved in writing by the Secretary of State before the placement starts.

(8) The number of hours for which a claimant is engaged in work is to be determined—

    (a) where no recognisable cycle has been established in respect of a claimant's work, by reference to the number of hours or, where those hours are likely to fluctuate, the average of the hours, which the claimant is expected to work in a week;

    (b) where the number of hours for which the claimant is engaged fluctuate, by reference to the average of hours worked over—

        (i) if there is a recognisable cycle of work, the period of one complete cycle (including, where the cycle involves periods in which the claimant does no work, those periods but disregarding any other absences);

        (ii) in any other case, the period of five weeks immediately before the date of claim or the date on which a superseding decision is made under section 10 (decisions superseding earlier decisions) of the Social Security Act 1998, or such other length of time as may, in the particular case, enable the claimant's average hours of work to be determined more accurately.

(9) For the purposes of determining the number of hours for which a claimant is engaged in work, that number is to include any time allowed to that claimant by the claimant's employer for a meal or for refreshment, but only where that claimant is, or expects to be, paid earnings in respect of that time.

[¹(9A) Where the amount determined by the calculation in paragraphs (3) and (4) would, but for this paragraph, include an amount of—
  (a) less than 50p, that amount shall be rounded up to the nearest 50p; or
  (b) less than £1 but more than 50p, that amount shall be rounded up to the nearest £1.]
(10) In this regulation—
[⁴ . . .]
[⁴ . . .]
"supervised work" means work done in accordance with paragraph (3) (a) or (b);
"volunteer" has the same meaning it has in regulation 43;
"work placement" means practical work experience with an employer, which is neither paid nor undertaken in expectation of payment.

AMENDMENTS

1. Social Security (Miscellaneous Amendments) Regulations 2011 (SI 2011/674) reg.16(5) (April 11, 2011).
2. Social Security (Miscellaneous Amendments) (No.3) Regulations 2010 (SI 2010/840) reg.9(10) (June 28, 2010).
3. Social Security (Miscellaneous Amendments) (No.3) Regulation 2013 (SI 2013/2536), reg.13(1) and (23) (October 29,2013).
4. Employment and Support Allowance (Exempt Work & Hardship Amounts) (Amendment) Regulations 2017 (SI 2017/205) reg.3 (April 3, 2017).

DEFINITIONS

"the Act"—see reg.2(1).
"claimant"—see WRA 2007 s.24(1).
"Contributions and Benefits Act"—see WRA 2007 s.65.
"employment"—see reg.2(1).
"relevant benefit"—see para.(10).
"self-employed earner"—see reg.2(1).
"specified work"—see paras (10), (4).
"supervised work"—see paras (10), (3) (a) or (b).
"voluntary organisation"—see reg.2(1).
"volunteer"—see para.(10) and reg.43(4).
"week"—see reg.2(1).
"work placement"—see para.(10).

GENERAL NOTE

4.142   This regulation needs to be read in conjunction with reg.40(1) which precludes entitlement to ESA in any week in which a claimant does work. "Work" for the purposes of that regulation is defined in reg.40(7) as any work done whether or not undertaken in expectation of payment. "Week" is a period of seven days beginning with Sunday (reg.40(7)). This regulation in contrast defines a variety of work which ranking as "exempt work" does not pursuant to reg.40(2)(f) preclude entitlement to ESA under the general preclusive rule in reg.40(1).

The regulation is part of the welfare to work strategy, of encouraging people to try out work, the better to enable a return to work.

The current categories of exempt work

4.143   Some embody an earnings limit, others both an earnings and hours limit. The matters of determining the hours of engagement and assessing earnings are examined further below, after considering the seven categories of exempt work:

(1) *Work for which the earnings in any week do not exceed £20 (para. (2)):* there is no hours limit as such here, but it is anticipated that in practice the effect of the minimum wage laws will mean that DWP staff will expect a claimant in this category to be working less than 5 hours a week. Its prime role is the encouragement of social contact.

(2) *Unpaid work for a charity or voluntary organization (para. (6)(a)):* Work done where the claimant is engaged by a charity or voluntary organization is exempt where he receives no payment of earnings and the Secretary of State is satisfied that it is reasonable for him to provide the service free of charge. "Charity" is not defined in the ESA Regs, so must bear the meaning it does in charity law. "Voluntary organization" means a body, other than a public or local authority, the activities of which are carried on otherwise than for profit (reg.2(1)).

(3) *Work done as a volunteer (paras (6)(b), (10)):* Voluntary work other than that covered by para.(6)(1)(a) is thus also protected where the claimant receives no payment of earnings and the Secretary of State is satisfied that it is reasonable for him to provide the service free of charge. "Volunteer" is defined in para.(10) by reference to reg.43(4) to embrace a person who is engaged in voluntary work otherwise than for a relative, where the only payment received by him or due to be paid to him by virtue of being so engaged is in respect of any expenses reasonably incurred by him in connection with that work. "Relative" is widely defined: it means a close relative, grand-parent, grand-child, uncle, aunt, nephew or niece (reg.2(1)). "Close relative" covers a parent, parent-in-law, son, son-in-law, daughter, daughter-in-law, step-parent, step-son, step-daughter, brother, sister, or the spouse of any of these persons, or if that person is one of an unmarried couple, the other member of that couple (reg.2(1)). There are no hours or earnings limits.

(3) *Supervised work (paras (3), (10)):* there are two categories here. First, work done with the supervision of bodies providing or finding work for disabled people (para.(3)(a)). The bodies in question are a public or local authority or a voluntary organisation (that is, a body, other than a public or local authority, whose activities are carried on otherwise than for profit (reg.2(1)). The second category covers work while a patient of a hospital or similar institution under medical supervision as part of a treatment programme. The patient must be an in-patient or a regularly attending out-patient (para. (3)(b)). Whichever of the two categories, the earnings from the work must not exceed 16 x National Minimum Wage a week (see further para.(9A)). On "hospital or similar institution", some guidance is given in DMG, paras 18031–18033, 24018–24023. But this is not binding on tribunals or courts.

(4) *Work done in the course of receiving assistance in pursuing self-employed earner's employment whilst participating in certain programmes or arrangements (para. (5)):* this makes it easier for people receiving ESA to attempt self employment. Test Trading allows people to try out 'self employment' for a period of up to 26 weeks. Its introduction prevents participants being regarded as in work with the possibility of a loss of benefit should earnings exceed the permitted work limits.

(5) *Permitted work for up to 16 hours a week where earnings do not exceed national minimum wage:* The work must be done for less than 16 hours a week (see further below) and the earnings in any week must not exceed 16 x National Minimum Wage (and note the rounding rule in para. (9A)). The previous 52-week restriction on undertaking permitted work for ESA claimants in the work-related activity group and the assessment phase of the benefit was abolished with effect from April 3, 2017, with a view to improving work incentives. As a result, ESA claimants are now able to continue to undertake permitted work while retaining all their benefit for an indefinite period.

(6) *approved, unpaid work placements (paras (7), (10)):* "Work placement" is practical work experience with an employer, which is neither paid nor taken on in expectation of payment (para.(10)). The work placement

must have been approved by the Secretary of State in writing prior to its commencement.

In determining the number of hours of engagement in work (paras (8), (9)) an averaging approach applies, varying according to whether there is or is not a recognizable cycle and whether the claimant's hours fluctuate (para.(8)). With regard to para.(8) (averaging of hours) and the non-applicability of the Computation of Earnings Regulations for the purpose of averaging earnings, see also *LB v Secretary of State for Work and Pensions (ESA)* [2019] UKUT 153 (AAC). The hours of engagement include time the employer allows for meals or refreshment where the claimant is, or expects to be, paid earnings in respect of that time (para.(9)).

The earnings limit—Computation of Earnings Regs not applicable here

4.144   Unlike the position with IB, ESA is not within the sphere of the SSCBA 1992 and so the Computation of Earnings Regs cannot apply. Calculation of earnings is to be done under the rules in the ESA Regs.

Effect of work on entitlement to contributory allowance where claimant is receiving certain regular treatment

4.145   **46.** Where a claimant who is entitled to a contributory allowance and is treated as having limited capability for work by virtue of regulation 26 works on any day during a week when the claimant is, in accordance with regulation 26, receiving certain regular treatment or recovering from that treatment, that work is to have no effect on the claimant's entitlement to the contributory allowance.

DEFINITIONS

    "claimant"—see WRA 2007 s.24(1).
    "contributory allowance"—see WRA 2007 s.1(7).
    "entitled"—see WRA 2007 s.24(1).
    "limited capability for work"—see WRA 2007 s.24(1).
    "week"—see reg.2(1), WRA 2007 s.24(1).

GENERAL NOTE

4.146   This (affording an exception to the preclusive rule on work in reg.40(1)) provides that those treated under reg.26 as having limited capability for work on days when receiving or recovering from certain regular treatments (e.g. chemotherapy), who work on other days of the week in which they receive or are recovering from such treatment such treatment, will not have their entitlement to CESA affected by doing that work. For the impact of such work on entitlement to IRESA, see the exclusionary "remunerative work" rules (WRA 2007, Sch.1 para.6(1)(e); reg.41) and, in terms of the IRESA "balance sheet", the impact of earnings on entitlement.

PART 8

CONDITIONALITY

CHAPTER 1

WORK-FOCUSED HEALTH-RELATED ASSESSMENT

Regs 47–53
4.147   Note that on June 24, 2010, in a letter to the JCP customer representative group, the DWP announced the suspension of the work-focused health related assessment for a

period of two years from July 19, 2010. It noted that ongoing external evaluation had shown mixed results for the assessment. Its two-year suspension affords an opportunity for DWP reconsideration of the assessment's purpose and delivery, as well as freeing up capacity to deal with the demands of re-assessing existing incapacity benefits customers as part of the process of migration to ESA or—for those who fail the limited capability for work assessment—denial of ESA, cancellation of the existing award of an incapacity benefit and effective transfer either to JSA or (if qualifying in another category than "incapable of work") to IS. See further the Migration Regulations: the Employment and Support Allowance (Transitional Provisions, Housing Benefit and Council Tax Benefit) (Existing Awards) (No. 2) Regulations 2010 (SI 2010/1907) (as amended). Note further that from June 1, 2011 the Regs governing the work-focused health related assessment (regs 47–49, 51–53, below) were revoked (see Employment and Support Allowance (Work-Related Activity) Regulations 2011 (SI 2011/1349) reg.11).

CHAPTER 2

WORK-FOCUSED INTERVIEWS

Requirement to take part in a work-focused interview

54.—(1) The Secretary of State may require a claimant who satisfies the requirements in paragraph (2) to take part in one or more work-focused interviews as a condition of continuing to be entitled to the full amount of employment and support allowance payable to the claimant.

4.148

(2) The requirements referred to in paragraph (1) are that the claimant—
  (a) is either—
    (i) entitled to an employment and support allowance; or
    (ii) a person in respect of whom the Secretary of State has made an award under regulation 146(1);
  (b) is not a member of the support group;
  (c) has not reached the age at which a woman of the same age as the claimant would attain pensionable age; [¹ ...]
  (d) is not only entitled to a contributory allowance payable at a nil rate [¹; and
  (e) is not a lone parent who is responsible for and a member of the same household as a child under one.]

(3) Any requirement to take part in a work-focused interview ceases to have effect if the claimant ceases to satisfy the requirements in paragraph (2).

AMENDMENT

1. Social Security (Work-focused Interviews for Lone Parents and Partners) (Amendment) Regulations 2011 (SI 2011/2428) reg.5(3) (October 31, 2011).

DEFINITIONS

"claimant"—see WRA 2007 s.24(1).
"contributory allowance"—see WRA 2007 ss.24(1), 1(7).
"member of the support group"—see WRA 2007 s.24(4).
"pensionable age"—see reg.2(1).
"work-focused interview"—see WRA 2007 s.12(7).

GENERAL NOTE

4.149   This regulation, read with WRA 2007 s.11 and regs 48–53, deals with the second aspect of "conditionality", the requirements imposed on most of those who fall outside the support group as not having limited capability for work-related activity. The policy is that ESA brings rights, responsibilities and opportunities to people with health conditions and disabilities by asking them to engage with Jobcentre Plus (and contracted providers in the private and voluntary sectors [PVS]) to work towards fulfilling their ambitions. The key to this is seen in the incorporation in membership of work-related activity group of ESA of an element of conditionality modelled on those applied in the Pathways to Work programme. This has a number of elements: (i) participation in a work-focused health related assessment (WFHRAt) (WRA 2007 s.11; regs 47–53); (ii) participation in a work-focused interview; and (iii) as resources permit (and not before 2011), undertaking work-related activity that increases the likelihood of getting a job (e.g. work trials). This regulation stipulates that as a condition of receiving the full amount of ESA, a claimant may be required to participate in one or more work-focused interviews, the second element of taking part in work-related activity (para.(1)). This requirement may, however, only be imposed on a claimant not in the support group, awarded ESA or an advance award of it under reg.146, who, whether male or female, has not reached the female pensionable age by reference to his/her date of birth, who is not merely entitled to CESA at a nil rate (e.g. because of abatement under WRA 2007 ss.2, 3) (para.(2), reg.2(1) and link to Pensions Act 1995, Sch.4, para.1) and who is not a lone parent with responsibility for a child under one in the same household. Should such a requirement have been imposed when those conditions were met, it will cease to have effect when the claimant no longer satisfies one or more of them (e.g. becomes a member of the support group because the health condition and it limiting effects have worsened, or has reached the exempting age, or whose ESA entitlement drops to CESA at a nil rate) (para.(3)).

Although WRA 2007 s.16 and reg.63 enable contracting out so as to bring expertise from the private and voluntary sectors (PVS) into the process of assisting claimants to prepare for and enhance their prospects of starting or returning to work, it is envisaged, however, that the first work-focused interview will always be with someone from Jobcentre Plus and will be held around the eighth week of the assessment period.

Note that failure, without good cause, to participate in a work-focused interview (regs 55, 57, 58, 61) is sanctioned initially by halving the amount of work-related activity component and eventually by reducing it to nil (reg.63), the reduction to cease after compliance has been induced or the requirement to participate has ceased to have effect under para.(3) (reg.64).

Work-focused interview

4.150   **55.** The purposes of a work-focused interview are any or all of the following—

(a) assessing the claimant's prospects for remaining in or obtaining work;

(b) assisting or encouraging the claimant to remain in or obtain work;

(c) identifying activities that the claimant may undertake that will make remaining in or obtaining work more likely;

(d) identifying training, educational or rehabilitation opportunities for the claimant which may make it more likely that the claimant will remain in or obtain work or be able to do so;

(e) identifying current or future work opportunities, including self-employment opportunities, for the claimant, that are relevant to the claimant's needs and abilities.

DEFINITIONS

"claimant"—see WRA 2007 s.24(1).
"training"—see reg.2(1).
"work-focused interview"—see WRA 2007 s.12(7).

GENERAL NOTE

Pursuant to WRA 2007, s.12(7) this regulation prescribes the purposes of a work-focused interview as any or all of those listed in paras (a)–(e).   **4.151**

Notification of interview

56.—(1) The Secretary of State must notify the claimant of the require-   **4.152**
ment to [¹take part in] the work-focused interview including details of the
date, time and [¹if required to attend in person, the] place of the interview.
(2) A work-focused interview may take place at a claimant's home if it
is determined that requiring the claimant to attend elsewhere would cause
undue inconvenience to, or endanger the health of, the claimant.
(3) The notification referred to in paragraph (1) may be in writing or otherwise.

AMENDMENT

1. Employment and Support Allowance (Work-Related Activity) Regulations
2011 (SI 2011/1349) reg.12 (June 1, 2011).

DEFINITIONS

"claimant"—see WRA 2007 s.24(1).
"work-focused interview"—see WRA 2007 s.12(7).

GENERAL NOTE

The Secretary of State must give proper notification to the claimant that he is   **4.153**
required to take part in the work-focused interview. This must include details of its
date, time and (if required to attend in person) place (para.(1)). The notification
need not be in writing (para.(2)). This is in marked contrast to other provisions
imposing requirements with respect to the three elements of the work capability
assessment (WCA) (see regs 22–24, 36–38, 49). So is the absence of any stipulation as to due period of notice. As to place, none is specified (a consequence of
ability to contract-out the interviews—reg.62). But the interview can take place at
the claimant's home if it is decided that requirement to attend elsewhere would
endanger his health or simply cause undue convenience.

Taking part in a work-focused interview

57.—(1) A claimant is regarded as having taken part in a work-focused   **4.154**
interview if the claimant—
  (a) [¹if required to attend in person,] attends for the interview at the
     place and at the date and time notified in accordance with regulation
     56;
[¹(aa) if not required to attend in person, is available and responds at the
     date and time notified in accordance with regulation 56 to any contact
     made at that time for the purpose of carrying out the interview;]
  (b) provides information, if requested by the Secretary of State, about
     any or all of the matters set out in paragraph (2);

(c) participates in discussions to the extent the Secretary of State considers necessary, about any or all of the matters set out in paragraph (3);

(d) [¹ . . .].

(2) The matters referred to in paragraph (1)(b) are—

(a) the claimant's educational qualifications and vocational training;

(b) the claimant's work history;

(c) the claimant's aspirations for future work;

(d) the claimant's skills that are relevant to work;

(e) the claimant's work-related abilities;

(f) the claimant's caring or childcare responsibilities; and

(g) any paid or unpaid work that the claimant is undertaking.

(3) The matters referred to in paragraph (1)(c) are—

(a) any activity the claimant is willing to undertake which may make obtaining or remaining in work more likely;

(b) any such activity that the claimant may have previously undertaken;

(c) any progress the claimant may have made towards remaining in or obtaining work;

(d) any work-focused health-related assessment the claimant may have taken part in; and

(e) the claimant's opinion as to the extent to which the ability to remain in or obtain work is restricted by the claimant's physical or mental condition.

AMENDMENT

1. Employment and Support Allowance (Work-Related Activity) Regulations 2011 (SI 2011/1349) reg.13 (June 1, 2011).

DEFINITIONS

"claimant"—see WRA 2007 s.24(1).
"work-focused health-related assessment"—see WRA 2007 s.11(7).
"work-focused interview"—see WRA 2007 s.12(7).

GENERAL NOTE

4.155   Failure, without good cause, to take part in a work-focused interview (regs 55, 57, 58, 61) is sanctioned initially by halving the amount of work-related activity component and eventually by reducing it to nil (reg.63), the reduction to cease after compliance has been induced or the requirement to participate has ceased to have effect under para.(3) (reg.64).

This regulation sets out when a claimant is to be regarded as having taken part: attendance at the proper place, date and time (para.(1)(a)) or, if not required to attend in person, is available and responds at the notified date and time to any contact made for the purpose of the interview (para.(1)(aa)); provision of the requisite information required by the Secretary of State (paras (1)(b), (2)); participation to such an extent as the Secretary of State considers necessary in discussion about the key matters stipulated in para.(3); and assisting the Secretary of State (in reality someone in Jobcentre Plus or a contractor or employee of a contractor) in drawing up an "action plan" as defined in reg.58.

Action plan

4.156   **58.**—*Revoked by Employment and Support Allowance (Work-Related Activity) Regulations 2011 (SI 2011/1349) reg.14 (June 1, 2011).*

Deferral of requirement to take part in a work-focused interview

59.—(1) A requirement to take part in a work-focused interview may be deferred or treated as having been deferred if at the time the work-focused interview is to take place, or was due to take place, such an interview would not at that time be or have been—

(a) of assistance to the claimant; or

(b) appropriate in the circumstances.

(2) A decision under paragraph (1) may be made at any time after the requirement to take part in the work-focused interview is imposed, including after the time that the work-focused interview was due to take place or took place.

(3) Where a requirement to take part in a work-focused interview is deferred, or treated as having been deferred, then the time that the work-focused interview is to take place must be re-determined.

4.157

DEFINITIONS

"claimant"—see WRA 2007 s.24(1).
"work-focused interview"—see WRA 2007 s.12(7).

GENERAL NOTE

This regulation enables deferral of a work-focused interview (or treating it as deferred) if holding it would not assist the claimant or otherwise be inappropriate (para.(1)). The decision on deferral can be made at any time after the requirement to take part was imposed on the claimant, whether before or after it was due to take place (para.(2)). If deferred, the matter of when such an interview is to take place has to be re-determined (para.(3)).

4.158

Requirement to take part in a work-focused interview not to apply

60. The Secretary of State may determine that a requirement on a claimant to take part in a work-focused interview is not to apply, or is to be treated as not having applied, if that interview would not be, or would not have been, of assistance because the claimant is or was likely to be starting or returning to work.

4.159

DEFINITIONS

"claimant"—see WRA 2007 s.24(1).
"work-focused interview"—see WRA 2007 s.12(7).

GENERAL NOTE

This enables lifting of the requirement to take part in a work-focused interview, whether before or after it was due to take place, where it would not be (or be likely to have been of assistance) because the claimant is or was likely to be starting or returning to work.

4.160

Failure to take part in a work-focused interview

61.—(1) A claimant who is required to take part in a work-focused interview but fails to do so must show good cause for that failure within 5 working days of the date on which the Secretary of State gives notification of that failure.

(2) The Secretary of State must determine whether a claimant who is

4.161

required to take part in a work-focused interview has failed to do so and, if so, whether the claimant has shown good cause for that failure in accordance with paragraph (1).

[[1](3) *Revoked in respect of failures on or after December 3, 2012. For text of provision prior to that date see the previous edition of this Volume.*]

DEFINITIONS

"claimant"—see WRA 2007 s.24(1).
"relative"—see reg.2(1).
"work-focused interview"—see WRA 2007 s.12(7).

GENERAL NOTE

4.162   Failure, without good cause, to participate in a work-focused interview (regs 55, 57, 58) is sanctioned initially by halving the amount of work-related activity component and eventually by reducing it to nil (reg.63), the reduction to cease after compliance has been induced or the requirement to participate has ceased to have effect under para.(3) (reg.64).

Contracting out certain functions relating to work-focused interviews

4.163   **62.**—(1) Any function of the Secretary of State specified in paragraph (2) may be exercised by, or by employees of, such person (if any) as may be authorised by the Secretary of State.

(2) The functions are any function under—

(a) regulation 54(1) (requirement to take part in a work-focused interview);
(b) regulation 56(1) and (2) (notification requirement);
(c) regulation 57(1)(b) and (c) (taking part in a work-focused interview);
(d) [[1]. . .];
(e) regulation 59(1) and (3) (deferral of requirement to take part in a work-focused interview);
(f) regulation 60 (requirement to take part in a work-focused interview not to apply).

AMENDMENT

1. Employment and Support Allowance (Work-Related Activity) Regulations 2011 (SI 2011/1349) reg.15 (June 1, 2011).

GENERAL NOTE

4.164   Pursuant to WRA 2007 s.16, which enables contracting-out, this regulation sets out in para.(2) functions of the Secretary of State under these regulations which can be exercise by an authorised contractor or the employees of such a contractor. The idea is to bring expertise from the private and voluntary sectors (PVS) into the process of assisting claimants to prepare for and enhance their prospects of starting or returning to work. It is envisaged, however, that the first work-focused interview will always be with someone from Jobcentre Plus and will be held around the eighth week of the assessment period. Note that sanctioning decisions (regs 63, 64) are not-contracted out, although clearly information provided by contractors will inform those decisions.

Reduction of employment and support allowance

63.—[¹(1) Where the Secretary of State has determined—   4.165
  (a) that a claimant who was required to take part in a work-focused interview has failed to do so and has failed to show good cause for that failure in accordance with regulation 61; or
  (b) that a claimant who was required to undertake work-related activity has failed to do so and has failed to show good cause for that failure in accordance with regulation 8 of the Employment and Support Allowance (Work-Related Activity) Regulations 2011,
("a failure determination") the amount of the employment and support allowance payable to the claimant is to be reduced in accordance with this regulation.]

[²(2) Subject to paragraph (3), the amount of the reduction in relation to each failure determination is 100% of the prescribed amount for a single claimant as set out in paragraph (1)(a) of Part 1 of Schedule 4.]

(3) In any benefit week, the amount of an employment and support allowance payable to a claimant is not, by virtue of this regulation, to be reduced—
  (a) below 10 pence;
  (b) in relation to more than—
    (i) one failure determination relating to work-related activity; and
    (ii) one failure determination relating to a work-focused interview; and
  (c) by more than 100% of the [² prescribed amount for a single claimant as set out in paragraph 1(a) of Part 1] of Schedule 4 in any circumstances.

(4) Where a claimant is entitled to both a contributory allowance and an income-related allowance, any reduction in the claimant's allowance must first be applied to the part of that allowance treated as attributable to the claimant's contributory allowance and only if there is any amount outstanding is it to be applied to the part of that allowance treated as attributable to the claimant's income-related allowance.

(5) For the purposes of determining the amount of any income-related allowance payable, a claimant is to be treated as receiving the amount of any contributory allowance [³including new style ESA] which would have been payable but for any reduction made in accordance with this regulation [³or section 11J of the Act respectively].

[² (6) Subject to paragraph (10), the reduction is to have effect for—
  (a) one week for each seven day period during which the claimant fails to meet a compliance condition; and
  (b) a further fixed period determined in accordance with paragraph (7).

[⁴ (7) The fixed period that applies in the circumstances described in the first column of the following table is set out in the second column.

Circumstances applicable to claimant's case	Fixed period
Where there has been no previous failure by the claimant that falls within paragraph (8)	1 week
Where there have been one or more previous failures by the claimant that fall within paragraph (8) and the date of the most recent previous failure is not within 52 weeks beginning with the date of the current failure	1 week
Where there have been one or more previous failures by the claimant that fall within paragraph (8) and the date of the most recent previous failure is within 52 weeks, but not within 2 weeks, beginning with the date of the current failure and the period of reduction applicable to the most recent previous failure is or, but for paragraph (3), would have been—	
(a) 1 week	2 weeks
(b) 2 weeks	4 weeks
(c) 4 weeks	4 weeks
Where there have been one or more previous failures by the claimant that fall within paragraph (8) and the date of the most recent previous failure is within 2 weeks beginning with the date of the current failure and the period of reduction applicable to the most recent previous failure is or, but for paragraph (3), would have been—	
(a) 1 week	1 week
(b) 2 weeks	2 weeks
(c) 4 weeks	4 weeks.]

(8) A previous failure falls within this paragraph if—
(a) it relates to a failure for which a reduction was imposed under this regulation, or would have been but for paragraph (3); [⁴ . . .]
(b) that failure occurred on or after 3rd December 2012; [⁴ . . .]
(c) [⁴ . . .].
(9) This paragraph applies where the claimant meets a compliance condition before the end of the period of one week after the date of the failure to which the failure determination relates.
(10) Where paragraph (9) applies, the claimant's employment and support allowance is reduced only for the fixed period set out in paragraph (7) applicable to the claimant.
(11) In this regulation—
"compliance condition" means—
(a) where the failure by the claimant relates to a requirement to take part in a work-focused interview, either—
(i) taking part in a work-focused interview, or
(ii) making an agreement with the Secretary of State to take part in a work-focused interview at an agreed date;
(b) where the failure by the claimant relates to a requirement to undertake work-related activity, either—
(i) undertaking the activity specified in the action plan, or
(ii) where so notified by the Secretary of State, undertaking an alternative activity, or
(iii) making an agreement with the Secretary of State to undertake the activity referred to in sub-paragraph (i) or (ii) at an agreed date;
"current failure" means a failure which may lead to a reduction under

this regulation in relation to which the Secretary of State has not yet determined whether the amount of the employment and support allowance payable to the claimant is to be reduced in accordance with this regulation.]

AMENDMENTS

1. Employment and Support Allowance (Work-Related Activity) Regulations 2011 (SI 2011/1349) reg.17 (June 1, 2011).
2. Employment and Support Allowance (Sanctions) (Amendment) Regulations 2012 (SI 2012/2756) reg.4 (December 3, 2012).
3. Universal Credit (Consequential, Supplementary, Incidental and Miscellaneous Provisions) Regulations 2013 (SI 2013/630) reg.37(1), (4) (April 29, 2013).
4. Social Security (Jobseeker's Allowance, Employment and Support Allowance and Universal Credit) (Amendment) Regulations 2016 (SI 2016/678) regulation 4 (July 25, 2016).

DEFINITIONS

"the Act"—see reg.2(1).
"claimant"—see WRA 2007 s.24(1).
"compliance condition"—see para.(11).
"contributory allowance"—see WRA 2007 ss.24(1), 1(7).
"current failure"—see para.(11).
"failure determination"—see para.(1).
"income-related allowance"—see WRA 2007 ss.24(1), 1(7).
"new style ESA"—see reg.2(1).
"work-focused health- related assessment"—see WRA 2007 s.11(7).
"work-focused interview"—see WRA 2007 s.12(7).

GENERAL NOTE

In accordance with WRA 2007 ss.12(3), 13(3), this regulation provides the sanction for failure without good cause to take part in a work-focused interview or work-related activity. The sanction, put simply, is a reduction in the amount of ESA to which the person would otherwise be entitled (para.(1)). On the face of the Act and the first paragraph of this regulation, that could be a reduction of ESA as a whole, even to nil. The legal reality—effected by the words "in accordance with the provisions of this regulation" in para.(1) and by paras (2) and (3)—is that the reduction in any benefit week is set at 100 per cent of the prescribed amount for a single claimant (see para.1(a), Pt 1, Sch.4), whatever the number of failures and whether relating to work-related interview or work-related activity or both, and cannot exceed that in any circumstances (para.(3)). Nor can this sanction of reduction take the claimant's entitlement in any benefit week below 10 pence (para.(3).

The current version of para.(2), requiring the sanction to be by way of a reduction amounting to the standard or basic rate for ESA, has been in force since December 3, 2012. Before that date the sanctions regime operated solely on the work-related activity component). That component was not subject to reduction after December 2012. However, the abolition by s.15 of the Welfare Reform and Work Act 2016 of the work-related activity component for (broadly speaking) new claims since April 3, 2017 means that if a new claimant in the work-related activity group is sanctioned they would presumably now lose the entirety of their standard rate of ESA.

The period of reduction is one week for each seven day period in which the claimant fails to meet a "compliance condition" (see para.(11)) *plus* a fixed period, varying according to whether the failure is a first, second or third or subsequent failure (paras (6), (7). However, where the claimant meets a compliance condition within a week of the failure at issue, only the fixed period

4.166

of reduction is to apply (paras (9), (10)). As regards the appropriate fixed period, looking at the current failure in the context of the previous 52 weeks, the period for which reduction is to be effected is set at one week for a first failure, two weeks for a second failure and four weeks for a third or subsequent failure (paras (7), (8)). A previous failure cannot be one occurring before December 3, 2012 (para. (8)).

Paragraphs (4) and (5) deal with the situation where the claimant's ESA is composed both of CESA and IRESA (a common situation). Reduction is to be effected first against the amount attributable to CESA and only if after that there is a balance of reduction still to be applied, against IRESA (para.(4)). However, even where CESA is thus reduced, for the purposes of deciding on the amount of IRESA when drawing up the IRESA "balance sheet" of "needs" and "resources", the claimant is to be treated as if he were receiving the full amount of CESA to which he would otherwise be entitled but for reduction in accordance with this regulation, and not the reduced amount of CESA left after the reduction demanded by this regulation has been effected (para.(5)).

Paragraph (7)

4.167   The purpose of the 2016 amendment, according to the accompanying Explanatory memorandum, was "to clarify the length of a sanction to be imposed on a claimant. In each case, the existing provisions do not meet the policy intention in a number of certain circumstances concerning multiple sanctions and this instrument rectifies that anomaly" (para.2.1). The policy intention was that in order to prevent anyone incurring lengthy penalties over a short period, a failure which occurs within two weeks of the most recent previous failure should incur a sanction of the same length as the sanction imposed for that previous failure, rather than the length of the sanction increasing. In addition, any sanction imposed for a failure more than 12 months before the failure currently under consideration should not increase the duration of the next sanction. However, DWP identified that the previous form of the regulation did not fully support this policy in specific, limited circumstances namely when a claimant has three or more sanctionable failures and either each occurred within 14 days of the next (and there are more than 14 days between the first and third) or the last two occurred within 14 days of each other (and there are more than 365 days between the first and third). The amendments were designed to ensure that in all cases, where a failure has occurred within 14 days of a previous one, the length of the subsequent sanction is for the same duration as the previous sanction so as to fully reflect the policy intention.

Regulation 64, below, sets out the circumstances in which a reduction imposed for a failure determination under this regulation is to cease.

Cessation of reduction

4.168   **64.**—[¹(1) Any reduction imposed as a result of a failure determination which resulted from a failure to undertake work-related activity in accordance with the Employment and Support Allowance (Work-Related Activity) Regulations 2011 ceases to have effect if—

   (a) [²*omitted*]
   (b) the claimant subsequently ceases to be subject to a requirement to undertake work-related activity; or
   (c) the Secretary of State decides it is no longer appropriate to require the person to undertake work-related activity at that time.

(1A) The Secretary of State must notify the person in writing—

   (a) [²*omitted*]
   (b) of any decision under paragraph (1)(c).]

(2) Any reduction imposed as a result of a failure determination which

resulted from a failure to take part in a work-focused interview ceases to have effect if—

    (a) [²*omitted*]

    (b) the claimant subsequently ceases to meet the requirements set out in regulation 54(2).

AMENDMENTS

1. Employment and Support Allowance (Work-Related Activity) Regulations 2011 (SI 2011/1349) reg.18 (June 1, 2011).

2. Employment and Support Allowance (Sanctions) (Amendment) Regulations 2012 (SI 2012/2756) reg.5 (December 3, 2012).

DEFINITIONS

"claimant"—see WRA 2007 s.24(1).   **4.169**

"failure determination"—see reg.63(1).

"work-focused interview"—see WRA 2007 s.12(7).

GENERAL NOTE

Any reduction in ESA effected in respect of a failure determination under reg.63   **4.170** ceases to have effect in the circumstances set out in this regulation.

As regards failure determinations in respect of work-related activity, the sanction ceases once the claimant is no longer subject to a requirement to undertake such activity (para.(1)(b)) or where the Secretary of State decides that his undertaking work-related activity is no longer appropriate at that time and notifies him of that in writing (paras (1)(c), (1A)).

As regards failure determinations in respect of work-focused interviews, the reduction ceases where the claimant no longer meets the requirements set by reg.54(2) (e.g. becomes a member of the support group) (para.(2)(b)).

[¹ Hardship payments

64A.—The Secretary of State must make a hardship payment to a claim-   **4.171** ant only where—

    (a) the Secretary of State is satisfied that the claimant is or will be in hardship unless a hardship payment is made;

    (b) the claimant's employment and support allowance has been reduced in accordance with regulation 63;

    (c) the claimant meets the conditions of entitlement to an income-related employment and support allowance;

    (d) the claimant completes and submits an application—

        (i) approved for the purpose by the Secretary of State, or in such other form as the Secretary of State accepts as sufficient, and

        (ii) in such manner as the Secretary of State determines; and

    (e) the claimant provides such information or evidence as the Secretary of State may require, in such manner as the Secretary of State determines.]

AMENDMENT

1. Employment and Support Allowance (Sanctions) (Amendment) Regulations 2012 (SI 2012/2756) reg.6 (December 3, 2012).

[¹ Circumstances in which a claimant is to be treated as being in hardship

4.172

64B. A claimant is to be treated as being in hardship if the claimant's partner, or a child or qualifying young person for whom the claimant or the claimant's partner is responsible, is or will be in hardship unless a hardship payment is made.]

AMENDMENT

1. Employment and Support Allowance (Sanctions) (Amendment) Regulations 2012 (SI 2012/2756) reg.6 (December 3, 2012).

[¹ Matters to be taken into account in determining hardship

4.173

64C.—(1) The Secretary of State must take the following matters into account in determining hardship—

(a) whether the claimant's partner or a person in the claimant's family satisfies the requirements for a disability premium specified in paragraphs 6 and 7 of Schedule 4, or an element of child tax credit in respect of a child or young person who is disabled or severely disabled within the meaning of regulation 8 of the Child Tax Credit Regulations 2002;

(b) the resources which are likely to be available to the household without a hardship payment, including resources from persons who are not members of the household, but excluding any payment referred to in paragraph (2);

(c) the difference between the resources referred to in sub-paragraph (b) and the amount of the hardship payment that the claimant would receive;

(d) whether there is substantial risk that the household will not have access to essential items (including food, clothing, heating and accommodation), or will have access to such essential items at con-siderably reduced levels, without a hardship payment; and

(e) the length of time that the factors set out in sub-paragraphs (b) to (d) are likely to continue.

(2) The payments to be excluded from the resources referred to in par-agraph (1)(b) are payments made under paragraph 7(1) or (2) of Schedule 8 (sums to be disregarded in the calculation of income other than earnings: child tax credit and child benefit) to the claimant or the claimant's partner in respect of a child or young person who is a member of the claimant's household or family.]

AMENDMENT

1. Employment and Support Allowance (Sanctions) (Amendment) Regulations 2012 (SI 2012/2756) reg.6 (December 3, 2012).

[¹ The amount of a hardship payment

4.174

64D.—(1) A hardship payment is 60% of the prescribed amount for a single claimant as set out in paragraph (1)(a) of Part 1 of Schedule 4.

(2) A payment calculated in accordance with paragraph (1) shall, if it is not a multiple of 5p, be rounded to the nearest such multiple or, if it is a multiple of 2.5p but not of 5p, to the next lower multiple of 5p.]

AMENDMENT

1. Employment and Support Allowance (Sanctions) (Amendment) Regulations 2012 (SI 2012/2756) reg.6 (December 3, 2012).

CHAPTER 4

NOTIFICATION

Notification under this Part

65.—(1) Where written notification is to be given in accordance with this Part, such notification may be sent by post.   **4.175**

(2) Any notification sent by post is to be taken to have been received on the second working day after posting.

GENERAL NOTE

This deals with notifications in respect of the conditionality elements in Pt 8 of these regulations. It stipulates that where written notifications are thereby required or envisaged (see regs 49(2),56(3)) they may be sent by post (para.(1)). If so the rule is that such notification is to be taken to have been received on the second working day after posting. (para.(2)).   **4.176**

CHAPTER 5

MODIFICATION OF THE ACT IN RELATION TO CLAIMS TO WHICH SECTION 5(1)(C) OF THE ADMINISTRATION ACT APPLIES

Modifications of the Act

66.—(1) Where a person has made a claim for an employment and support allowance to which section 5(1)(c) of the Administration Act applies, the Act applies with the following modifications.   **4.177**

(2) Section 11(1) of the Act applies—

(a) as if for sub-paragraph (a) there were substituted—

"(a) either—

(i) entitled to an employment and support allowance; or

(ii) a person who has made a claim for an employment and support allowance to which regulations under section 5(1)(c) of the Administration Act apply; and"; and

(b) as if for "continuing to be" there were substituted "being".

(3) Section 12(1) of the Act applies—

(a) as if for sub-paragraph (a) there were substituted—

"(a) either—

(i) entitled to an employment and support allowance; or

(ii) a person who has made a claim to which section 5 applies; and"; and

(b) as if for "continuing to be" there were substituted "being".

DEFINITIONS

"the Act"—see reg.2(1).
"Administration Act"—see WRA 2007 s.65.

GENERAL NOTE

4.178   This regulation alters the terms of WRA 2007 ss.11(1) ("work-focused health-related assessment") and 12(1) ("work-focused interview") where a person has made a claim for ESA which falls to be governed by the AA 1992 s.5(1)(c) (a claim made, or treated as made, for a period wholly or partly after the date on which it is made). In such cases, s.11(1) is to read (modifications in square brackets):

"(1) Regulations may make provision for or in connection with imposing on a person who is—
[(a) either—
       (i) entitled to an employment and support allowance; or
       (ii) a person who has made a claim for an employment and support allowance to which regulations under section 5(1)(c) of the Administration Act apply; and]
   (b) not a member of the support group,
a requirement to take part in one or more work-focused health-related assessments as a condition of [being] entitled to the full amount payable to him in respect of the allowance apart from the regulations."

Similarly, s.12(1) is to read (modifications in square brackets):

"(1) Regulations may make provision for or in connection with imposing on a person who is—
[(a) either—
       (i) entitled to an employment and support allowance; or
       (ii) a person who has made a claim to which section 5 applies; and]
   (b) not a member of the support group,
a requirement to take part in one or more work-focused interviews as a condition of [being] entitled to the full amount payable to him in respect of the allowance apart from the regulations."

PART 9

AMOUNTS OF ALLOWANCE

CHAPTER 1

PRESCRIBED AMOUNTS

Prescribed amounts

4.179   **67.**—(1) Subject to regulations 68, 69 [¹ . . .] (amounts in other cases, special cases [¹ . . .]), the amounts prescribed for the purposes of the calculation of the amount of an income related allowance under section 4(2)(a) of the Act in relation to a claimant are such of the following amounts as may apply in the claimant's case—
   (a) an amount in respect of the claimant or, if the claimant is a member of a couple, an amount in respect of both of them determined in accordance with paragraph 1(1), (2) or (3) of Schedule 4 (amounts) as the case may be;
   (b) the amount of any premiums which may be applicable to the claimant determined in accordance with Parts 2 and 3 of that Schedule (premiums);
   (c) any amounts determined in accordance with Schedule 6 (housing

costs) which may be applicable to the claimant in respect of [³ housing costs as prescribed] in that Schedule.

(2) Subject to regulation 69 (special cases) the amount prescribed for the purposes of the calculation of the amount of a claimant's contributory allowance under section 2(1)(a) of the Act is the amount determined in accordance with paragraph 1(1) of Schedule 4 as may apply in the claimant's case.

(3) Subject to regulation 69, the amount of the [² . . .] support component [² is] prescribed in Part 4 of Schedule 4.

AMENDMENTS

1. Social Security (Miscellaneous Amendments) (No. 5) Regulations 2009 (SI 2009/3228) reg.3(4)(a) (January 25, 2010).
2. Employment and Support Allowance and Universal Credit (Miscellaneous Amendments and Transitional and Savings Provisions) Regulations 2017 (SI 2017/204) reg.2(1) and (3) (April 3, 2017).
3. Loans for Mortgage Interest Regulations 2017 (SI 2017/725) reg.18 and Sch.5, para.1(a) (April 6, 2018).

MODIFICATION

Regulation 67 is modified by Sch.2, para.12 of the Employment and Support Allowance (Transitional Provisions, Housing Benefit and Council Tax Benefit) (Existing Awards) (No. 2) Regulations 2010 (SI 2010/1907) (as amended) for the purposes specified in reg.16(1). For details of the modification, see the text of those Regulations below.

DEFINITIONS

"claimant"—see WRA 2007 s.24(1).
"contributory allowance"—see WRA 2007 s.1(7).
"couple"—see reg.2(1).
"income related allowance"—see WRA 2007 s.1(7).

GENERAL NOTE

Paragraph (1)
This regulation is similar to reg.17 of the IS Regulations and reg.83 of the JSA Regulations. The applicable amounts are set out in Sch.4 below.   **4.180**

In the same manner as IS and JSA, this read with Sch.4 paras 1(1) (single claimant, age related), (2) (lone parent, age-related) or (3) (couple, age related) as appropriate, specifies the amounts applicable in respect of a claimant as regards IRESA: an amount for him and any partner (para.(1)(a)); applicable premiums (para.(1)(b), Sch.4 Pts 2 and 3); and applicable housing costs (para.(1)(c), Sch.6). This is, however, subject to regs 68 (amounts in other cases polygamous marriages), 69 (special cases) and 163 (urgent cases).

Paragraph (2)
This sets the prescribed amount (basic allowance) of CESA (WRA 2007 s.2(1)   **4.181**
(a)) by reference to Sch.4 para.1(1). There are two rates, a higher one for those aged 25 or over, or who have been awarded the support component, and a lower one for those aged under 25 (Sch.4, para.1(1)). As the support component is only awarded from the end of the assessment phase, all claimants aged under 25 receive the lower rate during that phase. Until April 3, 2015 all claimants, irrespective of age, received the higher rate once the assessment phase was over. Claimants to whom any of the circumstances in paragraphs 2 to 7 of Sch. 2 to the Employment and Support Allowance and Universal Credit (Miscellaneous Amendments and Transitional

and Savings Provisions) Regulations 2017 (SI 2017/204) (see below) have transitional protection from the change. It appears that this aspect of the April 3, 2017 changes was unintended. Regulation 7 of the Employment and Support Allowance (Miscellaneous Amendments and Transitional and Savings Provision) Regulations 2017 (SI 2017/581) reinstates the former law with effect from June 23, 2017.

For those terminally ill covered by reg.7(1)(a) the higher rate component is available from the start of the claim on the basis of terminal illness or the date of an application for revision or suppression on that basis.

The prescription of the amount is, however, subject to reg.69 (special cases). Note also that, whatever the amount of CESA thus set, it is, under WRA 2007 ss.2(1)(c) and 3, subject to reduction in respect of a variety of payments: pension payments (including permanent health insurance payments) (s.3(1)(a), (3); regs 72, 74 and 75); PPF periodic payments (s.3(1)(b), (3); reg.74); and prescribed payments to members of prescribed bodies carrying out public or local functions (currently limited to councillor's allowance and the bodies in the definition of councillor in reg.2(1)) (s.2(1)(c); regs 73, 76). The amount of CESA is also to be reduced by the amount of statutory maternity pay (s.2(2), (3); reg.80), statutory adoption pay (s.2(4), (5); reg.81) or additional statutory paternity pay (s.2(6), (7)); reg.82) to which the claimant is entitled during his period of limited capability for work.

Paragraph (3)

4.182   Subject to reg.69 (special cases), read with Sch.4, para.4, this specifies the amount of the support component. The former work-related activity component was abolished with effect from April 3, 2017, except for those claimants to whom any of the circumstances in paragraphs 2 to 7 of Sch.2 to SI 2017/204 apply: see below.

Polygamous marriages

4.183   **68.**—(1) Subject to regulation 69 [¹ . . .] (special cases [¹ . . .]), where a claimant is a husband or wife by virtue of a polygamous marriage the amounts prescribed for the purposes of the calculation of the amount of an income-related allowance under section 4(2)(a) of the Act are such of the following amounts as may apply in the claimant's case—

(a) an amount in respect of the claimant and the other party to the marriage determined in accordance with paragraph 1(3) of Schedule 4;

(b) an amount equal to the difference between the amounts specified in paragraph 1(3)(a) (couple where both aged 18 and over) and 1(1)(b) (single claimant aged 25 and over) of Schedule 4 in respect of each spouse additional to the marriage;

(c) the amount of any premiums which are applicable to the claimant determined in accordance with Parts 2 and 3 of that Schedule (premiums);

(d) any amounts determined in accordance with Schedule 6 (housing costs) which may be applicable to the claimant in respect of [² housing costs as prescribed] in that Schedule.

(2) In the case of a partner who is aged less than 18, the amount which applies in respect of that partner is nil unless—

(a) that partner is treated as responsible for a child; or

(b) that partner is a person who—

(i) had that partner not been a member of a polygamous marriage would have qualified for an income-related allowance; or

(ii) satisfies the requirements of section 3(1)(f)(iii) of the Jobseekers Act (prescribed circumstances for persons aged 16 but less than 18); or

(iii) is the subject of a direction under section 16 of that Act (persons under 18: severe hardship).

AMENDMENTS

1. Social Security (Miscellaneous Amendments) (No.5) Regulations 2009 (SI 2009/3228) reg.3(4)(b) (January 25, 2010).
2. Loans for Mortgage Interest Regulations 2017 (SI 2017/725) reg.18 and Sch.5, para.1(b) (April 6, 2018).

MODIFICATION

Regulation 68 is modified by Sch.2, para.13 of the Employment and Support Allowance (Transitional Provisions, Housing Benefit and Council Tax Benefit) (Existing Awards) (No.2) Regulations 2010 (SI 2010/1907) (as amended) for the purposes specified in reg.16(1). For details of the modification, see the text of those Regulations below.

DEFINITIONS

"the Act"—reg.2(1).
"claimant"—WRA 2007 s.24(1).
"couple"—reg.2(1).
"income-related allowance"—WRA 2007 s.24(1) and 1(7).
"Jobseekers Act"—reg.2(1).
"partner"—*ibid.*
"polygamous marriage"—*ibid.*
"single claimant"—*ibid.*

GENERAL NOTE

This regulation is similar to reg.18 of the IS Regulations and reg.84 of the JSA Regulations.   4.184

Special cases

69.—(1) In the case of a claimant to whom any paragraph in column (1)   4.185
of Schedule 5 applies (amounts in special cases), the amount in respect of the claimant is to be the amount in the corresponding paragraph in column (2) of that Schedule.

(2) In Schedule 5—
"partner of a person subject to immigration control" means a person—
(a) who is not subject to immigration control within the meaning of section 115(9) of the Immigration and Asylum Act; or
(b) to whom section 115 of that Act does not apply by virtue of regulation 2 of the Social Security (Immigration and Asylum) Consequential Amendments Regulations 2000; and
(c) who is a member of a couple and the member's partner is subject to immigration control within the meaning of section 115(9) of that Act and section 115 of that Act applies to the partner for the purposes of exclusion from entitlement to an income-related allowance;
"patient" means a person (other than a prisoner) who is regarded as receiving free in-patient treatment within the meaning of regulation 2(4) and (5) of the Social Security (Hospital In- Patients) Regulations 2005;
"person from abroad" has the meaning given in regulation 70;
"person in hardship" means a person who satisfies regulation 158 but only for a period not exceeding 6 weeks;

"prisoner" means a person who—

(a) is detained in custody pending trial or sentence on conviction or under a sentence imposed by a court; or

(b) is on temporary release in accordance with the provisions of the Prison Act 1952 or the Prisons (Scotland) Act 1989, other than a person who is detained in hospital under the provisions of the Mental Health Act 1983 or, in Scotland, under the provisions of the Mental Health (Care and Treatment) (Scotland) Act 2003 or the Criminal Procedure (Scotland) Act 1995.

[² (3) In Schedule 5 "person serving a sentence of imprisonment detained in hospital" means a person ("P") who satisfies either of the following conditions.

(4)   The first condition is that—

(a) P is being detained under section 45A or 47 of the Mental Health Act 1983 (power of higher courts to direct hospital admission; removal to hospital of persons serving sentences of imprisonment etc.); and

(b) in any case where there is in relation to P a release date within the meaning of section 50(3) of that Act, P is being detained on or before the day which the Secretary of State certifies to be that release date.

(5)   The second condition is that P is being detained under—

(a) section 59A of the Criminal Procedure (Scotland) Act 1995 (hospital direction); or

(b) section 136 of the Mental Health (Care and Treatment) (Scotland) Act 2003 (transfer of prisoners for treatment of mental disorder).]

AMENDMENTS

1. Social Security (Miscellaneous Amendments) (No.5) Regulations 2009 (SI 2009/3228) reg.3(4)(b) (January 25, 2010).

2. Social Security (Persons Serving a Sentence of Imprisonment Detained in Hospital) Regulations 2010 reg.5(2) (March 25, 2010).

MODIFICATION

The definition of "prisoner" in para.(2) is modified with effect from April 8, 2020 by reg.2(1) and (2)(d) of the Social Security (Coronavirus) (Prisoners) Regulations 2020 (SI 2020/409). The modification provides that the ESA Regulations 2008 "are to be read as if the definition of "prisoner" did not include a person on temporary release in accordance with the provisions of the Prison Act 1952". By reg.6 of SI 2020/409 (as amended by reg.2 of SI 2020/1156), , the modification will expire at the end of May 12, 2021.

DEFINITIONS

"claimant"—WRA 2007 s.24(1).
"couple"—reg.2(1).
"Immigration and Asylum Act"—*ibid.*
"income-related allowance"—WRA 2007 s.24(1) and 1(7).
"partner"—reg.2(1).

GENERAL NOTE

4.186   This regulation is similar to reg.21 of the IS Regulations and reg.85 of the JSA Regulations. Applicable amounts in special cases are prescribed by Sch.5 below.

Special cases: supplemental—persons from abroad

70.—(1) "Person from abroad" means, subject to the following provi-   4.187
sions of this regulation, a claimant who is not habitually resident in the
United Kingdom, the Channel Islands, the Isle of Man or the Republic of
Ireland.

(2) A claimant must not be treated as habitually resident in the United
Kingdom, the Channel Islands, the Isle of Man or the Republic of
Ireland unless the claimant has a right to reside in (as the case may be) the
United Kingdom, the Channel Islands, the Isle of Man or the Republic of
Ireland other than a right to reside which falls within paragraph (3) [8 or
(3A)].

(3) A right to reside falls within this paragraph if it is one which exists by
virtue of, or in accordance with, one or more of the following—

   (a) regulation 13 of the [8 Immigration (European Economic Area)
      Regulations 2016];

   (b) regulation 14 of those Regulations, but only in a case where the right
      exists under that regulation because the claimant is—
      (i) a jobseeker for the purpose of the definition of "qualified
         person" in regulation 6(1) of those Regulations; or
      (ii) a family member (within the meaning of regulation 7 of those
         Regulations) of such a jobseeker; [10 or]

  [4 [8 (bb) regulation 16 of those Regulations, but only in a case where the
      right exists under that regulation because the claimant satisfies the
      criteria in paragraph (5) of that regulation;]]

   (c) [10 ...]
   (d) [10 ...]
   (e) [10 ...]

[8 (3A) A right to reside falls within this paragraph if it exists by virtue
of a claimant having been granted limited leave to enter, or remain in, the
United Kingdom under the Immigration Act 1971 by virtue of—

   (a) Appendix EU to the immigration rules made under section 3(2) of
      that Act; [11 ...];

   (b) being a person with a Zambrano right to reside as defined in Annex
      1 of Appendix EU to the immigration rules made under section 3(2)
      of that Act.] [11; or

   (c) having arrived in the United Kingdom with an entry clearance that
      was granted under Appendix EU (Family Permit) to the immigration
      rules made under section 3(2) of that Act.]

[9 (3B) Paragraph (3A)(a) does not apply to a person who—

   (a) has a right to reside granted by virtue of being a family member of a
      relevant person of Northern Ireland; and

   (b) would have a right to reside under the Immigration (European
      Economic Area) Regulations 2016 if the relevant person of Northern
      Ireland were an EEA national, provided that the right to reside does
      not fall within paragraph (3).]

(4) A claimant is not a person from abroad if the claimant is—

[7 (za) a qualified person for the purposes of regulation 6 of the [8
      Immigration (European Economic Area) Regulations 2016] as a
      worker or a self-employed person;

  (zb) a family member of a person referred to in sub-paragraph (za) [9 ...];

  (zc) a person who has a right to reside permanently in the United

Kingdom by virtue of regulation 15(1)(c), (d) or (e) of those Regulations;]

[⁹ (zd) a family member of a relevant person of Northern Ireland, with a right to reside which falls within paragraph (3A)(a), provided that the relevant person of Northern Ireland falls within sub-paragraph (za), or would do so but for the fact that they are not an EEA national;]

[¹⁰ (ze) a frontier worker within the meaning of regulation 3 of the Citizens' Rights (Frontier Workers) (EU Exit) Regulations 2020;

(zf) a family member of a person referred to in sub-paragraph (ze), who has been granted limited leave to enter, or remain in, the United Kingdom by virtue of Appendix EU to the immigration rules made under section 3(2) of the Immigration Act 1971;]

(g) a refugee within the definition in Article 1 of the Convention relating to the Status of Refugees done at Geneva on 28th July 1951, as extended by Article 1(2) of the Protocol relating to the Status of Refugees done at New York on 31st January 1967;

[⁶ (h) a person who has been granted leave or who is deemed to have been granted leave outside the rules made under section 3(2) of the Immigration Act 1971 where that leave is—

(i) discretionary leave to enter or remain in the United Kingdom;

(ii) leave to remain under the Destitution Domestic Violence concession; or

(iii) leave deemed to have been granted by virtue of regulation 3 of the Displaced Persons (Temporary Protection) Regulations 2005;]

(i) a person who has humanitarian protection granted under those rules; [⁶ or]

(j) a person who is not a person subject to immigration control within the meaning of section 115(9) of the Immigration and Asylum Act and who is in the United Kingdom as a result of deportation, expulsion or other removal by compulsion of law from another country to the United Kingdom; [¹ . . .]

(k) [⁶ ...]

(l) [¹ [⁶ ...]]

[⁹ (5) In this regulation—

"EEA national" has the meaning given in regulation 2(1) of the Immigration (European Economic Area) Regulations 2016;

"family member" has the meaning given in regulation 7(1)(a), (b) or (c) of the Immigration (European Economic Area) Regulations 2016 except that regulation 7(4) of those Regulations does not apply for the purposes of paragraphs (3B) and (4)(zd);

"relevant person of Northern Ireland" has the meaning given in Annex 1 of Appendix EU to the immigration rules made under section 3(2) of the Immigration Act 1971.]

[¹⁰ (6) References in this regulation to the Immigration (European Economic Area) Regulations 2016 are to be read with Schedule 4 to the Immigration and Social Security Co-ordination (EU Withdrawal) Act 2020(Consequential, Saving, Transitional and Transitory Provisions) Regulations 2020.]

AMENDMENTS

1. Social Security (Habitual Residence) (Amendment) Regulations 2009 (SI 2009/362) reg.9 (March 18, 2009).

2. Social Security (Miscellaneous Amendments) (No. 3) Regulations 2011 (SI 2011/2425) reg.23(1) and (7) (October 31, 2011).

3. Treaty of Lisbon (Changes in Terminology or Numbering) Order 2012 (SI 2012/1809) art.3(1) and Sch.1 Pt.2 (August 1, 2012).

4. Social Security (Habitual Residence) (Amendment) Regulations 2012 (SI 2012/2587) reg.2 (November 8, 2012).

5. Social Security (Croatia) Amendment Regulations 2013 (SI 2013/1474) reg.7 (July 1, 2013).

6. Social Security (Miscellaneous Amendments) (No.3) Regulations 2013 (SI 2013/2536) reg.13(1) and (24) (October 29, 2013).

7. Social Security (Habitual Residence) (Amendment) Regulations 2014 (SI 2014/902) reg.7 (May 31, 2014).

8. Social Security (Income-related Benefits) (Updating and Amendment) (EU Exit) Regulations 2019 (SI 2019/872) reg.7 (May 7, 2019).

9. Social Security (Income-Related Benefits) (Persons of Northern Ireland – Family Members) (Amendment) Regulations 2020 (SI 2020/638) reg 7 (August 24, 2020).

10. Immigration and Social Security Co-ordination (EU Withdrawal) Act 2020 (Consequential, Saving, Transitional and Transitory Provisions) (EU Exit) Regulations 2020 (SI 2020/1309) reg 73 (December 31, 2020 at 11.00 pm).

11. Immigration (Citizens' Rights etc.) (EU Exit) Regulations 2020 (SI 2020/1372) reg.23 (December 31, 2020 at 11.00 pm).

MODIFICATION

Regulation 70 is modified by Sch.1, para.10A of the Employment and Support Allowance (Transitional Provisions, Housing Benefit and Council Tax Benefit) (Existing Awards) (No.2) Regulations 2010 (SI 2010/1907) as amended for the purposes specified in reg.6(1) of those Regulations. For the details of the modification, pp.1410-1452 of Vol.1 of the 2020/21 edition.

DEFINITION

"Immigration and Asylum Act"—reg.2(1).

GENERAL NOTE

See the commentary to the Immigration (European Economic Area) Regulations 2016 below.

4.188

Definition of non-dependant

71.—(1) In these Regulations, "non-dependant" means any person, except someone to whom paragraph (2), (3) or (4) applies, who normally resides with a claimant or with whom a claimant normally resides.

4.189

(2) This paragraph applies to—

(a) any member of the claimant's family;

(b) a child or young person who is living with the claimant but who is not a member of the claimant's household;

(c) a person who lives with the claimant in order to care for the claimant or for the claimant's partner and who is engaged for that purpose by a charitable or voluntary organisation which makes a charge to the claimant or the claimant's partner for the care provided by that person;

(d) the partner of a person to whom sub-paragraph (c) applies.

(3) This paragraph applies to a person, other than a close relative of the claimant or the claimant's partner—

(a) who is liable to make payments on a commercial basis to the claimant or the claimant's partner in respect of the person's occupation of the claimant's dwelling;

(b) to whom the claimant or the claimant's partner is liable to make payments on a commercial basis in respect of the claimant's occupation of that person's dwelling;

(c) who is a member of the household of a person to whom sub-paragraph (a) or (b) applies.

(4) Subject to paragraph (5), this paragraph applies to—

(a) a person who jointly occupies the claimant's dwelling and who is either—

(i) a co-owner of that dwelling with the claimant or the claimant's partner (whether or not there are other co-owners); or

(ii) jointly liable with the claimant or the claimant's partner to make payments to a landlord in respect of the person's occupation of that dwelling;

(b) a partner of a person to whom sub-paragraph (a) applies.

(5) Where a person is a close relative of the claimant or the claimant's partner, paragraph (4) applies to that person only if the claimant's, or the claimant's partner's, co-ownership, or joint liability to make payments to a landlord in respect of occupation of the dwelling arose either before 11th April 1988 or, if later, on or before the date on which the claimant or the claimant's partner first occupied the dwelling in question.

(6) For the purposes of this regulation a person resides with another only if they share any accommodation except a bathroom, a lavatory or a communal area but not if each person is separately liable to make payments in respect of occupation of the dwelling to the landlord.

(7) In this regulation "communal area" means any area (other than rooms) of common access (including halls and passageways) and rooms of common use in sheltered accommodation.

DEFINITIONS

"child"—reg.2(1).
"claimant"—WRA s.24(1).
"close relative"—*ibid.*
"family"—reg.2(1) and (3).
"partner"—reg.2(1).
"voluntary organisation"—*ibid.*
"young person"—*ibid.*

GENERAL NOTE

4.190   See the notes to reg.3 of the IS Regs.

CHAPTER 2

DEDUCTIONS FROM THE CONTRIBUTORY ALLOWANCE

Permanent health insurance

4.191   72. [*Omitted as not applying to income-related ESA*]

CHAPTER 3

STATUTORY PAYMENTS

PART 10

INCOME AND CAPITAL

CHAPTER 1

GENERAL

Calculation of income and capital of members of claimant's family and of a polygamous marriage

4.203

83.—(1) Subject to paragraph (4), the income and capital of a claimant's partner which by virtue of paragraph 6(2) of Schedule 1 to the Act is to be treated as income and capital of the claimant, is to be calculated in accordance with the following provisions of this Part in like manner as for the claimant; and any reference to the "claimant" is, except where the context otherwise requires, to be construed, for the purposes of this Part, as if it were a reference to the claimant's partner.

(2) Subject to the following provisions of this Part, the income paid to, or in respect of, and capital of, a child or young person who is a member of the claimant's family is not to be treated as the income or capital of the claimant.

(3) Subject to paragraph (5), where a claimant or the partner of a claimant is married polygamously to two or more members of the claimant's household—

  (a) the claimant is to be treated as possessing capital and income belonging to each such member; and

  (b) the income and capital of that member is to be calculated in accordance with the following provisions of this Part in like manner as for the claimant.

(4) Where at least one member of a couple is aged less than 18 and the applicable amount of the couple falls to be determined under paragraph 1(3)(e), (f), (g), (h) or (i) of Schedule 4 (amounts), the income of the claimant's partner is not to be treated as the income of the claimant to the extent that—

  (a) in the case of a couple where both members are aged less than 18, the amount specified in paragraph 1(3)(c) of that Schedule exceeds the amount specified in paragraph 1(3)(i) of that Schedule; and

  (b) in the case of a couple where only one member is aged less than 18, the amount specified in paragraph 1(3)(a) of that Schedule exceeds the amount which is specified in paragraph 1(3)(h) of that Schedule.

(5) Where a member of a polygamous marriage is a partner aged less than 18 and the amount which applies in respect of that partner under regulation 68(2) (polygamous marriages) is nil, the claimant is not to be treated as possessing the income of that partner to the extent that an amount in respect of that partner would have been included in the applicable amount if the partner had fallen within the circumstances set out in regulation 68(2)(a) or (b).

DEFINITIONS

  "child"—see reg.2(1).
  "couple"—*ibid.*
  "family"—*ibid.*
  "partner"—*ibid.*

"polygamous marriage"—*ibid.*
"young person"—*ibid.*; s.142 SSCBA.

GENERAL NOTE

This regulation contains the basic rule on aggregation of resources of the claimant   4.204
and any partner for the purposes of income-related ESA. It is similar to reg.23 of the
Income Support Regulations/reg.88 of the JSA Regulations 1996.

The rules governing income and capital for the purposes of income-related old
style ESA are very similar to those applying to income support and income-based
old style JSA. Where there are differences between the income support and the
income-based JSA provisions ESA generally follows the income support model. The
reader should therefore refer to the notes to the corresponding income support provision in Part II of this volume for further explanation of the provisions in this Part.

Income of participants in the self-employment route

84. Chapters 2, 3, 4, 6, 8 and 9 of this Part and regulations 132 to 137,   4.205
142 and 143 do not apply to any income which is to be calculated in accordance with Chapter 5 of this Part (participants in the self-employment route).

DEFINITION

"self-employment route"—see reg.2(1).

GENERAL NOTE

This is similar to reg.23A of the Income Support Regulations/reg.88A of the JSA   4.206
Regulations 1996.

[¹ [³ . . .]] Liable relative payments

85. Regulations 91 to 109, 111 to 117 and Chapter 10 of this Part do not   4.207
apply to any payment which is to be calculated in accordance with Chapter
8 of this Part ([²[⁴ . . .] liable relative payments]).

AMENDMENTS

1. Employment and Support Allowance (Miscellaneous Amendments)
Regulations 2008 (SI 2008/2428) reg.20(2)(a) (October 27, 2008).
2. Employment and Support Allowance (Miscellaneous Amendments)
Regulations 2008 (SI 2008/2428) reg.20(3) (October 27, 2008).
3. Social Security (Miscellaneous Amendments) (No.4) Regulations 2009 (SI
2009/2655) reg.11(4) (April 12, 2010).
4. Social Security (Miscellaneous Amendments) (No.4) Regulations 2009 (SI
2009/2655) reg.11(5) (April 12, 2010).

GENERAL NOTE

This is similar to reg.25 of the Income Support Regulations/reg.89 of the JSA   4.208
Regulations 1996.

Child support

86. [¹ . . .]   4.209

AMENDMENT

1. Employment and Support Allowance (Miscellaneous Amendments)
Regulations 2008 (SI 2008/2428) reg.20(4)(a) (October 27, 2008).

Calculation of income and capital of students

4.210   **87.** The provisions of Chapters 2 to 7 of this Part (income and capital) are to have effect in relation to students and their partners subject to the modifications set out in Chapter 10 of this Part (students).

DEFINITION

"partner"—see reg.2(1).

GENERAL NOTE

4.211   This is similar to reg.26 of the Income Support Regulations/reg.91 of the JSA Regulations 1996.

Calculation of income which consists of earnings of participants in exempt work

4.212   **88.** Notwithstanding the other provisions of this Part, regulations 91(2), 92 to 99 and 108(3) and (4) and Schedule 7 (sums to be disregarded in the calculation of earnings) are to apply to any income which consists of earnings which is to be calculated for the purposes of regulations 45(2) to (4) (exempt work—earnings limits).

GENERAL NOTE

4.213   The general rule is that a claimant who does any work in a week will not normally be entitled to old style ESA for that week (see reg.40(1)), but this does not apply to exempt work (see reg.40(2)(f)). See reg.45 for the rules for exempt work; in the case of work referred to in reg.45(2)-(4) this is subject to earnings limits. Regulation 88 is necessary because the exempt work provisions are relevant to both contributory and income-related ESA.

It provides that the following regulations apply for the purposes of calculating a claimant's earnings under the exempt work provisions in reg.45(2)-(4): reg.91(2) (period over which a payment is taken into account); reg.92 (calculation of earnings of self-employed earners); reg.93 (date on which income is treated as paid); reg.94 (calculation of weekly amount of income); reg.95 (earnings of employed earners); reg.96 (calculation of net earnings of employed earners); reg.97 (earnings of self-employed earners); reg.98 (calculation of net profit of self-employed earners); reg.99 (deduction of tax and contributions for self-employed earners); reg.108(3) and (4) (notional earnings) and Sch.7 (sums to be disregarded in the calculation of earnings). The broad effect is that earnings from exempt work (for both contributory and income-related ESA) will be assessed in the same way as earnings generally are for income-related ESA.

4.214   Note that if the claimant is doing exempt work, any earnings that do not exceed the relevant weekly limit under reg.45(2), (3) or (4) are disregarded (see para.5 of Sch.7). The limit is £20 or, in some circumstances, 16 x the national minimum wage hourly rate for adults aged 23 and over, subject to rounding up to the nearest 50p or £1 (thus, currently, from April 2021, £143 per week: see the note to the out-dated definition of "National Minimum Wage" in reg.2(1)). In addition, if the claimant's earnings from the exempt work are less than the relevant limit, the remainder of the disregard (up to a maximum of £20, can be applied to a partner's earnings (see paras 6 and 7 of Sch.7). If the claimant is undertaking exempt work and also has earnings from work as a member of the Disability Living Allowance Advisory Board or as a disability member of a tribunal, the £20 disregard of such earnings under para.7 of Sch.7 only applies to the extent that the claimant's earnings from exempt work are less than the relevant limit. Note that the Disability Living Allowance Advisory Board was abolished on February 7, 2013 by the Public Bodies (Abolition of the Disability Living Allowance Advisory Board) Order 2013, arts 1(2) and (3).

Calculation of income where pension payments, PPF periodic payments or councillor's allowance payable

89. [*Omitted as not relevant to income-related ESA.*]   4.215

CHAPTER 2

INCOME

Calculation of income

90.—(1) For the purposes of paragraph 6(1) of Schedule 1 to the Act   4.216
(conditions of entitlement to an income-related allowance), the income of a
claimant is to be calculated on a weekly basis—
  (a) by determining in accordance with this Part, other than Chapter 7,
       the weekly amount of the claimant's income; and
  (b) by adding to that amount the weekly income calculated under regu-
       lation 118 (calculation of tariff income from capital).

(2) For the purposes of paragraph (1) "income" includes capital treated
as income under regulation 105 (capital treated as income) and income
which a claimant is treated as possessing under regulations 106 to 109
(notional income).

(3) For the purposes of paragraph 10 of Schedule 2 to the Act (effect of
work), the income which consists of earnings of a claimant is to be calcu
lated on a weekly basis by determining the weekly amount of those earnings
in accordance with regulations 91(2), 92 to 99 and 108(3) and (4) and
Schedule 7.

(4) For the purposes of paragraph (3), "income which consists of earnings" includes income which a claimant is treated as possessing under regulation 108(3) and (4).

(5) For the purposes of pension payments, PPF periodic payments and
a councillor's allowance to which section 3 of the Act applies, the income
other than earnings of a claimant is to be calculated on a weekly basis
by determining in accordance with regulation 94(1), (2), (5) and (6) the
weekly amount of the pension payments, PPF periodic payment or a councillor's allowance paid to the claimant.

DEFINITIONS

  "claimant"—see reg.83(1).
  "councillor"—see reg.2(1).
  "councillor's allowance"—*ibid.*
  "pension payments"—see WRA 2007 s.3(3); regs 72 and 72A.
  "PPF periodic payment"—see WRA 2007 s.3(3).

GENERAL NOTE

  Paragraphs (1) and (2) are similar to reg.28 of the Income Support   4.217
Regulations/reg.93 of the JSA Regulations 1996. They confirm that all income
resources, including resources specifically treated as earnings or income, are to
be taken into account for the purposes of calculating entitlement to income-
related ESA.

Paragraphs (3) to (4)

Paragraph 10 of Sch.2 to the Welfare Reform Act 2007 provides for regulations to treat a person as not entitled to ESA because of undertaking work. See regs 40–46 which implement this for old style ESA. Under reg.45 certain categories of work are exempt; in the case of work referred to in reg.45(2)–(4) this is subject to earnings limits. Paragraph (3) provides that for the purpose of calculating a claimant's weekly earnings in these circumstances the following regulations apply: reg.91(2) (period over which a payment is taken into account); reg.92 (calculation of earnings of self-employed earners); reg.93 (date on which income is treated as paid); reg.94 (calculation of weekly amount of income); reg.95 (earnings of employed earners); reg.96 (calculation of net earnings of employed earners); reg.97 (earnings of self-employed earners); reg.98 (calculation of net profit of self-employed earners); reg.99 (deduction of tax and contributions for self-employed earners); reg.108(3) and (4) (notional earnings) and Sch.7 (sums to be disregarded in the calculation of earnings). See also reg.88 which makes similar provision. Paragraph (4) specifically provides that such earnings include notional earnings.

Paragraph (5)

4.219   This paragraph is not relevant to income-related ESA.

Calculation of earnings derived from employed earner's employment and income other than earnings

4.220   **91.**—(1) Earnings derived from employment as an employed earner and income which does not consist of earnings are to be taken into account over a period determined in accordance with the following provisions of this regulation and at a weekly amount determined in accordance with regulation 94 (calculation of weekly amount of income).

(2) Subject to the following provisions of this regulation, the period over which a payment is to be taken into account is to be—

(a) where the payment is monthly, a period equal to the number of weeks from the date on which the payment is treated as paid to the date immediately before the date on which the next monthly payment would have been so treated as paid whether or not the next monthly payment is actually paid;

(b) where the payment is in respect of a period which is not monthly, a period equal to the length of the period for which payment is made;

(c) in any other case, a period equal to such number of weeks as is equal to the number obtained (and any fraction is to be treated as a corresponding fraction of a week) by dividing—

(i) the net earnings; or

(ii) in the case of income which does not consist of earnings, the amount of that income less any amount paid by way of tax on that income which is disregarded under paragraph 1 of Schedule 8 (income other than earnings to be disregarded),

by the amount of an [¹ employment and support] allowance which would be payable had the payment not been made plus an amount equal to the total of the sums which would fall to be disregarded from that payment under Schedule 7 (earnings to be disregarded) or, as the case may be, any paragraph of Schedule 8 other than paragraph 1 of that Schedule, as is appropriate in the claimant's case, and that period is to begin on the date on which the payment is treated as paid under regulation 93 (date on which income is treated as paid).

(3) The period over which a Career Development Loan, which is paid pursuant to section 2 of the Employment and Training Act 1973, is to be taken into account is the period of education and training intended to be supported by that loan.

(4) Where grant income as defined in Chapter 10 of this Part has been paid to a claimant who ceases to be a full-time student before the end of the period in respect of which that income is payable and, as a consequence, the whole or part of that income falls to be repaid by that claimant, that income is to be taken into account over the period beginning on the date on which that income is treated as paid under regulation 93 (date on which income is treated as paid) and ending—

(a) on the date on which repayment is made in full;

(b) where the grant is paid in instalments, on the day before the next instalment would have been paid had the claimant remained a full-time student; or

(c) on the last date of the academic term or vacation during which that claimant ceased to be a full-time student,

whichever is the earlier.

[² [³ (4A)(a) This paragraph applies where earnings are derived by a claimant as a member of a reserve force prescribed in Part 1 of Schedule 6 to the Contributions Regulations—

(i) in respect of a period of annual continuous training for a maximum of 15 days in any calendar year; or

(ii) in respect of training in the claimant's first year of training as a member of a reserve force for a maximum of 43 days in that year.

(b) Earnings, whether paid to the claimant alone or together with other earnings derived from the same source, are to be taken into account—

(i) in the case of a period of training which lasts for the number of days listed in column 1 of the table in sub-paragraph (c), over a period of time which is equal to the number of days set out in the corresponding row in column 2 of that table; or

(ii) in any other case, over a period which is equal to the duration of the training period.

(c) This is the table referred to in sub-paragraph (b)(i)—

Column 1 *Period of training in days*	Column 2 *Period of time over which earnings are to be taken into account in days*
8 to 10	7
15 to 17	14
22 to 24	21
29 to 31	28
36 to 38	35
43	42]

(4B) The period over which earnings to which paragraph (4A) applies are to be taken into account shall begin on the date on which the payment is treated as paid under regulation 93.]

(5) Where, but for this paragraph—

(a) earnings not of the same kind are derived from the same source; and

(b) the periods in respect of which those earnings would fall to be taken into account overlap, wholly or partly,

those earnings are to be taken into account over a period equal to the aggregate length of those periods and that period is to begin with the earliest date on which any part of those earnings would otherwise be treated as paid under regulation 93.

(6) In a case to which paragraph (5) applies, earnings under regulation 95 (earnings of employed earners) are to be taken into account in the following order of priority—

(a) earnings normally derived from the employment;

(b) any payment to which paragraph (1)(b) or (c) of that regulation applies;

(c) any payment to which paragraph (1)(j) of that regulation applies;

(d) any payment to which paragraph (1)(d) of that regulation applies.

(7) Where earnings to which regulation 95(1)(b) to (d) applies are paid in respect of part of a day, those earnings are to be taken into account over a period equal to a day.

(8) Any earnings to which regulation 95(1)(j) applies which are paid in respect of, or on the termination of, part-time employment, are to be taken into account over a period equal to one week.

(9) In this regulation "part-time employment" means, if the claimant were entitled to income support, employment in which the claimant is not to be treated as engaged in remunerative work under regulation 5 or 6(1) and (4) of the Income Support Regulations (persons treated, or not treated, as engaged in remunerative work);

(10) For the purposes of this regulation the claimant's earnings and income which does not consist of earnings are to be calculated in accordance with Chapters 3 and 6 respectively of this Part.

AMENDMENTS

1. Social Security (Miscellaneous Amendments) Regulations 2009 (SI 2009/583), reg.10(3) (April 6, 2009).

2. Social Security (Miscellaneous Amendments) (No.2) Regulations 2012 (SI 2012/2575) reg.5(2) (November 5, 2012).

3. Social Security (Members of the Reserve Forces) (Amendment) Regulations 2015 (SI 2015/389) reg. 4(3) (April 6, 2015).

DEFINITIONS

"claimant"—see reg.83(1).

"employed earner"—see reg.2(1).

"first year of training"—*ibid.*

"full-time student"—*ibid.*

"grant income"—see reg.131(1).

GENERAL NOTE

4.221   This is similar to reg.29 of the Income Support Regulations/reg.94(1) to (5) and (10) of the JSA Regulations 1996. Paragraphs (6) to (9) of reg.94 of the JSA Regulations 1996 contain different provisions defining the length of the period for which a "compensation payment" is to be taken into account.

In relation to earnings to which paras (4A) and (4B) apply (earnings from training as a member of a reserve force), see the disregard in para.11A of Sch.7. This ignores such earnings to the extent that they would have the effect of reducing entitlement to income-related ESA to less than 10p per week.

Although the current form of para.(4A) refers to earnings "derived by a claimant", it seems likely that it is intended to primarily refer to the claimant's partner's earnings as a member of a reserve force, not the claimant's (for obvious reasons). The previous form of para.(4A) referred to such earnings that were "derived by a claimant's partner".

Calculation of earnings of self-employed earners

92.—(1) Except where paragraph (2) applies, where a claimant's income consists of earnings from employment as a self-employed earner the weekly amount of the claimant's earnings is to be determined by reference to the claimant's average weekly earnings from that employment—

(a) over a period of one year; or

(b) where the claimant has recently become engaged in that employment or there has been a change which is likely to affect the normal pattern of business, over such other period as may, in any particular case, enable the weekly amount of the claimant's earnings to be determined more accurately.

[1(2)(a) Where the claimant's earnings consist of any items to which this paragraph applies those earnings shall be taken into account over a period equal to such number of weeks as is equal to the number obtained (and any fraction shall be treated as a corresponding fraction of a week) by dividing the earnings by the amount of employment and support allowance which would be payable had the payment not been made plus an amount equal to the total of the sums which would fall to be disregarded from the payment under Schedule 7 (earnings to be disregarded) as is appropriate in the claimant's case;

(b) This paragraph applies to—

(i) royalties or other sums paid as a consideration for the use of, or the right to use, any copyright, design, patent or trade mark; or

(ii) any payment in respect of any book registered under the Public Lending Right Scheme 1982 or work made under any international public lending right scheme that is analogous to the Public Lending Right Scheme 1982,

where the claimant is the first owner of the copyright, design, patent or trademark, or an original contributor to the book or work concerned.]

(3) For the purposes of this regulation the claimant's earnings are to be calculated in accordance with Chapter 4 of this Part.

4.222

AMENDMENT

1. Social Security (Miscellaneous Amendments) Regulations 2009 (SI 2009/583) reg.10(3) (April 6, 2009).

DEFINITIONS

"claimant"—see reg.83(1).
"self-employed earner"—see reg.2(1).

GENERAL NOTE

This is similar to reg.30 of the Income Support Regulations/reg.95 of the JSA Regulations 1996.

4.223

Date on which income is treated as paid

4.224   **93.**—(1) Except where paragraph (2) [² . . .] applies, a payment of income to which regulation 91 (calculation of earnings derived from employed earner's employment and income other than earnings) applies is to be treated as paid—

(a) in the case of a payment which is due to be paid before the first benefit week pursuant to the claim, on the date on which it is due to be paid;

(b) in any other case, on the first day of the benefit week in which it is due to be paid or the first succeeding benefit week in which it is practicable to take it into account.

(2) Employment and support allowance, income support, jobseeker's allowance, maternity allowance, short-term or long-term incapacity benefit, [³ severe disablement allowance or universal credit] is to be treated as paid on [³ on any day] in respect of which it is payable.

(3) [² . . .]

[¹ (4) [² . . .]]

AMENDMENTS

1. Social Security (Miscellaneous Amendments) Regulations 2009 (SI 2009/583) reg.10(5) (April 6, 2009).

2. Social Security (Miscellaneous Amendments) Regulations 2011 (SI 2011/674) reg.16(7) (April 11, 2011).

3. Universal Credit (Consequential, Supplementary, Incidental and Miscellaneous Provisions) Regulations 2013 (SI 2013/630) reg.37(5) (April 29, 2013).

DEFINITIONS

"benefit week"—see reg.2(1).
"universal credit"—*ibid.*

GENERAL NOTE

4.225   This is similar to reg.31 of the Income Support Regulations/reg.96 of the JSA Regulations 1996.

Calculation of weekly amount of income

4.226   **94.**—(1) For the purposes of regulation 91 (calculation of earnings derived from employed earner's employment and income other than earnings) and Chapter 2 of Part 9 (deductions from contributory allowance), subject to paragraphs (2) to (8), where the period in respect of which a payment is made—

(a) does not exceed a week, the weekly amount is to be the amount of that payment;

(b) exceeds a week, the weekly amount is to be determined—

(i) in a case where that period is a month, by multiplying the amount of the payment by 12 and dividing the product by 52;

(ii) in a case where that period is 3 months, by multiplying the amount of the payment by 4 and dividing the product by 52;

[² (iii) in a case where that period is a year and the payment is an award of working tax credit, by dividing the payment by the number of days in the year and multiplying the result by 7;

(iiia) in a case where that period is a year and the payment is income other than an award of working tax credit, by dividing the amount of the payment by 52;]

(iv) in any other case by multiplying the amount of the payment by 7 and dividing the product by the number equal to the number of days in the period in respect of which it is made.

(2) Where a payment for a period not exceeding a week is treated under regulation 93(1)(a) (date on which income is treated as paid) as paid before the first benefit week and a part is to be taken into account for some days only in that week (the relevant days), the amount to be taken into account for the relevant days is to be calculated by multiplying the amount of the payment by the number equal to the number of relevant days and dividing the product by the number of days in the period in respect of which it is made.

(3) Where a payment is in respect of a period equal to or in excess of a week and a part thereof is to be taken into account for some days only in a benefit week (the relevant days), the amount to be taken into account for the relevant days is, except where paragraph (4) applies, to be calculated by multiplying the amount of the payment by the number equal to the number of relevant days and dividing the product by the number of days in the period in respect of which it is made.

(4) In the case of a payment of—

(a) maternity allowance, short-term or long-term incapacity benefit or severe disablement allowance, the amount to be taken into account for the relevant days is to be the amount of benefit payable in respect of those days;

(b) an employment and support allowance, income support or a job-seeker's allowance, the amount to be taken into account for the relevant days is to be calculated by multiplying the weekly amount of the benefit by the number of relevant days and dividing the product by 7.

(5) Except in the case of a payment which it has not been practicable to treat under regulation 93(1)(b) (date on which income is treated as paid) as paid on the first day of the benefit week in which it is due to be paid, where a payment of income from a particular source is or has been paid regularly and that payment falls to be taken into account in the same benefit week as a payment of the same kind and from the same source, the amount of that income to be taken into account in any one benefit week is not to exceed the weekly amount determined under paragraph (1)(a) or (b) of the payment which under regulation 93(1)(b) is treated as paid first.

(6) Where the amount of the claimant's income fluctuates and has changed more than once, or a claimant's regular pattern of work is such that the claimant does not work every week, the foregoing paragraphs may be modified so that the weekly amount of the claimant's income is determined by reference to the claimant's average weekly income—

(a) if there is a recognisable cycle of work, over the period of one complete cycle (including, where the cycle involves periods in which the claimant does no work, those periods but disregarding any other absences);

(b) in any other case, over a period of 5 weeks or such other period as may, in the particular case, enable the claimant's average weekly income to be determined more accurately.

(7) Where income is taken into account under paragraph (4) of regula-

tion 91 over the period specified in that paragraph, the amount of that income to be taken into account in respect of any week in that period is to be an amount equal to the amount of that income which would have been taken into account under regulation 132 (calculation of grant income) had the person to whom that income was paid not ceased to be a full-time student.

(8) Where any payment of earnings is taken into account under [¹paragraph (8)] of regulation 91 (calculation of earnings derived from employed earner's employment and income other than earnings), over the period specified in that paragraph, the amount to be taken into account is to be equal to the amount of the payment.

AMENDMENTS

1. Employment and Support Allowance (Miscellaneous Amendments) Regulations 2008 (SI 2008/2428) reg.8(1) (October 27, 2008).
2. Social Security (Miscellaneous Amendments) Regulations 2009 (SI 2009/583) reg.10(6) (April 6, 2009).

DEFINITIONS

"benefit week"—see reg.2(1).
"claimant"—see reg.83(1).
"full-time student"—see reg.2(1).

GENERAL NOTE

4.227   This is similar to reg.32 of the Income Support Regulations/reg.97 of the JSA Regulations 1996 (except that there is no equivalent of para.(8) in reg.97 as the JSA rules for the treatment of compensation payments made on the termination of part-time employment are different (see the note to reg.94(6)–(9) of the JSA Regs 1996)).

CHAPTER 3

EMPLOYED EARNERS

Earnings of employed earners

4.228   **95.**—(1) Subject to [¹paragraphs (2) and (3)], "earnings" means, in the case of employment as an employed earner, any remuneration or profit derived from that employment and includes—
(a) any bonus or commission;
(b) any payment in lieu of remuneration except any periodic sum paid to a claimant on account of the termination of the claimant's employment by reason of redundancy;
(c) any payment in lieu of notice;
(d) any holiday pay except any payable more than 4 weeks after the termination or interruption of employment;
(e) any payment by way of a retainer;
(f) any payment made by the claimant's employer in respect of expenses not wholly, exclusively and necessarily incurred in the performance of the duties of the employment, including any payment made by the claimant's employer in respect of—

    (i) travelling expenses incurred by the claimant between the claimant's home and place of employment;

   (ii) expenses incurred by the claimant under arrangements made for the care of a member of the claimant's family owing to the claimant's absence from home;

  (g) any award of compensation made under section 112(4) or 117(3)(a) of the Employment Rights Act 1996 (the remedies: orders and compensation, enforcement of order and compensation);

  (h) any payment or remuneration made under [⁴section] 28, 34, 64, 68 [⁴or] 70 of the Employment Rights Act 1996 (right to guarantee payments, remuneration on suspension on medical or maternity grounds, complaints to employment tribunals);

  (i) any such sum as is referred to in section 112(3) of the Contributions and Benefits Act (certain sums to be earnings for social security purposes);

  (j) where a payment of compensation is made in respect of employment which is part-time employment, the amount of the compensation;

  (k) the amount of any payment by way of a non-cash voucher which has been taken into account in the computation of a person's earnings in accordance with Part 5 of Schedule 3 to the Social Security (Contributions) Regulations 2001.

(2) "Earnings" are not to include—

  (a) subject to paragraph (3), any payment in kind;

  (b) any remuneration paid by or on behalf of an employer to the claimant in respect of a period throughout which the claimant is on maternity leave, paternity leave [⁵, shared parental leave] [⁶, parental bereavement leave] or adoption leave or is absent from work because the claimant is ill;

  (c) any payment in respect of expenses wholly, exclusively and necessarily incurred in the performance of the duties of the employment;

  (d) any occupational pension;

  (e) any lump sum payment made under the Iron and Steel Re-adaptation Benefits Scheme.

[² (f) any payment in respect of expenses arising out of the [³ claimant participating as a service user].]

(3) Paragraph (2)(a) is not to apply in respect of any non-cash voucher referred to in paragraph (1)(k).

(4) In this regulation—

"compensation" means any payment made in respect of, or on the termination of, employment in a case where a claimant has not received or received only part of a payment in lieu of notice due or which would have been due to the claimant had that claimant not waived the right to receive it, other than—

  (a) any payment specified in paragraph (1)(a) to (i);

  (b) any payment specified in paragraph (2)(a) to [³ (f)];

  (c) any redundancy payment within the meaning of section 135(1) of the Employment Rights Act 1996;

  (d) any refund of contributions to which that person was entitled under an occupational pension scheme; and

  (e) any compensation payable by virtue of section 173 of the Education Reform Act 1988;

"part-time employment" means, if the claimant were entitled to income support, employment in which the claimant is not to be treated as engaged in remunerative work under regulation 5 or 6(1) and (4) of the Income Support Regulations (persons treated, or not treated, as engaged in remunerative work).

AMENDMENTS

1. Employment and Support Allowance (Miscellaneous Amendments) Regulations 2008 (SI 2008/2428) reg.8(2) (October 27, 2008).
2. Social Security (Miscellaneous Amendments) (No. 4) Regulations 2009 (SI 2009/2655) reg.11(6) (October 26, 2009).
3. Social Security (Miscellaneous Amendments) (No.3) Regulations 2013 (SI 2013/2536) reg.13(26) (October 29, 2013).
4. Social Security (Miscellaneous Amendments) Regulations 2014 (SI 2014/591) reg.10(2) (April 28, 2014).
5. Shared Parental Leave and Statutory Shared Parental Pay (Consequential Amendments to Subordinate Legislation) Order 2014 (SI 2014/3255) art.20(7) (December 31, 2014).
6. Parental Bereavement Leave and Pay (Consequential Amendments to Subordinate Legislation) Regulations 2020 (SI 2020/354) reg.19(4) (April 6, 2020).

DEFINITIONS

"adoption leave"—see reg.2(1).
"claimant"—see reg.83(1).
"claimant participating as a service user"—see reg. 2(8).
"employed earner"—see reg.2(1).
"family"—*ibid.*
"occupational pension"—*ibid.*
"parental bereavement leave"—*ibid.*
"shared parental leave"—*ibid.*

GENERAL NOTE

4.229   The equivalent income support and old-style JSA are regs 35 and 98 respectively. This regulation adopts the model of reg.35 of the Income Support Regulations rather than reg.98 of the JSA Regulations 1996. For the differences between reg.98 and this regulation (and reg.35 of the Income Support Regulations), see the notes to reg.98 of the JSA Regulations 1996. Note also that unlike the equivalent provisions in reg.35 and reg.98, para.(1)(d) (which relates to holiday pay) does not contain any special rule relating to trade disputes.

Calculation of net earnings of employed earners

4.230   **96.**—(1) For the purposes of regulation 91 (calculation of earnings derived from employed earner's employment and income other than earnings) the earnings of a claimant derived from employment as an employed earner to be taken into account, subject to paragraph (2), are the claimant's net earnings.

(2) There is to be disregarded from a claimant's net earnings, any sum, where applicable, specified in paragraphs 1 to 12 of Schedule 7 (sums to be disregarded in the calculation of earnings).

(3) For the purposes of paragraph (1) net earnings are to be calculated by taking into account the gross earnings of the claimant from that employment less—

(a) any amount deducted from those earnings by way of—
  (i) income tax;
  (ii) primary Class 1 contributions under section 6(1)(a) of the Contributions and Benefits Act;

   (b) one-half of any sum paid by the claimant in respect of a pay period by way of a contribution towards an occupational or personal pension scheme.

DEFINITIONS

   "claimant"—see reg.83(1).
   "Contributions and Benefits Act"—see WRA 2007 s.65.
   "employed earner"—see reg.2(1).
   "occupational pension scheme"—*ibid.*
   "pay period"—*ibid.*
   "personal pension scheme"—*ibid.*

GENERAL NOTE

   This is similar to reg.36 of the Income Support Regulations/reg.99 of the JSA   **4.231**
Regulations 1996.

CHAPTER 4

SELF-EMPLOYED EARNERS

Earnings of self-employed earners

   97.—(1) Subject to paragraph (2), "earnings", in the case of employ-   **4.232**
ment as a self-employed earner, means the gross receipts of the employment and include any allowance paid under section 2 of the Employment
and Training Act 1973 or section 2 of the Enterprise and New Towns
(Scotland) Act 1990 to the claimant for the purpose of assisting the claimant in carrying on the claimant's business.

   (2) "Earnings" do not include—

   (a) where a claimant is involved in providing board and lodging accommodation for which a charge is payable, any payment by way of such
a charge;

   (b) any payment to which paragraph [¹28, 29 or 29A] of Schedule 8 refers
(payments in respect of a person accommodated with the claimant
under an arrangement made by a local authority or voluntary organisation[¹, payments] made to the claimant by a health authority, local
authority or voluntary organisation in respect of persons temporarily
in the claimant's care) [¹and any payments made to a claimant under
section 73(1)(b) of the Children and Young People (Scotland) Act
2014 (kinship care allowance)];

[² (ba) any payment made in accordance with section 26A of the Children
(Scotland) Act 1995 (duty to provide continuing care)—

     (i) to a claimant; or

     (ii) where paragraph (3) applies, to another person ("A") which A
passes on to the claimant;]

   (c) any sports award.

[² (3) This paragraph applies only where A—

   (a) was formerly in the claimant' s care;

   (b) is aged 16 or over; and

   (c) continues to live with the claimant.]

AMENDMENTS

1. Social Security and Child Support (Care Payments and Tenant Incentive Scheme) (Amendment) Regulations 2017 (SI 2017/995) reg.7(3) (November 7, 2017).

2. Social Security and Child Support (Care Payments and Tenant Incentive Scheme) (Amendment) Regulations 2017 (SI 2017/995) reg.13(3) (November 7, 2017).

DEFINITIONS

"board and lodging"—see reg.2(1).
"claimant"—see reg.83(1).
"self-employed earner"—see reg.2(1).
"sports award"—*ibid.*
"voluntary organisation"—*ibid.*

GENERAL NOTE

4.233   This is similar to reg.37 of the Income Support Regulations/reg.100 of the JSA Regulations. See the notes to reg.37 for the effect of the 2017 amendments and payments under s.73 of the Children and Young People (Scotland) Act 2014.

See those notes also for discussion of the effect of the receipt from May/June 2020 onwards of grants under the Coronavirus Self-Employment Income Support Scheme (SEISS), of payments in respect of any furloughed employees under the Coronavirus Job Retention Scheme (CJRS) and of other sorts of grants or loans under special coronavirus schemes. It is argued there that the true effect on the calculation of self-employed earnings in means-tested benefits apart from universal credit is not as has been suggested by the government.

Calculation of net profit of self-employed earners

4.234   **98.**—(1) For the purposes of regulation 92 (calculation of earnings of self-employed earners), the earnings of a claimant to be taken into account are to be—

(a) in the case of a self-employed earner who is engaged in employment on that self-employed earner's own account, the net profit derived from that employment;

(b) in the case of a self-employed earner whose employment is carried on in partnership or is that of a share fisherman within the meaning of the Social Security (Mariners' Benefits) Regulations 1975, that self-employed earner's share of the net profit derived from that employment less—

(i) an amount in respect of income tax and of National Insurance contributions payable under the Contributions and Benefits Act calculated in accordance with regulation 99 (deduction of tax and contributions for self-employed earners); and

(ii) one half of any premium paid in the period that is relevant under regulation 92 (calculation of earnings of self-employed earners) in respect of a personal pension scheme.

(2) There is to be disregarded from a claimant's net profit any sum, where applicable, specified in paragraphs 1 to 11 of Schedule 7.

(3) For the purposes of paragraph (1)(a) the net profit of the employment, except where paragraph (9) applies, is to be calculated by taking into account the earnings of the employment over the period determined under regulation 92 less—

(a) subject to paragraphs (5) to (7), any expenses wholly and exclusively defrayed in that period for the purposes of that employment;
(b) an amount in respect of—
  (i) income tax; and
  (ii) National Insurance contributions payable under the Contributions and Benefits Act,
  calculated in accordance with regulation 99 (deduction of tax and contributions for self-employed earners); and
(c) one half of any premium paid in the period that is relevant under regulation 92 in respect of a personal pension scheme.

(4) For the purposes of paragraph (1)(b), the net profit of the employment is to be calculated by taking into account the earnings of the employment over the period determined under regulation 92 less, subject to paragraphs (5) to (7), any expenses wholly and exclusively defrayed in that period for the purpose of that employment.

(5) Subject to paragraph (6), a deduction is not to be made under paragraph (3)(a) or (4) in respect of—
(a) any capital expenditure;
(b) the depreciation of any capital asset;
(c) any sum employed or intended to be employed in the setting up or expansion of the employment;
(d) any loss incurred before the beginning of the period determined under regulation 92 (calculation of earnings of self-employed earners);
(e) the repayment of capital on any loan taken out for the purposes of the employment;
(f) any expenses incurred in providing business entertainment.

(6) A deduction is to be made under paragraph (3)(a) or (4) in respect of the repayment of capital on any loan used for—
(a) the replacement in the course of business of equipment or machinery; and
(b) the repair of an existing business asset except to the extent that any sum is payable under an insurance policy for its repair.

(7) The Secretary of State will refuse to make a deduction in respect of any expenses under paragraph (3)(a) or (4) where the Secretary of State is not satisfied that the expense has been defrayed or, having regard to the nature of the expense and its amount, that it has been reasonably incurred.

(8) For the avoidance of doubt—
(a) a deduction is not to be made under paragraph (3)(a) or (4) in respect of any sum unless it has been expended for the purposes of the business;
(b) a deduction is to be made thereunder in respect of—
  (i) the excess of any VAT paid over VAT received in the period determined under regulation 92;
  (ii) any income expended in the repair of an existing asset except to the extent that any sum is payable under an insurance policy for its repair;
  (iii) any payment of interest on a loan taken out for the purposes of the employment.

(9) Where a claimant is engaged in employment as a child minder the net profit of the employment is to be one-third of the earnings of that employment, less—

    (a) an amount in respect of—
        (i) income tax; and
        (ii) National Insurance contributions payable under the Contributions and Benefits Act,
      calculated in accordance with regulation 99 (deduction of tax and contributions for self-employed earners); and
    (b) one half of any premium paid in respect of a personal pension scheme.

(10) Notwithstanding regulation 92 (calculation of earnings of self-employed earners) and the foregoing paragraphs, the Secretary of State may assess any item of a claimant's income or expenditure over a period other than that determined under regulation 92 as may, in the particular case, enable the weekly amount of that item of income or expenditure to be determined more accurately.

(11) For the avoidance of doubt where a claimant is engaged in employment as a self-employed earner and that claimant is also engaged in one or more other employments as a self-employed or employed earner any loss incurred in any one of the claimant's employments is not to be offset against the claimant's earnings in any other of the claimant's employments.

DEFINITIONS

    "claimant"—see reg.83(1).
    "Contributions and Benefits Act"—see WRA 2007 s.65.
    "employment"—see reg.2(1).
    "personal pension scheme"—*ibid.*
    "self-employed earner"—*ibid.*

GENERAL NOTE

4.235   This is similar to reg.38 of the Income Support Regulations/reg.101 of the JSA Regulations 1996 (except that there is no equivalent of reg.101(3) of the JSA Regulations which is concerned with calculating the amount of any earnings to be deducted from old style contribution-based JSA).

Deduction of tax and contributions for self-employed earners

4.236   **99.**—(1) Subject to paragraph (2), the amount to be deducted in respect of income tax under regulation 98(1)(b)(i), (3)(b)(i) or (9)(a)(i) (calculation of net profit of self-employed earners) is to be calculated on the basis of the amount of chargeable income and as if that income were assessable to income tax at the [¹ ...] [³ basic rate, or in the case of a Scottish taxpayer, the Scottish basic rate, of tax less only the personal reliefs to which the claimant is entitled under Chapters 2, 3 and 3A of Part 3 of the Income Tax Act 2007 as are appropriate to the claimant's circumstances].

(2) If the period determined under regulation 92 is less than a year the earnings to which the [¹basic rate] [³, or the Scottish basic rate,] of tax is to be applied and the amount of the personal reliefs deductible under [³ paragraph (1) are] to be calculated on a pro rata basis.

(3) The amount to be deducted in respect of National Insurance contributions under regulation 98(1)(b)(i), (3)(b)(ii) or (9)(a)(ii) is to be the total of—
    (a) the amount of Class 2 contributions payable under section [² 11(2)] or, as the case may be, [² 11(8)] of the Contributions and Benefits

Act at the rate applicable at the date of claim except where the claimant's chargeable income is less than the amount specified in section 11(4) of that Act ([² small profits threshold]) for the tax year in which the date of claim falls; but if the assessment period is less than a year, the amount specified for that tax year is to be reduced pro rata; and

(b) the amount of Class 4 contributions (if any) which would be payable under section 15 of that Act (Class 4 contributions recoverable under the Income Tax Acts) at the percentage rate applicable at the date of claim on so much of the chargeable income as exceeds the lower limit but does not exceed the upper limit of profits and gains applicable for the tax year in which the date of claim falls; but if the assessment period is less than a year, those limits are to be reduced pro rata.

(4) In this regulation "chargeable income" means—

(a) except where sub-paragraph (b) applies, the earnings derived from the employment less any expenses deducted under paragraph (3)(a) or, as the case may be, (4) of regulation 98;

(b) in the case of employment as a child minder, one-third of the earnings of that employment.

AMENDMENTS

1. Employment and Support Allowance (Miscellaneous Amendments) Regulations 2008 (SI 2008/2428) reg.8(3) (October 27, 2008).

2. Social Security (Miscellaneous Amendments No. 2) Regulations 2015 (SI 2015/478) reg.35 (April 6, 2015)

3. Social Security (Scottish Rate of Income Tax etc.) (Amendment) Regulations 2016 (SI 2016/233) reg.6(3) (April 6, 2016).

DEFINITIONS

"claimant"—see reg.83(1).
"Contributions and Benefits Act"—see WRA 2007 s.65.
"Scottish basic rate" – see reg.2(1).
"Scottish taxpayer" – *ibid.*

GENERAL NOTE

This is similar to reg.39 of the Income Support Regulations/reg.102 of the JSA Regulations 1996.   **4.237**

CHAPTER 5

PARTICIPANTS IN THE SELF-EMPLOYMENT ROUTE

Interpretation

100. In this Chapter "special account" means, where a claimant was   **4.238** carrying on a commercial activity in respect of which assistance is received under the self-employment route, the account into which the gross receipts from that activity were payable during the period in respect of which such assistance was received.

DEFINITIONS

"claimant"—see reg.83(1).
"self-employment route"—see reg.2(1).

GENERAL NOTE

4.239   This is similar to reg.39A of the Income Support Regulations/reg.102A of the JSA Regulations 1996.

Treatment of gross receipts of participants in the self-employment route

4.240   **101.** The gross receipts of a commercial activity carried on by a claimant in respect of which assistance is received under the self-employment route, are to be taken into account in accordance with the following provisions of this Chapter. [[34], or from a Grenfell Tower payment,]

DEFINITIONS

"claimant"—see reg.83(1).
"self-employment route"—see reg.2(1).

GENERAL NOTE

4.241   This is similar to reg.39B of the Income Support Regulations/reg.102B of the JSA Regulations 1996.

Calculation of income of participants in the self-employment route

4.242   **102.**—(1) The income of a claimant who has received assistance under the self-employment route is to be calculated by taking into account the whole of the monies in the special account at the end of the last day on which such assistance was received and deducting from those monies—

(a) an amount in respect of income tax calculated in accordance with regulation 103 (deduction in respect of tax for participants in the self-employment route); and

(b) any sum to which paragraph (4) refers.

(2) Income calculated pursuant to paragraph (1) is to be apportioned equally over a period which starts on the date the income is treated as paid under paragraph (3) and is equal in length to the period beginning with the day on which assistance was first received under the self-employment route and ending on the last day on which such assistance was received.

(3) Income calculated pursuant to paragraph (1) is to be treated as paid —

(a) in the case where it is due to be paid before the first benefit week in respect of which the participant or the participant's partner first claims an income-related allowance following the last day on which assistance was received under the self-employment route, on the day in the week in which it is due to be paid which corresponds to the first day of the benefit week;

(b) in any other case, on the first day of the benefit week in which it is due to be paid.

(4) This paragraph refers, where applicable in each benefit week in respect of which income calculated pursuant to paragraph (1) is taken into account

pursuant to paragraphs (2) and (3), to the sums which would have been disregarded under paragraph 7(1) of Schedule 7 had the income been earnings.

DEFINITIONS

> "benefit week"—see reg.2(1).
> "claimant"—see reg. 83(1).
> "self-employment route"—see reg.2(1).

GENERAL NOTE

This is similar to reg.39C of the Income Support Regulations/reg.102C of the JSA   **4.243**
Regulations 1996.

Deduction in respect of tax for participants in the self-employment route

103.—(1) The amount to be deducted in respect of income tax   **4.244**
under regulation 102(1)(a) (calculation of income of participants in the
self-employment route) in respect of the period determined under regulation 102(2) is to be calculated as if—

(a) the chargeable income is the only income chargeable to tax;

[²(b) the personal reliefs applicable to the person receiving assistance
under the self-employment route under Chapters 2, 3 and 3A of Part
3 of the Income Tax Act 2007 are allowable against that income;]
and

(c) the rate at which the chargeable income less the [² personal reliefs] is
assessable to income tax is the [¹ . . .] basic rate [², or in the case of
a Scottish taxpayer, the Scottish basic rate,] of tax.

(2) For the purpose of paragraph (1), the [² basic rate, or the Scottish
basic rate, of tax to be applied and the amount of personal reliefs deductible are], where the period determined under regulation 102(2) is less than
a year, to be calculated on a pro rata basis.

(3) In this regulation, "chargeable income" means the monies in the
special account at the end of the last day upon which assistance was
received under the self-employment route.

AMENDMENTS

1. Employment and Support Allowance (Miscellaneous Amendments)
Regulations 2008 (SI 2008/2428) reg.8(4) (October 27, 2008).

2. Social Security (Scottish Rate of Income Tax etc.) (Amendment) Regulations
2016 (SI 2016/233) reg.6(4) (April 6, 2016).

DEFINITIONS

> "self-employment route"—see reg.2(1).
> "Scottish basic rate"—*ibid.*
> "Scottish taxpayer"—*ibid.*

GENERAL NOTE

This is similar to reg.39D of the Income Support Regulations/reg.102D of the   **4.245**
JSA Regulations 1996.

CHAPTER 6

OTHER INCOME

Calculation of income other than earnings

4.246   **104.**—(1) For the purposes of regulation 91 (calculation of earnings derived from employed earner's employment and income other than earnings) [² [³ . . .]] the income of a claimant which does not consist of earnings to be taken into account will, subject to paragraphs (2) to (7), be the claimant's gross income and any capital treated as income under regulation 105 (capital treated as income).

(2) There is to be disregarded from the calculation of a claimant's gross income under paragraph (1), any sum, where applicable, specified in Schedule 8.

(3) Where the payment of any benefit under the benefit Acts is subject to any deduction by way of recovery the amount to be taken into account under paragraph (1) is to be the gross amount payable.

(4) [¹Paragraphs (5) and (5A) apply] where—

    (a) a relevant payment has been made to a claimant in an academic year; and

    (b) that claimant abandons, or is dismissed from, that claimant's course of study before the payment to the claimant of the final instalment of the relevant payment.

(5) [¹Where a relevant payment is made quarterly, the] amount of a relevant payment to be taken into account for the assessment period for the purposes of paragraph (1) in respect of a claimant to whom paragraph (4) applies, is to be calculated by applying the formula—

$$\frac{A - (B \times C)}{D}$$

where—

    A = the total amount of the relevant payment which that claimant would have received had that claimant remained a student until the last day of the academic term in which the person abandoned, or was dismissed from, the course, less any deduction under regulation 137(6) (treatment of student loans);

    B = the number of benefit weeks from the benefit week immediately following that which includes the first day of that academic year to the benefit week immediately before that which includes the day on which the claimant abandoned, or was dismissed from, that claimant's course;

    C = the weekly amount of the relevant payment, before the application of the £10 disregard, which would have been taken into account as income under regulation 137(3) had the claimant not abandoned or been dismissed from, the course and, in the case of a claimant who was not entitled to an income-related allowance immediately before that claimant abandoned or was dismissed from the course, had that claimant, at that time, been entitled to an income-related allowance;

    D = the number of benefit weeks in the assessment period.

[¹(5A) Where a relevant payment is made by two or more instalments in a quarter, the amount of a relevant payment to be taken into account for the assessment period for the purposes of paragraph (1) in respect of a person to whom paragraph (4) applies, shall be calculated by applying the formula in paragraph (5) but as if—

 A = the total amount of relevant payments which that person received, or would have received, from the first day of the academic year to the day the person abandoned the course, or was dismissed from it, less any deduction under regulation 137(6).]

(6) [¹In this regulation]—

"academic year" and "student loan" have the same meanings as for the purposes of Chapter 10 of this Part;

[¹"assessment period" means—

(a) in a case where a relevant payment is made quarterly, the period beginning with the benefit week which includes the day on which the claimant abandoned, or was dismissed from, the course and ending with the benefit week which includes the last day of the last quarter for which an instalment of the relevant payment was payable to that claimant;

(b) in a case where the relevant payment is made by two or more instalments in a quarter, the period beginning with the benefit week which includes the day on which the claimant abandoned, or was dismissed from, the course and ending with the benefit week which includes—

 (i) the day immediately before the day on which the next instalment of the relevant payment would have been due had the payments continued; or

 (ii) the last day of the last quarter for which an instalment of the relevant payment was payable to that claimant,

 whichever of those dates is earlier;]

"quarter" for the purposes of the definition of "assessment period" in relation to an academic year means a period in that year—

(a) beginning on 1st January and ending on 31st March;

(b) beginning on 1st April and ending on 30th June;

(c) beginning on 1st July and ending on 31st August; or

(d) beginning on 1st September and ending on 31st December;

"relevant payment" means either a student loan or an amount intended for the maintenance of dependants referred to in regulation 132(6) (calculation of grant income) or both.

(7) In the case of income to which regulation 91(4) (calculation of income of former students) applies, the amount of income to be taken into account for the purposes of paragraph (1) is to be the amount of that income calculated in accordance with regulation 94(7) (calculation of weekly amount of income) and on the basis that none of that income has been repaid.

(8) Subject to paragraph (9), for the avoidance of doubt there is to be included as income to be taken into account under paragraph (1)—

(a) any payment to which regulation 95(2) or 97(2) (payments not earnings) applies; or

(b) in the case of a claimant who is receiving support provided under section 95 or 98 of the Immigration and Asylum Act including support provided by virtue of regulations made under Schedule 9 to that Act, the amount of such support provided in respect of essential living needs of the claimant and the claimant's partner (if any) as is specified in regulations made under paragraph 3 of Schedule 8 to that Act.

(9) In the case of a claimant who is the partner of a person subject to immigration control and whose partner is receiving support provided under section 95 or 98 of the Immigration and Asylum Act including support provided by virtue of regulations made under Schedule 9 to that Act, there is not to be included as income to be taken into account under paragraph (1) the amount of support provided in respect of essential living needs of the partner of the claimant and the claimant's dependants (if any) as is specified in regulations made under paragraph 3 of Schedule 8 to the Immigration and Asylum Act.

[⁴ (10) Where a claimant is a member of a couple and the claimant's partner is receiving a contributory allowance, and that benefit has been reduced under regulation 63 or section 11J of the Act, the amount of the benefit to be taken into account is the amount as if it had not been so reduced.

(11) Where a claimant is a husband or wife by virtue of a polygamous marriage and the other party to the marriage or any spouse additional to the marriage is receiving a contributory allowance, and that benefit has been reduced under regulation 63 or section 11J of the Act, the amount of the benefit to be taken into account is the amount as if it had not been so reduced.]

AMENDMENTS

1. Social Security (Students and Miscellaneous Amendments) Regulations 2008 (SI 2008/1599) reg.7(2) (October 27, 2008).

2. Social Security (Miscellaneous Amendments) (No. 4) Regulations 2009 (SI 2009/2655) reg.11(7) (October 26, 2009).

3. Social Security (Miscellaneous Amendments) Regulations 2011 (SI 2011/674) reg.16(8) (April 11, 2011).

4. Social Security (Miscellaneous Amendments) (No.3) Regulations 2013 (SI 2013/2536) reg.13(27) (October 29, 2013).

DEFINITIONS

"academic year"—see reg.131(1).
"benefit week"—see reg.2(1).
"claimant"—see reg.83(1).
"couple"—see reg.2(1).
"full-time student"—*ibid.*
"partner"—*ibid.*
"student loan"—see reg.131(1).

GENERAL NOTE

4.247   This is similar to reg.40 of the Income Support Regulations/reg.103 of the JSA Regulations 1996 (except that there is no equivalent to para.(9) in reg.103 of the JSA Regulations).

Capital treated as income

4.248   **105.**—(1) Capital which is payable by instalments which are outstanding on—

(a) the first day in respect of which an income-related allowance is payable or the date of the determination of the claim, whichever is earlier; or

(b) in the case of a supersession, the date of that supersession,

is to be treated as income if the aggregate of the instalments outstanding and the amount of the claimant's capital otherwise calculated in accordance with Chapter 7 of this Part exceeds £16,000.

(2) Any payment received under an annuity is to be treated as income.

(3) Any earnings to the extent that they are not a payment of income are to be treated as income.

(4) Any Career Development Loan paid pursuant to section 2 of the Employment and Training Act 1973 is to be treated as income.

(5) Where an agreement or court order provides that payments are to be made to the claimant in consequence of any personal injury to the claimant and that such payments are to be made, wholly or in part, by way of periodical payments, any such periodical payments received by the claimant (but not a payment which is treated as capital by virtue of this Part), are to be treated as income.

DEFINITION

"claimant"—see reg.83(1).

GENERAL NOTE

This is similar to reg.104 of the JSA Regulations 1996/reg.41 of the Income Support Regulations (except that there is no equivalent to reg.41(4) (repayment of PAYE tax in trade dispute cases)).   4.249

Notional income—deprivation and income on application

106.—(1) A claimant is to be treated as possessing income of which the claimant has deprived himself or herself for the purpose of securing entitlement to an employment and support allowance or increasing the amount of that allowance, or for the purpose of securing entitlement to, or increasing the amount of, income support or a jobseeker's allowance.   4.250

(2) Except in the case of—

(a) a discretionary trust;
(b) a trust derived from a payment made in consequence of a personal injury;
(c) an employment and support allowance;
(d) a jobseeker's allowance;
(e) working tax credit;
(f) child tax credit;
(g) a personal pension scheme, occupational pension scheme or a payment made by the Board of the Pension Protection Fund where the claimant [² has not attained the qualifying age for state pension credit];
[¹(ga) any sum to which paragraph (9) applies;]
[³(gb) any sum to which regulation 137(4A) (treatment of student loans) applies;]
(h) any sum to which paragraph 43(2)(a) of Schedule 9 (capital to be disregarded) applies which is administered in the way referred to in paragraph 43(1)(a) of that Schedule;
(i) any sum to which paragraph 44(a) of Schedule 9 refers; or
(j) rehabilitation allowance made under section 2 of the Employment and Training Act 1973,

income which would become available to the claimant upon application being made but which has not been acquired by the claimant is to be treated as possessed by the claimant but only from the date on which it could be expected to be acquired were an application made.

(3) A claimant who has attained the [² qualifying age for state pension credit] is to be treated as possessing—

(a) the amount of any income from an occupational pension scheme, a personal pension scheme or the Board of the Pension Protection Fund—
   (i) for which no claim has been made; and
   (ii) to which the claimant might expect to be entitled if a claim for it were made;
(b) income from an occupational pension scheme which the claimant elected to defer,

but only from the date on which it could be expected to be acquired were an application for it to be made.

(4) This paragraph applies where a claimant [² who has attained the qualifying age for state pension credit]—

(a) is entitled to money purchase benefits under an occupational pension scheme or a personal pension scheme;
(b) fails to purchase an annuity with the funds available in that scheme; and
(c) either—
   (i) defers in whole or in part the payment of any income which would have been payable to the claimant by that claimant's pension fund holder; or
   (ii) fails to take any necessary action to secure that the whole of any income which would be payable to the person by that claimant's pension fund holder upon the person applying for it, is so paid; or
   (iii) income withdrawal is not available to the claimant under that scheme.

(5) Where paragraph (4) applies, the amount of any income foregone is to be treated as possessed by that claimant, but only from the date on which it could be expected to be acquired were an application for it to be made.

(6) The amount of any income foregone in a case where paragraph (4) (c)(i) or (ii) applies is to be the [⁵ rate of the annuity which may have been purchased with the fund] and is to be determined by the Secretary of State who will take account of information provided by the pension fund holder in accordance with regulation 7(5) of the Social Security (Claims and Payments) Regulations 1987.

(7) The amount of any income foregone in a case where paragraph (4) (c)(iii) applies is to be the income that the claimant could have received without purchasing an annuity had the funds held under the relevant occupational or personal pension scheme been held under a scheme where income withdrawal was available and is to be determined in the manner specified in paragraph (6).

(8) In paragraph (4), "money purchase benefits" has the meaning it has in section 181 of the Pension Schemes Act 1993.

[¹(9) Paragraphs (1) and (2) do not apply in respect of any amount of income other than earnings, or earnings derived from employment as an employed earner, arising out of the [⁴ claimant participating as a service user].]

AMENDMENTS

1. Social Security (Miscellaneous Amendments) (No. 4) Regulations 2009 (SI 2009/2655) reg.11(8) (October 26, 2009).

2. Social Security (Miscellaneous Amendments) (No. 2) Regulations 2010 (SI 2010/641) reg.12(4) (April 6, 2010).

3. Social Security (Miscellaneous Amendments) (No. 5) Regulations 2010 (SI 2010/2429) reg.11(2) (November 1, 2010).

4. Social Security (Miscellaneous Amendments) (No. 3) Regulations 2013 (SI 2013/2536) reg.13(28) (October 29, 2013).

5. Social Security (Miscellaneous Amendments No.4) Regulations 2017 (SI 2017/1015) reg.13 (November 16, 2017).

DEFINITIONS

"claimant"—see reg.83(1).
"claimant participating as a service user"—see reg.2(8).
"occupational pension scheme"—see reg.2(1).
"payment"—*ibid.*
"pension fund holder"—*ibid.*
"personal pension scheme"—*ibid.*
"the qualifying age for state pension credit"—*ibid.*

GENERAL NOTE

This is similar to reg.42(1)–(2CA) and (8ZA) of the Income Support Regulations reg.105(1)–(5A) and (15A) of the JSA Regulations 1996.   **4.251**

Note that under para.(1) persons who have deprived themselves of income will be caught by this rule if the purpose of the deprivation was to secure entitlement to or increase the amount of ESA *or income support or JSA*. This avoids the question that might otherwise have arisen on a claimant transferring from income support (or JSA) to ESA whether a deprivation which had only been for the purposes of income support (or JSA) could be caught by para.(1). The provision has not yet been extended to cover universal credit.

On para.(2)(gb) (which has no equivalent in the Income Support or JSA Regulations), see the note to reg.137.

Notional income—income due to be paid or income paid to or in respect of a third party

107.—(1) Except in the case of a discretionary trust, or a trust derived   **4.252** from a payment made in consequence of a personal injury, any income which is due to be paid to the claimant but—

(a) has not been paid to the claimant;

(b) is not a payment prescribed in regulation 8 or 9 of the Social Security (Payments on Account, Overpayment and Recovery) Regulations 1988 (duplication and prescribed payments or maintenance payments) and not made on or before the date prescribed in relation to it,

is, except for any amount to which paragraph (2) applies, to be treated as possessed by the claimant.

(2) This paragraph applies to—

(a) an amount which is due to be paid to the claimant under an occupational pension scheme but which is not paid because the trustees or managers of the scheme have suspended or ceased payments due to an insufficiency of resources;

(b) any amount by which a payment made to the claimant from an occupational pension scheme falls short of the payment to which the claimant was due under the scheme where the shortfall arises because the trustees or managers of the scheme have insufficient resources available to them to meet in full the scheme's liabilities; or

    (c) any earnings which are due to an employed earner on the termination of that employed earner's employment by reason of redundancy but which have not been paid to that employed earner.

(3) Any payment of income, other than a payment of income specified in [¹²paragraph (5) or (5A)], made to a third party in respect of a single claimant or the claimant's partner (but not a member of the third party's family) is to be treated—

    (a) in a case where that payment is derived from—

        (i) a payment of any benefit under the benefit Acts;

        (ii) a payment from the Armed Forces and Reserve Forces Compensation Scheme;

        (iii) a war disablement pension, war widow's pension or war widower's pension; or

        (iv) a pension payable to a person as a widow, widower or surviving civil partner under any power of Her Majesty otherwise than under an enactment to make provision about pensions for or in respect of persons who have been disabled or have died in consequence of service as members of the armed forces of the Crown,

    as possessed by that single claimant, if it is paid to the claimant or by the claimant's partner, if it is paid to the claimant's partner;

    (b) in a case where that payment is a payment of an occupational pension, a pension or other periodical payment made under a personal pension scheme or a payment made by the Board of the Pension Protection Fund, as possessed by that single claimant or, as the case may be, by the claimant's partner;

    (c) in any other case, as possessed by that single claimant or the claimant's partner to the extent that it is used for the food, ordinary clothing or footwear, household fuel, rent for which housing benefit is payable, or any housing costs to the extent that they are met under regulations 67(1)(c) or 68(1)(d) (housing costs), of that single claimant or, as the case may be, of the claimant's partner, or is used for any council tax or water charges for which that claimant or that partner is liable,

but, except where sub-paragraph (a) applies, this paragraph does not apply to any payment in kind to the third party.

(4) Any payment of income, other than a payment of income specified in [¹²paragraph (5) or (5A)], made to a single claimant or the claimant's partner in respect of a third party (but not in respect of another member of the claimant's family) is to be treated as possessed by that single claimant or, as the case may be, the claimant's partner, to the extent that it is kept or used by that claimant or used by or on behalf of the claimant's partner but, except where paragraph (3)(a) applies, this paragraph does not apply to any payment in kind to the third party.

(5) Paragraphs (3) and (4) do not apply in respect of a payment of income made—

    (a) under [⁴or by] the Macfarlane Trust, the Macfarlane (Special Payments) Trust, the Macfarlane (Special Payments) (No. 2) Trust, the Fund, the Eileen Trust[³, MFET Limited][⁶, the Skipton Fund, the Caxton Foundation][⁹, the Scottish Infected Blood Support Scheme][¹¹, an approved blood scheme][¹⁰, the London Emergencies Trust, the We Love Manchester Emergency Fund] [¹², the National Emergencies Trust] or [¹the Independent Living Fund (2006)];

(b) pursuant to section 19(1)(a) of the Coal Industry Act 1994 (concessionary coal); or

(c) pursuant to section 2 of the Employment and Training Act 1973 in respect of a person's participation—

    (i) in an employment programme specified in regulation 75(1)(a)(ii) of the Jobseeker's Allowance Regulations;

    (ii) in a training scheme specified in regulation 75(1)(b)(ii) of those Regulations;

    (iii) in the Intensive Activity Period specified in regulation 75(1)(a)(iv) of those Regulations;

    (iv) in a qualifying course within the meaning specified in regulation 17A(7) of those Regulations; or

[^{5} (ca) in respect of a person's participation in [^{7} a scheme prescribed in regulation 3 of the Jobseeker's Allowance (Schemes for Assisting Persons to Obtain Employment) Regulations 2013] or the Mandatory Work Activity Scheme; or]

(d) under an occupational pension scheme, in respect of a pension or other periodical payment made under a personal pension scheme or a payment made by the Board of the Pension Protection Fund where—

    (i) a bankruptcy order has been made in respect of the person in respect of whom the payment has been made or, in Scotland, the estate of that person is subject to sequestration or a judicial factor has been appointed on that person's estate under section 41 of the Solicitors (Scotland) Act 1980;

    (ii) the payment is made to the trustee in bankruptcy or any other person acting on behalf of the creditors; and

    (iii) the person referred to in paragraph (i) and that person's partner (if any) does not possess, or is not treated as possessing, any other income apart from that payment.

[^{12}(5A) Paragraphs (3) and (4) do not apply in respect of a payment of income which is a Grenfell Tower payment.]

(6) Where the claimant resides in a care home, an Abbeyfield Home or an independent hospital, or is temporarily absent from such a home or hospital, any payment made by a person other than the claimant or a member of the claimant's family in respect of some or all of the cost of maintaining the claimant or the claimant's partner in that home or hospital is to be treated as possessed by the claimant or the claimant's partner.

(7) In paragraph (2)(a) and (b) "resources" has the same meaning as in section 181(1) of the Pension Schemes Act 1993.

[^{2} (8) Paragraphs (1), (3) and (4) do not apply in respect of any amount of income other than earnings, or earnings derived from employment as an employed earner, arising out of the [^{8} claimant participating as a service user].]

AMENDMENTS

1. Employment and Support Allowance (Miscellaneous Amendments) Regulations 2008 (SI 2008/2428) reg.8(5) (October 27, 2008).

2. Social Security (Miscellaneous Amendments) (No. 4) Regulations 2009 (SI 2009/2655) reg.11(9) (October 26, 2009).

3. Social Security (Miscellaneous Amendments) (No. 2) Regulations 2010 (SI 2010/641) reg.12(3)(b) (April 6, 2010).

4. Social Security (Miscellaneous Amendments) (No. 2) Regulations 2010 (SI 2010/641) reg.12(5)(a) (April 6, 2010).

5. Social Security (Miscellaneous Amendments) (No. 2) Regulations 2011 (SI 2011/1707) reg.4(4)(b) and (5) (August 5, 2011).

6. Social Security (Miscellaneous Amendments) (No. 3) Regulations 2011 (SI 2011/2425) reg.23(8) (October 31, 2011).

7. Jobseeker's Allowance (Schemes for Assisting Persons to Obtain Employment) Regulations 2013 reg.15(b) (February 12, 2013).

8. Social Security (Miscellaneous Amendments) (No. 3) Regulations 2013 (SI 2013/2536) reg.13(29) (October 29, 2013).

9. Social Security (Scottish Infected Blood Support Scheme) Regulations 2017 (SI 2017/329) reg.8(3)(a) (April 3, 2017).

10. Social Security (Emergency Funds) (Amendment) Regulations 2017 (SI 2017/689) reg.8(3)(a) (June 19, 2017).

11. Social Security (Infected Blood and Thalidomide Regulations 2017 (SI 2017/870) reg.8(3)(a) (October 23, 2017).

12. Social Security (Income and Capital) (Miscellaneous Amendments) Regulations 2020 (SI 2020/618) reg.7(3) (July 15, 2020).

DEFINITIONS

"Abbeyfield Home"—see reg.2(1).
"approved blood scheme"—*ibid.*
"Armed Forces and Reserve Forces Compensation Scheme"—*ibid.*
"benefit Acts"—*ibid.*
"care home"—*ibid.*
"Caxton Foundation"—*ibid.*
"claimant"—see reg.83(1).
"claimant participating as a service user"—see reg.2(8).
"Eileen Trust"—see reg.2(1).
"family"—*ibid.*
"the Fund"—*ibid.*
"Grenfell Tower Payment"—*ibid.*
"independent hospital"—*ibid.*
"the Independent Living Fund (2006)"—*ibid.*
"the London Emergencies Trust"—*ibid.*
"Macfarlane (Special Payments) Trust"—*ibid.*
"Macfarlane (Special Payments) (No. 2) Trust"—*ibid.*
"Macfarlane Trust"—*ibid.*
"MFET Limited"—*ibid.*
"the National Emergencies Trust"—*ibid.*
"occupational pension"—*ibid.*
"occupational pension scheme"—*ibid.*
"ordinary clothing and footwear"—*ibid.*
"partner"—*ibid.*
"payment"—*ibid.*
"personal pension"—*ibid.*
"personal pension scheme"—*ibid.*
"Scottish Infected Blood Support Scheme"—*ibid.*
"single claimant"—*ibid.*
"Skipton Fund"—*ibid.*
"war disablement pension"—*ibid.*
"war widow's pension"—*ibid.*
"war widower's pension"—*ibid.*
"water charges"—*ibid.*
"the We Love Manchester Emergency Fund"—*ibid.*

GENERAL NOTE

4.253   This is similar to reg.42(3)–(4A), (8A) and (8ZA) of the Income Support Regulations/reg.105(6)–(11) and (15A), together with the definition of "resources" in reg.105(16), of the JSA Regulations 1996 (except that paras (3) and (4) do not contain any special provisions relating to trade disputes).

Notional income—other income

108.—(1) Where a claimant's earnings are not ascertainable at the time of the determination of the claim or of any revision or supersession the Secretary of State will treat the claimant as possessing such earnings as is reasonable in the circumstances of the case having regard to the number of hours worked and the earnings paid for comparable employment in the area.

4.254

(2) Where the amount of a subsistence allowance paid to a claimant in a benefit week is less than the amount of income-based jobseeker's allowance that claimant would have received in that benefit week had it been payable to the claimant, less 50p, the claimant is to be treated as possessing the amount which is equal to the amount of income-based jobseeker's allowance which the claimant would have received in that week, less 50p.

(3) Subject to paragraph (4), where—

(a) a claimant performs a service for another person; and

(b) that person makes no payment of earnings or pays less than that paid for a comparable employment in the area,

the Secretary of State is to treat the claimant as possessing such earnings (if any) as is reasonable for that employment unless the claimant satisfies the Secretary of State that the means of that person are insufficient for the person to pay, or to pay more, for the service.

(4) Paragraph (3) will not apply—

(a) to a claimant who is engaged by a charitable or voluntary organisation or who is a volunteer if the Secretary of State is satisfied in any of those cases that it is reasonable for the claimant to provide the service free of charge;

(b) in a case where the service is performed in connection with—

(i) the claimant's participation in an employment or training programme in accordance with regulation 19(1)(q) of the Jobseeker's Allowance Regulations, other than where the service is performed in connection with the claimant's participation in the Intensive Activity Period specified in regulation 75(1)(a)(iv) of those Regulations; or

(ii) the claimant's or the claimant's partner's participation in an employment or training programme as defined in regulation 19(3) of those Regulations for which a training allowance is not payable or, where such an allowance is payable, it is payable for the sole purpose of reimbursement of travelling or meal expenses to the claimant or the claimant's partner participating in that programme;

(c) to a claimant who is engaged in work experience whilst participating in—

(i) the New Deal for Lone Parents; or

(ii) a scheme which has been approved by the Secretary of State as supporting the objectives of the New Deal for Lone Parents; or

(d) to a claimant who is participating in a work placement approved in writing by the Secretary of State before the placement starts;

(e) in sub-paragraph (d) "work placement" means practical work experience with an employer, which is neither paid nor undertaken in expectation of payment.

[¹ (5) Paragraphs (1) and (3) do not apply in respect of any amount of income other than earnings, or earnings derived from employment as an employed earner, arising out of the [² claimant participating as a service user].]

AMDENDMENTS

1. Social Security (Miscellaneous Amendments) (No. 4) Regulations 2009 (SI 2009/2655) reg.11(10) (October 26, 2009).
2. Social Security (Miscellaneous Amendments) (No. 3) Regulations 2013 (SI 2013/2536) reg.13(30) (October 29, 2013).

DEFINITIONS

"benefit week"—see reg.2(1).
"claimant"—see reg.83(1).
"claimant participating as a service user"—see reg. 2(8).
"partner"—see reg.2(1).
"payment"—*ibid.*
"subsistence allowance"—*ibid.*
"voluntary organisation"—*ibid.*

GENERAL NOTE

4.255   This is similar to reg.42(5)–(6AA) and (8ZA) of the Income Support Regulations/ reg.105(11A)–(13A) and (15A), together with the definition of "work placement" in reg.105(16), of the JSA Regulations 1996. There are some differences in reg.105 of the JSA Regulations (e.g. there is no equivalent to para.(4)(c) which relates to lone parents).

Notional income—calculation and interpretation

4.256   **109.**—(1) Where a claimant is treated as possessing any income under regulation 106 or 107 the foregoing provisions of this Part are to apply for the purposes of calculating the amount of that income as if a payment had actually been made and as if it were actual income which the claimant does possess.

(2) Where a claimant is treated as possessing any earnings under regulation 108(1) or (3) the foregoing provisions of this Part are to apply for the purposes of calculating the amount of those earnings as if a payment had actually been made and as if they were actual earnings which the claimant does possess except that paragraph (3) of regulation 96 (calculation of net earnings of employed earners) does not apply and the claimant's net earnings are to be calculated by taking into account the earnings which the claimant is treated as possessing, less—

(a) where the period over which those earnings are to be taken into account is a year or more, an amount in respect of income tax equivalent to an amount calculated by applying to those earnings the [¹ . . .] [² basic rate, or in the case of a Scottish taxpayer, the Scottish basic rate, of tax in the year of assessment less only personal reliefs to which the claimant is entitled under Chapters 2, 3 and 3A of Part 3 of the Income Tax Act 2007 as are appropriate to the claimant's circumstances];

(b) where [² . . .] the period over which those earnings are to be taken into account is less than a year, the earnings to which the [¹basic rate] [², or the Scottish basic rate,] of tax is to be applied and the amount of the [²personal reliefs deductible under this paragraph are] to be calculated on a pro rata basis;

(c) where the weekly amount of those earnings equals or exceeds the lower earnings limit, an amount representing primary Class 1 contributions under section 6(1)(a) of the Contributions and Benefits Act, calculated by applying to those earnings the initial and main primary percentages in accordance with section 8(1)(a) and (b) of that Act; and

(d) one-half of any sum payable by the claimant in respect of a pay period by way of a contribution towards an occupational or personal pension scheme.

AMENDMENTS

1. Employment and Support Allowance (Miscellaneous Amendments) Regulations 2008 (SI 2008/2428) reg.8(6) (October 27, 2008).
2. Social Security (Scottish Rate of Income Tax etc.) (Amendment) Regulations 2016 (SI 2016/233) reg.6(5) (April 6, 2016).

DEFINITIONS

"claimant"—see reg.83(1).
"employed earner"—see reg.2(1).
"pay period"—*ibid*.
"payment"—*ibid*.
"Scottish basic rate" – *ibid*.
"Scottish taxpayer" – *ibid*.

GENERAL NOTE

This is similar to reg.42(7)–(8) of the Income Support Regulations/reg.105(14)–(15) of the JSA Regulations 1996.   4.257

CHAPTER 7

CAPITAL

Capital limit

110. For the purposes of paragraph 6(1)(b) of Schedule 1 to the Act as it applies to an income-related allowance (no entitlement to benefit if capital exceeds prescribed amount), the prescribed amount is £16,000.   4.258

DEFINITION

"the Act"—see reg.2(1).

GENERAL NOTE

This contains a similar provision to that in reg.45 of the Income Support Regulations/reg.107 of the JSA Regulations 1996.   4.259

Calculation of capital

111.—(1) For the purposes of [¹sections 1(2)] and 4 of, and Part 2 of Schedule 1 to, the Act as it applies to an income-related allowance, the capital of a claimant to be taken into account is, subject to paragraph (2), to be the whole of the claimant's capital calculated in accordance with this   4.260

Part and any income treated as capital under regulation 112 (income treated as capital).

(2) There is to be disregarded from the calculation of a claimant's capital under paragraph (1) any capital, where applicable, specified in Schedule 9.

AMENDMENT

1. Employment and Support Allowance (Miscellaneous Amendments) Regulations 2008 (SI 2008/2428) reg.8(7) (October 27, 2008).

DEFINITIONS

"the Act"—see reg. 2(1).
"claimant"—see reg.83(1).

GENERAL NOTE

4.261   This is similar to reg.46 of the Income Support Regulations/reg.108 of the JSA Regulations 1996. See e.g. *RB v SSWP (ESA)* [2016] UKUT 384 (AAC).

Income treated as capital

4.262   **112.**—(1) Any bounty derived from employment to which regulation 43(1)(e) and paragraph 12 of Schedule 7 apply and paid at intervals of at least one year is to be treated as capital.

(2) Any amount by way of a refund of income tax paid in respect of, or deducted from, profits or income chargeable to tax under the provisions in Part 2 of the Income Tax (Trading and Other Income) Act 2005 or Part 2 of the Income Tax (Earnings and Pensions) Act 2003 is to be treated as capital.

(3) Any holiday pay which is not earnings under regulation 95(1)(d) (earnings of employed earners) is to be treated as capital.

(4) Except any income derived from capital disregarded under paragraph 1, 2, 4 to 8, 10, 16, 43 or 44 of Schedule 9, any income derived from capital is to be treated as capital but only from the date it is normally due to be credited to the claimant's account.

(5) In the case of employment as an employed earner, any advance of earnings or any loan made by the claimant's employer is to be treated as capital.

(6) Any payment under section 30 of the Prison Act 1952 (payments for discharged prisoners) or allowance under section 17 of the Prisons (Scotland) Act 1989 (allowances to prisoners on discharge) is to be treated as capital.

(7) Any charitable or voluntary payment which is not made or not due to be made at regular intervals, other than one to which paragraph (8) applies, is to be treated as capital.

[¹(8) This paragraph applies to --
(a) any payment which is made under or by the Macfarlane Trust, the Macfarlane (Special Payments) Trust, the Macfarlane (Special Payments) (No.2) Trust, the Fund, the Eileen Trust, MFET Ltd, the Skipton Fund, the Caxton Foundation, the Scottish Infected Blood Support Scheme, an approved blood scheme, the London Emergencies Trust, the We Love Manchester Emergency Fund, the National Emergencies Trust or the Independent Living Fund (2006); or
(b) any Grenfell Tower payment.]

(9) Any arrears of subsistence allowance which are paid to a claimant as a lump sum are to be treated as capital.

AMENDMENTS

1. Social Security (Income and Capital) (Miscellaneous Amendments) Regulations 2020 (SI 2020/618) reg.7(4) (July 15, 2020).

DEFINITIONS

"approved blood scheme"—see reg.2(1).
"Caxton Foundation"—*ibid.*
"claimant"—see reg.83(1).
"Eileen Trust"—see reg.2(1).
"employed earner"—*ibid.*
"the Fund"—*ibid.*
"Grenfell Tower Payment"—*ibid.*
"the Independent Living Fund (2006)"—*ibid.*
"the London Emergencies Trust"—*ibid.*
"Macfarlane (Special Payments) Trust"—*ibid.*
"Macfarlane (Special Payments) (No. 2) Trust"—*ibid.*
"Macfarlane Trust"—*ibid.*
"MFET Limited"—*ibid.*
"the National Emergencies Trust"—*ibid.*
"Scottish Infected Blood Support Scheme"—*ibid.*
"Skipton Fund"—*ibid.*
"subsistence allowance"—*ibid.*
"the We Love Manchester Emergency Fund"—*ibid.*

GENERAL NOTE

This is similar to reg.48 of the Income Support Regulations/reg.110 of the JSA   **4.263**
Regulations 1996 (except that it does not contain any special provisions relating to trade disputes).

Calculation of capital in the United Kingdom

113. Capital which a claimant possesses in the United Kingdom is to be   **4.264**
calculated at its current market or surrender value less—
(a) where there would be expenses attributable to sale, 10%; and
(b) the amount of any incumbrance secured on it.

DEFINITION

"claimant"—see reg.83(1).

GENERAL NOTE

This is similar to reg.49 of the Income Support Regulations/reg.111 of the JSA   **4.265**
Regulations.

Calculation of capital outside the United Kingdom

114. Capital which a claimant possesses in a country outside the United   **4.266**
Kingdom is to be calculated—
(a) in a case in which there is no prohibition in that country against the transfer to the United Kingdom of an amount equal to its current market or surrender value in that country, at that value;

(b) in a case where there is such a prohibition, at the price which it
would realise if sold in the United Kingdom to a willing buyer,
less, where there would be expenses attributable to sale, 10% and the
amount of any incumbrance secured on it.

DEFINITION

"claimant"—see reg.83(1).

GENERAL NOTE

4.267   This is similar to reg.50 of the Income Support Regulations/reg.112 of the JSA
Regulations 1996.

Notional capital

4.268   **115.**—(1) A claimant is to be treated as possessing capital of which the
claimant has deprived himself or herself for the purpose of securing entitlement to an employment and support allowance or increasing the amount
of that allowance, or for the purpose of securing entitlement to, or increasing the amount of, income support or a jobseeker's allowance except—
   (a) where that capital is derived from a payment made in consequence of
       any personal injury and is placed on trust for the benefit of the claimant;
   (b) to the extent that the capital which the claimant is treated as pos-
       sessing is reduced in accordance with regulation 116 (diminishing
       notional capital rule);
   (c) any sum to which paragraph 43(2)(a) of Schedule 9 (capital to be
       disregarded) applies which is administered in the way referred to in
       paragraph 43(1)(a); or
   (d) any sum to which paragraph 44(a) of Schedule 9 refers.
   (2) Except in the case of—
   (a) a discretionary trust;
   (b) a trust derived from a payment made in consequence of a personal
       injury;
   (c) any loan which would be obtainable only if secured against capital
       disregarded under Schedule 9;
   (d) a personal pension scheme;
   (e) an occupational pension scheme or a payment made by the Board of
       the Pension Protection Fund where the claimant [⁴ has not attained
       the qualifying age for state pension credit]; or
   (f) any sum to which paragraph 43(2)(a) of Schedule 9 (capital to be
       disregarded) applies which is administered in a way referred to in
       paragraph 43(1)(a); or
   (g) any sum to which paragraph 44(a) of Schedule 9 refers,
any capital which would become available to the claimant upon application
being made but which has not been acquired by the claimant is to be treated
as possessed by the claimant but only from the date on which it could be
expected to be acquired were an application made.
   (3) Any payment of capital, other than a payment of capital specified in
[¹¹paragraph (5) or (5A)], made to a third party in respect of a single claimant
or the claimant's partner (but not a member of the third party's family) is to be
treated—
   (a) in a case where that payment is derived from—

    (i) a payment of any benefit under the benefit Acts;

    (ii) a payment from the Armed Forces and Reserve Forces Compensation Scheme;

    (iii) a war disablement pension, war widow's pension or war widower's pension; or

    (iv) a pension payable to a person as a widow, widower or surviving civil partner under any power of Her Majesty otherwise than under an enactment to make provision about pensions for or in respect of persons who have been disabled or who have died in consequence of service as members of the armed forces of the Crown,

as possessed by that single claimant, if it is paid to that claimant, or by the claimant's partner, if it is paid to that partner;

(b) in a case where that payment is a payment of an occupational pension, a pension or other periodical payment made under a personal pension scheme or a payment made by the Board of the Pension Protection Fund, as possessed by that single claimant or, as the case may be, by the claimant's partner;

(c) in any other case, as possessed by that single claimant or the claimant's partner to the extent that it is used for the food, ordinary clothing or footwear, household fuel, rent for which housing benefit is payable or any housing costs to the extent that they are met under regulation 67(1)(c) and 68(1)(d) (housing costs) of that single claimant or, as the case may be, of the claimant's partner, or is used for any council tax or water charges for which that claimant or partner is liable.

(4) Any payment of capital, other than a payment of capital specified in [¹¹paragraph (5) or (5A)] made to a single claimant or the claimant's partner in respect of a third party (but not in respect of another member of the claimant's family) is to be treated as possessed by that single claimant or, as the case may be, the claimant's partner, to the extent that it is kept or used by that claimant or used by or on behalf of the claimant's partner.

(5) Paragraphs (3) and (4) will not apply in respect of a payment of capital made—

(a) under [³or by] the Macfarlane Trust, the Macfarlane (Special Payments) Trust, the Macfarlane (Special Payments) (No. 2) Trust, the Fund, the Eileen Trust [², MFET Limited][¹, the Independent Living Fund (2006)], the Skipton Fund[⁶, the Caxton Foundation] [⁸, the Scottish Infected Blood Support Scheme][¹⁰, an approved blood scheme][⁹, the London Emergencies Trust, the We Love Manchester Emergency Fund] [¹¹, the National Emergencies Trust] or the London Bombings Relief Charitable Fund;

(b) pursuant to section 2 of the Employment and Training Act 1973 in respect of a claimant's participation—

    (i) in an employment programme specified in regulation 75(1)(a)(ii) of the Jobseeker's Allowance Regulations;

    (ii) in a training scheme specified in regulation 75(1)(b)(ii) of those Regulations; or

    (iii) in the Intensive Activity Period specified in regulation 75(1)(a)(iv) of those Regulations; or

    (iv) in a qualifying course within the meaning specified in regulation 17A(7) of those Regulations;

[⁵ (ba) in respect of a person's participation in [⁷ a scheme prescribed in regulation 3 of the Jobseeker's Allowance (Schemes for Assisting Persons to Obtain Employment) Regulations 2013] or the Mandatory Work Activity Scheme;]

(c) under an occupational pension scheme, in respect of a pension or other periodical payment made under a personal pension scheme or a payment made by the Board of the Pension Protection Fund where—

    (i) a bankruptcy order has been made in respect of the person in respect of whom the payment has been made or, in Scotland, the estate of that person is subject to sequestration or a judicial factor has been appointed on that person's estate under section 41 of the Solicitors (Scotland) Act 1980;

    (ii) the payment is made to the trustee in bankruptcy or any other person acting on behalf of the creditors; and

    (iii) the person referred to in paragraph (i) and that person's partner (if any) does not possess, or is not treated as possessing, any other income apart from that payment.

[[11](5A) Paragraphs (3) and (4) do not apply in respect of a payment of income which is a Grenfell Tower payment.]

(6) Where a claimant stands in relation to a company in a position analogous to that of a sole owner or partner in the business of that company, the claimant is to be treated as if that claimant were such sole owner or partner and in such a case—

(a) the value of the claimant's holding in that company, notwithstanding regulation 111 (calculation of capital), is to be disregarded; and

(b) the claimant will, subject to paragraph (7), be treated as possessing an amount of capital equal to the value or, as the case may be, the claimant's share of the value of the capital of that company and the foregoing provisions of this Chapter are to apply for the purposes of calculating that amount as if it were actual capital which the claimant does possess.

(7) For so long as the claimant undertakes activities in the course of the business of the company, the amount which the claimant is treated as possessing under paragraph (6) is to be disregarded.

(8) Where a claimant is treated as possessing capital under any of paragraphs (1) to (6), the foregoing provisions of this Chapter are to apply for the purposes of calculating its amount as if it were actual capital which the claimant does possess.

(9) For the avoidance of doubt a claimant is to be treated as possessing capital under paragraph (1) only if the capital of which the claimant has deprived himself or herself is actual capital.

AMENDMENTS

1. Employment and Support Allowance (Miscellaneous Amendments) Regulations 2008 (SI 2008/2428) reg.8(8) (October 27, 2008).

2. Social Security (Miscellaneous Amendments) (No. 2) Regulations 2010 (SI 2010/641) reg.12(3)(d) (April 6, 2010).

3. Social Security (Miscellaneous Amendments) (No. 2) Regulations 2010 (SI 2010/641) reg.12(5)(c) (April 6, 2010).

4. Social Security (Miscellaneous Amendments) (No. 2) Regulations 2010 (SI 2010/641) reg.12(6) (April 6, 2010).

5. Social Security (Miscellaneous Amendments) (No. 2) Regulations 2011 (SI 2011/1707) reg.4(6)(b) and (7) (August 5, 2011).

6. Social Security (Miscellaneous Amendments) (No. 3) Regulations 2011 (SI 2011/2425) reg.23(9) (October 31, 2011).

7. Jobseeker's Allowance (Schemes for Assisting Persons to Obtain Employment) Regulations 2013 (SI 2013/276) reg.15(b) (February 12, 2013).

8. Social Security (Scottish Infected Blood Support Scheme) Regulations 2017 (SI 2017/329) reg.8(3)(c) (April 3, 2017).

9. Social Security (Emergency Funds) (Amendment) Regulations 2017 (SI 2017/689) reg.8(3)(c) (June 19, 2017).

10. Social Security (Infected Blood and Thalidomide Regulations 2017 (SI 2017/870) reg.8(3)(c) (October 23, 2017).

11. Social Security (Income and Capital) (Miscellaneous Amendments) Regulations 2020 (SI 2020/618) reg.7(5) (July 15, 2020).

DEFINITIONS

"approved blood scheme"—see reg.2(1).
"Armed Forces and Reserve Forces Compensation Scheme"—*ibid.*
"benefit Acts"—*ibid.*
"Caxton Foundation"—*ibid.*
"claimant"—see reg.83(1).
"Eileen Trust"—see reg.2(1).
"family"—*ibid.*
"the Fund"—*ibid.*
"Grenfell Tower Payment"—*ibid.*
"the Independent Living Fund (2006)"—*ibid.*
"London Bombings Relief Charitable Fund"—*ibid.*
"the London Emergencies Trust"—*ibid.*
"Macfarlane (Special Payments) Trust"—*ibid.*
"Macfarlane (Special Payments) (No. 2) Trust"—*ibid.*
"Macfarlane Trust"—*ibid.*
"MFET Limited"—*ibid.*
"the National Emergencies Trust"—*ibid.*
"occupational pension"—*ibid.*
"occupational pension scheme"—*ibid.*
"ordinary clothing and footwear"—*ibid.*
"partner"—*ibid.*
"payment"—*ibid.*
"personal pension scheme"—*ibid.*
"the qualifying age for state pension credit"—*ibid.*
"Scottish Infected Blood Support Scheme"—*ibid.*
"single claimant"—*ibid.*
"Skipton Fund"—*ibid.*
"war disablement pension"—*ibid.*
"war widow's pension"—*ibid.*
"war widower's pension"—*ibid.*
"water charges"—*ibid.*
"the We Love Manchester Emergency Fund"—*ibid.*

GENERAL NOTE

This is similar to reg.51 of the Income Support Regulations /reg.113 of the JSA **4.269** Regulations 1996. See e.g. *RB v SSWP (ESA)* [2016] UKUT 384 (AAC).

Note that under para.(1) persons who have deprived themselves of capital will be caught by this rule if the purpose of the deprivation was to secure entitlement to or increase the amount of ESA *or income support or JSA*. This avoids the question that might otherwise have arisen on a claimant transferring from income support (or JSA) to ESA whether a deprivation which had only been for the purposes of income support (or JSA) could be caught by para.(1). The provision has not yet been extended to cover universal credit.

Diminishing notional capital rule

4.270   **116.**—(1) Where a claimant is treated as possessing capital under regulation 115(1) (notional capital), the amount which the claimant is treated as possessing—

(a) in the case of a week that is subsequent to—
    (i) the relevant week in respect of which the conditions set out in paragraph (2) are satisfied; or
    (ii) a week which follows that relevant week and which satisfies those conditions,
    is to be reduced by an amount determined under paragraph (2);

(b) in the case of a week in respect of which paragraph (1)(a) does not apply but where—
    (i) that week is a week subsequent to the relevant week; and
    (ii) that relevant week is a week in which the condition in paragraph (3) is satisfied,
    is to be reduced by the amount determined under paragraph (3).

(2) This paragraph applies to a benefit week or part-week where the claimant satisfies the conditions that—

(a) the claimant is in receipt of an income-related allowance; and

(b) but for regulation 115(1), the claimant would have received an additional amount of an income-related allowance in that benefit week or, as the case may be, that part-week,

and in such a case, the amount of the reduction for the purposes of paragraph (1)(a) is to be equal to that additional amount.

(3) Subject to paragraph (4), for the purposes of paragraph (1)(b) the condition is that the claimant would have been entitled to an income-related allowance in the relevant week, but for regulation 115(1), and in such a case the amount of the reduction is to be equal to the aggregate of—

(a) the amount of an income-related allowance to which the claimant would have been entitled in the relevant week but for regulation 115(1); and for the purposes of this sub-paragraph if the relevant week is a part-week that amount is to be determined by dividing the amount of an income-related allowance to which the claimant would have been so entitled by the number equal to the number of days in the part-week and multiplying the quotient by 7;

(b) the amount of housing benefit (if any) equal to the difference between the claimant's maximum housing benefit and the amount (if any) of housing benefit which the claimant is awarded in respect of the benefit week, within the meaning of regulation 2(1) of the Housing Benefit Regulations 2006 (interpretation), which includes the last day of the relevant week;

(c) the amount of council tax benefit (if any) equal to the difference between the claimant's maximum council tax benefit and the amount (if any) of council tax benefit which the claimant is awarded in respect of the benefit week which includes the last day of the relevant week, and for this purpose "benefit week" [[1] means a period of 7 consecutive days beginning on a Monday and ending on a Sunday].

(4) The amount determined under paragraph (3) is to be re-determined under that paragraph if the claimant makes a further claim for an income-

related allowance and the conditions in paragraph (5) are satisfied, and in such a case—

    (a) sub-paragraphs (a) to (c) of paragraph (3) will apply as if for the words "relevant week" there were substituted the words "relevant subsequent week"; and

    (b) subject to paragraph (6), the amount as re-determined is to have effect from the first week following the relevant subsequent week in question.

(5) The conditions are that—

    (a) a further claim is made 26 or more weeks after—

        (i) the date on which the claimant made a claim for an income-related allowance in respect of which the claimant was first treated as possessing the capital in question under regulation 115(1);

        (ii) in a case where there has been at least one re-determination in accordance with paragraph (4), the date on which the claimant last made a claim for an income-related allowance which resulted in the weekly amount being re-determined; or

        (iii) the date on which the claimant last ceased to be in receipt of an income-related allowance;

    whichever last occurred; and

    (b) the claimant would have been entitled to an income-related allowance but for regulation 115(1).

(6) The amount as re-determined pursuant to paragraph (4) is not to have effect if it is less than the amount which applied in that case immediately before the re-determination and in such a case the higher amount is to continue to have effect.

(7) For the purposes of this regulation—

"part-week" means a period to which Part 14 (periods of less than a week) applies;

"relevant week" means the benefit week or part-week in which the capital in question of which the claimant has deprived himself or herself within the meaning of regulation 115(1)—

    (a) was first taken into account for the purpose of determining the claimant's entitlement to an income-related allowance, a jobseeker's allowance or income support; or

    (b) was taken into account on a subsequent occasion for the purpose of determining or re-determining the claimant's entitlement to an income-related allowance, a jobseeker's allowance or income support on that subsequent occasion and that determination or re-determination resulted in the claimant's beginning to receive, or ceasing to receive, an income-related allowance, a jobseeker's allowance or income support;

and where more than one benefit week or part-week is identified by reference to paragraphs (a) and (b) of this definition the later or latest such benefit week or, as the case may be, the later or latest such part-week;

"relevant subsequent week" means the benefit week or part-week which includes the day on which the further claim or, if more than one further claim has been made, the last such claim was made.

Amendment

1. Council Tax Benefit Abolition (Consequential Provision) Regulations 2013 (SI 2013/458) reg.4 and Sch.2 para.8 (April 1, 2013).

DEFINITIONS

> "benefit week"—see reg.2(1).
> "claimant"—see reg.83(1).
> "week"—see reg.2(1).

GENERAL NOTE

4.271 This is similar to reg.51A of the Income Support Regulations/reg.114 of the JSA Regulations 1996.

Capital jointly held

4.272 **117.** Except where a claimant possesses capital which is disregarded under regulation 115(6) (notional capital), where a claimant and one or more persons are beneficially entitled in possession to any capital asset they are to be treated as if each of them were entitled in possession to the whole beneficial interest therein in an equal share and the foregoing provisions of this Chapter are to apply for the purposes of calculating the amount of capital which the claimant is treated as possessing as if it were actual capital which the claimant does possess.

DEFINITION

> "claimant"—see reg.83(1).

GENERAL NOTE

4.273 This is similar to reg.52 of the Income Support Regulations/reg.115 of the JSA Regulations 1996.

Calculation of tariff income from capital

4.274 **118.**—(1) Except where the circumstances prescribed in paragraph (3) apply to the claimant, where the claimant's capital calculated in accordance with this Part exceeds £6,000 it is to be treated as equivalent to a weekly income of £1 for each complete £250 in excess of £6,000 but not exceeding £16,000.

(2) Where the circumstances prescribed in paragraph (3) apply to the claimant and that claimant's capital calculated in accordance with this Part exceeds £10,000, it is to be treated as equivalent to a weekly income of £1 for each complete £250 in excess of £10,000 but not exceeding £16,000.

(3) For the purposes of paragraph (2) the prescribed circumstances are that the claimant lives permanently in—

(a) a care home or an independent hospital;

(b) an Abbeyfield Home; or

(c) accommodation provided under section 3 of, and Part 2 of the Schedule to, the Polish Resettlement Act 1947 (provision of accommodation in camps) where the claimant requires personal care by reason of old age, disablement, past or present dependence on alcohol or drugs, past or present mental disorder or a terminal illness and the care is provided in the home.

(4) For the purposes of paragraph (3), a claimant is to be treated as living permanently in such home, hospital or accommodation where the claimant is absent—

(a) from a home, hospital or accommodation referred to in sub-paragraph (a) or (b) of paragraph (3)—

    (i) in the case of a claimant over pensionable age, for a period not exceeding 52 weeks; and

    (ii) in any other case, for a period not exceeding 13 weeks;

(b) from accommodation referred to in sub-paragraph (c) of paragraph (3), where the claimant, with the agreement of the manager of the accommodation, intends to return to the accommodation in due course.

(5) Notwithstanding paragraphs (1) and (2), where any part of the excess is not a complete £250 that part is to be treated as equivalent to a weekly income of £1.

(6) For the purposes of paragraphs (1) and (2), capital includes any income treated as capital under [¹regulation 112 (income treated as capital)].

AMENDMENT

1. Employment and Support Allowance (Miscellaneous Amendments) Regulations 2008 (SI 2008/2428) reg.20(6) (October 27, 2008).

DEFINITIONS

"Abbeyfield Home"—see reg.2(1).
"care home"—*ibid.*
"claimant"—see reg.83(1).
"independent hospital"—see reg.2(1).

GENERAL NOTE

This is similar to reg.53 of the Income Support Regulations/reg.116 of the JSA   **4.275** Regulations 1996. It is not entirely clear why para.(4)(a) contains a separate rule for a claimant over pensionable age (reg.53(1C)(a) of the Income Support Regulations does the same but not reg.116 of the JSA Regulations), since claimants over pensionable age are not entitled to ESA (or income support or indeed JSA).

CHAPTER 8

[¹ [² . . .] LIABLE RELATIVE PAYMENTS]

AMENDMENTS

1. Employment and Support Allowance (Miscellaneous Amendments) Regulations 2008 (SI 2008/2428) reg.20(5) (October 27, 2008).
2. Social Security (Miscellaneous Amendments) (No.4) Regulations 2009 (SI 2009/2655) reg.11(5) (April 12, 2010).

Interpretation

119. In this Chapter—   **4.276**
[¹ [² . . .]]
"claimant" includes a young claimant;
[¹"claimant's family" shall be construed in accordance with section 137 of the Contributions and Benefits Act (interpretation of part 7 and supplementary provisions);
"housing costs" means those costs which may be met under paragraph 1(2) of Schedule 6;]
"liable relative" means—
    (a) a spouse, former spouse, civil partner or former civil partner of a claimant or of a member of the claimant's family;

(b) a parent of a child or young person who is a member of the claimant's family or of a young claimant;

(c) a person who has not been adjudged to be the father of a child or young person who is a member of the claimant's family or of a young claimant where that person is contributing towards the maintenance of that child, young person or young claimant and by reason of that contribution the claimant may reasonably be treated as the father of that child, young person or young claimant;

(d) a person liable to maintain another person by virtue of section 78(6)(c) of the Administration Act (liability to maintain) where the latter is the claimant or a member of the claimant's family,

and, in this definition, a reference to a child's, young person's or young claimant's parent includes any person in relation to whom the child, young person or young claimant was treated as a child or a member of the family;

[¹"ordinary clothing and footwear" means clothing and footwear for normal daily use but does not include school uniforms;]

"payment" means a periodical payment or any other payment made by or derived from a liable relative [¹ . . .] but it does not include any payment—

(a) arising from a disposition of property made in contemplation of, or as a consequence of—
 (i) an agreement to separate;
 (ii) any proceedings for judicial separation, divorce or nullity of marriage; or
 (iii) any proceedings for separation, dissolution or nullity in relation to a civil partnership;

(b) made after the death of the liable relative;

(c) made by way of a gift but not in aggregate or otherwise exceeding £250 in the period of 52 weeks beginning with the date on which the payment, or if there is more than one such payment the first payment, is made; and, in the case of a claimant who continues to be in receipt of an income-related allowance at the end of the period of 52 weeks, this provision is to continue to apply thereafter with the modification that any subsequent period of 52 weeks is to begin with the first day of the benefit week in which the first payment is made after the end of the previous period of 52 weeks;

[¹(d) made to a third party, or in respect of a third party, unless the payment is—
 (i) in relation to the claimant or the claimant's [² partner or is made or derived from a person falling within sub-paragraph (d) of the definition of liable relative]; and
 (ii) [³ . . .] in respect of food, ordinary clothing or footwear, fuel, [³ rent for which housing benefit is payable, housing costs to the extent that they are met under regulation 67(1)(c) or 68(1)(d) (housing costs),] council tax or water charges;]

(e) in kind;

(f) to, or in respect of, a child or young person who is to be treated as not being a member of the claimant's household under regulation 156 (circumstances in which a person is to be treated as being or not being a member of the same household);

(g) which is not a periodical payment, to the extent that any amount of that payment—

    (i) has already been taken into account under this Part by virtue of a previous claim or determination;

    (ii) has been recovered under section 74 of the Administration Act (income support and other payments) or is currently being recovered; or

    (iii) at the time the determination is made, has been used by the claimant except where the claimant has deprived himself or herself of that amount for the purpose of securing entitlement to an income-related allowance or increasing the amount of that allowance;

[² (h) to which paragraph 60 of Schedule 8 (sums to be disregarded in the calculation of income other than earnings) applies.]

"periodical payment" means—

(a) a payment which is made or is due to be made at regular intervals [¹ ...];

(b) in a case where the liable relative has established a pattern of making payments at regular intervals, any such payment;

(c) any payment [¹ [² ...] that does not exceed] the amount of an income-related allowance payable had that payment not been made;

(d) any payment representing a commutation of payments to which paragraph (a) or (b) of this definition applies whether made in arrears or in advance,

but does not include a payment due to be made before the first benefit week pursuant to the claim which is not so made;

"young claimant" means a person aged 16 or over but under 20 who makes a claim for an income-related allowance.

AMENDMENTS

1. Employment and Support Allowance (Miscellaneous Amendments) Regulations 2008 (SI 2008/2428) reg.20(7) (October 27, 2008).

2. Social Security (Miscellaneous Amendments) (No. 4) Regulations 2009 (SI 2009/2655) reg.11(11) (April 12, 2010).

3. Social Security (Miscellaneous Amendments) Regulations 2013 (SI 2013/443) reg.9(3) (April 2, 2013).

DEFINITIONS

"benefit week"—see reg.2(1).
"child"—*ibid.*
"claimant"—see reg.83(1).
"family"—see reg.2(1).
"young person"—*ibid.*

GENERAL NOTE

This is similar to reg.54 of the Income Support Regulations/reg.117 of the JSA Regulations 1996.

The amendments made to Ch.8 with effect from April 12, 2010 were as a consequence of the introduction of a total income disregard of child maintenance from that date, replacing the previous partial disregard (see the form of para.60 of Sch.8

4.277

introduced on April 12, 2010). Any lump sum payments of periodical child maintenance would retain their character as income for the periods to which they related, but could metamorphose into capital in so far as retained beyond those periods. Note that child maintenance under the child support legislation is now identified in para.60 of Sch.8, and is therefore excluded from the meaning of "payment" for the purposes of Ch.8 (para.(h) of the definition above). Chapter 8 therefore once again only deals with liable relative payments.

Treatment of [¹ [² . . .]] liable relative payments

4.278   **120.** Subject to regulation 121 (disregard of payments treated as not relevant income) [³ . . .] a payment—

(a) to the extent that it is not a payment of income, is to be treated as income;
(b) is to be taken into account in accordance with the following provisions of this Chapter.

AMENDMENTS

1. Employment and Support Allowance (Miscellaneous Amendments) Regulations 2008 (SI 2008/2428) reg.20(2)(b) (October 27, 2008).
2. Social Security (Miscellaneous Amendments) (No. 4) Regulations 2009 (SI 2009/2655) reg.11(4) (April 12, 2010).
3. Social Security (Miscellaneous Amendments) (No. 4) Regulations 2009 (SI 2009/2655) reg.11(12) (April 12, 2010).

DEFINITION

"payment"—*ibid.*

GENERAL NOTE

4.279   This is similar to reg.55 of the Income Support Regulations/reg.118 of the JSA Regulations 1996.

Disregard of payments treated as not relevant income

4.280   **121.** Where the Secretary of State treats any payment as not being relevant income for the purposes of section 74A of the Administration Act (payment of benefit where maintenance payments collected by Secretary of State), that payment is to be disregarded in calculating a claimant's income.

DEFINITIONS

"payment"—see reg.119.
"relevant income"—see reg.2(c), Social Security Benefits (Maintenance Payments and Consequential Amendments) Regulations 1996 (SI 1996/940).

GENERAL NOTE

4.281   This is similar to reg.55A of the Income Support Regulations/reg.119 of the JSA Regulations 1996.
For reg.2(c) of the Social Security Benefits (Maintenance Payments and Consequential Amendments) Regulations 1996 see Part II of this volume.

Period over which periodical payments are to be taken into account

4.282   **122.**—(1) The period over which a periodical payment is to be taken into account is to be—

(a) in a case where the payment is made at regular intervals, a period equal to the length of that interval;
(b) in a case where the payment is due to be made at regular intervals but is

not so made, such number of weeks as is equal to the number (and any fraction is to be treated as a corresponding fraction of a week) obtained by dividing the amount of that payment by the weekly amount of that periodical payment as calculated in accordance with regulation 124(4) (calculation of the weekly amount of a liable relative payment);

(c) in any other case, a period equal to a week.

(2) The period under paragraph (1) is to begin on the date on which the payment is treated as paid under regulation 125 (date on which a liable relative payment is to be treated as paid).

DEFINITION

"periodical payment"—see reg.119.

GENERAL NOTE

This is similar to reg.56 of the Income Support Regulations/reg.120 of the JSA Regulations 1996.

4.283

[¹ Period over which payments other than periodical payments are to be taken into account

123.—(1) The period over which a payment other than a periodical payment (a "non-periodical payment") is to be taken into account shall be determined as follows.

4.284

(2) Except in a case where paragraph (4) applies, the number of weeks over which a non-periodical payment is to be taken into account shall be equal to the number obtained by dividing that payment by the amount referred to in paragraph (3).

(3) The amount is the aggregate of £2 and—

(a) the amount of employment and support allowance that would be payable had no payment been made [² . . .].

(4) This paragraph applies in a case where a liable relative makes a periodical payment and a non-periodical payment concurrently and the weekly amount of the periodical payment (as calculated in accordance with regulation 124) is less than B.

(5) In a case where paragraph (4) applies, the non-periodical payment shall, subject to paragraphs (6) and (7), be taken into account over a period of the number of weeks equal to the number obtained by applying the formula—

$$\frac{A}{B-C}$$

(6) If the liable relative ceases to make periodical payments, the balance (if any) of the non-periodical payment shall be taken into account over the number of weeks equal to the number obtained by dividing that balance by the amount referred to in paragraph (3).

(7) If the amount of any subsequent periodical payment varies, the balance (if any) of the non-periodical payment shall be taken into account over a period of the number of weeks equal to the number obtained by applying the formula—

$$\frac{D}{B-E}$$

(8) The period under paragraph (2) or (4) shall begin on the date on which the payment is treated as paid under regulation 125 (date on which a liable relative payment is to be treated as paid) and the period under paragraph (6) or (7) shall begin on the first day of the benefit week in which the cessation or variation of the periodical payment occurred.

(9) Any fraction which arises by applying a calculation or formula referred to in this regulation shall be treated as a corresponding fraction of a week.

(10) In paragraphs (4) to (7)—

A = the amount of the non-periodical payment;

B = the aggregate of £2 and the amount of employment and support allowance that would be payable had the periodical payment not been made [² . . .];

C = the weekly amount of the periodical payment;

D = the balance (if any) of the non-periodical payment.

E = the weekly amount of any subsequent periodical payment.]

AMENDMENTS

1. Employment and Support Allowance (Miscellaneous Amendments) Regulations 2008 (SI 2008/2428) reg.20(9) (October 27, 2008).

2. Social Security (Miscellaneous Amendments) (No. 4) Regulations 2009 (SI 2009/2655) reg.11(13) (April 12, 2010).

DEFINITIONS

"liable relative"—see reg.119.
"payment"—*ibid.*
"periodical payment"—*ibid.*

GENERAL NOTE

4.285   This is similar to reg.57 of the Income Support Regulations/reg.121 of the JSA Regulations 1996.

Calculation of the weekly amount of a [¹ [² . . .]] liable relative payment

4.286   **124.**—(1) Where a periodical payment is made or is due to be made at intervals of one week, the weekly amount is to be the amount of that payment.

(2) Where a periodical payment is made or is due to be made at intervals greater than one week and those intervals are monthly, the weekly amount is to be determined by multiplying the amount of the payment by 12 and dividing the product by 52.

(3) Where a periodical payment is made or is due to be made at intervals and those intervals are neither weekly nor monthly, the weekly amount is to be determined by dividing that payment by the number equal to the number of weeks (including any part of a week) in that interval.

(4) Where a payment is made and that payment represents a commutation of periodical payments whether in arrears or in advance, the weekly amount is to be the weekly amount of the individual periodical payments so commuted as calculated under paragraphs (1) to (3) as is appropriate.

(5) The weekly amount of a payment to which regulation 123 (period over which payments other than periodical payments are to be taken into account) applies, is to be equal to the amount of the divisor used in calcu-

lating the period over which the payment or, as the case may be, the balance is to be taken into account.

AMENDMENTS

1. Employment and Support Allowance (Miscellaneous Amendments) Regulations 2008 (SI 2008/2428) reg.20(2)(c) (October 27, 2008).
2. Social Security (Miscellaneous Amendments) (No. 4) Regulations 2009 (SI 2009/2655) reg.11(4) (April 12, 2010).

DEFINITIONS

"payment"—see reg. 119
"periodical payment"—*ibid.*

GENERAL NOTE

This is similar to reg.58 of the Income Support Regulations/reg.122 of the JSA Regulations 1996.

4.287

Date on which a [¹ [² . . .]] liable relative payment is to be treated as paid

125.—(1) A periodical payment is to be treated as paid—

4.288

(a) in the case of a payment which is due to be made before the first benefit week pursuant to the claim, on the day in the week in which it is due to be paid which corresponds to the first day of the benefit week;

(b) in any other case, on the first day of the benefit week in which it is due to be paid unless, having regard to the manner in which an income-related allowance is due to be paid in the particular case, it would be more practicable to treat it as paid on the first day of a subsequent benefit week.

(2) Subject to paragraph (3), any other payment is to be treated as paid—

(a) in the case of a payment which is made before the first benefit week pursuant to the claim, on the day in the week in which it is paid which corresponds to the first day of the benefit week;

(b) in any other case, on the first day of the benefit week in which it is paid unless, having regard to the manner in which an income-related allowance is due to be paid in the particular case, it would be more practicable to treat it as paid on the first day of a subsequent benefit week.

(3) Any other payment paid on a date which falls within the period in respect of which a previous payment is taken into account, not being a periodical payment, is to be treated as paid on the first day following the end of that period.

AMENDMENTS

1. Employment and Support Allowance (Miscellaneous Amendments) Regulations 2008 (SI 2008/2428) reg.20(2)(d) (October 27, 2008).
2. Social Security (Miscellaneous Amendments) (No. 4) Regulations 2009 (SI 2009/2655) reg.11(4) (April 12, 2010).

DEFINITIONS

"benefit week"—see reg.2(1).
"payment"—see reg. 119
"periodical payment"—*ibid.*

GENERAL NOTE

4.289   This is similar to reg.59 of the Income Support Regulations/reg.123 of the JSA Regulations 1996.

Liable relative payments to be treated as capital

4.290   **126.** [¹ . . .]

AMENDMENT

1. Employment and Support Allowance (Miscellaneous Amendments) Regulations 2008 (SI 2008/2428) reg.20(4)(b) (October 27, 2008).

CHAPTER 9

CHILD SUPPORT

Treatment of child support maintenance

4.291   **127.** [¹ . . .]

AMENDMENT

1. Employment and Support Allowance (Miscellaneous Amendments) Regulations 2008 (SI 2008/2428) reg.20(4)(c) (October 27, 2008).

Calculation of the weekly amount of payments of child support maintenance

4.292   **128.** [¹ . . .]

AMENDMENT

1. Employment and Support Allowance (Miscellaneous Amendments) Regulations 2008 (SI 2008/2428) reg.20(4)(c) (October 27, 2008).

Date on which child support maintenance is to be treated as paid

4.293   **129.** [¹ . . .]

AMENDMENT

1. Employment and Support Allowance (Miscellaneous Amendments) Regulations 2008 (SI 2008/2428) reg.20(4)(c) (October 27, 2008).

Disregard of payments treated as not relevant income

4.294   **130.** [¹ . . .]

AMENDMENT

1. Employment and Support Allowance (Miscellaneous Amendments) Regulations 2008 (SI 2008/2428) reg.20(4)(c) (October 27, 2008).

CHAPTER 10

STUDENTS

Interpretation

131.—(1) In this Chapter—   4.295

"academic year" means the period of twelve months beginning on 1st January, 1st April, 1st July or 1st September according to whether the course in question begins in the winter, the spring, the summer or the autumn respectively but if students are required to begin attending the course during August or September and to continue attending through the autumn, the academic year of the course is to be considered to begin in the autumn rather than the summer;

"access funds" means—

(a) grants made under section [³68] of the Further and Higher Education Act 1992 [³ . . .] [⁹ or section 10 of the Higher Education and Research Act 2017] for the purpose of providing funds on a discretionary basis to be paid to students;

(b) grants made under sections 73(a) and (c) and 74(1) of the Education (Scotland) Act 1980;

(c) grants made under Article 30 of the Education and Libraries (Northern Ireland) Order 1993, or grants, loans or other payments made under Article 5 of the Further Education (Northern Ireland) Order 1997 in each case being grants, or grants, loans or other payments as the case may be, made for the purpose of assisting students in financial difficulties;

(d) discretionary payments, known as "learner support funds", which are made available to students in further education by institutions out of funds provided by the [⁵ [⁷ Secretary of State under section 14 of the Education Act 2002] or [⁸ . . .] under sections 100 and 101 of [⁷ the Apprenticeships, Skills, Children and Learning Act 2009]]; or

(e) Financial Contingency Funds made available by the Welsh Ministers;

"college of further education" means, in Scotland, an educational establishment by which further education is provided;

[² "contribution" means—

(a) any contribution in respect of the income of a student or any person which the Secretary of State, the Scottish Ministers or an education authority takes into account in ascertaining the amount of a student's grant or student loan; or

(b) any sums, which in determining the amount of a student's allowance or bursary in Scotland under the Education (Scotland) Act 1980, the Scottish Ministers or education authority takes into account being sums which the Scottish Ministers or education authority consider that it is reasonable for the following persons to contribute towards the holder's expenses—

(i) the holder of the allowance or bursary;

(ii) the holder's parents;

(iii) the holder's parent's spouse, civil partner or a person ordinarily living with the holder's parent as if he or she were the spouse or civil partner of that parent; or

(iv) the holder's spouse or civil partner;]
"course of advanced education" means—

(a) a course leading to a postgraduate degree or comparable qualification, a first degree or comparable qualification, a diploma of higher education or a higher national diploma; or

(b) any other course which is of a standard above advanced GNVQ, or equivalent, including a course which is of a standard above a general certificate of education (advanced level), a Scottish national qualification (higher or advanced higher);

"covenant income" means the income payable to a student under a Deed of Covenant by a person whose income is, or is likely to be, taken into account in assessing the student's grant or award;

"education authority" means a government department, [⁴a local authority as defined in section 579 of the Education Act 1996 (interpretation)], an education authority as defined in section 123 of the Local Government (Scotland) Act 1973, an education and library board established under Article 3 of the Education and Libraries (Northern Ireland) Order 1986, any body which is a research council for the purposes of the Science and Technology Act 1965 or any analogous government department, authority, board or body, of the Channel Islands, Isle of Man or any other country outside Great Britain;

"full-time course of advanced education" means a course of advanced education which is—

(a) a full-time course of study which is not funded in whole or in part by the [⁵ [⁷ Secretary of State under section 14 of the Education Act 2002][⁸ or under section 100 of the Apprenticeships, Skills, Children and Learning Act 2009]] or by the Welsh Ministers or a full-time course of study which is not funded in whole or in part by the Scottish Ministers at a college of further education or a full-time course of study which is a course of higher education and is funded in whole or in part by the Scottish Ministers;

(b) a course of study which is funded in whole or in part by the [⁵ [⁷ Secretary of State under section 14 of the Education Act 2002][⁸ or under section 100 of the Apprenticeships, Skills, Children and Learning Act 2009]] or by the Welsh Ministers if it involves more than 16 guided learning hours per week for the student in question, according to the number of guided learning hours per week for that student set out—

   [⁵ (i) in the case of a course funded by the [⁷ Secretary of State [⁹. . .]], in the student's learning agreement signed on behalf of the establishment which is funded by [⁸ the Secretary of State] for the delivery of that course; or]

   (ii) in the case of a course funded by the Welsh Ministers, in a document signed on behalf of the establishment which is funded by that Council for the delivery of that course; or

(c) a course of study (not being higher education) which is funded in whole or in part by the Scottish Ministers at a college of further education if it involves—

   (i) more than 16 hours per week of classroom-based or workshop-based programmed learning under the direct guidance of teaching staff according to the number of hours set out in a document signed on behalf of the college; or

(ii) 16 hours or less per week of classroom-based or workshop-based programmed learning under the direct guidance of teaching staff and it involves additional hours using structured learning packages supported by the teaching staff where the combined total of hours exceeds 21 per week, according to the number of hours set out in a document signed on behalf of the college;

"full-time course of study" means a full-time course of study which—

(a) is not funded in whole or in part by the [⁵ [⁷ Secretary of State under section 14 of the Education Act 2002][⁸ or section 100 of the Apprenticeships, Skills, Children and Learning Act 2009]] or by the Welsh Ministers or a full-time course of study which is not funded in whole or in part by the Scottish Ministers at a college of further education or a full-time course of study which is a course of higher education and is funded in whole or in part by the Scottish Ministers;

(b) a course of study which is funded in whole or in part by the [⁵ [⁷ Secretary of State under section 14 of the Education Act 2002][⁸ or section 100 of the Apprenticeships, Skills, Children and Learning Act 2009]] or by the Welsh Ministers if it involves more than 16 guided learning hours per week for the student in question, according to the number of guided learning hours per week for that student set out—

[⁵ (i) in the case of a course funded by the [⁷ Secretary of State [⁸ . . .], in the student's learning agreement signed on behalf of the establishment which is funded by [⁸ the Secretary of State] for the delivery of that course; or]

(ii) in the case of a course funded by the Welsh Ministers, in a document signed on behalf of the establishment which is funded by that Council for the delivery of that course; or

(c) is not higher education and is funded in whole or in part by the Scottish Ministers at a college of further education if it involves—

(i) more than 16 hours per week of classroom-based or workshop-based programmed learning under the direct guidance of teaching staff according to the number of hours set out in a document signed on behalf of the college; or

(ii) 16 hours or less per week of classroom-based or workshop-based programmed learning under the direct guidance of teaching staff and it involves additional hours using structured learning packages supported by the teaching staff where the combined total of hours exceeds 21 per week, according to the number of hours set out in a document signed on behalf of the college;

"full-time student" means a person who is not a qualifying young person or child within the meaning of section 142 of the Contributions and Benefits Act (child and qualifying young person) and who is—

(a) aged less than 19 and is attending or undertaking a full-time course of advanced education;

(b) aged 19 or over but under pensionable age and is attending or undertaking a full-time course of study at an educational establishment; or

(c) on a sandwich course;

"grant" (except in the definition of "access funds") means any kind of educational grant or award and includes any scholarship, studentship, exhibition, allowance or bursary but does not include a payment from access funds or any payment to which paragraph 13 of Schedule 8 or paragraph 52 of Schedule 9 applies;

"grant income" means—

(a) any income by way of a grant;

(b) in the case of a student other than one to whom paragraph (c) refers, any contribution which has been assessed whether or not it has been paid;

(c) in the case of a student who is a lone parent [⁶ , is a person who has no partner and who is responsible for and a member of the same household as a young person] or is a person to whom Part 4 applies, any contribution which has been assessed and which has been paid,

and any such contribution which is paid by way of a covenant is to be treated as part of the student's grant income;

"higher education" means higher education within the meaning of Part 2 of the Further and Higher Education (Scotland) Act 1992;

"last day of the course" means the date on which the last day of the final academic term falls in respect of the course in which the student is enrolled;

"period of study" means—

(a) in the case of a course of study for one year or less, the period beginning with the start of the course and ending with the last day of the course;

(b) in the case of a course of study for more than one year, in the first or, as the case may be, any subsequent year of the course, other than the final year of the course, the period beginning with the start of the course or, as the case may be, that year's start and ending with either—

(i) the day before the start of the next year of the course in a case where the student's grant or loan is assessed at a rate appropriate to the student's studying throughout the year or, if the claimant does not have a grant or loan, where a loan would have been assessed at such a rate had the claimant had one; or

(ii) in any other case the day before the start of the normal summer vacation appropriate to the student's course;

(c) in the final year of a course of study of more than one year, the period beginning with that year's start and ending with the last day of the course;

"periods of experience" means periods of work experience which form part of a sandwich course;

[¹⁰"postgraduate loan" means a loan to a student undertaking a postgraduate master's degree course or a postgraduate doctoral degree course pursuant to regulations made under section 22 of the Teaching and Higher Education Act 1998;]

"sandwich course" has the meaning prescribed in regulation 2(9) of the Education (Student Support) Regulations 2007, regulation 4(2) of the Education (Student Loans) (Scotland) Regulations 2007 or regulation 2(8) of the Education (Student Support) Regulations (Northern Ireland) 2007;

"standard maintenance grant" means—

(a) except where paragraph (b) or (c) applies, in the case of a student attending or undertaking a course of study at the University of London or an establishment within the area comprising the City of London and the Metropolitan Police District, the amount specified for the time being in paragraph 2(2)(a) of Schedule 2 to the Education (Mandatory Awards) Regulations 2003 ("the 2003 Regulations") for such a student;

(b) except where paragraph (c) applies, in the case of a student residing at the student's parent's home, the amount specified in paragraph 3(2) of Schedule 2 to the 2003 Regulations;

(c) in the case of a student receiving an allowance or bursary under the Education (Scotland) Act 1980, the amount of money specified for the relevant year appropriate for the student set out in the Student Support in Scotland Guide issued by the Student Awards Agency for Scotland, or its nearest equivalent in the case of a bursary provided by a college of further education or a local education authority;

(d) in any other case, the amount specified in paragraph 2(2) of Schedule 2 to the 2003 Regulations other than in paragraph (a) or (b) of that paragraph;

"student" means a person, other than a person in receipt of a training allowance, who is attending or undertaking a course of study at an educational establishment;

"student loan" means a loan towards a student's maintenance pursuant to any regulations made under section 22 of the Teaching and Higher Education Act 1998, sections [¹73(f)], 73B and 74 of the Education (Scotland) Act 1980 or article 3 of the Education (Student Support) (Northern Ireland) Order 1998 and is to include, in Scotland, amounts paid under regulation 4(1)(c) of the Students' Allowances (Scotland) Regulations 2007.

(2) For the purposes of the definition of "full-time student" in paragraph (1), a person is to be regarded as attending or, as the case may be, undertaking a full-time course of study, a full-time course of advanced education or as being on a sandwich course—

(a) subject to paragraph (3), in the case of a person attending or undertaking a part of a modular course which would be a full-time course of study for the purposes of this Part, for the period beginning on the day on which that part of the course starts and ending—

(i) on the last day on which the claimant is registered with the educational establishment as attending or undertaking that part as a full-time course of study; or

(ii) on such earlier date (if any) as the claimant finally abandons the course or is dismissed from it;

(b) in any other case, throughout the period beginning on the date on which the claimant starts attending or undertaking the course and ending on the last day of the course or on such earlier date (if any) as the claimant finally abandons it or is dismissed from it.

(3) For the purpose of sub-paragraph (a) of paragraph (2), the period referred to in that sub-paragraph is to include—

(a) where a person has failed examinations or has failed to successfully complete a module relating to a period when the claimant was attending or undertaking a part of the course as a full-time course of study, any period in respect of which the claimant attends or undertakes the course for the purpose of retaking those examinations or that module;

(b) any period of vacation within the period specified in that paragraph or immediately following that period except where the person has registered with the educational establishment to attend or undertake the final module in the course and the vacation immediately follows the last day on which the claimant is required to attend or undertake the course.

(4) In paragraph (2), "modular course" means a course of study which consists of two or more modules, the successful completion of a specified number of which is required before a person is considered by the educational establishment to have completed the course.

AMENDMENTS

1. Employment and Support Allowance (Miscellaneous Amendments) Regulations 2008 (SI 2008/2428) reg.8(9) (October 27, 2008).

2. Social Security (Miscellaneous Amendments) Regulations 2009 (SI 2009/583) reg.10(7) (April 6, 2009).

3. Social Security (Miscellaneous Amendments) (No. 4) Regulations 2009 (SI 2009/2655) reg.11(14) (October 26, 2009).

4. Local Education Authorities and Children's Services Authorities (Integration of Functions) (Local and Subordinate Legislation) Order 2010 (SI 2010/1172) art.5 and Sch.3, para.81 (May 5, 2010).

5. Apprenticeships, Skills, Children and Learning Act 2009 (Consequential Amendments to Subordinate Legislation) (England) Order 2010 (SI 2010/1941) reg.28(4) (September 1, 2010).

6. Social Security (Work-focused Interviews for Lone Parents and Partners) (Amendment) Regulations 2011 (SI 2011/2428) reg.5(4) (October 31, 2011).

7. Young People's Learning Agency Abolition (Consequential Amendments to Subordinate Legislation) (England) Order 2012 (SI 2012/956) art.22(4) (May 1, 2012).

8. Deregulation Act 2015 (Consequential Amendments) Order 2015 (SI 2015/971) art.2 and Sch.3 para.14(4) (May 26, 2015).

9. Higher Education and Research Act 2017 (Further Implementation etc.) Regulations 2019 (SI 2019/1027) reg.31(2) (August 1, 2019).

10. Social Security (Income and Capital) (Miscellaneous Amendments) Regulations 2020 (SI 2020/618) reg.7(6) (July 15, 2020).

DEFINITIONS

"training allowance"—see reg.2(1).
"young person"—*ibid.*

GENERAL NOTE

4.296 This is similar to reg.61 of the Income Support Regulations. Under old style JSA the definitions applying to full-time students are in a slightly different form. See reg.130 of the JSA Regulations 1996 for some of the definitions but the main ones are to be found in reg.1(3) and (3A)–(3E) of those Regulations (see further the note to reg.130 of the JSA Regulations 1996).

Note that in the definition of "grant income" the cases where a contribution will only be included if it is actually paid are a lone parent, a single person who is responsible for and a member of the same household as a young person or a person "to whom Part 4 applies". Since Part 4 concerns who is or is not to be treated as receiving education for the purposes of para.6(1)(g) of Sch.1 to the Welfare Reform

Act 2007 it is not clear what this reference means. If the aim is to mirror the income support definition of "grant income", the reference is presumably only intended to be to reg.18 in Part 4 (which provides that students who are entitled to a disability living allowance, personal independence payment or armed forces independence payment are not to be treated as receiving education for the purposes of para.6(1)(g) and so can qualify for income-related ESA). In this connection note that the equivalent provision for the treatment of student loans (see reg.137(5)(a)(ii)) only includes a student who is entitled to income-related ESA by virtue of reg.18.

See the note to reg.61 of the Income Support (General) Regulations 1987 for the operation of the new definition of "postgraduate loan".

Calculation of grant income

132.—(1) The amount of student's grant income to be taken into account, subject to paragraphs (2) and (3), is to be the whole of the student's grant income.

(2) There is to be disregarded from the amount of a student's grant income any payment—

(a) intended to meet tuition fees or examination fees;

(b) intended to meet additional expenditure incurred by a disabled student in respect of that student's attendance on a course;

(c) intended to meet additional expenditure connected with term time residential study away from the student's educational establishment;

(d) on account of the student maintaining a home at a place other than that at which the student resides while attending the course but only to the extent that the student's rent is not met by housing benefit;

(e) on account of any other person but only if that person is residing outside of the United Kingdom and there is no applicable amount in respect of that person;

(f) intended to meet the cost of books and equipment;

(g) intended to meet travel expenses incurred as a result of the student's attendance on the course;

(h) intended for the maintenance of a child dependant;

(i) intended for the child care costs of a child dependant;

[¹(j) of higher education bursary for care leavers made under Part III of the Children Act 1989 [⁵ or under Part 6 of the Social Services and Well-being (Wales) Act 2014].]

(3) Where a student does not have a student loan [⁴ or a postgraduate [⁶ . . .] loan] and is not treated as possessing [⁴ a student loan or a postgraduate [⁶ . . .] loan], there is to be excluded from the student's grant income—

(a) the sum of [²£303] per academic year in respect of travel costs; and

(b) the sum of [³£390] per academic year towards the costs of books and equipment,

whether or not any such costs are incurred.

(4) Subject to paragraph (6), a student's grant income except any amount intended for the maintenance of adult dependants under Part 3 of Schedule 2 to the Education (Mandatory Awards) Regulations 2003 is to be apportioned—

(a) subject to paragraph (7), in a case where it is attributable to the period of study, equally between the weeks in the period beginning with the benefit week, the first day of which coincides with, or immediately follows, the first day of the period of study and ending with

4.297

the benefit week, the last day of which coincides with, or immediately precedes, the last day of the period of study;

(b) in any other case, equally between the weeks in the period beginning with the benefit week, the first day of which coincides with, or immediately follows, the first day of the period for which it is payable and ending with the benefit week, the last day of which coincides with, or immediately precedes, the last day of the period for which it is payable.

(5) Any grant in respect of an adult dependant paid under section 63(6) of the Health Services and Public Health Act 1968 (grants in respect of the provision of instruction to officers of hospital authorities) and any amount intended for the maintenance of an adult dependant under the provisions referred to in paragraph (4) is to be apportioned equally over a period of 52 weeks or, if there are 53 benefit weeks (including part-weeks) in the year, 53 weeks.

(6) In a case where a student is in receipt of a student loan or where that student could have acquired a student loan by taking reasonable steps but had not done so, any amount intended for the maintenance of an adult dependant under provisions other than those referred to in paragraph (4) is to be apportioned over the same period as the student's loan is apportioned or, as the case may be, would have been apportioned.

(7) In the case of a student on a sandwich course, any periods of experience within the period of study is to be excluded and the student's grant income is to be apportioned equally between the weeks in the period beginning with the benefit week, the first day of which immediately follows the last day of the period of experience and ending with the benefit week, the last day of which coincides with, or immediately precedes, the last day of the period of study.

AMENDMENTS

1. Social Security (Miscellaneous Amendments) Regulations 2009 (SI 2009/583) reg.10(8) (April 6, 2009).

2. Social Security (Students and Miscellaneous Amendments) Regulations 2009 (SI 2009/1575) reg.2(2) and (4)(e) (September 1, 2009 (or if the student's period of study begins between August 1 and August 31, 2009, the first day of the period).

3. Social Security (Students and Miscellaneous Amendments) Regulations 2009 (SI 2009/1575) reg.2(3) and (4)(e) (September 1, 2009 (or if the student's period of study begins between August 1 and August 31, 2009, the first day of the period)).

4. Social Security (Treatment of Postgraduate Master's Degree Loans and Special Support Loans) (Amendment) Regulations 2016 (SI 2016/743) reg.5(3) (August 4, 2016).

5. Social Services and Well-being (Wales) Act 2014 and the Regulation and Inspection of Social Care (Wales) Act 2016 (Consequential Amendments) Order 2017 (SI 2017/901) art.13(2) (November 3, 2017).

6. Social Security (Income and Capital) (Miscellaneous Amendments) Regulations 2020 (SI 2020/618) reg.7(7) (July 15, 2020).

DEFINITIONS

"benefit week"—see reg.2(1).
"grant"—see reg.131(1).
"grant income"—*ibid.*
"period of study"—*ibid.*
"periods of experience"—*ibid.*
"postgraduate loan"—*ibid.*
"sandwich course"—*ibid.*

"student"—*ibid.*
"student loan"—*ibid.*

GENERAL NOTE

This is similar to reg.62 of the Income Support Regulations/reg.131 of the JSA   4.298
Regulations 1996. See the note to reg.62 for the effect of the new rule on "postgraduate loans".

Calculation of covenant income where a contribution is assessed

133.—(1) Where a student is in receipt of income by way of a grant   4.299
during a period of study and a contribution has been assessed, the amount
of the student's covenant income to be taken into account for that period
and any summer vacation immediately following is to be the whole amount
of the student's covenant income less, subject to paragraph (3), the amount
of the contribution.

(2) The weekly amount of the student's covenant income is to be determined—

(a) by dividing the amount of income which falls to be taken into
    account under paragraph (1) by 52 or, if there are 53 benefit weeks
    (including part-weeks) in the year, 53; and
(b) by disregarding from the resulting amount, £5.

(3) For the purposes of paragraph (1), the contribution is to be treated
as increased by the amount, if any, by which the amount excluded under
regulation 132(2)(g) (calculation of grant income) falls short of the
amount for the time being specified in paragraph 7(2) of Schedule 2 to the
Education (Mandatory Awards) Regulations 2003 (travel expenditure).

DEFINITIONS

"benefit week"—see reg.2(1).
"contribution"—see reg.131(1).
"covenant income"—*ibid.*
"grant"—*ibid.*
"grant income"—*ibid.*
"period of study"—*ibid.*
"student"—*ibid.*

GENERAL NOTE

This is similar to reg.63 of the Income Support Regulations/reg.132 of the JSA   4.300
Regulations 1996.

Calculation of covenant income where no grant income or no con-tribution is assessed

134.—(1) Where a student is not in receipt of income by way of a grant   4.301
the amount of the student's covenant income is to be calculated as follows—

(a) any sums intended for any expenditure specified in regulation 132(2)
    (a) to (e), necessary as a result of the student's attendance on the
    course, are to be disregarded;
(b) any covenant income, up to the amount of the standard mainte-
    nance grant, which is not so disregarded is to be apportioned equally
    between the weeks of the period of study and there is to be disre-
    garded from the covenant income to be so apportioned the amount

which would have been disregarded under regulation 132(2)(f) and (g) and (3) had the student been in receipt of the standard maintenance grant;

(c) the balance, if any, is to be divided by 52 or, if there are 53 benefit weeks (including part-weeks) in the year, 53 and treated as weekly income of which £5 is to be disregarded.

(2) Where a student is in receipt of income by way of a grant and no contribution has been assessed, the amount of the student's covenant income is to be calculated in accordance with paragraph (1), except that—

(a) the value of the standard maintenance grant is to be abated by the amount of the student's grant income less an amount equal to the amount of any sums disregarded under regulation 132(2)(a) to (e); and

(b) the amount to be disregarded under paragraph (1)(b) is to be abated by an amount equal to the amount of any sums disregarded under regulation 132(2)(f) and (g) and (3).

DEFINITIONS

"benefit week"—see reg.2(1).
"contribution"—see reg.131(1).
"covenant income"—*ibid.*
"grant"—*ibid.*
"grant income"—*ibid.*
"period of study"—*ibid.*
"student"—*ibid.*

GENERAL NOTE

4.302   This is similar to reg.64 of the Income Support Regulations/reg.133 of the JSA Regulations 1996.

Relationships with amounts to be disregarded under Schedule 8

4.303   **135.** No part of a student's covenant income or grant income is to be disregarded under paragraph 16 of Schedule 8 (charitable and voluntary payments).

DEFINITIONS

"covenant income"—see reg.131(1).
"grant income"—*ibid.*
"student"—*ibid.*

GENERAL NOTE

4.304   This is similar to reg.65 of the Income Support Regulations/reg.134 of the JSA Regulations.

Other amounts to be disregarded

4.305   **136.**—(1) For the purposes of ascertaining income other than grant income, covenant income and loans treated as income in accordance with regulation 137 (treatment of student loans), any amounts intended for any expenditure specified in regulation 132(2) (calculation of grant income) necessary as a result of the student's attendance on the course is to be disregarded but only if, and to the extent that, the necessary expenditure exceeds or is likely to exceed the amount of the sums disregarded under regulation 132(2) and (3),

133(3) (calculation of covenant income where a contribution is assessed), 134(1)(a) or (b) (calculation of covenant income where no grant income or no contribution is assessed) and 137(6) on like expenditure.

(2) Where a claim is made in respect of any period in the normal summer vacation and any income is payable under a Deed of Covenant which commences or takes effect after the first day of that vacation, that income is to be disregarded.

DEFINITIONS

"covenant income"—see reg.131(1).
"grant income"—*ibid.*

GENERAL NOTE

This is similar to reg.66 of the Income Support Regulations/reg.135 of the JSA Regulations 1996.

4.306

Treatment of student loans [⁴ and postgraduate [⁶ . . .] loans]

137.—(1) [⁴ A student loan and a postgraduate [⁶ . . .] loan are to be treated as income unless the loan] is a specified loan or award in which case it is to be disregarded.

4.307

(2) For the purposes of paragraph (1), a "specified loan or award" means—

[⁵(a) in relation to England, a loan made by the Office for Students under section 39 or 40 of the Higher Education and Research Act 2017;]

(b) in relation to Wales, a loan made by the Higher Education Funding Council for Wales under section 65 of the Further and Higher Education Act 1992;

(c) in relation to Scotland, a loan made by an educational institution from funds it has received under the Education (Access Funds) (Scotland) Regulations 1990;

(d) in relation to Northern Ireland, an award made by the Department for Employment and Learning under article 51 of the Education and Libraries (Northern Ireland) Order 1986.

(3) In calculating the weekly amount of the loan to be taken in account as income—

(a) in respect of a course that is of a single academic year's duration or less, a loan which is payable in respect of that period is to be apportioned equally between the weeks in the period beginning with—

(i) except in a case where paragraph (ii) applies, the benefit week, the first day of which coincides with, or immediately follows, the first day of the single academic year;

(ii) where the student is required to start attending the course in August or where the course is less than an academic year's duration, the benefit week, the first day of which coincides with, or immediately follows, the first day of the course,

and ending with the benefit week, the last day of which coincides with, or immediately precedes, the last day of the course;

(b) in respect of an academic year of a course which starts other than on 1st September, a loan which is payable in respect of that academic year is to be apportioned equally between the weeks in the period beginning with the benefit week, the first day of which coincides with, or immediately follows, the first day of that academic year and ending

with the benefit week, the last day of which coincides with, or immediately precedes, the last day of that academic year but excluding any
benefit weeks falling entirely within the quarter during which, in the
opinion of the Secretary of State, the longest of any vacation is taken;

(c) for the purposes of sub-paragraph (b), "quarter" is to have the same
    meaning as for the purposes of regulation 104(6) (calculation of
    income other than earnings);

(d) in respect of the final academic year of a course (not being a course
    of a single year's duration), a loan which is payable in respect of that
    final academic year is to be apportioned equally between the weeks
    in the period beginning with—

    (i) except in a case where paragraph (ii) applies, the benefit week,
        the first day of which coincides with, or immediately follows, the
        first day of that academic year;

    (ii) where the final academic year starts on 1st September, the
         benefit week, the first day of which coincides with, or immedi-
         ately follows, the earlier of 1st September or the first day of the
         autumn term,

    and ending with the benefit week, the last day of which coincides
    with, or immediately precedes, the last day of the course;

(e) in any other case, the loan is to be apportioned equally between the
    weeks in the period beginning with the earlier of—

    (i) the first day of the first benefit week in September; or

    (ii) the benefit week, the first day of which coincides with, or imme-
         diately follows, the first day of the autumn term,

    and ending with the benefit week, the last day of which coincides
    with, or immediately precedes, the last day of June,

and, in all cases, from the weekly amount so apportioned there is to be
disregarded £10.

(4) A student is to be treated as possessing a student loan [⁴ or a postgraduate [⁶ . . .] loan] in respect of an academic year where—

(a) a student loan [⁴ or a postgraduate [⁶ . . .] loan] has been made to
    that student in respect of that year; or

(b) [³ subject to paragraph (4A)] the student could acquire [⁴ a student
    loan or a postgraduate [⁶ . . .] loan] in respect of that year by taking
    reasonable steps to do so.

[³ (4A) A student is not to be treated as possessing any part of a student
loan [⁴ or a postgraduate [⁶ . . .] loan] which has not been paid to that student
in respect of an academic year where the educational institution at which the
student was attending a course has confirmed in writing that the student has
suspended attendance at the course due to a health condition or disability
that renders the student incapable of continuing that course.]

(5) Where a student is treated as possessing a student loan under paragraph (4), the amount of the student loan to be taken into account as
income is to be, subject to paragraph (6)—

(a) in the case of a student to whom a student loan is made in respect
    of an academic year, a sum equal to the maximum student loan the
    student is able to acquire in respect of that year by taking reasonable
    steps to do so and either—

    (i) in the case of a student other than one to whom paragraph (ii)
        refers, any contribution whether or not it has been paid to that
        student; or

(ii) in the case of a student who is entitled to an income-related allowance by virtue of being a student to whom regulation 18 (circumstances in which the condition that the claimant is not receiving education does not apply) applies;

(b) in the case of a student to whom a student loan is not made in respect of an academic year, the maximum student loan that would be made to the student if—

(i) the student took all reasonable steps to obtain the maximum student loan that student is able to acquire in respect of that year; and

(ii) no deduction in that loan was made by virtue of the application of a means test.

[⁴ (5A) Where a student is treated as possessing a postgraduate [⁶ . . .] loan under paragraph (4) in respect of an academic year, the amount of that loan to be taken into account as income shall be, subject to paragraph (6), a sum equal to 30 per cent. of the maximum postgraduate [⁶ . . .] loan the student is able to acquire in respect of that academic year by taking reasonable steps to do so.]

(6) There is to be deducted from the amount of income taken into account under paragraph (5) [⁴ or (5A)]—

(a) the sum of [¹£303] per academic year in respect of travel costs; and

(b) the sum of [²£390] per academic year towards the costs of books and equipment,

whether or not any such costs are incurred.

AMENDMENTS

1. Social Security (Students and Miscellaneous Amendments) Regulations 2009 (SI 2009/1575) reg.2(2) and (4)(e) (September 1, 2009 (or if the student's period of study begins between August 1 and August 31, 2009, the first day of the period)).

2. Social Security (Students and Miscellaneous Amendments) Regulations 2009 (SI 2009/1575) reg.2(3) and (4)(e) (September 1, 2009 (or if the student's period of study begins between August 1 and August 31, 2009, the first day of the period)).

3. Social Security (Miscellaneous Amendments) (No.5) Regulations 2010 (SI 2010/2429) reg.11(3) (November 1, 2010).

4. Social Security (Treatment of Postgraduate Master's Degree Loans and Special Support Loans) (Amendment) Regulations 2016 (SI 2016/743) reg.5(4) (August 4, 2016).

5. Higher Education and Research Act 2017 (Further Implementation etc.) Regulations 2019 (SI 2019/1027) reg.31(3) (August 1, 2019).

6. Social Security (Income and Capital) (Miscellaneous Amendments) Regulations 2020 (SI 2020/618) reg.7(8) (July 15, 2020).

DEFINITIONS

"academic year"—see reg.131(1).
"benefit week"—see reg.2(1).
"last day of the course"—see reg.131(1).
"postgraduate loan"—*ibid.*
"student"—*ibid.*
"student loan"—*ibid.*

GENERAL NOTE

Except in relation to the disregard of a "specified loan or award" (see paras (1) and (2)), this is similar to reg.136 of the JSA Regulations 1996/reg.66A of the

4.308

Income Support Regulations. See the notes to reg.66A, in particular for the effect of the new provisions on "postgraduate loans". Note however that the rules as to when the amount of the student loan will not include an assessed contribution if it has not been paid differ for each benefit: in the case of income-related ESA it applies if the student is entitled to disability living allowance, personal independence payment or armed forces independence payment (regs 137(5)(a)(ii) and 18); for income-based JSA it applies if the claimant qualifies for the disability premium; and in the case of income support it applies to disabled students and lone parents/lone foster parents.

Under para.(1) a "specified loan or award" (defined in para.(2)) is disregarded. Regulation 66A(1) of the Income Support Regulations and reg.136(1) of the JSA Regulations 1996 used to provide that a "hardship loan" (defined in para. (1A) of both sets of Regulations) was disregarded. However the words "unless it is a hardship loan in which case it shall be disregarded" were omitted from reg.66A(1)/reg.136(1), and regs 66A(1A) and 136(1A) were also omitted, with effect from November 17, 2008 by regs 2(10) and 4(9) respectively of the Social Security (Miscellaneous Amendments) (No. 6) Regulations 2008 (SI 2008/2767). According to the Explanatory Memorandum which accompanied these amending regulations these amendments were being made because hardship loans had not been payable since May 2004. It is not known why similar provision for a disregard of a "specified loan or award" has not been made in the Income Support/JSA Regulations.

The effect of para.(4A), inserted with effect from November 1, 2010, is that a student whose university/college has confirmed in writing that they "have suspended attendance at the course due to a health condition or disability that renders the student incapable of continuing that course" will not be treated as possessing any part of a student loan or a postgraduate loan that has not been paid to them. Nor will it count as notional income (see reg.106(2)(gb)). If the loan or any part of it has already been paid to them, it will count as income (see paras (1) and (4)(a)). No amendments equivalent to para.(4A) and reg.106(2)(gb) have been made to the Income Support/JSA Regulations 1996, presumably because the appropriate benefit for such a student to claim is old style ESA.

Treatment of payments from access funds

4.309   **138.**—(1) This regulation applies to payments from access funds that are not payments to which regulation 142(2) or (3) (income treated as capital) applies.

(2) A payment from access funds, other than a payment to which paragraph (3) applies, is to be disregarded as income.

(3) Subject to paragraph (4) and paragraph 39 of Schedule 8, any payments from access funds which are intended and used for food, ordinary clothing or footwear, household fuel, rent for which housing benefit is payable or any housing costs to the extent that they are met under regulation 67(1)(c) or 68(1)(d) (housing costs), of a single claimant or, as the case may be, of the claimant's partner, and any payments from access funds which are used for any council tax or water charges for which that claimant or partner is liable is to be disregarded as income to the extent of £20 per week.

(4) Where a payment from access funds is made—
  (a) on or after 1st September or the first day of the course, whichever first occurs, but before receipt of any student loan in respect of that year and that payment is intended for the purpose of bridging the period until receipt of the student loan; or
  (b) before the first day of the course to a person in anticipation of that person becoming a student,
that payment is to be disregarded as income.

DEFINITIONS

    "access funds"—see reg.131(1).
    "claimant"—see reg.83(1).
    "ordinary clothing or footwear"—see reg.2(1).
    "payment"—*ibid.*
    "single claimant"—*ibid.*
    "student"—see reg.131(1).
    "student loan"—*ibid.*

GENERAL NOTE

4.310   This is similar to reg.66B of the Income Support Regulations/reg.136A of the JSA Regulations 1996.

Treatment of fee loans

4.311   **139.** A loan for fees, known as a fee loan or a fee contribution loan, made pursuant to regulations made under Article 3 of the Education (Student Support) (Northern Ireland) Order 1998, section 22 of the Teaching and Higher Education Act 1998 or section 73(f) of the Education (Scotland) Act 1980, is to be disregarded as income.

GENERAL NOTE

4.312   This is similar to reg.66C of the Income Support Regulations/reg.136B of the JSA Regulations 1996.

[¹ Treatment of special support loans

139A. A special support loan within the meaning of regulation 68 of the Education (Student Support) Regulations 2011 is to be disregarded as income.]

AMENDMENT

    1. Social Security (Treatment of Postgraduate Master's Degree Loans and Special Support Loans) (Amendment) Regulations 2016 (SI 2016/743) reg.5(5) (August 4, 2016).

GENERAL NOTE

    See the note to reg.66D of the Income Support Regulations.

Disregard of contribution

4.313   **140.** Where the claimant or the claimant's partner is a student and, for the purposes of assessing a contribution to the student's grant or student loan, the other partner's income has been taken into account, an amount equal to that contribution is to be disregarded for the purposes of assessing that other partner's income.

DEFINITIONS

    "claimant"—see reg.83(1).
    "contribution"—see reg.131(1).
    "grant"—*ibid.*
    "partner"—see reg.2(1).
    "student"—see reg.131(1).
    "student loan"—*ibid.*

4.314 GENERAL NOTE

This is similar to reg.67 of the Income Support Regulations/reg.137 of the JSA Regulations 1996.

Further disregard of student's income

4.315 **141.** Where any part of a student's income has already been taken into account for the purposes of assessing that student's entitlement to a grant [¹, student loan or postgraduate [² . . .] loan], the amount taken into account is to be disregarded in assessing that student's income.

AMENDMENTS

1. Social Security (Treatment of Postgraduate Master's Degree Loans and Special Support Loans) (Amendment) Regulations 2016 (SI 2016/743) reg.5(6) (August 4, 2016).
2. Social Security (Income and Capital) (Miscellaneous Amendments) Regulations 2020 (SI 2020/618) reg.7(9) (July 15, 2020).

DEFINITIONS

"grant"—see reg.131(1).
"postgraduate loan"—*ibid.*
"student"—*ibid.*
"student loan"—*ibid.*

GENERAL NOTE

4.316 This is similar to reg.67A of the Income Support Regulations/reg.137A of the JSA Regulations 1996.

Income treated as capital

4.317 **142.**—(1) Any amount by way of a refund of tax deducted from a student's income is to be treated as capital.

(2) An amount paid from access funds as a single lump sum is to be treated as capital.

(3) An amount paid from access funds as a single lump sum which is intended and used for an item other than food, ordinary clothing or footwear, household fuel, rent for which housing benefit is payable or any housing costs to the extent that they are met under regulation 67(1)(c) or 68(1)(d), of a single claimant or, as the case may be, of the claimant's partner, or which is used for an item other than any council tax or water charges for which that claimant or partner is liable is to be disregarded as capital but only for a period of 52 weeks from the date of the payment.

DEFINITIONS

"access funds"—see reg.131(1).
"claimant"—see reg.83(1).
"ordinary clothing or footwear"—see reg.2(1).
"payment"—*ibid.*
"single claimant"—*ibid.*
"student"—see reg.131(1).

GENERAL NOTE

4.318 This is similar to reg.68 of the Income Support Regulations/reg.138 of the JSA Regulations 1996.

Disregard of changes occurring during summer vacation

143. In calculating a student's income there is to be disregarded any change in the standard maintenance grant occurring in the recognised summer vacation appropriate to the student's course, if that vacation does not form part of the student's period of study, from the date on which the change occurred up to the end of that vacation.

4.319

DEFINITIONS

"period of study"—see reg.131(1).
"standard maintenance grant"—*ibid.*
"student"—*ibid.*

GENERAL NOTE

This is similar to reg.69 of the Income Support Regulations/reg.139 of the JSA Regulations 1996.

4.320

PART 11

SUPPLEMENTARY PROVISIONS

CHAPTER 1

MISCELLANEOUS

Waiting days

144.—(1) A claimant is not entitled to an employment and support allowance in respect of [³ 7] days at the beginning of a period of limited capability for work.

4.321

(2) Paragraph (1) does not apply where—

(a) the claimant's entitlement to an employment and support allowance commences within 12 weeks of the claimant's entitlement to income support, state pension credit, a jobseeker's allowance, a carer's allowance [¹, statutory sick pay or a maternity allowance] coming to an end;

(b) the claimant is terminally ill and has—

    (i) made a claim expressly on the ground of being terminally ill; or

    (ii) made an application for supersession or revision in accordance with the Social Security and Child Support (Decisions and Appeals) Regulations 1999 which contains an express statement of being terminally ill; or

(c) the claimant has been discharged from being a member of Her Majesty's forces and 3 or more days immediately before that discharge were days of sickness absence from duty, which are recorded by the Secretary of State for Defence [¹, or

(d) the claimant is the other member of a couple to whom regulation 4I(2) of the Social Security (Claims and Payments) Regulations 1987 applies and the former claimant was not entitled to an employment and support allowance in respect of [³ 7] days at the beginning of the period of limited capability for work which relates to the former claimant's entitlement.

[²; or

(e) the claimant is entitled to an employment and support allowance by virtue of section 1B of the Act (further entitlement after time-limiting).]

AMENDMENTS

1. Employment and Support Allowance (Miscellaneous Amendments) Regulations 2008 (SI 2008/2428) reg.9(1) (October 27, 2008).

2. Employment and Support Allowance (Duration of Contributory Allowance) (Consequential Amendments) Regulations 2012 (SI 2012/913) reg.9(2) (May 1, 2012).

3. Social Security (Jobseeker's Allowance and Employment and Support Allowance) (Waiting Days) Amendment Regulations 2014 (SI 2014/2309), reg.2(2) (October 27, 2014).

MODIFICATION

Regulation 144 is disapplied by Sch.1, para.14 of the Employment and Support Allowance (Transitional Provisions, Housing Benefit and Council Tax Benefit) (Existing Awards) (No.2) Regulations 2010 (SI 2010/1907) (as amended) for the purposes specified in reg.6(1). For details of the modification, see the text of those Regulations on p.1577. The modification is further modified in those cases in relation to which universal credit has come into force—see the General Note to the 2010 Regulations.

DEFINITIONS

"claimant"—see WRA 2007, s.24(1).
"a member of Her Majesty's forces"—see reg.2(1).
"terminally ill"—see reg.2(1).

GENERAL NOTE

4.322   WRA 2007, s.22 and Sch.2 para.2 provide that "except in prescribed circumstances" a claimant cannot be entitled to ESA for a prescribed number of days at the beginning of a period of limited capability for work. This regulation originally set the number of these days of non-entitlement ("waiting days") at three. From October 27, 2014 that was increased to seven with respect to a new claim in respect of a waiting period starting on or after that date; regulation 4 of the amending instrument ensures that the changes made to reg.144 do not apply where a waiting period began before that date.

It further provides in para.(2) for the exceptions to that general rule:

- where entitlement to ESA begins within 12 weeks of entitlement to IS, SPC, JSA, carer's allowance or SSP coming to an end (sub-para.(a));

- terminally ill claimants (including those seeking revision or supersession on the basis of being terminally ill) (sub-para.(b));

- discharge from Her Majesty's forces where three or more days of recorded sickness absence from duty preceded it (sub-para.(c));

- the claimant is the other member of a couple to whom reg.4I of the Claims and Payments Regs applies (change of claimant during a period of limited capability for work) and the previous claimant had already served the waiting days (sub-para.(d));

- where for someone not in the support group entitlement to CESA ended because of the time limit set by WRA 2007 s.1A (currently 365 days), but further entitlement arises under s.IB of that Act because subsequent deterioration in health now places that person in the support group (sub-para.(e)).

In addition, the general rule is, of course, affected by the "linking rule" (on which see reg.145) in a case of intermittent incapacity where that rule fuses into one ostensibly separate spells of limited capability for work: the "waiting days" only have to be served once in a period of limited capability for work.

Linking rules

145.—(1) Any period of limited capability for work which is separated from another such period by not more than 12 weeks is to be treated as a continuation of the earlier period.

4.323

[¹ (2)–(5) *Revoked.*]

AMENDMENT

1. Employment and Support Allowance (Amendment of Linking Rules) Regulations 2012 (SI 2012/919), reg.5(6) (May 1, 2012).

DEFINITIONS

"child tax credit"—see reg.2(1).
"claimant"—see WRA 2007 s.24(1).
"qualifying remunerative work"—see reg.2(1).
"relevant tax credit conditions"—see para.(4).
"training"—see reg.2(1).
"week"—see reg.2(1).
"work or training beneficiary"—see reg.148.
"working tax credit"—see reg.2(1).

GENERAL NOTE

Linking rules are crucial for those suffering from intermittent incapacity. They impact, to the claimant's benefit, as regards "waiting days"; those days of non-entitlement (see para.(2) and ESA Regs, reg.144) only have to be served once in any period of limited capability for work. They are also relevant to determining the relevant benefit year and hence the appropriate tax years to which to have regard with respect to the application of the national insurance contribution conditions (see further the commentary to Sch.1 Pt 1 paras 1–3).

4.324

There is now only one linking rule: two ostensibly separate spells of limited capability for work will be fused into one where the separation period between the spells is not more than 12 weeks (para.(1)). This fusing does not, however, mean that days in the separation period thereby become ones of limited capability for work (*Chief Adjudication Officer v Astle* (Court of Appeal, judgment of March 17, 1999, available on LEXIS and noted in [1999] 6 J.S.S.L. 203). See further for more detail the commentary to SSCBA 1992, s.30C(1)(c) (the "linking" rule)). A period of limited capability for work can only be formed of days of actual limited capability for work and/or ones which the legislative scheme treats as ones of limited capability for work.

Advance awards

146.—(1) Where section 5 of the Act (advance award of income-related allowance) applies to a claim and the claimant satisfies the conditions in paragraph (3)—

4.325

    (a) the claim is to be treated as if made for a period from the relevant day; and

    (b) the Secretary of State may award an employment and support allowance from the relevant day.

(2) In this regulation the "relevant day" is the day after the end of a period

of 13 weeks beginning on the first day on which the claimant would be entitled to an income-related allowance if the claimant satisfied the condition in paragraph 6(1)(a) of Schedule 1 to the Act. (3) The conditions are that—

(a) the Secretary of State is of the opinion that unless there is a change of circumstances the claimant will satisfy the conditions set out in section 1(3)(b) to (f) of, and Part 2 of Schedule 1 to, the Act when an income-related allowance becomes payable under the award; and

(b) the claimant is treated as having limited capability for work under regulation 20, 25, 26, [¹ 30] or 33(2) (conditions for treating a person as having limited capability for work) for the period before an income-related allowance becomes payable under the award.

(4) Where an award is made under paragraph (1)—

(a) the award for an employment and support allowance will become payable on the date on which the claimant would have been entitled to a main phase employment and support allowance if the claimant had satisfied the condition in paragraph 6(1)(a) of Schedule 1 to the Act before the relevant day;

(b) sections 4(4)(a) and 4(5)(a) of the Act do not apply to that award.

AMENDMENT

1. Employment and Support Allowance (Miscellaneous Amendments) Regulations 2008 (SI 2008/2428) reg.9(2) (October 27, 2008).

DEFINITION

"claimant"—Welfare Reform Act 2007, s.24(1).
"income-related allowance"—Welfare Reform Act 2007, s.24(1) and 1(7).
"main phase employment and support allowance"—reg.2(1).

GENERAL NOTE

4.326   See the General Note to s.5 of the Welfare Reform Act 2007.

Recovery orders

4.327   **147.**—(1) Where an award of income-related allowance has been made to a claimant, the Secretary of State may apply to the court for a recovery order against the claimant's partner.

(2) On making a recovery order the court may order the partner to pay such amount at such intervals as it considers appropriate, having regard to all the circumstances of the partner and, in particular, the partner's income.

(3) Except in Scotland, a recovery order is to be treated for all purposes as if it were a maintenance order within the meaning of section 150(1) of the Magistrates Courts Act 1980.

(4) Where a recovery order requires the partner to make payments to the Secretary of State, the Secretary of State may, by giving notice in writing to the court which made the order, the liable person and the claimant, transfer to the claimant the right to receive payments under the order and to exercise the relevant rights in relation to the order.

(5) In paragraph 4, "the relevant rights" means, in relation to a recovery order, the right to bring any proceedings, take any steps or do any other thing under or in relation to the order.

"partner"—see reg.2(1).
"payment"—*ibid.*

GENERAL NOTE

See s.23 of the Welfare Reform Act 2007 and the note to that section.   4.328
This regulation is similar to reg.169 of the JSA Regulations 1996.

[¹ Claimants appealing a decision

147A.—[⁴ (1) This regulation applies where a claimant has made and is   4.329
pursuing an appeal against a relevant decision of the Secretary of State as
defined in regulation 30.]

(2) Subject to paragraph (3), where this regulation applies, a determination
of limited capability for work by the Secretary of State under regulation 19
shall not be made until the appeal is determined by the First-tier Tribunal.

(3) Paragraph (2) does not apply where either—

(a) the claimant suffers from some specific disease or bodily or mental
disablement from which the claimant was not suffering when entitlement began; or

(b) a disease or bodily or mental disablement from which the claimant
was suffering at that date has significantly worsened.

(4) Where this regulation applies and the Secretary of State makes a
determination—

(a) in a case to which paragraph (3) applies (including where the determination is not the first such determination) that the claimant does
not have or, by virtue of regulation 22 or 23, is to be treated as not
having limited capability for work; or

(b) subsequent to a determination that the claimant is to be treated as
having limited capability for work by virtue of a provision of these
Regulations other than regulation 30, that the claimant is no longer
to be so treated,

this regulation and regulation 30 apply as if that determination had not
been made.

(5) Where this regulation applies and—

(a) the claimant is entitled to an employment and support allowance
by virtue of being treated as having limited capability for work in
accordance with regulation 30;

(b) neither of the circumstances in paragraph (3) applies, or, subsequent
to the application of either of those circumstances, the claimant has
been determined not to have limited capability for work; and

(c) the claimant's appeal is dismissed, withdrawn [² , struck out or has
been discontinued in accordance with the provisions of regulation
33(10) of the Social Security and Child Support (Decisions and
Appeals) Regulations 1999 (notice of appeal),]

the claimant is to be treated as not having limited capability for work [² with
effect from the day specified in paragraph (5A).]

[² (5A) The day specified for the purposes of paragraph (5) is the first day
of the benefit week following the date on which the Secretary of State [³ ...]

(a) receives the First-tier Tribunal's notification that the appeal is dismissed, withdrawn or struck out, [³ ...]

(b) [³ ...]]

(6) Where a claimant's appeal is successful, subject to paragraph (7), any finding of fact or other determination embodied in or necessary to the decision of the First-tier Tribunal or on which the First-tier Tribunal's decision is based shall be conclusive for the purposes of the decision of the Secretary of State, in relation to an award made in a case to which this regulation applies, as to whether the claimant has limited capability for work or limited capability for work-related activity.

(7) Paragraph (6) does not apply where, due to a change of circumstances after entitlement to which this regulation applies began, the Secretary of State is satisfied that it is no longer appropriate to rely on such finding or determination.]

MODIFICATION

Regulation 147A is modified by Sch.2 para.15 of the Employment and Support Allowance (Transitional Provisions, Housing Benefit and Council Tax Benefit) (Existing Awards) (No. 2) Regulations 2010 (SI 2010/1907) (as amended) for the purposes specified in reg.16(1) of those Regulations. For details of the modifications, see the text of those Regulations on p.1577. The modification is further modified in those cases and in relation to which universal credit has come into force—see the General Note to the 2010 Regulations.

AMENDMENTS

1. Social Security (Miscellaneous Amendments) (No. 3) Regulations 2010 (SI 2010/840) reg.9(15) (June 28, 2010).

2. Social Security (Miscellaneous Amendments) (No. 3) Regulations 2011 (SI 2011/2425) reg.23(10) and (11) (October 31, 2011).

3. Social Security, Child Support, Vaccine Damage and Other Payments (Decisions and Appeals) (Amendment) Regulations 2013 (SI 2013/2380) reg.7(2) (October 28, 2013).

4. Employment and Support Allowance (Repeat Assessments and Pending Appeal Awards) (Amendment) Regulations 2015 (SI 2015/437) reg. 3(3) (March 30, 2015).

DEFINITION

"relevant decision"—see reg. 30(5).

GENERAL NOTE

4.330   Before June 28, 2010, reg.6 provided that where a claimant appealed against a decision that he did not have limited capability for work the assessment phase did not end until the appeal was determined by a tribunal. In addition, reg.3(j) of the Claims and Payments Regulations 1987 (see Vol.III in this series) provided that a claim was not required where a claimant had made and was pursuing an appeal against a decision that he did not have limited capability for work. Thus the effect of reg.3(j) was that a further award of ESA could be made when a claimant appealed, without the claimant having to make a claim, thereby allowing the claimant to continue to receive ESA (paid at the basic rate) pending the tribunal's decision on his appeal ("the pending appeal award"). This was, however, subject to the production of medical evidence, which was necessary so that the claimant could be treated as having limited capability for work under reg.30. The "six months rule" in reg.30(2)(b) was disapplied by reg.30(3) where the claimant's appeal against a decision that he did not have limited capability for work had not yet been determined by a tribunal (note, however, that where the appeal is against a decision that the claimant does not have limited capability for work in respect of a claim for ESA made on or after March 30, 2015, reg.30(3) now only applies where the claimant is appealing against a "relevant decision"—see the amendments to reg.30 made on March 30, 2015 and see below).

This procedure, however, raised a number of issues, for example, whether this prevented retrospective payment of the relevant component in the case of a successful appeal. This is because under s.2(2)(a) and (3)(a) and s.4(4)(a) and (5)(a) of the Welfare Reform Act 2007, one of the conditions of entitlement to the work-related activity/support component is that the assessment period has ended. It seems that in practice the DWP was paying the appropriate component from the beginning of the 14th week after the claimant's entitlement to ESA began if the appeal succeeded under the authority of ss.2(4)(b) and 4(6)(b) (see the advice given in paras 44647 to 44650 of Vol.8 of the *Decision Makers Guide*).

Another issue was the grounds for bringing the pending appeal award to an end, once the tribunal had made its decision on the appeal. In *CG v SSWP (ESA)* [2011] UKUT 384 (AAC) Judge Turnbull stated that he had "found considerable difficulty in trying to work out the effect of the legislation". The claimant in that case had appealed on June 3, 2009 against a decision made on May 26, 2009 that she did not have limited capability for work. A tribunal dismissed her appeal on February 1, 2010. As Judge Turnbull pointed out, this meant from February 1, 2010 reg.30(3) no longer applied. The consequence was that the claimant was no longer exempt from the condition in reg.30(2)(b) that it had not been determined in the six months preceding the date of claim that she did not have limited capability for work.

Judge Turnbull then went on to decide that in relation to a pending appeal award "date of claim" in reg.30(2)(b) should probably be read as referring to the date of the appeal against the decision that the claimant did not have limited capability for work (in this case June 3, 2009). In his view, it could not have been the intention that reg.30(2)(b) would never become applicable because there was no "date of claim" in relation to pending award appeals. He continued:

"9. ... The effect of the view which I prefer, therefore, is from 1 February 2010 the condition in reg. 30(2)(b) became applicable, and was not satisfied because it had, within 6 months before 3 June 2009 (the date of appeal – and therefore in my view the date of claim for this purpose) been determined that the Claimant did not have limited capability for work. The position was in my judgment therefore probably that from 1 February 2010 the Secretary of State was entitled to supersede and remove the Claimant's award of ESA from that date on the simple ground that the Claimant no longer fulfilled the conditions for being treated as not [*sic*] having limited capability for work.

10. ... Although the Secretary of State could have made a decision terminating entitlement simply by reason of the fact that the appeal had been dismissed on 1 February, I do not think that there was anything to stop the Secretary of State making a decision as to [...] whether the Claimant actually had limited capability for work. Further, the terms of reg. 21(1)(b) and (c), and reg. 21(2), would appear to have entitled the Secretary of State to make such a determination without requiring the claimant to fill in a further ESA 50 questionnaire, or submit to a further medical examination."

In this case the Secretary of State had in fact made a determination on actual limited capability for work when deciding to terminate the pending appeal award.

It will be noted that Judge Turnbull took the view that the Secretary of State was entitled to end the claimant's award of ESA from February 1, 2010 simply on the ground that the claimant no longer fulfilled the conditions for being treated as having limited capability for work. The Secretary of State, however, had submitted that the effect of reg.30(1)(a) was that the claimant continued to be entitled to be treated as having limited capability for work until it had been determined whether or not she actually had limited capability for work (this was the approach taken in DMG Memo 7/10, paras 23 and 24). Judge Turnbull, however, doubted whether this was right because in his view the intention must have been that a pending appeal award could be superseded by reason of the fact that the appeal had been decided. But in *TW v SSWP* [2012] UKUT 152 (AAC) (another pre-June 28, 2010 appeal)

Judge Jupp accepted that when terminating a pending appeal award it was necessary for the decision-maker to decide on the claimant's actual capability for work at the date of that decision.

Furthermore, case law on the operation of the comparable IB regulation (reg.28 of the Social Security (Incapacity for Work) (General) Regulations 1995 (SI 1995/311), see the 2010/11 edition of this Volume) held that where a claimant could not be treated as incapable of work because of a determination on incapacity within the previous six months, it was necessary to go on to determine whether the claimant was actually incapable of work (see *CIB/1031/2000*, *CIB/3106/2003* and *R(IB)8/04*). Judge Turnbull, however, did not refer to any of these decisions.

Introduction of reg.147A

4.331   With effect from June 28, 2010, however, reg.6 was revoked and replaced by reg.147A. Regulation 3(j) of the Claims and Payments Regulations was also amended from the same date. As amended, it provided that a claim for ESA was not required where the claimant's appeal "relates to a decision to terminate or not to award a benefit *for which a claim was made*" (emphasis added). In other words, reg.3(j) did not apply where the appeal related to a decision where a claim was not made because it was not required (under reg.3(j)). Without this amendment it would seem possible for ESA to have remained in payment indefinitely on the basis of continuous appeals, supported by a medical certificate, each time a pending appeal award came to an end.

Paragraph (1)

4.332   Up to March 30, 2015 reg.147A applied where a claimant had made and was pursuing an appeal against a decision that he did not have limited capability for work. The new form of reg.147A(1), however, only applies where the claimant has made and is pursuing an appeal against a "relevant decision of the Secretary of State as defined in regulation 30". Note that the new form only applies where the decision under appeal was in respect of a claim made, or treated as made, on or after March 30, 2015 (see reg.2 of the ESA (Repeat Assessment and Pending Appeal Awards) (Amendment) Regulations 2015 (SI 2015/437)).

A "relevant decision" is a decision that *first* determines that the claimant does not have limited capability for work, or *first* determines this after a previous decision (by the Secretary of State or on appeal) that the claimant does have limited capability for work (see reg.30(5)).

Thus reg.147A (and the other provisions discussed below) will no longer apply to appeals against repeat claims for ESA where the claim is made at any time on or after March 30, 2015, *unless* the claimant is suffering from a new condition or there has been a significant worsening of an existing condition (see reg.30(2)(b) and (4)).

What if there has been a previous decision that the claimant did not have limited capability for work but it is accepted that his condition has significantly worsened, or that he has a new condition, and so he is treated as having limited capability for work under reg.30, but he then fails the work capability assessment and appeals that decision? Although the position is not entirely clear, it is suggested that that decision *is* a "relevant decision" within the meaning of reg.30(5) because it is the first determination in relation to this new condition or significantly worsened condition. This does not, however, appear to be the view of the DWP (see example 4 at the end of DMG Memo 10/15).

The effect of the claimant appealing was that he could be awarded ESA without making a claim (reg.3(j) of the Claims and Payments Regulations). Note, however, that reg.3(j) was also amended on March 30, 2015. Where the appeal is against a decision that the claimant does not have limited capability for work in respect of a claim for ESA made on or after March 30, 2015, reg.3(j) only applies where the claimant is appealing against a "relevant decision". In other cases, the claimant will have to make a new claim for ESA.

In addition, the claimant could be treated as having limited capability for work until the appeal was determined—see reg.30(3) which disapplied the "six months rule" in reg.30(2)(b) where the claimant's appeal against a decision that he did not have limited capability for work had not yet been determined by a tribunal. However, reg.30(2)(b) and (3) were also amended on March 30, 2015. The effect is that reg.30(3) now only applies where the claimant is appealing against a "relevant decision".

These provisions therefore allow a new award to be made and basic rate ESA to be paid pending the determination of the appeal, *provided that* the claimant submits medical evidence in accordance with reg. 30(2)(a) so that he can be treated as having limited capability for work under reg.30(1) (and provided that he continues to satisfy the other conditions of entitlement to ESA), but in respect of claims for ESA made on or after March 30, 2015 this only applies where the claimant is appealing against a "relevant decision". According to para.37 of DMG Memo 33/10 the new award will normally begin on the day after the last day of entitlement under the award that is the subject of the appeal or the day the medical evidence begins, if later.

Note *AR v SSWP (ESA)* [2013] UKUT 358 (AAC) in which the claimant had misrepresented a material fact on her original claim form. The fact that no new claim was required meant that the Secretary of State was entitled to rely on the information provided in the original claim form when making the pending appeal award and so the misrepresentation on the original claim form remained an effective cause of the overpayment in relation to the pending appeal award.

Paragraphs (2) and (4)

The effect of para.(2) is that the Secretary of State will not make a determination of limited capability for work in relation to the pending appeal award until the appeal is decided by a tribunal.   **4.333**

Paragraph (2) does not apply, however, if the claimant's condition significantly worsens or he develops a new condition. This exception is necessary because without it the Secretary of State would not be able to decide that the claimant has limited capability for work on the basis of the new/worsened condition pending the determination of the appeal. Note, however, that in the case of a new/worsened condition, if the Secretary of State determines that the claimant does not have, or is to be treated under reg.22 (failure to return the limited capability for work questionnaire) or reg.23 (failure to attend a medical examination) as not having, limited capability for work, reg.147A and reg.30 will apply (para.(4)(a)). Regulation 147A and reg.30 will also apply if, having determined that the claimant is to be treated as having limited capability for work (*other* than under reg.30), the Secretary of State subsequently determines that he is no longer to be so treated (para.(4)(b)).

Note that para.(2) only applies until the appeal is determined by the First-tier Tribunal. Therefore it will not apply while a claimant pursues an appeal to the Upper Tribunal.

Paragraph (5)

If the claimant's appeal (in relation to his original/earlier claim) is then dismissed, withdrawn or struck out, the claimant will be treated as not having limited capability for work from the first day of the benefit week following the date on which the Secretary of State was notified by the First-tier Tribunal of its decision (paras (5) (c) and (5A)(a)). From October 31, 2011 this also applied if, before the appeal was submitted to the First-tier Tribunal, the claimant (or an authorised representative) notified the Secretary of State in writing that he did not wish the appeal to continue. In this case the claimant was treated as not having limited capability for work from the first day of the benefit week following the date on which the Secretary of State discontinued action on the appeal (paras (5)(c) and (5A)(b)). However, para.(5A) (b) was omitted with effect from October 28, 2013. This was due to the revocation of reg.33 of the Decisions and Appeals Regulations 1999 (SI 1999/991) with effect from October 28, 2013. This is because of the extension of "mandatory reconsideration" and "direct lodgement" of appeals to, inter alia, social security benefits that was introduced on October 28, 2013. See further the note to r.22 of the Tribunal   **4.334**

Procedure (First-tier Tribunal) (Social Entitlement Chamber) Rules 2008 (SI 2008/2685) in Vol. III of this series. It is not clear why a similar amendment has not been made to para.(5)(c).

The purpose of this provision is to provide a mechanism for bringing the decision awarding ESA pending the determination of the appeal to an end. Such a mechanism is needed because the tribunal will of course only have dealt with the question of whether the claimant had limited capability for work/work-related activity at the date of the decision under appeal to it; the tribunal's decision has no direct effect on the decision awarding ESA pending the determination of the appeal.

However, para.(5) will not apply if the claimant's condition has significantly worsened or he has developed a new condition (unless in such a case the Secretary of State has subsequently decided that the claimant does not have limited capability for work).

The claimant will of course have a right of appeal against a decision under para. (5) in the normal way.

What issues does a tribunal have to consider in relation to such an appeal? Paragraphs (5) and (5A) provide for a decision to be made that the claimant is to be treated as not having limited capability for work from the start of the benefit week following notification of the First-tier Tribunal's decision. (Until October 28, 2013 this provision also applied where the Secretary of State had discontinued action on an appeal under reg.33(10) of the Decisions and Appeals Regulations 1999.) The effect of such a decision is that the claimant will not be entitled to ESA.

However, in order for a decision to be made under paras (5) and (5A) all of the conditions in para.(5) have to be met. This includes the condition in para.(5)(b) that neither of the circumstances in para.(3) apply (or if either of them has applied, it has since been determined that the claimant does not have limited capability for work). The circumstances in para.(3) are that the claimant is suffering from a new disease or bodily or mental disablement or that a disease or bodily or mental disablement has significantly worsened. It is suggested that, in order to decide this, the work capability assessment ("WCA") has to be applied because if the claimant satisfies the WCA at the date of the decision under paras (5) and (5A) there will, by definition, have been a significant worsening by the date of that decision and so a circumstance in para.(3) *will* apply. See *CIB/1959/1997* and *CIB/2198/1997* referred to in the note to reg.30 which held that "significantly worsened", as regards the claimant's condition, must be related to what is now the WCA (and what was then the personal capability assessment), so that it will only have significantly worsened if it has done so to an extent that the claimant would satisfy what is now the WCA if he were subjected to it (although note *SK v SSWP* [2009] UKUT 121 (AAC) which doubted that the question of significant worsening required that a judgment be made as to whether the claimant might satisfy what was then the personal capability assessment (see para.8)). In this connection note also reg.21(1)(b) and (c) and (2) under which the Secretary of State can determine limited capability for work without requiring a claimant to complete an ESA 50 or submit to a medical examination. If the Secretary of State can so act, so can the tribunal. If the tribunal does decide that at the date of the decision under paras (5) and (5A) the claimant satisfied the WCA, the conditions for treating the claimant as not having limited capability for work under paras (5) and (5A) will not be met. In addition, as the tribunal has decided that the claimant has satisfied the WCA, the relevant component will be immediately payable, as the conditions in ss.2(2) and (3) or 4(4) and (5) of the Welfare Reform Act 2007 will inevitably be met as the assessment phase will have ended long ago (see also *SSWP v PT (ESA)* [2011] UKUT 317 (AAC); [2012] AACR 17).

But what if new evidence, which establishes that the claimant in fact satisfied the WCA at the time of the original disallowance and which was not before the tribunal which confirmed that disallowance, is presented to a tribunal hearing an appeal against a decision made under paras (5) and (5A)? In this situation the claimant's condition may not have significantly worsened or he may not have developed a new condition and so neither of the circumstances in para.(3) may apply. Is the effect of para.(5) that the claimant has to be treated as not having limited capability for work or can the tribunal consider the question of whether the claimant actually has limited capability for work/work-related activity at the date of the decision terminating the pending appeal award. See, by way of analogy, *CIB/1031/2000*, *CIB/3106/2003* and *R(IB)8/04* which held that where a tribunal found that a claimant could not be treated as being incapable of work under reg.28 of the Incapacity for Work Regulations (the comparable IB provision to reg.30), the tribunal should go on to consider whether the claimant had actual incapacity for work.

It could be argued that because para.(5) treats a person as *not* having limited capability for work (emphasis added) that the analogy does not apply and that a new claim for ESA is required. However, it is also arguable that all that para.(5) does is to undo the deeming of limited capability for work in reg.30 (see the other condition for the application of para.(5) that the claimant is entitled to ESA by virtue of reg.30 (para.(5)(a)) and that actual limited capability for work can (and should) be considered. Moreover, if a tribunal is not able to consider whether the claimant did have actual limited capability for work/work-related activity at the date of the decision terminating the pending appeal award, this could cause substantial unfairness in some situations. The claimant may well have not made a new claim for ESA, thinking that the whole matter would be resolved when the tribunal heard his appeal against the decision terminating his pending appeal award. Depending on the length of time before the appeal against the termination of the pending appeal award is heard, this could cause injustice if the claimant only becomes aware of the fact that he needs to make a new claim at that tribunal hearing. Paragraph (5) is a deeming provision and arguably should not be applied to require a claimant to be treated as not having limited capability for work where the evidence is clearly to the contrary and shows that the claimant has actual limited capability for work/work-related activities. It could be argued that reg.22 (failure to return the ESA 50) and reg.23 (failure to attend a medical examination) also treat a claimant as not having limited capability for work and yet it has not been suggested that the question of whether the claimant has actual limited capability for work needs to be considered when these regulations are applied. Regulations 22 and 23 are, however, penalty provisions for non-cooperation and it is suggested therefore merit a different approach.

Unfortunately the operation of reg.147A has led to considerable confusion in some cases. It is often not clear when a claimant appeals following the termination of his pending appeal award whether he wishes to appeal against that decision or against the tribunal's original/earlier decision (or both). This will require clarification with the claimant at an early stage. In addition, appeal submissions from the Department frequently do not make clear that this is an appeal against a decision terminating a pending appeal award, thus causing confusion for both the appellant and the tribunal.

Note also that the Department found it necessary (at the end of June 2012) to issue further guidance on the operation of reg.147A following requests from decision makers (see DMG Memo 26/12).

Paragraphs (6) and (7)
If the claimant's appeal (against the original/earlier decision) is successful, subject   **4.335** to any change of circumstances that has occurred since the claimant was awarded ESA pending the determination of his appeal, any finding of fact or determination by the tribunal will be conclusive for the purposes of the Secretary of State's decision in relation to the pending appeal award as to whether the claimant has limited capability for work/work-related activity (paras (6) and (7)). Note reg.3(5E) of the Decisions and Appeals Regulations 1999 (see Vol.III in this series) which allows revision of the pending appeal award if the appeal is successful. This is necessary so that the relevant component can be paid since the claimant will only have been paid ESA at the basic rate until the appeal was determined.

The result should therefore be that the claimant will be paid arrears of ESA, including the relevant component, from the beginning of the 14th week of his entitlement to ESA. It seems, however, that the DWP was not doing this where the claimant had claimed and been awarded JSA while the appeal was pending. This was apparently because of reg.31. Regulation 31 provided that a claimant who had claimed JSA and had a reasonable prospect of obtaining employment was to be treated as not having limited capability for work for the period of the JSA claim, even though it had been determined that he had (or was to be treated under regs 20, 25. 26 or 29 as having) limited capability for work. The DWP stated that reg.31 would be revoked and indeed this has happened (see reg.25(1) of the Employment and Support Allowance (Transitional Provisions, Housing Benefit and Council Tax Benefit) (Existing Awards) (No. 2) Regulations 2010 (SI 2010/1907) which revokes reg.31 with effect from October 1, 2010). For an argument as to why full payment of arrears of ESA was possible even before the revocation of reg.31 (based on reg.3(5A) of the Decisions and Appeals Regulations) see CPAG's *Welfare Rights Bulletin 218.*

See *NC v SSWP (ESA)* [2015] UKUT 147 (AAC) (in particular para. 42) as to the operation of paras (6) and (7) in circumstances where the claimant had limited capability for work as at the date of the decision under appeal but on the facts she ceased to do so two weeks later.

Note the modified form of reg.147A (and reg.30) which apply where the claimant is appealing against a conversion decision under the Employment and Support Allowance (Transitional Provisions, Housing Benefit and Council Tax Benefit) (Existing Awards) (No. 2) Regulations 2010 (SI 2010/1907) (as amended) which determined he did not have limited capability for work. See also the modified form of reg.3(j) of the Claims and Payments Regulations which applies in the case of appeals against conversion decisions. The effect is that a claimant who appeals against a conversion decision will be paid basic rate ESA from the date of his appeal.

The main difference under the modified form of reg.147A is that if the claimant's appeal is successful, his entitlement under reg.147A terminates at the start of the benefit week following the date on which the Secretary of State receives notification of the tribunal's decision (see the modified para.(6)). The claimant will be entitled to ESA (with the relevant component) under the conversion decision.

CHAPTER 2

WORK OR TRAINING BENEFICIARIES

4.336   *Regulations 148, 149, and 150 were revoked with effect from May 1, 2012 by reg.5(7) of the Employment and Support Allowance (Amendment of Linking Rules) Regulations 2012 (SI 2012/919).*

CHAPTER 3

TEMPORARY ABSENCE FROM GREAT BRITAIN

Absence from Great Britain

4.337   **151.**—(1) A claimant who is entitled to an employment and support allowance is to continue to be so entitled during a period of temporary absence from Great Britain only in accordance with this Chapter.

(2) A claimant who continues to be entitled to a contributory allowance during a period of temporary absence will not be disqualified for receiving that allowance during that period under section 18(4) of the Act.

DEFINITIONS

"claimant"—Welfare Reform Act 2007 s.24(1).
"contributory allowance"—Welfare Reform Act 2007 s.24(1) and 1(7).

GENERAL NOTE

Under s.1(3) of the Welfare Reform Act, it is a condition of entitlement to ESA 4.338 that the claimant should be "in Great Britain". However, para.5 of Sch.2 to that Act empowers the Secretary of State to "make provision . . . as to the circumstances in which a person is to be treated as being, or not being, in Great Britain".

In addition, those entitled to a contributory allowance are disqualified under s.18(4)(a) while they are absent from Great Britain "except where regulations otherwise provide". Paragraph 6 of Sch.2 to the Act provides that "regulations may provide that in prescribed circumstances a claimant who is not in Great Britain may nevertheless be entitled to a contributory allowance".

The regulations in this Chapter are made under those powers

Short absence

152. A claimant is to continue to be entitled to an employment and 4.339 support allowance during the first 4 weeks of a temporary absence from Great Britain if—

(a) the period of absence is unlikely to exceed 52 weeks; and
(b) while absent from Great Britain, the claimant continues to satisfy the other conditions of entitlement to that employment and support allowance.

GENERAL NOTE

See the commentary to reg.4(1) and (2) of the IS Regs. 4.340

Absence to receive medical treatment

153.—(1) A claimant is to continue to be entitled to an employment and 4.341 support allowance during the first 26 weeks of a temporary absence from Great Britain if—

(a) the period of absence is unlikely to exceed 52 weeks;
(b) while absent from Great Britain, the claimant continues to satisfy the other conditions of entitlement to that employment and support allowance;
(c) the claimant is absent from Great Britain solely—
    (i) in connection with arrangements made for the treatment of the claimant for a disease or bodily or mental disablement directly related to the claimant's limited capability for work which commenced before leaving Great Britain; or
    (ii) because the claimant is accompanying a dependent child in connection with arrangements made for the treatment of that child for a disease or bodily or mental disablement;
(d) those arrangements relate to treatment—
    (i) outside Great Britain;

    (ii) during the period whilst the claimant is temporarily absent from Great Britain; and

    (iii) by, or under the supervision of, a person appropriately qualified to carry out that treatment; and

(e) [¹ . . .]

(2) In paragraph (1)(d)(iii), "appropriately qualified" means qualified to provide medical treatment, physiotherapy or a form of treatment which is similar to, or related to, either of those forms of treatment.

AMENDMENT

1. Social Security (Miscellaneous Amendments) (No.4) Regulations 2009 (SI 2009/2655) reg.11(1) and (15) (October 26, 2009).

GENERAL NOTE

4.342   Where the temporary absence is in connection with receiving medical treatment for a condition related to the claimant's limited capacity for work, or because the claimant is accompanying a dependent child who is receiving medical treatment, ESA remains payable for the first 26 weeks of absence, as long as the total length of the absence is unlikely to exceed 52 weeks. From October 26, 2009, there is no longer any requirement to obtain the Secretary of State's permission before departure. Where the medical treatment abroad is paid for by the NHS, see reg.154 below.

Absence in order to receive NHS treatment

4.343   **154.** A claimant is to continue to be entitled to an employment and support allowance during any period of temporary absence from Great Britain if—

    (a) while absent from Great Britain, the claimant continues to satisfy the other conditions of entitlement to that employment and support allowance;

    (b) that period of temporary absence is for the purpose of the claimant receiving treatment at a hospital or other institution outside Great Britain where the treatment is being provided—

        (i) under section 6(2) of the Health Service Act (Performance of functions outside England) or section 6(2) of the Health Service (Wales) Act (Performance of functions outside Wales);

        (ii) pursuant to arrangements made under section 12(1) of the Health Service Act (Secretary of State's arrangements with other bodies), section 10(1) of the Health Service (Wales) Act (Welsh Ministers' arrangements with other bodies), paragraph 18 of Schedule 4 to the Health Service Act (Joint exercise of functions) or paragraph 18 of Schedule 3 to the Health Service (Wales) Act (Joint exercise of functions); or

        (iii) under any equivalent provision in Scotland or pursuant to arrangements made under such provision; [¹ . . .]

AMENDMENT

1. Social Security (Miscellaneous Amendments) (No. 3) Regulations 2010 (SI 2010/840) reg.9(1) and (16) (June 29, 2010).

GENERAL NOTE

4.344   See the commentary to reg.4(3A) of the IS Regs.

Absence of member of family of member of Her Majesty's forces

155.—(1) A claimant is to continue to be entitled to an employment and support allowance during any period of temporary absence from Great Britain if—

    (a) the claimant is a member of the family of a member of Her Majesty's forces and temporarily absent from Great Britain by reason only of the fact that the claimant is living with that member; [¹ . . .]

    (2) In this regulation "member of the family of a member of Her Majesty's forces" means the spouse, civil partner, son, daughter, step-son, step-daughter, father, father-in-law, step-father, mother, mother-in-law or step-mother of such a member.

4.344.1

AMENDMENT

1. Social Security (Miscellaneous Amendments) (No.3) Regulations 2010 (SI 2010/840) reg.9(1) and (17) (June 29, 2010).

CHAPTER 4

MEMBERSHIP OF HOUSEHOLD

Circumstances in which a person is to be treated as being or not being a member of the household

156.—(1) Subject to the following provisions of this regulation—

    (a) the claimant and the claimant's partner; and

    (b) where the claimant or the claimant's partner is responsible for a child or young person, that child or young person and any child of that child or young person,

are to be treated as being members of the same household.

4.345

(2) Paragraph (1) applies even where any of them is temporarily living away from the other members of the family.

(3) Paragraph (1) does not apply to a person who is living away from the other members of the family where—

    (a) that person does not intend to resume living with the other members of the family; or

    (b) that person's absence from the other members of the family is likely to exceed 52 weeks, unless there are exceptional circumstances (for example where the person is in hospital or otherwise has no control over the length of absence), and the absence is unlikely to be substantially more than 52 weeks.

(4) Paragraph (1) does not apply in respect of any member of a couple or of a polygamous marriage where—

    (a) one, both or all of them are patients detained in a hospital provided under section 4 of the Health Service Act (high security psychiatric services), section 4 of the Health Service (Wales) Act (high security psychiatric services) or section 102 of the National Health Service (Scotland) Act 1978 (state hospitals);

    (b) one, both or all of them are—

      (i) detained in custody pending trial or sentence upon conviction or under a sentence imposed by a court; or

      (ii) on temporary release in accordance with the provisions of the Prison Act 1952 or the Prisons (Scotland) Act 1989;

(c) the claimant is abroad and does not satisfy the conditions of Chapter 4 of this Part (temporary absence from Great Britain); or

(d) any one of them is permanently residing in a care home, an Abbeyfield Home or an independent hospital.

(5) A child or young person is not to be treated as a member of the claimant's household where that child or young person is—

(a) placed with the claimant or the claimant's partner by a local authority under [⁴ section 22C(2)] of the Children Act 1989 or by a voluntary organisation under section 59(1)(a) of that Act;

[³(aa) placed with the claimant or the claimant's partner by a local authority under section 81(2) of the Social Services and Well-being (Wales) Act 2014;]

(b) placed with the claimant or the claimant's partner prior to adoption;

(c) in accordance with a relevant enactment, boarded out with the claimant or the claimant's partner, whether or not with a view to adoption; or

(d) placed for adoption with the claimant or the claimant's partner pursuant to a decision under the [¹ Adoption and Children Act 2002] or the Adoption Agencies (Scotland) Regulations 1996.

(6) Subject to paragraphs (7) and (8), paragraph (1) does not apply to a child or young person who is not living with the claimant and who—

(a) in a case which does not fall within sub-paragraph (b), has been continuously absent from Great Britain for a period of more than four weeks commencing—

    (i) where that child or young person went abroad before the date of the claim for an employment and support allowance, on the date of that claim;

    (ii) in any other case, on the day which immediately follows the day on which that child or young person went abroad;

(b) where regulation 153 (absence to receive medical treatment) applies, has been continuously absent from Great Britain for a period of more than 26 weeks, that period commencing—

    (i) where that child or young person went abroad before the date of the claim for an employment and support allowance, on the date of that claim;

    (ii) in any other case, on the day which immediately follows the day on which that child or young person went abroad;

(c) has been an in-patient or in accommodation for a continuous period of more than 12 weeks commencing—

    (i) where that child or young person became an in-patient or, as the case may be, entered that accommodation, before the date of the claim for an employment and support allowance, with that date; or

    (ii) in any other case, with the date on which that child or young person became an inpatient or entered that accommodation, and, in either case, has not been in regular contact with either the claimant or any member of the claimant's household;

(d) is being looked after by, or in the care of, a local authority under a relevant enactment;

(e) has been placed with a person other than the claimant prior to adoption;

(f) has been boarded out under a relevant enactment with a person other than the claimant prior to adoption;

(g) has been placed for adoption pursuant to a decision under the [¹ Adoption and Children Act 2002] or the Adoption Agencies (Scotland) Regulations 1996; or

(h) is detained in custody pending trial or sentence upon conviction or under a sentence imposed by a court.

(7) Sub-paragraphs (a)(i), (b)(i) and (c)(i) of paragraph (6) do not apply in a case where immediately before the date of claim for an employment and support allowance the claimant was entitled to an income-based job-seeker's allowance or income support.

(8) A child or young person to whom any of the circumstances mentioned in sub-paragraphs (d) or (h) of paragraph (6) applies is to be treated as being a member of the claimant's household only for that part of any benefit week where that child or young person lives with the claimant.

(9) In this regulation—

"accommodation" means accommodation provided by a local authority in a home owned or managed by that local authority—

(a) under sections 21 to 24 of the National Assistance Act 1948 (provision of accommodation);

[² (aa) under Part 1 of the Care Act 2014 (care and support);]

(b) in Scotland, under section 13B or 59 of the Social Work (Scotland) Act 1968 (provision of residential or other establishment; [³ . . .]

[³ (ba)in Wales, under section 35 or 36 of the Social Services and Well-being (Wales) Act 2014; or]

(c) under section 25 of the Mental Health (Care and Treatment) (Scotland) Act 2003 (care and support services etc.), where the accommodation is provided for a person whose stay in that accommodation has become other than temporary; and

"voluntary organisation" has the meaning assigned to it in the Children Act 1989, or in Scotland, by section 94 of the Social Work (Scotland) Act 1968.

(10) For the purposes of these Regulations a person is responsible for a child or young person if that child or young person usually lives with that person.

AMENDMENTS

1. Employment and Support Allowance (Miscellaneous Amendments) Regulations 2008 (SI 2008/2428) reg.9(3) (October 27, 2008).

2. Care Act 2014 (Consequential Amendments) (Secondary Legislation) Order 2015 (SI 2015/643) art.2 and Sch. para.29(1) and (2) (April 1, 2015).

3. Social Services and Well-being (Wales) Act 2014 and the Regulation and Inspection of Social Care (Wales) Act 2016 (Consequential Amendments) Order 2017 (SI 2017/901) art.13(1) and (3) (November 3, 2017).

4. Social Services and Well-being (Wales) Act 2014 and the Regulation and Inspection of Social Care (Wales) Act 2016 (Consequential Amendments) Order 2017 (SI 2017/901) art.27(1) and (2) (November 3, 2017).

MODIFICATION

With effect from April 8, 2020, para.(4)(b)(ii) is modified by reg.3(1)(c) of the Social Security (Coronavirus) (Prisoners) Regulations 2020 (SI 2020/409). The modification provides that reg.156(4)(b)(ii) is to be read as if the words "the Prison Act 1952 or" were omitted. By reg.6 of SI 2020/409 (as amended by reg.2 of SI 2020/1156), the modification will expire at the end of May 12, 2021.

DEFINITIONS

"Abbeyfield Home"—reg.2(1).
"child"—*ibid.*
"claimant"—WRA 2007, s.24(1).
"family"—reg.2(1) and (3).
"income-based jobseeker's allowance"—*ibid.*
"income support"—*ibid.*
"independent hospital"—*ibid.*
"partner"—*ibid.*
"polygamous marriage"—*ibid.*
"relevant enactment"—*ibid.*
"young person"—*ibid.*

GENERAL NOTE

4.346   See the commentary to reg.16 of the IS Regs. Note however that the ESA has no equivalent of reg.15 of the IS Regs. Under para.(10) whether or not a person is responsible for a child or young person for the purpose of ESA depends upon whether the "child or young person usually lives with that person" rather than, for IS, who receives child benefit.

PART 12

DISQUALIFICATION

Disqualification for misconduct etc.

4.347   **157.**—(1) Subject to paragraph (3), paragraph (2) applies where a claimant—

(a) has limited capability for work through the claimant's own misconduct, except in a case where the limited capability is due to pregnancy or a sexually transmitted disease; or

(b) fails without good cause to attend for or submit to medical or other treatment (excluding vaccination, inoculation or major surgery) recommended by a doctor with whom, or a hospital or similar institution with which, the claimant is undergoing medical treatment, which would be likely to remove the limitation on the claimant's capability for work;

(c) fails without good cause to refrain from behaviour calculated to retard the claimant's recovery; or

(d) is, without good cause, absent from the claimant's place of residence without leaving word with the Secretary of State where the claimant may be found.

(2) A claimant referred to in paragraph (1) is to be disqualified for receiving an employment and support allowance for such period not exceeding 6 weeks as the Secretary of State may determine.

(3) Paragraph (1) does not apply where the claimant—

(a) is disqualified for receiving an employment and support allowance by virtue of regulations made under section [¹6B or] 7 of the Social

Security Fraud Act 2001; or
(b) is a person in hardship.

AMENDMENT

1. Social Security (Loss of Benefit) (Amendment) Regulations 2010 (SI 2010/1160) reg.12(2) (April 1, 2010).

DEFINITIONS

"claimant"—see WRA 2007 s.24(1).
"doctor"—see reg.2(1).
"medical treatment"—see reg.2(1).
"person in hardship"—see reg.158.
"week"—see reg.2(1).

GENERAL NOTE

Disqualification here represents an attempt to deny ESA to those whose behaviour has in some way brought about their limited capability for work, or has worsened it, or where the claimant has behaved inappropriately in some other way.

This regulation provides that (subject to the two exceptions in para.(3)), someone who falls within one of the several "heads" of disqualification examined below must be disqualified for receiving ESA. As under the sickness and invalidity benefits regime (on which see USI Regs reg.17, revoked from April 13, 1993— pp.737–40 of Bonner, Hooker and White, *Non-Means Tested Benefit: The Legislation* (1994)), and the incapacity benefit system, the maximum period imposable is six weeks. No minimum is specified (unlike disqualification in JSA where one week is specified—Jobseekers Act 1995 s.19(3)). Although, like JSA, ESA is in principle a weekly benefit, payment for less than a week is possible, so arguably the minimum should still be one day (the minimum unit for benefit purposes). While there have been some changes of wording from that in USI Regs reg.17, governing sickness and invalidity benefits disqualifications and from Incapacity for Work (General) Regulations 1995 reg.18, in so far as the wording remains the same as that incapacity benefit provision, case authorities on that regime and its predecessors remain authoritative. Some of the "heads" are subject to a "good cause" saving. The rule-making power to further define or restrict "good cause" has not been exercised in this context (WRA 2007 s.18(3)).

If one or more of the "heads" apply, there must be some disqualification: the discretion afforded by the regulation goes only to the length of the period (maximum six weeks). As with exercising the equivalent discretion for jobseeker's allowance purposes, the determining authorities must act judicially and consider each case in the light of its circumstances and give reasons for their choice of period (see *R(U) 8/74(T)*; *R(S) 1/87*; *CS/002/1990*, para.6). The same rules on considering and recording decisions on the matter would apply (*R(U) 4/87*). Some of the factors relevant in exercising the discretion in that context may equally be relevant here. The burden lies on the decision maker to show that the claimant falls clearly and squarely within the head of disqualification (*R(S) 7/83*). Where "good cause" is the issue, it falls to the claimant to establish that he had it (*R(S) 9/51*). *R(S) 1/87* made it abundantly clear that in the same case the same facts could put in issue more than one of the heads of disqualification in USI Regs reg.17(1). There the heads at issue were paras 17(1)(b) and (1)(d)(ii). The poorly completed record of the SSAT's decision did not make clear on which head they rested disqualification. This was an error of law, a breach of the duty to record reasons for the decision and the material facts on which it is based. Presumably as well as complying with this duty, a tribunal should also comply with *R(U) 2/71* where the case involves the Secretary of State relying on a head of disqualification not set out in the

4.348

appeal papers or the tribunal relying on a different ground to that relied on by the Secretary of State.

Paragraph (1)(a)

4.349   This penalises certain behaviour by the claimant. Disqualification must be imposed if his incapacity is due to his own misconduct, but two instances where incapacity may have arisen in consequence of what might otherwise be treated as sexual misconduct are expressly stated not to ground disqualification: (a) where the incapacity is due to a sexually transmitted disease; and (b) the case of pregnancy.

Misconduct has not been exhaustively defined. Presumably, by analogy with its use in the unemployment benefit and jobseeker's allowance contexts, it denotes conduct which is blameworthy, reprehensible and wrong. It is unclear in this context, whether merely reckless or negligent conduct will suffice. *R(S)2/53* has been thought to import a requirement of wilfulness, but this may be to read too much into a particular example of misconduct. In that case the Commissioner considered alcoholism, and upheld disqualification. Drinking to such an extent to endanger health raises a prima facie inference of misconduct which can only be rebutted if the claimant proves that the alcoholism was involuntary, the result of disease or disablement which destroyed his willpower, so that he was *unable* to refrain from excessive drinking. The particular evidence in that case of an anxiety state was insufficient to rebut the presumption. Whether in the current medical and social climate the provision could apply to incapacity through heavy smoking remains to be seen. The paragraph could have unfortunate implications for some AIDS victims such as intravenous drug users who become infected nonsexually.

Paragraph (1)(b)

4.350   This seems designed to deal with a specific aspect of behaviour which may contribute to further limited capability for work or hinder recovery. Disqualification must be imposed where the claimant fails to attend for or submit to medical or other treatment. The medical or other treatment must be recommended by a doctor with whom, or a hospital or similar institution with which, he is undergoing medical treatment and be such as would be likely to render him capable of work. This formulation may reverse *R(S) 3/57*, depending on the scope of "other treatment". There the blind claimant gave up a vocational training course when she became pregnant and refused to resume it thereafter; under USI Regs reg.17(1) (c) she had not refused treatment for her disablement since the course could have no effect on her blindness (para.6; *cf. R2/60SB*). Failure to attend for or submit to certain medical or other treatment is explicitly exempt from the sanction, namely failure to attend for or submit to vaccination or inoculation of any kind or to major surgery.

Establishing "good cause" for non-compliance precludes disqualification. In *R(S) 9/51* the claimant did so. Her non-attendance was founded on her own firm conviction that her religious beliefs (Christian Scientist) required her not to. It would not have been enough merely to establish membership of a sect whose religious rules forbade submission to treatment or examination.

Paragraph (1)(c)

4.351   Disqualification here penalises a claimant who fails to refrain from behaviour calculated to retard his recovery. "Calculated to retard his recovery" does not import an intention on his part to do so; the test is an objective one: was his behaviour likely to do so. Thus in *R(S) 21/52* the Commissioner upheld disqualification of the claimant, suffering from influenza bronchitis who was taken ill after undertaking a 60-mile drive when so suffering. However in *R(S) 3/57* (above para.(1)(b)) the course was irrelevant to recovery from blindness, so leaving and refusing to resume the course could not ground disqualification. Establishing good cause for the failure precludes disqualification. Mere ignorance of the rules is not good cause *(R(S) 21/52)*.

Paragraph (1)(d)

This requires the claimant not to be absent from his place of residence without leaving word as to where he can be found. It is designed to penalise those who deliberately seek to avoid the Department's visiting officers who may call as part of the Department's claims control mechanisms. It will only be invoked where visits have already proved ineffective, and as a matter of law the absence must have occurred during the currency of a claim. The rule cannot apply unless the claimant has a residence; it is not to be interpreted as imposing a requirement to have one *(R(S) 7/83)*, so claimants of no fixed abode cannot be caught by it. *R(S) 1/87* requires findings be made as to place of residence, any absence in the relevant period, and on whether the claimant had failed to leave word where he could be found. If those findings showed the claimant's absence from his residence without leaving word as to his whereabouts, it would then fall to the claimant to establish good cause for so acting (see para.12). A claimant's genuine difficulty in leaving word where he might be found was held to constitute good cause in *R(S) 6/55*. There the claimant lived with relatives who were out at work on the three occasions that the visiting officer called. The claimant was out in the park or at the cinema on those occasions, and there was no one with whom he could leave a message. His doctor had advised him to get out as much as possible. Mere ignorance of the rules is not good cause *(R(S) 21/52)*.

4.352

Exceptions (paragraph (3))

Someone disqualified under the specified fraud provision cannot be disqualified under this regulation (sub-para.(b)). Nor can someone who qualifies as a "person in hardship" as defined in reg.158 (sub-para.(b)).

4.353

Meaning of "person in hardship"

158.—(1) A claimant is a "person in hardship" if the claimant—

4.354

(a) has informed the Secretary of State of the circumstances on which the claimant relies to establish that fact; and

(b) falls within paragraph (2), (3) or (5).

(2) A claimant falls within this paragraph if—

(a) she is pregnant;

(b) a member of the claimant's family is pregnant;

(c) the claimant is a single claimant aged less than 18; or

(d) the claimant is a member of a couple and both members are aged less than 18.

(3) Subject to paragraph (4), the claimant falls within this paragraph if the claimant or the claimant's partner—

(a) is responsible for a child or young person who is a member of the claimant's household;

(b) has been awarded an attendance allowance [², the care component [³ , armed forces independence payment] or the daily living component];

(c) has claimed either attendance [², disability living allowance [³, armed forces independence payment] or personal independence payment] and the claim has not been determined;

(d) devotes a considerable portion of each week to caring for another person who—

(i) has been awarded an attendance allowance [², the care com-

ponent [³ , armed forces independence payment] or the daily
living component]; or

    (ii) has claimed either attendance allowance [², disability living
allowance [³, armed forces independence payment] or personal
independence payment] and the claim has not been determined; or

  (e) [¹ has attained the qualifying age for state pension credit].

(4) A claimant to whom paragraph (3)(c) or (3)(d)(ii) applies is a person
in hardship only for 26 weeks from the date of the claim unless the claimant
is a person in hardship under another provision of this regulation.

(5) The claimant falls within this paragraph where the Secretary of State
is satisfied, having regard to all the circumstances and, in particular, the
matters set out in paragraph (6), that unless an employment and support
allowance is paid, the claimant, or a member of the claimant's family, will
suffer hardship.

(6) The matters referred to in paragraph (5) are—

  (a) the resources which are likely to be available to the claimant and
the claimant's family and the length of time for which they might be
available; and

  (b) whether there is a substantial risk that essential items, including
food, clothing and heating, will cease to be available to the claimant
or a member of the claimant's family, or will be available at considerably reduced levels and the length of time for which this might be
so.

(7) In this regulation "care component" means the care component of
disability living allowance at the highest or middle rate prescribed under
section 72(3) of the Contributions and Benefits Act.

AMENDMENTS

1. Social Security (Equalisation of State Pension Age) Regulations 2009 (SI
2009/1488) reg.43 (April 6, 2010).

2. Personal Independence Payment (Supplementary Provisions and Consequential
Amendments) Regulations 2013 (SI 2013/388) reg.8 and Sch. para.40(1) and (4)
(April 8, 2013).

3. Armed Forces and Reserve Forces Compensation Scheme (Consequential
Provisions: Subordinate Legislation) Order 2013 (SI 2013/591) art.7 and Sch.
para.37(1) and (4) (April 8, 2013).

DEFINITIONS

"attendance allowance"—see reg.2(1).
"care component"—see para.(7).
"claimant"—see WRA 2007 s.24(1).
"Contributions and Benefits Act"—see WRA 2006 s.65.
"disability living allowance"—see reg.2(1).
"family"—see reg.2(1).
"person in hardship"—see para.(1).

GENERAL NOTE

4.355   The effect of this regulation is similar to reg.140 of the JSA Regulations.

Paragraph (1)

4.356   A person in hardship cannot be disqualified from receiving ESA under reg.157
(see para.(3)(b) of that regulation). This paragraph defines someone as a "person

in hardship" who notifies the Secretary of State of the circumstances relied on to establish this, so long as he satisfies the conditions set in paras (2), (3) or (5).

Paragraph (2)

This covers a claimant who is pregnant; a claimant where a family member is   4.357
pregnant; the claimant is single and under 18; and the claimant who is a member of
a couple and both the claimant and partner are under 18.

Paragraphs (3), (4)

This covers someone aged 60 or over; someone responsible for a child or young   4.358
person who is a member of his household someone who has been awarded attendance allowance (note the wider coverage of that term in reg.2(1)) or the care component (middle or higher rate) of disability living allowance (see para.(7)); and a
carer who devotes a considerable portion of a week to caring for another who has
been awarded attendance allowance (again note the wider coverage of that term in
reg.2(1)) or the care component of DLA at middle of higher rate (see para.(7)). The
paragraph also brings in, but only for 26 weeks unless the claimant also qualifies
under another head, someone who has claimed attendance allowance (again note
the wider coverage of that term in reg.2(1)) or middle or higher rate care component
of DLA (see para.(7)), but the claim remains undetermined, or the carer devoting a
substantial portion of the week to caring for someone in that position (paras (3)(c),
(d)(ii), (4)).

Paragraphs (5), (6)

These cover the claimant where the Secretary of State is satisfied that unless ESA   4.359
is paid, the claimant or a member of his family will suffer hardship. In considering
whether that is the case, he must have regard to all the circumstances, particularly
those set out in para.(6).

Treating a claimant as not having limited capability for work

159.—(1) Subject to paragraph (2), the claimant is to be treated as not   4.360
having limited capability for work if the claimant is disqualified for receiving
a contributory allowance during a period of imprisonment or detention in
legal custody if that disqualification is for more than 6 weeks.

(2) Where the claimant is entitled to an amount under paragraph 3 of
Schedule 5 (special cases: prisoners) during a period of imprisonment
or detention in legal custody, the claimant is to be treated as not having
limited capability for work from the day after the day on which entitlement
ended.

DEFINITIONS

"claimant"—see WRA 2007 s.24(1).
"contributory allowance"—see WRA 2007 s.1(7).

GENERAL NOTE

Those disqualified for contributory ESA under s.18(4) of the Welfare Reform Act   4.361
for more than six weeks because they are imprisoned or detained in custody are
treated by para.(1) as not having limited capability for work.

Under reg.69 and para.3(b) of Sch.5, a person may be entitled to income-related
ESA at a reduced rate while detained in custody pending trial or pending sentence
following conviction. In those circumstances, the person is treated by para.(2) as not
having limited capability for work from the day after that entitlement ends.

Exceptions from disqualification for imprisonment

4.362   **160.**—(1) Notwithstanding section 18(4)(b) of the Act, a claimant is not disqualified for receiving a contributory allowance for any period during which that claimant is undergoing imprisonment or detention in legal custody—

(a) in connection with a charge brought or intended to be brought against the claimant in criminal proceedings;

(b) pursuant to any sentence; or

(c) pursuant to any order for detention,

made by a court in such proceedings, unless paragraph (2) applies.

(2) This paragraph applies where—

(a) a penalty is imposed on the claimant at the conclusion of the proceedings referred to in paragraph (1); or

(b) in the case of default of payment of a sum adjudged to be paid on conviction a penalty is imposed in respect of such default.

(3) Notwithstanding section 18(4)(b) of the Act, a claimant [2 "C"] is not to be disqualified for receiving a contributory allowance, for any period during which C is undergoing detention in legal custody after the conclusion of criminal proceedings if it is a period during which [3 C is detained in a hospital or similar institution in Great Britain as a person suffering from mental disorder unless C satisfies either of the following conditions.

(4) The first condition is that—

(a) C is being detained under section 45A or 47 of the Mental Health Act 1983 (power of higher courts to direct hospital admission; removal to hospital of persons serving sentences of imprisonment etc.); and

(b) in any case where there is in relation to C a release date within the meaning of section 50(3) of that Act, C is being detained on or before the day which the Secretary of State certifies to be that release date.

(4A) The second condition is that C is being detained under—

(a) section 59A of the Criminal Procedure (Scotland) Act 1995 (hospital direction); or

(b) section 136 of the Mental Health (Care and Treatment) (Scotland) Act 2003 (transfer of prisoners for treatment of mental disorder).]

(5) For the purposes of this regulation—

(a) "court" means any court in the United Kingdom, the Channel Islands or the Isle of Man or in any place to which the Colonial Prisoners Removal Act 1884 applies or any naval court-martial, army court-martial or air force court-martial within the meaning of the Courts-Martial (Appeals) Act 1968 or the Courts-Martial Appeal Court;

(b) "hospital or similar institution" means any place (not being a prison, a young offender institution, a secure training centre, secure accommodation in a children's home [3, a place at which a secure accommodation service within the meaning of Part 1 of the Regulation and Inspection of Social Care (Wales) Act 2016 is being provided] or a remand centre, and not being at or in any such place) in which persons suffering from mental disorder are or may be received for care or treatment;

(c) "penalty" means a sentence of imprisonment or detention under section 90 or 91 of the Powers of Criminal Courts (Sentencing) Act

2000 [⁴or section 250 or 259 of the Sentencing Code], a detention and training order under [⁴section 100 of the Powers of Criminal Courts (Sentencing) Act 2000 or Chapter 2 of Part 10 of the Sentencing Code], a sentence of detention for public protection under section 226 of the Criminal Justice Act 2003 or an extended sentence under section 228 of that Act or, in Scotland, under section 205, 207 or 208 of the Criminal Procedure (Scotland) Act1995;

(d) in relation to a person who is liable to be detained in Great Britain as a result of any order made under the Colonial Prisoners Removal Act 1884, references to a prison must be construed as including references to a prison within the meaning of that Act;

(e) criminal proceedings against any person must be deemed to be concluded upon that person being found insane in those proceedings so that the person cannot be tried or that person's trial cannot proceed.

(6) Where a claimant outside Great Britain is undergoing imprisonment or detention in legal custody and, in similar circumstances in Great Britain, the claimant would, by virtue of this regulation, not have been disqualified for receiving a contributory allowance, the claimant is not disqualified for receiving that allowance by reason only of the imprisonment or detention.

AMENDMENTS

1. Employment and Support Allowance (Miscellaneous Amendments) Regulations 2008 (SI 2008/2428) reg.10 (October 27, 2008).
2. Social Security (Persons Serving a Sentence of Imprisonment Detained in Hospital) Regulations 2010 (SI 2010/442) reg.5(3) (March 25, 2010).
3. Social Security and Child Support (Regulation and Inspection of Social Care (Wales) Act 2016) (Consequential Provision) Regulations 2018 (SI 2018/228) reg.11(1) and (3) (April 2, 2018).
4. Sentencing Act 2020 Sch.24 para.366 (December 1, 2020).

DEFINITIONS

"claimant"—see WRA 2007 s.24(1).
"court"—see para.(5)(a).
"hospital or similar institution"—see para.(5)(b).
"penalty"—see para.(5)(c).
"prison"—see para.(5)(d).

GENERAL NOTE

Under s.18(4) of the WRA 2007, a claimant is disqualified for contributory ESA **4.363** while "undergoing imprisonment or detention in legal custody". This regulation establishes exceptions to that rule. Under paras (1) and (2), there is no disqualification while the claimant is in custody pending trial or sentence unless a penalty is imposed. Payment of contributory ESA is suspended under reg.161 below during the period when it is not known whether a penalty will eventually be imposed. By para.(6), the same rule is applied to claimants imprisoned outside Great Britain. Under para.(3), there is no disqualification where the claimant is compulsorily detained in hospital following the conclusion of criminal proceedings unless a prison sentence is imposed and the claimant is subsequently transferred to hospital under the specified legislation.

Suspension of payment of a contributory allowance during imprison-ment

4.364   **161.** [*Omitted as not applying to income-related ESA*]

PART 13

URGENT CASES

GENERAL NOTE

4.365   Part 13 (regs 162–164), which provided for 'urgent cases" payments of ESA to certain claimants who were treated as possessing notional income under reg.107, was revoked the Social Security (Miscellaneous Amendments) (No.5) Regulations 2009 (SI 2009/3228) reg.2 with effect from January 25, 2010.

The revocation was subject to two savings. The first covered any person to whom reg.162(2) applied (i.e. who was treated as possessing notional income) on January 24, 2010. The second covered any person who, on the same date, fell within para.1 of Pt 1 of the Schedule to the Social Security (Immigration and Asylum) Regulations 2000 (SI 2000/636). That paragraph relates to some persons subject to immigration control with limited leave to enter or remain in the UK and whose remittances from abroad had been disrupted. The second saving is necessary because such a person may not be affected by reg.107 on January 24, 2010, but might subsequently become so during the same period of limited leave. It applies for a period, or the aggregate of any periods, of 42 days within the period of limited leave or until the claimant ceases to fall within para.1 of Pt 1 of the Schedule to SI 2000/636. See regs 2(2)–(4) of SI 2009/3229 in Vol.II.

4.366   For the abolition of urgent cases payments generally, see the commentary to Pt VI of the Income Support Regulations in Vol.II.

PART 14

PERIODS OF LESS THAN A WEEK

Entitlement for less than a week—amount of an employment and support allowance payable

4.367   **165.**—(1) This regulation applies where the claimant is entitled to an employment and support allowance for a part-week and is subject to the following provisions of this Part.

(2) The amount payable by way of an income-related allowance in respect of that part-week is to be calculated by applying the formula—

(a) where the claimant has no income—

$$\frac{(N \times A)}{7}$$

or

(b) where the claimant has an income—

$$\frac{N \times (A - 1)}{7} - B$$

where—

A is the claimant's weekly applicable amount in the relevant week;

B is the amount of any employment and support allowance, jobseeker's allowance, income support, maternity allowance, incapacity benefit or severe disablement allowance payable to the claimant or the claimant's partner in respect of any day in the part-week;

I is the claimant's weekly income in the relevant week; and

N is the number of days in the part week.

(3) The amount payable by way of a contributory allowance in respect of a part-week is to be calculated by applying the formula—

$$\frac{(N \times X) - Y}{7}$$

where—

X is the amount calculated in accordance with section 2(1) of the Act;

Y is the amount of any widow's benefit, widowed parent's allowance, [¹ bereavement support payment under section 30 of the Pensions Act 2014], training allowance, carer's allowance and any increase in disablement pension payable in accordance with Part 1 of Schedule 7 to the Contributions and Benefits Act (Unemployability Supplement) payable in respect of any day in the part-week;

N is the number of days in the part-week.

(4) In this Part—

"part-week" means an entitlement to an employment and support allowance in respect of any period of less than a week;

"relevant week" means the period of 7 days determined in accordance with regulation 166.

AMENDMENT

1. Pensions Act 2014 (Consequential, Supplementary and Incidental Amendments) Order 2017 (SI 2017/422), art.31(2) (April 6, 2017).

GENERAL NOTE

This regulation is similar to reg.150 of the JSA Regs.   4.368

Relevant week

166.—(1) Where a part-week—   4.369

(a) is the whole period for which an employment and support allowance is payable, or occurs at the beginning of an award, the relevant week is the period of 7 days ending on the last day of that part-week; or

(b) occurs at the end of an award, the relevant week is the period of 7 days beginning on the first day of the part-week.

(2) Where a claimant has an award of an employment and support allowance and that claimant's benefit week changes, for the purpose of calculating the amounts of an employment and support allowance payable for the part-week beginning on the day after the last complete benefit week

before the change and ending immediately before the change, the relevant week is the period of 7 days beginning on the day after the last complete benefit week.

Definitions

    "benefit week"—reg.2(1).
    "claimant"—WRA 2007 s.24(1).
    "part-week"—reg.165(4).
    "relevant week"—*ibid.*

General Note

4.370   This regulation is similar to reg.152 of the JSA Regs.

Modification in the calculation of income

4.371   **167.** For the purposes of regulation 165 (entitlement for less than a week—amount of an employment and support allowance payable), a claimant's income and, in determining the amount payable by way of an income-related allowance, the income of any person which the claimant is treated as possessing under regulations made under section 17(3) of the Act, regulation 68 (polygamous marriages) or regulation 83 (calculation of income and capital of members of claimant's family and of a polygamous marriage), is to be calculated in accordance with Parts 10 (income and capital) and 13 (urgent cases) subject to the following changes—

    (a) any income which is due to be paid in the relevant week is to be treated as paid on the first day of that week;

    (b) in determining the amount payable by way of an income-related allowance, any jobseeker's allowance, employment and support allowance, income support [¹ , universal credit] maternity allowance, incapacity benefit or severe disablement allowance payable in the relevant week but not in respect of any day in the part-week is to be disregarded;

    (c) the amount referred to as B in regulation 165(2) is to be disregarded;

    (d) in determining the amount payable by way of a contributory allowance, any widow's benefit, training allowance, widowed parent's allowance, [² bereavement support payment under section 30 of the Pensions Act 2014], carer's allowance and any increase in disablement pension payable in accordance with Part 1 of Schedule 7 to the Contributions and Benefits Act (unemployability supplement) which is payable in the relevant week but not in respect of any day in the part-week is to be disregarded;

    (e) where the part-week occurs at the end of the claim—
        (i) any income; or
        (ii) any change in the amount of income of the same kind, which is first payable within the relevant week but not on any day in the part-week is to be disregarded;

    (f) where only part of the weekly balance of income is taken into account in the relevant week, the balance is to be disregarded.

Amendments

1. Universal Credit (Consequential, Supplementary, Incidental and Miscellaneous Provisions) Regulations 2013 (SI 2013/630) reg.37(1) and (6) (April 29, 2013).

2. Pensions Act 2014 (Consequential, Supplementary and Incidental Amendments) Order 2017 (SI 2017/422) art.31(3) (April 6, 2017).

GENERAL NOTE

This regulation is similar to reg.153 of the JSA Regs.   4.372

[¹ **Reduction in certain cases**
168.—(1) Where a disqualification is to be made in accordance with   4.373
regulation 157 in respect of a part-week, the amount referred to in paragraph (2) is to be payable by way of an employment and support allowance
in respect of that part-week.
(2) The amount mentioned in paragraph (1) is—
(a) one seventh of the employment and support allowance which would
have been paid for the part-week if—
(i) there was no disqualification under regulation 157; and
(ii) it was not a part-week; multiplied by
(b) the number of days in the part-week in respect of which no disqualification is to be made in accordance with regulation 157.]

AMENDMENT

1. Social Security (Miscellaneous Amendments) (No.3) Regulations 2013 (SI
2013/2536) reg.13(1) and (31) (October 29, 2013).

GENERAL NOTE

This regulation is similar to reg.154 of the JSA Regs.   4.374

Payment of a contributory allowance for days of certain regular treatment

169. [*Omitted as not applying to income-related ESA*]   4.375

SCHEDULE 1   **Regulation 2(2)**

HER MAJESTY'S FORCES

PART 1

PRESCRIBED ESTABLISHMENTS AND ORGANISATIONS

1. Any of the regular naval, military or air forces of the Crown.   4.376
2. Royal Fleet Reserve.
3. Royal Navy Reserve.
4. Royal Marines Reserve.
5. Army Reserve.
6. Territorial Army.
7. Royal Air Force Reserve.
8. Royal Auxiliary Air Force.
9. The Royal Irish Regiment, to the extent that its members are not members of any force
falling within paragraph 1.

PART 2

ESTABLISHMENTS AND ORGANISATIONS OF WHICH HER MAJESTY'S FORCES DO NOT CONSIST

10. Her Majesty's forces are not to be taken to consist of any of the establishments or organisations specified in Part 1 of this Schedule by virtue only of the employment in such establishment or organisation of the following persons—

(a) any person who is serving as a member of any naval force of Her Majesty's forces and who (not having been an insured person under the National Insurance Act 1965 and not having been a contributor under the Social Security Act 1975 or not being a contributor under the Contributions and Benefits Act) locally entered that force at an overseas base;

(b) any person who is serving as a member of any military force of Her Majesty's forces and who entered that force, or was recruited for that force outside the United Kingdom, and the depot of whose unit is situated outside the United Kingdom;

(c) any person who is serving as a member of any air force of Her Majesty's forces and who entered that force, or was recruited for that force, outside the United Kingdom, and is liable under the terms of engagement to serve only in a specified part of the world outside the United Kingdom.

GENERAL NOTE

4.377   See the commentary to the definition of "member of Her Majesty's forces" in reg.2(1).

IMPORTANT PRELIMINARY NOTE ABOUT SCHEDULES 2 (LIMTED CAPABILITY FOR WORK ASSESSMENT) AND 3 (LIMITED CAPABILITY FOR WORK-RELATED ACTIVITY ASSESSMENT)

4.378   Completely new Schedules were substituted on March 28, 2011 by the Employment and Support Allowance (Limited Capability for Work and Limited Capability for Work-Related Activity) (Amendment) Regulations 2011 (SI 2011/228) reg.4. Regulation 2 of those regulations sets out the cases to which the new Schedules apply. It provides:

"Application

2.—(1) These Regulations apply to:—

(a) a person who makes a claim for an employment and support allowance on or after 28 March 2011 (including a claim in respect of any period before that date);

(b) subject to paragraphs (2) and (3), a person who made a claim for an employment and support allowance before 28 March 2011 in respect of whom a determination is made on or after that date as to whether that person has or is to be treated as having limited capability for work under Part 5 of the ESA Regulations or as to whether that person has or is to be treated as having limited capability for work-related activity under Part 6 of those Regulations;

(c) subject to paragraphs (2) and (3), a person who is entitled to an employment and support allowance immediately before 28 March 2011 in respect of whom, on or after that date—

(i) the Secretary of State determines afresh under regulation 19(7) of the ESA Regulations whether the person has or is to be treated as having limited capability for work;

(ii) the Secretary of State determines afresh under regulation 34(4) of the ESA Regulations whether the person has or is to be treated as having limited capability for work-related activity; and

(d) subject to paragraphs (2) and (3), a notified person as defined by regulation 4 of the Reassessment Regulations in respect of whom a determination is made on or after 28 March 2011 as to whether that person has or is to be treated as having limited capability for work under Part 5 of the ESA Regulations or as to whether that person has or is to be treated as having limited capability for work-related activity under Part 6 of the ESA Regulations.

(2) Where, before 28 March 2011, a questionnaire relating to the previous version of Schedule 2 to the ESA Regulations was issued to a person in accordance with regulation 21(1)(b) of those Regulations (information required for determining capability for work), regulation 4(1) does not apply to that person for the purposes of making a determination as to limited capability for work under Part 5 of the ESA Regulations;

(3) Where, before 28 March 2011, a questionnaire relating to the previous version of Schedule 3 to the ESA Regulations was issued to a person in accordance with regulation 36(1)(a) of those Regulations (information required for determining capability for work-related activity) regulation 4(2) does not apply to that person for the purposes of making a determination as to limited capability for work-related activity under Part 6 of the ESA Regulations.

(4) In this regulation "the previous version of Schedule 2 to the ESA Regulations" and "the previous version of Schedule 3 to the ESA Regulations" mean those Schedules as they have effect immediately before the date on which these Regulations come into force.

(5) The provisions of paragraphs (2) to (4) do not apply to any determination made on or after 28 September 2011."

The text and commentary immediately following this Note is that operative from March 28, 2011, as amended from January 28, 2013.

[¹SCHEDULE 2   **Regulation 19(2) and (3)**   **4.379**

ASSESSMENT OF WHETHER A CLAIMANT HAS LIMITED CAPABILITY FOR WORK

PART 1

PHYSICAL DISABILITIES

(1) *Activity*	*(2)* *Descriptors*	*(3)* *Points*
1. [²Mobilising unaided by another person with or without a walking stick, manual wheelchair or other aid if such aid is normally, or could reasonably be, worn or used.]	1 (a) Cannot [³unaided by another person] either: (i) mobilise more than 50 metres on level ground without stopping in order to avoid significant discomfort or exhaustion; or (ii) repeatedly mobilise 50 metres within a reasonable timescale because of significant discomfort or exhaustion.	15
	(b) Cannot [³unaided by another person] mount or descend two steps [³...] even with the support of a handrail.	9
	(c) Cannot [³unaided by another person] either (i) mobilise more than 100 metres on level ground without stopping in order to avoid significant discomfort or exhaustion; or (ii) repeatedly mobilise 100 metres within a reasonable timescale because of significant discomfort or exhaustion.	9

(1) *Activity*	(2) *Descriptors*	(3) *Points*
	(d) Cannot [³unaided by another person] either:	6
	(i) mobilise more than 200 metres on level ground without stopping in order to avoid significant discomfort or exhaustion; or	
	(ii) repeatedly mobilise 200 metres within a reasonable timescale because of significant discomfort or exhaustion.	
	(e) None of the above [³applies].	0
2. Standing and sitting.	2 (a) Cannot move between one seated position and another seated position located next to one another without receiving physical assistance from another person.	15
	(b) Cannot, for the majority of the time, remain at a work station, either:	9
	(i) standing unassisted by another person (even if free to move around); or	
	(ii) sitting (even in an adjustable chair) [²; or	
	(iii) a combination of (i) and (ii),] for more than 30 minutes, before needing to move away in order to avoid significant discomfort or exhaustion.	
	(c) Cannot, for the majority of the time, remain at a work station, either:	6
	(i) standing unassisted by another person (even if free to move around); or	
	(ii) sitting (even in an adjustable chair) [²; or	
	(iii) a combination of (i) and (ii),] for more than an hour before needing to move away in order to avoid significant discomfort or exhaustion.	
	(d) None of the above apply	0
3. Reaching.	3 (a) Cannot raise either arm as if to put something in the top pocket of a coat or jacket.	15
	(b) Cannot raise either arm to top of head as if to put on a hat.	9
	(c) Cannot raise either arm above head height as if to reach for something.	6
	(d) None of the above apply.	0
4. Picking up and moving or transferring by the use of the upper body and arms.	(a) Cannot pick up and move a 0.5 litre carton full of liquid.	15
	(b) Cannot pick up and move a one litre carton full of liquid.	9
	(c) Cannot transfer a light but bulky object such as an empty cardboard box.	6

(1) Activity	(2) Descriptors	(3) Points
	(d) None of the above apply.	0
5. Manual dexterity.	5. [³(a) Cannot press a button (such as a telephone keypad) with either hand or cannot turn the pages of a book with either hand.]	15
	(b) Cannot pick up a £1 coin or equivalent with either hand.	15
	(c) Cannot use a pen or pencil to make a meaningful mark [³ with either hand].	9
	(d) Cannot [² single-handedly] use a suitable keyboard or mouse.	9
	(e) None of the above [³ applies].	0
[² 6. Making self understood through speaking, writing, typing, or other means which are normally, or could reasonably be, used, unaided by another person.]	6 (a) Cannot convey a simple message, such as the presence of a hazard.	15
	(b) Has significant difficulty conveying a simple message to strangers.	15
	(c) Has some difficulty conveying a simple message to strangers.	6
	(d) None of the above apply.	0
[² 7. Understanding communication by— (i) verbal means (such as hearing or lip reading) alone,	7. (a) Cannot understand a simple message [³,such as the location of a fire escape,] due to sensory impairment [³…].	15
[(ii) non-verbal means (such as reading 16 point print or Braille) alone, or	(b) Has significant difficulty understanding a simple message from a stranger due to sensory impairment.	15
(iii) a combination of (i) and (ii), using any aid that is normally, or could reasonably be, used, unaided by another person.]	(c) Has some difficulty understanding a simple message from a stranger due to sensory impairment.	6
	(d) None of the above [³ applies].	0
[² 8. Navigation and maintaining safety, using a guide dog or other aid if either or both are normally, or could reasonably be, used.]	8 (a) Unable to navigate around familiar surroundings, without being accompanied by another person, due to sensory impairment.	15
	(b) Cannot safely complete a potentially hazardous task such as crossing the road, without being accompanied by another person, due to sensory impairment.	15
	(c) Unable to navigate around unfamiliar surroundings, without being accompanied by another person, due to sensory impairment.	9
	(d) None of the above apply.	0
[² 9. Absence or loss of control whilst conscious leading to extensive evacuation of the bowel and/or bladder, other than enuresis (bed-wetting), despite the wearing or use of any aids or adaptations which are normally, or could reasonably be, worn or used.]	9 (a) At least once a month experiences: (i) loss of control leading to extensive evacuation of the bowel and/or voiding of the bladder; or (ii) substantial leakage of the contents of a collecting device sufficient to require cleaning and a change in clothing.	15

(1) Activity	(2) Descriptors	(3) Points
	(b) [² The majority of the time is at risk] of loss of control leading to extensive evacuation of the bowel and/or voiding of the bladder, sufficient to require cleaning and a change in clothing, if not able to reach a toilet quickly.	6
	(c) [³ Neither of the above applies.]	0
10. Consciousness during waking moments.	10 (a) At least once a week, has an involuntary episode of lost or altered consciousness resulting in significantly disrupted awareness or concentration.	15
	(b) At least once a month, has an involuntary episode of lost or altered consciousness resulting in significantly disrupted awareness or concentration.	6
	(c) None of the above apply.	0

PART 2

MENTAL, COGNITIVE AND INTELLECTUAL FUNCTION ASSESSMENT

(1) Activity	(2) Descriptors	(3) Points
11. Learning tasks.	11 (a) Cannot learn how to complete a simple task, such as setting an alarm clock.	15
	(b) Cannot learn anything beyond a simple task, such as setting an alarm clock.	9
	(c) Cannot learn anything beyond a moderately complex task, such as the steps involved in operating a washing machine to clean clothes.	6
	(d) None of the above apply.	0
12. Awareness of everyday hazards (such as boiling water or sharp objects).	12.(a) Reduced awareness of everyday hazards leads to a significant risk of: (i) injury to self or others; or (ii) damage to property or possessions such that [⁴the claimant requires] supervision for the majority of the time to maintain safety.	15
	(b) Reduced awareness of everyday hazards leads to a significant risk of (i) injury to self or others; or (ii) damage to property or possessions such that [⁴the claimant frequently requires] supervision to maintain safety	9
	(c) Reduced awareness of everyday hazards leads to a significant risk of: (i) injury to self or others; or (ii) damage to property or possessions such that [⁴the claimant occasionally requires] supervision to maintain safety.	6
	(d) None of the above apply.	0

(1) Activity	(2) Descriptors	(3) Points
13. Initiating and completing personal action (which means planning, organisation, problem solving, prioritising or switching tasks).	13 (a) Cannot, due to impaired mental function, reliably initiate or complete at least 2 sequential personal actions.	15
	(b) Cannot, due to impaired mental function, reliably initiate or complete at least 2 [⁴ sequential] personal actions for the majority of the time.	9
	(c) Frequently cannot, due to impaired mental function, reliably initiate or complete at least 2 [⁴ sequential] personal actions.	6
	(d) None of the above [⁴ applies].	0
14. Coping with change.	14 (a) Cannot cope with any change to the extent that day to day life cannot be managed.	15
	(b) Cannot cope with minor planned change (such as a pre-arranged change to the routine time scheduled for a lunch break), to the extent that overall day to day life is made significantly more difficult.	9
	(c) Cannot cope with minor unplanned change (such as the timing of an appointment on the day it is due to occur), to the extent that overall, day to day life is made significantly more difficult.	6
	(d) None of the above apply.	0
15. Getting about.	15 [²(a) Cannot get to any place outside the claimant's home with which the claimant is familiar.]	15
	(b) Is unable to get to a specified place with which the claimant is familiar, without being accompanied by another person.	9
	(c) Is unable to get to a specified place with which the claimant is unfamiliar without being accompanied by another person.	6
	(d) None of the above apply.	0
16. Coping with social engagement due to cognitive impairment or mental disorder.	16 (a) Engagement in social contact is always precluded due to difficulty relating to others or significant distress experienced by the [⁴ claimant].	15
	(b) Engagement in social contact with someone unfamiliar to the claimant is always precluded due to difficulty relating to others or significant distress experienced by the [⁴ claimant].	9
	(c) Engagement in social contact with someone unfamiliar to the claimant is not possible for the majority of the time due to difficulty relating to others or significant distress experienced by the [⁴ claimant].	6
	(d) None of the above [⁴ applies].	0
17. Appropriateness of behaviour with other people, due to cognitive impairment or mental disorder.	17 (a) Has, on a daily basis, uncontrollable episodes of aggressive or disinhibited behaviour that would be unreasonable in any workplace.	15

(1) *Activity*	(2) *Descriptors*	(3) *Points*
	(b) Frequently has uncontrollable episodes of aggressive or disinhibited behaviour that would be unreasonable in any workplace.	15
	(c) Occasionally has uncontrollable episodes of aggressive or disinhibited behaviour that would be unreasonable in any workplace.	9
	(d) None of the above apply.	0.]

AMENDMENTS

1. Employment and Support Allowance (Limited Capability for Work and Limited Capability for Work-Related Activity) (Amendment) Regulations 2011 (SI 2011/228) reg.4(1) (March 28, 2011).
2. Employment and Support Allowance (Amendment) Regulations 2012 (SI 2012/3096) reg.5(2) (January 28, 2013, subject to application, transitional and savings provisions in reg. 2 of this amending instrument, below, para.9.601).
3. Social Security (Miscellaneous Amendments) (No.3) Regulations 2013 (SI 2013/2536) reg.13(32) (October 29, 2013).
4. Social Security (Miscellaneous Amendments) (No.3) Regulations 2013 (SI 2013/2536) reg.13(33) (October 29, 2013).

DEFINITION

"claimant"—see WRA 2007 s.24(1).

GENERAL NOTE

I. A Note on the Background to the WCA and the new Schs 2 and 3 inserted on March 28, 2011

4.380   In 1995, a new test for incapacity for work was introduced: the "all work test". In 2000 this was renamed the personal capability assessment (PCA). This, like the "all work" test, lay at the heart of the reform effected by the Social Security (Incapacity for Work) Act 1994. According to Government, the results of two large scale evaluation studies to assess the validity and reliability of this essentially medical and functional test indicated:

> "that [it provided] a more effective means of assessing incapacity, which [would] help ensure that benefit is targeted on those people who are incapable of work, because of their medical condition" (DSS/Benefits Agency, *The medical assessment for incapacity benefit* (HMSO, 1994), p.35).

The "personal capability assessment" was one which—like the WCA—ignored the other personal/environmental factors governing access to employment by people with disabilities (R. Berthoud, "The 'medical' assessment of incapacity: a case study of the (lack of) influence of research on policy" [1995] 2 J.S.S.L. 61, at pp.70, 75). It did not measure people against the requirements of specific jobs (the "personal capability assessment" contained no definition of work for none was required given its nature). Its exclusionary effect would, it was thought by Berthoud, largely deny benefit to persons who probably were capable of work (*ibid.* at p.82). However, it was thought possible that some, who would have failed the previously applicable informal and more holistic test, might qualify as incapable on the AWT/PCA, while some, who failed the AWT/PCA, might well in fact be incapable of work.

The "personal capability assessment" was an assessment of the extent of the claimant's incapacity, by reason of some specific disease or bodily or mental disablement which he has, to perform the activities prescribed in the Schedule [to the IFW Regulations], entitled "disabilities which may make a person incapable of work" (IFW Regulations reg.24).

The new Work Capability Assessment (WCA) underpinning ESA followed similar lines, but embodied important changes to reflect the demands of the modern workplace, the development and availability of adaptive technology, and the legal obligations on employers to make reasonable adjustments better to accommodate those people with long term disabilities. In consequence, the 15 physical activities in the AWT/PCA were reduced to 11, in order to better reflect the activities that an employer might reasonably expect of his workforce. More radically, the mental health provisions in the IFW Regulations were thought not to be the most relevant to activities requisite for remaining in or returning to work. Consequently, the four activities dealing with mental functions in the AWT/PCA were increased to the ten activities in the original WCA with respect to mental, cognitive and intellectual function, reflecting a desire to deal better with the problems of a client group which made up some 41 per cent of the IB caseload.

The difficulties of applying the AWT/PCA are evident in a burgeoning case law. The difficulties of devising a test which accurately ascertains capability for work or for work-related activity are emphasized by ongoing review and the frequent amendments that are the subject of this commentary. Less than three years after its introduction, the WCA was thoroughly revised with new Schs 2 and 3 operating from March 28, 2011 for all new claims after that date, and for most determinations and assessments made after that date. The development of the WCA from the AWT/PCA and its recent revision are examined in some depth here on the basis that this will aid the task of decision-makers and tribunals, who must interpret and apply the wording of the activities and descriptors to the varied circumstances of individual cases, by casting light on the changes and their purpose. It is, of course, for decision-makers and tribunals to decide what the wording chosen to achieve those purposes actually means. Setting out the antecedents of the current provisions also highlights the continued application to similar or identical wording of pertinent case law authorities both on the AWT/PCA and the previous version of the WCA itself, which can be found in para.9.365 of the 2012/13 edition of this volume as updated by the 2012/13 Supplement.

The original WCA was devised by the DWP's Health Work and Wellbeing Directorate with input from two technical working groups, one focusing on mental health and learning difficulties, the other on physical function and conditions (hereinafter "review group"). The review group consisted of medical and other relevant experts. It examined how the incapacity benefits regime's Personal Capability Assessment (PCA) could be improved and updated so as to reflect the many changes since its inception:

> "in the prevalence of disabling conditions; in advances in medical science resulting in the availability of new and more effective medical interventions; and in the workplace environment. The Disability Discrimination Act, introduced after the PCA had been developed, has influenced the ability of employers to make reasonable adjustments to accommodate people with long term disabilities. It has also raised the expectations of disabled people that adjustments should be made to enable them to work."

The work of the review group fed into the drafting of the regulations on the WCA. After that first element had been developed work continued on the second and third elements of the WCA, although nothing has been published on this. Government anticipated that the WCA would "fail" some 60,000 claimants a year who would have "passed" the PCA (DWP, *Impact Assessment of the Employment and Support Allowance Regulations 2008—Public sector Impact Only* in *Explanatory Memorandum to Employment and Support Allowance Regulations 2008 (SI 2008/794) and the Employment and Support Allowance (Transitional Provisions) Regulations 2008 (SI 2008/795)*, p.9). Statistics from 2012 suggested that some 54 per cent of new claimants were found capable of work (DWP Press Release, April 24, 2012: see *http://www.dwp.gov.uk/newsroom/press-releases/2012/apr-2012/dwp042-12.shtml*), exceeding the DWP's expectations of 38 per cent (DWP, Explanatory Memorandum to the SSAC on the Amending Regulations: App 1a: Revising the WCA – assessment of impact, para.9). Figures published by the DWP in January 2014, however, indicated that 61% of new claimants with a completed claim were found to have limited capability of work. But the WCA is not merely an incapacity-based tool for determining entitlement to ESA. That remains true of its first element, but its second element is rather a more positive assessment considering ability to benefit from work-related activity with a view to promoting capacity for work. The first element is an assessment of limited capability to work (hereinafter the LCWA) (the subject of this Schedule). The second element is an assessment of limited capacity to engage in work-related activity (hereinafter LCWRA) (the subject of Sch.3). Both assessments will generally be conducted at the same time by the same health care professional. Those found not to have limited capacity for work-related activity (expected to be some 90 per cent of new claimants) were originally required to undergo the third element of the WCA: a work-focused health related assessment (WFHRAt).

In many cases, it was envisaged all three elements of the new WCA would be covered in a single appointment with a health care professional working for Atos Origin Medical Services (MS), the company which originally contracted with the DWP to deliver these assessments. However, the WFHRAt was suspended for a two-year period beginning July 19, 2010; ongoing external evaluation of it had shown mixed results, and the suspension affords an opportunity for the DWP to reconsider the assessment's purpose and delivery and frees up capacity to deal with the "migration" of existing incapacity benefits customers to ESA or a more appropriate benefit (typically JSA). The regs dealing with it were revoked from June 1, 2011.

Schedule 2 deals with the LCWA and establishing limited capability for work: the core element of entitlement to ESA. The vast majority of claimants for ESA will be subject to this first element of the new WCA through a face to face assessment with a trained healthcare professional testing the claimant against the activities and descriptors in the Schedule, in the light of the material in the claimant's questionnaire, any evidence from the GP and the professional's examination. Assessment will take place much earlier than in an equivalent claim for IB.

The Government's view remains that the overwhelming majority of customers are capable of some work, given the right support. The approach is designed to treat people in line with their capabilities, instead of making assumptions based on their condition. Hence, because the ESA tests are designed to assess which claimants can benefit from the help towards work afforded by work-related activity, to "write off" from the chance of work as few people as possible, very few groups are exempt from the LCWA: the terminally ill; those receiving treatment by way of intravenous, intraperitoneal or intrathecal chemotherapy; such of those recovering from such treatment as the Secretary of State is satisfied should be treated as having limited capability for work; (from March 28, 2011) those likely to receive such treatment in the next six months; those excluded or prevented from working as a carrier, or having been in contact with a case of relevant disease (food poisoning, infectious or notifiable diseases covered by a variety of public health enactments); pregnant women at a certain stage in pregnancy or where there is a serious risk of damage to their or their unborn child's health if they do not refrain from work (reg.20); and (from March 28, 2011) those who would be found to have limited capability for work-related activity under any of the descriptors in paras 15 and 16 of the revised Sch.3. Hospital inpatients (reg.25) and persons undergoing or recovering from certain regular treatments (e.g. plasmapheresis, radio therapy, dialysis, parenteral nutrition) for at least two days a week (reg.26) are also treated as having limited capability for work. All such persons are exempt from the information gathering requirements with respect to the LCWA (reg.21(3)).

Decision-makers have discretion in respect of all claimants on whether it is necessary in their case to complete the questionnaire or require more information than is provided by the claimant's doctor under the Medical Evidence Regs (reg.21(2)). Whether someone is required to undergo a medical examination is also a matter of decision-maker discretion (reg.23). Typically, most claimants will have to both complete the questionnaire (form ESA50) and undergo medical examination, usually at a medical examination centre, but sometimes in the claimant's home. Failure to do so, without good cause, is as usual sanctioned by treating the person as not having limited capability for work, thus denying benefit (regs 22–24). The Work Capability Assessment is a face-to-face meeting, lasting between 75 and 90 minutes, depending on whether just two or (originally) all three elements of the WCA are carried out. It explores how the claimant's illness or disability affects their ability to work and carry out day-to-day activity Each part of the assessment will be carried out by specially trained healthcare professionals (whether doctor or nurse) approved by the Secretary of State to assess these matters and report to the decision-maker, generally in the form of a computer-generated report.

The WRA 2007 stipulates merely that whether a person's capability for work is limited by his physical or mental condition and, if so, whether the limitation is such that it is not reasonable to require him to work is to be determined in accordance with regulations. ESA Regs, reg.19(1) elaborates that this is to be determined on the basis of a limited capability for work assessment (LCWA), that is by:

> "an assessment of the extent to which a claimant who has some specific disease or bodily or mental disablement is capable of performing the activities prescribed in Schedule 2 or is incapable by reason of such disease or bodily or mental disablement of performing those activities" (reg.19(2)).

This is familiar stuff for those who have worked with the AWT/PCA. The claimant is to be matched, in the light of all the evidence, by the decision-maker or tribunal against a reformulated range of activities and descriptors, and an appropriate "score" awarded. The threshold "score" for entitlement under the WCA remains 15 points, but as regards its computation, there are both "old" and "new" elements.

It is stressed that incapability to perform an activity must arise from a specific bodily disease or disablement, a specific mental illness or disablement, or as a direct result of treatment provided by a registered medical practitioner, for such a disease, illness or disablement (reg.19(5)). The extent of capability to perform a physical activity has, as with IB, to be assessed as if the claimant is wearing any prosthesis with which he is fitted or wearing or using any aid or appliance which is normally worn or used. In computing the score, where more than one descriptor in respect of a particular activity applies, only the highest is counted towards the total "score" (reg.19(4)). Otherwise one simply adds up the total of the particular scores in respect of each activity, whether physical or mental, to see if the threshold of 15 points is reached. If it is, or is exceeded, the claimant has established limited capability for work, grounding entitlement to the basic allowance in ESA. The matter may be determined afresh where the Secretary of State wishes to ascertain: (i) whether there has been a relevant change of circumstances in relation to the claimant's physical or mental condition; (ii) whether the previous decision was made in ignorance of, or was based on a mistake as to, some material fact; or at least three months have passed since the last decision (reg.19(7), (8)).

If the threshold score is not attained, limited capability for work has not been established, there can be no entitlement to ESA and the unsuccessful claimant (subject to retention of ESA pending appeal) will have to look for income maintenance, typically to JSA or, more rarely, IS.

The radical revision of Schs 2 and 3, effective March 28, 2011: Given the careful pre-   **4.381**
paratory work in devising the WCA, which came into being on October 27, 2008, it might be thought surprising that it was thought necessary to wholly replace Schs 2 and 3 with effect from March 28, 2011, especially as the precise wording of the original ESA Regs had further been honed even before they had entered into force. In fact, the process of review began very early in the operative life of the WCA, with a DWP-led review being announced in the December 2008 White Paper, *Raising Expectations* (Cm.7506). It was thought important that the WCA continued to "provide an up-to-date accurate assessment of a person's functional capability for work and work related activity" (Secretary of State's Statement in accordance with s.174(2) of the SSAA 1992). Led by officials in the DWP, the review began in March 2009, a mere six months after the introduction of ESA. The review, however, also involved representatives of stakeholder groups and employers, experts from the fields

of physical, mental and occupational health, and a member of the Social Security Advisory Committee attending in her personal capacity. This Departmental-led review (hereinafter "*Review*") reported in October 2009 and its report can be found online at *http://www.dwp.gov.uk/docs/work-capability-assessment-review.pdf*.

Representations were made by disability groups that some of the recommendations from that the *Review* did not adequately address their concerns. Consequently, the Secretary of State asked the Chief Medical Adviser (CMA) to undertake a further technical review, part of which involved work with representatives of those specialist disability groups which had been part of the group conducting the internal *Review*. This CMA honing with stakeholders (hereinafter "*CMA*") was published in March 2010 and can be found online as an addendum to the *Review* at *http://www. dwp.gov.uk/docs/work-capability-assessment-review.pdf*. This technical review, led by the CMA and taking into account the work done by the *Review* group, saw work undertaken by medical experts within the DWP "with the aim of ensuring that the recommendations of the internal review would lead to a revised WCA which would more accurately and fairly assess an individual's capability for work and thus their entitlement to benefits" (*CMA*, p.3). That technical review proposed a number of changes to the proposals of the internal review and those changes were accepted by the Secretary of State and embodied in the amending Regulations which inserted the new Schedules now under consideration. The draft amending Regulations were also the subject of consideration and report by the SSAC. Its unsupportive Report and recommendations as regards the new Schedules was considered by the Secretary of State. The SSAC Report, material submitted to it by the DWP explaining the draft Regulations, and the Secretary of State's reasons for rejecting the SSAC recommendations (hereinafter "*SSAC Report*") can be found online at *http://www. official-documents.gov.uk/document/other/9780108509698/9780108509698.pdf*).

This DWP-led review and subsequent CMA honing was distinct from the independent annual review envisaged by the WRA 2007 s.10. The first of those five statutory reviews was undertaken by Professor Michael Harrington and published in November 2010.

4.382   The DWP-led *Review* saw ESA as an "active benefit", a temporary benefit for the majority of claimants, providing support and encouragement to assist the journey of an individual from an ESA claimant into the workplace. The policy behind ESA is premised on a large body of research evidence (described by Harrington as "incontrovertible") which shows both that work is generally good for physical and mental health and well-being and also the converse—that there is a strong association between worklessness and ill-health, with prolonged time away from work rendering recovery and return to work progressively less likely. The *Review* considered that the WCA was generally working well:

> "There was broad consensus amongst the experts that the WCA was performing according to design. The descriptors used in the WCA were indeed reliably identifying individuals according to capability" (*Review*, para.4.1, p.16).

Despite involvement of stakeholders in that process it is clear that this view not altogether shared by them. The SSAC commented:

> "We recognise that any assessment of benefit entitlement that necessarily involves testing and scoring an individual's functional capabilities is going to be both potentially challenging and controversial. As many of our respondents have pointed out, the assessment process, and the experience of the benefit claimant, can be stressful and frustrating. We have also noted the concern expressed by respondents about the Department's conclusions with regard to the internal review of the WCA, and the manner in which they have been presented with regard to the current proposals. It appears to us that there is a disagreement of substance between the Department and the external stakeholders who participated in the review as to whether the WCA in its present form could be said to be working satisfactorily" (*SSAC Report*, para.6.2).

In particular, the SSAC thought that the view that the WCA was not working well was supported by the high rate of success on appeal (some 40 per cent of appeals are upheld) (*SSAC Report*, para.4.10). Harrington also found that the WCA:

> "is not working as well as it should. There are clear and consistent criticisms of the whole system and much negativity surrounding the process. There is strong evidence that the system can be impersonal and mechanistic, that the process lacks transparency and that a lack of communication between the various parties involved contributes to poor decision making and a high rate of appeals".

He did not, however, consider the system as "broken or beyond repair", and proposed a substantial series of recommendations to improve its effectiveness—all of which have been accepted by the Government—which would have a positive impact on the WCA process "making it fairer and more effective, changing perceptions so the WCA is seen as a positive first step towards work, and reducing the rate on appeals". He noted that more subjective conditions such as mental health and fluctuating conditions were difficult to assess so that "some of the descriptors used in the assessment may not adequately measure or reflect the full impact of such conditions on the individual's capability for work". He recommended for the second WRA 2007 s.10 review further work on the descriptors, particularly in assessing fluctuating conditions and, possibly, generalised pain. Harrington established a review group (composed of Mind, Mencap and the National Autistic Society to look in detail at the mental, intellectual and cognitive descriptors, to make recommendations to him about any refinements to the descriptors as a basis for his consideration of recommendations to be made to Ministers early in 2011. Like Harrington, the judicial review decision of the Upper Tribunal (AAC) in *MM & DM v SSWP* [2013] UKUT 259; [2016] AACR 11 also called for amendment of the testing procedures in mental health cases so as to increase the gathering of further medical evidence. See further the annotation to reg. 21, above, on the judicial review challenge under the Equality Act 2010 with respect to aspects of the decision-making process. The January 2013 changes do not respond to these pressures, however, but are rather the governmental response to a number of Upper Tribunal decisions seen as thwarting the policy intention behind the statutory provisions.

The substantial redrawing of Schs 2 and 3 effective from March 28, 2011 was designed to fulfil a number of aims or objectives: **4.383**

- Removing unnecessary complexities and overlaps in order to simplify the descriptors, to remove inappropriate double counting and to ensure ease of administration and greater transparency for the claimant.

- Expanding the support group in relation to certain mental function and communication problems.

- Improving the assessment of fluctuating conditions by ensuring that the effects of exhaustion and discomfort are recognised.

- Taking greater account of the effects of adaptations and aids in improving an individual's function so as more accurately to identify those lacking the capability to work rather than simply assuming lack of capability merely because of a particular functional impairment.

It was expected that the changes to the LCWA would increase by some five per cent the number of new claims not eligible for ESA, but that the revisions to the LCWRA would slightly increase the percentage of successful claims allocated to the support group (*Review*, para.5.2). The DWP-led review group tested the proposed new activities and descriptors through a detailed analysis of ESA cases. That analysis:

> "revealed that in the vast majority of cases experts thought that the new descriptors would result in appropriate changes in the entitlement decision. The descriptors were thought to be functioning as anticipated and providing a more concise and clearer assessment. The re-focusing of the physical function areas better

reflect the activities most applicable to the workplace. The mental function descriptors were found to be clearer and consequently minimised double scoring in addition to providing improved clarity.

The small number of cases that members felt would be inappropriately assessed resulted in further minor refinements of the descriptors" (*Review*, para.5.4).

The *Review* considered that while the existing WCA was working well, the wholesale revision effected would represent "a more robust and accurate evaluation of limited capability for work", because it was founded on recent experience with ESA, simplifying the LCWA, reflecting reasonable adaptation of the disabled to their disability and, because of the Disability Discrimination Act (now the Equality Act 2010), of the reasonable adjustment of workplaces and further consideration of the necessary functions of the modern workplace (*Review*, para.5.5).

The SSAC, in contrast was less sanguine, both about the original WCA and the proposed revisions to it. It saw the WCA as rigid and unnecessarily prescriptive, encouraging a focus on the claimant's specific condition or disability covered by the descriptors, rather than looking at their capability for work, and adaptation to their disability, holistically. A functional assessment cannot easily measure the significance of the many factors which in reality determine capability for work. It regarded the result of the WCA as essentially an expression of the judgment and opinion of the assessor, albeit something based on professional knowledge, training, experience and observation. It considered that some of the streamlining in the proposed new Schedules had removed some of the assessment's necessary subtleties without enhancing its relevance to the real world. It thought that theoretical work capability had not enabled significant numbers to move into work and called for a cost-benefit analysis of the end-to-end process of assessing an ESA claimant where in reality what was determined was not "benefit or work" but rather which out-of-work benefit (ESA or JSA) was the more appropriate. It reported:

"a widespread perception that, overall, rather than simplifying, streamlining and refining the test, these amendments will make it harder in practice for claimants to demonstrate that they have limited capacity for work or work related activity" (*SSAC Report*, para.4.3).

While it welcomed some of the changes (e.g. the extension of the "deemed" limited capability for work categories), the SSAC recommended that the DWP not proceed with the revisions to the Schs until these had been considered in the light of Harrington and the experience of the trial of the migration of IB claimants to ESA (*SSAC Report*, para.7.3).

In February 2011, having considered Harrington, the Secretary of State declined to do so. The amending Regulations were a carefully-crafted package following a thorough, holistic DWP-led review and CMA honing. The WCA would remain subject to ongoing review, but the Government must retain freedom to implement changes when it considers them necessary to improve the assessment without always awaiting the outcome of the next stage of the review process. (*SSAC Report*, Secretary of State's Response, para.24). The DWP Explanatory Memorandum to the SSAC on the amending Regulations indicated that it was expected that the changes to the mental, cognitive and intellectual function descriptors would have a minimal impact on the disallowance rate (para.4.6), but that overall the changes both to physical and mental descriptors would increase by five per cent the number of claimants being found capable of work (para.4.9). Changes to the LCWRA assessment would increase the numbers in the support group from 6.4 to 6.9 per cent (para.4.9).

The revised Schedules thus appear centrally as the product of the internal *Review* and *CMA* honing, rather than Harrington. The process whereby they came into being has been set out at some length, not only as background. The view taken in this commentary is that, while decision-makers and tribunals must focus on the wording of the Schedules, light can be thrown on particular activities and descriptors both by consideration of the reports that led to them and by consideration, where appropriate, of Upper Tribunal and other court decisions on the predecessors of the current WCA; the AWT/PCA from the incapacity benefits regime and from the pre-March 28, 2011 version of the WCA (see pp.1080–1114, paras 9.457–9.489).

The second Harrington report was published in November 2011: *An Independent Review of the Work Capability Assessment – year two.* This reported that "The WCA has, in my view, noticeably changed for the better. However there is still further to go" (p.7 para.5). The recommendations in the second report were aimed at improving the fairness and effectiveness of the assessment by better communications and sharing of information between all parts of the system, increasing and improving the transparency of the assessment, ensuring quality decisions were made and monitoring the impact of recommendations from the Independent Reviews. For the Government's Response, see Cm 8229 (also November 2011).

A year later the picture was very much the same. The third Harrington report was published in November 2012: *An Independent Review of the Work Capability Assessment – year three.* It reported that "real progress has been made but the pace and scope of the improvements has been slower than the Review would have hoped" (p.8 para. 6). The main areas where further changes were needed were continuing to improve communications with claimants and within DWP Operations, improve the face-to-face assessment and establishing quality dialogue between DWP and First-tier Tribunals. In addition, Harrington advocated keeping the Decision Maker central to the assessment process (and providing them with all the further documentary evidence they need to get the decision "right first time") and stressed the need to continually monitor changes to the WCA and to complete work that was under way on the descriptors. For the Government's Response, see Cm 8474 (also November 2012).

A number of relatively minor changes were made on October 29, 2013 to clarify the drafting of the descriptors and to align the Schedules in these Regulations with those in the ESA Regulations 2013 applicable to "new style" ESA (on which see Part XIII of this volume).

Dr Paul Litchfield conducted the final two reviews. His first was *An Independent Review of the Work Capability Assessment – year four* (December 2013). Dr Litchfield acknowledged at the outset that "the length and complexity of the process contributes to dissatisfaction and negative perceptions surrounding the assessment. People need to feel that they are being treated fairly when dealing with an organisation and it is their perception that drives attitudes and behaviours more than any objective assessment of what has happened" (p.7 para.3). On the WCA itself, he recommended that the DWP review its use of WCA scores, place less emphasis on the number attained and simply use the calculation to determine whether the threshold for benefit has been reached. Further recommendations were designed to improve objectivity, improve decision making and simplify the process. Other changes were suggested with a view to addressing the needs of claimants with mental health conditions. The Government did not publish its response until March 2014 (Cm 8843).

The last report was published in November 2014: *An Independent Review of the Work Capability Assessment – year five* (for the Government's Response see Cm 9014, February 2015). This fifth report contained a total of 33 further recommendations. The report recognised the difficulties created by the frequent changes to the WCA, noted the marked increase in the proportion of claimants being allocated to the support group and yet again emphasised the need to address negative perceptions of the WCA and to improve decision-making standards. The importance of meeting the needs of claimants with mental health problems and/or learning disabilities was also reiterated. The report also set out a number of principles which it recommended should be taken into account it was decided to undertake a fundamental redesign of the WCA, as had been recommended by the House of Commons Work and Pensions Committee in its report *Employment and Support Allowance and Work Capability Assessments* (HC 302, 2014).

Meanwhile the HC Public Accounts Committee has noted how the DWP has increasingly used third-party contractors to provide health and disability assessments *Contracted out health and disability assessments*, 33rd Report of 2015–16, HC 727). In 2005, the Department awarded a contract to Atos Healthcare (Atos) for Incapacity Benefit and, from 2008, ESA assessments. After Atos requested to exit the ESA contract early, the Centre for Health and Disability Assessments (CHDA), a wholly-owned subsidiary within MAXIMUS, took over ESA assessments from March 2015. The Committee noted that the DWP and its contractors have reduced the backlogs that previously existed; outstanding ESA assessments fell from 724,000 in early 2014 to 410,000 in August 2015. However, the Committee also considered that contractors' performance still does not meet claimants', the Department's and taxpayers' expectations, in particular with continuing concerns about the quality of assessments. Thus ESA assessments still take on average 23 weeks. In addition, a significant proportion of the assessment reports sampled by contractors (ranging from 7 per cent to 20 per cent) do not meet the contractual standard required and yet the DWP only returns less than 1 per cent of all assessment reports to contractors because they cannot be used to make a decision. As the DWP increases the number of assessments to be completed by contractors, the Committee states it must learn from past experience to ensure contractors are set challenging but realistic targets against which they are held to account. In addition, the Committee considered the DWP also needs to develop a competitive market for health and disability assessments to ensure that there are sufficient credible bidders for contracts as they come up for renewal.

For the latest and comprehensive Parliamentary report, see HC Work and Pensions Committee, *PIP and ESA Assessments*, Seventh Report of Session 2017-19 (HC 829, February 2018) and *PIP and ESA Assessments: claimant experiences*, Fourth Report of Session 2017-19 (HC 355, January 2018); the Government's response has been published by the Committee as its Eighth Special Report, *PIP and ESA assessments: Government Response to the Committee's Seventh Report of 2017–19*.

4.384   *The structure of the current Sch.2*: As with its predecessor, Sch.2 has two Parts. Part I deals with physical disabilities. Part II covers the mental, cognitive and intellectual function assessment.

Part I (physical disabilities) now contains only ten activities, rather than the eleven in the original Sch.2. They cover: mobilising; standing and sitting; reaching; picking up and moving or transferring by the use of the upper body and arms; manual dexterity; making oneself understood; understanding communication; navigation and maintaining safety; continence (absence or loss of control) other than enuresis; and consciousness during waking moments. The coverage and formulation of the activities and descriptors in the Schedule very much reflects the favoured principle of taking into account adaptations to condition and the use of suitable aids (e.g. walking stick, manual wheelchair, guide dog). This is on the basis that by accounting for any aids or adaptations which an individual may successfully and reasonably use to mitigate the disabling impact of their condition, their actual capability can the better be determined, and was thought to be consistent with the principle that as few people should be written off from re-engagement with work as possible merely because of their condition (*Review*, para.3.2). "Bending or kneeling" (Activity 3 in the original Sch.2) has been dropped. It was considered that activities 1–3 in the original Sch.2 (walking; standing and sitting; bending or kneeling) provided a significant level of overlap, whereby an individual (e.g. a wheelchair user) could score in each activity for what was in the modern workplace essentially the same disability, thus affording an inaccurate assessment of the individual's true level of functional limitation. "Bending or kneeling" was seen as:

> "an unnecessary requirement for the workplace. This is highlighted by the fact that wheelchair users who may be capable of work, may also be unable to bend or kneel. Changes to the [other] two activities [walking/mobilising; standing and sitting] mean that Bending or Kneeling is redundant as an activity. The removal of this activity is also in line with active encouragement in the workplace not to bend forward when lifting for health and safety reasons" (*Review*, para.4.3.1, p.19).

Activity 10 of the original Sch.2 (continence other than enuresis) has been short-
ened and simplified and is now Activity 9 in the new Sch.2.

Part II of Sch.2 (mental, cognitive and intellectual function assessment) contains
seven activities rather than the ten in the original WCA. They cover: learning tasks;
awareness of everyday hazards; initiating and completing personal action; coping
with change; getting about; coping with social engagement due to cognitive impairment or mental disorder; appropriateness of behaviour with other people, due to
cognitive impairment or mental disorder. It was thought that this revision and
reduction removed unnecessary complexities and overlaps.

II. The importance of the amendments effected on January 28, 2013

As reg.2 of the amending instrument makes clear (see para.9.614, below), these   **4.385**
apply to all claims made on or after January 28, 2013 and to most decisions made
on or after that date, whether the claim was made before that date or not. For a six
month period, however, some cases where questionnaires were sent out before that
date remained subject to the unamended regime, on which see the 2012/13 edition
of this volume.

The amendments relevant to the application of this Schedule concern the assessment process (reg.19(4), (5)); the wording of activities 1, 6, 7, 8, 9; and descriptors
2(b), (c), 5(d), 9(b) and 15(a).

As regards the assessment process, reg.19(4) now provides that in assessing
someone's capability to perform the activities in Pt 1 of this Schedule (physical
disabilities) the person is to be assessed as if fitted with or wearing any prosthesis
with which that person is normally fitted or normally wears, or, as the case may be,
wearing or using any aid or appliance which is normally, or could reasonably be
expected to be, worn or used. In addition, reg.19(5) brings in the requirement—
familiar from the IB regime—that Pt 1 of this Schedule (physical disabilities) must
be linked to incapability arising from a specific bodily disease or disablement or as
a direct result of treatment provided by a registered medical practitioner for such
a disease or disablement. Similarly it introduces the requirement that Pt 2 of this
Schedule (mental, cognitive and intellectual function assessment) must be linked
to incapability arising from a specific mental illness or disablement or as a direct
result of treatment provided by a registered medical practitioner for such an illness
or disablement. Under the previous wording of the paragraph (still applicable to
some cases after January 28, 2013—see reg.2 of the amending instrument, below,
para.9.614), there was no such link (*KP* v *SSWP (ESA)* [2011] UKUT 216 (AAC);
KN v *SSWP (ESA)* [2011] UKUT 229 (AAC); *RM* v *SSWP (ESA)* [2011] UKUT
454 (AAC); *AH* v *SSWP (ESA)* [2011] UKUT 333 (AAC)).

The changes to particular activities and descriptors are reflected in the commentary to each of them.

III Order of treatment in this commentary

In the nature of things, this is a lengthy annotation to a Schedule which lies at   **4.386**
the heart of determining the key question whether a claimant for ESA has limited
capability for work. It aims to identify and highlight key issues and concerns and to
indicate which features of a burgeoning case law on the AWT/PCA and the original
WCA remain of significance and assistance: (a) in approaching what is in essence
a similar task to those earlier regimes (matching a claimant's health condition to
a range of activities and descriptors and assigning a score); and (b) more specifically in interpreting and applying any similarly worded terms of the activities and
descriptors in the revised LCWA. The commentary is sub-divided as follows:

[A]   Approaching the interpretation of the Schedule as a whole.
[B]   Interpreting specific activities and descriptors: Pt I: physical disabilities.
[C]   Approaching Pt II: mental, cognitive and intellectual function assessment.

[A] Approaching the interpretation of the Schedule as a whole

4.387   *Evidence and attention to detail:* Decision-makers must pay very close attention to the precise wording of the activities and descriptors and to the matter of appropriate evidence to ground their findings (*CSIB/12/96*). Cases must be decided in the light of the totality of the evidence, medical or otherwise, including that from the claimant (*CIB/15663/1996*). His evidence does not require corroboration unless self-contradictory or improbable (*R(I) 2/51*). Differing medical opinions and reports must carefully be appraised, without rigid preconceptions on whether the report of the examining health professional is always to be preferred as more disinterested and informed than that of the claimant's GP or consultant, or vice versa (contrast *CIB/13039/1996* and *CIB/3968/1996* with *CIB/17257/1996*; *CW v SSWP (ESA)* [2011] UKUT 386 (AAC), para.24). Both types of evidence can, from different perspectives, prove valuable (*CIB/17257/1996*; *CIB/21/2002*). A tribunal is not *bound to* decide in the same way as any particular doctor certifies; when faced with a conflict of medical opinion, they are at liberty to prefer, giving reasons, one view rather than another (*R(S) 1/53*; *CSIB/684/1997*; *CSIB/848/1997*; *CIB/309/1997*; *R. v Social Security Commissioner Ex p. Dobie* (QBD, October 26, 1999)—but cf. *CIB/17257/1996*). But that does not warrant underestimating a DWPMS personal capability assessment report, which is based on a more intensive and detailed clinical examination and history-taking than the invalidity benefit system (*CIB/15663/1996*). To prefer a DWPMS doctor's report on the grounds that it is more detailed is not, as such, irrational (*R. v Social Security Commissioner Ex p. Dobie*, QBD (October 26, 1999)). A tribunal should not reject a claimant's appeal on the basis that he was "not a reliable or credible witness" without giving reasons for that finding (*CSIB/459/1997*). It should be made clear that the claimant's evidence has been considered, what account has been taken of it, and, if rejected, why it has been rejected (*CIB/309/1997*; *CW v SSWP (ESA)* [2011] UKUT 386 (AAC), para.24). Nor should a tribunal simply record acceptance of the DWPMS doctor's findings; rather it should make and record its own findings on the descriptors (*CSIB/459/1997*; *CIB/4232/2007*). The correct approach is to weigh all the evidence in the context of the case (*CIB/3620/1998*); *CIB/2308/2001*, para.20; *FR v SSWP (ESA)* [2015] UKUT 151 (AAC), paras 9–12). In *CIB/3074/2003* Commissioner Bano allowed the claimant's appeal because the tribunal had dismissed the appeal "on the basis of a formulaic endorsement of the examining medical practitioner's report", rather than looking at it in the light of its nature and the evidence as a whole. Although a tribunal cannot conduct a physical examination of the claimant, it can use all its senses, including ocular observation of the claimant during the hearing, when considering whether the LCWA is satisfied (*R1/01(IB) (T)*; *R4/99 (IB)*) and a tribunal medical member can properly look at x-rays put in evidence (*R(IB) 2/06*). Getting a claimant to roll up his trouser leg so that the tribunal could ascertain whether he had muscle wastage was impermissible (*MA v SSWP (ESA)* [2015] UKUT 290 (AAC), paras 14-19). Tribunals should also consider carefully evidence that the medical examination was perfunctory. Where a claimant criticises as inadequate a WCA examination, it would, however, be extremely unusual to use in such a case the tribunal's power to exclude otherwise admissible evidence on the basis that its admission would be unfair; but where, as usual, the report of that examination is admitted, questions about the adequacy of the report and the examination are relevant to the weight that the tribunal should accord to the report (*JM v SSWP (IB)* [2010] UKUT 386 (AAC), paras 18, 19). Equally, where the health practitioner's report disputes the claimant's account of his disabilities in his questionnaire, natural justice requires that tribunals hear the claimant's oral evidence about his condition, before deciding which account to prefer (*CIB/5586/1999*). Tribunals should be wary of adviser/representative revision of the picture painted by the claimant's questionnaire answers and the health professional's report, and should look for supporting evidence where such statements differ significantly from the claimant's original own assessment of his or her condition (*CIB/2913/2001*).

The issue of the claimant's credibility arose in *KN v SSWP (ESA)* [2016] UKUT 521 (AAC). Judge Gray held that the fact that a claimant did not make a complaint to the organisation responsible for the HCP did not undermine his or her credibility if the report and/or examination is subsequently criticised on any appeal: "There is no legal requirement for a complaint to be made in tandem with an appeal, and it seems to me wholly wrong to use the absence of such a complaint as a significant credibility pointer" (at para.24).

Now that assessments are carried out by a wider range of HCPs, consideration has been given to the weight that should be placed on their evidence, particularly in mental health cases, where the particular experience of the HCP lies in a non-mental health field.

In *(1) ST, (2) GF v SSWP (ESA)* [2014] UKUT 547 (AAC); [2015] AACR 23, a panel of three Upper Tribunal judges categorically rejected Judge Mark's comments in *JH v SSWP (ESA)* [2013] UKUT 269 (AAC), para.22—which it saw as *obiter*—as

> "wrong if and to the extent that they purport to create a rule of law or starting point that observations on mental health descriptors by HCP physiotherapists are of no probative value whatsoever or are highly likely or likely to have little probative value and thus should be accorded no or little weight by the decision maker and the First-tier tribunal" (para.33).

Instead the proper approach is that the probative value of an HCP physiotherapist's report is a matter for the decision maker or tribunal dealing with the case, just as it is with other reports and evidence.

The panel so held, firstly, because the legislation makes no distinction between an HCP's ability to deal with mental health descriptors as opposed to physical ones. It merely requires approval by the Secretary of State and registration with the appropriate regulatory body. So any such rule as Judge Mark's would frustrate the statutory framework (para.34). The panel's second rationale noted the difference between the LCW assessment (how a condition affects the claimant's functional capacity) and "a medical examination carried out as part of a process of diagnosis and treatment" (para.35), a distinction acknowledged in Professor Harrington's *First Review* of the ESA process. The panel thus considered that the medical examination carried out by a HCP for the LCW did not require that HCP to be a medical specialist in all the physical and mental problems that might be exhibited by a particular claimant. To require the HCP to be such a specialist "would create insurmountable problems for the assessment process" since many claimants have a variety of problems which might then require assessment in a particular case by several HCPs rather than one (para.35).

What is required, however, is that the HCP have an informed understanding of the claimant's medical conditions and the difficulties flowing from them. This requires adequate training and supervision. The panel had received detailed information on the current training process (see paras 11-19)—something not available to Judge Mark in *JH*—and, while not commenting on that programme, did observe that none of the independent reviews of the ESA assessment process had criticised the performance of physiotherapists relative to HCPs from other disciplines and that training for HCPs on mental health problems was being reviewed with the aim of increasing the knowledge of all HCPs (para.36).

There is, therefore, no need for a tribunal to adjourn for further particulars on the qualifications of the HCP in a particular case. The specialist tribunal with its medical member must "make its own findings having regard to all the evidence before it" (para.37). The correct starting point was that identified by Judge Ovey in an incapacity benefit appeal (*JF v SSWP (IB)* [2011] UKUT 385 (AAC) at para.25:

> "...the report is prepared by an HCP who has been trained (whether as part of the training as an HCP or through other training) at least to the level thought appropriate by the Department of Work and Pensions for carrying out examinations where mental health issues are raised. In other words the selection and training procedures ought to have produced an HCP who can conduct a mental

health examination competently. It follows that evidence that the HCP has not undergone separate specialist training should not of itself have any effect on the weight which the tribunal attaches to the report. . ."

The panel held that the weight to be accorded to any report "addressing the functional impact of any medical condition on a claimant" is a matter for the specialist tribunal which should consider

"(a) the level of the author's expertise (for example, an HCP or a consultant psychiatrist) and (b) the knowledge of the claimant possessed by the author (for example, knowledge gained from a one-off assessment or that gained as a treating clinician). Additionally the date of the evidence, its comprehensiveness, and its relevance to the issues the tribunal has to determine are also key matters for the tribunal to consider. Importantly the tribunal should explain its reasoning for attaching weight to one type or piece of evidence rather than to another" (para.38 of *ST/GF*).

In *ST* v *SSWP (ESA)* [2012] UKUT 469 (AAC), Judge Wright held that with respect to a decision to supersede an award of benefit on the basis of a new work capability assessment, natural justice and the right to a fair trial under art.6(1) ECHR required that the Secretary of State make available to the tribunal the previous work capability assessment (ESA85). In *CA* v *SSWP (ESA)* [2013] UKUT 442 (AAC), Judge Ward stated that it was likely to be an exceptional case in which a change in descriptors would exempt the Secretary of State from that duty, since a previous WCA assessment, particularly one close in time and where the condition in question is not said to be changing can prove of evidential value and assist the tribunal to assess the robustness of the latest assessment at issue, by giving a picture of the claimant's history and considering the descriptors thought by the previous HCP then to be relevant. It is ultimately for the tribunal what to make of that previous assessment. The scope and extent of the obligation of Secretary of State for Work and Pensions to produce previous medical reports, or records of them, in every case has now been considered by a three-judge panel of the Upper Tribunal in *FN* v *SSWP (SA)* [2015] UKUT 670 (AAC); [2016] AACR 24 (formerly *CSE/422/2013*, *CSE/435/2013* and *CSE/19/2014*). The panel broadly agreed with decisions such as *JC* v *DSD (IB)* [2011] NICom 177; [2014] AACR 30 and also both *ST* v *SSWP (ESA)* [2012] UKUT 469 (AAC) and *AM* v *SSWP (ESA)* [2013] UKUT 458 (AAC). The three-judge panel stressed that the previous adjudication history and associated evidence is not *always* relevant to an employment and support allowance appeal and that, even if the Secretary of State has not produced all the information and evidence that he should have produced with his response to an appeal, it does not necessarily follow that the First-tier Tribunal's decision will be wrong in law and liable to be set aside:

"79. ... We can envisage a situation where a First-tier Tribunal considers that it has sufficient relevant evidence before it to determine the issues arising in the appeal without the requirement to call for evidence which is missing because the Secretary of State has failed in his duty to provide it.
80. ... Our view is that the first choice for the tribunal should not be to adjourn but to get on with the task of determining the issues arising in the appeal when satisfied that it has the necessary relevant evidence before it. It might be the case that having weighed and assessed the appellant's oral evidence, the tribunal might be satisfied that the evidence is credible, should be accepted and the appeal be allowed ..."

In *CA* v *SSWP (ESA)* [2016] UKUT 523 (AAC) the claimant had failed a previous WCA, not appealed that decision and claimed and received JSA for nine months before making a further (and again unsuccessful) ESA claim. This time she appealed the adverse WCA decision, but did not mention the previous ESA assessment. Judge Lane, dismissing the further appeal, held that the FTT had not failed in its inquisitorial duty:

"15. Tribunals in the Social Entitlement Chamber are alert to legal and evidential matters that are relevant but which would be obscure to a layman. They are
accustomed to being proactive in a way that would be foreign in other Chambers.
But, as *FN* establishes, their proactivity is not boundless. A tribunal cannot pull
a rabbit out of a hat unless it is given a hat to work with. The hat, in this case, is
evidence from the appellant that there has been no change in their medical condition or disablement since a previous award or assessment."

See further the commentary in Vol III of this series to the Social Security and
Child Support (Decisions and Appeals) Regulations 1999 (SI 1999/991) reg.6(2)
(g) and (r) (Supersession of decisions) and to Tribunal Procedure (First-tier
Tribunal) (Social Entitlement Chamber) Rules 2008 (SI 2008/2685) r.24(1)–(5)
(Responses).

Where the claimant has complained about a medical examination and no response
to that has been received by the tribunal, or any relevant medical report is not before
the tribunal, it is appropriate to consider whether to adjourn., but it does not follow
that it must adjourn (*SA v SSWP (ESA)* [2013] UKUT 616 (AAC), per Judge
Mark):

"It needs to consider all the matters in issue in the complaint, the likelihood of
their being resolved or at least further illuminated by the report, the relevance of
the complaints to the matters before it and the likely relevance of any possible
response by ATOS in addition to any other relevant matters. Having considered all relevant matters it needs to decide whether it was better to proceed or
to adjourn in order to deal with the case fairly and justly in accordance with the
overriding objective in rule 2 of the Tribunal Procedure (First-tier Tribunal)
(SEC) Rules 2008 (see further *MA v SoS* [2009] UKUT 221 (AAC)). It also
needs to give reasons for its decision."

The computerised medical examination report is the end product of the system.
In that report statements or phrases can be produced mechanically by the software,
which produces relevant phrases from its memory bank, and, unless the examining
health professional using it is very careful, the statements in the report may not
necessarily represent actual wording chosen and typed in by him. This generates
an increased risk of accidental mistakes or discrepancies being left undetected in
the final product of the process. The need for careful appraisal of the computerized
report has been stressed by Commissioners Howell and Williams (*CIB/511/2005*;
CIB/476/2005; *CIB/1522/2005*; *CIB/0664/2005*; *CIB/3950/2007*; *CIB/1006/2008*).
It is submitted that reports under the revised WCA ought to be scrutinized even
more carefully because further glitches might have crept in during the necessary
software revision undertaken in a relatively short period of time.

Section 7 of the Electronic Communications Act 2000 has no application to the
computerised report form (*R(IB) 7/05*).

4.388

In *NH v SSWP (ESA)* [2014] UKUT 114 (AAC), concerns about the qualifications of the examining health care professional, a nurse, and the computerized
report combined so that Judge Williams had to set aside the decision superceding
entitlement which had been upheld by the tribunal:

"this report not only calls into question whether the nurse actually conducted
a mental health examination as reported or even read the report she submitted
before doing so but also more generally the evidential value of a report conducted
or purportedly conducted by a nurse when there is no indication that the nurse had
any specific qualifications to conduct that aspect of the examination. Was she aware
of the importance in this case of examining the mental health issues? Was she qualified to give the advice she gave about them? If so, why is this report so deficient in
that area? It also calls into question the validity of a report produced by a computer
programme that allows the operator to delete the whole of the relevant parts of the
report which should record results of a clinical physical examination so that there is
no "supporting medical evidence" while still generating unqualified opinions about
unexamined physical functions for which there is no such evidence" (para.10).

Judge Williams thought the case to be "one of the most disturbing examples of repeated failure fairly to assess the actual medical problems of an appellant that I have seen for some time. Indeed, it is disturbing enough to call aspects of the system itself into question" (para.18).

To reiterate: the first task is to decide from all the evidence in the case which descriptors apply, the second to calculate the scores. Decision-makers and tribunals must in the light of all relevant evidence identify the relevant health condition and consider carefully the full range of activities which may be impaired by it (*CIB/5797/1997*; *CIB/3589/2004*). Scoring should proceed from top to bottom, so as to properly identify the highest ranking descriptor in the range attached to the particular activity which can properly be said to apply to the claimant (*CIB/5361/1997*; reg.19(6)).

4.389   *The LCWA is not a snapshot—the need for an approach characterized by "reasonableness"*: The "sometimes" descriptors in the AWT/PCA were not carried over into ESA, but this merely means that there is no descriptor under which the claimant can score points simply because he is sometimes unable to perform the relevant activity. Their removal did not mean that there was no longer a need for the decision-makers to take into account whether the claimant can perform the relevant activity with some degree of repetition. That need subsists in relation to the WCA descriptors as in relation to its predecessors in the AWT/PCA (*AF v SSWP (ESA)* [2011] UKUT 61 (AAC), para.11; *AG v SSWP (ESA)* [2013] UKUT 77 (AAC), paras.14–18; *SAG v Department for Social Development (ESA)* [2012] AACR 6). Indeed such a requirement seems inherent in any test of capability for work designed to be attuned to the needs of the modern workplace and a level of activity an employer would expect. The Government emphasised that, like the PCA, the LCWA was not intended to be a simple snapshot. The review group whose work led to the original WCA rightly stressed that guidance to decision-makers and to the healthcare professionals involved in the assessments of capacity would indicate the factors to be taken into account in ascertaining whether a claimant can perform a particular function: ability to do it just once is not enough (the person must reliably be able to sustain or repeat the activity); distress, pain, and fatigue involved in carrying out the activity; and the detrimental effects of medication. The *Review* leading to the revised WCA commented:

"Individuals whose conditions fluctuate in an unpredictable manner may provide a more significant challenge in relation to employment as employers are less able to predict and manage their absence.

. . . [T]he WCA has afforded individuals greater opportunity to detail the variations in their condition, specifically in the questionnaire which they are asked to complete. Rather than a yes/no format, the potential responses also include 'it varies', and space is provided for the detailing of the variation.

In the course of the assessment itself, healthcare professionals take into account fluctuations which an individual may experience in their capability. The assessment seeks to identify whether an individual is capable of carrying out an activity reliably and repeatedly for the majority of the time. If an individual is unable to do so, then they are considered unable to carry out the activity at all, and will be awarded points accordingly" (para.4.10.1).

The *CMA* honing report also commented on fluctuating conditions, echoed this last point, and emphasised that:

"Guidance states that if an individual cannot complete an action safely, reliably and repeatedly they should be considered unable to complete it at all. Recognising the challenges associated with assessing fluctuating conditions, there is ongoing work which aims to enhance the training that healthcare professionals (HCPs) receive and ensure that advice in this area is comprehensive.

In recognition, however, of the importance of accurately assessing fluctuating conditions, changes have been suggested to certain descriptors where exertion is a significant component. This ensures that where an individual is unable to do something as a result of exhaustion experienced, rather than discomfort, that is captured in the assessment" (*CMA*, para.2.1).

Those changes to specific descriptors have been embodied in the revised Schedules.

But (save where embodied in specific descriptors and thus as specific legal elements) this approach is not just a matter of guidance. It is submitted that it is embodied in legal rules established by the extensive jurisprudence on approaching the very similar exercise in the PCA. The requirement is for ability to perform the specified activities with "reasonable regularity"; there must be an element of reasonableness in the approach to the question of what someone is or is not capable of doing, including consideration of his ability to perform the activities most of the time *(C1/95(IB)*; *CSIB/17/96)*, so that the question becomes whether the claimant would normally be able to perform the stated activity if and when called upon to do so *(CIB/13161/96*; *CIB/13508/96)*. The nature of a *specific* working environment and the matter of employability are both irrelevant *(C1/95*; *CIB/13161/96*; *CIB/13508/96)*, but there is some relationship between Sch.2 and the work context. In *AS v SSWP (ESA)* [2013] UKUT 587 (AAC), approved by the Northern Ireland Court of Appeal in *O'Neill v Department for Communities* [2018] NICA 29 (a ruling refusing permission to appeal), Judge Wikeley considered in some depth the nature of that relationship, stating that he accepted as correctly made a concession by the Secretary of State's representative.

"that the various activities in Schedule 2 have "a connection with the workplace", albeit that the descriptors are not concerned with any one specific working environment and do not bring in wider questions of employability. This concession properly reflects the direction of policy travel as embodied in legislative change in this area. The first clue is in the change of name; Parliament has approved the shift from the "personal capability assessment" in the incapacity benefit scheme to the "work capability assessment" under the ESA regime. The second clue lies in the drafting of the various activities and individual descriptors, and in particular the amendments which took effect on March 28, 2011 (see further the Explanatory Memorandum to the draft 2011 Regulations, sent to the Social Security Advisory Committee on 13 August 2010). Thus the first three activities in the original Schedule 2 to the ESA Regulations—walking, standing and sitting, bending or kneeling—were seen as providing a high degree of overlap for e.g. wheelchair users, so providing an inaccurate assessment of an individual's true level of functional limitation in the workplace. This resulted in a radical rewriting of the first activity, transforming it from "walking" to "mobilising", the specific inclusion of the "work station" test in the second activity (standing and sitting) and the abolition of the third activity (bending or kneeling) as being both an unnecessary and undesirable requirement in the modern workplace.

It follows that the activities and descriptors in Schedule 2 do not exist in some sort of artificial or parallel universe, entirely divorced from the real world of work. They have to be applied on their own terms, but understood against the backdrop of the modern workplace. In deciding whether a particular descriptor is met, decision makers and tribunals may therefore find it helpful to consider the claimant's ability to undertake the activity in question in a range of different working contexts. However, claimants will not be awarded a defined descriptor simply because they can show that it would apply to them if they were employed to do a particular job in a specific type of working environment.

This is entirely consistent with the well-established principle that decision makers and tribunals must consider whether a claimant can perform a particular activity with a reasonable degree of repetition, sometimes referred to as [the] "reasonable regularity" principle. This principle applies to the ESA scheme just as it did to the previous incapacity benefit regime. As Upper Tribunal Judge Turnbull has explained, "if the effect of performing the activity is likely to be to disable the claimant from performing it for a substantial period, that will need to be taken into account" (see *AF v Secretary of State for Work and Pensions* (ESA) [2011] UKUT 61 at para.11, approved and followed in *SAG v Department for Social Development* (ESA) [2012] AACR 6). Judge Nicholas Paines QC has described the principle in similar terms: "it is implicit in this that a description set out in a descriptor will not fit a claimant who can only perform the relevant task exceptionally or infrequently" *(AG v Secretary of State for Work and Pensions (ESA)* [2013] UKUT 77 (at para.18).

Within the legislative scheme as a whole, this principle only makes sense in the context of the needs of a modern workplace and the level of activity that an employer attuned to the requirements of disability discrimination law can reasonably expect. Plainly, the test is not about a high-pressure working environment, e.g. a call-centre with demanding targets or a factory production line with a fast-moving conveyor belt. Equally, however, the test is not about what the person can do in their own home and entirely in their own time and at their own pace, subject to no external constraints or pressures whatsoever. If reasonable regularity is judged by the latter criterion, then the test has ceased to be a test of "whether a claimant's capability for work is limited by the claimant's physical or mental condition within regulation 19(1) of the ESA Regulations" (paras 18-21).

Judge Wikeley further held that the Court of Appeal decision in *Charlton v SSWP* [2009] EWCA Civ 42 (reported as *R(IB) 2/09*), which in the context of ESA Regs 2008, reg.29 required an examination of the work required, does not assist in interpreting the Sch. descriptors (para.17).

Just as the failure to carry over to the WCA the "sometimes" descriptors which featured in the AWT/PCA did not remove this requirement of a reasonable degree of repetition of performance (see *AF v SSWP (ESA)* [2011] UKUT 61 (AAC), para.11; *SAG v Department for Social Development (ESA)* [2012] AACR 6), so it is submitted that the incorporation into specific descriptors of an "exertion" element does not remove the overall requirement of "reasonable regularity". It must govern the overall approach to assessment.

4.390 Where variable, intermittent and sporadic conditions and their impact on earning capacity are involved, difficult questions of judgment in assessing incapacity for work arise where the claimant can sometimes do things but at other times not. Neither the PCA nor the LCWA were designed to be a simple "snapshot". The system aims to assess the claimant's condition over a particular period, taking account of pain and fatigue *(CIB/14587/1996; CIB/13161/96; CIB/13508/96)*, fears for health and the medical advice received by the claimant *(CSIB/12/96)*. The questionnaire asks about variability—the claimant's own doctor can include material on this in the MED 4, and examining health care professionals with Medical Services have been trained to conduct examinations with these issues in mind. The structure of the legislative scheme, however, produces a problem. It embodies a test based on an examination on a particular day designed to provide information on, and assessment of, a claimant over a period of time. The "normality" approach as part of "reasonable regularity" deals with one aspect of the problem: the reference in *C1/95(IB)* to a claimant being able to accomplish a task most of the time is to be read as meaning "as and when called upon to do so". On this basis, one looks at the position which normally prevails in the period (see *CSIB/459/1997*, para.13; *CIB/911/1997*, paras 12, 13). The more difficult situation is where it is accepted that the claimant's condition is such that for certain periods he is able to cope satisfactorily with normal activities; the problem of the sporadic or intermittent condition. The problem generated significant disagreement among Commissioners on approach. The authoritative Tribunal of Commissioners' decision is *R(IB) 2/99(T)*, endorsed by a tribunal of Commissioners in Northern Ireland in *R1/02(IB) (T)*. *R(IB) 2/99* concerned the situation where a claimant suffered from a condition causing greater disability on some days than on others. The key question was whether the claimant was incapable of work under the PCA on days on which, if the days were viewed in isolation, he or she might not satisfy that test (para.2). While the Tribunal decision does not prescribe any one approach as *universally* applicable, the central thrust of the decision is to see as justified for the majority of cases, the "broad approach" typified by *CIB/6244/97* rather than the stricter "daily approach" exemplified by *CIB/13161/96* and *CIB/13508/96*. The Tribunal did not, however, find helpful the distinction drawn between "variable" and "intermittent" conditions in

CIB/6244/97. Moreover, the Tribunal recognised that in some cases at least—generally when looking backwards over a prolonged period in the course of which the claimant has only had "short episodes of disablement" (for example, in the dwindling number of cases where the First-tier Tribunal had to consider matters "down to the date of the hearing", or in "review or overpayment cases")—something akin to the meticulous approach in *CIB/13161/96* and *CIB/13508/96* along the lines of Commissioner Jacobs' approach to intermittent conditions in *CIB/6244/1997* would be appropriate (para.17).

The practical reality is that most cases which fall to be decided by the decision-maker in the Department do not concern entitlement to benefit for a past period. Generally, a decision on the award of benefit is "forward looking" and usually made for an indefinite period. Although the decision-maker must of course consider the period from the medical examination up to the date of his decision, that decision will rarely be concerned with entitlement to benefit for a substantial period in the past. While both the "broad" and the "daily basis" approaches are each consistent with the wording of the legislation, the "broad approach" is "the only approach that can sensibly be applied by a decision-maker, making what is in effect a prospective determination for an extended period" (para.11). The Tribunal considered the broader-based approach adopted in *R(A) 2/74* to the attendance allowance issue— was there a period *throughout* which the claimant could be said to be so severely disabled as to require at night prolonged or repeated attention in connection with bodily functions? The Tribunal decided that such an approach applied equally to incapacity benefit despite its daily basis. It noted (without using those statements to support its construction of the legislation) that such an approach accorded with ministerial statements in Parliament on the introduction of the all work test (for example, that the "all work test" (now the "personal capability assessment") is not a "snapshot"). Nonetheless, the Tribunal stressed that:

4.391

> "the words of the legislation cannot be ignored . . . [I]n those cases where relevant descriptors are expressed in terms that the claimant 'cannot', rather than 'sometimes cannot', perform the activity, one should not stray too far from an arithmetical approach that considers what the claimant's abilities are 'most of the time'—the phrase used in *C1/95(IB)*. Nevertheless, we agree that all the factors mentioned by counsel [neither of whom argued for a 'daily basis' approach]—the frequency of 'bad' days, the lengths of periods of 'bad' days and of intervening periods, the severity of the claimant's disablement on both 'good' and 'bad' days and the unpredictability of 'bad' days—are relevant when applying the broad approach. Thus a person whose condition varies from day to day and who would easily satisfy the 'all work test' on three days a week and would nearly satisfy it on the other four days might well be considered to be incapable of work for the whole week. But a person who has long periods of illness separated by periods of remission lasting some weeks during which he or she suffers no significant disablement, might well be considered to be incapable of work during the periods of illness but not to be incapable of work during the periods of remission, even if the periods of illness are longer than the periods of remission. Each case must be judged on its merits and . . . there are some cases where a claimant can properly be regarded as incapable of work both on days when the 'all work test' is clearly satisfied and on other days in between those days and that there are other cases where the claimant can be regarded as incapable of work only on 'bad days' . . ." (para.15).

That ESA is a weekly benefit, coupled with the demise of the "sometimes" descriptors, emphasises the continued authority and propriety of this approach to the LCWA tasks. Hence, as regards forward-looking decisions, claimants whose condition is such as only to satisfy the test on four or five days a month (albeit days of severe disablement) cannot, however unpredictable those days may be, properly be regarded as satisfying the test for the whole month. It thus may be that some claimants who are unemployable nonetheless are seen as "capable of work" under the PCA or the LCWA.

In *R1/02(IB)(T)*, a Northern Ireland tribunal of Commissioners endorsed the "broad brush" approach to variable conditions in *R(IB)2/99(T)*, but also laid emphasis on para.15 of it, set out above, with one reservation. They were unhappy with the phrase "the unpredictability of 'bad' days", commenting that those who decide cases:

> "will simply have to try to determine the likely patterns of functional limitation. Uncertainty as to the possibility of a future recurrence would not of itself usually be enough to satisfy the test which must be satisfied on the balance of probability at the time of the decision maker's decision" (para.26).

Applying para.15 of *R(IB)2/99* in *CIB/2620/2000*, Commissioner Bano held that the case before him (a sufferer from dysmenorrhoea) was one of the minority of cases in which the broad approach could not be applied, one where the claimant could only be considered incapable of work on "bad days".

4.392 *Making and recording decisions*: Setting rigorous standards for tribunals (cf. his approach to activity 3 in *CSIB/12/96*), Commissioner Walker in *CSIB 324/97* stipulated the following approach to making and recording decisions under the "all work" test [the predecessor of the IB PCA]:

> "the best and safest practice is for a tribunal to consider and make findings of fact about, first, the disability or disabilities, be they disease or bodily or mental problems, from which an individual has been proved on the evidence to suffer. Second, they should consider and make findings of fact about which, if any of the activities set out in the Schedule, are established to be adversely affected by any of those disabilities. Thirdly, and based upon appropriate findings of fact, in the case of each and every activity the tribunal should determine which descriptor best fits the case having regard to the evidence, in their view. Finally, in the reasons, they should explain why a particular activity has been held not to be adversely affected where there was a contention that it was so affected, and why a particular descriptor has been preferred to any other contended for" (para.11).

But that best and safest practice need not necessarily always be followed. For example, where the issue is whether or not the tribunal believes the claimant on a matter fundamental and relevant, if on reasonable grounds the tribunal did not believe the claimant when he alleged that his responses in the questionnaire were not accurate, then the finding that the tribunal did not believe that he had been mistaken when providing those responses covered in reality all the disputed areas raised at the hearing, and it was not necessary to record specific findings of fact on each of the activity questions brought up by the claimant (per Northern Ireland Chief Commissioner Martin in *C46/97(IB)*, drawing with approval on Deputy Commissioner Ramsay's decision in *CIB/16572/96*). In para.5 of *CIB/4497/1998*, Commissioner Rowland sets out useful guidance on the minimum requirements of giving reasons. He noted that:

> "a statement of reasons may be adequate even though it could be improved on and, in particular, a failure to observe the 'best and safest practice' recommended in *CSIB 324/97* . . . is not necessarily an error of law . . . What is required by way of reasoning depends very much on the circumstances of the case before the tribunal. Those challenging reasoning must explain its inadequacy and show the significance of the inadequacy."

Where a tribunal has heard oral evidence from a claimant on the effect of his/her condition, it must ensure that, when considering the report of the HCP, it makes clear what it makes of the claimant's evidence, whether that agrees or disagrees with findings in the HCP report (*YD v SSWP (IB)* [2010] UKUT 290 (AAC), para.12). In that case, Judge Turnbull also said that where the claimant has given oral evidence, a tribunal will not necessarily then have to deal with each of the mental health descriptors at issue, "although it may often be desirable to do so" (para.13).

When applying the principles to a particular case, it should be remembered that a First-tier Tribunal has an inquisitorial role (*CIB/14442/96*). It should be cautious about exercising that role when considering mental disablement (*CIB/14202/1996*, see head [C] below). Where the claimant is represented by a competent adviser (e.g. a Welfare Rights officer employed by a "responsible" local authority), a tribunal is entitled to proceed on the basis that the representative will put forward all relevant points on his client's behalf and to know the case that is being made for the client. The tribunal in such a case should not be expected to inquire further into the claimant's case; to require that would be to place an impossible administrative burden on tribunals (*CSIB/389/1998*). Overall, the tribunal's task is rendered easier now in that, because of the SSA 1998, the focus is on matters as at the date of the Secretary of State's decision rather than covering matters in the often lengthy period down to the date of the hearing (see further Vol.III: *Administration, Adjudication and the European Dimension*).

[B] Interpreting specific activities and descriptors: Pt I: physical disabilities

Note that from January 28, 2013, reg.19(4) provides that in assessing someone's   **4.393**
capability to perform the activities in this Part of this Schedule (physical disabilities) the person is to be assessed as if fitted with or wearing any prosthesis with which that person is normally fitted or normally wears, or, as the case may be, wearing or using any aid or appliance which is normally, or could reasonably be expected to be, worn or used. In addition, reg.19(5) brings in the requirement—familiar from the IB regime—that this Part of this Schedule (physical disabilities) must be linked to incapability arising from a specific bodily disease or disablement or as a direct result of treatment provided by a registered medical practitioner for such a disease or disablement.

Activity 1: Mobilising unaided by another person with or without a walking stick, manual wheelchair or other aid if such aid is normally, or could reasonably be, worn or used: On a preliminary note, there are of course important differences in the drafting of the mobility descriptors for ESA and PIP respectively. It follows that what may appear to be inconsistent decisions relating to a particular individual's ability to mobilise under ESA and PIP regimes may be more apparent than real. However, there may be circumstances in which on the facts the FTT needs to consider whether to adjourn to have sight of the relevant PIP reports etc when deciding an ESA appeal: see e.g. *JB v SSWP (ESA)* [2017] UKUT 20 (AAC). On the potential significance of an award of PIP to an ESA appeal concerned with mobilising unaided, see *AG v SSWP (ESA)* [2017] UKUT 413 (AAC), where Judge Hemingway ruled as follows on the comparability (if any) of a PIP award and an ESA award (at para.9):

> "The statutory tests are not the same. One is concerned with standing and moving and the other with mobilising which includes the possible use, where appropriate, of a manual wheelchair. Anyway a tribunal, whatever award has been made in respect of a different benefit, will be entitled to make its own decision with respect to entitlement to the benefit with which it is concerned on the appeal before it. It should not simply ignore the possible relevance of an award of a different benefit but that relevance is likely to be in relation to the possibility of there being further relevant evidence which might not be before the tribunal on the appeal and the appropriateness or otherwise of adjourning to get it."

See also *MH v SSWP (ESA)* [2018] UKUT 194 (AAC) where Judge Poole QC held that the tribunal did not act in error of law by failing to adjourn (or to record its reasons for not adjourning) for evidence about a PIP award, nor in either determining the ESA appeal without having before it that evidence or in failing directly to address the claimant's PIP award in its statement of reasons.

As Judge Rowland noted in *KB v SSWP (ESA)* [2014] UKUT 126 (AAC)

> "The scheme of this legislation is clear. For each of descriptors 1(a), (c) and (d), two questions must be asked. First, can the claimant mobilise more than the relevant distance without stopping. If the answer is "no", the descriptor is satisfied.

If the answer is "yes", the second limb must be considered and it must be asked whether the claimant can repeatedly mobilise the relevant distance. Again, if the answer is "no", the descriptor is satisfied. Only if the answer is "yes" to both questions is the descriptor not satisfied so that one must consider the next descriptor" (para.6).

To the same effect see *GC v SSWP (ESA)* [2014] UKUT 117 (AAC), applying *HD v SSWP (ESA)* [2014] UKUT 72 (AAC), a decision on Activity 1 in Sch.3.

The profound change here from the PCA/WCA is from "walking" to "mobilizing" and the removal of the "cannot walk at all" descriptor, thus encompassing adaptation to disability, namely manual wheelchair use. On wheelchair or other aids, the question is whether the wheelchair or other aid "could reasonably be worn or used" or "is normally worn or used". Until the decision of a panel of three Upper Tribunal judges in *SI v SSWP (ESA)* [2014] UKUT 308 (AAC); [2015] AACR 5, there was marked judicial disagreement on the range of factors to be taken into account in determining "reasonableness". Some judges favoured taking account of a broad range (see e.g. *M v SSWP (ESA)* [2012] UKUT 376; *NT v SSWP (ESA)* [2013] UKUT 360 (AAC); *BG v SSWP (ESA)* [2013] UKUT 504 (AAC)). Others saw as pertinent a narrower range of factors, focusing on a predominantly (and sometimes an exclusively) functional approach (see e.g. *TB v SSWP (ESA)* [2013] UKUT 408 (AAC); *AR v SSWP (ESA)* [2013] UKUT 417 (AAC); *MG v Department for Social Development (ESA)* [2013] NI Com 359). In *SI*, the panel of three Upper Tribunal judges held that the approach to be followed was the broader "in all the circumstances" one. The panel considered that

"if a person is in practice precluded from using an aid *for any reason and would on that ground be excluded from part of the job market*, it is unfair to assess his or her entitlement to ESA on the basis that he or she could use the aid" (para.58, emphasis supplied by commentator).

Like Judge Wikeley in *AS v SSWP (ESA)* [2013] UKUT 587 (AAC), the panel saw the LCWA as a functional one related to the circumstances of the modern workplace. Like the "cooking test" for disability benefits the WCA is a "thought experiment" so that the LCWA is applied "on the basis that the notional employer from whom the claimant might obtain employment has a modern workplace and is prepared to make reasonable adjustments in order to enable the claimant to be employed" (para.76).

Given that panel decision, it is submitted that the following factors or circumstances—identified from pre- and post-*SI* case law and *SI* itself—are ones of relevance, but this list is not advanced as an exhaustive one:—

- whether use of a wheelchair rather than crutches was medically suitable and had been suggested by medical personnel (*M v SSWP (ESA)* [2012] UKUT 376)—note, however,in contrast,, in a rare case where the claimant inappropriately used a wheelchair (on the medical evidence he did not need one), the tribunal was entitled to assess his ability to mobilize on the basis of his using the wheelchair (*MA v SSWP (ESA)* [2015] UKUT 290 (AAC), paras 23-31);

- whether or not the claimant had been referred for assessment for an NHS wheelchair as an aid to determining whether a wheelchair would normally be used by someone with the claimant's disabilities (*MG v Department for Social Development (ESA)* [2013] NI Com 359, paras 35–44; *TB v SSWP (ESA)* [2013] UKUT 408 (AAC)—although such a referral is not, however, conclusive of whether a wheelchair could in fact reasonably be used by the particular claimant (*TB*);

- whether in light of the claimant's condition and the availability of wheelchairs by local providers, the claimant would in reality have access to one (*M v SSWP (ESA)* [2012] UKUT 376).

If a claimant does not have a wheelchair, the panel in *SI* stated that Secretary of State should produce evidence on their availability, but it also considered that this would not in practice be problematic given the Access to Work scheme or similar schemes operated by Jobcentres. The panel were mistaken in that the Access to Work scheme does not cover wheelchairs (*CS v SSWP (ESA)* [2014] UKUT 519 (AAC), para.42). But, as noted in *BG v SSWP (ESA)* [2013] UKUT 504 (AAC), while "it is even possible that inability to afford a wheelchair may be relevant . . . it would not normally be so given their relative cheapness and their availability from the NHS and charities where reasonably required" (para.15);

- the claimant's home environment (*M v SSWP (ESA)* [2012] UKUT 376; *BG v SSWP (ESA)* [2013] UKUT 504 (AAC)), but in *SI* the panel thought its importance in this context is lessened by the fact that a manual wheelchair could be kept available at the workplace if the home environment does not enable its storage there. It is submitted that this approach focuses too much on the workplace itself, ignoring the issue of how such a claimant would be able to get to and from the workplace, something inherent as a focus in a number of the Sch.2 descriptors and the approach in *Charlton* to regs. 29 and 35.

The mobilization test is an actual rather than hypothetical test; "if the claimant had a manual wheelchair could he or she reasonably use it". As *SI* and the above factors show, the answer to this is not purely a matter of whether, when in the wheelchair, the claimant can mobilize. But even looking at the issue from a purely functional point of view, as Judge Williams made clear in *AR v SSWP (ESA)* [2013] UKUT 417 (AAC), reasonable use of a wheelchair involves several aspects of functional ability aside from the lower limbs. While there is no longer a "rising from sitting" activity in Sch.2, one must nonetheless consider it in the context of whether a wheelchair can reasonably be used. On a functional analysis, "can a claimant reasonably be expected to use a wheelchair (including getting into and out of it) without the aid of another person if he or she cannot reasonably be expected to handle the wheelchair whilst preparing to get into it, or after getting out of it?" (para.35). Unfortunately, the standard forms (ESA50 and ESA85) do not deal with such issues because they are no longer dealt with elsewhere in the Schedules. Tribunals must be wary of falling into the trap of assuming that every claimant who can reasonably use a wheelchair must thereby be able to propel it for more than 50 metres; this is especially so in a case where there is no evidence that the claimant in question has actually used a wheelchair under his own propulsion. Likewise the mere fact of a forthcoming assessment for wheelchair use is not evidence that a wheelchair could be reasonably used (*SG v SSWP (ESA)* [2018] UKUT 34 (AAC)). Note further that a powered wheelchair cannot be an "other aid" for the purposes of Activity 1; see *WT v SSWP (ESA)* [2016] UKUT 472 (AAC);[2017] AACR 16 at para.20.

Descriptor 1(a) is now coterminous with Activity 1 in Sch.3 on LCWRA. That the activity is now mobilising renders this aspect of the LCWA more difficult to satisfy than under the original WCA. Note that "severe discomfort" in the original Sch.2, thought to be ambiguous, has been replaced by "significant discomfort" as part of the CMA honing. Specific provision is made to deal with fluctuating conditions by including "exhaustion" as factor necessitating "stopping" mobilising and by including as an alternative in each of descriptors (a), (c) and (d), the idea of "cannot repeatedly mobilise . . . within a reasonable timescale".

Insofar as the descriptors deal with "walking" as a form of mobilising, no regard should be paid to the case law on "virtually unable to walk" in DLA (*CSIB/60/1996; LD v SSWP* [2009] UKUT 208 (AAC)). However, that there is an award of the mobility component of DLA or PIP is pertinent as regards an ESA claim in respect of this activity in that the *evidence* underpinning the award of that component can throw light on whether the descriptors for Activity 1 are satisfied, but whether it does so or nor depends on all the circumstances (e.g. the nature and date of the award as compared to the date of the ESA decision), so that a decision to adjourn or not for the

DLA papers is similarly dependent on circumstances (*DF v SSWP (ESA)* [2014] UKUT 129 (AAC); *ML v SSWP (ESA)* [2013] UKUT 174 (AAC); [2013] AACR 33; *MI v SSWP (ESA)* [2013] UKUT 447 (AAC); *GC v SSWP (ESA)* [2014] UKUT 117 (AAC) *MA v SSWP (ESA)* [2014] UKUT 185 (AAC); *JC v SSWP (ESA)* [2014] UKUT 257 (AAC)). A tribunal need not do so, however, where that evidence would add nothing of significance to the other evidence before the tribunal, for example, because the claimant's condition has fundamentally altered since that award or because that award was made in respect of a temporary condition (e.g. restrictions on walking due to an operation) no longer pertaining (*JC*, paras 4–7). A tribunal faced with evidence of a claimant's ability or lack thereof to walk to identified local shops known to the tribunal can draw appropriate inferences from the representative walking ability of the claimant having regard to what she regularly accomplished (*LD v SSWP* [2009] UKUT 208 (AAC)).

Unlike its immediate predecessor ("without stopping or severe discomfort"), descriptors (a), (c) and (d) stipulate "without stopping in order to avoid significant discomfort or exhaustion". While there is still no explicit requirement that the "significant discomfort" be caused by walking or otherwise mobilising, it would seem that since the stopping must be to avoid "severe discomfort", the reformulation may cast some doubt on the applicability to these reformulated descriptors of *AW v SSWP (ESA)* [2011] UKUT 75 (AAC), where Judge Ward held that the previous formulation covered a claimant whose discomfort was always there.

"Pausing" is to be equated with "stopping" for the purposes of descriptors (a), (c) and (d) (*GC v SSWP (ESA)* [2014] UKUT 117 (AAC), para.21; *DB v SSWP (ESA)* [2014] UKUT 471 (AAC), para.4). So that if a tribunal found that a claimant paused for a few seconds after 30 metres, it should go on to ask "why?" (*DB*, para.5). In addition a tribunal should not confine consideration merely to mobilising on foot but should also consider possible wheelchair use (*DB*, para.7).

In *DJ v SSWP (ESA)* [2016] UKUT 93 (AAC) Judge Wright was concerned with the terms of descriptor 1(b) before its amendment with effect from January 28, 2013. The issue was whether the words "unaided by another person" in that context were limited to physical aid by another person. Judge Wright concluded that no such limitation was in place as regards the pre-January 2013 version of the regulations (at para.45):

> "47. I do accept, however, the Secretary of State's argument that the aid from another person which is (and was) contemplated by activity 1 and descriptor 1(b) in Schedule 2 to the ESA Regs means active aid and does not cover passively standing by waiting to intervene if help were to become needed. It seems to me that this flows both (a) from the word "aid" as a verb, which has clear connotations of actively providing help to the other person rather than just standing by, as well as (b) the aid given by another person which would usually be necessary to help a claimant to carry out an activity when their incapability to do so is a mental restriction. Reassuring and cajoling the claimant so as to aid them to surmount their acute anxiety about using stairs will involve talking to them and perhaps hand movements rather than just standing behind or in front of them doing and saying nothing. The latter is not, in my judgment, another person providing aid to the claimant."

However, in holding that the words "unaided by another person" in descriptor 1(a) were not limited to *physical* aid by another person, Judge Wright specifically left open the question of whether the position was different on the terms of the descriptor *after* January 28, 2013, given the amendments at the same time to reg.19(5) (see para.45).

Activity 1: descriptors (a)(ii), (c)(ii) and (d)(ii): "*repeatedly mobilise [X metres] within a reasonable timescale:* In *AS* v *SSWP (ESA)* [2013] UKUT 587 (AAC), Judge Wikeley considered the meaning of this phrase, which he saw as a legislative variant on the case law principle of "reasonable regularity" (para. 28). He regarded as an "excellent starting point" Judge Jacobs's decision in *AH* v *SSWP (ESA)* [2013]

UKUT 118 (AAC) (noted fully in the annotation to Sch.3 activity/descriptor 1 (para.9.398)). From that case, he took two points. First of all, the need, when considering the "reasonable regularity" principle to focus on the particular wording of the descriptors so that in this context the use of "repeatedly in descriptors (a)(ii), (c)(ii) and (d)(ii) meant that the principle did not apply to limb (i) of each of those descriptors (para.27). Secondly, he took the point that it was important "where the legislative text contains irreducible terms, [to apply] the statutory language without any gloss" (para.29). Like Judge Jacobs, he took the view that it was not for the Upper Tribunal to proffer a precise definition of these terms, but considered that in this case the tribunal's findings went beyond the bounds envisaged by case law. The provisions of the Sch. had to be construed "against the background of a working environment" (see para.9.374, above). He continued:

"What might well be a reasonable timescale for the Appellant at home would not necessarily be a reasonable timescale in the workplace. The consequence of the tribunal's approach was to rob the word "repeatedly" of any real meaning, as the tribunal's findings would equally well meet a statutory test predicated on the activity in question being performed only "occasionally ... in the course of a day". Whilst I am not prepared to draw a precise line, I am satisfied that on any reasonable analysis this tribunal's conclusion was the wrong side of the line. The ability to perform a function in a working environment "repeatedly ... within a reasonable timescale" must be something more than "occasionally ... in the course of a day" (para.32).

In *CS v SSWP (ESA)* [2014] UKUT 519 (AAC), Judge White considered descriptor 1(a).He held that although the phrase "on level ground" appears only in para.(a)(i) and is absent from para.(a)(ii), "the only possible interpretation of the repeatability test is that it is on the same terms as the primary test. That is on level ground" (para.30). It is submitted that this interpretation must also govern paras (c) and (d).

A claimant's ability to mobilise *with* significant discomfort or exhaustion should be disregarded for the purposes of Activity 1: see *GL v Secretary of State for Work and Pensions (ESA)* [2015] UKUT 503 (AAC).

A tribunal's fact-finding (and the relevance to that process of a claimant's own estimate as to how far s/he can walk) was in issue in *MM v SSWP (ESA)* [2017] UKUT 236 (AAC). Judge Hemingway held that it is perfectly permissible for a tribunal to attach weight to the claimant's own estimate as to how long in terms of time (usually expressed in minutes) he/she is able to walk for. It is also permissible for a tribunal to extrapolate as to what such an estimate, if reliable, might translate into in terms of distance. However, there is no rule to say that where a time estimate is offered it has to be accepted unless there is something specific to contradict it or to suggest it is unreliable. Further, it may be appropriate for a tribunal to consider whether such an estimate is, or is not, likely to be reliable and to probe this in questioning with a claimant. There may be reason to think that time estimates as to journeys which are undertaken regularly might be more reliable than other estimates. Finally, "the tribunal was not required to make a precise finding as to exactly how many metres the claimant could mobilise for. Absolutely precise findings as to something like that will often, realistically, be simply impossible. All it was required to do was make a finding as to which category the claimant fell into as to the range of distances contained within the relevant set of descriptors" (at para.13).

Fact-finding was also an issue in *GZ v SSWP (ESA)* [2017] UKUT 447 (AAC). There the tribunal, dismissing the claimant's appeal found that she qualified for 6 points for mobilising, making the following finding: "We find that she cannot unaided by another person mobilise more than 200 metres on level ground without stopping in order to avoid significant discomfort or exhaustion, or repeatedly mobilise 200 metres within a reasonable timescale because of significant discomfort or exhaustion." Judge Mesher explained why such a finding, without defining which limb of descriptor 1(d) applied, was inadequate:

"6. That [error of law] is in the form of the tribunal's finding of fact in the middle of paragraph 17 of the statement of reasons which adopted the terms of descriptor 1(d) without saying which of the two alternatives within the descriptor was satisfied. That in my judgment is not good enough as a finding of fact, because of the relationship of descriptor 1(d) with descriptors 1(a) and (c). If the tribunal considered that the claimant fell only within descriptor 1(d)(ii), because she could mobilise for more than 200 metres without stopping but could not achieve 200 metres repeatedly within a reasonable timescale, that would necessarily entail that she did not satisfy 1(c)(i) (because she could mobilise more than 100 metres) and would perhaps make it unlikely that she could satisfy descriptor 1(c)(ii) on the basis of not being able to mobilise 100 metres repeatedly. However, if the tribunal considered that the claimant fell within descriptor 1(d)(i), because she could not mobilise more than 200 metres without stopping, that would not as a matter of logical necessity exclude satisfaction of descriptor 1(c). Thus it might be necessary for a tribunal to explain why it chose descriptor 1(d)(i) rather than 1(c)(i). But more pertinently for the present case, if a claimant can only mobilise without stopping for some distance between 100 metres and 200 metres, that does not exclude the possibility that the claimant, while able to mobilise more than 100 metres without stopping, cannot achieve 100 metres repeatedly within a reasonable timescale and so satisfies descriptor 1(c)(ii). The same could potentially be said in relation to descriptor 1(a)(ii) and 50 metres. As a result, while it may not be necessary to the award of 6 points under descriptor 1(d) to specify which alternative is satisfied, in terms of the required underlying findings of fact on the whole activity of mobilising it is necessary in any statement of reasons to be more specific. It seems to me that there are two ways out where descriptor 1(d) is satisfied. The tribunal can identify the distance that it finds that the claimant can mobilise without stopping in order to avoid significant discomfort or exhaustion without considering the issue of repetition. There can then be a firm factual basis, allied to whatever explanation is appropriate, for not applying descriptor 1(c) or 1(a) and in particular for not applying descriptor 1(c)(ii). Alternatively, if the tribunal is unable to be so specific, it may be sufficient for it to explain that, while not sure precisely how far the claimant can mobilise beyond 100 metres without stopping, it has expressly considered descriptor 1(c)(ii) and is satisfied (and why) that the claimant can repeatedly mobilise 100 metres within a reasonable timescale. The question of what sort of range of estimates would be acceptable would very much depend on the circumstances of particular cases. What in my judgment is plainly not sufficient is to make a finding of fact simply in the terms used in the present case and then to say nothing at all in the statement of reasons about descriptor 1(c)."

4.394   *Activity 2: standing and sitting:* The six scoring descriptors—which differentiated standing and sitting more clearly—in the original WCA have been reduced to three. This represents an amalgamation predicated on the modern workplace requiring an individual to remain at their work station long enough to do their job.

As regards descriptor (a), this looks to "without physical assistance from another person", rather than (as in the PCA) "without the help of another person", so ability to do so with encouragement from another person would preclude a score under this head. Ability only to move between one seated position and another located next to one another by using the seat or back of the chair to deliver the force necessary to move cannot score; the precluded assistance is merely "physical assistance from another person" (compare *(R(IB) 2/03)*.

As regards descriptors (b) and (c), there is now no requirement that the individual can both stand and sit; being able to do one or the other for the requisite length of time will preclude scoring under descriptors (b) and (c) (*MC v SSWP (ESA)* [2012] UKUT 324 (AAC); [2013] AACR 13, paras 4, 5; *EW v SSWP (ESA)* [2013] UKUT 228 (AAC), paras 9, 10), something put beyond any doubt by the addition from January 28, 2013 of sub-para.(iii) to descriptors 2(b) and (c). There is no longer any stipulation about the type of chair (it used to be "a chair with a high back and no arms" or "an upright chair")—this was thought unnecessary given the range of adaptable chairs available and the employers' legal duty to provide one as part of the obligation to make reasonable adjustments to the workplace to accommodate persons with disabilities.

While it should be noted that in *MM v Department for Social Development (ESA)* [2014] NI Com 48 a tribunal of three Northern Ireland Commissioners disagreed with Judge Wikeley's approach in *MC* to the interpretation of Activity 2 descriptors *prior to the January 2013 amendment*, that decision is of persuasive authority only and thus, in terms of judicial precedent, ranks lower than that of Judge Wikeley in *MC* which is directly binding in Great Britain (*CC v SSWP (ESA)* [2015] UKUT 62 (AAC)).

The decision of Judge Ward in *EC v SSWP (ESA)* [2015] UKUT 618 (AAC) considers the conflict in the case law on the pre-March 2011 version of the activity 2 descriptors. Judge Ward held that there were "compelling reasons" to depart from the decision of the Northern Ireland Tribunal of Commissioners in *MM v Department for Social Development (ESA)*. In doing so, he analysed a range of materials which shed light on the issues relevant to the interpretation of the Activity 2 descriptors:

"57. In conclusion, it seems to me that an argument based on informed interpretation, if relying on a committee report, needs to be based on its final form and to take into account other material which Parliament must be taken as having had in mind when approving the legislation. In the light of the totality of the material before me, I accept that the mischief at which the legislation was aimed, on this aspect, included ensuring that people who could remain at a workstation for the requisite period by combining sitting and standing would not get points. Seen against that background, the ambiguity in the use of the 'either ... or' construction in the descriptors in activity 2 between 2011 and 2013 would fall to be resolved in accordance with Judge Wikeley's obiter views in *MT*. The Tribunal of Commissioners in *MM* did not have the advantage that I have now had, through oral submissions and subsequent written submissions, of comprehensive examination of the background materials leading up to the making of the Regulations. In those circumstances, while I have applied a test of whether there is a 'compelling reason' to depart from the decision in *MM*, I have concluded that there is. With the benefit of those fuller submissions (which it appears were not made in *MC* or *MT* either) I conclude that a person who can remain at a workstation by a combination of sitting and standing for the requisite period is not entitled to points."

In addition, as regards descriptors (b) and (c), the meaning of "at a workstation" was considered by Judge Mitchell in *LC v SSWP (ESA)* [2015] UKUT 664 (AAC). The judge held that the First-tier Tribunal had erred in law by failing to address whether the claimant could fairly be said to have been capable of performing a job of work while remaining sat "at a workstation" in the light of her evidence that she needed to sit with one leg stretched rigidly out in front of her. Judge Mitchell concluded as follows:

"23. I conclude, therefore, that when descriptors 2(b) and 2(c) refer to a person remaining 'at a workstation' they refer to the person being orientated towards a workstation, whether sitting or standing, in such a manner that they may fairly be described as capable of performing a job of work. I do not think I need to go any further than this in interpreting the descriptor by, for example, attempting to define a workstation. I can leave it to the good sense of tribunals, using their knowledge of everyday life and their specialist expertise, to apply that test.
24. If, therefore, a person needs to sit with a rigidly outstretched leg so that s/he could not fairly be said to be capable of doing a job of work at a workstation, even with the benefits supplied by an adjustable chair, this would not amount to the person remaining sat 'at a work station'.

25. So far as section 20 of the Equality Act 2010 (reasonable adjustments) is concerned, I see no need for tribunals to try and predict how it might operate in a particular case. Attempting to identify the content of any particular reasonable adjustment divorced from a real world case is very difficult and liable to introduce unnecessary confusion and complexity. The question of what is reasonable is informed by two sets of variables: the characteristics of the disabled person and the entity obliged to make the adjustment. What might be reasonable for a small independent trader could well differ from what is required of a well-resourced multinational corporation. Instead, tribunals should simply rely on their own knowledge and expertise in applying the descriptors by envisaging the typical workstations and adjustable chairs with which I suspect we are all familiar."

Note again the replacement of "severe discomfort", thought to be ambiguous, with "significant discomfort" as part of CMA honing, and also the inclusion in descriptors (b) and (c) of "exhaustion" and "for the majority of the time" as one aspect of dealing with fluctuating conditions and the requirement of "reasonable regularity". The degree of discomfort must be such as to require the claimant to move away from the workstation; it is not enough if it merely disrupts, even very significantly, the claimant's concentration at the workstation (*DT v SSWP (ESA)* [2013] UKUT 244 (AAC) in the context of the pre-March 28, 2011 descriptors).

"Standing" does not mean standing stock-still. The normal person (the yardstick for applying the descriptors) does not do so for any length of time. As Commissioner Lloyd-Davies stated in *R(IB) 6/04*:

"The quasi-involuntary movements that most people make in standing for prolonged periods do not . . . count. Instead the tribunal should concentrate on how long a claimant can stand before needing or having to move around or sit down (usually because of pain in the back or legs)" (para.5).

4.395 *Activity (3): reaching*: this assesses a person's ability to raise their upper limbs above waist height. It also identifies those with very restricted shoulder movement. This is almost identical to the reaching Activity 4 in the original WCA, the only omission being that Activity 4 descriptor (b) ("cannot put either arm behind back as if to put on a coat or jacket"). That was thought inappropriate since, by not requiring ability to put both hands behind the back inadequately identified these limitations. Moreover, it was superfluous as this was not a required function in many workplaces.

Descriptor (b) scores only 9, as opposed to 15 under the AWT/PCA in the IB regime. It does not involve raising the upper arm above head level (*CIB 2811/1995*). In contrast, descriptor (c) ("cannot raise either arm above head height as if to reach for something") requires that more than a minimal amount of the arm must be above head level. Reaching involves a degree of stretching, and involves being able to raise the upper arm above shoulder level and to go at least some way towards straightening the arm in moving it towards a notional object" (*CIB 2811/1995*, para.7) so that a claimant with full elbow flexion could probably achieve the task in (b) but not (c).

4.396 *Activity 4: picking up and moving or transferring by use of the upper body or arms*: this is similar to the corresponding activity in the original WCA (Activity 5). Like their immediate predecessor, the formulations avoid previous ambiguity over the meaning of "carry", and make it clear that what is covered is picking up and moving, using the upper body and arms (compare *R(IB) 5/03*). The key difference is that under the original WCA the descriptors variously referred to the use of either hand (descriptors (a) and (b)) or of both hands together (descriptor (c)). They thus assumed only persons with two hands. The Review thought this inappropriate; two hands were not necessarily required to perform the activity:

"For example, an item may be transferred by wedging it against the body, or another limb, to achieve the same outcome. Many amputees chose not to have a prosthetic limb in order to retain the sensation of touch; however they remain able to complete the task" (para.4.3.2, p.23).

The new descriptors thus deliberately make no mention of hands thus rendering *MH v SSWP (ESA)* [2011] UKUT 492 (AAC) inapplicable here (see para.8). But as with its predecessor the wording of the activity (use of the upper body or arms) means that it is thus not sufficient only to focus on problems with arms. Problems with shoulder(s) or neck should also be taken into account (*TO'B v SSWP (ESA)* [2011] UKUT 461 (AAC)), as should the effect on a back condition (*AG v SSWP (ESA)* [2018] UKUT 137 (AAC).

This descriptor has been considered in two other cases, each dealing with whether the task can be achieved by someone with only one good arm, given that the descriptor, unlike its predecessors no longer stipulates using both hands together.

In *KH v SSWP (ESA)* [2014] UKUT 455 (AAC), Judge Mark accepted that the change in wording means that the use of both hands together is no longer essential, so that if a person could pick the box up and move it by the use of one arm and the upper body, that is by wedging it under the arm, that would suffice as capability to complete the task. But he rightly cautioned that not everyone can be expected to do that. It would depend on all the circumstances of the claimant's condition so that, in this particular case, he considered that the tribunal was entitled to conclude that this claimant "would reasonably require both arms to perform the task", especially so since the object in question is "bulky" (para.4).

In *MT v SSWP (ESA)* [2014] UKUT 548 (AAC), Judge Hemingway agreed with Judge Mark's approach in *KH*, accepting that in principle the task could sometimes be performed by someone with one arm in the way suggested. But he rightly commented that completion of the task is undoubtedly easier for those with two good arms and that it cannot simply be assumed, given the bulky size of the object in question, that someone with one good arm will be capable of accomplishing it (paras 18, 19). It is dependent on all the circumstances of the case. A tribunal should

> "offer some explanation as to how it concludes (if it does so conclude) that the task can be achieved by a claimant who is incapacitated in the way this appellant says he is. In the passage quoted above, the F-tT has not made it clear whether it thinks the appellant could use his left upper limb at all in attempting the task. On the assumption that it does not think he could, it has not explained how it thinks the task might practically be achieved with the use of the rest of his upper body and his right upper limb. Its finding that he is "resolute" does indicate its view that he has determination but that, of itself, will not always be sufficient for a claimant to overcome physical difficulties and does not, of itself, therefore, represent an adequate explanation for its ultimate conclusion. The task of an F-tT in such a case need not be regarded as an exacting one but the standard required has not, for the above reasons, been reached here" (para.20).

A different issue arose in *MK v SSWP (ESA)* [2016] UKUT 74 (AAC), namely whether the ½ or 1 litre carton full of liquid to be picked up and moved under descriptors 4(a) and (b) respectively is a closed or open carton. Judge Wright concluded that the context necessarily implied that it had to be read as a closed carton, and so spillage in the act of picking up and moving is not relevant. The descriptors are therefore limited to the tasks of "picking up" and "moving" and not the manner in which they are achieved (at para.24). However, this is subject to the following qualification:

> "20. Different considerations might apply where the activity of picking up and moving cannot be completed because the item is dropped or thrown away involuntarily before it is moved or transferred. Then issues of whether the activity can be carried out reliably and repeatedly might come in to play. I would accept that the movement or transfer needs to be to a specific place and cannot involve random and involuntary throwing of the item (even though in one sense it would nonetheless have moved if thrown). This is not, however, to do with manner in which the activity is carried out but whether the activity can in any reasonable sense be done at all."

It follows that "if balance and a steady hand are relevant considerations at all then they fall to be considered under manual dexterity and not picking up and moving" (at para.24).

4.397   *Activity 5: manual dexterity*: As compared with its immediate predecessor, gone are the descriptors dealing with a "star-headed" sink tap and doing up or undoing small buttons. The former was thought to have awarded individuals a disproportionately high number of points for an identified disability which was not necessarily an activity for functioning in the workplace, thus misidentifying affected individuals for ESA purposes. Also removed are the six-point descriptors to make scoring more equitable across the activities. Ability to use a pen and pencil now specifically requires ability to use either "to make a meaningful mark" whereas its predecessor had been interpreted to require ability to use either, with either hand, so as to write in a normal manner. The new formulation arguably requires less ability. Ability to do things with one hand was thought by the *Review* to show capability to perform the specified activity. As regards descriptor (d), use of a keyboard, this jarred with the approach taken by Judge May in *DW* v *SSWP (ESA)* [2010] UKUT 245 (AAC) where he considered a case where a claimant sometimes could physically use a keyboard using one hand, but was unable to do so using two, thus preventing him using "a shift key to form capital letters or for example the sign '@'" (para.3). The approach in the *Review* would suggest that inability to use the shift key does not score so long as the keyboard can be used with one hand. The insertion from January 28, 2013 of "single-handedly" gives effect to that policy intention.

Taking the interpretation implicit in Judge May's decision in *DW*, Judge Mark in *CL v SSWP (ESA)* [2013] UKUT 434 (AAC) thought that inability to use either a keyboard or a mouse is enough to score points; it was not necessary to show inability to use both. He approved Judge May's approach in *DW*, following *Moyna*, on the need to take a broad view on whether a claimant could or could not satisfy the descriptor, stating that there are no absolutes by reference to which "can" and "cannot" are to be defined. The fact that a claimant could use a mouse or keyboard to a limited extent does not mean that s/he can use it in the way it was intended to be used. He disagreed with this commentator's view in the annotation, above, that the reformulation of the descriptor jarred with Judge May's approach, with the Judge himself being able to use a conventional key board with one hand, but did, however, accept that only being able to use one hand was more difficult, would be slower and that, on a conventional keyboard, combinations of three keys (typically control, alt and delete) – often used for logging on and security or recovery purposes – would not be possible on a conventional keyboard. The principle of "reasonable regularity" may also have relevance (see *KE* v *Department for Social Development (ESA)* [2013] NI Com 59, a decision of Chief Commissioner Mullan, on the previous wording of the descriptor). Since the descriptor now refers to a suitable keyboard or mouse, it is a submitted that for a tribunal properly to decide on this descriptor it needs evidence on the nature of the keyboard or mouse envisaged.

The above interpretation arguably chimes with an approach of reading the words of the Schedule in the context of the "work environment" in the sense that it is looking to ability physically to use a normal or adapted computer although not to test "computer literacy" in the same way as descriptor 5(c) no longer tests ability to write in a meaningful manner. But , as Judge Wright held in *DG v SSWP (ESA)* [2014] UKUT 100 (AAC), that analogy with descriptor 5(c) surely means that descriptor 5(d) can be satisfied with a very low level of ability (e.g. using a mouse alone to insert a check in a tick box); that what is being tested is not overall use of a computer with a mouse; but rather—as with Judge Jacobs' "functional approach" in *GS v SSWP (ESA)* [2010] UKUT 244 (AAC) to the descriptor on doing up or undoing small buttons in the predecessor of the manual dexterity activity and the appropriate inference from the analogy with descriptor 5(c) as regards the use of a pen or pencil to make a meaningful *mark*—a very basic degree of dexterity "in terms of use of a suitable keyboard or mouse [reading the "or" conjunctively rather than disjunctively] (e.g. gripping the mouse and moving it over an icon or box and then using a finger to click on it and using the keyboard to type out letters, numbers or symbols" (para.48). In other words, descriptor 5(d), like 5(c), cannot be satisfied if the claimant can do one of the activities: "the nine points only fall to be awarded … if the claimant cannot do both of the tasks [set out in descriptor 5(d)]; in other words, he can do neither of them" (para.3). Judge Wright preferred the "functional approach" and considered *DW* and *CL* to be wrongly decided and, guided by *R(I)12/75,* declined to follow them (paras 3, 55). He saw this interpretation as consonant with that taken by then Commissioner Howell in *R(IB)3/02* ("bending or kneeling") and (building on that analysis) that by Judge Wikeley in *MC v SSWP (ESA)* [2012] UKUT 324; [2013] AACR 13 ("standing or sitting"). He respectfully disagreed with the view of the Chief Commissioner in Northern Ireland, Judge Martin, in *R1/03 (IB)* that "or" was generally to be read disjunctively and only rarely conjunctively, as not fully reflecting the nuances of the English language and failing to focus adequately on the import of the word "cannot" when used with "or". Underscoring all this, Judge Wright considered that the "conjunctive" interpretation meant that the descriptor properly assessed separately different types of "manual dexterity activities", albeit that there was some "crossover":

"The test of "use of a suitable [keyboard]" or "use of a mouse" focuses on the parts of the hands and fingers that are needed to use such an item. Thus with the suitable [keyboard] it is primarily looking at the power, sense and spacing in the finger or fingers of the hand so as to be able to press the buttons on the keyboard. Grip plays little or no role. On the other hand, the use of a mouse is likely to involve in part, different manual dexterity functions. The primary function may be to grip and then move the mouse, though the ability to click and click and drag, the cursor may also be important, so the flexing of fingers in the hand gripping the mouse is also likely to be important" (para.50).

In addition, if the legislative purpose had been to test the use of a keyboard with a mouse the descriptor could easily have been worded in that way.

Legally speaking, it is open to tribunal judges at either First-tier or Upper level, to choose which of these conflicting decisions to follow. Which is ultimately to be preferred will eventually be decided by the weight of authority or by one but not the other being reported in the AACR. It may be relevant that the issue was the subject of full argument by one of the parties in *DG* but not in *CL*. Perhaps this is an area requiring decision by a panel of three Upper Tribunal judges.

As Judge Mark notes in *KH v SSWP (ESA)* [2014] UKUT 455 (AAC), the disagreement between himself and Judge Wright remains to be resolved on another occasion. As described above, they disagree on whether scoring under this descriptor requires inability to use both these items of computer equipment (Judge Wright) or inability to use one (Judge Mark). But in *KH,* Judge Mark agrees with Judge Wright that it is not computer literacy that is being tested, but that rather

"what is being tested is the physical ability, so far as manual dexterity is concerned, to use a suitable keyboard or mouse. His description in paragraph 48 of his decision of the test is whether the mouse can be gripped and moved over an icon or box and then clicked and using the keyboard to type out letters, numbers and symbols. Again, I would not dissent from that, subject to questions relating to such matters as reasonable repetition and the effects of, for example, repetitive strain injury, and that the purpose of the so using the mouse or typing out letters etc. is to achieve certain results on the computer they are being used with. It is possible that a person may have sufficient control of the hands to be able to move and click the mouse or type letters but insufficient control to do so with any degree of accuracy or with any regularity or for any reasonable time.

When the descriptor speaks of using a keyboard or mouse, as Judge Wright's examples make clear, the use can only be to achieve results on a computer. It follows that in assessing whether hands are so lacking in dexterity as to score points on this descriptor it must be in relation to the operation of a computer. Why that scores the same number of points as not being able to make a meaningful mark with a pen or pencil is unclear, but what is clear is that even Judge Wright's description of what is required is far more demanding than a physical ability to make a cross on a piece of paper" (paras 10, 11).

In *SM v SSWP (ESA)* [2015] UKUT 617 (AAC) the appellant had been with congenital deformities to both hands, involving the fusion of certain fingers. One of the issues on the appeal was descriptor 5c: "cannot use a pen or pencil to make a meaningful mark with either hand". The claimant's appeal was allowed on a reg.29 point. However, Judge Ward expressed the following view:

"7. It follows that I have received only brief submissions from the parties about descriptor 5 (c). The tribunal found as fact that the claimant could write his signature. It certainly is an issue before me (I am not clear whether it was before the First-tier Tribunal) whether he can do so with reasonable regularity but that is something for the tribunal to which this case is remitted to explore. The claimant's representative draws attention to varies definitions of 'meaningful'. In my view descriptor 5(c) is not concerned with marks that are 'meaningful' in the sense of 'having great meaning, eloquent, expressive' (per Collins dictionary). That is a sense which might be appropriate when 'meaningful' is applied to, for instance, glances, but is not a natural sense when applied to something such as rudimentary as a mark with a pen or pencil. Rather, I consider that it in this context means 'having meaning' as opposed to 'not having meaning'. Further than that I prefer not to go in this case."

And see, to the same effect, Judge Jacobs in *SSWP v LH (ESA)* [2017] UKUT 475 (AAC):

"14. The mark has to be meaningful, so it must be capable of conveying some meaning and, inevitably, be a mark that is directed in the sense of the claimant having a meaning in mind. But that does not make the descriptor a test of intellectual capacity, which is the exclusive province of Part 2 of the Schedule (regulation 19(5)(b)). The level of the claimant's literacy is not in issue. This is a test of physical function, whereas literacy is a mental matter. And the test is limited to the claimant's fingers, hands and wrists, which are not related to literacy.
15. I agree with Judge Ward in *SM* that descriptor 5(c) is not concerned with the content of what is written. The only issue is whether it is meaningful. It has to be capable of conveying meaning. Random doodling or scribbling is not sufficient. It is not, though, necessary to convey any particular meaning. None is specified, so any meaning will do. It might be in the form of words, like a person's name or signature. Or it might be in the form of some symbol, such as a tick that could indicate agreement on a form or a cross that could indicate a vote at an election."

SM v SSWP (ESA) and *SSWP v LH (ESA)* were both followed and endorsed by Judge Wright in *NA v SSWP (ESA)* [2018] UKUT 399 (AAC). As regard descriptor 5(c), the judge stressed that the language of the test requires consideration to be given to the claimant's ability to use both the right and the left hand – so no points are scored if the person can carry out the function with at least one hand. In addition, the statutory test is not whether the person can write a word or a sentence with either hand (as under the old law) but rather the more limited test of not being able to make a meaningful mark with either hand. In that context, the use of the word 'cannot' in the descriptor requires attention to be given to a claimant's functional ability to make a meaningful mark with either hand across a range of potential situations. On the facts of the case, the tribunal's error lay in:

"its failure to consider in the round and across a number of potential or actual situations whether the claimant was unable with his right hand or his left hand to make a meaningful mark with a pen or pencil. For example, could he make the mark of a tick or a cross with either his right or his left hand on a census form or an election card? If he could, even if it was only with one hand, it is not apparent on what basis it could be concluded that he could not make a meaningful mark with either hand" (para.26).

Finally, Judge Mitchell has expressed the view (obiter) that the reference to a £1 coin in descriptor 5(b) includes "the £1 coin in the form in which it exists whenever the assessment is applied in an individual case" (para.26) and so can include the new-style £1 coin: *R v SSWP* [2018] UKUT 326 (AAC).

Activity 6: making self understood through speaking, writing, typing, or other means which are normally, or could reasonably be, used, unaided by another person: The imme-diate predecessor of this Activity dealt solely with communicating and making oneself understood through speech. The *Review* considered that the activities in the original WCA dealing with speech, hearing and vision, focused too much on the impairment rather than the disability it engendered. To do so was to ignore the adaptations that those with disabilities have made, thereby reducing their level of disability. Hence the removal of the "cannot speak at all" descriptor because that removed the message that those who cannot speak at all or only with very significant pain (see *CIB/4306/1999*) inherently cannot work. The *Review* consid-ered that speech was not the sole mode by which individuals conventionally make themselves understood, so the modes of communicating were broadened to reflect this. The yardstick now is ability to convey a simple message, such as the presence of a hazard, whether at all (descriptor (a)), or to strangers (descriptors (b) and (c)).

"Normally used" means normally used by people in the claimant's situation acting reasonably in all the circumstances (*CIB/14499/1996*).

Activity 7: Understanding communication by (i) verbal means (such as hearing or lip   **4.398**
reading) alone, (ii) non-verbal means (such as reading 16 point print or Braille) alone, or (iii) a combination of (i) and (ii), in each case using any aid that is normally, or could reasonably be, used, unaided by another person: The version of Activity 7 in force before January 28, 2013 was analysed by Judge Markus QC in *AT and VC v Secretary of State for Work and Pensions (ESA)* [2015] UKUT 445 (AAC); [2016] AACR 8. However, her decision is also relevant to the current formulation of the descrip-tors (see para.54). At the outset Judge Markus noted that the terms 'verbal' and 'non-verbal' are confusing 'because both forms of understanding in Activity 7 relate to verbal communications, in that the activity is about understanding words whether written or spoken'. Thus "'verbal' is used to mean 'spoken' and 'non-verbal' is used to mean 'written'" (para.37). Further, the drafting left it ambiguous as to "whether a claimant must be unable to understand or have difficulty in understanding commu-nication by both verbal and non-verbal means in order to satisfy the relevant descrip-tors, or whether inability/difficulty by only one of those means is sufficient" (para.1).

Judge Markus therefore considered the legislative history of Activity 7 and its antecedents. This led her to conclude "that in order to qualify under a relevant descriptor a claimant need be impaired in either hearing or vision (but not both) or, as amended, in understanding either spoken or written communication (but not both)" (para.48). The current formulation "is not much of an improvement on the previous wording" (para.50), but the judge was satisfied "that the word "alone" was inserted after each of (i) and (ii) with the intention of making clear that it is sufficient if a person is unable to understand a message by either verbal or non-verbal means" (para.51). Judge Markus's decision was followed in the context of the post-January 2013 version of the regulations by Judge Ward in *CM v SSWP (ESA)* [2016] UKUT 242 (AAC) (dealing with the parallel descriptor in a Sch.3 case).

The decisions in *AT and VC v SSWP (ESA)* [2015] UKUT 445 (AAC); [2016] AACR 6 and *CM v SSWP (ESA)* [2016] UKUT 242 (AAC) were followed by Judge Church in *RK v SSWP (ESA)* [2019] UKUT 345 (AAC), where it was held that a tribunal could find a claimant suffering from hearing loss was able to under-stand written communication even if she could only understand writing in Urdu: "The activities set out in Schedule 2 are broad proxies for the kinds of activities a claimant may be expected to do in a workplace or in getting to and from work, but any limitation in a claimant's ability to perform an activity which doesn't result from a health condition is not relevant to the assessment of their entitlement… A claimant cannot, therefore, score points for difficulties with communicating with others or understanding communication if the difficulty stems simply from the claimant and the (hypothetical) other people in question not speaking the same language" (at paras 14 and 15).

The predecessor of this dealt only with hearing. The reformulation here again, as with Activity 6, reflects the view that the activities in the original WCA dealing with speech, hearing and vision, focused too much on the impairment rather than the disability it engendered, sending an erroneous message that those who cannot hear at all are inherently unable to work. The yardstick now is that the claimant, due to sensory impairment, cannot understand a simple message, such as the location of a fire escape, either at all (descriptor (a)) or from a stranger (descriptors (b) and (c)). As regards reading 16 point print, what is being tested is the ability to understand a message contained in something with that size print.

4.399	*Activity 8: Navigation and maintaining safety, using a guide dog or other aid if either or both are normally, or could reasonably be, used:* The predecessor of this tested vision (visual acuity). The reformulation here again, as with Activity 6, reflects the view that the activities in the original WCA dealing with speech, hearing and vision, focused too much on the impairment rather than the disability it engendered, sending an erroneous message that those who cannot see at all are inherently unable to work. The key disabling features of visual impairment were thought by the *Review* to be inability or reduced ability, due to sensory impairment, to navigate and maintain safety. It was considered that these would be greater in unfamiliar surroundings, hence the gradations in scoring. Note that "crossing the road" is merely an example of "a potentially hazardous task" and not the sole context for descriptor (b) (*CC v SSWP(ESA)* [2015] UKUT 62 (AAC)).

"Normally used" means normally used by people in the claimant's situation acting reasonably in all the circumstances (*CIB/14499/1996*).

The policy intent behind the change in wording from January 28, 2013 was

"that this activity should examine the ability to understand communication sufficiently clearly to be able to comprehend a simple message by either verbal or non-verbal means or both. The descriptors may therefore apply if a claimant has hearing impairment alone, visual impairment alone or a combination of hearing and visual impairment" (Explanatory Memorandum, *http://www.legislation.gov.uk/uksi/2012/3096/pdfs/uksiem_20123096_en.pdf*)

The meaning of "due to sensory impairment" was touched on in *Secretary of State for Work and Pensions v AI (rule 17) (ESA)* [2017] UKUT 346 (AAC). Strictly the decision is not a binding authority as it is a decision consenting to the Secretary of State (SSWP) withdrawing his appeal to the Upper Tribunal on the meaning of "sensory impairment" under descriptor 8(b) in Sch. 2. The claimant had serious balance problems caused by Meniere's disease. The SSWP appealed to the Upper Tribunal on the ground that "sensory impairment" meant a direct impairment of one the five physical senses of sight, hearing, smell, taste and touch. The SSWP subsequently sought the Upper Tribunal's consent to withdraw the appeal, having obtained further expert evidence on the nature of Meniere's disease. However, this specialist evidence may be useful in other cases.

4.400	*Activity 9: Absence or loss of control whilst conscious leading to extensive evacuation of the bowel and/or bladder, other than enuresis (bed-wetting), despite the wearing or use of any aids or adaptations which are normally, or could reasonably be, worn or used:* This is a significant simplification compared to the original WCA and its coverage of "continence", although the new WCA does not use that term. Like its predecessors, this Activity does not directly deal with capability to work, but rather with matters of personal dignity and social acceptability; "the loss of dignity resulting from the associated soiling is considered severe enough to make it unreasonable to expect an individual with severe incontinence to work" (*Review*, p.33). As Judge Mitchell pointed out in *PC v SSWP (ESA)* [2015] UKUT 285 (AAC), descriptor (a) has a different logic to the other LCWA activities and descriptors. They relate directly to ability to perform tasks in the workplace. In contrast descriptor 9(a) is

"not about bodily and mental processes used to do work. A monthly incontinence event of the type prescribed is of itself unlikely to have any significant bearing on the performance of work tasks. There must be a different reason for the legislator deciding that anyone within descriptor 9(a) meets the condition of having limited capability for work. I think it is obvious that this is connected to the deeply personal and potentially embarrassing and distressing nature of significant continence problems" (para.30).

That is why the focus is on absence or loss of control, rather than mere urgency. The frequency of urination experienced by a diabetic because of the condition or medication is to be distinguished from urgency leading to a loss of control (*NH v SSWP (ESA)* [2011] UKUT 82 (AAC)). As regards descriptor (b) the requirement from January 28, 2013 is that the claimant is *for the majority of the time* at risk of loss of control. Note that it deals with "risk" and not the materialisation of that risk; there can be a risk without it ever materialising or doing so on only a few occasions (*NH v SSWP (ESA)* [2011] UKUT 82 (AAC)); *KB v SSWP (ESA)* [2014] UKUT 126 (AAC); *DG v SSWP (ESA)* [2015] UKUT 370 (AAC), paras 15–17)). The aspect of being unable to control the full voiding of the bladder essentially involves asking:

"no more than, if the appellant starts to urinate, will he be able to stop before his bladder is completely empty? The tribunal is most likely to be able to arrive at a reasoned conclusion on this by applying its expert knowledge to the surrounding evidence including the ESA50, GP and medical reports provided by the appellant or obtained by the tribunal, ESA85 (particularly the typical day) and lifestyle" (*NH v SSWP (ESA)* [2011] UKUT 82 (AAC), para.14).

In *NL v SSWP (ESA)* [2017] UKUT 397 (AAC), allowing the claimant's appeal, Judge Rowland considered it possible that the tribunal had:

"placed too much weight on the distinction between urgency and incontinence. The word 'continence', which at one time featured in the Schedules, no longer does so: the question is simply whether the claimant loses control, or is at risk of doing so, to the extent that he requires, or would require, cleaning and a change of clothing. Moreover, the words 'evacuation' of the bowel and 'voiding' of the bladder in descriptor 9(a)(i) need to be read in the light of descriptor 9(a)(ii) and I agree with the Secretary of State that the revised WCA Handbook (5 July 2016) accurately describes their effect –

'The descriptors relate to a substantial leakage of urine or faeces – such that there would be a requirement for the person to have a wash and change their clothing' (para.6)."

Judge Rowland added that "Descriptor 9(b) is satisfied when the claimant has only rare occasions of such a substantial leakage but is, for the majority of the time, at risk of having one unless able to reach a toilet quickly" (para.7).

An important starting point for these descriptors is that the "absence or loss of control" experienced must be "whilst conscious", on which see *CL v SSWP (ESA)* [2019] UKUT 39 (AAC). There Judge West held (at para.28) that:

"a claimant who loses control of his bowel or bladder whilst in a state of altered, as opposed to lost, consciousness, cannot score points under the descriptors linked to activity 9. If a person has lost consciousness, it clearly cannot be said that that person is "conscious" for the purposes of activity 9. A person who is in a state of altered consciousness, as a claimant may be when experiencing a seizure and possibly for a time in its aftermath, equally cannot be said to be "conscious" within the meaning of activity 9."

In *NH*, approved in *CP v SSWP (ESA)* [2011] UKUT 507 (AAC), Judge Lane sets out a number of helpful questions in para.14. That the yardstick is now "extensive evacuation of the bowel and/or voiding of the bladder" precludes, as did its predecessor, application of IB decisions bringing dribbling and leaking within the "loss of control" rubric (see e.g. *CSIB/880/2003*). Sufferers of stress incontinence may thus find it difficult to score. The necessary extent of the disability is measured by the need for "cleaning and a change of clothing". "Change of clothing" does not require a complete change since that would rarely be a consequence even of considerable levels of incontinence (*EM v SSWP (ESA)* [2014] UKUT 34 (AAC), paras 22, 23). Sanitary pads do not constitute "clothing" for this purpose. Nor, in this context, do disposable pants. In *EM*, Judge Mark said:

> "In practical terms, bearing in mind that the activity is dealing with matters of personal dignity and social acceptability, it appears to me that almost any change of clothing would count for this purpose since the soiled clothing would then have to be retained in the workplace for the rest of the day by the person who has soiled him or herself with the real risk of the clothing in question being seen or smelled by others in the workplace. If, however, pants are disposable, then in my view it would be likely to be the responsibility of the employer to ensure that there were facilities for them to be disposed of. Further it does not appear to me to have been intended that a change of disposable protective sanitary wear was to be relevant, since that would normally be needed in the event of the sort of accident contemplated by the descriptor. For those reasons, I would not consider that in most, if not all, circumstances a change of such wear was properly to be included in a change of clothing" (para.23).

Descriptor (a), through sub-para.(ii), recognises that the impact on the individual of such a need for cleaning and a change of clothing "is just as great where it results from leaking of a collecting device rather than loss of control of bladder or bowels". The precise scope of "collecting device" remains untested—does it include incontinence pads, or just catheter bags or stoma bags? The scope of "aids or adaptations" is not wholly clear; as Judge Mark noted in *EM*, the aids and adaptations envisaged might be thought mainly to cover internal devices, such as an artificial valve manually operated to open and close the bladder, which control such opening and closing or the evacuation of the bowel thus not embracing "sanitary pads and similar devices" since they "do not affect control over the evacuation of the bowel or the voiding of the bladder but only the consequences of such an event occurring" (para. 20). However, the wider wording ("aids or adaptations which are normally, or could reasonably be worn or used") suggests the terms are not so limited, so that "sanitary pads are aids which affect a claimant's ability to perform an activity in that their use may result in there being no need for a change of clothing" (para.20). In *PC v SSWP (ESA)* [2015] UKUT 285 (AAC), Judge Mitchell agreed with Judge Mark that "the aids and adaptations encompassed ...are limited" (para.20) to "those which prevent or minimise a loss of control" (para.38). A bucket thus cannot amount to an aid or adaptation. Nor can it amount to an "aid or appliance" for purposes of descriptors (a) and (b):

> "A bucket cannot reasonably be used in any workplace, apart from perhaps an incredibly unusual one like a one-person lighthouse, to deal with incontinence. That would run counter to, and undermine, the purpose of the continence activity and descriptors. It would be impossible to maintain dignity in those circumstances. The range of permissible aids and appliances must be restricted to achieve that aim and discounted if use in the workplace would be likely to expose an individual to the indignity against which these descriptors are designed to protect. But this does not mean that a less intrusive receptacle than a bucket must

be discounted, if it can be used by a person without that associated indignity. I have no idea whether such things exist" (para.39).

Nor is a bucket a "toilet" (ibid).

As with all its predecessors, applying these descriptors involves intrusive scrutiny of the lives of claimants, embracing intimate and embarrassing areas affecting a claimant's dignity. It is necessary to appreciate the nature of the problems of sufferers, the varied nature and disabling effects of irritable bowel syndrome (IBS) (see *CIB/14332/96*) the role of diet (*CSIB/889/1999*), and the nature and role of various urinary or fecal collecting devices. It is also necessary to define and apply carefully the terms used in the descriptors.

Aids or adaptations "normally used" means if the aid or adaptation in question is normally used by people in the claimant's situation acting reasonably in all the circumstances (*CIB/14499/1996*). In *LB* v *SSWP (ESA)* [2013] UKUT 352 (AAC), Judge Mark considered the use of aids or adaptations. He thought that the DWP guidance to decision-makers in Memo DMG 24/12, issued after Judge Levenson's decision in *RP* v *SSWP* [2011] UKUT (ESA) 449 (AAC) (noted in the annotation to reg.19(4) (see para.9.49), embodied a non-exhaustive set of useful matters to be considered in cases, but stressed, as does the guidance itself, that those set out are not the only factors which may be relevant. Judge Mark summarized the relevant parts of the guidance thus:

"In relation to those physical descriptors which specifically refer to the use of aids, including continence, it observes that decision makers should apply the test in a way that displays consistency between the work capability assessment as a whole and the assessment of each descriptor in particular (para.6). It goes on to state that the decision maker should establish whether the claimant normally uses an aid or appliance, and if not, whether the use of it has been prescribed or advised. If a claimant does not have an aid or appliance which they have been prescribed or advised to use, the decision maker should establish whether it would help the claimant, why they are not using one and whether the explanation is reasonable.

The guidance goes on to state that the decision maker must consider all the circumstances in deciding whether it would be reasonable to assess the claimant as using an aid that they have not been prescribed or that they have not been advised to use. Factors identified include whether (1) the claimant possesses the aid or appliance; (2) the claimant was given specific medical advice about managing their condition, and it is reasonable for them to continue to follow that advice; (3) the claimant would be advised to use an aid or appliance if they raised it with the appropriate authority such as a GP or occupational therapist; (4) if it is medically reasonable for them to use an aid or appliance; (5) the health condition or disability is likely to be of short duration; (6) an aid or appliance is widely available; (7) an aid or appliance is affordable in the claimant's circumstances; (8) the claimant is able to use and store the aid or appliance; and (9) the claimant is unable to use an aid or appliance due to their physical or mental health condition" (paras 11, 12).

He noted that the HCP had not carried out the recommended enquiries. Nor had the tribunal done so. It had referred to the claimant's urine well which he kept in his car as "an aid which he used". But this failed to address the fact it was only of use in the car and even there did not always prove adequate because he could not get to it in time or was not in a suitably quiet place to use it. It could not reasonably be expected to be used in non-private places (para.20). As regards the possible use of pads—which the claimant did not use because he felt shame at the continence problem at his age—Judge Ward stressed that while they could deal with post-urinary dribbling (which does not count for scoring purposes anyway), he was less clear how they could deal adequately with extensive evacuation of the bladder. Moreover—as an additional factor not mentioned in the DWP guidance—the tribunal should consider whether their use might actually exacerbate the problem of "accidents" where the claimant could reach a toilet in time "because they might increase the time required for the claimant to prepare himself to urinate" (para.22).

The descriptors should be applied bearing in the context of the claimant's personal circumstances and any mobility problems experienced by the claimant (*EM v SSWP (ESA)* [2014] UKUT 34 (AAC); *FR v SSWP (ESA)* [2015] UKUT 151 (AAC)). In *EM*, Judge Mark highlighted the error in the then guidance in the DWP Medical Services Handbook which stated that mobility problems should be ignored as regards this descriptor since those problems were dealt with elsewhere in Sch.2. He considered that

> "This statement is wholly misguided both in relation to the descriptor as it was at the time of the decision and as it now is. In descriptor 9(a)(i) the only question is whether at least once a month the claimant experiences loss of control leading to extensive evacuation of the bowel and/or voiding of the bladder sufficient to require cleaning and a change of clothes. The fact that this is because the claimant is unable to reach a toilet in time because of other physical problems is irrelevant, as one would expect bearing in mind that the purpose of the descriptor is to deal with questions of personal dignity and social acceptability. This is made even clearer, if that were possible, by the wording of descriptor 9(b) where the question is whether there is a risk of loss of control if not able to reach a toilet quickly. Loss of control at least once a month because the claimant cannot reach a toilet quickly plainly qualifies for 15 points if the other requirements are met" (para.25).

The guidance in that handbook has been revised to take account of *EM* (see *FR v SSWP (ESA)* [2015] UKUT 151 (AAC), para.21). Rightly so, since, as Judge Grey QC put it in *FR*:

> "The effect of the "loss of control" set out in descriptor 9 must be assessed in the light of an individual's personal circumstances. If, as a result of limited mobility, he or she is more adversely affected than someone who has greater mobility and an associated ability to better manage the effects of any threatened loss of control, this should be taken into account by the decision-maker. The alternative would be to divorce the assessment of this activity and the descriptors from the reality of an individual's ability to cope with their condition and to replace an assessment which is claimant-centred with one based on (here) the ability of a 'hypothetical', reasonably mobile individual to reach toilets. The activity seeks to assess the likelihood of loss of personal dignity and shame in the workplace associated with significant 'accidents'. It should make no difference whether soiling may occur because an individual's restricted mobility slows down the process of reaching a toilet, or because the loss of control is comparatively rapid. The effect on the individual and their ability to work is the same" (para.19).

For mobilising difficulties to be relevant to Activity 9 and its descriptors, however, there must exist an underlying problem of bowel or bladder functioning; mobilising difficulties alone are not enough. there must be a disease or disablement affecting the control mechanisms of bowel or bladder (*PC v SSWP (ESA)* [2015] UKUT 285 (AAC). paras 33-36, 45; *DG v SSWP (ESA)* [2015] UKUT 370 (AAC), para.18).

For a successful reasons challenge, see *VH v SSWP (ESA)* [2018] UKUT 290 (AAC) (at paras.15 and 16).

4.401   *Activity 10: Consciousness during waking moments:* The focus here is on "involuntary episodes of lost or altered consciousness" which result in "significantly disrupted awareness or concentration". If experienced at least once a week, 15 points are scored and thus limited capability for work established. If experienced at least once a month, six points are scored. With no reference now being made to "epileptic or similar seizures" and the descriptors referring to "significantly disrupted awareness or concentration", the strict and narrow approach in *R(IB) 2/07(T)* is no longer warranted. It cast doubt on earlier authorities on "altered consciousness", finding *CSIB/14/1996*, which had given hope to those who suffered severe headaches, to have been wrongly decided. *R(IB) 2/07(T)* required alteration of consciousness such that the sufferer was "incapable of any deliberate act". In *BB v SSWP (ESA)* [2011] UKUT 158 (AAC); [2012] AACR 2, Judge Ward considered that the Tribunal of Commissioners decision in *R(IB) 2/07(T)*, insofar as it created a test of severity of an episode of altered consciousness should be seen purely as a decision of the previous IB regime. The ESA regime, by providing a statutory yardstick of "results in significantly disrupted awareness or concentration", rendered inapplicable to ESA the test of being "incapable of any deliberate act" (para.14), and the matter of the meaning of the statutory phrase in the ESA regime should be considered "untrammeled as regards the extent of the effects of the episode" by *R(IB) 2/07(T)* (para.15).

In *CB v SSWP (ESA)* [2015] UKUT 287 (AAC), Judge Rowley considered "lost consciousness" self-explanatory in most cases. As regards "altered consciousness", she adopted the proposition set out in the Training and Development Handbook for HCPs, while recognizing that that work is in no way binding on decision-makers or tribunals:

"'Altered consciousness' implies that, although the person is not fully unconscious, there is a definite clouding of mental faculties resulting in loss of control of thoughts or actions" (PC, para. 10).

The matter of giving substance to the concepts "lost or altered consciousness resulting in significantly disrupted awareness or concentration" and applying them to the facts of disputed cases is very directly the task of the tribunal in the light of all the evidence. In the context of the similarly-worded activity 11 in the Sch. in force at March 27, 2011, *RA v SSWP (ESA)* [2010] UKUT 301 (AAC) considered that the transient and immediate effects of consuming alcohol should not count towards meeting the descriptors of this activity (para.10). Moreover alcohol dependence did not raise issues here since it ranked as a "mental condition" and not, as required, a physical disease or disablement (para.18). In that same context, in *AB v SSWP (ESA)* [2012] UKUT 151 (AAC) Judge Jacobs held that the effects of sleep apnoea were not covered. It takes effect only when asleep and not during waking moments, thus not directly affecting capability for work. Although sleep so interrupted because of the condition does, however, mean that a sufferer may be unrefreshed, tired and liable to fall asleep during the day because of natural tiredness, Judge Jacobs considered that this, even where due to a medical condition could not properly be described as involuntary but rather something subject to control, something we all experience. Nor did he consider it properly describable as disrupting awareness or concentration in this context.

In *JG v SSWP (ESA)* [2013] UKUT 496 (AAC), Judge Mark considered the case of a claimant whose drowsiness was a direct side effect of his Parkinson's medication. Applying ESA Regs 2008, reg.19(5)(c), it arose as a direct result of treatment by a medical practitioner for that disease. As tiredness induced by medication, it was thus distinguishable from the "natural tiredness" considered by Judge Jacobs in *AB v SSWP (ESA)* [2012 UKUT 151 (AAC). As regards Judge Jacobs's comments on "natural tiredness" in that case, Judge Ward agreed that in general it was something one can control and cannot in the context of descriptor (a) be described as "involuntary", but stated further that

"[i]t would not, however, be true of somebody suffering from narcolepsy, nor would it be true of somebody who has been administered a sedative designed to cause them to fall asleep, or which has that consequence. There will be occasions when the tiredness or drowsiness is so extreme that voluntary control is lost. Whether there are occasions when the claimant's medication results in such occasions, and if so, how frequently this occurs, is a matter for the tribunal to determine.

... [T]he descriptor clearly refers both to lost and altered consciousness. Sleep is a form of lost consciousness just as much as a state induced by an epileptic fit. A person is not awake if they have lost consciousness and the reference to 'remaining conscious during waking moments' or, as here, 'consciousness during waking moments' is plainly concerned with involuntary loss of consciousness of any type. I can see no difference between losing consciousness due to narcolepsy and losing consciousness due to any other cause. ... [D]rug induced drowsiness can, if severe enough, amount to or result in an involuntary episode of lost or altered consciousness resulting in significantly disrupted awareness or concentration. It is for the tribunal to investigate the cause, nature and extent of the problem and to determine whether there are occasions when the side effects of the claimant's medication have that effect on him, and if so, how frequently they occur" (paras 9–11).

In a Northern Ireland decision, *DM v Department for Social Development (ESA)* [2013] NI Com 17, following Judge Jacobs in *AB*, Commissioner Stockman considered that the "correct approach to the activity excludes considerations of periods of normal sleep. Falling asleep during the day does not equate to loss of consciousness" (para.24). *SY v SSWP (ESA)* [2016] UKUT 378 (AAC) confirms that falling asleep during the day due to the effects of a medical condition does not amount to "an involuntary episode of lost or altered consciousness" for the purpose of descriptors (a) or (b) of Activity 10.

[C] Approaching and interpreting specific descriptors: Pt II: mental, cognitive and intellectual function assessment

4.402   The terms of the activities and descriptors in Pt II are so different from those in the PCA that no specific IB case law on the PCA descriptors and activities can readily be made relevant. Not so, however, IB case law on the general approach to be taken, namely that, while a tribunal has an inquisitorial function, it should be cautious about exercising it when considering mental disablement (*CIB/14202/1996*), unless the matter has been raised beforehand and there is in addition some medical or other evidence on the point (*R(IB) 2/98*). Now that assessments are carried out by a wider range of HCPs, consideration has been given to the weight that should be placed on their evidence, particularly in mental health cases, where the particular experience of the HCP lies in a non-mental health field. In *JH v SSWP (ESA)* [2013] UKUT 269 (AAC), the claimant was assessed in a 15-minute interview by a HCP who was a physiotherapist. Judge Mark thought that when dealing with mental health problems:

"the opinion of the physiotherapist as to the conclusions to be drawn have no probative value whatsoever. This is because the physiotherapist has no professional expertise in mental health matters. Although the strict rules of evidence do not apply, a tribunal can only take into account evidence that has probative value" (para.22).

He thought that in such cases the disability analyst should have mental health qualifications. But he further noted that even where that is the case, "tribunals should beware of placing too much weight on such reports, based as they are on a very short interview with a claimant and without access to medical records" (para.23). In *ST & GF v SSWP (ESA)* [2014] UKUT 547 (AAC); [2015] AACR 23, a panel of three Upper Tribunal judges categorically rejected Judge Mark's comments—which it saw as *obiter*—as

"wrong if and to the extent that they purport to create a rule of law or starting point that observations on mental health descriptors by HCP physiotherapists are of no probative value whatsoever or are highly likely or likely to have little probative value and thus should be accorded no or little weight by the decision maker and the First-tier tribunal" (para.33).

Instead the proper approach is that the probative value of an HCP physiotherapist's report is a matter for the decision maker or tribunal dealing with the case, just as it is with other reports and evidence.

The panel so held, firstly, because the legislation makes no distinction between an HCP's ability to deal with mental health descriptors as opposed to physical ones. It merely requires approval by the Secretary of State and registration with the appropriate regulatory body. So any such rule as Judge Mark's would frustrate the statutory framework (para.34). The panel's second rationale noted the difference between the LCW assessment (how a condition affects the claimant's functional capacity) and "a medical examination carried out as part of a process of diagnosis and treatment" (para.35), a distinction acknowledged in Professor Harrington's *First Review* of the ESA process. The panel thus considered that the medical examination carried out by a HCP for the LCW did not require that HCP to be a medical specialist in all the physical and mental problems that might be exhibited by a particular claimant. To require the HCP to be such a specialist "would create insurmountable problems for the assessment process" since many claimants have a variety of problems which might then require assessment in a particular case by several HCPs rather than one (para.35).

What is required, however, is that the HCP have an informed understanding of the claimant's medical conditions and the difficulties flowing from them. This requires adequate training and supervision. The panel had received detailed information on the current training process (see paras 11-19)—something not available to Judge Mark in *JH*—and, while not commenting on that programme, did observe that none of the independent reviews of the ESA assessment process had criticised the performance of physiotherapists relative to HCPs from other disciplines and that training for HCPs on mental health problems was being reviewed with the aim of increasing the knowledge of all HCPs (para.36).

There is, therefore, no need for a tribunal to adjourn for further particulars on the qualifications of the HCP in a particular case. The specialist tribunal with its medical member must "make its own findings having regard to all the evidence before it" (para.37). The correct starting point was that identified by Judge Ovey in an incapacity benefit appeal (*JF v SSWP (IB)* [2011] UKUT 385 (AAC) at para.25:

". . .the report is prepared by an HCP who has been trained (whether as part of the training as an HCP or through other training) at least to the level thought appropriate by the Department of Work and Pensions for carrying out examinations where mental health issues are raised. In other words the selection and training procedures ought to have produced an HCP who can conduct a mental health examination competently. It follows that evidence that the HCP has not undergone separate specialist training should not of itself have any effect on the weight which the tribunal attaches to the report. . ."

The panel held that the weight to be accorded to any report "addressing the functional impact of any medical condition on a claimant" is a matter for the specialist tribunal which should consider:

"(a) the level of the author's expertise (for example, an HCP or a consultant psychiatrist) and (b) the knowledge of the claimant possessed by the author (for example, knowledge gained from a one-off assessment or that gained as a treating clinician). Additionally the date of the evidence, its comprehensiveness, and its relevance to the issues the tribunal has to determine are also key matters for the tribunal to consider. Importantly the tribunal should explain its reasoning for attaching weight to one type or piece of evidence rather than to another" (para.38 of *ST & GF*).

In *JS v SSWP (ESA)* [2011] UKUT 243 (AAC), Judge Ward, following *R(DLA) 2/01* and *R(DLA) 3/01*, held that evidence coming into existence after the date of the decision could be relied on so far as relevant to showing the circumstances pertaining at the date of the decision. Accordingly, here, where there was evidence of a recent diagnosis of depression, of recent weight loss, low weight and a very low body mass index (BMI), the tribunal in the exercise of its inquisitorial jurisdiction ought to have followed this up to see if this was a symptom of untreated depression or, at the very least, to have made clear in its reasons what it made of this evidence. There is only a very limited carry-over of case authorities on the original LCWA, given the degree of revision of activities and descriptors undertaken in the amending Regulations.

From January 28, 2013 reg.19(5) requires that incapability to perform the activities in this Part of this Schedule (mental, cognitive and intellectual function assessment) must be linked to incapability arising from a specific mental illness or disablement or as a direct result of treatment provided by a registered medical practitioner for such an illness or disablement. Under the previous wording of the paragraph (still applicable to some cases after January 28, 2013—see reg.2 of the amending instrument, below, para.9.614), there was no such link (*KP v SSWP (ESA)* [2011] UKUT 216 (AAC); [2012] AACR 5; *KN v SSWP (ESA)* [2011] UKUT 229 (AAC); *RM v SSWP (ESA)* [2011] UKUT 454 (AAC); *AH v SSWP (ESA)* [2011] UKUT 333 (AAC)), but the specific language of activities 16 and 17 then as now specifically required causation by cognitive impairment or mental disorder.

The revised LCWA contains only seven activities rather than the ten in the original LCWA. This revision and reduction were designed to remove unnecessary complexities and overlaps and prevent double scoring.

4.403 *Activity 11: Learning tasks*: This aims to identify individuals who have difficulty learning new tasks. The equivalent in the original LCWA covered learning and comprehension but the latter was considered superfluous by the *Review* on the basis that understanding how to do something was built in to the process of retaining that knowledge. The complexity of the task affords the necessary gradation between descriptors. Note that the instances given in each descriptor (setting an alarm clock (descriptors (a) and (b)); operating a washing machine to clean clothes (descriptor (c)) are merely examples.

See by analogy the guidance from Judge Rowley on this activity in the context of Sch.3 in *Secretary of State for Work and Pensions v AT (ESA)* [2017] UKUT 338 (AAC). Note also her observation that "the words 'due to cognitive impairment or mental disorder' do not appear in the descriptors for that activity, presumably because the activity falls under Part 2 of Schedule 2 which is headed 'mental, cognitive and intellectual function assessment.' In my judgment, nothing turns on the difference" (at para.9).

See also *TM v SSWP (ESA)* [2018] UKUT 9 (AAC), dealing with descriptor 11c, where Judge Wikeley observed (at para. 22) that "The method by which the person learns the task in question is irrelevant. They may be able to do so by reading the information booklet. They may be able to do so by having the necessary steps being demonstrated to them. The route is irrelevant. As [the Secretary of State's representative] neatly puts it, 'Reading a manual is just one way of learning to use something, show and tell is another'."

4.404 *Activity 12: Awareness of everyday hazards (such as boiling water or sharp objects):* The focus here is on significant risk of injury to people or damage to property or possessions (rather than, as originally proposed, on risk of significant injury or significant damage). "Everyday hazards" means commonplace or ordinary hazards that are similar in kind to boiling water and sharp objects; it does not extend to social hazards, e.g. the risk of financial exploitation or sexual abuse that a vulnerable claimant with low social intelligence may face because of her suggestibility (*RR v SSWP (ESA)* [2018] UKUT 143 (AAC)). The gradation between descriptors flows from the level of supervision required to manage the risk (supervision needed for: majority of time (15); frequently (9); occasionally (6)). The requisite "reduced awareness of the risks of everyday hazards" could stem from learning difficulties, affected concentration and self-awareness, or the effects of medication (*Review*, para.4.4.2).

4.405 *Activity 13: Initiating and completing personal action (which means planning, organization, problem solving, prioritizing or switching tasks):* The overall intention of the Activity is to assess someone's capability to carry out routine activity. Note the meaning of "personal action" set out in the Activity itself. This part of the revised LCWA seeks to combine in one activity disabilities covered by three activities in the original LCWA: memory and concentration; execution of tasks; initiating and sustaining personal action. This was done because the original three were perceived by the *Review* as each identifying the same disability, namely, the inability to complete a task. The amalgamation thus precludes the double or triple scoring available under the former LCWA. The descriptors focus on completion of at least two sequential tasks, since it was unlikely that in a work context an individual would only be required to undertake a single task. The gradation between descriptors (b) and (c) turns on how often verbal prompting from another is needed to complete the personal action ((b) "most of the time"; (c) "frequent"). The *Review* specifically stated that:

> "if the time it takes an individual to complete a task means it cannot be executed reliably and repeatedly, then they will be considered unable to do so" (p.45).

Conditions potentially involving this Activity were thought to be lapses in memory and concentration, due to fatigue, depression or neurological impairment, apathy, obsessive compulsive behaviours, overwhelming fear or delusions.

In *MW v SSWP (ESA)* [2014] UKUT 112 (AAC), a case of a claimant with obsessive compulsive disorder, Judge Rowland held that the tribunal had erred in law:

> "It neither addressed the consequences of the claimant's need constantly to check that what he had done was right nor paid sufficient attention to the precise language of the legislation. The main consequence of the claimant's disorder was that everything took much longer, but there is also evidence that, for instance, turning gas hobs on and off when cooking had resulted a build-up of gas and in him being a danger to himself to the extent that his mother had taken over his cooking from him. The material features of the legislation are, first, that it is not enough that the claimant can initiate and complete personal actions – he or she must be able to do so "reliably"—and, secondly, a finding that a person can sometimes reliably initiate or complete actions may rule out descriptor 13(a)—at least on a literal construction of that descriptor—but it leaves open the possibility of either of descriptors 13(b) or 13(c) being satisfied since those descriptors are satisfied if the claimant cannot reliably initiate or complete at least two [personal] actions "for the majority of the time" or "frequently".
>
> The word "reliably" makes it unnecessary to go as far as is argued on behalf of the claimant and hold that a person is to be treated as not being able to initiate and complete actions at all if he or she can do so only with excessive delay. The Secretary of State is right to argue that one should consider separately whether there is a difficulty in initiating an action and whether there is a difficulty in completing it and that in this case the difficulty lay in completing actions, although arguably the difficulty in completing the first action creates a difficulty in initiating the second. In any event, the practical point is that, if compulsive behaviour means that it takes an excessive amount of time to complete at least two actions, it can be said that the claimant cannot "reliably" complete them. The First-tier Tribunal did not consider whether that was, at least frequently, so in this case or, if it did, it gave inadequate reasons for its conclusion" (paras 6, 7).

Activity 13 was further considered by Judge Jacobs in *MP v Secretary of State for Work and Pensions (ESA)* [2015] UKUT 458 (AAC), where he noted it was "neither necessary nor appropriate to define 'personal action'. They are ordinary words that have to be given their normal meaning" (see *Moyna v Secretary of State for Work and Pensions* [2003] 1 W.L.R. 1929 at [24]). Accordingly, "At the risk of stating the obvious, it means something undertaken by someone on their own" (para.23). Judge Jacobs held that the tribunal "must apply common sense in deciding what constitutes an action. It is possible to render the legislation redundant by splitting an action into its component parts. The definition of Activity 13 recognises this by referring to 'tasks' as components of a single action" (para.28). See further the analysis at paras.30–41, including this passage at paras 34–35:

"34. The tribunal's decision on Activity 13 must relate only to actions that involve all these tasks. This does not mean that the tribunal must find evidence of an action involving all those tasks that the claimant cannot complete. It may be that there will be evidence from, say, dressing that shows the claimant being unable to plan by selecting appropriate clothing to wear outdoors, which can be put together with evidence from, say, cooking, that shows the claimant being unable to prioritise tasks. This specific evidence may have to be supplemented by inferences drawn from the nature of the claimant's condition or other factors.

35. This does not mean that the action considered need necessarily be complicated, so long as the tribunal takes all potential tasks into account. Take dressing as an example. Most of the time dressing may simply be routine. It may even involve nothing more than putting on the clothing selected and laid out by the claimant's partner. But it can require planning (deciding what to wear), organising (assembling the different items required), problem solving (finding an alternative item of clothing for something that is in the wash), prioritising (deciding whether it is more important to get dressed or to wash a particular item of clothing) or switching tasks (going to iron a shirt to wear). To put it differently. The tribunal must always be sure that the evidence on which it relies actually demonstrates an ability to undertake all the tasks required by the activity."

See, for a successful reasons challenge, *VH v SSWP (ESA)* [2018] UKUT 290 (AAC) (at paras.17-20).

4.406   *Activity 14: Coping with change:* This assesses ability to cope with change. The focus in descriptors (b) and (c) is now on whether the change is "planned" or "unplanned", rather than "expected", "unexpected" or "unforeseen". Decision-makers and tribunals should look at all the evidence about the person's daily life.

In mental health descriptor cases the context of a particular piece of evidence can be very important (see *PD v SSWP (ESA)* [2012] UKUT 255 (AAC)). In *GC v SSWP (ESA)* [2013] UKUT 405 (AAC) work-related stress had been the reason the claimant left his previous job as a driver. Being required to change his planned-out driving route part way through a shift, caused him stress, made him bad-tempered, such that he had to leave that job. The decision reflects Judge Ward's important reminder that different people have different abilities to cope with change.

On the evidence Judge Ward found the claimant's ability to cope with change very low and that he satisfied descriptor (c) and had limited capability for work.

What does "cope" mean? In *GC v SSWP (ESA)* [2013] UKUT 405 (AAC), Judge Ward considered it to be

"a word of general application. It significance in the present context is well expressed by a definition given in the Oxford English Dictionary (Online Edition) of 'To manage, deal (competently) with, a situation or problem'. It seems to me that a variety of human behaviours and responses may be indicative of a failure to "cope" in such a sense. Among them may be stress reactions and discomfort sufficient to require the intervention of another in circumstances where such intervention would not normally be expected" (para.6).

4.407   *Activity 15: Getting about:* The differential here between descriptors is one of familiarity. That was thought in the *Review* to ensure the work-related nature of the activity, since the workplace would be a familiar environment. From January 28, 2013, descriptor (a) reads: "cannot get to any place outside the claimant's home with which the claimant is familiar", rather than to "any specified place" thus attempting to make clear that the need is based on most places a claimant cannot get to rather than a single specified place, and aiming to give effect to a policy intention that this activity is to reflect inability to travel unaccompanied by someone for those individuals that are severely affected by a mental health condition (e.g. agoraphobia). "Any place outside the claimant's home" means more than simply beyond their front door. According to Judge Bano in *PC v Secretary of State for Work and Pensions (ESA)* [2015] UKUT 531 (AAC):

> "For my part, I do not consider that putting out the bins or going outside to have a cigarette amounts to 'getting about', even if there is a chance of meeting a neighbour or visitor to the building when doing so. In my judgment, descriptor 1 of Activity 15 requires an investigation of whether a claimant can go to a place outside the immediate vicinity of their home, and that in order to satisfy the descriptor it is not necessary for a claimant to establish that he or she cannot go beyond their front door" (para.8).

The other descriptors refer to "any specified place" or a "specified place", just as did those in Activity 18 in the original LCWA. This phraseology was considered in *DW v SSWP (ESA)* [2011] UKUT 79 (AAC). There, Judge Turnbull dealt with the case of a claimant, suffering from a stress-related illness brought about because of the circumstances of her dismissal from her previous employment, who was found by the tribunal to be fearful of seeing anyone involved with her former employment or reminders of it, such as vans or lorries and who would be unable to visit her employer's premises at all or, at best, accompanied. He took the view that this could not bring her within descriptors 18(a) (as originally worded) or 18(b):

> "the words 'cannot get to any specified place . . .' in 18(a) . . . clearly mean that there is no place with which the claimant is familiar (or would be familiar with if she went out) which she could get to on her own. The words 'is unable to get to a specified place . . . without being accompanied by another person on each occasion' in 18(b) . . . mean that the claimant always needs to be accompanied when getting to a familiar place" (para.15).

Evidence that a claimant had gone unaccompanied to familiar places and accompanied to an unfamiliar one where she was trembling and sweating cannot support a finding that she could go unaccompanied to an unfamiliar place (*LM v SSWP (ESA)* [2013] UKUT 552 (AAC)). See also *MC v SSWP (ESA)* [2015] UKUT 646 (AAC), discussed in the commentary to reg.19 above.

In *AB v SSWP (ESA)* [2016] UKUT 96 (AAC) the issue was whether, if a claimant undertakes a journey by taxi, is that claimant "accompanied" by the taxi driver. Judge Hemingway held that "if a claimant can only undertake a journey to an unfamiliar place by taxi because of a requirement of undertaking the journey in the presence of another person or because the assistance of that other person is required, then that journey is, for the purposes of the relevant descriptor, an accompanied one" (at para.12). The tribunal had therefore erred in law by assuming that a journey in a taxi would be an unaccompanied journey without enquiring into whether the presence of the taxi driver was essential or important to the appellant's ability to make a journey to a specified place with which he was unfamiliar.

See also *TM v SSWP (ESA)* [2018] UKUT 9 (AAC), where Judge Wikeley accepted a concession by the Secretary of State that reg.19(4) limits consideration of aids and appliances to the *physical health* descriptors in Part 1 of Sch.2. and so in the context of activity 15 the FTT should not have considered the claimant's ability to navigate by a mobile phone app.

Activity 16: Coping with social engagement due to cognitive impairment or mental **4.408** *disorder:* The primary aim here is to assess functional capability in terms of social contact with the ability to get around being dealt with by other activities. The gradation between descriptors (a), on the one hand, and (b) and (c), on the other, is that the latter two look to inability to engage with strangers, the former with anyone ("social contact is always precluded"). The *Review* thought familiarity an appropriate measure in relation to the workplace. That between (b) and (c) turns on whether that engagement is "never possible" (descriptor (b)) or "not possible for the majority of the time" (descriptor (c)). The preclusion of engagement (descriptor (a)) or the difficulty of engagement (descriptors (b) and (c)) must in each case be "due to difficulty relating to others or significant distress experienced by the individual being assessed for LCW". Contact which involves or would involve "significant distress" must be excluded from consideration" (*DW v SSWP (ESA)* [2014] UKUT 20 (AAC), para.4).

What does "cope" mean? In *GC* v *SSWP (ESA)* [2013] UKUT 405 (AAC), Judge Ward considered it to be:

> "a word of general application. It significance in the present context is well expressed by a definition given in the Oxford English Dictionary (Online Edition) of 'To manage, deal (competently) with, a situation or problem'. It seems to me that a variety of human behaviours and responses may be indicative of a failure to "cope" in such a sense. Among them may be stress reactions and discomfort sufficient to require the intervention of another in circumstances where such intervention would not normally be expected" (para.6).

In *LM* v *SSWP (ESA)* [2013] UKUT 552 (AAC), Judge Mark considered that descriptor (b) is satisfied if for the majority of the time, social engagement is always precluded (paras 12, 13). As regards descriptors (a) and (b) he could not read "always" as "often" or "for the majority of the time" (the term in descriptor (c)), but rather as "persistently or repeatedly". To say otherwise would have the odd result that a claimant could not satisfy descriptors (a) and (b) but, because of ESA Regs 2008, reg.34(2) would satisfy descriptor 13 in Sch.3 (see para.15). Judge Mark continued:

> "the tribunal is required to form an overall picture of the claimant's ability to engage in social conduct over a period and it does not appear to me that occasional very limited engagement in such conduct need prevent a tribunal concluding that overall the claimant is always unable to do so. To take an extreme example, a person in a coma who surfaces occasionally and is able to engage briefly during that period with familiar and unfamiliar persons before lapsing into unconsciousness should nevertheless be found in this context always to be unable to engage in social contact" (para.16).

He awarded the claimant points under descriptor (b).

See also, however, the annotation to reg.34(2) and the decision of the Court of Session in *SSWP v Brade* [2014] CSIH 39 XA81/13 (May 1,2014); [2014] AACR 29.

The precise scope of "social", of "engagement" and of "contact" has troubled Upper Tribunal Judges and generated different opinions. It has therefore recently been considered by a panel of three Upper Tribunal Judges, but to understand the panel's judgment it is necessary to first take on board the conflicting decisions.

In *KB* v *SSWP (ESA)* [2013] UKUT 152 (AAC), noted in the annotation to Sch.3, activity and descriptor 13 (see para.9.425), as regards "social engagement" and "social contact", Judge Parker, accepting the approach advanced by the Secretary of State's representative, thought "social" to be "a simple reference to relations with other human beings" carrying no connotations of "leisure, pleasure or mutuality", so that a tribunal could properly look at evidence about business visits or contacts with professionals, as well as with friends, relatives and strangers. It was not tied to contact in an informal setting (see paras 15–17). Judge Ward disagreed with this in *AR* v *SSWP (ESA)* [2013] UKUT 446 (AAC). It rendered "social" virtually otiose, placing the focus purely on "engagement with others". It also jarred with the ordinary meaning of the word in the Concise Oxford Dictionary, a meaning Judge Ward thought closer to the legislator's intention. Looking at the legislative history, he considered that the difficulties faced by those with autistic spectrum disorder were very much in mind. Material from the National Autism Society showed the difficulties faced in understanding the rules on social contact and distinguishing a "true friend" from a "pretend friend". Accordingly, in Judge Ward's view,

"social contact in this sense is not the same as contact for business or professional purposes. If one goes to a medical examination, or a tribunal hearing, the
rules are firmly established by the process and/or the person conducting it, and
are typically clearly defined, often in writing. If the person being examined or
whose case it is does not respond in a way that a person without disability might,
the person conducting it may because of their professional responsibilities be
expected within generous limits to accommodate the non-conforming response
and certainly not, as it were, to take a poorer view of, or attempt to avoid further
contact with, the person because of it. That is precisely what is lacking in the
social sphere, where people are free to interact on their own terms and to accept
the behaviour of another or to reject it, and largely do so on the basis of the sort of
unwritten rules to which the National Autism Society guidance makes reference,
an inability to respect which could, in the words of the descriptor, be an indication of "difficulty relating to others" (para.18).

In *LM* v *SSWP (ESA)* [2013] UKUT 552 (AAC), Judge Mark cited this paragraph
and gave it qualified support, stating that while he agreed that

"merely attending a medical examination or tribunal hearing does not establish
an ability to engage in social contact, but it does not follow that in the course of
that examination or hearing the party will not demonstrate an ability to respond
appropriately and engage in limited social contact despite the distress that the
meeting is causing and that such contact causes. The fact that a person is not so
far along the autistic spectrum as to be wholly unable to engage in social contact
does not mean that a person might not experience significant distress if required
to engage in such contact. A tribunal needs to assess the ability to engage in social
contact, which can be in any context, the extent to which a person has the capacity so to engage, the distress it causes when engagement occurs and the impact of
that distress on the ability so to engage" (para.18).

In *JM* v *SSWP (ESA)* [2014] UKUT 22 (AAC), Judge Gray endorsed Judge Ward's   **4.409**
view and added "the observation that because for the important purpose of benefit
entitlement, or indeed in order to effect treatment for a mental health condition, one
may be able to summon up reserves to attend such an appointment that may not be
sufficient in relation to a test which is of the ability to perform an activity reliably
and repeatedly" (para.16).
In *AP* v *SSWP (ESA)* [2013] UKUT 293 (AAC), Judge Turnbull considered
descriptor (c). He accepted that

"difficulty, from a mental point of view, in simply getting alone to the destina-
tion does not fall to be taken into account under activity 16 (unless the difficulty
getting there is itself due to problems with engaging in social contact (e.g. on
public transport)). In other words, a claimant does not qualify for points under
activity 16(c) merely because he could not put himself in most of the situations
where he might engage in social contact with someone unfamiliar, because he
could not leave the house unaccompanied in order to do so" (para.11).

"The difficulty with others" aspect of the descriptor envisaged the situation in
which it is the need to engage with others which caused the problem. In contrast,
however, the alternative—"significant distress experienced by the individual"—did
not, in his view,

"require that it is the need to interact with others which per se causes the distress.
… the wording is satisfied whatever the immediate cause of the distress may be,
provided that it is due to cognitive impairment or mental disorder, and that it
is sufficiently severe and occurs on sufficient occasions to prevent the claimant
engaging with others "for the majority of the time."
Thus, if the effect of having to leave his home unaccompanied, or to enter unfa-

miliar buildings, is to cause distress which prevents the claimant then being able to engage with someone unfamiliar, ... 16(c) could apply, even if the claimant would have been perfectly capable of engaging with that unfamiliar person if he had been accompanied by friend or family, or if he had been in familiar surroundings.

Thus, the Claimant in the present case was not in my judgment prevented from satisfying 16(c) merely because it was not the process of interacting with unfamiliar persons per se which caused her difficulty" (paras 12–14).

In *SSWP v LC (ESA)* [2014] UKUT 268 (AAC), Judge Williams agreed with Judge Ward's comments on "social contact" in *AR v SSWP (ESA)* [2013] UKUT 446 (AAC) and with Judge Mark's "persuasive analysis" of the meaning of "always" in *LM v SSWP (ESA)* [2013] UKUT 552 (AAC). Judge Williams considered that it "can be read as meaning "every day" but not "every moment", something important where the problems of a claimant are variable. His construction of "always" was, however, made without knowing of the decision of the Court of Session in *SSWP v Brade* [2014] AACR 29 (see annotation to ESA Regs 2008 reg.34(2)), and reads "always" somewhat more narrowly than the Court of Session which saw it as connoting "cannot 'for the majority of the time' engage". In addition, his decision was made before that in *JC v SSWP (ESA)* [2014] UKUT 352 (AAC); [2015] AACR 6 in which a panel of three Upper Tribunal Judges considered this activity and the case law on it, in particular the conflicting approaches of Judge Parker in *KB v SSWP (ESA)* [2013] UKUT 152 (AAC) and Judge Ward in *AR*, above. Insofar as other decisions are at variance with that of the Three-Judge Panel, *JC* is the authoritative decision to be followed.

In *JC*, the panel considered it "common ground" that the phrases "coping with social engagement" in the definition of the activity and "engagement in social contact" in the definition of the descriptor have the same meaning (para.6). It accepted the submission that "the Activities and their descriptors are intended to assess whether a person is able to engage with others for the purpose of work" (para.16). It also agreed with Judge Wikeley's comments in para.19 of his decision in *AS v SSWP (ESA)* [2013] UKUT 587 (AAC) that the activities and descriptors must be "applied on their own terms, but understood against the backdrop of the modern workplace" (para.16). The panel took the view that the differences between Judges Parker and Ward were less than appeared at first sight (para.22). Like Judge Ward it disagreed with Judge Parker that "social" simply meant "relations with other human beings" and did not "carry connotations of leisure and pleasure", but, unlike Judge Ward, did not accept that Parliament's intention was directed only at the difficulties in communication experienced by these with Autistic Spectrum Disorder (ASD) or similar difficulties, although it agreed that Parliament would have had the difficulties of those with ASD in mind (para.25). Instead, the causes "referred to in the Activities and their Descriptors" when read in the context of other relevant provisions in the legislation "show that the intention was not so confined but was directed to the possible impact of a wider range of impairments or disorders" (para.26). The panel saw the words of the definitions in the Activities and Descriptors at issue as a whole and the underlying statutory purposes as being "the most important factors that determine the nature and quality of the behaviour and communications covered by the Activities and their descriptors" (para. 27). Applying these factors requires decision-makers and tribunals to consider the following:

"(i) the range of meanings in common usage of the individual words that are used and so of "coping", "engagement", "social" and "contact" in the context of their combined effect,

(ii) the causes referred to in the Activities for the problems with coping with and engaging in social contact,

(iii) the causes referred to in the Descriptors and their link with the relevant cognitive impairment or mental disorder, and

(iv) the underlying purposes of the legislation and so of the assessments" (para.27).

Given the underlying purposes (whether a person is able to engage with others for the purpose of work and the context of the modern workplace), the panel could not endorse limitation to

"the nature and quality of the contact or engagement . . . to contact for pleasure or leisure or characterised by friendliness, geniality or companionship and so the choices that that involves [since such a limitation] would be surprising because that limitation (a) would exclude aspects of communication in the workplace, and (b) would not take proper account of the distinction in the descriptors between communication with people with whom the claimant is familiar and all communication. Indeed, it seems to us that points (a) and (b) dictate that the tests in the Activities and their Descriptors extend to contact for the purposes of work and so to contact with other characteristics and purposes that involve different degrees of choice or no choice because they relate to a structured situation or professional relationship (e.g. doctor and patient, lawyer and client)" (para.28).

On that basis the panel agreed with Judge Parker and the Secretary of State that, taken in isolation, "social" is a reference to "with other human beings" (para.29). However, since "social" is not isolated but qualifies "engagement" or "contact", this left open

"the nature and quality of the "engagement" or "contact" that is precluded or not possible for the given reasons and thus the assessment of what "engagement or contact with other people" the claimant can cope with due to his cognitive impairment or mental disorder" (para.30).

Key elements here, viewing "coping" and "engagement" in the context of the statutory purposes underlying assessment, were ones of "reciprocity, give and take, initiation and response" (para.32). These can be demonstrated not only by contact characterised by friendliness, geniality or companionship but also "without those elements (and the choices they involve) being present" such as "is often the case in the workplace and elsewhere", although those other contexts might also sometimes display them (para.32). The panel usefully pointed to examples which could equally demonstrate "the necessary degree of reciprocity, give and take, initiation and response": buying a ticket or groceries; contact with a medical examiner or other professional; conversation with a stranger on a park bench or elsewhere; or contact with the First-tier Tribunal itself (para.33). The panel saw the issues, fact finding and value judgements involved as eminently suitable for the First-tier Tribunal, and in the view of the panel: 4.410

"it is open to a decision maker to base his decision on an example or examples chosen from a wide range of situations. Whether the evidence and findings relating to the claimant's communications with others and behaviour in the chosen example or examples have the necessary degree of reciprocity, give and take, initiation and response raises issues of fact and degree and of judgment having regard to all the circumstances relating to them. As with other such issues, the authorities show that it is not practical or appropriate to identify the statutory criterion by reference to abstract examples or by reference to a general classification or description other than the statutory test" (para.34).

The proper approach for a tribunal in each case is to consider and determine how

"The nature and quality of the examples of communications and behaviour they take into account (and thus the reciprocity, give and take, initiation and response shown thereby) would, for the reasons given in the Activities and their Descriptors, be likely to be an effective barrier to the claimant working" (para.35).

The panel accepted that, because the conceptual test thus set out involves value judgments, this leaves "room for different decision-makers applying the right approach in the right way to reach different answers" (para.36 read with paras 9–12).

Good decision-making here involves carrying out the necessary fact-finding "separately from, although with an eye to, the value judgements that have to be applied to those findings" so as to identify and particularise "by reference to primary facts, the situations and events that will be taken into account and so the bedrock of the decision" (para.38). To reach their decision the tribunal must

"address and decide whether those findings show that:

(i) the claimant has cognitive impairment or mental disorder,
(ii) a causative link between that impairment or disorder and his difficulty relating to others or significant distress, and
(iii) a causative link between that difficulty and distress and a preclusion for all of the time or an impossibility for a majority of the time of contact with all other people, or those who are unfamiliar to the claimant, that has the necessary degree of reciprocity, give and take, initiation and response.

In addressing whether the contact with other people has the necessary nature and quality the tribunal should consider in each individual case how the nature and quality of the communications and behaviour would impact on the ability of the individual to work and so whether or not it would be an effective barrier to him working" (paras 38–39).

As regards the first case under appeal, the panel considered that the tribunal had erred in law in that it may not have understood or applied the statutory test correctly. It had seemed to be concerned about the claimant being able to be helped by someone. The panel did not consider that a person could properly be regarded "as able to engage in social contact if she or he can do so only if accompanied by someone, at least without further explanation as to how it is envisaged that that might be realistic in the workplace" (para.45). The matter was remitted for decision by another tribunal to be decided in light of the guidance proffered by the panel's decision. The panel found no error of law in the second case under appeal (paras 49–60).

4.411   *Activity 17: Appropriateness of behaviour with other people, due to cognitive impairment or mental disorder.* This was revised to remove some of the more negative phraseology of its predecessor, to find more "neutral" terms than "bizarre" or "outbursts". Gradation between descriptors is set in terms of the frequency of the episodes of the relevant behaviour: (a) "on a daily basis"; (b) "frequently"; (c) "occasionally". The episodes must in each case be "uncontrollable". In each case, the behaviour must be "aggressive or disinhibited". A key standard in each descriptor is whether this behaviour "would be unreasonable in any workplace".

As regards descriptor (a), in *WT v SSWP (ESA)* [2013] UKUT 556 (AAC), Judge Gray considered the meaning of "on a daily basis". While this was a decision dealing with identical wording in Sch.3, activity/descriptor 14, Judge Gray also applied it to descriptor (a), its "mirror descriptor". Rather than merely deploy a dictionary definition, he took the "mischief" approach to interpretation and reasoned thus:

"The mischief that the descriptor must be intended to remedy is the creation of an unsafe or otherwise unacceptable work environment for co-workers. The way in which the avoidance of that is accomplished is to exclude from the workplace those who, due to their mental health condition exhibit certain behaviour. If on virtually every day that they were at work they displayed such behaviour, would the fact that there were very rare days on which they did not prevent them from falling within the meaning of the descriptor? To answer "yes" to that question would not be to address the mischief. The descriptor must, then, be interpreted more widely than literally every day.

I fortify myself in this view because the ordinary meaning of the words "on a daily basis" seem to me to connote a lesser test than "every day". The phrase is not confined to events which happen literally every day. Someone might be said to read a particular newspaper on a daily basis even though there were periods when they did not, such as where they were abroad on holiday when it was not available. Walking the dog on a daily basis is an activity which may be interrupted by the ill-health of either dog or walker, but a short break would not change the very regular nature of the activity or make that description inapt.

The words "on a daily basis", then, in the context of schedule 3 descriptor 14, and its mirror descriptor under schedule 2, regulation 17 (a), means certainly more than for the majority of the time, that being the regulation 34 (2) test, and must mean more than frequently, that being the test of periodicity in regulation 17(b), but it does not mean literally every day or even on every working day. The essence is of this being an enduring position; one which is happening regularly, constantly or continually. It is for the tribunal to find the facts as to the frequency of the behaviour set out in the descriptor, and then apply this approach to those facts with their usual common sense" (paras 40-42).

As regards descriptor (c), in *KE v SSWP (ESA)* [2013] UKUT 370 (AAC), Judge Williams noted that "the incidence [of disinhibited behaviour] is at a lower level of occurrence but at a higher level of intensity than the previous test, although the underlying issue manifested by these forms of conduct is the same" (para.17). It now attracts three more points than its predecessor (9 rather than 6). The claimant had several times been required to leave the Jobcentre because of abusive and insulting things he said rather than did, "a classic form of disinhibited behaviour". As regards the criterion "unreasonable in any workplace, Judge Williams thought a Jobcentre unlikely to "apply a lower test than an employer would be expected to apply" (para.18).

In *WC v SSWP (ESA)* [2014] UKUT 363, Judge Rowley commended to tribunals considering descriptors under this Activity the following list of questions constituting a "methodical approach":

"(a) Does the claimant have cognitive impairment or mental disorder?

(b) If so, does that cause the claimant to behave in the way described by the descriptor, namely:

(i) Does the claimant have episodes of aggressive or disinhibited behaviour?
(ii) Are any such episodes uncontrollable?
(iii) How often do they occur (noting the words of the descriptor: "on a daily basis," "frequently," "occasionally,").
(iv) Would such behaviour be unreasonable in any workplace?" (para.10).

Judge Rowley, adopting Judge Gray's observations in the quotation from *WT*, considered that the relevant behaviour could include "sufficiently serious verbal aggression" since its use

"may well create an unacceptable work environment for co-workers, or indeed others with whom the person exhibiting the behaviour may come into contact in the workplace. It would be wrong to say that such conduct can never be enough to satisfy activity 17. Further, in my view it is not necessary for the claimant to have been involved in a fight or argument for activity 17 to apply. There may be examples where his or her behaviour has been aggressive or disinhibited but has not led to another person responding by fighting or arguing. Indeed, in many cases when faced with such behaviour, some people's natural reaction is to walk away. That does not necessarily make the aggressive or disinhibited behaviour any less serious, nor does it necessarily render it any more acceptable to co-workers or others in the workplace. In each case it will be for the tribunal to consider the evidence, find the facts and decide, in the light of those findings, whether a particular claimant's behaviour, whether physical or verbal, is sufficient to satisfy the relevant criteria" (para.16).

Moreover, since the wording of Activity 17 applies to "any workplace", he rejected as an "unnecessary gloss" on that wording the submission of the Secretary of State that "the claimant's behaviour would have to be considered unacceptable in an average workplace such as a call centre" (para.18).

It is vital to note that under ESA Regs 2008, reg.19(2), (5) incapability of performing the activity in respect of any descriptor in Pt 2 of Sch.2 must arise from a specific mental illness or disablement. Alcohol misuse in itself is not such a disablement. To rank as disablement the misuse of alcohol must rank as "alcohol dependency" in terms of the "constellation of markers" found in quotations from *R(DLA) 6/06* in the Three-Judge Panel's decision in *JG v SSWP (ESA)* [2013] UKUT 37 (AAC); [2013] AACR 23. Accordingly, in *DR v SSWP (ESA)* [2014] UKUT 188 (AAC); [2014] AACR 38, Judge May held the tribunal were right to hold that the descriptors did not apply. Moreover, he was persuaded that

"the volume of alcohol the claimant is said to drink on a daily basis would not in itself amount to the disinhibited behaviour referred to in descriptors 17(a) in Schedule 2 and 14 in Schedule 3. I see the force in Mr Webster's submission that disinhibited behaviour requires the context of an inhibition. I cannot see, and it has not been established, what the inhibition in this case is and how the drinking of a certain volume of alcohol amounts in itself to disinhibited behaviour. Disinhibited behaviour may result as a consequence of drinking specific quantities of alcohol but that is not the basis upon which the claimant's argument is put. Mr Orr seeks to widen "disinhibition" beyond the scope of what the statutory provisions can bear. The activity for both descriptors relates to the appropriateness of behaviour "with" other people, which suggests that the descriptor is intended to be applied in respect of behaviour which is more than the passive drinking of alcohol" (para.8).

[¹SCHEDULE 3   **Regulation 34(1)**

4.412   ASSESSMENT OF WHETHER A CLAIMANT HAS LIMITED CAPABILITY FOR WORK-RELATED ACTIVITY

Activity	*Descriptors*
[² 1. Mobilising unaided by another person with or without a walking stick, manual wheelchair or other aid if such aid is normally, or could reasonably be, worn or used.]	Cannot either: (a) mobilise more than 50 metres on level ground without stopping in order to avoid significant discomfort or exhaustion; or (b) repeatedly mobilise 50 metres within a reasonable timescale because of significant discomfort or exhaustion.
2. Transferring from one seated position to another.	Cannot move between one seated position and another seated position located next to one another without receiving physical assistance from another person.
3. Reaching.	Cannot raise either arm as if to put something in the top pocket of a coat or jacket.

Activity	Descriptors
4. Picking up and moving or transferring by the use of the upper body and arms (excluding standing, sitting, bending or kneeling and all other activities specified in this Schedule).	Cannot pick up and move a 0.5 litre carton full of liquid.
5. Manual dexterity.	[³Cannot press a button (such as a telephone keypad) with either hand or cannot turn the pages of a book with either hand.]
[² 6. Making self understood through speaking, writing, typing, or other means which are normally, or could reasonably be, used, unaided by another person.]	Cannot convey a simple message, such as the presence of a hazard.
[² 7. Understanding communication by: (i) verbal means (such as hearing or lip reading) alone, (ii) non-verbal means (such as reading 16 point print or Braille) alone, or (iii) a combination of (i) and (ii), using any aid that is normally, or could reasonably be, used, unaided by another person.]	Cannot understand a simple message [³,such as the location of a fire escape due to sensory impairment [³...] .
[² 8. Absence or loss of control whilst conscious leading to extensive evacuation of the bowel and/or voiding of the bladder, other than enuresis (bed-wetting), despite the wearing or use of any aids or adaptations which are normally, or could reasonably be, worn or used.]	At least once a week experiences: (a) loss of control leading to extensive evacuation of the bowel and/or voiding of the bladder; or (b) substantial leakage of the contents of a collecting device sufficient to require the individual to clean themselves and change clothing.
9. Learning tasks.	Cannot learn how to complete a simple task, such as setting an alarm clock, due to cognitive impairment or mental disorder.
10. Awareness of hazard.	Reduced awareness of everyday hazards, due to cognitive impairment or mental disorder, leads to a significant risk of: (a) injury to self or others; or (b) damage to property or possessions such that [³ the claimant requires] supervision for the majority of the time to maintain safety.
11. Initiating and completing personal action (which means planning, organisation, problem solving, prioritising or switching tasks).	Cannot, due to impaired mental function, reliably initiate or complete at least 2 sequential personal actions.
12. Coping with change.	Cannot cope with any change, due to cognitive impairment or mental disorder, to the extent that day to day life cannot be managed.
13. Coping with social engagement, due to cognitive impairment or mental disorder.	Engagement in social contact is always precluded due to difficulty relating to others or significant distress experienced by the [³ claimant].

1497

Activity	Descriptors
14. Appropriateness of behaviour with other people, due to cognitive impairment or mental disorder.	Has, on a daily basis, uncontrollable episodes of aggressive or disinhibited behaviour that would be unreasonable in any workplace.
15. Conveying food or drink to the mouth.	(a) Cannot convey food or drink to the claimant's own mouth without receiving physical assistance from someone else;
	(b) Cannot convey food or drink to the claimant's own mouth without repeatedly [³ stopping or] experiencing breathlessness or severe discomfort;
	(c) Cannot convey food or drink to the claimant's own mouth without receiving regular prompting given by someone else in the claimant's physical presence; or
	(d) Owing to a severe disorder of mood or behaviour, fails to convey food or drink to the claimant's own mouth without receiving:
	(i) physical assistance from someone else; or
	(ii) regular prompting given by someone else in the claimant's presence.
16. Chewing or swallowing food or drink.	(a) Cannot chew or swallow food or drink;
	(b) Cannot chew or swallow food or drink without repeatedly stopping, experiencing breathlessness or severe discomfort;
	(c) Cannot chew or swallow food or drink without repeatedly receiving regular prompting given by someone else in the claimant's presence; or
	(d) Owing to a severe disorder of mood or behaviour, fails to:
	(i) chew or swallow food or drink; or
	(ii) chew or swallow food or drink without regular prompting given by someone else in the claimant's presence.]

AMENDMENTS

1. Employment and Support Allowance (Limited Capability for Work and Limited Capability for Work-Related Activity) (Amendment) Regulations 2011 (SI 2011/228) reg.4(2) (March 28, 2011).
2. Employment and Support Allowance (Amendment) Regulations 2012 (SI

2012/3096) reg.5(2) (January 28, 2013, subject to application, transitional and savings provisions in reg.2 of this amending instrument, para.9.614).

3. Social Security (Miscellaneous Amendments) (No.3) Regulations 2013 (SI 2013/2536) reg.13(34) (October 29, 2013).

DEFINITIONS

"claimant"—see WRA 2007 s.24(1).

GENERAL NOTE

Establishing limited capability for work-related activity might be said to be the central condition of entitlement to support component. The assumption behind ESA is that the vast majority of claimants, if given the right support, are in fact capable of some work. Government anticipates that only some 10 per cent of claimants (those with more severe health conditions) will be entitled to the support component and so not be subject to work-related activity conditionality requirements. Entry to this protected support group depends on it being established—generally through a work-related activity assessment (LCWRA) of a more stringent nature than the LCWA covered by reg.19 and Sch.2—that the claimant has limited capability for work-related activity: the LCWRA is thus the second element in the revised Work Capability Assessment.

4.413

Entry to the support group is based on someone demonstrating that they have a severe level of functional limitation. Until January 28, 2013, this was established when by reason of the claimant's physical or mental condition, at least one of the range of descriptors in this revised Sch.3 to the ESA Regs applies to the claimant. From that date, reg.34(3A) provides that in deciding which descriptor applies, incapability must arise in respect of descriptors 1 to 8, 15(a), 15(b), 16(a) and 16 (b), from a specific bodily disease or disablement or as a direct result of treatment provided by a registered medical practitioner for such a disease or disablement (para. (3A)(a), (c)(i)). Similarly, as regards descriptors 9 to 14, 15(c), 15(d), 16(c) and 16 (d), incapability must arise from a specific mental illness or disablement; or as a direct result of treatment provided by a registered medical practitioner for such an illness or disablement (para.(3A)(b), (c)(i)). Note that for some cases after January 28, 2013, for a six month period, the previous version of reg.34 can be applicable (see reg.2 of the amending instrument, below, para.9.614). Under both original and amended forms of reg.34, assessment has to take account of prostheses, aids and appliances (para.(3)). It is submitted here that the key elements of IB case law and ESA case law which carry across into interpreting and applying the provisions in Sch.2 on the revised LCWRA will also apply here: decide in the light of the totality of the evidence, making a careful appraisal of differing medical reports; the need for careful attention to detail; the concept of reasonable regularity (the test is not a snapshot); relevant factors of pain, discomfort and of fears for the claimant's health; and the need carefully to approach conditions which vary and fluctuate. But here reg.34(2) makes clear that a:

"descriptor applies to a claimant if that descriptor applies to the claimant for the majority of the time or, as the case may be, on the majority of the occasions on which the claimant undertakes or attempts to undertake the activity described by that descriptor."

This, in broad terms appears to put on a statutory footing for the LCWRA assessment, the "reasonable regularity" test approved for incapacity benefit in *R(IB) 2/99* and by analogy applicable to ESA assessments (*EH v SSWP (ESA)* [2011] UKUT 21 (AAC), para.31). In considering issues under Sch.3, a tribunal should also consider the full ESA85 report and not simply the section stating the EMP's opinion on the Sch.3 issues, as well as other applicable medical evidence with respect to the claimant (*EH v SSWP (ESA)* [2011] UKUT 21 (AAC), paras

27–30, 41–44). The focus, as in Sch.2, should be on "the claimant's functional ability to perform the particular aspect of the activity covered by a descriptor" (*EH v SSWP (ESA)* [2011] UKUT 21 (AAC), para.38, approving Judge Jacobs's in *GS v SSWP (ESA)* [2010] UKUT 244 (AAC), para.14). On the importance of a consistent approach to the descriptors under Sch.2 and Sch.3 respectively, see *SSWP v JL (ESA)* [2018] UKUT 291 (AAC).

4.414 There is no scoring system and the criteria are deliberately more stringent than in the LCWA. In Committee, the Minister for Employment and Welfare Reform explained both characteristics:

> "The levels of functional limitation used in the descriptors for determining limited capability for work-related activity are greater because we intend to place in the support group only the minority of customers who are so severely impaired that it would not be reasonable to require them to undertake work-related activity . . . People with less severe functional limitations across a range of descriptors might score highly and be inappropriately included in the support group when they might benefit from work-related activity . . . A number of case studies were provided in the background information, which hon. Members will find helpful. [See DWP, *Welfare Reform Bill: Draft Regulations and Supporting Material* (January 2007), pp.13–17.] Under the revised PCA, someone with a moderate learning disability would score 50 points. They would be significantly above the 15-point threshold, but we clearly would not wish to put even someone with 50 points into the support group automatically, because we are determined to ensure that the new system does not write off people with learning disabilities. The technical groups considered all the options. A crude points-based system would have unintended consequences." (*Hansard*, Standing Committee A, October 19, 2006 (afternoon), col.120 (Mr Jim Murphy MP)).

In *CD v SSWP (ESA)* [2012] UKUT (AAC) 289; [2013] AACR 12, Judge Levenson considered the relationship between the terms of descriptors in Sch.2 and the correlative provision in Sch.3, albeit in the context of the Schedules as at March 27, 2011:

> "Irrespective of what the Minister told the relevant committee, looking at the wording of the legislation and regulations I cannot find any support for the Secretary of State's argument that a person qualifying under Sch.3 must inevitably be more severely impaired than one who qualifies under Sch.2. The claimant's reference to the reaching descriptors [now Sch.2 para.3(a); Sch.3, para.3] is persuasive on this point" (para.21).

In *CN v SSWP (ESA)* [2014] UKUT 286 (AAC), Judge Markus applied *CD v SSWP (ESA)* [2012] UKUT 289 (AAC); [2013] AACR 12 to find erroneous in law a tribunal decision finding the claimant not to have limited capability for work-related activity when it had accepted that he had limited capability for work without reviewing the basis on which the decision-maker had proceeded (he had used the "old" pre January 2011 Sch.2), since that limited capability was not disputed. Judge Markus accepted that there are more substantial differences in wording between the two relevant descriptors in this case than between those in issue in *CD*, but was of the opinion that a claimant who fell within old activity 16(a) would fall within new activity 13(a) in the current version of Sch.2 and so would also fall within activity 11 in Sch.3. Moreover a person who satisfies activity 17(a) under the old Sch.2 must satisfy activity 12 of the current Sch.3, as long as the inability is due to cognitive impairment or mental disorder.

There is an equivalent of the "exceptional circumstances" provision applicable to the limited capability for work question, considered above. A claimant who does not pass the LCWRA can nonetheless be treated as having the requisite limited capability for work-related activity grounding membership of the support group where, by reason of the specific disease or bodily or mental disablement from which s/he suffers, "there would be a substantial risk to the mental or physical health of any person if the claimant were found not to have limited capability for work-related activity" (reg.35(2)).

There were only 11 activities in the original Sch.3. They covered walking or moving on level ground; rising from sitting and transferring from one seated position to another; picking up and moving or transferring by means of the upper body and arms; reaching; manual dexterity; continence; maintaining personal hygiene; eating and drinking (conveying food or drink to the mouth and chewing or swallowing it); learning or comprehension in the completion of tasks; personal action (planning, organisation, problem solving, prioritising or switching tasks); and communication. The terms of the descriptors were also more stringent than in the LCWA, to avoid removing too many people from the group which affords incentive to engage in work-related activity and thus denying them the opportunity to take steps to make real their fundamental right to work. Thus, as regards walking, the single descriptor (since amended) could only be met where a claimant could not "walk" more than 30 metres without repeatedly stopping, experiencing breathlessness or severe dis-comfort. "Walk" covered walking with a walking stick, other aid or crutches, each if normally used; and embraced the claimant moving by manually propelling a wheel-chair. That on rising from sitting etc, required in effect that the claimant fulfilled two of the 15 point descriptors in the LCWA. Most, with counterparts in the LCWA, were couched in terms equivalent to the more difficult of their 15 point descriptors. That original Sch.2 will apply to all decisions made before March 28, 2011 and also beyond that date where ESA questionnaires had before that date been sent out to claimants or notified persons under the Migration Regulations (transferees from IB, IS (incapacity based) or SDA. But that concession on questionnaires sent out before March 28 will cease after six months (September 28, 2011) (see reg.2 of the amend-ing Regulations).

Those meeting the LCWRA test (or satisfying the "exceptional circumstances" provision) were placed in the support group and received the support component without having to satisfy work-related activity conditions, although they could voluntarily participate in those programmes. Their position could be reviewed peri-odically or where there had been a change of circumstances in the claimant's physi-cal or mental condition or it was thought that a previous determination was made in ignorance of or a mistake as to some material fact (reg.34(4), (5)). The threshold for membership of the support group was high; many claimants in receipt of the middle and higher rates of Disability Living Allowance (DLA) may not meet it. Those who fail to establish limited capability for work-related activity instead receive the work-related activity component.

Under the revised LCWRA assessment the subject of this commentary, now com-prising 16 activities, the threshold remains high, and the same basic rules on the support group continue to apply. But Government anticipated that the revisions and reformulations effected by the *Review* and *CMA* honing (see further the commentary to Sch.2, above) would mean a slight expansion of the numbers allocated to the support group because of a relaxed mobility descrip-tor (Activity 1 now aligns its requisite distance at 50 metres, as opposed to 30 metres, the same as its highest scoring LCWA counterpart), changes to the mental function assessment and the addition of another sensory impairment-related support group (*Review*, para.5.2). As regards Activities 1–15, each activity and single descriptor corresponds to descriptor (a) (usually the highest scoring but always the one hardest to satisfy) in the corresponding Activity in the LCWA in the revised Sch.2, above. Consequently, it is submitted that any case law on corresponding terms in those revised Sch.2 descriptors is applicable to those in Sch.3, as effective from March 28, 2011. Note, however, that the numbering does not correspond as between Schs 2 and 3. Thus in Sch.3 (LCWRA), there is no equivalent of Sch.2 (LCWA) activity 8 (Navigation and maintaining safety, using a guide dog or other aid if normally used), activity 10 (Consciousness during waking moments) or activity 15 (getting about). Similarly, there is in

Sch.2 (LCWA) itself, no equivalent of Sch.3 (LCWRA) multi-descriptor activities 15 (conveying food or drink to the mouth) or 16 (Chewing or swallowing food or drink). Instead, persons covered by those activities in the terms set out in Sch.3 (LCWRA) are from March 28, 2011 treated as having limited capability for work under ESA Regs, reg.20(g).

On the need to interpret the terms of both this Sch and Sch.2 against the background of a working environment, see the annotation to Sch.2 *(Approaching the Interpretation of the Schedule as a whole) (the LCWA is not a snapshot—the need for an approach characterized by "reasonableness")*.

Interpreting specific activities and descriptors

4.415   *Activity 1: "Mobilising unaided by another person with or without a walking stick, manual wheelchair or other aid if such aid can reasonably be used":* This descriptor contains two tests. As Judge Williams put it in *HD v SSWP (ESA)* [2014] UKUT 72 (AAC):

> "the "cannot either" … "or" wording is properly interpreted as meaning "one or the other of (a) and (b)". In other words, a claimant who can satisfy the Secretary of State or a tribunal that he or she cannot mobilise to the level of one or other of (a) and (b) is entitled to be regarded as meeting the descriptor as a whole even if he or she can mobilise to the extent that the other is met" (para.4, citing para.15 of his decision granting leave to appeal).

The Secretary of State accepted that interpretation *(ibid.,* para.5) to the same effect see *GC v SSWP (ESA)* [2014] UKUT 117 (AAC), applying *HD*, and *KB v SSWP (ESA)* [2014] UKUT 126 (AAC), both decisions on Activity 1 in Sch.2. In *AH v SSWP (ESA)* [2013] UKUT 118 (AAC); [2013] AACR 32, Judge Jacobs pointed up the difference in wording between descriptors 1(a) and 1(b). With 1(a), he saw it as impossible to read into it "the need for regularity" (para.14). In contrast the wording of 1(b), taking due account also of reg.34(2), demands mobilising "repeatedly", without "significant discomfort or exhaustion" and within a "reasonable timescale". Judge Jacobs saw these as "normal words in everyday use" and as being coloured by their context. But he saw

> "no reason why they should have a different meaning just because they appear in Schedule 3. The purpose of that Schedule is to identify claimants who are not required to take part in work-related activity. But it does so by reference to the nature and extent of their disabilities, not by reference to work-related activity itself. The effect of coming within Schedule 3 may differ from the effect of coming within Schedule 2, but the criteria for classifying claimants are the same. I am not going to attempt to define what these words mean. That would be wrong. It would be the wrong approach to statutory interpretation and would trespass impermissibly into the role of the First-tier Tribunal. It is not for the Upper Tribunal to give more specific content to the law than the language used in the legislation. The Upper Tribunal will not decide that 'repeatedly' means five times, ten times or any other number. Nor will the Upper Tribunal decide that 'reasonable timescale' means five seconds, five minutes or any other time.
>
> The correct approach was explained by Lord Upjohn in *Customs and Excise Commissioners v Top Ten Promotions Ltd* [1969] 1 W.L.R. 1163, at 1171:
>
>> 'It is highly dangerous, if not impossible, to attempt to place an accurate definition upon a word in common use; you can look up examples of its many uses if you want to in the Oxford Dictionary but that does not help on definition; in fact it probably only shows that the word normally defies definition. The task of the court in construing statutory language such as that which is before your Lordships is to look at the mischief at which the Act is directed and then, in that light, to consider whether as a matter of common sense and every day usage the known, proved or admitted or properly inferred facts of the particular case bring the case within the ordinary meaning of the words used by Parliament.'

The key to applying the words of Activity 1 lies in making findings of fact relevant to those words that are as specific as the evidence allows. And, if the claimant is present at the hearing, the tribunal should ensure that it obtains evidence that is sufficient to that purpose. Just to take one example: the tribunal should have probed Mr H's evidence that he 'could not repeatedly do 50 metres'. How far could he walk before stopping? What made him stop? How did he feel? How soon could he proceed? How often could he repeat that process? This was particularly important in this case, because of the content of Mr H's evidence to the tribunal. At least as it was recorded by the judge—the record of proceedings does not have to be verbatim—his evidence was expressed in the language of the Schedule. The tribunal had to obtain evidence that would allow it to assess Mr H's answers by reference to that language. It could not do that if the evidence repeated that language. The tribunal would at least need to know what Mr H meant by 'repeatedly', as he might not be using it in the same way as in Activity 1" (paras 18–21).

As regards "could reasonably be ... used", Upper Tribunal Judges are divided on the permissible range of matters to examine, and the issue of the proper approach to take is to be decided by a tribunal of three Upper Tribunal Judges. See further the annotation to Sch.2, Activity 1, above.

Activity 7: "understanding communication"; Descriptor "cannot understand a simpler message such as the location of a fire escape due to sensory impairment": In *AT and VC v SSWP (ESA)* [2015] UKUT 445 (AAC); [2016] AACR 8, Judge Markus QC was "satisfied that Activity 7 in Schedule 3 was intended to correspond with the highest descriptor in Activity 7 of Schedule 2" (para.53). Furthermore, as with Sch.2, Activity 7 (both in its current and previous formulations: see para 54) "applied to a claimant who was unable to communicate by either verbal means or non-verbal means and it was not necessary for the claimant to be unable to communicate by both means" (para.53). Judge Markus's decision was followed in the context of the post-January 2013 version of the regulations by Judge Ward in *CM v SSWP (ESA)* [2016] UKUT 242 (AAC). Both decisions were followed by Judge Church in *RK v SSWP (ESA)* [2019] UKUT 345 (AAC).   **4.416**

Activity 9: "learning tasks"; Descriptor: "Cannot learn how to complete a simple task, such as setting an alarm clock, due to cognitive impairment or mental disorder: See the following guidance from Judge Rowley on this activity in *Secretary of State for Work and Pensions v AT (ESA)* [2017] UKUT 338 (AAC):   **4.417**

"cannot learn"

3. The activity is concerned with a claimant's ability to "learn" a new task, i.e. their ability to absorb, understand and retain information. As the WCA Handbook recognises, different people learn in different ways. They may prefer to watch a visual demonstration, have verbal instruction or read instructions. An inability to learn using one method would not generally lead to an overall inability to learn a new task if another way could be employed.

"how to complete a simple task"

4. "Simple task" is not defined. It would be inappropriate for me to offer any further definition, save perhaps to note the obvious - a simple task is one which is easy and straightforward. It is unlikely to involve more than one or two steps.

"such as setting an alarm clock"

5. The words "such as" are important. They confirm that the illustration given – of setting an alarm clock – is merely an example. Other instances may need to be considered by decision makers and tribunals. Further examples are listed in the WCA Handbook:

> "Brushing teeth. This would involve remembering to put toothpaste onto a brush and brushing all areas of teeth.
> Washing. This would involve the ability to use soap/shower gel and wash their

body.
Brushing hair.
Turning on the television/using basic functions on the TV remote control.
Getting a glass of water."

Judge Rowley also stressed the further fundamental requirement that the inability to learn a simple task be "due to cognitive impairment or mental disorder", as reinforced by the requirements of reg.34(6)(b).

4.418   *Activity 12: "coping with change": Descriptor: "Cannot cope with any change, due to cognitive or mental disorder, to the extent that day to day life cannot be managed":* In *CH v SSWP (ESA)* [2013] UKUT 207 (AAC), Judge Fordham held that

> "the word 'any' brings in changes of differing degree of significance. An individual will fail if, the majority of the time: (a) they cannot cope with significant change but (b) they can cope with less significant change. That is the consequence of the word 'any' in descriptor 12. An individual will succeed if, the majority of the time they cannot cope with 'any' change, even a less significant change. It is not of itself fatal that the claimant can sometimes cope with a change" (para.7).

4.419   *Activity 13: "coping with social engagement due to cognitive impairment or mental disorder"; Descriptor: "engagement in social contact is always precluded due to difficulty relating to others or significant distress experienced by the individual":* In *KB v SSWP* (ESA) [2013] UKUT 152 (AAC), Judge Parker considered the relationship between this wording (the requisite of "always") and the stipulation in reg.34(2) that "a descriptor applies to a claimant if that descriptor applies to the claimant for the majority of the time or, as the case may be, on the majority of the occasions on which the claimant undertakes or attempts to undertake the activity described by that descriptor". Having looked at definitions of "always" in the *Concise Oxford Dictionary*, Judge Parker concluded that neither this activity and descriptor, nor its counterpart in Activity 16 of Sch.2 set out an "all or nothing test". Rather "always" here

> "means 'repeatedly' or 'persistent' or 'often'. A 'majority' may be constituted by events which happen only on 50.1% of the possible occasions, but a greater frequency is required by the use of the word 'always'. It is a question of degree, but a fact finding tribunal is eminently suited to applying these subtle nuances of difference in a common sense way. It suffices to say in the present case, that because a claimant attends one tribunal hearing, and his GP accepts that he comes to the surgery very occasionally, does not *necessarily* entail the conclusion, as the tribunal clearly considered that it did, that it 'cannot be said that engagement in social contact is always precluded'" (para.14).

Judge Fordham took much the same approach in *CH v SSWP (ESA)* [2013] UKUT 207 (AAC) (para.8).

As regards "social engagement" and "social contact", Judge Parker, accepting the approach advanced by the Secretary of State's representative, thought that "social" to be "a simple reference to relations with other human beings" carrying no connotations of "leisure, pleasure or mutuality", so that a tribunal could properly look at evidence about business visits or contacts with professionals, as well as with friends, relatives and strangers. It was not tied to contact in an informal setting (see paras 15–17). What conduct constitutes the necessary "contact" or engagement" is

> "a matter of fact and degree, likewise eminently suitable for consideration by a tribunal as a matter of common sense having regard to all the circumstances. At one end of the scale, if a claimant sat silently throughout his tribunal hearing then, outwith exceptional circumstances, a reasonable tribunal could hold that this did not amount to the necessary 'contact' or 'engagement'; similarly, monosyllabic responses in such a context is a borderline scenario. However, where, as here, the claimant communicated with the tribunal on an extensive basis, according to the

record, then a conclusion that such did not amount to any 'social engagement' or 'social contact' would have been irrational" (para.18).

See also the annotation to Sch.2, Activity 16 for Judge Mark's narrower view that "always" did not mean "often" (*LM v SSWP (ESA)* [2013] UKUT 552 (AAC)), and for Judge Ward's disagreement with Judge Parker's interpretation of "social" (*AR v SSWP (ESA)* [2013] UKUT 446 (AAC)) and Judge Mark's qualified support for Judge Ward's approach (*LM v SSWP (ESA)* [2013] UKUT 553 (AAC)). See also, however, the annotation to reg.34(2) and the decision of the Court of Session in *SSWP v Brade* [2014] CSIH 39 XA81/13 (May 1, 2014); [2014] AACR 29.

See further the annotation to Sch.2, Activity 16 and in particular the decision of the three-judge panel in *JC v SSWP (ESA)* [2014] UKUT 352 (AAC); [2015] AACR 6, which follows Judge Parker on the meaning of "social", identifies the key elements of "engagement" and "coping" as "reciprocity, give and take, initiation and response", and identifies the conceptual test to be applied and the decision-making process to be followed for its application by tribunals.

Activity 14: Appropriateness of behaviour with other people, due to cognitive impairment or mental disorder: descriptor: Has, on a daily basis, uncontrollable episodes of aggressive or disinhibited behaviour that would be unreasonable in any workplace.

In *WT v SSWP (ESA)* [2013] UKUT 556 (AAC), Judge Gray considered the meaning of "on a daily basis". Rather than merely deploy a dictionary definition, he took the "mischief" approach to interpretation and reasoned thus:

"The mischief that the descriptor must be intended to remedy is the creation of an unsafe or otherwise unacceptable work environment for co-workers. The way in which the avoidance of that is accomplished is to exclude from the workplace those who, due to their mental health condition exhibit certain behaviour. If on virtually every day that they were at work they displayed such behaviour, would the fact that there were very rare days on which they did not prevent them from falling within the meaning of the descriptor? To answer "yes" to that question would not be to address the mischief. The descriptor must, then, be interpreted more widely than literally every day.

I fortify myself in this view because the ordinary meaning of the words "on a daily basis" seem to me to connote a lesser test than "every day". The phrase is not confined to events which happen literally every day. Someone might be said to read a particular newspaper on a daily basis even though there were periods when they did not, such as where they were abroad on holiday when it was not available. Walking the dog on a daily basis is an activity which may be interrupted by the ill-health of either dog or walker, but a short break would not change the very regular nature of the activity or make that description inapt.

The words "on a daily basis", then, in the context of schedule 3 descriptor 14, and its mirror descriptor under schedule 2, regulation 17 (a), means certainly more than for the majority of the time, that being the regulation 34 (2) test, and must mean more than frequently, that being the test of periodicity in regulation 17(b), but it does not mean literally every day or even on every working day. The essence is of this being an enduring position; one which is happening regularly, constantly or continually. It is for the tribunal to find the facts as to the frequency of the behaviour set out in the descriptor, and then apply this approach to those facts with their usual common sense" (paras 40–42).

It is vital to remember that under ESA Regs 2008 reg.34(6)(b), incapability of performing the activity in respect of this descriptor must arise from a specific mental illness or disablement. Alcohol misuse in itself is not such a disablement. To rank as disablement the misuse of alcohol must rank as "alcohol dependency" in terms of the "constellation of markers" found in quotations from *R(DLA) 6/06* in para.44 of the Three-Judge Panel's decision in *JG v SSWP (ESA)* [2013] UKUT 37 (AAC); [2013] AACR 23 (see annotation to ESA Regs 2008 reg.19) Accordingly, in *DR v*

SSWP (ESA) [2014] UKUT 188 (AAC); [2014] AACR 38, Judge May held the tribunal were right to hold that the descriptor did not apply. Moreover, he was persuaded that:

> "the volume of alcohol the claimant is said to drink on a daily basis would not in itself amount to the disinhibited behaviour referred to in descriptors 17(a) in Schedule 2 and 14 in Schedule 3. I see the force in Mr Webster's submission that disinhibited behaviour requires the context of an inhibition. I cannot see, and it has not been established, what the inhibition in this case is and how the drinking of a certain volume of alcohol amounts in itself to disinhibited behaviour. Disinhibited behaviour may result as a consequence of drinking specific quantities of alcohol but that is not the basis upon which the claimant's argument is put. Mr Orr seeks to widen "disinhibition" beyond the scope of what the statutory provisions can bear. The activity for both descriptors relates to the appropriateness of behaviour "with" other people, which suggests that the descriptor is intended to be applied in respect of behaviour which is more than the passive drinking of alcohol" (para.8).

Activity 16: Chewing or swallowing food or drink: In *WC v SSWP (ESA)* [2015] UKUT 304 (AAC); [2016] AACR 1, Judge Wikeley held that (given that one cannot "chew" drink) "this phrase means, in effect, and adding words to ensure clarity of meaning", "cannot *either* chew *and* swallow food or *swallow* drink" (para. 1). That decision was considered by Judge Jacobs in *IC v SSWP (ESA)* [2015] UKUT 615 (AAC), where the specific question that arose was whether a claimant can satisfy either descriptor 16a or 16b on account of the difficulties he experiences as a result of his false teeth. Judge Jacobs held that there was simply no evidence that activity 16 could apply on the facts of the instant case, given the requirements of reg.34(6) (b); thus there was no evidence that the claimant's difficulties with his false teeth arose from a specific bodily disease or disablement or from treatment (para.13). Judge Jacobs continued, without deciding, to consider whether false teeth are and aid or appliance (within reg.34(3)(b)) or a prosthesis (within reg.35(3)(a)) (para.14). Judge Jacobs stressed further the importance of applying the statutory test, rather than a substitute test, and gave the following guidance:

> "16. This brings me to another way to frame the issue, which is to concentrate on the food rather than the chewing. As I put it in my preliminary observations: what sort of food is envisaged by the descriptor? Again, there is a range of possibilities. It is not necessary to be able to eat any food, from the most tender to the toughest. That would set too demanding a standard. But liquidised food is a liquid, more akin to a drink than food, and does not require chewing.
> 17. A third, and better, way to frame the issue is to take the whole expression and ask: what is involved in chewing food? That at least preserves the immediate context. It makes the expression as a whole the object of the enquiry, rather than its individual components. It does not, though, produce any clear answer.
> 18. On any formulation, it is important to remember the context, which is a test of whether a claimant's capability for work and for work-related activity is restricted sufficiently to qualify for an employment and support allowance. The disability need not have a direct effect on the performance of work or work-related activity, as feeding oneself is not going to be involved in either case. So the scope of the Activity cannot be calibrated by its effect in those contexts. Nevertheless the effect of satisfying a descriptor in terms of benefit entitlement indicates that the disability should be significant. It must be such that 'it is not reasonable to require' the claimant to undertake work or the activity, to use the language of section 8(1) and 9(1) of the Welfare Reform Act 2007. The passage in the WCA Handbook reflects that, although it is not presented (and must not be taken) as a comprehensive statement of the physical conditions that can lead to the disabilities in Activity 16(a) and (b)."

Regulations 67(1)(a) and (2) and 68(1)(a) and (b)

SCHEDULE 4

AMOUNTS

PART 1

PRESCRIBED AMOUNTS

1. The weekly amounts specified in column (2) in respect of each person or couple specified in column (1) are the weekly amounts specified for the purposes of regulations 67(1) and 68 (prescribed amounts and polygamous marriages).

4.420

(1)			*(2)*	
Person or Couple			*Amount*	
(1)		*Single claimant—*	(1)	
	(a)	who satisfies the conditions set out in section 2(2) [¹² . . .] or 4(4) [¹²...] of the Act [¹³ or who is a member of the work-related activity group];	(a)	[¹⁴ £74.70];
	(b)	aged not less than 25;	(b)	[¹⁴ £74.70];
	(c)	aged less than 25.	(c)	[¹⁴ £59.20];
(2)		Lone parent [⁶ or a person who has no partner and who is responsible for and a member of the same household as a young person]—	(2)	
	(a)	who satisfies the conditions set out in section 4(4) [¹²...] of the Act [¹³ or who is a member of the work-related activity group and satisfies the conditions set out in Part 2 of Schedule 1 to the Act];	(a)	[¹⁴ £74.70;
	(b)	aged not less than 18;	(b)	[¹⁴ £74.70];
	(c)	aged less than 18.	(c)	[¹⁴ £59.20];
(3)		*Couple—*	(3)	
	(a)	where both members are aged not less than 18;	(a)	[¹⁴ £117.40];
	(b)	where one member is aged not less than 18 and the other member is a person under 18 who—	(b)	[¹⁴ £117.40];
		(i) [³ if that other member had not been a member] of a couple, would satisfy the requirements for entitlement to income support other than the requirement to make a claim for it; or		
		(ii) [³ if that other member had not been a member] of a couple, would satisfy the requirements for entitlement to an income-related allowance; or		
		(iii) satisfies the requirements of section 3(1)(f)(iii) of the Jobseekers Act (prescribed circumstances for persons aged 16 but less than 18); or		
		(iv) is the subject of a direction under section 16 of that Act (persons under 18: severe hardship);		
	(c)	where the claimant satisfies the conditions set out in section 4(4) [¹² . . .] of the Act [¹³ or the claimant is a member of the work-related activity group and satisfies the conditions set out in Part 2 of Schedule 1 to the Act] and both members are aged less than 18 and—	(c)	[¹⁴ £117.40];
		(i) at least one of them is treated as responsible for a child; or		

(1) *Person or Couple*	(2) *Amount*
(ii) had they not been members of a couple, each would have qualified for an income-related allowance; or	
(iii) had they not been members of a couple the claimant's partner would satisfy the requirements for entitlement to income support other than the requirement to make a claim for it; or	
(iv) the claimant's partner satisfies the requirements of section 3(1)(f)(iii) of the Jobseekers Act (prescribed circumstances for persons aged 16 but less than 18); or	
(v) there is in force in respect of the claimant's partner a direction under section 16 of that Act (persons under 18: severe hardship);	
(d) where both members are aged less than 18 and—	(d) [¹⁴ £89.94];
(i) at least one of them is treated as responsible for a child; or	
(ii) had they not been members of a couple, each would have qualified for an income-related allowance; or	
(iii) had they not been members of a couple the claimant's partner satisfies the requirements for entitlement to income support other than a requirement to make a claim for it; or	
(iv) the claimant's partner satisfies the requirements of section 3(1)(f)(iii) of the Jobseekers Act (prescribed circumstances for persons aged 16 but less than 18); or	
(v) there is in force in respect of the claimant's partner a direction under section 16 of that Act (persons under 18: severe hardship);	
(e) where the claimant is aged not less than 25 and the claimant's partner is a person under 18 who—	(e) [¹⁴ £74.70];
(i) would not qualify for an income-related allowance if the person were not a member of a couple;	
(ii) would not qualify for income support if the person were not a member of a couple;	
(iii) does not satisfy the requirements of section 3(1)(f)(iii) of the Jobseekers Act (prescribed circumstances for persons aged 16 but less than 18); and	
(iv) is not the subject of a direction under section 16 of that Act (persons under 18: severe hardship);	
(f) where the claimant satisfies the conditions set out in section 4(4) [¹²...] of the Act [¹³ or the claimant is a member of the work-related activity group and satisfies the conditions set out in Part 2 of Schedule 1 to the Act] and the claimant's partner is a person under 18 who—	(f) [¹⁴ £74.70];
(i) would not qualify for an income-related allowance if the person were not a member of a couple;	

(1)		(2)
Person or Couple		*Amount*

(1) Person or Couple			(2) Amount
	(ii)	would not qualify for income support if the person [¹ were] not a member of a couple;	
	(iii)	does not satisfy the requirements of section 3(1)(f)(iii) of the Jobseekers Act (prescribed circumstances for persons aged 16 but less than 18); and	
	(iv)	is not the subject of a direction under section 16 of that Act (persons under 18: severe hardship);	
(g)		where the claimant satisfies the conditions set out in section 4(4) [¹²...] of the Act [¹³ or the claimant is a member of the work-related activity group and satisfies the conditions set out in Part 2 of Schedule 1 to the Act] and both members are aged less than 18 and paragraph (c) does not apply;	(g) [¹⁴ £74.70];
[¹ (h)		where the claimant is aged not less than 18 but less than 25 and the claimant's partner is a person under 18 who—	(h) [¹⁴ £59.20];
	(i)	would not qualify for an income-related allowance if the person were not a member of a couple;	
	(ii)	would not qualify for income support if the person were not a member of a couple;	
	(iii)	does not satisfy the requirements of section 3(1)(f)(iii) of the Jobseekers Act (prescribed circumstances for persons aged 16 but less than 18); and	
	(iv)	is not the subject of a direction under section 16 of that Act (persons under 18: severe hardship);]	
(i)		where both members are aged less than 18 and paragraph (d) does not apply.	(i) [¹⁴ £59.20].

Regulations 67(1)(b) and 68(1)(c)

PART 2

PREMIUMS

2. Except as provided in paragraph 4, the weekly premiums specified in Part 3 of this Schedule are, for the purposes of regulation 67(1)(b) and 68(1)(c), to be applicable to a claimant who satisfies the condition specified in paragraphs 5 to 8 in respect of that premium.

4.421

3. An enhanced disability premium in respect of a person is not applicable in addition to a pensioner premium.

4.—(1) For the purposes of this Part of this Schedule, once a premium is applicable to a claimant under this Part, a person is to be treated as being in receipt of any benefit—
   (a) in the case of a benefit to which the Social Security (Overlapping Benefits) Regulations 1979 applies, for any period during which, apart from the provisions of those Regulations, the person would be in receipt of that benefit; and
   (b) for any period spent by a person in undertaking a course of training or instruction provided or approved by the Secretary of State under section 2 of the Employment and Training Act 1973, or by [³ Skills Development Scotland] or Highlands and Islands Enterprise under section 2 of the Enterprise and New Towns (Scotland) Act 1990, or for any period during which the person is in receipt of a training allowance.
   [⁷ (2) For the purposes of the carer premium under paragraph 8, a claimant is to be treated

as being in receipt of a carer's allowance by virtue of sub-paragraph (1)(a) only if and for so long as the person in respect of whose care the allowance has been claimed remains in receipt of—

(a) attendance allowance;

(b) the care component of disability living allowance at the highest or middle rate prescribed in accordance with section 72(3) of the Contributions and Benefits Act; [⁸ . . .]

(c) the daily living component of personal independence payment at the standard or enhanced rate in accordance with section 78(3) of the 2012 Act] [⁸ ; or

(d) armed forces independence payment.]

Pensioner premium

4.422   **5.** The condition is that the claimant or the claimant's partner has attained the qualifying age for state pension credit.

Severe disability premium

4.423   **6.**—(1) The condition is that the claimant is a severely disabled person.

(2) For the purposes of sub-paragraph (1), a claimant is to be treated as being a severely disabled person if, and only if—

(a) in the case of a single claimant, a lone parent [⁶ , a person who has no partner and who is responsible for and a member of the same household as a young person] or a claimant who is treated as having no partner in consequence of sub-paragraph (3)—

    (i) the claimant is in receipt of the care component [⁷ , the daily living component] [⁸ , armed forces independence payment] [⁵ or attendance allowance];

    (ii) subject to sub-paragraph (4), the claimant has no non-dependants aged 18 or over normally residing with the claimant or with whom the claimant is normally residing; and

    (iii) no person is entitled to, and in receipt of, [¹¹ a carer's allowance or has an award of universal credit which includes the carer element] in respect of caring for the claimant;

(b) in the case of a claimant who has a partner—

    (i) the claimant is in receipt of the care component [⁷ , the daily living component] [⁸ , armed forces independence payment] [⁵ or attendance allowance];

    (ii) the claimant's partner is also in receipt of the care component [⁷ , the daily living component] [⁸ , armed forces independence payment] or attendance allowance or, if the claimant is a member of a polygamous marriage, all the partners of that marriage are in receipt of the care component [⁷ , the daily living component] [⁸ , armed forces independence payment] or attendance allowance; and

    (iii) subject to sub-paragraph (4), the claimant has no non-dependants aged 18 or over normally residing with the claimant or with whom the claimant is normally residing, and,

either a person is entitled to, and in receipt of, a carer's allowance [¹¹ or has an award of universal credit which includes the carer element] in respect of caring for only one of the couple or, in the case of a polygamous marriage, for one or more but not all the partners of the marriage or, as the case may be, no person is entitled to, and in receipt of, such an allowance [¹¹ or has such an award of universal credit] in respect of caring for either member of the couple or any partner of the polygamous marriage.

(3) Where a claimant has a partner who does not satisfy the condition in sub-paragraph (2)(b)(ii) and that partner is blind or severely sight impaired or is treated as blind or severely sight impaired that partner is to be treated for the purposes of sub-paragraph (2) as if the partner were not a partner of the claimant.

(4) For the purposes of sub-paragraph (2)(a)(ii) and (b)(iii) no account is to be taken of—

(a) a person receiving attendance allowance, [⁷ the daily living component] [⁸ , armed forces independence payment] or the care component;

(b) subject to sub-paragraph (7), a person who joins the claimant's household for the first time in order to care for the claimant or the claimant's partner and immediately before so joining the claimant or the claimant's partner was treated as a severely disabled person; or

(c) a person who is blind or severely sight impaired or is treated as blind or severely sight impaired.

(5) For the purposes of sub-paragraph (2)(b) a person is to be treated—

(a) as being in receipt of attendance allowance or the care component if the person would, but for the person being a patient for a period exceeding 28 days, be so in receipt;

(b) as being entitled to, and in receipt of, a carer's allowance [¹¹ or having an award of universal credit which includes the carer element] if the person would, but for the person for whom the person was caring being a patient in hospital for a period exceeding 28 days, be so entitled and in receipt [¹¹ of carer's allowance or have such an award of universal credit] .

[⁷(c) as being in entitled to, and in receipt of, the daily living component if the person would, but for regulations under section 86(1) (hospital in-patients) of the 2012 Act, be so entitled and in receipt.]

(6) For the purposes of sub-paragraph (2)(a)(iii) and (b), no account is to be taken of an award of carer's allowance [¹¹ or universal credit which includes the carer element] to the extent that payment of such an award is backdated for a period before the date on which the award is first paid.

(7) Sub-paragraph (4)(b) is to apply only for the first 12 weeks following the date on which the person to whom that provision applies first joins the claimant's household.

(8) In sub-paragraph (2)(a)(iii) and (b), references to a person being in receipt of a carer's allowance [¹¹ or as having an award of universal credit which includes the carer element] are to include references to a person who would have been in receipt of that allowance [¹¹ or had such an award] but for the application of a restriction under section [⁴ 6B or] 7 of the Social Security Fraud Act 2001 (loss of benefit provisions).

(9) [¹¹ (a)] In this paragraph—

[⁹ "blind or severely sight impaired" means certified as blind or severely sight impaired by a consultant ophthalmologist and a person who has ceased to be certified as blind or severely sight impaired where that person's eyesight has been regained is, nevertheless, to be treated as blind or severely sight impaired for a period of 28 weeks following the date on which the person ceased to be so certified;]

"the care component" means the care component of disability living allowance at the highest or middle rate prescribed in accordance with section 72(3) of the Contributions and Benefits Act.

[¹¹ (b) A person has an award of universal credit which includes the carer element if the person has an award of universal credit which includes an amount which is the carer element under regulation 29 of the Universal Credit Regulations 2013.]

Enhanced disability premium

7.—(1) Subject to sub-paragraph (2), the condition is that—   **4.424**
    (a) the claimant's applicable amount includes the support component; [⁷ . . .]
    (b) the care component of disability living allowance is, or would, but for a suspension of benefit in accordance with regulations under section 113(2) of the Contributions and Benefits Act or, but for an abatement as a consequence of hospitalisation, be payable at the highest rate prescribed under section 72(3) of that Act in respect of—
        (i) the claimant; or
        (ii) the claimant's partner (if any) who is aged less than the qualifying age for state pension credit [⁷ ; [⁸ . . .]
[⁸ (c)   the daily living component is, or would, but for regulations made under section 86(1) (hospital in-patients) of the 2012 Act, be payable at the enhanced rate under section 78(2) of that Act in respect of—
        (i) the claimant; or
        (ii) the claimant's partner (if any) who is aged less then the qualifying age for state pension credit"]; or
    (d) armed forces independence payment is payable in respect of—
        (i) the claimant; or
        (ii) the claimant's partner (if any) who is aged less than the qualifying age for state pension credit.]

(2) An enhanced disability premium is not applicable in respect of—
    (a) a claimant who—
        (i) is not a member of a couple or a polygamous marriage; and
        (ii) is a patient within the meaning of regulation 69(2) and has been for a period of more than 52 weeks; or
    (b) a member of a couple or a polygamous marriage where each member is a patient within the meaning of regulation 69(2) and has been for a period of more than 52 weeks.

Carer premium

8.—(1) Subject to sub-paragraphs (2) and (4), the condition is that the claimant or the   **4.425**
claimant's partner is, or both of them are, entitled to a carer's allowance under section 70 of the Contributions and Benefits Act.

(2) Where a carer premium is awarded but—

- (a) the person in respect of whose care the carer's allowance has been awarded dies; or
- (b) in any other case the person in respect of whom a carer premium has been awarded ceases to be entitled to a carer's allowance, the condition for the award of the premium is to be treated as satisfied for a period of 8 weeks from the relevant date specified in sub-paragraph (3).

(3) The relevant date for the purposes of sub-paragraph (2) is—

- (a) where sub-paragraph (2)(a) applies, the Sunday following the death of the person in respect of whose care a carer's allowance has been awarded or the date of death if the death occurred on a Sunday; or
- (b) in any other case, the date on which the person who has been entitled to a carer's allowance ceases to be entitled to that allowance.

(4) Where a person who has been entitled to a carer's allowance ceases to be entitled to that allowance and makes a claim for an income-related allowance, the condition for the award of the carer premium is to be treated as satisfied for a period of 8 weeks from the date on which—

- (a) the person in respect of whose care the carer's allowance has been awarded dies; or
- (b) in any other case, the person who has been entitled to a carer's allowance ceased to be entitled to that allowance.

Persons in receipt of concessionary payments

4.426   9. For the purpose of determining whether a premium is applicable to a person under paragraphs 6, 7 and 8, any concessionary payment made to compensate that person for the non-payment of any benefit mentioned in those paragraphs is to be treated as if it were a payment of that benefit.

Persons in receipt of benefit

4.427   10. For the purposes of this Part of this Schedule, a person is to be regarded as being in receipt of any benefit if, and only if, it is paid in respect of the person and is to be so regarded only for any period in respect of which that benefit is paid.

PART 3

WEEKLY AMOUNT OF PREMIUMS SPECIFIED IN PART 2

4.428   11.—

Premium	Amount
(1) Pensioner premium for a person to whom paragraph 5 applies who—	(1)
(a) is a single claimant and—	(a)
(i) [12 . . .];	(i) [12 . . .];
(ii) is entitled to the support component; or	(ii) [15 £63.00];
[12 (iii) is not entitled to the support component;]	(iii) [15 £102.40];
(b) is a member of a couple and—	(b)
(i) [12 . . .]	(i) [12 . . .];
(ii) is entitled to the support component; or	(ii) [15 £113.50];
[12 (iii) is not entitled to the support component;]	(iii) [15 £152.90];
(2) Severe disability premium—	(2)
(a) where the claimant satisfies the condition in paragraph 6(2)(a);	(a) [15 £67.30];
(b) where the claimant satisfies the condition in paragraph 6(2)(b)—	(b)

Premium	Amount
(i) if there is someone in receipt of a carer's allowance or if the person or any partner satisfies that condition only by virtue of paragraph 6(5);	(i) [¹⁵ £67.30];
(ii) if no-one is in receipt of such an allowance.	(ii) [¹⁵ £134.60].
(3) Carer premium.	(3) [¹⁵ £37.30]; in respect of each person who satisfies the condition specified in [¹ paragraph 8(1)].
(4) Enhanced disability premium where the conditions in paragraph 7 are satisfied.	(4)(a) [¹⁵ £17.20]; in respect of each person who is neither— (i) a child or young person; nor (ii) a member of a couple or a polygamous marriage, in respect of whom the conditions specified in paragraph 7 are satisfied; (b) [¹⁵ £24.60]; where the claimant is a member of a couple or a polygamous marriage and the conditions specified in [¹ paragraph 7] are satisfied in respect of a member of that couple or polygamous marriage.

Regulation 67(3)

PART 4

[¹² THE COMPONENT]

12. [¹² . . .].   4.429

13. The amount of the support component is [¹⁶ £39.40].

AMENDMENTS

1. Employment and Support Allowance (Miscellaneous Amendments) Regulations 2008 (SI 2008/2428) reg.14 (October 27, 2008).
2. Social Security (Miscellaneous Amendments) Regulations 2009 (SI 2009/583) reg.10(2) (April 6, 2009).
3. Social Security (Miscellaneous Amendments) (No.4) Regulations 2009 (SI 2009/2655) reg.11(1) and (16) (October 26, 2009).
4. Social Security (Loss of Benefit) Amendment Regulations 2010 (SI 2010/1160) reg.12(1) and (3) (April 1, 2010).
5. Social Security (Miscellaneous Amendments) (No.3) Regulations 2011 (SI 2011/2425) reg.23(14) (October 30, 2011).
6. Social Security (Work-focused Interviews for Lone Parents and Partners) (Amendment) Regulations 2011 (SI 2011/2428) reg.5(5) (October 30, 2011).
7. Personal Independence Payment (Supplementary Provisions and Consequential Amendments) Regulations 2013 (SI 2013/388) reg.8 and Sch., para.40(1) and (5) (April 8, 2013).
8. Armed Forces and Reserve Forces Compensation Scheme (Consequential Provisions: Subordinate Legislation) Order 2013 (SI 2013/591) art.7 and Sch., para.37(1) and (5) (April 8, 2013).

9. Universal Credit and Miscellaneous Amendments (No. 2) Regulations 2014 (SI 2014/2888) reg.3(7)(a) (November 26, 2014).

10. Welfare Benefits Up-rating Order 2015 (SI 2015/30) art.11(1) and Sch.4 (April 6, 2015).

11. Universal Credit and Miscellaneous Amendments Regulations 2015 (SI 2015/1754) reg.19 (November 4, 2015).

12. Employment and Support Allowance and Universal Credit (Miscellaneous Amendments and Transitional and Savings Provisions) Regulations 2017 (SI 2017/204) reg.2(1) and (4) (April 3, 2017).

13. Employment and Support Allowance (Miscellaneous Amendments and Transitional and Savings Provision) Regulations 2017 (SI 2017/581) reg.7(1) and (4) (June 23, 2017, subject to the transitional and savings provision in reg.10).

14. Social Security Benefits Up-rating Order 2021 (SI 2021/162) art 31(1) and (2) and Sch.11 (April 12, 2021).

15. Social Security Benefits Up-rating Order 2021 (SI 2021/162) art 31(1) and (4) and Sch.12 (April 12, 2021).

16. Social Security Benefits Up-rating Order 2021 (SI 2021/162) art 31(6)(b) (April 12, 2021).

GENERAL NOTE

4.430   See the commentary to reg.67 and to Sch.2 to the IS Regs.

Claimants who fall within paras 2 to 7 of Sch.2 to the Employment and Support Allowance and Universal Credit (Miscellaneous Amendments and Transitional and Savings Provisions) Regulations 2017 (see below), but who are not entitled to the support component, continue to be entitled to the work-related activity component on a transitional basis. From April 6, 2020, the weekly amount of the work-related activity component in such cases is £29.70: see art.31(6)(a) of SI 2021/162.

If a claimant with transitional protection is also entitled to the pensioner premium, it is paid at the following rates from April 12, 2020:

Single claimant entitled to the work-related activity component	£72.20
Single claimant entitled to the support component	£63.00
Single claimant entitled to neither component	£102.40
Member of a couple entitled to the work-related activity component	£123.20
Member of a couple entitled to the support component	£113.50
Member of a couple entitled to neither	£152.90

see art.31(5) and Sch.11, para.2 of SI 2021/162. The only circumstances in which a transitionally protected claimant would not be entitled to either the work-related activity component or the support component would seem to be during the assessment phase. Although that phase must have ended long ago in most cases, a rate of the premium that would be applicable continues to be prescribed.

Those who are awarded the support component (except for some in-patients) also become entitled to have the enhanced disability premium included in their applicable amount when their entitlement to IRESA is calculated (see paras.7(1)(a) and (2)). In some cases, this will mean that claimants who were previously only entitled to CESA (*i.e.*, because they were excluded from IRESA by the means test) become entitled to IRESA for the first time. For some of the procedural issues to which this can give rise, see *DJ v Secretary of State for Work and Pensions (ESA)* [2015] UKUT 342 (AAC). Note, in particular, that ESA is a single benefit and it is not necessary for someone who is already entitled to CESA to make a fresh claim to receive IRESA.

Regulation 69

SCHEDULE 5

SPECIAL CASES

PART 1

AMOUNTS PRESCRIBED FOR THE PURPOSES OF SECTION 4(2) OF THE ACT

Claimants without accommodation

1. A claimant who is without accommodation.　　1. The amount applicable to the claim-　　**4.431**
ant under regulation 67(1)(a).

Members of religious orders

2. A claimant who is a member of, and fully　　2. Nil.
maintained by, a religious order.

Prisoners

3. A claimant　　　　　　　　　　　　　　　　3.　　　　　　　　　　　　　　　　**4.432**
(a) except where sub-paragraph (b) applies,　　(a) Nil;
　　who is a prisoner;
(b) who is detained in custody pending trial　　(b) only such amount, if any, as
　　or sentence following conviction by a court.　　may be applicable under regulation
　　　　　　　　　　　　　　　　　　　　　　67(1)(c) and the amount of nil under
　　　　　　　　　　　　　　　　　　　　　　regulation 67(3).

Specified cases of temporarily separated couples

4. A claimant who is a member of a couple and　　4. Either—
who is temporarily separated from the claimant's
partner where—
(a)　　one member of the couple is—
　　(i)　　not a patient but is residing in a care　(a)　the amount applicable to the
　　　　home, an Abbeyfield Home or an　　　　claimant as a member of a couple
　　　　independent hospital; or　　　　　　　　under regulation 67(1); or
　　(ii)　resident in premises used for the
　　　　rehabilitation of alcoholics or drug
　　　　addicts; or
　　(iii)　resident in accommodation
　　　　provided under section 3 of and
　　　　Part 2 of the Schedule to, the Polish
　　　　Resettlement Act 1947 (provision of
　　　　accommodation in camps); or
　　(iv)　participating in arrangements for
　　　　training made under section 2 of
　　　　the Employment and Training Act
　　　　1973 or section 2 of the Enterprise
　　　　and New Towns (Scotland) Act
　　　　1990 or attending a course at an
　　　　employment rehabilitation centre
　　　　established under that section of the
　　　　1973 Act, where the course requires
　　　　the person to live away from the
　　　　dwelling occupied as the home; or
　　(v)　in a probation or bail hostel
　　　　approved for the purpose by the
　　　　Secretary of State; and

(b)   the other member of the couple is—
(i)   living in the dwelling occupied as the home; or
(ii)   a patient; or
       residing in a care home, an Abbeyfield Home or an independent hospital.
(iii) Home or an independent hospital.

(b)   the aggregate of the claimant's applicable amount and that of the claimant's partner assessed under the provisions of these Regulations as if each of them were a single claimant or [³ , a lone parent or a person who has no partner and who is responsible for and a member of the same household as a young person], whichever is the greater.

Polygamous marriages where one or more partners are temporarily separated

4.433   5. A claimant who is a member of a polygamous marriage and who is temporarily separated from a partner, where one of them is living in the home where the other member is—

(a)   not a patient but is residing in a care home, an Abbeyfield Home or an independent hospital; or

(b)   resident in premises used for the rehabilitation of alcoholics or drug addicts; or

5.   Either—

(a)   the amount applicable to the members of the polygamous marriage under regulation 68; or

(b)   the aggregate of the amount applicable for the members of the polygamous marriage who remain in the home under regulation 68 and the amount applicable in respect of those members not in the home calculated as if each of them were a single claimant or [³ , a lone parent or a person who has no partner and who is responsible for and a member of the same household as a young person], whichever is the greater.

(c)   attending a course of training or instruction provided or approved by the Secretary of State where the course requires the person to live away from home; or

(d)   in a probation or bail hostel approved for the purpose by the Secretary of State.

Couple where one member is abroad

4.434   6. Subject to paragraph 7, a claimant who is a member of a couple where one member of the couple is temporarily absent from the United Kingdom.

6.   For the first 4 weeks of that absence, the amount applicable to them as a couple under regulation 67(1) or 69, as the case may be, and thereafter, the amount applicable to the claimant in Great Britain under regulation 67(1) or 69, as the case may be, as if the claimant were a single claimant [³ , a lone parent, or as the case may be a person who has no partner and who is responsible for and a member of the same household as a young person].

Couple or member of couple taking child or young person abroad for treatment

7.— (1) A claimant who is a member of a couple where either—
  (a) the claimant or the claimant's partner is; or
  (b) both the claimant and the claimant's partner are, absent from the United Kingdom in the circumstances specified
  (2) in sub-paragraph (2).
For the purposes of sub-paragraph (1)
  (a) the specified circumstances are—
in respect of a claimant, those in regulation 153(1)(a), (b), (c)(ii), (d) and (e);

  (b) in respect of a claimant's partner, as if regulation 153(1)(a), (b), (c)(ii), (d) and (e) applied to that partner.

7. For the first 26 weeks of that absence, the amount applicable to the claimant under regulation 67(1) or 69, as the case may be and, thereafter, if the claimant is in Great Britain the amount applicable to the claimant under regulation 67(1) or 69, as the case may be, as if the claimant were a single claimant [³ , a lone parent, or as the case may be a person who has no partner and who is responsible for and a member of the same household as a young person].

4.435

Polygamous marriages where any member is abroad

8. Subject to paragraph 9, a claimant who is a member of a polygamous marriage where one or more members of the marriage are temporarily absent from the United Kingdom.

8. For the first 4 weeks of that absence, the amount applicable to the claimant under regulation 68 and 69, as the case may be, and thereafter, if the claimant is in Great
Britain the amount applicable to the claimant under regulations 68 and 69, as the case may be, as if any members of the polygamous marriage not in the United Kingdom were not a member of the marriage.

4.436

Polygamous marriage: taking child or young person abroad for treatment

9.—(1) A claimant who is a member of a polygamous marriage where one or more members of the marriage is absent from the United Kingdom in the circumstances specified in sub-paragraph (2).
(2) For the purposes of sub-paragraph (1) the specified circumstances are—
  (a) in respect of a claimant, those in regulation 153(1)(a), (b), (c)(ii), (d) and (e);
  (b) in respect of a claimant's partner or partners, as the case may be, as if regulation 153(1)(a), (b), (c)(ii), (d) and (e) applied to that partner or those [¹ partners].

9. For the first 26 weeks of that absence, the amount applicable to the claimant under regulations 68 and 69, as the case may be, and thereafter, if the claimant is in Great Britain the amount applicable to the claimant under regulations 68 and 69, as the case may be, as if any member of the polygamous marriage not in the United Kingdom were not a member of the marriage.

4.437

Partner of a person subject to immigration control

10.
  (a) A claimant who is the partner of a person subject to immigration control.

10.
  (a) The amount applicable in respect of the claimant only under regulation 67(1)(a) any amount which may be applicable to
the claimant under regulation 67(1)(b) plus the amount applicable to the claimant under regulation 67(1)(c) or, as the case may be, regulation 69.

4.438

(b) Where regulation 68 (polygamous marriages) applies and the claimant is a person—

   (i) who is not subject to immigration control within the meaning of section 115(9) of the Immigration and Asylum Act; or

   (ii) to whom section 115 of that Act does not apply by virtue of regulation 2 of the Social Security (Immigration and Asylum) Consequential Amendments Regulations 2000; and

   (iii) who is a member of a couple and one or more of the person's partners is subject to immigration control within the meaning of section 115(9) of that Act and section 115 of that Act applies to that partner or those partners for the purposes of exclusion from entitlement to income-related allowance.

(b) the amount determined in accordance with that regulation or regulation 69 in respect of the claimant and any partners of the claimant who are not subject to immigration control within the meaning of section 115(9) of the Immigration and Asylum Act and to whom section 115 of that Act does not apply for the purposes of exclusion from entitlement to an income-related allowance.

Person from abroad

4.439   11. Person from abroad.   11.   Nil.

PART 2

AMOUNTS PRESCRIBED FOR THE PURPOSES OF SECTIONS 2(1) AND 4(2) OF THE ACT

[² Persons serving a sentence of imprisonment detained in hospital

4.440   12. A person serving a sentence of imprisonment detained in hospital.   12. The amount applicable under regulation 67(2) and the amount of nil under regulation 67(3).

Patients]

4.441   13. Subject to paragraph 12, a single claimant who has been a patient for a continuous period of more than 52 weeks or, where the claimant is one of a couple, [⁴ each] member of the couple has been a patient for a continuous period of more than 52 weeks.   13. The amounts applicable under regulation 67(1)(a), (c) and (2) and the amount of nil under regulation 67(3).

Person in hardship

4.442   14. A claimant who is a person in hardship.   14. The amount to which the claimant is entitled under regulation 67(1)(a) and (2) or 68(1)(a) is to be reduced by 20%.

AMENDMENTS

1. Employment and Support Allowance (Miscellaneous Amendments) Regulations 2008 (SI 2008/2428) reg.15 (October 27, 2008).

2. Social Security (Persons Serving a Sentence of Imprisonment Detained in Hospital) Regulations 2010 (SI 2010/442) reg.5(4) (March 25, 2010).

3. Social Security (Work-focused Interviews for Lone Parents and Partners) (Amendment) Regulations 2011 (SI 2011/2428) reg.5(6) (October 30, 2011).

4. Social Security (Miscellaneous Amendments) (No. 3) Regulations 2013 (SI 2013/2536) reg.13(1) and (35) (October 29, 2013).

GENERAL NOTE

See the commentary to reg.67 and to Sch.7 to the IS Regs.   **4.443**

MODIFICATION

The word "prisoner" in para.(3)(a) is defined by reg.69(2). With effect from April 8, 2020, that definition is modified by reg.2(1) and (2)(d) of the Social Security (Coronavirus) (Prisoners) Regulations 2020 (SI 2020/409). The modification provides that the ESA Regulations 2008 "are to be read as if the definition of "prisoner" did not include a person on temporary release in accordance with the provisions of the Prison Act 1952". By reg.6 of SI 2020/409 (as amended by reg.2 of SI 2020/1156), the modification will expire at the end of May 12, 2021.

REGULATIONS 67(1)(c), 68[¹(1)](d)

SCHEDULE 6

HOUSING COSTS

Housing costs

1.—(1) Subject to the following provisions of this Schedule, the housing costs applicable to   **4.444**
a claimant are those costs—
  (a) which the claimant or, where the claimant has a partner, that partner is, in accordance with paragraph 4, liable to meet in respect of the dwelling occupied as the home which the claimant or that claimant's partner is treated as occupying; and
  (b) which qualify under [³² paragraph 18].
(2) In this Schedule—
  [²⁶ . . .]
"housing costs" means those costs to which sub-paragraph (1) refers;
  [²⁶ . . .]
  [³² . . .]
(3) For the purposes of this Schedule a disabled person is a person—
  [¹³ (a) (i) in respect of whom the main phase employment and support allowance is payable to the claimant or to a person living with the claimant; or
         (ii) where they are the claimant or a person living with the claimant, in respect of whom there would be entitlement to an employment and support allowance [²⁸ . . .], but for the application of section 1A of the Act (duration of contributory allowance);]
  (b) who, had that person in fact been entitled to income support, would have satisfied the requirements of paragraph 12 of Schedule 2 to the Income Support Regulations (additional condition for the disability premium);
  (c) aged 75 or over; [²⁰ . . .]
  (d) who is disabled or severely disabled for the purposes of section 9(6) of the Tax Credits Act (maximum rate) [²⁰ ; or
  (e) who is entitled to an award of universal credit [²⁹ and has limited capability for work or limited capability for work and work-related activity as construed in accordance with regulations 39 and 40 of the Universal Credit Regulations 2013.]]
[¹⁴ (3A) For the purposes of this Schedule a claimant is a "work or training beneficiary" on any day in a linking term where the claimant—
  (a) had limited capability for work–
        (i) for more than 13 weeks in the most recent past period of limited capability for work; or

(ii) for 13 weeks or less in the most recent past period of limited capability for work where the claimant became entitled to an award of an employment and support allowance by virtue of a conversion decision which took effect from the commencement of the most recent past period of limited capability for work;

(b) ceased to be entitled to an allowance or advantage at the end of that most recent past period of limited capability for work; and

(c) became engaged in work or training within one month of so ceasing to be entitled.

(3B) A claimant is not a work or training beneficiary if—

(a) the most recent past period of limited capability for work was ended by a determination that the claimant did not have limited capability for work; and

(b) that determination was on the basis of a limited capability for work assessment.

(3C) In sub-paragraphs (3A) and (3B)—

"allowance or advantage" means any allowance or advantage under the Act or the Contributions and Benefits Act for which entitlement is dependent on limited capability for work;

"conversion decision" has the meaning given in regulation 5(2)(a) of the Employment and Support Allowance (Transitional Provisions, Housing Benefit and Council Tax Benefit) (Existing Awards) (No.2) Regulations 2010;

"linking term" means a period of 104 weeks from the first day immediately following the last day in a period of limited capability for work;

"most recent past period of limited capability for work" means the period of limited capability for work which most recently precedes the period in respect of which the current claim is made, including any period of which that previous period is treated as a continuation by virtue of regulation 145(1) (linking rules); and

"work" means work, other than work under regulation 45 (exempt work), for which payment is made or which is done in expectation of payment.]

(4) For the purposes of sub-paragraph (3), a person will not cease to be a disabled person on account of that person being disqualified for receiving benefit or treated as not having limited capability for work by virtue of the operation of section 18(1) to (3) of the Act.

Remunerative work

4.445

2.—(1) Subject to [¹sub-paragraphs (2) to (8)], a [¹non-dependant (referred to in this paragraph as "person")] is to be treated for the purposes of this Schedule as engaged in remunerative work if that person is engaged, or, where the person's hours of work fluctuate, is engaged on average, for not less than 16 hours a week, being work for which payment is made or which is done in expectation of payment.

(2) Subject to sub-paragraph (3), in determining the number of hours for which a person is engaged in work where that person's hours of work fluctuate, regard is to be had to the average of hours worked over—

(a) if there is a recognisable cycle of work, the period of one complete cycle (including, where the cycle involves periods in which the person does no work, those periods but disregarding any other absences);

(b) in any other case, the period of 5 weeks immediately prior to the date of claim, or such other length of time as may, in the particular case, enable the person's weekly average hours of work to be determined more accurately.

(3) Where no recognisable cycle has been established in respect of a person's work, regard is to be had to the number of hours or, where those hours will fluctuate, the average of the hours, which that person is expected to work in a week.

(4) A person is to be treated as engaged in remunerative work during any period for which that person is absent from work referred to in sub-paragraph (1) if the absence is either without good cause or by reason of a recognised, customary or other holiday.

(5) A person is not to be treated as engaged in remunerative work on any day on which the person is on maternity leave, paternity leave [²⁵ shared parental leave] [³⁴ , parental bereavement leave] or adoption leave or is absent from work because the person is ill.

(6) For the purposes of this paragraph, in determining the number of hours in which a person is engaged or treated as engaged in remunerative work, no account is to be taken of any hours in which the person is engaged in an employment or a scheme to which regulation 43(1) (circumstances under which partners of persons entitled to an income-related allowance are not to be treated as engaged in remunerative work) applies.

(7) For the purposes of sub-paragraphs (1) and (2), in determining the number of hours for which a person is engaged in work, that number is to include any time allowed to that person by that person's employer for a meal or for refreshment, but only where that person is, or expects to be, paid earnings in respect of that time.

[¹(8) A person is to be treated as not being engaged in remunerative work on any day in which that person falls within the circumstances prescribed in regulation 43(2) (circumstances in which partners of claimants entitled to an income-related allowance are not to be treated as engaged in remunerative work).

(9) Whether a claimant or the claimant's partner is engaged in, or to be treated as being engaged in, remunerative work is to be determined in accordance with regulations 41 or 42 (meaning of "remunerative work" for the purposes of paragraph 6(1)(e) and (f) of Schedule 1 to the Act) as the case may be.]

Previous entitlement to other income-related benefits

3.—(1) Where the claimant or the claimant's partner was in receipt of, or was treated as being in receipt of, an income-based jobseeker's allowance or income support not more than 12 weeks before one of them becomes entitled to an income-related allowance or, where the claimant or the claimant's partner is a person to whom paragraph 15(2) or (13) (linking rules) refers, not more than 26 weeks before becoming so entitled and—   **4.446**
- (a) the applicable amount for that income-based jobseeker's allowance or income support included an amount in respect of housing costs [³² under paragraph 16 of Schedule 2] to the Jobseeker's Allowance Regulations or, as the case may be, [³² paragraph 17 of Schedule 3] to the Income Support Regulations; and
- (b) the circumstances affecting the calculation of those housing costs remain unchanged since the last calculation of those costs,

the applicable amount in respect of housing costs for an income-related allowance is to be the applicable amount in respect of those costs current when entitlement to an income-based jobseeker's allowance or income support was last determined.

(2) Where a claimant or the claimant's partner was in receipt of state pension credit not more than 12 weeks before one of them becomes entitled to [¹an income-related allowance] or, where the claimant or the claimant's partner is a person to whom paragraph 15(2) or (13) (linking rules) refers, not more than 26 weeks before becoming so entitled, and—
- (a) the appropriate minimum guarantee included an amount in respect of housing costs [³² under paragraph 13 of Schedule 2] to the State Pension Credit Regulations 2002; and
- (b) the circumstances affecting the calculation of those housing costs remain unchanged since the last calculation of those costs,

the applicable amount in respect of housing costs for an income-related allowance is to be the applicable amount in respect of those costs current when entitlement to state pension credit was last determined.

(3) Where, in the period since housing costs were last calculated for an income-based job-seeker's allowance, income support or, as the case may be, state pension credit, there has been a change of circumstances, other than a reduction in the amount of an outstanding loan, which increases or reduces those costs, the amount to be met under this Schedule must, for the purposes of the claim for an income-related allowance, be recalculated so as to take account of that change.

Circumstances in which a person is liable to meet housing costs

4. A person is liable to meet housing costs where—   **4.447**
- (a) the liability falls upon that person or that person's partner but not where the liability is to a member of the same household as the person on whom the liability falls;
- (b) because the person liable to meet the housing costs is not meeting them, the claimant has to meet those costs in order to continue to live in the dwelling occupied as the home and it is reasonable in all the circumstances to treat the claimant as liable to meet those costs;
- (c) in practice the claimant shares the housing costs with other members of the household none of whom are close relatives either of the claimant or the claimant's partner, and—
  - (i) one or more of those members is liable to meet those costs; and
  - (ii) it is reasonable in the circumstances to treat the claimant as sharing responsibility.

Circumstances in which a person is to be treated as occupying a dwelling as the home

5.—(1) Subject to the following provisions of this paragraph, a person is to be treated as occupying as the home the dwelling normally occupied as the home by that person or, if that   **4.448**

person is a member of a family, by that person and that person's family and that person is not to be treated as occupying any other dwelling as the home.

(2) In determining whether a dwelling is the dwelling normally occupied as the claimant's home for the purposes of sub-paragraph (1) regard must be had to any other dwelling occupied by the claimant or by the claimant and that claimant's family whether or not that other dwelling is in Great Britain.

(3) Subject to sub-paragraph (4), where a claimant who has no partner is a full-time student or is on a training course and is liable to make payments (including payments of mortgage interest or, in Scotland, payments under heritable securities or, in either case, analogous payments) in respect of either (but not both) the dwelling which that claimant occupies for the purpose of attending the course of study or the training course or, as the case may be, the dwelling which that claimant occupies when not attending that course, that claimant is to be treated as occupying as the home the dwelling in respect of which that claimant is liable to make payments.

(4) A full-time student is not to be treated as occupying a dwelling as that student's home for any week of absence from it, other than an absence occasioned by the need to enter hospital for treatment, outside the period of study, if the main purposes of that student's occupation during the period of study would be to facilitate attendance on that student's course.

(5) Where a claimant has been required to move into temporary accommodation by reason of essential repairs being carried out to the dwelling normally occupied as the home and that claimant is liable to make payments (including payments of mortgage interest or, in Scotland, payments under heritable securities or, in either case, analogous payments) in respect of either (but not both) the dwelling normally occupied or the temporary accommodation, that claimant must be treated as occupying as the home the dwelling in respect of which that claimant is liable to make those payments.

(6) Where a claimant is liable to make payments in respect of two (but not more than two) dwellings, that claimant must be treated as occupying both dwellings as the home only—

    (a) where that claimant has left and remains absent from the former dwelling occupied as the home through fear of violence in that dwelling or of violence by a former member of the claimant's family and it is reasonable that housing costs should be met in respect of both that claimant's former dwelling and that claimant's present dwelling occupied as the home;

    (b) in the case of a couple or a member of a polygamous marriage where a partner is a fulltime student or is on a training course and it is unavoidable that that student, or they, should occupy two separate dwellings and reasonable that housing costs should be met in respect of both dwellings; or

    (c) in the case where a claimant has moved into a new dwelling occupied as the home, except where sub-paragraph (5) applies, for a period not exceeding four benefit weeks from the first day of the benefit week in which the move occurs if that claimant's liability to make payments in respect of two dwellings is unavoidable.

(7) Where—

    (a) a claimant has moved into a dwelling and was liable to make payments in respect of that dwelling before moving in;

    (b) that claimant had claimed an income-related allowance before moving in and either that claim has not yet been determined or it has been determined but an amount has not been included under this Schedule and if the claim has been refused a further claim has been made within four weeks of the date on which the claimant moved into the new dwelling occupied as the home; and

    (c) the delay in moving into the dwelling in respect of which there was liability to make payments before moving in was reasonable and—

        (i) that delay was necessary in order to adapt the dwelling to meet the disablement needs of the claimant or any member of the claimant's family;

       (ii) the move was delayed pending [[15] local welfare provision or] the outcome of an application for a social fund payment under Part 8 of the Contributions and Benefits Act to meet a need arising out of the move or in connection with setting up the home in the dwelling, and—

          (aa) a member of the claimant's family is aged five or under;

          (bb) the claimant is a person in respect of whom the main phase employment and support allowance is payable;

          (cc) the claimant's applicable amount includes a pensioner premium;

          (dd) the claimant's applicable amount includes a severe disability premium; or

          (ee) a child tax credit is paid for a member of the claimant's family who is disabled or severely disabled for the purposes of section 9(6) of the Tax Credits Act; or

(iii) the claimant became liable to make payments in respect of the dwelling while that claimant was a patient or was in residential accommodation,

that claimant is to be treated as occupying the dwelling as the home for any period not exceeding four weeks immediately prior to the date on which that claimant moved into the dwelling and in respect of which that claimant was liable to make payments.

(8) This sub-paragraph applies to a claimant who enters residential accommodation—

(a) for the purpose of ascertaining whether the accommodation suits that claimant's needs; and

(b) with the intention of returning to the dwelling which that claimant normally occupies as the home should, in the event, the residential accommodation prove not to suit that claimant's needs,

and while in the accommodation, the part of the dwelling which that claimant normally occupies as the home is not let or sub-let to another person.

(9) A claimant to whom sub-paragraph (8) applies is to be treated as occupying the dwelling that the claimant normally occupies as the home during any period (commencing on the day that claimant enters the accommodation) not exceeding 13 weeks in which the claimant is resident in the accommodation, but only in so far as the total absence from the dwelling does not exceed 52 weeks.

(10) A claimant, other than a claimant to whom sub-paragraph (11) applies, is to be treated as occupying a dwelling as the home throughout any period of absence not exceeding 13 weeks, if, and only if—

(a) that claimant intends to return to occupy the dwelling as the home;

(b) the part of the dwelling normally occupied by that claimant has not been let or sub-let to another person; and

(c) the period of absence is unlikely to exceed 13 weeks.

(11) This sub-paragraph applies to a claimant whose absence from the dwelling that that claimant normally occupies as the home is temporary and—

(a) that claimant intends to return to occupy the dwelling as the home;

(b) the part of the dwelling normally occupied by that claimant has not been let or sub-let; and

(c) that claimant is—

(i) detained in custody on remand pending trial or, as a condition of bail, required to reside—

(aa) in a dwelling other than the dwelling that claimant occupies as the home; or

(bb) in premises approved under section 13 of the Offender Management Act 2007,

or, detained pending sentence upon conviction;

(ii) resident in a hospital or similar institution as a patient;

(iii) undergoing or, as the case may be, that claimant's partner or dependant child is undergoing, in the United Kingdom or elsewhere, medical treatment or medically approved convalescence, in accommodation other than residential accommodation;

(iv) following, in the United Kingdom or elsewhere, a training course;

(v) undertaking medically approved care of a person residing in the United Kingdom or elsewhere;

(vi) undertaking the care of a child whose parent or guardian is temporarily absent from the dwelling normally occupied by that parent or guardian for the purpose of receiving medically approved care or medical treatment;

(vii) a claimant who is, whether in the United Kingdom or elsewhere, receiving medically approved care provided in accommodation other than residential accommodation;

(viii) a full-time student to whom sub-paragraph (3) or (6)(b) does not apply;

(ix) a claimant other than a claimant to whom sub-paragraph (8) applies, who is receiving care provided in residential accommodation; or

(x) a claimant to whom sub-paragraph (6)(a) does not apply and who has left the dwelling that claimant occupies as the home through fear of violence in that dwelling, or by a person who was formerly a member of that claimant's family; and

(d) the period of that claimant's absence is unlikely to exceed a period of 52 weeks, or in exceptional circumstances, is unlikely substantially to exceed that period.

(12) A claimant to whom sub-paragraph (11) applies is to be treated as occupying the dwelling that claimant normally occupies as the home during any period of absence not exceeding 52 weeks beginning with the first day of that absence.

(13) In this paragraph—

"medically approved" means certified by a medical practitioner;

"patient" means a person who is undergoing medical or other treatment as an in-patient in a hospital or similar institution;

[³ "period of study" has the meaning given in regulation 131 (interpretation);]

"residential accommodation" means accommodation which is a care home, an Abbeyfield Home or an independent hospital;

"training course" means such a course of training or instruction provided wholly or partly by or on behalf of or in pursuance of arrangements made with, or approved by or on behalf of, Scottish Enterprise, Highlands and Islands Enterprise, a government department or the Secretary of State.

Housing costs not met

4.449

6.—(1) No amount may be met under the provisions of this Schedule—

(a) in respect of housing benefit expenditure; or

(b) where the claimant is living in a care home, an Abbeyfield Home or an independent hospital except where the claimant is living in such a home or hospital during a temporary absence from the dwelling the claimant occupies as the home and in so far as they relate to temporary absences, the provisions of paragraph 5(8) to (12) apply to that claimant during that absence.

(2)–(14) [³² . . .]

Apportionment of housing costs

4.450

7.—(1) Where the dwelling occupied as the home is a composite hereditament and—

(a) before 1st April 1990 for the purposes of section 48(5) of the General Rate Act 1967 (reduction of rates on dwellings), it appeared to a rating authority or it was determined in pursuance of subsection (6) of section 48 of that Act that the hereditament, including the dwelling occupied as the home, was a mixed hereditament and that only a proportion of the rateable value of the hereditament was attributable to use for the purpose of a private dwelling; or

(b) in Scotland, before 1st April 1989 an assessor acting pursuant to section 45(1) of the Water (Scotland) Act 1980 (provision as to valuation roll) has apportioned the net annual value of the premises including the dwelling occupied as the home between the part occupied as a dwelling and the remainder,

the amounts applicable under this Schedule are to be such proportion of the amounts applicable in respect of the hereditament or premises as a whole as is equal to the proportion of the rateable value of the hereditament attributable to the part of the hereditament used for the purposes of a private tenancy or, in Scotland, the proportion of the net annual value of the premises apportioned to the part occupied as a dwelling house.

(2) Subject to sub-paragraph (1) and the following provisions of this paragraph, where the dwelling occupied as the home is a composite hereditament, the amount applicable under this Schedule is to be the relevant fraction of the amount which would otherwise be applicable under this Schedule in respect of the dwelling occupied as the home.

(3) For the purposes of sub-paragraph (2), the relevant fraction is to be obtained in accordance with the formula—

$$\frac{A}{A + B}$$

where—

A is the current market value of the claimant's interest in that part of the composite hereditament which is domestic property within the meaning of section 66 of the Act of 1988;

B is the current market value of the claimant's interest in that part of the composite hereditament which is not domestic property within that section.

(4) In this paragraph—

"composite hereditament" means—

(a) as respects England and Wales, any hereditament which is shown as a composite hereditament in a local non-domestic rating list;

(b) as respects Scotland, any lands and heritages entered in the valuation roll which are part residential subjects within the meaning of section 26(1) of the Act of 1987;

"local non-domestic rating list" means a list compiled and maintained under section 41(1) of the Act of 1988;

"the Act of 1987" means the Abolition of Domestic Rates Etc. (Scotland) Act 1987;

"the Act of 1988" means the Local Government Finance Act 1988.

(5) Where responsibility for expenditure which relates to housing costs met under this Schedule is shared, the amounts applicable are to be calculated by reference to the appropriate proportion of that expenditure for which the claimant is responsible.

Existing housing costs

8.—[²⁶ . . .]   **4.451**

[²⁶ Housing costs]

9.—(1) Subject to the provisions of this Schedule, the [²⁶ . . .] housing costs to be met in   **4.452**
any particular case are—
    (a) where the claimant has been entitled to an employment and support allowance for a
        continuous period of 39 weeks or more, an amount—
          (i) [³² . . .]
          (ii) equal to any payments which qualify under paragraph 18(1)(a) to (c);
    (b) in any other case, nil.
(2) [³² . . .]
(3) Where a claimant or that claimant's partner ceases to be in receipt of or treated as being
in receipt of income support, income-based jobseeker's allowance or state pension credit and
one of them becomes entitled to an income-related allowance in a case to which [¹paragraph 3]
applies, the eligible capital for the time being owing is to be recalculated on each anniversary
of the date on which the housing costs were first met for whichever of the benefits concerned
the claimant or that claimant's partner was first entitled.
(4)–(7)[²⁶ . . .]

General exclusions from [²⁶ paragraph 9]

10.—(1) [²⁶ Paragraph 9] will not apply where—   **4.453**
    (a) [⁷ the claimant or the claimant's partner] has attained the qualifying age for state
        pension credit;
    (b) the housing costs are payments—
          (i) under a co-ownership agreement;
          (ii) under or relating to a tenancy or licence of a Crown tenant; or
          (iii) where the dwelling occupied as the home is a tent, in respect of the tent and the
             site on which it stands.
(2) In a case falling within sub-paragraph (1), the housing costs to be met are—
    (a) where paragraph (a) of sub-paragraph (1) applies, an amount—
          (i) [³² . . .]
          (ii) equal to the payments which qualify under paragraph 18;
    (b) where paragraph (b) of sub-paragraph (1) applies, an amount equal to the payments
        which qualify under paragraph 18(1)(d) to (f).

The calculation for loans

11. [³² . . .]   **4.454**

General provisions applying to [²⁶ . . .] housing costs

12.—[³² . . .]   **4.455**

The standard rate

13.—[³² . . .]   **4.456**

Excessive Housing Costs

14.—[³² . . .]   **4.457**

Linking rule

15.—(1) [⁹ . . .] for the purposes of this Schedule—   **4.458**
    (a) a claimant is to be treated as being in receipt of an income-related allowance during
        the following periods—
          (i) any period in respect of which it was subsequently determined that that claim-
             ant was entitled to an income-related allowance; and
          (ii) any period of 12 weeks or less or, as the case may be, 52 weeks or less, in respect

of which that claimant was not in receipt of an income-related allowance and which fell immediately between periods in respect of which—

    (aa) that claimant was, or was treated as being, in receipt of an income-related allowance;

    (bb) that claimant was treated as entitled to an income-related allowance for the purpose of sub-paragraph (9) or (10); or

    (cc) (i) above applies;

(b) a claimant is to be treated as not being in receipt of an income-related allowance during any period other than a period to which (a)(ii) above applies in respect of which it is subsequently determined that that claimant was not so entitled;

(c) where—

    (i) the claimant was a member of a couple or a polygamous marriage; and

    (ii) the claimant's partner was, in respect of a past period, in receipt of an income-related allowance for that claimant's partner and the claimant; and

    (iii) the claimant is no longer a member of that couple or polygamous marriage; and

    (iv) the claimant made a claim for an income-related allowance within 12 weeks or, as the case may be, 52 weeks, of ceasing to be a member of that couple or polygamous marriage,

the claimant must be treated as having been in receipt of an income-related allowance for the same period as the claimant's former partner had been or had been treated, for the purposes of this Schedule, as having been;

(d) where the claimant's partner's applicable amount was determined in accordance with paragraph 1(1) (single claimant) or paragraph 1(2) [[12] (lone parents etc.)] of Part 1 of Schedule 4 (prescribed amounts) in respect of a past period, provided that the claim was made within 12 weeks or, as the case may be, 52 weeks, of the claimant and that claimant's partner becoming one of a couple or polygamous marriage, the claimant is to be treated as having been in receipt of an income-related allowance for the same period as the claimant's partner had been or had been treated, for the purposes of this Schedule, as having been;

(e) where the claimant is a member of a couple or a polygamous marriage and the claimant's partner was, in respect of a past period, in receipt of an income-related allowance for that claimant's partner and the claimant, and the claimant has begun to receive an income-related allowance as a result of an election by the members of the couple or polygamous marriage, that claimant is to be treated as having been in receipt of an income-related allowance for the same period as that claimant's partner had been or had been treated, for the purposes of this Schedule, as having been;

(f) where the claimant—

    (i) is a member of a couple or a polygamous marriage and the claimant's partner was, immediately before the participation by any member of that couple or polygamous marriage in an employment programme specified in regulation 75(1)(a)(ii) of the Jobseeker's Allowance Regulations, in the Intensive Activity Period specified in regulation 75(1)(a)(iv) of those Regulations, in receipt of an income-related allowance and the claimant's applicable amount included an amount for the couple or for the partners of the polygamous marriage; and

    (ii) has, immediately after that participation in that programme, begun to receive an income-related allowance as a result of an election under regulation 4(3) of the Social Security (Claims and Payments) Regulations 1987 by the members of the couple or polygamous marriage,

the claimant is to be treated as having been in receipt of an income-related allowance for the same period as that claimant's partner had been or had been treated, for the purposes of this Schedule, as having been;

(g) where—

    (i) the claimant was a member of a family of a person (not being a former partner) entitled to an income-related allowance and at least one other member of that family was a child or young person;

    (ii) the claimant becomes a member of another family which includes that child or young person; and

    (iii) the claimant made a claim for an income-related allowance within 12 weeks or, as the case may be, 52 weeks, of the date on which the person entitled to an income-related allowance mentioned in paragraph (i) above ceased to be so entitled,

the claimant is to be treated as being in receipt of an income-related allowance for the same period as that person had been or had been treated, for the purposes of this Schedule, as having been.

(2) [⁹ . . .]

(3) For the purposes of this Schedule, where a claimant has ceased to be entitled to an income-related allowance because that claimant or that claimant's partner is—

    (a) participating in arrangements for training made under section 2 of the Employment and Training Act 1973 or section 2 of the Enterprise and New Towns (Scotland) Act 1990; or

    (b) attending a course at an employment rehabilitation centre established under that section, the claimant is to be treated as if that claimant had been in receipt of an income-related allowance for the period during which that claimant or that claimant's partner was participating in such arrangements or attending such a course.

(4) For the purposes of this Schedule, a claimant who has ceased to be entitled to an income-related allowance because—

    (a) that claimant or that claimant's partner was participating in an employment programme specified in regulation 75(1)(a)(ii) of the Jobseeker's Allowance Regulations, in the Intensive Activity Period specified in regulation 75(1)(a)(iv) of those Regulations or in an employment zone scheme; and

    (b) in consequence of such participation the claimant or the claimant's partner was engaged in remunerative work or had an income [¹¹ equal to or] in excess of the claimant's applicable amount as prescribed in Part 9,

will be treated as if the claimant had been in receipt of an income-related allowance for the period during which that claimant or that claimant's partner was participating in that programme or activity.

(5) Where, for the purposes of sub-paragraphs (1), (3) and (4), a claimant is treated as being in receipt of an income-related allowance, for a certain period, that claimant will, subject to sub-paragraph (6), be treated as being entitled to an income-related allowance for the same period.

(6) [³² . . .]

(7) For the purposes of this Schedule, in determining whether a claimant is entitled to or to be treated as entitled to an income-related allowance, entitlement to a contribution-based jobseeker's allowance immediately before a period during which that claimant or that claimant's partner is participating in an employment programme specified in regulation 75(1)(a)(ii) of the Jobseeker's Allowance Regulations, in the Intensive Activity Period specified in regulation 75(1)(a)(iv) of those Regulations is to be treated as entitlement to an income-related allowance for the purposes of any requirement that a claimant is, or has been, entitled to an income-related allowance for any period of time.

(8) For the purposes of this Schedule, sub-paragraph (9) applies where a claimant is not entitled to an income-related allowance by reason only that the claimant has—

    (a) capital exceeding £16,000; or

    (b) income [⁹ equal to or] exceeding the applicable amount which applies in that claimant's case; or

[⁹ (bb) an amount of contributory allowance payable in respect of a claimant under section 2 that is equal to, or exceeds, the applicable amount in the claimant's case; or]

    (c) both capital exceeding £16,000 and income exceeding the applicable amount which applies in that claimant's case.

(9) A claimant to whom sub-paragraph (8) applies is to be treated as entitled to an income-related allowance throughout any period of not more than 39 weeks which comprises only days—

    (a) on which that claimant is entitled to a contributory allowance, a contribution-based jobseeker's allowance, statutory sick pay or incapacity benefit; or

    (b) on which that claimant is, although not entitled to any of the benefits mentioned in paragraph (a) above, entitled to be credited with earnings equal to the lower earnings limit for the time being in force in accordance with regulation 8A or 8B of the Social Security (Credits) Regulations 1975.

[¹² (10) Subject to sub-paragraph (11), for the purposes of this Schedule, a claimant is to be treated as entitled to an income-related allowance throughout any period of not more than 39 weeks following the refusal of a claim for an income-related allowance made by or on behalf of the claimant, if the claimant is a person to whom sub-paragraph (8) applies and who is—

    (a) a lone parent;

    (b) a person who has no partner and who is responsible for and a member of the same household as a young person; or

    (c) a person who is described in paragraph 4 or 5 of Schedule 1B of the Income Support (General) Regulations (person caring for another person).]

(11) Sub-paragraph (10) will not apply in relation to a claimant mentioned in that sub-paragraph who, during the period referred to in that sub-paragraph—

    (a) is engaged in, or is treated as engaged in, remunerative work or whose partner is engaged in, or is treated as engaged in, remunerative work;

[¹(b) is in full-time education and in receipt of disability living allowance [¹⁸, armed forces independence payment] [¹⁶ or personal independence payment];]

    (c) is temporarily absent from Great Britain, other than in the circumstances specified in regulation 152 or 153(1)(c)(ii) (temporary absence from Great Britain).

(12) In a case where—

    (a) sub-paragraphs (9) and (10) apply solely by virtue of sub-paragraph (8)(b); and

    (b) the claimant's income includes payments under a policy taken out to insure against the risk that the policy holder is unable to meet [³² any payment which qualifies under paragraph 18],

sub-paragraphs (9) and (10) will have effect as if for the words "throughout any period of not more than 39 weeks" there will be substituted the words "throughout any period that payments are made in accordance with the terms of the policy".

(13) This sub-paragraph applies—

    (a) to a person who claims an income-related allowance, or in respect of whom an income-related allowance is claimed and who—

        (i) received payments under a policy of insurance taken out to insure against loss of employment, and those payments are exhausted; and

        (ii) had a previous award of an income-related allowance where the applicable amount included an amount by way of housing costs; and

    (b) where the period in respect of which the previous award of an income-related allowance was payable ended not more than 26 weeks before the date the claim was made.

(14) Where sub-paragraph (13) applies, in determining—

    (a) [²⁶ . . .]

    (b) for the purposes of paragraph 9(1) whether a claimant has been entitled to an income-related allowance for a continuous period of 39 weeks or more,

any week falling between the date of the termination of the previous award and the date of the new claim is to be ignored.

(15) In the case of a claimant who is a work or training beneficiary, the references in sub-paragraphs (1)(a)(ii), (1)(c)(iv), (1)(d) and (1)(g)(iii) to a period of 12 weeks is to be treated as references to a period of 104 weeks.

(16) For the purposes of sub-paragraph (1)(a)(ii), (1)(c)(iv), (1)(d) and (1)(g)(iii), the relevant period will be—

    (a) 52 weeks in the case of a person to whom sub-paragraph (17) applies;

    (b) subject to sub-paragraph (15), 12 weeks in any other case.

(17) This sub-paragraph applies, subject to sub-paragraph (18), in the case of a claimant who, on or after 27th October 2008, has ceased to be entitled to an income-related allowance because that claimant or that claimant's partner—

    (a) has commenced employment as an employed earner or as a self-employed earner or has increased the hours in which that claimant or that claimant's partner is engaged in such employment;

    (b) is taking active steps to establish that claimant or that claimant's partner in employment as an employed earner or as a self-employed earner under any scheme for assisting persons to become so employed which is mentioned in regulation 19(1)(r)(i) to (iii) of the Jobseeker's Allowance Regulations; or

    (c) is participating in—

        (i) a New Deal option;

        (ii) an employment zone programme; or

        (iii) the self-employment route; or

        (iv) the Intensive Activity Period specified in regulation 75(1)(a)(iv) of the Jobseeker's Allowance Regulations,

and, as a consequence, that claimant or that claimant's partner was engaged in remunerative work or had income [¹¹ equal to or] in excess of the applicable amount as prescribed in Part 9.

(18) Sub-paragraph (17) is only to apply to the extent that immediately before the day on which the claimant ceased to be entitled to an income-related allowance, that claimant's housing costs were being met in accordance with paragraph [²⁶ . . .] 9(1)(a) or would have been so met but for any non-dependant deduction under paragraph 19.

(19) For the purpose of determining whether the linking rules set out in this paragraph apply in a case where a claimant's former partner was entitled to state pension credit, any reference to an income-related allowance in this Schedule is to be taken to include also a reference to state pension credit.

(20) Where a person is one to whom regulation 6(5) of the Income Support Regulations (persons not treated as engaged in remunerative work) applies, the period prescribed in para-

graph (6) of that regulation is not to be included for the purposes of any linking rule or for determining whether any qualifying or other period is satisfied.

Loans on residential property

   16.—[³² . . .]   **4.459**

Loans for repairs and improvements to the dwelling occupied as the home

   17.—[³² . . .]   **4.460**

[³² Housing costs]

   18.—(1) Subject to the deduction specified in sub-paragraph (2) and the reductions appli-   **4.461** cable in sub-paragraph (5), there are to be met under this paragraph the amounts, calculated on a weekly basis, in respect of the following housing costs—
   (a) payments by way of rent or ground rent relating to a long tenancy;
   (b) service charges;
   (c) payments by way of rentcharge within the meaning of section 1 of the Rentcharges Act 1977;
   (d) payments under a co-ownership scheme;
   (e) payments under or relating to a tenancy or licence of a Crown tenant;
   (f) where the dwelling occupied as the home is a tent, payments in respect of the tent and the site on which it stands.
   (2) Subject to sub-paragraph (3), the deductions to be made from the weekly amounts to be met under this paragraph are—
   (a) where the costs are inclusive of any of the items mentioned in paragraph 6(2) of Schedule 1 to the Housing Benefit Regulations 2006 (payment in respect of fuel charges), the deductions prescribed in that paragraph unless the claimant provides evidence on which the actual or approximate amount of the service charge for fuel may be estimated, in which case the estimated amount;
   (b) where the costs are inclusive of ineligible service charges within the meaning of para- graph 1 of Schedule 1 to the Housing Benefit Regulations 2006 (ineligible service charges) the amounts attributable to those ineligible service charges or where that amount is not separated from or separately identified within the housing costs to be met under this paragraph, such part of the payments made in respect of those housing costs which are fairly attributable to the provision of those ineligible services having regard to the costs of comparable services;
   (c) any amount for repairs and improvements, and for this purpose the expression "repairs and improvements" has [³² the meaning in sub-paragraph (6)].
   (3) Where arrangements are made for the housing costs, which are met under this paragraph and which are normally paid for a period of 52 weeks, to be paid instead for a period of 53 weeks, or to be paid irregularly, or so that no such costs are payable or collected in certain periods, or so that the costs for different periods in the year are of different amounts, the weekly amount will be the amount payable for the year divided by 52.
   (4) Where the claimant or a member of the claimant's family—
   (a) pays for reasonable repairs or redecorations to be carried out to the dwelling they occupy; and
   (b) that work was not the responsibility of the claimant or any member of the claimant's family; and
   (c) in consequence of that work being done, the costs which are normally met under this paragraph are waived,
then those costs will, for a period not exceeding 8 weeks, be treated as payable.
   (5) Where in England and Wales an amount calculated on a weekly basis in respect of housing costs specified in sub-paragraph (1)(e) includes water charges, that amount is to be reduced—
   (a) where the amount payable in respect of water charges is known, by that amount;
   (b) in any other case, by the amount which would be the likely weekly water charge had the property not been occupied by a Crown tenant.
   [³² (6) For the purposes of sub-paragraph (2)(c), "repairs and improvements" means any of the following measures undertaken with a view to maintaining the fitness of the dwelling for human habitation or, where the dwelling forms part of a building, any part of a building containing that dwelling—
   (a) provision of a fixed bath, shower, wash basin, sink or lavatory, and necessary associ-

ated plumbing, including the provision of hot water not connected to a central heating system;

(b) repairs to existing heating system;

(c) damp proof measures;

(d) provision of ventilation and natural lighting;

(e) provision of drainage facilities;

(f) provision of facilities for preparing and cooking food;

(g) provision of insulation of the dwelling occupied as the home;

(h) provision of electric lighting and sockets;

(i) provision of storage facilities for fuel or refuse;

(j) repairs of unsafe structural defects;

(k) adapting a dwelling for the special needs of a disabled person; or

(l) provision of separate sleeping accommodation for persons of different sexes aged 10 or over but under the age of 20 who live with the claimant and for whom the claimant or the claimant's partner is responsible.]

Non-dependant deductions

4.462

19.—(1) Subject to the following provisions of this paragraph, the following deductions from the amount to be met under the preceding paragraphs of this Schedule in respect of housing costs are to be made—

(a) in respect of a non-dependant aged 18 or over who is engaged in any remunerative work, [³⁶ £102.85];

(b) in respect of a non-dependant aged 18 or over to whom paragraph (a) does not apply, [³⁶ £15.95].

(2) In the case of a non-dependant aged 18 or over to whom sub-paragraph (1)(a) applies because that non-dependant is in remunerative work, where the claimant satisfies the Secretary of State that the non-dependant's gross weekly income is—

(a) less than [³⁶ £149.00], the deduction to be made under this paragraph will be the deduction specified in sub-paragraph (1)(b);

(b) not less than [³⁶ £149.00] but less than [³⁶ £217.00], the deduction to be made under this paragraph will be [³⁵ £36.65];

(c) not less than [³⁶ £217.00] but less than [³⁶ £283.00], the deduction to be made under this paragraph will be [³⁵ £50.30];

(d) not less than [³⁶ £283.00] but less than [³⁶ £377.00], the deduction to be made under this paragraph will be [³⁵ £82.30];

(e) not less than [³⁶ £377.00] but less than [³⁶ £469.00], the deduction to be made under this paragraph will be [³⁶ £93.70].

[³² (2A) Where a non-dependant deduction is being made under the Loans for Mortgage Interest Regulations 2017, the amount of the deduction under sub-paragraph (1) or (2) is to be reduced by an amount equal to that non-dependant deduction.]

(3) Only one deduction is to be made under this paragraph in respect of a couple or, as the case may be, the members of a polygamous marriage, and where, but for this sub-paragraph, the amount that would fall to be deducted in respect of one member of a couple or polygamous marriage is higher than the amount (if any) that would fall to be deducted in respect of the other, or any other, member, the higher amount is to be deducted.

(4) In applying the provisions of sub-paragraph (2) in the case of a couple or, as the case may be, a polygamous marriage, regard will be had, for the purpose of sub-paragraph (2), to the couple's or, as the case may be, all the members of the polygamous marriage's, joint weekly income.

(5) Where a person is a non-dependant in respect of more than one joint occupier of a dwelling (except where the joint occupiers are a couple or members of a polygamous marriage), the deduction in respect of that non-dependant is to be apportioned between the joint occupiers (the amount so apportioned being rounded to the nearest penny) having regard to the number of joint occupiers and the proportion of the housing costs in respect of the dwelling occupied as the home payable by each of them.

(6) No deduction is to be made in respect of any non-dependants occupying the dwelling occupied as the home of the claimant, if the claimant or any partner of the claimant is—

[²⁴ (a) certified as blind or severely sight impaired by a consultant ophthalmologist, or who is within 28 weeks of ceasing to be so certified;]

(b) receiving in respect of that claimant or that claimant's partner either—

(i) an attendance allowance; [¹⁷ . . .]

(ii) the care component of the disability living allowance [¹⁷ ; [¹⁹ . . .]

(iii) the daily living component] [¹⁹ ; or

(iv) armed forces independence payment].

(7) No deduction is to be made in respect of a non-dependant—

   (a) if, although the [¹non-dependant] resides with the claimant, it appears to the Secretary of State that the dwelling occupied as the non-dependant's home is normally elsewhere;

   (b) if the non-dependant is in receipt of a training allowance paid in connection with youth training;

   (c) if the non-dependant is a full-time student during a period of study or, if the non-dependant is not in remunerative work, during a recognised summer vacation appropriate to the non-dependant's course;

   (d) if the non-dependant is aged under 25 and in receipt of income support, an income-based jobseeker's allowance or an income-related allowance [²⁸ and they are still in the assessment phase in accordance with regulation 4];

   (e) in respect of whom a deduction in the calculation of a rent rebate or allowance falls to be made under regulation 74 of the Housing Benefit Regulations 2006 (non-dependant deductions);

   [¹(f) to whom, but for paragraph (5) of regulation 71 (definition of non-dependant) paragraph (4) of that regulation would apply;]   **4.463**

   (g) if the non-dependant is not residing with the claimant because the non-dependant has been a patient for a period in excess of 52 weeks, or is a prisoner, and for these purposes—

      (i) "patient" has the meaning given in paragraph 5(13) and "prisoner" has the meaning given in regulation 69(2) (special cases); and

      (ii) in calculating a period of 52 weeks as a patient, any two or more distinct periods separated by one or more intervals each not exceeding 28 days is to be treated as a single period; [²¹ ...]

   (h) if the non-dependant is in receipt of state pension credit; [²¹ or

  (ha) if the non-dependant is aged less than 25 and is entitled to an award of universal credit which is calculated on the basis that the non-dependant does not have any earned income;]

   [²² (7ZA) For the purposes of sub-paragraph (7)(b)]

      "youth training" means—

      (i) arrangements made under section 2 of the Employment and Training Act 1973 or section 2 of the Enterprise and New Towns (Scotland) Act 1990; or

      (ii) arrangements made by the Secretary of State for persons enlisted in Her Majesty's forces for any special term of service specified in regulations made under section 2 of the Armed Forces Act 1966 (power of Defence Council to make regulations as to engagement of persons in regular forces),

   for purposes which include the training of persons who, at the beginning of their training, are under the age of 18.

   [²¹ (7A) For the purposes of sub-paragraph (7)(ha), "earned income" has the meaning given in regulation 52 of the Universal Credit Regulations 2013.]

(8) In the case of a non-dependant to whom sub-paragraph (2) applies because that nondependent is in remunerative work, there is to be disregarded from that non-dependant's gross income—

   (a) any attendance allowance [¹⁷ , disability living allowance [¹⁹ , armed forces independence payment] or personal independence payment] received by that non-dependant;

   (b) [³⁵ any Grenfell Tower payment or] any payment made under [⁵ or by] the Macfarlane Trust, the Macfarlane (Special Payments) Trust, the Macfarlane (Special Payments) (No. 2) Trust, the Fund, the Eileen Trust [⁴ , MFET Limited] [¹⁰ , the Skipton Fund, the Caxton Foundation] [³⁰, the Scottish Infected Blood Support Scheme] [³³, an approved blood scheme] [³¹, the London Emergencies Trust, the We Love Manchester Emergency Fund] [³⁵, the National Emergencies Trust] or [¹ the Independent Living Fund (2006)] which, had that non-dependant's income fallen to be calculated under regulation 104 (calculation of income other than earnings), would have been disregarded under paragraph 22 of Schedule 8 (income in kind); and

   (c) any payment which, had that non-dependant's income fallen to be calculated under regulation 104 would have been disregarded under paragraph 41 of Schedule 8 (payments made under certain trusts and certain other payments);

   [³³ (d) any payment made under or by a trust, established for the purpose of giving relief and assistance to disabled persons whose disabilities were caused by the fact that during their mother's pregnancy she had taken a preparation containing the drug known as Thalidomide, and which is approved by the Secretary of State.]

Continuity with income support, an income-based jobseeker's allowance or state pension credit

4.464
20.—(1) For the purpose of providing continuity between income support, an income-based jobseeker's allowance or state pension credit and an employment and support allowance—

    (a) [²⁶...]

    (b) had the award of an employment and support allowance been an award of income support or an income-based jobseeker's allowance and the housing costs which would then have been met would have included an additional amount met in accordance with paragraph 7 of Schedule 3 to the Income Support Regulations or, as the case may be, paragraph 18(1)(b) of Schedule 2 to the Jobseeker's Allowance Regulations (add back), an amount equal to that additional amount must be added to the housing costs to be met under this Schedule, but that amount must be subject to the same qualifications and limitations as it would have been had the award been of income support or an income-based jobseeker's allowance; and

    (c) subject to paragraph 15(20), for the purposes of any linking rule or for determining whether any qualifying or other period is satisfied, any reference to an employment and support allowance in this Schedule must be taken also to include a reference to income support, an income-based jobseeker's allowance or state pension credit.

    (2) [³²...]

AMENDMENTS

1. Employment and Support Allowance (Miscellaneous Amendments) Regulations 2008 (SI 2008/2428) reg.16 (October 27, 2008).

2. Social Security (Housing Costs Special Arrangements) (Amendment and Modification) Regulations 2008 (SI 2008/3195) reg.2(1)(a) and (2) (January 5, 2009).

3. Social Security (Miscellaneous Amendments) (No.4) Regulations 2009 (SI 2009/2655) reg.11(17)(a) (October 26, 2009).

4. Social Security (Miscellaneous Amendments) (No.2) Regulations 2010 (SI 2010/641) reg.12(3)(e) (April 6, 2010).

5. Social Security (Miscellaneous Amendments) (No.2) Regulations 2010 (SI 2010/641) reg.12(5)(d) (April 6, 2010).

6. Social Security (Miscellaneous Amendments) (No.4) Regulations 2009 (SI 2009/2655) reg.11(17)(b) (April 12, 2010).

7. Social Security (Miscellaneous Amendments) (No.3) Regulations 2010 (SI 2010/840) reg.9(18) (June 28, 2010).

8. Social Security (Housing Costs) (Standard Interest Rate) Amendment Regulations 2010 (SI 2010/1811) reg.2(1)(d) and (2) (October 1, 2010).

9. Social Security (Miscellaneous Amendments) Regulations 2011 (SI 2011/674) reg.16(11) (April 11, 2011).

10. Social Security (Miscellaneous Amendments) (No.3) Regulations 2011 (SI 2011/2425) reg.23(8) (October 31, 2011).

11. Social Security (Miscellaneous Amendments) (No.3) Regulations 2011 (SI 2011/2425) reg.23(15) (October 31, 2011).

12. Social Security (Work-focused Interviews for Lone Parents and Partners) (Amendment) Regulations 2011 (SI 2011/2428) reg.5(7) (October 31, 2011).

13. Employment and Support Allowance (Duration of Contributory Allowance) (Consequential Amendments) Regulations 2012 (SI 2012/913), reg.9(4) (May 1, 2012).

14. Employment and Support Allowance (Amendment of Linking Rules) Regulations 2012 (SI 2012/919), reg.5(8) (May 1, 2012).

15. Social Security (Miscellaneous Amendments) Regulations 2013 (SI 2013/443), reg.9(4) (April 2, 2013).

16. Personal Independence Payment (Supplementary Provisions and Consequential Amendments) Regulations 2013 (SI 2013/388), reg.8 and Sch., Part 2, para.40(6)(a) (April 8, 2013).

17. Personal Independence Payment (Supplementary Provisions and Consequential Amendments) Regulations 2013 (SI 2013/388), reg. 8 and Sch., Part 2, para.40(6)(b) (April 8, 2013).

18. Armed Forces and Reserve Forces Compensation Scheme (Consequential Provisions: Subordinate Legislation) Order 2013 (SI 2013/591), art.7 and Sch., para.37(6)(a) (April 8, 2013).

19. Armed Forces and Reserve Forces Compensation Scheme (Consequential Provisions: Subordinate Legislation) Order 2013 (SI 2013/591), art.7 and Sch., para.37(6)(b) (April 8, 2013).

20. Universal Credit (Consequential, Supplementary, Incidental and Miscellaneous Provisions) Regulations 2013 (SI 2013/630) reg.37(7)(a) (April 29, 2013).

21. Universal Credit (Consequential, Supplementary, Incidental and Miscellaneous Provisions) Regulations 2013 (SI 2013/630) reg.37(7)(b) (April 29, 2013).

22. Social Security (Miscellaneous Amendments) (No.3) Regulations 2013 (SI 2013/2536) reg.13(36) (October 29, 2013).

23. Social Security (Miscellaneous Amendments) Regulations 2014 (SI 2014/591) reg.10(3) (April 28, 2014).

24. Universal Credit and Miscellaneous Amendments (No. 2) Regulations 2014 (SI 2014/2888) reg.3(7)(b) (November 26, 2014).

25. Shared Parental Leave and Statutory Shared Parental Pay (Consequential Amendments to Subordinate Legislation) Order 2014 (SI 2014/3255) art.20(8) (December 31, 2014).

26. Social Security (Housing Costs Amendments) Regulations 2015 (SI 2015/1647) reg.4 (April 1, 2016).

27. Social Security Benefits (Adjustment of Amounts and Thresholds) Regulations 2016 (SI 2016/242) reg.7(3) (April 11, 2016).

28. Employment and Support Allowance and Universal Credit (Miscellaneous Amendments and Transitional and Savings Provisions) Regulations 2017 (SI 2017/204) regs 2(1) and (5) (April 3, 2017).

29. Employment and Support Allowance and Universal Credit (Miscellaneous Amendments and Transitional and Savings Provisions) Regulations 2017 (SI 2017/204) reg.7(1) and Sch.1, para.15 (April 3, 2017).

30. Social Security (Scottish Infected Blood Support Scheme) Regulations 2017 (SI 2017/329) reg.8(1) and (3)(d) (April 3, 2017).

31. Social Security (Emergency Funds) (Amendment) Regulations 2017 (SI 2017/689) reg.8(1) and (3) (June 19, 2017).

32. Loans for Mortgage Interest Regulations 2017 (SI 2017/725) reg.18 and Sch.5, para.1(c) (April 6, 2018).

33. Social Security (Infected Blood and Thalidomide) Regulations 2017 (SI 2017/870) reg.8(1) and (3) (October 23, 2017).

34. Parental Bereavement Leave and Pay (Consequential Amendments to Subordinate Legislation) Regulations 2020 (SI 2020/354) reg.19(1) and (5) (April 6, 2020).

35. Social Security (Income and Capital) (Miscellaneous Amendments) Regulations 2020 (SI 2020/618) reg.7(1) and (10) (July 15, 2020).

36. Social Security Benefits Up-rating Order 2021 (SI 2021/162) art 31(1) and (7) (April 12, 2021).

DEFINITIONS

"Abbeyfield Home"—see reg.2(1).
"armed forces independence payment"—*ibid.*
"attendance allowance"—*ibid.*
"care home"—*ibid.*

"Caxton Foundation"—*ibid.*
"child"—ibid.
"child support maintenance"—see reg.2(2).
"claimant"—see reg.83(1).
"couple"—see reg.2(1).
"Crown tenant"—*ibid.*
"daily living component"—*ibid.*
"dwelling occupied as the home"—*ibid.*
"Eileen Trust"—*ibid.*
"family"—*ibid.*
"full-time student"—*ibid.*
"the Fund"—*ibid.*
"housing benefit expenditure"—*ibid.*
"independent hospital"—*ibid.*
"the Independent Living Fund (2006)"—*ibid.*
"local welfare provision "—*ibid.*
"Macfarlane (Special Payments) Trust"—*ibid.*
"Macfarlane (Special Payments) (No. 2) Trust"—*ibid.*
"Macfarlane Trust"—*ibid.*
"maintenance assessment"—see reg.2(2).
"maintenance calculation"—*ibid.*
"MFET Limited"—see reg.2(1).
"non-dependant"—see reg.71.
"parental bereavement leave"—see reg.2(1).
"partner"—*ibid.*
"period of study"—*ibid.*
"personal independence payment"—*ibid.*
"polygamous marriage"—*ibid.*
"shared parental leave"—*ibid.*
"Skipton Fund"—*ibid.*
"training allowance"—*ibid.*
"universal credit"—*ibid.*
"water charges"—*ibid.*
"young person"—*ibid.*

GENERAL NOTE

4.465   Sch. 6 is similar to Sch.3 to the IS Regulations/Sch.2 to the JSA Regulations 1996 (where there are differences between those Schedules Sch.6 generally adopts the income support model) and, in common with those schedules has been heavily amended to restrict its scope following the abolition of benefit payments for mortgage interest and their replacement by repayable loans: see, generally, the commentary to Sch.3 to the IS Regulations in Vol.II and the Loans for Mortgage Interest Regulations in Vol.V.

The differences from Sch. 3 before those changes are set out in full on pp.1331-3 of Vol.I of the 2017-18 edition. Those that remain relevant following the changes are as follows:

- *Paragraph 2* defines when a non-dependant will be treated as in remunerative work for the purposes of Sch.6. This paragraph is necessary because the definition of remunerative work in regs 41 and 42 only applies to the claimant and the claimant's partner and does not apply for the purposes of Sch.6 (see the definition of "remunerative work" in reg.2(1)). See also para.2(9) which specifically provides that whether a claimant or a claimant's partner is engaged in, or is to be treated as engaged in, remunerative work is to be determined in accordance with regs 41 or 42.

- There is no equivalent to para.2(2) of Sch.3 (which relates to trade disputes).

- *Paragraph 15(20)* of this Schedule provides that any period during which a claimant qualifies for a "housing costs run-on" under reg.6(5) of the Income Support Regulations does not count for the purpose of any linking rules or determining whether any qualifying or other period is satisfied under this Schedule.

- There is no waiting period for housing costs if either the claimant's partner or the claimant has reached the qualifying age for state pension credit (para.10(1)(a)) this is the same rule as for JSA (see para.8(1)(a) of Sch.2 to the JSA Regulations 1996) and reflects the fact that it is possible to claim ESA or JSA if a claimant is under pensionable age (WRA 2007 s.1(3)(c), Jobseekers Act s.1(2)(h)), whereas the cut-off in the case of income support is the qualifying age for state pension credit (s.124(1)(aa) SSCBA).

Regulations 96(2), 98(2)

SCHEDULE 7

Sums to be Disregarded in the Calculation of Earnings

1.—(1) In the case of a claimant who has been engaged in remunerative work as an employed earner or, had the employment been in Great Britain, would have been so engaged—

    (a) any earnings, other than items to which sub-paragraph (2) applies, paid or due to be paid from that employment which terminated before the first day of entitlement to an income-related allowance;

    (b) any earnings, other than a payment of the nature described in [² sub-paragraph (2)(a) or (b)(ii)], paid or due to be paid from that employment which has not been terminated where the claimant is not—

        (i) engaged in remunerative work; or

        (ii) suspended from employment.

(2) This sub-paragraph applies to—

[² (a) any payment of the nature described in—

        (i) regulation 95(1)(e) (earnings of employed earners), or

        (ii) section 28, 64 or 68 of the Employment Rights Act 1966 (guarantee payments, suspension from work on medical or maternity grounds); and]

    (b) any award, sum or payment of the nature described in—

        (i) regulation 95(1)(g) or (i); or

        (ii) section 34 or 70 of the Employment Rights Act 1996 (guarantee payments and suspension from work: complaints to employment tribunals),

including any payment made following the settlement of a complaint to an employment tribunal or of court proceedings.

2.—(1) In the case of a claimant to whom this paragraph applies, any earnings (other than a payment of the nature described in [² paragraph 1(2)(a) or (b)(ii)] which relate to employment which ceased before the first day of entitlement to an income-related allowance whether or not that employment has terminated.

(2) This paragraph applies to a claimant who has been engaged in part-time employment as an employed earner or, had the employment been in Great Britain, would have been so engaged; but it does not apply to a claimant who has been suspended from employment.

3. If the claimant's partner has been engaged in remunerative work as an employed earner or, had the employment been in Great Britain, would have been so engaged, any earnings paid or due to be paid on termination of that employment by way of retirement but only if—

    (a) on retirement the partner is entitled to a retirement pension under the Contributions and Benefits Act; or

    (b) the only reason the partner is not entitled to a retirement pension under the Contribution and Benefits Act is because the contribution conditions are not satisfied.

4.466

[⁷ **3A.** If the claimant's partner has been engaged in remunerative work as an employed earner or, had the employment been in Great Britain, would have been so engaged, any earnings paid or due to be paid on termination of that employment by way of retirement but only if—

    (a) on retirement the partner is entitled to a state pension under Part 1 of the Pensions Act 2014; or

    (b) the only reason the partner is not entitled to a state pension under Part 1 of the Pensions Act 2014 is because the partner does not have the minimum number of qualifying years.]

4. In the case of a claimant who has been engaged in remunerative work or part-time employment as a self-employed earner or, had the employment been in Great Britain, would have been so engaged and who has ceased to be so employed, from the date of the cessation of the claimant's employment any earnings derived from that employment except earnings to which regulation 92(2) (royalties etc.) applies.

5. In the case of a claimant who is undertaking work which falls within one of the categories in regulation 45(2) to (4) any earnings derived from that work which do not exceed the limits specified for that work of £20 in regulation 45(2) or, as the case may be, [⁴ 16 x National Minimum Wage] in regulation 45(3) or (4).

[³ **5A.** In the case of a claimant who receives a payment to which regulation 92(2) applies, £20, except where regulation 45(2) to (4) applies to the claimant, in which case the amounts specified in paragraph 6 shall apply, but only up to a maximum of £20.]

6. Where regulation 45(2) to (4) applies to the claimant and that claimant's earnings are less than—

    (a) in a case to which regulation 45(2) applies, £20;

    (b) in a case to which regulation 45(3) and (4) applies, [⁴ 16 x National Minimum Wage],

the earnings of the claimant's partner are to be disregarded to the extent that the claimant's earnings are less than £20 or, as the case may be, [⁴ 16 x National Minimum Wage], but only up to a maximum of £20.

7.—(1) In a case to which this paragraph applies, £20; but notwithstanding regulation 83 (calculation of income and capital of members of claimant's family and of a polygamous marriage), if this paragraph applies to a claimant it will not apply to the claimant's partner except where, and to the extent that, the earnings of the claimant which are to be disregarded under this paragraph are less than £20.

(2) Subject to sub-paragraph (3), this paragraph applies in the case of a claimant to whom regulation 40(2)(a), (b) or (e), 43(1)(a), (d), (e) or (f), or (2) or 45(5) applies.

(3) Where a claimant is doing the work set out in regulation 40(2)(b) and is also undertaking any of the categories of work set out in regulation 45(2) to (4), this paragraph applies only to the extent that the claimant's earnings are less than the limit of—

    (a) £20 set out in regulation 45(2); or

    (b) [⁴ 16 x National Minimum Wage] set out in regulation 45(3) and (4),

as the case may be.

(4) This paragraph applies, in a case where the claimant's partner is in part-time employment and paragraph 6 does not apply.

8. Notwithstanding the foregoing provisions of this Schedule, where two or more payments of earnings of the same kind and from the same source are to be taken into account in the same benefit week, because it has not been practicable to treat the payments under regulation 93(1)(b) (date on which income treated as paid) as paid on the first day of the benefit week in which they were due to be paid, there is to be disregarded from each payment the sum that would have been disregarded if the payment had been taken into account on the date on which it was due to be paid.

9. Any earnings derived from employment which are payable in a country outside the United Kingdom for such period during which there is a prohibition against the transfer to the United Kingdom of those earnings.

10. Where a payment of earnings is made in a currency other than sterling, any banking charge or commission payable in converting that payment into sterling.

11. Any earnings which are due to be paid before the date of claim and which would otherwise fall to be taken into account in the same benefit week as a payment of the same kind and from the same source.

[⁵ **11A.**—(1) In the case of an income-related employment and support allowance, where earnings to which sub-paragraph (2) applies (in aggregate with the claimant's other income (if any) calculated in accordance with this Part) exceed the applicable amount (calculated as specified in section 4(2) and (3) of the Act) less 10 pence, the amount of those earnings corresponding to that excess.

(2) This sub-paragraph applies to earnings, in so far as they exceed the amount disregarded under paragraph 7, derived by the claimant's partner from employment as a member of any [⁶ . . .] reserve force prescribed in Part 1 of Schedule 6 to the Social Security (Contributions) Regulations 2001 in respect of annual continuous training for a maximum period of 15 days in any calendar year [⁶ or in respect of training in the claimant's first year of training as a member of a reserve force for a maximum of 43 days in that year.]]

12. In the case of a claimant who—
    (a) has been engaged in employment as a member of any [⁶ . . .] reserve force prescribed in Part 1 of Schedule 6 to the Social Security (Contributions) Regulations 2001; and
    (b) by reason of that employment has failed to satisfy any of the conditions for entitlement to an income-related allowance other than paragraph 6(1)(a) of Schedule 1 to the Act (income not in excess of the applicable amount),
any earnings from that employment paid in respect of the period in which the claimant was not entitled to an income-related allowance.

13. In the case of a person to whom paragraph (5) of regulation 6 of the Income Support Regulations applies, any earnings.

14. In this Schedule—
    "part-time employment" means, if the person were entitled to income support, employment in which the person is not to be treated as engaged in remunerative work under regulation 5 or 6(1) and (4) of the Income Support Regulations (persons treated, or not treated, as engaged in remunerative work);
    "remunerative work", for the purposes of this paragraph and paragraphs 1, 3 and 4, has the meaning prescribed in regulation 5, except for paragraphs (3B) and (4) of that regulation, of the Income Support Regulations.

AMENDMENTS

1. Social Security (Miscellaneous Amendments) (No.3) Regulations 2009 (SI 2009/2343) reg.5(4) (October 1, 2009).

2. Social Security (Miscellaneous Amendments) (No.4) Regulations 2009 (SI 2009/2655) reg.11(18) (October 26, 2009).

3. Social Security (Miscellaneous Amendments) (No.3) Regulations 2010 (SI 2010/840) reg.9(19) (June 28, 2010).

4. Social Security (Miscellaneous Amendments) Regulations 2011 (SI 2011/674) reg.16(12) (April 11, 2011).

5. Social Security (Miscellaneous Amendments) (No.2) Regulations 2012 (SI 2012/2575) reg.5(3) (November 5, 2012).

6. Social Security (Members of the Reserve Forces) (Amendment) Regulations 2015 (SI 2015/389) reg.4(4)(a) (April 6, 2015).

7. Pensions Act 2014 (Consequential, Supplementary and Incidental Amendments) Order 2015 (SI 2015/1985) art.31(3) (April 6, 2016).

DEFINITIONS

    "benefit week"—see reg.2(1).
    "couple"—*ibid.*
    "employed earner"—*ibid.*
    "family"—*ibid.*
    "first year of training"—*ibid.*
    "National Minimum Wage"—*ibid.*
    "partner"—*ibid.*
    "polygamous marriage"—*ibid.*

GENERAL NOTE

Paragraphs 1–4

4.467   Paragraphs 1 to 4 are similar to paras 1 to 3 of Sch.8 to the Income Support Regulations/paras 1 to 4 of Sch.6 to the JSA Regulations 1996. They contain the earnings disregards on the termination of "remunerative work" (defined in para.14) and on the stopping of "part-time employment" (also defined in para.14) before the claim, as well as on the cessation of self-employment. Note that the definitions of "remunerative work" and "part-time employment" largely (but not entirely) import the income support tests.

Paragraphs 5–7

4.468   The disregards in these paragraphs are different from those in Sch.8 to the Income Support Regulations/Sch.6 to the JSA Regulations 1996 because of the different rules for the effect of work on entitlement to ESA (see regs 40–46 for these rules).

The earnings limit for "exempt work" under reg.45(2) is £20. From April 11, 2011 the earnings limit for such work under reg.45(3) or (4), rather than being a set amount, is 16 x the national minimum wage for adults aged 25 and over (rounded up to the nearest 50p or £1, as the case may be—see reg.45(9A)). This change was introduced so as to avoid the need to amend the regulations each time the national minimum wage changes. At the current rate of the national minimum wage (in April 2021) the earnings limit for exempt work under reg.45(3) or (4), after taking account of the rounding up, is £143 (see the note to the out-dated definition of "National Minimum Wage" in reg.2(1)).

Paragraph 5 disregards earnings from exempt work up to the relevant limit. In addition, if the claimant's earnings from such work are less than the relevant limit, his partner's earnings are ignored to the extent of the spare amount below the relevant limit, subject to a maximum of £20 (para.6).

Under para.7 earnings from the following attract a £20 disregard:
  (i)   work undertaken by the claimant as a councillor, as a member of the Disability Living Allowance Advisory Board (abolished on February 7, 2013 by the Public Bodies (Abolition of the Disability Living Allowance Advisory Board) Order 2013, arts 1(2) and 3) or as a tribunal member with a disability qualification, during an emergency to protect another person, property or livestock, or while receiving assistance in pursuing self-employment under a government scheme;
  (ii) work undertaken by the claimant's partner as a childminder, as a councillor, as a part-time fire-fighter, auxiliary coastguard, part-time member of a lifeboat crew or member of the Territorial army, or where the partner is receiving assistance under the "self-employment route" (defined in reg.2(1)), or is not to be treated as in remunerative work under one of the categories in reg.43(2);
  (iii) part-time employment (defined in para.14) undertaken by the claimant's partner where the disregard under para.6 does not apply.

4.469   But note that a couple cannot have a total disregard of more than £20.

Note also that if a claimant who is working as a member of the Disability Living Allowance Advisory Board (now abolished, see above) or as a tribunal member with a disability qualification is also doing work that counts as exempt work under reg.45(2) to (4), the disregard under para.7 only applies to the extent that his earnings are less than the relevant limit for that exempt work.

Paragraph 5A

4.470   This provides for a £20 disregard to apply to royalties, copyright payments and public lending right payments. The wording of para.5A is not exactly clear but it seems that the intent is that if a disregard in respect of exempt work already applies, the disregard under para.5A will depend on the amount by which the claimant's earnings fall below the relevant permitted work earnings limit, subject to the £20 maximum (see DMG, para.50468).

Paragraph 11A

Under para.11A earnings of a claimant's partner as a member of a reserve force **4.471** from training (i) for a maximum of 43 days in the first year of training (see the definition of "first year of training" in reg.2(1)); or (ii) for a maximum of 15 days' annual continuous training in any calendar year are disregarded to the extent that they would have the effect of reducing entitlement to income-related ESA to less than 10p per week. This disregard is in addition to the £20 disregard of a partner's earnings as a member of a reserve force in para.7(2).

Note that the additional words added at the end of para.11A(2) on April 6, 2015 refer to "the *claimant's* first year of training as a member of a reserve force". However, it seems likely that this is intended to refer in this context to the claimant's *partner's* first year of such training.

The purpose of para.11A is to enable entitlement to ESA to continue while a claimant's partner is attending such training (note that a claimant's partner is not treated as in remunerative work for the purposes of ESA if s/he is engaged in employment as a member of a reserve force: see reg.43(1)(e)(vi)). See also reg.91(4A) for the periods that earnings from such training are taken into account. The relevant period begins on the date that the earnings are treated as paid under reg.93 (see reg.91(4B)).

Paragraphs 8-12

Paragraphs 8 to 12 are similar to paras 10 to 13 and 15A of Sch.8 to the Income **4.472** Support Regulations/paras 13–16 and 19 of Sch.6 to the JSA Regulations 1996.

Regulation 104(2)

SCHEDULE 8

Sums to be Disregarded in the Calculation of Income other than Earnings

1. Any amount paid by way of tax on income which is taken into account under regulation **4.473** 104 (calculation of income other than earnings).

[¹⁹ **1A.** Any payment in respect of any travel or other expenses incurred, or to be incurred, by the claimant in respect of that claimant's participation in [²³ a scheme prescribed in regulation 3 of the Jobseeker's Allowance (Schemes for Assisting Persons to Obtain Employment) Regulations 2013] or the Mandatory Work Activity Scheme.]

2. Any payment in respect of any expenses incurred, or to be incurred, by a claimant who is—
    (a) engaged by a charitable or voluntary organisation; or
    (b) a volunteer,
if the claimant otherwise derives no remuneration or profit from the employment and is not to be treated as possessing any earnings under regulation 108(3) (notional income).

[⁵ **2A.** Any payment in respect of expenses arising out of the [³² claimant participating as a service user].]

3. In the case of employment as an employed earner, any payment in respect of expenses wholly, exclusively and necessarily incurred in the performance of the duties of the employment.

4. In the case of a payment under Parts 11 to 12ZB [⁵² or 12ZD] of the Contributions and Benefits Act or any remuneration paid by or on behalf of an employer to the claimant who for the time being is unable to work due to illness or maternity or who is taking paternity leave [³⁵ shared parental leave] [⁵², parental bereavement leave] or adoption leave—
    (a) any amount deducted by way of primary Class 1 contributions under the Contributions and Benefits Act;

(b) one-half of any sum paid by the claimant by way of a contribution towards an occupational or personal pension scheme.

5. In Northern Ireland, in the case of a payment under Parts 11 to 12ZB of the Social Security Contributions and Benefits (Northern Ireland) Act 1992, or any remuneration paid by or on behalf of an employer to the claimant who for the time being is unable to work due to illness or maternity or who is taking paternity leave, [35 shared parental leave] [52, parental bereavement leave] or adoption leave—

(a) any amount deducted by way of primary Class 1 contributions under that Act;

(b) one-half of any sum paid by way of a contribution towards an occupational or personal pension scheme.

6. Any guardian's allowance.

7.—(1) Any child tax credit.

(2) Any child benefit.

[12 [16 (3) Any increase in respect of a dependent child or dependent young person under section 80 or 90 of the Contributions and Benefits Act.]]

8. Any mobility component of disability living allowance [27 or the mobility component of personal independence payment].

9. Any concessionary payment made to compensate for the non-payment of—

(a) any payment specified in paragraph 8 or 11;

(b) an [1income-related] employment and support allowance, income support [31, universal credit] or [1 an income-based jobseeker's allowance].

10. Any mobility supplement or any payment intended to compensate for the non-payment of such a supplement.

11. Any attendance allowance [28, the care component of disability living allowance or the daily living component].

12. Any payment to the claimant as holder of the Victoria Cross or George Cross or any analogous payment.

13.—(1) Any payment—

(a) by way of an education maintenance allowance made pursuant to—
(i) regulations made under section 518 of the Education Act 1996;
(ii) regulations made under section 49 or 73(f) of the Education (Scotland) Act 1980; or
(iii) directions made under section 73ZA of the Education (Scotland) Act 1980 and paid under section 12(2)(c) of the Further and Higher Education (Scotland) Act 1992; [22 . . .]

(b) corresponding to such an education maintenance allowance, made pursuant to—
(i) section 14 or section 181 of the Education Act 2002; or
(ii) regulations made under section 181 of that Act [22; or

(c) in England, by way of financial assistance made pursuant to section 14 of the Education Act 2002.]

(2) Any payment, other than a payment to which sub-paragraph (1) applies, made pursuant to—

(a) regulations made under section 518 of the Education Act 1996;

(b) regulations made under section 49 of the Education (Scotland) Act 1980; or

(c) directions made under section 73ZA of the Education (Scotland) Act 1980 and paid under section 12(2)(c) of the Further and Higher Education (Scotland) Act 1992;

in respect of a course of study attended by a child or a young person or a person who is in receipt of an education maintenance allowance [22 or other payment] made pursuant to any provision specified in sub-paragraph (1).

14. Any payment made to the claimant by way of a repayment under regulation 11(2) of the Education (Teacher Student Loans) (Repayment etc.) Regulations 2002.

15.—(1) Any payment made pursuant to section 2 of the Employment and Training Act 1973 (functions of the Secretary of State) or section 2 of the Enterprise and New Towns (Scotland) Act 1990 (functions in relation to training for employment etc.) except a payment—

(a) made as a substitute for an employment and support allowance [12 or a jobseeker's allowance];

(b) of an allowance referred to in section 2(3) of the Employment and Training Act 1973 or section 2(5) of the Enterprise and New Towns (Scotland) Act 1990;

(c) intended to meet the cost of living expenses which relate to any one or more of the items specified in sub-paragraph (2) whilst a claimant is participating in an education, training or other scheme to help the claimant enhance that claimant's employment prospects unless the payment is a Career Development Loan paid pursuant to section 2 of the Employment and Training Act 1973 and the period of education or training or the scheme, which is supported by that loan, has been completed; or

(d) made in respect of the cost of living away from home to the extent that the payment relates to rent for which housing benefit is payable in respect of accommodation which is not normally occupied by the claimant as that claimant's home.

(2) The items specified in this sub-paragraph for the purposes of sub-paragraph (1)(c) are food, ordinary clothing or footwear, household fuel, rent for which housing benefit is payable, or any housing costs to the extent that they are met under regulation 67(1)(c) or 68(1)(d) (housing costs), of the claimant or, where the claimant is a member of a family, any other member of the claimant's family, or any council tax or water charges for which that claimant or member is liable.

[[17] **15A.** Any payment made to the claimant in respect of any travel or other expenses incurred, or to be incurred, in complying with a requirement to undertake work-related activity.]

16.—(1) Subject to sub-paragraph (2) and paragraph 41, any relevant payment made or due to be made at regular intervals.

(2) Sub-paragraph (1) is not to apply to a payment which is made by a person for the maintenance of any member of that person's family or of that person's former partner or of that person's children.

(3) In this paragraph, "relevant payment" means—
(a) a charitable payment;
(b) a voluntary payment;
(c) a payment (not falling within sub-paragraph (a) or (b) above) from a trust whose funds are derived from a payment made in consequence of any personal injury to the claimant;
(d) a payment under an annuity purchased—
  (i) pursuant to any agreement or court order to make payments to the claimant; or
  (ii) from funds derived from a payment made,
in consequence of any personal injury to the claimant; or
(e) a payment (not falling within sub-paragraph (a) to (d) above) received by virtue of any agreement or court order to make payments to the claimant in consequence of any personal injury to the claimant.

17. Subject to paragraphs 39 and 40, £10 of any of the following, namely—
(a) a war disablement pension (except insofar as such a pension falls to be disregarded under paragraph 10 or 11);
(b) a war widow's pension or war widower's pension;
(c) a pension payable to a person as a widow, widower or surviving civil partner under any power of Her Majesty otherwise than under an enactment to make provision about pensions for or in respect of persons who have been disabled or have died in consequence of service as members of the armed forces of the Crown;
(d) a guaranteed income payment [[3] and, if the amount of that payment has been abated to less than £10 by a [[6] pension or payment falling within article 31(1)(a) or (b) of the Armed Forces and Reserve Forces (Compensation Scheme) Order 2005], so much of [[6] that pension or payment] as would not, in aggregate with the amount of [[6] any] guaranteed income payment disregarded, exceed £10];
(e) a payment made to compensate for the non-payment of such a pension or payment as is mentioned in any of the preceding sub-paragraphs;
(f) a pension paid by the government of a country outside Great Britain which is analogous to any of the pensions or payments mentioned in sub-paragraphs (a) to (d) above;
[[39] (g) a pension paid by a government to victims of National Socialist persecution;]
(h) any widowed mother's allowance paid pursuant to section 37 of the Contributions and Benefits Act;
(i) any widowed parent's allowance paid pursuant to section 39A of the Contributions and Benefits Act.

18. Where a claimant receives income under an annuity purchased with a loan which satisfies the following conditions—
(a) that the loan was made as part of a scheme under which not less than 90% of the pro-

ceeds of the loan were applied to the purchase by the person to whom it was made of an annuity ending with that person's life or with the life of the survivor of two or more persons (in this paragraph referred to as "the annuitants") who include the person to whom the loan was made;

(b) that the interest on the loan is payable by the person to whom it was made or by one of the annuitants;

(c) that at the time the loan was made the person to whom it was made or each of the annuitants had attained the age of 65 [49 or, if it was higher at that time, pensionable age];

(d) that the loan was secured on a dwelling in Great Britain and the person to whom the loan was made or one of the annuitants owns an estate or interest in that dwelling; and

(e) that the person to whom the loan was made or one of the annuitants occupies the accommodation on which it was secured as that person's home at the time the interest is paid,

the amount, calculated on a weekly basis equal to—

(i) where, or insofar as, section 369 of the Income and Corporation Taxes Act 1988 (mortgage interest payable under deduction of tax) applies to the payments of interest on the loan, the interest which is payable after deduction of a sum equal to income tax on such payments at the applicable percentage of income tax within the meaning of section 369(1A) of that Act;

(ii) in any other case the interest which is payable on the loan without deduction of such a sum.

19. Any payment made to the claimant by a person who normally resides with the claimant, which is a contribution towards that person's living and accommodation costs, except where that person is residing with the claimant in circumstances to which paragraph 20 or 21 refers.

4.474 **20.** Where the claimant occupies a dwelling as the claimant's home and the dwelling is also occupied by another person and there is a contractual liability to make payments to the claimant in respect of the occupation of the dwelling by that person or a member of that person's family—

(a) where the aggregate of any payments made in respect of any one week in respect of the occupation of the dwelling by that person or a member of that person's family, or by that person and a member of that person's family, is less than £20, the whole of that amount; or

(b) where the aggregate of such payments is £20 or more per week, £20.

21. Where the claimant occupies a dwelling as the claimant's home and the claimant provides in that dwelling board and lodging accommodation, an amount, in respect of each person for whom such accommodation is provided for the whole or any part of a week, equal to—

(a) where the aggregate of any payments made in respect of any one week in respect of such accommodation provided to such person does not exceed £20, 100% of such payments; or

(b) where the aggregate of any such payments exceeds £20, £20 and 50% of the excess over £20.

22.—(1) Subject to sub-paragraphs (2) and (3), except where regulation 104(8)(b) (provision of support under section 95 or 98 of the Immigration and Asylum Act including support provided by virtue of regulations made under Schedule 9 to that Act in the calculation of income other than earnings) or regulation 107(3)(a) (notional income) applies, any income in kind;

(2) The exception under sub-paragraph (1) will not apply where the income in kind [53 is a Grenfell Tower payment or] is received from the Macfarlane Trust, the Macfarlane (Special Payments) Trust, the Macfarlane (Special Payments) (No.2) Trust, the Fund, the Eileen Trust[8, MFET Limited][20, the Skipton Fund, the Caxton Foundation][40, the Scottish Infected Blood Support Scheme] [42, an approved blood scheme][41, the London Emergencies Trust, the We Love Manchester Emergency Fund] [53, the National Emergencies Trust] or [1the Independent Living Fund (2006)].

(3) The first exception under sub-paragraph (1) will not apply where the claimant is the partner of a person subject to immigration control and whose partner is receiving support provided under section 95 or 98 of the Immigration and Asylum Act including support provided by virtue of regulations made under Schedule 9 to that Act and the income in kind is support provided in respect of essential living needs of the partner of the claimant and the claimant's dependants (if any) as is specified in regulations made under paragraph 3 of Schedule 8 to the Immigration and Asylum Act.

(4) The reference in sub-paragraph (1) to "income in kind" does not include a payment to a third party made in respect of the claimant which is used by the third party to provide benefits in kind to the claimant.

23.—(1) Any income derived from capital to which the claimant is or is treated under regulation 117 (capital jointly held) as beneficially entitled but, subject to sub-paragraph (2), not income derived from capital disregarded under paragraph 1, 2, 4 to 8, 10 or 16 of Schedule 9.

(2) Income derived from capital disregarded under paragraph 2 or 4 to 8 of Schedule 9 but only to the extent of—

    (a) any mortgage repayments made in respect of the dwelling or premises in the period during which that income accrued; or

    (b) any council tax or water charges which the claimant is liable to pay in respect of the dwelling or premises and which are paid in the period during which that income accrued.

(3) The definition of "water charges" in regulation 2(1) is to apply to sub-paragraph (2) with the omission of the words "in so far as such charges are in respect of the dwelling which a person occupies as the home".

24. Any income which is payable in a country outside the United Kingdom for such period during which there is prohibition against the transfer to the United Kingdom of that income.

25. Where a payment of income is made in a currency other than sterling, any banking charge or commission payable in converting that payment into sterling.

26.—(1) Any payment made to the claimant in respect of a child or young person who is a member of the claimant's family—

    (a) pursuant to regulations under section 2(6)(b), 3 or 4 of the Adoption and Children Act 2002 or in accordance with a scheme approved by the Scottish Ministers under section 51A of the Adoption (Scotland) Act 1978 (schemes for payment of allowances to adopters) [18 or in accordance with an adoption allowance scheme made under section 71 of the Adoption and Children (Scotland) Act 2007 (adoption allowances schemes)];

    (b) which is a payment made by a local authority in pursuance of section 15(1) of, and paragraph 15 of Schedule 1 to, the Children Act 1989 (local authority contribution to a child's maintenance where the child is living with a person as a result of a [33 child arrangements] order) [7, or in Scotland section 50 of the Children Act 1975 (payments towards maintenance of children)];

    (c) which is a payment made by an authority, as defined in Article 2 of the Children (Northern Ireland) Order 1995, in pursuance of Article 15 of, and paragraph 17 of Schedule 1 to, that Order (contributions by an authority to child's maintenance);

    (d) in accordance with regulations made pursuant to section 14F of the Children Act 1989 (special guardianship support services).

(2) Any payment, other than a payment to which sub-paragraph (1)(a) applies, made to the claimant pursuant to regulations under section 2(6)(b), 3 or 4 of the Adoption and Children Act 2002.

27. In the case of a claimant who has a child or young person—

    (a) who is a member of the claimant's family; and

    (b) who is residing at an educational establishment at which that child or young person is receiving relevant education,

any payment made to that educational establishment, in respect of that child or young person's maintenance by or on behalf of a person who is not a member of the family or by a member of the family out of funds contributed for that purpose by a person who is not a member of the family.

[13 **28.** Any payment made to the claimant with whom a person is accommodated by virtue of arrangements made—

    (a) by a local authority under—

        [44(i) section 22C of the Children Act 1989 (ways in which looked after children are to be accommodated and maintained,]

        [43(ia) section 81(2) of the Social Services and Well-being (Wales) Act 2014 (ways in which looked after children are to be accommodated and maintained),]

        (ii) section 26 of the Children (Scotland) Act 1995 (manner of provision of accommodation to child looked after by local authority), or

        (iii) regulations 33 or 51 of the Looked After Children (Scotland) Regulations 2009 (fostering and kinship care allowances and fostering allowances); or

(b) by a voluntary organisation under section 59(1)(a) of the 1989 Act (provision of accommodation by voluntary organisations).]

29. Any payment made to the claimant or the claimant's partner for a person ("the person concerned"), who is not normally a member of the claimant's household but is temporarily in the claimant's care, by—

(a) a health authority;

(b) a local authority but excluding payments of housing benefit made in respect of the person concerned;

(c) a voluntary organisation;

(d) the person concerned pursuant to section 26(3A) of the National Assistance Act 1948;

[³⁰ (da) a clinical commissioning group;

(db) the National Health Service Commissioning Board; [³⁶...]]

(e) [³⁰...]

(f) a Local Health Board established under section 16BA of the National Health Service Act 1977 or by an order made under section 11 of the Health Service (Wales) Act [³⁶ or

(g) the person concerned where the payment is for the provision of accommodation in respect of the meeting of that person's needs under section 18 or 19 of the Care Act 2014 (duty and power to meet needs for care and support) [⁴³ or under section 35 or 36 of the Social Services and Well-being (Wales) Act 2014 (duty and powers to meet care and support needs of an adult)].]

[⁴⁵**29A.**— Any payment made to a claimant under section 73(1)(b) of the Children and Young People (Scotland) Act 2014 (kinship care assistance).]

30.—(1) Any payment made by a local authority in accordance with—

(a) section 17, 23B, 23C or 24A of the Children Act 1989;

(b) section 12 of the Social Work (Scotland) Act 1968; [⁴³...]

[³⁸ (c) section 22, 26A, 29 or 30 of the Children (Scotland) Act 1995 (local authorities' duty to promote welfare of children, duty to provide continuing care and provision of advice and assistance to certain [⁴³ young persons); or

(d) the following sections of the Social Services and Well-being (Wales) Act 2014—

(aa) section 37 or 38, but excluding any direct payment made in accordance with regulations made under section 51 of that Act, or

(bb) section 109, 110, 114 or 115.]]

(2) Subject to paragraph (3), any payment (or part of a payment) made by a local authority in accordance with section 23C of the Children Act 1989 [³⁸ or section 22, 26A or 29 of the Children (Scotland) Act 1995 (local authorities' duty to promote welfare of children, duty to provide continuing care and provision of advice and assistance for certain young persons] to a person ("A") which A passes on to the claimant.

(3) Sub-paragraph (2) applies only where A—

(a) was formerly in the claimant's care; and

[³⁸ (b) is aged 18 or over or, in the case of a payment or part of a payment made in accordance with section 26A of the Children (Scotland) Act 1995, aged 16 or over, and]

(c) continues to live with the claimant.

[⁴⁶**31.** Any payment received under an insurance policy taken out to insure against the risk of being unable to maintain repayments on a loan which qualifies under Part 1 of Schedule 1 to the Loans for Mortgage Interest Regulations 2017 (legacy benefit claimants and SPC claimants) and used to meet such repayments.]

32.—(1) Except where paragraph 31 (or 33) applies, and subject to sub-paragraph (2), any payment made to the claimant which is intended to be used and is used as a contribution towards—

(a) any payment due on a loan if secured on the dwelling occupied as the home which does not qualify under [⁴⁶Part 1 of Schedule 1 to the Loans for Mortgage Interest Regulations];

[⁴⁶(b) any charge which qualifies in accordance with paragraph 18 of Schedule 6 (housing costs) to these Regulations or any interest payment on a loan which qualifies under Part 1 of Schedule 1 to the Loans for Mortgage Interest Regulations, to the extent that the charge or payment is not met under these Regulations or by loan payments (as the case may be)];

(c) any payment due on a loan which qualifies under [⁴⁶Part 1 of Schedule 1 to the Loans for Mortgage Interest Regulations] attributable to the payment of capital;

(d) any amount due by way of premiums on—
   (i) an insurance policy taken out to insure against the risk of being unable to make the payments referred to in (a) to (c) above; or
   (ii) a policy of insurance taken out to insure against loss or damage to any building or part of a building which is occupied by the claimant as the claimant's home;
(e) the claimant's rent in respect of the dwelling occupied by the claimant as the home but only to the extent that it is not met by housing benefit; or the claimant's accommodation charge but only to the extent that the actual charge exceeds the amount payable by a local authority in accordance with Part 3 of the National Assistance Act 1948 [³⁶ or Part 1 of the Care Act 2014 (care and support) [⁴³ or Part 4 of the Social Services and Well-being (Wales) Act 2014 (meeting needs) other than direct payments made in accordance with regulations made under section 50 or 52 of that Act]].

(2) This paragraph does not apply to any payment which is treated as possessed by the claimant by virtue of regulation 107(3)(c).

[⁴⁶(3) In this paragraph—
(a) "Loans for Mortgage Interest Regulations" means the Loans for Mortgage Interest Regulations 2017;
(b) "loan payments" has the meaning given in the Loans for Mortgage Interest Regulations.]

33.—(1) Subject to sub-paragraph (2), any payment received under an insurance policy, other than an insurance policy referred to in paragraph 31, taken out to insure against the risk of being unable to maintain repayments under a regulated agreement as defined for the purposes of the Consumer Credit Act 1974 or under a hire-purchase agreement or a conditional sale agreement as defined for the purposes of Part 3 of the Hire-Purchase Act 1964.

(2) A payment referred to in sub-paragraph (1) is to only be disregarded to the extent that the payment received under that policy does not exceed the amounts, calculated on a weekly basis which are used to—
(a) maintain the repayments referred to in sub-paragraph (1); and
(b) meet any amount due by way of premiums on that policy.

34.—(1) Subject to sub-paragraphs (2) and (3), in the case of a claimant residing in a care home, an Abbeyfield Home or an independent hospital, any payment, except a charitable or voluntary payment disregarded under paragraph 16 made to the claimant which is intended to be used and is used to meet the cost of maintaining the claimant in that home or hospital.

(2) This paragraph does not apply to a claimant for whom accommodation in a care home, an Abbeyfield Home or an independent hospital is provided by
[³⁶ (a) a local authority under section 26 of the National Assistance Act 1948; or
(b) a person other than a local authority under arrangements made with the person by a local authority in the exercise of the local authority's functions under section 18 or 19 of the Care Act 2014 (duty and power to meet needs for care and support) [⁴³ or under section 35 or 36 of the Social Services and Well-being (Wales) Act 2014 (duty and powers to meet care and support needs of an adult)].]

(3) The amount to be disregarded under this paragraph is not to exceed the difference between—
(a) the claimant's applicable amount; and
(b) the weekly charge for the accommodation.

35. Any social fund payment made pursuant to Part 8 of the Contributions and Benefits Act.

[²⁵ **35A.** Any local welfare provision.]

36. Any payment of income which under regulation 112 (income treated as capital) is to be treated as capital.

37. Any payment under Part 10 of the Contributions and Benefits Act (pensioner's Christmas bonus).

38. Any payment which is due to be paid before the date of claim which would otherwise fall to be taken into account in the same benefit week as a payment of the same kind and from the same source.

39. The total of a claimant's income or, if the claimant is a member of a family, the family's income and the income of any person which the claimant is treated as possessing under regulation 83(3) (calculation of income and capital of members of claimant's family and of a polygamous marriage) to be disregarded under regulation 133(2)(b) and 134(1)(c) (calculation of covenant income), regulation 137(1) and (2) (treatment of student loans), regulation 138(3) (treatment of payments from access funds) and paragraph 17 is in no case to exceed £20 per week.

40. Notwithstanding paragraph 39 where two or more payments of the same kind and from the same source are to be taken into account in the same benefit week, there is to be disregarded from each payment the sum which would otherwise fall to be disregarded under this Schedule; but this paragraph is to apply only in the case of a payment which it has not been practicable to treat under regulation 93(1)(b) (date on which income is treated as paid) as paid on the first day of the benefit week in which it is due to be paid.

41.—(1) Any payment made under [⁹ or by] the Macfarlane Trust, the Macfarlane (Special Payments) Trust, the Macfarlane (Special Payments) (No. 2) Trust ("the Trusts"), the Fund, the Eileen Trust[⁸, MFET Limited][²⁰, the Skipton Fund, the Caxton Foundation][⁴⁰, the Scottish Infected Blood Support Scheme] [⁴², an approved blood scheme][⁴¹, the London Emergencies Trust, the We Love Manchester Emergency Fund][⁵³, the National Emergencies Trust] or [¹the Independent Living Fund (2006)].

[⁵³(1A) Any Grenfell Tower payment.]

(2) Any payment by or on behalf of a person who is suffering or who suffered from haemophilia, or who is or was a qualifying person which derives from a payment made under [⁹ or by] any of the Trusts to which sub-paragraph (1) refers[⁵³, or from a Grenfell Tower payment,] and which is made to or for the benefit of—

(a) that person's partner or former partner from whom that person is not, or where that person has died was not, estranged or divorced or with whom that person has formed a civil partnership that has not been dissolved or, where that person has died, had not been dissolved at the time of that person's death;

(b) any child who is a member of that person's family or who was such a member and who is a member of the claimant's family; or

(c) any young person who is a member of that person's family or who was such a member and who is a member of the claimant's family.

(3) Any payment by or on behalf of the partner or former partner of a person who is suffering or who suffered from haemophilia or who is or was a qualifying person provided that the partner or former partner and that person are not, or if either of them has died were not, estranged or divorced or, where the partner or former partner and that person have formed a civil partnership, the civil partnership has not been dissolved or, if either of them has died, had not been dissolved at the time of the death, which derives from a payment made under [⁹ or by] any of the Trusts to which sub-paragraph (1) refers[⁵³, or from a Grenfell Tower payment,] and which is made to or for the benefit of—

(a) the person who is suffering from haemophilia or who is a qualifying person;

(b) any child who is a member of that person's family or who was such a member and who is a member of the claimant's family; or

(c) any young person who is a member of that person's family or who was such a member and who is a member of the claimant's family.

(4) Any payment by a person who is suffering from haemophilia or who is a qualifying person, which derives from a payment under [⁹ or by] any of the Trusts to which sub-paragraph (1) refers, [⁵³ or from a Grenfell Tower payment,] where—

(a) that person has no partner or former partner from whom that person is not estranged or divorced or with whom that person has formed a civil partnership that has not been dissolved, nor any child or young person who is or had been a member of that person's family; and

(b) the payment is made either—

(i) to that person's parent or step-parent; or

(ii) where that person at the date of the payment is a child, a young person or a full-time student who has not completed full-time education and had no parent or step-parent, to that person's guardian,

but only for a period from the date of the payment until the end of two years from that person's death.

(5) Any payment out of the estate of a person who suffered from haemophilia or who was a qualifying person, which derives from a payment under [⁹ or by] any of the Trusts to which sub-paragraph (1) refers, [⁵³ or from a Grenfell Tower payment,] where—

(a) that person at the date of that person's death (the relevant date) had no partner or former partner from whom that person was not estranged or divorced or with whom that person had formed a civil partnership that had not been dissolved, nor any child or young person who was or had been a member of that person's family; and

(b) the payment is made either—

    (i) to that person's parent or step-parent; or

    (ii) where that person at the relevant date was a child, a young person or a full-time student who had not completed full-time education and had no parent or step-parent, to that person's guardian,

but only for a period of two years from the relevant date.

(6) In the case of a person to whom or for whose benefit a payment referred to in this paragraph is made, any income which derives from any payment of income or capital made under or deriving from any of the Trusts [53 or from a Grenfell Tower payment].

(7) For the purposes of sub-paragraphs (2) to (6), any reference to the Trusts is to be construed as including a reference to the Fund, the Eileen Trust[8, MFET Limited], the Skipton Fund[21, the Caxton Foundation][40, the Scottish Infected Blood Support Scheme] [42, an approved blood scheme][41, the London Emergencies Trust, the We Love Manchester Emergency Fund][53, the National Emergencies Trust] and the London Bombings Relief Charitable Fund.

42. Any payment made by the Secretary of State to compensate for the loss (in whole or in part) of entitlement to housing benefit.

43. Any payment made to a juror or a witness in respect of attendance at a court other than compensation for loss of earnings or for the loss of a benefit payable under the benefit Acts.

44. Any payment in consequence of a reduction of council tax under section 13 [26 , section 13A] or section 80 of the Local Government Finance Act 1992 (reduction of liability for council tax).

45.—(1) Any payment or repayment made—

  (a) as respects England, under regulation 5, 6 or 12 of the National Health Service (Travel Expenses and Remission of Charges) Regulations 2003 (travelling expenses and health service supplies);

  (b) as respects Wales, under regulation 5, 6 or 11 of the National Health Service (Travelling Expenses and Remission of Charges) (Wales) Regulations 2007;

  (c) as respects Scotland, under regulation 3, 5 or 11 of the National Health Service (Travelling Expenses and Remission of Charges) (Scotland) (No. 2) Regulations 2003 (travelling expenses and health service supplies).

(2) Any payment or repayment made by the Secretary of State for Health [47 and Social Care], the Scottish Ministers or the Welsh Ministers which is analogous to a payment or repayment mentioned in sub-paragraph (1).

46. Any payment made to such persons entitled to receive benefits as may be determined by or under a scheme made pursuant to section 13 of the Social Security Act 1988 in lieu of vouchers or similar arrangements in connection with the provision of those benefits (including payments made in place of healthy start vouchers, milk tokens or the supply of vitamins).

47. Any payment made either by the Secretary of State for Justice or by the Scottish Ministers under a scheme established to assist relatives and other persons to visit persons in custody.

48. Any payment (other than a training allowance) made, whether by the Secretary of State or by any other person, under the Disabled Persons (Employment) Act 1944 to assist disabled persons to obtain or retain employment despite their disability.

49. Any supplementary pension under article 23(2) of the Naval, Military and Air Forces Etc. (Disablement and Death) Service Pensions Order 2006 (pensions to widows, widowers or surviving civil partners) and any analogous payment made by the Secretary of State for Defence to any person who is not a person entitled under that Order.

[3 **50.**–(1) If the claimant is in receipt of any benefit under Part 2, 3 or 5 of the Contributions and Benefits Act, any increase in the rate of that benefit arising under Part 4 (increases for dependants) or section 106(a) (unemployability supplement) of that Act, where the dependant in respect of whom the increase is paid is not a member of the claimant's family.

(2) If the claimant is in receipt of any pension or allowance under Part 2 or 3 of the Naval, Military and Air Forces Etc. (Disablement and Death) Service Pensions Order 2006, any increase in the rate of that pension or allowance under that Order, where the dependant in respect of whom the increase is paid is not a member of the claimant's family.]

51. In the case of a pension awarded at the supplementary rate under article 27(3) of the Personal Injuries (Civilians) Scheme 1983 (pensions to widows, widowers or surviving civil partners), the sum specified in paragraph 1(c) of Schedule 4 to that scheme.

52.—(1) Any payment which is—   **4.475**

  (a) made under any of the Dispensing Instruments to a widow, [1widower or surviving

civil partner] of a person—
  (i) whose death was attributable to service in a capacity analogous to service as a member of the armed forces of the Crown; and
  (ii) whose service in such capacity terminated before 31st March 1973; and
  (b) equal to the amount specified in article 23(2) of the Naval, Military and Air Forces Etc. (Disablement and Death) Service Pensions Order 2006.

(2) In this paragraph "the Dispensing Instruments" means the Order in Council of 19th December 1881, the Royal Warrant of 27th October 1884 and the Order by His Majesty of 14th January 1922 (exceptional grants of pay, non-effective pay and allowances).

53. Any payment made [⁴. . .] under section 12B of the Social Work (Scotland) Act 1968 [¹⁰ , or under sections 12A to 12D of the National Health Service Act 2006 (direct payments for health care)] [³⁶ or under sections 31 to 33 of the Care Act 2014 (direct payments)] or under regulations made under section 57 of the Health and Social Care Act 2001 (direct payments) [⁴³, or in accordance with regulations made under section 50 or 52 of the Social Services and Well-being (Wales) Act 2014 (direct payments)].

54.—(1) Any payment specified in sub-paragraph (2) to a claimant who was formerly a student and who has completed the course in respect of which those payments were made.
(2) The payments specified for the purposes of sub-paragraph (1) are—
  (a) any grant income and covenant income as defined for the purposes of Chapter 10 of Part 10;
  (b) any student loan as defined in Chapter 10 of Part 10;
  (c) any contribution as defined in Chapter 10 of Part 10 which—
    (i) is taken into account in ascertaining the amount of a student loan referred to in paragraph (b); and
    (ii) has been paid.

55.—(1) Subject to sub-paragraph (2), in the case of a person who is receiving, or who has received, assistance under the self-employment route, any payment to the person—
  (a) to meet expenses wholly and necessarily incurred whilst carrying on the commercial activity;
  (b) which is used or intended to be used to maintain repayments on a loan taken out by that person for the purposes of establishing or carrying on the commercial activity,
in respect of which such assistance is or was received.
(2) Sub-paragraph (1) is to apply only in respect of payments which are paid to that person from the special account as defined for the purposes of Chapter 5 of Part 10.

56. Any payment made with respect to a person on account of the provision of after-care under section 117 of the Mental Health Act 1983 or section 25 of the Mental Health (Care and Treatment) (Scotland) Act 2003 or the provision of accommodation or welfare services to which Part 3 of the National Assistance Act 1948 refers or to which the Social Work (Scotland) Act 1968 refers, [³⁶ or the provision of care and support under Part 1 of the Care Act 2014 (care and support)] [⁴³, or the provision of care and support in respect of an adult under Part 4 of the Social Services and Well-being (Wales) Act 2014 (duty and powers to meet care and support needs of an adult)] which falls to be treated as notional income under paragraph (6) of regulation 107 (payments made in respect of a person living in a care home, an Abbeyfield Home or an independent hospital).

57.—(1) Any payment of a sports award except to the extent that it has been made in respect of any one or more of the items specified in sub-paragraph (2).
(2) The items specified for the purposes of sub-paragraph (1) are food, ordinary clothing or footwear, household fuel, rent for which housing benefit is payable or any housing costs to the extent that they are met under regulation 67(1)(c) or 68(1)(d) (housing costs), of the claimant or, where the claimant is a member of a family, any other member of the claimant's family, or any council tax or water charges for which that claimant or member is liable.
(3) For the purposes of sub-paragraph (2) "food" does not include vitamins, minerals or other special dietary supplements intended to enhance the performance of the person in the sport in respect of which the award was made;

58. Where the amount of a subsistence allowance paid to a person in a benefit week exceeds the amount of income-based jobseeker's allowance that person would have received in that benefit week had it been payable to that person, less 50p, that excess amount.

59. In the case of a claimant participating in an employment zone programme, any discretionary payment made by an employment zone contractor to the claimant, being a fee, grant, loan or otherwise.

[[11] **60.**—(1) Any payment of child maintenance made or derived from a liable relative where the child or young person in respect of whom the payment is made is a member of the claimant's family, except where the person making the payment is the claimant or the claimant's partner.

(2) In sub-paragraph (1)—

"child maintenance" means any payment towards the maintenance of a child or young person, including any payment made voluntarily and payments made under—

(a) the Child Support Act 1991;

(b) the Child Support (Northern Ireland) Order 1991;

(c) a court order;

(d) a consent order;

(e) a maintenance agreement registered for execution in the Books of Council and Session or the sheriff court books;

"liable relative" means a person listed in regulation 119 (interpretation) other than a person falling within sub-paragraph (d) of that definition.]

61. In the case of a person to whom paragraph (5) of regulation 6 of the Income Support Regulations (persons not treated as in remunerative work) applies, the whole of that person's income.

62. Any discretionary housing payment paid pursuant to regulation 2(1) of the Discretionary Financial Assistance Regulations 2001.

63.—(1) Any payment made by a local authority or by the Welsh Ministers, to or on behalf of the claimant or the claimant's partner relating to a service which is provided to develop or sustain the capacity of the claimant or the claimant's partner to live independently in the claimant's or the claimant's partner's accommodation.

(2) For the purposes of sub-paragraph (1) "local authority" includes, in England, a county council.

64. Any housing benefit to which the claimant is entitled.

65. [[24] . . .]

[[29] **66.** Any armed forces independence payment.]

[[54] **67.** Any direct payments within the meaning of section 49 of the Children and Families Act 2014 made to a claimant.]

[[40] **68.** Any bereavement support payment under section 30 of the Pensions Act 2014 except any such payment which is disregarded as capital under paragraph 11(1)(d) or 60 of Schedule 9.]

[[48] **69.** Any payment of carer's allowance supplement made under section 81 of the Social Security (Scotland) Act 2018.]

[[50] **70.** Any early years assistance given in accordance with section 32 of the Social Security (Scotland) Act 2018.]

[[51] **71.** Any funeral expense assistance given in accordance with section 34 of the Social Security (Scotland) Act 2018.]

[[54] **72.** Any Scottish child payment assistance given in accordance with [...] section 79 of the Social Security (Scotland Act 2018.

[[55] **73.** Any short-term assistance given in accordance with regulations made under section 36 of the Social Security (Scotland) Act 2018.

AMENDMENTS

1. Employment and Support Allowance (Miscellaneous Amendments) Regulations 2008 (SI 2008/2428) reg.18 (October 27, 2008).

2. Employment and Support Allowance (Miscellaneous Amendments) Regulations 2008 (SI 2008/2428) reg.20(10) (October 27, 2008).

3. Social Security (Miscellaneous Amendments) (No.7) Regulations 2008 (SI 2008/3157) reg.11(3) (January 5, 2009).

4. Social Security (Miscellaneous Amendments) Regulations 2009 (SI 2009/583) reg.10(9) (April 6, 2009).

5. Social Security (Miscellaneous Amendments) (No.4) Regulations 2009 (SI 2009/2655) reg.11(19)(a) (October 26, 2009).

6. Social Security (Miscellaneous Amendments) (No.4) Regulations 2009 (SI 2009/2655) reg.11(19)(b) (October 26, 2009).

7. Social Security (Miscellaneous Amendments) (No. 4) Regulations 2009 (SI 2009/2655) reg.11(19)(c) (October 26, 2009).

8. Social Security (Miscellaneous Amendments) (No. 2) Regulations 2010 (SI 2010/641) reg.12(3)(f) (April 6, 2010).

9. Social Security (Miscellaneous Amendments) (No. 2) Regulations 2010 (SI 2010/641) reg.12(5)(e) (April 6, 2010).

10. Social Security (Miscellaneous Amendments) (No. 2) Regulations 2010 (SI 2010/641) reg.12(7) (April 6, 2010).

11. Social Security (Miscellaneous Amendments) (No. 4) Regulations 2009 (SI 2009/2655) reg.11(19)(d) (April 12, 2010).

12. Social Security (Miscellaneous Amendments) (No. 3) Regulations 2010 (SI 2010/840) reg.9(20) (June 28, 2010).

13. Social Security (Miscellaneous Amendments) (No. 5) Regulations 2010 (SI 2010/2429) reg.11(4)(a) (November 1, 2010).

14. Social Security (Miscellaneous Amendments) (No. 5) Regulations 2010 (SI 2010/2429) reg.11(4)(b) (November 1, 2010).

15. Social Security (Miscellaneous Amendments) (No. 5) Regulations 2010 (SI 2010/2429) reg.11(4)(c) (November 1, 2010).

16. Social Security (Miscellaneous Amendments) Regulations 2011 (SI 2011/674) reg.16(13) (April 11, 2011).

17. Employment and Support Allowance (Work-related Activity) Regulations 2011 (SI 2011/1349) reg.19 (June 1, 2011).

18. Adoption and Children (Scotland) Act 2007 (Consequential Modi-fications) Order 2011 (SI 2011/1740) art.1 and Sch.1, para.47(4) (July 15, 2011).

19. Social Security (Miscellaneous Amendments) (No. 2) Regulations 2011 (SI 2011/1707) reg.4(8)(b) and (9) (August 5, 2011).

20. Social Security (Miscellaneous Amendments) (No. 3) Regulations 2011 (SI 2011/2425) reg.23(8) (October 31, 2011).

21. Social Security (Miscellaneous Amendments) (No. 3) Regulations 2011 (SI 2011/2425) reg.23(9) (October 31, 2011).

22. Social Security (Miscellaneous Amendments) (No. 3) Regulations 2011 (SI 2011/2425) reg.23(16) (October 31, 2011).

23. Jobseeker's Allowance (Schemes for Assisting Persons to Obtain Employment) Regulations 2013 (SI 2013/276) reg.15(b) (February 12, 2013).

24. Council Tax Benefit Abolition (Consequential Provision) Regulations 2013 (SI 2013/458) reg.3 and Sch.1 (April 1, 2013).

25. Social Security (Miscellaneous Amendments) Regulations 2013 (SI 2013/443) reg.9(5)(a) (April 2, 2013).

26. Social Security (Miscellaneous Amendments) Regulations 2013 (SI 2013/443) reg.9(5)(b) (April 2, 2013).

27. Personal Independence Payment (Supplementary Provisions and Consequential Amendments) Regulations 2013 (SI 2013/388) reg.8 and Sch., Pt 2, para.40(7)(a) (April 8, 2013).

28. Personal Independence Payment (Supplementary Provisions and Consequential Amendments) Regulations 2013 (SI 2013/388) reg.8 and Sch., Pt 2, para.40(7)(b) (April 8, 2013).

29. Armed Forces and Reserve Forces Compensation Scheme (Consequential Provisions: Subordinate Legislation) Order 2013 (SI 2013/591) art.7 and Sch., para.37(7) (April 8, 2013).

30. National Treatment Agency (Abolition) and the Health and Social Care Act 2012 (Consequential, Transitional and Saving Provisions) Order 2013 (SI 2013/235) art.11 and para.116(3) of Part 1 of Sch.2 (April 1, 2013).

31. Universal Credit (Consequential, Supplementary, Incidental and Miscellaneous Provisions) Regulations 2013 (SI 2013/630) reg.37(8) (April 29, 2013).

32. Social Security (Miscellaneous Amendments) (No.3) Regulations 2013 (SI 2013/2536) reg.13(37) (October 29, 2013).

33. Child Arrangements Order (Consequential Amendments to Subordinate Legislation) Order 2014 (SI 2014/852) art.16 (April 22, 2014).

34. Special Educational Needs (Consequential Amendments to Subordinate Legislation) Order 2014 (SI 2014/2103) art. 27(1) (September 1, 2014).

35. Shared Parental Leave and Statutory Shared Parental Pay (Consequential Amendments to Subordinate Legislation) Order 2014 (SI 2014/3255) art.20(9) (December 31, 2014).

36. Care Act 2014 (Consequential Amendments) (Secondary Legislation) Order 2015 (SI 2015/643) art.2 and Sch., para.29(3) (April 1, 2015).

37. Children and Young People (Scotland) Act 2014 (Consequential Modifications) Order 2016 (SI 2016/732) art.8(2) (August 5, 2016).

38. Social Security (Income-Related Benefits) Amendment Regulations 2017 (SI 2017/174) reg.7 (March 20, 2017).

39. Social Security (Scottish Infected Blood Support Scheme) Regulations 2017 (SI 2017/329) reg.8(3)(e) (April 3, 2017).

40. Pensions Act 2014 (Consequential, Supplementary and Incidental Amendments) Order 2017 (SI 2017/422) art.31(4) (April 6, 2017).

41. Social Security (Emergency Funds) (Amendment) Regulations 2017 (SI 2017/689) reg.8(3)(e) (June 19, 2017).

42. Social Security (Infected Blood and Thalidomide Regulations 2017 (SI 2017/870) reg.8(3)(e) (October 23, 2017).

43. Social Services and Well-being (Wales) Act 2014 and the Regulation and Inspection of Social Care (Wales) Act 2016 (Consequential Amendments) Order 2017 (SI 2017/901) art.13(4) (November 3, 2017).

44. Social Services and Well-being (Wales) Act 2014 and the Regulation and Inspection of Social Care (Wales) Act 2016 (Consequential Amendments) Order 2017 (SI 2017/901) art.27(3) (November 3, 2017).

45. Social Security and Child Support (Care Payments and Tenant Incentive Scheme) (Amendment) Regulations 2017 (SI 2017/995) reg.7(4) (November 7, 2017).

46. Loans for Mortgage Interest Regulations 2017 (SI 2017/725) Sch.5, as amended by Loans for Mortgage Interest and Social Fund Maternity Grant (Amendment) Regulations 2018 (SI 2018/307) reg.2(18)(b) (April 5, 2018).

47. Secretaries of State for Health and Social Care and for Housing, Communities and Local Government and Transfer of Functions (Commonhold Land) Order 2018 (SI 2018/378) Sch., para.21(o) (April 11, 2018).

48. Social Security (Scotland) Act 2018 (Consequential Modifications) Order 2018 (SI 2018/872) art.7 (September 3, 2018).

49. Social Security (Miscellaneous Amendments No.5) Regulations 2017 (SI 2017/1187) reg.8 (December 6, 2018).

50. Social Security (Scotland) Act 2018 (Best Start Grants) (Consequential Modifications and Saving) Order 2018 (SI 2018/1138) art.10(2) (December 10, 2018).

51. Social Security (Scotland) Act 2018 (Funeral Expense Assistance and Early Years Assistance) (Consequential Modifications and Savings) Order 2019 (SI 2019/1060) art.17(2) (September 16, 2019).

52. Parental Bereavement Leave and Pay (Consequential Amendments to Subordinate Legislation) Regulations 2020 (SI 2020/354) reg.19(6) (April 6, 2020).

53. Social Security (Income and Capital) (Miscellaneous Amendments) Regulations 2020 (SI 2020/618) reg.7(11) (July 15, 2020).

54. Social Security (Scotland) Act 2018 (Information-sharing and Scottish Child Payment) (Consequential Provision and Modifications) Order 2020 (SI 2020/482) art.8(2) (November 9, 2020).

55. Social Security (Scotland) Act 2018 (Young Carer Grants, Short-Term Assistance and Winter Heating Assistance) (Consequential Provision and Modifications) Order 2020 (SI 2020/989) art.14(2) (November 9, 2020).

DEFINITIONS

"Abbeyfield Home"—see reg.2(1).
"adoption leave"—*ibid.*
"approved blood scheme"—*ibid.*
"armed forces independence payment"—*ibid.*
"benefit week"—*ibid.*
"board and lodging"—*ibid.*
"care home"—*ibid.*
"Caxton Foundation"—*ibid.*
"child"—*ibid.*
"claimant"—see reg.83(1).
"claimant participating as a service user"—see reg.2(8).
"daily living component"—see reg.2(1).
"dwelling occupied as the home"—*ibid.*
"Eileen Trust"—*ibid.*
"employed earner"—*ibid.*
"employment zone"—*ibid.*
"family"—*ibid.*
"the Fund"—*ibid.*
"Grenfell Tower payment"—*ibid.*
"guaranteed income payment"—*ibid.*
"Immigration and Asylum Act"—*ibid.*
"independent hospital"—*ibid.*
"the Independent Living Fund (2006)"—*ibid.*
"local welfare provision"—*ibid.*
"the London Bombings Relief Charitable Fund"—*ibid.*
"the London Emergencies Trust"—*ibid.*
"Macfarlane (Special Payments) Trust"—*ibid.*
"Macfarlane (Special Payments) (No. 2) Trust"—*ibid.*
"Macfarlane Trust"—*ibid.*
"Mandatory Work Activity Scheme"—*ibid.*
"MFET Limited"—*ibid.*
"the National Emergencies Trust"—*ibid.*
"occupational pension scheme"—*ibid.*
"ordinary clothing or footwear"—*ibid.*
"parental bereavement leave"—*ibid.*
"partner"—*ibid.*
"payment"—*ibid.*
"personal independence payment"—*ibid.*
"personal pension scheme"—*ibid.*
"qualifying person"—*ibid.*
"Scottish Infected Blood Support Scheme"—*ibid.*
"self-employment route"—*ibid.*
"shared parental leave"—*ibid.*
"Skipton Fund"—*ibid.*
"sports award"—*ibid.*
"subsistence allowance"—*ibid.*
"training allowance"—*ibid.*
"universal credit"—*ibid.*
"voluntary organisation"—*ibid.*
"week"—*ibid.*
"the We Love Manchester Emergency Fund"—*ibid.*
"young person"—*ibid.*

GENERAL NOTE

This is similar to Sch.9 to the Income Support Regulations/Sch.7 to the JSA 4.476
Regulations 1996 (subject to some reordering and minor adjustments in the wording).
See the notes in this volume where there is no specific note about a provision below.

With effect from May 29, 2020, reg.26(1)(a) of the Victims' Payments Regulations
2020 (SI 2020/103) (see Part II) provides that a victims' payment or a lump sum
under those Regulations is to be disregarded as income or capital. Under the
Regulations payments are to be made to those injured in a "Troubles-related incident", which is defined in s.10(11) of the Northern Ireland (Executive Formation
etc) Act 2019 as "an incident involving an act of violence or force carried out in
Ireland, the United Kingdom or anywhere in Europe for a reason related to the constitutional status of Northern Ireland or to political or sectarian hostility between
people there".

See the notes to Sch.9 to the Income Support Regulations for the status of the
£500 payment from local authorities to certain people who are required by NHS
Test and Trace to self-isolate and the automatic April 2021 payment to recipients
of WTC. If, as suggested there, the former constitute "local welfare provision" (on
which see the notes to para.31A of Sch.9 to the Income Support Regulations), the
disregard for IRESA purposes is in para.35A. The payments to WTC recipients
appear to be capital, not income (see the notes to Sch.8 of the Income Support
Regulations).

Under para.7(3), inserted on June 28, 2010 and substituted on April 11, 2011,
child dependency increases that are still being paid with carer's allowance, retirement pension, incapacity benefit, severe disablement allowance or widowed parent's
allowance are disregarded. This is because income payable to or in respect of a child
is not taken into account in ESA as it does not include any entitlement for children.

The amendment to para.15(1)(a), also made on June 28, 2010, means that a
training allowance paid as a substitute for JSA is also not disregarded. Under the
previous form of para.15(1)(a) only a training allowance paid as a substitute for
ESA was not disregarded.

Note para.15A (inserted with effect from June 1, 2011) which provides for an
income disregard of travel and other expenses paid in connection with undertaking
work-related activity. For the capital disregard, see para.32A of Sch.9.

Paragraph 17

The amendment to sub-para.(g) in 2017 deals belatedly with the discrimination 4.477
identified by Judge Williams in *MN v Bury Council and SSWP (HB)* [2014] UKUT
187 (AAC), holding that compensation pension payments made by the Dutch
Government to victims of National Socialist persecution should be treated in the
same way as payments made under schemes administered by the Governments of
Germany and Austria for the purposes of calculating entitlement (in that case) to
working age housing benefit.

Paragraph 53

With effect from April 1, 2014, the disregard in para.53 is modified by art.2 of,
and para.14 of the Schedule to, the Social Care (Self-directed Support) (Scotland)
Act 2013 (Consequential Modifications and Savings) Order 2014 (SI 2014/513)
so that the words "as a direct payment as defined in section 4(2) of the Social Care
(Self-directed Support) (Scotland) Act 2013" are substituted for the words "under
section 12B of the Social Work (Scotland) 1968". However, under art.3 of the
Order, this modification does not apply if a payment is made under s.12B of the
1968 Act on or after April 1, 2014.

Paragraph 67

This provides for an income disregard of payments under s.49 of the Children and 4.478
Families Act 2014 (personal budgets and direct payments). Under s.49, parents of

a child/young person with an education, health and care plan ("an EHC plan") will have the option of a personal budget, through which they will have control over how some of the provision in the EHC plan will be delivered. EHC plans will gradually replace special educational needs statements and learning disability assessments in England.

Paragraph 68

The initial one-off lump sum payment of the new (from April 2017) and controversial bereavement support payment and any arrears of monthly payments included in the first monthly payment are disregarded as capital under paras 11(1) and 60 of Sch.9 for 52 weeks. Paragraph 68 disregards other monthly payments as income other than earnings. In so far as arrears retain their character as income rather than capital (see the notes to para.7 of Sch.10 to the Income Support Regulations) they would be disregarded under para.68.

Paragraph 70

Since the Scottish early years assistance, including the best start grants that came into operation on December 10, 2018, will take the form of lump sum payments, it would probably not constitute income in any event and need this disregard. The payments are disregarded as capital by para.63 of Sch.9.

Paragraph 71

Funeral expense assistance, disregarded as income by this paragraph, is implemented by the Funeral Expense Assistance (Scotland) Regulations 2019 (SSI 2019/292) (see Vol.IV of this series). See para.64 of Sch.9 for the disregard as capital.

Paragraph 72

The regulations referred to in para.84 are the Scottish Child Payment Regulations 2020 (SSI 2020/351) (see Vol.IV of this series), which provide for a payment of £10 per week (paid four-weekly in arrears) to claimants in receipt of a UK income-related benefit who are responsible for a child under the age of six. Applications and initial payments could not have effect before mid-February 2021. See para.11(1)(a) of Sch.9 for the disregard as capital of payments of arrears.

Paragraph 73

The regulations referred to in para.73 have not yet been made. The introduction of a scheme was originally planned for 2020, providing for payments to be made to claimants who have appealed against or requested redetermination of a determination to reduce or stop paying another form of assistance (initially in relation to the new child disability payments to replace DLA for the under-18s) under the 2018 Act. The plans were deferred until summer 2021 for a pilot of the child disability payment and the autumn for a full roll-out. It appears that the pilot scheme will be implemented in July 2021 and presumably regulations will be made to set up the short-term assistance scheme at the same time. See para.11(1)(a) of Sch.9 for the disregard as capital of payments of arrears.

Regulation 111(2)

SCHEDULE 9

CAPITAL TO BE DISREGARDED

4.479 1. The dwelling occupied as the home but, notwithstanding regulation 83 (calculation of income and capital of members of claimant's family and of a polygamous marriage), only one dwelling is to be disregarded under this paragraph.

[¹⁰ **1A.** Any payment in respect of any travel or other expenses incurred, or to be incurred, by the claimant in respect of that claimant's participation in [¹⁵ a scheme prescribed in regulation 3 of the Jobseeker's Allowance (Schemes for Assisting Persons to Obtain Employment)

Regulations 2013] or the Mandatory Work Activity Scheme, but only for 52 weeks beginning with the date of receipt of the payment.]

2. Any premises acquired for occupation by the claimant which that claimant intends to occupy as the home within 26 weeks of the date of acquisition or such longer period as is reasonable in the circumstances to enable the claimant to obtain possession and commence occupation of the premises.

3. Any sum directly attributable to the proceeds of sale of any premises formerly occupied by the claimant as the home which is to be used for the purchase of other premises intended for such occupation within 26 weeks of the date of sale or such longer period as is reasonable in the circumstances to enable the claimant to complete the purchase.

4. Any premises occupied in whole or in part by—
   (a) a partner or relative of a single claimant or any member of the family as the home where that person [5 has attained the qualifying age for state pension credit] or is incapacitated;
   (b) the former partner of a claimant as the home; but this provision is not to apply where the former partner is a person from whom the claimant is estranged or divorced or with whom the person formed a civil partnership that has been dissolved.

5. Where a claimant has ceased to occupy what was formerly the dwelling occupied as the home following the claimant's estrangement or divorce from, or dissolution of the claimant's civil partnership with, the claimant's former partner, that dwelling for a period of 26 weeks from the date on which the claimant ceased to occupy that dwelling or, where that dwelling is occupied as the home by the former partner who is [14 a lone parent or a person who has no partner and who is responsible for and a member of the same household as a young person,] for as long as it is so occupied.

6. Any premises where the claimant is taking reasonable steps to dispose of those premises, for a period of 26 weeks from the date on which the claimant first took such steps, or such longer period as is reasonable in the circumstances to enable the claimant to dispose of those premises.

7. Any premises which the claimant intends to occupy as the home, and in respect of which that claimant is taking steps to obtain possession and has sought legal advice or has commenced legal proceedings, with a view to obtaining possession, for a period of 26 weeks from the date on which the claimant first sought such advice or first commenced such proceedings whichever is earlier, or such longer period as is reasonable in the circumstances to enable the claimant to obtain possession and commence occupation of those premises.

8. Any premises which the claimant intends to occupy as the home to which essential repairs or alterations are required in order to render them fit for such occupation, for a period of 26 weeks from the date on which the claimant first takes steps to effect those repairs or alterations, or such longer period as is reasonable in the circumstances to enable those repairs or alterations to be carried out and the claimant to commence occupation of the premises.

9. Any future interest in property of any kind, other than land or premises in respect of which the claimant has granted a subsisting lease or tenancy, including sub-leases or sub-tenancies.

10.—(1) The assets of any business owned in whole or in part by the claimant and for the purposes of which that claimant is engaged as a self-employed earner or, if the claimant has ceased to be so engaged, for such period as may be reasonable in the circumstances to allow for disposal of any such asset.

(2) The assets of any business owned in whole or in part by the claimant where that claimant—
   (a) is not engaged as self-employed earner in that business by reason of some disease or bodily or mental disablement; but
   (b) intends to become engaged (or, as the case may be, re-engaged) as a self-employed earner in that business as soon as the claimant recovers or is able to become engaged, or reengaged, in that business,
for a period of 26 weeks from the date on which the claim for an income-related allowance is made, or is treated as made, or, if it is unreasonable to expect the claimant to become engaged or re-engaged in that business within that period, for such longer period as is reasonable in the circumstances to enable the claimant to become so engaged or re-engaged.

(3) In the case of a person who is receiving assistance under the self-employment route, the assets acquired by that person for the purpose of establishing or carrying on the commercial activity in respect of which such assistance is being received.

(4) In the case of a person who has ceased carrying on the commercial activity in respect of which assistance was received as specified in sub-paragraph (3), the assets relating to that activity for such period as may be reasonable in the circumstances to allow for disposal of any such asset.

11.—(1) Subject to sub-paragraph (2), any arrears of, or any concessionary payment made to compensate for arrears due to the non-payment of—

    (a) any payment specified in paragraph [35[368, 10, 11, 66, 72 or 73] of Schedule 8] (other income to be disregarded);

    (b) an income-related allowance, an income-related benefit or an income-based jobseeker's allowance [18, universal credit], child tax credit or working tax credit;

    (c) any discretionary housing payment paid pursuant to regulation 2(1) of the Discretionary Financial Assistance Regulations 2001,

    [23(d) bereavement support payment under section 30 of the Pensions Act 2014,]

    [33(e) maternity allowance under section 35 of the Contributions and Benefits Act (state maternity allowance for employed or self-employed earner),]

but only for a period of 52 weeks from the date of the receipt of the arrears or of the concessionary payment.

(2) In a case where the total of any arrears and, if appropriate, any concessionary payment referred to in sub-paragraph (1) relating to any one of the specified payments, benefits or allowances, amounts to £5,000 or more (referred to in this sub-paragraph and in sub-paragraph (3) as the "relevant sum") and is—

    [30(a) paid in order to rectify, or to compensate for—

      (i) an official error as defined in regulation 1(2) of the Social Security and Child Support (Decisions and Appeals) Regulations 1999, or

      (ii) an error on a point of law; and]

    (b) received by the claimant in full on or after 14th October 2001,

sub-paragraph (1) is to have effect in relation to such arrears or concessionary payment either for a period of 52 weeks from the date of receipt, or, if the relevant sum is received in its entirety during the award of an income-related allowance, for the remainder of that award if that is a longer period.

(3) For the purposes of sub-paragraph (2), "the award of an income-related allowance" means—

    (a) the award either of an income-related allowance, income support [18, universal credit] or of an income-based jobseeker's allowance in which the relevant sum (or first part thereof where it is paid in more than one instalment) is received; and

    (b) where that award is followed by one or more further awards which in each case may be either of an income-related allowance, income support [18, universal credit] or of an income-based jobseeker's allowance and which, or each of which, begins immediately after the end of the previous award, such further awards until the end of the last such award, provided that for any such further awards the claimant—

      (i) is the person who received the relevant sum;

      (ii) is the partner of the person who received the relevant sum, or was that person's partner at the date of that person's death; [18 ...]

      (iii) in the case of a joint-claim jobseeker's allowance, is a joint-claim couple either member or both members of which received the relevant sum [18; or

      (iv) in a case where universal credit is awarded to the claimant and another person as joint claimants, either the claimant or the other person, or both of them, received the relevant sum].

12. Any sum—

    (a) paid to the claimant in consequence of damage to, or loss of, the home or any personal possession and intended for its repair or replacement; or

    (b) acquired by the claimant (whether as a loan or otherwise) on the express condition that it is to be used for effecting essential repairs or improvements to the home,

and which is to be used for the intended purpose, for a period of 26 weeks from the date on which it was so paid or acquired or such longer period as is reasonable in the circumstances to enable the claimant to effect the repairs, replacement or improvements.

13. Any sum—

    (a) deposited with a housing association as defined in section 1(1) of the Housing Associations Act 1985 or section 338(1) of the Housing (Scotland) Act 1987 as a condition of occupying the home;

(b) which was so deposited and which is to be used for the purchase of another home, for the period of 26 weeks or such longer period as is reasonable in the circumstances to complete the purchase.

14. Any personal possessions except those which had or have been acquired by the claimant with the intention of reducing that claimant's capital in order to secure entitlement to an employment and support allowance, a jobseeker's allowance or to income support or to increase the amount of those benefits.

15. The value of the right to receive any income under an annuity and the surrender value (if any) of such an annuity.   **4.480**

16. Where the funds of a trust are derived from a payment made in consequence of any personal injury to the claimant or the claimant's partner, the value of the trust fund and the value of the right to receive any payment under that trust.

17.—(1) Any payment made to the claimant or the claimant's partner in consequence of any personal injury to the claimant or, as the case may be, the claimant's partner.
(2) But sub-paragraph (1)—
(a) applies only for the period of 52 weeks beginning with the day on which the claimant first receives any payment [²in consequence of that personal injury];
(b) does not apply to any subsequent payment made to the claimant in consequence of that injury (whether it is made by the same person or another);
(c) ceases to apply to the payment or any part of the payment from the day on which the claimant no longer possesses it;
(d) does not apply to any payment from a trust where the funds of the trust are derived from a payment made in consequence of any personal injury to the claimant.
(3) For the purpose of sub-paragraph (2)(c), the circumstances in which a claimant no longer possesses a payment or a part of it include where the claimant has used a payment or part of it to purchase an asset.

18. The value of the right to receive any income under a life interest or from a life rent.

19. The value of the right to receive any income which is disregarded under paragraph 9 of Schedule 7 or paragraph 24 of Schedule 8 (earnings or other income to be disregarded).

20. The surrender value of any policy of life insurance.

21. Where any payment of capital falls to be made by instalments, the value of the right to receive any outstanding instalments.

22.—(1) Any payment made by a local authority in accordance with—
(a) section 17, 23B, 23C or 24A of the Children Act 1989;
(b) section 12 of the Social Work (Scotland) Act 1968; [²⁷ . . .]
[²¹ (c) section 26A, 29 or 30 of the Children (Scotland) Act 1995 (local authorities' duty to provide continuing care and provision of advice and assistance for certain [²⁷ young persons); or
(d) the following sections of the Social Services and Well-being (Wales) Act 2014—
(aa) section 37 or 38, but excluding any direct payment made in accordance with regulations made under section 51 of that Act, or
(bb) section 109, 110, 114 or 115.]]
(2) Subject to paragraph (3), any payment (or part of a payment) made by a local authority in accordance with section 23C of the Children Act 1989 [²¹ or section 26A or 29 of the Children (Scotland) Act 1995 (local authorities' duty to promote welfare of children, duty to provide continuing care and provision of advice and assistance for certain young persons)] to a person ("A") which A passes on to the claimant.
(3) Sub-paragraph (2) applies only where A—
(a) was formerly in the claimant's care; and
[²¹ (b) is aged 18 or over or, in the case of a payment or part of a payment made in accordance with section 26A of the Children (Scotland) Act 1995, aged 16 or over, and]
(c) continues to live with the claimant.

23. Any social fund payment made pursuant to Part 8 of the Contributions and Benefits Act.

[¹⁶ **23A.** Any local welfare provision.]

24. Any refund of tax which falls to be deducted under section 369 of the Income and Corporation Taxes Act 1988 (mortgage interest payable under deduction of tax) on a payment of relevant loan interest for the purpose of acquiring an interest in the home or carrying out repairs or improvements in the home.

25. Any capital which under regulation 105 or 137 (capital treated as income or treatment of student loans) is to be treated as income.

26. Where a payment of capital is made in a currency other than sterling, any banking charge or commission payable in converting that payment into sterling.

27.—(1) Any payment made under [⁷or by] the Macfarlane Trust, the Macfarlane (Special Payments) Trust, the Macfarlane (Special Payments) (No. 2) Trust ("the Trusts"), the Fund, the Eileen Trust[⁶, MFET Limited][¹, the Independent Living Fund (2006)], the Skipton Fund[¹², the Caxton Foundation][²², the Scottish Infected Blood Support Scheme] [²⁵, an approved blood scheme][²⁴, the London Emergencies Trust, the We Love Manchester Emergency Fund][³⁴, the National Emergencies Trust] or the London Bombings Relief Charitable Fund.

[³⁴(1A) Any Grenfell Tower payment or any payment made by the Child Migrants Trust (registered charity number 1171479) under the scheme for former British child migrants.]

(2) Any payment by or on behalf of a person who is suffering or who suffered from haemophilia or who is or was a qualifying person, which derives from a payment made under [⁷ or by] any of the Trusts to which sub-paragraph (1) refers[³⁴, or from a Grenfell Tower payment,] and which is made to or for the benefit of—

(a) that person's partner or former partner from whom the person is not, or where that person has died was not, estranged or divorced or with whom the person has formed a civil partnership that has not been dissolved or, where that person has died, had not been dissolved at the time of that person's death;

(b) any child who is a member of that person's family or who was such a member and who is a member of the claimant's family; or

(c) any young person who is a member of that person's family or who was such a member and who is a member of the claimant's family.

(3) Any payment by or on behalf of the partner or former partner of a person who is suffering or who suffered from haemophilia or who is or was a qualifying person provided that the partner or former partner and that person are not, or if either of them has died were not, estranged or divorced or, where the partner or former partner and that person have formed a civil partnership, the civil partnership has not been dissolved or, if either of them has died, had not been dissolved at the time of the death, which derives from a payment made under [⁷ or by] any of the Trusts to which sub-paragraph (1) refers[³⁴, or from a Grenfell Tower payment,] and which is made to or for the benefit of—

(a) the person who is suffering from haemophilia or who is a qualifying person;

(b) any child who is a member of that person's family or who was such a member and who is a member of the claimant's family; or

(c) any young person who is a member of that person's family or who was such a member and who is a member of the claimant's family.

(4) Any payment by a person who is suffering from haemophilia or who is a qualifying person, which derives from a payment under [⁷ or by] any of the Trusts to which sub-paragraph (1) refers, [³⁴ or from a Grenfell Tower payment,] where—

(a) that person has no partner or former partner from whom the person is not estranged or divorced or with whom the person has formed a civil partnership that has not been dissolved, nor any child or young person who is or had been a member of that person's family; and

(b) the payment is made either—

(i) to that person's parent or step-parent; or

(ii) where that person at the date of the payment is a child, a young person or a full-time student who has not completed full-time education and had no parent or step-parent, to that person's guardian,

but only for a period from the date of the payment until the end of two years from that person's death.

(5) Any payment out of the estate of a person who suffered from haemophilia or who was a qualifying person, which derives from a payment under [⁷ or by] any of the Trusts to which sub-paragraph (1) refers, [³⁴ or from a Grenfell Tower payment,] where—

(a) that person at the date of that person's death (the relevant date) had no partner or former partner from whom the person was not estranged or divorced or with whom the person had formed a civil partnership that had not been dissolved, nor any child or young person who was or had been a member of that person's family; and

    (b) the payment is made either—
        (i) to that person's parent or step-parent; or
       (ii) where that person at the relevant date was a child, a young person or a full-time student who had not completed full-time education and had no parent or step-parent, to that person's guardian,
but only for a period of two years from the relevant date.

(6) In the case of a person to whom or for whose benefit a payment referred to in this paragraph is made, any capital resource which derives from any payment of income or capital made under or deriving from any of the Trusts [34 or from a Grenfell Tower payment].

(7) For the purposes of sub-paragraphs (2) to (6), any reference to the Trusts is to be construed as including a reference to the Fund, the Eileen Trust[6, MFET Limited], the Skipton Fund[12, the Caxton Foundation] [22, the Scottish Infected Blood Support Scheme] [25, an approved blood scheme] [24, the London Emergencies Trust, the We Love Manchester Emergency Fund] [34, the National Emergencies Trust] or the London Bombings Relief Charitable Fund.

28. The value of the right to receive an occupational or personal pension.

29. The value of any funds held under a personal pension scheme.

30. The value of the right to receive any rent except where the claimant has a reversionary interest in the property in respect of which rent is due.

31. Any payment in kind [34which is a Grenfell Tower payment or] made by a charity or under the Macfarlane Trust, Macfarlane (Special Payments) Trust, the Macfarlane (Special Payments) (No. 2) Trust, the Fund, the Eileen Trust[6, MFET Limited] [11, the Skipton Fund, the Caxton Foundation] [22, the Scottish Infected Blood Support Scheme] [25, an approved blood scheme] or [2the Independent Living Fund (2006)].

32. Any payment made pursuant to section 2 of the Employment and Training Act 1973 or section 2 of the Enterprise and New Towns (Scotland) Act 1990, but only for the period of 52 weeks beginning on the date of receipt of the payment.

[9 **32A.** Any payment made to the claimant in respect of any travel or other expenses incurred, or to be incurred, in complying with a requirement to undertake work-related activity but only for 52 weeks beginning with the date of receipt of the payment.]

33. Any payment made by the Secretary of State to compensate for the loss (in whole or in part) of entitlement to housing benefit.

34. Any payment made to a juror or a witness in respect of attendance at a court other than compensation for loss of earnings or for the loss of a benefit payable under the benefit Acts.

35. Any payment [2in consequence of a reduction] of council tax under section 13 [17 , section 13A] or, as the case may be, section 80 of the Local Government Finance Act 1992 (reduction of liability for council tax), but only for a period of 52 weeks from the date of the receipt of the payment.

36. Any grant made to the claimant in accordance with a scheme under section 129 of the Housing Act 1988 or section 66 of the Housing (Scotland) Act 1988 (schemes for payments to assist local housing authorities and local authority tenants to obtain other accommodation) which is to be used—
    (a) to purchase premises intended for occupation as the claimant's home; or
    (b) to carry out repairs or alterations which are required to render premises fit for occupation as the claimant's home,
for a period of 26 weeks from the date on which the claimant received such a grant or such longer period as is reasonable in the circumstances to enable the purchase, repairs or alterations to be completed and the claimant to commence occupation of those premises as the claimant's home.

37.—(1) Any payment or repayment made—
    (a) as respects England, under regulation 5, 6 or 12 of the National Health Service (Travel Expenses and Remission of Charges) Regulations 2003 (travelling expenses and health service supplies);
    (b) as respects Wales, under regulation 5, 6 or 11 of the National Health Service (Travelling Expenses and Remission of Charges) (Wales) Regulations 2007;
    (c) as respects Scotland, under regulation 3, 5 or 11 of the National Health Service

(Travelling Expenses and Remission of Charges) (Scotland) (No. 2) Regulations 2003 (travelling expenses and health service supplies);
but only for a period of 52 weeks from the date of receipt of the payment or repayment.

(2) Any payment or repayment made by the Secretary of State for Health [²⁹ and Social Care], the Scottish Ministers or the Welsh Ministers which is analogous to a payment or repayment mentioned in sub-paragraph (1); but only for a period of 52 weeks from the date of receipt of the payment or repayment.

38. Any payment made to such persons entitled to receive benefits as may be determined by or under a scheme made pursuant to section 13 of the Social Security Act 1988 in lieu of vouchers or similar arrangements in connection with the provision of those benefits (including payments made in place of healthy start vouchers, milk tokens or the supply of vitamins) but only for a period of 52 weeks from the date of receipt of the payment.

[⁴ **38A.** Any payment made under Part 8A of the Social Security Contributions and Benefits Act 1992 (entitlement to health in pregnancy grant).]

39. Any payment made either by the Secretary of State for Justice or by the Scottish Ministers under a scheme established to assist relatives and other persons to visit persons in custody, but only for a period of 52 weeks from the date of receipt of the payment.

40. Any arrears of supplementary pension which is disregarded under paragraph 49 of Schedule 8 (sums to be disregarded in the calculation of income other than earnings) or of any amount which is disregarded under paragraphs 51 or 52 of that Schedule, but only for a period of 52 weeks from the date of receipt of the arrears.

41. Any payment (other than a training allowance) made, whether by the Secretary of State or by any other person, under the Disabled Persons (Employment) Act 1944 to assist disabled persons to obtain or retain employment despite their disability.

42. Any payment made by a local authority under section 3 of the Disabled Persons (Employment) Act 1958 [²⁷or under Part 4 of the Social Services and Well-being (Wales) Act 2014] to homeworkers assisted under the Blind Homeworkers' Scheme.

4.481   **43.**—(1) Any sum to which sub-paragraph (2) applies and—
   (a) which is administered on behalf of a person by the High Court or the County Court under Rule 21.11(1) of the Civil Procedure Rules 1998 or by the Court of Protection;
   (b) which can only be disposed of by order or direction of any such court; or
   (c) where the person concerned is under the age of 18, which can only be disposed of by order or direction prior to that person attaining age 18.
   (2) This sub-paragraph applies to a sum which is derived from—
   (a) an award of damages for a personal injury to that person; or
   (b) compensation for the death of one or both parents where the person concerned is under the age of 18.

44. Any sum administered on behalf of a person in accordance with an order made under section 13 of the Children (Scotland) Act 1995, or under Rule 36.14 of the Ordinary Cause Rules 1993 or under Rule 128 of the Ordinary Cause Rules, where such sum derives from—
   (a) an award of damages for a personal injury to that person; or
   (b) compensation for the death of one or both parents where the person concerned is under the age of 18.

45. Any payment to the claimant as holder of the Victoria Cross or George Cross.

46. In the case of a person who is receiving, or who has received, assistance under the self-employment route, any sum which is acquired by that person for the purpose of establishing or carrying on the commercial activity in respect of which such assistance is or was received but only for a period of 52 weeks from the date on which that sum was acquired.

47.—(1) [²Any payment of a sports award] for a period of 26 weeks from the date of receipt of that payment except to the extent that it has been made in respect of any one or more of the items specified in sub-paragraph (2).
   (2) The items specified for the purposes of sub-paragraph (1) are food, ordinary clothing or footwear, household fuel, rent for which housing benefit is payable or any housing costs to the extent that they are met under regulation 67(1)(c) or 68(1)(d) (housing costs), of the claimant or, where the claimant is a member of a family, any other member of the claimant's family, or any council tax or water charges for which that claimant or member is liable.

(3) For the purposes of sub-paragraph (2) "food" does not include vitamins, minerals or other special dietary supplements intended to enhance the performance of the person in the sport in respect of which the award was made.

48. In the case of a claimant participating in an employment zone programme, any discretionary payment made by an employment zone contractor to the claimant, being a fee, grant, loan or otherwise, but only for the period of 52 weeks from the date of receipt of the payment.

49. Any arrears of subsistence allowance paid as a lump sum but only for the period of 52 weeks from the date of receipt of the payment.

50. Where an ex-gratia payment of £10,000 has been made by the Secretary of State on or after 1st February 2001 in consequence of the imprisonment or internment of—
  (a) the claimant;
  (b) the claimant's partner;
  (c) the claimant's deceased spouse or deceased civil partner; or
  (d) the claimant's partner's deceased spouse or deceased civil partner,
by the Japanese during the Second World War, £10,000.

51. In the case of a person to whom paragraph (5) of regulation 6 of the Income Support Regulations (persons not treated as in remunerative work) applies, the whole of the claimant's capital.

52.—(1) Any payment—
  (a) by way of an education maintenance allowance made pursuant to—
      (i) regulations made under section 518 of the Education Act 1996;
      (ii) regulations made under section 49 or 73(f) of the Education (Scotland) Act 1980;
      (iii) directions made under section 73ZA of the Education (Scotland) Act 1980 and paid under section 12(2)(c) of the Further and Higher Education (Scotland) Act 1992; [¹³ . . .]
  (b) corresponding to such an education maintenance allowance, made pursuant to—
      (i) section 14 or section 181 of the Education Act 2002; or
      (ii) regulations made under section 181 of that Act [¹³ ; or
  (c) in England, by way of financial assistance made pursuant to section 14 of the Education Act 2002.]
  (2) Any payment, other than a payment to which sub-paragraph (1) applies, made pursuant to—
  (a) regulations made under section 518 of the Education Act 1996;
  (b) regulations made under section 49 of the Education (Scotland) Act 1980; or
  (c) directions made under section 73ZA of the Education (Scotland) Act 1980 and paid under section 12(2)(c) of the Further and Higher Education (Scotland) Act 1992,
in respect of a course of study attended by a child or a young person or a person who is in receipt of an education maintenance allowance [¹³ or other payment] made pursuant to any provision specified in sub-paragraph (1).

53.—(1) Subject to sub-paragraph (2), the amount of any trust payment made to a claimant or a member of a claimant's family who is—
  (a) a diagnosed person;
  (b) the diagnosed person's partner or the person who was the diagnosed person's partner at the date of the diagnosed person's death;
  (c) a parent of a diagnosed person, a person acting in the place of the diagnosed person's parents or a person who was so acting at the date of the diagnosed person's death; or
  (d) a member of the diagnosed person's family (other than that person's partner) or a person who was a member of the diagnosed person's family (other than that person's partner) at the date of the diagnosed person's death.
  (2) Where a trust payment is made to—
  (a) a person referred to in sub-paragraph (1)(a) or (b), that sub-paragraph will apply for the period beginning on the date on which the trust payment is made and ending on the date on which that person dies;
  (b) a person referred to in sub-paragraph (1)(c), that sub-paragraph will apply for the period beginning on the date on which the trust payment is made and ending two years after that date;

(c) a person referred to in sub-paragraph (1)(d), that sub-paragraph will apply for the period beginning on the date on which the trust payment is made and ending—
    (i) two years after that date; or
    (ii) on the day before the day on which that person—
      (aa) ceases receiving full-time education; or
      (bb) attains the age of 20,
whichever is the latest.

(3) Subject to sub-paragraph (4), the amount of any payment by a person to whom a trust payment has been made, or of any payment out of the estate of a person to whom a trust payment has been made, which is made to a claimant or a member of a claimant's family who is—
(a) the diagnosed person's partner or the person who was the diagnosed person's partner at the date of the diagnosed person's death;
(b) a parent of a diagnosed person, a person acting in the place of the diagnosed person's parents or a person who was so acting at the date of the diagnosed person's death; or
(c) a member of the diagnosed person's family (other than that person's partner) or a person who was a member of the diagnosed person's family (other than that person's partner) at the date of the diagnosed person's death,
but only to the extent that such payments do not exceed the total amount of any trust payments made to that person.

(4) Where a payment as referred to in sub-paragraph (3) is made to—
(a) a person referred to in sub-paragraph (3)(a), that sub-paragraph will apply for the period beginning on the date on which that payment is made and ending on the date on which that person dies;
(b) a person referred to in sub-paragraph (3)(b), that sub-paragraph will apply for the period beginning on the date on which that payment is made and ending two years after that date;
(c) a person referred to in sub-paragraph (3)(c), that sub-paragraph will apply for the period beginning on the date on which that payment is made and ending—
    (i) two years after that date; or
    (ii) on the day before the day on which that person—
      (aa) ceases receiving full-time education; or
      (bb) attains the age of 20,
whichever is the latest.

(5) In this paragraph, a reference to a person—
(a) being the diagnosed person's partner;
(b) being a member of the diagnosed person's family; or
(c) acting in the place of the diagnosed person's parents,
at the date of the diagnosed person's death will include a person who would have been such a person or a person who would have been so acting, but for the diagnosed person residing in a care home, an Abbeyfield Home or an independent hospital on that date.

(6) In this paragraph—
"diagnosed person" means a person who has been diagnosed as suffering from, or who, after that person's death, has been diagnosed as having suffered from, variant Creutzfeldt-Jakob disease;
"relevant trust" means a trust established out of funds provided by the Secretary of State in respect of persons who suffered, or who are suffering, from variant Creutzfeldt-Jakob disease for the benefit of persons eligible for payments in accordance with its provisions;
"trust payment" means a payment under a relevant trust.

54. The amount of a payment, other than a [³ war disablement pension, war widow's pension or war widower's pension], to compensate for the fact that the claimant, the claimant's partner, the claimant's deceased spouse or deceased civil partner or the claimant's partner's deceased spouse or deceased civil partner—
(a) was a slave labourer or a forced labourer;
(b) had suffered property loss or had suffered personal injury; or
(c) was a parent of a child who had died,
during the Second World War.

55.—(1) Any payment made by a local authority or by the Welsh Ministers, to or on behalf of the claimant or the claimant's partner relating to a service which is provided to develop or sustain the capacity of the claimant or the claimant's partner to live independently in the claimant's or the claimant's partner's accommodation.

(2) For the purposes of sub-paragraph (1) "local authority" includes, in England, a county council.

56. Any payment [²⁰ made as a direct payment under Part 1 of the Care Act 2014 (care and support) or] made under [⁴ . . .] regulations made under section 57 of the Health and Social Care Act 2001 or under section 12B of the Social Work (Scotland) Act 1968[⁸, or under sections 12A to 12D of the National Health Service Act 2006 (direct payments for health care)[²⁷, or in accordance with regulations made under section 50 or 52 of the Social Services and Well-being (Wales) Act 2014 (direct payments)]].

57. Any payment made to the claimant pursuant to regulations under section 2(6)(b), 3 or 4 of the Adoption and Children Act 2002.

58. Any payment made to the claimant in accordance with regulations made pursuant to section 14F of the Children Act 1989 (special guardianship support services).

[¹⁹ **59.** Any direct payments within the meaning of section 49 of the Children and Families Act 2014 made to a claimant.]

[²³ **60.** Any bereavement support payment in respect of the rate set out in regulation 3(2) or (5) of the Bereavement Support Payment Regulations 2017 (rate of bereavement support payment), but only for a period of 52 weeks from the date of receipt of the payment.]

[²⁶ **61.** Any payment made under or by a trust, established for the purpose of giving relief and assistance to disabled persons whose disabilities were caused by the fact that during their mother's pregnancy she had taken a preparation containing the drug known as Thalidomide, and which is approved by the Secretary of State.]

[²⁸[³¹ **62.** Any payment made to a claimant under section 73(1)(b) of the Children and Young People (Scotland) Act 2014 (kinship care assistance).]]

[³¹ **63.** Any early years assistance given in accordance with section 32 of the Social Security (Scotland) Act 2018.]

[³²**64.** Any funeral expense assistance given in accordance with section 34 of the Social Security (Scotland) Act 2018.]

[³⁵**65.** Any assistance given in accordance with the Carer's Assistance (Young Carer Grants) (Scotland) Regulations 2019.]

[³⁶**66.** Any winter heating assistance given in accordance with regulations made under section 30 of the Social Security (Scotland) Act 2018.]

AMENDMENTS

1. Employment and Support Allowance (Miscellaneous Amendments) Regulations 2008 (SI 2008/2428) reg.8(8) (October 27, 2008).
2. Employment and Support Allowance (Miscellaneous Amendments) Regulations 2008 (SI 2008/2428) reg.19 (October 27, 2008).
3. Social Security (Miscellaneous Amendments) (No.7) Regulations 2008 (SI 2008/3157) reg.11(4) (January 5, 2009).
4. Social Security (Miscellaneous Amendments) Regulations 2009 (SI 2009/583) reg.10(10) (April 6, 2009).
5. Social Security (Equalisation of State Pension Age) Regulations 2009 (SI 2009/1488) reg.44 (April 6, 2010).
6. Social Security (Miscellaneous Amendments) (No.2) Regulations 2010 (SI 2010/641) reg.12(3)(g) (April 6, 2010).
7. Social Security (Miscellaneous Amendments) (No.2) Regulations 2010 (SI 2010/641) reg.12(5)(f) (April 6, 2010).
8. Social Security (Miscellaneous Amendments) (No.2) Regulations 2010 (SI 2010/641) reg.12(7) (April 6, 2010).
9. Employment and Support Allowance (Work-related Activity) Regulations 2011 (SI 2011/1349) reg.20 (June 1, 2011).
10. Social Security (Miscellaneous Amendments) (No.2) Regulations 2011 (SI 2011/1707) reg.4(10)(b) and (11) (August 5, 2011).
11. Social Security (Miscellaneous Amendments) (No.3) Regulations 2011 (SI 2011/2425) reg.23(8) (October 31, 2011).

12. Social Security (Miscellaneous Amendments) (No.3) Regulations 2011 (SI 2011/2425) reg.23(9) (October 31, 2011).

13. Social Security (Miscellaneous Amendments) (No.3) Regulations 2011 (SI 2011/2425) reg.23(16) (October 31, 2011).

14. Social Security (Work-focused Interviews for Lone Parents and Partners) (Amendment) Regulations 2011 (SI 2011/2428) reg.5(8) (October 31, 2011).

15. Jobseeker's Allowance (Schemes for Assisting Persons to Obtain Employment) Regulations 2013 (SI 2013/276) reg.15(b) (February 12, 2013).

16. Social Security (Miscellaneous Amendments) Regulations 2013 (SI 2013/443) reg.9(6)(a) (April 2, 2013).

17. Social Security (Miscellaneous Amendments) Regulations 2013 (SI 2013/443) reg.9(6)(b) (April 2, 2013).

18. Universal Credit (Consequential, Supplementary, Incidental and Miscellaneous Provisions) Regulations 2013 (SI 2013/630) reg.37(9) (April 29, 2013).

19. Special Educational Needs (Consequential Amendments to Subordinate Legislation) Order 2014 (SI 2014/2103) art.27(2) (September 1, 2014).

20. Care Act 2014 (Consequential Amendments) (Secondary Legislation) Order 2015 (SI 2015/643) art.2 and Sch., para.29(4) (April 1, 2015).

21. Children and Young People (Scotland) Act 2014 (Consequential Modifications) Order 2016 (SI 2016/732) art.8(3) (August 5, 2016).

22. Social Security (Scottish Infected Blood Support Scheme) Regulations 2017 (SI 2017/329) reg.8(3)(c) (April 3, 2017).

23. Pensions Act 2014 (Consequential, Supplementary and Incidental Amendments) Order 2017 (SI 2017/422) art.31(5) (April 6, 2017).

24. Social Security (Emergency Funds) (Amendment) Regulations 2017 (SI 2017/689) reg.8(3)(f) (June 19, 2017).

25. Social Security (Infected Blood and Thalidomide Regulations 2017 (SI 2017/870) reg.8(3)(f) (October 23, 2017).

26. Social Security (Infected Blood and Thalidomide Regulations 2017 (SI 2017/870) reg.8(5) (October 23, 2017).

27. Social Services and Well-being (Wales) Act 2014 and the Regulation and Inspection of Social Care (Wales) Act 2016 (Consequential Amendments) Order 2017 (SI 2017/901) art.13(5) (November 3, 2017).

28. Social Security and Child Support (Care Payments and Tenant Incentive Scheme) (Amendment) Regulations 2017 (SI 2017/995) reg.7(5) (November 7, 2017).

29. Secretaries of State for Health and Social Care and for Housing, Communities and Local Government and Transfer of Functions (Commonhold Land) Order 2018 (SI 2018/378) Sch., para.21(o) (April 11, 2018).

30. Social Security (Treatment of Arrears of Benefit) Regulations 2018 (SI 2018/932) reg.7 (September 11, 2018).

31. Social Security (Scotland) Act 2018 (Best Start Grants) (Consequential Modifications and Saving) Order 2018 (SI 2018/1138) art.10(3) (December 10, 2018).

32. Social Security (Scotland) Act 2018 (Funeral Expense Assistance and Early Years Assistance) (Consequential Modifications and Savings) Order 2019 (SI 2019/1060) art.17(3) (September 16, 2019).

33. Social Security (Capital Disregards) (Amendment) Regulations 2019 (SI 2019/1314) reg.7(2) (October 31, 2019).

34. Social Security (Income and Capital) (Miscellaneous Amendments) Regulations 2020 (SI 2020/618) reg.7(12) (July 15, 2020).

35. Social Security (Scotland) Act 2018 (Young Carer Grants, Short-Term Assistance and Winter Heating Assistance) (Consequential Provision and Modifications) Order 2020 (SI 2020/989) art.7 (November 9, 2020).

36. Social Security (Scotland) Act 2018 (Young Carer Grants, Short-Term Assistance and Winter Heating Assistance) (Consequential Provision and Modifications) Order 2020 (SI 2020/989) art.20 (November 9, 2020).

DEFINITIONS

"Abbeyfield Home"—see reg.2(1).
"approved blood scheme"—*ibid.*
"care home"—*ibid.*
"Caxton Foundation"—*ibid.*
"child"—*ibid.*
"claimant"—see reg.83(1).
"dwelling occupied as the home"—see reg.2(1).
"Eileen Trust"—*ibid.*
"employment zone"—*ibid.*
"family"—*ibid.*
"the Fund"—*ibid.*
"Grenfell Tower payment"—*ibid.*
"independent hospital"—*ibid.*
"the Independent Living Fund (2006)"—*ibid.*
"local welfare provision"—*ibid.*
"the London Bombings Relief Charitable Fund"—*ibid.*
"the London Emergencies Trust"—*ibid.*
"lone parent"—*ibid.*
"Macfarlane (Special Payments) Trust"—*ibid.*
"Macfarlane (Special Payments) (No. 2) Trust"—*ibid.*
"Macfarlane Trust"—*ibid.*
"Mandatory Work Activity Scheme"—*ibid.*
"MFET Limited"—*ibid.*
"the National Emergencies Trust"—*ibid.*
"occupational pension"—*ibid.*
"ordinary clothing or footwear"—*ibid.*
"partner"—*ibid.*
"payment"—*ibid.*
"personal pension scheme"—*ibid.*
"policy of life insurance"—*ibid.*
"qualifying person"—*ibid.*
"relative"—*ibid.*
"Scottish Infected Blood Support Scheme"—*ibid.*
"self-employed earner"—*ibid.*
"self-employment route"—*ibid.*
"single claimant"—*ibid.*
"Skipton Fund"—*ibid.*
"sports award"—*ibid.*
"subsistence allowance"—*ibid.*
"training allowance"—*ibid.*
"universal credit"—*ibid.*
"the We Love Manchester Emergency Fund"—*ibid.*
"young person"—*ibid.*

GENERAL NOTE

This is similar to Sch.10 to the Income Support Regulations/Sch.8 to the JSA **4.482** Regulations 1996 (subject to some reordering and minor adjustments in the wording). See the notes to Sch.10 where there is no specific note about a provision below.

With effect from May 29, 2020, reg.26(1)(a) of the Victims' Payments Regulations 2020 (SI 2020/103) (see Part II) provides that a victims' payment or a lump sum under those Regulations is to be disregarded as capital or income. Under the Regulations payments are to be made to those injured in a "Troubles-related incident", which is defined in s.10(11) of the Northern Ireland (Executive Formation etc) Act 2019 as "an incident involving an act of violence or force carried out in

Ireland, the United Kingdom or anywhere in Europe for a reason related to the constitutional status of Northern Ireland or to political or sectarian hostility between people there".

See the notes to Sch.10 to the Income Support Regulations for detailed discussion of the status of the £500 NHS Test and Trace payments to those self-isolating and of the April 2021 £500 payments to WTC recipients.

Paragraphs 47 to 49 of Sch.10 to the Income Support Regulations have not been reproduced in this Schedule as they are no longer relevant.

Note that in para.14 the disregard of the value of personal possessions does not apply if they have been acquired in order to reduce capital so as to gain entitlement to, or increase the amount of, ESA, *JSA or income support*. This avoids the question that might otherwise have arisen on a claimant transferring from income support (or JSA) to ESA whether, if the acquisition had only been for the purposes of income support (or JSA), the disregard in para.14 applies.

Note that under para.32A payments of travel or other expenses paid in connection with undertaking work-related activity that count as capital are disregarded but only for 52 weeks from the date of receipt. For the income disregard see para.15A of Sch.8.

Paragraph 31

4.483   Note that there has been no amendment to para.31 equivalent to that made with effect from June 19, 2017 in para.27(1) and (7).

Paragraph 56

4.484   With effect from April 1, 2014, the disregard in para.56 is modified by art.2 of, and para.14 of the Schedule to, the Social Care (Self-directed Support) (Scotland) Act 2013 (Consequential Modifications and Savings) Order 2014 (SI 2014/513) so that the words "as a direct payment as defined in section 4(2) of the Social Care (Self-directed Support) (Scotland) Act 2013" are substituted for the words "under section 12B of the Social Work (Scotland) 1968". However, under art.3 of the Order, this modification does not apply if a payment is made under s.12B of the 1968 Act on or after April 1, 2014.

Paragraph 59

4.485   This provides for a capital disregard of payments under s.49 of the Children and Families Act 2014 (personal budgets and direct payments). See further the note to para.67 of Sch.8 which provides for an income disregard of such payments.

Paragraph 60

4.486   The initial one-off lump sum payment of the new (from April 2017) and controversial bereavement support payment is disregarded as capital under this provision for 52 weeks from the date of receipt. The insertion of sub-para.(d) into para.11(1) secures the disregard as capital of payments of arrears of monthly payments, also for 52 weeks from the date of receipt. In so far as arrears of monthly payments retain their character as income rather than capital (see the notes to para.7 of Sch.10 to the Income Support Regulations) they would be disregarded under para.68 of Sch.8.

Paragraph 62

4.487   This paragraph has now formally been given its correct number. See the note to para.74 of Sch.10 to the Income Support Regulations for payments under s.73 of the Children and Young People (Scotland) Act 2014.

Paragraph 63

Scottish early years assistance, including the best start grants in operation from   **4.488**
December 10, 2018, is also disregarded as income by para.70 of Sch.8.

Paragraph 64

Funeral expense assistance, disregarded as capital by this paragraph, is imple-   **4.489**
mented by the Funeral Expense Assistance (Scotland) Regulations 2019 (SSI
2019/292) (see Vol.IV of this series). See para.71 of Sch.8 for the disregard as
income.

Paragraph 65

Under the specified regulations (SSI 2019/324, in operation from October 21,
2019: see Vol.IV of this series), young carer grants of (from April 2021) £308.15,
limited to one a year, are payable in Scotland to carers aged 16 to 18 who care for
at least 16 hours a week over a 13-week period for a person who normally receives
a disability benefit. There appears to have been a gap during which grants were not
disregarded as capital, since para.65 did not come into force until November 9,
2020. No disregard as income has been introduced, but no doubt the grants are in
their nature payments of capital.

Paragraph 66

The relevant regulations under s.30 of the Social Security (Scotland) Act 2018
are the Winter Heating Assistance for Children and Young People (Scotland)
Regulations 2020 (SSI 2020/352, in operation from November 9, 2020: see Vol.IV
of this series), which initially provide an automatic annual grant in November 2020
to a family of £200 (£202 for 2021) for each child entitled to the highest rate of the
care component of DLA in the week of September 21–27, 2020. No disregard as
income has been introduced, as the grant plainly constitutes capital.

The Employment and Support Allowance Regulations 2008

(SI 2008/794) (AS AMENDED)

SCHEDULES 2 AND 3, AS IN FORCE AT MARCH 27, 2011.

These govern all decisions made on or before that date. The degree to which   **4.490**
these provisions cover some decisions taken after that date is set out in regulation
2 of the Employment and Support Allowance (Limited Capability for Work and
Limited Capability for Work- Related Activity) (Amendment) Regulations 2011 (SI
2011/228), set out in para.9.365 in the previous edition of this volume. The provisions may still be relevant in a very small number of appeals. For their text see the
previous edition of this Volume as updated by the 2012/13 Supplement

The Employment and Support Allowance (Transitional Provisions) Regulations 2008

(SI 2008/795) (*as amended*)

The Secretary of State for Work and Pensions in exercise of the powers conferred by section 25(2)(b) and (c) and 29 of, and paragraphs 1(1), 2 and 3(b), (c) and (d) of Schedule 4 to, the Welfare Reform Act 2007, makes the following Regulations which are made by virtue of, or consequential on, the provisions of the Welfare Reform Act 2007 and which are made before the end of a period of 6 months beginning with the coming into force of those provisions.

Citation, commencement and interpretation

4.492   **1.**—(1) These Regulations may be cited as the Employment and Support Allowance (Transitional Provisions) Regulations 2008.

(2) This regulation and regulations 2, 3 and 4 shall come into force on 27th July 2008.

(3) Regulation 5 shall come into force on 27th October 2008.

(4) In these Regulations "income support on the grounds of disability" means income support awarded to a person to whom regulation [¹ . . .] 13(2)(b) or (bb) of, or paragraph 7(a) or (b), 10, 12 or 13 of Schedule 1B to, the Income Support (General) Regulations 1987 (prescribed categories of person) applies.

AMENDMENT

1. Employment and Support Allowance (Miscellaneous Amendments) Regulations 2008 (SI 2008/2428) reg.42 (October 27, 2008).

DEFINITION

"income support on the grounds of disability"—see para.(4).

GENERAL NOTE

4.493   This regulation entered into force on July 27, 2008, three months before the main ESA scheme became operative.

Claim for existing award

4.494   **2.**—(1) A claim for incapacity benefit, severe disablement allowance or income support on the grounds of disability, whenever made, in respect of a period which begins on or after the appointed day, is to be treated as a claim for an employment and support allowance.

(2) Paragraph (1) does not apply to

(a) [² ...]

(b) [² ...]

(c) [² ...]

[¹(d) a claim for income support on the grounds of disability made by a claimant who is entitled to incapacity benefit or severe disablement allowance; or

(e) a claim for incapacity benefit made by a claimant who is entitled to income support on the grounds of disability.]

(3) Paragraph (1) does not apply insofar as a claim is treated as a claim for severe disablement allowance, maternity allowance or carer's allowance under regulation 9(1) of and Part 1 of Schedule 1 to, the Social Security (Claims and Payments) Regulations 1987 (claims treated as claimed in addition or in the alternative).

AMENDMENTS

1. Employment and Support Allowance (Transitional Provisions) (Amendment) Regulations 2008 (SI 2008/2783) reg.2 (October 26, 2008).
2. Employment and Support Allowance (Transitional Provisions, Housing Benefit and Council Tax Benefit) (Existing Awards) (No. 2) Regulations 2010 (SI 2010/1907) reg.24 (January 31, 2011).

DEFINITIONS

"appointed day"—see WRA 2007 s.29, Sch.4, para.11.
"claimant"—see WRA 2007 s.24(1).
"incapacity benefit"—see WRA 2007 s.29, Sch.4, para.11.
"income support on the grounds of disability"—see reg.1(4).
"severe disablement allowance"—see WRA 2007 s.29, Sch.4, para.11.

GENERAL NOTE

This regulation entered into force on July 27, 2008, three months before October 27, 2008, the "appointed day" when WRA 2007 s.1 and the main ESA provisions became operative (see WRA 2007 s.29 Sch.4 para.11, and the Welfare Reform Act 2007 (Commencement No.6 and Consequential Provisions) Order 2008 (SI 2008/787) art.2(4). **4.495**

It deals with claims for one or more of the benefits in the already existing incapacity benefits' regime: incapacity benefit; severe disablement allowance (limited, of course, only to those entitled to it immediately before April 6, 2001) and "income support on the grounds of disability". This last covers claims for income support by someone to whom regulation 13(2)(b) or (bb) of, or para.7(a) or (b), 10, 12 or 13 of Sch.1B to, the Income Support (General) Regs 1987 (prescribed categories of person) applies (that is someone claiming IS as a person incapable of work; as a disabled or deaf student; or as a blind person).

Paragraph (1) provides that a claim for any such benefit made on or after October 27, 2008 (the "appointed day") is to be treated as one for ESA. To this there are two exceptions:

(1) *Where a person entitled to incapacity benefit or severe disablement allowance claims income support on the grounds of disability and a person who is entitled to income support on the grounds of disability claims incapacity benefit (para.(2)(d), (e)).*

Memo DMG 40/08 gives an example (IB entitlement enabling IS claim):

"Sue has been in receipt of IB for several years. She is not entitled to IS because her partner Mark is in remunerative work. Mark is made redundant in November 2008, and Sue claims IS on the grounds of disability. The DM makes a determination that Sue's claim is not treated as a claim for ESA, and decides the claim for IS accordingly."

(2) Where a claim is treated as a claim for severe disablement allowance, maternity allowance or carer's allowance under reg.9(1) of and Pt 1 of Sch.1 to, the Social Security (Claims and Payments) Regs 1987 (claims treated as claimed in addition or in the alternative).

See further the commentary to that regulation in Vol.III.

Claim by person entitled or potentially entitled to existing award

4.496   **3.**—(1) A person who is entitled to an existing award is excluded from making a claim for an employment and support allowance.

(2) A claim for an employment and support allowance made by a person who would be entitled to an existing award if that person made a claim described in regulation 2(2), is to be treated as a claim for that award.

DEFINITION

"existing award"—see WRA 2007 s.29 Sch.4 para.11.

GENERAL NOTE

4.497   This regulation entered into force on July 27, 2008, three months before October 27, 2008, the "appointed day" when WRA 2007 s.1 and the main ESA provisions became operative (see WRA 2007 s.29 Sch.4 para.11, and the Welfare Reform Act 2007 (Commencement No.6 and Consequential Provisions) Order 2008 (SI 2008/787), art.2(4).

Paragraph (1) deals with claims for ESA by someone entitled to an "existing award", that is, one or more of the benefits in the already existing incapacity benefits' regime: incapacity benefit; severe disablement allowance (limited, of course, only to those entitled to it immediately before April 6, 2001) and "income support on the grounds of disability" (WRA 2007 s.29, Sch.4, para.11). This last covers claims for income support under by someone to whom 13(2)(b) or (bb) of, or para.7(a) or (b), 10, 12 or 13 of Sch.1B to, the Income Support (General) Regs 1987 (prescribed categories of person) applies (that is someone claiming IS as a person incapable of work; as a disabled or deaf student; or as a blind person).

Paragraph (1) provides that someone so entitled cannot be entitled to ESA. That and an existing award are mutually exclusive.

Paragraph (2) extends that preclusion to those who claim ESA but would be entitled to an "existing award" (IB, SDA or incapacity/disability-based IS, as the case may be) if they made a "linked" claim for it as envisaged by reg.2(2).

Paragraph (1) receives some consideration in *CG v SSWP* (ESA) [2011] UKUT 167 (AAC), principally in terms of it setting out arguments advanced by the Secretary of State on its application (see para.2 of the decision). Judge May considered that he did not need to comment on those arguments since he was able to decide the appeal on another basis. In this case the claimant had appealed a decision denying him ESA as no longer having limited capability for work on re-assessment. The tribunal upheld that decision of the Secretary of State but purported also to allow an appeal in respect of Incapacity Benefit/credits, that success invalidating any ESA claim. Judge May held that this was outside the jurisdiction of the tribunal and it had thus erred in law. What the tribunal should have done was to determine the ESA appeal before them on the basis as to whether there were any grounds for the Secretary of State to supersede the existing award of ESA and in the event that they were so satisfied to then determine the ESA appeal on its merits, that is, whether the claimant satisfied the conditions for ESA. It would then be for the Secretary of State to determine what he wished to do in the light of that decision.

In *SSWP v C'OC (ESA)* [2011] UKUT 447 (AAC), Judge Wikeley agreed with submissions made by the Secretary of State largely following the lines of the approach taken by Judge May in *CG v SSWP (ESA)* [2011] UKUT 167 (AAC). Here there was no entitlement to an existing award because there had within the previous six months been a disallowance of incapacity benefit following a PCA (ESA Regs 2008 reg.30(2)). Moreover the claimant's appeal was against a supersession decision whereas the First-tier tribunal had focussed on the original decision of the Secretary of State to award ESA, a decision not under appeal, so that the tribunal thus acted outside its jurisdiction.

Claim for period before appointed day

4. Where—   4.498
(a) (i) before the appointed day a person purports to make a claim, or
    (ii) on or after the appointed day a person makes a claim,
    for an employment and support allowance for a period beginning before the appointed day; and
(b) it appears to the Secretary of State that the person would be entitled to incapacity benefit or income support on the grounds of disability if that person made a claim for it in accordance with section 1(1)(a) of the Administration Act, the purported claim or claim may be treated by the Secretary of State as a claim in the alternative for incapacity benefit or income support on the grounds of disability.

DEFINITIONS

"appointed day"—see WRA 2007 s.29 Sch.4 para.11.
"incapacity benefit"—see WRA 2007 s.29 Sch.4 para.11.
"income support on the grounds of disability"—see reg.1(4).

GENERAL NOTE

This regulation entered into force on July 27, 2008, three months before October   4.499
27, 2008, the "appointed day" when WRA 2007 s.1 and the main ESA provisions became operative (see WRA 2007 s.29, Sch.4, para.11, and the Welfare Reform Act 2007 (Commencement No.6 and Consequential Provisions) Order 2008 (SI 2008/787) art.2(4).

It deals with a claim for ESA made before October 27, 2008 (the "appointed day) or after that but for a period prior to the appointed day. No entitlement to ESA can arise until October 27, 2008. So such a claim can either be rejected or, under this regulation, instead treated by the Secretary of State as a claim in the alternative for incapacity benefit or income support on the grounds of disability (IS as a person incapable of work; as a disabled or deaf student; or as a blind person). But it can only be so treated if the Secretary of State is satisfied that he would have been entitled to one of those benefits has a claim been made for it.

Transitional protection in relation to the Jobseekers Act 1995

5. In relation to a person who—   4.500
(a) is entitled to an existing award; or
(b) would be entitled to an existing award if that person made a claim described in regulation 2(2),
the Jobseekers Act 1995 shall continue to have effect as if paragraphs 12(2), (5)(b) and (6) of Schedule 3 to the Welfare Reform Act 2007 had not come into effect.

DEFINITIONS

"existing award"—see WRA 2007 s.29 Sch.4 para.11.

GENERAL NOTE

4.501   An "existing award" is an award of one or more of the benefits in the already existing incapacity benefits' regime: incapacity benefit; severe disablement allowance (limited, of course, only to those entitled to it immediately before April 6, 2001) and "income support on the grounds of disability" (WRA 2007 s.29, Sch.4, para.11). This last covers claims for income support under by someone to whom reg.6(4)(a) or 13(2)(b) or (bb) of, or para.7(a) or (b), 10, 12 or 13 of Sch.1B to, the Income Support (General) Regs 1987 (prescribed categories of person) applies (that is someone claiming IS as a person incapable of work; as a disabled worker; as a disabled or deaf student; or as a blind person). This regulation deals with those entitled to an existing award or who would be if they claimed it in respect of a "linked" period under reg.2(2). It provides that in respect of them the Jobseekers Act 1995 continues to have effect as if the changes effected by the specified provisions in WRA 2007 Sch.3 had never taken effect. In short, read the relevant Jobseekers Act provisions as laid out in the 2008/09 edition of Vol.II.

The Social Security (Housing Costs Special Arrangements) (Amendment and Modification) Regulations 2008

(SI 2008/3195)

Made by the Secretary of State for Work and Pensions under ss.123(1)(a), 135(1), 137(1) and 175(1) and (3) and (4) of the Social Security Contributions and Benefits Act 1992, ss.4(5), 35(1) and 36(2) and (4) of the Jobseekers Act 1995, ss.2(3)(b), 17(1) and 19(1) of the State Pension Credit Act 2002, and ss.4(2)(a) and (3), 24(1) and 25(2), (3) and (5) of the Welfare Reform Act 2007.

REGULATIONS REPRODUCED

PART 3

MODIFICATIONS RELATING TO CERTAIN PERSONS WHO CLAIM A RELEVANT
BENEFIT AFTER 4ᵀᴴ JANUARY 2009

GENERAL NOTE

The modifications to the rules for housing costs for income-related ESA made by   **4.503**
these Regulations only apply to certain claimants. See the note to Sch.6 to the ESA
Regulations.

The modifications relating to waiting periods made by these Regulations were
revoked on April 1, 2016 by the Social Security (Housing Costs Amendments)
Regulations 2015 (SI 2015/1647), subject to a saving provision in reg.8 of those
Regulations: see below. However, the modifications which concern the capital limit
for eligible loans (together with the time limit for receipt of housing costs in the case
of JSA) continue in effect.

Citation, commencement and interpretation

1.— (1) These Regulations may be cited as the Social Security (Housing   **4.504**
Costs Special Arrangements) (Amendment and Modification) Regulations
2008.

(2) Regulations 4 to 6, in so far as they relate to a particular person, come
into force on the first day of the first benefit week to commence for that
person on or after 5ᵗʰ January 2009.

(3) The remaining provisions of these Regulations come into force on 5ᵗʰ
January 2009.

(4) In these Regulations—
    "benefit week" has the same meaning as in—
        (a) regulation 2(1) of the Employment and Support Allowance
        Regulations, where the relevant benefit is an employment and
        support allowance;
    [(b) and (c) omitted as not relating to ESA]
    "housing costs" has the same meaning as in paragraph 1(1) (housing
    costs) of—
        (a) Schedule 6 to the Employment and Support Allowance
        Regulations, where the relevant benefit is an employment and
        support allowance;
    [(b) and (c) omitted as not relating to ESA]
    "relevant benefit" means—
        (a) an employment and support allowance;
        (b) income support;
        (c) a jobseeker's allowance;
    "the Employment and Support Allowance Regulations" means the
    Employment and Support Allowance Regulations 2008;
    [Remaining definitions omitted as not relating to ESA]

PART 2

MODIFICATIONS RELATING TO CERTAIN CLAIMANTS WHO ARE ENTITLED
TO A RELEVANT BENEFIT ON 4ᵀᴴ JANUARY 2009

Application

4.505 **3.**—(1) This Part applies in relation to a person who—

(a) is entitled to a relevant benefit on 4ᵗʰ January 2009; and

(b) on or after that date falls within paragraph (3) or (4).

(2) This Part ceases to apply in relation to a person who makes a further claim to the same, or claims another, relevant benefit after 4ᵗʰ January 2009.

(3) A person falls within this paragraph if, apart from these Regulations, the housing costs to be met in the benefit week that includes 4ᵗʰ January 2009 would be nil in that person's case because [¹ that person] has not been entitled to the relevant benefit concerned for the period mentioned in sub-paragraph (1)(a) in any of the following provisions—

(a) paragraph 8 (existing housing costs) or paragraph 9 (new housing costs) of Schedule 6 to the Employment and Support Allowance Regulations;

[(b) and (c) omitted as not relating to ESA]

(4) A person falls within this paragraph if [¹ that person] has been entitled to a relevant benefit for a continuous period, which includes 4th January 2009, for at least 8 weeks but less than 26 weeks under any of the provisions mentioned in paragraph (5) as in force apart from these Regulations.

(5) The provisions are—

(a) paragraph 8(1)(b) (existing housing costs) or paragraph 9(6) (new housing costs) of Schedule 6 to the Employment and Support Allowance Regulations;

[(b) and (c) omitted as not relating to ESA]

AMENDMENT

1. Social Security (Housing Costs Special Arrangements) (Amendment) Regulations 2009 (SI 2009/3257) reg.2 (January 5, 2010).

Modification of the Employment and Support Allowance Regulations

4.506 **4.** Schedule 6 (housing costs) to the Employment and Support Allowance Regulations applies in relation to a person to whom this Part applies as if—

(a) [¹ . . .]

(b) [¹ . . .]

(c) in paragraph 12(4) (general provisions applying to new and existing housing costs) the reference to "£100,000" were to "£200,000";

(d) [¹ . . .]

AMENDMENT

1. Social Security (Housing Costs Amendments) Regulations 2015 (SI 2015/1647), reg.7(1) (April 1, 2016). Note that the revocation of these paragraphs is subject to the saving provision in reg.8 of SI 2015/1647. See p.1585 for this saving provision.

Saving

7.[¹ . . .]   4.507

AMENDMENT

1. Social Security (Housing Costs Amendments) Regulations 2015 (SI 2015/1647), reg.7(1) (April 1, 2016). Note that the revocation of this regulation is subject to the saving provision in reg.8 of SI 2015/1647. See p.1585 for this saving provision.

PART 3

MODIFICATIONS RELTING TO CERTAIN PERSONS WHO CLAIM A RELEVANT BENEFIT AFTER 4ᵀᴴ JANUARY 2009

Application and interpretation

[¹ **8.**—(1) This Part applies on and after 5th January 2010 to a person   4.508
("C") who—
   (a) claims a relevant benefit after 4th January 2009; and
   (b) satisfies any of the following conditions.
(2) The first condition is that Part 2 applied to C at any time.
(3) The second condition is that this Part (as it has effect on and after 5th January 2010) applied to C in relation to a previous award.
(4) The third condition is that—
   (a) neither C nor C's partner has been awarded a relevant benefit as the result of an earlier claim (whether the award was made before or on or after 5th January 2009);
   (b) neither C nor C's partner is in receipt of state pension credit before the date on which C's claim is made or treated as made; and
   (c) C does not fall to be treated under a linking rule as being in continuous receipt of the benefit to which C's claim relates in respect of a period which begins on or before 4th January 2009 and which ends immediately before the date on which C's claim is made or is treated as made.
(5) The fourth condition is that—
   (a) C is not in receipt of a relevant benefit immediately before the date on which a claim made by C after 4th January 2009 is made or treated as made;
   (b) neither C nor C's partner is in receipt of state pension credit before that claim is made or treated as made;
   (c) C or C's partner was awarded a relevant benefit as the result of a claim made or treated as made before that claim; and
   (d) C does not fall to be treated under a linking rule as being in continuous receipt of a relevant benefit during the period which falls immediately between the date on which a claim to which this provision relates is made or treated as made and the last period to occur before that date in respect of which C was in receipt of a relevant benefit (whether as a single person or as a member of a couple or polygamous marriage).

(6) The fifth condition is that—

(a) C or C's partner is in receipt of state pension credit before the date on which any claim for a relevant benefit made by C or C's partner after 4th January 2009 is made or treated as made; and

(b) none of the following provisions apply in relation to any such claim—

　　(i) paragraph 3(2) (previous entitlement to other income-related benefits) of Schedule 6 (housing costs) to the Employment and Support Allowance Regulations;

　　(ii) paragraph 1A(1A) (previous entitlement to income-based job-seeker's allowance, income-related employment and support allowance or state pension credit) of Schedule 3 (housing costs) to the Income Support Regulations;

　　(iii) paragraph 1A(1ZA) or (1B) (previous entitlement to income support, income-related employment and support allowance or state pension credit) of Schedule 2 (housing costs) to the Jobseeker's Allowance Regulations.

(7) In this regulation—

a "linking rule" means a provision of—

(a) paragraph 15 (linking rule) of Schedule 6 (housing costs) to the Employment and Support Allowance Regulations,

(b) paragraph 14 (linking rule) of Schedule 3 (housing costs) to the Income Support Regulations, or (as the case may be)

(c) paragraph 13 (linking rule) of Schedule 2 (housing costs) to the Jobseeker's Allowance Regulations;

"partner" has the same meaning as in regulation 1(3) (citation, commencement and interpretation) of the Jobseeker's Allowance Regulations.]

AMENDMENT

1. Social Security (Housing Costs Special Arrangements) (Amendment) Regulations 2009 (SI 2009/3257) reg.4 (January 5, 2010).

Modification of the Employment and Support Allowance Regulations

4.509　　**9.** Schedule 6 (housing costs) to the Employment and Support Allowance Regulations applies in relation to a person to whom this Part applies as if—

(a) [¹ . . .]

(b) [¹ . . .]

(c) [¹ . . .]

(d) [¹ . . .]

(e) [¹ . . .]

(f) in paragraph 12 (general provisions applying to new and existing housing costs)—

　　(i) [¹ . . .]

　　(ii) [¹ . . .]

　　(iii) in sub-paragraph (4), the reference to "£100,000" were to "£200,000";

(g) [¹ . . .]

(h) [¹ . . .]

(i) [¹ . . .]

AMENDMENT

1. Social Security (Housing Costs Amendments) Regulations 2015 (SI 2015/1647), reg.7(1) (April 1, 2016). Note that the revocation of most of this regulation (with the exception of para.(f)(iii)) is subject to the saving provision in reg.8 of SI 2015/1647: see below.

The Employment and Support Allowance (Transitional Provisions, Housing Benefit and Council Tax Benefit) (Existing Awards) (No. 2) Regulations 2010

(SI 2010/1907) *(as amended)*

These Regulations provided for claimants who were previously entitled to incapacity benefit, income support on the basis of incapacity or disability, or severe disablement allowance to be migrated to employment and support allowance. That process should now have completed (with those claimants who are currently entitled to income-related ESA awaiting a further migration to UC) and it is no longer necessary for the Regulations to be included in the current edition of this work.

However, the Regulations remain in force (see pp.1410-1452 of Vol.I of the 2020/21 edition) and it is (just) possible that there may still be cases in which claimants have been missed by the migration process and to which they still apply.

4.509.1

The Employment and Support Allowance (Work-Related Activity) Regulations 2011

(SI 2011/1349) *(as amended)*

In accordance with section 26(1)(b) of the Welfare Reform Act 2007, and section 8(3) of the Welfare Reform Act 2009, a draft of this instrument was laid before Parliament and approved by a resolution of each House of Parliament.

The Secretary of State for Work and Pensions makes the following Regulations in exercise of the powers conferred by sections 9 and 10 of the Social Security Act 1998, and sections 11, 12(1) and (2), 13, 14, 15, 16, 17(3)(b), 24(1) and 25 of the Welfare Reform Act 2007.

In accordance with section 173(1) of the Social Security Administration Act 1992, the Secretary of State has obtained the agreement of the Social Security Advisory Committee that proposals in respect of these Regulations should not be referred to them.

4.509.2

ARRANGEMENT OF REGULATIONS

PART 1

GENERAL

4.510

PART 2

WORK-RELATED ACTIVITY

PART 3

CONTRACTING OUT

PART 4

AMENDMENTS TO THE ESA REGULATIONS

PART 5

AMENDMENT TO THE SOCIAL SECURITY AND CHILD SUPPORT (DECISIONS AND APPEALS) REGULATIONS 1999

PART 1

GENERAL

Citation and commencement

1. These Regulations may be cited as the Employment and Support   4.511
Allowance (Work-Related Activity) Regulations 2011 and shall come into
force on 1st June 2011.

GENERAL NOTE

For an instructive analysis of the complications and difficulties in challenging   4.512
decisions made under the conditionality regime introduced into ESA by these regulations see *LM v SSWP (ESA)* [2016] UKUT 360 (AAC).

Interpretation

2.—(1) In these Regulations—   4.513
"the Act" means the Welfare Reform Act 2007;
"the ESA Regulations" means the Employment and Support Allowance
    Regulations 2008;
"action plan" means an action plan issued in accordance with regulation
    5;
"carer's allowance", "child", [¹ ...] "medical treatment" and "working
    day" have the meaning given in regulation 2(1) of the ESA
    Regulations.
(2) For the purpose of these Regulations where a written notice is given
by sending it by post it is taken to have been received on the second working
day after posting.

AMENDMENT

1. Social Security (Work-focused Interviews for Lone Parents and Partners)
(Amendment) Regulations 2011 (SI 2011/2428) reg.7 (October 31, 2011).

PART 2

WORK-RELATED ACTIVITY

Requirement to undertake work-related activity

3.—(1) The Secretary of State may require a person who satisfies the   4.514
requirements in paragraph (2) to undertake work-related activity as a condition of continuing to be entitled to the full amount of employment and
support allowance payable to that person.
(2) The requirements referred to in paragraph (1) are that the person—
(a) is required to take part in, or has taken part in, one or more work-
    focused interviews pursuant to regulation 54 of the ESA Regulations;
(b) is not a lone parent who is responsible for and a member of the same
    household as a child under the age of [¹ 3];
(c) is not entitled to a carer's allowance; and

(d) is not entitled to a carer premium under paragraph 8 of Schedule 4 to the ESA Regulations.

(3) A requirement to undertake work-related activity ceases to have effect if the person becomes a member of the support group.

(4) A requirement imposed under paragraph (1)—

(a) must be reasonable in the view of the Secretary of State, having regard to the person's circumstances; and

(b) may not require the person to—

(i) apply for a job or undertake work, whether as an employee or otherwise; or

(ii) undergo medical treatment.

(5) A person who is a lone parent and in any week is responsible for and a member of the same household as a child under the age of 13, may only be required to undertake work-related activity under paragraph (1) during the child's normal school hours.

AMENDMENT

1. Income Support (Work-Related Activity) and Miscellaneous Amendments Regulations 2014 (SI 2014/1097) reg.15 (April 27, 2014).

GENERAL NOTE

4.515   Regulation 3 provides that the Secretary of State may require certain ESA claimants (who fall within para.(2)) to undertake work-related activity as a condition of continuing to be entitled to be paid their full ESA. However, by para.(4)(a) the requirement imposed under para.(1) "must be reasonable, in the view of the Secretary of State, having regard to the person's circumstances". Further, a claimant who fails to comply with such a requirement must show "good cause" within five working days of notice of such failure (see reg.8(1)). In *LM v SSWP (ESA)* [2016] UKUT 360 (AAC) Judge Wright ruled as follows (at para.37):

". . . satisfaction of regulation 8 of the ESA 2011 Regs requires the Secretary of State's decision maker, and the First-tier Tribunal on an appeal from such a decision to be satisfied, in a case or where the issue arises, that the requirement was reasonable on the circumstances of the claimants case, as a claimant cannot 'fail' to meet a requirement where there was in law no lawful requirement."

Furthermore, in accordance with normal principles, later evidence as to what a claimant's circumstances were "obtaining at [that] time", even if not known to the decision maker at the time of the decision, could still be taken into account under s.12(8)(b) of the Social Security Act 1998. As to whether issues arise for determination under regulation 3 (reasonable requirement) or reg.8 (good cause), this will depend on all the circumstances. According to Judge Wright (at para.43):

". . . If a claimant in his or her appeal letter or at the appeal hearing says the requirement was not reasonable having regard to his circumstances (or some such words, the exact statutory wording obviously does not need to be used) then the First-tier Tribunal will need to determine that issue in deciding the appeal. On the other hand, an appeal written by a welfare rights officer which focuses solely on arguing that the reasons given within the five days amount to good cause and where the surrounding evidence does not suggest that the particular requirement was other than a reasonable one for the particular appellant, would probably not be an appeal giving rise to an issue under regulation 3(4)(a) to be determined."

Directions about work-related activity

4.—(1) The circumstances in paragraph (2) are the circumstances pre-   4.516
scribed for the purposes of section 15(1)(a) of the Act.

(2) The circumstances referred to in paragraph (1) are that—

(a) the person has been identified by the Secretary of State as having a
barrier to work and in the view of the Secretary of State has refused
to address that barrier; and

(b) the Secretary of State considers that the activity specified in the
direction given under section 15(1) of the Act is a prerequisite to the
person's ability to obtain or remain in work.

Notification of work-related activity and action plans

5.—(1) The Secretary of State must notify a person of a requirement to   4.517
undertake work-related activity by including the requirement in a written
action plan given to the person.

(2) The action plan must specify—

(a) the work-related activity which the person is required to undertake;
and

(b) any other information that the Secretary of State considers appropriate.

GENERAL NOTE

As to what is required by the provision that "the action plan must *specify*" (empha-   4.518
sis added) see the discussion by Judge Wright in *LM v SSWP (ESA)* [2016] UKUT
360 (AAC) at paras 31 and 34(i), although the point did not need to be resolved in
the particular circumstances of that appeal.

Requirement to undertake work-related activity at a particular time not to apply

6. The Secretary of State may determine that a requirement as to the   4.519
time at or by which work-related activity is to be undertaken is not to apply,
or is to be treated as not having applied, if in the view of the Secretary of
State it would be, or would have been, unreasonable to require the person
to undertake the activity at or by that time.

GENERAL NOTE

For a provisional analysis of the scope and effect of reg.6 in the decision-making   4.520
and appellate contexts, and whether decisions under regulation 6 are appealable, see
the discussion by Judge Wright in *LM v SSWP (ESA)* [2016] UKUT 360 (AAC)
at paras 13–17, although the point did not need to be resolved in the particular circumstances of that appeal (see paras 29 and 35).

Reconsideration of action plans

7.—(1) A person may request reconsideration of an action plan.   4.521

(2) On receipt of a request the Secretary of State must reconsider the
action plan.

(3) A decision of the Secretary of State following a request must be in
writing and given to the person.

Failure to undertake work-related activity

4.522   **8.**—(1) A person who is required to undertake work-related activity but fails to do so must show good cause for the failure within 5 working days of the date on which the Secretary of State gives notice of the failure.

(2) The Secretary of State must determine whether a person who is required to undertake work-related activity has failed to do so and, if so, whether the person has shown good cause for the failure.

(3) [*¹Omitted.*]

AMENDMENT

1. Employment and Support Allowance (Sanctions) (Amendment) Regulations 2012 (SI 2012/2756) reg.7(2) (December 3, 2012, in respect of failures on or after that date (see reg.1 of the amending regs.)).

PART 3

CONTRACTING OUT

Contracting out

4.523   **9.**—(1) Any function of the Secretary of State specified in paragraph (2) may be exercised by, or by employees of, such person (if any) as may be authorised by the Secretary of State.

(2) The functions are—

(a) any function under—

    (i) regulation 3 (requirement to undertake work-related activity);

    (ii) regulation 5 (notification of work-related activity and action plans);

    (iii) regulation 6 (requirement to undertake work-related activity not to apply);

    (iv) regulation 7 (reconsideration of action plans);

(b) any function under [¹regulation 64(1)(c) and (1A)(b)] of the ESA Regulations (decisions in relation to cessation of reduction);

[¹(c) any function relating to a compliance condition under regulation 63(11) (compliance condition: notifications and agreements).]

AMENDMENT

1. Employment and Support Allowance (Sanctions) (Amendment) Regulations 2012 (SI 2012/2756) reg.7(3) (December 3, 2012, in respect of failures on or after that date (see reg.1 of the amending regs.)).

PART 4

AMENDMENTS TO THE ESA REGULATIONS

4.524   *Amendments to regs 2(1), 56, 57. 58, 61–64 and Schs 8 and 9 of the ESA Regulations effected by regs 10, 12–13 and 15–20 of this SI have been taken into account in preparing the text of those Regs in this Volume.*

The revocation of regs 47–49, 51–53 and 58 of the ESA Regulations effected by regs 11 and 14 of this SI have been taken into account in preparing the text of those Regs in this Volume.

PART 5

AMENDMENT TO THE SOCIAL SECURITY AND CHILD SUPPORT (DECISIONS AND APPEALS) REGULATIONS 1999

Amendment to the Social Security and Child Support (Decisions and Appeals) Regulations 1999

21. *The amendment effected to regulation 1(3) of the Social Security and Child Support (Decisions and Appeals) Regulations 1999 (interpretation) ("failure determination"), has been taken into account in Vol. III: Administration, Adjudication and the European Dimension.*   4.525

The Employment and Support Allowance (Amendment) Regulations 2012

(SI 2012/3096)

The Secretary of State for Work and Pensions makes the following   4.526
Regulations in exercise of the powers conferred by sections 8(1), (2), (3) and (5), 9(1), (2) and (3), 24(1) and 25(2) and (5) of, and paragraphs 1 and 9 of Schedule 2 to, the Welfare Reform Act 2007.

In accordance with section 173(1)(b) of the Social Security Administration Act 1992, the Secretary of State has obtained the agreement of the Social Security Advisory Committee that proposals in respect of these Regulations should not be referred to them.

REGULATIONS REPRODUCED

1.   Citation, commencement and interpretation
2.   Application, transitional and savings provisions

Citation, commencement and interpretation

1.— (1) These Regulations may be cited as the Employment and Support   4.527
Allowance (Amendment) Regulations 2012 and come into force on 28th January 2013.

(2) In these Regulations—

"the ESA Regulations" means the Employment and Support Allowance Regulations 2008; and

"the commencement date" means the date on which these Regulations come into force.

Application, transitional and savings provisions

4.528   **2.**—(1) Subject to paragraphs (2) and (3), these Regulations apply to—

(a) a person who makes a claim for an employment and support allowance on or after the commencement date (including a claim in respect of any period beginning before that date);

(b) a person who made a claim for an employment and support allowance before the commencement date in respect of whom a determination is made on or after that date—

(i) as to whether that person has or is to be treated as having limited capability for work under Part 5 of the ESA Regulations, or

(ii) as to whether that person has or is to be treated as having limited capability for work-related activity under Part 6 of those Regulations;

(c) a person who is entitled to an employment and support allowance immediately before the commencement date in respect of whom, on or after that date—

(i) the Secretary of State determines afresh under regulation 19(7) of the ESA Regulations whether the person has or is to be treated as having limited capability for work;

(ii) the Secretary of State determines afresh under regulation 34(4) of the ESA Regulations whether the person has or is to be treated as having limited capability for work-related activity; and

(d) a notified person within the meaning of regulation 4 of the Employment and Support Allowance (Transitional Provisions, Housing Benefit and Council Tax Benefit) (Existing Awards) (No.2) Regulations 2010 in respect of whom a determination is made on or after the commencement date as to whether that person—

(i) has or is to be treated as having limited capability for work under Part 5 of the ESA Regulations, or

(ii) is to be treated as having limited capability for work-related activity under Part 6 of those Regulations.

(2) Where a person has been issued with a questionnaire which relates to the provisions of Schedule 2 of the ESA Regulations as they had effect immediately before the commencement date, regulation 5 does not apply for the purposes of making a determination on or after that date as to that person's limited capability for work under Part 5 of the ESA Regulations and, for those purposes, the provisions of Schedule 2 of the ESA Regulations are to continue to apply in respect of that person as they had effect immediately before the commencement date.

(3) Where a person has been issued with a questionnaire which relates to the provisions of Schedule 3 of the ESA Regulations as they had effect immediately before the commencement date, regulation 6 does not apply for the purposes of making a determination on or after that date as to that person's limited capability for work under Part 6 of the ESA Regulations and, for those purposes, the provisions of Schedule 3 of the ESA Regulations are to continue to apply in respect of that person as they had effect immediately before the commencement date.

(4) The provisions of paragraphs (2) to (3) do not apply to any determination made in respect of a person on or after 28th July 2013.

DEFINITIONS

"the commencement date"—see reg.1(2).
"the ESA Regulations" —see reg.1(2).

GENERAL NOTE

This sets the scope of application of the various changes to the ESA Regs effected on January 28, 2013 and taken account of in the text and commentary to those Regulations. Basically, the amended provisions apply to all claims on or after that date and to most decisions on ESA entitlement taken on or after that date (para. (1)). For a six month "period of grace", however, ending on July 28, 2013, those issued with questionnaires based on one or other of the pre-January 28 Schs to those Regulations will have their assessment governed by the relevant pre-January 28 Sch. (paras (2)-(4)).

4.529

The Social Security (Housing Costs Amendments) Regulations 2015

(SI 2015/1647)

Made by the Secretary of State for Work and Pensions under ss.123(1)(a), 135(1), 137(1) and 175(1), (3) and (4) of the Social Security Contributions and Benefits Act 1992, ss.4(5), 35(1) and 36(2) and (4) of the Jobseekers Act 1995, ss.4(2)(a), 24(1) and 25(2), (3) and (5) of the Welfare Reform Act 2007 and ss.11(4) and (5)(b), 40, 42(1), (2) and (3) of, and para.1 of Sch.6 to, the Welfare Reform Act 2012.

4.530

[In force April 1, 2016]

Saving provision

8.—(1) This regulation applies to a person ("P") where, for the purpose of determining whether P's entitlement to a relevant benefit includes an amount for housing costs, the Secretary of State determines that P is entitled or required to be treated as entitled to one or more relevant benefits for a continuous period which includes 31st March 2016.

4.531

(2) Where this regulation applies to P, the provisions of—
(a) Schedule 6 to the Employment and Support Allowance Regulations 2008;
(b) Schedule 3 to the Income Support (General) Regulations 1987; and
(c) Schedule 2 to the Jobseeker's Allowance Regulations 1996,
as modified by the Social Security (Housing Costs Special Arrangements) (Amendment and Modification) Regulations 2008 are to have effect in relation to P as if the amendments made by regulations 2 to 4 of these Regulations and the revocation made by regulation 7(1) had not been made.

(3) Where this regulation applies to P, the provisions of Schedule 5 to the Universal Credit Regulations 2013 are to have effect in relation to P as if the amendments made by regulations 5 and 6 of these Regulations had not been made.

(4) In this regulation, "relevant benefit" means—
(a) an employment and support allowance under Part 1 of the Welfare Reform Act 2007;

(b) income support under the Income Support (General) Regulations 1987;

(c) a jobseeker's allowance under the Jobseeker's Allowance Regulations 1996; and

(d) universal credit under Part 1 of the Welfare Reform Act 2012.

GENERAL NOTE

4.532   See the notes to the Social Security (Housing Costs Special Arrangements) (Amendment and Modification) Regulations 2008 above and to Sch. 6 to the ESA Regulations.

The Employment and Support Allowance and Universal Credit (Miscellaneous Amendments and Transitional and Savings Provisions) Regulations 2017

(SI 2017/204)

In Force April 3, 2017

4.533   The Secretary of State for Work and Pensions makes the following Regulations in exercise of the powers conferred by sections 12(1), 17(4), 18(3), 19(2)(d), 25(a) and 42(3)(a) of the Welfare Reform Act 2012 and sections 15(4) and (5) and 34(1) of the Welfare Reform and Work Act 2016.

In accordance with section 173(5)(b) of the Social Security Administration Act 1992, this instrument contains only regulations made by virtue of, or consequential upon, sections 15, 16, 17 and 34 of the Welfare Reform and Work Act 2016 and is made before the end of the period of 6 months beginning with the coming into force of those sections.

In accordance with section 176(1) of the Social Security Administration Act 1992 the Secretary of State has consulted with organisations appearing to him to be representative of the authorities concerned.

GENERAL NOTE

4.534   Parts 1–3 of, and Sch.1 to, these Regulations, taken together with ss.15–17 of the Welfare Reform and Work Act 2016, abolish the work-related activity component of ESA (and the LCW element of universal credit) with effect from April 3, 2017 and make a number of consequential amendments. However, for ESA, the abolition is subject to the transitional and savings provisions in Sch.2, Pt.1, to which effect is given by reg.2. Part 2 of the Schedule contains equivalent provisions for universal credit and is reproduced in Vol.II.

Under Pt.1 of Sch.2, claimants who are found to have—or are treated as having—limited capability for work, but not limited capability for work-related activity, continue to be entitled to the work-related activity component in the following circumstances:

• A claim for ESA is made before April 3, 2017 and that claim results in an award of ESA (para.2).

Paragraph 2 does not contain any conditions about when, or by whom, the award is made, so an award that does not include the support component made by the FTT or UT in (say) April 2018 on a claim made before April 3, 2017 will entitle the claimant to the work-related activity component. Nor is there any condition about the date from which the award of ESA must be effective. This leads to consequences that may not have been intended. For example, C claims ESA on March 31, 2017 at a time when she is a person subject to immigration control. However, she is granted indefinite leave to remain with effect from April 10, 2017 and, on April 17, 2017, the Secretary of State decides the claim and awards ESA, Para.2 appears to require that the award should include the work-related activity component because C "has made . . . a claim for ESA before 3rd April 2017 and that claim [has resulted] in an award of ESA" even though the award will be effective from April 10, 2017, a week after the work-related activity component was otherwise abolished.

- A claim for ESA is made after April 3, 2017, but the resulting period of limited capability for work is treated as having begun before that date under the linking rules in reg.145 of the ESA Regulations or reg.86 of the ESA Regulations 2013 (para.3), which provide that any such period which is separated from another by 12 weeks or less is to be treated as a continuation of the earlier period.

- A person with an "existing award" (i.e., of incapacity benefit, severe disablement allowance or income support on the basis of incapacity or disability: see WRA 2007, Sch.4, para.11) becomes a notified person under reg.4 of SI 2010/1907 (para.4). The consequence is that any claimant who is migrated from one of those benefits to ESA, but who is not awarded the support component, will be entitled to the work-related activity component.

- A claim for ESA is made after April 3, 2017 but is treated as covering a period before that date by virtue of reg.19 of the Claims and Payments Regulations or reg.28 of the Claims and Payments Regulations 2013, with the result that benefit becomes payable before April 3, 2017 (para.5).

- A claim for ESA is made after April 3, 2017 but the first day of the claimant's assessment phase began before 3rd April 2017 by virtue of reg.5 of the ESA Regulations or reg.6 of the ESA Regulations 2013 (para.6).

  It is difficult to see what para.6 adds to para.3 (see the second bullet point above). A claimant's assessment phase can only begin sooner than the date of claim by virtue of reg.5 or reg.6 if the current period of limited capability for work is treated as a continuation of an earlier period under reg.145 of the ESA Regulations or reg.86 of the ESA Regulations 2013. In those circumstances, the work-related activity component continues in existence by virtue of para.3, so that para.6 appears to be otiose.

- A claimant who was entitled to ESA before April 3, 2017 becomes entitled to maternity allowance immediately after the award of ESA ends and then re-claims ESA within 12 weeks after entitlement to maternity allowance ends.

Citation and commencement

1. These Regulations may be cited as the Employment and Support Allowance and Universal Credit (Miscellaneous Amendments and Transitional and Savings Provisions) Regulations 2017 and come into force on 3rd April 2017.

4.535

PART 4

CONSEQUENTIAL, TRANSITIONAL AND SAVINGS PROVISIONS

Consequential, transitional and savings provisions

4.536   7.—(1)[Omitted]
(2) Schedule 2 contains transitional and savings provisions.

Regulation 7(2)

SCHEDULE 2

TRANSITIONAL AND SAVINGS PROVISIONS

PART 1

EMPLOYMENT AND SUPPORT ALLOWANCE: TRANSITIONAL AND SAVINGS PROVISIONS

Transitional and savings provisions: General

4.537   1.—(1) The amendments made by regulations 2 and 3, paragraphs 1 to 9 of Schedule 1 and by section 15(1) to (3) of the Welfare Reform and Work Act 2016 (which amend sections 2 and 4 of the Welfare Reform Act 2007) do not apply where any of the circumstances in paragraphs 2 to 7 apply.
(2) In this Part—
"assessment phase" has the same meaning as in the Welfare Reform Act 2007;
[¹ "claim"] means [¹ . . .] a claim for an employment and support allowance [¹ made] in accordance with regulations 4ZC, 4G, 4H and 4I of the Social Security (Claims and Payments) Regulations 1987 or regulations 13 to 17 of the Universal Credit, Personal Independence Payment, Jobseeker's Allowance and Employment and Support Allowance (Claims and Payments) Regulations 2013;
"employment and support allowance" means an allowance under Part 1 of the Welfare Reform Act 2007;
"ESA Regulations 2008" means the Employment and Support Allowance Regulations 2008;
"ESA Regulations 2013" means the Employment and Support Allowance Regulations 2013.

Claimants who have made a claim for employment and support allowance before 3rd April 2017

4.538   2. The first circumstance is where the claimant has made or is treated as having made a claim for an employment and support allowance before 3rd April 2017 and that claim results in an award of employment and support allowance.

Claimants who had been found to have limited capability for work before 3rd April 2017

3. The second circumstance is where the claimant's period of limited capability for work began on or after 3rd April 2017 and is treated as a continuation of an earlier period of limited capability for work which began before 3rd April 2017 by virtue of—
(a) regulation 145 of the ESA Regulations 2008; or
(b) regulation 86 of the ESA Regulations 2013.

4.539

Claimants on Incapacity Benefits who have or will become notified persons

4. The third circumstance is where the claimant [¹ has been,] is or becomes a notified person within the meaning of regulation 4 of the Employment and Support Allowance (Transitional Provisions, Housing Benefit and Council Tax Benefit) (Existing Awards) (No. 2) Regulations 2010 and a determination is effective as to whether that person—
(a) has or is to be treated as having limited capability for work under Part 5 of the ESA Regulations 2008;
(b) has or is to be treated as having limited capability for work under Part 5 of the ESA Regulations 2013;
(c) has or is to be treated as having limited capability for work-related activity under Part 6 of the ESA Regulations 2008; or
(d) has or is to be treated as having limited capability for work-related activity under Part 6 of the ESA Regulations 2013.

4.540

Claimants where their award becomes payable before 3rd April 2017

5. The fourth circumstance is where the claimant becomes entitled to an employment and support allowance before 3rd April 2017 by virtue of—
(a) regulation 19(1) and paragraph 16 of Schedule 4 to the Social Security (Claims and Payments) Regulations 1987; or
(b) regulation 28 of the Universal Credit, Personal Independence Payment, Jobseeker's Allowance and Employment and Support Allowance (Claims and Payments) Regulations 2013.

4.541

Claimants where their assessment phase begins before 3rd April 2017

6. The fifth circumstance is where the first day of the claimant's assessment phase began before 3rd April 2017 by virtue of—
(a) regulation 5 of the ESA Regulations 2008; or
(b) regulation 6 of the ESA Regulations 2013.

4.542

Claimants where they have been entitled to maternity allowance

7. The sixth circumstance is where—
(a) a claimant was entitled to a maternity allowance under section 35 of the Social Security Contributions and Benefits Act 1992 and the end of that award is within 12 weeks beginning with the date that the claim for an employment and support allowance is made; and
(b) immediately prior to their entitlement to a maternity allowance

4.543

beginning the claimant was previously entitled to an employment and support allowance before 3rd April 2017.

AMENDMENT

1. Employment and Support Allowance (Miscellaneous Amendments and Transitional and Savings Provision) Regulations 2017 (SI 2017/581) reg.9 (June 23, 2017).

The Employment and Support Allowance (Miscellaneous Amendments and Transitional and Savings Provision) Regulations 2017

(SI 2017/581)

In Force June 23, 2017

ARRANGEMENT OF REGULATIONS

The Secretary of State for Work and Pensions makes the following Regulations in exercise of the powers conferred by sections 15(4) and (5) and 34(1) of the Welfare Reform and Work Act 2016.

In accordance with section 173(5)(b) of the Social Security Administration Act 1992, this instrument contains only regulations made by virtue of, or consequential upon section 15 of the Welfare Reform and Work Act 2016 and is made before the end of the period of 6 months beginning with the coming into force of this section.

In accordance with section 176(1) of the Social Security Administration Act 1992 the Secretary of State has consulted with organisations appearing to him to be representative of the authorities concerned.

GENERAL NOTE

4.545   These Regulations make a number of technical amendments to clarify issues that have arisen in relation to the abolition of the work-related activity component with effect from April 3, 2017 (see SI 2017/204 above). The amendments made by regs 2-9 have been incorporated in the appropriate places in the text. Reg.10 provides that—unsurprisingly—the amendments made by regs 2-8 do not apply to those who have transitional protection from the changes in SI 2017/204. Reg.9 has not been included in that transitional and savings provision because it makes technical amendments to the extent of that transitional protection given by SI 2017/204 Sch.2, Pt.1.

Citation and commencement

4.546   1. These Regulations may be cited as the Employment and Support Allowance (Miscellaneous Amendments and Transitional and Savings Provision) Regulations 2017 and come into force on 23rd June 2017.

Transitional and savings provision

10. The amendments made by regulations 2 to 8 of these Regulations do not apply where any of the circumstances in paragraph 2 to 7 of Schedule 2 (transitional and savings provisions) to the Employment and Support Allowance and Universal Credit (Miscellaneous Amendments and Transitional and Savings Provisions) Regulations 2017, as amended by regulation 9 of these Regulations apply.

4.547

PART V

UC COMMENCEMENT ORDERS

The Welfare Reform Act 2012 (Commencement No.9 and Transitional and Transitory Provisions and Commencement No.8 and Savings and Transitional Provisions (Amendment)) Order 2013

(SI 2013/983) (C. 41) (AS AMENDED)

The Secretary of State, in exercise of the powers conferred by section 150(3) and (4)(a), (b)(i) and (c) of the Welfare Reform Act 2012, makes the following Order:

ARRANGEMENT OF ARTICLES

23. Amendment of the Welfare Reform Act 2012 (Commencement No 8 and Savings and Transitional Provisions) Order 2013
24. Appeals relating to ESA and JSA

Schedule 1 Postcode districts
Schedule 2 Universal credit provisions coming into force in relation to certain claims and awards
Schedule 3 Commencement of repeals in Part 1 of Schedule 14 to the Act
Schedule 4 Modifications of the Transitional Provisions Regulations 2010
Schedule 5 The Gateway Conditions

GENERAL NOTE

5.2   This Commencement Order ("the Commencement No.9 Order") was the first to "roll out" the universal credit scheme. Originally it had to be read together with the Transitional Provisions Regulations 2013. This Order accordingly brought into force, albeit for limited purposes only, provisions of the WRA 2012 that related to both the introduction of universal credit and the abolition of income-related ESA and income-based JSA. This was achieved by reference to the specific categories of cases set out in arts. 3 and 4. However, these provisions applied only to four post-code districts in Manchester, Oldham and Stockport (or "the relevant districts"; see Sch.1) as from April 29, 2013 (also the date on which the Transitional Provisions Regulations 2013 came into force). The justification for the limited "roll out" was that it would "facilitate an evaluation of the Universal Credit business processes and information technology functionality in a live environment before it is rolled out nationally from October 2013" (*Explanatory Memorandum to the Transitional Provisions Regulations 2013*, Para.7.64).
        In this Order and its following companions (see further below), an award of ESA under Part 1 of the Welfare Reform Act 2007, in a case where income-related ESA has been abolished (i.e. in a Pathfinder area), is referred to as a "new style ESA award". Likewise an award of JSA under the Jobseekers Act 1995, in a case where income-based JSA has been abolished, is referred to as a "new style JSA award". Conversely an award of ESA under Part 1 of the Welfare Reform Act 2007, in a case where income-related ESA has not been abolished, is referred to as an "old style ESA award". Similarly an award of JSA under the Jobseekers Act 1995, in a case where income-based JSA has not been abolished, is referred to as an "old style JSA award".
        This Order was initially followed by the Commencement No.11 Order (certain postcodes in Wigan ("the No.2 relevant districts") and Oldham and Warrington ("the No.3 relevant districts") as from July 1, 2013), the Commencement No.13 Order (certain postcodes in Hammersmith, Manchester and Wigan ("the No.4 relevant districts") as from October 28, 2013) and the Commencement No.14 Order (certain postcodes in Rugby, Inverness and Perth ("the No.5 relevant districts") as from November 25, 2013). Further Commencement Orders duly followed.
        In addition, of course, a claimant who lived in one of the four originally specified postcode districts had also to be a member of the Pathfinder Group, i.e. be a person who met the requirements of regulations 5 to 12 of the Transitional Provisions Regulations 2013. However, as noted above the No.9 Commencement Order (along with the No.11, 13, 14 and 16 Commencement Orders) was amended by the Welfare Reform Act 2012 (Commencement No.9, 11, 13, 14, 16 and 17 and Transitional and Transitory Provisions (Amendment)) Order 2014 (SI 2014/1661). In conjunction with these changes, the Transitional Provisions Regulations 2013 were revoked and replaced by the Universal Credit (Transitional Provisions) Regulations 2014 (SI 2014/1230). At the same time, the "Pathfinder Group" conditions, previously contained in regs.5 to 12 of the Transitional Provisions Regulations 2013 were omitted from the Transitional Regulations 2014. Instead, similar conditions (known

as the "gateway conditions") appeared in Sch.5 to the Commencement No.9 Order as inserted by art.16 of (SI 2014/1661).

Citation

1. This Order may be cited as the Welfare Reform Act 2012 (Commencement No.9 and Transitional and Transitory Provisions and Commencement No.8 and Savings and Transitional Provisions (Amendment)) Order 2013.

5.3

Interpretation

2.—(1) In this Order—

"the Act" means the Welfare Reform Act 2012 (apart from in Schedule 4);

"the 1995 Act" means the Jobseekers Act 1995;

"the 2007 Act" means the Welfare Reform Act 2007;

"the amending provisions" means the provisions referred to in article 4(1)(a) to (c);

[¹] [⁴ "claimant"—

(a) in relation to an employment and support allowance, has the same meaning as in Part 1 of the Welfare Reform Act 2007, save as mentioned in article 5(1A);

(b) in relation to a jobseeker's allowance, has the same meaning as in the Jobseekers Act 1995 (as it applies apart from the amendments made by Part 1 of Schedule 14 to the Act that remove references to an income-based jobseeker's allowance), save as mentioned in article 5(1A);

(c) in relation to universal credit, has the same meaning as in Part 1 of the Act

"appointed day" means the day appointed for the coming into force of the amending provisions in accordance with article 4(3);]

"the Claims and Payments Regulations 1987" means the Social Security (Claims and Payments) Regulations 1987;

"the Claims and Payments Regulations 2013" means the Universal Credit, Personal Independence Payment, Jobseeker's Allowance and Employment and Support Allowance (Claims and Payments) Regulations 2013;

"contribution-based jobseeker's allowance" means a contribution-based allowance under the 1995 Act as it has effect apart from the amendments made by Part 1 of Schedule 14 to the Act that remove references to an income-based allowance;

"contributory employment and support allowance" means a contributory allowance under Part 1 of the 2007 Act as it has effect apart from the amendments made by Schedule 3, and Part 1 of Schedule 14, to the Act that remove references to an income-related allowance;

[¹ "conversion decision" has the meaning given by the 2010 Transitional Regulations;]

"the Decisions and Appeals Regulations 2013" means the Universal Credit, Personal Independence Payment, Jobseeker's Allowance and Employment and Support Allowance (Decisions and Appeals) Regulations 2013;

[⁵ "the Digital Service Regulations 2014" means the Universal Credit (Digital Service) Amendment Regulations 2014;]

5.4

[⁶ "disability living allowance" means an allowance under section 71 of the Social Security Contributions and Benefits Act 1992;]

"employment and support allowance" means an employment and support allowance under Part 1 of the 2007 Act;

"the ESA Regulations 2008" means the Employment and Support Allowance Regulations 2008;

"the ESA Regulations 2013" means the Employment and Support Allowance Regulations 2013;

[¹ [³ . . .]

"First-tier Tribunal" has the same meaning as in the Social Security Act 1998;

"gateway conditions" means the conditions specified in Schedule 5;

"housing benefit" means housing benefit under section 130 of the Social Security Contributions and Benefits Act 1992;]

"income-based jobseeker's allowance" means an income-based jobseeker's allowance under the 1995 Act;

"income-related employment and support allowance" means an income-related allowance under Part 1 of the 2007 Act;

[¹ "income support" means income support under section 124 of the Social Security Contributions and Benefits Act 1992;]

"jobseeker's allowance" means an allowance under the 1995 Act;

[¹ [² "joint claimants"], in relation to universal credit, has the same meaning as in Part 1 of the Act;]

"the JSA Regulations 1996" means the Jobseeker's Allowance Regulations 1996;

"the JSA Regulations 2013" means the Jobseeker's Allowance Regulations 2013;

[¹ "new style ESA" means an employment and support allowance under Part 1 of the 2007 Act as amended by the provisions of Schedule 3, and Part 1 of Schedule 14, to the Act that remove references to an income-related allowance and "new style ESA award" shall be construed accordingly;

"new style JSA" means a jobseeker's allowance under the 1995 Act as amended by the provisions of Part 1 of Schedule 14 to the Act that remove references to an income-based allowance and "new style JSA award" shall be construed accordingly;

"old style ESA" means an employment and support allowance under Part 1 of the 2007 Act as it has effect apart from the amendments made by Schedule 3, and Part 1 of Schedule 14, to the Act that remove references to an income-related allowance and "old style ESA award" shall be construed accordingly;

"old style JSA" means a jobseeker's allowance under the 1995 Act as it has effect apart from the amendments made by Part 1 of Schedule 14 to the Act that remove references to an income-based jobseeker's allowance and "old style JSA award" shall be construed accordingly;]

[⁶ "personal independence payment" means an allowance under Part 4 of the Act;]

"relevant districts" means the postcode districts specified in Schedule 1;

[¹ "single claimant", in relation to universal credit, has the same meaning as in Part 1 of the Act;

"state pension credit" means state pension credit under the State Pension Credit Act 2002;

"tax credit" (including "child tax credit" and "working tax credit") has the same meaning as in the Tax Credits Act 2002;]

[¹ . . .];

"the 2010 Transitional Regulations" means the Employment and Support Allowance (Transitional Provisions, Housing Benefit and Council Tax Benefit)(Existing Awards)(No.2) Regulations 2010.

[¹ "the 2014 Transitional Regulations" means the Universal Credit (Transitional Provisions) Regulations 2014;

"the Universal Credit Regulations" means the Universal Credit Regulations 2013;

"Upper Tribunal" has the same meaning as in the Social Security Act 1998.]

[¹ (2) For the purposes of this Order—

(a) the Claims and Payments Regulations 2013 apply for the purpose of deciding—

(i) whether a claim for universal credit is made or is to be treated as made; and

(ii) the date on which such a claim is made; and

(b) where a couple is treated, in accordance with regulation 9(8) of the Claims and Payments Regulations 2013, as making a claim for universal credit, references to the date on which the claim is treated as made are to the date of formation of the couple.]

AMENDMENTS

1. Welfare Reform Act 2012 (Commencement No.9, 11, 13, 14 and 16 and Transitional and Transitory Provisions (Amendment)) Order 2014 (SI 2014/1452) art.4 (June 16, 2014).

2. Welfare Reform Act 2012 (Commencement No.9, 11, 13 14, 16 and 17 and Transitional and Transitory Provisions (Amendment)) Order 2014 (SI 2014/1661) art. 4(1) (June 30, 2014).

3. Welfare Reform Act 2012 (Commencement No.9, 11, 13, 14, 16 and 17 and Transitional and Transitory Provisions (Amendment) (No.2)) Order 2014 (SI 2014/1923) art. 4(2) (July 28, 2014).

4. Welfare Reform Act 2012 (Commencement No.9, 11, 13 14, 16, 17 and 19 and Transitional and Transitory Provisions (Amendment)) Order 2014 (SI 2014/3067) art.6(2)(a) (November 24, 2014).

5. Welfare Reform Act 2012 (Commencement No.20 and Transitional and Transitory Provisions and Commencement No.9 and Transitional and Transitory Provisions (Amendment)) Order 2014 (SI 2014/3094) art.7(2)(a) (November 26, 2014).

6. Welfare Reform Act 2012 (Commencement No.9, 11, 13, 14, 16, 17 and 19 and Transitional and Transitory Provisions (Amendment)) Order 2015 (SI 2015/32) art.4(2) (January 26, 2015).

Day appointed for commencement of the universal credit provisions in Part 1 of the Act

3.—(1) 29th April 2013 is the day appointed for the coming into force of- 5.5

(a) sections 29 (delegation and contracting out), 37(1), (2), (8) and (9) (capability for work or work-related activity), 38 (information) and 39(1), (2), (3)(b) and (c) (couples) of the Act;

(b) the following paragraphs of Schedule 2 to the Act (universal credit:

amendments) and section 31 of the Act (supplementary and consequential amendments) in so far as it relates to those paragraphs, in
so far as they are not already in force—
  (i) paragraphs 1, 2, 32 to 35, 37 to 42, 52 to 55 and 65;
  (ii) paragraphs 4, 8, 10 to 23, 25 and 27 to 31 and paragraph 3 in
  so far as it relates to those paragraphs; and
  (iii) paragraphs 44, 45, 47, 49, 50(2) and 50(1) in so far as it relates
  to 50(2), and paragraph 43 in so far as it relates to those paragraphs and sub-paragraphs; and
(c) paragraph 1 of Schedule 5 to the Act (universal credit and other
working-age benefits) and section 35 of the Act in so far as it relates
to that paragraph.
(2) The day appointed for the coming into force of the provisions of the
Act listed in Schedule 2, in so far as they are not already in force, in relation
to the case of a claim referred to in paragraph (3)(a) to (d) and any award
that is made in respect of such a claim, and in relation to the case of an
award referred to in paragraph (3)(e) or (f), is the day appointed in accordance with paragraph (4).
  [¹ (3) The claims and awards referred to are—
(a) a claim for universal credit where, on the date on which the claim is
made, the claimant resides in one of the relevant districts and meets
the gateway conditions;
[²(b) a claim for universal credit where—
  (i) in the case of a single claimant, the claimant gives incorrect
  information regarding the claimant residing in a relevant district or meeting the gateway conditions and the claimant does
  not reside in such a district or does not meet the gateway conditions on the date on which the claim is made;
  (ii) in the case of joint claimants, either or both of the joint claimants gives or give incorrect information regarding his or her (or
  their) residing in such a district or meeting the gateway conditions and one or both of them does not or do not reside in such
  a district or does not or do not meet those conditions on the
  date on which the claim is made; and
  (iii) after a decision is made that the single claimant is, or the joint
  claimants are, entitled to universal credit and one or more payments have been made in respect of the single claimant or the
  joint claimants, the Secretary of State discovers that incorrect
  information has been given regarding residence or meeting the
  gateway conditions.]
(c) a claim for universal credit that is treated as made by a couple in
the circumstances referred to in regulation 9(8) of the Claims and
Payments Regulations 2013 (claims for universal credit by members
of a couple) where the claim complies with paragraph (7);
[²(d) a claim for universal credit by a former member of a couple who were
joint claimants of universal credit, whether or not the claim is made
jointly with another person, where the former member is not exempt
from the requirement to make a claim by virtue of regulation 9(6)
of the Claims and Payments Regulations 2013 (claims for universal
credit by members of a couple), where the claim is made during the
period of one month starting with the date on which notification is
given to the Secretary of State that the former joint claimants have

ceased to be a couple, and where the claim complies with paragraph (8);]
(e) an award of universal credit that is made without a claim in the circumstances referred to in regulation 6(1) or (2) of the Claims and Payments Regulations 2013 (claims not required for entitlement to universal credit in some cases) where the circumstances referred to in paragraph (9) apply; and
(f) an award of universal credit that is made without a claim in the circumstances referred to in regulation 9(6), (7) or (10) of the Claims and Payments Regulations 2013 (claims for universal credit by members of a couple) where the circumstances referred to in paragraph (9) apply.]
(4) The day appointed in relation to the cases of the claims and awards referred to in paragraph (2) is—
(a) in the case of a claim referred to in paragraph (3)(a) to (d), the first day of the period in respect of which the claim is made or treated as made;
(b) in the case of an award referred to in paragraph (3)(e) or (f), the first day on which a person is entitled to universal credit under that award.
(5) [¹ . . .];
(6) For the purposes of paragraph (4)(a), where the time for making a claim for universal credit is extended under regulation 26(2) of the Claims and Payments Regulations 2013, the reference to the first day of the period in respect of which the claim is made or treated as made is a reference to the first day of the period in respect of which the claim is, by reason of the operation of that provision, timeously made or treated as made.
[¹ (7) A claim that is treated as made by a couple in the circumstances referred to in regulation 9(8) of the Claims and Payments Regulations 2013 complies with this paragraph where, on the date on which the claim is treated as made, the member of the couple who did not previously have an award of universal credit [³ . . .] is not entitled to state pension credit.
(8) A claim by a former member of a couple that is made in the circumstances referred to in paragraph (3)(d) complies with this paragraph where, on the date on which the claim is made, [³ neither the former member nor his or her partner (if any) is entitled to state pension credit].
(9) The circumstances referred to are where the relevant person is not entitled to state pension credit and, save where an award of universal credit is made in the circumstances referred to in regulation 9(7) of the Claims and Payments Regulations 2013, his or her partner (if any) is not entitled to [³ state pension credit].
(10) For the purposes of paragraph (9), "relevant person" means—
(a) where an award of universal credit is made in the circumstances referred to in regulation 6(1) or (2) of the Claims and Payments Regulations 2013, the former claimant referred to in that regulation 6(1);
(b) where an award of universal credit is made in the circumstances referred to in paragraph (6) of regulation 9 of the Claims and Payments Regulations 2013, [³ as that paragraph has effect apart from the amendments made by the Digital Service Regulations 2014,] the member of the former couple referred to in that paragraph;

[³(ba) where an award of universal credit is made in the circumstances referred to in paragraph (6) of regulation 9 of the Claims and Payments Regulations 2013, as that paragraph has effect as amended by the Digital Service Regulations 2014, the former joint claimant of universal credit to whom a new award of universal credit is made as referred to in sub-paragraph (a) or (b) of that paragraph;]

(c) where an award of universal credit is made in the circumstances referred to in paragraph (7) of regulation 9 of the Claims and Payments Regulations 2013, each of the joint claimants referred to in that paragraph;

(d) where an award of universal credit is made in the circumstances referred to in paragraph (10) of regulation 9 of the Claims and Payments Regulations 2013, the surviving partner referred to in that paragraph.

[³ (10A) In paragraph (3)—

(a) in sub-paragraph (c), the reference to regulation 9(8) of the Claims and Payments Regulations 2013 is a reference to that provision both as it has effect as amended by the Digital Service Regulations 2014 and as it has effect apart from that amendment;

(b) in sub-paragraph (d), the reference to regulation 9(6) of the Claims and Payments Regulations 2013 is a reference to that provision as it has effect apart from the amendment made by the Digital Service Regulations 2014;

(c) in sub-paragraph (f), the reference to regulation 9(6) of the Claims and Payments Regulations 2013 is a reference to that provision both as it has effect as amended by the Digital Service Regulations 2014 and as it has effect apart from that amendment.]

(11) For the purposes of paragraphs (8) and (9), "partner" means a person who forms part of a couple with the person in question, where "couple" has the same meaning as it has in section 39 of the Act.]

AMENDMENTS

1. Welfare Reform Act 2012 (Commencement No.9, 11, 13, 14 and 16 and Transitional and Transitory Provisions (Amendment)) Order 2014 (SI 2014/1452) art.5 (June 16, 2014).

2. Welfare Reform Act 2012 (Commencement No.9, 11, 13, 14, 16 and 17 and Transitional and Transitory Provisions (Amendment) (No.2)) Order 2014 (SI 2014/1923) art. 4(3) (July 28, 2014).

3. Welfare Reform Act 2012 (Commencement No.20 and Transitional and Transitory Provisions and Commencement No.9 and Transitional and Transitory Provisions (Amendment)) Order 2014 (SI 2014/3094) art.7(2)(b) (November 26, 2014).

DEFINITIONS

"the Act"–art. 2(1).
"the Claims and Payments Regulations 2013"–*ibid.*
"relevant districts"–*ibid.*
"the Transitional Regulations"–*ibid.*

GENERAL NOTE

Paragraph (1)
This brings into force various provisions relating to universal credit (including   **5.6**
some supplementary and consequential provisions set out in Sch.2 to the 2012 Act)
on April 29, 2013.

Paragraph (2)
This tortuously worded provision has the effect of bringing into force those pro-   **5.7**
visions relating to universal credit in Part 1 of the WRA 2012, as set out in Sch.2,
where one of the different categories of case referred to in art.3(3) applies. These
relate to claims for UC and any resulting award as well as to awards of universal
credit without a claim.

Paragraph (3)
This specifies the various situations in which para.(2) has the effect of applying   **5.8**
the new universal credit rules.

Sub-Paragraph (3)(a)
This covers the situation where a person makes a claim for universal credit in   **5.9**
respect of a period that begins on or after April 29, 2013 where that individual
both resides in a "relevant district" at the time that the claim is made and meets the
gateway conditions.

Sub-Paragraph (3)(b)
Where a person claims universal credit and incorrectly states that they live in a   **5.10**
relevant district, that person remains subject to the new regime.

Sub-Paragraph (3)(c)
This covers the case of a single person who becomes a member of a couple where   **5.11**
the other member was already entitled to universal credit.

Sub-Paragraph (3)(d)
Where a couple separate, and the member of the couple who is not exempt from   **5.12**
making a claim for universal credit makes a claim within a period of one month, the
new rules apply.

Sub-Paragraph (3)(e)
A person may be awarded universal credit without making a claim as a result of   **5.13**
changes in their income within six months of their income being such that they were
not previously entitled to universal credit.

Sub-Paragraph (3)(f)
Again, a person may be awarded universal credit without making a claim where   **5.14**
a couple cease to be a couple and an award is made to the member of the couple
who is exempt from making a claim. Similarly, an award of universal credit may be
made without a claim to a couple where the members of the couple were previously
entitled to the new benefit as single claimants. In addition, the new regime applies
where an award of universal credit is made without a claim to a member of a couple
where the other member of the couple has died.

Paragraphs (4) – (11)
These make supplementary provision dealing with the effective date of universal   **5.15**
credit claims and awards under the preceding rules.

[¹ [² [³ Incorrect information regarding residence in a relevant district or meeting the gateway conditions

5.16   **3A.**—(1) This article applies where a claim for universal credit is made and it is subsequently discovered that the single claimant or either or both of two joint claimants gave incorrect information regarding his or her (or their) residing in one of the relevant districts or meeting the gateway conditions and the conditions referred to in paragraph (2) are met.

(2) The conditions referred to are that, on the date on which the claim was made, the claimant—

   (a)   did not reside in one of the relevant districts (unless paragraph (3) applies); or

   (b)   did reside in one of the relevant districts but did not meet the gateway conditions.

(3) This paragraph applies where the claimant resided in an area apart from the relevant districts with respect to which the provisions of the Act referred to in Schedule 2 were in force in relation to a claim for universal credit and the conditions (if any) that applied to such a claim, for those provisions to come into force, were met.

(4) Where the discovery is made before the claim for universal credit has been decided—

   (a)   the claimant is to be informed that the claimant is not entitled to claim universal credit;

   (b)   if the claimant (or, in the case of joint claimants, either of them) makes a claim for old style ESA, old style JSA or income support ("the specified benefit") and the date on which that claim is made (as determined in accordance with the Claims and Payments Regulations 1987) is after the date on which the claim for universal credit was made, but no later than one month after the date on which the information required by sub-paragraph (a) was given—

      (i)   the claim for the specified benefit is to be treated as made on the date on which the claim for universal credit was made or the first date on which the claimant would have been entitled to the specified benefit if a claim had been made for it on that date, if later; and

      (ii) any provision of the Claims and Payments Regulations 1987 under which the claim for the specified benefit is treated as made on a later date does not apply;

   (c)   if the claimant (or, in the case of joint claimants, either of them) makes a claim for housing benefit and the date of that claim (as determined in accordance with the Housing Benefit Regulations 2006 or, as the case may be, the Housing Benefit (Persons who have attained the qualifying age for state pension credit) Regulations 2006 (together referred to as "the Housing Benefit Regulations")) is after the date on which the claim for universal credit was made, but no later than one month after the date on which the information required by sub-paragraph (a) was given—

      (i)   the claim for housing benefit is to be treated as made on the date on which the claim for universal credit was made or the first date on which the claimant would have been entitled to housing benefit if a claim had been made for it on that date, if later; and

    (ii) any provision of the Housing Benefit Regulations under which the claim for housing benefit is treated as made on a later date does not apply;

(d) if the claimant (or, in the case of joint claimants, either of them) makes a claim for a tax credit and that claim is received by a relevant authority at an appropriate office (within the meaning of the Tax Credits (Claims and Notifications) Regulations 2002 ("the 2002 Regulations")) during the period of one month beginning with the date on which the information required by sub-paragraph (a) was given—

    (i) the claim for a tax credit is to be treated as having been received by a relevant authority at an appropriate office on the date on which the claim for universal credit was made or the first date on which the claimant would have been entitled to a tax credit if a claim had been so received on that date, if later; and

    (ii) any provision of the 2002 Regulations under which the claim is treated as having been made on a later date does not apply.

(5) Where the discovery is made after a decision has been made that the claimant is entitled to universal credit, but before any payment has been made—

(a) that decision is to cease to have effect immediately, by virtue of this article;

(b) the claimant is to be informed that they are not entitled to claim universal credit; and

(c) sub-paragraphs (b) to (d) of paragraph (4) apply.

(6) Where the discovery is made after a decision has been made that the claimant is entitled to universal credit and one or more payments have been made in respect of the claimant, the decision is to be treated as a decision under section 8 of the Social Security Act 1998.

(7) For the purposes of paragraph (4), a person makes a claim for old style ESA or old style JSA where he or she makes a claim for an employment and support allowance or a jobseeker's allowance and the claim is subject to Part 1 of the 2007 Act or the 1995 Act respectively as those provisions have effect apart from the amendments made by the amending provisions.]]]

Amendments

1. Welfare Reform Act 2012 (Commencement No.9, 11, 13, 14 and 16 and Transitional and Transitory Provisions (Amendment)) Order 2014 (SI 2014/1452) art.5 (June 16, 2014).

2. Welfare Reform Act 2012 (Commencement No.9, 11, 13 14, 16 and 17 and Transitional and Transitory Provisions (Amendment)) Order 2014 (SI 2014/1661) art. 4(3) (June 30, 2014).

3. Welfare Reform Act 2012 (Commencement No.9, 11, 13, 14, 16 and 17 and Transitional and Transitory Provisions (Amendment) (No.2)) Order 2014 (SI 2014/1923) art. 4(4) (July 28, 2014).

Definitions

"the 1995 Act"–see art. 2(1).
"the 2007 Act"–*ibid.*
"the 2002 Regulations"–para.(4)(d).
"the Act"–see art.2(1).
"the amending provisions"–*ibid.*

"the Claims and Payments Regulations 1987"–*ibid*.
"claimant"–*ibid*.
"employment and support allowance"–*ibid*.
"gateway conditions"–*ibid*.
"housing benefit"–*ibid*.
"the Housing Benefit Regulations"–para.(4)(c).
"income support"–see art.2(1).
"jobseeker's allowance"–*ibid*.
"joint claimants"–*ibid*.
"old style ESA"–*ibid*.
"old style JSA"–*ibid*.
"relevant districts"–*ibid*.
"single claimant"–*ibid*.
"the specified benefit"–para.(4)(b).
"tax credit"–see art.2(1).

GENERAL NOTE

5.17   This makes provision for the position where a person claims universal credit and provides incorrect information as to their place of residence or their compliance with the gateway conditions. This article is similar to reg.13 of the revoked 2013 Transitional Regulations.

Day appointed for the abolition of income-related employment and support allowance and income-based jobseeker's allowance

5.18   [¹4.—(1) The day appointed for the coming into force of—
(a) section 33(1)(a) and (b) and (2) of the Act (abolition of benefits);
(b) paragraphs 22 to 26 of Schedule 3 to the Act (abolition of benefits: consequential provisions) and section 33(3) of the Act in so far as it relates to those paragraphs; and
(c) the repeals in Part 1 of Schedule 14 to the Act (abolition of benefits superseded by universal credit) that are referred to in Schedule 3,
in relation to the case of a claim referred to in paragraph (2)(a) to (d) and (g) and any award that is made in respect of such a claim, and in relation to the case of an award referred to in paragraph (2)(e) and (f), is the day appointed in accordance with paragraph (3).
(2) The claims and awards referred to are—
(a) a claim for universal credit, an employment and support allowance or a jobseeker's allowance where, on the date on which the claim is made [² or treated as made], the claimant—
    (i) resides in one of the relevant districts; and
    (ii) meets the gateway conditions;
[² (b) a claim for universal credit where—
    (i) in the case of a single claimant, the claimant gives incorrect information regarding the claimant residing in a relevant district or meeting the gateway conditions and does not reside in such a district or does not meet the gateway conditions on the date on which the claim is made;
    (ii) in the case of joint claimants, either or both of the joint claimants gives or give incorrect information regarding his or her (or their) residing in such a district or meeting those conditions and one or both of them does not or do not reside in such a district or does not or do not meet those conditions on the date on which the claim is made; and

    (iii) after a decision is made that the single claimant is, or the joint claimants are, entitled to universal credit and one or more payments have been made in respect of the single claimant or the joint claimants, the Secretary of State discovers that incorrect information has been given regarding residence or meeting the gateway conditions;]

(c) a claim for universal credit that is treated as made by a couple in the circumstances referred to in regulation 9(8) of the Claims and Payments Regulations 2013 (claims for universal credit by members of a couple) where the claim complies with article 3(7) and [³ . . .] ;

[²(d) a claim for universal credit by a former member of a couple who were joint claimants of universal credit, whether or not the claim is made jointly with another person, where the former member is not exempt from the requirement to make a claim by virtue of regulation 9(6) of the Claims and Payments Regulations 2013 (claims for universal credit by members of a couple), where the claim is made during the period of one month starting with the date on which notification is given to the Secretary of State that the former joint claimants have ceased to be a couple, and where the claim complies with article 3(8);]

(e) an award of universal credit that is made without a claim in the circumstances referred to in regulation 6(1) or (2) of the Claims and Payments Regulations 2013 (claims not required for entitlement to universal credit in some cases) where the circumstances referred to in article 3(9) apply;

(f) an award of universal credit that is made without a claim in the circumstances referred to in regulation 9(6), (7) or (10) the Claims and Payments Regulations 2013 (claims for universal credit by members of a couple) where the circumstances referred to in article 3(9) apply; and

(g) a claim for an employment and support allowance or a jobseeker's allowance [² other than one referred to in sub-paragraph (a) that is made or treated as made] —

    (i) during the relevant period by a single claimant of universal credit or, in the case of joint claimants of universal credit, by either of the joint claimants, where the single claimant has made or the joint claimants have made, or been treated as having made, a claim for universal credit within sub-paragraphs (a) to (d);

    (ii) during the relevant period by a single claimant of universal credit or, in the case of joint claimants of universal credit, by either of the joint claimants, where the single claimant has been awarded, or the joint claimants have been awarded, universal credit without a claim within sub-paragraph (e) or (f);

    (iii) by a person who is entitled to make a claim for universal credit in the circumstances referred to in sub-paragraph (d) but has not yet done so; or

    (iv) by a person who may be entitled to an award of universal credit in the circumstances referred to in sub-paragraph (e) or (f) but where no decision has yet been made as to the person's entitlement.

(3) Subject to paragraph (4), the day appointed in relation to the cases referred to in paragraph (2) is—

(a) in the case of a claim referred to in paragraph (2)(a) to (d) and (g), the first day of the period in respect of which the claim is made or (in the case of a claim for universal credit) treated as made;

(b) in the case of an award referred to in paragraph (2)(e) or (f), the first day on which a claimant is entitled to universal credit under that award.

(4) In relation to the case of a claim referred to in paragraph (2)(c) (claim for universal credit treated as made by a couple), where the member of the couple referred to in regulation 9(8)(b) of the Claims and Payments Regulations 2013 ("new claimant partner") was entitled during the prior period to an old style ESA award or an old style JSA award, the new claimant partner was at that time a member of a couple and the award included an amount in respect of the new claimant partner and his or her partner ("P"), the day appointed in relation to that case is the day after the day on which the new claimant partner and P ceased to be a couple for the purposes of the ESA Regulations 2008 or the JSA Regulations 1996 as the case may be.

(5) For the purposes of paragraph (4), the "prior period" means the period beginning with the first day of the period for which the claim for universal credit is treated as made and ending with the day before the day on which the claim for universal credit is treated as made.

(6) In paragraph (1), the reference to the case of a claim for universal credit referred to in paragraph (2)(a) to (d) (and any award made in respect of the claim), or of an award of universal credit referred to in paragraph (2) (e) and (f), includes a reference to—

(a) a case where a notice under regulation 4 of the 2010 Transitional Regulations (the notice commencing the conversion phase in relation to an award of incapacity benefit or severe disablement allowance) is issued to a single claimant or in the case of joint claimants, either of those claimants, during the designated period;

(b) where sub-paragraph (a) does not apply, a case where a conversion decision is made during that period in relation to an award of incapacity benefit or severe disablement allowance to which a single claimant or in the case of joint claimants, either of those claimants, is entitled; and

(c) where sub-paragraphs (a) and (b) do not apply, a case where the effective date of a conversion decision in relation to such an award occurs during that period (where "effective date" has the same meaning as in the 2010 Transitional Regulations),

and any award of an employment and support allowance that is made consequent on a conversion decision that relates to the notice referred to in sub-paragraph (a), the conversion decision referred to in sub-paragraph (b) or the conversion decision referred to in sub-paragraph (c), as the case may be.

(7) For the purposes of paragraph (6), the designated period means—

(a) in relation to a claim for universal credit referred to in paragraph (2) (a), (b)(i) [², (ii)] or (d), any period when a decision has not yet been made on the claim;

(b) in relation to a claim for universal credit that is treated as made as referred to in paragraph (2)(c), any period when no decision has yet been made as to the joint claimants' entitlement;

(c) any period, subsequent to the period referred to in sub-paragraph (a) or (b), when the single claimant or joint claimants is or are entitled to an award of universal credit in respect of the claim; and

(d) in relation to an award of universal credit referred to in paragraph (2) (e) or (f), any period when the single claimant or joint claimants to whom the award was made is or are entitled to that award.]

[³ (8) In paragraph (2)—

(a) in sub-paragraph (c), the reference to regulation 9(8) of the Claims and Payments Regulations 2013 is a reference to that provision both as it has effect as amended by the Digital Service Regulations 2014 and as it has effect apart from that amendment;

(b) in sub-paragraph (d), the reference to regulation 9(6) of the Claims and Payments Regulations 2013 is a reference to that provision as it has effect apart from the amendments made by the Digital Service Regulations 2014;

(c) in sub-paragraph (f), the reference to regulation 9(6) of the Claims and Payments Regulations 2013 is a reference to that provision both as it has effect as amended by the Digital Service Regulations 2014 and as it has effect apart from that amendment.]

[⁴ [⁵(9)] For the purposes of paragraph (1), the reference to the case of a claim for universal credit referred to in paragraph (2)(a) to (d) (and any award made in respect of the claim), or of an award of universal credit without a claim referred to in paragraph (2)(e) and (f), includes a reference to an old style ESA award or an old style JSA award that exists (or, as a result of an act as referred to in [⁵ paragraph (10)], is later found to have existed at that time) immediately before the day appointed (as referred to in paragraph (3) or (4)) in relation to that claim or award without a claim.

[⁵ (10)] For the purposes of [⁵ paragraph (9)], the acts referred to are–

(a) the revision of a decision that the claimant was not entitled to old style ESA or old style JSA; or

(b) an appeal to the First-tier Tribunal, the Upper Tribunal or a court against such a decision.]

AMENDMENTS

1. Welfare Reform Act 2012 (Commencement No.9, 11, 13, 14 and 16 and Transitional and Transitory Provisions (Amendment)) Order 2014 (SI 2014/1452) art.6 (June 16, 2014).

2. Welfare Reform Act 2012 (Commencement No.9, 11, 13, 14, 16 and 17 and Transitional and Transitory Provisions (Amendment) (No.2)) Order 2014 (SI 2014/1923) art. 4(5) (July 28, 2014).

3. Welfare Reform Act 2012 (Commencement No.20 and Transitional and Transitory Provisions and Commencement No.9 and Transitional and Transitory Provisions (Amendment)) Order 2014 (SI 2014/3094) art.7(2)(c) (November 26, 2014).

4. Welfare Reform Act 2012 (Commencement No.9, 11, 13, 14, 16, 17 and 19 and Transitional and Transitory Provisions (Amendment)) Order 2015 (SI 2015/32) art.4(3) (January 26, 2015).

5. Welfare Reform Act 2012 (Commencement No.22 and Transitional and Transitory Provisions) Order 2015 (SI 2015/101) art.7(2)(a) (February 11, 2015).

DEFINITIONS

"the Act"–art. 2(1).
"the Claims and Payments Regulations 2013"–*ibid.*
"employment and support allowance"–*ibid.*

"income-based jobseeker's allowance"–*ibid.*
"income-related employment and support allowance"–*ibid.*
"jobseeker's allowance"–*ibid.*
"relevant districts"–*ibid.*
"the Transitional Regulations"–*ibid.*
"the 2010 Transitional Regulations"–*ibid.*

General Note

Paragraph (1)
5.19   This brings into force provisions relating to the abolition of both income-related ESA and income-based JSA. This includes the repeal of various provisions relating to the abolished allowances as set out in Sch.3. However, these provisions are only brought into force where one of the various different categories of case set out in Paragraph (2) applies.

Paragraph (2)
5.20   This sets out the various categories of case affected by the amendments made by para.(1).

Paragraph (2)(a)
5.21   Where a person (i) resides in a relevant district (see Sch.1); (ii) meets the gateway conditions; and (iii) makes a claim for universal credit, ESA or JSA, then the amendments made by para.(1) above govern both the claim and any award made in respect of that claim.

Paragraph (2)(b)
5.22   This covers the situation here a person claims universal credit and incorrectly states that they live in a relevant district, or provides incorrect information as to their meeting the Pathfinder Group conditions. Such a claim remains within the universal credit regime despite the error.

Paragraph (2)(c)
5.23   This is analogous to art.3(3)(c).

Paragraph (2)(d)
5.24   This is analogous to art.3(3)(d).

Paragraph (2)(e)
5.25   This is analogous to art.3(3)(e).

Paragraph (2)(f)
5.26   This is analogous to art.3(3)(f).

Provisions that apply in connection with the abolition of income-related employment and support allowance and income-based jobseeker's allowance under article 4

5.27   [¹ 5.—(1) [². ..] [³ In determining, for the purposes of article 4(2)(a), whether a claim for an employment and support allowance or a jobseeker's allowance meets the gateway conditions, Schedule 5 is to be read as though—
  (a) any reference in that Schedule to making a claim for universal credit included a reference to making a claim for an employment and support allowance or a jobseeker's allowance as the case may be; and
  (b) the reference in paragraph 4 to a single claimant, or to joint claimants, of universal credit was a reference to a person who would be a single claimant of universal credit or to persons who would be joint

claimants of universal credit, if the claimant of an employment and support allowance or a jobseeker's allowance had made a claim for universal credit.

(1A) For the purposes of article 4(2)(a), where a claim for an employment and support allowance or a jobseeker's allowance is made by a couple or a member of a couple, any reference in article 4(2)(a) or Schedule 5 (save in paragraph 4 of that Schedule) to "the claimant" is a reference to each member of the couple.

(1B) For the purposes of paragraph (1A), "couple" has the same meaning as it has in section 39 of the Act.]

(2) [⁴. ...]

(3) For the purposes of article 4(2)(g), "relevant period" means—

    (a) in relation to a claim for universal credit within article 4(2)(a) to (d), any UC claim period, and any period subsequent to any UC claim period in respect of which the single claimant or the joint claimants is or are entitled to an award of universal credit in respect of the claim;

    (b) in relation to an award of universal credit within article 4(2)(e) or (f), any period when the single claimant or the joint claimants to whom the award was made is or are entitled to the award.

(4) For the purposes of paragraph (3)(a), a "UC claim period" is a period when—

    (a) a claim for universal credit within article 4(2)(a), (b)(i) [², (ii)] or (d) has been made but a decision has not yet been made on the claim;

    (b) a claim for universal credit within article 4(2)(c) has been treated as made and no decision has yet been made as to the joint claimants' entitlement; or

    (c) a decision has been made that a single claimant or joint claimants is or are not entitled to universal credit and—

        (i) the Secretary of State is considering whether to revise that decision under section 9 of the Social Security Act 1998, whether on an application made for that purpose, or on the Secretary of State's own initiative; or

        (ii) the single claimant or the joint claimants has or have appealed against that decision to the First-tier Tribunal and that appeal or any subsequent appeal to the Upper Tribunal or to a court has not been finally determined.

[⁵ (5) For the purposes of article 4(2)(a) and (g), the Claims and Payments Regulations 1987 apply, subject to paragraphs (6) and (7), for the purposes of deciding–

    (a) whether a claim for an employment and support allowance or a jobseeker's allowance is made; and

    (b) the date on which the claim is made or treated as made.

(6) Subject to paragraph (7),–

    (a) a person makes a claim for an employment and support allowance or a jobseeker's allowance if he or she takes any action which results in a decision on a claim being required under the Claims and Payments Regulations 1987; and

    (b) it is irrelevant that the effect of any provision of the Claims and Payments Regulations 1987 is that, for the purposes of those Regulations, the claim is made or treated as made at a date that is earlier than the date on which that action is taken.

(7) Where, by virtue of–

(a) regulation 6(1F)(b) or (c) of the Claims and Payments Regulations 1987, in the case of a claim for an employment and support allowance; or

(b) regulation 6(4ZA) to (4ZD) and (4A)(a)(i) and (b) of those Regulations, in the case of a claim for a jobseeker's allowance,

a claim for an employment and support allowance or a jobseeker's allowance is treated as made at a date that is earlier than the date on which the action referred to in paragraph (6)(a) is taken, the claim is treated as made on that earlier date.]

(8) For the purposes of article 4(3)(a)—

(a) in the case of a claim for universal credit, where the time for making a claim is extended under regulation 26(2) of the Claims and Payments Regulations 2013 (time within which a claim for universal credit is to be made), the reference to the first day of the period in respect of which the claim is made is a reference to the first day of the period in respect of which the claim is, by reason of the operation of that provision, timeously made;

(b) in the case of a claim for an employment and support allowance or a jobseeker's allowance, where the time for making a claim is extended under regulation 19 of, and Schedule 4 to, the Claims and Payments Regulations 1987, the reference to the first day of the period in respect of which the claim is made is a reference to the first day of the period in respect of which the claim is, by reason of the operation of those provisions, timeously made.]

AMENDMENTS

1. Welfare Reform Act 2012 (Commencement No.9, 11, 13, 14 and 16 and Transitional and Transitory Provisions (Amendment)) Order 2014 (SI 2014/1452) art.7 (June 16, 2014).

2. Welfare Reform Act 2012 (Commencement No.9, 11, 13, 14, 16 and 17 and Transitional and Transitory Provisions (Amendment) (No.2)) Order 2014 (SI 2014/1923) art. 4(6) (July 28, 2014).

3. Welfare Reform Act 2012 (Commencement No.9, 11, 13 14, 16, 17 and 19 and Transitional and Transitory Provisions (Amendment)) Order 2014 (SI 2014/3067) art.6(2)(b) (November 24, 2014).

4. Welfare Reform Act 2012 (Commencement No.20 and Transitional and Transitory Provisions and Commencement No.9 and Transitional and Transitory Provisions (Amendment)) Order 2014 (SI 2014/3094) art.7(2)(d) (November 26, 2014).

5. Welfare Reform Act 2012 (Commencement No.9, 11, 13, 14, 16, 17 and 19 and Transitional and Transitory Provisions (Amendment)) Order 2015 (SI 2015/32) art.4(4) (January 26, 2015).

DEFINITIONS

"the Claims and Payments Regulations 1987"–art. 2(1).
"the Claims and Payments Regulations 2013"–*ibid.*
"income-based jobseeker's allowance"–*ibid.*
"income-related employment and support allowance"–*ibid.*
"jobseeker's allowance"–*ibid.*
"the Transitional Regulations"–*ibid.*

GENERAL NOTE

5.28   These provisions supplement and further define the provisions of art.4.

[¹ Transitional provision where Secretary of State determines that claims for universal credit may not be made: effect on claims for employment and support allowance and jobseeker's allowance

5A.—(1) Where a person makes a claim for an employment and support allowance or a jobseeker's allowance at a time when they would not be able to make a claim for universal credit by virtue of a determination under regulation 4(1) of the 2014 Transitional Regulations (claims for universal credit may not be made in an area or category of case) [⁴, or by virtue of regulation [⁵ 4A of those Regulations (restriction on claims for universal credit by persons entitled to a severe disability premium) [⁶ ...] [⁷ or article 4(11) of the Welfare Reform Act 2012 (Commencement No. 32 and Savings and Transitional Provisions) Order 2019 (no claims for universal credit by frontier workers)] [² and where the amending provisions would otherwise have come into force in relation to the claim by virtue of article 4(2)(a) or any corresponding provision in any order made under section 150(3) of the Act other than this Order], then—

5.29

    (a) in relation to a claim for an employment and support allowance, Part 1 of the 2007 Act and the Welfare Reform Act 2009 are to apply as though the amending provisions and the provisions referred to in article 7(1)(c), (d) and (f) had not come into force in relation to the claim;

    (b) in relation to a claim for a jobseeker's allowance, the 1995 Act, the Social Security Administration Act 1992(2) and the Social Security Act 1998(3) are to apply as though the amending provisions and the provisions referred to in article 7(1)(a), (b) and (e) had not come into force in relation to the claim.]

    [² (2) Paragraph (1) does not apply in relation to a claim for an employment and support allowance ("ESA") or a jobseeker's allowance ("JSA") where the claim is made or treated as made—

    (a) where the claimant of ESA or JSA has made or been treated as having made a claim for universal credit ("UC") within article 4(2) (a) to (d) (whether or not the claim for UC is made jointly with another person), or has been awarded UC without a claim within article 4(2)(e) or (f) (whether or not the award is made to the claimant of ESA or JSA and another person as joint claimants), during the "relevant period" in relation to that claim or award as referred to in article 5(3)(a) or (b);

    (b) where the claimant of ESA or JSA has made a claim for UC within any provision of an order made under section 150(3) of the Act, apart from this Order, that corresponds to article 4(2)(a) or (b) (whether or not the claim for UC is made by the claimant of ESA or JSA and another person as joint claimants), during the "relevant period" in relation to that claim as referred to in the provision of that order that corresponds to article 5(3)(a); or

    (c) at a time when the claimant of ESA or JSA may be entitled to an award of UC without a claim in the circumstances referred to in article 4(2) (e) or (f) (whether or not the award may be made to the claimant of ESA or JSA and another person as joint claimants) but where no decision has yet been made as to the claimant's entitlement.]

    [³ (3) For the purposes of this article, paragraphs (5) to (7) of article 5 apply for the purpose of deciding—

(a) whether a claim for ESA or JSA is made; and

(b) the date on which the claim is made or treated as made.]

AMENDMENTS

1. Welfare Reform Act 2012 (Commencement No.9, 11, 13, 14 and 16 and Transitional and Transitory Provisions (Amendment)) Order 2014 (SI 2014/1452) art.8 (June 16, 2014).

2. Welfare Reform Act 2012 (Commencement No.19 and Transitional and Transitory Provisions and Commencement No.9 and Transitional and Transitory Provisions (Amendment)) Order 2014 (SI 2014/2321) art.7 (September 15, 2014).

3. Welfare Reform Act 2012 (Commencement No.23 and Transitional and Transitory Provisions) Order (2015/634) art.8(5) (March 18, 2015).

4. Welfare Reform Act 2012 (Commencement No.9 and 21 and Transitional and Transitory Provisions (Amendment)) Order 2017 (SI 2017/483) art.2(2) (April 6, 2017).

5. Universal Credit (Transitional Provisions) (SDP Gateway) Amendment Regulations 2019 (SI 2019/10) reg.3(1) (January 16, 2019).

6. Universal Credit (Restriction on Amounts for Children and Qualifying Young Persons) (Transitional Provisions) Amendment Regulations 2019 (SI 2019/27) reg.4(1) (February 1, 2019).

7. Welfare Reform Act 2012 (Commencement No. 32 and Savings and Transitional Provisions) Order 2019 SI 2019/167) art.5(2)(a) (February 1, 2019).

GENERAL NOTE

5.30   This provision has the effect that where a person claims ESA or JSA, and they would *not* be able to claim universal credit by virtue of a determination made by the Secretary of State that a claim for universal credit may not be made in a specified class of case or area (see reg.4(1) of the 2014 Transitional Regulations), then Part 1 of the Welfare Reform Act 2007, the Jobseekers Act 1995 and other relevant provisions apply in relation to the ESA or JSA claim as if the amending provisions had not come into force (see para.(1), subject to the exceptions in paras.(2)).

Transitional provision: where the abolition of income-related employment and support allowance and income-based jobseeker's allowance is treated as not applying

5.31   **6.**—(1) Paragraph (2) applies where—

(a) a person has or had a new style ESA award or a new style JSA award ("the award") [¹ by virtue of the coming into force of the amending provisions under any secondary legislation];

(b) in respect of all or part of the period to which the award relates, the person—

(i) makes a claim, or is treated as making a claim, for universal credit; or

(ii) makes an application to the Secretary of State for supersession of the decision to make the award, on the basis of a relevant change of circumstances that would relate to the grounds for entitlement to an income-related employment and support allowance or an income-based jobseeker's allowance if the amending provisions had not come into force [¹ ...];

(c) if the amending provisions had not come into force under [¹ ...] and, in the case of a claim for universal credit, an application for supersession of the decision to make the award had been made, the person would be entitled to an income-related employment and support allowance or an income-based jobseeker's allowance, as the case may be, with respect to the period for which the claim for universal credit or application for supersession is made;

(d) where the person makes an application for supersession of the decision to make the award, the period in respect of which the application is made does not include any period in respect of which the person has been awarded universal credit; [¹ and]

[¹(e)(i) on the date on which the claim for universal credit is made, or the application for supersession is received, as the case may be, the claim does not, or, in the case of an application for supersession, a claim for universal credit by the person would not, fall within any case (including a case with respect to which an award of universal credit may be made without a claim) in relation to which the provisions of the Act referred to in Schedule 2 are in force ("the UC commencement case"); or

(ii) on that date, the claim for universal credit does, or, in the case of an application for supersession, a claim for universal credit by the person would, fall within the UC commencement case, but the claim does or would fall within a case (including a case that relates in whole or in part to residence in an area) that is the subject of a determination made by the Secretary of State under regulation 4(1) of the 2014 Transitional Regulations (determination that claims for universal credit may not be made) [²[³ or the claim is or would be one to which regulation 4A of those Regulations (restriction on claims for universal credit by persons entitled to a severe disability premium) or article 4(11) of the Welfare Reform Act 2012 (Commencement No. 32 and Savings and Transitional Provisions) Order 2019 (no claims for universal credit by frontier workers) applies]].]

(2) Where this paragraph applies, then, in relation to the award and with effect from the first day of the period in respect of which the claim is made or treated as made, or the application for supersession is made, the 1995 Act or Part 1 of the 2007 Act, as the case may be, is to apply as though the amending provisions had not come into force [¹ ...].

(3) For the purposes of paragraph (1) [¹ ...]—

(a) the Claims and Payments Regulations 2013 apply for the purpose of deciding—

(i) whether a claim for universal credit is made or is to be treated as made; and

(ii) the day on which the claim is made or is to be treated as made; [¹ ...]

(b) [¹ ...].

(4) For the purposes of paragraph (2), the reference to the period in respect of which the application for supersession is made is a reference to the period beginning with the day from which the superseding decision takes effect in accordance with section 10(5) of the Social Security Act 1998 and regulation 35 of, and Schedule 1 to, the Decisions and Appeals Regulations 2013 (effectives dates: Secretary of State decisions).

(5) For the purposes of paragraph (2), the reference to the first day of the period in respect of which the claim for universal credit is made or treated as made, in a case where the time for making a claim for universal credit is extended under regulation 26(2) of the Claims and Payments Regulations

2013, is a reference to the first day of the period in respect of which the claim is, by reason of the operation of that provision, timeously made or treated as made.

[[1] (6) For the purposes of this article, "secondary legislation" means an instrument made under an Act.]

AMENDMENTS

1. Welfare Reform Act 2012 (Commencement No.9, 11, 13, 14 and 16 and Transitional and Transitory Provisions (Amendment)) Order 2014 (SI 2014/1452) art.9 (June 16, 2014).
2. Welfare Reform Act 2012 (Commencement No.9 and 21 and Transitional and Transitory Provisions (Amendment)) Order 2017 (SI 2017/483) art.2(3) (April 6, 2017).
3. Welfare Reform Act 2012 (Commencement No. 32 and Savings and Transitional Provisions) Order 2019 SI 2019/167) art.5(2)(b) (February 1, 2019).

DEFINITIONS

"the 1995 Act"–art. 2(1).
"the 2007 Act"–*ibid.*
"the amending provisions"–*ibid.*
"the award"–para.1(a)
"the Claims and Payments Regulations 2013"–art.2(1).
"employment and support allowance"–*ibid.*
"the Decisions and Appeals Regulations 2013"–*ibid.*
"income-based jobseeker's allowance"–*ibid.*
"income-related employment and support allowance"–*ibid.*
"jobseeker's allowance"–*ibid.*
"new style ESA award"–*ibid.*
"new style JSA award"–*ibid.*
"relevant districts"–*ibid.*
"the Transitional Regulations"–*ibid.*

GENERAL NOTE

5.32   This makes transitional provision for cases where the conditions in para.(1) are met. These all concern cases where the claimant either moves out of a relevant district or is not in the Pathfinder Group. In these cases, the award is treated as though the provisions in art.4(1)(a)-(c) above had not come into force (para.(2); see further art.9(2)). In consequence the person concerned will be able to claim an existing benefit, i.e. income-related ESA or income-based JSA, once again. The six conditions set out in Para.(1) are (in summary) that (a) the claimant has a new style ESA award or new style JSA award; (b) they make a claim for universal credit or applies for supersession of the decision to make the award; (c) they would otherwise be entitled to income-related ESA or income-based JSA; (d) any award of universal credit has come to an end; (e), any claim for universal credit does not fall within the category of a "UC commencement case" or, if so, is the subject of a determination made by the Secretary of State under reg.4(1) of the 2014 Transitional Regulations. Paras.(3)-(5) make supplementary provision for paras.(1) and (2).

Day appointed for commencement of provisions relating to claimant responsibilities with respect to employment and support allowance and jobseeker's allowance, and transitional provisions

5.33   7.—(1) The day appointed for the coming into force of—
(a) section 44(2) of the Act and section 44(1) of the Act in so far as it relates to section 44(2) (claimant commitment for jobseeker's allowance);

(b) section 49(2) and (3) to (5) of the Act (and section 49(1) of the Act in so far as it relates to those provisions) (claimant responsibilities for jobseeker's allowance);

(c) section 54(2) of the Act (and section 54(1) of the Act in so far as it relates to that provision) (claimant commitment for employment and support allowance);

(d) section 57(2), (4), (5) and (9) of the Act (and section 57(1) of the Act in so far as it relates to those provisions) (claimant responsibilities for employment and support allowance);

(e) the repeals in Part 4 of Schedule 14 to the Act (jobseeker's allowance: responsibilities after introduction of universal credit); and

(f) the repeals in Part 5 of Schedule 14 to the Act (employment and support allowance: responsibilities after introduction of universal credit),

in so far as they are not already in force, is, in relation to a particular case, the day on which the amending provisions come into force, under any secondary legislation, in relation to that case.

[¹ (2) Where, under any secondary legislation, in relation to a new style JSA award, the 1995 Act applies as though the amending provisions had not come into force, then, with effect from the day on which the 1995 Act so applies, the 1995 Act, the Social Security Administration Act 1992 and the Social Security Act 1998 are to apply in relation to the award as though the provisions referred to in paragraph (1)(a), (b) and (e) had not come into force.

(3) Where, under any secondary legislation, in relation to a new style ESA award, Part 1 of the 2007 Act applies as though the amending provisions had not come into force, then, with effect from the day on which Part 1 of the 2007 Act so applies, Part 1 of the 2007 Act and the Welfare Reform Act 2009 are to apply in relation to the award as though the provisions referred to in paragraph (1)(c), (d) and (f) had not come into force.]

(4) For the purposes of paragraphs (1) to (3), "secondary legislation" means an instrument made under an Act.

AMENDMENTS

1. Welfare Reform Act 2012 (Commencement No.11 and Transitional and Transitory Provisions and Commencement No.9 and Transitional and Transitory Provisions (Amendment)) Order 2013 (SI 2013/1511) art.6 (July 1, 2013).

DEFINITIONS

"the Act"–art. 2(1).
"the 1995 Act"–*ibid.*
"the 2007 Act"–*ibid.*
"the amending provisions"–*ibid.*
"employment and support allowance"–*ibid.*
"jobseeker's allowance"–*ibid.*
"new style ESA award"–*ibid.*
"new style JSA award"–*ibid.*
"secondary legislation"–para.(4).

GENERAL NOTE

This provides for the appointed day and transitional provisions for the measures in the WRA 2012 that relate to claimant responsibilities in relation to a new style ESA award or a new style JSA award.

5.34

Day appointed for commencement of provisions concerning consideration of revision before appeal

5.35   **8.** 29th April 2013 is the day appointed for the coming into force of paragraphs 1 to 11 and 15 to 18 of Schedule 11 to the Act (power to require consideration of revision before appeal) and section 102(6) of the Act in so far as it relates to those paragraphs, to the extent that those provisions are not already in force.

DEFINITIONS

"the Act"–art.2(1).

GENERAL NOTE

5.36   This simply brings into force those provisions of Sch.11 to the Act concerning consideration of revision before appeal.

Transitional provision: conversion of incapacity benefits

5.37   **9.**—(1) Subject to paragraph (2), where the amending provisions come into force under article 4(1) in relation to the case of a claim referred to in article 4(2)(a) to (d) [¹ or (g)] and any award made in respect of the claim, or the case of an award referred to in article 4(2)(e) or (f), the 2010 Transitional Regulations are to apply in relation to that case as if the modifications set out in Schedule 4 were made.

(2) Where article 6(2) applies in relation to a new style ESA award (such that the award continues as an old style ESA award), the 2010 Transitional Regulations are to apply in relation to the award, in its continuation as an old style ESA award, as if those modifications had not been made.

AMENDMENTS

1. Welfare Reform Act 2012 (Commencement No.9, 11, 13, 14 and 16 and Transitional and Transitory Provisions (Amendment)) Order 2014 (SI 2014/1452) art.10 (June 16, 2014).

DEFINITIONS

"the amending provisions"–art.2(1).
"new style ESA award"–*ibid.*
"old style ESA award"–*ibid.*
"the 2010 Transitional Regulations"–*ibid.*

GENERAL NOTE

5.38   The introduction of universal credit was always going to be complicated. That complexity has been made worse by the fact that many existing awards of ESA have not been assessed for conversion, sometimes described as "reassessment", to ESA, even though that process began on October 11, 2010. This regulation allows for transitional provisions whereby, in relation to cases with respect to which art.4 has come into force, the Transitional Provisions Regulations 2010 are to be read as if the amendments set out in Sch.4 were made. Those amendments substitute references to provisions that apply to new style ESA awards, including the ESA Regulations 2013.

[¹ Transition from old style ESA]

5.39   **10.**—[¹ (1) This article applies where a person—
(a) makes, or is treated as making, a claim for an employment and

support allowance and, under article 4, Part 1 of the 2007 Act, as amended by the provisions of Schedule 3, and Part 1 of Schedule 14, to the Act that remove references to an income-related allowance, applies in relation to the claim; or

(b) (i) has an old style ESA award immediately before the appointed day in relation to a case of a claim for universal credit referred to in article 4(2)(a) to (d) (and any award made in respect of the claim), or an award of universal credit referred to in article 4(2)(e) or (f); and

(ii) the old style ESA award consists of or includes a contributory employment and support allowance (which allowance therefore continues as a new style ESA award),

and, in the case of sub-paragraph (a), the condition referred to in paragraph (1A) is satisfied.

(1A) The condition is that—

(a) the person previously made, or was treated as having made, a claim for an employment and support allowance and Part 1 of the 2007 Act, as it has effect apart from the provisions of Schedule 3, and Part 1 of Schedule 14, to the Act that remove references to an income-related allowance, applied in relation to the claim;

(b) a notice was issued to the person under regulation 4 of the 2010 Transitional Regulations and Part 1 of the 2007 Act, as that Part has effect apart from the provisions of Schedule 3, and Part 1 of Schedule 14, to the Act that remove references to an income-related allowance, applied in relation to the notice; or

(c) the person previously had a new style ESA award and article 6(2) applied in relation to the award (which award therefore continued as an old style ESA award).]

(2) Where this article applies, the ESA Regulations 2013 are to be read as if—

(a)(i) in the definitions of "period of limited capability for work" in regulations 2 (interpretation) and 3 (further interpretation), the reference to a period throughout which a person has, or is treated as having, limited capability for work included a reference to a period throughout which the person in question had, or was treated as having, limited capability for work under the ESA Regulations 2008; and

(ii) the reference, in the definition in regulation 2, to regulation 28 of the Claims and Payments Regulations 2013 (time within which a claim for employment and support allowance is to be made) included a reference to regulation 19 of, and Schedule 4 to, the Claims and Payments Regulations 1987 (prescribed times for claiming benefit);

(b) in regulation 6 (the assessment phase–previous claimants)—

(i) any reference to an employment and support allowance included a reference to an old style ESA award; and

(ii) in paragraph (2)(b)(v) and (c)(iii), the reference to regulation 26 (conditions for treating a claimant as having limited capability for work until a determination about limited capability for work has been made) included a reference to regulation 30 of the ESA Regulations 2008 (conditions for treating a claimant as having limited capability for work until a determination about limited capability for work has been made);

(c) in regulation 7 (circumstances where the condition that the assessment phase has ended before entitlement to the support component [³ . . .] arises does not apply)—

    (i) any reference to an employment and support allowance included a reference to an old style ESA award; and

    (ii) in paragraph (3)(b)(iv), (c)(iii), (c)(iv) and (d)(iii), the reference to regulation 26 included a reference to regulation 30 of the ESA Regulations 2008;

(d) in regulation 11 (condition relating to youth–previous claimants), any reference to an employment and support allowance included a reference to an old style ESA award;

(e) in regulation 15 (determination of limited capability for work)—

    (i) the reference in paragraph (7)(a) to a claimant having been determined to have limited capability for work included a reference to such a determination made under Part 5 of the ESA Regulations 2008; and

    (ii) the reference in paragraph (7)(b) to a person being treated as having limited capability for work included a reference to a person being so treated under regulation 20 (certain claimants to be treated as having limited capability for work), 25 (hospital patients), 26 (claimants receiving certain regular treatment) or 29 (exceptional circumstances) of the ESA Regulations 2008;

(f) in regulation 26 (conditions for treating a claimant as having limited capability for work until a determination about limited capability for work has been made)—

    (i) in paragraph (2)(b), the reference to regulation 18 (failure to provide information in relation to limited capability for work) and 19 (claimant may be called for a medical examination to determine whether the claimant has limited capability for work) included a reference to regulation 22 (failure to provide information in relation to limited capability for work) and 23 (claimant may be called for a medical examination to determine whether the claimant has limited capability for work) of the ESA Regulations 2008; and

    (ii) in paragraph (4)(c), the reference to regulation 18 included a reference to regulation 22 of the ESA Regulations 2008;

(g) in regulation 30(4) (determination of limited capability for work-related activity), the reference to a determination about whether a claimant has, or is to be treated as having or not having, limited capability for work-related activity included such a determination that was made under Part 6 of the ESA Regulations 2008; [¹ . . .]

[¹(ga) in regulation 39(6) (exempt work), the reference to an employment and support allowance included a reference to an old style ESA award;

(gb) in regulation 85(2)(a) (waiting days), where a claimant was entitled to an old style ESA award with effect from the first day of a period of limited capability for work by virtue of regulation 144(2)(a) of the ESA Regulations 2008 and, with effect from [² a day between the second and the seventh day of that period (including the second and the seventh day)], that award continued as a new style ESA award in the circumstances referred to in paragraph (1)(b) of this article, the reference to an employment and support allowance included a reference to the old style ESA award;]

(h) in regulation 87(1) (claimants appealing a decision), the reference to a determination that the claimant does not have limited capability for work under the ESA Regulations 2013 included a reference to such a determination under the ESA Regulations 2008.

(i) in regulation 89 (short absence), where—

(i) a claimant had an old style ESA award in the circumstances referred to in paragraph (1)(b) of this article;

(ii) a temporary absence from Great Britain commenced when regulation 152 of the ESA Regulations 2008 applied to the claimant; and

(iii) the first 4 weeks of the temporary absence had not ended immediately before the first day of entitlement to the new style ESA award,

the initial words of regulation 89 included a reference to the claimant being entitled to the new style ESA award during the remainder of the first 4 weeks of the temporary absence that commenced when regulation 152 of the ESA Regulations 2008 applied to the claimant;

(j) in regulation 90 (absence to receive medical treatment), where—

(i) a claimant had an old style ESA award in the circumstances referred to in paragraph (1)(b) of this article;

(ii) a temporary absence from Great Britain commenced when regulation 153 of the ESA Regulations 2008 applied to the claimant; and

(iii) the first 26 weeks of the temporary absence had not ended immediately before the first day of entitlement to the new style ESA award,

the initial words of paragraph (1) of regulation 90 included a reference to the claimant being entitled to the new style ESA award during the remainder of the first 26 weeks of the temporary absence that commenced when regulation 153 of the ESA Regulations 2008 applied to the claimant;

(k) in regulation 93 (disqualification for misconduct etc)—

(i) in paragraph (3), for "Paragraph (2) does" there were substituted "Paragraphs (2) and (5) do"; and

(ii) after paragraph (4) there were inserted—

"(5) Subject to paragraph (3), a claimant is to be disqualified for receiving an employment and support allowance for any period determined by the Secretary of State under regulation 157(2) of the Employment and Support Allowance Regulations 2008(3) less any days during that period on which those Regulations applied to the claimant.

(6) Where paragraph (5) applies to a claimant, paragraph (2) is not to apply to that claimant with respect to any matter referred to in paragraph (1) that formed the basis for the claimant's disqualification under regulation 157(2) of the Employment and Support Allowance Regulations 2008.";

(l) in regulation 95 (treating a claimant as not having limited capability for work), the existing words became paragraph (1) and—

(i) at the beginning of paragraph (1), there were inserted "Subject to paragraph (2),"; and

(ii) after paragraph (1), there were inserted—

"(2) A claimant is to be treated as not having limited capability for work if—

(a) under Part 1 of the Act as it has effect apart from the amendments made by Schedule 3, and Part 1 of Schedule 14, to the Welfare Reform Act 2012 that remove references to an income-related allowance ("the former law"), the claimant was disqualified for receiving a contributory employment and support allowance during a period of imprisonment or detention in legal custody;

(b) Part 1 of the Act as amended by the provisions of Schedule 3, and Part 1 of Schedule 14, to the Welfare Reform Act 2012 that remove references to an income-related allowance ("the current law") applied to the claimant with effect from a day that occurred during the period of imprisonment or detention in legal custody referred to in sub-paragraph (a) and during the period of six weeks with effect from the day on which the claimant was first disqualified as referred to in sub-paragraph (a); and

(c) the total of—

(i) the period for which the claimant was disqualified for receiving a contributory employment and support allowance during the period of imprisonment or detention in legal custody when the former law applied to the claimant; and

(ii) the period for which the claimant was disqualified for receiving an employment and support allowance during the period of imprisonment or detention in legal custody when the current law applied to the claimant,

amounts to more than six weeks."]

[¹ (3) Subject to paragraph (4), where this article applies, the 2007 Act is to be read as though—

(a) the reference to an employment and support allowance in section 1A(1) and (4) to (6);

(b) the first reference to an employment and support allowance in section 1A(3); and

(c) the first reference to an employment and support allowance in section 1B(4),

included a reference to a contributory employment and support allowance.

(4) Where this article applies and the 2010 Transitional Regulations apply to a person, paragraph (3)(c) becomes paragraph (3)(b) and, for paragraph (3)(a) and (b), there is substituted—

"(a) in section 1A as substituted by the 2010 Transitional Regulations—

(i) the reference to an employment and support allowance in section 1A(1), (4) and (5); and

(ii) the first reference to an employment and support allowance in section 1A(3); and".

(5) Where this article applies and a claimant—

(a) had an old style ESA award in the circumstances referred to in paragraph (1)(b); and

(b) the old style ESA award had not been preceded by a new style ESA award in the circumstances referred to in paragraph (1A)(c), the 2007 Act is to be read as if, in section 24(2), the beginning of the assessment phase (subject to section 24(3)) was the first day of the period for which the claimant was entitled to the old style ESA award.]

AMENDMENTS

1. Welfare Reform Act 2012 (Commencement No.11 and Transitional and Transitory Provisions and Commencement No.9 and Transitional and Transitory Provisions (Amendment)) Order 2013 (SI 2013/1511) art.8 (July 1, 2013).

2. Welfare Reform Act 2012 (Commencement No.9, 11, 13 14, 16, 17 and 19 and Transitional and Transitory Provisions (Amendment)) Order 2014 (SI 2014/3067) art.7(a) (November 24, 2014).

3. Employment and Support Allowance and Universal Credit (Miscellaneous Amendments and Transitional and Savings Provisions) Regulations 2017 (SI 2017/204) reg.7 and Sch.1 para.9(2) (April 3, 2017).

DEFINITIONS

"the amending provisions"–art. 2(1)
"appointed day"–*ibid.*
"the Claims and Payments Regulations 1987"–*ibid.*
"the Claims and Payments Regulations 2013"–*ibid.*
"contributory employment and support allowance"–*ibid.*
"employment and support allowance"–*ibid.*
"the ESA Regulations 2008"–*ibid.*
"the ESA Regulations 2013"–*ibid.*
"new style ESA award"–*ibid.*
"old style ESA award"–*ibid.*

GENERAL NOTE

This makes transitional provisions for assessments of limited capability for work **5.40** or for work and work-related activity where a person has a new style ESA award and previously had an old style ESA award. Article 11 deals with the converse position.

So, for example, under the new style ESA award the definition of a period of limited capability for work includes a period throughout which the claimant had, or was treated as having, limited capability for work for the purposes of old style ESA (para.(2)(a)). Similarly, where the old style and new style awards link, then days of entitlement to old styled ESA in the linked award are included in calculating the end of the assessment phase (para.(2)(b)). To the same end, any earlier period of limited capability for work under the old style ESA award is counted in working out whether the work related activity component or support component is payable from the first day of entitlement (para.(2)(c)). Likewise, the six months rule for the purposes of treating a claimant as having limited capability for work until a further determination is made includes having limited capability for work (or being treated as such) under an old style ESA award (subs.(2)(f)).

[¹ Transition from new style ESA]

11.—[¹ (1) This article applies where a person— **5.41**
  (a) makes, or is treated as making, a claim for an employment and support allowance and Part 1 of the 2007 Act, as it has effect apart from the provisions of Schedule 3, and Part 1 of Schedule 14, to the Act that remove references to an income-related allowance, applies in relation to the claim; or
  (b) has a new style ESA award and article 6(2) applies in relation to the award (which award therefore continues as an old style ESA award),

and, in the case of sub-paragraph (a), the condition referred to in paragraph (1A) is satisfied.

(1A) The condition is that—

(a) the person previously made, or was treated as having made, a claim for an employment and support allowance and, under article 4, Part 1 of the 2007 Act, as amended by the provisions of Schedule 3, and Part 1 of Schedule 14, to the Act that remove references to an income-related allowance, applied in relation to the claim;

(b) a notice was issued to the person under regulation 4 of the 2010 Transitional Regulations and, under article 4, Part 1 of the 2007 Act, as amended by the provisions of Schedule 3, and Part 1 of Schedule 14, to the Act that remove references to an income-related allowance, applied in relation to the notice; or

(c) the person previously—

   (i) had an old style ESA award immediately before the appointed day in relation to a case of a claim for universal credit referred to in article 4(2)(a) to (d) (and any award made in respect of the claim), or an award of universal credit referred to in article 4(2) (e) or (f); and

   (ii) the old style ESA award consisted of or included a contributory employment and support allowance (which allowance therefore continued as a new style ESA award).]

(2) Where this article applies, the ESA Regulations 2008 are to be read as if—

(a)(i) in the definitions of "period of limited capability for work" in regulation 2(1) and (5) (interpretation), the reference to a period throughout which a person has, or is treated as having, limited capability for work included a reference to a period throughout which the person in question had, or was treated as having, limited capability for work under the ESA Regulations 2013; and

   (ii) the reference, in the definition in regulation 2(1), to regulation 19 of the Claims and Payments Regulations 1987 (time for claiming benefit) included a reference to regulation 28 of the Claims and Payments Regulations 2013 (time within which a claim for an employment and support allowance is to be made);

(b) in regulation 5 (the assessment phase–previous claimants)—

   (i) any reference to an employment and support allowance included a reference to a new style ESA award; and

   (ii) in paragraph (2)(b)(v) and (c)(iii), the reference to regulation 30 (conditions for treating a claimant as having limited capability for work until a determination about limited capability for work has been made) included a reference to regulation 26 of the ESA Regulations 2013 (conditions for treating a claimant as having limited capability for work until a determination about limited capability for work has been made);

(c) in regulation 7 (circumstances where the condition that the assessment phase has ended before entitlement to the support component [5 . . .] arises does not apply)—

   (i) any reference to an employment and support allowance included a reference to a new style ESA award; and

   (ii) in paragraph (1B)(b)(iv), (c)(iii), (c)(iv) and (d)(iii), the reference to regulation 30 included a reference to regulation 26 of the ESA Regulations 2013;

(d) in regulation 10 (condition relating to youth – previous claimants), any reference to an employment and support allowance included a reference to a new style ESA award;

(e) in regulation 19 (determination of limited capability for work)—

   (i) the reference in paragraph (7)(a) to a claimant having been determined to have limited capability for work included a reference to such a determination made under Part 4 of the ESA Regulations 2013; and

   (ii) the reference in paragraph (7)(b) to a person being treated as having limited capability for work included a reference to a person being so treated under regulation 16 (certain claimants to be treated as having limited capability for work), 21 (hospital patients), 22 (claimants receiving certain treatment) or 25 (exceptional circumstances) of the ESA Regulations 2013;

(f) in regulation 30 (conditions for treating a claimant as having limited capability for work until a determination about limited capability for work has been made)—

   (i) in the initial words of paragraph (2)(b), the reference to regulation 22 (failure to provide information in relation to limited capability for work) and 23 (claimant may be called for a medical examination to determine whether the claimant has limited capability for work) included a reference to regulation 18 (failure to provide information in relation to limited capability for work) and 19 (claimant may be called for a medical examination to determine whether the claimant has limited capability for work) of the ESA Regulations 2013; and

   (ii) in [² paragraph (4)(c)], the reference to regulation 22 included a reference to regulation 18 of the ESA Regulations 2013;

(g) in regulation 34(4) (determination of limited capability for work-related activity), the reference to a determination about whether a claimant has, or is to be treated as having or not having, limited capability for work-related activity included such a determination that was made under Part 5 of the ESA Regulations 2013; [¹ . . .]

[¹(ga) in regulation 45(10) (exempt work), the reference to an employment and support allowance included a reference to a new style ESA award;

(gb) in regulation 144(2)(a) (waiting days), where the claimant was entitled to a new style ESA award with effect from the first day of a period of limited capability for work by virtue of regulation 85(2)(a) of the ESA Regulations 2013 and, with effect from [⁴ a day between the second and the seventh day of that period (including the second and the seventh day)], that award continued as an old style ESA award in the circumstances referred to in paragraph (1)(c) of this article, the reference to an employment and support allowance included a reference to the new style ESA award;]

(h) in regulation 147A(1) (claimants appealing a decision), the reference to a determination that the claimant does not have limited capability for work included a reference to such a determination under the ESA Regulations 2013.

(i) in regulation 152 (short absence), where—

   (i) a claimant had a new style ESA award in the circumstances referred to in paragraph (1)(b) of this article;

   (ii) a temporary absence from Great Britain commenced when regulation 89 of the ESA Regulations 2013 applied to the claimant; and

   (iii) the first 4 weeks of the temporary absence had not ended immediately before the first day of entitlement to the old style ESA award,

the initial words of regulation 152 included a reference to the claimant being entitled to the old style ESA award during the remainder of the first 4 weeks of the temporary absence that commenced when regulation 89 of the ESA Regulations 2013 applied to the claimant;

  (j) in regulation 153 (absence to receive medical treatment)—

   (i) a claimant had a new style ESA award in the circumstances referred to in paragraph (1)(b) of this article;

   (ii) a temporary absence from Great Britain commenced when regulation 90 of the ESA Regulations 2013 applied to the claimant; and

   (iii) the first 26 weeks of the temporary absence had not ended immediately before the first day of entitlement to the old style ESA award,

the initial words of paragraph (1) of regulation 153 included a reference to the claimant being entitled to the old style ESA award during the remainder of the first 26 weeks of the temporary absence that commenced when regulation 90 of the ESA Regulations 2013 applied to the claimant;

  (k) in regulation 157 (disqualification for misconduct etc)—

   (i) in paragraph (3), for "Paragraph (2) does" there were substituted "Paragraphs (2) and (4) do"; and

   (ii) after paragraph (3) there were inserted—

"(4) Subject to paragraph (3), a claimant is to be disqualified for receiving an employment and support allowance for any period determined by the Secretary of State under regulation 93(2) of the Employment and Support Allowance Regulations 2013 less any days during that period on which those Regulations applied to the claimant.

(5) Where paragraph (4) applies to a claimant, paragraph (2) is not to apply to that claimant with respect to any matter referred to in paragraph (1) that formed the basis for the claimant's disqualification under regulation 93(2) of the Employment and Support Allowance Regulations 2013."; [² . . .]

  (l) in regulation 159 (treating a claimant as not having limited capability for work), the existing words became paragraph (1) and—

   (i) at the beginning of paragraph (1), there were inserted "Subject to paragraph (2),"; and

   (ii) after paragraph (1), there were inserted—

"(2) A claimant is to be treated as not having limited capability for work if—

  (a) under Part 1 of the Act as amended by the provisions of Schedule 3, and Part 1 of Schedule 14, to the Welfare Reform Act 2012 that remove references to an income-related allowance ("the former law"), the claimant was disqualified for receiving an employment and support allowance during a period of imprisonment or detention in legal custody;

  (b) Part 1 of the Act as it has effect apart from the amendments made by Schedule 3, and Part 1 of Schedule 14, to the Welfare Reform Act 2012 that remove references to an income-related allowance ("the current law") applied to the claimant with effect from a day that occurred during the period of imprisonment or detention in legal custody referred to in sub-paragraph (a) and during the period of six weeks with effect from the day on which the claimant was first disqualified as referred to in sub-paragraph (a); and

(c) the total of—

    (i) the period for which the claimant was disqualified for receiving an employment and support allowance during the period of imprisonment or detention in legal custody when the former law applied to the claimant; and

    (ii) the period for which the claimant was disqualified for receiving a contributory employment and support allowance during the period of imprisonment or detention in legal custody when the current law applied to the claimant,

amounts to more than six weeks."]; [³ and

(m) in Schedule 6 (housing costs), in paragraphs 8(1) and 9(1), each reference to an employment and support allowance included a reference to new style ESA.]

[¹ (3) Subject to paragraph (4), where this article applies, the 2007 Act is to be read as though—

(a) the reference to a contributory allowance in section (1A)(1) and (4) to (6);

(b) the first reference to a contributory allowance in section (1A)(3); and

(c) the first reference to a contributory allowance in section 1B,

included a reference to a new style ESA award.

(4) Where this article applies and the 2010 Transitional Regulations apply to a person, paragraph (3)(c) becomes paragraph (3)(b) and, for paragraph (3)(a) and (b), there is substituted—

"(a) in section 1A as substituted by the 2010 Transitional Regulations—

    (i) the reference to a contributory allowance in section 1A(1), (4) and (5); and

    (ii) the first reference to a contributory allowance in section 1A(3); and".

(5) Where this article applies and a claimant—

(a) had a new style ESA award in the circumstances referred to in paragraph (1)(b); and

(b) the new style ESA award had not been preceded by an old style ESA award in the circumstances referred to in paragraph (1A)(c),

section 24(2) of the 2007 Act is to be read as if the beginning of the assessment phase (subject to section 24(3)) was the first day of the period for which the claimant was entitled to the new style ESA award.]

AMENDMENTS

1. Welfare Reform Act 2012 (Commencement No.11 and Transitional and Transitory Provisions and Commencement No.9 and Transitional and Transitory Provisions (Amendment)) Order 2013 (SI 2013.1511) art.9 (July 1, 2013).

2. Welfare Reform Act 2012 (Commencement No.13 and Transitional and Transitory Provisions) Order 2013 (SI 2013/2657) art. 5(a) (October 29, 2013).

3. Welfare Reform Act 2012 (Commencement No.9, 11, 13, 14 and 16 and

Transitional and Transitory Provisions (Amendment)) Order 2014 (SI 2014/1452) art.11 (June 16, 2014).

4. Welfare Reform Act 2012 (Commencement No.9, 11, 13 14, 16, 17 and 19 and Transitional and Transitory Provisions (Amendment)) Order 2014 (SI 2014/3067) art.7(a) (November 24, 2014).

5. Employment and Support Allowance and Universal Credit (Miscellaneous Amendments and Transitional and Savings Provisions) Regulations 2017 (SI 2017/204) reg.7 and Sch.1 para.9(3) (April 3, 2017).

DEFINITIONS

"the Claims and Payments Regulations 1987"–art. 2(1)
"the Claims and Payments Regulations 2013"–*ibid.*
"employment and support allowance"–*ibid.*
"the ESA Regulations 2008"–*ibid.*
"the ESA Regulations 2013"–*ibid.*
"new style ESA award"–*ibid.*
"old style ESA award"–*ibid.*

GENERAL NOTE

5.42   This makes transitional provisions for assessments of limited capability for work or for work and work-related activity where a person has an old style ESA award and previously had a new style ESA award. Article 10 deals with the converse position. The modifications are to similar effect as in Art.10.

[¹Transition from old style JSA

5.43   **12.**—(1) This article applies where a person—
(a) makes, or is treated as making, a claim for a jobseeker's allowance and, under article 4, the 1995 Act, as amended by the provisions of Part 1 of Schedule 14 to the Act that remove references to an income-based jobseeker's allowance, applies in relation to the claim; or
(b) (i) has an old style JSA award (whether or not the award was made to the person as a member of a joint-claim couple) immediately before the appointed day in relation to a case of a claim for universal credit referred to in article 4(2)(a) to (d) (and any award made in respect of the claim), or an award of universal credit referred to in article 4(2)(e) or (f); and
(ii) the old style JSA award consists of or includes a contribution-based jobseeker's allowance (which allowance therefore continues as a new style JSA award),
and, in the case of sub-paragraph (a), the condition referred to in paragraph (2) is satisfied.
(2) The condition is that the person previously—
(a) made, or was treated as having made, a claim for a jobseeker's allowance (whether or not as a member of a joint-claim couple) and the 1995 Act, as it has effect apart from the provisions of Part 1 of Schedule 14 to the Act that remove references to an income-based jobseeker's allowance, applied in relation to the claim; or
(b) had a new style JSA award and article 6(2) applied in relation to the award (which award therefore continued as an old style JSA award).
(3) Where this article applies, the JSA Regulations 2013 are to be read as if—

(a) in regulation 15(3)(b) (victims of domestic violence), the reference to regulation 15 applying to the claimant included a reference to the claimant having been treated as being available for employment under regulation 14A(2) or (6) of the JSA Regulations 1996;

(b) in regulation 36(1) (waiting days), where a person was entitled to an old style JSA award with effect from the first day of a jobseeking period by virtue of regulation 46(1)(a) of the JSA Regulations 1996 and, with effect from [² a day between the second and the seventh day of that period (including the second and the seventh day)], that award continued as a new style JSA award in the circumstances referred to in paragraph (1)(b) of this article, the reference to a job-seeker's allowance included a reference to the old style JSA award;

(c) in regulation 37 (jobseeking period)—

   (i) the jobseeking period in relation to a claimant included any period that, under regulation 47 of the JSA Regulations 1996 (jobseeking period), forms part of the jobseeking period for the purposes of the 1995 Act; and

   (ii) in paragraph (3), the reference to a day that is to be treated as a day in respect of which the claimant was entitled to a jobseeker's allowance included a reference to any day that, under regulation 47(4) of the JSA Regulations 1996, is to be treated as a day in respect of which the claimant was entitled to a contribution-based jobseeker's allowance;

(d) in regulation 41 (persons temporarily absent from Great Britain), where a person had an old style JSA award in the circumstances referred to in paragraph (1)(b) of this article, the reference in paragraph (2)(b), (3)(a) and (c), (5)(a) and (6)(b) to entitlement to a jobseeker's allowance included a reference to the old style JSA award; and

(e) in regulation 46 (short periods of sickness), after paragraph (5) there were inserted—

"(6) Where—

(a) a person has been treated under regulation 55(1) of the Jobseeker's Allowance Regulations 1996 as capable of work or as not having limited capability for work for a certain period; and

(b) these Regulations apply to that person with effect from a day ("the relevant day") within that period,

the person is to be treated for the part of that period that begins with the relevant day as capable of work or as not having limited capability for work.

(7) Where paragraph (6) applies to a person and the conditions in paragraph (1)(a) to (c) are fulfilled in relation to that person on any day within the part of a period referred to in paragraph (6), the requirement of paragraph (1) to treat the person as capable of work or as not having limited capability for work is to be regarded as satisfied with respect to the fulfilment of those conditions on that day.

(8) For the purposes of paragraph (3), where paragraph (6) applies to a person, paragraph (3) is to apply to the person as though the preceding provisions of this regulation had applied to the person with respect to the person having been treated for a period, under regulation 55(1) of the Jobseeker's Allowance Regulations 1996 and paragraph (6), as capable of work or as not having limited capability for work.".

(4) Where this article applies, the 1995 Act is to be read as though, in

section 5 of the 1995 Act, the reference to a jobseeker's allowance in subsection (1) and the first reference to a jobseeker's allowance in subsection (2) included a reference to a contribution-based jobseeker's allowance.

(5) For the purposes of this article, "joint-claim couple" has the meaning given in section 1(4) of the 1995 Act.]

AMENDMENTS

1. Welfare Reform Act 2012 (Commencement No.11 and Transitional and Transitory Provisions and Commencement No.9 and Transitional and Transitory Provisions (Amendment)) Order 2013 (SI 2013/1511) art.10 (July 1, 2013).
2. Welfare Reform Act 2012 (Commencement No.9, 11, 13 14, 16, 17 and 19 and Transitional and Transitory Provisions (Amendment)) Order 2014 (SI 2014/3067) art.7(a) (November 24, 2014).

DEFINITIONS

"the amending provisions"–art. 2(1).
"the appointed day"–*ibid.*
"contribution-based jobseeker's allowance"–*ibid.*
"jobseeker's allowance"–*ibid.*
"joint-claim couple"—see para.(5).
"the JSA Regulations 1996"–art. 2(1).
"the JSA Regulations 2013"–*ibid.*
"new style JSA award"–*ibid.*
"old style JSA award"–*ibid.*

GENERAL NOTE

5.44   This makes transitional provisions for the continuity of jobseeking periods where a person has a new style JSA award and previously had an old style JSA award. Article 13 deals with the converse position.

[¹Transition from new style JSA

5.45   **13.**—(1) This article applies where a person—
(a) makes, or is treated as making, a claim for a jobseeker's allowance (whether or not as a member of a joint-claim couple) and the 1995 Act, as it has effect apart from the provisions of Part 1 of Schedule 14 to the Act that remove references to an income-based jobseeker's allowance, applies in relation to the claim; or
(b) has a new style JSA award and article 6(2) applies in relation to the award such that it continues as an old style JSA award,
and, in the case of sub-paragraph (a), the condition referred to in paragraph (2) is satisfied.
(2) The condition is that the person previously—
(a) made, or was treated as having made, a claim for a jobseeker's allowance and, under article 4, the 1995 Act, as amended by the provisions of Part 1 of Schedule 14 to the Act that remove references to an income-based jobseeker's allowance, applied in relation to the claim; or
(b)(i) had an old style JSA award immediately before the appointed day in relation to a case of a claim for universal credit referred to in article 4(2)(a) to (d) (and any award made in respect of the claim), or an award of universal credit referred to in article 4(2)(e) or (f); and

   (ii) the old style JSA award consisted of or included a contributory employment and support allowance (which allowance therefore continued as a new style JSA award).

(3) Where this article applies, the JSA Regulations 1996 are to be read as if—

[²(za) in regulation 11, the references in paragraph (2)(a) and (b) to a jobseeker's allowance included a reference to new style JSA;]

   (a) in regulation 14A (victims of domestic violence), for the purposes of paragraph (3)(b) of that regulation, a person had been treated as available for employment on a day (under paragraph (2) of that regulation) where regulation 15 of the JSA Regulations 2013 applied to that person on that day;

[²(aa) in regulation 17A(7), in paragraph (a) of the definition of "benefit", the reference to a jobseeker's allowance included a reference to new style JSA;

  (ab) in regulation 19(1)(r), the reference to a jobseeker's allowance included a reference to new style JSA;]

   (b) in regulation 46 (waiting days)—

     (i) where a person was entitled to a new style JSA award with effect from the first day of a jobseeking period by virtue of regulation 36(1) of the JSA Regulations 2013 and, with effect from [³ a day between the second and the seventh day of that period (including the second and the seventh day)], that award continued as an old style JSA award in the circumstances referred to in paragraph (1)(b) of this article, the reference to a jobseeker's allowance in paragraph (1)(a) included a reference to the new style JSA award; and

     (ii) the second reference to a jobseeker's allowance in paragraph (1)(d) included a reference to a new style JSA award;

   (c) in regulation 47 (jobseeking period)—

     (i) the jobseeking period in relation to a claimant included any period that, under regulation 37 of the JSA Regulations 2013 (jobseeking period) forms part of the jobseeking period for the purposes of the 1995 Act; and

     (ii) in paragraph (4), the reference to any day that is to be treated as a day in respect of which the claimant was entitled to a contribution-based jobseeker's allowance included a reference to a day that, under regulation 37(3) of the JSA Regulations 2013 (jobseeking period), is to be treated as a day in respect of which the claimant was entitled to a jobseeker's allowance;

   (d) in regulation 50 (persons temporarily absent from Great Britain), where a person had a new style JSA award in the circumstances referred to in paragraph (1)(b) of this article, the reference in paragraph (2)(b), (3)(a) and (c), (5)(a) and (c), (6AA)(a) and (6D)(b) to entitlement to a jobseeker's allowance included a reference to the new style JSA award; [² . . .]

   (e) in regulation 55 (short periods of sickness), after paragraph (5) there were inserted—

"(6) Where—

   (a) a person has been treated under regulation 46(1) of the Jobseeker's Allowance Regulations 2013 as capable of work or as not having limited capability for work for a certain period; and

(b) these Regulations apply to that person with effect from a day ("the relevant day") within that period,

the person is to be treated for the part of that period that begins with the relevant day as capable of work or as not having limited capability for work.

(7) Where paragraph (6) applies to a person and the conditions in paragraph (1)(a) to (c) are fulfilled in relation to that person on any day within the part of a period referred to in paragraph (6), the requirement of paragraph (1) to treat the person as capable of work or as not having limited capability for work is to be regarded as satisfied with respect to the fulfilment of those conditions on that day.

(8) For the purposes of paragraph (3), where paragraph (6) applies to a person, paragraph (3) is to apply to the person as though the preceding provisions of this regulation had applied to the person with respect to the person having been treated for a period, under regulation 46(1) of the Jobseeker's Allowance Regulations 2013 and paragraph (6), as capable of work or as not having limited capability for work.".

[²(f) in paragraphs 6(1) and 7(1) of Schedule 2 (housing costs), each reference to a jobseeker's allowance included a reference to new style JSA; and

(g) in paragraph 13 of Schedule 2 (housing costs)—

    (i) in paragraph (a) of sub-paragraph (1) (apart from sub-paragraph (ii)(bb) of that paragraph), each of the references to a jobseeker's allowance included a reference to new style JSA;

    (ii) in sub-paragraph (1)(b), the reference to a jobseeker's allowance included a reference to new style JSA; and

    (iii) in sub-paragraph (1)(c)(iv) and (f)(iii), the reference to the making of a claim for a jobseeker's allowance included a reference to the making of a claim for a jobseeker's allowance where the 1995 Act, as it has effect as amended by the amending provisions, applied to the claim and the new style JSA award that resulted from the claim continued as an old style JSA award by virtue of article 6 of this Order.]

(4) Where this article applies, the 1995 Act is to be read as though, in section 5 of the 1995 Act, the reference to a contribution-based jobseeker's allowance in subsection (1) and the first reference to a contribution-based jobseeker's allowance in subsection (2) included a reference to a new style JSA award.

(5) For the purposes of this article, "joint-claim couple" has the meaning given in section 1(4) of the 1995 Act.]

AMENDMENTS

1. Welfare Reform Act 2012 (Commencement No.11 and Transitional and Transitory Provisions and Commencement No.9 and Transitional and Transitory Provisions (Amendment)) Order 2013 (SI 2013.1511) art.11 (July 1, 2013).

2. Welfare Reform Act 2012 (Commencement No.9, 11, 13, 14 and 16 and Transitional and Transitory Provisions (Amendment)) Order 2014 (SI 2014/1452) art.12 (June 16, 2014).

3. Welfare Reform Act 2012 (Commencement No.9, 11, 13 14, 16, 17 and 19 and Transitional and Transitory Provisions (Amendment)) Order 2014 (SI 2014/3067) art.7(a) (November 24, 2014).

"contribution-based jobseeker's allowance"–art. 2(1).
"jobseeker's allowance"–*ibid.*
"joint-claim couple"—see para.(5).
"the JSA Regulations 1996"–art. 2(1).
"the JSA Regulations 2013"–*ibid.*
"new style JSA award"–*ibid.*
"old style JSA award"–*ibid.*

GENERAL NOTE

This makes transitional provisions for the continuity of jobseeking periods where   5.46
a person has an old style JSA award and previously had a new style JSA award.
Article 12 deals with the converse position.

Sanctions: transition from old style ESA in case of a new award

14.—(1) This article applies where—   5.47
  (a) a person is entitled to a new style ESA award and they were previ-
      ously entitled to an old style ESA award that was not in existence
      immediately before the first day on which the person in question is
      entitled to the new style ESA award; and
  (b) immediately before the old style ESA award terminated, payments
      were reduced under regulation 63 of the ESA Regulations 2008
      (reduction of employment and support allowance).
  (2) Where this article applies—
  (a) the failure which led to reduction of the old style ESA award ("the
      relevant failure") is to be treated for the purposes of Part 8 of the
      ESA Regulations 2013, as a failure which is sanctionable under
      section 11J of the 2007 Act (sanctions);
  (b) the new style ESA award is to be reduced in relation to the relevant
      failure, in accordance with the provisions of this article and Part 8 of
      the ESA Regulations 2013 as modified by this article; and
  (c) the reduction referred to in sub-paragraph (b) is to be treated, for the
      purposes of the ESA Regulations 2013, as a reduction under section
      11J of the 2007 Act.
  (3) The reduction period for the purposes of the ESA Regulations 2013
is to be the number of days which is equivalent to the length of the fixed
period applicable to the person under regulation 63 of the ESA Regulations
2008 in relation to the relevant failure, minus—
  (a) the number of days (if any) in that fixed period in respect of which
      the amount of the old style ESA award was reduced; and
  (b) the number of days (if any) in the period starting with the day after
      the day on which the old style ESA award terminated and ending
      with the day before the first day on which the person is entitled to the
      new style ESA award.
  (4) Accordingly, regulation 51 of the ESA Regulations 2013 (general
principles for calculating reduction periods) applies in relation to the relevant failure as if—
  (a) in paragraph (1), for the words "in accordance with regulations
      52 and 53" there were substituted the words "in accordance with
      article 14 of the Welfare Reform Act 2012 (Commencement No.9
      and Transitional and Transitory Provisions and Commencement

No.8 and Savings and Transitional Provisions (Amendment)) Order 2013"; and

(b) in paragraph (3), for the words "in accordance with regulation 52 or 53" there were substituted the words "in accordance with article 14 of the Welfare Reform Act 2012 (Commencement No.9 and Transitional and Transitory Provisions and Commencement No.8 and Savings and Transitional Provisions (Amendment)) Order 2013".

DEFINITIONS

"the 2007 Act"–art. 2(1).
"employment and support allowance"–*ibid.*
"the ESA Regulations 2008"–*ibid.*
"the ESA Regulations 2013"–*ibid.*
"new style ESA award"–*ibid.*
"old style ESA award"–*ibid.*

GENERAL NOTE

5.48   This makes transitional provision in relation to sanctions where a person has a new style ESA award and previously had an old style ESA award and was subject to sanctions.

Sanctions: transition from old style ESA in case of a continuing award

5.49   **15.**—(1) This article applies where—

(a) the amending provisions have come into force under article 4(1) in relation to the case of a claim for universal credit referred to in [¹ article 4(2)(a)] to (d) (and any award that is made in respect of the claim) or an award of universal credit referred to in article 4(2)(e) or (f);

(b) the person in question had an old style ESA award immediately before the appointed day which consisted of or included a contributory allowance (which allowance therefore continues as a new style ESA award); and

(c) immediately before the appointed day, payments under that award were reduced in accordance with regulation 63 of the ESA Regulations 2008 (reduction of employment and support allowance).

(2) Where this article applies—

(a) the failure which led to reduction of the old style ESA award ("the relevant failure") is to be treated for the purposes of Part 8 of the ESA Regulations 2013, as a failure which is sanctionable under section 11J of the 2007 Act (sanctions);

(b) on and after the appointed day, the award (in its continuation as a new style ESA award) is to be reduced in relation to the relevant failure, in accordance with the provisions of this article and Part 8 of the ESA Regulations 2013 as modified by this article; and

(c) the reduction referred to in sub-paragraph (b) is to be treated, for the purposes of the ESA Regulations 2013, as a reduction under section 11J of the 2007 Act.

(3) The reduction period for the purposes of the ESA Regulations 2013

is to be the number of days which is equivalent to the length of the fixed period applicable to the person under regulation 63 of the ESA Regulations 2008 in relation to the relevant failure, minus the number of days (if any) in that period in respect of which the amount of the old style ESA award was reduced.

(4) Accordingly, regulation 51 of the ESA Regulations 2013 (general principles for calculating reduction periods) applies in relation to the relevant failure as if—

(a) in paragraph (1), for the words "in accordance with regulations 52 and 53" there were substituted the words "in accordance with article 15 of the Welfare Reform Act 2012 (Commencement No.9 and Transitional and Transitory Provisions and Commencement No.8 and Savings and Transitional Provisions (Amendment)) Order 2013"; and

(b) in paragraph (3), for the words "in accordance with regulation 52 or 53" there were substituted the words "in accordance with article 15 of the Welfare Reform Act 2012 (Commencement No.9 and Transitional and Transitory Provisions and Commencement No.8 and Savings and Transitional Provisions (Amendment)) Order 2013".

AMENDMENT

1. Welfare Reform Act 2012 (Commencement No.9, 11, 13, 14 and 16 and Transitional and Transitory Provisions (Amendment)) Order 2014 (SI 2014/1452) art.13 (June 16, 2014).

DEFINITIONS

"the 2007 Act"–art. 2(1)
"the amending provisions"–*ibid*.
"the appointed day"–*ibid*.
"employment and support allowance"–*ibid*.
"the ESA Regulations 2008"–*ibid*.
"the ESA Regulations 2013"–*ibid*.
"new style ESA award"–*ibid*.

GENERAL NOTE

This makes transitional provision in relation to sanctions where a person has an award of universal credit and previously had an old style ESA award which was subject to sanctions.

5.50

Escalation of sanctions: transition from old style ESA

16.—(1) This article applies where a person is entitled to a new style ESA award and, at any time previously, the person was entitled to an old style ESA award.

5.51

(2) Where this article applies, for the purposes of determining the reduction period under regulation 52 of the ESA Regulations 2013 (low-level sanction) in relation to a sanctionable failure by the person to whom the new style award referred to in paragraph (1) was made, other than a failure which is treated as sanctionable under article 14 or 15—

(a) a reduction of a new style ESA award in accordance with article 14 or 15 as the case may be; and

(b) a reduction of an old style ESA award under the ESA Regulations 2008 which did not result in a reduction under article 14 or 15,

is, subject to paragraph (3), to be treated as arising from a sanctionable failure for which the reduction period which applies is the number of days which is equivalent to the length of the fixed period which applied under regulation 63 of the ESA Regulations 2008 (reduction of employment and support allowance).

(3) In determining a reduction period under regulation 52 of the ESA Regulations 2013 in accordance with paragraph (2), no account is to be taken of—

(a) a reduction of a new style ESA award in accordance with article 14 or 15, as the case may be, if, at any time after that reduction, the person was entitled to an old style ESA award, an old style JSA award or income support;

(b) a reduction of an old style ESA award under the ESA Regulations 2008 if, at any time after that reduction, the person was entitled to universal credit, a new style ESA award or a new style JSA award, and was subsequently entitled to an old style ESA award, an old style JSA award or income support.

DEFINITIONS

"employment and support allowance"–art. 2(1).
"the ESA Regulations 2008"–*ibid.*
"the ESA Regulations 2013"–*ibid.*
"new style JSA award"–*ibid.*
"old style ESA award"–*ibid.*
"old style JSA award"–*ibid.*

GENERAL NOTE

5.52   This ensures that any previous old style ESA fixed period reductions are taken into account when deciding the appropriate reduction period for the purposes of new style ESA award.

Sanctions: transition from old style JSA in case of a new award

5.53   17.—(1) This article applies where—

(a) a person is entitled to a new style JSA award and they were previously entitled to an old style JSA award that was not in existence immediately before the first day on which the person in question is entitled to the new style JSA award;

(b) immediately before that old style award terminated, payments were reduced under section 19 (as it applied both before and after substitution by the Act) (before substitution: circumstances in which a jobseeker's allowance is not payable; after substitution: higher-level sanctions) or 19A (other sanctions) of the 1995 Act, or under regulation 69B of the JSA Regulations 1996 (the period of a reduction under section 19B : Claimants ceasing to be available for employment etc.); and

(c) if the old style JSA award was made to a joint-claim couple within the meaning of the 1995 Act and the reduction related to—

(i) in the case of a reduction under section 19 as it applied before substitution by the Act, circumstances relating to only one member of the couple; or

    (ii) in the case of a reduction under section 19 as it applied after substitution by the Act, a sanctionable failure by only one member of the couple,

the new style JSA award was made to that member of the couple.

(2) Where this article applies—

(a) the circumstances or failure which led to reduction of the old style JSA award (in either case "the relevant failure") is to be treated, for the purposes of the JSA Regulations 2013, as—

    (i) a failure which is sanctionable under section 6J of the 1995 Act (higher-level sanctions), where the reduction was under section 19 of the 1995 Act; or

    (ii) a failure which is sanctionable under section 6K of the 1995 Act (other sanctions), where the reduction was under section 19A of the 1995 Act or regulation 69B of the JSA Regulations 1996;

(b) the award of new style JSA is to be reduced in relation to the relevant failure, in accordance with the provisions of this article and Part 3 of the JSA Regulations 2013 (sanctions), as modified by this article; and

(c) the reduction is to be treated, for the purposes of the JSA Regulations 2013, as a reduction under section 6J or, as the case may be, section 6K of the 1995 Act.

(3) The reduction period for the purposes of the JSA Regulations 2013 is to be the number of days which is equivalent to the length of the period of reduction of a jobseeker's allowance which is applicable to the person under regulation 69, 69A or 69B of the JSA Regulations 1996, minus—

(a) the number of days (if any) in that period in respect of which the amount of a jobseeker's allowance was reduced; and

(b) the number of days (if any) in the period starting with the day after the day on which the old style JSA award terminated and ending with the day before the first day on which the person is entitled to a new style JSA award.

(4) Accordingly, regulation 18 of the JSA Regulations 2013 (general principles for calculating reduction periods) applies in relation to the relevant failure as if—

(a) in paragraph (1), for the words "in accordance with regulations 19, 20 and 21", there were substituted the words "in accordance with article 17 of the Welfare Reform Act 2012 (Commencement No.9 and Transitional and Transitory Provisions and Commencement No.8 and Savings and Transitional Provisions (Amendment)) Order 2013"; and

(b) in paragraph (3), for the words "in accordance with regulation 19, 20 or 21", there were substituted the words "in accordance with article 17 of the Welfare Reform Act 2012 (Commencement No.9 and Transitional and Transitory Provisions and Commencement No.8 and Savings and Transitional Provisions (Amendment)) Order 2013".

DEFINITIONS

"the Act"–art.2(1).
"the 1995 Act"–*ibid.*
"jobseeker's allowance"–*ibid.*
"the JSA Regulations 1996"–*ibid.*

"the JSA Regulations 2013"–*ibid.*
"new style JSA award"–*ibid.*
"old style JSA award"–*ibid.*

GENERAL NOTE

5.54   This makes transitional provision in relation to sanctions where a person has a new style JSA award and previously had an old style JSA award and was subject to sanctions.

Sanctions: transition from old style JSA in case of a continuing award

5.55   **18.**—(1) This article applies where—

(a) the amending provisions have come into force under article 4(1) in relation to the case of a claim for universal credit referred to in [¹ article 4(2)(a)] to (d) (and any award that is made in respect of the claim) or an award of universal credit referred to in article 4(2)(e) or (f);

(b) the person in question had an old style JSA award immediately before the appointed day which consisted of or included a contribution-based allowance (which allowance therefore continues as a new style JSA award);

(c) immediately before the appointed day, payments under that award were reduced under section 19 (as it applied both before and after substitution by the Act) (before substitution: circumstances in which a jobseeker's allowance is not payable; after substitution: higher-level sanctions) or 19A (other sanctions) of the 1995 Act, or under regulation 69B of the JSA Regulations 1996) (the period of a reduction under section 19B : Claimants ceasing to be available for employment etc.); and

(d) if the old style JSA award was made to a joint-claim couple within the meaning of the 1995 Act and the reduction related to—

(i) in the case of a reduction under section 19 as it applied before substitution by the Act, circumstances relating to only one member of the couple; or

(ii) in the case of a reduction under section 19 as it applied after substitution by the Act, a sanctionable failure by only one member of the couple,

the new style JSA award was made to that member of the couple.

(2) Where this article applies—

(a) the circumstances or failure which led to reduction of the old style JSA award (in either case "the relevant failure") is to be treated, for the purposes of the JSA Regulations 2013, as—

(i) a failure which is sanctionable under section 6J of the 1995 Act (higher-level sanctions), where the reduction was under section 19 of the 1995 Act; or

(ii) a failure which is sanctionable under section 6K of the 1995 Act (other sanctions), where the reduction was under section 19A of the 1995 Act or regulation 69B of the JSA Regulations 1996;

(b) the award (in its continuation as a new style JSA award) is to be reduced in relation to the relevant failure, in accordance with the provisions of this article and Part 3 of the JSA Regulations (sanctions), as modified by this article; and

(c) the reduction is to be treated, for the purposes of the JSA Regulations 2013, as a reduction under section 6J or, as the case may be, section 6K of the 1995 Act.

(3) The reduction period for the purposes of the JSA Regulations 2013 is to be the number of days which is equivalent to the length of the period of reduction of a jobseeker's allowance which is applicable to the person under regulation 69, 69A or 69B of the JSA Regulations 1996, minus the number of days (if any) in that period in respect of which the amount of a jobseeker's allowance was reduced.

(4) Accordingly, regulation 18 of the JSA Regulations 2013 (general principles for calculating reduction periods) applies in relation to the relevant failure as if—

(a) in paragraph (1), for the words "in accordance with regulations 19, 20 and 21", there were substituted the words "in accordance with article 18 of the Welfare Reform Act 2012 (Commencement No.9 and Transitional and Transitory Provisions and Commencement No.8 and Savings and Transitional Provisions (Amendment)) Order 2013"; and

(b) in paragraph (3), for the words "in accordance with regulation 19, 20 or 21", there were substituted the words "in accordance with article 18 of the Welfare Reform Act 2012 (Commencement No.9 and Transitional and Transitory Provisions and Commencement No.8 and Savings and Transitional Provisions (Amendment)) Order 2013".

AMENDMENT

1. Welfare Reform Act 2012 (Commencement No.9, 11, 13, 14 and 16 and Transitional and Transitory Provisions (Amendment)) Order 2014 (SI 2014/1452) art.13 (June 16, 2014).

DEFINITIONS

"the Act"–art. 2(1).
"the 1995 Act"–*ibid.*
"the amending provisions"–*ibid.*
"the appointed day"–*ibid.*
"jobseeker's allowance"–*ibid.*
"the JSA Regulations 1996"–*ibid.*
"the JSA Regulations 2013"–*ibid.*
"new style JSA award"–*ibid.*
"old style JSA award"–*ibid.*

GENERAL NOTE

This is the JSA equivalent to reg.15.   5.56

Escalation of sanctions: transition from old style JSA

19.—(1) This article applies where a person is entitled to a new style JSA   5.57
award and, at any time previously, the person was entitled to an old style JSA award.

(2) Where this article applies, for the purposes of determining the applicable reduction period under regulation 19 (higher-level sanction), 20 (medium-level sanction) or 21 (low-level sanction) of the JSA Regulations

2013 in relation to a sanctionable failure by the person other than a failure which is treated as sanctionable by virtue of article 17 or 18—

    (a) a reduction of a new style JSA award in accordance with article 17 or 18; and

    (b) a reduction of an old style JSA award under section 19 (as it applied both before and after substitution by the Act) or 19A of the 1995 Act, or under regulation 69B of the JSA Regulations 1996, which did not result in a reduction under article 17 or 18,

is, subject to paragraph (3), to be treated as arising from a sanctionable failure for which the reduction period is the number of days which is equivalent to the length of the period which applied under regulation 69, 69A or 69B of the JSA Regulations 1996.

(3) In determining a reduction period under regulation 19 (higher-level sanction), 20 (medium-level sanction) or 21 (low-level sanction) of the JSA Regulations 2013 in accordance with paragraph (2), no account is to be taken of—

    (a) a reduction of a new style JSA award in accordance with article 17 or 18 if, at any time after that reduction, the person was entitled to an old style JSA award, an old style ESA award or income support;

    (b) a reduction of an old style JSA award under section 19 (as it applied both before and after substitution by the Act) or 19A of the 1995 Act, or under regulation 69B of the JSA Regulations 1996, if, at any time after that reduction, the person was entitled to universal credit, a new style JSA award or a new style ESA award, and was subsequently entitled to an old style JSA award, an old style ESA award or income support.

DEFINITIONS

    "the Act"–art. 2(1).
    "the 1995 Act"–*ibid.*
    "the JSA Regulations 1996"–*ibid.*
    "the JSA Regulations 2013"–*ibid.*
    "new style JSA award"–*ibid.*
    "old style ESA award"–*ibid.*
    "old style JSA award"–*ibid.*

GENERAL NOTE

5.58   This is the JSA equivalent to reg.16.

Termination of sanctions under a new style ESA or JSA award

5.59   **20.**—(1) Paragraph (2) applies where—

    (a) a new style ESA award or new style JSA award terminates while there is an outstanding reduction period (within the meaning of regulation 55 of the ESA Regulations 2013 (reduction period to continue where award of employment and support allowance terminates) or regulation 23 of the JSA Regulations 2013 (reduction period to continue where award of jobseeker's allowance terminates)) and the claimant becomes entitled to an old style ESA award, an old style JSA award or income support during that period; or

    (b) article 6(2) applies to a new style ESA award or new style JSA award (such that it continues as an old style ESA award or an old style JSA award) and there is such an outstanding reduction period on the last day of the period of the new style ESA award or new style JSA award.

(2) Where this paragraph applies—

(a) regulation 55 of the ESA Regulations 2013 or regulation 23 of the JSA Regulations 2013, as the case may be, are to cease to apply; and

(b) the reduction period is to terminate on the first day of entitlement to an old style ESA award, old style JSA award or income support as the case may be.

DEFINITIONS

"employment and support allowance"–art.2(1).
"the ESA Regulations 2013"–*ibid.*
"jobseeker's allowance"–*ibid.*
"the JSA Regulations 2013"–*ibid.*
"new style ESA award"–*ibid.*
"new style JSA award"–*ibid.*
"old style JSA award"–*ibid.*

GENERAL NOTE

This provides that where a claimant has a new style ESA (or new style JSA) **5.60** award, is subject to sanctions and subsequently becomes entitled to an old style ESA (or old style JSA) award or income support, then the sanctions cease to have effect.

Transitory provisions: appeals

21.—(1) Paragraph (2) applies where— **5.61**

(a) the amending provisions have come into force under article 4(1) in relation to the case of a claim referred to in article 4(2)(a) to (d) (and any award that is made in respect of the claim) or the case of an award referred to in article 4(2)(e) or (f);

(b) the person is sent notice of a decision relating to a new style ESA award or a new style JSA award; and

(c) the date of notification with respect to that decision is before 28th October 2013.

(2) Where this paragraph applies, the provisions mentioned in paragraph (3) apply for the purposes of any appeal in relation to that decision as if regulation 55 of the Decisions and Appeals Regulations 2013 (consequential amendments) did not apply in that person's case.

(3) The provisions referred to are the following provisions of the Social Security and Child Support (Decisions and Appeals) Regulations 1999—

(a) regulation 32 (late appeals);

(b) regulation 33 (notice of appeal); and

(c) regulation 34 (death of a party to an appeal).

(4) For the purposes of paragraph (1), "the date of notification" means the date on which the decision notice was posted to the person's last known address by the Secretary of State.

DEFINITIONS

"the amending provisions"–art.2(1).
"the Decisions and Appeals Regulations 2013"–*ibid.*
"new style JSA award"–*ibid.*

GENERAL NOTE

5.62   This makes limited transitory provision with respect to appeals where a person is sent a notice relating to a new style ESA award or a new style JSA award before October 29, 2013.

Transitional provision: references to contributory employment and support allowance and contribution-based jobseeker's allowance

5.63   **22.**—Where the amending provisions have come into force under article 4(1) in relation to the case of a claim referred to in article 4(2)(a) to (d) [¹ or (g)] (and any award that is made in respect of the claim) or the case of an award referred to in article 4(2)(e) or (f), then, in relation to such a case, any reference in the Social Security Administration Act 1992 or the Social Security Contributions and Benefits Act 1992 to—

　　(a) a contributory employment and support allowance is to be read as if it included a reference to a new style ESA award; and

　　(b) a contribution-based jobseeker's allowance is to be read as if it included a reference to a new style JSA award.

AMENDMENT

　　1. Welfare Reform Act 2012 (Commencement No.9, 11, 13, 14 and 16 and Transitional and Transitory Provisions (Amendment)) Order 2014 (SI 2014/1452) art.14 (June 16, 2014).

DEFINITIONS

　　"the amending provisions"–*ibid.*
　　"contribution-based jobseeker's allowance"–*ibid.*
　　"contributory employment and support allowance"–*ibid.*
　　"new style JSA award"–*ibid.*

GENERAL NOTE

5.64   This provision seeks to ensure that new style ESA and JSA awards are to be treated to all intents and purposes as awards of a contributory employment or support allowance or to a contribution-based jobseeker's allowance respectively. It does so by providing that, in relation to a case with respect to which art.4 has come into force, references in the SSAA 1992 and the SSCBA 1992 are to be construed as if they included a reference to a new style ESA award or to a new style JSA award respectively.

Amendment of the Welfare Reform Act 2012 (Commencement No 8 and Savings and Transitional Provisions) Order 2013

5.65   **23.**—(1) Article 5 of the Welfare Reform Act 2012 (Commencement No 8 and Savings and Transitional Provisions) Order 2013 (appointed day and saving for provisions relating to overpayments) is amended as follows.

　　(2) In paragraph (3)(a), at the beginning insert "subject to paragraph (3A),".

　　(3) After paragraph (3) insert—

　　"(3A) In so far as section 105(1) of the 2012 Act inserts section 71ZB(1) (b) and (c) of the 1992 Act, those paragraphs come into force on 29th April 2013 only in so far as they relate respectively to a new style JSA award and a new style ESA award.".

(4) In paragraph (6), for "those benefits have been claimed before 29th April 2013" substitute "they relate respectively to an old style JSA award and an old style ESA award".

(5) After paragraph (6) add—

"(7) In this article, "old style JSA award", "new style JSA award", "old style ESA award" and "new style ESA award" have the same meaning as in article 2(1) of the Welfare Reform Act 2012 (Commencement No.9 and Transitional and Transitory Provisions and Commencement No.8 and Savings and Transitional Provisions (Amendment)) Order 2013.".

DEFINITIONS

"the appointed day"–art. 2(1).
"new style JSA award"–*ibid.*
"old style ESA award"–*ibid.*
"old style JSA award"–*ibid.*

GENERAL NOTE

This amends art.5 of the Commencement No.8 Order as regards overpayments. **5.66** It is intended to make it clear that the new rules applying to overpayments of employment and support allowance and of jobseeker's allowance under the WRA 2012 apply only to overpayments of a new style ESA award and a new style JSA award respectively (para.(3)). The amendments also clarify that the old rules relating to overpayments of those benefits will continue to apply to overpayments of an old style ESA award and an old style JSA award respectively (para.(4)).

[¹ Appeals relating to ESA and JSA

24.—(1) This article applies where, after an award of universal credit has **5.67** been made to a claimant (where that award is made by virtue of the coming into force of the provisions of the Act referred to in Schedule 2, under any secondary legislation) —

(a) an appeal against a decision relating to the entitlement of the claimant to an old style ESA award or an old style JSA award is finally determined; or

(b) a decision relating to the claimant's entitlement to such an award is revised under section 9 of the Social Security Act 1998 ("the 1998 Act") or superseded under section 10 of that Act.

(2) Where this article applies, the Secretary of State is to consider whether it is appropriate to revise under section 9 of the 1998 Act the decision in relation to entitlement to universal credit or, if that decision has been superseded under section 10 of that Act, the decision as so superseded (in either case, "the UC decision").

(3) Where it appears to the Secretary of State to be appropriate to revise the UC decision, it is to be revised in such manner as appears to the Secretary of State to be necessary to take account of—

(a) the decision of the First-tier Tribunal, Upper Tribunal or court, or, as the case may be, the decision relating to entitlement to an old style ESA award or an old style JSA award, as revised or superseded; and

(b) any finding of fact by the First-tier Tribunal, Upper Tribunal or court.

(4) For the purposes of this article, "secondary legislation" means an instrument made under an Act.]

AMENDMENT

1. Welfare Reform Act 2012 (Commencement No.9, 11, 13, 14 and 16 and Transitional and Transitory Provisions (Amendment)) Order 2014 (SI 2014/1452) art.15 (June 16, 2014).

GENERAL NOTE

5.68   This makes provision relating to the possible revision of a decision to make a universal credit award in the situation where an appeal against a decision not to award old style ESA or old style JSA is made after a universal credit award has been made.

SCHEDULE 1

POSTCODE DISTRICTS

5.69   1. M43
2. OL6
3. OL7
4. SK16

Article 3(2)

SCHEDULE 2

UNIVERSAL CREDIT PROVISIONS COMING INTO FORCE IN RELATION TO CERTAIN CLAIMS AND AWARDS

5.70   1. Section 1 (universal credit).
2. Section 2(1) (claims).
3. Section 3 (entitlement).
4. Section 4(1) and (4) (basic conditions).
5. Section 5 (financial conditions).
6. Section 6 (restrictions on entitlement).
7. Section 7(1) and (4) (basis of awards).
8. Section 8 (calculation of awards).
9. Section 9(1) (standard allowance).
10. Section 10(1) (responsibility for children and young persons).
11. Section 11(1) and (2) (housing costs).
12. Section 12(1) and (2) (other particular needs or circumstances).
13. Section 13 (work-related requirements: introductory).
14. Section 14 (claimant commitment).
15. Section 15(1) and (4) (work-focused interview requirement).
16. Section 16 (work preparation requirement).
17. Section 17(1), (2), (3)(a) to (e), (4) and (5) (work search requirement).
18. Section 18 (work availability requirement).
19. Section 19(1), (2)(a) to (c), (5) and (6) (claimants subject to no work-related requirements).
20. Section 20 (claimants subject to work-focused interview requirement only).
21. Section 21 (claimants subject to work preparation requirement).
22. Section 22 (claimants subject to all work-related requirements).
23. Section 23 (connected requirements).
24. Section 24(2), (3) and (4) (imposition of requirements).
25. Section 26(1) to (5) (higher-level sanctions).
26. Section 27(1) to (3) and (6) to (8) (other sanctions).

SCHEDULE 3

COMMENCEMENT OF REPEALS IN PART 1 OF SCHEDULE 14 TO THE ACT

Short title and chapter	Extent of repeal
Jobseekers Act 1995 (c.18)	Section 1(2A) to (2D) and (4). In section 2, in subsection (3C)(d), "contribution-based". Sections 3 to 3B.
	In section 4— (a) in subsection (1), "contribution-based"; (b) subsections (3), (3A) and (6) to (11A).
	Section 4A.
	In section 5— (a) in the heading and in subsection (1) "contribution-based"; (b) in subsection (2), "contribution-based" in the first two places; (c) in subsection (3), "contribution-based".
	Section 13.
	Sections 15 to 17. In section 17A(10), the definition of "claimant".
	Section 23.
	Sections 26.
	In section 35(1)— (a) in the definition of "claimant", the words from "except" to the end; (b) the definitions of "contribution-based jobseeker's allowance", "income-based jobseeker's allowance", "income-related employment and support allowance", "joint-claim couple", "joint-claim jobseeker's allowance" and "the nominated member".
	In section 38— (a) in subsections (3) and (4), "contribution-based"; (b) subsection (6).
	In Schedule 1— (a) in paragraph 6(1), "contribution-based"; (b) paragraphs 8 and 8A; (c) paragraphs 9 to 10; (d) in paragraph 11(1), "contribution-based"; (e) in paragraph 16(1) and (2)(d), "contribution-based"; (f) paragraph 18(b) and (c).
Welfare Reform and Pensions Act 1999 (c.30)	In Schedule 7, paragraphs 2(3) and (4), 4, 5(3) and (4), 6, 9 to 11, 15 and 16.
	In Schedule 8, paragraph 29(2).

Short title and chapter	Extent of repeal
State Pension Credit Act 2002 (c.16)	In Schedule 2, paragraphs 36 to 38.
Income Tax (Earnings and Payments) Act 2003 (c.1)	In Schedule 6, paragraphs 228 to 230.
Civil Partnership Act 2004 (c.33)	In Schedule 24, paragraphs 118 to 122.
Welfare Reform Act 2007 (c.5)	In section 1— (a) in subsection (2), in the opening words, "either"; (b) in subsection (2)(a), "Part 1 of" and "that Part of"; (c) subsection (2)(b) and the preceding "or"; (d) in subsection (3)(f), the words from "(and" to "allowance)"; (e) in subsection (3A), "Part 1 of"; (f) in subsection (6), the definition of "joint-claim jobseeker's allowance"; (g) subsections (6A) and (7). In subsection 1A— (a) in the heading "contributory"; (b) in subsections (1) (in both places), (3) and (4), "Part 1 of". Section 1B(2). In section 2, in the heading, "contributory". In section 3, in the heading, "contributory". Sections 4 to 6. Section 23. In section 24(1), the definitions of "contributory allowance" and "income-related allowance". In section 26(1)(a), "or 4(4)(c) or (5)(c)". Section 27(2)(a) and (4). In Schedule 1— (a) the heading to Part 1; (b) Part 2. In Schedule 2— (a) in the headings to paragraphs 6 and 7, "Contributory allowance:"; (b) paragraph 8; (c) paragraph 11(b) and (c); (d) paragraph 12, so far as not otherwise repealed.
Welfare Reform Act 2009 (c.24)	In Part 3 of Schedule 7, the entry relating to the Civil Partnership Act 2004.

SCHEDULE 4

MODIFICATIONS OF THE 2010 TRANSITIONAL REGULATIONS

5.72   1. The 2010 Transitional Regulations are to be read as if the amendments set out in this Schedule were made.

2. (1) Regulation 2 (interpretation) is amended as follows.

(2) In paragraph (1)—

(a) insert at the appropriate places in the alphabetical order of the definitions—

""the Claims and Payments Regulations" means the Universal Credit, Personal

Independence Payment, Jobseeker's Allowance and Employment and Support Allowance (Claims and Payments) Regulations 2013;";

""the Decisions and Appeals Regulations" means the Universal Credit, Personal Independence Payment, Jobseeker's Allowance and Employment and Support Allowance (Decisions and Appeals) Regulations 2013;";

""the ESA Regulations" means the Employment and Support Allowance Regulations 2013;";

  (b) omit—
    (i) the definition of "income-related allowance";
    (ii) paragraphs (a) to (d) of the definition of "relevant deduction";
  (c) in the definition of "benefit week", for "the 2008 Regulations" substitute "the ESA Regulations".

(3) In paragraph (3), omit "or awards".

3. In regulation 4 (the notice commencing the conversion phase), omit paragraph (6).

4. In regulation 5 (deciding whether an existing award qualifies for conversion)—
  (a) in paragraph (1), omit "or awards";
  (b) in paragraph (2)(a), for "or awards qualify" substitute "qualifies";
  (c) in paragraph (2)(b), for "or awards do" substitute "does";
  (d) in paragraph (6)(b), omit "or awards".

5. In regulation 6(2) (application of certain enactments for purpose of making conversion decisions)—
  (a) for sub-paragraphs (b) and (c), substitute—
    "(b) the ESA Regulations;
    (c) regulation 38(2) and (3) of the Claims and Payments Regulations (evidence and information in connection with an award);";
  (b) for sub-paragraph (e), substitute—
    "(e) the Decisions and Appeals Regulations."

6. In regulation 7 (qualifying for conversion)—
  (a) in paragraph (1)—
    (i) omit "or awards";
    (ii) for "qualify" substitute "qualifies";
  (b) in paragraphs (2)(b) and (3)(b), for "regulation 30 of the 2008 Regulations" substitute "regulation 26 of the ESA Regulations".

7. In regulation 8(1) (amount of an employment and support allowance on conversion), for "the 2008 Regulations" substitute "the ESA Regulations".

8. In regulation 9(1) (determining entitlement to a transitional addition)—
  (a) for "or awards qualify" substitute "qualifies";
  (b) omit "or 11(2) (transitional addition: income support)".

9. In regulation 10 (transitional addition: incapacity benefit or severe disablement allowance)—
  (a) in paragraph (1), omit "(and for these purposes it is irrelevant whether the person is also entitled to any existing award of income support)";
  (b) in paragraph (4)(a), for "paragraph (2) of regulation 67 of the 2008 Regulations (prescribed amounts for purpose of calculating a contributory allowance)" substitute "paragraph (1) of regulation 62 of the ESA Regulations (prescribed amounts)".

10. Omit regulation 11 (transitional addition: income support).

11. In regulation 12 (regulations 10 and 11: supplementary)—
  (a) in the title, for "Regulations 10 and 11" substitute "Regulation 10";
  (b) in paragraph (1), for "regulations 10 and 11" substitute "regulation 10";
  (c) in paragraph (2), for "Amounts A and C are" substitute "Amount A is" and for "Amounts B and D are" substitute "Amount B is";
  (d) for paragraph (3)(a), substitute—
    "(a) by virtue of an order made under section 150 of the Administration Act (annual up-rating of benefits), there is an increase in the weekly rate which, in accordance with regulation 10(3) (transitional addition: incapacity benefit or severe disablement allowance), is to be used to calculate Amount A; and";
  (e) in paragraph (4)(a), for "paragraph (3)(a)(i) or (ii)" substitute "paragraph (3)(a)";
  (f) in paragraphs (3) and (4), omit "or C" and "or applicable amount (as the case may be)".

12. In regulation 13(3) (the effective date of a conversion decision), omit "or awards".

13. In regulation 14 (conversion decision that existing award qualifies for conversion)—
  (a) in paragraph (1)—
    (i) for "Subject to paragraph (2A), paragraphs (2) to (6)" substitute "Paragraphs (2) to (5)";

(ii) for "or awards qualify" substitute "qualifies";

(b) for paragraph (2), substitute—

"(2) On the effective date of the conversion decision P's existing award is by virtue of this paragraph converted into, and shall have effect on and after that date as, a single award of an employment and support allowance of such amount as is specified in the conversion decision.";

(c) omit paragraphs (2A), (2B) and (6);

(d) in paragraph (4), omit "or awards";

(e) for paragraph (7), substitute—

"(7) In this regulation paragraphs (2) to (5) are subject to regulation 17 (changes of circumstances before the effective date).".

14. In regulation 15 (conversion decision that existing award does not qualify for conversion)—

(a) in paragraph (1)—

(i) for "Subject to paragraphs (2A) and (4), paragraphs (2), (3) and (6)" substitute "Subject to paragraph (4), paragraphs (2) and (3)";

(ii) for "or awards do" substitute "does";

(b) for paragraph (2), substitute—

"(2) P's entitlement to an existing award of incapacity benefit or severe disablement allowance shall terminate by virtue of this paragraph immediately before the effective date of P's conversion decision.";

(c) omit paragraphs (2A), (2B) and (6);

(d) in paragraph (4)(a)—

(i) for "the 2008 Regulations" substitute "the ESA Regulations";

(ii) in paragraph (i), for "regulation 22(1) (failure to provide information or evidence requested in relation to limited capability for work)" substitute "regulation 18(1) (failure to provide information in relation to limited capability for work)";

(iii) in paragraph (ii), for "regulation 23(2) (failure to attend for a medical examination to determine whether the claimant has limited capability for work)" substitute "regulation 19(2) (claimant may be called for a medical examination to determine whether the claimant has limited capability for work)";

(e) in paragraph (5)—

(i) in sub-paragraph (c), omit "or awards";

(ii) in sub-paragraph (d), omit "or those existing awards";

(f) for paragraph (7), substitute—

"(7) In this regulation paragraphs (2) and (3) are subject to regulation 17 (changes of circumstances before the effective date).".

15. In regulation 16 (application of other enactments applying to employment and support allowance)—

(a) in paragraph (1A)(b), for "regulation 145(1) of the 2008 Regulations" substitute "regulation 86 of the ESA Regulations";

(b) in paragraph (2)(e)(ii), for "the 2008 Regulations" substitute "the ESA Regulations";

(c) in paragraph (2)(e)(iii), omit "(being regulations consequentially amended by regulations made under Part 1 of the 2007 Act)".

16. In regulation 17 (changes of circumstances before the effective date)—

(a) omit "or awards" in both places where it occurs;

(b) in paragraph (a)(ii)—

(i) omit "regulation 14(2B)(a) (termination of an existing award of incapacity benefit or severe disablement allowance where entitlement to award of income support continues),";

(ii) for "(termination of existing awards which do not qualify for conversion)" substitute "(termination of an existing award which does not qualify for conversion)";

(c) omit paragraph (c).

17. In regulation 18 (reducing the transitional addition: general rule), for paragraph (2) substitute—

"(2) For the purposes of paragraph (1), a relevant increase is an increase in any amount applicable to the person under regulation 62(1) or (2) of the ESA Regulations, which is not excluded by paragraph (3).".

18. In regulation 21 (termination of transitional addition)—

(a) in paragraph (1)(b)—

(i) for ", (3), (3A) and (4)" substitute ", (3) and (3A)"and (4)";

    (ii) omit "an employment and support allowance (entitlement to which arises from sections 1(2)(a) or 1(2)(b) of the 2007 Act), or to" and "or to an income-related allowance";

(b) omit paragraph (4);

(c) in paragraph (5)(a), for "regulation 145(1) of the 2008 Regulations (linking rules)" substitute "regulation 86 of the ESA Regulations (linking period)";

(d) in paragraph (5)(c)(ii), for "regulation 30 of the 2008 Regulations" substitute "regulation 26 of the ESA Regulations";

(e) in paragraph (5A)(c), for "regulation 145(1) of the 2008 Regulations (linking rules)" substitute "regulation 86 of the ESA Regulations (linking period)";

(f) omit paragraph (6);

(g) in paragraph (7)—

    (i) for ", 1A and 2" substitute "and 1A";

    (ii) omit "or additions, as the case may be," in both places where it occurs;

    (iii) for "an allowance which is referred to in paragraph (1)(b)" substitute "a contributory allowance".

19. In regulation 22 (disapplication of certain enactments following conversion decision), omit paragraphs (c) and (d).

20. In Schedule 1 (modification of enactments: making conversion decisions)—

(a) in paragraph 2(a), for the modified section 1(2) substitute—

"(2) Subject to the provisions of this Part, a notified person is entitled to an employment and support allowance if the person satisfies the basic conditions and is entitled to an existing award of incapacity benefit or severe disablement allowance.";

(b) for paragraph 6, substitute—

"6. Schedule 1 to the 2007 Act is to be read as if paragraphs 1 to 6 were omitted.";

(c) in the heading to Part 2, for "the 2008 Regulations" substitute "the ESA Regulations";

(d) in paragraph 10, for "Regulation 30" substitute "Regulation 26";

(e) omit paragraph 10A;

(f) in paragraph 11, for "Regulation 75" substitute "Regulation 68";

(g) in paragraph 12, for "Regulation 144" substitute "Regulation 85";

(h) in the sub heading to Part 3, for "Social Security (Claims and Payments) Regulations 1987" substitute "The Claims and Payments Regulations";

(i) in paragraph 13—

    (i) for "Regulation 32 of the Social Security (Claims and Payments) Regulations 1987" substitute "Regulation 38 of the Claims and Payments Regulations";

    (ii) in sub-paragraph (a), for "paragraph (1)" substitute "paragraph (2)";

    (iii) in sub-paragraph (b), for "paragraph (1A)" substitute "paragraph (3)".

21. (1) Schedule 2 (modification of enactments: after the conversion phase) is amended as follows.

(2) In paragraph 2—

(a) in sub-paragraph (a), in the modified section 1(2)–

    (i) in paragraph (a), for "or awards into a single award of an employment and support allowance;" substitute "into an award of an employment and support allowance; and";

    (ii) omit paragraph (c) and for "; and" at the end of paragraph (b) substitute ",";

(b) in sub-paragraph (b) in the modified section 1(7)—

  [¹ (i) for the definition of "contributory allowance" substitute—

"employment and support allowance" means an employment and support allowance to which a person is entitled by virtue of the Employment and Support Allowance (Transitional Provisions, Housing Benefit and Council Tax Benefit) (Existing Awards)(No.2) Regulations 2010 which was based on an award of incapacity benefit or severe disablement allowance to which the person was entitled.] and for "; and" following that definition substitute "."];

    (ii) omit the definition of "income-related allowance".

[¹ (2A) In paragraph 2A—

(a) in paragraph (1), omit "contributory"; and

(b) in paragraph (2), in the substituted section 1A

    (i) in paragraphs (1) and (3) to (5), for " a contributory allowance" substitute "an employment and support allowance"; and

    (ii) in paragraph (3), omit "Part 1 of".]

(3) In paragraph 3(b), for "regulation 147A of the 2008 Regulations" substitute "regulation 87 of the ESA Regulations".

(4) Omit paragraphs 4 and 4A.

(5) In paragraph 6A—
  (a) in sub-paragraph (a), after paragraph (iv) insert "and";
  (b) in sub-paragraph (b), for "; and" substitute ".";
  (c) omit sub-paragraph (c).
(6) In the heading to Part 3, for "the 2008 Regulations" substitute "the ESA Regulations".
(7) In paragraph 8, for "regulation 147A of the 2008 Regulations" substitute "regulation 87 of the ESA Regulations".
(8) In paragraph 10, for "regulation 30" substitute "regulation 26".
"(9) For paragraph 11, substitute—
      11. Regulation 39 (exempt work) is to be read as if, in the definition of "work
      period" in paragraph (6), after "referred to in paragraph (1)(c)", in both places
      where it occurs, there were inserted ", or any work done in accordance with regula-
      tion 17(4)(a) of the Social Security (Incapacity for Work)(General) Regulations
      1995.
(10) For paragraph 12, substitute—"
      "**12.** Regulation 62 (prescribed amounts) is to be read as if, in paragraph (1), for
      sub-paragraphs (a) and (b) there were substituted—
  (a)(i) where the claimant satisfies the conditions set out in section 2(2) or (3) of the
          Act, [²£74.70]; or
     (ii) where the claimant does not satisfy the conditions set out in section 2(2) or (3)
          of the Act—
  (aa) where the claimant is aged not less than 25, [²£74.70]; or
  (bb) where the claimant is aged less than 25, [²£59.20]; and
  (b)   the amount of any transitional addition to which the person is entitled under
        regulation 10 of the Employment and Support Allowance (Transitional Provisions,
        Housing Benefit and Council Tax Benefit) (Existing Awards) (No.2) Regulations
        2010."
(9) Omit paragraph 13.
(10) In paragraph 14—
  (a) for "Regulation 75" substitute "Regulation 68";
  (b) for "paragraph 38" substitute "paragraph 11".
(11) In paragraph 15—
  (a) in the introductory words, for "Regulation 147A" substitute "regulation 87";
  (b) in the inserted regulation—
      (i)   in the description of the number of the regulation, for "147A.—" substitute
             "87.—";
      (ii)   in paragraph (2), for "regulation 19" substitute "regulation 15";
      (iii) in paragraph (4)(a), for "regulation 22 or 23" substitute "regulation 18 or 19";
      (iv)   for "regulation 30", in all places where it occurs, substitute "regulation 26";
      (v)   in paragraph (5)(c), for the words from ", struck out" to "(notice of appeal)",
             substitute "or struck out";
      (vi)   in paragraph (5A), for "either—" and sub-paragraphs (a) and (b), substitute
             "receives the First-tier Tribunal's notification that the appeal is dismissed, with-
             drawn or struck out.".
(12) Omit paragraph 16.
(13) In the sub-heading before paragraph 17, for "Social Security (Claims and Payments)
Regulations 1987" substitute "The Claims and Payments Regulations".
(14) In paragraph 17, for "The Social Security (Claims and Payments) Regulations 1987"
substitute "The Claims and Payments Regulations".
(15) For paragraph 18 substitute—
      "**18.** Regulation 7 (claims not required for entitlement to an employment and
      support allowance in certain cases) is to read as if—
  (a) the existing provisions were renumbered as paragraph (1);
  (b) after paragraph (1) there were inserted—
(2) It is also not to be a condition of entitlement to an employment and support allowance
that a claim be made for it where any of the following conditions are met—
  (a) the claimant—
      (i)   has made and is pursuing an appeal against a conversion decision made by virtue
             of the Employment and Support Allowance (Transitional Provisions, Housing
             Benefit and Council Tax Benefit) (Existing Awards) (No.2) Regulations 2010
             which embodies a determination that the beneficiary does not have limited
             capability for work; or
      (ii)   was entitled to an employment and support allowance by virtue of the

Employment and Support Allowance (Transitional Provisions, Housing Benefit and Council Tax Benefit) (Existing Awards) (No.2) Regulations 2010 and has made and is pursuing an appeal against a later decision which embodies a determination that the claimant does not have limited capability for work; or

(b) the claimant is entitled to an existing award which is subject to conversion under the Employment and Support Allowance (Transitional Provisions, Housing Benefit and Council Tax Benefit) (Existing Awards) (No.2) Regulations 2010." "

(16) In paragraph 19, for "regulation 26C" substitute "regulation 51".

(17) In paragraph 20—

(a) for "regulation 32(1B)" substitute "regulation 38(4)";

(b) in sub-paragraph (a), for the words "sub-paragraph (a)" substitute "sub-paragraph (b)";

(c) in sub-paragraph (b), for "(ab)" substitute "(bb)".

(18) Omit paragraph 21.

(19) In paragraph 22, for "Schedule 9B" substitute "Schedule 7".

(20) In paragraph 22A, in the inserted text omit paragraph (2B).

(21) In paragraph 23, in the inserted text omit paragraph (2B).

(22) In paragraph 24, in the inserted text omit paragraph (2B).

(23) In paragraph 25, in the inserted text omit paragraph (2B).

(24) In the sub-heading before paragraph 25A, for "Social Security and Child Support (Decisions and Appeals) Regulations 1999" substitute "Universal Credit, Personal Independence Payment, Jobseeker's Allowance and Employment and Support Allowance (Decisions and Appeals) Regulations 2013".

(25) In paragraph 25A—

(a) in sub-paragraph (1), for "Regulation 3 of the Social Security and Child Support (Decisions and Appeals) Regulations 1999 (revision of decisions)" substitute "Regulation 5 of the Universal Credit, Personal Independence Payment, Jobseeker's Allowance and Employment and Support Allowance (Decisions and Appeals) Regulations 2013 (revision on any grounds)";

(b) in sub-paragraph (1)(b), for "paragraph (9)(a)" substitute "paragraphs (2)(a) and (h)";

(c) for sub-paragraph (1)(c), substitute—

"(c) in paragraph (2)(a), for "in the case of an advance award under regulation 32, 33 or 34 of the Claims and Payment Regulations 2013" there were substituted, "in the case of an advance award under regulation 32, 33 or 34 of the Claims and Payment Regulations 2013 or a conversion decision within the meaning of regulation 5(2)(a) of the Employment and Support Allowance (Transitional Provisions, Housing Benefit and Council Tax Benefit) (Existing Awards) (No.2) Regulations 2010".";

(d) for sub-paragraph (2), substitute—

"(2) Regulation 23(1)(a) of those Regulations (change of circumstances) is to be read as if for "in the case of an advance award under regulation 32, 33 or 34 of the Claims and Payments Regulations 2013" there were substituted "in the case of an advance award under regulation 32, 33 or 34 of the Claims and Payments Regulations 2013 or a conversion decision within the meaning of regulation 5(2)(a) of the Employment and Support Allowance (Transitional Provisions, Housing Benefit and Council Tax Benefit) (Existing Awards) (No.2) Regulations 2010." "

(26) Omit paragraph 27.

22. In Schedule 3—

(a) for "The Social Security (Claims and Payments) Regulations 1987" substitute "the Claims and Payments Regulations";

(b) for " The Social Security and Child Support (Decisions and Appeals) Regulations 1999" substitute "the Decisions and Appeals Regulations".

AMENDMENTS

1. Welfare Reform Act 2012 (Commencement No.11 and Transitional and Transitory Provisions and Commencement No.9 and Transitional and Transitory Provisions (Amendment)) Order 2013 (SI 2013/1511) art.7 (July 1, 2013).

2. Social Security Benefits Uprating Order 2021 (SI 2021/162) para.32(3) (April 12, 2021).

(ii) in relation to Wales, a person who is approved as a foster parent under the Fostering Services (Wales) Regulations 2003;

(iii) in relation to Scotland, a person who is approved as a kinship carer or a foster carer under the Looked After Children (Scotland) Regulations 2009 [⁴;

(c) "young person" means a person–

(i) who is not a child but who is under the age of 20; and

(ii) for whom the claimant would be responsible for the purposes of regulation 4 of the Universal Credit Regulations, if the person were a qualifying young person within the meaning of regulation 5 of those Regulations.]

Other requirements

5.79   **7.** The claimant—

[² (a) must not be carrying on a trade, profession or vocation in respect of which he or she receives self-employed earnings (within the meaning of regulation 57 of the Universal Credit Regulations) and must declare that he or she does not expect to carry on such a trade, profession or vocation during the period of one month starting with the date on which the claim for universal credit is made;]

(b) must not be receiving education or undertaking a course of training of any kind and must declare that he or she does not intend to engage in education or training of any kind (other than where required to do so by the Secretary of State, or by agreement with the Secretary of State, in connection with an award of universal credit) during the period of one month starting with the date on which the claim for universal credit is made;

(c) must not have—

(i) a deputy appointed by the Court of Protection under Part 1 of the Mental Capacity Act 2005 ("the 2005 Act");

(ii) a receiver appointed under Part 7 of the Mental Health Act 1983 and treated as a deputy by virtue of the 2005 Act; or

(iii) any other person acting on the claimant's behalf in relation to the claim for universal credit;

(d) must have a national insurance number;

[⁴ (e) must have an account with a bank, a building society, the Post Office, or a Credit Union (within the meaning of the Credit Unions Act 1979] [⁵ or, in the case of joint claimants(2), either member of the couple must have such an account] [²;

(f) must not be—

(i) a company director, within the meaning of the Companies Act 2006; or

(ii) a member of a limited liability partnership, within the meaning of the Limited Liability Partnerships Act 2000.]

Declarations

5.80   **8.** [³ (1)] [² A] declaration which is required by paragraph 2(3)(c), 4(1) , [³ 4(2)] or 7(a) or (b) is to be made by such method as may be required by the Secretary of State in relation to the person by whom it is to be made.]

[³ (2) A declaration which is required by paragraph 4(2) in relation to a couple may be made on behalf of the couple by both members of the couple or by either of them.]

AMENDMENTS

1. Welfare Reform Act 2012 (Commencement No.9, 11, 13, 14 and 16 and Transitional and Transitory Provisions (Amendment)) Order 2014 (SI 2014/1452) art.16 (June 16, 2014).

2. Welfare Reform Act 2012 (Commencement No.9, 11, 13 14, 16 and 17 and Transitional and Transitory Provisions (Amendment)) Order 2014 (SI 2014/1661) art. 4(4) (June 30, 2014).

3. Welfare Reform Act 2012 (Commencement No.9, 11, 13, 14, 16 and 17 and Transitional and Transitory Provisions (Amendment) (No.2)) Order 2014 (SI 2014/1923) art. 4(7) (July 28, 2014).

4. Welfare Reform Act 2012 (Commencement No.9, 11, 13, 14, 16, 17 and 19 and Transitional and Transitory Provisions (Amendment)) Order 2015 (SI 2015/32) arts.4(5) and 5 (January 26, 2015).

5. Welfare Reform Act 2012 (Commencement No.24 and Transitional and Transitory Provisions and Commencement No.9 and Transitional and Transitory Provisions (Amendment)) Order 2015 (SI 2015/1537) art.5(2)(a) (July 21, 2015).

GENERAL NOTE

Paragraph 4

One of the gateway conditions is that a single claimant must declare that their   5.81
earned income for the next month "is not expected to exceed" a set figure (originally
£330, now £338). The question on the original on-line claim form is subtly different, namely "Are you expecting take-home pay of £330 or more in the next month?"
See AM v SSWP (UC) [2017] UKUT 131 for a discussion of the difficulties this
may create. As Judge Rowland observed:

'25. The Secretary of State argues that, because those who are uncertain are
not confident that they will receive take-home pay of £330 or more in the next
month, the correct answer for them to give on the claim form is no. I accept that,
as a matter of very strict logic, that is so and that therefore the advice given to
the claimant on 20 July 2015 was, strictly speaking, correct insofar as it explained
which answer on the claim form was appropriate. However, it seems to me to be
unlikely that this claimant is the only one to have read the option no as requiring
him to declare that he expected not to receive take-home pay of £330 or more
in the next month even though he had no such clear expectation. People do not
always distinguish between I am not expecting take-home pay of £330 or more in
the next month and I am expecting not to receive take-home pay of £330 or more
in the next month. Without some guidance, the claim form is apt to confuse and
a cautious person may prefer to answer "yes" rather than "no" so as to avoid an
apparent under-declaration that might be construed as deliberately misleading.'

Judge Rowland further held as a matter of law as follows (at para.23):

'23. Whether or not "highly likely" is the right phrase, I accept that in both paragraph 4(1) of Schedule 5 to the Commencement No.9 Order and in the question posed on the claim form, "expect" or "expecting" is used in the sense of the
person concerned being reasonably confident about what will happen.'

The Welfare Reform Act 2012 (Commencement No.11 and Transitional and Transitory Provisions and Commencement No.9 and Transitional and Transitory Provisions (Amendment)) Order 2013

(SI 2013/1511) (C. 60) (AS AMENDED)

*The Secretary of State, in exercise of the powers conferred by section 150(3) and (4)(a),
(b)(i) and (c) of the Welfare Reform Act 2012, makes the following Order:*

ARRANGEMENT OF ARTICLES

relation to claimant responsibilities with respect to employment and support allowance and jobseeker's allowance

GENERAL NOTE

5.83 Note that the text of this Commencement Order is not included in its entirety in this volume as it is now unlikely to give rise to live appeals. The full text can be found in the 2019/20 edn of this book at paras 3.183-3.212.

This Commencement Order ("the Commencement No.11 Order") extended the universal credit scheme to certain postcode districts in Wigan ("the No.2 relevant districts") and Manchester, Oldham and Warrington ("the No.3 relevant districts") as from July 1, 2013. The Order accordingly brought into force in those areas the provisions of the WRA 2012 that relate to both the introduction of universal credit and the abolition of income-related ESA and income-based JSA. This was achieved by reference to the specific categories of cases set out in arts.3 and 4. In addition, of course, the claimant had to fall within the Pathfinder Group, i.e. be a person who meets the requirements of regs.5 to 12 of the Transitional Provisions Regulations 2013 (or now meet the "gateway conditions" as set out in Sch.5 to the Commencement No.9 Order (as amended)).

An award of ESA under Part 1 of the Welfare Reform Act 2007, in a case where income-related ESA has been abolished, is referred to as a "new style ESA award". Likewise an award of a JSA under the Jobseekers Act 1995, in a case where income-based JSA has been abolished, is referred to as a "new style JSA award". Conversely an award of ESA under Part 1 of the Welfare Reform Act 2007, in a case where income-related ESA has not been abolished, is referred to as an "old style ESA award". Similarly an award of JSA under the Jobseekers Act 1995, in a case where income-based JSA has not been abolished, is referred to as an "old style JSA award".

This Order also amended certain transitional provisions in the Commencement No.9 Order.

The Welfare Reform Act 2012 (Commencement No.13 and Transitional and Transitory Provisions) Order 2013

(SI 2013/2657) (C.103) (AS AMENDED)

The Secretary of State, in exercise of the powers conferred by section 150(3) and (4)(a), (b)(i) and (c) of the Welfare Reform Act 2012, makes the following Order:

ARRANGEMENT OF ARTICLES

5.84   1. Citation
      2. Interpretation

3.   Day appointed for commencement of the universal credit provisions in Part 1 of the Act
4.   Day appointed for the abolition of income-related employment and support allowance and income-based jobseeker's allowance
5.   Amendment of the No.9 Order
6.   Application of the No.9 Order

Schedule: The No.4 relevant districts

GENERAL NOTE

This Commencement Order ("the Commencement No.13 Order") extended   5.85
the universal credit scheme to certain postcode districts in West London
(Hammersmith), Manchester and Wigan ("the No.4 relevant districts") as from
October 28, 2013. In addition, of course, the claimant had initially to fall within the
Pathfinder Group, i.e. be a person who met the requirements of regs.5 to 12 of the
Transitional Provisions Regulations 2013, and subsequently the gateway conditions
in Sch.5 to the Commencement No.9 Order.
    Note that the text of this Commencement Order is not included in its entirety in
this volume as it is now unlikely to give rise to live appeals. The full text can be found
in the 2019/20 edn of this book at paras 3.213-3.235.

The Welfare Reform Act 2012 (Commencement No.14 and Transitional and Transitory Provisions) Order 2013

SI 2013/2846 (C.114) (AS AMENDED)

The Secretary of State, in exercise of the powers conferred by section 150(3) and (4)(a), (b)(i) and (c) of the Welfare Reform Act 2012, makes the following Order:

ARRANGEMENT OF ARTICLES

1.   Citation   5.86
2.   Interpretation
3.   Day appointed for commencement of the universal credit provisions in Part 1 of the Act
4.   Day appointed for the abolition of income-related employment and support allowance and income-based jobseeker's allowance
5.   Application of the No.9 Order

Schedule: The No.5 relevant districts

GENERAL NOTE

This Commencement Order ("the Commencement No.14 Order") extended the   5.87
universal credit scheme to certain postcode districts in Rugby, Inverness and Perth
("the No.5 relevant districts") as from November 25, 2013. In addition, of course,
the claimant had to fall within the Pathfinder Group, i.e. be a person who met the
requirements of regs.5 to 12 of the Transitional Provisions Regulations 2013, later
the "gateway conditions" (see Sch.5 to the Commencement No.9 Order). Note that
the text of this Commencement Order is not included in its entirety in this volume

as it is now unlikely to give rise to live appeals. The full text can be found in the 2019/20 edn of this book at paras 3.236-3.254.

The Welfare Reform Act 2012 (Commencement No.16 and Transitional and Transitory Provisions) Order 2014

SI 2014/209 (C. 7) (AS AMENDED)

The Secretary of State, in exercise of the powers conferred by section 150(3) and (4)(a), (b)(i) and (c) of the Welfare Reform Act 2012, makes the following Order:

ARRANGEMENT OF ARTICLES

5.88
1. Citation
2. Interpretation
3. Day appointed for commencement of the universal credit provisions in Part 1 of the Act
4. Day appointed for the abolition of income-related employment and support allowance and income-based jobseeker's allowance
5. Application of the No.9 Order
6. Day appointed for the coming into force of section 139 of the Act

Schedule: The No.6 and No.7 relevant districts

GENERAL NOTE

5.89   This Commencement Order ("the Commencement No.16 Order") extended the universal credit scheme to certain postcode districts in Bath and Harrogate ("the No.6 relevant districts") as from February 24, 2014 and to others in Shotton ("the No.7 relevant districts") as from April 7, 2014. In addition, of course, the claimant had to fall within the Pathfinder Group, i.e. be a person who met the requirements of regs.5 to 12 of the Transitional Provisions Regulations 2013, later the "gateway conditions" (see Sch.5 to the Commencement No.9 Order). Note that the text of this Commencement Order is not included in its entirety in this volume as it is now unlikely to give rise to live appeals. The full text can be found in the 2019/20 edn of this book at paras 3.255-3.267.

The Welfare Reform Act 2012 (Commencement No.9, 11, 13, 14 and 16 and Transitional and Transitory Provisions (Amendment)) Order 2014

(SI 2014/1452) (C.56)

The Secretary of State, in exercise of the powers conferred by section 150(3) and (4)(a), (b)(i) and (c) of the Welfare Reform Act 2012(1), makes the following Order:

ARRANGEMENT OF ARTICLES

PART 1

CITATION, INTERPRETATION AND APPLICATION

PART 2

AMENDMENT OF THE NO.9 ORDER

PART 3

AMENDMENT OF THE NO.11, 13, 14 AND 16 ORDERS

5.91   Note that the text of this Commencement Order is not included in its entirety in this volume as it is now unlikely to give rise to live appeals. However, the exception is that the myriad amendments made to the Commencement No.9 Order by Pt 2 of this Order are incorporated above in the text of the relevant Order. The full text of this Order can be found in the 2019/20 edn of this book at paras 3.268-3.274.

The Welfare Reform Act 2012 (Commencement No.17 and Transitional and Transitory Provisions) Order 2014Welfare Reform Act 2012 (Commencement No.17) Order 2014

SI 2014/1583 (C. 61) (AS AMENDED)

The Secretary of State, in exercise of the powers conferred by sections 150(3) and (4)(a), (b)(i) and (c) of the Welfare Reform Act 2012, makes the following Order:

ARRANGEMENT OF ARTICLES

5.92   1.   Citation
2.   Interpretation
3.   Day appointed for commencement of the universal credit provisions in Part 1 of the Act
4.   Day appointed for the abolition of income-related employment and support allowance and income-based jobseeker's allowance
5.   Application of the No.9 Order

Schedule: Postcode Districts and part-districts

GENERAL NOTE

5.93   This Commencement Order ("the Commencement No.17 Order") extended the universal credit scheme to certain postcode districts and as from various dates in areas known as the No.8, No.9, No.10, No.11, No.12 and No.13 relevant districts (see Schedule). All the scheduled postcode districts were in the North West. In addition, of course, the claimant had to fall within the Pathfinder Group, i.e. be a person who met the requirements of regs.5 to 12 of the Transitional Provisions Regulations 2013, later the "gateway conditions" (see Sch.5 to the Commencement No.9 Order).

For an example of an Upper Tribunal appeal involving a case subject to this Commencement Order, see *AM v SSWP (UC)* [2017] UKUT 131 (and especially paragraphs 12–14). Note that the text of this Commencement Order is not included in its entirety in this volume as it is now unlikely to give rise to live appeals. The full text can be found in the 2019/20 edn of this book at paras 3.275-3.287.

The Welfare Reform Act 2012 (Commencement No.9, 11, 13, 14, 16 and 17 and Transitional and Transitory Provisions (Amendment)) Order 2014

(SI 2014/1661) (C.69)

The Secretary of State, in exercise of the powers conferred by sections 150(3) and (4)(a), (b)(i) and (c) of the Welfare Reform Act 2012, makes the following Order:

ARRANGEMENT OF ARTICLES

GENERAL NOTE

Note that the text of this Commencement Order is not included in its entirety in this volume as it is now unlikely to give rise to live appeals. The text of this Order can be found in the 2019/20 edn of this book at paras 3.288-3.297.

5.94

The Welfare Reform Act 2012 (Commencement No.9, 11, 13, 14, 16 and 17 and Transitional and Transitory Provisions (Amendment) (No.2)) Order 2014

(SI 2014/1923) (C.88)

The Secretary of State, in exercise of the powers conferred by section 150(3) and (4)(a), (b)(i) and (c) of the Welfare Reform Act 2012, makes the following Order:

ARRANGEMENT OF ARTICLES

5.95

GENERAL NOTE

Note that the text of this Commencement Order is not included in its entirety in this volume as it is now unlikely to give rise to live appeals. The full text of this Order can be found in the 2019/20 edn of this book at paras 3.298-3.309. The main change made by this Order was the removal of the condition that a claimant had to be single in order for the universal credit provisions to come into force where a claim is made for universal credit (and for the amending provisions to come into force where a claim is made for universal credit, ESA or JSA). This meant that as from July 28, 2014, the universal credit provisions (and the amending provisions) came into force where a claim is made by members of a couple where they reside in an area covered by the relevant Commencement Orders and each member meets

5.96

the remaining gateway conditions. These provisions were already in force for claims made by members of a couple who resided in certain areas by virtue of the Welfare Reform Act 2012 (Commencement No.9, 11, 13 14, 16 and 17 and Transitional and Transitory Provisions (Amendment)) Order 2014 (SI 2014/1661). To reflect the fact that the universal credit provisions (and the amending provisions) came into force where a claim is made by a couple who reside in one of the "relevant districts", art.4 makes consequential changes to articles 3, 4 and 5 of the Commencement No.9 Order and inserts a new article 3A into that Order.

The Welfare Reform Act 2012 (Commencement No.19 and Transitional and Transitory Provisions and Commencement No.9 and Transitional and Transitory Provisions (Amendment)) Order 2014

(SI 2014/2321) (C.99) (AS AMENDED)

The Secretary of State makes the following Order in exercise of the powers conferred by sections 150(3) and (4)(a), (b)(i) and (c) of the Welfare Reform Act 2012:

ARRANGEMENT OF ARTICLES

GENERAL NOTE

5.98   Note that the text of this Commencement Order is not included in its entirety in this volume as it is now unlikely to give rise to live appeals. The full text of this Order can be found in the 2019/20 edn of this book at paras 3.310-3.332. This Commencement Order ("the Commencement No.19 Order") extended the UC scheme to certain postcode districts in a wide range of different areas in the North West of England (known as the No.14, No.15, No.16, No.17, No.18, No.19, No.20, No.21, No.22, No.23, No.24, No.25, No.26 or No.27 relevant districts – see Schedule). In addition, of course, the claimant must meet the gateway conditions in Sch.5 to the Commencement No.9 Order.

The Welfare Reform Act 2012 (Commencement No.9, 11, 13 14, 16, 17 and 19 and Transitional and Transitory Provisions (Amendment)) Order 2014

SI 2014/3067 (C.129)

The Secretary of State for Work and Pensions makes the following Order in exercise of the powers conferred by sections 150(3) and (4)(a), (b)(i) and (c) of the Welfare Reform Act 2012:

GENERAL NOTE

The main effect of this Order was to amend the Commencement No.11 and the **5.100** Commencement No.17 Orders so as to modify the "gateway conditions" specified in Sch.5 to the Commencement No.9 Order by (in large part) removing the condition that a claimant must not have responsibility for children or young persons in a case where the claimant resides in certain postcode districts or part-districts in the North West of England (as covered by those Commencement No.11 and No.17 Orders). As a consequence the provisions listed in Sch.2 to the No.9 Order come into force where, on the date on which a claim for universal credit is made, the claimant resides in one of those postcode districts or part-districts and meets the modified gateway conditions. Note that the text of this Commencement Order is not included in its entirety in this volume as it is now unlikely to give rise to live appeals. The full text of this Order can be found in the 2019/20 edn of this book at paras 3.333–3.341.

The Welfare Reform Act 2012 (Commencement No.20 and Transitional and Transitory Provisions and Commencement No.9 and Transitional and Transitory Provisions (Amendment)) Order 2014

(SI 2014/3094) (C.133)

The Secretary of State for Work and Pensions makes the following Order in exercise of the powers conferred by sections 150(3) and (4)(a), (b)(i) and (c) of the Welfare Reform Act 2012:

GENERAL NOTE

5.102   Note that the text of this Commencement Order is not included in its entirety in this volume as it is now unlikely to give rise to live appeals. The full text of this Order can be found in the 2019/20 edn of this book at paras 3.342-3.350. This Commencement Order ("the Commencement No.20 Order") extended the universal credit scheme to the part postcode district in Sutton (SM5 2) known as "the No.28 relevant district". This applied for a limited test period only, namely November 26, 2014 until December 20, 2014. In this instance there was no further requirement that the claimant had to meet the gateway conditions (in Sch.5 to the Commencement No.9 Order). This was because this extension involved the testing of the enhanced digital (or full) service for universal credit for the full scope of universal credit households in a limited area (i.e. the part postcode SM5 2). See also the Universal Credit (Digital Service) Amendment Regulations 2014 (SI 2014/2887), introduced with effect from 26 November 2014, which were limited to any claimant who lived in the digital trial area and who was referred to as a 'Digital service claimant'. There is no Schedule to this Commencement Order as the relevant part postcode area is simply defined by reference to the definition of "the No.28 relevant district" in art.2(1). Provision for universal credit new claims in Sutton was subsequently resumed under the Commencement No.21 Order.

The Welfare Reform Act 2012 (Commencement No.9, 11, 13, 14, 16, 17 and 19 and Transitional and Transitory Provisions (Amendment)) Order 2015

(SI 2015/32) (C.3)

The Secretary of State for Work and Pensions makes the following Order in exercise of the powers conferred by section 150(3) and (4)(a) and (b)(i) of the Welfare Reform Act 2012:

ARRANGEMENT OF ARTICLES

5.103
1.   Citation
2.   Interpretation
3.   Amendment of the No.9, No.11, No.13, No.14, No.16, No.17 and No.19 Orders: cases to which the amendments apply
4.   Amendment of the No.9 Order
5.   Amendment of paragraphs 4 and 7 of Schedule 5 to the No.9 Order
6.   References to provisions of the No.9 Order amended by articles 4 and 5
7.   Amendment of the No.11 Order – gateway conditions
8.   Amendment of the No.17 Order – gateway conditions
9.   Amendment of the No.11 Order, No.13 Order, No.14 Order, No.16 Order, No.17 Order and No.19 Order – consequential amendment

GENERAL NOTE

5.104   This Commencement Order provided for the introduction of universal credit claims from claimants with children in all live service areas. This was implemented in two stages, with effect from January 26 and March 2, 2015. Thus Art.4 amended Sch.5 to the Commencement No.9 Order so that there is no longer a general condition that a claimant must not have responsibility for children or young persons. In its place is a condition that a claimant must not have responsibility for certain children and young persons (e.g. most children or young persons who are looked after by a local authority and children or young persons who are entitled to DLA or PIP). Article 3(1) in turn provides that those amendments to permit claims by those with responsibility for children came into effect on January 26, 2015 where a claimant resides in any of the areas covered by the Commencement No.9 Order. In addition, these changes also come into effect on the same date where a claimant resides in the areas covered by the Commencement No.11, No.13, No.14, No.16 and No.17 Orders (save for postcode districts and part-districts BL1 to BL4, BL5 1, BL5 3, BL6 4, BL6 9 and M26 3 in the No.9 relevant districts and the No.13 relevant districts (other than postcode part-district CH62 9). Article 3(2) meanwhile provides that the same changes came into effect on March 2, 2015 where a claimant resides in postcode districts and part-districts in the No.9 relevant districts listed above or in one of the No.13 relevant districts, covered by the Commencement No.17 Order, or in the areas covered by the Commencement No.19 Order. Note that the text of this Commencement Order is not included in its entirety in this volume as it is now unlikely to give rise to live appeals. The full text of this Order can be found in the 2019/20 edn of this book at paras 3.351-3.361.

The Welfare Reform Act 2012 (Commencement No.21 and Transitional and Transitory Provisions) Order 2015

(SI 2015/33) (C.4)

The Secretary of State for Work and Pensions makes the following Order in exercise of the powers conferred by section 150(3) and (4)(a), (b)(i) and (c) of the Welfare Reform Act 2012:

ARRANGEMENT OF REGULATIONS

5.105

GENERAL NOTE

This Order (the Commencement No.21 Order) provided for the resumption of universal credit new claims in Sutton as from January 28, 2015, following the pilot in place there from November 26 to December 19, 2014 (by virtue of the Commencement No.20 Order).

5.106

Citation

1. This Order may be cited as the Welfare Reform Act 2012 (Commencement No.21 and Transitional and Transitory Provisions) Order 2015.

5.107

Interpretation

5.108   **2.**—(1) In this Order–
"the Act" means the Welfare Reform Act 2012;
"the 1998 Act" means the Social Security Act 1998;
"the amending provisions" means the provisions referred to in article
   4(1)(a) to (c) of the No.9 Order (day appointed for the abolition of
   income-related employment and support allowance and income-based
   jobseeker's allowance);
"claimant"–
(a) in relation to an employment and support allowance, has the same
    meaning as in Part 1 of the Welfare Reform Act 2007, save as men-
    tioned in article 5(1A) of the No.9 Order as applied by article 4(7)
    of this Order;
(b) in relation to a jobseeker's allowance, has the same meaning as in
    the Jobseekers Act 1995 (as it applies apart from the amendments
    made by Part 1 of Schedule 14 to the Act that remove references
    to an income-based jobseeker's allowance), save as mentioned in
    article 5(1A) of the No.9 Order as applied by article 4(7) of this
    Order;
(c) in relation to universal credit, has the same meaning as in Part 1 of
    the Act;
"the Claims and Payments Regulations 2013" means the Universal
   Credit, Personal Independence Payment, Jobseeker's Allowance
   and Employment and Support Allowance (Claims and Payments)
   Regulations 2013;
"employment and support allowance" means an employment and
   support
allowance under Part 1 of the Welfare Reform Act 2007;
"First-tier Tribunal" has the same meaning as in the 1998 Act;
"jobseeker's allowance" means a jobseeker's allowance under the
   Jobseekers Act 1995;
"joint claimants", in relation to universal credit, has the same meaning as
   in Part 1 of the Act;
"the No.9 Order" means the Welfare Reform Act 2012 (Commencement
   No.9 and Transitional and Transitory Provisions and Commencement
   No.8 and Savings and Transitional Provisions (Amendment)) Order
   2013;
"the No.28 relevant district" means the postcode part-district SM5 2;
"single claimant", in relation to universal credit, has the same meaning as
   in Part 1 of the Act;
[¹...]
"Upper Tribunal" has the same meaning as in the 1998 Act.
(2) For the purposes of this Order, the Claims and Payments Regulations
2013 apply for the purpose of deciding–
(a) whether a claim for universal credit is made; and
(b) the date on which such a claim is made.

Amendment

1. Welfare Reform Act 2012 (Commencement No.23 and Transitional and
Transitory Provisions) Order 2015 (SI 2015/634) art.9(2) (June 10. 2015).

Day appointed for the coming into force of the universal credit provisions

3.—(1) The day appointed for the coming into force of the provisions of the Act listed in Schedule 2 to the No.9 Order, in so far as they are not already in force, in relation to the case of a claim referred to in paragraph (2), and any award that is made in respect of the claim, is the day appointed in accordance with paragraph (3).

5.109

(2) The claims referred to are–

(a) a claim for universal credit that is made on or after 28th January 2015 in respect of a period that begins on or after 28th January 2015 where, on the date on which the claim is made, the claimant resides in the No.28 relevant district [1 . . .];

(b) a claim for universal credit that is made on or after 28th January 2015 in respect of a period that begins on or after 28th January 2015 where–

(i) in the case of a single claimant, the claimant gives incorrect information regarding the claimant residing in the No.28 relevant district [1 . . .] and the claimant does not reside in that district [1 . . .] on the date on which the claim is made;

(ii) in the case of joint claimants, either or both of the joint claimants gives or give incorrect information regarding his or her (or their) residing in that district [1 . . .] and one or both of them does not or do not reside in that district [1 . . .] on the date on which the claim is made,

and after a decision is made that the single claimant is, or the joint claimants are, entitled to universal credit and one or more payments have been made in respect of the single claimant or the joint claimants, the Secretary of State discovers that incorrect information has been given regarding such residence [1 . . .].

(3) The day appointed in relation to the case of a claim referred to in paragraph (2), and any award that is made in respect of the claim, is the first day of the period in respect of which the claim is made.

(4) Article 3(6) of the No.9 Order applies for the purposes of paragraph (3) as it applies for the purposes of article 3(4)(a) of the No.9 Order.

(5) Article 3A of the No.9 Order applies in connection with a claim for universal credit where a single claimant, or, as the case may be, either or both of joint claimants, gives or give incorrect information regarding his or her (or their) residing in the No.28 relevant district [1 . . .], as it applies in connection with the giving of incorrect information regarding a claimant residing in one of the relevant districts (as defined in the No.9 Order) [1 . . .].

AMENDMENT

1. Welfare Reform Act 2012 (Commencement No.23 and Transitional and Transitory Provisions) Order 2015 (SI 2015/634) art.9(3) (June 10, 2015).

DEFINITIONS

"claimant"–see art.2(1).
"joint claimant"–*ibid.*
"single claimant"–*ibid.*

"No.9 Order"–*ibid.*
"No.28 relevant district"–*ibid.*
"specified condition"–*ibid.*

Day appointed for the abolition of income-related employment and support allowance and income-based jobseeker's allowance

S.110

4.—(1) The day appointed for the coming into force of the amending provisions, in relation to the case of a claim referred to in paragraph (2), and any award that is made in respect of the claim, is the day appointed in accordance with paragraph (3).

(2) The claims referred to are–

(a) a claim for universal credit that is made on or after 28th January 2015 in respect of a period that begins on or after 28th January 2015 where, on the date on which the claim is made, the claimant resides in the No.28 relevant district [² . . .];

(b) a claim for universal credit that is made on or after 28th January 2015 in respect of a period that begins on or after 28th January 2015 where–

   (i) in the case of a single claimant, the claimant gives incorrect information regarding the claimant residing in the No.28 relevant district [² . . .] and the claimant does not reside in that district [² . . .] on the date on which the claim is made;

   (ii) in the case of joint claimants, either or both of the joint claimants gives or give incorrect information regarding his or her (or their) residing in that district [² . . .] and one or both of them does not or do not reside in that district [² . . .] on the date on which the claim is made,

and after a decision is made that the single claimant is, or the joint claimants are, entitled to universal credit and one or more payments have been made in respect of the single claimant or the joint claimants, the Secretary of State discovers that incorrect information has been given regarding such residence [² . . .];

(c) a claim for an employment and support allowance or a jobseeker's allowance that is made or treated as made on or after 28th January 2015 where, on the date on which the claim is made or treated as made, the claimant resides in the No.28 relevant district [² . . .];

(d) a claim for an employment and support allowance or a jobseeker's allowance other than one referred to in sub-paragraph (c) that is made or treated as made during the relevant period by a single claimant of universal credit or by either of two joint claimants of universal credit who has or have made a claim for universal credit within sub-paragraph (a) or (b).

(3) The day appointed in relation to the case of a claim referred to in paragraph (2), and any award that is made in respect of the claim, is the first day of the period in respect of which the claim is made.

(4) For the purposes of paragraph (2)(d), "relevant period" means, in relation to a claim for universal credit within paragraph (2)(a) or (b), any UC claim period, and any period subsequent to any UC claim period in respect of which the claimant is entitled to an award of universal credit in respect of the claim.

(5) For the purposes of paragraph (4), a "UC claim period" is a period when–

(a) a claim for universal credit within sub-paragraph (a) of paragraph (2), or within sub-paragraph (b)(i) or (ii) of that paragraph, has been made but a decision has not yet been made on the claim; or

(b) a decision has been made that the claimant is not entitled to universal credit and–

    (i) the Secretary of State is considering whether to revise that decision under section 9 of the 1998 Act, whether on an application made for that purpose, or on the Secretary of State's own initiative; or

    (ii) the claimant has appealed against that decision to the First-tier Tribunal and that appeal or any subsequent appeal to the Upper Tribunal or to a court has not been finally determined.

(6) [¹ Paragraphs (6), (7), (9) and (10)] of article 4 of the No.9 Order apply in relation to a claim for universal credit referred to in paragraph (2) (and any award that is made in respect of the claim) as they apply in relation to a claim for universal credit referred to in sub-paragraphs (a) and (b) of article 4(2) of the No.9 Order (and any award that is made in respect of the claim).

(7) Paragraphs (1A) and (1B) of article 5 of the No.9 Order apply for the purposes of paragraph (2)(c) as they apply for the purposes of article 4(2)(a) of the No.9 Order (but as if the references in paragraph (1A) to Schedule 5 to the No.9 Order were omitted).

(8) Paragraphs (5) to (7) of article 5 of the No.9 Order apply for the purposes of sub-paragraphs (c) and (d) of paragraph (2) as they apply for the purposes of subparagraphs (a) and (g) of article 4(2) of the No.9 Order.

(9) Article 5(8) of the No.9 Order applies for the purposes of paragraph (3) as it applies for the purposes of article 4(3)(a) of the No.9 Order.

AMENDMENTS

1. Welfare Reform Act 2012 (Commencement No.22 and Transitional and Transitory Provisions) Order 2015 (SI 2015/101), art.7(2)(b) (February 11, 2015).

2. Welfare Reform Act 2012 (Commencement No.23 and Transitional and Transitory Provisions) Order 2015 (SI 2015/634) art.9(4) (June 10, 2015).

DEFINITIONS

"the amending provisions"–see art.2(1).
"claimant"–*ibid.*
"employment and support allowance"–*ibid.*
"First-tier Tribunal"–*ibid.*
"jobseeker's allowance"–*ibid.*
"joint claimant"–*ibid.*
"No.9 Order"–*ibid.*
"No.28 relevant district"–*ibid.*
"relevant period"–para.(4).
"specified condition"–see art.2(1).
"UC claim period"–para.(5).
"Upper Tribunal"–see art.2(1).

Application of the No.9 Order

5.111   **5.** Articles 9 to 22 of the No.9 Order apply in connection with the coming into force of the amending provisions in relation to the case of a claim referred to in article 4(2), and any award made in respect of the claim, as they apply in connection with the coming into force of the amending provisions in relation to the case of a claim referred to in sub-paragraph (a), (b) or (g) of article 4(2) of the No.9 Order and any award made in respect of the claim.

DEFINITIONS

> "the amending provisions"–see art.2(1).
> "No.9 Order"–*ibid.*

Transitional provision: claims for housing benefit, income support or a tax credit

5.112   **6.**—(1) Except as provided by paragraphs [¹1(2) to (5) and (11)], a person may not make a claim for housing benefit, income support or a tax credit (in the latter case, whether or not as part of a Tax Credits Act couple) on any date where, if that person made a claim for universal credit on that date (in the capacity, whether as a single person or as part of a couple, in which he or she is permitted to claim universal credit under the Universal Credit Regulations 2013), the provisions of the Act listed in Schedule 2 to the No.9 Order would come into force under article 3(1) and (2)(a) of this Order in relation to that claim for universal credit.

(2) Paragraph (1) does not apply to a claim for housing benefit in respect of specified accommodation [⁴ or temporary accommodation].

(3) Paragraph (1) does not apply to a claim for housing benefit [⁹ ...] where–

[⁵ [⁸ (a) in the case of a claim for housing benefit, the claim is made by a member of a State Pension Credit Act couple who has reached the qualifying age for state pension credit, where the other member has not reached that age, and entitlement begins, or in the case of claims made in advance of entitlement is to begin—

  (i) before 15th May 2019; or

  (ii) on or after 15th May 2019 where one of the savings in the sub-paragraphs of article 4(1) of the Welfare Reform Act 2012 (Commencement No. 31 and Savings and Transitional Provisions and Commencement No. 21 and 23 and Transitional and Transitory Provisions (Amendment)) Order 2019 applies to that person and the saving has not ceased to have effect under article 4(2) of that Order, and

entitlement to housing benefit is to be construed in accordance with article 2 of that Order;]]

  (b) [⁹ ...]

(4) Paragraph (1) does not apply to a claim for a tax credit where a person or persons makes or make a claim for child tax credit or working tax credit and on the date on which he or she (or they) makes or make the claim he or she (or they) [⁹ has or have an award of working tax credit or child tax credit respectively]

(5) Paragraph (1) does not apply to a claim for a tax credit where a person [⁹ has or had, or persons have or had, an award of] child tax credit or

working tax credit in respect of a tax year and that person or those persons makes or make (or is or are treated as making) a claim for that tax credit for the next tax year.

[⁹ (6) In paragraph (4), the reference to a person having an award of a tax credit includes where the person is "treated as being entitled to a tax credit" in the circumstances referred to in regulation 11(1) and (2)(a) to (ca) of the Universal Credit (Transitional Provisions) Regulations 2014 but as if, in regulation 11(1), for "For the purposes of regulations 7(7) and 8(4)" there were substituted "For the purposes of article 6(4) of the Welfare Reform Act 2012 (Commencement No. 21 and Transitional and Transitory Provisions) Order 2015".]

(7) Subject to paragraph (8), for the purposes of this article–

(a) a claim for housing benefit, income support or a tax credit is made by a person on the date on which he or she takes any action which results in a decision on a claim being required under the relevant Regulations; and

(b) it is irrelevant that the effect of any provision of the relevant Regulations is that, for the purpose of those Regulations, the claim is made or treated as made on a date that is earlier than the date on which that action is taken.

(8) Where under the provisions referred to in paragraph (9), a claim for housing benefit or income support is treated as made at a date that is earlier than the date on which the action referred to in paragraph (7)(a) is taken, the claim is treated as made on that earlier date.

(9) The provisions referred to are–

(a) in the case of a claim for housing benefit, regulation 83(4E), (4F), (5)(d) or (8) of the Housing Benefit Regulations 2006 ("the 2006 Regulations") or, as the case may be, regulation 64(5F), (5G), (6)(d) or (9) of the Housing Benefit (Persons who have attained the qualifying age for state pension credit) Regulations 2006 ("the 2006 (SPC) Regulations")); or

(b) in the case of a claim for income support, [² regulation 6(1A)(b) or 6A] of the Social Security (Claims and Payments) Regulations 1987.

(10) For the purposes of this article–

(a) "couple" (apart from in the expressions "State Pension Credit Act couple" and "Tax Credit Act couple"), has the meaning given in section 39 of the Act;

(b) "housing benefit" means housing benefit under section 130 of the Social Security Contributions and Benefits Act 1992;

(c) "income support" means income support under section 124 of the Social Security Contributions and Benefits Act 1992;

(d) "qualifying age for state pension credit" means the qualifying age referred to in section 1(6) of the State Pension Credit Act 2002;

(e) the "relevant Regulations" means–

(i) in the case of a claim for housing benefit, the 2006 Regulations or, as the case may be, the 2006 (SPC) Regulations;

(ii) in the case of a claim for income support, the Social Security (Claims and Payments) Regulations 1987;

(iii) in the case of a claim for a tax credit, the Tax Credits (Claims and Notifications) Regulations 2002;

(f) "specified accommodation" means accommodation to which one or more of sub-paragraphs (2) to (5) of paragraph 3A of Schedule 1 to the Universal Credit Regulations 2013 applies;

(g) "state pension credit" means state pension credit under the State Pension Credit Act 2002;

(h) "State Pension Credit Act couple" means a couple as defined in section 17 of the State Pension Credit Act 2002;

(i) "tax credit" (including "child tax credit" and "working tax credit") and "tax year" have the same meanings as in the Tax Credits Act 2002;

(j) "Tax Credits Act couple" means a couple as defined in section 3(5A) of the Tax Credits Act 2002[⁴;

(k) "temporary accommodation" means accommodation which falls within Case 1 or Case 2 under paragraph 3B of Schedule 1 to the Universal Credit Regulations].

[¹ (11) Paragraph (1) does not apply to a claim for housing benefit, income support or a tax credit where, by virtue of a determination made under regulation 4 [³, or by virtue of regulation [⁶ 4A [⁷...]] [⁷...],] of the Universal Credit (Transitional Provisions) Regulations 2014, [⁹ or by virtue of article 4(11) of the Welfare Reform Act 2012 (Commencement No. 32 and Savings and Transitional Provisions) Order 2019] the person in question would be prevented from making a claim for universal credit as referred to in that paragraph.]

AMENDMENTS

1. Welfare Reform Act 2012 (Commencement No.23 and Transitional and Transitory Provisions) Order 2015 (SI 2015/634) art.9(5) (March 18, 2015).

2. Welfare Reform Act 2012 (Commencement No.23 and Transitional and Transitory Provisions) (Amendment) Order 2015 (SI 2015/740) art.2(b) (March 18, 2015).

3. Welfare Reform Act 2012 (Commencement No.9 and 21 and Transitional and Transitory Provisions (Amendment)) Order 2017 (SI 2017/483) art.3 (April 6, 2017).

4. Welfare Reform Act 2012 (Commencement No. 9, 21 and 23 (Amendment), Commencement No. 11, 13, 17, 19, 22, 23 and 24 (Modification), Transitional and Transitory Provisions) Order 2018 (2018/138) art.6(2) (April 11, 2018).

5. Welfare Reform Act 2012 (Commencement No. 31 and Savings and Transitional Provisions and Commencement No. 21 and 23 and Transitional and Transitory Provisions (Amendment)) Order 2019 (SI 2019/37) art.5(2) (January 15, 2019).

6. Universal Credit (Transitional Provisions) (SDP Gateway) Amendment Regulations 2019 (SI 2019/10) reg.3(2) (January 16, 2019).

7. Universal Credit (Restriction on Amounts for Children and Qualifying Young Persons) (Transitional Provisions) Amendment Regulations 2019 (SI 2019/27) reg.4(2) (February 1, 2019).

8. Welfare Reform Act 2012 (Commencement No. 31 and Savings and Transitional Provisions and Commencement No. 21 and 23 and Transitional and Transitory Provisions (Amendment)) Order 2019 (SI 2019/37) art.5 (January 15. 2019).

9. Welfare Reform Act 2012 (Commencement No. 32 and Savings and Transitional Provisions) Order 2019 (SI 2019/167) art 5(3) (February 1, 2019).

DEFINITIONS

"the 2006 Regulations"–para.(9)(a).
"the 2006 (SPC) Regulations"–*ibid.*
"child tax credit"–para.10(i).
"couple"–para.(10)(a).
"housing benefit"–para.(10)(b).
"income support"–para.(10)(c).

"qualifying age for state pension credit"–para.10(d).
"relevant Regulations"–para.10(e).
"specified accommodation"–para.10(f).
"state pension credit"–para.10(g).
"State Pension Credit Act couple"–para.10(h).
"tax credit"–para.(10)(i).
"Tax Credits Act couple"–para.10(j).
"working tax credit"–para.10(i).

The Welfare Reform Act 2012 (Commencement No.22 and Transitional and Transitory Provisions) Order 2015

(SI 2015/101) (C.6)

The Secretary of State for Work and Pensions makes the following Order, in exercise of the powers conferred by section 150(3) and (4)(a), (b)(i) and (c) of the Welfare Reform Act 2012:

ARRANGEMENT OF REGULATIONS

1. Citation   5.113
2. Interpretation
3. Day appointed for the coming into force of the universal credit provisions
4. Day appointed for the abolition of income-related employment and support allowance and income-based jobseeker's allowance
5. Application of the No.9 Order
6. Modification of the Universal Credit (Digital Service) Amendment Regulations 2014
7. Technical amendment — numbering in the 2015 Amendment Order

GENERAL NOTE

Note that the text of this Commencement Order is not included in its entirety   5.114
in this volume as it is now unlikely to give rise to live appeals. The full text of this
Order can be found in the 2019/20 edn of this book at paras 3.370-3.379. This
Order made provision for the first phase of the national expansion of universal credit
claims for single claimants for various dates (depending on the district concerned)
between February 16 and July 20, 2015. It is important also to note that this Order
has been subsequently modified for certain purposes by the Commencement No.26
and No.27 Orders, as well as by the Modification Order 2016.

The Welfare Reform Act 2012 (Commencement No.23 and Transitional and Transitory Provisions) Order 2015

(SI 2015/634) (C.32)

The Secretary of State for Work and Pensions makes the following Order in exercise of the powers conferred by section 150(3) and (4)(a), (b)(i) and (c) of the Welfare Reform Act 2012:

ARRANGEMENT OF ARTICLES

1. Citation   5.115

GENERAL NOTE

5.116   This Commencement Order ("the Commencement No.23 Order") provided for the expansion of universal credit to further postcode areas in the London Boroughs of Sutton, Croydon and Southwark in three phases. These a were the No.50, No.51 and No.52 relevant districts. Thus e.g. under art.3(1) and (2)(a), the universal credit provisions came into force in relation to a claim for universal credit, and any award that is made in respect of the claim, where the claim was made on or after March 18, 2015 with respect to a period that begins on or after that date and, on the date on which the claim was made, the claimant resides in one of the "No.50 relevant districts". The same provision was made for claims made on or after June 10, 2015 where the claimant resided in one of the "No.51 relevant districts" and for claims made on or after November 4, 2015 where the claimant resides in one of the "No.52 relevant districts".

Citation

5.117   **1.** This Order may be cited as the Welfare Reform Act 2012 (Commencement No.23 and Transitional and Transitory Provisions) Order 2015.

Interpretation

5.118   **2.**—(1) In this Order—
"the Act" means the Welfare Reform Act 2012;
"the amending provisions" means the provisions referred to in article 4(1)(a) to (c) of the No.9 Order (day appointed for the abolition of income-related employment and support allowance and income-based jobseeker's allowance);
"claimant"—
(a) in relation to an employment and support allowance, has the same meaning as in Part 1 of the Welfare Reform Act 2007, save as mentioned in article 5(1A) of the No.9 Order as applied by article 4(7) of this Order;
(b) in relation to a jobseeker's allowance, has the same meaning as in the Jobseekers Act 1995 (as it applies apart from the amendments made by Part 1 of Schedule 14 to the Act that remove references to an income-based jobseeker's allowance), save as mentioned in

article 5(1A) of the No.9 Order as applied by article 4(7) of this Order;

(c) in relation to universal credit, has the same meaning as in Part 1 of the Act;

"the Claims and Payments Regulations 1987" means the Social Security (Claims and Payments) Regulations 1987;

"employment and support allowance" means an employment and support allowance under Part 1 of the Welfare Reform Act 2007;

"jobseeker's allowance" means a jobseeker's allowance under the Jobseekers Act 1995;

"joint claimants", in relation to universal credit, has the same meaning as in Part 1 of the Act;

"the No.9 Order" means the Welfare Reform Act 2012 (Commencement No.9 and Transitional and Transitory Provisions and Commencement No.8 and Savings and Transitional Provisions (Amendment)) Order 2013;

"the No.11 Order" means the Welfare Reform Act 2012 (Commencement No.11 and Transitional and Transitory Provisions and Commencement No.9 and Transitional and Transitory Provisions (Amendment)) Order 2013;

"the No.13 Order" means the Welfare Reform Act 2012 (Commencement No.13 and Transitional and Transitory Provisions) Order 2013;

"the No.14 Order" means the Welfare Reform Act 2012 (Commencement No.14 and Transitional and Transitory Provisions) Order 2013;

"the No.16 Order" means the Welfare Reform Act 2012 (Commencement No.16 and Transitional and Transitory Provisions) Order 2014;

"the No.17 Order" means the Welfare Reform Act 2012 (Commencement No.17 and Transitional and Transitory Provisions) Order 2014;

"the No.19 Order" means the Welfare Reform Act 2012 (Commencement No.19 and Transitional and Transitory Provisions and Commencement No.9 and Transitional and Transitory Provisions (Amendment)) Order 2014;

"the No.21 Order" means the Welfare Reform Act 2012 (Commencement No.21 and Transitional and Transitory Provisions) Order 2015;

"the No.22 Order" means the Welfare Reform Act 2012 (Commencement No.22 and Transitional and Transitory Provisions) Order 2015;

"the No.50 relevant districts" means the postcode part-districts SM6 7 and SM6 8;

"the No.51 relevant districts" means the postcode part-districts CR0 4 and SM6 9;

"the No.52 relevant districts" means the postcode part-districts CR0 2 and SE1 5;

"single claimant", in relation to universal credit, has the same meaning as in Part 1 of the Act.

(2) For the purposes of this Order, the Universal Credit, Personal Independence Payment, Jobseeker's Allowance and Employment and Support Allowance (Claims and Payments) Regulations 2013 apply for the purpose of deciding—

(a) whether a claim for universal credit is made; and

(b) the date on which such a claim is made.

(3) For the purposes of this Order, the Claims and Payments Regulations

1987 apply, subject to paragraphs (4) and (5), for the purposes of deciding—

    (a) whether a claim for an employment and support allowance or a jobseeker's allowance is made; and

    (b) the date on which the claim is made or treated as made.

(4) Subject to paragraph (5), for the purposes of this Order—

    (a) a person makes a claim for an employment and support allowance or a jobseeker's allowance if he or she takes any action which results in a decision on a claim being required under the Claims and Payments Regulations 1987; and

    (b) it is irrelevant that the effect of any provision of those Regulations is that, for the purposes of those Regulations, the claim is made or treated as made at a date that is earlier than the date on which that action is taken.

(5) Where, by virtue of—

    (a) regulation 6(1F)(b) or (c) of the Claims and Payments Regulations 1987, in the case of a claim for an employment and support allowance; or

    (b) regulation 6(4ZA) to (4ZD) and (4A)(a)(i) and (b) of those Regulations, in the case of a claim for a jobseeker's allowance,

a claim for an employment and support allowance or a jobseeker's allowance is treated as made at a date that is earlier than the date on which the action referred to in paragraph (4)(a) is taken, the claim is treated as made on that earlier date.

Day appointed for the coming into force of the universal credit provisions

5.119   **3.**—(1) The day appointed for the coming into force of the provisions of the Act listed in Schedule 2 to the No.9 Order, in so far as they are not already in force, in relation to the case of a claim referred to in paragraph (2), and any award that is made in respect of the claim, is the day appointed in accordance with paragraph (3).

(2) The claims referred to are—

    (a) a claim for universal credit that is made on or after 18th March 2015 in respect of a period that begins on or after 18th March 2015 where, on the date on which the claim is made, the claimant resides in one of the No.50 relevant districts;

    (b) a claim for universal credit that is made on or after 10th June 2015 in respect of a period that begins on or after 10th June 2015 where, on the date on which the claim is made, the claimant resides in one of the No.51 relevant districts;

    (c) a claim for universal credit that is made on or after 4th November 2015 in respect of a period that begins on or after 4th November 2015 where, on the date on which the claim is made, the claimant resides in one of the No.52 relevant districts;

    (d) a claim for universal credit that is made on or after the date referred to in any of subparagraphs (a) to (c), in respect of a period that begins on or after that date where—

        (i) in the case of a single claimant, the claimant gives incorrect information regarding the claimant residing in a district as referred to in the sub-paragraph in question and the claimant does not reside in such a district on the date on which the claim is made;

(ii) in the case of joint claimants, either or both of the joint claimants gives or give incorrect information regarding his or her (or
their) residing in such a district and one or both of them does
not or do not reside in such a district on the date on which the
claim is made, and after a decision is made that the single claimant is, or the joint claimants are, entitled to universal credit
and one or more payments have been made in respect of the
single claimant or the joint claimants, the Secretary of State
discovers that incorrect information has been given regarding
residence.

(3) The day appointed in relation to the case of a claim referred to in
paragraph (2), and any award that is made in respect of the claim, is the first
day of the period in respect of which the claim is made.

(4) Article 3(6) of the No.9 Order applies for the purposes of paragraph
(3) as it applies for the purposes of article 3(4)(a) of the No.9 Order.

(5) Article 3A of the No.9 Order applies in connection with a claim for
universal credit where a single claimant, or, as the case may be, either or
both of joint claimants, gives or give incorrect information regarding his or
her (or their) residing in one of the No.50, No.51 or No.52 relevant districts, as it applies in connection with the giving of incorrect information
regarding a claimant residing in one of the relevant districts (as defined in
the No.9 Order).

DEFINITIONS

"the Act"–see art.2(1).
"claimant"–*ibid.*
"joint claimant"–*ibid.*
"single claimant"–*ibid.*
"No.9 Order"–*ibid.*
"the No.50 relevant districts"–*ibid.*
"the No.51 relevant districts"–*ibid.*
"the No.52 relevant districts"–*ibid.*

GENERAL NOTE

See by analogy the commentary to art.3 of the Commencement No.22 Order.   5.120

Day appointed for the abolition of income-related employment and support allowance and income-based jobseeker's allowance

4.—(1) The day appointed for the coming into force of the amending   5.121
provisions, in relation to the case of a claim referred to in paragraph (2),
and any award that is made in respect of the claim, is the day appointed in
accordance with paragraph (3).

(2) The claims referred to are—
(a) a claim for universal credit that is made on or after 18th March 2015
in respect of a period that begins on or after 18th March 2015 where,
on the date on which the claim is made, the claimant resides in one
of the No.50 relevant districts;
(b) a claim for universal credit that is made on or after 10th June 2015
in respect of a period that begins on or after 10th June 2015 where,
on the date on which the claim is made, the claimant resides in one
of the No.51 relevant districts;

    (c) a claim for universal credit that is made on or after 4th November 2015 in respect of a period that begins on or after 4th November 2015 where, on the date on which the claim is made, the claimant resides in one of the No.52 relevant districts;

    (d) a claim for universal credit that is made on or after the date referred to in any of subparagraphs (a) to (c), in respect of a period that begins on or after that date where—

        (i) in the case of a single claimant, the claimant gives incorrect information regarding the claimant residing in a district as referred to in the sub-paragraph in question and the claimant does not reside in such a district on the date on which the claim is made;

        (ii) in the case of joint claimants, either or both of the joint claimants gives or give incorrect information regarding his or her (or their) residing in such a district and one or both of them does not or do not reside in such a district on the date on which the claim is made, and after a decision is made that the single claimant is, or the joint claimants are, entitled to universal credit and one or more payments have been made in respect of the single claimant or the joint claimants, the Secretary of State discovers that incorrect information has been given regarding residence;

    (e) a claim for an employment and support allowance or a jobseeker's allowance that is made or treated as made on or after 18th March 2015 where, on the date on which the claim is made or treated as made, the claimant resides in one of the No.50 relevant districts;

    (f) a claim for an employment and support allowance or a jobseeker's allowance that is made or treated as made on or after 10th June 2015 where, on the date on which the claim is made or treated as made, the claimant resides in one of the No.51 relevant districts;

    (g) a claim for an employment and support allowance or a jobseeker's allowance that is made or treated as made on or after 4th November 2015 where, on the date on which the claim is made or treated as made, the claimant resides in one of the No.52 relevant districts;

    (h) a claim for an employment and support allowance or a jobseeker's allowance other than one referred to in sub-paragraphs (e) to (g) that is made or treated as made during the relevant period by a single claimant of universal credit or by either of two joint claimants of universal credit who has or have made a claim for universal credit within any of subparagraphs (a) to (d).

(3) The day appointed in relation to the case of a claim referred to in paragraph (2), and any award that is made in respect of the claim, is the first day of the period in respect of which the claim is made.

(4) For the purposes of paragraph (2)(h), "relevant period" means, in relation to a claim for universal credit within any of sub-paragraphs (a) to (d) of paragraph (2), any UC claim period, and any period subsequent to any UC claim period in respect of which the claimant is entitled to an award of universal credit in respect of the claim.

(5) For the purposes of paragraph (4), a "UC claim period" is a period when—

    (a) a claim for universal credit within any of sub-paragraphs (a) to (c) of paragraph (2), or within sub-paragraph (d)(i) or (ii) of that paragraph, has been made but a decision has not yet been made on the claim; or

(b) a decision has been made that the claimant is not entitled to universal credit and—

(i) the Secretary of State is considering whether to revise that decision under section 9 of the Social Security Act 1998, whether on an application made for that purpose, or on the Secretary of State's own initiative; or

(ii) the claimant has appealed against that decision to the First-tier Tribunal and that appeal or any subsequent appeal to the Upper Tribunal or to a court has not been finally determined.

(6) Paragraphs (6), (7), (9) and (10) of article 4 of the No.9 Order apply in relation to a claim for universal credit referred to in paragraph (2) (and any award that is made in respect of the claim) as they apply in relation to a claim for universal credit referred to in sub-paragraphs (a) and (b) of article 4(2) of the No.9 Order (and any award that is made in respect of the claim).

(7) Paragraphs (1A) and (1B) of article 5 of the No.9 Order apply for the purposes of subparagraphs (e) to (g) of paragraph (2) as they apply for the purposes of article 4(2)(a) of the No.9 Order (but as if the references in paragraph (1A) to Schedule 5 to the No.9 Order were omitted).

(8) Article 5(8) of the No.9 Order applies for the purposes of paragraph (3) as it applies for the purposes of article 4(3)(a) of the No.9 Order.

DEFINITIONS

"the amending provisions"–see art.2(1).
"claimant"–*ibid.*
"employment and support allowance"–*ibid.*
"jobseeker's allowance"–*ibid.*
"joint claimant"–*ibid.*
"No.9 Order"–*ibid.*
"the No.50 relevant districts"–*ibid.*
"the No.51 relevant districts"–*ibid.*
"the No.52 relevant districts"–*ibid.*
"relevant period"–para.(4).
"UC claim period"–para.(5).

Transitory provision – application of the "specified condition" for a period

5.—(1) Paragraphs (2) to (4) apply in relation to a case where a claim for universal credit, an employment and support allowance or a jobseeker's allowance is made on or after 18th March 2015 and before 10th June 2015.   5.122

(2) Where this paragraph applies, article 2(1) of this Order applies as if, after the definition of "single claimant" there were inserted—

";

"specified condition" means the condition that a claimant is a British citizen who—

(a) has resided in the United Kingdom throughout the period of two years ending with the date on which the claim for universal credit is made; and

(b) has not, during that period, left the United Kingdom for a continuous period of four weeks or more.".

(3) Where this paragraph applies, article 3 of this Order applies as if it were amended as follows—

(a) in sub-paragraph (a) of paragraph (2), after "relevant districts" insert "and meets the specified condition";

(b) in sub-paragraph (d)(i) of paragraph (2)—

    (i) after "in question" insert "or meeting the specified condition"; and

    (ii) after "in such a district" insert "or does not meet that condition";

(c) in sub-paragraph (d)(ii) of paragraph (2)—

    (i) after "residing in such a district" insert "or meeting the specified condition"; and

    (ii) after "reside in such a district" insert "or does not or do not meet that condition";

(d) in the closing words of sub-paragraph (d) of paragraph (2), after "regarding residence" insert "or meeting the specified condition as the case may be";

(e) in paragraph (5)—

    (i) after "No.52 relevant districts" insert "or meeting the specified condition"; and

    (ii) after "the No.9 Order)" insert "or meeting the gateway conditions (as defined in the No.9 Order)".

(4) Where this paragraph applies, article 4 of this Order applies as if it were amended as follows—

(a) in sub-paragraphs (a) and (e) of paragraph (2), after "relevant districts" insert "and meets the specified condition";

(b) in sub-paragraph (d)(i) of paragraph (2)—

    (i) after "in question" insert "or meeting the specified condition"; and

    (ii) after "in such a district" insert "or does not meet that condition";

(c) in sub-paragraph (d)(ii) of paragraph (2)—

    (i) after "residing in a such a district" insert "or meeting the specified condition"; and

    (ii) after "reside in such a district" insert "or does not or do not meet that condition";

(d) in the closing words of sub-paragraph (d) of paragraph (2), after "regarding residence" insert "or meeting the specified condition".

DEFINITIONS

"employment and support allowance"–see art.2(1).
"jobseeker's allowance"–*ibid*.

Application of the No.9 Order

5.123   **6.** Articles 9 to 22 of the No.9 Order apply in connection with the coming into force of the amending provisions in relation to the case of a claim referred to in article 4(2), and any award made in respect of the claim, as they apply in connection with the coming into force of the amending provisions in relation to the case of a claim referred to in sub-paragraph (a), (b) or (g) of article 4(2) of the No.9 Order and any award made in respect of the claim.

"the amending provisions"–see art.2(1).
"No.9 Order"–*ibid.*

Transitional provision: claims for housing benefit, income support or a tax credit

7.—(1) Except as provided by paragraphs (2) to (6), a person may not make a claim for housing benefit, income support or a tax credit (in the latter case, whether or not as part of a Tax Credits Act couple) on any date where, if that person made a claim for universal credit on that date (in the capacity, whether as a single person or as part of a couple, in which he or she is permitted to claim universal credit under the Universal Credit Regulations 2013), the provisions of the Act listed in Schedule 2 to the No.9 Order would come into force under article 3(1) and [¹ (2)(a) to (c) of this Order in relation to that claim] for universal credit.

(2) Paragraph (1) does not apply to a claim for housing benefit, income support or a tax credit where, by virtue of a determination made under regulation 4 [², or by virtue of regulation [⁵ 4A [⁶...]] [⁶...],] of the Universal Credit (Transitional Provisions) Regulations 2014, [⁷ or by virtue of article 4(11) of the Welfare Reform Act 2012 (Commencement No. 32 and Savings and Transitional Provisions) Order 2019] the person in question would be prevented from making a claim for universal credit as referred to in that paragraph.

(3) Paragraph (1) does not apply to a claim for housing benefit in respect of specified accommodation [³ or temporary accommodation].

(4) Paragraph (1) does not apply to a claim for housing benefit [⁷...] where—

[⁴ [⁹ (a) in the case of a claim for housing benefit, the claim is made by a member of a State Pension Credit Act couple who has reached the qualifying age for state pension credit, where the other member has not reached that age, and entitlement begins, or in the case of claims made in advance of entitlement is to begin—
  (i) before 15th May 2019; or
  (ii) on or after 15th May 2019 where one of the savings in the sub-paragraphs of article 4(1) of the Welfare Reform Act 2012 (Commencement No. 31 and Savings and Transitional Provisions and Commencement No. 21 and 23 and Transitional and Transitory Provisions (Amendment)) Order 2019 applies to that person and the saving has not ceased to have effect under article 4(2) of that Order, and
entitlement to housing benefit is to be construed in accordance with article 2 of that Order;]]
(b) [⁷...]

(5) Paragraph (1) does not apply to a claim for a tax credit where a person or persons makes or make a claim for child tax credit or working tax credit and on the date on which he or she (or they) makes or make the claim he or she (or they) [⁷ has or have an award of working tax credit or child tax credit respectively].

(6) Paragraph (1) does not apply to a claim for a tax credit where a person [⁷ has or had, or persons have or had, an award of] child tax credit or working tax credit in respect of a tax year and that person or those persons

makes or make (or is or are treated as making) a claim for that tax credit for the next tax year.

[⁷ (7) In paragraph (5), the reference to a person having an award of a tax credit includes where the person is "treated as being entitled to a tax credit" in the circumstances referred to in regulation 11(1) and (2)(a) to (ca) of the Universal Credit (Transitional Provisions) Regulations 2014 but as if, in regulation 11(1), for "For the purposes of regulations 7(7) and 8(4)" there were substituted "For the purposes of article 7(5) of the Welfare Reform Act 2012 (Commencement No 23 and Transitional and Transitory Provisions) Order 2015".]

(8) Subject to paragraph (9), for the purposes of this article—

(a) a claim for housing benefit, income support or a tax credit is made by a person on the date on which he or she takes any action which results in a decision on a claim being required under the relevant Regulations; and

(b) it is irrelevant that the effect of any provision of the relevant Regulations is that, for the purpose of those Regulations, the claim is made or treated as made on a date that is earlier than the date on which that action is taken.

(9) Where under the provisions referred to in paragraph (10), a claim for housing benefit or income support is treated as made at a date that is earlier than the date on which the action referred to in paragraph (8)(a) is taken, the claim is treated as made on that earlier date.

(10) The provisions referred to are—

(a) in the case of a claim for housing benefit, regulation 83(4E), (4F), (5)(d) or (8) of the 2006 Regulations or, as the case may be, regulation 64(5F), (5G), (6)(d) or (9) of the the 2006 (SPC) Regulations; or

(b) in the case of a claim for income support, [¹ regulation 6(1A)(b) or 6A] of the Claims and Payments Regulations 1987.

(11) For the purposes of this article—

(a) "couple" (apart from in the expressions "State Pension Credit Act couple" and "Tax Credit Act couple"), has the meaning given in section 39 of the Act;

(b) "housing benefit" means housing benefit under section 130 of the Social Security Contributions and Benefits Act 1992;

(c) "income support" means income support under section 124 of the Social Security Contributions and Benefits Act 1992;

(d) "qualifying age for state pension credit" means the qualifying age referred to in section 1(6) of the State Pension Credit Act 2002;

(e) "the 2006 Regulations" means the Housing Benefit Regulations 2006;

(f) "the 2006 (SPC) Regulations" means the Housing Benefit (Persons who have attained the qualifying age for state pension credit) Regulations 2006;

(g) "the relevant Regulations" means—

(i) in the case of a claim for housing benefit, the 2006 Regulations or, as the case may be, the 2006 (SPC) Regulations;

(ii) in the case of a claim for income support, the Claims and Payments Regulations 1987;

(iii) in the case of a claim for a tax credit, the Tax Credits (Claims and Notifications) Regulations 2002;

(h) "specified accommodation" means accommodation to which one or more of subparagraphs (2) to (5) of paragraph 3A of Schedule 1 to the Universal Credit Regulations 2013 applies;

(i) "State Pension Credit Act couple" means a couple as defined in section 17 of the State Pension Credit Act 2002;

(j) "tax credit" (including "child tax credit" and "working tax credit") and "tax year" have the same meanings as in the Tax Credits Act 2002;

(k) "Tax Credits Act couple" means a couple as defined in section 3(5A) of the Tax Credits Act 2002 [³;

(l) "temporary accommodation" means accommodation which falls within Case 1 or Case 2 under paragraph 3B of Schedule 1 to the Universal Credit Regulations].

AMENDMENTS

1. Welfare Reform Act 2012 (Commencement No.23 and Transitional and Transitory Provisions) (Amendment) Order 2015 (SI 2015/740), art.2(a) (March 17, 2015).

2. Social Security (Restrictions on Amounts for Children and Qualifying Young Persons) Amendment Regulations 2017 (2017/376) reg.4 (April 6, 2017).

3. Welfare Reform Act 2012 (Commencement No. 9, 21 and 23 (Amendment), Commencement No. 11, 13, 17, 19, 22, 23 and 24 (Modification), Transitional and Transitory Provisions) Order 2018 (2018/138) art.6(3) (April 11, 2018).

4. Welfare Reform Act 2012 (Commencement No. 31 and Savings and Transitional Provisions and Commencement No. 21 and 23 and Transitional and Transitory Provisions (Amendment)) Order 2019 (SI 2019/37) art.5(2) (January 15, 2019).

5. Universal Credit (Transitional Provisions) (SDP Gateway) Amendment Regulations 2019 (SI 2019/10) reg.3(3) (January 16, 2019).

6. Universal Credit (Restriction on Amounts for Children and Qualifying Young Persons) (Transitional Provisions) Amendment Regulations 2019 (SI 2019/27) reg.4(3) (February 1, 2019).

7. Welfare Reform Act 2012 (Commencement No. 32 and Savings and Transitional Provisions) Order 2019 (SI 2019/167) art 5(4) (February 1, 2019).

8. Welfare Reform Act 2012 (Commencement No. 31 and Savings and Transitional Provisions and Commencement No. 21 and 23 and Transitional and Transitory Provisions (Amendment)) Order 2019 (SI 2019/37) art.5 (January 15, 2019).

DEFINITIONS

"the 2006 Regulations"–para.(11)(e).   **5.125**
"the 2006 (SPC) Regulations"–para.(11)(f).
"child tax credit"–para.11(j).
"couple"–para.(11)(a).
"housing benefit"–para.(11)(b).
"income support"–para.(11)(c).
"qualifying age for state pension credit"–para.11(d).
"relevant Regulations"–para.11(g).
"specified accommodation"–para.11(h).
"State Pension Credit Act couple"–para.11(i).
"tax credit"–para.(11)(j).
"Tax Credits Act couple"–para.11(k).
"working tax credit"–para.11(j).

Amendment of the Welfare Reform Act 2012 (Commencement No.9 and Transitional and Transitory Provisions and Commencement No.8 and Savings and Transitional Provisions (Amendment)) Order 2013

5.126   **8.**—(1) Paragraphs (2) and (3) apply in relation to a case where a claim for universal credit is made on or after 18th March 2015.

(2) Where this paragraph applies, in article 3A(3) of the No.9 Order, at the end insert "(and a determination had not been made under regulation 4 of the Universal Credit (Transitional Provisions) Regulations 2014, preventing a claim for universal credit being made with respect to the area in question or the category of case in question)".

(3) Where this paragraph applies, any reference in the No.11 Order, the No.13 Order, the No.14 Order, the No.16 Order, the No.17 Order, the No.19 Order, the No.21 Order or the No.22 Order to article 3A of the No.9 Order is a reference to that article as amended by paragraph (2).

(4) Paragraph (5) applies in relation to a case where a claim for an employment and support allowance or a jobseeker's allowance is made on or after 18th March 2015.

(5) Where this paragraph applies, for paragraph (3) of article 5A of the No.9 Order substitute—

> "(3) For the purposes of this article, paragraphs (5) to (7) of article 5 apply for the purpose of determining—
> (a) whether a claim for ESA or JSA is made; and
> (b) the date on which the claim is made or treated as made.".

Amendment of the Welfare Reform Act 2012 (Commencement No.21 and Transitional and Transitory Provisions) Order 2015

5.127   **9.**—(1) Paragraphs (2) to (4) apply in relation to a case where a claim for universal credit, an employment and support allowance or a jobseeker's allowance is made on or after 10th June 2015.

(2) Where this paragraph applies, in article 2(1) of the No.21 Order, omit the definition of "specified condition".

(3) Where this paragraph applies, article 3 of the No.21 Order is amended as follows—

(a) in paragraph (2)(a), omit "and meets the specified condition";

(b) in sub-paragraph (b) of paragraph (2)—

> (i) in paragraph (i), omit "or meeting the specified condition" and "or does not meet the specified condition";
> (ii) in paragraph (ii), omit "or meeting the specified condition" and "or does not or do not meet the specified condition"; and
> (iii) in the closing words, omit "or meeting the specified condition as the case may be"; and

(c) in paragraph (5), omit "or meeting the specified condition" and "or meeting the gateway conditions (as defined in the No.9 Order)".

(4) Where this paragraph applies, article 4 of the No.21 Order is amended as follows—

(a) in sub-paragraphs (a) and (c) of paragraph (2), omit "and meets the specified condition"; and

(b) in sub-paragraph (b) of paragraph (2)—

(i) in paragraph (i), omit "or meeting the specified condition" and "or does not meet the specified condition";

(ii) in paragraph (ii), omit "or meeting the specified condition" and "or does not or do not meet the specified condition"; and

(iii) in the closing words, omit "or meeting the specified condition as the case may be".

(5) With effect from 18th March 2015, article 6 of the No.21 Order is amended as follows—

(a) in paragraph (1), for "(2) to (5)" substitute "(2) to (5) and (11)";

(b) in paragraph (9)(b), for "regulation 6(1A)(b)" substitute "regulations 6(1A)(b) and 6A"; and

(c) after paragraph (10) insert—

> "(11) Paragraph (1) does not apply to a claim for housing benefit, income support or a taxcredit where, by virtue of a determination made under regulation 4 of the Universal Credit (Transitional Provisions) Regulations 2014, the person in question would be prevented from making a claim for universal credit as referred to in that paragraph.".

Modification of the Universal Credit (Digital Service) Amendment Regulations 2014

10. With effect from 18th March 2015, the Universal Credit (Digital Service) Amendment Regulations 2014 have effect as if, in regulation 5(3)(a) of those Regulations (savings), for "the postcode part-district SM5 2" there were substituted "one of the postcode part-districts CR0 2 and CR0 4, SM5 2, SM6 7 to SM6 9 and SE1 5".   5.128

Modification of the Universal Credit (Surpluses and Self-employed Losses) (Digital Service) Amendment Regulations 2015

11. With effect from 18th March 2015, the Universal Credit (Surpluses and Self-employed Losses) (Digital Service) Amendment Regulations 2015 have effect as if, in regulation 4(3)(a) of those Regulations (savings), for "the postcode part-district SM5 2" there were substituted "one of the postcode part-districts CR0 2 and CR0 4, SM5 2, SM6 7 to SM6 9 and SE1 5."   5.129

The Welfare Reform Act 2012 (Commencement No.23 and Transitional and Transitory Provisions) (Amendment) Order 2015

(2015/740) (C.39)

The Secretary of State for Work and Pensions makes the following Order in exercise of the powers conferred by section 150(3) and (4)(a), (b)(i) and (c) of the Welfare Reform Act 2012:

ARRANGEMENT OF ARTICLES

5.130   Note that the text of this Commencement Order is not included in this volume as it is now unlikely to give rise to live appeals. The full text of this Order can be found in the 2019/20 edn of this book at paras 3.394-3.396.

The Welfare Reform Act 2012 (Commencement No.24 and Transitional and Transitory Provisions and Commencement No.9 and Transitional and Transitory Provisions (Amendment)) Order 2015

(SI 2015/1537) (C.87)

The Secretary of State makes the following Order, in exercise of the powers conferred by section 150(3) and (4)(a), (b)(i) and (c) of the Welfare Reform Act 2012:

ARRANGEMENT OF ARTICLES

5.131   1. Citation
        2. Interpretation
        3. Day appointed for the coming into force of the universal credit provisions
        4. Day appointed for the abolition of income-related employment and support allowance and income-based jobseeker's allowance
        5. Amendment of the No.9 Order and cases to which the amendment applies
        6. Application of the No.9 Order
        7. Modification of the Universal Credit (Digital Service) Amendment Regulations 2014
        8. Revocation of modification of the Universal Credit (Digital Service) Amendment Regulations 2014
        9. Modification of the Universal Credit (Surpluses and Self-Employed Losses) (Digital Service) Amendment Regulations 2015

GENERAL NOTE

5.132   Note that the text of this Commencement Order is not included in its entirety in this volume as it is now unlikely to give rise to live appeals. The full text of this Order can be found in the 2019/20 edn of this book at paras 3.397-3.408. The broad effect of this Commencement Order ("the Commencement No.24 Order") was to complete the national expansion of universal credit claims for single claimants in a series of stages from September 21, 2015 through to April 25, 2016.

Article 2 of the Order defines the gateway conditions, which are the requirements to be met to make a claim for universal credit. These are set out in Sch.5 to the Commencement No.9 Order (as amended). Article 5 of this Order amends para.7(e) of Sch.5 to allow the gateway condition requiring a universal credit claimant to have a particular type of account to be met in the case of a claim by a couple if either member of the couple has such an account.

It should be noted that para.(a) of the definition of the gateway conditions in Art.2 of this Order causes them to have effect apart from the amendments to Sch.5 made by art.4(5)(b) of the Welfare Reform Act 2012 (Commencement No.9, 11, 13, 14, 16, 17 and 19 and Transitional and Transitory Provisions (Amendment)) Order 2015 (S.I. 2015/32). That Order removed the condition that a claimant must not (at least for the great majority of cases) have responsibility for children or young persons. That particular gateway condition is reapplied for claims made with respect to the areas to which this Order applies. The gateway conditions are further modified by para.(b) of the definition and para.(3) to require that a claimant must be single, with consequent changes to alter or omit provisions relevant only to couples including the amendment by art.5 noted above ("the modified gateway conditions").

Article 3 then brought into force provisions relating to universal credit in Part 1 of the Act as set out in Sch.2 to the Commencement No.9 Order, in relation to a number of different types of cases and at different dates.

The Welfare Reform Act 2012 (Commencement No.25 and Transitional and Transitory Provisions) Order 2015

(2015/1930) (C.118)

The Secretary of State for Work and Pensions makes the following Order in exercise of the powers conferred by section 150(3) and (4)(a), (b)(i) and (c) of the Welfare Reform Act 2012:

ARRANGEMENT OF ARTICLES

GENERAL NOTE

Note that the text of this Commencement Order is not included in its entirety in this volume as it is now unlikely to give rise to live appeals. The full text of this Order can be found in the 2019/20 edn of this book at paras 3.409-3.418. This Commencement Order provided for the expansion of universal credit to further designated postcodes in the London Borough of Sutton as from December 2, 2015 (see the definition of "the designated postcodes" in art.2(1)).

The Welfare Reform Act 2012 (Commencement No.26 and Transitional and Transitory Provisions and Commencement No.22, 23 and 24 and Transitional and Transitory Provisions (Modification)) Order 2016

(2016/33) (C.3)

The Secretary of State for Work and Pensions makes the following Order in exercise of the powers conferred by section 150(3) and (4)(a), (b)(i) and (c) of the Welfare Reform Act 2012:   **5.134**

ARRANGEMENT OF ARTICLES

GENERAL NOTE

5.135   Note that the text of this Commencement Order is not included in its entirety
in this volume as it is now unlikely to give rise to live appeals. The full text of this
Order can be found in the 2019/20 edn of this book at paras 3.419-3.435. The effect
of this Commencement Order was to provide for the introduction of the universal
credit digital or full service in postcodes administered by Sutton, London Bridge,
Hounslow and Croydon jobcentres with effect from January 27, 2016 and February
24, 2016.

The Welfare Reform Act 2012 (Commencement No.27 and Transitional and Transitory Provisions and Commencement No.22, 23 and 24 and Transitional and Transitory Provisions (Modification)) Order 2016

(SI 2016/407) (C.20)

The Secretary of State for Work and Pensions makes the following Order in exercise of the powers conferred by section 150(3) and (4)(a), (b)(i) and (c) of the Welfare Reform Act 2012:

ARRANGEMENT OF ARTICLES

Note that the text of this Commencement Order is not included in its entirety   **5.137**
in this volume as it is now unlikely to give rise to live appeals. The full text of this
Order can be found in the 2019/20 edn of this book at paras 3.436-3.448. This
Commencement Order provided for the further expansion of the universal credit
digital or full service in various designated postcode areas with effect from March
23, 2016 (Croydon, London Bridge and Musselburgh) and April 27, 2016 (Purley,
Thornton Heath and Great Yarmouth).

The Welfare Reform Act 2012 (Commencement No.13, 14, 16, 19, 22, 23 and 24 and Transitional and Transitory Provisions (Modification)) Order 2016

(SI 2016/596) (C.41)

The Secretary of State for Work and Pensions makes the following Order in   **5.138**
exercise of the powers conferred by section 150(3) and (4)(a), (b)(i) and (c) of
the Welfare Reform Act 2012:

ARRANGEMENT OF ARTICLES

Note that the text of this Commencement Order is not included in its entirety in   **5.139**
this volume as it is now unlikely to give rise to live appeals. The full text of this Order
can be found in the 2019/20 edn of this book at paras 3.449-3.462. This Order,

amending and modifying a range of earlier Commencement Orders, provides for the expansion of the full or digital universal credit service in a number of designated postcode areas with effect from May 25, June 29 and July 27, 2016.

The Welfare Reform Act 2012 (Commencement No.19, 22, 23 and 24 and Transitional and Transitory Provisions (Modification)) Order 2016

(SI 2016/963) (C.86)

The Secretary of State for Work and Pensions makes the following Order in exercise of the powers conferred by section 150(3) and (4)(a), (b)(i) and (c) of the Welfare Reform Act 2012:

ARRANGEMENT OF ARTICLES

GENERAL NOTE

Note that the text of this Commencement Order is not included in its entirety   5.141
in this volume as it is now unlikely to give rise to live appeals. The full text of this
Order can be found in the 2019/20 edn of this book at paras 3.463-3.522. This
Commencement Order provided for the expansion of the full Universal Credit
service (or 'Digital Service' in the legislation) to postcodes administered by a total of
20 jobcentres on a weekly basis between October 5, and December 14, 2016 (along
with a number of minor variations to the existing roll-out).

The Welfare Reform Act 2012 (Commencement No.11, 13, 16, 22, 23 and 24 and Transitional and Transitory Provisions (Modification)) Order 2017

(SI 2017/57) (C.5)

The Secretary of State for Work and Pensions makes the following Order in exercise of the powers conferred by section 150(3) and (4)(a), (b)(i) and (c) of the Welfare Reform Act 2012:

ARRANGEMENT OF ARTICLES

19. Modification of the No.23 Order: claims for housing benefit, income support or a tax credit

SCHEDULE   POSTCODE DISTRICTS AND PART-DISTRICTS

GENERAL NOTE

Note that the text of this Commencement Order is not included in its entirety in this volume as it is now unlikely to give rise to live appeals. The full text of this Order can be found in the 2019/20 edn of this book at paras 3.523-3.575. This Commencement Order provided for the expansion of the full Universal Credit service (or 'Digital Service' in legislation) to postcodes administered by a total of 15 jobcentres on a weekly basis between February 1 and April 26, 2017.

The Welfare Reform Act 2012 (Commencement No.9 and 21 and Transitional and Transitory Provisions (Amendment)) Order 2017

(SI 2017/483) (C.44)

The Secretary of State for Work and Pensions makes the following Order in exercise of the powers conferred by section 150(3) and (4)(a), (b)(i) and (c) of the Welfare Reform Act 2012:

ARRANGEMENT OF ARTICLES

5.143
1. Citation
2. Amendment of the Welfare Reform Act 2012 (Commencement No.9 and Transitional and Transitory Provisions and Commencement No.8 and Savings and Transitional Provisions (Amendment)) Order 2013
3. Amendment of the Welfare Reform Act 2012 (Commencement No.21 and Transitional and Transitory Provisions) Order 2015

GENERAL NOTE

5.144   Note that the text of this Commencement Order is not included in this volume as it is now unlikely to give rise to live appeals. The full text of this Order can be found in the 2019/20 edition of this book at paras 3.576-3.579.

The Welfare Reform Act 2012 (Commencement No. 19, 22, 23 and 24 and Transitional and Transitory Provisions (Modification)) Order 2017

(SI 2017/584) (C. 53)

Made 24th April 2017

The Secretary of State for Work and Pensions makes the following Order in exercise of the powers conferred by section 150(3) and (4)(a), (b)(i) and (c) of the Welfare Reform Act 2012:

ARRANGEMENT OF ARTICLES

GENERAL NOTE

Note that the text of this Commencement Order is not included in its entirety in this volume as it is now unlikely to give rise to live appeals. The full text of this Order can be found in the 2019/20 edition of this book at paras 3.580-3.620. This Commencement Order provided for the expansion of the full Universal Credit service (or 'Digital Service' in legislation) to postcodes administered by a total of 13 jobcentres on a weekly basis between May 3 and June 28, 2017.

The Welfare Reform Act 2012 (Commencement No. 29 and Commencement No. 17, 19, 22, 23 and 24 and Transitional and Transitory Provisions (Modification)) Order 2017

2017 No. 664 (C. 56)

Made 19th May 2017

The Secretary of State for Work and Pensions makes the following Order in exercise of the powers conferred by section 150(3) and (4)(a), (b)(i) and (c) of the Welfare Reform Act 2012:

ARRANGEMENT OF ARTICLES

GENERAL NOTE

This Commencement Order provided for the expansion of the full Universal Credit service (or 'Digital Service' in legislation) to postcodes administered by a total of 30 jobcentres on a weekly basis between July 5 and 19, 2017, although in some postcodes on a phased basis until September 2017. Note that the text of this Commencement Order is not included in its entirety in this volume as it is now unlikely to give rise to live appeals. The full text of this Order can be found in the 2019/20 edition of this book at paras 3.621-3.682.

The Welfare Reform Act 2012 (Commencement No. 17, 19, 22, 23 and 24 and Transitional and Transitory Provisions (Modification)) Order 2017

2017 No. 952 (C. 86)

Made 28ᵗʰ September 2017

The Secretary of State for Work and Pensions makes the following Order in exercise of the powers conferred by section 150(3) and (4)(a), (b)(i) and (c) of the Welfare Reform Act 2012:

ARRANGEMENT OF ARTICLES

5.147   1. Citation
2. Interpretation
3. Modification of the No. 17 Order, the No. 19 Order, the No. 22 Order and the No. 24 Order: removal of the gateway conditions

4. Modifications of the No. 17 Order, the No. 19 Order, the No. 22 Order and the No. 24 Order in consequence of removal of the gateway conditions

5. Modification of the No. 23 Order: claims for housing benefit, income support or a tax credit

SCH   POSTCODE DISTRICTS AND PART-DISTRICTS WHERE GATEWAY CONDITIONS REMOVED

GENERAL NOTE

This Commencement Order provided for the expansion of the full Universal Credit service (or 'Digital Service' in legislation) to further postcodes between October 4, 2017 and January 24, 2018. Note that the text of this Commencement Order is not included in its entirety in this volume as it is now unlikely to give rise to live appeals. The full text of this Order can be found in the 2019/20 edn of this book at paras 3.683-3.689.

The Welfare Reform Act 2012 (Commencement No. 9, 21 and 23 (Amendment), Commencement No. 11, 13, 17, 19, 22, 23 and 24 (Modification), Transitional and Transitory Provisions) Order 2018

2018 No. 138 (C. 13)

Made 2nd February 2018

The Secretary of State for Work and Pensions makes the following Order in exercise of the powers conferred by section 150(3) and (4)(a), (b)(i) and (c) of the Welfare Reform Act 2012:

ARRANGEMENT OF ARTICLES

GENERAL NOTE

This Commencement Order provided for the expansion of the full Universal Credit service (or 'Digital Service' in legislation) to further postcodes between February 7 and April 25, 2018. It also provided for universal credit claimants living in temporary accommodation to claim housing benefit instead of the universal credit housing element from April 11, 2018. Note that the text of this Commencement

Order is not included in its entirety in this volume as it is now unlikely to give rise to live appeals. The full text of this Order can be found in the 2019/20 edn of this book at paras 3.690-3.698.

The Welfare Reform Act 2012 (Commencement No. 17, 19, 22, 23 and 24 and Transitional and Transitory Provisions (Modification)) Order 2018

SI 2018/532 (C.43)

Made 26th April 2018

5.149 *The Secretary of State for Work and Pensions makes the following Order in exercise of the powers conferred by section 150(3) and (4)(a), (b)(i) and (c) of the Welfare Reform Act 2012:*

ARRANGEMENT OF ARTICLES

1. Citation
2. Interpretation
3. Modification of the No. 17 Order, the No. 19 Order, the No. 22 Order and the No. 24 Order: removal of the gateway conditions
4. Modifications of the No. 17 Order, the No. 19 Order, the No. 22 Order and the No. 24 Order in consequence of removal of the gateway conditions
5. Modification of the No. 23 Order: claims for housing benefit, income support or a tax credit
SCH POSTCODE DISTRICTS AND PART-DISTRICTS WHERE GATEWAY CONDITIONS REMOVED

GENERAL NOTE

5.150   This Order modified a series of prior Commencement Orders (as listed in art.2(1)), which in turn brought into force provisions of the WRA 2012 relating to universal credit and the abolition of IR-ESA and IB-JSA. Articles 3 and 4 of each of those prior Commencement Orders brought into force provisions in Part 1 of the WRA 2012 Act, as set out in Sch. 2 to the No. 9 Commencement Order, and provisions of the 2012 Act relating to the abolition of the two legacy benefits. Article 3 of this Order modified the provisions of the prior Commencement Orders as set out in the first column of the table in the Schedule. The effect was that the restrictions on claiming universal credit (i.e. the gateway conditions specified in Sch. 5 to the No. 9 Commencement Order) no longer applied. The modified provisions were specified by reference to the postcode districts and part-districts listed in the corresponding entry in the second column of the table. The modifications applied by reference to residence in those areas where claims were made for universal credit, ESA or JSA on or after the dates in the corresponding entry in the third column of the table. Article 4 of this Order made consequential modifications to several similar provisions in each of the prior Commencement Orders to remove references to meeting the gateway conditions. One consequence of the gateway conditions no longer applying was that claims by couples became possible for the first time in certain of the specified postcodes, namely those for which the universal credit provisions were commenced under the No. 22 Commencement Order and the No. 24 Commencement Order for single UC claimants only. Article 5 modified art. 7 of the No.23 Commencement Order such that, where the gateway conditions no longer applied to claims for universal credit (by virtue of art. 3 of this Order), a person could not (save in specified cases) make a claim for housing benefit, income support or a tax credit on a date on which, if that person made a claim for universal credit on that date, the universal credit provisions would come into force under the provisions in question.

Citation

1. This Order may be cited as the Welfare Reform Act 2012 (Commencement No. 17, 19, 22, 23 and 24 and Transitional and Transitory Provisions (Modification)) Order 2018.

5.151

Interpretation

2.—(1) In this Order—

5.152

"claimant"—

(a) in relation to an employment and support allowance, has the same meaning as in Part 1 of the Welfare Reform Act 2007;

(b) in relation to a jobseeker's allowance, has the same meaning as in the Jobseekers Act 1995 (as it applies apart from the amendments made by Part 1 of Schedule 14 to the Welfare Reform Act 2012 that remove references to an income-based jobseeker's allowance);

(c) in relation to universal credit, has the same meaning as in Part 1 of the Welfare Reform Act 2012;

"the Claims and Payments Regulations 1987" means the Social Security (Claims and Payments) Regulations 1987;

"employment and support allowance" means an employment and support allowance under Part 1 of the Welfare Reform Act 2007;

"jobseeker's allowance" means a jobseeker's allowance under the Jobseekers Act 1995;

"the No. 17 Order" means the Welfare Reform Act 2012 (Commencement No. 17 and Transitional and Transitory Provisions) Order 2014;

"the No. 19 Order" means the Welfare Reform Act 2012 (Commencement No. 19 and Transitional and Transitory Provisions and Commencement No. 9 and Transitional and Transitory Provisions (Amendment)) Order 2014;

"the No. 22 Order" means the Welfare Reform Act 2012 (Commencement No. 22 and Transitional and Transitory Provisions) Order 2015;

"the No. 23 Order" means the Welfare Reform Act 2012 (Commencement No. 23 and Transitional and Transitory Provisions) Order 2015;

"the No. 24 Order" means the Welfare Reform Act 2012 (Commencement No. 24 and Transitional and Transitory Provisions and Commencement No. 9 and Transitional and Transitory Provisions (Amendment)) Order 2015.

(2) For the purposes of this Order, the Universal Credit, Personal Independence Payment, Jobseeker's Allowance and Employment and Support Allowance (Claims and Payments) Regulations 2013 apply for the purpose of deciding—

(a) whether a claim for universal credit is made; and

(b) the date on which the claim is made.

(3) For the purposes of this Order, the Claims and Payments Regulations 1987 apply, subject to paragraphs (4) and (5), for the purposes of deciding—

(a) whether a claim for an employment and support allowance or a job-seeker's allowance is made; and

(b) the date on which the claim is made or treated as made.

(4) Subject to paragraph (5), for the purposes of this Order—

(a) a person makes a claim for an employment and support allowance or a jobseeker's allowance if that person takes any action which results in a decision on a claim being required under the Claims and Payments Regulations 1987; and

(b) it is irrelevant that the effect of any provision of those Regulations is that, for the purposes of those Regulations, the claim is made or treated as made at a date that is earlier than the date on which that action is taken.

(5) Where, by virtue of—

(a) regulation 6(1F)(b) or (c) of the Claims and Payments Regulations 1987, in the case of a claim for an employment and support allowance; or

(b) regulation 6(4ZA) to (4ZD) and (4A)(a)(i) and (b) of those Regulations, in the case of a claim for a jobseeker's allowance,

a claim for an employment and support allowance or a jobseeker's allowance is treated as made at a date that is earlier than the date on which the action referred to in paragraph (4)(a) is taken, the claim is treated as made on that earlier date.

Modification of the No. 17 Order, the No. 19 Order, the No. 22 Order and the No. 24 Order: removal of the gateway conditions

5.153   3.—The provisions specified in the first column of the table in the Schedule have effect as though the reference in those provisions to meeting the gateway conditions were omitted, in respect of a claim for universal credit that is made, or a claim for an employment and support allowance or a jobseeker's allowance that is made or treated as made, by reference to the claimant's residence in any postcode district or part-district specified in the corresponding entry in the second column, on or after the date specified in the corresponding entry in the third column.

Modifications of the No. 17 Order, the No. 19 Order, the No. 22 Order and the No. 24 Order in consequence of removal of the gateway conditions

5.154   4.—(1) This article applies in respect of claims in relation to which provisions of the No. 17 Order, the No. 19 Order, the No. 22 Order and the No. 24 Order are modified by article 3.

(2) Where this article applies, the following modifications also have effect—

(a) those made to the No. 17 Order by article 10(2) of the Welfare Reform Act 2012 (Commencement No. 29 and Commencement No. 17, 19, 22, 23 and 24 and Transitional and Transitory Provisions (Modification)) Order 2017; and

(b) those made to the No. 19 Order, the No. 22 Order and the No. 24 Order by articles 13(2), 14(2) and 15(2) respectively of the Welfare Reform Act 2012 (Commencement No. 19, 22, 23 and 24 and Transitional and Transitory Provisions (Modification)) Order 2016.

Modification of the No. 23 Order: claims for housing benefit, income support or a tax credit

5.—(1) This article applies to claims in relation to which the provisions referred to in paragraph (2)(a) to (d) are modified by article 3.

(2) Where this article applies, article 7 of the No. 23 Order (prevention of claims for housing benefit, income support or a tax credit) applies as though the reference in paragraph (1) of that article to article 3(1) and (2)(a) to (c) of that Order included a reference to—

(a) paragraph (1) and sub-paragraphs (g), (i) and (k) of paragraph (2) of article 3 of the No. 17 Order;

(b) paragraph (1) and sub-paragraphs (a), (b), (d), (f), (h), (j), (k), (m) and (n) of paragraph (2) of article 3 of the No. 19 Order;

(c) paragraph (1) and sub-paragraphs (a), (c), (e) to (j), (l) to (n), (p) to (r) and (t) of paragraph (2) of article 3 of the No. 22 Order; and

(d) paragraph (1) and sub-paragraphs (a) to (d), (f) to (u), (w) to (y), (bb) and (cc) of paragraph (2) of article 3 of the No. 24 Order.

Article 3

SCHEDULE

POSTCODE DISTRICTS AND PART-DISTRICTS
WHERE GATEWAY CONDITIONS REMOVED

5.155

5.156

Provisions modified	Postcode			Date
Articles 3(2)(t) and 4(2)(mm) and (nn) of the No. 22 Order	LL22 7.	LL22 9.		2nd May 2018
Articles 3(2)(c) and 4(2)(e) and (f) of the No. 24 Order	CV23 1.			2nd May 2018
Articles 3(2)(f) and 4(2)(k) and (l) of the No. 24 Order	B45 9.			2nd May 2018
Articles 3(2)(j) and 4(2)(s) and (t) of the No. 24 Order	NE6 4. NE26 1 to NE26 3. NE30.	NE12. NE28.	NE25 8. NE29.	2nd May 2018
Articles 3(2)(k) and 4(2)(u) and (v) of the No. 24 Order	LN7.			2nd May 2018
Articles 3(2)(t) and 4(2)(mm) and (nn) of the No. 24 Order	NE13 6.	NE25 9.	NE27.	2nd May 2018
Articles 3(2)(cc) and 4(2)(eee) and (fff) of the No. 24 Order	IV2 8.	MK43 1 and MK43 2.		2nd May 2018

Articles 3(2)(f) and 4(2)(k) and (l) of the No. 22 Order	SY8 2.	SY8 3.		9th May 2018
Articles 3(2)(h) and 4(2)(o) and (p) of the No. 22 Order	SY1. SY4 1 to SY4 3. SY6. SY11. SY14 7. TF12.	SY2. SY4 5. SY10 1. SY12. TF9 1. WV16.	SY3. SY5 6 to SY5 8. SY10 8. SY13. TF9 3.	9th May 2018
Articles 3(2)(n) and 4(2)(aa) and (bb) of the No. 22 Order	SY4 4. TF11 9.	TF9 2. TF13 6.	TF9 4.	9th May 2018
Articles 3(2)(t) and 4(2)(mm) and (nn) of the No. 22 Order	LL14 5.			9th May 2018
Articles 3(2)(a) and 4(2)(a) and (b) of the No. 24 Order	WV15 5			9th May 2018
Articles 3(2)(b) and 4(2)(c) and (d) of the No. 24 Order	IP14.			9th May 2018
Articles 3(2)(c) and 4(2)(e) and (f) of the No. 24 Order	HG14 7. NG24. NN10.	NG22 0. NG25.	NG23 6. NN9 6.	9th May 2018
Articles 3(2)(f) and 4(2)(k) and (l) of the No. 24 Order	SY5 0. SY10 7.	SY5 9. SY10 9.	SY9.	9th May 2018
Articles 3(2)(h) and 4(2)(o) and (p) of the No. 24 Order	IP20, IP23.	IP21. NR15 2.	IP22.	9th May 2018
Articles 3(2)(i) and 4(2)(q) and (r) of the No. 24 Order	IP6 8.			9th May 2018
Articles 3(2)(k) and 4(2)(u) and (v) of the No. 24 Order	NG23 7.			9th May 2018
Articles 3(2)(l) and 4(2)(w) and (x) of the No. 24 Order	TF11 8.	WV15 6.		9th May 2018
Articles 3(2)(r) and 4(2)(ii) and (jj) of the No. 24 Order	WV5 7.			9th May 2018
Articles 3(2)(s) and 4(2)(kk) and (ll) of the No. 24 Order	NG23 5.			9th May 2018

1700

Articles 3(2)(i) and 4(2)(i) of the No. 17 Order	L10 0. L10 8. L33 0 to L33 2. L35 1 to L35 3. L36 0 to L36 4.	L10 2 and L10 3. L28 3 to L28 7. L33 5 to L33 9. L35 5. L36 6 to L36 9.	L10 6. L32. L34. L35 7.	16th May 2018
Articles 3(2)(a) and 4(2)(a) of the No. 19 Order	L33 3 and L33 4. OL10. OL12 9. OL16.	M24 0 to M24 2. OL11. OL15 0.	M24 5 and M24 6. OL12 6. OL15 8.	16th May 2018
Articles 3(2)(b) and 4(2)(b) of the No. 19 Order	L10 1. L14. L36 5.	L10 4 and L10 5. L28 0 and L28 1. M24 4.	L10 7. L28 8.	16th May 2018
Articles 3(2)(d) and 4(2)(d) of the No. 19 Order	OL12 0.	OL12 7.		16th May 2018
Articles 3(2)(c) and 4(2)(e) and (f) of the No. 22 Order	EN5 1 and EN5 2. HA8 4. N2 8. N20. NW9 0 and NW9 1.	EN5 5. HA8 9. N3. NW4 NW9 5 to NW9 8	HA8 0. N2 2. N12. NW7. NW11.	16th May 2018
Articles 3(2)(i) and 4(2)(q) and (r) of the No. 22 Order	DG1. DG4 DG7. DG9. DG12.	DG2. DG5. DG8 0 and DG8 1. DG10. DG13.	DG3. DG6. DG8 7 to DG8 9. DG11. DG14.	16th May 2018
Articles 3(2)(l) and 4(2)(w) and (x) of the No. 22 Order	E10 7.	E10 9.	E17.	16th May 2018
Articles 3(2)(t) and 4(2)(mm) and (nn) of the No. 22 Order	EN4 8 and EN4 9. N18 9.	N9 0 and N9 1.	N18 2.	16th May 2018
Articles 3(2)(a) and 4(2)(a) and (b) of the No. 24 Order	DG16 5. L10 9.	EN4 0. N18 3.	EN5 3 and EN5 4. OL15 9.	16th May 2018
Articles 3(2)(c) and 4(2)(e) and (f) of the No. 24 Order	HA8 5 to HA8 8.	ML12 6.	NW9 9.	16th May 2018
Articles 3(2)(d) and 4(2)(g) and (h) of the No. 24 Order	DG8 6.			16th May 2018
Articles 3(2)(i) and 4(2)(q) and (r) of the No. 24 Order	EH27. EH47. EH52. EH55.	EH28. EH48. EH53. FK1 2.	EH29. EH49 6. EH54. ML7 5.	16th May 2018
Articles 3(2)(w) and 4(2)(ss) and (tt) of the No. 24 Order	N2 0.	N2 9.		16th May 2018

Articles 3(2)(cc) and 4(2)(eee) and (fff) of the No. 24 Order	NW9 4.			16th May 2018
Articles 3(2)(l) and 4(2)(w) and (x) of the No. 22 Order	PL22. PL25.	PL23. PL26.	PL24.	23rd May 2018
Articles 3(2)(p) and 4(2)(ee) and (ff) of the No. 22 Order	PL27. PL30. PL33. TR3 6. TR6.	PL28. PL31. TR1. TR4.	PL29. PL32. TR2. TR5.	23rd May 2018
Articles 3(2)(t) and 4(2)(mm) and (nn) of the No. 22 Order	TR7.	TR8.	TR9.	23rd May 2018
Articles 3(2)(b) and 4(2)(c) and (d) of the No. 24 Order	GU47 0. RG10 8. RG41. SL1 7.	GU47 9. RG12. RG42. SL5 8.	RG10 0. RG40. RG45. SL6 1 to SL6 9.	23rd May 2018
Articles 3(2)(i) and 4(2)(q) and (r) of the No. 24 Order	SL8.			23rd May 2018
Articles 3(2)(u) and 4(2)(oo) and (pp) of the No. 24 Order	SL5 0.	SL5 7.	SL5 9.	23rd May 2018
Articles 3(2)(y) and 4(2)(ww) and (xx) of the No. 24 Order	RG21. RG24. RG27.	RG22. RG25. RG28 9.	RG23. RG26. RG29.	23rd May 2018
Articles 3(2)(l) and 4(2)(w) and (x) of the No. 22 Order	DA11 0.	DA11 7.	DA12.	30th May 2018
Articles 3(2)(d) and 4(2)(g) and (h) of the No. 24 Order	DA13 0. ME3. ME7.	ME1. ME4. ME8.	ME2. ME5.	30th May 2018
Articles 3(2)(h) and 4(2)(o) and (p) of the No. 24 Order	LS25 6. YO11. YO14.	YO8 3 to YO8 5. YO12. YO21.	YO8 8 and YO8 9. YO13. YO22.	30th May 2018
Articles 3(2)(o) and 4(2)(cc) and (dd) of the No. 24 Order	DN14 0.			30th May 2018
Articles 3(2)(p) and 4(2)(ee) and (ff) of the No. 24 Order	CT18. CT21. DA13 9. TN29.	CT19. DA10. TN25 5 to TN25 7. TN26 2.	CT20. DA11 8 and DA11 9. TN28.	30th May 2018

Articles 3(2)(t) and 4(2)(mm) and (nn) of the No. 24 Order	NE31. NE34. SR6 7.	NE32. NE35.	NE33. NE36.	30th May 2018
Articles 3(2)(a) and 4(2)(a) and (b) of the No. 22 Order	BS20.	BS49.		6th June 2018
Articles 3(2)(j) and 4(2)(s) and (t) of the No. 22 Order	LL24. LL27. LL30. LL34.	LL25. LL28. LL31.	LL26. LL29. LL32.	6th June 2018
Articles 3(2)(l) and 4(2)(w) and (x) of the No. 22 Order	TR14.	TR15.	TR16.	6th June 2018
Articles 3(2)(p) and 4(2)(ee) and (ff) of the No. 22 Order	TR17. TR20.	TR18. TR26.	TR19. TR27.	6th June 2018
Articles 3(2)(r) and 4(2)(ii) and (jj) of the No. 22 Order	CF31. CF34.	CF32 7 to CF32 9. CF36.	CF33.	6th June 2018
Articles 3(2)(t) and 4(2)(mm) and (nn) of the No. 22 Order	LL2 8. TR11.	TR3 7. TR12.	TR10. TR13.	6th June 2018
Articles 3(2)(a) and 4(2)(a) and (b) of the No. 24 Order	BN5. RH10 4 to RH10 9. RH12 5. RH15. RH18. RH20 2 to RH20 4. TN7.	BN6. RH11. RH13. RH16. RH19 1 RH20 9	RH10 1. RH12 1 and RH12 2. RH14 9. RH17. RH19 4. TB6.	6th June 2018
Articles 3(2)(d) and 4(2)(g) and (h) of the No. 24 Order	RH20 1.	TN3 9.		6th June 2018
Articles 3(2)(f) and 4(2)(k) and (l) of the No. 24 Order	L33.			6th June 2018
Articles 3(2)(g) and 4(2)(m) and (n) of the No. 24 Order	BS1. BS4. BS9 1. BS40 6 to BS40 9.	BS2. BS6 5. BS13. BS41.	BS3. BS8. BS14.	6th June 2018
Articles 3(2)(l) and 4(2)(w) and (x) of the No. 24 Order	PO30. PO38. PO41. SO40 9.	PO31. PO39. SO40 4. SO45.	PO32. PO40. SO40 7.	6th June 2018
Articles 3(2)(m) and 4(2)(y) and (z) of the No. 24 Order	BN45.			6th June 2018

Articles 3(2)(s) and 4(2)(kk) and (ll) of the No. 24 Order	RH6 6. RH12 3 and RH142 4.	RH7 9. RH14 0.	RH10 3. RH19 2 and RH19 3.	6th June 2018
Articles 3(2)(t) and 4(2)(mm) and (nn) of the No. 24 Order	CF32 0.			6th June 2018
Articles 3(2)(x) and 4(2)(uu) and (vv) of the No. 24 Order	CF35.			6th June 2018
Articles 3(2)(cc) and 4(2)(eee) and (fff) of the No. 24 Order	RH12 0.			6th June 2018
Articles 3(2)(f) and 4(2)(k) and (l) of the No. 22 Order	HR1. HR6. SY8 1.	HR2. HR9 5 and HR9 6.	HR4. SY7 0.	13th June 2018
Articles 3(2)(g) and 4(2)(m) and (n) of the No. 22 Order	IP25. PE37.	NR19,	NR20 4.	13th June 2018
Articles 3(2)(i) and 4(2)(q) and (r) of the No. 22 Order	EH38. EH45. TD3. TD6. TD9 1, TD11.	EH43. TD1. TD4. TD7. TD9 7 to TD9 9. TD13.	EH44. TD2. TD5. TD8. TD10. TD14.	13th June 2018
Articles 3(2)(j) and 4(2)(s) and (t) of the No. 22 Order	HR9 7.			13th June 2018
Articles 3(2)(a) and 4(2)(a) and (b) of the No. 24 Order	TD9 0.			13th June 2018
Articles 3(2)(f) and 4(2)(k) and (l) of the No. 24 Order	DE5 DE56 4. HR3. HR8 1.	DE55 1. DE56 9. HR5. SY7 8.	DE56 0 and DE56 1. DE75. HR7. SY8 4.	13th June 2018
Articles 3(2)(g) and 4(2)(m) and (n) of the No. 24 Order	LN12 2. LN13 9. PE23.	LN12 9. NG16 2 to NG16 5. PE24.	LN13 3. PE22 8. PE25.	13th June 2018
Articles 3(2)(h) and 4(2)(o) and (p) of the No. 24 Order	NR20 3.			13th June 2018
Articles 3(2)(j) and 4(2)(s) and (t) of the No. 24 Order	DE55 2 to DE55 7. S42 5 and S42 6.	DE56 2. S45.	NG16 6.	13th June 2018

Articles 3(2)(l) and 4(2)(w) and (x) of the No. 24 Order	NR20 5.			13th June 2018
Articles 3(2)(p) and 4(2)(ee) and (ff) of the No. 24 Order	LE1. LE4. LE7. LE9 6. LE18.	LE2. LE5. LE8 4 to LE8 6. LE9 9. LE19.	LE3. LE6. LE9 1 to LE9 3. LE17 4 and LE17 5. LE87.	13th June 2018
Articles 3(2)(q) and 4(2)(gg) and (hh) of the No. 24 Order	ST1. ST4 1 to ST4 3. ST9. ST12.	ST2. ST6 1 to ST6 4. ST10. ST13.	ST3. ST6 6 to ST6 9. ST11.	13th June 2018
Articles 3(2)(w) and 4(2)(ss) and (tt) of the No. 24 Order	PE32 2.			13th June 2018
Articles 3(2)(bb) and 4(2)(ccc) and (ddd) of the No. 24 Order	KY13 0. PH2. PH5. PH8. PH11. PH14. PH17.	KY14. PH3. PH6. PH9. PH12. PH15. PH18.	PH1. PH4. PH7. PH10. PH13. PH16.	13th June 2018
Articles 3(2)(g) and 4(2)(m) and (n) of the No. 22 Order	TN23. TN26 1. TN30.	TN24. TN26 3.	TN25 4. TN27 0.	20th June 2018
Articles 3(2)(a) and 4(2)(a) and (b) of the No. 24 Order	DH1. DH6 1. DL5 4 and DL5 5. DL17.	DH2. DH6 4 and DH6 5. DL5 7.	DH3 2 to DH3 4. DH7. DL16.	20th June 2018
Articles 3(2)(d) and 4(2)(g) and (h) of the No. 24 Order	TN27 8.			20th June 2018
Articles 3(2)(g) and 4(2)(m) and (n) of the No. 24 Order	KT1. KT3 5. KT9 2. TW1. TW10. TW12 3.	KT2. KT5. SW13 TW2. TW11.	KT3 3. KT6 7. SW14. TW9. TW12 1.	20th June 2018
Articles 3(2)(h) and 4(2)(o) and (p) of the No. 24 Order	EC1A. EC1R 3. EC1V 7 and EC1V 8. N1 8. N19 3 and N19 4. SW1E. SW1V. SW1Y. W1C. W1G. W1K. W1U. W9 2. WC2N.	EC1M 4 to EC1M 7. EC1V 0. EC1Y. N5 1. NW8 8 and NW8 9. SW1H. SW1W. W1A. W1D. W1H. W1S. W1W. WC2E. WC2R.	EC1R 0 and EC1R 1. EC1V 2 and EC1V 4. N1 1 and N1 2. N7 6 to N7 8. SW1 A. SW1P. SW1X. W1B. W1F. W1J. W1T 3. W2. WC2H 7.	20th June 2018

Articles 3(2)(j) and 4(2)(s) and (t) of the No. 24 Order	DL1. DL4 2.	DL2 2 and DL2 3. DL5 6.	DL3. DL12 8.	20th June 2018
Articles 3(2)(k) and 4(2)(u) and (v) of the No. 24 Order	BD1. BD3 9. BD5. BD8. BD12. BD15. BD18. BD20 9.	BD2. BD4 6 and BD4 7. BD6. BD9. BD13. BD16. BD20 0. BD21.	BD3 0. BD4 9. BD7. BD10 8 and BD10 9. BD14. BD17. BD20 5 and BD20 6. BD22.	20th June 2018
Articles 3(2)(l) and 4(2)(w) and (x) of the No. 24 Order	DL2 1.	TS21 2.		20th June 2018
Articles 3(2)(o) and 4(2)(cc) and (dd) of the No. 24 Order	KT3 4. SW19 1 to SW19 5.	KT3 6. SW19 7 to SW19 9.	KT4 8.	20th June 2018
Articles 3(2)(q) and 4(2)(gg) and (hh) of the No. 24 Order	BD3 8.	BD4 0.	BD10 0.	20th June 2018
Articles 3(2)(s) and 4(2)(kk) and (ll) of the No. 24 Order	IG1. IG4. IG7 4. KT4 7. RM3. RM7. RM13.	IG2. IG5. IG8 0 and IG8 1. RM1. RM5. RM11. RM14 1 and RM14 2.	IG3. IG6. IG8 7 and IG8 8. RM2. RM6 4. RM12. RM14 9.	20th June 2018
Articles 3(2)(u) and 4(2)(oo) and (pp) of the No. 24 Order	KT6 4 to KT6 6.	KT9 1.	TW12 2.	20th June 2018
Articles 3(2)(w) and 4(2)(ss) and (tt) of the No. 24 Order	EC1M 3. N1C. N6. N19 5. NW8 6 and NW8 7. W9 1. WC1E. WC1R. WC2A. Wc2H 8 and WC2H 9.	EC1 N. N1 0. N7 0. NW1 1 to NW1 6. W1T1 and W1T 2. WC1A. WC1H. WC1V. WC2B.	EC1R 4 and EC1R 5. N1 9. N7 9. NW8 0. W1T4 to W1T 7. WC1B. WC1N. WC1X. WC2H 0.	20th June 2018
Articles 3(2)(y) and 4(2)(ww) and (xx) of the No. 24 Order	EC1V 1. N4.	EC1V 9. N5 2.	N1 3.	20th June 2018
Articles 3(2)(m) and 4(2)(y) and (z) of the No. 22 Order	AB41 8. AB44. AB53 4 to AB53 6.	AB42. AB45 1.	AB43. AB45 3.	27th June 2018

Articles 3(2)(a) and 4(2)(a) and (b) of the No. 24 Order	CF46. CF48 3 and CF48 4. NP7 8 and NP7 9. NP16.	CF47. NP7 0 and NP7 1. NP12 4. NP25.	CF48 1. NP7 5 and NP7 6. NP15. NP26.	27th June 2018
Articles 3(2)(f) and 4(2)(k) and (l) of the No. 24 Order	NP7 7.	NP8.		27th June 2018
Articles 3(2)(i) and 4(2)(q) and (r) of the No. 24 Order	AB37. AB54. IV30. IV36.	AB38. AB55. IV31.	AB45 2. AB56. IV32.	27th June 2018
Articles 3(2)(x) and 4(2)(uu) and (vv) of the No. 24 Order	CF48 2.			27th June 2018
Articles 3(2)(e) and 4(2)(i) and (j) of the No. 22 Order	CO1. CO4 0. CO5 7 and CO5 8.	CO2. CO4 3.	CO3. CO4 5.	4th July 2018
Articles 3(2)(g) and 4(2)(m) and (n) of the No. 22 Order	CO4 9.	CO11 2.	CO12.	4th July 2018
Articles 3(2)(a) and 4(2)(a) and (b) of the No. 24 Order	CO7 7. SO21 1 and SO21 2. SP9.	CO7 9. SO22. SP10.	SO20. SO23. SP11 7 to SP11 9.	4th July 2018
Articles 3(2)(b) and 4(2)(c) and (d) of the No. 24 Order	CO5 0. CO11 1.	CO6 3 and CO6 4.	CO7 6.	4th July 2018
Articles 3(2)(c) and 4(2)(e) and (f) of the No. 24 Order	CO5 9. HA2 HA7.	CO6 1. HA3.	HA1. HA5 5.	4th July 2018
Articles 3(2)(d) and 4(2)(g) and (h) of the No. 24 Order	BN11. BN14. BN17. BN44. PO10 8. PO20.	BN12. BN15. BN18. GU28. PO18. PO21.	BN13. BN16. BN43. GU29. PO19. PO22.	4th July 2018
Articles 3(2)(g) and 4(2)(m) and (n) of the No. 24 Order	HA5 1 to HA5 3.	HA6 1.		4th July 2018
Articles 3(2)(h) and 4(2)(o) and (p) of the No. 24 Order	EX10. EX13. EX16. EX24. EX33. EX36. EX39.	EX11. EX14. EX19. EX31. EX34. EX37.	EX12. EX15. EX22 7. EX32. EX35. EX38.	4th July 2018

1707

Articles 3(2)(j) and 4(2)(s) and (t) of the No. 24 Order	HA5 4.	HA6 2 and HA6 3.		4th July 2018
Articles 3(2)(m) and 4(2)(y) and (z) of the No. 24 Order	BN42.			4th July 2018
Articles 3(2)(p) and 4(2)(ee) and (ff) of the No. 24 Order	CT1. CT3 4. CT6.	CT2. CT4.	CT3 1 and CT3 2. CT5.	4th July 2018
Articles 3(2)(r) and 4(2)(ii) and (jj) of the No. 24 Order	SE4. SE8 3 and SE8 4. SE23.	SE6 4. SE13. SE26.	SE6 9. SE19 2 and SE19 3. SO24 0.	4th July 2018
Articles 3(2)(y) and 4(2)(ww) and (xx) of the No. 24 Order	RG28 7. SP11 0.	SO21 3. SP11 6.	SO24 9.	4th July 2018
Articles 3(2)(cc) and 4(2)(eee) and (fff) of the No. 24 Order	CO4 6.			4th July 2018
Articles 3(2)(n) and 4(2)(aa) and (bb) of the No. 22 Order	LE11.	LE12 7 and LE12 8.		11th July 2018
Articles 3(2)(b) and 4(2)(c) and (d) of the No. 24 Order	LE12 9.			11th July 2018
Articles 3(2)(g) and 4(2)(m) and (n) of the No. 24 Order	PE11.	PE12 2.	PE12 6 to PE12 9.	11th July 2018
Articles 3(2)(j) and 4(2)(s) and (t) of the No. 24 Order	S21 1 to S21 3.	S43 3.	S44.	11th July 2018
Articles 3(2)(l) and 4(2)(w) and (x) of the No. 24 Order	CV1. CV4. CV7 7. S26. S61 3 and S61 4. S66. TS17 0. TS18. TS21 1. TS23.	CV2. CV5. CV8 3. S60. S62. TS15. TS17 5 and TS17 6. TS19. TS21 3.	CV3. CV6. S25. S61 1. S65. TS16. TS17 8. TS20. TS22.	11th July 2018
Articles 3(2)(m) and 4(2)(y) and (z) of the No. 24 Order	PE6 0.			11th July 2018

Articles 3(2)(o) and 4(2)(cc) and (dd) of the No. 24 Order	DN14 4 to DN14 9. HU13 3. HU17. S61 2. YO16.	HU10. HU14 HU18. YO8 6. YO25.	HU13 0. HU15. S21 4 and S21 5. YO15. YO43.	11th July 2018
Articles 3(2)(p) and 4(2)(ee) and (ff) of the No. 24 Order	DE1. DE6 9. DE23. SE72 2.	DE3. DE21. DE24. DE73 6 and DE73 7.	DE6 1 to DE6 4. DE22. DE65.	11th July 2018
Articles 3(2)(r) and 4(2)(ii) and (jj) of the No. 24 Order	TS17 7.	TS17 9.		11th July 2018
Articles 3(2)(s) and 4(2)(kk) and (ll) of the No. 24 Order	DE74.	LE12 5.		11th July 2018
Articles 3(2)(u) and 4(2)(oo) and (pp) of the No. 24 Order	HU4 7.	HU13 9.		11th July 2018
Articles 3(2)(w) and 4(2)(ss) and (tt) of the No. 24 Order	PE12 0.			11th July 2018
Articles 3(2)(g) and 4(2)(g) of the No. 17 Order	PR0. PR4 4 and PR4 5. PR25 1 to PR25 3.	PR1. PR5 4 and PR5 5. PR25 9.	PR2. PR11. PR26 6.	18th July 2018
Articles 3(2)(i) and 4(2)(i) of the No. 17 Order	L35 0. WA9. WA11 8 and WA11 9.	L35 4. WA10. WA12.	L35 8 and L35 9. WA11 0.	18th July 2018
Articles 3(2)(k) and 4(2)(k) of the No. 17 Order	CW12 1 and CW12 2. SK9.	CW12 4. WA16.	CW12 9.	18th July 2018
Articles 3(2)(a) and 4(2)(a) of the No. 19 Order	WA11 7.			18th July 2018
Articles 3(2)(f) and 4(2)(f) of the No. 19 Order	SK10.	SK11 6 to SK11 9.		18th July 2018
Articles 3(2)(h) and 4(2)(h) of the No. 19 Order	PR4 0.			18th July 2018
Articles 3(2)(j) and 4(2)(j) of the No. 19 Order	L35 6.			18th July 2018
Articles 3(2)(k) and 4(2)(k) of the No. 19 Order	PR5 0. PR6. PR26 7 to PR26 9.	PR5 6. PR7.	PR5 8. PR25 4 and PR25 5.	18th July 2018

Articles 3(2)(m) and 4(2)(m) of the No. 19 Order	PR3.			18th July 2018
Articles 3(2)(n) and 4(2)(aa) and (bb) of the No. 22 Order	SK11 0.			18th July 2018
Articles 3(2)(q) and 4(2)(gg) and (hh) of the No. 22 Order	B74 2 and B74 3. WS2. WS5 3.	WS1 1 to WS1 3. WS3 1 to WS3 3. WS9 0 and WS9 1.	WS1 9. WS4. WS9 8.	18th July 2018
Articles 3(2)(a) and 4(2)(a) and (b) of the No. 24 Order	CW12 3.			18th July 2018
Articles 3(2)(f) and 4(2)(k) and (l) of the No. 24 Order	NP13. NP23.	NP22 3 and NP22 4.	NP22 9.	18th July 2018
Articles 3(2)(g) and 4(2)(m) and (n) of the No. 24 Order	BS5 7 and BS5 8 BS7 8.	BS6 6 and BS6 7.	BS6 9.	18th July 2018
Articles 3(2)(i) and 4(2)(q) and (r) of the No. 24 Order	B43 7.			18th July 2018
Articles 3(2)(j) and 4(2)(s) and (t) of the No. 24 Order	WS1 4.			18th July 2018
Articles 3(2)(l) and 4(2)(w) and (x) of the No. 24 Order	BS5 0. BS16 3.	BS5 6. WS3 5.	BS5 9.	18th July 2018
Articles 3(2)(n) and 4(2)(aa) and (bb) of the No. 24 Order	BS7 9.	BS16 1 and BS16 2.		18th July 2018
Articles 3(2)(r) and 4(2)(ii) and (jj) of the No. 24 Order	WS10 8.			18th July 2018
Articles 3(2)(g) and 4(2)(g) of the No. 17 Order	BL0 9. BL9 0. M25 1. M26 1 and M26 2.	BL8 1 to BL8 3. BL9 5. M25 3. M26 4.	BL8 9. BL9 8 and BL9 9. M25 9. M45.	25th July 2018
Articles 3(2)(a) and 4(2)(a) of the No. 19 Order	BL9 7.			25th July 2018
Articles 3(2)(b) and 4(2)(b) of the No. 19 Order	M7 4. M22 0 to M22 2. M23.	M8. M22 5. M25 0.	M9. M22 8 and M22 9. M25 2.	25th July 2018

Articles 3(2)(d) and 4(2)(d) of the No. 19 Order	BL9 6.			25th July 2018
Articles 3(2)(j) and 4(2)(j) of the No. 19 Order	M22 4.			25th July 2018
Articles 3(2)(k) and 4(2)(k) of the No. 19 Order	BL8 4.			25th July 2018
Articles 3(2)(n) and 4(2)(n) of the No. 19 Order	CA1. CA4. CA7 0. CA8 0 and CA8 1. CA11.	CA2. CA5. CA7 5. CA8 9. CA16.	CA3. CA6. CA& 7 to CA7 9. CA10 1 to CA10 3. CA17.	25th July 2018
Articles 3(2)(g) and 4(2)(m) and (n) of the No. 22 Order	CO7 0. CO13. CO16.	CO7 5. CO14.	CO7 8. CO15.	25th July 2018
Articles 3(2)(l) and 4(2)(w) and (x) of the No. 22 Order	E4 6. E11 4. SS8.	E4 8 and E4 9. E11 9.	E10 5 and E10 6. SS7.	25th July 2018
Articles 3(2)(g) and 4(2)(m) and (n) of the No. 24 Order	DH4. NE37 9. SR2. SR5 2 to SR5 5.	DH5. NE38. SR3. SR5 9.	NE37 1 and NE37 2. SR1. SR4.	25th July 2018
Articles 3(2)(o) and 4(2)(cc) and (dd) of the No. 24 Order	BR1 1 to BR1 3. BR3 3 to BR3 6. BR5. SE20.	BR1 9. BR3 9. BR6. TN16 3.	BR2. BR4. BR7.	25th July 2018
Articles 3(2)(p) and 4(2)(ee) and (ff) of the No. 24 Order	BR8. DA2. DA9.	DA1 1 and DA1 2. DA3. TN14 7.	DA1 9. DA4. TN15 6 and TN15 7	25th July 2018
Articles 3(2)(q) and 4(2)(gg) and (hh) of the No. 24 Order	E4 7. SS6.		SS4. SS5.	25th July 2018
Articles 3(2)(r) and 4(2)(ii) and (jj) of the No. 24 Order	BR1 4 and BR1 5. DA1 5.	BR3 1. SE6 1 to SE6 3.	DA1 3.	25th July 2018
Articles 3(2)(s) and 4(2)(kk) and (ll) of the No. 24 Order	E6 1. E6 9. E12. E16. IG8 9.	E6 3. E7. E13. E18.	E6 5 to E6 7. E11 1 to E11 3. E15. E20 1 and E20 2.	25th July 2018
Articles 3(2)(t) and 4(2)(mm) and (nn) of the No. 24 Order	CA8 2. SR5 1.	CA9 3. SR6 0.	NE37 3. SR6 8 and SR6 9.	

Articles 3(2)(y) and 4(2)(ww) and (xx) of the No. 24 Order	E20 3.		25th July 2018

The Welfare Reform Act 2012 (Commencement No. 17, 19, 22, 23 and 24 and Transitional and Transitory Provisions (Modification) (No. 2)) Order 2018

SI 2018/881 (C.68)

Made 19th July 2018

5.157 *The Secretary of State for Work and Pensions makes the following Order in exercise of the powers conferred by section 150(3) and (4)(a), (b)(i) and (c) of the Welfare Reform Act 2012:*

ARRANGEMENT OF ARTICLES

GENERAL NOTE

5.158 This Commencement Order follows the same format and has the same effect as the Welfare Reform Act 2012 (Commencement No. 17, 19, 22, 23 and 24 and Transitional and Transitory Provisions (Modification)) Order 2018 (SI 2018/532) except for different postcode districts and part districts.

Citation

5.159 **1.** This Order may be cited as the Welfare Reform Act 2012 (Commencement No. 17, 19, 22, 23 and 24 and Transitional and Transitory Provisions (Modification) (No. 2)) Order 2018.

Interpretation

5.160 **2.**—(1) In this Order—
"claimant"—
(a) in relation to an employment and support allowance, has the same meaning as in Part 1 of the Welfare Reform Act 2007;
(b) in relation to a jobseeker's allowance, has the same meaning as in the Jobseekers Act 1995 (as it applies apart from the amendments

made by Part 1 of Schedule 14 to the Welfare Reform Act 2012 that remove references to an income-based jobseeker's allowance);

(c) in relation to universal credit, has the same meaning as in Part 1 of the Welfare Reform Act 2012;

"the Claims and Payments Regulations 1987" means the Social Security (Claims and Payments) Regulations 1987;

"employment and support allowance" means an employment and support allowance under Part 1 of the Welfare Reform Act 2007;

"jobseeker's allowance" means a jobseeker's allowance under the Jobseekers Act 1995;

"the No. 17 Order" means the Welfare Reform Act 2012 (Commencement No. 17 and Transitional and Transitory Provisions) Order 2014;

"the No. 19 Order" means the Welfare Reform Act 2012 (Commencement No. 19 and Transitional and Transitory Provisions and Commencement No. 9 and Transitional and Transitory Provisions (Amendment)) Order 2014;

"the No. 22 Order" means the Welfare Reform Act 2012 (Commencement No. 22 and Transitional and Transitory Provisions) Order 2015;

"the No. 23 Order" means the Welfare Reform Act 2012 (Commencement No. 23 and Transitional and Transitory Provisions) Order 2015;

"the No. 24 Order" means the Welfare Reform Act 2012 (Commencement No. 24 and Transitional and Transitory Provisions and Commencement No. 9 and Transitional and Transitory Provisions (Amendment)) Order 2015.

(2) For the purposes of this Order, the Universal Credit, Personal Independence Payment, Jobseeker's Allowance and Employment and Support Allowance (Claims and Payments) Regulations 2013 apply for the purpose of deciding—

(a) whether a claim for universal credit is made; and

(b) the date on which the claim is made.

(3) For the purposes of this Order, the Claims and Payments Regulations 1987 apply, subject to paragraphs (4) and (5), for the purposes of deciding—

(a) whether a claim for an employment and support allowance or a jobseeker's allowance is made; and

(b) the date on which the claim is made or treated as made.

(4) Subject to paragraph (5), for the purposes of this Order—

(a) a person makes a claim for an employment and support allowance or a jobseeker's allowance if that person takes any action which results in a decision on a claim being required under the Claims and Payments Regulations 1987; and

(b) it is irrelevant that the effect of any provision of those Regulations is that, for the purposes of those Regulations, the claim is made or treated as made at a date that is earlier than the date on which that action is taken.

(5) Where, by virtue of—

(a) regulation 6(1F)(b) or (c) of the Claims and Payments Regulations 1987, in the case of a claim for an employment and support allowance; or

(b) regulation 6(4ZA) to (4ZD) and (4A)(a)(i) and (b) of those Regulations, in the case of a claim for a jobseeker's allowance,

a claim for an employment and support allowance or a jobseeker's allowance is treated as made at a date that is earlier than the date on which the action referred to in paragraph (4)(a) is taken, the claim is treated as made on that earlier date.

Modification of the No. 17 Order, the No. 19 Order, the No. 22 Order and the No. 24 Order: removal of the gateway conditions

5.161   **3.** The provisions specified in the first column of the table in the Schedule have effect as though the reference in those provisions to meeting the gateway conditions were omitted, in respect of a claim for universal credit that is made, or a claim for an employment and support allowance or a jobseeker's allowance that is made or treated as made, by reference to the claimant's residence in any postcode district or part-district specified in the corresponding entry in the second column, on or after the date specified in the corresponding entry in the third column.

Modifications of the No. 17 Order, the No. 19 Order, the No. 22 Order and the No. 24 Order in consequence of removal of the gateway conditions

5.162   **4.**—(1) This article applies in respect of claims in relation to which provisions of the No. 17 Order, the No. 19 Order, the No. 22 Order and the No. 24 Order are modified by article 3.

(2) Where this article applies, the following modifications also have effect—

(a) those made to the No. 17 Order by article 10(2) of the Welfare Reform Act 2012 (Commencement No. 29 and Commencement No. 17, 19, 22, 23 and 24 and Transitional and Transitory Provisions (Modification)) Order 2017; and

(b) those made to the No. 19 Order, the No. 22 Order and the No. 24 Order by articles 13(2), 14(2) and 15(2) respectively of the Welfare Reform Act 2012 (Commencement No. 19, 22, 23 and 24 and Transitional and Transitory Provisions (Modification)) Order 2016.

Modification of the No. 23 Order: claims for housing benefit, income support or a tax credit

5.163   **5.**—(1) This article applies to claims in relation to which the provisions referred to in paragraph (2)(a) to (d) are modified by article 3.

(2) Where this article applies, article 7 of the No. 23 Order (prevention of claims for housing benefit, income support or a tax credit) applies as though the reference in paragraph (1) of that article to article 3(1) and (2)(a) to (c) of that Order included a reference to—

(a) paragraph (1) and sub-paragraphs (c) and (i) of paragraph (2) of article 3 of the No. 17 Order;

(b) paragraph (1) and sub-paragraphs (b) to (h) and (j) to (n) of paragraph (2) of article 3 of the No. 19 Order;

(c) paragraph (1) and sub-paragraphs (a), (c) to (e), (g) to (k), (m) to (q), and (t) of paragraph (2) of article 3 of the No. 22 Order; and

(d) paragraph (1) and sub-paragraphs (a) to (d), (f) to (y), (aa) and (cc) of paragraph (2) of article 3 of the No. 24 Order.

SCHEDULE

POSTCODE DISTRICTS AND PART-DISTRICTS
WHERE GATEWAY CONDITIONS REMOVED

5.164

Provisions modified	Postcodes			Date
Articles 3(2)(i) and 4(2)(q) and (r) of the No. 22 Order	SW11 2 SW15 9	SW15 2 SW17 6 and SW17 7	SW15 4 SW18 1 to SW18 3	5th September 2018
Articles 3(2)(j) and 4(2)(s) and (t) of the No. 22 Order	CF81 NP11 3 and NP11 4 NP24	CF83 2 to CF83 4 NP11 6 and NP11 7	CF83 8 and CF83 9 NP12 0 to NP12 3	5th September 2018
Articles 3(2)(a) and 4(2)(a) and (b) of the No. 24 Order	CF82			5th September 2018
Articles 3(2)(f) and 4(2)(k) and (l) of the No. 24 Order	NP11 5	NP22 5		5th September 2018
Articles 3(2)(g) and 4(2)(m) and (n) of the No. 24 Order	SW15 1	SW15 3	SW15 5 and SW15 6	5th September 2018
Articles 3(2)(h) and 4(2)(o) and (p) of the No. 24 Order	EX7 SA63 SA66 SA69 SA72 TQ7 TQ10 TQ12 5 and TQ12 6	SA61 SA64 SA67 SA70 SA73 TQ8 TQ11 TQ13	SA62 SA65 SA68 SA71 TQ6 TQ9 TQ12 1 to TQ12 3 TQ14	5th September 2018
Articles 3(2)(i) and 4(2)(q) and (r) of the No. 24 Order	HP9 HP12 HP15 SL2 3 and SL2 4 SL9 7 to SL9 9	HP10 HP13 HP16 SL7	HP11 HP14 SL0 SL9 1	5th September 2018
Articles 3(2)(j) and 4(2)(s) and (t) of the No. 24 Order	SL9 0			5th September 2018
Articles 3(2)(l) and 4(2)(w) and (x) of the No. 24 Order	BS9 2 to BS9 4	BS10 5	BS11	5th September 2018

Articles 3(2)(n) and 4(2)(aa) and (bb) of the No. 24 Order	BS7 0 BS34	BS10 6 and BS10 7 BS35	BS32	5th September 2018
Articles 3(2)(o) and 4(2)(cc) and (dd) of the No. 24 Order	SW17 0	SW18 4 and SW18 5	SW19 6	5th September 2018
Articles 3(2)(p) and 4(2)(ee) and (ff) of the No. 24 Order	TQ1 TQ4	TQ2 TQ5	TQ3 TQ12 4	5th September 2018
Articles 3(2)(x) and 4(2)(uu) and (vv) of the No. 24 Order	CF83 1			5th September 2018
Articles 3(2)(g) and 4(2)(m) and (n) of the No. 22 Order	IP24 PE21	IP27 0 PE22 9	PE20 1 and PE 20 2	12th September 2018
Articles 3(2)(n) and 4(2)(aa) and (bb) of the No. 22 Order	SK13 SK23	SK17 6 and SK17 7	SK22	12th September 2018
Articles 3(2)(a) and 4(2)(a) and (b) of the No. 24 Order	NR16 2			12th September 2018
Articles 3(2)(c) and 4(2)(e) and (f) of the No. 24 Order	NG15 9 NG19 6 NG21	NG18 NG19 9 NG22 8 and NG22 9	NG19 0 NG20 0 NG70	12th September 2018
Articles 3(2)(f) and 4(2)(k) and (l) of the No. 24 Order	B60 B78 1 HR8 2 WR13	B61 CV9 HR8 9 WR14	B76 0 CV13 6 WR8 0	12th September 2018
Articles 3(2)(g) and 4(2)(m) and (n) of the No. 24 Order	LN11 PE22 0	LN12 1 PE22 7	LN13 0	12th September 2018
Articles 3(2)(j) and 4(2)(s) and (t) of the No. 24 Order	DE4 SK17 0	DE45 SK17 8 and SK17 9	NG19 7	12th September 2018
Articles 3(2)(k) and 4(2)(u) and (v) of the No. 24 Order	DN10 4 PE20 3	DN21	LN8 6	12th September 2018

Articles 3(2)(u) and 4(2)(oo) and (pp) of the No. 24 Order	CB6 3	CB7		12th September 2018
Articles 3(2)(w) and 4(2)(ss) and (tt) of the No. 24 Order	CB6 1 and CB6 2 PE14	IP26 PE15	PE13 PE16	12th September 2018
Articles 3(2)(o) and 4(2)(cc) and (dd) of the No. 22 Order	G51 1 to G51 3	G51 9	G52 1	19th September 2018
Articles 3(2)(q) and 4(2)(gg) and (hh) of the No. 22 Order	G51 4 PA1 PA2 9 PA5 PA8 PA12	G52 2 to G52 4 PA2 PA3 PA6 PA9	G52 9 PA2 6 and PA2 7 PA4 PA7 PA10	19th September 2018
Articles 3(2)(s) and 4(2)(kk) and (ll) of the No. 24 Order	PA2 8			19th September 2018
Articles 3(2)(v) and 4(2)(qq) and (rr) of the No. 24 Order	G83 7 PA21 PA24 PA27 PA30 PA33 PA36 PA41 PA44 PA47 PA60 PA63 PA66 PA69 PA72 PA75 PA78	G84 PA22 PA25 PA28 PA31 PA34 PA37 PA42 PA45 PA48 PA61 PA64 PA67 PA70 PA73 PA76	PA20 PA23 PA26 PA29 PA32 PA35 PA38 PA43 PA46 PA49 PA62 PA65 PA68 PA71 PA74 PA77	19th September 2018
Articles 3(2)(i) and 4(2)(i) of the No. 17 Order	M27 0 M28	M27 5 M30	M27 8 and M27 9 M38	26th September 2018
Articles 3(2)(g) and 4(2)(g) of the No. 19 Order	L16 L18 3 and L18 4 L24 0 to L24 3 L26	L17 0 L18 6 to L18 9 L24 6 to L249 L27	L17 5 and L17 6 L19 L25	26th September 2018
Articles 3(2)(j) and 4(2)(j) of the No. 19 Order	L24 4 and L24 5			26th September 2018
Articles 3(2)(l) and 4(2)(l) of the No. 19 Order	M1 M5 M27 4	M2 M6 M27 6	M3 M7 1 to M7 3 M50	26th September 2018

Articles 3(2)(m) and 4(2)(m) of the No. 19 Order	LA5 0 LA8 LA11 9 M44	LA6 1 and LA6 2 LA9 LA22	LA7 LA11 6 LA23	26th September 2018
Articles 3(2)(k) and 4(2)(u) and (v) of the No. 22 Order	HS1 HS4 HS7 KW15 LA10 5 ZE3	HS2 HS5 HS8 KW16 ZE1	HS3 HS6 HS9 KW17 ZE2	26th September 2018
Articles 3(2)(n) and 4(2)(aa) and (bb) of the No. 22 Order	BN7 BN10	BN8 5 and BN8 6 BN25	BN9 TN22	26th September 2018
Articles 3(2)(o) and 4(2)(cc) and (dd) of the No. 22 Order	G5 G43 G53 6	G41 G44 5 G53 9	G42 G44 9	26th September 2018
Articles 3(2)(p) and 4(2)(ee) and (ff) of the No. 22 Order	TR21 TR24	TR22 TR25	TR23	26th September 2018
Articles 3(2)(a) and 4(2)(a) and (b) of the No. 24 Order	BN8 4			26th September 2018
Articles 3(2)(c) and 4(2)(e) and (f) of the No. 24 Order	G44 4			26th September 2018
Articles 3(2)(h) and 4(2)(o) and (p) of the No. 24 Order	EX1 EX4 EX8 EX18	EX2 EX5 EX9 EX20	EX3 EX6 EX17 EX21	26th September 2018
Articles 3(2)(i) and 4(2)(q) and (r) of the No. 24 Order	HP5 HP8 HP19 HP22 MK18	HP6 HP17 HP20 HP27	HP7 HP18 HP21 MK17 0	26th September 2018
Articles 3(2)(l) and 4(2)(w) and (x) of the No. 24 Order	BH21 6 BH25 SO42	BH23 8 BH31 SP6	BH24 SO41	26th September 2018
Articles 3(2)(s) and 4(2)(kk) and (ll) of the No. 24 Order	G44 3 G76 0 G78	G46 G76 6 to G76 8	G53 7 G77	26th September 2018
Articles 3(2)(y) and 4(2)(ww) and (xx) of the No. 24 Order	PO1 PO4 PO7	PO2 PO5 PO8	PO3 PO6	26th September 2018

Articles 3(2)(o) and 4(2)(cc) and (dd) of the No. 24 Order	SE7 SE9 9 SE12 2	SE9 1 SE10 0 and SE10 1 SE18	SE9 5 and SE9 6 SE10 9	3rd October 2018
Articles 3(2)(q) and 4(2)(gg) and (hh) of the No. 24 Order	CM21 0 and CM21 1 EN11 SG3 SG5 9 SG9 SG12	CM22 7 SG1 SG4 SG6 SG10 SG13	CM23 SG2 SG5 1 and SG5 2 SG8 1 SG11 SG14	3rd October 2018
Articles 3(2)(r) and 4(2)(ii) and (jj) of the No. 24 Order	SE3 SE12 0 TS1 TS4 TS8	SE9 2 to SE9 4 SE12 8 and SE12 9 TS2 TS5	SE10 8 SE28 TS3 TS7 8	3rd October 2018
Articles 3(2)(u) and 4(2)(oo) and (pp) of the No. 24 Order	SG7	SG8 5	SG8 8 and SG8 9	3rd October 2018
Articles 3(2)(y) and 4(2)(ww) and (xx) of the No. 24 Order	E2 E9	E5 N1 4 to N1 7	E8 N16	3rd October 2018
Articles 3(2)(f) and 4(2)(k) and (l) of the No. 24 Order	LD1 LD4 LD7 LL36 SY15 SY18 SY21	LD2 LD5 LD8 SA9 SY16 SY19 SY22	LD3 LD6 LL35 SY10 0 SY17 SY20 9	10th October 2018
Articles 3(2)(h) and 4(2)(o) and (p) of the No. 24 Order	SY20 8			10th October 2018
Articles 3(2)(k) and 4(2)(u) and (v) of the No. 24 Order	LS29 0	LS29 7 to LS29 9		10th October 2018
Articles 3(2)(q) and 4(2)(gg) and (hh) of the No. 24 Order	BD3 7 LS1 LS4 LS7 LS10 LS13 LS16 LS18 LS21 LS24 8 and LS24 9 LS26 0 LS29 6	BD4 8 LS2 LS5 LS8 LS11 LS14 LS17 1 LS19 LS22 LS25 3 LS27 WF3 2	BD11 1 LS3 LS6 LS9 LS12 LS15 LS17 5 to LS17 9 LS20 LS23 LS25 5 LS28	10th October 2018

Articles 3(2)(t) and 4(2)(mm) and (nn) of the No. 24 Order	CF61 CF64	CF62 CF71	CF63	10th October 2018
Articles 3(2)(aa) and 4(2)(aaa) and (bbb) of the No. 24 Order	LS26 8	WF3 1		10th October 2018
Articles 3(2)(g) and 4(2)(m) and (n) of the No. 22 Order	IP11 IP13 6 IP16	IP12 IP13 9 IP17	IP13 0 IP15	17th October 2018
Articles 3(2)(n) and 4(2)(aa) and (bb) of the No. 22 Order	NN14 2 NN16 0	NN14 6 NN16 8 and NN16 9	NN15	17th October 2018
Articles 3(2)(q) and 4(2)(gg) and (hh) of the No. 22 Order	WS3 4 WS9 9	WS7 4	WS8 6	17th October 2018
Articles 3(2)(b) and 4(2)(c) and (d) of the No. 24 Order	IP13 7 and IP13 8 NR26	NR11 8 NR27	NR25	17th October 2018
Articles 3(2)(c) and 4(2)(e) and (f) of the No. 24 Order	B94 CV23 8 CV33 CV47 NN16 6	CV8 1 and CV8 2 CV31 CV34 NN14 1 WR1	CV23 0 CV32 CV35 8 NN14 3 and NN14 4 WR4 9	17th October 2018
Articles 3(2)(d) and 4(2)(g) and (h) of the No. 24 Order	WR3 WR7	WR4 0 WR9 0	WR5 1 WR9 8 and WR9 9	17th October 2018
Articles 3(2)(f) and 4(2)(k) and (l) of the No. 24 Order	WR2 WR9 7	WR5 2 and WR5 3 WR6		17th October 2018
Articles 3(2)(g) and 4(2)(m) and (n) of the No. 24 Order	NG16 1			17th October 2018
Articles 3(2)(l) and 4(2)(w) and (x) of the No. 24 Order	CV35 7 NR3 NR6 NR9 NR12 7 and NR12 8 NR15 1 NR18	NR1 NR4 NR7 NR10 NR13 4 to NR13 6 NR16 1 WS8 7	NR2 NR5 NR8 NR11 7 NR14 NR17	17th October 2018
Articles 3(2)(r) and 4(2)(ii) and (jj) of the No. 24 Order	WV12	WV13		17th October 2018

Articles 3(2)(s) and 4(2)(kk) and (ll) of the No. 24 Order	LE12 6 NG3 NG6 NG11 NG14 5	NG1 NG4 NG7 NG12 NG15 5 to NG15 8	NG2 NG5 1 and NG5 2 NG8 NG13 8 and NG13 9	17th October 2018
Articles 3(2)(u) and 4(2)(oo) and (pp) of the No. 24 Order	CB1 CB4 CB22 CB25 9 PE27 PE28 4 and PE28 5 SG8 0	CB2 CB5 CB23 PE19 PE28 0 PE28 9 SG8 6 and SG8 7	CB3 CB21 5 and CB21 6 CB24 PE26 1 PE28 2 PE29	17th October 2018
Articles 3(2)(w) and 4(2)(ss) and (tt) of the No. 24 Order	PE26 2	PE28 3		17th October 2018
Articles 3(2)(g) and 4(2)(m) and (n) of the No. 24 Order	HA4 UB7 UB10	UB3 UB8 UB11	UB4 UB9 4 and UB9 5	24th October 2018
Articles 3(2)(j) and 4(2)(s) and (t) of the No. 24 Order	UB9 6			24th October 2018
Articles 3(2)(l) and 4(2)(w) and (x) of the No. 24 Order	PO33 PO36	PO34 PO37	PO35	24th October 2018
Articles 3(2)(n) and 4(2)(aa) and (bb) of the No. 24 Order	BS15 BS30 GL9	BS16 4 to BS16 7 BS36 GL12 8	BS16 9 BS37 GL13	24th October 2018
Articles 3(2)(r) and 4(2)(ii) and (jj) of the No. 24 Order	DA1 4 DA7 DA15 DA18 GU14 GU34 9 GU52	DA5 DA8 DA16 GU11 GU30 GU35 SE2	DA6 DA14 DA17 GU12 4 GU34 1 to GU34 3 GU51	24th October 2018
Articles 3(2)(s) and 4(2)(kk) and (ll) of the No. 24 Order	CR3 6 and CR3 7 GU3 1 and GU3 2 GU6 GU9 GU26 KT18 KT21 KT23 RH2 RH5 RH7 6 SM7 1 and SM7 2	GU1 GU4 8 GU7 GU10 GU27 KT19 KT22 2 KT24 RH3 RH6 0 RH8 SM7 9	GU2 GU5 GU8 GU12 6 KT17 KT20 KT22 7 to KT22 9 RH1 RH4 RH6 7 to RH6 9 RH9	24th October 2018

Articles 3(2)(t) and 4(2)(mm) and (nn) of the No. 24 Order	LU1	LU2	LU5 5 and LU5 6	24th October 2018
Articles 3(2)(u) and 4(2)(oo) and (pp) of the No. 24 Order	GU3 3 GU21 GU24	GU4 7 GU22 KT14 6	GU12 5 GU23	24th October 2018
Articles 3(2)(w) and 4(2)(ss) and (tt) of the No. 24 Order	N8 N17	N10 N22	N15 3 to N15 5	24th October 2018
Articles 3(2)(y) and 4(2)(ww) and (xx) of the No. 24 Order	GU34 4 and GU34 5 N15 6			24th October 2018
Articles 3(2)(o) and 4(2)(cc) and (dd) of the No. 22 Order	G1 2 G4 G13 G21 G33 6	G2 G11 G14 G22	G3 G12 G20 G23	31st October 2018
Articles 3(2)(i) and 4(2)(q) and (r) of the No. 24 Order	AB10 AB13 AB16 AB23 AB31 AB34 AB39 AB51	AB11 AB14 AB21 AB24 AB32 AB35 AB41 6 and AB41 7 AB52	AB12 AB15 AB22 AB25 AB33 AB36 AB41 9 AB53 8	31st October 2018
Articles 3(2)(m) and 4(2)(y) and (z) of the No. 24 Order	G61	G62	G64 1 to G64 3	31st October 2018
Articles 3(2)(c) and 4(2)(c) of the No. 17 Order	BL1 BL4 BL6 4	BL2 BL5 1 BL6 9	BL3 BL5 3 M26 3	7th November 2018
Articles 3(2)(b) and 4(2)(b) of the No. 19 Order	L15	L18 0 to L18 2	L18 5	7th November 2018
Articles 3(2)(c) and 4(2)(c) of the No. 19 Order	L1 L6 0 and L6 1 L7 L17 7 to L17 9	L2 L6 3 and L6 4 L8	L3 L6 6 to L6 9 L17 1 to L17 4	7th November 2018
Articles 3(2)(e) and 4(2)(e) of the No. 19 Order	BL5 2			7th November 2018
Articles 3(2)(k) and 4(2)(k) of the No. 19 Order	BL6 5 to BL6 7	BL7		7th November 2018

Articles 3(2)(o) and 4(2)(cc) and (dd) of the No. 24 Order	S1 S4 S6 3 S9 S12 S32 S35 8 and S35 9	S2 S5 0 S7 S10 S14 S33	S3 S5 5 to S5 7 S8 S11 S17 S35 0 to S35 4	7th November 2018
Articles 3(2)(t) and 4(2)(mm) and (nn) of the No. 24 Order	NE20 NE61 NE65 7 and NE65 8 NE67 NE70 TD15	NE23 NE63 NE66 5 NE68 NE71	NE25 0 NE64 NE66 9 NE69 TD12	7th November 2018
Articles 3(2)(x) and 4(2)(uu) and (vv) of the No. 24 Order	CF37 CF40 CF43 CF72	CF38 CF41 CF44	CF39 CF42 CF45	7th November 2018
Articles 3(2)(n) and 4(2)(aa) and (bb) of the No. 22 Order	TF1 TF4 TF7	TF2 TF5 TF8	TF3 TF6 TF10 7	14th November 2018
Articles 3(2)(q) and 4(2)(gg) and (hh) of the No. 22 Order	NG5 0	NG5 7		14th November 2018
Articles 3(2)(a) and 4(2)(a) and (b) of the No. 24 Order	SY7 9			14th November 2018
Articles 3(2)(d) and 4(2)(g) and (h) of the No. 24 Order	DY10 1 and DY10 2 DY12 1 DY14 0 WR12	DY10 4 DY12 3 WR10	DY11 6 and DY11 7 DY13 8 and DY13 9 WR11	14th November 2018
Articles 3(2)(f) and 4(2)(k) and (l) of the No. 24 Order	DY12 2 WR8 9	DY13 0 WR15	DY14 8 and DY14 9	14th November 2018
Articles 3(2)(g) and 4(2)(m) and (n) of the No. 24 Order	NG9 1	NG9 3 to NG9 9		14th November 2018
Articles 3(2)(i) and 4(2)(q) and (r) of the No. 24 Order	B21 8 B66 B69 DY4	B43 5 and B43 6 B67 B70 WS5 4	B65 9 B68 B71 WS10 0	14th November 2018
Articles 3(2)(j) and 4(2)(s) and (t) of the No. 24 Order	MK16 8 NN2 NN5 NN12 OX17	MK19 NN3 NN7 1 to NN7 3 NN13 6 and NN13 7 WS10 7	NN1 NN4 NN7 9 NN13 9 WS10 9	14th November 2018

Articles 3(2)(k) and 4(2)(u) and (v) of the No. 24 Order	LN4 3 and LN4 4	LN10 6	NG32 3	14th November 2018
Articles 3(2)(l) and 4(2)(w) and (x) of the No. 24 Order	DY10 3	DY11 5	TF10 8 and TF10 9	14th November 2018
Articles 3(2)(s) and 4(2)(kk) and (ll) of the No. 24 Order	NG5 3 to NG5 6 NG4 6	NG5 8 and NG5 9	NG9 2	14th November 2018
Articles 3(2)(w) and 4(2)(ss) and (tt) of the No. 24 Order	PE30 PE33 PE36	PE31 6 and PE31 7 PE34 PE38	PE32 1 PE35	14th November 2018
Articles 3(2)(d) and 4(2)(d) of the No. 19 Order	BB4 BB9 4 and BB9 5 BB18 9 OL13	BB8 BB9 7 to BB9 9 BL0 O	BB9 0 BB18 5 OL12 8	21st November 2018
Articles 3(2)(j) and 4(2)(j) of the No. 19 Order	SK1 SK4 SK7	SK2 SK5 SK8	SK3 SK6 SK12	21st November 2018
Articles 3(2)(k) and 4(2)(k) of the No. 19 Order	BB9 6			21st November 2018
Articles 3(2)(n) and 4(2)(n) of the No. 19 Order	BB7			21st November 2018
Articles 3(2)(a) and 4(2)(a) and (b) of the No. 22 Order	BB18 6			21st November 2018
Articles 3(2)(c) and 4(2)(e) and (f) of the No. 22 Order	NW2 1 NW6 9	NW2 4 to NW2 7 NW6 6 and NW6 7 NW10 2 and NW10 3 NW10 8 and NW10 9		21st November 2018
Articles 3(2)(e) and 4(2)(i) and (j) of the No. 22 Order	ME14 ME17 1	ME15 ME16 8 ME17 3 and ME17 4 ME18 6		21st November 2018
Articles 3(2)(g) and 4(2)(m) and (n) of the No. 22 Order	ME17 2			21st November 2018
Articles 3(2)(h) and 4(2)(o) and (p) of the No. 22 Order	DE13 0 ST14 7	DE13 8 ST14 9	DE14	21st November 2018

Articles 3(2)(q) and 4(2)(gg) and (hh) of the No. 22 Order	NG15 0	NG17 0 to NG17 3	NG17 5 to NG17 9	21st November 2018
Articles 3(2)(t) and 4(2)(mm) and (nn) of the No. 22 Order	NW10 4	NW10 7		21st November 2018
Articles 3(2)(a) and 4(2)(a) and (b) of the No. 24 Order	TN12 9			21st November 2018
Articles 3(2)(b) and 4(2)(c) and (d) of the No. 24 Order	NN8 2 to NN8 6	NN8 9		21st November 2018
Articles 3(2)(c) and 4(2)(e) and (f) of the No. 24 Order	NG17 4 NN29	NN8 1	NN9 5	21st November 2018
Articles 3(2)(d) and 4(2)(g) and (h) of the No. 24 Order	ME6 ME18 5 TN1 TN3 8 TN10 TN13 TN15 8 and TN15 9 TN27 9	ME16 0 ME19 TN2 TN4 TN11 TN14 5 and TN14 6 TN17	ME16 9 ME20 TN 3 0 TN9 TN12 5 to TN12 8 TN15 0 TN18	21st November 2018
Articles 3(2)(f) and 4(2)(k) and (l) of the No. 24 Order	DE11 DE13 9 ST15 ST17 9 ST21	DE12 6 DE15 ST16 ST18 0	DE12 8 ST14 8 ST17 4 ST20	21st November 2018
Articles 3(2)(h) and 4(2)(o) and (p) of the No. 24 Order	NW10 5	W10 4		21st November 2018
Articles 3(2)(j) and 4(2)(s) and (t) of the No. 24 Order	DE6 5 NN6 0	NG19 8 ST14 5	NG20 8 and NG20 9	21st November 2018
Articles 3(2)(l) and 4(2)(w) and (x) of the No. 24 Order	ST17 0 WS6 WS15 1 and Ws15 2	ST18 9 WS11 WS15 4	ST19 WS12 WS15 9	21st November 2018
Articles 3(2)(o) and 4(2)(cc) and (dd) of the No. 24 Order	TN16 1			21st November 2018

Articles 3(2)(p) and 4(2)(ee) and (ff) of the No. 24 Order	DE73 5	DE73 8		21st November 2018
Articles 3(2)(r) and 4(2)(ii) and (jj) of the No. 24 Order	WV11 9			21st November 2018
Articles 3(2)(s) and 4(2)(kk) and (ll) of the No. 24 Order	TN8	TN16 2		21st November 2018
Articles 3(2)(t) and 4(2)(mm) and (nn) of the No. 24 Order	LU3 LU6 SG15 SG18	LU4 LU7 SG16 SG19 1	LU5 4 SG5 3 and SG5 4 SG17	21st November 2018
Articles 3(2)(u) and 4(2)(oo) and (pp) of the No. 24 Order	SG19 2 and SG19 3			21st November 2018
Articles 3(2)(w) and 4(2)(ss) and (tt) of the No. 24 Order	NW2 2 and NW2 3 W9 3	NW61 and NW6 2	NW6 5	21st November 2018
Articles 3(2)(d) and 4(2)(gg) and (hh) of the No. 22 Order	EH1 EH4 EH7 EH10 4 to EH10 6 EH12 EH15 G60 G82 1 to G82 4 G83 3	EH2 EH5 EH8 EH10 9 EH13 EH16 5 and EH16 6 G81 1 to G81 4 G82 9	EH3 EH6 EH9 EH11 EH14 EH17 7 G81 6 G83 0	28th November 2018
Articles 3(2)(i) and 4(2)(q) and (r) of the No. 22 Order	EH10 7	EH16 4	EH17 8	28th November 2018
Articles 3(2)(m) and 4(2)(y) and (z) of the No. 22 Order	G83 9			28th November 2018
Articles 3(2)(i) and 4(2)(q) and (r) of the No. 24 Order	EH30			28th November 2018
Articles 3(2)(m) and 4(2)(y) and (z) of the No. 24 Order	G81 5			28th November 2018

Articles 3(2)(r) and 4(2)(ii) and (jj) of the No. 24 Order	GU31	GU32	GU33	28th November 2018
Articles 3(2)(u) and 4(2)(oo) and (pp) of the No. 24 Order	GU15 GU18 GU25 KT7 KT11 KT14 7 KT16 TW16 TW19	GU16 GU19 GU46 KT8 KT12 KT14 9 KT22 0 TW17 TW20	GU17 GU20 GU47 7 and GU47 8 KT10 KT13 KT15 TW15 TW18	28th November 2018
Articles 3(2)(v) and 4(2)(qq) and (rr) of the No. 24 Order	G63 0	G82 5	G83 8	28th November 2018
Articles 3(2)(w) and 4(2)(ss) and (tt) of the No. 24 Order	TS6 TS9 6 TS12	TS7 0 TS10 TS13	TS7 9 TS11 TS14	28th November 2018
Articles 3(2)(y) and 4(2)(ww) and (xx) of the No. 24 Order	PO9 PO12 PO15 SO31 0 and SO31 1 SO32 3	PO10 7 PO13 PO16 SO31 6 and SO31 7	PO11 PO14 PO17 SO31 9	28th November 2018
Articles 3(2)(aa) and 4(2)(aaa) and (bbb) of the No. 24 Order	LS25 1 and LS25 2 LS26 9 WF3 3 and WF3 4 WF6 WF9	LS25 4 WF1 WF4 WF7 WF10	LS25 7 WF2 WF5 WF8 WF11	28th November 2018
Articles 3(2)(c) and 4(2)(c) of the No. 19 Order	L4 0 to L4 4 L62	L4 7 L6 5	L5	5th December 2018
Articles 3(2)(f) and 4(2)(f) of the No. 19 Order	L4 6	L4 8 and L4 9	L11	5th December 2018
Articles 3(2)(g) and 4(2)(g) of the No. 19 Order	L12	L13		5th December 2018
Articles 3(2)(h) and 4(2)(h) of the No. 19 Order	FY5	FY6	FY7	5th December 2018
Articles 3(2)(m) and 4(2)(m) of the No. 19 Order	FY1 FY4 LA12 LA15 LA18 LA21	FY2 FY8 LA13 LA16 LA19 PR4 1 to PR4 3	FY3 LA11 7 LA14 LA17 LA20	5th December 2018

Articles 3(2)(c) and 4(2)(e) and (f) of the No. 22 Order	HA0 2 to HA0 4	HA9	NW10 0 and NW10 1	5th December 2018
Articles 3(2)(o) and 4(2)(cc) and (dd) of the No. 22 Order	G1 1 G15 G33 1 to G33 5 G40 G69 6 to G69 8	G1 3 to G1 5 G31 G33 9 G45	G1 9 G32 G34 G69 1	5th December 2018
Articles 3(2)(t) and 4(2)(mm) and (nn) of the No. 22 Order	HA0 1			5th December 2018
Articles 3(2)(a) and 4(2)(a) and (b) of the No. 24 Order	HP1 LL58 LL62 LL65 LL68 LL71 LL74 LL77 7 and L77 8 WD7	HP2 LL60 LL63 LL66 LL69 LL72 LL75 LL78	HP3 9 LL61 LL64 LL67 LL70 LL73 LL76 WD6	5th December 2018
Articles 3(2)(b) and 4(2)(c) and (d) of the No. 24 Order	CM0 CM1 9 CM9 4 and CM9 5	CM1 to CM1 3 CM2 CM9 8	CM1 6 and CM1 7 CM3 5 to CM3 8 CM11 1	5th December 2018
Articles 3(2)(c) and 4(2)(e) and (f) of the No. 24 Order	CM1 4 CM9 6	CM3 1	CM3 3 and CM3 4	5th December 2018
Articles 3(2)(f) and 4(2)(k) and (l) of the No. 24 Order	LL59	LL77 9		5th December 2018
Articles 3(2)(h) and 4(2)(o) and (p) of the No. 24 Order	SA35 SA38 SA43 SA45 SA48 SY25	SA36 SA41 SA44 6 SA46 SY23	SA37 SA42 SA44 9 SA47 SY24	5th December 2018
Articles 3(2)(i) and 4(2)(q) and (r) of the No. 24 Order	HP4 2 and HP4 3 MK2 MK5 MK8 MK11 MK14 MK16 6	HP23 MK3 MK6 MK9 MK12 MK15 MK16 9	MK1 MK4 MK7 MK10 MK13 MK16 0 MK46	5th December 2018
Articles 3(2)(j) and 4(2)(s) and (t) of the No. 24 Order	HP3 0	HP3 8		5th December 2018

Articles 3(2)(q) and 4(2)(gg) and (hh) of the No. 24 Order	CM5 EN9 3	CM16 IG10	EN9 1	5th December 2018
Articles 3(2)(s) and 4(2)(kk) and (ll) of the No. 24 Order	IG7 5 and IG7 6	IG9	RM4	5th December 2018
Articles 3(2)(t) and 4(2)(mm) and (nn) of the No. 24 Order	HP4 1	MK17 8 and MK17 9		5th December 2018
Articles 3(2)(w) and 4(2)(ss) and (tt) of the No. 24 Order	NW1 0 NW5	NW1 7 to NW1 9 NW6 3 and NW6 4	NW3	5th December 2018
Articles 3(2)(g) and 4(2)(m) and (n) of the No. 22 Order	CB8 1	IP28 6 and IP28 7		12th December 2018
Articles 3(2)(h) and 4(2)(o) and (p) of the No. 22 Order	CW2 5 ST5 5 to ST5 9	CW3 9 ST7 1	ST5 2 and ST5 3 ST7 8	12th December 2018
Articles 3(2)(n) and 4(2)(aa) and (bb) of the No. 22 Order	ST7 3	ST8 6	ST8 9	12th December 2018
Articles 3(2)(b) and 4(2)(c) and (d) of the No. 24 Order	NR12 0 NR21 7 and NR21 8	NR12 9 NR24	NR21 0 NR28	12th December 2018
Articles 3(2)(f) and 4(2)(k) and (l) of the No. 24 Order	LL23 LL39 LL42 LL45 LL48 LL52 LL55 SA14 SA17 SA20 SA33	LL37 LL40 LL43 LL46 LL49 LL53 LL56 SA15 SA18 SA31 ST5 4	LL38 LL41 LL44 LL47 LL51 LL54 LL57 SA16 SA19 SA32	12th December 2018
Articles 3(2)(h) and 4(2)(o) and (p) of the No. 24 Order	SA34 SA44 4 and SA44 5	SA39	SA40	12th December 2018
Articles 3(2)(l) and 4(2)(w) and (x) of the No. 24 Order	NR11 6			12th December 2018

Articles 3(2)(o) and 4(2)(cc) and (dd) of the No. 24 Order	S5 8 and S5 9 S6 9 S36 1 to S36 4	S6 1 and S6 2 S13	S6 4 to S6 6 S20	12th December 2018
Articles 3(2)(q) and 4(2)(gg) and (hh) of the No. 24 Order	ST4 4 to ST4 9 ST7 4	ST5 0 and ST5 1 ST8 7	ST6 5	12th December 2018
Articles 3(2)(t) and 4(2)(mm) and (nn) of the No. 24 Order	CA8 7 NE24 NE43 NE46 NE49 NE65 9	NE19 NE26 4 NE44 NE47 NE62 NE66 1 to NE66 4	NE22 NE42 5 and NE42 6 NE45 NE48 NE65 0	12th December 2018
Articles 3(2)(u) and 4(2)(oo) and (pp) of the No. 24 Order	CB8 0 HU1 HU4 6 HU6 HU9 HU16 IP28 8	CB8 7 to CB8 9 HU2 HU4 9 HU7 HU11 HU19	CB25 0 HU3 HU5 HU8 HU12 HU20	12th December 2018
Articles 3(2)(w) and 4(2)(ss) and (tt) of the No. 24 Order	IP27 9 NR23	NR21 9 PE31 8	NR22	12th December 2018
Articles 3(2)(cc) and 4(2)(eee) and (fff) of the No. 24 Order	All further postcode districts and part-districts in England and Wales, and Scotland			12th December 2018

The Welfare Reform Act 2012 (Commencement No. 31 and Savings and Transitional Provisions and Commencement No. 21 and 23 and Transitional and Transitory Provisions (Amendment)) Order 2019

SI 2019/37

Made 14th January 2019

5.165   *The Secretary of State for Work and Pensions makes the following Order in exercise of the powers conferred by section 150(3) and (4)(a), (b)(i) and (c) of the Welfare Reform Act 2012*

ARRANGEMENT OF ARTICLES

GENERAL NOTE

Articles 1 and 2 of this Commencement Order are introductory and arts. 3 and 4 are concerned with state pension credit and do not directly affect this volume. Article 5 amends art.6(3)(a) of the No.21 and art.7(4)(a) of the No.23 Commencement Orders relating to the introduction of universal credit to supplement the provisions of those Orders that prevent claims to housing benefit by a member of a mixed-age couple of state pension credit qualifying age. Claims are prevented in the same cases as that member is excluded from entitlement to state pension credit, allowing for the savings cases in art.4(1) whilst they continue under art.4(2). Articles 6 and 7 make transitional provision in housing benefit cases and for parties to a polygamous marriage.

5.166

The High Court has ruled that the exclusion of mixed-age couples from pension credit is neither discriminatory nor in breach of the public sector equality duty (PSED): see *R (on the application of Prichard) v SSWP* [2020] EWHC 1495 (Admin), where the claimant was due to reach state pension age on July 6, 2020, but his wife would not do so for a further 6 years. As a result of the changes outlined above, the couple would have to continue to claim working-age benefits until 2026 and would be £65,000 worse off than they would have been had the changes not been made. Both the claimant and his wife had serious illnesses and were in receipt of disability benefits. The couple would be classed as a 'no-conditionality mixed-age couple' as the claimant was over pension age and his wife received carer's allowance (and so she would not be subject to any work-related requirements). On the application for judicial review, Laing J held that the Secretary of State had had appropriate regard to the relevant equality needs under the PSED (see further Equality Act 2010, s.149). She further held that the policy in question, in its application to no-conditionality mixed-age couples, was not manifestly without reasonable foundation. It followed that "the differential treatment of which the claimant complains is not a breach of article 14 (whether read with article 8 or with A1P1), and, therefore, that the 2019 Order, which provides for the commencement of paragraph 64 of the 2012 Act (and by that route, of section 4(1A) of the SPCA) is not incompatible with the claimant's Convention rights" (at [136]).

Citation

1. This Order may be cited as the Welfare Reform Act 2012 (Commencement No. 31 and Savings and Transitional Provisions and Commencement No. 21 and 23 and Transitional and Transitory Provisions (Amendment)) Order 2019.

5.167

Interpretation

2.—(1) In this Order—
[1"the 1992 Act" means the Social Security Contributions and Benefits Act 1992;]
"the 2002 Act" means the State Pension Credit Act 2002;
"the 2012 Act" means the Welfare Reform Act 2012;

5.168

"the appointed day" means the day referred to in article 3;
[¹...];
[²"assessment period", in relation to universal credit entitlement, has the same meaning as in regulation 21 of the Universal Credit Regulations 2013;]
"the Housing Benefit SPC Regulations" means the Housing Benefit (Persons who have attained the qualifying age for state pension credit) Regulations 2006;
"the No. 21 Order" means the Welfare Reform Act 2012 (Commencement No. 21 and Transitional and Transitory Provisions) Order 2015;
"the No. 23 Order" means the Welfare Reform Act 2012 (Commencement No. 23 and Transitional and Transitory Provisions) Order 2015;
"polygamous marriage" has the same meaning as in regulation 3(5) of the Universal Credit Regulations 2013;
"the qualifying age for state pension credit" has the same meaning as in the 2002 Act;
"secondary legislation" has the same meaning as in Part 1 of the 2012 Act;
"state pension credit" has the same meaning as in the 2002 Act.
[¹(1A) In this Order, "couple" has the same meaning as in the 2002 Act, save—
  (a) in reference to entitlement to housing benefit, where it has the same meaning as in Part VII of the 1992 Act; and
[²(b) in article 7(3), in relation to references to persons being treated as a couple in accordance with article 7(2)(a)(ii), where it has the meaning referred to in article 7(2)(a)(ii).]
  (2) In this Order—
  (a) "mixed-age couple" means a couple, one member of which has attained the qualifying age for state pension credit and the other of which has not; and
  (b) the definition in sub-paragraph (a) includes a polygamous marriage where at least one party to the marriage has attained the qualifying age for state pension credit and at least one has not.
  (3) Save as stated to the contrary in article 6(2) [¹and article 8(2)(b)], all references in this Order to claims or entitlement to housing benefit are to claims or entitlement under the Housing Benefit SPC Regulations only.
  (4) In this Order—
  (a) a person is entitled to state pension credit or housing benefit on any day where the person has made a claim for that benefit and the conditions of entitlement are met in relation to that person, regardless of whether, respectively, entitlement begins on a later day under—
    (i) regulation 16A (date of entitlement under an award of state pension credit for the purpose of payability and effective date of change of rate) of the Social Security (Claims and Payments) Regulations 1987; or
    (ii) regulation 57 (date on which entitlement is to commence) of the Housing Benefit SPC Regulations; and
  (b) [¹save in article 7(3)(a),] a reference to claiming or entitlement to state pension credit or housing benefit as part of a [¹mixed-age] couple is a reference to [¹a person claiming or] being so entitled, on the basis that [¹the person] is a member of a couple or [¹...] a polygamous marriage.

AMENDMENTS

1. Welfare Reform Act 2012 (Commencement No. 31 and Savings and Transitional Provisions (Amendment)) Order 2019 (SI 2019/935) art.2(2) (May 14, 2019).
2. Universal Credit (Persons who have attained state pension credit qualifying age) (Amendment) Regulations 2020 (SI 2020/655) reg.7(2) (November 25, 2020).

Appointed day

3. 15th May 2019 is the appointed day for the coming into force of paragraph 64 (universal credit amendments: insertion of section 4(1A) into the 2002 Act) of Schedule 2 to the 2012 Act, and section 31 of the 2012 Act in so far as it relates to that paragraph.

5.169

Savings

4.—(1) Subject to paragraph (2), the 2002 Act shall have effect as though section 4(1A) (exclusion of mixed-age couples from state pension credit) had not come into force in relation to a member of a mixed-age couple who, on the day before the appointed day and as part of that couple, is entitled to—

5.170

(a) state pension credit;
(b) housing benefit; or
(c) state pension credit and housing benefit.

(2) The savings in the sub-paragraphs of paragraph (1) shall cease to have effect in relation to the member of the mixed-age couple referred to on any day after the appointed day when that person is not entitled to either state pension credit or housing benefit as part of the same mixed-age couple.

Transitional provision: termination of awards of housing benefit

6.—(1) The awards of housing benefit referred to in paragraph (2) are to terminate on the day referred to in paragraph (3), subject to paragraph (4).

5.171

(2) The awards are those where entitlement under the Housing Benefit SPC Regulations as part of a mixed-age couple begins on or after the appointed day and where the awards are made—

(a) at any time, under the Housing Benefit Regulations 2006 or the Housing Benefit SPC Regulations, to a person who, after the award, becomes a member of a mixed-age couple;
(b) at any time, under the Housing Benefit Regulations 2006, to a person who is a member of a mixed-age couple, where the award subsequently ceases to be subject to those Regulations and becomes subject to the Housing Benefit SPC Regulations; or
(c) on or before the day of making of this Order, to a person who claimed in advance of attaining the qualifying age for state pension credit.

(3) The termination takes effect—

(a) in the case of an award referred to in paragraph (2)(a) or (b), on the later of the appointed day and the day entitlement under the Housing Benefit SPC Regulations as part of a mixed-age couple takes effect on the award, as a change of circumstances, in accordance with the Housing Benefit and Council Tax Benefit (Decisions and Appeals) Regulations 2001; or

(b) in the case of an award referred to in paragraph (2)(c), on the day after the day of making of this Order.

(4) Paragraph (1) does not apply to awards in respect of specified accommodation or temporary accommodation, as defined respectively in sub-paragraphs (h) and (l) of article 7(11) of the No. 23 Order.

Transitional provision: [¹ application [²to housing benefit] of the rules in universal credit for treatment of couples and] polygamous marriages

5.172

7.—[²(1) Paragraph (3) applies where a person ("P"), who has attained the qualifying age, would otherwise not be entitled to either state pension credit or universal credit, because—

(a) but for that paragraph, P would be a member of the same household as a partner who has not attained the qualifying age and therefore a member of a mixed-age couple, who—
   (i) is prevented from claiming housing benefit under article 6 of the No. 21 Order or article 7 of the No. 23 Order; or
   (ii) has an award of housing benefit terminated under article 6; and
(b) P is neither entitled to universal credit jointly with that partner, nor entitled to universal credit as a single person, in one of the cases set out in paragraph (2).

(2) The cases are where P is not entitled to universal credit because P has attained the qualifying age and—

(a) any of the following paragraphs of regulation 3 of the Universal Credit Regulations 2013 (couples) applies, and in the case of paragraph (ii) below, one of the following circumstances applies—
   (i) paragraph (3) (treatment of certain couples – universal credit may only be claimed as a single person);
   (ii) paragraph (4) (treatment of polygamous marriages), so that P is not entitled to universal credit because P may only claim universal credit either as one of two parties to a polygamous marriage to be treated as a couple and the other party has also attained the qualifying age, or as a remaining party to such a marriage to be treated as single;
   (iii) paragraph (6) (absence from the household – universal credit may only be claimed as a single person); or
(b) P lost joint entitlement to universal credit as part of a mixed-age couple due to one of the following changes of circumstances taking effect from a date (namely the first day of the universal credit assessment period in which the change occurred) that is earlier than when, but for paragraph (3), the same change would take effect for the purposes of housing benefit, those changes being where—
   (i) P and their partner are no longer a couple;
   (ii) P is party to a marriage that is no longer polygamous and P's remaining spouse has attained the qualifying age.

(3) Where this paragraph applies—
(a) P and their partner who are to be treated as a non-polygamous couple in accordance with paragraph (2)(a)(ii), or who are no longer parties to a polygamous marriage in accordance with paragraph (2)(b)(ii), are to be treated as members of the same household as each other but not of that of any party (or parties) with whom they are

not part of a couple in accordance with those provisions and one of them may claim or remain entitled to housing benefit as part of that couple; or

(b) P who is to be treated as single in accordance with paragraph (2)(a) (i) to (iii), or is single in accordance with paragraph (2)(b)(i), is to be treated as though P is not a member of the same household as any party (or parties) with whom P is not part of a couple in accordance with those provisions and may claim or remain entitled to housing benefit as a single person,

where paragraph (2)(a) applies, with effect from the date on which the relevant paragraph of regulation 3 of the Universal Credit Regulations 2013 first applies to C, or, where paragraph (2)(b) applies, with effect from the date referred to in paragraph (2)(b) on which C lost universal credit entitlement.]

AMENDMENTS

1. Welfare Reform Act 2012 (Commencement No. 31 and Savings and Transitional Provisions (Amendment)) Order 2019 (SI 2019/935) art.2(3) (May 14, 2019).
2. Universal Credit (Persons who have attained state pension credit qualifying age) (Amendment) Regulations 2020 (SI 2020/655) reg.7(3) (November 25, 2020).

[¹Transitional provision: where restrictions on claims for universal credit are in place

8.—(1) This article applies to a member of a mixed-age couple who, 5.173 further to articles 3 to 7, is excluded from entitlement to state pension credit or housing benefit, and is also prevented from claiming universal credit by virtue of—

(a) regulation 4 of the Universal Credit (Transitional Provisions) Regulations 2014 (claims for universal credit may not be made in an area or category of case);

(b) regulation 4A of those Regulations (restriction on claims for universal credit by persons entitled to a severe disability premium); or

(c) article 4(11) of the Welfare Reform Act 2012 (Commencement No. 32 and Savings and Transitional Provisions) Order 2019 (no claims for universal credit by frontier workers).

(2) Where this article applies, the member of the mixed-age couple who has attained the qualifying age for state pension credit is, for the purposes of an award of benefit referred to in the following sub-paragraphs to that member, to be treated as—

(a) meeting the basic condition of entitlement (upper age limit) for—
  (i) income support, in section 124(1)(aa) of the 1992 Act;
  (ii) a jobseeker's allowance, in section 1(2)(h) of the 1995 Act; or
  (iii) an employment and support allowance, in section 1(3)(c) of the 2007 Act; and

(b) not having attained that age for housing benefit, for the purposes of regulation 5 of the Housing Benefit Regulations 2006 and regulation 5 of the Housing Benefit SPC Regulations, so that the Housing Benefit Regulations 2006 apply to the assessment of the award.

(3) This article continues to apply until the award of benefit referred to in paragraph (2)(a) or (b) terminates, regardless of whether paragraph (1)(a), (b) or (c) continues to apply throughout the award.

(4) Where a member of a mixed-age couple who has attained the qualifying age for state pension credit is entitled to income support by virtue of paragraph (2)(a)(i), references to a claimant's partner in paragraphs 9 and 9A (conditions for pensioner premium) and in paragraph 10 (condition for higher pensioner premium) of Schedule 2 to the Income Support (General) Regulations 1987 have effect as though they were references to the claimant.

(5) In this article—

"the 1995 Act" means the Jobseekers Act 1995;

"the 2007 Act" means the Welfare Reform Act 2007;

"employment and support allowance" means an employment and support allowance under Part 1 of the 2007 Act as it has effect apart from the amendments made by Schedule 3, and Part 1 of Schedule 14, to the 2012 Act that remove references to an income-related employment and support allowance;

"income support" has the same meaning as in Part VII of the 1992 Act;

"jobseeker's allowance" means a jobseeker's allowance under the 1995 Act as it has effect apart from the amendments made by Part 1 of Schedule 14 to the 2012 Act that remove references to an income-based jobseeker's allowance.]

AMENDMENT

1. Welfare Reform Act 2012 (Commencement No. 31 and Savings and Transitional Provisions (Amendment)) Order 2019 (SI 2019/935) art.2(4) (May 14, 2019).

The Welfare Reform Act 2012 (Commencement No. 32 and Savings and Transitional Provisions) Order 2019

SI 2019/167

Made 31st January 2019

5.174 *The Secretary of State for Work and Pensions makes the following Order in exercise of the powers conferred by section 150(3) and (4)(a), (b)(i) and (c) of the Welfare Reform Act 2012:*

ARRANGEMENT OF ARTICLES

1. Citation and Interpretation
2. Commencement of provisions on abolition of tax credits
3. Savings
4. Appointed day – coming into force of universal credit provisions and abolition of income-related employment and support allowance and income-based jobseeker's allowance: persons resident outside Great Britain
5. Amendment of the No. 9, No. 21 and No. 23 Orders

5.175 GENERAL NOTE

This is no ordinary Commencement Order. Article 2 in effect repeals (as from February 1, 2019) Part 1 of the Tax Credits Act 2002 by commencing s.33(1)(f) of the WRA 2012, which abolishes child tax credit and working tax credit. However, these repeals are subject to the important savings provisions set out in Art.3. Meanwhile, Art.4 commences the provisions of Part 1 of the WRA 2012 that relate to universal credit and the abolition of both IR-ESA and IB-JSA for specified categories of cases. Art.5 simply makes consequential amendments to the No.9, 21 and 23 Commencement Orders, and are incorporated into those provisions in the text above.

Citation and Interpretation

1.—(1) This Order may be cited as the Welfare Reform Act 2012 (Commencement No. 32 and Savings and Transitional Provisions) Order 2019. 5.176

(2) In this Order—

"the Act" means the Welfare Reform Act 2012;

"the 2002 Act" means the Tax Credits Act 2002;

"the 2015 Order (N.I.)" means the Welfare Reform (Northern Ireland) Order 2015;

"the No. 8 Order (N.I.)" means the Welfare Reform (Northern Ireland) Order 2015 (Commencement No. 8 and Transitional and Transitory Provisions) Order 2017;

"the No. 9 Order" means the Welfare Reform Act 2012 (Commencement No. 9 and Transitional and Transitory Provisions and Commencement No. 8 and Savings and Transitional Provisions (Amendment)) Order 2013;

"the No. 21 Order" means the Welfare Reform Act 2012 (Commencement No. 21 and Transitional and Transitory Provisions) Order 2015;

"the No. 23 Order" means the Welfare Reform Act 2012 (Commencement No. 23 and Transitional and Transitory Provisions) Order 2015;

"the Claims and Payments Regulations 1987" means the Social Security (Claims and Payments) Regulations 1987;

"couple" means a couple as defined in section 3(5A) of the 2002 Act;

"employment and support allowance" means an employment and support allowance under Part 1 of the Welfare Reform Act 2007;

"jobseeker's allowance" means a jobseeker's allowance under the Jobseekers Act 1995;

"joint-claim couple" has the same meanings as in the Jobseeker's Act 1995;

"Her Majesty's forces" has the same meaning as in the Armed Forces Act 2006;

"mixed-age couple" means a couple, one member of which has attained the qualifying age and the other of which has not;

"polygamous unit" means a polygamous unit within the meaning of the Tax Credits (Polygamous Marriages) Regulations 2003;

"qualifying age" means the qualifying age for state pension credit as defined in section 1(6) of the State Pension Credit Act 2002;

"single claimant" means a person who makes a single claim for a tax credit as referred to in section 3(3)(b) of the 2002 Act;

"tax credit" (including "child tax credit" and "working tax credit") have the same meanings as in the 2002 Act and "tax year" has the same meaning as in Part 1 of that Act;

"UC age condition" means the condition in section 4(1)(b) of the Act for Great Britain or Article 9(1)(b) of the 2015 Order (N.I.) for Northern Ireland, subject to any exceptions in any instrument made under the Act or 2015 Order (N.I.);

"UC couple" means a couple as defined in section 39 of the Act for Great Britain or Article 45 of the 2015 Order (N.I.) for Northern Ireland (in article 4, as defined in that section 39);

"UC joint claimants" means joint claimants as defined in section 40 of the Act for Great Britain or Article 46 of the 2015 Order (N.I.) for Northern Ireland (in article 4, as defined in that section 40);

"UC provisions" means the provisions listed in Schedule 2 to the No. 9 Order;

"UC single claimant" means a single claimant as defined in section 40 of the Act for Great Britain or Article 46 of the 2015 Order (N.I.) for Northern Ireland (in article 4, as defined in that section 40);

"UC transitional provisions" means the orders made under section 150(3) of the Act or Article 2(2) of the 2015 Order (N.I.) that commence the UC provisions, or the provisions listed in Schedule 1 to the No. 8 Order (N.I.), respectively, and the regulations made under Schedule 6 to the Act or Schedule 6 to the 2015 Order (N.I.).

(3) In this Order—

(a) "frontier worker" means a person, other than a person referred to in sub-paragraph (b), who is in Great Britain for the purposes of section 4(1)(c) of the Act but who does not reside in Great Britain or Northern Ireland;

(b) the person referred to is a crown servant or member of Her Majesty's forces posted overseas (where "crown servant" and "posted overseas" have the same meanings as in regulation 10 of the Universal Credit Regulations 2013).

Commencement of provisions on abolition of tax credits

5.177   **2.** The day appointed for the coming into force of section 33(1)(f) of the Act (abolition of tax credits) and the repeal of Part 1 of the 2002 Act (but not Schedule 1 or 3), by Part 1 of Schedule 14 to the Act, is 1st February 2019.

GENERAL NOTE

5.178   Article 2, which extends to both Great Britain and Northern Ireland, commences s.33(1)(f) of the WRA 2012 , which abolishes child tax credit and working tax credit, and the repeal of Part 1 of the Tax Credits Act 2002 (but not Sch. 1 or 3), by Part 1 of Sch. 14 to the Act, on February 1, 2019, subject to the savings referred to below. In particular, art. 3 contains a saving for existing awards of a tax credit – e.g. one that has effect for a period that includes January 31, 2019. In these cases, s.33(1)(f) is treated as if it had not come into force.

Savings

5.179   **3.**—(1) Section 33(1)(f) of the Act, and the repeal of Part 1 of the 2002 Act (but not Schedule 1 or 3) by Part 1 of Schedule 14 to the Act, shall be treated as though they had not come into force, in relation to a case as referred to in paragraph (2), (3), (4), (5) or (9).

(2) The case referred to is the case of an award of a tax credit that has effect for a period that includes 31st January 2019.

(3) The case referred to is the case of an award of a tax credit where the period for which it has effect begins on or after 1st February 2019 and where the claim for the award is made by—

(a) a single claimant who is, or a couple both members of which are, aged under the qualifying age on the day that the claim is made;

(b) a mixed-age couple which is also a UC couple on that day; or

(c) a polygamous unit which on that day consists wholly of persons who, ignoring any restrictions on claiming universal credit in the UC transitional provisions, could claim universal credit, and meet the UC age condition, as—

    (i) UC joint claimants and one or more UC single claimants; or

    (ii) a number of UC single claimants.

(4) The case referred to is the case of an award of a tax credit where the period for which it has effect begins on or after 1st February 2019 and where the claim for the award is made by—

(a) a mixed-age couple apart from one referred to in paragraph (3)(b); or

(b) a polygamous unit apart from one referred to in paragraph (3)(c),

where, on the day on which the claim is made, a member of the couple, or a member or members of the polygamous unit, would be able to claim universal credit were it not for restrictions on claiming universal credit in the UC transitional provisions.

(5) The case referred to is a case, not falling within paragraph (3) or (4), of—

(a) an award of child tax credit where the period for which it has effect begins on or after 1st February 2019 and where, on the day on which the claimant or claimants of the award makes or make the claim for it, he or she (or they) has or have an award of working tax credit;

(b) an award of working tax credit where the period for which it has effect begins on or after 1st February 2019 and where, on the day on which the claimant or claimants of the award makes or make the claim for it, he or she (or they) has or have an award of child tax credit;

(c) an award of child tax credit or working tax credit where the period for which it has effect begins on or after 1st February 2019 and where the claimant or claimants who makes or make the claim for the award had an award of the same type of tax credit for the previous tax year to the tax year for which the award is made.

(6) For the purposes of paragraph (5)(a) and (b)—

(a) a person is to be treated as having an award of working tax credit with effect from the start of a tax year ("current tax year") even though a decision has not been made under section 14 of the 2002 Act in respect of a claim for that tax credit for that tax year, if the person had an award of working tax credit for the previous tax year and any of the cases specified in paragraph (7) applies; and

(b) a person is to be treated as having an award of child tax credit with effect from the start of a tax year ("current tax year") even though a decision has not been made under section 14 of the 2002 Act in respect of a claim for that tax credit for that tax year, if the person had an award of child tax credit for the previous tax year and any of the cases specified in paragraph (7) applies.

(7) The cases are—

(a) a final notice has not been given to the person under section 17 of the 2002 Act in respect of that previous tax year;

(b) a final notice has been given, which includes provision by virtue of subsections (2) and (4) of section 17, or a combination of those subsections and subsection (6) of that section and—

    (i) the date specified in the notice for the purposes of section 17(2) and (4) or, where different dates are specified, the later of them, has not yet passed and no claim for a tax credit for the current tax year has been made, or treated as made; or

    (ii) a claim for a tax credit has been made, or treated as made, on or before the date mentioned in paragraph (i), but no decision has been made in relation to that claim under section 14(1) of the 2002 Act;

  (c) a final notice has been given, no claim for a tax credit for the current tax year has been made, or treated as made, and no decision has been made under section 18(1) of the 2002 Act in respect of entitlement to a tax credit for the previous tax year;

  (d) a final notice has been given and the person made a declaration in response to a requirement included in that notice by virtue of section 17(2)(a), (4)(a) or (6)(a), or any combination of those provisions—

    (i) by the date specified on the final notice;

    (ii) if not in accordance with paragraph (i), within 30 days following the date on the notice to the person that payments of a tax credit under section 24(4) of the 2002 Act have ceased due to the person's failure to make the declaration by the date specified in the final notice; or

    (iii) if not in accordance with paragraph (i) or (ii), before 31st January in the tax year following the period to which the final notice relates and, in the opinion of Her Majesty's Revenue and Customs, the person had good reason for not making the declaration in accordance with paragraph (i) or (ii).

(8) In this article, a reference to the date on which a claim for a tax credit is made is a reference to the date on which such a claim is made or treated as made as provided for in the Tax Credits (Claims and Notifications) Regulations 2002.

(9) The case referred to is the case of an award of a tax credit that had effect for a period that ended on or before 30th January 2019.

GENERAL NOTE

5.180   Article 2 above brings into force on February 1, 2019 s.33(1)(f) of the WRA 2012 which provides for the abolition of both child tax credit and working tax credit. Article 2 is subject to the savings provisions in art.3, which specifies five cases to which s.33(1)(f) does not apply. In these cases, s.33(1)(f) is treated as if it had not come into force.

Case 1 – article 3(2)
    Case 1 applies to an award of a tax credit that has effect for a period that includes January 31, 2019. Since most tax credits awards are made for the entire tax year, the effect is that the majority of tax credits recipients for tax year 2018/19 will be unaffected by the commencement of s.33(1)(f).

Case 2 – article 3(3)
    Case 2 applies to an award of a tax credit for a period beginning on or after February 1, 2019 where:

  (a) the claim for the tax credit was made by a single claimant, couple or polygamous unit; and

  (b) the single claimant, both members of the couple or all members of the polygamous unit could claim universal credit and meet the relevant age condition (in s.4 of the Welfare Reform Act 2012).

Case 3 – article 3(4)
    Case 3 applies to an award of child tax credit or working tax credit that has effect for a period beginning on or after February 1, 2019 where:

    (a) the claim is made by a couple or a polygamous unit where only one member of the couple, or only some members of the polygamous unit, could claim universal credit and meet the age condition, and

    (b) where the member or members who could claim universal credit, and meet the age condition, cannot claim universal credit by virtue of restrictions in a transitional provisions order made under section 150(3) of the 2012 Act or regulations made under Sch.6 to that Act.

Cases 2 and 3 – persons who could claim Universal Credit

Cases 2 and 3 refer to a person who could claim universal credit. The Universal Credit (Transitional Provisions) Regulations 2014 (SI 2014/1230) set out the categories of person who are capable of claiming universal credit. The general rule is that a person who is able to make a claim for universal credit is unable to claim a tax credit (art.7 of the No.23 Commencement Order. Cases 2 and 3 operate as exemptions to this general rule.

Case 4 – article 3(5)

Case 4 applies to an award, not falling with Case 2 or Case 3, for a period beginning on or after February 1, 2019, of:

    (a) child tax credit where, on the date of claim, the person/s have an award of working tax credit; and

    (b) working tax credit where, on the date of claim, the person/s have an award of child tax credit;

    (c) either tax credit where the claimant/s had an award of the same type of tax credit for the previous tax year.

For these purposes, a person is treated as having an award of tax credit even if a decision on a claim for tax credit under s.14 of the Tax Credits Act 2002 is awaited, in the cases described in art.3(7).

Case 5 – article 3(9)

Case 5 applies to an award of a tax credit that had effect for a period that ended on or before January 30, 2019.

Appointed day – coming into force of universal credit provisions and abolition of income-related employment and support allowance and income-based jobseeker's allowance: persons resident outside Great Britain

4.—(1) The day appointed for the coming into force of the UC provisions, in so far as they are not already in force, in relation to the case of a claim referred to in paragraph (2), and any award that is made in respect of the claim, is the day appointed in accordance with paragraph (3).   5.181

(2) The claim referred to is a claim for universal credit that is made on or after 1st February 2019 in respect of a period that begins on or after 1st February 2019 where, on the date that the claim is made, the claimant (in the case of UC joint claimants, either claimant) resides outside Great Britain.

(3) The day appointed in relation to the case of a claim referred to in paragraph (2), and any award that is made in respect of the claim, is the first day of the period in respect of which the claim is made.

(4) Article 3(6) of the No. 9 Order applies for the purposes of paragraph (3) as it applies for the purposes of article 3(4)(a) of the No. 9 Order.

(5) The day appointed for the coming into force of the provisions referred to in article 4(1)(a) to (c) of the No. 9 Order, in so far as they are not already in force, in relation to the case of a claim referred to in paragraph

(6), and any award that is made in respect of the claim, is the day appointed in accordance with paragraph (7).

(6) The claims referred to are—

(a) a claim for universal credit that is made on or after 1st February 2019 in respect of a period that begins on or after 1st February 2019 where, on the date that the claim is made, the claimant (in the case of UC joint claimants, either claimant) resides outside Great Britain;

(b) a claim for an employment and support allowance or a jobseeker's allowance that is made on or after 1st February 2019 in respect of a period that begins on or after 1st February 2019 where, on the date that the claim is made, the claimant (in the case of a claim for a jobseeker's allowance by a joint-claim couple, or a claim for either allowance by a person who would form part of a UC couple for the purposes of universal credit, either member of the couple) resides outside Great Britain;

(c) a claim for an employment and support allowance or a jobseeker's allowance other than one referred to in sub-paragraph (b) that is made or treated as made during the relevant period by a UC single claimant or by either of two UC joint claimants who has or have made a claim for universal credit under sub-paragraph (a).

(7) The day appointed in relation to the case of a claim referred to in paragraph (6), and any award that is made in respect of the claim, is the first day of the period in respect of which the claim is made.

(8) Paragraphs (6), (7), (9) and (10) of article 4 of the No. 9 Order apply in relation to a claim for universal credit referred to in paragraph (6)(a) (and any award that is made in respect of the claim) as they apply to a claim for universal credit referred to in sub-paragraph (a) or (b) of article 4(2) of the No. 9 Order (and any award that is made in respect of the claim).

(9) Article 5(8) of the No. 9 Order applies for the purposes of paragraph (7) as it applies for the purposes of article 4(3)(a) of the No. 9 Order.

(10) Article 7 of the No. 23 Order applies as though the reference in paragraph (1) of that article to article 3(1) and (2)(a) to (c) of that Order included a reference to paragraphs (1) and (2).

(11) No claim may be made for universal credit on or after 1st February 2019 by a UC single claimant who is, or UC joint claimants each of whom is, a frontier worker.

(12) Articles 9 to 22 of the No. 9 Order apply in connection with the coming into force of the provisions referred to in article 4(1)(a) to (c) of the No. 9 Order, in relation to the case of a claim referred to in paragraph (6), and any award made in respect of the claim, as they apply in connection with the coming into force of those provisions in relation to the case of a claim referred to in sub-paragraph (a) or (g) of article 4(2) of the No. 9 Order and any award that is made in respect of the claim.

(13) In this article—

(a) "claimant"—

(i) in relation to an employment and support allowance, has the same meaning as in Part 1 of the Welfare Reform Act 2007;

(ii) in relation to a jobseeker's allowance, has the same meaning as in the Jobseeker's Act 1995 (as it applies apart from the amendments made by Part 1 of Schedule 14 to the Act that remove references to an income-based jobseeker's allowance), save as mentioned in paragraph (6)(b);

    (iii) in relation to universal credit, has the same meaning as in Part 1 of the Act, save as mentioned in paragraph (2) and (6)(a);

(b) "relevant period" means, in relation to a claim for universal credit within paragraph (6)(a), any UC claim period, and any period subsequent to any UC claim period in respect of which the claimant is entitled to an award of universal credit in respect of the claim;

(c) "UC claim period" means a period when—

    (i) a claim for universal credit within paragraph (6)(a) has been made but a decision has not yet been made on the claim; or

    (ii) a decision has been made that the claimant is not entitled to universal credit and—

        (aa) the Secretary of State is considering whether to revise that decision under section 9 of the Social Security Act 1998, whether on an application made for that purpose or on the Secretary of State's own initiative; or

        (bb) the claimant has appealed against that decision to the First-tier Tribunal and that appeal, or any subsequent appeal to the Upper Tribunal or a court, has not yet been finally determined;

(d) the Universal Credit, Personal Independence Payment, Jobseeker's Allowance and Employment and Support Allowance (Claims and Payments) Regulations 2013 apply for the purpose of deciding—

    (i) whether a claim for universal credit is made;

    (ii) the date on which such a claim is made;

(e) the Claims and Payments Regulations 1987 apply, subject to sub-paragraphs (f) and (g), for the purpose of deciding—

    (i) whether a claim for an employment and support allowance or a jobseeker's allowance is made; and

    (ii) the date on which the claim is made or treated as made;

(f) subject to sub-paragraph (g)—

    (i) a person makes a claim for an employment and support allowance or a jobseeker's allowance if he or she takes any action which results in a decision on a claim being required under the Claims and Payments Regulations 1987; and

    (ii) it is irrelevant that the effect of any provision of those Regulations is that, for the purposes of those Regulations, the claim is made or treated as made at a date that is earlier than the date on which that action is taken;

(g) where, by virtue of—

    (i) regulation 6(1F)(b) or (c) of the Claims and Payments Regulations 1987, in the case of a claim for an employment and support allowance; or

    (ii) regulation 6(4ZA) to (4ZD) and (4A)(a)(i) and (b) of those Regulations, in the case of a claim for a jobseeker's allowance,

a claim for an employment and support allowance or a jobseeker's allowance is treated as made at a date that is earlier than the date on which the action referred to in sub-paragraph (f)(i) is taken, the claim is treated as made on that earlier date.

GENERAL NOTE

5.182   Article 4, which extends to Great Britain only, commences the provisions in Part 1 of the WRA 2012 that relate to universal credit and the abolition of IR-ESA and IB-JSA for the cases set out in this article.

Article 4(1) and (2) bring into force the provisions relating to universal credit (listed in Schedule 2 to the No.9 Commencement Order 2013 in relation to a claim for universal credit that is made on or after February 1, 2019 with respect to a period that begins on or after that date, where the claimant (in the case of joint claimants, either of them) resides outside Great Britain. This includes a Crown servant or a member of Her Majesty's forces posted overseas. Article 4(5) and (6) bring into force the provisions of the Act relating to the abolition of the two legacy benefits in relation to a claim for universal credit, ESA or JSA that is made on or after February 1, 2019 with respect to a period that begins on or after that date, where the claimant (in the case of joint claimants, either of them) resides outside Great Britain. Article 4(10) applies provisions in art.7 of the No. 23 Commencement Order to the commencement of the universal credit provisions such that a claim may not be made for housing benefit, income support or a tax credit where under this Order a claim may be made for universal credit, subject to the exceptions stated. Article 4(11) provides that a claim for universal credit may not be made by a single claimant or joint claimants where the claimant or each of the joint claimants is a "frontier worker" (see art.1(3)(a)).

Amendment of the No. 9, No. 21 and No. 23 Orders

5.183   **5.—**

GENERAL NOTE

5.184   The amendments made by art.5 to the No. 9, No. 21 and No. 23 Orders with effect from February 1, 2019 have been incorporated in the text of those Orders (above).

The Welfare Reform Act 2012 (Commencement No. 33) Order 2019

SI 2019/1135 (C. 34)

Made: 17th July 2019

The Secretary of State for Work and Pensions makes the following Order in exercise of the powers conferred by section 150(3) of the Welfare Reform Act 2012:

Citation

5.185   **1.**   This Order may be cited as the Welfare Reform Act 2012 (Commencement No. 33) Order 2019.

Appointed day

5.186   **2.** The appointed day for the coming into force of section 36 of, and Schedule 6 to, the Welfare Reform Act 2012 in so far as they are not already in force, is the day after this Order is made.

GENERAL NOTE

This Order brings into force, on the day after it is made, the remaining regulation-making powers in Sch.6 to the Welfare Reform Act 2012. The Schedule enables the Secretary of State to make provision by regulations for the purpose of, or in connection with, replacing existing benefits (see s.33 of that Act, which specifies the "existing benefits" that are to be replaced) with universal credit.

5.187

PART VI

TRANSITIONAL, SAVINGS AND MODIFICATIONS PROVISIONS

The Income Support (Transitional) Regulations 1987

(SI 1987/1969)

These regulations have been omitted in order to save space and because they are now only likely to be relevant to a very few cases. For the full text of these Regulations, see Vol. II of Social Security Legislation 2000. Special transitional additions payable under reg. 15 were increased by 0.5% from April 12, 2021 by art. 22 of SI 2021/162.

6.1

The Income Support (General) Amendment No.6 Regulations 1991

(SI 1991/2334) (AS AMENDED)

Made by the Secretary of State under ss. 22(1) and 84(1) of the Social Security Act 1986 and s. 166(1) to (3A) of the Social Security Act 1975

[IN FORCE NOVEMBER 11, 1991]

Saving Provision in relation to Severe Disability Premium

4.—(1) The provisions of this regulation are subject to regulation 5.

6.2

(2) Where paragraph (3), (4), (5) or (6) applies to a claimant, sub-paragraph (2)(a)(ii), or, as the case may be, sub-paragraph (2)(b)(iii) of paragraph 13 of Schedule 2 to the General Regulations shall have effect as if the relevant amendment had not been made.

(3) This paragraph applies to a claimant who satisfied both the qualifying conditions in the week immediately preceding 21st October 1991.

(4) This paragraph applies to a claimant—

(a) who satisfied both the qualifying conditions in at least one of the eight weeks immediately preceding 21st October 1991, but did not satisfy either or both of those conditions in the week immediately preceding that date; and

(b) who in a week commencing not more than eight weeks after the date on which he last satisfied both the qualifying conditions, would again have satisfied both those conditions if the relevant amendment had not been made.

(5) This paragraph applies to a claimant—

(a) who ceased to be entitled to income support because he became engaged in remunerative work for a period not exceeding the permitted period determined in accordance with regulation 6 and that period had commenced but had not ended before 21st October 1991; and

(b) who satisfied both the qualifying conditions in the week ending on the day before the first day of that period commenced; and

(c) who in the week which commences on the day immediately following the day on which that period ends, would again have satisfied both the qualifying conditions if the relevent amendment had not been made.

(6) This paragraph applies to a claimant—

(a) who satisfied both the qualifying conditions immediately before he—

(i) participated in arrangements for training made under section 2 of the Employment and Training Act 1973 or section 2 of the Enterprise and New Towns (Scotland) Act 1990; or

(ii) attended a course at an employment rehabilitation centre established under section 2 of the Employment and Training Act 1973,

and he had begun the training or joined the course before 21st October 1991 and was still continuing with the training or course at that date; and

(b) who in the week which commences on the day immediately following the last day he attended the training or course, would again have satisfied both the qualifying conditions if the relevant amendment had not been made.

(7) The "qualifying conditions" means the two qualifying conditions set out in paragraph (8)(a) and (b) below.

(8) For the purposes of paragraph (7)—

(a) the first qualifying condition is that the claimant—

(i) has made a claim for income support which has not been determined, but had it been determined and an award made, his applicable amount would have included severe disability premium; or

(ii) has a current award of income support and the applicable amount appropriate to that award includes severe disability premium; or

(iii) has a current award of income support and has before 21st October 1991 made an application in writing in accordance with section 104(2) of the Social Security Act requesting a review of that award, where the ground, or one of the grounds for review, is that—

(aa) he has become a co-owner with a close relative of the dwelling which he and that close relative jointly occupy as their home; or

(bb) he has become jointly liable with a close relative to make payments to a landlord in respect of the dwelling which he and that close relative jointly occupy as their home,

whether or not there are other co-owners or other persons jointly liable to make such payments and, if revised, the applicable amount appropriate to the award includes severe disability premium in respect of a period prior to that date;

(b) the second qualifying condition is that the person is—

(i) a co-owner, with a close relative, of the dwelling he and that close relative jointly occupy as their home, whether or not there are other co-owners; or

(ii) jointly liable, with a close relative, to make payments to a landlord in respect of the dwelling he and that close relative jointly occupy as their home, whether or not there are other persons jointly liable to make such payments.

[1(9) For the purposes of paragraph (8)(b) and regulation 5(2)(b), where a person has satisfied the second qualifying condition, but his circumstances change so that he no longer satisfies it, he shall nonetheless be treated as satisfying it for so long as he is a person to whom paragraph (10) applies.

(10) This paragraph applies to a person—

(a) who was, together with a close relative of his, either a co-owner of, or jointly liable to make payments to a landlord in respect of, the dwelling which he and that close relative jointly occupied as their home; and

(b) who has since become, with that close relative or any other close relative, either—

    (i) jointly liable to make payments to a landlord in respect of that dwelling or any other dwelling; or

    (ii) a co-owner of that dwelling or any other dwelling,

    which he and the close relative jointly occupy as their home (whether or not there are other co-owners, or other persons jointly liable to make such payments).]

AMENDMENT

1. Income-related Benefits Schemes (Miscellaneous Provisions) Amendment Regulations 1991 (SI 1991/2695) reg.5 (December 27, 1991).

DEFINITIONS

"claimant"—see Income Support Regulations reg.2(1).
"close relative"—*ibid.*
"dwelling occupies as the home"—*ibid.*
"partner"—*ibid,*
"permitted period"—see reg.6.
"relevant amendment"—see General Note.
"remunerative work"—see Income Support Regulations reg.2(1).
"Social Security Act"—*ibid.*

GENERAL NOTE

The "relevant amendment" is the amendment to the definition of non-dependant in reg.3 of the Income Support Regulations with effect from November 11, 1991, by reg.2 of these Regulations (reg.1(3)). These Regulations were made on October 21, 1991, which is why that is the date used in reg.4 to fix the transitional protection. Regulation 4 allows existing claimants to continue to receive the benefit of the severe disability premium where they previously met the new conditions for joint occupiers of the home, except that the joint occupation was with a close relative.

Regulation 5 defines when the protection of reg.4 ceases to apply.

6.3

Circumstances in which regulation 4 ceases to apply

5.—(1) Regulation 4 shall cease to apply to a claimant, or his partner, on the relevant day and shall not apply on any day thereafter.

(2) The relevant day is the first day after a period of eight consecutive weeks throughout which—

(a) subject to paragraph (3), he is not entitled to income support; or

(b) he is unable to satisfy, or be treated as satisfying, the second qualifying condition.

(3) For the purpose of calculating a period in excess of eight weeks in paragraph (2)(a) above the following periods shall be disregarded—

(a) where the claimant, or his partner, becomes engaged in remunerative

6.4

work, any period during which he, or his partner, was not entitled to income support, not exceeding the permitted period determined in accordance with regulation 6;

(b) any period during which the claimant, or his partner, was participating in arrangements for training made under section 2 of the Employment and Training Act 1973 or section 2 of the Enterprise and New Towns (Scotland) Act 1990 or attending a course at an employment rehabilitation centre established under section 2 of the Employment and Training Act 1973.

DEFINITIONS

"claimant"—see Income Support Regulations reg.2(1).
"partner"—*ibid.*
"permitted period"—see reg.6.
"qualifying condition"—see reg.4(7).

Definition of "permitted period" for the purposes of regulations 4 and 5

6.5   **6.**—(1) For the purposes of regulations 4(5) and 5(3)(a), where a claimant has ceased to be entitled to income support because he or his partner became engaged in remunerative work, [¹ . . .] the permitted period shall be a period of 12 consecutive weeks.
(2) [¹ . . .]
(3) [¹ . . .]

AMENDMENT

1. Income Support (General) (Jobseeker's Allowance Consequential Amendments) Regulations 1996 (SI 1996/206) reg.31 (October 7, 1996).

DEFINITIONS

"claimant"—see Income Support Regulations reg.2(1).
"partner"—*ibid.*
"relevant education"—see Income Support Regulations reg.12.
"remunerative work"—see Income Support Regulations reg.2(1).
"student"—*ibid.*

The Income Support (General) Amendment No.3 Regulations 1993

(SI 1993/1679)

Made by the Secretary of State under ss.135(1), 136(5)(b), 137(1) and 175(1) to (4) of the Social Security Contributions and Benefits Act 1992

[In force August 2, 1993]

6.6   **2.**—(4) In the case of a claimant who was entitled to income support by virtue of regulation 70 of the Income Support Regulations for the benefit week which includes 2nd August 1993, then in respect of each day after that date on which the claimant's entitlement to income support continues, regulation 70 shall continue to apply in his case as if the preceding provisions of this regulation had not been made.

GENERAL NOTE

See the notes to reg.70(3) in the 1995 edition of J. Mesher and R. Wood, *Income-related Benefits: the Legislation*. Regulation 70(3) was amended by reg.2(1)–(3) of these Regulations on August 2, 1993.

6.7

Saving

4.—(1) In the case of a claimant who was entitled to income support for the benefit week which included 2nd August 1993 then, but subject to paragraph (3), in respect of each day after that date on which the claimant's entitlement to income support continues, Schedule 3 to the Income Support Regulations shall continue to apply in his case as if regulation 3 of these Regulations had not been made.

6.8

(2) Heads (c) to (f) of sub-paragraph (9) of paragraph 7 of Schedule 3 to the Income Support Regulations shall apply to paragraph (1) above as they apply to sub-paragraph (1) of paragraph 7, but with the modification that for the words "in receipt of income support", wherever they occur, there were substituted the words "entitled to income support" and that the words "Subject to sub-paragraphs (10) and (11)" were omitted.

(3) In its application to any loan taken out or increased after 2nd August 1993 Schedule 3 to the Income Support Regulations shall have effect as amended by regulation 3 of these Regulations.

(4) Paragraphs (1) and (3) above shall apply as from 11th April 1994 as if for the references to "2nd August 1993" wherever they occur there were substituted references to "11th April 1994".

GENERAL NOTE

See the notes to para.7(6B)–(6F) of the former Sch.3 to the Income Support Regulations in the 1995 edition of J. Mesher and P. Wood, *Income-related Benefits: the Legislation*. Paragraph 7 of the former Sch.3 was amended by reg.3 of these regulations on August 2, 1993. See also notes to para.11(4)–(11) of the new Sch.3.

6.9

The Income-related Benefits Schemes (Miscellaneous Amendments) (No.3) Regulations 1994

(SI 1994/1807)

Made by the Secretary of State under ss.131(3)(b), 135(1), 137(1) and (2) (i) and 175(1), (3) and (4) of the Social Security Contributions and Benefits Act 1992

[In force August 1, 1994]

GENERAL NOTE

See the amendment to reg.21(3) of the Income Support Regulations inserted by reg.4(1) of these Regulations.

6.10

These regulations were revoked by reg.11(1)(a) of the Social Security (Persons From Abroad) Amendment Regulations 2006 (SI 2006/1026) with effect from April 30, 2006.

The Disability Working Allowance and Income Support (General) Amendment Regulations 1995

(SI 1995/482) (AS AMENDED)

Made by the Secretary of State under ss.124(1)(d)(i) and (3), 129(2B) (b) and (c) and (8), 135(1), 137(1) and 175(1), (3) and (4) of the Social Security Contributions and Benefits Act 1992 and s.12(1) of the Social Security (Incapacity for Work) Act 1994

[In force April 13, 1995]

Transitional provisions with respect to the Income Support Regulations

6.11
19.—(1) Sickness benefit shall be a qualifying benefit for the purposes of regulation 9(2)(a)(i) of the Income Support Regulations, and for this purpose "sickness benefit" means sickness benefit under section 31 of the Social Security Contributions and Benefits Act 1992 as in force on 12th April 1995.

(2) Where the disability premium was applicable to a claimant on 12th April 1995 by virtue of paragraph 12(1)(b) of Schedule 2 to the Income Support Regulations as in force on that date, the disability premium shall continue to be applicable to that claimant for so long as paragraph 12(1)(b) (i) of that Schedule applies to him.

(3) Paragraph (2) shall not apply to a claimant to whom paragraph 12(1) (b)(i) of Schedule 2 to the Income Support Regulations has ceased to apply for a period of more than 56 continuous days.

(4) Where on 12th April 1995 paragraph 5 of Schedule 1 to the Income Support Regulations (persons incapable of work) as in force on that date applied to a claimant, but the disability premium was not applicable to him, that claimant shall be treated for the purposes of paragraph 12(1) of Schedule 2 to the Income Support Regulations as if, throughout the period that paragraph 5 of Schedule 1 had applied to him, paragraph 12(1)(b)(i) of Schedule 2 applied to him.

(5) [² Where it is determined on or after 13th April, 1995] that a claimant fails to satisfy the incapacity for work test, in accordance with regulations made under section 171C of the Contributions and Benefits Act (the all work test), on its first application to the claimant concerned, and the claimant, immediately prior to [¹13th April 1995], was either—
  (a) incapable of work and had been so for a continuous period of 28 weeks in circumstances to which paragraph 5 of Schedule 1 of the Income Support Regulations refers (persons incapable of work not required to be available for employment); or
  (b) in receipt of invalidity benefit or severe disablement allowance,
then, in a case in which either regulations 8(2A) or 11(2A) of the Income Support Regulations applies (persons not required to be available for employment and registration for employment), notwithstanding regulation 22(1A) and (5A) of the Income Support Regulations (reductions in applicable

amounts), the amount of any income support to which the claimant is entitled shall be calculated in accordance with regulation 17 of those Regulations.
   [¹(6) Where—
   (a) a determination of the amount of a person's benefit has been made
        in a case to which paragraph (5) of this regulation, as originally
        made, had effect; and
   (b) an appeal to which regulation 8(2A) or 11(2A) of the Income
        Support Regulations (persons not required to be available or regis-
        tered for employment) refers, remains outstanding on 2nd October
        1995;
the amount of any benefit to which he is entitled shall continue to be determined under paragraph (5), as originally made, until the determination of
the appeal.]

AMENDMENTS

   1. Income-related Benefits Schemes and Social Security (Claims and Payments)
(Miscellaneous Amendments) Regulations 1995 (SI 1995/2303) reg.8(2) (October
2, 1995).
   2. Social Security Act 1998 (Commencement No.9 and Savings and Consequential
and Transitional Provisions) Order 1999 (SI 1999/2422 (C.61)) art.3(12) and
Sch.11 (September 6, 1999).

Savings with respect to the Income Support Regulations

   20.—(1) Where a person was not required to be available for employ-   6.12
ment on 12th April 1995 by virtue of regulation 8(2) of the Income Support
Regulations as in force on that date, that regulation shall continue to apply in
that person's case as if regulation 6 of these Regulations had not been made.
   (2) Where a claimant was not required to register for employment on 12th
April 1995 by virtue of regulation 11(2) of the Income Support Regulations
as in force on that date, that regulation shall continue to apply in that claimant's case as if regulation 8 of these Regulations had not been made.
   (3) Where a claimant appeals against a decision of an adjudication officer
that he is not incapable of work, and that decision was made on or before
12th April 1995, regulations 8 and 11 of the Income Support Regulations
shall apply in that claimant's case as if these Regulations had not been made.
   (4) Where the higher pensioner premium was applicable to a claimant on, or at any time during the 8 weeks immediately preceding, 12th
April 1995 by virtue of paragraph 12(1)(c)(i) of Schedule 2 to the Income
Support Regulations as in force on that date, paragraph 12 of that Schedule
shall continue to apply in that claimant's case as if regulation 16 of these
Regulations had not been made.

GENERAL NOTE

   These transitional and saving provisions relate to some of the amendments made   6.13
to the Income Support Regulations as a consequence of the introduction of incapacity benefit and the new tests for deciding incapacity for work from April 13, 1995.
See the notes to reg.22A of, and paras 24–25 of Sch.1B to, the Income Support
Regulations.
   Regulation 19(5) was amended on October 2, 1995 to make it clear that it only
applied to people who had been incapable of work for 28 weeks or in receipt of

invalidity benefit or severe disablement allowance immediately before April 13, 1995 (and not to people who were so incapable, etc. by the date of the adjudication officer's decision). Regulation 19(6) allows payment of full income support under the previous form of reg.19(5) to those whose appeals are outstanding on October 2, 1995 until the appeal has been determined. This should mean the final determination of the appeal, e.g. if it is taken to the Social Security Commissioner (now Upper Tribunal).

See the further transitional protection in reg.27(3) of the Income Support (General) (Jobseeker's Allowance Consequential Amendments) Regulations 1996 (p.1759).

The Income-related Benefits Schemes (Miscellaneous Amendments) Regulations 1995

(SI 1995/516)

Made by the Secretary of State under ss.123(1)(a) to (c), 128(5), 129(4) and (8), 135(1), 136(3), (5)(a) and (b), 137(1), (2)(c) and (d)(i) and 175(1), (3) and (4) of the Social Security Contributions and Benefits Act 1992

[IN FORCE APRIL 10, 1995]

Saving

6.14   **28.**—(1) In the case of a claimant who was entitled to income support for the benefit week which included 9th April 1995 then, but subject to paragraph (3), in respect of each day after that date on which the claimant's entitlement to income support continues, Schedule 3 to the Income Support Regulations shall continue to have effect as though regulation 25(c) of these Regulations had not been made.

(2) Heads (c) to (f) of sub-paragraph (9) of paragraph 7 of Schedule 3 to the Income Support Regulations shall apply to paragraph (1) above as they apply to sub-paragraph (1) of paragraph 7, but with the modification that for the words "in receipt of income support", wherever they appear, there were substituted the words "entitled to income support" and that the words "Subject to sub-paragraphs (10) and (11)" were omitted.

(3) In its application to any loan taken out or increased after 9th April 1995, Schedule 3 to the Income Support Regulations shall have effect as amended by regulation 25(c) of these Regulations.

DEFINITION

"claimant"—see Income Support Regulations reg.2(1).

GENERAL NOTE

6.15   See the notes to para.7(6B)–(6F) of the former Sch.3 to the Income Support Regulations in the 1995 edition of J. Mesher and P. Wood, *Income-related Benefits: the Legislation*. Paragraph 7(6C) of the former Sch.3 was amended by reg.25(c) of these Regulations on April 10, 1995. See also the notes to para.11(4)–(11) of the new Sch.3.

The Social Security (Income Support and Claims and Payments) Amendment Regulations 1995

(SI 1995/1613)

Made by the Secretary of State under ss.135(1), 136(5)(b), 137(1) and 175(1) and (3)–(5) of the Social Security Contributions and Benefits Act 1992 and ss.5(1)(p). 15A(2), 189(1) and (4) and 191 of the Social Security Administration Act 1992

[In force October 2, 1995]

Revocations and savings

5.—(2) The revocation by paragraph (1) above and Schedule 4 to these Regulations of any provision previously amended or substituted but subject to a saving for existing beneficiaries does not affect the continued operation of those savings.

6.16

GENERAL NOTE

See the notes to para.11(4)–(11) of Sch.3 to the Income Support Regulations.

6.17

The Income Support (General) Amendment and Transitional Regulations 1995

(SI 1995/2287)

Made by the Secretary of State under ss.135(1), 137(1) and 175(1) and (3) to (5) of the Social Security Contributions and Benefits Act 1992

[In force October 2, 1995]

Transitional protection

3.—(1) Where a claimant for income support whose applicable amount, in the benefit week which included 1st October 1995, included an amount in respect of the interest on a loan or part of a loan by virtue of paragraph 7(6), 7(7) or 8(1)(a) of Schedule 3 to the Income Support Regulations (housing costs) ("the former paragraphs") as then in force and that loan or part of a loan is not a qualifying loan for the purposes of paragraphs 15 and 16 of Schedule 3 to the Income Support Regulations, paragraphs (2) and (3) shall have effect in his case.

6.18

(2) A loan or part of a loan to which paragraph (1) applies shall qualify as a loan to which paragraph 15 or 16, as the case may be, of Schedule 3 to the Income Support Regulations applies, for as long as any of the former paragraphs would have continued to be satisfied had it remained in force and the claimant remains in receipt of income support or is treated as being in receipt of income support.

(3) Heads (a), (c) and (e) of sub-paragraph (1) of paragraph 14 of Schedule 3 to the Income Support Regulations shall apply to paragraph (2) above as they apply to Schedule 3, but as if the words "Subject to sub-paragraph (2)" at the beginning were omitted.

DEFINITION

"claimant"—see Income Support Regulations reg.2(1).

GENERAL NOTE

6.19   See the note to para.7 of Sch.3 to the Income Support Regulations.

The Income-related Benefits Schemes and Social Security (Claims and Payments) (Miscellaneous Amendments) Regulations 1995

(SI 1995/2303)

Made by the Secretary of State under ss.123(1), 124(1)(d), 129(3), 130(2) and (4), 135(1), 136(1) and (3)–(5), 137(1) and (2)(b), (d), (h), (i) and (l) and 175(1) and (3)–(6) of the Social Security Contributions and Benefits Act 1992 and ss.5(1)(h), (i) and (o), 6(1)(h) and (i) and 189 of the Social Security Administration Act

[In force October 2, 1995]

Transitional provision with respect to the Income Support Regulations

6.20   **8.**—(1) In determining whether a claimant is entitled to income support on or after 2nd October 1995 and whether he satisfies the provisions of either—
  (a) regulation 4(2)(c)(v) of the Income Support Regulations(temporary absence from Great Britain); or
  (b) paragraph 7 of Schedule 1 to those Regulations (disabled students not required to be available for work);
in a case where the claimant, for a period up to and including 12th April 1995, was continuously incapable of work for the purposes of paragraph 5 of Schedule 1 to the Income Support Regulations, as it was then in force, that period of incapacity shall be treated as forming part of a subsequent period of incapacity beginning not later than 7th June 1995 to which the provisions referred to in paragraphs (a) or (b) above refer and which is continuous to the date of the determination in question.

DEFINITION

"claimant"—see Income Support Regulations reg.2(1).

GENERAL NOTE

6.21   See the notes to reg.4(2)(c)(v) of the Income Support Regulations. For para.7 of Sch.1 see the 1996 edition of J. Mesher and P. Wood, *Income-related Benefits: the Legislation.*

The Income Support (General) (Jobseeker's Allowance Consequential Amendments) Regulations 1996

(SI 1996/206) (AS AMENDED)

Made by the Secretary of State under s.40 of the Jobseekers Act 1995 and ss.124(1)(e), 137(1) and 175(1) to (4) of the Social Security Contributions and Benefits Act 1992

[In force October 7, 1996]

Transitional provisions

27.—(1) Where on 6th October 1996 or at any time during the eight weeks immediately preceding that date paragraph 4(1) of Schedule 1 to the principal Regulations (persons caring for another person) as in force on that date applied to a claimant, or would have applied to him if he had made a claim for income support the claimant shall be treated for the purposes of paragraphs 5 and 6 of Schedule 1B to the principal Regulations as if, throughout the period that paragraph 4(1) of Schedule 1 applied or would have applied to him, paragraph 4 of Schedule 1B had applied or would have applied to him.

(2) Where on 6th October 1996 paragraph 5 of Schedule 1 to the principal Regulations (persons incapable of work) as in force on that date applied to a claimant, the claimant shall be treated for the purposes of regulation 4(2)(c)(v) of and paragraph 10 of Schedule 1B to the principal Regulations as if, throughout the period that paragraph 5 of Schedule 1 applied to him, paragraph 7 of Schedule 1B had applied to him.

(3) Where—

(a) a determination of the amount of a person's benefit has been made in a case to which regulation 19(5) of The Disability Working Allowance and Income Support (General) Amendment Regulations 1995 as originally made had effect (amendments consequential on the coming into force of the Social Security (Incapacity for Work) Act 1994: transitional provisions); and

(b) an appeal to which regulations 8(2A) or 11(2A) of the principal Regulations as in force on 2nd October 1995 referred (persons not required to be available or registered for employment), has still to be determined,

regulation 22A(1) of the principal Regulations (reduction in applicable amount where the claimant is appealing against a decision that he is not incapable of work) shall not apply to that person.

DEFINITION

"claimant"—see Income Support Regulations reg.2(1).

GENERAL NOTE

These transitional provisions relate to the some of the changes made to the income support scheme as a result of the introduction of JSA on October 7, 1996. On para.(3) see the notes to regs 19 and 20 of the Disability Working Allowance and

6.22

6.23

Income Support (General) Amendment Regulations 1995 on p.1754 and reg.22A of the Income Support Regulations.

Continuity with jobseeker's allowance

6.24   **32.**—In determining whether a person is entitled to income support [¹or is to be treated as being in receipt of income support or whether any amount is applicable or payable—

    (a) entitlement to an income-based jobseeker's allowance shall be treated as entitlement to income support for the purposes of any requirement that a person is or has been entitled to income support for any period of time; and

    (b) a person who is treated as being in receipt of income-based jobseeker's allowance shall be treated as being in receipt of income support for the purposes of any requirement that he is or has been treated as being in receipt of income support for any period of time.]

AMENDMENT

    1. Income-related Benefits Schemes and Social Fund (Miscellaneous Amendments) Regulations 1996 (SI 1996/1944) reg.12 (October 7, 1996).

GENERAL NOTE

6.25   Paragraph (a) of this important provision allows entitlement to income-based JSA to count as entitlement to income support for the purposes of satisfying any requirement that the person is or has been entitled to income support for any period of time. Paragraph (b) has the same effect where the requirement is that the person is or has been treated as being in receipt of income support. This could be relevant, for example, in relation to waiting periods or the linking rules for payment of housing costs. For the JSA provision see para.18(1)(c) of Sch.2 to the JSA Regulations 1996; for the ESA provision see para.20(1)(c) of Sch.6 to the ESA Regulations 2008 in Vol.I of this series.

The Income-related Benefits and Jobseeker's Allowance (Personal Allowances for Children and Young Persons) (Amendment) Regulations 1996

(SI 1996/2545)

Made by the Secretary of State under ss.128(1)(a)(i) and (5), 129(1)(c) (i) and (8), 135(1), 136(3) and (4), 137(1) and 175(1), (3) and (4) of the Social Security Contributions and Benefits Act 1992 and ss.4(5), 35(1) and 36(1), (2) and (4) of the Jobseekers Act 1995

[In force April 7, 1997].

Transitional provisions

6.26   **10.**—(1) Where, in relation to a claim for income support, jobseeker's allowance, housing benefit or council tax benefit, a claimant's weekly applicable amount includes a personal allowance in respect of one or more children or young persons who are, as at the day before the appropriate date these Regulations come into force for the purpose of those benefits in accordance with regulation 1 of these Regulations (referred to in this regulation as "the appropriate date"), aged 11, 16 or 18, the provisions specified in regulation 2(7) of these Regulations shall have effect, for the period specified in paragraph (2) below, as if regulation 2 of these Regulations had not been made.

(2) The period specified for the purposes of paragraph (1) above shall be, in relation to each particular child or young person referred to in that paragraph, the period beginning on the appropriate date and ending—

(a) where that child or young person is aged 11 or 16 as at the day before the appropriate date, on 31st August 1997;

(b) where that young person is aged 18 as at the day before the appropriate date, on the day preceding the day that young person ceases to be a person of a prescribed description for the purposes of regulation 14 of the Income Support Regulations, regulation 76 of the Jobseeker's Allowance Regulations, regulation 13 of the Housing Benefit Regulations or regulation 5 of the Council Tax Benefit Regulations.

DEFINITIONS

"child"—see SSCBA s.137(1).
"claimant"—see Income Support Regulations reg.2(1).
"young person"—see Income Support Regulations regs 2(1) and 14.

GENERAL NOTE

See the notes to para.2 of Sch.2 to the Income Support Regulations. Paragraph 2 of Sch.2 and para.2 of Sch.1 to the JSA Regulations 1996 were amended by reg.2 of these Regulations on April 7, 1997.   **6.27**

The weekly amount for a person aged not less than 18 in sub-para.(d) of the previous form of para.2 of Sch.2 and para.2 of Sch.1 to the JSA Regulations was increased to £38.90 from April 7, 1997 (Social Security Benefits Up-rating Order 1997 (SI 1997/543) art.18(4) and 24(4)). The weekly amounts in sub-paras (a), (b) and (c) were also increased and were the same as the amounts in sub-paras (a), (b) and (c) of the 1997 form of the respective paras.

The Social Security Amendment (Capital Limits and Earnings Disregards) Regulations 2000

(SI 2000/2545) (AS AMENDED)

Made by the Secretary of State under ss.123(1)(a), (d) and (e), 134(1), 136(2) and (5)(b) and (d), 137(1) and 175(1), (3) and (4) of the Social Security Contributions and Benefits Act 1992 and ss.12(4)(b) and (d), 13(1) and (3), 35(1) and 36(1), (2) and (4) of the Jobseekers Act 1995

[In force April 9, 2001]

Saving

4.—[¹ . . .], paragraph 4(4)(c) of Schedule 8 to the Income Support Regulations and paragraph 5(4)(c) of Schedule 6 to the Jobseeker's Allowance Regulations shall have effect as if regulation 3 above had not been made in a case where the claimant was entitled, by virtue of   **6.28**

sub-paragraph (2) or (3) of those paragraphs as in force immediately before the coming into force of these Regulations, to a disregard of £15.

AMENDMENT

1. Housing Benefit and Council Tax Benefit (Consequential Provisions) Regulations 2006 (SI 2006/217) reg.3 and Sch.1 (March 6, 2006).

GENERAL NOTE

6.29   See the note to para.4 of Sch.8 to the Income Support Regulations. Paragraph 4 of Sch.8 and para.5 of Sch.6 to the JSA Regulations 1996 were amended by reg.3 of, and the Sch. to, these Regulations on April 9, 2001.

The Child Support (Consequential Amendments and Transitional Provisions) Regulations 2001

(SI 2001/158) (AS AMENDED)

Made by the Secretary of State under s.29(2) of the Child Support, Pensions and Social Security Act 2000

[In force in relation to a particular case on the date on which s.1 of the 2000 Act comes into force in relation to that type of case]

PART III

SAVINGS

Savings for particular cases

6.30   **10.**—[¹ (Z1) This regulation is subject to the Child Support (Transitional Provisions) Regulations 2000.]

(1) Where, in respect of a particular case there is a maintenance assessment the effective date of which is before the date that these Regulations come into force with respect to that type of case ("the commencement date"), these Regulations shall not apply for the purposes of—

(a) *[omitted]*;

(b) the Income Support Regulations, in relation to a person who is entitled to income support for a period beginning on or before the day before the commencement date;

(c) the Jobseeker's Allowance Regulations, in relation to a person who is entitled to a jobseeker's allowance for a period beginning on or before the day before the commencement date; and

(d) *[omitted]*.

(2) These Regulations shall not apply with respect to the Income Support Regulations and the Jobseeker's Allowance Regulations in relation to a person who is entitled to income support or a jobseeker's allowance, as the case may be, for a period beginning on or before the day before the commencement date.

AMENDMENT

1. Child Support (Transitional Provision) (Miscellaneous Amendments) Regulations 2003 (SI 2003/347) reg.2(3) and (4)(b) (March 3, 2003).

GENERAL NOTE

These regulations made amendments to regs 60A and 60C(6)(a) of, and para.14(2) of Sch.3 to, the Income Support Regulations and to regs 125 and 128(6) (a) of, and para.13(2) of Sch.2 to, the JSA Regulations 1996. See the note to reg.60A of the Income Support Regulations in the 2008/09 edition of this volume.

6.31

The Social Security (Working Tax Credit and Child Tax Credit) (Consequential Amendments) Regulations 2003

(SI 2003/455) (AS AMENDED)

Made by the Secretary of State under ss.1(1C) and 189(1) of the Social Security Administration Act 1992, ss.22(5), 122(1), 123(1)(a), (d) and (e), 124(1)(e), 135(1), 136(1), (3), (4) and (5), 137(1), 138(1)(a), (2) and (4), and 175(1) and (3) to (5) of the Social Security Contributions and Benefits Act 1992, ss.4(5), 12, 13(2), 35(1), 36(2) and (4) of the Jobseekers Act 1995

Citation, commencement and interpretation

1.—(1) These Regulations may be cited as the Social Security (Working Tax Credit and Child Tax Credit) (Consequential Amendments) Regulations 2003 and this regulation shall come into force on 1 April 2003.

6.32

(2) Subject to paragraph (5), in a case where a claimant for income support—

(a) has a child or young person who is a member of his family for the purposes of his claim for income support, and

(b) is awarded, or his partner is awarded, a child tax credit for a period beginning before 6 April 2004,

regulation 7 shall have effect from the first day of the first benefit week to commence for that claimant on or after the day from which that award of child tax credit begins and regulation 2 and Schedule 1 shall have effect from the first day of the first benefit week to commence for that claimant on or after 6 April 2004.

(3) Subject to [¹ paragraphs (4A) to (5)], in a case where a claimant for income support—

(a) has a child or young person who is a member of his family for the purposes of his claim for income support, and

(b) has not been awarded, or his partner has not been awarded, a child tax credit for a period beginning before 6 April 2004,

regulations 2 and 7 and Schedule 1 shall have effect from the first day of the first benefit week to commence for that claimant on or after the day on which his, or his partner's, award of child tax credit begins.

(4) Subject to [¹ paragraphs (4A) to (5)], in a case where paragraph (2) (a) or (3)(a) does not apply to a claimant for income support, regulation 2 and Schedule 1 shall have effect from the first day of the first benefit week to commence for that claimant on or after 6 April 2004.

[¹ (4A) the case of a person who makes a claim for income support on or after 8th September 2005, regulation 2 and Schedule 1 shall have effect from the date that claim is made.

(4B) Subject to paragraph (4C), in the case of a claimant for income support who applies on or after 8th September 2005 for an amount to be included in his applicable amount in respect of a child or young person, regulation 2 and Schedule 1 shall have effect from the date of that application.

(4C) Paragraph (4B) shall not apply to a claimant for income support who already has an amount included in his applicable amount in respect of a child or young person on the date he makes the application referred to in that paragraph.]

(5) *[Omitted.]*

(6) Subject to [¹ paragraphs (8A) to (9)], in a case where a claimant for a jobseeker's allowance—

  (a) has a child or young person who is a member of his family for the purposes of his claim for jobseeker's allowance, and

  (b) is awarded, or his partner is awarded, a child tax credit for a period beginning before 6 April 2004, regulation 8 shall have effect from the first day of the first benefit week to commence for that claimant on or after the day from which that award of child tax credit begins and regulation 3 and Schedule 2 shall have effect from the first day of the first benefit week to commence for that claimant on or after 6th April 2004.

(7) Subject to [¹ paragraphs (8A) to (9)], in a case where a claimant for a jobseeker's allowance—

  (a) has a child or young person who is a member of his family for the purposes of his claim for jobseeker's allowance, and

  (b) has not been awarded, or his partner has not been awarded, a child tax credit for a period beginning before 6th April, 2004.

regulations 3 and 8 and Schedule 2 shall have effect from the first day of the first benefit week to commence for that claimant on or after the day on which his, or his partner's, award of child tax credit begins.

(8) Subject to [¹ paragraphs (8A) to (9)], in a case where paragraph (6)(a) or (7)(a) does not apply to a claimant for jobseeker's allowance, regulation 3 and Schedule 2 shall have effect from the first day of the first benefit week to commence for that claimant on or after 6 April 2004.

[¹ (8A) In the case of a person who makes a claim for a jobseeker's allowance on or after 8th September 2005, regulation 3 and Schedule 2 shall have effect from the date that claim is made.

(8B) Subject to paragraph (8C), in the case of a claimant for a jobseeker's allowance who applies on or after 8th September 2005 for an amount to be included in his applicable amount in respect of a child or young person, regulation 3 and Schedule 2 shall have effect from the date of that application.

(8C) Paragraph (8B) shall not apply to a claimant for a jobseeker's allowance who already has an amount included in his applicable amount in respect of a child or young person on the date he makes the application referred to in that paragraph.]

(9)–(10) *[Omitted.]*

(11) In paragraphs (2) to (5) and regulation 7, the expressions "benefit week", "claimant" and "partner" have the same meaning as in regulation 2(1) of the Income Support Regulations and in paragraphs (6) to (9) and regulation 8, the expressions "benefit week" and "partner" have

the same meaning as in regulation 1(3) of the Jobseeker's Allowance Regulations.

(12) In these Regulations—

[Omitted].

"the Income Support Regulations" means the Income Support (General) Regulations 1987; and

"the Jobseeker's Allowance Regulations" means the Jobseeker's Allowance Regulations 1996.

2.–6. *[Omitted.]* 6.33

AMENDMENT

1. Social Security (Tax Credit) Regulations 2005 (SI 2005/2294) reg.2(2) (September 8, 2005).

Income Support—transitional arrangements

7.—(1) [¹ Subject to paragraph (2) and regulation 31(3) of the Income 6.34 Support Regulations,] in the case of a claimant for income support who makes a claim, or whose partner makes a claim, for a child tax credit, the Secretary of State shall treat that claimant's income as including an amount equivalent to the amount of child tax credit to which he, or his partner, is entitled for the period specified in pargraph (3).

(2) In a case where a claimant for income support—

(a) has a child or young person who is a member of his family for the purposes of his claim for income support; and

(b) is, or has a partner who is, aged not less than 60.

the Secretary of State shall, [¹ in the benefit week which begins on or includes 5 October 2003, disregard from his income an amount equivalent to the amount of child tax credit to which he is entitled.]

(3) For the purposes of [¹ paragraph (1)], the specified period begins on the first day of the first benefit week to commence for that claimant on or after 7 April 2003, or the date the award of child tax credit begins if later, and ends on the day before the first day of the first benefit week to commence for that claimant on or after 6 April 2004.

(4) In the case of a claimant for income support who applies for an applicable amount under regulation 17 or 18 of the Income Support Regulations on or after 7 April 2003 in respect of a child or young person who is a member of his family, the Secretary of State shall treat that claimant's income as including an amount equivalent to the amount of child benefit to which he, or his partner, is entitled in respect of that child or young person for the period specified in paragraph (5).

(5) For the purposes of paragraph (4), the specified period begins on the first day of the first benefit week to commence for that claimant on or after the date from which his claim includes that applicable amount and ends on—

(a) in a case where the claimant, or his partner, is awarded child tax credit for a period beginning before 6th April 2004, the first day of the first benefit week to commence for that claimant on or after 6 April 2004;

(b) in the case where the claimant, or his partner, is awarded child tax credit for a period beginning on or after 6th April 2004 the first day of the first benefit week to commence for that claimant on or after the day that award of child tax credit begins; or

(c) the first day of the first benefit week in which his applicable amount in respect of that child or young person ends, if earlier.

(6) [³. . .]

(7) [³. . .]

AMENDMENTS

1. Social Security (Working Tax Credit and Child Tax Credit) (Consequential Amendments) (No.3) Regulations 2003 (SI 2003/1731) reg.6 (August 8, 2003).

2. Social Security (Miscellaneous Amendments) Regulations 2004 (SI 2004/565) reg.11 (April 12, 2004).

3. Social Security (Miscellaneous Amendments) Regulations 2011 (SI 2011/674) reg.11(a) (April 11, 2011).

Jobseeker's allowance—transitional arrangements

6.35   **8.**—(1) [¹ Subject to regulation 96(3) of the Jobseeker's Allowance Regulations,] in the case of a claimant for jobseeker's allowance who makes a claim, or whose partner makes a claim, for a child tax credit, the Secretary of State shall treat that claimant's income as including an amount equivalent to the amount of child tax credit to which he, or his partner, is entitled for the period specified in pararaph (2).

(2) For the purposes of paragraph (1) the specified period begins on the first day of the first benefit week to commence for that claimant on or after 7 April 2003, or the date that award of child tax credit begins if later, and ends on the day before the first day of the first benefit week to commence for that claimant on or after 6 April 2004.

(3) In the case of a claimant for jobseeker's allowance who applies for an applicable amount under regulation 83 or 84 of the Jobseeker's Allowance Regulations on or after 7 April 2003 in respect of a child or young person who is a member of his family, the Secretary of State shall treat the claimant's income as including an amount equivalent to the amount of child benefit to which he, or his partner, is entitled in respect of that child or young person for the period specified in paragraph (4).

(4) For the purposes of paragraph (3), the specified period begins on the first day of the first benefit week to commence for that claimant on or after the date from which his claim includes that applicable amount and ends on—

(a) in a case where the claimant, or his partner, is awarded child tax credit for a period beginning before 6 April 2004, the first day of the first benefit week to commence for that claimant on or after 6 April 2004;

(b) in a case where the claimant, or his partner, is awarded child tax credit for a period beginning on or after 6 April 2004, the first day of the first benefit week to commence for that claimant on or after the day on which that award of child tax credit begins; or

(c) the first day of the first benefit week in which his applicable amount in respect of that child or young person ends, if earlier.

(5) [³. . .]

(6) [³. . .]

AMENDMENTS

1. Social Security (Working Tax Credit and Child Tax Credit) (Consequential Amendments) (No.3) Regulations 2003 (SI 2003/1731) reg.6(1) and (3) (August 8, 2003).

2. Social Security (Miscellaneous Amendments) Regulations 2004 (SI 2004/565) reg.11 (April 12, 2004).

3. Social Security (Miscellaneous Amendments) Regulations 2011 (SI 2011/674) reg.11(b) (April 11, 2011).

GENERAL NOTE

These regulations make transitional provisions for IS and JSA claimants who are responsible for a child or young person and who are also awarded child tax credit (see Vol.IV) which was introduced on April 7, 2003.

6.36

It is intended that starting from April 6, 2004, IS and JSA will become "adults only" benefits with all means-tested state financial help towards the cost of bringing up a child being met through child tax credit. To this end, reg.2 and Sch.1 and reg.3 and Sch.2 (which are referred to above) amend, respectively, the IS Regulations and the JSA Regulations 1996 from that date (except in "transitional cases"—see the note to reg.17 of the Income Support Regulations) so as to abolish the family premium and personal allowances for children and young persons and child-related premiums.

Regulations 7(1)–(3) and 8(1)–(2) deal with the period between April 7, 2003 and April 6, 2004. The general rule is that child tax credit counts as income for income support and JSA so that the claimant does not receive a double benefit.

Note that regs 7(6)–(7) and 8(5)–(6) provided for a £10.50 disregard of child benefit in respect of a child under one in transitional cases to mirror the "baby element" in child tax credit. However these paragraphs were revoked with effect from April 11, 2011 in line with the abolition of the child tax credit baby element from April 6, 2011.

6.37

Regulation 1(5), (9) and (10) which are not reproduced here amend other regulations with effect from April 7, 2003. Their effect is noted in the text of those regulations where appropriate.

In *R(IS) 3/05* the Commissioner acknowledges that there were several problems in working out the meaning of reg.7(1) but on the facts of that case he saw no difficulty in interpreting reg.7(1) as deeming the claimant's income to include the amount equivalent to that contained in the operative award of child tax credit. The main issue was whether the claimant had made a valid claim for child tax credit (the claimant having discovered that he would be better off not claiming child tax credit); the Commissioner decided that an effective claim had been made.

However, the Commissioner did have to grapple with the meaning of reg.7(1) in *CIS/1064/2004*. The claimant, who had two young children, had been awarded working tax credit and child tax credit for the period April 6, 2003 to April 5, 2004. However she had stopped working, it seems in early August 2003 (it was not exactly clear when). This resulted in a change in the tax credit decisions. The award of working tax credit was stopped and the overpayment of working tax credit that was said to have arisen was set off against the child tax credit that remained payable, leaving very little in payment. But, when calculating her income support the maximum amount of child tax credit was taken into account. The claimant appealed. The tribunal reluctantly dismissed her appeal, deciding that as reg.7(1) used the word "entitled", rather than "paid", and as a person who is in receipt of income support is entitled to the maximum award of child tax credit (see ss.7(2) and 13(1) of the Tax Credits Act 2002 and reg.4 of the Tax Credits (Income Thresholds and Determination of Rates) Regulations 2002 (SI 2002/2008) in Vol. IV of this series), it was the amount of that entitlement that had to be taken into account.

6.38

In a very detailed analysis the Commissioner firstly rejects the claimant's contention that reg.7(1) did not apply where a person who already had an award of child tax credit made a claim for income support during the tax year 2003/2004 but only applied where a person who was already in receipt of income support applied for child tax credit. He decided that the order in which the claims were made did not matter. He then went on to consider the application of reg.7(1) in the claimant's case. Identifying the effect of reg.7(1) was, in his view, "a matter of considerable difficulty and complexity". However, he concludes that the most natural reading of reg.7(1) was that it required identification of the amount of child tax credit to which the particular claimant was actually "entitled" week by week during the period that was in question for income support purposes. It did not simply deem the claimant to be receiving the maximum amount of child tax credit for the children for whom she was responsible. However, the question remained of what was meant by "is entitled". The Commissioner concluded that it referred to the amount of child tax credit attributable, in accordance with the most recent award or amended award made by the Board, to the period from the effective date of the award or amended award to the end of the tax year. This result was consistent with the overall scheme of decision-making under the Tax Credits Act 2002. It also had the merit of being consistent with the general principle that the income support scheme was designed to meet financial needs when they arose through a shortfall in resources available at the time in question.

Applying this to the facts of the claimant's case, the Commissioner finds that the Board must have made a decision under s.28(5) of the 2002 Act (because the child tax credit had been reduced to recoup the overpayment of working tax credit), although he thought that there must also have been a use of the duty under reg.12(3) of the Tax Credits (Payments by the Board) Regulations 2002 (SI 2002/2173) (see Vol.IV in this series) to adjust the amount of the child tax credit payment in consequence of the amendment of the child tax credit award. Therefore, as there had been an amended award, the effect of reg.7(1) and (3) was that the clamant had to be treated as receiving an amount of income equivalent to the amount of child tax credit to which she was entitled under that amended award. The result was that it was the amount of child tax credit that she was actually receiving that was to be taken into account in calculating her income support. Note that the Commissioner left open how reg.7(1) and (3) applied in a case where the award of child tax credit had not been amended but by some administrative action there had simply been an adjustment of the amount paid without an amendment of the award.

6.39   The final question was how much of the amount under the amended child tax credit award was to be taken into account for the period specified in reg.7(1) and (3). The answer to this was to be found in reg.31(3) of the Income Support Regulations, although this did not supply a complete rule for the taking into account of income arising from awards of child tax credit and working tax credit. This was because it does not say how a weekly amount of income is to be derived from the amount of a tax credit award. The Commissioner therefore considered that reg.32 of the Income Support Regulations, substituting for the word "payment" in that regulation the amount of the tax credit award or amended award, should be applied (either directly or by a process of analogy to flesh out reg.31(3)). The period of the most recent child tax credit or working tax credit award had to be considered. Thus, where there had been an amended award, the period over which the amount of the amended award would be taken into account would be only the period after the effective date of the amendment. The weekly amount so calculated had then to be taken into account, but only from the first day of the benefit week identified under reg.31(3). The weekly amount had to be attributed to all the benefit weeks in the period after the effective date of the amendment to the end of the tax year, regardless of the way in which payments of tax credit were actually being made. If a tax credit award was terminated or amended later in the year there would either no longer be any amount to be taken into account or there would have to be a fresh application of reg.31(3)(b) or (c).

Note also *CSTC/326/2005* which holds that a claimant who was in receipt of income support and transferring to child tax credit could only be awarded child tax credit from the date of his claim – it could not be backdated for three months. For further discussion of this case see Vol.IV in this series.

The Social Security (Housing Costs Special Arrangements) (Amendment and Modification) Regulations 2008

(SI 2008/3195) (AS AMENDED)

Made by the Secretary of State for Work and Pensions under ss.123(1)(a), 135(1), 137(1) and 175(1) and (3) and (4) of the Social Security Contributions and Benefits Act 1992, ss.4(5), 35(1) and 36(2) and (4) of the Jobseekers Act 1995, ss.2(3)(b), 17(1) and 19(1) of the State Pension Credit Act 2002, and ss.4(2)(a) and (3), 24(1) and 25(2), (3) and (5) of the Welfare Reform Act 2007.

GENERAL NOTE

The modifications to the rules for housing costs for income support, income-   6.41
based JSA, income-related ESA and state pension credit made by these Regulations only apply to certain claimants, even after the January 2010 amendments. See the note to Sch.3 to the Income Support Regulations under *"Modifications to the waiting periods and the cap on loans for certain claimants from January 5, 2009"* and *"Further Modifications from January 5, 2010"*.

The modifications relating to waiting periods made by these Regulations were revoked on April 1, 2016 (subject to a saving provision: see p.1776) but the modifications which concern the capital limit for eligible loans (together with the time limit for receipt of housing costs in the case of JSA) continue in effect.

Citation, commencement and interpretation

6.42   **1.**—(1) These Regulations may be cited as the Social Security (Housing Costs Special Arrangements) (Amendment and Modification) Regulations 2008.

(2) Regulations 4 to 6, in so far as they relate to a particular person, come into force on the first day of the first benefit week to commence for that person on or after 5ᵗʰ January 2009.

(3) The remaining provisions of these Regulations come into force on 5ᵗʰ January 2009.

(4) In these Regulations—

"benefit week" has the same meaning as in—

    [(a) omitted as not relating to income support, income-based JSA or state pension credit]

    (b) regulation 2(1) of the Income Support Regulations, where the relevant benefit is income support;

    (c) regulation 1(2) of the Jobseeker's Allowance Regulations, where the relevant benefit is a jobseeker's allowance;

"housing costs" has the same meaning as in paragraph 1(1) (housing costs) of—

    [(a) omitted as not relating to income support, income-based JSA or state pension credit]

    (b) Schedule 3 to the Income Support Regulations, where the relevant benefit is income support;

    (c) Schedule 2 to the Jobseeker's Allowance Regulations, where the relevant benefit is a jobseeker's allowance;

"relevant benefit" means—

    (a) an employment and support allowance;

    (b) income support;

    (c) a jobseeker's allowance;

[Definition omitted as not relating to income support, income-based JSA or state pension credit]

"the Income Support Regulations" means the Income Support (General) Regulations 1987;

"the Jobseeker's Allowance Regulations" means the Jobseeker's Allowance Regulations 1996;

"the State Pension Credit Regulations" means the State Pension Credit Regulations 2002.

PART 2

MODIFICATIONS RELATING TO CERTAIN CLAIMANTS WHO
ARE ENTITLED TO A RELEVANT BENEFIT ON
4ᵀʰ JANUARY 2009

Application

6.43   **3.**—(1) This Part applies in relation to a person who—

    (a) is entitled to a relevant benefit on 4ᵗʰ January 2009; and

    (b) on or after that date falls within paragraph (3) or (4).

(2) This Part ceases to apply in relation to a person who makes a further claim to the same, or claims another, relevant benefit after 4ᵗʰ January 2009.

(3) A person falls within this paragraph if, apart from these Regulations, the housing costs to be met in the benefit week that includes 4ᵗʰ January 2009 would be nil in that person's case because [¹ that person] has not been entitled to the relevant benefit concerned for the period mentioned in sub-paragraph (1)(a) in any of the following provisions—

[(a) omitted as not relating to income support or income-based JSA]
- (b) paragraph 6 (existing housing costs) or paragraph 8 (new housing costs) of Schedule 3 to the Income Support Regulations;
- (c) paragraph 6 (existing housing costs) or paragraph 7 (new housing costs) of Schedule 2 to the Jobseeker's Allowance Regulations.

(4) A person falls within this paragraph if [¹ that person] has been entitled to a relevant benefit for a continuous period, which includes 4ᵗʰ January 2009, for at least 8 weeks but less than 26 weeks under any of the provisions mentioned in paragraph (5) as in force apart from these Regulations.

(5) The provisions are—

[(a) omitted as not relating to income support or income-based JSA]
- (b) paragraph 6(1)(b) (existing housing costs) or paragraph 8(4) (new housing costs) of Schedule 3 to the Income Support Regulations;
- (c) paragraph 6(1)(b) (existing housing costs) or paragraph 7(6) (new housing costs) of Schedule 2 to the Jobseeker's Allowance Regulations.

AMENDMENT

1. Social Security (Housing Costs Special Arrangements) (Amendment) Regulations 2009 (SI 2009/3257) reg.2 (January 5, 2010).

Modification of the Income Support Regulations

5.—Schedule 3 (housing costs) to the Income Support Regulations applies in relation to a person to whom this Part applies as if—   6.44
- (a) [¹ . . .]
- (b) [¹ . . .]
- (c) in paragraph 11(5) (general provisions applying to new and existing housing costs) the reference to "£100,000" were to "£200,000";
- (d) [¹ . . .]

AMENDMENT

1. Social Security (Housing Costs Amendments) Regulations 2015 (SI 2015/1647) reg.7(1) (April 1, 2016). Note that the revocation of these paragraphs is subject to the saving provision in reg.8 of SI 2015/1647. See p.1776 for this saving provision.

Modification of the Jobseeker's Allowance Regulations

6.—Schedule 2 (housing costs) to the Jobseeker's Allowance Regulations applies in relation to a person to whom this Part applies as if—   6.45
- (a) after paragraph 4 (housing costs not met) there were inserted—

"Housing costs: limitation applicable to qualifying loans

4A.—(1) Subject to sub-paragraphs (2) and (3), no amount may be met in respect of housing costs under paragraph 14 or 15 where   6.46

the claimant has been in receipt of housing costs under either or both of those paragraphs for a total of 104 weeks.

(2) No week in which the appropriate amount specified in paragraph 10(4) is £100,000 in relation to that claimant is to count towards the 104 week total.

(3) Sub-paragraph (1) does not apply where—

    (a) the claimant or his [¹ . . .] partner or, if the claimant is a member of a joint-claim couple, the other member of the couple, was previously entitled to income support or employment and support allowance; and

    (b) 12 weeks or less has elapsed since the last day of that entitlement and the first day of entitlement to a jobseeker's allowance.

[²(4) In determining whether the exemption provided for in sub-paragraph (3) applies, where the claimant or his partner or, if the claimant is a member of a joint-claim couple, the other member of the couple was in receipt of a jobseeker's allowance immediately before becoming entitled to income support by virtue of regulation 6(6) of the Income Support Regulations, no account shall be taken of entitlement arising by virtue of that regulation.]"

    (b) [³ . . .]
    (c) [³ . . .]
    (d) in paragraph 10(4) (general provisions applying to new and existing housing costs) the reference to "£100,000" were to "£200,000";
    (e) [³ . . .]

AMENDMENTS

1. Social Security (Housing Costs Special Arrangements) (Amendment) Regulations 2009 (SI 2009/3257) reg.3 (January 5, 2010).

2. Social Security (Miscellaneous Amendments) (No.3) Regulations 2011 (SI 2011/2425) reg.26(2) (October 31, 2011).

3. Social Security (Housing Costs Amendments) Regulations 2015 (SI 2015/1647) reg.7(1) (April 1, 2016). Note that the revocation of these paragraphs is subject to the saving provision in reg.8 of SI 2015/1647. See p.1776 for this saving provision.

Saving

6.47   **7.**—[¹ . . .]

AMENDMENT

1. Social Security (Housing Costs Amendments) Regulations 2015 (SI 2015/1647) reg.7(1) (April 1, 2016). Note that the revocation of this regulation is subject to the saving provision in reg.8 of SI 2015/1647. See p.1776 for this saving provision.

PART 3

MODIFICATIONS RELATING TO CERTAIN PERSONS WHO CLAIM A RELEVANT BENEFIT AFTER 4TH JANUARY 2009

Application and interpretation

6.48   [¹**8.**—(1) This Part applies on and after 5th January 2010 to a person ("C") who—

(a) claims a relevant benefit after 4th January 2009; and

(b) satisfies any of the following conditions.

(2) The first condition is that Part 2 applied to C at any time.

(3) The second condition is that this Part (as it has effect on and after 5th January 2010) applied to C in relation to a previous award.

(4) The third condition is that—

(a) neither C nor C's partner has been awarded a relevant benefit as the result of an earlier claim (whether the award was made before or on or after 5th January 2009);

(b) neither C nor C's partner is in receipt of state pension credit before the date on which C's claim is made or treated as made; and

(c) C does not fall to be treated under a linking rule as being in continuous receipt of the benefit to which C's claim relates in respect of a period which begins on or before 4th January 2009 and which ends immediately before the date on which C's claim is made or is treated as made.

(5) The fourth condition is that—

(a) C is not in receipt of a relevant benefit immediately before the date on which a claim made by C after 4th January 2009 is made or treated as made;

(b) neither C nor C's partner is in receipt of state pension credit before that claim is made or treated as made;

(c) C or C's partner was awarded a relevant benefit as the result of a claim made or treated as made before that claim; and

(d) C does not fall to be treated under a linking rule as being in continuous receipt of a relevant benefit during the period which falls immediately between the date on which a claim to which this provision relates is made or treated as made and the last period to occur before that date in respect of which C was in receipt of a relevant benefit (whether as a single person or as a member of a couple or polygamous marriage).

(6) The fifth condition is that—

(a) C or C's partner is in receipt of state pension credit before the date on which any claim for a relevant benefit made by C or C's partner after 4th January 2009 is made or treated as made; and

(b) none of the following provisions apply in relation to any such claim—

(i) paragraph 3(2) (previous entitlement to other income-related benefits) of Schedule 6 (housing costs) to the Employment and Support Allowance Regulations;

(ii) paragraph 1A(1A) (previous entitlement to income-based jobseeker's allowance, income-related employment and support allowance or state pension credit) of Schedule 3 (housing costs) to the Income Support Regulations;

(iii) paragraph 1A(1ZA) or (1B) (previous entitlement to income support, income-related employment and support allowance or state pension credit) of Schedule 2 (housing costs) to the Jobseeker's Allowance Regulations.

(7) In this regulation—

a "linking rule" means a provision of—

(a) paragraph 15 (linking rule) of Schedule 6 (housing costs) to the Employment and Support Allowance Regulations,

(b) paragraph 14 (linking rule) of Schedule 3 (housing costs) to the Income Support Regulations, or (as the case may be)

(c) paragraph 13 (linking rule) of Schedule 2 (housing costs) to the Jobseeker's Allowance Regulations;

"partner" has the same meaning as in regulation 1(3) (citation, commencement and interpretation) of the Jobseeker's Allowance Regulations.]

AMENDMENT

1. Social Security (Housing Costs Special Arrangements) (Amendment) Regulations 2009 (SI 2009/3257) reg.4 (January 5, 2010).

Modification of the Income Support Regulations

6.49   **10.**—Schedule 3 (housing costs) to the Income Support Regulations applies in relation to a person to whom this Part applies as if—

(a) [¹ . . .]
(b) [¹ . . .]
(c) [¹ . . .]
(d) [¹ . . .]
(e) [¹ . . .]
(f) in paragraph 11 (general provisions applying to new and existing housing costs)—
    (i) [¹ . . .]
    (ii) [¹ . . .]
    (iii) in sub-paragraph (5), the reference to "£100,000" were to "£200,000";
(g) [¹ . . .]
(h) [¹ . . .]

AMENDMENT

1. Social Security (Housing Costs Amendments) Regulations 2015 (SI 2015/1647) reg.7(1) (April 1, 2016). Note that the revocation of most of this regulation (with the exception of para.(f)(iii)) is subject to the saving provision in reg.8 of SI 2015/1647. See p.1776 for this saving provision.

Modification of the Jobseeker's Allowance Regulations

6.50   **11.**—Schedule 2 (housing costs) to the Jobseeker's Allowance Regulations applies in relation to a person to whom this Part applies as if—

(a) [³ . . .]
[¹(b) after paragraph 4 (housing costs not met) there were inserted—

"Housing costs: limitation applicable to qualifying loans

6.51   **4A.**—(1) Except as mentioned below, no amount may be met in respect of housing costs under paragraph 14 or 15 after the claimant has been in receipt of housing costs under either or both of those paragraphs ("relevant housing costs") for a cumulative total of 104 weeks, beginning on or after 5th January 2009.

(2) Sub-paragraphs (3) to [²(7)] apply for the purposes of sub-paragraph (1).

(3) No week in which the appropriate amount specified in paragraph 10(4) is £100,000 in relation to the claimant is to count towards the 104 week total.

(4) Where sub-paragraph (5) applies to the claimant, relevant housing costs awarded to him in respect of a previous award of a jobseeker's allowance are to be disregarded.

(5) This sub-paragraph applies to the claimant where he does not fall to be treated under paragraph 13 (linking rule) as being in receipt of a jobseeker's allowance for a continuous period beginning with the first day of the last period in respect of which he was not in receipt of a jobseeker's allowance and ending immediately before his most recent claim is made or is treated as made.

(6) Sub-paragraph (1) does not apply where—

    (a)   the claimant or his partner or, if the claimant is a member of a joint-claim couple, the other member of the couple, was entitled to an employment and support allowance or income support before one of them becomes entitled to a jobseeker's allowance; and

    (b)   12 weeks or less has elapsed since the last day of that entitlement and the first day of entitlement to a jobseeker's allowance.]

[² (7) In determining whether the exemption provided for in sub-paragraph (6) applies, where the claimant or his partner or, if the claimant is a member of a joint-claim couple, the other member of the couple was in receipt of a jobseeker's allowance immediately before becoming entitled to income support by virtue of regulation 6(6) of the Income Support Regulations, no account shall be taken of entitlement arising by virtue of that regulation.]"

    (c) [³ . . .]
    (d) [³ . . .]
    (e) [³ . . .]
    (f) [³ . . .]
    (g) in paragraph 10 (general provisions applying to new and existing housing costs)—

        (i) [³ . . .]
        (ii) [³ . . .]
        (iii) in sub-paragraph (4), the reference to "£100,000" were to "£200,000";

    (h) [³ . . .]
    (i) [³ . . .]
    (j) [³ . . .]

AMENDMENTS

1. Social Security (Housing Costs Special Arrangements) (Amendment) Regulations 2009 (SI 2009/3257) reg.5 (January 5, 2010).

2. Social Security (Miscellaneous Amendments) (No.3) Regulations 2011 (SI 2011/2425) reg.26(3) (October 31, 2011).

3. Social Security (Housing Costs Amendments) Regulations 2015 (SI 2015/1647) reg.7(1) (April 1, 2016). Note that the revocation of most of this regulation (with the exception of paras (b) and (g)(iii)) is subject to the saving provision in reg.8 of SI 2015/1647. See p.1776 for this saving provision.

PART 4

MODIFICATIONS RELATING TO CERTAIN PERSONS WHO CLAIM STATE
PENSION CREDIT

Modifications relating to certain persons who claim State Pension Credit

6.52 **12.**—(1) This Part applies where—
(a) a person becomes entitled to state pension credit;
(b) that person or that person's partner ceases to be entitled to a relevant benefit;
(c) that person or [¹ that person's] partner is a person to whom
[¹ —
(i) Part 2 applies, or
(ii) Part 3 (as it has effect, in relation to the person or that person's partner, on and after 5th January 2010) applies or would have applied had the person claiming state pension credit remained entitled to a relevant benefit.]
(d) the last day on which the person or [¹ that person's] partner was entitled to a relevant benefit was no more than 12 weeks before—
(i) except where head (ii) applies, the first day of entitlement to state pension credit; or
(ii) where the claim for state pension credit was treated as made on a day earlier than the day on which it was actually made ("the actual date"), the day which would have been the first day of entitlement to state pension credit had the claim been treated as made on the actual date; and
(e) in the period immediately before the date on which the person's entitlement to the relevant benefit ended, [¹ that person's] applicable amount included an amount in respect of housing costs under any of the provisions mentioned below.
(2) The provisions are—
(a) paragraph 16 (loans on residential property) or 17 (loans for repairs and improvements to the dwelling occupied as the home) of Schedule 6 to the Employment and Support Allowance Regulations;
(b) paragraph 15 (loans on residential property) or 16 (loans for repairs and improvements to the dwelling occupied as the home) of Schedule 3 to the Income Support Regulations;
(c) paragraph 14 (loans on residential property) or 15 (loans for repairs and improvements to the dwelling occupied as the home) of Schedule 2 to the Jobseeker's Allowance Regulations.
(3) Paragraph 8(2) (general provisions applying to housing costs) of Schedule 2 to the State Pension Credit Regulations is to apply in relation to a person to whom this Part applies as if the reference to "£100,000" were to "£200,000".

AMENDMENT

6.53 1. Social Security (Housing Costs Special Arrangements) (Amendment) Regulations 2009 (SI 2009/3257) reg.6 (January 5, 2010).

The Income Support (Prescribed Categories of Person) Regulations 2009

(SI 2009/3152)

With effect from December 30, 2009, reg.2 of these Regulations revoked   **6.54**
reg.13(2)(b) and (bb) of, and paras 7(a) and (b), 10, 12 and 13 of Sch.1B to,
the Income Support Regulations, subject to a saving provision for certain claimants.
See the 2015/16 edition of this book for these Regulations and the notes to them.

The Social Security (Miscellaneous Amendments) (No.5) Regulations 2009

(SI 2009/3228)

Made by the Secretary of State under ss.123(1)(a), 124(1)(e), 135(1),   **6.55**
136(3), (4) and (5)(a), (b) and (c), 137(1) and (2)(d), and 175(1), (3) and
(4) of the Social Security Contributions and Benefits Act 1992, ss.4(5), 12(1),
(2) and (4)(a), (b) and (c), 13, 35(1) and 36(1), (2) and (4) of, and paras
1(2)(b) and 8A of Sch.1 to, the Jobseekers Act 1995, s.115(3), (4) and (7),
166(3) and 167(1) of the Immigration and Asylum Act 1999, and ss.17(1), (2)
and (3)(a), (b) and (c), 24(1), 25(1), (2), (3) and (5) of, and para.6(3)(b)
of Sch.1 to, the Welfare Reform Act 2007.

[In force January 25, 2010]

Citation, commencement and interpretation

1.—(1) These Regulations may be cited as the Social Security   **6.56**
(Miscellaneous Amendments) (No.5) Regulations 2009.

(2)–(3) . . .

(4) In this regulation—

. . .

"the Employment and Support Allowance Regulations" means the
    Employment and Support Allowance Regulations 2008;
"the Immigration and Asylum Regulations" means the Social Security
    (Immigration and Asylum) Consequential Amendments Regulations
    2000;
"the Income Support Regulations" means the Income Support (General)
    Regulations 1987; and
"the Jobseeker's Allowance Regulations" means the Jobseeker's
    Allowance Regulations 1996.

Abolition (subject to savings) of urgent case payments

2.—(1) Subject to paragraphs (2) to (4), the following provisions are   **6.57**
revoked—

(a) Part 6 of the Income Support Regulations (urgent cases);
(b) Part 10 of the Jobseeker's Allowance Regulations (urgent cases);
(c) regulation 12(3) of the Immigration and Asylum Regulations (tran-
    sitional arrangements and savings);

(d) Part 13 of the Employment and Support Allowance Regulations (urgent cases).

(2) The provisions referred to in paragraph (1) ("the relevant provisions") continue to have effect in relation to a person who, on the day before the day on which these Regulations come into force, is a person ("P") to whom regulation 70(2)(b) of the Income Support Regulations, regulation 147(2)(b) of the Jobseeker's Allowance Regulations or (as the case may be) regulation 162(2) of the Employment and Support Allowance Regulations applies.

(3) Where on the day before the day on which these Regulations come into force P falls within paragraph 1 of Part 1 of the Schedule to the Immigration and Asylum Regulations, the relevant provisions continue to have effect in relation to P until—

(a) the expiry of the period, or the aggregate of any periods, of 42 days during any one period of leave to which paragraph 1 of Part 1 of that Schedule applies, or

(b) the day on which P no longer falls within paragraph 1 of Part 1 of that Schedule,

whichever shall first occur.

(4) In any other case, the relevant provisions continue to have effect in relation to P until the day on which regulation 70(2)(b) of the Income Support Regulations, regulation 147(2)(b) of the Jobseeker's Allowance Regulations or (as the case may be) regulation 162(2) of the Employment and Support Allowance Regulations ceases to apply to P.

GENERAL NOTE

6.58 See the commentary to Pt 6 (regs 70–72) of the Income Support Regulations.

Abolition of urgent case payments: supplementary provisions

6.59 3.—. . .

Revocation (subject to savings) of provisions specifying that certain persons are to be treated as not engaged in remunerative work

6.60 4.—(1) Subject to paragraphs (3) to (7), the following provisions are revoked—

(a) in the Income Support Regulations—
　　(i) regulation 6(4)(a) and (d) (persons not treated as engaged in remunerative work), and
　　(ii) paragraphs 8 and 9 of Schedule 1B (prescribed categories of persons);

(b) in the Jobseeker's Allowance Regulations—
　　(i) regulation 53(c) and (h) (persons treated as not engaged in remunerative work), and
　　(ii) paragraphs 7 and 8 of Schedule A1 (categories of members of a joint-claim couple who are not required to satisfy the conditions in section 1(2B)(b));

(c) regulation 43(2)(a) and (d) of the Employment and Support Allowance Regulations (circumstances under which partners of claimants entitled to an income-related allowance are not to be treated as engaged in remunerative work).

(2) . . .

(3) Paragraphs (4) to (6) apply to a person ("P") who in respect of a period which includes the day before the date on which these Regulations come into force—

(a) is entitled to a specified benefit (irrespective of whether P claims the benefit before, on or after that day), and

(b) falls within one of the provisions referred to in paragraph (1).

(4) Where the specified benefit is income support, regulation 6(4)(a) and (d) of, and paragraphs 8 and 9 of Schedule 1B to, the Income Support Regulations continue to have effect in relation to P's entitlement to that benefit.

(5) Where the specified benefit is a jobseeker's allowance, regulation 53(c) and (h) of, and paragraphs 7 and 8 of Schedule A1 to, the Jobseeker's Allowance Regulations continue to have effect in relation to P's entitlement to that benefit.

(6) Where the specified benefit is an employment and support allowance, regulation 43(2)(a) and (d) of the Employment and Support Allowance Regulations continue to have effect in relation to P's entitlement to that benefit.

(7) The provisions saved by paragraphs (4), (5) and (6) continue to have effect in relation to P's entitlement to the specified benefit until the day on which—

(a) P first ceases to fall within a provision referred to in paragraph (1), or,

(b) P first ceases to be entitled to that benefit,

whichever shall first occur.

(8) In this regulation "specified benefit" means income support, a job-seeker's allowance or an employment and support allowance.

GENERAL NOTE

See the commentary to reg.6 of the Income Support Regulations.   **6.61**

The Social Security (Lone Parents and Miscellaneous Amendments) Regulations 2012

(SI 2012/874)

Made by the Secretary of State for Work and Pensions under ss. 2(A)(1), 189(1), (4) and (5) and 191 of the Social Security Administration Act 1992, ss. 123(1), 124(1)(c), 137(1) and 175(1) and (3) to (5) of the Social Security Contributions and Benefits Act 1992, ss. 6(4), 7(4), 35(1) and 36(2) of the Jobseekers Act 1995 and ss. 2(4)(a), 4(6)(a) and 24(1) of the Welfare Reform Act 2007.

[In force May 21, 2012]

Savings and transitional provisions applicable to certain lone parents following a full-time course

7.—(1) This regulation applies to a lone parent if the following condi-   **6.62**
tions are met.

(2) The first condition is that—

(a) immediately before the specified day the lone parent was entitled to income support and fell within paragraph 1 (lone parents) of Schedule 1B (prescribed categories of person) to the Income Support Regulations;

(b) no other paragraph of Schedule 1B applies to the lone parent; and

(c) on and after the specified day, the lone parent is responsible for and a member of the same household as—

    (i) a single child aged 5 or over, or

    (ii) more than one child where the youngest child is aged 5 or over.

(3) The second condition is that immediately before the specified day, and on and after that day, the lone parent is also—

(a) a full-time student attending or undertaking a full-time course of advanced education, a full-time course of study or a sandwich course, or

(b) following a full-time course of training or instruction provided pursuant to arrangements made by the Secretary of State or pursuant to a scheme which has been approved by the Secretary of State as supporting the objectives set out in section 2 of the Employment and Training Act 1973.

(4) This regulation does not apply, or (as the case may be) it ceases to apply, to a lone parent if the lone parent makes a further claim for income support on or after the specified day.

(5) Where this regulation applies to a lone parent—

(a) paragraph 1 of Schedule 1B to the Income Support Regulations as in force in relation to the lone parent at the beginning of the period of study referred to in paragraph (3)(a) shall continue to have effect in relation to the lone parent for so long as the lone parent remains a full-time student;

(b) paragraph 1 of Schedule 1B to the Income Support Regulations as in force at the beginning of the particular course of training or instruction referred to in paragraph (3)(b) shall continue to have effect in relation to the lone parent for so long as the lone parent is following that full-time course; and

(c) any requirement to take part in a work-focused interview every 13 weeks in accordance with regulation 2ZA of the Lone Parents Regulations or regulation 4A of the Jobcentre Plus Regulations shall continue to apply in relation to the lone parent at a time when, apart from this paragraph, the requirement would cease to apply because the lone parent's child's or youngest child's, age exceeds the age specified in those regulations.

(6) For the purposes of this regulation—

"full-time course of advanced education", "full-time course of study" and "sandwich course" have the same meaning as in regulation 61 of the Income Support Regulations;

"full-time student" and "period of study" have the same meaning as in regulation 2(1) of the Income Support Regulations;

"specified day" means 21st May 2012.

GENERAL NOTE

6.63   See the note to para.1 of Sch.1B to the Income Support Regulations.

(SI 2014/1097)

The Income Support (Work-Related Activity) and Miscellaneous Amendments Regulations 2014

(SI 2014/1097)

Made by the Secretary of State for Work and Pensions under ss. 2A(1), (3), (6) and (8), 2D(1), (4)(a), (b), (d), (f) and (h) and (5) to (9)(c), 2E(3)(a) and (b), (4) and (5)(a) and (d), 2G(2)(a) and (4), 2H, 189(1) and (4) to (6) and 191 of the Social Security Administration Act 1992, ss. 9(1), 10(3) and (6) and 84 of the Social Security Act 1998, ss. 11E(1)(a), 13(2)(a), 24(1) and 25(2) and (3) of the Welfare Reform Act 2007 and ss. 20(1)(a), 21(1)(b) and (5), 40 and 42(2) and (3) of the Welfare Reform Act 2012.

[In force April 28, 2014]

REGULATIONS REPRODUCED

PART 1

GENERAL

PART 2

WORK-RELATED ACTIVITY

GENERAL NOTE

See the note to para. 1 of Sch. IB to the Income Support Regulations.   **6.65**

PART 1

GENERAL

Citation, commencement and interpretation

1.—(1) These Regulations may be cited as the Income Support   **6.66**

(Work-Related Activity) and Miscellaneous Amendments Regulations 2014 and come into force on the day after the day on which they are made.

(2) In these Regulations—

"action plan" means an action plan given in accordance with regulation 3;

"working day" means any day other than a Saturday, a Sunday, Christmas Day, Good Friday or a day which is a bank holiday under the Banking and Financial Dealings Act 1971.

PART 2

WORK-RELATED ACTIVITY

Requirement to undertake work-related activity

6.67   **2.**—(1) The Secretary of State may require a person who satisfies the conditions in paragraph (2) to undertake work-related activity as a condition of continuing to be entitled to the full amount of income support payable apart from these Regulations.

(2) The conditions referred to in paragraph (1) are that the person—

(a) is entitled to income support;

(b) is subject to a requirement imposed under section 2A of the Social Security Administration Act 1992;

(c) is not a lone parent of a child under the age of 3; and

(d) falls within paragraph 1(1) of Schedule 1B to the Income Support (General) Regulations 1987 and no other paragraph within that Schedule.

(3) A requirement imposed under paragraph (1)—

(a) must be reasonable in the view of the Secretary of State, having regard to the person's circumstances; and

(b) may not require the person to apply for a job or undertake work, whether as an employee or otherwise.

Notification of work-related activity

6.68   **3.**—(1) The Secretary of State must notify a person of a requirement to undertake work-related activity by including the requirement in a written action plan which is given to the person.

(2) The action plan must contain—

(a) particulars of the work-related activity which the person is to undertake; and

(b) any other information that the Secretary of State considers appropriate.

Requirement to undertake work-related activity at a certain time not to apply

6.69   **4.**—The Secretary of State may determine that a requirement as to the time at, or by, which work-related activity is to be undertaken is not to apply, or is to be treated as not having applied, if in the view of the Secretary of State it would be, or would have been, unreasonable to require the person to undertake the activity at or by that time.

Reconsideration of action plans

5.—(1) A person may request the reconsideration of an action plan.   6.70
(2) On receipt of a request the Secretary of State must reconsider the
action plan.
(3) A decision of the Secretary of State following a request must be in
writing and given to the person.

Failure to undertake work-related activity

6.—(1) A person who is required to undertake work-related activity but   6.71
fails to do so must show good cause for the failure before the end of five
working days beginning with the date on which the Secretary of State gives
notice to the person of the failure.
(2) The Secretary of State must determine whether a person who is
required to undertake work-related activity has failed to do so and, if so,
whether the person has shown good cause for the failure.
(3) In a case where within one month of the date on which the Secretary
of State gave notice to a person of their failure to undertake work-related
activity—
  (a) the person brings new facts to the attention of the Secretary of State
      which could not reasonably have been brought to the attention of
      the Secretary of State within the period specified in paragraph (1);
      and
  (b) those facts show that the person had good cause for failing to under-
      take work-related activity,
paragraph (1) applies with the modification that for the words "five
working days" there is substituted "one month".
(4) Where a notice under paragraph (1) is sent by post it is taken to have
been received on the second working day after it is sent.

Good cause

7.—Matters to be taken into account by the Secretary of State in   6.72
determining whether a person has shown good cause for failing to undertake work-related activity for the purposes of regulation 6(2) include that—
  (a) the person misunderstood the requirement to undertake work-
      related activity due to any learning, language or literacy difficulties of
      the person or any misleading information given to the person by the
      Secretary of State;
  (b) the person was attending a medical or dental appointment, or accom-
      panying someone for whom they have caring responsibilities to such
      an appointment, and that it would have been unreasonable, in the
      circumstances, for the person to undertake work-related activity;
  (c) the person had difficulties with their normal mode of transport and
      that no reasonable alternative was available;
  (d) the established customs and practices of the religion to which the
      person belongs prevented the person undertaking work-related activ-
      ity on that day or at that time;
  (e) the person was attending an interview with an employer with a view
      to obtaining employment;
  (f) the person was pursuing employment opportunities as a self-
      employed earner;

(g) the person, a dependant of the person or someone for whom the person provides care suffered an accident, sudden illness or relapse of a physical or mental health condition;

(h) the person was attending the funeral of a close friend or relative on the day fixed for the work-related activity;

(i) a disability from which the person suffers made it impracticable to attend at the time fixed for the work-related activity;

(j) the availability of child care.

Reduction of income support

6.73   **8.**—(1) Subject to paragraph (4), where the Secretary of State has determined that a person who was required to undertake work-related activity has failed to do so and has not shown good cause for that failure in accordance with regulation 6 (failure to undertake work-related activity), the amount of income support payable to the person is to be reduced in accordance with paragraph (2).

(2) Subject to paragraphs (3) and (4), the amount of the reduction of income support in relation to each failure is 20 per cent. of the amount applicable in respect of a single claimant for income support aged not less than 25 as prescribed in paragraph 1(1)(e) of Schedule 2 to the Income Support (General) Regulations 1987.

(3) In any benefit week, the amount of income support payable to a person is not, by virtue of paragraph (1), to be reduced below 10 pence.

(4) The amount of income support payable to a person is not to be reduced in accordance with paragraph (1) if that amount—

(a) is, at the time a determination falls to be made in respect of the current failure, being paid at a reduced rate in accordance with paragraphs (1) and (2), regulations 7(3) and 8 of the Social Security (Work-focused Interviews for Lone Parents) and Miscellaneous Amendments Regulations 2000 or regulation 12(2) (c) of the Social Security (Jobcentre Plus Interviews) Regulations 2002; and

(b) was last reduced not more than two weeks before the date of the current failure.

(5) In this regulation—

"benefit week" means any period of seven days corresponding to the week in respect of which income support is due to be paid;

"current failure" means a failure which, in relation to a person, may lead to a reduction in income support under paragraph (1) in relation to which the Secretary of State has not yet determined whether the amount of income support payable to the person is to be reduced in accordance with those paragraphs.

Circumstances where reduction under regulation 8(1) and (2) ceases to have effect

6.74   **9.**—(1) The reduction in income support set out in regulation 8(1) in respect of a failure to undertake work-related activity ceases to have effect in respect of a person from whichever is the earlier of—

(a) the date on which the person is no longer required to take part in a work-related activity as a condition of continuing to be entitled to the full amount of benefit which is payable apart from these Regulations; or

(b) the first day of the benefit week in which the person satisfies a compliance condition.

(2) In paragraph (1)(b), "compliance condition" means a requirement to—

(a) undertake work-related activity; or

(b) take part in a work-focused interview.

Restrictions on availability

10.—(1) Subject to paragraph (2), a person to whom regulation 2 applies may restrict the times at which they are required to undertake work-related activity.

(2) A person may not restrict the times at which they are required to undertake work-related activity by virtue of paragraph (1) to exclude—

(a) their child's normal school hours; or

(b) any period during which the person entrusts temporary supervision of their child to a person over the age of 18, not including any form of health care for the child.

Contracting out

11.—(1) Any function of the Secretary of State under this Part specified in paragraph (2) may be exercised by, or by employees of, such person (if any) as the Secretary of State may authorise for that purpose.

(2) The functions are any function under—

(a) regulation 2 (requirement to undertake work-related activity);

(b) regulation 3 (notification of work-related activity);

(c) regulation 4 (requirement to undertake work-related activity at a certain time not to apply);

(d) regulation 5 (reconsideration of action plans).

The Shared Parental Leave and Statutory Shared Parental Pay (Consequential Amendments to Subordinate Legislation) Order 2014

(2014/3255)

In force in accordance with art. 1(2) and (3)

The Secretary of State makes the following Order in exercise of the powers conferred by section 135(3) and 136(1) and (2) of the Children and Families Act 2014.

Citation and commencement

1.-(1) This Order may be cited as the Shared Parental Leave and Statutory Shared Parental Pay (Consequential Amendments to Subordinate Legislation) Order 2014.

(2) The provisions of this Order specified in article 37 come into force on 31st December 2014.

(3) The remaining provisions of this Order come into force on 5th April 2015

6.75

6.76

6.77

Amendment of Miscellaneous Regulations

6.78   **2.-34.** *[Omitted—Where relevant the amendments have been noted in the text of the Universal Credit Regulations (above) and in Vols I-IV]*

Transitional provisions

6.79   **35.**-(1) The amendments made by this Order in those articles which come into force on 5th April 2015 in accordance with 1(3) (amendments relating to references to ordinary and additional paternity leave and to ordinary and additional statutory paternity pay) do not have effect in relation to—

(a) ordinary statutory paternity pay which is paid;

(b) additional statutory paternity pay which is paid;

(c) a period in respect of which additional statutory paternity pay is payable which begins, or continues;

(d) ordinary paternity leave which is taken; or

(e) additional paternity leave which is taken;

on or after 5th April 2015.

(2) In this article—

"additional paternity leave" means leave under section 80AA or 80BB of the Employment Rights Act 1996;

"additional statutory paternity pay" means pay under section 171ZEA or 171ZEB of the Social Security Contributions and Benefits Act 1992;

"ordinary paternity leave" means leave under section 80A or 80B of the Employment Rights Act 1996;

"ordinary statutory paternity pay" means pay under section 171ZA or 171ZB of the Social Security Contributions and Benefits Act 1992.

36.   *[Omitted as relating solely to Northern Ireland]*

Provisions coming into force on 31st December 2014

6.80   **37.** The provisions specified in article 1(2) are—

(a) this article;

(b) article 1;

(c)-(y) *[Omitted]*

(z) article 28(1), (2)(c), (3)(c) and (4)(c) and (d);

(aa)-(hh) *[Omitted]*

(gg) article 35;

(hh) *[Omitted]*.

GENERAL NOTE

6.81   This Order makes consequential amendments to secondary legislation following the introduction of shared parental leave and statutory shared parental pay in place of additional paternity leave and additional statutory paternity pay by Part 7 of the Children and Families Act 2014. Those amendments that come into force on April 5, 2015 are subject to the transitional provisions in art.35.

The Social Security (Housing Costs Amendments) Regulations 2015

(SI 2015/1647)

Made by the Secretary of State for Work and Pensions under ss.123(1)(a), 135(1), 137(1) and 175(1), (3) and (4) of the Social Security Contributions and Benefits Act 1992, ss.4(5), 35(1) and 36(2) and (4) of the Jobseekers Act 1995, ss.4(2)(a), 24(1) and 25(2), (3) and (5) of the Welfare Reform Act 2007 and ss.11(4) and (5)(b), 40, 42(1), (2) and (3) of, and para.1 of Sch.6 to, the Welfare Reform Act 2012.

[In force April 1, 2016]

Citation and commencement

1. These Regulations may be cited as the Social Security (Housing Costs   6.82
Amendments) Regulations 2015 and come into force on 1st April 2016.

Amendment of the Income Support (General) Regulations 1987, the Jobseeker's Allowance Regulations 1996 and the Employment and Support Allowance Regulations 2008

2-4. *[Omitted]*   6.83

Amendment of the Universal Credit Regulations 2013

5. *[Omitted – see the amendments to para.5(2)(a) and (b) of Sch. 5 to the   6.84
Universal Credit Regulations 2013 in Pt. III]*

Amendment of the Universal Credit (Transitional Provisions) Regulations 2014

6. *[Omitted – see the amendment to reg. 29 of the Universal Credit   6.85
(Transitional Provisions) Regulations 2014 in Pt. IV]*

Revocation

7. *[Omitted as not relevant to universal credit]*   6.86

Saving provision

8.—(1) This regulation applies to a person ("P") where, for the purpose   6.87
of determining whether P's entitlement to a relevant benefit includes an
amount for housing costs, the Secretary of State determines that P is entitled or required to be treated as entitled to one or more relevant benefits for
a continuous period which includes 31st March 2016.

(2) Where this regulation applies to P, the provisions of—

(a) Schedule 6 to the Employment and Support Allowance Regulations
2008;

(b) Schedule 3 to the Income Support (General) Regulations 1987;
and

(c) Schedule 2 to the Jobseeker's Allowance Regulations 1996,

as modified by the Social Security (Housing Costs Special Arrangements)
(Amendment and Modification) Regulations 2008 are to have effect in
relation to P as if the amendments made by regulations 2 to 4 of these
Regulations and the revocation made by regulation 7(1) had not been
made.

(3) Where this regulation applies to P, the provisions of Schedule 5 to
the Universal Credit Regulations 2013 are to have effect in relation to P as
if the amendments made by regulations 5 and 6 of these Regulations had
not been made.

(4) In this regulation, "relevant benefit" means—

(a) an employment and support allowance under Part 1 of the Welfare
Reform Act 2007;

(b) income support under the Income Support (General) Regulations 1987;

(c) a jobseeker's allowance under the Jobseeker's Allowance Regulations 1996; and

(d) universal credit under Part 1 of the Welfare Reform Act 2012.

The Employment and Support Allowance (Miscellaneous Amendments and Transitional and Savings Provision) Regulations 2017

(SI 2017/581)

IN FORCE JUNE 23, 2017

REGULATIONS REPRODUCED

6.88   1.   Citation and commencement
2–9.   *[Omitted]*
10.   Transitional and savings provision

GENERAL NOTE

6.89   These Regulations make a number of technical amendments to clarify issues that have arisen in relation to the abolition of the work-related activity component of ESA with effect from April 3, 2017 (see SI 2017/204 in Vol. I). The amendments made by regs 2-9 have been incorporated in the appropriate places in the text. Reg.10 provides that—unsurprisingly—the amendments made by regs 2-8 do not apply to those who have transitional protection from the changes in SI 2017/204. Regulation 9 has not been included in that transitional and savings provision because it makes technical amendments to the extent of the transitional protection given by SI 2017/204 Sch.2, Pt.1.

The Secretary of State for Work and Pensions makes the following Regulations in exercise of the powers conferred by ss. 15(4) and (5) and 34(1) of the Welfare Reform and Work Act 2016.

In accordance with section 173(5)(b) of the Social Security Administration Act 1992, this instrument contains only regulations made by virtue of, or consequential upon s.15 of the Welfare Reform and Work Act 2016 and is made before the end of the period of 6 months beginning with the coming into force of this section.

In accordance with s.176(1) of the Social Security Administration Act 1992 the Secretary of State has consulted with organisations appearing to him to be representative of the authorities concerned.

Citation and commencement
6.90   1. These Regulations may be cited as the Employment and Support Allowance (Miscellaneous Amendments and Transitional and Savings Provision) Regulations 2017 and come into force on 23rd June 2017.

Transitional and savings provision
10. The amendments made by regulations 2 to 8 of these Regulations do not apply where any of the circumstances in paragraph 2 to 7 of Schedule 2 (transitional and savings provisions) to the Employment and Support Allowance and Universal Credit (Miscellaneous Amendments and Transitional and Savings Provisions) Regulations 2017, as amended by regulation 9 of these Regulations apply.

PART VII

THE RIGHT TO RESIDE

The Immigration (European Economic Area) Regulations 2016

(SI 2016/1052)

REGULATIONS REPRODUCED

These Regulations were revoked in their entirety by, s. 1 of, and Sch. 1, para. 2(2) to, the Immigration and Social Security Co-ordination (EU Withdrawal) Act 2020 with effect from December 31, 2020 at 11.00 pm. However, for the purposes of entitlement to benefit and for certain categories of claimant, a number of individual regulations are continued in effect–often in amended form–by the Citizens' Rights (Application Deadline and Temporary Protection) (EU Exit) Regulations 2020 (SI 2020/1209) and the Immigration and Social Security Co-ordination (EU Withdrawal) Act 2020 (Consequential, Saving, Transitional and Transitory Provisions) (EU Exit) Regulations 2020 (SI 2020/1309). Only those regulations that continue to have effect in those circumstances are reproduced below. For the text of the Regulations as it stood immediately before they were revoked, see pp. 948-1063 of Vol V of the 2020/21 edition.

PART 1

PRELIMINARY

PART 2

EEA RIGHTS

PART 3

RESIDENCE DOCUMENTATION

PART 7

GENERAL

SCHEDULES

GENERAL NOTE

7.2   *The United Kingdom's withdrawal from the European Union*

The United Kingdom left the European Union on January 31, 2020 at 11.00 pm. Section 1 of the European Union (Withdrawal) Act 2018 ("the Withdrawal Act") repealed the European Communities Act 1972 at that date and time: see the definition of "exit day" in s.20(1) of the Withdrawal Act as supplemented by s.20(2)–(5) and reg.2 of the European Union (Withdrawal) Act 2018 (Exit Day) (Amendment) (No. 3) Regulations 2019 (SI 2019/1423).

However, s.1A and 1B of the Withdrawal Act (inserted by ss.1 and 2 of the European Union (Withdrawal Agreement) Act 2020 ("the Withdrawal Agreement Act")) which came into force at the same date and time (see the European Union (Withdrawal Agreement) Act 2020 (Commencement No.1) Regulations 2020 (SI 2020/75) provided that, despite the repeal of the 1972 Act:

-    it continued to have effect in domestic UK law during the "implementation period" "as it [had] effect in domestic law ... immediately before exit day": see s.1A(1), and (2) of the Withdrawal Agreement Act; and

- EU-derived domestic legislation also continued to have effect in domestic UK law during the implementation period "as it [had] effect in domestic law ... immediately before exit day": see s.1B(1) and (2) of the Withdrawal Agreement Act.

The Implementation Period ended on December 31, 2020 at 11.00 pm. As a result, ss.1A and 1B of the Withdrawal Act expired and (subject to what is said below about the Withdrawal Agreement itself) EU law ceased to have effect in the UK except to the extent that it had been retained as part of UK domestic law by sections 2-7 of the Withdrawal Act and subordinate legislation made under that Act. These regulations ("the 2016 Regulations") were not so retained. Rather, they were revoked by s.1 of, and Sch.1, para.2(2) to, the Immigration and Social Security Co-ordination (EU Withdrawal) Act 2020.

The consequence for the right to reside test is that, with four exceptions, the free movement rights of EEA nationals in relation to the UK have come to an end. The rights of EEA nationals under UK immigration law have become the same as those of nationals of other states that are not in the Common Travel Area ("CTA"). Any non-CTA national who does not have either indefinite leave to remain (including settled status under EUSS: see below), or limited leave to remain that does not fall within the categories set out in s.115(9)(b)-(d) of the Immigration and Asylum Act 1999 (including pre-settled status under EUSS), is likely to be a "person subject to immigration control" as defined in the amended s.115(9) (see. Vol.II) and is excluded from entitlement to benefit by s.115(1) unless one of the exceptions in the amended Social Security (Immigration and Asylum) Consequential Amendments Regulations 2000 (SI 2000/636) (again, see Vol.II), applies.

The four exceptions referred to above are as follows: 7.3

1. Nationals of the Common Travel Area

The Channel Islands and the Isle of Man were never part of the EU or EEA and the rights of Island nationals in the CTA remain unchanged. The Republic of Ireland continues to be part of the CTA and the rights of Irish citizens have been confirmed by s.3ZA of the Immigration Act 1971 as inserted by s.2(2) of Immigration and Social Security Co-ordination (EU Withdrawal) Act 2020 immediately after 11.00 pm on December 31, 2020. That section provides that "[a]n Irish citizen does not require leave to enter or remain in the United Kingdom, unless" an order restricting that right has been made under paras (2)-(4).

2. EEA nationals and their family members with "pre-settled" status

EU nationals who wish to continue to live in the UK after the end of the 7.4 Implementation Period are required to apply under the EU Settlement Scheme ("EUSS") in Appendix EU to the Immigration Rules.

Applicants who can satisfy the Home Office that they meet the criteria in paras EU11 or EU12 of the Appendix, and that they should not be refused on grounds of suitability (paras EU15 and EU16), are given indefinite leave to remain (also known in this context as "settled status"). Those who have been granted settled status have a right to reside in the UK that counts for the purposes of all income-related benefits.

Applicants who do not qualify for settled status will be given limited leave to remain for five years (also known as "pre-settled status") if they meet the criteria in para.EU14. Those with pre-settled status may apply for settled status as soon as they meet the criteria in paras EU11 or EU12.

Subject to what is said about the *Fratila and Tanase* and *CG* cases (below) the limited leave to remain granted to those with pre-settled status does not, on its own, count for the purpose of the right to reside test for any means-tested benefit: see reg.21AA(3A)(a) of the IS Regulations, reg.85A(3A)(a) of the JSA Regulations 1996, reg.2(3A)(a) of the SPC Regulations 2002, reg.70(3A)(a) of the ESA Regulations 2008 and reg.9(3)(c)(i) of the Universal Credit Regulations.

However, those with pre-settled status—technically those who are "members of the post-transition period group" as defined by reg.1(2) of SI 2020/1309—may nevertheless have other rights of residence that *do* count for the purposes of the right to reside test. That is because the provisions of social security law that establish the test (other than reg.9 of the Universal Credit Regulations 2013, but see the General Note to that provision) have been amended to state that references in those Regulations to the 2016 Regulations "are to be read with Schedule 4 to the Immigration and Social Security Co-ordination (EU Withdrawal) Act 2020 (Consequential, Saving, Transitional and Transitory Provisions) Regulations 2020". Those Regulations save some provisions of the 2016 Regulations (often in a modified form) for the purposes of access to benefits and as they relate those with pre-settled status. See the text of, and commentary to, the affected regulations (below) for further details.

The effect is that those with pre-settled status who have a right to reside under the saved and modified 2016 regulations to satisfy the right to reside test as long as the particular right counts for the purpose of that benefit. So, for example, a person with pre-settled status who retains worker status while temporarily incapable of work is potentially entitled to universal credit.

But what of those whose *only* right to reside derives from their pre-settled status? In *R (Fratila and Tanase) v Secretary of State for Work and Pensions* [2020] EWHC 998 (Admin), the High Court (Swift J) upheld the validity of reg.9(3)(c)(i) of the Universal Credit Regulations in the face of a submission that it discriminated unlawfully on the grounds of nationality contrary to art.18 TFEU. On appeal, however, the Court of Appeal, by a majority (McCombe and Moylan LJJ, Dingemans LJ dissenting), reversed that decision: see *Fratila and Tanase v Secretary of State for Work and Pensions* [2020] EWCA Civ 1741. The majority held that the exclusion from benefit of those whose only right of residence was their pre-settled status amounted to unlawful discrimination on the grounds of nationality contrary to Art.18 TFEU. The Supreme Court gave the Secretary of State permission to appeal. However, before the Supreme Court appeal (UKSC 2021/0008) was heard, the Grand Chamber of the CJEU decided a preliminary reference from an appeal tribunal in Northern Ireland. That is probably because an appeal tribunal in Northern Ireland has made a preliminary reference to the CJEU (*CG v Department for Communities* (Case C-709/20) that raised similar issues. The questions referred to the CJEU were:

"Is Regulation 9(3)(c)(i) of The Universal Credit Regulations (Northern Ireland) 2016 ..., which excludes from entitlement to Social Security benefits EU nationals with a domestic right of residence (Limited Leave to Remain) [in this case 'pre-settled status' under the Appendix EU of the UK Immigration Rules] unlawfully discriminatory (either directly or indirectly) pursuant to Article 18 of the Treaty on the Functioning of the European Union and inconsistent with the UK's obligations under the European Communities Act 1972?
If the answer to question 1 is in the affirmative, and Regulation 9(3)(c)(i) of The Universal Credit Regulations (Northern Ireland) 2016 is held to be indirectly discriminatory, is Regulation 9(3)(c)(i) of The Universal Credit Regulations (Northern Ireland) 2016 justified pursuant to Article 18 of the Treaty on the Functioning of the European Union and inconsistent with the UK's obligations under the European Communities Act 1972?"

and the Grand Chamber ruled as follows:

"Article 24 of [the Citizenship Directive] must be interpreted as not precluding the legislation of a host Member State which excludes from social assistance economically inactive Union citizens who do not have sufficient resources and to whom that State has granted a temporary right of residence, where those benefits are guaranteed to nationals of the Member State concerned who are in the same situation.

However, provided that a Union citizen resides legally, on the basis of national law, in the territory of a Member State other than that of which he or she is a national, the national authorities empowered to grant social assistance are required to check that a refusal to grant such benefits based on that legislation does not expose that citizen, and the children for which he or she is responsible, to an actual and current risk of violation of their fundamental rights, as enshrined in Articles 1, 7 and 24 of the Charter of Fundamental Rights of the European Union. Where that citizen does not have any resources to provide for his or her own needs and those of his or her children and is isolated, those authorities must ensure that, in the event of a refusal to grant social assistance, that citizen may nevertheless live with his or her children in dignified conditions. In the context of that examination, those authorities may take into account all means of assistance provided for by national law, from which the citizen concerned and her children are actually entitled to benefit."

The Supreme Court will now need to decide how to apply the ruling in *CG* to the facts of *Fratila and Tanase*.

3.   *EEA nationals and their family members who have yet to apply under the EU*
     Settlement Scheme or whose applications have yet to be determined.

The position of those who are eligible to apply under EUSS (*i.e.*, those   7.5
EEA nationals who were living in the UK immediately before the end of the Implementation Period) but who have not yet done so, or who have done so but are waiting for a decision, is governed by the Citizens' Rights (Application Deadline and Temporary Protection) (EU Exit) Regulations 2020 (SI 2020/1209).

Those regulations establish two periods, a "grace period" for applying under the EU Scheme that expired on June 30, 2021, and a "relevant period", which for those who have made a timeous application, begins immediately after the grace period and lasts until the application is finally determined. During the grace period, parts of the 2016 Regulations continue in effect, usually in a modified form, as they apply to a "relevant person" (as defined in reg.3(6) of SI 2020/1209: see below). During the relevant period, they apply, again usually in a modified form, to a person who has made an in-time application (as defined in reg.4(6):see below) and who, immediately before the end of the Implementation Period, was either lawfully resident in the United Kingdom by virtue of the 2016 Regulations or had a right of permanent residence in the United Kingdom under those Regulations: see reg.4(2). See the text of, and commentary to, the affected regulations (below) for further details.

On August 6, 2021, the government announced that:

"The Home Office has put in place comprehensive arrangements to enable those with reasonable grounds for missing the deadline to apply to the EUSS.
While the numbers applying late have been small compared to pre-deadline application numbers, to provide further reassurance to late applicants the government will protect their rights until their application and any appeal is decided.
The government will also take a similar approach with joining family members, who will have temporary protection for three months after their arrival in the UK and pending the outcome of an EUSS application made during that period (and of any appeal)": see https://www.gov.uk/government/news/temporary-protection-for-more-applicants-to-the-settlement-scheme.

It is not absolutely clear whether the reassurance is intended to extend to all late applicants or only those "with reasonable grounds for missing the deadline", although, the tenor of the announcement suggests the former. Whichever represents the policy intention, further legislation will be needed to implement it but, at the time of going to press, none has been introduced.

4.   *Those with directly effective rights under the Withdrawal Agreement*

Section 7A of the Withdrawal Act (inserted by s.5 of the Withdrawal Agreement   7.6
Act) gives direct effect to those rights "created by" or "arising under" the Withdrawal Agreement "as in accordance with the withdrawal agreement are without further enactment to be given legal effect or used in the United Kingdom". Furthermore, by section 7A(3),"[e]very enactment (including an enactment contained in this Act) is to be read and has effect subject to those directly effective rights. If therefore, SI 2020/1209 or SI 2020/1309 have not implemented the Withdrawal Agreement in

a way that gives full effect to those rights, an EEA National may be able to derive rights of residence directly from the Citizens Rights provisions in Part 2 of the Withdrawal Agreement itself. The existence, and extent, of any such rights will be established by case law.

The law following the end of the Implementation Period

7.7   Only those regulations that continue to have effect for the purposes of access to benefits by virtue of SI 2020/1209 and SI 2020/1309 are reproduced below. The remainder of this note, and the commentary to the individual regulations discusses the law as so preserved and not, where different, the law that applied during the Implementation Period.

For the text of, and commentary to, the Regulations as they stood immediately before they were revoked, see pp.948-1063 of Vol V of the 2020/21 edition.

These Regulations ("the 2016 Regulations") implement Directive 2004/38/EC "on the right of citizens of the Union and their family members to move and reside freely within the territory of the Member States" ("the Citizenship Directive"): see Vol.III. They therefore govern whether EEA nationals and their family members have a right to reside for the purposes of universal credit IS, HB, income-based JSA, SPC, child benefit, CTC and income-related ESA.

In the commentary to these Regulations, references to numbered articles (*e.g.,* "art.7") are to the Citizenship Directive unless the contrary is stated.

Introduction and historical background

7.8   Claimants who are "persons from abroad" as defined in reg.21AA of the IS Regulations, reg.85A of the JSA Regulations and reg.70 of the ESA Regulations are not entitled to IS, JSA or ESA. This is because they are treated as a special case with an applicable amount of nil (see para.17 of Sch.7 to the IS Regulations, para.14 of Sch.5 to the JSA Regulations and para.11 of Sch.5 to the ESA Regulations). For child benefit, SPC, and universal credit, the same result is achieved by treating such claimants as "not in Great Britain" (see reg.23(2) of the Child Benefit (General) Regulations 2006, reg.2 of the SPC Regulations and reg.9 of the Universal Credit Regulations) and, therefore, as failing to satisfy the conditions of entitlement in, respectively, s.146(2) of SSCBA 1992, s.1(2)(a) of SPCA 2002 and s.4(1)(c) of WRA 2012. Similarly, CTC claimants with no right to reside are treated as "not in the United Kingdom" (reg.3(5) of the Tax Credits (Residence) Regulations 2003) and, therefore, as having no entitlement to claim under s.3 TCA 2002.

From the introduction of the IS and HB Schemes in April 1988 until the Immigration and Asylum Act 1999 came into force on April 3, 2000, the exclusion of "persons from abroad" from benefit was the principal mechanism for denying income-related benefits to those claimants who were considered to have insufficiently close links with Great Britain. The approach was extended to community charge benefit when that benefit was introduced on April 1, 1990 and then to CTB, JSA and ESA when they were introduced on April 1, 1993, October 7, 1996 and October 27, 2008 respectively.

Originally, the definition of "person from abroad" was in reg.21(3) of the IS Regulations. It was a wide definition and encompassed those who did not have leave to enter or remain in the UK or whose leave had been granted on a sponsorship undertaking or was conditional upon not having recourse to public funds (see pp.164–167 of the 1999 edition of Mesher & Wood, *Income-related Benefits: the Legislation* for further details).

That definition was widened on August 1, 1994 by the introduction of the "habitual residence test". That test was aimed principally at EEA nationals (although it affects many others) but EC law prohibiting discrimination against the citizens of other Member States meant that, to be valid, it had to apply to British citizens as well. One of the results of the change was therefore that, for the first time, a British citizen could be excluded from income-related benefits as a "person from abroad".

In the early days of the test there were a number of challenges to its validity both on the grounds that it was *ultra vires* s.124(1) of the Contributions and Benefits Act and as being unlawful under EC law. However, these challenges were all unsuccessful (see pp.290–291 of the 1999 edition of Mesher and Wood, *Income-related Benefits: the Legislation*).

Subsequently, in *Couronne v Crawley BC and Secretary of State for Work and Pensions* [2007] EWCA Civ 1086, the Court of Appeal held that the test did not discriminate unlawfully against British Citizens from the Chagos Islands in comparison with British Citizens of Irish ethnic or national origin either under the Race Relations Act 1976 or art.14 and art.8 and or art.1 First Protocol ECHR. In that case, the appellants had been unlawfully prevented by the British government from returning to their homeland but the Court held that it was not irrational for the habitual residence test to be applied to them.

With effect from April 3, 2000, the definition of "person from abroad" was narrowed to such an extent that only the habitual residence test remained. Most claimants who had previously fallen within other heads of the definition were re-categorised as "persons subject to immigration control" and excluded from income-related benefits by s.115 of the Immigration and Asylum Act 1999.   **7.9**

On May 1, 2004, 10 additional countries joined the EU and the habitual residence test was supplemented by the introduction (as reg.21(3G) of the IS Regulations, reg.85(4B) of the JSA Regulations and reg.2(2) of the SPC Regulations) of the "right to reside" test. The test was also applied to child benefit and child tax credit by amendments to reg.23 of the Child Benefit Regulations and reg.3 of the Tax Credits (Residence) Regulations 2003.

In addition, the Accession (Immigration and Worker Registration) Regulations 2004 (SI 2004/1219) ("the A8 Regulations") established a registration scheme which imposed greater restrictions on the rights of "A8 Nationals" (see below) to reside in the UK as workers or jobseekers than applied to the nationals of other member States.

From that point on, EEA nationals who did not have a legal right to reside—very broadly, those who had never been, or (in certain circumstances) were no longer, economically active and were not the family members of people who were, or had been, economically active—ceased to be regarded as habitually resident unless they had the benefit of transitional protection, and stood no chance of becoming habitually resident in the future, irrespective of their intentions and the length of time for which they had actually lived in the UK.

On April 30, 2006, the Citizenship Directive came into force and repealed the previous Directives upon which EC immigration law had been based. The Citizenship Directive was implemented in UK domestic law by the Immigration (European Economic Area) Regulations 2006 ("the 2006 Regulations").

On the same day, the right to reside test was revised to reflect the new EU Law and the definition of "person from abroad" was moved from reg.21 to reg.21AA of the IS Regulations, and from reg.85 to reg.85A of the JSA Regulations.

On January 1, 2007, Bulgaria and Romania joined the EU and the Accession (Immigration and Worker Authorisation) Regulations 2006 (SI 2006/3317) ("the A2 Regulations") (see below) established an authorisation scheme which restricted the rights of "A2 nationals" (see below) to reside in the UK as workers or jobseekers. With effect from the same day, the right to reside test was further amended.   **7.10**

On May 1, 2009 (although, at the time, the law purported to end the A8 Scheme on May 1, 2011: see the discussion of *Secretary of State for Work and Pensions v Gubeladze* [2019] UKSC 31 below), the A8 States became full members of the EU and their nationals ceased to be subject to additional restrictions on their right to reside in the UK (i.e., over and above those that apply to the nationals of other EU states) from that date. Whether previous periods of residence were lawful under the former A8 Scheme remains relevant to whether an A8 national has acquired a permanent right of residence (see reg.7A of the 2006 Regulations).

On July 1, 2013, Croatia joined the EU and the Accession of Croatia (Immigration and Worker Authorisation) Regulations 2013 (SI 2013 No. 1460) (see below) established a further authorisation scheme which restricted the rights of Croatian nationals to reside in the UK as workers or jobseekers (see below), along similar lines to the A2 scheme.

On January 1, 2014, Bulgaria and Romania became full members of the EU and their nationals ceased to be subject to additional restrictions on their right to reside in the UK (i.e., over and above those that apply to the nationals of other EU states) from that date. Whether previous periods of residence were lawful under the former A8 Scheme remains relevant to whether an A8 national has acquired a permanent right of residence (see reg.7B of the 2006 Regulations).

Also on January 1, 2014, the habitual residence test for jobseeker's allowance was amended to include an additional requirement that the claimant should have been living in the Common Travel Area for the past three months.

On February 1, 2017, the 2006 Regulations (other than regs 7A and 7B) were consolidated and revoked by the 2016 Regulations. There is a table of equivalences in Sch.7 to the Regulations.

On July 1, 2018, Croatian nationals became full members of the EU and their nationals ceased to be subject to additional restrictions on their right to reside in the UK (i.e., over and above those that apply to the nationals of other EU states) from that date. Whether previous periods of residence were lawful between July 1, 2013 and June 30, 2018 remains relevant to whether a Croatian national has acquired a permanent right of residence.

On January 31, 2020 at 11.00 pm, the United Kingdom left the EU. However, the EU and domestic law relating to the right to reside test was preserved during the implementation period: see under the heading, *The United Kingdom's withdrawal from the European Union*, above.

Overview

7.11   Given that background, the framework of the law is now as follows:

(1) under s.115(1) and (3) of the Immigration and Asylum Act 1999, a "person subject to immigration control" is not entitled to a wide range of benefits including income support, income-based jobseeker's allowance, income-related ESA, state pension credit, universal credit and social fund payments. However, EEA nationals and their family members cannot fall within the definition of "person subject to immigration control" in s.115(9), EEA nationals because they are expressly excluded and family members because they do not require leave to enter or remain in the UK: see s.7 of the Immigration Act 1988;

(2) this general rule is subject to the limited exceptions that are set out in the Social Security (Immigration and Asylum) Consequential Amendments Regulations 2000 (SI 2000/636—see below);

(3) even if a claimant is not a "person subject to immigration control", he may nevertheless be a "person from abroad" if he is not habitually resident in the Common Travel Area ("CTA") (i.e. the UK, Channel Islands, Isle of Man and Republic of Ireland). This includes British and Irish nationals;

(4) claimants who are nationals of EEA countries (other than the UK and the Republic of Ireland), or of Switzerland, only satisfy the habitual residence test if they have a "right to reside" in the CTA—see reg.21AA(2).

For a more detailed discussion of points (1) and (2) above, see the notes to SI 2000/636.

Subject to what is said about the burden of proof in *Kerr v Department for Social Development* [2004] UKHL 23 (*R 1/04 (SF)*), it is for the Secretary of State to prove that a claimant is not habitually resident, rather than for the claimant to show that he is, although it is preferable to resolve any doubts by enquiring further into the facts rather than relying on the burden of proof—see *R(IS) 6/96*.

EEA nationals

Although, conceptually, the "right to reside" test applies to all claimants, the legal framework explained above means that, as a matter of practice, it will only affect nationals of the EEA states and their family members (including, in exceptional cases, the parents of British children: see reg.16(5)). This is because non-EEA nationals will either have a right of abode in the UK, in which case, they will obviously also have a right to reside here; or they will have some type of leave to remain here, in which case, they will have a right to reside here for the duration of that leave—and any extension of it (although they will not necessarily be entitled to income-related benefits); or they will be illegal entrants or overstayers, in which case they are already excluded from benefit as persons subject to immigration control so that the additional requirement that they have should have the right to reside before being entitled to benefit has no practical effect.

By contrast, under s.7 of the Immigration Act 1988, EEA nationals do not usually require leave to enter or remain in the UK and, in principle, "must be admitted to the United Kingdom if [they produce], on arrival, a valid national identity card or passport issued by an EEA state" (see reg.11). It is therefore possible for EEA nationals to be admitted to the UK who have no legal right to reside here: whether or not they have such a right depends on EU Law.

The EEA now consists of the 27 EU countries (namely Austria, Belgium, Bulgaria, Croatia, Cyprus, the Czech Republic, Denmark, Estonia, Finland, France, Germany, Greece, Hungary, Ireland, Italy, Latvia, Lithuania, Luxembourg, Malta, the Netherlands, Poland, Portugal, Romania, Slovakia, Slovenia, Spain and Sweden) together with Norway, Liechtenstein and Iceland.

Nationals of Norway, Liechtenstein and Iceland have the same rights of residence in the UK as EU nationals: see the definition of "EEA national" in reg.2 below.

The rights of A8 nationals (i.e., nationals of the Czech Republic, Estonia, Hungary, Latvia, Lithuania, Poland, Slovakia and Slovenia, which joined the EU on May 1, 2004), of A2 nationals (i.e., nationals of Bulgaria and Romania), and of Croatian nationals, to reside in the UK as workers or work seekers were once more restricted than for nationals of most other Member States. The A8 restrictions applied from May 1, 2004 until April 30, 2009—but see the discussion of *Secretary of State for Work and Pensions v Gubeladze* [2019] UKSC 31—and the A2 restrictions applied from January 1, 2007 to December 31, 2013. The Croatian restrictions applied from July 1, 2013 to June 30, 2018. The former restrictions remain relevant to the question whether the residence of an A8, A2 or Croatian national during those periods counts towards the acquisition of a permanent right of residence.

The rights of Croatian, A8 and A2 nationals are considered in more detail below.

British nationals

British nationals have a right of abode in the UK (see s.2(1)(a) of the Immigration Act 1971 and *R(PC)2/07*) and therefore automatically have a right to reside in the CTA.

In some circumstances—for example, the treatment of family members—EU Law is more favourable to the nationals of other Member States than domestic UK law is to British nationals. In such circumstances, British nationals cannot rely upon their status as EU citizens to obtain the more favourable treatment unless the unfavourable treatment is the consequence of having exercised an EU right, such as the rights to freedom of movement or establishment.

For similar reasons, British nationals who have not exercised any EU right are subject to the habitual residence test as it applies to non-EEA nationals (see below) because they cannot take advantage of the exemptions in para.(4)(a)–(e). For the position of British nationals who are also nationals of another EEA State see the discussion of the *McCarthy* case below.

For the rights of non-British nationals who are parents of British children, see reg.16(5).

7.12

7.13

Irish and Island nationals

7.14   Ireland, the Channel Islands and the Isle of Man are part of the CTA and their nationals automatically have a right to reside in the UK. However, the Channel Islands and the Isle of Man are not part of the EU or the EEA (see *SSWP v JG (RP)* [2013] UKUT 300 (AAC) at para.34) and their nationals are subject to the habitual residence test as it applies to non-EEA nationals (see the commentary to reg.21AA of the IS Regulations). The exemptions in para.(4)(a)–(e) cannot apply to them. There are reciprocal agreements between the UK and the Isle of Man (SI 2016/187) and Jersey and Guernsey (SI 1994/2802).

As Ireland is a member of the EU, Irish nationals in the UK may well be exercising EU rights and therefore have a right to reside under EU law in addition to their rights under domestic UK law. Therefore, even though Irish nationals have a right to reside, it may be to their advantage to establish that they fall within one of the EU categories in para.(4)(a)–(e) in order to obtain exemption from the habitual residence test. Those Irish nationals who are unable to establish such an exemption will be subject to the habitual residence test as it applies to non-EEA nationals.

The special treatment accorded by the UK to Irish nationals, but not accorded to citizens of other member States, which might otherwise be thought to be contrary to the various prohibitions in EU law against discrimination on the ground of nationality, is lawful because the provision for Irish citizens is protected by art.2 of the Protocol on the Common Travel Area (Protocol 20 annexed to the TFEU and TEU). That article states that the United Kingdom and Ireland "may continue to make arrangements between themselves relating to the movement of persons between their territories" and provides that nothing in articles 26 and 77 of the Treaty on the Functioning of the European Union or in any other provision of that Treaty or of the Treaty on European Union or in any other measure adopted under them shall affect any such arrangements: see *Patmalniece v SSWP* [2011] UKSC 11 at paras 54–61.

Complications sometimes arise because, before January 1, 2005, the domestic law of the Republic of Ireland entitled anyone born on the island of Ireland (i.e. including Northern Ireland) to Irish citizenship, irrespective of the nationality of their parents or the existence of any other connection with the Republic. In particular, non-EEA nationals have sometimes arranged for a child to be born in Northern Ireland (or in the Republic) so as to obtain a right to reside in the UK by virtue of that child's Irish citizenship. It is clear from the decision of the ECJ in *Zhu and Chen v Home Secretary* (Case C–200/02) that this stratagem will sometimes work as far as immigration law is concerned. But its success depends upon the parents and child being self-sufficient and having health insurance (see *W(China) v Home Secretary* [2006] EWCA Civ 1494) and it will therefore be of limited efficacy in establishing a right to reside for the purpose of entitlement to income-related benefits.

Gibraltar

7.15   The status of Gibraltar was explained by Upper Tribunal Judge White in *SSWP v JG (RP)* (above) at paras 29-32.

> "29.   Gibraltar was ceded in perpetuity by Spain to Great Britain under the Treaty of Utrecht 1713. It is a British Crown Colony. It is not part of the United Kingdom. This separate status is recognized under national law, international law and European Union law.
>
> 30.   In Case C-145/04 *Spain v United Kingdom* [2006] ECR I-7917, the Court of Justice described the status of Gibraltar as follows:
>
> > '19.   In Community law, Gibraltar is a European territory for whose external relations a Member State is responsible within the meaning of Article 299(4) EC and to which the provisions of the EC Treaty apply. The Act concerning the conditions of accession of the Kingdom of Denmark, Ireland and the United Kingdom of Great Britain and Northern Ireland and the adjustments to the Treaties (OJ 1972 L 73, p. 14) provides, however, that certain parts of the Treaty are not to apply to Gibraltar.'

31.   European Union law on citizenship of the Union and the free movement of persons applies to Gibraltar.

32.   The Family Allowances, National Insurance and Industrial Injuries (Gibraltar) Order 1974 (SI 1974 No 555) ("the Gibraltar Order") provides:

'1.   Any reference in the following paragraphs to a territory shall be construed as a reference to the territory of the United Kingdom or Gibraltar or both as the case may be and any reference to a child shall be construed as a reference to any person for whom family allowances are payable under the legislation in question.

2(a).   Any person shall have the same rights and liabilities in relation to social security other than family allowances, as he would have had if the United Kingdom and Gibraltar had been separate Member States of the European Economic Community.

For the purpose of giving effect to paragraph (a) above the same procedures shall so far as is practicable be adopted in relation to the person and benefit concerned as would have been applicable had the United Kingdom and Gibraltar been such separate Member States.'"

Nationals of Norway, Iceland and Liechtenstein:

Nationals of the three EEA states that are not EU members enjoy the same   7.16
rights as EU citizens by virtue of the EEA Treaty (also known as the "Oporto Agreement"): see *Ullusow v Secretary of State for Work and Pensions* [2007] EWCA Civ 657 (July 5, 2007, CA, Sir Andrew Morritt C., Lloyd and Moses L.JJ.) overturning *CPC/2920/2005* in which a tribunal of Commissioners held that, on a true interpretation of the Oporto Agreement, Directive 90/364 only conferred a right to reside on those (non-EU) EEA nationals who are seeking to exercise a right of establishment (i.e. to set up a business in the UK).

The 2016 Regulations do not distinguish between EEA nationals who are EU citizens and those who are not. The exemptions in reg.21AA(4) of the IS Regulations, reg.85A(4) of the JSA Regulations, and reg.2(4) of the SPC Regulations apply to nationals of Iceland, Liechtenstein and Norway, and to their family members (see reg.7), as if they were EU nationals (see reg.10(e) of SI 1026/2006).

Swiss nationals

Switzerland is not a member of either the EU or the EEA. However, since June   7.17
1, 2002, Swiss nationals have had rights of residence in Britain that are similar to those enjoyed by EEA nationals. Those rights are conferred by the Luxembourg Agreement (*Agreement between the European Community and its Member States, of the one part, and the Swiss Confederation, of the other, on the Free Movement of Persons,* Luxembourg, June 21, 1999, Cm.5639).

Before April 30, 2006, that agreement was implemented as a matter of domestic law by the Immigration (Swiss Free Movement of Persons) (No.3) Regulations 2002 (SI 2002/1241). From that date, SI 2002/1241 was revoked and reg.2(1) of the 2006 Regulations deemed Switzerland to be an EEA state, even though it is not actually one. That approach is continued in the 2016 Regulations. In addition, the exemptions in reg.21AA(4) of the IS Regulations, reg.85A(4) of the JSA Regulations, and reg.2(4) of the SPC Regulations apply to Swiss nationals, and to their family members (see reg.7), as if they were EU nationals (see reg.10(e) of SI 2006/1026).

The effect is that Swiss nationals have the full range of rights conferred on EEA nationals by the 2016 Regulations. Switzerland is also a party to the European Social Charter (see immediately below), but that Charter does not confer any additional right to reside on Swiss nationals.

Turkish nationals and nationals of the Republic of Northern Macedonia

Although not EEA States, Turkey has ratified the European Convention on Social   7.18
and Medical Assistance ("the ECSMA Agreement") and the European Social

Charter, and the Republic of Northern Macedonia has ratified the Social Charter. In some circumstances, this will have the effect that Turkish and Northern Macedonian nationals are not excluded from benefit as "persons subject to immigration control" (see the commentary to SI 2000/636). However, the right to reside and habitual residence tests remain applicable (*CH/2321/2007*) and neither the ECSMA Agreement nor the Social Charter confers any direct right of residence or right to benefit: see *Yesiloz v Camden LBC and SSWP* [2009] EWCA Civ 415 (R(H) 7/09. This is because, as the Commissioner pointed out at para.6 of *CIS/1773/2007*, the ECSMA Agreement "requires the Contracting Powers to enact legislation conferring rights to benefit but it does not confer those rights itself. In the United Kingdom, it is for Parliament to give effect to ECSMA through domestic legislation" (see also para.24 of *CJSA/4705/999*, *CIS/259/2008* and paras 27–40 of the decision of the Court of Appeal in *Abdirahman v Secretary of State for Work and Pensions* [2007] EWCA Civ 657). Therefore, it is not possible for an ECSMA national who is not also an EEA national to assert in the domestic courts of the UK that legislation breaches the UK's international obligations under ECSMA: s/he can only rely on the rights conferred by domestic law. The same is true of the Social Charter (see para.39 of *Abdirahman*).

The Citizenship Directive

7.19   The phrase "right to reside" is not defined in social security legislation and whether or not a claimant has such a right therefore falls to be determined by the ordinary rules of immigration law and, in particular, EU Law.

That Law changed with effect from April 30, 2006 when the Citizenship Directive came into force and it is therefore necessary to ascertain the period with which one is dealing in order to know which law to apply. Readers are referred to pp.298-306 of Vol. II of the 2006 edition, and to the Updating Material for those pages in the Supplement to that edition, for a full discussion of the law as it stood before April 30, 2006.

The purpose of the Citizenship Directive is to extend the rights of EU citizens. Therefore, arguments suggesting that the rights it confers are less extensive than those conferred by the former law need to be treated with caution. As the ECJ held in Case C-127/08 *Metock v Minister for Justice, Equality and Law Reform* at para.59:

> "As is apparent from recital 3 in the preamble to Directive 2004/38, it aims in particular to 'strengthen the right of free movement and residence of all Union citizens', so that Union citizens cannot derive less rights from that directive than from the instruments of secondary legislation which it amends or repeals."

The only exception to this principle in UK law occurred in the decision of the Court of Appeal in *State for Work and Pensions v Elmi* [2011] EWCA Civ 1403 (see below). However the principle appears to have been ignored rather than disapplied in that case.

The changes in EU Law from April 30, 2006 were reflected by amendments to domestic social security law and, in particular, the introduction of reg.21AA and of reg.85A of the JSA Regulations, and the substitution of a new reg.2 in the SPC Regulations.

The most important conceptual change in the domestic law is that, whereas, before April 30, 2006, any right of residence was sufficient to satisfy the right to reside test, it is now necessary to ask whether the particular right of residence enjoyed by the claimant counts for the purpose of the particular benefit that s/he has claimed (see para.(3) of each of those Regulations). For example, the initial right of residence (see below) does not count for the purposes of any income-related benefit and the extended right of residence enjoyed by jobseekers only counts for the purposes of JSA.

The personal scope of the Citizenship Directive

7.20   By art.3(1) of the Citizenship Directive, it applies to "all Union citizens who move to or reside in a Member State other than that of which they are a national, and to their family members . . . who accompany or join them". For the definition of "family members", see reg.7.

The rights under the Citizenship Directive are extended to the nationals of the other EEA States and to Switzerland by, respectively, the Oporto Agreement and the Luxembourg Agreement (see above). The commentary to these Regulations will therefore follow the Regulations themselves by describing the beneficiaries of the Directive as "EEA nationals" and their family members.

It follows the words "who move to or reside in a Member State other than that of which they are a national" in art.3(1) that, whatever rights they may have under the EU *Treaties*, EU citizens do not have rights *under the Citizenship Directive* against the Member States of which they are nationals unless they have exercised their rights to freedom of movement to live in another EU state.

The leading case on this point is *McCarthy v Secretary of State for the Home Department* (Case C-434/09). Mrs McCarthy was a dual British/Irish citizen who was born in, and had always lived in, the UK. She was in receipt of social security benefits. She married a Jamaican citizen who did not have leave to remain in the UK. She then obtained an Irish passport and she and her husband applied for a residence permit and a residence document as, respectively, an EU citizen and the family member of an EU citizen. Those applications were refused, on the basis that Mrs McCarthy was not a qualifying person (see below). On appeal, the Supreme Court referred the following question to the ECJ for a preliminary ruling:

> "1.   Is a person of dual Irish and United Kingdom nationality who has resided in the United Kingdom for her entire life a 'beneficiary' within the meaning of Article 3 of [the Citizenship Directive]?"

The ECJ reformulated that question and answered as follows:

> "—   Article 3(1) of [the Citizenship Directive] must be interpreted as meaning that that directive is not applicable to a Union citizen who has never exercised his right of free movement, who has always resided in a Member State of which he is a national and who is also a national of another Member State."

Note, however, that the Citizenship Directive is not the only source of rights of residence. Such rights can arise directly under arts 20, 21 and 45 of TFEU, under EU Regulations (particularly, Regulation 492/2011, formerly Regulation 1612/68), and under the domestic law of the UK. Such rights do not necessarily depend upon the exercise by the EU citizen of his or her free movement rights. In particular:

- an EU citizen who has never exercised his/her rights of free movement, who has always resided in a Member State of which s/he is a national may, exceptionally, derive rights against such a Member State under art.21 TFEU where the application of measures by that Member State would have the effect of depriving him or her of "the genuine enjoyment of the substance of the rights conferred by virtue of his [or her] status as a Union citizen or of impeding the exercise of his [or her] right of free movement and residence within the territory of the Member States: see the discussion of *Zambrano* below.

- until October 15, 2012, a British citizen who is a dual national of another EU State, was able to derive rights from his or her other nationality under domestic UK law (i.e. the 2006 Regulations) where those Regulations were more favourable to him or her than EU law would be (see the decisions of the Upper Tribunal in *SSWP v AA* [2009] UKUT 249 (AAC) and HG v SSWP (SPC) [2011] UKUT 382 (AAC). However, from October 16, 2012, the 2006 Regulations were amended by SI 2012/1547 to reflect the Citizenship Directive as interpreted in *McCarthy*. The changes, which effectively reverse the decisions of the Upper Tribunal referred to above, are subject to transitional protection set out in para.9 of Sch.6.

The position of British nationals who are also nationals of another EEA State (and of their family members) has recently changed as a result of the decision of the Grand Chamber of the CJEU in *Lounes Secretary of State for the Home Department (Case C-165/16)*.

The Court was considering circumstances in which Ms O, a Spanish national, had exercised her rights to freedom of movement to live and work in the UK and become a naturalised British citizen, while retaining her Spanish nationality. She subsequently married Mr Lounes who was an Algerian national and, under domestic immigration law, an illegal overstayer. Mr Lounes then applied for the issue of a residence card as a family member of an EEA national (i.e., under reg.18). That application was refused and he was served with notice of a decision to remove him from the UK as an overstayer.

Under the 2016 Regulations, an EEA national who becomes a naturalised British citizen ceases to be an "EEA National" as defined in see reg.2(1). Therefore third country national family members cannot derive a right of residence as his/her family member.

The Grand Chamber ruled that the UK was correct to say that Ms O (and Mr Lounes) ceased to be beneficiaries of the Directive when she became British. However, Mr Lounes derived a right of residence directly from Art 21(1) TFEU "on conditions which must not be stricter than those provided for by [the]Directive". The Court's formal ruling was in the following terms:

> "[The Citizenship Directive] must be interpreted as meaning that, in a situation in which a citizen of the European Union (i) has exercised his freedom of movement by moving to and residing in a Member State other than that of which he is a national, under Article 7(1) or Article 16(1) of that directive, (ii) has then acquired the nationality of that Member State, while also retaining his nationality of origin, and (iii) several years later, has married a third-country national with whom he continues to reside in that Member State, that third-country national does not have a derived right of residence in the Member State in question on the basis of [the Citizenship Directive].
>
> The third-country national is however eligible for a derived right of residence under Article 21(1) TFEU, on conditions which must not be stricter than those provided for by [the Citizenship Directive] for the grant of such a right to a third-country national who is a family member of a Union citizen who has exercised his right of freedom of movement by settling in a Member State other than the Member State of which he is a national."

The Lounes principle is not confined to cases in which the family member is a third-country national. It also applies where s/he is an EEA national: see ODS v SSWP (UC) [2019] UKUT 192 (AAC) and AS v SSWP (UC) [2018] UKUT 260 (AAC) at paras 31-36.

The *Lounes* principle does not, however, apply where the EU National worked in the UK and became a naturalised British citizen before the EU before Member State of which she is a national acceded to the EU: see the decision of the Immigration Appeals Chamber of the Upper Tribunal in *Kovacevic (British citizen – Art 21 TFEU) Croatia* [2018] UKUT 273 (IAC). Ms Kovacevic is a national of Croatia who lawfully entered the UK in 1995 and naturalised as a British citizen in 2007 (i.e., before Croatia acceded to the EU on 1 July 2013). Since arriving in the UK, she had resided and worked lawfully under UK domestic law and she retained her Croatian nationality following naturalisation. In June 2014, (i.e., after Croatia acceded to the EU) she married an Algerian national. The Upper Tribunal distinguished *Lounes*. Although she was a dual British/Croatian national, Ms Kovacevic had neither lived nor worked in the UK in the exercise of her Treaty rights. Her rights were therefore analogous to those of the Mrs McCarthy in *McCarthy v Secretary of State for the Home Department* C-434/09 and no right arose under art.21.

"Residence" and "lawful presence"

7.21   Lawful presence is not the same as a right of residence. A claimant who is lawfully present in the UK (i.e. who has been admitted under the right of entry in reg.11 of the 2016 Regulations, is in fact present in the UK, and would have an immediate right of re-entry if ever removed) does not *ipso facto* have a right to reside (see *Abdirahman* and *Ulluslow*).

Whether a claimant is lawfully present in the UK is, however, relevant for other social security purposes (see, in particular, the commentary on the ECSMA Agreement and the European Social Charter in the General Note to SI 2000/636).

Meaning of "right to reside"

"Right to reside" is defined by reg.2(1) as meaning "a right to reside in the United Kingdom under these Regulations (or where so specified, a right to reside under a particular regulation)".

7.22

However, these Regulations implement the Citizenship Directive and may sometimes do so imperfectly, in which case a right to reside for social security purposes will arise by virtue of the Directive and will take precedence over domestic UK immigration law. Conversely, there are a number of occasions when these Regulations confer rights that have no equivalent in the Directive. These Regulations must therefore be understood in the context of the relevant EU law.

The starting point must be that under art.20 of the Treaty on the Functioning of the European Union ("TFEU") (formerly art.17 of the EC Treaty ("TEC")) "[e]very person holding the nationality of a Member State shall be a citizen of the Union" and that, under art.21 (ex-art.18 TEC).

"1. Every citizen of the Union shall have the right to move and reside freely within the territory of the Member States, subject to the limitations and conditions laid down in this Treaty and by the measures adopted to give it effect. . .."

It is also of potential relevance that, under art.18 (Ex-art.12 TEC):

"Within the scope of application of this Treaty, and without prejudice to any special provisions contained therein, any discrimination on grounds of nationality shall be prohibited"

and that, under art.45 (Ex-art.39 TEC):

"1. Freedom of movement for workers shall be secured within the Community. 2. Such freedom of movement shall entail the abolition of any discrimination based on nationality between workers of the Member States as regards employment, remuneration and other conditions of work and employment. 3. It shall entail the right, subject to limitations justified on grounds of public policy, public security or public health:. . .

    (c)   to stay in a Member State for the purpose of employment in accordance with the provisions governing the employment of nationals of that State laid down by law, regulation or administrative action;

    (d)   to remain in the territory of a Member State after having been employed in that State, subject to conditions which shall be embodied in implementing regulations to be drawn up by the Commission."

The "limitations and conditions" authorised by art.20(1) are contained in the Citizenship Directive, see art.1(a) and (c). In that context, the drafting of the Citizenship Directive can often seem confusing because it appears to *grant* rights subject to limitations and conditions, rather than to *limit* rights that have already been conferred by the Treaty. However, except in relation to the right of permanent residence (which does not derive directly from the Treaty), the Directive has to be read on the basis that Treaty rights only apply to the extent set out. The circumstances in which it is possible to go behind the Directive and derive a right of residence directly from the Treaty are now extremely narrow: see below).

Compatibility of the right to reside test with EU law

In the past, it has been controversial whether the right to reside test, both as it affects A8 and A2 nationals, and as it affects some economically-inactive nationals of all Member States, is fully in accordance with EU law. However, that controversy has been put to rest by the decisions of the Court of Appeal of England and Wales

7.23

in *Abdirahman* (above) and *Kaczmarek v SSWP* [2008] EWCA Civ 1310; (also reported as R(IS) 5/09), of the House of Lords in *Zalewska v Department for Social Development* [2008] UKHL 67, (also reported as R 1/09(IS)), and by the decisions of the Supreme Court in *Patmalniece v SSWP* [2011] UKSC 11 and *Mirga v Secretary of State for Work and Pensions* [2016] UKSC 1.

Abdirahman was the appeal against the decisions of the tribunal of Commissioners in *CIS/3573/2005* and *CH/2484/2005*. The challenge was to the right to reside test as a whole. Mrs Abdirahman was a Swedish national who, at the time under consideration had not been economically active in the UK and did not have a right to reside under the Citizenship Directive or the 2006 Regulations. She argued that she had a right to reside as a citizen of the European Union under art.21 TFEU (ex-art.18 TEC) and that the right to reside test discriminated against her on the grounds of nationality contrary to art.18 TFEU (ex-art.12 TEC). Both those arguments were rejected. Her art.21 (ex-art.18) right was "subject to the limitations and conditions laid down in [the] Treaty and by the measures adopted to give it effect" and on the authority of the *Trojani* case (above) and of a number of previous Court of Appeal decisions, including *W (China) v Secretary of State for the Home Department* (below), that article did not confer a right of residence in circumstances where the limitations imposed by the relevant Directive (in that case Directive 90/364) were not satisfied. Although the right to reside test was discriminatory, that discrimination was not "within the scope of application of the Treaty" because art.12 did not extend to cases in which there was no right to reside under either the Treaty or the relevant domestic law. Moreover, even if art.12 were engaged, the discrimination was in any event justified by the need to prevent benefit tourism and as an aspect of immigration control.

In *Kaczmarek*, the claimant had been economically active for a period of three years in the past but was no longer so. She relied on a passage from the judgment in *Trojani* (para.43) in submitting that "a citizen of the Union who is not economically active may rely on art.12 EC [now art.18 TFEU] where he has been lawfully resident in the host Member State for a certain time or possesses a residence permit" (emphasis added). However, the Court decided that "the reference to 'a certain time' is a reference to specific qualifying periods which give rise to an express right of residence".

Zalewska was about the validity of one aspect of the former registration scheme for A8 nationals (and, by implication, the equivalent provisions of the former authorisation scheme for A2 nationals and the current authorisation scheme for Croatian nationals). Specifically, it concerned the position of an A8 national who worked lawfully in the UK but became involuntarily unemployed or temporarily incapable of work before completing 12 months' lawful work. Any other EEA national would be regarded in those circumstances as a "person retaining the status of worker" with an entitlement to benefit. However, the effect of the former A8 Regulations was that an A8 national in that position was treated as a "workseeker" with no such entitlement. By the time the appeal reached the House of Lords, the issue was whether that treatment amounted to the unlawful denial of a social advantage that was available to UK nationals (i.e. contrary to art.7(2) of the former Regulation 1612/68). This, in turn depended on whether the exclusion from benefit was a proportionate exercise of the authority given by the relevant derogation in the Treaty of Accession. Although that derogation did not mention art.7 of Regulation 1612/68, it was not necessary to do so because, if the A8 scheme was proportionate, an A8 national who did not comply with it was not a worker for the purposes of art.7 and was therefore not entitled to its protection. Their Lordships decided by a majority (Lords Hope, Carswell and Brown, Baroness Hale and Lord Neuberger dissenting) that the A8 scheme was compatible with the EU law principle of proportionality. See also in this context the decision of the Court of Appeal in England and Wales in *R. (D) v Secretary of State for Work and Pensions* [2004] EWCA Civ 1468 (October 11, 2004, CA, Mummery and Kay L.JJ.) and *CIS/3232/2006*.

Patmalniece was concerned with the application of the "Equality of Treatment" provisions of art.3 of the former Regulation 1408/71 to the claimant's claim for

SPC. In that case, the claimant was within the personal scope of the Regulation and SPC was within the material scope. It therefore could not be said, as had been held in *Abdirahman*, that the subject matter of the appeal was not within the scope of the anti-discrimination provision in question. Relying on the decision of the ECJ in *Bressol v Gouvernement de la Communauté Française*, Case C-73/08, the Supreme Court held unanimously that the right to reside test was indirectly rather than directly discriminatory. Regulation 2 of the SPC Regulations was said to impose:

> "a composite test, one element of which [i.e., the right to reside test] could be satisfied by a person who was not a national of the host Member State only if he met certain additional conditions but which every national of the host member state would automatically satisfy"

and that the effect of the conditions in that regulation (i.e. both the right to reside test and the habitual residence test) had to be looked at cumulatively. It was not directly discriminatory on grounds of nationality but, as it put nationals of other member States at a particular disadvantage, it was indirectly discriminatory and needed to be justified. By a majority (Lord Walker dissenting), it found that discrimination to be justified by:

> "the principle that those who are entitled to claim social assistance in the host Member State should have achieved a genuine economic tie with it or a sufficient degree of social integration as a pre-condition for entitlement to it"

and that justification was not undermined by the more favourable treatment accorded by the UK to Irish nationals because of art.2 of Protocol 20 to the TFEU and TEU (the Protocol on the Common Travel Area, see above).

The decision in *Patmalniece* applies to child benefit and child tax credit as it does to other social security benefits. In *AS v HMRC (CB)* [2013] NICom 15, the Chief Commissioner of Northern Ireland distinguished *Patmalniece* and held that the right to reside test in reg.27(3) of the Child Benefit (General) Regulations 2006 (i.e. of the Northern Ireland regulations which is equivalent to reg.23(4) of the GB regulations) is unlawfully discriminatory on the grounds of nationality contrary to art.3 of Regulation 1408/71. However, the Court of Appeal in Northern Ireland allowed HMRC's appeal (*HM Revenue & Customs v Spiridonova* [2014] NICA 63) and confirmed the validity of the test.

That leaves the question of whether it is possible to derive a right of residence directly from art.21(1) TFEU (ex-art.18(1) TEC) in circumstances where no such right is expressly conferred by the Citizenship Directive or the Regulations. In *Kaczmarek*, the Court followed the approach adopted by the Commissioner in that case (*CIS/2538/2006*), namely that there is no direct right of residence under art.21 unless the denial of such a right would offend the general principles of community law and, in particular, the principle of proportionality. In such cases, there may be a freestanding right of residence under art.21(1). However, the Citizenship Directive provides the benchmark for proportionality (even in cases arising before that Directive came into force) and art.21(1) cannot be interpreted so as to confer rights that go beyond the Citizenship Directive except where it can be shown that there is a lacuna in the Directive.

For examples of post-Kaczmarek decisions on proportionality see *SSWP v DWP* [2009] UKUT 17 (AAC), *SSWP v IM-M* [2009] UKUT 71 (AAC), *SSWP v CA* [2009] UKUT 169 (AAC), *RM v SSWP (IS)* [2010] UKUT 238 (AAC), *SSWP v PS-B (IS)* [2016] UKUT 511 (AAC), *SSWP v AC (UC)* [2017] UKUT 130 (AAC) and *JK v SSWP (SPC)* [2017] UKUT 179 (AAC). Cases in which a right to reside is conferred on the basis that it is disproportionate to apply the normal rules will be exceptional. For examples, see *R(IS) 4/09* and *JK* (above). *AC* holds that "the circumstances in which a lacuna may be avoided must relate to a potential gap in the EU legislation" rather than under domestic law. However, this is difficult to reconcile with *JK*.

More recently, the issue of proportionality has been considered again by the Supreme Court in *Mirga v Secretary of State for Work and Pensions* [2016] UKSC

1. The claimant was a Polish national who had come to the UK in 1998 at the age of 10 with her parents and siblings. The family went back to Poland in 2002 but returned to the UK in June 2004. After completing her education, the claimant started work in April 2005. Her first period of work of seven months was registered under the former worker registration scheme for A8 nationals but the two subsequent short periods were not. She left home in June 2006, having fallen out with her father because she was pregnant (her mother had died in October 2004). Her claim for income support made in August 2006 was refused on the ground that she did not have a right to reside. The Court of Appeal ([2012] EWCA Civ 1952) rejected the argument that in these circumstances the refusal of income support was disproportionate and therefore offensive to EU law. The Court relied, firstly, on *Zalewska* and, secondly, on the distinction drawn in para. 5 of *Kaczmarek* between lawful presence and right to reside. The protection of the claimant's fundamental rights did not require that she be accorded a right of residence. She was lawfully present, and if the Home Office decided to remove her, would have a right of appeal against that decision and be able to raise any argument based on fundamental rights arising out of EU law or Art. 8 ECHR at that point. On further appeal, the Supreme Court upheld the decision of the Court of Appeal. On the issue of proportionality, the Court decided, following the judgments of the CJEU in *Dano v Jobcenter Leipzig* (C-333/13) and *Jobcenter Berlin Neukölln v Alimanovic* (Case C-67/14), that the provisions of Directive 2004/38/EC "guarantees a significant level of legal certainty and transparency in the context of the award of social assistance by way of basic provision while complying with the principle of proportionality" so that an examination of proportionality in the context of an individual case was not necessary, except (possibly) in exceptional cases, of which Ms Mirga's case was not one.

For examples of cases decided by the Upper Tribunal after the decision of the Supreme Court in *Mirga*, see *MM v SWP (ESA)* [2017] UKUT 437 (AAC) and *LO v SSWP (IS)* [2017] UKUT 440 (AAC) both of which demonstrate how very exceptional a claimant's circumstances would have to be to fall into the (possible) category of exceptional cases in which an individual consideration of those circumstances might be required by the principle of proportionality. For guidance on how to approach issues of proportionality following *Kaczmarek* and *Mirga*, see *JS v SSWP (IS)* [2019] UKUT 135 (AAC).

The UK case law which holds that there is no general right for EEA nationals who are not economically active to reside in a member state of which they are not a national is reinforced by the Grand Chamber of the ECJ in *Dano v Jobcenter Leipzig* (C-333/13). The court ruled that: "Article 24(1) of Directive 2004/38/EC ..., read in conjunction with Article 7(1)(b) thereof, and Article 4 of Regulation No 883/2004, ... must be interpreted as not precluding legislation of a Member State under which nationals of other Member States are excluded from entitlement to certain 'special non-contributory cash benefits' within the meaning of Article 70(2) of Regulation No 883/2004, although those benefits are granted to nationals of the host Member State who are in the same situation, in so far as those nationals of other Member States do not have a right of residence under Directive 2004/38 in the host Member State." The Court's decision received considerable publicity in the UK but does not actually change the law as it was previously understood: economically inactive EEA nationals who are without sufficient resources do not have a right to reside and so are not entitled to social assistance.

PART 1

PRELIMINARY

Citation and commencement

7.24 **1.** [¹ ...]

AMENDMENT

1. Immigration and Social Security Co-ordination (EU Withdrawal) Act 2020 (c.20), s.1 and Sch.1, para.2(2) (December 31 2020 at 11.00 pm).

GENERAL NOTE

For the purposes of entitlement to benefits, the revocation of reg.1 is not subject to any saving provisions.

7.25

General interpretation

2.—(1) In these Regulations—

"the 1971 Act" means the Immigration Act 1971;

"the 1999 Act" means the Immigration and Asylum Act 1999;

"the 2002 Act" means the Nationality, Immigration and Asylum Act 2002;

"the 2006 Regulations" means the Immigration (European Economic Area) Regulations 2006;

"the 2016 Act" means the Immigration Act 2016;

"civil partner" does not include—

(a) a party to a civil partnership of convenience; or

(b) the civil partner ("C") of a person ("P") where a spouse, civil partner or durable partner of C or P is already present in the United Kingdom;

"civil partnership of convenience" includes a civil partnership entered into for the purpose of using these Regulations, [¹or any other right conferred by the EU Treaties], as a means to circumvent—

(a) immigration rules applying to non-EEA nationals (such as any applicable requirement under the 1971 Act to have leave to enter or remain in the United Kingdom); or

(b) any other criteria that the party to the civil partnership of convenience would otherwise have to meet in order to enjoy a right to reside under these Regulations [¹or the EU Treaties];

"Common Travel Area" has the meaning given in section 1(3) of the 1971 Act;

"decision maker" means the Secretary of State, an immigration officer or an entry clearance officer (as the case may be);

"deportation order" means an order made under regulation 32(3) [² or under section 5(1) of the Immigration Act 1971];

"derivative residence card" means a card issued to a person under regulation 20;

"derivative right to reside" means a right to reside under regulation 16;

"document certifying permanent residence" means a document issued under regulation 19(1);

"durable partner" does not include—

(a) a party to a durable partnership of convenience; or

(b) the durable partner ("D") of a person ("P") where a spouse, civil partner or durable partner of D or P is already present in the United Kingdom and where that marriage, civil partnership or durable partnership is subsisting;

"durable partnership of convenience" includes a durable partnership entered into for the purpose of using these Regulations, [¹or any other right conferred by the EU Treaties], as a means to circumvent—

(a) immigration rules applying to non-EEA nationals (such as any

7.26

applicable requirement under the 1971 Act to have leave to enter or
remain in the United Kingdom); or
(b) any other criteria that the party to the durable partnership of convenience would otherwise have to meet in order to enjoy a right to
reside under these Regulations [¹or the EU Treaties];
"EEA decision" means a decision under these Regulations that concerns—
(a) a person's entitlement to be admitted to the United Kingdom;
*[Editorial note: This is the pre-revocation wording of sub-para. (b) that contin-
ues to apply to those with pre-settled status]*
(b) a person's entitlement to be issued with or have renewed, or not to
have revoked, an EEA family permit, a registration certificate, residence card, derivative residence card, document certifying permanent
residence or permanent residence card (but does not include a decision to reject an application for the above documentation as invalid);
*[Editorial note: This is the modified wording of sub-para. (b) that now applies
to claimants for whom reg.2 is saved by SI 2020/1209]*
(b) a person's entitlement to be issued with or have renewed, or not to
have revoked, an EEA family permit [⁵ ...] (but does not include
a decision to reject an application for the above documentation as
invalid);
(c) a person's removal from the United Kingdom; or
(d) the cancellation, under regulation 25, of a person's right to reside in
the United Kingdom,
but does not include [³ ...] a decision to [⁴ refuse] an application under
regulation 26(4) (misuse of a right to reside: material change of circumstances), or any decisions under regulation 33 (human rights considerations
and interim orders to suspend removal) or 41 (temporary admission to
submit case in person);
"EEA family permit" means a document issued under regulation 12;
[² "EEA national" means—
(a) a national of an EEA State who is not also a British citizen; or
(b) a national of an EEA State who is also a British citizen and who prior
to acquiring British citizenship exercised a right to reside as such a
national, in accordance with regulation 14 or 15,
save that a person does not fall within paragraph (b) if the EEA State of
which they are a national became a member State after that person acquired
British citizenship.]
"EEA State" means—
(a) a member State [³ . . .]; or
(b) Liechtenstein, Iceland, Norway or Switzerland;
"entry clearance" has the meaning given in section 33(1) of the 1971 Act;
"entry clearance officer" means a person responsible for the grant or
refusal of entry clearance;
"exclusion order" means an order made under regulation 23(5) [⁴ or
directions issued by the Secretary of State for a person not to be given
entry to the United Kingdom on the grounds that the person's exclusion is conducive to the public good];
"indefinite leave", "immigration laws" and "immigration rules" have the
meanings given in section 33(1) of the 1971 Act;
"marriage of convenience" includes a marriage entered into for the
purpose of using these Regulations, [¹or any other right conferred by
the EU Treaties], as a means to circumvent—

(a) immigration rules applying to non-EEA nationals (such as any applicable requirement under the 1971 Act to have leave to enter or remain in the United Kingdom); or

(b) any other criteria that the party to the marriage of convenience would otherwise have to meet in order to enjoy a right to reside under these Regulations [¹or the EU Treaties];

"military service" means service in the armed forces of an EEA State;

"permanent residence card" means a document issued under regulation 19(2);

"qualifying EEA State residence card" means a valid document called a "Residence card of a family member of a Union Citizen" issued under Article 10 of Council Directive 2004/38/EC (as applied, where relevant, by the EEA agreement) by any EEA State (except Switzerland) to a non-EEA family member of an EEA national as proof of the holder's right of residence in that State;

"registration certificate" means a certificate issued under regulation 17;

"relevant EEA national" in relation to an extended family member has the meaning given in regulation 8(6);

"residence card" means a card issued under regulation 18;

"right to reside" means a right to reside in the United Kingdom under these Regulations (or where so specified, a right to reside under a particular regulation);

"spouse" does not include—

(a) a party to a marriage of convenience; or

(b) the spouse ("S") of a person ("P") where a spouse, civil partner or durable partner of S or P is already present in the United Kingdom.

(2) Section 11 of the 1971 Act (construction of references to entry) applies for the purpose of determining whether a person has entered the United Kingdom for the purpose of these Regulations as it applies for the purpose of determining whether a person has entered the United Kingdom for the purpose of that Act.

AMENDMENT

Regulation 2 was revoked by s.1 of, and Sch.1, para.2(2) to, the Immigration and Social Security Co-ordination (EU Withdrawal) Act 2020 with effect from December 31, 2020 at 11.00 pm. The text given above is of the regulation as saved and modified for the purposes of entitlement to benefit by: 7.27

- (For those EEA nationals with pre-settled status) reg.83 of, and Sch.4, paras 2, 3 and 4(a) of the Immigration and Social Security Co-ordination (EU Withdrawal) Act 2020 (Consequential, Saving, Transitional and Transitory Provisions) (EU Exit) Regulations 2020 (SI 2020/1309); and

- (For those EEA nationals who had a right of residence in the UK under EU law immediately before December 30, 2020 at 11.00 pm, but who have neither settled nor pre-settled status) by regs 3(2), 4(3) and 5(a) of the Citizens' Rights (Application Deadline and Temporary Protection) (EU Exit) Regulations 2020 (SI 2020/1209).

Square brackets with superscript numbers in the text refer to the Modifications section below and not, as elsewhere in this work, to amendments. For the amendments that were made to reg.2 before its revocation see pp.965-968 of Vol.V of the 2020/21 edition.

MODIFICATIONS

1. By Sch.4, para.4(a)(i) and (ii) to SI 2020/1309 and regs 3(2), 4(3) and 5(a)(i) and (ii) of SI 2020/1209 all instances of the words "or any other right conferred by the EU Treaties" and of the words "or the EU Treaties" are to be read:
(aa) in so far as they relate to things done on or after exit day but before commencement day [*i.e.*, December 31, 2020 at 11.00 pm], were a reference to a right conferred by the EU Treaties so far as they were applicable to and in the United Kingdom by virtue of Part 4 of the EU withdrawal agreement;
(bb) in so far as they relate to things done on or after commencement day, were omitted;
2. SI 2020/1309, Sch.4, para.4(a)(iii). This modification applies to those with pre-settled status only. SI 2020/1209 contains no equivalent provision.
3. SI 2020/1309, Sch.4, para.4(a)(iv); SI 2020/1209, regs 3(2), 4(3) and 5(a)(iv).
4. SI 2020/1309, Sch.4, para.4(a)(v). This modification applies to those with pre-settled status only. SI 2020/1209 contains no equivalent provision.
5. SI 2020/1209, regs 3(2), 4(3) and 5(a)(iv).

DEFINITIONS

"extended family member"—see reg.8.
"family member"—see reg.7.

GENERAL NOTE

7.28 *Paragraph (1)*: Most of these definitions are either self-explanatory or are discussed in the commentary to the regulations where the defined terms are used. The following merit comment here.

"*Common Travel Area*" is defined by reference to Immigration Act 1971 s.1(3) which states:

"(3) Arrival in and departure from the United Kingdom on a local journey from or to any of the Islands (that is to say, the Channel Islands and Isle of Man) or the Republic of Ireland shall not be subject to control under this Act, nor shall a person require leave to enter the United Kingdom on so arriving, except in so far as any of those places is for any purpose excluded from this subsection under the powers conferred by this Act; and in this Act the United Kingdom and those places, or such of them as are not so excluded, are collectively referred to as 'the common travel area'."

See also Immigration Act 1971 s.11(2) and (4) (quoted in the commentary to para.(2) below) and *Irish and Island Nationals* in the General Note to these Regulations, above.

"*entry clearance*" is defined by Immigration Act 1971 s.33(1) as meaning "a visa, entry certificate or other document which, in accordance with the immigration rules, is to be taken as evidence or the requisite evidence of a person's eligibility, though not a British citizen, for entry into the United Kingdom (but does not include a work permit)".

"*indefinite leave*" is defined by Immigration Act 1971 s.33(1) as meaning "leave under this Act to enter or remain in the United Kingdom . . . which is not . . . limited as to duration".

"*immigration laws*" is defined by Immigration Act 1971 s.33(1) as meaning "this Act and any law for purposes similar to this Act which is for the time being or has (before or after the passing of this Act) been in force in any part of the United Kingdom and Islands".

"*immigration rules*" is defined by Immigration Act 1971 s.33(1) as meaning the rules laid down under s.3(2) of that act. Section 3(2) is in the following terms:

"(2) The Secretary of State shall from time to time (and as soon as may be) lay before Parliament statements of the rules, or of any changes in the rules, laid down by him as to the practice to be followed in the administration of this Act for regulating the entry into and stay in the United Kingdom of persons required by this Act to have leave to enter, including any rules as to the period for which leave is to be given and the conditions to be attached in different circumstances; and section 1(4) above shall not be taken to require uniform provision to be made by the rules as regards admission of persons for a purpose or in a capacity specified in section 1(4) (and in particular, for this as well as other purposes of this Act, account may be taken of citizenship or nationality).

If a statement laid before either House of Parliament under this subsection is disapproved by a resolution of that House passed within the period of forty days beginning with the date of laying (and exclusive of any period during which Parliament is dissolved or prorogued or during which both Houses are adjourned for more than four days), then the Secretary of State shall as soon as may be make such changes or further changes in the rules as appear to him to be required in the circumstances, so that the statement of those changes be laid before Parliament at latest by the end of the period of forty days beginning with the date of the resolution (but exclusive as aforesaid)."

The text of the current immigration rules can be found online at *https://www.gov. uk/guidance/immigration-rules* and an archive of previous versions of the rules is at *https://www.gov.uk/government/collections/archive-immigration-rules*.

"indefinite leave" is defined by Immigration Act 1971 s.33(1) as meaning "leave under this Act to enter or remain in the United Kingdom . . . which is not . . . limited as to duration".

Paragraph 2 requires that the question whether a person has entered the United Kingdom for the purpose of the 2016 Regulations should be determined in accordance with Immigration Act 1971 s.11. That section is in the following terms:

"Construction of references to entry, and other phrases relating to travel.

11.—(1) A person arriving in the United Kingdom by ship or aircraft shall for purposes of **7.29** this Act be deemed not to enter the United Kingdom unless and until he disembarks, and on disembarkation at a port shall further be deemed not to enter the United Kingdom so long as he remains in such area (if any) at the port as may be approved for this purpose by an immigration officer; and a person who has not otherwise entered the United Kingdom shall be deemed not to do so as long as he is detained under the powers conferred by Schedule 2 to this Act or section 62 of the Nationality, Immigration and Asylum Act 2002 or by section 68 of the Nationality, Immigration and Asylum Act 2002 or on immigration bail within the meaning of Schedule 10 to the Immigration Act 2016.

(2) In this Act "disembark" means disembark from a ship or aircraft, and "embark" means embark in a ship or aircraft; and, except in subsection (1) above,

    (a) references to disembarking in the United Kingdom do not apply to disembarking after a local journey from a place in the United Kingdom or elsewhere in the common travel area; and

    (b) references to embarking in the United Kingdom do not apply to embarking for a local journey to a place in the United Kingdom or elsewhere in the common travel area.

(3) Except in so far as the context otherwise requires, references in this Act to arriving in the United Kingdom by ship shall extend to arrival by any floating structure, and "disembark" shall be construed accordingly; but the provisions of this Act specially relating to members of the crew of a ship shall not by virtue of this provision apply in relation to any floating structure not being a ship.

(4) For purposes of this Act "common travel area" has the meaning given by section 1(3), and a journey is, in relation to the common travel area, a local journey if but only if it begins and ends in the common travel area and is not made by a ship or aircraft which—

    (a) in the case of a journey to a place in the United Kingdom, began its voyage from, or has during its voyage called at, a place not in the common travel area; or

    (b) in the case of a journey from a place in the United Kingdom, is due to end its voyage in, or call in the course of its voyage at, a place not in the common travel area.

(5) A person who enters the United Kingdom lawfully by virtue of section 8(1) above, and seeks to remain beyond the time limited by section 8(1), shall be treated for purposes of this Act as seeking to enter the United Kingdom."

Continuity of residence

7.30   **3.**—(1) This regulation applies for the purpose of calculating periods of continuous residence in the United Kingdom under these Regulations.

(2) Continuity of residence is not affected by—

(a) periods of absence from the United Kingdom which do not exceed six months in total in any year;

(b) periods of absence from the United Kingdom on compulsory military service; or

(c) one absence from the United Kingdom not exceeding twelve months for an important reason such as pregnancy and childbirth, serious illness, study or vocational training or an overseas posting.

(3) Continuity of residence is broken when—

(a) a person serves a sentence of imprisonment;

(b) a deportation or exclusion order is made in relation to a person; or

(c) a person is removed from the United Kingdom under these Regulations [¹ or the Immigration Acts].

(4) Paragraph (3)(a) applies, in principle, to an EEA national who has resided in the United Kingdom for at least ten years, but it does not apply where the Secretary of State considers that—

(a) prior to serving a sentence of imprisonment, the EEA national had forged integrating links with the United Kingdom;

(b) the effect of the sentence of imprisonment was not such as to break those integrating links; and

(c) taking into account an overall assessment of the EEA national's situation, it would not be appropriate to apply paragraph (3)(a) to the assessment of that EEA national's continuity of residence.

AMENDMENT

Regulation 3 was revoked by s.1 of, and Sch.1, para.2(2) to, the Immigration and Social Security Co-ordination (EU Withdrawal) Act 2020 with effect from December 31, 2020 at 11.00 pm. The text given above is of the regulation as saved and modified for the purposes of entitlement to benefit by:

- (For those EEA nationals with pre-settled status) reg.83 of, and Sch.4, paras 2, 3 and 4(b) of the Immigration and Social Security Co-ordination (EU Withdrawal) Act 2020 (Consequential, Saving, Transitional and Transitory Provisions) (EU Exit) Regulations 2020 (SI 2020/1309); and

- (For those EEA nationals who had a right of residence in the UK under EU law immediately before December 30, 2020 at 11.00 pm, but who have neither settled nor pre-settled status) by regs 3(2), 4(3) and 5(b) of the Citizens' Rights (Application Deadline and Temporary Protection) (EU Exit) Regulations 2020 (SI 2020/1209).

Square brackets with superscript numbers in the text refer to the Modifications section below and not, as elsewhere in this work, to amendments. For the amendments that were made to reg.3 before its revocation see p.970 of Vol.V of the 2020/21 edition.

MODIFICATIONS

1. SI 2020/1309, Sch.4, para.4(b). This modification applies to those with pre-settled status only. Regs regs 3(2), 4(3) and 5(b) of SI 2020/1209 save reg.3 without modification.

DEFINITIONS

"EEA national"—see reg.2(1).
"exclusion order"—*ibid.*
"military service"—*ibid.*

GENERAL NOTE

Continuity of residence is relevant to the acquisition of a permanent right of resi-   **7.31**
dence under art.16(1) and (2) and reg.15(1)(a) and (b). Regulation 3 implements
art.16(3)

Paragraph (2): Continuity of residence is not affected by absence on military service,
absences for any reason that do not in total exceed six months in any year or by a single
absence of no more than 12 months "for an important reason such as pregnancy and
childbirth, serious illness, study or vocational training or an overseas posting".

As is clear from the quoted words, that list is not exhaustive. In *Babajanov v
Secretary of State for the Home Department (Continuity of residence – Immigration
(EEA) Regulations 2006)* [2013] UKUT 513 (IAC), the Upper Tribunal held that
when deciding whether absence for a non-listed reason falls within art.16(3), the
purpose of the absence needs to be considered and should involve compelling
events and/or an activity linked to the exercise of Treaty rights in the UK.

Absences within art.16(3)/reg.3(2) do not break continuity of residence, but
do they count towards the five-year period required by art.16(1) and reg.15(1)(a)
and (b)? In *CIS/2258/2008* at para.17 the Commissioner held that they did not.
However, in *Idezuna (EEA—permanent residence) Nigeria* [2011] UKUT 474 (IAC)
the Immigration Appeals Chamber of the Upper Tribunal held—without expressly
addressing the point or being referred to *CIS/2258/2008*—that the appellant had
acquired a permanent right of residence through a period of five years' continuous
residence beginning on April 23, 2004 and ending on April 23, 2009 even though
there was evidence that he had been absent from the UK for two periods including
one from October 29, 2006 to December 17, 2006. Previous editions have suggested that the reasoned decision of the Commissioner in *CIS/2258/2008* should be
followed in preference to *Idezuna*. However, the weight of authority now favours the
opposite conclusion. In *Babajanov* (above), a two-judge panel of the Immigration
Appeals Chamber of the Upper Tribunal held that the right of permanent residence
is capable of being established whilst a national of a Member State or a family
member of that national is outside the host country. If that is correct, it follows that
periods of absence within art.16(3)/reg.3(2) do count towards the five-year period.

Under reg.15(1)(a) and (b), a permanent right of residence is conferred
on EEA nationals and their family members who have "resided in the United
Kingdom in accordance with these Regulations for a continuous period of five
years". In *Secretary of State for the Home Department v Ojo* [2015] EWCA Civ 1301,
the Court of Appeal held that "[t]he acquisition of a permanent right of residence
depends on continuous residence in a qualifying status". It is therefore not possible
for a claimant who has resided in the UK continuously, but whose residence has not
been continuously legal—in the sense of being in accordance with the Regulations—
to aggregate separate periods of legal residence to achieve a total of five years. The
decision of the Upper Tribunal in *OB v SSWP (ESA)* [2017] UKUT 255 (AAC)
and, to the extent that it followed *OB*, in *AP v SSWP (IS)* [2018] UKUT 307
(AAC), were per incuriam and wrongly decided: see *Cardiff CC v HM (HB)* [2019]
UKUT 271 (AAC).

Imprisonment – paras (3) and (4): Any period during which an EEA national is
serving a sentence of imprisonment in this country is not to be included when calculating whether he has resided in the United Kingdom for a continuous period and
breaks continuity of residence so that a the person must reside lawfully for five years
after his or her release from prison before acquiring a permanent right of residence:
Onuekwere v Secretary of State for the Home Department (Case C-378/12); *Secretary of
State for the Home Department v MG* (Case C-400/12), *HR (Portugal) v Secretary of
State for the Home Office* [2009] EWCA Civ 371; *Carvalho v Secretary of State for the*

Home Department [2010] EWCA Civ 1406; *Jarusevicius (EEA Reg 21—effect of imprisonment)* [2012] UKUT 120 (IAC) and *SO (imprisonment breaks continuity of residence) Nigeria* [2011] UKUT 164 (IAC). For the purposes of para.(3)(a), a "sentence of imprisonment" includes a sentence of detention in a Young Offenders' Institution: see *Secretary of State for the Home Department v Viscu* [2019] EWCA Civ 1052.

However, an EEA national does not cease to be a qualified person as a result of being detained in a hospital pursuant to an order of the court under the Mental Health Act 1983, having not been convicted of any criminal offence: *JO (qualified person – hospital order – effect) Slovakia* [2012] UKUT 237(IAC).

"Worker", "self-employed person", "self-sufficient person" and "student"

7.32
4.—(1) In these Regulations—

(a) "worker" means a worker within the meaning of Article 45 of the Treaty on the Functioning of the European Union;

(b) "self-employed person" means a person who is established in the United Kingdom in order to pursue activity as a self-employed person [¹ within the meaning of] Article 49 of the Treaty on the Functioning of the European Union;

(c) "self-sufficient person" means a person who has—

(i) sufficient resources not to become a burden on the social assistance system of the United Kingdom during the person's period of residence; and

(ii) comprehensive sickness insurance cover in the United Kingdom;

(d) "student" means a person who—

(i) is enrolled, for the principal purpose of following a course of study (including vocational training), at a public or private establishment which is—

(aa) financed from public funds; or

(bb) otherwise recognised by the Secretary of State as an establishment which has been accredited for the purpose of providing such courses or training within the law or administrative practice of the part of the United Kingdom in which the establishment is located;

(ii) has comprehensive sickness insurance cover in the United Kingdom; and

(iii) has assured the Secretary of State, by means of a declaration, or by such equivalent means as the person may choose, that the person has sufficient resources not to become a burden on the social assistance system of the United Kingdom during the person's intended period of residence.

(2) For the purposes of paragraphs (3) and (4) below, "relevant family member" means a family member of a self-sufficient person or student who is residing in the United Kingdom and whose right to reside is dependent upon being the family member of that student or self-sufficient person.

(3) In sub-paragraphs (1)(c) and (d)—

(a) the requirement for the self-sufficient person or student to have sufficient resources not to become a burden on the social assistance system of the United Kingdom during the intended period of residence is only satisfied if the resources available to the student or self-sufficient person and any of their relevant family members are sufficient to avoid the self-sufficient person or student and all their relevant family members from becoming such a burden; and

(b) the requirement for the student or self-sufficient person to have comprehensive sickness insurance cover in the United Kingdom is only satisfied if such cover extends to cover both the student or self-sufficient person and all their relevant family members.

(4) In paragraph (1)(c) and (d) and paragraph (3), the resources of the student or self-sufficient person and, where applicable, any of their relevant family members, are to be regarded as sufficient if—

(a) they exceed the maximum level of resources which a British citizen (including the resources of the British citizen's family members) may possess if the British citizen is to become eligible for social assistance under the United Kingdom benefit system; or

(b) paragraph (a) does not apply but, taking into account the personal circumstances of the person concerned and, where applicable, all their relevant family members, it appears to the decision maker that the resources of the person or persons concerned should be regarded as sufficient.

(5) For the purposes of regulation 16(2) (criteria for having a derivative right to reside), references in this regulation to "family members" includes a "primary carer" as defined in regulation 16(8).

AMENDMENT

Regulation 4 was revoked by s.1 of, and Sch.1, para.2(2) to, the Immigration and Social Security Co-ordination (EU Withdrawal) Act 2020 with effect from December 31, 2020 at 11.00 pm. The text given above is of the regulation as saved and modified for the purposes of entitlement to benefit by:

- (For those EEA nationals with pre-settled status) reg.83 of, and Sch.4, paras 2, 3 and 4(c) of the Immigration and Social Security Co-ordination (EU Withdrawal) Act 2020 (Consequential, Saving, Transitional and Transitory Provisions) (EU Exit) Regulations 2020 (SI 2020/1309); and

- (For those EEA nationals who had a right of residence in the UK under EU law immediately before December 30, 2020 at 11.00 pm, but who have neither settled nor pre-settled status) by regs 3(2), 4(3) and 5(c) of the Citizens' Rights (Application Deadline and Temporary Protection) (EU Exit) Regulations 2020 (SI 2020/1209).

Square brackets with superscript numbers in the text refer to the Modifications section below and not, as elsewhere in this work, to amendments. For the amendments that were made to reg.4 before its revocation see pp.971-973 of Vol.V of the 2020/21 edition.

MODIFICATIONS

1. SI 2020/1309, Sch.4, para.4(c); SI 2020/1209 regs 3(2), 4(3) and 5(c).

DEFINITIONS

"decision maker"—see reg.2(1).
"derivative right to reside"—see regs 2(1) and 16.
"family member"—see reg.7.
"primary carer"—see reg.16(8).
"right to reside"—see reg.2(1).

GENERAL NOTE

Workers, self-employed persons, self-sufficient persons and students are all "qualified persons" as defined in reg.6 and have an extended right of residence by virtue of art.7(1) and reg.14 that counts for the purposes of entitlement to all income-

7.33

related benefits. They are also exempt from the habitual residence test under reg.21AA(4)(za) of the IS Regs, reg.85(4)(za) of the JSA Regulations, reg.2(4)(za) of the SPC Regulations, reg.70(4)(za) of the ESA Regulations 2008 and reg.9(4)(a) of the Universal Credit Regulations.

Worker

7.34   *Paragraph (1)(a)* defines "worker" as meaning a worker within the meaning of art.45 TFEU (ex-39 TEC), which is reproduced in Vol.III. That definition is not as helpful as it appears, because neither that Treaty nor the measures that have implemented it (including the Citizenship Directive) include a definition of the term "worker" and case law makes it clear that it means different things in different contexts and sometimes even in different parts of the same Regulation (see Case C–85/96 *Martinez Sala v Freistaat Bayern*; Case C–138/02 *Collins v Secretary of State for Work and Pensions* [2005] Q.B. 145 (reported as *R(JSA) 3/06* and *CJSA/1475/2006*). However, the reference to art.45 TFEU in the definition does make it clear that the word is to be interpreted in accordance with EU law and hence in accordance with the established case law of the ECJ. A number of principles can be derived from those cases:

- The term "worker" has a Community meaning and may not be defined by reference to the national laws of Member States (Case C–75/63 *Hoekstra (née Unger) v Bestuur der Bedrijfsvereniging voor Detailhandel en Ambachten* [1964] E.C.R. 177).

- As a concept that defines the field of application of one of the fundamental freedoms guaranteed by the Treaty, it may not be interpreted restrictively (Case C–53/81 *Levin v Staatssecretaris van Justitie* [1982] E.C.R. 1035).

- The term applies to those who are employees rather than self-employed. For these purposes "the essential characteristic of an employment relationship is that for a certain period a person performs services for and under the direction of another person in return for which he receives remuneration" (Case C–357/89 *Raulin v Minister Van Onderwijs en Wetenschappen* [1992] E.C.R. I-1027 at para.10). However, the existence of a legally-binding employment relationship is not conclusive of whether the employee is a worker (Case C–344/87 *Bettray v Staatssecretaris Van Justitie* [1989] E.C.R. 1621). A person who has been a worker, but is no longer employed, may retain worker status under art.7(3) and reg.6(2): see the commentary to reg.6, below.

- The requirement that a "worker" should receive remuneration means that voluntary activity is not "work" for these purposes (*CIS/868/2008* and *CIS/1837/2006*). Similarly, a person who receives carer's allowance for caring for a severely disabled person is not providing services for remuneration and so is not a worker for the purposes of art.7(1)(a) of the Citizenship Directive: see *JR v SSWP (IS) and JR v Leeds CC and another (HB)* [2014] UKUT 154 (AAC).

- The concept extends to part-time workers but only to the extent that the work undertaken is "effective and genuine. . . to the exclusion of activities on such a small scale as to be regarded as purely marginal and ancillary" (*Levin*, at para.17).

- As long as the work undertaken, is "effective and genuine" in this sense, it is irrelevant whether it "yields an income lower than that which, in the [host] state, is considered as the minimum required for subsistence, whether that person supplements the income from his activity as an employed person with other income so as to arrive at that minimum or is satisfied with means of support lower than the said minimum" (*Levin*, at para.18). Moreover, "where a national of a Member State pursues within the territory of another Member State by way of employment activities which may in themselves be regarded as effective and genuine work, the fact that he claims financial assistance payable out of the public funds of the latter Member State in order to supplement the income he receives from those activities does not exclude him from the provisions of community law relating to freedom of movement for workers" (Case C–139/85 *Kempf v Staatssecretaris Van Justitie* [1986] E.C.R. 1741 (formal ruling of the Court)).

- The motives which may have prompted the worker to seek employment in another Member State are irrelevant provided s/he pursues, or wishes to pursue, an effective and genuine activity (*Levin*, at para.23).

- In assessing whether a person is a worker, account should be taken of all the occupational activities s/he has undertaken in the host State (although activities pursued in other Member States do not count) (*Raulin*). In principle, there seems to be no reason why this should not include work done during a claimant's previous stay in the UK (even if on this occasion the person has not yet obtained employment) although this will depend on the length of time which has passed since the previous stay, the circumstances in which that employment came to an end, and the extent to which it can be said that the work now sought is connected to the work previously undertaken—see also the discussion of *Collins*, below.

Whether work undertaken by a particular claimant is, on the facts, "effective and genuine" within the case law of the ECJ is a matter for the national courts (i.e. the First-tier Tribunal and, on appeal, the Upper Tribunal) (*Levin*, at para.13).

Traditionally, the "effective and genuine" test was thought to present a low threshold. It excluded cases of abuse (i.e. relationships not really entered into for the purpose of pursuing economic activity but for the sole purpose of obtaining some other advantage: see the Advocate General in *Raulin* at para.9) and cases in which the work undertaken was not really economic activity at all (such as the rehabilitative work in *Bettray*) or "if it is done pursuant to some other relationship between the parties which is not an employment relationship, as where a lodger performs some small task for his landlord as part of the terms of his tenancy" (see the decision of the Court of Appeal in *Barry v London Borough of Southwark* [2008] EWCA Civ 1440 at para.20). Although the duration of the work is a relevant factor (*Raulin*), work undertaken for very short periods and for a very few hours a week has been held to qualify. For example, in *R(IS) 12/98* an au pair who had worked for five weeks (being paid £35 for a 13-hour week, plus free board and lodging) was held to be a worker.

However, there was a difference of opinion between Commissioners over whether, for work to be effective and genuine, the claimant's hours of work and earnings (or, in the case of a jobseeker (see the commentary to reg.6, below), the prospective hours of work and earnings) had to be such that s/he was not eligible to claim social assistance: see pp.312–313 of Vol.II of the 2010/11 edition. The current position is that, whilst the level of the claimant's hours and earnings are a relevant factor, the decision cannot be taken on a formulaic basis, and the correct approach is to consider what is proportionate, taking into account all relevant matters: see *SS v Slough Borough Council* [2011] UKUT 128 (AAC) at para.25.

The issue of sufficiency of earnings has also been considered by the ECJ in Cases C-22/08 and C-23/08 *Vatsouras and Koupatantze v Arbeitsgemeinschaft (ARGE) Nürnberg 900* and Case C-14/09 *Hava Genc v Land Berlin*. In the former case, the Court stated:

"27. Neither the origin of the funds from which the remuneration is paid nor the limited amount of that remuneration can have any consequence in regard to whether or not the person is a 'worker' for the purposes of Community law (see Case 344/87 *Bettray* [1989] ECR 1621, paragraph 15, and Case C-10/05 *Mattern and Cikotic* [2006] ECR I-3145, paragraph 22).

28. The fact that the income from employment is lower than the minimum required for subsistence does not prevent the person in such employment from being regarded as a 'worker' within the meaning of Article 39 EC (see Case 53/81 *Levin* [1982] ECR 1035, paragraphs 15 and 16, and Case C-317/93 *Nolte* [1995]

ECI-4625, paragraph 19), even if the person in question seeks to supplement that remuneration by other means of subsistence such as financial assistance drawn from the public funds of the State in which he resides (see Case 139/85 *Kempf* [1986] ECR 1741, paragraph 14)."

In the latter, it reiterated that:

"20. Neither the origin of the funds from which the remuneration is paid nor the limited amount of that remuneration, nor indeed the fact that the person in question seeks to supplement that remuneration by other means of subsistence such as financial assistance drawn from the public funds of the State in which he resides, can have any consequence in regard to whether or not the person is a 'worker' for the purposes of European Union law (see, to that effect, Case 139/85 *Kempf* [1986] ECR 1741, paragraph 14; Case 344/87 *Bettray* [1989] ECR 1621, paragraph 15; and Case C-10/05 *Mattern and Cikotic* [2006] ECR I-3145, paragraph 22)."

In *CSIS/467/2007*, the Commissioner held that the claimant's physical incapacity to do the work she had undertaken and the fact that she had been dismissed from it after a short period were relevant to the issue of whether the work was effective and genuine.

Even though s/he will not be a "worker", person who is engaged in work that is not effective and genuine may still be a jobseeker if s/he satisfies the conditions in art.7(3) and reg.6. As the duration of work is a factor that is relevant to whether the work is effective and genuine, it is possible that work which would not have been regarded as effective and genuine at the outset will become so through repetition. In other words, a jobseeker can become a worker through the passage of time while s/he continues in a job. Guidance on this issue was given by the Upper Tribunal in *NE v SSWP* [2009] UKUT 38 (AAC). The claimant had worked for 15 hours in December 2004 and (possibly) for three weeks for an agency in January 2005 before claiming IS in July 2005. Judge Rowland stated:

"9. The issue in a case like the present may be said to be whether the claimant has genuinely and effectively (to borrow that phrase from its usual context) become a worker rather than a workseeker. I do not accept [counsel for the claimant]'s submission that agency work is by its nature ancillary and insufficient to confer on a claimant the status of worker. Although agency work is often temporary and for short periods, it is not necessarily so. However, I do accept that a distinction is to be drawn between temporary employment for a short period and indefinite employment that has been curtailed prematurely. Where work is undertaken for what is expected from the outset to be for a very short period and is known to be temporary, the person concerned is obliged to keep looking for work and often he or she cannot realistically be said to have become established in work and to have ceased to be a workseeker. It does not follow that all agency workers always remain workseekers. Where short periods of temporary work are not separated by longer periods of no work, it will often be appropriate to regard the person concerned as having become a worker rather than a workseeker. There will be cases where work that is temporarily is nonetheless for a prolonged period or where there is a high likelihood of further work being obtained and, in particular, many agency workers will be able to show that the agency has regularly found them work albeit for short periods and they have, for practical purposes, become established members of the national workforce. On the other hand, where a person has worked only intermittently for very short periods, as in *CIS/1793/2007*, the claimant is more likely to have remained a workseeker because the work performed has been marginal. The case-law shows that whether work is marginal is a matter of judgement on the facts of each case. In *Ninni-Orasche v Bundesminister für Wissenschaft, Verkehr und Kunst* (Case C-413/01) [2003] E.C.R. I-13187, the Court did not rule out the possibility that work under a fixed-term contract for two and a half months might be marginal and ancillary."

The duration of work was also an issue in *Barry*, in which a citizen of the Netherlands was held to be a worker on the basis of having done two weeks' work as a steward at the All England Tennis Championships at Wimbledon for which he was paid £789.86 net. See, however, the comments of Judge Rowland at para.8 of *NE v SSWP.*

An employee undertaking genuine and effective work is a worker for the purposes of the Citizenship Directive even if employed under a contract that is performed illegally (e.g., because the employer does not account to HMRC for the PAYE and national insurance contributions due on the employee's wages): see *JA v SSWP (ESA)* [2012] UKUT 122 (AAC) (CE/2190/2011) at paras 15–20. Similarly, undeclared work by a person claiming benefit can still be genuine and effective, see *Barry* at paras 28, 31 and 45 and *NE v SSWP* at para.4.

A person may acquire worker status by virtue of work done as a victim of illegal people trafficking: see *EP v SSWP (JSA)* [2016] UKUT 445 (AAC).

Minimum earnings threshold

Although there has been no change in the law governing whether work is effective and genuine, there was a change in the administrative practice followed by the DWP when deciding that issue with effect from March 1, 2014. The change was set out in DMG Memo 1/14 which establishes a "Minimum Earnings Threshold". The DWP will accept that claimants who have had average gross earnings of at least the primary earnings threshold for national insurance contributions (£157 pw in 2017/18, £162 in 2018/19, £166 in 2019/20, £183 in 2020/21and £184 in 2021/22) the three months before the claim are (or were) in effective and genuine work, without making further enquiries. The circumstances of claimants who do not meet that threshold, or have not done so for a continuous period of three months before the claim, will be investigated in more detail. 7.35

Contrary to the way in which the change was misrepresented in the press, the law does not require that a claimant must earn at least £155 pw before s/he can be accepted as being in effective and genuine work: see *RF v London Borough of Lambeth* [2019] UKUT 52 (AAC).

Self-employed person

Paragraph 1(b) defines "self-employed person" as meaning a person who is established in the United Kingdom in order to pursue activity as a self-employed person in accordance with art.49 TFEU (ex-43 TEC), which is reproduced in Vol.III. That definition is narrower than the equivalent definition in the 2000 Regulations, which included the words "or who seeks to do so" at the end. It follows that to have an extended right of residence as a self-employed person it is not sufficient to arrive in the UK with the wish to establish oneself. It is necessary to have taken active steps to pursue self-employment. This accords with the previous law; see *R(IS) 6/00*, para.31 (a case on the former Directive 73/148). Exactly what steps will suffice to give rise to the extended right of residence will depend upon the particular circumstances of individual cases. 7.36

RM v SSWP (IS) [2014] UKUT 401 (AAC), [2015] AACR 11 contains guidance on the concept of self-employment in EU law.

It is not necessary to register as self-employed with HMRC in order to have a right to reside as a self-employed person (see *SSWP v IM-M* [2009] UKUT 71 (AAC)). However, registration with HMRC is evidence of self-employed status.

The Upper Tribunal has decided that, as is the case for work as an employee, activity as a self-employed person must be "effective and genuine", rather than "marginal or ancillary" in order to give rise to a right of residence (see *Bristol City Council v FV (HB)* [2011] UKUT 494 (AAC) (CH/2859/2011), in which Judge Rowland upheld a decision of the First-tier tribunal that the activities of a Big Issue seller were effective and genuine and amounted to self-employment). The authority cited for that proposition, namely *Jany v Staatssecretarie van Justitie* (Case C-268/99) at para.33 is equivocal, as are the authorities from which *Jany* is itself derived: see *Deliège v Ligue Francophone de Judo and others* (Joined Cases C-56/91 and C-191/97) at paras 52–55 and *Steymann v Staatssecretaris van Justitie* (Case 196/87) at paras 14–15. Nevertheless, it is suggested that *Bristol City Council* is correctly decided on the point. For a case in which self-employed work was held by the Upper Tribunal not to be effective and genuine, see *SSWP v HH (SPC)* [2015] UKUT 583 (AAC).

Jany was considered further by the Upper Tribunal (Judge E Mitchell) in *N v HMRC (CHB)* [2021] UKUT 28 (AAC) in which it was held, at para.1, that "[a] street musician, or busker, as that undertaking is conventionally understood, cannot be a self-employed person for the purposes of establishing a right to reside in the UK under EU law". To be self-employed, the claimant's husband had to satisfy each of the three cumulative *Jany* principles, namely that the relevant activity was:

"— outside any relationship of subordination concerning the choice of that activity, working conditions and conditions of remuneration;
— under that person's own responsibility; and
— in return for remuneration paid to that person directly and in full."

A street musician could not do so because (at para.90):

"For conditions of remuneration to exist, they must be agreed (and, in the light of condition (1), be outside any relationship of subordination). Whether the route taken is via condition (1) or condition (3), in my judgment the *Jany* test requires some kind of *agreement as to remuneration*" (added emphasis),

and (at paragraph 93):

"his activity did not involve any agreement as to remuneration: there could not have been any common advance understanding or meeting of minds as to the amount of remuneration. The giving of donations by passers-by does not involve a common understanding as to the amount of remuneration provided to the street musician, and there is also a good argument that, for the same reason, it does not involve remuneration at all. It is a matter of pure chance whether the sum provided matches the musician's expectation.

Or as HMRC's submission succinctly put it (at para.77) his activity was "not carried out in return for remuneration, only in the hope of donation".

In so deciding, Judge Mitchell preferred the ECJ's decision in *Jany* over its earlier decision in *Roosmalen v Bestuur van de Bedrijfsvereniging voor de Gezondheid, Geestelijke en Maatschappelijke Belangen*, Case C-300/84.

Fostering is not self-employment (see *SSWP v SY (IS)* [2012] UKUT 233 (AAC) at paras 10–11). Similarly, a person who receives carer's allowance for caring for a severely disabled person is not providing services for remuneration and so is not a self-employed person for the purposes of art.7(1)(a) of the Citizenship Directive: see *JR v SSWP (IS) and JR v Leeds CC and another (HB)* [2014] UKUT 154 (AAC).

For the circumstances in which a person who has ceased self-employment retains the status of a "self-employed person" see the commentary to reg.6, below.

Self-sufficient persons

7.37   The status of "self-sufficient person" is governed by paras (1)(c), (3) and (4). The general rule (in para.(1)(c)) is that, to count as self-sufficient, a person must have "sufficient resources not to become a burden on the social assistance system of the United Kingdom during the person's period of residence" (para.(1)(c)(i)) and "comprehensive sickness insurance cover in the United Kingdom" (para.(1)(c)(ii)). That definition follows art.7(1)(b) of the Citizenship Directive.

Social assistance

7.38   The decision of the ECJ in *Pensionsversicherungsanstalt v Brey* Case C-140/12 holds (at para.61) that "social assistance":

"must be interpreted as covering all assistance introduced by the public authorities, whether at national, regional or local level, that can be claimed by an individual who does not have resources sufficient to meet his own basic needs and the needs of his family and who, by reason of that fact, may become a burden on the public finances of the host Member State during his period of residence which could have consequences for the overall level of assistance which may be granted by that State".

Further, the fact that a benefit is a special non-contributory cash benefit for the purposes of Regulation (EC) 883/2004 does not prevent its being social assistance for the purposes of art.7(1)(b) of the Citizenship Directive (*ibid.* at para.58). In *Brey*, an Austrian benefit called the *Ausgleichzulage* (compensatory supplement), which appears to be similar to state pension credit, was held (at para.62) to be social assistance. Housing benefit and the former council tax benefit are also social assistance *SG v Tameside Metropolitan Borough Council (HB)* [2010] UKUT 243 (AAC) at para.50. However, tax credits may not be (see *R (A, B and C) v Secretary of State for the Home Department* [2013] EWHC 1272 at para.46, although the observations were made when granting permission to apply for judicial review and are therefore not binding).

Burden
"Burden" in para.(1)(c)(i) and art.7(1)(b) means "unreasonable burden": see Recitals (10) and (16) to the Citizenship Directive and *Brey*, above, paras 53-54, 57 and generally. The Court in Brey places particular emphasis (at para.72) on whether "the difficulties which a beneficiary of the right of residence encounters are temporary" as a relevant factor in assessing whether the grant of a social security benefit could place a burden on the host Member State's social assistance system as a whole.

7.39

Sufficient resources
The person's resources are "sufficient" if (taking into account the resources of any relevant family member) they exceed the maximum level of resources which a British citizen and his family members may possess if he is to become eligible for social assistance under the United Kingdom benefit system; or, if that is not the case, it appears those resources should be regarded as sufficient "taking into account the personal situation of the person concerned and, where applicable, any family members": see para.(4), which follows art.8(4).

7.40

If a person "has" sufficient resources then, with one exception, the origin of those resources is irrelevant. So, for example, where accommodation is made available to a claimant by a third party, the claimant "is in principle entitled to have that taken into account towards determining the sufficiency of their resources" (*SG v Tameside MBC* (HB) [2010] UKUT 243 (AAC). at paras 51-52, following the decision of the ECJ in Case C-408/03 *Commission v Kingdom of Belgium*). This includes the earnings of a spouse or partner who is a third-country national: see *Singh and others v Minister for Justice and Equality* (Case C-218/14).

The exception is that a person who has earnings, but who is nevertheless not a worker, cannot rely upon those earnings to establish self-sufficiency (*VP v SSWP (JSA)* [2014] UKUT 32 (AAC) at para.92, agreeing with the Chief Commissioner for Northern Ireland in *AS v HMRC (CB)* [2013] NICom 15 at para.110 and with the former Asylum and Immigration Tribunal in *MA & Others (EU national; self-sufficiency; lawful employment) Bangladesh* [2006] UKAIT 90 at para.44).

It will often seem self-evident that a person who has been driven by circumstances to claim an income-related benefit, no longer satisfies that definition of a "self-sufficient person". However, the decision in *Brey* means that that consequence does not follow automatically. There may be cases in which a person can assert that, although they are without resources at present, they should still be regarded as self-sufficient because their claim for benefit does not represent an unreasonable burden on the social assistance system of the United Kingdom. The reasoning underlying that conclusion is stated at paras 63-78 of *Brey*:

7.41

"63. . . . the fact that a national of another Member State who is not economically active may be eligible, in light of his low pension, to receive [a social assistance] benefit could be an indication that that national does not have sufficient resources to avoid becoming an unreasonable burden on the social assistance system of the host Member State for the purposes of Article 7(1)(b) of [the Citizenship] Directive . . ..

64. However, the competent national authorities cannot draw such conclusions without first carrying out an overall assessment of the specific burden which granting that benefit would place on the national social assistance system as a whole, by reference to the personal circumstances characterising the individual situation of the person concerned.

65. First, it should be pointed out that there is nothing in [the Citizenship] Directive . . . to preclude nationals of other Member States from receiving social security benefits in the host Member State . . ..

66. On the contrary, several provisions of that directive specifically state that those nationals may receive such benefits. Thus, as the Commission has rightly pointed out, the very wording of Article 24(2) of that directive shows that it is only during the first three months of residence that, by way of derogation from the principle of equal treatment set out in Article 24(1), the host Member State is not to be under an obligation to confer entitlement to social assistance on Union citizens who do not or no longer have worker status. In addition, Article 14(3) of that directive provides that an expulsion measure is not to be the automatic consequence of recourse to the social assistance system of the host Member State by a Union citizen or a member of his family.

67. Second, it should be noted that the first sentence of Article 8(4) of [the Citizenship] Directive . . . expressly states that Member States may not lay down a fixed amount which they will regard as 'sufficient resources', but must take into account the personal situation of the person concerned. Moreover, under the second sentence of Article 8(4), the amount ultimately regarded as indicating sufficient resources may not be higher than the threshold below which nationals of the host Member State become eligible for social assistance, or, where that criterion is not applicable, higher than the minimum social security pension paid by the host Member State.

68. It follows that, although Member States may indicate a certain sum as a reference amount, they may not impose a minimum income level below which it will be presumed that the person concerned does not have sufficient resources, irrespective of a specific examination of the situation of each person concerned . . ..

69. Furthermore, it is clear from recital 16 in the preamble to [the Citizenship] Directive 2004/38 that, in order to determine whether a person receiving social assistance has become an unreasonable burden on its social assistance system, the host Member State should, before adopting an expulsion measure, examine whether the person concerned is experiencing temporary difficulties and take into account the duration of residence of the person concerned, his personal circumstances, and the amount of aid which has been granted to him.

70. Lastly, it should be borne in mind that, since the right to freedom of movement is – as a fundamental principle of EU law – the general rule, the conditions laid down in Article 7(1)(b) of [the Citizenship] Directive . . . must be construed narrowly . . . and in compliance with the limits imposed by EU law and the principle of proportionality . . ..

71. In addition, the margin for manoeuvre which the Member States are recognised as having must not be used by them in a manner which would compromise attainment of the objective of [the Citizenship] Directive . . ., which is, inter alia, to facilitate and strengthen the exercise of Union citizens' primary right to move and reside freely within the territory of the Member States, and the practical effectiveness of that directive . . ..

72. By making the right of residence for a period of longer than three months conditional upon the person concerned not becoming an 'unreasonable' burden

on the social assistance 'system' of the host Member State, Article 7(1)(b) of [the Citizenship] Directive . . ., interpreted in the light of recital 10 to that directive, means that the competent national authorities have the power to assess, taking into account a range of factors in the light of the principle of proportionality, whether the grant of a social security benefit could place a burden on that Member State's social assistance system as a whole. [The Citizenship] Directive . . . thus recognises a certain degree of financial solidarity between nationals of a host Member State and nationals of other Member States, particularly if the difficulties which a beneficiary of the right of residence encounters are temporary . . ..

. . .

75. It can be seen from paragraphs 64 to 72 above that the mere fact that a national of a Member State receives social assistance is not sufficient to show that he constitutes an unreasonable burden on the social assistance system of the host Member State.

76. As regards the legislation at issue in the main proceedings, it is clear from the explanation provided by the Austrian Government at the hearing that, although the amount of the compensatory supplement depends on the financial situation of the person concerned as measured against the reference amount fixed for granting that supplement, the mere fact that a national of another Member State who is not economically active has applied for that benefit is sufficient to preclude that national from receiving it, regardless of the duration of residence, the amount of the benefit and the period for which it is available, that is to say, regardless of the burden which that benefit places on the host Member State's social assistance system as a whole.

77. Such a mechanism, whereby nationals of other Member States who are not economically active are automatically barred by the host Member State from receiving a particular social security benefit, even for the period following the first three months of residence referred to in Article 24(2) of the Citizenship Directive . . ., does not enable the competent authorities of the host Member State. . . to carry out – in accordance with the requirements under, inter alia, Articles 7(1)(b) and 8(4) of that directive and the principle of proportionality – an overall assessment of the specific burden which granting that benefit would place on the social assistance system as a whole by reference to the personal circumstances characterising the individual situation of the person concerned.

78. In particular, in a case such as that before the referring court, it is important that the competent authorities of the host Member State are able, when examining the application of a Union citizen who is not economically active and is in Mr Brey's position, to take into account, inter alia, the following: the amount and the regularity of the income which he receives; the fact that those factors have led those authorities to issue him with a certificate of residence; and the period during which the benefit applied for is likely to be granted to him. In addition, in order to ascertain more precisely the extent of the burden which that grant would place on the national social assistance system, it may be relevant, as the Commission argued at the hearing, to determine the proportion of the beneficiaries of that benefit who are Union citizens in receipt of a retirement pension in another Member State."

Brey was considered by the Upper Tribunal in *VP v SSWP (JSA)* [2014] UKUT 32 (AAC). For the reasons given are paras 71-79 of his decision, Judge Ward held that "*Brey* is concerned with what follows where a right of residence has arisen in the first place": it does not operate to confer a right of residence on a claimant who has not previously had such a right. **7.42**

Judge Ward also expressed the view (at para.84) that the requirement for a person to have sufficient resources not to become a burden on the social assistance system of the United Kingdom "during his period of residence" meant that:

"a person wishing to assert self-sufficiency at the beginning of a five year period (with a view to subsequent permanent residence) would have to point to "resources" to see them through five years. . . . [i]t may often be the case . . . that consideration is only given to the topic at the end of the five year period when a right of permanent residence is asserted (whether as part of a benefit claim or otherwise). . . . In my view the question, whenever asked, remains: was the person at the beginning of year 1 – and in principle at any other times in the period – able to show sufficient resources to meet the test? I do not accept that a person who could not meet the test on that basis could simply lie low for five years and through a combination of luck and an unusually frugal lifestyle avoid being any kind of burden to the social assistance system and then argue that they have retrospectively shown that they had throughout had the resources to be self-sufficient."

In *Gusa v Minister for Social Protection, Attorney General, Ireland* (Case C-442/16), Advocate General Wathelet recommended that the Court should rule that art.16(1) of the Citizenship Directive confers a right of permanent residence on a Member State national who has resided in the territory of the host Member State for an uninterrupted period of five years without relying on the social assistance system of that host Member State. However, the Court did not follow that recommendation.

The requirement for (in para.64 of *Brey*) for "an overall assessment of the specific burden which granting that benefit would place on the national social assistance system as a whole, by reference to the personal circumstances characterising the individual situation of the person concerned" may seem to conflict with the subsequent decisions of the CJEU in *Dano v Jobcenter Leipzig* (C-333/13), *Jobcenter Berlin Neukölln v Alimanovic* (Case C-67/14) and *Vestische Arbeit Jobcenter Kreis Recklinghausen v Garcia-Nieto and others* (C-299/14) and with the decision of the Supreme Court in *Mirga v Secretary of State for Work and Pensions* [2016] UKSC 1 (see below). However, those decisions were dealing with a different issue. None of the claimants in *Dano, Alimanovic, Garcia-Nieto* or *Mirga* was claiming to be self-sufficient. They all accepted—or were the subject of final findings of fact—that they did not fall within any head of art.7. Rather they argued that the principle of equal treatment required that they should receive social assistance in a Member State of which they were not a national on the same basis as those who were nationals of that State, which in turn raised the question of the scope of the derogation in art.24(2). Such derogations have to be applied proportionately but the CJEU and Supreme Court held that the Citizenship Directive itself ensured proportionality, so that there was no need for an individual assessment in such cases. That is very different from saying that an individual assessment is not required when a claimant is saying that he has a right of residence under art.7(1)(b) in circumstances where art.8(4) provides that:

> "Member States may not lay down a fixed amount which they regard as "sufficient resources", *but must take into account the personal situation of the person concerned*" (emphasis added).

In other words, by requiring an individual assessment of the "unreasonable burden" question in the context of a claim to be self-sufficient, Brey does no more than give effect to what the Citizenship Directive says.

Comprehensive sickness insurance

7.43 *SG v Tameside MBC (HB)* also considered the requirement for "comprehensive sickness insurance". In that appeal, the claimant, a Polish national who had been living in Sweden for many years and was receiving Swedish invalidity benefit in the UK under the provisions of the former Regulation (EEC) No. 1408/71. The Upper Tribunal accepted a concession from the Secretary of State that the claimant could rely on the UK's right to the reimbursement of healthcare costs under arts 27–34 of that Regulation and art.95 of Regulation (EEC) No. 574/72 as meeting the requirement for comprehensive sickness insurance. However, in *SSWP v HH (SPC)* [2015] UKUT 583 (AAC), it was emphasised that, under art.28a of Regulation

1408/71 the Member State competent in respect of pensions was only responsible for the costs of healthcare "to the extent that the pensioner and members of his family would have been entitled to such benefits under the legislation [of that Member State] if they resided in the territory of [that] Member State". Whether a claimant and her/his family members would have been so entitled was a question of foreign law that had to be proved by evidence: see paras 5-6 of *HH*.

The rights of reimbursement referred to in *SG v Tameside MBC (HB)* are now to be found in arts 35 and 41 of Regulation (EC) 883/2004 and arts 62-86 of Regulation (EC) 987/2009.

In *SSWP v GS(PC)* [2016] UKUT 394 (AAC), [2017] AACR 7, the Upper Tribunal considered the position of an Italian National who held an EHIC card issued by Italy which entitled him to medical benefits in kind (*i.e.,* in this case, NHS treatment) "during a stay in the territory of another Member State": see art.19 of Regulation (EC) 883/2004 (equivalent to art.22(1)(a) of the former Regulation (EEC) 1408/71) and art.25 of Regulation (EC) 987/2009 (equivalent to art.21 of Regulation (EEC) 574/72). In some circumstances, the UK would have been entitled to seek reimbursement from Italy for the costs of any such treatment. But whether those circumstances exist in any given case raises complicated issues of law and fact, particularly as to whether the UK has become the competent state—in which case no reimbursement would be possible—and at what point a "stay" (defined by art.1(k) of Regulation (EC) 883/2004 as meaning "temporary residence") becomes "residence" (defined by art.1(j) as meaning "habitual residence"): see the decision of the CJEU in *I v Health Service Executive* C-255/13. In *GS*, Judge Ward held that the claimant had become habitually resident in the UK and that the UK therefore would have had no right to seek reimbursement of NHS costs from Italy merely because he held an EHIC card. However, Judge Ward added (at para.40):

> "10. It does not however follow from what I have said that there are no circumstances in which reliance could be placed on an EHIC as amounting to CSIC. The conditions governing the scope of the coverage must be considered and applied to the circumstances of the case. While, as C-255/13–with its exceptional facts–demonstrates, very lengthy periods would not necessarily always be precluded from constituting a "stay", it will be for temporary–and so, in practice though not as a matter of law, probably shorter–periods that such reliance is most likely to be possible."

In the absence of a right to reimbursement from another Member State, the ability to obtain free medical treatment under the National Health Service does not amount to comprehensive sickness insurance (see *Ahmad v Secretary of State for the Home Department* [2014] EWCA Civ 988; *FK (Kenya) v Secretary of State for the Home Department* [2010] EWCA Civ 1302; *W (China) and X (China) v Secretary of State for the Home Department* [2006] EWCA Civ 1494 and *VP v SSWP (JSA)* [2014] UKUT 32 (AAC) at paras 98-105).

It follows from the decision in *Ahmad* that the observations made by Judge Rowland in *SSWP v SW (IS)* [2011] UKUT 508 (AAC) at [20] and by the Chief Commissioner of Northern Ireland in *AS v HMRC (CB)* at para.128 (xi) and (xii) do not correctly state the law.

There may, however, be further developments on this issue following the decision of the Grand Chamber of the CJEU in *A v Latvijas Republikas Veselības ministrija* (Case C-535/19). A. is an Italian national, who moved to Latvia to join his spouse, a Latvian national, and their two children. He applied to be affiliated to the Latvian public sickness insurance system and issued with a European Health Insurance Card, but that application was refused. The Grand Chamber ruled that the refusal was contrary to EU law:

> "1. Article 3(1)(a) of Regulation (EC) No 883/2004 ...as amended by Regulation (EC) No 988/2009 ..., must be interpreted as meaning that medical care, financed by the State, which is granted, without any individual and discretionary assessment of personal needs, to persons falling within the categories of recipients

defined by national legislation, constitutes 'sickness benefits' within the meaning of that provision, thus falling within the scope of Regulation No 883/2004, as amended by Regulation No 988/2009.

2. Article 11(3)(e) of Regulation No 883/2004, as amended by Regulation No 988/2009, read in the light of Article 7(1)(b) of [the Citizenship] Directive, must be interpreted as precluding national legislation which excludes from the right to be affiliated to the public sickness insurance scheme of the host Member State, in order to receive medical care financed by that State, economically inactive Union citizens, who are nationals of another Member State and who fall, by virtue of Article 11(3)(e) of Regulation No 883/2004, as amended by Regulation No 988/2009, within the scope of the legislation of the host Member State and who are exercising their right of residence in the territory of that State under Article 7(1)(b) of that directive.

Article 4 and Article 11(3)(e) of Regulation No 883/2004, as amended by Regulation No 988/2009, and Article 7(1)(b) and Article 24 of [the Citizenship] Directive must be interpreted, by contrast, as not precluding the affiliation of such Union citizens to that system from not being free of charge, in order to prevent those citizens from becoming an unreasonable burden on the public finances of the host Member State.

The final quoted paragraph is interesting because (once the double negative is resolved) it says that the host Member State need not allow affiliation to its public sickness insurance scheme to be "free of charge". That is not the same as a requirement that the affiliated person should have comprehensive sickness insurance. In relation to the right of Member States not to make affiliation free of charge, the Court observed (at para.59):

"... as the Advocate General stated in point 124 of his Opinion, the host Member State may make the affiliation to its public sickness insurance system of an economically inactive Union citizen, residing in its territory on the basis of Article 7(1)(b) of [the Citizenship Directive] subject to conditions intended to ensure that that citizen does not become an unreasonable burden on the public finances of that Member State. Such conditions may include the conclusion or maintaining by that citizen of comprehensive private sickness insurance, enabling the reimbursement to that Member State of the health expenses it has incurred for that citizen's benefit, *or the payment, by that citizen, of a contribution to that Member State's public sickness insurance system.* In that context, it is nevertheless for the host Member State to ensure that the principle of proportionality is observed and, therefore, that it is not excessively difficult for that citizen to comply with such conditions.

It can only be a matter of time before it is argued that, in the light of the decision in *A*, a person who does not have sickness insurance but who is able to pay a contribution to (in the UK context) the National Health Service by having sufficient resources to pay any NHS charges as they fall due, should be treated as having comprehensive sickness insurance for the purposes of art.7(1)(b).

Note, finally, that in *VI v Commissioners for Her Majesty's Revenue and Customs* (Case C-247/20), an appeal tribunal in Northern Ireland has referred the following questions to the CJEU:

"Is a child EEA Permanent Resident required to maintain Comprehensive Sickness Insurance in order to maintain a right to reside, as s/he would as a self-sufficient person, pursuant to Regulation 4(1) of the 2016 Regulations?

Is the requirement, pursuant to Regulation 4(3)(b) of The Immigration (European Economic Area) Regulations 2016 (that Comprehensive Sickness Insurance cover in the United Kingdom is only satisfied for a student or self-sufficient person, with regard to Regulation 16(2)(b)(ii) of The Immigration (European

Economic Area) Regulations 2016, if such cover extends to both that person and all their relevant family members), illegal under EU law in light of Article 7(1) of [the Citizenship Directive] and the jurisprudence of the Court of Justice of the European Union in paragraph 70 of *Teixeira* C-480/08?

Following the decision in paragraph 53 of *Ahmad v. Secretary of State for the Home Department* [2014] EWCA Civ 988, are the Common Travel Area reciprocal arrangements in place regarding Health Insurance cover between the United Kingdom and the Republic of Ireland considered 'reciprocal arrangements' and therefore constitute Comprehensive Sickness Insurance for the purposes of Regulation 4(1) of the 2016 Regulations?"

At the time of going to press, no date has been announced for the delivery of the Advocate General's opinion.

Students

Under the definition in para.(1)(d), the students who have a right of residence are those who are "enrolled, for the principal purpose of following a course of study (including vocational training), at a public or private establishment which is ... financed from public funds; or ... otherwise recognised by the Secretary of State as an establishment which has been accredited for the purpose of providing such courses or training within the law or administrative practice of the part of the United Kingdom in which the establishment is located".

7.44

It is necessary for students to make a declaration to the Secretary of State (or satisfy him in some other manner) that they have sufficient resources to avoid them (and any family members) becoming a burden on the social assistance system of the United Kingdom" (see reg.4(1)(d)). For the level of resources that is sufficient, and the approach to be taken where a student claims an income-related benefit, see the note on "self-sufficient persons" (above).

It is also necessary for students to have comprehensive sickness insurance cover in the United Kingdom (see the discussion under *Comprehensive sickness insurance*, above). From April 6, 2015 such insurance must cover family members as well as the student (see the amendment to reg.4(2) and (3) of the 2006 Regulations by reg.4 of SI 2015/694 and para.(3)(b)).

In *CIS/419/2007*, the Commissioner held that a Polish single parent intercalating student who was not looking for work does not have a right of residence under the former Directive 93/96/EEC.

Paragraph (5): see the commentary to reg.16, below.

7.45

"Worker or self-employed person who has ceased activity"

5.—(1) In these Regulations, "worker or self-employed person who has ceased activity" means an EEA national who satisfies a condition in paragraph (2), (3), (4) or (5).

7.46

(2) The condition in this paragraph is that the person—

(a) terminates activity as a worker or self-employed person and—

    (i) had reached the age of entitlement to a state pension on terminating that activity; or

    (ii) in the case of a worker, ceases working to take early retirement;

(b) pursued activity as a worker or self-employed person in the United Kingdom for at least 12 months prior to the termination; and

(c) resided in the United Kingdom continuously for more than three years prior to the termination.

(3) The condition in this paragraph is that the person terminates activity in the United Kingdom as a worker or self-employed person as a result of permanent incapacity to work; and—

(a) had resided in the United Kingdom continuously for more than two years immediately prior to the termination; or

(b) the incapacity is the result of an accident at work or an occupational disease that entitles the person to a pension payable in full or in part by an institution in the United Kingdom.

(4) The condition in this paragraph is that the person—

(a) is active as a worker or self-employed person in an EEA State but retains a place of residence in the United Kingdom and returns, as a rule, to that place at least once a week; and

(b) immediately prior to becoming so active in the EEA State, had been continuously resident and continuously active as a worker or self-employed person in the United Kingdom for at least three years.

(5) A person who satisfied the condition in paragraph (4)(a) but not the condition in paragraph (4)(b) must, for the purposes of paragraphs (2) and (3), be treated as being active and resident in the United Kingdom during any period during which that person is working or self-employed in the EEA State.

(6) The conditions in paragraphs (2) and (3) as to length of residence and activity as a worker or self-employed person do not apply in relation to a person whose spouse or civil partner is a British citizen.

(7) Subject to regulation 6(2), periods of—

(a) inactivity for reasons not of the person's own making;

(b) inactivity due to illness or accident; and

(c) in the case of a worker, involuntary unemployment duly recorded by the relevant employment office,

must be treated as periods of activity as a worker or self-employed person, as the case may be.

AMENDMENT

Regulation 5 was revoked by s.1 of, and Sch.1, para.2(2) to, the Immigration and Social Security Co-ordination (EU Withdrawal) Act 2020 with effect from December 31, 2020 at 11.00 pm. However, for the purposes of entitlement to benefit, the regulation was saved in an unmodified form by:

- (For those EEA nationals with pre-settled status) reg.83 of, and Sch.4, paras 2, 3 and 4(d) of the Immigration and Social Security Co-ordination (EU Withdrawal) Act 2020 (Consequential, Saving, Transitional and Transitory Provisions) (EU Exit) Regulations 2020 (SI 2020/1309); and

- (For those EEA nationals who had a right of residence in the UK under EU law immediately before December 30, 2020 at 11.00 pm, but who have neither settled nor pre-settled status) by regs 3(2), 4(3) and 5(d) of the Citizens' Rights (Application Deadline and Temporary Protection) (EU Exit) Regulations 2020 (SI 2020/1209).

DEFINITIONS

"civil partner"—see reg.2(1).
"EEA national"—*ibid.*
"EEA State"—*ibid.*
Self-employed person—see reg.4(1)(b).
"spouse"—*ibid.*
"worker"—see reg.4(1)(a).

GENERAL NOTE

Workers and self-employed persons who have ceased activity have a permanent right of residence under reg.15(1)(c) and art.17, even if they have lived in the UK for less than five years. This regulation implements the conditions established by art.17 for the exercise of that right.

7.47

There are three routes to the status of a worker or self-employed person who has ceased activity. They are set out in paras (2) to (4).

Paragraph (2) implements art.17(1)(a). It applies to people who have resided continuously in the UK for more than three years and worked in the UK as a worker or a self-employed person for at least 12 months and who then "terminate activity as a worker or self-employed person"—or, in plain English, retire. To qualify under this paragraph, the former worker or self-employed person must have reached state pension age before terminating activity or, if s/he was a worker, have ceased working to take early retirement. In *AT v Pensionsversicherungsanstalt* (Case C-32/19) the CJEU rejected an interpretation of art.17, under which the requirements of a year's work and three years' residence only applied to those taking early retirement and not those ceasing work after reaching retirement age. It follows that para.(2) correctly implements art.17(a) of the Directive.

Ceasing paid employment to take early retirement requires a definitive step by the worker or self-employed person to leave the labour market and one which involves a positive decision by the worker or self-employed person to take early retirement. It is not simply a status that may be identified retrospectively by the application of hindsight. How such a positive decision is shown will be a matter for the evidence in the individual case. It may, most obviously, be shown by the person accessing some early retirement allowance or pension from an employer or private/occupational pension provider: see *JP v SSWP (ESA)* [2018] UKUT 161 (AAC) at para.39.

Paragraph (3) implements art.17(1)(b). It applies to people terminating activity as a worker or self-employed person as a result of permanent incapacity for work. The former worker or self-employed person must also either have resided continuously in the UK for more than two years before terminating activity or have become permanently incapable of work as a result of an accident at work or an occupational disease that entitles him or her to "a pension payable in full or in part by an institution in the United Kingdom". It is suggested that industrial injuries disablement benefit would amount to such a pension as would employment and support allowance. However, public service pensions payable following early retirement on medical grounds may also count as—depending on the meaning of "institution"—a private occupational pension payable in those circumstances.

Paragraph (4) implements art.17(1)(c). It applies to cross-border workers.

Legal or actual residence?

The word "reside" in Article 17(1)(a) of the Citizens Directive and reg.5 means "actually reside" and not "legally reside": see the decision of the Supreme Court in Secretary of State for Work and Pensions v Gubeladze [2019] UKSC 31 (at paras 76-92) overruling the decision of the Court of Appeal ([2017] EWCA Civ 1751) and upholding the decision of Upper Tribunal Judge Ward in TG v SSWP (PC) [2015] UKUT 50 (AAC). The earlier decision of Upper Tribunal Judge Jacobs in ID v SSWP (IS) [2011] UKUT 401 (AAC), which is to the contrary effect, is no longer good law.

7.48

"Qualified person"

6.—(1) In these Regulations—
"jobseeker" means an EEA national who satisfies conditions A, B and, where relevant, C;

7.49

"qualified person" means a person who is an EEA national and in the United Kingdom as—

(a) a jobseeker;
(b) a worker;
(c) a self-employed person;
(d) a self-sufficient person; or
(e) a student;

"relevant period" means—

(a) in the case of a person retaining worker status under paragraph (2)(b) or self-employed person status under paragraph (4)(b), a continuous period of six months;
(b) in the case of a jobseeker, 91 days, minus the cumulative total of any days during which the person concerned previously enjoyed a right to reside as a jobseeker, not including any days prior to a continuous absence from the United Kingdom of at least 12 months.

(2) A person who is no longer working must continue to be treated as a worker provided that the person—

(a) is temporarily unable to work as the result of an illness or accident;
(b) is in duly recorded involuntary unemployment after having been employed in the United Kingdom for at least one year, provided the person—
    (i) has registered as a jobseeker with the relevant employment office; and
    (ii) satisfies conditions A and B;
(c) is in duly recorded involuntary unemployment after having been employed in the United Kingdom for less than one year, provided the person—
    (i) has registered as a jobseeker with the relevant employment office; and
    (ii) satisfies conditions A and B;
(d) is involuntarily unemployed and has embarked on vocational training; or
(e) has voluntarily ceased working and has embarked on vocational training that is related to the person's previous employment.

(3) A person to whom paragraph (2)(c) applies may only retain worker status for a maximum of six months.

(4) A person who is no longer in self-employment must continue to be treated as a self-employed person provided that the person—

(a) is temporarily unable to engage in activities as a self-employed person as the result of an illness or accident;
(b) is in duly recorded involuntary unemployment after having worked as a self-employed person in the United Kingdom for at least one year provided the person—
    (i) has registered as a jobseeker with the relevant employment office; and
    (ii) satisfies conditions D and E;
(c) is in duly recorded involuntary unemployment after having worked as a self-employed person in the United Kingdom for less than one year, provided the person—
    (i) has registered as a jobseeker with the relevant employment office; and
    (ii) satisfies conditions D and E;

    (d) is involuntarily no longer in self-employment and has embarked on vocational training; or

    (e) has voluntarily ceased self-employment and has embarked on vocational training that is related to the person's previous occupation.

(4A) A person to whom paragraph (4)(c) applies may only retain self-employed person status for a maximum of six months.

(4B) Condition D is that the person—

    (a) entered the United Kingdom as a self-employed person or in order to seek employment as a self-employed person; or

    (b) is present in the United Kingdom seeking employment or self-employment, immediately after enjoying a right to reside under sub-paragraphs (c) to (e) of the definition of qualified person in paragraph (1) (disregarding any period during which self-employed status was retained pursuant to paragraph (4)(b) or (c)).

(4C) Condition E is that the person provides evidence of seeking employment or self-employment [¹ . . .]

(5) Condition A is that the person—

    (a) entered the United Kingdom in order to seek employment; or

    (b) is present in the United Kingdom seeking employment, immediately after enjoying a right to reside under sub-paragraphs (b), (d) or (e) of the definition of qualified person in paragraph (1) (disregarding any period during which worker status was retained pursuant to paragraph (2)(b) or (c)).

(6) Condition B is that the person provides evidence of seeking employment and [¹ , when determining whether the person is a jobseeker,] having a genuine chance of being engaged.

(7) A person may not retain the status of—

    (a) a worker under paragraph (2)(b);

    (b) a jobseeker; or

    (c) a self-employed person under paragraph (4)(b)]

for longer than the relevant period without providing compelling evidence of continuing to seek employment and [¹ , where that person is a jobseeker] having a genuine chance of being engaged.

(8) Condition C applies where the person concerned has, previously, enjoyed a right to reside under this regulation as a result of satisfying Conditions A and B or, as the case may be, conditions D and E

    (a) in the case of a person to whom paragraph (2)(b) or (c) or (4)(b) or (c) applied, for at least six months; or

    (b) in the case of a jobseeker, for at least 91 days in total,

unless the person concerned has, since enjoying the above right to reside, been continuously absent from the United Kingdom for at least 12 months.

(9) Condition C is that the person has had a period of absence from the United Kingdom.

(10) Where condition C applies—

    (a) paragraph (7) does not apply; and

    (b) condition B or, as the case may be, condition E has effect as if "compelling" were inserted before "evidence".

AMENDMENT

Regulation 6 was revoked by s.1 of, and Sch.1, para.2(2) to, the Immigration and Social Security Co-ordination (EU Withdrawal) Act 2020 with effect from

December 31, 2020 at 11.00 pm. The text given above is of the regulation as saved and modified for the purposes of entitlement to benefit by:

- (For those EEA nationals with pre-settled status) reg.83 of, and Sch.4, paras 2, 3 and 4(e) of the Immigration and Social Security Co-ordination (EU Withdrawal) Act 2020 (Consequential, Saving, Transitional and Transitory Provisions) (EU Exit) Regulations 2020 (SI 2020/1309); and

- (For those EEA nationals who had a right of residence in the UK under EU law immediately before December 30, 2020 at 11.00 pm, but who have neither settled nor pre-settled status) by regs 3(2), 4(3) and 5(e) of the Citizens' Rights (Application Deadline and Temporary Protection) (EU Exit) Regulations 2020 (SI 2020/1209).

Square brackets with superscript numbers in the text refer to the Modification section below and not, as elsewhere in this work, to amendments. For the amendments that were made to reg.6 before its revocation see pp.985-987 of Vol.V of the 2020/21 edition.

MODIFICATION

1. SI 2020/1309, Sch.4, para.4(e); SI 2020/1209 regs 3(2), 4(3) and 5(e).

DEFINITIONS

"EEA national"—see reg.2(1).
"right to reside"—*ibid.*
"Self-employed person"—see reg.4(1)(b).
"self-sufficient person"—see reg.4(1)(c).
"student"—see reg.4(1)(d).
"worker"—see reg.4(1)(a).

GENERAL NOTE

7.50   Regulation 6 specifies the categories of EEA National who are "qualified persons", namely jobseekers, workers, self-employed persons, self-sufficient persons and students. Qualified persons have an extended right of residence under reg.14 and residence as a qualified person counts towards the continuous period of five years' residence required by reg.15(1)(a) for the acquisition of a permanent right of residence. They are also exempt from the habitual residence test (see reg.21AA(4) of the IS Regulations, reg.85A(4) of the JSA Regulations 1996, and reg.2(4) of the SPC Regulations and reg.9(4) of the Universal Credit Regulations).

British nationals are not "EEA nationals" for the purposes of the 2016 Regulations even if they are dual nationals of another Member State (see the definition of that phrase in reg.2(1)). From October 16, 2012, they can only be "qualified persons" if they benefit from the transitional provisions in para.9 of Sch.6.

For commentary on who counts as a worker, self-employed person, self-sufficient person or a student, see the General Note to reg.4.

Persons who retain the status of worker and "jobseekers"

7.51   Under para.(2) it is possible for people who were, but are not now, workers to retain that status. EEA nationals who have not previously worked in the UK—or who have ceased to be members of the UK labour market since they last worked here—but are looking for work potentially have a right to reside as "jobseekers".

The use of "jobseeker" in this context is unfortunate. In domestic UK social security law, "jobseeker" is used colloquially to describe anyone who claims JSA or, possibly, jobseeking credits. But such a person may be a worker (because part-time work may be genuine and effective but the claimant may be looking for full-time employment), a person who has retained worker status, or a "jobseeker" in the sense described above. The rights of residence that attach to each of those categories are different and it is therefore important not to assume that a person is a "jobseeker" merely because they are claiming JSA.

In particular, it can be difficult to distinguish those who are retaining worker status on the basis of involuntary employment and those who are "mere" jobseekers. However, the rights of the two groups are markedly different because Member States are not obliged to pay social assistance to nationals of other member states whose only right of residence is as a jobseeker, and in that respect, are not obliged to treat jobseekers equally with their own nationals (see *Jobcenter Berlin Neukölln v Alimanovic* (Case C-67/14)). In practice this means that:

- A right to reside as a jobseeker (or the family member of a jobseeker) only counts for the purposes of JSA. This is because the UK seems to accept that JSA is not social assistance but a benefit designed to facilitate access to the labour market and, therefore, the UK has to treat EEA nationals equally in relation to it. In contrast, those who retain worker status *also* have a right to reside for the purposes of ESA, IS, SPC, housing benefit and, increasingly, importantly, universal credit. Jobseekers do not. (Note, in this context, that the Housing Benefit (Habitual Residence) Amendment Regulations 2014 (SI 2014/539), which removed entitlement to housing benefit from jobseekers with effect from April 1, 2014 is neither *ultra vires*—see the decision of the three-judge panel of the UT in *IC v Glasgow City Council and SSWP (HB)* [2016] UKUT 321 (AAC), [2017] AACR 1—nor contrary to the ECHR: see the decision of the Court of Appeal in Northern Ireland in *Stach v Department for Communities and Department for Work and Pensions* [2020] NICA 4.)

- If a person who retains worker status becomes ill, s/he may continue to retain worker status on the basis that s/he is temporarily incapable of work. This means s/he can receive ESA. If a jobseeker becomes too ill to work, s/he ceases to be entitled to JSA and cannot receive ESA because s/he does not have a right to reside that counts for ESA purposes.

- To qualify for JSA, jobseekers have to show that they are actually habitually resident in the UK. This means that jobseekers are also subject to the three-months' test (see the commentary to reg.21AA of the IS Regulations). Those who retain worker status do not have to be actually habitually resident (although they often will be) because they are exempt from the HRT (see reg.85A(4)(za) of the JSA Regulations 1996) and do not need to have lived in the UK for the past three months.

Given the importance of the distinction and the potential for confusion, previous editions of this work have fought a rearguard action to retain the use of the word "work-seeker", which, before the Citizenship Directive, was the word used to describe those who are now called "jobseekers". More than ten years later, the time has come to admit defeat and this edition now uses "jobseeker" except when quoting directly from cases in which the judge has used "workseeker". However, a surrender over nomenclature does not mean that the distinction between jobseekers who claim JSA and workers (including those retaining that status) who claim JSA is any less important.

Retaining worker status

The rules about retaining worker status relate to people who do not have subsisting contracts of employment. Those who are still employed, even though, temporarily, they are not actually working, *e.g.,* because of illness or pregnancy or because they have been laid off, continue to be "workers" and therefore do not need to rely on the rules (see *CS v SSWP* [2009] UKUT 16 (AAC) and *CIS/185/2008* at para.8).

Although the Citizenship Directive and the 2016 Regulations contain detailed rules about the circumstances in which worker status is retained, the underlying principle by which those rules should be interpreted is whether the former worker continues to be in the labour market. As was explained by the Commissioner in *CIS/3789/2006* (at para.8):

7.52

"... It may seem harsh, but the status of a "worker" is accorded only to those actually engaged in economic activity in the labour market or as self-employed persons at the material time. Accepting that this description can extend to those temporarily unable to be at their work because of illness or accident, or an involuntary spell of unemployment, it is still not apt to include a person who has withdrawn from employment voluntarily and has been and remains economically inactive, neither in work nor seeking it: albeit for entirely proper and understandable practical reasons such as having had to take a break from the world of work because of the breakdown of a relationship and the continuing family responsibilities of having a young child under school age to look after and another one on the way"

See also the observations of the Court of Appeal to similar effect at paras 21 and 22 of *SSWP v Dias*.

Former workers who retain that status are treated as workers by these Regulations and are therefore qualified persons with an extended right of residence under reg.14. They are also exempt from the habitual residence test (see reg.21AA(4)(c), reg.85A(4) of the JSA Regulations, reg.2(4)(c) of the SPC Regulations, reg.70(4)(c) of the ESA Regulations 2008 and reg.9(4)(a) of the Universal Credit Regulations).

Whether worker status has been retained can involve a detailed analysis of the facts of the case. Tribunals need to investigate the issues and make proper findings of fact (see *SSWP v IR* [2009] UKUT 11 (AAC)).

In domestic UK law, the question is governed by reg.6(2), and (5) –(7), which implements art.7(3).

Temporarily unable to work

7.53   As used in reg.6(2)(a), inability to work is a concept of EU law and must be interpreted the same way throughout the EU (*CIS/4304/2007*). It therefore does not depend upon the domestic legislation governing incapacity benefits in the individual member States. The Commissioner stated (at para.35):

"The context provides some guidance. It ensures continuity of worker status for someone who would otherwise be employed or looking for work. That employment or search for employment provides the touchstone against which the claimant's disabilities must be judged. The question is: can she fairly be described as unable to do the work she was doing or the sort of work that she was seeking?"

The meaning of "temporarily" was considered by the Commissioner in *CIS/3890/2005*. The tribunal had taken the view that a temporary incapacity was one "which had a certainty of recovery". The Commissioner stated:

"5. ... The tribunal was entitled to take the view that the condition from which the claimant was suffering was a permanent one. However, it does not follow that incapacity was not temporary, if the claimant was to be regarded as incapable of work at all. The fact that the claimant had returned to work was sufficient to show that the condition was not one that would permanently incapacitate the claimant in respect of all work. (Although the return to work was after the date of the Secretary of State's decision, it was evidence that could be taken into account in considering what could have been anticipated at the date of that decision.) However, it is reasonable to consider a person to be incapable of work for a period after he or she has become incapable of following previous employment, even if there is other work that he or she might undertake. Moreover, the British system in respect of incapacity benefit deems a person to be incapable of work for benefit purposes if a personal capability assessment is satisfied and also pending such an assessment. Such a person may not actually be incapable of work and may be looking for a job. If such a person is not to be treated as incapable of work for the purposes of the 2000 Regulations, there would arise the question whether that person should be treated as a workseeker instead. However, there are practical difficulties in treating a person who is entitled to benefit on the basis of incapacity as a workseeker, not the least of which is arranging for registration as being available for work. There is therefore much to be said for what appears to be implied in the Secretary of State's submission, which is that a person should be treated as incapable of work if entitled to benefits on that basis.

6. It seems to me that the tribunal erred in assuming that because the claimant may have had a permanent disability, she was necessarily permanently incapable of work or, alternatively, in failing to consider whether she was a workseeker if she was not incapable of work. I therefore set aside the tribunal's decision and I accept the Secretary of State's suggestion that I should find that the claimant was temporarily incapable of work. . .".

In *Secretary of State for the Home Department v FB* [2010] UKUT 447 (IAC), a two-judge panel of the Upper Tribunal held that a "temporary" incapacity is one that is not "permanent". See also the decisions of the Court of Appeal in *De Brito v Secretary of State for the Home Department* [2012] EWCA Civ 709 (at para.33), *Konodyba v Royal Borough of Kensington & Chelsea* [2012] EWCA Civ 982 (at paras 18-23) and in *Samin v City of Westminster* [2012] EWCA Civ 1468 where the relevant law was summarised as follows (para.31):

"Temporary is to be contrasted with permanent. The question is one of fact in every case; plainly the circumstances which will fall to be examined will vary infinitely. It will generally be helpful to ask whether there is or is not a realistic prospect of a return to work. It will generally not be helpful to ask if the interruption is indefinite; an indefinite absence from work may well not be temporary, but it might be, for example if an injured man is awaiting surgery which can be expected to restore him to fitness to work, but the date when it will be available is uncertain".

The meaning of "temporarily unable to work" was further considered by the Upper Tribunal (Judge Jacobs) in *HK v SSWP* [2017] UKUT 421 (AAC). After quoting from para.35 in his previous decision, CIS/4304/2007 he added:

"4. ... In other words, the claimant's ability to work has to be decided as a purely factual matter without regard to the particular tests applied by domestic legislation, in this case the employment and support allowance legislation. This is subject to two qualifications.

5. First, there is a difference between the test that has to be applied and the evidence that is relevant to the test. Accordingly, the way that the employment and support allowance legislation would apply to the claimant may be relevant as evidence of inability to work.

6. Second, there is a difference between the basis of the right to reside and the entitlement to benefit. If the claimant wishes to claim for a period before the date when he submitted his claim, his entitlement during that period will be determined by the domestic legislation."

The temporary incapacity for work must be the result of an illness or accident suffered by the EEA national and not, for example, the illness of a dependent child—*CIS/3182/2005*.

Pregnancy

The position of pregnant women requires particular mention here.   7.54

Some pregnant women who are EEA nationals will be entitled to benefits that are not subject to the right to reside test or because they satisfy that test:

- A woman who has worked may have an entitlement to statutory maternity pay, maternity allowance or, in some very limited circumstances, incapacity benefit (none of which depends on her having a right to reside).

- A woman who still has a contract of employment but takes time off to give birth will still be a "worker" (in the same way as a person who takes leave for other reasons) and will therefore not need to show that she has "retained" that status (see *CIS/185/2008* at para.8 and *CIS/4237/2007* in which an A8 national was held to be legally working while on maternity leave).

However, for other women a problem arises because of the conditions of entitlement for IS, JSA and ESA under domestic law.

Under para.14 of Sch.1B to the IS Regulations, a woman falls within a prescribed category if she is "incapable of work by reason of pregnancy" and also during the period from eleven weeks before the expected week of confinement until seven weeks after the end of the pregnancy. Women in this category may claim IS but, subject to what is said below, may also claim JSA if they can satisfy the labour market conditions. Regulations 20(d) and (f) of the ESA Regulations (see Vol.I) treat pregnant women as having limited capability for work either if working would endanger their health or the health of the unborn child or (in the case of women with no entitlement to statutory maternity pay or maternity allowance) from the sixth week before the expected week of confinement and the fourteenth day after the actual date of confinement. A woman who is treated as having limited capability for work may not claim JSA and, if she is to be entitled to an income-related benefit at all, must claim either IS or ESA.

But many pregnant women who are EEA nationals will be unable to make such a claim. Those who have never worked in the UK (or have worked but since withdrawn from the labour-market) will, at most, have a right to reside as a jobseeker (in the narrow sense described below) and that right does not count for the purposes of IS or ESA. Women who have worked in the UK but who give up their jobs because of their pregnancies, or those who—when they became pregnant—were involuntarily unemployed (see below) and claiming JSA as a person who had retained worker status, need to rely on art.7 of the Citizenship Directive or reg.6(2)(a). In the past, they could not always do so. In an individual case a pregnant woman might be suffering from an illness by reason of her pregnancy (see *CIS/731/2007*) but pregnancy *per se* is not an "illness or accident" (*CIS/4010/2006* and the judgment of the ECJ in *Saint Prix* (below) at paras 29–30). The question therefore arises whether a woman who gives up employment (or the search for employment in cases where she was previously retaining worker status on the basis of involuntary unemployment) can retain (or continue to retain) worker status simply by virtue of being pregnant.

The answer to that question is yes. In *Saint Prix v Secretary of State for Work and Pensions* (Case C-507/12) [2014] AACR 18, the claimant was a French national who had worked until she was nearly six months pregnant but then gave up because the demands of her job had become too strenuous for her. She spent about a week looking for less strenuous work and then, at the beginning of the eleventh week before her expected date of confinement, she claimed income support. She returned to work three months after the premature birth of her child.

The Secretary of State refused her income support claim on the ground that she had no longer retained worker status. An appeal tribunal upheld her appeal against that decision. However, the Upper Tribunal (*JS v SSWP (IS)* [2010] UKUT 131 (AAC) upheld the Secretary of State's appeal as did the Court of Appeal (*JS v Secretary of State for Work and Pensions* [2011] EWCA Civ 806, [2012] AACR 7). The claimant then appealed to the Supreme Court, which referred the following questions to the CJEU (see *Saint Prix v Secretary of State for Work and Pensions* [2012] UKSC 49):

"1. Is the right of residence conferred upon a 'worker' in Article 7 of the Citizenship Directive to be interpreted as applying only to those (i) in an existing employment relationship, (ii) (at least in some circumstances) seeking work, or (iii) covered by the extensions in article 7(3), or is the Article to be interpreted as not precluding the recognition of further persons who remain 'workers' for this purpose?

2. (i) If the latter, does it extend to a woman who reasonably gives up work, or seeking work, because of the physical constraints of the late stages of pregnancy (and the aftermath of childbirth)?

(ii) If so, is she entitled to the benefit of the national law's definition of when it is reasonable for her to do so?"

The CJEU answered those questions by ruling that:

"Article 45 TFEU must be interpreted as meaning that a woman who gives up work, or seeking work, because of the physical constraints of the late stages of pregnancy and the aftermath of childbirth retains the status of 'worker', within the meaning of that article, provided she returns to work or finds another job within a reasonable period after the birth of her child."

The Court's reasoning is set out at paras 38–46 of its judgment:

"38. . . . it cannot be argued, contrary to what the United Kingdom Government contends, that Article 7(3) of [the Citizenship] Directive lists exhaustively the circumstances in which a migrant worker who is no longer in an employment relationship may nevertheless continue to benefit from that status.

39. In the present case, . . . Ms Saint Prix was employed in the territory of the United Kingdom before giving up work, less than three months before the birth of her child, because of the physical constraints of the late stages of pregnancy and the immediate aftermath of childbirth. She returned to work three months after the birth of her child, without having left the territory of that Member State during the period of interruption of her professional activity.

40. The fact that such constraints require a woman to give up work during the period needed for recovery does not, in principle, deprive her of the status of 'worker' within the meaning Article 45 TFEU.

41. The fact that she was not actually available on the employment market of the host Member State for a few months does not mean that she has ceased to belong to that market during that period, provided she returns to work or finds another job within a reasonable period after confinement . . ..

42. In order to determine whether the period that has elapsed between childbirth and starting work again may be regarded as reasonable, the national court concerned should take account of all the specific circumstances of the case in the main proceedings and the applicable national rules on the duration of maternity leave, in accordance with Article 8 of Council Directive 92/85/EEC of 19 October 1992 on the introduction of measures to encourage improvements in the safety and health at work of pregnant workers and workers who have recently given birth or are breastfeeding . . .

43. The approach adopted in paragraph 41 of the present judgment is consistent with the objective pursued by Article 45 TFEU of enabling a worker to move freely within the territory of the other Member States and to stay there for the purpose of employment . . ..

44. As the Commission contends, a Union citizen would be deterred from exercising her right to freedom of movement if, in the event that she was pregnant in the host State and gave up work as a result, if only for a short period, she risked losing her status as a worker in that State.

45. Furthermore, it must be pointed out that EU law guarantees special protection for women in connection with maternity. In that regard, it should be noted that Article 16(3) of [the Citizenship] Directive provides, for the purpose of calculating the continuous period of five years of residence in the host Member State allowing Union citizens to acquire the right of permanent residence in that territory, that the continuity of that residence is not affected, inter alia, by an absence of a maximum of 12 consecutive months for important reasons such as pregnancy and childbirth.

46. If, by virtue of that protection, an absence for an important event such as pregnancy or childbirth does not affect the continuity of the five years of residence in the host Member State required for the granting of that right of residence, the physical constraints of the late stages of pregnancy and the immediate

aftermath of childbirth, which require a woman to give up work temporarily, cannot, a fortiori, result in that woman losing her status as a worker."

Tribunals must therefore assess whether the woman has claimed IS or ESA because she gave up work, or seeking work, because of the physical constraints of the late stages of pregnancy and the aftermath of childbirth and, if so, whether—taking into account paras 40–42 of the judgment—she remains in the labour market. In *SSWP v SFF, ADR v SSWP, CS v LB Barnet & SSWP* [2015] UKUT 502, the Upper Tribunal considered a number of legal and practical issues arising from that assessment namely:
  (a) What is the nature of the *Saint Prix* right: in particular, is it a right to be assessed prospectively or retrospectively?
  (b) To whom is the *Saint Prix* right available?
  (c) When does a *Saint Prix* right start?
  (d) How long does the "reasonable period" last?
  (e) Does a woman have to return to work (or find another job) or will a return to seeking work suffice?
  (f) Can a *Saint Prix* right contribute to the period of time necessary to acquire the right of permanent residence under art.16 of Directive 2004/38?
Judge Ward answered those questions as follows:
  (a) The *Saint Prix* right is to be assessed prospectively. The proviso in para.41 of the CJEU's judgment—namely that in order to retain worker status a formerly-pregnant woman should "[return] to work or find another job within a reasonable period after confinement"—did not create "a condition precedent to the [*Saint Prix*] right coming into existence, which would have the consequence that the existence of the right could only be assessed retrospectively, but . . . a condition subsequent for terminating it where it is not met . . .". The issue was "primarily one of the woman's intention, but subject to the special protection conferred by the CJEU's judgment". Approaching it in that way "means that a woman is protected by her worker status until such time, not exceeding the end of the "reasonable period" contemplated by para.47 of *Saint-Prix*, as she by her words or actions shows an intention not to be part of the employment market": see para.22 of *SFF*. This approach avoids the potential problem with s.12(8)(b) of the Social Security Act 1998, *i.e.*, that any return to work will often occur after the date of the decision under appeal.
  (b) As is implicit in the CJEU's decision itself—and as was not in dispute in before the Upper Tribunal—the *Saint Prix* right is available to women who have exercised the right of freedom of movement for workers and have been employed in a Member State other than that of their residence and to those who by meeting the conditions of Article 7(3) retain worker status while looking for work. It has yet to be decided whether a "jobseeker" in the EU sense—*i.e.*, a woman who has never previously worked in the UK or who, having worked in the UK, has left the labour market but is now seeking work—can avail herself of the right. That is because none of the claimants in *SFF* fell within that category.
  (c) Judge Ward ruled that "the 11th week before the expected date of childbirth which appears as the earliest permitted commencement of a maternity pay period and for payment of maternity allowance and, more importantly, as the start of the period when a claimant for income support fulfils, without more, the requirement to fall within a "prescribed category" of person . . . provides a convenient yardstick by which to assess whether the test is fulfilled but one that is capable of being displaced in particular cases".
  (d) Contrary to the guidance issued by the Secretary of State in DMG Memo 25/14—which had advised decision makers that the maximum reasonable period was the 26 weeks during which a woman is entitled to ordinary maternity leave—Judge Ward ruled that the reasonable period is to be

determined taking account of the 52-week period covered by the rights to ordinary and additional maternity leave and of the circumstances of the particular case: see para.35. He added:

> "As a matter of practice rather than of law, it seems likely that it will be an unusual case in which the period is other than the 52 week period".

(e) A return to seeking work will suffice. Judge Ward accepted (at para.39) a submission from the Secretary of State, that:

> "if a woman with rights under Article 7(3)(b) or (c) had to find a job within the reasonable period after childbirth rather than merely returning to qualifying work seeking, then she would have to do more as the result of leaving the labour market temporarily because of pregnancy and the aftermath of childbirth than if she had remained as a person with retained worker status under Article 7(3)(b) or (c)."

The same was true of a woman who was in employment at the beginning of the reasonable period but whose job had come to an end during that period (para.40). The reference in the CJEU's judgment to a condition that a woman "returns to work or finds another job" could be explained by the fact that that is what had happened on the facts of *Saint Prix* (para.41).

(f) The *Saint Prix* right does count towards the continuous period of legal residence necessary to acquire the right of permanent residence. The Secretary of State did not dispute that in *SFF* and therefore the reason why it is so is not explained. It is because a woman exercising the *Saint Prix* right retains worker status while she does so. Therefore, that period counts towards the qualifying residence period for the permanent right of residence in the same way as any other period of residence as a retained-status worker.

Note that receipt of maternity allowance does not lead to a woman automatically abandoning her worker status: see *Secretary of State for Work and Pensions v MM (IS)* [2015] UKUT 128 (AAC) at para.57.

Where a pregnant woman was formerly *self*-employed – and where self-employment does not continue while she is on maternity leave: see *HMRC v GP (final decision)* below – it remains to be decided whether *Saint Prix* can apply. In *HMRC v HD (CHB) (Second interim decision)* [2018] UKUT 148 (AAC), Judge Ward decided to refer the following question (or one substantially in the same form) to the CJEU:

> "In circumstances where an EU citizen who is a national of one Member State (i) is present in another Member State (the host Member State), (ii) has been active as a self-employed person within the meaning of Article 49 TFEU in the host Member State, (iii) was paid a maternity allowance from May 2014 (a point at which she considered herself less able to work on account of pregnancy), (iv) has been found to have ceased to be in genuine and effective self-employed activity from July 2014, (v) gave birth in August 2014, and (vi) did not return to genuine and effective self-employed activity in the period following the birth and prior to claiming jobseekers' allowance as a jobseeker in February 2015:
>
> > Must Article 49 TFEU be interpreted as meaning that such a person, who ceases self-employed activity in circumstances where there are physical constraints in the late stages of pregnancy and the aftermath of childbirth, retains the status of being self-employed, within the meaning of that Article, provided she returns to economic activity or seeking work within a reasonable period after the birth of her child?"

Where a pregnant woman is wrongly advised to claim IS or ESA rather than JSA, see the discussion below.

Saint-Prix is a case which should be treated as being unique to the special circumstances with which it was concerned, *i.e.*, pregnancy. It is not an authority that provides any basis for drawing analogies with its circumstances: see *JS v SSWP (IS)* [2019] UKUT 135 (AAC) at para.33. In that case, the claimant—a Polish national—was told by social services that he had to give up work to look after his children or they would be take into care. However, he did not retain worker status by analogy with *Saint Prix*.

Involuntary unemployment

7.55   The provisions on involuntary unemployment in reg.6 of the 2016 Regulations purport to implement art.7(3)(b)–(d) of the Citizenship Directive. Until December 31, 2013, the equivalent provisions of the 2006 Regulations were more generous to claimants than art.7(3) strictly required. The provisions were substantially amended with effect from January 1, 2014, July 1, 2014 and November 10, 2014 and there must now be a question as to whether they are more restrictive than art.7(3) permits.

For the position until December 31, 2013, see pp.321-325 of Vol.II of the 2013-2014 edition. The position from January 1, 2014 to June 30, 2014 is set out at p.329 of Vol.II of the 2014–2015 edition. From July 1, 2014, the domestic law of the UK is as follows.

Under para.(2)(b) and (c), as drafted, EEA nationals who have ceased to be workers retain worker status if they are in duly recorded involuntary unemployment provided they have registered as a jobseeker with the relevant employment office and satisfy two conditions, namely Condition A and Condition B.

Condition A is that they either entered the United Kingdom in order to seek employment or are present in the United Kingdom seeking employment, immediately after enjoying a right to reside as a worker, a self-employed person, a self-sufficient person, or as a student: see para.(5). When applying the "immediately after" test, "any period during which worker status was retained" is disregarded.

Condition B is that they "can provide evidence that [they are] seeking employment and [have] a genuine chance of being engaged": see reg.6(6).

Under para.(2)(c) and (3), EEA nationals who have been employed in the UK for less than a year, cannot retain worker status for longer than six months.

Under reg.6(2)(b) and (7), EEA nationals who have been employed in the UK for at least a year may retain the status of worker for longer than six months but only if they can provide "compelling evidence" that they are continuing to seek employment and have a genuine chance of being engaged.

However, in *KH v Bury MBC and SSWP* [2020] UKUT 50 (AAC), the Upper Tribunal (Judge Wright) held that, for those who had worked in the UK for at least a year—i.e., those within reg.6(2)(b)—the requirement to provide evidence of "having a genuine chance of being engaged" was contrary to EU law and that the FTT had erred by applying reg.6(2)(b)(ii) (as it relates to Condition B) and (7) to such a claimant. The judge accepted the submission made by CPAG on behalf of the appellant as follows:

> "38.   The crux of the appellant's argument, which I accept, is that EU law draws a distinction between mere workseekers (i.e. what are termed 'jobseekers' under regulation 6(1)(a) of the 2006 EEA Regs), primarily those who have never worked in the Member State in which they are seeking work, and those who have worked in the Member State in question (here the UK) and have become 'workers' by so doing and who then retain that worker status by remaining in the labour market and looking for work.
>
> 39.   For the latter group … their status as persons who have worked in the Member State is recognised by the differing periods for which that status may be retained depending on the length of time they previously worked in the Member State. A person who has worked for less than a year retains the status of worker for no less than six months under Article 7(3)(c) of the Directive, provided he or she is involuntarily unemployed and has registered as a jobseeker with the relevant employment office. The person who has worked for more than one year has no temporal limitation on the period when his or her worker status may be maintained under Article 7(3)(b), provided he or she is involuntarily unemployed and has registered as a jobseeker with the relevant employment office. The retention for this second category of person is indefinite. But beyond this, those who have

been employed for more than a year are entitled under EU law to retain worker status for as long as they remain involuntarily employed in the labour market and registered as a jobseeker at the employment office. It is no part of meeting those requirements, however, that such a person must show they have a genuine chance of being engaged in employment. By contrast, the test of a genuine chance of being engaged in employment is an appropriate means of identifying whether mere workseekers continue to have a connection with the Member State's employment or labour markets."

By implication, the decision in *KH* also applies to those who have worked in the UK for less than a year during the six month period specified in reg.6(3). However, for the reasons given in the passage quoted above, it does not apply to those who are jobseekers (in the narrow meaning of "mere workseekers").

The Secretary of State was given permission to appeal to the Court of Appeal against the decision in *KH*, but it is understood that the appeal will not be pursued.

EEA nationals who cease to retain worker status under the six months rule but remain in the UK and continue to seek work will become "jobseekers" (see below) if they continue to satisfy Condition A (as they inevitably will), Condition B and (where relevant) an additional condition ("Condition C").

The meaning of "voluntary" (and hence "involuntary") unemployment was considered by the Commissioner in *CIS/3315/2005*. Following *R(IS) 12/98*, he held that the term:

"... must be regarded as focussing on the question whether the claimant is still in the labour market rather than on the circumstances in which he or she ceased to be employed, although the latter may be relevant as evidence as to whether the clamant is still genuinely in the labour market".

It was therefore unnecessary for the claimant to argue that she was forced to give up her job by her circumstances and therefore did not give it up voluntarily and, depending on those circumstances—for example, if she were unable to work or be available for work because of child care responsibilities—such an argument would be detrimental to her case.

An EU citizen who retains worker status by virtue of reg.6(2)(b) will not lose that worker status merely because his or her JSA is disallowed on the grounds of "not actively seeking work: see *SSWP v WN (rule 17)* [2018] UKUT 268 (AAC).

"Duly recorded" and "registered as a jobseeker"

The Commissioner in *CIS/3315/2005* also considered the requirement (in the 2000 Regulations) that such unemployment should be "duly recorded by the relevant employment office" and accepted a concession from the Secretary of State that the requirement was met by an income support claimant who declared that s/he was seeking work at the first opportunity (in this case in answer to a question on the "Right To Reside Stencil"). The Commissioner left open the question of whether an income support claimant who was in fact looking for work but, for some reason, answered "no" to that question would nevertheless meet the requirement.

The position from April 30, 2006 was less clear but has now been clarified. From that date, it was no longer sufficient for claimants to be in "duly recorded involuntary unemployment": they also had to have "registered as a jobseeker with the relevant employment office" (arts 7(3)(b) and (c) of the Citizenship Directive and reg.6(2)(b) of the 2006 Regulations). In *CIS/3799/2007* (paras 17 and 18) and *CIS/184/2008*, the Secretary of State did not repeat the concession that had been made in *CIS/3315/2005*. The Commissioner held that, in order to satisfy the additional requirement of registration as a jobseeker with the relevant employment office, a claimant must claim JSA rather than IS. However, in *SSWP v FE* [2009] UKUT 287 (AAC) a Three-Judge Panel decided (by a majority, Walker J., CP, and Judge Ward, Judge Howell QC dissenting) that claiming JSA or registering for NI credits were not the only means of "registering as a jobseeker". Summarising its conclusions, the majority stated:

7.56

"29. We conclude that the Secretary of State has not shown that the UK has defined specific mechanisms as being the only ways in which an individual can, for the purposes of Article 7(3)(c) "register as a jobseeker with the relevant employment office". That being so, the tribunal was entitled to hold that the Secretary of State's factual concessions meant that the claimant succeeded in her appeal. In summary:

a. What the Directive contemplates is that a claimant has done what is needed in order to have his or her name recorded as looking for work by the relevant employment office

b. Whether or not this has been done is a question of fact

c. There is no rule of law that such registration can be effected only by way of registering for jobseeker's allowance or national insurance credits, less still only by successfully claiming one or other of those benefits

d. Nor was there at the material time an administrative practice to that effect (even assuming—without deciding—that to be a lawful way of implementing the Directive)

e. Successfully claiming jobseeker's allowance or national insurance credits will no doubt provide sufficient evidence to satisfy Article 7(3)(c); but

f. Those who are able to show not merely that they were seeking work, but that they had done what is needed in order to have their name recorded as looking for work by the relevant employment office—will meet the registration requirement of Article 7(3)(c).

g. It being conceded that the claimant had stated on the Habitual Residence Test documents that she was seeking work and that the extent of the work being sought was sufficient, it follows that she met the relevant test."

Therefore, the claimant who (as the Secretary of State conceded, the relevant documents having been lost) had ticked the "Yes" box on the HRT2 form in response to the question "Are you looking for work in the UK?" and was actually seeking work retained her former worker status. The decision of the majority of the Upper Tribunal in *SSWP v FE* was subsequently upheld by the Court of Appeal in *Secretary of State for Work and Pensions v Elmi* [2011] EWCA Civ 1403, [2012] AACR 22.

This issue highlights the unfortunate consequences that can flow from the use of the word "jobseeker" to denote what the French text of the Citizenship Directive describes as a *demandeur d'emploi* and what EU law previously described as a "workseeker": see above. If the English text had required those who wished to retain worker status to register "as a workseeker" with the relevant employment office, no one would have thought that requirement necessarily involved making a claim for JSA.

The decision in *FE* means that former workers who retain worker status may be entitled to claim IS. However, they would be much better advised to claim JSA. The risk with claiming IS is that the efforts of IS claimants' to find work are not actively monitored by the Department. It will therefore be up to them to prove that they satisfy Conditions A and B (above) and (where relevant) Condition C (below). If they are unable to do so, they will be classed as jobseekers, and therefore not entitled to IS.

Participation in a work-focused interview by an IS claimant does not amount to or involve registration for work: see *SSWP v ZW* [2009] UKUT 25 (AAC). The decision was doubted by Maurice Kay LJ in *Elmi* (at para.20) but has not been overruled and remains binding, at least on the First-tier Tribunal.

Two further issues arise. The first is whether, in order to satisfy the requirement of registration, the claim for JSA (or IS) must be made immediately after the cessation of employment. The second concerns the position of the, mostly female, claimants who are wrongly advised by the DWP to claim IS or ESA rather than JSA.

The first issue was considered by the Commissioner in *CIS/1934/2006* (at para.8) and *CIS/0519/2007* and by the Upper Tribunal in *SSWP v IR (IS)* [2009] UKUT 11 (AAC), *SSWP v MK (IS)* [2013] UKUT 163 (AAC) and *VP v SSWP (JSA)* [2014] UKUT 32 (AAC) (AAC), [2014] AACR 25. In *IR*, the judge stated (at para.15):

"There is still a question of the speed with which the claim must be made. A gap between becoming involuntarily unemployed and claiming jobseeker's allowance is not necessarily fatal. Whether it is significant or not will depend on the length of the gap and the reasons for it. Put into the legal terms of EC analysis, the question is whether the gap shows that the claimant has withdrawn from the labour market. A claimant may take a few days to think about the future or to rest after a stressful period leading to redundancy. That may be consistent with remaining in the labour market. In contrast, a claimant who decides to spend six months backpacking in the Australian outback before looking for work has clearly left the labour market for the time being. The tribunal must investigate this issue at the rehearing."

However, *IR* was a decision on the pre-Directive law under which it was only necessary for claimants to establish that they were in duly-recorded involuntary unemployment. The Upper Tribunal has decided that, because the Citizenship Directive introduced an additional requirement that a claimant should be "registered as a jobseeker with the relevant unemployment office", the appropriate test is now whether there has been "undue delay" in so registering (*VP* at paras 51-57, following *MK* at para.69).

The law as stated in *VP* and *MK* is problematic. The concept of "undue delay" is not found in the Citizenship Directive or the 2016 Regulations. Further, the basis for the conclusion that *IR* does not apply after the Citizenship Directive came into force appears to be the decision of the Court of Appeal in *Elmi*. In that case, the majority of the Upper Tribunal had concluded that words requiring registration "as a jobseeker with the relevant employment office" did not add anything to the pre-April 2006 law. A clear majority of the Court (Moses LJ at para.26 and Baron J. at para.29) held that that conclusion was incorrect and that registration as a job-seeker was an additional requirement. However, the majority decision of the Upper Tribunal was based on the authority of the ECJ in *Metock* that "Union citizens cannot derive less rights from that directive than from the instruments of secondary legislation which it amends or repeals" (see above). It is implicit in the Court of Appeal decision that the majority of the Upper Tribunal was wrong to follow *Metock*. However, no explanation is given why that is the case: *Metock* is not even mentioned either in the Court of Appeal decision or in the minority decision of the Upper Tribunal with which, on this point, the Court of Appeal agreed.

What amounts to undue delay will depend heavily on the facts of individual cases. However, in *SSWP v MM (IS)* [2015] UKUT 128 (AAC) the Upper Tribunal held that a delay of five weeks did not amount to undue delay where the claimant did not claim JSA while she waited to see if she would get more work from her agency and made a claim promptly as soon as it became apparent that there was no further work. And in *FT v (1) LB of Islington and (2) SSWP (HB)* [2015] UKUT 121 (AAC)) the Secretary of State and the local authority accepted that the same was true of a delay of six weeks. The claimant had previously obtained jobs quickly, had savings to tide her over and had provided specific details of her steps to find work during the period between the end of her previous employment and her registration as a jobseeker.

As to the second issue, EEA nationals who are looking for work in the UK would always have been well-advised to claim JSA rather than IS. But people are not always well-advised. In particular, lone parents, and women in the late stages of pregnancy (see above), are often advised to claim IS or ESA rather than JSA. As pointed out in *SSWP v CA* [2009] UKUT 169 (AAC), it will usually be incorrect for Jobcentre staff to advise lone parents and pregnant women to claim income support rather than jobseeker's allowance, even if they are CTA nationals. As the judge explained:

"18. In cases where the claimant is a British or Irish citizen, or has leave to remain in the UK, there may be circumstances in which it is correct for Jobcentre staff to advise a lone parent who is receiving jobseeker's allowance to cease her jobsearch and claim income support instead.

19.   However, such cases are likely to be few and far between because:

(a) even if the lone parent would be entitled to income support, ceasing to sign on may affect her eventual entitlement to retirement pension by making her ineligible for unemployment credits under regulation 8A of the Social Security (Credits) Regulations 1975 and forcing her instead to rely upon the less advantageous rules for home responsibilities protection; and

(b) in any event, it is government policy that lone parents should be encouraged and assisted to seek work.

20. In cases where the right to reside is an issue, such advice will almost always be incorrect. The structure of the right to reside test means that a lone parent who is an EEA national (other than a citizen of the United Kingdom or Ireland) will only be entitled to income support if they have acquired a permanent right of residence or are the separated (but not divorced) spouse of another EEA national who has right to reside in the UK."

If the EEA national has never been on JSA and is wrongly advised to claim IS, the only remedy is to seek compensation either under the Department's *Financial Redress for Maladministration* scheme (details of which can be found on its website) or, less easily, through the courts as damages for negligent misstatement. However, where the claimant was already on JSA and has been wrongly advised to cease claiming that benefit and claim IS instead, s/he should appeal against the decision to terminate the JSA claim (which will often not have been notified expressly) as well as the refusal of IS (see para.5 of *CIS/571/2007* and paras 29–32 of *CIS/4144/2007*). Note that an extension of time may be necessary. The claimant should argue that s/he did not give informed consent to the withdrawal of the JSA award. In addition, the power to supersede a decision awarding benefit is just that, a power not a duty. Claimants should argue that for the Secretary of State to exercise that power so as to disadvantage a claimant for having relied on the advice of his own staff would be an abuse of power contrary to the principle in *CIS/6249/1999* (see para.32 of *CIS/4144/2007*).

Vocational Training

7.57   In *SSWP v EM* [2009] UKUT 146 (AAC), Judge Rowland held (at para.10) that what is now reg.6(2)(d) of the 2016 Regulations gives effect to art.7(3)(d) of Directive, which in turn codifies the effects of *Lair* and *Raulin*. It applies:

"... only where a person has to retrain in order to find work reasonably equivalent to his or her former employment. Like regulation 6(2)(b), it does not look back at the circumstances in which the person has become unemployed, although that may be part of the background; it is concerned with the situation where a person cannot reasonably be expected to be in the labour market because there is no appropriate market. That is not the case here. Jobs in education have obvious attractions for parents with young children, but the claimant in the present case could have looked for work equivalent to her former employment."

The claimant, who had worked in a chicken-processing factory and had left to train as a teaching assistant, was therefore not "involuntarily unemployed" within what is now reg.6(2)(d) and could not rely upon what is now reg.6(2)(e) because her training was not "related to [her] previous employment".

"Jobseekers"

7.58   The right to reside granted by regs 6(1)(a) and 14 to "a jobseeker" is not conferred by the Citizenship Directive but is derived directly from art.45 TFEU (ex. art.39 TEC) (see Case C–292/89 *R. v Immigration Appeal tribunal Ex p. Antonissen* [1991] E.C.R. I-745).

Since July 1, 2014, "jobseeker" has been defined for the purposes of the 2016 Regulations (and the 2006 Regulations) by para.(1) as "a person who satisfies conditions A, B and, where relevant, C". Condition A is described above in the discussion of retention of worker status.

Condition B is that is that the person provides evidence of seeking employment and having a genuine chance of being engaged. Following the decision of the Upper Tribunal in *KH v Bury MBC and SSWP* [2020] UKUT 50 (AAC), the Condition only applies to jobseekers (in the narrow EU sense of that word). In *KH*, Judge Wright held that the requirement to provide evidence of "having a genuine chance of being engaged" in order to retain worker status was contrary to EU law and that the FTT had erred by applying reg.6(2)(b)(ii) (as it relates to Condition B) and (7) to such a claimant. It therefore follows that no question arises as to what evidence retained status workers must provide to establish a genuine chance of being engaged.

Condition B does, however, apply to jobseekers. The "genuine chance of being engaged" test is a derived from para.21 of the decision of the ECJ in *R v Immigration Appeal Tribunal ex p. Antonissen* (Case C-292/89) which first established that a limited right of residence to seek work in another Member State was part of the principle of free movement of workers.

The Secretary of State can assess whether there is a genuine chance of being engaged using the evidence supplied by the claimant to demonstrate that the domestic law "labour market" conditions of entitlement to JSA are satisfied. However, it may be necessary for HMRC to apply the test without such detailed evidence in order to determine entitlement to child benefit: see, further, *DD v HMRC and SSWP (CB)* [2020] UKUT 66 (AAC).

Further, by para.(7) a person cannot remain a jobseeker for more than the "relevant period" of "91 days, minus the cumulative total of any days during which the person concerned previously enjoyed a right to reside as a jobseeker, not including any days prior to a continuous absence from the United Kingdom of at least 12 months" (see para.(1)) without providing "compelling" evidence of continuing to seek employment and having a genuine chance of being engaged.

The way in which the requirements to have a genuine chance of being engaged and to provide compelling evidence of that chance were applied in practice by the DWP was considered by the Upper Tribunal (Judge Ward) in *SSWP v MB (JSA)* (and linked cases) [2016] UKUT 372 (AAC), [2017] AACR 6, in which the claimants were all jobseekers. The DWP had implemented the requirement for "compelling evidence" administratively by the establishment of a "genuine prospects of work" test ("GPoW"). That test treated "genuine prospects of work" as synonymous with "a genuine chance of being engaged" and as effectively requiring either a definite job offer of genuine and effective work or that there had been a change of circumstances which made it likely that the claimant will receive a job offer imminently.

However, following *MB*, this does not reflect the law. To begin with, the legal test in reg.6 requires a jobseeker to show that s/he has "a genuine chance of being engaged" rather than that s/he has genuine prospects of work. Judge Ward confirmed that the rights of jobseekers under EU law are derived from what is now art.45 TFEU as interpreted by the decision of the ECJ in *Antonissen*. There is no requirement in *Antonissen* that a genuine chance of being engaged must be established by evidence that is more "compelling" than would usually be required. Moreover, as Lord Hoffmann stated in *Re B (Children)* [2008] UKHL 35 at para.13:

"13. [T]here is only one civil standard of proof and that is proof that the fact in issue more probably occurred than not."

Applying that principle, Judge Ward stated:

"54. The test under *Antonissen* remains whether a person has "genuine chances of being engaged" and that is a matter which falls to be decided on the civil standard of proof. In assessing whether a person has genuine chances of being engaged, the (flexible) principle that "regard should be had, to whatever extent appropriate, to inherent probabilities" (*Re B*) is available to a tribunal. However, that is a matter of "common sense, not law" per Lord Hoffmann. ...

56.   If regulation 6(7) of the 2006 Regulations does not go beyond the process which *Re B* permits and requiring *Antonissen* to be fully applied in accordance with its terms, then in my judgment it is unexceptionable. It does not detract from the Community interpretation of who is a "worker" and does not interpret the term, as regards jobseekers, any more restrictively than the Court of Justice already has. It may be said that on that view the requirement for "compelling evidence" does not add anything, save for making express to decision-makers and tribunals what was the case anyway, but that is not necessarily an inappropriate purpose for legislation.

57.   What in my view the amendment cannot do and does not do is anything more than that. In particular, it cannot raise the bar for what constitutes a genuine chance (or chances) of being engaged higher than it falls to be set in accordance with *Antonissen*, which I have sought to interpret in this decision. ... Insistence on 'compelling' evidence may, if care is not taken, all too easily result in raising the bar above the level I have found to be required, namely chances that are founded on something objective and offer real prospects of success in obtaining genuine and effective work within a reasonable period."

Judge Ward also made the following points about the way in which whether or not a jobseeker has a genuine chance of being engaged should be assessed.

- "Genuine" is an everyday word. In the context of a chance, it "implies both the need for the chance to be founded on something objective (i.e., it is genuine as opposed to illusory or speculative) but also something about the likelihood that the chance will come to fruition". "What is contemplated are chances that, as well as being founded on something objective, offer real prospects of success in obtaining work".

- There has to be a genuine chance of being engaged in work that is "genuine and effective" (i.e., in the *Levin* sense).

- A "genuine chance of being engaged" is not something that can only be satisfied if the person can point to a particular job.

- A "chance" is something which by its nature necessitates a degree of looking forward. Qualifications that the person has obtained, or is in the process of obtaining, in the UK may be relevant.

- There is no absolute time limit on a right under *Antonissen*. A Member State may wish to conduct more frequent reviews after a certain time but that must be distinguished from only granting the right for a set period of time. There is nothing to stop a Member State conducting a review after 6 months but nor is there anything in EU law which permits any kind of step change in what has to be proved at that (or any other) point.

- However, a tribunal will need to take a period of 6 months (or indeed longer) unsuccessful jobseeking into account, along with other factors, in assessing whether a person did have "genuine chances" as at the date that needs to be looked at.

In *OS v SSWP (JSA)* [2017] UKUT 107 (AAC), Judge Ward confirmed that where a claimant obtains employment after the date of the Secretary of State's decision refusing jobseeker's allowance, that circumstance can be taken into account as evidence that she had a genuine chance of being engaged as at the date of that decision. Section 12(8)(b) of the Social Security Act 1998, which prevents the First-tier Tribunal from considering circumstances not obtaining at the date of the decision under appeal, "does not preclude inferences being drawn from events which occurred after the decision date about circumstances obtaining when, or before, the decision was made: see, inter alia, R(DLA) 2/01 and 3/01".

The relationship between the inaccurately-named "genuine prospects of work" test and participation in the New Enterprise Allowance ("NEA") scheme was considered by the Upper Tribunal in *EG v SSWP (JSA)* [2018] UKUT 285 (AAC). Judge Poole QC accepted a concession by the Secretary of State that the First-tier Tribunal had erred in law by failing 'to consider the implications of the claimant's participation in the NEA scheme in relation to whether he had a genuine prospect of work and retained jobseeker's status" but rejected the claimant's submission that, while participating in the scheme he did not have to show that he had a genuine chance of being engaged.

As far as any right to reside the claimant may have had as a jobseeker is concerned, the decision cannot be faulted. However, it is strongly arguable that the First-tier Tribunal erred more fundamentally by failing to consider whether his participation in the NEA scheme had given rise to a separate right of residence as a self-employed person. The NEA scheme is established under Jobseekers Act 1995, s.17A and the Jobseeker's Allowance (Schemes for Assisting Persons to Obtain Employment) Regulations 2013. And, as its name suggests, it is designed to help people into self-employment. Regulation 3(5) of those Regulations states that it is "designed to assist a claimant into self-employed earner's employment comprising guidance and support provided by a business mentor, access to a loan to help with start-up costs (subject to status) and a weekly allowance for a period of 26 weeks once the claimant starts trading." It is implicit in the definition that a claimant may have begun to trade as a self-employed person but still be participating in the NEA scheme: it cannot be assumed that, just because a claimant is claiming jobseeker's allowance and participating in a scheme under s.17A, he can only have a right of residence as a jobseeker. The point is a potentially important one for claimants. Claimants who are self-employed persons have a right of residence that counts for the purposes of all working-age means-tested benefits, not just JSA, and so can claim HB if they live in rented accommodation and can claim ESA if they become ill.

Condition C is that "the person has had a period of absence from the United Kingdom" (see para.(9)).

By para.(8), Condition C applies:

"where the person concerned has, previously, enjoyed a right to reside under [regulation 6] as a result of satisfying conditions A and B—

    (a) in the case of a person to whom paragraph (2)(b) or (ba) applied, for at least 6 months; or

    (b) in the case of a jobseeker for at least 91 days in total.

unless the person concerned has, since enjoying the above right to reside, been continuously absent from the United Kingdom for at least 12 months."

The length of the period of absence is not specified. In particular, para.(8) does not say that the period of absence must be at least 12 months. It only says that Condition C does not apply at all where there has been a continuous absence for 12 months or more.

A period of absence of more than three months may have the effect that the claimant will not be entitled to JSA immediately on return to the UK: see the commentary to reg.21AA of the IS Regulations.

The decision in SSWP v RR (IS)

Previous editions drew attention to the fact that unnecessarily broad language in the decision of a Three-Judge Panel in *SSWP v RR (IS)* [2013] UKUT 21 (AAC) seemed to have blurred the distinction between "workers" and "jobseekers" by suggesting that anyone who could bring themselves within art.39 TEC (which would include *Antonissen* jobseekers) are thereby workers for the purposes of art.7(1)(a) of the Citizenship Directive: for more details, see pp.344-345 of Vol.II of the 2015/16 edition. However, *RO v SSWP (JSA)* [2015] UKUT 533 (AAC), confirms that *RR* is not authority for that proposition. *RR* remains authority that a national of another EEA state who comes to the UK in order to take up an offer of employment but has not yet been able to take it up for medical reasons and has therefore never

7.59

worked in the UK, she has a right to reside under art.39(3)(a) and (b) TEC (now art.45 TFEU) as the holder of a job offer—at least while the job offer was being kept open for her—and so was a worker for the purposes of art.7(1)(a) of the Citizenship Directive.

Pre-accession work

7.60   In *CIS/1833/2006*, the Commissioner held, applying the decision of the ECJ in Case C-171/91 *Tsiotras v Landeshauptstadt Stuttgart*, that work undertaken by a Maltese national in the UK before Malta acceded to the EU on May 1, 2004 did not count for the purposes of the predecessor to reg.6(2). However, that position decision cannot stand in the light of the subsequent decision of the Grand Chamber of the CJEU in *Ziolkowski and Szeja* (see below).

Retaining self-employed status

7.61   A person who has ceased self-employment because they are temporarily incapable of work retains the status of a "self-employed person" in the same way as a worker (see above and art.7(3)(a) of the Citizenship Directive).

In the past, however, the view was taken that a formerly self-employed person did not retain self-employed status during periods of involuntary unemployment: see in *SSWP v RK* [2009] UKUT 209 (AAC) and *R. (Tilianu) v Secretary of State for Work and Pensions* [2010] EWCA Civ 1397.

That view is no longer tenable. In *Gusa v Minister for Social Protection, Ireland, Attorney General* (Case C-442/16), the CJEU ruled that:

> "Article 7(3)(b) of [the Citizenship Directive] must be interpreted as meaning that a national of a Member State retains the status of self-employed person for the purposes of Article 7(1)(a) of that directive where, after having lawfully resided in and worked as a self-employed person in another Member State for approximately four years, that national has ceased that activity, because of a duly recorded absence of work owing to reasons beyond his control, and has registered as a jobseeker with the relevant employment office of the latter Member State."

That ruling reflects the facts of the individual case. Paragraph 45 of the judgment makes it clear that it applies whenever anyone has been self-employed for over a year. And the decision of Judge Ward in *SB v SSWP* (UC) [2019] UKUT 219 (AAC), following the decision of the CJEU in *Tarola v Minister of Social Protection* (Case C-483/17), holds that the *Gusa* principle also applies where the claimant has been self-employed for less than a year (although, in those circumstances, self-employed status is retained for "no less than six months" (i.e., in the same way as worker status is retained by an EEA national who has been employed for less than a year).

Such a person retains self-employed status and is not a jobseeker (*i.e.*, in the EU sense). S/he can therefore claim social assistance (i.e., IS. HB, IRESA, SPC and, importantly, UC).

The decisions in *RK* and *Tilianu* cannot be reconciled with the decision in *Gusa* and are therefore no longer good law.

On July 24, 2018, reg.6 was amended by SI 2018/801, reg.2 and Sch., para.2, to bring domestic UK law into line with EU law as set out in *Gusa*. New paras (4)(b)-(e) and (4A)-(4C) have the effect that a formerly self-employed person retains self-employed status in the same circumstances that a formerly employed person retains worker status, the only difference being that Conditions D and E (equivalent to Conditions A and B for former workers) can be satisfied by seeking self-employment as well as employment.

However, the issue whether a formerly self-employed person has to retain self-employed status only arises if that person has actually ceased to be self-employed. That is a question of fact in each case: see the decisions of the Upper Tribunal in *RJ v SSWP (JSA)* [2011] UKUT 477 (AAC), [2012] AACR 12; *SSWP v AL (JSA)* [2010] UKUT 451 (AAC) and *SSWP v JS* [2010] UKUT 240 (AAC). In the last of those cases, Judge Jacobs stated (at para.5):

"5.   I do not accept that a claimant who is for the moment doing no work is necessarily no longer self-employed. There will commonly be periods in a person's self-employment when no work is done. Weekends and holiday periods are obvious examples. There may also be periods when there is no work to do. The concept of self-employment encompasses periods of both feast and famine. During the latter, the person may be engaged in a variety of tasks that are properly seen as part of continuing self-employment: administrative work, such as maintaining the accounts; in marketing to generate more work; or developing the business in new directions. Self-employment is not confined to periods of actual work. It includes natural periods of rest and the vicissitudes of business life. This does not mean that self-employment survives regardless of how little work arrives. It does mean that the issue can only be decided in the context of the facts at any particular time. The amount of work is one factor. Whether the claimant is taking any other steps in the course of self-employment is also relevant. The claimant's motives and intentions must also be taken into account, although they will not necessarily be decisive."

Similarly, in *HMRC v GP (final decision)* [2017] UKUT 11 (AAC) (one of two cases with that neutral citation: see *HD* below), Judge Ward accepted that a pregnant woman could retain self-employed status while on maternity leave. Whether or not that status is retained is a question of fact (paras 10 and 23–34). For the position where a pregnant woman does not continue to be self-employed see the discussion of *HMRC v HD (interim decision)* [2017] UKUT 11 (AAC) (above).

"Family member"

7.—(1) In these Regulations, "family member" means, in relation to a person ("A")—   7.62
- (a) A's spouse or civil partner;
- (b) A's direct descendants, or the direct descendants of A's spouse or civil partner who are either—
  - (i) aged under 21; or
  - (ii) dependants of A, or of A's spouse or civil partner;
- (c) dependent direct relatives in A's ascending line, or in that of A's spouse or civil partner.

(2) Where A is a student residing in the United Kingdom otherwise than under regulation 13 (initial right of residence), a person is not a family member of A under paragraph (1)(b) or (c) unless—
- (a) in the case of paragraph (1)(b), the person is the dependent child of A or of A's spouse or civil partner; or
- (b) A also falls within one of the other categories of qualified person mentioned in regulation 6(1).

(3) A person ("B") who is an extended family member and has been issued with an EEA family permit, a registration certificate or a residence card must be treated as a family member of A, provided—
- (a) B continues to satisfy the conditions in regulation [² 8(1A),] 8(2), (3), (4) or (5); and
- (b) the EEA family permit, registration certificate or residence card remains in force.

(4) A must be an EEA national unless regulation 9 applies (family members [¹ and extended family members] of British citizens).

AMENDMENT

Regulation 7 was revoked by s.1 of, and Sch.1, para.2(2) to, the Immigration and Social Security Co-ordination (EU Withdrawal) Act 2020 with effect from

December 31, 2020 at 11.00 pm. However, for the purposes of entitlement to benefit, the regulation was saved in an unmodified form by:

- (For those EEA nationals with pre-settled status) reg.83 of, and Sch.4, paras 2, 3 and 4(f) of the Immigration and Social Security Co-ordination (EU Withdrawal) Act 2020 (Consequential, Saving, Transitional and Transitory Provisions) (EU Exit) Regulations 2020 (SI 2020/1309); and

- (For those EEA nationals who had a right of residence in the UK under EU law immediately before December 30, 2020 at 11.00 pm, but who have neither settled nor pre-settled status) by regs 3(2), 4(3) and 5(f) of the Citizens' Rights (Application Deadline and Temporary Protection) (EU Exit) Regulations 2020 (SI 2020/1209).

DEFINITIONS

"civil partner"—see reg.2(1).
"EEA family permit"—see regs 2(1) and 12.
"EEA national"—see reg.2(1).
"qualified person"—see reg.6(1).
"registration certificate"—see regs 2(1) and 17.
"residence card"—see regs 2(1) and 18.
"spouse"—see reg.2(1).
"student"—see reg.4(1)(d).

GENERAL NOTE

7.63   The "family members" of a qualified person and of a person with a permanent right of residence have an extended right of residence in the UK: see reg.14(2). In addition residence as such a family member counts towards the continuous period of five years' residence required by reg.15(1)(a) and (b) for the acquisition of a permanent right of residence. In *CIS/1685/2007*, the Commissioner held that, in an appropriate case, a tribunal must consider whether the claimant has a right of residence as a family member of a qualified person as well as considering his/her rights as a qualified person. See also *CIS/2431/2006*.

Family members who are EEA nationals can become qualified persons in their own right by, for example, looking for or accepting work.

Family members

7.64   Regulation 7 reflects the definition of the phrase "family member" in art.2(2). Under art.3(1), the family members of an EEA national are "beneficiaries" of (*i.e.*, are within the personal scope of) the Citizenship Directive, even if they are not themselves EEA Nationals.

Paragraph (1) provides that, except where the qualified person only has a right of residence as a student, the phrase means the qualified person's spouse or civil partner, the "direct descendants" (i.e. children, grandchildren, etc.) of the qualified person (or of the spouse or civil partner) who are either their dependants or are under the age of 21, and "dependent direct relatives in the ascending line", i.e. parents and grandparents, etc. of the qualified person (or of the spouse or civil partner).

A child who has been placed in the permanent legal guardianship of a citizen of the Union under the Algerian *kafala* system (and—by implication—any other type of guardianship that does not create the legal relationship of parent and child), is not a "direct descendant of the guardian and therefore cannot derive a right of residence as a "family member" of the guardian. However:

"… it is for the competent national authorities to facilitate the entry and residence of such a child as one of the other family members of a citizen of the Union pursuant to Article 3(2)(a) of [the Citizenship Directive], read in the light of Article 7 and Article 24(2) of the Charter of Fundamental Rights of the European Union, by carrying out a balanced and reasonable assessment of all the current and relevant circumstances of the case which takes account of the various interests in play and, in particular, of the best interests of the child concerned. In the event that it is established, following that assessment, that the child and its guardian, who is a citizen of the Union, are called to lead a genuine family life and that that child is dependent on its guardian, the requirements relating to the fundamental right to respect for family life, combined with the obligation to take account of the best interests of the child, demand, in principle, that that child be granted a right of entry and residence in order to enable it to live with its guardian in his or her host Member State."

see the decision of the Grand Chamber of the CJEU in *SM v Entry Clearance Officer* (Case C-129/18).

Paragraph (2) provides that, where the qualified person's sole right of residence is as a student, only the qualified person's spouse or civil partner and their dependent children count as "family members" after the initial period of three months has expired.

"Spouse" does not include a party to a UK same sex marriage under the Marriage (Same Sex Couples) Act 2013: see the Marriage (Same Sex Couples) Act 2013 (Consequential and Contrary provisions and Scotland) Order 2014 (SI 2014/560), art.3 and Sch.2, Pt 2. (The phrase "EU instruments" used in that Schedule is defined in Sch.1 to the European Communities Act 1972 (as amended) as "any instrument issued by an EU institution".) However, a party to a same sex marriage might nevertheless be a "family member" within art.2(2)(b) of the Citizenship Directive, (*i.e.*, the provision that treats civil partners as family members).

Moreover, it has recently become clear that that in certain circumstances, a third-country national same-sex spouse of an EEA national will have a right of residence under art.21 TFEU: see *Coman, Hamilton & Anor. v Inspectoratul General pentru Imigrări & Ors* (Case C-673/16). Mr Coman is a dual national of Romania and the USA. He met Mr Hamilton, a US citizen in New York and lived with him there. He then moved to Brussels to work as a parliamentary assistant at the European Parliament. The couple were married in Brussels. In due course, Mr Coman wished to return to Romania. However, Romania neither permits same-sex marriage, nor recognises same-sex marriages contracted elsewhere. It therefore did not accept that Mr Hamilton was Mr Coman's family member and refused him a right of residence. However, the Grand Chamber of the CJEU ruled as follows:

"1. In a situation in which a Union citizen has made use of his freedom of movement by moving to and taking up genuine residence, in accordance with the conditions laid down in Article 7(1) of [the Citizenship] Directive ..., in a Member State other than that of which he is a national, and, whilst there, has created and strengthened a family life with a third-country national of the same sex to whom he is joined by a marriage lawfully concluded in the host Member State, Article 21(1) TFEU must be interpreted as precluding the competent authorities of the Member State of which the Union citizen is a national from refusing to grant that third-country national a right of residence in the territory of that Member State on the ground that the law of that Member State does not recognise marriage between persons of the same sex.

2. Article 21(1) TFEU is to be interpreted as meaning that, in circumstances such as those of the main proceedings, a third-country national of the same sex as a Union citizen whose marriage to that citizen was concluded in a Member State in accordance with the law of that state has the right to reside in the territory of the Member State of which the Union citizen is a national for more than three months. That derived right of residence cannot be made subject to stricter conditions than those laid down in Article 7 of [the Citizenship] Directive ...."

"Spouse" and "civil partner" are defined by reg.2(1) as not including a party to a marriage of convenience or a civil partnership of convenience. Those definitions also exclude parties to polygamous and quasi-polygamous relationships: where either party to a marriage or civil partnership has a spouse, civil partner, or "durable partner" (see regs 2(1) and 8) already present in the UK, other spouses, civil partners and durable partners do not count as family members.

The spouse of a qualified person retains that status until finally divorced (Case C–267/83 *Diatta v Land Berlin* [1985] E.C.R. 567). By the same reasoning, the civil partner of a qualified person should retain that status until the partnership is finally dissolved. For the circumstances in which the former spouse or civil partner of a qualified person can retain a right of residence in the UK following divorce or dissolution of the partnership, see the General Note to reg.10.

Paragraph (3). Some people who do not satisfy the criteria, may nevertheless fall within the definition of "extended family member": see reg.8. Such people are treated as family members as long as reg.8 continues to apply to them and they have been issued with an EEA family permit, registration certificate or residence card that remains in force. See further, the General Note to reg.8.

Paragraph (4) provides that, with one exception, reg.7 only applies to the family members of EEA nationals. As the definition of EEA National in reg.2(1) excludes British citizens, the effect is that the family members of British citizens have no rights under the 2016 Regulations, require leave to enter and remain, and are subject to the more restrictive provisions in Pt 8 of the Immigration Rules. The exception is that, in the circumstances set out in reg.9, the family members of a British citizen are treated as if they were the family members of an EEA national. See further the General Note to reg.9.

Dependency

7.65   The requirement that certain family members should be "dependent" on the EEA national or his/her spouse has been considered by the Court of Appeal in *Jeleniewicz v SSWP* [2008] EWCA Civ 1163 reported as R(IS) 3/09 and by the Commissioner in *CIS/2100/2007* and *CPC/1433/2008.*

In *Jeleniewicz*, the Court upheld a finding by the Commissioner (in *CIS/1545/2007*) that (under the law as it stood before April 30, 2006) where a student had contact with his daughter twice a week and made irregular payments towards her maintenance averaging £10 per week, the daughter did not have a right to reside as his dependent child (and the daughter's mother did not have a right to reside as the daughter's primary carer). It was not enough that there should be some emotional dependency. There must be material support which, though not necessarily financial, must provide for or contribute towards, the basic necessities of life.

In *CIS/2100/2007*, the Commissioner reviewed the ECJ case law (Case C–316/85 *Centre Public D'Aide Sociale de Courcelles v Lebon* [1987] E.C.R. 2811, Case C–200/02 *Chen v Secretary of State for the Home Department* [2005] Q.B. 325 and Case C–1/05 *Jia v Migrationsverket* [2007] Q.B. 545) and concluded as follows:

"44. In summary, the case law is authority for these propositions:

- A person is only dependent who actually receives support from another.

- There need be no right to that support and it is irrelevant that there are alternative sources of support available.

- That support must be material, although not necessarily financial, and must provide for, or contribute towards, the basic necessities of life."

"Material support" does not include emotional or social support or linguistic support (i.e., translation) : see *SSWP v MF (SPC)* [2018] UKUT 179 (AAC).

In *Pedro v SSWP* [2009] EWCA Civ 1358, the Court of Appeal (Mummery, Sullivan and Goldring L.JJ.) (an appeal from the decision of the Deputy Commissioner in *CPC/1433/2008*) considered whether, to be dependent, the family member had to prove that they needed the support of the EEA national or their spouse in the country of origin rather than in the host Member State. In *Jia*, the Grand Chamber of the ECJ held that dependence in the country of origin was required for the purposes of the former Directive 73/148 on the freedom of establishment and provision of services. However, the Court—in reliance on *Metock* (see above)—confined the application of *Jia* to cases arising under the pre-April 30, 2006 law. Therefore it was only necessary for Mrs Pedro to prove that she was dependent on her son in the United Kingdom in order to be a "dependent direct relative in the ascending line" for the purposes of art.2(2)(d) of the Citizenship Directive. Giving the judgment of the Court, Goldring L.J. stated:

> "67. Article 2(2) [i.e., of the Citizenship Directive] does not specify when the dependency has to have arisen. Neither does it require that the relative must be dependent in the country of origin. Article 3(2)(a), on the other hand, requires actual dependency at a particular time and place. That difference, as I have said, is reflected by Article 8(5)(d) as compared with 8(5)(e). It cannot be an accident of drafting. It contemplates, as it seems to me, that where in an Article 2(2)(d) case reliance is placed on dependency, it can be proved by a document from the host state without input from the state of origin. Taking Article 2(2)(d) together with Article 8(5)(d) suggests that dependency in the state of origin need not be proved for family members. It is sufficient if, as is alleged here, the dependency arises in the host state."

The authority of *Pedro* may be somewhat compromised because it does not refer to the decision of the Court of Appeal (Sullivan, Ward and Etherton L.JJ.) in *SM (India) v Entry Clearance Officer* [2009] EWCA Civ 1426 which was given approximately two weeks earlier. In *SM (India)*, the Court applied *Jia* to a post-April 30, 2006 case: the appeal was stated to be against the refusal to issue the appellants with "EEA family permits under Regulation 12 of the Immigration (European Economic Area) Regulations 2006". The decision in *SM (India)* was given after the hearing in *Pedro* but before judgment in that case was handed down. However, it cannot be that the Court in *SM (India)* was unaware of the issue in *Pedro* because Sullivan L.J. was a member of both panels. The decisions can be reconciled on the basis that *SM (India)* was about entry clearance and therefore inevitably involved people who had yet to come to the UK. In such circumstances, the only type of dependence that could arise was dependence in the country of origin, so that the possibility or reliance on dependence in the UK did not arise. The aspect of *Jia* that was in issue in *SM (India)* was whether dependence had to arise as a matter of necessity or whether it could be a matter of choice. Therefore the Court in *SM (India)* was not dealing with the issue that had to be considered in *Pedro* and which led the Court in that case to confine the operation of *Jia* to circumstances arising before April 30, 2006.

Dependency is a question of fact. If one person is in fact dependent on another, the reasons why that is so are irrelevant. *Entry Clearance Officer, Manila v Lim (EEA – dependency)* [2013] UKUT 437 (IAC) concerned a Malaysian citizen, aged 60, who owned a three-bedroom house in Malaysia (valued at £80,000) and had savings of approximately £55,000 in an Employers Provident Fund based on her past employment, which she was entitled to withdraw. However, she wished to leave her savings and her house to her children and grandchildren and so relied on remittances from her daughter, who was married to a Finnish national working in the UK. Judge Storey confirms that, subject to there being no abuse of rights, the jurisprudence of the Court of Justice allows for dependency of choice and that there was no discernible reason why this should not include dependency of choice in the form of choosing not to live off savings. Similarly in *Reyes v Migrationsverket* (Case C-423/12) the ECJ confirmed that there was no need to determine the reasons for the dependence. Ms Reyes was a Philippines citizen born in 1987 who moved to

Sweden in March 2011 to join her mother who was married to a Norwegian. Her mother had moved to Germany to work when she was three years old and had regularly sent money to support her family in the Philippines. The Court ruled that Ms Reyes did not have to show that she had tried to find work or subsistence support in the Philippines in order to establish her dependency, nor did the fact that Ms Reyes was well placed to obtain employment and intended to start work affect the interpretation of dependency. The ECJ did refer to the fact that following *Jia* it was necessary for Ms Reyes to have been dependent in the country from which she had come (*cf. Pedro* above). However, on the facts, Ms Reyes was dependent in the Philippines so the point cannot have been essential to the Court's reasoning.

Note that, even in those categories of family member where dependence on the qualified person forms part of the definition, it is not necessary for the family member to live in the same household as the qualified person in order to have a right of residence. This is important because family breakdown will often be the reason the family member claims an income-related benefit.

"Extended family member"

7.66   **8.**—(1) In these Regulations "extended family member" means a person who is not a family member of an EEA national under regulation 7(1)(a), (b) or (c) and who satisfies a condition in paragraph (1A), (2), (3), (4) or (5).

    (1A) The condition in this paragraph is that the person—

      (a) is under the age of 18;

      (b) is subject to a non-adoptive legal guardianship order in favour of an EEA national that is recognised under the national law of the state in which it was contracted;

      (c) has lived with the EEA national since their placement under the guardianship order;

      (d) has created family life with the EEA national; and

      (e) has a personal relationship with the EEA national that involves dependency on the EEA national and the assumption of parental responsibility, including legal and financial responsibilities, for that person by the EEA national.

    (2) The condition in this paragraph is that the person is—

      (a) a relative of an EEA national; and

      (b) residing in a country other than the United Kingdom and is dependent upon the EEA national or is a member of the EEA national's household; and either—

        (i) is accompanying the EEA national to the United Kingdom or wants to join the EEA national in the United Kingdom; or

        (ii) has joined the EEA national in the United Kingdom and continues to be dependent upon the EEA national, or to be a member of the EEA national's household.

    (3) The condition in this paragraph is that the person is a relative of an EEA national and on serious health grounds, strictly requires the personal care of the EEA national or the spouse or civil partner of the EEA national.

    (4) The condition in this paragraph is that the person is a relative of an EEA national and would meet the requirements in the immigration rules (other than those relating to entry clearance) for indefinite leave to enter or remain in the United Kingdom as a dependent relative of the EEA national.

    (5) The condition in this paragraph is that the person is the partner (other than a civil partner) of, and in a durable relationship with, an EEA

national or the child (under the age of 18) of that partner and is able to prove this to the decision maker.

(6) In these Regulations, "relevant EEA national" means, in relation to an extended family member—

(a) referred to in paragraph (2), (3) or (4), the EEA national to whom the extended family member is related;

(b) referred to in paragraph (5), the EEA national who is the durable partner of the extended family member.

(7) In paragraphs (2), (3) and (4)], "relative of an EEA national" includes a relative of the spouse or civil partner of an EEA national.

[Editorial note: This is the modified wording of para. (8) that now applies to those with pre-settled status]

(8) [¹ ...]

[Editorial note: This is the modified wording of para. (8) that now applies to claimants for whom reg. 8 is saved by SI 2020/1209]

(8) Where an extensive examination of the personal circumstances of the applicant is required under these Regulations, it must include examination of the following—

(a) the best interests of the applicant, particularly where the applicant is a child;

(b) the character and conduct of the applicant; and

(c) [² ...]

AMENDMENT

Regulation 8 was revoked by s.1 of, and Sch.1, para.2(2) to, the Immigration and Social Security Co-ordination (EU Withdrawal) Act 2020 with effect from December 31, 2020 at 11.00 pm. The text given above is of the regulation as saved and modified for the purposes of entitlement to benefit by:

• (For those EEA nationals with pre-settled status) reg.83 of, and Sch.4, paras 2, 3 and 4(g) of the Immigration and Social Security Co-ordination (EU Withdrawal) Act 2020 (Consequential, Saving, Transitional and Transitory Provisions) (EU Exit) Regulations 2020 (SI 2020/1309); and

• (For those EEA nationals who had a right of residence in the UK under EU law immediately before December 30, 2020 at 11.00 pm, but who have neither settled nor pre-settled status) by regs 3(2), 4(3) and 5(g) of the Citizens' Rights (Application Deadline and Temporary Protection) (EU Exit) Regulations 2020 (SI 2020/1209).

Square brackets with superscript numbers in the text refer to the Modifications section below and not, as elsewhere in this work, to amendments. For the amendments that were made to reg.8 before its revocation see pp.1008-1009 of Vol.V of the 2020/21 edition.

MODIFICATIONS

1. SI 2020/1309, Sch.4, para.4(g).
2. SI 2020/1209, regs 3(2), 4(3) and 5(g).

DEFINITIONS

"civil partner"—see reg.2(1).
"decision maker"—*ibid.*
"durable partner"—*ibid.*
"EEA family permit"—see regs 2(1) and 12.

"EEA national"—see reg.2(1).
"entry clearance"—*ibid.*
"family member"—see reg.7.
"immigration rules"—see reg.2(1).
"registration certificate"—see regs 2(1) and 17.
"relevant EEA national"—see General Note.
"residence card"—see regs 2(1) and 18.
"spouse"—*ibid.*

GENERAL NOTE

7.67   Under art.3(2), a host Member State is required, in accordance with its national legislation, to facilitate entry and residence for "any other family members, irrespective of their nationality, not falling under the definition in [art.2(2): see the General Note to reg.7 above] who, in the country from which they have come, are dependants or members of the household of the Union citizen having the primary right of residence, or where serious health grounds strictly require the personal care of the family member by the Union citizen" and for "the partner with whom the Union citizen has a durable relationship, duly attested". Regulation 8, taken together with reg.7(3), implements the UK's obligations under art.3(2) by treating "extended family members" as if they were family members as long as they have a valid EEA family permit (see reg.12(4) and (5)), registration certificate (see reg.17(5) and (6)) or residence card (see reg.18.(4) and (5)).

The requirement for an extended family member to have been issued with one of those documents in order to have a right of residence, reflects the fact that the obligation imposed by art.3(2) on Member States is not to allow extended family members rights of free movement but only to facilitate entry and residence in accordance with national law. It follows that, for extended family members, the issue of an EEA family permit, registration certificate or residence card is constitutive of the right to reside. The right only exists if the host state grants it. The issue of a family permit, registration certificate or residence card is the mechanism by which the UK grants the right (see *CIS/612/2008*). This is in contrast to the usual situation in which the issue of a residence document under the Citizenship Directive is merely evidence of a right that has arisen independently: see the General Note to Pt 3. Note, however, that although the issue of an EEA family permit, registration certificate or residence card is a necessary condition of the right to reside, it is not sufficient. Under reg.7(3), a tribunal considering a right to reside appeal involving an extended family member must be satisfied both that a relevant residence document has been issued and that the conditions in paras (2)–(5) (see below) continue to be satisfied.

The UK is not obliged to issue an EEA family permit, registration certificate or residence card to every extended family member. However, art.3(2) also requires that "[the] host Member State shall undertake an extensive examination of the personal circumstances and shall justify any denial of entry or residence to these people". In *Secretary of State for the Home Department v Rahman* (Case C-83/11) the Grand Chamber of the CJEU ruled that:

"1. On a proper construction of Article 3(2) of [the Citizenship Directive]:

– the Member States are not required to grant every application for entry or residence submitted by family members of a Union citizen who do not fall under the definition in Article 2(2) of that directive, even if they show, in accordance with Article 10(2) thereof, that they are dependants of that citizen;

– it is, however, incumbent upon the Member States to ensure that their legislation contains criteria which enable those persons to obtain a decision on their application for entry and residence that is founded on an extensive

examination of their personal circumstances and, in the event of refusal, is justified by reasons;
- the Member States have a wide discretion when selecting those criteria, but the criteria must be consistent with the normal meaning of the term 'facilitate' and of the words relating to dependence used in Article 3(2) and must not deprive that provision of its effectiveness; and
- every applicant is entitled to a judicial review of whether the national legislation and its application satisfy those conditions."

Extended family members who are EEA nationals can become qualified persons in their own right by, for example, looking for or accepting work.

Extended family member

Paragraph (1). "Extended family member" is defined by para.(1) as a person who   7.68
is not a family member of an EEA national (*i.e.,* as defined in reg.7) and satisfies at least one of the five conditions in paras (1A) to (5).

Paragraph (1A) sets out the first condition. It applies to a person who is under 18, is "subject to a non-adoptive legal guardianship order in favour of an EEA national that is recognised under the national law of the state in which it was contracted" and who meets the other specified criteria.

Paragraph (2) sets out the second condition. The drafting is not as clear as it might be, because of the problem with the opening words of para.(2)(b) identified below. Overall, it is important to remember that the 2016 Regulations are primarily about immigration. It follows that para.(2) is mainly concerned with circumstances in which the putative extended family member is outside the UK and wishes to enter in order to accompany or join the EEA national.

However, for social security purposes, the issue whether someone is an extended family member can only arise once they have arrived in the UK. In such a case, the position is governed by para.(2)(a) and (b)(ii). To qualify as an extended family member, the person must be "a relative of the EEA national" who has formerly resided in a country other than the UK and was either dependent on the EEA national, or a member of the EEA national's household in that country, and has joined the EEA national in the UK and continues to be dependent on him/her or to be a member of his/her household. "Relative" is not defined and therefore bears its normal meaning.

Although the opening words of para.(2)(b) are in the present tense (*"residing* in a country other than the United Kingdom") they must also include *former* residence in such a country. This is required by the express words of art.3(2) ("the country from which they have come") and also because any other interpretation would make para.(2)(b)(ii) meaningless by requiring the putative extended family member to have joined the EEA national in the UK and to be still residing in a country other than the UK at the same time.

The words "and continues to be dependent" in what is now para.(2)(b)(ii) require the non-EEA national to establish that there has not been a break in his or her dependency on the EEA national: see *Chowdhury (Extended family members: dependency)* [2020] UKUT 188 (IAC). The same is presumably also the case where the non-EEA national is a member of the EEA national's household. If so, there would seem to be no reason why the non-EEA national should not move from dependency to household membership (or vice versa) without breaking continuity.

VN (EEA rights – dependency) Macedonia [2010] UKUT 380 (IAC) confirms (without expressly addressing the point made above) that the decision in *Pedro* (see the General Note to reg.7 above) does not apply to extended family members with the effect that, to establish a right of residence, extended family members are required to show both dependence in the country from which they have come and dependence in the UK.

In *Soares v Secretary of State for the Home Department* [2013] EWCA Civ 575 the Court of Appeal held that the predecessor to para.(2)(aa) and (b)(ii) require dependence on, or household membership of, the EEA national him/herself. Dependence on, or household membership of, the EEA national's spouse or civil partner does not count for this purpose. However, para.(7) provides that the phrase "relative of an EEA national" includes a relative of the spouse or civil partner of an EEA national where, before February 1, 2017, a person has been issued with an EEA family permit, a registration certificate or a residence card on the basis of being an extended family member and, since the most recent issue of such a document been continuously resident in the UK. This is a puzzling provision and has no equivalent in the 2006 Regulations. Given the decision in *Soares*, there should not be anyone who has been granted a UK residence document on the basis of being an extended family member of the spouse or civil partner of an EEA national. Presumably, the purpose is to protect the *status quo* in cases where such a mistake has been made.

It is not necessary for the putative extended family member to establish the prior and present connection with the EEA national in the same capacity. So, for example, a relative who was a member of the EEA national's household (but not a dependant) before coming to the UK and is now dependant on the EEA national (but not a household member) within the UK satisfies the definition (see *Dauhoo (EEA Regulations—reg.8(2))* [2012] UKUT 79 (IAC)). However, it is necessary that the situation of dependence (or household membership) must have existed "in the country from which the family member concerned comes" and must have done so "at the very least at the time when [the extended family member] applies to join the Union citizen on whom he is dependent": see the paras 32–35 of the decision of the CJEU in *Secretary of State for the Home Department v Rahman & Others* (Case C-83/11). See also *CIS/612/2008* and *AP and FP (Citizens Directive Article 3(2); discretion; dependence) India* [2007] UKAIT 48.

Paragraph (3) sets out the third condition. It is that the putative extended family member "is a relative of an EEA national and on serious health grounds, strictly requires the personal care of the EEA national". Again, subject to para.(7), the putative extended family member must be related to the EEA national and not the EEA national's spouse or civil partner: see the discussion of *Soares* above.

Paragraph (4) sets out the fourth condition, namely that the putative extended family member "is a relative of an EEA national and would meet the requirements in the immigration rules (other than those relating to entry clearance) for indefinite leave to enter or remain in the United Kingdom as a dependent relative of the EEA national". This condition has no express equivalent in art.3(2) but is implicit in the obligation to facilitate entry and residence in accordance with national law and in the principle of equal treatment in art.24. The UK could hardly be said to be "facilitating" the entry or residence of an extended family member, or treating the EEA national equally, if it were not to allow a right of residence on the same, very strict, terms that apply to the family members of British citizens.

Paragraph (5) sets out the final condition. The putative extended family member qualifies if he or she is "the partner (other than a civil partner) of, and in a durable relationship with, an EEA national, and is able to prove this to the decision maker." The wording is broad enough to cover irregular, but durable, relationships between both heterosexual and same sex partners.

"Durability" was considered by the Commissioner in *CIS/612/2008*. It was stated that:

> "36. 'Durable' has an element of ambiguity. It may mean that it has lasted or that it is capable of lasting. Too much should not be made of this. If the focus is on the past, the length of time for which the partnership has survived will not be the only factor that is relevant. The circumstances will be as important as the duration of the relationship. Survival in times of wealth, health and good fortune is less an indication of durability than survival in terms of poverty, poor health and misfortune. And if the focus in on the present and future, the fact that it has lasted may, depending on the circumstances, be very good evidence that it is and will remain durable.

37. 'Durable' governs the relationship, not the partnership. However, the relationship has to be with the partner. It may, and usually will, have existed before the couple became partners and evidence of the relationship at that time is relevant to its durability.

38. Subject to these points, the durability of a relationship is an issue of fact."

"Durable partner" is defined by reg.2(1) as not including "a party to a durable partnership of convenience" or to those in a quasi-polygamous durable partnership. "Durable partnership of convenience" is further defined as including:

"a durable partnership entered into for the purpose of using these Regulations, or any other right conferred by the EU Treaties, as a means to circumvent—

(a) immigration rules applying to non-EEA nationals (such as any applicable requirement under the 1971 Act to have leave to enter or remain in the United Kingdom); or

(b) any other criteria that the party to the durable partnership of convenience would otherwise have to meet in order to enjoy a right to reside under these Regulations or the EU Treaties".

However, it is difficult to see how any partnership that fell within that definition could satisfy the criteria for assessing durability in *CIS/612/2008*.

Paragraph (6). The phrase "relevant EEA national" is not used in reg.8, other than to define that phrase as it appears in other regulations. It means the EEA national to whom the extended family member is related, or of whom s/he is the durable partner.

Family members [² and extended family members] of British citizens

9.—(1) If the conditions in paragraph (2) are satisfied, these Regulations apply to a person who is the family member ("F") of a British citizen ("BC") as though the BC were an EEA national [¹ and BC is to be treated as satisfying any requirement to be a qualified person].

(1A) These Regulations apply to a person who is the extended family member ("EFM") of a BC as though the BC were an EEA national if—

(a) the conditions in paragraph (2) are satisfied; and

(b) the EFM was lawfully resident in the EEA State referred to in paragraph (2)(a)(i).

(2) The conditions are that—

(a) BC—

(i) is residing in an EEA State as a worker, self-employed person, self-sufficient person or a student, or so resided immediately before returning to the United Kingdom; or

(ii) has acquired the right of permanent residence in an EEA State;

(b) F or EFM and BC resided together in the EEA State;

(c) F or EFM and BC's residence in the EEA State was genuine

(d) either—

(i) F was a family member of BC during all or part of their joint residence in the EEA State;

(ii) F was an EFM of BC during all or part of their joint residence in the EEA State, during which time F was lawfully resident in the EEA State; or

(iii) EFM was an EFM of BC during all or part of their joint residence in the EEA State, during which time EFM was lawfully resident in the EEA State;

(e) genuine family life was created or strengthened during F or EFM and BC's joint residence in the EEA State and

7.69

(f) the conditions in sub-paragraphs (a), (b) and (c) have been met concurrently.

(3) Factors relevant to whether residence in the EEA State is or was genuine include—

(a) [¹ ...]

(b) the length of F or EFM and BC's joint residence in the EEA State;

(c) the nature and quality of the F [² or EFM] and BC's accommodation in the EEA State, and whether it is or was BC's principal residence;

(d) the degree of F or EFM and BC's integration in the EEA State;

(e) whether F's or EFM's first lawful residence in the EU with BC was in the EEA State.

(4) This regulation does not apply—

(a) where the purpose of the residence in the EEA State was as a means for circumventing any immigration laws applying to non-EEA nationals to which F or EFM would otherwise be subject (such as any applicable requirement under the 1971 Act to have leave to enter or remain in the United Kingdom);

(b) ...

(5) Where these Regulations apply to F or EFM, BC is to be treated as holding a valid passport issued by an EEA State for the purposes of the application of these Regulations to F or EFM.

(6) In paragraph (2)(a)(ii), BC is only to be treated as having acquired the right of permanent residence in the EEA State if such residence would have led to the acquisition of that right under regulation 15, had it taken place in the United Kingdom.

(7) [¹ ...]

AMENDMENT

Regulation 9 was revoked by s.1 of, and Sch.1, para.2(2) to, the Immigration and Social Security Co-ordination (EU Withdrawal) Act 2020 with effect from December 31, 2020 at 11.00 pm. The text given above is of the regulation as saved and modified for the purposes of entitlement to benefit by:

- (For those EEA nationals with pre-settled status) reg.83 of, and Sch.4, paras 2, 3 and 4(h) of the Immigration and Social Security Co-ordination (EU Withdrawal) Act 2020 (Consequential, Saving, Transitional and Transitory Provisions) (EU Exit) Regulations 2020 (SI 2020/1309); and

- (For those EEA nationals who had a right of residence in the UK under EU law immediately before December 30, 2020 at 11.00 pm, but who have neither settled nor pre-settled status) by regs 3(2), 4(3) and 5(h) of the Citizens' Rights (Application Deadline and Temporary Protection) (EU Exit) Regulations 2020 (SI 2020/1209).

Square brackets with superscript numbers in the text refer to the Modification section below and not, as elsewhere in this work, to amendments. For the amendments that were made to reg.9 before its revocation see pp.1008-1009 of Vol.V of the 2020/21 edition.

MODIFICATION

1. SI 2020/1309, Sch.4, para.4(h); SI 2020/1209 regs 3(2), 4(3) and 5(h)

DEFINITIONS

"the 1971 Act"—see reg.2(1).
"EEA national"—*ibid.*

"EEA State"—*ibid.*
"extended family member"—see reg.8.
"family member"—see reg.7.
"immigration laws"—*ibid.*
"jobseeker"—see reg.6(1).
"qualified person"—*ibid.*
"Self-employed person"—see reg.4(1)(b).
"self-sufficient person"—see reg.4(1)(c).
"student"—see reg.4(1)(d).
"worker"—see reg.4(1)(a).

GENERAL NOTE

The Citizenship Directive does not confer an automatic right of residence on 7.70
the third-country national family members of EEA nationals in the Member State
of nationality. However, where the EEA national has resided with a third country
national family member in a member state of which the EEA national is not a
national, while exercising rights under art.7, the Member State of nationality must
grant the third-country national family member a derived right of residence on
the EEA national's return: see *R v Immigration Appeal Tribunal and Surinder Singh,
ex p. Secretary of State for the Home Department* (Case C-370/90); *Minister voor
Vreemdelingenzaken en Integratie v Eind* (Case C-291/05) and *O and B v Minister voor
Immigratie, Integratie en Asiel* (Case C-456/12). That principle is implemented in UK
domestic law by reg.9.

Regulation 9 in (more or less) its present form was inserted in the 2006
Regulations by reg.44 and Sch.5 with effect from November 25, 2016 because the
UK government considered that, as it was previously worded, the regulation was
open to abuse and was being used to circumvent the family reunification provisions
of domestic UK immigration law (which are less generous than the rules for the
family members or EEA nationals exercising their rights of free movement here).
Adopting the approach of the CJEU in the *O and B* case, there is now a requirement (in para.(2)(c)) that the residence of the British citizen and the family member
in the other EEA state should have been "genuine" and para.(3) lists a number of
factors that must be taken into account when deciding whether that is the case.
In addition, an anti-abuse provision in para.(4)(a) disapplies the regulation where
"the purpose of the residence in the EEA State was as a means for circumventing
any immigration laws applying to non-EEA nationals to which F would otherwise
be subject (such as any applicable requirement under the 1971 Act to have leave to
enter or remain in the United Kingdom)": see, *e.g., Kaur v Secretary of State for the
Home Department* [2020] EWCA Civ 98.

Before March 28, 2019, para.(4)(b) also disapplied the Regulation where the
third-country national was only a "family member" by virtue of the rules treating
"extended family members" as family members. However, that restriction became
unsustainable following the decision in following the decision of in the CJEU in
Banger v Secretary of State for the Home Department (Case C-89/17). In *Banger
(Unmarried Partner of British National)* [2017] UKUT 125 (IAC), the Immigration
Appeals Chamber of the Upper Tribunal referred the following questions:

"(1) Do the principles contained in the decision in Immigration Appeal Tribunal
and Surinder Singh, ex parte Secretary of State for the Home Department
(Case C-370/90) [1992] operate so as to require a Member State to issue or,
alternatively, facilitate the provision of a residence authorisation to the non-
Union unmarried partner of a EU citizen who, having exercised his Treaty right
of freedom of movement to work in a second Member State, returns with such
partner to the Member State of his nationality?
(2) Alternatively, is there a requirement to issue or alternatively, facilitate the
provision of such residence authorisation by virtue of European Parliament and

Council Directive 2004/38/EC on the right of citizens of the Union and their family members to move and reside freely within the territory of the Member States ("the Directive")?

(3) Where a decision to refuse a residence authorisation is not founded on an extensive examination of the personal circumstances of the Applicant and is not justified by adequate or sufficient reasons is such decision unlawful as being in breach of Article 3(2) of the Citizens Directive?

(4) Is a rule of national law which precludes an appeal to a court or tribunal against a decision of the executive refusing to issue a residence card to a person claiming to be an extended family member compatible with the Directive?

The CJEU answered those questions as follows:

1. Article 21(1) TFEU must be interpreted as requiring the Member State of which a Union citizen is a national to facilitate the provision of a residence authorisation to the unregistered partner, a third-country national with whom that Union citizen has a durable relationship that is duly attested, where the Union citizen, having exercised his right of freedom of movement to work in a second Member State, in accordance with the conditions laid down in [the Citizenship] Directive ..., returns with his partner to the Member State of which he is a national in order to reside there.
2. Article 21(1) TFEU must be interpreted as meaning that a decision to refuse a residence authorisation to the third-country national and unregistered partner of a Union citizen, where that Union citizen, having exercised his right of freedom of movement to work in a second Member State, in accordance with the conditions laid down in [the Citizenship] Directive ..., returns with his partner to the Member State of which he is a national in order to reside there, must be founded on an extensive examination of the applicant's personal circumstances and be justified by reasons.
3. Article 3(2) of [the Citizenship] Directive ... must be interpreted as meaning that the third-country nationals envisaged in that provision must have available to them a redress procedure in order to challenge a decision to refuse a residence authorisation taken against them, following which the national court must be able to ascertain whether the refusal decision is based on a sufficiently solid factual basis and whether the procedural safeguards were complied with. Those safeguards include the obligation for the competent national authorities to undertake an extensive examination of the applicant's personal circumstances and to justify any denial of entry or residence.

With effect from March 28, 2019, reg.3(4) and (5) of SI 2019/468 amended reg.9 so as to bring domestic UK law into line with EU law as set out in *Banger*. The new para.(1A) gives extended family members of British citizens the same rights as British citizens, provided only that the extended family member was lawfully resident in the state in which the British citizen was residing in accordance with his or her rights under art.7 of the Citizenship Directive: see para.(1A)(b).

The right of facilitation recognised by the CJEU in *Banger* is not subject to the limitations on the right recognised in the *O and B* case. So, it is not necessary for a *Banger* durable partner to have made an application to the immigration authorities of the Member State in which the relationship was formed or strengthened under art.3(2) of the Directive or, to have obtained an immigration decision from those authorities based on that provision: see the decision of the Court of Appeal (Underhill, Sharp and Sales LJJ) in *Secretary of State for the Home Department v Christy* [2018] EWCA Civ 2378.

In *NY-v-Department for Communities (JSA)* [2021] NI Com 9 the claimant, a German national in a durable partnership with a British National had entered the UK in 2005, before the Citizenship Directive came into force. However. Mr Commissioner Stockman held that, as the source of the *Banger* right was art.21 TFEU rather than the Directive, the principle in *Banger* had to apply by analogy to the relevant law before Directive 2004/38/EC, namely art.10(2) of Regulation 1612/68. That Article required Member States to facilitate the admission of "any member of the family not coming within the provisions of paragraph 1 if dependent on the worker referred to above or living under his roof in the country whence he comes". It followed that the versions of the 2016 Regulations in force before March 2019, the 2006 Regulations and the Immigration (European Economic Area) Regulations 2000 had all failed to implement EU law correctly. Accordingly, the claimant had a *Banger* right of residence which, as a directly enforceable EU right, took precedence over domestic UK law.

By contrast, in *GA v SSWP (SPC)* [2018] UKUT 172 (AAC), the claimant was an Italian national. On the assumed facts, he had met and married a British citizen while she was living and working in Italy in 1968. They moved to the UK in 1969 and the claimant had worked in the UK from 1970 to 2000, when he left the UK. In the meantime, the couple had separated but did not divorce. The claimant returned to the UK in 2013 and the couple were finally divorced in March 2015. Judge Markus QC held that in those circumstances, the Surinder Singh principle did not apply because, at the time the British Citizen was working in Italy, and at the time of her return to the UK with her husband, the UK was not a member of the (then) EEC and so was not exercising her Treaty rights to freedom of movement on either occasion.

In *HK v SSWP (PC) [2020] UKUT 73* (AAC), the issue was whether the words "these Regulations apply to a person who is the family member ("F") of a British citizen ("BC") as though the BC were an EEA national" had the effect that BC had to be the equivalent of a qualified person or a person with a right of permanent residence in order for F to acquire a right to reside. Judge Ward summarised the facts as follows:

"2.   The background is that the appellant (Mr K) is an Austrian national. His wife, Mrs K, is a British citizen. It is common ground that in 1979, before the couple had met, Mrs K went to Germany to work and did so for many years, eventually accruing a right of permanent residence there under [the Directive]. It was while living and working in Germany that she met and married Mr K. In November 2014, by which time Mrs K was not in good health, they moved to live in Scotland, initially living on savings and the pension from Mr K's job in Germany and staying with a relative. In around April 2018, ... the couple applied for social housing, housing benefit and council tax reduction and Mr K applied for state pension credit. Under section 1(2) of the State Pension Credit Act 2002 and Regulations 2(1) and 2(2) of the State Pension Credit Regulations 2002/1792, it is a condition of entitlement that a claimant has a qualifying right to reside. On 30 July 2018 the Secretary of State decided that Mr K did not have such a right and so his claim was refused."

The reason for the refusal was that, if regulation 9(1) is read literally and the 2016 Regulations applied to her "as though [she] were an EEA national", then she would not have had a right to reside herself and Mr K could therefore have no better right as her family member. Mrs K was above state pension credit age, ill, and would not have fallen within any of the categories of "qualified person" in reg.6. Neither would she have a right of permanent residence in the UK under reg.15 because she had not lived in the UK as a qualified person for a continuous period of five years. As a matter of immigration law, she did not need those rights because she had a right of abode as a British citizen. Nevertheless, if the 2016 Regulations were applied to her "as though [she] were an EEA national", then she did not have them.

Relying in particular on the decision of the CJEU in *Minister voor Vremdelingenzaken en Integratie v RNG Eind* (C-456/12), Judge Ward held at [44] that "reg 9(1) is to be interpreted as not requiring, as part of how "these Regulations apply", "BC" to fulfil the condition of being a "qualified person" under reg.6". The reasoning behind that conclusion is summarised at [31]:

"31.   The requirement is to apply the Directive "by analogy", a somewhat ill-defined process. We know, however, that, whatever this means, it does not extend to the ability to impose a requirement to be economically active upon return (*Eind*), even though either that, or being a student or self-sufficient, would be a requirement if one was starting *ab initio* in another Member State. Nor can it be the case that the conditions imposed could derogate from the effectiveness of allowing a person who has acquired a right of permanent residence elsewhere to return with the family member concerned (*O and B* at [45]), as would occur if a condition were to be imposed requiring the citizen to re-qualify for permanent residence by a further 5 years as a qualified person before reliance could be placed on the second limb of reg 14(2) . . . . This view is consistent with the idea, seen in both *Eind* and *O and B*, that what earned the Union citizen's ability to confer a derived right upon his family member was his initial exercise of freedom of movement rights to go to another Member State to an extent which passes the *O and B* tests of strengthening family life there.

Finally Judge Ward observed (at [44]):

"While the issue has been raised in these proceedings only tangentially, I cannot see that the condition in reg 14(2) could be applied so as to require the returning British citizen to have a right of permanent residence (as if under the Directive) either".

Dual national: national of an EEA State who acquires British citizenship

7.71

9A.—(1) In this regulation "DN" means a person within paragraph (b) of the definition of "EEA national" in regulation 2(1).

(2) DN who comes within the definition of "qualified person" in regulation 6(1) is only a qualified person for the purpose of these Regulations if DN—

(a) came within the definition of "qualified person" at the time of acquisition of British citizenship; and

(b) has not at any time subsequent to the acquisition of British citizenship lost the status of qualified person.

(3) Regulation 15 only applies to DN, or to the family member of DN who is not an EEA national, if DN satisfies the condition in paragraph (4).

(4) The condition in this paragraph is that at the time of acquisition of British citizenship DN either—

(a) was a qualified person; or

(b) had acquired a right of permanent residence in accordance with these Regulations.

AMENDMENT

Regulation 9A was revoked by s.1 of, and Sch.1, para.2(2) to, the Immigration and Social Security Co-ordination (EU Withdrawal) Act 2020 with effect from December 31, 2020 at 11.00 pm. However, for the purposes of entitlement to benefit, the regulation was saved in an unmodified form by:

- (For those EEA nationals with pre-settled status) reg.83 of, and Sch.4, paras 2, 3 and 4(i) of the Immigration and Social Security Co-ordination (EU Withdrawal) Act 2020 (Consequential, Saving, Transitional and Transitory Provisions) (EU Exit) Regulations 2020 (SI 2020/1309); and

- (For those EEA nationals who had a right of residence in the UK under EU law immediately before December 30, 2020 at 11.00 pm, but who have neither settled nor pre-settled status) by regs 3(2), 4(3) and 5(i) of the Citizens' Rights (Application Deadline and Temporary Protection) (EU Exit) Regulations 2020 (SI 2020/1209).

Definitions

"EEA national"—see reg.2(1).
"qualified person"—see reg.6.
"right of permanent residence"—see reg.15.

General Note

Regulation 9A was inserted with effect from July 24, 2018 by SI 2018/801 in order to bring domestic law into line with EU law as set out by the CJEU in *Toufik Lounes v Secretary of State for the Home Department* (Case C-165/16): see, further, the discussion under the heading, *The personal scope of the Citizenship* Directive, in the introductory General Note to these Regulations.

Paragraph (1) defines "DN" (obviously short for "dual national") as meaning a person within para.(b) of the definition of "EEA National" in reg.2(1), namely "a national of an EEA State who is also a British citizen and who prior to acquiring British citizenship exercised a right to reside as such a national, in accordance with regulation 14 or 15".

Paragraph (2) provides that such a dual national is only a "qualified person" within reg.6 if s/he was a qualified person when s/he acquired British citizenship and has not lost that status at any time since. The consequence, which is not spelled out in the regulation, is that where the dual national satisfies those requirements, his or her family members and extended family members have the same rights as the family members and extended family members of any qualified person.

Paragraphs (3) and (4) provide that neither the dual national, nor his or her non-EEA family members, are treated as having a permanent right of residence under reg.15 unless the dual national was either a qualified person, or had acquired a permanent right of residence, when s/he acquired British citizenship. This does not affect the dual national who, *ex hypothesi*, is a British citizen (see note to para.(1) above). However, it may restrict the circumstances in which family members and extended family members may derive a permanent right of residence from the dual national.

"Family member who has retained the right of residence"

10.—(1) In these Regulations, "family member who has retained the right of residence" means, subject to paragraphs (8) and (9), a person who satisfies a condition in paragraph (2), (3), (4) or (5).

7.72

(2) The condition in this paragraph is that the person—
(a) was a family member of a qualified person or of an EEA national with a right of permanent residence when the qualified person or the EEA national with the right of permanent residence died;
(b) resided in the United Kingdom [¹ lawfully] for at least the year immediately before the death of the qualified person or the EEA national with a right of permanent residence; and
(c) satisfies the condition in paragraph (6).

(3) The condition in this paragraph is that the person—
(a) is the direct descendant of—
   (i) a qualified person or an EEA national with a right of permanent residence who has died;
   (ii) a person who ceased to be a qualified person on ceasing to reside in the United Kingdom;
   (iii) the spouse or civil partner of the qualified person or EEA national described in sub-paragraph (i) immediately preceding that qualified person or EEA national's death; or
   (iv) the spouse or civil partner of the person described in sub-paragraph (ii); and
(b) was attending an educational course in the United Kingdom imme-

diately before the qualified person or the EEA national with a right of permanent residence died, or ceased to be a qualified person, and continues to attend such a course.

(4) The condition in this paragraph is that the person is the parent with actual custody of a child who satisfies the condition in paragraph (3).

(5) The condition in this paragraph is that the person ("A")—

(a) ceased to be a family member of a qualified person or an EEA national with a right of permanent residence on the termination of the marriage or civil partnership of A;

(b) was residing in the United Kingdom in accordance with these Regulations at the date of [² . . .] the termination;

(c) satisfies the condition in paragraph (6); and

(d) either—

(i) prior to the initiation of the proceedings for the termination of the marriage or the civil partnership, the marriage or civil partnership had lasted for at least three years and the parties to the marriage or civil partnership had resided in the United Kingdom for at least one year during its duration;

(ii) the former spouse or civil partner of the qualified person or the EEA national with a right of permanent residence has custody of a child of that qualified person or EEA national;

(iii) the former spouse or civil partner of the qualified person or the EEA national with a right of permanent residence has the right of access to a child of that qualified person or EEA national, where the child is under the age of 18 and where a court has ordered that such access must take place in the United Kingdom; or

(iv) the continued right of residence in the United Kingdom of A is warranted by particularly difficult circumstances, such as where A or another family member has been a victim of domestic violence whilst the marriage or civil partnership was subsisting.

(6) The condition in this paragraph is that the person—

(a) is not an EEA national but would, if the person were an EEA national, be a worker, a self-employed person or a self-sufficient person under regulation 6; or

(b) is the family member of a person who falls within paragraph (a).

(7) In this regulation, "educational course" means a course within the scope of Article 10 of Council Regulation (EU) No. 492/2011.

(8) A person ("P") does not satisfy a condition in paragraph (2), (3), (4) or (5) if, at the first time P would otherwise have satisfied the relevant condition, P had a right of permanent residence under regulation 15.

(9) A family member who has retained the right of residence ceases to enjoy that status on acquiring a right of permanent residence under regulation 15.

AMENDMENT

Regulation 10 was revoked by s.1 of, and Sch.1, para.2(2) to, the Immigration and Social Security Co-ordination (EU Withdrawal) Act 2020 with effect from December 31, 2020 at 11.00 pm. The text given above is of the regulation as saved and modified for the purposes of entitlement to benefit by:

- (For those EEA nationals with pre-settled status) reg.83 of, and Sch.4, paras 2, 3 and 4(j) of the Immigration and Social Security Co-ordination (EU Withdrawal) Act 2020 (Consequential, Saving, Transitional and Transitory Provisions) (EU Exit) Regulations 2020 (SI 2020/1309); and

- (For those EEA nationals who had a right of residence in the UK under EU law immediately before December 30, 2020 at 11.00 pm, but who have neither settled nor pre-settled status) by regs 3(2), 4(3) and 5(j) of the Citizens' Rights (Application Deadline and Temporary Protection) (EU Exit) Regulations 2020 (SI 2020/1209).

Square brackets with superscript numbers in the text refer to the Modifications section below and not, as elsewhere in this work, to amendments. For the amendments that were made to reg.10 before its revocation see pp.1019-1020 of Vol.V of the 2020/21 edition.

MODIFICATIONS

1. SI 2020/1309, Sch.4, para.4(j)(i). This modification applies to those with pre-settled status only. SI 2020/1209 contains no equivalent provision. The word "lawfully" in the modified form of para.(2)(b) replaced the words "in accordance with these Regulations". The paragraph is saved in its unmodified form for the purposes of SI 2020/1209 and as it applies to residence in the United Kingdom before December 31, 2020 at 11.00 pm.

2. SI 2020/1309, Sch.4, para.4(j)(ii);); SI 2020/1209 regs 3(2), 4(3) and 5(j)

DEFINITIONS

"civil partner"—see reg.2(1).
"EEA national"—*ibid.*
"family member"—see reg.7.
"qualified person"—see reg.6(1).
"self-employed person"—see reg.4(1)(b).
"self-sufficient person"—see reg.4(1)(c).
"spouse"—see reg.2(1).
"worker"—see reg.4(1)(a).

GENERAL NOTE

Regulation 10 implements arts 12 and 13. A family member who has retained the right of residence has an extended right of residence in the UK for as long as s/he retains that status (see reg.14(3)). In addition residence as a family member who has retained the right of residence counts towards the continuous period of five years' residence required by reg.15(1)(a) and (b) for the acquisition of a permanent right of residence. Note that a family member who has already acquired a right of permanent residence (i.e., by residing with the EEA national for a continuous period of five years) does not need to rely on—and is not subject to the restrictions in—reg.10: see *MS v SSWP* (ESA) [2020] UKUT 235 (AAC) (and also para.(9)). 7.73

Family member who has retained the right of residence

Paragraph (1). "Family member who has retained the right of residence" is defined by para.(1). The phrase means a person—other than a person with a right of permanent residence (see para.(8))—who satisfies at least one of four conditions. 7.74

Paragraph (2) sets out the first condition. It applies to those who were family members of a qualified person, or of an EEA national with a permanent right residence, when that person died and who had resided in the UK in accordance with the 2016 Regulations for at least a year immediately before the death. This only applies where the person seeking to retain the right of residence either:

- is not an EEA national, but would qualify as a worker, a self-employed person or a self-sufficient person if s/he were;

- or is a family member of such a person,

(see para.(6)). In other words, to retain the right of residence by satisfying para. (2), the former family member must be economically active or the family member of someone else who is. The first option excludes EEA nationals because an EEA national who would qualify as a worker, a self-employed person or a self-sufficient person would be a qualified person with an extended right of residence in any event and would not need to have such a right under reg.10.

Paragraph (3) sets out the second condition. It applies to the direct descendants of a qualified person, or of an EEA national with a permanent right residence, who has died or ceased to be a qualifying person on ceasing to reside in the UK (or of the spouse or civil partner of such a qualified person) who were attending an educational course (within the scope of art.10 of regulation 492/2011 (formerly art.12 of Regulation 1612/68): see para.(7)) in the UK immediately before the qualified person died or ceased to live in the UK and who continue to attend such a course.

Paragraph (4) sets out the third condition. It applies to parents who have "actual custody" of a child who satisfies the conditions in para.(3).

Paragraph (5) sets out the fourth condition. It applies to former spouses or civil partners of a qualified person, or of an EEA national with a permanent right residence (a "former spouse or partner"), who were residing in the UK on the date when the marriage or civil partnership came to an end, where either:

- the marriage or civil partnership had lasted for at least three years before the commencement of the legal proceedings to terminate it and the parties had both resided in the UK for at least one year during its duration. The decision of the CJEU in *Singh and others v Minister for Justice and Equality* (Case C-218/14) holds that art.13(2) of the Citizenship Directive (which is implemented by para.(5)) only applies where the qualified person or EEA national with a permanent right of residence was still resident in the host member State at the time when the divorce proceedings (or proceedings to terminate the civil partnership) were commenced; or

- the former spouse or partner has custody of a child of the qualified person, or of the EEA national with a permanent right residence, or a right of access to such a child that, by court order, can only take place in the UK; or

- there are "particularly difficult circumstances" that warrant the former spouse or partner continuing to have a right of residence in the UK. The example that is given is where the former spouse or partner or another family member has "been a victim of domestic violence while the marriage or civil partnership was subsisting"

As with para.(2), para.(5) only applies where the person seeking to retain the right of residence is not an EEA national, but would qualify as a worker, a self-employed person or a self-sufficient person if s/he were, or is a family member of such a person (see para.(6) and the commentary to para.(2) above).

Residence in the UK before February 1, 2017 counts as residence in accordance with the 2016 Regulations if it was in accordance with the 2000 Regulations or the 2006 Regulations (see Sch.6, para.8).

For the date on which a marriage or civil partnership ends, see the commentary to reg.7 above.

PART 2

EEA RIGHTS

Right of admission to the United Kingdom

7.75   *[Editorial note: The text of reg.11 below applies <u>only</u> to claimants for whom the regulation is saved by SI 2020/1209. The regulation has been revoked for those with pre-settled status]*

11.—(1) An EEA national must be admitted to the United Kingdom on arrival if the EEA national produces a valid national identity card or passport issued by an EEA State.

(2) A person who is not an EEA national must be admitted to the United Kingdom if that person is—

(a) [¹ . . .]

(b) a family member of an EEA national, a family member who has retained the right of residence, a person who meets the criteria in paragraph (5) or a person with a right of permanent residence under regulation 15 and produces on arrival—

   (i) a valid passport; and

   (ii) a valid EEA family permit, residence card, derivative residence card or permanent residence card.

(3) An immigration officer must not place a stamp in the passport of a person admitted to the United Kingdom under this regulation who is not an EEA national if the person produces a residence card, a derivative residence card [¹ or a permanent residence card].

(4) [¹ . . .]

(5) The criteria in this paragraph are that a person ("P")—

(a) previously resided in the United Kingdom under regulation 16(3) and would be entitled to reside in the United Kingdom under that regulation were P in the country;

(b) is accompanying an EEA national to, or joining an EEA national in, the United Kingdom and P would be entitled to reside in the United Kingdom under regulation 16(2) were P and the EEA national both in the United Kingdom;

(c) is accompanying a person ("the relevant person") to, or joining the relevant person in, the United Kingdom and—

   (i) the relevant person is residing, or has resided, in the United Kingdom under regulation 16(3); and

   (ii) P would be entitled to reside in the United Kingdom under regulation 16(4) were P and the relevant person both in the United Kingdom;

(d) is accompanying a person who meets the criteria in sub-paragraph (b) or (c) ("the relevant person") to the United Kingdom and—

   (i) P and the relevant person are both—

     (aa) seeking admission to the United Kingdom in reliance on this paragraph for the first time; or

     (bb) returning to the United Kingdom having previously resided there pursuant to the same provisions of regulation 16 in reliance on which they now base their claim to admission; and

   (ii) P would be entitled to reside in the United Kingdom under regulation 16(6) were P and the relevant person there; or

(e) is accompanying a British citizen to, or joining a British citizen in, the United Kingdom and P would be entitled to reside in the United Kingdom under regulation 16(5) were P and the British citizen both in the United Kingdom.

(6) Paragraph (7) applies where—

(a) a person ("P") seeks admission to the United Kingdom in reliance on paragraph (5)(b), (c) or (e); and

(b) if P were in the United Kingdom, P would have a derived right to reside under regulation 16(8)(b)(ii).

(7) Where this paragraph applies a person ("P") must only be regarded as meeting the criteria in paragraph (5)(b), (c) or (e) where P—

  (a) is accompanying the person with whom P would on admission to the United Kingdom jointly share care responsibility for the purpose of regulation 16(8)(b)(ii); or

  (b) has previously resided in the United Kingdom pursuant to regulation 16(2), (4) or (5) as a joint primary carer and seeks admission to the United Kingdom in order to reside there again on the same basis.

(8) But this regulation is subject to regulations 23(1), (2), (3) and (4) and 31.

(9) A person is not entitled to be admitted by virtue of this regulation where that person is subject to a decision under regulation 23(6)(b) (removal decision).

AMENDMENT

Regulation 11 was revoked by s.1 of, and Sch.1, para.2(2) to, the Immigration and Social Security Co-ordination (EU Withdrawal) Act 2020 with effect from December 31, 2020 at 11.00 pm and, for those with pre-settled status, SI 2020/1309 contains no savings provision.

The text given above is of the regulation as saved and modified for the purposes of entitlement to benefit for those EEA nationals who had a right of residence in the UK under EU law immediately before December 30, 2020 at 11.00 pm, but who have neither settled nor pre-settled status, by regs 3(2), 4(3) and 6(a) of the Citizens' Rights (Application Deadline and Temporary Protection) (EU Exit) Regulations 2020 (SI 2020/1209).

Square brackets with superscript numbers in the text refer to the Modification section below and not, as elsewhere in this work, to amendments. For the amendments that were made to reg.11 before its revocation see pp.1022-1023 of Vol.V of the 2020/21 edition.

MODIFICATION

1. SI 2020/1209, regs 3(2), 4(3) and 6(a).

DEFINITIONS

"derivative residence card"—see regs 2(1) and 20.
"EEA family permit"—see regs 2(1) and 12.
"EEA national"—see reg.2(1).
"EEA State"—*ibid*.
"family member"—see reg.7.
"family member who has retained the right of residence"—see reg.10.
"permanent residence card"—see regs 2(1) and 19(2).
"qualifying EEA State residence card"—see reg.2(1).
"residence card"—see regs 2(1) and 18.
"right to reside"—see reg.2(1).

GENERAL NOTE

7.76
Regulation 11 is about rights of entry, rather than rights of residence and therefore does not require detailed commentary in a publication about social security. It is, however, worth noting that it is the right of EEA nationals and their family members to enter the UK without leave under Immigration Act 1988 s.7 and reg.11 that means they are not excluded from entitlement to benefits as "persons subject to immigration control" under Immigration and Asylum Act 1999, s.115.

Issue of EEA family permit

[Editorial note: This is the modified wording of reg.12 that now applies to   7.77
claimants for whom the regulation is saved by SI 2020/1209]

12.—(1) An entry clearance officer must issue an EEA family permit to
a person who applies for one if the person is a family member of an EEA
national and—

(a) the EEA national—

    (i) is residing in the United Kingdom in accordance with these
Regulations; or

    (ii) will be travelling to the United Kingdom within six months of
the date of the application and will be an EEA national residing
in the United Kingdom in accordance with these Regulations
on arrival in the United Kingdom; and

(b) the family member will be accompanying the EEA national to the
United Kingdom or joining the EEA national there.

(2) An entry clearance officer must issue an EEA family permit to a
person who applies and provides evidence demonstrating that, at the time
at which the person first intends to use the EEA family permit, the person—

(a) would be entitled to be admitted to the United Kingdom because
that person would meet the criteria in regulation 11(5); and

(b) will (save in the case of a person who would be entitled to be admitted to the United Kingdom because that person would meet the
criteria for admission in regulation 11(5)(a)) be accompanying to, or
joining in, the United Kingdom any person from whom the right to
be admitted to the United Kingdom under the criteria in regulation
11(5) is derived.

(3) An entry clearance officer must issue an EEA family permit to—

(a) a family member who has retained the right of residence; or

(b) a person who is not an EEA national but who has acquired the right
of permanent residence under regulation 15.

(4) An entry clearance officer may issue an EEA family permit to an
extended family member of an EEA national (the relevant EEA national)
who applies for one if—

[¹ (aa) the extended family member satisfies the condition in paragraph (5)
of regulation 8;]

(a) the relevant EEA national satisfies the condition in paragraph (1)(a);

(b) the extended family member wants to accompany the relevant EEA
national to the United Kingdom or to join that EEA national there;
and

(c) in all the circumstances, it appears to the entry clearance officer
appropriate to issue the EEA family permit.

(5) Where an entry clearance officer receives an application under paragraph (4) an extensive examination of the personal circumstances of the
applicant must be undertaken by the Secretary of State and if the application is refused, the entry clearance officer must give reasons justifying the
refusal unless this is contrary to the interests of national security.

(5A) An EEA family permit issued under this regulation may be issued
in electronic form.

(6) An EEA family permit issued under this regulation must be issued
free of charge and as soon as possible.

(7) But an EEA family permit must not be issued under this regulation if
the applicant or the EEA national concerned is not entitled to be admitted

to the United Kingdom as a result of regulation 23(1), (2) or (3) or falls to be excluded in accordance with regulation 23(5).

(8) An EEA family permit must not be issued under this regulation to a person ("A") who is the spouse, civil partner or durable partner of a person ("B") where a spouse, civil partner or durable partner of A or B holds a valid EEA family permit.

Amendment

Regulation 12 was revoked by s.1 of, and Sch.1, para.2(2) to, the Immigration and Social Security Co-ordination (EU Withdrawal) Act 2020 with effect from December 31, 2020 at 11.00 pm with effect from December 31, 2020 at 11.00 pm.

The text given above is of the regulation as saved and modified for the purposes of entitlement to benefit for those EEA nationals who had a right of residence in the UK under EU law immediately before December 30, 2020 at 11.00 pm, but who have neither settled nor pre-settled status, by regs 3(2), 4(3) and 6(b) of the Citizens' Rights (Application Deadline and Temporary Protection) (EU Exit) Regulations 2020 (SI 2020/1209).

For those with pre-settled status, the revocation of reg.12 was not subject to any saving provision *for the purposes of access to benefits*. Savings provisions do, however, exist for *immigration purposes*: see reg.83 and Sch.3, para.3(1) and (2) of SI 2020/1309 below.

Square brackets with superscript numbers in the text refer to the Modification section below and not, as elsewhere in this work, to amendments. For the amendments that were made to reg.12 before its revocation see pp.1024-1025 of Vol.V of the 2020/21 edition.

Modification

1. SI 2020/1209, regs 3(2), 4(3) and 6(b).

Definitions

"civil partner"—see reg.2(1).
"durable partner"—*ibid.*
"EEA family permit"—see General Note to Pt.3.
"EEA national"—see reg.2(1).
"entry clearance officer"—*ibid.*
"extended family member"—see reg.8.
"family member"—see reg.7.
"family member who has retained the right of residence"—see reg.10.
"relevant EEA national"—see regs 2(1) and 8(6).
"spouse"—see reg.2(1).

General Note

7.78   See the General Note to Pt 3.

Initial right of residence

7.79   **13.**—(1) An EEA national is entitled to reside in the United Kingdom for a period not exceeding three months beginning on the date of admission to the United Kingdom provided the EEA national holds a valid national identity card or passport issued by an EEA State.

(2) A person who is not an EEA national but is a family member who has retained the right of residence or the family member of an EEA national residing in the United Kingdom under paragraph (1) is entitled to reside in the United Kingdom provided that person holds a valid passport.

(3) An EEA national or the family member of an EEA national who is an unreasonable burden on the social assistance system of the United Kingdom does not have a right to reside under this regulation.

[Editorial note: This is the modified wording of para. (4) that now applies to those with pre-settled status]

(4)   A person who otherwise satisfies the criteria in this regulation is not entitled to a right to reside under this regulation [¹ if that person is subject to a deportation order or exclusion order unless that order] is set aside, revoked or otherwise no longer has effect.

[Editorial note: This is the modified wording of para. (4) that now applies to claimants for whom reg.13 is saved by SI 2020/1209]

(4)   A person who otherwise satisfies the criteria in this regulation is not entitled to a right to reside under this regulation where the Secretary of State or an immigration officer has made a decision under regulation 23(6)(b) (decision to remove on grounds of public policy, public security or public health), 24(1) (refusal to issue residence documentation etc),25(1) (cancellation of a right of residence), 26(3) (misuse of right to reside) [², 27A (decisions taken on conducive grounds)] or 31(1) (revocation of admission) or an order under regulation 23(5) (exclusion order) or 32(3) (deportation order), unless that decision or order, as the case may be, is set aside, revoked or otherwise no longer has effect.

AMENDMENT

Regulation 13 was revoked by s.1 of, and Sch.1, para.2(2) to, the Immigration and Social Security Co ordination (EU Withdrawal) Act 2020 with effect from December 31, 2020 at 11.00 pm. The text given above is of the regulation as saved and modified for the purposes of entitlement to benefit by:

- (For those EEA nationals with pre-settled status) reg.83 of, and Sch.4, paras 2, 3 and 4(k) of the Immigration and Social Security Co-ordination (EU Withdrawal) Act 2020 (Consequential, Saving, Transitional and Transitory Provisions) (EU Exit) Regulations 2020 (SI 2020/1309); and

- (For those EEA nationals who had a right of residence in the UK under EU law immediately before December 30, 2020 at 11.00 pm, but who have neither settled nor pre-settled status) by regs 3(2), 4(3) and 6(c) of the Citizens' Rights (Application Deadline and Temporary Protection) (EU Exit) Regulations 2020 (SI 2020/1209).

Square brackets with superscript numbers in the text refer to the Modification section below and not, as elsewhere in this work, to amendments. For the amendments that were made to reg.13 before its revocation see pp.1025-1026 of Vol.V of the 2020/21 edition.

MODIFICATIONS

1. SI 2020/1309, Sch.4, para.4(k).
2. SI 2020/1209, regs 3(2), 4(3) and 6(c).

DEFINITIONS

"EEA national"—see reg.2(1).
"EEA State"—*ibid.*
"family member"—see reg.7.
"family member who has retained the right of residence"—see reg.10.
"right to reside"—see reg.2(1).

GENERAL NOTE

7.80   Regulation 13 implements art.6. It permits EEA nationals, and their non-EEA national family members, to reside in the UK for up to three months for any reason. That right is subject to reg.13(3)(b) (implementing art.14) and therefore ceases if either the EEA national or the family member "becomes an unreasonable burden on the social assistance system of the United Kingdom".

Rights of residence under the Citizenship Directive normally carry with them the right to equal treatment under art.24. However, the right to equal treatment that accompanies the initial right of residence is subject to a derogation in art.24(2) which states that "the host Member State shall not be obliged to confer entitlement to social assistance during the first three months of residence". In *Vestische Arbeit Jobcenter Kreis Recklinghausen v Garcia-Nieto* and others (C-299/14), the CJEU confirmed that neither art.24, nor the principle of equality of treatment in art.4 of Regulation (EC) No 883/2004, prevented Member States from excluding those whose only right of residence arose under art.6 of the Citizenship Directive from entitlement to special non-contributory cash benefits (see art.70(2) of Regulation No 883/2004) which also constitute "social assistance" within the meaning of Article 24(2). In such circumstances, (following *Alimanovic* (C-67/14) and distinguishing *Brey* (C-140/12): see further below) it was unnecessary to carry out an individual assessment of the circumstances of the person concerned.

In accordance with those derogations, reg.21AA(3)(a) and (c) of the IS Regulations, reg.85A(3) of the JSA Regulations, reg.70(a) and (c) of the ESA Regulations, reg.2(3)(a) and (c) of the SPC Regulations, and reg.9(3)(a) of the Universal Credit Regulations provide that the initial right of residence does not qualify a claimant to any of those benefits.

However, under domestic law, though not EU law, residence pursuant to reg.13 is "in accordance with these regulations" within reg.15(1)(a) and therefore counts towards the period of five years' continuous residence required by that regulation for the acquisition of a permanent right of residence: see *GE v SSWP (ESA)* [2017] UKUT 145 (AAC), [2017] AACR 34.

Extended right of residence

7.81   **14.**—(1) A qualified person is entitled to reside in the United Kingdom for as long as that person remains a qualified person.

(2) A person ("P") who is a family member of a qualified person residing in the United Kingdom under paragraph (1) or of an EEA national with a right of permanent residence under regulation 15 is entitled to remain in the United Kingdom for so long as P remains the family member of that person or EEA national.

(3) A family member who has retained the right of residence is entitled to reside in the United Kingdom for so long as that person remains a family member who has retained the right of residence.

[Editorial note: This is the modified wording of para. (4) that now applies to those with pre-settled status]

(4)   A person who otherwise satisfies the criteria in this regulation is not entitled to a right to reside in the United Kingdom under this regulation [¹ if that person is subject to a deportation order or exclusion order unless that order] is set aside, revoked or otherwise no longer has effect.

[Editorial note: This is the modified wording of para. (4) that now applies to claimants for whom reg. 14 is saved by SI 2020/1209]

(4)   A person who otherwise satisfies the criteria in this regulation is not entitled to a right to reside in the United Kingdom under this regulation where the Secretary of State or an immigration officer has made a decision under regulation 23(6)(b), 24(1), 25(1), 26(3) [², 27A] or 31(1),

or an order under regulation 23(5) (exclusion order) or 32(3) (deportation order), unless that decision or order, as the case may be, is set aside, revoked or otherwise no longer has effect.

AMENDMENT

Regulation 14 was revoked by s.1 of, and Sch.1, para.2(2) to, the Immigration and Social Security Co-ordination (EU Withdrawal) Act 2020 with effect from December 31, 2020 at 11.00 pm. The text given above is of the regulation as saved and modified for the purposes of entitlement to benefit by:

- (For those EEA nationals with pre-settled status) reg.83 of, and Sch.4, paras 2, 3 and 4(l) of the Immigration and Social Security Co-ordination (EU Withdrawal) Act 2020 (Consequential, Saving, Transitional and Transitory Provisions) (EU Exit) Regulations 2020 (SI 2020/1309); and

- (For those EEA nationals who had a right of residence in the UK under EU law immediately before December 30, 2020 at 11.00 pm, but who have neither settled nor pre-settled status) by regs 3(2), 4(3) and 6(d) of the Citizens' Rights (Application Deadline and Temporary Protection) (EU Exit) Regulations 2020 (SI 2020/1209).

Square brackets with superscript numbers in the text refer to the Modification section below and not, as elsewhere in this work, to amendments. For the amendments that were made to reg.14 before its revocation see pp.1026-1027 of Vol.V of the 2020/21 edition.

MODIFICATION

1. SI 2020/1309, Sch 4, para.4(l),
2. SI 2020/1209, regs 3(2), 4(3) and 6(d).

DEFINITIONS

"EEA national"—see reg.2(1).
"family member"—see reg.7.
"family member who has retained the right of residence"—see reg.10.
"qualified person"—see reg.6(1).
"right to reside"—see reg.2(1).

GENERAL NOTE

Regulation 14 implements art.7. It establishes an extended right of residence for three categories of people: 7.82

- qualified persons (para.(1));

- family members of qualified persons or of EEA nationals with a permanent right of residence (para.2); and

- family members who have retained the right of residence (para.(3)).

Those categories are discussed in detail in the General Notes to regs 4, 6, 7 and 10 above.

Where an extended right of residence exists, it does so in addition to any initial or permanent right of residence that may exist during the same period.

The extended right of residence conferred on a "family member who has retained the right of residence" by para.(3) is not a right that is excluded by reg.21AA(3)(b)(ii) of the IS Regulations (or, by parity of reasoning, by the equivalent provisions of the JSA Regulations, the SPC Regulations, the ESA Regulations and the UC Regulations): see the decision of the Inner House of the Court of Session in *Slezak v Secretary of State for Work and Pensions* [2017] CSIH 4, [2017] AACR 21.

Right of permanent residence

7.83   **15.**—(1) The following persons acquire the right to reside in the United Kingdom permanently—

  (a) an EEA national who has resided in the United Kingdom [¹ lawfully] for a continuous period of five years;

  (b) a family member of an EEA national who is not an EEA national but who has resided in the United Kingdom with the EEA national [¹ lawfully] for a continuous period of five years;

  (c) a worker or self-employed person who has ceased activity;

  (d) the family member of a worker or self-employed person who has ceased activity, provided—

    (i) the person was the family member of the worker or self-employed person at the point the worker or self-employed person ceased activity; and

    (ii) at that point, the family member enjoyed a right to reside on the basis of being the family member of that worker or self-employed person;

  (e) a person who was the family member of a worker or self-employed person where—

    (i) the worker or self-employed person has died;

    (ii) the family member resided with the worker or self-employed person immediately before the death; and

    (iii) the worker or self-employed person had resided continuously in the United Kingdom for at least two years immediately before dying or the death was the result of an accident at work or an occupational disease;

  (f) a person who—

    (i) has resided in the United Kingdom [¹ lawfully] for a continuous period of five years; and

    (ii) was, at the end of the period, a family member who has retained the right of residence.

(2) Residence in the United Kingdom as a result of a derivative right to reside does not constitute residence for the purpose of this regulation.

(3) The right of permanent residence under this regulation is lost through absence from the United Kingdom for a period exceeding two years.

[Editorial note: This is the modified wording of para. (4) that now applies to those with pre-settled status]

(4) A person who satisfies the criteria in this regulation is not entitled to a right to permanent residence in the United Kingdom [² if that person is subject to a deportation order or exclusion order unless that order] is set aside, revoked or otherwise no longer has effect.

[Editorial note: This is the modified wording of para. (4) that now applies to claimants for whom reg. 15 is saved by SI 2020/1209]

(4) A person who satisfies the criteria in this regulation is not entitled to a right to permanent residence in the United Kingdom where the Secretary of State or an immigration officer has made a decision under regulation 23(6)(b), 24(1), 25(1), 26(3) [³, 27A] or 31(1), or an order under regulation 23(5) (exclusion order) or 32(3) (deportation order), unless that decision or order, as the case may be, is set aside, revoked or otherwise no longer has effect.

AMENDMENT

Regulation 15 was revoked by s.1 of, and Sch.1, para.2(2) to, the Immigration and Social Security Co-ordination (EU Withdrawal) Act 2020 with effect from December 31, 2020 at 11.00 pm. The text given above is of the regulation as saved and modified for the purposes of entitlement to benefit by:

- (For those EEA nationals with pre-settled status) reg.83 of, and Sch.4, paras 2, 3 and 4(m) of the Immigration and Social Security Co-ordination (EU Withdrawal) Act 2020 (Consequential, Saving, Transitional and Transitory Provisions) (EU Exit) Regulations 2020 (SI 2020/1309); and

- (For those EEA nationals who had a right of residence in the UK under EU law immediately before December 30, 2020 at 11.00 pm, but who have neither settled nor pre-settled status) by regs 3(2), 4(3) and 6(e) of the Citizens' Rights (Application Deadline and Temporary Protection) (EU Exit) Regulations 2020 (SI 2020/1209).

Square brackets with superscript numbers in the text refer to the Modifications section below and not, as elsewhere in this work, to amendments. For the amendments that were made to reg.15 before its revocation see pp.1027-1026 of Vol.V of the 2020/21 edition.

MODIFICATIONS

1. SI 2020/1309, Sch.4, para.4(m)(i). This modification applies to those with pre-settled status only. SI 2020/1209 contains no equivalent provision.
It provides that in so far as reg.15 applies to residence in the United Kingdom after December 31, 2020 at 11.00 pm, it is modified "as if the EEA Regulations 2016 (with the modifications set out in this paragraph [*i.e.*, para.4 of Sch.4]) had been in force at all relevant times and as if for the words "in accordance with these Regulations" in each place they occur there were substituted "lawfully".
2. SI 2020/1309, Sch.4, para.4(m)(ii).
3. SI 2020/1209, regs 3(2), 4(3) and 6(e).

DEFINITIONS

"derivative right to reside"—see regs 2(1) and 16.
"EEA national"—see reg.2(1).
"family member"—see reg.7.
"family member who has retained the right of residence"—see reg.10.
"right to reside"—see reg.2(1).
"self-employed person"—see reg.4(1)(b).
"worker"—see reg.4(1)(a).
"worker or self-employed person who has ceased activity"—see reg.5.

GENERAL NOTE

Regulation 15 implements arts 16 and 17 of the Citizenship Directive. It establishes a permanent right of residence for five categories of people: **7.84**

- EEA nationals who have "resided in the UK in accordance with these Regulations for a continuous period of five years";

- family members of an EEA national who have resided in the UK with the EEA national "in accordance with these Regulations for a continuous period of five years". This category only applies where the family member is not an EEA national him or herself: otherwise there would be a permanent right of residence because of the previous category;

- a "worker or self-employed person who has ceased activity" and the family members of such a person;

- (in certain circumstances) family members of workers or self-employed persons who have died;

- (in certain circumstances) people who were formerly "family members who ha[d] retained the right of residence".

Those whose right of residence arises under paras (1)(c)–(e) (i.e., those who fall within the third and fourth of the five categories set out above) are exempt from the habitual residence test (and therefore also from the right to reside test) under reg.21AA(4)(zb) of the IS Regulations, reg.85A(4)(zb) of the JSA Regulations 1996, and reg.2(4)(zb) of the SPC Regulations and reg.9(4)(zb) of the Universal Credit Regulations. Those whose right arises under paras (1)(a), (b) and (f) (*i.e.,* on the basis of five years' continuous residence) are not automatically exempt but will almost inevitably have been living in the UK for considerably longer than would be required to become actually habitually resident.

Paragraphs (1)(a) and (b) – Continuous residence

7.85   Residence "in accordance with" these Regulations includes certain types of residence before February 1, 2017 including residence under the 2006 Regulations, the 2000 Regulations, and before October 2, 2000, in accordance the Immigration (European Economic Area) Order 1994 (see below).

For continuity of residence, see the commentary to reg.3.

Legal residence—Ziolkowski and Szeja:

7.86   The question of what type or types of residence can form the basis of a permanent right to reside under art.16 of the Citizenship Directive was once an area of considerable legal uncertainty (see pp.334-340 of Vol.II of 2011–12 edition). The problem arose because although reg.15 requires that the period of five years' continuous residence should have been "in accordance with" what are now the 2016 Regulations, art.16 merely provides that the EEA national should have "resided legally" for that period. As it is possible for EEA national to reside legally in the UK without such residence being in accordance with the 2016 Regulations, it was unclear whether reg.15 correctly implemented art.16 and, if not, what other types of lawful residence would give rise to the permanent right.

However, the law has been clarified—at least in relation to this point—by the decision of the Grand Chamber of the ECJ in *Tomasz Ziolkowski v Land Berlin* and *Barbara Szeja, Maria-Magdalena Szeja, Marlon Szeja v Land Berlin* (Joined Cases C-424/10 and C-425/10). In the light of that decision, it now appears that reg.15 not only fully implements art.16 but—at least as regards the rights of jobseekers—is more generous to certain EEA nationals than art.16 strictly requires.

In *Ziolkowski and Szeja*, the appellants in the proceedings before the *Bundesverwaltungsgericht* (the German Federal Administrative Court) were Polish nationals who had lived in Germany since 1989 and 1988 respectively. At that time, Poland had not acceded to the EU and both were granted residence permits on humanitarian grounds under German domestic law. Although Mr Ziolkowski (at least) had worked in Germany in the past, by the time Poland acceded to the EU on May 1, 2004, neither was in employment or had sufficient resources to support him or herself economically so as not to be a burden on the German social assistance system. In 2005, both applied to the State of Berlin to extend their residence permits under German domestic law or to issue a residence permit under EU law. Those applications were refused on the basis that the applicants were unable to support themselves financially and did not have a right of residence under EU law. Mr Ziolkowski and Mrs Szeja appealed and it was ultimately argued on their behalf that they had resided legally in Germany under German domestic law (i.e., by virtue of the residence permits) for a continuous period in excess of five years before Poland acceded to the EU and that—following the principle in *Lassal* (see below)— each acquired a right of permanent residence under art.16 when the Citizenship Directive came into force on April 30, 2006. The *Bundesverwaltungsgericht* took the view that residence which was lawful under national law alone did not amount to legal residence for the purposes of art.16. It nevertheless referred the following questions to the ECJ:

"1. Is the first sentence of Article 16(1) of Directive 2004/38 to be interpreted as conferring on Union citizens who have resided legally for more than five years in the territory of a Member State on the basis of national law alone, but who did not during that period fulfil the conditions laid down in Article 7(1) of Directive 2004/38, a right of permanent residence in that Member State?

2. Are periods of residence by Union citizens in the host Member State which took place before the accession of their Member State of origin to the European Union also to be counted towards the period of lawful residence under Article 16(1) of Directive 2004/38?"

The ECJ answered those questions as follows:

"1. Article 16(1) of [the Citizenship] Directive ... must be interpreted as meaning that a Union citizen who has been resident for more than five years in the territory of the host Member State on the sole basis of the national law of that Member State cannot be regarded as having acquired the right of permanent residence under that provision if, during that period of residence, he did not satisfy the conditions laid down in Article 7(1) of the directive.

2. Periods of residence completed by a national of a non-Member State in the territory of Member State before the accession of the non-Member State to the European Union must, in the absence of specific provisions in the Act of Accession, be taken into account for the purpose of the acquisition of the right of permanent residence under Article 16(1) of Directive 2004/38, provided those periods were completed in compliance with the conditions laid down in Article 7(1) of the directive."

It follows that *Lekpo-Bozua v Hackney LBC* [2010] EWCA Civ 909 and *Okafor v Secretary of State for the Home Department* [2011] EWCA Civ 499 are correctly decided. It also follows that previously binding UK authority to the effect that pre-accession residence cannot count towards the five-year period (including *GN (EEA Regulations: Five years' residence) Hungary* [2007] UKAIT 73 and *CPC/3764/2007* at para.18) should no longer be followed.

The Court's reasoning on the first question is set out at paras 31–51 of its judgment as follows:

- Article 16 made no express reference to the law of the Member States for the purpose of determining how the phrase "resided legally" was to be interpreted, that phrase must be regarded "as designating an autonomous concept of EU law which must be interpreted in a uniform manner throughout the Member States" (paras 31–33).

- As the Citizenship Directive contained no definition of that phrase, its meaning must be determined by considering, among other things, the context in which it occurs and the purposes of the rules of which it forms part. The aim of the Directive was to facilitate and strengthen the exercise of each EU citizen's right to move and reside freely within the territory of the Member States by providing a single legislative act codifying and revising the instruments of EU law which preceded the Citizenship Directive. But the subject matter of the Citizenship Directive, as was apparent from art.1(a) and (b), concerned the conditions governing the exercise of that right and the right of permanent residence (paras 34–37).

- The Citizenship Directive introduced a gradual system as regards the right of residence in a host Member State (para.38).

- First, for periods of residence of up to three months, art.6 limits the conditions and formalities of the right of residence to the requirement to hold a valid identity card or passport and the requirement, under art.14(1), for the EU citizen and any family members not to become an unreasonable burden on the social assistance system of the host Member State (para.39).

- Then, for periods of residence of longer than three months, the right is subject to the conditions set out in art.7(1) and, under art.14(2), is retained only if the EU citizen and any family members satisfy those conditions. Recital 10 in the preamble to the Citizenship Directive in particular showed that those conditions are intended, inter alia, to prevent nationals of other Member States becoming an unreasonable burden on the social assistance system of the host Member State. (para.40).

- Finally, EU citizens acquire the right of permanent residence after residing legally for a continuous period of five years in the host Member State and that right is not subject to the conditions referred to above. Recital 17 in the preamble states that such a right should be laid down for all EU citizens and their family members who have resided in the host Member State 'in compliance with the conditions laid down in this Directive' during a continuous period of five years without becoming subject to an expulsion measure. The *travaux préparatoires* showed that the relevant part of recital 17 was included "in order to clarify the content of the term "legal residence"" for the purpose of art.16(1) (paras 41–42).

- Further the Citizenship Directive stated explicitly that, to acquire a permanent right of residence, family members of an EU citizen who retain a right of residence following the death of the EU citizen; or his or her departure from the host State; or following divorce, annulment of marriage or the termination of a registered partnership must satisfy the conditions in art.7(1) (see arts 12, 13 and 18) (paras 43–44).

- It follows that "resided legally" in art.16(1) of the Citizenship Directive should be construed as meaning residence which complies with the conditions laid down in the Citizenship Directive, in particular those set out in art.7(1). Consequently, a period of residence which complies with the law of a Member State but does not satisfy the conditions in art.7(1) cannot be regarded as a "legal" period of residence within the meaning of art.16(1) (paras 45–47).

- Article 37 of the Citizenship Directive does not affect that analysis. It simply provides that the Directive does not preclude the laws of the Member States from introducing provisions that are more favourable than those established by the Directive. That does not mean that such provisions must be incorporated into the system introduced by the Citizenship Directive. It is for each Member State to decide not only whether it will introduce more favourable provision but also the conditions to which the more favourable rules are subject and, in particular, the legal consequences of a right of residence granted on the basis of national law alone (paras 47–50).

On the second question (i.e. that concerning pre-accession residence), the Court reasoned that, on the Accession of a new Member State, the principle is that EU law applies to that State in full from the outset unless there are express derogations which establish transitional provisions. Nationals of any Member State may rely on EU law as regards the present effects of circumstances which existed previously including circumstances which arose before the accession of a Member State to the EU (e.g., *Saldanha and MTS* (Case C-122/96) [1997] E.C.R. I-5325, at para.14; *Österreichischer Gewerkschaftsbund* (Case C-195/98) [2000] E.C.R. I-10497, at para.55; and *Duchon* (Case C-290/00) [2002] ECR I-3567 at para.44)). As there are no transitional provisions that are relevant to the question, art.16(1) can be applied to the present and future effects of situations arising before the accession of the Member State of which the EU citizen is a national to the EU. Although periods of residence completed in the territory of the host Member State by a national of another State before the accession of the latter State to the EU do not fall within the scope of EU law but solely within the domestic law of the host Member State, provided the person concerned can demonstrate that such periods were completed in compliance with the conditions laid down in art.7(1) of Directive, taking such periods into account from the date of accession of the Member State of nationality to the EU does not give retroactive effect to art.16, but simply gives present effect to situations which arose before the date of transposition of that Directive.

Residence from April 30, 2006:

Following *Ziolkowski and Szeja*, the position as regards residence for periods from April 30, 2006 (when the Citizenship Directive came into force) may be summarised as follows.

7.87

Such residence is "legal" for the purposes of art.16(1)—and therefore counts towards the acquisition of a right of permanent residence—only if the person whose residence is under consideration satisfies the conditions in art.7(1) of the Citizenship Directive (i.e. if that person is a worker (or has retained that status), self-employed (or has retained that status), self-sufficient, a student or a family member of someone who falls into those categories).

Therefore residence that is lawful solely by virtue of rights enjoyed:

- as a jobseeker (i.e. under art.45 TFEU (ex-art.39 TEC): see *R. v IAT Ex p. Antonissen*, Case C-292/89); or

- as the child of a migrant worker or former migrant worker who has established him or herself in education (i.e. under art.10 of Regulation 492/2011 (formerly art.12 of Regulation 1612/68) or as the primary carer of such a child (i.e. under the principles established in *Ibrahim* and *Teixeira*). See further *Okafor* at para.31; or

- under arts 20 and 21 TFEU (including the rights enjoyed by some parents of British children under the principle established in *Zambrano*: see below); or

- (to the extent that the resident does not satisfy the conditions in art.7(1)) under the domestic law of the UK.

is **not** "legal" for the purposes of art.16(1) and does not count towards the acquisition of a right of permanent residence.

In *Ziolkowski and Szeja* none of the applicants had any of the rights of residence listed immediately above. Thus the question of whether residence pursuant to such rights is "legal" for the purposes of art.16 was not strictly before the Court. However, it was subsequently confirmed by the ECJ at paras 32–48 of *Alarape and Tijani v Secretary of State for the Home Department* (Case C–529/11) that:

> "Periods of residence in a host Member State which are completed by family members of a Union citizen who are not nationals of a Member State solely on the basis of Article 12 of Regulation No 1612/68, as amended by Directive 2004/38, where the conditions laid down for entitlement to a right of residence under that directive are not satisfied, may not be taken into consideration for the purposes of acquisition by those family members of a right of permanent residence under that directive."

However, although residence as a jobseeker does not count towards the acquisition of a permanent right of residence under EU law, it counts towards the acquisition of such a right under the more favourable provisions of para.(1): see below. The more favourable provisions of reg.15 apply only to residence as a jobseeker and not to residence in any of the other capacities listed above.

Residence before April 30, 2006

7.88   As is apparent from the Court's answer to the second question in *Ziolkowski and Szeja*, it is also possible for certain types of residence during periods before the Citizenship Directive came into force on April 30, 2006 to count towards the acquisition of the right of permanent residence after that date.

Where the member State of nationality was a member of the EU at the time when the claimant was resident in the UK, the decision of the ECJ in *Secretary of State for Work and Pensions v Lassal* (Case C-162/09) holds that pre-Directive residence will count towards the five-year period, if it is "in accordance with earlier European Union law instruments". In *Alarape and Tijani v Secretary of State for the Home Department*, the ECJ confirmed that that phrase only refers to the instruments that were repealed by, and consolidated in, the Citizenship Directive and does not include instruments, such as art.12 of Regulation 1612/68 (now art.10 of Regulation 492/2011), which are unaffected by the Citizenship Directive.

Where the member State of nationality was not a member of the EU at the time when the claimant was resident in the UK, *Ziolkowski and Szeja* holds that—in the absence of specific provisions in the Act of Accession—pre-Directive residence counts towards the five-year period if it was "in compliance with the conditions laid down in Article 7(1) of the [Directive]". Previously binding UK authority to the effect that pre-accession residence cannot count towards the five year period (including *R(IS) 3/08* and *CPC/3764/2007*) should no longer be followed.

This aspect of the decision in *Ziolkowski and Szeja* raises two further issues:

- First, there is the obvious conceptual problem about how residence can have been "in compliance with" the conditions in art.7(1) at a time when that provision was not in force and the resident's state of nationality was not even a member of the EU. The answer to that problem can be found in the Court's insistence that it was not applying art.16 retrospectively but rather giving present and future effect to circumstances which had arisen in the past. Articles 7(1) and 16(1) exist now. Although the Citizenship Directive as a whole may only affect those who are "beneficiaries" as defined by art.3(1), none of the, relatively well-established, criteria for establishing whether the conditions in art.7(1) are satisfied require that the person to whom they are applied should be an EU citizen at the relevant time. If, for example, it is possible to conclude that a Polish national was a self-employed person in May 2004, there is no reason why one cannot also conclude that she was a self-employed person during the previous month, or year, or years and therefore say that, during that period, she satisfied the condition that is now laid down in art.7(1)(a). Analysed in that way, the difficulties are likely to be evidential rather than conceptual.

- However that analysis leads to the second issue, namely that the narrow criteria for establishing whether the conditions in art.7(1) are satisfied do not require that the residence or work under consideration must also have been legal under the domestic law of the host state at the time. Suppose that the same Polish national referred to in the previous bullet point entered the UK illegally in March 2001 and worked here illegally on a self-employed basis for a continuous period ending on or before April 2006. Presumably she did not acquire a permanent right of residence as soon as the Citizenship Directive came into force on April 30, 2006, but nothing in *Ziolkowski and Szeja* actually says otherwise. The contrary outcome could, perhaps, be achieved by holding that a person in that position was not resident at all but only present, so that even if her activities would otherwise bring her within art.7(1), there would still be no "residence" for the purposes of art.16. Some support for that approach can be found in *R(IS) 3/08* which holds that temporary admission as an asylum seeker does not amount to a right of residence and *SSWP v LS (IS)* [2012] UKUT 207 (AAC).

The 2006 Regulations were amended with effect from July 16, 2012 to codify what was said in *Ziolkowski and Szeja* about pre-accession residence. Under para.6(3)(a) of Sch.4 to those Regulations, the codified right became conditional on the person concerned having had leave to enter or remain in the UK at the relevant time. That provision has now been consolidated as para.8(3)(b) of Sch.6. The codification refers to residence "in accordance with these Regulations" (para.8(3)(c) of Sch.6) and will therefore include jobseekers in addition to people who come within art.7 of the Citizenship Directive.

Loss of the *Lassal* right

Once the inchoate permanent right of residence conferred by *Lassal* has accrued,   7.89
it can potentially be lost by:

- a period of absence from the UK (see *Lassal* at paras 56–58); or

- a period of residence in the UK that was not legal (i.e. in the sense that it was not "in accordance with earlier European Union law instruments") (see *Secretary of State for the Home Department v Dias* (Case C-325/09) at paras 62–66); between the date on which the five years' continuous residence was completed and April 30, 2006.

Although there is no ECJ authority on the point, it seems probable that the inchoate right of permanent residence based on pre-Directive, pre-accession, residence that was recognised in *Ziolkowski and Szeja*, will be lost in the same circumstances as the *Lassal* right.

That conclusion in *Lassal* that the inchoate right can be lost through absence from the UK is unexceptionable. As the Court rightly points out, any other interpretation would have required Member States "to grant the right of permanent residence. . . even in cases of prolonged absences which [called] into question the link between the person concerned and the host Member State".

However, the rule was extended by analogy in *Dias* to cover situations in which a concluded period of five years' lawful residence before April 30, 2006 is followed by a period of residence for which there is no legal basis. The Court ruled that:

"periods of residence of less than two consecutive years, completed on the basis solely of a residence permit validly issued pursuant to Directive 68/360, without the conditions governing entitlement to a right of residence having been satisfied, which occurred before 30 April 2006 and after a continuous period of five years' legal residence completed prior to that date, are not such as to affect the acquisition of the right of permanent residence under Article 16(1) of Directive 2004/38."

The ECJ's justification for that ruling was that:

"64. . . .it should be noted, as the Advocate General has stated in points 106 and 107 of her Opinion, that the integration objective which lies behind the acquisition of the right of permanent residence laid down in Article 16(1) of Directive 2004/38 is based not only on territorial and time factors but also on qualitative elements, relating to the level of integration in the host Member State.
65. As the situations are comparable, it follows that the rule laid down in Article 16(4) of Directive 2004/38 must also be applied by analogy to periods in the host Member State completed on the basis solely of a residence permit validly issued under Directive 68/360, without the conditions governing entitlement to a right of residence of any kind having been satisfied, which occurred before 30 April 2006 and after a continuous period of five years' legal residence completed prior to that date."

The analogy drawn by the ECJ is false or, at any rate, is not inevitably true. Leaving a country for a period of two consecutive years obviously reduces one's level of integration in that country. The same cannot be said of Mrs Dias' decision to remain in the country but to spend time looking after her child instead of working, even if that decision meant that she left the labour market for a period. On the contrary, the process of raising a child in the UK probably increases one's level of integration in British society. One could go further. It is arguable that even claiming UK social security benefits involves being integrated in Britain: the process necessitates interacting with institutions of the state and involves doing something that almost every UK citizen will do at some time during his or her life. Finally, as it stands the analogy proves too much. It is being asserted that two years of economic inactivity is to be equated with two years' absence from the host State, but if that were the case before April 30, 2006 it is equally the case after that date. If, therefore, the analogy were correct, the implication would be that those who acquired a permanent right of residence after April 30, 2006 should be deprived of that right after two years of economic inactivity in the same way as they would be after two years' absence.

The passages from the Advocate General's opinion in *Dias* (to which the Court refers) explain the analogy on a slightly different basis:

> "106. First, the integration objective which lies behind Article 16 of the directive is based not only on territorial and time factors but also on qualitative elements. It therefore seems to me quite possible that unlawful conduct of a Union citizen may diminish his integration in the host State from a qualitative point of view. In so far as a Union citizen, following a period of legal residence in the host Member State, remains without a right of residence based on European Union law or national law in the host Member State, and the national authorities do not grant leave to remain, that can clearly in my view be taken into account from the perspective of integration.
> 107.   Second, the principle of equal treatment also supports that point of view. A Union citizen who complies with the law, who did not remain unlawfully contrary to the wishes of the host Member State in that State, would not be entitled to a right of permanent residence on 30 April 2006 following absence for more than two years, pursuant to Article 16(4) of Directive 2004/38. It does not seem justified to reward a Union citizen who does not comply with the law."

At least in the UK, the premise on which those passages are based is incorrect. An EEA national who stays in the UK after a positive right of residence comes to an end is not acting unlawfully. S/he commits no criminal offence; remains lawfully present here; is not, without more, subject to removal; and, if removed, would have an immediate right of re-entry. Even if it is the case that "unlawful conduct" can diminish the level of integration, no unlawful conduct occurs in these circumstances. For that reason, treating a period of lawful presence after the acquisition of an inchoate right of residence as neutral, rather than as potentially preventing the right from crystallising, would not involve "rewarding" a Union citizen who does not comply with the law.

The 2006 Regulations were amended with effect from July 16, 2012 by (SI 2012/1547) to reflect the Citizenship Directive as interpreted in *Dias*. The amended Regulations provide for the automatic loss of the *Lassal* right after two years' residence that is not in accordance with the Regulations. The 2016 Regulations have consolidated that rule at para.8(4)(b) of Sch.6.

The position of jobseekers and their family members under UK domestic law

7.90   As noted above, jobseekers do not satisfy the conditions in art.7(1) of the Citizenship Directive and therefore, under EU law as declared in *Ziolkowski and Szeja*, residence as a jobseeker—though lawful by virtue of art.45 TFEU—does not count towards the acquisition of the permanent right of residence under art.16(1). The same is true of residence as the family member of a jobseeker.

However, domestic UK law is more favourable to jobseekers and their family members. Since April 30, 2006, first reg.6 of the 2006 Regulations and now reg.6 of these Regulations have included jobseekers in the definition of as "qualified persons". They therefore have an extended right of residence under reg.14. The consequence is that residence as a jobseeker, or as the family member of a jobseeker, is "in accordance with these regulations" for the purposes of reg.15(1) so that if it lasts for a continuous period of five years—or, more probably, forms part of a continuous period of five years throughout which the claimant was a qualified person for a number of different reasons (or a family member of such a person)—the claimant will acquire a permanent right of residence by virtue of that regulation: see *GE v SSWP (ESA)* [2017] UKUT 145 (AAC), [2017] AACR 34.

The definition of "jobseeker" in reg.6 does not contain any requirement to register as a jobseeker. Therefore it is suggested that periods during which a claimant can show that s/he was seeking employment and had a genuine chance of being engaged will count towards the five-year period even if s/he was not claiming JSA or jobseeking credits.

Regulation 5 of the 2000 Regulations, did not expressly include "jobseekers" in the definition of "qualified person". However, "workers" were so included and "worker" was defined as meaning "a worker within the meaning of Article 39 of the EC Treaty". "Worker" in art.39 TEC (now art.45 TFEU) has a wider meaning than it has in art.7 of the Citizenship Directive. It is therefore arguable that a jobseeker who would have been treated as "worker" under art.39 was a qualified person with a right of residence under reg.14(1) of those Regulations and that family members of such a jobseeker had a right of residence under reg.14(2). As already noted, the types of residence before April 30, 2006 specified in para.8 of Sch.6 count towards the five-year period in reg.15.

A8 and A2 nationals

The A8 Regulations have largely been revoked. The text immediately before revocation is set out at pp.792–798 of Vol.II of the 2011/2012 edition and detailed commentary is to be found at paras 2.274–2.276 of Vol.II of the 2016/17 edition. However, the Regulations remain relevant to the acquisition of a permanent right of residence under paras (1)(a) and (b) because residence that was not within the A8 Regulations is not "in accordance with" the 2016 Regulations: see reg.7A of the 2006 Regulations and Sch.6, para.(8). The same is true of the A2 Regulations (above): see reg.7B of the 2006 Regulations. However, as the A2 Scheme required prior authorisation for work done by Bulgarian and Romanian nationals, it now raises fewer practical problems than the A8 Regulations, which only required that work employment should be registered with the Home Office once it had commenced; a requirement that was often overlooked.

7.91

Until recently, the main issues arising under the A8 Regulations concerned their legality and duration.

As to legality, in *RP v SSWP* [2016] UKUT 422 (AAC); [2019] AACR 6, the Upper Tribunal (Judge Ward) referred the following questions to the CJEU:

"Did Annex XII of the Treaty of Accession permit Member States to exclude Polish nationals from the benefits of Article 7(2) of the Workers Regulation and Article 7(3) of the Citizenship Directive where the worker, though he had belatedly complied with the national requirement that his employment be registered, had not yet worked for an uninterrupted registered twelve month period?

If the answer to the first question is "no," may a Polish national worker in the circumstances in question 1 rely on Article 7(3) of the Citizenship Directive which concerns retention of worker status?"

The CJEU answered question 1 as follows (see *Prefeta v Secretary of State for Work and Pensions* (C-618/16)):

"Chapter 2 of Annex XII to the Act concerning the conditions of accession of the [A8 States, Cyprus, and Malta] and the adjustments to the Treaties on which the European Union is founded, must be interpreted as permitting, during the transitional period provided for by that act, the United Kingdom . . . to exclude a Polish national, such as Mr Rafal Prefeta, from the benefits of Article 7(3) of [the Citizenship Directive], when that person has not satisfied the requirement imposed by national law of having completed an uninterrupted 12-month period of registered work in the United Kingdom."

The A8 Regulations were therefore in accordance with EU law.

As to duration, in *Secretary of State for Work and Pensions v Gubeladze* [2019] UKSC 31 at paras 1-75, the Supreme Court upheld the decisions of the Court of Appeal ([2017] EWCA Civ 1751) and Upper Tribunal Judge Ward in *TG v SSWP (PC)* [2015] UKUT 50 (AAC) that the two-year extension of the A8 accession period from May 1, 2009 to April 30, 2011 by the Accession (Immigration and Worker Registration) (Amendment) Regulations 2009 (SI 2009/892) was not compatible with EU law because it was not a proportionate exercise of the UK's powers under the Treaty of Accession. It follows that, from May 1, 2009, the rights of A8 nationals to reside in the UK as workers or jobseekers were the same as for other EU citizens (other than A2 nationals) and were no longer subject to restriction. The decision is of potential benefit to A8 nationals who need to rely on residence during that period to establish a permanent right of residence: see, e.g., *AM v SSWP (ESA)* [2019] UKUT 215 (AAC).

Finally, in *SSWP v NZ (ESA) (Third interim decision)* [2017] UKUT 0360 (AAC), the Upper Tribunal (Judge Ward) decided that neither the Accession (Immigration and Worker Registration) Regulations 2004 nor any other provision effected a valid derogation from art.17 of the Directive. As a person who would—but for the impact of the worker registration scheme—otherwise on any view have been a worker, the claimant's inability to point to 12 months of registered work did not preclude her from relying on art.17 if she could satisfy its remaining conditions.

Paragraphs (1)(c) and (d)– worker or self-employed person who has ceased activity and their family members

7.92   See the commentary to regs 5 and 7.

The family members of a worker or self-employed person who has ceased activity only acquire a permanent right of residence to the extent that they were family members of the worker or self-employed person at the time s/he ceased activity and had a right of residence in that capacity at that time. These rules prevent family members who join the worker or self-employed person in the UK after s/he has retired—and, it would seem, those who become family members by marriage or birth after that date—from acquiring a permanent right of residence immediately. However, such a person would have an extended right of residence under reg.14(2) and would acquire a permanent right of residence under reg.15(1)(b) after five years' continuous residence in the UK pursuant to that right.

Paragraph (1)(e) – Family members of workers or self-employed persons who have died:

7.93   A family member (see reg.7) of a worker or self-employed person who has died has a permanent right of residence where the family member resided with the deceased person immediately before his or her death, and either:

- the deceased person had resided continuously in the UK for at least two years immediately before his death; or

- the death was the result of an accident at work or an occupational disease.

Paragraph (1)(f) – Family members who have retained the right of residence

7.94   A person who has lived in the UK in accordance with the 2016 Regulations for a continuous period of five years acquires a permanent right of residence if, at the end of that period, s/he is a family member who has retained the right of residence.

In practice, this category only affects non-EEA nationals: an EEA national who had lived in the UK in accordance with the 2016 Regulations for a continuous period of five years would acquire a permanent right of residence under para.(1)(a), irrespective of whether s/he was a family member who has retained the right of residence at the end of that period.

For the definition of "family member who has retained the right of residence" see reg.10. One consequence of that definition is that the permanent right of residence conferred by para.(1)(f) replaces rather than supplements, the extended right of residence granted by reg.14(3). Under reg.10(8), the acquisition of the permanent right of residence brings an end to the person's former status as a family member who has retained the right of residence; by ceasing to hold that status, the person loses his or her former rights under reg.14(3).

Paragraph (2) – Derivative right to reside
Residence under a derivative right to reside (see reg.16) does not count as residence for the purpose of para.(1). 7.95

Paragraph (3) – Loss of the permanent right of residence
Paragraph (3) implements art.16(4). The right of permanent residence is lost if the EEA national is absent from the UK for more than two years. 7.96

Derivative right to reside

16.—(1) A person has a derivative right to reside during any period in which the person— 7.97
  (a) is not an exempt person; and
  (b) satisfies each of the criteria in one or more of paragraphs (2) to (6).
(2) The criteria in this paragraph are that—
  (a) the person is the primary carer of an EEA national; and
  (b) the EEA national—
    (i) is under the age of 18;
    (ii) resides in the United Kingdom as a self-sufficient person; and
    (iii) would be unable to remain in the United Kingdom if the person left the United Kingdom for an indefinite period.
(3) The criteria in this paragraph are that—
  (a) any of the person's parents ("PP") is an EEA national who resides or has resided in the United Kingdom;
  (b) both the person and PP reside or have resided in the United Kingdom at the same time, and during such a period of residence, PP has been a worker in the United Kingdom; and
  (c) the person is in education in the United Kingdom.
(4) The criteria in this paragraph are that—
  (a) the person is the primary carer of a person satisfying the criteria in paragraph (3) ("PPP"); and
  (b) PPP would be unable to continue to be educated in the United Kingdom if the person left the United Kingdom for an indefinite period.
(5) The criteria in this paragraph are that—
  (a) the person is the primary carer of a British citizen ("BC");
  (b) BC is residing in the United Kingdom; and
  (c) BC would be unable to reside in the United Kingdom or in [¹ an] EEA State if the person left the United Kingdom for an indefinite period.
(6) The criteria in this paragraph are that—
  (a) the person is under the age of 18;
  (b) the person does not have leave to enter, or remain in, the United Kingdom under the 1971 Act but see paragraph (7A);
  (c) the person's primary carer is entitled to a derivative right to reside in the United Kingdom under paragraph (2), (4) or (5); and
  (d) the primary carer would be prevented from residing in the United Kingdom if the person left the United Kingdom for an indefinite period.
(7) In this regulation—
  (a) "education" excludes nursery education but does not exclude educa-

tion received before the compulsory school age where that education is equivalent to the education received at or after the compulsory school age;

(b) "worker" does not include a jobseeker or a person treated as a worker under regulation 6(2);

(c) an "exempt person" is a person—

(i) who has a right to reside under another provision of these Regulations;

(ii) who has the right of abode under section 2 of the 1971 Act;

(iii) to whom section 8 of the 1971 Act, or an order made under subsection (2) of that section, applies; or

(iv) who has indefinite leave to enter or remain in the United Kingdom but see paragraph (7A).

(7A) Leave to enter, or remain in, the United Kingdom under the 1971 Act which has been granted by virtue of Appendix EU to the immigration rules is not to be treated as leave for the purposes of paragraph (6)(b) or (7)(c)(iv).

(8) A person is the "primary carer" of another person ("AP") if—

(a) the person is a direct relative or a legal guardian of AP; and

(b) either—

(i) the person has primary responsibility for AP's care; or

(ii) shares equally the responsibility for AP's care with one other person.

(9) In paragraph (2)(b)(iii), (4)(b) or (5)(c), if the role of primary carer is shared with another person in accordance with paragraph (8)(b)(ii), the words "the person" are to be read as "both primary carers".

(10) Paragraph (9) does not apply if the person with whom care responsibility is shared acquired a derivative right to reside in the United Kingdom as a result of this regulation prior to the other person's assumption of equal care responsibility.

(11) A person is not be regarded as having responsibility for another person's care for the purpose of paragraph (8) on the sole basis of a financial contribution towards that person's care.

[Editorial note: This is the modified wording of para. (12) that now applies to those with pre-settled status] (12) A person does not have a derivative right to reside [² if that person is subject to a deportation or exclusion order unless that order] unless that decision is set aside or otherwise no longer has effect.

[Editorial note: This is the modified wording of para. (12) that now applies to claimants for whom reg. 16 is saved by SI 2020/1209]

(12) A person does not have a derivative right to reside where the Secretary of State or an immigration officer has made a decision under regulation 23(6)(b), 24(1), 25(1), 26(3) [³, 27A] or 31(1), unless that decision is set aside or otherwise no longer has effect.

Amendment

Regulation 16 was revoked by s.1 of, and Sch.1, para.2(2) to, the Immigration and Social Security Co-ordination (EU Withdrawal) Act 2020 with effect from December 31 2020 at 11.00 pm. The text given above is of the regulation as saved and modified for the purposes of entitlement to benefit by:

- (For those EEA nationals with pre-settled status) reg.83 of, and Sch.4, paras 2, 3 and 4(n) of the Immigration and Social Security Co-ordination (EU

Withdrawal) Act 2020 (Consequential, Saving, Transitional and Transitory Provisions) (EU Exit) Regulations 2020 (SI 2020/1309); and

- (For those EEA nationals who had a right of residence in the UK under EU law immediately before December 30, 2020 at 11.00 pm, but who have neither settled nor pre-settled status) by regs 3(2), 4(3) and 6(f) of the Citizens' Rights (Application Deadline and Temporary Protection) (EU Exit) Regulations 2020 (SI 2020/1209).

Square brackets with superscript numbers in the text refer to the Modification section below and not, as elsewhere in this work, to amendments. For the amendments that were made to reg.16 before its revocation see pp.1038-1039 of Vol.V of the 2020/21 edition.

MODIFICATION

1. SI 2020/1309, Sch.4, para.4(n)(i); SI 2020/1209 regs 3(2), 4(3) and 6(f)(i).
2. SI 2020/1309, Sch.4, para.4(n)(ii).
3. SI 2020/1209 regs 3(2), 4(3) and 6(f)(ii).

DEFINITIONS

"the 1971 Act"—see reg.2(1).
"derivative right to reside"—see reg.2(1) and the General Note.
"EEA national"—see reg.2(1).
"EEA State"—*ibid.*
"jobseeker"—see reg.6(1).
"right to reside"—see reg.2(1).
"self-sufficient person"—see reg.4(1)(c).
"worker"—see reg.4(1)(a).

GENERAL NOTE

Regulation 16 codifies a number of different decisions of the CJEU by conferring a "derivative right of residence" for various categories of people whose rights do not arise directly under the Citizenship Directive but have been held to arise from the TFEU or from other provisions of EU law, notably art.10 of Regulation (EU) 492/2011. Under para.(1), a person has a derivative right of residence during any period in which s/he is not an exempt person and satisfies all criteria in one or more of paras (2)–(7).   **7.98**

Residence pursuant to a derivative right to reside does not count as residence within reg.15 and therefore does not lead to a permanent right of residence.

Paragraphs (1)(a) and (7) – Exempt persons   **7.99**
"Exempt person" is defined by para.(7) as a person who has a right to reside under another provision of these Regulations, or is a British citizen or a Commonwealth citizen with the right of abode, or is entitled to enter or remain in the UK under s.8 Immigration Act 1971 (Exceptions for seamen, aircrews and other special cases), or has indefinite leave to remain. The effect of that definition, taken with para.(1)(a) is that a derivative right to reside is a right of last resort. People with most other rights of residence do not qualify for a derivative right to reside. For a practical example, see *SSWP v MH (IS)* [2016] UKUT 526 (AAC).

Primary carers of self-sufficient children
Paragraph (2) applies to a person who is the primary carer (as defined in para.(8)) of an EEA national aged under 18, who is living in the UK as a self-sufficient person and would be unable to remain in the United Kingdom if that person left the UK for an indefinite period. It therefore consolidates the decision of the ECJ in *Zhu and Chen v Home Secretary* (Case C–200/02).   **7.100**

In *Bajratari v Secretary of State for the Home Department* [2017] NICA 74, the question arose whether a child's resources could be "sufficient" where they were derived from work undertaken unlawfully (i.e., without the necessary work permit) by a third-country national parent. The Court of Appeal in Northern Ireland referred the following questions to the CJEU:

> "[i] Can income from employment that is unlawful under national law establish, in whole or in part, the availability of sufficient resources under Article 7(1) (b) of the Citizens Directive?
>
> [ii] If 'yes', can Article 7(1) (b) be satisfied where the employment is deemed precarious solely by reason of its unlawful character?"

The reference has been registered at the CJEU as Case C-93/18 and Advocate General Szpunar has issued an opinion recommending that the Court should answer those questions as follows:

> "Article 7(1)(b) of [the Citizenship Directive] must be interpreted as meaning that a young child who is a Union citizen has sufficient resources not to become a burden on the social assistance system of the host Member State during his period of residence where, in circumstances such as those of the case in the main proceedings, those resources are provided from income derived from the activity unlawfully carried on in that Member State, without a residence or work permit, by the child's father, a national of a third country."

At the time of going to press, no date had been fixed for the delivery of the Court's judgment.

Regulation 4(5) provides that "[for] the purposes of regulation 16(2) (criteria for having a derivative right to reside), references in this regulation to "family members" includes a "primary carer" as defined in regulation 16(8). What this means is that the comprehensive sickness insurance that the EEA national must have in order to be a self-sufficient person must cover his or her primary carers as well.

Children of migrant workers in education

7.101   Paragraph (3) applies to a person who is the child of a migrant worker or former migrant worker and who is in education (as defined in reg.7(a)) in the UK. It therefore codifies the decision of the ECJ in *Baumbast and R v Secretary of State for the Home Department* (Case C-413/99). It is not necessary for the child to be self-sufficient or to have comprehensive sickness insurance.

However, it is necessary for the child to satisfy all the requirements of the paragraph. In *JS v SSWP (ESA)* [2016] UKUT 314 (AAC), the Upper Tribunal (Judge Wright) held (in relation to the equivalent, though differently worded, provisions of reg.15A of the 2006 Regulations) that those requirements are not met where it is one of the child's grandparents, rather than a parent, who was the EEA national who had been a worker in the UK. That was so even though, under the definition in para.(8), a grandparent can be the child's "primary carer" for the purposes of paras (4)-(6).

Similarly, it is not sufficient for the EEA national who has been a worker in the UK to be a person who is not the child's biological parent and is not in a legally recognised relationship with the parent: see *IP v SSWP* [2015] UKUT 691 (AAC) and *OFNATS v Ahmed* (Case C-45/12). It is also necessary for there to have been a period when the child lived in the UK and the parent was a worker here: see *Bolton MBC v HY (HB)* [2018] UKUT 103 (AAC).

The right codified in para.(3) does not extend to the children of EEA nationals who have been self-employed in the UK but have not been workers: see the decisions of the CJEU in *Secretary of State for Work and Pensions v Czop* (Case C-147/11) and of the Court of Appeal in *Hrabkova v Secretary of State for Work and Pensions* [2017] EWCA Civ 794. Ms Hrabkova has been refused permission to appeal to the Supreme Court (ref: UKSC 2018/0018).

Primary carers of children of migrant workers in education

7.102   Paragraph (4) codifies the right of residence established for the primary carers of the children of migrant workers who are in education in the UK that was established by the ECJ in *Ibrahim v London Borough of Harrow* (Case C-310/08) and *Teixeira v*

London Borough of Lambeth (Case C-480/08). Again the primary carer does not need to be self-sufficient or to have comprehensive sickness insurance. However, under the definition of "primary carer" in para.(8), the carer does have to be a "direct relative" of the child. In *MS v SSWP (IS)* [2016] UKUT 348 (AAC), the Upper Tribunal (Judge Jacobs) held that this did not include the child's elder brother, even though he had been appointed her legal guardian. Guardianship creates rights and responsibilities but it does not create a parental relationship. The position would probably be different if the putative primary carer were the child's adoptive parent.

The right does not extend to the primary carers of children who have not established themselves in education even where the child has a right of residence as the family member of an EEA national who is a worker: see *AM v SSWP and City and County of Swansea Council* [2019] UKUT 361 (AAC).

Where primary carers are also jobseekers (in the EU sense of that term), they cannot be denied social assistance on the basis of the derogation in art.24(2) of the Citizenship Directive (see Vol.III). Their rights as primary carer (and also the rights of the child) arise under arts 7(2) and 10 of Regulation (EU) No. 492/2011 (formerly Regulation (EEC) No 1612/68) and are independent of any right of residence as a jobseeker. Art.24(2) only derogates from the right to equal treatment under art.24(1) which, in turn, only applies to "Union citizens residing *on the basis of this Directive* in the host Member State" (added emphasis) and therefore does not apply to rights arising under Regulation No. 492/2011 or Regulation (EC) No. 883/2004: see the decision of the Grand Chamber of the CJEU in *Jobcenter Krefeld – Widerspruchsstelle v JD* (Case No. C-181/19).

Carers of British citizens

Paragraph (5) codifies the right of residence for some people who care for British   7.103
citizens derived from art.21 TFEU by the Grand Chamber of the CJEU in *Zambrano v Office national de l'emploi (ONEm)* (Case C-34/09). In *DM v SSWP (PIP)* [2019] UKUT 26 (AAC), Upper Tribunal Judge Ward accepted a concession from the Secretary of State that "Regulation 16(5) of the Immigration (European Economic Area) Regulations 2016 (and regulation 15A(4A) of the 2006 Regulations) applies to carers of adult British citizens as well as children, and this reflects the relevant EU case law": see also the decision of the High Court (Lane J.) in *R (Hamid Saeed) v Secretary of State for the Home Department* [2018] EWHC 1707 (Admin).

Under reg.9(3) of the Universal Credit Regulations, reg.21AA(3) of the IS Regulations, reg.85A(3) of the JSA Regulations 1996, reg.2(4) of the SPC Regulations and reg.23(4)(b)(i) of the Child Benefit Regulations 2006 (see *HMRC v AD (CHB)* [2020] UKUT 353 (AAC)), the *Zambrano* right of residence has not counted for the purposes of any social security benefit since November 8, 2012. That position was confirmed by the decision of the Supreme Court in *R (HC) v Secretary of State for Work and Pensions and others* [2017] UKSC 73.

Other children of primary carers

Where the primary carer with a derivative right of residence under paras (2), (4)   7.104
or (5) is also the primary carer of another child (who is not an exempt person) and who does not have leave to enter or remain in the UK, the other child will have a derivative right of residence under para.(6) if the primary carer would not be able to remain in the UK if the other child left the UK for an indefinite period.

PART 3

RESIDENCE DOCUMENTATION

GENERAL NOTE

It is unnecessary for a publication about social security law to go into detail about   7.105
the various documents issued to those with rights under these Regulations. Those documents were:

- a registration certificate

  Registration certificates were issued by the Secretary of State under reg.17 to qualified persons, to EEA nationals who were family members of a qualified person or an EEA national with the right of permanent residence, and to family members who had retained the right of residence. They may also be issued to extended family members who were EEA nationals.

- a residence card

  Residence cards were issued by the Secretary of State under reg.18 to the family members of a qualified person or an EEA national with the right of permanent residence, but who were not themselves EEA nationals. They could also be issued to extended family members who were not EEA nationals.

- a document certifying permanent residence

  Documents certifying permanent residence are issued by the Secretary of State under reg.19 to EEA nationals with a right of permanent residence.

- a permanent residence card

  Permanent residence cards were issued by the Secretary of State under reg.19 to those with a right of permanent residence who were not EEA nationals.

- a derivative residence card

  Derivative residence cards were issued by the Secretary of State under reg.20 to those (whether EEA nationals or not) who had a derivative right to reside under reg.16.

- an EEA family permit

  EEA family permits were issued by entry clearance officers under reg.12 to family members of EEA national who were outside the UK and wished to accompany the EEA national to the UK or to join him or her here, to family members who had retained the right of residence, and to people who were not EEA nationals but had a right of permanent residence under reg.16. They could also be issued to extended family members.

The main value of these documents in social security cases is as evidence that the Home Office had accepted the claimant had a right to reside. However, it must be born in mind that—except in the case of extended family members: see reg.8—regs 17–20 all provide that the documents to which they refer are:

"(a) proof of the holder's right to reside on the date of issue;
(b) no longer valid if the holder ceases to have a right to reside under these Regulations; [and]
(c) invalid if the holder never had a right to reside under these Regulations."

This follows the ruling of the CJEU in *Dias v Secretary of State for Work and Pensions* (Case C-325/09), [2012] AACR 36. The Court held, confirming the provisional view expressed by the Court of Appeal (*Secretary of State for Work and Pensions v Dias* [2009] EWCA Civ 807), that the mere possession of a (former) residence permit did not make the claimant's residence "legal" for the purposes of art.16(1) of the Citizenship Directive. The ECJ's formal answer to the question referred by the Court of Appeal was that:

"periods of residence completed before 30 April 2006 on the basis solely of a residence permit validly issued pursuant to Directive 68/360, without the conditions governing entitlement to any right of residence having been satisfied, cannot be regarded as having been completed legally for the purposes of the acquisition of the right of permanent residence under Article 16(1) of Directive 2004/38" and its reasoning is summarised succinctly at para.54 of its judgment:

"... the declaratory character of residence permits means that those permits merely certify that a right already exists. Consequently, just as such a declaratory character means that a citizen's residence may not be regarded as illegal, within the meaning of European Union law, solely on the ground that he does not hold a residence permit, it precludes a Union citizen's residence from being regarded as legal, within the meaning of European Union law, solely on the ground that such a permit was validly issued to him."

A registration certificate did not have retrospective effect (*CIS/4237/2007*, para.9).

Issue of registration certificate

17.—(1) The Secretary of State must issue a registration certificate to a qualified person immediately on application and production of—

   (a) a valid national identity card or passport issued by an EEA State; and

   (b) proof that the applicant is a qualified person.

(2) In the case of a worker, confirmation of the worker's engagement from the worker's employer or a certificate of employment is sufficient proof for the purposes of paragraph (1)(b).

(3) The Secretary of State must issue a registration certificate to an EEA national who is the family member of a qualified person or of an EEA national with a right of permanent residence under regulation 15 immediately on application and production of—

   (a) a valid national identity card or passport issued by an EEA State; and

   (b) proof that the applicant is such a family member.

(4) The Secretary of State must issue a registration certificate to an EEA national who is a family member who has retained the right of residence on application and production of—

   (a) a valid national identity card or passport; and

   (b) proof that the applicant is a family member who has retained the right of residence.

(5) The Secretary of State may issue a registration certificate to an extended family member not falling within regulation 7(3) who is an EEA national on application if—

   (a) the application is accompanied or joined by a valid national identity card or passport;

   (b) the relevant EEA national is a qualified person or an EEA national with a right of permanent residence under regulation 15; and

   (c) in all the circumstances it appears to the Secretary of State appropriate to issue the registration certificate.

(6) Where the Secretary of State receives an application under paragraph (5) an extensive examination of the personal circumstances of the applicant must be undertaken by the Secretary of State and if the application is refused, the Secretary of State must give reasons justifying the refusal unless this is contrary to the interests of national security.

(7) A registration certificate issued under this regulation must state the name and address of the person registering and the date of registration.

(8) A registration certificate is—

   (a) proof of the holder's right to reside on the date of issue;

   (b) no longer valid if the holder ceases to have a right to reside under these Regulations;

7.106

(c) invalid if the holder never had a right to reside under these Regulations.

(9) This regulation is subject to regulations 24 (refusal to issue or renew and revocation of residence documentation) and 25 (cancellation of a right of residence).

AMENDMENT

Regulation 17 was revoked by s.1 of, and Sch.1, para.2(2) to, the Immigration and Social Security Co-ordination (EU Withdrawal) Act 2020 with effect from December 31 2020 at 11.00 pm. For the purposes of access to benefits, the revocation was not subject to any savings. Savings provisions do, however, exist for immigration purposes: see reg.83 and Sch.3, para.3(3) of SI 2020/1309 below.

DEFINITIONS

"EEA national"—see reg.2(1).
"EEA State"—*ibid.*
"extended family member"—see reg.8.
"family member"—see reg.7.
"family member who has retained the right of residence"—see reg.10.
"qualified person"—see reg.6(1).
"registration certificate"—see reg.2(1) and the General Note to Pt 3.
"relevant EEA national"—see regs 2(1) and 8(6).
"right to reside"—see reg.2(1).
"worker"—see reg.4(1)(a).

Issue of residence card

7.107   **18.**—(1) The Secretary of State must issue a residence card to a person who is not an EEA national and is the family member of a qualified person or of an EEA national with a right of permanent residence under regulation 15 on application and production of—

(a) a valid passport; and
(b) proof that the applicant is such a family member.

(2) The Secretary of State must issue a residence card to a person who is not an EEA national but who is a family member who has retained the right of residence on application and production of—

(a) a valid passport; and
(b) proof that the applicant is a family member who has retained the right of residence.

(3) On receipt of an application under paragraph (1) or (2) and the documents that are required to accompany the application the Secretary of State must immediately issue the applicant with a certificate of application for the residence card and the residence card must be issued no later than six months after the date on which the application and documents are received.

(4) The Secretary of State may issue a residence card to an extended family member not falling within regulation 7(3) who is not an EEA national on application if—

(a) the application is accompanied or joined by a valid passport;
(b) the relevant EEA national is a qualified person or an EEA national with a right of permanent residence under regulation 15; and
(c) in all the circumstances it appears to the Secretary of State appropriate to issue the residence card.

(5) Where the Secretary of State receives an application under paragraph (4) an extensive examination of the personal circumstances of the applicant must be undertaken by the Secretary of State and if the application is refused, the Secretary of State must give reasons justifying the refusal unless this is contrary to the interests of national security.

(6) A residence card issued under this regulation is valid for—

(a) five years from the date of issue; or

(b) in the case of a residence card issued to the family member or extended family member of a qualified person, the envisaged period of residence in the United Kingdom of the qualified person,

whichever is the shorter.

(7) A residence card—

(a) must be called "Residence card of a family member of a Union Citizen";

(b) is proof of the holder's right to reside on the date of issue;

(c) is no longer valid if the holder ceases to have a right to reside under these Regulations;

(d) is invalid if the holder never had a right to reside under these Regulations.

(8) This regulation is subject to regulations 24 and 25.

AMENDMENT

Regulation 18 was revoked by s.1 of, and Sch.1, para.2(2) to, the Immigration and Social Security Co-ordination (EU Withdrawal) Act 2020 with effect from December 31 2020 at 11.00 pm. For the purposes of access to benefits, the revocation was not subject to any savings. Savings provisions do, however, exist for immigration purposes: see reg.83 and Sch.3, para.3(4) of SI 2020/1309 below.

For the amendments that were made to reg.18 before its revocation see pp.1045-1046 of Vol.V of the 2020/21 edition.

DEFINITIONS

"EEA national"—see reg.2(1).
"extended family member"—see reg.8.
"family member"—see reg.7.
"family member who has retained the right of residence"—see reg.10.
"qualified person"—see reg.6(1).
"relevant EEA national"—see regs 2(1) and 8(6).
"residence card"— see reg.2(1) and the General Note to Pt 3.
"right to reside"— see reg.2(1).

Issue of a document certifying permanent residence and a permanent residence card

19.—(1) The Secretary of State must, as soon as possible, issue an EEA national with a right of permanent residence under regulation 15 with a document certifying permanent residence on application and the production of—

(a) a valid national identity card or passport issued by an EEA State; and

(b) proof that the EEA national has a right of permanent residence.

(2)   The Secretary of State must issue a person who is not an EEA national who has a right of permanent residence under regulation 15 with a permanent residence card no later than six months after an application is received and the production of—

7.108

(a) a valid passport; and

(b) proof that the person has a right of permanent residence.

(3) Subject to paragraph (4) a permanent residence card is valid for ten years from the date of issue and must be renewed on application.

(4) A document certifying permanent residence and a permanent residence card is—

(a) proof that the holder had a right to reside under regulation 15 on the date of issue;

(b) no longer valid if the holder ceases to have a right of permanent residence under regulation 15;

(c) invalid if the holder never had a right of permanent residence under regulation 15.

(5) This regulation is subject to regulations 24 and 25.

AMENDMENT

Regulation 19 was revoked by s.1 of, and Sch.1, para.2(2) to, the Immigration and Social Security Co-ordination (EU Withdrawal) Act 2020 with effect from December 31 2020 at 11.00 pm. For the purposes of access to benefits, the revocation was not subject to any savings. Savings provisions do, however, exist for immigration purposes: see reg.83 and Sch.3, para.3(5) of SI 2020/1309 below.

DEFINITIONS

"document certifying permanent residence"— see reg.2(1) and the General Note to Pt 3.
"EEA national"—see reg.2(1).
"EEA State"—*ibid.*
"permanent residence card"— see reg.2(1) and the General Note to Pt 3.
"right to reside"— see reg.2(1).

Issue of a derivative residence card

7.109   **20.**—(1) The Secretary of State must issue a person with a derivative residence card on application and on production of—

(a) a valid national identity card issued by an EEA State or a valid passport; and

(b) proof that the applicant has a derivative right to reside under regulation 16.

(2) On receipt of an application under paragraph (1) the Secretary of State must issue the applicant with a certificate of application as soon as possible.

(3) A derivative residence card issued under paragraph (1) is valid until—

(a) the date five years from the date of issue; or

(b) any earlier date specified by the Secretary of State when issuing the derivative residence card.

(4) A derivative residence card issued under paragraph (1) must be issued as soon as practicable.

(5) A derivative residence card is—

(a) proof of the holder's derivative right to reside on the day of issue;

(b) no longer valid if the holder ceases to have a derivative right to reside under regulation 16;

(c) invalid if the holder never had a derivative right to reside under regulation 16.

(6) This regulation is subject to regulations 24 and 25.

AMENDMENT

Regulation 20 was revoked by s.1 of, and Sch.1, para.2(2) to, the Immigration and Social Security Co-ordination (EU Withdrawal) Act 2020 with effect from December 31 2020 at 11.00 pm. For the purposes of access to benefits, the revocation was not subject to any savings. Savings provisions do, however, exist for immigration purposes: see reg.83 and Sch.3, para.3(6) of SI 2020/1309 below.

DEFINITIONS

"derivative residence card"— see reg.2(1) and the General Note to Pt 3.
"derivative right to reside"—see regs 2(1) and 16.
"EEA State"—see reg.2(1).
"right to reside"—*ibid.*

Procedure for applications for documentation under this Part and regulation 12

[Editorial note: This is the modified wording of reg.21 that now applies to claim-   **7.110**
ants for whom that regulation is saved by SI 2020/1209]

21.—(1) An application for [¹ . . .] an EEA family permit under regulation 12, must be made—

(a) online, submitted electronically using the relevant pages of www.gov.uk; or

(b) by post or in person, using the relevant application form specified by the Secretary of State on www.gov.uk.

(2)   All applications must—

(a) be accompanied by the evidence or proof required by [¹ . . .] regulation 12 [¹ . . .] within the time specified by the Secretary of State on www.gov.uk; and

(b) be complete.

(3) [¹ . . .]

(4) When an application is submitted otherwise than in accordance with the requirements in this regulation, it is invalid and must be rejected.

(4A) An application for [¹ . . .] an EEA family permit under regulation 12, is invalid where the person making the application is subject to a removal decision made under regulation 23(6)(b), a deportation order made under regulation 32(3) or an exclusion order made under regulation 23(5).

(5) [¹ . . .]

(6) [¹ . . .]

AMENDMENT

Regulation 21 was revoked by s.1 of, and Sch.1, para.2(2) to, the Immigration and Social Security Co-ordination (EU Withdrawal) Act 2020 with effect from December 31 2020 at 11.00 pm. The text given above is of the regulation as saved and modified for the purposes of entitlement to benefit and as it relates to those EEA nationals who had a right of residence in the UK under EU law immediately before December 30, 2020 at 11.00 pm, but who have neither settled nor pre-settled status, by regs 3(2), 4(3) and 6(g) of the Citizens' Rights (Application Deadline and Temporary Protection) (EU Exit) Regulations 2020 (SI 2020/1209).

For those EEA nationals with pre-settled status, reg.21 is saved for immigration purposes without modification: see reg.83 and Sch.3, paras 3 and 6(l) of SI 2020/1309 below

For the amendments that were made to reg.21 before its revocation (and the wording that is saved for immigration purposes) see pp.1047-1048 of Vol.V of the 2020/21 edition.

MODIFICATION

1. SI 2020/1209 regs 3(2), 4(3) and 6(g).

DEFINITIONS

"derivative residence card"—see regs 2(1) and 20.
"EEA family permit"—see regs 2(1) and 12.
"EEA national"—see reg.2(1).
"extended family member"—see reg.8.
"family member"—see reg.7.
"residence card"—see regs 2(1) and 18.

Verification of a right of residence

7.111   22.—(1) This regulation applies where the Secretary of State—

(a) has reasonable doubt as to whether a person ("A") has a right to reside or a derivative right to reside; or

(b) wants to verify the eligibility of a person ("A") to apply for an EEA family permit [¹ . . .].

(2) Where this regulation applies, the Secretary of State may invite A to—

(a) provide evidence to support the existence of a right to reside or a derivative right to reside (as the case may be), or to support an application for an EEA family permit [¹ . . .]; or

(b) attend an interview with the Secretary of State.

(3) If A purports to have a right to reside on the basis of a relationship with another person ("B"), (including, where B is a British citizen, through having lived with B in another EEA State), the Secretary of State may invite B to—

(a) provide information about their relationship or residence in another EEA State; or

(b) attend an interview with the Secretary of State.

(4) If without good reason A or B (as the case may be)—

(a) fails to provide the information requested;

(b) on at least two occasions, fails to attend an interview if so invited;

the Secretary of State may draw any factual inferences about A's entitlement to a right to reside as appear appropriate in the circumstances.

(5) The Secretary of State may decide following the drawing of an inference under paragraph (4) that A does not have or ceases to have a right to reside.

(6) But the Secretary of State must not decide that A does not have or ceases to have a right to reside on the sole basis that A failed to comply with this regulation.

(7) This regulation may not be invoked systematically.

AMENDMENT

Regulation 22 was revoked by s.1 of, and Sch.1, para.2(2) to, the Immigration and Social Security Co-ordination (EU Withdrawal) Act 2020 with effect from December 31 2020 at 11.00 pm. The text given above is of the regulation as saved and modified for the purposes of entitlement to benefit and as it relates to those EEA nationals who had a right of residence in the UK under EU law immediately before December 30, 2020 at 11.00 pm, but who have neither settled nor pre-settled status, by regs 3(2), 4(3) and 6(h) of the Citizens' Rights (Application Deadline and Temporary Protection) (EU Exit) Regulations 2020 (SI 2020/1209).

For those EEA nationals with pre-settled status, reg.22 is saved for immigration purposes without modification: see reg.83 and Sch.3, paras 3 and 6(m) of SI 2020/1309 below, revocation (and the wording that is saved for immigration purposes).

For the amendments that were made to reg.22 before its revocation, see pp.1048-1049 of Vol.V of the 2020/21 edition.

7.112

MODIFICATION

1. SI 2020/1209 regs 3(2), 4(3) and 6(h).

DEFINITIONS

"derivative right to reside"—see regs 2(1) and 16.
"EEA family permit"—see regs 2(1) and 12.
"EEA State"—see reg.2(1).
"right to reside"—*ibid.*

PART 7

GENERAL

Effect on other legislation

43. Schedule 3 (effect on other legislation) has effect.

7.113

AMENDMENT

Regulation 43 was revoked by s.1 of, and Sch.1, para.2(2) to, the Immigration and Social Security Co-ordination (EU Withdrawal) Act 2020 with effect from December 31 2020 at 11.00 pm. The text given above is of the regulation as saved for the purposes of entitlement to benefit and as it relates to those EEA nationals who had a right of residence in the UK under EU law immediately before December 30, 2020 at 11.00 pm, but who have neither settled nor pre-settled status, by regs 3(2), 4(3) and 10(a) of the Citizens' Rights (Application Deadline and Temporary Protection) (EU Exit) Regulations 2020 (SI 2020/1209). There are no relevant savings provisions for those EEA nationals with pre-settled status.

Substitution of regulation 9 of the 2006 Regulations

44. [¹ ...]

7.114

AMENDMENT

1. Regulation 46(a) (January 31, 2017).

GENERAL NOTE

Unlike the other provisions of these Regulations, reg.55 and Sch.5 came into force on November 25, 2016 (see reg.1(2)(a)). They inserted a new reg.9 into the 2006 Regulations (see pp.175–6 of the Supplement to the 2016/17 edition). The inserted regulation was in the same terms as reg.9 of these Regulations. Accordingly, when the main provisions in these Regulations came into force on February 1, 2017 (thereby revoking the 2006 Regulations), reg.46 below revoked reg.44 and Sch.5. Regulation 46 was itself revoked by s.1 of, and Sch.1, para.2(2) to, the Immigration and Social Security Co-ordination (EU Withdrawal) Act 2020 with effect from December 31 2020 at 11.00 pm.

7.115

Revocations, savings, transitory and transitional provisions and consequential modifications

7.116   45. Schedule 4 (revocations and savings), Schedule 6 (transitional provisions) and Schedule 7 (consequential modifications) have effect.

AMENDMENT

Regulation 45 was revoked by s.1 of, and Sch.1, para.2(2) to, the Immigration and Social Security Co-ordination (EU Withdrawal) Act 2020 with effect from December 31 2020 at 11.00 pm. The text given above is of the regulation as saved for the purposes of entitlement to benefit and as it relates to those EEA nationals who had a right of residence in the UK under EU law immediately before December 30, 2020 at 11.00 pm, but who have neither settled nor pre-settled status, by regs 3(2), 4(3) and 10(b) of the Citizens' Rights (Application Deadline and Temporary Protection) (EU Exit) Regulations 2020 (SI 2020/1209). The regulation is not saved in so far as it relates to Part 1 of Schedule 4.

There are no relevant savings provisions for those EEA nationals with pre-settled status.

GENERAL NOTE

The combined effect of reg.45 and Sch.6, and the former reg.44 and Sch.5 was that:

- All decisions made on or after 1 February 2017 were to be treated as having been made under the 2016 Regs, whatever the date of the application;

- Regulation 9 of the 2016 Regs applied to all decisions made on or after 25 November 2016 whatever the date of the application;

- In all other respects the 2006 Regulations applied if the application was made before 25 November 2016 *and* the decision was made before 1 February 2017:

see the decision of the Immigration and Asylum Chamber of the Upper Tribunal in *Oksuzoglu (EEA appeal – "new matter")* [2018] UKUT 385 (IAC).

For a discussion of the effect of Schedule 7, see *HMRC v AD (CHB)* [2020] UKUT 353 (AAC).

Revocation of regulation 44 and Schedule 5

7.117   46. The following are revoked—
(a) regulation 44;
(b) Schedule 5.

GENERAL NOTE

7.118   See the General Note to reg.44, above.

Regulation 27

SCHEDULE 1

CONSIDERATIONS OF PUBLIC POLICY, PUBLIC SECURITY AND THE FUNDAMENTAL INTERESTS OF SOCIETY ETC.

7.119   *Omitted*

SCHEDULE 2

APPEALS TO THE FIRST-TIER TRIBUNAL

Omitted   7.120

SCHEDULE 3

EFFECT ON OTHER LEGISLATION

Leave under the 1971 Act

1. Where a person has leave to enter or remain under the 1971 Act which   7.121
is subject to conditions and that person also has a right to reside under these
Regulations, those conditions do not have effect for as long as the person
has that right to reside.

Person not subject to restriction on the period for which they may remain

2.—(1) For the purposes of the 1971 Act and British Nationality Act   7.122
1981, a person who has a right of permanent residence under regulation
15 must be regarded as a person who is in the United Kingdom without
being subject under the immigration laws to any restriction on the period
for which the person may remain.

(2) But a qualified person, the family member of a qualified person,
a person with a derivative right to reside and a family member who has
retained the right of residence must not, by virtue of that status, be so
regarded for those purposes.

Carriers' liability under the 1999 Act

3. *Omitted*   7.123

AMENDMENT

Schedule 3 was revoked by s.1 of, and Sch.1, para.2(2) to, the Immigration
and Social Security Co-ordination (EU Withdrawal) Act 2020 with effect from
December 31 2020 at 11.00 pm. The text given above is of the Schedule as saved
for the purposes of entitlement to benefit and as it relates to those EEA nationals
who had a right of residence in the UK under EU law immediately before December
30, 2020 at 11.00 pm, but who have neither settled nor pre-settled status, by regs
3(2), 4(3) and 10(c) of the Citizens' Rights (Application Deadline and Temporary
Protection) (EU Exit) Regulations 2020 (SI 2020/1209).

There are no relevant savings provisions for those EEA nationals with pre-settled
status.

DEFINITIONS

"the 1971 Act"—see reg.2(1).
"the 1999 Act"—*ibid.*
"derivative right to reside"—see regs 2(1) and 16.
"family member"—see reg.7.
"family member who has retained the right of residence"—see reg.10.
"immigration laws"—see reg.2(1).
"qualified person"—see reg.6(1).
"right to reside"—see reg.2(1).

SCHEDULE 4

REVOCATIONS AND SAVINGS

PART 1

TABLE OF REVOCATIONS

7.124   **1.** *Omitted*

PART 2

SAVINGS AND MODIFICATIONS

Accession member States: savings and modifications

7.125   **2.**—(1) Regulations 7A and 7B of the 2006 Regulations (arrangements for accession member States) continue to have effect in relation to any EEA national to whom they applied immediately before 1st February 2017.

(2) Where regulations 7A and 7B continue to have effect—

(a) they do so with the following modifications—

(i) in paragraph (3) of regulation 7A and paragraph (4) of regulation 7B, as though the references to treating periods of involuntary unemployment duly recorded by the relevant employment office as periods of work for the purposes of regulation 5(7)(c) of the 2006 Regulations were to treating such periods of involuntary unemployment as periods of work for the purposes of regulation 6(2) of these Regulations; and

(ii) as though the references to regulations 6(2) (persons who continue to be treated as a worker) and 15 (right of permanent residence) were references to those provisions in these Regulations; and

(b) these Regulations have effect save that regulation 17 (issue of registration certificate) has effect as though, in paragraph (9), for "regulation 24" there were substituted "regulations 7A and 7B of the 2006 Regulations and regulation 24 of these Regulations".

Appeals

7.126   **3.**—(1) Notwithstanding the revocation of the 2006 Regulations by paragraph 1(1), those Regulations continue to apply—

(a) in respect of an appeal under those Regulations against an EEA decision which is pending (within the meaning of regulation 25(2) of the 2006 Regulations) on 31st January 2017;

(b) in a case where a person has, on 31st January 2017, a right under those Regulations to appeal against an EEA decision.

(2) For the purposes of this paragraph, "EEA decision" has the meaning given in regulation 2 of the 2006 Regulations and the definition of "EEA decision" in regulation 2 of these Regulations does not apply.

AMENDMENT

Schedule 4 was revoked by s.1 of, and Sch.1, para.2(2) to, the Immigration and Social Security Co-ordination (EU Withdrawal) Act 2020 with effect from December 31 2020 at 11.00 pm. The text given above is of Pt. 2 of the Schedule as saved for the purposes of entitlement to benefit and as it relates to those EEA nationals who had a right of residence in the UK under EU law immediately before December 30, 2020 at 11.00 pm, but who have neither settled nor pre-settled status, by regs 3(2), 4(3) and 10(d) of the Citizens' Rights (Application Deadline and Temporary Protection) (EU Exit) Regulations 2020 (SI 2020/1209).

There are no relevant savings provisions for those EEA nationals with pre-settled status.

DEFINITIONS

"the 2006 Regulations"—see reg.2(1).
"EEA decision"—see General Note.
"EEA national"—see reg.2(1).
"registration certificate"—see regs 2(1) and 17.

GENERAL NOTE

In para.3, "EEA decision" is defined by reg.2 of the 2006 Regulations as follows: 7.127

"'EEA decision' means a decision under these Regulations that concerns—

(a) a person's entitlement to be admitted to the United Kingdom;
(b) a person's entitlement to be issued with or have renewed, or not to have revoked, a registration certificate, residence card, derivative residence card, document certifying permanent residence or permanent residence card;
(c) a person's removal from the United Kingdom; or
(d) the cancellation, pursuant to regulation 20A, of a person's right to reside in the United Kingdom;"

rather than by reg.2 (see sub-para.(2)). The difference is that the 2006 definition does not include the words, "(but does not include a decision that an application for the above documentation is invalid)" in head (b) or the full-out exclusory words:

"but does not include a decision to refuse to issue a document under regulation 12(4) (issue of an EEA family permit to an extended family member), 17(5) (issue of a registration certificate to an extended family member) or 18(4) (issue of a residence card to an extended family member), a decision to reject an application under regulation 26(4) (misuse of a right to reside: material change of circumstances), or any decisions under regulation 33 (human rights considerations and interim orders to suspend removal) or 41 (temporary admission to submit case in person);"

at the end.

Regulation 44

SCHEDULE 5

TRANSITORY PROVISIONS

[Revoked by reg.46(b) with effect from January 31, 2017]

GENERAL NOTE

See the commentary to reg.44, above. 7.128

Regulation 45

SCHEDULE 6

TRANSITIONAL PROVISIONS

Interpretation

1.—(1) In this Schedule, "permission to be temporarily admitted in order 7.129
to make submissions in person" means—

(a) in relation to the 2006 Regulations, permission to be temporarily admitted under regulation 29AA(2) of the 2006 Regulations;

(b) in relation to these Regulations, permission to be temporarily admitted under regulation 41(2).

(2) References to documents applied for or issued under the 2006 Regulations are to those documents as defined in regulation 2(1) of the 2006 Regulations.

Existing documents

7.130   **2.**—(1) An EEA family permit issued under regulation 12 of the 2006 Regulations before 1st February 2017 is to be treated as an EEA family permit issued under regulation 12 of these Regulations.

(2) Any document issued or treated as though issued under Part 3 of the 2006 Regulations is to be treated as though issued under Part 3 of these Regulations.

(3) Nothing in this paragraph extends the validity of any document issued under the 2006 Regulations beyond that document's original period of validity.

Verification of a right of residence

7.131   **3.** Where, before 1st February 2017, the Secretary of State had invited a person to provide evidence or information or to attend an interview under regulation 20B of the 2006 Regulations (verification of a right of residence), the Secretary of State's invitation is to be treated as though made under regulation 22 of these Regulations.

Outstanding applications

7.132   **4.**—(1) An application for—

(a) an EEA family permit;

(b)–(f) [¹ . . .]; or

(g) permission to be temporarily admitted in order to make submissions in person;

made but not determined before 1st February 2017 is to be treated as having been made under these Regulations.

(2) But regulation 21 and the words in parentheses in paragraph (b) of the definition of an EEA decision in regulation 2(1) are of no application to such an application made before 1st February 2017

Removal decisions, deportation orders and exclusion orders under the 2006 Regulations

7.133   **5.**—(1) A decision to remove a person under regulation 19(3)(a), (b) or (c) of the 2006 Regulations must, upon the coming into force of Part 4 of these Regulations in its entirety, be treated as a decision to remove that person under regulation 23(6) (a), (b) or (c) of these Regulations, as the case may be.

(2) A deportation order made under regulation 24(3) of the 2006 Regulations must be treated as a deportation order made under regulation 32(3) of these Regulations.

(3) Until the coming into force of Part 4 in its entirety, a deportation

order to which sub-paragraph (2) applies has effect until revoked by the Secretary of State.

(4) An exclusion order made under regulation 19(1B) of the 2006 Regulations must, upon the coming into force of Part 4 in its entirety, be treated as though having been made under regulation 23(5) of these Regulations.

(5) A person removed under regulation 19(3)(a) of the 2006 Regulations before 1st February 2017 is to be taken into account for the purposes of regulation 26(2).

(6) Where sub-paragraph (5) applies to a person, regulation 26 has effect as though the references to "12" were to "36".

Certification under regulations 24AA and 29AA of the 2006 Regulations

6.—(1) Where the Secretary of State certified under regulation 24AA   7.134
of the 2006 Regulations (human rights considerations and interim orders to suspend removal) that a person's removal from the United Kingdom would not be unlawful under section 6 of the Human Rights Act 1998 (public authority not to act contrary to the Human Rights Convention), the removal of that person is to be treated as though certified under regulation 33 of these Regulations.

(2) Where sub-paragraph (1) applies, certification treated as though given under regulation 33 does not amount to certification under that regulation for the purposes of paragraph 2(1)(b) of Schedule 2 to these Regulations (appeals to the First tier Tribunal).

(3) Where the Secretary of State granted a person permission to be temporarily admitted to the United Kingdom to make submissions in person under regulation 29AA of the 2006 Regulations, that permission is to be treated as though given under regulation 41 of these Regulations.

(4) A person temporarily admitted to the United Kingdom in order to make submissions in person under regulation 29AA(6) of the 2006 Regulations is to be treated as though having been temporarily admitted under regulation 41(6) of these Regulations.

Appeals to the Commission

7. *Omitted*   7.135

Periods of residence prior to the coming into force of these Regulations

8.—(1) Any period of time during which an EEA national ("P") resided   7.136
in the United Kingdom in accordance with the conditions listed in sub-paragraphs (2) or (3) is to be taken into account for the purpose of calculating periods of residence in the United Kingdom in accordance with these Regulations.

(2) The condition in this paragraph is that P resided in, or was treated as though having resided in, the United Kingdom in accordance with—

(a) the Immigration (European Economic Area) Regulations 2000; or
(b) the 2006 Regulations.

(3) The condition in this paragraph is that P resided in the United Kingdom in circumstances where—

(a) P was a national of a State which at that time was not an EEA State;

(b) P had leave to enter or remain in the United Kingdom under the 1971 Act for the duration of P's residence; and

(c) P would have been residing in the United Kingdom in accordance with these Regulations, had P's State of origin been an EEA State at that time, and had these Regulations been in force.

(4) Any period during which P resided in the United Kingdom in circumstances which met the conditions in sub-paragraph (2) or (3) is not to be taken into account for the purposes of sub-paragraph (1) where that residence was followed by a period of at least two continuous years during which—

(a) P was absent from the United Kingdom; or

(b) P's residence in the United Kingdom—

    (i) did not meet the conditions in sub-paragraph (2) or (3); or

    (ii) was not otherwise in accordance with these Regulations.

Preservation of transitional provisions in relation to family members of dual nationals

7.137

9.—(1) Where—

(a) the right of a family member ("F") to be admitted to, or reside in, the United Kingdom pursuant to these Regulations depends on a person ("P") being an EEA national;

(b) P would be an EEA national if P was not also a British citizen; and

(c) any of the criteria in sub-paragraphs (2), (3) and (4) is met;

P will, notwithstanding the effect of the definition of an EEA national in regulation 2, be regarded as an EEA national for the purpose of these Regulations.

(2) The criterion in this sub-paragraph is met where F was on 16th July 2012 a person with the right of permanent residence in the United Kingdom under the 2006 Regulations.

(3) Subject to sub-paragraph (5), the criterion in this sub-paragraph is met where F—

(a) was on 16th July 2012 a person with a right of residence in the United Kingdom under the 2006 Regulations; and

(b) on 16th October 2012—

    (i) held a valid registration certificate or residence card issued under the 2006 Regulations;

    (ii) had made an application under the 2006 Regulations for a registration certificate or residence card which had not been determined; or

    (iii) had made an application under the 2006 Regulations for a registration certificate or residence card which had been refused and in respect of which an appeal under regulation 26 of the 2006 Regulations could be brought while the appellant was in the United Kingdom (excluding the possibility of an appeal out of time with permission) or was pending (within the meaning of section 104 of the Nationality, Immigration and Asylum Act 2002(5), as it applied on 16th July 2012).

(4) Subject to sub-paragraph (6), the criterion in this sub-paragraph is met where F—

(a) had, prior to 16th July 2012, applied for an EEA family permit pursuant to regulation 12 of the 2006 Regulations; or

(b) had applied for and been refused an EEA family permit and where, on 16th July 2012, an appeal under regulation 26 of the 2006

Regulations against that decision could be brought (excluding the possibility of an appeal out of time with permission) or was pending (within the meaning of section 104 of the Nationality, Immigration and Asylum Act 2002 Act, as it applied on 16th July 2012).

(5) The criterion in sub-paragraph (3) is not met in a case to which sub-paragraph (3)(b)(ii) or (iii) applies where no registration certificate or residence card was, in fact, issued pursuant to that application.

(6) The criterion in sub-paragraph (4) is not met where—

(a) F was issued with an EEA family permit pursuant to an application made prior to 16th July 2012 but F had not been admitted to the United Kingdom within six months of the date on which it was issued; or

(b) no EEA family permit was, in fact, issued pursuant to that application.

(7) Where met, the criteria in sub-paragraphs (2), (3) and (4) remain satisfied until the occurrence of the earliest of the following events—

(a) the date on which F ceases to be the family member of P; or

(b) the date on which F's right of permanent residence is lost.

(8) P will only continue to be regarded as an EEA national for the purpose of considering the position of F under these Regulations.

AMENDMENT

Schedule 6 was revoked by s.1 of, and Sch.1, para.2(2) to, the Immigration and Social Security Co-ordination (EU Withdrawal) Act 2020 with effect from December 31 2020 at 11.00 pm. The text given above is of the Schedule as saved and modified for the purposes of entitlement to benefit and as it relates to those EEA nationals who had a right of residence in the UK under EU law immediately before December 30, 2020 at 11.00 pm, but who have neither settled nor pre-settled status, by regs 3(2), 4(3) and 10(e) of the Citizens' Rights (Application Deadline and Temporary Protection) (EU Exit) Regulations 2020 (SI 2020/1209).

There are no relevant savings provisions for those EEA nationals with pre-settled status.

Square brackets with superscript numbers in the text refer to the Modification section below and not, as elsewhere in this work, to amendments. For the amendments that were made to reg.16 before its revocation see pp.1053-1057 of Vol.V of the 2020/21 edition.

MODIFICATION

1. SI 2020/1209 regs 3(2), 4(3) and 10(e).

DEFINITIONS

"the 1971 Act"—see reg.2(1).
"the 2006 Regulations"—*ibid.*
"derivative residence card"—see regs 2(1) and 20.
"deportation order"—see reg.2(1).
"document certifying permanent residence"—see regs 2(1) and 19(1).
"EEA decision"—see reg. 2(1).
"EEA family permit"—see regs 2(1) and 12.
"EEA national"—see reg.2(1).
"EEA State"—*ibid.*
"exclusion order"—*ibid.*
"family member"—see reg.7.
"permanent residence card"—see regs 2(1) and 19(2).
"registration certificate"—see regs 2(1) and (17).
"residence card"—see regs 2(1) and 18.

SCHEDULE 7

CONSEQUENTIAL MODIFICATIONS

7.138   **1.**—(1) Unless the context otherwise requires—
  (a) any reference in any enactment to the 2006 Regulations, or a provision of the 2006 Regulations, has effect as though referring to these Regulations, or the corresponding provision of these Regulations, as the case may be;
  (b) but—
    (i) any reference to a provision of the 2006 Regulations in column 1 of the table has effect as though it were a reference to the corresponding provision of these Regulations listed in column 2; and
    (ii) any reference to a provision of the 2006 Regulations with no corresponding provision in these Regulations ceases to have effect.

(2) Unless otherwise specified in the table, sub-divisions of the provisions of the 2006 Regulations listed in column 1 correspond to the equivalent sub-division in the corresponding provision of these Regulations.

(3) This paragraph is of no application where the reference to the 2006 Regulations had the effect of amending the 2006 Regulations. Additionally this paragraph has no application to amendments to the 2006 Regulations made under Schedule 5 of these Regulations.

TABLE OF EQUIVALENCES

7.139

(1)	*(2)*	*(3)*
Provision in the 2006 Regulations	*Corresponding provision in these Regulations*	*Description of provision*
1	1(1) to (2)	Citation and commencement
2(3)	2(2)	General interpretation
3(3)	3(3)(c)	Continuity of residence
4(2)	4(2) and (3)	"Worker", "self-employed person", "self-sufficient person" and "student"
4(4)	4(2) and (4)	
6(2)(ba)	6(2)(c)	"Qualified person"
6(2)(c)	6(2)(d)	
6(2)(d)	6(2)(e)	
6(2A)	6(3)	
6(3)	6(4)	
6(4) and 6(8)	Relevant definitions in 6(1)	
6(9)	6(8)	
6(10)	6(9)	
6(11)	6(10)	

(1)	(2)	(3)
Provision in the 2006 Regulations	*Corresponding provision in these Regulations*	*Description of provision*
8(2)	8(2) and (7)	Extended family member
8(3)	8(3) and (7)	
9(1)	9(1) and (7)	Family members of British citizens
9(3)(a) to (c)	9(3)(a) to (e)	
9(4)	9(5)	
11(4)(ba)	11(4)(c)	Right of admission to the United Kingdom
11(4)(c)	11(4)(d)	
12(1A)	12(2)	Issue of EEA family permit
12(1B)	12(3)(a)	
12(2)	12(4)	
12(3)	12(5)	
12(4)	12(6)	
12(5)	12(7)	
12(6)	12(8)	
14(5)	14(4)	Extended right of residence
15(1A)	15(2)	Right of permanent residence
15(2)	15(3)	
15(3)	15(4)	
15A	16	Derivative right to reside
15A(1)	16(1)	
15A(2)	16(2)	
15A(3)	16(3)	
15A(4)	16(4)	
15A(4A)	16(5)	
15A(5)	16(6)	
15A(6)	16(7)	
15A(7)	16(8)	
15A(7A)	16(9)	
15A(7B)	16(10)	
15A(8)	16(11)	
15A(9)	16(12)	
16	17	Issue of registration certificate
16(8)	17(9)	
17	18	Issue of residence card
17(6A)	18(7)	
18	19	Issue of a document certifying permanent residence and a permanent residence card
18(5)	19(4)(b)	
18(6)	19(5)	

(1)	(2)	(3)
Provision in the 2006 Regulations	*Corresponding provision in these Regulations*	*Description of provision*
18A	20	Issue of a derivative residence card
18A(5)	20(6)	
19	23	Exclusion and removal from the United Kingdom
19(1A)	23(2)	
19(1AB)	23(3)	
19(1B)	23(5)	
19(2)	23(4)	
19(3)	23(6)	
19(4)	23(7)(a)	
19(5)	23(7)(b)	
20	24	Refusal to issue or renew and revocation of residence documentation
20(1A)	24(2)	
20(2)	24(3)	
20(3)	24(4)	
20(4)	24(5)	
20(5)	24(6)	
20(6)	24(7)	
20A	25	Cancellation of a right of residence
20B	22	Verification of a right of residence
20B(8)	Relevant definition in 2(1)	
21	27	Decisions taken on public policy, public security and public health grounds
21(5)	27(5) and (8) and Schedule 1	
21A	28	Application of Part 4 to persons with a derivative right to reside
21A(1)	28(2)	
21A(2)	28(1)	
21A(3)(c)	28(2)(a)	
21A(3)(d)	28(2)(b)	
21A(3)(f)	28(2)(c)	
21A(3)(g)	28(2)(d)	
21B	26	Misuse of a right to reside
21B(1)	26(1) and (2)	
21B(2)	26(3)	
21B(3)	26(4)	
21B(4)	26(5)	
21B(5)	26(6)	
21B(6)	Relevant definition in 2(1)	

(1)	*(2)*	*(3)*
Provision in the 2006 Regulations	*Corresponding provision in these Regulations*	*Description of provision*
22	29	Person claiming right of admission
23	30	Person refused admission
23A	31	Revocation of admission
24	32	Person subject to removal
24A	34	Revocation of deportation and exclusion orders
24A(1)	34(1) and (2)	
24A(2)	34(3)	
24A(3)	34(4)	
24A(4)	34(5)	
24A(5)	34(6)	
24AA	33	Human rights considerations and interim orders to suspend removal
25	35	Interpretation of Part 6
26	36	Appeal rights
26(2A)	36(3)	
26(3)	36(4)	
26(3A)	36(5)	
26(4)	36(8)	
26(5)	36(7)	
26(6)	36(9)	
26(7)	36(10)	
26(8)	36(11)	
27	37	Out of country appeals
27(1)(zaa)	37(1)(b)	
27(1)(aa)	37(1)(c)	
27(1)(b)	37(1)(d)	
27(1)(c)	37(1)(e)	
27(1)(ca)	37(1)(f)	
27(1)(d)	37(1)(g)	
28	38	Appeals to the Commission
28(8)	38(8) and (9)	
28A	39	National security: EEA Decisions
29	40	Effect of appeals to the First-tier Tribunal or Upper Tribunal
29(4A)	40(5)	
29(5)	40(6)	
29A	42	Alternative evidence of identity and nationality
29AA	41	Temporary admission in order to submit case in person

(1)	(2)	(3)
Provision in the 2006 Regulations	*Corresponding provision in these Regulations*	*Description of provision*
30	43	Effect on other legislation
31	45 and 46	Revocations etc.
Schedule 1	Schedule 2	Appeals to the First-tier Tribunal
Schedule 1, paragraph 1	Schedule 2, paragraph 2	
Schedule 1, paragraph 2	Schedule 2, paragraph 3	
Schedule 2	Schedule 3	Effect on other legislation
Schedule 2, paragraph 1(2)	Schedule 3, paragraph 1	
Schedule 2, paragraph 3	Schedule 3, paragraph 3	
Schedule 2, paragraph 4	Schedule 2, paragraph 2	

AMENDMENT

Schedule 7 was revoked by s.1 of, and Sch.1, para.2(2) to, the Immigration and Social Security Co-ordination (EU Withdrawal) Act 2020 with effect from December 31 2020 at 11.00 pm. The text given above is of Pt. 2 of the Schedule as saved for the purposes of entitlement to benefit and as it relates to those EEA nationals who had a right of residence in the UK under EU law immediately before December 30, 2020 at 11.00 pm, but who have neither settled nor pre-settled status, by regs 3(2), 4(3) and 10(f) of the Citizens' Rights (Application Deadline and Temporary Protection) (EU Exit) Regulations 2020 (SI 2020/1209).

There are no relevant savings provisions for those EEA nationals with pre-settled status.

DEFINITION

"the 2006 Regulations"—see reg.2(1).

SCHEDULE

CONSEQUENTIAL AMENDMENTS

[Omitted.]

SI 2021/1209

The Citizens' Rights (Application Deadline and Temporary Protection) (EU Exit) Regulations 2020

IN FORCE DECEMBER 31, 2020 AT 11.00 PM

REGULATIONS REPRODUCED

PART 1

PRELIMINARY

1. Citation, commencement and interpretation   **7.140**

PART 2

DEADLINE FOR APPLICATIONS

2. Deadline for applications

PART 3

SAVING OF THE EEA REGULATIONS 2016 ETC. DURING THE GRACE PERIOD AND
WHILST APPLICATIONS ARE FINALLY DETERMINED

3. Grace period
4. Applications which have not been finally determined by the application deadline
5-6. [*Noted in the text of the 2016 Regulations where relevant*]
7-9. [*Omitted*]
10. [*Noted in the text of the 2016 Regulations where relevant*]
11. Entitlement to benefits and public services
12. Modification of other enactments
13. Evidencing status

The Secretary of State makes the following Regulations in exercise of the powers conferred by section 7(1) and (4) of, and paragraph 12 of Schedule 4 to, the European Union (Withdrawal Agreement) Act 2020.

These are the first regulations to be made under paragraphs (b), (c), (d), (e), (f) and (g) of section 7(1) of that Act. In accordance with paragraph 1(1) of Schedule 4 to that Act, a draft of these Regulations was laid before and approved by a resolution of each House of Parliament.

GENERAL NOTE

See the commentary to the modified Immigration (European Economic Area)   **7.141**
Regulations 2016 (above) and to s.115 of the Immigration and Asylum Act 1999 and the Social Security (Immigration and Asylum) Consequential Amendments Regulations 2000 in Vol.II.

PART 1

PRELIMINARY

Citation, commencement and interpretation

7.142   1.—(1) These Regulations may be cited as the Citizens' Rights (Application Deadline and Temporary Protection) (EU Exit) Regulations 2020 and come into force on IP completion day.

(2) In these Regulations—

"the EEA Regulations 2016" mean the Immigration (European Economic Area) Regulations 2016;

"application deadline" has the meaning given in regulation 2.

PART 2

DEADLINE FOR APPLICATIONS

Deadline for applications

7.143   2. The end of 30 June 2021 is the deadline for submission of an application for residence status ("application deadline") that applies for the purposes of the following provisions—

(a) the first sub-paragraph of Article 18(1)(b) of the withdrawal agreement;

(b) the first sub-paragraph of Article 17(1)(b) of the EEA EFTA separation agreement, and

(c) the first sentence of Article 16(1)(b) of the Swiss citizens' rights agreement.

GENERAL NOTE

7.143.1   On August 6, 2021, the government made the following announcement relating to those EEA nationals who failed to meet the 30 June 2021 imposed by reg.2 for applying under EUSS:

> "The Home Office has put in place comprehensive arrangements to enable those with reasonable grounds for missing the deadline to apply to the EUSS.

> While the numbers applying late have been small compared to pre-deadline application numbers, to provide further reassurance to late applicants the government will protect their rights until their application and any appeal is decided.

> The government will also take a similar approach with joining family members, who will have temporary protection for three months after their arrival in the UK and pending the outcome of an EUSS application made during that period (and of any appeal)": see https://www.gov.uk/government/news/temporary-protection-for-more-applicants-to-the-settlement-scheme.

It is not absolutely clear whether the reassurance is intended to extend to all late applicants or only those "with reasonable grounds for missing the deadline", although, the tenor of the announcement suggests the former. Whichever represents the policy intention, further legislation will be needed to implement it but, at the time of going to press, none has been introduced.

PART 3

SAVING OF THE EEA REGULATIONS 2016 ETC. DURING THE GRACE PERIOD AND WHILST APPLICATIONS ARE FINALLY DETERMINED

Grace period

3.—(1) This regulation has effect if the EEA Regulations 2016 are revoked on IP completion day (with or without savings). 7.144

(2) The provisions of the EEA Regulations 2016 specified in regulations 5 to 10 continue to have effect (despite the revocation of those Regulations) with the modifications specified in those regulations in relation to a relevant person during the grace period.

(3) The provisions specified in regulation 11 apply in relation to a relevant person during the grace period as if any reference to the EEA Regulations 2016 or any provision of those Regulations are to the Regulations or provision of the Regulations as continued in effect and modified by regulations 5 to 10.

(4) The enactments specified in regulation 12 apply in relation to a relevant person during the grace period with the modifications specified in that regulation.

(5) For the purposes of this regulation—

(a) the grace period is the period beginning immediately after IP completion day and ending with the application deadline;

(b) a person is to be treated as residing in the United Kingdom at any time which would be taken into account for the purposes of calculating periods when the person was continuously resident for the purposes of the EEA Regulations 2016 (see regulation 3);

(c) a person who does not have the right to reside in the United Kingdom permanently is to be treated as having such a right if the person had a right of permanent residence in the United Kingdom under those Regulations (see regulation 15) and who, immediately before IP completion day, has been absent from the United Kingdom for a continuous period of 5 years or less (disregarding any period of absence before the person acquired the right of permanent residence).

(6) In this regulation—

"EEA document" means—

(a) an EEA family permit issued under regulation 12 of the EEA Regulations 2016;

(b) a registration certificate issued under regulation 17 of those Regulations, or (c) a residence card issued under regulation 18 of those Regulations;

"family member"—

(a) has the same meaning as in paragraph (1) of regulation 7 of the EEA Regulations 2016 (read with paragraph (2) of that regulation) as those Regulations had effect immediately before IP completion day, and

(b) includes an extended family member within the meaning of regulation 8 of those Regulations as they had effect immediately before IP completion day if that person—

(i) immediately before IP completion day satisfied the condition in regulation 8(5) of those Regulations (durable partner), or

(ii) holds a valid EEA document (regardless of whether that document was issued before or after IP completion day);

"relevant family member", in relation to a person ("P"), means a family member who—

(a) was a family member of P immediately before IP completion day;
(b) is P's child and—
   (i) the child's other parent is a relevant person or has leave to enter or remain in the United Kingdom by virtue of residence scheme immigration rules(1);
   (ii) the child's other parent is a British citizen;
   (iii) P has sole or joint rights of custody of the child in the circumstances set out in the last point of Article 10(1)(e)(iii) of the withdrawal agreement or the last point of Article 9(1)(e)(iii) of the EEA EFTA separation agreement, or
   (iv) P falls within Article 10(1)(e)(iii) of the Swiss citizens' rights agreement (children of beneficiaries of that agreement);
(c) becomes a family member of P after IP completion day by virtue of being issued with an EEA document (see paragraph (b)(ii) of the definition of "family member"), or
(d) is the spouse or civil partner of P and P is a national of Switzerland;
"relevant person" means a person who does not have (and who has not, during the grace period, had) leave to enter or remain in the United Kingdom by virtue of residence scheme immigration rules and who—
(a) immediately before IP completion day—
   (i) was lawfully resident in the United Kingdom by virtue of the EEA Regulations 2016, or
   (ii) had a right of permanent residence in the United Kingdom under those Regulations (see regulation 15), or
(b) is not a person who falls within sub-paragraph (a) but is a relevant family member of a person who immediately before IP completion day—
   (aa) was lawfully resident in the United Kingdom by virtue of the EEA Regulations 2016, or
   (bb) had a right of permanent residence in the United Kingdom under those Regulations (see regulation 15).

Applications which have not been finally determined by the application deadline

7.145   4.—(1) This regulation has effect if the EEA Regulations 2016 are revoked on IP completion day (with or without savings).
(2) This regulation applies to a person ("the applicant") who—
(a) has made an in-time application (see paragraph (6)), and
(b) immediately before IP completion day—
   (i) was lawfully resident in the United Kingdom by virtue of the EEA Regulations 2016, or
   (ii) had a right of permanent residence in the United Kingdom under those Regulations (see regulation 15).
(3) The provisions of the EEA Regulations 2016 specified in regulations 5 to 10 continue to have effect (despite the revocation of those Regulations) with the modifications specified in those regulations in relation to the applicant during the relevant period.
(4) The provisions specified in regulation 11 apply in relation to the applicant during the relevant period as if any reference to the EEA Regulations 2016 or any provision of those Regulations are to the Regulations or provision of the Regulations as continued in effect and modified by regulations 5 to 10.

(5) The enactments specified in regulation 12 apply in relation to the applicant during the relevant period with the modifications specified in that regulation.

(6) For the purposes of this regulation—

(a) an in-time application is an application for leave to enter or remain in the United Kingdom by virtue of residence scheme immigration rules which—

    (i) is valid under residence scheme immigration rules;

    (ii) is made on or before the application deadline, and

    (iii) has not been withdrawn;

(b) the relevant period begins immediately after the application deadline and ends—

    (i) if the applicant is, by virtue of the in-time application, granted leave to enter or remain in the United Kingdom, on the day on which that leave is granted;

    (ii) if a decision is taken not to grant any leave to enter or remain in the United Kingdom in response to the applicant's application and the applicant does not appeal against that decision, on the first day on which the applicant is no longer entitled to appeal against that decision (ignoring any possibility of an appeal out of time with permission);

    (iii) if a decision is taken not to grant any leave to enter or remain in the United Kingdom in response to the applicant's application and the applicant brings an appeal against that decision, on the day on which that appeal is finally determined, withdrawn or abandoned, or lapses under paragraph 3 of Schedule 1 to the Immigration (Citizens' Rights Appeals) (EU Exit) Regulations 2020;

(c) a person is to be treated as residing in the United Kingdom at any time which would be taken into account for the purposes of calculating periods when the person was continuously resident for the purposes of the EEA Regulations 2016 (see regulation 3);

(d) a person who does not have the right to reside in the United Kingdom permanently is to be treated as having such a right if the person had a right of permanent residence in the United Kingdom under those Regulations (see regulation 15) and who, immediately before IP completion day, has been absent from the United Kingdom for a continuous period of 5 years or less (disregarding any period of absence before the person acquired the right of permanent residence).

(7) For the purposes of paragraph (6)(b)(iii)—

(a) an appeal is not finally determined while (as the case may be)—

    (i) an application for permission to appeal under section 11 or 13 of the Tribunals, Courts and Enforcement Act 2007 could be made or is awaiting determination;

    (ii) permission to appeal under either of those sections has been granted and the appeal is awaiting determination;

    (iii) an appeal has been remitted under section 12 or 14 of that Act and is awaiting determination;

    (iv) any of the following applications could be made—

        (aa) an application for leave to appeal under section 7 of the applied 1997 Act;

> > (bb) an application for a certificate under section 7B of the applied 1997 Act;
> >
> > (cc) an application for permission to appeal under section 7C of the applied 1997 Act, or
> >
> > (v) leave to appeal under section 7, or permission to appeal under section 7C, of the applied 1997 Act has been granted and the appeal is awaiting determination;
>
> (b) an appeal is to be treated as abandoned if the appellant is granted leave to enter or remain in the United Kingdom by virtue of residence scheme immigration rules;
>
> (c) an appeal is not to be treated as abandoned solely because the appellant leaves the United Kingdom.

(8) For the purposes of paragraph (7), "the applied 1997 Act" means the Special Immigration Appeals Commission Act 1997 as it applies for the purposes of the Immigration (Citizens' Rights Appeals) (EU Exit) Regulations 2020 by virtue of Part 2 of Schedule 1 to those Regulations.

Provisions relating to definitions etc.

7.146   5. [*Noted in the text of the 2016 Regulations where relevant*]

Provisions relating to residence rights

7.147   6. [*Noted in the text of the 2016 Regulations where relevant*]

Provisions relating to powers of refusal of admission and removal etc.

7.148   7. [*Omitted*]

Provisions relating to procedures in relation to EEA decisions

7.149   8. [*Omitted*]

Provisions relating to appeals

7.150   9. [*Omitted*]

Miscellaneous provisions

7.151   10. [*Noted in the text of the 2016 Regulations where relevant*]

Entitlement to benefits and public services

7.152   11. The provisions specified in this regulation are—

(a) regulation 21AA (special cases: supplemental – persons from abroad) of the Income Support (General) Regulations 1987;

(b) [*Omitted*]

(c) regulation 85A (special cases: supplemental – persons from abroad) of the Jobseeker's Allowance Regulations 1996;

(d) [*Omitted*]

(e) regulation 2 (persons not in Great Britain) of the State Pension Credit Regulations 2002;

(f) regulation 3 (circumstances in which a person is treated as not being in the United Kingdom) of the Tax Credits (Residence) Regulations 2003;

(g) [*Omitted*]
[¹ (ga) regulation 7 (funeral payments: entitlement) of the Social Fund Maternity and Funeral Expenses (General) Regulations 2005;]
(gb)-(n) [*Omitted*]
   (o) regulation 70 (special cases: supplemental – persons from abroad) of the Employment and Support Allowance Regulations 2008;
   (p) [*Omitted*]
(q)-(s) [*Omitted*]
(t)   regulations 2 (interpretation) and 9 (persons treated as not being in Great Britain) of the Universal Credit Regulations 2013;
(u)-(y) [*Omitted*]

AMENDMENT

1.   Immigration and Social Security Co-ordination (EU Withdrawal) Act 2020 (Consequential, Saving, Transitional and Transitory Provisions) (EU Exit) Regulations 2020 (SI 2020/1309) reg.49 (December 31, 2020 at 11.00 pm)

Modification of other enactments

12.—(1) The following enactments with the modifications set out below are specified for the purposes of regulations 3 and 4—   7.153
(a)-(f) [Omitted]
   (g) section 7(1) of the Immigration Act 1988 (persons exercising Community rights and nationals of member States)(c), as it had effect immediately before IP completion day, with the modification that "of an enforceable EU right or" were omitted;
   (h) section 10 of the Immigration and Asylum Act 1999 (removal of persons unlawfully in the United Kingdom), as it had effect immediately before IP completion day, with the modification that in subsection (5) "of an enforceable EU right or" were omitted;
   (i) section 115 of that Act (exclusion from benefits), as it had effect immediately before IP completion day;
(j)-(p) [*Omitted*]
   (q) Part 2 of the Schedule to the Social Security (Immigration and Asylum) Consequential Amendments Regulations 2000 (persons not excluded from certain benefits under section 115 of the Immigration and Asylum Act 1999), as it had effect immediately before IP completion day;
(r)-(w) [*Omitted*]
(2)   Any reference in another enactment to a person who, under the Immigration Act 1971, requires leave to enter or remain in the United Kingdom (including section 13 of the Asylum and Immigration Act 1996) is to be read in light of paragraph (1)(g) above (application with modification of section 7 of the Immigration Act 1988).

Evidencing status

13. Where any question arises as to whether a person is or was lawfully resident in the United Kingdom at a particular point in time by virtue of the EEA Regulations 2016 (including as continued in effect and modified by these Regulations) for the purposes of these Regulations, it is for the individual in question to prove that they were.   7.154

2020 No. 1309

The Immigration and Social Security Co-ordination (EU Withdrawal) Act 2020 (Consequential, Saving, Transitional and Transitory Provisions) (EU Exit) Regulations 2020

REGULATIONS REPRODUCED

PART 1

INTRODUCTION

PART 2

IMMIGRATION

[*Omitted*]

PART 3

ACCESS TO BENEFITS AND SERVICES

[*Amendments noted in the text of the amended regulations*]

PART 4

NATIONALITY

[*Omitted*]

PART 5

SAVING PROVISION IN CONNECTION WITH THE EC ASSOCIATION AGREEMENT WITH TURKEY

[*Omitted*]

PART 6

SAVING PROVISION IN CONNECTION WITH THE IMMIGRATION (EUROPEAN ECONOMIC AREA) REGULATIONS

PART 8

TRANSITIONAL AND FURTHER SAVING PROVISION

[*Omitted*]

SCHEDULES

SCHEDULES 1 AND 2—[*Omitted*]

SCHEDULE 3—SAVING PROVISION IN CONNECTION WITH THE IMMIGRATION
(EUROPEAN ECONOMIC AREA) REGULATIONS 2016

SCHEDULE 4—SAVING PROVISION IN RELATION TO ACCESS TO BENEFITS
AND SERVICES

SCHEDULE 5—[*Omitted*]

IN FORCE DECEMBER 31, 2020 AT 11.00 PM.

The Secretary of State makes the following Regulations in exercise of
the power conferred by sections 5 and 8(5) of the Immigration and Social
Security Co-ordination (EU Withdrawal) Act 2020.

PART 1

INTRODUCTION

Citation, commencement and extent

1.—(1) These Regulations may be cited as the Immigration and Social   7.155
Security Co-ordination (EU Withdrawal) Act 2020 (Consequential, Saving,
Transitional and Transitory Provisions) (EU Exit) Regulations 2020.

(2) These Regulations come into force at the time and on the date when
paragraph 2(2) of, and Schedule 1 to, the 2020 Act comes into force for all
purposes except for—

- (a) regulations 47, 48 and 49 which come into force immediately before
  that time and date;
- (b) regulation 20(7) and (8) which come into force on 1st December
  2020;
- (c) regulations 3, 7, 12(3) and (4),14,15(3), 16, 20(5) and (6), 31, 36,
  37 and 40 to 44 which come into force on 1st July 2021.

(3) Any provision of these Regulations which amends, repeals or revokes
an enactment has the same extent as the enactment amended, repealed or
revoked (ignoring extent by virtue of an Order in Council under any of the
Immigration Acts).

(4) Any saving, transitional or transitory provision in these Regulations
has the same extent within the United Kingdom as the provision to which
it relates.

Interpretation – General

7.156   2. In these Regulations—
"the 2020 Act" means the Immigration and Social Security Co-ordination
(EU Withdrawal) Act 2020;
"commencement day" means the time at and date on which the
Immigration (European Economic Area) Regulations 2016 are revoked for
all purposes.

PART 2

IMMIGRATION

7.157   [*Omitted*]

PART 3

ACCESS TO BENEFITS AND SERVICES

7.158   [*Amendments noted in the text of the amended regulations*]

PART 4

NATIONALITY

7.159   [*Omitted*]

PART 5

SAVING PROVISION IN CONNECTION WITH THE EC ASSOCIATION
AGREEMENT WITH TURKEY

7.160   [*Omitted*]

PART 6

SAVING PROVISION IN CONNECTION WITH THE IMMIGRATION (EUROPEAN
ECONOMIC AREA) REGULATIONS

**Saving provision in connection with the Immigration (European
Economic Area) Regulations 2016**

7.161   82.   Schedule 3 has effect.

PART 7

SAVING PROVISION IN CONNECTION WITH THE IMMIGRATION ACCESS TO
BENEFITS AND SERVICES

Saving provision in connection with access to benefits and services

7.162   83. Schedule 4 has effect.

PART 8

TRANSITIONAL AND FURTHER SAVING PROVISION

[*Omitted*]   **7.163**

SCHEDULES

SCHEDULES 1 AND 2

[*Omitted*]   **7.164**

REGULATION 82

SCHEDULE 3

SAVING PROVISION IN CONNECTION WITH THE IMMIGRATION (EUROPEAN
ECONOMIC AREA) REGULATIONS 2016

1. In this Schedule "EEA Regulations 2016" means the Immigration (European   **7.165**
Economic Area) Regulations 2016 and, unless provided otherwise, refers to those
Regulations as they had effect immediately before they were revoked.

Deportation and exclusion orders
2.—(1) Any deportation order made or treated as having been made by virtue of   **7.166**
the EEA Regulations 2016 continues to apply for the period specified in the order
or until revoked.

(2) Any deportation order made by virtue of the EEA Regulations 2016 as they
are continued in effect by the Citizens' Rights (Application Deadline and Temporary
Protection) (EU Exit) Regulations 2020 continues to apply for the period specified
in the order or until revoked.

(3) Any exclusion order made or treated as having been made by virtue of the
EEA Regulations 2016 continues to apply for the period specified in the order or
until revoked.

(4) Any exclusion order made by virtue of the EEA Regulations 2016 as they are
continued in effect by the Citizens' Rights (Application Deadline and Temporary
Protection) (EU Exit) Regulations 2020 continues to apply for the period specified
in the order or until revoked.

(5) Regulation 34(3) to (6) of the EEA Regulations 2016 (revocation of deportation and exclusion orders) continue to apply—

   (a) in respect of any deportation order or exclusion order within sub-paragraph
      (1) or (3) with the modification that in paragraph (3), after "deportation or
      exclusion order" there were inserted "made on the grounds of public policy,
      public security or public health in accordance with regulation 27";

   (b) in respect of any deportation order or exclusion order within sub-paragraph
      (2) or (4) with the modifications that—

      (i) in paragraph (3), after "deportation or exclusion order" there were
         inserted "made on the grounds of public policy, public security or
         public health in accordance with regulation 27";

      (ii) after paragraph (6) there were inserted—

"(7) An application for revocation of a deportation order made on conducive
grounds in accordance with regulation 27A is to be considered in accordance with
the immigration rules that apply in relation to an application for revocation of a
deportation order made by virtue of section 3 of the Immigration Act 1971.".

(6) This paragraph does not apply to the extent that the provisions specified in paragraph (5) continue to apply to a deportation or exclusion order by virtue of the Citizens' Rights (Application Deadline and Temporary Protection) (EU Exit) Regulations 2020.

Pending applications for documentation under the EEA Regulations 2016

7.167 3.—(1) Regulation 12 of the EEA Regulations 2016 (issue of EEA family permit), continues to apply for the purposes of considering and, where appropriate, granting an application for a family permit which was validly made in accordance with the EEA Regulations 2016 before commencement day.

(2) Regulation 12 of the EEA Regulations 2016 also continues to apply for the purposes of considering and, where appropriate, granting an application for a family permit which was validly made after commencement day in accordance with the EEA Regulations 2016 as they are continued in effect by the Citizens' Rights (Application Deadline and Temporary Protection) (EU Exit) Regulations 2020.

(3) Regulation 17 of the EEA Regulations 2016 (issue of registration certificate), continues to apply for the purposes of considering and, where appropriate, granting an application for a registration certificate which was validly made in accordance with the EEA Regulations 2016 before commencement day.

(4) Regulation 18 of the EEA Regulations 2016 (issue of residence card), continues to apply for the purposes of considering and, where appropriate, granting an application for a residence card which was validly made in accordance with the EEA Regulations 2016 before commencement day.

(5) Regulation 19 of the EEA Regulations 2016 (issue of a document certifying permanent residence and a permanent residence card), continues to apply for the purposes of considering and, where appropriate, granting an application for a document certifying permanent residence or a permanent residence card, which was validly made in accordance with the EEA Regulations 2016 before commencement day.

(6) Regulation 20 of the EEA Regulations 2016 (issue of a derivative residence card), continues to apply for the purposes of considering and, where appropriate, granting an application for a derivative residence card which was validly made in accordance with the EEA Regulations 2016 before commencement day.

Application of EEA Regulations 2016 to pending applications

7.168 4.—(1) Subject to sub-paragraph (2) the provisions of the EEA Regulations 2016 specified in paragraph 6 continue to apply (despite the revocation of those Regulations) with the modifications specified for the purposes of determining whether an application referred to in paragraph 3 should be granted.

(2) The provisions specified in paragraph 6 do not apply to the extent that the provisions of the EEA Regulations 2016 specified in that paragraph continue to apply to an application within paragraph 3(2) by virtue of the Citizens' Rights (Application Deadline and Temporary Protection) (EU Exit) Regulations 2020.

Existing appeal rights and appeals

7.169 5.—(1) Subject to sub-paragraph (4), the provisions of the EEA Regulations 2016 specified in paragraph 6 continue to apply—

    (a) to any appeal which has been brought under the Immigration (European Economic Area) Regulations 2006 and has not been finally determined before commencement day,

    (b) to any appeal which has been brought under the EEA Regulations 2016 and has not been finally determined before commencement day,

    (c) in respect of an EEA decision, within the meaning of the EEA Regulations 2016, taken before commencement day, or

    (d) in respect of an EEA decision, within the meaning of the EEA Regulations

2016 as they continue in effect by virtue of these Regulations or the Citizens' Rights (Application Deadline and Temporary Protection) (EU Exit) Regulations 2020, which is taken on or after commencement day.

(2)   For the purposes of paragraph (1)—

(a) an appeal is not to be treated as finally determined while a further appeal may be brought and, if such a further appeal is brought, the original appeal is not to be treated as finally determined until the further appeal is determined, withdrawn or abandoned; and

(b) an appeal is not to be treated as abandoned solely because the appellant leaves the United Kingdom.

(3) The revocation of the EEA Regulations 2016 does not affect the application of the Immigration (European Economic Area) Regulations 2006 to an appeal that falls within paragraph 3(1) of Schedule 4 to the EEA Regulations 2016.

(4) The provisions specified in paragraph 6 do not apply to the extent that the provisions of the EEA Regulations 2016 specified in paragraph 6 continue to apply to an appeal or EEA decision by virtue of the Citizens' Rights (Application Deadline and Temporary Protection) (EU Exit) Regulations 2020.

Specified provisions of the EEA Regulations 2016

6.—(1) The specified provisions of the EEA Regulations 2016 are—   7.170

(a) regulation 2 (general interpretation) with the following modifications—

(i) as if all instances of the words "or any other right conferred by the EU Treaties"—

(aa) in so far as they relate to things done on or after exit day but before commencement day, were a reference to a right conferred by the EU Treaties so far as they were applicable to and in the United Kingdom by virtue of Part 4 of the EU withdrawal agreement;

(bb) in so far as they relate to things done on or after commencement day, were omitted;

(ii) as if all instances of the words "or the EU Treaties"—

(aa) in so far as they relate to things done on or after exit day but before commencement day, were a reference to the EU Treaties so far as they were applicable to and in the United Kingdom by virtue of Part 4 of the EU withdrawal agreement;

(bb) in so far as they relate to things done on or after commencement day, were omitted;

(iii) as if, at the end of the definition of "deportation order", there were inserted "or under section 5(1) of the Immigration Act 1971";

(iv) as if, in the definition of "EEA State", the words ", other than the United Kingdom" were omitted; and

(v) as if, at the end of the definition of "exclusion order", there were inserted "or directions issued by the Secretary of State for a person not to be given entry to the United Kingdom on the grounds that the person's exclusion is conducive to the public good";

(b) regulation 3 (continuity of residence) with the modification that, at the end of paragraph (3)(c), there were inserted "or the Immigration Acts";

(c) regulation 4 ("worker", "self-employed person", "self-sufficient person" and "student") with the modification that, in paragraph (1)(b), for "in accordance with" there were substituted "within the meaning of";

(d) regulation 5 ("worker or self-employed person who has ceased activity");

(e) regulation 6 ("qualified person") with the following modifications—

(i) in paragraph (4C), "and having a genuine chance of being engaged" were omitted;

   (ii) in paragraph (6), after "employment and" there were inserted ", when determining whether the person is a jobseeker,";

   (iii) in paragraph (7), after "continuing to seek employment and" there were inserted ", where that person is a jobseeker";

 (f) regulation 7 ("family member");

 (g) regulation 8 ("extended family member");

 (h) regulation 9 (family members and extended family members of British citizens) with the following modifications—

   (i) in paragraph (1), at the end there were inserted "and BC is to be treated as satisfying any requirement to be a qualified person";

   (ii) sub-paragraph (a) of paragraph (3) were omitted;

   (iii) paragraph (7) were omitted;

 (i) regulation 9A (dual national: national of an EEA State who acquires British citizenship);

 (j) regulation 10 ("family member who has retained the right of residence") with the following modifications—

   (i) in paragraph (2)(b), in so far as it applies to residence in the United Kingdom after commencement day, for "in accordance with these Regulations" there were substituted "lawfully";

   (ii) in paragraph (5)(a), "the initiation of proceedings for" were omitted;

 (k) regulation 11 (right of admission to the United Kingdom);

 (l) regulation 21 (procedure for applications for documentation under this Part and regulation 12);

 (m) regulation 22 (verification of a right of residence);

(n)-(bb) [*Omitted*]

Nationality, Immigration and Asylum Act 2016 - saving in relation to appeals

7.171 7. [*Omitted*]

Regulation 83

SCHEDULE 4

SAVING PROVISION IN RELATION TO ACCESS TO BENEFITS AND SERVICES

7.172 1. In this Schedule—

 (a) "EEA Regulations 2016" means the Immigration (European Economic Area) Regulations 2016(128) as they had effect immediately before they were revoked;

 (b) "member of the post-transition period group" means a person who has limited leave to enter, or remain in, the United Kingdom granted by virtue of residence scheme immigration rules within the meaning given by section 17 of the European Union (Withdrawal Agreement) Act 2020.

 2. For the purposes of the provisions specified in paragraph 3 the provisions of the EEA Regulations 2016 specified in paragraph 4 continue to have effect in relation to a person who is a member of the post-transition period group, with the specified modifications, despite the revocation of those Regulations by the 2020 Act.

 3. The provisions specified in this paragraph are—

 (a) regulation 21AA (special cases: supplemental–persons from abroad) of the Income Support (General) Regulations 1987;

 (b) [*Omitted*]

(c) regulation 85A (special cases: supplemental–persons from abroad) of the Jobseeker's Allowance Regulations 1996;
(d) [*Omitted*]
(e) [*Omitted*]
(f) regulation 2 (persons not in Great Britain) of the State Pension Credit Regulations 2002;
(g) [*Omitted*]
(h) regulation 3 (circumstances in which a person is treated as not being in the United Kingdom) of the Tax Credits (Residence) Regulations 2003;
(i) regulation 7 (funeral payments: entitlement) of the Social Fund Maternity and Funeral Expenses (General) Regulations 2005;
(j)-(n) [*Omitted*]
(o) regulations 23 (circumstances in which person treated as not being in Great Britain) and 27 (circumstances in which person treated as not being in Northern Ireland) of the Child Benefit (General) Regulations 2006;
(p)-(q) [*Omitted*]
(r) regulation 70 (special cases: supplemental – persons from abroad) of the Employment and Support Allowance Regulations 2008;
(s)-(v) [*Omitted*];
(w) regulations 2 (interpretation) and 9 (persons treated as not being in Great Britain) of the Universal Credit Regulations 2013(151);
(x)-(bb) [*Omitted*]
4. [*Noted in the text of the 2016 Regulations where relevant*]

Continued application of section 7(1) of the Immigration Act 1988 for purposes of housing legislation
5. [Omitted]   7.173

SCHEDULE 5

TRANSITIONAL AND FURTHER SAVING PROVISION

[*Omitted*]   7.174

INDEX

LEGAL TAXONOMY
FROM SWEET & MAXWELL

This index has been prepared using Sweet and Maxwell's Legal Taxonomy. Main index entries conform to keywords provided by the Legal Taxonomy except where references to specific documents or non-standard terms (denoted by quotation marks) have been included. These keywords provide a means of identifying similar concepts in other Sweet & Maxwell publications and online services to which keywords from the Legal Taxonomy have been applied. Readers may find some minor differences between terms used in the text and those which appear in the index. Suggestions to *sweetandmaxwell.taxonomy@thomson.com*.

(All references are to paragraph number)

A2 and A8 nationals
See **Foreign nationals**
Abbeyfield Home
employment and support allowance, 4.4
income support, 2.3
Absence
income support, 2.67–2.73
jobseeker's allowance, 3.157–3.165
"Academic year"
definition, 2.476
Access to learning fund
income support
definition, 2.475
generally, 2.516–2.518
income treated as capital, 2.525–2.526
jobseeker's allowance
definition, 3.385
generally, 3.401–3.402
Action plans
generally, 1.358–1.359
work-focused interviews, 4.156
work-related activities
generally, 4.517–4.518
reconsideration, 4.521
Regulations, 6.70
Actively seeking employment
actively seeking work test
generally, 1.112–1.123
part-week test, 3.95–3.96
touchstone test, 3.89–3.94
carers, 3.108–3.109
deemed circumstances
carers, 3.108–3.109
Coronavirus, and, 3.98
domestic violence, 3.68–3.71
during first 13 weeks, 3.101–3.102
full-time students, 3.105–3.106
generally, 3.97–3.100
laid-off workers, 3.103–3.104
lone parents with children aged 5, 3.107
short time workers, 3.103–3.104
voluntary workers, 3.108–3.109
domestic violence, 3.68–3.71

during first 13 weeks, 3.101–3.102
full-time students, 3.105–3.106
generally, 1.112–1.123
laid-off workers, 3.103–3.104
lone parents with children aged 5 not in
full-time education, 3.107
part-week test, 3.95–3.96
short time workers, 3.103–3.104
students, 3.105–3.106
touchstone test, 3.89–3.94
voluntary workers, 3.108–3.109
young people, 3.214–3.215
Adoption leave
employment and support allowance,
4.4
jobseeker's allowance, 3.3
"Advance of earnings"
income support, 2.393
jobseeker's allowance, 3.350–3.351
Advance payments
employment and support allowance
generally, 4.325–4.326
statutory provisions, 1.338–1.339,
1.422, 1.433
Aggregation
income-related benefits, 1.46–1.50
income support, 2.200–2.215
jobseeker's allowance, 3.292–3.293
Air crew
employment and support allowance,
4.4, 4.5
Appeals
deductions from income support
community charge, 2.896
council tax, 2.934
fines, 2.912
income support
applicable amounts, 2.195–2.199
generally, 2.565, 2.602–2.604
jobseekers' agreements, 1.139
transitional provision
JSA, 5.67–5.68
miscellaneous, 5.61–5.62

1931

refuses to apply for vacant work,
1.206–1.210
Regulations (1996), 3.229–3.232
sanctionable conduct,
1.185–1.213–1.215
sexual offences outside employment,
1.190
voluntarily leaves employment without
good reason, 1.195–1.205
other sanctions
generally, 1.218–1.233
Regulations, 3.233–3.234
misconduct causing loss of employment as
employed earner
'employed earner', 1.186–1.187
evidence, 1.192–1.194
examples, 1.191
generally, 1.186–1.187
'lost his employment', 1.186–1.187
meaning of misconduct, 1.188–1.190
proof, 1.192–1.194
scope of misconduct, 1.188–1.190
sexual offences, 1.190
voluntarily leaves employment without
good reason
domestic circumstances, 1.205
early retirement, 1.199
generally, 1.195
grievances about work , 1.204
'just cause', 1.200
onus of proof, 1.197
personal circumstances, 1.205
Regulations, 3.246–3.247
'such employment', 1.196
'voluntarily leaves', 1.198
'without good reason', 1.200–1.203
voluntary redundancies, 3.246–3.247
young people, 3.222–3.226
Registration certificates
general note, 7.105
issue, 7.106
procedure for applications, 7.110
verification of right of residence, 7.111
Rehabilitation
allowances
jobseeker's allowance, 3.339–3.341
Relatives
income support
close relative, 2.11
generally, 2.3
jobseeker's allowance
close relative, 3.25
generally, 3.3
"Relevant education"
income support
cessation of qualification, 2.109
child, 2.107
entitlement conditions, 2.110–2.126
'full-time education', 2.108
general note, 2.106
generally, 2.105
qualifying young person, 2.107–2.108
Regulations, 2.105–2.109

jobseeker's allowance
generally, 1.285, 1.306
Regulations, 3.177–3.180
Religious groups
income support, 2.159
Religious orders
See **Religious groups**
"Remunerative work"
carers, 2.93–2.98
child minders, 2.93–2.98
councillors, 2.93–2.98
income support
'employment', 2.99
generally, 2.546, 2.585
persons treated as engaged in,
2.74–2.92
persons treated as not engaged in,
2.93–2.98
jobseeker's allowance
generally, 3.166–3.169
meaning, 3.3
persons treated as engaged in,
3.170–3.174
persons treated as not engaged in,
3.175–3.176
persons treated as engaged in
engaged in work, 2.79
generally, 2.74–2.92
'remunerative', 2.77–2.78
seasonal workers, 2.84–2.85
self-employment, 2.89
term-time only workers, 2.86–2.88
persons treated as not engaged in
carers, 2.93–2.98
child minders, 2.93–2.98
councillors, 2.93–2.98
lone parents, 2.93–2.98
sports awards, 2.93–2.98
training allowances, 2.93–2.98
voluntary work, 2.93–2.98
'remunerative', 2.77–2.78
seasonal workers, 2.84–2.85
self-employment, 2.89
sports awards, 2.93–2.98
term-time only workers, 2.86–2.88
training allowances, 2.93–2.98
voluntary work, 2.93–2.98
Repeatedly mobilise
See **Descriptors for incapacity**
Reserve forces
income support, 2.6–2.7
Residence
See also **Foreign nationals**
deadline for applications, 7.143
derivative right
carers of British children, 7.103
children of migrant workers in
education, 7.101
documentation, 7.109
exempt persons, 7.99
generally, 7.97–7.98
introduction, 7.95
issue of residence cards, 7.109